ENCYCLOPEDIA OF AFRICAN AMERICAN RELIGIONS

Religious Information Systems (Vol. 9)

Garland Reference Library of Social Science (Vol. 721)

Religious Information Systems
J. Gordon Melton
General Editor

Religious Bodies in the United States: A Directory
by J. Gordon Melton

Religious Information Sources: A Worldwide Guide
by J. Gordon Melton and Michael A. Köszegi

Magic, Witchcraft, and Paganism in America:
A Bibliography
Second Edition
by J. Gordon Melton and Isotta Poggi

The African-American Holiness Pentecostal Movement:
An Annotated Bibliography
by Sherry Sherrod DuPree

Holy Ground: A Study of the American Camp Meeting
by Kenneth O. Brown

The Cult Controversy: A Guide to Sources
by J. Gordon Melton

Encyclopedic Handbook of Cults in America
Revised and Updated
by J. Gordon Melton

Islam in North America: A Sourcebook
edited by Michael A. Köszegi and J. Gordon Melton

Encyclopedia of African American Religions
edited by Larry G. Murphy,
J. Gordon Melton, and Gary L. Ward

Exposing Cults: Understanding the Rise
of Gurus in North America
by David Christopher Lane

A Guide to the End of the World: Popular Eschatology in America
by Jon R. Stone

ENCYCLOPEDIA OF
AFRICAN AMERICAN RELIGIONS

edited by
Larry G. Murphy
J. Gordon Melton
Gary L. Ward

RELIGIOUS INFORMATION SYSTEMS

Garland Publishing, Inc.
New York & London
1993

Library of Congress Cataloging-in-Publication Data

Encyclopedia of African American religions / edited by Larry Murphy,
    J. Gordon Melton, Gary L. Ward.
        p. cm. — (Religious information systems ; vol. 9) (Garland reference
library of social science ; vol. 721)
    Includes bibliographic references and index.
    ISBN 0-8153-0500-1
    1. Afro-Americans—Religion—Encyclopedias. 2. Afro-American
churches—Encyclopedias. 3. United States—Religion—Encyclopedias.
I. Murphy, Larry (Larry G.) II. Melton, J. Gordon. III. Ward, Gary L.
IV. Series. V. Series: Garland reference library of social science ; vol. 721.
BR563.N4E53   1993
200'.89'96073—dc20   93-7224
                                                                         CIP

Printed on acid-free, 250-year-life paper
Manufactured in the United States of America

To my son

Ayinde Murphy,

the response to our praise

Table of Contents

TABLE OF CONTENTS

TABLE OF CONTENTS

TABLE OF CONTENTS

TABLE OF CONTENTS

John Thomas Walker
Orris George Walker, Jr.
Wyatt Tee Walker
Paris Arthur Wallace
William Jacob Walls
Alexander Walters
Clara Mae Ward
Samuel Ringgold Ward
Thomas Marcus Decatur Ward
Andrew Jackson Warner
Booker Taliaferro Washington
Dennis Comer Washington
Joseph Reed Washington, Jr.
Wilbur Thornton Washington
William A. Washington
Charles Emory Rogers Waters
Edward Waters
Ethel Waters
Edgar Benton Watson
Thomas Watson
Way of the Cross Church of Christ

Alexander Walker Wayman
Samuel Weir
Wesleyan Church
Western University
Phillis Wheatley
Alfred Edward White
Woodie Walter White
Wilberforce University
Wiley College
William Reid Wilkes
Albert Cecil Williams
Arthur Benjamin Williams, Jr.
Elizabeth Barbara Williams
George Washington Williams
Lacey Kirk Williams
Milton A. Williams
Noah W. Williams
Peter Williams, Jr.
Peter Williams, Sr.
Riley Felman Williams
Robert Simeon Williams

Smallwood Edmund Williams
Joseph Willis
Gayraud Stephen Wilmore, Jr.
Frank Theodore Wilson, Sr.
Arthur Walter Womack
Women in the Pulpit, African American
John Wesley Wood
George Washington Woodbey
Cornelia Wright
Harold Louis Wright
Nathan Wright, Jr.
Richard Robert Wright, Jr.
Theodore Sedgwick Wright

X–Y
Xavier University
Yahweh ben Yahweh
Yahweh's Temple
Andrew Jackson Young
George Benjamin Young
Roy Lee Young

Contributors

Lillian E. Ashcraft-Easton
Department of History
Bowling Green State University

Hans Baer
Department of Sociology and Anthropology
University of Arkansas at Little Rock

Keith A. Burton[*]
Garrett-Evangelical Theological Seminary

John Henderson Cartwright
Department of Social Ethics
Boston University School of Theology

Olivia M. Cloud
Black Church Development Section
Baptist Sunday School Board
Southern Baptist Convention

David D. Daniels, III
Field of History
McCormick Theological Seminary

Cyprian Davis
Department of Church History
St. Meinrad's School of Theology

Sherry Sherrod DuPree
Santa Fe Community College Library
Gainesville, Florida

James Evans
President
Colgate Rochester Theological Seminary

Leroy Fitts
First Baptist Church
Baltimore, Maryland

Jacquelyn Grant
Black Woman in Church and Society
Interdenominational Theological Center

Allen C. Guelzo
Department of History
Eastern College

Philip A. Harley
Professor Emeritus
Garrett-Evangelical Theological Seminary

Sylvia M. Jacobs
Department of History and Social Science
North Carolina Central University

Alonzo Johnson
Department of Religious Studies
University of South Carolina

Michael A. Köszegi
Research Associate
Institute for the Study of American Religion

CONTRIBUTORS

Othal Hawthorne Lakey
Bishop
Christian Methodist Episcopal Church

Roger D. Launius
Reorganized Church of Jesus Christ of Latter Day
    Saints

Philip Charles Lucas
Department of Religious Studies
Stetson University

William B. McClain
Department of Homiletics
Wesley Theological Seminary

Cristel Manning*
Department of Religious Studies
University of California—Santa Barbara

Portia K. Maultsby
African American Studies Department
African American Arts Institute
Indiana University

Michael L. Mickler
Department of Church History
Unification Theological Seminary

Ella Pearson Mitchell
Department of Homiletics
Interdenominational Theological Center

Henry H. Mitchell*
Department of Homiletics
Interdenominational Theological Center

Isotta Poggi
Institute for the Study of American Religion

Elizabeth Pullen*
Department of Religious Studies
University of California—Santa Barbara

Kenneth B. Smith
President
Chicago Theological Seminary

Jon R. Stone
Department of Religion and Philosophy
University of North Iowa

Herman E. Thomas
Department of Religious Studies
University of North Carolina at Charlotte

Harold Dean Trulear
Dean
New York Theological Seminary

Gayraud S. Wilmore
Professor Emeritus, Editor of the *Journal of the
Interdenominational Theological Center*

*In doctoral program

Introduction

The *Encyclopedia of African American Religions* is the most comprehensive reference work to date covering African American religious leaders and groups, and the major issues raised by the development of African American religious life. It has grown out of a conversation between myself and Larry Murphy at an American Academy of Religion meeting several years ago. Out of my own work in compiling reference works, I suggested that there was a real need for such an encyclopedic volume and expressed some surprise that given the vitality of Black studies during the last two decades that no one had attempted doing it. Larry responded that he had been giving the same idea some thought over the years but had never acted upon it beyond some preliminary collection of materials. Given the convergence of our concern, we decided to give it a try. An initial list of some 800 entries was prepared and we divided the work load. We also recruited Gary L. Ward, who had joined the staff of the Institute for the Study of American Religion in 1988 and in whose work I had great confidence, to join us. Then we began to create a list of specialists whom we could ask to assist us by writing some of the key articles.

Biographical Entries

Our first task was the definition of the volume. Our area of coverage would be the broad spectrum of African American religions both past and present. As such we needed to provide entries on the major African American religious leaders. Very early in the project we decided to include an entry on each of the bishops of the African Methodist Episcopal Church, the African Methodist Episcopal Zion Church, and Christian Methodist Episcopal Church, and the founders and major national leaders of the several African American Baptist conventions. We also wanted to include biographical entries on the founders of the larger African American churches and religious groups. Beyond those more obvious criteria, we would have to make some judgments about those outstanding religious leaders to be included.

We then turned to the issue of African American leaders in predominantly White churches and religious groups. We agreed to provide entries on all of the African American bishops of the Episcopal Church and the United Methodist Church (and its antecedent bodies). Again we would have to make some hard judgments about prominent leaders in non-episcopal churches such as the American Baptist Churches in the U.S.A. and the Reformed Church in America.

Finally, as regards the biographical entries, we made a conscious decision to be diligent in searching out African American women who had made prominent contributions to the development of the religious community and document their accomplishments. We also sought out female scholars as contributors to the *Encyclopedia*.

Organizational Entries

Above and beyond the biographical entries, we included an entry on each of the African American denominations and religious groups and on the more prominent religious organizations. This goal is obviously a heuristic one, but, drawing from the files of the Institute for the Study of American Religion, the major research facility monitoring African American religious groups over the past generation, we have been able to compile a list of several hundred Christian denominations and religious bodies which show the broad participation of African Americans across the spectrum of American religious life, from orthodox Christianity to Eastern religions to African-based religions. We also wanted to tell the story of the emergence of African constituencies in the larger predominantly White denominations.

Among the most important of Black religious organizations are the Black institutions of higher learning. The great majority of these either are religiously sponsored or were founded as religious schools. Because of the demise of many of these schools, not to mention the development of many into secular state-supported institutions, there is the danger that their history will be lost or ignored. We quickly discovered that no comprehensive list of these schools had ever been compiled, and thus we set out to create such a list and include entries on each college, university, Bible school, or seminary. Even though we have discovered and generated entries on over 100 such schools, the list is not yet complete, and we continued to locate missing schools right up to the closing date for new additions to the text.

Broad Coverage

Having sketched out our area of coverage, we had to set some boundaries to what was becoming an overwhelming task. We first decided to limit our coverage to the United States and not attempt covering the work of African American groups overseas. We have had to make a few exceptions, as missionary work in Africa and the Caribbean Islands has on occasion been crucial to the developing churches in the United States. For example, the first African American bishops in the predominantly White churches were assigned to serve outside the country in places such as Liberia and Haiti. It is our hope that the work of African American churches overseas and the development of affiliated religious groups can be treated fully in a later volume.

We also agreed to place strict limitations on our treatment of the efforts of White churches and church leaders to minister in the Black community, the development of social action programs on racial justice, and the White churches' response to the presence of African Americans in their midst. To keep faith with this criterion, we decided to exclude biographical entries on White church and religious leaders, even though some White people, from Methodist William Capers to Roman Catholic John R. Slattery, had greatly altered the direction of African American religion. Their contributions have been covered in the context of the story of the development of those black religious organizations they most affected.

In like measure, we decided to put aside a primary treatment of slavery except as it impinged upon the story of the creation of religious life within the African American community. Slavery and the various efforts at abolition is the single area of the African American experience which has been given the most comprehensive attention in the literature and a set of reference books already covers the slavery controversy.

Having agreed upon the area of concern to be targeted, we began to write and commission others to write the entries (topics, organizations, and people) for inclusion in the *Encyclopedia*. The initial list of 800 grew throughout the period we worked on the project to a final list of **some 1200 entries**. Initially, Ward assumed responsibility for the biographical entries and wrote the great majority of them. The *Encyclopedia* features biographical sketches of 773 people. Melton took primary responsibility of the many articles on the several hundred black religious organizations. This section includes 341 entries, the majority of which he authored, though most of the longer articles on the major African American groups were authored by specialists who had done particular research on them.

Murphy agreed to take charge of the 30 or so major topical entries from the Civil Rights Movement to the status and role of women. He also took charge of recruiting and/or writing the articles on the major African denominations (AME, AMEZ, National Baptist, etc.) and the White churches with a significant Black membership.

Special Features

Two special features highlight this volume. During the process of compiling the *Encyclopedia*, we became aware of just how much new information we were generating as well as how much more well-known data we were assembling for the first time under one cover. It seemed that compiling a chronological list of the major events in black religious history would be a meaningful contribution. The resulting **Chronology** appears below in the introductory material.

Secondly, to allow direct contact with the currently existing religious organizations discussed in the text, a **Directory** of all the churches and groups for which an entry appears has been attached at the end of this text.

Indexing/Cross-Indexing

In order to make this volume as user friendly as possible, a set of indices has been included. There is a complete subject/organization/personal name index. Secondly, there is a cross index of all of the biographical entries by the church or religious tradition with which the person is identified. Thus one can turn to the "Biographical Cross-

Index" and quickly locate all of the Presbyterians or Pentecostals profiled in the *Encyclopedia*. Finally, major entries mentioned throughout the text are in boldface type.

Bibliography/Sources

Very early in the planning stages of this work, the editors proposed to compile a bibliography for inclusion in this work. However, as the work progressed, we saw that such a bibliography would not be as useful as attaching relevant references to each article. Such references will allow the user quickly to discover additional items which expand upon the topic under discussion. However, we have compiled a selective bibliography of the major texts on African American religion and the major religious traditions. The selective bibliography constitutes a basic working library of African American religious studies.

Acknowledgments

The compiling of this *Encyclopedia* has proved a massive undertaking and could not have been done without the cooperation of many. Primary thanks must go to the many contributors of the articles included in the text. They have shared of their special expertise and have made this volume a far stronger work than it could have been if the writing had been left exclusively to the three editors.

Second only to the contributors, however, is the staff of the Library of the University of California—Santa Barbara under the leadership of University Librarian Joseph Boissé. This volume was largely compiled from the Black Studies Collection and the American Religions Collection (ARC) of UCSB. We offer special thanks to Black Studies Librarian Sylvia Curtis and Library Assistant M. Alyce Harris who made their materials available for our use and went above and beyond the call of duty in assisting our search for information.

The ARC at UCSB was established in 1985 when the Institute for the Study of American Religion turned over its collection of books and files to the care of the Library's Special Collections Department. The ARC contains a significant set of materials on Black religious groups which had been gathered over the years and continues to grow.

The combined ARC and Black Studies Collection at UCSB, though relatively unheralded, constitute one of the better libraries in African American religion in the United States. Copies of the majority of the items cited in the text may be found at UCSB.

Finally, we offer our special thanks to Isotta Poggi of the Institute for the Study of American Religion staff who worked on the *Encyclopedia* at every stage, prepared the Directory and Index, and did much of the final checking and verification on the text.

J. Gordon Melton
September 1992

A Final Note

The editors completed their work on this volume with a sense of satisfaction that we had compiled the most comprehensive encyclopedic work on African American religion possible at this time. However, we were also aware that additional new entries to this volume were being suggested right up to our writing deadline. And then as editing of the articles proceeded other new entries were suggested. Thus we ended our writing phase with a decision to prepare a supplement in the near future. Not only would such a proposal allow us extra time to locate data on some important figures about whom biographical information had been elusive, track down the missing black schools, and discover additional denominations and religious groups, but it would allow the readership of this volume the opportunity to make suggestions for inclusion of people, organizations, and subjects we might have overlooked. We invite suggestions for additional entries or comments on improving the *Encyclopedia* in future editions. Address your comments to the editors:

J. Gordon Melton
Gary L. Ward
Institute for the Study of American
Religion
Box 90709
Santa Barbara, CA 93190

Larry G. Murphy
Garrett-Evangelical Theological
Seminary
2121 Sheridan Road
Evanston, IL 60201

Abbreviations

AAB	Burle, William Jeremiah. *American Authors and Books*. New York: Crown Publishers, 1962.
AAE	*Afro-American Encyclopedia*. 10 vols. North Miami, FL: Educational Book Publishers, 1974.
AAP	Penn, Irvine Garland. *The Afro-American Press and Its Editors*. Springfield, MA: Wiley & Co., 1891.
AARS	Williams, Ethel, and Clifton Brown, eds. *Afro-American Religious Studies: A Comprehensive Bibliography with Locations in American Libraries*. Metuchen, NJ: Scarecrow Press, 1972.
ACAB	Wilson, James Grant, and John Fiske, eds. *Appleton's Cyclopaedia of American Biography*. New York: Appleton, 1888.
ACC	Hart, James D. *A Companion to California*. New York: Oxford University Press, 1978.
ALNA	Dreer, Herman. *American Literature by Negro Authors*. New York: Macmillan, 1950.
AMECMIM	Foster, J. Curtis, Jr. *The African Methodist Episcopal Church Makes Its Mark in America*. Nashville, TN: African Methodist Episcopal Church Publishing House, 1976.
AMEZC	Walls, William J. *The African Methodist Episcopal Zion Church*. Charlotte, NC: A.M.E. Zion Publishing House, 1974.
AMS	Gaines, Wesley J. *African Methodism in the South*. 1890. Rept.: Chicago: Afro-Am. Press, 1969.
AMSC	James, Frederick C. *African Methodism in South Carolina: A Bicentennial Focus*. Tappan, NY: Custombook, Inc., for the Seventh Episcopal District, A.M.E. Church, 1987.
ANT	Warfel, Harry R. *American Novelists of Today*. New York: American Book Co., 1951.
AWW	Faust, Langdon Lynne. *American Women Writers: A Critical Reference Guide from Colonial Times to the Present*. New York: Ungar, 1983.
BA	Burkett, Randall, and Richard Newman, eds. *Black Apostles: Afro-American Clergy Confront the Twentieth Century*. Boston, MA: G. K. Hall, 1978.
BAA	Brignano, Russell C. *Black Americans in Autobiography*. Durham, NC: Duke University Press, 1984.
BAB	Blackett, R. J. M. *Beating Against the Barriers: Biographical Essays in Nineteenth-Century Afro-American History*. Baton Rouge, LA: Louisiana State University Press, 1986.
BAC	Christopher, Maurine. *Black Americans in Congress*. Revised ed. New York: T. Y. Crowell Co., 1976.
BAMEC	Wright, Richard, Jr. *The Bishops of the African Methodist Episcopal Church*. Nashville, TN: A.M.E. Church Sunday School Union, 1963.
BAW	Matthews, Geraldine O. *Black American Writers, 1773–1949*. Boston, MA: G. K. Hall, 1975.
BAWPP	Rush, Theressa Gunnells, Carol Myers, and Esther Arata. *Black American Writers Past and Present*. Metuchen, NJ: Scarecrow Press, 1975.
BDA-AAM	Southern, Eileen. *Biographical Dictionary of African-American and African Musicians*. Westport, CT: Greenwood Press, 1982.
BDA-AHP	DuPree, Sherry Sherrod. *Biographical Dictionary of African-American, Holiness-Pentecostals, 1880–1990*. Washington, DC: Middle Atlantic Regional Press, 1989.
BDACSL	Melton, J. Gordon. *Biographical Dictionary of American Cult and Sect Leaders*. New York: Garland Publishing, 1986.
BDAE	Ohles, John F. *Biographical Dictionary of American Educators*. 3 vols. Westport, CT: Greenwood Press, 1978.
BDBPC	David, Jay. *Black Defiance: Black Profiles in Courage*. New York: William Morrow & Co., 1972.
BDCALC	Mickelson, Arnold R., ed. *A Biographical Directory of Clergymen of the American Lutheran Church*. Minneapolis, MN: Augsburg Publishing House, 1972.
BDNM	Williams, Ethel. *Biographical Directory of Negro Ministers*. 1st ed.: 1965; 2nd ed.: 1970; 3rd ed.: Boston, MA: G. K. Hall, 1975.

BDSA	Knight, Lucian Lamar. *Biographical Dictionary of Southern Authors*. Atlanta, GA: The Martin & Hoyt Co., 1929. Rpt. Detroit, Michigan: Gale Research Co., 1978.
BDUMB	*Biographical Directory of United Methodist Bishops, Spouses, and Widows*. Office of the Secretary of the Council of Bishops, 1988.
BE	*The Brethren Encyclopedia*. 3 vols. Philadelphia, PA and Oak Brook, IL: The Brethren Encyclopedia, 1983.
BGM	Fauset, Arthur Huff. *Black Gods of the Metropolis*. Philadelphia, PA: University of Pennsylvania Press, 1944.
BGRC	Lapp, Rudolph M. *Blacks in Gold Rush California*. New Haven, CT: Yale University Press, 1977.
BGWC	Burgess, John M. *Black Gospel/White Church*. New York: Seabury Press, 1982.
BH	Jones, Charles Edwin. *Black Holiness*. Metuchen, NJ: The American Theological Library Association and Scarecrow Press, 1987.
BHAC	Thorpe, Earl E. *Black Historians: A Critique*. New York: Morrow, 1971.
BHBA	Toppin, Edgar Allen. *A Biographical History of Blacks in America Since 1528*. New York: McKay, 1971.
BHONH	Drotning, Phillip T. *Black Heroes in Our Nation's History*. New York: Cowles Book Company, 1969.
BJH	Brotz, Howard. *The Black Jews of Harlem: Negro Nationalism and the Dilemmas of Negro Leadership*. New York: Schocken Books, 1964.
BLA	White, John. *Black Leadership in America 1895–1968*. 2nd ed. London and New York: Longman, 1990.
BLC	Mezle, S. Okechukwu, and Ram Desai, eds. *Black Leaders of the Centuries*. Buffalo, NY: Black Academy Press, Inc., 1970.
BLTC	Franklin, John Hope. *Black Leaders of the Twentieth Century*. Urbana, IL: University of Illinois Press, 1982.
BMC	Bechler, Le Roy. *The Black Mennonite Church in North America, 1886–1986*. Scottdale, PA and Kitchener, ON: Herald Press, 1986.
BMIC	Nichols, Charles H., ed. *Black Men in Chains: Narratives by Escaped Slaves*. New York and Westport: Lawrence Hill & Co., 1972.
BN	Essien-Udom, E. U. *Black Nationalism: A Search for an Identity in America*. Chicago: University of Chicago Press, 1962.
BNA	Bracey, John H., Jr., August Meier, and Elliott Rudwick, eds. *Black Nationalism in America*. Indianapolis, IN: Bobbs-Merrill Co., 1970.
BP	Metcalf, George R. *Black Profiles*. New York: McGraw-Hill, 1968.
BPAW	Golder, Morris E. *The Bishops of the Pentecostal Assemblies of the World, Inc.* Indianapolis, Indiana: The Author, 1980, and an updated addendum, circa 1988.
BPEAR	Kaplan, Sidney and Emma N. Kaplan. *The Black Presence in the Era of the American Revolution*. Revised ed. Amherst, MA: University of Massachusetts Press, 1989.
BPJ	Swift, David E. *Black Prophets of Justice: Activist Clergy Before the Civil War*. Baton Rouge. LA: Louisiana State University Press, 1989.
BPL	Tucker, David M. *Black Pastors and Leaders: Memphis, 1819–1972*. Memphis, TN: Memphis State University Press, 1975.
BPMC	McClain, William B. *Black People in the Methodist Church: Whither Thou Goest?* Cambridge, MA: Schenkman Publishing Co., 1984.
BPUSA	Bennett, Lerone, Jr. *Black Power U.S.A.: The Human Side of Reconstruction, 1867–1877*. Chicago: Johnson Publishing Co., 1967.
BR	Thornbrough, Emma Lou. *Black Reconstructionists*. Englewood Cliffs, NJ: Prentice-Hall, 1972.
BRBR	Wilmore, Gayraud S. *Black Religion and Black Radicalism*. 2nd ed. Maryknoll, NY: Orbis Books, 1983.
BSC	Washington, Joseph R., Jr. *Black Sects and Cults*. Garden City, NY: Doubleday & Company, 1972.
BTFTMC	Griffin, Paul R. *Black Theology as the Foundation of Three Methodist Colleges: The Educational Views and Labors of Daniel Payne, Joseph Price, and Isaac Lane*. Lanham, MD: University Press of America, 1984.
BW	Katz, William Loren. *The Black West*. Garden City, NY: Doubleday & Company, 1971.
BWA	Barksdale, Richard, and Keneth Kinnamon, eds. *Black Writers of America*. New York: Macmillan Company, 1972.
BWASS	Metzger, Linda. *Black Writers: A Selection of Sketches from Contemporary Authors*. Detroit, MI: Gale Research Company, 1989.
BWMH	Jackson, George F. *Black Women Makers of History: A Portrait*. Sacramento, CA: Dome Printing & Publishing, 1975.

BWNCAL	Loewenberg, Bert James. *Black Women in Nineteenth-Century American Life*. University Park, PA: Pennsylvania State University Press, 1976.
BWR	Richardson, Marilyn. *Black Women and Religion: A Bibliography*. Boston, MA: G. K. Hall & Co., 1980.
BWTC	Pease, Jane H. and William H. Pease. *Bound with Them in Chains: A Biographical History of the Antislavery Movement*. Westport, CT: Greenwood Press, 1972.
CA	*Contemporary Authors*. Detroit, MI: Gale Research Company, 1962–.
CAA	Foy, Felician A., ed. *Catholic Almanac 1992*. Huntington, IN: Our Sunday Visitor Publishing Division, 1991.
CB	*Current Biography*. New York: H. W. Wilson Co., 1940–.
CBL	Fax, Elton C. *Contemporary Black Leaders*. New York: Dodd, Mead, & Co., 1970.
CCAN	Gillard, John T. *The Catholic Church and the American Negro*. Baltimore, MD: St. Joseph's Society Press, 1929.
CEAMEC	Wright, Richard R., Jr. *Centennial Encyclopedia of the African Methodist Episcopal Church*. Philadelphia, PA: Book Concern of the A.M.E. Church, 1916.
CH	Bergman, Peter M. *The Chronological History of the Negro in America*. New York: Harper & Row, 1969.
CMECTY	Harris, Eula W., and Maxie H. Craig. *Christian Methodist Episcopal Church Through the Years*. Revised ed. Jackson, TN: Christian Methodist Episcopal Church Publishing House, 1965.
CR	Blackwell, Earl, ed. *Celebrity Register*. New York: Simon and Schuster, 1973.
CRACG	Adams, A. John and Joan Martin Burke, eds. *Civil Rights: A Current Guide to the People, Organizations, and Events*. New York: R. R. Bowker Co., 1970.
CRS	D'Emilio, John. *The Civil Rights Struggle: Leaders in Profile*. New York: Facts on File, 1979.
DAA	Adams, Oscar Fay. *Dictionary of American Authors*. New York: Houghton, 1897.
DAB	Johnson, Allen, and Dumas Malone, eds. *Dictionary of American Biography*. 10 vols. New York: Charles Scribner's Sons, 1931. 8 supplements, 1944–1988.
DANB	Logan, Rayford W., and Michael R. Winston, eds. *Dictionary of American Negro Biography*. New York: W. W. Norton, 1982.
DARB	Bowden, Henry Warner. *Dictionary of American Religious Biography*. Westport, CT: Greenwood Press, 1977.
DAS	Press, Jaques Cattell, ed. *Directory of American Scholars*. 8th ed. New York: R. R. Bowker Co., 1982.
DCB	*Dictionary of Canadian Biography*. 12 vols. Toronto: University of Toronto Press, 1966–1990.
DNAADB	Wallace, William Stewart. *Dictionary of North American Authors Deceased Before 1950*. Detroit, MI: Gale Research, 1968.
DPCM	Burgess, Stanley M., and Gary B. McGee, eds. *Dictionary of Pentecostal and Charismatic Movements*. Grand Rapids, MI: Regency Reference Library, Zondervan Publishing Co., 1988.
EAB	Garraty, John A., ed. *Encyclopedia of American Biography*. New York: Harper & Row, 1974.
EAJ	Paneth, Donald. *Encyclopedia of American Journalism*. New York: Facts on File, 1983.
EAMEC	Wright, Richard R., Jr. *Encyclopedia of the African Methodist Episcopal Church*. 2nd ed. Philadelphia, PA: Book Concern of the A.M.E. Church, 1947.
EBA	Low, W. Augustus, and Virgil A. Clift, eds. *Encyclopedia of Black America*. New York: McGraw-Hill, 1981.
EBAP	Robinson, William H., Jr. *Early Black American Poets*. Dubuque, IA: William C. Brown Co., 1971.
ELC	Bodensieck, Julius, ed. *The Encyclopedia of the Lutheran Church*. 3 vols. Minneapolis, MN: Augsburg Publishing House, 1965.
ENB	Freeman, Edward A. *The Epoch of Negro Baptists and the Foreign Mission Board, National Baptist Convention, U.S.A., Inc*. 1953; rpt. New York: Arno Press, 1980.
EPP	Hartshorn, William Newton. *An Era of Progress and Promise, 1863–1910*. Boston, MA: Priscilla Publishing Co., 1910.
ERS	Hill, Samuel S., ed. *Encyclopedia of Religion in the South*. Macon, GA: Mercer University Press, 1984.
ESB	*Encyclopedia of Southern Baptists*. 3 vols. Nashville, TN: Broadman Press, 1958. Suppl. 1982.
ESH	Roller, David C., and Robert W. Twyman, eds. *Encyclopedia of Southern History*. Baton Rouge, LA: Louisiana State University Press, 1979.
EWM	Harmon, Nolan, ed. *The Encyclopedia of World Methodism*. 2 vols. Nashville, TN: The United Methodist Publishing House, 1974.
FAW	McHenry, Robert. *Famous American Women*. New York: Dover, 1983.
FFF	Garrett, Romeo B. *Famous First Facts About Negroes*. New York: Arno Press, 1972.
FNHA	Hughes, Langston. *Famous Negro Heroes of America*. New York: Dodd, Mead, 1958.

GBA	Richardson, Benjamin A., and William A. Fahey. *Great Black Americans*. 2nd ed. New York: Thomas Y. Crowell Co., 1976.
GBB	Boddie, Charles Emerson. *God's "Bad Boys."* Valley Forge, PA: Judson Press, 1972.
GMBS	Major, Gerri. *Gerri Major's Black Society*. Chicago: Johnson Publishing Co., 1976.
GMC	Foley, Albert Sidney. *God's Men of Color: The Colored Catholic Priests of the United States, 1854–1954*. New York: Farrar, Strauss, 1955.
GNPP	Adams, Russell. *Great Negroes Past and Present*. 3rd ed. Chicago: Afro-American Publishing Co., 1969.
GRM	Burkett, Randall K. *Garveyism as a Religious Movement*. Metuchen, NJ: Scarecrow Press, 1978.
HAMEC	Gregg, Howard D. *History of the African Methodist Episcopal Church*. Nashville, TN: A.M.E. Sunday School Union, 1980.
HAMECH	Payne, Daniel A. *History of the African Methodist Episcopal Church*. Nashville, TN: Publishing House of the A.M.E. Sunday School Union, 1891.
HAMEZC	Bradley, David Henry, Sr. *A History of the A.M.E. Zion Church*. 2 vols. Nashville, TN: The Parthenon Press, 1956, 1970.
HAMEZCIA	Moore, John Jamison. *History of the A.M.E. Zion Church in America*. York, PA: Teachers' Journal Office, 1884.
HBB	Fitts, Leroy. *A History of Black Baptists*. Nashville, TN: Broadman Press, 1985.
HBBUS	Banks, William L. *A History of Black Baptists in the United States*. Philadelphia, PA: The Author, 1987.
HBCUS	Davis, Cyprian. *The History of Black Catholics in the United States*. New York: Crossroads, 1990.
HCGCH	Cobbins, Otho B. *History of the Church of God in Christ (Holiness), U.S.A., 1895–1965*. New York: The Author, 1966.
HCMEC	Lakey, Othal Hawthorne. *The History of the C.M.E. Church*. Memphis, TN: The C.M.E. Publishing House, 1985.
HCMECA	Phillips, Charles Henry. *The History of the Colored Methodist Episcopal Church in America*. New York: Arno Press, 1972.
HH	Brown, Hallie Q., ed. *Homespun Heroines and Other Women of Distinction*. Freeport, NY: Books for Libraries Press, 1971.
HNB	Robinson, Wilhelmena S. *Historical Negro Biographies*. International Library of Negro Life and History. New York: Publishers Co., 1967.
HNC	Woodson, Carter G. *The History of the Negro Church*. Washington, DC: Associated Publishers, 1921.
HNRA	Williams, George Washington. *History of the Negro Race in America*. 2 vols. New York: Bergman Publishers, 1968.
HPAW	Golder, Morris E. *History of the Pentecostal Assemblies of the World*. Indianapolis, IN: The Author, 1973.
HPM	Synan, Vinson. *The Holiness-Pentecostal Movement in the United States*. Grand Rapids, MI: Eerdmans, 1971.
HUBA	Williams, Ethel, and Clifton Brown. *The Howard University Bibliography of African and Afro-American Religious Studies*. Wilmington, DE: Scholarly Resources, 1977.
IAAH	Reid, Robert Henry, Jr. *Irony of Afro-American History*. Nashville, TN: A.M.E. Publishing House, 1984.
IB	Ward, Gary, Bertil Persson, and Alan Bain. *Independent Bishops: An International Directory*. Detroit, MI: Apogee Books, 1990.
IBAW	Spradling, Mary Mace, ed. *In Black and White: Afro-Americans in Print*. 3rd ed. Detroit, MI: Gale Research, 1985.
IBAWCB	Campbell, Dorothy W. *Index to Black American Writers in Collective Biographies*. Littleton, CO: Libraries Unlimited, Inc., 1983.
IBS	Rountree, Louise Marie. *An Index to Biographical Sketches and Publications of the Bishops of the AME Zion Church*. Salisbury, NC: Carnegie Library, Livingstone College, 1963.
IDAW	Lanker, Brian. *I Dream a World: Portraits of Black Women Who Changed America*. New York: Stewart, Tabori & Chang, 1989.
IP	Lee, George L. *Interesting People: Black American History Makers*. Jefferson, NC: McFarland & Co., 1976.
IPAA	Sherman, Joan R. *Invisible Poets: Afro-Americans of the Nineteenth Century*. 2nd ed. Urbana and Chicago: University of Chicago Press, 1989.
IVR	Hammond, Lily Hardy. *In the Vanguard of a Race*. New York, 1922.
IWW	Ireland, Norma Olin. *Index to Women of the World From Ancient to Modern Times*. Westwood, MA: F. W. Faxon Co., 1970.
LBAS	Shockley, Ann Allen. *Living Black American Scholars*. New York: R. R. Bowker Co., 1973.

LC	Lueker, Erwin L., ed. *Lutheran Cyclopedia*. Revised ed. St. Louis, MO: Concordia Publishing House, 1975.
LCAN	Krebs, Ervin E. *The Lutheran Church and the American Negro*. Columbus, OH: Board of American Missions, American Lutheran Church, 1950.
LV	Franklin, Robert Michael. *Liberating Visions: Human Fulfillment and Social Justice in African-American Thought*. Minneapolis, MN: Fortress Press, 1990.
LW	McHenry, Robert. *Liberty's Women*. Springfield, MA: G & C Merriam Co., 1980.
MB	Leete, Frederick DeLand. *Methodist Bishops*. Nashville, TN: The Parthenon Press, 1948.
MBRL	Young, Henry J. *Major Black Religious Leaders*. 2 vols. Nashville, TN: Abingdon, 1977–79.
ME	*The Mennonite Encyclopedia*. 5 vols. Scottdale, PA and Waterloo, Ont.: Herald Press, vols. 1–4, 1959; vol. 5, 1990.
MM	Simmons, William J. *Men of Mark*. Cleveland, OH: George M. Rewell & Co., 1887. Rpt. Arno Press and New York Times, 1968.
MSB	Wormley, Stanton L., and Lewis H. Fenderson, eds. *Many Shades of Black*. New York: William Morrow & Co., 1969.
NA	*Negro Almanac*. 5th ed. Detroit, MI: Gale Research Company, 1989.
NAH	Cromwell, John W. *The Negro in American History*. Washington, DC: The American Negro Academy, 1914.
NAW	James, Edward T., ed. *Notable American Women*. 3 vols. Cambridge, MA: Belknap Press of Harvard University Press, 1971.
NAWMP	Sicherman, Barbara, and Carol Hurd Green, eds. *Notable American Women: The Modern Period*. Cambridge, MA: Belknap Press of Harvard University Press, 1980.
NBAW	Smith, Jessie Carney, ed. *Notable Black American Women*. Detroit, MI: Gale Research Company, 1991.
NBH	Brawley, Benjamin G. *Negro Builders and Heroes*. Chapel Hill, NC: The University of North Carolina Press, 1937.
NBHUSA	Jordan, Lewis Garnett. *Negro Baptist History, USA 1750–1930*. Nashville, TN: The Sunday School Publishing Board, 1930.
NBPH	Boone, Theodore S. *Negro Baptists in Pictures and History*. Detroit, MI: The Voice of Destiny, 1964.
NCAB	*National Cyclopedia of American Biography*. 63 vols. permanent series, 13 vols. current series. New York: James T. White & Co., 1896–.
NCW	Scally, Mary Anthony. *Negro Catholic Writers, 1900–1943*. Grosse Point, MI: Walter Romig, Publisher, 1945.
NEA	Loggins, Vernon. *Negro Author: His Development in America to 1900*. Port Washington, NY: Kennikat Press, 1931, 1964.
NG	Brawley, Benjamin. *The Negro Genius*. New York: Dodd, Mead & Co., 1937.
NHM	Shaw, J. Beverly F. *The Negro in the History of Methodism*. Nashville, TN: The Parthenon Press, 1954.
NIOY	Shofner, Jerrell H. *Nor Is It Over Yet: Florida in the Era of Reconstruction, 1863–1877*. Gainesville, FL: The University Presses of Florida, 1974.
NM	Moonie, Louise, ed. *Newsmakers: The People Behind Today's Headlines*. Detroit, MI: Gale Research Company, 1985–.
NNW	Majors, Monroe A. *Noted Negro Women: Their Triumphs and Activities*. 1893; Rept.: Freeport, NY: Books for Libraries Press, 1971.
NNY	Ottley, Roi, and William J. Weatherby, eds. *Negro in New York*. Dobbs Ferry, NY: Oceana Publications, 1967.
NPT	Broderick, Francis, and August Meier, eds. *Negro Protest Thought in the Twentieth Century*. New York: Bobbs-Merrill, 1965.
NSE	Wish, Harvey, ed. *The Negro Since Emancipation*. Englewood Cliffs, NJ: Prentice-Hall, Inc., 1964.
NV	Bardolph, Richard. *The Negro Vanguard*. New York: Vintage Press, 1959.
NWAC	Ottley, Roi. *New World A-Coming*. New York: Arno Press, 1968.
NYB	*Negro Year Book*. Tuskegee Institute, AL: Negro Year Book Publishing Co., (variantly) 1912–1952.
NYTBS	*New York Times Biographical Service*. New York: New York Times, 1970–.
NYTO	*New York Times Obituary Index*. 2 vols. New York: New York Times, 1970, 1980.
OBMS	Pegues, Albert W. *Our Baptist Ministers and Schools*. Springfield, MA: Wiley & Co., 1892.
OBS	Hemesath, Caroline. *Our Black Shepherds*. Washington, DC: Josephite Pastoral Center, 1987.
OHYAMEZC	Hood, James Walker. *One Hundred Years of the African Methodist Episcopal Zion Church*. New York: A.M.E. Zion Book Concern, 1895.
OHYNF	Bontemps, Arna. *100 Years of Negro Freedom*. New York: Dodd, Mead & Co., 1961.

ONL	Boulware, Marcus H. *The Oratory of Negro Leaders: 1900–1968*. Westport, CT: Negro Universities Press, 1969.
OS	Diamonstein, Barbaralee, ed. *Open Secrets: Ninety-Four Women in Touch with Our Time*. New York: The Viking Press, 1972.
OTSB	*One Thousand Successful Blacks*. Ebony Success Library. Chicago: Johnson Publishing Co., 1973.
PATN	Murray, Andrew E. *Presbyterians and the Negro—A History*. Philadelphia, PA: Presbyterian Historical Society, 1966.
PBGB	Wagner, Clarence M. *Profiles of Black Georgia Baptists*. Atlanta, GA: Bennett Brothers Printing Co., 1980.
PBP	Haskins, James. *Profiles in Black Power*. Garden City, NY: Doubleday & Company, 1972.
PHCGC	Cornelius, Lucille J. *The Pioneer History of the Church of God in Christ*. N.p.: The Author, 1975.
PHNA	Hughes, Langston, and Milton Meltzer. *A Pictorial History of the Negro in America*. 3rd ed. Eds. Eric Lincoln, and Milton Meltzer. New York: Crown Publishers, 1968.
PIC	Ovington, Mary White. *Portraits in Color*. New York: The Viking Press, 1927.
PNW	Dannett, Sylvia G. L. *Profiles of Negro Womanhood, 1619–1900*. 2 vols. New York: Educational Heritage, 1964.
PP	Bennett, Lerone, Jr. *Pioneers in Protest*. Chicago: Johnson Publishing Co., 1968.
RAM	Singleton, George A. *The Romance of African Methodism: A Study of the African Methodist Episcopal Church*. New York: Exposition Press, 1952.
RCM	Lakey, Othal Hawthorne. *The Rise of "Colored Methodism;" a Study of the Background and the Beginnings of the Christian Methodist Episcopal Church*. Dallas, TX: Crescendo Book Publications, 1972.
REAW	Lamar, Howard R., ed. *The Reader's Encyclopedia of the American West*. New York: Thomas Y. Crowell Co., 1977.
RLA	Schwarz, J. C., ed. *Religious Leaders of America*. Vol. II. New York: The Author, 1942.
RLOA	Melton, J. Gordon. *Religious Leaders of America*. Chicago: Gale Research, 1991.
SBAA	Page, James Allen. *Selected Black American Authors*. Boston, MA: G. K. Hall, 1977.
SBIAA	Cook, Richard B. *The Story of the Baptists in All Ages*. Baltimore, MD: H. M. Wharton, 1884.
SCA	Jackson, Joseph H. *A Story of Christian Activism: The History of the National Baptist Convention, U.S.A., Inc.* Nashville, TN: Townsend Press, 1980.
SFAY	Lewis, Helen M., and Meharry H. Lewis, eds. *Seventy-Fifth Anniversary Yearbook of the Church of the Living God, the Pillar and Ground of Truth, Inc., 1903–1978*. Nashville, TN: General Headquarters, Church of the Living God, the Pillar and Ground of Truth, 1978.
SNB	Pelt, Owen D., and Ralph Lee Smith. *The Story of the National Baptists*. New York: Vantage Press, 1960.
SOTT	Sterling, Dorothy, ed. *Speak Out in Thunder Tones: Letters and Other Writings by Black Northerners, 1787–1865*. Garden City, New York: Doubleday & Co., 1973.
SS	Andrews, William L., ed. *Sisters of the Spirit: Three Black Women's Autobiographies of the Nineteenth Century*. Bloomington, IN: Indiana University Press, 1986.
TAO	Embree, Edwin R. *Thirteen Against the Odds*. New York: The Viking Press, 1944.
TCBD	Johnson, Rossiter, ed. *The Twentieth Century Biographical Dictionary of Notable Americans*. Boston, MA: The Biographical Society, 1904.
TCNL	Culp, D. W., ed. *Twentieth Century Negro Literature*. 1902; Rept.: Miami, FL: Mnemosyne Publishing Co., 1969.
TCSAPR	Lippy, Charles H., ed. *Twentieth-Century Shapers of American Popular Religion*. Westport, CT: Greenwood Press, 1989.
TNA	Jenness, Mary. *Twelve Negro Americans*. Freeport, NY: Books for Libraries Press, 1936.
TP	Hollenweger, Walter J. *The Pentecostals*. Trans. R. A. Wilson. Minneapolis, MN: Augsburg Publishing House, 1972.
TSW	Rollins, Charlene Hill. *They Showed the Way: Forty American Negro Leaders*. New York: Thomas Y. Crowell, 1964.
VBA	Foner, Philip S. *Voice of Black America*. New York: Simon & Schuster, 1972.
WB	Daniel, Sadie Iola. *Women Builders*. Revised by Charles H. Wesley and Thelma D. Perry. Washington, DC: Associated Publishers, 1970.
WGMC	Rogers, J. A. *World's Great Men of Color*. 2 vols. New York: Macmillan, 1972.
WITW	Bennett, Lerone, Jr. *Wade in the Water: Great Moments in Black History*. Chicago: Johnson Publishing Co., 1979.

WRA   Ruether, Rosemary Radford, and Rosemary Skinner Keller, eds. *Women and Religion in America.* 3
           vols. San Francisco: Harper & Row, 1981–1986.
WRF   Cain, Alfred E. *The Winding Road to Freedom.* New York: Educational Heritage, 1965.
WWA   *Who's Who in America.* 47 vols. Wilmette, IL: Marquis Who's Who, 1899–.
WWABA   *Who's Who Among Black Americans.* Through the 5th ed., Lake Forest, IL: Educational
           Communications, Inc. 6th ed. Chicago, IL: Gale Research Company, 1990–91.
WWAM   Price, Carl F., ed. *Who's Who in American Methodism.* New York: E. B. Treat & Co., 1916.
WWAW   *Who's Who of American Women.* 17 vols. Wilmette, IL: Marquis Who's Who, 1958–.
WWC   Schwarz, J. C., ed. *Who's Who in the Clergy.* Vol. I. New York: The Author, 1936.
WWCA   *Who's Who in Colored America.* New York: Who's Who in Colored America Corp., 1927, 1931, 1940.
WWCR   Mather, Frank Lincoln. *Who's Who of the Colored Race.* 1915; Rept.: Detroit, MI: Gale Research
           Company, 1976.
WWE   *Who's Who in the East.* 23 vols. Chicago, IL: Marquis Who's Who, 1943–.
WWF   Reifert, Gail, and Eugene M. Dermody. *Women Who Fought: An American History.* Norwalk, CA:
           Dermody, 1978.
WWMC   *Who's Who in the Methodist Church.* Nashville, TN: Abingdon Press, 1966.
WWR   *Who's Who in Religion.* Chicago: Marquis Who's Who, 1975–76; 2nd ed. 1977; 3rd ed.: 1985.
WWW   *Who's Who in the World.* Chicago: Marquis Who's Who, 1970–.
WWWA   *Who Was Who in America With World Notables.* Vols. 1–9 plus Historical Volume. Wilmette, IL:
           Marquis Who's Who, 1897–.
WWWANAA   *Who Was Who Among North American Authors 1921–1939.* 3 vols. Detroit, MI: Gale Research
           Company, 1976.

Religion in the African American Community

by

Larry G. Murphy

The form of the present volume represents the first salient fact about the religious experience of Africans in the North American Diaspora—it has a sweep and diversity of expression which make it *encyclopedic*. No single religious tradition comprehends it; no facile interpretive principle explains it. Indeed, the extensive table of contents to this volume suggests rather than exhausts the scope of the subject.

African American religion as a subject of intellectual inquiry is relatively new to the academic arena. Well into the twentieth century there were still relatively few White scholars who considered Black people and their cultural life to qualify for serious study. This was a reflection both of the prevailing negative American assessment of the worth of African American life and the prevailing Euro/Anglo-centric character of American scholarship. On the other hand, the proscriptive laws and institutional policies of the nation inhibited Black access to academic training, academic positions, or, as importantly, the sense of freedom to be engaged in intellectual pursuits. There were notable exceptions on both sides. Melville Herskovits made the study of Black life, from the African continent to the Western Diaspora, his central work, establishing the perhaps unparalleled Africana Collection of research materials at Northwestern University. Black scholars Martin Delaney, Edward Blyden, George Washington Williams, W. E. B. DuBois, Carter G. Woodson, and E. Franklin Frazier, among others, laid early, significant foundations for exploring and understanding the unfolding tapestry of African American life. Woodson, in fact, sought to bring cooperative intentionality to this undertaking by initiating in 1915 the organization of the Association for the Study of Negro Life and History. This consortium of researchers and writers, still vitally active today, has been responsible for the publication for some 76 years of the respected quarterly *The Journal of Negro History*. And it was Woodson who initiated the observance of an annual Negro History Week, now celebrated as African American History Month. In this tradition have stood such distinguished scholars as Benjamin Mays, Joseph Nicholson, John Hope Franklin, and Charles S. Johnson. Their work was complemented by persons such as Arthur Schomburg and Jesse Moorland, who gathered large volumes of materials on African American life into what are now major research collections.

The social revolution in Black America in the 1950s and 1960s, with its emphasis on Black identity and Black pride of heritage, engendered a flowering in the study of African American history and culture. Black studies departments were organized at universities across the nation. Black students began opting term projects, then area concentrations, then whole degree programs that focused on African and African American subject matter. Not only was there a sense of freedom to be so engaged but the sense that liberation—existential, intellectual, and even social/political—would ultimately result.

This ferment in the Black community sparked, in some cases, and complemented in others, social movements in many sectors of the American populace, movements toward a broader ostensible social inclusivity and institutional recognition of the diverse elements in our national makeup. Thereby, African American subject matter began to achieve an academic "legitimacy" both for Black scholars and for an increasing number of Whites. A generation of scholars has emerged which, building on the work of their pioneering predecessors, has retrieved substantial amounts of research data and produced provocative volumes on African American life and history.

xxxi

The study of African American religion has been a prime beneficiary of this process. Most students of Black life have recognized the centrality of religion historically in Black communities. Thus it has been the object of primary data collection and has been a component in narrative interpretations of Black social and institutional dynamics.

The developments here described have prepared the ground for professors Albert Raboteau and David Wills to collaborate with a cadre of colleagues today toward the production of a major, multi-volume documentary history of African American religion. Thus, also, is possible an *encyclopedia* with thousands of entries on individuals, movements, and organizations spanning the religious spectrum.

In conceptualizing the present volume it was clear to the editors that the organizing subject was *religious history* as opposed to what has traditionally been called *church history*. For church history suggests an examination of *Christian* denominations and formal institutions. African Americans do, indeed, have their own ecclesiastical institutions (e.g., the African Methodist Episcopal Church, the National Baptist Convention, USA, Inc., the Church of God in Christ) which could be chronicled over long periods—more than two centuries back, in some cases. But moving in this direction would exclude the religious life of the majority of Black people during most of this country's history, because Blacks were not affiliated *en masse* with official denominational structures until just after the Civil War. Furthermore, as this volume will demonstrate, African American religious life has never been confined solely to the Christian tradition. It has found expression in Islam, Judaism, Hinduism, Vodun, New Thought, and many other religious modalities, some created *de novo*.[1] The scope is widened still more because even when African Americans adhere in name to existing religious traditions, the reality of the Diaspora is that, as William Watty points out,

> Everywhere, creolization has taken place to a greater or lessor degree. Voodoo in Haiti is not the Voodoo in Dahomey. Shango in Trinidad is not the Shango of Yorubaland, the Black Muslims are a far cry from Mecca, the Black Jews are not recognized in Zion. Each has represented an accommodation on the part of Black People to historical situations in varying degrees in selection and rejection.

Watty goes on to include in this assessment the Black Christian churches in the US, which also evolved in distinction from their larger White Christian context. While acknowledging the reactive dimension of alienation and protest in this process of evolving, Watty focuses on what is for him the more determinative, pro-active dynamic, saying,

> These [churches] are not some unfortunate aberrations of or deviations from some pre-supposed universal Christianity but, on the contrary, represent the essence of Christianity, which is only authenticated as it is accommodated, [as it] reckons with the scandal and the glory of particularity.[2]

Finally, a real dynamism of religion in the African American community has often come from individuals and groups of persons acting out of religious conviction but acting on their own, rather than at the behest of a religious institution or judicatory, even when they were so affiliated. *Religious history*, then, because it is broad and encompassing, takes in the variety of both institutional and noninstitutional religious developments which are essential parts of the story of African American life.

Religion in African American Life

A characterization of African Americans commonly offered by Black and White commentators, alike, is that they are "a religious people." To what degree is such a designation accurate? Contemporary research is revealing increasing evidence of African religious beliefs and behaviors that survived enslavement and transportation to the Americas, in spite of the conscious attempt of the slavery system to obliterate all cultural memory and sense of group identity. Survival and reconstruction of African traditions has been much more obvious and complete in Latin America and the Caribbean than in the US. The descriptive reporting of Florestan Fernandes and Donald Pierson on Brazil, Zora Neale Hurston on Jamaica, Maya Deren on Haiti, and many others, shows just how much this is so [though one must bear in mind William Watty's observation concerning the creolization of these traditions].

In the U.S., the reassertion of African cultural systems was expressly not tolerated. Yet scholars are discovering the glitches in the enforcement of this intolerance. Clear Africanisms are to be found in the African Americans' diet, dress, language, musical instrumentation and composition, styles of labor, thought patterns, religio-philosophical ideas and values, and many other areas. These are identified and discussed in the writings of Herskovits, John

Blassingame, and Albert Raboteau, among others. A suggestive sampling is given in the present volume in the entry by Lillian Ashcraft-Eason, treating Blacks in the colonial period. One sees, then, the demonstration of Margaret Mead's point that cultures are resilient, having the power of continuity to survive invasive assault. And, suggests Mead, even in situations of extensive systemic disruption, cultural fragments may survive by adapting new forms as the vehicles for old meanings and infusing old forms with new meanings.[3]

Thus, some Africans transported to North America must have arrived with elements of traditional African religion intact, or at least as usable fragmentary resources. From the early days of slavery up to the present, one could find practitioners of traditional African religious ceremonies and quasi-religious conjuring arts. One could also find persons acting out of a remembered Muslim heritage.

Now there was a deep ambivalence among Anglo Christians concerning evangelization of African slaves due, to fear of its consequences for the security of the slavery system and for the continued subordination of Blacks. After all, by common custom in the West, Christians were not to hold other Christians in involuntary servitude. As these fears were allayed by civil and ecclesiastical decrees, evangelization increasingly occurred.

A number of factors, including the ongoing resistance of slave owners and the perennial shortage of clergy to service even the White population, prevented evangelization from ever becoming anything like universal. W. E. B. DuBois estimated the ratio of confessing slave Christians at approximately one in ten. Others have set the number somewhat higher, e.g., one in six.[4] In either case, the minority percentage perhaps represents both the limited extent of gospel contact and also the differential response of slaves to the presentation of the Christian message. Some were convicted by the preaching and became authentic converts; some preferred to continue in whatever mode of religious adaptation on which they had already settled; others rejected the Christian message, either because of the slavery-supporting form in which it typically was presented or because of the identification of the messenger with the slavery system itself.

And yet, Judeo-Christian language, symbols, and images were integrated into the larger cultural framework in which all US residents, slave or free, lived their lives, and all, ultimately, were influenced thereby. Looking back, then, to the matter of African Americans as "a religious people," one is led to say that this perception is owing not so much to any actual greater inherent religious sensibility or theistic orientation among Africans and their Diaspora descendants. Rather, it would seem that religion's function of addressing issues of identity, security, and purposiveness has had a much more engaging pertinence for African Americans than for some other groups, given the nature of their historical status and their treatment in the American context. Depersonalized by an external definition as chattel/property; marginalized in social intercourse; excluded by statute and common practice from participation in the privileges and institutional processes of the nation; their physical existence, itself, devalued and under continuous threat, even from the enforcers of the law—these challenges have been cast in the very serviceable categories of religion and addressed through the primary, sometimes sole agencies of advocacy at their disposal, namely, the churches and other religious institutions.

In the constraining, inhibiting context in which most of African America has lived for most of its history, religion has been an arena of freedom. Religion happens internally, beyond society's proscriptive reach. In its institutional expression, whether the "invisible institution" of the slaves or the more formal, overt structures of free persons, there has been afforded to Blacks a level of ownership and self-determination, indeed self-articulation, largely unavailable in any other sphere before the present time. Hence the centrality of religious institutions in African American community life. Further, such authors as Richard Wright and Howard Thurman, in their autobiographies, have spoken of the role of the Black Church in providing a sense of place and belonging, of personal meaningfulness and existential stability to its members.

Not all persons in Black communities have been subscribers to the confessions of the various religious institutions nor consistent participants in their associational life. At least one study has shown that in such overt expressions of religiosity as church attendance, Black people hardly, if at all, exceed other segments of the population.[5] Yet, by and large, Black Americans have inherited a religious vocabulary, primarily Judeo-Christian, which colors and adds grace notes to their articulation of their reality. They have inherited a religious conceptual framework, largely Judeo-Christian but informed by residual African categories and filtered through their American experience. Through this framework their reality is interpreted and understood and issues of present well-being and ultimate destiny are addressed.

Religion among African Americans has been more than a stratagem for survival and psych-emotional stability. It has been an appropriate, authentic response to what they have experienced as a benevolent, transcendent Being—a response of wonder and trust, of awe and gratitude. That response has been creatively particularized, as illustrated by entries in this volume by James Evans on Black Theology; Henry Mitchell on Black preaching; Portia Maultsby on Black sacred music; the entry by the editors on Black Judaism; and the introductory essay by John Cartwright on the religiously rooted social activism of Martin Luther King, Jr. While particularizing from existing models, African Americans have shown religious innovation, also, in theological formulation, organizational design, and the application of religion to the challenges and promises of life. This will be seen many times in the pages of this volume.

Beyond the Present Work

A religious history of African American people has yet to be written. Important works have been produced examining the development of a distinctive Afro-Christian tradition during the colonial and national periods among slaves and free Blacks. Notable examples are Carter G. Woodson's early *History of the Negro Church*; W. E. B. DuBois' Atlanta University Study on *The Negro Church*; Albert Raboteau's *Slave Religion*. Such works have tended to focus upon Blacks in evangelical Protestantism, with some lesser attention to other streams of tradition, mainly Christian. Helpful histories have been done on the rise and organizational development of independent Black denominational bodies, especially Methodist and Baptist, though not all groups have been the subjects of recent or updated works. Many Black sub-groups and caucuses in predominantly White denominations have been treated. For instance, Gayraud Wilmore has published on Black Presbyterians; Cyprian Davis on Black Catholics; William B. McClain on Blacks in United Methodism. Other specialized works have examined Black Muslims; Black Pentecostals; Blacks in Spiritualism, Eastern religions, the occult; Black religious nationalism; and more. Provocative thematic works have highlighted what their authors believed to be key trajectories in Black religion. In two examples, Leonard Barrett in a book of the same name spoke of a "soul force" in Black religion; Mechal Sobel sought to trace out an African American "sacred cosmos." Writers in a variety of disciplines have explored the development of aspects of Black religion such as theology, music, preaching, social philosophy, institutional management, and gender roles.

A few writers have attempted to encompass African American religious history in an interpretative paradigm. For instance, Gayraud Wilmore wrote of it as the successive ebb and flow of "radicalism," in terms of the activist, prophetic Judeo-Christian stream of social transformation. Vincent Harding's recent two volume work on the social history of African Americans sees religion as a core element of the story. He employs the image of a river to represent Black people as they move with variable but determined force toward freedom.

Sociologists have compiled and analyzed the data on Black religious beliefs and behaviors and on the social milieux in which these have been operative. E. Franklin Frazier set the terms for much of the early discussion about the nature of the Black religion in America. It was he who coined the phrase "invisible institution" to refer to church-type activities among the slaves. Benjamin Mays and Joseph Nicholson undertook major sociological research in the 1930s to illuminate Black church life and Black understandings of God. Most recently, C. Eric Lincoln and Lawrence Mamiya replicated the Mays/Nicholson study on an even grander scale. The resulting volume of history and sociological analysis entitled *The Black Church in the African American Experience* has been broadly acclaimed as a major extension of knowledge and understanding on the subject.

Yet, Lincoln and Mamiya treat only the seven historic Black Christian denominations. The persistent and intriguing fact of African American religious life is its wide-ranging diversity, well beyond mainline Protestant Christianity, and its depth of conviction across the range. A religious history of the African American people that is conscientiously inclusive must meet the challenge that its subject is *encyclopedic*. It is the hope of the present editors that this volume will illumine the task, serve as a useful resource on its own, and point directions for work yet to be done.

References

1. The comprehensive chronicling of Black religious groups really began in the several issues of the *Religious Census* issued by the United States Department of Commerce. That project was dropped following the 1936 issue. It was revived in 1977 and 1979 by *The Directory of Religious Bodies in the United States* (New York: Garland, 2nd ed., 1992) and the *Encyclopedia of American Religions* (Detroit: Gale Research, 4th ed., 1993) authored by J. Gordon Melton. These volumes, periodically updated, provide entries on all of the Black denominations and religious groups within the larger coverage of American religions. Melton has also recently completed a companion volume, *Religious Organizations of America* (Detroit: Gale Research) which also includes

comprehensive coverage of Black religious organizations. Melton's work has been joined by the valuable *Directory of African American Religious Bodies* edited by Wardell J. Payne (Washington, DC: Howard University Press, 1991) which provides a primary focus on those people and organizations functioning primarily within the Black community.

2. William Watty, "Black Religion in the Caribbean—Present and Future." Paper delivered at the Annual Meeting of the Society for the Study of Black Religion, Kingston, Jamaica, November 25, 1986.

3. Cf. Mead, *Culture and Commitment* (Garden City, NY: Natural History Press/Doubleday & Co., 1970): Chap. 1.

4. Cf. Gunnar Myrdal, *An American Dilemma* (New York: Harper and Bros., 1944): 860; W. E. B. DuBois, *The Negro Church* (Atlanta: Atlanta University Press, 1903).

5. Cf. C. Eric Lincoln and Lawrence H. Mamiya, *The Black Church in the African American Experience* (Durham, NC: Duke University Press, 1990): 382.

Martin Luther King, Jr.
and
Modern African American Religion

by

John Henderson Cartwright

[*Editors note:* In compiling this *Encyclopedia*, the editors came to the conclusion that African American history (both secular and sacred) could be divided into three periods. The dividing line between the first and second era was provided by the Civil War, the Emancipation Proclamation, and the new opportunities they initiated. The dividing line between the second and third period was the civil rights movement of the 1950s and 1960s. That movement was carried by the unique gestalt of ideas articulated by Martin Luther King, Jr. The vitality of African American life in the last generation, it could be argued, grows out of the continuance of King's life and work through those who consider themselves his students, and the reaction to him by those who considered his perspective and program limited or ultimately a failure. In either case, King stands as the dividing line of modern Black history. Hence, we asked John Cartwright, one of the major interpreters of King's life, to prepare this summary of his thought and its religious roots.]

Undoubtedly, Martin Luther King, Jr., was both one of the most influential and one of the most controversial figures of the twentieth century. All indications suggest that he will remain so for the foreseeable future. He was a young man of 39 years when an assassin's bullet took his life on Thursday, April 4, 1968. His entire ministry had been in the service of civil rights and equal justice for the poor and oppressed, regardless of race, creed, or color.

Choosing to enter the full-time pastoral ministry while completing his doctorate in systematic theology at Boston University, King accepted a call in 1954 to become pastor of Dexter Avenue Baptist Church in Montgomery, Alabama. Approximately one year later, when Mrs. Rosa Parks refused to give up her seat on a city bus and the Blacks of Montgomery rose up in protest, the youthful King was thrust into a leadership role which he would carry for the remainder of his life.

Though options to preach or teach in the North were open to them, both Martin and his spouse, **Coretta Scott King**, accepted the call from Dexter Avenue Baptist Church in the spirit of sacrificial vocation. "We agreed," he said, "that, in spite of the disadvantages and inevitable sacrifices, our greatest service would be rendered in our native South. We came to the conclusion that we had something of a moral obligation to return—at least for a few years." Thus, the two of them shared the ministry, the cause, and the sacrifices fully together.

Of the variety of images that come to mind when one mentions the name of Martin Luther King, Jr.—champion of civil rights, head of the **Southern Christian Leadership Conference** (S.C.L.C.), orator, Nobel Peace laureate, disciple of Mahatma Gandhi—perhaps the only image that truly would do justice to the whole of his personhood is simply that of a committed Christian minister. Of course, there are those who maintain that he perverted the Christian message, and conversely, those who feel that he captured its very essence. Whatever the case, there can be no doubt but that he based his words and deeds on his Christian convictions. The numerous and all too frequent distortions and misrepresentations of King's life and message, by friend and foe alike, can be attributed in large measure to a failure to recognize this cardinal fact and its entailments.

Thus, it was neither King the humble humanitarian nor King the rootless radical who challenged the status quo of the 1950s and 60s. Rather, it was King the committed Christian who, firmly grounded in that tradition, reminded his Christian brothers and sisters that:

> You have a dual citizenry. You live both in time and eternity. Your highest loyalty is to God, and not to the mores or the folkways, the state or the nation, or any man-made institution. If any earthly institution or custom conflicts with God's will, it is your Christian duty to oppose it. You must never allow the transitory, evanescent demands of man-made institutions to take precedence over the eternal demands of the Almighty God.

Likewise the point of departure of King's social philosophy and vision of the goal of human society was fundamentally religious, rooted in his personal faith in God and in the power of love to transform the hearts and minds of all God's children, regardless of race, creed, status, or nationality. Furthermore, despite the degree of influence on him by non-Christian sources—e.g., the classical philosophers, Karl Marx, and especially Mahatma Gandhi—the fact remains that his "intellectual" categories were drawn almost exclusively from Christian theology and morality.

A Christian Social Ideal

King referred to his conception of the Christian social ideal as the "Beloved Community." Although King does not specifically account for his use of the expression "Beloved Community," the term was a part of the popular theological vocabulary of the Boston University School of Theology during the period when he was in attendance there as a doctoral student (1951–1955). As a technical term, however, the Beloved Community can be traced to the philosophical writings of Josiah Royce (1855–1916) who, along with his teacher, R. H. Lotze, played a major role in the development of the school of thought that is called "personal idealism" or "personalism." King would have been well acquainted with Royce, for Boston University was a center for personalism and three of the leading personalists of that time—Edgar S. Brightman, Peter A. Bertocci, and L. Harold DeWolf—were King's primary instructors, with DeWolf also serving as his major professor. King tells of their influence:

> It was mainly under these teachers that I studied personalistic philosophy—the theory that the clue to the meaning of ultimate reality is found in personality. This personal idealism remains today my basic philosophical position.

The debt to Royce not only for the term, Beloved Community, but also for a great deal of its meaning for King is apparent from the following passage expressing Royce's idea of the universal community:

> All morality, namely, is, from this point of view, to be judged by the standards of the BELOVED COMMUNITY, of the ideal Kingdom of Heaven. Concretely stated, this means that you are to test every course of action not by the question: What can we find in the parables or in the Sermon on the Mount which seems to us more or less directly to bear upon this special matter? The central doctrine of the Master was: 'So act that the Kingdom of Heaven may come.' This means: So act as to help, however you can, and whenever you can towards making mankind one loving brotherhood, whose love is not a mere affection for morally detached individuals, but a love of the unity of its own life upon its own divine level, and a love of individuals in so far as they can be raised to communion with this spiritual community itself.

Royce goes on to stress both loyalty and sacrifice. For him, loyalty is "the Will to Believe in something eternal, and to express that belief in the practical life of a human being." But what would loyalty be without trial? To be loyal to the ideal of the Beloved Community one finds the universal meaning of sacrifice. "So the sacrifice of Christ is emulated by the death of each individual man—death to selfishness . . . the death thus died by membership in the 'Beloved Community,' means the sacrifice of individual desires in the interest of the ideal brotherhood of all."

Although these themes were to become central ingredients in King's conception of the Beloved Community, he cites as the major influence Walter Rauschenbusch's interpretation of the Kingdom of God and its relationship to the idea of an inclusive human community. King stated that he indeed found the theological basis for his social concern in the thought of Rauschenbusch—in his emphasis on Christian social responsibility and his insistence that the gospel at its best deals with the whole man, not only his soul but also his body; not only his spiritual well-being but his material well-being. This is no doubt true, but it is equally true that King was not explicitly aware of the salient influence of Royce on Rauschenbusch. Not only in general did Royce's philosophy influence him considerably. Rauschenbusch acknowledged his debt to Royce's *The Problem of Christianity* in aiding him to arrive at a solidaristic view of society and an interpretation of many traditional Christian doctrines in social terms. In any case, the central and all-pervading theme for Rauschenbusch was the Kingdom of God. The Kingdom is the social ideal of Christendom; it was also the first and most essential dogma of the Christian faith. Thus the Kingdom was both a religious and a social doctrine: religious in that it is "divine in its origin, progress and consummation, and is the continuous revelation of the power, the righteousness, and the love of God;" social in that the Kingdom is "always both present and future . . . always coming, always pressing in on the present, always big with possibility, and always inviting immediate action" that promotes the progressive unity of mankind.

The organic centrality of the doctrine of the Kingdom led Rauschenbusch to conclude that the Christian religion, itself, is essentially corporate and communal in character. He stated, therefore, that the fundamental purpose of Christianity is "to transform human society into the Kingdom of God by regenerating all human relations and reconstituting them in accordance with the will of God." Hence the Kingdom is synonymous with a transformed and regenerated society; for, in the words of his classic definition, it is "humanity organized according to the will of God" and "the organized fellowship of humanity acting under the impulse of love."

King was quite sympathetic with this outlook, although he was at odds with Rauschenbusch on two counts. First, he felt that Rauschenbusch had fallen victim to the nineteenth-century "cult-of-inevitable progress" which led him to a superficial optimism concerning man's nature. Secondly, he thought that Rauschenbusch came perilously close to identifying the Kingdom of God with a particular social and economic system. Nevertheless, King acknowledged his indebtedness to Christian liberalism in general and to Walter Rauschenbusch in particular for giving him a theological basis for the social concern which had already grown up in him as a result of his early experiences of racial and economic injustice. The overwhelming evidence supports the view that these sources, furthermore, were the basis both for King's "I have a dream" general theme and for his idea of the Beloved Community in particular.

This is not to say, however, that there were no other influences in the development of the idea of the Beloved Community. Indeed, King was an eclectic thinker with a greater genius for synthesizing extant ideas than creating them. He read all of the influential historical thinkers in dialectical fashion and attempted in his own mind to synthesize the partial truths and partial errors that he found there. Thus the idea of the Beloved Community is comprised of some primary elements taken from several sources. The Christian liberalism of the "Social Gospel" variety provided the theological foundations; the personal idealism of Brightman, DeWolf, et. al., contributed philosophical foundations; the philosophy of nonviolence of Henry David Thoreau and Mahatma Gandhi provided the means; and the "Christian realism" of Reinhold Niebuhr, with its emphasis on the human capacity for evil and its pessimism about human effort in attaining social ideals qualified both King's optimism about its historical attainment and his attitude toward the kind of tactics needed for its fulfillment.

Following Rauschenbusch, however, King directly related all of his social and theological concerns to the central place he assigned to the Beloved Community. Underlying all of King's thought and activity was this vision of the Beloved Community and the hope that one day an inclusive human community would be actualized.

Despite the ubiquity of the idea of the Beloved Community in King's writings and speeches, nowhere did he attempt to delineate or systematize fully his vision. In general it can be said, however, that for King: 1) the Beloved Community would be the ideal corporate expression of the Christian faith; and, 2) it is a fully integrated and inclusive community of love and justice and brotherhood. Indeed, after the formation in 1957 of the Southern Christian Leadership Conference, King described the purpose of that organization as follows: "The ultimate aim of S.C.L.C. is to foster and create the 'beloved community' in America . . . S.C.L.C. works for integration. Our ultimate goal is genuine intergroup and interpersonal living—integration."

Although the concept of "integration" was conceived within the context of racial conflict in America, King saw in this idea the total interrelatedness of the whole human family. It included not only all races, but also all classes, all ethnic groups, all nations, and all religions; for "we are tied together in the single garment of destiny, caught in an inescapable network of mutuality." Therefore, "no man is an island" and "do not ask for whom the bells toll," as King would so often summarize in quoting from the father of metaphysical poetry, Canon John Donne.

He was equally aware that there is a moral difference between integration and desegregation. For him, desegregation is at bottom negative because it only eliminates discrimination in those areas of social life that can be corrected by law. Integration, on the other hand, is much more inclusive and positive in that it implies the loving acceptance of individuals and groups into the total range of human activities. Thus desegregation cannot be the hallmark of the Beloved Community because at best it will only create "a society where men are physically desegregated and spiritually segregated, and where elbows are together and hearts apart. It gives us social togetherness and spiritual apartness. It leaves us with a stagnant equality of sameness rather than a constructive equality of oneness."

Finally, as with Rauschenbusch, King could not envision the Beloved Community apart from the question of economic justice. This must be a society that is not only free from the malformation of persons resulting from racial hatred but also free from the "malformation of persons resulting from economic injustice and exploitation." And because he believed that injustice anywhere is a threat to justice everywhere, economic and social liberation is basically a matter of justice and not of race. He was concerned that justice not be seen apart from the indivisibility of human existence. Thus to King, the Beloved Community would reflect the intention of God that all his children should have the physical as well as the spiritual necessities of life.

King never attached a label to his economic views, although he was certainly influenced by Karl Marx and other critics of capitalism. Obviously he needed not search further for a revolutionary economic posture since Protestant liberalism had already convinced him of the radical and revolutionary quality of a "properly conceived" Christian faith. However, his rather thoroughgoing egalitarian and somewhat socialist approach to questions of wealth and property could allow one to label him a "democratic socialist." He said, for example, "life is sacred. Property is intended to serve life, and no matter how much we surround it with rights and respect, it has no personal being. It is part of the earth man walks on; it is not man."

In any case, he rejected both doctrinaire capitalism and doctrinaire communism in terms of the goal of the Beloved Community. He stated, rather, in typical King fashion, that "the Kingdom of God is neither the thesis of individual enterprise nor the antithesis of collective enterprise, but a synthesis which reconciles the truth of both."

In singling out the matter of economic justice within the idea of the Beloved Community, King combined two traditional Biblical themes—the "holiness of the poor" and the "blessed community." One might conclude in this regard that in King's social thought, Blacks became the embodiment of "the poor" and integration represented the vision of "the holy community." Furthermore, for King these two elements—the holy oppressed and the blessed community—are not merely interrelated; they are inseparable. Without the vision of restored community, the poor are relegated to perpetual alienation from political participation and made the objects of charity and social service programs.

In summary, King's own description of his vision of the Beloved Community will suffice:

> The dream is one of equality of opportunity, of privilege and property widely distributed; a dream of a land where men will not take necessities from the many to give luxuries to the few; a dream of a land where men do not argue that the color of a man's skin determines the content of his character; a dream of a place where all our gifts and resources are held not for ourselves alone but as instruments of service for the rest of humanity . . . where every man will respect the dignity and worth of all human personality, and men will dare to live together as brothers . . . Whenever it is fulfilled, we will emerge from the bleak and desolate midnight of man's inhumanity to man into the bright and glowing daybreak of freedom and justice for all of God's children.

The Beloved Community and the Kingdom of God

It is noteworthy that one finds an absence of explicit reference to and explication of the doctrine of the Kingdom of God in the writings of King. However, references to the idea of the Beloved Community occur throughout his writings and occupy a central place in them. The explanation for this fact is undoubtedly that for King the Beloved Community and the Kingdom of God are synonymous.

It is additionally plausible that King intentionally substituted one for the other in order to avoid any identification of his idea of the Kingdom with the more traditional idea of an other-worldly realm quite removed from this earth. Credence for this point of view is enhanced by the tenor of a rare passage from King on the meaning of the Kingdom of God for him.

> Jesus took over the phrase 'the Kingdom of God,' but he changed its meaning. He refused entirely to be the kind of a Messiah that his contemporaries expected. Jesus made love the mark of sovereignty. Here we are left with no doubt as to Jesus' meaning. The Kingdom of God will be a society in which men and women live as children of God should live. It will be a kingdom controlled by the law of love . . . Many have attempted to say that the ideal of a better world will be worked out in the next world. But Jesus taught men to say, "Thy will be done in earth, as it is in heaven." Although the world seems to be in bad shape today, we must never lose faith in the power of God to achieve His purpose.

From this passage it is also clear that King and Rauschenbusch agreed completely that the Kingdom is "humanity organized according to the will of God." The idea of the Kingdom, furthermore, was seen by both as corrective not only to the error of spiritualizing the Kingdom by projecting it into the world-to-come, but also the error of identifying the Kingdom with a particular social or political philosophy.

Moreover, for King it was especially important that the controlling concept of the Kingdom be that of "community." Indeed, one could characterize his whole theology as a theology of community. Pivotal to that theology is a doctrine of creation which purports that persons were not only made in the image of God but also, and of equal importance, they were made for relationship. Just as the Imago Dei became the basis for the individual's dignity and worth, created relatedness becomes the basis for community. Since we are all children of the same Father-Creator, we are all one family, one community, inseparably bound together. Segregation, therefore, is so profoundly wrong because it denies relationship, just as does anything else which perverts or destroys community. Therefore, to oppose inclusive community is to resist the very laws of God's created order. King even interpreted the crucifixion-resurrection-pentecost events in terms of community:

> The Cross is the eternal expression of the length to which God will go in order to restore broken community. The resurrection is a symbol of God's triumph over all the forces that seek to block community. The Holy Spirit is the continuing community-creating reality that moves through history.

From this central idea of community, King drew two further conclusions which became basic to both his idea of the Beloved Community and to his active ministry. The first was the conviction that there cannot be community without social justice. For him, the Hebrew prophets, in proclaiming that Yahweh is a just and righteous God who requires justice and righteousness from his children, were not merely voicing a demand for conformity of humanity of God. They were enunciating a prerequisite for the existence of community. Without the justice and righteousness of peace, freedom, equality, and harmony, community becomes sounding brass and tinkling cymbal. Thus community and justice are welded of necessity. Community without justice is hollow; justice without community is blind. The former begets colonialism; the latter, paternalism. Both are denials of the intention of the Creator.

The second conclusion emerging from the idea of community was framed around the New Testament concept of *agape* (love). Contrasting *agape* with the other two words for love in the Greek New Testament (eros and philia), King thought *agape* to be the essence of the Christian Gospel. It is characterized by "understanding, redeeming good will for all men. It is an overflowing love which is purely spontaneous, unmotivated, groundless, and creative. It is not set in motion by any quality or function of its object. It is the love of God operating in the human heart."

This concept of *agape* allowed King to make the critical distinction between that which underlies community and that which creates and sustains it. Justice undergirds community but cannot create it. Justice, King would say, may help to form an inclusive neighborhood, but only love can produce an inclusive neighborliness. It is the only force that can bring community into existence because its inherent unselfishness leads to cooperation instead of competition and conflict. In sum, *agape* is "love in action. *Agape* is love seeking to preserve and create community. It is insistence on community even when one seeks to break it. *Agape* is willing to sacrifice in the interest of mutuality. *Agape* is a willingness to go to any length to restore community." Thus it becomes clear why King was so insistent on going beyond the justice of desegregation to the love of integration, beyond association to community—the Beloved Community of the Kingdom of God.

The Realization of the Beloved Community

The demands of the Gospel, as King saw them, propelled him into his pilgrimage toward nonviolence. This was no journey for a dilettante, but rather a sober and careful attempt at the formulation of comprehensive and coherent social philosophy grounded in the metaphysics of a personal God, a Christian systematic theology, and an ethics of the dignity and worth of all human personality. This fundamentally religious vision of the goal of human society was rooted also in King's deep personal faith in God and in the power of love which he believed could transform the hearts and minds of all God's children, regardless of race, creed, status, or nationality.

The main original theological contribution of King's tragically shortened career was his remarkably consistent translating of his positive theological tenets into action. In this process he related his theological beliefs in an authentic and original way to various social theories and movements. At Boston University his theoretical position was being crystallized but not tested in action. One could say, therefore, that a fundamental aspect of Montgomery, of Selma, of Birmingham and all the rest was their being test-grounds—proving grounds, if you will—for the adequacy of his theological position. On such battlefields one's ideals are either smashed or strengthened, abandoned or defended, compromised or held steadfast.

In the thinking through of so comprehensive a dream as that which King envisioned, and assuming as he did, intellectual categories and concepts derived almost exclusively from Christian theology and morality, three fundamental problems become the foci of this constructive activity.

The first was that of developing and articulating a social vision as the goal of our earthly striving. Thus, King asked: "From a Christian perspective, what kind of society must human society be when human society truly becomes?" The Beloved Community, which was discussed earlier, became the central focus in this regard.

The second problem involved methodology. Given his belief that means and ends must cohere, King asked: "By what 'legitimate' means can we transform our social existence in light of the present condition of humanity?"

The last problem centered in King's belief that the essence of the Christian Gospel is love, which is a translation of *agape*. Given both the commandment to love and a sin-sick world, King asked: "How can love become incarnate without becoming at the same time either some kind of sentimentality or, as with the Kantian categorical imperative, a sublime but unrealizable and frustrating 'ought'?"

These latter two problems put into focus the matter of achieving the goal of the Beloved Community. Once again, the starting point for King was the connectedness of all life. In the closing chapter of *Where Do We Go from Here: Chaos or Community?*, King speaks eloquently of the moral solidarity of the human race.

> From time immemorial human beings have lived by the principle that 'self-preservation is the first law of life.' But this is a false assumption. I would say that other-preservation is the first law of life precisely because we cannot preserve self without being concerned about preserving other selves.

This follows from the fact that deeply woven into the fiber of our religious tradition is the conviction that persons are made in the image of God, and that they are souls of infinite metaphysical value. If we accept this as a profound moral fact, we cannot be content to see our fellow human beings hungry, to see them victimized with ill-health, when we have the means to help them.

We must recognize, said King, that all persons are truly interdependent. "Every nation is an heir of a vast treasury of ideas and labor to which both the living and the dead of all nations have contributed. Whether we realize it or not, each of us lives eternally 'in the red.' We are everlasting debtors to known and unknown men and women." All life, therefore, in a profound sense, is interrelated. In materialistic economic terms, mankind is the unit of cooperation. In spiritual and moral terms, humanity is the unit of uplift, betterment and respect.

In this call to transcend the petty boundaries of class, race, sex, nationality, etc., as a moral duty to the norm of universal community and humanity, King was essentially attempting to provide the moral foundations for the transition from a limited perspective and exclusiveness to the idea of universal community.

Universal community for King means several things. In the first place, it means a continued emphasis on both the personal and the social aspects of religion. The idea of the self-sufficient soul must never be allowed to subsume the meaning of the Gospel. As King stated,

> We must come to see that the Christian gospel is a two-way road. On the one side, it seeks to change the souls of persons and thereby unite them with God; on the other side it seeks to change the environmental conditions of men so that the soul will have a chance after it is changed. Any religion that professes to be concerned with the souls of persons and yet is not concerned with the economic and social conditions that strangle them [is barbarous].

Secondly, inclusive community points to the vision of mankind becoming "one world" as a condition of peace, if not survival. King states,

> We have inherited a large house, a great 'world house' in which we have to live together—black and white, Easterner and Westerner, Gentile and Jew, Catholic and Protestant, Moslem and Hindu—a family unduly separated in ideas, culture and interest, who, because we can never again live apart, must somehow live with each other in peace.

King believed that peace is heavily dependent on our loyalties becoming more ecumenical rather than sectional:

> Our loyalties must transcend our race, our tribe, our class, and our nation; and this means that we must develop a world perspective. No individual can live alone, and as long as we try, the more we are going to have war in this world. Now the

judgment of God is upon us, and we must either learn to live together as brothers and sisters or we are all going to perish together as fools.

At King's funeral, Benjamin Mays pointed to King's motif of "one world community:" "He [King] was supra-race, supra-nation, supra-denomination, supra-class, supra-culture. . . He belonged to the world and to mankind. Now he belongs to posterity."

Finally, universal community entails the idea of Christian vocation and commitment. In a 1965 interview with Alex Haley, King was recounting mistakes that he had made in leading the civil rights movement. He sorrowfully reported that,

the most pervasive mistake . . . was in believing that because our cause was just, we could be sure that the white ministers of the South, once their Christian consciences were challenged, would rise to our aid. I felt that white ministers would take our cause to the white power structures. I ended up, of course, chastened and disillusioned. As our movement unfolded, and direct appeals were made to white ministers, most folded their hands—and some even had stands against us.

King was then asked if he disagreed with their stated reason for refusing help, which was that it is not the proper role of the church to "intervene in secular affairs." King responded most emphatically in the affirmative and went on to elaborate.

The essence of the Epistles of Paul is that Christians should rejoice at being deemed worthy to suffer for what they believe. The projection of a social gospel, in my opinion, is the true witness of a Christian life. This is the meaning of the true ekklesia—the inner, spiritual church. The Church once changed society. It was then a thermostat of society. But today I feel that too much of the church is merely a thermometer, which measures rather than molds popular opinion.

The laxity of the white church and of white ministers was particularly painful to King, especially when one remembers that his "Letter from a Birmingham Jail" (1963) was addressed to a group of white clergymen who had publicly criticized King for "unwise and untimely" demonstrations. Later on, King reflects.

I will remain true to the church as long as I live. But the laxity of the white church collectively has caused me to weep tears of love. There cannot be deep disappointment without deep love. Time and time again in my travels, as I have seen the outward beauty of white churches, I have had to ask myself, "What kind of people worship there? Who is their God? Is their God the God of Abraham, Isaac, and Jacob, and is their Savior the Savior who hung on the cross at Golgotha? Where were their voices when a black race took upon itself the cross of protest against human injustice to their fellow humans? Where were their voices when defiance and hatred were called for by white persons who sat in these very churches?" My optimism about help from the white church was shattered; and on too many occasions since, my hopes for the white church have been dashed.

King died still nurturing an amazement at the sheer amount of hypocrisy within the Christian Church.

Finally, the idea of nonviolence was for King the key concept that linked not only the methodology of inclusive community with the commandment to love, but also reconciled the often polar norms of love, power, and justice. Put into a simple formula it can still be stated as follows: What is needed is a realization that power without love is reckless and abusive and that love without power is sentimental and anemic. Power at its best is love implementing the demands of justice. Justice at its best is love correcting everything that stands against love. There is nothing essentially wrong with power. The problem is that in most situations power is unequally distributed. This has led Black Americans, for example, in the past to seek their goals through love and moral suasion devoid of power and white Americans to seek their goals through power devoid of love and conscience. This is the often-seen occurrence of the confrontation of immoral power and powerless morality. Inclusive community must have as a prerequisite, therefore, some means of sharing power. And since authentic community can exist only on the strength of goodwill and mutuality, the means for attaining the end of community must be inherently benevolent. Nonviolence is the only such means. It is both loving and confrontational, respectful and principled, judging and redeeming.

In his first book, *Stride Toward Freedom*, King recounts his "Pilgrimage to Nonviolence." Conspicuously absent from that account, however, is any mention of **Howard Thurman**, noted Black Baptist preacher and mystic who was a contemporary and friend of Martin's parents and who was Dean of the Chapel at Boston University during King's matriculation as a doctoral student.

Interestingly, as early as 1935, Thurman was searching for a means by which he could operationalize the love-ethic in the struggle for wholeness and community. Thus began his pilgrimage to nonviolence. Luther Smith states that,

> The development of a philosophy of non-violent protest for the Black struggle is a foremost achievement of his [Thurman's] social witness. Here Thurman makes a signal contribution to providing a method for change in American race relations. He has done more than any other person to articulate the ethical and spiritual necessity for Blacks' civil liberties struggle to be grounded in the principles of non-violence.

Indeed there is a profound affinity between Thurman and his younger contemporary, Martin Luther King, Jr., with regard to the explication of nonviolence. Five common points can be identified from their various writings:

1. That nonviolent resistance is not a method for cowards, for it does resist evil.
2. That it does not seek to humiliate the opponent, but to win understanding and friendship.
3. That the attack is directed against forces of evil rather than against the persons doing the evil.
4. That it willingly accepts suffering without retaliation, including violence.
5. That it avoids not only external physical violence but also internal violence of the spirit.

Thurman saw, as did King, that those principles would tend to introduce new possibilities for reconciliation between the oppressed and the powerful. They would permit love to enter conflict creatively and thus to address the real problem—the spiritual ills of separation, fear, hate, and deception.

On the subject of King and Thurman, it is interesting to note that there is a good deal of speculation regarding the probable influence of Thurman on King. Such speculation stems in part from the report by historian/journalist Lerone Bennett, Jr., that while interviewing King during the 1956 Montgomery bus boycott, he noticed a copy of Thurman's *Jesus and the Disinherited* in King's briefcase. This report makes even more curious the fact that King does not refer explicitly to Thurman in any of his speeches or writings.

Another writer suggests that Thurman might have been the first person to sow the seed of "nonviolent suffering" in the mind of Black Americans. S. P. Fullwinder goes so far as to credit Thurman with indirect responsibility for introducing King to the nonviolent ethic. That scenario goes something like this. Thurman, while Dean of Rankin Chapel at Howard University, went to India and met with Gandhi, who strongly influenced his thinking. Upon his return to Howard University, Thurman urged President Mordecai Johnson of Howard to make the pilgrimage to India in order to hear first-hand Gandhi's views on nonviolence. When President Johnson returned from India, he lectured at Fellowship House in Philadelphia on the Gandhian ethic of love and nonviolence. Martin Luther King, Jr., was in the congregation on that occasion and wrote later in his account of his "Pilgrimage to Nonviolence" that he began to study seriously the usefulness of the nonviolent ethic after hearing Johnson's lecture on Gandhi. For his part, however, Thurman, in his autobiography *With Head and Heart*, never mentions any serious conversation with King about the nonviolent ethic, even though both were at Boston University in the mid 1950s.

Unquestionably both King and Thurman held quite similar views regarding nonviolence and the love ethic. Both dedicated their ministries to revealing the possibilities for community. Both tried to practice the love ethic within their respective arenas of ministry and both with the same designation of the same goal—the beloved community.

Whatever the case may be, King acknowledged that he was so motivated and electrified by Mordecai Johnson's portrayal of the life and teachings of Gandhi that he immediately embarked on a study of Gandhi's writings. He began to have a keen appreciation for the concept of "Satyagraha," which means truth-force or love-force, and its potential in the area of social reform. King went on to state that "it was in this Gandhian emphasis on love and nonviolence that I discovered the method for social reform that I had been seeking," that nonviolence was "the only morally and practically sound method open to oppressed people in their struggle for freedom," and that "Gandhi was probably the first person in history to lift the love ethics of Jesus above mere interaction between individuals to a powerful and effective social force on a large scale."

This was to serve him well in the storm that gathered during his Montgomery ministry. In *Stride Toward Freedom*, he recalls:

When I went to Montgomery as a pastor, I had not the slightest idea that I would later become involved in a crisis in which nonviolent resistance would be applicable. I neither started the protest nor suggested it. I simply responded to the call of the people for a spokesman. When the protest began, my mind, consciously or unconsciously, was driven back to the Sermon on the Mount, with its sublime teachings on love, and to the Gandhian method of nonviolent resistance.

Now in speaking about Christian love, King was quick to acknowledge that it may never be completely fulfilled. He recognized that "men have a tragic inclination to yield to selfish impulses, but one always has the capacity to strive for love. It always remains the regulating ideal." Fundamentalists tend to take everything in the Bible literally, King argued; yet when pressed, most of them write off the phrase "Love your enemies" as unrealistic. Although King himself wrote off a literal view of the virgin birth, he insisted that Jesus' words, as reported in the New Testament, be interpreted literally.

In doing so, he has made what many clergypersons and others consider a singular contribution to modern religious thought. Using the words of Jesus and the example of Gandhi in India, King became one of the first and certainly the foremost in articulating the concept of nonviolent resistance for Christianity in America and, more importantly, in organizing and campaigning for social reform using nonviolent methods and discipline.

Generally speaking, King was a liberal-optimist on the question of the actualization of the "Beloved Community" within history. Whatever naive optimism in this regard he once harbored, the "Christian realism" of Niebuhr had purged. Nevertheless, he found in the social gospel and in personalism an optimism concerning the divine nature which balanced the Niebuhrian pessimistic emphasis on the potential for evil in human nature. This optimism bolstered his faith in the power of God to achieve His purpose among humanity and within history as well as the possibilities of human beings when they allow themselves to become co-workers with God. Thus, to whatever extent the "Kingdom will come," it will be a product of human effort and God's help.

It is difficult to see how King could have come to any other conclusion given his firm conviction that the universe is on the side of justice and righteousness and that as we struggle to defeat the forces of evil, the God of the universe struggles with us. He often said to his followers:

The believer in nonviolence has deep faith in the future. This faith is another reason why the nonviolent resister can accept suffering without retaliation. For he knows that in his struggle for justice he has cosmic companionship . . . Whether we call it an unconscious process, an impersonal Brahman, or a Personal Being of matchless power and infinite love, there is a creative force in this universe that works to bring the disconnected aspects of reality into a harmonious whole.

In the main, King placed less emphasis on the specific question of actualization than on the attributes and qualities which persons must acquire in order to hasten the coming of the Beloved Community and insure its survival. Cardinal among these is the adoption of nonviolence, not merely as a policy or tactic, but as a moral imperative. In the struggle for community, only nonviolence acts to reestablish the wholeness of community and reconciles oppressor with the oppressed. In this regard, there is the implication in King that the Beloved Community would gradually emerge as the by-product of the practice of nonviolence and the realization of wider and wider degrees of social cooperation.

He further stressed the need for loyalty and devotion in pursuit of community. He knew fully well that fulfillment may be nourished by hope but is attained through tenacious work. Each stride toward the goal requires sacrifice, suffering, and struggle. One must be willing to suffer for the sake of others, express love (*agape*) to its fullest extent, and live with devotion, concern for justice, rightness, and harmony with God.

Thus out of King's faith in the power of God, love, and nonviolence to reconcile persons to each other and to God emerged his dream of the Beloved Community—admittedly a "dream," but for King, the committed servant of God, it was the only one that was worthy of the struggle.

References

Branch, Taylor. *Parting the Waters: America in the King Years 1954–63*. New York: Simon and Schuster, Inc., 1988. 1064 pp.

Garrow, David J. *Bearing the Cross: Martin Luther King, Jr. and the Southern Christian Leadership Conference*. New York: William Morrow, 1986. 800 pp.

King, Martin Luther, Jr. *Stride Toward Freedom*. New York: Harper and Row, 1958. 230 pp.

———. *Strength to Love.* New York: Harper and Row, 1963. 146 pp.

———. *Where Do We Go From Here: Chaos or Community?* New York: Harper and Row, 1967. 209 pp.

Smith, Kenneth L., and Ira G. Zepp, Jr. *Search for the Beloved Community: The Thinking of Martin Luther King, Jr.* Valley Forge, PA: Judson Press, 1974. 159 pp.

Symposium #2: "The Philosophical and Theological Influences in the Thought and Action of Martin Luther King Jr." *Debate and Understanding* 1, 3 (1977): 171–216.

Womanist Theology:
Black Women's Experience
as a Source for
Doing Theology

by

Jacquelyn Grant

Introduction

Black theology and other Third World theologies of liberation have shown through their challenge of the methodologies of classical theologies that experience of the dominant culture has been the invisible crucible for theologizing. They have demonstrated that theology is not unrelated to socio-political realities of existence, and that historically it has been used to maintain the social and political advantages of the status quo. The portrayal of the universal God was such that an affirmation of this meant a simultaneous negation of all others' cultural perceptions of the divinity, as well as a negation of those very cultures. Nowhere was this more clear than in the area of Christian foreign missions where conversion to Christianity implicitly meant deculturalization and acceptance of the western value system on the part of Asians, Africans, and Latin Americans. Upon conversion, one had to withdraw from indigenous ways of imaging the divine reality, and embrace foreign, western ways which often served to undergird oppressive religious, social and political structures.

This is true not only in the foreign missions field but also in the western world; it is reflected in the ways in which oppressors deal with oppressed people within their own territory. We see this with respect to Third World people in the first world context as well as with respect to women. The experiences of Black Women provided especially insightful sources for doing theology.

An illustration emerging out of Black theology and Feminist theology will make the point. Theologians in both these camps propose an alternative understanding, for example, of Christian love.

James Cone in an early work makes a distinction between a nonthreatening love of many Christians and the radical love of Jesus which demands justice.

> There is no place in Christian theology for sentimental love—love without risk or cost. Love demands all, the whole of one's being. Thus, for the Black [person] to believe the Word of God about [God's] love revealed in Christ, he/she must be prepared to meet head-on the sentimental "Christian" love of whites, which would make him/her a nonperson.[1]

Cone insists that one cannot practice Christian love and at the same time practice racism. He argues:

> It seems that whites forget about the necessary interrelatedness of love, justice, and power when they encounter Black people. Love becomes emotional and sentimental. This sentimental, condescending love accounts for their desire to "help" by relieving the physical pains of the suffering Blacks so they can satisfy their own religious piety and keep the poor powerless. But the new Blacks, redeemed in Christ, must refuse their "help" and demand that Blacks be confronted as persons. They must say to whites that authentic love is not "help," not giving Christmas baskets, but working for

political, social, and economic justice, which always means a redistribution of power. It is a kind of power which enables the Blacks to fight their own battles and thus keep their dignity. "Powerlessness breeds a race of beggars."[2]

Black people do not need a love which functions contrary to the establishment of Black personhood. This understanding of love was just recently affirmed by Black theologians (lay and clergy, professional and non-professional) in Southern Africa in their challenge to the church through *The Kairos Document*. They cautioned, "we must also remember that the most loving thing we can do for both the oppressed and for our enemies who are oppressors is to eliminate the oppression, remove the tyrants from power and establish a just government for the common good of all the people."[3] Here, love is not defined in the interest of those who wish to maintain the present status quo. But it is defined from the point of view of those on the underside of history—the victims of the oppressors' power.

In a similar vein, feminists challenge traditional understandings of love. Valerie Saiving Goldstein expresses her suspicions of traditional theological works in the following way:

I am no longer certain as I once was that, when theologians speak of "man," they are using the word in its generic sense. It is, after all, a well-known fact that theology has been written almost exclusively by men. This alone should put us on guard, especially since contemporary theologians constantly remind us that one of man's strongest temptations is to identify his own limited perspective with universal truth.[4]

Lifting up the Christian notion of sin and love, Goldstein suggests that it would be equally unsatisfactory to impose universal understanding on those concepts. The identification of these notions with self-assertion and selflessness respectively, functions differently in masculine experience and feminine experience. She explains further:

Contemporary theological doctrines of love have been constructed primarily upon the basis of masculine experience and thus view the human condition from the male standpoint. Consequently, these doctrines do not provide an adequate interpretation of the situation of women—nor, for that matter, of men, especially in light of certain fundamental changes taking place in our own society.[5]

Because of their feminine character, for women love takes the form of nurturing, supporting and servicing their families. Consequently, if a woman believes

the theologians, she will try to strangle their impulses in herself. She will believe that, having chosen marriage and children and thus being face to face with the needs of her family for love, refreshment, and forgiveness, she has no right to ask anything for herself but must submit without qualification to the strictly feminine role.[6]

For women too, the issue is one of personhood—are women to deny who they are in order to be saved?

Goldstein then argues that when experience in theology is scrutinized, we will discover that because it has been synonymous with masculine experience, it is inadequate to deal with the situation of women.

In other words, Black theologians and feminist theologians have argued that the universalism which classical theologians attempt to uphold represents merely the particular experiences of the dominant culture. Blacks identify that experience as White experiences; and women identify it as a male experience. The question then is, if universalism is the criteria for valid theology, how is such universalism achieved?

What will be explored here is how Black women's experiences can provide some insights into this question. In doing so, Black women not only join Blacks and feminists in their challenge of theology but they also provide an internal critique for Black men as well as for White women. In this paper, I will focus primarily upon Black women's experience as related to the development of feminist theology. (In a rather limited way, I have addressed the issue of Black women's experiences and Black theology in an article entitled "Black Theology and The Black Woman."[7] That subject certainly has not been exhausted and shall be treated in more substantive ways in the future.)

But here I am interested in engaging feminist theology with reference to its constructive efficacy for Black women, given the peculiarities of their experiences. The results will be the beginnings of a theology from a Black Woman's perspective, with special reference to Christology.

In order to create a common starting point, let's begin with a synopsis of the basic tenets of feminist theology. First, feminist theology seeks to develop a *wholistic theology*. Feminist theology rejects the traditional forms of oppressive and one-sided, male-dominated theologies which arise out of patriarchal religion(s).[8] Women have begun to see that their continuous oppression in the church and society has its basis in these patriarchal religion(s). Historically, the theologies of religions have emerged out of the experiences of men, making the theologies representative thereof. Because humanity is comprised of both men and women, feminist theologians seek to develop a more wholistic perspective in theology.

Second, in seeking to produce a wholistic perspective in theology, feminist theologians call for the *eradication of social/sexual dualisms* in human existence which are inherent in patriarchy. A patriarchy is characterized by male-domination and female submission and subordination. In such a society, men are considered strong, intelligent, rational and aggressive; women are considered weak, irrational, and docile.

A third function of feminist theology is to conceptualize *new and positive images of women*. Throughout history, including the history of theology, women have been portrayed in negative ways. They have been sources of evil (snakes), authors of trickery (witches), and stimulants (therefore causes) for the sexual perversions of men (temptresses and prostitutes). These negative images must be changed to reflect reality.

Finally, feminist theology must *evaluate male-articulated understandings of the Christian faith*. Doctrines developed in a system of patriarchy merely perpetuate patriarchal structures. As the patriarchal theological system is challenged, so are the doctrines, e.g., God, Jesus Christ, the Fall and the Church.

Emerging Black Feminist Perspective

It has been argued by many Blacks that the women's liberation movement is a White middle-class movement. Therefore, it is believed to be totally irrelevant to the situation of Black women since the majority of them are not middle-class.

Brenda Eichelberger gives several reasons for Black women's non-involvement in feminist causes. Among them are such things as class differences, the lack of Black women's knowledge about the real issues involved and the suspicion that the middle-class White Women's movement is divisive to the Black community, which claims prior allegiance.[9] In spite of these and other negative responses to the White women's liberation movement, there has been a growing feminist consciousness among many Black women and Black men. This consciousness is coupled by the increased willingness of Black women to undertake an independent analysis of sexism, thereby creating an emerging Black perspective on feminism. Black feminism grows out of Black women's tri-dimensional reality of race/sex/class. It holds that full human liberation cannot be achieved simply by the elimination of any one form of oppression. Consequently, real liberation must be "broad in the concrete";[10] it must be based upon a multi-dimensional analysis.

Recent writings by secular Black feminists have challenged White feminist analysis and Black race analysis, particularly by introducing data from Black women's experience that has been historically ignored by White feminists and Black male liberationists.

In only a few of them do Black women employ only a gender analysis to treat Black women's reality. Whereas Ntozake Shange focuses chiefly upon sexism, Michelle Wallace, like Alice Walker, presumes that White racism has had an adverse effect upon the Black community in a way that confuses and reinforces the already existing sexism. Sharon Harley, Rosalyn Terborg-Penn, Paula Giddings and Gloria Wade-Gayles all recognize the inclusiveness of the oppressive reality of Black women as they endure racism, sexism and economic oppression. Barbara Smith, Gloria Hull, Bell Hooks and Angela Davis particularly explore the implications of this tri-dimensional oppression of Black women. In so doing, Black women have either articulated Black feminist perspectives or developed grounds for doing so.[11] These perspectives, however, have not led to the resolution of tensions between Black women and White women, and they even brought to the forefront some tensions between Black women and Black men.

On the contrary, the possibly irreparable nature of these tensions is implied in Walker's suggestion that the experience of being a Black woman or a White woman is so different that another word is required to describe the liberative efforts of Black women. Her suggestion that the word "womanist" is more appropriate for Black women is derived from the sense of the word as it is used in Black communities:

Womanist, from womanish (Opp. of "girlish," i.e. frivolous, irresponsible, not serious). A Black feminist or feminist of color. From the Black folk expression of mothers to female children, "You acting womanish," i.e., like a woman. Usually referring to outrageous, audacious, courageous or willful behavior. Wanting to know more and in greater depth than is considered "good" for one. Interest in grown-up doings. Acting grown up. Being grown up. Interchangeable with another Black folk expression: "You trying to be grown." Responsible. In charge. Serious.[12]

Womanists were Sojourner Truth, Jarena Lee, Amanda Berry Smith, Ida B. Wells, Mary Church Terrell, Mary McCloud Bethune and countless others not remembered in any historical study. A womanist then is a strong Black woman who has sometimes been mislabeled a domineering castrating matriarch. A womanist is one who has developed survival strategies in spite of the oppression of her race and sex in order to save her family and her people. Walker's womanist notation suggests not "the feminist," but the active struggle of Black women that makes them who they are. For some Black women that may involve being feminine as traditionally defined, and for others it involves being masculine as stereotypically defined. In any case, womanist means being and acting out who you are and interpreting the reality for yourself. In other words, Black women speak out for themselves. As a Black feminist critic Barbara Christian explains, referring to Audre Lorde's poem about the deadly consequence of silence, Black women must speak up and answer in order to validate their own experience. This is important even if only to ourselves. It is to the womanist tradition that Black women must appeal for the doing of theology.

The Beginnings of a Womanist Theology, with Special Reference to Christology

Womanist theology begins with the experiences of Black women as its point of departure. These experiences include not only Black women's activities in the larger society but also in the churches, and reveals that Black women have often rejected the oppressive structure in the church as well.

These experiences provide a context which is significant for doing theology. Those experiences had been and continue to be defined by racism, sexism and classism and therefore offer a unique opportunity and a new challenge for developing a relevant perspective in the theological enterprise. This perspective in theology which I am calling womanist theology draws upon the life and experiences of some Black women who have created meaningful interpretations of the Christian faith.

Black women must do theology out of their tri-dimensional experience of racism/sexism/classism. To ignore any aspect of this experience is to deny the holistic and integrated reality of Black womanhood. When Black women say that God is on the side of the oppressed, we mean that God is in solidarity with the struggles of those on the underside of humanity, those whose lives are bent and broken from the many levels of assault perpetrated against them.

In a chapter entitled "Black Women: Shaping Feminist Theory," Hooks elaborates on the interrelationship of the threefold oppressive reality of Black women and shows some of the weaknesses of White feminist theory. Challenging the racist and classist assumptions of White feminism, Hooks writes:

> Racism abounds in the writings of white feminists, reinforcing white supremacy and negating the possibility that women will bond politically across ethnic and racial boundaries. Past feminist refusal to draw attention to and attack racial hierarchy suppressed the link between race and class. Yet class structure in American society has been shaped by the racial politics of white supremacy."[13]

This means that Black women, because of oppression determined by race and their subjugation as women, make up a disproportionately high percentage of the poor and working classes. However, the fact that Black women are a subjugated group even within the Black community and the White women's community does not mean that they are alone in their oppression within those communities. In the women's community poor White women are discriminated against, and in the Black community, poor Black men are marginalized. This suggests that classism, as well as racism and sexism, has a life of its own. Consequently, simply addressing racism and sexism is inadequate to bring about total liberation. Even though there are dimensions of class which are not directly related to race or sex, classism impacts Black women in a peculiar way which results in the fact that they are most often on the bottom of the social and economic ladder. For Black women doing theology, to ignore classism would mean that their theology is no different from any other bourgeois theology. It would be meaningless to the majority of Black women, who are themselves poor. This means that addressing only issues relevant to middle-class women or Blacks will simply not do. The daily struggles of poor Black women serve as the gauge for the verification of the claims of womanist theology. Anna Julia Cooper makes a relevant point.

> Women's wrongs are thus indissolubly linked with all undefended woes, and the acquirement of her "rights" will mean the supremacy of triumph of all right over might, the supremacy of the moral forces of reason, and justice, and love in the government of the nations of earth.[14]

Black women's experience must be affirmed as the crucible for doing womanist theology. It is the context in which we must decide theological questions. More specifically, it is within the context of this experience that Black women read the Bible. A (brief) look at Black women's use of the Bible indicates how it is their experiences which determine relevant questions for them.

The Bible in the Womanist Tradition

Theological investigation into the experiences of Christian Black women reveals that Black women considered the Bible to be a major source of religious validation in their lives. Though Black women's relationship with God preceded their introduction to the Bible, the Bible gave some content to their God-consciousness.[15] The source for Black women's understanding of God as creator, sustainer, comforter, and liberator took on life as they agonized over their pain, and celebrated the hope that as God delivered the Israelites, they would be delivered as well. The God of the Old and New Testament became real in the consciousness of oppressed Black women. Of the use of the Bible, Fannie Barrier Williams quite aptly said:

> Though the Bible was not an open book to the Negro before emancipation, thousands of the enslaved men and women of the negro race learned more than was taught to them. Thousands of them realized the deeper meanings, the sweeter consolations and the spiritual awakenings that are part of the religious experiences of all Christians.[16]

In other words, though Black people in general and Black women in particular were politically impotent, religiously controlled, they were able to appropriate certain themes of the Bible which spoke to their reality. For example, Jarena Lee, a nineteenth century Black woman preacher in the African Methodist Episcopal Church, constantly emphasized the theme "Life and Liberty" in her sermons which were always biblically based. This interplay of scripture and experience was exercised expressly by many Black women. An ex-slave woman revealed that when her experience negated certain oppressive interpretations of the Bible given by white preachers, she, through engaging the biblical message for herself, rejected them. Consequently she also dismissed white preachers who distorted the message in order to maintain slavery. Her grandson, Howard Thurman, speaks of her use of the Bible in this way:

> "During the days of slavery," she said, "the master's minister would occasionally hold services for the slaves. Always the white minister used as his text something from Paul, 'Slaves be obedient to them that are your masters . . . as unto Christ.' Then he would go on to show how, if we were good and happy slaves, God would bless us. I promised my Maker that if I ever learned to read and if freedom ever came, I would not read that part of the Bible."[17]

What we see here is perhaps more than a mere rejection of a White preacher's interpretation of the Bible: it is an exercise in internal critique of the Bible. The liberating message of the gospel is seen as over against the oppressive elements in the Bible. The truth which the Bible brought was undeniable, though perception of it was often distorted in order to support the monstrous system of oppression. Sarcastically responding to this tendency, Fannie Barrier Williams admonished, "do not open the Bible too wide." Biblical interpretation, realized Williams, a non-theologically trained person, had at its basis the prior agenda of White America. She therefore argued:

> Religion, like every other force in America, was first used as an instrument and servant of slavery. All attempts to Christianize the negro were limited by the important fact that he was property of valuable and peculiar sort, and that the property value must not be disturbed, even if his soul were lost. If Christianity could make the negro docile, domestic and less an independent and fighting savage, let it be preached to that extent and no further.[18]

A false, pernicious, demoralizing gospel could only be preached if the Bible was not opened wide enough, lest one sees the liberating message of Jesus as summarized in Luke 4:18. The Bible must be read and interpreted in the light of Black women's own oppression and God's revelation within that context. The womanist must, like Sojourner, "compare the teachings of the Bible with the witness" in them.[19]

To do Womanist theology, then, we must read and hear the Bible and engage it within the context of our own experience. This is the only way that it can make sense to people who are oppressed. Black women of the past did not hesitate in doing this and we must do no less.

Jesus in the Womanist Tradition

Having opened the Bible wider than many White people, Black people, in general, and Black women in particular, found a Jesus who they could claim, and whose claim for them was one of affirmation of dignity and self-respect.

In the experience of Black people, Jesus was "all things."[20] Chief among these however was the belief in Jesus as the divine co-sufferer, who empowers them in situations of oppression. For Christian Black women in the past, Jesus was their central frame of reference. They identified with Jesus because they believed that Jesus identified with them. As Jesus was persecuted and made to suffer undeservedly, so were they. His suffering culminated in the crucifixion. Their crucifixion included rapes, and husbands being castrated (literally and metaphorically), babies being sold, and other cruel and often murderous treatments. But Jesus' suffering was not the suffering of a mere human, for Jesus was understood to be God incarnate. As Harold Carter observed of Black prayers in general, there was no difference made between the persons of the Trinity, Jesus, God, or the Holy Spirit. All of these proper names for God were used interchangeably in prayer language. Thus, Jesus was the one who speaks the world into creation. He was the power behind the Church.[21] Black women's affirmation of Jesus as God meant that White people were not God. One old slave woman clearly demonstrates this as she prayed:

> Dear Massa Jesus, we all uns beg Ooner [you] come make us a call dis yere day. We is nutting but poor Etiopian women and people ain't tink much 'bout we. We ain't trust any of dem great high people for come to we church, but do' you is de one great Massa, great too much dan Massa Linkum, you ain't shame to care for we African people.[22]

Implicit in the description "nothing but poor Black women" and what follows is the awareness of the public devaluation of Black women. But in spite of that Jesus is presented as a confidant who could be trusted while White people could not be trusted. This woman affirmed the contribution of Abraham Lincoln to the emancipation of Blacks, but rejected Mr. Lincoln as her real or ultimate master. Quite a contrast to the master's (slave owner's) perception of him/herself.

This slave woman did not hesitate to identify her struggle and pain with those of Jesus. In fact, the common struggle made her know that Jesus would respond to her beck and call.

> Come to we, dear Massa Jesus. De sun, he hot too much, de road am dat long and boggy (sandy) and we ain't got no buggy for send and fetch Ooner. But Massa, you 'member how you walked dat hard walk up Calvary and ain't weary but tink about we all dat way. We know you ain't weary for to come to we. We pick out de torns, de prickles, de brier, de backsliding' and de quarrel and de sin out of you so dey shan't hurt Ooner pierce feet no more.[23]

The reference to "no buggy" to send for Jesus brings to mind the limited material possessions of pre- and post-Civil War Blacks. In her speech, "Ain't I a Woman?" Sojourner Truth emphasized that Black women were not helped into carriages as were White women.[24] In the prayer, this woman speaks of that reality wherein most Blacks didn't even have carriages or buggies. For had she owned one, certainly she'd send it to fetch Jesus. Here we see the concern for the comfort and the suffering of Jesus. Jesus suffers when we sin—when we backslide or when we quarrel. But still Jesus is identified with her plight. Note that Jesus went to the cross with this Black woman on his mind. He was thinking about her and all others like her. So totally dedicated to the poor, the weak, the downtrodden, the outcast that in this Black woman's faith, Jesus would never be too tired to come. As she is truly among the people at the bottom of humanity, she can make things comfortable for Jesus even though she may have nothing to give him—no water, no food—but she can give tears and love. She continues:

> Come to we, dear Massa Jesus. We all uns ain't got no good cool water for give you when you thirsty. You know, Massa, de drought so long, and the well so low, ain't nutting but mud to drink. But we gwine to take de 'munion cup and fill it wid de tear of repentance, and love clean out of we heart. Dat all we hab to gib you, good Massa.[25]

The material or physical deprivation experienced by this woman did not reduce her desire to give Jesus the best. Being a Black woman in the American society meant essentially being poor, with no buggy, and no good cool water. Life for Black women was indeed bad, hot and at best muddy. Note that there is no hint that their condition results from some divine intention. Now, whereas I am not prepared to say that this same woman or any others in that church the next day would have been engaged in political praxis by joining such movements as Nat Turner's rebellion or Denmark Vesey's revolt, it is clear that her perspective was such that the social, political and economic orders were believed to be sinful and against the will of the real master, Jesus.

For Black women, the role of Jesus was revealed as they encountered him in their experience as one who empowers the weak. In this vein, Jesus was such a central part of Sojourner Truth's life that all of her sermons made him the starting point. When asked by a preacher if the source of her preaching was the Bible, she responded "No honey, can't preach from de Bible—can't read a letter."[26] Then she explained: "When I preaches, I has jest one text to preach from, an I always preaches from this one. My text is, "When I found Jesus!"[27] In this sermon Sojourner Truth recounts the events and struggles of life from the time her parents were brought from Africa and sold "up an' down, an' hither an' yon. . . ."[28] to the time that she met Jesus within the context of her struggles for dignity of Black people and women. Her encounter with Jesus brought such joy that she became overwhelmed with love and praise:

> Praise, praise, praise to the Lord! An' I begun to feel such a love in my soul as I never felt before—love to all creatures. An' then, all of a sudden, it stopped, an' I said, Dar's de white folks that have abused you, an' beat you, and an' abused your people—think o' them! But then there came another rush of love through my soul, an' I cried out loud—"Lord, I can love even white folks![29]

This love was not a sentimental, passive love. It was a tough, active love that empowered her to fight more fiercely for the freedom of her people. For the rest of her life she continued speaking at abolition and women's rights gatherings, where she condemned the horrors of oppression.

The Womanist Traditions and Christological Reflections

More than anyone, Black theologians have captured the essence of the significance of Jesus in the lives of Black people which to an extent includes Black women. They all hold that the Jesus of history is important for understanding who he was and his significance for us today. By and large they have affirmed that this Jesus is the Christ, that is, God incarnate. They have argued that in the light of our experience, Jesus meant freedom.[30] They have maintained that Jesus means freedom from the sociopsychological, psychocultural, economic and political oppression of Black people. In other words, Jesus is a political messiah.[31] "To free [humans] from bondage was Jesus' own definition of his ministry."[32] This meant that as Jesus identified with the lowly of his day, he now identifies with the lowly of this day, who in the American context are Black people. The identification is so real that Jesus Christ in fact becomes Black. It is important to note that Jesus' blackness is not a result of ideological distortion of a few Black thinkers, but a result of careful Christological investigation. Cone examines the sources of Christology and concludes that Jesus is Black because "Jesus was a Jew." He explains:

> It is on the basis of the soteriological meaning of the particularity of his Jewishness that theology must affirm the christological significance of Jesus' present blackness. He is black because he was a Jew. The affirmation of the Black Christ can be understood when the significance of his past Jewishness is related dialetically to the significance of his present blackness. On the other hand, the Jewishness of Jesus located him in the context of the Exodus, thereby connecting his appearance in Palestine with God's liberation of oppressed Israelites from Egypt. Unless Jesus were truly from Jewish ancestry, it would make little theological sense to say that he is the fulfillment of God's covenant with Israel. But on the other hand, the blackness of Jesus brings out the soteriological meaning of his Jewishness for our contemporary situation when Jesus' person is understood in the context of the Cross and resurrection. Without negating the divine election of Israel, the Cross and resurrection are Yahweh's fulfillment of his original intention for Israel. . . .[33]

The condition of Black people today reflects the cross of Jesus. Yet the resurrection brings the hope that liberation from oppression is immanent. The resurrected Black Christ signifies this hope.

Cone further argues that this christological title, "The Black Christ," is not validated by its universality, but, in fact, by its particularity. Its significance lies in whether or not the christological title "points to God's universal will to liberate particular oppressed people from inhumanity."[34] These particular oppressed peoples to which Cone refers are characterized in Jesus' parable on the last Judgment as "the least." "The least in America are literally present in Black people."[35] This notion of "the least" is attractive because it descriptively locates the condition of Black women. "The least" are those people who have no water to give, but offer what they have, as the old slave woman cited above says in her prayer. Black women's experience in general is such a reality. Their tri-dimensional reality renders their particular situation a complex one. One could say that not only are they the oppressed of the oppressed, but their situation represents "the particular within the particular."

But is this just another situation that takes us deeper into the abyss of theological relativity? I would argue that it is not, because it is in the context of Black women's experience where the particular connects up with the universal. By this I mean that in each of the three dynamics of oppression, Black women share in the reality of a broader community. They share race suffering with Black men; with White women and other Third World women they are victims of sexism; and with poor Blacks and Whites, and other Third World peoples, especially women, they are disproportionately poor. To speak of Black women's tri-dimensional reality, therefore, is not to speak to Black women exclusively, for there is an implied universality which connects them with others.

Likewise, with Jesus Christ, there was an implied universality which made him identify with others—the poor, the woman, the stranger. To affirm Jesus' solidarity with the "least of the people" is not an exercise in romanticized contentment with one's oppressed status in life. For as the resurrection signified that there is more to life than the cross of Jesus Christ, for Black women it signifies that their tri-dimensional oppressive existence is not the end, but it merely represents the context in which a particular people struggle to experience hope and liberation. Jesus Christ thus represents a three-fold significance; first he identifies with the "little people," Black women, where they are; secondly, he affirms the basic humanity of these, "the least;" and thirdly, he inspires active hope in the struggle for resurrected, liberated existence.

To locate the Christ in Black people is a radical and necessary step, but understanding of a Black women's reality challenges us to go further. Christ among the least must also mean Christ in the community of Black women. William Eichelberger was able to recognize this as he further particularized the significance of the Blackness of Jesus by locating Christ in Black women's community. He was able to see Christ not only as Black male but also as Black female.

> God, in revealing Himself and His attributes from time to time in His creaturely existence, has exercised His freedom to formalize His appearance in a variety of ways. . . . God revealed Himself at a point in the past as Jesus the Christ a Black male. My reasons for affirming the Blackness of Jesus of Nazareth are much different from that of the white apologist. . . . God wanted to identify with that segment of mankind which had suffered most, and is still suffering. . . . I am constrained to believe that God in our times has updated His form of revelation to western society. It is my feeling that God is now manifesting Himself, and has been for over 450 years, in the form of the Black American Woman as mother, as wife, as nourisher, sustainer and preserver of life, the Suffering Servant who is despised and rejected by men, a personality of sorrow who is acquainted with grief. The Black Woman has borne our griefs and carried our sorrows. She has been wounded because of American White society's transgressions and bruised by white iniquities. It appears that she may be the instrumentality through whom God will make us whole. [36]

Granted, Eichelberger's categories for God and woman are very traditional. Nevertheless, the significance of his thought is that he is able to conceive of the Divine reality as other than a Black male messianic figure.

Even though Black women have been able to transcend some of the oppressive tendencies of White male (and Black male) articulated theologies, careful study reveals that some traditional symbols are inadequate for us today. The Christ understood as the stranger, the outcast, the hungry, the weak, the poor, makes the traditional male Christ (Black and White) less significant. Even our sisters of the past had some suspicions about the effects of a male image of the divine, for they did challenge the oppressive use of it in the church's theology. In so doing, they were able to move from a traditional oppressive Christology, with respect to women, to an egalitarian Christology. This kind of egalitarian Christology was operative in Jarena Lee's argument for the right of women to preach. She argued ". . . the Saviour died for the woman as well as for the man."[37] The crucifixion was for universal salvation, not just for male salvation or, as we may extend the argument to include, not just for White salvation. Because of this, Christ came and died, no less for the woman as for the man, no less for Blacks as for Whites. For Lee, this was not an academic issue, but one with practical ramification.

> If the man may preach, because the Savior died for him, why not the woman? Seeing he died for her also. Is he not a whole Saviour, instead of half one? as those who hold it wrong for a woman to preach, would seem to make it appear.[38]

Lee correctly perceives that there is an ontological issue at stake. If Jesus Christ were a Saviour of men then it is true the maleness of Christ would be paramount.[39] But if Christ is the Savior of all, then it is the humanity—the wholeness—of Christ which is significant.

Sojourner was aware of the same tendency of some scholars and church leaders to link the maleness of Jesus and the sin of Eve with the status of women and she challenged this notion in her famed speech "Ain't I A Woman?"

Then that little man in black there, he says women can't have much rights as men, 'cause Christ wasn't a woman! Where did your Christ come from? Where did your Christ come from? From God and a woman. Man had nothing to do with Him.

If the first woman God ever made was strong enough to turn the world upside down alone, these women together ought to be able to turn it back, and get it right side up again! And now they is asking to do it, the men better let them.[40]

I would argue, as suggested by both Lee and Sojourner, that the significance of Christ is not his maleness, but his humanity. The most significant events of Jesus Christ were the life and ministry, the crucifixion, and the resurrection. The significance of these events, in one sense, is that in them the absolute becomes concrete. God becomes concrete not only in the man Jesus, for he was crucified, but in the lives of those who will accept the challenge of the risen Saviour—the Christ. For Lee, this meant that women could preach; for Sojourner, it meant that women could possibly save the world; for me, it means today this Christ, found in the experience of Black women, is a Black woman.

Conclusion

I have argued that Black women's tri-dimensional reality provides a fertile context for articulating a theological perspective which is wholistic in scope and liberating in nature. The theology is potentially wholistic because the experience out of which it emerges is totally interconnected with other experiences. It is potentially liberating because it rests not on one single issue which could be considered only a middle-class issue relevant to one group of people, but it is multi-faceted. Thus, the possibility for wholistic theology is more likely. Feminist theology as presently developed is limited by virtue of the experience base for feminist theology. That is, when feminists say that experience is the crucible for doing [feminist] theology, they usually mean White women's experience. With few exceptions, feminist thinkers do their analysis primarily, and in some circles exclusively, based on the notion that because sexism is the longest and most universal form of oppression, it should claim priority.[41]

Black women, by and large, have not held this assumption. Many have claimed that because of the pervasiveness of racism, and because of its defining character for black life in general, racism is most important. Though Sojourner Truth never did develop a sophisticated social analysis, she was aware of the fact that she (and her poor people) were poor because she was Black, and perhaps poorer because she was a woman. I say "perhaps" simply because in the slave economy one could argue that there was relatively little distinction between the property status of slaves by virtue of gender; women were no less property than men. As property, they were a part of the material distributed, rather than participants in the inevitable (system of) material distribution. Thus as indicated above in the black woman's prayer, material possessions of blacks were limited. In a sense one could say that by virtue of one's race, one was slave and by virtue of that status one was poor.

Still as we see the issues today, class distinctions which have emerged even in the Black community, and sex differences, which have taken on new forms of institutionalization, must be addressed. For liberation to become a reality, race, sex, and class must be deliberately confronted. Interconnected as they are, they all impinge greatly on the lives of Black women. Overwhelming as are these realities, Black women do not feel defeated. For Jarena Lee observed the hope of the struggle is based on the faith that Jesus died (and was raised) for the woman as well as the man. This realization gave inspiration for the struggle. Black women today inside and outside of the church still bring an optimistic spirit as reflected in the conclusion of Maya Angelou's poem, "Still I Rise":

> Out of the hut of history's shame
> I rise
> Up from a past that's rooted in pain
> I rise
> I'm a Black ocean, leaping and wide,
> Welling and Swelling, I bear in the tide
> leaving behind nights of terror and fear
> I rise
> Into a daybreak that's wondrously clear
> I rise
> Bringing the gifts that my ancestors gave

I am the dream and the hope of the slave.
I rise.
I rise.
I rise.[42]

Endnotes:

1. James H. Cone, *Black Theology and Black Power* (New York: The Seabury Press, 1969): 53–54.

2. Ibid., 53–54.

3. The Kairos Theologians, *The Kairos Document: Challenge to the Church*, 2nd ed. (Braarnfontein, South Africa: Skotaville Publishers, 1985; Rept.: Grand Rapids, MI: William B. Eerdmans Publishing Company, 1986): 24–25.

4. Valerie Saiving Goldstein, "The Human Situation of a Feminist," *The Journal of Religion* 40 (April 1960): 100.

5. Ibid.

6. Ibid.

7. Jacquelyn Grant, "Black Theology and The Black Woman," in *Black Theology: A Documentary History, 1966–1979*, eds. Gayraud S. Wilmore and James H. Cone (New York: Orbis Books, 1979): 418–433.

8. See Sheila D. Collins. *A Different Heaven and Earth: A Feminist Perspective on Religion* (Valley Forge, PA: Judson Press, 1974); Mary Daley, *Beyond God the Father: Toward a Philosophy of Women's Liberation* (Boston, MA: Beacon Press, 1973); Mary Daley, *The Church and the Second Sex: With a New Feminist Post Christian Introduction by the Author* (New York: Harper Bros., 1975).

9. Brenda Eichelberger, "Voice of Black Feminism," *Quest: A Feminist Quarterly* III (Spring, 1977): 16–23.

10. This phrase is used by Anna Julia Cooper, *A Voice From the South* (Xenia, Ohio: Abdine Publishing House, 1852; Rept.: Westport, CT: Negro Universities Press, 1969), cited by Bell Hooks, *Ain't I A Woman: Black Women and Feminism* (Boston, MA: South End Press, 1981): 193–194. I use it here to characterize Black women's experience. To be concerned about Black women's issues is to be *concrete*. Yet because of their interconnectedness with Black men (racism), White women (sexism) and the poor (classism), it is also to be, at the same time, concerned with broad issues.

11. See Ntozake Shange, *For Colored Girls Who Have Considered Suicide When the Rainbow is Enuf.* (New York: Macmillan Company, 1975); Michelle Wallace, *Black Macho and the Myth of the Superwoman* (New York: Dial Press, 1978); Alice Walker, *The Color Purple* (New York: Harcourt, Brace and Jovanovich Publishers, 1982); and *In Search of Our Mothers' Gardens* (San Diego, CA: Harcourt, Brace and Jovanovich Publishers, 1983); Sharon Harley and Rosalyn Terborg-Penn, eds. *Afro-American Women* (New York: Kennikat Press, 1978); Paula Giddings, *When and Where I Enter* (New York: William Morrow and Company, Inc., 1984); Gloria Wade-Grayles, *No Crystal Stair: Visions of Race and Sex in Black Women's Fiction* (New York: Pilgrim Press, 1984); Bell Hooks, *Feminist Theory: From Margin to Center* (Boston: South End Press, 1984); Barbara Smith, Gloria Hull, and Patricia Scott, *All the Women Are White, and All the Blacks Are Men, But Some of Us Are Brave* (New York: The Feminist Press, 1982); Angela Y. Davis, *Women, Race and Class* (New York: Vintage Book, 1981).

12. Walker, in *Search of Our Mothers' Gardens*, xi.

13. Hooks, *Feminist Theory*, 3.

14. Cooper, *A Voice from the South*, 19.

15. Cecil Wayne Cone, *Identity Crisis in Black Theology* (Nashville, TN: African Methodist Episcopal Church Press, 1975), passim, especially chapter III.

16. Bert James Lowenberg and Ruth Bogin, eds., *Black Women in Nineteenth-Century American Life: Their Words, Their Thoughts, Their Feelings* (University Park, PA: The Pennsylvania State University Press, 1976): 267.

17. Howard Thurman, *Jesus and the Disinherited* (Nashville, TN: Abingdon Press, 1949): 30–31.

18. Lowenberg and Bogin, *Black Women in Nineteenth-Century American Life*, 265.

19. Olive Gilbert, *Sojourner Truth: Narrative and Book of Life* (1850 and 1875; Rept.: Chicago: Johnson Publishing Co., 1970), p. 83.

20. Harold A. Carter, *The Prayer Tradition of Black People* (Valley Forge: Judson Press, 1976), 50. Carter, in referring to traditional Black prayer in general, states that Jesus was revealed as one who "was all one needs!"

21. Ibid.

22. Ibid., 49

23. Ibid.

24. Sojourner Truth. "Ain't I A Woman?" in Mariam Schneir, ed., *Feminism: The Essential Historical Writings* (New York: Vintage Books, 1972).

25. Carter, *The Prayer Tradition*, 49.

26. Gilbert, *Sojourner Truth*, 118.

27. Ibid., 119.

28. Ibid.

29. Ibid.

30. James Deotis Roberts, *A Black Political Theology* (Philadelphia, PA: The Westminster Press, 1974): 138. See especially chapter 5. See also Noel Leo Erskine, *Decolonizing Theology: A Caribbean Perspective* (New York: Orbis Books, 1980): 125.

31. Roberts, *A Black Political Theology*, p. 133.

32. Albert Cleage, *The Black Messiah* (New York: Sheed and Ward, 1969): 92.

33. James H. Cone, *God of the Oppressed* (New York: Seabury Press, 1975): 134.

34. Ibid., 135.

35. Ibid., 136.

36. William Eichelberger, "Reflections on the Person and Personality of the Black Messiah," *The Black Church* II (n.d.): 54.

37. Jerena Lee, *The Life and Religious Experiences and Journal of Mrs. Jerena Lee: A Colored Lady Giving an Account of Her Call to Preach* (Philadelphia, PA: n.p., 1836): 15–16.

38. Ibid., 16.

39. There is no evidence to suggest that Black women debated the significance of the maleness of Jesus. The fact is that Jesus Christ was a real, crucial figure in their lives. However, recent feminist scholarship has been important in showing the relation between the maleness of Christ and the oppression of women.

40. Truth, "Ain't I A Woman?," in Schneir, op. cit., 94.

41. This question is explored further in Jacquelyn Grant, *The Development and Limitation of Feminist Theology: Toward an Engagement of Black Women's Religious Experience and White Women's Religious Experience* (New York: Union Theological Seminary, Ph.D. dissertation, 1985).

42. Maya Angelou, *And Still I Rise* (New York: Random House, 1978): 42.

A Chronology
of
African American Religion

The 1600s

1618 — Angela, an African, arrives at Point Comfort, Virginia, on the ship *Treasurer.* European name suggests baptism prior to arrival.

1619 — 20 Black people arrive in Virginia at Jamestown as indentured servants. The term of service for indentured servants, Black or White, was usually seven years, after which they became free and able to participate in the economic, social, and political life.

1623 — The first colonial baptism of a Black person, a child, takes place in the Anglican church in Jamestown. He is given the name Anthony.

1639 — Dutch Reformed Church in New Amsterdam (New York City) begins baptizing Black people.

1641 — An African woman, unnamed, is accepted into full membership of the Congregational Church in Dorchester, Massachusetts.

1667 — Through a series of actions beginning in 1667, the status of Black people converted to Christianity is clarified. Conversion to Christianity does not grant freedom.

1669 — Emmanuel, a 50–year-old African American, is baptized in the Lutheran Church in New York on Palm Sunday.

1670 — By Virginia legislative action, Black people lose their voting rights and in the future ". . . all servants, not being Christians," brought into Virginia by sea were declared slaves for life.

1672 — The Black population in the colonies now numbers in the thousands. The changing conditions of life have led to the founding of isolated "Maroon" communities of former slaves in the interior of Virginia. Virginia offers a bounty for captured Maroons, who have been raiding White communities for supplies.

1688 — The Friends (Quakers) of Germantown, Pennsylvania, a group of former Mennonites, issue the first protest of slavery in the Western Hemisphere, in a letter to the Philadelphia Monthly Meeting of the Society of Friends.

The 1700s

1700 — There are an estimated 28,000 Black people in the British American Colonies.

1704 — Elias Neau, a Frenchman in New York City, opens a catechism school for Black slaves.

1738 — October 16, Peter Böhler lands in Savannah to begin Moravian mission to the slave population in South Carolina.

1743 — Quassey, a member of the Baptist congregation in Newport, Rhode Island, is the first African American Baptist.

— Society for the Propagation of the Gospel in Foreign Parts (Church of England) opens a school for African Americans in Charleston, South Carolina.

1747 — Presbyterians begin mission to slaves in Hanover, Virginia.

1750 — Quaker Anthony Benezet opens school for African Americans in Philadelphia.

1757 — Rev. Samuel Davies, a White Presbyterian minister, baptizes 150 African Americans (slaves), the first received into the Presbyterian Church.

1758 — The first documented African American Baptist congregation is founded in Mecklenburg County, Virginia, on the plantation of William Byrd.

1760 — Poet Jupiter Hammon publishes *Salvation by Christ with Penitential Cries*.

1764 — The first Methodist society in America, organized by Robert Strawbridge (White) in Frederick County, Maryland, has Black charter members, including a slave named Anne Switzer. Two years later, a woman known only as Betty joined four others in a class meeting that grew to become John Street Methodist Church, the first Methodist congregation in New York City. This congregation vies with one in Virginia as the first Methodist church in the United States.

1771 — Upon his arrival in New York, Joseph Pilmoor, the first Methodist preacher sent to America, discovers Black members of St. John's Methodist Church.

1772 — Methodist preacher Francis Asbury begins traveling to various Methodist centers through the Southern and Middle colonies and finds numerous Black people worshipping with the societies.

— Black people are admitted to membership in the Baptist congregations in Providence, Rhode Island, and Boston, Massachusetts.

— Phillis Wheatley publishes *Poems on Various Subjects, Religious and Moral*, the first book of poetry by an African American.

1773 — An itinerant Black Baptist preacher named Palmer baptizes a group of slaves at Silver Bluff, Aiken County, South Carolina, and forms them into a church, the second regularly formed Black Baptist church in North America. Included in the group is David George who becomes the church's preacher. George Liele, another itinerant Black Baptist preacher, who was ordained on May 20, occasionally speaks at Silver Bluff and for other groups along the coast of Georgia and South Carolina.

1776 — The third oldest Baptist church in the Colonies is established at Williamsburg, Virginia.

1778 — At some point in 1778 or 1779, George Liele takes advantage of the loose social controls during the Revolutionary War and forms a Black Baptist church in Savannah, Georgia.

1782 — British evacuate Savannah. Liele ordains Andrew Bryan before leaving.

— Lemuel Hayes is ordained in the Congregational Church and becomes the first African American to pastor a predominantly White congregation.

1783 — January, George Liele arrives in Jamaica, where he becomes an indentured servant of the governor.

— Baptists Moses Baker and George Givens travel as missionaries to the West Indies.

1784 — George Liele completes his period of indenture and begins preaching in Kingston.

1786 — African Americans are members of the first sunday school organized in America. It was formed by Methodist Bishop Francis Asbury in Maryland in the home of David Crenshaw.

1787 — Richard Allen, Absalom Jones, and others withdraw from St. George Methodist Church, Philadelphia. They organize the first independent Black society in America, the Free Black Society.

1790 — Census reveals 59,557 free Black people and 697,624 slaves, of whom 292,627 reside in Virginia.

— Henry Evans organizes a Methodist church, named Evans Chapel in his honor, in Fayetteville, North Carolina. He is regarded as the father of Methodism in the Fayetteville area.

— Two Baptists, Hector Peters and Sampson Colbert, undertake a missionary journey to West Africa.

1791 — Williamsburg Church is admitted to predominantly White Dover Baptist Association.

1792 — David George travels to Sierra Leone with 1,196 other Black people and founds church in Freetown.

1793 — Jesse Peter becomes the first pastor of the First African Church, Augusta, Georgia.

— Richard Allen publishes his autobiography, the first by an African American.

— Catherine Ferguson, an African American, founds the first Sunday School in New York City in her home. It later moves to a church on Murray Street and is known as the Murray Street Sunday School for the next forty years. The student body was interracial.

1794 — The African Episcopal Church of St. Thomas is formed in Philadelphia under the leadership of Absalom Jones. It is the first African American Anglican congregation.

— July 29, Bethel African Methodist Episcopal Church is dedicated in Philadelphia by Bishop Francis Asbury.

1795 — Absalom Jones is ordained as a deacon in the Protestant Episcopal Church.

— Andrew Bryan builds Baptist church in Savannah, Georgia.

1796 — Black Methodist leaders in New York City petition to organize a church for African Methodists.

1799 — Richard Allen becomes the first African American ordained (as a deacon) by the Methodists.

— Harry Hosier is ordained a deacon in the Methodist Church by Bishop Francis Asbury.

1800–1859

1800 — Census counts 895,602 slaves.

— An estimated 25 percent of all Methodists and Baptists in the United States are African Americans.

— Methodist Episcopal Church officially authorizes ordination of Black ministers as deacons.

1801 — New York African Methodists incorporate with a Black board of trustees, a step in the formation of the African Methodist Episcopal Zion Church.

— John Chavis becomes a missionary to the slaves, the first African American home missionary commissioned by the Presbyterian Church in the U.S.

1804 — Thomas Paul converts and organizes Joy Street Baptist Church in Boston, Massachusetts.

— Absalom Jones is ordained a priest in the Episcopal Church.

1805 — Peter Spencer leads a withdrawal of Black members from Asbury Methodist Episcopal Church, Wilmington, Delaware. They form Ezion MEC.

1806 — Stone Street, or African Church, Mobile, Alabama, is formed by this year.

1807 — The First African Presbyterian Church is founded in Philadelphia under the pastoral leadership of John Gloucester, a former slave.

1808 — The U.S. Congress moves to stop the slave trade.

1809 — Thomas Paul forms the Abyssinian Baptist Church in New York City.

— African Baptist Church is organized in Philadelphia.

— John Gloucester is appointed as a missionary by the Presbyterian Church. He is ordained in Tennessee in 1911 and then called to Philadelphia to organize a congregation.

1813 — African Union Church is formed under Peter Spencer by former members of the Ezion Methodist Episcopal Church in Wilmington, Delaware.

1815 — Richmond African Baptist Missionary Society is organized by Lott Carey and Collin Teague.

1816 — Bethel Church in Philadelphia separates completely from the Methodist Episcopal Church. African Methodists in Baltimore also separate from the White Methodists under the leadership of Daniel Coker. At a gathering in Philadelphia, the African Methodist Episcopal Church is formed. It is the oldest African American organization currently in existence.

— April 11, Richard Allen is consecrated as bishop of the African Methodist Episcopal Church by Bishop Francis Asbury.

— American Colonization Society is founded by Robert Finley. Black leaders protest its announced program.

— St. Philip's Episcopal Church organized in New York City.

— John Stewart, Methodism's first home missionary, begins his ministry to the Wyandot Indians in Ohio.

1819 — Richard Allen endorses the call to the ministry of Jarena Lee, who begins a career as a traveling missionary.

1820 — Legislation against slave trade is strengthened.

— Daniel Coker sails for Africa as an unofficial missionary for the African Methodist Episcopal Church.

— Simeon Jocelyn, a White man, organizes a group of African Americans for religious instruction. The group eventually becomes the Dixwell Avenue Congregational Church, the first African American Congregational Church.

1821 — A second group of free Blacks arrives in Sierra Leone.

— Zilpha Elaw begins preaching as an unordained evangelist for the Methodist Episcopal Church.

— Lott Carey sails for Africa as a missionary for the Baptists.

— First Conference of African Methodist Episcopal Zion Church in New York City elects James Varick as its bishop.

— Samuel Cornish founds First Colored Presbyterian Church of New York.

1822 — Plot for an insurrection led by Denmark Vasey is discovered in Charleston, South Carolina. Black religious activity in the city is severely repressed. African Methodist Episcopal Church members migrate to Philadelphia.

— Lane Seminary (Ohio) students debate abolition and colonization.

— Liberia founded.

— St. James First African Church organizes in Baltimore, Maryland, the first Episcopal Church for African Americans in a slave state.

1826 — The first congregation of Black Baptists in New Orleans, Louisiana, is organized.

1827 — African Methodist Episcopal Church societies are formed in Canada.

— *Freedom's Journal*, the first African American periodical, is established by Rev. Samuel Cornish and John P. Russworm.

— Scipio Beaneo begins AME church mission work in Haiti. Several minor stations are established.

1828 — Morris Brown is elected as the second African Methodist Episcopal Church bishop.

— Oblate Sisters of Providence, the first African American religious order, is founded in Baltimore, Maryland.

— Theodore S. Wright graduates from Princeton Theological Seminary, the first African American seminary graduate.

1829 — William Capers, a White Methodist minister, is appointed as a missionary to plantation-bound slaves.

— Temple Street African Congregational Church is formed as the first Congregational Church for African Americans.

1830 — Census reports 2,009,043 slaves in the United States.

— September 20–24, Richard Allen presides at the first National Negro Convention which convenes in Philadelphia. Among the attendees are the Revs. Samuel Cornish, Peter Williams, and J. W. C. Pennington.

1831 — Slave preacher Nat Turner leads rebellion in which 60 White people are killed.

1832 — In reaction to Nat Turner insurrection, repressive slave codes, including provisions against the operation of churches among slaves, are enacted across the South.

— Presbyterian minister Charles Colcock Jones is appointed missionary for the Association for the Religious Instruction of Negroes.

— New York annual conference of the AME Church votes to send a missionary to Canada.

1833 — Oberlin College founded.

1834 — The Providence Baptist Association, the first African American Baptist association, is formed in Ohio.

1837 — Meeting resistance to her call to preach, Rebecca Jackson leaves the AME Church.

1838 — The Union Baptist Association is formed in Ohio.

1839 — The Colored Baptist Association and Friends to Humanity (later renamed the Wood River Baptist Association) is formed in Illinois.

— Daniel Payne is ordained by the Frankean Synod (Lutheran).

1840s — President John Tyler invites Bishop Daniel Payne to the White House to preach the funeral sermon for his recently deceased servant.

1840 — Morris Brown organizes the Upper Canada Conference of the African Methodist Episcopal Church among fugitive slaves in Canada.

— The American Baptist Missionary Convention is organized at the Abyssinian Baptist Church in New York City.

— The American and Foreign Anti-Slavery Society is organized.

— The AME Church General Conference establishes the Canadian annual conference.

1841 — November, First Colored Presbyterian Church of Washington, D.C., established by J. F. Cook, Sr.

— The African Methodist Episcopal Church launches the first African American magazine, the *Review*.

1842 — November 21, the Congregation of the Sisters of the Holy Family, a religious order of African American nuns, Harriette Delille, Juliet Gaudin, Josephine Charles, and a Miss Abbot, is founded in New Orleans.

1845 — Southern churchmen gather in Charleston, South Carolina, to prioritize a Christian mission to the slaves.

— Wood River Baptist Church is organized in Illinois.

1846 — Congregationalists form the American Missionary Association to labor among the slaves.

1850 — September 18, fugitive slave laws are passed.

1853 — The first Y.M.C.A. for African American residents of Washington, D.C., is opened.

— The Western Colored Baptist Convention is organized by African American Baptists west of the Mississippi River.

1854 — James Augustus Healy is ordained in Paris at Notre Dame Cathedral, the first African American Roman Catholic priest.

— The Presbyterian Church establishes Ashnun Institute (now Lincoln University) in Lincoln, Pennsylvania, the first institution for higher learning for African Americans.

1856 — African Methodist work in Canada is set apart as British Methodist Episcopal Church.

1857 — March 6, the Dred Scott decision is handed down.

1858 — Francis Burns, the first Black bishop of the Methodist Episcopal Church, is elected to serve over the Liberia Conference.

— Thomas Frye (Tennessee) and Michael Coble (North Carolina) are licensed to preach by the Lutheran Church.

1859 — Rebecca Jackson organizes an African American Shaker group in Philadelphia.

— October 16, John Brown leads raid on Harper's Ferry.

1860–1899

1860 — Census reports 3,953,760 slaves in the United States.

1861 — April 12, Civil War begins with the firing on Fort Sumter.

1863 — January 1, Lincoln issues Emancipation Proclamation.

— March 11, Wilberforce University is founded as first African American-controlled college in the United States. Daniel Payne becomes the first African American college president.

— In May the African Methodist Episcopal Church reenters South Carolina on the heels of Northern troops.

— African Methodist Bishop Henry McNeal Turner becomes the first African American chaplain in the United States Army.

— Bishop Daniel Payne travels to Tennessee and in December accepts two congregations into the African Methodist Episcopal Church.

1864 — February 21, St. Francis Xavier Catholic Church is dedicated as the first parish for African Americans of the Roman Catholic Church.

— The African Methodist Episcopal Church enters Eastern North Carolina, and later in the year organizes the North Carolina Conference.

— The Western Colored Baptist Convention reorganizes as the Northwestern and Southern Baptist Convention.

1865 — February 12, Henry Highland Garnet becomes the first African American to enter the chambers of the House of Representatives and the first to deliver a sermon to that body. His sermon commemorated the adoption of the Thirteenth Amendment to the U.S. Constitution.

— March 3, Abraham Lincoln signs the bill creating the Freedman's Bureau.

— April 9, General Robert E. Lee surrenders, thus ending the Civil War.

— The Union Church of Africans merges with the First Colored Methodist Protestant Church.

— African Methodist Episcopal Church organizes South Carolina Conference.

— Louisiana African American Baptists organize first Baptist association in the South.

— December 18, the Thirteenth Amendment, abolishing slavery in the United States, is ratified.

1866 — April 9, Civil Rights Act bestows full citizenship on African Americans. It is reinforced by the Fourteenth Amendment, ratified June 16.

— Three Baptist associations in the Northern and Western states form Consolidated Baptist Association.

— Alabama and North Carolina Baptists form state conventions.

— Methodist Episcopal Church, South, moves to organize remaining Black members in what will become the Colored Methodist Episcopal Church.

— In July Octavius Brooks Frothingham, speaking for the Unitarians, attacks sectarian religious teachers in the South working with the Freedman's Union Commission.

— Reacting in part to Frothingham, in August, Methodists gather for organizing convention of the Freedman's Aid Society of the Methodist Episcopal Church.

1867 — Black leaders of the Christian Church (Disciples of Christ) organize the American Evangelizing and Education Association. That same year the Disciples organize the Freedman's Missionary Society.

— February 2, Patrick Francis Healy becomes the first African American Jesuit priest.

— March 2, Reconstruction Act passed over presidential veto.

1869 — Rev. Henry McNeal Turner becomes the first African American postmaster. He was appointed by President Grant to a post in Macon, Georgia.

— Colored (now Second) Cumberland Presbyterian Church organized by African American members of the Cumberland Presbyterian Church.

1870 — Colored (now Christian) Methodist Episcopal Church is organized December 15 at Jackson, Tennessee. William H. Miles and Richard A. Vanderhorst are elected bishops.

— The Commission on Home Missions to Colored People supersedes the Freedman's Commission of the Episcopal Church.

— African Methodist minister Rev. Hiram Rhoades Revels becomes the first African American elected to the U.S. Senate.

1871 — Women's Baptist Foreign Missionary Society of the West is organized at Chicago. It commissions Louise C. Fleming as its first missionary to Africa.

— The Jubilee Singers from Fisk University introduce African American sacred music to the general public.

1874 — August, New England Baptist Missionary Convention organized.

— Patrick Healy becomes president of Georgetown University, the first Black president of a Catholic university.

— Women's Parent Mite Missionary Society formed by the women of the Northern conferences of the African Methodist Episcopal Church.

— November 8, James T. Holly is consecrated bishop for the Eglise Orthodoxe Apostolique Haitienne by bishops of the Episcopal Church.

1875 — James A. Healy is appointed bishop of Portland, the first African American Roman Catholic bishop.

1876 — About this year, the Christian Faith Bands, the first of the independent African American Holiness groups, is founded. The Bands would later accept Pentecostalism and become the Church of God (Apostolic).

1877 — Radical Reconstruction ends with the withdrawal of the last Federal troops from the South.

— Synodical Conference (Lutheran) begins mission to the Freemen. John F. Doesher (White) is appointed as a missionary.

1878 — National Convention of Church of Christ (Disciples of Christ) is organized by African American members.

— Mathilda Beasley founds the Third Order of St. Francis, a Roman Catholic order for the African American nuns and opens orphanage in Savannah, Georgia.

— July 3, St. Paul's Colored Lutheran Church is organized in Little Rock, Arkansas. Its building is dedicated on August 18, at which time 23 are baptized. A month later its school opens. This is the first Lutheran Church organized by African Americans.

1880 — Baptist Foreign Mission Convention is organized at Montgomery, Alabama, on November 24. William H. McAlpine is elected its first president.

— Ladies Home and Foreign Missionary Society formed by the African Methodist Episcopal Zion Church's General Conference.

1882 — Episcopal priest George F. Bragg begins publications of the *Lancet*.

— Reformed Zion Apostolic Church is organized.

1883 — Episcopal priest Alexander Crummell founds the Conference of Church Workers Among Colored People.

— Baptist Women's Educational Convention of the State of Kentucky founded in Louisville.

1884 — Commission on Catholic Missions among the Colored People and the Indians is instituted by the Third Plenary Council of the American hierarchy of the Roman Catholic Church.

— Rev. Samuel David Ferguson becomes the first African American bishop of the Episcopal Church. He was assigned to Liberia.

1885 — African Methodist minister Benjamin W. Arnett is elected to the legislature of Ohio, the first Black person elected from a predominantly White district.

— Jane Williams is the first African American woman ordained in the Church of God (Anderson, Indiana).

1886 — August 25, American National Baptist Convention is founded at St. Louis, Missouri.

— April 24, Augustus Tolton is ordained in Rome as a priest of the Roman Catholic Church.

1888 — St. Joseph's Seminary, a major seminary, is founded in Baltimore, Maryland, by the Society of St. Joseph to train priests for the Roman Catholic priesthood.

1889 — Charles M. Kinney is the first African American ordained by the Seventh-day Adventist Church.

— Epiphany Apostolic College, a minor seminary, is founded in Baltimore, Maryland, by the Society of St. Joseph for the training of African American priests for the Roman Catholic Church.

— January 1–4, First Catholic Afro-American Congress convenes in Washington, D.C.

— William Christian founds the Church of the Living God (Christian Workers for Fellowship), one of the first churches to teach that Jesus was a Black man.

— Rabbi Leon Richelieu organizes the Moorish Zionist Temple in New York City, the first Black Jewish congregation.

1890 — Christian Church (Disciples of Christ) places its African American work under a new Board of Negro Education and Evangelism.

— Mother Katherine Drexel (White) founds the Blessed Sacrament Sisters for Indians and Colored People.

1893 — Formation of National Baptist Educational Convention at Washington, D.C.

1894 — The AMEZ Church ordains Julia A. J. Foote as a deacon, the first African American woman so acknowledged.

— Repeal of a section of the Emancipation Act dealing with voting rights launches a new wave of legal measures aimed at segregating Blacks and Whites.

— C. P. Jones and Charles H. Mason found the Church of God in Christ.

1895 — May 19, Mary Jane Small becomes the second female deacon in the AMEZ Church.

— September 24, three Baptist conventions merge to form the National Baptist Convention of the U.S.A.

1896 — Supreme court rules in *Plessy vs. Ferguson* and establishes the "separate but equal" principle which undergirds segregation of the races in schools and other social structures across the South.

— William S. Crowdy organizes the Church of God and Saints of Christ in Lawrence, Kansas.

— Southern women of the AME Church, excluded from the leadership of the Women's Mite Society, organize the Women's Home and Foreign Missionary Society.

1897 — Lott Carey Baptist Home and Foreign Missionary Convention is formed December 16.

— March, Episcopal priest Alexander Crummell founds the American Negro Academy, the first African American association dedicated to scholarship and the arts.

— National Baptist Publishing Board incorporated.

1898 — AMEZ Church ordains Mary Jane Small, the wife of missionary bishop John B. Small, as an elder, the first female elder in the Church.

1900–1955

1900 — Christian Church (Disciples of Christ) disbands the Board of Negro Education and Evangelism and transfers responsibility for African American ministry to Christian Woman's Board of Missions.

— The first African American branch of the Y.M.C.A. in New York City is formed by Charles Thomas Walker.

— Reverdy C. Ransom creates the first institutional church in the Black community, in Chicago's Southside.

— August 31, Women's Auxiliary to Lott Carey Baptist Home and Foreign Missionary Convention founded.

— September 15, Women's Convention of the National Baptist Convention of the U.S.A. is established.

— Christ's Sanctified Holy Church founded in 1904 in Louisiana.

— AMEZ Church ordains Julia A. J. Foote as an elder, the first to serve in the United States.

1903 — Eliza Healy becomes the first African American assigned as the superior of a convent of a Roman Catholic religious order.

1906 — Episcopal Church creates the American Church Institute for Negroes to raise financial support for its African American educational enterprises.

— April 9, the Azusa Street Revival is launched when the "Spirit" falls on Jennie Evans Moore and Edward S. Lee. From this revival over the next three years, Pentecostalism is spread around the world.

— Apostolic Faith Mission Church of God, possibly the first organized Pentecostal denomination, is founded in Alabama by F. W. Williams.

— Pentecostal Assemblies of the World is organized in Los Angeles.

— The Roman Catholic Church extends its efforts in the African American community by establishing the Catholic Board for Mission Work among Colored People.

1907 — At a gathering of Primitive Baptists in Huntsville, Alabama, the National Primitive Baptist Convention of the U.S.A. is organized.

— Charles H. Mason breaks with former Holiness colleague C. P. Jones and reorganizes the Church of God in Christ as a Pentecostal denomination.

1908 — Healing of Mary Lewis Tate leads to formation of Church of the Living God, the Pillar and Ground of Truth, an early Pentecostal body in Alabama.

— William J. Seymour and Charles H. Mason hold revival services in Washington which lead to the formation of the Apostolic Faith Church of God.

— W. E. Fuller of Atlanta, Georgia, organized the African American membership of the Fire-Baptized Holiness Church as the Colored Fire-Baptized Holiness Church (now the Fire-Baptized Holiness Church of God of the Americas).

1909 — Knights of Peter Claver, a Roman Catholic fraternity, is formed in Mobile, Alabama, to assist African American Catholics.

— The Young Woman's Society of the AMEZ Church begins in the home of Victoria Richardson in Salisbury, North Carolina.

1911 — Martha Cunningham Dolby is ordained as possibly the first woman and among the very few African American ministers in the Church of the Brethren.

— Mother Lizzie Roberson is appointed Overseer of Woman's Work in the four-year-old Church of God in Christ.

1913 — Noble Drew Ali launches the Moorish Science Temple of America with a center in Newark, New Jersey.

1915 — September 9, National Baptist Convention (Unincorporated) is formed.

— September, Xavier University is opened by the Blessed Sacrament Sisters for Indiana and Colored People in New Orleans, Louisiana, the only Roman Catholic Church college in the United States for African Americans.

1917 — African American members of the Disciples of Christ organize at the National Convention of the Church of Christ (changed in 1942 to National Christian Missionary Convention).

— William Thomas Phillips founds the Ethiopian (now Apostolic) Overcoming Holy Church of God in Mobile, Alabama.

— Woman's Connectional Missionary Society (now the Woman's Missionary Council) is authorized by the general conference of the Colored (now Christian) Methodist Episcopal Church. Mattie Elizabeth Colemen is elected its first president.

1918 — Rev. Edward T. Demby becomes the first African American bishop elected by the Episcopal Church and assigned service in the United States. He is named suffragan bishop of Arkansas and the Southwest.

— Women's Missionary Council is given official recognition by the general conference of the CME Church.

1919 — Robert C. Lawson leaves the Pentecostal Assemblies of the World, moves to New York City, and founds the Church of Our Lord Jesus Christ of the Apostolic Faith. Among the issues raised by Lawson is the acceptance of women into the ministry of the Pentecostal Assemblies of the World.

— Wentworth Arthur Matthew formed the Commandment Keepers Congregation of the Living God, a Black Jewish group in Manhattan.

1920 — Matthew W. Clair, Sr., and Robert E. Burns become the first African American bishops elected by the Methodist Episcopal Church for service in the United States.

— November, St. Augustine's Seminary, Greenville, Mississippi, is opened by the Society of the Divine Word as the only seminary of the Roman Catholic Church dedicated to the training of African Americans for the priesthood.

1921 — September 2, George Alexander McGuire organizes the African Orthodox Church. He is consecrated archbishop on September 28 in Chicago.

— George Edmund Haynes founds the Department of Race Relations of the Federal Council of Churches.

1922 — Endich Theological Seminary opened by the African Orthodox Church.

1923 — September 16, St. Augustine's Seminary opens in its new permanent home in Bay St. Louis, Mississippi, by the Society of the Divine Word as the major seminary for the training of African American priests by the Roman Catholic Church.

1924 — Pentecostal minister Samuel M. Crouch, Sr., of Dallas, Texas, becomes the first African American radio preacher.

— Beth B'nai Abraham founded in New York City by Rabbi Arnold Josiah Ford.

1925 — A college (now Xavier University) opens in New Orleans, Louisiana, the first college for African Americans founded by the Roman Catholic Church.

1926 — Mordecai Johnson becomes the first African American president of Howard University.

1931 — Xavier University is the first (and only) Roman Catholic university for African Americans.

1932 — Samuel Gimes begins his 35–year leadership of the Pentecostal Assemblies of the World.

— June 7, Judge Lewis J. Smith dies unexpectedly a week after sentencing Father Divine to a jail term. From his cell, Father Divine, when questioned about the occurrence replies, "I hated to have to do it."

— Louis Gregory becomes member of National Spiritual Assembly, the governing body for the Baha'i Faith in the United States.

1935 — Mary McLeod Bethune leads in the consolidation of several women's organizations into the National Council of Negro Women.

1936 — Alexander Preston Shaw elected bishop of the Methodist Episcopal Church.

1939 — Three predominantly White branches of Methodism unite. As part of the plan of union, the church is divided into five regional jurisdictions, while African American members are set apart in a nongeographical Central Jurisdiction.

— Carnella Jamison (Barnes) is ordained by the Christian Church (Disciples of Christ), the only African American Female minister in the denomination.

1941 — Bethune-Cookman College becomes a four-year senior college, and Mary McLeod Bethune the first African American female college president.

— Joseph Oliver Bowers is consecrated as first twentieth-century African American bishop of the Roman Catholic Church. He is assigned to duty in Africa.

1944 — June 28, James Russell Brown becomes the first African American commissioned officer in the chaplaincy in the U.S. Navy.

— The two women's societies of the AME Church merge to form the Women's Missionary Society.

— Baptist minister Adam Clayton Powell, Jr., becomes the first African American elected to Congress from the state of New York. He continues as pastor of the Abyssinian Baptist Church in Harlem during his lengthy political career.

1946 — February 18, James H. Lark is ordained as the first African American minister in the Mennonite Church.

1954 — Supreme Court rules in *Brown vs. Board of Education* and reverses "separate but equal" principle. Ruling becomes the starting point for a generation of civil rights activity.

— Dr. James Joshua Thomas becomes pastor of Mott Haven Reformed Church in the Bronx, New York, the first Black minister to become pastor of a Reformed Church congregation.

— September 26, James H. Lark is consecrated as the first African American bishop of the Mennonite Church.

1955–1969

1955 — December 1, Rosa Parks refuses to move to the "colored" section of a Montgomery bus. On December 5, Rev. Martin Luther King, Jr., leads a boycott of the buses by the city's African American community. The event launches the Civil Rights Movement.

1956 — General conference of the Methodist Church passes legislation to begin the process of eliminating the Central Jurisdiction.

— Career of Prophet Jones, founder of the Church of Universal Triumph/The Dominion of God, begins decline following arrest and trial for gross indecency.

1957 — March, Southern Christian Leadership Conference formed.

— Rev. Archibald J. Carey, Jr., becomes the first Black to head a White House committee, the President's Committee on Government Employment Policy.

— President Eisenhower enforces integration of Central High School in Little Rock, Arkansas.

— Bible Way Church of Our Lord Jesus Christ World Wide founded by former leaders of the Church of Our Lord Jesus Christ of the Apostolic Faith.

1958 — Johnnie Colemon is the first African American ordained by the Unity School of Christianity, a New Thought metaphysical denomination founded in 1889.

— Sallie A. Crenshaw becomes the first African American in the United Methodist tradition ordained as an elder (in the Central Tennessee Conference of what was then the Methodist Church [1939–1968]).

1960 — Era of nonviolent sit-in demonstrations begins in Greensboro, North Carolina.

— May 16, S. Dorme Lartey becomes the first native African to be elected as a bishop of the African Methodist Episcopal Church.

1961 — First of the Freedom Rides.

— James Meredith enters University of Mississippi.

— Baptist followers of Martin Luther King, Jr., leave the National Baptist Convention, U.S.A., to form the Progressive National Baptist Convention. Timothy Moses Chambers is elected as its first president.

1962 — John Melville Burgess consecrated as suffragan bishop of Massachusetts, the first African American to be assigned to a predominantly White diocese in the Episcopal Church.

— Afro-Peruvian monk Martin de Porres is canonized by the Roman Catholic Church.

1963 — 16th Street Baptist Church in Birmingham, Alabama, is bombed and four children are killed.

— Martin Luther King, Jr., and S.C.L.C. target Birmingham for demonstrations.

— National Black Evangelical Association founded.

1964 — December 10, Martin Luther King, Jr., is awarded Nobel Peace prize.

— Edler G. Hawkins is the first African American selected as moderator of the United Presbyterian Church (now a part of the Presbyterian Church [U.S.A.]).

— Civil Rights Bill passed by Congress.

— Malcolm X resigns from Nation of Islam.

— As part of the process of dissolving the all Black Central Jurisdiction, the Methodist Church assigns African American Bishops James S. Thomas and Prince Taylor, Jr., to predominantly White episcopal areas in the North Central and North Eastern Jurisdictions.

1965 — February 21, Malcolm X is assassinated.

— March 21, Civil Rights march from Selma to Montgomery, Alabama, begins.

— July 24–26, S.C.L.C. targets Chicago for demonstrations.

— African Americans in the Watts section of Los Angeles riot.

— Harold Perry becomes the first twentieth-century African American named as a bishop of the Roman Catholic Church for service in this century. He is assigned as auxiliary of New Orleans.

— Trudy Trimm becomes the first female pastor accepted in the National Baptist Convention, U.S.A., Inc.

1966 — January, Harold S. Perry is consecrated as the Roman Catholic auxiliary bishop of New Orleans, the first African American bishop assigned to a position in the United States since Bishop Healy in the 1870s.

— Martin Luther King, Jr., returns to Chicago for further demonstrations in the summer.

— June 26, James Meredith leads march in Jackson, Mississippi. Stokely Carmichael articulates concept of "Black Power," a term coined by author Richard Wright in 1954 as book title.

— National Committee of Negro Churchmen release statement on "Black Power." Responding to that statement, and later spurred by the assassination of Martin Luther King, Jr., (1968), African American leaders in several predominantly White denominations begin to organize caucuses. Over the next four years the American Baptist Black Caucus, Black Affairs Council (Unitarian Universalist Association), Black Council (Reformed Church in America), Black Leadership Conference (Presbyterian Church in the U.S.), Black Methodists for Church Renewal, Black Presbyterians United (United Presbyterian Church in the U.S.A.), Ministers for Racial and Social Justice (United Church of Christ), Union of Black Episcopalians, and United Black Christians (United Church of Christ) are organized by African Americans in the major White Protestant denominations. Roman Catholics organize the National Black Catholic Clergy Caucus, the National Black Sisters' Conference, the National Black Lay Catholic Conference, and the National Office for Black Catholics.

1967 — Mrs. Robert Clayton is elected as the first African American president of the National Young Women's Christian Association.

— Jaramogi Abebe Agyeman (Albert Cleage, Jr.) launches the Black Christian Nationalist Movement at the Shrine of the Black Madonna in Detroit on Easter Sunday.

1968 — April 4, Martin Luther King, Jr., assassinated in Memphis, Tennessee.

— Ralph Abernathy, King's successor as head of SCLC, leads Poor People's March on Washington.

— On July 6, Washington Square United Methodist Church in New York City becomes the first major organization to respond to James Forman's demand for Black reparations by donating $15,000 to the National Black Economic Development Conference.

— Episcopal Church votes to give James Forman $200,000.

1969 — May 17, Thomas Kilgore, Jr., is elected the first African American president of the American Baptist Churches in the U.S.A.

— B. Barton McIntyre is named a Lt. Colonel in the Salvation Army, the highest rank ever attained by an African American.

— Rev. Johnnie Colemon is elected president of the Association of Unity Churches.

— Rev. Ike founds the United Church and Science of Living Institute in Boston.

— Clarence 13X, founder of the Nation of the Five Percent, a Nation of Islam splinter, is shot and killed.

— John Melville Burgess becomes the Episcopal Church's bishop of Massachusetts in 1969.

1970–Present

1970 — Donald M. Payne becomes the first African American head of the national council of the Young Men's Christian Association.

— Society for the Study of Black Religion is founded; Charles Shelby Rooks is named as the first president.

1971 — May, Clarie Collins Harvey becomes the first African American president of Church Women United.

— Supreme Court overturns conviction of Muhammad Ali on draft evasion charges.

— June 19, ground is broken for the monument to Mary McLeod Bethune in Washington, D.C.'s Lincoln Square, the first monument to an African American person on public land in the nation's capital.

1972 — Association for the Study of Black History votes to change its name to the Association of African American History.

— Shirley Caesar wins Grammy Award for her song "Put Your Hand in the Hand of the Man from Galilee."

— December 7, W. Sterling Cary becomes the first African American president of the National Council of Churches of Christ in the U.S.A.

1973 — Dorothy Morris becomes the first female presiding elder in the AME Church (Guyana Conference).

1974 — Charles Shelby Rooks becomes the president of Chicago Theological Seminary, the first African American named president of a White seminary.

— Alice M. Henderson is the first female (either Black or White) to receive assignment as a chaplain in the U. S. Army.

— Katie G. Cannon becomes the first African American female ordained in the Presbyterian Church.

— Lawrence W. Bottoms becomes the first African American named as moderator of the Presbyterian Church in the U.S., now part of the Presbyterian Church (U.S.A.).

1975 — February 25, Elijah Muhammad dies and is succeeded as head of the Nation of Islam by his son, W. D. Muhammad.

— July 1, W. D. Muhammad opens membership in the Nation of Islam to all races.

— Martin Luther King, Sr., is the first African American to address a joint session of the Alabama state legislature.

1976 — Thelma Cornelia Adair is the first African American woman elected as moderator of the United Presbyterian Church in the U.S.A., now a part of the Presbyterian Church (U.S.A.).

1977 — Joseph L. Howze is the first African American Roman Catholic in this century to serve as a diocesan bishop.

— January 8, Pauli Murray becomes the first African American woman ordained to the priesthood by the Episcopal Church.

1978 — The Church of Jesus Christ of Latter-day Saints opens church membership and priesthood to Black people.

— December 10, Fr. Emerson J. Moore is named a Prelate of Honor to Pope Paul VI, the first African American so honored.

— Sandra Wilson is ordained to the Episcopal ministry and becomes the first African American female minister appointed to pastor a congregation.

1979 — Walter D. Dennis elected suffragan bishop of New York in the Episcopal Church.

1983 — January 27, Moses Anderson consecrated as a bishop in the Roman Catholic Church.

— Cornelia Wright becomes the first female appointed as a presiding elder to serve in the United States by the AME Church.

1984 — Bishop Philip R. Cousin begins his term as the first African American president of the National Council of Churches of Christ in the U.S.A.

— Leontine T. C. Kelly is the first African American woman elected as a bishop of a major denomination (United Methodist Church).

1987 — May 21, the National Black Catholic Congress convenes in Washington, D.C.

1988 — March 15, Eugene A. Marino is named archbishop of Atlanta, the first African American Roman Catholic archbishop.

— National Missionary Baptist Convention of America founded by former members of the National Baptist Convention of America.

1989 — Barbara C. Harris is consecrated as the first African American female bishop in the Episcopal Church and the first female bishop in the Worldwide Anglican Communion.

— Joan Salmon Campbell becomes the first African American female selected as moderator of the Presbyterian Church (U.S.A.).

— James A. Forbes is named pastor of Riverside Church, New York City.

1991 — February 20, AME Bishop Vinton R. Anderson becomes the first African American elected as a president of the World Council of Churches.

"Is Christ free? Did he come to preach liberty to the captives? Is his gospel the jubilee trumpet that proclaims the liberty of the world? Did Jesus pray, preach, travel, weep, agonize and die, and rise again, that liberty, in body and soul, should be enjoyed by every child of Adam, of every clime, country, and colour; then to be like Jesus in heart and life, in principle and practice, in desire and object, we must be free, and others must be free, and all must be free. O how delightful to strive to make human and immortal souls like Jesus Christ!"

Paul Quinn, Bishop
African Methodist Episcopal Church
1834

A

ABEL, ELIJAH (July 25, 1810–December, 1884), early elder of the **Church of Jesus Christ of Latter-day Saints**, was born in Maryland. Little is known of Abel's early life, even his exact birth place being disputed in the several records. However, in 1832, just two years after the church was founded, he converted, moved to the church's headquarters in Kirkland, Ohio, and was baptized by Ezekiel Roberts. He was one of the few African American members of the church. In 1836 he was admitted to the Melchizedek priesthood, a step through which all Mormon males are expected to pass, and was licensed as a minister of the gospel. Then in December of that year, he was promoted to the rank of a seventy (administrator) and given a patriarchal blessing. The blessing was unusual. In most such blessings, members were named as a descendant of one of the Old Testament patriarchs. The non-White Abel was declared an orphan and was told, "Thou shalt be made equal to thy brethren, and thy soul be white in eternity and thy robes glittering."

During the late 1830s Abel became a missionary for the church in New York and Canada. He ran into trouble in St. Lawrence County, New York, when he was accused of murdering a woman and five children. He was able to prove himself innocent and nothing came of the charges. In 1839 he moved to Nauvoo, Illinois, where the church headquarters had been relocated. At this time there were only about a dozen African Americans in the church membership. Latter-day Saints were basically opposed to slavery and did not own slaves. Abel was a carpenter and also was appointed as the town's undertaker. For a time he lived in the home of church founder Joseph Smith, Jr.

In 1842 Abel moved to Cincinnati. He married Mary Ann Adams, with whom he had three children, and followed his carpentry trade. Then in 1843 he became the object of the attention of a regional conference of the Cincinnati branch. The visiting elders who conducted the meeting expressed concern about his visibility and the possibility that he might present himself as the equal of White members. A resolution was adopted limiting his activities to work among other African Americans. This resolution is cited as the first instance in which race was used as a criterion for limiting the activities of a church member. Meanwhile, in 1849, Brigham Young, who had led the church to Utah following the murder of the church's founder, declared Black people ineligible for the priesthood. The Utah legislature adopted a set of "black laws" designed to assign a defined lesser status to Black residents.

Abel moved to Utah in 1853, and his skills as a carpenter were put to use in the construction of the temple. He also found his position in the church challenged. Though a priest and minister, he was not allowed to have his marriage sealed in the temple, an important step which married Mormons believe sets their marriage in eternity. In spite of the problems with the church, he settled in Salt Lake City as a member of the Mill Creek Ward. An additional five children were born. He supplemented his income for a brief period by managing a hotel. His wife died in 1877.

In 1880 Abel applied to John Taylor, who had succeeded Brigham Young as the church's president, to go through the temple endowments ceremony. The Council of the Twelve (who rule the church along with the president), refused his request. Though turned back, he remained a member in good standing and in 1883 was appointed to go on a mission in Ohio and Canada. While on the mission, his health failed and he returned to Utah at the beginning of December 1884. He died two weeks later. It has been hypothesized that his going on the mission was to show his loyalty to the church and to demonstrate his worthiness to go through the long-sought temple ceremony.

Abel is remembered as representative of the church's early acceptance of African Americans, and his career coincides with the church's slide into those racial practices which were to dominate it until the 1960s.

Bringhurst, Newell G. "Elijah Abel and the Changing Status of Blacks within Mormonism." *Dialogue* 12 (Summer 1979). Reprinted in Lester E. Bush, Jr., and Armand L. Mauss, eds. *Neither White nor Black*. Medvale, UT: Signature Books, 1984. 249 pp.

———. *Saints, Slaves, and Blacks: The Changing Place of Black People within Mormonism*. Westport, CT: Greenwood Press, 1981. 254 pp.

ABERNATHY, RALPH DAVID (March 11, 1926–April 17, 1990), civil rights leader and close colleague of Martin Luther King, Jr., was born in Linden, Alabama, the tenth of twelve children in the family of farmers William L. and Louivery (Bell) Abernathy. After serving overseas in the Army, Abernathy was ordained a Baptist minister in 1948, in 1950 received a B.S. degree from Alabama College in Montgomery, and an M.A. degree in sociology at Atlanta University in 1951. That same year he accepted the position of pastor of the First Baptist Church in Montgomery, Alabama. He married Juanita Odessa Jones, a teacher, on August 31, 1952. In 1954 **Martin Luther King, Jr.**, whom Abernathy had already come to know through the Ebenezer Baptist Church in Atlanta, arrived in Montgomery as pastor of the Dexter Avenue Baptist Church.

Abernathy gained a high public profile when he called for a citywide boycott of the segregated bus system in response to the arrest on December 1, 1955, of Rosa Parks who refused to give up her seat to a White person. Abernathy also suggested the organization of the Montgomery Improvement Association (MIA) as a permanent body for coordinating the protest. King, although relatively new to Montgomery, was elected to head the MIA, and Abernathy accepted a secondary position on the executive board and program committee. This seemed to set the pattern for their future working relationship, in which King was always in the limelight. Abernathy, however, claimed not to have felt a rivalry with King. They remained very close, and King rarely made a major decision without Abernathy at his side.

The bus boycott lasted 381 days, until the Supreme Court decision of November 13, 1956, against bus segregation was delivered by federal marshals to city officials on December 20. Abernathy's home and church were subsequently bombed on January 10, 1957. Abernathy was away at the time, and his wife and baby daughter were unharmed, though the house was damaged and the church had to be completely rebuilt. That same month the **Southern Christian Leadership Conference** (S.C.L.C.) was founded, King being elected president and Abernathy financial secretary-treasurer.

The S.C.L.C. was the means by which nonviolent resistance to segregation practices was carried beyond Montgomery to other cities in the South. In 1961 Abernathy, in order to be closer to the Atlanta headquarters of the S.C.L.C., resigned his pastorate in Montgomery and became pastor of the West Hunter Street Baptist Church in Atlanta (affiliated with the **American Baptist Churches in the U.S.A.**), where he remained for the rest of his career.

As a leader of voter registration drives, and various forms of civil disobedience, Abernathy was often subject to abuse and arrest; he was in jail together with King a total of seventeen times. He was one of seven Black leaders who met with President Kennedy on September 19, 1963, to discuss the aftermath of the bomb which killed four Black girls at a Birmingham church on September 15. He was a key leader in all the major civil rights actions of the 1960s, including the famous march from Selma to Montgomery in March, 1965. That same year, at King's request, Abernathy was made vice-president-at-large of the S.C.L.C.

On April 4, 1968, King was assassinated, and Abernathy was soon installed as the new president of the S.C.L.C. The major immediate task was to continue the planning for the Poor People's Campaign, which involved bringing poor people in caravans from many parts of the country to an encampment called Resurrection City in Potomac Park, Washington, D.C. In the next several years of his leadership, there were other major S.C.L.C. actions, including a second Poor People's Campaign in 1969, a successful voter registration drive in Greene County, Alabama in 1969, the organization of Operation Breadbasket in Atlanta, and a 100–mile march in Georgia in 1970 to protest police brutality. Nevertheless, the S.C.L.C. grew weaker and weaker. In December 1971, **Jesse Jackson** left the organization to promote his own group, **Operation PUSH**, and took most of the S.C.L.C. Chicago chapter with him. By 1973 S.C.L.C.'s income had dropped from over $2,000,000 per year to about $500,000, and many employees had to be dropped. Abernathy tried to resign on July 9, 1973, but the board of directors would not accept it, and he remained president until February 1977. He ran unsuccessfully in that year for the Georgia congressional seat vacated when Andrew Young was appointed as U.S. ambassador to the United Nations.

After leaving the S.C.L.C., Abernathy slowly grew estranged from many of the other civil rights leaders, particularly King's widow, Coretta Scott King, voicing objections to a 1978 television depiction of King's life on the grounds that it did not give proper credit to other conference leaders, and in 1980 supporting Ronald Reagan's campaign for President, based on assurances that Blacks would be given high government posts. In the following two campaigns, however, he supported Jesse Jackson's candidacy. Nevertheless, he was not invited to participate in the 1986 ceremonies to mark the first national Martin Luther King, Jr., national holiday. Finally, in 1989 Abernathy published his autobiography, *And the Walls Came Tumbling Down*, which told of King's adulterous behavior. He defended the inclusion of this information by noting that others had already discussed the matter publicly. Despite the disagreements with others in the civil rights community in his later years, at his death he was remembered as a faithful and courageous leader.

Abernathy, Ralph. *And the Walls Came Tumbling Down*. New York: Harper and Row, 1989. 640 pp.

———. "The Nonviolent Movement: The Past, the Present, and the Future." In Rhoda L. Goldstein, ed. *Black Life and Culture in the United States*. New York: Thomas Y. Crowell Co., 1971, 180–209.

"King Aide Abernathy Dies at 64," *Houston Chronicle* (April 18, 1990).

"Ralph Abernathy, Aid to Dr. King, Dies," *Los Angeles Times* (April 18, 1990).

WWABA (80–81), *EBA, CB* (68), *NYTO, CRS, WWR* (75, 77), *NA, RLOA, IP*.

ADAIR, THELMA CORNELIA (b. 1922), first African American female elected Moderator of the United Presbyterian Church, was born in Lincoln County, North Carolina, one of five children in the family of Robert James and Violet (Wilson) Davidson. Her father was a Baptist minister and educator and her mother was a school teacher, mortician, and community organizer. Adair's first years were on the campus of Western Union Baptist Academy in Spindale, North Carolina, where her father was principal and superintendent and her mother was a teacher. At about her fifth birthday, her father became principal of Davidson High School in Kings Mountain, North Carolina, and pastor of several Baptist churches on a circuit. The children in the family regularly crossed denominational boundaries, participating in the activities of all the churches in town, including Baptist, CME, AME, AMEZ, Presbyterian, and Sanctified. Adair's elementary education was at the school where her father was principal, and her secondary education was at Lincoln Academy, a boarding school three miles away, run by the American Mission Society of the Congregational Church.

A few days before her thirteenth birthday, she entered Barber-Scotia Junior College for women in Concord, North Carolina, related to the Presbyterian Church. She then went to Bennett College for Women, related to the Methodist Episcopal Church. During the summer months she taught in public schools. Upon graduation, her first full-time job was at Mt. Carmel Junior High School near Lancaster, South Carolina, teaching math, science, and history to poor, rural children of very limited experience. She was paid $50 per month, and was required to visit every family and attend church in the community.

Soon she married Eugene Adair, a Presbyterian minister and Sunday School missionary, left her job, and began traveling with him throughout North and South Carolina, organizing Sunday Schools, building chapels, conducting Vacation Church Schools, etc. Together they had three children. In 1942 they sold their car and used the money to go to New York. He entered Union Theological Seminary and she entered Teachers' College at Columbia University. While she worked on her Ph.D. in Education, the then-president of Union Theological Seminary, Henry Sloan Coffin, asked the couple to open the Mt. Morris Presbyterian Church in Harlem that had closed after the White congregation left. From that point on she had one foot in the social ministry of that church and the other in education, becoming a professor of education at Queens College, University of the City of New York.

She specialized in early childhood education and wrote books such as *A Lap to Sit On, School and Community, Parents and the Day Care Center*, and *When We Teach Fours and Fives*. She organized and directed Day Care Centers for the children of migrant farm workers and in New York City for the children of working parents. She organized and directed Head Start programs, and formulated programs for the Queens College Child Parents Center in Jamaica, Long Island. She has been a teacher and consultant internationally, with the Peace Corps, Operation Crossroads Africa, UNESCO, and numerous universities.

In the United Presbyterian Church in the USA, since 1983 a constituent part of the **Presbyterian Church (U.S.A.)**, she was a ruling elder in the Mt. Morris Presbyterian Church and a leader in **Black Presbyterians United**, but did not gain wide fame until May 1976, when she became the first Black woman Moderator of the church's General Assembly (the 188th). There had been two previous Black moderators, Edler Hawkins in 1964 and Clinton Marsh in 1973, but not even any Black women candidates until Adair.

Widgeon, Pam. "Dr. Thelma Adair Elected Presbyterian Moderator." *Afro-American* (May 25, 1976): 1, 5.

Wilson, Frank T., ed. "Living Witnesses: Black Presbyterians

in Ministry, Part III." *Journal of Presbyterian History* 55 (Summer 1977): 180–238.
IBAW.

ADAMS, C. C. (b. 1895), was for years corresponding secretary of the Foreign Mission Board of the **National Baptist Convention of the U.S.A., Inc.** He also pastored a church in Philadelphia, and for a number of years was president of the Pennsylvania Baptist State Convention. He was chair of the Foreign Mission Board before being elected corresponding secretary in 1941. In 1944 he published a small book entitled *Negro Baptists and Foreign Missions*, and he made three extended trips to the Convention's mission stations in Africa between 1945 and 1950. In 1948 Adams was knighted by the Liberian government for his service in that country, and especially for the role of the Foreign Mission Board in the work of the Carrie V. Dyer Memorial Hospital. He continued as secretary of the Foreign Mission Board into the 1960s, supervising over sixty mission stations in Africa.

Adams, C. C., and Marshall A. Talley. *Negro Baptists and Foreign Missions*. Philadelphia, PA: The Foreign Mission Board of the National Baptist Convention, U.S.A., Inc., 1944. 84 pp.
"The Baptists." *Ebony* 4 (October 1949): 28–33.
AARS, HUBA, SNB, SCA.

ADAMS, CHARLES G. (b. December 13, 1936), internationally known Baptist minister, was born in Detroit, Michigan, the son of Charles Nathaniel and Clifton Verdelle (Gilchrist) Adams. He attended Fisk University in Nashville, Tennessee, from 1954 to 1956, and received his B.A. from the University of Michigan in 1958. On August 4, 1963, he married Florence Layne, with whom he has had two children. He received his S.T.B. in 1964 from Harvard Divinity School in Boston, Massachusetts, as a Rockefeller Fellow.

Adams was ordained in 1961 as a member of the **National Baptist Convention, U.S.A., Inc.,** but soon affiliated with the **Progressive National Baptist Convention, Inc.,** founded that year. It broke away from the National Baptist Convention of the U.S.A., Inc., over issues of length of tenure for officers and support for the civil rights movement. From 1962 to 1969 he pastored the Concord Baptist Church in Boston. In 1967 he founded and then presided over a community housing project, Concord Baptist Homes. From 1969 to the present he has pastored Hartford Memorial Baptist Church in Detroit, Michigan.

He has led his church into involvement in a wide variety of social action ministries, including a credit union, tutorial services for high school and college students, and the Agape House. The Agape House provides a free medical clinic, a food co-op, free legal counseling, a print shop and school, an auto shop and school, and other services. Beginning in 1971 Adams headed the Michigan chapter of the **Southern Christian Leadership Conference**, and in 1973 he became chair of the Detroit Satellite of **Operation PUSH** (People United to Save Humanity) founded by Rev. **Jesse Jackson**. He is a life member of the N.A.A.C.P. and has served on the boards of numerous community service organizations, including the Mayor's Health Care Advocacy Commission; Greater Detroit Opportunities Industrialization Centers; and Detroit Commission on Community Relations.

In addition to his other responsibilities, Adams has maintained a steady stream of published writings. Since 1970 he has been a columnist for the *Michigan Chronicle*, and since 1970 he has also been editor of *Baptist Progress*. He has published articles in several journals, and in 1976 published a book, *Equality Under the Law*. Since 1972 he has been chair of the board of trustees of Shaw College in Detroit, and has been active in the Michigan Academy of Arts and Letters. In 1969 he was a lecturer at Andover Newton Theological Seminary in Andover, Massachusetts, and since then has lectured in many schools across the country. He is also in high demand as a preacher, and has been a pulpit guest in major churches in the United States and South Africa. In 1984 *Ebony* magazine named him one of America's fifteen top Black preachers. He holds honorary doctorates from Morris Brown College, the University of Michigan, and several other schools.

Adams, Charles G. "The Burden of the Black Religion." *Tempo* 2 (December 15–January 1, 1970): 15.
———. *Equality Under the Law*. Valley Forge, PA: Judson Press, 1976.
———. "Some Aspects of Black Worship." *Andover Newton Quarterly* 11 (January 1971): 124–138.
"America's Fifteen Greatest Black Preachers." *Ebony* (September 1984): 27–33.
HUBA, AARS, WWR (75–76).

ADAMS, JOHN HURST (b. November 27, 1929), 87th bishop of the **African Methodist Episcopal Church** (AME), was born in Columbia, South Carolina, the son of Eugene Avery and Charity A. (Nash) Adams. His father (d.1969) was an AME minister, and Adams was named after Bishop **John Hurst** (1863–1930). He received his B.A. from Johnson C. Smith College in Charlotte, North Carolina in 1948, was ordained deacon in 1949 and elder in 1952. He went on to Boston University School of Theology, where he received his S.T.B. in 1951 and S.T.M. in 1953. He later did advanced studies at Harvard University and Union Theological Seminary in New York City. In 1949, while still in seminary, he was assistant pastor of the Charles Street AME Church in Boston, Massachusetts. In 1950 he was assigned as pastor of the Bethel AME Church in Lynn, Massachusetts. In 1952 he became a professor at Wilberforce University and its related Payne Theological Seminary in Ohio.

On August 25, 1956, he married Dolly Jacqueline Desselle, with whom he had three children. That year Wilberforce gave him an honorary D.D. degree as he left to be president of Paul Quinn College in Waco, Texas. While in Texas, he served as State Education Director of the National Association for the Advancement of Colored People (N.A.A.C.P.). In 1956 Gayraud Stephen Wilmore led in the founding of the National Committee of Negro Churchmen (now the **National Conference of Black Churchmen**), and Adams was a charter member who wrote many of the position papers for the organization.

In 1962 he left Texas to be pastor of the First AME Church in Seattle, Washington. During his six years there he became widely known as a champion of civil rights, leading a movement to equalize all the facilities in Seattle. He was honored in 1964 as Man of the Year by B'nai B'rith Northwest, and in 1965 was named Man of the Year by the Seattle and Northwest Area Urban League. In 1965 he organized and chaired the Freedom Patrol Movement. In 1968 he went to Grant Memorial AME Church in the Watts community of Los Angeles, California. There he once again was active in a wide variety of community activities. He was presiding officer of the Los Angeles Black Political Convention, which empowered citizens in the choice of civil office candidates. He was president of the Ujima Development Corporation, which underwrote a new black-owned community in Los Angeles, with a 500–unit housing complex, medical center, small businesses, and education program. He lectured in theology and preaching at the School of Theology in Claremont, California.

At the 1972 General Conference in Dallas, Texas, Adams was elected on the first ballot, and eventually seven other bishops were elected at that historic General Conference. He was first assigned to the Tenth Episcopal District in Texas, shifting to the Second District (Maryland, Washington, D.C., Virginia, North Carolina) in 1980. He has served on the National Conference of Black Churchmen, the national board of Black United Funds, the National Council of Churches, and **Operation PUSH** (People United to Save Humanity). In 1984, *Ebony* magazine named him one of the top fifteen Black preachers in America.

"America's Fifteen Greatest Black Preachers." *Ebony* 39 (September 1984): 27–33.
WWABA (88), *AMECMIM, BDNM* (75), *WWR* (85), *EBA, AMSC, HAMEC, FEDHR.*

AENON BIBLE SCHOOL. A **Pentecostal Assemblies of the World** (PAW) school. Like most Pentecostal churches during the first half of the twentieth century, the Pentecostal Assemblies of the World did not place a high priority on education for ministers, their emphasis being upon the movement and leading of the Holy Spirit in the life of the believer. It was thought by many that the work of the Holy Spirit could be stifled, and often was, by education. Within the PAW the cause of ministerial education was led by Bishop **Karl F. Smith** (1892–1972), for many years pastor of the Church of the Apostolic Faith in Columbus, Ohio.

As World War II approached, Smith argued for the founding of an educational institution at the annual conventions of the PAW. In 1940, Smith and LeBaugh H. Stansbury were given permission to establish a school. A school was opened in Columbus, Ohio, at the beginning of 1941, and classes were held in Smith's church. Smith chose the name Aenon, meaning "waters of refreshing." The course lasted only eight weeks. Property was purchased in 1944 which allowed the school not only expanded classroom facilities but provided dormitory space for resident students.

Disaster struck in 1947 when fire destroyed the upper stories of the building and water inflicted severe damage on the first floor. Classes were moved back to the church while the school was repaired. However, expansion continued and with the growth of the faculty, a new two-year curriculum was initiated in 1948. Two years later a full four-year course was introduced. Smith served as president during this time.

The school has had a tenuous existence at times, but has survived through the years. In 1981 it was moved to Indianapolis, Indiana, into the Assemblies' new headquarters complex. In 1978 a branch of the school was opened in Philadelphia.

Golder, Morris E. *History of the Pentecostal Assemblies of the World.* Indianapolis, IN: The Author, 1973. 195 pp.

AFRICAN AMERICAN CATHOLIC CONGRE-GATION. A church in the Roman Catholic tradition. The African American Catholic Congregation grew out of the tension of a rising visible Black presence in the **Roman Catholic Church** in America in the last half of the twentieth century and the problems of the church in accommodating to that presence. The subject of that tension, in this case, was **George A. Stallings** (b. 1948). Stallings had been raised as a Roman Catholic and as a teenager decided to go into the priesthood. After completing his education in Rome, he was ordained in 1974. His first appointment was St. Teresa of Avila Roman Catholic Church, an African American parish in the archdiocese of Washington (D.C.). At the same time he became a lecturer at St. Mary's Seminary in nearby Emmitsburg, Maryland, and at the Washington Theological Union.

Stalling appeared to be launched on a successful career as both a parish priest and teacher. His early years coincided with the gradual emergence of African American Catholic organizations, many of which, such as the **National Black Catholic Clergy Caucus**, were headquartered in Washington. However, as years passed he became increasingly and openly critical of both his archbishop, James Hickey, and of the Roman Catholic Church in general. He saw each as possessed of an intense racism.

In 1988, to respond to Stallings and to quiet some of the criticism, Hickey moved him from the parish to a new assignment as a special evangelist for the archdiocese for work within the Black community. However, the move only served to heighten the rhetoric and the relationship between the archbishop and his priest worsened. Soon afterward Stallings quit the church and founded a rival congregation, the Imani Temple (so called after the Swahili word for "faith"). With his every move of media interest, he soon was able to found additional congregations in nearby states.

Unable to reconcile his differences with Hickey, on May 12, 1990, he was consecrated by Archbishop Richard W. Bridges of the independent American National Catholic Church. He now possessed apostolic orders through the lineage of the Old Catholic movement (which had broken with Rome in the nineteenth century following the changes made by Vatican I). The Old Catholic Church allows its priests to marry, and has in more recent years been very lenient in accepting divorced and remarried people into full communion and allowing artificial birth control. The African American Catholic Congregation fully accepted this distinction.

The Congregation inherited the social activism so evident during the early years of Stallings ministry and has moved to establish a variety of social service and social justice ministries in the predominantly Black community of Washington, D.C.

Grogan, David. "A Black Catholic Priest's Renegade Church Stirs an Unholy Furor." *People* 32, 5 (July 31, 1989): 26–28.

Historical and Doctrinal Digest of the African American Catholic Congregation. Washington, DC: African American Catholic Congregation, 1990. 16 pp.

AFRICAN AMERICAN UNITARIAN UNIVER-SALIST MINISTRY. A Unitarian Universalist Association organization. The African American Unitarian Universalist Ministry was originally conceived by the Affirmative Action Task Force created by the African American ministers of the Unitarian Universalist Association's Department of Ministry. It was founded in 1988 by Mark D. Morrison-Reed and William E. Jones. Morrison-Reed had earlier authored an attack upon the racism in the Unitarian Universalist Association in his *Black Pioneers in a White Denomination* (1984).

As presently constituted the relatively new agency is charged with producing African American-oriented materials for use in Unitarian Universalist churches. They are preparing worship materials, theological reflections on liberation theology, and historical and descriptive brochures. The ministry has 20 members drawn from among Black ministers, education directors, and denominational staff. Headquarters is in Boston, Massachusetts.

AFRICAN ISLAMIC MISSION. A Muslim group. The African Islamic Mission is an African American orthodox Muslim organization which emerged in the 1970s in Brooklyn, New York. It is headquartered in the Al Masjid Al Jaaami'a under the leadership of Imam Alhaji Obaba Muhammadu. The mission is most noted for its development of a black history publication series which includes reprints of many rare and hard to find books on the origins of African people.

Introduction to Islam: The First and Final Religion. Brooklyn, NY: African Islamic Mission, n.d. 16 pp.

AFRICAN METHODIST EPISCOPAL CHURCH. A Methodist organization. The movement of African American Methodism to institutionalized form dates from at least as early as 1786, scarcely two years after the founding of U.S. Methodism, itself. In that year,

Black Christians in Baltimore voluntarily had begun meeting for prayer and devotions separate from the Whites in the Methodist church with which they were affiliated. In that same year, **Richard Allen**, a former slave from Delaware, now a licensed Methodist preacher, organized some forty-two Black Philadelphians into prayer meetings and a Methodist society. With the support of three other Blacks—**Absalom Jones**, William White, and Dorus Ginnings—Allen initiated the building of a house of worship. However, in the face of strong opposition from the White Methodist clergy stationed in Philadelphia, both the building effort and the separate devotional meetings were discontinued.

Tension between Black and White Methodists in Philadelphia surfaced once again the following year. In November of 1787, Allen, Jones, and other Blacks arrived at the city's St. George Methodist Church for Sunday worship and were directed to a newly built gallery for seating. Mistakenly moving to the "White" area of the gallery, they were pulled from their knees during prayer by ushers insisting they move to the proper section. Instead, at prayer's end, several Blacks left the sanctuary as a group and, says Allen, ". . . they were no more plagued with us in the church." Over the next few years, the group met under the name of the Free African Society, inaugurating among African Americans nationwide the formation of mutual aid societies for support in material crises and for social and religious interaction. They also began, under Allen and Jones, an effort to raise funds through public subscription for the erection of a house of worship. In spite of strong opposition from St. George's clergy and the threat to read them out of church membership, the effort proceeded and a building was constructed.

Allen and Jones felt that it was desirable to align the group with the Methodist Church, even in the face of hostility, for, as Allen phrased it, "No religious sect or denomination would suit the capacity of the colored people as well as the Methodists; for the plain and simple gospel suits best for any people." The decision of a majority of the new society, though, was to affiliate with the Church of England [Episcopal]. Thus, in 1794 the congregation and the building which housed it became the St. Thomas African Episcopal Church. Absalom Jones was ordained as the first Black Protestant priest in the U.S. and became pastor to St. Thomas'.

Richard Allen purchased, with his own funds, a blacksmith shop and fitted it up for a church. It was dedicated, also in 1794, by Methodist bishop Frances Asbury as the Bethel Church. There, Allen and others like him who "could not be anything else but a Methodist" found their devotional home. Allen provided informal leadership to the congregation, and in 1799 he was ordained a deacon in the Methodist Church by Bishop Asbury—the first Black person to be granted that rank. Nonetheless, Bethel was officially served by White clergy appointed by the Methodist conference.

In Baltimore, Blacks at the two White churches formed an independent Colored Methodist Society after they had been put in galleries and not allowed to receive communion until after the Whites had been served. In several other cities in the region Blacks had experienced disaffection from Methodist congregations with whom they had affiliated and had withdrawn into separated worship groupings. Conflicts continued between the Philadelphia group and the conference over the quality and sensitivity of clergy assigned to them and also over the ownership of church property. The recognition of widespread, common concerns among Black Methodists led to a call in April, 1816, for all such separated bodies to convene to consider legal independence. Sixteen representatives from five congregations met at Bethel, Philadelphia. They voted to organize themselves under the name the African Methodist Episcopal Church. They sued for independence before the Supreme Court of Pennsylvania and were granted their plea. **Daniel Coker** was elected bishop of the new body but declined, and Richard Allen became the first bishop to serve the denomination.

The new church affirmed its Methodist heritage by adopting a system of church government patterned closely after that of the mother church. A quadrennial General Conference, comprised of clergy and lay delegates from every region the church serves establishes church policy, enacts legislation, and approves a budget for the coming quadrennial period. The General Board of the General Conference serves as trustee/custodian of all church properties. The Judicial Council is the supreme court of appeals for all disputes arising within the operation of the church. The bishops are the top-level administrative officers of the church. They preside over geographic districts approximately balanced for parity among the bishops in terms of numbers of constituents and churches. Today there are nineteen such episcopal districts worldwide.

The work of the denomination is managed through annual conferences, which are geographic/administrative subdivisions of episcopal districts. Bishops preside over the meetings of the annual conferences in their districts. Here, clergy and laity report on their labors in ministry for the year past, plan and set the budget for the work of the ensuing year. Also at the annual conferences bishops appoint clergy to the churches they will serve for the year. Theoretically, all clergy are subject to relocation each year; that is the essence of the Methodist term *itinerant* ("traveling") clergy. But the pattern of annual reassignment which, indeed, once pertained has lengthened, so that clergy may now serve several years in one station before "promotion" or the matching of a pastor's gifts with the needs of a particular congregation elsewhere suggest a move is in order. Annual conferences are further divided into *presiding elder districts*, supervised by clergy of the same title, appointed by the bishops as their assistants.

The laws and operating procedures by which the AME Church is governed, as well as its doctrinal affirmations, are contained in the *Book of Discipline*. Like church structure, it closely parallels that of the Methodist Episcopal Church (now **United Methodist Church**). In matters of faith it adheres to Methodism's Twenty-Five Articles.

The AME Church historically has seen a particular responsibility for ministering to African Americans. But, like the other Black Methodist bodies, it understands its larger mission to be universal. The ranks of its lay and clergy membership have always been open to all persons.

In its *Book of Discipline*, the AME Church sets forth its understanding of its "Mission and Purpose," as follows:

> . . . to minister to the spiritual, intellectual, physical and emotional needs of all people by spreading Christ's liberating gospel by word and deed. Each local church of the African Methodist Episcopal Church shall engage in carrying out the spirit of the original Free African Society out of which the A.M.E. Church evolved.

In keeping with this statement, it is common to find local congregations sponsoring, in addition to worship and Bible study, programs for health care, counseling, hunger relief, youth guidance and recreation, cultural enrichment, and economic development. Many AME congregations establish school facilities and sponsor housing for the elderly and other persons of limited income.

Evangelism was an early emphasis of the denomination. In 1827, Scipio Bean was sent as a missionary to Haiti. In the post Civil-War years AME clergy evangelized Native Americans in the Southwestern states and established churches in Mexico. The Rev. (later Bishop) **Henry McNeal Turner** planted African Methodism in South Africa just before the turn of the century. Today the church is represented in over twenty African countries, in England, Canada, Jamaica, Haiti, the Dominican Republic, the Virgin Islands, the Windward Island, Guyana, and Surinam. The church

holds membership in the National Council of Churches, the World Council of Churches, and, through its Caribbean congregations, in the Caribbean Conference of Churches.

Another early, strong emphasis was education. Over the years and widely across the nation the denomination has sponsored numerous schools, colleges, seminaries, and training institutes. Prominent among those at the collegiate level are Wilberforce and Allen Universities, Paul Quinn, Shorter, Bonner-Campbell, Edward Waters, Kittrel, Payne, and Morris Brown colleges. Seminaries include Payne, in Xenia, OH, and Turner, in Atlanta, GA. At least three Job Corps vocational training centers are hosted on AME properties. And several schools, from the primary grades through the collegiate level, are also sponsored by the church in Africa and the Caribbean. Among these are the Monrovia College and Industrial Training School in Monrovia, Liberia, and the School of Religion in Johannesburg, South Africa.

As of 1991 there were some 3,000,000 members in the worldwide African Methodist Episcopal Church, served by 6500 clergy in over 6200 congregations. Communication across this broad religious network occurs through several publications, including the *Christian Recorder* and the *Quarterly Review*, respectively the oldest newspaper and magazine continuously published by black people in the world; the *Voice of Missions;* the *Women's Missionary Magazine;* the *Journal of Christian Education;* and the *Secret Chamber.*

Aptheker, Herbert. *A Documentary History of the Negro People in the United States.* 2 vols. New York: The Citadel Press, 1968.

Gregg, Howard D. *History of the African Methodist Episcopal Church: The Black Church in Action.* Nashville, TN: The AMEC Sunday School Union, 1980. 523 pp.

Lincoln, C. Eric, and Lawrence Mamiya. *The Black Church in the African American Experience.* Durham, NC: Duke University Press, 1990. 519 pp.

Melton, J. Gordon, ed. *The Encyclopedia of American Religions.* 3rd Edition. Detroit, MI: Gale Research, Inc., 1989. 1102 pp.

Norwood, Frederick, ed. *Sourcebook of American Methodism.* Nashville, TN: Abingdon Press, 1982. 683 pp.

Payne, Wardell J., ed. *Directory of African American Religious Bodies: A Compendium by the Howard University School of Divinity.* Washington, DC: Howard University Press, 1991. 363 pp.

AFRICAN METHODIST EPISCOPAL ZION CHURCH. A Methodist organization. The desire for non-discriminatory access to the Communion table and to itinerant ministry in the Methodist Episcopal Church led Black New Yorkers in the John Street Methodist Church to seek a separate arena of church life. Led by **James Varick**, in 1796 they requested and were granted permission by Bishop Frances Asbury to conduct services of worship among themselves. A hall was rented and a Methodist congregation was formed; it became chartered in 1801 as the African Methodist Episcopal Church of the City of New York, known also as Zion Church. The congregation was served by a White pastor, William Stillwell, who was appointed to this charge, along with John Street Church, by the Methodist Conference. Stillwell later served concurrently the Asbury Church, a Black congregation which emerged out of an 1813 split in Zion Church.

A legal action by White Methodist clergy in New York in 1820 seeking greater clergy control over church properties caused considerable anxiety among Zion members regarding the security of their church property. As a result, a series of meetings on the subject led to the decision in July of that year to "decline receiving any further services from [the Methodist Conference clergy] as respects our church government." William Stillwell, who had, himself, led a schism in the conference over the same issue, was retained as Zion's pastor.

Then, in June of 1821, representatives from Zion, Asbury, and other churches in New York, Connecticut, and Pennsylvania met in New York, under the leadership of James Varick, to form an independent Black Methodist body. In 1822 Varick was elected the first "bishop" (the term used at the time being "superintendent").

The 1848 General Conference of this body voted to add "Zion" to its name in honor of the first congregation and in order to distinguish the denomination clearly from **Richard Allen**'s **African Methodist Episcopal Church** based in Philadelphia.

From its start in New York, the AMEZ Church came to achieve a concentration of strength in North Carolina (where its publication department, archives, and General Secretary are now located.) Growth during the 19th century prior to the Civil War was only modest. Yet the church counted some noteworthy African Americans among its membership, including **Sojourner Truth**, Frederick Douglass, **Harriet Tubman**, and Jermain Loguen. The Rev. (later bishop) **John J. Moore** pioneered the church's work on the West Coast, beginning in the 1850s. He firmly planted Zion in the Far West and also distinguished himself as an educator, journalist/publisher, and leading advocate for Black social and political advancement. He was succeeded on the Coast by other strong clergy who further advanced the work, persons such as **Alexander Walters** and **C. Calvin Pettey** (both later to become bishops.) Pettey organized an emigration movement of Zion members from North Carolina to a colony he established in Northern California.

Following the war, Zionites contended with AMEs for the recruitment into membership of the millions of ex-slaves and for the acquisition of the many church properties abandoned by Southerners or confiscated by the Union Army. In 1868 Bishop **J. J. Clinton** organized the Tennessee Annual Conference. The Texas Conference was organized by Bishop **Thomas H. Lomax** in 1883, and the Oklahoma Conference by Bishop C. C. Pettey in 1897. At century's end, Zion claimed some 350,000 members in the U.S., Africa, South America, and the West Indies.

Because of their affinity to Methodism, Zion's founders adopted, with only minor modifications, the *Book of Discipline*, Twenty-Five Articles of Religion, and the ecclesiastical structure of the mother church. The latter includes the system of quadrennial General Conferences, geographical episcopal districts (presently 13), Annual Conferences, and Presiding Elders as supervisory staff serving under the bishops. The work of the church is distributed among several boards, agencies and departments: Publications; Christian Education; Church Extension; Home Missions; Overseas Missions; Women's Home and Overseas Missionary Society; Bureau of Evangelism; Historical Society; Public Relations and Social Service; Council of Laity. A longstanding commitment to education has produced numerous schools and seminaries, including Livingstone College, Salisbury, North Carolina; Clinton Junior College, Rock Hill, South Carolina; Lomax-Hannon Junior College, Greenville, Alabama; and Hood Theological Seminary, Salisbury, North Carolina. The weekly *Star of Zion* newspaper, well over a century old, is the principal journal of the denomination, which also publishes through its Publishing House and Book Concern the *Quarterly Review*, the *Missionary Seer* (monthly), the *Church School Herald*, and a complete line of church school literature.

The evangelical commitment of the AMEZ Church is pursued under the auspices of its Bureau of Evangelism, established in 1920. Mission efforts have planted Zion congregations in Haiti, the Bahamas, Jamaica, South America, Liberia, and England. Other aspects of the church's sense of mission and ministry are expressed through the AMEZ Health Center, in Hot Springs, Arkansas, and through the Laymen's Council.

The role of women in the life of the church is one place where Zion Methodism took the lead. With the ordination of **Julia Foote** and **Mary Small** to deacon and then full elder status between 1894 and 1900, the AME Zion church was the second among all Methodist bodies (after the Primitive Methodists) to recognize women's ordained religious vocation.

Today the African Methodist Episcopal Zion Church claims some 1.3 million members in 6057 churches served by over 6200 clergy. It holds membership in both the National Council of Churches and the World Council of Churches.

The AMEZ Church has entered serious merger negotiations with another branch of Black Methodism, the **Christian Methodist Episcopal Church**. The General Conferences of the two bodies have approved the merger; it awaits final approval by the annual conferences. At this writing, however, there does not appear to be active movement in this direction.

Bradley, David H., Sr. *A History of the A.M.E. Zion Church*. 2 vols. Nashville, TN: Parthenon Press, 1956, 1970.

Lincoln, C. Eric, and Lawrence Mamiya. *The Black Church in the African American Experience*. Durham, NC: Duke University Press, 1990. 519 pp.

Melton, J. Gordon. *The Encyclopedia of American Religions*. 3rd Edition. Detroit, MI: Gale Research, Inc., 1989. 1102 pp.

Norwood, Frederick, ed. *Sourcebook of American Methodism*. Nashville, TN: Abingdon Press, 1982. 683 pp.

Payne, Wardell J., ed. *Directory of African American Religious Bodies: A Compendium by the Howard University School of Divinity*. Washington, DC: Howard University Press, 1991. 363 pp.

Walls, William J. *The African Methodist Episcopal Zion Church: Reality of the Black Church*. Charlotte, NC: AME Zion Publishing House, 1974. 669 pp.

AFRICAN MISSIONS AND THE AFRICAN AMERICAN CHRISTIAN CHURCHES. At the beginning of the nineteenth century, American Protestant missionary societies began to focus on foreign mission work. White Congregationalists, Baptists, Methodists, Episcopalians, and Presbyterians all had organized foreign mission societies by 1840. The first foreign mission society in the United States was the interdenominational American Board of Commissioners for Foreign Missions (ABCFM), formed in 1810. However, with the rise of denominationalism, all the non-Congregationalists withdrew from the ABCFM and founded their own separate mission societies.

A number of American mission societies began to support mission work in Africa in the early nineteenth century. By that date, Africa was seen as a legitimate area for proselytizing, and American-based churches established mission stations there. American boards regarded Africans as "uncivilized and un-Christian" and they sought financial support from congregations at home by evoking a picture of the ignorant, unclothed, diseased, and generally benighted African.

The idea that "civilization" meant Westernization enjoyed a special vogue in mid-nineteenth century missiology. Christianity and "civilization" were inseparable. Racially inferior Africans could never attain the heights of Western "civilization"; they might receive all the spiritual blessings of Christianity but still remain within their own inferior culture. Therefore, any study of Christianity in Africa since 1800 must involve an analysis of these perceptions.

During the American Protestant missionary movement in Africa, Black Americans assumed a role in the evangelization of Africa. Many African Americans accepted the contemporary theory of "providential design," the idea that Blacks had been brought to America for slavery so that they might be Christianized and "civilized" to return to Africa with the light of "civilization." Basically, African Americans endorsed the Western image of Africa as a "Dark Continent."

In the latter half of the nineteenth century European governments shifted their interest in Africa from the slave trade to colonization. Hence, the late nineteenth and early twentieth centuries witnessed the partitioning of Africa with the subsequent establishment of European colonial rule. During this period, a small segment of the African American community addressed themselves to the issue of the impact of European colonialism in Africa. Generally, they concluded that as long as the interests and welfare of Africans were being considered, European activities on the continent could be beneficial to Africa and Africans.

Black Americans also supported mission work in Africa, believing that this religious and cultural exposure would help make the continent more acceptable to the world. Neither the Black masses nor their leaders have ever forgotten their ancestral homeland and during the height of the missionary movement, Black churches expressed their interest in the continent by sending missionaries there, just as White churches were doing. After 1870 African Americans could not resist the call to serve, and Black churches became involved in African mission work. Although African Americans were assigned to fields other than Africa by both White and Black church boards, the majority saw their destiny in Africa and volunteered to work there.

The earliest plan contemplated for the use of Black American missionaries in Africa was the one proposed by Samuel Hopkins of Newport, Rhode Island. Soon after his installation in 1770, Hopkins, a prominent clergy of the First Congregational Church of Newport, formulated a plan that contained both missionary and emigration features. Actually, the missionary tradition had its roots in the emigration movement. Hopkins' plan called for the selection and education of American free Blacks as Christian ministers who would then emigrate to Africa and teach Africans the doctrines and duties of Christianity.

Two candidates, both members of the First Congregational Church, were selected to be trained for this purpose and went to Princeton University (Princeton, New Jersey) to study theology in order to prepare themselves as missionaries. With the British occupation of Newport during the American Revolutionary War, Hopkins' pastoral work was interrupted. He was unable to put his plan into effect. After 1791 Hopkins sought to renew his plan, but his death in 1803 ended his emigration-missionary dreams. At that time none of his emigrant-missionaries had completed their education. However, it is believed that at least two of his candidates later went to Liberia under a similar plan of the American Colonization Society (ACS).

On December 28, 1816 the constitution of the ACS was adopted. The ACS was dedicated to repatriating Blacks to Africa but it also was committed to African mission work. The philosophy of the ACS carried a strong missionizing theme. As such, a free Black minister of the **African Methodist Episcopal Church** (AME) emigrating to Liberia became the first African American missionary in Africa.

On February 6, 1820 **Daniel Coker**, from Baltimore, Maryland, along with ninety others, left New York harbor, on the ship the *Elizabeth*, as the first party of emigrants sent to what would become Liberia by the ACS. Coker was sent to Africa, a year before **Lott Carey**, as a missionary with a subsidy from the Maryland Colonization Society. Daniel Coker was the first African American to leave for Africa with a clear missionary purpose, although he had not been appointed by any particular missionary board. Ten days after the ship left New York, Coker organized the first foreign branch of the AME Church on board the ship. Coker first settled in Liberia but later transferred to Sierra Leone.

In 1815 Lott Carey helped to establish the Richmond African Baptist Missionary Society and was elected recording secretary. Carey, born a slave, purchased his freedom and eventually became a leader in the First Baptist Church of Richmond. On May 1, 1819 Carey was appointed as a missionary by the General Missionary Convention of the Baptist Denomination in the United States of America for Foreign Missions. It had been formed in 1814, but soon was known as the Triennial Convention because it met every three years. The Triennial Convention was later renamed the American Baptist Foreign Mission Society and is today the **American Baptist Churches in the U.S.A.** This appointment set the stage for the beginning of Baptist mission work in Africa. Carey, then, was also both an emigrant and a missionary.

The First Baptist Church of Monrovia was organized in Richmond on January 11, 1821 by ACS emigrants who twelve days later sailed to Africa on the *Nautilus*. The group first settled in Sierra Leone because ACS agents had not yet purchased land in Liberia. However, in 1822 they moved to Cape Mesurado, the first settlement in Liberia and the present-day site of Monrovia. Carey established the first Baptist church in Monrovia, Providence Baptist Church.

The Methodists: Independent Black-led churches began mission activity in Africa in the nineteenth century and began to appoint Blacks as missionaries in their ancestral homeland. The largest number of African American missionaries sent to Africa by Black boards went during the late nineteenth and early twentieth centuries.

The AME Church was organized as a separate branch of Methodism in 1816. Its foreign mission outreach began in 1820 when Daniel Coker organized the first AME Church in Sierra Leone. That church, however, was abandoned after Coker's death. In 1822 Charles Butler was appointed the first official AME missionary but he never left the United States for his assignment. John Boggs became the earliest commissioned AME missionary to reach Africa in 1824, serving in Liberia. However, there is no available information on the extent of the work that he established.

In 1844 the General Conference of the AME Church authorized the organization of the Parent Home and Foreign Missionary Society as the central agency for the operation of missions, but the society did not begin to function actively until 1864, when a Board of Missions was established and a Secretary of Missions elected. Ultimately, two women's auxiliaries were formed. In 1874 the Woman's Parent Mite Missionary Society was organized in Philadelphia. The Woman's Home and Foreign Missionary Society was established in South Bend, Indiana in 1898 as a result of Bishop **Henry McNeal Turner**'s visit to South Africa where he saw the need for Black missionaries, and because of southern AME women's dissatisfaction with northern leadership in the Mite Missionary Society. The Woman's Parent Mite Missionary Society supported the work of the church in Haiti, Santo Domingo, Liberia, Sierra Leone, Barbados, Demarara, the Bahamas, the Virgin Islands, Trinidad, and Jamaica. The Woman's Home and Foreign Missionary Society supervised AME missions in southern Africa.

Africa was set apart as a foreign mission field by the General Conference of the AME Church in 1856 and John R. V. Morgan was appointed missionary pastor to Liberia. Little is known of his activities except that he returned to the United States because his work was not supported by the church.

The first permanent AME mission in Africa was established in 1878. On April 21 of that year Samuel E. Flegler sailed from Charleston to Liberia on the *Azor* with over 206 other South Carolinian emigrants. Flegler led this AME congregation to Liberia where they settled at Brewerville, sixty miles in the interior of Liberia. Their settlement marked the formal beginning of AME churches in Africa. Initially sponsored by the Morris Brown AME Church in Charleston, the Liberian AME Church eventually was recognized by the national church conference. Flegler returned to South Carolina in 1881.

The permanent work of the AME Church in Sierra Leone began in 1886 when John Richard Frederick was appointed as the first officially sponsored AME missionary to that country. Frederick was sent to Africa by the New England Conference of the AME Church but most of his financial support was contributed by the Ohio Conference. He sailed on November 20, 1886.

Frederick was quite successful during his first few years in Sierra Leone and he soon spread his work into the interior. He was the first AME missionary to work extensively with indigenous Africans rather than with emigrants. After his arrival in Sierra Leone in 1887 he worked with educational and social welfare projects.

Frederick became friends with the West Indian emigrant **Edward Blyden**, who was living in Sierra Leone at the time. With Blyden and James "Holy" Johnson, Frederick helped found the Dress Reform Society, which had the goal of encouraging westernized Africans to reject European dress in favor of traditional African attire. Frederick remained one of Blyden's closest friends and was chosen to preach the sermon at Blyden's funeral in 1912.

Frederick got along well with Africans, so much so that some interior ethnic groups pleaded for him to open a mission station in their towns. He began training Africans as missionaries and also as ministers. He founded Bethel AME Church and Allen AME Church in Sierra Leone. In 1890 Frederick started AME missions at Mange and Magbele. He adjusted well to Sierra Leone and remained there for the rest of his life.

By 1897 Frederick had become disillusioned over AME commitment to support the mission in Sierra Leone. He felt that he was faced with a lack of moral and financial support from the AME Church and withdrew from the church. He joined the British Wesleyan Methodist Church.

The year after Frederick's arrival in Sierra Leone in 1887, Sarah Gorham, fifty-six years of age, became the first woman missionary of the AME Church appointed to a foreign field. In 1880 Gorham visited relatives who had emigrated to Liberia and she spent a year traveling throughout the country preaching and comforting the needy. It was on this trip that she became interested in African mission work. She returned to the United States in 1881 and settled in Boston, Massachusetts where she joined Charles Street AME Church.

In 1888 Gorham offered her services to the AME Church as a missionary. Although sponsored by the AME Woman's Parent Mite Missionary Society, most of Gorham's financial support, like John Frederick's, came from the Ohio Conference.

Soon after her arrival in Freetown, Sierra Leone in September of 1888 Gorham traveled to Magbele, where she was active in the Allen AME Church. She worked at Magbele, one hundred miles from Freetown, among Temne women and girls. It was at Magbele that she established the Sarah Gorham Mission School, which gave both religious and industrial training. In 1891 she traveled to the United States to recuperate and regain her health. She later returned to Sierra Leone.

In July of 1894 Gorham was bedridden with malaria and died on August 10 in Freetown. On her tombstone was the following inscription: "She was early impressed that she should go to Africa as a missionary and that her life['s] work should be there. She crossed the ocean five times, and ended her mission on the soil and among the people she so desired to benefit."

In November of 1891 Bishop Turner reached Freetown and organized the Sierra Leone Annual Conference in the Zion AME Church. This was the first annual conference of the church established in Africa. Two weeks later he initiated the Liberia Annual Conference in Muhlenberg.

The years between 1892 and 1900 also witnessed the rise and growth of the AME Church in South Africa. The late nineteenth and early twentieth centuries saw the emergence of the independent church movement, or Ethiopianism, in South Africa. European missionaries in South Africa unwittingly sowed the seeds of discontent among African religious leaders by refusing to promote an indigenous clergy to positions of responsibility and by not heeding the African cries for self-determination in church government. During the early 1880s African evangelists began to secede from established churches in South Africa. The seeds of Ethiopianism had been sown. On November 5, 1893, Mangena Maake Mokone formed his own church, the Ethiopian Church.

In 1895 the Ethiopian Church of South Africa began negotiations for affiliation with the American-based AME Church. The Ethiopian Church believed that union with the AME Church would help the Ethiopian Church evangelize the continent of Africa. On June 19, 1896, the Ethiopian Church of South Africa became the Fourteenth Episcopal District of the AME Church, with James Mata Dwane as general superintendent of that district. Bishop Turner visited the recently constituted Fourteenth District in 1898 and ordained more than fifty AME ministers.

However, the failure of the AME Church to fund a proposed training school in the Cape Colony for educating South African AME church members, and the belief that the Ethiopian Church's absorption into the AME Church undercut the Ethiopian spirit of self-reliance led Dwane to secede from the AME Church on October 6, 1899. In 1900, Dwane's group, the Order of Ethiopia, was accepted into the Anglican Church.

In 1900 **Levi Jenkins Coppin** was elected the first bishop of South Africa and was assigned to the Fourteenth Episcopal District (Cape Colony and the Transvaal). Coppin was born free in Frederick Town, Maryland on December 24, 1848. His mother was a very religious woman who gave him religious training and taught him to read and write. He was graduated from Protestant Episcopal Divinity School (Philadelphia, Pennsylvania) in 1887. The son of AME parents, Coppin joined the church in 1865, was licensed to preach in 1876, ordained deacon in 1879 and elder in 1880, and elected the thirtieth bishop in 1900. In 1881 he married his second wife, Fanny Jackson.

Fanny M. Jackson Coppin, one of America's first Black women to be graduated from college, was born a slave in Washington, D.C. in 1837. After her Aunt Sarah Clark bought her freedom, she was educated in Massachusetts and Rhode Island, then earned an A.B. degree in 1865 and an A.M. degree in 1890 from Oberlin College (Oberlin, Ohio). Between 1865 and 1902 she taught at and eventually became principal of the Institute for Colored Youth in Philadelphia. From 1883 to 1892 she served as president of the AME's Woman's Home and Foreign Missionary Society.

Levi Coppin first arrived in Cape Town alone on February 19, 1901, and departed for the United States on December 26. In November 1902 he returned with his wife, Fanny Coppin. Missionary headquarters were located in Cape Town, although the Coppins frequently traveled into the interior.

Levi Coppin was prohibited by the South African government from visiting the Orange Free State and Transvaal Republics, but he traveled throughout Cape Colony and into Basutoland (today Botswana) and Southern Rhodesia (today Zimbabwe) to establish missions and spread the Gospel. He married almost one hundred couples and baptized over a hundred adults and children. During their stay in South Africa, Fanny Coppin directed most of her attention in Cape Town and the rural areas to organizing Black South African women into Women's Christian Temperance Union societies and into women's Mite Missionary Societies.

One of the permanent results of the Coppins' missionary stay in South Africa was the establishment of Bethel Institute at Cape Town. An old building was converted into a school and mission house. They left South Africa in the Spring of 1904. A Fanny Jackson Coppin Girls' Hall was named in Fanny Coppin's honor at Wilberforce Institute in Evaton, South Africa.

By the beginning of the twentieth century the AME church was definitely mission-minded. The church was united in an effort to support the cause of missions in Africa and elsewhere.

The second largest independent Black Methodist denomination in the United States in the nineteenth century was the **African Methodist Episcopal Zion Church** (AMEZ). A conference in October 1820 officially organized the AMEZ denomination. In 1876 the AMEZ Church began its foreign missionary activities in Liberia. In that year Andrew Cartwright of North Carolina arrived at Brewerville. On January 7, 1876 Cartwright, his mother, Mary Cartwright, his first wife, Rosanna Cartwright (full name unknown) of Elizabeth City, North Carolina, and their two daughters, Anne Marie and Lucy Cartwright, emigrated to Liberia.

Andrew Cartwright combined the positions of emigrant and missionary even though the AMEZ Church did not officially sponsor his mission. He organized the first AMEZ churches on the African continent in Brewerville on February 7, 1878, and in Clay Ashland in November 1878. He also established a mission at Cape Palmas in 1879. By 1880 he reported another church at Antherton.

Andrew Cartwright sent a formal report to the AMEZ General Conference assembled in Montgomery, Alabama, in 1880. It was at this meeting that concrete plans for AMEZ work in Africa were made with the formation of the General Home and Foreign Mission Board and the Ladies' Mission Society. The church-sponsored Livingstone College in Salisbury, North Carolina, was encouraged to train missionaries for Africa.

Andrew Cartwright returned to America in order to arouse the mission interest of the members of his denomination. At the AMEZ General Conference of 1884 he officially was confirmed as the church's first missionary to Liberia. Cartwright's first wife had died in Liberia in 1880, and before he left the United States he married Carrie Annie S. (full name unknown) of Plymouth, North Carolina in 1885/1886. The two returned to Liberia.

In 1886, Andrew Cartwright organized a church at Cape Palmas, but shortage of funds caused it to close. Two years later he started the first foreign mission school of the AMEZ Church, with both male and female students. Carrie Cartwright worked as a missionary teacher in the school.

Andrew Cartwright felt that he should have been acknowledged by the AMEZ Church as superintendent of African missions, but the church's response was that there was no need for the election of a missionary bishop at that time. The church viewed him as a poor administrator who had not expanded the mission. Andrew Cartwright served in Liberia until his death in Liberia on January 14, 1903, but his mission never grew much beyond an individual effort.

However, in 1896 **John Bryan Small** was elected AMEZ bishop to Africa, the West Indies, and three home conferences. Small was born and educated in Barbados. He joined the British army as a clerk and was stationed in the West African country of the Gold Coast (today Ghana) for three years, but he also traveled along the western coast from Sierra Leone to Nigeria. He resigned from the army because of British policies toward the Asante kingdom. On a number of occasions in the nineteenth century the British had battled with the Asante, who wanted to prevent foreign domination of the coastal trade.

In 1871 Small came to the United States, joined the AMEZ Church, and pursued his original career as a preacher. In 1896 the church decided to appoint a bishop to Africa, the West Indies, and three home conferences, and because of Small's experience in Africa, he was elected. He chose as his ecclesiastical motto, "For bleeding Africa."

On June 22, 1896 Bishop Small and his wife, **Mary Julia Blair Small**, left the United States. As bishop, John Small visited Sierra Leone, Liberia, and the Gold Coast but he centered his work in the Gold Coast. His most outstanding contribution to AMEZ mission work in Africa was his efforts to train indigenous African church leadership. He discouraged the church from

sending more Black American missionaries to Africa and concentrated upon sending young Africans to be trained as missionaries at the AMEZ Church's Livingstone College. Between 1897 and 1900 Small had enrolled at least four students from the Gold Coast at Livingstone College. The most notable was James E. K. Aggrey who was destined to become famous in the twentieth century as an educator and African nationalist.

Under Bishop Small's administration, AMEZ work in Africa took on new life. Steady and substantial progress was made in the formation of new organizations and the establishment of schools. By 1900 the mission could claim one school with forty-five students, and two churches with seventy-one full members. In 1901 Small founded the Zion *Missionary Seer* in the Gold Coast to stimulate work in foreign fields. Bishop Small returned to the United States in 1904. He died on January 15, 1915, with these words from his deathbed: "Don't let my African work fail."

By the beginning of the twentieth century the AMEZ Church had established itself in the Gold Coast. There had developed in the church a widespread interest in missionary expansion in Africa. Like the AME Church, the AMEZ Church concentrated on adding African members from already converted English-speaking areas such as Liberia, Sierra Leone, the Gold Coast, or South Africa.

This was not the case with the smaller Black Methodist church. In the early twentieth century the Colored Methodist Episcopal (CME) Church would join with the Methodist Episcopal Church, South (MECS) to open a mission station in French-speaking Belgian Congo (today Zaire).

The Methodist Episcopal Church (today a constituent part of the United Methodist Church) was one of the earliest missionary societies in Africa. The church sent its first missionary, Melville Beveridge Cox, to Liberia in 1833. But Cox died four months after his arrival, with his dying words forming the backbone of future American Methodist missionary work in Africa: "Though a thousand fall, let not Africa be given up." With the division of the Methodist Episcopal Church in 1844, the Liberian field fell to the Methodist Episcopal Church, North. Thereafter, the Methodist Episcopal Church, South (MECS) did not initiate African mission work until 1910.

The CME Church (today the **Christian Methodist Episcopal Church**), was organized in Jackson, Tennessee on December 15, 1870. At its inception the church was made up of ex-slaves who had been members of the MECS. The CME Church sought cooperation and assistance from southern Whites and continued close association with the MECS. The CME

Women's Missionary Society was founded in May 1894 at Fort Valley, Georgia, by **Lucius Holsey** and it became an organized missionary department in July of 1898.

For two decades before 1910, leaders of the Southern Presbyterian Church repeatedly had asked the MECS to enter the Congo and cooperate with them in the evangelization of Central Africa. The Southern Presbyterian Church's African adventure had begun in 1890 when two pioneer missionaries—a White, Samuel N. Lapsley, and a Black, William Henry Sheppard—established the American Presbyterian Congo Mission at Luebo. Four years before the beginning of World War I, the MECS decided to investigate the possibility of sending missionaries to Africa and asked the CME Church to join in the effort. Neither the MECS nor the CME Church had missions in Africa at this time.

Certainly, one of the considerations of the MECS was the desirability of securing the cooperation of the CME Church prior to entering African mission work. The MECS would furnish a large share of the financial support and a portion of the leadership while the CME Church would furnish the principal number of workers. As one CME minister explained, "the purpose of the great Methodist Episcopal Church, South is to do its bit for African missions through the Colored Methodist Episcopal Church! If we furnish the men and women, the parent Church will furnish the means." Basically, this statement summarized the proposed relationship that the MECS and the CME Church were to have in Africa, and the nature of the union.

At the sixtieth meeting of the Board of Missions of the MECS, held in Nashville, Tennessee in May 1906, a resolution was adopted affirming that the members of the board supported the opening of a mission in Africa, and the matter was referred to committee. From 1906 to 1910, the church discussed and studied the issue, resulting in a number of young men and women of the MECS volunteering for missionary service. At the same time, interest was stimulated among the students and faculty of the CME's Paine College in Augusta, Georgia, which led to a discussion of the role of the CME Church in the evangelization of Africa, and the possibility of cooperation between the MECS and the CME Church in the opening of a mission in Africa. These events were followed by an offer for service by Reverend John W. Gilbert, professor of Greek at Paine College and assistant secretary of the Board of Education for work among Blacks of the MECS.

During the 1910 General Conference of the CME Church, which convened at Augusta, Georgia, Dr. W. R. Lambuth, Fraternal Messenger to the CME Church from the MECS, delivered an address which suggested that the CME Church should cooperate with the MECS in establishing a mission in Africa. At the end of Lambuth's speech, resolutions were adopted requesting the College of Bishops of the CME Church to appoint a committee to investigate the plan. Lambuth felt that professor Gilbert's offer, along with two other Paine College graduates, to serve in Africa immensely strengthened the appeal to both churches.

When the Board of Missions of the MECS met in 1910, the secretary presented the report of the committee to which had been referred the question of opening a mission in Africa. The committee resolved that the Board of Missions should take immediate and definite steps toward the establishment of a mission in Africa and confer with the CME Church concerning an alliance in this missionary effort. Gilbert, Fraternal Delegate to this conference from the CME Church, was invited to address the board on this subject. The committee's report was adopted unanimously.

The resolution of the committee was endorsed by the 1910 General Conference of the MECS. Still, by the 1911 annual meeting, no further action had been taken to inaugurate these recommendations. The College of Bishops, however, appointed Lambuth to lead an expedition to Africa. A Board of African Missions was set up to raise funds and secure qualified candidates for the proposed mission. Lambuth arranged to visit Central Africa in 1911.

For the two Methodist churches, Lambuth of the MECS and Gilbert of the CME Church were the logical persons to make the trip to Africa. Accordingly, the MECS in 1911 commissioned the pair to proceed to the Congo to investigate the possibility of establishing a mission in the country. This action represented the first biracial attempt to cooperate in the formation of an American mission in Africa, although there were many examples of interracial collaboration through the use of Black and White missionaries, such as the Southern Presbyterian Church in the Congo or the American Board of Commissioners for Foreign Missions (Congregationalist) in Angola and Southern Rhodesia.

Walter Russell Lambuth was born on November 10, 1854, in Shanghai, China, the son of missionary parents, James William and Mary Isabella McClellan Lambuth. He earned a B.D. degree and an M.D. degree in the United States, and served intermittently from 1877 to 1891 as a medical missionary of the MECS in China and Japan. On May 16, 1910, at the sixteenth General Conference of the church, Lambuth was elected bishop. Three days later he was ordained. Bishop Lambuth died at Yokohama, Japan, on September 26, 1921.

John Wesley Gilbert was born on January 9, 1865, in Hephzibah, Georgia, to Gabriel and Sarah (full name unknown) Gilbert, farm hands. Early in his teens Gilbert went to Augusta, Georgia where he entered the public schools and later was the first student at and a graduate of Paine Institute. He also studied at the Atlanta Baptist Seminary (now Morehouse College; Atlanta, Georgia) and Brown University (Providence, Rhode Island), and at the American School of Classics in Athens, Greece. Gilbert, in 1888, became the first Black teacher at Paine Institute and College, where he taught Greek. In 1895 he entered the ministry of the CME Church. From 1913 to 1914, he served as the third president of Miles College (Birmingham, Alabama). Reverend Gilbert died in Augusta, Georgia on November 18, 1923.

The relationship between the MECS, the CME Church, and Paine College was noteworthy. Paine Institute was established in 1882 at Augusta, Georgia, and chartered in 1883, adopting its present name in 1903. Its original mission was to train African American ministers and teachers. It represented a unique experiment in southern interracial cooperation. It was assisted financially and was operated by both the CME and the MECS. Almost from its beginning, Paine's faculty was interracial and international. The trustees were chosen equally from both churches. It was understandable, then, that out of this environment would come an attempt at Methodist missionary union in Africa.

For Lambuth and Gilbert, the years 1911–1912 were spent in travel and study. Gilbert, the CME Church's first commissioned missionary to Africa, met Lambuth in London and they sailed for the Congo from Antwerp, Belgium, on October 14, 1911. They arrived at Matadi, on the Lower Congo River, twenty-one days later, on November 5. The following morning they began a two day railroad journey to Stanley Pool where they remained for ten days. From this point they traveled nearly nine hundred miles by boat on the Upper Congo, Kasai, and Lulua Rivers, reaching the American Presbyterian Congo Mission at Luebo on December 7. They were welcomed at Luebo and observed the results of twenty-one years of missionary work.

After spending two weeks at Luebo, and with the advice of the Presbyterian missionaries, Lambuth and Gilbert, with sixty carriers, started inland to find a location for their new mission. On February 1, 1912, after a forty-one day march by foot, they reached the village of Wembo Niama (or Wembo Nyama) in the Atetela region. The village of Chief Wembo Niama was located about four degrees south of the equator between the twenty-fourth and twenty-fifth degrees longitude and bounded by the Lubefu, Lomami, and Lukanye Rivers. Lambuth and Gilbert were invited to the house of the chief where they remained for four days. Because of the

urgings of the chief, and the belief that the hand of God had shaped their course, the two church leaders determined to plant the mission station at this place. Lambeth and Gilbert, after seven months in the Congo, returned to the United States in the Spring of 1912.

Upon their return, Bishop Lambuth reported at the sixty-seventh meeting of the Board of Missions of the MECS that there was a great opportunity in the Congo for evangelization. He revealed that Belgian authorities were friendly and seemed willing to grant Americans the privileges of missionary work among Africans. A land concession had been ceded to the church in the Atetela region.

Gilbert, after his arrival in the U.S., offered himself to the Board of Missions of the MECS as a candidate for African mission work and was accepted. Both Lambuth and Gilbert assumed that Gilbert would go back to the Congo to help establish the mission. For a while after 1912, the CME Church continued to be eager about cooperating with the MECS in this venture.

The MECS's Congo Mission was launched officially at the meeting of the Board of Missions in May 1913. The work was to begin in the village of Wembo Niama. Three White missionaries and their wives were accepted by the Committee on Candidates and scheduled to sail for Europe in late 1913 in order to hear lectures on tropical life, the care of health, and missionary methods and policies. Bishop Lambuth was to join the group in Antwerp and then they would all proceed to the Congo. With these missionaries, and "with the entrance into that field at a later date of Prof[essor] and Mrs. J. W. Gilbert, representatives of the Colored Methodist Episcopal Church," Lambuth believed that the MECS would be able to establish a strong and viable mission.

On November 8, 1913, Bishop Lambuth and the party of six missionaries set sail from Antwerp, Belgium, without Professor Gilbert, to open the MECS's Congo Mission. They arrived at Matadi on November 28 and reached Luebo on Christmas Eve day. With the full cooperation of the nearby American Presbyterian Congo Mission, the Methodist Episcopal Congo Mission was organized on February 12, 1914, at Wembo Niama, and the missionary dream of the MECS in Africa became a reality.

At the 1914 General Conference of the CME Church in St. Louis, Reverend Gilbert made an appeal for CME cooperation with the MECS. But despite Gilbert's plea, and a prior interest in placing Africa under special episcopal superintendency, by the time the CME Church met in 1914, it was indifferent to the idea. This spirit of detachment made it impossible for the conference to recommend a bishop for Africa, despite assurances from the MECS that it would assist the CME Church in supervision of the African work.

At the 1918 meeting of the General Conference of the CME Church, the body turned its attention to the development of educational programs, an area that the church always had given first priority. In 1918 Reverend Gilbert was elected the first editor of Sunday School materials of the CME Church. In the 1922 episcopal address CME bishops spoke of African missions, affirming, "we wish to say, with all emphasis, that we are in thorough sympathy with [the idea of missions], but we do not see where we can get men and money for such an enterprise at this time, when other older and better equipped churches find it a trying task to foster the missions which they have projected in that land [Africa]." Obviously, the idea of a union between the CME Church and the MECS was dead by this date.

As it was conceived, the unification scheme of an African mission of the MECS and the CME Church never had a chance of getting beyond the planning stages. Although Bishop Lambuth and Professor Gilbert made a propitious trip to the Congo, nothing ever could have come of the idea of combining MECS finances with CME Church labor. In spite of the initial support of both churches, probably the greatest obstacle was the Belgian government, which refused to issue permits to African Americans seeking to reside in the Belgian Congo.

As early as 1878 King Leopold of Belgium and his concessionary companies had shown an interest in using African Americans as workers in the Congo. However, during the 1890s two African Americans—the historian, George Washington Williams, and the missionary, William Henry Sheppard—led a campaign which depicted Leopoldian rule in the Congo as exploitative. This did not ensure an attitude of trust of Black Americans by Congo authorities. The reluctant Belgian government had been forced to assume control of the Congo in 1908, after years of worldwide condemnation of the atrocities of the Leopoldian regime. In addition, in 1909 Sheppard, of the American Presbyterian Congo Mission, was tried in Leopoldville for libel against a Belgian concessionary company operating in the Congo. Although Sheppard was found innocent, soon after the trial he returned to the United States permanently. From this date onward, Belgian officials discouraged and limited Black American missionaries from work in the Congo. Bolstering their exclusionary policy were recent uprisings in Kenya, Nyasaland (today Malawi), South Africa, Southwest Africa (today Namibia), and Tanganyika (today Tanzania), some of which the European colonialists erroneously tied to African

American missionary activity. This atmosphere helps to explain why the Belgians dissuaded American churches from using African Americans in their African missions, particularly well educated Blacks such as Gilbert.

There is also evidence that such an interracial enterprise was opposed by some leaders in the MECS and the CME Church. One CME member explained why: "Perhaps the colored church was not quite ready for such responsibility. Perhaps the White church was not quite Christian enough to treat Negroes as brothers as Bishop Lambuth had done." In the end, it was not feasible to carry out the plan of cooperation between the MECS and the CME Church. The suspicions of the Belgian government and the attitude of some MECS and CME Church administrators help to explain why the scheme of the two churches in 1911–1912 to open a Congo mission never materialized.

The Baptists: Black American Baptists also became involved in African mission work in the nineteenth century. The result of this missionary consciousness among Black Baptists was the organization and spread of many independent regional organizations throughout the United States, including the Providence Baptist Association formed in 1835 and based in Ohio; the Wood River Baptist Association created in 1838 in Illinois; the General Association of Western States and Territories organized in 1873; and the New England Baptist Missionary Convention established in 1874.

In 1840 Black Baptists from the New England and middle Atlantic states met to organize the first national Black Baptist missionary group, the **American Baptist Missionary Convention**. The second national Black Baptist missionary organization, the Northwestern and Southern Baptist Convention, was formed in 1864 to serve those areas not reached by the American Baptist Missionary Convention. In 1866 the American Baptist Missionary Convention and the Northwestern and Southern Baptist Convention joined to form the **Consolidated American Baptist Missionary Convention**. Although the Consolidated Baptists had home missions they made no efforts in foreign missions. In 1878 the work of the Consolidated American Baptist Missionary Convention terminated and in 1880 the **Baptist Foreign Mission Convention of the United States** (BFMC) was organized.

Interest among Black Baptists in African missions came from the efforts at organization from southern Black Baptists, particularly in the southeastern states of South Carolina, North Carolina, and Virginia. In 1878, the Baptist Educational, Missionary, and Sunday-School Convention of South Carolina, founded in 1866, resolved unanimously to send a missionary to Africa.

The group selected Harrison N. Bouey as its missionary appointee. Bouey was born on August 4, 1849 in Columbia County, Georgia but he grew up in Augusta. He was converted in 1870, ordained in 1876, and completed the theology course at Augusta Institute (moved to Atlanta in 1879 to become Atlanta Baptist Seminary; today Morehouse College). He worked as a public school teacher in Augusta.

On April 21, 1878 Bouey, a bachelor, sailed to Liberia on the *Azor* with the group of 206 South Carolina emigrants including the AME missionary Samuel E. Flegler. Bouey retorted: "Go to Africa? Yes, my Lord commands, and I am afraid not to go." During his two year stay in Monrovia, Bouey worked among the Gola people. While there he helped construct a road outside Royesville, eighteen miles northwest of Monrovia, which came to be called the "Bouey Road." Bouey also helped organize the Liberia Baptist Missionary Convention. The two Baptist churches established by the South Carolina emigrants were accepted into the Liberia Baptist Missionary Convention in December 1879. Bouey returned to the United States in 1880. He settled in Selma, Alabama, and served as the first vice president of the BFMC.

In April 1882 Bouey married Laura P. Logan of Charleston, South Carolina. He served as pastor and superintendent of missions for Missouri Baptists. After the death of his wife in 1897 Bouey again sailed to Africa in January 1902 but returned to America in 1905. On December 11, 1906, Bouey and three of his four sons returned to Africa. His elder son later joined them. Bouey continued to work in Liberia as a National Baptist Convention missionary until his death on December 15, 1909 at Cape Mount. He was buried on the banks of Lake Peause alongside Hattie J. Pressley and, allegedly, Henderson McKinney, although McKinney's grave has not been found there.

In 1879 the Black Baptist State Convention of North Carolina followed the lead of South Carolina and appointed James O. Hayes as a missionary to Liberia. Hayes went to Africa as a missionary-emigrant, as had Lott Carey and Harrison Bouey.

Hayes had been born in eastern North Carolina. He was one of the first students to enter Shaw University (Raleigh, North Carolina), graduating from the scientific department in May 1879. Hayes did not sail to Liberia until June 1881. He was one of the founders and the first teacher of Ricks Institute in Montserrado County. In 1883 he married Ada Ellen Merritt.

When the Lott Carey Foreign Mission Convention (LCC) opened its first mission in Brewerville, Liberia, in 1897, Hayes became its first missionary. He had affiliated with the convention immediately after its founding that year. Hayes pastored a church in Brewerville to which an industrial school was added to train Liberian youth. He served as a member of the Liberia Baptist Missionary Convention.

During the years 1880 to 1883 the BFMC laid the foundations for future missionary endeavors and the movement for African missions gained momentum. From 1883 to 1886 the African mission movement of the BFMC experienced success. In 1883 the BFMC commissioned six missionaries to Liberia: William W. Colley and his wife (full name unknown), James H. and Hattie J. Harris Pressley, John J. Coles, and Henderson McKinney.

William W. Colley headed this mission party, which sailed in December 1883. Colley was born a slave on February 12, 1847, probably in Winchester, Virginia. He attended Richmond Institute and was graduated in 1887 (chartered in 1876, name changed to Richmond Theological Seminary in 1886, united with Wayland Seminary in 1897 under the name Virginia Union University). Colley was accepted for African mission work in 1875 by the Southern Baptist Convention and worked at Lagos and Abeokuta in southern Nigeria. In Lagos he helped erect a chapel and residence. When he was recalled in 1879 the Lagos mission had twenty-four members.

Back in the United States Colley helped organize the BFMC and served as its first corresponding secretary from November 1880 to December 1883, when he sailed to Liberia. In Liberia the six pioneer missionaries established the Bendoo Baptist Mission at Grand Cape Mount among the Vai people of western Liberia. Colley began publication, at his own expense, of the periodical *African Missions*. He returned to America in 1886 because of poor health.

James Pressley, also a graduate of Richmond Institute, and Hattie Pressley of Virginia arrived in Liberia in December 1883 with the BFMC pioneer party. Hattie Pressley helped with the establishment of the Bendoo Baptist Mission. Reverend Pressley organized a Baptist church among the Vai people and baptized more than one hundred persons.

But the mission had problems from the beginning, the foremost one was health. Hattie Pressley was pregnant when she arrived in Liberia but she lost the baby. And less than a year after their arrival Hattie Pressley died of fever on August 15, 1884. She was the first BFMC missionary to die in Africa and was buried in Liberia.

Reverend Pressley was sick most of his two years in Liberia. Weakened by periodic bouts with fever and disheartened by his child's and wife's deaths, he returned to the United States in 1885 as an invalid. In a poem entitled "The Cry of the Heathen," published in 1896, Reverend Pressley emphasized a continuing need for missions by erroneously portraying Africa as devoid of any religious development:

Hear the voice of Ethiopia
Coming from that distant land;
Would you answer to that crying?
Give to them a helping hand.
Don't you hear that heathen mother,
Praying to the gods of stone?
Trying to heal a heart of trouble,
A heart by sin and sorrow torn.

In this land we have our Jesus,
Who will save us when we die;
When we leave this world of trouble
We shall live with Him on high.
But they know no God of mercy,
Who will hear them when they pray;
There they have no loving Jesus,
Who will take their sins away.
Thus they die in awful darkness,
Die without the Gospel light;
Die without the love of Jesus,
Die and sink to endless night.
If you cannot go and teach them,
You can help those who are there,
You can with a cry of pity,
Carry them to God in prayer.

John J. Coles was born on April 26, 1856 in Shattersburg, Virginia. Coles entered Richmond Institute in 1878 and was graduated five years later, in 1883. He was licensed to preach by the Baptist Church on July 14, 1878 and ordained on November 4, 1883. On December 1, 1883, he sailed to Liberia with the BFMC pioneer party. Coles was assisted financially by the New York Colonization Society.

Coles and McKinney entered Liberia College to study Arabic under Edward Blyden. Coles was first stationed at the Bendoo Baptist Mission and was elected president of the mission on January 20, 1885. Having learned the Vai language, he preached to the people without an interpreter. A book that Coles wrote during his mission work in Liberia, *Africa in Brief*, was published in 1886. The same year he returned to America, traveling throughout the South lecturing on the need for financial support of the BFMC Liberian mission.

While on furlough in the United States he met and on December 21, 1886 married Lucy A. Henry of Memphis, Tennessee. The pair traveled to Liberia in

early 1887 accompanied by four other missionaries, Edgar (or Egbert) B. and Mattie E. (full name unknown) Topp and James J. Diggs and his wife (full name unknown). Upon his return to Liberia John Coles was assigned to the Bendoo and Jundoo stations where he organized and maintained a school for African boys. Lucy Coles aided her husband in the work at the Bendoo and Jundoo stations where she taught at the mission school.

The ill health of Reverend Coles forced the couple to leave Africa in 1893. Financial problems forced the Bendoo Baptist Mission to be closed after their departure. The old mission houses were sold for lumber. Upon their return to the United States, John Coles was elected the third corresponding secretary of the BFMC but he died a few months after his election. Lucy Coles was elected to finish his unexpired term, which she did until 1895 when the **National Baptist Convention, U.S.A., Inc.** was organized.

The sixth and final missionary who was commissioned by the BFMC in 1883 was Henderson (nickname Hence) McKinney. McKinney was born in Edwards, Mississippi, in 1860. In May 1883 the first graduation was held at Natchez Seminary and McKinney was one of the first seven students to receive a high school diploma. The coeducational school was founded at Natchez, Mississippi in 1877 and was operated as a private church school by the American Baptist Home Mission Society until 1938. In the fall of 1883 Natchez Seminary was moved to Jackson, Mississippi, and by common consent, the institution's name was changed to Jackson College, in honor of Andrew Jackson, for whom Jackson, Mississippi was named (today, Jackson State University; Jackson, Mississippi).

On December 1, 1883, McKinney traveled to Africa in the party with William Colley. McKinney also was supported by the New York Colonization Society. Before his departure, McKinney cautioned: "Fear not the African climate, for God in the form of man visited Africa long ago."

McKinney received additional seminary training, and learned Arabic at Liberia College under the West Indian emigrant Edward Blyden. In 1884 McKinney was appointed as an active missionary. He opened the Marfa station near Grand Cape Mount. On April 15, 1887, McKinney died at his post. He had set out on a mission tour in the interior of Liberia and apparently died in a ferry accident. A Liberian chief had entrusted to McKinney a young Liberian man to be sent to the United States to be educated. But before final arrangements could be completed, McKinney died. Edgar (or Egbert) Topp later brought the young man to

Jackson College as the school's first foreign student. From 1887 to 1894, a time of nationwide economic difficulty, the African mission movement of the BFMC declined because of the limitation of financial resources.

In 1895 the Baptist Foreign Mission Convention of the United States joined with the American National Baptist Convention (organized in 1886) and the Baptist National Educational Convention (established in 1893) to form the National Baptist Convention of America (NBC). The National Baptist Convention split into two conventions in 1915, the National Baptist Convention and the National Baptist Convention of the U.S.A., Incorporated.

R. A. Jackson, an independent Baptist missionary in South Africa, affiliated with the National Baptist Convention in 1896. Jackson, a Baptist preacher from Arkansas, financed his own way to South Africa in 1894 and established a mission at Cape Town. He later was joined by Joseph I. Buchanan, a Black sailor from Baltimore, Maryland.

As an independent missionary, Jackson traveled 25,000 miles into the interior, and within four years he had founded five mission stations. In 1896 the NBC agreed to sponsor Reverend Jackson as their superintendent of South African work. His brightest convert, John Tule, was elected an official missionary by the NBC and later was educated in the United States. Tule and his American-born wife, Mamie Branton Tule of North Carolina, returned to South Africa in 1897 as missionaries of the NBC and the Lott Carey Convention.

In July 1897 Jackson and his wife (full name unknown) took a six month furlough in the United States. For a short time in 1898 Jackson defected to the Lott Carey Convention because of inadequate financial support from the NBC. But by 1900 Jackson had withdrawn from the LCC. The Jacksons remained at their post until October 1906 when they permanently returned to the United States.

In 1897, a majority of the Virginia and North Carolina delegates of the newly formed National Baptist Convention met in Washington, D.C., where they set up the Lott Carey Foreign Mission Convention (later the Lott Carey Baptist Home and Foreign Mission Convention). Separation centered on the issues of the declining importance of foreign missions in the National Baptist Convention, and a desire by these delegates for Black control of mission work without any cooperation with White Baptists.

In the early years the LCC cooperated with other Baptist boards engaged in mission work in foreign fields. In 1900 the LCC agreed to join with the American Baptist Missionary Union (ABMU) to mutually support Reverend Clinton Boone and Eva Boone in the Congo.

Clinton Caldwell Boone was born on May 9, 1873 in Winton, North Carolina. At the age of nineteen he entered Waters Normal Institute in Winton. Scholarships helped him to complete Waters Institute and Richmond Theological Seminary. He was graduated from the seminary on May 21, 1900 with a B.D. degree. It was probably in Richmond that he met Eva Roberta Coles, his first wife, and Rachel A. Tharps, his second wife, both of whom were graduates of Hartshorn Memorial College (Richmond), which was opened in 1883. On January 16, 1901 Boone married his first wife.

Eva Roberta Coles was born on January 8, 1880 in Charlottesville, Virginia. Although it has been claimed in some publications that she was the daughter of the missionary couple John J. and Lucy A. Henry Coles, this was not likely since the Coleses did not marry until December 21, 1886. Coles taught in Charlottesville before marrying Clinton Boone.

The Boones left New York on April 13, 1901 reaching the Palabala station in the Katanga province of the Congo on May 24. They went out under the auspices of the ABMU (today the American Baptist Churches in the U.S.A.) in cooperation with the LCC.

Clinton Boone preached and taught the Congolese in their own language. Eva Boone took charge of the infant class and conducted the kindergarten. She was one of the first ABMU missionaries to advance the idea of a sewing school. Despite the difficulty of enlisting African women, who saw sewing as men's work, Eva Boone enrolled more than forty women in her sewing group before her death. After several weeks of illness, brought on by a poisonous bite, Eva Boone died on December 8, 1902, barely twenty-two years old, and was buried at Palabala.

In 1905 Clinton Boone was transferred to Lukunga, where he assisted in building a new station. He spent five years in the Congo and in 1906 he returned to America. He took the medical course at Leonard Medical School, Shaw University (Raleigh, North Carolina), which he completed in 1910.

The same year Boone traveled to Liberia as a LCC medical missionary. He first was stationed at Brewerville but later was transferred to Monrovia where he opened a day school. In 1918 he became minister of Providence Baptist Church, which had been organized in 1822 by Lott Carey.

After nine years in Liberia, he returned to the United States and allegedly took a course in mechanical dentistry at Bodee Dental School (New York City). Boone received training both as a physician and a dentist at the expense of the LCC. His education equipped him as one of the best-prepared missionaries ever sent out by any convention.

In 1919 Boone married Rachel Tharps. Rachel A. Tharps was born in Richmond, Virginia. After graduation from Hartshorn Memorial College, she became a school teacher in Richmond. The Boones traveled to Monrovia, Liberia in 1920 as LCC missionaries. Clinton Boone worked as a medical and dental missionary, and as pastor of Providence Baptist Church. Rachel Boone opened a school in the city.

The Boones and their two children (both born in Liberia) left the country in 1926 and returned to America permanently. Reflecting on his mission work in Africa, Boone reminisced: "I do not regret a single sacrifice that I have made for the redemption of Africa and if I had ten thousand other lives I would be delighted to spend them all to lift up the fallen and care for the dying in Africa."

In 1908 the LCC agreed to co-sponsor, with the NBC, D. E. Murff in South Africa. D. E. Murff was born on May 17, 1857 in Laurensville, Mississippi. He attended Wayland Seminary (opened in Washington, D.C. in 1865, moved to Richmond, Virginia in 1899 after merging into Virginia Union University). On December 11, 1906 Reverend Murff sailed to South Africa with his wife Mattie E. Wilson Murff, who had been born in Natchez, Mississippi on May 15, 1867. The Murffs took up NBC work in Cape Town.

During his superintendency, Reverend Murff assisted in laying the foundation for the Shiloh Baptist Church and finished building a school house. Mattie Murff was a faithful and efficient assistant to her husband. The couple returned to America in July 1910 because of impaired health.

Also in 1908 the LCC appointed three new missionaries to Liberia. Cora and William Thomas sailed to Liberia as LCC missionaries in December 1908, arriving in January 1909. G. D. Gayles arrived in mid-1909.

Cora Ann Pair was born in Knightdale, Wake County, North Carolina on September 8, 1875. She was graduated from Shaw University (Raleigh, North Carolina) in 1895 with a higher English diploma. Between 1904 and 1906, she took post-graduate courses in missionary training at the theological school of Fisk University (Nashville, Tennessee). Before going to Africa Pair acted as principal of an orphanage for Black children in Oxford, North Carolina. In November 1908 Cora Pair married William Thomas.

William Henry Thomas was born on March 31, 1881 in Duncans Parish of Trelawny, Jamaica. He completed his elementary and secondary education in Jamaica but came to the United States as a young man to continue his higher education. He was graduated from Shaw University in 1908 with an A.B. degree and B.Th.

degree. Pair and Thomas had met at Shaw University. Cora Thomas was sponsored by the Woman's Baptist Missionary Convention of North Carolina.

The couple was stationed at Brewerville. Shortly after their arrival, William Thomas became a naturalized Liberian citizen. At Brewerville, Reverend Thomas served as LCC superintendent of the mission as well as a preacher and teacher. For thirty-three years he served as principal of the Baptist boarding high school in Brewerville. He extended the work of the convention into journalism and for a while operated the only printing press among Black Baptists in Liberia. In 1909 he began publication of the *Watchman*, a monthly paper of the Brewerville station.

Cora Thomas encouraged the LCC mission board to establish an industrial school, which was later named the Lott Carey Mission School. She taught hundreds of boys and girls and young women and men at the school. After Reverend Thomas' death on September 4, 1942 Cora Thomas was appointed superintendent of the mission, succeeding her husband. She served in that capacity for four years. In 1946 she left Liberia because of failing health. Cora Thomas returned to Liberia in 1951 with the Lott Carey Pilgrimage Group. After a severe attack of malaria, she died at Brewerville on May 10, 1952. She was buried on the Lott Carey Mission School campus next to her husband.

The third missionary that the LCC appointed to Liberia in 1908 was G. D. Gayles of Baltimore, Maryland. Gayles' travel expenses were paid by Baptists in his home city. He arrived in Liberia in mid-1909 and was also stationed at Brewerville.

The paucity of financial resources of the LCC and NBC tended to limit their missionary activities in Africa. By 1915 the LCC had placed most of its American-born missionaries in West Africa, primarily in Liberia. In that country the LCC could build upon the foundation laid by James Hayes. NBC missionaries, by that date, had served in South Africa, Liberia, and Nyasaland.

The African mission work of African American churches changed after 1920. By the end of World War I, European imperialists had occupied all of the continent of Africa except for Liberia and Ethiopia. These colonialists believed that the African American presence in Africa caused unrest among Africans. European officials felt that Black missionaries were dangerous to the maintenance of law and order in Africa because Africans might identify with their better educated and more politically conscious brothers and sisters. The European powers feared that these Black American missionaries might unwittingly, or wittingly, encourage political revolts among Africans. By that date, the general consensus of European governments in Africa was that African American missionaries upset the status quo and caused too many disruptions to warrant their effectiveness in the "civilizing mission" in Africa.

During the forty year period between 1920 and 1960 very few Black American missionaries not already stationed in Africa were assigned there by White boards. Black boards continued to send African American missionaries to Africa, but their efforts basically were confined to several countries. After 1960 Black Americans were again appointed as missionaries to Africa, but by that date African indigenous missionaries made up the majority of missionaries on the continent and these Africans replaced foreign missionaries.

Between 1820 and 1980, from 250,000 to 350,000 Americans served as missionaries in Africa. Black Americans represented an infinitesimal percentage of that figure. During this period probably no more than six hundred African Americans, sent out by over two dozen missionary societies served in sub-Saharan countries. About half of these were sent out by Black church boards. Of the total six hundred, at least half were women, with about two-thirds of these unmarried commissioned missionaries and one-third "missionary wives." Over 50 percent of all the Black American missionaries who were stationed in Africa before 1980 served in Liberia and another 25 percent served in three other West African countries, Ghana, Nigeria, and Sierra Leone.

African Americans served as missionaries in a total of twenty sub-Saharan countries. Because language was a crucial determinant to placement, thirteen of these colonies or countries were English-speaking. There were five French-speaking colonies and two Portuguese-speaking colonies with Black American missionaries. None were assigned to German, Italian, or Spanish-speaking colonies.

The significance of the mission work of African American churches in Africa was that it helped to bridge the chasm between Africans on the continent and African Americans that had been created by the slave trade. Black boards had fewer missionaries stationed in Africa than White boards because less financial resources were available for mission support. Therefore, since a smaller number of missionaries were sent to Africa by Black boards during the nineteenth and twentieth centuries, in comparison to the numbers sent by White boards, any contribution that these missionaries of Black boards made to African mission work was as individuals more so than in a collective or denominational sense.

Regardless of how historians assess the impact of the mission movement on Africa, African American churches felt that they had a "special" relationship and "special" obligation to Africa and Africans. This belief was a significant if not the determinative factor in their motivations for African mission work, and in their continued interest and multiple activities on the continent.

Adams, C. C., and Talley, Marshall A. *Negro Baptists and Foreign Missions*. Philadelphia, PA: Foreign Mission Board of the National Baptist Convention, U.S.A., Inc., 1944. 94 pp.

Berry, Lewellyn L. *A Century of Missions of the African Methodist Episcopal Church, 1840–1940*. New York: Gutenberg Printing Co., 1942. 333 pp.

Boone, Clinton C. *Congo As I Saw It*. New York: J. J. Little and Ives Co., 1927. 96 pp

———. *Liberia As I Know It*. Richmond, VA: 1929. 152 pp. Rept.: Westport, CT: Negro Universities Press, 1970. 152 pp.

Bradley, David Henry. *A History of the AME Zion Church*. 2 vols. Nashville, TN: Parthenon Press, 1956, 1970.

Cade, John. *Holsey: The Incomparable*. New York: Pageant Press, 1964. 221 pp.

Calhoun, E. Clayton. *Of Men Who Ventured Much and Far: The Congo Quest of Dr. Gilbert and Bishop Lambuth*. Atlanta, GA: Institute Press, 1961. 153 pp.

Cannon, James. *History of Southern Methodist Missions*. Nashville, TN: Cokesbury Press, 1926. 356 pp.

Cauthen, Baker J., ed. *Advance: A History of Southern Baptist Foreign Missions*. Nashville, TN: Broadman Press, 1970. 329 pp.

Chirenje, J. Mutero. *Ethiopianism and Afro-Americans in Southern Africa, 1883–1916*. Baton Rouge, LA: Louisiana State University Press, 1987. 231 pp.

Colclough, Joseph C. *The Spirit of John Wesley Gilbert*. Nashville, TN: Cokesbury Press, 1925.

Coles, John J. *Africa in Brief*. New York: New York Freeman Steam Printing Establishment, 1886.

Coppin, Fanny Jackson. *Reminiscences of School Life and Hints on Teaching*. Philadelphia, PA: AME Book Concern, 1913. 191 pp. Rept.: New York: Garland Publishing, 1987. 191 pp.

Coppin, Levi J. *Observations of Persons and Things in South Africa, 1900–1904*. Philadelphia, PA: AME Book Concern, 1904. 205 pp.

Fitts, Leroy. *Lott Carey: First Black Missionary to Africa*. Valley Forge, PA: Judson Press, 1978. 159 pp.

Freeman, Edward A. *The Epoch of Negro Baptists and the Foreign Mission Board*. Kansas City, MO: Central Seminary Press, 1953. 301 pp.

Gregg, Howard D. *History of the African Methodist Episcopal Church: The Black Church in Action*. Nashville, TN: AMEC Sunday School Union, 1980. 523 pp.

Harvey, William J., III. *Bridges of Faith Across the Seas: The*

Story of the Foreign Mission Board, National Baptist Convention, USA, Inc. Philadelphia: Foreign Mission Board, National Baptist Convention, U.S.A., Inc., 1989. 523 pp.

Hervey, G. Winfred. *The Story of Baptist Missions in Foreign Lands.* St. Louis, MO: Chancy R. Barns, 1884.

Hood, J. W. *One Hundred Years of the African Methodist Episcopal Church.* New York: A.M.E. Book Concern, 1895

Jacobs, Sylvia M., ed. *Black Americans and the Missionary Movement in Africa.* Westport, CT: Greenwood Press, 1982. 255 pp.

Jenifer, John T. *Centennial Retrospect History of the African Methodist Episcopal Church.* Nashville, TN: AME Sunday School Union, 1916. 454 pp.

Jordan, Artishia Wilkerson. *The African Methodist Episcopal Church in Africa.* N.p., n.d.

Jordan, Lewis Garnett. *In Our Stead: Facts About Foreign Missions.* Philadelphia, PA: 1913.

———. *Negro Baptist History, U.S.A.* Nashville, TN: Sunday School Publishing Board, 1930. 394 pp.

———. *On Two Hemispheres.* Nashville, TN: 1935.

———. *Pebbles From An African Beach.* Philadelphia, PA: Lisle-Carey Press, 1918.

———. *Up the Ladder in Foreign Missions.* Nashville, TN: National Baptist Publishing Board, 1901. 269 pp.

Lakey, Othal Hawthorne. *The Rise of "Colored Methodism." A Study of the Background and the Beginnings of the Christian Methodist Episcopal Church.* Dallas, TX: Crescendo Book Publications, 1972. 128 pp.

Lambuth, Walter Russell. *Winning the World for Christ: A Study in Dynamics.* New York: Fleming H. Revell Company, 1915. 245 pp.

Martin, Sandy D. *Black Baptists and African Missions.* Macon, GA: Mercer University Press, 1989. 242 pp.

McAfee, Sara Jane. *History of the Woman's Missionary Society in the Colored Methodist Episcopal Church.* Jackson, TN: Publishing House C.M.E. Church, 1934.

Merriam, Edmund F. *A History of American Baptist Missions.* Philadelphia, PA: American Baptist Publication Society, 1900.

Payne, Daniel A. *History of the AME Church.* Nashville, TN: Publishing House of the AME Sunday School Union, 1891. 218 pp.

Pelt, Owen D., and Smith, Ralph Lee. *The Story of the National Baptists.* New York: Vantage Press, 1960. 272 pp.

Pinson, William W. *Walter Russell Lambuth, Prophet and Pioneer.* Nashville, TN: Cokesbury Press, 1925. 261 pp.

Reeve, Thomas E. *In Wembo Nyama's Land, A Story of the Thrilling Experiences in Establishing the Methodist Mission Among the Atetela.* Nashville, TN: Publishing House of the M.E. Church, South, 1923.

Rux, Mattie, and Ransome, Mary M. *History of the Woman's Auxiliary to the Lott Carey Baptist Foreign Mission Convention, 1900–1956.* n.p., n.d.

Smith, Charles Spencer. *A History of the African Methodist Episcopal Church.* Philadelphia, PA: Book Concern of the AME Church, 1922. 570 pp.

Tupper, Henry Allen. *Foreign Missions of the Southern Baptist Convention.* Philadelphia, PA: American Baptist Publication Society, 1880.

Walls, William Jacob. *The African Methodist Episcopal Zion Church: Reality of the Black Church.* Charlotte, NC: AME Zion Publishing House, 1974. 669 pp.

Williams, Walter L. *Black Americans and the Evangelization of Africa, 1877–1900.* Madison, WI: University of Wisconsin Press, 1982. 259 pp.

Sylvia M. Jacobs

AFRICAN ORTHODOX CHURCH.

AFRICAN ORTHODOX CHURCH. An Eastern Orthodox church. The African Orthodox Church (AOC) represents the coming together of three distinct movements in the early twentieth century, each of which became focused in the ecclesiastical career of **George Alexander McGuire**, founder and archbishop of the church. The first movement was the struggle for recognition by the African American members of the (Protestant) **Episcopal Church**. By World War I, a significant element of the debate within the Episcopal Church swirled around the election of African American bishops to serve in the United States (several had already been elected to serve outside the country). Several different proposals were put forward, among them the so-called Arkansas Plan, named for Arkansas Bishop William M. Brown, who proposed it. He called for the establishment of a sister church headed by Black bishops to serve the then African American constituency of the Episcopal Church. Eventually, suffragan bishops (assistant bishops), without right of succession, were elected. McGuire had become an Episcopal priest in 1897 and had an outstanding career for the next twenty years. In 1905 he was appointed archdeacon for colored work in Arkansas under Bishop Brown. This was the highest post available to an African American in the Episcopal Church at the time. A decade later he would be among the candidates whose names were considered for the post of suffragan bishop of Arkansas.

The second force contributing to the formation of the African Orthodox Church was the migration of numerous West Indians into the United States during the first two decades of the twentieth century and the formation of a West Indian community within the larger African American community in New York City in the years immediately after World War I. McGuire was born and raised in Antigua. As a young man he became a minister with the Moravian Church and later the

Methodist Church. In the 1890s he moved to the United States and was reordained as an Episcopalian minister. He became increasingly irritated with the Episcopal church's inability to respond positively to the striving for equality of African Americans. For a short period he dropped out of the ministry to attend medical school. Finishing his medical degree in 1910, the following year he became field secretary of the American Church Institute for Negroes for two years. He then returned to Antigua as a missionary. While in Antigua he began to follow the career of **Marcus Garvey** and following Garvey's move to America and his founding of the American chapter of the Universal Negro Improvement Association, McGuire also returned to the United States.

Back in the United States McGuire began to associate with other West Indians, a circle of which formed around him. The circle grew to include such people as **William E. J. Robertson** (Jamaica), **Reginald Grant Barrow** (Barbados), **Edmund Robert Bennett** (Antigua), **William Russell Miller** (Tobago), and **Hubert Augustus Rogers** (Dutch West Indies). These men would all become important figures in AOC history.

Finally, McGuire had available to him an independent Catholic episcopacy agreeable to consecrating him to the office of bishop in the apostolic lineage. Like many before him, McGuire had become increasingly frustrated with the White-dominated Episcopal Church. He was ready to leave. Previously, African ministers who left the church had only Methodist, Baptists, or a variety of sectarian groups to join. The possibility of joining or creating a church with a historic episcopacy was not present. However, in 1915, independent Archbishop Joseph René Vilatte had founded the American Catholic Church, and, before the year was out had consecrated Frederick E. J. Lloyd to the episcopacy. Like McGuire, Lloyd almost became an Episcopal bishop.

McGuire's frustration with the Episcopal Church reached a breaking point in 1919. He joined the **Reformed Episcopal Church** with the intention of founding a congregation for West Indians in New York City and soon established as the Church of the Good Savior. In January 1921, he severed relations with the Reformed Episcopal Church and founded an Independent Episcopal Church. He organized the first congregation, The Church of the Good Shepherd, in New York City, and others followed his lead. At a gathering in 1921, he was elected bishop. He then sought consecration as bishop from a number of sources including the Roman Catholic Church and the Russian Orthodox Church. Finally he heard of Archbishop Vilatte and in September of that year traveled to Chicago. In the sanctuary of the American Catholic Church of Our Lady of Good Death he was consecrated. Robertson, who accompanied him, was ordained to the priesthood. He returned to New York and was enthroned as bishop of the African Orthodox Church.

Unlike many of the independent Catholic churches, the African Orthodox Church grew into a denomination of substance. During the two years following his break with the Episcopal Church, parishes had been established in Brooklyn, New York; Pittsburgh; New Haven, Connecticut; Nova Scotia; Cuba; and Santa Domingo. Endich Theological Seminary was opened, and soon additional congregations emerged in Philadelphia, Boston, the Bahamas, and Florida. The growth led to the election of the second bishop of the church, William E. J. Robertson, in 1923. Arthur S. Trotman and Reginald G. Barrow were added in 1924 and 1925 respectively. The church became truly international in 1927 with the incorporation of a group of South Africans under the leadership of Daniel W. Alexander.

All through the period of formation of the AOC, McGuire had remained active in the U.N.I.A. In 1920 he was elected Chaplain-General of the U.N.I.A. and was given the title of "Archbishop of Ethiopia." He emerged as a spokesperson of Ethiopianism and began to envision the possibility of a worldwide church for Black people. In this regard in 1921 he authored two small volumes: *The Universal Negro Catechism* and *The Universal Negro Ritual*.

Under McGuire's leadership, the church prospered. An order of deaconesses was initiated. In 1931 a new headquarters building was purchased and dedicated as Holy Cross AOC Cathedral. McGuire died in 1934, and was succeeded by William E. J. Robertson, then presiding in Miami and residing over the Church's Southern Jurisdiction. The year after McGuire's death a controversy arose in New York. Over the next three years several bishops were suspended from their positions and formed rival churches. Bishop Barrow formed the **African Orthodox Church of New York and Massachusetts**. Bishop Trotman, taking advantage of the fact that the AOC had incorporated in Florida rather than New York, formed the African Orthodox Church, Inc. Judgment in the resultant lawsuit was rendered in 1938. The dissidents were enjoined from either using the name African Orthodox Church (in any form) or claiming a connection with McGuire. They reorganized as the **Holy African Church**, but informally continued as the African Orthodox Church, there rarely being more than one congregation in any state of either faction.

New York City remained the center of the church's

strength. However, on the heels of the lawsuit, Bishop Hubert A. Rogers resigned from the church and took two of the parishes, St. Leonard's and St. Augustine's, into the **North American Old Roman Catholic Church**. Archbishop Carfora, head of the N.A.O.R.C.C., even established the African Apostolic Catholic Church and placed Rogers at its head in an attempt to woo more AOC congregations into his fold. The plan was dropped in 1945 when an agreement on inter-communion between the AOC and the N.A.O.R.C.C. was worked out. Rogers eventually succeeded Carfora.

Robertson continued as head of the AOC until his death in 1962. He was succeeded by Richard Grant Robinson. Trotman emerged as the leader of the Holy African Church. He was succeeded by Robert A. Valentine (1945–1954), Frederick A. Toote (1954–1959) and Gladstone St. Clair Nurse.

Robinson and Nurse were able to complete a union between the two churches, which reunited in 1964. Robinson died in 1967 and Nurse succeeded him as primate. Nurse was succeeded in 1976 by Archbishop **William R. Miller** and in 1981 Miller was succeeded by Archbishop **Stafford J. Sweething**, the current Primate.

Under McGuire, a substantial church was built. Over the next generation, much of the glory faded, though there were still some strong parishes. The school has had a precarious position going in and out of existence. In 1983 the church had 17 parishes and 5,100 members. Since that time, Bishop **G. Duncan Hinkson**, pastor of the parish in Chicago, St. Augustine's, has left to found the **African Orthodox Church of the West**.

Newman, Richard. "The Origins of the African Orthodox Church." In *The Negro Churchman*. Millwood, NY: Kraus Reprint Co., 1977. Introductory essay from the reprints of the AOC magazine.

Terry-Thompson, A. C. *The History of the African Orthodox Church*. N.p.: 1956. 139 pp.

Trela, Jonathan. *A History of the North American Old Roman Catholic Church*. Scranton, PA: The Author, 1979. 124 pp.

AFRICAN ORTHODOX CHURCH OF NEW YORK AND MASSACHUSETTS.

An Eastern Orthodox church. The African Orthodox Church of New York and Massachusetts was founded by **Reginald Grant Barrow** (b. 1889), formerly a bishop in the **African Orthodox Church** (AOC). Barrow had been active in the founding of the AOC and was elected to the episcopacy and consecrated as a bishop in 1925. He was a close associate of Archbishop **George A. McGuire**, the AOC Primate until McGuire's death in 1934.

During the interim immediately after McGuire's death, the affairs of the AOC were managed by Very Rev. **Frederick A. Toote**, the Vicar General. Protests and challenges to his handling of the office led to a schism. Barrows, Toote, and AOC Bishops **Arthur Stanley Trotman** and **Robert Arthur Valentine**, and others established the African Orthodox Church in New York and Massachusetts and claimed to be the continuing McGuire body. The issue went to court. Before the adjudication process was completed, Grant suspended Trotman, who in turn founded a third body, the African Orthodox Church, Incorporated (The AOC had not yet moved to incorporate). In 1938, the court ruled against both Barrow and Trotman and enjoined them from using the name African Orthodox Church or to claim a tie to McGuire.

Trotman reorganized his following as the **Holy African Church** and it eventually absorbed what was left of Barrow's group. The Holy African Church reunited with the AOC in 1964.

Terry-Thompson, A. C. *The History of the African Orthodox Church*. N.p.: 1956. 139 pp.

Trela, Jonathan. *A History of the North American Old Roman Catholic Church*. Scranton, PA: The Author, 1979. 124 pp.

AFRICAN ORTHODOX CHURCH OF THE WEST.

An Eastern Orthodox church. The African Orthodox Church in the West continued the ministry of the **African Orthodox Church** begun in Chicago after World War II. St. Augustine's Church was formed in 1955 by the Rev. **G. Duncan Hinkson**, a physician, and eleven charter members. Originally meeting in rented facilities, in 1959 they purchased a building on Chicago's southside which was named St. Augustine's Church. Hinkson was consecrated in 1959, and St. Augustine's became a Cathedral. For many years the church was the center for African Orthodoxy in the city.

Then in 1984, Hinkson broke with the African Orthodox Church and organized a new jurisdiction which he called the African Orthodox Church of the West. Since the issues which led to the break were administrative, the doctrine and practice of the parent body were retained. Shortly after founding the new jurisdiction, Hinkson consecrated **Franzo W. King** and assigned him to lead the work in San Francisco, where he now heads the One Mind Temple, described as an Evolutionary Transitional Body of Christ. The San Francisco Church has gained some notice for its designation of the late jazz musician John Coltrane as a saint.

AFRICAN THEOLOGICAL ARCHMINISTRY.

The African Theological Archministry was founded in 1955 as the Order of Damballah Hwedo Ancestor Priests by Walter Eugene King (b. 1928). Raised a Baptist, King left the Church and began a search for a new religious faith in Africa. In 1954 he went to Haiti and discovered **Voodoo** (or Vodun). He returned to Harlem and founded the Order of Damballah Hwedo Ancestor Priests as a religious group practicing Voodoo, the version of traditional African religion which has survived in Haiti. Four years later he traveled to Matanzas, Cuba, and was initiated in the Orisha-Vodu African priesthood, a form of Afro-Cuban religion commonly called Santeria. Following this visit, the Order was superseded by the Shango Temple (named after a prominent Yoruban deity). In 1960 he incorporated the African Theological Ministry and a short time later the Shango Temple became known as the Yoruban Temple.

Since that time, King and those drawn into the Ministry have attempted to practice the ancient faith of the Yorubans of present-day Nigeria. They think of its as the "rainforest version" of the ancient Egyptian religion. It is similar to and underlies Santeria, but makes no attempt to identify African gods with Christian saints. It is a polytheistic system (though acknowledging an underlying unitive force) and worship emphasizes the appeasement of the deities. The main deity is Shango [or Chango], and the pantheon includes Elegba, the god of luck; Ogun, the god of metal; Ifa, the god of divination; and Eshu, the trickster and messenger of the gods.

In 1970, some of the members of the temple moved to a rural spot in South Carolina near Sheldon and created Oyotunji, a model Yoruban village. Only Yoruban (no English) is spoken before noon each day. Visitors are treated as if they have entered a foreign country. King began a thorough reform of the movement along Yoruban lines. In 1972 he traveled to Nigeria and was initiated into the Ifa priesthood. He returned and was proclaimed oba-king (Alashe) of the village. He is known today as Oba Efuntola Oseijeman Adelabu Adefunmi I. He presided over the first Parliament of Oyotunji chiefs and landowners and in 1973 founded the *Igbimolosha* or priest council. As ruler of Oyotunji, King Efuntola resides in a palace constructed for him. He has a number of wives and many children.

While Oyotunji has become the center of the Ministry, it is by no means its only center. The New York Temple has remained open and in the 1980s it published the more substantive works produced by the movement. There are schools to train priests in both New York and South Carolina. There are an estimated 19 centers in various locations around the country and the Ministry reports some 10,000 adherents, only 200 of whom reside at Oyotunji, which has become a pilgrimage site for African Americans from across the nation.

Adefunmi I, Oba Efuntola Oseijeman Adelabu. *The Gods of Africa.* Sheldon, SC: Great Benin Books, 1960. 23 pp.

———. *Olorisha: A Guidebook into Yoruba Religion.* Sheldon, SC: Orisha Academy of the Yoruba Village of Oyotunji, 1982. 35 pp.

Canet, Carlos. *Oyotunji.* Miami, FL: Editorial AIP, n.d. 14 pp.

Edwards, Gary, and John Mason. *Onje Fun Orisha (Food for the Gods).* New York: Yoruba African Theological Archministry, 1981. 143 pp.

Hunt, Carl M. *Oyotunji Village: The Yoruba Movement in America.* Washington, DC: University Press of America, 1979. 130 pp.

Mason, John. *Osanyin.* New York: Yoruba Theological Archministry, 1983. 48 pp.

AFRICAN UNION FIRST COLORED METHODIST PROTESTANT CHURCH.

An African American Methodist denomination. The African Union First Colored Methodist Protestant Church was formed in 1866 by the merger of the African Union Church and the First Colored Methodist Protestant Church. The African Union Church is one of two bodies which can be traced to 1805 and the establishment of Ezion Methodist Church in Wilmington, Delaware. Ezion was formed by a group of Black members of Asbury, the local congregation of the Methodist Episcopal Church. The Black members, led by **Peter Spencer** (1782–1843) and William Anderson (d. 1843), were offended at being made to worship in a segregated balcony and forced to take communion after the Whites. Without leaving the Methodist Episcopal Church, they formed a separate congregation and constructed their own building where they could freely exercise their spiritual gifts. For the next decade, the minister assigned to Wilmington preached at both Asbury and Ezion.

In 1812, James Bateman was appointed to Asbury and Ezion and soon afterward he and the very independent leaders at Ezion were in the midst of a major conflict. Bateman dismissed the trustees and class leaders. A lawsuit resulted, but before it was settled, the Black members simply walked away and founded a new congregation, this time completely independent of the Methodist Episcopal Church. The Union Church of

Africans thus became the first of the several African American Methodist churches to establish an independent structure, three years prior to the formation of the African Methodist Episcopal Church in Philadelphia.

The new church also chose a congregational form of governance and rejected the episcopal office so prominent in their parent body. Spencer was ordained by the congregation as their minister. Slowly the church grew as congregations were organized throughout the Northeast. The church suffered one major split, in 1850, when a disagreement arose over the institution of bishops. Those who wanted bishops left to form the **Union American Methodist Episcopal Church**. The Union Church of Africans emerged out of the conflict as the African Union Church.

Meanwhile, the Methodist Episcopal Church had suffered several other schisms including that of another democratic group which rejected episcopal authority. The Methodist Protestant Church separated in the late 1820s. Around 1840, members of the African Methodist Episcopal Church who had come to reject the episcopal office left that church and reorganized using the Methodist Protestant Church as their model. They chose the name First Colored Methodist Protestant Church. In 1866, soon after the Civil War, the First Colored Methodist Protestant Church merged with the African Union Church.

The African Union First Colored Methodist Protestant Church inherited and followed the 25 Articles of Religion common to all of Methodism. It altered them by placing the Apostles Creed at the beginning as article one and deleting the article on the Rulers of the United States. Otherwise the church follows Methodist emphases on faith in Jesus Christ and the activity of the free grace of God in all people. The church has a congregational polity. For many years the leading officials of the church, elected by the general conference, were the president and vice-president. In 1966, however, the church created the office of senior bishop and junior bishop, though neither office carries any of the traditional prerogatives of the bishopric. The church is organized into districts (currently three in number). The mission work of the church has been placed in the care of the women members. There were in 1988 approximately 6,500 members in 35 churches.

Baldwin, Lewis V. *Invisible Strands in African Methodism*. Metuchen, NJ: Scarecrow Press, 1983. 288 pp.
———. *The Mark of a Man: Peter Spencer and the African Union Methodist Tradition*. Lanham, MD: University Press of America, 1987. 87 pp.
Russell, Daniel James. *History of the African Union Methodist Protestant Church*. Philadelphia, PA: Union Star Book and Job Printing and Publishing House, 1920. 66 pp.

AFRICAN UNIVERSAL CHURCH. A Holiness Pentecostal church. The African Universal Church is one of two churches which grew out of the ministry of Laura Adorkor Koffey (or Kofi) (1893?–1928), generally remembered as Mother Koffey by those who knew her. Mother Koffey was a Princess, the daughter of a tribal ruler in what is today Ghana. As a young woman in Africa, she was converted to Pentecostalism and soon afterward felt called to preach. She became a preacher in 1924. Her call was accompanied by a number of dreams and visions in which she was visited by God, whom she referred to as her "Old Man God." God wished her to come to America. She arrived at the beginning of 1926. She made her headquarters in the South, but occasionally journeyed north and was briefly associated with **Marcus Garvey**'s Universal Negro Improvement Association, then on its final decline. Beginning in the fall of 1926 she preached her way from New Orleans to Mobile to Jacksonville, Florida. (Koffey's critics told a much different story. They claimed that she had been born in Athens, Georgia, and had simply traveled widely prior to her appearance in 1927. It would be the 1960s before the truth of Koffey's own account was definitively verified.)

In 1927, in Jacksonville, Florida, the African Universal Church was organized. It is a trinitarian Pentecostal body with a strong emphasis on healing and the soon return of Jesus Christ. It teaches members to expect four marked spiritual experiences, justification, sanctification, the baptism of fire, and the baptism of the Holy Spirit. The baptism of fire is available to the Spirit-filled believer. The baptism of the Holy Spirit is for the sanctified. The ordinances of baptism and the Lord's Supper are kept, but water is not used for the baptism and wine is not served during the Lord's supper.

Along with her religious message, Koffey emphasized the connection of African Americans with the people of contemporary Africa. She had plans to develop a business located in Jacksonville which would provide a commercial tie between America and her homeland. She was arrested in Atlanta on much the same charge that had stopped Garvey, taking money for a fraudulent commercial scheme. Then on March 8, 1928, she was assassinated while preaching to a crowd in Miami, Florida.

Following the assassination, the church reorganized and continued. The church is headed by an archbishop (for many years Clarence C. Addison), and regional overseers. There is also a senior mother who oversees district mothers who in turn oversee parish mothers. Also following the assassination there was a split in the church, with a group in Florida and Alabama separating. They are now known as the **African Universal Church, Inc.**

In 1934, the Commercial League Corporation, a self help company in the spirit of the Universal Negro Improvement Association, was formed. Among other functions, it provides insurance for church members. Addison, who led the church for over 40 years, was a Black nationalist and anti-integrationist. As such, during the 1960s he opposed the goals of the civil rights movement and found some approval from conservative White political groups.

Headquarters of the church for many years were in Webster, New Jersey. In 1970 there were approximately 100 congregations, but in recent years, contact had been broken and data on the current status of the group is not available.

Mother's Sacred Teachings. Jacksonville, FL: The Mafro Ile-Ife, n.d. 76 pp.

AFRICAN UNIVERSAL CHURCH, INC. A
Holiness Pentecostal church. The African Universal Church, Inc. is one of two churches which grew out of the ministry of Laura A. Koffey (or Kofi), better known as Mother Koffey. Mother Koffey preached throughout the South for several years (1926–1928) until her assassination in 1928 in Miami. Following the assassination, some of her followers in Florida and Alabama reorganized.

The history of the group during its early decades is fragmentary, but many of the local centers became autonomous churches disconnected from the movement as a whole. Emerging as a prominent leader continuing to keep alive Koffey's teachings and memory during the 1930s was E. B. Nyombolo, an African who had been attracted to the Church while living in America. He headed what was termed the Missionary African Universal Church, founded the Ile-Ife Institute in Jacksonville, Florida, and edited a periodical, *The African Messenger*. He also published the *African Universal Hymnal*, *Mother's Closet Prayer Book*, *Mother's Sacred Teachings*, and a volume of *Mother's Sayings*. In keeping with the church's message of self-help, an intentional community was created near Daphne City, Alabama, in the 1940s. Adorkaville, a second church community, was opened in Jacksonville.

In 1953 a reorganization of the churches, which had over the years drifted apart, occurred and three churches came together in a new corporate structure: St. Adorkor

African Universal Church, Miami, Florida; St. Adorkor African Universal Church, Hollywood, Florida; and the African Universal Church, Jacksonville, Florida. Elder John Dean was elected as the first chairman of the general assembly. He served until 1958 and was succeeded by Deacon Clifford Hepburn (1958–1970), Sister Gloria Hepburn (1970–1974) and Deacon Audley Sears, Sr. (1974–present).

Important to the life of the church during this time, in 1968 Ernest Sears, a member, traveled to Ghana in an attempt to locate Mother Koffey's family. An earlier attempt in the 1930s had left unanswered charges that Koffey had lied about her African background. However, Sears made contact with the family, who had never been informed of the assassination in 1928, and upon his return brought Koffey's nephew with him.

At present the African Universal Church, Inc. has seven affiliated congregations in Florida and Alabama. Headquarters is in West Hollywood, Florida. In the late 1970s, contact was reestablished with the church in Daphne City, Alabama. Doctrine is like that of the **African Universal Church**.

African Universal Hymnal. Jacksonville, FL: Missionary African Universal Church, 1961. 68 pp.
The Church: Why Mother Established the Church and What It Stands For. Jacksonville, FL: The Ile-Ife, n.d. 15 pp.
Kofi, Laura Adorka. *Mother's Sacred Teachings*. Jacksonville, FL: The Mafro Ile-Ife, n.d. 76 pp.
———. *Mother's Sayings*. Jacksonville, FL: Missionary African Universal Church, n.d. 20 pp.
Payne, Wardell J., ed. *Directory of African American Religious Bodies: A Compendium by the Howard University School of Divinity*. Washington, DC: Howard University Press, 1991. 363 pp.

AFRO-AMERICAN MISSIONARY CRUSADE. An
independent Evangelical Christian missionary organization. The Afro-American Missionary Crusade is a small agency formed in 1947 by a group of Evangelicals who wished to support Montrose Waite, a missionary formerly with the Christian and Missionary Alliance for work in West Africa. In 1951 Montrose opened the Bopolu Bible Mission, elementary school, in Liberia. Facilities were soon expanded to include a orphanage, medical dispensary, and agricultural assistance office. The headquarters office in Philadelphia, raises financial support for the Bopolu center, its only missionary station.

Goddard, Burton L. *The Encyclopedia of Modern World Missions*. Camden, NJ: Thomas Nelson & Sons, 1967. 742 pp.

AFRO-AMERICAN ORTHODOX CHURCH. An Orthodox church. The Afro-American Orthodox Church was a small liturgical church founded in the late 1930s by Bishop George A. Brooks who had been consecrated by **Reginald Grant Barrow** of the African **Orthodox Church of New York and Massachusetts**. It was similar in faith and practice to the **African Orthodox Church**. Little is known of its subsequent fate.

Trela, Jonathan. *A History of the North American Old Roman Catholic Church.* Scranton, PA: The Author, 1979. 124 pp.

THE AFRO-AMERICAN SOCIAL RESEARCH ASSOCIATION. The Afro-American Social Research Association was formed in the 1970s by a Black man who has taken the designation "The Spirit of Truth." That designation came as a result of his receiving a series of messages from one he believes to be the Creator. Many of these messages have been incorporated into a book, *"The Spirit of Truth," Doom Days.*

The Spirit of Truth teaches that God gave the earth to and for all people but that his intentions have been corrupted by wicked people taking control. A major sign of the control of the wicked is the monetary system, the destruction of which The Spirit of Truth advocates. In the face of continued wickedness, the Creator has also announced his plans to devastate the earth in the near future with a comet.

The Spirit of Truth has also announced the formation of the United Countries of the Solar System which has petitioned the United Nations to denounce the monetary system and return the earth's resources to the use of all people in their struggle to survive.

The association is headquartered in Jacksonville, Florida.

Melton, J. Gordon. *Encyclopedia of American Religions.* Detroit, MI: Gale Research Company, 1989. 1100 pp.

AGYEMAN, JARAMOGI ABEBE (b. June 13, 1911), founder of the Black Christian Nationalist Movement and the **Pan African Orthodox Christian Church**, was born in Indianapolis, Indiana, the son of Albert Buford Cleage, Sr., one of the first Black physicians at Detroit General Hospital, and Pearl Reed. His birth name was Albert Buford Cleage, Jr., but since 1972 he has been known as Jaramogi Abebe Agyeman, a Swahili name which means "liberator, blessed man, savior of the nation." He received his A.B. degree from Wayne State University, Detroit, in 1937, supporting himself as a case worker (1931–1938) for the Department of Public

Welfare. In 1939 he decided to enter the ministry and went on to earn a B.D. from Oberlin School of Theology in Ohio. He married Doris Graham, whom he later divorced after having two daughters.

He was ordained as a Congregationalist (in 1957 becoming part of the United Church of Christ) minister and pastored the Candler Memorial Congregational Church in Lexington, Kentucky (1942–43), the Church for the Fellowship of All People in San Francisco, California (1943–44), and St. John's Congregational Church in Springfield, Massachusetts (1946–51). In 1951 he returned to Detroit to be the minister of St. Mark's Community (Presbyterian) Church. At this point he began to struggle with a new sense of race consciousness, Detroit being a center for new Black movements such as the **Nation of Islam**. He began to read **Marcus Garvey** and other Black nationalists, and slowly developed a new theology. He came to believe that Europeans had painted a false picture of Jesus as a White man and universal savior, when in fact the Hebrews were Black people, including Jesus and his mother. Jesus as a Black Messiah, Agyeman believes, came specifically to free Blacks from the oppression of the gentiles (Whites).

By 1953 Agyeman (Cleage) had changed sufficiently in his outlook that he took three hundred members from St. Mark's Community Church and began a new church, the Central Congregational Church. In this new setting, he continued to develop his ideas and ministry. He disavowed individualism and defined salvation as a corporate experience. On Easter Sunday 1967, a large oil painting called, "The Black Madonna" was unveiled in the sanctuary, and Agyeman (Cleage) called for a Black theology to fill out what the painting symbolized. In January, 1968, the church, by this time counting one thousand members, was officially renamed the Shrine of the Black Madonna. Also begun was the Black Christian Nationalist Movement, designed to rebuild the Black Nation. Agyeman (Cleage) was by this time a recognized Black power spokesperson in Detroit, and became a significant player in the actions to rebuild the city after the destructive riots in the summer of 1967. His militant stances, however, were disavowed by many moderate Black leaders.

In April, 1970, the Black Christian Nationalist Movement held its first convention and pledged to make the Black church a revolutionary force. Congregations around the country soon identified with the Shrine of the Black Madonna. Connections with the United Church of Christ were broken in late 1972 and a new denomination, the Pan African Orthodox Christian Church (at first called the **Black Christian Nationalist Church**, Inc.), was born. Agyeman (Cleage) published his views in several books, primarily in *The Black Messiah* (1968) and *Black Christian Nationalism* (1972). In recent years he has concentrated on the building of his organization and has carried a low public profile.

"The Black Christian Nationalist Church." *Black World* 23 (January 1974): 88–89.

Cleage, Albert B., Jr. *Black Christian Nationalism: New Directions for the Black Church.* New York: William Morrow, 1972. 312 pp.

———. *The Black Messiah.* New York: Sheed and Ward, 1968. 278 pp.

———. "The Black Messiah and the Black Revolution." In James J. Gardiner and J. Deotis Roberts, Sr., eds. *Quest for a Black Theology.* Philadelphia, PA: United Press, 1971, 1–21.

Cleage, Albert B., Jr., and George Breitman. *Myths About Malcolm X: Two Views.* New York: Merit Publishers, 1968. 30 pp.

"Interview: Al Cleage on Black Power." *United Church Herald* 11 (February 1968): 26–30.

Rhodes, Rhoda J. "Black UCC Clergyman Organizes New Denomination." *A.D.* (UCC edition) 1 (November 1972): 52.

Serrin, William. "Cleage's Alternative." *Reporter* (New York) 38 (May 30, 1968): 29–30.

Ward, Hiley H. *Prophet of the Black Nation.* Philadelphia, PA: Pilgrim Press, 1969. 222 pp.

PBP, WWABA (85), HUBA, IBAW, EBA, CA (65–68), OTSB, LBAS, RLOA, BRBR, IBAWCB, MBRL.

AHMADIYYA MOVEMENT IN ISLAM. An Islamic movement with numerous African-American members. The Ahmadiyya Movement in Islam was founded in northern India (now Pakistan) in the 1880s by Hazrat Mirza Ghulam Ahmad (1835–1908). It developed as a revival movement to support the spread of Islam and was for many years accepted as part of orthodox Islam. Ahmad reported an early vision of the extension of Islam into America and the first of his books was translated into English in 1910. Following World War I, proselytizing efforts began in North America, and in 1921 a center was opened in Chicago by Dr. Mufti Muhammad Sadiq. He began a magazine, *Muslim Sunrise.*

The Ahmadiyya Movement was not intended to be a predominantly Black movement; however, its appearance coincided with the massive migration of Blacks to the North following World War I and the rising popularity of the **Moorish Science Temple of America.** The great majority of converts were African Americans, though there was no intent to target them exclusively, and most of the centers were located in the middle of Black communities. As the movement developed, little attempt was made to recruit outside of the Black community and not until the massive immigration of Asian Indians in the 1970s did the American branch of the movement develop a significant non-Black membership.

The Ahmadiyya Movement has insisted upon its oneness with orthodox Islam, yet it holds to several unique ideas, and in the 1950s was declared heretical by the Pakistani government. That assessment is now held by orthodox Muslim community. Most importantly, in his key book, *Barahin-i-Ahmaditah*, Ahmad declared himself to be the mahdi, the expected returning prophet and savior of the Muslims. It is assumption of the role of Prophethood, a status equal to Muhammad, which led to the movement's designation as heretical. Also, Ahmad believed that Jesus had not died on the cross but had survived his ordeal and migrated to Kashmir where he lived a long life. There is a tomb in Kashmir which is identified as the burial place of one Issa, whom many identify as the Christians' Jesus. That Jesus lived and died a natural death led to the conclusion that the Second Coming of the Christ must be in the person of another person like Jesus. Ahmad also assumed that messianic role and the American branch of the movement circulates a number of publications detailing their particular understanding of Jesus.

The movement is headquartered in Washington, D.C. Affiliated centers can be found in approximately 30 cities in the United States with an additional 18 centers in Canada. It should also be noted that there is a second branch of the Ahmadiyya movement, the Ahmadiyya Anjuman Ishaat Islam Lahore, Inc., with headquarters in Newark, California. This branch denies that Ahmad ever intended to assume a status equal to Muhammad. Coming to America only in the 1970s, it has not moved into the Black community in the way the older branch has.

Faber-Kaiser, Andreas. *Jesus Died in Kashmir.* London: Gordon & Cremonesi, 1976. 184 pp.

Khan, Muhammad Zafrulla. *Ahmadiyyat: The Renaissance of Islam.* London: Tabshir Publications, 1978. 360 pp.

Koszegi, Michael A., and J. Gordon Melton. *Islam in North America: A Sourcebook.* New York: Garland Publishing, 1992. 372 pp.

Nadwi, S. Abul Hasan Ali. *Qadianism: A Critical Study.* Lucknow, India; Islamic Research and Publications, 1972. 167 pp. A critical appraisal from an orthodox Islamic perspective.

ALABAMA LUTHERAN COLLEGE. *See:* **CONCORDIA COLLEGE.**

ALI, NOBLE DREW (January 8, 1886–July 20, 1929), founder of the **Moorish Science Temple of America**, was born in North Carolina, and grew up with the name Timothy Drew. Though poor, and with little formal education, he was able to travel to various parts of the world in the early years of the twentieth century. He was most impressed with Islamic lands and their relative lack of racial prejudice. He came to the conclusion that the American Blacks were Moors, the descendants of the Moabites of Canaan, and that their true homeland was Morocco.

He returned to America with a new interpretation of American history. He believed that prior to the Revolution Blacks in the colonies freely flew the red Moorish flag, and that this was the real "cherry tree" cut down by George Washington. It was the Continental Congress in 1779, he thought, that condemned the Blacks to slavery and conspired to rob them of their Moorish memory and identity. In 1912 he requested President Woodrow Wilson to release the Moorish flag, which he claimed was hidden in a safe in Independence Hall in 1776.

He founded his first temple in 1913 in Newark, New Jersey, where he had worked as an expressman, and soon the movement spread to Pittsburgh, Detroit, and numerous other cities. By this time he was known as Noble Drew Ali; he said that this name was given him by Sultan Abdul Asis Abn Saud during a visit to Mecca. To join the temple required only the acceptance of a Moorish identity and a one dollar donation. In 1925 the headquarters was established in Chicago, and in 1926 the organization was incorporated in Illinois as the Moorish Temple of Science, a name changed two years later to the Moorish Science Temple of America.

In 1927 Ali published *The Holy Koran*, a sixty-page statement of beliefs bearing little similarity to the orthodox Islamic scripture, the *Holy Koran* (or *Qu'ran*). It was not generally distributed, but kept in confidence among the membership. Ali's book had as a major source *The Aquarian Gospel of Jesus Christ* by Spiritualist Levi Dowling, with some chapters owing also to *Infinite Wisdom*, a 1923 book published by the deLaurence Company purporting to be derived from ancient Tibetan manuscripts. Ali evidently struck some of the right chords; by 1928 he had seventeen subordinate temples (to the one in Chicago) in fifteen states.

This, however, was also a time of strife in the organization. Some leaders were growing rich by selling products such as Old Moorish Healing Oil and Moorish Purifier Bath Compound. Drew moved to expel these people, including his business manager, Claude D. Green. Green was killed in March 1929 and the police arrested Ali, though he had been out of town at the time of the death. Five months later Ali died, and the cause of death was never determined. Some have suggested that the combination of the upcoming trial and treatment at the hands of the police led to his demise. Others suggest that Green's partisans are to blame. In any case, Ali was succeeded by R. German Ali, who led the organization for many years. Wallace Fard, one of the members, left the movement, claiming to be the reincarnation of Ali, and began what came to be known as the **Nation of Islam** (and later the American Muslim Mission).

Calverley, Edwin E. "Negro Muslims in Hartford." *The Muslim World* 55 (October 1965): 340–345.
Simpson, Frank T. "The Moorish Science Temple and Its 'Koran.'" *The Moslem World* 37 (January 1947): 56–61.
BGM, EBA, BN, IBAW, CH, BDACSL, BSC, RLOA.

ALLEN, ALEXANDER JOSEPH (September 22, 1887–November 21, 1956), 62nd bishop of the **African Methodist Episcopal Church** (AME), was born in Columbus, Georgia, the son of George W. and Phoebe (Harvey) Allen. His father was well-known as a General Officer in the AME Church, the editor (for twenty-eight years) of its periodical, the *Southern Christian Recorder*. Allen grew up attending public schools in Girard, Alabama. He was converted at age twelve and was elected Sunday School superintendent at age sixteen. He graduated with a B.A. in 1910 from Clark University in Atlanta, Georgia, and was licensed to preach by the Quarterly Conference of St. James AME Church in Columbus, Georgia, on June 9, 1911, by William Decker Johnson (later a bishop himself).

From 1911 to 1913 Allen was executive secretary of the Ninth Street Y.M.C.A. in Columbus, Georgia. In 1913 he joined the New England Annual Conference, and served until 1915 as the executive secretary of the Goffe Street Y.M.C.A. in New Haven, Connecticut. He took advantage of the proximity of the Yale University Divinity School and did some graduate work there. He was ordained deacon at the Charles Street AME Church in Boston, Massachusetts, on June 6, 1915, by Bishop Evans Tyree. Just a few weeks later, on June 30, 1915, he married Jewett Washington, and together they had four sons.

He was assigned to the Second AME Church in Boston from 1915 to 1917. This was a storefront church of 23 members on Camden Street that is now known as Grant AME Church. For a few months in 1917 he was at North Adams AME Church in Northampton, Massachusetts. He was ordained elder in Newport, Rhode Island, on June 13, 1917, again by Bishop Tyree. During that summer he pastored the AME Church in Jamestown, Rhode Island, and then was appointed to Payne AME Church in Connellsville, Pennsylvania, where he stayed until 1921. He was appointed to Mount Vernon AME Church in Columbus, Ohio, from 1921 to 1926, and while there was a two-term president of the local chapter of the N.A.A.C.P. He spent a year at Allen AME Church in Portsmouth, Ohio, and then was at Allen AME Church in Dayton, Ohio, from 1927 to 1931. During those years he was president of the Connectional Council of the AME Church.

In 1931 he was named divisional secretary of the American Bible Society (A.B.S), with headquarters in Cleveland, Ohio, a position he held for nine years. He became very active in community issues as a board member of the Cleveland Y.M.C.A. and the Urban League. He served as vice-president of the Church Union of Cleveland, which represented all the Protestant churches. At the Detroit General Conference in May 1940, he was elected bishop, and was consecrated on May 12, 1940. He was assigned to the newly created Sixteenth Episcopal District embracing the Caribbean Islands and the Guyanas in South America. Many churches were established as he and his family came to know and love the people.

In 1948 he was assigned to the Third Episcopal District, a familiar area of Ohio, western Pennsylvania, and West Virginia. He chaired the board of trustees of Wilberforce University in Ohio, and helped revitalize both it and the related Payne Theological Seminary. He authored the ministerial plan known as the Richard Allen Mutual Insurance Association. He was director of the Dunbar Life Insurance Company and the Quincy Savings and Loan Association, and was the recipient of many awards and honors. He was a delegate to the First Assembly of the World Council of Churches in Amsterdam, at the World Council of Methodism at Oxford, England, in 1951, and the Third Faith and Order Assembly of the World Council of Churches at Lund, Sweden, in 1952. He was a member of the executive committee of the Federal Council of Churches (now National Council of Churches). At the 1956 General Conference he was assigned to the Fourth Episcopal District, composed of several midwestern states, and died in that office six months later.

EAMEC, HAMEC, RLA, EWM, BAMEC, NCAB (46).

ALLEN, JOHN CLAUDE (April 5, 1899–February 6, 1975), 28th bishop of the **Christian Methodist Episcopal Church** (CME), was born in Talladega, Alabama, the fifth of six sons of Benjamin and Dollie Garrett Allen. He was converted at age twelve and joined the Jacobs CME Church in Talladega. He served as Class Leader and Sunday School Superintendent, and received his B.A. degree at Talladega College before moving to Detroit, Michigan in 1919. There he joined St. James CME Church and was much influenced by its pastor, E. M. Dozier. In 1926 he acknowledged his call to ministry and was licensed to preach. That same year he married Rosa Martin.

He pastored a number of churches in Michigan until he was called to finish the term of a presiding elder for the Chicago District who had passed away. When that term ended in 1934, he was assigned to Israel Metropolitan CME Church in Gary, Indiana. He thought the assignment would only be for one year, but ended up staying for twelve years. During that time, in the midst of the Depression, he tripled the membership to over 1,000 and built a large, new, brick sanctuary. This was an astonishing accomplishment that brought him church-wide attention. He was also a leader in the community, serving from 1935 to 1945 as president of the Gary Interdenominational Ministerial Alliance. He founded both the Gary Council of Churches and the Urban League of Northwest Indiana.

At the 1946 General Conference in St. Louis, Missouri, Allen was elected General Secretary of Kingdom Extension. He remained in Gary, Indiana, serving in many community capacities, and was the first Black ever to serve on the Gary School Board, from 1949 to 1956. During this time faculties began integrating, Blacks entered top administrative posts, and the first Black women became principals. At the 1950 General Conference he introduced the successful resolution to begin mission work along the west coast of Africa. During his twelve-year tenure as Secretary of Kingdom Extension, thirty-four new congregations were organized and more than one hundred churches were purchased, rebuilt, paid out of debt, or reclaimed. This outstanding achievement, wrought largely in the Far West, led to his being elected bishop at the 1954 General Conference in Memphis, Tennessee.

During his first four years as bishop he remained in Kingdom Extension to finish the work he had begun. In 1959 he dedicated the first CME Church in Alaska, Lewis Temple in Fairbanks. In 1958 he was assigned to the Third Episcopal District, composed of ten states in the Midwest. During the next sixteen years his accomplishments were again noteworthy: seven new churches were organized, seventy-seven churches were built, purchased, or remodeled, 277 parsonages were added, and nine other churches were given significant miscellaneous aid. He became known as the "Great Expansionist." His first wife died in 1963, and he married Sarah B. Gray on April 24, 1964. He retired at the May, 1974 General Conference in Philadelphia, Pennsylvania. He died less than a year later, and was survived by his wife and one daughter.

Doyle, Bertram W. "A Saga of Faithfulness: The Eulogy Delivered for the Funeral of Bishop John Claude Allen." *Christian Index* 108 (March 6, 1975): 6, 7, 14.
"The Life and Times of Bishop J. Claude Allen." *Christian Index* 108 (March 6, 1975): 4.
EWM, CMECTY.

ALLEN, LINEUNT SCOTT (b. May 4, 1918), a bishop of the **United Methodist Church**, was born in Meridian, Mississippi, the son of Louis and Mable (Fiedler) Allen. He received his B.A. in 1940 from Clark College in Atlanta, Georgia and his B.D. in 1942 from Gammon Theological Seminary in Atlanta. He was ordained a deacon in the Methodist Church in 1939 and became an elder in 1942. On February 19, 1942 he married Sarah Charles Adams.

His first pastorate was George Oliver Methodist Church in Atlanta, Georgia, in 1938–39. Further pastorates included Grace Methodist Church in Covington, Georgia (1939–41); Eastpoint Methodist Church in Fairborn, Georgia (1941–42); Asbury Methodist Church in Savannah, Georgia (1942–48); and Central Methodist Church in Atlanta (1948–56). In 1956 he was also an instructor in Philosophy and Religion at Clark College. From 1956 to 1967 he was editor of the *Central Christian Advocate*. During this time he earned his M.A. from Northwestern University/Garrett Theological Seminary (1961).

On August 19, 1967, Allen was consecrated bishop for what, at that time, was the non-geographical Central Jurisdiction, the all-black structure within the Methodist Church. He was assigned to the Gulf Coast Episcopal Area composed of Central Alabama, Florida, Mississippi, and Upper Mississippi. In 1968 the Methodist Church merged with the Evangelical United Brethren and became the United Methodist Church. At the same time the Central Jurisdiction was eliminated and the black bishops were integrated into the new system. From 1968 to 1976 Allen presided over the Holston Episcopal Area, and from 1976 to 1984 he headed the Charlotte (North Carolina) Episcopal Area. From 1976 to 1984 he also served on the General

Conference Standing Administrative Committee on Correlation and Editorial Revision. He retired in 1984 and has since formed a Center for Ministerial Exchange, Education, and Training for Inclusiveness and Open Itineracy at Gammon Theological Seminary. He has received several honorary degrees and citations. He has been president of the General Commission on Religion and Race, the General Commission on Archives and History, and the World Division of the General Board of Global Ministries. He has served as trustee of Bennett College, Bethune-Cookman College, Brevard College, Greensboro College, High Point College, Pfeiffer College, and the Lake Junaluska Assembly of the Southeastern Jurisdiction.

Allen, L. Scott. "Toward Preserving the History of the Central Jurisdiction." *Methodist History* 7 (October 1968): 24–30.
HUBA, AARS, WWMC, EWM, WWA (84–85), *BDUMB.*

ALLEN, RICHARD (February 14, 1760–March 26, 1831), founder of the Free African Society and the **African Methodist Episcopal Church**, was born in Philadelphia, Pennsylvania, to slave parents owned by Benjamin Chew. Chew was a lawyer, and about 1767 a decline in his practice occasioned the selling of the Allen family to the Sturgis family near Dover, Delaware. About the age of seventeen Allen was converted to Methodism, and with the permission of his owner joined the local Methodist Society. The owner was a kindly man and, due to Allen's influence, was himself eventually responsive to the Methodist message. He came to believe it wrong to hold slaves, and offered that Allen and his brother could purchase their freedom for $2,000 Continental currency or 60 British pounds worth of gold and silver currency. The two were released to earn this money, and Allen worked as a woodcutter, bricklayer, and wagon driver, finally purchasing his freedom sometime about the end of the Revolutionary War.

After the war he traveled around Delaware, New Jersey, and Pennsylvania, preaching the gospel and working odd jobs for support. He was very bright, gaining on his own a knowledge of reading and writing. He was present at the organizing "Christmas Conference" of American Methodism in Baltimore, Maryland, in December 1784. He traveled for a time in 1785 with Richard Whatcoat on the Baltimore circuit, and Francis Asbury, the head of American Methodism, often gave him additional preaching assignments. In February 1786, he went to Philadelphia and began efforts with **Absalom Jones** and other African American members of St. George's Methodist Church to preach to the Blacks of that city. Their efforts were not supported by that largely White congregation, which restricted their gatherings and segregated them in worship. Allen began a Black prayer group and considered starting an all-Black congregation, but the idea was opposed by both Whites and Blacks. Acutely aware of the tenuous positions of free Blacks, Allen, Jones, and others organized the Free African Society on April 12, 1787. This was the first independent African American society in the United States, and was dedicated to mutual aid and the abolition of slavery.

At a Sunday worship service in November 1787, Allen and the other Blacks were directed upstairs to the gallery, instead of the usual seats along the outer wall of the main floor. Then during the opening prayer, they were interrupted by the sexton, who said they were in the wrong part of the gallery. They walked out of St. George's with a new determination to build a church specifically for Blacks. Although the pastor of St. George's vigorously opposed this endeavor, they received aid from several prominent people, including the physician Benjamin Rush. The Free African Society served as the initial gathering point, adding Quaker-like times of silence to their regular meetings, an innovation which Allen opposed. When the time came to decide on the affiliation of the church they planned to build, Allen and Absalom Jones voted for Methodist, but the rest, disenchanted with Methodism, voted for the Episcopal Church. Such a church was built, and Jones remained to become its priest, the first Black American Episcopal priest. Allen reclaimed an old blacksmith's shop on Lombard, near Sixth Street, and fixed it up as a chapel so that those Blacks who preferred Methodism would have a place to worship.

In 1793 a yellow fever epidemic swept Philadelphia and Allen was among those Black leaders of the Free African Society recruited to help tend to the sick and the dead. This work consumed the better part of their time for some months, calling for heroic sacrifices, often in the face of abusive treatment, and delaying work on the church. On July 29, 1794 (twelve days after Jones' St. Thomas African Episcopal Church was dedicated), the chapel was officially dedicated by Bishop Asbury as Bethel Church. The name came from the dedication prayer offered by a White minister, John Dickens, who prayed that the church "might be a Bethel to the gathering of thousands of souls." Since that time, many churches in the Allen lineage have used Bethel in their name.

This was not the end of their problems, however. Since the church was part of the Methodist connection, it had to deal with various people in the hierarchy who would do it damage. Also, since Allen was not ordained and the church could not afford to pay much, it had to accept a series of visiting White preachers. Allen was the unofficial leader of the church, and organized a day school at the church in 1795. Asbury ordained Allen a deacon in 1799, which made Allen the first ordained Black in the Methodist Church, and finally in a position to pastor the Bethel Church himself. He was not in the itinerant system, however, and was under the authority of the Philadelphia elder. He could not celebrate the Lord's Supper or perform baptisms or weddings outside the appointment or when the elder was available to officiate. This worked so long as the elder gave Allen a large measure of autonomy. When a Virginian, James Smith, came to St. George's in 1805 and became the new ruling elder, problems reappeared. The congregation reduced its vulnerability to takeover by amending its charter with a two-thirds vote of its members, a valid move for a civil corporation. The state supreme court approved the document, known as the "African Supplement," on March 16, 1807. The document basically removed authority from the elder and placed it in the hands of the congregation's trustees. None of this would have been necessary if Allen had been made an elder, and Allen reassured the Annual Conference that independence was not the goal, only the degree of self-regulation enjoyed by White congregations. Bishop Asbury did not contest it.

The matter might have rested there, but for other complications. Bishop Asbury backed off from his original support for Black clergy and for abolition. After ordaining eight additional local Black deacons for New York, Baltimore, and Philadelphia between 1806 and 1809, he stopped the practice, and refused to ordain any Black an elder. Conceding the power of southern Methodists, Asbury approved expurgated versions of the *Discipline* in 1804 and 1808 in which passages against slavery were removed. A lawsuit by a disgruntled member of Bethel, backed by White Methodists, forced a sheriff's sale of the church on June 12, 1815, but Allen was the highest bidder and successfully held on to the property. In December of that year, at the New Year's Eve service, the new elder, Robert Burch, sought to preach at Bethel without asking for trustee approval, and the congregation blocked his entrance. This was an ironic circle of events for Black-White Methodist relations in Philadelphia. Burch petitioned the state supreme court for redress, but the judges ruled in favor of the church and its "African Supplement." This legally freed Allen's church from restraints, but by now independence from White Methodists was seemingly inevitable. A number of other Black groups had similarly seceded from their White congregations in New York, New Jersey, Delaware, and Maryland, and were seeking a means of self-direction.

On April 7, 1816, the first convention of these separated African American groups (sixteen in number) was held in Philadelphia, with Allen presiding. They decided to create the African Methodist Episcopal Church (AME), and Allen was ordained an elder and consecrated as its first bishop on April 11, 1816. Among those participating in the ceremony was Absalom Jones, by this time an Episcopal priest. Allen remained as the pastor of Bethel AME Church until his death, and although promised an annual salary of $500, accepted only $80 a year. His main source of income was from a boot and shoe business and other enterprises. He oversaw the continual building of the church, organizing the New York Conference in 1820 and authorizing the Pittsburgh or Western Conference in 1830. The president of Haiti in 1824 requested that the AME Church be planted there, offering to donate a large plot of land. A delegation was sent, beginning the international spread of the church.

Allen's leadership extended well beyond the bounds of the church. He and Jones were founding members of the African Masonic Lodge in 1798. In 1804 he organized the "Society of Free People of Color for Promoting the Instruction and School Education of Children of African Descent." In 1809 he and Jones founded the Society for the Suppression of Vice and Immorality. The American Colonization Society was founded in 1816, and Allen vigorously opposed its program of resettling free Blacks in Africa. He helped Jones and others organize a conference against it in January 1817. On September 15, 1830, shortly before his death, he presided over the first "Convention of the Colored Men of the United States," with twenty-seven elected delegates from seven states and thirteen honorary delegates. It was held at Bethel AME Church and was the first secular movement toward the betterment of Black life in America. It also revealed Allen as the first national Black leader.

Allen's most intimate legacy was his family. We know little of Flora, his first wife, with whom he had no children. He married Sarah about 1800, and had with her six children. His public legacy is matched by few others. He wrote a number of pamphlets on abolition and other themes, and an autobiography as well. He is revered as the father of the AME Church and for his pioneering example of self-determination. His influence spread far beyond the AME Church, and representations of him are found in Black homes across the United States and Africa. The statue of him in Fairmount Park, Philadelphia, dedicated on June 12, 1876, was the first statue created by American Blacks to commemorate one of their own people.

Alexander, E. Curtis. *Richard Allen: The First Exemplar of African Methodist Education*. New York: ECA Associates, 1985. 172 pp.

Allen, Richard. *The Life, Experience, and Gospel Labors of the Rt. Rev. Richard Allen*. 1793; Rept.: Philadelphia, PA: Lee & Yeocum, 1888. 69 pp.

Bragg, George Freeman. *Richard Allen and Absalom Jones*. Baltimore, MD: The Church Advocate Press, 1915. 16 pp.

George, Carol V. R. *Segregated Sabbaths: Richard Allen and the Emergence of Independent Black Churches 1760–1840*. New York: Oxford University Press, 1973. 205 pp.

Gravely, Will B. "African Methodisms and the Rise of Black Denominationalism." In Russell E. Richey and Kenneth E. Rowe, eds. *Rethinking Methodist History: A Bicentennial Historical Consultation*. Nashville, TN: Kingswood Books, An Imprint of the United Methodist Publishing House, 1985, 111–124.

Jones, Absalom, and Richard Allen. *A Narrative of the Proceedings of the Black People During the Late Awful Calamity in Philadelphia in 1793, and a Refutation of Some Censures, Thrown Upon Them in Some Late Publications*. Philadelphia, PA: William W. Woodard, 1794. 28 pp.

Mathews, Marcia M. *Richard Allen*. Baltimore, MD: Helicon, 1963. 151 pp.

Wesley, Charles H. *Richard Allen: Apostle of Freedom*. 1935; 2nd edition. Washington DC: Associated Publishers, 1969. 303 pp.

BHBA, MM, HNB, DANB, DAB (1), *EWM, DARB, MBRL, BAMEC, PP, CH, PHNA, NBH, ACAB, NCAB* (13), *HAMEC, RAM, TSW, GNPP, NV, HNC, EBA, HAMECH, IBAW, AARS, BAW, HUBA, NA, BP, WRF, BPEAR, EAMEC, AMECMIM, SOTT, AAE, NYB* (1925–26).

ALLEN UNIVERSITY. An **African Methodist Episcopal Church** school. Allen University dates to 1870 when, at a meeting of the Columbia District of the South Carolina Conference of the African Methodist Episcopal Church, an agreement was reached to begin a school. With approval of the annual conference the land was secured and opened as Payne Institute. In 1880, following the assignment to South Carolina of Bishop **William F. Dickerson**, one of the most educated leaders of the church, plans were made to begin a university in Columbia. Payne Institute was merged into the new venture which was called Allen University after the church's first bishop. A theological department, soon renamed the William F. Dickerson Theological Seminary after the school's founder, was included in the original organization of the institution. As was common for the post-Civil War schools in the south, teacher training proved a significant part of the early curriculum, and Allen supplied many teachers for the state's public schools.

Smith, Charles Spencer. *A History of the African Methodist Episcopal Church*. Philadelphia, PA: Book Concern of the AME Church, 1922. 570 pp.

ALLEYNE, CAMERON CHESTERFIELD (September 3, 1880–March 24, 1955), 44th bishop of the **African Methodist Episcopal Zion Church** (AMEZ), was born in Bridgetown, Barbados, British West Indies, the son of Robert Henry and Amelia Anne (Clarke) Alleyne. He attended Naprima College in Trinidad from 1899 to 1903, and from there went to Tuskegee Institute in Alabama from 1903 to 1904, where he finished his B.A. He was ordained deacon on October 5, 1904, and began a pastorate in Anniston, Alabama. He married Lucille Annie Washington on June 29, 1905, with whom he had one child. He was ordained elder on December 12, 1905.

After leaving Anniston he served at St. Elmo, Tennessee, from 1905 to 1908, followed by the John Wesley Church in Washington, D.C. from 1908 to 1912, and People's Church (now Hood Memorial Church) in Providence, Rhode Island, from 1912 to 1916. In 1916 he was elected editor of the *A.M.E. Zion Quarterly Review*, a position he held until 1924, while continuing to pastor in local churches. From 1916 to 1917 he was at Grace Church in Charlotte, North Carolina, and from 1917 to 1924 he ministered in New Rochelle, New York.

At the General Conference in 1924, five bishops were elected, the largest single group in the history of the denomination. Alleyne was one of those, and was consecrated to the bishopric on May 20, 1924. He was the first person ever elected to that office by a unanimous vote of the General Conference. He was assigned to the newly organized Twelfth District as the denomination's first resident bishop in Africa, and from 1924 to 1928 he and his wife lived there, tending to the Zion churches in Liberia, Nigeria, Ghana, and elsewhere. Alleyne is credited with the rejuvenation of these missions, which had fallen into some disarray. His replacement in Africa in 1928 was William Walter Matthews.

In 1928 Alleyne was assigned the Seventh Episcopal District, which he served until 1936, when he moved to the Sixth Episcopal District of the church, covering Philadelphia, Baltimore, New Jersey, Tennessee, South America, and the Virgin Islands. He retained this position until his death, making his residence in Philadelphia. He was known as a progressive leader, and was a strong advocate of education. He was a trustee of Livingstone College in Salisbury, North Carolina; Shorter College in Little Rock, Arkansas; and Payne Seminary in Wilberforce, Ohio. He had great success in home missions, supervising an extensive evangelism and building campaign in the Philadelphia and Baltimore Conferences. He was called the greatest expansionist of the church of his generation. Livingstone College gave him an honorary M.A. in 1915, and Howard University in Washington, D.C. gave him an honorary D.D. in 1924.

During World War II Alleyne represented the AMEZ Church on the Commission of Army and Navy Chaplains. His wife died soon after the General Conference of May 1944, and he married Bettye Lee Roberts in June 1946. He published several books, the most well-known being his first book, *Gold Coast at a Glance* (1931). His autobiographical work is *Twenty-Five Years in the Episcopacy* (1950).

"The Anthology of the AME Zion Bishops." *Star of Zion* 57 (September 28, 1933): 1, 6.
"Bishop Cameron Chesterfield Alleyne." *A.M.E. Zion Quarterly Review* 59, No.3 (1949): 106–107.
"Bishop Cameron Chesterfield Alleyne." *A.M.E. Zion Quarterly Review* 77, No.4 (1965): 199–200.
"Bishop C.C. Alleyne Marries." *Star of Zion* 70 (June 13, 1946): 1, 8.
"The Magnificent Qualities of Our Bishops: Part 5." *Star of Zion* 70 (July 11, 1946): 1, 8.
"New Era of Zion Methodism." *Star of Zion* 48 (August 7, 1924): 1, 5.
Alleyne, Cameron Chesterfield. *Gold Coast at a Glance*. New York: The Hunt Printing Co., 1931. 143 pp.
———. *Highways That Lead to God*. Philadelphia: Sixth Episcopal District, A.M.E. Zion Church, 1941. 73 pp.
———. *Twenty-Five Years in the Episcopacy*. 1950.
HAMEZC, NYTO, IBSP, AARS, HUBA, AMEZC, RLA.

ALPHA AND OMEGA PENTECOSTAL CHURCH OF GOD OF AMERICA. A Trinitarian Holiness Pentecostal church. The Alpha and Omega Pentecostal Church was founded by Rev. Magdalene Mabe Phillips, (b.1905) formerly a minister of the United Holy Church of America. When the church was originally founded in 1945 Phillips and the eight original members assumed the name Alpha and Omega Church of God Tabernacle. Phillips was followed in leadership by **Charles E. Waters, Sr.,** but he left in 1964 to found the **True Fellowship Pentecostal Church of God of America**.

He was succeeded by Rev. John Mabe, the founder's brother.

The church follows the holiness pentecostal doctrine of its parent body. It teaches that believers are justified at the time they accept Christ. Subsequently they may, by the power of the Holy Spirit, be sanctified. Sanctified people may also receive the baptism of the Holy Spirit, evidenced by speaking in tongues. Members follow a holiness code which prohibits the use of tobacco, alcohol and narcotics, either immodest or ostentatious dress, and divorce. Baptism is by immersion. The church is small, its congregations all located in the greater Baltimore metropolitan area. There are several hundred members.

Piepkorn, Arthur J. *Profiles in Belief.* Vol. III. New York: Harper & Row, 1979. 262 pp.

ALSTORK, FRANK WESLEY (June 16, 1885–July 5, 1948), 52nd bishop of the **African Methodist Episcopal Zion Church** (AMEZ), was born in Coatapa, Alabama, one of seven children born to Alonzo Gary and Elizabeth Alstork. His father was a minister in the AMEZ Church, and his uncle, John Wesley Alstork, was also a bishop in the church. He grew up in the Big Zion Church in Mobile, Alabama, and later attended the Little Hope Chapel in Mobile, where he was licensed to preach at age twenty. Two years later, on December 1, 1907, he was ordained a deacon and joined the West Alabama Conference. He was assigned a small church in Talladega, where he was attending Talladega College.

After completing his time at Talladega, he then was assigned to Midland City, Alabama, followed by Hurtsboro, Alabama, and St. Mark's Church in St. Louis. In 1914 he married Willie Gertrude Kemp; they had no children. His next position was as presiding elder in the Missouri Conference. Returning to the local church pastorate, he went to Smith Memorial Church in Du Quoin, Illinois, where he built a sanctuary, followed by the Metropolitan AMEZ Church in Birmingham, Alabama. In 1927 he went to the Union Wesley Church in Washington, D.C., leaving it in 1940 after a second unsuccessful bid for the episcopacy. He moved to the Wesley Church in Philadelphia, Pennsylvania. At the 1944 General Conference in Detroit, he was elected bishop, and was consecrated on May 14, 1944.

As bishop he was assigned to the Tenth Episcopal District (covering Alabama) until 1948, when he was moved to the Eighth Episcopal District (covering conferences in Virginia and North Carolina). He was a strong advocate of Black rights and dignity, and was in the forefront of the battle against police brutality. He was committed to the values of education, and served as trustee at Lomax-Hannon College in Greenville, Alabama, at the Dinwiddie Normal and Industrial College in Virginia, and of Livingstone College in Salisbury, North Carolina. He also was a member of the International Council of Religious Education and the Fraternal Council of Churches. An automobile accident in Washington, D.C., on May 24, 1948, inflicted injuries which eventually proved fatal, tragically ending his fruitful ministry.

"Alstork, Watson Elected Bishops." *Star of Zion* 68 (May 25, 1944): 1.
"Bishop Alstork in Auto Wreck—Dies." *Star of Zion* 72 (July 22, 1948): 6.
"Frank Wesley Alstork." *Journal of Negro History* 33 (October 1948): 502–503.
IBSP, AMEZC, HAMEZC.

ALSTORK, JOHN WESLEY (September 1, 1852–July 23, 1920), 28th bishop of the **African Methodist Episcopal Zion Church** (AMEZ), was born in Talladega, Alabama, the son of Frank and Mary Jane Alstork. He attended Longwood Institute beginning in 1868, and was soon an assistant teacher. He entered Talladega College in 1871, and married Mamie Meta Lawson on May 26, 1872. In 1873, at the age of twenty-one, he joined the AMEZ Church.

He was licensed to preach in 1878, and joined the Alabama Conference of the church in 1879. He was ordained deacon in the East Alabama Conference on November 26, 1882, and appointed to Thompson Chapel in Opelika, Alabama. Bishop **James W. Hood** ordained him an elder on November 30, 1884, at which point he was appointed to a prestigious church, Clinton Chapel (also known as Old Ship Church) in Montgomery, Alabama. He was very successful in this pastorate, paying off the mortgage and building a new parsonage.

In 1889 he was elected presiding elder of the Montgomery District, which he served for three years. In 1892 he became presiding elder of the Greenville District, and was there for four years. In 1893 he founded Greenville College (which he renamed **Lomax-Hannon Industrial College** in 1904). By this time he was a regular delegate to General Conference. He was elected bishop at the 1900 General Conference in Washington, D.C., and was consecrated on May 20, 1900. He was the church's first bishop from Alabama, and was so popular he was the first bishop elected by acclamation.

As a bishop he was widely known. He frequently traveled in Cuba, and asked that it be included in his episcopal supervision, which was granted. He was a delegate to the Ecumenical Methodist Conference in 1901 in London and again in 1911 in Toronto. In 1904 he was assigned to the Alabama Episcopal District. He was trustee for a number of schools, including Livingstone College, the State Normal School, Hale Infirmary, Longridge Academy, and the Industrial and Orphan School in Macon. He became Grand Master of the York Rite Masons, and held several other prominent Masonic offices. In 1911 he organized the South Alabama Conference, and in 1912 the Cahaba Conference. His scholarship was held in high regard, and he was a member of the Sociological Congress. Livingstone College granted him an honorary D.D. degree in 1892, and Princeton Normal and Industrial College in Indiana granted him an honorary LL.D. degree in 1908. Six months after his wife died, his own life ended suddenly while he was addressing a Sunday School Convention in Searcy, Alabama.

Alstork, John Wesley. "Greatest Need of the Negro Race." In W. N. Hartshorn, ed. *An Era of Progress.* Boston, MA: Priscilla Publishing Co., 1910, p. 400.
"Bishop John Wesley Alstork." *A.M.E. Zion Quarterly Review* 64, 2 (1953): 103–104.
EWM, AMEZC, HAMEZC, AARS, WWCR, IBSP.

AMERICAN ASSOCIATION FOR ETHIOPIAN JEWS. The American Association for Ethiopian Jews, the primary organization in America supporting the cause of Ethiopian Jews, was founded in 1974 by the merger of The American Pro-Falasha Committee and the Friends of Beta-Israel Community in Ethiopia. The American Pro-Falasha Committee was established in 1922 by Jacques Faitlovitch (1880–1955) an Orthodox Jew who had become interested in the Falashas through his teacher Joseph Halevy. Around the turn of the century he made the first of several trips to Ethiopia to visit the Falasha communities and report on their condition to the Jewish world at large. Convinced that they were true Jews, and concerned about the inroads being made by Christian missionaries, he appealed for assistance.

Rebuffed by the Jewish community in Europe, on his own he created a "mission" to counter the effects of the Christian missionaries and established two schools to train Falasha children. In 1906 he set up a support committee in Italy which was later transferred to Germany and in 1922 it became the Pro-Falasha Committee in the United States. He was able to garner the support of such leading Jewish voices as Cyrus Adler and Israel Goldstein. Faitlovitch served as executive secretary of the committee for the rest of his life.

The Italian invasion of Ethiopia stopped efforts to assist the Falashas until after World War II. Meanwhile Faitlovitch became an Israeli citizen and assisted the first movement of Falashas to Israel.

The Friends of the Beta-Israel Community in Ethiopia was started by Dr. Greanum Berger, who has brought a new level of activism in demands for support for the Falashas. Berger's enthusiastic championing of the cause led to the merger of his organization with the older committee in 1974. Since that time the new American Association for Ethiopian Jews has launched a program to inform Jews around the world of the plight of Ethiopian Jews, a minority in a hostile environment, to place the rescue of the Ethiopian Jews as a priority on the agenda of the world Jewish community, and to lead in the movement of Ethiopian Jews to Israel. A major gain was made in 1975 when Israel recognized the Falashas as Jews according to the Law of Return of 1950, meaning they could settle in Israel and be granted full citizenship. The work of the association has taken on a more urgent tone with the widespread reports of persecution since the assumption of power by a Marxist regime in 1975. Between 1948 and 1979, only about 300 Ethiopian Jews had made the trek to Israel. By 1990 approximately 1,200 Falashas had been brought to Israel through the association's efforts. It continues to work for those remaining in Ethiopia.

The association is headquartered in Washington, D.C. It publishes a quarterly newsletter, *Release.*

Avraham, Shmuel. *Treacherous Journey: My Escape from Ethiopia.* New York: Shapolsky Publishing, 1986. 178 pp.
Gruber, Ruth. *Rescue: The Exodus of the Ethiopian Jews.* New York: Atheneum, 1987. 234 pp.
Rapoport, Louis. *The Lost Jews: Last of the Ethiopian Falashas.* New York: Stein and Day, 1980. 252 pp.

AMERICAN BAPTIST BLACK CAUCUS. An **American Baptist Churches in the U.S.A.** organization. The American Baptist Black Caucus was founded in 1968 as the Black American Baptist Churchmen. The name was changed in 1981. The caucus is one of a number of African American organizations which were formed in the late 1960s following the organization of the National Committee of Negro Churchmen (now the **National Conference of Black Churchmen**). The National Committee was attempting to respond positively to the issues of Black economic power which had been raised so powerfully in the mid-1960s and to address what seemed to be the limitations of the nonviolent action program espoused by **Martin Luther King, Jr.**

It is estimated that over 480,000 members (approximately 30 percent of the membership) in the American Baptist Churches are African American. It is this constituency which the caucus represents and addresses. It has as a major goal the bridging of the gap between Black and White ministers and members. It has also built a program which seeks the churches' cooperation in scholarship aid for minority students, supplying resources for the inner city, opening positions for Blacks in denominational posts and employment, and support for Black schools. It has developed a placement service for pastors seeking positions and churches seeking pastors.

The caucus is headquartered in the office of the president. As presidents are elected annually, that office changes locations frequently; however, the caucus may be contacted through the American Baptist offices in Valley Forge, Pennsylvania. The caucus publishes a semi-annual *Black Caucus Newsletter* and a monthly periodical, *ABC TAB*.

AMERICAN BAPTIST CHURCHES IN THE U.S.A. A Baptist church. The American Baptist Churches in the U.S.A., organized in 1907 as the Northern Baptist Convention, continues the organizational life of Baptists in the United States from the colonial period. From its inception, the denomination changed its name twice: American Baptist Convention (1950) and American Baptist Churches in the U.S.A. (1972). The emergence of the convention brought together in a single coordinating body three major boards and emphases—Overseas Witness, National Ministries, and Education and Publication. These were the outgrowth of the American Baptist Publication Society, American Baptist Home Mission Societies and the General Missionary Convention of the Baptist Denomination for Foreign Missions.

During the early organizational years of American Baptist life, White Baptists in the North took a lively interest in the conversion of slaves and the evolution of African American Baptist life. Moreover, African Americans actually attained membership in the denomination. The early style of church life, especially on the local levels, was bi-racial. With the organization of separate, African American Baptist churches in Boston, New York and other parts of the North, the new churches united with existing Baptist associations and societies of the general Baptist denomination. This relationship remained rather solid until African American Baptists decided to organize their own associations, state conventions, regional conventions and eventually a separate denomination.

With the organization of African American Baptist associations and conventions, White American Baptists adopted a program of cooperation with the separate groups. However, the period between 1832 and 1865 witnessed a time of relative inactivity on the part of American Baptists because of the controversy over slavery. Very little was done on the behalf of African American Baptists by the American Baptist Home Mission Society. It was not until the post-Civil War era that American Baptists renewed their interest in African Americans. They became especially interested in the plight of the freedmen in the South. Accordingly, by 1870, American Baptists were operating schools for freedmen in several cities. Among these schools were Wayland Seminary, Washington, D.C.; Richmond Theological Seminary, Richmond, Virginia; Shaw University, Raleigh, North Carolina; Roger Williams University, Nashville, Tennessee; Leland University, New Orleans, Louisiana; Benedict College, Columbia, South Carolina; and Spelman Seminary, Atlanta, Georgia. Some of these schools were jointly supported by African American Baptists in the respective states. These Home Mission schools educated most of the leadership of African American Baptists until the integration of the predominantly White seminaries in the early twentieth century.

The Women's Home Mission Society of New England and the Church Edifice Work of the American Baptist Convention also played key roles in the development of African American Baptist life. Both provided funds for the organization and development of churches. In 1882, the Church Edifice work spent $10,237.38 among African American Baptist churches in the South. Hence, the rapid development of these churches was partly a cooperative ministry between African American and White Baptists.

African American Baptists responded rather warmly to these overtures of assistance on the part of American Baptists. Because the color line was not radically drawn in the North, African American Baptists maintained an affinity with their White colleagues in the North. In fact, some of their churches continued to remain vital parts of the ministry of the American Baptist Convention as well as the **National Baptist Convention, U.S.A., Inc.** The statistical data in the minutes of the National Baptist Convention for 1926 reflects that there were 410 African American Baptist Churches with 116,137 members in the convention in 1926. These churches were located in twenty-three of the northern and northwestern states of the nation. In 1926, 323 of the 627 African American Baptist churches aligned with the American Baptist Convention were located in the major cities of the North and the Northwest. However, the convention made little or no effort to increase the number of these churches.

By the middle of the twentieth century, the American Baptist Convention experienced a significant decline in White membership. Partly to offset such a decline in numbers, the convention launched a more aggressive program to increase its membership. Gradually, the convention looked to African American Baptists as a potential source of new members. William Thomas Mckee, Field Counselor for the Ministers and Missionaries Benefit Board, and E. B. Hicks became pioneers in the recruitment of African American Baptist Churches to dually align themselves with the American Baptist Convention and one of the Black Baptist conventions.

William Mckee used the vehicle of the Ministers and Missionaries Benefit Board as a strong appeal to the African Baptist pastors to unite with the convention in order to receive much needed benefits. The vast majority of African American Baptist pastors had no retirement benefits and health programs offered through their local churches. The National Baptists had very little to offer in terms of such benefits. Hence, African American Baptist pastors gradually looked to the Ministers and Missionaries Benefit Board for these much needed services. This trend gradually spread to the southern parts of the nation. In 1961, letters welcoming three African American Baptist Churches were read before the American Baptist Convention. The churches which applied and received membership were the New Hope Baptist Church, Dallas, Texas, with 472 members; Ebenezer Baptist Church, Richmond, Virginia, with 1200 members; and, the New Shiloh Baptist Church, Baltimore, Maryland, with 1,400 members. Since these churches were outside the normal area of convention operation, the American Baptist Convention offered the American Baptist Home Mission Societies as the official channel through which these churches would be served by the convention.

In 1965, E. B. Hicks made American Baptists more aware of the potential of greater cooperation with African American Baptists. He inspired the Community Witness Program, Division of Church Missions, American Baptist Home Mission Societies to sponsor one national and six regional inclusive church workshops. These workshops had a threefold purpose: (1) to build bridges of understanding between the three major divisions of the American culture—Caucasian, Negro, and Spanish-speaking; (2) to help change the stereotyped images that the different groups have of one another; and (3) to work toward the development of inclusive churches, where people learn to serve and worship together in multi-racial communities throughout the nation. These workshops brought a new awakening to the American Baptist Convention.

By 1968, the Black Churchmen of the American Baptist Convention issued a demand for greater representation in the higher administrative levels of the convention. Subsequently, the convention gradually opened its boards to African American Baptists. The convention was well on its way to becoming the most racially inclusive fellowship in America.

With the rapid increase of African American churches in the South aligning themselves with the American Baptist Convention (hereafter known as the American Baptist Churches in the U.S.A.), E. B. Hicks saw the need for a new organizational structure in the South. As previously mentioned, the Home Mission Societies was the only channel through which these churches had representation. A Committee of the Southern Caucus at the American Baptist Convention was appointed to organize the work of the American Baptist Churches in the South. Among the most influential African American members of the committee were Rev. Kelly Miller Smith, pastor of the First Baptist Church Capitol Hill, Nashville, Tennessee; Rev. Barry Hopkins of Richmond, Virginia; Rev. Marcus Garvey Wood, pastor of Providence Baptist Church, Baltimore, Maryland; and Rev. Leroy Jordan, pastor of the First Baptist Church, Tulsa, Oklahoma. On April 10–12, 1970, the actual organizational meeting for the Southern Region of the American Baptist Churches in the U.S.A. took place at the Myers Park Baptist Church, Charlotte, North Carolina. Rev. E. B. Hicks became the first executive minister of the new organization of American Baptists. Both African American and White Baptist Churches united with the southern regional organization. Rev. E. B. Hicks was careful to lead the new Southern Region to be just in its racially inclusive policy of leadership.

The American Baptist Churches of the South (ABCOTS) originally consisted of one hundred thirty-one churches. The first president was Rev. J. B. Henderson, pastor of Bank Street Memorial Baptist Church, Norfolk, Virginia. Other officers reflected the policy of racial inclusivity. However, the majority of the churches were African American Baptists.

In 1976, Rev. E. B. Hicks retired from the office of executive minister of ABCOTS. He was succeeded by Rev. James E. Peters, Jr., who continued the basic program of Rev. E. B. Hicks. In 1979, Peters resigned and was succeeded by Rev. Walter Leroy Parrish, II. Under the new leadership, the Southern Region has grown in stewardship and influence on the broader American Baptist denomination.

The policy of racial inclusivity of the American Baptist Churches in the U.S.A. has been unprecedented in American denominational life. In 1970, the convention elected Rev. **Thomas Kilgore, Jr.**, pastor of Second Baptist Church, Los Angeles, California, to serve as its first African American president. Subsequently, the convention elected other Africans to the presidency, including Harold Davis (1989) and Rev. James A. Scot, pastor of Bethany Baptist Church, Newark, N.J. (1991). A representative number of African American Baptists have served in top leadership positions within the denomination.

Currently, the American Baptist Churches composition is 60 percent White, 37 percent African American Baptists and 3 percent Hispanic, Asian or Native American. The total denominational membership of the convention is approximately 5,730 congregations with 1.6 million members in the United States and Puerto Rico.

The American Baptist. Special issue. September/October, 1989.

Baptist Home Missions in North America. New York: Baptist Home Mission Rooms, 1883. 544 pp.

Everett, Harvey A., and Paul L. Stagg. *A Report on Organizing a Region in the South*, a Proposal by the Committee on Organizing the Work of the American Baptist Churches in the South, Appointed by the Southern Caucus at the American Baptist Convention. January, 1970. 21 pp.

Fitts, Leroy. *A History of Black Baptists*. Nashville, TN: Broadman Press, 1985. 368 pp.

Leroy Fitts

AMERICAN BAPTIST THEOLOGICAL SEMINARY.

A Baptist school. In the years before 1913, Drs. **Lacey K. Williams**, O. L. Bailey, and C. B. Bailey, all prominent leaders within the **National Baptist Convention, U.S.A., Inc.**, began to talk about the possibility of founding a new convention-supported seminary. In 1913, the idea was presented to both the National Baptist Convention and the Southern Baptist Convention (SBC). The proposal followed years of discussion within the SBC on how to assist Black Baptist ministers, and led by E. Y. Mullins, the convention responded to the proposal by establishing a committee to work with the Black Baptists in the establishment of such a school.

A joint committee between the two conventions worked for over a decade. Not only were there intense disagreements over the location and control of the school, but World War I further delayed negotiations. Finally, Nashville was agreed upon as a site. The school was to remain in the hands of the National Baptist Convention from which the president and two-thirds of the board would be drawn. The school opened in 1924 and the following year **Sutton E. Griggs** was called as president. In 1934 the property of the former Roger Williams University was acquired as the site of a new campus. Dr. J. M. Nabrit, who became president in 1936, immediately put the new site to use by opening a National Baptist Missionary Training School and a retirement home for Black ministers on campus.

The seminary stands as one of the models of Black/White cooperation with each supplying needed resources. Board membership is now equally divided between the two conventions. Over the years, as the school has grown, the SBC has contributed the greater percentage of the financial support for the school, and initiated a scholarship program to annually pay tuition and expenses for the majority of the students at the seminary, while members of the National Baptist Convention continue to supply the majority of the administrative and intellectual leadership.

Baker, Robert A. *The Southern Baptist Convention and Its People, 1607–1972*. Nashville, TN: Broadman Press, 1974. 477 pp.

Fitts, Leroy. *A History of Black Baptists*. Nashville, TN: Broadman Press, 1985. 368 pp.

AMERICAN CATHOLIC CHURCH (SYRO-ANTIOCHEAN).

An Old Catholic church. The American Catholic Church (Syro-Antiochean) grew out of a significant doctrinal split in the American Catholic Church. In the late 1930s, Percy Wise Clarkson became the primate of the American Catholic Church, an independent Catholic church in the Western Roman tradition, which had been established by Archbishop Joseph Renè Vilatte early in the twentieth century. Clarkson, however, had absorbed strong occult leaning from his study of Theosophy and began to lead the church into the orbit of the theosophically inclined Liberal Catholic Church. Among the people who rejected the direction to which Clarkson pointed was Bishop **Ernest Leopold Peterson** (d. 1959). In the early 1940s. Peterson withdrew from Clarkson's jurisdiction and established the American Catholic Church (Syro-Antiochean) which for many years was headquartered in Miami, Florida. Peterson was succeeded by Herbert Wilkie whom he had consecrated in 1950. There has been no sign of the church in recent years and it is believed defunct.

AMERICAN MUSLIM MISSION. *See:* **Nation of Islam**.

AMERICAN NATIONAL BAPTIST CONVENTION.

A Baptist organization. The American National Baptist Convention (ANBC) was a cooperative missionary society and one of several Black Baptist organizations that joined to form the **National Baptist Convention, U.S.A., Inc.** in 1895.

After the **Baptist Foreign Mission Convention** was established in 1880 to help foster national support for African missions, one of its earliest and most persistent problems was the hesitancy on the part of its more influential Black pastors to band together with Whites. These church leaders believed that African missions were the sole province of African American Baptists. Arguing against this position was **William J. Simmons**, a Black Baptist minister who maintained that cooperation with rather than the exclusion of Whites would better serve the cause of the African mission. In addition, Simmons and other Black Baptists thought that an organization that united the efforts of Blacks in all foreign missions would likewise bring success to the Christian mission. Accordingly, Simmons called together interested clergy and laypersons to coordinate considering how best to implement these strategies. Six hundred delegates met on August 25, 1886 and launched the American National Baptist Convention. Simmons himself was elected first president of the ANBC and served until his untimely death in 1890 at the age of forty. Unfortunately, the vision of a unified effort in foreign missions was not to be realized in the ANBC. Even so, the ANBC did direct African American Baptists along the path toward greater unity of purpose in missions.

The ANBC joined with the American National Baptist Convention, the Baptist Foreign Mission Convention, and the National Baptist Educational Convention in 1895 to form the National Baptist Convention.

Fitts, Leroy. *A History of Black Baptists*. Nashville, TN: Broadman Press, 1985. 368 pp.

Jackson, Joseph H. *A Story of Christian Activism: The History of the National Baptist Convention, U.S.A., Inc.* Nashville, TN: Townsend Press, 1980. 790 pp.

Martin, Sandy D. *Black Baptists and African Missions*. Macon, GA: Mercer University Press, 1990. 242 pp.

Pelt, Owen D., and Ralph Lee Smith. *The Story of the National Baptists*. New York: Vantage Press, 1960. 272 pp.

Jon R. Stone

AMMONS, EDSEL ALBERT (b. February 17, 1924), a bishop of the **United Methodist Church**, was born in Chicago, Illinois, the son of Albert Clifton and Lila Kay (Sherrod) Ammons. From 1943 to 1946 he was in the Army Quartermaster Corps. He received his B.A. in 1948 from Roosevelt University in Chicago, Illinois. He was ordained deacon in 1947 and elder in 1949, and from 1949 to 1954 pastored the St. Mark **African Methodist Episcopal Zion Church** (AMEZ) in Chicago. On August 18, 1951, he married June Billingsley, with whom he had six children. In 1954–55 he pastored the St. John AMEZ Church in Highland Falls, New York, then returned to Chicago. From 1951 to 1956 he was also a social case worker for the Department of Welfare, Cook County, Illinois. In 1956 he completed his B.D. at Garrett-Evangelical Theological Seminary in Evanston, Illinois.

In 1957 Ammons left the AMEZ and joined the Rock River Annual Conference of the Methodist Church under the influence of Bishop Charles W. Brashares. From 1957 to 1963 he pastored the Whitfield Methodist Church (now the Ingleside-Whitfield Methodist Parish) in Chicago. From 1958 to 1961 he was vice-president of the Chatham-Avalon Community Council. From 1963 to 1966 he was Director of Urban Ministries for the Rockford District in Illinois, and from 1966 to 1968 he was a part of the program staff for the Rock River Annual Conference. From 1968 to 1976 he was on the faculty of Garrett-Evangelical Theological Seminary. In 1972–73 he was executive director of the Educational and Cultural Institute of Black Clergy in Chicago. In 1975 he earned his D.Min. from Chicago Theological Seminary.

In 1976 Ammons was elected bishop and assigned to the Michigan Episcopal Area. He was president of the General Board of Discipleship from 1980 to 1984 and during the 1988–1992 chaired the Health and Welfare Ministries Department of the General Board of Global Ministries. In 1984 he was assigned to the West Ohio Episcopal Area. He is the recipient of several honorary degrees. He retired in 1992.

Ammons, Edsel A. *My Membership Vows*. Nashville, TN: Discipleship Resources, 1984. 28 pp.

———. *Voluntarism and the Church: Implications for Black/White Relations in the United Methodist Church*. Evanston, IL: Bureau of Social and Religious Research, Garrett-Evangelical Theological Seminary, 1976. 17 pp.

WWABA (92–93), *WWA* (90–91), *BDNM* (75), *BDUMB*.

AMOS, WALTER HANSEL (March 16, 1908–January 2, 1975), 32nd bishop of the **Christian**

Methodist Episcopal Church (CME), was born in Milan, Tennessee, the son of E. F. B. and Alice E. Amos. His father was a minister in the CME Church, so he grew up in various parsonages according to his father's assignments. He received his college degree at Lane College in Jackson, Tennessee, and became a physical education instructor at Manassas High School in Memphis, Tennessee. He also for a time was principal of Henderson-Rosenwald School in Henderson, Tennessee, and was director of athletics at Miles College in Birmingham, Alabama. He married Alice N. Mason, eldest daughter of Bishop C. H. Mason of the Church of God in Christ. They had one child who died in 1949 at the age of four.

In 1934, at a Youth Conference in Oklahoma City, Oklahoma, he received a call to ministry. He was ordained a deacon in 1936 and began his ministry at the Moody Chapel CME Church in Memphis. He later moved to the Rock of Ages CME Church in Memphis, and then the Jubilee Temple CME Church in Chicago, Illinois. While there he took graduate courses at Garrett Bible Institute (now Garrett-Evangelical Theological Seminary) in Evanston, Illinois, and at the University of Chicago School of Divinity. In 1945 he moved to St. John CME Church in Detroit, Michigan, where he served for seventeen years. He was instrumental in moving the church from its previous location at St. Aubin and Maple to its present location, where great commitment and sacrifice created a new structure. He also studied at Wayne University in Detroit, earning an M.A. degree, and took Ph.D.-level courses at the University of Michigan in Ann Arbor.

Amos was elected bishop at the May, 1962 General Conference in St. Louis, Missouri. He was assigned to the Ninth Episcopal District, which included the California, New Mexico-Arizona, and Oklahoma-Muskogee Conferences. During his tenure the Alaska-Pacific Conference was organized, and the mission program in Alaska rejuvenated. In 1962 he became chair of the General Board of Pensions for the church, and led in establishing the church's first Insurance-Pension Plan. In 1966 he was a delegate to the World Ecumenical Methodist Conference in London, England. He served in many other capacities, including as vice-president of the California Council of Churches, and as a part of the Commission on Social Welfare of the National Council of Churches. At the 1974 General Conference he was assigned to the Third Episcopal District in the Midwest, but died six months into that work.

"A Message From the College of Bishops: Bishop Walter Hansel Amos, March 16, 1908–January 2, 1975." *Christian Index* 108 (January 23, 1975): 7.
"The Obituary for Bishop Walter Hansel Amos." *Christian Index* 108 (January 23, 1975): 8.
BDNM (75), CMECTY, EWM.

ANDERSON, DUKE WILLIAM (April 10, 1812–February 17, 1873), Baptist minister and teacher, was born near Lawrenceville, Illinois. His father was a White soldier who soon thereafter died fighting in the Indian wars, and his mother was a Black woman who struggled to bring up her two sons by herself on the farm. The family received a stipend from the father's military service, which enabled Anderson to obtain a basic education at an Illinois rural school.

He learned quickly and at age seventeen began to teach school. The following year, on September 30, 1830, he married Ruth Ann Lucas, with whom he had five children. He taught for one more year, then settled down on a farm he purchased. On September 4, 1839, his wife died giving birth to their fifth child, who also died. He soon sold the farm, began teaching again, and eventually moved the family to Alton, Illinois, where he married Mary Jane Ragens on August 17, 1842. He had two more children with her.

Soon after the death of his first wife Anderson experienced conversion, and in Alton he joined the African Methodist Episcopal Church (AME), as there was no Black Baptist church available. In 1843 the church experienced a split, with many members, including Anderson, forming a Baptist church. He now felt himself called to the ministry, was ordained in 1844, and began to preach in various places in the area. In 1845 he purchased an eighty-acre farm about five miles from Alton, spearheading a new community for which he was parson, schoolmaster, and justice of the peace. Soon a Baptist church was built, the Salem Baptist Church on Wood River, which organized the Wood River Baptist Association with nearby churches, Anderson being the first Moderator. This association gradually extended its connections throughout the state of Illinois, and its annual gathering became a statewide event.

In 1852, at the height of his leadership in Wood River, Anderson sold the farm and left for Quincy, Illinois, where he felt he could give his children a better education. There he once again took up farming, preaching, and became active in the Underground Railroad. Despite the dangers involved, he lectured all over the state against slavery, and his tremendous presence and speaking abilities enabled him to overcome even combative audiences. He was three times chosen State Missionary by the State Missionary Society. A pro-slavery mob from Missouri burned the Missionary Institute School, where two of his children were students, and the family had to move again to find suitable education.

About 1854 Anderson accepted the pastorate of a Baptist church in Buffalo, New York, an anti-slavery stronghold where he could educate his children. After a very successful stay there, in late 1857 he accepted a new position at the Groghan Street Baptist Church in Detroit, Michigan. On October 23, 1860, his second wife passed away, and on March 18, 1861, he married Mrs. Eliza Julia Shad of Chatham, Canada. Soon after the end of the Civil War he became pastor of the 19th Street Baptist Church of Washington, D.C., and almost overnight was a widely recognized leader in that city. He was elected a trustee of Howard University, of the Freedman's Savings Bank and Trust Company, and in 1871 was elected Commissioner of the Washington Asylum. He was a justice of the peace from April 8, 1869, to April 9, 1872. The membership of the church grew such that in March 1871 the old house of worship had to be abandoned and a new one was completed at the same site on Nineteenth and I Streets on November 19, 1871. Many high officials from the government were in attendance, and a letter from the President was read. Anderson's funeral a few years later brought the largest attendance to a funeral Washington had ever seen, save for that of Abraham Lincoln.

HNRA, IBAW.

ANDERSON, FELIX SYLVESTER (October 3, 1893–May, 1983), 64th bishop of the **African Methodist Episcopal Zion Church** (AMEZ), was born in Wilmington, North Carolina, the son of Charles and Betty (Foye) Anderson. In 1899 the family moved to Boston, Massachusetts, where Anderson attended Rice and Dwight elementary schools and English high school. He was converted on February 10, 1910, at the Columbus Avenue AMEZ Church in Boston, and soon decided to train for the ministry. He preached his trial sermon in August, 1913, at Clinton Chapel Church in Charlotte, North Carolina. He was ordained a deacon on November 15, 1915, and an elder on November 17, 1917. He graduated from Livingstone College in Salisbury, North Carolina, in 1920, with a B.A. He married Bessie B. Bizzell on April 28, 1920, with whom he had six children. One of his children, **Herman Anderson**, also became a bishop. He spent 1920–1921 at Hood Theological Seminary, also in Salisbury, and

attended Western Theological Seminary in Pittsburgh from 1922 to 1924.

Anderson's schooling was supported by his ministry, in which he had been active since 1913. He worked in the Rocky Creek Circuit, the Maineville Circuit, the Smith Grove Circuit, the Liberty Circuit, and elsewhere, all in North Carolina. He then went to First AMEZ Church in Providence, Rhode Island. Corresponding to his attendance at Western Theological Seminary, he then served at Mt. Washington in Pittsburgh, and Trimble Chapel in Oakdale, Pennsylvania. His next church was at Mt. Lebanon in Elizabeth City, North Carolina, where he also served as teacher at P.W. Moore High School in Elizabeth City from 1929 to 1931. He then went to Kadesh in Edenton, North Carolina, and Hunter Chapel in Tuscaloosa, Alabama. These were followed by Shaw Metropolitan in Atlanta, Georgia, Union Chapel in Athens, Georgia, St. Peter's in Southern Pines, North Carolina, Big Zion in Mobile, Alabama, and Broadway Temple in Louisville, Kentucky.

It was while he was at Broadway Temple that he gained a high public profile. From 1954 to 1960 he served three terms in the Kentucky State Legislature, representing the 42nd District. He was the first Black Democrat elected to the Kentucky assembly, and the fourth Black overall to sit in that legislature. His most notable action during that time was the authoring in 1954 of a desegregation bill that he saw through to successful passage. In January 1958, he became the first Black in the history of Kentucky to sit as chair of a standing committee (Suffrage, Elections, and Constitutional Amendments). This work catapulted him into the bishopric in 1960, where he served for twelve years in the South and in Kentucky. He retired at the 1972 General Conference.

"Biographical Sketch." *Star of Zion* 91 (April 25, 1968): 1–3.
Ray, Stepney S. "Dr. Felix S. Anderson Endorsed for the Bishopric." *Star of Zion* 83 (May 12, 1960): 5, 6.
"Rev. Felix Anderson." *Star of Zion* 82 (April 30, 1959): 8.
"Zion Bids Farewell to Bishop Felix S. Anderson." *Star of Zion* 107 (May 26, 1983): 2.
"Zion Mourns the Loss of Bishop Felix S. Anderson." *Star of Zion* 107 (May 19, 1983): 1.
AMEZC, HAMEZC, WWABA (90), *IBSP.*

ANDERSON, HERMAN LEROY (b. February 23, 1923), 77th bishop of the **African Methodist Episcopal Zion Church** (AMEZ), was born in Wilmington, North Carolina, the son of Felix Sylvester and Bessie Bernice (Bizzell) Anderson. His father was a minister in the

AMEZ Church and became a bishop in 1960. Anderson attended Wiliston High School in Wilmington, and then earned a B.S. degree at Tuskegee Institute, Alabama in 1943. After service in the Navy during World War II, he became a self-employed fuel business operator, and married Ruth Rosetta Rogers on July 6, 1946, with whom he had three children. From 1947 to 1953 he was a teacher in the Wilmington school system, and from 1953 to 1956 he was a mail carrier in Wilmington. During this time he was licensed to preach, and performed some pastoral duties at Luke AMEZ Church in Belmont, North Carolina.

In 1956 he began his ministerial career full-time by becoming pastor of Hood Memorial AMEZ Church in Belmont, North Carolina. At the same time, he entered Hood Theological Seminary, from which he gained his B.D. degree in 1959. In 1959 he was assigned to St. James AMEZ Church in Ithaca, New York. In 1962 he was transferred to Soldiers Memorial AMEZ Church in Salisbury, North Carolina, where he stayed for a decade. In 1972 he moved to Broadway Temple AMEZ Church in Louisville, Kentucky.

In 1976, Anderson was elected General Secretary-Auditor of the denomination, and served for four years, based in Charlotte, North Carolina. In 1980 he was elected bishop, thus following in his father's footsteps. He was assigned to the Ninth Episcopal District, covering the California, Southwest Rocky Mountain, Oregon-Washington, Alaska, Pee Dee, and West Alabama Annual Conferences. His wife serves as Missionary Supervisor of the district.

Anderson serves in numerous capacities. He is a trustee of Livingstone College in Salisbury, North Carolina, is chair of the Commission on Pan-Methodist Cooperation, and is on the Committee on Social Concerns, World Methodist Council. He is part of the Congress of National Black Children, the N.A.A.C.P., and in 1984 became director of the Congress of National Black Churches.

"Vignettes of Our Bishops: Bishop Herman L. Anderson." *Star of Zion* 111 (December 3, 1987): 7.
WWR (85), *BDNM* (70).

ANDERSON, MOSES B. (September 9, 1928–), a bishop of the **Roman Catholic Church**, was born in Selma, Alabama, the oldest of six children in the family of Henry and Nancy (King) Anderson. During the Depression years the family became destitute and his father left to find work. Anderson irregularly attended the Clark school or the Payne Presbyterian Institute, as most of his time was spent functioning as the father of

the family. He mowed lawns to help bring income to the household, and was an active member of the Ebenezer Baptist Church choir. By the time he entered Knox Academy High School he was a regular student, and he excelled in all areas. For three successive years he was elected president of his class, he was on the varsity basketball team, and at graduation in 1949 he was valedictorian.

While in high school friends introduced him to the Don Bosco Boys' Club, a Catholic organization with games and activities that he enjoyed. He became more and more interested in Catholic beliefs, took a series of private instructions, and finally was baptized into that faith on May 25, 1949. The director of the club, an Edmundite priest named Nelson Ziter, encouraged his ambitions toward the priesthood and found him a scholarship to Xavier University in New Orleans, Louisiana, the only predominantly African American Catholic university in the Western Hemisphere. While there, a patron, Mrs. Helen Beriswell, decided to pay all of his expenses in his preparation for the priesthood.

In 1951 Anderson left Xavier for the one-year novitiate of the Fathers of St. Edmund in Putney, Vermont, and made his religious profession on August 22, 1952. He then finished his last two years of undergraduate study at the Edmundite College of St. Michael in Winooski, Vermont, graduating with honors in 1954, a major in philosophy. He enrolled in St. Edmund's Seminary in Burlington, Vermont, for the four-year course in theology, and was ordained a priest on May 30, 1958. For one year he was assigned as associate pastor of Our Lady of Consolation Church in Charlotte, North Carolina, with the distinction of being the first Black priest in the state. In 1960 he was a lecturer in theology at St. Michael's College in Winooski, Vermont, and from 1961 to 1965 he pastored St. Catherine's Church in Elizabeth City, North Carolina. From 1966 to 1968 he was Associate Professor of Theology at St. Michael's College, in 1969 becoming Vice President for Student Affairs.

From 1971 to 1981 Anderson was Associate Professor of Theology and Director of Spiritual Affairs at Xavier University in New Orleans, where he initiated a number of new programs. He established a Religious Center which stressed African American culture. In one of the two chapels, the room was filled with symbols and artifacts of African and African-American culture. He began large, outdoor worship experiences called "Soul Masses," with spirituals, hand-clapping, and foot-stomping. He urged students not to deny their heritage, but to "praise the Lord through their Blackness." In 1981 the Superior General of his order appointed him pastor of the 150-member All Saints Church in Anniston,

Alabama, in the diocese of Birmingham, and again had the distinction of being the first Black priest in the state. He was only there for one year, but made strongly-felt changes in worship, adding such things as a banner in the sanctuary depicting a Black crucified Christ, and in the All Saints School, raising money for a new kindergarten school.

On December 7, 1982 a press conference in Detroit announced that Anderson had been chosen Auxiliary (assistant) Bishop of Detroit, Michigan. He was consecrated for that task on January 27, 1983, becoming the first member of the Society of St. Edmund to become a bishop. He was assigned specifically to the West Region of the Archdiocese of Detroit, including the Westside Inner City, Grand River, Farmington-Southfield, West Detroit, and North-West Wayne vicariates. He has been among those leading the way in the Catholic Church toward remaking the church's image and treatment of Blacks. On January 23, 1985 he participated with other bishops in a demonstration against apartheid near the South African embassy in Washington, D.C.

WWR (85), *WWABA* (90–91), *OBS.*

ANDERSON, VINTON RANDOLPH (July 11, 1927–), the first African-American president of the World Council of Churches and the 92nd bishop of the **African Methodist Episcopal Church** (AME), was born in Somerset, Bermuda, the son of Ruth Gladys Anderson. He was orphaned and then adopted by Charles L. and Frances Ratteray. He came to the United States in 1947 to go to college. He was ordained in 1951, and in 1952 he received both his B.A. from Wilberforce University in Ohio and a B.D. from the related Payne Theological Seminary.

His first ministerial assignment was at St. Mark AME Church in Topeka, Kansas, from 1952 to 1953. On October 29, 1952, he married Vivienne L. Cholnondeley, with whom he had four children. The next year he went to Brown Chapel AME Church in Parsons (1953–1955), then to St. Luke AME Church in Lawrence (1955–1959), and St. Paul AME Church in Wichita (1959–1964), all in Kansas. While at St. Paul's he earned an M.A. in Philosophy at the University of Kansas (1962), and was first vice-president of the Wichita Branch of the N.A.A.C.P. He gained distinction as the first black chair of the Wichita Council of Churches. In 1961 he was a delegate to the World Ecumenical Methodist Conference in Oslo, Norway. In 1963 he was part of the President's Commission on

Equal Employment Opportunities. In 1964 he went to another St. Paul's, this time in St. Louis, Missouri, where he stayed for eight years. That year he was awarded an honorary D.D. degree from Paul Quinn College in Waco, Texas. He was appointed representative of the AME Church to the Commission of Higher Education of the National Council of Churches. In 1966 he was again a delegate to the World Ecumenical Methodist Conference, in London, England. He attended again in Colorado in 1971 and in Hawaii in 1981. In 1970 he became a naturalized citizen of the United States.

At the General Conference in 1972 Anderson was elected bishop, the first native of Bermuda elevated to the bishopric in any denomination. He was assigned to the Ninth Episcopal District, set in Alabama. That year he was part of a team visiting New Zealand and Australia sponsored by the World Council of Churches Program to Combat Racism. From 1976 to 1984 he was moved to another Episcopal District composed of Ohio, West Virginia, and Pennsylvania, and from 1984 to 1990 he was Director of the church's Office of Ecumenical Relations and Urban Affairs, based in St. Louis, Missouri.

In 1990 he was assigned to the Fifth Episcopal District. He has been active on many fronts, receiving the N.A.A.C.P.'s Distinguished Service Award and the Urban League's Award of Merit. He has served on the Board of Trustees or Board of Directors of the Urban Training Center in Chicago; Daniel Payne College in Birmingham, Alabama; Wilberforce University in Ohio; and Payne Theological Seminary in Ohio. He is known as the compiler of the first *Book of Worship* for the AME Church, and since 1977 has been chair of Worship and Liturgy for the Consultation on Church Union (C.O.C.U.). He has served as First Vice President, North American Region, of the World Methodist Council. He is currently vice-president of both the Consultation on Church Union and the **Congress of National Black Churches**. On February 20, 1991 Anderson was elected president of the World Council of Churches at the Seventh Assembly held in Canberra, Australia. He is the first African-American to gain that office and will serve a seven-year term.

"On the Cover: Vinton Randolph Anderson." *A.M.E. Church Review* 106 (April–June 1991): 2.
"A Salute to Bishop Vinton R. Anderson." *A.M.E. Church Review* 106 (April–June 1991): 6.
WWABA (88), *WWR* (75–76), *BDNM* (70), *EBA, IBAW, HAMEC, FEDHR.*

ANDERSON, WILLIAM T. (August 20, 1859–August 21, 1934), physician, minister, and Army officer, was born into slavery in Seguin, near San Antonio, Texas. He and his mother moved to Galveston, Texas, during the Civil War, where he stayed for most of his childhood. As a young man he felt a call to the ministry and joined the Texas Conference of the **African Methodist Episcopal Church** (AME). The church sent him to Wilberforce University in Ohio for three years to get a better education. Thanks to a banker benefactor, Stephen Watson, he was able to stay to earn a Theology Certificate in 1886 and go on to the Homeopathic Medical College of Cleveland, Ohio, from which he graduated in 1888. He married Sada J. Anderson.

From 1888 to 1897 Anderson was pastor of AME churches in Urbana and Lima, the Warren Chapel AME Church in Toledo, and St. John's AME Church in Cleveland, Ohio, which was the largest AME church in the state. On August 16, 1897, President McKinley appointed him chaplain of the 10th Cavalry, U.S. Army, with the rank of captain. He arrived at the 10th Cavalry's headquarters at Fort Assinniboine, Montana, in November, 1897, and while there served also as post treasurer, librarian, and school superintendent. In April, 1898 the group was ordered to the Chickamauga staging area in preparation for the Spanish-American War in Cuba, but Anderson remained behind for three months as quartermaster, commissary, signal and engineer ordnance, exchange officer, and commander of the fort. This made him among the first Blacks ever to command an American military post.

In late July, 1898, he joined the troops in Santiago, Cuba, shortly after the 10th Cavalry had played a significant role in the Battle of Las Guasimas and the charge up San Juan Hill. Anderson was able to save a number of lives with his medical training, working against fever and dysentery. He often went into Cuban cities, assisting the Red Cross and working toward the establishment in that country of the Y.M.C.A. He spent several months immediately after the short war at several forts along the Texas and Alabama Gulf Coast. During this time he worked with Herschel Cashin, a recorder in the United States Land Office in Huntsville, Alabama, writer Charles Alexander, surgeon Arthur M. Brown of the 10th Cavalry, and Sgt. Horace Bivins, also of the 10th Cavalry, in producing a book on the heroism of Black soldiers in the Cuban campaign, called *Under Fire with the Tenth Cavalry* (1899).

In mid-1899 Anderson and the 10th Cavalry returned to Manzanillo, Cuba as part of the occupying forces, remaining until April, 1902. From 1902 to 1907 he was at Fort Mackintosh, Texas, and Fort Robinson in the Pine Ridge area of Nebraska. In both these places he helped organize a Y.M.C.A. for the troops as a forum for discussing racial problems and for managing their own affairs. In April, 1907, the 10th Cavalry was moved to Fort William McKinley in the Philippines. In August, 1907, Anderson was promoted to major, only days after completing the necessary ten years of service. At that point he was one of the highest ranking Blacks in the regular Army, and for the entire first decade of the twentieth century he was the only Black chaplain in the U.S. Army. While at Fort McKinley he commanded the U.S. Morgue, located in Manila.

On January 10, 1910, he returned to the United States at Fort Ethan Allen in Vermont, and shortly thereafter retired on disability due to a fever originally contracted in Cuba in 1898. He returned to Wilberforce to be accountant and secretary to the bishop of the Third Episcopal District of the AME Church. In September, 1916 he became pastor of the Warren Chapel AME Church in Toledo, Ohio, where he had previously ministered for a time. In September, 1918 he left that position to serve in the Quartermaster Corps of the U.S. Army, but World War I ended only a few weeks later and he moved to Cleveland. For the remainder of his career he returned to another previous position, pastor of St. John's AME Church in Cleveland. He was very well known in the community, and the weekly *Cleveland Gazette* reported regularly on his activities.

Cashin, Herschel, William T. Anderson, et al. *Under Fire with the Tenth U.S. Cavalry.* New York: F. T. Neely, 1899. 361 pp.

Levstik, Frank R. "William T. Anderson: Army Officer, Doctor, Minister, and Writer." *Negro History Bulletin* 40 (January–February 1977): 662–663.

DANB, IBAW.

ANSAARU ALLAH COMMUNITY. A Black Muslim group. The Ansaaru Allah Community was founded in 1967 in Brooklyn, New York, by As Sayyid Al Imaan Isa Al Haahi Al Madhi (born Dwight York), but claims its authority from two previous movements. Primarily, the Community continues the traditions of the nineteenth-century Sudanese leader, Muhammad Ahmad Ibn Abdullah (1845–1885), best known for his defeat of the British at Khartoun, who is considered the true Madhi and successor to the prophet Muhammad. Authority is also claimed from **Shaikh Daoud**, founder of the Muslim Mosque, who died in 1980.

According to the Community, As Siyyid Al Imaan Isa Al Haahi Al Madhi is the third successor of the Madhi, the first successor being As Sayyid Abdur Rahman Mahammad Al Madhi and the second, As

Sayyid Al Haadi Abdur Muhammad Rahman Al Madhi. Originally the community was known as the Ansaaru Pure Sufis. They briefly assumed a designation as Nubians in 1968, the next year becoming known as Nubian Islaamic Hebrews, the name they carried through most the 1970s. Each name change has been accompanied by a modification of the community's dress and further clarification of its mission and goals. Important in the development of the movement was the "Opening of the Seventh Seal" (a reference to the biblical book of Revelation 8:1) in 1970. This event was signaled by the formalization of the organization of the Ansaaru Allah Community, the movement into a new headquarters building, and the purchase of a press from which has flowed numerous publications. 1970 was the hundredth year after the Madhi established his community on Abba Island on the Nile River.

The Community teaches that Adam and Eve were Nubians (i.e., Black people). There were no pale (white) people until after the flood when Ham was cursed for his homosexual desires. Ham's punishment was the development of leprosy, not upon himself, but upon his fourth son, Canaan. Thus pale people, known as Canaanites, derived from this curse, and Nubians are not allowed to mix their blood with members of such peoples.

Abraham, a descendent of Noah, became the father of two nations, one through his son Isaac (the Israelites) and the other through his son Ishmael. The Israelites were enslaved for 430 years in Egypt. It was later predicted that the Ishmaelites would be enslaved in a land not their own for 400 years. That prophecy has come true as Nubians were enslaved in the Americas and other places around the world.

The Ansaaru believe in Allah (they do not use the term "God") who is Alone in his Oneness and Power. They accept the *Tawrah* (the Jewish Bible or Old Testament), the *Zubuwr* (the Psalms of David), the *Injiyl* (The Christian New Testament) and the *Holy Qur'aan* as authoritative texts for teaching.

Following the establishment of its headquarters in 1970, the Nubian Mission grew rapidly. By 1972, centers were functioning in Albany, New York; Philadelphia, Pennsylvania; Connecticut; and Texas. A number of other centers were opened in the East and South within the following year. In 1973 As Sayyid traveled to Trinidad and succeeded in opening an initial center. Subsequently centers have been opened in Jamaica, Puerto Rico, Guyana, and Tobago.

The success of the Ansaaru has prompted some polemics with the larger Sunni Muslim community. Critics have, for example, accused As Sayyid Al Imaan Isa Al Haadi Al Madhi of changing his birth date from 1935 to 1945 in order to coincide with the hundredth anniversary of the Madhi's birthdate. They have also charged that he has made false claims of his relationship to the Madhi and the movement which he founded. He has in turn charged the Sunni with hypocrisy and watering down the religion of Islam.

Headquarters of the Ansaaru Allah community is in Brooklyn. There are centers in Black communities around the world. They have established a publishing and literature distribution system, the Tents of Kedar.

As Sayyid Isa Al Haadi Al Madhi. *Muhammad Ahmad: The Only True Madhi!* Brooklyn, NY: Ansaru Allah Community, n.d. 47 pp.

———. *Thus Says Imaan Isa.* 2 vols. Brooklyn, NY: Ansaaru Allah Publications, 1988.

———. *What Is a Muslim?* Brooklyn, NY: Ansaaru Allah Community, 1979. 37 pp.

———. *Whatever Happened to the Nubian Islamic Hebrew Mission?* Brooklyn, NY: Original Tents of Kedar, 1989. 315 pp.

Phillips, Abu Ameenah Bilal. *The Ansar Cult in America.* Riyadh, Saudi Arabia: Tawheed Publications, 1988. 198 pp. An attack upon the Ansaaru Allah Community from a Sunni Muslim position.

ANTIOCH ASSOCIATION OF METAPHYSICAL SCIENCE. A New Thought metaphysical church. The Antioch Association of Metaphysical Science is one of the first African American groups to appropriate the metaphysical teachings of the New Thought movement. The Association was founded by Dr. H. Lewis Johnson (b. 1890). Dr. Johnson was born and raised in Georgia of Christian parents. In the 1920s, she moved to Detroit, Michigan. She gathered a small group and in 1930 organized St. Ruth Holy Science Church. The Association was founded in 1932 and over the next decades, five additional congregations were created and active by 1965.

The Association teaches metaphysical or mental science. It believes that natural law produces all that is. Every person is a mystic sensitive to the "vibration of spiritual influences." It believes in the power of spiritual law to heal and bring prosperity to those who attune to it.

APOSTLE CHURCH OF CHRIST IN GOD. An Apostolic Pentecostal church. The Apostle Church of Christ in God was formed in 1940 by former leaders of the Church of God (Apostolic). At the time, Bishop Thomas Cox, the founder of the Church of God was ill and unable to function. His role was being filled by Bishop Eli Neal. Neal had assumed a somewhat dictatorial stance and rarely consulted with or listened to other ministers in the Church. After some consideration, five elders, J. C. Richardson, Sr., J. W. Audrey, Jerome Jenkins, W. R. Bryant, and J. M. Williams, established the Church of Christ in God. Headquarters were located in Winston-Salem, North Carolina. Three congregations were a part of the original organization. J. W. Audrey was elected as the first bishop. The church grew through the 1940s and in 1952 J. C. Richardson (b. 1910) was elected as the church's second bishop. In 1956 Audrey retired and Richardson succeeded him as presiding bishop.

Bishop Richardson emphasized church growth and the church expanded steadily. He began a magazine, the *Apostolic Gazette* (later the *Apostolic Journal*). He initiated an educational fund to assist members attending college. In 1961 he entered seminary as a means not only to improve his education but to encourage other ministers to do likewise. The progress of the church continued through the 1960s, but in 1971 the church experienced a major schism when several ministers and churches left and reorganized under Bishop Audrey. The remnant continued and through the 1970s was able to resume a growth pattern.

The church is, like its parent, an Apostolic Pentecostal body. It affirms the existence of one God (and by implication denies the orthodox Christian idea of the Trinity). God's name is Jesus. Baptism is done in the name of Jesus, rather than with the more common formula of "Father, Son and Holy Spirit." As a Pentecostal Church, it teaches believers to seek the baptism of the Holy Spirit evidenced by speaking in tongues.

In 1980 the Church had 25 churches and 2,150 members.

Richardson, James C., Jr. *With Water and Spirit: A History of Black Apostolic Denominations in the U.S.* Winston-Salem, NC: The Author, 1980. 151 pp.

APOSTOLIC ASSEMBLIES OF CHRIST. An Apostolic Pentecostal church. The Apostolic Assemblies of Christ grew out of the situation created by the death of Bishop **Samuel N. Hancock**, the founder and presiding bishop of the **Pentecostal Churches of the Apostolic Faith**. The traditional teachings of the Apostolic Faith affirm that there is one God and that Jesus is his name. Hancock had held to the idea that Jesus was simply the son of God. This deviation from Apostolic teaching was tolerated in Hancock's case. He

had been a respected leader in the **Pentecostal Assemblies of the World** prior to forming the Pentecostal Church of the Apostolic Faith. Following his death in 1963, Bishop Willie Lee, pastor of Christ Apostolic Temple in Indianapolis, Indiana, who agreed with him on his understanding of Jesus, became the presiding bishop. What had been tolerated in Hancock was not in Lee's case. In 1964, a split occurred, and for the next four years there were two groups which shared the name Pentecostal Church of the Apostolic Faith. One group, headed by Bishop Elzie Young had possession of the charter, and kept the former name of the organization.

Lee died in 1968 and in 1970 his followers reorganized under the leadership of Bishop G. M. Boone as the Apostolic Assemblies of Christ. The new church is congregationally organized as a loose association of congregations and against any centralized control. By 1980 there were approximately 23 congregations and 3,500 members.

Richardson, James C., Jr. *With Water and Spirit: A History of Black Apostolic Denominations in the U.S.* Winston-Salem, NC: The Author, 1980. 151 pp.

APOSTOLIC CHURCH OF CHRIST. An Apostolic Pentecostal church. During the 1960s Bishop Johnnie Draft was an overseer in the **Church of God (Apostolic)** and pastor of St. Peter's Church, the headquarters church of the denomination. However, in 1969 he resigned from St. Peter's and left the Church. With Elder Wallace Snow, he founded the Apostolic Church of Christ. The reason for their defection was never stated. They established headquarters in Winston-Salem and soon purchased a new headquarters building. Over the first decade, the Church established six congregations and has a reported 300 members.

The Church follows the non-Trinitarian Christian doctrine of its parent body. It affirms One God whose name is Jesus. Baptism is by immersion in the name of Jesus. It teaches the attainability by believers of the baptism of the Holy Spirit, with evidence of speaking in tongues.

Richardson, James C., Jr. *With Water and Spirit: A History of Black Apostolic Denominations in the U.S.* Winston-Salem, NC: The Author, 1980. 151 pp.

APOSTOLIC FAITH CHURCH OF GOD AND TRUE HOLINESS. A Holiness Pentecostal church. In 1946 Charles W. Lowe, founder and for over 35 years leader of the **Apostolic Faith Churches of God** separated from the main body of the Church and with one congregation organized the Apostolic Faith Church of God and True Holiness. He was succeeded by Bishop Levi Butts, and more recently by Bishop Oree Keyes. Bishop Keyes has been very active in seeking to unite the various factions which have developed from the original work begun by Bishops Seymour and Lowe. He helped form the **United Fellowship Convention of the Original Azusa Street Mission** which includes five similar churches.

In 1990 The Apostolic Faith Church of God in True Holiness had 24 congregations. Headquarters is in Jefferson, Ohio.

DuPree, Sherry Sherrod. *The African American Holiness Pentecostal Movement: An Annotated Bibliography*. New York: Garland Publishing, 1993.

APOSTOLIC FAITH CHURCH OF GOD GIVING GRACE. A Holiness Pentecostal church. The Apostolic Faith Church of God Giving Grace was founded in the mid-1960s as the New Jerusalem Apostolic Faith Churches of God. Its founders, Bishop Rufus A. Easter and Mother Lillie P. Williams, were formerly associated with the Apostolic Faith Churches of God. There was no doctrinal dispute in the break and the Church follows the doctrine of the parent body. Bishop Easter was succeeded by Bishop Geanie Perry, the current leader of the Church. The Church supports the New Jerusalem Rest Home and a Helping Hand Community Food Bank. Headquarters is in Warrenton, North Carolina. In 1990 there were 12 churches.

DuPree, Sherry Sherrod. *The African American Holiness Pentecostal Movement: An Annotated Bibliography*. New York: Garland Publishing, 1993.

APOSTOLIC FAITH CHURCH OF GOD LIVE ON. A Holiness Pentecostal church. The Apostolic Faith Church of God Live On is one of several groups which originated in the Apostolic Faith Church of God founded in 1909 by Bishop **William J. Seymour** and Charles W. Lowe. It was founded in 1952 by Bishop Jesse Handshaw, Bishop Willie P. Cross, and Elder R. T. Butts, all formerly of the **Apostolic Faith Church of God and True Holiness**, the branch of the church headed by Lowe at that time. No doctrinal matters were at issue, and the church follows the beliefs and practices of its parent body. Bishop Handshaw was succeeded by Bishop Richard Cross, the present leader of the Church.

Headquarters is in Hopewell, Virginia. In 1990 the church had approximately 25 affiliated congregations. The church published two periodicals, *The Guiding Light*, and the *Crusade*.

The Church has joined with other branches of the Apostolic Faith Church to form the **United Fellowship Convention of the Original Azusa Street Mission** which meets annually.

DuPree, Sherry Sherrod. *The African American Holiness Pentecostal Movement: An Annotated Bibliography*. New York: Garland Publishing, 1993.

Payne, Wardell J., ed. *Directory of African American Religious Bodies: A Compendium by the Howard University School of Divinity*. Washington, DC: Howard University Press, 1991. 363 pp.

APOSTOLIC FAITH CHURCHES OF A LIVING GOD. An Apostolic Pentecostal church. The Apostolic Faith Churches of A Living God originated in 1979 through the coming together of seven congregations in South Carolina which had left the **Apostolic Faith Churches of God**. The Church were called together by Bishop Leroy Williams who had in the 1960s been the president of the South Carolina District Young People's Union of the Apostolic Faith Church of God. The present head of the church is Bishop Richard C. Johnson., Sr. The cause of the split was administrative, not doctrinal, hence the Churches retain the same beliefs and practices of the parent church.

Headquarters is in Columbia, South Carolina. The church publishes a periodical, *Union Newsletter*. They hold an annual convention each summer.

Payne, Wardell J., ed. *Directory of African American Religious Bodies: A Compendium by the Howard University School of Divinity*. Washington, DC: Howard University Press, 1991. 363 pp.

APOSTOLIC FAITH CHURCHES OF GOD. A Holiness Pentecostal group. The Apostolic Faith Churches of God dates to 1909 when **William J. Seymour**, pastor of the mission on Azusa Street in Los Angeles from which the Pentecostal Movement had been spread around the United States, and **Charles H. Mason**, founder of the **Church of God in Christ**, visited Washington, D.C. Among the people affected by their new teachings of Pentecostalism was Charles W. Lowe of Handsom, Virginia. He founded the Apostolic Faith Church of God, loosely affiliated with Seymour's organization in Los Angeles. Over the years other congregations were founded, some of which became the sources of new denominations. The Church was finally chartered in Maryland in 1938 (the same year the Los Angeles center was permanently dissolved).

In 1945 Bishop Lowe separated from the main body of the Apostolic Faith Churches of God and while keeping the original name, added the words "and True Holiness" to it. The main body of the Church then reorganized and elected Bishop Rossie Cleveland Grant, who was succeeded by Bishop George Buchanan White. Following White was Bishop George W. Parks. Parks discontinued the previous corporation and operated as an unincorporated fellowship of churches. His successor, Bishop Lois Cleveland Grant, reincorporated as the Apostolic Faith Churches of God. Bishop Grant was succeeded by Bishop Abraham Urquhart and Stephen Douglas Willis, Sr., the present presiding bishop.

The Apostolic Faith Churches of God have joined with other branches of the Church originally founded by Seymour and Lowe in the **United Fellowship Convention of the Original Azusa Street Mission**.

Headquarters is located in Franklin Virginia. They hold an annual convention each August.

DuPree, Sherry Sherrod. *The African American Holiness Pentecostal Movement: An Annotated Bibliography.* New York: Garland Publishing, 1993.

Payne, Wardell J., ed. *Directory of African American Religious Bodies: A Compendium by the Howard University School of Divinity.* Washington, DC: Howard University Press, 1991. 363 pp.

APOSTOLIC FAITH MISSION CHURCH OF GOD.

An Apostolic Pentecostal church. The modern Pentecostal Movement is generally thought of as emerging out of the revival at the Azusa Street Mission in Los Angeles under the leadership of **William J. Seymour**. The revival lasted for three years (1906–1908) during which time many people attended from all over the country and carried the unique beliefs and practices being espoused there to their home. Among the first who attended and received the baptism of the Holy Spirit evidenced by his speaking in tongues was F. W. Williams (d. 1923). Returning to the South, Williams spread the message of the revival in Mississippi and then Alabama. In Mobile a revival was occasioned by his preaching. One entire congregation of Primitive Baptists accepted his message and turned their church building over to him as the first meeting hall for what would become a new church. The Apostolic Faith Mission Church was formally organized in the summer of 1906 as an outpost of the church in Los Angeles.

In 1915, the Apostolic or Oneness message swept through Pentecostal circles. This new teaching essentially denied the traditional doctrine of the Trinity and affirmed the existence of One God whose name was Jesus. Accompanying the message was the practice of baptizing people in the Name of Jesus rather than with the trinitarian formula of "Father, Son and Holy Spirit." Williams was among the first to accept the Apostolic message. He broke with Seymour and reorganized his following as the Apostolic Faith Mission Church of God.

The Church follows essential Apostolic teachings. It forbids the use of intoxicants including alcohol, narcotics and tobacco. Members are encouraged to marry within the faith. Spiritual healing is emphasized. The Church is headed by a Senior Bishop and a Cabinet of Executive Officers made up of the bishops, overseers, and the general secretary. Women are accepted into the ordained ministry. By 1984, the church had 17 congregations and approximately 1,500 members. Most of the membership is in Alabama.

Piepkorn, Arthur C. *Profiles in Belief.* Vol. 3. San Francisco: Harper & Row, 1979. 262 pp.

APOSTOLIC HOLINESS CHURCH OF AMERICA.

A Holiness Pentecostal church. The Apostolic Holiness Church of America was founded in 1927 in Mount Olive, North Carolina, by a group of former members of the **Apostolic Faith Church of God** originally founded by Bishops **William J. Seymour** and Charles Lowe. The group included Elders J. M. Barns, W. M. D. Atkins, Ernest Graham, J. M. McKinnon, and Sisters Sarah Artis and Emma Spruel. Doctrine is like other branches of the movement as all the issues at stake in the separation were administrative.

In 1973 the Church went through a constitutional revision under its present presiding bishop, Isaac Ryals, assisted by W. R. Turner, I. W. Hicks, Jessie Budd, Shirley Clark, and E. V. Ethridge. The Church is headquartered in Fremont, North Carolina. In 1990 it had ten affiliated congregations.

APOSTOLIC OVERCOMING HOLY CHURCH OF GOD.

An Apostolic Pentecostal church. The Apostolic Church of God was founded by William Thomas Phillips (1893–1973) who would lead the church for 59 years. Raised a Methodist, as a young man he developed a concern for holy living which led him to the study of the Bible. He was converted to the message of **Pentecostalism** and through him he received the teachings of the Apostolic Oneness perspective.

Phillips was ordained in 1913. In 1916 he began a new direction as an independent evangelist. A year later, the people who had responded to his ministry asked him to form a new church over which he would be the bishop. The church was named the Ethiopian Overcoming Holy Church of God. The Church was formed just as spreading news of Ethiopia was causing many within the African American community to identify with it. It retained that name until 1941 when it adopted its present name, a reflection of the fact that some Whites had joined the Church.

The Church follows the non-Trinitarian Oneness Apostolic position. It rejects the hint of tritheism in the traditional doctrine of the Trinity and strongly affirms its belief in One God whose name is Jesus. Out of that belief it baptizes by immersion in the name of Jesus only. It teaches that such baptism is necessary for salvation. God, Jesus, acts upon the baptized believer to baptize in the Spirit (signaled by the believer speaking in tongues) and to sanctify him/her as they become more holy over their lifetime. The church prays for divine healing of the sick, and practices both foot washing and tithing.

The church is congregationally organized though led by a person designated as "bishop." The presiding bishop leads the annual general assembly. There have been only two presiding bishops to date, Phillips and his successor, **Jasper Roby**. He is assisted by several associate bishops. *The People's Mouthpiece* is the church's magazine. In 1988 the church had approximately 200 churches and 12,000 members.

Arrington, Juanita R. *A Brief History of the Apostolic Overcoming Holy Church of God, Inc., and Its Founder*. Birmingham, AL: Forniss Printing Company, 1984.

Doctrine and Discipline. Birmingham, AL: Apostolic Overcoming Holy Church of God, 1985.

ARKANSAS BAPTIST COLLEGE. A Baptist school. The origins of Arkansas Baptist College, Little Rock, Arkansas, can be traced to the convention of African American Baptists in Arkansas in 1884. Approval was give to a plan to open the Baptist Institute for the training of ministers which began in November of that year at the Mount Zion Baptist Church. Rev. J. P. Lawson, a White Baptist minister from Joplin, Missouri, led the school for the next three years, but when funds were exhausted, the school closed.

Within a few months, those interested in the continuation of a school arranged for facilities at Mount Pleasant Baptist Church and located Rev. Harry Woodstall, a missionary with the American Baptist Home Mission Society, who assisted in the reorganization of the institution. A new corporation was established and the school reopened as the Arkansas Baptist College. A lot was purchased and the school building erected.

Beginning with an initial ministerial course, the college later added a normal curriculum. Still later, in this century, a full liberal arts curriculum was created. The school continues as an independent Black Baptist college accredited by the North Central Association of Colleges and Schools.

Fitts, Leroy. *A History of Black Baptists*. Nashville, TN: Broadman Press, 1985. 368 pp.

ARMSTRONG, JOSIAH HAYNES (May 30, 1842– March 23, 1898), 24th bishop of the **African Methodist Episcopal Church** (AME), was born in Lancaster County, Pennsylvania. Little is known of his early life. He entered the Union Army in 1863 as a private and soon rose to the rank of a non-commissioned officer. He served as cook, teamster, and when permitted, as a soldier. He was converted in 1868, at age 26, in Jacksonville, Florida, by the preaching of William Bradwell. He was ordained a deacon the following year by Bishop **John M. Brown**, and joined the Florida Conference. He was ordained an elder in 1870.

He served churches in Bellville, Lake City, and Jasper, Florida, building sanctuaries in each place. In Jasper he was also a school teacher. In 1877 he was presiding elder of the Live Oak District. In 1878 he was elected secretary of the Florida Conference. He served two terms in the Florida Legislature as representative from Columbia County. He became good friends with **Abraham Grant**, and transferred to Texas at about the same time he did, in 1878. Both rose rapidly in the church, and Grant was elected a bishop in 1888.

Armstrong was assigned as pastor of Reedy Chapel in Galveston, where he led in remodeling the facility. He next served Bethel AME Church in Dallas, followed by a church in Austin. He was secretary of his Conference in Texas for eleven years, and also served a term as presiding elder of the Houston District. In 1892 he was elected financial secretary of the denomination, and in the 1896 General Conference at Wilmington, North Carolina, he was elected a bishop. He was assigned to the Tenth Episcopal District set in Texas. After a little less than two years, he died in Galveston, Texas. There is a church named for him in New Castle, Delaware.

BAMEC, HAMEC, EWM, CEAMEC.

ARNETT, BENJAMIN WILLIAM, JR. (March 6, 1838–October 7, 1906), seventeenth bishop of the **African Methodist Episcopal Church** (AME) and Ohio state legislator, was born in Brownsville, Pennsylvania, of Black and Scotch-Irish ancestry. His father, Benjamin William Arnett, Sr., was an active member of the AME Church, and purchased the first lot on which the Brownsville church was built. Arnett, Jr., assisted in the family income by working on various river steamboats, and waiting tables in hotels. He experienced conversion on February 14, 1856, and joined the AME Church. Shortly after he turned twenty, a tumor forced the amputation of a leg, but this did not change the pace of his life, as he married Mary Louisa Gordon later that year, on May 25, 1858.

An industrious young man, Arnett, Jr., educated himself sufficiently to obtain a teacher's certificate on December 19, 1863, whereupon he became the only Black teacher in Fayette County, Pennsylvania. On March 30, 1865 he received a license to preach, and two years later decided to make church work his career. He transferred to the Ohio Conference and received his first appointment on April 19, 1867, at the Walnut Hills AME Church near Cincinnati, where he also taught at the local school. He was ordained a deacon on April 30, 1868, and an elder on May 12, 1870.

Serving a number of churches in Ohio, he rose steadily in prominence. In 1872 he was first elected as an Ohio Annual Conference delegate to General Conference, and was elected its assistant secretary. He became secretary of the General Conference in 1876 and in May, 1880, became financial secretary (re-elected in 1884). In this latter position he was responsible for the publication of the annual *Budget* of the AME Church, large volumes which contained not only statistics, but historical and cultural information, and which he continued to edit through 1904. Although the *Budget* is his most famous publication, he also authored a number of other works, including *Colored Sunday Schools* (1896).

Arnett, Jr.'s energies were put to use, not just in the church, but in a variety of social settings. He was very active in the YMCA, vice-president of the Anti-Saloon League of America, and part of the National Equal Rights League headed by Frederick Douglass. His oratorical abilities made him a sought-after speaker for Republican party activities beginning in the 1870s. He was chaplain of the Republican State Convention of Ohio in 1880 and chaplain of the National Republican Convention at St. Louis in 1896. He was active in the Masons, achieving the Sublime Degree Master Mason in August, 1875. In fall, 1885, he was elected as representative of Greene County, Ohio, to the Ohio Legislature, and during his term successfully introduced a bill abolishing the state's "Black laws." At this time he became friends with William McKinley, Jr., and maintained that connection during McKinley's later term as President (1897–1901).

In 1888 he was elected bishop on the first ballot and was assigned to the Seventh Episcopal District (South Carolina and Florida), which he served until 1892. From there he moved to the Fourth Episcopal District, including states in the Midwest and Northwest (1892–1900), the Third Episcopal District, including Ohio, California, and Pittsburgh (1900–1904), and the First Episcopal District (1904–1906), including New York and other northeastern states. In 1893 he was a representative to the World's Parliament of Religions in Chicago, and presided over the September 15 session, for which leadership the AME Church gave him a gold medal. During his term in the Third Episcopal District, he established a home at Wilberforce University in Ohio on a ten-acre estate which he called "Tawawa Chimney Corner," for the nearby Indian Tawawa Springs. His residence there until his sudden death of uremic poisoning enhanced the position of Wilberforce and the related Payne Theological Seminary as the intellectual and cultural center of the AME Church, as he hosted many visitors and collected a superior library.

Arnett, Benjamin W., ed. *The Budget.* Xenia, OH: Torchlight Printing Co., 1881.
———. *Colored Sunday Schools.* Nashville: AME Sunday School Union, 1896.
———. "The Northwest Territory." Address at the Music Hall, Chicago, Oct. 11, 1899. *Ohio Archaeological and Historical Quarterly* 8 (1900): 433–64.
———. *The Poetical Works of James Madison Bell.* Lansing, MI: Press of Wynkoop, Hallenbeck, Cranford Co., 1901. 208 pp.
———. *The Wilberforce Alumnal.* Xenia, OH: Gazette Office, 1885. 64 pp.
Coleman, Lucretia H. Newman. *Poor Ben: A Study of Real Life.* Nashville: AME Sunday School Union, 1890. 220 pp.
DANB, EWM, BAMEC, HUBA, NYTO, MM, NCAB, RLOA, CEAMEC.

ARTER, JARED MAURICE (January 27, 1850–192?), educator and Missionary Baptist minister, was born into slavery in Harper's Ferry, West Virginia, the son of Jeremiah and Hannah Frances (Stephenson) Arter. His father died from a fall in 1857. Arter was nine years old when John Brown made his famous raid on Harper's Ferry. In the fall of 1864 his mother, her new husband, and their total of nine children moved to Washington,

D.C. There Arter worked for some months in a flour mill, then as a bellboy in Dyer's Hotel. In the spring of 1865 he was bound to service to a business man in Newfield, New York in return for education and training. Mr. Ayers ran a grocery, clothing, and drug store in the village and took Arter in as one of the family. About a year later the family moved to Ithaca, New York, on an orchard farm. Arter attended public schools several months each year in Newfield and then in Ithaca. About 1869 he was released from his service and returned to Washington, D.C., moving on shortly to West Virginia.

He worked various manual labor jobs until October, 1873, when both he and his brother William enrolled at Storer College in Harper's Ferry. That fall he experienced conversion and joined the Baptist Church. In the fall of 1879 Arter entered the freshman class of Pennsylvania State College in Bellefonte, Pennsylvania, the first Black student at that institution. The next two years he taught school to earn money, then in the fall of 1882 he entered the sophomore class of Hillsdale College in Michigan, where he received his B.A. in 1885. He then taught school again in the Rippon District, West Virginia and was ordained a Baptist minister. In 1887 he went to Storer College as a teacher and minister of the college church. On June 3, 1890, he married Emily Carter, with whom he had three children.

In 1891 he left Storer to enroll in the University of Chicago Theological Seminary, where he earned his B.D. in 1894. Shortly after graduation he was ordained for another denomination, the **National Baptist Convention, U.S.A., Inc.**, and accepted a teaching position at the Baptist Theological Seminary in Lynchburg, Virginia, beginning January 1, 1895. He taught Civics, Latin, Physics, and Rhetoric and also traveled as financial agent for the school. He left the seminary in 1898 and in 1899 was principal of the Hagerstown, Maryland, public school. On January 1, 1900, he began teaching at Morgan College in Lynchburg, Virginia, but in March left to take a long-awaited position as head of the new J. S. Manning Bible School in Cairo, Illinois, where he stayed for eight years. 1907 was a difficult year which saw the death of his brother William, his wife Emily, and his youngest son.

On September 1, 1908 he became president of West Virginia Industrial School, Seminary and College, and principal of Hill Top Graded School in Hill Top, West Virginia. He was officially installed in this position in an extra session of the West Virginia Baptist State Convention. On December 2, 1908 most of the school was burned to the ground, but it was slowly rebuilt with the help of businessmen who enlarged the school's land to a full fifty acres. In the meantime school was conducted in an old public school building nearby. During this time he married again, to Maggie Wall. Some buildings were partially rebuilt by 1914, but the trustees, instead of proceeding, decided to close the school for three years until all indebtedness was paid off, and thus Arter's administration ended on June 15, 1915.

He then pastored the Baptist Church of Sun, West Virginia and was principal of the Fayetteville Graded School. In the fall of 1916 he was recalled to the pastorate of the Storer College Church in Harper's Ferry, with duties also including teaching Bible classes. In the summer of 1918 he delivered a sermon to **Nannie H. Burroughs'** National Training School for Women and Girls in Washington, D.C. He resigned from Storer on October 9, 1921 to take a position as head of the ministerial department at Simmons University in Louisville, Kentucky, but a sudden illness sent him to the hospital for many weeks. In his recovery he wrote his autobiography, *Echoes from a Pioneer Life.*

Arter, Jared Maurice. *Echoes from a Pioneer Life.* Atlanta, Georgia: A. B. Caldwell Publishing Co., 1922. 126 pp.
WWCR.

ASSEMBLIES OF GOD, GENERAL COUNCIL OF THE. The Assemblies of God is a Pentecostal denomination founded in 1914. It drew together a number of predominantly White Pentecostal churches which had developed over the previous eight years since the revival at the Azusa Street Mission had launched the movement on its way. The interracial fellowship so evident at the Mission began to dissolve very quickly and as the movement spread across the United States, local congregations tended to be racially exclusive.

As a national organization, the Assemblies were almost totally White, but not entirely. From the beginning there were a few African American congregations and racially-mixed congregations. In 1915, a year after its formation, the General Council granted ministerial credentials to Ellsworth S. Thomas (d. 1936). Thomas had been ordained by R. E. Erdmann, an independent Black minister in Buffalo, New York. As pastor of a church in Binghamton, New York, Thomas visited the initial Assemblies gathering in 1914, but did not affiliate immediately. He regularly spoke at Council meetings over the next 20 years. Other African American pastors tended to come from the Northeast, where the majority of predominantly Black congregations existed. Among early pastors were J. Edward Howard and Cornelia Jones Robertson. One factor limiting their proliferation was the spread outside of the Deep South of the **Church of God in Christ,** an

African American Pentecostal group who doctrine was very similar to that of the Assemblies of God. Not only was there a natural tendency of African Americans to gravitate to the Church of God in Christ, but the Assemblies at times encouraged it, though several ministers such as Isaac Neeley were sent to African as missionaries.

In 1939, the Eastern District ordained an African American preacher named Ellison, pastor of a congregation in the Bronx, New York. The Assemblies congregation he served had applied for his ordination. He was supported by Robert Brown. Brown as pastor of a large congregation in New York City was the most influential pastor who developed a record over the years of supporting African American presence in the church. The matter of his credentials was referred to the General Presbytery. The Presbytery ruled that it was generally disapproving of ordaining any Black men, but if they were ordained they were to be given a license to preach only within the bounds of their district. The matter kept surfacing. For example, in 1945 Bruce Gibson, who had been given his license in 1933 as pastor of a congregation in the Seattle, Washington, area, had left to affiliate with the Church of God in Christ. He spoke at the Council session on behalf of its building an all-Black fellowship within its boundaries. At the time he had founded a Bible school which was training Black ministers. Over stiff Southern opposition the proposal was accepted, but was never acted upon.

In 1951, Bob Harrison applied for a license in the California-Nevada Conference. Just completing his college work, Harrison had been the first African American to attend the Assemblies Bethany Bible College in Santa Cruz, California. His licensing was refused on the grows of it being against Assemblies policy. At the time it was noted that Harrison's grandmother, Cornelia Robertson, had at one time been as licensed minister with the Assemblies. The case was appealed to the Executive Presbytery. The case remained in limbo as the issue was pushed back and forth between California and the Assemblies' headquarters in Missouri. In 1957 Harrison finally received a license to preach, but the question of ordination was left unresolved. Then in 1962, Baptist evangelist Billy Graham, invited Harrison to join his gospel team. Somewhat embarrassed, the Assemblies moved quickly to ordain Harrison.

Harrison's ordination was different from those few others that had occurred over the years; it was highly publicized. It was also soon followed by the publication of *The Cross and the Switchblade*, the best-selling story of David Wilkerson, the Assemblies pastor who had left

his congregation in 1958 to work among the Black and Hispanic gangs of New York. His remarkable effort at changing lives led to numerous speaking engagements in which he would bring his converts along to minister at Assemblies congregations across the church. Some of those young people became the first African Americans to speak in many of the Assemblies congregations. One of Wilkerson's associates, Thurman Faison, went on to develop a congregation in Harlem and then one in Chicago. Through the 1960s both Harrison and Faison regularly called the Assemblies attention to their neglect of African Americans. Their words were heard by leaders very much aware that the Assemblies had targeted successfully almost every ethnic group in the country except African Americans. This neglect had been based in part on what has been termed the "Sisterhood myth," the idea that the Assemblies had a sister organization, the Church of God in Christ, which functioned as the Assemblies' missionary arm to African Americans and hence relieved the Assemblies of any responsibility in that direction. That myth has been challenged in recent decades by those who have noted any lack of a coordinated action, even contact, between the two organizations and the significant difference of doctrine, especially on the issue of holiness and sanctification.

A change of policy toward African American ministry came with the emergence of Spencer Jones. Jones was the first African American to enroll and graduate from Central Bible College, the Assemblies school in Springfield, Missouri. He became pastor of an integrated congregation in Springfield, before taking over the Southside Tabernacle which Faison had founded in Chicago. Placed on the National Home Missions Board, he was given support to initiate inner-city evangelism efforts. In 1981 he called the first Inner City Pastors Conference, which had the added effect of organizing the Black clergy into a fellowship group within the Assemblies and providing a context for their regular meeting. Through the conference, Jones set into place a goal-oriented program of ministry, pastor training, and church formation in urban African American communities across the United States.

Through the 1980s, the Assemblies of God joined the Seventh-day Adventists and the United Methodists as the most racially and ethnically inclusive churches in America. In doing so, ministry to and by African Americans has become a vital part of the Assemblies' life. Not only has the inner-city program continued, but African Americans have been appointed to national staff and ministry posts quite apart from the concerns of pastoral and missional concerns directly with African

Americans. While remnants of racism remain, the more obvious steps highlighted by the Civil Rights movement of the 1960s have been taken.

"Inner City Children Are Hurting: Ministry to Them Must Be Hastened." *Mission America Newsletter* 7, 3 (November 1989): 2.

Kenyon, Howard N. "Black Ministers in the Assemblies of God." *Assemblies of God Heritage* 7, 1 (Spring 1987): 10–13, 20.

Wilkerson, David. *The Cross and the Switchblade*. New York: Bernard Geis Associates, 1963. 218 pp.

ASSOCIATED CHURCHES OF CHRIST (HOLINESS). A Holiness church. Bishop **William Washington**, an African American Holiness minister who had been working within a predominantly White Holiness association, moved to Los Angeles in 1915. He continued to work primarily within White Holiness circles for a period, but then founded an African American congregation which he incorporated as an independent organization. In 1917, **C. P. Jones**, the founder of the **Church of Christ (Holiness), U.S.A.** came to Los Angeles and conducted a revival meeting. At that time the two leaders worked out an agreement which allowed them to cooperate. Jones then settled in Los Angeles and founded Christ Temple Church.

The Jones/Washington accord lasted for a quarter of a century, but in 1946 began to fall apart. The leaders on the West Coast accused the leadership in the higher levels of the church back in the East (where the church had expanded greatly after the northern migration following World War I) of manipulating some problems in ways unacceptable to them. Hence in 1947 most of the West Coast Churches withdrew. Already incorporated as the Associated Churches of Christ (Holiness), they reorganized under Washington and continued as a separate body. As neither doctrine nor basic polity questions were at issue, the church continued to follow the beliefs, organization, and practices which were operative before the split. As the name implies, the Associated Churches of Christ (Holiness) is a Holiness church in the Wesleyan tradition. There is a belief in the experience of sanctification in which the believer is made perfect in love and given the power to lead a holy life.

The Church is headquartered in Los Angeles. It a small association with less than twenty congregations.

ASSOCIATION OF BLACK DIRECTORS OF CHRISTIAN EDUCATION. An ecumenical organiza-

tion. The Association of Black Directors of Christian Education was founded in 1989 as a support organization for directors of Christian education in African American churches. Dr. Colleen Burchett was elected president of the new organization.

In order to carry its goal of preparing educators for the needs of the 1990s and beyond, the Association divided itself into eleven geographical regions, and each region has developed a focus on a particular area of concern including Black history, Black family life, and evangelism, or social problems such as genocide and drugs.

The headquarters of the Association is in Chicago, Illinois. It issues a quarterly *ABDCE Newsletter*. There are approximately 35 members.

Payne, Wardell J., ed. *Directory of African American Religious Bodies: A Compendium by the Howard University School of Divinity*. Washington, DC: Howard University Press, 1991. 363 pp.

ASTROLOGICAL METAPHYSICAL OCCULT REVELATORY ENLIGHTENMENT (AMORE) CHURCH. The Astrological Metaphysical Occult Revelatory Enlightenment Church was formed in July 1972 by Rev. Charles Robert Gordon (b. 1931), formerly a minister in the **African Methodist Episcopal Zion Church**. Following his theological education, he served churches in Heath Springs, South Carolina; Sewickley, Pennsylvania; Flint, Michigan; and Waterbury, Connecticut. He was designated bishop and Spiritual Primate of the AMORE Church.

The AMORE Church is grounded in the Judeo-Christian tradition and the Bible, but incorporates ideas and practices which are biblical, but which have not generally been approved of by mainline churches. The members of the church are taught astrology, numerology, mental telepathy, yoga, graphology, and the other psychic disciplines. The church also teaches a belief in reincarnation and karma. God is viewed impersonally and anthropomorphic images of God are discouraged.

The headquarters of the AMORE Church has not been located since the mid-1980s and its current status is unknown.

Melton, J. Gordon. *Encyclopedia of American Religions*. Detroit, MI: Gale Research Company, 1989. 1100 pp.

ATKINSON COLLEGE. An **African Methodist Episcopal Zion Church** school. Atkinson College was founded in 1889 in Madisonville, Kentucky, as the Madisonville High School. The lead in the establishment of the school came from Bishop **Thomas H. Lomax**, the church's most notable leader in educational endeavors during his episcopal tenure. The school has a very unstable beginning, but in 1894 secured the support of a wealthy White man, John B. Atkinson, who donated substantial sums to the school. In 1896 the school was incorporated as the Atkinson Literary and Industrial College. The school continued until 1936.

Walls, William J. *The African Methodist Episcopal Zion Church: Reality of the Black Church.* Charlotte, NC: AMEZ Publishing House, 1974. 669 pp.

ATTWELL, JOSEPH SANDIFORD (July 1, 1831–October 8, 1881), pioneer minister and missionary of the (Protestant) **Episcopal Church**, was born in Barbados, British West Indies. After a common school education he spent three years at Codrington College, B.W.I. In 1863 he came to the United States and entered the Theological Seminary of the Protestant Episcopal Church at Philadelphia, from which he graduated in 1866. During this initial time in the United States he also collected funds to help people emigrate to Liberia in Africa. He was successful in collecting about $20,000, and was instrumental in founding the settlement of Crozerville in Liberia.

After graduating from seminary Attwell was the first Black person ordained deacon for the Protestant Episcopal Church in Kentucky. After serving two years there as a missionary, establishing several churches, he went to Petersburg, Virginia, where he was ordained priest in 1868 and made rector of St. Stephen's Protestant Episcopal Church and head of its parish school. In 1873 he moved to be rector of St. Stephen's Protestant Episcopal Church in Savannah, Georgia, where he remained for two years.

In October, 1875, he was installed as rector of historic St. Philip's Protestant Episcopal Church in New York City, which had been founded in 1818 by **Peter Williams, Jr.** Attwell stayed there the rest of his life, and his pastorate was marked by great success. When he passed away after six years he left behind a widow and three small boys. Two of his well-known successors in that church were **Hutchens Chew Bishop**, from 1886 to 1933, and his son, **Shelton Hale Bishop**, from 1933 to 1962.

NYTO, NYB (1912).

AUSAR AUSET SOCIETY. The Ausar Auset Society is a Rosicrucian organization which began as a chapter of the Rosicrucian Anthroposophical League. Rosicrucianism is an occult philosophy based in Western mystery traditions. It experienced a rebirth in the West in the last half of the nineteenth-century. Among those who developed modern Rosicrucian traditions was theosophist Max Heindel, the teacher of Samuel Richard Parchment, the founder the Rosicrucian Anthroposophical Society.

R. A. Straughn, the leader of the New York chapter of the Rosicrucian Anthroposophical Society, had been a student of ancient Egypt. Among his earliest accomplishments was the authorship of a manual of instruction for the Society utilizing Egyptian themes, *The Realization of Neter Nu.* Through the 1980s, Straughn began to use the religious name, Ra Un Nefer Amen I and the Rosicrucian Anthroposophical Society was superseded by the Ausar Auset Society. Ra Un Nefer Amen I (also known as Shekhem Ur Shekhem) increasingly turned his attention exclusively to the Black community in an effort to teach them their African/Egyptian heritage and the ancient wisdom of their tradition. Among the first problems he attacked was that of divorce within the Black community. In the *Black Woman's, Black Man's Guide to a Spiritual Union*, he offered insights from African cosmology to counter the corruptions of Western marriage relationships.

In 1980 Straughn began a periodical, *The Oracle of Tehuti* (more recently superseded by *Metu Neter*). Through the 1980s, beginning with *Health Teachings of the Ageless Wisdom* (1980), he authored a number of books concerned with alternative approaches to health for Afro-Americans. Texts have concentrated upon homeopathic, nutritional, and herbal means to health.

Progressive attempts to appropriate the ancient African/Egyptian teachings culminated in 1990 in the *Metu Neter: The Great Oracle of Tehuti and the Spiritual System of Spiritual Cultivation.* In *Metu Neter*, Ra Un Nefer Amen I laid out the basic axioms underlying African cosmology over against that of the West. He taught that humans live in a world that was created, and is maintained, by the unified working of a multiplicity of agencies and the world is composed of a multiplicity of entities unified through a web of interdependence. *Metu Neter* also contains instructions for an oracle (system of divination) based upon this insight.

The work of the Society is centered upon the Bronx, New York, where the headquarters is located, but the literature has circulated widely through the Black community.

Straughn, R. A. (Ra Un Nefer Amen). *Black Woman's, Black Man's Guide to a Spiritual Union.* Bronx, NY: Oracle of Thoth, 1981. 140 pp.

———. *Meditation Techniques of the Kabalists, Vedantins and Taoists.* Bronx, NY: Maat Publishing Co., 1976. 166 pp.

———. *Metu Neter: The Great Oracle of Tehuti and the Egyptian System of Spiritual Cultivation.* Bronx, NY: Khamit Publishing Co., 1990. 441 pp.

———. *The Oracle of Thoth.* Bronx, NY: Oracle of Thoth Publishing Company, 1977. 168 pp.

———. *The Realization of Neter Nu: A Kabalistical Guide to the Realization of Self.* Brooklyn, NY: Maat Publishing Company, 1976. 98 pp.

"Be loyal to your own. If there be faults, seek to correct them; but lend your heart and hand to the development and support of what is your own, designed for the highest good of you and your children."

E. M. Brawley, Baptist Educator
1890

B

BABER, GEORGE WILBUR (August 29, 1898–December 26, 1970), 63rd bishop of the **African Methodist Episcopal Church** (AME), was born in Cleveland, Ohio, the son of William and Emma Effie (Griffin) Baber. His father, a native of Canada, was a minister in the AME Church, and the family moved a number of times as he was appointed to different churches. Baber experienced conversion in 1911 and was licensed to preach in 1919. Also in 1919 he married Alma Maria Wims, with whom he had five children. After being educated in the Michigan public schools, he received his B.A. from Payne Theological Seminary at Wilberforce University in Ohio, and his B.D. from Chicago Theological Seminary. He was ordained deacon in 1922 and elder in 1924.

His first pastorate of record was at the LaPorte AME Church in Indiana, from 1924 to 1927, where he built a new church building and purchased a parsonage. From 1927 to 1929 he was at the AME Church in Michigan City, Indiana, where he again built a new church, this one with a gymnasium. At the Benton Harbor AME Church in Michigan from 1928 to 1931 he built another church and paid for it. From 1931 to 1934 he was assigned to the AME Church in Flint, Michigan, where he rebuilt the church. His major reputation was created at the Ebenezer AME Church in Detroit. During his tenure (1934–1944), he increased the membership from 500 to over 6,000 and purchased and paid for a large, new church structure that hosted the General Conference in 1940. It was the last church building in which all the daily sessions of an AME General Conference could be housed. He is one of the few AME ministers who ever built, rebuilt, or bought a new church in every one of his charges. In 1937 he was a delegate to the Conference on Life and Work in London, England.

On the basis of his outstanding record Baber was elected bishop in 1944 and assigned to the Seventeenth Episcopal District (South Africa). In 1945 he was reassigned to the Arkansas area succeeding Bishop **George E. Curry**, and in 1946 was reassigned to the Baltimore area succeeding Bishop **Monroe H. Davis**. From 1948 to 1956 he headed the Fourth Episcopal District (Michigan, Minnesota, Indiana, Illinois). In 1955 his first wife died and he then married Mrs. Elvira Mayfield Derrick of Louisiana. From 1956 to 1964 he was assigned to the First Episcopal District (New York, New Jersey, New England, Bermuda, Pennsylvania), and from 1964 to the end of his career he headed the Second Episcopal District (Maryland, Virginia, North Carolina, and Washington, D.C.).

As bishop he continued his church-building reputation, with many churches built in the various regions under his supervision. In the Fourth Episcopal District he founded Camp Baber near Cassopolis, Michigan, and was a member of several community organizations, including the Detroit Interracial Committee; the Welfare Board of Flint, Michigan; and Home Federal Savings and Loan Association. In the First Episcopal District he organized "The Walk to Emmaus," a service in which the audience is only men, and "A Night in White," a service among the women's missionary groups. These and other programs were credited with increasing church membership and significantly lifting morale.

He was a delegate to the World Methodist Conferences in Oxford, England (1951) and Oslo, Norway (1961), and to the World Council of Churches Assembly in New Delhi, India in 1961. For many years, beginning in 1952, he was on the Advisory Board of the American Bible Society, and he was active in the N.A.A.C.P. In 1960–61 Baber was president of the Bishops' Council, and from 1960 to 1962 he was chair of the general board. In about 1962 he participated with Bishop Corson, president of the World Council of Methodism, in the opening communion service of the Philadelphia Annual Conference of the Methodist Church. This was the first time that an AME bishop and a White Methodist bishop had joined together in communion. He was active in various social and political issues, and in 1968 publicly expressed his support for Hubert H. Humphrey's presidential candidacy. He was known as a balanced leader and often played the role of peacemaker in the church. A housing project was named for him in Baltimore, Maryland.

EBA, HAMEC, WWWA (5), *EWM, BDNM* (70), *NYTO, BAMEC.*

BAGNALL, ROBERT WELLINGTON (October 14, 1883–1943), an **Episcopal Church** priest and N.A.A.C.P. official, was born in Norfolk, Virginia, the son of Robert and Sophronia (Harrison) Bagnall. He attended public schools and then Mission College in Norfolk, Virginia. His father was an Episcopal priest, and he decided to follow in those footsteps. He graduated from Bishop Payne Divinity School in Virginia in 1903 and was ordained a priest in the Protestant Episcopal Church that year.

His first appointment was to Epiphany Episcopal Church in Blackstone, Pennsylvania, from 1903 to 1904. From 1904 to 1906 he was principal of Croom Normal and Industrial School and rector of St. Simon's Episcopal Church in Croom, Maryland. On July 11, 1906 he married Lillian Anderson; there were no children. He was rector of St. Andrew's Episcopal Church in Cleveland, Ohio, from 1906 to 1911, where he paid off the mortgage, remodeled the building, and doubled the membership. From 1911 to 1921 he headed St. Matthew's Episcopal Church in Detroit, Michigan, where again he built up the membership and finances, despite eliminating the rented pew system.

In the Detroit parish Bagnall began to work with the problems of the stream of migrants from the South. In 1911 he joined a local protest group and reorganized it as an N.A.A.C.P. branch. From that point on he was a significant civil rights leader. He was successful in persuading the Ford Motor Company to hire more Blacks and in eliminating Jim Crow laws in Ypsilanti schools. He worked against police brutality in Detroit and the passage of an anti-intermarriage bill in 1913, and for the passage of the Michigan Civil Rights Bill. In 1918 he was appointed an N.A.A.C.P. district organizer, and in the next three years he founded twenty-five new chapters in Michigan and Ohio. In 1919 an accusation of immorality in his church sent him to court, where he was fully exonerated of any wrongdoing.

In 1921 Bagnall was hired as a full-time director of branches for the N.A.A.C.P. and over the next twelve years reorganized the whole branch system. He traveled an estimated 10,000 miles per year, spending an average of 100 days per year on the road, a very taxing schedule. He also wrote a number of pamphlets, such as *The Psychology of the K.K.K* (1924) and *The New Abolition* (1925). His work is given credit for much of the strength and enthusiasm of the branches, the source of most of the organization's revenue. He was nationally known as an orator whose power came more from his ability to muster relevant facts to support a deep social conscience than from a facility with words. He also was associated with a more radical civil rights group, the Friends of Negro Freedom, becoming its first executive officer in 1920. The group was sponsored by the *Messenger* magazine, and Bagnall served on the magazine's staff from 1923 to 1926. He also contributed articles to the *Survey*, the *Nation*, the *World Tomorrow*, *Opportunity*, the *Crisis*, and the *Southern Workman*. He strongly opposed **Marcus Garvey**'s Black nationalist movement, and wrote a famous caricature of Garvey in the March 1923 issue of the *Messenger*. He and others urged Attorney General Harry M. Daugherty to proceed quickly with the charge against Garvey of mail fraud.

At the end of 1931, after a year of internal dissension and shrinking budgets, Bagnall was let go, an unfortunate end to that chapter of his life. On May 15, 1933, he became rector of St. Thomas' Episcopal Church in Philadelphia, Pennsylvania, where he remained for the rest of his life. His participation in the N.A.A.C.P. from this time was minimal, and he concentrated his efforts on his church. He successfully eliminated its debt and strengthened the membership, maintaining an ever-positive and effective ministry into the last years of his career.

WWC, WWCA (38–40), *DANB, WWCR.*

BAILEY, ANNE PENNY LEE (September 22, 1894– December 18, 1975), an evangelist and supervisor of women's work for the **Church of God in Christ**, was born in Temple, Texas, the daughter of Rev. and Mrs. Felix Garrett. Her father was a Baptist minister, and at the age of twelve she had an experience of conversion and joined the Baptist church. In 1915 she accepted the Pentecostal ideas concerning sanctification (a belief in the total cleansing available to the believer) and the baptism of the Holy Spirit (an experience of the indwelling of the Holy Spirit initially evidenced by speaking in tongues), and joined the Church of God in Christ. She took the lead in preaching the Pentecostal faith among African Americans in Arkansas, Kansas,

Missouri, and Illinois. She was an accomplished musician, a talent which greatly aided her evangelistic message.

In the 1920s, Mother Bailey's work was concentrated in Buffalo, New York, New York City, and the surrounding states of New Jersey, Connecticut, and Massachusetts. She attended the first convocation in New Jersey for leaders in the church called by Elder J. F. Bryant and Mother Lula Cox in 1921. As a result of her work, in 1927, she was named state supervisor (of women's work) for Maryland. In 1928 responsibilities were added for Delaware and Washington, D.C. In 1943 she succeeded Lula Cox as supervisor for New Jersey. That same year she married John S. Bailey, a bishop in the church residing in Detroit, Michigan. In 1964 Bailey succeeded Mother **Lillian Coffey** as international supervisor of women's work for the Church of God in Christ, a position she retained for the rest of her life. She died in Detroit, and was succeeded by **Mattie Carter McGlothen**.

BALL, WILLIAM FRANKLIN (August 3, 1906–January 8, 1984), 77th bishop of the **African Methodist Episcopal Church** (AME), was born at Remley's Point, near Mt. Pleasant, South Carolina, the only son of Charles F. and Delia (Blake) Ball. After a couple of years the family moved to Florida, and Ball was converted on June 30, 1911, in Grant Memorial AME Church in Jacksonville. As he grew up, he served as Sunday School teacher, class leader, steward, usher, and president of the A.C.E. League. He experienced a call to preach in 1919, at the young age of thirteen, and was licensed to preach in 1922 by the pastor, James Murray. After graduating from Stanton High School he went to Edward Waters College, where he earned the B.A. degree, and also attended Walker Business College. At Wilberforce University/Payne Theological Seminary in Ohio he earned the B.D. degree.

He was admitted into the East Florida Annual Conference in 1925 and ordained a deacon in 1926 at the St. James AME Church in Jacksonville by Bishop **John Hurst**. In 1927 he married Agnes Marie Moton, with whom he had two children. His first pastorates were at the Marietta Mission, the Middleburg Mission, and the Yukon Mission, each with less than forty members. He preached for seven years before he could earn enough from church work alone to support his family. He supplemented his income by working as an insurance agent. Other Florida pastorates were at Callahan Station, Plant City Station, and Green Cove. He became friends during this time with **Henry Young**

Tookes, and when Tookes was elected bishop in 1932 and assigned to the 13th Episcopal District (Kentucky and Tennessee), Ball followed him.

His next appointments were at the Providence AME Church in Memphis, Tennessee; Burks Chapel in Paducah, Kentucky; and St. Paul AME Church in Chattanooga, Tennessee. In 1938 he celebrated paying the St. Paul church out of debt. In 1940 Bishop Tookes was assigned to the Florida District, and Ball once again followed him back to Florida. Ball was assigned to the Grant Memorial AME Church in Jacksonville, where he had spectacular success, adding over 1,250 members during his pastorate. This brought him wide recognition, and he was nominated for bishop first in 1948 and again in 1952, each time receiving a substantial number of votes. In 1953 he was made presiding elder of the West Jacksonville District, now under **Bishop Gregg**. His next appointment was Bethel AME Church in Miami, the largest AME church in southern Florida. While there he completed the church edifice and added hundreds of members.

At the General Conference in 1956 he was elected bishop and assigned the 18th Episcopal District, and soon thereafter also the 17th Episcopal District, both fairly recently created districts in South Africa. Again he lived up to his reputation as a revival preacher with a specialty in evangelism by building two new churches in Swaziland, one in Basutoland, eight in Southern Rhodesia, and four in Northern Rhodesia (Rhodesia now being Zambia). In 1960 he was assigned to the Tenth District (Texas), then later the Eleventh District, followed by the Eighth Episcopal District (Mississippi and Louisiana). He was suspended from his episcopal duties during the quadrennium 1972–1976, but then resumed his office. At the time of his death he presided over the 13th Episcopal District (Kentucky and Tennessee). There are churches named for him in Africa and Texas.

"How Candidate Won Bishopric." *Ebony* 12 (August 1956): 20.
"In Memoriam: Bishop W. F. Ball, Sr." *AME Christian Recorder* 133 (January 9, 1984): 1.
HAMEC, BDNM (70), *EWM, BAMEC, AMSC.*

BAPTIST FOREIGN MISSION CONVENTION. A Baptist organization. The Baptist Foreign Mission Convention (BFMC) was a cooperative national missionary organization and one of three national Black Baptist organizations that joined in 1895 to form the **National Baptist Convention, U.S.A., Inc.**

Since the 1840s, interest in African missions had been the bond that strengthened cooperative work among Black Baptists. But with the demise of the **Consolidated American Baptist Missionary Convention** in 1878, national cooperation in African missionary work among African American Baptists suffered greatly. Concerned over flagging support for the African mission, **William W. Colley**, an African missionary with the Southern Baptist Convention, returned to the United States in 1880 to campaign for renewed national cooperation among Black Baptists. On November 24, 1880, Colley convened a conference with 150 other Baptist leaders in Montgomery, Alabama. From these meetings came the Baptist Foreign Mission Convention, a national convention whose focus would eventually go even beyond the African mission to include other foreign missions as well. **William H. McAlpine** was chosen as first president of the BFMC, with Colley its corresponding secretary. Vice-presidents were also elected from eleven states.

Though the success of this national cooperative missions movement among African Americans was slow at first, the leaders of the BFMC were eventually able to unite all other groups behind its banner, all, that is, except the **New England Baptist Missionary Convention**, its chief rival, and the Baptist African Mission Convention. The BFMC later joined with the **American National Baptist Convention** and the **National Baptist Educational Convention** in 1895 to form the National Baptist Convention, U.S.A., Inc.

Fitts, Leroy. *A History of Black Baptists.* Nashville, TN: Broadman Press, 1985. 368 pp.

Jackson, Joseph H. *A Story of Christian Activism: The History of the National Baptist Convention, U.S.A., Inc.* Nashville, TN: Townsend Press, 1980. 790 pp.

Pelt, Owen D., and Ralph Lee Smith. *The Story of the National Baptists.* New York: Vantage Press, 1960. 272 pp.

Jon R. Stone

BAPTISTS, AFRICAN AMERICAN. The largest religious group among African Americans is the Baptist. The predominantly African American seven-million member **National Baptist Convention, U.S.A., Inc.**, is the fourth largest religious denomination in the United States. In addition, three other predominantly African American Baptist associations report a membership in the millions: the **National Baptist Convention of America**, the **National Missionary Baptist Convention of America**, and the **Progressive National Baptist Convention**.

The Baptist movement emerged in stages within the larger Puritan movement in England in the early seventeenth century and was soon brought to the United States. The first churches were in New England, but before the end of the century congregations were established in the Middle colonies and as far south as Charleston, South Carolina. The Baptists profited greatly from the First Great Awakening in the 1740s. White Baptists tended to be from the lower end of the economic scale and Blacks, both free and slave, were frequently included as members in the congregations, and many of the Baptists, even in the South, opposed slavery. John Leland, a Baptist minister, was the most prominent advocate of an antislavery stance.

While most Black Baptists worshipped in integrated congregations, as early as 1758, the first African American Baptist congregation was founded in Lunenburg (now Mecklenburg), Virginia. It was located on the plantation of William Byrd III, in the Bluestone River, from which the church was named. It was constituted by two White preachers, Phillip Mulkey and William Murphy, associates of Shubael Stearns. This initial congregation was scattered a year later, and the church discontinued. The congregation was reconstituted in 1772 at which time four Black preachers were ordained: Moses, Benjamin, and Thomas Gardiner (three brothers), and a fourth known only as Farrell.

Though the Lunenburg church was first, the Silver Bluff church in South Carolina is of more importance. It provided the genesis of a number of congregations along the South Carolina/Georgia coast and led to the development of the Baptist church in the West Indies. As early as 1774, **George Liele** had emerged in the area as a Baptist preacher. Then in 1775, a White preacher named Palmer (possibly Wait Palmer, who had twenty years earlier baptized Shubael Stearns, who had brought the Separatist Baptist movement into the area) formally constituted the congregation. Meanwhile, in 1777 Liele started a second congregation at Savannah. In 1778, with the Revolutionary War raging around them, a group of members of the Silver Bluff congregation moved to Savannah and joined Liele's congregation there. The remainder of the Silver Bluff congregation moved to Augusta, Georgia, in 1891 where under Jesse Peter, they formed the Springfield Baptist Church. Then in 1782 Liele left Georgia for Jamaica where he founded the Baptist church in the West Indies. The congregation in Savannah continued in a somewhat unstable fashion until 1788 when Andrew Bryan arrived and it was reorganized under his care. In 1790 it joined the Georgia Baptist Association. Over the next two years the church grew to include some 250 members. In 1802, when it joined with two predominantly White churches to form the Savannah River Baptist Association, the church had over 800 members. Early in the new century, the African Baptist Church of Savannah spawned two congregations, Second Colored Baptist Church and Great Ogeechee Baptist Church, both constituted in 1802.

In 1818 the Savannah River Association divided. Five Black churches and six mixed churches then constituted the Sunbury Baptist Association. Though the majority of members of the churches of Association were Black, records indicate that it was largely controlled by the White members. The Black churches remained members of the Association until 1864 and the following years joined with congregations in Florida and South Carolina to create the Zion Baptist Association.

Records have been discovered of approximately a dozen African American Baptist congregations (all in the South) established prior to 1800, and there is every reason to believe that there were a number for whom the records have yet to be surfaced. In addition, over a hundred more known congregations formed prior to the Civil War. Some remained independent, others joined the predominantly White associations. Congregations spread across the South during the first half of the nineteenth century, though their growth was strongly inhibited by the prohibitions on the religious life of Black people following the several prominent slave insurrections, especially those of Denmark Vesey in 1822 and **Nat Turner** in 1831.

Black Baptists in the North. The first African American Baptist congregation in the North, the Joy Street church under the leadership of Thomas Paul, was constituted in 1805. Two years later, Paul's leadership became crucial in negotiating the formation of the Abyssinian Church in New York City by 16 former members of Gold Street Baptist Church. These two pioneering congregations were soon joined by churches in Philadelphia (1808), Trenton, New Jersey (1812), Wood River, Illinois (1818), and Albany, New York (1821).

It is in the Midwest and Northeast that the first all-Black associations began to form. In 1835 six congregations formed the Providence Baptist Association, and five years later a second Union Association appeared. In 1839 the Colored Baptist Association (later Wood River) in Illinois (then representing three congregations) became the second all-Black association. It grew and in 1849 split, the churches in southern Illinois forming the Mount Olive Association.

In 1840, the Abyssinian Church hosted representatives of the Zion Baptist Church (also in New York City) and the Union Church in Philadelphia, who formed the American Baptist Missionary Convention (ABMC). The Convention focused African Americans' concern for missions in Africa. It grew to include Baptists from across the Northern states and even some from southern churches, and thus became an important force in creating a national network of Black Baptists. The ABMC was joined by the Western Colored Baptist Convention, a similar group uniting congregations in the Western states. These two groups united in 1867 to form the Consolidated American Baptist Convention.

After the War. Following the Civil War, the Baptist movement among African American expanded rapidly. That expansion was accompanied by the struggles to develop national organizations and some level of autonomy from White domination and control. Forty years of concentration on a set of issues revolving around the dominant concerns of education and missions would lead to the formation of the National Baptist Convention in 1895, heralded by the creation of the Consolidated Convention just two years after the war. The first steps, for most Baptists, however, were more immediate. The new freedoms necessitated a massive educational effort at all levels to a people denied even the opportunity to learn the basics or reading and writing. Slowly schools were created across the South. Colleges, whose first task was to teach potential scholars the rudiments of letters and numbers so they could read the Bible, grew into high schools and then junior and senior colleges.

At first, the African American community needed the assistance of the Whites, many of whom shared generously. However, those who gave the money, also generally wished to keep control of the institutions created with that money. Thus Black Baptists were constantly faced with different forms of the issue of accepting White money or struggling to build and control their own institutions. While for many, the basic issue would be resolved with the formation of the National Baptist Convention, it in fact would continue over the control of Black schools into the last half of the twentieth century.

A major step to mobilize African American Baptists nationally came in 1880 with the formation of the Baptist Foreign Mission Convention. It was joined in 1886 by the **American National Baptist Convention** and in 1893 by the **National Baptist Educational Convention**. These three bodies united in 1895 to form the National Baptist Convention, U.S.A., Inc. Throughout the twentieth century, the story of Black Baptists would largely center upon the new convention and the several conventions which split from it, and the continuing relationship of African Americans with the northern White Baptists (now the **American Baptist Churches in the U.S.A.**), an account of which is summarized in their entries in this *Encyclopedia*.

Jackson, J. H. *A Story of Christian Activism: The History of the National Baptist Convention, U.S.A., Inc.* Nashville, TN: Townsend Press, 1980. 790 pp.

McBeth, H. Leon. *The Baptist Heritage.* Nashville, TN: Broadman Press, 1987. 850 pp.

Pelt, Owen D., and Ralph Lee Smith. *The Story of the National Baptists.* New York: Vantage Press, 960. 272 pp.

Sobel, Mechal. *Trabelin' On: The Slave Journey to an Afro-Baptist Faith.* Westport, CT: Greenwood Press, 1979. 454 pp.

BARAKA, (IMAMU) AMIRI (b. October 7, 1934), playwright, poet, educator, and for a time Imamu (clergy) of the **Kawaida** faith, was born Everett LeRoi Jones in Newark, New Jersey. His father, Coyt LeRoi Jones, was a postal superintendent and his mother, Anna (Russ) Jones, was a social worker. He grew up attending a Baptist Church in Newark and was exceptionally bright. He graduated from Barringer High School at the young age of fifteen and entered the Newark campus of Rutgers University on a scholarship.

He felt out of place at Rutgers and transferred to Howard University in Washington, D.C. Although he was happier there, he saw what he called the "Negro sickness," accepting a belief in Black inferiority, demonstrated in such practices as not allowing jazz in the music department. He received his B.A. in English in 1954 and joined the Air Force, stationed most of the time as a sergeant in a Strategic Air Command post in Puerto Rico. There he witnessed the "White sickness," where the function of being an oppressor is itself oppressing and deforming. Upon return to Newark he found no jobs available and moved to the Village in New York City and got a position at the *Record Changer* magazine. There he met Hettie Cohen, a White Jewish woman, whom he married on October 13, 1958; they had two daughters.

In New York he furthered the writing he had begun in the military service. In addition to poetry and prose, he started composing stage drama, and slowly gained recognition. He was a John H. Whitney Fellow in 1960–61 and a Guggenheim Fellow in 1965–66. From 1963 to 1965 he taught courses in post-1945 American poetry and in writing at the New School for Social Research and in the summer of 1964 taught a course at the University of Buffalo. From 1958 to 1963 he and his wife published *Yugen*, a journal devoted to the literary cutting edge. He also edited *The Floating Bear*, another important introducer of new poets, and numerous other transitory literary periodicals. He was editor for Totem Press and Corinth Books, and his major editorial work was *The Moderns: An Anthology of New Writing in America*. His first published collection of poems was *Preface* (1961), followed by *The Dead Lecturer* (1964). In 1965 he published the autobiographical novel, *The System of Dante's Hell*.

He became known to the wider public primarily through his plays. With Diane DiPrima and others he founded the American Theatre for Poets in 1961. The plays he produced over the next several years have been called "the beginning of Black Theater." His play, *Dutchman*, ran at the Cherry Lane Theatre from March 24, 1964 to February, 1965, to critical acclaim, and won the Obie Award as the best off-Broadway play of the year. Commentators suggested he was on the way to inheriting James Baldwin's mantle as the leading Black writer. About this time he began conducting the newly founded Black Arts Repertory Theatre/School (BART/S) in Harlem. He supervised the production of many plays and cultural events designed to educate participants from age seven and up to "a new pride in their color." Many described these productions as "anti-White."

His own personal journey, including his growing Black consciousness, led to a divorce from his wife in August 1965, and by 1966 he had left New York altogether and eventually founded Spirit House (also known as Heckalu Community Center) in Newark, New Jersey. Spirit House began as the headquarters of non-professional actors performing plays by Black playwrights and evolved into a community service headquarters with play productions on weekends and everything from a primary school to sports and meetings during the week. Baraka (Jones) founded Jihad (Holy War) Productions as the agency to handle many of his smaller publications and those of other aspiring Black writers. In the summer of 1967 he was arrested during the Newark riots for allegedly carrying weapons and resisting arrest, but he said he was framed and brutalized by the police. He was convicted and sentenced to more than two years in prison, but the conviction was overturned in 1968 and he spent only about a week in jail. The original judge had spent court time denouncing Baraka's (Jones') poetry and philosophy, which the American Civil Liberties Union and others criticized as inappropriate.

Shortly after the arrest, Baraka (Jones) was

converted to Islam through a group of Black Sunni Muslims, and he was given the Arabic name of Ameer Barakat, meaning Blessed Prince. He did not remain with this group for long, being influenced also by the moral teachings of **Nation of Islam** head **Elijah Muhammad**; by the traditional West African faith of the Yorubans; and by West Coast neo-African leader **Ron (Maulana) Karenga**. In the spring of 1967 Baraka (Jones) taught at San Francisco State College, and while on the West Coast was inspired by Karenga's methods of organizing the Black community. An integral part of this was Kawaida, a word meaning "customary, or traditionally adhered to, by Black people." Kawaida is a creative blend of African and Islamic religious elements in a form geared to support a Black cultural nationalism. Use of the Swahili language is considered a crucial part of the process.

Kawaida is based upon Seven Principles, or Nguzo Saba, which are Umoja (Unity), Kujichagulia (Self-Determination), Ujima (Collective Work and Responsibility), Ujamaa (Cooperative Economics), Nia (Purpose), Kuumba (Creativity), and Imani (Faith). Baraka became an Imamu (Swahili for "spiritual leader") of the Kawaida faith, and under Karenga's influence changed Ameer to Amiri and Barakat to Baraka, retaining the same meaning through a Swahilized pronunciation. In August 1967 he married Amini Baraka (Sylvia Wilson) in a Yoruba ceremony with a Yoruba priest named Nana Oserjeman. He had five more children with Ms. Baraka, who also brought two daughters from a previous marriage.

With some modifications, Baraka's program of cultural nationalism and Kawaida became much like Karenga's on the West Coast. The teachers at Spirit House taught its principles, and the Black Community Development and Defense Organization (B.C.D.), which he founded in January 1968, was based upon it. Members dropped their "slave" names in favor of "traditional" names, abstained from tobacco, drugs, and alcohol, and observed the rules of courtesy, propriety, and sharing. B.C.D. was one of about forty organizations that made up the Committee for a United Newark (C.U.N.). In 1970 Baraka helped candidate Kenneth Gibson become Newark's first Black mayor. Later in 1970 the ties with Karenga were broken. Baraka became secretary general of the National Black Political Assembly and in 1972 became chair of the Congress of Afrikan Peoples (C.A.P.), a politically oriented united front group formed out of the Black Power Congress in Atlanta, Georgia, in September, 1970. Over time he grew frustrated with the "backward" elements in Kawaida, including a strong male chauvinism, and by 1974 was attempting to formulate a "revolutionary Kawaida," with an emphasis on Pan-Africanism and Marxist/socialism. On October 7, 1974, he publicly announced his dropping of cultural nationalism and acceptance of socialism. C.A.P. was officially changed to a Marxist-Leninist organization. He dropped his association with Kawaida.

Over the years he has been a prolific author and noted jazz and blues critic as well as teacher. In 1977–78 he was a visiting lecturer in Afro-American Studies at Yale University in New Haven, Connecticut, and in 1983 he became associate professor in African Studies at the State University of New York at Stony Brook (S.U.N.Y.), achieving professor status in 1985. In the late 1980s he taught at Rutgers University as well, and sought a permanent position there, but was denied tenure. Many students demonstrated against the decision, saying that it was driven by the controversial nature of his positions rather than the quality of his writing or teaching. In 1981 he received the National Endowment for the Arts Poetry Award and in 1985 received the New Jersey Council for the Arts Drama Award.

Axios, Costa. *Papa Doc Baraka: Fascism in Newark.* New York: National Caucus of Labor Committees, 1973. 36 pp.

Baraka, Imamu Amiri. *The Autobiography of LeRoi Jones/ Amiri Baraka.* New York: Freundlich Books, 1984. 329 pp.

———. *The Baptism and the Toilet.* New York: Grove Press, 1967. 62 pp.

———. *Black Music.* New York: William Morrow & Co., 1970. 221 pp.

———. *Blues People; Negro Music in White America.* New York: William Morrow & Co., 1963. 244 pp.

———. *Three Books by Imamu Amiri Baraka (LeRoi Jones): The System of Dante's Hell, Tales, and The Dead Lecturer.* New York: Grove Press, 1967.

Benston, Kimberly. *Baraka: The Renegade and the Mask.* New Haven, CT: Yale University Press, 1976. 290 pp.

———, ed. *Imamu Amiri Baraka: A Collection of Critical Essays.* Englewood Cliffs, NJ: Prentice-Hall, 1978. 195 pp.

Brown, Lloyd W. *Amiri Baraka.* Boston, MA: Twayne Publishing Co., 1980. 180 pp.

Harris, William J. *The Poetry and Poetics of Amiri Baraka: The Jazz Aesthetic.* Columbia, MO: University of Missouri Press, 1985. 174 pp.

Hudson, Theodore R. *From LeRoi Jones to Amiri Baraka: The Literary Works.* Durham, NC: Duke University Press, 1973. 222 pp.

———. *A LeRoi Jones (Amiri Baraka) Bibliography.* Washington, DC: N.p., 1971. 18 pp.

Lacey, Henry C. *To Raise, Destroy, and Create: The Poetry,*

Drama, and Fiction of Imamu Baraka. Troy, NY: Whitston Publishing Co., 1981. 205 pp.

Llorens, David. "Ameer (LeRoi Jones) Baraka." *Ebony* 24 (August 1969): 75–83.

Richards, Sandra L. *Sweet Meat from LeRoi: The Dramatic World of Amiri Baraka.* Palo Alto, CA: Stanford University Dissertation, 1979. 249 pp.

BHBA, IBAWCB, BNA, CH, CRS, WWABA (90–91), CRACG, SBAA, BWA, CA (21–24), CB (1970), EBA, AARS, IBAW, HUBA.

BARBER, JESSE BELMONT (November 2, 1893–January 27, 1979), national executive in the United Presbyterian Church in the U.S.A., since 1983 a constituent part of the **Presbyterian Church, (U.S.A.),** was born in Charlotte, North Carolina, the fifth child of John and Cecelia (Lyles) Barber. His father died three months before he was born, and his mother brought him up in a devoutly religious environment. After receiving his basic education in the Charlotte area, he went to Lincoln University in Pennsylvania, receiving his A.B. in 1915, and his S.T.B. and M.A. both in 1918.

His first pastorate was from 1918 to 1922 at Grace Presbyterian Church in Seattle, Washington. During that time he took some additional studies at the University of Washington in Seattle. From 1922 to 1924 he served as a Sunday School missionary in his home town of Charlotte. He married Mae Valeria Fortune on September 30, 1923, with whom he had one child, Jesse Belmont, Jr., who later became a well-known physician. In 1926 Barber became pastor of the Leonard Street Presbyterian Church and director of the parochial school, Newton Institute, in Chattanooga, Tennessee. The Board of National Missions of the Presbyterian Church in the U.S.A. soon decided to close Newton Institute, and a community center was opened instead. This center had a kindergarten, nursery, and health clinic, staffed by volunteers.

His pastorate there was marked by progress and innovation. He urged the church to elect women as elders and to support the National Association for the Advancement of Colored People (N.A.A.C.P.). He was a founding member of the Interracial Committee of Chattanooga, a notably effective organization. In 1941 he left that position to be dean of Lincoln University's theological seminary in Pennsylvania. There he developed a strong field education program and became Associate Director of the Institute for Racial and Cultural Relations.

In 1950 he became a staff member of the Board of National Missions, and succeeded Albert B. McCoy as head of the work with the Blacks in the South. When the Board was reorganized later, he was appointed Assistant Secretary of Evangelism. In 1952 he updated his master's thesis and published it with the title, *Climbing Jacob's Ladder: Story of the Work of the Presbyterian Church U.S.A. Among the Negroes.* He was also the author of a number of articles in denominational journals and for a number of years was editor of *New Advance,* a semi-monthly magazine published by the Unit to Work with Colored People.

In 1960, two years after the Presbyterian Church in the U.S.A. merged with the United Presbyterian Church in North America to form the United Presbyterian Church in the U.S.A., he reached mandatory retirement age, and left the national position to serve as Minister of Visitation in Siloam Presbyterian Church in Brooklyn, New York. He continued in this ministry until health problems forced him to retire in 1974.

Barber, Jesse Belmont. *Climbing Jacob's Ladder: Story of the Work of the Presbyterian Church U.S.A. Among the Negroes.* New York: Board of National Missions, Presbyterian Church in the U.S.A., 1952. 103 pp.

Wilson, Frank T., ed. "Living Witnesses: Black Presbyterians in Ministry, Part III." *Journal of Presbyterian History* 55 (Summer 1977): 180–238.

CA (85–88), WWCA (38–40), HUBA, AARS.

BARBER-SCOTIA COLLEGE. A **Presbyterian Church (U.S.A.)** school. Barber-Scotia College, Concord, North Carolina, began as Scotia Seminary, a girl's school founded in 1867 by Dr. Duke Dorland with the cooperation of the Freedman's Committee of the Presbyterian Church, U.S.A. (now a constituent part of the **Presbyterian Church (U.S.A.).** Dorland associated his work with the Catawba Presbytery, formed in 1866 by the African American churches in North Carolina affiliated with Northern Presbyterians. It opened its doors with one teacher and ten pupils and featured an elementary, secondary, and teacher training curriculum. In 1916 it added a junior college curriculum and became known as Scotia Women's College. Over the years the elementary and high school programs were dropped.

In 1930 Scotia merged with Barber Memorial College of Anniston, Alabama, and assumed its present name. Barber Memorial College was founded in 1896 by Margaret Marr Barber and was named for her late husband, Phineas N. Barber, who had left money to found a boarding school for African American girls. The elementary curriculum expanded to include normal courses for the training of school teachers. In 1924 the college course was added and the first six grades discontinued. The local community was greatly disappointed when the college was suddenly transferred six years later.

In 1932, Dr. Leland Stewart Cozart, the first African American president, assumed leadership of the merged school. He would give the institution 32 years of outstanding service. He oversaw the discontinuance of the high school (1934), the development from a junior college to a four-year senior college (1944), and the accreditation by the Southern Association of College and Secondary Schools (1954). The school also became co-educational in 1954, the first male student also being the first White student.

Parker, Inez Moore. *The Rise and Decline of the Program of Education for Black Presbyterians of the United Presbyterian Church U.S.A., 1865–1970.* San Antonio, TX: Trinity University Press, 1977. 319 pp.

BARBOUR, JOSEPHUS PIUS, SR. (June 8, 1894–January 10, 1974), long-time editor of the *National Baptist Voice*, the official organ of the **National Baptist Convention, U.S.A., Inc.**, was born in Galveston, Texas, the son of Alfred and Ellen Barbour. He received his B.A. in 1917 from Morehouse College in Atlanta, Georgia, and later his B.D. from Crozer Theological Seminary in Chester, Pennsylvania. He married Olee Littlejohn, with whom he had three children.

After a time as a teacher at Tuskegee Institute in Alabama, he accepted the pastorate of Calvary Baptist Church in Chester, Pennsylvania, where he remained the rest of his life. Over the years Barbour rose through the ranks of the denomination and joined the executive board. About 1956 he became editor of the *National Baptist Voice*, a highly influential position he held for the rest of his life. He was highly regarded for his abilities as thinker, theologian, philosopher, and writer.

SCA, BDNM (70), NYTO.

BARBOUR, RUSSELL CONWELL (December 8, 1897–August 10, 1944), Baptist minister and long-time editor of the *National Baptist Voice*, the official organ of the **National Baptist Convention of the U.S.A., Inc.**, was born in Nashville, Tennessee, one of five children in the family of Alfred and Ellen (MacBeth) Barbour. He was named after Russell Herman Conwell, the Baptist minister who became famous both as the creator of the "Acres of Diamonds" sermon and as the founder

of Temple University in Philadelphia. Barbour's father was a Baptist minister, and he baptized him at the age of ten. Barbour attended Houston Junior College in Texas, received his B.A. from Morehouse College in Atlanta, Georgia, in 1920, and did some graduate work the following year at Colgate University in Hamilton, New York. He was ordained on August 25, 1921, and immediately began an eight-year pastorate of the Macedonia Baptist Church in Galveston, Texas, from 1921 to 1929, succeeding his father's ministry there. On September 11, 1926 he married Lillian Lewis; they had no biological offspring and adopted two children.

In Galveston he emerged as a civil rights leader, beginning with the fight for voters' rights against such obstacles as the poll tax. In 1930 he moved to the pastorate of the First Baptist Church (Capitol Hill) of Nashville, Tennessee. Shortly afterwards he also became editor of the *National Baptist Voice*. He maintained both his pastorate and his editorial duties until his death, and he became one of the most well-known persons in the whole denomination.

Though by nature rather retiring and even-tempered, his editorials were often charged with emotion and scathing criticisms. He dealt fairly with those who responded with equal criticism and printed their remarks on the front page. The passionate exchanges in the paper made it popular reading and actually a unifying force in the convention. In 1943, for example, he published a very heated exchange between himself and **Adam Clayton Powell, Sr.**, over his review of Powell's book, *Picketing Hell*. Barbour regretted the multiple divisions of Black Baptists and hoped to be a force towards more unity among the several conventions.

In addition to his church and paper, Barbour also served as a theology professor at the American Baptist Theological Seminary in Nashville and as chaplain of the Tennessee Agricultural and Industrial State University (now Tennessee State University), also in Nashville. The First Baptist Church was broad enough in its views of its place in the community to thus share the time and talents of Barbour. When Barbour's funeral was conducted at that church on August 15, 1944, it is said that the congregation represented the greatest assembly of National Baptist leadership ever gathered outside the convention itself. It is not clear why he passed away at such an early age (47); some have surmised that he was simply worn out by accepting too many speaking engagements and other responsibilities. His influence on the denomination was a lasting one.

GBB, RLA, NYTO.

BARKER, VIRGIL M. (1879–August 30, 1974), a bishop of the **Church of God in Christ** (COGIC), was born and raised in Drew County, Arkansas. He experienced salvation in 1901 and sanctification the following year. As a young man he attended Branch Normal College at Pine Bluff, Arkansas. During his student days he encountered Pentecostalism and was baptized with the Holy Spirit as evidenced in his speaking in tongues and affiliated with the Church of God in Christ which had been established that year by **Charles H. Mason**. He began preaching during his last year of college and following graduation in 1908 began preaching full time. In 1910 he married Ruth Flernoy. Two years later Mason encouraged his move to Kansas City, Missouri, where Barker founded the State Temple Church of God in Christ, the first COGIC congregation in the area. The church became the center for the dissemination of Pentecostalism through the African American community in Missouri, Kansas, Iowa, and Nebraska.

Memorable in his early years of ministry was a revival meeting in 1915 in Moberly, Missouri, in which 75 people were converted and experienced the baptism of the Holy Spirit and out of which six became preachers. In 1917 Mason appointed him overseer of Iowa, Nebraska, and Western Missouri, a position he retained for three decades. In 1947, his title was changed to bishop, and in the face of a growing church, his territory was divided, and he remained the leader over Western Missouri. He stayed in that position for the rest of his life. Following the national reorganization of COGIC in the 1960s under Presiding Bishop James O. Patterson, Barker was named as a member of the church's board of directors.

Barker was an early promoter of missions in the church and in 1926 was appointed vice-president of the newly formed national Missionary Board. Also, as one of the more educated leaders in the church, he developed a deep commitment to educational and youth work. In 1929 he hosted the first national gathering of the Young People Willing Workers, COGIC's youth organization. Over the years, the sunday school program grew in connection with the Y.P.W.W. and was only separated in the 1950s. In 1951 Barker hosted COGIC's first National Sunday School Convention.

Cornelius, Lucille J. *The Pioneer History of the Church of God in Christ.* N.p.: The Author, 1975. 102 pp.

DuPree, Sherry Sherrod. *Biographical Dictionary of African American Holiness-Pentecostals, 1880–1990.* Washington, DC: Middle Atlantic Regional Press, 1989. 386 pp.

Patterson, J. O., German R. Ross, and Julia Mason Atkins. *History and Formative Years of the Church of God in Christ with Excepts from the Life of Its Founder—Bishop C. H. Mason.* Memphis, TN: Church of God in Christ Publishing House, 1969. 143 pp.

BARNES, CARNELLA JAMISON (b. January 11, 1911), pioneer minister of the **Christian Church (Disciples of Christ)** and former president of the United Christian Missionary Society, was born in Edwards, Mississippi, the youngest of eight children in the family of Samuel and Anna (Harris) Jamison. The family farmed their own land and, although poor, never went hungry. Her mother died when she was five and her father later married Roberta Perry. Barnes grew up attending the Friendship Baptist Church with her family. At age fourteen she was accepted as a boarding student at the mostly White Southern Christian Institute. From the beginning she financed this with her own wages, making cream and butter in the school's milk room.

After earning an A.A. degree from the school Barnes became an elementary school teacher. After about three years she enrolled in Talladega College in Alabama on a scholarship, where she achieved a B.A. in elementary education. This increased her salary considerably when she returned to teaching. As an adult she became a member of the predominantly White Disciples of Christ Church (which became the Christian Church [Disciples of Christ] in 1957) and became heavily involved in its United Christian Missionary Society (U.C.M.S.). Eventually she became president of the U.C.M.S. and moved to its headquarters in Indianapolis, Indiana. She did not let entrenched racism and sexism stop her, and while in this position attended Chicago Theological Seminary. She earned an M.A. in religious education and was ordained a minister in 1939, one of the few women ministers and perhaps the only Black woman minister in the denomination at that time.

In 1945 she moved to Los Angeles, California, as the executive secretary of the Avalon Community Center, the first Black community center in that city. There she met and married Anderson B. Barnes, with whom she had three children. In 1952 she ran for a seat on the Los Angeles City Board of Education. Opponents accused her of communist sympathies, but she still garnered over 100,000 votes, a milestone event for a Black woman candidate. In 1962 she joined the newly founded Department of Senior Citizens Affairs in Los Angeles, and worked her way up the ranks from coordinator to supervising coordinator, then to assistant director, and finally to deputy director. When she left this position in 1976 she continued her work in this area as a program consultant with the Los Angeles County Area Agency on Aging until retirement in 1979. She was instrumental in creating the Senior Adult Camp, Older American Recognition Day, Affiliated Committees on Aging, and the Southern California Interfaith Coalition on Aging. She organized the first chapter of the American Association of Retired Persons (A.A.R.P.) in Los Angeles County and began the first Senior Citizens Observation of Negro History Week.

Her many achievements on behalf of the needs of the elderly earned her many honors and awards, including the Disciple of the Year Award from the Christian Church (Disciples of Christ), the Rosa Parks Award from the **Southern Christian Leadership Conference** and the Martin Luther King Legacy Association. She has served as president of the Los Angeles branch of Church Women United and as president of the International Christian Women's Fellowship of the Disciples of Christ Church. In 1988 Barnes came out of retirement to be program director of Respite Care/Transportation, part of the Watts Health Foundation's Senior Services Center. She is also chair of the Division of Mission Strategy and Outreach of the United Christian Church in Los Angeles and maintains an active presence in numerous other organizations.

NBAW.

BARNWELL, HENRY S. (August 1, 1881–March 1, 1942), a Congregational Church minister, was born in Charleston, South Carolina. Growing up in Charleston, he attended high school at Avery Institute and following his graduation in 1899 he left for Alabama to attend Talladega College, a Congregational Church institution. While there he served the college church as his minister. He graduated in 1903 and on January 29, 1904, was ordained to the ministry in his home church in Charleston. He then became pastor of the church at Lake Charles, Louisiana, and in 1910 began five successful years at Thomasville, Georgia.

In 1915 Barnwell left the pastorate to become principal of Fessenden Academy, a school sponsored by the Congregationalists' American Missionary Association (AMA), which oversaw the Black Cogregational churches in the South. He was in Florida in 1919 when the AMA completed its reorganization of the Black churches into four districts under a single superintendent. In 1921 Barnwell was called to become the district superintendent for Alabama, Kentucky, and Tennessee. He quickly emerged as the most aggressive of the several superintendents and as the health of the work's superintendent, **Alfred E. Lawless**, began to fail, Barnwell was called to Atlanta as his assistant. Gradually he took over all of the administrative duties

and in 1927, when Lawless finally was forced to retire, became the new superintendent.

Barnwell inherited an almost impossible situation. Most of the over 100 Black Congregational churches were poor, small, and isolated in rural areas. They were also segregated from any effective contact with White Congregational churches which might be in geographical proximity. Most were receiving money to support their minister's salary. There had been a continual loss of membership as members joined the exodus to the North. When the Depression began, budgets for Southern work were cut significantly. Shortly after assuming full control of the Atlanta office, Barnwell was faced with the results of an AMA study of Black churches receiving aid from the denomination. The AMA moved to close some churches and discontinue aid to others.

Following the merger in 1931 of the Congregational and Christian Churches (now a part of the **United Church of Christ**), the Black churches of the former Christian Church were added to Barnwell's territory. The number of churches almost tripled and the territory was increased to include Virginia (where the Christian Church had been strongest) and the northern states of New York, New Jersey, and Pennsylvania. Also aggravating the situation was the cultural distinctiveness of the two groups of churches, the Congregational churches being from a more staid tradition with an educated ministry and the Christian churches from a revivalistic tradition with less emphasis on formal training for their ministers. Then in 1936 the entire work was transferred from the AMA to the denomination's Board of Home Missions.

Through the 1930s, the Black churches under Barnwell's superintendency show a steady marked decline year by year. He is credited with doing all that was possible in an assignment which was beyond the ability of any one person. Also the AMA was more oriented toward strengthening local church programs and improving their church schools than to evangelism and church growth. The Board of Home Missions, on the other hand, emphasized evangelism. Only after the problems created by the merger and the transfer of authority to the new board did the decline stop.

Barnwell served until his death on Sunday, March 1, 1942, on his way to speak at the church in Goldsboro, North Carolina. He was succeeded by J. Stanley Taylor. The congregations with which Barnwell worked are now part of the **United Church of Christ**.

Taylor, J. Stanley. *A History of the Black Congregational Christian Church of the South.* New York: United Church Press, 1978. 175 pp.

BARROW, REGINALD GRANT (September 24, 1889–1979) was the founder of the **African Orthodox Church of New York and Massachusetts**. Little is known of Barrow's life prior to his joining the **African Orthodox Church** in the early 1920s. He was born in Barbados and at some point migrated. He was the third bishop elected by the church and was consecrated by Archbishop **George Alexander McGuire** on September 8, 1925, assisted by Bishops **William E. J. Robertson** and **Arthur Stanley Trotman**.

Barrow was a close associate of McGuire, but shortly after McGuire's death in 1934, he split with the church. Joined by others, he formed the rival African Orthodox Church in New York and Massachusetts. He worked actively to fight a lawsuit which was brought by the African Orthodox Church to prevent the use of their name by Barrow and those associated with him. The court ruled against Barrow and soon afterward his church was absorbed in another AOC splinter, the **Holy African Church**, which had been established by Trotman, whom Barrow had kicked out of his jurisdiction.

Barrow continued to function as a bishop in the Northeast for many years. The aggressive pro-Black policy which brought the African Orthodox Church into existence a half century before was evident in Barrow's appearance at the 1960 meeting of the Committee to Present the Truth about the Name "Negro," a early organization assisting the transition away from derogatory names applied to African Americans. Later in the 1960s he retired to Barbados where his son has served a term as Prime Minister. As there was no AOC work on the island, and he wished to remain active, he eventually contacted the local bishop of the Roman Catholic Church and in 1970 was received into that church as a priest. He resumed his ministry in a Roman Catholic parish until his death in 1979.

Terry-Thompson, A. C. *The History of the African Orthodox Church.* N.p.: 1956. 139 pp.

Trela, Jonathan. *A History of the North American Old Roman Catholic Church.* Scranton, PA: The Author, 1979. 124 pp.

BARROW, WILLIE B. TAPLIN (b. December 7, 1924), Church of God minister and former national executive director of **Operation PUSH** (People United to Serve Humanity), was born in Burton, Texas, one of six children in the family of Nelson Taplin and his wife. Her father was a rural pastor in the **Church of God (Anderson, Indiana)**, and she decided to follow in those footsteps. After graduating from a Texas high school she went to the Warner Pacific School of Theology in Portland, Oregon. There she gave early evidence of her leadership by being elected president of the Student Council and founding the first Black Church of God in Portland. She then studied for a time at the Moody Bible Institute in Chicago, Illinois, and the Central Conservatory of Music before shifting to the University of Monrovia, Liberia, where she completed her doctorate of divinity. She married Clyde Barrow, a native of Honduras and a former labor leader there. They had one son, now deceased.

Back in the United States Barrow became associate pastor and member of the board of trustees of the Vernon Park Church of God in Chicago, where she has since remained. Known to many as the "Little Warrior," she has been active in numerous causes which reflect her belief that issues of social justice belong among the concerns of a minister. In 1943 she joined the National Urban League and in 1945 she joined the National Council of Negro Women. In the 1960s she joined in the struggle for civil rights and began working closely with Jesse Jackson. In 1969 they led a campaign to highlight the problem of hunger in Chicago. She was state coordinator for the Illinois Coalition Against Hunger and was a member of the Special Hunger Task Force. She also spent time as Special Projects Director for Operation Breadbasket, a program of the **Southern Christian Leadership Conference** (S.C.L.C.). In 1969 she was named Chicago's Woman of the Year.

After **Jesse Jackson** founded Operation PUSH in 1971 to promote economic and political advances for the poor, Barrow was immediately involved. She was instrumental in organizing a number of major actions, including the Spring Offensive of April 4, 1973, a cooperative, nationwide demonstration among over seventy-five organizations to protest President Nixon's budget cuts. In the mid-1970s she became the organization's first female national vice-president. When Jackson had to vacate the presidency in 1984 to run for President of the United States, Barrow was one of those who took turns filling that position. In 1986 she became president on a more settled basis and during Jackson's 1988 bid for the highest political office in the land Barrow was a loyal member of his core staff. She retired from leading Operation PUSH in 1989 and returned to the position of vice-president and chief consultant.

NBAW, WWABA (92–93), *NA, IBAW.*

BASS, RICHARD OLIVER (b. June 24, 1923), 47th bishop of the **Christian Methodist Episcopal Church** (CME), was born in Nashville, Tennessee, the son of D. W. and Ethel M. (McCorkle) Bass. He received his

B.A. from Lane College in Jackson, Tennessee, in 1947 and finished his B.D. at Garrett Biblical Institute (now Garrett-Evangelical Theological Seminary) in Evanston, Illinois, in 1950. From 1944 to 1948 he was president of the National Youth Conference of the CME Church (Greenville County). He married Edith V. Thomas, with whom he had two children.

His first regular pastoral assignment was to Young's Chapel in Raleigh, North Carolina, where he stayed from 1950 to 1951. He was at Sidney Park CME Church in Columbia, South Carolina, from 1951 to 1956, and at Israel CME Church in Greenville, South Carolina, from 1956 to 1958. In 1958 he went to another Israel CME Church, this one in Gary, Indiana. In Gary he was a member of the board of the local chapter of the Urban League. He was also a leader of the ministerial association and received an award from the Michigan-Indiana Conference of the church for Fellowship and Cooperation Among Churches.

In 1962 he moved to Lewis Metropolitan CME Church in Los Angeles, California, where he stayed for thirteen years and began to make a significant name for himself in the denomination. He directed the Annual Conference's Christian Education program for his entire time in Los Angeles. He was a member of the executive board of the **Southern Christian Leadership Conference** (S.C.L.C.) West, and taught at leadership training schools across the country. From 1970 to 1972 he was president of the Los Angeles branch of the N.A.A.C.P. He was on the board of directors of the Los Angeles Urban League from 1972 to 1975, and also served on the board of directors of the Los Angeles Council of Churches. He chaired both the Commission on Housing, Los Angeles, and the Commission on Public Affairs, Los Angeles.

In 1975 Bass moved northward to the prestigious Beebe Memorial CME Cathedral in Oakland, California. There he also became highly involved in the community. In 1979 his church received the Church of the Year Award from the Oakland N.A.A.C.P. In 1980 he was on the board of directors of the Bay Area Black United Fund. A few years later he accepted an invitation to serve as professor and chaplain at Texas College in Tyler, Texas, part of the Dallas-Fort Worth Conference of the church. He was holding this position when he was elected bishop on the second ballot at the General Conference in Birmingham, Alabama, in 1986. He was assigned to the Fifth Episcopal District (the Alabama Conferences; Florida Conference, and Haitian Mission).

"Actions of the 31st General Conference in Birmingham, Alabama." *Christian Index* 119 (May 1, 1986): 3.
WWABA (80–81), *BDNM* (75).

BAY RIDGE CHRISTIAN COLLEGE. A **Church of God (Anderson, Indiana)** school. Bay Ridge Christian College, Kendleton, Texas, is a small school founded in 1961 by the **Church of God (Anderson, Indiana)** to serve its African American membership. The idea for the school originated with J. Horace Germany, a White minister who moved to Mississippi in 1952 with the idea of starting a self-help program for training Black ministers. It is controlled by the Church's predominantly Black Southern Association.

Smith, John W. V. *The Quest for Holiness & Unity.* Anderson, IN: Warner Press, 1980. 502 pp.

BEARDEN, HAROLD IRVIN (March 8, 1910–March 19, 1990), 83rd bishop of the **African Methodist Episcopal Church** (AME), was born in Atlanta, Georgia, the son of Lloyd and Mary (DaCosta) Bearden. He was ordained deacon in the AME Church in 1930 and elder in 1931. On June 12, 1931 he married Lois Minerva Mathis, with whom he had six children. He received his B.A. in 1933 from Morris Brown College in Atlanta, and his B.D. in 1951 from Turner Theological Seminary in Atlanta.

His first pastorate was at Fountain Chapel AME Church in Atlanta, beginning in 1928. Subsequent pastorates, all of them in Georgia, included St. John AME Church in Atlanta; Austell Circuit in Austell; Greater Bethel AME Church in Blandtown; Turner Chapel AME Church in Marietta; First AME Church in Athens; St. James AME Church in Columbus; and St. Paul AME Church in Atlanta. He was national grand chaplain of the N.A.A.C.P. from 1948 to 1956 and in 1958–59 he was president of the Atlanta branch of the N.A.A.C.P. From 1960 to 1962 he was a presiding elder, and from 1962 to 1964 he pastored Big Bethel AME Church in Atlanta.

On May 17, 1964 Bearden was elected bishop and that year received the Alumnus of the Year award from Morris Brown College. He was assigned to the Seventeenth Episcopal District (Central Africa), where he was the only AME bishop ever to live in Zambia in its rural area with the Zambians. From 1968 to 1972 he was assigned to the Fourteenth Episcopal District (West Africa). From 1972 to 1976 he was assigned to the Third Episcopal District, during which time he was president of the board of trustees of Wilberforce University in Ohio.

From 1976 to 1980 he headed the Sixth Episcopal District (including Georgia). He was secretary of the Council of Bishops in 1972–73 and president in 1973–74. He was chair of the board of trustees of both Morris

Brown College and Turner Theological Seminary from 1976 to 1980. He was also active in the Atlanta Y.M.C.A. and the Civic League. In 1978 he received the Outstanding Citizen Award from the Georgia State Senate, and that year was chaplain for the Atlanta Braves. From 1980 to 1984 he was on special assignment, and he retired in 1984.

WWR (75–76), OTSB, WWABA (80–81), WWA (84–85), BDNM (75), EWM, HAMEC, FEDHR.

BEASLEY, MATHILDA (c.1834–December 20, 1903), the first African American **Roman Catholic Church** nun in Georgia, was born in New Orleans, Louisiana, the daughter of a French Creole mother of color and an Indian father. She is reported to have been orphaned at an early age, but other details of her early life are not known. In 1857, at age twenty-three, she married Abraham (or Abram) Beasley, a prosperous free Black who owned a restaurant and produce market and also sold slaves. Although her husband sold slaves, she was apparently not of the same mind. She remembered acts of kindness done for her by some Blacks as a young orphan, and she secretly taught classes for Black boys and girls in 1859–60, when it was illegal to do so. A group of Franciscan nuns came to Savannah from Minnesota in the early 1870s, and at that point she became interested in the Franciscan Order. Soon she gave away all her property for the founding of the St. Francis Home for Colored Orphans.

After her husband's death in 1878, Beasley turned over the rest of her inherited property to the Sacred Heart Church. She went to England to study as a novitiate, and returned to the United States a Franciscan nun, the first Black nun in Georgia. She supervised the newly founded order for Black sisters, the Third Order of St. Francis, and its St. Joseph Colored Orphan Asylum in Savannah. The work of this small group was exceedingly difficult, with little in the way of financial support from the church. By 1896 it had only five sisters and nineteen girls. About 1900 the order was suppressed by the bishop and its work taken over by the Missionary Franciscan Sisters of the Immaculate Conception.

In 1901 Mother Beasley was given a small, private cottage on the property of the Sacred Heart Church in Savannah. It is not known whether it was simply her choice to live separately from the other members of the order or whether there were racial considerations involved. She spent much of her time sewing various articles and turning over the earnings to help the poor Black population of Savannah. While she often would

not be seen a day or two at a time during the week, she never missed an early Mass on Sunday, and when she did, a group of nuns hurried over to her cottage. She had passed away early that morning after arranging her burial clothes and few possessions in her room and while in prayer before the altar of her private chapel.

PNW, NYTO, AAE, IBAW, BWR, HBCUS.

BECKETT, WILLIAM WESLEY (August 17, 1857–1927), 40th bishop of the **African Methodist Episcopal Church** (AME), was born into slavery in Edisto Island, South Carolina, the son of Thomas and Martha Beckett. He was converted in 1870, at the age of sixteen, and joined the AME Church in 1871. His undergraduate education was at Clark University in Atlanta, Georgia. He married Mary E. Glenn on January 21, 1877, with whom he had eight children. He was licensed to preach in 1878 at Edisto Island. From 1882 to 1884 he was a member of the South Carolina State Legislature. He joined the South Carolina Annual Conference at Georgetown in 1884 and received his first appointment at Union Circuit. From 1885 to 1886 he was at the Brunson Circuit, and was ordained a deacon in 1886. During his short time in Brunson he built Ward Chapel for $1,800. He pastored the Sheldon Circuit from 1887 to 1889, and entered Gammon Theological Seminary in Atlanta in 1888. He did not have a church assignment during his last years in seminary, and he graduated in 1892 with a B.D. degree.

Upon graduation from seminary he did not immediately take another church appointment, but rather spent two years under federal appointment as Inspector of the Port of Charleston, South Carolina. In 1894 he was presiding elder of the Beaufort District, and in 1895 was at Emanuel Station. In his one year at Emanuel Station he raised $12,000, much of which went to pay off a mortgage. From 1896 to 1900 he was presiding elder of the Mt. Pleasant District, and pastored Cain's Chapel (St. Luke's) in Charleston from 1900 to 1904. About 1900 he was an agent of the Jeannes Fund for the improvement of rural schools in the South. He was at the Morris Brown Station from 1904 to 1908, during which time he was also a member of the Church Extension Board. He remodeled the church in 1905 at a cost of $5,000 and bought a parsonage in 1907 for $2,500.

He was noted for his evangelizing strengths, and in 1908 was elected Secretary of Missions for the denomination, a position he held until 1912. During that time he was editor of the Voice of Missions. In 1911 he took some graduate courses at Columbia University in New York. In 1912 he became president of Allen University in Columbia, South Carolina, which gave him an honorary D.D. degree. He was elected a bishop on the second ballot on May 18, 1916, at the General Conference in Kansas City. He was assigned to work in South Africa and braved the submarine-infested waters of World War I in order to carry out his task. In 1920 he was assigned to the Eighth Episcopal District (Mississippi) and in 1924 went to cover the Seventh Episcopal District (South Carolina). He did not live to finish that term.

BAMEC, CEAMEC, EWM, WWWA (vol.4), HAMEC, AMSC.

BECRAFT, ANN MARIE (1805–December 16, 1833), educator and among the first African American nuns in the **Roman Catholic Church**, was born in Georgetown, Washington, D.C. Her father, William Becraft, formerly a slave in the household of Charles Carroll of Carrollton, was for many years the chief steward of the Union Hotel in Georgetown, and a beloved person known to many. He raised her in the Roman Catholic faith. About 1812 Becraft went to her first school, run by Henry Potter, for one year. She then attended Mrs. Billings school until 1820. At that point, though only fifteen years old, she founded her own school for Black girls on Dunbarton Street in Georgetown.

This school was a great success and gained a fine reputation in the area. In 1827, when she was twenty-two, her beauty and character so impressed Father Vanlomen, the priest of Holy Trinity Catholic Church, that he helped her move into a much larger facility on Fayette Street, opposite the Georgetown Convent. There the school was reopened as both a boarding and day school and received much sympathetic assistance from the convent sisters. On Sunday mornings she would lead her 30–35 students to services at Holy Trinity Catholic Church. The school continued to run smoothly, but Becraft began to feel the need for a life of greater religious dedication.

In August 1831, she turned the school over to one of her star former pupils and went to Baltimore to join the Oblate Sisters of Providence at Our Lady of Mount Providence Convent. She entered the novitiate on September 8 and the following September, in 1832, took her vows with the name Sister Mary Aloysius. She was the ninth **Oblate Sister of Providence**. The order had been founded by Fr. Nicholas Joubert and **Elizabeth Lange** for the education of Black children. Becraft then

taught at the convent school, continuing her passion for teaching, until her premature death in 1833.

HNRA, AAE, IBAW, BWR, NNW, PNW, CH, HBCUS.

BEEBE, JOSEPH A. (June 25, 1832–June 6, 1903), 3rd bishop of the **Christian Methodist Episcopal Church** (CME), formerly the Colored Methodist Episcopal Church, was born into slavery in Fayetteville, North Carolina, one of seventeen children of African parents. His father, Edward Carven, was one of the first Methodist Episcopal Church, South (MECS), preachers in Fayetteville (his mother's name is unknown). He experienced conversion in 1849, at the age of seventeen, and joined the MECS. He was licensed to preach in 1851, becoming the fourth in a line of preachers in his family. He learned the shoemaker's trade, and was a favorite of the pious White mistress, who gave him a basic education. On his own he extended this knowledge until he became an acknowledged intellectual leader as well as one of the most gifted pulpit orators. He married Cornelia Bookrum on December 30, 1858.

At the end of the Civil War he joined the **African Methodist Episcopal Zion Church** (AMEZ) and was ordained a deacon in 1865 and an elder in 1866 by Bishop **Joseph J. Clinton**. He served the AMEZ Church in Edenton, North Carolina, from 1865 to 1868 and counted one thousand persons saved by his ministry. In 1868 he was assigned to Washington, North Carolina. In 1871 he joined the newly organized CME Church under Bishop **William Henry Miles**, who appointed him presiding elder of the Washington District of the North Carolina Conference. The following year he was appointed presiding elder of the Edenton District of the same conference. In March, 1873, he was a delegate to the General Conference and was selected Recording Secretary. Before the conference was over, however, he was also elected bishop on a nearly unanimous vote. He served as bishop for thirty years, and in 1892 succeeded Miles as senior bishop.

CMECTY, EWM, HCMEC, HCMECA, RLOA.

BELIN, HENRY ALLEN, JR., 104th bishop of the **African Methodist Episcopal Church** (AME), was born in Oakdale, Louisiana, the son of Henry Allen, Sr., and Beatrice (Boney) Belin. His father was an AME minister in the Eighth Episcopal District for more than sixty years. Belin Jr. attended the public schools in Baton Rouge, Louisiana. He received his B.A. and Th.D.

from Leland College in Baker, Louisiana, and his M.S. from the Lampton School of Religion in Jackson, Mississippi. He married Lucinda Crawford, with whom he has had three children.

Belin served a number of churches in the Eighth and Thirteenth Episcopal Districts, including Payne Chapel AME Church in Nashville, Tennessee. He also was selected for a term as a presiding elder. In 1972 he was elected secretary-treasurer of the AME Church Sunday School Union, where he served with distinction for the next twelve years. During this time he oversaw the construction of the new million-dollar publishing house headquarters in Nashville and the remodeling of the John Avery Apartments. In 1984 he completed one of many major publishing efforts with the AME Church Bicentennial *Hymnal*. That year he was elected bishop at the General Conference in Kansas City, Missouri, and assigned to the Fifteenth Episcopal District, covering South Africa. In 1988 he was assigned to the Twelfth Episcopal District, with headquarters in North Little Rock, Arkansas.

FEDHR.

BELL, WILLIAM AUGUSTUS (February 16, 1882–January 23, 1961), president of Miles College and General Secretary of Christian Education of the **Christian Methodist Episcopal Church** (CME), was born in Elbert County, Georgia, one of six children of Mary Jane (Thompson) and Luther H. A. Bell. He grew up in the local St. Paul CME Church, joining as a young boy. His father was a leader in the first effort to project lay work in an organized, connectional way. He graduated from the High School Department of Paine College in Augusta, Georgia, in 1901. From that point until 1904 he left to earn money for further education, and for a time was valet to a wealthy gentleman. In the meantime, he took correspondence courses, which enabled him to enter the Junior College class at Paine in the fall of 1904. He received his B.A. in 1906, and then did some graduate work at Columbia University in New York City. He supported himself through school by serving for a number of years as the private secretary of Bishop **R. S. Williams**.

In 1908 he became a mathematics instructor at Miles College in Birmingham, Alabama. He was appointed president of the college in 1912, and the following year went to Paine College as dean. On September 3, 1913, he married Helen Matile Caffey, with whom he had three children. In 1917 he resigned this position to do Y.M.C.A. work with those in the armed services. In 1919 he became executive secretary of the Southeastern Region of the Interchurch World Movement, and then in 1922 he joined the Service Company of Atlanta, Georgia, as a business executive. During this time he joined the Butler Street CME Church, pastored by H. W. Evans, and was a leader in the rebuilding work done there.

At one point, Bell was the youngest layperson ever elected as a delegate to General Conference. He was elected Secretary of the General Conference at Kansas City in 1926, and held that position for over twenty-five years. He was the first layperson to hold that office. In 1930 he returned to Paine College as its field secretary. In 1934 he was hired by the CME Church as its General Secretary of Christian Education. In 1936 he was appointed president of Miles College in Birmingham, Alabama.

Bell was known as a bridge-builder, between races, between denominations, between young and old. For many years he was the secretary of the Commission on Cooperation and Council between the former MECS and the CME Church. In 1952 he was elected chair, the only CME member to occupy that position in all the years of the commission's life. In his later years he had health difficulties, which caused him to relinquish his title as Secretary of the General Conference at the General Conference in 1954. The General Conference then elected him honorary secretary for life. Before his death, he had already tendered his resignation to the Board of Trustees of the college, to be effective May, 1961.

"Bishop W. A. Bell: A Sketch of His Life." *Christian Index* 94 (May 4, 1961): 1, 14.

Carter, G. H. "Dr. William Augustus Bell." *Christian Index* 94 (February 2, 1961): 1, 14.

Graham, W. L. "W. A. Bell and the Church's Interracial Emphasis." *Christian Index* 94 (May 4, 1961): 1.

Gray, Madison B. "William Augustus Bell-Student at Paine College, Unwritten History." *Christian Index* 94 (May 4, 1961): 5.

WWWA (vol.4), *WWCA* (38–40).

BELL, WILLIAM YANCY (February 23, 1887–April 10, 1962), 20th bishop of the **Christian Methodist Episcopal Church** (CME), was born in Memphis, Tennessee, the son of John H. and Cordelia (McCoy) Bell. He attended public schools in Memphis and joined the church in 1898. He received his B.A. degree from Lane College in Jackson, Tennessee, in 1907, working his way through school as a porter for White families. He then moved to Chicago to join a brother, and took a job at a post office with an eye toward working his way through Rush Medical College. When he realized that African Americans could not advance in the postal service, despite civil service laws, he had to choose another course. He went to Evanston, Illinois, where in 1915 he received both an M.A. from Northwestern University and a B.D. from Garrett Biblical Institute (now Garrett-Evangelical Theological Seminary). He later noted that his ambition was often stimulated by racial affronts, which were rarely in short supply. As a young boy, for example, he once saw a naked, freshly lynched Black hanging from a tree. His anger and energies were directed through a religious context, and he followed in his father's footsteps in becoming a CME minister. He was ordained a deacon in 1912. On June 26, 1913 he married Annabelle Compton, with whom he had three children.

Following his graduation from Garrett, he was ordained elder and assigned to New Hope CME Church in Evanston, where he had previously done pastoral work. From 1916 to 1917 he was a professor of classical languages at Lane College. From 1918 to 1919 he was a chaplain in the U.S. Army. In 1919 he founded Williams Institutional CME Church (named after the Church's senior bishop **Robert S. Williams**) in Harlem, New York City, to help meet the needs of the Blacks migrating north. It was built on a grand scale, covering a full city block, and he remained as pastor for nine years. He also remained dedicated to his educational training, interrupted by the outbreak of World War I, which had prevented his utilizing a Northwestern scholarship for study abroad. He went instead to Yale University, thanks partly to a Carroll Cutler Fellowship, and received his Ph.D. in Semitic Languages in 1924. In 1928 he accepted a position at Gammon Theological Seminary in Atlanta, Georgia, as professor of New Testament. In the year 1932–1933 he was visiting professor of Biblical Interpretation at Morris Brown College in Atlanta, and then he returned to Gammon. In 1935 he went to Howard University in Washington, D.C. as professor of Old Testament.

At the 1938 General Conference in Hot Springs, Arkansas, Bell was elected bishop. As bishop his assignments covered variously the Annual Conferences in Georgia, Florida, and Ohio. In Georgia he revitalized the CME presence there, and rejuvenated Holsey Academy, making it a secondary school for the education of ministers. His final assignment was the Seventh Episcopal District, composed of the Carolinas and the northeastern seaboard states. His first wife died while the children were still young, and in 1947 he married Ruby May Hall, with whom he had two more

children. In 1958 he became senior bishop, and served briefly once again as pastor of Williams Institutional CME Church.

In 1961 a glaucoma condition necessitated cutting back on his responsibilities, and the New York-Washington Conference was assigned to Bishop Luther Stewart. From September 1961 to his death he served without compensation as the pastor of the Ebenezer CME Church in South Boston, Virginia. One of the projects of his later years was an interdenominational shrine in South Boston, where numerous life-size murals depicting Christian themes frame a three-acre lake and a small, log chapel.

Bell, William Yancy, ed. and tr. *The Mutawakkili of as-Suyuti.* Cairo, Egypt: Nile Mission Press, 1926.

"Bishop William Yancy Bell." *Christian Index* 96 (May 3, 1962): 3.

Coles, Joseph C., Jr. "Remembering Bishop William Yancy Bell." *Christian Index* 116 (January 15, 1983): 5, 6.

NV, CMECTY, RLA, WWWA (vol.4), *WWCA* (38–40), *EWM, IBAW.*

BEMAN, AMOS G. (c.1812–1874), a pioneer Congregational Church minister, was born in Colchester, Connecticut. His father, Jehiel Beman, was the son of a freed slave and worked as a shoemaker in Colchester before the **African Methodist Episcopal Zion Church** (AMEZ) sent him to Middletown, Connecticut in 1830. There he became minister of Cross Street AMEZ Church, the only African American church in Middletown. Beman was active with his father in community involvement, and in the summer of 1831 was chosen secretary of the Middletown meeting of Blacks to protest the **American Colonization Society** and the underlying notion of American Blacks moving to Liberia. In 1833 he was elected secretary of the Black Home Temperance Society, of which his father was president.

Beman had hoped to enter Wesleyan University in Middletown after Charles B. Ray was accepted as a student, but the trustee action in the fall of 1832 which led to Ray's leaving dashed Beman's plans. A sympathetic White student, Samuel Dole, agreed to tutor Beman in his room at Wesleyan, but hostile students soon forced the sessions off campus. Even then, threatened violence cut short the lessons after a total of six months. In 1833 Beman walked the twenty miles to Hartford, was certified to teach, and was immediately employed in the one school for African Americans, conducted in the African Congregational Church on

Talcott Street. He taught there for four years, during which time he began thinking of entering the ministry. Besides the example of his father, in Hartford he had been impressed by AMEZ minister Hosea Easton, who had lobbied (unsuccessfully) for Hartford to establish a Black high school, and had published an influential treatise on the church's duty toward the civil condition of the Black people.

In 1836 he entered Oneida Theological Institute in Whitesboro, near Utica, New York. The other three Blacks in the mostly White entering class were **Henry Highland Garnet**, **Alexander Crummell**, and **Amos Freeman**. After only one year Beman apparently ran out of money and was forced to return to his teaching position in Hartford. About a year after that he was examined by the Hartford North Association of Congregational Ministers, which recommended he be licensed. He then (1838) left for New Haven, Connecticut, where he pastored the Temple Street African Congregational Church, becoming the first full-time, licensed Black minister serving a Black church in the city. The Temple Street Church was the first Congregational church for Blacks in the country, and was founded in 1829 by Simeon S. Jocelyn, a White minister. Connecticut was, during Beman's time, arguably the most hostile state in New England toward African Americans, with sixteen anti-abolitionist and anti-Black mobs counted between 1833 and 1837 alone. That Beman was able to be a significant leader for many years without being the subject of direct violence is testimony to his considerable skills. His predecessor, Jocelyn, had been constantly threatened.

Beman was ordained as an evangelist in March 1839, by the Congregational clergy of New Haven, who also ordained and installed him as a settled minister in the fall of 1941. He was married by this time, and had one daughter. His church was a busy center of activity, a focal point for protest meetings as well as education and mutual assistance. He was becoming a major figure in statewide Black gatherings on temperance and civil rights, and at regional and national Black conferences. In 1840 he was elected vice-president of the Connecticut State Temperance and Moral Reform Society, which struggled to gain the franchise for Blacks. In 1841 he spent several weeks in Portland, Maine, helping establish the Abyssinian Congregational Church on Sumner Street. In 1843 he was elected president of the national Black convention in Buffalo, and spoke in opposition to the proposed endorsement of Henry H. Garnet's controversial "Address to the Slaves."

Beman was a powerful orator who evoked great praise from both White and Black listeners. He was a regular columnist in various Black papers, including Charles Ray's *Colored American*, and at one point had a short-lived paper of his own, the *Herald of Justice*. Over the years he took his church into involvement in the Underground Railroad. As part of his temperance efforts, abstinence from alcohol was a requirement of membership in his congregation. Lack of proper financial support from his basically well-off congregation caused him to consider an offer in 1843 from the Second African Presbyterian Church in Philadelphia, but he did not accept, and his own situation gradually improved. In 1848 the church membership stood at 177, about 20 percent of the adult Blacks in the city. In 1846 he helped found the Second Congregational Church in Pittsfield, Massachusetts. In 1850 he considered and declined an offer from the First African Presbyterian Church in Philadelphia. In 1855 he declined an offer from the Fifteenth Street Presbyterian Church in Washington, D.C. Despite depending heavily upon White funding for easing his church's indebtedness, Beman criticized fellow Congregational minister Horace Bushnell for his racist remarks, and otherwise continued to speak his own mind.

In 1856 he began to do a significant amount of traveling as a preacher and itinerant abolitionist speaker, although he retained his church position. In 1856 and 1857 he lost his wife and two children to typhoid fever. In early 1858 he resigned from the Temple Street Church and became pastor of the Abyssinian Congregational Church he had helped found in Portland, Maine. A few months later he married Eliza Kennedy of New Haven, a White widow with two children. The marriage caused considerable uproar in both New Haven and Portland, but this seems to have passed. In June 1859, after tripling the church's membership, Beman left to take a full-time position with the American Missionary Association. This ended in 1861, but he continued lecturing, and for two years (1863–1865) pastored a small Presbyterian/ Congregational church in Greenport, Long Island. Here his wife died of cancer in 1864. From 1865 to September, 1866, Beman pastored the Mount Zion Congregational Church in Cleveland, Ohio, and then began work in the South under the Presbyterian Home Missions Committee. About 1869 he settled in Connecticut again, and from 1870 to 1872 was the supply pastor for the Second Congregational Church in Pittsfield, Massachusetts. He married again in 1871, this time to a Black woman, and was chaplain of the Connecticut Senate for a session in 1872.

CH, BPJ, SOTT.

BEN HILL UNITED METHODIST CHURCH. The Ben Hill United Methodist Church in Atlanta, Georgia is reportedly the largest African American congregation of the United Methodist Church in the United States with a membership of well over 6,000 and a staff of more than 43 full-time and part-time individuals employed.

Originally an all-White congregation, Ben Hill Methodist Church was founded as Wesley Chapel in a log cabin in 1853. In 1926, the members voted to move to the Ben Hill area of greater Atlanta. Demographic changes in the 1960s transformed the Ben Hill area into a predominantly Black community. Rather than close down the church and move, the leaders of Ben Hill Methodist accepted the challenge of integration and opened its doors to the surrounding African American community. The transition in 1974 from a White to a Black congregation brought with it a period of dynamic growth. Under the leadership of Cornelius Henderson, the church's first Black pastor, the membership increased tenfold, swelling from 400 in 1974 to 4,000 by 1986. Membership growth has continued under Henderson's successor, Walter Kimbrough, increasing from 5,300 in 1987 to 6,000 in 1989.
Community outreach through a variety of social and educational programs forms the centerpoint of Ben Hill Methodist's vision for urban ministry. These programs, including a credit counseling ministry and a school, are a food pantry, blood bank, and aid to the homeless, all of which feature lay member involvement.

Mohney, Ralph, and Neil Mohney. Parable Churches: Stories of United Methodism's Ten Fastest Growing Churches. Nashville, TN: Discipleship Renewal, 1989. 36 pp.

Jon R. Stone

BENEDICT COLLEGE. An **American Baptist Churches in the U.S.A.** school. Benedict College gave focus to the educational efforts of the American Baptist Home Mission Society in South Carolina. It was founded as Benedict Institute in Columbia, South Carolina, in 1870 and named after the husband of Mrs. B. A. Benedict whose initial donation allowed the purchase of the land upon which the school was built. Two curricula dominated the college, the training of teachers for the public schools and the training of ministers. In 1924 the school was incorporated as Benedict College. Unlike a number of other schools begun by the society, Benedict remained affiliated with the American Baptist Churches in the U.S.A., though

the administration of the school is now largely in the hands of Black leaders.

Fitts, Leroy. *A History of Black Baptists.* Nashville, TN: Broadman Press, 1985. 368 pp.

BENNETT, EDMUND ROBERT (March 19, 1875– May 14, 1949), bishop of the **African Orthodox Church**, was born in St. John's City, Antigua, in the West Indies. When he was still a child, his family moved to Baltimore, Maryland. He entered the Baltimore Normal School and graduated in 1890. Because he was only 15 years old, the school system would not accept him as a teacher, so he went to work for Claggett Chapel, a private Episcopalian school. During these years he also became a lay reader at St. James, the old Episcopal congregation for African Americans in Baltimore. He was finally able to pursue his education at Hoffman Hall in Nashville, Tennessee, and at St. Mark's Academy in Memphis, before being allowed to enter Nashotah House, the **Episcopal Church** seminary in Wisconsin.

He graduated in 1896 and was ordained. As a student he had started St. Philip's Mission in St. Paul, Minnesota, and this became his first assignment as a priest. A year later he became the priest of St. Mark's Church in Wilmington, Delaware. While there, in 1898 he married Marguerite May Fields. He was given a D.D. degree from North Carolina State College.

In 1909 he was named rector of St. Philip's Church in Jacksonville, Florida, and archdeacon of the state of Florida. At this time the church was struggling with the entrance of African Americans into the episcopacy. The church's first solution was the creation of suffragan bishops without the right of succession. Bennett turned down the offer to become suffragan of Florida. A short time later, he moved to New Jersey as pastor of St. Augustine Parish, and in 1914 to St. Philip's Church in Buffalo, New York.

In 1925 he moved to Philadelphia where he served at St. John the Divine. While there he met **George A. McGuire**, primate of the African Orthodox Church (AOC). McGuire convinced Bennett to leave the Episcopal Church and join in the new venture. In 1928, shortly after the move, he was elected auxiliary bishop of New York and consecrated by McGuire the following year. After McGuire died in 1934, he assumed additional duties as dean of Endich Seminary. In 1938 he was designated the successor of **William E. J. Robertson**, the primate. The following year he was elevated as Archbishop-Primate of the Western Province of the

AOC and named bishop of Brooklyn and Long Island. He was enthroned in 1940. He headed the church for the next nine years. He was succeeded as primate by Archbishop **Richard Grant Robinson**.

Terry-Thompson, A. C. *The History of the African Orthodox Church.* N.p.: 1956. 139 pp.

BENNETT, ROBERT AVON, JR. (b. January 11, 1933), a priest of the (Protestant) **Episcopal Church** and seminary professor, was born in Baltimore, Maryland, the son of Irene Julie (Harris) and Robert Avon Bennett, Sr. He received his B.A. in 1954 from Kenyon College in Gambier, Ohio and his S.T.B. in 1966 from General Theological Seminary in New York City. On May 23, 1959, he married Patricia Ann Greg, with whom he had at least two children. Sometime after 1977 he married Marceline M. Donaldson, and from their union four children were born.

He was ordained deacon in 1958 and priest in 1959. His first church appointment was as assistant priest at St. James' Episcopal Church in Baltimore, Maryland, from 1958 to 1963. From 1959 to 1963 he was also chaplain at Morgan State College in Baltimore, and from 1963 to 1965 he was a fellow and tutor at General Theological Seminary. From 1965 to 1968 he was an instructor at the Episcopal Divinity School in Cambridge, Massachusetts, becoming assistant professor of Old Testament in 1968, associate professor in 1974, and later full professor. In 1974 he completed his Ph.D. at Harvard University.

From 1973 to 1977 he was a trustee of the Absalom Jones Theological Institute and the Interndenominational Theological Center in Atlanta, Georgia. Since 1982 he has been vice-chair of the Standing Liturgical Commission of the Episcopal Church and a member of the Lectionary Committee of the National Council of Churches. Since 1984 he has been a member of the Final Selection Committee of the Fund for Theological Education. He has a number of published writings, including *The Bible for Today's Church* (1979).

Bennett, Robert A. "Africa and the Biblical Period." *Harvard Theological Review* 64 (October 1971): 483–500.
———. *The Bible for Today's Church.* New York: Seabury Press, 1979. 305 pp.
———. "Biblical Hermeneutics and the Black Preacher." *Journal of the Interdenominational Theological Center* 1 (Spring 1974): 38–53.
———. "Black Episcopalians: A History from the Colonial Period to the Present." *Historical Magazine of the Protestant Episcopal Church* 43 (September 1974): 231–245.
———. *Sharing the Vision: The Church's Teaching Series Reader.* New York: Seabury Press, 1980. 123 pp.
HUBA, BDNM (75), *WWABA* (92–93), *WWR* (77).

BENNETT COLLEGE. A **United Methodist Church** school. Following the Civil War, the Freedman's Aid Society of the Methodist Episcopal Church set education for the former slaves as a top priority. Bennett College was established in 1873 in Greensboro, North Carolina, with an initial gift of $10,000 from Lyman Bennett, a White man from Troy, New York. The school operated as a coeducational liberal arts college for several generations, during which time it gained a reputation for sending its graduates into the professions.

During the years after World War I, the school suffered greatly from overcrowding and a major fire which destroyed several of the buildings. In 1926 the college was reorganized as a woman's college, since which time it has grown and prospered. The Methodist Episcopal Church went through two mergers in 1939 and 1968 and is now a constituent part of the United Methodist Church. Bennett became one of the first of the post-Civil War schools to qualify for accreditation by the Southern Association of Schools and Colleges.

Stowell, Jay S. *Methodist Adventures in Negro Education.* New York: Methodist Book Concern, 1922. 190 pp.

BETHEA, JOSEPH BENJAMIN (b. September 9, 1932), a bishop of the **United Methodist Church**, was born in Dillon, South Carolina, the son of Rufus Emery and Ella Blumer (Johnson) Bethea. He received his B.A. in 1953 from Claflin College in Orangeburg, South Carolina, and his B.D. in 1956 from Gammon Theological Seminary in Atlanta, Georgia. He was ordained deacon in 1954 and elder in 1956. On June 7, 1958, he married Shirley Ann Cundiff, with whom he had one daughter.

His first pastorate was in Walhalla, South Carolina (1953–54), followed by Ninety Six, South Carolina (1954–56); Elkin, North Carolina (1956–61); and St. Paul Methodist Church in Reidsville, North Carolina (1961–65). From 1965 to 1968 he was a district superintendent based in Richmond, Virginia, and during this time, from 1966 to 1968, he did post-graduate studies at Union Theological Seminary in Richmond. All of his appointments up to this point took place within the Central Jurisdiction, a non-geographical, all-Black structure within the Methodist Church. In 1968 the

Methodist Church merged with the Evangelical United Brethren Church to become the United Methodist Church, and the Central Jurisdiction was dissolved. From 1968 to 1972 Bethea pastored the St. Matthews United Methodist Church in Greensboro, North Carolina.

From 1972 to 1977 Bethea directed the Black Studies Center at Duke University Divinity School in Durham, North Carolina. He served at one point as chair of **Black Methodists for Church Renewal**. From 1977 to 1983 he was a district superintendent of the Rockingham District, North Carolina, and in 1980–81 was a lecturer at Duke Divinity School. From 1983 to 1986 he was administrative assistant to the bishop in Raleigh, North Carolina, and was district superintendent of the Raleigh District from 1986 to 1988. He was chair of the North Carolina Regional Commission on Higher Education and Campus Ministry. From 1981 to 1988 he was a member of the executive committee of the World Methodist Council. In 1988 he was elected bishop, and has since covered the Columbia Episcopal Area in South Carolina. He has served on the General Board of Church and Society and the General Commission on Religion and Race (of which he was vice-chair in 1988).

Bethea, Joseph B. "The Black Church: 1973." *The Duke Divinity School Review* 39 (Winter 1974): 21–26.
WWMC, WWR (85), *WWA* (90–91), *HUBA, BDUMB.*

BETHUNE, MARY McLEOD (July 10, 1875–May 18, 1955), Methodist educator and for a time one of the most influential women in the United States, was born in Mayesville, South Carolina, the fifteenth of seventeen children. Her parents, Samuel and Patsy (McIntosh) McLeod, were slaves until Emancipation, and carried the surname of their former owners. The family worked a five-acre farm and struggled to send her to the local Presbyterian Mission School for Negroes. Her teacher, Emma Wilson, seeing her potential, found a sponsor in Mary Crissmon, a White Quaker schoolteacher in Denver, Colorado, to support her further education at Scotia Seminary in Concord, North Carolina, a Presbyterian school for African American girls with a faculty composed of both Whites and Blacks. She graduated in 1894 and moved on to the Bible Institute for Home and Foreign Missions (later the Moody Bible Institute) in Chicago, where she was the only African American student, graduating the following year.

Bethune had grown up in a fervently Christian home (Methodist Episcopal Church), and for most of her childhood had envisioned herself as a missionary to Africa. Now identifying as a Presbyterian and applying to the Board of Missions of the Presbyterian Church, U.S.A., she found to her dismay that there was no such position for a Black woman. She instead found a teaching job (1896–1897) at the Haines Normal and Industrial Institute in Augusta, Georgia. Lucy Laney, the Black founder and principal of that school, convinced her that service among the African Americans of the United States was an equally worthy and needed calling. She next accepted a position (1897–98) at the Kindell Institute in Sumter, South Carolina, where she met Albertus Bethune and married him in May, 1898. After a brief move to Savannah where their only child, Albert, was born, they moved in late 1899 to Palatka, Florida, where Bethune opened a Presbyterian mission school. Later she decided to resettle in Daytona Beach, and on October 3, 1904, she opened the Daytona Normal and Industrial Institute with only $1.50 in capital. By this time her marriage to Albertus, who did not share her missionary zeal, had dissolved.

Her efforts to build the school in the face of all odds were indefatigable. In less than two years she had 250 pupils, mostly girls. She bought a town dump, nicknamed "Hell's Hole," for $5 down and in 1907 moved into the first building on that property. In 1912 she persuaded James N. Gamble, son of the founder of Procter and Gamble, to serve as chair of the school board, and he was instrumental in the further growth of the school. By 1923 it had 300 students on a campus with eight buildings and a farm on twenty acres. In that year the Methodist Episcopal Church, North, became a sponsor of the school and merged it with the all-male Cookman Institute in Jacksonville, doubling its size. Bethune was named president (a position she held until December 1942), and in 1929 the new school was officially renamed Bethune-Cookman College. In 1932 it was accredited as a junior college, and in 1936 the high school department was discontinued. In 1941 the school was accredited as a four-year college (still Methodist-related), making Bethune the first Black woman to have founded and headed a four-year college in the United States.

Meanwhile, Bethune had been lending her energies to a wide number of other projects. In 1920 she became vice-president of the Commission on Interracial Cooperation of the National Urban League. From 1924 to 1928 she was president of the National Association of Colored Women (NACW); in 1935 she united the major Black women's groups into the National Council of Negro Women (NCNW), which she headed until December, 1949. She was an important supporter of the Southern Conference for Human Welfare, an officer of the National Association for the Advancement of Colored People (NAACP), and wrote numerous journal and newspaper articles. She returned to her Methodist roots in 1923 and quickly became a major figure in the church. She was a delegate to General Conference from 1928 to 1944 and served on numerous boards. She favored the 1939 reunion of the North and South branches of the Methodist Episcopal Church, but opposed the Plan of Union, with its call for all Blacks to be placed in a non-geographic Central Jurisdiction.

In 1935 she was appointed to the National Advisory Committee to the National Youth Administration (NYA), and soon was director of the Division of Negro Affairs in the NYA. A friend of Eleanor Roosevelt, she was one of the few Blacks with regular access to the White House, and the first Black woman to head a federal office. Concerned to further Black interests beyond the NYA, in August 1936, she organized the Federal Council on Negro Affairs, an informal group of Black government officials who met weekly at her home. She left government work when the NYA ceased operation in 1944. In her later years Bethune was the recipient of many honors; Ida Tarbell selected her as one of the fifty greatest women in the United States. In 1952 she finally went to Africa (Liberia), not as a missionary, but as an envoy personally chosen by President Truman. In 1974 a national memorial was erected in her honor in Washington, D.C.

Bethune, Mary McLeod. "Certain Unalienable Rights." In Rayford Logan, ed. *What the Negro Wants*. Chapel Hill, NC: University of North Carolina Press, 1944. 352 pp.

————. "My Last Will and Testament." *Ebony* (Aug.1955): 105–110.

Finkelstein, Louis, ed. *Thirteen Americans: Their Spiritual Autobiographies*. New York: Harper and Row, 1953. 296 pp.

Halassa, Malu. *Mary McLeod Bethune*. New York: Chelsea House Publishing Co., 1989. 111 pp.

Holt, Rackham. *Mary McLeod Bethune, A Biography*. New York: Doubleday, 1964. 306 pp.

Peare, Catherine Owens. *Mary McLeod Bethune*. New York: Doubleday, 1951. 219 pp.

Ross, B. Joyce. "Mary McLeod Bethune and the National Youth Administration: A Case Study of Power Relationships in the Black Cabinet of Franklin D. Roosevelt." *Journal of Negro History* 60 (Jan. 1975): 1–28.

Smith, Elaine M. "Mary McLeod Bethune and the National Youth Administration." In Mabel E. Deutrich and Virginia C. Purdy, eds. *Clio Was a Woman: Studies in the History of American Women*. Washington, DC: Howard University Press, 1980. 352 pp.

Sterne, Emma Gelders. *Mary McLeod Bethune*. New York: Knopf, 1957. 268 pp.

Young, Jacqueline Ann. *A Study of the Educational Philosophies of Three Pioneer Black Women*. New Brunswick, NJ: Rutgers University Doctoral Thesis, 1987. 149 pp.

DRB, DANB, EWM, NAWMP, DAB (Sup.5), *EBA, ERS, CB* (42), *NA, NCAB* (49), *HNB, BHBA, WWCA* (38–40), *DARB, NBH, WB, TSW, WWCR, AWW, PNW, TAO, NWAC, ONL, RLOA, GBA, BLTC, NBAW*.

BETHUNE-COOKMAN COLLEGE. A United Methodist Church school. Bethune-Cookman College, now located in Daytona Beach, Florida, was the result of a merger of two schools, Cookman Institute and Daytona Normal and Industrial School for Girls. Cookman Institute, named after Methodist holiness preacher Alfred Cookman, who gave money for the school's initial building, was the first Black college in the state of Florida and for many years its only one. It was founded in 1873 in Jacksonville, Florida, by Rev. S. B. Darnell. Originally it served a broad constituency of children, young college students, and older people denied an education during the last decades of the slave era. Its curriculum stretched from elementary through post-high school industrial training, and was designed to send graduates to Clark University and/or Gammon Theological Seminary. It operated both a day and night school. Destroyed in the Jacksonville Fire of 1900, the school relocated to the edge of Jacksonville, rebuilt, and served several hundred students each year until its merger in 1923.

The Daytona Normal and Industrial School for Girls was founded in 1904 in Daytona Beach, Florida, by **Mary McLeod Bethune** (1875–1955), a devout Methodist, remembered today as one of the great educators of the twentieth century. Bethune taught school in the South for almost a decade prior to founding her college with money she made selling ice cream and homemade pies. She kept the school going by putting a significant amount of time into fundraising. The school operated as an independent venture until the merger in 1923 at which time the Methodist Episcopal Church assumed some responsibility for the new school.

The present name of the school was adopted in 1931. During the next decade, in spite of the hardships of the Depression, Bethune built it into a four-year liberal arts college, the transformation being complete by 1941. During this time (1936–1943), Bethune served on the National Youth Administration, and was able to recruit Eleanor Roosevelt to the school's board of trustees. Her long tenure as president of the school came to an end in 1942 with her retirement. The school is now owned and sponsored by the General Board of Education of the United Methodist Church.

Harmon, Nolan B., ed. *Encyclopedia of World Methodism*. 2 vols. Nashville, TN: United Methodist Publishing House, 1974.

Stowell, Jay S. *Methodist Adventures in Negro Education*. New York: Methodist Book Concern, 1922. 190 pp.

BEVEL, JAMES LUTHER (b. October 19, 1936), minister of the **American Baptist Churches in the U.S.A.** who gained public recognition as one of **Martin Luther King, Jr.**'s key leaders of the **Southern Christian Leadership Conference** (S.C.L.C.), was born in Itta Bena, Laflore County, Mississippi. He was ordained into the Baptist ministry in 1959 and entered the American Baptist Theological Seminary in Nashville, Tennessee. While in school he became active in the civil rights movement, participating in 1960 in Nashville's first sit-in protest. He married Diane Judith Nash, with whom he had two children.

He was chair of the Nashville Student Movement in 1960–61 and pastor in Dixon, Tennessee, from 1959 to 1961. He graduated from seminary in 1961 and helped found the Student Non-Violent Coordinating Committee (S.N.C.C.). He served as its field secretary in Mississippi and was a founder of the Mississippi Free Press in 1961. In 1962 he directed the action program of the Albany Movement in Georgia, where S.N.C.C. joined with the S.C.L.C. to protest the trial of freedom riders. Bevel liked what he saw of the S.C.L.C. and in 1963 joined it as Alabama project coordinator. He led the statewide drive to register Black voters in the spring and summer of 1965. Many of the marches were broken up by police, and he suffered head injuries in March, 1965, at the hands of Selma police. He often assisted King in communicating with S.N.C.C. and other groups that frequently had conflicting agendas and strategies.

In 1966 King chose Bevel to head the Chicago S.C.L.C., which involved coordinating the activities of one hundred neighborhood action groups in the ghetto. Attempting to reverse the pattern of money flowing out of the ghetto and not in, he led a boycott of four dairy companies that refused to hire Blacks. He also held protests against housing discrimination. His most famous saying is related to the work of the S.C.L.C.: "Christ got the movement started; we are just trying to keep it going."

Bevel was an early opponent of the war in Vietnam,

and in 1963 received the Peace Award of the War Resisters League. In 1965 he urged the creation of an "international peace army" that would join the forces of civil rights and anti-war activists. In early 1967 he persuaded King to openly condemn the Vietnam war, which initially led to much criticism. In January, 1967 he became the leader of the Spring Mobilization Committee to End the War in Vietnam, and helped organize the large demonstrations in New York and San Francisco on April 15. As many as 125,000 participated in the New York demonstration, including King.

Bevel spent the rest of 1967 on leave from the S.C.L.C. concentrating on anti-war activities, then returned in early 1968. He was in Memphis when King was assassinated in April of 1968 and led the planned march on behalf of the city's striking sanitation workers. One month later he was a leader in the S.C.L.C.'s Poor People's Campaign in Washington, D.C. He later coordinated activities in Philadelphia and was an aide for **Ralph Abernathy**, King's successor in the S.C.L.C. Since that time he has continued to serve that organization.

"Dr. King Carries Fight to Northern Slums." *Ebony* 21 (April 1966): 94–102.

"The Men Behind Martin Luther King." *Ebony* 20 (June 1965): 164–173.

WWABA (90–91), *CRS, CRACG, IBAW*.

BIBLE WAY CHURCH OF OUR LORD JESUS CHRIST WORLD WIDE. An Apostolic Pentecostal church. Prior to 1957 some leaders of the **Church of Our Lord Jesus Christ of the Apostolic Faith** had raised the issue of the autocratic leadership of **R. C. Lawson**, the church's bishop. They had suggested that Lawson consider sharing the leadership and among other requests had asked him to consecrate more bishops for the growing denomination. Lawson refused, and in 1957 a number of the leading ministers and their churches left to form the Bible Way Churches of Our Lord Jesus Christ. Among the leaders of the new church were **Smallwood Edmond Williams** (1907–1991), John S. Beane, McKinley Williams, Winfield S. Showell, and Joseph Moore. They were consecrated by **John S. Holly**, a bishop of the **Pentecostal Assemblies of the World**. They chose Williams, for many years the general secretary of the parent body, as their new presiding bishop. The name of the church was taken from the name of the congregation Williams had led in Washington, D.C.

Williams has been credited for taking the lead

among Apostolic church groups in the development of a social service and social justice ministry. He led the church to become involved in Washington politics, sponsored the construction of a supermarket near his church, encouraged the development of a housing complex, and worked for more job opportunities within the African American community. His book, *Significant Sermons* (1970), was largely concerned with a Christian response to social problems. Williams also emphasized education as signaled by his opening and maintaining a Bible school adjacent to the headquarters church in Washington. In this effort he was greatly aided by Dr. **James I. Clark**, remembered as the denomination's great pioneer educator.

The Church follows the non-Trinitarian Pentecostal doctrine of its parent body which emphasizes that Jesus is God and baptizes in the name of Jesus only.

Beginning with 70 churches, by 1980 there were 300 congregations and 250,000 members.

Official Directory, Rules and Regulations of the Bible Way Church of Our Lord Jesus Christ World Wide, Inc. Washington, DC: Bible Way Church of Our Lord Jesus Christ World Wide, 1973.

Richardson, James C., Jr. *With Water and Spirit: A History of Black Apostolic Denominations in the U.S.* Martinsville, VA: The Author, 1980. 151 pp.

Williams, Smallwood Edmond. *Significant Sermons.* Washington, DC: Bible Way Church Press, 1970. 164 pp.

———. *This Is My Story.* Washington, DC: Wm. Willoughby Publishers, 1981. 195 pp.

BIBLE WAY PENTECOSTAL APOSTOLIC CHURCH. An Apostolic Pentecostal church. The Bible Way Pentecostal Church emerged in 1957 during the same disruption which split the **Church of Our Lord Jesus Christ of the Apostolic Faith** and led to the formation of the **Bible Way Church of Our Lord Jesus Christ World Wide**. It was formed by Curtis P. Jones (d. 1976) who had begun his career as a pastor in the **Church of God (Apostolic)**. In 1933 he was sent to Roanoke, Virginia, to begin a new church. Later in the decade, however, he rejected the leadership of the church's new bishop, Thomas J. Cox, and left to join with **Robert C. Lawson**, the bishop of the Church of Our Lord Jesus Christ of the Apostolic Faith. He also assumed pastoral responsibility for St. Paul Apostolic Church in Henry County, Virginia.

In 1957 a growing protest against Lawson's autocratic policies, especially his refusal to appoint other bishops, culminated in a number of leading pastors leaving his jurisdiction and forming a new denomination. Jones left during this period, but did not unite with the new Bible Way Church. Instead, in 1960 he joined with two other independent congregations to form a new body, the Bible Way Pentecostal Apostolic Church. Since that time a fourth congregation as been added to their association.

The church follows the Jesus Only non-Trinitarian position of its parent body. Headquarters is in Roanoke, Virginia.

Richardson, James C., Jr. *With Water and Spirit: A History of Black Apostolic Denominations in the U.S.* Martinsville, VA: The Author, 1980. 151 pp.

BIBLE WAY TRAINING SCHOOL. A **Bible Way Church of Our Lord Jesus Christ Worldwide** school. The Bible Way Training School was founded in Washington, D.C., in 1945 by **Smallwood E. Williams**. At the time Williams was a pastor in the **Church of Our Lord Jesus Christ of the Apostolic Faith**. However, in 1957 he left the church and led in the founding of the Bible Way Church. The school became the training school for the new denomination.

BILLOUPS, EDWARD DOYLE (b. December 16, 1896), a vice-president of the **National Baptist Convention, U.S.A., Inc.,** was born in West Baton Rouge, Louisiana, the son of Luke and Julia (Prince) Billoups. He received his B.Th. in 1912 from Baton Rouge College. He married Helen Rucker, with whom he had four children. From 1922 up to about 1970 he pastored the New St. John Baptist Church in Baton Rouge.

From 1946 to 1964 he was president of the Louisiana State Baptist Convention and was president of the Interdenominational Alliance in Baton Rouge from 1948 to about 1970. In 1951 he became president of the board of trustees of Leland College. In 1953, when **Joseph H. Jackson** was elected the new 13th president of the National Baptist Convention, U.S.A., Inc., Billoups was elected one of four regional vice-presidents at-large. He was also an active member of the N.A.A.C.P. and served on the advisory boards of Union Theological Seminary in New Orleans, Louisiana, and United Theological Seminary in Monroe, Louisiana.

SCA, BDNM (70).

BISHOP, CECIL (b. May 12, 1930), 78th bishop of the **African Methodist Episcopal Zion Church** (AME), was born in Pittsburgh, Pennsylvania, the son of Ross Mance and Diana Briggs (Wilson) Bishop. In 1953 he married Wilhelmina Jones, who also attended Knoxville College in the music department. He graduated from Knoxville College in Tennessee in 1954, and began pastoring the Center Grove AME Church in Tobaccoville, North Carolina. He attended Hood Theological Seminary in Salisbury, North Carolina from 1954 to 1956, was ordained deacon in 1955 and elder in 1957. From 1957 to 1960 he pastored the Clinton AMEZ Church in Rockville, Maryland. At the same time he was pursuing graduate degrees at Howard University School of Religion in Washington, D.C., receiving a B.D. in 1958, and Wesley Theological Seminary in Washington, D.C., where he received his S.T.M. in 1960.

In 1960 Bishop was assigned to Trinity AME Zion Church in Greensboro, North Carolina, where he began to gain a wide reputation. He became a member of the North Carolina State Advisory Committee of the U.S. Commission on Civil Rights, and chaired the Greensboro Housing Authority. Within the denomination he became director of the Division of Preaching Ministries (Department of Evangelism) and a member of the Board of Home Missions. He also served as a professor at Bennett College in Greensboro and an assistant professor at Hood Theological Seminary. About 1975 he moved to the prestigious John Wesley AMEZ Church in Washington, D.C.

At the General Conference in May, 1980, he was elected bishop and assigned to the Twelfth Episcopal District in West Africa. His first wife died on April 29, 1982, and he later married Marlene Yvette Adams of San Francisco. In 1984 Bishop was transferred to the Tenth Episcopal District, composed of four Annual Conferences within the state of Alabama. As bishop he has chaired the denomination's Board of Evangelism and the Board of Worship and Ritual, and has been represented in such organizations as the World Council of Churches and the **Congress of National Black Churches**. In November, 1985, he received the John Wesley Society Award at Graduates' Days at Wesley Theological Seminary in Washington, D.C. The award was founded in 1964 to pay tribute to graduates who had given outstanding service to the ministry and mission of the church.

"Bishop Bishop Receives Wesley Award." *Star of Zion* 110 (November 28, 1985): 1.
"Dr. Bishop Seeks Episcopacy." *Star of Zion* 104 (April 3, 1980): 1, 16.
"Memorial Services Held in D.C. for Mrs. Bishop." *Star of Zion* 106 (May 13, 1982): 1, 7.
"Vignettes of Our Bishops: Bishop Cecil Bishop." *Star of Zion* 111 (December 10, 1987): 7.
BDNM (70), *OTSB, WWABA* (85).

BISHOP, HUTCHENS CHEW (October 26, 1858–May 17, 1937), pioneer **Episcopal Church** priest, was born in Baltimore, Maryland. His parents were active members in the Chapel of St. Mary, an Episcopal congregation for African Americans. Bishop sang in the choir and was an acolyte, and the rector, Calbraith B. Perry, took a special interest in him. Under Perry's guidance, Bishop trained for entry into the ministry. In 1878 he became the first African American student allowed to enroll at General Theological Seminary in New York City, and graduated with his B.D. in 1881.

His "high church" convictions ran into obstacles in the era of the controversies engendered by the Oxford Movement, and he could not be ordained in Baltimore. He established residence in Albany, New York, where there was a sympathetic bishop, and was ordained a deacon in the (Protestant) Episcopal Church by William Croswell Doane in 1882. After a year's service in the cathedral at Albany, he was ordained a priest on May 24, 1883. He was then free to return to Baltimore and be assistant priest in the Chapel of St. Mary, where he stayed for about a year. From 1884 to 1886 he was assistant rector of St. Mark's (Protestant) Episcopal Church in Charleston, South Carolina.

On January 1, 1886, he was made rector of historic St. Philip's (Protestant) Episcopal Church in New York City, founded in 1818 by **Peter Williams, Jr.** He served continuously in this church, as its fourth rector, for the next forty-seven years, increasing the congregation's reputation as a major force in the city. By 1915 the church was famous as the wealthiest Black church in America, with basic church property and land worth $225,000, and a number of apartment buildings worth $620,000.

The church underwent a number of changes during Bishop's tenure. In 1856 the church had already moved from Centre Street to Mulberry Street near Bleecker, and the draft riots of 1863 damaged the church and closed it for a time. Shortly after Bishop's arrival the church decided to move again, due to population shifts, and on June 21, 1886, the first worship service was held at the 25th Street building. In 1896 a parish house and rectory were built at 127 West 30th Street, five blocks from the church, and there a number of new organizations was born, including the St. Christopher Club, the St. Agnes Club, and the young men's guild.

These organizations played a vital role in the growth of the church. The St. Christopher Club, for instance, for boys between twelve and sixteen, sponsored sport teams, glee clubs, and dramatics. In 1908 it had the first Black basketball team in the country. It was the first Black club to sponsor amateur boxing, and sent one of its own to an American Olympic team. In 1928 the church gained its first Boy Scout Troop, and by 1930 had over 300 boys in four troops.

In 1908 Bishop, with great foresight, understood the new Black movement into Harlem, and began to oversee the purchase of property on West 133rd and 134th Streets. The present church and parish house were built there beginning in 1910, and the new sanctuary was dedicated on March 25, 1911. During the Depression, Bishop organized a social center to help ease some of the burdens so many were under. His son, **Shelton Hale Bishop**, also became a priest, and took over the parish upon Bishop's retirement in 1933.

Bishop, Shelton Hale. "A History of St. Philip's Church, New York City." *Historical Magazine of the Protestant Episcopal Church* 15 (1946): 298–317.
WWCR, NYTO.

BISHOP, SHELTON HALE (February 26, 1889–August 24, 1962), well-known priest of St. Philip's (Protestant) **Episcopal Church** in Harlem, New York City, was born in New York City, the son of Estelle Gilliam and **Hutchens Chew Bishop**. His father was, since 1886, the priest of St. Philip's, a church already famous as the wealthiest Black church in America, and Bishop knew from early childhood that he, too, wanted to be an Episcopal priest. He was active in all aspects of St. Philip's, beginning as an acolyte at age seven. He attended Columbia University, receiving his B.A. in 1911, the year St. Philip's moved from 25th Street to West 134th Street, and graduated from the **Episcopal Church**'s General Theological Seminary in New York City in 1914.

He was ordained a deacon in the Cathedral of St. John the Divine on June 7, 1914, and became a priest on July 4, 1915. During that time he was curate at St. Thomas' (Protestant) Episcopal Church in Chicago. His first position as a priest was at St. Augustine's (Protestant) Episcopal Church in Pittsburgh, Pennsylvania, from 1915 to 1916. From 1916 to 1923 he served at the Church of the Holy Cross, also in Pittsburgh. He also did some graduate work in religious education at the University of Pittsburgh. In 1923 he returned to his home parish at St. Philip's as senior curate, and during this time did graduate work at Columbia University's Teacher's College, receiving an M.A. in 1927. His new concepts of church school and religious education replaced the traditional Sunday School at the church almost immediately, and he took the title of Director of Religious Education. The church's educational system became a widely copied model. In 1933 he succeeded his father as rector of St. Philip's.

In 1933 the Depression was causing a financial crisis in the church. It had previously depended upon income from investment property, but real estate values had crashed. Almost overnight the budget of the church was cut from $50,000 to $15,000, and then to $12,000. Many believed the church would go under, but Bishop found ways to keep the doors open. During his overall tenure as rector, St. Philip's grew in membership and stature, the annual budget increasing from $12,000 to $91,000. During that same time, however, the once-posh neighborhood around the church in Harlem changed to that of poverty-stricken tenements. Under his leadership the church accepted these changes and worked to reach out to all people with relevant services. In 1952 the church surpassed St. Bartholomew's Episcopal Church on Park Avenue and Trinity Episcopal Church at Broadway and Wall Street as the largest Episcopal church in the nation. At that time it counted 3,707 members, almost all Black, with about 60 percent of British West Indies stock.

St. Philip's gained a reputation for innovative groups and programming. In 1946 the Lafargue Clinic was founded in a collaboration by Bishop, psychiatrist Fredric Wertham, and Black author Richard Wright. This was the first basically free psychiatric facility in Harlem, and by 1952 a volunteer staff of over 25 was providing help two nights a week to anyone who asked, for 25 cents per session (if possible), averaging some sixty people a week. The clinic received donations from around the country to support this ministry. The church developed 22 organizations, including its own accredited credit union. The church began a community center offering programs dealing with drug and alcohol addiction, regular classes in modern dance, painting, and ceramics, a story hour for children, weekly dances for teenagers, and an annual street fair. For church retreats and vacations, St. Philip's owned Camp Great Neck in Tunkannock, Pennsylvania.

Bishop was the first Black to serve on a diocesan standing committee in U.S. Episcopal history. Although known as a "moderate churchman," some of the things he did were highly unusual. He kept church staff salaries low "so we can identify ourselves with the majority, not minority of the congregation." His own salary was a mere $400 a month in 1952. In the 1940s the immediate area around the church was terrorized by constant gang warfare. Bishop personally went to both of the gangs, the "Sabers" and the "Slicksters." His mediating activity was successful enough that the gang activity in the area was eventually virtually eliminated.

Bishop was known as a pacifist, and in 1945 issued a statement with others denying that compulsory military training was "approved by most Negro leaders." In 1954, *Ebony* magazine named Bishop one of the ten best Black preachers in America. He retired in 1957 at the age of 67, and moved with his wife to a home on Oahu, Hawaii. There he took the vicar's post at St. John's Episcopal Church at Kula, and also served as occasional replacement for priests in the area on furlough. In 1959 he published his major written piece, *The Wonder of Prayer*.

Bishop, Shelton Hale. "A History of St. Philip's Church, New York City." *Historical Magazine of the Protestant Episcopal Church* 15 (1946): 298–317.
———. *The Romance of the Negro.* New York: N.p., 1910.
———. *The Wonder of Prayer.* Greenwich, CT: Seabury Press, 1959. 95 pp.
"Five Plans for Retirement." *Ebony* 13, 14 (June 1958): 50–56.
"Great Negro Preachers." *Ebony* 9, 10 (July 1954): 26–30.
"Harlem's St. Philip's." *Time* 59 (January 7, 1952): 50–52.
"Harlem's St. Philip's Tops in U.S. Membership." *Ebony* 7, 8 (November 1952): 60–66.
"St. Philip's Bishop." *Newsweek* 41 (May 18, 1953): 100.
NYTO, IBAW, HUBA, AARS, WWC.

BISHOP, WILLIAM HAYWOOD (1793–June, 1873), 5th bishop of the **African Methodist Episcopal Zion Church** (AMEZ), was born in Maryland, but the family soon moved to Troy, New York. There are conflicts on his dates, but according to the most recent history by **William Walls**, Bishop joined the New York Conference of the church as a licensed preacher on May 18, 1826. He was ordained deacon on May 21, 1827, and elder on May 18, 1828. He was elected bishop at the Eighth General Conference in June, 1852, and was consecrated on July 4, 1852. He was assigned the area including New York, Genesee, and Canada West. The two other bishops, **George Galbreath** and **George Spywood**, were assigned to their areas, all on an equal standing. Arrangements previous to 1852 had one head bishop (general superintendent) and assistant bishops, but the 1852 conference passed a resolution changing

that for the time being, in deference to claims by Galbreath.

When Galbreath died in 1853, Bishop decided that the decision for episcopal equality no longer applied, and declared that he held a superior position to that of Spywood. The result was a controversy in which most of the church, largely in the South and West, followed Bishop in forming the Wesleyan Methodist Episcopal Church. The split might have remained permanent, but a Lycoming County, Pennsylvania, court case around late 1854 issued a stunning defeat to the Bishop faction over the possibility of retaining control over some of the denomination's property. Both sides then had an interest in reuniting, which was accomplished on June 6, 1860. Bishop was reelected as a bishop, and continued in that office until his retirement in 1868.

HAMEZC, EWM, AMEZC, OYHAMEZC, NHM, IBSP.

BISHOP COLLEGE. An **American Baptist Churches in the U.S.A.** school. In the 1870s, Dr. Nathan Bishop, previously a secretary of the American Baptist Home Mission Society, let it be known that he had $10,000 which he would contribute toward the founding of a school for Black people in the state of Texas. Unusually for the time, Baptists of the Southern Baptist Convention, the American Baptist Home Mission Society (northern Baptists, now the American Baptists Churches in the U.S.A.), and **National Baptist Convention, U.S.A., Inc.** pooled resources to found Bishop College in Marshall, Texas, and the first board of trustees drew its members from the three groups. The founding of the college was also a signal that Southern Baptists had recovered enough from the war that they felt able to contribute significantly to the aid of the Freedmen.

While essentially a college with professional training in law and medicine, the school provided elementary and high school education and basic education for adults who had never been able to learn to read and write. In 1892, Bishop affiliated with Shaw University and Richmond Theological Seminary (now Virginia Union University), which began to accept graduates to complete their professional training in theology, law, and medicine.

During the twentieth century, African Americans began to move into administrative and faculty positions. The first Black president was Dr. Joseph H. Rhoads. Rhoads completed the discontinuance of the high school. During his administration the college emerged as a senior college of the first rank, and one of the two colleges west of the Mississippi River accredited by the

Southern Association of Colleges and Schools when it first accepted Black schools in 1957. During his long tenure (1929–1951), besides leading the school through the years of the Depression, he also oversaw the development of a master's degree program in education (1947, and more recently discontinued), a junior college extension program in Dallas (1947), and the **Lacy Kirk Williams** Ministers' Institute. The Institute provides short term training programs for ministers and church workers.

Following Rhoads in another long tenure as president was Dr. M. K. Curry, Jr., who expanded the faculty and program and in 1961 oversaw the movement of the college to Dallas, Texas. In its new home the school became a charter member of the Dallas-Fort Worth Metropolitan InterUniversity Council and the Southwest Center for Advanced Studies, two co-operative associations. However, recently, the school was dissolved and its campus sold to Paul Quinn College, which at the time of the sale moved to Dallas from Waco, Texas.

Fitts, Leroy. *A History of Black Baptists.* Nashville, TN: Broadman Press, 1985. 368 pp.

BISHOP PAYNE DIVINITY SCHOOL. An **Episcopal Church** school. The Bishop Payne Divinity School dates to the fall of 1878 when the Virginia Theological School (of the Protestant Episcopal Church) opened a branch adjacent to St. Stephen's Episcopal Church in Petersburg, Virginia. St. Stephen's had grown out of the missionary work of three women in the employ of the church's Freedmen Commission. Rev. Thomas Spencer, rector of St. John's Episcopal Church, was placed in charge of the school. Its first class had six pupils. The school, besides educating Black Episcopalians, attracted the ministers of the **Reformed Zion Union Episcopal Church** (a Black Methodist denomination). After several years the school was set aside as an independent institution. It was named for Bishop **John Payne**, the first bishop of the church's African Mission. After his death, his widow worked at the school.

The school almost closed in 1890 but was revived by the appointment of its first African American professor, Rev. John Wesley Johnson, who also happened to be the school's first graduate. Among the major assets he brought to the school was his ability to recruit a steady supply of students to insure the school's existence for another generation. In 1906 the church placed the school under the general oversight of the American Institute for Negroes, which the church had created to assist in the stable funding of the several schools for Black people which it operated. The institute also set the standard of instruction for the school.

Bragg, George F. *History of the Afro-American Group of the Episcopal Church.* Baltimore, MD: Church Advocate Press, 1922. 319 pp.

BLACK AFFAIRS COUNCIL. A Unitarian Universalist Association agency. The Black Affairs Council was established by the Unitarian Universalist Association in 1968, as part of a quadrennial effort to raise $250,000 to empower Black Unitarian Universalists in particular and Black people in general. The move came prior to the 1969 **Black Manifesto** which called upon White and Black churches to raise large sums of money for Black economic development. The establishment of the Council coincided with an Association resolution supporting Black people in their quest for positions of leadership in both religion and the secular culture. During 1972 the funding for racial justice issues was placed in the hands of the various program agencies of the Association.

BLACK AND WHITE ACTION. An organization which operated within the Unitarian Universalist Association. Active in the 1960s and 1970s, Black and White Action was an association of Unitarian Universalists working to create an inclusive, open, and just church and society. The Association was headquartered in Oakland, California, and it had chapters around the United States. Its activities included the publication of papers on institutional racism, mobilization of the Black community through voter registration drives, providing scholarships to African American ministerial students, and organization of various interracial activities.

BLACK CONCERNS WORKING GROUP. A Unitarian Universalist Association agency. The Unitarian Universalist Association's Black Concerns Working Group continues the organization's concern for racial justice manifest in its first assembly in 1961. During the 1960s and 1970s several organizations were formed to implement actions on different issues. However, in 1983, a perception of continuing racism within the association prompted the formation of the Working Group to offer guidance within the association on eliminating remnants of racism wherever they might be and mobilizing the association to actions intent upon influencing political leaders to work for the elimination of racism.

BLACK COUNCIL—REFORMED CHURCH IN AMERICA. During the late 1960s, African American members of most of the major denominations formed caucuses within their respective bodies. Blacks with the **Reformed Church in America** did not move quickly to organize until June 6, 1969, when **James Forman**, head of the **National Black Economic Development Conference**, and his supporters moved into the national offices of the Reformed Church and shut down normal operations. The "sit-in" was on behalf of the **Black Manifesto** which he had presented to the churches a month previously. The manifesto demanded that each of the White denominations pay reparations to be used in economic development within the African American community because of their cooperation in the oppression of Black people over the centuries.

The Reformed Church appointed an ad hoc committee to respond to the manifesto. Among its recommendations was the formation of the Black Council. Such a council was formed in August by Elders Clyde Watts, John Ashby, and Edgar Dillard. Rev. B. Moses James was elected as its first chairperson. There is now an annual lectureship in his honor sponsored by the organization. It was given an initial grant of $100,000. The council has remained as a program agency of the church to administer funds and manage minority affairs.

The council is headquartered in New York at the Interchurch Center on Riverside Drive. There are some 45 African American congregations in the denomination. It publishes the monthly *Black Caucus RCA*.

Payne, Wardell J., ed. *Directory of African American Religious Bodies: A Compendium by the Howard University School of Divinity.* Washington, DC: Howard University Press, 1991. 363 pp.

BLACK JUDAISM. Black Judaism is the popular designation of modern Africans and African Americans who follow a variety of the Jewish faith. Among African Americans, the first Black Jews were a few converts to Judaism during the nineteenth century, the most famous being Old Billy who regularly attended the synagogue in Charleston, South Carolina, during the first half of the nineteenth century. Then in 1867 Joseph Helévy went to Ethiopia to visit the **Falashas**, Africans who considered themselves to be the descendants of the Queen of Sheba and Jews. The existence of the Falashas was known in the West, but little information was popularly available. The story of his discoveries was widely circulated.

The Falashas were not, of course, the only Black Jews around the world. Less known are the Lemba people, the Black Jews of Southern Africa whose territory is in Zimbabwe and the Transvaal. The Zafy Ibrahim (descendants of Abraham) reside in Madagascar, and the Djo-tongo in Surinam. And some of the Black Jews of Yemen have migrated to and settled in Israel.

African American Jewish Groups. By the end of the nineteenth century, several preachers had arisen in the African American community who were telling their audiences that the Jews of the Old Testament were Black people. Most prominent of these was William Christian, founder of the **Church of the Living God (Christian Workers for Fellowship)**. He was followed by several preachers who took the idea even further by suggesting that Black people were the descendants of the biblical Israelites, the Lost Tribes of Israel, an idea which gained immediate support from the previous attachment of former slaves with the biblical story of the Jewish captivity. Possibly the first of these prophets was F. S. Cherry, who settled in Philadelphia at the beginning of the twentieth century and organized the **Church of God (Black Jews)**. The more important prophet, however, was **William S. Crowdy** of Lawrence, Kansas. Following an intense visionary experience Crowdy organized the eclectic **Church of God and Saints of Christ** in 1896 and during the first years of the new century carried it to Black communities in the Midwest and Northeast. He eventually settled in Philadelphia.

Early in the twentieth century the idea of "Black Jews" was wedded to that of Black nationalism, the concept of the Black people as a culture and nation who should possess a land of their own in which they ruled themselves. Judaism became an element in an ethnic gestalt which identified them as a people. Most of the groups which arose through the twentieth century absorbed Black nationalist ideas, but varied widely in their tactics. Some quietly withdrew and assumed a very low profile, while others became militant activists.

Two factors undergirded the growth of Black Judaism early in the century. First, in 1904 Jacques Faitlovitch made his initial visit among the Falashas of

Ethiopia. The Abyssinian Jews became his life long crusade. His aim was to reconnect the Falashas and the worldwide Jewish community. His activity had the side effect of reviving interest in Ethiopia among African Americans. Within the Black community Ethiopian became synonymous with Black and "Ethiopianism" an expression of Black nationalism. Second, in 1916 **Marcus Garvey** arrived in the United States from Jamaica to gather American support for the Universal Negro Improvement Association (U.N.I.A.).

Black Judaism, Ethiopianism, and the Garvey movement came together in the career of **Arnold Josiah Ford**. Like Garvey, a West Indian, Ford arrived in America in 1912. He became an early Garvey supporter and compiled the U.N.I.A. hymnal, *The Universal Ethiopian Hymnal*, and co-authored the text of the organization's national anthem, "Ethiopia, Land of our Fathers." Sometime around 1924, Ford founded Beth B'nai Abraham, a Black Jewish nationalist congregation in New York City. About the same time he met Arthur Wentworth Matthew, leader of the **Commandment Keepers Congregation of the Living God**. Matthew had started as a Pentecostal minister but had absorbed Black Jewish ideas both from his contact with White Jews and his association with Garvey. In 1930 Ford left the United States to live out his life in Ethiopia. He turned his followers over to Matthew's care.

The several congregations of Black Jews existed through the next generation and were eventually joined by a number of new movements which grew up during the ferment within the Black community during the 1960s. Two of these groups emerged in Chicago, a city which had a history of support for Black Jewish ideas. The **Original Hebrew Israelite Nation** was founded in the 1960s by Rabbi Ben Ammi Carter and Shaleah. From headquarters in the A-Beta Center on Chicago's south side, Carter called for a return to the Holy Land, now the new state of Israel. In 1968 a group was able to migrate to Israel and were soon joined by several hundred others all claiming citizenship under the law of return. By 1980 there were some 1,500 members in Israel. Their arrival initiated a lengthy negotiation with the Israeli government.

The House of Judah was founded in Chicago in 1965 by Prophet William A. Lewis. In 1971 Lewis moved his following to rural Michigan where they lived quietly until 1983 when a young boy was killed by his mother who was disciplining him. Following a lengthy litigation which saw the mother imprisoned, the group resettled in rural Alabama.

A third important Black Jewish group founded at the end of the decade was the **Nation of Yahweh (Hebrew Israelites)**. The Nation was formed by Hulon Mitchell, Jr., a former member of the Nation of Islam. Mitchell, known as **Yahweh ben Yahweh**, believes himself to be Yahweh's son and the savior and deliverer of his people. From headquarters in Miami, Florida, the movement spread across America in the 1970s and 1980s.

Each of the 1960s Black Jewish groups assumed a highly militant stance both within the Black community and in the face of the White community. Each also has encountered several legal problems which have disrupted their life. Members of the Original Hebrew Israelite Nation were arrested in a series of raids in the early 1980s and eventually charged in a massive conspiracy to steal and use passports, blank checks, credit cards, and airline tickets. The life of the House of Judah was disrupted by charges of systematic child abuse. In 1992, Yahweh ben Yahweh and some of his followers were convicted of murder and several lesser crimes and have received lengthy prison terms. This history of illegal activity, violence, and resultant confrontation with the law has done much to slow the growth of Black Judaism in recent years.

Black Jews/White Jews. The existence of Black religious groups claiming to be Jews, both the various Black groups around the world and the newer African American groups, created a host of problems for the larger White Jewish community. At the more theoretical level they became another challenge to White Jewish identity and the ways of telling the story of Jewish history. On a more practical level, especially since the founding of the state of Israel and its articulation of the Law of Return, which allows any Jew to emigrate to the country, Black Jews of all varieties have arrived to claim their rights and privileges. In the United States, Blacks calling themselves Jews or wishing to convert to Judaism have forced different agencies to create policy decisions on how to deal with them.

Some African Americans have gone through a formal conversion process as described in Jewish law and have gained at least a modest acceptance in the White Jewish community. The most famous such converted African American in the last generation was entertainer Sammy Davis, Jr. In more recent years there have arisen new Jewish congregations consisting entirely of African Americans who have gone through the formal process of conversion to Judaism and who have been recognized within the Jewish Community. Among these are the Congregation Zichron Rabbi Eliazer Meskin, in Brooklyn, New York; Congregation Mount Horeb in New York City; and Adat Beyt Mosheh Congregation in Mullica Township, New Jersey.

Short of formal conversion, some Jews have

worked to build bridges between the Black and White Jewish communities. A prime example of such endeavors was the short-lived **Hatzaad Harishon** (The First Step), founded in 1964 by Ya'akov Gladstone, which brought members of the two communities together for dialogue and celebration. During the 1970s the American Jewish Congress operated a Jewish-Black Information Center (since closed) which kept interested people informed on a wide range of issues between the the Black and Jewish community including that of Black Jews.

Other members of the White Jewish community have become concerned with the fate of the Falashas and have tried to mobilize support for them in the form of direct aid and in lobbying for a more open policy toward them by the state of Israel. This effort began in the 1920s with the formation of the American Pro-Falasha Committee founded by Faitlovitch but gained renewed momentum with the founding of the Friends of Beta-Israel Community in Ethiopia by Dr. Graenum Berger in 1965. These two groups merged in 1974 as the **American Association for Ethiopian Jews**.

Through most of the twentieth century, the Black community and the White Jewish community have shared a common history as oppressed peoples, and Jewish leaders (both religious and secular) took a prominent role in the civil rights movement. However, that relationship has been under significant attack since the 1970s as Black leaders have identified leaders of the White Jewish community as oppressors more than as fellow sufferers. Black Jewish leaders, frustrated at the very limited recognition they have received from the Jewish community in the 1960s, saw the situation as a sign of an entrenched racism which denied Jewish teachings about a lack of a color barrier in the Jewish faith. The community's racism was most clearly perceived in the refusal to allow Blacks to attend Jewish schools and the Jewish community's lack of support for the Falashas.

Christian Black Jews. To round out the picture of Black Judaism, it is necessary to speak of two other groups, neither strictly Black Jews, but both borrowing heavily from Black Jewish themes. The **Pan African Orthodox Christian Church** began in 1953 in Detroit when a group of Black Presbyterians left their building behind and reorganized as Central Congregational Church, affiliated with the **United Church of Christ**. Their pastor was Albert B. Cleage, Jr. Cleage, a community activist, slowly led the church into an acceptance of a radical Black theology, which drew heavily on Black Jewish themes. Most startling has been the reimaging

of Christianity as an intensely Afro-American faith. Cleage, who changed his name to **Jaramogi Abebe Agyeman**, speaks of a Black Jesus, has opened several churches dedicated to the Black Madonna, and mobilized his following as the **Black Christian Nationalist Movement**.

Finally, the **Rastafarians** of Jamaica adopted numerous Black Jewish ideas. They, for example, accept the story told in the Jewish Bible (the Old Testament) as the history of Black people, though they claim Ethiopia, not Israel, as their homeland. In recent years, a number of Rastafarians have appeared in most major United States cities.

ben-Jochannan, Yosef. *We the Black Jews: Witness to the "White Jewish Race" Myth.* New York: Alkebulan Books and Education Materials Associates, 1983. 408 pp.

Berson, Lenora E. *The Negroes and the Jews.* New York: Random House, 1971. 436 pp.

Hughley, Ella J. *The Truth about Black Biblical Hebrew-Israelites (Jews).* Springfield Gardens, NY: Hughley Publications, 1982. 68 pp.

Malcioln, Jóse V. *How the Hebrews Became Jews.* New York: U. B. Productions, 78. 35 pp.

Parfitt, Tutor. *The Thirteenth Gate: Travels Among the Lost Tribes of Israel.* Bethesda, MD: Adler & Adler, 1987. 167 pp.

BLACK MANIFESTO. The Black Manifesto is a document created in 1968/69 by **James Forman** and members of a Black revolutionary group, the League of Revolutionary Black Workers. Forman, a former executive director of the Student Nonviolent Coordinating Committee, was invited to address the 1969 **National Black Economic Development Conference** sponsored by the **Interreligious Foundation for Community Organization** (IFCO), an organization established by the social action agencies of various churches and the American Jewish Committee. Forman came to the occasion with an intense anticlericalism, Marxist economic theory, and a belief that the churches were a significant force in the oppression of Black people.

Forman presented the Black Manifesto on April 26 at the IFCO conference. It called for the White churches and synagogues of America to pay $500,000,000 in reparations, said money to be used for economic development and training within the African American community. Its outline of projects for funding included several publishing houses, a university, a land bank, Black-controlled television networks, and seed money through which more capital could be developed. The manifesto called for Black people to disrupt the activities of the denominations, including worship services, until the demands were met.

While received with quiet approval by the IFCO, on Sunday, May 4, Forman took the proposal to New York City and interrupted the service at Riverside Church to read it. The initial disruptive act, which was followed by others, gained him nationwide attention, and the various agencies which funded IFCO began meeting to draft responses. Local churches and regional and state judicatories also gave consideration to the manifesto in their summer meetings.

The church response was largely consistent. First, most church leaders rejected the revolutionary tone and Marxist overlay of the document and many, but by no means all, rejected the idea of reparations. Second, most church leaders also saw the basic demand for assistance for the Black community was justified and they made efforts to reconsider allocations of funds to respond positively to the manifesto's demands. At the denominational level the amount of reallocated money ran into the hundreds of thousands of dollars.

Third, as a whole, while a percentage of the money was given to IFCO, the majority of it went to related projects over which the denominations had direct control. Much of the money went to fund the many African American caucus groups which had sprung into existence in all of the major denominations in 1967–68. These included the **American Baptist Black Caucus**, the **Black Council of the Reformed Church in America**, **Black Methodists for Church Renewal**, **Ministers for Racial and Social Justice**, **National Black Presbyterian Caucus**, **National Office for Black Catholics**, **Union of Black Episcopalians**, and **United Black Christians**.

Meanwhile, as the denominations were developing their response, IFCO backed away from its tacit approval of the document and noted that it had never been officially approved as an IFCO policy statement. That move left Forman's organization, the National Black Economic Development Conference, isolated. IFCO indicated that only money given to it with specific instructions to pass on to BEDC would be granted to Forman. By the summer of 1970, only slightly more than $300,000 had been given to BEDC.

While rejected in theory, the Black Manifesto had left an enduring legacy in the continued funding of African American organizations within the major denominations.

Forman, James. *The Making of Black Revolutionaries.* New York: Macmillan Company, 1972. 568 pp.

Lovelace, John A. "The Black Manifesto." *Christian Advocate* 13, 14 (July 10, 1969): 3, 21.
Wogaman, Philip. "Testing the Rhetoric of the Black Manifesto." *Christian Advocate* 13, 17 (September 4, 1969): 9–10.

BLACK METHODISTS FOR CHURCH RENEWAL (BMCR). A caucus of African American members within the **United Methodist Church**. Black Methodists for Church Renewal continues the long struggle for justice, equality, and power within the Methodist Episcopal Church (now a constituent part of the United Methodist Church) which dates to 1787 and the breakaway movement from St. George's ME Church led by **Richard Allen**, William White and **Absalom Jones**. That struggle entered a new phase in 1969.

The year 1969 was racing to a cataclysmic encounter with history. The issue had its roots in the urban crises of the 50s and 60s. Disillusionment, despair and disaffection within the Black community, indeed the whole community, had produced bad fruit in gunfire, smoke, and violence in city after city across America. A series of factors and events was sending shock waves through the church, including the restlessness of indigenous groups and adolescent gangs; police violence; rising fear of Black and White citizens in our cities; the feeling of impotence among Black leaders in the face of Black youths' challenging threats; disgracefully inadequate salaries and unimaginative and irrelevant church planning; the rise and influence of the **Nation of Islam** (Black Muslims); resistance to school desegregation; growing economic violence; political powerlessness; and the death of Dr. **Martin Luther King, Jr**.

The urban crisis was a clear challenge to Black Church leadership, a call to Black leadership for accountability, new styles of ministry and mission if we were to survive in our ghettoes, and new models of hope for community living not heretofore known.

New slogans, "Black Power," "Black Pride," etc., were strident and renewed calls to Black America to free itself from the shackles of racism, economic oppression, and violence in pursuit of freedom. This thrust led, in turn, to the birthing of the Black Caucus within the Methodist Church on December 13, 1969.

It began when Dr. Philip A. Harley, pastor of St. James United Methodist Church, Chicago, Illinois, invited several of his colleagues, Dr. **Edsel A. Ammons**, Dr. Harry Gibson, district superintendent of Western District, Dr. Maceo D. Pembroke, pastor of St. Mark United Methodist Church, and the Reverend Roy Neal to talk about these events. Each clearly understood the call to a new style of urban ministry resulting in a consensus in the reading of the signs of the times. There was also hesitancy and anxiety over the unorthodoxy of the proposed course of action.

At the time Ammons was the Black clergy serving on the Northern Illinois Conference Program Council staff. His principal task was to serve as the urban analyst to interpret and assist local churches to understand and develop an urban mission and ministry thrust. The group assembled on December 13 urged him to send out a call to all the Black clergy sisters and brothers. The clergy responded to a person. Thus began long hours of meetings, heated debates and prolonged historical and theological reflection and review. These meetings lasted well into the night. The caucus identified and heralded the arrival of a new day for the Black church. A distinct logos was proposed and a statement of identity hammered out. The group saw themselves as Black Americans first, children of God by election, United Methodists by choice, and local church persons by calling. Critical theological treatises were written, discussed, refined, until they arrived at a consensual articulation of theory and practice. The Rev. Roy Neal and Dr. John Porter were the principal writers.

Two events seem to capture this moment in the caucus' history. The first was a meeting at the home of the Western District Superintendent, Dr. Harry Gibson, Oak Park, Illinois, in the fall of 1967, where many long hours of discussion engaged the most creative efforts of the caucus. The Old Testament image of the prophet was the style adopted by the caucus. The emerging position papers became foundational statements for the Black Caucus (the yet unborn Black Methodists for Church Renewal). The second came later in this same year, 1967, in the form of the Detroit rebellion—the shootout at the Rev. **C. L. Franklin**'s New Light Baptist Church. The seriousness of the urban crisis and the necessity of a response were thrust upon sensitive Black leaders of the Methodist Church, indeed upon the whole Christian Church.

With the position papers completed and with the image of the shootout before them, over 100 Methodist pastors serving the city of Chicago attended a specially called meeting held at the Chicago Temple (First United Methodist Church). The question was raised and debated, "How shall we respond to this burgeoning urban disaster?" Subsequently, the Black Caucus engaged in marathon sessions with then Bishop Thomas M. Pryor, Dr. Merlyn Northfelt, and the Cabinet (i.e., the district superintendents of the conference) around a number of issues.

In June of 1968 Ammons left the conference Program Council staff to join the faculty of Garrett

Theological Seminary, Evanston, Illinois. His replacement by another Black person was important to the caucus as it had become one of the caucus' non-negotiable positions. The caucus advanced several candidates for the appointment, none of whom were acceptable to the bishop and cabinet. Gibson, a member of the cabinet, supported by Pembroke and Dr. Willie B. Clay, proposed Harley for the position. Members of the Black Caucus, facing a deadline and the intransigence of the Bishop and Cabinet on this point, acquiesced and Dr. Harley was appointed. This action was the first victory for the caucus in confrontation politics. So the Black Caucus prepared for the 1969 Northern Illinois Annual Conference armed with political stratagems, a sense of self-worth, and a sense that it moved "with GOD's hand on us."

At the conference, the Black Caucus, led by the Reverends Richard Lawrence and William T. Carter, engaged in negotiation defining church missional priorities to address urban crises and to extend more collegial respect, power, and recognition to the church's Black constituency. These were heady times. In Detroit, Michigan, just three months earlier, **James Forman** presented to his **Black Economic Development Conference** a "**Black Manifesto**," in which the churches of America were identified with the evil cabal of capitalism and corporate America. The church, said the manifesto, was guilty of racism and, as such, must set for the nation the example of reconciliation and reparations. The James Forman Manifesto came to the attention of the conference during this session and the conference leadership tried to interpose the Black Caucus and its demands between the imperative of a response, as a conference, to Forman's demands and the legitimate demands of its Black constituency. Speaking on behalf of the Black Caucus, the Reverends Carter and Lawrence broke off any further negotiations, thereby freeing the Northern Illinois Conference to respond to the demands "of our brother," James Forman. They urged the conference to deal with Forman with institutional integrity, while holding the caucus claims as distinct from the larger issues raised by the Black Manifesto.

The Birth of BMCR. To deal with the Black Manifesto, the Northern Illinois Annual Conference called for a special session to convene in the fall. On December 11, 1969, clergy of the Northern Illinois Conference met at the Chicago Temple to approve a $300,000 program aimed at strengthening the church's work in the Black and Hispanic communities. This proposal was received by the Black clergy and their supporters as a bold attempt to head off and co-opt the movement and initiative of the newly formed Black Caucus. Dr. Merlyn Northfelt, Program Coordinator, was the principal author of this proposal. Harley, Carter and Gibson voiced their rejection of the plan, and the caucus demanded full and complete jurisdiction of these funds and their use.

The Black Caucus was seeking empowerment within the Annual Conference, and moved on the faith and hope that the people would support it. Nothing like this had ever happened before to test the loyalty of people called Black Methodists. Were they Black people first, children of God by election, and United Methodists by choice? The atmosphere at the special session was one of excitement, bitterness and anguish. Harsh words, bitter feelings, all symbolic of the times, were spoken but the Black Caucus never lost its cool or commitment to the task. Indeed, it was in the charged, hopeful atmosphere of this meeting that in the course of the caucus's discussions the name Black Methodists for Church Renewal emerged. Meanwhile, on the national level, events were moving at a hectic pace, as other elements of the United Methodist Church which had been formed in the midst of the crisis, made an effort to respond to the Black Manifesto.

Black Methodists for Church Renewal. Black Methodists for Church Renewal, born out of the urban crisis, also emerged amid massive changes in Methodism. In 1968 the Methodist Church (1939–1968) completed its lengthy merger negotiations with the Evangelical United Brethren which led to the formation of the United Methodist Church. Also, in response to the civil rights movement, the Methodist Church (1939–1968) had made substantial steps to eliminate the all-Black Central Jurisdiction and merge the churches of its member conferences into the predominantly White geographical conferences.

In response to the **Black Manifesto** which demanded $500,000,000 from the churches for economic development within the Black community, the new United Methodist Church's Board of Missions voted an initial $300,000 to be administered by the Black members of the board and the Black United Methodist bishops. The board had turned to BMCR for advice on their actions. In response, BMCR also issued a petition to the 1970 special session of the general conference, called to complete the unfinished business of the merger. The petition listed demands which included $10.5 million dollars for BMCR, $10 million for the several predominantly Black United Methodist colleges, and a million dollar loan fund for African American students. They also asked for a 30 percent representation on all the boards and agencies of the church. At the time, Blacks made up six percent of the church's membership.

While the general conference approved only some of the demands of the BMCR petition, several of the annual conferences made a significant change in their budget and priorities by approving financial support for BMCR. Among the most prominent was the Missouri West Conference which voted approximately $500,000 to be given to that conference's unit of BMCR.

Over the succeeding years BMCR has been the principal organization serving the Black ministers and clergy of United Methodism. It has provided the platform from which Black members could address their concerns to the church as a whole and has fought to enlist the church's support for its twelve Black colleges, the strengthening of African American congregations, and the recruitment of Blacks into full-time Christian service. It regularly works for the elimination of surviving racist structures in the church's organization and life. Many Black ministers and lay people give BMCR the credit for preserving their association with the United Methodist Church through the early years of the 1970s when the pull of Black separatism was at its height. Harry V. Arichardson has also noted that as the organization matured, it was able to turn from a somewhat single-minded attention to protest toward cooperation with the church in implementing its goals.

BMCR is headed nationally by a board of directors. Most annual conferences also have local BMCR units. It publishes the *NOW Newsletter* from its headquarters in Dayton, Ohio.

Campbell, James F. "Lawson Led BMCR Sets Goals." *Christian Advocate* 14, 5 (March 5, 1970): 24.
Lovelace, John A. "Black Groups Becoming Strategic." *Christian Advocate* 13, 12 (June 12, 1969): 24.
Richardson, Harry V. *Dark Salvation.* Garden City, NY: Doubleday & Company, 1976. 324 pp.
Various working and position papers produced by the Black Caucus, Northern Illinois Conference.

Philip A. Harley

BLACKWELL, ANNIE WALKER (August 21, 1862–December 7, 1922), a missionary executive with the **African Methodist Episcopal Zion Church** (AMEZ), was born in Chester, South Carolina, the oldest daughter of Dublin Isaiah and Mathilda (Potts) Walker. Her father was a minister who, after the Civil War, associated with the AMEZ Church and became a presiding elder. Blackwell graduated from Scotia

Seminary in Concord, North Carolina, and became a schoolteacher, working variously in Statesville, Charlotte, and Chester. On December 7, 1887, she married a minister in the church, **George Lincoln Blackwell**, who later became a bishop. Together they had two children, both of whom died.

Both Blackwell and her husband were mission-minded, and she channelled most of her considerable energies into the Woman's Home and Foreign Missionary Society (W.H.F.M.S.) of the AMEZ Church. In 1902 she was named assistant corresponding secretary of the W.H.F.M.S., as well as editor of the women's column in the *Star of Zion*, the major denominational journal. She later became associate editor of the *Missionary Seer*. The W.H.F.M.S. had labored slowly since its inception in 1880, and suffered from a general lack of membership and enthusiasm. Blackwell reported to the bishops in 1904 her prescription for a new start. She urged that the society be removed from the interference of local pastors and the hierarchy, making it completely controlled by the women, and that it be given full authority as the women's auxiliary of the Mission Board of the church. At the 1904 General Conference, her position was supported by her election as corresponding secretary of the W.H.F.M.S., and by the election of her husband as a bishop. Under her leadership (the corresponding secretary position in this organization having more impact than that of president) the W.H.F.M.S. grew significantly, gaining chapters in most local churches. She is credited with implementing the idea of life memberships and Life Matrons as a means of gaining commitment and money for the missions of the church, and the first Life Member was enrolled in 1906. In 1907 friends contributed enough to make her the gift of a life membership in the W.H.F.M.S. She and Victoria Richardson then turned their attention to organizing the Young Woman's Society, a missionary organization for the younger church members.

Her executive competence and oratorical abilities made her a very popular figure, and she was reelected to her office in every succeeding General Conference until her death, a span of eighteen years. She was editor for four years of the *Women's Christian Temperance Union Tidings*, and was president of the Staff Auxiliary of Douglass Hospital in Philadelphia. She was a delegate to the Methodist Ecumenical Conference in Toronto, Canada, in 1911, and Governor John K. Tener appointed her a delegate to the National Civic Movement Convention in Kansas City, Missouri, in 1914. Her life upheld her motto, which was, "Keep everlastingly at it." She died suddenly on her thirty-fifth wedding anniversary, while at home in Philadelphia tending to her ailing husband.

AMEZC, HAMEZC, OHYAMEZC, RLOA, WWCR.

BLACKWELL, GEORGE LINCOLN (July 3, 1861–March 20, 1926), 32nd bishop in the **African Methodist Episcopal Zion Church** (AMEZ), was born into slavery in Henderson, North Carolina, one of eleven children born to Hailey and Catherine (Wyche) Blackwell. In part, because of the size of his family, he went to live with relatives in Granville County, near Oxford, North Carolina. He was converted in 1876, at the age of fifteen, and joined the Union AMEZ Church. He became an active member and quickly assumed a leadership role in the congregation. As his involvement increased, he decided to enter the ministry.

In 1880 he was licensed to preach, and joined the North Carolina Conference in 1881. He was then assigned the Morehead City circuit, where he built a church. The following year he was relieved of his pastoral duties in order to attend Livingston College, though in 1883 he took an assignment to the Manchester circuit to earn tuition money. He maintained this assignment for over a year, traveling fortnightly a distance of almost two hundred miles to reach the circuit. He was ordained deacon on February 18, 1884, and at the Annual Conference again gave up preaching to devote more time to his studies. He was ordained elder on February 22, 1885, and in May was assigned to Moore's Chapel in Lincolnton. In 1886 he went to Mt. Pleasant (Center Street) in Statesville, North Carolina, while still attending college. He married Anne E. Walker on December 7, 1887, and graduated with his A.B. degree, with honors, in 1888.

He then transferred to the New England Conference and served in Bridgeport, Connecticut (1888–89) and Cambridgeport, Massachusetts (1889–91). In 1889 he entered Boston University School of Theology, graduating with the S.T.B. degree in 1892. Meanwhile, in May, 1891, he was assigned to the North Russell Street AMEZ Church in Boston. After graduation he was assigned to the Big Wesley AMEZ Church in Philadelphia. In 1893 he became Dean of the Theological Department at Livingstone College, remaining until 1896. In 1893 he published his first book, *The Model Homestead; Three Pointed, Practical and Picturesque Sermons on the Parable of the Prodigal Son*. In 1896 he moved to Charlotte, North Carolina, as the editor of Sunday School literature and general agent for and manager of the AMEZ Publishing House. In

1900 he was promoted to General Secretary of that enterprise, and in 1904 became Missionary Secretary of the denomination. He was elected bishop at the General Conference in 1908, and was consecrated on May 20, 1908.

As bishop, he is credited with significantly advancing the work of the church, being skilled in preaching, administrating, and publicizing alike. Evangelism was a priority for him, and he edited the *Missionary Seer* beginning in 1904. He was a delegate to the Ecumenical Methodist Conference in London in 1901, and again in Toronto in 1911. He was a trustee of Livingstone College. He enjoyed writing and literature, and was a member of the International Longfellow Society. After his first book, he published two others, *Cloaks of Sin* (1904) and *Man Wanted* (1907). After eighteen years in the episcopacy, overseeing the Second Episcopal District (composed of Albemarle, Allegheny, and Virginia Conferences), he died at his home in Philadelphia.

Blackwell, George Lincoln. *Cloaks of Sin*. N.p., 1904.
———. *Man Wanted*. N.p., 1907.
———. *The Model Homestead; Three Pointed, Practical and Picturesque Sermons on the Parable of the Prodigal Son*. Boston: Marshall Printers, 1893. 76 pp.
"New Era of Zion Methodism." *Star of Zion* 48 (August 7, 1924): 1, 5.
"Rev. G. L. Blackwell, A.B., S.T.B." *Star of Zion* 50 (March 25, 1926): 1, 5.
AMEZC, WWCR, HAMEZC, AARS, HUBA, BAW, IBAW, IBSP.

BLAKE, CHARLES EDWARD (b. August 5, 1940) nationally known **Church of God in Christ** pastor and bishop, was born in North Little Rock, Arkansas, the son of Lula Mae Champion and Junious Augustus Blake. He preached his first sermon on July 25, 1956, at the age of sixteen, and early on seemed headed for a career in the ministry. He received his B.A. in 1962 from California Western University (United States International University) in San Diego, California, and that year was ordained a minister in the Church of God in Christ. On July 11, 1964, he married Mae Lawrence, with whom he had three children. He received his M.Div. in 1965 from the Interdenominational Theological Center in Atlanta, Georgia, and later pursued graduate studies at the Claremont Graduate School in Claremont, California, and Fuller Theological Seminary, in Pasadena, California.

From 1962 to 1963 he was co-pastor of the Greater Jackson Memorial Church of God in Christ in San Diego. In 1963–64 he was pastor of the Marietta Church of God in Christ in Marietta, Georgia. He was very active in the crisis which hit the Church of God in Christ in 1965 following the death of **Charles H. Mason**, the church's founder. From 1965 to 1970 he was vice-president of the Publication Board and chair of the Christian Education Board, Youth Department. From 1966 to 1971 he was editor of youth literature for the denomination. From 1969 to the present he has been pastor of the West Angeles Church of God in Christ in Los Angeles, California.

Over the years Blake has become a powerful force within the denomination, holding a number of influential positions. Since 1971 he has been a trustee of both the Interdenominational Theological Center and the Charles Harrison Mason Theological Seminary, both in Atlanta, Georgia. Since 1973 he has been superintendent of the Southern California Jurisdiction of the Church of God in Christ, and since 1975 has served as special aide to the Chair of the General Assembly of the Church of God in Christ. He has been chair of the Social and Political Concerns Committee and the Institute Committee, both in the Church of God in Christ Jurisdiction of Southern California. He has written a number of books and pamphlets, including *The Church of God in Christ: Its Organizational Crisis* (1965) and *Hope and Help for the Homosexual*. He is widely known as an outstanding orator, and as his congregation has grown he has been in great demand as a preacher and lecturer around the country. In 1984 *Ebony* magazine named him one of America's best Black preachers. In 1985 he was named bishop of the Southern California jurisdiction of the church.

"America's Fifteen Greatest Black Preachers." *Ebony* 39 (September 1984): 27–33.
Blake, Charles E. *The Church of God in Christ: Its Organizational Crisis*. N.p.: 1965. 20 pp.
WWR (75–76), *BH*.

BLAKELY, GEORGE WAYMAN (August 30, 1905– c. August, 1972), a bishop of the **African Methodist Episcopal Church** (AME), was born in Ashley County, Arkansas, the son of Richard and Alice Blakely. He attended the public schools in Ashley County, and became a full member of Pleasant Grove AME Church in Thebes, Arkansas, at the age of twelve. He was licensed to preach in Bethel AME Church in North Little Rock, Arkansas, in 1918, where he attended Shorter College. He was admitted to the South Arkansas Annual

Conference in Warren in November, 1919. He married Annie Marion King on June 26, 1922, with whom he had no children. He was ordained a deacon in October, 1923, in Kansas City, Missouri, and was assigned to the Turner Mission AME Church in Kansas City while still attending school. He was ordained elder in September, 1925, in Pueblo, Colorado, by Bishop **A. J. Carey, Sr**. He received his B.A. from Western University in Quindaro, Kansas in 1924, and spent 1925 pastoring at the Mt. Olive AME Church in Sheridan, Wyoming. There he raised money to remodel the parsonage. In 1926 he went on to Iliff School of Theology in Denver, Colorado, where he received his B.D. in 1928, while pastoring at the Ward Mission in Denver.

After graduation from seminary Blakely was assigned to the Ward Chapel AME Church in Junction City, Kansas, where he stayed only a year, followed by one year at Bethel AME Church in Leavenworth, Kansas, and one year at St. John AME Church in Pine Bluff, Arkansas. In the first two of these stops he paid up mortgages and improved the parsonages. At St. John's he repaired the church and built a new, brick parsonage. From 1931 to 1935 he was at Visitor's Chapel AME Church in Hot Springs, Arkansas, where he repurchased the church after it was sold out of the connection. He then managed to pay off the bills for the organ, the new furniture for the parsonage, and complete remodeling the church basement. The following year he was presiding elder of the Monticello District.

From 1936 to 1937 he pastored Carter Chapel AME Church in Helena, Montana, where he bought new pews and renovated the parsonage. He was presiding elder of the Pine Bluff District in 1937–1938 and of the Little Rock District in 1938–1939. From 1939 to 1953 he pastored Big Bethel AME Church in Little Rock, Arkansas, where he paid the $21,000 principal debt in only four years. He remodeled the church basement and kitchen, installed rooms for recreation and education, placed a neon sign and cross above the church, put on a new roof, and remodeled the parsonage. His first wife died on March 13, 1943, and he married Vera Corrine Doyle in 1945, with whom he had two children. He was a delegate to the first meeting of the World Council of Churches in Amsterdam in 1948. He was vice-president of the Arkansas Branch of the **National Fraternal Council of Negro Churches** and was on the executive committee of the Urban League. He became one of the first Black members of a grand jury in Pulaski County, Arkansas, since Reconstruction, and was one of the first Black members of the State Central Committee of the Republican Party.

In 1953 Blakely was assigned to St. Paul AME Church in St. Louis, Missouri, where his reputation continued to grow. In 1962 he was a delegate to the World Methodist Ecumenical Council in Oslo, Norway. At the General Conference in Cincinnati, Ohio, in 1964 he was elected bishop. He was consecrated on May 17, 1964, and assigned to the 16th Episcopal District (Caribbean-South America area), maintaining his residence in St. Louis. He was retired for health reasons in 1972.

EAMEC, BDNM (70), *EBA, EWM, HAMEC.*

BLYDEN, EDWARD WILMOT (August 3, 1832–February 7, 1912), author, educator, diplomat, and Presbyterian minister, was born in St. Thomas, Virgin Islands, Danish West Indies, where most Blacks were still slaves. His free parents were from the Ibo tribe and were members of the Dutch Reformed Church. His mother, Judith, was a schoolteacher and his father, Romeo, a tailor. Blyden attended primary school in Charlotte Amalie, the capital. In 1842 the family moved to Porto Bello, Venezuela, for two years. Upon return to St. Thomas his sizable intellect and powers came to the attention of Rev. John P. Knox, the White American pastor of the Dutch Reformed Church in Charlotte Amalie. Blyden, under his tutelage, decided to become a minister and to pursue college training in the United States.

In May, 1850, Blyden went to the United States but was refused admission in several theological seminaries because of his color. The New York Colonization Society, however, paid his way in 1851 to Liberia, Africa, where he was able to enroll in the new Alexander High School, a Presbyterian institution in the capital city of Monrovia. That year he became editor of the *Liberia Herald*. In 1856 he published the first of many pamphlets, *A Voice from Bleeding Africa*, which attacked slavery and emphasized the capabilities of Black people. The introduction to his second pamphlet, *A Vindication of the African Race* (1857) was written by **Alexander Crummell**, the well-known Black Episcopal priest who was in Liberia at the time as a missionary. Blyden was soon recognized as a major Pan-African theorist/spokesperson.

In 1856 he married Sarah Yates, from a wealthy mulatto family (ironic considering his later feelings about mulattoes), with whom he had three children. He became disenchanted with the marriage, and about 1876, without getting a divorce, began a well-known intimate relationship with Anna Erskine, a schoolteacher from Louisiana. When he later advocated polygamy as a natural expression of African personality and culture, many denounced him for attempting merely to rationalize his own personal behavior.

In 1858 Blyden was ordained a Presbyterian minister and named principal of Alexander High School. In the spring and summer of 1861 he traveled to England and the United States seeking support for Liberian education. In 1861 and again in 1880 he was the Liberian Commissioner to the General Assembly of the American Presbyterian Church. Although Blyden held no college degree, he had a thorough mastery of Latin and Greek (and other languages) and became in 1862 Professor of Classics at Liberia College, holding that position until 1871. For part of this time, from 1864 to 1866, he was also Secretary of State, and in that role tried unsuccessfully to end the border dispute with Sierra Leone and with somewhat more success to attract American emigrants. He felt that American Blacks would have more success seeking freedom in Africa than in the United States. In an effort to make the college more relevant to Africa's Muslim population, he studied Arabic and in 1867 added it to the curriculum. During the 1860s he attacked the mulatto ruling elite as bigoted and unpatriotic, and began to lead a Black faction in opposition. He came to hold the controversial position that mulattoes did not belong in the Black race. In May 1871 he barely escaped being lynched by his political enemies and spent the next two years in Sierra Leone.

In Sierra Leone he continued his normal high level of activity. He founded and edited the *Negro* (1872–74), a weekly newspaper which championed a cultural nationalism. He called for African control of institutions, the establishment of a nonsectarian African Christian Church, and a secular, independent African University. He wanted Great Britain to be constructive in its African presence, and to counter the effects of its rulership as a colonial power, and urged it to help build in Sierra Leone a real national infrastructure. He returned to Liberia in October 1873 and from 1875 to 1877 was once again principal of Alexander High School.

In 1877 he was appointed by President James Payne as Liberia's ambassador to Britain, the first ambassador to that country in Liberia's history. For the next two years he spent much of his time in London working on, among other things, ending the border dispute with Sierra Leone and obtaining investments for a railroad into Liberia's interior; in neither venture was he successful. He was, however, tremendously successful in social circles. He was the toast of every elite group, being well-known for his writings, humanitarian stances, and wit. He saw himself as working on behalf of Black people everywhere, seeking to create in Liberia, the only

independent nation in Africa besides Ethiopia, a new start.

In January 1880 he was offered the presidency of Liberia College, a position he eagerly accepted. He wanted to remake the curriculum to stress relevance to African culture, history, and agriculture. For a variety of reasons, including too many other projects (he was Minister of the Interior from 1880 to 1882) and too many long trips to America, this agenda did not become reality and the college dismissed him in 1884. In 1885 he was a candidate for the presidency of the republic, but lost to the incumbent, Hilary W. Johnson.

For the rest of his life Blyden lived mostly in Sierra Leone. He was employed in Liberia a few more times for short periods, as ambassador to Britain (five months in 1892), as professor at Liberia College (fourteen months in 1900–01), and as ambassador to Britain and France (five months in 1905). In 1886 he relinquished his credentials as a Presbyterian minister and declared himself to be a nonsectarian representative of Christ, a "Minister of Truth." In 1887 his major book, *Christianity, Islam, and the Negro Race* was published, and he lived largely off the income from his writings, lectures, and private tutoring. In December 1890 he was called to Lagos to settle a dispute with the Church Missionary Society, which had taken over work on the Niger Mission and had dismissed the Black religious workers and condemned their previous efforts. Blyden recommended the establishment of a nonsectarian African church in order to avoid similar conflicts. This did not happen, but Blyden's influence did lead to the establishment in Lagos of the United Native African Church in August 1891.

In 1896–97 Blyden was agent for Native Affairs for Lagos, and in this capacity opened a government school for Muslim youth. His longstanding interest in Islam began to take a greater role in his life. He saw Islam as a very positive force in Africa, with a history of making no differentiations on the grounds of color. He felt that it transcended national barriers in Africa with less cultural disruption than Christianity, and encouraged learning and scholarship. From 1901 to 1906 Blyden was director of Muslim education in Sierra Leone, and in his last years he spent much of his time privately teaching Muslim youth English and other topics. He never became a Muslim himself, but rather saw his role as a bridge between Christians and Muslims. African Muslims held him in high esteem and allowed him some latitude in this role. One of his last publications was a pamphlet called *African Life and Customs* (1908), which has been judged "the first important attempt at sociological analysis of African society as a whole."

Blyden was a major figure of his time on many levels—political, religious, cultural. In Africa he was called "the highest intellectual representative and the greatest defender and uplifter of the African race." About six hundred of his letters to more than fifty individuals and institutions in many countries survive, and constitute an invaluable research source for a time and region that tend to lack good documentation. Although he did not live in the United States, he visited it at least eight times and had a significant impact upon many American leaders. Because of his connection with the American Colonization Society (a group supported by many Southern slaveholders) and his anti-mulatto bias, many American Blacks distrusted him. This was generally overcome, however, by respect for his scholarly defense of Blacks everywhere and for the ease with which he moved among world leaders. His critique of Christianity in America as perverted and used to degrade and enslave Blacks was a catalyst for greater theological reflection.

Benjamin, George J. *Edward W. Blyden: Messiah of Black Revolution.* New York: Vantage Press, 1979. 92 pp.

Blyden, Edward Wilmot. *African Life and Customs.* London: C. M. Phillips, 1908. 91 pp.

———. *The African Problem, and Other Discourses Delivered in America in 1890.* London: W. B. Whittingham, 1890. 104 pp.

———. *Africa's Offering; Being Addresses, Sermons, etc., by Edward W. Blyden.* New York: J. A. Gray, 1862. 167 pp.

———. *Christianity, Islam, and the Negro Race.* 1888; Rept.: Edinburgh: University Press, 1967. 423 pp.

———. *From West Africa to Palestine.* Freetown, Sierra Leone: T. J. Sawyer, 1873. 201 pp.

Hargreaves, J. D. "Blyden of Liberia." *History Today* 19 (August 1969): 568–573.

Jones, Wilbur Devereux. "Blyden, Gladstone, and the War." *Journal of Negro History* 49 (January 1964): 56–61.

Holden, Edith. *Blyden of Liberia.* New York: Vantage Press, 1966. 1040 pp.

Lynch, Hollis R., ed. *Black Spokesman: Selected Published Writings of Edward Wilmot Blyden.* New York: Humanities Press, 1971. 354 pp.

———. *Edward Wilmot Blyden: Pan-Negro Patriot, 1832–1912.* London: Oxford University Press, 1967. 272 pp.

———. "Edward W. Blyden: Pioneer West African Nationalist." *Journal of African History* 6 (1965): 373–388.

———, ed. *Selected Letters of Edward Wilmot Blyden.* New York: Kraus-Thomson Organization Press, 1978. 530 pp.

HNB, AAE, ACAB, NYTO, NAH, MBRL, MM, DANB, IBAW, IBAWCB, AARS, HUBA.

BODDIE, CHARLES EMERSON (b. June 13, 1911), prominent minister of the **American Baptist Churches in the U.S.A.** and seminary president, was born in New Rochelle, New York, the son of Jacob Benjamin and Mary Gertrude (Smith) Boddie. His father was a well-known Baptist preacher. He was ordained a Baptist minister in 1932 and in 1933 received his B.A. from Syracuse University in New York. He then went to Colgate Rochester Divinity School, where he received his B.D. in 1936. On September 9, 1935, he married Mary Lavinia Johnson, with whom he had two children.

He served pastorates in Elmira, New York, from 1935 to 1939, followed by Huntington, West Virginia (1939–42) and Rochester, New York (1942–56). While in Rochester he continued his education, receiving an M.A. in 1949 from the University of Rochester. In 1951 he received a D.D. from Keuka College in Keuka Park, New York. From 1956 to 1961 he was a staff member in the missionary personnel department of the American Baptist Foreign Mission Society, and in this position toured all over the world, inspecting mission stations. From 1961 to 1963 he served as secretary of the public relations department. In 1963 he accepted the position of president of the American Baptist Theological Seminary in Nashville, Tennessee, where he remained until retirement in June 1980.

In 1965 he was Lane Lecturer at New Orleans Baptist Theological Seminary and in 1968 he was the Faulkner Lecturer at Tennessee State University. He was widely sought as a speaker at schools, camps, and chautauquas. He was a member of the Board of Education and Publication of the American Baptist Convention. In 1970 he was briefly a part of the Southern Baptist Convention's African Baptist Evangelistic Campaigns, through which he toured Africa. His first wife having passed away, he married Mabel Bell Crooks on July 4, 1970. She brought with her two daughters from a previous marriage. In 1974 he became a member of the board of directors of the National Conference of Christians and Jews. He authored two books, *Giant in the Earth* (1944), about his father, and *God's Bad Boys* (1972), composed of biographical sketches of prominent Black Baptist ministers.

Boddie, Charles Emerson. *Giant in the Earth: A Biography.* Berne, IN: Berne Witness Co., 1944.

———. *God's "Bad Boys."* Valley Forge, PA: Judson Press, 1972. 125 pp.

CA (65–68), *AARS, HUBA, IBAWCB, WWR* (75–76).

BODDIE, JAMES TIMOTHY (September 16, 1900– November 22, 1963), a leading Baptist preacher, was born in Darby, Pennsylvania, the youngest of five children in the family of Jacob Benjamin and Martha (Branch) Boddie. Only two of those children survived past infancy. At the age of two, Boddie was in danger of dying from whooping cough, but was healed by a visit from Prophet Andrew Jones, a friend of the family. Boddie's mother passed away shortly afterwards and his father later married Mary Gertrude Smith. His father was a Baptist minister, said to have been one of the best preachers of his day. After attending New Rochelle High School in New Rochelle, New York, Boddie soon felt the call to follow in his father's footsteps.

After holding jobs for a time in the post office and a laundry, he was ready to begin in the ministry. His first official sermon was so impressive that he was both licensed to preach and ordained a minister on the same day in 1918, perhaps the first time such a thing had happened in the history of Black Baptists. The home church where his father preached, Bethesda Baptist Church of New Rochelle, sent him to Virginia Seminary and College in Lynchburg, Virginia. While there in 1923 he was assistant pastor at Second Calvary Baptist Church in Norfolk, Virginia. For a short time in 1924 he was assistant pastor at Bethesda Baptist Church in New Rochelle, New York, and from 1924 to 1926 he was pastor of the Forest Level Baptist Church in Forest, Virginia. He received his B.A. in 1925 from Virginia Theological Seminary and then enrolled at Rochester Theological Seminary in New York, where he was president of the student body. He graduated with his B.D. in 1928.

From 1927 to 1929 he pastored the Union Baptist Church in Lackawanna, New York. On June 24, 1928 the married Emery M. Moore, with whom he had four children. From 1929 until 1939 he pastored the Union Baptist Church in Baltimore, Maryland, where he carried out an extensive program of community service. In 1931, during the Depression, the church fed and clothed over 5,000 people. For three years, from 1939 to 1942, he was pastor of the Mount Zion Baptist Church in Philadelphia, Pennsylvania. Then he accepted the pastorate of the New Shiloh Baptist Church in Baltimore, where he remained for twenty-one years until his death.

This was an extremely large and vigorous church, where his considerable powers of preaching and organization could have full range. Although for much of his career he was associated with the **National Baptist Convention, U.S.A., Inc.**, and even served for a time as a national-level officer and on the state level as president, the internal strife led him to break

completely from convention alliance. After a while he returned to those wider connections, only this time with the mostly White American Baptist Convention (A.B.C), with which a well-known half-brother, Charles Emerson Boddie, was associated. He was active in the formation of the Caucus of the A.B.C. representing the **American Baptist Churches in the U.S.A.**, in the South.

This association with the A.B.C. represented another change he made over the years. For much of his life he was so angry at the injustices done by White people that this awareness was "dangerously close to making him an anglophobe." His experiences at Rochester Theological Seminary helped ease some of that, but it took many years after that to slowly work through his feelings to a point of greater discernment. Only then was he able to consider associating with the A.B.C. His reputation among both Whites and Blacks was such that he was in constant demand around the country as a preacher and lecturer. In 1954 he was a delegate to the Baptist World Alliance meeting in London. Eventually, his grueling schedule and diabetes got the best of him, and at his funeral were many of the leading citizens of the state.

GBB, WWCA (38–40).

BONNER, ISAIAH HAMILTON (July 27, 1890– September 5, 1979), 68th bishop of the **African Methodist Episcopal Church** (AME), was born in Camden, Alabama, the son of Richard and Priscilla Bonner. While growing up he attended the Camden Academy and the Miller's Ferry Normal and Industrial School. He was very active in his local AME church, serving in most of its available offices. He was licensed to preach at Bethel AME Church in Knoxville, Tennessee, in May, 1910, and joined the East Tennessee Annual Conference in 1911. He received his B.A. in 1912 from Knoxville College, and his B.D. from the same school in 1914. He was ordained deacon in 1913 and elder in 1920. He married Nannie Jones, with whom he had three children.

His first pastorate was at the AME church in South Pittsburg, Tennessee, from 1913 to 1914. His next known pastorate was at the eight-member Chicasaw Mission in 1919–20. From 1921 to 1923 he pastored Quinn Chapel AME Church in Uniontown, Alabama (163 members), followed by Metropolitan AME Church in Mobile, Alabama, in 1924–25 (202 members); Cherry Street AME Church in Dothan, Alabama, from 1926 to 1929 (360 members); St. John AME Church in Montgomery, Alabama, from 1929 to 1936 (1038 members); presiding elder of the Montgomery District in 1937; Brown Chapel AME Church in Selma, Alabama, in 1938–39 (721 members); and Bethel AME Church in Mobile, Alabama, from 1940 to 1948 (1,115 members).

He was in the ministry for seven years before he had a self-supporting church, and survived only by teaching school. His ministries were very successful, paying off mortgages at many of the churches, taking in 765 members overall, and counting 230 conversions. He was on the financial board of the denomination from 1930 to 1936. In 1948 he was elected bishop and was assigned to the Fifteenth Episcopal District, adding the Seventeenth District in June, 1948. Both were in Africa, and he supervised the building of seventeen churches in those districts, as well as Bonner Hall at Wilberforce Institute in the Transvaal. From 1952 to 1960 he was assigned to the Seventh District (South Carolina), and from 1960 to 1968 he headed the Ninth District (Alabama). From 1968 to 1976 he was assigned to the Eighth District (Louisiana), retiring in 1976.

For many years Bonner was chair of the board of trustees of Daniel Payne College in Birmingham, Alabama, where he built Bonner-Gaston Hall. During his tenure the college was admitted into full membership in the Southern Association of Colleges in 1957, the first AME college to achieve that distinction. He was also chair of the board of trustees of Allen University in Columbia, South Carolina, from 1956 to 1960. He chaired the Missionary Board of the denomination from 1952 to 1956. In 1958 he was part of a five-member delegation that went to South Africa to celebrate the 60th anniversary of the establishment of the AME Church there. He was active in Montgomery's Civic League, and was president of Alabama's State Interdenominational Alliance for three years. In 1960 he was secretary of the Bishops' Council, and in 1961–62 was its president. He was the first native Alabamian to be president of the Bishops' Council. There are several churches named for him in South Africa and one in Bessemer, Alabama.

EWM, HAMEC, OTSB, BDNM, BAMEC.

BONNER, WILLIAM LEE (b. 1929?), presiding bishop of the **Church of Our Lord Jesus Christ of the Apostolic Faith,** was born in Boldwen County, Georgia, one of five children of Emmett and Janie Bonner. As a teenager he moved to New York City. He associated with the Church of our Lord Jesus Christ of the Apostolic Faith and was ordained by **R. C. Lawson,** its presiding bishop. He also married Ethel Mae Smith,

Lawson's secretary. Lawson named Bonner junior pastor of the headquarters church in New York. He also served as chauffeur for Bishop Lawson. Then in 1945 he was replaced as junior pastor by Maurice Hunter and assigned as pastor of the Green Avenue Church of Our Lord Jesus Christ in Brooklyn, New York. He was thus not part of the staff when the new headquarters complex was opened that year. He later noted that at the time he received a revelation from God that he would be presiding bishop one day. In 1947 he was sent to Detroit as pastor of the denomination's lead church in the state.

Ten years later, Bonner faced the issues raised by a group of church leaders, most notably **Smallwood Williams,** who complained that Lawson's leadership had become too dictatorial and that he had not increased the number of bishops as the church had grown and expanded. As Lawson stood firm, the group left to found the **Bible Way Church of Our Lord Jesus Christ World Wide.** Bonner remained loyal to Lawson. Three years later Lawson died and was succeeded by **Hubert Spencer.** Bonner became pastor of the headquarters church in New York City. Spencer died after only three years in office. Following a brief period of transition, Bonner was named the third presiding bishop of the Church.

As presiding bishop Bonner has initiated several firsts. He instituted a retirement pension program for aged ministers, the first such program among Apostolic churches. He also began a missionary program to establish at least one congregation in every state. To accomplish that goal, he has diverted denominational money to support home missionaries. Previously, the support of such pioneers was born by themselves. Under his direction the church has resumed its growth which was stalled at the time of the Bible Way defection.

Richardson, James C., Jr. *With Water and Spirit: A History of Black Apostolic Denominations in the U.S.* Winston-Salem, NC: The Author, 1980. 151 pp.

BOONE, THEODORE SYLVESTER (b. December 28, 1896), prominent Baptist minister and author, was born in Winchester, Texas, the son of Alexander Lorenzo and Ida (Chaney) Boone. He attended Terrell High School in Terrell, Texas, and for one year (1915) was at Prairie View College in Prairie View, Texas. From 1915 to 1918 he attended Bishop College in Marshall, Texas, then received his B.A. in 1918 from Des Moines College in Des Moines, Iowa. From 1918 to 1920 he attended the University of Iowa at Iowa City, and received his LL.B. in 1922 from the Chicago Law

School in Illinois. On December 27, 1921, he married Ruby Beatrice Alexander. He practiced law in Indianapolis, Indiana from 1922 to 1924 and received his M.A. in 1924 from Arkansas Baptist College in Little Rock, Arkansas.

His first pastorate was at the 8th Street Baptist Church in Temple, Texas, from 1924 to 1931. In 1924 he became editor-chief of the *Western Star*, the periodical of the Baptist Missionary and Education Convention in Texas. He also edited that organization's Women's Auxiliary periodical, *Open Door*. From 1931 to 1936 he pastored Mt. Gilead Baptist Church in Fort Worth, followed by the Greater Mt. Gilead Baptist Church from 1936 to 1944. In 1933 he received the Most Famous Negro Citizen Award of Fort Worth. He edited the *Fort Worth Light*. From 1938 to 1945 he was a lecturer at Bishop College. In 1944 he became the pastor of the well-known King Solomon Missionary Baptist Church in Detroit, Michigan, where he remained for the rest of his career. From 1939 to 1953 he was director of the Historical Commission and was historiographer of the **National Baptist Convention, U.S.A., Inc.** He authored several major books, including *The Philosophy of Booker T. Washington* (1939), *A Social History of Negro Baptists* (1952), and *The Negro Baptist in Pictures and History; A Negro Baptist Historical Handbook* (1964).

Boone, Theodore S. *Loyalty Unparalleled and Sacrifice Unstinted; Brother Branham with Dr. Williams.* Detroit, MI: N.p., 1948. 70 pp.

———. *Negro Baptist Chief Executives in National Places.* Detroit, MI: N.p., 1948. 70 pp.

———. *The Negro Baptist in Pictures and History; A Negro Baptist Historical Handbook.* Detroit, MI: Voice of Destiny, 1964. 54 pp.

———. *"Old Chief," Alexander Lorenza Boone, D.D., LL.D.; A Biography by His Son, Theodore Sylvester Boone.* Houston, TX: The Western Star Publishing Co., 1927. 64 pp.

———. *The Philosophy of Booker T. Washington.* Fort Worth, TX: Manney Printing Co., 1939. 311 pp.

———. *A Social History of Negro Baptists.* Detroit, MI: Historical Commission, National Baptist Convention, U.S.A., 1952. 98 pp.

HUBA, BAW, AARS, WWCA (38–40), *EBA, BDNM* (70).

BOOTH, LAVAUGHN VENCHAEL

BOOTH, LAVAUGHN VENCHAEL (b. January 7, 1919), organizer, first vice-president and later president of the **Progressive National Baptist Convention**, was born in Collins, Mississippi, the son of Frederick Douglas and Mamie (Powell) Booth. He earned his B.A. in 1940 from Alcorn A & M College in Mississippi, his B.D. in 1943 from Howard University in Washington, D.C., and an M.A. in 1945 from the University of Chicago Divinity School. On June 3, 1943 he married Georgia Anna Morris, with whom he had five children.

His first pastorate was at the First Baptist Church in Warrenton, Virginia (1942–43), followed by the First Baptist Church in Gary, Indiana (1944–52), and Zion Baptist Church in Cincinnati, Ohio (1952–84). Over the years he became one of a group of Baptist clergy unhappy with the **National Baptist Convention, U.S.A., Inc.** Its president, **Joseph H. Jackson**, had overseen a rules change in 1957 to allow for an unlimited number of successive terms in office, which offended a number of people. He also supported a conservative policy of "gradualism" in relation to the achievement of civil rights, which went against the grain of many of the more activist clergy.

In 1961 Booth was the leading organizer of a breakaway organization, the Progressive National Baptist Convention, U.S.A., Inc., which advocated strong support for the civil rights movement and a democratic election of officers with limited tenure. Its initial organizational meeting was held on November 14–15, 1961, at his Zion Baptist Church in Cincinnati, Ohio. Among the two dozen or so of the founding clergy members was **Martin Luther King, Jr.** The first president of the new organization was T. M. Chambers and Booth was the first vice-president, serving in that position until 1969. In 1968 he accomplished another first as the first Black trustee of the University of Cincinnati.

From 1970 to 1975 he was a vice-president of the Baptist World Alliance and at the same time, 1971 to 1974, he was president of the Progressive National Baptist Convention. In 1972 he founded Martin Luther King Sunday and in 1974 he organized and then chaired the Cincinnati Black Bank. He is a member of the board of directors of the Martin Luther King Jr. Center and is a member of the board of management of the American Bible Society. In 1978 he published a book-length tribute to Baptist leader **Lacey Kirk Williams**. In 1984 he founded and has since pastored the Olivet Baptist Church of Silverton, Ohio.

Booth, L. V. *"Crowned with Glory and Honor": The Life of Rev. Lacey Kirk Williams.* Hicksville, NY: Exposition Press, 1978. 246 pp.

———. *Who's Who in Baptist America.* Cincinnati, OH: Western Printing Co., 1960.

BDNM (75), HBB, WWABA (90–91), WWR (75), AARS, HUBA.

BORDERS, WILLIAM HOLMES (b. February 24, 1905), nationally known Baptist minister and charter member of the **Progressive National Baptist Convention**, was born in Macon, Georgia, the seventh child of James Buchanan and Leila (Birdsong) Borders. His father was the minister of Swift Creek Baptist Church, and at age eight Borders felt the call to follow in those footsteps. His mother died when he was twelve and soon his father began to have physical problems that prevented regular work. Borders got a job as substitute mail carrier at the post office and earned enough money to support the family. He also saved enough to get him into college, and he enrolled at Morehouse College in Atlanta, Georgia. He was so poor by his third year, despite working at many jobs outside class, that he could not pay tuition and was told to leave the campus. He kept attending classes, however, and Dr. Samuel Archer, the dean of men, respected his persistence and quietly helped him. When he had completed all his requirements Dr. Archer helped convince the president, Dr. John Hope, to let him graduate on the promise he would pay back what was owed the school. He thus earned his B.A. in 1929. He then got a scholarship to Garrett Biblical Institute (now Garrett Theological Seminary) in Evanston, Illinois, where he was introduced to the "Social Gospel" and learned new ways of thinking theologically. He married Julia Pate on January 1, 1931, with whom he had two children. He earned a B.D. from Garrett in 1932, and then earned an M.A. in 1936 from the University of Chicago.

While in seminary he took his first pastorate at the Second Baptist Church in Evanston. In 1937, while working on his doctorate, he was offered the position of professor at Morehouse College (variously teaching courses in ethics, Bible, and philosophy of religion), and decided to take it as a means of exiting from the Second Baptist Church, where things were not going well. Once back in Atlanta he was an occasional guest preacher at the nearby Wheat Street Baptist Church. This was a difficult time for that congregation; the church had been destroyed by fire in 1917 and after a great struggle the basement was built for a new building, but the Depression hit and no further construction was possible. On November 17, 1937, the struggling 400–member group asked Borders to be the new pastor.

In his own experience from his first pastorate, he knew the only way to connect with people as a pastor was to make religion relevant to their real needs and experiences, and he determined to serve as "my brother's keeper." He created a stir in the church by immediately advertising in the surrounding slum for people to attend church, regardless of their clothing or condition. He created another stir by making public the state of giving at the church. Soon he managed to stop a potential riot near the church where a trolley-car conductor was trying to enforce the laws forcing Blacks to use only the rear door. Word began to spread about this new pastor and attendance and giving began to rise. The church had turned a corner.

Under his direction the congregation began a comprehensive program of service in the community. With renewed confidence the building program began again. In 1939 a large steel and stone sanctuary was finished and in 1954 a religious education and community center was completed. The community center was one of the largest ever built in America by a Black congregation and together with the rest of the church occupied an entire city block. It staffed a nursery school with degree-holding teachers, offered adult education classes, meetings for Alcoholics Anonymous, and scores of other programs, all without regard to denominational affiliation. In 1956 the church founded its own credit union and soon had 715 accounts and assets over $250,000.

Borders gained a wide reputation as someone not afraid to get involved in social and political issues. In 1939 he went to the mayor of Atlanta and, as spokesman for five thousand registered Black voters, asked for a Black policeman. The request was rudely refused. Some months later, after leading a voter registration drive, he returned with the same request and a list of an additional fifteen thousand registered Black voters. The same mayor then reportedly said, "Reverend Borders, how many Negro policemen do you people want?" In 1941 Borders began a radio program in which he criticized the lack of equal police protection and civil rights. He also campaigned for decent hospital care, recreational facilities, and salaries. By the early 1950s this was the second-highest rated radio program in the city. One result of the publicity was that the church was able to open a job placement center.

In 1945 he led the movement that resulted in the hiring of Black bus drivers. In 1946, after four Blacks were lynched in Monroe, Georgia, he raised money in the church to pay for their burial and to post a $5,000 reward for information leading to the conviction of those responsible. He also pressured the town for a criminal investigation, but no one would talk. In 1954 *Ebony* magazine named Borders one of the nation's ten best Black preachers. His well-known motto was "I'm Somebody," and he had become known as "the Prophet of Wheat Street." In 1957 he chaired the committee to desegregate the bus system, and by plan was arrested with five other clergy for violating the segregation laws. This initiated the court case that eventually forced the integration of buses, and Borders was co-chair of the committee that subsequently oversaw the integration of restaurants, hotels, and other facilities. By this time the congregation counted some 5,000 members.

In 1957 he was expelled from the **National Baptist Convention, U.S.A., Inc.**, after he protested the actions of President **Joseph H. Jackson**, and in 1961 he participated in the formation of the Progressive National Baptist Convention, Inc. In 1959 Borders led the church in purchasing a 287–acre farm about twenty miles outside of Atlanta to use as a summer camp. The White neighbors did not like the prospect and hassled the church to sell the property to them. Several buildings were mysteriously burned, and finally in 1961 the church sold it for twice the original price. In 1961 he led the church in acquiring an adjoining twenty-two acre site which had been cleared by the Atlanta Housing Authority for slum renewal. Instead of the property going to someone who did not care for the previous tenants or for the neighborhood, it went to the church. On this property was built a 520–unit housing project called Wheat Street Gardens, the first of its kind in the nation, and a Black architect and Black construction firm were involved. Groundbreaking was on April 26, 1963, and on May 26, 1964, the first families moved in. In 1967 a Black-owned shopping center was added.

In 1968, after the assassination of Dr. **Martin Luther King, Jr.**, new racial tensions were in the air. A Methodist minister, Frank Roughton, suggested that the Christian Council of Metropolitan Atlanta put on a passion play, *Behold the Man*, that he had written. He further suggested renting the Atlanta Stadium for the performance and possibly casting a Black man in the role of Jesus. The council agreed that this could go a long way toward easing the tensions of the city. After much searching, Rev. Roughton chose Borders to portray Jesus. The thoroughly integrated cast numbered 500 and the choir had 2,000 voices. The play was produced in September, and was a stunning success. In 1969 Borders again broke new ground by hiring a White Methodist minister, Frank Howard, as associate pastor. Unfortunately, he was murdered by a robber in 1971. In 1972 a fourteen-story retirement center was completed by the church. In 1976 Borders published *Preaching the Gospel*, one of a number of books by his hand. He retired in 1989.

Borders, William Holmes. *Men Must Live as Brothers: Twenty Sermons Which Were First Preached in the Wheat Street Baptist Church, Atlanta.* Atlanta, GA: N.p., 1947. 243 pp.
———. *Sermons.* Philadelphia: Dorrance and Company, 1939. 90 pp.
———. *Seven Minutes at the "Mike" in the Deep South.* Atlanta, GA: B. F. Logan Press, 1943. 83 pp.
———. *Thunderbolts.* Atlanta, GA: Morris Brown College Press, 1942. 50 pp.
English, James W. *The Prophet of Wheat Street.* Published in 1967 as *Handyman of the Lord.* Elgin, IL: David C. Cook Publishing Co., 1973. 205 pp.
"God's Mighty Fortress." *Ebony* 12 (July 1956): 86–90.
"Great Negro Preachers." *Ebony* 10 (July 1954): 26–30.
"Miracle in Atlanta—A Black Christ." *Ebony* 24 (December 1968): 33–40.
Young, Henry J., ed, with contributions by Borders et al. *Preaching the Gospel.* Philadelphia, PA: Fortress Press, 1976. 89 pp.
BAW, HUBA, AARS, IBAW, IBAWCB, HBB, OTSB, EBA, WWABA (80–81), RLA, MSB.

BOWEN, JOHN WESLEY EDWARD, JR. (September 24, 1889–July 12, 1962), the ninth African American non-missionary bishop of the Methodist Episcopal Church (now a part of the **United Methodist Church**), was born in Baltimore, Maryland, the son of Ariel Serena Hedges and **John Wesley Edward Bowen, Sr.** His father was recognized by many as the preeminent Black Methodist Episcopal minister of his day, was a candidate for bishop on several occasions, and was a professor at Gammon Theological Seminary in Atlanta beginning in 1893. At the time of Bowen Jr.'s birth, however, Bowen, Sr., was pastor of the Centennial Methodist Episcopal Church in Baltimore.

Bowen Jr. was a student at the prestigious Philips Exeter Academy in New Hampshire from 1904 to 1907, then received his B.A. in 1911 from Wesleyan University in Middletown, Connecticut, and his M.A. in 1913 from Harvard University in Cambridge, Massachusetts. He taught at New Orleans College in 1913–14 and at Tuskegee Institute in Alabama in 1916–17. He was ordained deacon in the Atlanta Conference of the Methodist Episcopal Church in 1917 and taught at Walden College in Nashville (now Central Tennessee College) in 1917–18. He was ordained elder in 1918 and in 1918–19 he was a U.S. Army chaplain.

From 1919 to 1922 Bowen was field agent for the Board of Sunday Schools, and from 1922 to 1924 was on the faculty at Claflin College in Orangeburg, South Carolina. His first pastorate was in Jackson, Mississippi, from 1925 to 1929, followed by Trinity Methodist

Episcopal Church in New Orleans, Louisiana (1929–31); Shreveport, Louisiana (1931–35); and Grace Methodist Episcopal Church in New Orleans (1935–36). From 1936 to 1942 he was district superintendent of the New Orleans District, and from 1942 to 1944 he pastored the First Street Methodist Episcopal Church in New Orleans. From 1944 to 1948 he edited the *Central Christian Advocate*.

In 1939 the Methodist Episcopal Church merged with the Methodist Episcopal Church (South) and the Methodist Protestant Church to form the Methodist Church. At that time the nineteen Black conferences, regardless of location, became part of the Central Jurisdiction. Bowen was elected bishop in 1948 by the Central Jurisdiction and served the Atlantic Coast Episcopal Area until his retirement in 1960. The previous non-missionary Black bishops of the church were **Robert E. Jones** (elected 1920), **Matthew W. Clair, Sr.** (elected 1920), **Alexander Preston Shaw** (elected 1936), **William A. C. Hughes** (elected 1940), **Lorenzo H. King** (elected 1940), **Edward W. Kelly** (elected 1944), **Robert N. Brooks** (elected 1944), and **Willis J. King** (elected 1944). He visited the Holy Land and Africa in 1951 and in 1954 visited India and Pakistan. He was active in the N.A.A.C.P., the Y.M.C.A., and the Urban League. He served as a trustee of Clark College, Gammon Theological Seminary, Claflin College, and Bethune-Cookman College.

WWWA (4), *EWM*.

BOWEN, JOHN WESLEY EDWARD, SR. (December 3, 1855–July 20, 1933), a Methodist Episcopal minister and the first African American to serve as a regular professor at Gammon Theological Seminary, was born in New Orleans, Louisiana, the son of Rose Simon and Edward Bowen. His father, a successful carpenter and builder, had moved to New Orleans from Washington, D.C. When Bowen was three years old his father purchased both him and his mother out of slavery. When Bowen was thirteen he entered the preparatory department of New Orleans University, a school for Blacks newly founded by the Methodist Episcopal Church. At age seventeen he entered the university proper, and that year also experienced conversion at a Methodist revival meeting. He joined the Methodist Episcopal Church (now part of the **United Methodist Church**) and nine months later was licensed as a local preacher. He received his B.A. in 1878 with the school's first graduating class.

From 1878 to 1882 he taught Latin and Greek at Central Tennessee College (formerly Walden College). He then entered Boston University's School of Theology, where he earned his B.S.T. in 1885. During that same period (1882–85) he pastored the Revere Street Methodist Episcopal Church in Boston. He stayed on at the seminary to receive the Ph.D. in 1887, among the first Ph.D.s to be earned by a Black person in the United States. From 1885 to 1888 he pastored St. John's Methodist Episcopal Church in Newark, New Jersey. On September 14, 1886, he married Ariel Serena Hedges, with whom he had four children. In 1888–89 he pastored the Centennial Methodist Episcopal Church in Baltimore, Maryland, while also teaching church history at Morgan College in Baltimore. In that city he conducted a revival which reportedly saw 735 conversions.

From 1889 to 1892 Bowen pastored Asbury Methodist Episcopal Church in Washington, D.C., and was also professor of Hebrew at Howard University from 1890 to 1892. In 1892–93 he was field secretary for the Stewart Missionary Society in the church, but in 1893 was called to the chair of Historical Theology at Gammon Theological Seminary in Atlanta, Georgia. He was the first African American to hold a full professorship at Gammon, and remained there for the rest of his career. For some years Gammon was the only theological seminary in the country existing solely to train Black clergy. In 1893 Bowen was the recipient of the first honorary D.D. degree given by Gammon to an African American. In his years at Gammon he was recognized as the leading Black minister of the Methodist Episcopal Church, and was a prominent, but unsuccessful candidate for bishop at the 1896, 1900, and 1904 General Conferences. He was also widely known as a supporter of a broad range of projects to enhance the lives and prospects of African Americans.

In December 1895 Bowen was the main organizer of a three-day Congress on Africa, from which was subsequently published a volume of addresses and proceedings, edited by Bowen. From 1892 to 1900 Bowen was a member of the national board of control of the Epworth League, the youth and young adult ministry organization of the church. Even after that time he remained an important leader of the Black section of the Epworth League, and in 1902 organized the *Negro Young People's Christian and Educational Congress*, complete with subsequent published addresses. He strongly opposed the segregation of Black clergy and laity in the Methodist system, a segregation that was made more explicit in 1939 when the Methodist Episcopal Church merged with the Methodist Episcopal Church, South, and the Methodist Protestant Church to form the Methodist Church. From 1939 to 1968, when a further merger created the United Methodist Church, the nineteen Black conferences, regardless of location, became part of the Central Jurisdiction. Bowen also opposed segregation in public transportation and for some time had a platform for his views as co-editor of the well-regarded *Voice of the Negro*, and also the *Negro, the Stewart Missionary Magazine*.

Bowen was a delegate to the World Methodist Conferences in Washington, D.C. (1891) and London (1901). His first wife died in 1904 and on May 24, 1906, he married Irene L. Smallwood. He was president of Gammon Theological Seminary from 1906 to 1910 and was vice-president, in addition to his teaching duties, from 1910 until his retirement in 1932. Bowen's significant stature as skilled pulpit orator, statesman, and educator helped pave the way for the first African American non-missionary bishops elected in the Methodist Episcopal Church, **Robert E. Jones** and **Matthew Wesley Clair, Sr.**, both in 1920. One of Bowen's children, **John Wesley Edward Bowen, Jr.**, was himself elected bishop in 1948.

Bowen, John Wesley Edward, ed. *Africa and the American Negro. Addresses and Proceedings of the Congress on Africa, Held Under the Auspices of the Stewart Missionary Foundation for Africa of Gammon Theological Seminary, in Connection with the Cotton States and International Exposition, December 13–15, 1895*. Atlanta, GA: Gammon Theological Seminary, 1896. 242 pp.

———. *An Appeal for Negro Bishops, but no Separation*. New York: Eaton & Mains, 1912. 88 pp.

———. *An Appeal to the King; the Address Delivered on Negro Day in the Atlanta Exposition, October 21, 1895*. Atlanta, GA: N.p., 1895. 7 pp.

Penn, I. Garland, and John W. E. Bowen, eds. *The United Negro: His Problems and His Progress*. Atlanta, GA: D. E. Luther Publishing Co., 1902. 600 pp.

———. *What Shall the Harvest Be? A National Sermon; or, A Series of Plain Talks to the Colored People of America, on Their Problems*. Washington, DC: Stafford Printing Co., 1892. 87 pp.

HUBA, AARS, BAW, TCNL, NBH, HNB, AAE, WWCR, WWCA (30–32), DANB, NCAB (14), EBA, IBAWCB, IBAW.

BOWENS, JOSEPH THOMAS (b. April 14, 1918), the bishop and general president of the **United Holy Church in America**, was born in Wilson, North Carolina, the son of Sallie Stevens and Horace Bowens. His father was an active minister in the church and pastored three churches in and around Wilson, North Carolina. Following high school, Bowens attended Temple University and the New Era Theological Seminary. He later did post-graduate work at the University of Maryland. He had had an initial experience of faith in his teens and acknowledged a call to the ministry in 1939. He preached his first sermon in 1940, was ordained in 1941, and named assistant pastor of the Mt. Pisgah United Holy Church in Philadelphia, Pennsylvania (thus facilitating his attendance at Temple University). He married Clara Washington in October 1942 and a month later began a two-year period of service in the Army.

After his discharge from the Army in 1944, Bowens returned to Mt. Pisgah and Philadelphia. In 1950 he became pastor of Faith Tabernacle in Washington, D.C., a position he has retained in addition to his general church responsibilities. His broader leadership was initially demonstrated both in his evangelistic endeavors (being one of the best orators in the church) and his missionary endeavors. From 1951 to 1961 he served as the church's Representative of Foreign Affairs. He traveled widely developing the church in Africa, the Barbados, Trinidad, Haiti, and the Philippines. In 1961 he was named a bishop of the church. In 1962 he was named vice-president of the Northern District.

In 1972 Bowens became second vice-general president of the church. He continued his missionary endeavors and devoted particular attention to the spread of the church in Africa. He was in Africa in 1980 when called to the general presidency.

As general president of the United Holy Church, he immediately let it be known that he planned an extensive outreach by the church into the surrounding culture. His vision for the United Holy Church had two main thrusts—a self-conscious effort to plant churches in places where no United Holy Church congregations presently existed and the development of community service outreach programs by presently existing congregations. He led in the movement of the church into Alaska and the development of a headquarters complex in Greensboro, North Carolina. Especially close to his heart, he has conducted an extensive building program for the church in Liberia. Finally, he has articulated plans for the development of a church-owned apartment complex and education system.

Gregory, Chester W. *The History of the United Holy Church of America, Inc., 1886–1986*. Baltimore, MD: Gateway Press, 1986. 275 pp.

BOWERS, JOSEPH OLIVER (b. March 28, 1910), the first African American priest whose consecration as a bishop in the **Roman Catholic Church** occurred in the United States, was born in Roseau, Dominica, British West Indies (**James A. Healy**, the first American Black Catholic bishop, was consecrated in Rome). Bowers' father was the headmaster at one of the public schools in the city and saw to it that Bowers received an excellent education. In 1928, at the age of eighteen, he enrolled in St. Augustine's Seminary in Bay St. Louis, Mississippi. This school had been founded in 1920 by the **Society of the Divine Word** to train missionary priests for service abroad and among Blacks and Mexicans in the United States. It was the only all-Black Catholic seminary in the country. He completed the junior college course in 1931 at the top of his class. He moved to East Troy, Wisconsin, where he entered the class of novices, and served as the organist for the choir.

He returned to Bay St. Louis after he had taken his initial vows into the Society of the Divine Word in 1933. He continued in his progress toward the priesthood, studying theology and philosophy. He became fluent in German, French, Italian, Greek, and Latin, as well as English. He had some editorial responsibilities for *St. Augustine's Messenger*, a popular missions magazine, and wrote a number of articles for it, focusing on Roman Catholic relationships with Black people. He was ordained a priest in Rome on January 22, 1939, and assigned to the society's foreign mission on the Gold Coast of West Africa, for which Bowers had volunteered. In Africa he quickly mastered several of the local dialects (Ga, Twi, and Ewe) and served in an itinerant capacity until he was made head of the Koforidua Church. He wrote several articles about his experiences there.

In March, 1948 Bowers left Africa for Rome, where he took advanced studies in canon law, receiving a doctorate in that subject in 1952. While working on that degree he was able to exercise the pastoral office at various places in Europe. In 1951 he spent some time as an assistant in a large White parish in Liverpool, England, run by English Jesuits. He noted that this was his most pleasant experience in a mixed ministry.

In late April, 1953, Cardinal Spellman consecrated Bowers as a bishop near St. Augustine's Seminary. Bowers was assigned to the Accra diocese in Africa, covering 38,000 Catholics and 196 schools. He was the first Black to be consecrated in the Society of the Divine Word. James Augustine Healy was the first Black American Catholic bishop, consecrated in 1875. Because Healy was consecrated in Rome, however, Bowers was the first Black consecrated bishop in the United States. After Healy the next American Black who was consecrated bishop was **Harold R. Perry** in 1966. Bowers' consecration ceremony took place in Our Lady of the Gulf Church in Bay St. Louis, Mississippi, a

church which had never permitted a Black priest to say Mass until the day of the consecration. Before Bowers left for Accra he ordained two Black priests at St. Augustine Seminary, the first time in the United States that Black priests were ordained by a Black bishop. At that time there were 68 Black priests in the United States. Bowers stated that he felt it fundamental to the future of Africa that the church establish a native clergy.

"The Birth of a Bishop." *Ebony* 8 (August 1953): 25–33.
"First Negro Bishop." *Newsweek* 41 (May 4, 1953): 60.
Bowers, Joseph O. "Hail the New Chief!" *St. Augustine's Messenger* 20 (March 1942): 58–59.
———. "Our Colored Catholic Neighbors." *St. Augustine's Messenger* 18 (March 1940): 32–34.
NCW, GMC, HUBA, IBAW.

BOWLES, EVA DEL VAKIA (January 24, 1875–June 14, 1943), prominent Young Women's Christian Association (Y.W.C.A.) officer, was born in Albany, Athens County, Ohio, the first child of John Hawes and Mary Jane (Porter) Bowles. This was a family of "firsts," as her father was possibly the first Black railway postal clerk in Ohio, and her paternal grandfather, the Rev. John Randolph Bowles, a Baptist minister, was said to have been the first Black teacher to receive a salary from the Ohio public school fund. In 1883 the family moved to Columbus, Ohio, where she moved through the public school system, finding a special interest in music. She received some higher education at Ohio State University and Columbia University, and was prepared to teach music to the blind. She was employed, however, by the American Missionary Association as the first Black teacher in Chandler Normal School, Lexington, Kentucky. She went on to teach also at St. Augustine's School in Raleigh, North Carolina, and St. Paul's Normal and Industrial Institute in Lawrenceville, Virginia.

In 1905 Bowles was called to New York to run a new project which became the 137th Street Branch Y.W.C.A., for some years the largest Black branch in the country. She was the first paid Black Y.W.C.A. secretary in America. In 1908 she took a training course at the School of Philanthropy, decided to move back to her hometown, and accepted a position as a caseworker for the Associated Charities of Columbus, Ohio. She was the first Black professional in this field. In 1913 she was asked to return to New York as a part of the National Board of the Y.W.C.A., in charge of the urban work with Black girls and women. In 1917 she was placed in charge of the Colored Work Committee of the Y.W.C.A.'s War Work Council. Her major task was to set up recreational facilities for the use of Black women entering industry for the first time. Such centers were built in industrial areas and near Army camps. She also established fifteen "hostess houses" on military bases; the one at Camp Upton in Yaphank, New York, earned Theodore Roosevelt's respect such that he designated $4,000 of his Nobel Peace Prize to be distributed by Bowles.

In 1919 Bowles wrote a report on the accomplishments of this work, adding her philosophy of the position of Blacks in the Y.W.C.A. as a whole. She was a vigorous opponent of those who wished to create a formal, separate "colored department," but neither did she want the Black work to be subordinate to a White headquarters. Instead, she preferred that the Y.W.C.A. integrate on all levels. The various articles she wrote for the Y.W.C.A.'s *Association Monthly* and *Woman's Press* were further channels for the expression of her perspective. When the Council on Colored Work was discontinued in 1931 as a separate entity, this was a distinct victory for her goals. Nevertheless, in 1932 the National Board's reorganization plan appeared to her to reduce significantly the higher level roles for Blacks, and she resigned in protest.

Bowles worked briefly as an executive for the National Colored Merchants Association, and then returned to Ohio as secretary of the West End Branch of the Cincinnati Y.W.C.A. In 1940 she was a Harlem organizer for the Wendell Wilkie Republican presidential campaign. She died of cancer on a family visit in Virginia and was buried in Columbus, Ohio.

Speer, Emma Bailey. "Eva D. Bowles," *Woman's Press* XXVI (July 1932): 431.

DANB, NAW, WWCA, RLOA.

BOWMAN, THEA (1939–March 30, 1990), educator, Catholic nun, and gospel singer, was born in Canton, Mississippi, the granddaughter of a slave. Not much has been published about her early life. She spoke of entering the **Roman Catholic Church** in the 1940s, and later became the only Black member of the Franciscan Sisters of Perpetual Adoration. She gained a national reputation for urging the Catholic Church to embrace the culture of African Americans. Bowman was director of the Office of Intercultural Affairs for the Diocese of Jackson, Mississippi, and helped to found and was a faculty member of the Institute of Black Catholic Studies at Xavier University in New Orleans, Louisiana. In 1985 she edited a study called *Families: Black and Catholic, Catholic and Black: Readings, Resources, and Family Activities.* She helped organize the 1987 Black Catholic Congress.

In 1988 she recorded an album of fifteen spirituals, "Sister Thea: Songs of My People," representative of the songs she sang around the country to raise awareness of Black Catholic culture and heritage. In 1989 the Sister Thea Bowman Black Catholic Educational Foundation was established by Mary Lou Jennings and Thomas F. X. Hoar, to provide financial support for Black Catholic students at all educational levels. That year she received the U.S. Catholic Award. She died of breast and bone cancer less than two months before she was to be the first African-American to receive the Laetare Medal from the University of Notre Dame. The medal, the oldest and most prestigious award given to American Catholics, was awarded to her posthumously on May 20.

Bowman, Thea, ed. *Families: Black and Catholic, Catholic and Black: Readings, Resources, and Family Activities.* Washington, DC: Commission on Marriage and Family Life, Department of Education, U.S. Catholic Conference, 1985. 153 pp.

"Deaths." *The Christian Century* 107 (May 9, 1990): 490.

Donnelly, Mary Queen. "Sister Thea Bowman (1937–1990)." *America* (April 28, 1990): 420–421.

"Sister Thea Bowman, Singing Nun, Dies of Cancer at 52." *Jet* 78 (April 16, 1990): 14.

WWABA (92–93), *NYTBS* (1990).

BOYD, HENRY ALLEN (April 15, 1876–May 28, 1959), head of the National Baptist Publication Board for almost forty years, was born in Grimes County, Texas, one of nine children born to **Richard Henry Boyd** and Hattie Moore. His father, a former slave, put together a multifaceted career as a Baptist minister and entrepreneur, and Boyd caught that spirit of personal and community achievement. As a teenager he was the first Black hired as a clerk at the San Antonio post office.

In 1895 the **National Baptist Convention, U.S.A., Inc.** was founded and the following year Boyd's father was elected secretary of the Home Mission Board. Boyd's father moved to Nashville for that job, and also founded the National Baptist Publishing Board in January, 1897. Soon Boyd, his wife, and young daughter moved from San Antonio to join his father in Nashville in the publishing work. In 1904 Boyd was ordained a Baptist minister and saw his role, like that of his father, as one of bolstering Black pride and providing general moral and cultural uplift to the Black community.

In 1905 new Jim Crow laws in Nashville led to a Black boycott of the streetcars, and the Boyds began a new Black newspaper, the *Nashville Globe,* to help spread the news of the day. While his father provided the financial initiative for the paper, Boyd was responsible for its regular management and cultivation, a typical pattern for their various enterprises. The paper was published weekly for forty years, and was often instrumental in pushing through reforms and affecting political campaigns. Its success led Boyd to serve as an organizer of and corresponding secretary for the National Negro Press Association.

Two other Boyd businesses which were located in the publishing building were the National Baptist Church Supply Company, which built church furniture, and the National Negro Doll Company, which produced Black dolls. When Boyd's father died in 1922, he formally took over the businesses he was not already managing, including the One Cent Savings Bank and Trust (now the Citizens Saving Bank and Trust Company), which he guided safely through the Depression, and the Supreme Liberty Life Insurance Company of Chicago. One of Boyd's major interests was higher education for Blacks, and largely through his influence the Tennessee Agricultural and Industrial State School (now Tennessee State University) was founded in 1911 and located in Nashville. He served as trustee for both Meharry Medical College and Fisk University.

The relationship of the National Baptist Publication Board with the National Baptist Convention was an informal one in the beginning. Over time, some convention leaders grew concerned over the fact that the publishing facilities and the published materials themselves were in the name of Richard Henry Boyd. They were also aware that the elder Boyd intended to pass on to the younger Boyd the publishing house as an inheritance, and they moved to restructure everything via incorporation. The Boyds fought this in court and won, and in 1915 they withdrew the publishing house from the National Baptist Convention, U.S.A., Inc., and placed it in the service of a new rival organization, the **National Baptist Convention of America**. After Boyd's death, the publishing house and the rest of the business empire was passed to his nephew, Theophilus Bartholomew Boyd, Jr.

Boyd, Richard H. *A Story of the National Baptist Publishing Board*. Nashville, TN: National Baptist Publishing Board, 1915. 145 pp.

Lamon, Lester C. *Black Tennesseans, 1900–1930*. Knoxville, TN: University of Tennessee Press, 1977. 320 pp.

DANB, NYTO, WWCR, RLOA.

BOYD, RICHARD HENRY (March 15, 1843–August 23, 1922), founder of the National Baptist Publishing Board, was born a slave on the Gray plantation in Nexubee County, Mississippi. His mother's name was Indiana Dixon, but Boyd was given the name Dick Gray. In 1849 the Gray family moved to Washington County, Texas, and during the Civil War several family members, including the plantation master, were killed fighting for the Confederacy. After these deaths Boyd was made manager of the plantation, but after Emancipation he left and tried his hand at several trades. In 1867 he changed his name to Richard Henry Boyd and worked to learn how to read and write. In 1869 he entered Bishop College in Marshall, Texas, and although he did not graduate, he was ordained a Baptist minister and married Hattie Moore.

In 1870 Boyd organized the first African American Baptist association in Texas with six churches. During his twenty-six years of ministry there, he pastored several churches and represented Texas Baptists at the Centennial Exposition in 1876. In 1895 the **National Baptist Convention, U.S.A., Inc.** was founded and the following year Boyd moved to Nashville to serve as secretary of the Home Missions Board. By January, 1897, he was able to found the National Baptist Publishing Board, which issued the first series of Baptist literature for Blacks in the United States.

Besides the Baptist Publishing House, Boyd was active in other enterprises designed to provide both business success and service to the Black community. He founded the National Negro Doll Company in 1911 as one of the first companies to make Black dolls, and the National Baptist Church Supply Company, which built church furniture and other items. He organized the One Cent Savings Bank and Trust (now the Citizens Savings Bank and Trust Company) in 1904 and served as its president until 1922. In 1905–06 he created the *Nashville Globe*, a newspaper to serve the Blacks in that area, begun in response to new Jim Crow laws and in support of organized resistance to them. This paper was published on a weekly basis for over forty years and played a significant role in political contests and social reform.

The National Baptist Publishing Board proved immensely successful, with a building valued at over $350,000 in 1912 and with an output of over 128 million periodicals by 1915. Boyd was a prolific author himself, writing or editing some fifteen volumes, perhaps the most important being *A Story of the National Baptist Publishing Board* (1915).

The relationship between the board and the National Baptist Convention, however, did not fare so well. The board was originally set up as Boyd's business, with a clear but informal connection to the convention. Some convention leaders became concerned that everything in the publishing house, including the published material, was in Boyd's name, and that one of his sons, **Henry Allen Boyd**, was set to receive it all as an inheritance. They tried, through incorporation, to gain control of the publishing house, but lost in the courts. In 1915 Boyd withdrew from the National Baptist Convention of the U.S.A., Inc., and associated the publishing house with a new, rival organization, the **National Baptist Convention of America**. After his death from a stroke, the publishing house and other businesses were passed on to his son, Henry Allen Boyd.

Chicago Defender (Sept. 2, 1922): 1,2.
Nashville Banner (Aug. 24, 1922): 7.
Nashville Tennessean (Aug. 24, 1922).
Boyd, Richard Henry. *Ancient and Modern Sunday School Methods.* Nashville TN: National Baptist Publishing Board, 1909. 80 pp.
————. *Baptist Sunday School Catechism.* Nashville, TN: National Baptist Publishing Board, 1899.
————. *Baptist Pastor's Guide and Parliamentary Rules.* Nashville, TN: National Baptist Publishing Board, 1900. 62 pp.
————. *The Separate or "Jim Crow" Car Laws or Legislative Enactments of Fourteen Southern States.* Nashville, TN: National Baptist Publishing Board, 1909. 67 pp.
————. *A Story of the National Baptist Publishing Board.* Nashville, TN: National Baptist Publishing Board, 1915. 145 pp.
DANB, DAB, HNB, WWACB, DNAADB, WWCR, NBHUSA, RLOA, SCA, BMS, HBB.

BOYDTON INSTITUTE. A Christian and Missionary Alliance and Church of Christ (Holiness), U.S.A. school. The **Christian and Missionary Alliance** is a Holiness body founded in 1897. It has concentrated its missionary endeavors on foreign work and has thus done little in home missions in general and among African Americans in particular. During the first half of this century, the Alliance did support two schools in the South, Lovejoy Institute at Mills Springs, South Carolina, and the Mary B. Mullen School, in Ayr, North Carolina. However, in 1911 it took over Boydton Institute, originally established in 1879, and operated it as an academy and Bible school for African Americans for over a decade. It was noted as having especially flourished in the early 1920s under superintendent Charles S. Morris. In 1923, the Alliance gave the school to the **Church of Christ (Holiness)** who continued to operate it until the Depression forced its closure in 1929.

Cobbins, Otho Beale. *History of the Church of Christ (Holiness), U.S.A., 1895–1965.* Chicago: National Publishing Board, Church of Christ (Holiness), U.S.A., 1966. 446 pp.
Ekvall, Robert B., et. al. *After Fifty Years: A Record of God's Working through the Christian and Missionary Alliance.* Harrisburg, PA: Christian Publications, 1934. 278 pp.

BRADLEY, DAVID HENRY, SR. (September 20, 1905–September 24, 1979), long-time editor of the *A.M.E. Zion Quarterly Review*, was born in Franklin, Pennsylvania, a son of Daniel Francis and Cora A. (Brewer) Bradley. His paternal grandfather had been freed from slavery on March 10, 1836, and his father was an **African Methodist Episcopal Zion Church** (AMEZ) minister. His mother's father was a free citizen who served in the Civil War. The family home was in Bedford, Pennsylvania, but they were more often elsewhere, as Bradley's father went from church to church in both Pennsylvania and Ohio. His father died in 1921, and Bradley graduated from the Bedford high school in 1925.

With the aid of a Job Mann Trust scholarship for future ministers, he attended Livingstone College in Salisbury, North Carolina, graduating in 1929 with honors. In 1932 he received an M.A. from the University of Pittsburgh. His thesis was "The Federal Elections Bill of 1890," concerning the final effort of the Republican party to get the Black vote in the South. While in college his first pastorate was in Mercer, Pennsylvania, followed by churches in West Bridgewater, Bellevue, and Altoona, all in Pennsylvania. He married Harriette Marie Jackson, with whom he had two children.

In 1933, after graduation, Bradley returned to Livingstone College as professor of history, where he stayed for two years. In 1935 he became the pastor of Ridgewood AMEZ Church in New Jersey, and remained there for fourteen years. For most of that time (1936–1948) he also served as the Conference Director of Christian Education. While in New Jersey he continued his studies at the Washington Square College of New York University, completing his Ph.D. in 1942. At the 1948 General Conference he was elected editor of the *A.M.E. Zion Quarterly*, the minister's journal of the church. He was reelected by acclamation every four years thereafter until his death. As part of his work with the journal, he was elected Assistant Secretary of Christian Education by the Joint Boards of Christian Education, and in this capacity represented the denomination on the Committee on Administration and Leadership of the National Council of Churches

(N.C.C.). He was also involved in the old National Christian Teaching Mission and the Central Department of Educational Evangelism of the N.C.C. He represented the denomination in the early days of the Protestant Film Commission and worked with the special group involved in the interchurch project, Cooperative Curriculum Development. In 1956, in complement to his other responsibilities, he was elected the first salaried secretary of the worldwide A.M.E. Zion Historical Society.

Bradley gained additional recognition through his publications. In 1946 he wrote a number of articles on the early history of the denomination which were intended to buttress his dissertation work. In 1956 these papers were collected and expanded into the first volume of the two-volume *History of the AME Zion Church*. The second volume was published in 1970, and together they constituted a landmark event, the first such history of the denomination in over seventy years. He was a contributor to both Cully's *Westminster Dictionary of Christian Education* (1963) and Nolan Harmon's *Encyclopedia of World Methodism* (1974).

He was a delegate to many world Methodist conferences, including the 13th World Methodist Council/Conference in Dublin, Ireland, in 1976, where he was named treasurer of the World Methodist Historical Society. His residence was in Bedford, Pennsylvania, where he served a small congregation, the Mt. Pisgah AMEZ Church, without pay for over 20 years.

Bradley, David H., Jr. "A Personal Statement Given at the Memorial Service for Dr. David H. Bradley Sr." *A.M.E. Zion Quarterly Review* 91 (Fall 1979): 152–153.

Bradley, David H., Sr. "Francis Asbury and the Development of African Churches in America." *Methodist History* 10 (October 1971): 3–29.

———. *A History of the AME Zion Church*. 2 vols. Nashville: Parthenon Press, 1956–1970.

"David H. Bradley." *Star of Zion* 82 (October 15, 1959): 5.

"Dr. David H. Bradley, Sr. Passes." *Star of Zion* 103 (October 25, 1979): 4

Dunston, Alfred G., Jr. "Bradley, the Academician." *A.M.E. Zion Quarterly Review* 91 (Fall 1979): 155–157.

Foggie, Charles H. "Eulogy for Dr. David H. Bradley, Sr." *A.M.E. Zion Quarterly Review* 91 (Fall 1979): 150–151.

Hilliard, William Alexander. "Dr. David Henry Bradley Sr., As Administrative Assistant and Presiding Elder." *A.M.E. Zion Quarterly Review* 91 (Fall 1979): 154.

Untitled Sketch of David Bradley's Life. *A.M.E. Zion Quarterly Review* 91 (Fall 1979): 148–149.

EWM, HAMEZC, BDNM (75), HUBA, AARS.

BRAGG, GEORGE FREEMAN, JR. (January 25, 1863–March 12, 1940), a priest in the **Episcopal Church**, author, and civil rights leader, was born in Warrenton, North Carolina, the son of George Freeman and Mary Bragg, strong Episcopalians. In 1865 the family moved to Petersburg, Virginia, to be near his paternal grandmother, Caroline Wiley Bragg, the former house slave of an Episcopal priest. She and Bragg, Sr., helped found St. Stephen's Church for Negroes in Petersburg in 1867. Bragg, Jr., attended St. Stephen's Parish and Normal School and held various jobs on the side. In 1879 he entered the Theological School for Negroes in Petersburg, a branch of the Virginia Theological Seminary in Alexandria, though a conflict with the school rector led to his expulsion in 1880. Bragg, Jr., then spent some time as a teacher in Staunton, Virginia, and private tutors helped him further his own theological education. He was active in both church and community, and in 1882 began publishing the *Lancet*, one of the first Black weeklies in Virginia. For most of the rest of his life he was publishing some kind of periodical, typesetting and printing it all on machinery in his own home. In 1884 he was chosen as an honorary commissioner of the New Orleans Exposition. In 1885, thanks to a change in rectors, he reentered the Theological School for Negroes (renamed Bishop Payne Divinity School in 1886). In 1886 he began a new magazine, the *Afro-American Churchman* (later called the *Church Advocate*), and was ordained a deacon on January 12, 1887. Later that year, on September 20, he married Nellie Hill, with whom he would have four children. He was ordained a priest on December 19, 1888, in St. Luke's Church, Norfolk, where he was assigned.

His achievements at St. Luke's were considerable. He not only built up the congregation and its facilities, he founded the Industrial School for Colored Girls, built the Holy Innocents Mission (later renamed Grace Church), and created what came to be called the St. James Mission in Portsmouth. On November 17, 1891, he was assigned to the St. James Church in Baltimore, a troubled and financially insolvent parish.

Within only a few years the church had many more members, a new building and property, a new rectory, and was solvent. As before, Bragg, Jr.'s outreach into society was as impressive as his parish work. He began a new magazine with his printing press, the *Ledger*. In 1899 he founded the Maryland Home for Friendless Colored Children, and promoted advanced ideas for the care of these children. He was a leader in the struggle to get Black teachers at Black schools in Baltimore. For a time he was closely allied with Booker T. Washington, but later came to feel that Washington's approach to civil rights issues was too conservative. He instead became a supporter of William E. B. DuBois and the Niagara Movement, a predecessor of the N.A.A.C.P.

Although Bragg, Jr., felt that the Episcopal Church was a leader in interracial cooperation, he was a regular critic of the discriminatory practices he saw in it. He was also an important historian of Blacks in Maryland and in the Episcopal Church, the author of numerous pamphlets and *The History of the Afro-American Group of the Episcopal Church* (1922). He was passed over for bishop in 1911, despite the recommendation of the U.S. minister to Haiti, and again in 1917, despite being the apparently popular choice among the Black clergy.

Baltimore News-Post (March 12, 1940): 26.

Bragg, George Freeman, Jr. *A Bond-Slave of Christ: Entering the Ministry Under Great Difficulties.* N.p.: 1912. 16 pp.

————. *The First Negro Priest on Southern Soil.* Baltimore, MD: Church Advocate Press, 1909. 72 pp.

————. *The History of the Afro-American Group in the Episcopal Church.* Baltimore, MD: Church Advocate Press, 1922. 319 pp.

————. *The Men of Maryland.* Baltimore, MD: Church Advocate Press, 1914. 135 pp.

————. *The Story of Old St. Stephen's, Petersburg, Virginia.* Baltimore: Church Advocate Press, 1906(?). 72 pp.

WWCA (38–40), EBA, DANB, HUBA, WWCR, RLOA.

BRANHAM, JOHN L. (b. c.1913), well-known Baptist radio preacher, was born in Texas and reared in Chicago, Illinois, the youngest son of Rev. J. H. Branham, a prominent Baptist minister. He graduated from Morehouse College in Atlanta, Georgia, and received a call to St. Paul Baptist Church in Los Angeles, California. At the time, St. Paul's was a struggling congregation in an inadequate building. Branham married a Los Angeles social worker named Ethel.

Branham began a radio program over KFWB and the Armed Forces Network overseas. With considerable oratorical skills, he built an audience of over one million for his Sunday evening show, "Echoes of Eden." The new following enabled him to begin a fundraising drive for a new church structure, which was finally completed in 1951. The project cost $550,000 and included a snack bar, barbecue pit, elevator controlled pulpit, powder rooms, and a parking lot for 300 cars. The main auditorium was sound proofed and set up to seat 750 people. The church advertised a new slogan, "Love for Everybody," and boasted an integrated congregation, with one-fourth of the membership White.

In 1952 Branham gained some unwanted publicity when Hazel Simpson, a controversial "ex-bookie queen," shot him. A grand jury ruled the incident an accident, but the church had to face public questions about what was an awkward situation at best. In 1955 another scandal broke when Mack Shepherd, a church usher, charged that his daughter, 21–year-old Rosaretha Shepherd, who was working as Branham's personal secretary, had been seduced by Branham. Eight Black market records had hit Los Angeles filled with recorded sexually oriented telephone conversations supposedly including Branham, Rosaretha, and others. Shepherd said the records confirmed his earlier suspicions, but both Branham and the daughter said the voices were not theirs and they were not involved together. In three separate church votes the membership overwhelmingly supported Branham and declared the matter closed.

"Branham Denies Voice on Questionable Records." *Ebony* 10 (March 1955): 97–103.

"Top Radio Ministers." *Ebony* 4 (July 1949): 56–61.

IBAW.

BRAWLEY, EDWARD McKNIGHT (March 18, 1851–January 13, 1923), leading Baptist minister and president of Selma University in Selma, Alabama, was born in Charleston, South Carolina, to James M. and Ann L. Brawley. His parents were free Blacks who gave him every opportunity possible. At the age of ten, when his former school closed, they sent him to Philadelphia, where he attended grammar school and the Institute for Colored Youth. He was baptized in April, 1865, at the Shiloh Baptist Church in Philadelphia. From 1866 to 1869 he worked as a shoemaker's apprentice in Charleston, and in 1870 he entered Howard University in Washington, D.C. as its first full-time theology student. Three months later, however, preferring a full college education, he transferred to Bucknell University in Lewisburg, Pennsylvania, as its first Black student. When he graduated in 1875, the local White Baptist church where he was working ordained him a minister.

The mostly White American Baptist Publication Society immediately hired Brawley as a missionary to the Blacks in South Carolina. In only two years, he took the few operating Baptist associations he found, reorganized them, organized new ones, created a Sunday School convention in every association, and brought them all together in a state convention. For the next six years, as corresponding secretary and financial agent, he directed the work of the state convention, adding mission work in Africa and the support of ministerial candidates in school. In January, 1877, he married Mary W. Warick, a Howard University graduate, but near the end of the year both she and their infant daughter died. In 1878 he received an M.A. degree from Bucknell University. In December, 1879, he married Margaret Dickerson, with whom he had four children. He edited the *Baptist Pioneer* for three years.

In October, 1883, on the advice of his doctor, Brawley resigned from his position and accepted the presidency of Alabama Normal and Theological School. In the space of one year he doubled the number of students, upgraded the curriculum, added a college-level department, and had the school renamed Selma University. It is said that he spent half of his salary helping poor students. The ill health of his second wife led him to resign this position in late 1886 and return to South Carolina, where he accepted the presidency of Morris College. In January, 1887, he began publishing and editing the *Baptist Tribune*, a weekly denominational magazine. He also began work again for the American Baptist Publication Society as the district secretary for the Atlantic Coast District. From this association came his most important publication, *The Negro Baptist Pulpit* (1890), perhaps the first such collection of Black theological and denominational writing.

This was also a time of great ferment among Black Baptists, who were finding the means to join their efforts together. Brawley was a key figure in the 1886 formation of the American National Baptist Convention, and in 1891 served a year as its president. In 1895 the American National Baptist Convention became a constituent part of the new National Baptist Convention, renamed in 1915 the **National Baptist Convention, U.S.A., Inc.** From 1912 to 1920 Brawley was pastor at the White Rock Baptist Church in Durham, North Carolina. He served the last years of his life, from 1920 until his death, as professor of Old Testament history and evangelism at Shaw University in Raleigh, North Carolina.

Brawley, Edward McKnight, ed. *The Aggressiveness of Baptists*. Petersburg, VA: n.p., 1890.
———. *Church Finances*. Fernandina, FL: Fernandina Publishing Co., 1903.
———, ed. *The Negro Baptist Pulpit*. Philadelphia, PA: American Baptist Publication Society, 1890. 300 pp.
———. *Sin and Salvation: A Textbook on Salvation*. Revised by Benjamin Brawley. Philadelphia, PA: Judson Press, 1925. 23 pp.
MM, DANB, HUBA, RLOA, SCA, TCNL, OBMS.

BRAXTON, DANIEL R. (b. c.1890), pioneer Lutheran minister, was working as a cook in a Baltimore, Maryland restaurant when he became interested in the Lutheran Church and its ministry. Superintendent Herbert F. Richards personally provided him with theological and missionary instruction, and he was ordained in St. Mark's Lutheran Church in Baltimore about 1917, among the first Blacks ordained in the Lutheran Church. His first position was in Jackson, Mississippi, where he became the first resident pastor of a Black mission church begun by Richards in 1915. An old church building on North Blair Street was purchased, and church services, a Sunday School, and Christian day school were provided.

In 1920 Braxton conceived a plan to start a mission school in nearby Georgetown, but it evidently did not come to pass. He left the work about 1925, and in the 1930s was the pastor of the mission work in Montgomery, Alabama. In 1947 he pastored St. Philip's Mission in Prattville, Alabama. Little more is known about his career.

LCAN.

BRAXTON, EDWARD KENNETH (b. June 28, 1944), priest and theologian of the **Roman Catholic Church**, was born in Chicago, Illinois, the son of Mr. and Mrs. Cullen L Braxton, Sr. He received his B.A. in 1966, M.A. in 1968, S.T.B. in 1968, Ph.D. in 1975, and S.T.D. in 1976; the names of the schools are not available. He taught at Harvard University in 1976–77 and at Notre Dame University in 1977–78. From 1978 to 1981 he was chancellor for theological affairs and personal theology for the Archdiocese of Washington, D.C. In 1982–83 he was scholar in residence at Rome North American College. Since that time he has been director of the Catholic Student Center at the University of Chicago and official theological consultant with William H. Sadlier, Inc. in New York City.

Braxton is a member of the **National Black Catholic Clergy Caucus**, American Academy of Religion, and Catholic Theological Society of America. He has served on the board of directors of St. Mary of the Lake Seminary in Chicago, and is on the Catholic Bishops' Committee on Liturgy and Doctrine. He was the keynote speaker at the 43rd International Eucharistic Congress in Nairobi, Kenya, and a speaker at the historic **National Black Catholic Congress** in Washington, D.C., in 1987. He has published one book, *The Wisdom Community* (1980). In 1991 he assumed the pastoral leadership of St. Catherine's of Siena-St. Lucy parish in Oak Park, Illinois.

Braxton, Edward K. *The Wisdom Community*. New York: The Paulist Press, 1980. 222 pp.
WWABA (92–93), *IBAW*.

BRAY, JAMES ALBERT (August 23, 1870–September 1, 1944), educator and 18th bishop of the **Christian Methodist Episcopal Church** (CME), then known as the Colored Methodist Episcopal Church, was born in Carnesville, Georgia, the eldest of Andrew Jackson and Mary Frances (Webster) Bray's six children. He attended the public schools in Franklin County, Georgia, went to high school in Athens, Georgia, and received his B.A. at Atlanta University in 1893. He did not have the ministry in mind at that time, and he went into teaching, becoming president of the Georgia State Teachers' Association in 1898–1899. About this time he began seeking pastoral duties, and was ordained a deacon in 1900 and elder in 1901. On April 23, 1902, he married Mattie B. Davis, with whom he had one daughter.

From 1902 to 1903 he pastored Trinity CME Church in Augusta, Georgia, and at the same time he was the principal of W. Broad High School in Athens, Georgia, and made it the first high school for Blacks in the state. In 1902 he represented the CME Church at the Negro Congress in Atlanta. In 1903 he accepted the position of president of Lane College in Jackson, Tennessee, where he stayed for four years. In 1904 he received an honorary M.A. degree from Atlanta University, and in the summer of 1906 he took graduate courses at Harvard University. In 1907 he assumed the presidency of Miles Memorial College in Birmingham, Alabama. In 1909 he received an honorary LL.D. degree from Wilberforce University in Ohio. His first wife passed away, and on December 28, 1910, he married Martha Freeman Childs, with whom he had one more daughter, who did not survive him. In 1911 he was a delegate to the World Methodist Ecumenical Conference in Toronto, Canada.

In 1912 he left Miles College to be presiding elder of the North Alabama Conference, where he served for two years. In 1914 he was elected General Secretary of Education for the CME Church, a position he held for twenty years. During this time he was instrumental in obtaining large contributions for the denomination's colleges, and also secured the help of the Methodist Episcopal Church, South, for the promotion of Leadership Training Schools churchwide, for ministers and other church workers. He was the first to go to educational foundations for financial aid for the church colleges. He edited a journal called *Voice of the People*.

At the May 1934 General Conference in St. Louis, Missouri, he was elected bishop and assigned to the Episcopal District covering the Carolinas and Florida. He also became president of the church's Board of Religious Education. From 1938 until his death he presided over the Episcopal District which included Missouri, Arkansas, Illinois, and Louisiana, and he made his home in Chicago. Among many other activities, he served with distinction as president of the **National Fraternal Council of Negro Churches**.

Bray, James Albert. *A Challenge to World Christianity. An Address Delivered by Bishop James A. Bray at the Meeting of the Fraternal Council of Negro Churches, Cleveland, Ohio, August 21, 1935*. Jackson, TN: CME Publishing House, 1935. 16 pp.
———. *Survey of the Colleges and Schools of the Colored Methodist Episcopal Church*. N.p.: J. W. Perry, n.d. 16 pp.
CMECTY, RLA, EWM, WWCR, NYTO.

BRIGHT, JOHN DOUGLAS, SR. (October 10, 1917–July 2, 1972), 79th bishop of the **African Methodist Episcopal Church** (AME), was born in Americus, Georgia, the youngest of seven children in the family of Turner E. and Estella (Williams) Bright. His father was an upholsterer who passed away in 1931, and his mother, who passed away in 1959, took in washing and did hairdressing and sewing to help support the family. Bright was converted in childhood at the Campbell AME Church in Americus, led by its pastor, E. N. Martin. He attended McKay Hill School in Americus and after his father died went to New York City to live with a brother. There he completed his first two years of high school and joined the Bethel AME Church. With its help and the aid of the Conference Missionary Society he was able to go to Wilberforce University in Ohio in September, 1937, finish high school in its preparatory department, and stay on to study for the ministry. He graduated in 1942 with both a B.A. from Wilberforce and a B.D. from the related Payne Theological Seminary. He married Vida Mae Harris on July 30, 1942, with whom he had two children.

He was ordained a deacon in 1937, while still in school, and given his first pastorate at the Wayman AME Church in South Charleston, Ohio. From 1938 to 1940 he divided his time between three churches: Wayman AME Church in Hillsboro, Wayman AME Church in Bainbridge, and Shorter Chapel AME Church in Greenfield, all in Ohio. He was ordained elder in 1939 by Bishop **Reverdy C. Ransom**, who took him under his wing at Wilberforce and later, when close to death, laid his mantle upon him. From 1940 to 1942 he was at Lee Chapel AME Church in Cincinnati, and from 1942 to 1943 he served at St. Paul AME Church in Lima, Ohio.

At this point Bright moved to Pennsylvania, where he was assigned by Bishop Ransom to Bethel AME Church in Pittsburgh from 1943 to 1948. This was Bright's first big church, and he proved himself by, among other things, paying off the debt, purchasing a new parsonage, and increasing the membership. He then went to Allen AME Church in Philadelphia from 1948 to 1950, when he was assigned to the prestigious Mother Bethel AME Church in Philadelphia. At that time the church was in trouble, but he worked through the difficulties. At the time he arrived, this historic birthplace of the AME Church was in bad repair and was called simply Bethel AME Church. During his tenure women gained the right to vote on congregational matters, the name of the church was changed to Mother Bethel AME Church, the structure was renovated, a new organ was installed, a parsonage was purchased, a reserve fund was created, a building for a museum was acquired, and membership increased. In the 1953 Annual Conference he was instrumental in getting a woman ordained as a deacon.

In 1960 he was elected bishop and assigned to the 17th Episcopal District in Central Africa. In two short years seven new churches were built and much else was accomplished. From 1962 to 1964 he presided over the 12th Episcopal District (Arkansas and Oklahoma), where he served as chair of the Board of Trustees of Shorter College in Little Rock, Arkansas. In May, 1964, he was assigned to the First Episcopal District, covering Philadelphia, the Northeast, and Bermuda, where he remained until his death. Again during his tenure he displayed his strengths in church finance and expansion, building up treasuries and churches. In 1965 he led a delegation of one hundred clergy to participate in **Martin Luther King, Jr.**'s march from Selma to Montgomery. From 1967 to 1968 he served in Philadelphia as a member of the Commission on Human Relations. From 1969 to 1971 he was vice-president of the Philadelphia Housing Development Corporation. In May, 1970, he was elected president of the church's Council of Bishops, for a one-year term. In 1970 he was elected the first president of the National Committee of Negro Churchmen (now the **National Conference of Black Churchmen**). In 1971 he was the only Black chaplain sent by the Boy Scouts of America to the 13th World Boy Scout Jamboree in Tokyo, Japan. In 1971 and again in 1972 he was named by *Ebony Magazine* as one of the one hundred most influential Blacks in America. In 1971–1972 he was on the President's Special Advisory Council to the U.S. Senate Committee

on Aging and the Aged. He passed away in Dallas, Texas, the site of that year's General Conference.

Bright, John Douglas, Sr. "Central Africa and African Methodism." *AME Church Review* 94 (July–September 1968): 63–68.

———. "Speech Delivered by Bishop John D. Bright of the Twelfth Episcopal District." *AME Church Review* 80 (April–June 1964): 28–31.

"Profile of the New President of the Council of Bishops, 1970–1971." *AME Church Review* 100 (August–September 1970): 1.

BDNM (70), EWM, EBA, NCAB (vol.57), BAMEC, HAMEC, HUBA.

BROADIE, B. H. (b. c.1903), has received little attention despite his fame as a radio preacher. He began his career as a barber, and about 1941 gained a public profile by starting a twice-every-Sunday program over WHBI in Newark, New Jersey. The show originated from services held at his Gospel Tabernacle Church in Newark. He urged his very large audience to receive healings by placing one hand on the radio and the other on the problem part of the body. Much of his audience was in the Deep South, from where hundreds of listeners sent him letters each week. He was known as "The World's Wonder Radio Preacher."

"Top Radio Preachers." *Ebony* 4 (July 1949): 56–61.

BROOKINS, H. HARTFORD (b. June 8, 1925), civil rights activist and 91st bishop of the **African Methodist Episcopal Church** (AME), was born in Yazoo County, Mississippi. After briefly attending Campbell College in Buies Creek, North Carolina, he transferred northward. He received his B.A. in 1949 from Wilberforce University in Ohio and his B.D. in 1950 from Payne Theological Seminary at Wilberforce. He married Helene Winona Howard, with whom he had one son.

From 1950 to 1959 he pastored the St. Paul AME Church in Wichita, Kansas, and from 1959 to 1972 he pastored the First AME Church in Los Angeles, California. Both pastorates were extremely successful and he built a reputation as an excellent preacher and church builder. In Wichita he was the first Black president of the Wichita Inter-Racial Ministerial Alliance. During the 1960s he was a close friend of **Martin Luther King, Jr.**, and for a time was president of King's **Southern Christian Leadership Conference**

(S.C.L.C.) Western Region. He founded the Martin Luther King, Jr., Student Fund and organized the first Interfaith Service at the Hollywood Bowl in 1971. He relocated the First AME Church in Los Angeles and built a new, multi-million dollar sanctuary. He also added hundreds of new members to the rolls. He helped organize the committees that successfully elected the first Black city council member and the first Black mayor, Tom Bradley.

From the Los Angeles pastorate Brookins was elected bishop in 1972 and assigned to the 17th Episcopal District (Central Africa) from 1972 to 1976. From 1976 to 1984 he headed the 5th Episcopal District, based in Los Angeles, and created the "People's Trust Fund," which assists Black entrepreneurs who have been denied bank loans, enables churches to obtain low-interest loans, provides scholarship money to Black theology students, and offers emergency help to the poor. From 1984 to 1988 he was assigned to the 12th Episcopal District, based in Little Rock, Arkansas, and then was assigned to the 2nd Episcopal District, based in McLean, Virginia. He is married to Bonita Brookins, the president of Park Lane Associates, a public relations firm in Los Angeles.

As bishop, Brookins has continued his leadership activities in the realm of civil rights. In 1974 he was a delegate to the 6th Pan-African World Congress in Tanzania. He has been a strong supporter of Jesse Jackson's **Operation PUSH** (People United to Serve Humanity), and has served as chair of its national board of directors as well as chair of the Ecumenical Ministers Committee of PUSH. In 1985 he received the Image Award from the National Association for the Advancement of Colored People (N.A.A.C.P.), and has received numerous other awards and honors.

WWA (84–85), *WWABA* (92–93), *HAMEC*, *BDNM* (70), *FEDHR*.

BROOKS, HENRY CHAUNCEY (c. 1895–1968) was the founder of the **Way of the Cross Church of Christ**. Brooks was born and grew up in Franklinton, North Carolina. In 1917 he moved to Washington, D.C. He married Willie Shaw Dunston, with whom he had ten children. At some point, he was converted to Pentecostalism and then to the non-Trinitarian Apostolic Jesus Only teaching which emerged in Pentecostalism in 1915. By 1926 he had felt a call to preach and went to New York to present himself to Bishop **Robert C. Lawson** whose **Church of Our Lord Jesus Christ of the Apostolic Faith** was the most prominent Jesus Only

church on the East Coast. He asked Lawson to give him a ministerial license. Lawson refused but suggested that he return to Washington and work for a period with J. T. Morris, who had begun an Apostolic congregation in Washington affiliated with the **Pentecostal Assemblies of the World**.

Instead of associating with Morris, Brooks, his wife, and four other people founded an independent congregation, the Way of the Cross Church, in February 1927. With the assistance of his brother-in-law, John Luke Brooks, he founded a second congregation in Henderson, North Carolina. Impressed with his ability, in 1928 Lawson ordained Brooks and took his congregations under his Church of Our Lord Jesus Christ of the Apostolic Faith. By this time, another congregation affiliated with Lawson had been founded in Washington by **Smallwood E. Williams**. They worked as colleagues until 1933 when Lawson pressed to have the two congregations merge. Unwilling to agree, Brooks dropped his affiliation with Lawson and founded the Way of the Cross Church of Christ as an independent denomination.

For the rest of his life, Brooks served as the Supreme Bishop of the Way of the Cross churches and continued as pastor of the Washington, D.C., headquarters church. In his more than thirty years of leadership, he led in the establishment of congregations along the East Coast. He died in Washington in 1968 and was succeeded by J. L. Brooks.

DuPree, Sherry Sherrod. *Biographical Dictionary of African-American Holiness-Pentecostals, 1880–1990*. Washington, DC: Middle Atlantic Regional Press, 1989. 386 pp.

Richardson, James C., Jr. *With Water and Spirit: A History of Black Apostolic Denominations in the U.S.* Martinsville, VA: The Author, n.d. 151 pp.

BROOKS, JOHN DELAWARE (October 7, 1803–1874), 12th bishop of the **African Methodist Episcopal Zion Church** (AMEZ), was born in Baltimore, Maryland. Not much is known about his family or early childhood. He was ordained a deacon on June 11, 1843, and elder on May 4, 1845. He served a number of churches, with both failure and success. His pastorates did not generally grow in membership because he was very strict in his enforcement of Methodist discipline. In the early 1860s he was pastor of the Zion Wesley Church in Washington, D.C., and at one point he refused to serve communion to some prominent members whose jewelry or finery he found offensive. The result was a split in the church and the founding of St. Paul AME

Church. His success was the other side of this coin. His strictness was a sign for his many followers of his high moral character, piety, and the courageous ability to prefer a small number of strongly committed Christians to a church full of lukewarm members.

His standing as a serious minister of high principles enabled his election as bishop in 1864; he was consecrated on May 30. Unfortunately, after his first four years he upset more people, and some asked for his resignation. He offered to resign, but a compromise was reached, whereby he remained inactive during the next four-year assignment, which was to the mission field on the Pacific coast. In 1872 he retired and became chair of the Book Concern, a position he held until his death two years later at his home in York, Pennsylvania.

OHYAMEZC, AMEZC, HAMEZC, IBSP.

BROOKS, ROBERT NATHANIEL (May 8, 1888–August 2, 1953), college president and a bishop of the Methodist Church (now the **United Methodist Church**), was born in Hollis, North Carolina, the son of John and Louvinia (Schanck) Brooks. He received his B.A. in 1911 from Bennett College in Greensboro, North Carolina, and his B.D. in 1914 from Gammon Theological Seminary in Atlanta, Georgia. He was ordained deacon in 1915 and elder in 1917, serving parishes in North Carolina. In 1918 he completed his M.A. at Garrett Biblical Institute at Northwestern University in Evanston, Illinois. From 1918 to 1920 he was secretary for the denomination's Board of Sunday Schools, based in the Washington Conference. On September 3, 1919, he married Edith Crogman.

In 1920–21 Brooks was president of Haven Teacher's College in Meridian, Mississippi, and in 1921–22 he was president of Central Alabama College in Birmingham, Alabama. From 1922 to 1926 he was president of Samuel Huston College in Austin, Texas, and during his last year in the position (1925–26) he did post-graduate work at Union Theological Seminary in New York City. From 1926 to 1936 he was professor of Church History at Gammon Theological Seminary, and in 1931–32 did further studies at Oxford University in England. From 1936 to 1939 he was editor of the Southwestern edition of the *Christian Advocate*, a church periodical based in New Orleans, Louisiana. In 1939 the Methodist Episcopal Church merged with the Methodist Episcopal Church, South and the Methodist Protestant Church to form the Methodist Church. At that time the nineteen Black conferences, regardless of location, became part of the non-geographical Central

Jurisdiction. The name of the church periodical Brooks was editing changed, and from 1940 to 1944 he edited the *Central Christian Advocate*.

In 1944 Brooks was elected bishop by the Central Jurisdiction and was assigned to the New Orleans Episcopal Area, where he remained the rest of his career. As bishop he served as chair of the Committee on Negro Education of the Board of Education, was president of the college of bishops of the Central Jurisdiction, and served on numerous committees. He was president of the Methodist Federation for Social Action from 1947 to 1949 and was president of the board of trustees of Rust College and Samuel Huston College. He was also a trustee of Bennett College and Dillard University. From April to September 1947 he was sent to Africa to review and appraise the church's work there, and from June to September 1948 visited the mission stations in South America under the auspices of the Board of Foreign Missions. In New Orleans he established the Lafon Old Folks Home and the People's Methodist Community Center.

WWC, MB, WWWA (3), EWM, NYTO.

BROOKS, WALTER HENDERSON (August 30, 1861–July 7, 1945), Baptist minister and temperance leader, was born into slavery in Richmond, Virginia, the fifth of nine surviving children of Albert R. Brooks and Lucy Goode. His mother was a member of the Baptist Church in Richmond. His father was able to work in his own business and make an annual payment to his owner, rather than work on the plantation. His father earned enough to purchase his wife Lucy's freedom (she was on a different plantation) in 1862, and some of the children's at various times in the next few years. Lucy arranged to have Brooks and his brother David purchased by the tobacco firm of Turbin & Yarbrough, who placed them with her as boarders. Later an arrangement was made to hire them for hotel work, until Emancipation in 1865 freed them. Their father was educated, with a sizable library, and taught Brooks to read and write.

Brooks attended Wilberforce Institute in Carolina Mills, Rhode Island, for about one year, then entered the preparatory school of Lincoln University in Oxford, Pennsylvania, in 1866. In December 1867 he was converted and joined the new Ashmun Presbyterian Church at the university. Because of his mother's influence, he later left the Presbyterians and was baptized in 1873 by Rev. James Holmes of the Richmond Baptist Church (later the First African Baptist

Church). He graduated from Lincoln University with a B.A. in 1872 and stayed to enroll in the theological school. After one year, however, he had to leave for lack of funds, and took a job as a clerk in the Richmond post office. He married Eva Holmes, daughter of the Baptist minister, on April 21, 1874, and they had nine children together.

Soon after the marriage, Brooks left the post office to be a Sunday School missionary in Virginia for the American Baptist Publication Society of Philadelphia. He held this position for several years, until 1877, although he was not officially licensed to preach until December 24, 1876. He was chaplain of the Anti-Saloon League of the District of Columbia from 1875 to 1882. From April, 1877 to October, 1880 he was pastor of the Second African Baptist Church of Richmond. At that point he went to New Orleans, Louisiana, as a Sunday School missionary for the American Baptist Publication Society.

On November 12, 1882, he became pastor of the prestigious 19th Street Baptist Church in Washington, D.C., associated with the **National Baptist Convention, U.S.A., Inc.** There he remained for over six decades, until his death. By this time, through his speaking abilities on behalf of missions and temperance, he had won a national reputation. His preaching was dignified and scholarly, and he did not encourage emotional displays. He promoted strict moral discipline and created a church active in helping others. He was the first vice-president of the Bethel Literary and Historical Association in Washington, D.C., and published books of poetry. He had an active interest in Black Baptist history, and wrote a pamphlet, *The Silver Bluff Church; A History of Negro Baptist Churches in America*, in 1910; two articles on similar subject matter were published in 1922. His first wife died in 1912, and he married Florence H. Swann in 1915.

He lived into his nineties and became a revered senior spokesman. For years Lincoln University honored him as its oldest living graduate. He was a member of the National Baptist Foreign Mission Board in Philadelphia, and was a trustee for several schools, including Nannie H. Burrough's National Training School for Women and Girls and the Virginia Theological Seminary and College in Lynchburg.

Brooks, Walter Henderson. "The Evolution of the Negro Baptist Church." *Journal of Negro History* 7 (January 1922): 11–22.

———. *The Pastor's Voice: A Collection of Poems.* Washington, DC: The Associated Publishers, 1945. 391 pp.

———. "The Priority of the Silver Bluff Church and Its Promoters." *Journal of Negro History* 7 (April 1922): 172–196.

———. "Religion." An address at the Washington Conference on the Race Problem in the United States, for the National Sociological Society. In *How to Solve the Race Problem.* Washington, DC: Beresford, Printer, 1904, 212–227.

———. *The Silver Bluff Church; A History of Negro Baptist Churches in America.* Washington, DC: Press of R. L. Pendleton, 1910. 47 pp.

DANB, ENB, WWCR, EBA, HUBA, AARS, BAW, TCNL, OBMS.

BROOKS, WILLIAM SAMPSON (1865–1931), 44th bishop of the **African Methodist Episcopal Church** (AME), was born in Calvert County, Maryland, the son of Robert and Margie Rebecca Brooks. He grew up on a farm and attended the public school in Prince Fredericktown, the county seat of Calvert County. In 1886 he enrolled in the Centenary Biblical Institute (now Morgan State College) in Baltimore, Maryland, and was a student there for seven years. He graduated in 1892 from the theological department and then enrolled in the collegiate department, getting as far as the end of his sophomore year.

His first pastorate was at the AME Church in Minneapolis, Minnesota, during which he built two churches, St. James and St. Peter's. In 1895 he made his first trip abroad, visiting Great Britain, Norway, and Sweden. He had long had a special interest in Swedish language and culture and took the opportunity to make further studies. He was a guest preacher and lecturer on numerous occasions and undertook a special study in the British Museum in London under Professor Clapp of Edinburgh, Scotland.

Immediately upon his return to the United States later that year Brooks was ordained elder and assigned to Wayman Chapel AME Church on North Division Street in Chicago, where he stayed two years. He published an account of his journey abroad, called *What a Black Man Saw in a White Man's Country*. In 1897 he married Susan Williams, his organist and choir director; there were no children. Shortly afterwards he was appointed to St. Peter's AME Church in Minneapolis, Minnesota, where he stayed three years. From 1900 to about 1905 he pastored St. Stephen's AME Church in Chicago, Illinois. In June, 1904, he was a delegate to the Fourth World's Sunday School Convention in Jerusalem. Sailing with a Black Baptist minister from Kentucky, he visited all over the area, including Constantinople, Athens, Gibraltar, and

Nazareth. He later wrote a book about this trip, *Footprints of a Black Man; the Holy Land* (1915).

From about 1905 to about 1910 Brooks was appointed to St. Paul AME Church in Des Moines, Iowa, where he had great success and began building his reputation as an unsurpassed money-raiser. From there he had a short stay at St. Paul AME Church in Nashville, Tennessee, but even in that time managed to raised large amounts of money and add a substantial number of members. In 1912 he was sent to St. Paul AME Church in St. Louis, Missouri, a church struggling under a $14,000 debt. With strict organization of the membership, Brooks led a single-day fund drive on May 5, 1912, which raised $5,000, an unprecedented sum for any Black church in the country. One year later, on May 19, 1913, it raised $7,541.85, and soon the debt was gone. This gave him a nationwide reputation.

In 1917 he moved to St. Paul AME Church in Wichita, Kansas, for a few months, until he was shifted to Bethel AME Church in Baltimore, Maryland. He was sent to Bethel for the specific purpose of reducing a $90,000 debt that several previous pastors had been unable to handle. In less than three years he had paid off the entire amount, and the astounding achievement catapulted him into the bishopric. He was elected bishop on May 13, 1920, and consecrated three days later. Brooks requested to be assigned to Africa, only the second bishop, besides **H. M. Turner**, ever to request such an assignment.

Before he left for Africa Brooks toured the United States, telling people of his vision for the mission work of the church, and raising money for the task. In Liberia he almost immediately purchased twenty acres and personally helped build Monrovia College. In 1924 he requested a reassignment to Africa, which was granted, and he was able to follow up on his work. Other land purchased by him later became among the most valuable African properties held by the church. His wife died in Africa, and the Susan Brooks Memorial AME Church in Monrovia is named for her. In 1928 the General Conference passed a resolution moving all the bishops, and Brooks was assigned to Texas. In 1931 he married Elizabeth C. Carter of New Bedford, Massachusetts. He passed away later that same year. He left a legacy in church missions that will long be remembered.

Brooks, William Sampson. *Footprints of a Black Man; the Holy Land.* St. Louis, MO: Eden Publishing House, 1915. 317 pp.

———. *What a Black Man Saw in a White Man's Country: Some Account of a Trip to the Land of the Midnight Sun.* Minneapolis, MN: Harrison & Smith, 1899. 59 pp.

BAMEC, EWM, HAMEC, BAW.

BROOMFIELD, OREE, SR. (b. May 19, 1927), 45th bishop of the **Christian Methodist Episcopal Church** (CME), was born in Simpson County, Mississippi, near Magee, one of eight children in the family of Freddie Manson and Hettie (Thomas) Broomfield. He joined the Duckworth Chapel CME Church in Taylorsville, Mississippi, at an early age, and served variously as superintendent of the Sunday School, steward, and class leader before he was licensed to preach. He graduated from the Smith County Training School, and served in the Navy during World War II. He received the B.A. degree from Mississippi Industrial College in Holly Springs, Mississippi, in 1954. He married Wylene A. Parham, with whom he has had three children.

While he was at college received his first pastoral appointment, at the Hebron Chapel CME Church in Holly Springs, from 1952 to 1954. After graduation he went on to Gammon Theological Seminary in Atlanta, Georgia, where he obtained the B.D. degree in 1957. He pastored churches during this time as well, the Rock of Ages CME Church in Augusta from 1954 to 1956, and the Emmanuel Chapel CME Church and New Harmony Circuit in West Point, Georgia, from 1956 to 1958. From 1958 to 1964 he was assigned to the Anderson Chapel CME Church in Holly Springs, and for most of that time was also professor of religion and philosophy at Mississippi Industrial College. From 1959 to 1962 he was president of Marshall County Voters' League. In 1964 he spent a brief time at St. John CME Church in Washington, D.C.

In 1965 he was assigned to Cleaves Memorial CME Church in Oklahoma City, Oklahoma, staying until 1975. He was president of the Oklahoma Branch of the N.A.A.C.P. from 1972 to 1974. In 1972 he received a D.D. degree from Phillips University in Enid, Oklahoma. He next moved to Cedar Crest CME Cathedral in Dallas, Texas, where he continued to build a solid reputation. He served on the Dallas Public School Advisory Council for the Smooth Integration of the Schools, and was also adjunct professor of Religion and Philosophy at Bishop College in Dallas. For a time he was vice-president of the Greater Dallas Community of Churches. Within the denomination, he served twice on the Episcopal Committee and participated in the Long-Range Planning Committee. He was elected bishop at General Conference on the second ballot, May 9, 1982. He was assigned to the Tenth Episcopal District (Liberia; Ghana; Nigeria; and Lagos Conferences), then about 1984 shifted to the Seventh Episcopal District

(Carolina; and New York-Washington Conferences), where he has since remained.

"Bishop Oree Broomfield, Sr." *Christian Index* 115 (May 15, 1982): 4.
WWABA (75–76), *BDNM* (75).

BROWN, CALVIN SCOTT (March 23, 1859–194?), founder of the Waters Training Institute, founder and head of the **Lott Carey Baptist Foreign Mission Convention**, and later a leader in the **National Baptist Convention of America**, was born in Salisbury, North Carolina, the son of Henry and Flora (Pon) Brown. He received a solid schooling at a Friends institution until age seventeen, when his father died. He obtained a first grade teacher's certificate and found a teaching job to support his widowed mother, three sisters, and one brother. In 1879 he was able to enter Shaw University in Raleigh, North Carolina, and in 1886 received both a B.A. and B.D. as valedictorian of his class. In school he was already editor of the *Samaritan Journal*, the periodical of the Good Samaritan (fraternal) Order of North Carolina. He headed this organization for a number of years. On December 8, 1886, he married Amaza Jenette Drummond, with whom he had nine children.

Upon graduation **Henry Martin Tupper**, the founder of Shaw University, asked Brown to visit Winton, North Carolina, and ascertain its suitability for a secondary school to serve as a feeder for Shaw. Brown returned to Tupper some days later and sadly reported that conditions there were decidedly unfavorable. Tupper then gave him a $10 bill and told him to go back and start a school with that money. Brown gained the pastorate of a large Baptist church in Winton, where that same year he began the process of creating the Waters Training School. To advertise the project he founded a monthly paper called the *Chowan Pilot*, and in less than eighteen months a two-story, 60 x 30 foot building was completed. In the summer of 1887 he merged the *Chowan Pilot* with a new paper, the *Baptist Pilot*, begun by the North Carolina Ministerial Union, for which he was chosen editor. He purchased a printing press and office space on behalf of the Ministerial Union and began publishing this bi-weekly paper without any previous training in typesetting. It was the only paper published in Winton and was read by a majority of both White and Black citizens.

All this time, of course, Brown was principal of the Waters Training School, which slowly grew until, in 1928, it counted more than 450 students and property worth $80,000. Brown served as pastor of a number of prominent churches in North Carolina, and continued his education. In 1898 he received his D.D. from Shaw, and in 1900 completed his M.A. He was also part of the growing movement to unify the Black Baptist foreign missions endeavors, begun by the Foreign Mission Board in 1880 and the **National Baptist Convention, U.S.A., Inc.**, (N.B.C.) in 1895. The N.B.C., however, saw fit to eliminate all Virginians from its foreign mission board, despite the fact that Virginians had been leaders in African missions, and also moved the headquarters from Richmond, Virginia, to Louisville, Kentucky. The N.B.C. also decided to produce its own educational materials rather than depend upon the northern White American Baptist Publication Society.

Brown and others were deeply concerned about the N.B.C.'s ability to conduct foreign missions without the Virginians and also questioned the wisdom of creating an independent publications house. Brown believed that Blacks had not reached the point where they could adequately sustain such independent ventures, and did not want to appear ungrateful to the White Baptists for the tremendous humanitarian and religious works they had done for post-Civil War Blacks in the South. For moral, theological, and practical reasons Brown felt that Blacks and Whites should cooperate at least in the realm of religion. Thus in 1897 Brown helped found and then led a break-away group, the Lott Carey Baptist Foreign Mission Convention (L.C.C.). Brown was also president of the North Carolina Baptist Convention, a member of the L.C.C.

By 1905 the relationship between the N.B.C. and the L.C.C. had once again become amicable and the two reunited. The L.C.C. retained its existence as a distinct foreign mission group within the N.B.C. with the right to enter into cooperative arrangements with any other Baptist group. In 1915 the controversy over ownership of the publishing house led to a split between the N.B.C. and the unincorporated National Baptist Convention of America, and eventually (in 1924) the L.C.C. became the foreign mission arm of the unincorporated group. Brown continued to lead the L.C.C. for the rest of his career. In 1924 Brown represented the L.C.C. and the National Baptist Convention of America at the World Baptist Convention in Stockholm, Sweden. Over the years he toured Europe five times and visited Africa once.

Martin, Sandy D. "The Debate Over Interracial Cooperation Among Black Baptists in the African Mission Movement, 1895–1905." *The Journal of the Interdenominational Theological Center* 13 (Spring 1986): 291-303.
WWCA (38–40), *EBA, AAP, SNB, HBB, WWCR, OBMS*.

BROWN, DILLARD HOUSTON (June 20, 1912–November 19, 1969), the seventh Black bishop consecrated by the (Protestant) **Episcopal Church** (in America), was born in Marietta, Georgia, the son of Dillard Houston and Anna Rebecca (Robinson) Brown. He attended high school in Detroit, Michigan, then received his B.A. in 1936 from Morehouse College in Atlanta, Georgia, and his M.Th. in 1939 from the University of Southern California. He attended the Episcopal Church's General Theological Seminary in New York City in 1939–40, was ordained deacon in May 1940 and priest in June 1941. On February 13, 1942, he married Sarah Virginia Ross, with whom he had two daughters.

His first church assignment was as curate at St. Martin's Episcopal Church in New York City, from 1940 to 1942. From 1943 to 1946 he was vicar of the Church of the Incarnation in Jersey City, New Jersey, and he was rector of St. Luke's Episcopal Church in Washington, D.C., from 1946 to 1961. In 1961 he was elected bishop coadjutor of the Missionary District of Liberia, and in 1964 he succeeded Bravid W. Harris as diocesan bishop of Liberia. Brown's career was tragically cut short when he was assassinated in his office. The alleged assassin was a 63–year-old Biafran named Justin M. Obi, an unemployed chemistry professor who used to be a faculty member at the Episcopal Church-run Cuttington College in Suacoco, Liberia. There was no known motive for the shooting. Brown was remembered as a wise leader who was respected and loved by his constituency.

BDNM (65), *NYTO*, *ECA* (1962).

BROWN, EDWARD LYNN (b. April 2, 1936), 46th bishop of the **Christian Methodist Episcopal Church** (CME), was born in Madison County, Tennessee, the son of Willie T. and Ocie (Royal) Brown. He received his B.A. from Lane College in Jackson, Tennessee, in 1960, and his B.D. from the Interdenominational Theological Center in Atlanta, Georgia, in 1963. He married Gladys D. Stephens, with whom he has had two children.

He supported his way through college by pastoring churches, all in Tennessee. The first appointment was New Hope CME Church in Gibson County from 1957 to 1958, when he moved to St. Paul CME Church in Bolivar, Tennessee. In 1961 he went to Greenwood CME Church in Memphis, staying until 1967, when he was appointed to Mt. Pisgah CME Church, also in Memphis. He stayed at Mt. Pisgah for the next eleven years, where he gained a reputation for leadership and

community involvement. Among other responsibilities he was chair of the Advisory Committee of the Memphis Community Education Project. He was the recipient of numerous awards, including a commendation from the Community Action Agency in 1970, the mayor's Certificate for Service to the City of Memphis in 1971, the Memphis Urban League's award for Outstanding Community Service in 1973, and the Memphis N.A.A.C.P.'s award for Outstanding Service, also in 1973.

During this time he became heavily involved in the denomination's education program, serving as Associate Dean of the Joint Pastors' Institute and Dean of the South Memphis District Board of Christian Education. He was accepted as a writer for the General Board of Christian Education of the CME Church and co-authored a Bible study booklet called *Reconciliation: A Mission of the Christian Church*. In 1978 he left Mt. Pisgah to be General Secretary of the Board of Publication Services of the church. This position gave him an even higher profile, and at the General Conference in Birmingham in 1986, he was elected bishop on the second ballot. He was assigned to the Ninth Episcopal District (Muskogee, Oklahoma; Arizona-New Mexico; North and South California; and Alaska-Pacific Conferences), where he has since remained.

"New Bishops Elected." *Christian Index* 119 (May 1, 1986): 3.
WWABA (90–91), *BDNM* (75).

BROWN, EGBERT ETHELRED (July 11, 1875–February 17, 1956), founder of the first Unitarian church in Harlem, was born in Falmouth, Jamaica, the eldest of five children born to James and Florence Brown. Though he was a bright child, his father's position as an auctioneer did not bring enough money to finance any higher education, and at the age of nineteen Brown joined Jamaica's civil service, placing third in the national entrance exam. In 1898 he married Ella, with whom he had six children. In 1899 he became first clerk of the treasury, but his government career was destroyed in 1907 when he was dismissed for using public funds to help cover family expenses. The resulting personal crisis led him into a decision to enter the ministry.

Brown's religious path had already taken a distinctive turn. Raised an Episcopalian, as a teenager he turned to Unitarianism as a protest against orthodox trinitarian teaching. He was helped in his development by his Unitarian uncle, but there were no Unitarian churches nearby, and for a while he attended no church.

In 1895 he became the organist for the Montego Bay Wesleyan Methodist Church, a position he held until 1907. At that time, still a Unitarian at heart, he briefly considered the more immediately available ministry in the newly begun **African Methodist Episcopal Church** mission in Jamaica. Correspondence with Meadville Theological School (Unitarian) in Chicago, Illinois, however, led to his acceptance at that school, with scholarship aid, despite the uncertain professional future of a Black Unitarian.

After facing a number of obstacles, he arrived at Meadville in September, 1910. His program went well, and he was ordained in June, 1912. He returned to Jamaica and attempted to start a Unitarian congregation in Montego Bay. Unitarian officials, however, were doubtful about the success of this venture, and did not consistently back him, eventually dropping all support. The mission failed, and Brown took his family to Harlem, New York City, in early 1920. On March 7, 1920, he founded the Harlem Community Church (Unitarian), meeting in various halls. The group of about thirty met every other Sunday evening, and Brown supplemented his income by working variously as a hotel elevator operator, speaker for the Socialist Party, and magazine office secretary.

The Unitarian Association continued to block his progress, and at one point dropped him from the membership roster as a nuisance. There were other trials as well; his wife became mentally ill, his oldest son committed suicide in 1929, and in 1934 he was forced onto public relief. Even so, he was a leader in the Harlem Tenants League, the Federation of Jamaican Organizations, and other community groups. He continued his ministry, and when a new Association official investigated in 1937, he found an active membership of forty-four, and an attendance of nearly twice that.

At this point, finally, the church gained financial support under the Department of Unitarian Extension and Church Maintenance. Brown began receiving a retirement pension in 1939, but continued to minister to his church until his death. His church did not survive him, interested persons going instead to the larger Community Church of New York, which added a Black minister of education in 1947. Although visible outward success eluded him, Brown made a lasting impact on many in his cause of liberal religion.

Morrison-Reed, Mark D. *Black Pioneers in a White Denomination.* Boston, MA: Beacon Press, 1984. 217 pp. *NYTO, HUBA, RLOA.*

BROWN, HALLIE QUINN (March 10, c.1850–September 16, 1949), educator, civil rights leader, and representative of the **African Methodist Episcopal Church** (AME), was born in Pittsburgh, Pennsylvania, the fifth of six children in the family of Thomas Arthur and Frances Jane (Scroggins) Brown. Her mother was a freed slave and her father, also a freed slave, was a riverboat agent. In 1864 or 1865 the family moved to a farm in Chatham, Ontario, Canada, for her mother's health.

After acquiring a basic education in Canada the family sent her in 1868 to Wilberforce University, the AME Church institution in Ohio. The rest of the family moved there in 1870 and built a home, now called Homewood Cottage. She graduated with a B.S. in 1873, and then taught children in plantation schools in Mississippi and South Carolina during Reconstruction. She also taught adults to read with at least enough sufficiency to understand the Bible. She held teaching positions in the city public schools of Yazoo, Mississippi, and Columbia, South Carolina, but was compelled to return North in 1875. She taught night school for adult migrants from the South in Dayton, Ohio, for the next four years.

Owing to ill health she was forced to give up teaching for a time, but Bishop **Daniel Payne** of the AME Church sponsored a lecture tour of the South for her, and she spoke in many cities on behalf of Wilberforce University. She took a course in Dayton from Professor Robinson of the Boston School of Oratory. This polished her presentations and she thereafter had more success in her public elocutionary readings. She was one of the first Black women to make a living as an elocutionist. In 1880 she published her first book, *Bits and Odds: A Choice Selection of Recitations.* About this time the Wilberforce (later Stewart) Concert Company was formed, and she traveled with the group as a reader for four seasons, receiving nothing but praise.

In 1885 Brown became dean of Allen University in Columbia, South Carolina, holding that position for two years. In 1886, after several years of summer classes, she graduated from the Chautauqua Lecture School. In 1892–93 she was dean of women at Tuskegee Institute in Alabama, and in 1893 was appointed professor of elocution at Wilberforce University. Also in 1893 she was a principal founder of the Colored Women's League of Washington, D.C., the first national organization for Black women. In 1894 that group helped form the National Association of Colored Women.

In 1894 Brown began a tour of Europe which was

to last six years. She lectured in all the major cities of Great Britain and on the continent, often speaking on Black life in America and including folklore and songs. One of her favorite subjects for recitation was the writing of Paul Laurence Dunbar. She sometimes spoke on behalf of Wilberforce University, seeking financial support. There was a natural connection with her audiences on that topic, since William Wilberforce had been a British abolitionist. She also lectured in support of the British Women's Temperance Association. In 1895 she spoke at the World's Women's Christian Temperance Union in London. On July 7, 1899, she was a guest of Queen Victoria for tea at Windsor Castle. She attended the International Congress of Women in London in 1899, strengthening an espousal of women's rights and suffrage which began when she heard Susan B. Anthony speak at Wilberforce. In 1900 she asked the AME Church to elect her Secretary of Education, but was unsuccessful.

From 1900 to 1903 she was again professor of elocution at Wilberforce; then from 1903 to 1906 she traveled and spoke, making more trips abroad. After 1906 she returned to her professorship full-time. She became a member of the board of trustees of Wilberforce and regularly taught a Sunday School class of college students. In 1910 she went once again to Europe as representative of the Women's Parent Missionary Society of the AME Church to the World Missionary Conference in Edinburgh, Scotland, in June. On this trip she continued to seek funds for Wilberforce University, and Emery Hall was a direct result, named for the mother of a London philanthropist.

From 1905 to 1912 she was president of the Ohio State Federation of Women's Clubs. From 1915 to 1919 she taught freshman English at Wilberforce. She founded and chaired the Scholarship Fund of the National Association of Colored Women, and was the seventh president of that organization from 1920 to 1924. In 1922 she met with Senators Shortbridge, Lodge, and McCormick and President Harding to appeal for the passage of a national anti-lynching bill. She took an active role in the 1924 presidential campaign on behalf of Calvin Coolidge, addressing the Republican National Convention in Cleveland, Ohio, and directing the Colored Women's Activities at the campaign's Chicago national headquarters.

She was a tireless crusader for both the rights of Blacks and of women. In May 1925, at the All-American Musical Festival of the International Council of Women meeting in Washington, D.C., she told the assembly very pointedly how poorly she thought of the segregated seating and warned that unless the policy was changed she and the Black musicians scheduled to take

part would leave, and they did. In 1926 she published perhaps her most well-known book, *Homespun Heroines and Other Women of Distinction*. Named for her are a community house in St. Paul, Minnesota, and the library of Central State University in Wilberforce, Ohio. She never married. Despite her international fame as an elocutionist, nothing was written about her work in the field until 1975.

Brown, Hallie Quinn. *Bits and Odds: A Choice Selection of Recitations.* 1880.
————. *First Lessons in Public Speaking.* 1920.
————. *Homespun Heroines and Other Women of Distinction.* Xenia, OH: The Aldine Publishing Co.,1926. 248 pp.
————. *Pen Pictures of Pioneers of Wilberforce.* Xenia, OH: Aldine Publishing Co., 1937. 96 pp.
————. *Tales My Father Told and Other Stories.* Wilberforce, OH: N.p., 1925. 24 pp.
McFarlin, Annjennette S. "Hallie Quinn Brown: Black Woman Elocutionist." *The Southern Speech Communication Journal* 46 (Fall 1980): 72–82.
BAW, IBAW, WWCR, HUBA, AARS, IBAWCB, NA, CH, HNB, AAE, WB, NNW, DANB, FAW, BDAE, PNW, NAW, NBAW.

BROWN, JAMES RUSSELL (b. October 28, 1909), first Black Navy chaplain and for many years General Secretary of the **African Methodist Episcopal Church** (AME), was born in Guthrie, Oklahoma, the son of John Ellis and Nannie A. Brown. The family moved to Wichita, Kansas, where he attended Wichita High School East. He was licensed to preach in 1929 and joined the Kansas Annual Conference in 1930. He received a B.A. in 1932 from Friends University in Wichita, earning money on the side as a lifeguard at McKinley Park. He married Helba Long of Wichita. He enrolled in Howard University's School of Religion in Washington, D.C., where he received his B.D. in 1935. His thesis paper was entitled, "An Examination of the Thesis that Christianity in its Genesis was a Technique of Survival for an Underprivileged Minority." He was ordained deacon in 1933 and elder in 1935.

After some further study at the Chicago Theological Seminary, in 1937 he became a teacher at Bishop Williams School of Religion in Quindaro, Kansas, and was promoted to dean in 1940. In 1938 he became a trustee of both Western University in Quindaro and Douglass Hospital. He both taught at the seminary and pastored St. Luke AME Church in Kansas City (1938–44). He built the church structure in 1940 and paid off the mortgage in 1943. By this time the United States was at war. Although the Army had Black officers and chaplains as early as the Civil War, the Navy had not followed suit. In 1942 officials began looking for a suitable Black Navy chaplain, and Bishops Noah Wellington Williams and John Andrew Gregg recommended Brown for the position. Finally, on June 28, 1944, Brown became the first Black commissioned officer in the Navy Chaplain's Corps. In this position he saw overseas duty on Guam in the South Pacific.

After his tour of duty, Brown was assigned to the Shorter AME Church in Denver, Colorado. While there he did additional studies at Iliff School of Theology and was the first Black appointed as a member of the Citizen's Labor Management Commission of the City and County of Denver. He was also the first Black to become a member of the Governor's Human Relations Commission in the State of Colorado. Later, he served a church in Kansas and became the first Black on the Anti-Discrimination Commission of the State of Kansas. About 1960 he became General Secretary of the denomination and remained in that office, based in Chicago, Illinois, until his retirement in 1976. For a time he taught at the City College of San Francisco and in the 1970s he pastored St. Paul AME Church in St. Louis, Missouri.

Brown, James Russell. "An Examination of the Thesis that Christianity in its Genesis was a Technique of Survival for an Underprivileged Minority." B.D. Paper, School of Religion, Howard University, 1935.

Silvera, John D. *The Negro in World War II.* New York: Arno Press, 1969. 120 pp.

IBAW, AMECMIM, AARS, HUBA, EAMEC.

BROWN, JAMES WALTER (July 19, 1872–February 27, 1941), 49th bishop of the **African Methodist Episcopal Zion Church** (AME), was born in Elizabeth City, North Carolina, the son of Jesse R. and Araminta (Griffin) Brown. After attending the State Normal School in Elizabeth City, he went to Shaw University in Raleigh, North Carolina, graduating with a B.A. in 1893. He was assistant principal in the State Normal School in Elizabeth City from 1893 to 1899, when he decided to enter the ministry. He went to Lincoln University in Oxford, Pennsylvania, and graduated in 1903 with both an M.A. and an S.T.B. degree. He was ordained deacon on May 17, 1903, and assigned to Media and South Bethlehem, Pennsylvania, in the Philadelphia-Baltimore Conference, where he built a church. In October 1903 he married Martha Hill.

He was ordained elder on May 21, 1905, and transferred to the Western New York Conference, where he pastored Memorial AME Zion Church in Rochester, and also built a sanctuary, at a cost of $25,000, and

acquired other property for the church as well. Livingstone College, in Salisbury, North Carolina, gave him an honorary D.D. degree in 1912. In 1913 he was appointed to the Mother Zion Church in New York City. This prestigious church had recently been through a crisis which depleted the membership, and almost pushed them out of their meeting place. He led them to purchase the property on 136th Street, where they worshipped in a makeshift setting until a huge, Gothic structure was built in 1925 at a cost of $450,000. His first wife died in 1928, and he married Andrades Lindsay on August 5, 1930.

He was consecrated a bishop on May 20, 1936, and assigned to the Eleventh Episcopal District, comprised of all foreign work in Africa, the Virgin Islands, and South America. In this capacity, he and his wife made two trips to West Africa, visiting all the mission stations in the Gold Coast, Nigeria, and Liberia, and overseeing the construction of new schools and churches. Twice he was a delegate to the National Republican Convention, and at the Convention in Cleveland, Ohio, in 1936, became the first Black to offer the opening prayer. In 1940 he was assigned to the Tenth Episcopal District, comprising the African Conference, North-Central Texas Conference, and Oklahoma Conference. He was a member of the National Negro Business League, Odd Fellows, the National League on Urban Conditions Among Negroes, and served on the board of the Y.M.C.A. Colored Branch, New York. His tenure as bishop was tragically cut short by a fatal accident as he crossed a busy street in New York City, near the Mother Zion Church.

"Bishop J. W. Brown Dies in Auto Accident." *Star of Zion* 65 (February 27, 1941): 1.

"Bishop James Walter Brown." *A.M.E. Zion Quarterly Review* 51, 2 (1941): 83–84.

"Obituary for Bishop J.W. Brown." *Star of Zion* 65 (March 6, 1941): 5.

RLA, AMEZC, HAMEZC, WWCR, WWCA (38–40), IBAW.

BROWN, JOHN MIFFLIN (September 8, 1817– March 16, 1893), eleventh bishop of the **African Methodist Episcopal Church** (AME), was born in Cantwell's Bridge (now called Odessa), New Castle County, Delaware. Not much is known about his family; his grandfather was a Methodist minister and his mother was also Methodist. He was born a mulatto and attended a Methodist Sunday School and a private day school taught by a friendly White woman. He apparently did not live with his original family after the age of ten, when he moved to Wilmington, Delaware to live with the family of William A. Seals, a Quaker.

In Wilmington he at first attended the Presbyterian church and Sunday School, but disliked being confined to the gallery because of his color. He then went to the Roman Catholic Sunday School, where he was graciously received. Father Carroll, the priest, offered to send him to the African American Catholic school in Baltimore, Maryland, but Brown preferred not to abandon in any long-term fashion his Methodist heritage. After two years in Wilmington an older sister in Philadelphia brought him there and placed him in the home of a Dr. Emerson and attorney Henry Chester. While he did service chores around the house, they in turn gave him educational instruction and religious training. While with them he attended St. Thomas' Colored Protestant **Episcopal Church**.

In 1835, at the age of eighteen, he moved to the home of Frederick H. Hinton and became his apprentice in the barbering trade. In January of the following year, he experienced conversion and joined the Bethel AME Church in Philadelphia. In the evenings he began private studies toward the ministry with a local minister. He attended a manual labor school briefly in Amherst, Massachusetts, returned to Philadelphia for a short time, then left for Poughkeepsie, New York, where he went to another school conducted by Rev. Nathaniel Blount, and worked in a barber shop. In the summer of 1838 he worked in a New York City barber shop, and that fall he enrolled in Wesleyan Academy in Wilbraham, Massachusetts, and spent two years preparing for college. In the summer of 1840 his health became poor and he returned to Philadelphia to recuperate. As he could, he continued with private studies of Latin and Greek under Rev. Harris of the local Presbyterian church.

In the fall of 1841 he entered Oberlin College in Ohio, but was unable to complete a degree. Having a relatively advanced education, however, he moved to Detroit and opened in the fall of 1844 the first school for Black children in the history of that city. After the death of the local AME pastor, Brown was appointed acting minister of that church from 1844 to 1847. Under his leadership a lot was purchased and a sanctuary constructed. In September 1849 he joined the Ohio Conference, was ordained a deacon, and was assigned to the AME Church in Columbus, Ohio. He was also appointed principal of Union Seminary, the first school owned and operated by the AME Church. It was begun in 1844 by action of the General Conference and located at first in the Columbus AME Church, then moved to a 120–acre farm about twelve miles from the city. In his

three years there Brown increased the enrollment from three to one hundred, but its future remained in doubt. In 1856, when the church acquired Wilberforce University, the farm was sold and the assets of Union Seminary were merged with the new institution.

On February 13, 1852, he married Mary Louise Lewis, with whom he had eight children. Later that year, in August, he was appointed to Allen Station in Pittsburgh, Pennsylvania. After only a few months he joined the Indiana Conference and went to the mission in New Orleans, Louisiana, arriving on September 29, 1852. During his five years in New Orleans he built Morris Brown Chapel, purchased Trinity Chapel, and was imprisoned at least five times for allowing slaves to attend worship. For three of those years he pastored the original St. James AME Church, and was responsible for beginning congregations in nearby Algiers and Covington. In April, 1857 he was transferred to Asbury Chapel in Louisville, Kentucky, where he stayed for a year. In May, 1858 he went to Bethel AME Church in Baltimore, where he added 700 members and remodeled the church at a cost of over $5,000. During this time he became editor of the *Repository of Religion, Literature, Art and Science*. From 1861 to 1863 he was at the Ebenezer AME Church in Baltimore, and in December, 1863 he was sent to Brite Street AME Church. While at that church he was also responsible for mission work, and accompanied Bishops Payne and Wayman to Virginia to start St. John's AME Church in Norfolk.

In 1864 he was briefly editor of the church's journal, the *Christian Recorder*, but left it when later in the year he was elected secretary of the Parent Home and Foreign Missionary Society of the AME Church. In the next four years raised $10,000 for the establishment of schools and churches in the South. At the General Conference in Washington, D.C. in 1868, Brown was elected bishop, and was consecrated on May 25. He was assigned to the Seventh Episcopal District (South Carolina, Georgia, Florida, and Alabama), organizing the Alabama Conference on July 25, 1868, in the basement of the Methodist Episcopal Church, South, in Selma, Alabama. In 1871 he helped organize Payne College in Cokesbury, South Carolina, now Allen University in Columbia, South Carolina.

From 1872 to 1876 he supervised the Sixth Episcopal District (Tennessee, Arkansas, Louisiana, and Texas), during which time he began the school that later became Paul Quinn College in Waco, Texas. He organized the West Texas, South Arkansas, West Tennessee, Denver (CO), and Columbia (SC) conferences, and helped organize the North Georgia Conference in 1872. From 1876 to 1880 he was assigned the Second Episcopal District (Baltimore, Virginia, North and South Carolina), from 1880 to 1884 he headed the First Episcopal District (Philadelphia, New York, New England, New Jersey), from 1884 to 1888 the Fourth Episcopal District (Missouri, North Missouri, Kansas, Illinois, Iowa, and California), and from 1888 to 1892 the Fourth Episcopal District (Indiana, Illinois, Michigan, and Iowa). He was a delegate to the first World Methodist Ecumenical Conference in London in 1881 and the second conference in Washington, D.C. in 1891. He was known as an eloquent, learned, friendly gentleman who was popular with all classes, and passed away at his home in Washington, D.C. There are at least 29 churches named for him in fifteen states.

Brown, John Mifflin. *The Priesthood.* Quadrennial Sermon, 16th General Conference, Baltimore, 1884.

———. *Sermon by Bishop John M. Brown, on the Necessity of Ministerial Education, Delivered to the Students of Wilberforce University and the Ministers of the Seventh Episcopal District.* Philadelphia, PA: Stanford, 1870. 24 pp.

DAB (vol. 2), *MM, DANB, BAMEC, WWWA* (H), *RAM, CEAMEC, HAMEC, IBAW, EWM, AARS.*

BROWN, MORRIS (January 8, 1770–May 9, 1849), second bishop of the **African Methodist Episcopal Church** (AME), was born free in Charleston, South Carolina, of mixed parentage. The group of free Blacks in Charleston was largely exempted from the usual restrictions because of the close blood ties most of them had with the aristocratic Whites of the area. He was able to gain some amount of basic education, was converted at an early age in one of the White Methodist churches in town, and immediately gained a license to preach. He earned his living as a shoemaker. In 1816 a dispute over burial grounds led to the founding of a separate Black Methodist society, of which Brown was the leader. He married Maria (last name unknown), with whom he had six children.

Brown was ordained a deacon in 1817, one year after **Richard Allen** founded the AME Church in Philadelphia, Pennsylvania. In 1818 Allen ordained Brown an elder and the Charleston Black Methodist society was brought into the AME Church. With the title of Emanuel AME Church, it was the first AME church in the South, and Brown was its first minister. Bethel Methodist Church gave the group its old sanctuary in which to meet. Brown used his prosperous shoe business and the church as bases from which to help numerous slaves purchase their freedom and make their way north. In 1821 he was imprisoned for a year for his efforts. In

1822 Denmark Vesey, a strong layperson in the church, led his unsuccessful insurrection, and the authorities suspected significant church involvement. The now over 1800-member church was closed, and Brown, fearing for his safety, fled to Philadelphia, where he became Richard Allen's close assistant.

He was appointed assistant pastor of Bethel AME Church in 1825, assistant bishop to Allen in 1826, and was consecrated bishop on May 25, 1828. In August, 1830, at Hillsboro, Ohio, he organized the Pittsburgh or Western Conference, comprising all the territory between the Allegheny Mountains and the Mississippi River. After Allen passed away in 1831 Brown was the sole bishop until Edward Waters was consecrated in 1836. In July, 1840, he organized the Canada Conference, and on October 2, 1840, at Blue River, Indiana, he organized the Indiana Conference. At the 1844 General Conference, future bishop **Daniel Payne** agitated for a regular course of study for ministers, and Brown was instrumental in persuading the church to agree.

In 1844, while in Canada on episcopal work, Brown suffered a stroke, causing a paralysis from which he never recovered. The Philadelphia Conference retired him in 1845, but he remained as active as possible. By the time of his death the AME Church was organized in fourteen states with six annual conferences, three bishops, sixty-two elders, and 17,375 members, twice the membership of the church at the end of Richard Allen's life. Morris Brown College in Atlanta, Georgia, is named for him, as are several churches, including Morris Brown AME Church at 13 Morris Street in Charleston, South Carolina.

DAB (vol. 2), *BAMEC, DANB, CEAMEC, WWWA* (H), *AMSC, ERS, CH, HAMEC, IBAW, EWM, RAM.*

BROWN, ROBERT TURNER (February 14, 1860–September 15, 1933), 13th bishop of the **Christian Methodist Episcopal Church** (CME) (then known as the Colored Methodist Episcopal Church), was born in Courtland County, Alabama, the son of James and Eliza (Sanders) Brown. His father died when he was two, and at the age of seven he and his mother went to live on his uncle's farm. There he learned to read and write, despite his uncle's death only a few years later. He experienced conversion and joined the local CME church under Rev. W. R. Palmer. He was licensed to preach on February 19, 1879, by Rev. R. T. Thirgood and entered Central Tennessee College later that year. He was unable to continue through the whole course at the college, probably because of lack of money, and took a church appointment.

His first pastorate was at Gadsden, Alabama, where he was ordained deacon by Bishop Miles in 1881. From there he went to Hopkinsville, Kentucky, where Bishop **W. H. Miles** ordained him elder on October 15, 1882. From Hopkinsville he was transferred to the Indian Territory, where he spent two years with marked success. In 1884 he was elected editor of the church's journal, the *Christian Index*, holding that position for eight years. During that time he enrolled in Meharry Medical College in Nashville, Tennessee, where he received his B.A. in 1889. He then transferred to Walden University, also in Nashville, where he received his M.A. in 1892.

About 1892 he became dean of Lane College in Jackson, Tennessee, where he stayed for five years. In 1893 he published his major written work, *Doctrines of Christ and His Church*. About 1897 he became president of the Board of Missions of the CME Church. He also at some point served as president of the Board of Evangelists of the CME Church. From 1915 to 1919 he served as president of Miles Memorial College in Birmingham, Alabama. In September, 1921 he was a delegate to the Fifth World Methodist Ecumenical Conference in London. At the 1922 General Conference in St. Louis, Missouri, at the age of sixty-two, he was elected bishop. As bishop he headed the regions of Alabama, West Florida, and British West Indies, where he was instrumental in establishing a church in Trinidad. He was noted as a polished preacher.

Brown, Robert Turner. *The Doctrines of Christ and the Church*. Jackson, TN: CME Church Publishing House, 1893. 275 pp.
EWM, CMECTY, WWCA (30–32), *BAW, EBA*.

BROWN, STERLING NELSON (November 21, 1858– ?), educator and Congregationalist minister, was born in Roane County, Tennessee. He attended the first free public school ever offered in his county. While still a boy he experienced conversion and began to preach, leading a number of revivals. In Kingston, Tennessee, it is reported that due to his preaching every child in school, numbering over one hundred, was converted, as were a large number of the adults in town. He enrolled at Fisk University in Nashville, Tennessee, in 1875, where he remained for the next sixteen years. Many summers he earned tuition money by teaching, and towards the end of his college career the summers were spent supplying pulpits around the South. At some point he married and became the father of six children.

He graduated with a B.A. in 1885, and on June 1, 1885 he was ordained as the minister of Mount Zion Congregational Church in Cleveland, Ohio. While there he continued his studies at Oberlin Theological Seminary, earning a B.D. in 1888. Under his leadership the church increased its small flock to the extent that it was able to tear down the old place of worship and build a beautiful new one. On April 1, 1889, Brown accepted a call from the Plymouth Congregational Church in Washington, D.C., where he remained for a successful eight years. In 1892 he augmented this work as professor in the Theological Department of Howard University in Washington, D.C.

In January 1897, he founded a new church, Park Temple Congregational Church, in the northeast section of Washington, D.C. It soon developed into a healthy, growing church, and on October 1, 1901, it merged with Lincoln Congregational Church to become Lincoln Temple Congregational Church, with Brown as pastor. This new arrangement of a large main church and a branch church was unusual, but seemed to work. He maintained his teaching at Howard University, becoming professor of the English Bible. For three years he was an influential member of the Washington Board of Education. In 1907 he published his major written work, *Bible Mastery*.

In 1913 he resigned from the church work to devote himself more fully to teaching at Howard, where he expanded his duties to be director of extension work and correspondence study. He was very successful in business as president of Oak Park Realty Co., and owned a 100–acre farm in Maryland.

Brown, Sterling Nelson. *Bible Mastery*. Washington, DC: Merchants' Printing Co., 1907. 244 pp.
BAW, HUBA, IBAWCB, NBH, TCNL, WWCR.

BROWN, WILLIAM CORNELIUS (June 24, 1877– January 2, 1964), 48th bishop of the **African Methodist Episcopal Zion Church** (AMEZ), was born in Chowan County, near Edenton, North Carolina, the son of Whitman and Fannie Maria (Blount) Brown. He attended the State Normal School in Elizabeth City, North Carolina, and early on made a decision to enter the ministry. He became a lay preacher in Canaan's Temple Church in Chowan County before moving to the northeast, where he attended Boston University for a time. In 1900 he enrolled in Westbrook Seminary in Portland, Maine, and joined the New England Conference in 1901 at Providence, Rhode Island, where he was ordained deacon on May 5, 1901. He was assigned to the Portland Mission Church while still attending school, and is credited with saving a deteriorating situation at that church, the only Black church at the time in Maine. He married Gertrude Capehart on December 29, 1901, and graduated from seminary in 1904. He was ordained elder on June 12, 1904.

After staying at the Portland Church for a time, he then pastored the Creswell Circuit in the Virginia Conference, Kadesh Chapel in Edenton, North Carolina (also building the Columbia Mission in Columbia, North Carolina), Walters Memorial Church in Bridgeport, Connecticut, and Varick Memorial Church in New Haven, Connecticut. While at the latter church, he attended Yale University in 1912. He then was assigned to the John Wesley church in Washington, D.C., where he built the present structure. In 1920 he was assigned to the prestigious First Church (Fleet Street) in Brooklyn, New York, where he stayed for the next sixteen years. Here he firmly established his reputation, not only in building up the church, but in other arenas as well. He became director of the Brooklyn Branch, Urban League, and was regarded as one of the foremost leaders of the city. He was also president of the Acquiring Realty Corporation and director of the Supreme Liberty Life Insurance Company.

At the 1936 General Conference he was elected bishop, and was consecrated on May 20, 1936. He was assigned to the Texas and Oklahoma areas. With an established reputation for business acumen, he founded the Brotherhood Pension Service for the clergy. He was later assigned to the Pacific Coast area, where both he and his wife suffered long and difficult illnesses, but recovered sufficiently to make a strong contribution to the extension of the church in the West. He was next assigned to the Missouri and Kentucky Conferences, where he was serving when he retired to his home in Brooklyn in May, 1960.

"The Magnificent Qualities of Our Bishops: Part 7." *Star of Zion* 70 (August 22, 1946): 1, 8.
"Rites Held for Bishop Brown." *Star of Zion* 87 (April 2, 1964): 1, 5.
"Sidelights on the Character of Bishop W. C. Brown." *Star of Zion* 65 (July 31, 1941): 1.
"William Cornelius Brown." *Star of Zion* 82 (May 7, 1959): 5.
AMEZC, HAMEZC, WWCA (38–40).

BROWNE, GEORGE DANIEL (b. December 17, 1933), a bishop of the **Episcopal Church**, was born in Liberia, West Africa. His paternal grandfather was a high priest of one of the traditional religions of Africa, and his maternal grandfather was an Episcopal priest in Liberia. Browne received his B.S. in education in 1958 and his B.D. in 1962 from Cuttington College and Divinity School in Liberia. After graduation he came to the United States and in 1964 earned his Masters of Sacred Theology at the Episcopal Theological Seminary in Alexandria, Virginia. He married Clavender Agnes, with whom he had six children.

Browne was ordained deacon on December 30, 1962 and priest on July 21, 1963. Over the next seven years he was in charge of several congregations, was superintendent and chaplain of the diocese's only all-girl school, and chaplain and instructor in religion at Cuttington College. He published a number of items as historiographer of the diocese. He served on numerous church committees and was a member of the Board of Examining Chaplains. Due to the sudden death of Bishop Dillard Brown in 1969, a special convocation of the Liberian Church was held on April 1, 1970, at which time Browne was elected the tenth Episcopal bishop of Liberia, and one of the youngest Episcopal bishops in history. He was the first bishop elected under the special provision made by the House of Bishops to permit overseas districts to elect their own bishops if they so choose. Browne was consecrated on August 6, 1970.

Browne, George D. "History of the Protestant Episcopal Mission in Liberia up to 1838." *Historical Magazine of the Protestant Episcopal Church* 39 (March 1970): 17-27.
HUBA, AARS, EBA, ECA (1971).

BRUCE, ROBERT BLAIR (June 26, 1861–July 9, 1920), 35th bishop of the **African Methodist Episcopal Zion Church** (AMEZ), was born in Charlie Hope, Brunswick County, Virginia. Little is known of his parents; he was raised on a farm by a grandmother and uncle, who permitted him to attend school on rainy days. At about ten years of age he experienced conversion and joined Solomon's Temple at Charlie Hope. As he grew a little older he craved additional education, and regularly walked seven miles to a school in Lawrenceville, until he had achieved a basic education.

He joined the Virginia Conference of the AMEZ Church in 1884, and about 1886 enrolled in Payne Divinity School at Petersburg, Virginia. He was ordained deacon on September 5, 1886, and after graduation transferred to the Western North Carolina Conference, where he pastored in Winston-Salem for two years. He was ordained elder on November 20, 1892. In 1894 he went to Grace Church, Charlotte, where he served for five years and began building the present structure. He next went to the Little Rock

Church, also in Charlotte, for one year, and then the Soldiers Memorial in Salisbury for two years.

About 1903 he became editor of the AME Zion Sunday School periodicals, a position he held for more than twenty years. He was a firm believer in the benefits of the church producing its own literature, and was a major force in establishing and building up the church's publishing abilities. He functioned for many years as a presiding elder in the Charlotte area, though he was never officially appointed as such. For a few years he was dean of the Theological Seminary at Livingstone College in Salisbury.

At the 1916 General Conference in Louisville, Kentucky, he was the second of four bishops elected, and was consecrated on May 19, 1916. He was bishop for only four years before his death, during which time, however, he began constructive work in his assigned areas of Georgia and South Carolina.

"Sense-Economy." *Star of Zion* 102 (June 22, 1978): 2. *AMEZC, HAMEZC.*

BRYAN, ANDREW (1737–October 6, 1812), pioneer Baptist preacher, was born into slavery at Goose Creek, South Carolina. He was later brought to Savannah, Georgia, where he was converted by the preaching of **George Liele**, a Black Baptist. Liele baptized both Bryan and his wife, Hannah, just before he left Savannah with the British in 1782. Bryan began leading prayer meetings, then some months later began preaching to Black and White audiences in the region. His owner, Jonathan Bryan, agreed to this activity insofar as the preaching seemed inoffensive. Edward Davis, a wealthy White landowner, allowed a rough building to be constructed on his land at Yamacraw (Brampton) for meetings. Other slaveholders were not as optimistic about the value of letting Blacks congregate so freely, and disrupted their worship. Bryan was forced to hold the meetings in the swamps, persevering until Abraham Marshall, minister of Kiokee Baptist Church in Columbia County, agreed to baptize the members and organize them into a church, which was done on January 20, 1788, at the Brampton Barn. With such a duly constituted congregation in place, Bryan was "called" to its pastorate, and Marshall ordained him.

This new status, and Bryan's increasing popularity, brought more persecution upon the church, and both Bryan and his brother, Sampson, were severely whipped and put in prison, accused of plotting insurrection. His owner managed to get them released, and Bryan continued his preaching in the safety of the plantation barn. Opposition continued until the authorities ruled that the worship was lawful between sunrise and sunset. In 1790 the congregation joined the Georgia Baptist Association, and Lot No. 12, North Oglethorpe Ward, was purchased on June 1, 1790, at what is now Mill Street and Indian Street Lane. About this time, Bryan gained his freedom, and he was also able to buy freedom for his wife and daughter. With the help of sympathetic White preachers and others, Lot No. 7, Middle Oglethorpe Ward, was purchased on September 4, 1793. A parsonage for Bryan was built on part of this lot in 1794, and a church was finished on the other part of the lot in 1795. This was called at the time the Colored Baptist Church.

Bryan's congregation soon grew to several hundred members, and he decided to use some of that membership to organize another church, the Second Colored Baptist Church, in 1799. He placed a slave, Henry (Francis) Cunningham, as its pastor, who was soon enabled to purchase his freedom. In a similar way the Ogeechee Colored Baptist Church was later organized in a nearby area. A letter to a colleague in 1800 said that he was sixty-three, which places his birth year.

When Bryan died in 1812, the predominantly White Savannah Baptist Association had only praise for him and his ministry. His nephew, **Andrew Marshall**, succeeded him in the pulpit. In 1823 the local Baptist Association, in which the Blacks had no real voice, summarily changed the names of the Black churches, substituting "African" for "Colored." In 1832, in the aftermath of **Nat Turner**'s rebellion in 1831, Black churches in the South were suspect and their activities limited and persecuted. During this upheaval, a split developed in Bryan's original church over the apparent friendliness Andrew Marshall showed to the doctrines of Alexander Campbell, founder of the Disciples of Christ. Marshall and many members withdrew to a former White Baptist church building in Franklin Square that then became First African Baptist Church. Other members went to Second African or Ogeechee Baptist Church, and only about two hundred remained at the original church, led at first by Deacon Adam Johnson, and then by Rev. Thomas Anderson. Anderson applied to the local Baptist Association for readmission to the fellowship, and this was granted. They were given the name Third African Baptist Church to avoid confusion with Marshall's renegade group. In 1837 Marshall and his First African Baptist Church were readmitted into the Baptist Association. In 1865, after Emancipation, the Third African Baptist Church renamed itself the First Bryan Baptist Church. Both it and the First African Baptist Church have claimed primacy as "the" church founded by Liele and Bryan. A committee of the African

Missionary Baptist State Convention in 1888 decided that "the church organized at Brampton Barn, three miles southwest of Savannah, Jan. 20, 1788, is the First African Baptist Church of today." On the other hand, the First Bryan Baptist Church is still on Lot No. 7, the lot on which Bryan built his church in 1795.

Davis, John W. "George Liele and Andrew Bryan, Pioneer Negro Baptist Preachers." *Journal of Negro History* 2 (April 1918): 119–127.

Love, Emanuel King. *History of the First African Baptist Church, From its Organization, January 20, 1788 to July 1, 1888.* Savannah, GA: The Morning News Printing Co., 1888. 360 pp.

PBGB, IBAW, HBB, ERS, CH, HBBUS, HNC, SNB, ENB, SCA, NBH, PHNA, DANB, BPEAR, NYB (1925–26).

BRYANT, HARRISON JAMES (November 20, 1899–c. September 1, 1989), 82nd bishop of the **African Methodist Episcopal Church** (AME), was born in Keithville Village, near Georgetown, South Carolina, one of eight children in the family of Richard and Annie (Tucker) Bryant. His father died when he was in the sixth grade, and he had to drop out of school and work in the rice fields to help support the family. When he was seventeen and working at a sawmill, he had a dream in which the Lord urged him to go preach. He became very active in St. Stephens AME Church in Georgetown, and was elected president of the Allen Christian Endeavor League. In this role he had to speak to high school students, but his poor grammar was met with laughter. Instead of shrinking from the task, he was motivated to return to school. In 1920, at the age of twenty-one, he enrolled in Howard High School in Georgetown. His younger brothers and sisters were embarrassed by his presence there, but he graciously encouraged them to pretend they did not know him. He did house and yard work to support himself at school. For the rest of his life he would be an advocate of life long learning.

After graduating from high school he received a license to preach and began pastoring at St. Stephen's AME Church in 1923. His first assignment after being ordained deacon was at Jones Chapel AME Church in Lexington (1926–1927), followed by Chappelle Station AME Church in Columbia (1927–1932), both in South Carolina. He was ordained an elder in 1929, and was also enrolled at Allen University in Columbia, receiving his B.A. in 1932. He went on to receive his B.D. at Payne Theological Seminary at Wilberforce University in Ohio, in 1935. He pastored at the nearby First AME

Church in Xenia from 1932 to 1935. From 1935 to 1936 he was at Riverview AME Church in Little Rock, Arkansas, where he also was dean of Jackson Theological Seminary at Shorter College. On June 11, 1936, he married Edith Drusesella Holland, with whom he had six children.

After the marriage he was assigned to St. Paul AME Church in Zanesville, Ohio, where he stayed for three years. From 1939 to 1942 he was at another St. Paul AME Church, this time at Lexington, Kentucky. From 1942 to 1949 he pastored at St. John's AME Church in Baltimore, Maryland, where he rebuilt the church after a disastrous fire and paid it out of debt. From 1949 to 1964 he served at the prestigious Bethel AME Church, also in Baltimore. From 1960 to 1962 he was vice-president of the Maryland Council of Churches. He was very active in civil rights issues and was known in Congress. At the General Conference in 1964 he was elected bishop and assigned to the 15th Episcopal District (South Africa and Namibia), maintaining his residence in Baltimore. From 1968 to 1976 he served the 5th Episcopal District (Western United States) and located his residence in California.

In 1976 he retired and moved to Baltimore, Maryland, where he could attend the church he formerly led, Bethel, which at the time was pastored by his son, **John R. Bryant**. John Bryant has since (1988) been elected a bishop, and Bryant thus became the first living AME bishop to have a son elected to the bishopric, even elected from the same pastorate.

"Bishop Bryant's Life is a Christian Story." *A.M.E. Christian Recorder* 134 (March 25, 1985): 1, 6.

"On the Cover: In Memoriam, Bishop Harrison J. Bryant." *A.M.E. Church Review* 105 (October–December 1989): 2.

"Retired AME Bishop H.J. Bryant Funeral Held in Baltimore." *Star of Zion* 113 (November 9, 1989): 3, 10.

"A Tribute to Bishop Harrison James Bryant." *A.M.E. Church Review* 105 (October–December 1989): 5

OTSB, EAMEC, EWM, WWABA (90–91), *WWR* (75–76), *BDNM* (70), *AMSC, HAMEC, FEDHR.*

BRYANT, J. E. (1879–1939) an overseer with the **Church of God in Christ**, was born in Jasper County, Texas. His father was a Baptist preacher and the family active in church. He and his brothers and sisters experienced salvation as children. His father died when he was 18, and abandoning plans for an education, he went to work on the family farm to care for the family. He gradually fell away from the church. He married

Lula Adams and they would eventually have nine children.

Bryant was once again drawn to faith in a Baptist church in 1905. The next three years were ones of longing for a deeper experience of the Christian life. In 1908 he began teaching school. That year also proved to be the time he began a more intense life of faith. He heard Judge King, a minister with **Christ's Sanctified Holy Church**, a small African American Holiness church which had been founded in Louisiana a few years previously. While convinced that King was preaching about the holiness experience he, Bryant, did not yet move into the new level of Christian life. He did, however, enter the ministry. He was licensed to preach by the Baptists and two years later was ordained and elected moderator of the Lone Star Baptist Association.

In the summer of 1910 his wife became seriously ill. Acting on his wife's urging, he sent for the members of the Holiness church to pray for her. During their visit, she was miraculously healed and experienced sanctification, the experience of complete cleansing by the power of the Holy Spirit, the definitive experience of Holiness. A month later Bryant also experienced sanctification. As a result he associated with Christ's Sanctified Holy Church and in 1911 was reordained as a Holiness minister. He preached holiness for the next four years until 1915 when he also experienced the baptism of the Holy Spirit as evidenced by his speaking in tongues and became a member of the Church of God in Christ.

He soon moved into a leadership position with the Church of God in Christ, and was chosen to pioneer work in New England. He was appointed overseer (a title later changed to bishop) of Maine. From his home in Orange, New Jersey, he worked for the rest of his life building the church in the Northeast.

DuPree, Sherry Sherrod. *Biographical Dictionary of African-American Holiness-Pentecostals, 1880–1990.* Washington, DC: Middle Atlantic Regional Press, 1989. 386 pp.

Patterson, J. O., German R. Ross, and Julia Mason Atkins. *History and Formative Years of the Church of God in Christ with Excerpts from the Life of Its Founder—Bishop C. H. Mason.* Memphis, TN: Church of God in Christ Publishing House, 1969. 143 pp.

BRYANT, JOHN RICHARD (b. June 8, 1943), 106th bishop of the **African Methodist Episcopal Church** (AME), was born in Baltimore, Maryland, one of six children in the family of Harrison J. and Edith (Holland) Bryant. His father was a minister of the AME Church,

and was elected bishop in 1964. Bryant decided to follow in his father's footsteps, graduating from Morgan State College in Baltimore in 1965, and gaining his M.Th. from Boston School of Theology in 1970. He married Cecilia Williams, with whom he has had two children.

His first pastoral appointment was during seminary, at the Bethel AME Church in Fall River, Massachusetts, from 1968 to 1970. In 1970 he went to St. Paul AME Church in Cambridge, Massachusetts. During this time he became widely known in the denomination and community. He received the Springfield Outstanding Churchman Award from the Boston Jaycees and the Black Male Role-Model Award. He served on the Education Commission of the National Council of Churches, participated in Cambridge Model Cities, and founded and chaired the Black Empowerment Committee of Cambridge. He was a leader in the Boston Urban League. He studied at Colgate Rochester Divinity School, making a study tour in West Africa with its Black Church Studies program in the summer of 1972, and earning his D.Min. in 1975.

About 1976 he was appointed to Bethel AME Church in Baltimore, Maryland, remaining until 1988. There he continued his pattern of leadership, serving on the board of regents of Morgan State College and on the board of the National Committee of Black Churchmen (now the **National Conference of Black Churchmen**). He served on the Education Commission of the AME Church, on the Black Ecumenical Commission, and on the board of the Ecumenical Institute. He was president of Bethel Bible Institute, a board member of the World Methodist Council on Evangelism, and a board member of Freedom House, Inc. His sermons were broadcast on two television stations and four radio stations, and he received the Boston School of Theology's Outstanding Alumni Award.

At the General Conference in 1988 he was elected bishop, becoming the first bishop of the AME Church with a living father who was also bishop. His father passed away the following year. Bryant was assigned to the 14th Episcopal District covering Liberia.

WWABA (90–91), *BDNM* (75).

BUNTON, HENRY CLAY (b. October 19, 1903), 33rd bishop of the **Christian Methodist Episcopal Church** (CME), was born in a two-room log cabin near the village of Coker, Tuscaloosa County, Alabama, the sixth of twelve children in the family of Isaac and Sarah Lou (Noland) Bunton. His parents were pious Methodists and poor tenant farmers. His mother died after the ninth child, when Bunton was about seven, and his father married Mary Ella Blissett. She brought a son from a previous marriage, and the new couple had two more children.

He had a near-fatal case of whooping cough as a young child, and its effects lingered into adulthood. He attended an elementary school from about seven to ten years of age, and did not return to school until age twenty-two, when urged to do so by Rev. R. A. Kirk, the presiding elder of the Tuscaloosa District. As a teenager he worked in sawmills, coal mines, and railroads, and in 1922, at the age of nineteen, he married Estelle McKinney, with whom he had four children. Although he attended church, he avoided joining one for fear that he would then have to become a preacher, and he had not had many positive experiences with preachers. Finally, on June 2, 1924, he experienced conversion and soon joined the CME Church.

He entered Miles College in Birmingham, Alabama, in 1925 and was assigned to the sixth grade level. By this time he not only had a family to care for, but did not have the encouragement of his local church or community for going back to school. To support his family he continued working on the farm, tended the school's boiler, and was the school's night watchman. He received his first church appointment in 1926, to the as-yet nonexistent Avondale Mission Church. After three months he had fifteen regulars at home worship. He then went to Valley Creek, to a one-family church, where he stayed for two years. In 1928 he was ordained deacon in the North Alabama Conference and assigned to Dolomite, a mining camp near Birmingham, with sixteen members. In 1929 he was assigned to Little Rock CME Church at Cate City, east of Birmingham, with 30–40 members. In 1930 he was ordained elder and moved to Shady Grove CME Church in the Englewood section of Fairfield, staying about two years. In 1932 he was assigned to Miles Chapel on the Miles College campus. By about this time he was able to finish high school and two years at the college level at Miles before needing to take a break from studies and restore his family life.

About 1934, at the invitation of Bishop **James A. Bray**, he transferred to the East Florida Conference and was assigned to the Florencevilla-Winterhaven CME Church. One year later he went to Stewart Memorial CME Church in St. Petersburg, where he stayed four years. In 1937 he constructed the first educational building in the history of the denomination. The money for it was donated by a White woman, a Miss Fridgen. In 1939 he was assigned to St. James CME Church in Tallahassee, where he took the opportunity to attend Florida A & M University and receive his B.A. in 1941. At one point the bishop offered him a better church, provided he left school; he did not accept the offer. Still, in 1941 he went to the Carter Tabernacle CME Church in Orlando, the second biggest CME church in Florida. During his two years there a large debt was paid off. In 1942 he transferred to the Bullock Temple Church in Little Rock, Arkansas, the largest CME church in the state.

World War II interrupted his church work, and he became a chaplain in the U.S. Army in April, 1943. He was assigned to Camp Van Dorn in Mississippi, and on November 5, 1943, the unit sailed for England. With the rank of Major, he was part of the invasion of Normandy in June 1944. He returned to the U.S. on November 5, 1945, and the church assigned him to Sparks Chapel CME Church in Dallas, Texas. He wanted to attend Perkins School of Theology at Southern Methodist University, but it did not at the time accept Black students. The dean, Eugene Hawk, said that if Bunton could find as many as six Blacks who could take courses on a graduate level, he would arrange for it. Bunton found twelve, including himself, and classes began. In the second year they were integrated into the regular classes, but were still not considered officially registered. Blacks were not officially admitted until the fall of 1948. In addition to his church and school work, Bunton was part-time Y.M.C.A. Boy's Work Secretary for two of these years.

In the summer of 1950 he studied at Garrett Biblical Institute (now Garrett-Evangelical Theological Seminary in Evanston, Illinois, and then entered Iliff School of Theology in Denver, Colorado. Iliff gave him credit for the work done at Perkins, and he received his Th.M. in 1952. From 1952 to 1953 he was Director of Leadership Training, Adult Work, under the Board of Christian Education of the CME Church, and a writer of Sunday School literature. From 1953 to 1962 he pastored the prestigious Mt. Olive Cathedral CME Church in Memphis, Tennessee. In Memphis he was president of the Ministers and Citizens League, organized to get Blacks registered to vote. About 1958 he was elected president of the Ministerial Alliance of Memphis and Shelby County. In January, 1958, his first wife died, and he later married a widow, Alfreda Gibbs Carpenter. In 1959 he ran unsuccessfully for a Board of Education position. He was a charter member of the executive board of the **Southern Christian Leadership Conference** (S.C.L.C.) until 1962, when he was elected bishop.

After being elected bishop on May 17, 1962, at the

General Conference in St. Louis, Missouri, he was assigned to work on the East Coast (7th Episcopal District), and also became chair of the Publishing Board of the CME Church. In 1966 he shifted to the Conference in Ghana and Nigeria, serving until 1972, when he moved to the Seventh Episcopal District (Washington, D.C., South Carolina, and elsewhere along the Eastern Seaboard). He was automatically retired in 1978, though he was called to complete Bishop **Joseph Johnson**'s term in the Fourth Episcopal District (Louisiana and Mississippi) up to May, 1982.

Bunton, Henry Clay. *A Dreamer of Dreams: An Autobiography.* The Author, 1983[?]. 209 pp.
EBA, WWR (75–76), *EWM, BDNM* (75), *WWABA* (90–91), *CMECTY, OTSB.*

BURGESS, JOHN MELVILLE (b. March 11, 1909), the first Black **Episcopal Church** bishop to be assigned to a primarily White American diocese and the first to head a diocese in the United States, was born in Grand Rapids, Michigan, the son of Theodore Thomas and Ethel Inez (Beverly) Burgess. His father was a dining-car waiter on the Pere Marquette Railroad. Burgess waited tables in a fraternity house to work his way through the University of Michigan, where he earned a B.A. in 1930 and an M.A. in 1931, both in sociology. Although his own early life had been removed from the more overt and brutal racism of the South, by this time he had become aware of tremendous evil pervading all of American society. He decided that the Christian gospel offered the surest solution, and thus went to the Episcopal Theological School in Cambridge, Massachusetts, graduating with his B.D. in 1934. He was ordained deacon on June 29, 1934, and priest on January 25, 1935.

His first parish assignment was St. Philip's (Protestant) Episcopal Church in Grand Rapids, Michigan, where he served from 1934 to 1939. He then went to St. Simon of Cyrene Woodlaw (Protestant) Episcopal Church in Cincinnati, Ohio, from 1939 to 1946. On August 2, 1945, he married Esther J. Taylor, with whom he had two children. From 1946 to 1956 he was chaplain at Howard University in Washington, D.C. During part of that time, 1952 to 1956, he was also canon at the Washington Cathedral under Woodrow Wilson's grandson, Francis Sayre, dean of the cathedral. In 1952 he was a delegate to the World Council of Churches Central Committee meeting in Lucknow, India, and in 1961 attended the World Council of Churches Assembly in New Delhi, India. From 1956 to

1962 he was archdeacon of Boston and supervisor of the Episcopal City Mission.

On December 8, 1962 Burgess was consecrated suffragan (assistant) bishop of Massachusetts, the first Black Episcopal suffragan bishop of a primarily White diocese. Arkansas and North Carolina had previously had Black Episcopal suffragan bishops whose supervision was limited to non-White parishes. He was chosen suffragan bishop over four White candidates on the first ballot at a convention of diocesan priests in September 1962. He noted that year that the church needed to take a hard look at its relationship to Blacks and the issue of civil rights, and saw his task as helping the church move in the appropriate direction.

In 1969 Burgess was elected the successor (coadjutor) bishop to retiring Bishop Stokes, becoming diocesan bishop of Massachusetts on January 17, 1970. There were previous Black Episcopal bishops who presided over a diocese, but they were assigned to Liberia, in Africa. Burgess was the first one to preside over a diocese in the United States. He was active on the general board of the National Council of Churches and the general board of the Massachusetts Civil Liberties Union. He served on numerous denominational committees and was trustee for both Deaconess Hospital in Boston and St. Augustine's College in Raleigh, North Carolina. He retired in 1976 to serve as assistant professor at Yale Divinity School in New Haven, Connecticut. In 1982 he published *Black Gospel/White Church.*

"Boston's Negro Bishop." *Time* 80 (December 21, 1962): 37-38.
Burgess, John M. *Black Gospel/White Church.* New York: Seabury Press, 1982. 108 pp.
OTSB, IBAW, WWABA (92–93), *EBA, AAE, WWR* (77), *BDNM* (75), *BHBA, NA, MSB.*

BURNS, FRANCIS (December 5, 1809–April 18, 1863), the first African American elected a bishop (for missionary work abroad only) within the Methodist Episcopal Church (now a part of the **United Methodist Church**), was born in Albany, New York. His parents were so poor that when Burns was four or five years old he was indentured to a Methodist farmer named Atwood in Greene County, New York. Atwood saw to his basic education in public schools, and Burns experienced conversion at age fifteen. He joined the Methodist Episcopal Church and soon wanted to become a minister. He was licensed as a local preacher for the Windham Circuit, but his education was insufficient yet for ordination, and he had to remain with Atwood until age twenty-one.

When he gained his freedom at the end of 1830 officials of the Missionary Society in New York advised him to engage in studies with the goal of being a missionary to Liberia. This may have been the time when he attended the Lexington Heights Academy in New York, where he was the first Black student. This may have been one of the first occasions in the country that a Black student attended a White school. In September, 1834 he sailed for Liberia, landing on October 18. He joined the Liberia Conference of the Methodist Episcopal Church in 1838, and his first appointment was as a teacher at Cape Palmas. From 1840 to 1842 he was an assistant on the Bassa Circuit and in 1843 he began working in Monrovia.

In 1844 Burns returned to the United States, where on June 16 he was ordained deacon in Brooklyn, New York, and later on the same day was ordained elder at the Mulberry Street Methodist Episcopal Church in Manhattan, Bishop Janes officiating. He then returned to Liberia, where he was presiding elder of the Cape Palmas District (one of two districts in Liberia) for about ten years. In 1851 the Missionary Board asked him to found the Monrovia Seminary and superintend the mission there, which he did with much success. He also served as president of the Liberia Conference and editor of *Africa's Summary*. The 1856 General Conference made a provision for a missionary bishop in Africa, and in 1858 the Liberia Conference elected Burns for that position. He made the trip to the United States, where on October 14, 1858, Bishops E. S. Janes and Osmon Baker consecrated him at the Genessee Conference in Perry, New York. He returned to Liberia, where he served for five more years. When his health failed, on the advice of a physician he again went to the United States, where he passed away in Baltimore, Maryland, three days after his arrival and three months after the Emancipation Proclamation. He was buried in Monrovia.

EWM, NCAB (13), *ACAB, BAHA, MB.*

BURROUGHS, NANNIE HELEN (May 2, 1878?– May 20, 1961), educator and a founder of the Woman's Convention of the **National Baptist Convention, U.S.A., Inc.,** was born in Orange, Virginia, the eldest of two daughters in the family of John and Jennie (Poindexter) Burroughs. Both her sister and her father died when she was very young, and at age five her mother took her to Washington, D.C., where her mother found a job as a cook. Burroughs graduated from the M Street High School in 1896 with honors. She had studied business and domestic science and had organized the Harriet Beecher Stowe Literary Society.

Although the Washington, D.C. public school system did hire Black teachers, she was apparently too dark-skinned for their preference, and could not find a position as a domestic science teacher. She then determined that some day she would have a school not bound by such politics. She spent a year in Philadelphia as assistant editor of a Baptist paper, the *Christian Banner*, then received high marks on a civil service exam and returned to Washington expecting to be hired as a clerk. She was told there were no openings for "a colored clerk," and was forced to find other work as a janitor and then as a bookkeeper. She never married.

In 1900 Burroughs moved to Louisville, Kentucky, accepting a position as secretary for the Foreign Mission Board of the National Baptist Convention, U.S.A., Inc. While serving in that capacity she also organized the Woman's Industrial Club, which served moderately priced lunches in the downtown business district to working Blacks of Louisville, and in the evenings conducted classes. She taught the evening classes in typing, shorthand, bookkeeping, millinery, sewing, handicrafts, and cooking, for any member paying ten cents per week. She was eventually able to increase tuition, hire other teachers, and free herself to supervise the classes.

Later that year the annual meeting of the denomination was held in Richmond, Virginia, and she addressed the delegates with a speech entitled, "How the Sisters are Hindered from Helping." She was a tall, impressive woman with a gift for public speaking, and the speech stirred the whole convention. As a result the National Baptist Woman's Convention was founded at that meeting as an auxiliary to the National Baptist Convention, U.S.A., Inc., and she was elected its corresponding secretary. It convened its first annual convention in September, 1901, showing a bank account of $15. This organization and its work, which was primarily to reinforce Christian missions, immediately took over her life. She quickly began pressing also for a home mission of a training school for girls, which did not materialize for a number of years.

As primary spokesperson for the Woman's Convention, Burroughs traveled far and wide to advertise its work and gather financial support. The Woman's Convention raised $1,000 in her first year after 1901 and $50,000 in 1920. She was not afraid to speak out on political issues, and in 1902 issued "An Appeal to the Christian White Women of the Southland" to help work toward equal treatment in public transportation. Her reputation for eloquence was firmly established with her successful speech on "Women's Work" at the First Baptist World Alliance meeting in London in 1905. In 1907 the Woman's Convention finally was willing to purchase a six-acre site with a farmhouse in northeast Washington, D.C., selected by Burroughs as the ideal place for the National Training School for Women and Girls. The school opened on October 19, 1909, free of debt thanks to Burroughs' money-raising in Louisville. Initially, the school had eight staff people and seven students, but by the end of the first year had 31 students. The board of trustees was set up as bi-racial, with most members being women. The trustees also eventually became self-perpetuating, without direct connection with the parent denominational body. Burroughs fought for this freeing format for years with the officials of the church. For decades it was the only boarding school for Black girls north of Richmond, Virginia, and the only school established by a national organization of Black women.

Burroughs' nationwide lectures and fundraising, almost entirely among Blacks, provided most of the support money for the school, her mother, and later Alice Smith, a student who came to the school in 1928 and became Burroughs' assistant and confidante. In 1934, after being closed for a few years during the Depression, the school was renamed the National Trade and Professional School for Women and Girls. By this time the school had more land and more buildings, and had educated over 2,000 women. Burroughs emphasized, not just industrial and academic training, but the development of the whole character. She termed her program the "School of the 3 Bs—the Bible, bath, and broom: clean life, clean body, clean home," all aspects of her vision of the Christian woman and racial advancement.

Her motto was "We specialize in the wholly impossible," and she dared a number of innovations. She trained women not only in the traditional disciplines of sewing and typing, but also offered courses in printing, shoe repair, and barbering. She established a department of Black history and required students to take at least one course in it. She was careful not to exclude academic subjects in the effort to be practical, and believed it was possible to attain a classical and industrial education simultaneously. She was particularly concerned that her students receive careful training in grammar and other language skills. She modeled a literate life for them, not only through her professional lecturing, but through the regular publication of articles in journals such as the *Afro-American*, the *Voice*, the *Southern Workman*, and the *Pittsburgh Courier*. Her articles spoke of Black pride and the importance of an active use of "ballots and dollars" to fight racism. In 1944 she became editor of *The Worker*, published by the Woman's Convention.

Burroughs was active in the club movement among Black women and helped **Hallie Q. Brown**, president of the National Association of Colored Women from 1920 to 1924, gain for that organization jurisdiction over the maintenance of the Frederick Douglass Home in Washington, D.C., on August 12, 1922. Burroughs also founded the National Association of Wage Earners with Mary M. Bethune as vice-president. During the Depression, when the school was closed, Burroughs organized a self-help cooperative in the community around the school that provided rent-free facilities for a medical clinic and other businesses. Later called Cooperative Industries, Inc., it became a permanent organization under her management. She was a supporter of the 19th Street Baptist Church in Washington, D.C., headed by the famous Rev. **Walter Henderson Brooks**, who served as a trustee of her school.

In 1948, after 48 years, she left her position as corresponding secretary of the Woman's Convention and became president, holding that position until her death. She led the organization to establish a retreat home in Washington, D.C., for missionaries returning from work (in 1964 given as a gift by the Woman's Convention to the Foreign Mission Board) and to build a camp in Michigan for the youth department. In her last years she was hampered by diabetes, arthritis, and heart disease. In 1964 the board of trustees of the school changed the old format of the curriculum and reopened it as the Nannie Helen Burroughs School for elementary-age students. In 1975 Mayor Walter E. Washington proclaimed May 10 to be Nannie Helen Burroughs Day in the District of Columbia.

"Baptist Women Maintain D.C. Missionary Retreat." *Ebony* 20 (December 1964): 82–84.

Brooks, Evelyn. "Religion, Politics, and Gender: The Leadership of Nannie Helen Burroughs." *The Journal of Religious Thought* 44 (Winter–Spring 1988): 7–22.

Burroughs, Nannie Helen. *Grow . . . A Handy Guide for Progressive Church Women*. Washington, DC: National Baptist Convention of the U.S.A., Inc., n.d. 47 pp.

———. *Making Your Community Christian*. Washington, DC: Woman's Convention, auxiliary to the National Baptist Convention, n.d. 100 pp.

———. *A Manual for Sunshine Band Leaders. Methods—*

Programs. Washington, DC: Woman's Convention, n.d. 76 pp.

———. *The Slabtown District Convention; A Comedy in One Act*. Washington, DC: N.p., 1926. 44 pp.

———. *What Do You Think?* Washington, DC: N.p., 1950.

Lindley, Susan. "'Neglected Voices' and *Praxis* in the Social Gospel." *The Journal of Religious Ethics* 18 (Spring 1990): 75–102.

Pickens, William. *Nannie Burroughs and the School of the Three B's*. New York: N.p., 1921. 43 pp.

NA, IBAW, PNW, AARS, HUBA, BAW, CH, IBAWCB, AAE, SNB, SCA, HBB, WB, WWCR, WWCA (38–40), *IVR, DANB, NAWMP, BWR, NBAW*.

BUTLER, CHARLES W. (b. May 4, 1922), a leading minister of the **Progressive National Baptist Convention**, was born in Dermott, Arkansas. He earned a B.A. in 1939 from Philander Smith College in Little Rock, Arkansas, and a B.D. in 1949 from Union Theological Seminary in New York City. From 1943 to 1946 he served in the military for World War II.

His first church position was as associate pastor of the St. James Presbyterian Church in New York City, from 1947 to 1950. In 1950–51 he was a released-time teacher for the New York City Mission Society and a teacher in the Baptist Center of New York City. Also in 1951 he did residence work for a Ph.D. at Columbia University in New York City. From 1951 to 1954 he was a professor of Biblical Literature and Religion at Morehouse College in Atlanta, Georgia. From 1954 to 1963 he pastored the Metropolitan Baptist Church in Detroit, Michigan, and from 1963 to the present he has been pastor of the New Calvary Baptist Church in Detroit.

Butler has been a leader in his denomination and in many community activities in Detroit. From 1962 to 1964 he was president of the Progressive National Baptist Convention of Michigan. From 1978 to the present he has been a trustee of the Interdenominational Theological Center and the Morehouse School of Religion in Atlanta, Georgia. From 1983 to 1987 he was first vice-president of the Baptist Pastors Council of Detroit, and since 1987 has been its president. In 1970 he helped organize the First Independent National Bank of Detroit. In 1976 he was chair of the Police Commission of the City of Detroit, and from 1980 to 1986 was a member of the advisory board of Michigan Consolidated Gas Company, Detroit. From 1982 to 1984 he was national president of the Progressive National Baptist Convention, the religious group with the seventh largest Black membership in the United States. In 1988

he was chair of the board of directors of the **Congress of National Black Churches**.

"The One Hundred Most Influential Black Americans." *Ebony* 39 (May 1984): 29–34.

"Ten Religious Groups with the Biggest Black Membership." *Ebony* 39 (March 1984): 140–144.

WWABA (92–93).

BUTLER COLLEGE. A Baptist school. Butler College, Tyler, Texas, began in 1903. It was founded as the East Texas Baptist Industrial Academy by the East Texas Baptist Association, and the moderator of the Association, Rev. C. M. Butler, became the president of the school. He continued in that role until his death in 1924. Originally the Academy was a combined elementary and high school and only developed a junior college curriculum in the 1920s. Following Butler's death, the elementary program was dropped and the name changed to Butler College. It developed a co-operative relation with Bishop College, and regularly fed graduates to its campus.

Hard hit by the Depression, Butler turned to the Texas Baptist Convention (affiliated with the Southern Baptist Convention). Partial ownership of the college was offered in return for financial support. The convention responded and has since provided a portion of the funds for the college's operation. Following World War II, in 1947 the college was able to expand into a four-year senior college.

Fitts, Leroy. *A History of Black Baptists*. Nashville, TN: Broadman Press, 1985. 368 pp.

BYRD, VERNON RANDOLPH (b. 1931), 105th bishop of the **African Methodist Episcopal Church** (AME), was born in Enoree County, South Carolina. He was called to preach at the age of twelve and was a licensed preacher at age seventeen. He is a graduate of Allen University in Columbia, South Carolina, and has done graduate studies at Boston University in Massachusetts. He married Theora Lindsey, with whom he has had four children.

His first pastorate was at Macedonia AME Church in Seaford, Delaware (1954–59), followed by St. Paul AME Church in Hamilton, Bermuda (1959–66), where he first jumped into the public spotlight. While in Bermuda he was instrumental in quelling a riot and was thereby honored by the Queen of England with an honorary M.B.E. degree. He was president of the

Bermuda Ministerial Association and an arbitrator between the government and the local Bermuda Industrial Union. In 1966–67 he served a term as presiding elder in the Newark District of the New Jersey Annual Conference. In 1967 he was assigned to the Macedonia AME Church in Camden, New Jersey, where he stayed for three years. From 1970 to 1979 he pastored Morris Brown AME Church in Philadelphia, Pennsylvania, and from 1979 to 1984 he pastored St.

James AME Church in Newark, New Jersey. In 1984 he was elected bishop at the General Conference in Kansas City, Missouri, and assigned to the Fourteenth Episcopal District in West Africa. One of the many projects he initiated there was the Frank Curtis Cummings Health Clinic in Monrovia, Liberia. In 1988 he was assigned to the Thirteenth Episcopal District.

AMSC, FEDHR.

"But, believing that to get the right men into the right places is a 'consummation most devoutly to be wished,' it is a matter of serious concern to us to see our youth, with just as decided diversity of talent as any other people, all herded together into three or four occupations. It is cruel to make a teacher or a preacher of a man who ought to be a printer or a blacksmith, and that is exactly what we are now obliged to do."

Fanny M. Jackson Coppin
African Methodist Educator
1913

C

C. H. MASON THEOLOGICAL SEMINARY. A **Church of God in Christ** school. The C. H. Mason Theological Seminary, Atlanta, Georgia, was founded in 1970 as the ministerial training school for the Church of God in Christ. It was one of the first projects of Bishop **James O. Patterson**, the church's presiding bishop, and part of a large effort to build a higher education program. The school was established in Atlanta to be a part of the Interdenominational Theological Center, the cooperative graduate school founded some years earlier.

Sherry Sherrod DuPree

CAESAR, SHIRLEY (b. October 13, 1938), minister of the **Mount Calvary Holy Church of America** and prominent gospel singer, was born in Durham, North Carolina, the tenth of twelve children in the family of Jim and Hallie Caesar. Her father, "Big Jim," was a professional singer in the Just Come Four gospel quartet. She grew up in the strict environment of the Mount Calvary Holy Church of America denomination. After her father's death when she was six (other sources say twelve) years old she needed to begin her own career as a gospel singer quickly to support her invalid mother, Hallie (d.1986). Turning professional when she was about fourteen, she toured the church circuit on weekends and during the summer. Known as "Baby Shirley," she sang with a number of groups, including The Charity Singers, and with the gospel preacher Leroy Johnson. She managed to finish high school in the Durham public schools and later studied business education at North Carolina State College (now North Carolina Central University) and Shaw University in Raleigh, North Carolina.

At the age of twenty, in 1958, Caesar became a full-time singer and joined the Caravans under the leadership of Albertina Walker. The group made several recordings and Caesar thus gained her first national exposure and experience. In 1961, while still a part of the Caravans, she added to her repertoire by becoming an evangelist. In 1966 she formed her own group, the Shirley Caesar Singers, and moved from Chicago back to Durham. In this new phase of her career she integrated preaching and singing into a seamless presentation that is her trademark. Like Mahalia Jackson, she has refused to sing secular songs, but sings in a contemporary "rock-gospel" style. After Jackson passed the height of her popularity in the 1950s and early 1960s, Caesar was one of the heirs to her gospel "crown." In 1976 she signed a million-dollar contract with Roadshow Records. Caesar has been called "the leading female gospel singer of her generation" and "the reigning queen of evangelistic gospel singing." She is certainly among the most sought-after and successful of the current gospel singers and has appeared across the United States and Europe. At only five feet tall, she gives the impression of a small fireball of energy.

Caesar maintains her activities in the non-singing ministry as well. She is co-pastor of the Mount Calvary Holy Church in Winston-Salem, North Carolina. Her co-pastor is her husband, Bishop Harold Ivory Williams, one of the leaders of the denomination, whom she married in about 1983. In 1987 Caesar won a seat on the Durham City Council and has been known to cancel appearances if they conflict with a council meeting. She is founder and director of the Calvary and Shirley Caesar Outreach Ministries, which opened in 1969 to provide various necessities to poor families. During her travels she often visits hospitals and senior citizens' homes to pray for people.

She has recorded at least twenty-six albums and received the 1972 Grammy Award for "Put Your Hand in the Hand of the Man from Galilee." She has won six Grammy Awards altogether, more than any other gospel singer. She received the People's Choice Award in 1975 and 1977 and the Dove Award in 1982. In 1975 and at least two other times *Ebony* magazine named her the best female gospel singer. In 1985 she received the

Image Award from the National Association for the Advancement of Colored People (N.A.A.C.P.) and in 1986 she received the Lifetime Achievement Award from S.E.S.A.C. music publishers. In 1989 *Billboard* magazine listed her as the number one artist for the year and her album, Live in Chicago, as the number one album. Her best-known songs include "Sweeping Through the City," "Running for Jesus," "No Charge," "Don't Drive Your Mama Away," "Sailing on the Sea of Your Love," "Put Your Hand in the Hand of the Man from Galilee," "Hold My Mule," and "Martin," a song dedicated to the memory of Martin Luther King, Jr.

"'First Lady' of Gospel." *Ebony* 32 (September 1977): 98–106.

"Gospel Music: A Shout of Black Joy." *Ebony* 27 (May 1972): 161–168.

"Shirley Caesar: Putting the Gospel Truth into Politics." *Ebony* 44 (December 1988): 66–70.

NBAW, BDA-AAM, WWABA (92–93), *BWR, IBAW.*

CAIN, RICHARD HARVEY (April 28, 1826–January 18, 1887), 14th bishop of the **African Methodist Episcopal Church** (AME), was born free in Greensboro County, West Virginia, the son of a Cherokee Indian mother and an African father. In 1831 the family moved to Gallipolis, Ohio, then to Portsmouth, Ohio, where he gained a basic education and worked on Ohio River steamships. He was converted in Portsmouth in 1841, and joined the Methodist Episcopal Church. He moved to Hannibal, Missouri, in 1844, where he was licensed to preach, but he became dissatisfied with the church, which had yet to authorize the ordination of Blacks. He soon returned to Ohio, this time to Cincinnati, and joined the African Methodist Episcopal Church.

He was assigned a church in Muscatine, Iowa, then part of the Indiana Conference, which he joined in 1854. He was ordained deacon by Bishop W. P. Quinn in 1859, and left the pastorate in 1860 for a year's study at Wilberforce University in Ohio. In 1861 he was transferred to the New York Conference to pastor Bridge Street Church in Brooklyn. He was ordained elder by Bishop **Daniel Payne** in 1862. In 1865 he and his wife, Laura, were sent to the South Carolina Conference, where he immediately reorganized Emanuel AME Church in Charleston, among the newly freed Blacks. Emanuel Church had been closed since 1822, when Denmark Vesey was thought to have planned his insurrection in its sanctuary.

In Charleston, Cain immediately became involved in Reconstruction activities. In just a few months, the Colored People's Convention was held at the church, and marked the first major movement for Black leadership in the South. By the fall of 1866 he was editor of the *South Carolina Leader*, the first postwar Black-run newspaper in the state. In 1868 its name was changed to the *Missionary Record*, and he remained as editor until the end of its run in 1872. He was a member of the constitutional convention in 1868 which revised South Carolina's laws. In July, 1868, he was elected to a four-year term as state senator from the Charleston district. In 1872 he was elected to represent South Carolina in the Forty-Third Congress (House of Representatives), and served from March 4, 1873, to March 3, 1875. Wilberforce University gave him an honorary D.D. degree in 1873. He did not run for Congress in 1874, since his at-large seat was abolished, but ran and was reelected in 1876 as congressman from the Second District. He made some memorable speeches on behalf of civil rights and honest politics, and introduced some major pieces of legislation, but none passed. He left Congress in March 1879.

In addition to his political activity, Cain was also successful in his church work. The Emanuel Church gained a large membership, and he is credited with beginning a sizable number of other churches in the Charleston area. Cain was elected bishop at the 1880 General Conference, and was assigned to the Ninth Episcopal District, which included the Louisiana, Texas, and West Texas Conferences. During this time he helped organize and served as the second president of Paul Quinn College in Waco, Texas. He organized the North Louisiana Conference on December 28, 1882, and the Central Texas Conference in December, 1883. In 1884 he was assigned to the First Episcopal District, which included the Philadelphia, New York, New Jersey, and New England Annual Conferences. There he served admirably for the remaining few years of his life. Churches have since been named for him in several states, and both Emanuel and Morris Brown churches in Charleston have marble memorials to him in their sanctuaries.

Cain, Richard Harvey. *Bishop's Pastoral Letter to Ministers and Members of the AME Church, August 20, 1880.* Typescript.

———. *Civil Rights Bill, Speech of Hon. Richard H. Cain, of South Carolina, Delivered in the House of Representatives, Saturday, Jan. 24, 1874.* N.p., n.d.

EWM, BAC, BPUSA, ACAB, CH, HNB, BR, EBA, BAMEC, RAM, HAMEC, MM, DAB (2), *DANB, NCAB* (11), *HUBA, IBAW, BAW, CEAMEC, AMECMIM, AMSC, AAP.*

CALDWELL, JOSIAH SAMUEL (August 2, 1862–April 7, 1935), 30th bishop of the **African Methodist Episcopal Zion Church** (AMEZ), was born in Charlotte, Mecklenburg County, North Carolina, the son of Dice and Martha (Howie) Caldwell. Work on the farm prevented his attendance at school more than a few months each year, but he spent many nights studying on his own. He married Ella Melchor in January 1881. Later that year, at age nineteen, he was converted at a camp meeting at Zion Hill in Concord, North Carolina, and joined the AMEZ Church. Two years later, in 1883, he decided to enter the ministry, and was licensed to preach. He enrolled in Livingstone College in Salisbury that fall, reportedly riding a mule to the campus, and alternated time between class work and work on the farm. He joined the Central North Carolina Conference in 1884, and was ordained a deacon on November 21, 1886. He graduated from college in May 1888, and was ordained elder later that year, on November 9.

His first church assignment was at Pineville, North Carolina, followed over the years by China Grove and Mt. Lebanon Church in Elizabeth City, both in North Carolina. Next was the Oak Street Church in Petersburg, Virginia, followed by the prestigious Big Wesley Church in Philadelphia, Pennsylvania. For a few months he also pastored Mother Zion Church in New York City in a circuit with Big Wesley, until the New York Conference was able to meet and fill the Mother Zion position in a regular manner. From 1900 to 1904, while at Big Wesley, Caldwell served as financial secretary of the denomination. In 1901 he was a delegate to the Ecumenical Methodist Conference in London. In 1902 he published two articles, one on finances of the church and the other on Young People's Societies.

At the 1904 General Conference he was elected bishop, and was consecrated on May 19, 1904. He was known as the "balance wheel" among the bishops, always holding a steady course. His financial acumen helped stabilize the church, and he was among the pioneer leaders of the Christian Endeavor Movement. He became known as a singer, and was particularly linked to such songs as "When the Saints Go Marching In," "Don't You Let Nobody Turn You Around," "Prayer is the Key to the Kingdom," and "There's Plenty Good Room in My Father's Kingdom."

He published a book of sermons in 1908, and an article, "The Greatest Need of the Negro Race," in a 1910 anthology. He was elected chair of the bishops in February, 1911, and later that year was once again a delegate to the Ecumenical Methodist Conference, this time at Toronto. He was again a delegate at the Conference in London in 1921, the year he became senior bishop. He was a trustee of Livingstone College

in Salisbury, North Carolina, Atkinson College in Madisonville, Kentucky, and Douglas Hospital in Philadelphia. After thirty-one years as a bishop, a little over a year after his wife's death, he passed away, and was survived by two daughters and one son.

"Bishop Caldwell Dead." *Star of Zion* 59 (April 11, 1935): 4.
Caldwell, Josiah S. "Financial Department of the AME Zion Church." In *The United Negro*. I. G. Penn, ed. Atlanta, GA: Luther, 1902, pp. 524f.
———. "Greatest Need of the Negro Race." In *An Era of Progress and Promise*. W. N. Hartshorn, ed. Boston, MA: Priscilla Publishing Co., 1910, pp. 399f.
———. "Young People's Societies as a Religious Force in the Church." In *The United Negro*. I. G. Penn, ed. Atlanta, GA: Luther, 1902, pp. 524f.
"New Era of Zion Methodism." *Star of Zion* 48 (August 7, 1924): 1, 5.
"Zion's Senior Bishops During the Twentieth Century." *Star of Zion* 104 (March 27, 1980): 1, 2.
WWCA (30–32), *WWCR, EBA, HAMEZC, AMEZC, AARS, HUBA.*

CALLENDER, EUGENE ST. CLAIR (b. January 21, 1926), civil rights activist and Presbyterian minister, was born in Boston, Massachusetts, the son of Arthur St. Clair and Eva Valeria (Graham) Callender. He received his B.A. in 1947 from Boston University and his B.D. in 1950 from Westminster Theological Seminary in Philadelphia, Pennsylvania. He married Lemoine DeLeaver, an administrator at Barnard College in New York City, with whom he had three children.

From 1950 to 1953 he was the associate pastor of the Second Christian Reformed Church in Paterson, New Jersey, and then did graduate work at Union Theological Seminary in New York City from 1953 to 1955. In 1955 he founded the Mid-Harlem Community Parish and led it until 1959. From 1959 to 1961 he was associate minister at the prestigious Church of the Master on 122nd Street in New York City, and from 1961 through 1965 was its senior minister. During this time he was co-chair of the Harlem Neighborhoods Association and vice-president of the New York branch of the N.A.A.C.P. He served on the board of directors of both Harlem Youth Opportunities Unlimited and Sheltering Arms Children Service.

He was also Moderator of the Presbytery of New York City of the United Presbyterian Church in the U.S.A., which in 1983 became a constituent part of the **Presbyterian Church U.S.A.** He chaired the Citywide Coordinating Committee that drafted the proposal for HARYOU-Act (Harlem Youth Action), the nation's first federal program for youth in the ghettoes. In 1967 he was on the President's Task Force on Manpower and Urban Unemployment, and was executive director of the New York Urban League.

In 1965 he became deputy administrator of the Housing and Development Administration of New York City. On August 21, 1969, he was elected president of the New York Urban Coalition, and took a leave of absence from his city position. He was a frequent lecturer at schools and colleges and hosted a weekly television show in New York City called "Positively Black." In 1971 he returned to pastor the Church of the Master, remaining there through 1984. From 1985 to 1989 he was the chief administrative officer of an agency in Albany, New York. In 1989 he retired and became interim pastor at the 100–member North Presbyterian Church on W. 155th Street in New York City.

"Organizations and Leaders Campaigning for Negro Goals in the United States." *New York Times* (August 10, 1964): 16. *EBA, IBAW, CRACG, BDNM* (70).

CAMPBELL, JABEZ PITT (February 5, 1815–August 9, 1891), eighth bishop of the **African Methodist Episcopal Church** (AME), was born free in Slaughter Neck, Delaware, the son of Anthony and Catharine Campbell. His father was a licensed preacher in the AME Church, and Campbell experienced conversion in 1825, joining the church under Rev. James Towson of the Lewistown Circuit. At one point his father was forced to give Campbell as collateral security to one of his debtors, and when he was unable to pay the debt, Campbell was in danger of being taken into servitude. At about the age of twelve, he ran away to Pennsylvania to avoid that fate, but was apprehended and sold for a term of years. After serving four and a half years, he purchased the last two and by the age of eighteen was free again.

He made his home with his mother in Philadelphia and joined the Bethel AME Church in 1833. He began studying in the early mornings, before work, eager for a thorough education. He preached his first sermon in Bethany AME Church in Holmesburg, Pennsylvania, in September 1838, and was licensed to preach on September 10, 1839. He was sent to open up New England to the AME Church and worked there until June 1843. His work laid the foundation for what became the New England Conference. Bishop Morris Brown ordained him deacon on June 20, 1841, and elder on June 20, 1843. From 1843 to 1847 he was assigned to Albany, New York, and on October 23, 1844, he

married Estella Medley. In 1847 he obtained a teaching position in Hudson, New York, and until 1850 also pastored congregations of the Wesleyan Methodist Connection both there and in Albany.

From 1850 to 1853 Campbell was assigned to the AME Church in Buffalo, New York, followed by the Union AME Church, Philadelphia (1854–1856). In 1854 he was also assigned the duties of general book steward and editor of the *Christian Recorder*, the newly established journal of the denomination. His first wife died, and in 1855 he married a widow, Mary Ann Akins (Shire). From 1856 to 1858 he was able to concentrate on his book and editing duties without a church appointment. From 1858 to 1860 he was appointed to Wesley AME Church in Philadelphia, followed by Trenton Circuit (1860–1862), Bethel AME Church in Philadelphia (1862–1863), Waters Chapel AME Church in Baltimore, Maryland (1863–1864), and finally St. John AME Church in Ebenezer, Baltimore. After only one month in Ebenezer, Campbell was elected bishop on the second ballot at General Conference and consecrated on May 23, 1864.

As bishop he was assigned to mission work in Mississippi, Arkansas, Louisiana, and California. He was the first AME bishop to visit California, and organized the California Conference at Sacramento on April 6, 1865. He organized the Louisiana Conference at New Orleans on November 1, 1865; and the Arkansas Conference at Little Rock, on November 19, 1868. From 1868 to 1872 he headed the First Episcopal District (Philadelphia, New Jersey, New York, and New England), and from 1872 to 1876 he covered the North and South Carolina, Baltimore, and Virginia Conferences. In 1876 he was a delegate to the General Conference of the Wesleyan Connection in England. From 1876 to 1880 he was assigned to the Florida, Georgia, Alabama, and Mississippi Conferences. He organized the North Mississippi Conference at Coldwater, on November 15, 1877; the East Florida Conference at Palatka, in February, 1878; and the North Alabama Conference at Florence on December 11, 1878.

From 1880 to 1884 he covered the Fifth Episcopal District (Kentucky and Tennessee), organizing the West Kentucky Conference at Paducah in October, 1880. He headed the Third Episcopal District (Indiana, Michigan, Ohio, and West Virginia) from 1884 to 1888, organizing the Michigan Conference at Battle Creek on August 24, 1887. He served as president of the board of trustees, Wilberforce University in Ohio, during this time. He was the first AME bishop to visit Haiti, and organized both the Haiti Annual Conference at Port-au-Prince in May, 1887, and the San Domingo Annual Conference the same month. He ended his career in the Second

Episcopal District (Baltimore, Virginia, and North Carolina). Campbell College in Jackson, Mississippi, has been named for him, as have numerous churches. His learning and wisdom were such that he was known as "the theologian of the denomination" during his lifetime.

Steward, Theophilus Gould. *Genesis Reread; or, The Latest Conclusions of Physical Science, Viewed in Their Relation to Mosaic Record. By T. G. Steward. To which is Added an Important Chapter on the Direct Evidences of Christianity, by Bishop J. P. Campbell.* Philadelphia, PA: AME Book Rooms, 1885.
HUBA, AARS, IBAW, BAMEC, MM, ACAB, HAMEC, EWM, CEAMEC, AAP.

CAMPBELL COLLEGE. An **African Methodist Episcopal Church** (AME) school. Campbell College, Jackson, Mississippi, was founded in 1887 as two separate schools, one located in Vicksburg and the other in Friar's Point, Mississippi. In 1898, however, under the guidance of Bishop **W. B. Derrick**, the two schools were united and Jackson chosen as a site for the new campus. By World War II the school served over 600 pupils annually, but has more recently been disbanded.

At some point between the world wars, Campbell absorbed Lampton College, formerly of Alexandria, Louisiana. Lampton originated in a school started by Bishop Abraham Grant in 1890 in Delphi, Texas. The school was destroyed by fire in 1907 and abandoned. However, in 1908 **Edward Wilkinson Lampton** was elected to the episcopacy and assigned to Louisiana. He revived the school and moved it to Alexandria. The school was named after the bishop who died in 1910 after only two years in office.

Smith, Charles Spencer. *A History of the African Methodist Episcopal Church.* Philadelphia, PA: Book Concern of the AME Church, 1922. 570 pp.
Wright, R. R. *The Encyclopedia of the African Methodist Episcopal Church.* Philadelphia, PA: Book Concern of the AME Church, 1947. 688 pp.

CAMPHOR, ALEXANDER PRIESTLY (August 9, 1865–December 11, 1919), the fourth African American missionary bishop of the Methodist Episcopal Church, was born in Soniat, Jefferson Parish, Louisiana, the son of Perry and Elizabeth (Washington) Camphor. At the time of his birth his father had already died and his mother gave him to Stephen Priestly, her pastor, so that he might have an education. Priestly adopted him and his mother helped with the purchase of books and such

as she was able. He attended Leland University in 1879–80 and then New Orleans University, where he received his B.A. in 1889 and M.A. in 1892. He then enrolled in Gammon Theological Seminary in Atlanta, Georgia, where he earned his B.D. in 1895. On November 19, 1895, he married Mamie Anna Rebecca Weathers, a nurse and teacher; there were apparently no children.

From 1889 to 1893 Camphor was professor of Mathematics at New Orleans University. In 1895 he joined the Delaware Conference of the Methodist Episcopal Church and pastored Janes Methodist Episcopal Church in Germantown, Pennsylvania. In 1896 he was pastor of St. John's Methodist Episcopal Church in Orange, New Jersey. Wanting to be a missionary in Africa he went to Liberia in 1897, and from 1898 until 1907 was president of the College of West Africa in Monrovia. He was also the United States Vice-Consul General for Liberia from 1902 to 1907.

He returned to the United States in 1908 to serve as president of Central Alabama Institute in Birmingham, where he remained for the next eight years. By this time he was a widely known and respected figure throughout the denomination. He was a delegate to the General Conferences of 1904 and 1912 and attended the World Missionary Conference at Edinburgh, Scotland, in 1910. He was active in the African Society, the Freedman's Aid Institution, and the Southern Sociological Congress. In 1909 he published *Missionary Story Sketches, Folklore from Africa.* He was a trustee of both the College of West Africa and Central Alabama Institute. In 1916 he was elected bishop for missionary service in Liberia, to which he then returned. The three African American missionary bishops in the Methodist Episcopal Church before him were **Francis Burns**, **John W. Roberts**, and **Isaiah B. Scott**. Camphor passed away only three years after his election. He was buried in New Orleans.

Camphor, Alexander P. *Missionary Story Sketches, Folklore from Africa.* New York: Eaton and Mains, 1909. 346 pp.
———. *Our Work in Liberia, West Africa: Its Need of Help.* S.L.: S.n., 1902 (?). 32 pp.
———. *Questionnaire Concerning Life, Thought, and Religion of African Natives: With Special Reference to Those of Liberia.* Monrovia, Liberia: Methodist Mission Press, 1923. 17 pp.
EWM, WWWA (1), WWAM, MB, BAW, HUBA, AARS, WWCR.

CANNON, KATIE GENEVA (b. January 3, 1950), Presbyterian minister and ethicist, was born in Concord, North Carolina, the daughter of Esau and Corine Lytle Cannon. She received her B.S. in 1971 in elementary education from Barber-Scotia College in Concord, then shifted her focus toward religion. She received a scholarship from the Rockefeller Protestant Foundation Fund for Theological Education and enrolled at Johnson C. Smith Seminary in Atlanta, Georgia. There she won the Isaac R. Clark Preaching Award from the Interdenominational Theological Center in 1973 and received her M.Div. in 1974. From 1975 to 1977 she was the first Black female pastor of Ascension Presbyterian Church. From 1977 to 1980 she was on the faculty of New York Theological Seminary and part of an ongoing ecumenical dialogue with Third World theologians. In 1982 she became editor of *Que Pasa*. She continued to work on further degrees with the help of another scholarship from the Fund for Theological Education, and as a Ford Foundation Fellow (1976–77) and Roothbert Fellow (1981–83). In 1983 she received her Ph.D. in Christian Ethics from Union Theological Seminary in New York.

Since then Cannon has been associate professor of Christian Ethics at the Episcopal Divinity School in Cambridge, Massachusetts, and since 1984 has served on the board of directors of the Women's Theological Center in Boston. In 1983–84 she was visiting professor at Harvard Divinity School and was visiting professor at Wellesley College in 1991. From 1986 to 1991 she was on the board of directors of the World Alliance of Reformed Churches Presbyterian and Congregational. She is a member of numerous organizations, including the Society for the Study of Black Religion and the American Academy of Religion. In 1985 she published *God's Fierce Whimsy: Christian Feminism and Theological Education*, her first book. In 1988 she broke new ground with *Black Womanist Ethics*. This book was described by Cheryl J. Sanders as "the first [ethics] text to be published by a Black woman professionally trained in theological ethics; the first book by any ethicist to ascribe authoritative status particularly to Black woman's experience as a ground of truth; and the first to apply a thoroughgoing ethical method to the study of Black women's literature."

Cannon, Katie G. *Black Womanist Ethics*. Atlanta, GA: Scholars Press, 1988. 183 pp.

———. *God's Fierce Whimsy: Christian Feminism and Theological Education*. New York: Pilgrim Press, 1985. 226 pp.

———. *Resources for a Constructive Ethic for Black Women: With Special Attention to the Life and Work of Zora Neale Hurston*. New York: Ph.D. Thesis, Union Theological Seminary, 1983. 258 pp.

Sanders, Cheryl J. "Black Women: Moral Agents." *Christianity and Crisis* 49 (December 11, 1989): 391–392. WWABA (92–93).

CARDOZO, FRANCIS LOUIS (January 1, 1837–July 22, 1903), Congregational minister, educator, and politician, was born free in Charleston, South Carolina, the son of Jacob N. Cardozo, a White Jewish economist and journalist, and a half-Black, half-Indian mother. At the age of five he was sent to a boarding school, where he remained until age twelve. At that point he became an apprentice carpenter for five years, followed by four years as a journeyman carpenter.

In 1858, at the age of twenty-one, he took $1,000 he had saved and went to the University of Glasgow, Scotland, where he studied for four years. While there, he took fifth place in Latin and seventh in Greek. He supplemented the money he brought with him by earnings during vacations and a scholarship of $1,000 he won in competition with the graduates of four colleges, which allowed him to attend another three years at Presbyterian seminaries in London and Edinburgh. In May, 1864, he returned to the United States to pastor the Temple Street Congregational Church in New Haven, Connecticut. That year he married Catherine Rowena Howell of New Haven, with whom he had four sons and two daughters, both of whom died in infancy.

In June, 1865, after only one year in the ministry, he decided he could be of more use in teaching, and offered his services to the **American Missionary Association** (A.M.A.), the benevolent society established by the Congregational Church to assist the Freedmen. The association agreed to send him to his hometown of Charleston, where his brother, Thomas W. Cardozo, had already begun the Lewis Tappan Night School under A.M.A. auspices. Unfortunately, Thomas had become embroiled in a scandal following an affair with one of his students, and soon after Louis arrived, Thomas was fired and Louis assigned as his replacement. In October 1865, Cardozo (Louis) opened a new school, Saxton School, which soon had one thousand students. He recruited both Black and White teachers, both locally and from the north through the A.M.A. His aim was to elevate the school to a normal school, which happened in the fall of 1866. He still saw himself in many ways as a minister, and in accord with A.M.A. policy, preached as opportunity allowed and incorporated religion classes into the school's curriculum.

In January 1868, Cardozo was elected a delegate to the state constitutional convention under Reconstruction, at which he was chair of the Committee on Education, and planned a statewide system of public schools. Since the convention met in Charleston, he was still able to supervise the school, but politics began consuming more and more of his time, and he felt compelled to tender his resignation to the A.M.A. effective May 1, 1868. Before this date, however, he was able to move the school into a new two-story brick building and the faculty into a new mission home. This was accomplished with the financial help of Charles Avery of Philadelphia, and the school was renamed Avery Normal Institute. For many years thereafter it was considered the premier school for Blacks in South Carolina.

On August 1, 1868, Cardozo was elected Secretary of State. In 1870 he was reelected, but after about six months, he resigned the position in favor of being a professor of Latin at Howard University in Washington, D.C. The governor suggested that instead of resigning, he appoint a deputy secretary to perform most of the functions, a suggestion that was accepted. He taught at Howard until March 1872, when his friends persuaded him to run for State Treasurer, to which he was elected on August 1, 1872. He was reelected to this office in 1876, but the fall of Republican Reconstruction caused him to give up the office on April 11, 1877. His abilities, integrity, and reputation in public office remained intact despite great opposition and scrutiny. In 1877 the governor and others recommended him for the presidency of Howard University, though this was not to be.

After the collapse of Reconstruction he obtained an appointment at the Treasury Department in Washington, D.C., where he stayed for six years, until he became principal of the Colored Preparatory High School in 1884. He remained as principal of the successor school, M Street High School, when it was inaugurated in 1891, and retired in 1896. He had introduced business courses at the high school, and a business high school which opened in 1928 in Washington, D.C. was named in his honor.

Cardozo, Francis L. *Finances of the State of South Carolina.* Columbia, SC: Daily Union-Herald, 1873. 16 pp.

Richardson, Joe M. "Francis L. Cardozo: Black Educator During Reconstruction." *Journal of Negro Education* 48 (1979): 73–83.

Sweat, Edward F. "Francis L. Cardoza [sic]: Profile of Integrity in Reconstruction Politics." *Journal of Negro History* 46 (October 1961): 217–232.

HNB, BPUSA, BR, IBAW, BHBA, ESH, MM, DANB.

CAREY, ARCHIBALD JAMES, JR. (February 29, 1908–1981), politician, judge, and **African Methodist Episcopal Church** (AME) minister, was born in Chicago, Illinois, the son of **Archibald J, Carey, Sr.,** and Elizabeth Hill (Davis) Carey. His father, also an AME minister and for years a major leader in the Chicago area, became a bishop in 1920. Carey, Jr., received a B.S. in 1929 from the Lewis Institute in Chicago and a B.D. in 1932 from Garrett Biblical Institute (now Garrett-Evangelical Theological Seminary) in Evanston, Illinois. He married Hazel Carey, with whom he had one child.

He was ordained in 1930 as a fourth generation AME minister and pastored the Woodlawn AME Church in Chicago from 1930 to 1949. After finishing his B.D. he enrolled at the Kent College of Law in Chicago, achieving his LL.B. in 1935. In 1936 he was admitted to the Illinois bar and began a private practice of law, eventually becoming a partner in the law firm of Prescott, Taylor, Carey, and Cooper. In 1947 he made a successful bid for the 3rd Ward alderman's seat on the Chicago City Council, which he held until 1955. In 1949 he was assigned to Quinn Chapel AME Church in Chicago, where his own father had been the minister from 1898 to 1904. He remained at Quinn Chapel until 1967, during which time he continued his political career, and became well-known as a civil rights advocate.

In 1952 Carey was speaker at the Republican National Convention and campaigned for Dwight D. Eisenhower. As a result, in 1953 he was appointed an alternate delegate to the 8th General Assembly of the United Nations and in 1954 received a Citizens Award from the University of Chicago. Also in 1954 *Ebony* magazine named him one of the nation's ten best Black preachers. From 1955 to 1961 he served as a member of the President's Committee on Government Employment Policy. He chaired that committee after 1957, the first Black to chair a White House committee. From 1957 to 1966 he was president of the board of directors of Illinois Federal Savings & Loan Association.

In 1966 he became a judge of the Circuit Court of Cook County, Illinois, a position he held until retirement in 1980. By 1967 it was clear he could no longer also continue his pastoral work, and he left the church position, though he was named pastor emeritus of Quinn Chapel. He was a lifetime trustee of Garrett Theological Seminary and trustee emeritus of the Interdenominational Theological Center in Atlanta, Georgia. He taught legal ethics at John Marshall Law School in Chicago and lectured at Roosevelt University in Chicago.

"Great Negro Preachers." *Ebony* 10 (July 1954): 26–30.
"What Happened to Hell?" *Ebony* 16 (January 1961): 47–52.
IBAW, BAMEC, OTSB, AAE, WWABA (90–91), *EBA.*

CAREY, ARCHIBALD JAMES, SR. (August 25, 1868–March 23, 1931), 43rd bishop of the **African Methodist Episcopal Church** (AME), was born in Atlanta, Georgia, the son of Jefferson Alexander and Anna (Bell) Carey. His father and grandfather were AME ministers, and he grew up in a religious atmosphere. At the age of nine he experienced conversion to Christianity. In 1888, while in college, he was licensed to preach and joined the North Georgia Annual Conference. He received his B.A. in 1889 from Atlanta University. He was ordained deacon in 1889 and elder in 1890. On December 18, 1890 he married Elizabeth Hill Davis, with whom he had five children.

His first pastorate was at Bethel AME Church in Atlanta, Georgia, followed by Mt. Zion AME Church in Jacksonville, Florida (1895–98), and then Quinn Chapel AME Church in Chicago, Illinois from 1898 to 1904. In 1904 he hosted the General Conference at Quinn Chapel, which made him a high profile denominational figure. From 1904 to 1909 he pastored Bethel AME Church in Chicago, and from 1909 to 1920 served the Institutional AME Church in Chicago.

During his twenty-two years of pastoring in Chicago, Carey became a very influential figure in city life. Under Mayor William Thompson he gained several key political posts, including Chief Examiner of Claims and Civil Service Commissioner. From the latter position he was able to secure more Black police officers and punish officers who mistreated Black prisoners. Because of his work attitudes on the police force perceptively changed. In 1915 he headed the Illinois Exposition celebrating fifty years of Black freedom and progress. During World War I he was chaplain of the 8th Illinois Regiment and chair of Draft Board No. 5 in Chicago. He was renowned as a skilled orator and regularly took prophetic stances against the injustices done to Blacks.

Carey was elected bishop on May 13, 1920 and assigned to the Fourteenth Episcopal District (Kentucky and Tennessee), and in 1928 was shifted to the Fourth Episcopal District, which included Illinois. From 1920 to 1922 he was a member of the Illinois Constitutional Convention. He was chair of the denomination's Financial Board and a trustee of Wilberforce University in Ohio. He was also chancellor of Turner Normal College in Shelbyville, Tennessee. In 1921 he read a paper at the World Conference of Methodism in London. Carey Temple in Chicago is named in his honor. A son, **Archibald James Carey, Jr.,** became a well-known minister, judge, and political official.

IBAW, WWWA (1), *EBA, HAMEC, EWM, WWCA* (30–32), *BAMEC.*

CAREY, LOTT (c.1780–November 10, 1828), pioneering Baptist preacher sometimes called the "Father of West African Missions," was born into slavery in Charles City County, Virginia. He lived on the estate of William A. Christian and was the only child of his parents, about whom little is known. His mother was not particularly pious, though his father was a respected member of a local Baptist church. He married about 1800, but his wife died about 1812. In 1804 Carey (sometimes spelled Cary) was hired out by the year as a laborer in the Shockhoe tobacco warehouse at Richmond. There his reputation as an intemperate troublemaker only increased. One Sunday in 1807 he was converted as he sat in the gallery listening to a sermon on Nicodemus from the third chapter of John, and was baptized by Rev. John Courtney of the First Baptist Church of Richmond.

Now a changed man, Carey spent all of his spare time learning to read, write, and preach. He was given a license to preach by the Baptists and preached among the slaves on the nearby plantations. He obtained a position as a shipping clerk, and his work in the warehouse was so exemplary he was allowed to sell small amounts of waste tobacco for his own benefit. By saving these bits of money and with the help of sympathizers, in 1813 he bought his freedom and the freedom of his two children with $850. He remained in his warehouse position earning $700 per year in salary, a large amount at the time, and remarried in 1815.

The First Baptist Church apparently allowed the Black members to meet separately, and Carey became the minister of the over 800–member African Baptist Church of Richmond. In 1815, two White Baptists, William Crane and David Roper, opened a night school for Blacks in the church gallery. Crane was very interested in African mission work, and one result was the awakening of that interest in his Black students, and the formation that same year of the Richmond African Baptist Missionary Society. Crane represented the society at the General Missionary Convention of the Baptist Church (founded in 1814) and elsewhere, a necessity to protect the Black group from the suspicion of insurrection. The formation of the society had a far-reaching impact, and within a couple of years the African Baptists of Philadelphia, Pennsylvania, and Petersburg, Virginia, had formed African Missionary Societies. Soon Carey and another newly freed colleague, Colin Teague, were determined to go to Africa themselves as missionaries.

Carey was received by the Baptist Board of Foreign Missions on May 1, 1819, and also by the American Colonization Society, though neither had funds yet to pay for any action. Carey was not so much in accord with the American Colonization Society's philosophy as he was interested in mission work and seeing the land of his heritage. Thanks largely to money raised by the Richmond African Baptist Missionary Society itself, in 1820 the Baptist Board of Foreign Missions voted funds to send both Carey and Colin Teague to Africa. Carey was so valuable at the warehouse that he was offered $200 more per year in salary to stay; nevertheless, the little group set sail on January 23, 1821, under the aegis of both the American Colonization Society and the Baptist Board of Foreign Missions. Carey is often mentioned as the first Black American missionary in Africa, but **David George** had founded a Baptist church in Sierra Leone in 1792. George, it is true, had been living in Canada for the previous ten years, and did not travel under the auspices of any missionary society. However, **Daniel Coker**, an AME minister, was sent to Africa under the auspices of the Maryland Colonization Society in early 1820, about one year before Carey set sail.

The group landed in Sierra Leone forty-four days later, but the purchase of the land that would become Liberia had not yet been completed, and they were forced to work in the fields, almost as slaves again, with other would-be settlers. Carey's second wife died there. Not until February 7, 1822, were they able to land at Cape Mesurado (now Monrovia), and even then the conditions were terrible. Carey, with no particular medical training, was the creditable Health Officer of the colony for almost two years, in a climate which produced much illness. Many of the settlers were killed in attacks by the indigenous Africans, which continued for about two years. Slave traders continued to work nearby. About mid-1823 Colin Teague returned to Sierra Leone.

In October 1825, a meeting house was dedicated, the Providence Baptist Church of Monrovia, with about seventy converts. This was the first Baptist church building in Liberia. A day school of twenty-one pupils had begun in Monrovia on April 18, 1825, and had forty-five pupils by 1827, when Carey moved the school to Grand Cape Mount. In September, 1826, Carey was elected vice-agent of the now 1200-person colony, despite earlier disagreements with the principal agent, Jehudi Ashmun. When Ashmun returned to the United States in March, 1828, for his health, the administration was left in Carey's hands, and Ashmun recommended that Carey be made the permanent administrator.

On November 8, 1828, Carey and others were working in an ammunitions warehouse, preparing for possible renewed hostilities with the native people, when a candle was knocked over and the building exploded. Carey survived for only two days. He was renowned as a brilliant preacher and a courageous gentleman, and left a legacy revered by many as the foundation of future Baptist missionary efforts. The Lott Carey Foreign Mission Convention was founded in December, 1897 by breakaway members of the National Baptist Convention, U.S.A.

Fisher, Mark Miles. "Lott Cary, the Colonizing Missionary." *Journal of Negro History* 7 (October 1922): 380–418.

Davis, Stanley A. *This Is Liberia*. New York: William-Frederick Press, 1953. 151 pp.

Fitts, Leroy. *Lott Carey: First Black Missionary to Africa*. Valley Forge, PA: Judson Press, 1978. 159 pp.

Gurley, Ralph Randolph. *Life of Jehudi Ashmun, Late Colonial Agent in Liberia. With an Appendix Containing Extracts from His Journal and Other Writings; With a Brief Sketch of the Life of the Rev. Lott Cary*. Washington, DC: J. C. Dunn, 1835. 160 pp.

"Recognition at Last for Missions' Other Carey." *Christianity Today* 25 (February 20, 1981): 45.

Taylor, James Barnett. *Biography of Elder Lott Cary*. Baltimore, MD: Armstrong & Berry, 1837. 97 pp.

SCA, HBB, HBBUS, ENB, SNB, LC, DANB, MM, AARS, HUBA, IBAW, SBIAA, NAH, OBMS.

CARROLL, EDWARD GONZALEZ (b. January 7, 1910), a bishop of the **United Methodist Church**, was born in Wheeling, West Virginia, the son of Julius Sylvester and Florence (Dungee) Carroll. He received his B.A. in 1930 from Morgan State College (now University) in Baltimore, Maryland, and his B.D. in 1933 from Yale University in New Haven, Connecticut. On July 3, 1934 he married Phenola Valentine, with whom he had two children. He was ordained deacon in the Washington Conference in 1933 and elder in 1935.

His first pastorate was at Mt. Washington, Maryland, in 1933–34, followed by Salem, Virginia, in 1934–35. In 1935–36 he was a member of the World Student Christian Federation "Pilgrimage of Friendship" to India, Burma, and Ceylon, a mission chaired by theologian **Howard Thurman**. In 1936–37 Carroll pastored in Grafton, West Virginia, and from 1937 to 1941 was a professor of Ethics and Philosophy at Morgan State College. During that time he continued his own studies and in 1941 received an M.A. from Columbia University in New York City. From 1941 to 1945 he was a chaplain in the U.S. Army. From 1945 to 1949 he was associate secretary of the National Student Y.M.C.A. From 1949 to 1953 he was associate pastor and director of Christian Education at St. Mark's Methodist Church in New York City, followed by pastorates at Epworth Methodist Church in New York

City (1953–55) and Sharp Street Memorial Methodist Church in Baltimore, Maryland (1955–62). He was district superintendent of the Washington District from 1962 to 1965 and of the Washington West District from 1965 to 1968. From 1963 to 1965 he was also vice-president of the Greater Washington Council of Churches.

In 1968 the Methodist Church merged with the Evangelical United Brethren to form the United Methodist Church. With that merger the Central Jurisdiction, the non-geographical segregated structure for Black members, was eliminated, and Black clergy and bishops were integrated into the whole structure. Carroll was appointed the pastor of Marvin Memorial United Methodist Church in Silver Spring, Maryland, where he stayed for four years. In July, 1972 Carroll was elected bishop and assigned to the Boston Episcopal Area, where he remained until retirement in 1980. He was a trustee of Boston University from 1972 to 1980. He has been active in a number of groups, including the North Conway Institute, Common Cause, and the Disciplined Order of Christ. He was on the board of directors of Sibley Hospital in Washington, D.C.; Wesley Theological Seminary; the Baltimore Urban League; and the N.A.A.C.P. In 1980–81 he was visiting professor and bishop in residence at Boston University School of Theology. He was interim director of Black Methodists for Church Renewal in 1981–82 and interim director of the Morgan Christian Center at Morgan State University in Baltimore in 1983–84.

Carroll, Edward Gonzalez. "The Washington Conference: Early Period, 1864–1915." In Gordon Pratt Baker, ed. *Those Incredible Methodists*. Baltimore, MD: Commission on Archives and History, Baltimore Conference, 1972, 284–313.

———. "Developing Culturally and Racially Inclusive Local Churches." In the Convocation on Urban Life in America, ed. *The Church in Urban America*. New York: National Division of the Board of Missions of the Methodist Church, 1966, 150–164.

———. "The Military Chaplain." In John Oliver Nelson, ed. *We Have This Ministry*. New York: International Committee of Young Men's Christian Associations, 1946, 58–66.

———. "Spiritual Training in the Seminary." *Nexus, Alumni Magazine of Boston University School of Theology* 16 (Winter 1972–73): 6–7.

WWR (77), EBA, HUBA, BDNM (75), WWMC, WWA (80–81), WWABA (92–93), BDUMB.

CARTER, NATHANIEL (c.1875–March 3, 1904), pioneer Lutheran minister, arrived in Baltimore, Maryland, from Virginia in 1892, and became interested in the fledgling Black mission being conducted by the Lutheran Church there. He was trained for the ministry by Rev. William Harley and other local Lutheran ministers and was ordained in 1896, as one of the first Blacks ordained in the Lutheran Church. About that time the need for a chapel was apparent, and since Carter had been taught German, the language still in use in most Lutheran congregations, he was able to make a tour of the Lutheran churches in the Midwest to raise money. This mission was successful, and in 1897 the chapel was built at 512 N. Eden Street, St. Philip's Evangelical Lutheran Church. Carter remained the pastor of the congregation until his death seven years later. The congregation is now affiliated with the Evangelical Lutheran Church in America.

LCAN.

CARTER, RANDALL ALBERT (January 1, 1867– February 6, 1954), eleventh bishop of the **Christian Methodist Episcopal Church** (CME), then known as the Colored Methodist Episcopal Church, was born in Fort Valley, Georgia, the son of Tobias and Grace (Chivers) Carter. He attended the public schools in Columbia, South Carolina, and in 1884 graduated from Allen University High School in Columbia. He joined the South Carolina Conference of the CME Church in 1887 at Green Pond. Later that year he entered Paine College in Augusta, Georgia, and transferred to the Georgia Conference. In 1889 he attended the first Epworth League Convention in Indianapolis. He married Jane S. Hooks on April 22, 1891, with whom he had one daughter. That same year he graduated with his B.A. degree.

His first church assignment of record was at the Butler Street Station in Atlanta, Georgia, in 1892. From 1893 to 1894 he pastored at the Barnsville CME Church, and the following four years were spent as presiding elder. From 1898 to 1903 he was appointed the first Secretary of the Epworth League in the CME Church. From 1903 to 1914 he returned to the position of presiding elder under Bishop **L. H. Holsey**, who made him a close aide. From 1898 to 1914 he was the leader of the Georgia delegation to General Conference, and served for more than twenty years as a member of the Committee on Episcopacy. In 1901 he was a delegate to the World Ecumenical Methodist Conference in London, and made an extended trip to visit the rest of Europe.

At the General Conference in St. Louis, Missouri in May 1914, Carter was elected bishop by more votes than any candidate in the history of the church had received. His first assignment was covering the conferences in Texas and Mississippi. He became the president of the board of trustees of Texas College in Tyler, Texas, and put the college on a solid financial foundation. His leadership made it the largest church-related college west of the Mississippi River. In 1919 he moved to Chicago, Illinois, and made it his home for the rest of his career, in which he covered jurisdictions including Washington, D.C., and Georgia.

Carter was known as the "Little Giant" and the "Great Expansionist," and the existence of over 250 churches is credited to his work. Next to his zeal for church growth was his commitment to education; his support of Texas College, Paine College, and other colleges was well-known, as was his leadership on the executive committee of the Association for the Study of Negro Life and History, founded by Carter Godwin Woodson. He published a number of works, including *Morning Meditations and Other Selections* (1917), *Feeding Among the Lilies* (1923), *Canned Laughter* (1923), *Brief Study of the Hebrew Prophets* (1937), and *Gathered Fragments* (1939). He was a delegate again to the World Ecumenical Methodist Conference that met in Toronto in 1921, and served many years on the executive committee of the Federal Council of Churches (now National Council of Churches). In the late 1940s his wife and daughter passed away, and he later married Helen Word.

Carter, Randall Albert. *A Brief Study of the Hebrew Prophets.* Jackson, TN: Colored Methodist Publishing House, 1937. 72 pp.

———. *Canned Laughter.* Cincinnati, OH: Caxton Press, 1923. 212 pp.

———. *Feeding Among the Lilies.* Cincinnati, OH: Caxton Press, 1923. 290 pp.

———. *Gathered Fragments.* Nashville, TN: The Parthenon Press, 1939. 278 pp.

———. *Morning Meditations and Other Selections.* Atlanta, GA: Foote & Davies Co., 1917.

———. "What the Negro Church Has Done." *Journal of Negro History* 11 (January 1926): 1–7.

"Randall Albert Carter." *Journal of Negro History* 39 (April 1954): 158–160.

AARS, BAW, HUBA, EBA, WWCA (38–40), RLA, WWCR, WWWA (H), CMECTY, EWM.

CARY, WILLIAM STERLING (b. August 10, 1927), first Black president of the National Council of Churches, was born in Plainfield, New Jersey, the son of Andrew J. and Sadie (Walker) Cary. He attended a predominantly White high school where he was very popular. At one point he ran for an office in student government and appeared to have won by a large margin, but the dean told him he lost. This incident prompted Cary's decision to attend a Black college. In 1948 he was ordained a minister with the American Baptist Convention (now the **American Baptist Churches in the U.S.A.**). He received his B.A. in 1949 from Morehouse College in Atlanta, Georgia, and his M.Div. in 1952 from Union Theological Seminary in New York City. At Union he was the first elected Black student body president. On July 11, 1953, he married Marie Phillips, with whom he had four children.

From 1953 to 1955 he was the pastor of Butler Memorial Presbyterian Church in Youngstown, Ohio, followed by the Church of the Open Door in Brooklyn, New York City (1955–58). By this time he had decided against maintaining his American Baptist Convention affiliation and in 1958 switched to the **United Church of Christ**. He thus pastored Grace Congregational Church in New York City from 1958 to 1968. In 1968 he took an administrative position as Associate Conference Minister of the Metropolitan New York Conference, United Church of Christ, holding that position for four years, the first Black to serve in that office. He was responsible for supervising the work in over one hundred congregations. During this time he was a member of the general board of the National Council of Churches and vice-president of the Protestant Council of New York.

On December 7, 1972, Cary was elected president of the National Council of Churches, the first African American to fill that position. After that term of office (1972–75) he was elected to a term as vice-president of the National Council of Churches (1975–78). He then moved to Hinsdale, Illinois, to be Conference Minister of the Illinois Conference of the United Church of Christ (U.C.C.). During his time in the national spotlight he gained a reputation as a champion of civil rights. He was an anti-war activist and advocated welfare reform, low-income housing, and strict enforcement of fair employment statutes. He attempted to moderate between those of liberal and conservative theological persuasions.

Cary has received many honorary degrees and has served in many influential capacities. He has been national chair of the Racial Justice Commission of the U.C.C. and on the executive committee of the Church's Office of Communication. He was vice-chair of the Coalition for Human Needs and Budget Priorities and on the board of directors of the National Federation of Settlements and Neighborhood Centers. He chaired the Commission on Regional and Local Ecumenism and was vice-chair of the Washington Coalition on Human

Needs and Budget Priorities. He served on President Ford's 17-member Advisory Committee on Refugees.

Bennett, Lerone, Jr. "Black Firsts." *Ebony* 37 (March 1982): 128–133.
WWABA (80–81), *WWR* (75–76), *BDNM* (75), *OTSB, CR, NA, EBA*.

CATHOLIC AFRO-AMERICAN CONGRESS MOVEMENT

In the late nineteenth century, as the Roman Catholic Church expanded, many Black people joined the church and several structures were created to serve their interests. Among these was a periodical, *The American Catholic Tribune*. Its editor Daniel Rudd began to promote the idea of a meeting of African American Catholics during the 1880s, and he found support from the likes of John R. Slattery, head of the **St. Joseph Society of the Sacred Heart**, who headed a mission effort in the Black community. The first Afro-American Congress was held in Washington, D.C., January 1–4, 1889. Fr. **Augustus Tolton**, the first Black priest to serve in America, celebrated the opening mass.

The congresses met annually for the next four years. The 1893 meeting was held in conjunction with the gathering of Roman Catholics for the World Parliament of Religions in Chicago. Other congresses met in Cincinnati (July 8–10, 1890); Philadelphia (July 5–7, 1892); and Baltimore (October 8–11, 1894). At each meeting the number of attendees grew and the level of activism on questions of racism increased. In 1893 the congress established a committee of grievances to document incidents of racism in the church.

After the 1894 meeting, however, the congresses were discontinued. They seem to have threatened the hierarchy of the church which had opposed any sign of lay organization and involvement (much less of African American lay organization) in the management of the church, an area over which they assumed complete hegemony. Also, by the mid-1890s, the church was in the midst of the Americanist controversy. Liberal churchmen were attempting to create an indigenous Catholic Church that included Black members and Black leadership. The liberal Americanists, who had most championed the cause of Black Catholics, lost as the controversy proceeded, and with their loss, the Black membership suffered a significant decrease in influence.

The congress idea was revived in the 1980s with the assistance of Bishop **John H. Ricard** and a new series of meetings initiated with the opening of the **National Black Catholic Congress** in 1987. It considered itself as continuing the previous congresses and thus counted itself as the sixth such congress.

Spaulding, David. "The Negro Catholic Congresses, 1889–1984." *Catholic Historical Review* 55 (October 1969): 337–57.

CATHOLIC NEGRO-AMERICAN MISSION BOARD

A **Roman Catholic Church** organization. One of the older structures by which the Roman Catholic Church relates to the African American community, the Catholic Negro-American Mission Board was founded in 1907 as the Catholic Board for Mission Work among the Colored People. It supplies financial support for nuns and lay teachers in African American Catholic schools in the south, especially those located in the poorer communities. Headquarters are in Washington, D.C., where the board works closely and shares staff with the **Commission for Catholic Missions among the Colored People and the Indians**.

CAUTHEN, JOSEPH DIXON

(February 21, 1887–September, 1974), 62nd bishop of the **African Methodist Episcopal Zion Church** (AMEZ), was born in Heath Springs, Kershaw County, South Carolina, one of thirteen children of Peter Cauthen and his wife (whose name is unknown). Life on the farm did not afford much time for schooling, and he attended Lancaster Normal and Industrial School, a boarding school, only beginning with the seventh grade. His parents could only contribute fifty cents toward this education. He completed his high school work at Clinton Junior College in Rock Hill, South Carolina. He joined the South Carolina Conference in 1912, and was licensed to preach at the Mt. Olive AME Zion Church in Rock Hill in 1913. He was ordained deacon on November 26, 1916, and later transferred to the Western North Carolina Conference, where he was ordained elder on November 14, 1920. He married Ruth Smith in 1921, who passed away in 1929. They had one child, Joseph Jr., born in 1928. Cauthen's college and theological work were completed at Livingstone College in Salisbury, North Carolina, where he received his B.A. degree in 1923. He also received a B.D. degree from the related Hood Theological Seminary in Salisbury.

Cauthen held pastorates in York County, South Carolina; Grover, North Carolina; and Cedar Grove Circuit, Gethsemane, Charlotte, North Carolina. In Charlotte he built a large parsonage and greatly increased the church membership. He then was assigned to State Street AMEZ Church in Mobile, Alabama, where he met Georgia Little, whom he married in 1940. This union brought a daughter, Muriel. He was in Mobile during the Depression, and voluntarily cut his salary from $175 to $125 a month. He used the difference to assist people through those difficult times. He was also able to purchase two houses for use as a recreation center, and made improvements on the church building. In 1931 Livingstone College granted him an honorary D.D. degree. He next served Varick AME Zion Church in Philadelphia, where he paid off a $15,000 mortgage, improved the church property, and bought a parsonage. He then moved to Metropolitan AME Zion Church in Norfolk, Virginia on November 25, 1949.

Cauthen was elected bishop at the 1956 General Conference, and was consecrated on May 13, 1956. He served with distinction as bishop the remainder of his career, marred only by the death of his second wife in January, 1964. His sentiments and actions were especially geared toward the service of his beloved Livingstone College. He was on its Board of Trustees for sixteen years.

Dabney, Thomas L. "Pastor Given 50 Cents in School May Be Bishop." *Star of Zion* 74 (October 25, 1951): 6.

Shipman, Dr. F. George. "Bishop Cauthen Made Impact on Schools." *Star of Zion* 97 (October 3, 1974): 1, 2.

Stephens, Raymond E. "Joseph Dixon Cauthen." *Star of Zion* 82 (October 8, 1959): 5.

AMEZC, HAMEZC, EWM.

CAUTION, TOLLIE LEROY, SR. (b. August 20, 1902), national officer in the (Protestant) **Episcopal Church**, was born in Baltimore, Maryland, the son of Gustave Orville and Blanche (Johnson) Caution. He grew up attending the historic St. James Episcopal Church under its famous rector, **George Freeman Bragg, Jr.** He received his B.A. in 1926 from Lincoln University in Pennsylvania and his S.T.B. in 1929 from Philadelphia Divinity School. He later did some graduate work at the University of Pennsylvania. He married Cora Marie Gosnell, with whom he had one child.

He was ordained in 1930 and was assigned to various Episcopal parishes in Maryland, Pennsylvania, and New York. His churches were characterized by creative work in liturgics and choral music. In 1945 he succeeded Bishop **Bravid Harris** in the office of Secretary for Negro Work in the National Council of the Episcopal Church, serving until 1952. In 1953 he became assistant director of the department of Domestic Missions.

From the knowledge gathered in these two positions Caution became the foremost authority on the relationship of the Episcopal Church to the Black community. He was a trustee for many schools, including St. Augustine's College in Raleigh, North Carolina; Voorhees College in Denmark, South Carolina; Okolona College in Okolona, Mississippi; Payne Divinity School; Philadelphia Divinity School; and Fort Valley College Center in Fort Valley, Georgia. He directed summer schools of Religious Education for St. Augustine's, Voorhees, and Okolona Colleges. He was an active member of the N.A.A.C.P. and the Southern Christian Leadership Conference (S.C.L.C.).

Unfortunately, Caution worked in an environment of "liberal" Whites who seemed to take for granted that they knew best and would be the ones setting policy and strategy. Many decisions were made without consulting him. Finally, he eliminated the awkward situation by taking an early retirement in 1957. He then found a position as executive secretary of the Division of Racial Minorities of the American Church Institute for Negroes (A.C.I.N.). The A.C.I.N. was founded in 1906 by the (Protestant) Episcopal Board of Missions to oversee and promote the church's schools for Blacks in the South. This position allowed him to continue his involvement with the Black Episcopal schools.

Caution, Tollie L. "Protestant Episcopal Church: Policies and Rationale Upon Which Support of its Negro Colleges is Predicated." *Journal of Negro Education* 29 (Summer 1960): 274–283.

BDNM (70), *BGWC, HUBA, AARS, IBAW.*

CENTER OF BEING. A Hindu group. The Center of Being is a Hindu organization incorporated in 1979. It is led by an African American, Her Holiness Sri Marashama Devi, generally referred to affectionately as *Mataji* (Mother) by her followers. Little is known of Mataji's early life. She was born in the United States around 1950. According to her followers, she was born enlightened, but voluntarily gave up her enlightened state at the age of twelve in order to experience the separation from the Divine experienced by most people and to work through the process of reunion. The next twelve years were ones of many spiritual experiences during which she saw Shiva, a prominent Hindu deity, who became her *guru* (teacher). She regained the enlightened state when she was 24.

Not long after she regained enlightenment, a few people recognized her attainment and began to seek her out. She took these people as students. The first of her students was given the name Baba Prem Ananda. Mataji and Anandaji formed the Center of Being in 1979. Mataji began to teach publicly in 1980. In 1984 the first issue of *Lila*, a quarterly journal, was issued. The center is headquartered in Los Angeles.

CENTRAL ALABAMA INSTITUTE. A Methodist Episcopal Church school. The Central Alabama Institute was founded as the Rust Normal Institute in Huntsville, Alabama, in 1872. As its name implies, it specialized in the training of teachers for the public schools. In 1904 it was moved to Birmingham, Alabama, and renamed the Central Alabama Institute.

In Birmingham, the Institute was headed by a series of outstanding Black educators. **Alexander Priestly Camphor** had taken post-graduate work at both Columbia University and the University of Chicago. After a tour as a missionary in Africa, he became president of the Institute in 1908 and remained in Birmingham until his election as bishop for Liberia in 1916. He was succeeded by the equally well-educated J. B. F. Shaw, who remained at the Institute for five years before moving to the presidency of **Haven Institute** in Mississippi. The last president of the Institute was R. N. Brooks, a graduate of Northwestern University. He came to Birmingham in 1921. Shortly after Brooks took over, the school returned to Huntsville as Alabama Central College, but was forced to close in 1923.

Stowell, Jay S. *Methodist Adventures in Negro Education*. New York: Methodist Book Concern, 1922. 190 pp.

CHAMBER OF HOLY VOODOO. The Chamber of Holy Voodoo was an organization which functioned in the 1970s and 1980s from New York City and offered to teach **Voodoo** to students by mail. The basic course offered to train students for the priesthood and teach healing, exorcism, and the process of spirit possession (Voodoo being a religion which emphasizes and values the ability to be possessed of the spirits). After more than a decade of public activity, the organization withdrew from public sight and its present status is unknown.

CHAMBERS, SINGLETON ROBERT (c.1909– ?), well-known radio preacher, entered the ministry at age thirteen. After studies at Tennessee State University, he eventually became head of the Evangelist Temple in Kansas City, Kansas, affiliated with the **Church of God in Christ**. About 1933 he began a radio program heard in two broadcasts over stations in Kansas City and Little Rock, Arkansas, that by the late 1940s claimed 200,000 listeners, two-thirds of them White. Chambers is said to have healed some 14,000 people, many of them by prayer over the telephone.

"Top Radio Ministers." *Ebony* 4 (July 1949): 56–61.
BH.

CHAMBERS, TIMOTHY MOSES (June 18, 1895–November, 1977), first president of the **Progressive National Baptist Convention**, was born in Mt. Pleasant, Texas, the son of Cicero Clarence and Jerreline Wade Chambers. After graduating from Fort Worth I & M College, he received his B.Th. in 1920 from Bishop College in Dallas, Texas. He married Hazel Catherine Thomas, with whom he had five children. He served in Texas for many years and was president of the Baptist Missionary and Educational Convention in Texas from 1945 to 1950. In 1947 he preached at the Baptist World Alliance meeting in Copenhagen, Denmark. About 1950 he moved to Los Angeles, California, where he pastored the Zion Hill Baptist Church.

By this time Chambers was quite well-known in the **National Baptist Convention, U.S.A., Inc.** (N.B.C. U.S.A.), and was elected president of the Constitutional Baptist State Convention, California/Nevada. He was president of the Los Angeles Interdenominational Ministerial Alliance in 1956. In 1961, when the Progressive National Baptist Convention was founded as a splinter from the N.B.C.U.S.A. over issues of officer tenure and support for the civil rights movement, Chambers was elected its first president and served from 1961 to 1966. In 1966 he left the Zion Hill church to organize and pastor the Roger Williams True Love Baptist Church in Los Angeles, where he remained for the rest of his career. He was also famous for his popular radio program, "Sweet Hour of Prayer," which ran for fourteen years.

BDNM (75), *HBB, EBA*.

CHAPPELLE, RICHARD ALLEN, SR. (b. February 25, 1934), 108th bishop of the **African Methodist Episcopal Church** (AME), was born in Miami, Florida, the son of Mitchell Peter and Mabel Juanita Chappelle. He received his B.S. from Bethune-Cookman College in Daytona Beach, Florida, and his D.D. from Lee Theological Seminary. On November 5, 1966 he married Barbara Jeanne Chappelle, with whom he has had three children.

His first pastorate was in Fellsmere, Florida (1965–67). He subsequently served churches in Gifford, Florida (1967–69); Riviera Beach, Florida (1969–73); Melbourne, Florida (1973–75); and Orlando, Florida (1975–76). From 1960 to 1973 he was a member of the Board of Public Instruction of Broward County, Florida, and from 1974 he was president of the Melbourne branch of the N.A.A.C.P. In 1976 he was elected general secretary for the AME denomination, a position he held for the next twelve years. In 1988 Chappelle was elected bishop and assigned to the Seventeenth Episcopal District.

WWA (80–81).

CHAPPELLE, WILLIAM DAVID (November 16, 1857–June 15, 1925), 37th bishop of the **African Methodist Episcopal Church** (AME), was born into slavery near Winnsboro, in Fairfield County, South Carolina, one of eleven children in the family of Henry and Patsy (McCrory) Chappelle. He spent much of his childhood working on the farm, though during Reconstruction he was able to attend a school run by Northern women. He was so eager to learn that he cut wood at night and carried it to town on his head, using the money he earned to buy his first book.

In 1875 he entered the Fairfield Normal Institute headed by Rev. Willard Richardson for the Presbyterian Church. That year he was converted at the Wayman Chapel AME Church in his home town, which his family had joined following the Civil War. On December 18, 1875, he married Eliza A. Ayers, with whom he had three children. In 1880 he graduated from the Fairfield Normal Institute and made the highest marks on the examination for a teaching certificate that had yet been made by a Black applicant to teach in the county. He was given a school near Winnsboro through the winter of 1880–1881.

Besides being a teacher, Chappelle decided to become a minister. He was licensed to preach in the AME Church in 1880, and joined the Columbia Annual Conference in November 1881. The next month, with only $50 to his name, he enrolled in Allen University in Columbia. He found a great friend in Bishop **William F. Dickerson**, who gave him a room in his own home, part-time work, and the occasional use of a horse. Even so, he often had to walk the sixteen miles on Sundays to his preaching assignment. In May, 1882, he was assigned Pine Grove Mission in Lexington County. He was ordained a deacon in 1883, and in 1885 an elder.

In 1884 he was assigned the Rock Hill Circuit in Littletown, where he stayed for three years. In 1887 he graduated with honors and received his B.A. from Allen University, the AME school in Columbia, South Carolina. His next assignment was King's Chapel in Pendleton. He stayed there for about four years during which time he succeeded in leading the congregation to build a new structure. Beginning about 1891 he became presiding elder of the Manning District, holding that position for four years. He then served five years as presiding elder of the Orangeburg District. In 1895 he received an M.A. from Allen University and taught

some classes as a professor. In 1897 he was appointed for two years as president of Allen University, holding that office concurrently with being presiding elder of the Orangeburg District. During that time he donated his presiding elder's salary to the university. On May 17, 1899, his wife died, and a year later on April 25, 1900, he married Rosina Palmer, with whom he had two more children.

In May, 1900 he was elected secretary-treasurer of the Sunday School Union. His new position involved his moving to Nashville, Tennessee, where he assumed the task of editing the literature of the Sunday School for the whole denomination. He found the department in deplorable condition, $6,000 in debt with no printing capability. The literature being used was from the Methodist Episcopal Church, South. By 1908, his final year in that position, he was able to report that the Sunday School Union was out of debt, had a printing outfit valued at $25,000, and held $1,000 toward the building of a new headquarters. In 1908 he returned to South Carolina and once again became president of Allen University, a position he held for the next four years.

At the General Conference in Kansas City, Missouri, in May 1912, Chappelle was elected bishop and was assigned to the 12th Episcopal District (Arkansas and Oklahoma). From 1916 until his death he served in his native South Carolina. Named for him is Chappelle Hall at Allen University.

EAMEC, WWWA (vol.1), *CEAMEC, EWM, HAMEC, WWCR, BAMEC, EBA, AMSC, TCNL.*

CHAVIS, JOHN (c. 1763–June 13, 1838), educator and preacher with the Presbyterian Church in the United States, lived an obscure early life. Most sources suggest a birthplace near Oxford in Granville County, North Carolina, but he appeared as a young boy in Mecklenburg County, Virginia. His father's identity is unknown, his mother's name is said to have been Lottie, and he had one brother, Anthony. Chavis was not a slave, but was likely the indentured servant of attorney John Milner. Milner perhaps saw to his basic education, and seems at any rate to have seen intellectual promise in him, for at his death in 1773 he willed Chavis his Greek and Latin volumes. William Willie, the Presbyterian minister in Sussex, Virginia, may have seen to Chavis' education after Milner's passing.

Chavis enlisted in the Fifth Virginia Regiment on December 29, 1778, under Captain May Cunnington. He served three years as a soldier, and then apparently returned to his home. The Mecklenburg County tax list of 1789 showed that he was a free Black, employed as a tutor, and had property consisting of one horse. He was said to have been a student under president John Witherspoon's supervision at the College of New Jersey (later called Princeton University) from about 1792 to 1794. Sometime during the following six years he was able to pursue "a regular course of academic studies" at Washington Academy in Lexington, Virginia (later called Washington and Lee University). He married a woman named Frances.

He was licensed to preach on November 19, 1800, by the presbytery of Lexington, Virginia, and in 1801 the General Assembly of the Presbyterian Church in the United States commissioned him to be a missionary to the slaves. He was the first Black Presbyterian home missionary. He ministered to slaves in Maryland, Virginia, and North Carolina, settling generally in North Carolina in 1805, and joining the Orange presbytery. About 1807 he left the missionary trail and opened a school in Raleigh, teaching White students during the day for $2.50 per quarter and Black students at night for $1.75 per quarter. He continued to preach frequently, moving freely among both White and Black Presbyterians.

Chavis' school was said to be the best preparatory school in the state, and was attended by children of many of the most prominent families of the area. Former students included Willie P. Mangum, U.S. Senator; Priestly H. Mangum, his brother; Archibald and John Henderson, sons of Chief Justice Henderson; and Charles Manly, Governor of North Carolina. Chavis was active politically as a Federalist. He favored the 1828 Protective Tariff Act and opposed Andrew Jackson as a backwoodsman without "blood or training." The year following the Nat Turner Rebellion of 1831, it became unlawful for Blacks to preach or teach in North Carolina, which deprived Chavis of his means of livelihood. He referred to the rebellion as "that abominable insurrection in Southampton." In 1833 the Orange Presbytery decided to help support him as a "superannuated licentiate." In the summer of 1835 the Presbyterian General Assembly took away his right to vote on church matters.

One year before his death, Chavis wrote a booklet, *Chavis' Letter Upon the Atonement of Christ*, which sold well and helped the presbytery provide for his support and that of his wife after his death. A housing project and a park in Raleigh are named for him.

Bontemps, Arna. "Even Money on John Chavis." *Common Ground* 10 (Autumn 1949): 36–39.

Franklin, John Hope. *The Free Negro in North Carolina, 1790–1863*. Chapel Hill, NC: University of North Carolina Press, 1943. 271 pp.

Knight, Edgar W. "Notes on John Chavis." *North Carolina Historical Review* 7 (1930): 326–345.

Shaw, George Clayton. *John Chavis, 1763–1838, a Remarkable Negro Who Conducted a School in North Carolina for White Boys and Girls*. Binghamton, NY: Vail-Ballou Press, 1931. 60 pp.

Smith, Charles Lee. *The History of Education in North Carolina*. Washington, DC: Gortt Printing Office, 1888. 180 pp.

NBH, CH, EBA, PHNA, HNB, DAB (2), BHBA, DANB, NCAB (7), BDAE, IBAW, BPEAR, NAH, NYB (1925–26).

CHERRY, FRANK S. (? –1965), founder of the **Church of God (Black Jews)**, was born somewhere in the South. Little is known of his family or early life. He said that he never went to school, and often derided the manners and thoughts of highly educated people. As an adult he worked as a common laborer and railway employee, and then gained a job as a seaman, and traveled over much of the world. He claimed that in a foreign land God appeared to him in a vision, appointed him a prophet, and sent him back to America.

He founded the Church of God on Nicholas Street in north Philadelphia, Pennsylvania, teaching that Blacks are the true Israel, the first Jews being Blacks, and that Jesus was a Black man. He criticized White Jews as frauds, and said that the first White man was Gehazi, who received his whiteness as a curse (II Kings 5:27). The church observes baptism, but Passover is substituted for the Lord's Supper. Divorce and pork are not allowed, and photographs of members are also forbidden (considered as graven images). Cherry was conversant with both Hebrew and Yiddish, and taught Hebrew to his followers. He became well-known for his preaching abilities and colloquialisms. He built a congregation of about 400 members, and was succeeded after his death by his son, Benjamin Cherry.

BSC, BGM, BH, BJH.

CHRIST HOLY SANCTIFIED CHURCH OF AMERICA. A Holiness Pentecostal church. Christ Holy Sanctified Church of America was founded in 1910 in Keatchie, Louisiana, by Sarah A. King and a Bishop Judge. It was incorporated the next year in Memsfield, Louisiana. It grew out of the same movement which had produced **Christ's Sanctified Holy Church** in Louisiana several years previously.

Judge was succeeded by Bishop Ulysses King of Oakland, California, and more recently E. L. McBride, the present leader. The church supports Christ Holy Sanctified School, an industrial school. Headquarters are in Fort Worth, Texas.

CHRISTIAN CHURCH (DISCIPLES OF CHRIST). The Christian Church (Disciples of Christ) is one of three denominations which grew out of the several reformation movements begun on the American frontier in the early nineteenth century by Barton Stone, Walter Scott, Thomas Campbell, and Alexander Campbell. The reformers had a desire to "restore" New Testament Christianity over against the growing fragmentation of denominationalism which they saw occurring around them. They desired to unite simply as Christians without denominational labels and sectarian beliefs. The effect, however, was to build a new denomination which has over the years split into three, the other two being the Churches of Christ (Non-instrumental) and the Christian Church and Churches of Christ.

The seminal event in the beginning of the Restoration movement was the great Cane Ridge Revival in Kentucky in 1801. African Americans were present at the revival and were to be found among the membership of the Cane Ridge Christian Church and other early Disciples congregations. Many of these were slaves of church members. Both Barton Stone and Alexander Campbell were slave owners and the emerging church offered no critique of slavery. Thomas Campbell did react to Southern laws limiting or preventing the preaching to slaves and at one point in 1819 moved his residence from Kentucky to Pennsylvania so as not to be hampered. The organization of Black members followed the common patterns. Some churches had separate balconies, some allowed Black members to sit in the back of the church hall, and some opened the church windows for Black members to listen from outside the building. In a minority of cases, Black members were organized into a separate fellowship whose services were held at a different hour from those of the White congregation.

A few African Americans were trained as preachers and assigned some leadership roles, especially as the church grew in the free states. One notable early African preacher was Alexander Campbell (no relation to the founder of the movement) who was converted at Cane Ridge. He was freed to become a preacher to the slaves. He moved to Lexington, Kentucky, and attended Transylvania University (a Disciples school) and founded a church at Midway, Kentucky. He was eventually able to purchase the freedom of his wife and

children and his son, Alexander Campbell II, became a minister.

The Disciples movement also intruded into the early development of the African American Baptists (the group which the Disciples most closely resembled). In 1832 Alexander Campbell was invited to speak at the African Baptist Church in Savannah which had been founded by **George Liele**. The church had over 2,500 members and was a member of the Sudbury Baptist Association. The church's pastor, **Andrew C. Marshall**, publicly declared his adherence to a number of Campbell's particular views. In reaction, the association charged him with Campbellism, the equivalent of charging him with heresy, and ordered that the church be dissolved. The church voted its overwhelming support of Marshall. The minority, some 155 members, were given the building. The 2,600 supporters of Marshall purchased another building and reorganized as the independent First African Church. It seems that his flirtation with Campbell's ideas was brief, however, as the church was readmitted to the Sudbury Association in 1837 and Marshall continued his popular ministry until his death in 1856.

Following the Civil War, many of the African American members of the Disciples congregations withdrew from the church and joined the Baptists or one of the African Methodist groups. Those who stayed began to organize separate congregations and as these were constituted state associations emerged, among the first being Kentucky (1872), Missouri (1974), Mississippi (1884) and Arkansas (1988). The strongest work of the Disciples among African Americans was in North Carolina where a group of Free Will Baptist Churches affiliated with the Disciples. Almost one third of African American Disciples reside in that state and have their own unique ways, including the practice of foot washing. In 1867 Rufus Conrad, a Disciples missionary, called a national meeting of African American Disciples at Nashville. The cooperative effort he initiated, however, soon failed because of lack of financial support by the Disciples. It was superseded by a second effort in 1878 known as the National Convention of Churches of Christ. H. Malcolm Ayers and Preston Taylor (1849–1931) emerged as the most prominent leader of the convention which was able to gather periodically through the end of the century. Preston Taylor, pastor of a church in Mt. Sterling, Kentucky, was appointed as a national evangelist in 1883. Three years later he settled in Nashville as pastor of the Gay Street Christian Church, but left the pastorate two years later to open a funeral business. He emerged as the major spokesperson of Black Disciples seeking some equity of access to the national church.

The American Christian Missionary Society (A.C.M.C.), whose loose organization slowed the development of cooperative national programs, responded to the condition of the Freedmen in 1872 by passing a resolution calling attention to the educational needs of the former slaves. The resolution led to the opening of the Louisville Bible School in Kentucky the next year and efforts begun to create the more substantial Southern Christian Institute which opened in 1882 in Edwards, Mississippi. Over the next several decades, several other schools, some short-lived, were opened.

In 1889 the A.C.M.S. appointed J. W. Jenkins, a Black man, as superintendent of African American work and in 1890 created the Board of Negro Education and Evangelization. The board was headquartered at Louisville. The control of the Southern Christian Institute was turned over to the board, which directed its activity for the next decade. Then in 1900, the entire program with African Americans was assigned to the Christian Woman's Board of Missions. The first visible result of the new structuring was the formation of Jarvis Christian College in Hawkins, Texas.

In 1917 the International Convention of the Disciples of Christ was organized. That event, along with a longstanding desire of African American leaders to have a regular opportunity for consultation and fellowship on the national level, occasioned the calling of the first national convention of African American Christian churches in Nashville. By this time, most of the White churches in the south had separated from the northern churches and reorganized as the Churches of Christ. Those Black churches that wished to remain in fellowship with the Disciples formed the National Convention of the Church of Christ and chose Preston Taylor as their first president. The agreement was reached to meet annually as an auxiliary of the annual International Convention of the Disciples of Christ. In 1942 the convention changed its name to the National Christian Missionary Convention. The convention picked up the publication of the *Christian Plea*, the most stable periodical for African American Disciples, which had been published by Southern Christian Institute since 1889, and for many years published it from their headquarters in Indianapolis.

The National Christian Missionary Convention developed education, missionary and women's programs over the next decades. In 1945 the convention requested the formation of a joint committee to coordinate the work of the convention and those White agencies which still had responsibility for work in the African American community. The committee was established and the fund used in supporting the field workers of the International Convention's United Christian Missionary Society turned over to it. This signaled the step-by-step process of integrating the structures of the International Convention on the national level. As new boards and agencies were formed, their leadership was integrated as a matter of course.

In 1968, the International Convention of the Disciples of Christ went through a complete restructuring and emerged as the Christian Church (Disciples of Christ). The restructuring brought a new unifying structure to the national agencies which had been established over the years by the Disciples. As a result the National Christian Missionary Convention met for the last time in 1969 and voted to merge into the General Assembly of the Christian Church (Disciples of Christ). A national convocation of the Christian Church continued to oversee the continuing business of the former National Convention. It met biennially. In 1971 the Assembly created the Committee on Black Work to promote work in the African American community. The administrative secretary of the National Convocation serves as chairperson of the committee and as assistant to the convention's president.

The appointment of the Committee on Black Work came as the Disciples were developing a response to the Civil Rights movement. In 1968 a new program, "Reconciliation," was developed and a Fund for Reconciliation established. In 1969, in response to the **Black Manifesto**, the church doubled its commitment to the Fund for Reconciliation from two to four million and set up an investment committee to invest endowments and surplus monies in minority controlled banks and businesses.

Currently structured into the national organization, Black Disciples continue as a small minority voice within the larger predominantly White Christian church.

Garrison, Winfred Ernest, and Alfred T. DeGroot. *The Disciples of Christ: A History*. St. Louis, MO: Bethany Press, 1948. 592 pp.

McAllister, Lester G., and William Tucker. *Journey in Faith: A History of the Christian Church (Disciples of Christ)*. St. Louis, MO: Bethany Press, 1975. 506 pp.

CHRISTIAN METHODIST EPISCOPAL CHURCH. The Christian Methodist Episcopal Church, referred to most commonly as the CME Church, arose out of the context of American slavery, the aftermath of the Civil War, and the problems of Reconstruction. It was organized in Jackson, Tennessee on December 16, 1870, as the Colored Methodist Episcopal Church in America by African Americans who, while slaves, had been preachers and members of the Methodist Episcopal Church, South (MECS), and who, attendant upon their freedom, requested from that church their own separate and independent religious organization. At the beginning of the Civil War there were 207,766 colored members of the MECS, the overwhelming majority of whom were slaves. In 1866, 78,742 of such members remained. Those who remained did so in order to establish their own church, "looking forward to our own ecclesiasticism" was the way Bishop-to-be **Isaac Lane** phrased it.

In accordance with disciplinary processes current at the time, the MECS granted the request of those former slave members, authorizing ordination of Black preachers, establishment of quarterly conferences, creation of annual conferences, and the organization of a separate ecclesiastical jurisdiction if the colored members desired it. Additionally, the MECS, authorized that all of its property utilized by its colored members be transferred to the new colored jurisdiction. The Organizing General Conference of the CME Church consisted of forty-one African American men representing eight annual conferences throughout the South. They elected **William H. Miles** from Kentucky and **Richard H. Vanderhorst** from Georgia the first bishops of the newest branch of Methodism. They were ordained to the high office by the Senior Bishop of the MECS, Robert Paine.

At the time of its organization the CME Church was located in the Southern United States where the vast majority of African Americans lived. Soon thereafter it began to follow the migration of its people along the Eastern Seaboard, into the Southwest and Midwest, and after the turn of the century had congregations on the Pacific Coast. Presently the Christian Methodist Episcopal Church is a major denomination of the African American tradition of American Methodism. It entered the 1990s with more than 800,000 communicant members, 3,000 congregations and 3,200 clergypersons throughout the United States, Nigeria, Ghana, Liberia, Haiti, and Jamaica.

The CME Church has from its inception considered the social, economic, and educational conditions of African Americans a central part of its mission. Its very existence as an independent religious institution resulted from the drive for self-determination on the part of persons only a few years removed from the shackles of slavery. Helping to provide education for African American youth has been essential to its missional activity, with some 22 educational institutions under its auspices at one time or another during its history, the most notable being Paine College, Augusta, Georgia; Lane College, Jackson, Tennessee; Miles College,

Birmingham, Alabama; and Texas College, Tyler, Texas. The CME Church has been at the forefront of the struggle for civil rights. Its pastors and lay members have been involved in all of the civil rights organizations and movements, serving as national and local officers, and as community leaders.

The Christian Methodist Episcopal Church has produced outstanding leaders for the church, the race, and the nation. **Lucius H. Holsey**, a prolific thinker and writer is said by his biographer to have provided the model for W. E. B. Dubois' development of the **Crisis Magazine**, official journal of the N.A.A.C.P.; Isaac Lane, a noted educator who was the founder of Lane College; **Charles Henry Phillips**, who led the fight against Jim Crow Laws in Kentucky in the early 1890s; **William Yancy Bell**, outstanding scholar, graduate of Yale Divinity School, and Dean of the Howard School of Religion; **Channing H. Tobias**, who served for several years as Chairman of the Board of the N.A.A.C.P.; Attorney Donald L. Hollowell, who served as legal counsel in Atlanta for many civil rights demonstrators, including **Martin Luther King, Jr.**; and **B. Julian Smith**, the noted leader in the ecumenical movement who helped to organize the National Council of Churches and the World Council of Churches.

Lakey, Othal Hawthorne. *The History of the C.M.E. Church.* Memphis, TN: The C.M.E. Publishing House, 1985. 683 pp.
Phillips, Charles Henry. *The History of the Colored Methodist Episcopal Church in America.* New York: Arno Press, 1972. 247 pp.

Othal Hawthorne Lakey

CHRIST'S SANCTIFIED HOLY CHURCH. A Holiness Pentecostal church. Christ's Sanctified Holy Church had its beginning when a band of White Holiness people from Virginia held meetings in West Lake, Louisiana, in 1903. C. E. Rigmaiden, a member of the **Christian Methodist Episcopal Church** (then known as the Colored MEC), had an experience of sanctification and began preaching. A group which included Dempsey Perkins, A. C. Mitchell, James Briller, Sr., and Lizzie Pleasant began to meet together. In 1904 they were organized as the Colored Church South, but over the next decade the church assumed its present name. It also absorbed Pentecostal teachings and began to associate the baptism of the Holy Spirit with speaking in tongues.

The church has several distinct beliefs; among them, it holds to one baptism, the Spirit's baptism, and hence does not practice water baptism. It is opposed to marriage with the non-sanctified and the use of tobacco and alcohol. It has opened the ministry to male and female alike.

Headquarters of the church is in Jennings, Louisiana. In 1957 there were 30 churches and 600 members. No more recent report has been obtained.

Religious Bodies: 1936. 3 vols. Washington, DC: United States Department of Commerce, Bureau of the Census, 1941.

Jones, Charles Edwin. *Black Holiness: A Guide to the Study of Black Participation in Wesleyan Perfectionist and Glossolalic Pentecostal Movements.* Metuchen, NJ: American Theological Library Association/Scarecrow Press, 1987. 388 pp.

CHURCH OF CHRIST HOLINESS UNTO THE LORD.

A Holiness Pentecostal church. The Church of Christ Holiness Unto the Lord was founded in 1926 in Savannah, Georgia, but grew out of the ministry of **William J. Seymour** of the Apostolic Faith Mission in Los Angeles, the original center from which the Pentecostal movement was disseminated around the United States. It was founded by a group led by Bishop Milton Solomon Bishop (d.1952) and included his wife, Saul Keels and his wife, Dora Brown, and others. The church's present leader, Bishop Moses Lewis, became General Overseer in 1979. The church follows the Holiness Pentecostal teachings as expounded by Seymour. In 1990 it had 35 affiliated congregations. Headquarters remain in Savannah. The church is affiliated with the **United Fellowship Convention of the Original Azusa Street Mission** which sponsors an annual gathering of those churches in the Eastern United States which grew out of Seymour's evangelistic activity.

DuPree, Sherry Sherrod. *The African American Holiness Pentecostal Movement: An Annotated Bibliography.* New York: Garland Publishing, 1993.

CHURCH OF CHRIST (HOLINESS), U.S.A.

A Holiness church. The Church of Christ (Holiness), U.S.A., was founded in 1907 but traces its history to 1894 when **Charles Price Jones** and **Charles H. Mason** founded the **Church of God in Christ**. Both Jones and Mason were Baptist ministers who had been converted to Methodist Holiness teachings. Holiness taught that Christians may, through an act of the Holy Spirit, experience sanctification, the baptism of the Holy Spirit, through which they are made perfect in love. This doctrine was anathema to the Baptists and, as a result,

both Jones and Mason were disfellowshipped. The church grew slowly for more than a decade. Then in 1907 Mason attended the revival he had heard about in Los Angeles and began preaching the new insights of Pentecostalism. While many accepted his new ideas, many others, including Jones, did not. Jones and those who wished to continue in their holiness perspective left and reorganized as the Church of Christ (Holiness). Jones set himself the task of building the denomination anew.

The Church follows Methodist doctrine but emphasizes the second work of grace in the life of believers which sanctifies them and makes them holy. At one point the church almost merged with the predominantly White **Church of the Nazarene**, but racism ultimately blocked the effort. That same racism had stopped the Church of Christ from having close relationships with the other large Holiness bodies.

The Church of Christ (Holiness) is episcopally organized. There is a senior bishop and seven diocese each headed by a bishop. A national convention meets biennially. In 1984 there were 170 congregations and approximately 10,000 members. Headquarters is in Jackson, Mississippi.

Cobbins, Otho B. *History of the Church of Christ (Holiness), U.S.A.* New York: 1966.

CHURCH OF GOD (ANDERSON, INDIANA).

A Holiness church. The Church of God was one of the first of several independent Holiness church fellowships formed in the last half of the nineteenth century. It was started in 1880 by Daniel S. Warner, formerly a minister of the General Eldership of the Churches of God in North America. As part of the holiness message Warner preached, he placed great emphasis upon the unity of the Church of God and decried sectarian religious organizations. It was clearly understood that the Church of God was an inclusive interracial fellowship. During the early years of the movement, African Americans were converted and integrated congregations developed. Among the early African American converts was **William J. Seymour**, who would later become one of the founders of modern Pentecostalism. Black ministers also served on the denominational boards and agencies created in the early twentieth century. The church's interracial character was fully illustrated in the publication in 1901 of William G. Schell's *Is the Negro a Beast?*, a refutation of Charles Carroll's popular propagandistic *The Negro as Beast.*

As the movement spread, Charleston, South Carolina, became an important center. The work began within the African American community and the first Black, Jane Williams, emerged as head of the congregation. From her congregation in Charleston the work spread to North Carolina, Georgia, Alabama, and Florida, and Williams worked hand-in-hand with both Black and White colleagues. By the second decade of the new century, however, the racial attitudes of the surrounding community had infiltrated the church to the extent that through the decade segregation would overcome the experiences of racial harmony many had experienced. Beginning in New York in 1909, congregational divisions along racial lines moved through the church. Both Chicago and Detroit split in 1915. These divisions resulted in the formation of segregated structures at the state, regional and national level.

By several stages, the National Association of the Church of God developed into the national organization for African American members of the Church of God. The Association grew out of a camp meeting which was first held in Western Pennsylvania in 1917. It attracted people from Pennsylvania and Ohio and gradually from further and further away. First known as the Western Pennsylvania and Eastern Ohio Camp Ground Association, as it grew, it later became the National Association of the Church of God, and took on many features of a separate national denominational structure for Black members. In 1933, *The Shinning Light*, a periodical for Black members, began publication.

The segregated situation in the church began to be reversed in the 1960s. At that time there were 396 Black churches and 20,700 members, slightly less than 20 percent of the total membership. In 1961, **Bay Ridge College** for African Americans was opened at Kendleton, Texas. The following year, Gabriel P. Dixon, a Black minister, was elected as vice-chairman of the General Ministerial Assembly (1962–66). In 1964 the church received the report of the Study Commission on Race Relations which it had been created in 1957. A statement which grew out of the report set the church decidedly against the segregated structures which then afflicted it at every level. Work on implementing the resolve of the statement (and another passed in 1968) has been slow but steady.

In 1967 the mission work of the National Association was integrated with that of the Mission Board of the church. In the five year period following the acceptance of the 1964 report, a 90 percent increase of African American members in national positions in the church could be seen. Through the 1970s and 1980s, further steps at creating an inclusive fellowship have proceeded. For example, in 1977, out of a study of Bay

City College, a comprehensive plan for a Black Ministerial Education Program was initiated.

Callen, Barry L., ed. *The First Century: Church of God Reformation Movement.* 2 vols. Anderson, IN: Warner Press, 1979.

CHURCH OF GOD (APOSTOLIC). An Apostolic Pentecostal church. The Church of God (Apostolic) began as a Holiness church in 1897 under the leadership of Elder Thomas J. Cox. Originally called the Christian Faith Band, it was formed at the Zion Hill Church of God in Danville, Kentucky. Shortly after the turn of the century Elder Cox learned of the Pentecostal experience and during the years of World War I met Robert C. Lawson, then a pastor with the Pentecostal Assemblies of the World. From him he learned and later accepted the Apostolic theological position which rejected the traditional doctrine of the Trinity. Apostolic Pentecostalism, sometimes called "Jesus Only," believes that the doctrine of the Trinity is inherently tritheistic. The Apostolics emphasize monotheism, and claim that the name of the One God is Jesus. Therefore, they baptize members in the name of "Jesus only" rather than the traditional trinitarian formula of "Father, Son and Holy Spirit."

In 1915 the name of the church was changed to the Church of God (Apostolic). Cox led the church until his death in 1943. He was succeeded by two co-presiding bishops, Eli N. Neal, pastor of a church in Winston-Salem, North Carolina, and M. Gravely. Gravely was disfellowshipped several years later after his divorce and remarriage. Neal served until 1964 and was succeeded by Love Odom (1964–66), David E. Smith (1966–74), and R. K. Hash (1975–).

Headquarters of the Church of God (Apostolic) is in Winston-Salem Church. In 1980 the church had 43 churches and 15,000 members. The church experienced one major schism in the last years of Bishop Cox's administration during which time he was unable to function, and Bishop Neal assumed his administrative role.

Richardson, James C., Jr. *With Water and Spirit: A History of Black Apostolic Denominations in the U.S.* Martinsville, VA: The Author, n.d. 151 pp.

CHURCH OF GOD (BLACK JEWS). Early Black Jewish organization. One of numerous organizations which call themselves the Church of God, this organization was founded around the beginning of the twentieth century by Prophet **F. S. Cherry**, as the first of the modern Black Jewish groups. Cherry was a self-educated man, and as he was maturing learned some Hebrew and Yiddish. His career began with a vision in which the Lord appointed him as a prophet. Overseas at the time, he returned to the United States, settled in Philadelphia and began the work.

Cherry strongly differentiated his community from that of the larger Jewish community, the Black Christian community, and the newly emerging **Moorish Science Temple of America**. He believed that the original Jews were Black, and descended from the biblical Jacob, who was Black. The "white" Jews were the result of a curse placed on Gehazi (who in II Kings 5:27 is mentioned as having been afflicted with leprosy). He also believed that the "yellow" race was a result of White and Black people intermarrying. Cherry also denounced the Christian clergy, who he saw as educated fools. He believed that God was Black and that Jesus Christ was a Black man. As the Moorish Science Temple arose, he countered their contention that American Black people were descended from the ancient Moabites. Cherry cited Genesis 19:30–37 as evidence that the Moabites were unworthy ancestors for Black people to adopt.

The Church of God met on the Sabbath (Saturday). A liturgical year was established with New Year's celebrated in April at Passover. Celebrating Christian holidays was forbidden. The group had a certain apocalyptic hope, believing that at the end of the century, Jesus would return to institute the millennium.

Never a large organization, the Church of God has not been seen for more than a decade and its present status is unknown. It may be defunct.

Fauset, Arthur Huff. *Black Gods of the Metropolis: Negro Religious Cults in the Urban North.* Philadelphia, PA: University of Pennsylvania Press, 1944. 128 pp.

CHURCH OF GOD (CLEVELAND, TENNESSEE).

A Holiness Pentecostal church. The Church of God (Cleveland, Tennessee) can be traced to a Holiness revival in the mountains of eastern Tennessee in the mid-1880s. However the character of the present-day church was really set by the introduction of Pentecostalism by G. B. Cashwell in 1908. Cashwell had been to the revival at Azusa Street in Los Angeles at which the experience of speaking in tongues was tied to the concept of the baptism of the Holy Spirit. The Church of God became the primary Pentecostal group to emerge among White Holiness people in the South.

From eastern Tennessee the movement spread in all directions across the old Confederacy.

At the 1913 annual assembly, a report was received noting that two Church of God congregations of African Americans were active in Florida. They were placed under the White state overseer. In 1915, because of the development of African American congregations, Edmund S. Burr, the first African American ordained by the church and former missionary to the Bahamas, was made overseer of the Black congregations, but in 1917 that experiment ended, and they were returned to the guidance of the White overseer. For a number of years all of the African American congregations in the Church of God were in Florida. In 1922 the elder's council again appointed a Black minister, Thomas F. Richardson, as overseer of the African American churches.

In 1926 a committee of Black ministers, C. F. Bright, David LaFleur, and G. C. Sapp made a report to the church assembly. Rev. Bright, their chairman, requested, "We . . . feel somewhat embarrassed and handicapped to the extent we cannot make the progress that we really desire, and we are asking you brethren, with the consent of all our brethren present at this Assembly, if there can be any way formulated by which we can arrange better to take care of our affairs among the colored work." The resultant response of the assembly was to create a second assembly for the African American members and leadership which would be led by an overseer which they would choose. David LaFleur was chosen. It was further agreed that the church periodical would have a column in which to promote the Black ministries.

By this time, however, Black congregations had arisen in the North and the ministers of the northern churches vigorously protested the segregation into a separate assembly and refused to participate. A compromise was reached in which it was agreed that each congregation and minister could choose to participate in either the African American Assembly, the regular general assembly, or both, as they saw fit.

After World War II, Black leaders began to assert themselves. In 1952 they noted that their overseer was not allowed to sit in on the meetings of the church's supreme council. A seat *without vote* was granted. Then in 1958, the church decided to appoint a White person as the overseer of the Black churches. Announcement of the move at the Black assembly brought a flood of negative reaction, but the appointment remained. Few protested by leaving the church.

Tensions grew, however, as the situation across the South changed. In the early 1960s a debate developed over admitting Black students to Lee College. Then in 1965, J. T. Roberts, who had won the respect of many of his Black colleagues, resigned. The supreme council appointed another White minister, David L. Lemons. Again there was an angry reaction for Black members. At the supreme council meeting in 1966, Roberts presented a resolution calling for the church to integrate. The council passed the resolution on to the general assembly, which accepted it. The church disbanded all of its segregated structures at the national and regional level and removed all references to "colored" work from its minutes, one of the very few Southern-based predominantly White religious organizations which integrated in the 1960s. At about the same time, Lee College opened its doors to Black students.

Over the next two decades Black leaders pushed to make the integration functional at the highest levels of the church, and gradually national staff positions have been opened at every level of church life. Finally in 1986 the first African American was appointed to the supreme council.

Conn, Charles W. *Like a Mighty Army: Moves the Church of God.* Cleveland, TN: Church of God Publishing House, 1955. 380 pp.

Crews, Mickey. *The Church of God: A Social History.* Knoxville, TN: University of Tennessee Press, 1990. 260 pp.

CHURCH OF GOD (SANCTIFIED CHURCH). A Holiness church. The Church of God (Sanctified Church) dates to the early years of the Holiness movement begun by **Charles P. Jones** and **Charles H. Mason** in the 1890s. That church was generally called the **Church of God in Christ**, but informally was known simply as the Holiness Church and the Church of God. Among the associates of Jones and Mason during this time was Elder Charles W. Gray. He established the first church in Nashville, Tennessee, affiliated with Jones and Mason. Then in 1907 Mason accepted Pentecostalism and he and Jones parted company. Jones reorganized and incorporated his work as the Church of Christ (Holiness), U.S.A. Elder Gray, while in basic doctrinal agreement with Jones, decided not to affiliate his work with the new corporation and to continue his endeavor in Nashville under the name Church of God (Sanctified Church).

The Church of God grew peacefully until the late 1920s when a move to incorporate the church arose. Advocates of incorporation also called for consolidating the work under a board of directors. The issue came to a head in 1927. The idea was approved and a board

selected. It included Elders J. L. Rucker, R. A. Manter, R. L. Martin, M. S. Sowell, B. Smith, and G. A. Whitley. The board now directs the church at the denominational level. Elder Gray protested the change and in the end left the church and with his followers reorganized as the **Original Church of God (or Sanctified Church)**.

Doctrinally, the Church of God follows the teachings of the Holiness Movement, which believes in a second work of grace in the life of the believer which makes him/her holy. The Church of God differs from its parent body over polity. The Church of Christ (Holiness), U.S.A. is organized episcopally. The Church of God adopted a loose congregational polity which allows each church to act independently, especially in the matter of calling and dismissing its minister.

Headquarters of the church is in Nashville, Tennessee. At last report in the early 1970s, there were some 5,000 members in 60 congregations.

CHURCH OF GOD (WHICH HE PURCHASED WITH HIS OWN BLOOD). A Holiness church. The Church of God (Which He Purchased with His Own Blood) was founded in Oklahoma City, Oklahoma, in 1953 by William Fizer, formerly a minister with the **Church of the Living God (Christian Workers for Fellowship)**. Fizer developed a number of doctrinal differences with the Church of the Living God over the Lord's Supper. Basically, Fizer rejected the original teaching of the Church of the Living God's founder **William Christian** that water was to be used in the Lord's Supper. Fizer began to use grape juice (or wine). He also observed the Lord's Supper each Sunday.

The Church of God, like its parent body, is non-pentecostal, meaning it does not practice speaking in tongues. It teaches that the Holy Spirit is given to those who lead a holy life. It observes three ordinances, the Lord's Supper, baptism in the name of the Father, Son and Holy Spirit, and foot washing. Holiness is emphasized and members refrain from the use of tobacco and alcohol. Divine healing is taught, but doctors are consulted by the ill.

The church is headquartered in Oklahoma City. It is headed by the Chief Bishop and the several overseers.

CHURCH OF GOD IN CHRIST. A Holiness Pentecostal church. With over 5,900,000 members, the Church of God in Christ is the largest Pentecostal church in North America. It was founded by **Charles Price Jones** and **Charles Harrison Mason**. At the age of 18, Jones (1865–1949) moved to Memphis, Tennessee, where he was converted, joined Locust Grove Baptist Church, and was baptized by Elder J. D. Petty, in Crittenden County, Arkansas. He was licensed to preach in 1887, and moved to Helena, Arkansas, where he came under the watchful eye of Rev. **E. C. Morris**, later president of the **National Baptist Convention**. He attended Arkansas Baptist College, and in 1895 became pastor of Mt. Helm Baptist Church in Jackson, Mississippi.

Mason (1866–1961) grew up at Plummersville, Arkansas. He was baptized by his brother I. S. Nelson, a Baptist preacher, pastor of Mt. Olive Missionary Baptist Church. In 1892, he received a local license to preach, entered Arkansas Bible College, and after three months, left school to become a Baptist preacher. In 1895, on a visit to Jackson, Mississippi, Mason met Jones. Both had been strongly affected by the Holiness movement which had been spreading through the South since the end of the Civil War, and soon became friends. The next year because of their insistence upon the deeper spiritual experience of entire sanctification as a second work of grace (the basic experience of the Holiness people) they were rejected by their own Baptist church and association. Jones and Mason conducted a successful holiness revival in an abandoned cotton gin building owned by Dane Watson in Lexington, Mississippi, in February 1896, and formed the first local Church of God. In March 1897, Mason was walking the streets of Little Rock, Arkansas, when the Lord revealed to him the name, "The Church of God in Christ," through the scriptures I Thessalonians 2:14 and I Thessalonians 1:1. Mason and Jones moved their headquarters to Memphis, Tennessee, and in 1897, the Church of God in Christ was legally chartered and incorporated. This was the first Holiness church in the United States to obtain such a charter. Jones assumed leadership of the church as general overseer and presiding elder, and Mason was the support and co-leader. As a spiritual team, Jones became known for his hymns, and Mason for his preaching and teaching abilities.

The Emergence of Pentecostalism: In 1906 news spread to Memphis of the Azusa Street Revival in Los Angeles, California. This revival had broken out in an African American Holiness mission, soon to be named the Apostolic Faith Mission Church, located in an abandoned African Methodist Episcopal Church, under the leadership of **William Joseph Seymour**. The revival was built around the teaching and experience of the baptism in the Holy Ghost as initially evidenced by speaking in tongues. Any of the "saints," those who had

experienced sanctification, identified that experience with the baptism of the Holy Spirit, but Seymour taught that the baptism, the filling with the Holy Spirit, was an empowering that one knew they had received when they spoke in an unknown tongue.

The Azusa Street Revival attracted all races of people from all parts of the world. In March 1907, Mason, J. D. Young, and J. A. Jeter journeyed to Los Angeles. At Azusa Street, Mason and Young received the baptism in the Holy Ghost, but Jeter did not share the experience. When Mason, Young, and Jeter arrived in Memphis, the church was already divided over the doctrine. Jones was against the belief, and he and Mason struggled over its acceptability.

In August of 1907, the General Assembly of the Church of God in Christ met in Jackson, Mississippi. Following a discussion of the future of the church which lasted for three days and nights, the assembly withdrew the right hand of fellowship from Mason and all who promulgated the Pentecostal doctrine of speaking in tongues. Mason left the assembly with about half of the ministers and members, and reorganized as the first General Assembly of the Pentecostal Church of God in Christ. The ministers who helped form the new church were **E. R. Driver**, Justus Bowe, R. R. Booker, **W. M. Roberts**, R. E. Hart, D. W. Welch, A. A. Blackwell, E. M. Page, R. H. I. Clark, J. D. Young, James Brewer, Daniel Spearman, and H. H. Boone. Mason was named the chief apostle. For two years, Jones and Mason were in lawsuits over the name of the church and control of properties. In 1909, the courts allowed Mason and his followers to keep the charter and the name, Church of God in Christ. Jones and his followers became the **Church of Christ (Holiness) U.S.A.** and continued as a Holiness church.

The formal organization of the Church of God in Christ proved an important organizational step for the developing Pentecostal movement in the Mid-South and Midwest. Many Black and White Pentecostal preachers who were not members of the Church of God in Christ were ordained by Mason and/or given ministerial credentials from the Church of God in Christ between 1907 to 1919. The credentials allowed the independent ministers to function as pastors and to gain some of the standard benefits such as half-price train tickets. It became most important when World War I started, as it allowed them (and many were pacifists) to relate to the draft board. This was the only chartered, incorporated Pentecostal denomination in the nation. The church began to ordain both Black and White ministers from independent congregations, which did not have a recognized ecclesiastical body to ordain them.

To accommodate the White ministers, Mason issued a "gentleman's agreement" whereby they could issue Church of God in Christ credentials. In Memphis, there was a "White" Church of God in Christ, located at 930 Louisiana Street. William B. Holt (White) formally joined the Church of God in Christ, and was appointed superintendent of Spanish missions in California. Holt also served as secretary to Mason, in 1918.

In 1914 a number of the White Pentecostal ministers, many of whom held credentials from the Church of God in Christ, organized the General Council of the **Assemblies of God**. The Assemblies differed doctrinally from the Church of God in Christ (and the other Pentecostal denominations of the time) in that they had rejected the Wesleyan emphasis upon holiness and the sanctification experience, prior to receiving the baptism of the Holy Spirit. However, the Assemblies enjoyed cordial early relationships with the Church of God in Christ, and Mason attended and preached at the organizing convention of the Assemblies of God in Hot Springs, Arkansas, in 1914.

Through this period, following the lead set at Azusa Street, the revivals were frequently integrated, but a problem developed from the White people who felt hindered, by the stringent Southern social mores, in coming to the altar to "tarry" for the Holy Ghost with Black people. In Savannah, Georgia, for example, in 1912 when the White and Black Holiness Pentecostals worshiped in revivals, they were segregated by a large rope. The White side was covered with a sawdust floor, the Black side had no covering over the dirt floor. When the shouting began, a cloud of dust would cover the area. The missionary said, "God controlled the air, we all coughed and got dusty." In the spring of 1916, Mason was invited by the authorities of Nashville, Tennessee, to hold a camp meeting for the White people. A Brother Martin (White) paid all expenses for the auditorium that seated 7,000. Reportedly, God worked wonders, many were baptized in the Holy Ghost and many were healed.

World War I. The Church of God in Christ doctrine forbids the shedding of blood, a belief that created unavoidable conflict with the draft of men into the military. By 1918 the southern White populace expressed a growing fear that German agents were stirring Blacks to disloyalty or even revolt. In 1918, Mason's forthright stand against war led to his arrest in Lexington, Mississippi. He was eventually forced to leave town. Then on April 18, 1918, in Blythville, Arkansas, Rev. Jesse Payne, an elder in the Church of God in Christ, was tarred and feathered at night for alleged seditious remarks concerning the president of the United States and World War I. After Payne was tarred

and feathered he was forced to repeat the soldier's oath, and promised to talk Liberty Bonds and Red Cross to the end of his life and the end of the war. His pacifism misunderstood as disloyalty, Mason moved to clarify his position. On June 23, 1918, he addressed a large baptismal gathering at North Memphis on June 23, 1918, and preached a sermon entitled "The Kaiser in the Light of the Scriptures." He ended his sermon in prayer that the "German hordes" would be driven back in defeat behind their borders, in anticipation of the Prince of Peace who would come when men beat swords into plowshares and studied war no more. Mason also found scriptural approval for the purchase of Liberty Bonds in Matthew 5:42, and personally raised more than $3,000 for the government. Mason sent a telegram to President Wilson after the draft act was passed, in which he explained the church's doctrine. Mason stated that the church supported Liberty Bonds, War Stamps, and the Red Cross drives.

Church Polity. At the founding of the church in 1907, Mason was designated "General Overseer and Chief Apostle." He was given absolute authority in matters of doctrine and church organization, including the appointment of state overseers. In 1933, five overseers were consecrated to the office of bishop by Mason: I. S. Stafford (Detroit); E. M. Page (Dallas); **W. M. Roberts** (Chicago); **R. F. Williams** (Cleveland); and O. T. Jones, Sr. (Philadelphia). On November 18, 1961, Mason died in Detroit at the age of 95. Succeeding Mason through what proved to be a stormy transition period was Bishop **O. T. Jones, Sr.** (1891–1972) from Philadelphia. Jones was in power from 1962 to 1968. In November of 1968, Bishop **J. O. Patterson, Sr.** (1912–1989), the son-in-law of Mason, became the leader of the church. Patterson was given the title of presiding bishop. Bishop **Louis Henry Ford** (c.1924–) from Chicago succeeded Patterson as presiding bishop in December of 1989.

Following the death of Bishop Mason, the Church of God went through a reorganization at the highest levels which included the promulgation in 1972 of a new constitution. The General Assembly is now the legislative and doctrinal authority of the church. The delegation of the General Assembly includes the General Board, all jurisdictional bishops, all pastors and elders, jurisdictional supervisors of women's work, two district missionaries, one lay delegate from each jurisdictional assembly, and designated foreign delegates. The General Assembly meets twice a year, April and November. The General Assembly functions as the supreme judicial body of the church. Under the General Assembly are: the Board of Bishops, composed of all the bishops of the church, and the General Board, composed of twelve bishops elected by the General Assembly from the Board of Bishops for four years which serves as the executive arm of the church.

The presiding bishop is elected from the General Board by the General Assembly. The presiding bishop, acting in concert with the General Board, appoints all bishops, department heads, and national officers, except the general secretary, financial secretary, and treasurer who are elected by the General Assembly. Bishops (prior to 1957 called overseers) are selected by the presiding bishop from among the ordained elders of jurisdiction the bishop is to head. Jurisdictional assemblies meet twice per year or at the discretion of the bishop. Within the jurisdictions are districts, each headed by a district superintendent appointed by the jurisdictional bishop. Pastors usually start their own congregations and there is a tradition of family members continuing the church after the death of the founder. Women are not ordained to the ministry but may serve as missionaries appointed by their pastors and licensed at the jurisdictional level by the bishop. Women often start new congregations which are then turned over to elders as pastors.

Organizational Development: Within a few years of the founding of the church, three schools were opened. In 1918 Sister Pinkie Duncan and Professor James Courts (d. 1926) initiated what became the Saints Industrial School and Academy in the basement of the St. Paul Church of God in Christ in Lexington, Mississippi. The school prospered under the able leadership of Arenia Conelia Mallory (1905–1977), the second leader of the Lexington School. Mallory was accredited with many firsts for her part of the state, including the establishment of a junior college for Blacks in Holmes County. Mallory retired in June 1976, and the school closed in 1983. (The school is being remodeled and is projected to reopen in 1993.)

The Page Normal Industrial and Bible Institute was founded in 1919 by E. M. Page, James Courts, and "the Saints" of the Church of God in Christ in Hearne, Texas. Mrs. E. F. Bradly served as principal of the school. Geridge, Arkansas was the home of Justus Bowe's school.

In 1911, **Lizzie Woods Roberson** (1860–1945), then matron of the Baptist Academy in Dermott, Arkansas, was appointed by Mason as the leader of the Women's Department of the Church of God in Christ according to Jeremiah 9:17–20. Roberson established the prayer and Bible bands, sunshine bands, and sewing circles. Roberson gave Mason funds to open the first

bank account for the Church of God in Christ. During the 1920, the Women's Department assumed a major role in developing the missionary thrust of the church, supporting more than twelve mission outposts in foreign fields. Today, it underwrites one-third of the budget of the General Church.

Roberson, a legendary figure in the church, was succeeded as National Supervisor of Women in 1945 by the equally capable Mother **Lillian B. Coffey** (1896–1964). Coffey was known for nurse, home, and foreign missions programs. Under Coffey, the women of the church began to wear fashionable clothes, furs, costume jewelry, and feathers. Coffey was succeeded by Mother **Mattie Carter McGlothen**.

The Young People's Willing Workers began in 1914 with the appointment of Elder M. C. Green as the first national president. Under Bishop O. T. Jones, Sr., the YPWW became a standard feature in almost every Church of God in Christ congregation.

Foreign missions were initiated by the church in 1922 when Elder Paucius opened the first Church of God in Christ in Haiti in the home of Joseph and Mary St. Juste. In 1925, the Home and Foreign Mission Board was activated and the next year it sent Mrs. Mattie McCauley of Tulsa, Oklahoma, to Trinidad, West Indies. Elder Cornelius Hall, a native of Turks Island, evangelized his area. Work in Africa was opened in 1929 by Missionary Elizabeth White. By 1939, the overseas work had grown to the point that A. B. McEwen (1874–1969) was appointed Bishop of Foreign Fields. Today the church has two million members in Africa alone.

In 1946, the headquarters building of the Church of God in Christ was completed. Riley Williams was the overseer of building Mason Temple. James Delk, a White elder in the Church of God in Christ from Kentucky, was instrumental in helping to get the steel for the building of Mason Temple in Memphis. During World War II it was hard to get steel because it was used for military equipment. Delk went to Washington, D.C., to ask for the steel; it was granted. Delk then supervised the shipment of steel from the steel mill to Memphis. The Mason Temple convention hall was the largest building constructed and owned by a black religious group in the United States.

On April 3, 1968, Rev. **Martin Luther King, Jr.,** gave his last speech at the Mason Temple, Church of God in Christ. This sermon, "I Have Been to the Mountaintop," was delivered the night before his assassination on April 4th. The church had several members involved in the garbage strike which had brought King to Memphis.

Music and the Church: The Church of God in Christ has been known for music from its beginning. Cofounder C. P. Jones was a hymn writer and today his hymns such as "Jesus Only" can be found in *His Fullness Songs* (first published in 1906, revised in 1977). The Church of God hymnal, *Yes, Lord*, has several of Jones' hymns.

Over the years, many gospel musicians got their start in the Church of God in Christ. The first gospel singers were unaccompanied by music, only hand clapping, tambourines, washboards and handmade instruments. Elder F. W. McGee (d. 1972), from Chicago, was an overseer of Iowa with 25 churches in the Church of God in Christ. McGee accompanied himself on the piano and often included a cornet, guitar, and drums. His records had a swinging, jazzy flavor. McGee was Victor Records' most successful preacher of sermons and singing between 1926 and 1931. A guitar was not permitted in non-Pentecostal churches, and musicians often called them "starvation boxes," because the religious musicians would starve to death if they did not play in a sanctified church. In the Church of God in Christ all instruments were welcomed.

Elder Utah Smith (1906–1965), national evangelist of the Church of God in Christ, evangelized with the preaching and playing of his guitar; he was known for his famous song "Two Wings." Arizona Drane (1904–1964), was a blind gospel singer and piano player who was encouraged by **Samuel M. Crouch, Sr.** (1896–1976), a bishop in the Church of God in Christ, to evangelize and travel. Among the duets in the 1950s were the Boyer Brothers, Horace and James, who popularized "Take your Troubles to Jesus," and The O'Neil Twins, from St. Louis. Mattie Moss Clark organized the Southwest Michigan State Choir of the Churches of God in Christ in 1958. This choir has recorded, and has over 300 members. Sara Jordon Powell, Director of the Fine Arts Department of the Church of God in Christ, brings a classical touch, singing hymns, spirituals, and gospel. Today, contemporary gospel music is being restructured by the likes of BeBe and CeCe Winans, **Andrae Crouch**, and Deniece Williams, to name a just a few of those rooted in the Church of God in Christ.

Current Statistics: The Church of God in Christ is headquartered in Memphis, Tennessee. Bishop Louis H. Ford presides over the 5,900,000 million members in 15,300 congregations in the United States. There are also some two million members in Africa and additional work in the West Indies, Canada, and Europe. There are two major periodicals, *Whole Truth* and *The Voice of Missions*.

Clemons, Ithiel. "The Church of God in Christ." In Vinson Synan. *The 20th Century Pentecostal Explosion.* 1987.

Cornelius, Lucille J. *The Pioneer: History of the Church of God in Christ.* N.p.: The Author, 1975.

DuPree, Sherry Sherrod. *The African-American Holiness Pentecostal Movement: An Annotated Bibliography.* New York: Garland Publishing, 1993.

———. *Biographical Dictionary of African American Holiness Pentecostals, 1880–1990.* Washington, DC: Middle Atlantic Regional Press, 1989. 386 pp.

An Introduction to the Church of God in Christ: History, Theology, and Structure. N.p.: compiled by the Second Jurisdiction of Arkansas, Church of God in Christ., n.d. 66 pp.

Kelley, Frances Burnett, and German R. Ross. *Here Am I, Send Me: the Dramatic Story of Presiding Bishop J. O. Patterson, Challenging and Bold Leader of the Church of God in Christ.* Memphis, TN: 1970.

Mason, Elise W. *From the Beginning of Bishop C. H. Mason and the Early Pioneers of the Church of God in Christ.* Memphis, TN: 1991.

Mason, Mary Esther. *The History and Life Work of Elder C.H. Mason, Chief Apostle and his Co-Laborers.* Memphis, TN: Church of God in Christ Publishing House, n.d. 93 pp.

Official Manual with the Doctrine and Discipline of the Church of God in Christ. Memphis, TN: Church of God in Christ Publishing House, 1973.

Patterson, J. O., German Ross, and Julia Mason Atkins. *History and Formative Years of the Church of God in Christ with Excerpts from the Life and Works of Its Founder, Bishop C. H. Mason.* Memphis, TN: Church of God in Christ Publishing House, 1969. 143 pp.

Simmons, Dovie Marie. *Down Behind the Sun: The Story of Arenia Conelia Mallory.* Memphis, TN: 1983.

Sherry Sherrod DuPree

CHURCH OF GOD IN CHRIST, CONGREGATIONAL.

A Holiness Pentecostal church. Elder Justus Bowe had a stormy history with the **Church of God in Christ**. He was one of the original members of the church in 1907 when it separated from the Holiness work of **Charles P. Jones** and established as a Pentecostal group under **Charles H. Mason**. He was placed in charge of its work in Arkansas. During the two years after the church's founding, because of some lawsuits with Jones' **Church of Christ, Holiness**, Mason directed his leadership around the country not to formally organize. Bowe went ahead and solidified his organization in Arkansas, and as a result, all of the church's property was lost. However, he was forgiven his error and welcomed back into the church's leadership.

Through the 1920s, the church's organization was developed under the strong guidance of Mason, who named overseers for each territory. Bowe, was appointed to Arkansas. However, by 1932, Bowe had become convinced that the correct way to organize the church was congregationally, i.e., with each congregation owning its own property. That conclusion ran counter to the direction of the Church of God in Christ which was very centralized. Unable to reach an agreement, Bowe left and in 1932 founded the Church of God in Christ, Congregational. It agreed with its parent body on almost every point of doctrine and practice other than the matter of organizational structure. It did propose a doctrine of conscientious objection to war.

Bowe served as senior bishop of the church for 14 years, but in 1946 worked out a reconciliation with the Church of God in Christ. He had come to feel that he should return, since he was one of the founders and he resigned as senior bishop of the new church he had originally started. Bowe was succeeded as senior bishop by Elder George S. Black. Black had originally joined the church in 1934 after leaving the Church of God in Christ over a disagreement on the necessity of tithing.

The church has grown steadily during the last half of the twentieth century. In 1971 it reported 43 churches. In 1990 there were 59 congregations. Headquarters is in East St. Louis, Illinois.

DuPree, Sherry Sherrod. *The African American Holiness Pentecostal Movement: An Annotated Bibliography.* New York: Garland Publishing, 1993.

Jones, Charles Edwin. *Black Holiness: A Guide to the Study of Black Participation in Wesleyan Perfectionist and Glossolalic Pentecostal Movements.* Metuchen, NJ: American Theological Library Association/Scarecrow Press, 1987. 388 pp.

Black, George, William Walker, and E. Jones. *Manual.* East St. Louis, IL: Church of God in Christ, Congregational, 1948.

CHURCH OF GOD IN CHRIST, INTERNATIONAL. A Holiness Pentecostal church. Following the death of founder **Charles H. Mason**, the **Church of God in Christ** experienced a period of turmoil and organizational crisis which was only settled by a constitutional convention in 1968 and the emergence of **J. O. Patterson** as the new presiding bishop. In 1969, 14 bishops left the church and reorganized at Kansas City, Missouri, as the Church of God in Christ, International. Bishop Illie L. Washington became their first presiding bishop. The church initially claimed over a thousand churches (the congregations in the 14 areas previously served by the bishops) but had reduced that number to 300 congregations by the early 1970s, a more correct indication of the number of churches which actually followed the bishops into schism.

Jefferson was succeeded by Carl Williams, the present presiding bishop, in the late 1970s. The church is like its parent body in belief and practice, there being no doctrinal dispute involved in the separation. Headquarters is in Brooklyn, New York. In 1982 it reported 200,000 members in 300 congregations.

CHURCH OF HAKEEM. A New Thought group. The Church of Hakeem was a short-lived religious grouping which appeared on the West Coast of the United States in the late 1970s. It grew out of the prosperity teaching of Hakeem Abdul Rasheed (born Clifton Jones). By the early 1970s, Hakeem had absorbed the teachings of what is commonly referred to as "prosperity consciousness," a belief that prosperity (like health) is derived from a change of consciousness toward a more positive mental attitude. He first put these teachings into practice in a weight-reduction clinic. The clinic was closed by the State of California when it was disclosed that he used his teachings, rather than standard forms of diet and exercise, to promote the loss of fat. He was charged with the unlicensed practice of "psychology," a practice strictly regulated by the state.

The Church of Hakeem became an immediate success. Within a year of its founding early in 1978, it had centers across California from San Diego to Sacramento. It attracted many people who heard of its promise of a large return on a relatively small investment. Unfortunately, the church's program was built around a posey scheme, a standard confidence racket. In May 1979, Hakeem was indicted for fraud, and former members filed a class action suit against the church. Hakeem's conviction and the subsequent movement by the Internal Revenue Service against the church assured its dissolution.

CHURCH OF JESUS CHRIST OF LATTER-DAY SAINTS. The Church of Jesus Christ of Latter-day Saints is the largest of the several churches which grew out of the revelations received by Joseph Smith, Jr., in the early nineteenth century. The revelations began with an encounter with two personages (later identified as God the Father and Jesus Christ) and included the reception of a set of gold plates upon which was written a book later published as *The Book of Mormon. The*

Book of Mormon told a story of two groups of people who migrated from the Middle East to inhabit North America. Their descendants are the American Indians.

It was claimed that *The Book of Mormon* was the translation of a text originally written in Reformed Egyptian. Smith also translated two other pieces, Egyptian writings later published as "The Book of Moses" and "The Book of Abraham" and published as *The Pearl of Great Price*. Finally, Smith had continuing revelations throughout his years as the leader of the church. These were gathered into a volume first published in 1833 as the *Book of Commandments* (later reissued as the *Doctrine and Covenants*). All three books are accepted as scripture by the church. It should be noted that the *Doctrine and Covenants* is an open book in that the church believes that its president can receive new revelations at any time, and on occasion he has.

Shortly after the church was formed and *The Book of Mormon* published in 1830, African Americans joined. The first seems to have been a man known only as Black Peter. He first appears in Kirkland, Ohio, where the Church first gathered soon after its formation. A controversial figure in the church, he had a series of revelations including one suggesting that he could fly. To prove the truth of his theory, he jumped off a cliff. He was not hurt but lost faith in his flying ability. Catching the ethos of the church, he asked to marry a member, but Smith had no revelation allowing him to do so. Instead Smith had a revelation against false and competing revelations and Black Peter was cut off from the church.

The next year **Elijah Abel** joined the church and in 1832 he was ordained an elder and admitted into the Mormon priesthood (into which all Mormon males were expected to enter as a matter of course). However, Abel soon advanced to the rank of "Seventy," a leadership position in the church. He also received a patriarchal blessing (which generally carried some statement of the believer's relationship to an Old Testament personage). Abel continued as a member in good standing for the rest of his long life. Approximately ten African Americans joined the church during the 1930s, and at least one of these, Walker Lewis of Lowell, Massachusetts, was admitted to the priesthood.

Mormons set out to convert the world, but any evangelistic activity among Black people was hindered not only by shared racist attitudes among the church members but the laws operative in Northern states against the movement of free Black people which would have made it difficult (though not impossible) for Black converts to join the mobile Saints who moved their headquarters from Kirkland, Ohio, to Missouri, and then to Nauvoo, Illinois, during the first fifteen years of the church's existence.

Openness to accepting African American members began to change during the 1830s in Missouri. While the Mormons were not abolitionists, they were against slavery and did not participate in its practice. It has been noted that an element of the opposition they received from their Missouri neighbors was the accusation that they were abolitionists and trying to draw African Americans to the state. At this time, a racial theory begins to be articulated in the church's official documents. The most significant, "The Book of Moses," was completed in 1833. This volume, considered a supplement to the biblical book of Genesis, saw Cain, the rejected son of Adam, and his wicked descendants as Black people. Though not literally stated, "The Book of Moses" hinted that "blackness" was a curse God placed upon the disobedient. "The Book of Moses" also saw Ham, identified by many biblical commentators as the ancestor of the Black people of the earth, as cursed with perpetual servitude and implied that Black skin color was an element of the curse.

"The Book of Abraham" reinforced these ideas by identifying the Egyptians (with whom the Israelites contended) as the descendants of Ham. The Book of Abraham also talks of one Pharaoh who was a righteous man, but because of the curse upon him, was not allowed into the priesthood. "The Book of Moses" and "The Book of Abraham" were to foster an identification of people who opposed God's work in the Bible as Black people.

Smith at one time believed that Blacks who converted would eventually become part of one universal White race. From 1833 on, however, the belief in racial "regeneration" was set aside and more weight given to the permanent curse placed upon the descendants of Ham. Smith's statement would later grow into new policies concerning Black people within the church. During Smith's lifetime the racial theories which were in the process of developing did not lead to a change in the general anti-slavery stance of the church. In 1844, Smith's presidential platform contained a program for the gradual elimination of slavery in the land.

The Brigham Young Era: In 1844 Smith was assassinated, and the church he founded was thrown into a period of chaos. In relatively short order, the Mormons were forced out of Nauvoo, Illinois, and began their long trek to Salt Lake City. Following a struggle for control of the church, Brigham Young emerged as the new church president. Under Young, a policy of exclusion of Black people from the priesthood would become institutionalized in the church. The first statements leading to this new policy seem to have occurred in reaction to the disturbance caused by William McCary, an African American member briefly associated with the church in 1847. A few months after he joined, McCary began to have private revelations. He was expelled from the church and then set up a rival movement which drew a few members away from the church.

In the fall of 1847, Young first articulated a belief that Black people were not eligible to participate in various temple ordinances. In 1847 he made a clear statement that God cursed Cain's descendants with Black skin and denied them the priesthood. To deny them the priesthood carried with it a denial of participation in the ordinances of the temple which Mormons viewed generally as a key part of their eternal relationship with God. Among the important temple ceremonies is "sealing," in which couples are married for all eternity. In the 1850s Young would make Mormon policy public in a series of speeches in which he developed the idea of the curse of Cain.

Once settled in Utah, the Mormon-controlled state legislature passed a series of laws limiting Black people's access to the government and in 1852 passed a specific ordinance prohibiting Black/White inter-marriage. That same year, slavery was legalized in Utah. The institutionalization of denial of the priesthood to Black people and the passing of Black laws by the legislature served to limit the development of a Black community in Utah and Black participation in the church as a whole.

The position first articulated by Smith was reinforced over the years by the succeeding church presidents. The continued petitions of the few Black members to be allowed to marry in the temple gave both John Taylor and Joseph F. Smith the occasion to restate the church's teaching. Taylor was called upon to rule upon the petition of **Elijah Abel** and of Jane Manning James. James had been separated from her husband in 1869. She became especially concerned for her situation as Mormon doctrine assigns females a role in the afterlife according to the status of the husband to which they have been sealed.

Change in the Twentieth Century: The policy of denying the priesthood to Black people stood through the first half of the twentieth century and was only rarely questioned or even mentioned. It took on a new element as the international Mormon missionary enterprise developed. Areas dominated by Black populations, including the Black communities of the American South, were avoided by church workers.

Church leaders had to confront several new situations on the mission field. In 1932, for example, it was discovered that a Black man in Hawaii had been ordained in the belief that he was native Hawaiian. Four years later it was discovered that two Mormon elders had African ancestry. In 1947 the same situation emerged in New Zealand.

Then, during the 1940s, as part of the exodus of Black people out of the South, Utah's Black population doubled. In 1949 church president George Albert Smith publicly reasserted the church's longstanding position. During the same period, the state moved to institute segregated structures including the official definition of a section of Salt Lake City as a "Negro district." In spite of the policy, a few Black people opted to become members of the church. In 1956 one of the church's apostles, Mark A. Peterson, suggested that where a number of Black families joined, a segregated chapel for their worship services should be created.

In the 1950s, the church's position on Blacks in the priesthood began to be challenged, and in the 1960s, a matter of open debate among church members. The Mormon journal, *Dialogue*, founded in 1966, printed many of the articles reexamining the issue out of both theological and historical research.

In the 1960s Salt Lake City became the site of a variety of civil rights demonstrations. In 1963 planned demonstrations at the church's General Conference were canceled when the church issued a statement supportive of civil rights for all. That same year, David O. Oliver, an African American attorney in Salt Lake City, published an attack on the church's racial policies. Then in 1965 a new attack upon the priesthood doctrine was launched. While started by African American critics outside the church, it garnered support within.

As the challenge to the church's policy mounted, African American church members joined the debate. In 1970 Alan Gerald Cherry defended the church as the receptacle of truth and pushed aside the priesthood question. Two years later, an even stronger statement appeared. Wynetta Willis Martin, in *A Black Mormon Tells Her Story*, recounted her acceptance of the priesthood policy and even included a lengthy defense of it written by a White man. These two books were countered by the actions of Douglas A. Wallace, a Mormon High Priest from Vancouver, Washington, who took it upon himself to ordain Larry Lester, an African American member, to the priesthood. Wallace was disfellowshipped and his actions declared null and void.

Additional Pressures. Among the more important pressures on the church came from the emergence of several of its members as presidential candidates in the mid-1960s. Especially in 1967 and 1968, George Romney was repeatedly called upon to defend the church. The collapse of his presidential campaign took the church off of the hot seat until 1976 when Morris Udall ran for the presidency.

Concurrent with the pressure put on the church by the Romney and Udall races for the presidency, the church began to grow significantly overseas. In 1946, O. J. Umordak of Nigeria requested information on the church. Ignored, he persisted, and in 1959 the Church sent representatives to Africa and in 1963 opened a mission in Nigeria. This mission altered the older policy of avoiding evangelism in predominantly Black communities. The mission proved a disaster, however, as the Nigerian government was made aware of the priesthood policy and denied the missionaries residency visas.

Work in Brazil, which began among Brazilians of Portuguese ancestry, soon ran into the very mixed racial heritage of the population. As the church grew, word reached Salt Lake City that people with African ancestry were being ordained to the priesthood. At the same time the complex racial mix in the land made it often impossible to separate those with African ancestry from the rest.

The church began to make programmatic response to all the pressure put upon it. In 1971 it created the Genesis group to provide a ministry for some 200 Black members in Salt Lake City. Three apostles were appointed as a committee to deal with the church "Negro problem." Brigham Young University began to desegregate, especially in its sports program.

The pressures moving the Church to change its practices culminated in June 1978 when the First Presidency of the church announced that a revelation had been received and that forthwith all people will be admitted to the priesthood irregardless of race or color. At the same time the church moved quickly to act upon the new policy by initiating a missionary program in the Black communities of the United States and Africa. Within a few days Joseph Freeman, Jr. became the first Black to be ordained to the priesthood under the new policy. Later in the year the first African American stake president was named.

The 1978 announcement ended the public controversy surrounding the Church and inaugurated an era of church growth in West Africa. In the United States, while some Blacks have joined, they remain a tiny minority in an otherwise White organization.

Bringhurst, Newell G. *Saints, Slaves, and Blacks: The Changing Place of Black People within Mormonism.* Westport, CT: Greenwood Press, 1981. 254 pp.

Bush, Lester E., Jr., and Armand L. Mauss, ed. *Neither White nor Black: Mormon Scholars Confront the Race Issue in a Universal Church.* Midvale, UT: Signature Books, 1984. 249 pp. Contains an extensive bibliography on the debate over the status of African Americans in the Church.

Cherry, Alan Gerald. *It's You and Me, Lord!* Provo, UT: Trilogy Arts, 1970. 64 pp.

Lund, John Lewis. *The Church and the Negro.* Salt Lake City, UT: Paramount Publishers, 1967. 129 pp.

Oliver, David H. *A Negro on Mormonism.* Salt Lake City, UT: The Author, 1963. 54 pp.

Stewart, John J. *Mormonism and the Negro.* Orem, UT: Bookmark, 1960. 54 pp.

CHURCH OF OUR LORD JESUS CHRIST OF THE APOSTOLIC FAITH. An Apostolic Pentecostal church. The Apostolic movement began in 1915 and had its first major success when the **Pentecostal Assemblies of the World** accepted its message. The first schism in the movement occurred only four years later when **Robert C. Lawson** left the Assemblies to form the Church of Our Lord Jesus Christ of the Apostolic Faith. In 1913, Lawson was healed of what had been diagnosed as a terminal illness by **Garfield T. Haywood**, the Bishop of the Pentecostal Assemblies of the World. He founded churches in Texas, Missouri, and Ohio before moving to New York in 1919. There he broke with Haywood and formed the Church of the Lord Jesus Christ of the Apostolic Faith. Significant in Lawson's decision to form the new church was his inability to accept women ministers and a rather uncompromising stand on divorce and remarriage.

The new church began to grow in the Northeast as Lawson, by all reports an excellent preacher, carried his evangelical activity to other cities. At least one minister, **Karl F. Smith**, who succeeded Lawson as pastor in Columbus, Ohio, joined the new church and in 1923, when a new organizational structure was adopted, Smith became its executive secretary. Lawson threw himself into the emerging postwar African American community in New York. In the 1920s he began a radio show which attracted many new members. He organized funeral homes, a day nursery, a book store, a publishing concern, and a record store. He pioneered education among the Apostolic churches by founding the Church of Christ Bible Institute in 1926. He also moved to assist with the continuing problem of basic education for Black children in the South by establishing the R. C. Lawson Institute in Southern Pines, North Carolina, a combined elementary and secondary school. He also extended the church internationally through his trips to the West Indies in the 1930s. Having outgrown the

1,100-seat facilities in which Lawson's New York congregation had met, the headquarters church moved in the 1940s into a former Loew's theatre.

The major crisis for the church came in 1957. As the church had spread, Lawson, who had control of the church, had appointed state bishops. Regretting his giving them that title, he changed it to State Overseers. During the 1950s, however, a number of leaders began to complain that Lawson needed to share the power more and as a symbol of that sharing, appoint others as bishops. Lawson rejected that move. As a result a number of his leading ministers and 70 churches left and reorganized as the **Bible Way Church of Our Lord Jesus Christ World Wide**. At the time Lawson was in his last years. He died in 1961 and was succeeded by Bishop **Hubert Spencer** (1961–63) who is credited with proving crucial healing following the break, and **William L. Bonner**. Bonner started the church's retirement plan, a new idea among Apostolics, and initiated a new church extension program with a stated goal of planting at least one congregation in every state.

Doctrinally, the church is a non-Trinitarian Apostolic Pentecostal body. It affirms traditional Christian biblical teachings, but denies the doctrine of the Trinity. Instead it affirms the One God whose name it believes to be Jesus. It baptizes by immersion in the name of Jesus only, a practice it believes necessary for salvation. Women ministers are not allowed.

In 1988, the church had approximately 500 churches and 30,000 members.

CHURCH OF THE BRETHREN. A German-American Christian pietist church. The Brethren originated in Germany in the early eighteenth century and in the face of persecution migrated to Pennsylvania prior to the American Revolution. The Brethren opposed the slave trade and as early as 1782 admonished one member to set free a slave he owned and provide for her children. In 1797 the Brethren officially called upon the few members who owned slaves to free them as a condition of their continued membership in good standing in the fellowship.

Black people may have joined the Brethren in the late eighteenth century, though the continued use of the German language was a strong barrier. In both 1835 and 1845 inquiries were sent to the Brethren's conference concerning the advisability of accepting Black members. The problem was raised by the Brethren's practice of the holy kiss. In both cases the conference voted to affirm full membership for the Blacks, and asked the Black members to be patient with what it saw as the "weaker" Brethren, i.e., those who were troubled by

their presence. At least one Black preacher was commissioned prior to the Civil War. **Samuel Weir** did evangelistic work in Ohio where several congregations resulted from his preaching. Among those who joined in this period was John T. Lewis, later a farmer in New York, and longtime friend of Mark Twain.

Through the last decades of the nineteenth century, a concentration of Black members persisted in southern Ohio, but efforts to win Black members were limited. The Church of the Brethren were never a large body, they were decidedly ethnic in orientation, and most importantly, gave priority to foreign missions over home missions. Thus much of the work among Black people in the nineteenth century was lost due to a lack of continuity in leadership. Some Black families, however, have remained members of the Church of the Brethren and the Fellowship of Grace Brethren Churches, a fundamentalist Brethren denomination founded in the 1930s.

The Brethren Encyclopedia. 3 vols. Philadelphia, PA: The Brethren Encyclopedia, Inc., 1983.

CHURCH OF THE LIVING GOD (CHRISTIAN WORKERS FOR FELLOWSHIP) (CWFF). A Holiness church. William Christian was a Baptist who like his colleague **Charles H. Mason** accepted the teachings of the Holiness Movement. His speculation, however, led him into different directions, especially after Mason's acceptance of Pentecostalism in 1906, and in 1889 Christian formed the Church of the Living God in Wrightsville, Arkansas.

Like the **Church of God in Christ**, the Church of the Living God assumed a basic Holiness perspective. It accepted the idea of sanctification, the experience of being cleansed by the Holy Spirit, as a basic norm for Christian believers. When he encountered the Pentecostal teachings, which identified the baptism of the Holy Spirit with speaking in tongues, Christian rejected it, but not totally. He did not believe that speaking in tongues was evidential of the baptism, but allowed speaking in tongues as it might occur.

Among its distinctive ideas are its teachings on church ordinances. The church has three ordinances, baptism by immersion, the Lord's supper using unleavened bread and water (rather than wine or grape juice), and foot washing. Each ordinance is performed only once. It also believes that the Lord's Prayer is the only prayer to be prayed by Christians.

Christian is best remembered for being one of the first to teach that Jesus Christ and many biblical characters were in fact Black people. From biblical texts such as Psalms 119:83, Job 30:30, and Numbers 12:11, he taught that Abraham, David, Job, Jeremiah and Moses' wife were all Black. Jesus was considered to be Black because he was of the lineage of Abraham and David. Christian promulgated these ideas at a time when some White Baptists were debating whether or not Black people were fully human. Christian went on to emphasize that the church should not make a difference among people because of their race (Galatians 3:28).

Christian was succeeded in leadership by his wife Ethel L. Christian, and then his son, John L. Christian. The fourth bishop was F. C. Scott. The church is now headed by Bishop W. E. Crumes. Headquarters of the church is in Cincinnati, Ohio. In 1985 the church reported 42,000 members in 170 churches.

DuPree, Sherry Sherrod. *The African American Holiness Pentecostal Movement: An Annotated Bibliography.* New York: Garland Publishing, 1993.

Hollenweger, Walter J. *Black Pentecostal Concepts: Interpretations and Variations.* Geneva, Switz.: World Council of Churches, 1970. 70 pp.

Jones, Charles Edwin. *Black Holiness: A Guide to the Study of Black Participation in Wesleyan Perfectionist and Glossolalic Pentecostal Movements.* Metuchen, NJ: American Theological Library Association/Scarecrow Press, 1987. 388 pp.

CHURCH OF THE LIVING GOD, THE PILLAR AND GROUND OF THE TRUTH. A Pentecostal church. **Mary Lewis Tate** (1871–1930) was by all accounts a remarkable woman. Poor and the mother of two, she had a call to preach. In 1903 she started her religious work at Steele Springs, Tennessee, and for the next five years she traveled north through the Ohio Valley and south into Alabama. Her work in Alabama coincided with the initial spread of the Pentecostal message concerning the baptism of the Holy Spirit and the accompanying experience of speaking in tongues.

In 1908 she was taken ill, and many thought she would die. Instead she experienced a miraculous healing and in the process was given the baptism of the Holy Spirit and spoke in tongues (the definitive Pentecostal experience). As a result of her experiences she called a meeting in Greenville, Alabama, of these who had been affected by her ministry. The meeting lasted for several weeks during the summer. Over 100 people received the baptism of the Holy Spirit, and the Church of the Living God, The Pillar and Ground of the Truth was organized. She was named chief overseer and conducted her first ordinations of ministers for the new church.

Most of the small groups which had formed during her earlier ministry accepted the Pentecostal message and became congregations of the church. By 1919 there were congregations across the eastern United States. That year the congregation in Philadelphia left the church to found the **House of God Which Is the Church of the Living God, the Pillar and Ground of the Truth** (one of two churches with that name). However, Tate continued to build the church through the rest of her life.

In 1931, following Tate's death, church leaders were unable to reach a consensus over who should be the new chief overseer. They finally solved the problem by naming three overseers over three districts of the church. However, each eventually became independent and three distinct churches resulted. Among the three was Tate's son F. E. Lewis. He came to head what was most clearly the continuing Church of the Living God, the Pillar and Ground of the Truth. Lewis led the Church until his death in 1968 and was succeeded by Bishop Helen M. Lewis.

All three branches of the movement are Trinitarian Pentecostals. They teach a Wesleyan Protestant doctrine centered upon the necessity of salvation through faith in Christ. Church members expect to be sanctified by the Holy Spirit and be cleansed from outward sin and made perfect in love. They also expect to receive the baptism of the Holy Spirit and speak in tongues. Baptism is by immersion and foot washing is practiced as a third ordinance.

The church is organized episcopally and is headed by the chief overseer and the other bishops. An annual general assembly is the highest legislative body. There is a publishing concern, The New and Living Way Publishing House. In 1988 there were approximately 2,000 members.

The two other people appointed as overseers in 1931 were M. F. L. Keith (widow of Bishop W. C. Lewis, Tate's other son) and B. L. McLeod. Keith's groups eventually reorganized as the **House of God, Which is the Church of the Living God, the Pillar and Ground of the Truth without Controversy (Keith Dominion)**. McLeod's following became known as the **Church of the Living God, the Pillar and Ground of the Truth, Which He Purchased with His Own Blood.**

CHURCH OF THE LIVING GOD, THE PILLAR AND GROUND OF THE TRUTH (GENERAL ASSEMBLY). A Holiness church. The Church of the Living God, the Pillar and Ground of the Truth (General Assembly) is one of several groups which grew out of the original **Church of the Living God (Christian Workers for Fellowship)** founded in 1889 in Arkansas by William Christian. That Church grew and spread through the African American communities in mid-America, but suffered a number of schisms. In 1902, one such schism took the name Church of the Living God (Apostolic Church). In 1908 it was reorganized by Apostle Charles W. Harris as the General Assembly, Church of the Living God. In 1924, at a gathering in Athens, Texas, the Harris group united with another group of the same name.

Meanwhile, around World War I, still another group derived from the Church of the Living God was incorporated under the leadership of Bishop Arthur Joseph Hawthorne. E. J. Cain emerged as a leader of the church and in 1925 led in its reorganization. Then in 1926 he led the church to merge with the Harris group, taking the name Church of the Living God, the Pillar and Ground of the Truth (General Assembly). The merged church established headquarters in Oklahoma City, where it supported the Booker T. Washington Home for the Aged. It also supported the Edmondson Institute, a school and orphans' home in Athens, Texas.

In the years after the merger, a number of congregations left the church. E. J. Cain led one group of congregations into the **Church of the Living God, The Pillar and Ground of the Truth of Muskogee, Oklahoma**, a church with similar roots. The loss of congregations left the strength of the church in Texas. Headquarters were moved to Dallas, where they remain.

Jones, Charles Edwin. *Black Holiness: A Guide to the Study of Black Participation in Wesleyan Perfectionist and Glossolalic Pentecostal Movements*. Metuchen, NJ: American Theological Library Association/Scarecrow Press, 1987. 388 pp.

CHURCH OF THE LIVING GOD, THE PILLAR AND GROUND OF THE TRUTH OF MUSKOGEE, OKLAHOMA.

A Holiness church. The Church of The Living God, the Pillar and Ground of the Truth of Muskogee, Oklahoma, originated in Pine Bluff, Arkansas, 1895 when John Christian, the brother of William Christian, parted company. John, who had helped his brother found the **Church of the Living God (Christian Workers for Fellowship)** had developed several differences, among them concerning prayer. William taught that the Lord's Prayer was the only prayer a Christian believer need pray.

Early in the new century the church absorbed the Church of the Living God of Earlsboro, Pottawatomie County, Oklahoma. While the church was not a large

body, it had congregations scattered in the Midwest, Southwest and in California. Current headquarters of the church is in Decatur, Illinois. Bishop Herbert Dickerson is the current leader of the group.

Jones, Charles Edwin. *Black Holiness: A Guide to the Study of Black Participation in Wesleyan Perfectionist and Glossolalic Pentecostal Movements*. Metuchen, NJ: American Theological Library Association/Scarecrow Press, 1987. 388 pp.

CHURCH OF THE LIVING GOD, THE PILLAR AND GROUND OF THE TRUTH, WHICH HE PURCHASED WITH HIS OWN BLOOD.

A Holiness Pentecostal church. In 1931, following the death of **Mary Lewis Tate**, the founder of the **Church of the Living God, the Pillar and Ground of the Truth**, church leaders were unable to reach a consensus on who should succeed her as head of the organization. They resolved the dispute by appointing three different leaders to head three regions of the church. Eventually, each region became independent of the other. Among the three leaders was Bruce L. McLeod. He led what was informally known as the McLeod Dominion, until his death in 1936. He was succeeded by his widow Mattie Lou McLeod, who led the church for many years. In more recent years the church has become known as the Church of the Living God, the Pillar and Ground of the Truth, Which He Purchased with His Own Blood.

The Church is headquartered in Indianapolis, Indiana.

Payne, Wardell J., ed. *Directory of African American Religious Bodies: A Compendium by the Howard University School of Divinity*. Washington, DC: Howard University Press, 1991. 363 pp.

CHURCH OF THE LORD JESUS CHRIST OF THE APOSTOLIC FAITH.

An Apostolic Pentecostal church. In the early 1930s, **Sherrod C. Johnson**, a minister of the **Church of Our Lord Jesus Christ of the Apostolic Faith**, protested what he saw as the too liberal policies of the church's founder **Robert C. Lawson**. The controversy focused upon the appearance of females and the observance of holidays. Johnson argued for very conservative dress for females which included neither jewelry or straightened hair, nor makeup. He also suggested that women should wear cotton stockings, knee-length dresses and head coverings. He just as staunchly opposed the observance of Christmas, Lent, and Easter, all of which he had come to feel were pagan celebrations. In 1933 he broke with Lawson and founded the Church of the Lord Jesus Christ of the Apostolic Church. Johnson led the church until his death in 1961. He was succeeded by **S. McDowell Shelton**, who led the church until his recent death.

The church is one of the more conservative Oneness Pentecostal churches. It demands an exacting formula for baptism which must be in the name of the "Lord Jesus," rather than simply "Jesus" or "Jesus Christ." The church also teaches that one must have the baptism of the Holy Spirit, as evidenced by speaking in tongues, in order to have the new birth. As might be expected in light of the issues involved in its founding, the church has a strict behavior code, especially in matters of dress. Remarriage after divorce is prohibited. Women ministers and teachers are not allowed.

The church is led by its "Bishop, Apostle, and Chief Overseer." There is an annual convention. Headquarters is in a large complex built during the tenure of Bishop Shelton. A monthly magazine, *The Whole Truth*, serves the denomination. There is also a large radio ministry, also called "The Whole Truth." A widespread mission program has carried the church throughout the west Indies, Africa, and into Europe and the Middle East. In 1980 there were approximately 100 congregations.

CHURCH OF THE NAZARENE. A Holiness church. The Church of the Nazarene is a Holiness church begun in Los Angeles in 1895. Over the next several decades, it brought together a number of independent Holiness movements from various parts of the United States. It adopted its present name in 1919. That same year, C. B. Jernigan, chairman of the foreign missions committee, recommended that provision be made for evangelizing African Americans in the South, but there was little response. In what was primarily a White denomination, predominantly Black congregations emerged over the years, but no particular evangelistic or educational activity for African Americans occurred until 1944 when the Department of Home Missions recommended an evangelistic program. A new "Colored district" was established under the leadership of Roy. T. Williams, one of the church's general superintendents. The effort had a slow start as Williams died in 1946 and his successor J. B. Chapman died in 1947. Hardy C. Powers then headed the work.

In 1947 the first annual meeting of representatives of the Black churches was held. Five churches and three pastors were reported. The following year it was noted that African American work was being carried on in ten of the church's districts, primarily in the South. There were twelve Black ministers. That year, the first visible product of the new concern was opened, the Nazarene Training Institute, in Institute, West Virginia, a suburb of Charleston. The institute was located across the street from West Virginia State College for the Colored.

In 1953 the Black churches were put together in a new non-geographical Gulf Central District, which included congregations in twelve states. Lon Chambers, a White minister, was named superintendent. The sixth annual meeting of the representatives of the Black churches became the first meeting of the new district.

The institute and district were established just before sentiment was absorbed from the changing consciousness in the country to discontinue racially segregated work in the church. As a result, the institute was merged into the Nazarene Bible College in 1970 and the district dissolved in 1972, at which time there were 20 churches and missions in the districts. In the church as a whole there were 64 predominantly Black churches and over 500 congregations reporting African American members and attendees. To prevent the loss of program emphasis of the disbanded district, a Negro Advisory Committee (now the Council of Black Churchmen) was created. It meets annually and advises the Department of Home Missions on the ministry needs of the African American membership. The council now has a budget to create and administer a wide variety of programs from ministerial training to evangelistic efforts.

Hurn, R. W. *Black Evangelism—Which Way from Here?* Kansas City, MO: Nazarene Publishing House, 1974. 70 pp.

Purkiser, W. T. *Called Unto Holiness II: The Story of the Nazarenes, The Second Twenty Five Years.* Kansas City, MO: Nazarene Publishing House, 1983. 256 pp.

CHURCH OF UNIVERSAL TRIUMPH/THE DOMINION OF GOD. A Holiness church. Among the most well-known leaders in the Black community in the mid-twentieth century was Prophet Jones. Born **James Francis Marion Jones** (1908–1971) in Birmingham, Alabama, he was raised in one of the original Black Holiness churches, **Triumph the Church and Kingdom of God in Christ**. In 1938 the church sent him to Detroit to begin work. He became quite successful but ran into conflict with church headquarters in Alabama. Members of the church had begun to shower Jones with gifts. The church moved to claim the gifts for itself. Jones said they were his. Unable to reach an agreement, Jones broke with the church and founded the independent Church of Universal Triumph/The Dominion of God. As the leader of the church, Jones assumed the title of His Holiness Dr. James F. Jones, D.D., Universal Dominion Ruler. Most referred to him simply as Prophet Jones.

The new church was an immediate success and Jones soon had followers in the Black community in most of the large cities. The gifts made Jones a wealthy man. Among his possessions, which he flaunted before newsmen, were a white mink coat, five Cadillacs, a 54-room mansion, jewelry, perfumes, and a lavish wardrobe. Jones built a variant on traditional Holiness teachings based upon his claims to be in contact with God who gave him supernatural powers. God regularly instructed him in the form of a breeze fanning his ear. Sitting on a dais before his congregation, he would invite individuals to approach him and whisper their needs into his ear. He would in turn respond with some personal advice based upon his contact with the Deity. The many gifts lavished upon Jones came from people helped in these personal moments.

Jones' spectacular success was interrupted in 1956 when the Detroit police raided his home to arrest him and charge him with gross indecency. In a subsequent trial he was acquitted but in the meantime had lost a large percentage of his support, and his work entered a period of decline. He died in 1971, by which time his following was concentrated in Detroit and Chicago. He was succeeded as ruler of the Dominion by the Rev. Lord James Schaffer. Schaffer now heads the church with the assistance of the dominion council and the board of trustees. Headquarters remains in Detroit.

The church continues its Holiness emphases by demanding its members follow a strict behavior code. They are not allowed to use tobacco, alcohol, coffee, tea, and drugs, and refrain from playing games of any kind. They do not fraternize with people outside the church and do not marry without the consent of the "ruler" of the Dominion. There is an element of millennialism and it is believed that all who are alive in the year 2000 will become immortal and live forever in a heaven-like earth.

Kobler, John. "Prophet Jones: Messiah in Mink." *Saturday Evening Post* (March 5, 1955): 21, 74, 76.

CHURCHES OF GOD, HOLINESS.

A Holiness church. The Church of God, Holiness emerged in the 1920s out of the **Church of Christ (Holiness), U.S.A.** In 1914 King Hezekiah Burrus (d. 1963) was sent to Atlanta, Georgia, by **Charles P. Jones** to begin work for the Church of Christ. Starting with eight people, he was quite successful and quickly built a large congregation. He also led a revival in Norfolk, Virginia, which resulted in a second congregation being formed.

By 1920 his congregation was able to host the national convention of the church. However soon after that meeting, Burrus broke with Jones and founded the Churches of God, Holiness. There being no doctrinal difference in the split, the Churches of God retained the teachings of its parent body. Bishop Burrus was succeeded by his son Bishop Titus Paul Burrus.

There is a strong episcopal government. The church is headed by its bishop. The bishop appoints the state overseers who in turn assign all the pastors. The highest legislative authority is the national convention. Headquarters were established in Atlanta, Georgia. There is no recent report on membership. In 1967 there were 42 churches and some 25,000 members.

CLAFLIN COLLEGE.

A **United Methodist Church** school. Educational efforts began in South Carolina by the Methodist Episcopal Church immediately after the Civil War. The first need being that of training ministers, Baker Theological Institute was opened in 1866 in Charleston. Three years later, with money from Lee Claflin and his son Governor William Claflin of Massachusetts, the former campus of the Orangeburg Female College at Orangeburg, South Carolina, was purchased, and Claflin University opened. Baker became the theological department of the new school. The school prospered, especially after the state located the South Carolina Agricultural and Mechanical College on adjacent property. The two school operated almost as one until forced to separate in 1896. Claflin's Normal Department was especially fruitful in turning out teachers for the state's public school.

The first generation of success is largely attributed to the work of L. M. Dunton, who served as president from 1884 to 1922. It was during his tenure, in 1914, that the school adopted its more appropriate present name.

Through the nineteenth century, the school was largely staffed by White instructors and administrators and funded by wealthy White patrons, though as early as 1870 William H. Crogman became the first Black instructor and the first Black person in the employ of the Freedman's Aid Bureau as a teacher. During the early decades of the twentieth century, some changes were noticeable as Black faculty were hired and in 1922 J. B. Randolph became the school's first Black president. He served until 1945. Gradually, the South Carolina Conference took an increasing responsibility for the welfare of the college.

Jenkins, Warren M. *Steps Along the Way.* Columbia, SC: Socamead Press, 1967. 87 pp.

CLAIR, MATTHEW WALKER, JR. (August 12, 1890–July 10, 1968), a bishop of the Methodist Church (now the **United Methodist Church**), was born in Harper's Ferry, West Virginia, the son of Fannie Meade Walker and **Matthew Wesley Clair, Sr.** In 1920 his father was one of the first two Black ministers in the Methodist Church elected bishop for a regular, non-missionary service. Clair Jr. attended Syracuse University in New York in 1909–10, received his B.A. in 1915 from Howard University in Washington, D.C. and his S.T.B. in 1918 from Boston University School of Theology in Massachusetts. He was ordained in 1917. During World War I he was a chaplain for the 320th Labor Bn. in the U.S. Army. On November 25, 1920 he married Ethel Christian Smith, with whom he had two daughters.

His first pastorate was in Beford, Virginia (1918), followed by Martinsburg, West Virginia (1919); Roanoke, Virginia (1920–24); Daytona Beach, Florida (1924–25); and Denver, Colorado (1925–28). While in Denver he attended Iliff School of Theology and received his S.T.M. from there in 1927. In 1929 he served on the staff of the Board of Home Missions of the denomination. From 1929 to 1936 he was at a church in Indianapolis, Indiana; then from 1936 to 1940 he was professor of Practical Theology at Gammon Theological Seminary in Atlanta, Georgia. In 1940 he was appointed the minister of St. Mark Methodist Church in Chicago, Illinois, where he stayed for the next twelve years. During this time he solidified his own large reputation in the church, apart from his father's legacy. In 1947 he contributed the chapter "Methodism and the Negro" in a collection of essays called *Methodism.*

In 1952 Clair was elected bishop by the Central Jurisdiction, the segregated, non-geographical structure which had been established within the Methodist Church in 1939. This was the first time in the history of the Methodist Church that a bishop's son became a bishop. For the first four years most of his work was in reviewing and evaluating Methodist work in various parts of the world. He went to Africa from January to April 1954, and was a delegate to the Southeast Asia Central Conference in Singapore in 1956. In 1956 he was appointed to the St. Louis Episcopal Area, where he stayed for the rest of his career. This new assignment did not prevent him, however, from continuing a regular pattern of international visitation. He was asked by the council of bishops to review Methodist work in Central and South America from September to December 1958. In 1961 he toured Methodist work in Europe and was a fraternal delegate to the founding conference of the Ghana Methodist Church in July, 1961.

Clair served on the General Board of Education, the Board of Social Concerns, the Commission on Promotion and Cultivation, the Commission on Church Union (C.O.C.U.), and was chair of the Commission to Study Faith and War in the Nuclear Age. He was president of the board of trustees of Philander Smith College in Little Rock, Arkansas, and was on the board of the National Council of Churches. He was also on the board of directors of the E. Stanley Jones Union. From 1960 to 1962 he was president of the college of bishops of the Central Jurisdiction. He retired in 1964 to his home in St. Louis, and barely lived to see the dismantling of the Central Jurisdiction as a part of the 1968 merger of the Methodist Church and the Evangelical United Brethren to form the United Methodist Church.

Clair, Matthew W., Jr. "Methodism and the Negro." In William K. Anderson, ed. *Methodism.* Nashville, TN: The Methodist Publishing House, 1947, 240–250.
———. *Sociological Origins of the Negro Ministry in the United States.* Denver, CO: Iliff School of Theology Thesis, 1927.
EWM, WWMC, BDNM (70), *WWWA* (8), *AARS, HUBA.*

CLAIR, MATTHEW WESLEY, SR. (October 21, 1865–June 28, 1943), one of the first two African Americans elected as a (non-missionary) bishop in the Methodist Episcopal Church (now a part of the **United Methodist Church**), was born in Union, West Virginia, the son of Anthony and Ollie (Green) Clair. He experienced conversion at age fifteen, and was soon licensed to preach at the Simpson Methodist Episcopal Church in Charleston, West Virginia. He went to Morgan College (now State University) in Baltimore, Maryland, receiving his degree in 1889. Upon graduation he was admitted to the Washington Conference (a Black conference in the Methodist Episcopal Church) as a deacon and assigned to the Harper's Ferry Methodist Episcopal Church, West Virginia. Later that year, on November 12, he married Fannie Walker, with whom he had five sons.

He stayed at Harper's Ferry until 1893, when he moved to a church in Staunton, Virginia. In 1896 he was assigned to Ebenezer Church in Washington, D.C., where he stayed for only one year before becoming presiding elder of the Washington District, a position he held until 1902. In that year he became minister of Asbury Church in Washington, D.C., a prestigious Black church. During his long pastorate there he was elected a delegate to the General Conference twice (1904 and

1916) and oversaw the building of a new 1,800-seat sanctuary. In 1911 Howard University gave him an honorary Doctor of Divinity degree, as did Morgan College in 1918. In 1919–1920 he served as district superintendent of the Washington District, and once again went to General Conference in 1920. At that historic conference, Clair and **Robert E. Jones** were elected as the first two Black Methodist bishops who were not limited to work in Africa. Morgan College added to the celebration by awarding him an honorary Doctor of Laws degree.

Although Clair could have served in one of the nineteen Black conferences of the church in the United States, he was sent to direct the mission work in Monrovia, Liberia, Africa. During his eight years there he traveled far and wide, often preaching to isolated groups through interpreters. The president of Liberia appointed him to the national board of education, and he served on the American Advisory Commission of the Booker Washington Agricultural and Industrial Institute of Liberia. On a visit to the United States for the General Conference in 1924, he led the public prayer when President Calvin Coolidge dedicated the statue of Francis Asbury in Washington, D.C. Clair's first wife, Fannie, died on February 27, 1925, and he married Eva F. Wilson on November 2, 1926.

In 1928 Clair returned permanently to the United States to serve as bishop of the Covington, Kentucky, Episcopal Area, which covered Black conferences in the Midwest. That same year Wilberforce University in Ohio gave him an honorary Doctor of Laws degree. He retired in 1936, and stayed at his home in Covington. During his career he was a member of the Federal Council of Churches (now the National Council of Churches), and president of the board of trustees of Philander Smith College in Little Rock, Arkansas. He is the only bishop in the history of American Methodism to have a son also become a bishop.

WWCA (38–40), *IBAW, NYTO, WWC, EBA, EWM, MB, RLOA.*

CLARK, CAESAR A. W. (b. December 13, 1914), nationally known Baptist preacher, was born in Shreveport, Louisiana. He earned the B.A. degree in 1946 from Bishop College in Dallas, Texas, and later received many honorary degrees. After pastoring a number of churches in Louisiana and Tennessee, in 1950 he became the pastor of Good Street Baptist Church in Dallas, Texas, where he has remained ever since. He was married and had one son.

Two parts of his career have in particular vaulted him into national prominence. For many years, dating from the 1950s, he has been editor of the *National Baptist Voice*, a very influential position. He has also received acclaim as a brilliant orator. At least six times he has been selected as Eminent Guest Speaker at the **National Baptist Convention of America**, although his own affiliation is with the **National Baptist Convention, U.S.A., Inc.**, for which he has long been a member of the board of directors. He has preached as evangelist all over the country and has lectured at numerous colleges and universities. He preached in Liberia in 1972 and in 1980 represented his denomination as a preacher in the Soviet Union. In 1984 *Ebony* magazine named him one of America's fifteen best Black preachers. He has recorded more than twenty albums of sermons.

Clark has also been a pioneer in the holistic ministry of his church. In 1964, feeling that something needed to be done for the housing needs of Blacks in Dallas, he led the church to purchase the Good Haven Apartments. With the help of government funds the complex was renovated to include central air conditioning for 332 apartments. This partnership with federal funds later became an accepted trend in the ministries of other Black Baptist churches. Single for many years, Clark married Carolyn Elaine Bunche on April 16, 1987. He has been a trustee of Bishop College and an important fundraiser for its work. He has also been president of the Baptist Missionary and Education Convention of Texas.

"America's Fifteen Greatest Black Preachers." *Ebony* 39 (September 1984): 27–33.
WWABA (92–93), *HBB, SCA.*

CLARK, JAMES I., SR. (1901–March 13, 1972), a bishop of the **Bible Way Church of Our Lord Jesus Christ World Wide**, was born on the island of Trinidad in the West Indies. He migrated to the United States as a teenager and lived in New York City with his aunt. Shortly after World War I, he met **Robert C. Lawson**, who had moved to New York to establish the **Church of Our Lord Jesus Christ of the Apostolic Faith**. Under Lawson he was saved, baptized in the Holy Spirit as evidenced by his speaking in tongues, and called to the ministry. He married and he and his wife Rachel had 13 children.

He went on to become one of the more educated leaders of the church. He attended Shelton Bible College in Cape May, New Jersey (a Bible Presbyterian school founded by the Rev. Carl McIntyre), and the Institute of Religion and Social Studies, a joint program of Columbia University and the Jewish Theological Seminary. He eventually obtained his Th.D. from the American Divinity School. Clark pastored in Chester, Pennsylvania, and Paterson, New Jersey, before returning to New York City. In 1940 he became the dean of the Christ Bible Institute, the training school for the church's ministers.

In 1956 Clark joined with **Smallwood Williams** and other leaders of the church in protest of some of the policies of Lawson who had led the Church of Our Lord Jesus Christ of the Apostolic Faith since its establishment. They were most concerned about Lawson's refusal to share the leadership power and responsibilities. The following year Clark became one of the founders of the Bible Way Church of Our Lord Jesus Christ World Wide, and brought his New York parish, Christ Temple, with him. He also opened Christ Temple Bible Institute.

Clark was named a bishop in the Bible Way Church and continued to lead the New York work for the rest of his life. He died in New York City in 1972. He was succeeded by his son, Bishop James I. Clark, Jr., the present pastor of Christ Temple.

DuPree, Sherry Sherrod. *Biographical Dictionary of African-American Holiness-Pentecostals, 1880–1990.* Washington, DC: Middle Atlantic Regional Press, 1989. 386 pp.

CLARK COLLEGE. A United Methodist Church school. Clark College began as a school for Black children which met at Clark Chapel in Atlanta, Georgia. The name Clark refers to Bishop Davis W. Clark, the head of the Freedman's Aid Bureau for the Methodist Episcopal Church and one of the most active proponents of church education programs for former slaves. The little school took great strides once it had gained the attention of Bishop Gilbert Haven. In conjunction with Bishop Henry W. Warren, one of the major promoters of industrial education during this period and later president of Boston University, Haven secured 600 acres on the edge of Atlanta and opened the new Clark University on the site in 1880. Warren contributed resources for two of the buildings. After the first generation, the industrial education emphasis began to give way to the liberal arts curriculum.

In 1882 a chair of theology was created at Clark University which quickly evolved into a department of theology. It was separated from Clark as the Gammon School of Theology (later Gammon Theological Seminary) in 1888.

Clark remained on campus until 1941, shortly after the 1939 merger of the Methodist Episcopal Church and the Methodist Episcopal Church, South. That year it moved into the city to become part of the Atlanta University complex. It had previously changed its name from University to College.

Stowell, Jay S. *Methodist Adventures in Negro Education.* New York: Methodist Book Concern, 1922. 190 pp.

CLAYBORN, JOHN HENRY (December 2, 1882– June 17, 1954), 64th bishop of the **African Methodist Episcopal Church** (AME), was born in Spring Hill, near Arkadelphia, Arkansas, the eldest of nine children in the family of David T. and Martha Clayborn. His parents were members of the Spring Hill AME Church, which he joined after conversion at the age of nine. Over the following years he served that church faithfully as superintendent of the Sunday School, trustee, steward, and class leader. He attended Arkadelphia public schools and Philander Smith high school and college. He married Lula Bertha Mitchell in 1902, with whom he had six children.

He was licensed to preach at Bradshaw, Arkansas, in 1903, and joined the West Arkansas Annual Conference in 1904. He was assigned to the Bragg Circuit in 1905, and to the Onlaska Circuit in 1905–06. In 1906, after being ordained deacon, he went to the Glenville Circuit, followed by the Young Circuit in 1907. In 1908 Bishop **B. F. Lee** ordained him elder at Camden, Arkansas, and assigned him to the New Edinburg Circuit. He then pastored the Manchester Circuit (1910), Stamps AME Church (1911–12), and the St. James AME Church in Texarkana (1913). In all these assignments he was noted for substantial increases in membership. Among his accomplishments, he organized what is now called Clayborn Chapel in Pickens, built the Walnut Lake church, and paid the mortgages at both St. Phillips in Magnolia and St. James in Texarkana. He helped support himself by teaching in various public schools for about twenty-five years.

In 1914 he began a seventeen-year stretch of being a presiding elder. From 1914 to 1916 he was presiding elder of the Dumas District in South Arkansas, and from 1916 to 1919 was at the Fordyce District in Central Arkansas. There he took the opportunity to enter Shorter College and its related Jackson Theological Seminary in North Little Rock, Arkansas, receiving both his B.A. and B.D. in 1918. After covering other districts, he was at Magnolia District in West Arkansas from 1926 to 1929, and Helena District in East Arkansas from 1930 to 1931.

In 1932 the General Conference in Cleveland, Ohio, elected Clayborn editor and manager of the *Southern Christian Recorder*, which was then in a deplorable condition. In the next eight years he brought the number of subscribers up to 10,000 and bought and paid for an $18,000 printing plant. In 1936 he gave over $100 from the proceeds from the paper to church dependents. In 1940 he gave over $1,000 to the church for aid to retirees, widows, and orphans. In 1940 he ran for bishop but was not elected, and was not re-elected editor of the *Southern Christian Recorder*, defeated by **E. C. Hatcher**. On his return to Arkansas, however, he was appointed president of Shorter College, holding that position until 1944.

At the General Conference in Philadelphia, on May 9, 1944, Clayborn was elected bishop on the fifth ballot with 962 votes, the largest number up to that point ever given to a bishopric candidate. He was the first native of Arkansas to become an AME bishop. He was assigned to the 14th Episcopal District (West Africa), and was the first AME bishop to fly to Africa. He was also the only AME bishop to work in Africa during World War II. He organized Clayborn College in Ghana, the W. Sampson Brooks Industrial School in Monrovia, Liberia, and changed the Shaffer Day School in Arthington, Liberia, into the Shaffer-Smith Elementary School. He greatly aided Monrovia College, founded twenty years before by Bishop Brooks.

In 1946 he was elected president of the ecumenical **National Fraternal Council of Negro Churches**. He was assigned by the AMEs to oversee parts of the 2nd and 12th Episcopal Districts (Oklahoma, North Carolina, and Virginia), and from 1948 to 1952 covered the 13th Episcopal District (Tennessee and Kentucky). He closed The Goodwill Center and the R. R. Wright School of Religion in Memphis, sold the property, and bought a large Presbyterian church at Hernando and Pontotoc in Memphis for what is now known as Clayborn Temple AME Church. In the summer of 1951 he was a delegate to the Eighth Ecumenical Methodist Conference at Oxford, England, and on July 7, 1951, opened a session of the Republican National Convention in Chicago with prayer. He passed away several years later at his home in Little Rock, Arkansas.

RLA, BAMEC, HAMEC, EWM, EAMEC, WWWA (vol.3).

CLEAVES, NELSON CALDWELL (October 7, 1865–December 31, 1930), 12th bishop of the **Christian Methodist Episcopal Church** (CME), then known as the Colored Methodist Episcopal Church, was born in Oakland, Tennessee, the son of Lilburn and Ann Cleaves. He attended public school in Fayette County, and entered the private school of William Penn Liston about 1883. He was converted and joined the local CME church on September 12, 1882. He received a B.A. in 1887 from Lane College in Jackson, Tennessee, and later attended Fisk University in Nashville, but had to drop out in his final year on the advice of his physician.

From 1887 to 1889 he was the principal of city schools in Minden, Louisiana, and in 1889–90 founded the Minden High School. He married Jennie E. Lane on August 27, 1889, with whom he had four children. From 1890 to 1892 he was head of the English Department at Lane College. In the fall of 1893 he joined the West Tennessee Conference at Dyersburg, and was assigned to the South Jackson Circuit for one year. He then pastored in Humboldt from 1894 to 1895, in Clarksville from 1896 to 1898, and in Memphis from 1899 to 1901. At this point he transferred to Washington, D.C., where he served the Israel Metropolitan CME Church from 1902 to 1905. While there he was elected president of the Interdenominational Ministers' Alliance. He was assigned to the Sydney Park CME Church in Columbia, South Carolina, from 1906 to 1914.

At the General Conference in St. Louis, Missouri, in May 1914, Cleaves was elected bishop, and was assigned to the 7th Episcopal District, making his home in Jackson, Tennessee. He later covered other areas, and his home for most of the rest of his career was in St. Louis, Missouri. He was president of the Board for Superannuated Preachers, Widows, and Orphans of the CME Church, and was a delegate to and speaker at the Fifth Ecumenical Methodist Conference in London in September, 1921. He was president of the board of trustees of Miles Memorial College in Birmingham, Alabama, and of Mississippi Industrial College in Holly Springs, Mississippi.

WWCR, CMECTY, EWM, WWWA (vol.4), *WWCA* (30–32).

CLEMENT, GEORGE CLINTON (December 23, 1871–October 23, 1934), 37th bishop of the **African Methodist Episcopal Zion Church** (AMEZ), was born near Mocksville, Davie County, North Carolina, the youngest of six children born to Albert Turner and Eveleanor (Carter) Clement. Both of his parents were former slaves, and his father was a minister in the AMEZ Church. After attending public schools in his home county, he decided to follow in his father's footsteps and joined the Annual Conference as a licensed preacher on September 15, 1888, serving a number of churches. He was ordained a deacon on December 10, 1893, and was assigned to the church in Cleveland, North Carolina, in 1894, as he also entered Livingstone College, in Salisbury, North Carolina. He pastored the Second Creek Circuit in Zeb, from 1895 to 1897, and from 1897 to 1898 he was at the China Grove Church in Charlotte. He received his B.A. from Livingstone College in May, 1898. That same month, on May 25, 1898, he married Emma Clarissa Williams, with whom he had eight children, one of whom died at an early age.

He was assigned to Grace Church, in Charlotte, North Carolina, from 1898 to 1899, and then to Soldier's Memorial Church in Salisbury from 1899 to 1900. At that point he transferred to Louisville, Kentucky, where he led the Twelfth Street Church from 1900 to 1904. He purchased the valuable property on which the Broadway Temple Church was later built. He was elected editor of the church's journal, the *Star of Zion*, in 1904, and held that position until 1916. In 1904 Livingstone College gave him an honorary M.A., followed by an honorary D.D. in 1906. From 1914 to 1916 he was also manager of the A.M.E. Zion Publication House in Charlotte, North Carolina.

At the General Conference in 1916, Clement was elected bishop, consecrated on May 19. He was assigned to the Third Episcopal District, which he served until his death, maintaining his residence in Louisville, Kentucky. He was a trustee of the A.M.E. Zion Publication House, Livingstone College, and Atkinson College. For thirteen years (1921–1934) he was chair of the Committee on Church and Race Relations of the Federal (now National) Council of Churches, and he was a member of the executive committee of the Methodist Ecumenical Council. Having already been a delegate to the Ecumenical Methodist Conference in Toronto in 1911, he was also a delegate at the conference in London in 1921 and Atlanta in 1931. He was part of the Southern Inter-Racial Commission.

At a time when it was very unpopular for a Black to be a Democrat, Clement was one, in the hope that he could make a positive difference and not allow the Republicans to take Blacks for granted. At one point he refused a diplomatic post offered by President Woodrow Wilson. In 1925 he authored *Boards for Life's Building*. Several of his children became quite well-known in the church, and one, Rufus Early Clement, became president of Atlanta University.

Alleyne, Cameron C. "Eulogy to Bishop George Clinton Clement." *Star of Zion* 58 (November 1, 1934): 1, 5.
"Anthology of the AME Zion Bishops." *Star of Zion* 57 (September 28, 1933): 1, 6.
"Bishop Clement Passes." *Star of Zion* 58 (October 25, 1934): 1.
"Bishop G. C. Clement Translated." *Star of Zion* 58 (October 25, 1934): 4.
Clement, George Clinton. *Boards for Life's Building*. Cincinnati, OH: Caxton Press, 1924. 156 pp.
"George Clinton Clement." *Journal of Negro History* 20 (January 1935): 117–118.
"New Era of Zion Methodism." *Star of Zion* 48 (August 7, 1924): 1, 5.
AARS, BAW, HAMEZC, AMEZC, WWCA (30–32), WWWANAA, NCAB (vol. 36), WWCR, EBA.

CLEMENT, RUFUS EARLY (June 26, 1900–November 7, 1967), an **African Methodist Episcopal Zion** (AMEZ) minister and president of Atlanta University, was born in Salisbury, North Carolina, the son of George Clinton and Emma Clarissa (Williams) Clement. His father became a bishop in the AMEZ Church in 1916. After attending public schools in Charlotte, North Carolina, Clement went to Livingstone College in Salisbury, North Carolina, graduating as valedictorian with his B.A. in 1919. That year he was ordained a deacon. On December 23, 1919, he married Pearl Anne Johnson, with whom he had one daughter. By then he was enrolled at Garrett Biblical Institute (now Garrett-Evangelical Theological Seminary) in Evanston, Illinois, where he also continued part-time pastoring of local churches. He was ordained elder in 1921. He received his B.D. in 1922, and also studied concurrently at nearby Northwestern University, from which he earned an M.A. in 1922.

Upon graduation he joined the faculty of Livingstone College as a history teacher, becoming dean of the school in 1925. While he was dean Livingstone College became an accredited institution. From 1925 to 1928 he pastored the Bethel AMEZ Church in Kannapolis, North Carolina. In 1928–29 he studied on a fellowship at Northwestern University, earning his Ph.D. in 1930. From 1929 to 1931 he pastored the Sandy Ridge AMEZ Church in Landis, North Carolina, about seventeen miles from Salisbury. In 1931 he went to the newly founded Louisville Municipal College in Kentucky, and as dean helped organize the school, remaining until it was an accredited four-year college. In 1937 he succeeded John Hope as president of Atlanta University in Georgia, where he stayed for the rest of his life. During his administration the university's standards and reputation were greatly enhanced. It was placed on the approved list of the Association of American Universities and elected to membership in the Southern Association of Colleges and Secondary

Schools. The endowment increased from $3 million to $11 million, and enrollment rose from about one hundred to about 900 students. In 1964 Atlanta University joined with Clark, Morehouse, Morris Brown, and Spelman Colleges and Gammon Theological Seminary to form the Atlanta University Center. This allowed expanded services through shared facilities and personnel while keeping costs down.

His leadership was felt in many arenas. He was a founder of the Midwestern Athletic Association, serving as its first president from 1932 to 1957. From 1937 to 1942 he was on the executive committee of the Commission on Interracial Cooperation, and then was on the executive board of its successor organization, the Southern Regional Council. He was a delegate of the AMEZ Church to the World Methodist Conference at Oxford University, England, in 1951. He was second vice-chair of the American Council on Education in 1945–46, and a member of its Commission on International Affairs. He was a trustee of several colleges and was director of the Citizens Trust Company. He was elected to the Atlanta Board of Education in 1953, the first Black to hold such a position since 1871, and in 1966 was reelected to his fourth consecutive term.

Clement contributed to the *Dictionary of American Biography* and wrote numerous articles, mostly on Black education, for a variety of periodicals. He was a founder of (in 1940) and contributing editor to *Phylon*, a social science journal and review of race and culture. He was director of the National Public Housing Conference from 1939 to 1943, and was a director of the Atlanta Urban League. His strength of character is illustrated by an incident in 1940, when he was told by a White policeman that he would be shot entering a Whites-only area at a train station. Clement replied: "If I get shot, I'll get shot in the back." He was a leader of and major fundraiser for the United Negro College Fund. Among many awards and commendations, the editor of *Time* magazine in 1966 selected him as one of the fourteen most influential university presidents in America.

Bacote, Clarence A. *The Story of Atlanta University; a Century of Service, 1865–1965*. Atlanta, GA: Atlanta University Press, 1969. 449 pp.

Clement, Rufus E. "The Church School as a Factor in Negro Life." *Journal of Negro History* 12 (January 1927): 5–12.

"Death Notice." *Time* 90 (November 17, 1967): 102.

"Education: The Extracurricular Clout of Powerful College Presidents." *Time* 87 (February 11, 1966): 64–65.

AARS, HUBA, IBAW, NYTO, EBA, RLA, EWM, AAE, BDAE, CB (1946), WWCA (38–40).

CLEVELAND, JAMES (December 5, 1931–February 9, 1991), Baptist minister and major gospel recording artist, was born in Chicago, Illinois. He began singing in church choirs at an early age and first gained recognition when he sang a soprano solo at age eight with the choir of Chicago's Pilgrim Baptist Church, where his grandmother was a member. He taught himself to play the piano, and later studied gospel piano with "Little" Lucy Smith, organist for the **Roberta Martin** Singers. Early influences on his vocal style included **Mahalia Jackson** and the members of the Roberta Martin Singers—Myrtle Scott, Eugene Smith, and Robert Anderson. For a while he was Mahalia Jackson's paperboy.

Roberta Martin encouraged his own songwriting attempts and sang his "Grace is Sufficient" at the 1955 National Baptist Convention meeting. She published it for him, and the song became very popular. In the late 1940s and 1950s Cleveland was a part of a number of groups, including the Thorn Gospel Crusaders, The Caravans, the Gospelaires, and the Roberta Martin Singers. Often he served as pianist-arranger. About 1959 he formed the Gospel Chimes, with which he first began to gain national recognition. In 1960 he recorded "The Love of God" with the Voices of Tabernacle Choir of Detroit, Michigan, which was tremendously successful. In 1963 he formed the James Cleveland Singers and did further recordings with them and the 300–voice Angelic Choir of Nutley, New Jersey. More hits such as "Peace Be Still" (1963), "God Specializes," "He's Using Me," and "The Man, Jesus," solidified his reputation as the "Crown Prince of Gospel," and "King of Gospel."

From time to time during the early years he would preach as a licensed minister of the **Church of God in Christ**. In the early 1960s he was ordained as a Baptist minister and moved to Los Angeles, California, to pastor the New Greater Harvest Baptist Church. Later he founded and the Cornerstone Institutional Baptist Church in Los Angeles, which he pastored for the rest of his life. He made some recordings of his sermons. In 1966 the James Cleveland Singers performed at the famed Theatre Olympia in Paris for two weeks, then had command performances in Monaco before Prince Rainier and Princess Grace. In 1968 he founded the Gospel Music Workshop of America, with annual conventions in different cities across the country. In 1973 in Chicago about 10,000 musicians attended its workshops in all aspects of church music. In the late 1960s he organized the Southern California Community Choir and the Gospel Girls.

Cleveland continued to tour through the 1970s, with bookings made a year in advance and an income in six figures. In 1975 he received the National Association of Negro Musicians Award and in 1976 he received the N.A.A.C.P. Image Award. In 1973 he appeared in the film, *Save the Children*. He influenced many gospel singers, such as Aretha Franklin, Jesse Dixon, and William "Billy" Preston. He was one of the few gospel recording artists to have a set salary from the record company, rather than depending solely on royalties. In 1968, five years after "Peace Be Still" was recorded, it was still the biggest selling record for Savoy Records. He has written more gospel songs (at least 300) and made more recordings (46 albums, eight gold, one Grammy) than any other gospel figure of his generation. Many of his compositions have become standards in the field. He was the first Black gospel artist to have his name placed in the Hollywood Walk of Fame.

Cleveland's health began to fail in 1990. As his condition worsened, he outlined a plan for the continuance of the congregation. The plan included selling the building and the congregation moving into more economical facilities. Unfortunately he slipped into a coma before signing the document. The resulting turmoil following Cleveland's death has left the future of Cornerstone very much in doubt.

"James Cleveland: King of Gospel." *Ebony* 24 (November 1968): 74–82.

McGraw, Carol. "Church Split by Death of Leader." *Los Angeles Times* (July 5, 1991).

"A Week of Gospel Happiness." *Ebony* 28 (November 1972): 86–92.

OTSB, WWABA (90–91), *HUBA, IBAW, BDA-AAM.*

CLINTON, GEORGE WYLIE (March 28, 1859–May 12, 1921), 25th bishop of the **African Methodist Episcopal Zion Church** (AMEZ), was born into slavery in Cedar Creek Township, Lancaster County, South Carolina, the son of Jonathan and Rachel (Patterson) Clinton. His father died when he was only two years old, and then he and his mother lived with grandparents until he was sixteen. For a short time after Emancipation he had access to free education; then those schools were closed and he studied at a "subscription school" under a West Indies teacher hired by local Blacks.

In 1874 he entered South Carolina University at Columbia, when it was opened to Blacks, and won a $200 scholarship for four years. In 1876, however, the new Democratic governor, Wade Hampton, forced all Blacks to withdraw from the university, and Clinton returned home to teach, with a first-grade certificate. He also obtained a job as clerk in the office of C. P. Pelham, Auditor of Lancaster County, and also studied law at the

firm of Allison & Connors. After less than one year of studying law, some additional time reading the Bible led to a call to the ministry.

Clinton was licensed to preach in the AMEZ Church on February 14, 1879, and then divided his time between teaching and the church. He was variously principal of both Lancaster High School and Industrial Institute and of the Howard Grade School of Union, South Carolina. He founded a private school at Rock Hill, South Carolina, out of which developed the highly regarded Clinton Institute. He joined the South Carolina Conference in November 1881, and was appointed to Chester. He took the opportunity to enroll at Brainard College in the same town, and finished his undergraduate work, graduating with high honors. He began to write articles for a number of periodicals, becoming part of the editorial staff of the denomination's journal, the *Star of Zion*, about 1883.

He transferred in November 1888 from the South Carolina Conference to the Allegheny Conference, and was appointed to the prestigious John Wesley AME Church in Pittsburgh, Pennsylvania. There he built a large parsonage, purchased a new pipe organ, and hosted the 1892 General Conference. In May, 1890, he began the *Afro-American Spokesman*, at that time the only paper published by Blacks in the Pittsburgh-Allegheny area. At about the same time he started the *Quarterly* as a journal for the AME Zion clergy. Having made it a going concern, in 1892 he handed it over to the General Conference, which renamed it the *A.M.E. Zion Quarterly Review*. That same General Conference elected him editor of the *Star of Zion*, a position he held until 1896, increasing its circulation significantly. That publication was centered at Charlotte, North Carolina, and he took the opportunity to study at Livingstone College in Salisbury, North Carolina, earning an M.A. degree in 1894.

At the 1896 General Conference Clinton was elected bishop by the largest vote ever received up to that point by a candidate, and his already significant stature was raised to a national level. He was appointed to the Seventh Episcopal District, including Tennessee, Missouri, Mississippi, and California. He continued to make his home in Charlotte, however, and was a trustee of Livingstone College and Dinwiddie Institute. For eight years he was president of the board of trustees of Atkinson Literary and Industrial College. He was a member of the American Negro Academy, was vice-president of the International Sunday School Association, and was president of the Negro Young People's Religious and Educational Congress. He was a delegate to the Ecumenical Methodist Conferences of 1891, 1901, and 1911. He married Annie M. Kimball on May 30, 1899, but she died shortly after bearing a son. On February 6, 1901, he married Marie Louise Clay, with whom there were no other children. He was a leader in the Interracial Commission of the South and in that of the Federal (now National) Council of Churches. He authored several books, the most well-known being *Christianity Under the Searchlight* (1909). He became senior bishop in 1917 after the death of **Alexander Walters**.

Clinton, George W. *Christianity Under the Searchlight*. Nashville, TN: National Baptist Publishing Board, 1909. 321 pp.

———. "The Church and Modern Industry." In Elias B. Sanford. *Federal Council of the Churches in America*. New York: Revell Press, 1919, 65ff.

———. "Evangelism." In Arcadius S. Trawick, ed. *The New Voice in Race Adjustments*. New York: Student Volunteer Movement, 1914, 107–112.

———. *The Three Alarm Cries*. N.p., 1906.

———. *Tuskegee Lectures*. N.p., 1907.

"Of Historical Note: George Wylie Clinton." *A.M.E. Zion Quarterly Review* 85 (Winter 1973): 185.

"Zion's Senior Bishops During the Twentieth Century." *Star of Zion* 104 (March 27, 1980): 1–2.

AARS, BAW, HUBA, IBAW, IBAWCB, AAP, BDSA, TCNL, AMEZC, HAMEZC, DAB (vol.2), EWM, NYTO, NA, WWCR.

CLINTON, ISOM CALEB (May 22, 1830–October 18, 1904), 23rd bishop of the **African Methodist Episcopal Zion Church** (AMEZ), was born into slavery in Cedar Creek Township, Lancaster County, South Carolina. His owner, Irvin Clinton, also owned his mother, Camie Clinton, but his father, Lewis McDonald, was free. Irvin Clinton was a prominent lawyer, and saw that Clinton received an education. Clinton was so gifted and personable that he became foreman of the estate and manager of business affairs, continuing in that role even after Emancipation in 1865.

While still a slave he was licensed to preach, and led Blacks in worship on Sunday afternoons in the same church where the Whites worshiped in the morning. In 1866 his former owner allowed him to organize Mount Carmel Church in a separate house on the plantation. The church doubled as a public school, one of the first in the area for Black children. When Bishop Joseph J. Clinton entered the region on behalf of the AMEZ Church, he found teacher-preacher Clinton ready to join in the work, and ordained him deacon in the morning and elder in the afternoon of March 24, 1867. That same day the South Carolina Conference was organized.

Clinton became presiding elder in 1872, and that same year was elected treasurer of Lancaster County. When the new Democratic governor, Wade Hampton, was elected in 1876, he complimented Clinton by retaining him in that office for several months, when no other Republican treasurer was given the same privilege. Clinton remained presiding elder until 1892, and through his efforts as minister and presiding elder some thirty churches were established. In 1887 Livingstone College in Salisbury, North Carolina, presented him with an honorary D.D. degree. During his last four years as presiding elder he was also General Steward. He was elected bishop at the General Conference in 1892, and was consecrated on May 18.

The Mount Carmel Church grew to be one of the most well-known churches in the area, and for years one of the largest camp meetings in the South was held there. Nothing is known of Clinton's wife; one of his sons became a prominent physician and another son became a presiding elder. Clinton passed away at his home in Lancaster, South Carolina.

HAMEZC, OHYAMEZC, AMEZC.

CLINTON, JOSEPH JACKSON (October 3, 1823–May 24, 1881), 10th bishop of the **African Methodist Episcopal Zion Church** (AMEZ), was born in Philadelphia, Pennsylvania. He was fortunate to have an unusually fine early education, studying first at the famous Mr. Bird's school in Philadelphia and then at the Allegheny Institute. He experienced conversion at age fifteen, and was licensed as a local preacher at age seventeen, in 1840. In 1843 he joined the Philadelphia Annual Conference as an itinerant preacher, was ordained a deacon in 1845 and an elder in 1846. He married Letitia Sisco on October 22, 1844, with whom he had ten children, six of whom survived him. He served AMEZ churches in Trenton, New Jersey; Georgetown, Washington, D.C.; Pittsburgh, Pennsylvania; Allegheny City (now Avery Memorial Church), Pennsylvania; and Philadelphia, Pennsylvania. In 1855 he transferred to the Baltimore Conference to pastor the church in Baltimore.

Soon after the 1852 General Conference a split in the church occurred, largely over the managing of episcopal duties and roles. The majority of the church followed Bishop **William Howard Bishop** in forming the Wesleyan Methodist Episcopal Church. The split might have remained permanent, but a Lycoming County, Pennsylvania court case around late 1854 made it clear that the Bishop faction could not hope to retain any AMEZ property. Both sides were then interested in reuniting. While the AME Zion Church had its General Conference in 1856 in Philadelphia, Clinton was part of the Wesleyan Methodist Episcopal Church General Conference in Williamsburg, where he was elected bishop to assist William Howard Bishop. This election made Clinton the youngest bishop in the history of the church, at age 32 years and nine months, consecrated on June 30, 1856. The two groups reunited on June 6, 1860, and Clinton was reelected bishop (then called general superintendent) at each succeeding General Conference until 1880, when it was decided to make the bishopric a lifetime appointment, and all the current bishops received that designation.

In 1862 he was assigned to the Philadelphia and newly created Southern Annual Conferences. He was at first discouraged by this assignment, and wrote out his resignation. Melvina Fletcher, governess in the household of Montgomery Blair, President Lincoln's Postmaster General, and a loyal member of Zion Wesley (Metropolitan) Church in Washington, D.C., heard of his state of mind and went to talk to him in the fall of 1863. When he protested that he had no minister nor one dollar to take on his mission, she promised to raise $300 if he tore up his resignation. This she did, and Clinton was enabled to send five men to the mission field in 1863–64.

Clinton has since gone down as the unsurpassed expansionist in the history of the church, and the first bishop to the South. Under his leadership thirteen annual conferences were organized, 100,000 students were added to the Sunday Schools, and over 700 itinerant preachers were added to rolls. Against the wishes of the church in Bridgeport, Connecticut, Clinton removed **James Walker Hood** from that assignment in January 1864 and sent him to North Carolina as the first regular missionary to the South. The legendary success of Hood in North Carolina unlocked the future of the denomination and marked Clinton as an administrator of rare vision. He passed away at his home in Atlantic City, New Jersey, after a protracted illness.

"Bishop Joseph J. Clinton." *A.M.E. Zion Quarterly Review* 61 (1951): 181–182.
AMEZC, HAMEZC (vol.1), *OHYAMEZC, HAMEZCIA, EWM, TCBD, ACAB.*

CLINTON JUNIOR COLLEGE. An **African Methodist Episcopal Zion Church** (AMEZ) school. Clinton Junior College was founded in 1894 at Rock Hill, South Carolina, by two leading AMEZ ministers, Ner A. Crockett, the presiding elder of the Yorkville District, and W. M. Robinson, the pastor of Clinton Chapel AMEZ Church. They named the school after their bishop, **Isom Caleb Clinton**. In 1896 they presented their efforts to the denomination's general conference which designated it as a connectional institution. Crockett served as its first president and was successful in assembling many of the leading members of the church to serve on the school's board of trustees. Crockett served until 1908 and with the school firmly established turned the position over to Robert James Boulware, who was president until his death in 1931.

The loss of Boulware almost killed the school, which like many similar institutions suffered greatly due to the Great Depression. In fact, the school was forced to close briefly until the denomination's Board of Christian Education stepped in and recruited James Stephen Stanbeck to reopen it. Stanbeck served several years without a fixed salary commitment until health forced him to resign. He was succeeded by C. T. Hinton under whom the school began to recover and stabilize. Since that time it had a fruitful half century as a church-supported junior college.

Walls, William J. *The African Methodist Episcopal Church: Reality of the Black Church.* Charlotte, NC: A.M.E. Zion Publishing House, 1974. 669 pp.

COBB, HELENA BROWN (January 24, 1870– September 7, 1915), educator and missionary leader of the **Christian Methodist Episcopal Church** (CME), then known as the Colored Methodist Episcopal Church, was born in Monroe County, Georgia, the only daughter of Jonah and Louvonia Brown. She attended public schools in Monroe and Pike Counties, and in the fall of 1883 entered Stoors School in Atlanta, Georgia. In 1885 she enrolled in Atlanta University, and graduated on May 28, 1891, with high honors. For six years she was principal of the public schools at Milner, and for one year was assistant principal of the public school in Columbus, Georgia. She taught for seven years at the Haines Normal School in Marshallville, and was principal there for three years. She married Andrew J. Cobb, a CME minister, on December 19, 1899.

She was very active in the CME Church, and was one of the first women to want a Missionary Department for women in the church. She was one of the leaders in fighting for the recognition of the work and interests of women at the 1902 General Conference meeting in Nashville, Tennessee. In November 1902, she was unanimously elected by the Central Georgia Conference as president of the Conference Mission Society. In 1904 Bishop L. H. Holsey suggested the creation of a magazine called *Woman's Missionary Age*, and at the

General Conference at Memphis, Tennessee in May, 1906, Cobb was unanimously elected its first editor-in-chief. Her writing and management of the magazine, later called simply *Missionary Age*, gave it a wide circulation throughout the country.

From her position as president of the Conference Mission Society she opened the Helena B. Cobb Industrial Institute for Girls in 1908. It was located on eight acres of land in Barnesville, Georgia, donated by W. K. Wilkinson, a local White man. It was established to provide religious, moral, intellectual, domestic, and social training for Black girls, and was the only school of its kind owned and operated only by Blacks in the South. It was also the only school for girls under the auspices of the CME Church. Board and tuition were $7.00 per month.

In 1910 Cobb was elected president of the newly organized Inter-Conference Missionary Movement, and in 1914 was named its official lecturer. She was in great demand everywhere as a speaker, and was the author of a pamphlet known as "Our Women—A Sketch of Their Work." She did not succeed in her lifetime in creating a church-wide Missionary Council for women, but was instrumental in developing the groundswell of interest which led to its founding at the General Conference at Chicago, Illinois, in 1918 with **Mattie E. Coleman** its first president. Cobb achieved a reputation as the leading advocate of women's rights in the church, and for many years was arguably the most widely known and influential woman in the denomination.

HCMEC, CMECTY.

COBBS, CLARENCE H. (c.1908–1979), famous radio preacher, was born in Tennessee. In 1929 he moved with his wife Nana and their family to Chicago where he founded the First Church of Deliverance, a Spiritual church. The congregation affiliated with the **Metropolitan Spiritual Church of Christ**. He was ordained in September 1929. In 1934 he began a morning radio broadcast over station WSBC. He was only the second Black minister to have a show in Chicago. In 1935 the show moved to WIND, and in later to WCFL where it remained through the 1970s. By the late 1940s his church counted some 20,000 members and his Sunday night radio programs were heard by an estimated one million people, making him perhaps the most popular Black radio preacher of his day.

In 1943 Cobbs became the president of the Metropolitan Spiritual Churches of Christ, a position he retained for the rest of his life. In 1945 the church was destroyed by fire, but the large congregation was quickly able to rebuild. The new sanctuary was ready for use in the summer of 1946. He was known for a preaching style which mixed slang with the general theme of "Jesus is the light of the world." Cobbs' position gained him a life of luxury, with an expensive, three-story Michigan Avenue home, three cars, and a lace robe reportedly as costly as that worn by Pope Pius XII. Cobbs used his status to urge on his followers toward their goals, saying such things as, "It makes no difference what you think of me, but it makes a lot of difference what I think of you."

Affectionally known simply as "Preacher," Cobbs developed a strong community service interest; he led the congregation in building a community center, convalescent home, and children's center.

50th Anniversary: Rev. Clarence H. Cobbs, First Church of Deliverance (souvenir book). Chicago: First Church of Deliverance, 1979. Unpaged.
"Top Radio Ministers." *Ebony* 4 (July 1949): 56–61.

COFFEY, LILLIAN BROOKS (1896–1964), the national and international Supervisor of the Women's Department of the **Church of God in Christ** (COGIC), grew up in Memphis, Tennessee, and attended the early Church of Christ Sunday school which was opened across the street from her home. She experienced salvation as a youth under the ministry of COGIC founder **Charles H. Mason** who was a friend of her grandfather and like him a Baptist minister. Orphaned at an early age, Coffey found a new earthly father in Mason. She moved into the church offices and for 21 years managed it along with financial secretary Sister Jessie Strickland. On occasion, she traveled with him and preached and taught as an evangelist. Among her early accomplishments was the founding of the Lillian Brooks Coffey Rest Home in Detroit.

Women's work in the church was organized originally by **Lizzie Roberson**. Along with Mason, Mother Roberson trained Coffey, who appointed her as the Assistant Mother of the women's work. Following Roberson's death in 1945, Mother Coffey became the supervisor of the women's work. Under her leadership, the national organization which Roberson had built gained an international perspective and became the backbone of the church's missionary endeavor. At the time of Mother Roberson's death, the organization had spread through the church, but it was Mother Coffey's task to build the program for women into a vital resource for serving the church's missionary endeavor.

In 1951 she organized the first women's International Convention in Los Angeles. The convention set as its goal the evangelization of women in the foreign mission fields and the raising of money to support the church's mission program. She organized the "Lillian Coffey train" to carry conventioneers from Los Angeles to Chicago. The train not only raised financial support for the developing mission program, but gave the women who took the trip a new experience of the freedoms available to them in World War II America. The mission program developed as she appointed a mission director and developed a stewardess board to gather and send clothes and food overseas. In 1953 she led the effort of the women to build a home for Bishop Mason and his family in Memphis adjacent to the church's headquarters.

Marking her administration in the early 1960s, Coffey led a group of women on a tour of the White House where they were greeted by President John F. Kennedy. In 1964, the women's convention was in Albany, New York, with a post-convention trip to the New York World's Fair. It was to be her last convention as she died a few weeks later. She was succeeded by Mother **Anne Bailey**.

Cornelius, Lucille J. *The Pioneer History of the Church of God in Christ.* N.p.: The Author, 1975. 102 pp.

DuPree, Sherry Sherrod. *Biographical Dictionary of African-American Holiness-Pentecostals, 1880–1990.* Washington, DC: Middle Atlantic Regional Press, 1989. 386 pp.

COKER, DANIEL (c.1780–c.1846), one of the founders of the **African Methodist Episcopal Church** (AME) and the founder of the West African Methodist Church, was born in Baltimore County, Maryland, the son of an English, White indentured servant, Susan Coker, and a slave father, Edward Wright. He was classified as a slave, credited as the child of a mulatto woman on a neighboring plantation, and grew up with the name Isaac Wright. He was reared with his White half-brothers, children of his mother's first marriage. He attended the local school as his half-brothers' valet; this was not cruelty on their part, but the only way his siblings could find to give him access to education. Finally, perhaps with the aid of his brothers, he escaped to New York and, to avoid slave hunters, adopted the new name of Daniel Coker. He was also helped by the fact that he had a very light complexion and could pass for white.

In New York he continued to study on his own and came into contact with the Methodists. He was converted, began to preach, and decided to return to Baltimore to see his family. Once in Baltimore in 1801 he had to remain in hiding until a plan for his freedom

could be arranged. Four free Blacks, Charles Hackett, Nathaniel Gillaird, William Watts, and George Murray, provided the money for his purchase, which was made by the famous Quaker abolitionist John Needles, who immediately freed him. Michael Coate, a Methodist minister in Baltimore, also assisted in this process.

Coker joined a separate Black Methodist society upon his arrival in Baltimore (already in existence for several years), and urged other Black Methodists to do the same. In 1802 a deed created the Sharp Street Methodist Church, the first Black church building in Baltimore, and Coker was ordained a deacon by Bishop Francis Asbury in 1808. From 1802 to 1816 Coker also taught in the African Academy School connected with the Sharp Street Methodist Church. This was the first school for Blacks in Baltimore taught by a Black teacher, and was later known as the Daniel Coker School. In 1810 he published perhaps his best-known work, *A Dialogue Between a Virginian and an African Minister*, in which he brilliantly countered typical arguments against emancipation.

Concurrently with **Richard Allen**'s similar experiences in Philadelphia, Coker and other Methodist Blacks in Baltimore increasingly felt the sting of segregationist practices in the church. Although Black trustees owned and controlled the property on Sharp Street and by 1812 a building for the Asbury African Church, they depended upon the White elders for sacramental function and final disciplinary authority. Apparently there was difficulty in getting the elders to pay sufficient attention to the needs of the Black congregants for the pastoral office. In 1815 Coker led a group of several hundred into a complete separation from the White Methodists. This became known as the African Methodist Bethel Society, which at first rented a former Presbyterian church on Saratoga Street, later moving to a property on Fish Street. In April, 1816, Coker represented the Bethel church at Richard Allen's meeting in Philadelphia, where the AME Church was founded. He served as vice-chair and secretary of the meeting, and was nominated and elected on April 9, 1816, as the first bishop of the AME Church. Perhaps because of controversy over his light skin color, he resigned the position the following day, before he was consecrated, and Richard Allen was elected in his place. Coker returned to be the minister at the Baltimore Bethel church, now affiliated with the AME denomination. The congregation soon numbered over one thousand. Parts of the Sharp Street and Asbury congregations remained in their locations, still connected with the White Methodists.

On April 17, 1818, for unknown reasons, Coker was expelled from the church. At the next Baltimore Annual

Conference he appealed for reinstatement, which was granted. He was sent to Africa as a missionary with a subsidy from the Maryland Colonization Society, leaving on February 6, 1820, about one year before **Lott Carey**, who is sometimes thought to have been the first Black American missionary to Africa. Carey's ship, in fact, brought Coker's wife and children to join him. Both Carey and Coker were there many years after **David George**, an American living in Canada, who went as a missionary to Sierra Leone in 1792. Soon after Coker and company arrived at Sherbro Island, all three agents of the Maryland Colonization Society died, and Coker gained full responsibility for the eighty-eight free Black emigrants and the society property. Since conditions for a settlement were not yet present, most of the group went to the British colony, Sierra Leone. In 1820 he published Part One of his African journal, Part Two of which has apparently been lost.

When new agents from the American Colonization Society arrived on March 8, 1821, Coker's administration ended, and he may have expected as reward for his good work a position of some authority in the area to be settled as Liberia. The American Colonization Society, however, merely thanked him for his leadership and sent some money. He decided not to venture on to Liberia after all, but remained in Sierra Leone. The governor promptly appointed him superintendent of the village of Hastings, founded in 1819 as a settlement for Africans freed from slave ships. He organized Methodist societies in collaboration with the Wesleyan Methodist Church. When a split in the church developed, Coker became the superintendent of the independent group, which took the name West African Methodist Church. A large church building was erected of stone in nearby Freetown, and the new denomination was established on firm footing. The exact date of his death is unknown. One source says that Coker died of malaria in 1835, but the date given above is more common.

Coan, Josephus R. "Daniel Coker: 19th Century Black Church Organizer, Educator and Missionary." *Journal of the Interdenominational Theological Center* 3 (Fall 1975): 17–31.

Coker, Daniel. *A Dialogue Between a Virginian and an African Minister.* Baltimore, MD: Benjamin Edes, 1810. 43 pp.

——. *Journal of Daniel Coker, A Descendant of Africa, From the Time of Leaving New York, on the Ship Elizabeth, Capt. Sebor, on Voyage for Sherbro, in Africa, in Company with Three Agents and about Ninety Persons of Colour.* Baltimore, MD: Edward J. Coale, supported by the Maryland Auxiliary Colonization Society, 1820. 52 pp.

——. *Sermon Delivered Extempore in the African Bethel Church in the City of Baltimore, on the 21st of January, 1816, To a Numerous Concourse of People, on Account of the Coloured People Gaining Their Church (Bethel) in the Supreme Court of the State of Pennsylvania, by the Rev. D. Coker, Minister of Said Church.* Baltimore, MD: Printed at the Corner of East Street and Calhoun's Alley, 1816. 14 pp.

Gravely, Will B. "African Methodism and the Rise of Black Denominationalism." In Russell E. Richey and Kenneth E. Rowe, eds. *Rethinking Methodist History: A Bicentennial Historical Consultation.* Nashville, TN: Kingswood Books, An Imprint of the United Methodist Publishing House, 1985, 111–124.

DANB, CEAMEC, IBAW, BAW, AARS, HUBA, RAM.

COLEMAN, CAESAR DAVID (b. October 4, 1919), bishop of the **Christian Methodist Episcopal Church** (CME), was born in Pickens, Mississippi, the son of Ira Lee and Eddye (Love) Coleman. His father was a CME minister, and Coleman thus grew up moving from church to church, according to his father's assignment. During World War II he was a commissioned officer in the U.S. Armed Forces. He attended Mary Holmes Junior College in West Point, Mississippi, and then went to Mississippi Industrial College in Holly Springs, Mississippi, where he received both his B.A. and M.A. in 1947. He received his B.D. at Lincoln University in Pennsylvania in 1950.

In 1952 he was appointed to the Miles Chapel CME Church in Sardis, Mississippi, where he stayed until 1957. During that same time he was also professor of philosophy and religion at Mississippi Industrial College. He married Elizabeth Luellen on November 11, 1955, with whom he had one son, who became a CME minister. From 1956 to 1958 he was presiding elder of the North Mississippi Conference. In 1958 he was elected executive secretary of the General Board of Christian Education for the CME Church, with headquarters located in Chicago, Illinois. One of his major accomplishments in this position was helping to found the Interdenominational Theological Center in Atlanta, Georgia, in 1960 and serving on its board of trustees until 1976. He also authored several books, including *The CME Primer, Beyond Blackness to Destiny,* and *Organizational Manual and Guide for Christian Youth Fellowship.*

At the General Conference in May 1974, Coleman was elected bishop and assigned to the Eighth Episcopal District, covering the Texas conferences, with headquarters in Dallas. That year he became chair of the board of trustees of Texas College in Tyler, Texas, and from 1978 to 1986 was chair and chief endorser of the

Commission on the Chaplaincy. He also served as vice-president of the **National Congress of Black Churches** from 1982 to 1986, and treasurer of the Texas Conference of Churches during the same period.

On July 2, 1986, he was installed as the senior bishop (president and chief executive officer) of the CME Church, remaining situated in the Eighth Episcopal District. That year he was named one of the one hundred most influential Blacks in the country by *Ebony* magazine. He became patron bishop of the Women's Missionary Council of the CME Church beginning in 1986, and in 1988 was proclaimed Outstanding Minister by the Dallas Interdenominational Ministers' Alliance.

Coleman, Caesar D. "Agenda for the Black Church." *Religious Education* 64 (November–December 1969): 441–446.
———. *Beyond Blackness to Destiny.* Memphis, TN: CME Church Publishing House, 1969. 152 pp.
———. "Christian Methodist Episcopal Church: The Rationale and Policies upon Which Support of its College Is Predicated." *Journal of Negro Education* 29 (Summer 1960): 315–318.
"New Senior Bishop Installed." *The Christian Index* 119 (May 1, 1986): 3.
WWR (85), WWABA (90–91), AARS, HUBA.

COLEMAN, CHARLES CECIL (February 22, 1906–July 17, 1958), 63rd bishop of the **African Methodist Episcopal Zion Church** (AMEZ), was born in Key West, Florida, the son of Charles C. and Clara Albury Coleman. His father ran a tailor shop and his mother died during his early childhood. Much of his rearing was done by his devoted grandmother, who saw to his Christian training at the Cornish Chapel AMEZ Church in Key West. He joined the church at age fourteen. After graduating from Douglas High School in Key West, he was ordained deacon on November 30, 1924. The following year he entered Livingstone College in Salisbury, North Carolina, where he received his B.A. in 1929, valedictorian of his class. Upon graduation he married Alcestis McCullough; there were no children.

His first church assignment was in the West Central North Carolina Conference at Cedar Grove Circuit in Gold Hill. He later pastored St. James AMEZ Church in Southport, North Carolina; Clinton Chapel AME Zion Church in New Bern, North Carolina; Metropolitan AMEZ Church in Atlanta, Georgia; Monticello AMEZ Church in Monticello, Arkansas; St. Paul AMEZ Church in Little Rock, Arkansas; Clinton Chapel AMEZ Church in Union, South Carolina; Metropolitan AMEZ Church in Clinton, South Carolina; and State Street AMEZ

Church in Mobile, Alabama. In 1949 he earned a Ph.D. in sociology from McKinley-Roosevelt University in Chicago, Illinois. The same year he published his Ph.D. dissertation, *Patterns of Race Relations in the South*.

At the General Conference in Pittsburgh, Pennsylvania, in 1956, Coleman was elected bishop. He was assigned to the Twelfth Episcopal District, comprising the Louisiana, Arkansas, North Arkansas, and Oklahoma Conferences, and set up episcopal residence in Oklahoma City, Oklahoma. He was known as an eloquent preacher and clear thinker, with high principles and ideals. He passed away after only two years in the episcopacy.

"Bishop Charles Cecil Coleman." *A.M.E. Zion Quarterly Review* 68 (1959): 208.
Coleman, Charles C. *Patterns of Race Relations in the South.* New York: Exposition Press, 1949. 44 pp.
"Obituary of Charles Cecil Coleman, 63rd Bishop, AME Zion Church." *Star of Zion* 81 (September 4, 1958): 1, 2.
HAMEZC, AMEZC, BAW, HUBA, AARS.

COLEMAN, CLINTON REUBEN (b. December 4, 1916), 72nd bishop of the **African Methodist Episcopal Zion** Church (AMEZ), was born in Coden, Alabama, in the southern part of Mobile County. He was converted as a young man in the Clinton Chapel AMEZ Church, and later went northward to attend Livingstone College in Salisbury, North Carolina. While in college he entered the itinerant system through the West Central North Carolina Conference in 1936, and was assigned to Parker's Chapel Circuit in Concord. He married Ethel Gill, with whom he had four children.

After receiving his B.A. in 1939 he remained in Salisbury to attend the related Hood Theological Seminary, but was not able to complete a degree at that time. His other churches were Union Chapel AMEZ Church in Albermarle, North Carolina; St. Stephen AMEZ Church in Hamlet, North Carolina; and Evans Metropolitan AMEZ Church in Fayetteville, North Carolina. His ministry wrought success wherever he went, and his reputation grew. His last local church assignment was to the well-known Pennsylvania Avenue AMEZ Church in Baltimore, Maryland. While there, he completed the seminary program he had begun so many years before, receiving his M.Div. from Howard University School of Religion, Washington, D.C., in 1971. His thesis paper was a study of ministry in the Black ghetto context of his own Pennsylvania Avenue church.

At the General Conference in 1972 Coleman was elected bishop and assigned to the Fifth Episcopal

District, covering the Michigan, Virginia, Tennessee, and Trinidad-Tobago Annual Conferences. He established his episcopal residence in Baltimore, Maryland. After twenty year of service, her retired in 1992.

Coleman, Clinton R. *A Study of a Black Ghetto Church, the Pennsylvania Avenue AME Zion Church, Baltimore, Maryland*. Washington, DC: School of Religion, Howard University, MDiv. paper 1971.

"Vignettes of Our Bishops: Bishop Clinton R. Coleman." *Star of Zion* 111 (November 12, 1987): 5.

HUBA, AARS, AMEZC, WWR (85).

COLEMAN, MATTIE ELIZABETH (July 3, 1870– July, 1942), first president of the Woman's Missionary Council of the **Christian Methodist Episcopal Church** (CME), was born near Gallatin, Tennessee, the oldest of four children in the family of Howard (Coleman?), a minister in the **African Methodist Episcopal Church**. She experienced conversion and joined the church at age twelve. She finished high school at age fifteen and went to Central Tennessee College (later called Walden University). She had an excellent voice, and was a member of both the Walden Chorale Society and the female quartet.

In 1902 she married P. J. Coleman, a minister of the CME Church, and joined that denomination. She earned a degree in medicine from Meharry Medical College in 1906, and established a medical practice in Clarksville, Tennessee, where her husband was pastor of the Wesley Chapel CME Church. She was very concerned about the poor, and was always providing medical care to those otherwise unable to receive it, and providing food, clothing, and shelter when necessary out of her own means. It was in this context that her missionary interests took shape, and she first became known in this regard as president of the Clarksville District Missionary Society.

She was a strong advocate for the creation of the Woman's Missionary Council (known at first as the Woman's Connectional Missionary Society), and the General Conference in Chicago in 1918 finally gave permission for it. It was formally organized on September 3, 1918, and Coleman was elected its first president. Under her founding leadership, this group evolved into the strongest and most dedicated organization in the whole CME Church. She was in great demand as a speaker, and for many years was one of the most visible and influential women in the church.

For several years she was dean of women at Lane College in Jackson, Tennessee, and helped found the Nashville Bethlehem Center. She served as Medical Examiner of the Court of Calanthe, Tennessee, for more than twenty years, and in 1932 became the first graduate in Dental Hygiene at Meharry Medical College. She was the first Black woman physician to become State Tuberculosis Advisor and Counselor. She continued as head of the Woman's Missionary Council until 1939, and then devoted her attentions as head of the State Vocational School for Girls, until her death. Named for her is a church in Knoxville, Tennessee.

CMECTY, EWM, HCMEC.

COLEMON, JOHNNIE, founder of the **Universal Foundation for Better Living**, a New Thought metaphysical denomination serving a predominantly Black constituency, was born in Mississippi, the daughter of John Haley and Lula Haley Parker. She grew up in Mississippi in the 1920s as a member of the Methodist Church and graduated from Union Academy in Columbus, Mississippi. She then attended Wiley College, a Methodist school in Marshall, Texas, from which she received a B.A. She taught school in Canton, Mississippi, for six years and then moved to Chicago, where she worked as a price analyst in the Chicago Market Center.

In 1953 Colemon was told by a doctor that she had a terminal illness. He gave her six months to live. It was at this time she was introduced to the teachings of the Unity School of Christianity by her mother, who had been reading its literature for many years. She moved to Kansas City and enrolled as a full-time student at the school. Within six months all signs of her disease had vanished; however, she now had to face segregated barriers at the school. She was not permitted to live on campus at Unity Village, some fifteen miles from Kansas City, and was not allowed to eat in the school cafeteria. For over three years she commuted daily and brought a sack lunch. Then during her last year, she threatened to quit, and within a short time accommodations were made for her to live and dine on campus. Ordained in 1956 she returned to Chicago and organized Christ Unity Temple, the first predominantly Black Unity congregation.

By 1963 Christ Unity Temple, with some 20 members, moved into its own building. The church continued to grow and in the early 1970s Colemon was elected as the first Black president of the Association of Unity Churches. In 1974, her first husband having died, she married Don Nedd, founder of the Brooklyn Truth Center for Better Living. That same year, in spite of her leadership role in Unity and complaining of the organization's continuing racism, she broke with the school and association and formed the independent Christ Universal Temple for Better Living. She also opened a metaphysical school, the Johnnie Colemon Institute, to train New Thought ministers. As other ministers were trained and, following her example, went out to form their own congregations, the Universal Foundation for Better Living was incorporated as a new New Thought denomination. By the late 1980s there were 23 member congregations.

By 1978 Colemon was speaking at three services each Sunday to a audience in excess of 1,000 people. She began to plan for a larger church. In 1981 she began her television show, "Better Living with Johnnie Colemon." Her increasing duties heightened the need to consolidate her work under one roof. In 1985, on land acquired on Chicago's far south side, she opened a new Christ Universal Temple, which includes an auditorium that seats over 3,500, the school, and television facilities. While it was under construction both her husband and mother died.

During the 1980s Colemon emerged as one of the most prominent Black Chicago ministers and has served in a variety of positions in the city.

Colemon, Johnnie. *From the Founder's Desk.* Chicago, IL: Universal Foundation for Better Living, 1987. 67 pp.
———. *"It Works If You Work It."* 2 vols. Chicago: Universal Foundation for Better living, n.d.
Poinsett, Alex. "Rev. Johnnie Colemon's Dream Church." *Ebony* 40, 12 (December 1985), 74–80.

COLERIDGE, CLARENCE NICHOLAS (b. November 27, 1930), a bishop of the **Episcopal Church**, was born in Georgetown, Guyana, the son of Charles and Ina (DeWeever) Coleridge. He attended Lincoln University in Pennsylvania in 1950–51, received his B.A. in 1954 from Howard University in Washington, D.C., and received his M.Div. in 1960 from Drew Theological Seminary in Madison, New Jersey. He then spent a year at General Theological Seminary in New York City and was ordained deacon in January, 1961 and priest in January, 1962. On September 8, 1962 he married Euna Jervis, with whom he had two daughters.

In 1961–62 Coleridge was curate at St. Philip's Episcopal Church in New York City, and from 1962 to 1964 was curate at St. George's Episcopal Church in Brooklyn, New York. While at St. George's he was a part-time chaplain at Sea View Hospital on Staten Island. From 1966 to 1981 he was rector of St. Mark's Episcopal Church in Bridgeport, Connecticut. During this time he continued his education and received his Master of Social Work degree from the University of

Connecticut in 1973 and his D.Min. degree in Psychology, Pastoral Care, and Counseling from the Andover-Newton School of Theology in Newton, Massachusetts. From 1973 to 1977 he was a part-time pastoral counselor at Episcopal Social Service, and then served part-time as director of the Unicorn counseling service of the Episcopal Social Service, in which he administered a statewide network of counselors. In 1980 he was elected chair of the Connecticut Urban Caucus, and that same year was chosen Man of the Year by the National Council of Negro Women.

On May 16, 1981, Coleridge was elected bishop and assigned as suffragan bishop of the Diocese of Connecticut. Since 1981 he has also served as director of Pastoral Development of the Episcopal Church and director of the Governor's Task Force on Racial Justice.

WWA (84–85), *ECA* (1982), *BDNM* (75).

COLES, JOSEPH CARLYLE, JR. (b. February 15, 1926), a bishop of the **Christian Methodist Episcopal Church** (CME), was born in Washington, D.C., the son of Joseph Carlyle, Sr., and Rubie (Banks) Coles. He received his B.A. in 1947 from Howard University in Washington, D.C. and his B.D. from that institution's School of Religion in 1950. He married Geneva Rose Hamilton, with whom he had three children.

His first pastorate was at St. Paul's CME Church in Halifax, Virginia, in 1949–50, followed by Ebenezer CME Church in South Boston, Virginia (1950–53); Lane Metropolitan CME Church in Cleveland, Ohio (1953–63); and Williams Institutional CME Church in New York City (1963–74). During these last two pastorates he gained a national reputation, serving also as dean of the denomination's Ohio Leadership Training School (1955–59); member of the Cleveland Board of Education (1962–63); president of the Methodist Ministerial Alliance in Cleveland (1959–61); and on the executive committee of the Cleveland N.A.A.C.P. In New York City he furthered his education, receiving his S.T.M. degree in 1971 from New York Theological Seminary. From 1971 he was an adjunct instructor at Ramapo College in New Jersey.

In 1974 Coles was elected bishop and assigned to the Sixth Episcopal District, with headquarters in Atlanta, Georgia (covering the Jamaican Mission and the four Georgia conferences), where he has since remained. Since 1979 he has been on the executive board of the World Methodist Council and also since 1979 has been on the board of directors of the Southern Christian Leadership Conference. From 1982 to 1984 he was president of the Georgia Christian Council. He is a trustee of Atlanta University Center, Interdenominational Theological Center, Phillips School of Theology, and Paine College.

"Bright Young Men of God." *Ebony* 11 (March 1956): 17–23.
WWABA (92–93), *BDNM* (75).

COLLEY, WILLIAM W. (February 12, 1847–1909), the founder of the **Baptist Foreign Mission Convention** in 1880, was born in Prince Edward County, Virginia. He was the son of a Scottish preacher and a Native American woman. Thus, he was not an African-American, but he was apparently viewed almost universally as one during his lifetime and beyond. He never publicly discussed his origins, and we only know of his birth parents through the admissions of his widow. He was baptized in September 1870 and joined the Grand Hill Baptist Church in Richmond, Virginia. He attended Richmond Institute and was ordained in Alexandria, Virginia, in 1873.

In 1875 he went to Africa as a missionary with the Foreign Mission Board of the Southern Baptist Convention. He returned to the United States in 1879 and immediately spoke to Black Baptist leaders throughout the South of his conviction that more Black missionaries needed to be sent to Africa. In order to accomplish this a new level of intercongregation organization had to be created and Colley sent out the call for a national meeting. On November 24, 1880, about 150 persons from eleven states met in Montgomery, Alabama. Colley was temporary chair and was reportedly overcome with emotion as he began the proceedings. At this event the Foreign Mission Convention of the United States of America was founded, the first national-level organization of Black Baptists in the country. **William H. McAlpine** was elected the first president and Colley was elected corresponding secretary at an annual salary of $1,000. In 1883 Colley and five others were sent to establish a missionary program in Liberia, West Africa. They settled in Vey country, some forty miles from Monrovia, and organized two missions, Bendoo and Jundoo. One source suggests that Colley and his wife perished from hardship and disease, along with most of the other missionaries, by 1893. It appears, however, that he lived on until 1909, probably living in the United States after 1893. Colley has been called "the first of a great new group of Negro leaders that rose in the Baptist Church during the latter part of the nineteenth century."

SCA, EBA, SNB, HBB, IBAW.

COLLINS, GEORGE NAPOLEON (June 8, 1899–February, 1972), 80th bishop of the **African Methodist Episcopal Church** (AME), was born in Quincy, Florida, the son of Charles C. and Fannie (Armstead) Collins. He first felt the call to preach at age seven and experienced conversion about the age of sixteen. His mother and sister both passed away in 1914. In 1915 he was licensed to exhort in the Mt. Zion AME Church in Daytona Beach, Florida. In 1917 he enrolled in Edward Waters College in Jacksonville, Florida. He finished a high school-level education in June 1922, and in June 1926 he graduated from the school's college department and from B. F. Lee Seminary, receiving both a B.A. and B.D. He was helped to remain in school through a combination of scholarships, church grants, and part-time work at St. Paul AME Church in Jacksonville, from 1919 to 1924. In 1925 he married Lottie Phyllis Miller, with whom he had four children.

From 1925 to 1926 he pastored the St. James AME Church in Commers Mill, Jacksonville, Florida, followed by the St. James AME Church in Miami (1926–28); Mt. Moriah AME Church in Cocoa (1928–29); St. Mark AME Church in Orlando (1929–31); Mt. Zion AME Church in Daytona Beach (1931–33); Mt. Hermon AME Church in Ft. Lauderdale (1933–40); St. Paul AME Church in Tampa (1940–41), all in Florida. He pastored Visitors' Chapel AME Church in Hot Springs, Arkansas, from 1941 to 1944. His first wife passed away in 1933 and in 1941 he married Oneida Byrdie Mickens. He was a trustee of Edward Waters College from 1933 to 1941, and was a trustee of Shorter-Flipper-Curry College from 1941 to 1952. In 1945 he was appointed to Avery AME Church in Oklahoma City, Oklahoma, then in about 1952 went to Union Bethel AME Church in New Orleans, Louisiana.

Collins was presiding elder of the Central New Orleans District when he was elected bishop at the General Conference in May 1964. He was assigned to the Eighteenth Episcopal Conference (Basutoland, Bechuanaland, Swaziland, South Africa, and Portuguese East Africa). He later covered the Eleventh and Twelfth (Arkansas and Oklahoma) Episcopal Districts. He was killed in an auto accident in 1972 while returning from the funeral of a friend.

Collins, George N. "African Methodism Adventures in Missions, Four Years in Africa." *The African Methodist Episcopal Church Review* 92 (January–March 1968): 79–82.
EWM, HAMEC, BDNM (70), *BAMEC.*

COLONIAL ERA, AFRICAN AMERICAN CHRISTIANS DURING THE.

The beginnings of Christianity among those Africans who lived along its Atlantic coast south of the Sahara began with the European explorers. While the scope of the West Africans' exposure to Christianity in the sixteenth century is uncertain, by the mid-1500s, Portuguese and Spanish adventurers and the English Captain John Hawkins had introduced Africans to Christianity along the Gulf of Guinea. The involvement of Catholic nations in the transatlantic slave trade led to the presence of African Catholics residing in the Americas early in the sixteenth century, and it is not only possible but probable that some West Africans had knowledge of Christianity prior to their enslavement in the North American colonies.

The Spanish Era in the Americas. The earliest Africans to arrive in the English North American colonies had Christian names. This suggests that they had been baptized and named in transit, in accordance with the Spanish tradition. One of the first of these, Angela, arrived at Point Comfort, Virginia, on the ship *Treasurer*, circa 1618. Isabell and Anthony were among those first twenty Africans who landed in Jamestown, Virginia, in 1619. In 1622, an African woman with the name Mary was brought into Virginia on the *Margrett and John*. Records indicated that Mary married an African with the name Anthony Johnson; he had been transported to Virginia in 1621.

Although they undoubtedly worked in the capacity of indentured servants, the civil status of the first Africans in colonial Anglo-America was accordingly "made nebulous by a mixture of Spanish and English law, whereby a Spanish subject who had been christened or baptized was by that act enfranchised or set free under English law and admitted to the privileges" of a free person. If, indeed, these first Africans in North America had been baptized by their Spanish captors, there would be legal and moral force to the argument that, as Christians, they should be free in English territories.

In the British Colonies. One of the first baptisms in English colonial North America was that of William, son of the Africans Isabell and Anthony referred to above in the 1619 disembarkation. The document recorded in the 1624/25 parish Church records reads: "Anthony, Negro, Isabell, a Negro, and William, her child, baptized." Whether or not this was a family baptism into Christianity is unclear. Probably William only was ceremonially baptized as the first child born to African parents in North America. Under English law William should have been set free. The New England Puritans searched the Scriptures for its identification of Africans. New Englanders considered themselves to be privileged by God to own slaves. They held the notion that Africans were an accursed people, the descendants of Ham whom it was quite proper to destroy or enslave. Even Roger Williams, the radical Puritan-turned-Baptist, condoned slavery on the basis of this Puritan interpretation of Scriptures.

After thirty-nine Africans arrived in Boston in 1638, one of them, an enslaved woman, was received into the Puritan Church at Dorchester, Massachusetts, in 1641. Massachusetts was the first English colony to record the acceptance of an adult of African ancestry into full Christian fellowship while identifying her as a slave. In his memoirs John Winthrop noted that the woman, whom he did not identify by name, was baptized and communed into the Puritan congregation after having proven her "true godliness" over several years.

Slaveowners continued to question the wisdom of Christianizing their bondspeople only to have them successively sue for their emancipation on the basis of their being Christians. As the slaveowners' interest in permitting Africans to be Christianized was receding, the conversion rate among them proceeded at a trickle. In recognition of this social reality in 1660, King Charles II urged the Council for Foreign Plantations to accept responsibility for Christianizing African slaves and Indians.

On the Quaker front, George Fox (founder of the Quaker Movement) urged his followers to give the slaves religious instruction and to take them to meetings. Quakers were the only seventeenth century Christian denomination to propose that enslaved Africans be educated and freed with compensation after a period. Aware of the Quaker position, in 1672 the Virginia colony enacted legislation that forbade Black attendance at Quaker meetings. In the Carolinas, Black attendance at meetings continued until as late as 1699. Quakers reported in this same year that "there was great openness and tenderness in North Carolina [meetings]." Following the Germantown (Pennsylvania) Friends' Remonstrance of 1688 against even a limited term of enslavement, antislavery sentiment intensified among the Quakers.

Quaker sentiments and kingly decrees to the contrary, the pace of Christianizing Africans did not accelerate noticeably among the colonists for two main reasons: 1) local slaveowners were uneasy about what would be the state's disposition on their right to own Christianized slaves, and 2) slaveowners believed they lost profits when giving slaves time off to prepare for Christianization. To seventeenth century Protestants, Christianizing meant catechizing (offering religious instruction). Slaveowners thought of this process as an economic detriment to work schedules. Even on Sundays slaves generally were required to work either for their masters or, when allotted individual garden plots, for themselves.

The King's interest in slave conversions, however, did impress upon slaveowners the need to contend for settlement of the question. Not treating the issue of slave conversions but trying to safeguard ownership of enslaved Africans, in 1662 the Virginia colony enacted codes declaring "that all children borne in this country shall be held bond or free only according" to the mother's civil status, not mentioning her religious condition. Massachusetts soon followed suit. In 1664, Maryland became the first colony to pass legislation specifically guaranteeing that an enslaved African's civil status was unaffected by circumstances of baptism. Yet, the issue of the civil status of Christianized African slaves was not settled, and the nagging reality persisted that in all English colonies civil status was interrelated to and often determined by one's religious affiliation.

Thus, New York colonists understood that slaves and Christians were mutually exclusive groups. In 1665 the New York colony enacted a law stating that any Christian who has not sold her/himself into captivity shall not be kept in slavery. Anglican colonists then appealed to the Bishop of London (under whose jurisdiction the American colonies resided) for a decisive ruling. The Bishop reversed the impact of the New York code on Anglicans, stating that although an enslaved African might adopt Christianity, his/her conversion would not result in manumission. Accepting that cue, the Virginia legislature passed a statute in 1667 declaring that baptism of slaves did not exempt from bondage. The New York colony followed suit in 1674.

While the issue of securing slave property against incursions of Christianity was settled in the slaveowner's favor, the loss of economic profit that could result from the process of religious instruction so that slaves could be accepted into the Anglican and Puritan churches continued to plague slaveowners. The colonists seemed so disinclined to Christianize slaves that the Crown again in 1680, 1682, and 1686 instructed colonial governors "to do all within their power to facilitate and encourage the Conversion of Negroes and Indians to Christianity." However, only an occasional African was converted and taken into church membership.

Slavery and Witchcraft. Even the witchcraft mania, which had stormed New England, beginning in 1647 in Connecticut and climaxing in 1692 at Salem, did not inspire the colonists to Christianize slaves. Puritans, believing "powers of the devil could be executed by human witches," seemed particularly prone to this witchcraft mania. A Black woman servant named Marja was one of its first victims. Marja was accused of conspiring with two men to burn down a building in Roxbury, Massachusetts. She alone was executed by burning at the stake. The severity of the punishment was an apparent indication that paranoia had set into the colony and that social instability prevailed there.

In Salem, witchcraft was compounded by a decline in old-fashioned piety and by conflicting social interests. A major character in the Salem hysteria was a half-Indian, half-African slave woman named Tituba, whom the town's pastor had imported from Barbados. The hysteria ended with trials during which twenty residents were executed. One hundred fifty others, including Tituba and another Negro servant, Mary Black, were jailed. Both were later released, and Tituba was sold to pay for her jail expenses. Court documents claimed that her quick confession "exorcised" the evil spirits from her body and saved her life. Clemency for Tituba suggests that the real source of the furor was elsewhere. It lends credence to recent interpretations which indicate that no small amount of the confusion was touched off by conflicting class interests and religious tensions in the Puritan town. Some Puritans thought the epidemic was related to their failure to put forth a concerted effort to Christianize African people. In 1693 in the wake of the Salem trials, a group of slaves in Massachusetts requested that Cotton Mather organize them into a body for weekly religious instruction and worship.

Blame for witchcraft mania can be spread around. In *The World They Made Together*, Mechal Sobel maintains that if there were Africanisms, there were seventeenth- and eighteenth-century Europeanisms akin to Africanisms, and the African and European cultures in contact influenced each other. There had been a long period of intensive racial interaction within the seventeenth-century colonies. There were Africans living in small numbers together with Whites in great intimacy, sometimes in the same house, often doing the same work side by side, and sharing the same churches. This resulted in an American culture that was deeply affected by both Western and African values, and their interpenetration began to take place very early, beginning with the arrival of the first Africans into colonial Anglo-America.

West Africans brought with them to America a closely shared set of perceptions despite their ethnic diversity. Sterling Stuckey has persuasively argued, in *Slave Culture*, that while their Gods, family structures, languages, folkways, and mores differed, West Africans shared a basic worldview that made possible their melding into one Afro-American culture under the impact of slavery. Among the cultural elements which the West Africans brought with them to America was their mutual belief in spirit power. The natural order was seen as having special powers to which humans could have access through rituals, amulets, potions, and special artifacts and signs.

Keith Thomas, in *Religion and the Decline of Magic*, contends that seventeenth-century Englishmen viewed power as connected to land, wells, and trees and other natural places. Catholic priests blessed trees, wells, and land. Although the Anglican and Catholic Churches often objected to them by the seventeenth century, these practices continued so that guardian spirits in which people believed could be propitiated. In places like Droitwich, Derbyshire, Nantwich, and Worcestershire in England, patron saints or forefathers were petitioned to help the living, and in some communities local forefathers were canonized as saints who could be petitioned to help the living. Many colonists decorated their houses with charms, and signs, fertility figures and protective images so witches could not access their houses through danger points. In the more rational seventeenth and eighteenth centuries, English people of all classes continued to believe in witches, ghosts, magic, and charms.

The Society for the Propagation of the Gospel. Undoubtedly it was this general malaise of superstitious thought and belief in the workings of supernatural forces that the enlightened Euro-Christians in Anglo-America wanted to root out of the colonies. Despite the complaints of missionaries and other members of the clergy that immorality, wickedness, and superstitious thinking among White colonists impacted Africans, it was not until 1701 that the leadership within the Church of England authorized a systematic drive to evangelize and teach among the slaves. This missionary movement, called the Society for the Propagation of the Gospel in Foreign Parts (SPG), was largely the work of Thomas Bray who had been appointed commissary in Maryland in 1695. Headquartered in London, the SPG was financially independent of local church parishes in the colonies. It was organized with the intention that its missionaries would bypass the usual financial problems and local politics that individual clergymen encountered in Anglican parishes and take its efforts more successfully into slave communities. Only in Maryland and Virginia was the Anglican Church firmly established in the eighteenth century. Therefore, the overarching plan of the SPG was to expand the enlightened influence of Anglican outreach to all of the colonies.

The SPG launched its campaign under the shadow of colonial legislation that had been passed by the Maryland and Virginia colonies guaranteeing that a slave's status was unaffected by baptism. The advent of the SPG coincided with rising importations of slaves from Africa, and colonists were complaining that they felt overrun by "outlandish" Africans. In 1698, the Royal African Company's monopoly was ended by act of Parliament. In the wake of this action shippers with smaller vessels threw themselves into the fray and flooded the colonies with Africans. Fearful of slave revolts and finding themselves overwhelmed with the African presence, slaveowners found new excuses for failing to permit their slaves to be instructed. They complained that linguistic and cultural gaps could not be overcome sufficiently to really convert masses of Africans brought to them directly from the continent.

In its response to the colonists, SPG clergy became apologists for slavery by arguing that Christianity would make better slaves and that slavery was consistent with Christianity. Often the clergy appealed to profit motives of the slaveowners by pointing out that "converted slaves do better for their Masters profit than formerly, for they are taught to serve out of Christian Love and Duty." Although the SPG had broadly based institutional support only in Anglican dominated colonies, its purpose was so threatening to slaveowners that at least six colonial legislatures had passed acts by 1706 denying that baptism altered the condition of a slave "as to his bondage or freedom." In the face of continued resistance, in 1727 the Bishop of London gave the civil laws religious sanction by issuing an edict that endorsed them. The SPG intensified its outreach efforts by 1) seeking funds in England for financing the missionary outreach and 2) publishing tracts and sermons and sending them out to missionaries and catechists. While it sought to convert Blacks, however, the SPG not only was an apologist for slavery but also owner of over three hundred slaves who worked its plantations in Barbados and South Carolina.

The New England Congregationalists, feeling that the Anglican Church was not reformed enough, and having removed itself from England to avoid its dominance, were suspicious of Anglican reasons for establishing a missionary arm of the Church in America. Puritans, therefore effectively kept the Blacks away from the SPG missionaries. In 1729, the SPG missionary in Boston reported only one black convert, a slave. In 1750, this same missionary boasted of having baptized "five Negro children, one of whom was a slave," during the seven months preceding his report.

The New Englanders not only resisted evangelism among the slaves by SPG missionaries but they also spurned the missionizing efforts of their own clergy. In *Magnalia Christi*, Cotton Mather criticized those Puritan slaveholders who "deride, neglect, and oppose all our means of bringing their poor Negroes unto our Lord." There were areas of encouragement, nonetheless, if improving the numbers of Christianized Africans was what counted as much, if not more than, actual conversions. In 1738, after several groups of New England Congregationalists had converted to Anglicanism, the General Assembly of the Colony of Connecticut answered "yes" to the question of whether "infant slaves of Christian masters may be baptized in their master's right." The assembly stated that the masters should promise to bring the children up in the ways of religion and should feel obligated to offer them for baptism.

Meanwhile SPG missionaries in Maryland and Virginia complained that their commission to catechize Africans continued to be severely hampered by the planters' reluctance and outright resistance, by the large sizes of parishes, by the scarcity of clergy, by linguistic and cultural difficulties with African-born slaves. Slaveowners indicated that besides the fear of losing profits, they were concerned that Christianized slaves might threaten the status quo in the master-slave relationship by claiming spiritual if not civil equality. There was no positive law in the colonies obliging the slaveowners to instruct slaves in Christian doctrines. Hence, the most recalcitrant slaveowners were hardly to be persuaded by the SPG clergy to embrace a cause which might be injurious to their self-interests.

Not all masters were opposed to the conversion process, and some missionaries were resoundingly successful in their efforts to convert enslaved Africans. An SPG minister in Accomako, Virginia, (an Anglican colony) reported to the Bishop of London that he had baptized about two hundred slaves. The only North American mainland colony passionately to embrace the SPG was South Carolina. The SPG entered South Carolina (another Anglican colony) in 1702, and in 1704 the legislature encouraged ministers to settle in the colony by granting them land and the right to hold Negroes as slaves.

So confident were they in the benefits of religious instruction that some missionaries, like Samuel Thomas of Goose Creek, South Carolina, presumed that there was a link between Christianization and literacy. Thomas reported that in 1702, he had taught twenty slaves to read while instructing them in the Christian faith. A missionary to St. Andrew's Parish in South Carolina, from 1711 to 1717, praised two White female parishioners and slaveowners for their instructing large numbers of Blacks while Christianizing them. When examined, these slaves declared their faith and explained the chief articles of the religion. They recited from memory the Apostle's Creed, the Lord's Prayer, and the Ten Commandments. The missionary baptized fourteen of this group on the same Sunday.

The carefulness with which Africans were scrutinized prior to being admitted to baptism by some SPG missionaries was reflected in a statement by Francis LeJau who said, "I could easily multiply the number of slaves proselyted to Christianity but I put off their baptism and the receiving some persons to the holy table till we have a good testimony and proof of their life and conversation." Because he did not want slaves to seek baptism hoping to be freed, LeJau drafted a declaration, for those about to be baptized, which read: "You declare in the presence of God and before this Congregation that you do not ask for the holy baptism out of any design to free yourself from the Duty and Obedience that you owe to your master while you live, but merely for the good of Your Soul and to partake of the graces and Blessings promised to the members of the Church of Jesus Christ."

Roman Catholics in Louisiana. The Protestants had no monopoly on Christianizing and instructing enslaved Africans in North America. Bienville's Code, directing masters to instruct slaves in the doctrines of the Church, coincided with the SPG work. Like ministers from the SPG, Catholic priests reported a number of obstacles to missionary work among slaves. In addition to those which also plagued the Protestants was that of the Catholics' not having enough boats to travel the waterways to plantations where slaves were most numerous.

In the urban areas of Louisiana, there were opportunities for Blacks to receive somewhat thorough religious instruction. An example is seen among Blacks in New Orleans in 1727, the year in which the Ursuline nuns came into the area. They supplemented missionary work of the priests with that of the Ursuline Convent and served as a center for the instruction of Black Catholics from 1730–1824. Unlike the Protestants, Catholic slaveowners could not protest that baptism could mandate emancipation. Catholics had a history of sponsoring slaves for baptism. Parish church registered baptisms of Blacks and mulattos, showing that they occurred frequently during the French colonial period. In the Capuchin missions, large numbers of enslaved Africans were baptized in a single day, sometimes as many as seventy-five to one hundred, although large scale baptisms call into question the thoroughness of Christian preparation.

Religious Schools. Colonial Protestants thought Catholic emphasis on the efficacy of the sacraments was mechanistic. The Reformed emphasis on the individual's relationship to God, on searching the Scriptures, and on discerning the workings of grace within one's heart tended to de-emphasize the mediative role of sacrament-oriented worship. In addition, a theological emphasis upon the scriptural and the sermonic word undergirded a strong educational program.

The notion that religious instruction was requisite to Christian conversion was the inspiration behind several schools organized for Africans by SPG missionaries and associates. Elias Neau was one of the first of these missionary-schoolmasters. He organized a school for Blacks in New York City in 1704. In 1705, Neau had enrolled 27 Black women and 16 Black men from nine different households. He gave some of them two catechisms and other books. In 1707, Neau reported to SPG headquarters that he had over one hundred pupils enrolled. There were more than two hundred students in 1708.

Subsequent to Neau's success and following his death, Dr. Bray's Associates (an organization founded in memory of Thomas Bray the Commissary to Maryland) was organized in 1731 specifically to educate and convert Blacks to Anglicanism. The SPG and the Associates opened schools for Blacks in the colonies of Virginia, the Carolinas, Pennsylvania, New York, and New Jersey. The total number of schools was small, but the successes were notable.

Upon the advice of Alexander Garden (the Bishop of London's Commissary in South Carolina) that Blacks be trained as teachers, the SPG opened a school on September 12, 1743. It lasted over twenty years, despite the Stone River Rebellion in 1739 and the South Carolina legislature's adoption of a strict law against teaching slaves to write.

A community of Moravians, under the leadership of Count von Zinzendorf, settled in Georgia in 1735. From that base, they launched a campaign to convert Africans and Indians. The Moravians' goal was to help Africans become literate so that they could read the Bible. They preceded SPG and other missionaries in Georgia in these endeavors. The SPG and Bray's Associates did not support the work of lay catechists in the instruction of Blacks in Georgia until after slaves legally were admitted to the colony in 1749.

Subsequent to the Moravian initiative, the SPG appointed Joseph Ottolenghe to be its catechist in Georgia. He was an Italian-born convert from Judaism who disembarked in Savannah in 1751. He proposed to give slaves instruction three times a week, at the end of their workday, so that he could teach them to read the Bible for themselves, to recite the Lord's Prayer, the

Apostle's Creed, and a portion of the Catechism. He preached to them on the Being of a God, or the Life and Death of the Christ, or upon some other event or story taken out of the Bible. This work was terminated in 1759, after the Reverend Bartholomew Zouberbuhler, Rector of Christ Church in Savannah, argued in 1758 that itinerant catechists should be sent out to the plantations so that more slaves could be reached.

The SPG sometimes made special appeals for male students and provided an all-male leadership role model. Women were excluded from the ecclesiastical ranks, which was in keeping with Euro-Christian patriarchal traditions. Missionaries and catechists directed lessons in reading and writing to particularly apt male youths, grooming them to become teachers (tutors) among other Black slaves. Many women and girls, nevertheless, were numbered among the converts of SPG missionaries and instructors. A group of New York City White women opened a school in 1712 to train Black women, hoping they would become socially responsible and assimilable. Making Africans assimilable generally translated into acculturating them.

There were enlightened slaves who had not received religious instruction and who by Western standards were illiterate and backwards. Yet, many of these had heightened sensibilities that provoked them to offer penetrating insights into the behavior of White Christians. The Reverend Francis Varnod, minister to St. George's Parish in South Carolina, observed in 1724 that the slaves were "sensible that as we are Christians, we do not act accordingly." He observed a Negro male, about 14, who had never been instructed comment on his mistress' behavior. On her way to church, she had blamed him for some thing which had gone wrong. He was overheard saying, "'My mistress can curse and go to church.'" He thereby indicated his understanding that her behavior did not become an avowed Christian.

Blacks were aware, moreover, of the hypocrisy involved in admonishing slaves that a man should keep one wife and a woman one husband until death parted them. They realized that such admonitions could not be adhered to when masters separated them for any reason and traded them away from each other. Missionaries complained to slaveowners and to SPG headquarters about polygamous tendencies, i.e. male separations from women who either could not or had not given birth as a result of their mating and taking other wives and the women's frequent changing of husbands. Their consternation inspired legislation to regularize marriage procedures and to control perceived immorality among slaves, without circumventing an owners' privilege of separating married couples at his/her pleasure. The clergy complained, though, that White settlers, like the mistress referred to above, frequently were poor exemplars of Christian virtue.

Despite the minor upsurge of conversions among Africans owing largely to efforts of SPG missionaries, throughout the seventeenth century and into the first decades of the eighteenth century, the American colonists restricted the religious activities and assemblies among Blacks—both free and enslaved. The colonists seemed especially anxious to control those Blacks who were identified with Christian institutions and worship. These restrictions became more formalized after public funerals were banned in the Northern Neck region of Virginia late in the seventeenth century. Whites outlawed African religious practices as well, alleging that they, like Christian activities, provided opportunities for slaves to revolt.

The Great Awakening. Until the wave of revivals known as the First Great Awakening (1730–1780), Africans who were Christianized were beneficiaries of rudimentary education that accompanied religious instruction. By emphasizing personal religious experience, rather than formal instruction, as the requisite for acceptance to Christian fellowship, the Awakening made the Christianization of Black people more expedient and acceptable to slaveowners.

The isolated local revivals with which the Great Awakening began were consolidated into one movement under the preaching of Methodist preacher George Whitefield in 1739. Not requiring religious instruction, these evangelical revivals gave Africans their first opportunity for widespread participation in Christianity in Anglo-North America. The preaching of the Awakening included narratives of Bible stories and was coupled with opportunities for personal participation in worship services through singing, praying, and testifying. The combination of personal religious experience and personal participation struck a responsive chord in the African. The revival leader often commented on the Black participation in the revivals and that some appeared to have been truly born again.

Among Presbyterian evangelical preachers, Samuel Davies (future president of the College of New Jersey, now Princeton) experienced considerable success in his efforts to evangelize Negroes. He had a ministry to seven congregations in Hanover County, Virginia, beginning in 1748. He believed that "more than 1,000 Negroes attended on his ministry at different places where he alternately officiated."

In 1754, Shubal Stearns, a convert from Congregationalism to Baptist evangelicalism, under the influence of Whitefield, relocated with his brother-in-law from Connecticut to Virginia. Riding on the twin crests of spiritual zeal and physical energy, they preached and improvised on worship styles from Virginia to Georgia. In the old Anglican areas, they replaced learning the catechism with yearning for an ecstatic, personal experience. These ministers further invigorated services by calling for energetic singing.

Stearns and his colleagues were immensely popular. During revivals of the First Great Awakening (1740–1780) in the South, the Baptist Church was constituted by the socially dispossessed—poor Whites and Blacks, who were proud members in the Church of the lowly and persecuted. Large Black memberships in mixed congregations were not unusual, particular, in the poorer White churches in the South during the colonial period.

Although Blacks were in virtually all churches during the eighteenth century, these early Great Awakening congregations tended not to list their members by color or race. Some of these did list slaves separately. However, the full names of less than a dozen of these earliest Black American Christians have been recorded in history. Jupiter Hammon (Long Island, born circa 1720) and Phillis Wheatley (Boston, circa 1753–1784) are two of the few early Christians whose full names are known. Both of them are remembered primarily as domestic slaves and poets who accommodated slaveowners and were favored. Hammon, who was converted under the influence of Wesleyan evangelicals, devoted himself to the study of the Bible and preached among fellow slaves, exhorting them to become Christians and to rely on the Lord to secure their freedom. Phillis Wheatley was taken into membership at Boston's Old South Meeting House around 1769. By the time she was eighteen in 1772, White Congregationalists considered her to be a fully converted, zealous Christian. Her writings, when analyzed from the conversionary perspective, indicate that Phillis rejoiced in the psychological succor of her Christian faith and had little awareness of or appreciation for her African heritage. In this respect, hers was not a unique response, particularly among family favorites like Hammon and herself. Missionaries of the period said of slave converts generally, "They will ever bless God for their knowing good things which they knew not before [their enslavement in America]." Wheatley's fondness for evangelicalism is memorialized in her elegy on George Whitefield and in letters to her friend, Arbour Tanner, who lived in Newport, Rhode Island.

Full names of a few free black Christians who were born during the colonial period are known. **John Marrant**, for example, was reared in Georgia but born free in New York in 1755. Like Marrant, **Lemuel**

Haynes, **John Chavis**, and **Henry Evans** all were born during the colonial period but launched their ministerial careers in the Early National period of United States history.

Black Churches. Throughout the colonial period the majority of Blacks remained only minimally touched by Christianity. Those with most opportunity to become church members were free Blacks, favored slaves, household servants, slave artisans, and urban slaves. Slaves in remote rural areas had less opportunity to attend church, but this did not mean they were totally ignorant of Christianity, since they might have been included in family prayer circles, Bible reading, and other religious instruction. Revivalism helped to bring Blacks to Christianity in large enough numbers to make the founding of Black churches possible during the period of the First Great Awakening.

The only clearly independent Black churches founded during the colonial period were Baptist. The structure of the Baptist organization, with its governance via local church autonomy, was more conducive to the precarious autonomy of Black Christians and Black preachers than were the systems of government in other denominations. The first known Black Baptist Church, the African Baptist or "Bluestone" Church, was organized in 1758 on William Byrd's plantation near the Bluestone River in Mecklenburg, Virginia. Over the next generation others were formed in South Carolina, Virginia, and Georgia.

These churches, although initially organized under the direction of White ministers or drawn out of White congregations, attracted large numbers of Blacks in part because of the White southern Baptist's affinity for African-like religious practices. Consequently, the first independent Black Baptist members felt comfortable enough to join the predominantly White churches and to later pattern their orders of worship and creeds on those in the White churches.

Second to the Baptist Church, Blacks in the South were attracted to the revivals of the Methodist societies. They attended in large numbers and became part of Methodism's mixed membership. In the Methodist Movement, White ministers led emotional revivals and meetings in which Blacks and Whites together were "dying" and being reborn in African-style celebrations. John Marrant documented this phenomenon in his account of his own conversion experience in his memoirs. Ministers reported that it was common for men and women to fall down as dead under an exhortation. So electric was the atmosphere that hundreds of Blacks were said to have tears streaming down their faces when hearing sermons from Ezekiel's vision of the dry bones or how Black men and women themselves counted as members in the "glorious army" of God.

Free Black southerners and slaves sometimes were frequently charter members of the local mixed Methodist societies. Although Methodism was not separated from the Anglican Church prior to 1784, Methodist societies were formed in New York, Virginia, and North Carolina by 1766. When the very first Methodist society was organized in 1766, a Black woman was amongst its members.

Significant in mobilizing Black Baptists and Methodists was the Black preacher who memorized extensive portions of the Bible to teach the African in America. Four slaves who were preachers—Moses, Benjamin, and Thomas Gardiner, and Farrell—might have been ordained in 1774 by John Michaels, a White preacher in the Baptist church on the Byrd plantation in Virginia. Prior to the Revolutionary War, George Liele and Andrew Bryan were recognized as exhorters (preaching assistants) by White missionaries. Black men like them undoubtedly had been exhorting for some time and, when given an opportunity, they had assembled Christians under their leadership—first in the "Invisible Churches" of the enslaved, then in the racially mixed and predominantly White churches, and finally in the Black-organized churches. Active participation by Blacks as exhorters in the Awakening revivals concerned some Whites in the North and in the South. After the Revolutionary War ended and Black preachers began to be licensed by White ministers, the question of the propriety of Blacks preaching to Whites continued to linger.

W. E. B. DuBois recognized that some of the earliest Christian preachers and exhorters were former African priests with unusual gifts of leadership and persuasion. They led highly charged and emotional services, with the mourners bench, the "shout songs," handclapping, holy dancing, and sermons full of fervor and imagery. There was emphasis on personal religious experience as a sign of conversion and spiritual joy, on messages of salvation, hope, and the prospect of escape from earthly woes—all of which appealed to the enslaved masses and repressed free persons.

Dubois thought some African priests among the enslaved may also have been a constant menace to the Christianizing work among Blacks. In the absence of concerted efforts to help slaves improvise or adopt new faiths in the eighteenth-century, these priests became important figures on plantations. They began to function as interpreters of the supernatural, comforters of the sorrowing, and expositors of the longings, disappointments, and resentments of a bonded people.

One source of this genre of Black preacher was Dahomey, where dynastic quarrels had caused some chief priests and diviners to be sold as slaves. According to Melville Herskovits the most intransigent of these African priests were those from the river cults, for the most compliant priests were retained in Dahomey so as not to incur the wrath of the gods. Those men and women who had either learned their priestly craft in Africa, or who were taught by someone else who had, were the first religious leaders recognized by the slaves. Coming from among them, they appealed to the Black masses—all of whom were socially disinherited and generally enslaved, poor, and unlettered—in ways in which White preachers could not.

African American Christian Worldview. Because there is sparse Black testimony from the colonial period, scholars can only speculate about the ways in which Blacks during that period interpreted Christianity to fit the worldviews inherited from their African past. Henry Mitchell, author of *Black Belief*, stated that on a very general level Western Africanity and European Christianity (Protestant as well as Catholic) shared some important beliefs. A basic Christian doctrine which would not have seemed foreign to most Africans was belief in God as Supreme Creator of the world. The divine sonship of Jesus and the divinity of the third person of the Trinity, the Holy Spirit, would have seemed intelligible to many Africans accustomed to a plurality of divinities.

The notion of the Afterlife where evil suffers and good triumphs, along with the concept of sin as wrongdoing that deserves divine anger and punishment, was held in many African societies. That adoration and prayer were owed by humans to God would have seemed obvious to Africans, since the essence of their worship consisted of honoring the Supreme Being through the deities and ancestors. Many Blacks accepted the idea of a single Heaven for all people while assuming that the kinship line would continue in Heaven and that the afterlife would begin immediately at death.

According to the author of *Black Religion and Black Radicalism*, Gayraud Wilmore, although differences abounded there were enough similarities for slaves to find common ground between their beliefs and those of White Christians. This common ground gnaws at the foundation of the theory that the Africans' acceptance of Christianity required the adoption of a totally alien worldview. Sometimes Black Christians melded African and Christian beliefs into one whole. They made amulets in three parts to represent the Trinity. Many blacks became sin-sick prior to conversion, indicating their thinking that sin was causational. Conversion allowed them to be healed by Christ.

Most enslaved Africans were not afraid to die, for death became healing and liberating. In *Slave Religion*, Raboteau has observed that many new arrivals believed that after death their spirits would return to the traditional spirit abode near their homelands. As more Blacks converted to Christianity, Heaven became their new collective homeland. It was where Christian, and even some non-Christian, forefathers and foremothers were expected to meet them in the Afterlife.

The markings of African retentions within the Black Christian Churches are clearest in eighteenth century Black funerals and burials. Funerals were very important to Black Christians as they had been to their African forebears. Sometimes two funerals were favored, and the two-funerals custom was African. During the funerals, the soul's departure from the body was celebrated. Black Christians still believed that the souls of the departed would leave messages on the way to the grave and during the funeral. An improper funeral might cause the soul to haunt the living, for funerals prepared the spirit of the deceased for entry into the world of the ancestors. Sometimes funeral services were performed two or three weeks after the corpse was buried.

Grave markings among eighteenth-century Black Christians likewise were African-oriented. Black southern Christians made West-African-style grave markings by mounding graves, placing homemade markers and objects used by the deceased on them, scraping graves, decorating them with shells, and covering graves with gravesheds. There was much weeping and wailing at the graveside by Black Christians so that the spirit of the deceased could be sent off to the new home. This contrasted with Whites who had come to believe grief should be displayed in moderation. Probably during the colonial period, one could have identified numerous African retentions within the Black Christian worship services. According to some missionaries and members of the clergy, Africanisms obviously persisted among the Christianized Blacks, both slave and free.

This issue of African retentions in the Christian churches led to two conflicting theses. E. Franklin Frazier in the *Negro Church in America* suggested that African retentions in areas of the former English American colonies are negligible as Africans were almost totally stripped of culture in the process of their enslavement and by their embrace of Christianity. Countering Frazier, in *The Myth of the Negro Past*, Melville Herskovits argued that the system of slavery did not destroy African culture and that a considerable number of Africanisms continue to define African

American culture in the United States. Wilmore and Raboteau, taking a middle position, have concluded that it only seemed that the African religious heritage was lost in the North American colonies. Especially does this appear so when Black religion in the United States is compared with the Afro-cults of Brazil and the Caribbean. As Raboteau has noted, indifference, reluctance, and hostility to the conversion of Blacks in the first century of slavery in America assured that some forms of African religious belief and behavior would be continued. Besides a variety of factors such as the geographical remoteness of slaves from the predominant European culture in the Piedmont areas and Sea Islands, urban versus rural residency, domestic versus field and other task-oriented work, and the ratio of country-born slaves to those directly from Africa also determined differences in degrees of African retention in religion in Latin and British America.

On the Eve of the Revolution. In *African Americans in the Colonial Era*, Donald Wright commented that "it is ironic but instructive that, generally speaking, the more closely Blacks worshipped with Whites, the less they wanted to become 'Christians' worshiping with Whites. In New England where social interaction across racial lines was the longest and Christian proselytizing was strongest, the majority of Africans remained outside the White church during the First Great Awakening. Only 3% of Newport, Rhode Island's, Blacks were Christians in good standing in 1775, and only a quarter of them attended church at all. Although the Reverend Samuel Hopkins attributed the absence of Black folk in the churches to "'the deepest [African] prejudices against the Christian religion,'" the prejudice seems more to have been the result of New England Whites segregating Blacks in churches. In New England, slaves sat in segregated galleries, corners, or rear pews. At times the White people were inside the chapel, and the Black people were outside. Black Puritans were buried in segregated graveyards. They generally were not allowed to participate in matters related to governance.

Festering pockets of opposition against slave conversions and against gathering slaves for religious meetings persisted into the 1770s and 1780s. Whites with this mind-set questioned motives behind the Black affinity to revivalism out of the suspicion that the enslaved would foment uprisings and other bids for emancipation under the cloak of Christian worship. They took steps to limit opportunities for Blacks to meet in large groups. In 1770, Georgia forbade slave assemblies under penalty of "twenty-five stripes with a whip, switch, or cow-skin." This trend continued into later decades.

C. Eric Lincoln summarized the status of blacks in colonial Anglo-America's religious institutions. He asserted that for the most part, the Africans in America were "untaught and unchurched." Those who were "churched," he contended, were assigned a place of contempt in the religious world to mirror the place they had in the secular world. God became the Anglo-American God, justifying White inhumanity and inhumane conditions of racial separation and discrimination. Despite the White hostility and hypocrisy, Blacks joined the Christian denominations and over a period of time successfully crafted them into Black ones.

The earliest statistics on church membership were compiled in the post-colonial period. They suggest that at least modest numbers of Blacks continued to seek membership in the Protestant churches of the new United States of America, despite the continuation of slavery and the slave trade. When the Methodists began keeping racially separate statistics in 1786, there were 1,890 Blacks (10% of the Methodist membership). About a decade later (1797), nearly one-fourth (or 12,215) of all Methodists were Blacks. The majority of these were in Maryland, Virginia, and North Carolina. Among the Baptists in 1793, 18–19,000 Blacks constituted one-fourth of the 73,471 Baptist members.

During the colonial period, the Black Church was never completely without White control and monitoring. That's why the "Invisible Churches" and the independent Black churches were organized to give Black worshipers a modicum of privacy from White observation and domination. Black Christians had a "sense of ethnic differentness" which bound them together in spiritual and physical community. It is to this ethnic identity and the experience of enslavement that Michael R. Bradley referred when he stated that the formation of the Negro church is the key to the beginning of Afro-American community and culture. The independent Black Church movement drew Africans in America together from disparate and distant quarters, during and following the period of the Revolutionary War, into a Christian community replete with an ethnic identity and burgeoning self-autonomy.

Assad, Maurice. "The African Coptic Orthodox Church." A paper presented during the Pan African Christian Church Conference at the Interdenominational Theological Center (ITC), Atlanta, Georgia, July 1988.

Boyer, Paul, and Stephen Nissenbaum. *Salem Possessed: The Social Origins of Witchcraft.* Cambridge, MA: Harvard University Press, 1974. 231 pp.

Bradley, Michael R. "The Role of the Black Church in Colonial Slave Society." *Louisiana Studies* 14 (1975).

Burr, Lincoln George. *Narratives of the Witchcraft Cases, 1648–1702.* New York: Scribner's and Sons, 1914.

Cadbury, Henry J. "Negro Membership in the Society of Friends." *Journal of Negro History* 21 (April 1936).

Clifton, Denzil T. "Anglicanism and Negro Slavery in Colonial America." *Historical Magazine of the Protestant Episcopal Church* 39 (1970).

Copher, Charles B. "The Bible and the African Experience." A paper presented during the Pan African Christian Church Conference at ITC, Atlanta, Georgia, July 1988.

Ernest, Joseph B. *The Religious Development of the Negro in Virginia.* Charlottesville, VA.: The Mitchie Company, Printers, 1914.

Force, Peter, ed. *Tracts and Other Papers, Relating Principally to the Origin, Settlement, and Progress of the Colonies in North America from the Discovery of the Country to the Year 1776.* Vols. 2 & 3. New York: 1947.

Frazier, E. Franklin. *The Negro Church in America.* Liverpool, England: University of Liverpool, 1964. 90 pp.

Greene, Lorenzo J. *The Negro in Colonial New England.* New York: Atheneum, 1968. 404 pp.

Heartman, Charles F. ed. *Phillis Wheatley: Poems and Letters.* New York: The Author, 1915. 44 pp. Rept.: Miami: Mnemosyne Publishing Co., 1969.

Hening, William W. *Statutes at Large: Laws of Virginia.* Vol. 1. New York: Barton, 1832.

Herskovits, Melville J. *The Myth of the Negro Past.* Boston, MA: Beacon Press, 1941. 374 pp.

Higginbotham, Jr., A. Leon. *In the Matter of Color: Race and the American Legal Process, The Colonial Period.* New York: Oxford University Press, 1978. 512 pp.

Jochannan, ben Yosef A. A. *Black Man of the Nile and His Family.* Baltimore, MD: Black Classic Press, 1989. 428 pp.

Klingberg, Frank J. *Anglican Humanitarianism in Colonial New York.* Philadelphia, PA: Church Historic Society, 1940. 245 pp.

———, ed. *Carolina Chronicle of Dr. Francis LeJau, 1706–1717.* Berkeley, CA: University of California Press, 1956. 220 pp.

Lewis, Roscoe E. *The Negro in Virginia.* New York: Hastings House, 1940. 380 pp.

Lincoln, C. Eric. *Race, Religion, and the Continuing American Dilemma.* New York: Hill & Wang, 1984. 282 pp.

Mather, Cotton. *Diary of Cotton Mather, 1691–1724.* Boston, MA: The Society, 1911–1912.

Matthews, Alice E., "The Religious Experience of Southern Women," In Rosemary Radford Ruether and Rosemary Skinner Keller, eds. *Women and Religion in America: The Colonial and Revolutionary Periods.* San Francisco, CA: Harper and Row, 1983.

McClain, William B. *Black People in the Methodist Church: Whither Goest Thou?* Cambridge, MA: Schenkman Publishing Co., 1984. 159 pp.

Mitchell, Henry H. *Black Belief: Folk Beliefs of Black in America and West Africa.* New York: Harper & Row, 1975. 171 pp.

———. *Black Preaching.* Philadelphia, PA: Lippincott, 1970. 248 pp.

Murray, Heller. *Black Names: Origins and Usage.* Boston, MA: G.K. Hall & Co., 1975. 561 pp.

Piersen, William D. In *Black Yankees: the Development of an Afro-American, Sub-Culture in 18th Century New England.* Amherst, MA: University of Massachusetts, 1988. 237 pp.

Raboteau, Albert, *Slave Religion: The "Invisible Institution" in the Old South.* New York: Oxford University Press, 1978. 382 pp.

Records of Salem Witchcraft 1. Roxbury, 1864.

Roediger, David R. "Funerals in the Slave Community," *The Massachusetts Review* 22 (Spring 1981).

Sernett, Milton C., ed. *Afro-American Religious History: A Documentary Witness.* Durham, NC: Duke University Press, 1985. 505 pp.

Scherer, Lester B. *Slavery and the Churches in Early America, 1619–1819.* Grand Rapids, MI: William B. Eerdmans Publishing Company, 1975. 163 pp.

Snowden, Frank M., Jr. *Blacks in Antiquity.* Cambridge, Massachusetts: The Belknap Press of Harvard University, 1970. 164 pp.

Sobel, Mechal. *Trabelin' On: The Slave Journey to an Afro-Baptist Faith.* Westport CT: Greenwood Press, 1979. 454 pp.

———. *The World They Made Together: Black and White Values in Eighteenth-century Virginia.* Princeton, NJ: Princeton University Press, 1987. 364 pp.

Webb, (Ashcraft-Eason) Lillian, "Black Women and Religion in the Colonial Period." In Rosemary Radford Fuether and Rosemary Skinner Keller, eds. *Women and Religion in America: The Colonial and Revolutionary Periods.* San Francisco, CA: Harper and Row, 1983.

Whitefield, George, *Memoirs.* London, 1772.

Wilmore, Gayraud S. *Black Religion and Black Radicalism: Interpretation of the Religious History of Afro-American People.* Garden City, NJ: Anchor Books, 344 pp.

Wright, Donald R. *African Americans in the Colonial Era: From African Americans in the Colonial Area: From African Origins through the American Revolution.* Arlington Heights, IL: Harlan Davidson, Inc. 1990. 184 pp.

Yesehaq, Archbishop, "The Ethiopian Orthodox Church." A paper presented during the Pan African Christian Church conference at ITC, Atlanta, Georgia, July 1988.

Lillian E. Easton-Ashcraft

COLONIZATION, EMIGRATION, AND THE AMERICAN COLONIZATION SOCIETY. The

colonization movement in the United States was a nineteenth-century movement primarily supported by Anglo-Americans to return Blacks to Africa. The American Society for Colonizing Free People of Color in the United States (or American Colonization Society) was organized in Washington, D.C. by the (White) Presbyterian minister Robert Finley. It was enthusiastically embraced both by some Baptist and Methodist clergymen as a means for emancipating slaves and for expanding missionary work into Africa. Many of these Whites saw colonization as the only way to abolish slavery, a better alternative to the "galling chains" of Black servitude that they were unable to break through years of moralistic preaching. In addition to ending slavery and helping Blacks flee from White racism, some supporters of the colonization movement also hoped to show their White detractors that Blacks could govern themselves, thus demonstrating that freed slaves were no threat to civilized society.

But questions were raised from the outset concerning the motives of the society's supporters, many of whom were prominent supporters of slavery and themselves slaveholders. At Finley's request, free Blacks met at Bethel African Methodist Church in Philadelphia in January 1817 to discuss the colonization movement. Though interested in African missions, the leaders of America's Black churches were not at all enthusiastic about the efforts by Whites— North and South—to colonize West Africa with Black freemen. **Richard Allen**, founder of the **African Methodist Episcopal Church** (AME), and others at the meeting drafted a letter of protest. They saw the colonization movement as a veiled attempt by slaveholders to tighten their grip on slavery by deporting free Blacks and thus preventing them from gaining manumission for their fellow African-Americans.

There were African Americans who did support colonization. Some free Blacks had entertained the thought of emigrating en masse to the Caribbean Island of Haiti, to lower California, or elsewhere in the Far West. Also, the sizable number of free Blacks and fugitive slaves in the provinces of Canada made colonization there a feasible step toward non-White West Africa. A Black Quaker named **Paul Cuffe** had successfully voyaged to Western Africa with about forty fellow African-American emigrants in 1815. Cuffe believed that Blacks could only control their lives and destinies in their own land, far from the racial oppression of White America. **Lott Carey**, pioneer missionary to Liberia. Carey believed that though they be free, Blacks would never be able to rise to the level of or earn the respect of Whites. **Daniel Coker**, a founder with Allen of the AME Church, espoused colonization as a means

of securing political and religious freedom and escaping racial harassment. He was among the first to sail to Liberia in 1820 under the auspices of the Colonization Society. (A more substantial AME presence in West Africa did not appear until the 1850s, however.)

As abolitionism heated up in the North, supporters of colonization, especially in the Methodist churches, met their first significant White detractors. With fiery zeal, abolitionists assailed the motives of the colonizationists as being far from pure. William Lloyd Garrison, among others, charged that, in intent, the American Colonization Society was anti-Black and pro-slavery. In *Thoughts on African Colonization* (1832), Garrison argued that colonizationists were racists in that they wanted to separate the races and that colonization efforts perpetuated slavery in that they called for the deportation of *free* Blacks, not the emancipation of Black slaves.

In response, many supporters of the colonization movement, including Wilbur Fisk, president of Wesleyan University, believed that colonization was the most sensible and least volatile means of ending slavery. Colonizationists felt that the abolitionists did not truly appreciate Southern sensitivity to the issue of slavery or the delicate political and ecclesiastical relations between the North and South. Colonization was therefore the last best hope for securing the freedom of the slaves without disrupting the union of the churches or the union between the states. The abolitionist assaults on the colonization movement seriously undercut its efforts after the 1830s.

African-American interest in self-initiated emigration reemerged after Black hopes were disappointed in the Kansas-Nebraska Act (1854), the Dred Scott Decision (1857), the unsuccessful raid by John Brown (1859), and even at the election of Abraham Lincoln (1860), which promised to split the country in two, giving Southern slaveholders complete and unbridled mastery over the lives and fortunes of Blacks in the South, a prospect free Blacks fought and died to prevent.

After the Civil War, with the issue of the plight of slaves no longer at stake, emigration initiatives periodically reappeared to serve various concerns. For example, in 1901 **African Methodist Episcopal Church** Bishop **Henry M. Turner** called a meeting in Nashville at which the Colored National Emigration Association was formed. The association's attempts to purchase a ship to take African Americans to Liberia raised a storm of controversy which eventually led Turner to abandon the scheme. Another burst of enthusiasm came a decade later in connection with **Marcus Garvey** and the Universal Negro Improvement

Association. With the motto, "One God! One aim! One destiny!," Garvey sought to unite people of African descent at home and abroad for the redemption of Africa from colonialism and the establishment of a worldwide confraternity of Africans with a country and government absolutely their own. In the 1920s, with Garvey in jail, the **African Universal Church** would try to revive Garvey's program. These latter emigration plans only rarely caught the attention of more than a few African Americans, the great majority of whom had always seen their future in the United States.

Essien-Udom, E. U. *Black Nationalism.* New York: Dell Publishing Company, 1962. 448 pp.

Jackson, J. H. *A Story of Christian Activism: The History of the National Baptist Convention, U.S.A., Inc.* Nashville, TN: Townsend Press, 1980. 790 pp.

Lincoln, C. Eric. *The Black Experience in Religion.* Garden City, NJ: Doubleday & Company (Anchor Books), 1974. 369 pp.

Mathews, Donald G. *Slavery and Methodism: A Chapter in American Morality: 1780–1845.* Princeton, NJ: Princeton University Press, 1965. 329 pp.

Sernett, Milton C. *Black Religion and American Evangelicalism.* Metuchen, NJ: Scarecrow Press, 1975. 320 pp.

Wilmore, Gayraud S. *Black Religion and Black Radicalism.* Garden City, NJ: Anchor Books, 1973. 344 pp.

Jon R. Stone

COLTRANE, ALICE. *See:* **TURIYASANGITA-NANDA, SWAMI.**

COMMANDMENT KEEPERS CONGREGATION OF THE LIVING GOD. A Black Jewish synagogue. **Black Judaism** found some of its earliest support among West Indian people who had settled in the United States. Among these was **Wentworth Arthur Matthew** (1892–1973). Born in Lagos, West Africa, he had migrated to St. Kitts in the British West Indies as a youth and then in 1911 settled in New York City. There he became a Pentecostal minister with the **Church of the Living God, the Pillar and Ground of Truth** and active in the **Marcus Garvey's Universal Negro Improvement Association** (U.N.I.A.). While a Pentecostal minister he had his first encounter with White Jews by whom he was deeply influenced. He left the Church of the Living God, and in 1919 founded the Commandment Keepers: Holy Church of the Living God, over which he was named bishop.

In 1924 **Arnold Josiah Ford**, also a leader in Garvey's movement, founded Beth B'nai Abraham, a synagogue in New York City. Through their mutual association in the U.N.I.A., Ford and Matthew became friends and Ford assisted Matthew's further transition toward a more orthodox form of Judaism. Responding to the Ethiopianism in the U.N.I.A. and the spread of news about the **Falashas** (the Black Jews of Ethiopia), in 1930, Ford left America for Ethiopia, and his congregation merged into the Commandment Keepers. Matthew kept abreast of events in Ethiopia, and in 1935, following the ascension of Haile Selassie as Ethiopia's emperor, Matthew declared his congregation to be American Falashas and claimed authority for the new emperor to operate.

Matthew attempted to align his congregation with Orthodox Jewish practice. He learned and taught Hebrew. He instituted the Sabbath and kept the standard Jewish holidays. Kosher food regulations were imposed. However, he retained a few practices from his former Christian experience—foot washing, spiritual healing, and gospel hymns. He also incorporated elements of conjuring, the folk magic of southern Blacks, into what he termed Kabbalistic Science.

Matthew claimed that Black people were the real Jews (i.e., the Falashas) who had had their identity suppressed during the years of slavery. He taught that the Jewish patriarchs were Black. He also rejected Christianity as a White man's religion and especially disapproved of what he termed "niggeritions," by which he meant the loud and emotional excesses which had come to characterize much worship within the Black churches, especially Pentecostal ones.

Matthew continued to lead the congregation into the last half of the twentieth century. He found his leading student in the person of his grandson, David M. Dore, who he sent to Yeshiva University's High School for Boys. Following his graduation in 1972, Dore attended Erna Michael College. Meanwhile, upon the death of Matthew in 1973, Dore became the new rabbi at the congregation. Dore earned his diploma at Erna Michael College and moved on to work at Yeshiva University. In 1977 he became the second Black person to graduate from Yeshiva. Dore currently leads the congregation which has several centers in New York and surrounding states. There are an estimated 3,000 members.

Brotz, Howard M. *The Black Jews of Harlem.* New York: Schocken Books, 1970.

Ehrman, Albert. "Black Judaism in New York." Journal of *Ecumenical Studies* 8, 1 (Winter 1971): 103–114.

———. "The Commandment Keepers: A Negro Jewish Cult in America Today." *Judaism* 8, 3 (Summer 1959): 266–70.

Ottley, Roi. *New World A-Coming.* Boston, MA: Houghton Mifflin Company, 1943. 364 pp.

COMMISSION FOR CATHOLIC MISSIONS AMONG THE COLORED PEOPLE AND THE INDIANS.

A **Roman Catholic Church** agency. The Commission for Catholic Missions among the Colored People and the Indians is one of the oldest currently existing agencies through which the Roman Catholic Church relates to the Black community. Since it came into existence in 1884, especially in the last generation, it has been joined by a variety of organizations through which the predominantly White church and the Black Catholic community relate to each other. The primary function of the commission has become the distribution of funds received annually from the churchwide Black and Indian Mission Collection. These funds support workers in Black communities and on Native American reservations to assist in the compiling of statistical data on Black and Native American ministries.

COMMISSION FOR RACIAL JUSTICE.

A **United Church of Christ** agency. The Commission on Racial Justice was formed in 1967 as an official church agency to pursue the cause of racial justice both in the church and in society. The formation of the commission was a major first agenda item for the United Church's Black clergy caucus which had met informally in 1966 and had formalized their organization in 1967 as **Ministers for Racial and Social Justice**. There are an estimated 50,000 African American members in the United Church.

The commission began work immediately and joined in a 1967 voter registration drive in Chicago. That same year it initiated a Special Higher Education Program to assist Black students to make up economic and academic deficiencies. It has cooperated with Ministers for Racial and Social Justice and **United Black Christians** on numerous projects over the past two decades. The commission issues a newsletter, *Racial Justice Alerts,* and the weekly *Civil Rights Journal* which as a printed item is reproduced in several hundred newspapers and as an audiotape heard over 200 radio stations.

The commission can point to a number of accomplishments in its quarter century of existence. It helped form the National Black Leadership Roundtable, which draws representation from over 500 Black organizations and convenes meetings periodically to discuss the issues before the African American

community. It also conducted a national survey on hazardous wastes in poor and minority communities which has aided some to obtain some relief from the government.

The commission is centered at the United Church of Christ headquarters in Cleveland, Ohio, but has regional offices in Illinois, North Carolina, and Washington, D.C.

Payne, Wardell J., ed. *Directory of African American Religious Bodies: A Compendium by the Howard University School of Divinity.* Washington, DC: Howard University Press, 1991. 363 pp.

CONCORDIA COLLEGE.

A Lutheran school. Once the Lutherans, through the Synodical Conference, moved into the Black communities in the South following the Civil War, they found Alabama a fruitful mission field. During the first two decades of this century the mission expanded rapidly. In 1919 the leaders of the mission petitioned the Conference to establish a normal school for the training of teachers. After several delays, Alabama Lutheran College was opened in 1922 in Selma, Alabama. Its initial instruction was at the high school level. In 1925, following the closing of Luther College in New Orleans, the Synodical Conference gave money of the expansion of the school and an elementary department was added.

The school was founded by Professor R. Otho L. Lyn, a Black teacher. In 1922 the Conference passed a resolution to the effect that all of the teachers of the school would be Black people.

In 1966 the Synodical Conference dissolved in a doctrinal conference, and all of its member denominations except the Lutheran Church-Missouri Synod withdrew. The Missouri Synod, which had previously supplied most of the leadership for the Southern mission officially took control of and assumed responsibility for the Alabama Lutheran College. In the meantime, the school evolved into a junior college with an associated high school academy. As the public school system developed, the elementary school was discontinued. More recently, Alabama Lutheran College was absorbed into the denomination's Concordia College system which has campuses at various locations around the United States.

Drewes, Christopher F. *Half a Century of Lutheranism Among Our Colored People.* St. Louis, MO: Concordia Publishing House, 1927. 111 pp.

CONE, JAMES HAL (August 5, 1938–), **African Methodist Episcopal Church** theologian and educator, was born in Fordyce, Arkansas, the son of Charlie M. and Lucille Cone. After attending Shorter College for two years, he moved to Philander Smith College in Little Rock, Arkansas, where he received the B.A. degree in 1958. Following a strong interest in religion, he attended Garrett Theological Seminary, a **United Methodist Church** school in Evanston, Illinois, from which he received a B.D. degree in 1961. Cone went on to receive the Ph.D. in the history and literature of religion in 1965 at Northwestern University, in the Garrett-Northwestern joint Ph.D. program. He married Rose Hampton, with whom he had four children.

Cone began his teaching career as an assistant professor at Philander Smith College in 1964, at which time he was also assistant minister at the Woodlawn African Methodist Episcopal Church. He became assistant professor at Adrian College in Michigan in 1966, and assistant professor at Union Theological Seminary in New York City in 1969, where he has remained, achieving full professor status in 1973. In 1977 the seminary named him Charles A. Briggs Professor of Systematic Theology.

In the summer after Martin Luther King, Jr.'s death, Cone wrote *Black Theology and Black Power*. This book was for him a conversion journey from a white, European theology to a Black theology, and introduced the term "Black theology" into religious discourse. He followed this volume quickly with *A Black Theology of Liberation* (1970). Together they set the tone for his work, which has focused on the liberation of Blacks from oppression, both religiously and culturally. He has placed his thinking in the context of what he sees to be the primary theme of Jesus and of the Bible in general, a conscious solidarity with the poor and oppressed. This means, for Cone, that God, in Jesus, a Jew, concretely identified Godself in history with the oppressed and demonstrated God's willingness to suffer for the liberation of oppressed humanity. Over the years Cone has forged a number of links with liberation theologians, for instance in Latin America and among women, who share his general approach, but who speak out of the distinct concerns of their own communities. These concerns of other oppressed people have in turn shaped the expression of Cone's own theology.

Cone has maintained a prolific publication output. In addition to a steady stream of articles in journals ranging from *Theological Education* to *Ebony*, his work has included *The Spirituals and the Blues* (1972), and *Speaking the Truth: Ecumenism, Liberation, and Black Theology* (1986), among others. *My Soul Looks Back* (1982) has autobiographical elements, as he recounts many of the formative events in his spiritual development. His most recent book is *Martin & Malcolm & America: A Dream or a Nightmare* (1991). *Black Theology and Black Power* has been translated into a number of languages. In a career still far from over, his books have already made a significant impact not only on Black religious thinking, but on a wide spectrum of theological reflection.

Cone, James H. *Black Theology and Black Power*. New York: Seabury Press, 1969. 165 pp.
——. *A Black Theology of Liberation*. Philadelphia: Y. B. Lippincott & Co., 1970. 254 pp.
——. *Martin & Malcolm & America: A Dream or a Nightmare*. Maryknoll, New York: Orbis Books, 1991. 358 pp.
——. *My Soul Looks Back*. Nashville: Abingdon Press, 1982. 144 pp.
——. *Speaking the Truth: Ecumenism, Liberation, and Black Theology*. Grand Rapids, Michigan: W. B. Eerdmans Publishing Co., 1986. 167 pp.
——. *The Spirituals and the Blues*. New York: Seabury Press, 1972. 152 pp.
WWABA (88), EBA, BDNM (75), SBAA, HUBA, CA (33–36), DAS, OTSB, LBAS, RLOA, MBRL.

CONFERENCE OF CHURCH WORKERS AMONG COLORED PEOPLE. An **Episcopal Church** organization. In 1883, the Episcopal bishops and an number of leading White priests and lay people from the southern states held a conference at Sewanee, Tennessee, to discuss the ministry of the church in regard to African Americans. The conference drew up a plan for segregating Black church members. As a result of the Sewanee meeting, Rev. **Alexander Crummell** called the African American clergy together in New York City several months later. They organized to oppose the Sewanee Plan, and spearheaded its defeat a few weeks later at the church's general convention. It was also decided to meet annually and for many years the conference continued. Crummell became the editor of the conference's periodical, the *Church Advocate*.

In 1886 a change was made in the Conference makeup as two White ministers who worked in the African American community arrived to attend the conference. Their presence led to other White clergy being invited to future meetings. That conference also drafted legislation for the general convention asking for the establishment of the Church Commission on Work among Colored People. The general conference concurred and the commission was created.

The conference, whose gatherings continued well into the twentieth century, met in varying locations around the country. They raised Black consciousness throughout the church, built a community of interest among the widely separated African American congregations, and made the African American clergy known to the church members.

Bragg, George F. *History of the Afro-American Group of the Episcopal Church*. Baltimore, MD: Church Advocate Press, 1922. 319 pp.

CONGRESS OF NATIONAL BLACK CHURCHES. An ecumenical association. The Congress of National Black Churches is an association of six of the largest of the predominantly Black denominations originally brought together to explore their common interests and the possibility of common ventures. The six churches are the **African Methodist Episcopal Church**, **Christian Methodist Episcopal Church**, **Church of God in Christ**, **National Baptist Convention, U.S.A., Inc**, **National Missionary Baptist Convention of America**, and the **Progressive National Baptist Convention**. Bishop **John Hurst Adams** of the African Methodist Episcopal Church is credited with founding the Congress. Financial support for their initial coming together was supplied by a grant from the Lilly Endowment, Inc. More recently the Congress has been able to interest other corporate and private funding sources in a growing list of projects.

At their initial meetings, the representatives of the several denominations quickly identified four areas of common interest—evangelism, economic development, theological education, and media/communication resources, and these became the subject of early projects. These have been followed by projects focused on, among other issues, drug and alcohol abuse, rising insurance for local churches, and family life in African American communities. Among the more creative programs have been an effort to build intellectual and educational values in children (Project SPIRIT) and the National Fellowship Program, which offers pastors an opportunity to gain experiences in a related secular field through ten-month intern programs).

The Congress is headquartered in Washington, D.C. In 1988 Dr. Charles W. Butler, pastor of New Calvary Baptist Church in Detroit, Michigan, succeeded Bishop Adams as the chairman of the board of the Congress.

CONNER, JAMES MAYER (March 9, 1865–1925), 39th bishop of the **African Methodist Episcopal Church** (AME), was born into slavery in Winston County, Mississippi, the son of William and Mariah Conner. He experienced conversion and joined the AME Church in 1881, and was licensed to preach the following year. In 1883 he entered the itinerant system in the North Mississippi Conference and was sent to the Aberdeen Mission, where he bought land and built a new church. In 1884 he was ordained both deacon and elder by Bishop **Thomas M. D. Ward**. He married Glovenia L. Stewart on December 24, 1886, with whom he had five children.

After serving churches in Okolona (1884) and Stormsville (1885), he went to Forest City, Arkansas (1886), where he built a church. In 1887 he was assigned to Osceola, Arkansas, where he built another church, and then built yet another church at Newport, Arkansas (1888–89). He served many years as a presiding elder, beginning with four years on the Forest City District, from 1889 to 1893. He then was pastor for two years at Hot Springs, Arkansas, where he paid the church out of debt. From 1896 to 1897 he was presiding elder of the Little Rock (Arkansas) District, followed by the Vicksburg (Mississippi) District (1897–1901). From 1901 to 1905 he served the Bethel AME Church in Little Rock, Arkansas, where he bought a lot and built the parsonage. From 1905 to 1908 he was a pastor at Fort Smith, Arkansas. This was followed by two more stints as presiding elder, on the Jonesboro (Arkansas) District (1908–1910) and the Little Rock District (1910–1912). In each place he greatly enlarged the membership and giving to the Annual Conference.

Along the way he gained a higher education, with a Bachelor of Sacred Theology in 1891 from the National University of Chicago and another degree in 1897 from the American Institute of Sacred Literature at the University of Chicago. In 1905 he earned a B.D. from Shorter College in North Little Rock, Arkansas. From 1904 to 1912 he was on the financial board of the denomination. At the 1912 General Conference at Kansas City, Missouri, Conner was elected bishop and assigned to the Eighth Episcopal District (Mississippi and Louisiana). He built Conner Hall at Campbell College in Jackson, Mississippi, and organized the Northwest Mississippi Annual Conference. He built two modern buildings at Lampton College in Alexandria, Louisiana. From 1916 to 1920 he was assigned to the Twelfth Episcopal District (Arkansas, Oklahoma), and during this time founded Flipper-Key-Davis University in Tullahassee, Oklahoma, and established an agricultural college at Smale, Monroe, Arkansas. From 1920 to 1924 he covered the Fifteenth Episcopal District (Ontario, Michigan, Bermuda, Nova Scotia).

He served as president of the executive board and

of the alumni association of Shorter College, and published a number of magazines over the years, including the *Little Rock Reporter*, *Arkansas Statesman*, and *Conner's Magazine*. He also authored several books, namely, *Outlines of Christian Theology*, *Doctrines of Christ*, and *Elements of Success*. For seven years he was head of the Business Men's League of Arkansas. He was a delegate to the Ecumenical Methodist Conference in Toronto in 1911. His style of leadership was created in the context of the South, and in Michigan the people thought it too geared toward white approval. By 1924 his health was deteriorating and he retired, passing away one year later. He was credited with bringing some six thousand people into the church.

Conner, James Mayer. *Doctrines of Christ; or, the Teachings of Jesus Christ*. Little Rock, Arkansas: Shorter University, 1897. 204 pp.
———. *Elements of Success*. Philadelphia: AME Book Concern, 1911.
———. *Outlines of Christian Theology; or Theological Hints*. Little Rock, Arkansas: Brown, 1896. 300 pp.
WWWA (vol.4), *WWCR, EWM, CEAMEC, BAMEC, HAMEC, AARS, HUBA, BAW*.

CONSOLIDATED AMERICAN BAPTIST MISSIONARY CONVENTION. A Baptist organization.

The Consolidated American Baptist Missionary Convention (CABMC) was the first truly national African-American Baptist Convention, combining several regional conventions. Cooperative movements among Black Baptists began as early as 1840 with the organization in New York of the American Baptist Missionary Convention (ABMC). Though its strong emphasis on foreign missionary work led to a measure of stress within the ABMC, the spirit of cooperative Christian endeavor spread West and South over the next two decades.

Near the end of the Civil War, Black Baptists from these regions met in St. Louis to strengthen further their cooperative ties, with the result that the Northwestern Baptist Convention and the Southern Baptist Convention were created. Two years later, in 1866, these two conventions joined with the American Baptist Convention to form the Consolidated American Baptist Missionary Convention. In 1867, William Troy, then minister of the Second Baptist Church of Richmond, Virginia, was elected its first president.

The purpose of the CABMC was to unite Black Baptists throughout the United States in their support of missions, rather than divide that support among several regional conventions. During its first conference in Nashville in 1867, however, Troy successfully moved that the CABMC organize itself into district associations for easier management, a move that planted seeds of the CABMC's own failure. When after some delay, the motion was put into effect in 1872, two of the associations that the motion's implementation created—the General Association of Western States and Territories and the **New England Baptist Missionary Convention** (1874)—soon began to rival the very national convention they were established to assist. That is, these new associations emphasized and strengthened the very regionalism and the local independent activity that the founders of the CABMC sought to avoid. Unable to rein in the rival associations it created, the CABMC disbanded after 1878.

Fitts, Leroy. *A History of Black Baptists*. Nashville, TN: Broadman Press, 1985. 368 pp.
Jackson, Joseph H. *A Story of Christian Activism: The History of the National Baptist Convention, U.S.A., Inc.* Nashville, TN: Townsend Press, 1980. 790 pp.
Pelt, Owen D., and Ralph Lee Smith. *The Story of the National Baptists*. New York: Vantage Press, 1960. 272 pp.

Jon R. Stone

COOK, JOHN FRANCIS, SR. (c.1810–March 21, 1855),

educator and pioneer Presbyterian minister, was born into slavery in Washington, D.C. About the time he was sixteen, his aunt, Aletha Tanner, purchased his freedom. She had established a vegetable market near Lafayette Square in Washington, D.C., where her master had allowed her to earn her own income beyond her regular duties. She eventually earned enough to buy her own freedom as well as that of over twenty relatives and friends. Once Cook gained his freedom he apprenticed himself to a shoemaker and worked toward repaying his aunt. He may have briefly attended one of the few schools for Black children in the area, called the Smothers School after Henry Smothers, the Black teacher who founded it and ran it until 1825. Smothers was succeeded until 1834 by another Black man, John W. Prout.

He finished his apprenticeship in 1831, but dislocated his shoulder, making it hard to work full-time as a shoemaker. He obtained a job as assistant messenger in the office of the United States Land Commissioner, and in his spare time improved upon the rudimentary reading and writing skills he had already learned. His diligence in self-study was remarkable, and soon the Land Commissioner, Elisha Hayward, hired him for clerical work. In August 1834, he left that work and succeeded John Prout as head of the school, which he promptly renamed Union Seminary. This enterprise appeared to go well, and he had one hundred students in the winter and fifty in the summer.

Unfortunately, in September 1835, after only one year there, Snow's Riot occurred in Washington, part of the wave of anti-Black sentiment aroused by the Nat Turner Rebellion of 1831. Along with many other Black establishments, Cook's school was attacked and partially destroyed. Cook himself escaped harm only by having already left town. He did not immediately return, and joined many other Blacks in moving northward to more hospitable areas. He ended up in the Columbia, Pennsylvania, home of William Whipper, well-known Black reformer and lumber merchant. For about a year he conducted a school in Columbia, and then returned to Washington in September 1836, to reopen Union Seminary. He repaired the buildings and soon the enrollment was back to former levels. His reputation by that time was not only local, but national, as he had frequently participated in several of the various conventions of black people organized during the period, beginning with the Fourth Convention for the Improvement of the Free People of Colour, in June 1834 in New York. At the Fifth Convention in Philadelphia in 1835, Cook was secretary and thus a visible component.

It is not clear exactly when and why Cook became interested in the Presbyterian Church. For much of his life he was related to the **African Methodist Episcopal Church**, one of the founders of Union Bethel AME Church in Washington, D.C. (later called the Metropolitan AME Church), and apparently also was a licensed preacher. The predominantly White Fourth Presbyterian Church in town had run a Sabbath school for Black children for many years and for this reason encountered some hostility after Snow's Riot. John C. Smith, previously in Georgetown, arrived to pastor that church in 1839, and was not sympathetic to those who wanted to close the school. On the other hand, he did not desire continued hostility toward the church. He offered the solution of creating a separate congregation of Black Presbyterians who would then be responsible for their own Sabbath school.

One source indicates that Smith had been a friend and counselor of Cook for twenty years, and it may be that Smith convinced him that this would be an ideal opportunity to combine teaching with ministry. In any case, the First Colored Presbyterian Church of Washington was organized in November 1841, by Smith, and worship was conducted in Cook's schoolhouse. Cook was a charter member, and began intensive study for the ministry. Smith governed the church until Cook could take over. The presbytery of the District of Columbia formally received the church, later called the Fifteenth Street Presbyterian Church, on May 3, 1842. Cook was elected its pastor on July 13, 1843, preached his trial sermon later the same day, and was ordained the following day. He was the first Black ordained Presbyterian minister in the District of Columbia. By the time of his ordination the congregation had already doubled in size from its founding number of twenty-one to forty-two.

Cook pastored the Fifteenth Street Presbyterian Church until his death, at the same time continuing to supervise his successful school. He also had a large family of four sons and two daughters, from a first marriage to an Afro-Indian woman, Jane Mann, and after her death to Jane LeCount, from Philadelphia's Black upper class. In 1846, largely due to Cook's efforts, the Harmony Cemetery was established for Blacks in Washington. He organized a Total Abstinence Society in the congregation, and was a charter member of the first association of Black clergy in the District of Columbia, with **Daniel Payne** (AME Church) and L. Collins (AMEZ Church). John Smith remained a strong supporter and helped significantly in fundraising efforts to pay the debt on the old building and put up another one. The music of the church, under the direction of John H. Fleet, another pioneer Black educator, became well-known and another means of gaining donations. The cornerstone of the new building was laid in early 1852, and by the time of Cook's death the congregation numbered 120, with many of the most prominent Black citizens of the area.

After Cook's death the school was run variously by John Francis Cook, Jr. or George F. T. Cook, both Oberlin-educated, until June 1867, when public schools opened up to take its place. Almost all of his children were successful, and became part of Washington's elite Black class. Helen Appo Cook, for example, was a founder of the National Association of Colored Women. The Harmony Cemetery was later relocated in Maryland, maintaining strong ties with many Black families in Washington, D.C. The Fifteenth Street Presbyterian Church remained Cook's greatest legacy, growing in strength and influence. One of his most famous pastoral successors was **Francis J. Grimke**.

Gatewood, Willard, Jr. "John Francis Cook, Antebellum Black Presbyterian." *American Presbyterians* 67 (Fall 1989): 221–229.
IBAW, AAE, HNB, HNRA.

COPELAND, MARY SHAWN (b. August 24, 1947), **Roman Catholic Church** sister and theologian, was born in Detroit, Michigan, the daughter of John and Geraldine (Billingslea) Copeland. She received her B.A. in 1969 from Madonna College in Livonia, Michigan, and made her initial vows with the Dominican Sisters of Adrian in August, 1971.

She taught high school from 1969 to 1971 and from 1971 to 1976 was executive director of the **National Black Sisters' Conference** (N.B.S.C.). In 1971 she received the KAWAIDA Award from the N.B.S.C. In 1974 she was named one of the Outstanding Young Women of America and received the Sojourner Truth Award from the Black Woman's Community Development Foundation. In 1976–77 she was program director of the Black Theology Project—Theology in the Americas and in August, 1977, made her final vows in the Dominican order.

Copeland has been a board member of the Catholic Committee on Urban Ministry, the National Coalition of American Nuns, and the **National Office for Black Catholics**. She has published a number of reviews in such periodicals as *Black Scholar* and *Sisters Today*, and a chapter in *Models of Formation from an Afrikan Frame of Reference*.

WWABA (92–93), *ACWW* (80–81).

COPPIN, FANNY M. JACKSON (1837–January 21, 1913), educator and missionary, was born a slave in Washington, D.C., the daughter of Lucy Jackson. A free aunt, Sarah Clark, saved her small income until she could afford to buy Coppin's freedom for $125. She went to live with another aunt in New Bedford, Massachusetts, where she did hired housework and obtained occasional schooling. At fourteen she went to live with yet another aunt in Newport, Rhode Island, where she gained employment as a household servant for the historic Calvert family. In her six years with them, she grew very fond of the Calverts and gained enough further education to pass the entrance exam to Rhode Island State Normal School.

From there she entered Oberlin College in Ohio in 1860, where she studied several languages and prepared for a teaching career. In 1863 she was the first Black to be chosen a student-teacher for the preparatory classes, and she was quickly popular in that role. In her last year she was elected class poet and organized an evening class for the benefit of newly freed Blacks moving into Ohio. In 1865 she became one of the few female Black college graduates in the country. She was immediately hired by the Quaker-related Institute for Colored Youth in Philadelphia to teach Greek, Latin, and advanced mathematics.

A change in school leadership in 1869 soon led to Coppin taking the position of principal, another first for a Black woman in education; she held that office over thirty years. She became convinced that the school needed to provide practical training beyond the classics, and in 1871 introduced a more broad, normal school curriculum. Within a few years, most of the graduates were finding teaching positions. The Philadelphia Centennial Exposition of 1876 was the catalyst for another innovation at the school. Realizing the demand for industrial skills and the lack of sufficient training available to Blacks, Coppin began campaigning for funds to create an industrial department at the school. In 1888 the $40,000 necessary was reached, and the following year the new building was opened with training in ten different trades.

In 1881 she married **Levi Jenkins Coppin**, pastor of the Philadelphia Bethel Church and future bishop of the **African Methodist Episcopal Church** (AME). Her marriage brought her into a new sphere of activity. She became president of the Women's Home and Foreign Missionary Society of the AME Church, and was its delegate in 1888 to the Centenary of Missions Conference in London. There, she spoke proudly of the accomplishments of Black women missionaries, and carried that same message to the 1893 World's Fair in Chicago and to women's groups across the country.

Her husband was elected a bishop in 1900 and assigned to Cape Town, South Africa. She took the necessary time to close out her responsibilities at the school, and formally resigned in the summer of 1902 to join her husband in South Africa. Despite her age she traveled widely in the new land, organizing mission groups and encouraging the women. By the time they returned to Philadelphia in 1904, her health was deteriorating significantly, and she spent most of her remaining years confined to the home. Still having an active mind, however, she wrote the autobiographical *Reminiscences of School Life, and Hints on Teaching*, published in the year of her death. The school she nurtured for so long is today Cheyney State College.

Coppin, Fanny M. Jackson. *Reminiscences of School Life, and Hints on Teaching*. Philadelphia: AME Book Concern, 1913. Rpt. New York: Garland, 1987. 191 pp.

Coppin, Levi Jenkins. *Unwritten History*. Philadelphia, 1913. Rpt. New York: Negro Universities Press, 1968. 375 pp.

Perkins, Linda M. *Fanny Jackson Coppin and the Institute for Colored Youth, 1865–1902*. New York: Garland Publishing, 1987. 347 pp.

Young, Jacqueline Ann. *A Study of the Educational*

Philosophies of Three Pioneer Black Women. New Brunswick, New Jersey: Rutgers University Doctoral Thesis, 1987. 149 pp.

HH, HNB, NA, EBA, DANB, NAW, BWR, BWNCAL, WB, IWW, LW, BDAE, PNW, RLOA, IP, NAH, AAP, NBAW, BWMH.

COPPIN, LEVI JENKINS (December 24, 1848–June 25, 1924), 30th bishop of the **African Methodist Episcopal Church** (AME), was born to John and Jane (Lilly) Coppin, free Blacks in Frederickstown, Maryland. His mother provided for him and his seven siblings a role-model of religious devotion, and also took pains to teach them how to read and write. She taught other Blacks in the area as well, although she had to do so in secret, such education being against the law at the time. In 1865, when their church, which soon affiliated denominationally with the AME Church, openly began a school, Coppin was its first teacher.

That same year, Coppin had a conversion experience and began to yearn for more education in order to study the Bible. In search of financial means, in 1869 he moved first to Philadelphia and then to Wilmington, Delaware. There he joined the Bethel AME Church and was soon director of its choir. In September, 1875, he married Martha Grinnage, a schoolteacher, but eighteen months later both she and their nine-month-old boy died. Coppin meanwhile, after a failed business venture, moved toward the ministry. He was licensed to preach in 1876, and in 1877 moved to full-time with an appointment to the Philadelphia City Mission, a three-point charge. Two years later he was ordained deacon and appointed as assistant minister at the Bethel Church in Philadelphia. When the senior minister there died, Coppin succeeded him in the post, and was ordained elder in 1881. In that same year he married Fanny M. Jackson, principal of the Philadelphia Institute for Colored Youth, and was transferred to the Baltimore Bethel Church.

In 1884 Coppin requested a move to the small Allen Chapel in Philadelphia, which both allowed him to be closer to his wife's work and time to study at the Protestant Episcopal Divinity School in West Philadelphia, from which he graduated in 1887. From 1888 to 1896 he was editor of the *A.M.E. Church Review*, an influential denominational journal. In 1896 he fell short of votes as a candidate for bishop, and instead became minister, once again, of the Philadelphia Bethel Church. At the 1900 General Conference he was elected bishop and assigned to the Fourteenth District, Cape Town, South Africa. There, major tasks were orienting the Ethiopian churches to the AME Church and establishing missions.

In 1904 the Coppins returned to the family home in Philadelphia, from which base he tended to his assignments. From 1904 to 1908 his was the Seventh District (South Carolina and Alabama); from 1908 to 1912 the Second District (North Carolina, Virginia, Washington, D.C., and Maryland); from 1912 to 1916 briefly the Second District (again) and then the Seventh District (again); from 1916 to his death the Fourth District (a number of middle states and parts of Canada). In September, 1908, he represented the Black denominations at the 225th Anniversary of the founding of Philadelphia. In January, 1913, Fanny Jackson died after a long illness.

On August 1, 1914, Coppin married his third wife, Melissa Evelyn Thompson, a Philadelphia physician. A year and a half later, Theodosia was born, his one surviving child. He authored a number of works, including an autobiography, *Unwritten History* (1919). He also composed a number of hymns, including "The Church is Moving On," and "Our Father's Church." He was one of the founders of the Frederick Douglass Hospital, the N.A.A.C.P., the Constitution League, the Women's Christian Alliance, and other groups.

Coppin, Levi J. *The Key to Scriptural Interpretation.* Philadelphia: Publishing House of the AME Church, 1895. 209 pp.

———. *Letters From South Africa.* Philadelphia: AME Book Concern, 1904. 210 pp.

———. *Observations of Persons and Things in South Africa, 1900–1904.* Philadelphia: AME Book Concern, 1905. 205 pp.

———. *The Relation of Baptized Children to the Church.* Philadelphia: AME Publication Department, 1890. 106 pp.

———. *Unwritten History.* Philadelphia, 1913. Rpt. New York: Negro Universities Press, 1968. 375 pp.

DANB, EWM, HAMEC, BAMEC, HUBA, DAA, WWCR, RLOA, CEAMEC, AAP.

CORNISH, SAMUEL ELI (1795–November 6, 1858), Presbyterian minister and founder of the first Black periodical in the United States, was born to free parents in Sussex County, Delaware. He had two brothers who became **African Methodist Episcopal Church** ministers. He went north to Philadelphia in 1815 and was soon active in John Gloucester's First African Presbyterian Church. About 1817 he was presented to the Philadelphia Presbytery, sponsored by **John Gloucester** and Ezra Ely, pastor of the Pine Street

Presbyterian Church. The presbytery agreed to take him under its care, and assigned four ministers to oversee his studies, since he "had not received a regular education." The ministers also arranged for his room and board to allow full-time concentration on his studies. He was finally given the same examination as white candidates, and was licensed to preach in October, 1819. Actually, he had already been preaching for at least a year, once each Sunday, due to John Gloucester's illness. He was the first Black Presbyterian minister to undergo the same kind of rigorous examination as the white clergy.

After licensing, Cornish spent six months as a missionary to slaves on Maryland's Eastern Shore. In 1820 he was recruited by the New York Evangelical Missionary Society of Young Men to establish a mission in New York City's Bancker Street area. At first he was very successful, and after about a year founded on Rose Street the First Colored Presbyterian Church of New York. In 1824, with a membership numbering eighty, he was ordained and officially installed as pastor. That same year a new building was erected at Elm and Canal streets, and in 1824 he married Jane Livingston, with whom he had four children. Although the new brick sanctuary was made possible by contributions from white Presbyterians, their promises to help long-term with mortgage payments proved empty, and the church had to be sold in 1826. The presbytery voiced continued confidence in Cornish, and helped him find rented space for the congregation. He was placed in the awkward position of going to the various white churches again to request support. By this time, too, his main interest was elsewhere.

Mordecai M. Noah, editor of the *Enquirer* and other papers, was conducting a slanderous crusade, questioning the integrity and morality of New York's Black community. Black leaders gathered in 1827 to discuss the problem, and Cornish and John B. Russworm, perhaps the first Black college graduate in America (Bowdoin, 1826), were assigned the task of creating a weekly paper that would both defend the community's honor and give expression to its own needs and experiences. The first issue of *Freedom's Journal* appeared on March 16, 1827, the first Black periodical in the United States. This paper was immensely important in lifting the spirits of Blacks and revealing the prejudices of the white papers. Long before William Lloyd Garrison, Cornish and Russworm advocated immediate emancipation for slaves and full civil rights for all Blacks.

Cornish took heavy criticism from influential Presbyterian whites for his strong articles against the American Colonization Society. This, of course, only made his church fundraising efforts more difficult. Because the Blacks had previously had no publishing outlets, Cornish's stance was particularly powerful in revealing for the first time the antagonism of most Blacks toward the colonization efforts. He was also strongly supportive of educational opportunities. In September 1827, his original six-month commitment as editor came to an end, and he left the paper in Russworm's hands, becoming an agent for the New York Manumission Society's African Free Schools. The combination of his church's poor financial condition and his other pursuits led him to resign his pastorate in the spring of 1828. **Theodore Wright** would later take over the church and build on Cornish's foundation. In March 1829, Russworm announced his backing of the American Colonization Society and the idea of the return to Africa. Most of the Black community was outraged by what was perceived as a "sell-out," and he was quickly forced to resign. Cornish was called back to the editorship, and renamed the paper *The Rights of All*, debuting in May 1829. This lasted only into October. His other main editorial position was for the *Weekly Advocate*, which he soon renamed the *Colored American*, from mid-1837 to mid-1839.

After 1830, Cornish supported himself mainly through itinerant preaching and holding the occasional pastorate. He pastored Gloucester's church in Philadelphia in 1831–32, and then returned to the New York area. The American Anti-Slavery Society was founded in May 1833, and Cornish was one of four Blacks on the executive committee. Also in 1833 Cornish and Wright founded the Phoenix Society to increase the educational, employment, and cultural opportunities of Blacks. Cornish was employed as general agent, his salary being contributed by philanthropist Arthur Tappan. In 1838, reacting to his children's experience of prejudice in New York, being denied entrance to any of the Presbyterian schools, he moved the family first to Belleville, New Jersey, and then in 1840 to Newark, New Jersey. For all his efforts to improve his children's lives, his experience as a father was marked by tragedy. His two daughters each died at age twenty-two, one after a long illness, and one of his two sons drowned at age ten.

In May 1840, he joined Theodore Wright and others in withdrawing from the American Anti-Slavery Society and forming the American and Foreign Anti-Slavery Society, which opposed Garrisonian radicalism. By this time, however, his political influence in various reform groups was on the wane. He pastored the Negro Presbyterian Church in Newark in 1843. His wife died in 1844, and he returned to New York City the following year, where he organized Emmanuel Church and pastored it until 1847. Plagued by poor health for many of his adult years, he moved to Brooklyn in 1855, where he died three years later.

"The Black Press: 150 Years Old." *Ebony* 32 (April 1977): 112–113.

Cornish, Samuel E. *The Colonization Scheme Considered in its Rejection by the Colored People in its Tendency to Uphold Caste, in its Unfitness for Christianizing and Civilizing the Aborigines of Africa, and for Putting a Stop to the African Slave-Trade: In a Letter to the Hon. Theodore Frelinghuysen and the Hon. Benjamin F. Butler*. Newark, NJ: A Guest, 1840. 26 pp.

Pease, Jane H. and William H. *Bound with Them in Chains: A Biographical History of the Antislavery Movement*. Westport, CT: Greenwood Press, 1972. 334 pp.

Swift, David E. "Black Presbyterian Attacks on Racism: Samuel Cornish, Theodore Wright and Their Contemporaries." *Journal of Presbyterian History* 51 (Winter 1973): 433–470.

Wolseley, R. E. "Samuel E. Cornish—Pioneer Black Journalist and Pastor." *The Crisis* 83 (October 1976): 288–289.

DANB, BPJ, EBA, HNB, BHBA, NG, PHNA, PP, CH, IBAW, AARS, HUBA, BAW, SBAA, PATN, SOTT, BWTC.

COTTRELL, ELIAS (January 31, 1853–December 5, 1937), 7th bishop of the **Christian Methodist Episcopal Church** (CME), then known as the Colored Methodist Episcopal Church, was born in Holly Springs, Marshall County, Mississippi, the son of Daniel and Ann (Mull) Cottrell. His parents were not churchgoers, but his father, who was his first teacher, taught him the Lord's Prayer and how to read the Bible. By 1873 Cottrell was already advanced enough to teach in a private school. In August 1874, he experienced conversion, and joined the CME Church in August 1875. He was licensed to preach by Rev. Beverly Ford in November 1875. He joined the itinerant system two months later in the North Mississippi Conference, and was appointed to the Olive Branch Circuit. There he remained for three years, and was credited with more than three hundred conversions. He was ordained deacon by Bishop Miles on January 7, 1877, and ordained elder on December 5, 1878. He preached at the 1878 General Conference, giving reportedly the best sermon and making a strong impression.

In December 1878, he was transferred to the Tennessee Conference and stationed at the Capers CME Chapel in Nashville. While there he took a course in theology at Walden University in Nashville in 1879. He married Catherine Davis on January 1, 1880, with whom he had at least one child. In November 1880, he transferred back to the North Mississippi Conference, and was appointed to the Lamar Mission. The church was too small to support his family, and he farmed and took other work to add to the income. He continued to hold local church appointments until May 1882, when the General Conference elected him as Book Agent for the denomination, an office he held until 1886. As this was not a full-time position, he continued to pastor local churches, and was appointed at that time to the Byhalia Circuit. He remained there until 1884, when he went to the Verona CME Church.

In 1885 he transferred to the West Tennessee Conference and was appointed to Jackson Station. He later was presiding elder of the Brownsville District, and pastor of both Collins CME Chapel in Memphis and the Dyersburg CME Church. At the General Conference of May, 1890, Cottrell was elected Commissioner of Education for the denomination. At the next General Conference, in 1894, he was elected bishop, and spent most of his tenure as bishop assigned to the Mississippi Episcopal District, maintaining his residence in Holly Springs, Mississippi. He served also in various years, usually in addition to his Mississippi responsibilities, in Texas (1894–1897), Tennessee (1898–1901), the Indian Mission (1902–1905), Alabama (1902–1905), Florida (1914–1917), Louisiana (1914–1922), Tennessee (1922–1925), and Arkansas (1930–1933), when he retired.

One of his major accomplishments was the founding of the Mississippi Industrial College in Holly Springs in 1905. He continued to guide the school as trustee, general manager, and treasurer. He was senior bishop for the last five years of his episcopacy.

WWCR, WWC, CMECTY, EWM, WWCA (38–40), HCMEC, WWWA (vol.1), EBA.

COUSIN, PHILIP ROBERT (b. March 26, 1933), former president of the National Council of Churches and 96th bishop of the **African Methodist Episcopal Church** (AME), was born in Pittston, Pennsylvania, the son of Rev. Sylvester and Mary Cousin. He grew up in West Palm Beach, Florida, received his B.A. from Central State University in Wilberforce, Ohio, his M.The. from Boston University School of Theology, and his D.Min. from Colgate-Rochester Divinity School in New York. He married Margaret Joan Cousin, with whom he had five children.

He was ordained deacon in 1952, then entered the U.S. Army as a 2nd Lieutenant. He was ordained elder in 1955 and pastored churches in Norfolk, Virginia, Danville, Virginia, and Riviera Beach, Florida. From 1960 to 1965 he was president of Kittrell College in

North Carolina. From 1966 to 1976 he pastored St. Joseph CME Church in Durham, North Carolina. During that time he chaired Durham's Human Relations Commission (1968–69); chaired the North Carolina Voter Education Project (1968–76); was trustee for Lincoln Hospital (1966–72); was trustee of Fayetteville State University (1972–76); chair of the Political Committee of the Durham Commission on Affairs of Black People (1966–76); a member of the Durham County Board of Social Services (1970–76); and a member of the Durham County Board of Education (1972–76). In 1972 he received the Martin Luther King Fellowship in Black Church Studies, in connection with his studies at Colgate-Rochester.

Cousin was elected bishop in 1976 and was assigned to the Ninth Episcopal District, with headquarters in Birmingham, Alabama. In 1984 he was assigned to the Eleventh Episcopal District, with headquarters in Jacksonville, Florida. He presently serves the First Episcopal District with offices in Philadelphia. As bishop he has served on the board of directors of the **Southern Christian Leadership Conference** and as a trustee of Edward Waters College in Florida. His most prominent position has been as president of the National Council of Churches (N.C.C.), from 1984 to 1987. In 1984 he filled the unexpired term of the previous president, who had resigned, and in 1985 he was elected to serve the three-year term of 1985 through 1987. Since that time, the N.C.C. has switched to a four-year administrative cycle, with two different two-year presidents. Through this combination of circumstances, Cousin thus served longer as president of the N.C.C. than anyone else in the history of the organization. He was also the first N.C.C. president elected from a primarily African-American denomination.

Cousin, Philip. "Response." In Richard John Neuhaus, ed. *Speaking to the World: Four Protestant Perspectives.* Washington, D.C.: Ethics and Public Policy Center, 1983. 30 pp.
WWABA (92–93), *WWR* (85), *FEDHR.*

CRENSHAW CHRISTIAN CENTER SCHOOL OF MINISTRY.

The Crenshaw Christian Center School of Ministry began as an idea suggested to the school's founder, **Frederick K. C. Price,** by Pentecostal minister Kenneth Hagin as Hagin spoke of the founding of his ministerial school in Tulsa, Oklahoma. The idea germinated for a decade until the movement of the Crenshaw Christian Center, the independent Pentecostal Church pastored by Price, into the abandoned Los Angeles campus of Pepperdine University. In 1985 the school was opened. From the beginning the school had a strong evening program to accommodate applicants who were unable to quit their jobs and attend classes in the day.

Graduates of the school have assumed positions in the 16,000+ membership Crenshaw Christian Center and other churches of similar orientation in California, and some have started new congregations.

CROUCH, ANDRAE (b. July 1, 1942), Pentecostal gospel singer, was born in Los Angeles California, the son of Rev. and Mrs. Benjamin Crouch. His father pastored in the **Church of God in Christ** (COGIC). His great uncle, **Samuel M. Crouch, Sr.,** was a prominent COGIC bishop. It is said that Crouch's musical career began when he was eleven years old. His father had been invited to become the pastor of a congregation with no musical program. He was in a quandary, but called Andrae to him and prayed that God would give his son the gift of music. Two weeks later he was playing a hymn on the piano. Within a short time he began to direct the choir and play the piano in church. Like his uncle, Andrae's father also developed a radio show on which Andre performed with a trio composed of himself and a brother and his twin sister.

After high school Crouch attended Valley Junior College in San Fernando, California, and L.I.F.E. Bible College in Los Angeles (sponsored by the International Church of the Foursquare Gospel). While in school he sung with a church-related group, the Cogics. Around 1968 he became associated with Assembly of God minister David Wilkerson, who had organized a ministry to the gangs in New York. Crouch formed and toured with a choir of former drug addicts on behalf of Teen Challenge. He left Teen Challenge in 1969 and began the Disciples. Over the next decade he became one of the most popular gospel singers in America and the author of a number of hit gospel songs which were recorded by other artists. Part of his appeal came from his blending rock, pop, and country-Western into the traditional gospel sound. His early albums include *Take the Message Everywhere* (1969), *Keep on Singing* (1970), and *Soulfully* 1971. In 1974 he recorded a live album in Carnegie Hall and later another in London.

By 1990 Crouch had won six Grammy and three Dove Awards. He had performed around the world and received an Oscar nomination for the music he composed for the film "The Color Purple." He published his autobiography, *Through It All,* in 1974.

Crouch, Andrae. *Through It All.* Waco, TX: Word Books, 1974. 148 pp.

DuPree, Sherry Sherrod. *Biographical Dictionary of African-American Holiness-Pentecostals.* Washington, DC: Middle Atlantic Regional Press, 1989. 386 pp.

WWA.

CROUCH, SAMUEL M., SR. (October 2, 1896–August 14, 1976), was the first known Black radio preacher. Not much is known about his early life. He began preaching when still a teenager and soon he was pastor of the Wayside **Church of God in Christ** in Fort Worth, Texas. In 1924 he began the historic radio program over a local Fort Worth station. About 1935 he left Texas to pastor the Emmanuel Church of God in Christ in Los Angeles, California, where he remained for the rest of his life.

He held many positions of honor and service. From 1968 to 1972 he was second assistant bishop of the Church of God in Christ and from 1972 to 1976 he was first assistant bishop of the denomination. He was a member of the advisory board of the World Pentecostal Conference and was chancellor of Charles Harrison Mason Bible College in Los Angeles, California. He maintained a mission home in Fontana, California, as a rent-free residence for missionaries and church workers. In Ontario, California, he built Emmanuel Ontario Gardens, an apartment complex with a chapel for senior citizens.

"Top Radio Ministers." *Ebony* 4 (July 1949): 56–61.

BH, PHCGC, BPL, BDA-AHP.

CROWDY, WILLIAM SAUNDERS (1847–August 4, 1908), the founder of the Church of God and Saints of Christ, one of the first Black Jewish groups, was born into slavery, at Charlotte Hall, St. Mary's County, Maryland, the son of Basle and Sarah Ann Crowdy. In 1863 he joined the Union Army. After the war he moved to Guthrie, Oklahoma, and purchased a 100-acre farm. He joined the Baptist church. He stayed in Guthrie for many years, but in the 1890s moved to Kansas City, Missouri, and became a hotel cook. He also met and married Lovey Yates Higgins. Soon returning to the Guthrie farm, he had a vision that became the basis of a new church movement.

The vision, which occurred in 1893, began with a group of tables covered with filth. Each table was labeled with the name of a different church. Then a white table, the Church of God and Saints of Christ,

appeared. Subsequently, Crowdy was given the rules and guidelines, the "7 Keys," of what he took to be instructions to found a new movement, the true church.

About 1895 he went on his first preaching tour, to Texas followed the next year by a trip to Chicago. While in Chicago he was inspired to formally organize his church. He moved to Lawrence, Kansas, and there on November 8, 1896, he formed the Church of God and Saints of Christ. Within two years there were 29 congregations in Kansas and surrounding states. He returned to Chicago to launch the church in Illinois and slowly worked his way east.

During these years Crowdy delivered a number of sermons which were published and which have set the belief and practice of the group. He tried to synthesize Judaism and Christianity. He adopted the practice of observing Passover and other Jewish holidays and worship on the Sabbath. He taught that Black people were the ten lost tribes of Israel. He retained the practice of foot washing from his Baptist heritage.

In 1900 he moved to Philadelphia, where over a period of several years he built a congregation of 1,500 members. The Passover was first observed in Philadelphia. He established a printing press and began a periodical, the *Weekly Prophet.* He also married again, to Saint Hallie Brown, the assistant grand secretary. He later came to denounce the practice of remarriage and subsequently left his second wife and returned to his first one. In 1903, a smallpox epidemic broke out in Philadelphia, and at the urging of his followers, Crowdy moved to Washington, D.C.

During his Washington years, he appointed his nephew Joseph Wesley Crowdy, Calvin S. Skinner, and William Henry Plummer as his successors. In 1907 while in Newark, New Jersey, Crowdy suffered a stroke. He never recovered his health and died the following year in Washington, D.C.

Crowdy did not finish the development of the church which has in the years since his death moved toward the further incorporation of Jewish beliefs and practices as originally advocated by Crowdy.

Crowdy, William Saunders. *The Bible Gospel Told: The Revelation of God Revealed.* Washington, DC: Church of God and Saints of Christ, 1902.

———. *The Bible Story Revealed.* Belleville, VA: Church of God and Saints of Christ, 1902.

Walker, Beersheba Crowdy. *The Life and Works of William Saunders Crowdy.* Philadelphia: Elfreth Walker, 1955. 62 pp.

Wynia-Trey, Elly. *The Church of God and Saints of Christ: A Black Judeo-Christian Movement Founded in Lawrence,*

Kansas in 1896. Lawrence, KS: University of Kansas, A. B. Honors Thesis, 1988. 150 pp.

CRUMMELL, ALEXANDER (March 3, 1819–September 12, 1898), a priest and educator in the Episcopal Church, was born in New York City to Boston Crummell, of royal African heritage, and a mother whose ancestors had long been free Blacks in America. He attended the African Free School on Mulberry Street in Manhattan, and from 1831 to 1835 was at the Canal Street High School. At that point he and some friends went to Canaan, New Hampshire, to attend a new interracial school, but within a few months the townspeople destroyed the buildings and drove away the students and faculty. From 1836 to 1839 Crummell attended the Oneida Institute in Whitesboro, New York.

Crummell decided to seek ordination in the Episcopal Church, and in 1839 applied to General Theological Seminary in New York City, but was rejected for his color. He instead studied privately with several leading priests in Boston and Providence. He was prominent in anti-slavery activities and the Negro Convention Movement. In 1840 he drafted the petition to the New York state legislature to remove restrictions on the Black vote. In 1842 he was ordained a deacon by Bishop Griswold of Massachusetts, and in 1844 he was ordained a priest by Bishop Lee of Delaware.

The only position he could find in the church was in New York, organizing a new congregation of poor Blacks. Thwarted in his attempts to raise money for this church, he was encouraged to try fundraising in England. He did so from 1848 to 1853, where he traveled widely, preaching and lecturing. Sponsors enabled him to study in Queen's College, Cambridge, from which he graduated in 1853. He raised money for the New York church, but never returned there himself, as a physician had advised him to seek a warm climate. Instead he went to Liberia, Africa, as an Episcopal missionary.

Crummell devoted himself to Liberia, becoming a citizen and establishing many churches. About this time he got married. In 1858 he became principal of the Mount Vaughn High School at Cape Palmas, and in 1861 moved to the faculty of Liberia College at Monrovia. Over the years he made several visits to the United States through the American Colonization Society to promote Black emigration and investment in Liberia. During this time he published *The Relations and Duties of Free Colored Men in America to Africa* (1861) and *The Future of Africa* (1862). In 1866 differences with the administration led to his dismissal from Liberia College, and he began to form his own school. Soon, however, political unrest placed his life and that of his son in jeopardy, and in 1872 he left for the United States.

Settled in Washington, D.C., Crummell founded St. Luke's Episcopal Church. As the senior Black priest in the Episcopal Church, he led the movement for increased recognition and participation of Blacks in the church, particularly in the upper levels. In 1883 he founded the **Conference of Church Workers Among Colored People**. His first wife having died in the 1870s, he married Jennie M. Simpson on September 28, 1880. He retired from the church in 1894, and in that year published his autobiography, *Alexander Crummell, 1844–1894: The Shades and Lights of a Fifty Years' Ministry*. He taught at Howard University from 1895 to 1897, where he emphasized his belief that it was the responsibility of educated Blacks to raise up their people. His last major accomplishment was the 1897 founding of the American Negro Academy in Washington, D.C., as a forum where an elite group of forty scholars could support each other's efforts as leaders in the Black community.

Akpan, M.B. "Alexander Crummell and His African 'Race-Work': An Assessment of His Contributions in Liberia to Africa's 'Redemption,' 1853–1873." *Historical Magazine of the Protestant Episcopal Church* XLV (March 1976): 177–199.

Crummell, Alexander. *Alexander Crummell, 1844–1894: The Shades and Lights of a Fifty Years' Ministry.* St. Luke's Church, Washington, D.C.: R. L. Pendleton, Printer, 1894. 31 pp.

———. *Africa and America: Addresses and Discourses.* Springfield, Massachusetts: Wiley & Co., 1891. 466 pp.

———. *The Future of Africa.* New York: Charles Scribner, 1862. 354 pp.

———. *The Greatness of Christ and Other Sermons.* New York: Thomas Whittaker, 1882. 352 pp.

———. *The Relations and Duties of Free Colored Men in America to Africa.* Hartford, CT: Lockwood & Co., 1861. 54 pp.

DuBois, W. E. B. *The Souls of Black Folk.* Chicago: A. C. McClurg & Co., 1903. 264 pp.

Moses, Wilson Jeremiah. *Alexander Crummell: A Study of Civilization and Discontent.* New York: Oxford University Press, 1989. 380 pp.

Oldfield, John R. *Alexander Crummell (1819–1898) and the Creation of an African-American Church in Liberia.* Lewiston, NY: Edwin Mellon Press, 1990. 165 pp.

Rigsby, Gregory U. *Alexander Crummell: A Pioneer in Nineteenth-Century Pan-African Thought.* New York: Greenwood Press, 1987. 231 pp.

Scruggs, Otey M. *We the Children of Africa in This Land: Alexander Crummell*. Washington, D.C.: Department of History, Howard University, 1972. 25 pp.

MM, EBA, DANB, SBAA, DARB, DNAADB, DAA, AAB, ACAB (supp. 7), HNC, RLOA, BNA, NBH, NG, MBRL, GNPP, BRBR, NAH, NEA, SOTT, NYB (1925–26), BGWC, BWA.

CUFFE, PAUL (January 17, 1759–September 7, 1817), Society of **Friends (Quakers)** leader, sea captain, entrepreneur, and Pan-Africanist, was born in Cuttyhunk, near New Bedford, Massachusetts. He was the seventh of ten children in the family of Cuffe Slocum, a former slave who had purchased his freedom, and Ruth Moses, an Indian woman. Both parents were Quakers, though they were not allowed to be formal members. His father passed away in 1772 and soon Cuffe was on his own as a sailor on a whaling boat. Cuffe and most of his siblings eventually adopted their father's given name as the family surname.

During the War of Independence Cuffe was a maritime trader and blockade runner, a dangerous endeavor in which he several times lost everything to pirates. In 1780 Cuffe and a brother, John, protested the fact that they and other Blacks were taxed on the family property without the right to vote or be otherwise represented, an issue that the colonists were fighting about in relationship to the British authorities. Cuffe was briefly imprisoned for nonpayment of back taxes, but a compromise was worked out, and the tax issue was temporarily settled. The arguments raised by Cuffe helped lead to the 1783 Massachusetts law by which Blacks finally gained legal rights and privileges. On February 25, 1783, Cuffe married Alice Pequit, a local Indian woman from his mother's Wampanoag tribe.

Cuffe's business enterprises were guided by the Quaker attention to frugality, zeal, and honesty, and he prospered with a series of small sailing vessels. In 1787 he became part-owner with brother-in-law Michael Wainer of a twenty-five-ton schooner named *Sunfish*, his first whaling-sized ship. In 1795 he launched the sixty-nine-ton *Ranger*, and embarked on a daring port-of-call to Vienna, Maryland, in slave territory where free Blacks were always in danger. In the port the sight of a Black captain and an all-Black crew raised much excitement, and some sought to have the captain seized. Cuffe's credentials, however, were so impeccable that the authorities had no choice but to do business with him, and the fears of his presence subsided. He left the port with a full load of $1,000 worth of Indian corn, and paved the way for future dealings in the South. By 1800 Cuffe had landholdings of some 200 acres, a gristmill,

and total assets of $10,000. At this time he was the most successful Black entrepreneur in America.

In the mid-1790s Cuffe built a school on his property and hired a teacher, primarily for the benefit of the fifteen children in his extended family, but he opened the enrollment to any others who wished to come, making it one of the first integrated schools in the country. In 1806 he dedicated his largest ship yet, the 268–ton *Alpha*, which traded goods as far away as Scandinavia. In January 1808, President Jefferson's Embargo Act forbade international maritime trade and required whalers to post double bonds. In March 1808, Cuffe formally joined the Westport (Massachusetts) Meeting of Friends. Until the maritime embargo was lifted in June, 1809, Cuffe had the opportunity to consider the advantages of a shipping concern based in the British colony of Sierra Leone, West Africa, which at the same time would enable a Christian mission to the African natives and support to those African-Americans who wished to emigrate to Africa. A renewal of the embargo solidified these plans. In 1810 Cuffe was a delegate to the New England Yearly Meeting in Newport, the first Black delegate to any Yearly Meeting of Quakers.

On December 27, 1810, Cuffe sailed from Philadelphia for Sierra Leone to see firsthand what the business and philanthropic prospects were. He arrived on March 1, 1811, and after an initially poor impression began to warm to the possibilities of a triangular African trade involving Sierra Leone, the United States, and England. In July 1811, he went to England to meet with authorities there, and made a deep impression on the general public as the formidable Black captain of trade. He returned to Sierra Leone in November. He founded the Friendly Society of Sierra Leone, basically a Black cooperative trading society that encouraged Quaker virtues of temperance and frugality. Cuffe returned to the United States in April 1812, but deteriorating Anglo-American relations led to the seizure of his ship and cargo. With the support of many prominent people he met with President James Madison and was able to settle the matter.

The War of 1812 provided another obstacle to Cuffe's plans, and he managed to have a bill presented in Congress to enable him to carry on trade with and emigration to Sierra Leone despite the present circumstances. After much discussion the bill lost by seven votes. The war finally ended with the Treaty of Ghent on December 24, 1814, and plans were once again set in motion. Cuffe captained the seventy-foot brig *Traveller*, which left for Sierra Leone on December 8, 1815, filled with cargo and thirty-eight emigrants.

This was the first Black-initiated emigration movement from the United States. Once in Sierra Leone, Cuffe's reception by the governor was not altogether hospitable, but he succeeded in settling the emigrants and providing much encouragement and support to other residents with whom he already had relationships.

Cuffe returned to the United States in the spring of 1816, having lost about $8,000 on the trip, thanks to the lack of a British trading license and the absence of sufficient philanthropic support. In New York he named several New York ships and captains still involved in the slave trade, an action which led to the stifling of that activity and praise of Cuffe's character. Feeling that perhaps only in Africa could Blacks "rise to be a people," Cuffe continued to try to provide means of emigration to those who desired it, He was, however, unimpressed by the new **American Colonization Society**, which purported to pursue that very goal, but catered to racist motives. Cuffe was pained that the American Colonization Society took to using his name and reputation to advance its divisive goals, but thought that if that society offered any benefit whatever to the African cause, such benefit would outweigh any other consideration. He passed away before Liberia, a new African nation wrought by Black Americans, became a reality.

Atkin, Mary Gage. *Paul Cuffe and the African Promised Land*. Nashville, TN: Thomas Nelson, 1977. 160 pp.

Harris, Sheldon H. *Paul Cuffe: Black America and the Africa Return*. New York: Simon and Schuster, 1972. 288 pp.

Ives, Kenneth, ed. *Black Quakers: Brief Biographies*. Chicago: Progresiv Publishr, 1991. 155 pp.

Loomis, Sally. "The Evolution of Paul Cuffe's Black Nationalism." *Negro History Bulletin* 37 (October/November 1974): 298–302.

Salvador, George Arnold. *Paul Cuffe, the Black Yankee, 1759–1817*. Reynolds-De Walt Printing, 1969. 76 pp.

Thomas, Lamont D. "Memoirs of an African Captain." *Negro History Bulletin* 43 (January 1980): 11–12.

————. *Rise to be a People*. Urbana: University of Illinois Press, 1986. 187 pp.

WWWA (H), *AAE, GNPP, EBA, DANB, DAB, EAB, HNB, MM, NBH, IBAW*.

CUMBERLAND PRESBYTERIAN CHURCH OF AMERICA.

A Presbyterian church. Known until the summer of 1992 as the Second Cumberland Presbyterian Church in U.S., the Cumberland Presbyterian Church of America was formed in 1874 but the story of the church begins with the founding of the Cumberland Presbyterian Church in the early nineteenth century. As the church grew and spread, not only did White converts bring their slaves into the orb of the church, but a slave mission, similar to that of the Methodist Episcopal Church was established. As a result, by the time of the Civil War, some 20,000 Black people were Church members.

After the war, both Black and White leaders began to debate the future of the Freedmen in the Church. Almost immediately, the Church accelerated the education of Black ministers. Then, in October 1868 a convention of Black members became the occasion for Black ministers to discuss the possibility of a separate Black organization. Rev. Moses Weir, the leading spokesperson for the Black members and later a missionary to Liberia, raised the issue of establishing a separate church at the 1869 general assembly of the Cumberland Presbyterian Church. He argued that Black Cumberland Presbyterians could minister and evangelize the Freedmen as a separate organization and that the White church could help with financial assistance and further educational efforts. The assembly responded by passing legislation looking toward such a separate church.

The new church formed in stages. Beginning in 1871, all-Black synods began to be organized in Tennessee, Kentucky and Texas. Then in 1874, representatives from the synods met in Nashville, Tennessee, for the first general assembly of what was originally called the Colored Cumberland Presbyterian Church. Of the 20,000 members in 1860, approximately 3,000 remained.

The Church continues the Armenian theological perspective of the parent body and adopted a modified Westminster Confession of Faith which recognized free will's role in human salvation (over against a hard predestinarian position of traditional Presbyterianism). In 1984 the church completed a revision of its Confession of Faith. The church's highest judicatory is the general assembly. The church is divided into four synods, 15 presbyteries, and 153 congregations. There are approximately 15,000 members, the greatest concentration being in North Alabama and East Tennessee.

Campbell, Thomas H. *Good News on the Frontier*. Memphis, TN: Frontier Press, 1965.

CUMMINGS, FRANK CURTIS

(b. April 4, 1929), 95th bishop of the **African Methodist Episcopal Church** (AME), was born in Minter, Alabama, the Edmond and Annie (Moultrie) Cummings. He received his B.A. in 1949 from Daniel Payne College in

Birmingham, Alabama, and his B.D. in 1952 from Seattle Pacific College. On March 5, 1954, he married Martha Coleen Colly, with whom he had one daughter.

His first pastorate was in Alridge, Alabama (1948–49), followed by Bremerton, Washington (1952–53); Santa Barbara, California (1954–60); and St. Louis, Missouri (1960–68). In 1968 he was elected secretary-treasurer of the Church Extension Department of the AME Church, a position he held for the next eight years. During this time he created an insurance program for the churches and properties of the denomination worldwide. From 1965 to 1971 he was also vice-chair of the St. Louis Civil Service Commission. In 1976 Cummings was elected bishop. His first assignment was to the Eighth Episcopal District (covering Louisiana and Mississippi). More recently he moved to the First Episcopal District, with headquarters in Philadelphia, Pennsylvania.

He is founder and president of Allen Travel Service, based in Washington, D.C., and is president of the board of directors of West End Hospital Association. He has spearheaded a $10 million capital campaign to build an Episcopal District headquarters building in Philadelphia. In 1987 he published *The First Episcopal District's Historical Review of 200 Years of African Methodism*, a significant work covering the lives of many bishops and numerous programs and institutions of the AME Church.

Cummings, Frank C., John H. Dixon, Henry A. Wynn, Thelma M. Singleton-Scott, and Patricia A. P. Green. *The First Episcopal District's Historical Review of 200 Years of African Methodism*. Philadelphia, PA: First Episcopal District, African Methodist Episcopal Church, 1987. 512 pp. *WWA* (90–91), *WWR* (85).

CUMMINGS, JAMES L. (December 2, 1926–October 3, 1982), 40th bishop of the **Christian Methodist Episcopal Church** (CME), was born in Allenville, Kentucky, the son of Andrew and Fannie (Robbie) Cummings. He experienced conversion at the age of nine in Madisonville, Kentucky, where he attended primary school. The family later moved to Indianapolis, Indiana, where he graduated from Crispus Attucks High School. He received his B.A. from Lane College in Jackson, Tennessee, in 1948, and then attended Indiana University Law School, but left upon considering a call to the ministry. He married Barbara Jean Patton in 1950, with whom he had one daughter.

His first church assignment was at Northside CME Church in Indianapolis, from 1951 to 1953. This was followed by Christ CME Church in Norfolk, Virginia,

from 1953 to 1954, and Trinity CME Church in Indianapolis from 1954 to 1966. While at Trinity he enrolled in Christian Theological Seminary at Butler University, Indianapolis, Indiana, receiving his M.Div. in 1959. He served on the Indianapolis City Council from 1963 to 1969 and was on the city's Zoning Board from 1960 to 1963. His first wife died, and in 1956 he married Norma Jeannette Cravens; there were no further children. In 1959 he was cited in *Ebony* magazine as the first black minister in America to institute a church-sponsored Dial-A-Prayer. He served a term as president of the Indianapolis Ministerial Association. He built a new church building and purchased a parsonage.

In 1966 he was assigned to the historic Lane Tabernacle CME Church in St. Louis, Missouri, where he stayed for the next twelve years, long enough to burn the church mortgage. He served on the Eden Seminary Board of Directors beginning in 1969 and was the fraternal delegate to the 1976 **African Methodist Episcopal Church** General Conference. In 1970 he was elected to the St. Louis Board of Education, and was Board President in 1975–76. He was part of the East-West Gateway Coordinating Council from 1969 to 1973.

At the May 1978 General Conference he was elected bishop on the second ballot and assigned to the Second Episcopal District, at that time composed of the Ohio, Kentucky, Nigeria, and Ghana Conferences. In 1979, after the death of Bishop **Norris Curry**, he was assigned to the Ninth Episcopal District (seven western states), which he was serving at his death. In November, 1981, he was elected First Vice President of the National Council of Churches (N.C.C.) by its Governing Board, meeting in Cleveland, Ohio. With seventeen other N.C.C. representatives he travelled to the People's Republic of China at the invitation of the China Christian Council and the Protestant Three-Self Patriotic Movement. He was committed to the goal of the union of the A.M.E., A.M.E. Zion, and C.M.E. Churches. A heart attack at age fifty-five cut short his bright career.

"Bishop J. L. Cummings Is Dead At Age 55." *Star of Zion* 106 (October 21, 1982): 1.

"Bishop James L. Cummings Dies October 3 at Age 55." *Christian Index* 115 (October 15, 1982): 3–4.

"Bishop James L. Cummings: The Obituary." *Christian Index* 115 (October 15, 1982): 10.

"Our 40th Bishop—James L. Cummings." *Christian Index* 111 (May 11, 1978): 7.

Satterwhite, John H. "Bishop James L. Cummings: In Memoriam." *A.M.E. Zion Quarterly Review* 94 (January 1983): 49.

BDNM (75), *WWABA* (80–81).

CURRY, GEORGE EDWARD (1899–November, 1951), 60th bishop of the **African Methodist Episcopal Church** (AME), was born in Edgefield, South Carolina, the son of Andrew and Louise (Williams) Curry. He attended the public schools in Groverton, Georgia, and experienced conversion as a young man in Ward AME Church in Augusta, Georgia. He served in most of the offices available in the local church, including choir director and president of the A.C.E. League. He married in 1919; there were no children. He entered the building trade and was the designer/builder of the B. F. Lee Theological Seminary building in 1925. He lost a hand in an accident, but moved into the contracting part of the trade.

After becoming quite wealthy as a builder, Curry decided to enter the ministry. He attended Turner Theological Seminary at Morris Brown College in Atlanta, Georgia, and received his B.D. from B. F. Lee Theological Seminary at Edward Waters College in Jacksonville, Florida. He served a number of churches in Florida and was presiding elder for a time. He continued to use his building knowledge as superintendent of the facilities and grounds and as treasurer of Edward Waters College. In 1937 Curry was made manager of the A.M.E. Book Concern in Philadelphia, Pennsylvania, and in 1939 personally purchased the $110,000 mortgage on the Book Concern property.

At the 1940 General Conference his report on the Book Concern was attacked as false on thirteen points, but he was exonerated and elected bishop. He was assigned to West Africa, but refused to go. Bishop **Edward J. Howard** died in 1941 and afterward Curry was assigned to replace him in the Twelfth Episcopal District (Arkansas and Oklahoma). He made much of his wealth and openly claimed that he had "bought the bishopric." At some point he lost his wife in a fire which destroyed his home. In 1945 he was suspended on the charge of mishandling funds. The Council of Bishops in June, 1946, found him guilty but restored his position. A special called session of the General Conference in November, 1946, tried him again, found him guilty, and expelled him. He did not contest the decision, later rejoined the church, and tried to run a recreation park in Jacksonville, Florida. He suffered a number of reverses, however, and died in relative poverty.

EWM, HAMEC, AMSC, BAMEC.

CURRY, NORRIS SAMUEL (August 16, 1910–May 7, 1979), 31st bishop of the **Christian Methodist Episcopal Church** (CME), was born in Naples, Morse County, Texas, the son of Lonnie and Fannie (Hervey) Curry. His pastoral ministry began in 1928 in the East Texas Conference, later moving to the Central Texas Conference. In June 1933, he married Mary Cleopatra Reynolds, with whom he had two children. He attended Wiley College before graduating with his B.A. from Texas College in Tyler, Texas, in 1942. In 1944 he transferred to the New Jersey Conference, staying until 1949, except for the year 1947, when he was a teacher at Texas College. In 1949 he moved to Los Angeles, California, to pastor the prestigious Phillips Temple CME Church. During his nine years at Phillips a $210,000 building campaign was conducted, the church mortgage was burned, the educational building was built, and a new parking lot dedicated.

At the General Conference in May 1958, Curry was elected editor of the *Christian Index*, the denomination's newspaper. While editor he organized the Allen Temple CME Church in Compton, California, in 1961, which was later renamed in his honor. He was elected bishop on May 17, 1962, and assigned to the Fourth Episcopal District (Louisiana and Mississippi). In 1966 he was assigned to the Eighth Episcopal District (Texas), making his residence in Dallas, Texas. He became chair of the Texas College Board of Trust, and was instrumental in helping that college through a period of construction and transition, culminating with accreditation by the Southern Association of Secondary Schools and Colleges about 1969. In 1974 he was assigned to the Ninth Episcopal District (seven western states), which he was serving at his death. He was a trustee at several colleges and chair of the General Board of Lay Activities. In this latter position he wrote *The Laymen's Manual, CME Church*. His other writings include "Evangelistic Understanding of Spirit, Law, and Discipline in the Methodist Way," and "The Methodist Preacher: Prophet, Priest, and Pastor."

Curry gained an international reputation through his activities in ecumenical bodies, beginning as a delegate to the World Methodist Council in 1951 in Oxford, England. When Wesley's Chapel in London, England, was in danger of being demolished, Curry was a leader in the United States fundraising. He was a delegate to various National Council of Churches and World Council of Churches gatherings. At the 13th World Methodist Conference in Dublin, Ireland, in 1976, he was elected president of the World Methodist Council, the highest position available in international Methodism. On November 2, 1978, he was a featured speaker in Wesley's Chapel and the following day was a dinner guest of the Speaker of the British House of Commons.

"Bishop Norris Samuel Curry: The Obituary." *Christian Index* 112 (May 24, 1979): 6.

"The Death of Bishop Curry: 'He Fell But Knew No Fear!'" *Christian Index* 112 (May 10, 1979): 9.

Savage, Horace C. "Bishop Norris Curry: As I Knew Him." *Christian Index* 112 (May 24, 1979): 8.

AARS, HUBA, BDNM (75), *EWM, WWABA* (80–81), *EBA, CMECTY.*

"There are thousands who call me God—millions of them—there are millions of people who call me the devil, but I produce God and shake the earth with it."

"I teach that God has the right to manifest Himself through any person or thing He may choose. If my followers, however, believe that I am God and in so doing they are led to reform their lives and experience joy and happiness, why should I prevent them from doing so?"

Father Major J. Divine, Founder
Peace Mission Movement

D

DANIEL PAYNE COLLEGE. An **African Methodist Episcopal Church** (AME) school. Daniel Payne College, Birmingham, Alabama, was founded as Payne University in Selma, Alabama in 1889 by the several annual conferences in the state. The enthusiastic support of Brown Chapel AME Church, whose members helped construct the original building, assisted the school to open quickly once the financial support was secured. It was named for **Daniel A. Payne**, a prominent AME bishop. Through the remaining years of the nineteenth century, it operated out of a single building and served commuting students only, as there were no dorm facilities. Such facilities were opened soon after the turn of the century and for the next two decades the school experienced steady growth.

In 1912 newly elected Bishop **Joshua H. Jones** was assigned to Alabama and under his strong influence the department of theology was reorganized, and the training of ministers became a central focus of the school. The school was moved to a new campus in Birmingham, Alabama, in 1923. The school prospered through the 1920s, but was forced to close for two years (1930–32) due to the Depression.

In 1940, Bishop **D. Ward Nichols** was assigned to Alabama. He took an immediate interest in the welfare of the college. He led in the move to change its name from Payne University to Daniel Payne College, a designation more descriptive of its work. He worked to rid the school of a large debt that had been accumulated since its reopening and encouraged the expansion of both faculty and student body, and the construction of new facilities. His efforts led to full accreditation by the state of Alabama and placed the school in a position to join the first group of Black schools accredited by the Southern Association of Colleges in 1957.

Payne's campus was located adjacent to the Birmingham Airport. In more recent years the expansion of the airport facilities forced the movement of the entire campus to a new location in another part of the city.

Gregg, Howard D. *History of the African Methodist Episcopal Church: The Black Church in Action.* Nashville, TN: African Methodist Episcopal Sunday School Union, 1980. 524 pp.

Smith, Charles Spencer. *A History of the African Methodist Episcopal Church.* Philadelphia, PA: Book Concern of the AME Church, 1922. 570 pp

Wright, R. R. *The Encyclopedia of the African Methodist Episcopal Church.* Philadelphia, PA: Book Concern of the AME Church, 1947. 688 pp.

DAUGHTRY, HERBERT DANIEL (b. January 13, 1931), the national presiding minister of the House of the Lord Church, a predominantly Black Pentecostal denomination, was born in Savannah, Georgia, the son of Alonzo Austin Daughtry who in 1903 had left the ministry of the **United House of Prayer for All People** (led by **C. M. "Sweet Daddy" Grace**) to found the House of the Lord Church. Daughtry's childhood was spent in Georgia, but in 1942 the family moved to New York where congregations were begun in Harlem and in Brooklyn. He married Karen Smith. In 1952 the elder Daughtry died and, following eight years when the church was led by Mother Inez Conroy, Daughtry assumed the position of national presiding minister.

As the church's leader, Daughtry immediately became involved in community affairs. During the 1960s he worked with the Congress of Racial Equality and Operation Breadbasket in the struggle for community control of schools. In 1969 he became the chairman of Ministers Against Narcotics. In 1977 he helped create the Coalition of Concerned Leaders and Citizens to Save Our Youth and was the founder of the Commission on African Solidarity.

Daughtry has been a leader among Pentecostals at the international level. As early as 1969 he participated in the U.S. Conference of the World Council of Churches (held at Bush Hill Falls, Pennsylvania) and began three years' work with the council's Commission on World Mission and Evangelism on the quadrennial theme of "Salvation Today."

During the 1980s Daughtry expanded his leadership internationally. In 1980 he helped form the National Black United Front. He participated in the International Conference on Sanctions Against South Africa. His travels took him to a number of key tension spots around the globe, including Northern Ireland, Cuba, and East Germany. In the meantime he has overseen the growth of the House of the Lord Church which has become a national denomination.

Burgess, Stanley M., and Gary B. McGee, eds. *Dictionary of Pentecostal and Charismatic Movements*. Grand Rapids, MI: Zondervan Publishing House, 1988. 914 pp.

Daughtry, Herbert. *The House of the Lord Pentecostal Church: Official Orientation Material*. Brooklyn, NY: House of the Lord, n.d.

DAVAGE, MATTHEW SIMPSON (July 16, 1879–1976), Methodist Episcopal Church educator, was born in Shreveport, Louisiana, the son of Samuel and Harriett (Lee) Davage. After attending the public schools in Shreveport he went to New Orleans University (now Dillard University), graduating with a B.A. in 1900 and an M.A. in 1907. On August 10, 1904, he married Alice Vera Armstead.

He was for a number of years business manager of the Methodist Episcopal periodical *Southwestern Christian Advocate*, based in New Orleans, Louisiana. He then began a remarkable career as president of a number of colleges. He was the first Black president of Rust College in Holly Springs, Mississippi, holding that position from 1920 to 1924. From 1924 to 1941 Davage was president of Clark University in Atlanta, Georgia, an historically Black school founded by the Methodist Episcopal Church in 1867. Davage was its second Black president. Beginning about 1944 he was president of Samuel Huston College (Methodist) in Austin, Texas, and when it merged with Tillotson College (Congregationalist) in 1952, he was named the first president of the combined institution (Huston-Tillotson College) by unanimous vote. He was president of Huston-Tillotson from 1952 to 1955.

Davage was a well-known figure in national and international Methodist circles. He was treasurer of the Ecumenical Methodist Council, Western Section, for two quadrennia and was a delegate to the World Methodist Ecumenical Conferences of 1931, 1947, and 1951. He was treasurer of the Gulfside Advance Assembly Movement and chair of the Committee on Rules and the Committee on Expense and Agenda of the Central Jurisdiction (the all-Black Methodist structure that existed from 1939 to 1968). He was a member of the Commission on Church Union and was a part of the 1939 Uniting Conference which merged the Methodist Episcopal Church, the Methodist Episcopal Church, South, and the Methodist Protestant Church to form the Methodist Church.

Davage was one of the senior members of the Methodist Board of Publication and a member of the Administrative Board of the Commission on Christian Higher Education of the Association of American Colleges. He was a delegate to eleven General Conferences. After retirement he and his wife lived on the campus of Dillard University in New Orleans.

WWCR, EWM, WWAM.

DAVIS, MONROE HORTENSIUS (c.1886–February 9, 1953), 53rd bishop of the **African Methodist Episcopal Church** (AME), was born in Marion, South Carolina, the son of Monroe and Judith (Franklin) Davis. He attended Allen University in Columbia, South Carolina, and it was about that time that he was ordained deacon (1905) and then elder (1906). He received his B.D. from Drew University in Madison, New Jersey, and his B.A. from Howard University in Washington, D.C. On September 29, 1910, he married Catherine Beckett, with whom he had two children.

His pastorates included Wayman AME Church in Winnsboro, South Carolina; Bethel AME Church in Madison, New Jersey; Campbell AME Church in Washington, D.C.; Allen AME Church in Washington, D.C.; and St. John AME Church in Baltimore, Maryland. He was elected bishop in 1928 and assigned to West Africa. In 1931 he was assigned to the Second Episcopal District. For a number of years he was secretary of the Council of Bishops. He has been described as a persuasive preacher, kind to his friends, and a "terror" to his opponents.

About 1945 he was tried by a committee in Richmond, Virginia, on charges of malfeasance and misappropriation of funds. He was found guilty and suspended until the meeting of the Virginia Annual Conference, when his case was reviewed and he was restored. Further charges were then brought and he was tried again at a special session of the General Conference in November, 1946, at Little Rock, Arkansas. He was suspended again until the regular meeting of the General Conference in May, 1948. At that time he was put on the inactive list of bishops with no assignment, but at full salary. He was retired in 1952 and passed away a year later.

Davis, Monroe H. *The Dogmas and Precepts of the Fathers.* Nashville, TN: AME Sunday School Union, 1948. 107 pp. *AARS, HUBA, RLA, AMSC, HAMEC, EWM, BAMEC.*

DAVIS, NOAH (March, 1804–1866), Civil War era Baptist minister in Baltimore, Maryland, was born into slavery in Madison County, Virginia, the son of John and Jane Davis. They lived on the estate of Robert Patten, and John Davis was the head miller of Patten's grain mill, a responsible and respected position. Patten ran into financial difficulty, however, and had to sell the mill. John Davis lost his position, but gained his freedom in compensation, though the rest of the family still belonged to Patten. He allowed the family to move to Culpepper County about 1816, where they began farming. Noah Davis became an apprentice carpenter.

In 1818, at the age of fourteen, Davis went to Fredericksburg and apprenticed with boot and shoemaker Thomas Wright. During the following years he gained a passion for alcohol and other unfortunate habits from his fellow apprentices, but remained a trustworthy employee and learned to read and write. He spent time reading the Bible and began to contemplate his spiritual life. Finally he experienced conversion and was baptized into the Fredericksburg Baptist Church on September 19, 1831. In the church he met and married his wife, also a slave. Soon he was elected a deacon of the church and felt a call to the ministry. He was licensed to preach, but knew he needed more education and that meant freedom. Patten agreed to sell him his freedom for $500, and also agreed to let Davis travel to obtain the money. In June 1845, Davis left on a four-month trip that would take him through Philadelphia, New York, and Boston, but was still short by $200.

Soon, however, the **Southern Baptist Convention** offered to pay the remainder if he took a new position as missionary among the Blacks of Baltimore. Rev. Moses Clayton, a former slave, had founded the First Colored People's Baptist Church in 1836, and the plan was to capitalize on this beginning. Davis agreed to the position, although it meant he had to leave his wife and seven children, all still in slavery. He arrived in Baltimore in 1847 and was ordained for the work. He worked steadily under trying circumstances, teaching a Sunday School in his boarding house room. With the help of friends, on November 5, 1851, he purchased the freedom of his wife and two children for $600 and a bond for at least $200 more. To pay the rest of the bond he hired out one of his daughters as a domestic for $300

in advance, and insured his own life for $500. By the end of 1851 he had a grand total of fifteen members in his mission. There is no record of any attempt to stop Davis from preaching.

With the help of the Maryland Baptist Union, the Saratoga Street African Baptist Church was built and then dedicated on February 18, 1855. By that time the membership had grown to thirty. The church soon opened a day school, which at one time counted over one hundred students. He again traveled to various points in the Northeast to raise money to purchase the rest of his family, and in 1859 published his autobiography, *A Narrative of the Life of Rev. Noah Davis, a Colored Man*, to raise more money for this purpose. He apparently was successful. The church reached a high point in about 1857, when it reported seventy-one members, but in 1860 the Southern Baptist Convention withdrew its support, and the Civil War redirected most other monies. Davis became very ill, but kept the church going for six more years. Finally, the mortgage was foreclosed and the building sold. On his deathbed, Davis instructed the congregation to transfer to the Union Baptist Church, which they did. Davis is remembered as one of a large class of Black leaders whose accomplishments were not so exceptional as to gain them the fame others enjoyed, but whose work was heroic and meaningful nonetheless.

Davis, Noah. *A Narrative of the Life of Rev. Noah Davis, a Colored Man.* Baltimore, MD: J. F. Weishampel, 1859. 86 pp. *HBB, CH, BAW, AARS, BAHA.*

DAY, WILLIAM HOWARD (October 19, 1825– December 3, 1900), educator and general secretary of the **African Methodist Episcopal Zion Church** (AMEZ), was born in New York City, the son of John and Eliza (Dixon) Day. His primary education was in the private school of Rev. Frederick Jones, and then he attended the public high school in Northampton, Massachusetts. In high school he learned the printing trade working in the office of the *Northampton Gazette*. In 1842 he was examined in Latin and Greek by the Rev. Beriah Green, president of Whitestown Institute in New York, which allowed him to go to Oberlin College in Ohio, where he again passed a stiff entrance examination in Latin, Greek, and algebra. He supported himself through college as a printer, and graduated with his B.A. in 1947, the only Black in a class of fifty.

Upon graduation he moved to Cleveland where he was employed as a printer and worked politically to repeal Ohio's Black Laws. He was elected secretary of the National Convention of Colored Freemen at the Cleveland convention of 1848, and in 1853 was elected a vice-president with Frederick Douglass. In 1850 the state Convention of Colored Freemen sent him to plead their case before the state constitutional convention, and the Black Laws were repealed. He joined the *Cleveland Daily True Democrat* (later called the *Leader*) in 1851 as compositor, becoming mailing clerk and local editor in 1852. In 1853 he became editor of the *Aliened American* (later called the *People's Exposition*), a paper established at the insistence of several state conventions of freemen. In 1852 he called together the Black veterans of the War of 1812, who were publicly honored for the first time. In 1854 Day was appointed librarian of the Cleveland Library Association, the forerunner of the public library system.

In 1856 he moved to Canada and began teaching among the 50,000 Black Americans who had moved there. The next year he was elected professor of language by two colleges. He continued to work as a printer as well, and published John Brown's constitution for the new United States, in case his Harper's Ferry raid (1859) were to be successful. Being in possession of the document indicates that Day may have had some connection with Brown's conspiracy, but he remained free by his staying in Canada. In 1858 he was elected president of the National Board of Commissioners of Colored People of Canada and the United States. In 1859, at the invitation of Rev. William King of Canada, he went to England, Ireland, and Scotland to raise money to build a church and four schoolhouses in the Elgin settlement at Buxton, Canada. King and Day together raised 7,000 British pounds ($35,000 at that time) for this purpose. While in England he was called as a preacher, and spent the better part of three years there serving a congregation. In 1862 he was offered the Latin tutorship at Lincoln, England.

A meeting in England with African American explorer Martin R. Delany and Professor Campbell of the Institute for Colored Youth in Philadelphia resulted in the founding of the African Aid Society, which operated well into the twentieth century. While in England, Day was also a popular lecturer on the issues of the Civil War, and was hosted by a number of government leaders.

Upon his return to the United States about 1865 he worked with the Freedman's Aid Association and became an inspector-general of schools for refugees and freedmen in Maryland and Delaware. In 1866 he also began serving as editor of *Zion's Standard and Weekly Review*, a New York City paper run by the AMEZ Church. After the Virginia Annual Conference was established, he was ordained deacon and elder by Bishop

Joseph Clinton in 1866, and from 1867 to 1869 was superintendent of schools in the district of Maryland and Delaware under the United States government. He founded 140 schools, hired 150 teachers, and enrolled 7,000 students. In 1869 he risked his life registering Black voters in Wilmington, Delaware, and his efforts resulted in a change in the representation of Delaware's lower house. He then apparently served as a minister in local churches.

In 1872 Day moved to Harrisburg, Pennsylvania, and became a clerk in the corporation department of the auditor-general's office, holding that position until 1875. He continued his publishing interests as editor of a weekly paper, *Our National Progress*. He was elected general secretary of the AMEZ General Conference in 1867, 1888, 1892, 1896, and 1900. In 1878 he was elected to the Harrisburg school board from the Eighth Ward, the first Black to serve in that capacity. He was reelected in 1881 and was its president from 1891 to 1893, perhaps the first Black school board president in any predominantly White American community. It did not happen again in Harrisburg until 1969. After serving local churches around Harrisburg and transferring from the Virginia Conference, Day was appointed presiding elder of the Baltimore District in 1885, resigning in 1886 to become general missionary and intellectual instructor of the conference. Ill health forced him to leave the school board in 1898 and reduce his other commitments. He died in 1900, and was survived by his wife (name unknown) and no children. A high school and housing project in Harrisburg have been named for him.

Davis, Russell H. *Memorable Negroes in Cleveland's Past.* Cleveland, OH: The Western Reserve Historical Society, 1969. 58 pp.
"William Howard Day." *A.M.E. Zion Quarterly Review* 77 (Summer 1965): 61.
MM, DANB, IBAW, IBAWCB, AMEZC, AAP, EWM, SOTT, BAB.

DEAN, JENNIE (1852–1913), educator and home missionary, was born into slavery in Prince William County, Virginia, the daughter of Charles and Annie Dean. After the Civil War Dean moved to Washington, D.C. to earn money to help pay for a family farm near Sudley Springs, Virginia. On weekend trips home she went about establishing Sunday Schools and missions and set up industrial training for the youth, though her own education was marginal.

Eventually she settled permanently back in Prince William County and dedicated her life to missionary work among the Black population. Her concern was a broad one that encompassed both social and religious needs. She spent the first part of her career (apart from her regular job) focusing on religion, and among other things founded the Mount Calvary Church. Her father built a temporary structure to house the congregation and she spearheaded the fund drive that finally created a permanent church, dedicated in 1880.

About 1890 Dean turned her attention to the need for industrial education for Blacks in that area and organized a drive that drew upon interested people from as far away as New York and New England. The result was the Manassas Colored Industrial School, dedicated in September, 1894, with abolitionist Frederick Douglass the keynote speaker. Dean additionally showed her concern for the development of the next generation by speaking to groups as often as she could about proper social behavior. In 1896 she wrote a pamphlet called "Jennie Dean's Rules for Good Behavior Among Her People." Her admonitions were often contained in such statements as "Don't Address an Audience with Your Hands in Your Pockets," "Don't Turn Your Back on the Speaker," and "Politeness at Home and Abroad." The school prospered and by 1911 had eleven teachers and nine buildings on 215 acres. In 1933 it became part of the public school system. Dean remains a stellar example of someone who accomplished much with very little.

Lewis, Stephen Johnson. *Undaunted Faith: The Story of Jennie Dean, Missionary, Teacher, Crusader, Builder.* Catlett, VA: Circuit Press, 1942. 122 pp.

NBAW.

DE BAPTISTE, RICHARD

DE BAPTISTE, RICHARD (November 11, 1831–April 21, 1901), a Baptist minister who emerged as one of the most prominent organizers of Black Baptists in the decades following the Civil War, was born a free man in Fredericksburg, Virginia, the son of Eliza and William De Baptiste. His grandfather, an immigrant from France, had been a Revolutionary War veteran. His father, the owner of a construction company, saw to his education. In 1840 the family moved to Detroit, where they attended Second Baptist Church. The pastor, Rev. Samuel Davis, continued De Baptiste's education. In 1855 he married Georgianna Brische. Three years later, the church gave De Baptiste a license to preach. He was ordained in 1860 at Mount Pleasant, Ohio, where he had moved to pastor the Negro Baptist Church and teach school. In 1863 he moved to Chicago as pastor of the Olivet Baptist Church.

At the time De Baptiste moved to Chicago, the Olivet Church had approximately 100 members, but under his leadership it developed a school and soon became the church home of an increasing number of immigrants from the South. There were almost 500 members by 1868 when he oversaw the building of a new 800-seat sanctuary. When the church was destroyed by fire in 1874, he built a three-story structure as its replacement. As the pastor of Chicago's largest Black church, De Baptiste's voice reverberated through the Black Baptist community. He emerged during the war years as an advocate of Black separation and the formation of all-Black associations (the basic unit of organization above the congregational level for Baptists). He led Olivet into the Woods Creek Baptist Association, the oldest all-Black association in Illinois. As the war came to a close he moved swiftly to bring the churches of the South and Midwest into a single organization and in 1864 organized the Southern and Northwest [Baptist] Convention and then led it in 1866 to unite with the American Missionary Convention (centered in New England) to form the **Consolidated American Baptist Convention**. This convention, the first truly national African American Baptist organization, was a forerunner of the present **National Baptist Convention, U.S.A., Inc.** As president from 1867 to 1873, he promoted its fledgling missionary program in the West and in Haiti and was a corresponding editor for the convention's *National Observer.*

De Baptiste's career peaked in the late 1860s and early 1870s. Beginning with the death of his wife in 1872, he experienced a number of setbacks. In the late 1870s, the membership of Olivet declined and the organization of the Consolidated Convention was in disarray. In 1878 he became the editor of the *Conservator,* Chicago's first African American newspaper. However, by 1881, his children's health was failing, and the membership of Olivet declined to the point he had to resign as pastor. During the 1880s he continued a double career as the pastor of several small Baptist churches and as a journalist. For a while he was a corresponding editor for the *St. Louis Monitor,* and the *Baptist Herald* of Keokuk, Iowa. In 1884 he founded the *Western Herald,* but it did not survive for very long, and he edited the *Baptist Observer,* in Chicago, for a while. He died in Chicago having been left behind by the movement he had done so much to build.

Fisher, Mark Miles. *The History of Olivet Baptist Church of Chicago.* Chicago: M.A. Thesis, University of Chicago, 1922.

Logan, Rayford W., and Michael R. Winston, eds. *Dictionary of American Negro Biography.* New York: W. W. Norton & Co., 1982. 680 pp.

DEBERRY, WILLIAM NELSON (August 29, 1870–January 20, 1948), nationally known Congregational minister, was born in Nashville, Tennessee, the son of Caswell and Charlotte (Mayfield) DeBerry, both former slaves. His father was a railroad shop worker and also a lay preacher in the Baptist Church. DeBerry attended public school until he was about fourteen and began to work full-time. After only a summer's work, however, a friend persuaded him to join him at Fisk University. DeBerry struggled to complete the program, but each year he won a scholarship which he was able to supplement with money earned by working odd jobs during the school year and fulltime each summer. After finishing the preparatory department and beginning the college department he worked mostly as a teacher in the summers, with one summer as a Pullman porter.

After receiving his B.S. in 1896 he briefly considered a medical career, but then decided on the ministry. He felt that it was his role to help raise the level of ministry and religion above what he considered the ignorant emotionalism with which he grew up. He went to Oberlin Theological Seminary in Ohio, where he again earned a scholarship. He earned a B.D. in 1899. On September 6, 1899, he married Amanda McKissack, with whom he had two children. By this time he was associated with the Congregational Church, and wanted to go to a congregation in the South. There was no opening, and instead he went to St. John's Congregational Church in Springfield, Massachusetts, where he remained for 22 years.

When DeBerry arrived, St. John's had about one hundred members, and under his leadership it slowly grew. The Congregational Missionary Association, instead of sending him South, sent him on regular speaking tours to White churches in the North. He spoke very effectively on the need for the support of Black missions in the South, and raised considerable money for that effort. DeBerry eventually convinced his congregation to undertake a major expansion project of the church facilities so as to become a seven-day-a-week program center. Included in the new building was a printing press and employment center for men. Next door was constructed the parish home for working girls and an employment center for women. Over the years the church gained a large apartment building and a number of homes so that twenty-eight families could be sheltered. Later a 54–acre farm in East Brookfield, Massachusetts, was deeded to the church and became Camp Atwater.

The church's social service arm, St. John's Institutional Activities, Inc., was organized in 1911 and soon won national acclaim. It was patterned along the lines of the social services philosophy of the National Urban League, founded the same year. In 1917 it became an affiliate of the National Urban League. The organization was pioneering in its structure and effectively touched the large community of Blacks in Springfield. In 1914 Lincoln University granted him an honorary D.D. degree. In 1915 Fisk University made him a trustee, the first alumnus to serve in that capacity. About 1921 the Interchurch World Movement did a study of American churches and found that St. John's had "the most efficient system of organization and work of any church in the group surveyed, regardless of race or denomination."

In 1919 DeBerry was elected second assistant moderator of the National Council of Congregational Churches of Christ in America. In 1925 he was elected recording secretary of the American Missionary Association, and was reelected three successive times. In 1927 he received the William E. Harmon Foundation first place award for "distinguished service in religion among Negroes of the United States." In 1928 the city of Springfield gave him the William Pynchon Medal for "distinguished public service."

By 1930 the social service work had grown to such an extent that it needed to separate from the church as an independent entity. DeBerry resigned from the pastorate in order to devote himself to this work, which was redesigned as the Dunbar Community League, Inc. The League now had a sizable professional staff to oversee the many programs. There were personal visits to homes for individual and social adjustment problems. There were boys' and girls' clubs, a playground, music department, women's center, and many other services. DeBerry himself was involved in almost every significant activity of the Springfield Black community. He served on the boards of many local agencies and was also appointed to regional and state boards and commissions, often as the first Black person. In particular he served on the Springfield Board of Public Welfare and on the State Committee on Religious and Interracial Understanding. His first wife passed away, and in 1943 he married Louise Scott. He was widely sought as a speaker and was acclaimed as "one of the greatest churchmen of his time." He retired in 1947, but continued to direct Camp Atwater.

DeBerry, William N. "The Possibilities of the Negro Institutional Church." *Durham Fact Finding Conference* 2 (April 1929): 18–19.

———, ed. *Sociological Survey of the Negro Population of Springfield, Mass.* Springfield, MA: The Dunbar Community League, 1940.

"William Nelson DeBerry." *Journal of Negro History* 33 (July 1948): 384–385.

Williams, Charles H. "The Negro Church and Recreation."
Southern Workman 55 (February 1926): 58–69.
NYTO, NBH, WWCA (38–40), *HUBA, WWWA* (2), *RLA, DANB, EBA, IVR.*

DELANY, HENRY BEARD (1858–April 14, 1928), the fourth Black priest consecrated bishop by the **Episcopal Church** in the United States, was born in Florida and grew up a Methodist. As a young man he enrolled in St. Augustine's School (later St. Augustine's College), an Episcopal institution in Raleigh, North Carolina. While there he converted to the Episcopal Church and met his wife, Nanny J. Delany, with whom he had at least eight children. While she became a teacher at St. Augustine's, he eventually became its vice-principal. It was in that position that the bishop of North Carolina, the Rt. Rev. Dr. Cheshire, elevated Delany to be Archdeacon for the Colored Work of the diocese. Finally, on November 21, 1918, Delany was consecrated suffragan bishop of North Carolina. The three previous Black bishops of the Episcopal Church were James T. Holly (1874), Samuel D. Ferguson (1885), and Edward T. Demby (1918). Delany was the second Black bishop, after Demby, to be assigned to work within the United States.

Bragg, George F. *History of the Afro-American Group of the Episcopal Church.* Baltimore, MD: Church Advocate Press, 1922. 319 pp.
"Mrs. Henry Delany, Bishop's Widow, 95." *New York Times* (June 4, 1956): 29.
EBA, ECA (1929).

DELILLE, HENRIETTE (1813–November 16, 1862), the founder of the **Sisters of the Holy Family**, was born in New Orleans, the youngest of three children in the family of Jean Baptiste Delille-Sarpy, a White Creole, and his mistress, Marie Joseph "Pouponne" Dias, a free Black woman. Henriette Delille's Black relatives were Creoles, that is, French-speaking Roman Catholics descended from the original French colonists in that part of the country. A number owned sizable properties and a number, like herself, were quite light-skinned. The free Creoles of color in Louisiana held a unique social status in pre-Civil War years, and advantages tended to increase with the lightness of the skin.

Delille was apparently reared to follow her mother in the widely accepted system of concubinage between wealthy White men and free women, Black or White, with fine breeding. She was schooled in the social graces and the arts. At about the age of eleven she first met Sister Saint Marthe Fontier, the only member of the French religious order of the Dames Hospitalier then living in New Orleans. She opened a school on Barracks Street in about 1824 for young Black women and Delille was interested. By about 1826 she was heavily involved both in teaching and in various missionary activities such as visiting the sick, feeding the poor, and praying.

The school and mission center closed about 1827 and Sister Fontier went back to France, but Delille and close friend Juliette Gaudin, another free Creole of color, maintained their strong religious interests. Delille began to rebel against her future occupation and condemned extramarital relationships. This created great stress in the family and her mother finally suggested that she go to a nunnery in France, but Delille was determined to remain in New Orleans. In 1832 her mother had a nervous breakdown and the courts saw to Delille's care until 1835, when Delille was declared of legal age. In 1836 she, Juliette Gaudin, and others tried to form a religious community under the leadership of Marie Jeanne Aliquot, a French-born woman. The city and the Catholic hierarchy did not warm to its interracial character, and it was dropped.

In 1837 Father Etienne Jean François Rousselon arrived from France and the group asked him to be their advisor/advocate/patron. He was named the pastor of the new St. Augustine's Catholic Church in a Creole suburb, and asked permission to found a society of free Black women (no Whites) under the leadership of Delille. This was granted, and the group may be dated from 1842, when St. Augustine's church building was completed. This was the second Black American Catholic order, after the **Oblate Sisters of Providence** (1829, led by **Mary Elizabeth Lange**). Father Rousselon had envisioned this Sisters of the Holy Family to be a contemplative order. At the beginning it consisted of Delille, Gaudin, Josephine Charles, and Aliquot (secretly), and they had in mind a great deal more than contemplation. In 1847 the state required the incorporation of non-profit societies, and a lay Association of the Holy Family was formed to support the work of the women. With the help of some wealthy patrons a hospice was built in 1849 on Saint Bernard Street and the following year a convent and school were opened on Bayou Road.

In 1852 Delille, Gaudin, and Charles made their novitiate at Saint Michael's, a school for White girls, and said their final vows. The city of New Orleans seems to have accepted their order, although it closed other Black religious groups, such as St. James African Methodist Episcopal Church. This acceptance may have been because the Sisters of the Holy Family participated in the unique Creole social status and it was under White supervision. Under Delille's leadership the group grew and flourished. It became an integral part of the city's social support system, especially during the various epidemics of the 1850s and 60s. The sisters cared for the sick and orphaned of both races, and in 1860 an annex to the hospice was opened on Dauphine Street. After Delille died in late 1862 it looked for a time as though the order would fold, but it experienced renewal after the Civil War. They were permitted to wear habits in 1872, opened other convents and schools, and remain in force today. The order entered Delille in the process that leads to the consideration of sainthood by the **Roman Catholic Church**.

Detige, Audrey Marie. *Henriette Delille, Free Woman of Color.* New Orleans, LA: Sisters of the Holy Family, 1976.

Hart, Mary Francis Borgia. *Violets in the King's Garden: A History of the Sisters of the Holy Family of New Orleans.* New Orleans, LA: The Sisters of the Holy Family, 1976. 137 pp.

NBAW, HBCUS, BWR, IBAW.

DELIVERANCE EVANGELISTIC CENTERS. A Pentecostal church. At one point in the 1950s, 28–year old Arturo Skinner was contemplating suicide but was prevented by what he believed to be the voice of God who said to him, "Arturo, if you but turn around, I'll save your soul, heal your body, and give you a deliverance ministry." He entered a period of fasting and prayer during which time he had a number of visions and dreams. He also consecrated his life to the ministry, though initially he did not understand the nature of a "deliverance" (or healing) ministry.

He opened his first center in Brooklyn, New York, and as others were drawn to his work, he created additional centers and ordained ministers to head them. He welcomed women into the ministry.

The teachings of the Deliverance Evangelistic Centers are in agreement with those of the Pentecostal movement. The Trinity and the divinity of Christ are affirmed. Believers can expect to receive the baptism of the Holy Spirit evidenced by their speaking in tongues. Skinner, who died in 1975, was succeeded by Ralph Nickels. Headquarters is in Newark, New Jersey. Congregations are concentrated in New York, New Jersey, Pennsylvania, and Washington, D.C.

DELIVERANCE EVANGELISTIC CHURCH. A Pentecostal church. The Deliverance Evangelistic Church was founded in 1960 as an independent prayer group which engaged in evangelistic endeavors in Philadelphia. After a year of informal activity, the group, under the leadership of Rev. Dr. Benjamin Smith, Sr., settled in a permanent location and formally organized as the Deliverance Evangelistic Church. As the movement grew, other churches were founded, primarily in Pennsylvania and New Jersey.

The church set itself three goals: to evangelize people to Christ, to teach the word of God so that believers might mature spiritually, and to prepare believers for worship and service. Service to the community has been especially emphasized and as the church grew it developed a broad spectrum of social ministry to the poor through the redistribution of clothing, food, and shelter, and through visitation to hospitals, prisons, nursing homes and shut-ins.

The church has developed a radio broadcast and has founded the Deliverance Evangelistic Bible Institute and the youth Bible School. The church choirs have produced several albums.

Headquarters of the church is in Philadelphia. Dr. Smith, the founder, continues as the pastor of the organization. In 1990 the church reported 32 congregations and 83,000 members. Missionary work is supported in Liberia, Haiti, and India. It publishes a magazine, *Evangel*. There is an annual convention each summer.

Smith has envisioned the construction of "Deliverance Village," a building complex that would include a 7,000 seat auditorium, a Christian medical center, a Christian elementary and high school, and a home for the aged. To date, a part of the complex has been completed and opened, and construction on the auditorium began in 1989.

Payne, Wardell J., ed. *Directory of African American Religious Bodies: A Compendium by the Howard University School of Divinity.* Washington, DC: Howard University Press, 1991. 363 pp.

DEMBY, EDWARD THOMAS (February 13, 1869–October 14, 1957), the third Black priest consecrated bishop by the (Protestant) **Episcopal Church** in the United States, was born in Wilmington, Delaware, the son of Thomas and Mary Elizabeth (Tippit) Demby. He grew up in Wilmington and then in Philadelphia, Pennsylvania. He attended the Century Biblical Institute (later called Morgan College) in Baltimore, Maryland, then went to Lincoln University in Pennsylvania and Howard University in Washington, D.C. (1892–93). He received his B.D. in 1893 from Wilberforce University in Ohio and his S.T.D. in 1894 from the University of Chicago.

From 1894 to 1896 Demby was dean of Paul Quinn College in Waco, Texas, an institution of the African Methodist Episcopal Church. About 1896 he converted to the Episcopal Church. He was confirmed by Bishop Spaulding of Colorado, who sent him to Tennessee, where he was ordained deacon in 1898 and priest in 1899. He was rector of St. Paul's Episcopal Church in Mason, Tennessee (1899–1900), followed by St. Augustine's Episcopal Church in Kansas City, Missouri (1900–02). On September 17, 1902, he married Antoinette M. Riggs, who was the first Black registered nurse in Cleveland. Other pastorates included St. Michael's Episcopal Church in Cairo, Illinois (1903); St. Peter's Episcopal Church in Key West, Florida (1903–07); and Emmanuel Episcopal Church in Memphis, Tennessee (1907–15). In 1912 he was made Archdeacon of the Colored Work of the Diocese of Tennessee. From 1912 to 1918 he was principal of Hoffman-St. Mary's Industrial Institution in Keeling, Tennessee.

On September 29, 1918, Demby was consecrated Suffragan Bishop of Arkansas, with responsibility for Black church members and activities in Arkansas, Tennessee, Oklahoma, Kansas, New Mexico, and Texas. He remained in this position until his retirement in 1939. He was the third Black bishop of the Episcopal Church, following **James T. Holly** (1874) and **Samuel D. Ferguson** (1885), and was the first to have an assignment in the United States. He was the author of several books.

Demby, Edward Thomas. *A Bird's-Eye View of Exegetical Studies: The Writings of St. Paul and St. James.* Waco, TX: Paul Quinn College Print., 1896. 56 pp.
————. *The Mission of the Episcopal Church Among the Negroes of the Diocese of Arkansas.* Little Rock, AR: N.p., 190–.
HAAG, EBA, HUBA, AARS, BAW, NYTO, RLA, IBAW, IBAWCB, WWCA (38–40).

DENNIS, WALTER DECOSTER (b. August 23, 1932), suffragan bishop in the **Episcopal Church**, was born in Washington, D.C., the son of Walter, Sr., and Helen (Maddox) Dennis. He received his B.A. in 1952 from Virginia State College in Petersburg, Virginia, his M.A. in North American history and constitutional law in 1953 from New York University in New York City, and his S.T.B. in 1956 from General Theological Seminary in New York City.

He was ordained deacon in June 1956, and that summer was curate of St. Philip's Episcopal Church in Brooklyn, New York. From September 1956 to 1960 he was an assistant at the Cathedral Church of St. John the Divine in New York City. During this time, from 1956 to 1958, he did additional studies at New York University and advanced to Ph.D. candidacy. In June 1958, he was ordained to the priesthood. From September 1960 to July 1965 he was vicar of St. Cyprian Episcopal Church in Hampton, Virginia, and also served as assistant adjunct professor of American history and constitutional law at Hampton Institute (1961–65). In 1965 he returned to the Cathedral Church of St. John the Divine as canon residentiary, remaining there for fourteen years. He also began an adjunct professorship in Christian Ethics at General Theological Seminary.

Dennis has served on many boards and commissions relating to his topics of special interest—drugs, abortion, homosexuality, juvenile justice, and racism. While at St. John the Divine he planned and directed a number of conferences in these fields. He is on the board of directors of the Abortion Repeal Association; the Institute for the Study of Human Resources; and the National Organization for the Reform of Marijuana Laws. From 1975 to 1979 he was an adjunct professor of Christian ethics at General Theological Seminary in New York City. He has long been a member of the Union of Black Episcopalians and the convenor of the Black caucus of the diocese of New York. On October 5, 1979, he was consecrated as suffragan (assistant) bishop of the diocese of New York, where he has since remained. He has served on the Bishop's Committee on Taxation and the Committee on Social Concerns, and is a member of the Church's National Task Force on Hunger. He has authored a number of articles.

WWABA (90–91), *WWR* (85), *IBAW, BDNM* (75), *BGWC.*

DERRICK, WILLIAM BENJAMIN (July 27, 1843– April 15, 1913), 23rd bishop of the **African Methodist Episcopal Church** (AME), was born on the island of Antigua, West Indies, the son of Thomas J. Derrick, a White Scotch planter, and Eliza Derrick, a West Indian. He went to a private school when very young, and after two years was admitted to a public school at Gracefield under the auspices of the Moravians, attending from 1848 to 1856. In the spring of 1856 he was sent to a "select" high school for three years. In 1859 he was apprenticed to a blacksmith, but went to sea soon after completing his training. On May 6, 1860, on his first voyage to the United States, the ship was run aground in a storm, but managed to make it to New York. In America Derrick sailed on many ships, including a trip to London, England, in 1861. He returned to the United States that year, entered the U.S. Navy for a three-year term, and was assigned to the flagship Minnesota. He was also in the famous battle between the Monitor and Merrimac in 1862. He joined the newly founded St. John's AME Church in Norfolk, Virginia, in 1864, during the brief time it was led by soon-to-be bishop **John M. Brown**, and was licensed to preach the same year. He married Mary E. White, who lived but a short time; there were no children.

He joined the itinerant ministry in 1867, pastoring at Mt. Pisgah in the District of Columbia. He was ordained a deacon in 1868 and was transferred in 1869 to the Virginia Conference, serving as its assistant secretary while managing an impoverished mission in the Allegheny Mountains. In 1870 he was ordained an elder by Bishop **Alexander Wayman** and appointed to the church at Staunton, Virginia, serving also as presiding elder of the Staunton District. He was first elected as a delegate to General Conference in 1872, and went to every General Conference thereafter. In 1875 he was appointed to the church at Richmond, Virginia, and in 1877 became presiding elder of the Richmond District. By this time he was already a popular Republican political leader, and in the 1876 presidential campaign spoke at a mass meeting in New York City with James Blaine and Senator Foraker.

In 1879 Derrick left Richmond and about this time married his second wife, Lillian M. Derrick, with whom there were no children. He took her with him to visit his birthplace in the West Indies. After some weeks there they returned and he transferred to the New York Annual Conference, taking the church in Salem, New Jersey, followed by an assignment in Albany, New York. In June, 1884, he was nominated as a presidential elector-at-large by the Republican State Committee, but was opposed by many. John J. Freeman, the Black editor of the *Progressive American* argued that Derrick had never become a naturalized citizen of the United States and therefore could not serve in that position. Derrick responded that he had taken the oath of allegiance at the time of his military service, but declined the nomination anyway to help coordinate the denomination's centennial celebration. His final local church was the Sullivan Street AME Church in New York City, a large church of over 1,000 members which he served while also a presiding elder. In 1890 he was elected Missionary Secretary of the denomination and established his headquarters in the Bible House in New York City, lending it prestige. He was re-elected in 1892, and in 1896 was elected bishop on the first ballot. He was assigned to the Eighth Episcopal District (Mississippi and Arkansas), and was one of the founders of Campbell College. He headed the First Episcopal District (Pennsylvania) from 1900 to 1904, followed by the

Third Episcopal District (Ohio, Pittsburgh, West Indies, South America, and West Africa) from 1904 to 1908. His second wife died in 1907. His final assignment was to the Third Episcopal District (changing composition to include Ohio, Pittsburgh, West Virginia, Nova Scotia, and Bermuda) from 1908 to 1912. In 1909, he married Clara E. Henderson Jones, widow of a Chicago lawyer.

In 1906 he was called to help fill the unexpired term of Bishop **Charles Spencer Smith** in South Africa (Thirteenth Episcopal District) and restore a troubled situation. While there, he founded the Lillian Derrick Institute at Evaton, out of which grew the present Wilberforce Institute, about twenty-eight miles south of Johannesburg. He was a delegate to the World Methodist Conference of 1901 in London and again in 1911 in Toronto, Canada. He was known as a stirring and powerful orator, and had particular success with an address called "The Two Flags—the Stars and Stripes and the Union Jack," which helped restore goodwill between the United States and Great Britain.

Derrick, William Benjamin. *Testimony in the United States Industrial Commission. Reports of the Industrial Commission on Immigration, Including Testimony With Review and Digest and Special Reports.* Washington, DC: Government Printing Office, 1901.

———. "The Work of Evangelization Among the Negroes." In Elias B. Sanford, ed. *Church Federation: Inter-Church Conference of Federation, New York, November 15–21, 1905.* New York: Fleming H. Revell Co., 1906, 520–524.

AARS, HUBA, HAMEC, EWM, NYTO, CEAMEC, BAMEC, AAE, MM.

DICKERSON, WILLIAM FISHER (January 15, 1844–December 20, 1884), 13th bishop of the **African Methodist Episcopal Church** (AME), was born in Woodbury, New Jersey, the son of Henry and Sophia Dickerson. His father was a minister in the AME Church. In 1861 Dickerson experienced conversion and the following year moved to New York City and joined the Sullivan Street AME Church. He held many positions as a layperson, including class leader, musical director in the Sunday School, and chorister of the church choir. Deciding to follow in his father's footsteps and be a minister, he became a licensed exhorter and then a local preacher. He married Isabella Demarest, with whom he had several children.

He enrolled at Lincoln University in Pennsylvania in 1865 and the Rev. H. J. Rhodes at Oxford, Pennsylvania, renewed his license to preach in 1867. He was ordained deacon in 1868. He graduated in 1870 and that same year joined the itinerant ministry in the New

York Annual Conference as one of the few formally educated preachers in the denomination. He was appointed to a small congregation in Elizabeth, New Jersey, where he had a successful one-year stay. He was ordained elder in 1871, and assigned for the next two years to Providence, Rhode Island. Bishops **Jabez Campbell**, **James Shorter**, **Alexander Wayman**, and **Daniel Payne** were grooming him for a rapid rise up the ecclesiastical ladder. In 1873 he was moved to the Charles Street AME Church in Boston, Massachusetts. During his two-year stay there he produced reportedly the largest revival ever conducted in Boston among Blacks. He was a strong advocate of support for the young Wilberforce University in Xenia, Ohio, which gave him an honorary D.D. degree in 1873. He was elected regional secretary for the New England Annual Conference.

In 1876 Bishop Payne appointed Dickerson to the Bethel AME Church in New Haven, Connecticut, and one year later promoted him to the prestigious Sullivan Street AME Church in New York City. While some thought him too young for such an assignment, he proved them wrong by his talented administration and superb preaching, which brought many converts. He inaugurated the "Thinker's Course of Lectures" to introduce parishioners to literature, theology, and philosophy. Guest lecturers included such luminaries as **Francis Grimke** and **Hallie Quinn Brown**. In 1880 he was elected bishop on the second ballot at the age of 36, the youngest bishop ever elected in the AME Church. He was also the first AME bishop with a B.A. degree. He was assigned to the Sixth Episcopal District (South Carolina, Columbia, North Georgia, and Georgia Annual Conferences) from 1880 to 1884, establishing his home in Columbia, South Carolina. As a northerner in the fast-growing southern portion of the church, his authority was often tested. Nevertheless, despite this and despite his brief episcopacy, he made significant attempts to build up the southern wing of the AME Church. He founded Allen University in Columbia, South Carolina, in 1880, as a successor to Payne Institute in Cokesbury, South Carolina, and was its president until his death. In 1881 he helped found Morris Brown College in Atlanta, Georgia. He was president of Wilberforce University board of trustees from 1882 to 1884. He organized the Macon, Georgia, Conference on January 31, 1883, at Sanderville, and organized Kittrell College. He was a delegate to the First World Methodist Conference in London, England, in 1881. A heart condition cut short his career less than one month before his 41st birthday. Churches are named for Dickerson in Millsboro, Delaware, Frostburg, Maryland, and Lake City, South Carolina.

Dickerson, Dennis C. "William Fisher Dickerson: Northern Preacher/Southern Prelate." *Methodist History* 23 (April 1985): 135–152.

Dickerson, William F. *A Eulogy Upon the Life, Character, and Death of Rev. Lorenzo Westcott . . . Delivered Before Garnet Literary Association, the Faculty, Students and Friends in Lincoln University . . . November 7, 1879.* Lincoln University, Chester Co., PA., Garnet Literary Association, 1879. 40 pp.

CEAMEC, HAMEC, EWM, BAMEC, ACAB, TCBD.

DILLARD UNIVERSITY. A school jointly sponsored by the **United Church of Christ** and **United Methodist Church**. Dillard University, New Orleans, Louisiana, was founded in 1930 by the merger of New Orleans University and Straight College. New Orleans University began in 1865 as the Thompson Bible Institute in Bayou Teche, Louisiana, a school to train ministers to read and write. Former slaves, while being allowed to perfect their pulpit skills, had not been allowed to learn basic reading and writing skills and thus could not read the Bible. The Thompson school was superseded a few years later by the Newman Normal School, founded by John P. Newman (later a bishop) in New Orleans. Finally, in 1873, the Freedman's Aid Bureau, through Joseph C. Hartzell (later bishop) of the Methodist Episcopal Church, chartered New Orleans University which superseded the Normal School. Among the surviving documents from the founding days of the school are the moving comments of Rev. Emperor Williams who spoke at the groundbreaking ceremony.

> I wonder if this is the world I was born in! For twenty years I was a slave on these streets. It was a penitentiary offense to educate a Negro. I have seen my fellow servants whipped for trying to learn; but, today, here I am on this great avenue in this great city with the bishops and elders and people of the Methodist Episcopal Church speaking at the breaking of ground where a building is to be erected for the education of my people. I wonder if this is the world I was born in!

The school went on to specialize in teacher training, and produced many of the leading Black Methodist educators of the early twentieth century, including several college presidents. In 1889 Flint Medical College was organized as a department at the school and a pharmacy department was soon added. These continued until World War I when both were merged into Meharry Medical College.

Straight College was founded in 1869 in New Orleans by the Congregational Church's American

Missionary Association, one of several similar colleges and part of an extensive educational system which included a number of elementary and high schools. Straight trained many of the church's Black ministers through the nineteenth and twentieth century. Since the 1930 merger with New Orleans University to form Dillard University, the school has retained relationships with both the Methodists (the United Methodist Church) and the Congregationalists (now a constituent part of the **United Church of Christ**). The school was named for James Hardy Dillard, who had worked in Black educational efforts for many years.

Stowell, Jay S. *Methodist Adventures in Negro Education.* New York: Methodist Book Concern, 1922. 190 pp.

DISNEY, RICHARD RANDOLPH (June 24, 1830– April 18, 1891), 15th bishop of the **African Methodist Episcopal Church** (AME), was born in North East, Cecil County, Maryland. His parents had previously been slaves, but were free at the time of his birth. His father died when he was eight, and he was apprenticed to the barber trade. He later moved to Springfield, Massachusetts to enroll in Osgood Seminary. He was licensed to preach in the AME Church in 1856, graduated with honors from the seminary in 1857, and joined the Annual Conference. He was ordained deacon in 1858 and elder in 1860.

He was sent to do missionary work in Chatham, Ontario, Canada, and there joined the British Methodist Episcopal (B.M.E.) Church, which had separated from the AME Church in 1856, with Willis Nazrey as bishop. Disney held pastorates in Peel, Buxton, Windsor, Hamilton, St. Catherines, Toronto, and Chatham, and finally became book steward and editor for the church. Bishop Nazrey died on August 22, 1875, and on November 21, 1875 Disney was elected his successor. He led the B.M.E. Church in renewed talks with the AME Church and in 1884 the two groups were reunited.

In the AME Church Disney was assigned to the Tenth Episcopal District (Demerara, South America, Bermuda, Ontario, and Nova Scotia Conferences), composed of all the conferences that had come from the B.M.E. Church. From 1888 to 1891 he headed the Eighth Episcopal District (Mississippi, North Mississippi, Arkansas, and the South Arkansas and West Arkansas Annual Conferences). Churches in Philadelphia, Pennsylvania, and Greenville, Mississippi, are named for him.

HAMEC, EWM, BAMEC, ACAB.

DIVINE, FATHER MAJOR JEALOUS (1877?– September 10, 1965), founder of the **Peace Mission Movement**, was one of the more mysterious and elusive of public figures. He did not discuss his origins, and neither did his followers. There is some evidence that he was born George Baker in 1877 in Savannah, Georgia, but nothing conclusive. His followers claim that he married his first wife, Penninah (Sister Penny), on June 6, 1882. At various times he is considered to have been associated with Sam Morris (Father Jehoviah), and with John Hickerson (Bishop St. John the Divine). All three men were in Brooklyn, New York, shortly before 1919, when reliable biographical information about Divine is first available.

In 1919, Divine established himself, his wife, and twenty followers in Sayville, Long Island, New York, the substantive beginning of his Peace Mission Movement, though that name was not used until the 1930s. He was able to find many of his followers domestic jobs in the surrounding estates, and he preached a gospel of hard work, honesty, sobriety, equality, sexual abstinence, and himself as the Second Coming of Christ. He was known for "forbidding" sickness and death in his home, and providing free, or nearly free, meals and shelter for anyone who asked. Whites were invited to join, and some did, including some with wealth. In 1930, formerly known as Major Jealous Divine, he took the name Father Divine.

As his fame grew, literally busloads of people would travel to see him on the weekends, and the police took him and some eighty followers to court on November 15, 1931, as a "public nuisance." Divine pleaded not guilty, and after a jury trial ending May 25, 1932, found him guilty, the judge sentenced him on June 4 to the maximum one year in jail and a $500 fine. Three days later, on June 7, 1932, the apparently healthy judge, Lewis J. Smith, died of a heart attack, and Divine was quoted as saying, "I hated to do it." The conviction was soon reversed, and Divine's reputation as one who personally controlled cosmic forces was set. His followers still celebrate June 7.

In 1933 Divine moved the headquarters to Harlem, New York City, and on November 4, mayoral candidate Fiorello LaGuardia walked into a banquet and announced, "I came here tonight to ask Father Divine's advice and counsel," indicating significant political influence. The Peace Mission (no real estate or bank accounts were in Divine's name) became the owner of many hotels and businesses in several states, adding to the ability to provide jobs, shelter, and income. Divine attempted to alleviate social ills not only through these means, but through various forms of social agitation as well. In January 1936, he proposed a "Righteous Government Platform," and over 6,000 delegates from many social and political backgrounds came to a meeting to develop and sign the platform. Between 1936 and 1940 he lobbied strongly for a federal anti-lynching law. Divine's strength was such that he emerged relatively unscathed from a number of lawsuits, allegations, and scandals. In 1938 the Peace Mission acquired the Krum Elbow estate in Hyde Park and Divine became a neighbor of the Roosevelts. In 1941 he moved to a Philadelphia mansion on seventy-three acres, through the generosity of a White disciple, John De Voute, who sold the property to the Church in 1953.

The Peace Mission did not hold traditional worship services; at meals there were songs and occasional sermons. He promised his followers heaven on earth, and the rich, communal banquet table was the major religious symbol. The feasts were intended to recreate the daily communions of early Christianity, which time, for Divine, provided the defining practices of the religion. On April 29, 1946, several years after the death of his first wife, Divine married a young, White, Canadian woman named Edna Rose Ritching. Following his own teaching, their marriage was platonic. He said that the spirit of his first wife was transferred to her, as was his own spirit. This laid the foundation for her leadership after his death, at which time the movement's holdings were estimated to be worth $10 million.

Burnham, Kenneth E. *God Comes to America.* Boston: Lambeth Press, 1979. 167 pp.

Divine, Mother. *The Peace Mission Movement.* Philadelphia, PA: Imperial Press, 1982. 191 pp.

Harris, Sara and Harriet Crittenden. *Father Divine, Holy Husband.* Garden City, NY: Doubleday, 1953. Revised as *Father Divine.* New York: Collier Books, 1971. 377 pp.

Hoshor, John. *God in a Rolls Royce.* New York: Hillman, Curl, 1936. 272 pp.

Parker, Robert A. *The Incredible Messiah: The Deification of Father Divine.* Boston: Little, Brown, 1937. 323 pp.

Weisbrot, Robert. *Father Divine and the Struggle for Racial Equality.* Urbana, IL: University of Illinois Press, 1983. 241 pp.

HNB, BHBA, NYTO, BDA-AHP, NA (89), EBA, BH, DANB, DARB, BA, BDACSL, BGM, NWAC, ONL, RLOA, BSC, TCSAPR.

DIVINE WORD, SOCIETY OF THE. A religious order of the **Roman Catholic Church.** Along with St. Joseph's Society of the Sacred Heart, the missioners of the Society of the Divine Word have been a major force in the Catholic Church's work within the African American community. The Society was founded in 1875 at Steyl, the Netherlands, by Arnold Janssen, as a missionary order. By 1905, when it received final approval by the Pope, it had approximately 2,000 members, the largest percentage of which were lay brothers.

The Order began work in America in 1897, and the original members settled near Northrook, Illinois, then a rural community near Chicago. In 1905, the Society began work in Merigold, Mississippi, the first of its missionary ventures among Southern Blacks. Over the next half century, the Society founded more than 50 parishes in Texas, Mississippi, Arkansas, Missouri, and Louisiana, and beyond the South in California and New Jersey. It also opened 40 parochial schools for African American youth.

Noteworthy of its many projects was the formation of **St. Augustine's Seminary**, at Bay St. Louis, Mississippi, for the training of African American Catholic priests. At a time when only one or two seminaries in the whole country would admit Blacks, its work became vital for the develop of a priesthood to serve the growing Black Catholic community. The complex of work at Bay St. Louis became the headquarters of the society's Southern Province. It publishes *St. Augustine's Catholic Messenger* on behalf of the African American apostolate.

DIXON, EDWARD H. (c.1910– ?), pioneer Lutheran minister, grew up in Tuscaloosa, Alabama, and attended the Lutheran school at the Dobler Institute in Tuscaloosa. He took further training at Woodville Lutheran Normal College in Woodville, Ohio; at Emmanuel Lutheran College (Missouri Synod) in Greensboro, North Carolina; and at Capital University in Columbus, Ohio. He left school to pursue other work, and then returned to Capital University, finishing seminary in 1947. He pastored St. Philip's Lutheran Church (American Lutheran Church) in Columbus, Ohio, until 1949, when he went to Philadelphia to found Christ Lutheran Church. He remained as pastor there into the 1970s.

LCAN, EBA.

DIXON, ERNEST THOMAS, JR. (b. October 13, 1922), college president and a bishop of the **United Methodist Church**, was born in San Antonio, Texas. He graduated from Samuel Houston College in 1943 and that summer received his first appointment to a mission church in Brackettville, Texas. About that time he married Lois Freddie Brown, with whom he had four children. In 1945 he completed his B.D. from Drew Theological Seminary, the United Methodist school in Madison, New Jersey, and was ordained deacon. During his seminary years, he worked as an assistant pastor at churches in Harlem, New York, and in Summit, New Jersey.

In 1945 Dixon became Director of Religious Extension Service at Tuskegee Institute in Alabama, where he stayed for six years. The last two of those years he was also co-founder and co-pastor of Bowen Memorial Church at Tuskegee and instructor of Rural Church Work at Gammon Theological Seminary in Atlanta, Georgia. In 1946 he was ordained elder. In 1951–52 he was executive secretary for the Conference Board of Education of the West Texas Conference of the Central Jurisdiction. In 1952 Dixon moved to Nashville, Tennessee to join the staff of the General Board of Education, where he stayed for thirteen years.

From 1965 to 1969 Dixon was president of Philander Smith College in Little Rock, Arkansas, and from 1969 to 1972 he was a staff member in charge of coordination, research, and planning for the denomination's General Program Council, based in Dayton, Ohio. In 1972 he was elected bishop and assigned to the Kansas Episcopal Area. From 1972 to 1976 he served as president of the General Board of Higher Education and Campus Ministry. In 1977 his first wife died, and on May 18, 1979, he married Ernestine Gray Clark. In 1980 he was assigned to the San Antonio Episcopal Area. He is the recipient of numerous honorary degrees. After twelve years of service in Texas, in 1992 he retired.

BDUMB.

DIXON, LOUIE H. (1894–October 22, 1991), a bishop of the **Church of the Living God (Christian Workers for Fellowship)**, was born in Arkansas. As a young man he encountered the Church of the Living which had been formed in his home state by the Rev. William Christian. He became a minister and in 1924 moved to Chicago. He went to work for Armour and Co., from which he retired in 1959. He and his wife Prudie had three daughters.

In 1929 he founded the first congregation of the Church, Temple No. 120, in the city, in the living room of one of the four original members. While otherwise holding down a full-time job, he built the church in the city and founded two other temples. In 1962 he was consecrated as a bishop in the Church. He passed away in Chicago following 62 years of service as pastor of the Temple.

Heise, Kenan. "Bishop Louie Dixon; Led Church of the Living God." *Chicago Tribune* (October 23, 1991).

DOLBY, MARTHA CUNNINGHAM (October 28, 1878–October 21, 1956), perhaps the first woman minister in the **Church of the Brethren**, was born in Cottage Grove, Howard County, Indiana. Both of her parents belonged to the German Baptist Brethren faith. She was baptized at age sixteen and graduated from high school in 1899. Her father, Richard Cunningham, did not approve of women in college, but with her brother, Joe, she enrolled anyway in the Bible Department of Manchester College, Indiana, in 1900. She worked in the college kitchens to pay her way.

In 1903 she was sent by the General Mission Board of the Church of the Brethren to establish a church among Blacks in Palestine, Arkansas. Her father had sent money to the board towards a mission in the South. Mattie Cunningham, as she was popularly known, established a Sunday School for children, but ill health from a malarial infection forced her to leave Arkansas in 1906. She went to southern Ohio and worked among Black churches there. In 1907 she married Newton Dolby, with whom she had six children. Newton's father, Wiley Dolby, was a former Baptist minister who had converted to the Church of the Brethren and pastored in the area of Jeffersonville, Ohio. In 1907, after the marriage, Dolby and her husband were both installed as deacons in the Frankfort Church of the Brethren. On December 30, 1911, Dolby was installed into the ministry, one of the first women to become a minister in the Church of the Brethren.

After some years in Ohio, the family moved to Mt. Morris, Illinois, and then in 1917 to Urbana, Ohio, where they settled at the Springfield Church of the Brethren, some twelve miles from their home. In 1924 a new administration in the congregation, driven by racial prejudice, asked Dolby to leave. She then joined a Methodist church, where she ministered for the next nine years. Her husband died in 1926 and was buried in Urbana. His passing forced her to take in washing and ironing in addition to her ministry in order to support the family. From 1936 until her death she was the first resident minister of the Church of God (Black) in Urbana.

BE, IP.

DORSEY, THOMAS ANDREW (July 1, 1899– ?), Baptist minister and the "Father of Modern Black Gospel Music," was born in Villa Rica, Georgia, the son of Thomas Madison and Etta (Plant) Dorsey. His father was a Baptist revivalist preacher, and the family moved to Atlanta in 1910. Dorsey moved to Chicago in 1918 and worked at steel mills and music gigs to earn money to attend the Chicago Musical College (also called Chicago School of Composition and Arranging) for three years. With that solid foundation, he became a successful blues musician and composer. Known as "Georgia Tom," he traveled with the Whispering Syncopators and then was the piano player and band leader for famous blues artist Ma Rainey. He wrote more than 200 blues songs, including "Stormy Sea Blues," "Last Minute Blues," and the music for "It's Tight Like That."

Eventually he began to return to the music of his church heritage, and combined the traditional Black church music of the 1920s with blues chords, jazzy syncopation, improvisation, and emotional interpretation. The result was a new form of church music and Dorsey coined the term, "gospel music." This music was similar to some of the songs composed by **Charles A. Tindley** between 1900 and 1906, but was less dependent upon spirituals. Dorsey's first gospel song, "Someday, Somewhere," was written in 1921, but for a long time he could not interest anyone in the new music, just as Tindley's music took a long time to catch on. Finally in 1929 Dorsey began to get orders for "If You See My Savior." In 1931 he founded the first ever "gospel choir" at the Ebenezer Baptist Church in Chicago, and with colleague **Sallie Martin** and others founded in 1932 the National Convention of Gospel Choirs and Choruses, related to the **National Baptist Convention, U.S.A., Inc.**, which still holds annual gatherings. Martin traveled the country with Dorsey singing his songs to his accompaniment and organizing gospel choirs. They were a popular duo until about 1940, when Dorsey began traveling with **Mahalia Jackson**.

In 1932 his wife and infant son died, and shortly thereafter he wrote "Precious Lord, Take My Hand," his most successful song. In 1932 he moved from the Ebenezer Baptist Church to the Pilgrim Baptist Church, where he was music director. On February 17, 1941, he married Kathryn Mosely, with whom he had two children. Over the course of his career he wrote well over 400 gospel songs, and John Charles Thomas' rendition of "Peace in the Valley" in the 1940s became the first gospel song to make the "Hit Parade." Other famous songs included "There'll Be Peace," "I Will Put My Trust in the Lord," and "The Lord Has Laid His Hands on Me." So many of his songs became standards and million-plus sellers that Mahalia Jackson called him "the Irving Berlin of the religious field." He did much to shape the piano style of gospel music and to promote the careers of singers like Mahalia Jackson. In 1943 he wrote an autobiography, *My Ups and Downs*. He was sometimes confused with famous White bandleader Tommy Dorsey, and once they received each other's royalty checks.

Dorsey became a legend in his own time, and was in constant demand. In 1959 he composed the music for a 17-part television series on the Civil War, called "Ordeal by Fire." He ran the Thomas A. Dorsey Gospel Songs Music Publishing Company, the first publishing house for the promotion of Black American gospel music. His music was endorsed by the National Baptist Convention, U.S.A., Inc., although initially many clergy resisted Dorsey's mix of nightclub rhythms with church environment. In 1964 he was ordained a minister and functioned as assistant minister at the Pilgrim Baptist Church. In 1979 he was the first Black person elected to the Nashville Song Writers Association International Hall of Fame, and in 1981 was named to the Georgia Music Hall of Fame.

Banks, Lacy J. "Gospel Music: A Shout of Black Joy." *Ebony* 27 (May 1972): 161–168.

"King of the Gospel Writers." *Ebony* 18 (November 1962): 122–127.

Dorsey, Thomas A. *My Ups and Downs*. 1943.

Dorsey, Thomas A., Kathryn Dorsey, and Julia Mae Smith, eds. *Dorsey's Songs of the Kingdom*. Chicago: Thomas A. Dorsey, 1951. 64 pp.

NMA, WWA (78–79), AAE, ERS, BDA-AHP, IBAW.

DOUGLAS, FLOYD IGNATIUS (1887–1951), a bishop of the **Pentecostal Assemblies of the World** (PAW), was born in Nelson County, Kentucky. Douglas was reared as a Roman Catholic, but converted to Evangelical Protestantism, received the Pentecostal baptism of the Holy Spirit (as evidenced by speaking in tongues, the definitive experience of **Pentecostalism**), and was called to preach during a turbulent 1911. Shortly thereafter he became a member of the PAW and founded its first congregation in Louisville, Kentucky. He lived through the doctrinal change in 1915 in which the PAW accepted the new non-Trinitarian Jesus Only theology which had spread through the Pentecostal community.

In 1919 Douglas appears on the list of field superintendents responsible for Kentucky. When the position of field superintendent was abolished in 1920, he emerged as one of the 24 general elders of the PAW.

In 1923, when the organization was again altered and leadership placed in a relatively small board of presbyters, Douglas's name was not among the group, made up primarily of White members; however, he remained a prominent leader. He would begin to come into his own two years later. In the meantime, in 1924, Douglas moved to Los Angeles to become the pastor of the Apostolic Faith Home Assembly.

Until 1925, the Assemblies was an interracial fellowship with Black and White leaders and members working together. In 1924, however, the White members left to found the Pentecostal Ministerial Alliance. In response the PAW, now a predominantly Black organization, reorganized without the legislation which had been passed to appease the White leadership. Douglas's name was on the roster of district elders. In 1925 the Assemblies made its most radical organization change by adopting an episcopal government and electing five bishops, with provisions for enlarging the board of bishops in the near future. When that enlargement was made in 1928, Douglas was among those elected.

In 1931, Bishop **Garfield T. Haywood**, whose dynamism had largely held the Assemblies together during the ever-changing turbulent 1920s, died in 1931. On the heels of his death the Pentecostal Ministerial Alliance presented a plan for the reuniting of the PAW with its former White members. Many of the members and leaders wanted the return of the Assemblies to its fully integrated structure. As a result they left to found the Pentecostal Assemblies of Jesus Christ. When the dust settled, only two bishops remained of the board as constituted in 1928, A. William Lewis, a White man, and Douglas. They picked up the pieces and at a special meeting in March 1932 again reorganized.

In 1932, **Samuel J. Grimes** was elected as a third bishop and appointed as presiding bishop of the Assemblies. He would lead the PAW for the next thirty years. At this point Douglas's responsibilities became focused upon California, and he assumed responsibility for the development of the church on the West Coast. He was regularly returned to the bishop's office in the Assemblies' periodic elections for the rest of his life. He died in Los Angeles following a quarter century of work.

Golder, Morris E. *The Bishops of the Pentecostal Assemblies of the World.* Indianapolis, IN: The Author, 1980. 69 pp.

———. *History of the Pentecostal Assemblies of the World.* Indianapolis, IN: The Author, 1973. 195 pp.

DOYLE, BERTRAM WILBUR (July 3, 1897–December, 1980), 25th bishop of the **Christian Methodist Episcopal Church** (CME), was born in Lowndesboro, Alabama, one of four sons of Henry Sebastian and Anna Magnolia (Walker) Doyle. His father was a minister in the CME Church, and the family moved often. Doyle received his primary school education in Kerrville, Texas, and later attended the high school division of Wiley College in Marshall, Texas, from which he graduated in 1916. He then entered Ohio Wesleyan University in Delaware, Ohio, and on August 12, 1918, married Pansy Ray Stewart, with whom he had five children. He graduated from Ohio Wesleyan in 1921 and later, despite multiple other responsibilities, earned degrees from the University of Chicago (M.A., 1924 and Ph.D., 1934) and from Lane College in Jackson, Tennessee (D.D., 1934).

He taught sociology and economics at Samuel Houston College in Huntsville, Texas, from 1921 to 1922, and then sociology and psychology at Claflin College in Orangeburg, South Carolina, from 1922 to 1924. He pastored the St. Luke Presbyterian Church in Orangeburg from 1922 to 1923. He was ordained a deacon in the CME Church in 1924, and that year moved to teach at Clark University in Atlanta, Georgia. From 1925 to 1927 he was Dean of Paine College in Augusta, Georgia, and from 1926 to 1927 pastored the Macedonia CME Church in Allendale, South Carolina, about forty miles from the college. In 1926 he was Regional Director of the Georgia State Colored Teacher's Association, and from 1926 to 1927 was vice president of the National Association of Deans and Registrars in Colored Schools. In 1927 he became professor of sociology at Fisk University in Nashville, Tennessee, serving also as Dean of Men from 1928 to 1930. From 1929 to 1930 he pastored St. Luke's CME Church in Nashville.

Doyle remained at Fisk until 1937, when he was elected Secretary of Education for the CME Church, with headquarters in Louisville, Kentucky. He remained in that position until 1950, and was also Dean of Louisville Municipal College from 1942 to 1950. In 1937 his Ph.D. dissertation in sociology was published as *The Etiquette of Race Relations in the South: A Study in Social Control.* In 1948 he was president of the National Association of Deans and Registrars. At the General Conference in May, 1950, he was elected bishop and assigned to the Seventh Episcopal District, followed by the Sixth Episcopal District in 1954, the Eighth Episcopal District (Texas) in 1958, and the Second Episcopal District in 1966. He was a member of the executive committee of the World Methodist Council from 1951 to 1971, and led the CME Church delegation to the World Methodist Conference in Oslo, Norway, in 1961, and in London in 1966. He was chair of the board of trustees of Texas College in Tyler, Texas, from 1958 to 1966. He was senior bishop of the church from 1962 to 1970, when he retired.

Doyle, Bertram Wilbur. *The Etiquette of Race Relations in the South: A Study in Social Control.* Chicago: The University of Chicago Press, 1937. 249 pp.
———. *A Study of Business and Employment Among Negroes in Louisville, by Associates of Louisville Community College, University of Louisville, Louisville Urban League, Central Colored High School.* Louisville, KY: N.p., 1944. 92 pp.
"The Life of Bishop B. W. Doyle." *The Christian Index* 113 (December 15, 1980): 4.
IBAW, BAW, IBAWCB, HUBA, AARS, CMECTY, WWABA (80–81), *BDNM* (70), *EWM, EBA, WWCA* (38–40), *WWW* (78–79), *NYB* (1925–26).

DREW, TIMOTHY. *See:* **ALI, NOBLE DREW**.

DRIVER, EDDIE R. (? –1958) was the pioneer minister of the **Church of God in Christ** on the West Coast. Little is known of his early life, but at some point early in this century he became a minister in the church. He attended the first general assembly of the church in 1907. In 1914 he traveled to Los Angeles and preached the first sermons by a COGIC minister in the state. He returned home for his wife and before the year was out had settled in Los Angeles. He founded Saints Home Church, the denomination's Mother Church for the Southwest, and began an evangelistic ministry. He was named overseer for the states of California, Oregon, Washington, Arizona, and New Mexico. By 1919 he had founded 11 churches.

Driver would lead COGIC in California for over 35 years as overseer and later as bishop. In 1940 **Samuel M. Crouch**, long time pastor in Los Angeles, was consecrated bishop, and the aging and ill Driver turned over the administration of the district to him. Driver lived long enough to see his son, Louis M. Driver, consecrated as the bishop for Southern California, a new district which had been carved out of the growing West Coast work.

International Annual Holy Convocation Diamond Jubilee [Souvenir Program]. Memphis, TN: Church of God in Christ, 1982. 428 pp.

DUMAS, P. C. (c.1910– ?), pioneer Lutheran minister, grew up in Alabama and entered the Lutheran Church after attending one of the Christian day schools offered by the Synodical Conference (the agency covering mission work among Blacks). He was educated in church and public schools and then served as teacher and lay missionary in Tuscaloosa, Alabama, under the Synodical Conference. In 1928 he moved to Booth, Alabama, and worked for the American Lutheran Church under the Joint Synod of Ohio. During the next five years he worked variously there and in Prattville and Clanton (both in Alabama) and Jackson, Mississippi.

In 1933 he moved to Chicago, Illinois, where he continued religious supply work and was employed as a postal worker. During World War II he was assistant to Lutheran Chaplain John Plueger in Europe, and decided to become a minister. He did additional studies at Wilberforce University in Xenia, Ohio, and at Lutheran Theological Seminary at Capital University in Columbus, Ohio. He was ordained at St. James Evangelical Lutheran Church in Chicago, Illinois, pastored by another Black Lutheran, Robbin Skyles, on December 15, 1946. In January, 1947, he began pastoral work in Montgomery, Prattville, Booth, Wetumpka, and Clanton, Alabama. He later took additional courses at Alabama Lutheran Bible Institute and Alabama State College. In 1948 he was able to focus his energies at Trinity Lutheran Church in Montgomery, and remained there into the 1950s.

LCAN.

DUNSTON, ALFRED GILBERT, JR. (b. June 25, 1915), 68th bishop of the **African Methodist Episcopal Zion Church** (AMEZ), was born in Coinjock, North Carolina, the son of Alfred Gilbert and Cora Lee (Charity) Dunston. He was converted in Elizabeth City, North Carolina, and decided to become a minister. After receiving his B.A. (1935) from Livingstone College in Salisbury, North Carolina, he preached his trial sermon on September 4, 1935, at the Mt. Lebanon AME Zion Church, Elizabeth City. In 1936 he joined the Western North Carolina Conference and began pastoring at the Mt. Sinai AMEZ Church in Advance, North Carolina. He was ordained deacon in July, 1937, and transferred to the St. John AMEZ Church in Tomasville, North Carolina. In June, 1938, he was ordained elder.

In 1939 he was assigned to the Wallace Temple AMEZ Church in Bayonne, New Jersey, and took the opportunity to take graduate courses at Drew University in Madison, New Jersey, in 1939 and in 1941. He married Permilla R. Flack on June 18, 1940, and they had three children. He and Permilla later divorced. From 1941 to 1943 he was the minister of Price Memorial

AMEZ Church in Atlantic City, New Jersey, followed by service in the 92nd Infantry Division as chaplain in World War II. He won a citation for meritorious service in support of combat troops in the Po Valley Campaign. From 1946 to 1948 he pastored the Wallace Chapel AMEZ Church in Summit, New Jersey, from 1946 to 1948. Dunston then transferred to the Logan Temple AMEZ Church in Knoxville, Tennessee, where he stayed until 1952. From 1952 to 1963 he was assigned to the prestigious Big Wesley AMEZ Church in Philadelphia, Pennsylvania, where his reputation was developed across the church. He served on the board of directors of the Western Community House in Philadelphia beginning in 1956, and in 1963 was co-founder of Opportunities Industrialization Center. In 1958 he narrated the film, "The Rising New Africa," and in 1963 narrated a television documentary, "The Run From Race." From 1960 to 1963 he was a member of the Selective Patronage Movement in Philadelphia, and during the same period one of the directors of the Philadelphia Council of Churches. He was a trustee of Berea College and was a member of the Commission on Human Relations in Philadelphia.

At the 1956 General Conference Dunston (with others) was ruled ineligible as a candidate for the episcopacy, based on an irregular marital status (divorced). The controversy continued for the next eight years, but in 1964 General Conference the body voted to place Dunston's name on the ballot, and both he and **Charles Foggie**, also divorced, were subsequently elected bishops. Dunston was consecrated on May 21 and assigned to the Fourth Episcopal District (Nigeria and Liberia). He lived in Philadelphia, and in 1974 published *Black Man in the Old Testament and Its World*. In 1979 he became a teacher for the Institute for Black Ministries. In about 1980 he was assigned to the Second Episcopal District (North Carolina, New England, New Jersey, Albermarle, and Virgin Island Conferences). In 1984 *Ebony* magazine named him one of America's top fifteen Black preachers.

"America's Fifteen Greatest Black Preachers." *Ebony* 39 (September 1984): 27–33.

"Vignettes of Our Bishops: Bishop Alfred Gilbert Dunston, Jr." *Star of Zion* 111 (October 22, 1987): 7.

HAMEZC, WWABA (90–91), *WWR* (85), *EWM, AMEZC, BDNM* (75), *EBA*.

"We told him if he turned us out contrary to the rules of discipline, we should seek further redress. We told him we were dragged off our knees in St. George's church, and treated worse than heathens; and we were determined to seek out for ourselves, the Lord being our helper. He told us we were not Methodists, and left us."

Richard Allen, Founder
African Methodist Episcopal Church
1793

E

EASTERN ORTHODOX CATHOLIC CHURCH IN AMERICA. An Eastern Orthodox church. The Eastern Orthodox Catholic Church was begun in 1927 in New York City by Samuel Durbin Benedict and Edwin Wallace Hunter, who founded the Evangelical Catholic Church of New York. That year they consecrated John Thomas Beckles who, as Mar Thomas Theophilus, moved to found an independent jurisdiction which he called the Evangelical Orthodox Catholic Church in America. In 1933 Beckles was consecrated sub conditione by William Frederick Tyarcks, a White man but also a bishop of the **African Orthodox Church**. Beckles established his work in Harlem not far from a center opened in 1932 by **John More-Moreno**.

More-Moreno, a West Indian, had been ordained in 1932 in the Holy Eastern Orthodox Catholic and Apostolic Church in North America. The church grew out of a plan by Archbishop Aftimios Ofeish, who headed the Syrian work of the Russian Orthodox Church, to create an American multi-ethnic Orthodox church which would eventually incorporate all of Eastern Orthodoxy in North America. The plan was scuttled by the Russian Church after the Episcopal Church, which was giving heavy financial support to the poverty-stricken Russians, expressed its strong disapproval. Ofeish left the Russian jurisdiction to pursue his vision. Leadership of the church fell to Sophronios Bishara who ordained More-Moreno.

More-Moreno opened the Church of the Redeemer on Lenox Avenue in Harlem. In 1933 Bishara consecrated him, and the church became the Cathedral of Our Saviour. Bishara died in 1934. All the other bishops having either died or been deposed, More-Moreno inherited the corporation and became its ruling bishop.

During the 1930s, More-Moreno and Beckles met and became close friends. In 1943 More-Moreno was reconsecrated by Beckles, at which time he assumed the ecclesiastical name Mar Chrysostomos. In 1948 Beckles died, and More-Moreno became the ruling bishop and Patriarch of the Eastern Orthodox Catholic Church in America. He headed the church until his death in 1958. Shortly before he died he consecrated Gregory R. P. Adair, who succeeded him as ruling bishop, and John Adair. Gregory Adair was succeeded in the 1980s, by Dismas Markle, the present leader of the jurisdiction, who had been consecrated by Adair in 1981. Headquarters of the church is in central Florida at Sanford. In 1974 the church reported four active congregations.

Persson, Bertil. *The Apostolic Episcopal Ministry, Archbishop Arthur W. Brooks and Christ's Church by the Sea: Its Memory and Appreciation.* Solna, Sweden: The Author, 1989. 117 pp.

EDWARD WATERS COLLEGE. An **African Methodist Episcopal Church** (AME) school. Edward Waters College continues the education thrust initiated in Florida in 1866, immediately after the Civil War and the entrance of the AME Church into the state. The school was located on a 640–acre tract at Live Oak, Florida. It was chartered in 1872 as Brown Theological Institute, but renamed Brown University in 1874. However, in 1875, the school was lost in a lawsuit. Then in 1883, a second school was started in Jacksonville. Members of the local Mount Zion AME Church contributed their labors to erect the first building. It was called the East Florida Conference High School and later renamed Florida Scientific and Divinity High School. This school was lost in the 1901 fire which destroyed much of Jacksonville.

After the fire, the school was reopened in rented facilities. It was renamed after the church's third bishop, Edward Waters, and began the climb to become a college in fact as well as name. Giant steps were taken during the ten-year presidency of Bishop **John Hurst**. A theological department was opened in 1904.

Smith, Charles Spencer. *A History of the African Methodist Episcopal Church*. Philadelphia: Book Concern of the AME Church, 1922. 570 pp.

Wright, R. R. *The Encyclopedia of the African Methodist Episcopal Church*. Philadelphia, PA: The Book Concern of the AME Church, 1947. 688 pp.

EICHELBERGER, JAMES WILLIAM, JR. (August 30, 1886–January 24, 1967), General Secretary of Religious Education for the **African Methodist Episcopal Zion Church** (AMEZ), was born in Columbia, South Carolina, the son of James Washington and Josephine (Myers) Eichelberger. His mother passed away when he was young, and his father, a minister of the AMEZ Church, married Anzaniah M. Hartwell in 1892. He attended Howard Graded School in Columbia for only one month, after which his stepmother taught him at home for four years, until he enrolled in Allen University in Columbia, South Carolina, in 1896. He graduated from the normal department in 1900 and shifted into the college department. He was converted during a week of prayer services at Allen University in February 1900. He was then admitted to full membership in the Jones Chapel AMEZ Church on Main Street in Columbia.

In the fall of 1902 he transferred to Livingstone College in Salisbury, North Carolina, graduating with his B.A. in 1904. He was then employed briefly as a printer in the A.M.E. Zion Publishing House at Charlotte, North Carolina, until he gained a faculty position later that year at Clinton Institute (now College) at Rock Hill, South Carolina. In 1905 he attended the International Sunday School Convention of Toronto, Canada, which galvanized his previous interest in religious education and was the beginning of a new career direction. In 1907 he attended the Fifth World's Sunday School Convention in Rome, Italy, for which he was also the official representative of the AMEZ Church, though he had to provide his own funding for the trip. That year he left the teaching position and until 1909 managed a printing office in Columbia, South Carolina. In 1908 he was a delegate to General Conference for the first time, and continued to be a delegate for the rest of his life.

In 1909 he was elected principal of Walters Institute in Warren, Arkansas, where he stayed for the next dozen years. During these years the school's campus was greatly enlarged with additional land and buildings, and he founded the Civic League of Warren. He married Hattie Belle Miller on August 30, 1911, with whom he had one child. He continued developing his interest and skill in religious education, attending the Sixth World's

Sunday School Convention in Washington, D.C., and then in 1913 the Seventh World's Sunday School Convention in Zurich, Switzerland.

At the 1916 General Conference Eichelberger was elected General Superintendent of Sunday Schools for the AMEZ Church, a half-time position. In 1917 he originated and published the *Sunday School Bulletin*, which ran until 1924, when it was succeeded by the *Church School Herald*, which Eichelberger published until 1932. In 1920 the position was made full-time and he resigned from the Walters Institute, moving to Chicago, Illinois, the Christian Education headquarters of several denominations. He became a member of the Greater Walters AMEZ Church in Chicago. In 1921 he began coursework at Northwestern University in Chicago and completed his M.A. in religious education two years later.

At the 1924 General Conference the Sunday School and the Varick Christian Endeavor were merged and Eichelberger was elected to the new position of Director of Religious Education. He began work on a Ph.D., attending Northwestern again from 1925 to 1928, but only completed the first chapter of his dissertation, which was published as *The Religious Education of the Negro* (1931). At the 1932 General Conference all the offices of education in the denomination were combined, and he was elected General Secretary of the Christian Education Department, a position he held for the rest of his life. His first wife having passed away, he married Helen Herndon in 1938.

Eichelberger's long tenure at the helm of the church's Sunday School/Religious Education work gained him a high reputation and wide recognition, which he utilized in many arenas. He was a vice-president of the Executive Committee of the International Council of Religious Education and was a member of the Division of Christian Education of the National Council of Churches. He was a delegate to three Assemblies of the World Council of Churches (Amsterdam, 1948; Evanston, Illinois, 1954; and New Delhi, India, 1961). He was a part of the Chicago Inter-Racial Committee beginning in 1932. He was a trustee of Livingstone College and authored several booklets and manuals for the church.

Eichelberger, James William. "African Methodist Episcopal Church: The Rationale and Policies Upon Which Maintenance of its Colleges is Based." *Journal of Negro Education* 29 (Summer 1960): 323–329.

———. *The Religious Education of the Negro; an Address Delivered at the International Convention of Religious Education, Toronto, Canada, June 26, 1930, by James W. Eichelberger, Jr*. Chicago: The Herald Press, 1931. 16 pp.

"James William Eichelberger." *Star of Zion* 90 (March 9, 1967): 2.
WWCA (38–40), EWM, RLA, BAW, AARS, WWCR.

EIKERENKOETTER, FREDERICK J., II (b. June 1, 1935), founder of the **United Church and Science of Living Institute**, was born in Ridgeland, South Carolina, the son of Frederick Joseph, Sr., and Rema Estelle (Matthews) Eikerenkoetter. His father was a Baptist minister, architect, and builder, carrying a Dutch surname meaning "acorn carrier," and his mother was the local elementary school teacher. He received a call to the ministry at age fourteen and at age sixteen, although raised a Baptist, he became assistant pastor of the Bible Way Pentecostal Church in Ridgeland. He graduated from high school in 1952 and was so poor that additional schooling seemed out of the question. He received a scholarship, however, and in 1956 he earned a B.Th. from the American Bible College in New York City. From 1956 to 1958 he was a chaplain with the U.S. Air Force.

He then began work as a standard evangelist and faith healer, founding the United Church of Jesus Christ for All People back in Ridgeland. In 1962 he established the United Christian Evangelistic Association as the corporate vehicle of his ministry, which he still maintains. On February 7, 1964, he married Eula Mae Dent, with whom he had one child. Later that year he left Ridgeland and founded the Miracle Temple in Boston, experiencing great success as a healer. About 1965 he developed new ideas that seemed influenced by the New Thought movement, with its teachings of prosperity through mind-power, though he later claimed to have developed these ideas himself.

In 1966 he left Boston to set up a ministry in an abandoned movie theater on 125th Street in Harlem, New York City. His full name was awkwardly large for the marquee, and he became popularly known as Rev. Ike. He began to counsel followers to abandon a "pie-in-the-sky" theology of future rewards and to seek instead the good life now. He decided that preaching about hell was ineffectual, as most people are already in hell and are trying to get out. He began to describe God as less someone or somewhere else and more the real person in the self, adding that focusing on the self allows God to work. He urges visualization as a means of instilling successful thought in the mind, a first step toward abundant living. His work represents a major inroad of New Thought into the Black community.

In 1969 he moved out of Harlem into a block-sized former Loew's movie house on 175th Street in Manhattan's Washington Heights. He then founded the United Church and Science of Living Institute as the denominational name for his major settled congregation there. The building also houses his school, the Science of Living Institute. The United Church in New York soon developed an over 5,000–a-week average attendance, but most of his followers are not so organizationally affiliated. They were brought into relation with his work by preaching tours across the country, and by a gradually developed national radio network of over eighty stations and about twenty television stations. They are evident by the audiences he draws, by donations, and by subscriptions to his various offerings. He was the first Black minister to be seen on a regular nationwide television show. In 1972 he claimed 1,400,000 people to whom he sent a quarterly newsletter, *The Study Guide of the Science of Living*, and biweekly magazine called *Action!*.

Rev. Ike tells his followers to believe that "All that God is, I am," and "The lack of money is the root of all evil." He has said that the "best thing you can do for the poor is not to be one of them. And if you must do something, teach the poor how to do something for themselves." A method he offers to achieve one's goals of prosperity is the "Blessing Plan," by which one pledges money to his organization as an outward sign of one's inward belief that one deserves and seeks an abundant life. One then receives letters of financial advice. He receives many prayer requests each week and has built a Miracle Prayer Tower in New York with a Star of Faith on top. He reports answers to prayer as not only including financial rewards but also physical healing and family reconciliation.

He is in great demand as a guest speaker. In May 1973, he was a visiting lecturer in the department of psychiatry in Harvard Medical School; in January, 1975 he spoke at the University of Alabama; in November, 1975 he spoke at Atlanta University Center, and in 1977 he spoke at Rice University in Houston, Texas. He is a life member of the N.A.A.C.P. He has authored a number of pamphlets, including *How to Live Life More Abundantly* and *Where Does God Live?* In 1982 he reported that more than seven million people worldwide receive his quarterly magazine and that more than seventy million have ordered the red prayer cloths he advertises to be sent at no charge. He now has toned down his flamboyant image, spends less time on the road, and more time teaching classes in his school.

Eikerenkoetter, Frederick J. *Rev. Ike's Secrets for Health, Happiness, and Prosperity, for You: A Science of Living Study Guide.* 2nd ed. New York: F. Eikerenkoetter; Brookline, MA: Distributed by Science of Living Publications, 1982. 280 pp.

Murray, Virgie W. "Rev. Ike." *Sepia* 1 (February 1981): 79–82.

"Rev. Ike Preaches About the Profits." *Newsweek* 100 (December 20, 1982): 16.

Sanders, Charles L. "The Gospel According to Rev. Ike." *Ebony* 32 (December 1976): 148–154.

Tyler, Timothy. "That T-Bone Religion." *Time* 100 (December 11, 1972): 97.

WWABA (90–91), *IBAW*, *NYTBS* (75), *BH*, *WWR* (85).

EKEMAM, SAMUEL CHUKUKANNE (b. June 27, 1942), 83rd bishop of the **African Methodist Episcopal Zion Church** (AMEZ), was born in Ogwa Owerri, Biafra, the son of Josiah Akujobi and Catherine Mba Ekemam. He was ordained as a minister in the AMEZ Church and taught in the Owerri Schools from 1961 to 1963, and in the Port Harcourt Province of the church, Ahoada, in 1964. From 1964 to 1966 he was general secretary of the Ogwa Protestant Association. He married Faustina Akubuiro Ifechukwu.

In 1967 he went to the United States to attend school, supporting himself through pastoral assignments, serving the Doggetts Grove AMEZ Church in Forest City from 1967 to 1968 and the Hopewell AMEZ Church in Harris, North Carolina, from 1969 to 1970. His coursework was at Livingstone College in Salisbury, North Carolina, where he received his B.A. in 1970, taking some courses also at the related Hood Theological Seminary. In 1971 he moved to New Haven, Connecticut, where he became pastor of the Evers Memorial AMEZ Church while attending Yale University, receiving his M.A. in 1972.

Ekemam then returned to Africa, where he served as Deputy Field Superintendent of the Central Nigeria Conference and Presiding Elder of the ABA District of the Central Nigeria Conference. In 1987 he began several nursery schools, now known as Varick Zion Academy, and part of Ekemam's program called "Catch Them Young." At the 1988 General Conference he was elected bishop, becoming the second native of Africa in the history of the denomination to become a bishop. At that General Conference the 13th Episcopal District was created, covering the Liberia, Nigeria, Rivers, and Central Nigeria Annual Conferences, and Ekemam was assigned to this district. About 1989 he registered the AMEZ Church with the Nigerian government, allowing it to receive deeds to government-allocated property. He maintains his headquarters in Imo State.

"Bishop Ekemam Receives Investiture in Homeland." *Star of Zion* 112 (October 6, 1988): 1, 2.

"Bishop S. Chuka Ekemam Declares 1990 as 'the Year of the Holy Spirit.'" *Star of Zion* 114 (May 3, 1990): 8, 9.

"Three Bishops Consecrated at Little Rock AME Zion." *Star of Zion* 112 (August 18, 1988): 1, 2.

BDNM (75).

ELAW, ZILPHA (c.1790– ?), a pioneer woman Methodist Episcopal evangelist, was born near Philadelphia, Pennsylvania, one of three children (of 22 brothers and sisters) who survived. Her mother died when she was twelve years old, after giving birth to a twenty-second child. Elaw was then sent to live with Pierson and Rebecca Mitchel and their Quaker family until she was eighteen. Her father died when she was about fourteen. While she was with the Piersons she experienced conversion and saw a vision of Jesus. That year, 1808, she joined the Methodist Episcopal Church. In 1810 she married Joseph Elaw, a fuller by trade, with whom she had a daughter. About 1815 his business required a move to Burlington, New Jersey. The marriage was a difficult one in many ways because he was not so interested in religion. In 1816 she fell and received serious internal injuries from which she nearly died.

In 1817 she attended a camp meeting and expressed her first public prayer. People responded to her words, and soon she saw that this was something she may have been gifted to do. For the next several years she visited with many people on spiritual matters and saw numerous conversions. In 1819 she was again near death with an illness and had a vision of future health and a new call to come to a camp meeting. About a year later the camp meeting happened and there she received the divine word to go and preach. She subsequently received the approval and support of the elders and began to do so, but what she termed jealousy soon turned most of her Black class-members against her. Neither was her husband pleased with her preaching, but she continued. His health began to decline, until he passed away on January 27, 1823.

Elaw then was forced to find a servant's position until her own health declined again. At that point she opened a small school for Black children in her home and it slowly grew with the help of Quaker friends. After about two years she felt the call to venture forth preaching. In 1827 she left her daughter with relatives and went to Philadelphia, where she was so warmly received that she gained new courage to continue on to New York. She returned to Burlington in April 1828, with enough money to pay all her debts. After a few days she began a preaching tour of Maryland,

Washington, D.C., and the South. The power of her preaching combined with the novelty of a Black woman as a public speaker made her a sensation wherever she went.

In 1830 she made her way to the northeastern states, where she continued her pattern of winning over even hostile congregations and individuals. She was known to criticize the "artificial delicacy and respectability" of White Christians whose racism and immorality was often hid behind a veil of piety. She answered criticisms of a woman as preacher by referring to biblical figures such as Phoebe and Priscilla and the sometimes "extraordinary directions" of the Holy Spirit. In Nantucket, Massachusetts, about 1833, she was bedridden for eight months and at one point seemed about to die. About the time of her recovery her daughter married and settled there. After more journeys she joined her daughter and newborn child from about December, 1834 to July, 1835. She then had another preaching tour of fifteen months, and returned to Nantucket for a settled period of about three years. During this time, in 1837, she had a vision which confirmed a previous intimation that she would someday go to England.

In 1839 she made a tour of the southern states and began to receive contributions toward a trip to England. Arrangements were finally made and she sailed from New York in July, 1840. She spent at least six years there as an evangelist, and possibly the end of her days. In 1846 she published her autobiography, *Memoirs of the Life, Religious Experience, Ministerial Travels and Labours of Mrs. Zilpha Elaw, an American Female of Colour.*

Elaw, Zilpha. *Memoirs of the Life, Religious Experience, Ministerial Travels, and Labours of Mrs. Zilpha Elaw, an American Female of Colour.* London: The Author, 1846.
AARS, HUBA, IBAW, BWR, SS, NBAW.

EMBRY, JAMES CRAWFORD (November 2, 1834–August 16, 1897), 25th bishop of the **African Methodist Episcopal Church** (AME), was born in Knox County, Indiana, of Baptist parents who had migrated from South Carolina. He grew up on a farm, was converted in 1855 in Galena, Illinois, and was licensed to preach the following year by the Rev. F. Meyers of the AME Church. Having received a good basic education, he was able to make a living as a teacher prior to turning all his energies to the church. Early in the Civil War he was a hand on a supply boat in U.S. Grant's army in Kentucky and Tennessee. He joined the Annual Conference in August 1864, led by Bishop Quinn. He was ordained deacon in 1866 and elder in 1870, holding

numerous church appointments over the years. On November 19, 1872, he married Oregon P. Franklin, with whom he had five children.

In 1876 he was elected Secretary of Education for the denomination, serving until 1879, when he was made financial secretary upon the death of J.H.W. Burley, holding that office until 1884. In 1881 he was a delegate to the World Methodist Conference in London. From 1884 to 1896 he was Business Manager, during which time he built the Publishing House on Pine Street in Philadelphia, installed new printing machinery, and increased the circulation of the *Christian Recorder*. He was a great encourager of literary endeavors, and saw to it that the church's publishing efforts were supported by the most influential and educated leaders of the church. In 1890 he published *Digest of Christian Theology*, which for nearly fifty years was a standard book in the training of AME clergy. In 1892 he published a revised AME Church hymnal, which remained the official hymnal until 1954. About the same time he purchased the *Southern Christian Recorder* from Bishop **Henry McNeal Turner**, who had founded it in 1889 and personally owned it. At some point his first wife died, and he later married again, and had one son, Richard.

In 1896 Embry was elected bishop, reportedly largely on the basis of his tremendous service with the Book Concern. He was assigned to the Seventh Episcopal District (South Carolina and Florida), but did not live to complete the four-year assignment. The AME church in Ogden, Utah, is named for him.

Embry, James Crawford. *Digest of Christian Theology, Designed for Use of Beginners, in the Study of Theological Science.* Philadelphia, PA: AME Book Concern, 1890. 293 pp.
———. *"Our Father's House" and Family, Past, Present, and Future.* Philadelphia, PA: AME Book Concern, 1893. 95 pp.
DNAADB, CEAMEC, HAMEC, EWM, TCBD, BAMEC, ACAB (vol. 2), BAW, AARS, HUBA.

EMMANUEL. First African American Lutheran baptized in America. The first baptism of a Black person into the Lutheran Church in what is now the United States occurred in New Amsterdam (now New York City) on Palm Sunday, 1669. While Lutherans had been in the colonies for some years, organization of congregations proceeded slowly. However, in March 1669, Rev. Johnanes Fabricius arrived from Holland to organize the small band of New Amsterdam Lutherans and to begin to preach and administer the sacraments.

During the Palm Sunday service that year, while twelve members of the congregation were set aside for various offices, one new member was baptized. Fabricius recorded the incident in his letter home, "I also baptized a Negro of about 50 years more or less." The congregation wrote also, ". . . on Dominica Palmarum a 50 year old Negro was baptized and named Emmanuel." Unfortunately, nothing more is known of this first convert of Lutheranism in America.

vanLaer, Arnold J. H., trans. *The Lutheran Church in New York, 1649–1772: Records of the Lutheran Church Archives at Amsterdam, Holland.* New York: New York Public Library, 1946. 277 pp.

EMMANUEL TABERNACLE BAPTIST CHURCH APOSTOLIC FAITH.

An Apostolic Pentecostal church. The Emmanuel Tabernacle Baptist Church Apostolic Faith began in 1916 (incorporated 1917) in Columbus, Ohio. Columbus was an early center of the non-Trinitarian Apostolic movement which had originated in 1913 and spread through the still youthful Pentecostal movement. The new church was founded by Rev. (later Bishop) Martin Rawleigh Gregory (1885–1960). Gregory had been called to the ministry as a 17-year-old youth. He was educated at Colgate University and became a Baptist minister in 1903. In 1914 he moved to Columbus, Ohio, where he encountered Pentecostalism in its Apostolic form. His adoption of Pentecostalism led to a break with the Baptist Church.

Gregory was assisted in the founding of the Emmanuel Tabernacle by two females who had worked with him in the Baptist Church, Lela Grant and Bessie Dockett. He came very early to believe that women should share equally in the preaching of God's word, and as bishop of the church, Gregory opened the ordained ministry to women, the first Apostolic church to do so. As the church grew, and a board of bishops was created, women were elevated to the episcopacy.

The church holds to an Apostolic non-Trinitarian theology. Jesus is the name of the One God and baptism is done in the name of Jesus only. The church also practices foot washing.

Headquarters of the church remains in Columbus, Ohio. The current leader, Bishop H. C. Clark, is a female. An annual meeting is held each summer in Columbus. In 1990 there were approximately 30 congregations.

Payne, Wardell J., ed. *Directory of African American Religious Bodies: A Compendium by the Howard University School of Divinity.* Washington, DC: Howard University Press, 1991. 363 pp.

ENDICH THEOLOGICAL SEMINARY.

An **African Orthodox Church** seminary. Endich Theological Seminary, New York, New York, was founded by Archbishop **George A. McGuire** for the purpose of training priests for the African Orthodox Church. The school opened in 1922 with twelve students and three faculty members. Joining McGuire were Rev. (later Bishop) J. J. Van Loo and a Rev. Bridgeman. Van Loo taught English and Bridgeman taught Latin, Greek, and Hebrew. McGuire taught the theological courses. The seminary had a tenuous existence in the chaotic years following Archbishop McGuire's death but experienced a revival in the mid-1930s when Bishop **Edmond R. Bennett** became dean.

Through the years the school has waxed and waned as the church experienced periods of more or less slow growth. It often operated as a correspondence school. At times it was known as the Bishop McGuire Theological Seminary and College.

EPISCOPAL CHURCH.

The African American presence in what is now known as the Episcopal Church (formerly known as the Protestant Episcopal Church in the U.S.A.) dates from 1624, when the Church of England began baptizing enslaved Africans in the American colonies. While work with Blacks was nominal in the seventeenth century, some Anglican clergy did seek to do earnest evangelism among Blacks toward the century's end. This intention came to concrete focus with the organization, in 1701, of the "Society for the Propagation of the Gospel in Foreign Parts," whose expressed purpose was religious outreach to Blacks and Native Americans. Because the Church of England used a written form of liturgy, the efforts of the society included literacy training as well as religious appeal. Over 300 missionary teachers and clergy served the society during the next eighty years.

In 1779, the Protestant Episcopal Church in the United States of America was organized following its separation from the Church of England as a result of U.S. independence. Few Blacks remained in the new Episcopal Church, preferring to seek racially autonomous groups as opposed to accepting segregated seating in White parishes. The first Black parish was founded in Philadelphia in 1794. It was comprised primarily of former Methodists who had experienced humiliation and abuse as members of St. George's Methodist Episcopal Church. In 1787, they had formed

The Free African Society, a mutual aid society dedicated to educational, economic, and community uplift. The Society also had a religious component. Their leaders, **Absalom Jones** and **Richard Allen**, were both licensed preachers in the Methodist Episcopal Church, and exhorted the members to remain in the Methodist connection, albeit as an independent congregation. However, the body decided to affiliate with the Episcopal Church, with the condition of self rule. Allen dissented, and went on to found the **African Methodist Episcopal Church** (AME). Jones, who had been born a slave in Delaware, reluctantly agreed to make the change to the Episcopal Church and was made pastor, being ordained deacon in 1795 and priest in 1804. He continued to work with Allen in community affairs, and participated in Allen's consecration as the first bishop of the African Methodist Episcopal Church in 1816.

Though they did not parallel in numbers the rise of independent Black Methodist churches, there did develop several Black Episcopal parishes, primarily in Northeastern cities: St. Philip's, New York City (1819), St. James, Baltimore (1824), Christ Church, Providence (1843), St. Luke's, New Haven (1844), Crucifixion, Philadelphia (1847), St. Matthew's, Detroit (1851), and St. Philip's, Newark (1856). Most of these parishes had Black priests and vestries. Most also established schools and were active in fighting segregation in their respective cities. Several had to battle for the right to have voting representation in the General Convention. For instance, St. Thomas', Philadelphia, did not win that right until 1863. The churches also took an active role in the anti-slavery and abolitionist movements. St. Matthew's, Detroit, was a terminus on the Underground Railroad.

The growth of the Episcopal church among *southern* Blacks was quite different. The vast majority of Black Episcopalians in the South were enslaved members of their masters' parishes, or members of "slave parishes" established on plantations. If members of masters' parishes, they would normally meet at a time other than the regular Sunday service. All slave parishes were under the direct supervision of White clerical and lay leadership. The largest numbers were in South Carolina and Georgia, although Louisiana had some thirty-one slave parishes with thirty-six hundred members by 1855. In several urban areas, congregations were established for free and enslaved Blacks, under the supervision of White clergy and vestries. Calvary, Charleston, South Carolina (1848), St. Stephen's, Savannah (1856), and Chapel of the Good Shepherd, Mobile (1857), typified such efforts.

The Post Civil War Era. After the Civil War southern

Blacks left the Episcopal Church in droves. Evangelization efforts of Black Methodist and Baptist groups combined with the desire for self-determination by Black Episcopalians to produce a grand exodus. By some estimates, ninety percent of the exodus went to Black Methodist denominations. The AME, AMEZ and the CME Churches were particularly attractive to newly freed men and women, bringing together much of the liturgical sensibilities of Episcopal worship, while allowing for more cultural expression, as well as self-governance. In Charleston one sizeable group of Blacks affiliated with the newly formed (1873) Reformed Episcopal denomination. Organized in a "missionary" relationship to the Northern based denomination, between five hundred and one thousand communicants called the new church home in 1875, with several men received for ordination. Fairly obscure in Black church history, this branch of South Carolinian Episcopalians had grown in number to about three thousand by 1990, virtually half the small denomination's entire membership.

In 1865 the General Convention organized a Freedman's Commission paralleling some of the missionary efforts of Northern White denominations in the South. However its most lasting efforts were not in evangelization, but rather in education, having reached over 5,000 students before its demise in 1906. Schools were begun in Virginia, the Carolinas, Georgia, Florida and Kentucky, though the only surviving school of the Commission's efforts is St. Augustine's College (1867) in North Carolina. While it was not begun by the Commission, St. Paul's College (1888) emerged from the same missionary impulse, much of which had centered in Central Virginia by that time.

The Commission also spearheaded relief efforts to ease poverty among freedmen and women through donations of clothing and household items, as well as finances to feed and house the poorest among them.

Among the Northern Black leadership the missionary impulse had taken a different direction. Riding the rising tide of Black Nationalism and the early crest of Pan Africanism, Black church leaders focused on ministry to Liberia and Haiti. **James Theodore Holly**, believing that the best potential for Black self governance and progress lay in the Republic of Haiti, led a migration of New England Blacks to that Caribbean country in 1861, and established the Orthodox Apostolic Church, the first independent church established in the Anglican Communion in a non-English speaking area. In 1874 he was consecrated as the first African American bishop in the church, and in 1878 became the first Black to preach at Westminster Abbey. In 1885, **Samuel Ferguson** was made Bishop of Liberia and became the first Black to sit in the House of Bishops.

However the central figure in the nationalist/missionary efforts of the post Civil War era was **Alexander Crummell**. Refused admission to the General Theological Seminary of the Episcopal Church in New York, Crummell attended Andover Seminary in Massachusetts and was ordained to the ministry there in Boston. After further study in England, Crummell went to Liberia as parish priest and professor at the College of Liberia. Subsequent to his return to the United States in 1873, he founded St. Luke's parish in Washington, D.C., and brought the spirit of Pan Africanism to his work within the Episcopal Church in the United States. Crummell was an important thinker, speaker and writer in the Pan African movement. His sermons often reflected his commitment to Africa as the Black American's homeland, and called for serious investment in the progress of Blacks in Africa and the Americas. A co-founder of the American Negro Academy in 1897, he had a tremendous influence on the scholarly development of a young Harvard-trained thinker who happened to be baptized at St. Luke's, New Haven some years earlier, one W.E.B. DuBois.

In 1883 Crummell organized the Conference of Church Workers Among Colored People. That same year, the Conference successfully fought a plan to establish separate, disenfranchised "missionary districts" for Blacks in each diocese, and in 1886 led the church into the establishment of a Commission for Work Among Colored People. This Commission was instrumental in the regular publication of *The Church Advocate*, a journal of Black concerns. It also established King Hall, a seminary for the training of Black priests, under the leadership of Howard University professor William Tunnell. King Hall later closed, as Blacks were encouraged to go to Bishop Payne Divinity School (1878), a segregated branch of Virginia Theological Seminary. Payne was named for a White man who was the first bishop of Liberia.

The Commission met annually well into the twentieth century. It consisted mostly of Black persons, clergy and lay, but there were also some White persons involved with ministries in the Black community. It was a primary resource for strengthening the churches' work in those communities. The Commission continued its fight for justice in the general church, supporting a compromise plan in 1907 that would have established a national bishop for "Negrowork" with the designation "suffragan." The General Convention voted down the proposal, opting instead to set up "suffragans" in individual dioceses. Removing the office from the national church and tying it to the regions effectively slowed the process and diluted the power of the development of a Black episcopacy. Only in 1918 did any diocese name a Black suffragan—**Edward Demby** in Arkansas and **Henry Delany** in North Carolina; all other appointments went to White clerics. In addition to their parish work, both men had distinguished careers as educators, Demby at Paul Quinn College (an African Methodist school in Texas) and Delany at St. Augustine's. Yet the effectiveness of each man's episcopacy was circumscribed by White control and racism. The only other Black suffragan consecrated was **T. Momolu Gardiner** of Liberia.

By the 1920s the Conference of Church Workers was well established, and the number of Black congregations had risen to over 280. St. James, Baltimore, rector **George Freeman Bragg**, was diligent in his work as editor of *The Church Advocate*, and in 1922 published a book-length history of Blacks in the Episcopal church. The Episcopal Church formalized its relationship with Voorhees Junior College, which had been founded some twenty years earlier. Priest Arthur Myron Cochran published a setting of the Communion mass set to the music of Negro spirituals in 1925. Jamaican born Henry Laird Phillips received continued acclaim as archdeacon for colored work in Philadelphia. Brooklyn priest George Frazier Miller had been recognized for leadership in the Black labor movement, having assisted A. Philip Randolph in the organization of the National Association for the Promotion of Labor Unionism among Workers. This generation of leadership was succeeded by men such as **Tollie L. Caution, Sr.**, who served as Secretary for Negro Work for the National Church from 1945–52. He succeeded **Bravid W. Harris**, who became the first Black diocesan Bishop of Liberia, and then assistant director of the department of Domestic Missions.

It should be noted that much of the increase in Black membership in the Episcopal Church during this period came from the increased immigration of Anglicans from the Caribbean. Among their number, leaders such as Archdeacon Philips and **Alexander McGuire** made their impact on the church. Maguire later left the Episcopal Church to oversee the **African Orthodox Church**, a religious expression of **Marcus Garvey**'s Universal Negro Improvement Association.

The rise of the civil rights movement and the growing racial consciousness of the 1950s and 1960s were not without Black Episcopal contributions. Good Shepherd parish was part of the Montgomery Improvement Association. Episcopal clergy in Philadelphia were involved in the early development of **Leon Sullivan**'s Opportunities Industrialization Centers. **Nathan Wright**, of the diocese of Newark, was a central figure in the Black Power Conferences of the late 1960s, and several Episcopal church leaders were instrumental in the development of the National Committee of Negro Churchmen (now the **National Conference of Black Churchmen**). The ecumenical spirit of Black Episcopalians saw Thomas Logan elected to the board of directors of the Hampton Ministers' Conference and to the founding of the Absalom Jones Theological Institute as a constituent member of the Interdenominational Theological Center in 1972.

Within the church, the Episcopal Society of Cultural and Racial Unity was founded to foster interracial dialogue and activism. In 1967 the General Convention established a special program to address concerns arising from Black economic and self-determination efforts. In 1968 the Union of Black Episcopalians was started as a caucus movement within the Church, continuing the ministry of the Conference of Churchworkers. The Office for Negro Work has developed into the Office of Black Ministries, which has published *The Linkage* since 1984. Important consultations and conferences sponsored by Black Episcopalians in this era include a major theological consultation at the University of the South in 1978 and participation in an international Conference on Afro-Anglicanism at Codrington College, Barbados, in 1985. Then in 1989, the Black bishops held a consultation in Santo Domingo, from which was issued the document, *But We See Jesus: A Pastoral Letter from the Black Episcopal Bishops to the Clergy and Laity of the Episcopal Church.* Important theological voices which emerged in this period include Robert Bennett, J. Carleton Hayden, Kortright Davis, **Pauli Murray**, and Robert Hood.

Three Black bishops were consecrated in the 1960s, including **John Burgess** of Massachusetts. Elected suffragan in 1962, he became in 1970 the first Black diocesan bishop in the continental United States. By 1992, there were twenty-four Black bishops in the Protestant Episcopal Church, along with over four hundred fifty priests, thirty-three deacons, and an estimated quarter of a million communicants.

Finally, a Black parish was the site of the first ordination of female clergy in the Episcopal Church. These "irregular ordinations" (so called because they were not formally recognized until 1976) were held at the Church of the Advocate, Philadelphia, in 1974, where Paul Washington, a staunch community activist, was rector. A Black laywoman served as the crucifer in the procession for this historic event. She became, in 1988, the first female bishop in the Episcopal Church, the Anglican Communion, and all the churches that claim apostolic succession. Her name is **Barbara Harris**.

Bennett, Robert. "Black Episcopalians: A History from the Colonial Period to the Present." *The Historical Magazine of the Protestant Episcopal Church* 43, 3 (Sept. 1974):231–245.

Bragg, George Freeman. *The History of the Afro-American Group of the Episcopal Church.* New York: Johnson Reprint Corp, 1968. 319 pp.

Burgess John M., ed. *Black Gospel/White Church.* New York: Seabury, 1982. 108 pp.

Hayden, J. Carleton. "Conversion and Control: Dilemma of Episcopalians in Providing for the Religious Instruction of Slaves in Charleston, South Carolina, 1845–1860." *The Historical Magazine of the Protestant Episcopal Church* 40, 2 (June 1971):143–170.

———. "After the War: The Mission and Growth of the Episcopal Church among Blacks in the South, 1865–1877" *The Historical Magazine of the Protestant Episcopal Church* 42, 4 (Dec. 1973):403–427.

Jackson, Irene. "Music Among Blacks in the Episcopal Church: Some Preliminary Considerations." In *Lift Every Voice and Sing: A Collection of Afro-American Spirituals and Other Songs.* New York: Church Hymnal Corporation, 1981, pp. xvii–xxvii.

St. Luke's Journal of Theology (proceedings of Black Theological consultation) 22 (Sept. 1979).

Harold Dean Trulear

EPISCOPAL COMMISSION FOR BLACK MINISTRIES. An **Episcopal Church** agency. Founded in 1973, the Episcopal Commission for Black Ministries inherits the tradition of a series of structures established by the church over the years since the Civil War, each reflecting a maturing opinion concerning the role of African Americans in this large and somewhat aristocratic church. In 1865 the general convention created the Freedman's Commission to coordinate its missionary and benevolent ministries with the former slaves in the South. The commission was given permanent status within the Church's Board of Missions in 1870 as the Commission on Home Missions to Colored People.

Under the commission, African American churches were founded and nourished, schools were created, and ministers trained. An organized African American presence was evident from 1883 on when the annual Conference on Church Workers Among Colored People began to meet. In 1886 it petitioned the general convention to create a Church Commission for Work among Colored People which the church enacted. Then in 1906 the Board of Missions created the American

Church Institute for Negroes to provide additional support for the several African American schools.

The work of and with African Americans remained with the institute and the Board of Missions through the 1960s. Then in 1973, in response to the Civil Rights movement, the 1968 formation of the Union of Black Clergy and Laity (now the **Union of Black Episcopalians**), and the new Black consciousness present in both the secular world and the church, the Episcopal Commission for Black Ministries was created. Membership is composed of Black members of the church from across the United States. It serves as an official voice for Black people within the church and funnels church funds to assist developing congregations. The commission publishes a directory of Black clergy annually, and periodically convenes the Black Diocesan executives. The commission is headquartered at the church headquarters building in New York City.

Bragg, George F. *History of the Afro-American Group of the American Episcopal Church.* Baltimore, MD: Church Advocate Press, 1922. 319 pp.

EPPS, SAINT PAUL LANGLEY (b. February 18, 1916), a minister of the United Presbyterian Church, now a part of the **Presbyterian Church (U.S.A.),** general church officer, was born in Norfolk, Virginia, the son of William and Azarina Epps. His parents were active in the **African Methodist Episcopal Church** (AME), but through his paper route he developed a friendship with B. B. Evans, the minister of the local United Presbyterian Church. As a teenager he joined the United Presbyterian Church, but remained involved in the AME youth activities. Already as a young man he knew he wanted to be a minister.

Rev. Evans helped find scholarship funds to put Epps through college, and he graduated from Knoxville College, Tennessee, in 1939. He then entered Pittsburgh-Xenia Seminary in Pittsburgh, Pennsylvania, graduating in 1942. He married Kathryn Gilliam, with whom he had three children. In his final year of seminary, he was a student pastor at the Bidwell Presbyterian Church in Pittsburgh, but upon graduation felt that he needed to return to a ministry in the South. He was ordained in the United Presbyterian Church of North America, now a constituent part of the Presbyterian Church (U.S.A.) in August, 1942, and accepted a call to the Henderson United Presbyterian Church in Henderson, North Carolina. Henderson Institute, a mission school, was related to the church, and he also taught history there. During his four-and-a-half-year pastorate, he expanded the church beyond its milieu of the school and into the surrounding community.

In September 1946, instead of accepting a fellowship at Yale Divinity School for post-graduate study, he moved to Los Angeles, California, under the auspices of the denomination's American Board of Missions to begin the first of that church's congregations west of the Mississippi River under Black leadership. He settled in the newly developing Bel-Vue community, next to Watts, and the church property consisted of at first only a parsonage, garage, and vacant lot. Because of the community's lack of connection with Presbyterianism, the church was organized as the Bel-Vue Community Church. The church grew rapidly; in 1949 the sanctuary was dedicated and its mortgage was burned in 1957, when work on the educational unit was begun. Community outreach was significant, and Epps was a leader in the Bel-Vue Improvement League, bringing city services into the community. The church pioneered a program to help people establish credit and for acquiring scholarship aid for students.

During this time he gained a high profile in the denomination, serving as Moderator of both the Presbytery of Los Angeles and the Synod of California. He moderated the meeting at which the merger with the Presbyterian Church in the United States of America was agreed upon (the merger occurred in 1958). In 1964 he left Los Angeles to become part of the General Council staff in New York as Secretary for Services to Synods and Presbyteries in the Department of Interpretation and Stewardship. He was assigned to the Synods of the Dakotas, Iowa, Nebraska, and Colorado, and under his leadership per capita giving increased. In 1967 he joined the staff of the Division of Evangelism of the Board of National Missions as the Associate for Racial Ministries. This often involved helping White churches to adjust to changing neighborhoods and to learn to relate to non-White constituents.

In 1970 Epps became executive director of the new National Committee on the Self Development of People, a church-sponsored means of assisting poor people in achieving their goals. In 1979 he left New York to be interim pastor of the 180–member Rocky Mount Church in North Carolina. In 1981, at age 65, he moved to Windsor, North Carolina, formally entering retired status in 1988.

Wilson, Frank T., ed. "Living Witnesses: Black Presbyterians in Ministry, Part III." *Journal of Presbyterian History* 55 (Summer 1977): 180–238.
BDNM.

ESTELL, ERNEST COBLE (January 12, 1894–November 16, 1964), well-known Baptist preacher (**National Baptist Convention of the U.S.A., Inc.**), was born in Decherd, Tennessee, the eldest of three sons born to Robert Cole and Sarah Estell. As a young man Estell experienced conversion and was baptized into the Baptist Church. After attending the public schools in Decherd he graduated from the Summit High School in St. Louis, Missouri, where he joined the First Baptist Church. He took some courses from Alabama A & M College and graduated from Simmons University in Louisville, Kentucky, receiving the B.Th. degree. He married Leona Casey, with whom he had nine children.

He held a number of positions in the Boy Scouts of America, the Y.M.C.A., community organizations, interdenominational organizations, and several levels of Baptist denominational work. About 1925 he received a call to the ministry and his first pastorate was at Bethel Baptist Church in Drakesboro, Kentucky. In 1927 he moved to the Tabernacle Baptist Church in Dayton, Ohio, where he spent a very successful ten years. In 1930, his first wife having passed away, he married Lee Ella Payne.

On January 1, 1938, he arrived in Dallas, Texas, to pastor the prestigious St. John Baptist Church, where he remained the rest of his life. Under his leadership the church grew to a congregation of some 4,000 with an institutional program covering a wide range of activities seven days a week. On December 7, 1941, (Pearl Harbor Day) they had their first Sunday in a huge, new facility on Allen and Guillot Streets. As vice-president of the National Baptist Sunday School and Training Union Congress, he helped build that organization into one that matched delegate strength with the parent National Baptist Convention, U.S.A., Inc., which he also served as a member of the executive board. He was a trustee of Bishop College in Dallas and faithfully worked on its behalf.

In 1960 Estell was a delegate to the Baptist World Alliance meeting in Rio de Janeiro, Brazil. In 1961 Estell presented the resolution to the National Baptist Convention to renominate for president **Joseph H. Jackson**, who had led the convention as president since 1953. Jackson won, despite the concerted efforts of **Gardner C. Taylor** and others. One result was the breakaway formation that year of the **Progressive National Baptist Convention**. Estell was known as a powerful, evangelical preacher who went after sinners. He did not just attack the "safe" sins of drinking or cursing, but was very vocal about the sins of injustice and racial inequality. The effort to provide housing that would enhance Black self-esteem led to the crowning achievement of his career, the building of a three-million-dollar housing complex with luxury units, called Estell Village. This astounding project was just being completed when Estell passed away.

SCA, HBB, GBB.

ETHIOPIAN ORTHODOX CHURCH IN THE UNITED STATES OF AMERICA. A non-Chalcedonian Orthodox Church. Christians in Ethiopia trace their relationship to Christianity to the baptism of the Ethiopian eunuch by Philip mentioned in the Book of Acts 8:26–39. The next mention, however, is to the arrival of Bishop Frumentius around 352 C.E. Frumentius was not an Ethiopian, but as the story goes, he was shipwrecked there as a youth and grew up in the ancient kingdom of Axum. Having been raised a Christian prior to the shipwreck, around 341, he traveled to Egypt to ask for a bishop for Ethiopia. Athanasius of Alexandria responded by making Frumentius that bishop and sending him back to his adopted homeland. In the 350s, Frumentius was able to convert King Ella Amida and his court to Christianity which he signaled to the country and the world by placing a cross on the country's coins (the first known incident of a cross being placed on a coin). Frumentius was called *Abuna* (Our Father), a title still used by the primates of the Ethiopian Church, and was referred to by the people as *Anba Salama* (the Father of Peace).

The church was firmly established in Ethiopia by the arrival of a number of monks from Egypt. Because Egypt became the source of the church's arrival in Ethiopia, the church tended to become dependent upon Egypt, and events in the next century drove them even closer together. Following the conversion of Constantine, the long process of imposing not only Christianity, but a particular form of Christianity upon the Empire was launched. In 451, opinions expressed by Cyril I of Alexandria were condemned by the Council meeting at Chacedon. Cyril argued that Jesus Christ basically possessed one nature, divine. His opponents said Christ possessed two natures, human and divine. Those who agreed with Cyril were declared heretics and were suppressed throughout the Roman Empire. However, in those lands outside the reach of the Empire, including Egypt, Armenia and Ethiopia, monophysitism, the belief in one nature, survived as the "orthodox" view. Thus Egypt became aligned against the churches in the old Roman Empire. The controversy also allowed the Egyptian and Ethiopian churches to retain their own liturgies which varied substantially from that of the Greek Orthodox Church.

In the seventh century, the Muslims invaded and

conquered Egypt. The Coptic (Egyptian) Church was disestablished, but assigned a place in the new kingdom rather than being destroyed. Ethiopia continued to accept Egypt's senior position, at least in outward form, the Egyptians continued to send Abunas to Ethiopia, and both churches began to develop a culture cut off from that of the Christian lands of the Mediterranean. One element of this culture was the emergence of a tribe of "Jews" who seized control of the government for a brief period in the tenth century. This period is remembered in the Ethiopian church by its Saturday sabbath celebrations, the acceptance of the apocrypha as scripture, the designation of Old Testament figures as saints, the practice of male circumcision, and the adoption of a clean/unclean food code. The Muslims' surrounding of Ethiopia was uncomfortable, but Ethiopia had a special place in Islam because of the refuge provided Muhammad at one point by the Ethiopian emperor. It was not until the sixteenth century that Muslim invaders moved through the country and, seeing the strongly representational art of the Christians, destroyed much of its religious culture as idolatrous artifacts. A century later there was an attempt to impose Roman Catholicism on the land which led to a civil war and the banishment of the Catholics from the land.

Throughout their history, though invaded and abused, the Ethiopians were able to stay independent and to keep their Christianity alive. A new aeon began in 1893 when Menelik II established a new capital city, Addis Ababa, and began to build a new united nation and church. That process was accelerated under his successor, the now legendary Haile Selassie, who became emperor in 1928. A year after he ascended the throne, five native bishops were consecrated. In 1944 he founded a church theological college. In July 1948 he worked out an agreement with the Coptic Patriarch of Alexandria in Cairo for an independent Ethiopian Orthodox Church. The church became a charter member of the World Council of Churches at its initial gathering later that year. In 1959 the first Ethiopian was consecrated as Abuna for the Ethiopian Orthodox Church.

The Ethiopian Church in America. Most of the Orthodox churches like the Ethiopian Church, such as the Bulgarian, Armenian, or Serbian Orthodox church, came to North America as members of these churches migrated from their native land and took up residence in the United States and Canada. Such was not the case with the Ethiopian Church. There have been almost no Ethiopians residing in the United States in the twentieth century. Rather, the development of the Ethiopian Church came as African Americans turned to Ethiopia.

Throughout the twentieth century the image of Ethiopia had been placed as a positive powerful image before African Americans, especially during the years of the **Marcus Garvey** movement. Coupled with the hallowed references to Ethiopia in scripture, it is no wonder that the word began to attract religious sentiments to it. After World War I Jacques Faitlovitch made the United States the center of a pro-Falasha movement which raised the issue of the Black Jews of Ethiopia for the growing Black community in Northern cities. In 1921 bishop-to-be **George Alexander McGuire**, author of the *Universal Negro Catechism* for Garvey's **Universal Negro Improvement Association**, identified the "Black group of the human family" as Ethiopians. Among the movements growing out of Garvey's work was the Ethiopia Pacific Movement founded by Mittie Gordon in Chicago in 1932.

In 1937 the Ethiopian World Federation, Incorporated, was founded by Maluku E. Bayen, a nephew of Emperor Haile Selassie, to solicit aid for Ethiopia during the Italo-Ethiopian War. He worked in the Black communities of New York to raise money before founding a branch in Chicago in 1938. The federation may have been directly responsible for the founding of an Ethiopian Church. During World War II, an Archbishop Edwin H. Collins appeared in Harlem as the leader of an Ethiopian Coptic Orthodox Church (Western Hemisphere) headquartered on Lenox Avenue. In May 1944 he sponsored a program to celebrate the defeat of the Italian Army in Ethiopia. No further information on either the origin of the church or its eventual fate is available.

In the 1950s, Most Rev. Abuna Gabre Kristos Mikael, an African-American, established an independent Orthodox jurisdiction under the authority of Archbishop Walter A. Propheta, a White man who led the American Orthodox Catholic Church. Following the gaining of full independence for the Ethiopian Church by the consecration of an Ethiopian as the church's abuna, Bishop Mikael traveled to Addis Ababa to meet Abuna Basilios who ordained him in the Ethiopian Church and raised him to the rank of Chorepistopas. He then returned to the United States with a group of three priests and five deacons who were to pursue advanced study and also assist in the founding of a branch of the Ethiopian Orthodox Church in America. The group of priests were under the leadership of Fr. Laike Mandefro.

The experience of working with Bishop Mikael proved unsatisfactory and soon after the group's arrival in the United States, Mandefro and the priests broke with Mikael and established their work independently under the authority of Arbuna Theophilos, who succeeded Arbuna Basilios. They began to gather a congregation of Ethiopian Americans and other African Americans in Brooklyn, New York. The work prospered and headquarters in Addis Ababa recognized their accomplishments by raising Mandefro to the rank of archimandrite and placing him in charge of what was termed the Ethiopian Orthodox Church in the West. In 1974 this church affiliated with the National Council of Churches, but has never become a full member.

With the church firmly planted, in 1970 Mandefro was sent to Jamaica to repeat the process. Over the next decade churches were planted across the island in major population centers—Kingston, Montego Bay, Ocho Rios, Linsted, and St. Ann. The Jamaican branch is affiliated with the Caribbean Council of Churches.

The American branch of the Ethiopian Orthodox Church in the United States, that branch recognized by Addis Ababa, is headquartered in the Bronx, New York, at Holy Trinity Ethiopian Church. In the mid-1980s it reported 34 parishes and approximately 5,000 members. The Jamaican branch reported 7 parishes, 3 missions, and 10,000 members.

Following the break with Mandefro, Bishop Mikael did not abandon his mission. Rather he picked up his relationship to the American Orthodox Catholic Church and continued on. He was able to recruit some African American priests and through the next decade established three parishes in New York and Pennsylvania and missions overseas in Trinidad and Mexico. The Ethiopian Orthodox Coptic Church, Diocese of North and South America is headquartered in Brooklyn, New York. It has tried unsuccessfully to reestablish relationships with the Patriarch in Addis Ababa, but in the meantime pursues its ministry independently.

Essien-Udom noted in 1962 the presence of James R. Lawson, the leader of the United African Nationalists Movement and member of the Ethiopian Orthodox Coptic Church. In 1954 Lawson had been awarded a medal by Haile Selassie and had subsequently become an advocate of African independence. He published a periodical, *African News and Views: The Voice of Africa in America*.

Essien-Udom, E. U. *Black Nationalism: A Search for Identity in America*. New York: Dell, 1962. 448 pp.

Molnar, Enrico S. *The Ethiopian Orthodox Church*. Pasadena, CA: Bloy House Theological School, 1969. 25 pp.

Simon, M. K. *The Ethiopian Orthodox Church*. Addis Ababa, Ethiopia: N.p., 195?.

EVANGEL TEMPLE. *See:* **INTERNATIONAL EVANGELICAL CHURCH AND MISSIONARY ASSOCIATION**.

EVANS, HENRY (1740–1810), pioneer Methodist Episcopal Church preacher, was born to free parents from Virginia. He became a shoemaker and licensed Methodist preacher. In about 1780, on his way to Charleston, South Carolina, he stopped in Fayetteville, North Carolina. He was so dismayed at the depraved character of the slaves that he decided to stop for a time and preach among them. At first the authorities stopped the practice, considering it a disturbing element. He continued preaching, however, holding services in the surrounding sandhills, and moving from place to place to avoid violence from the Whites. Three times he swam across the partly frozen Cape Fear River to preach. In time there appeared a noticeable improvement in the manners and morals of the Black population and the authorities began to permit Evans to preach freely in town.

In about 1790 a rough building was constructed to house the congregation wrought by his work, and seats were reserved for Whites in the rear. Within a few years the number of Whites and Blacks grew so large that sheds had to be built on the sides to accommodate the people. This was the first Methodist church in Fayetteville. In many ways it became the center of attention in town and visitors felt obligated to stay long enough to hear Evans preach at least once. He was considered the best preacher of his time in that part of the territory. Methodist bishop Francis Asbury visited the church several times.

Evans lived in a room in back of the chancel and ran the congregation until about 1806, when ill health forced him to turn the congregation over to preachers appointed by Asbury. In a will dated December 9, 1809, he gave the part of the building and lot used for religious purposes to the Methodist Episcopal Church. The residential part of the property, he stipulated, would go to the church only upon the death of his widow. On the Sunday before his death he weakly made his way to the sanctuary and gave a final exhortation to the congregation.

EWM, IBAW, CH, NYB (1912).

EXUM, JOHN MADISON (January 3, 1909–November 28, 1984), 38th bishop of the **Christian Methodist Episcopal Church** (CME), was born in

Memphis, Tennessee, the son of John W. and Lena (Turner) Exum. His parents were charter members of the Greenwood CME Church in Memphis, and gave him a strong religious upbringing. Over the years as a layperson he served as Sunday School superintendent, steward, trustee, lay leader of the South Memphis District, delegate to several General Conferences, national secretary of the Connectional Laymen's Council, and auditor of the CME Church. He worked during this time as a Memphis mail-carrier, and was married to Lola Thelma Gibbs, with whom he had one daughter.

His first pastorate upon deciding to enter the ministry was at Rock of Ages CME Church in Memphis, from 1942 to 1944. He then was transferred to Cleaves Memorial CME Church in Denver, Colorado, where he also enrolled in the University of Denver, receiving his B.A. in 1947. He stayed in Denver to attend Iliff School of Theology, where he and John Hawkins were the only two Blacks in the student body. In addition to his studies and responsibilities to the Cleaves congregation, he was presiding elder of the Denver District.

Exum graduated with his Th.M. in 1950, and was assigned to the Jamison Memorial Temple CME Church in Kansas City, Missouri, where he stayed until 1959. While there he did graduate work in pastoral counseling at the University of Kansas. His next churches were Grace CME Church in Detroit, Michigan (1959–1961), Carter Metropolitan CME Church in Detroit, Michigan, Miles Memorial CME Church in Washington, D.C., and Lane Chapel CME Church in Tupelo, Mississippi. In addition to his pastoral successes, his profile was enhanced in the denomination as editor of the *Christian Index*, the official periodical.

He was elected bishop at the 1974 General Conference in Philadelphia, Pennsylvania, and assigned to the First Episcopal District (Tennessee and Arkansas). He was chair of the board of trustees of Lane College in Jackson, Tennessee, from 1974 to 1982, when he retired. He was also a trustee of five housing projects, Collins Chapel Hospital, Memphis Theological Seminary, and the John Madison Exum Towers, a senior citizen housing project in Memphis that he called the "crowning achievement" of his episcopal career. In late 1982 he was recalled out of retirement to finish the term of the late Bishop **James Cummings** in the Tenth Episcopal District (Africa), and in the few short months of his tenure organized a new Annual Conference in Liberia. He is remembered as a committed ecumenist, and at the time of his death in 1984 was president of the Pan-Methodist Bicentennial Committee, charged with planning the 200–year anniversary celebration of American Methodism among the various American Methodist and Wesleyan churches.

"Bishop John Madison Exum." *The Christian Index* 117 (December 1, 1984): 2, 3.

"CME Bishop John Madison Exum Dead at Age 75." *Star of Zion* 109 (December 20, 1984): 1, 2.

"School for Preachers." *Ebony* 5–6 (September 1950): 55–58.

WWR (85), BDNM (75), IBAW.

"If the women of the Churches are made to feel that they are personally responsible for the salvation of the world, and are enlisted to labor by the side of men, it will not be many years before a revolution will be felt all over this broad land, and the heathen will no longer walk in darkness, but will praise God, the light of their salvation."

Mary V. Cook, Baptist Educator
1890

F

FAITH BIBLE CHURCH. Faith Bible Church has been conceived as nondenominational even though the founder and presiding bishop, Dr. Lewis T. Tait, Sr., was consecrated by Bishop **Samuel Kelsey** of the **Church of God in Christ**, a Holiness Pentecostal body. However, the beliefs of the church are explicitly non-Pentecostal. The church was organized in 1959 in Washington, D.C., as a single congregation, the Faith Church of God in Son. Tait was consecrated three years later, and the present name of the church adopted. Affiliated ministers have developed their congregations in association with Faith Bible Church.

The church is committed to a basic orthodox Christian faith, while leaving wide latitude for interpretation. The Trinity, the inspiration of the Bible, the deity of Christ, the salvation through grace, the regenerative work of the Holy Spirit, and the resurrection are affirmed, in language derived from the Apostles Creed. Departing from a Pentecostal heritage, the Church asserts that the baptism of the Holy Spirit occurs at the time a sinner trusts Jesus and receives Him in their heart. Women are fully accepted in the ministry, and presently constitute 50 percent of the senior clergy.

Headquarters is in Washington, D.C. In 1990 there were six congregations and 3,000 members in Washington, D.C., and South Carolina. The church has an annual convention in Washington at which business is conducted, and an annual women's convention in South Carolina.

FAITH TABERNACLE COUNCIL OF CHURCHES, INTERNATIONAL. A Pentecostal church. The Faith Tabernacle Council of Churches, International was founded as the Faith Tabernacle Corporation of Church in Portland, Oregon, in 1962 by Bishop Louis W. Osborne, Sr. Osborne began the organization after a vision in which he caught and carried a light which gradually grew in intensity, thus allowing him to lead followers down the correct pathway.

The council is basically an Apostolic Pentecostal organization, but Osborne has emphasized the need for the preaching of the gospel and for fellowship and freedom. He has organized the council as an association of autonomous congregations. The council charters congregations and ordains ministers, but conformity of belief by ministers and churches is not demanded. While the council provides congregations with a set of "Guidelines for Christian Development," there is no requirement that the guidelines be followed.

Headquarters of the council is in Portland, Oregon. It publishes a periodical, the *Light of Faith*. There is an annual meeting each summer. In 1990 it reported 55 congregations including several churches in South Africa and Zimbabwe.

Payne, Wardell J., ed. *Directory of African American Religious Bodies: A Compendium by the Howard University School of Divinity.* Washington, DC: Howard University Press, 1991. 363 pp.

FALASHAS. *See:* **AMERICAN ASSOCIATION OF ETHIOPIAN JEWS.**

FARD, WALLACE D. (? –1934?), founder of the **Nation of Islam**, grew up in obscurity. There is no evidence to support his own claims that he was born in Mecca in 1877, the son of a wealthy member of the tribe of Koreish, the tribe of the Prophet Muhammad. Nor is there documented evidence of any other part of his life prior to his appearance in Detroit in July of 1930, during the Depression, when he began selling door-to-door in the Black community silks and other articles with purported origins in Africa. He combined this merchandizing with preaching about the "home country" of Africa and about Islam as the true religion of Blacks. He apparently had been a member of **Noble Drew Ali**'s **Moorish Science Temple of America**, which flourished in Chicago, Detroit, and other cities in the 1920s until Ali's death in 1929. Fard reportedly even claimed to be a reincarnation of Ali. The Nation of Islam later dated the founding of the Lost-Found Nation of Islam by Fard from July 4, 1930.

Fard soon gained a large following, as many as 8,000, and a hall was hired as the headquarters of the Temple of Islam. He wrote two manuals for instruction, *The Secret Ritual of the Nation of Islam*, which he taught orally, and *Teaching for the Lost-Found Nation of Islam in a Mathematical Way*. He added to Noble Drew Ali's teachings a number of his own ideas culled from sources as diverse as the writings of Joseph Rutherford (the founder of Jehovah's Witnesses), and Van Loon's *Story of Mankind*. He said that Blacks were the original people and that a scientist had genetically separated out the white part of their makeup, representing their weak and evil parts. The white people thus created soon took over and were granted 6,070 years of rulership. This would be overturned by Black hegemony in 1984.

Fard, sometimes called "the Prophet," organized the Fruit of Islam, a semi-military organization for protection, fraternity, and discipline, and a Muslim Girls' Training Corps Class for teaching home economics and proper Muslim behavior for women. He also founded the University of Islam, an elementary and secondary school. The school did not meet the standards of the Detroit Board of Education, which initiated some action against it, but the potential backlash from the Black community kept those efforts to a minimum. He took the name of Muhammad and urged his followers to substitute an "X" for their last names in repudiation of the slave heritage the names represented.

In 1934 Fard disappeared mysteriously and was succeeded by his chief assistant minister, Elijah (Poole) Muhammad. Under the leadership of **Elijah Muhammad** and with the assistance of **Malcolm X**, the Nation of Islam grew to be a significant force in Black America. For years the Nation of Islam annually celebrated Savior's Day around the beginning of March in observance of Fard's birthday. Elijah Muhammad taught that Allah (God) had appeared in the person of Fard to function as "the 'Messiah' of the Christians and the 'Mahdi' of the Muslims." After Elijah Muhammad died in February 1975, his son W. D. Muhammad took over the organization and in March 1976, announced that Fard was still alive. Despite the fact that Fard had long since been presumed dead, Muhammad claimed that "I can go to the telephone and dial his number anytime I want to." Little more was heard about Fard's

existence, however, and in 1980 the name of the organization was changed to the American Muslim Mission to reflect a philosophic change toward a more orthodox Muslim position.

Williams, Dennis A. and Elaine Sciolino. "Rebirth of the Nation." *Newsweek* 87 (March 15, 1976): 33.
DANB, CH, BN, BNA, IBAW, BHBA.

FARRAKHAN, LOUIS (b. May 11, 1933), founder of one of the several groups known as the **Nation of Islam**, was born in New York City's Bronx area as Louis Eugene Walcott. His Jamaican-born parents soon moved the family to the Roxbury district of Boston. Farrakhan (Walcott) showed remarkable abilities as a honor student and track star at Boston English High School, and was active in the **Episcopal Church**. His mother encouraged his musical aptitude and his skill at the violin became well known. He attended Winston Salem Teachers College in North Carolina for two years, then dropped out to pursue an entertainment career as singer/musician. He married Betsy Walcott, with whom he subsequently had nine children.

In 1953, while playing the nightclub circuit, doing mostly calypso and country songs, he was introduced to the world of Black Muslims. His interest grew, and in 1955 he attended a Muslim Saviour's Day Convention in Chicago, and heard Elijah Muhammad, head of the Nation of Islam, speak for the first time. Muhammad was already aware of Farrakhan and his leadership potential, and invited him to give himself fully to the movement. Farrakhan soon gave up show business, registered with the Nation of Islam's New York Temple, and became a part of the Fruit of Islam (FOI), the group's fraternal/security unit. He dropped his last name as a remnant of slave society (a common Black Muslim practice) and became known as Louis X.

Farrakhan rose swiftly through the ranks and was transferred to the Boston Temple as FOI Captain, subsequently becoming the temple's minister as well. After Malcolm X broke from the Nation of Islam in 1964, Louis X was returned to New York and made minister of Temple No. 7. About this time, **Elijah Muhammad** gave him the name Farrakhan. Muhammad never explained the meaning of this name, though "khan" in Arabic means "ruler." In 1975 Elijah Muhammad died, and leadership was passed to his son, Wallace, now known as **Warith Deen Muhammad**, who put Farrakhan into a national post in Chicago. Farrakhan had become part of the Muhammad family through the marriage of two of his daughters to a grandson and nephew of Elijah Muhammad. Over the next three years the Nation of Islam dropped many of its distinctive practices and moved into the mainstream of Islamic tradition, even changing its name to the American Muslim Mission. Disturbed by the changes, particularly the one allowing Whites as members, Farrakhan left the group in 1978 and began his own Nation of Islam, returning to the practices of Elijah Muhammad.

As leader of the new Nation of Islam, Louis Farrakhan is also known as Abdul Haleem Farrakhan. He has utilized his charismatic personality and considerable oratorical skills, particularly through radio programs, to rebuild a following of over 5,000 people with numerous mosques, based in Chicago. He jumped into the awareness of the larger public as a vocal supporter of **Jesse Jackson**'s **Operation PUSH**, and in 1984 of Jackson's presidential campaign. Some of his remarks, however, were widely seen as anti-Semitic, and Jackson's relations with the Jewish community were thereby further strained. Since that time, Farrakhan has concentrated on building his own organization and promoting his vision of Black economic and political power. In 1985 he began a nationwide tour to advertise P.O.W.E.R. (People Organized and Working for Economic Rebirth). With a $5 million loan from Libya, P.O.W.E.R. planned to develop an economically independent Black population, much as Elijah Muhammad had envisioned years before. In 1986 Farrakhan began a program focusing upon developing spiritual beliefs (as opposed to evangelism) and ties with Muslim countries around the world. He initiated a program of Qur'anic study for his followers, but has maintained an active apocalypticism.

Farrakhan, Louis. *Back Where We Belong: Selected Speeches*. Eds. Joseph D. Eure and Richard M. Jerome. Philadelphia: PC International Press, 1989. 302 pp.

———. *The Meaning of F.O.I.* Chicago: The Honorable Elijah Muhammad Educational Foundation, 1983. 20 pp.

———. *Seven Speeches*. New York: Ministry Class, Muhammad's Temple No. 7, 1974. 151 pp.

———. *Warning to the Government of America*. Chicago: The Honorable Elijah Muhammad Educational Foundation, 1983. 55 pp.

The Honorable Louis Farrakhan: A Minister for Progress. New York: Practice Press, 1987. 54 pp.

Lee, Martha and Thomas Flanagan. "The Black Muslims and the Fall of America: An Interpretation Based on the Failure of Prophecy." *Journal of Religious Studies* 16(1989): 140–156.

Mamiya, Lawrence H. "From Black Muslim to Bilalian: The Evolution of a Movement." *Journal for the Scientific Study of Religion* 21 (1982): 138–152.

Page, Clarence. "Deciphering Farrakhan." *Chicago* 33 (August 1984): 130–135.

Schwartz, Alan M. "Louis Farrakhan." *ADL Facts* 29 (Spring 1984): 1–23.

WWABA (88, 90), HUBA, RLOA.

FEDERATED COLORED CATHOLICS OF THE UNITED STATES. An early twentieth-century African American **Roman Catholic Church** organization. Federated Colored Catholics in the United States began in 1917 as an informal gathering of Black Roman Catholics in the home of Dr. **Thomas Wyatt Turner** (1877–1978), a professor of biology at Howard University, and a member of St. Augustine's Roman Catholic Church in Washington, D.C. Turner steered the discussion at the several meetings to the role of Black people in Catholicism. The informal gathering led to the formation of a Committee Against the Extension of Race Prejudice in the church and a letter-writing campaign directed to the Catholic press. The group also worked to find job placements for Black Catholics during World War I.

As the committee operated over the next two years, it assumed a new name as the Committee for the Advancement of Colored Catholics. Steps toward a more formal organization were taken in 1923 and a permanent structure created the following year. Encouraged by favorable comments made by members of the hierarchy, and with the active cooperation of the National Catholic Welfare Conference, the group held a national convention in 1925 at which time the Federated Colored Catholics of the United States was formally organized and Turner elected its first president. Support for the Cardinal Gibbons Institute, a secondary school serving Black pupils in Maryland, was adopted as an organization project.

Turner installed a policy of cooperation with the hierarchy of the church. Under his disciplined guidance of the organization it grew to incorporate 72 chapters by 1931. The group also continually approached the hierarchy on various issues such as allowing Black students to attend Catholic University in Washington, D.C. Its effectiveness was limited both by the dominant racism it encountered and the anxiety of the church over any organized activity by lay members.

In 1932, the issue of the organization's name, which had been raised on several occasions, came to a head. Some complained that the word "Colored" implied the very exclusiveness and separateness the organization was trying to overcome. Bowing to pressure, the name was changed to the National Catholic Federation for the Promotion of Better Race Relations. This name change signaled a subtle but important shift in emphasis within the organization from racial solidarity and uplift to building interracial harmony. The debate which followed the name change revealed deep personal and ideological differences which would lead to a split. At the same convention, Turner was not reelected to the presidency.

Actual control of the National Catholic Federation for the Promotion of Better Race Relations was retained by those opposed to Turner. Its strength was in the Midwest. In 1933 it changed its name to the National Catholic Interracial Federation. Turner's supporters, primarily in the East, returned to their previous name, Federated Colored Catholics. In 1934, members in New York formed a third organization, the Catholic Interracial Council. It was offered and assumed control of the federation's old periodical, now called the *Interracial Review*. The New York group survived and became a voice in the era of the church's concentration on interracial activity that carried it into the civil rights era of the 1960s.

Neither of the two branches of the old federation could regain the vitality of the years before the split. The Eastern group would survive until 1952, but was no longer an effective voice in altering church policy.

Nickels, Marilyn Wenzke. *Black Catholic Protest and the Federated Colored Catholics, 1971–1933: Three Perspectives on Racial Justice.* New York: Garland Publishing, 1988. 325 pp.

FELTUS, HENRY (December 15, 1877–1950), an early overseer (now bishop) of the **Church of God in Christ** (COGIC), was born in Centerville, Wilkerson County, Mississippi, on the Emery Plantation. His parents were Baptists and he experienced salvation as a 16–year old teenager in that church. He fell away from the church as a young man, but in 1905 first heard a Holiness minister preach the message of sanctification. In 1907 he responded to message and was sanctified by the Holy Spirit. The Holiness message set him at odds with the Baptists and he became the center of a Holiness congregation. He also became a Holiness preacher and began to travel around speaking and calling other congregations into existence, the first being founded in Gloster, Mississippi.

In 1910 he met **Charles H. Mason** in Baton Rouge, Louisiana. Several years previously, Mason had been one of the first to receive the baptism of the Holy Spirit, as evidenced by speaking in tongues, at the initial Pentecostal revival in Los Angeles. He shared the message with Feltus who immediately responded to it and associated himself with Mason's Church of God in Christ. In 1912 he moved to Louisiana as pastor of the Baton Rouge COGIC congregation.

In 1914 Feltus was made overseer (bishop) of the work in Louisiana. Under his leadership the church developed 25 congregations and moved into permanent facilities. Feltus passed the mantle of leadership to his son, Overseer/Bishop John Henry Feltus, who like his father organized an additional 25 congregations in Louisiana.

DuPree, Sherry Sherrod. *Biographical Dictionary of African-American Holiness Pentecostals, 1880–1990.* Washington, DC: Middle Atlantic Regional Press, 1989. 386 pp.

Mason, Mary Esther. *The History and Life Work of Elder C. H. Mason and His Co-Laborers.* N.p.: n.d. 93 pp.

Patterson, J. O., German R. Ross, and Julia Mason Atkins. *History and Formative Years of the Church of God in Christ with Excerpts from the Life and Works of its Founder—Bishop C. H. Mason.* Memphis, TN: Church of God in Christ Publishing House, 1969. 143 pp.

FERGUSON, CATHERINE (c.1779–July 11, 1854), Presbyterian founder of perhaps the first local church-related Sunday School in New York, was born into slavery on board a schooner sailing from Virginia to New York City. Her mother had been sold to a Presbyterian elder in New York City and worked for that man, known to history as "R. B.," for the next seven or eight years. At that point she was sold away and mother and daughter never saw each other again.

Her mother had bequeathed to her a strong religious sensitivity, and at age fourteen she approached John Mitchell Mason, the pastor of the Old Scotch Presbyterian Church on Cedar Street in lower Manhattan, to "talk about her soul." The discussion went well, and Ferguson began a life long relationship with Mason and that church. At about age seventeen, with the help of two church women, she was freed from slavery, and the following year she married. Little is known about the marriage except that the two children she bore did not survive to maturity, and her husband also apparently passed away before she was twenty.

At about the time of her marriage, circa 1797, she formally joined the church. The church was not of one mind about accepting her presence, and to take her first communion Rev. Mason had to escort her personally to the table. Eventually her gentle spirit won over the congregation and gained their full support. She earned a living by baking large cakes for social occasions and small cakes that she sold around the neighborhood. She became familiar with the children of the area and on Sundays would gather them into her house for Scripture lessons. Although she could neither read nor write, she knew large sections of the Bible by heart and could oversee the memorization and recitation aspects of the sessions. She had certain church members teach the children how to read and write with the Bible.

Her pioneering work took place in the context of the infant Sunday School movement, which dates from 1780 in Gloucester, England, and arrived in the United States after 1800. At an undetermined time, probably between 1810 and 1814, Rev. Mason invited Ferguson to base her Sunday School at his church, and it was thereafter known as the Murray Street Sabbath School. Although some have claimed that it was the first Sunday School in New York City, it seems that several independent schools were established before that time. Hers may, however, have been the first officially tied directly to a local congregation. During her lifetime the average attendance at Ferguson's school was between forty and fifty, with a student body that included both Blacks and Whites and both children and adults.

In addition to supervising the Sunday School, Ferguson took in orphans and destitute children and cared for them until permanent homes could be found. Over a forty-year period she took in about forty-eight children, both Black and White. Some of these children were unwed mothers, and Ferguson's establishment was among the first to provide for them. Every Friday she conducted a prayer meeting in her home, and in the last several years of her life added meetings on Sunday afternoons as well. She became something of a local legend in her own time, and it was said that in the vicinity of her home at 74 Thompson Street, "the whole aspect of the neighborhood was changed." When asked if she had saved any money over the years, she replied, "How could I, when I gave away all I earned?" When she passed away of cholera, her obituary was written up in both the *New York Times* and the *New York Daily Tribune*. Named in her honor, the Katy Ferguson Home for Unwed Mothers in New York City was founded in 1920.

Hartvik, Allen. "Catherine Ferguson, Black Founder of a Sunday-School." *Negro History Bulletin* 35 (December 1972): 176–177.
HH, DANB, AAE, HNB, NBAW, BWR, IBAW.

FERGUSON, SAMUEL DAVID (January 1, 1842– August 3, 1916), the second African American bishop consecrated by the **Episcopal Church** (in America) and the first Black bishop to sit in the Episcopal Church's House of Bishops, was born in Charleston, South Carolina, the son of Edward and Rosaine Elizabeth Ferguson. His father was a Baptist deacon and his mother was a Roman Catholic, but Ferguson was baptized as an infant by Episcopal Bishop Gadsden, at a time when Ferguson was seriously ill. At the age of six Ferguson moved with his parents to Liberia, West Africa, setting sail on May 6, 1848. His father soon passed away and his mother sought help from Bishop John Payne, who assumed responsibility for Ferguson's education in the mission schools.

In 1862 Ferguson became teacher of the boys' boarding school at the Cavalla Mission Station. In April 1863 he married Mary Leonora Montgomery. In 1863 he became principal of Mount Vaughan High School in Cape Palmas, where he remained for ten years. During this time he was ordained deacon (December 28, 1865) and priest (March 17, 1867). In 1868 he added to his school duties by becoming rector of St. Mark's Episcopal Church in Cape Palmas, where he had already been an assistant since he had been ordained deacon. His first wife passed away, and in July 1879 he married Sarah Elizabeth Brown. For many years he was president of the Council of Advice for the Episcopal bishop.

After the resignation of Bishop Charles C. Penick in 1883, the Episcopal Church decided to have a Black assistant bishop resident in Liberia to carry out the regular episcopal duties there. Ferguson was elected in 1884 to be that person, and was consecrated in Grace Episcopal Church, New York City, on June 24, 1885. He was the first Black Episcopal bishop for Liberia and the first Black member of the American House of Bishops and of the General Convention. Although **James T. Holly** was the first Black priest consecrated as bishop by the Episcopal Church (1874), this was technically a service done on behalf of the independent Eglise Orthodoxe Apostolique Haitienne. Holly thus was not a member of the House of Bishops and was not assigned a number in the succession of American bishops. To Ferguson, therefore, belongs the honor of being the first Black bishop of the Episcopal Church in the United States, number 139 in the succession of American bishops.

Ferguson's record as bishop was outstanding. From 1885 to 1907 there were 7,688 persons baptized and 3,949 confirmed, both figures several times greater than in the period of 1835 to 1885. By 1907 about 65 percent of the communicants were native Africans, and that group accounted for eleven of the twenty-seven Episcopal clergy in Liberia. In 1885 there had been only ten clergy altogether. He founded Cuttington Collegiate and Divinity School in Cape Palmas in 1889 to prepare ministerial candidates; it was basically a merger of the Hoffman Training Institution at Cavalla and the Mount

Vaughan High School in Cape Palmas. (Cuttington Collegiate and Divinity School was closed in 1929, rebuilt in Suacoco in 1948 and reopened in 1949 under the administration of Bishop **Bravid W. Harris**). Ferguson established a medical mission under Paulus Moort, a priest and physician from the Danish Virgin Islands, and oversaw the creation of Bromley Girls' School in 1909. After Ferguson's death in 1916 there was not another Black Episcopal bishop for Liberia until **T. M. Gardiner**, in 1921. However, the great respect that grew around the person of Ferguson and his work helped convince the Episcopal Church to consecrate a Black person for work in the United States, which occurred for the first time with **Edward T. Demby** in 1918.

Dunn, D. Elwood. "The Episcopal Church in Liberia Under Experimental Liberian Leadership: 1884–1916." *Anglican and Episcopal History* 58 (March 1989): 3–36.

Ferguson, Samuel D. *Double Anniversary Sermon of the Thirty Years' Episcopate of Bishop Samuel David Ferguson, D.D., June 24, 1885–1915; Fifty Years of His Ministry, Dec. 31, 1865–1915, Preached in St. Mark's Church, June 27, 1915.* N.p. 8 pp.

————. *Liberia and the Colonization Society.* Address Delivered Before the Pennsylvania Colonization Society, October 29, 1893. Philadelphia, PA: n.p., 1893. 16 pp.

————. *The Twentieth Century Calendar and Handbook of Liberia.* Liverpool, Lib.: J.A. Thompson & Co., n.d.

————. *Warning from the Watchtower to the Citizens of Liberia.* Cape Palmas, Liberia: P. E. Mission Program Office, 1913. 19 pp.

Hayden, J. Carleton. "Afro-Anglican Linkages, 1701–1900: Ethiopia Shall Soon Stretch Out Her Hands Unto God." *The Journal of Religious Thought* 44 (Summer–Fall 1987): 25–34.

BAW, HAAG, NYTO, EBA, ACAB, WWWA (1), *NCAB* (13), *IBAW, WWCR.*

FERRILL, LONDON (? –1854), an early Baptist minister, emerged in the records early in the nineteenth century as a slave of Anna Winston of Hanover County, Virginia. He would later claim descent from a royal line of African rulers. At the age of twelve, he had a conversion experience which followed his near death in the water. Freed a few years later, he moved to Kentucky, where in 1817 he presented himself for membership at the all-White First Baptist church of Lexington in spite of an independent Black Baptist congregation being available to him. He began preaching at the church and gathered a congregation primarily of younger free Blacks. In 1922 his group established an all-Black church and applied for a relationship to the Elkhorn Baptist Association. The Association approved his ordination and organized the First African Church. By the 1850s, the church had become the largest congregation of any denomination in the state, with over 1,820 members. He served the congregation for 32 years.

Hill, Samuel S. *Encyclopedia of Religion in the South.* Macon, GA: Mercer University Press, 1984. 878 pp.

FIRE BAPTIZED HOLINESS CHURCH OF GOD OF THE AMERICAS. A Holiness Pentecostal church. The Fire-Baptized Holiness Church of God of the Americas grew out of the Fire-Baptized movement within the Holiness movement of the 1890s. The movement had begun with the preaching of Benjamin Irwin for the idea of the third blessing awaiting Holiness people, the first two being justification (acceptance by God) and sanctification (holiness). The third blessing was a baptism of fire which would result in personal power and enthusiasm to live the Christian life. When the first Fire Baptized Holiness Association (now a constituent part of the International Pentecostal Holiness Church) was formed in 1898, W. O. Fuller was the only African American among the charter members. He set out to build the African American constituency. By 1908 over 900 African Americans had affiliated.

As the association grew contemporaneously with the enactment of new Jim Crow laws, and the number of Black members increased, it experienced increasing difficulties in locating facilities for biracial meetings. Feeling the discrimination, Fuller led the Black members to disassociate from the association and in 1908 they formed an independent organization, the Colored Fire Baptized Holiness Church. That name was changed in 1922 by the dropping of the word Colored and in 1926 by the addition "of the Americas." The White association gave them all of the property which had been accumulated for their use. Fuller was elected bishop.

Fuller led the church until his death in 1958. In 1912 the Fuller Normal and Industrial School was founded in Atlanta. It moved to Toccoa, Georgia, a year later, and after a decade there was relocated to Greenville, South Carolina, where it remains. Fuller Press was established in Atlanta. Fuller was succeeded by Bishop C. C. Childes. Congregations are concentrated in Georgia and South Carolina, but may be found throughout the eastern half of the United States. Headquarters is in Atlanta. In 1978 there were 775 congregations. *True Witness* is published semi-annually.

Discipline. F.B.H. *Church of God of the Americas.* Atlanta, GA: Fuller Press, 1962. 100 pp.

FISHER, CARL ANTHONY (b. November 24, 1945), a bishop of the **Roman Catholic Church**, was born in Pascagoula, Mississippi, one of twelve children in the family of Peter William and Evelyn Gertrude (Grant) Fisher. He grew up as a Roman Catholic and wanted to become a priest at an early age. In 1967 he joined the Society of St. Joseph, an order working for the development of African Americans in the church and society. He received his B.A. in 1968 from St. Joseph's Seminary College in Washington, D.C., and from 1968 to 1971 was a chaplain in the U.S. Navy, the first Black Catholic chaplain in that branch of the armed forces. He finished his M.Th. in 1970 at Oblate College in Washington, D.C. In 1971 he attended the University of Southern Mississippi, and finished his M.S.P.R. in 1974 from American University in Washington, D.C. While in school, in 1971 he was a counselor employee representative for Litton Industries and in 1972 was a management training specialist for Chevron Oil Company. He also worked as a consultant for minority affairs for the Standard Oil Company while in Mississippi.

He was ordained priest on June 2, 1973, and from 1973 to 1982 he was director of the Department of Vocations for the Society of St. Joseph. During the same period Fisher was associate editor of the *Josephite Harvest* magazine and associate pastor of St. Veronica's Catholic Church in Baltimore, Maryland. From 1982 to 1987 he pastored the oldest Black Catholic church in the country, St. Francis Xavier Catholic Church in Baltimore. The announcement of his appointment to the bishopric was made on December 19, 1986, and he was consecrated Auxiliary Bishop of Los Angeles, California, on February 23, 1987. Described as theologically conservative, he became the first Black Catholic bishop in the western United States, assigned specifically to the San Pedro Pastoral Region. The Los Angeles region has about 100,000 Black Catholics. He has been a frequent guest on the popular Los Angeles radio program, "Religion on the Line," and about 1989 began a regular column in a secular Long Beach newspaper.

"Carl A. Fisher, S.S.J., Auxiliary Bishop of Los Angeles." *America* 164 (April 13, 1991): 416–420.
WWABA (92–93), CAA, WWR (77), BDNM (75).

FISHER, ELIJAH JOHN (August 2, 1858–July 31, 1915), educator and national officer of the **National Baptist Convention of the U.S.A., Inc.**, was born into slavery in La Grange, Georgia, the next to youngest of eight boys in a family of seventeen (surviving) children born to Miles and Charlotte (Amos) Fisher, the property of a Dr. Ridley. In the summer of 1863 Union Army soldiers freed all the slaves on Ridley's plantation, but the Fisher (a name they took at that time, after a former decent master) family stayed on for another year, until they could make a down payment on a 48–acre farm. Meanwhile Elijah Fisher experienced conversion and was baptized in the First Baptist Church on October 19, 1863.

Miles Fisher was often a lay preacher on Sundays at the First Baptist Church of La Grange; the Black congregation met there after the White congregation had finished. He passed away in the spring of 1875, one year after making the last payment on the farm. In 1876 Elijah Fisher was forced to sell the farm to meet a court obligation and found a mining job in Anniston, Alabama. On September 25, 1877 he married Florida Neely, with whom he had five children. About six months later he became a butler for a Colonel A. T. Tyler in Anniston, a welcome change from the grime and sweat of the mines.

He was licensed to preach in 1879 but decided to teach in a country school instead of preaching. He had gained a smattering of education over the years, enough to get by in that position. He soon saved enough money to enroll in Atlanta Baptist College (now Morehouse College), where he spent about a year. On April 3, 1880, he had just made arrangements to teach at a school in Long Cane and was trying to catch the train when his overcoat caught on the tracks and pulled him under the train. He lost his left leg, a toe on the right foot and a finger on his right hand, but managed to survive the ten-mile trip to receive medical attention.

After recovery he was able to teach at one of the La Grange county summer schools. He became such a popular teacher that the school session was increased to a full eight months and an assistant teacher was employed. The name of the school was changed to La Grange Baptist Seminary and Fisher was its principal and head teacher. Soon, however he decided to leave the schoolroom and heed a call to the ministry, and was ordained on May 10, 1882. His first church was in Threats Grove, Troup County, Georgia, and other early churches included Macedonia Baptist Church near La Grange and Mount Zion Baptist Church in Whitefield Crossing (now Louise), Georgia. In the fall of 1883 he became pastor of the First Baptist Church in Anniston, Alabama, where in two years he eliminated a heavy debt and secured a large sum of money to build a new church. He was elected president of the Sunday School Convention of Northeast Alabama and moderator of the Rushing Spring Association.

Fisher's fine work in building up churches became well known and in 1885 he was chosen assistant secretary of the Missionary Baptist Convention of Georgia and moderator of the Western Union Association. During his two-year term of office he supervised the creation of a Sunday School convention and supported the La Grange Baptist Seminary. In 1887 he was called to the pastorate of the 300–member First Colored Baptist Church of La Grange, of which he had long been a member.

On October 1, 1889, he began as pastor of Mount Olive Baptist Church in Atlanta, which he took because he knew he would also have a chance to further his education. He immediately enrolled in Atlanta Baptist Seminary and was allowed to enter the senior class. He graduated from the Theological Department in 1890. Meanwhile, although Mount Olive Baptist Church was located in the worst part of town, he more than doubled the membership to more than six hundred in only three years. He eliminated the debt, bought a pipe organ, new pews, and a parsonage, and built a belfry and vestibule.

In 1893, while remaining pastor at Mount Olive, he was again elected moderator of the Western Union Association, a group connected with the State Baptist Convention, and served a three-year term. In November 1895, he was master of ceremonies for Baptist Day at the Cotton States International Exposition in Atlanta. Also in 1895 was the historic convention in Atlanta which merged the **Baptist Foreign Mission Convention** with the **American National Baptist Convention** and the **National Baptist Educational Convention** to form the National Baptist Convention, U.S.A., Inc. At this meeting Fisher first gained national attention and prominence, representing some of the more progressive elements in the church.

From 1895 to 1897 Fisher served the short-lived Georgia General Missionary and Educational Convention as president of the executive board and managing editor of its periodical, the *Rome Journal*. He supported the continued backing of the White American Baptist Home Mission Society in the operation of Spelman Seminary and Atlanta Baptist College, and served as a trustee of Spelman. He assumed more and more visibility in Atlanta, assuming in about 1897 the editorship of the newly founded *Atlanta Tribune*. He regularly promoted the organization of Black enterprises, often with his own money, all this while remaining the pastor of Mount Olive Baptist Church.

In 1901 he left Atlanta to pastor the Spruce Street Baptist Church in Nashville, Tennessee. Its building had burned to the ground the previous year, but in 1902 he led in the creation of a large new church and added two hundred to the membership. In the summer of 1902 he studied Greek and Hebrew at the University of Chicago, Illinois, and visited a number of the churches in the area. On October 20, 1902, the 600–member Olivet Baptist Church in Chicago invited him to pastor there. He accepted, despite the blossoming success in Nashville and the tremendous financial and morale problems facing Olivet. The first two years there were very trying, with internal church strife leading to lawsuits and much dissension. Nevertheless the church emerged very strong, and Fisher played an influential role in city politics, helping to clean up his part of town.

In September 1905, the church hosted the National Baptist Convention, U.S.A., Inc., which significantly boosted the image of the congregation. The following month the finishing touches were put on its large new building and the membership had climbed to about 2,000. The church began a seven-day-a-week service program and by 1908 was feeding over 50 destitute people a day. In about 1909 Fisher founded the Bethlehem Baptist Association of Chicago and Vicinity, which became one of the largest such groups in the state. In the summer of 1910 he was chair of the denominational delegation to the World's Missionary Conference in Edinburgh, Scotland. By that time the congregation had grown to 3,100 and was the largest Protestant congregation north of the Mason-Dixon Line. In 1912 he represented the denomination at the World's Baptist Alliance meeting in Philadelphia, Pennsylvania.

As the church became more self-directing he was able to spend more time traveling as speaker and representative. He was not afraid to take political sides on behalf of the Republican party and publicly criticized **Booker T. Washington** for not speaking out against lynchings. His motto was "Be somebody, do something, have something." In 1912 he founded and was president of the Chicago Religious Training Seminary as a school for ordained and lay Baptist training, held in his church. Within a year the school found a permanent home on Wabash Avenue and Fisher relinquished the presidency for the position of trustee.

He chaired the committee that drafted the constitution of the General Baptist State Convention of Illinois, and at the end of 1913 was elected its president. He was also president of the Western Baptist Convention, one of the incorporators of the National Baptist Publishing Board, and for over ten years was a vice-president of the **National Baptist Convention,**

U.S.A., Inc. He was such a force that it was commonly conceded that the convention would have split in 1914 had it not been for his efforts. Unfortunately he grew ill in 1915 and was not able to prevent that split in the convention that year which produced the National Baptist Convention of America. He passed away that summer, leaving a 3900–member church and a massive legacy of achievement. His son **Miles Mark Fisher** became a prominent Baptist minister and wrote the story of his father's life.

Fisher, Miles Mark. *The Master's Slave, Elijah John Fisher: A Biography*. Philadelphia, PA: The Judson Press, 1922. 194 pp.

NA, IBAW, WWCR, SCA.

FISHER, HENRY LEE (1874–1947), bishop and president of the **United Holy Church of America**, was born in Salisbury, North Carolina. The family later moved to Wilmington, North Carolina, where Fisher had a conversion experience at the age of eighteen and joined what two years later would be organized as the Holy Church of North Carolina. He soon was an ordained preacher, and became an effective evangelist in the area. In 1904 he traveled to Durham, North Carolina, to deliver the dedication sermon for the Durham Tabernacle, and to lead a revival campaign. This revival lasted a month and was so successful that he was invited to be the pastor of the new church, later renamed the Gospel Tabernacle. He remained at the Gospel Tabernacle for the rest of his career, making it one of the key churches in the growing Holy Church network, known from 1900 to 1910 as the Holy Church of North Carolina and Virginia. He married Annie Fisher.

Fisher quickly became a leading force in the denomination, aided by tackling such projects as the *Standard Manual for Holy Churches* (1910). The publication of the manual coincided with the church's name change to Holy Church of America. In 1916 he was named bishop of the Southern District and president of the church, the name of which changed again in that year to its present title, the United Holy Church of America. In 1918 he led the church in its formal incorporation as a nonprofit organization.

Fisher's priority as head of the church was its expansion through evangelism and missions. He supported the women's annual Home and Foreign Missionary Convention and organized the Missionary Department. After World War I, membership expanded in the north, and in 1920 he organized the Northern District. That same year he obtained from the **Christian and Missionary Alliance** the gift of Boynton Institute

in Boynton, Virginia, which the church began using as a training school. Missionary work was active, not only in the United States, but abroad, and from 1924 to 1928 Fisher traveled over 40,000 miles to support the missions in California, Bermuda, and Barbados. His wife, Annie, died about 1938, and he later married Inez Fisher.

Fisher's ministry carried the church through two world wars, and from its small, regional beginnings to a national and even international presence. As his work came to a close, he wrote a history of the church, *The History of the United Holy Church of America, Inc.*, a book he was uniquely qualified to put together. After his death, Gospel Tabernacle was renamed Fisher Memorial Church.

Fisher, Henry Lee. *The History of the United Holy Church of America, Inc.* Durham, NC: The Author, 194– . 55 pp.

———. *Standard Manual for Holy Churches*. Durham, NC: 1910. Reprinted Eden, NC: Dalcoe Printing Co., 1975. 45 pp.

Gregory, Chester W. *The History of the United Holy Church of America, Inc., 1886–1986*. Baltimore, MD: Gateway Press, 1986. 275 pp.

Turner, William Clair. *The United Holy Church of America: A Study in Black Holiness-Pentecostalism*. Durham, NC: Duke University, Ph.D. Dissertation, 1984. 221 pp.

BDA-AHP, BH, RLOA.

FISHER, MILES MARK (October 29, 1899–December 14, 1970), prominent Baptist minister, educator, and historian, was born in Atlanta, Georgia, the son of Florida Neely and **Elijah John Fisher**. He grew up in Chicago, where his father was minister of the Olivet Baptist Church, and it appeared from an early date that he would follow in those footsteps. He received his B.A. in 1918 from Morehouse College in Atlanta, Georgia, at which point he was ordained and began work as a YMCA camp secretary. From 1919 to 1920 he was pastor of the International Baptist Church in Chicago, and from 1921 to 1922 of the Zion Baptist Church in Racine, Wisconsin. The latter position allowed him to work on his B.D., which he received in 1922 from the Northern Baptist Theological Seminary in Lombard, Illinois, and on his M.A., completed also in 1922 from the University of Chicago. That same year he was an English instructor at Virginia Union University.

From 1923 to 1928 he pastored the Elam Baptist Church in Charles City County, Virginia, the Second Liberty Baptist Church, New Kent County, Virginia, and assisted at the Fourth Baptist Church in Richmond, Virginia, from 1924 to 1927. Also from 1923 to 1928 he was J. B. Hoyt professor of church history and New

Testament Greek at Virginia Union University's Richmond Theological Seminary. During this time he wrote *The Master's Slave—Elijah John Fisher* (1922) and *Virginia Union University and Some of Her Achievements* (1924). From 1928 to 1932 he was at the Sixteenth Street Baptist Church in Huntington, West Virginia. On September 6, 1930, he married Ada Virginia Foster, with whom he had six children.

In 1933 he became pastor of the well-known White Rock Baptist Church in Durham, North Carolina, where he remained for the rest of his career. He maintained his prodigious work schedule, teaching church history at Shaw University from 1934 to 1965, and pioneering the addition of Black history courses. Among the many items he wrote during this period were *A Short History of the Baptist Denomination* (1933) and his major work, *Negro Slave Songs in the United States* (1953), which won the American Historical Association prize for the outstanding historical volume of 1953. In that book, a further development of his dissertation, he argued that many of the slave songs were not simply religious, but were songs of protest and this-worldly freedom as well. The success of that book reflected his training in church history under William Warren Sweet at the University of Chicago Divinity School, which gave him his Ph.D. in 1948.

His church work earned him numerous awards, as well. In 1954 *Ebony* magazine named him one of the nation's ten best Black preachers, and noted that four-fifths of the congregation's 1,500 members turned out to hear him each Sunday. In 1956 the National Recreation Association gave him its Fiftieth Anniversary Award in honor of the White Rock Baptist Church's outstanding weekday recreation program for the community youth. He retired in 1964 and received the title of Pastor Emeritus.

Fisher, Miles Mark. *Lott Carey*. Philadelphia, PA: Foreign Mission Board, N.B.C. Publishers, 1921. 51 pp.

———. *The Master's Slave—Elijah John Fisher*. Philadelphia, PA: Judson Press, 1922. 194 pp.

———. *Negro Slave Songs in the United States*. New York: Cornell University Press, 1953. 223 pp.

———. *A Short History of the Baptist Denomination*. Nashville, TN: Sunday School Publication Board, 1933. 188 pp.

———. *Virginia Union University and Some of Her Achievements*. Richmond, VA: Brown Print Shop, 1924. 110 pp.

NCAB (56), WWCA (38–40), NYTO, BDA-AHP, EBA, BH, ERS, SBAA, CA (perm.series), RLOA.

FISHER, RICHARD LAYMON (September 28, 1934–October 25, 1991), a bishop in the **African Methodist Episcopal Zion Church** (AMEZ), was born in Evanston, Illinois, the son of the Rev. W. Frederic and Julia E. Fisher, both graduates of Livingstone College in Salisbury, North Carolina. After moving through the Evanston public school system, Fisher attended Boston University, graduating with his B.S. in 1956, then receiving his S.T.B. from Boston University School of Theology in 1959. While in college he served as assistant pastor in Mother Walls Memorial AMEZ Church, Boston, from 1954 to 1956. He married Joan Spratley, with whom he had two children.

Upon graduation from seminary he returned to the local church as pastor of Campbell Chapel AMEZ Church in Indianapolis, Indiana, from 1959 to 1960, followed by eleven years (1961–1972) at the Martin Temple AMEZ Church in Chicago, Illinois, and twelve years (1972–1984) at Washington Metropolitan AMEZ Church in St. Louis, Missouri. In each of these positions his work was marked by success; in St. Louis he increased the membership, renovated the church, paid off a mortgage, acquired an 18–unit apartment building, purchased a parsonage, completed a 192–unit housing development, and applied for 147 units of elderly housing. In 1974 he became chair of the Urban League of St. Louis, and was active in numerous other service organizations.

At the 1984 General Conference, Fisher was elected bishop on July 26, on the third ballot, and assigned to the Eleventh Episcopal District (Arkansas, Florida, Texas, Oklahoma, Arizona, and South Carolina Annual Conferences). He maintained his residence in St. Louis, and was active in such groups as the St. Louis Board of Education Citizens Task Force. He was a member of the Governing Board of the National Council of Churches and was on the board of trustees of the National Urban League, Livingstone College, and Clinton Junior College.

Armstrong, James David. "Bishop Richard Laymon Fisher: A Tribute." *The A.M.E. Zion Quarterly Review* 104 (January 1992): 2–3.

"Two Bishops Elected at General Conference." *Star of Zion* 108 (August 2, 1984): 1, 2.

"Vignettes of Our Bishops: Bishop Richard L. Fisher." *Star of Zion* 111 (December 17, 1987): 8.

"Two Bishops Elected at General Conference." *Star of Zion* 108 (August 2, 1984): 1, 2.

"Vignettes of Our Bishops: Bishop Richard L. Fisher." *Star of Zion* 111 (December 17, 1987): 8.

WWABA (90–91), WWR (85).

FISK JUBILEE SINGERS. The Fisk Jubilee Singers were formed by George L. White, an instructor at Fisk University during the 1870s. At the beginning of the decade, the school was in trouble financially, and White proposed that a group of his more talented singers be organized to go on a concert tour to raise money for the school. The original group consisted of eight singers, a pianist, and two helpers. The first tour occurred in 1871 and emphasized music popular in the White community, the audience to which the concerts were pitched. Leaving on October 6, the group headed to **Oberlin College**, where the National Council of Congregational Churches was holding its annual meeting. Henry Ward Beecher then invited them to Plymouth Congregational Church in Brooklyn, New York, and introduced them to his many contacts in New York and New England. A New York newspaper calling them the "Nigger Minstrels" prompted White to finally select a name for the group. He chose Jubilee Singers, a reference to the biblical year of jubilee.

While concentrating on White music in the beginning, the group soon realized that public response centered upon the slave music of the antebellum South. The slave songs, later termed "spirituals," quickly became the backbone of the Singers' concerts. The New England tours over the next four years added thousands of dollars to the Fisk treasury. In 1874 the group had a successful tour of England and Germany. By 1880, when the group disbanded, some $150,000 had been added to the Fisk treasury and made possible the school's significant revival in the 1880s.

The Fisk Jubilee Singers prompted other schools to send out similar singing groups. In 1873 Hampton Institute sent a choir on tour and in later years Tuskegee followed suit. Also on several occasions there were attempts to revive the Jubilee Singers at Fisk, though none of the later groups had their success. As an additional major consequence, the success of the Jubilee Singers called attention to the vast body of spirituals and led to the creation of structures to collect, study, and preserve them.

Work, John Wesley. *Folk Songs of the American Negro.* Nashville, TN: Fisk University, 1915. 132 pp.

FISK UNIVERSITY. One of a number of schools originally founded under the auspices of the American Missionary Association (A.M.A.), an agency of the Congregational Churches (now an integral part of the **United Church of Christ**). Fisk University, Nashville, Tennessee, was founded in 1866 by John Ogden, Erastus M. Cravath and Edward P. Smith, all White men. Smith,

an A.M.A. field secretary, was instructed to develop a school for the former slaves in Nashville and, with the assistance of the two other founders, secured a former Union Army hospital. Like many of the Freedman schools, it concentrated on the elementary and high school grades with a goal of training African American teachers. Two hundred enrolled soon after the school opened. It was incorporated in 1867 as Fisk University, as the founders planned to build a first-rate institution of higher learning. The normal school opened in 1867, and the first college courses were taught in 1871. For the rest of the century the high school and normal school fed students into the slowly emerging college. A boarding arrangement was developed in which students resided with the faculty.

Ogden led the school for its first quadrennium and was succeeded by Adam K. Spence who is generally credited with building the college department into the quality institution it has remained. The school suffered financial problems, however, as Spence was inept at fundraising. His career and the school, however, was saved by the 1871 tour of the **Fisk Jubilee Singers**, a group of students who gave concerts of African American songs of the slave era. They were an instant success and not only in America but in Europe.

With the money raised by the Fisk Singers, under President E. M. Cravath the school began to move away from a church supported school to become a private liberal arts university. Under his leadership, a new campus was built and the college department given priority over the elementary and secondary schools. Fisk experienced a watershed in 1925 when students and alumni joined to oust Fayette A. McKenzie from the presidency. He was replaced by Thomas E. Jones and an era of marked growth began. Jones was succeeded in 1946 by Charles S. Johnson, the school's first Black president. Through the 1980s, the school served approximately 500 students annually.

Richardson, Joe M. *A History of Fisk University, 1865–1946.* University, AL: University of Alabama Press, 1980. 227 pp.

FLIPPER, JOSEPH SIMEON (February 22, 1859–October 10, 1944), 33rd bishop of the **African Methodist Episcopal Church** (AME), was born into slavery in Atlanta, Georgia, son of Festus and Isabella (Buckhalter) Flipper, on the plantation of Ephraim G. Ponder. As a child he attended Big Bethel AME Church in Atlanta with his parents. Flipper was among the first students to enroll in Atlanta University, attending the primary and secondary departments from 1869 to 1876. He then taught school in Thomaston, Georgia, as one of the first Black teachers in Georgia. He was converted in March 1877, and joined the St. Thomas AME Church under Rev. S. W. Drayton. He was licensed as a local preacher in 1879, teaching by this time at Groverville (now Key) in Brooks County, and was admitted to the Georgia Annual Conference of the AME Church in January, 1880. He married Amanda Slater on February 24, 1880, with whom he had three children. His brother, Henry O. Flipper, was the first Black graduate of West Point Military Academy, in 1877.

His first church assignment was the Groverville Circuit, from 1880 to 1881, then the Boston Circuit, Georgia, from 1881 to 1882. He was ordained deacon in January 1882, and assigned to Darien, Georgia, until 1883, when he taught school for a year in Cairo and Whigham, Georgia. In January 1884 he was ordained elder and assigned to Quitman, Georgia, staying until 1886, when he transferred to the North Georgia Conference and was appointed to Big Bethel AME Church in Athens, Georgia, the largest church in the state, staying until 1889. He was the youngest pastor ever put in charge of that church, and raised more money during his tenure than had ever been raised in any church in the state.

From 1889 to 1892 he was pastor of Pierce Chapel AME Church in Athens, Georgia, and was presiding elder of the Athens District from 1892 to 1895. He was then at Allen Temple AME Church in Atlanta (1895–1899) and St. Paul's AME Church in Atlanta (1899–1903). In 1892 he became a member of the Episcopal Committee of the denomination, remaining in that role the rest of his life and serving as chair from 1900 to 1904. He was known as a strong supporter of the laity, and in 1900 prevented ministers from representing the laity on the Episcopal Committee. He was also a member of the Finance Board from 1900 to 1908. In 1903 he was appointed dean of Turner Theological Seminary at Morris Brown College in Atlanta, and was president of the college from 1904 to 1908. At one point he was president of the Citizens Trust Company of Atlanta.

In May, 1908 Flipper was elected bishop and assigned to the Ninth Episcopal District (Oklahoma and Arkansas). He visited places no bishop had ever before visited, and increased the membership. In 1912 he was sent to the Sixth Episcopal District (Georgia), where he served for sixteen years with many accomplishments. He organized the Morris Brown University System, composed of Central Park College in Savannah, Payne College in Cuthbert, and Morris Brown in Atlanta, and strengthened each of these constituent parts. He organized the S. W. Conference on December 10, 1912, and the Macon Conference on December 9, 1914. His

first wife having died, he married a widow, Susie Rembert (Erwin) on April 14, 1922.

From 1928 to 1936 he served the Eleventh Episcopal District (Florida), where he once again increased the membership and expanded Edward Waters College. In 1936 he was appointed to the Thirteenth District (Kentucky and Tennessee), but the sudden death of Bishop W. D. Johnson caused him to be quickly moved to the Seventh District (South Carolina), where he served from 1936 to 1944. There he established the Joseph Simeon Flipper Library, a beautiful stone building that remained one of his many legacies. Most of his personal books were willed to Turner Theological Seminary's library. He was regarded as one of the great authorities on AME Church law, and advocated a "supreme court" for the denomination. He was known as "Big Brother" and "Honest Joe." He became senior bishop in 1934, and was bishop for 36 years and five months, a term second in length only to Bishop Payne.

Flipper, Joseph Simeon. *Episcopal Address.* Nashville, TN: A.M.E. Sunday School Union, 1920. 78 pp.

———. *What Should Be the Attitude of the Negro Toward the Prevailing Sentiment Relative to His Education?* Atlanta, GA: Herald Publ. Co., 1908. 7 pp.

BAMEC, EAMEC, CEAMEC, WWCR, RLA, EWM, EBA, WWCA (38–40), WWWA (vol.2), NYTO, NCAB (vol.14), TCNL, BAW.

FLORIDA MEMORIAL COLLEGE. A Baptist school. Florida Memorial College was founded in 1879, one of several schools begun in the South by the American Baptist Home Missionary Society. It originally opened in Live Oak, Florida, as the Florida Baptist Institute for Negroes. In 1892 a second school, the Florida Normal and Industrial Institute, was opened at Jacksonville. It soon became known as the Florida Baptist Academy. In 1917 the school at Live Oak absorbed the Florida Baptist Academy, and the merged school moved to St. Augustine where it became the Florida Normal and Industrial Institute. The move into larger facilities allowed it to begin offering college courses. The gradual shift from secondary to college education occurred in stages over the next generation. The first class to graduate from the full four-year curriculum was in 1945. In 1950 the school became known as the Florida Normal and Industrial College and in 1963 assumed its present name. That same year it opened its doors to all races. In 1968 it moved to a new campus in Miami.

Today Florida Memorial College is a four-year liberal arts college, and it continues under the sponsorship of the **American Baptist Churches in the U.S.A.**

FOGGIE, CHARLES HERBERT (b. August 4, 1912), 69th bishop of the **African Methodist Episcopal Zion Church** (AMEZ), was born in Sumter, South Carolina, the son of James Legree and Mary (Lee) Foggie. He grew up in Boston, Massachusetts, affiliating with the Columbus Avenue AMEZ Church as a youth, but not being very interested in it. At one point he dropped out of high school, hoping for a career as a dancing entertainer. In 1931 he went with his mother to a Mother's Day service and felt as if the sermon were directed at him personally. He soon felt called to the ministry, was licensed to preach, and served one year as an assistant to Dr. Charles C. Williams in the Columbus Avenue church. He joined the New England Conference the following year and was assigned to attend school. While in school, he was ordained deacon on June 17, 1934, and elder on June 21, 1936.

He received his B.A. from Livingstone College in Salisbury, North Carolina, in 1936, and was assigned to the Wadsworth Street AMEZ Church in Providence, Rhode Island, from 1936 to 1939. During this time he began work at Boston University in Massachusetts, earning an M.A. in social ethics in 1938. It cost him $2.25 a week for a round trip from Boston to Providence, and the church paid him only $2.00 a week. He then went to Rush AMEZ Church in Cambridge, Massachusetts, closer to the Boston University School of Theology, earning his S.T.M. in 1939. In 1944 he was assigned to the prestigious Wesley Center AMEZ Church in Pittsburgh, Pennsylvania, where he stayed for 24 years and established his reputation. During his tenure a parsonage was built, the church was completed and decorated, and a large mortgage was eliminated. He served on the Mayor's Housing Committee, on the Race Relations Commission, and several other organizations. While in Pittsburgh he also met Madeline S. Sharpe, whom he married on January 9, 1952, and with whom he had one daughter.

At the General Conference in May, 1968 Foggie was elected bishop and assigned to the Twelfth Episcopal District (Arkansas, North Arkansas, Oklahoma, Georgia, Texas, and South Georgia Conferences). He had first been nominated for the episcopacy in 1956, but was ruled ineligible because of an irregular marital status. Not until 1964 was his name allowed to be placed on the ballot, which opened the way for his election at the following General Conference. He maintained his residence in Pittsburgh, and continued his involvement in the city. He has been president of the Pittsburgh N.A.A.C.P., on the Mayor's Advisory Committee on the Poverty Program, and chair of the board of directors of the Housing Authority.

In 1972 he was assigned to the Fifth Episcopal District, and in about 1984 was shifted to the Third Episcopal District (Allegheny, Ohio, Philadelphia, Baltimore, Guyana, and Barbados Conferences). He was secretary of the Board of Bishops, secretary of the board of trustees of Livingstone College, and chair of the Board of Home Missions. He received the Martin Luther King, Jr., Award and the Home Mission Evangelistic Award. He chaired the North American Section Worship Commission of the World Methodist Council, and was part of the Leadership Conference on Civil Rights. He retired in 1988.

"Dr. Charles Herbert Foggie Elected Bishop." *Star of Zion* 91 (June 13, 1968): 4.

Ellis, William W. "Fifty Years of Ministry in Zion: The Anniversary of Charles Herbert Foggie." *A.M.E. Zion Quarterly Review* 98 (October 1986): 4–7.

Fauntroy, Walter E. "Tribute to Bishop Charles Herbert Foggie." *A.M.E. Zion Quarterly Review* 98 (October 1986): 10–11.

Foggie, Charles H. "Retirement Notes in the Philadelphia and Baltimore Conference of the AME Zion Church, Washington, D.C., May 25, 1988." *A.M.E. Zion Quarterly Review* 99 (July 1988): 2–8.

"Vignettes of Our Bishops: Bishop Charles Herbert Foggie." *Star of Zion* 111 (October 29, 1987): 5.

WWABA (90–91), AMEZC, BDNM (75), WWR (85), EWM, HAMEZC.

FOOTE, JULIA A. J. (1823– ?), the first woman ordained a deacon in the **African Methodist Episcopal Zion Church** (AMEZ) was born into slavery in Schenectady, New York. Her father had been born free but was kidnapped as a child and enslaved. Over time he was able to purchase himself, his wife, and their first child (at that time their only child) out of slavery. They later joined the Methodist Episcopal Church and had to endure being forced into certain seats in the gallery and waiting until all the Whites had been served in order to receive communion.

There were no schools available for Black children, and Foote did not even learn the alphabet until she was nine years old. At the age of ten she was sent to live with the Prime family in the country. There she was able to attend the local rural school and gained a basic education. She returned to her own family at about the age of twelve and soon they moved to Albany, New York, where her parents joined the **African Methodist**

Episcopal Church (AME). She experienced conversion at the age of fifteen, and considered herself a "brand plucked from the burning," saved from a sinful life that she had felt herself so close to falling into. Nevertheless, she continued to experience inward conflicts and trauma, especially after an accident which cost her the sight of one eye.

After a time Foote learned about the complete sanctification taught among Holiness people, and eventually found that condition for herself. About a year later she married George Foote (the timing is difficult to ascertain), although he was not yet sanctified himself. They moved to Boston, where she spent most of the time alone while he worked away during the week in Chelsea. He later found a job as a seaman, on the ocean for six months at a time. She joined the local AME Church and began telling its members of her Holiness beliefs. She prayed and exhorted in many homes and made visitations in the hospital. After a time she had a vision in which she was told to go and preach the gospel. She had always been against women preachers and so resisted the call for several months, until another vision convinced her to respond.

Great opposition was raised to her decision to preach, and she was excommunicated from her congregation. She appealed to higher levels in the church, but was not heard. Shortly afterwards she returned to her parents' home in Binghamton, New York, where she was accepted and had some success evangelizing. In June of 1844(?) she attended the General Conference of the AME Church in Philadelphia, where she saw a motion to allow women clergy shouted down. She went to Ithaca, New York, in February 1845, where there was great division in the AME Church as to whether to allow her to preach. Finally another meeting place was obtained for her services. She continued her travels and preaching, mostly in New York. Some months later she heard of the death of her husband.

In 1849 she was asked by **Daniel Payne**, later bishop of the AME Church, to come visit in Baltimore, Maryland, and she spent some time in that area. In June 1850 she went to Pittsburgh, Pennsylvania, then on to Columbus, Ohio; Detroit, Michigan; Canada, and elsewhere. In about 1852 she settled in Cleveland, Ohio. In 1879 she published *A Brand Plucked from the Fire: An Autobiographical Sketch*. Not much more information is available about her work. After many years of labor she was finally ordained, but not in the AME Church. In 1884 Bishop **James Walker Hood** of the AMEZ Church ordained her a deacon in the New York Annual Conference, the first woman deacon in the history of the denomination. The second woman deacon,

Mrs. Mary J. Small, was not ordained until 1895. Foote was ordained an elder in 1900.

Foote, Julia A. J. *A Brand Plucked from the Fire: An Autobiographical Sketch.* Cleveland, OH: W. F. Schneider, 1879. 124 pp.
BAW, AARS, IBAW, BWR, HAMEZC, SS.

FORBES, JAMES ALEXANDER (b. September 6, 1935), the first African American senior pastor of the famous Riverside Church in New York City, was born in Burgaw, North Carolina, the son of James A. and Mable Forbes. He received his B.S. in chemistry in 1957 from Howard University in Washington, D.C., and his B.D. in 1962 from Union Theological Seminary. He married Bettye Jeanne Franks, with whom he has had one son.

He was ordained into the **Original United Holy Church International** and served a number of charges, including Binkley Memorial Baptist Church; St. John's United Holy Church in Richmond, Virginia; Holy Trinity Church in Wilmington, North Carolina; and St. Paul Holy Church in Roxboro, North Carolina. He continued to work on his education, receiving a D.Min. in 1975 from Colgate-Rochester Divinity School (as a U.S. Fellow of the Martin Luther King, Jr. Black Church Studies Program); a Certificate in Clinical Pastoral Education in 1975 from the Medical College of Virginia; and an S.T.D. in 1983 from Dickinson College in Carlisle, Pennsylvania.

Over the years he gained a reputation as a formidable preacher and as one who tried to combine a Pentecostal heritage with a progressive social activism. The title of his D.Min. thesis was *A Pentecostal Approach to Empowerment for Black Liberation* (1975). In 1976 he was named Brown-Sockman Associate Professor of Preaching at Union Theological Seminary in New York City, serving also as assistant pastor of the Forbes Temple United Holy Church in Jamaica, New York. In 1984 *Ebony* magazine named him one of the top fifteen Black preachers in America. About that same time he was promoted to Joe R. Engle Professor of Preaching at Union. He began to travel widely, preaching and lecturing at colleges and other settings around the country and internationally. He began serving on the board of directors of the Original United Holy Church International; the Inter-Collegiate Pentecostal Conference International; the **National Conference of Black Churchmen**; and many other organizations. In 1986 he delivered the highly coveted Lyman Beecher Lecture Series at Yale Divinity School.

On February 5, 1989, Forbes was named the first

Black senior pastor in the history of the Riverside Church, founded in Manhattan's Upper West Side in the 1920s by John D. Rockefeller, Jr. This church, with a membership of some 2,500 and an annual budget of $6,000,000, is considered by many the most prestigious pulpit in mainline Protestantism. It is affiliated with both the **American Baptist Churches in the U.S.A.** and the **United Church of Christ**, and Forbes thus now carries an ordination also with the American Baptist Churches. Forbes succeeded the famous preacher and social activist William Sloan Coffin, who went on to be the national director of Sane/Freeze, a group working to stop the development of nuclear weapons. Coffin's pastorate was not without controversy, and Forbes was chosen as someone who could heal rifts by combining a vigorous spiritual leadership as well as a social justice ministry. The Riverside Church has also worked hard to implement its belief in an inclusive church, and about one-third of its membership is now Black and Hispanic. Forbes was seen as the ideal candidate to solidify the church's commitment to inclusivity and pluralism. In 1989 he published his first major book, *The Holy Spirit and Preaching*.

"America's Fifteen Greatest Black Preachers." *Ebony* 39 (September 1984): 27–33.

Dyson, Michael. "New Days, Great Traditions: James Forbes at Riverside." *Christianity and Crisis* 49 (March 6, 1989): 52.

"Forbes Called to Riverside." *Christian Century* 106 (February 22, 1989): 201.

Forbes, James Alexander. *The Holy Spirit and Preaching*. Nashville, TN: Abingdon Press, 1989. 111 pp.

———. "How to Be Black and Christian Too." In M. A. Warren, ed. *Black Preaching: Truth and Soul*. Washington, DC: N.p., 1977, 79–96.

———. "Ministry of Hope from a Double Minority." *Theological Education* 9 (Summer 1973, supp.): 305–316.

———. *A Pentecostal Approach to Empowerment for Black Liberation*. Rochester, NY: D.Min. Thesis, Colgate Rochester Divinity School, 1975. 139 pp.

———. "Shall We Call This Dream Progressive Pentecostalism?" *Spirit* 1 (1977): 12–15.

BH, BDNM (70), NA.

FORD, ARNOLD JOSIAH (1890?–1935?), rabbi and co-composer of the Universal Ethiopian Anthem, was born in Barbados, British West Indies, the son of Edward Thomas Ford and Elizabeth Augusta (Braithwaite) Ford. He was educated in the Barbados public schools, showed a special aptitude for music, and as a young man became a music teacher in the British Navy. His father was an evangelical preacher, but when Ford moved to the United States in 1912, he dropped his Christian associations.

From 1912 to 1920 Ford was bandmaster of the New Amsterdam Musical Association in New York City, and was one of the founders of the Clef Club. Perhaps during this time he became acquainted with some of the Black Jewish groups that were present in Harlem. He began to identify himself as an Ethiopian Jew, and studied Hebrew and the Jewish tradition. In 1917 **Marcus Garvey**, another West Indian, arrived in New York City and organized the Universal Negro Improvement Association (UNIA). Ford met Garvey in that year, was drawn to his "Back to Africa" ideas, and joined the UNIA as its bandmaster and choirmaster. In that office he composed numerous hymns which expressed the religious aspects of Garveyism. They depicted Africa as the paradise lost, to which the exiled Blacks must return and help restore. He wrote the music and assisted Ben Burrell in the text of the National Anthem of the UNIA, "Ethiopia, Land of Our Fathers." Ford compiled and wrote much of the official hymnbook of the UNIA, *The Universal Ethiopian Hymnal*.

Ford tried to convince Garvey to adopt Judaism as the official religion of the UNIA, but Garvey refused to do so. Some biographers have written that this and other differences led to the expulsion of Ford from the UNIA in 1923, but there is evidence that he continued to be a part of UNIA events beyond that time. In 1924 Ford founded the Beth B'nai Abraham Congregation in New York City. As its rabbi, he taught that all Africans are blood Hebrews, although forced exposure to Christianity has blunted the memory of their true heritage. Knowledge of Ethiopian Jews, called **Falashas**, was spread in the 1920s through the fundraising efforts of Jacques Faitlovich of the University of Geneva. Ford felt the existence of the Falashas confirmed his beliefs, and after a meeting with Faitlovich in about 1929, determined to go to Ethiopia himself. This move became especially attractive when the Beth B'nai Abraham Congregation collapsed financially and lost its property. In 1930 he left what remained of his work to **Wentworth A. Matthew**, head of the Commandment Keepers Ethiopian Hebrew Congregation, and sailed for Ethiopia with his common-law wife, Mignon, and family.

He arrived in Ethiopia shortly after the coronation of Haile Selassie in November, 1930. Not much is known of his time there, except that he apparently made use of his musical expertise by teaching music, repairing instruments, and entertaining. He died sometime soon after the invasion of Ethiopia by Italy in 1935. His widow helped found the Princess Zännäbä Wärq school in Addis Ababa in the early 1940s.

Ehrman, Albert. "Explorations and Responses: Black Judaism in New York." *Journal of Ecumenical Studies* 8 (Winter 1971): 103–114.

Ford, Arnold Josiah, ed. *The Universal Ethiopian Hymnal.* New York: Beth B'nai Abraham Publishing Co., n.d.

Kobre, S. S. "Rabbi Ford." *Reflex* (January 1929): 25–29.

Landes, Ruth. "Negro Jews in Harlem." *Jewish Journal of Sociology* 9 (December 1967): 175–189.

WWCA (30–32), BDA-AHP, BDACSL, BJH, BA, GRM, NWAC, RLOA.

FORD, GEORGE A. (b. 1898), a bishop of the **African Orthodox Church** (AOC), was born and raised in Barbados. He attended Byroe Vocational School and became a journeyman tradesman with a variety of skills. He came to the United States in the 1920s where he met Bishop **Reginald G. Barrow** of the African Orthodox Church who was also from Barbados. He joined the church in 1926 and entered **Endich Theological Seminary**. He was ordained a deacon in 1933 and a priest in 1938.

Ford was a deacon at the time of the major schism in the AOC. In the mid-1930s, by several steps, Barrow led in the formation of what became known as the **Holy African Church**. Ford joined in the new group and in 1939 organized Christ Church, a parish in Brooklyn which he served for many years. In 1940 he returned to school and during the next three years improved his skills in drafting, woodwork, and power mechanics at Brooklyn Technical High School. That same year he became the general secretary of the Holy African Church, a post he would hold for the next 16 years. In 1956 he entered New York University and in 1964 was awarded his B.A. in vocational education. While finishing his college work, in 1957 he was elevated to the office of monsignor by Bishop **Gladstone S. Nurse**.

In 1964, Bishop Nurse finished an agreement which allowed the reunion of the AOC and the Holy African Church. With the rest of the church, Ford moved back into the African Orthodox Church. In 1971 he was installed as the Dean of St. Michael's Pro-Cathedral in Brooklyn by Bishop **Noel Smith**. Then in 1979, already in his eighties, Ford was elected to the bishopric and consecrated November 17, 1979, by Bishop Nurse assisted by Bishop **Frederick A. Toote**. He was named bishop of Massachusetts and Canada.

"In Profile." *The Trumpet: the Official Organ of the African Orthodox Church* 2, 2 (November 1980): 19–20.

FORMAN, JAMES (b. October 4, 1928), author of the **Black Manifesto** of 1969, was born in Chicago, Illinois, the son of Octavia Allen and Jackson Forman. As a child, Forman was sent to his grandmother's in Mississippi where he remained until school age. In 1932 his mother married John Rufus, and they brought him to Chicago. Forman grew up as James Rufus and only later learned that Rufus was his stepfather. Though Forman's mother was an active member of the **African Methodist Episcopal Church**, she placed him in St. Anselm's Roman Catholic School for the first five grades. He was proud of his Protestantism during these years, though upset at being denied honors because of it. He even briefly considered entering the ministry, but was offended by his experiences of the realities of church politics. In the end he dropped out of church entirely and became anticlerical. After finishing high school, he attended Wilson Junior College for one term before joining the Air Force in 1947.

Forman's four years in the Air Force merely strengthened the Black consciousness which had been growing since his elementary school days when he first learned of his racial difference from the dominant society. The number of racial incidents he experienced also led to increased occasions in which he fought back. After leaving the Air Force in 1951 he entered the University of Southern California. His career at USC was abruptly interrupted one evening when, having left the library, he was picked up by the Los Angeles Police. His brutalization at their hands led to a nervous breakdown and he spent several years recovering from it. He had married during his service days, and his illness finished what had already become a strained relationship.

By 1954 he had recovered his health and he entered Roosevelt University. As the civil rights movement gained momentum, he became a central figure in the student debate on the emerging issues, especially the virtues of nonviolence as a tactic for social change. He graduated in 1957 and spent a year at Boston University working on a master's degree in African affairs. During this time he became even more impressed over the power of nonviolent social action, having seen it work for African leader Nwane Nkrumah. After finishing school, Forman settled in Chicago as a teacher and began to actively involve himself in various civil rights incidents in the South. In 1960 the Student Nonviolent Coordinating Committee (SNCC), destined to be one of the more important of the groups active in the civil rights movement, was formed, and in 1961 it called Forman to be its executive director. He remained in that post into 1964 and was active in its leadership through the rest of the decade. His developing perspective is illustrated in his book, *Sammy Younge, Jr.: The First Black College Student to Die in the Black Liberation Movement* (1968).

Forman's experiences in SNCC and his growing impatience with the course of the civil rights movement readied him to receive with some enthusiasm the call for Black Power which emerged in the mid-1960s. He had by this time come to the conclusion that revolutionary change (systemic social change) was necessary and that such change required the taking of economic power by the Black community. The rise of Black Power also provided Forman with the high point of his career.

The positive response to the call for Black Power, in the economic sense, led to the formation of a number of new organizations. Among these were the National Committee of Negro Churchmen (now the **National Conference of Black Churchmen**) founded in 1966 primarily by Black leaders in the churches associated with the National Council of Churches, especially those who held positions in the major predominantly White denominations. The formation of the committee also led in 1967 and 1968 to the organization of the African American clergy and lay leadership in almost all of the major White denominations. By the beginning of 1968 such caucuses were firmly in place among the American Baptists, United Methodists, United Presbyterians, the United Church of Christ, and Roman Catholics. A child of the churches was **Interreligious Foundation for Community Organization** (IFCO), founded in 1967, which awarded funds to groups for community organizing. It was supported by a number of the predominantly White Protestant churches, several national Roman Catholic organizations, and the Unitarian Universalists, as well as the American Jewish Committee.

In 1968 Forman participated in the formation of the **National Black Economic Development Conference** (BEDC) (later the word National was deleted from the title). Through this committee, Forman took the lead in preparing the "Black Manifesto." He had by this time developed a Marxist interpretation of the social situation and believed that the Christian churches were instruments of Black capitalist oppression. The manifesto, written as a document for IFCO, called for $500,000,000 in reparations to be used to fund a number of programs from publishing houses to a Black

university. It also called upon African Americans to disrupt the activities (including the worship services) of the churches and synagogues as a way to force payment. Forman saw BEDC as the organization to implement the demands, with the money being channeled through IFCO. Approved, at least tacitly by the IFCO conference in April 1969, Forman went to New York and on May 4 attracted the nation's attention by interrupting the service at the prestigious Riverside Church to read the manifesto.

As might be expected the document caused a round of controversy. Most of IFCO's backers moved to reorder priorities in light of its demands, but over the ensuing months a number of changes occurred. IFCO backed away from the manifesto, especially its more radical language. The churches, on the other hand, began to respond with large grants, but most of these did not go to IFCO but to the various African American caucus groups. As a whole the money which did go to IFCO did not go to Forman and the BEDC. By the summer of 1970, BEDC had received only $300,000, which was used for administration and to start a publishing house, whose first major publication was a text by Forman on political philosophy.

Following the demise of the debates over the manifesto, Forman and the BEDC have faded into relative obscurity. Forman turned his attention to writing his autobiography, *The Making of Black Revolutionaries*, which appeared in 1972 (rev. ed., 1982).

Forman, James. *The Making of Black Revolutionaries*. New York: Macmillan Publishing, 1972. 568 pp. Rept.: Washington, DC: Open Hand Pub., 1985. 568 pp.

———. *The Political Thought of James Forman*. Detroit, MI: Black Star Publishing, 1970. 190 pp.

———. *Sammy Younge, Jr.: The First Black College Student to Die in the Black Liberation Movement*. New York: Grove Press, 1968. 282 pp.

Zinn, Howard. *SNCC: the New Revolutionaries*. Boston: Beacon Press, 1964. 286 pp.

FOUNTAIN, WILLIAM ALFRED (October 29, 1870–April 23, 1955), educator and 46th bishop of the **African Methodist Episcopal Church** (AME), was born in Elberton, Georgia, the eldest of eighteen children in the family of Richard and Virginia Fountain. He attended Elberton public schools and was converted in April 1888, while attending Clark College in Atlanta, subsequently joining the Allen Temple AME Church in Atlanta, Georgia. As a layperson he held the offices of class leader, steward, trustee, and Sunday School superintendent. He graduated from the secondary department of Allen University in Columbia, South Carolina, in 1892.

He was both licensed to preach and ordained deacon in 1892 and was assigned to the Pindergrass Mission AME Church from 1892 to 1893. He married Jessie Williams on June 29, 1894, with whom he had one child. He was at Bethel AME Church in Athens, Georgia from 1893 to 1895 and at Grant Chapel AME Church in Washington, Georgia from 1895 to 1897. In 1898 he was assigned to Turner Chapel AME Church in Marietta, about twenty miles from Atlanta, where he enrolled at Morris Brown College, earning his B.A. in 1900. His first wife died in September 1898, and on October 24, 1899, he married Julia T. Allen, with whom he had four children. He became presiding elder of the Athens District in 1901, while he continued his studies at Turner Theological Seminary in Atlanta, earning his B.D. in 1902.

From 1905 to 1907 he was assigned to Allen Temple AME Church in Atlanta, followed by St. Stephens AME Church in Wilmington, North Carolina in 1908, and the Steward Chapel AME Church in Macon, Georgia, from 1908 to 1911. His ministry was very successful in every location, and he paid off the mortgages at six different churches. He organized the Second AME Church and built St. Luke AME Church, both in Washington, Georgia. In 1911 he became president of Morris Brown University and chancellor of the Morris Brown University System, consisting of Payne College in Cuthbert, Central Park Normal and Industrial College in Savannah, and Morris Brown University in Atlanta.

At the 1920 General Conference Fountain was elected bishop and assigned to the 18th Episcopal District, covering territory from California to the West Indies and South America. In 1924 he was assigned to the Ninth Episcopal District (Alabama and Louisiana Conferences), and in 1928 he was assigned to the Sixth Episcopal District (Georgia). In 1948 he was shifted to the Twelfth Episcopal District (Arkansas and Oklahoma Conferences), and from 1951 to 1952 returned to the Ninth District. He was a trustee of both Morris Brown University and Wilberforce University in Ohio, Morehouse College in Atlanta, and Daniel Payne College in Cuthbert, Georgia.

During his tenure in Georgia, the membership reached the largest of any other Episcopal District, and funding was equally high. He enabled Morris Brown College, which was nearly bankrupt in 1928, to become the largest AME college by 1948. He sold the old site of the college, secured new grounds, and organized money-raising efforts that garnered an endowment of

$500,000. He became senior bishop after the death of Bishop **Joseph S. Flipper** in October 1944, and chaired the "After-the-War Planning Committee" of the denomination. He organized the AME Church in Vancouver, Canada, and added 1,000 members in St. Croix in the Virgin Islands. It is estimated that in his career there were approximately 5,000 conversions by his preaching. He went blind during 1950–51, and was retired in 1952. Named for him are "Fountain Drive" in S. W. Atlanta, Fountain High Schools in Georgetown, British Guiana and in San Juan, Trinidad, and AME churches in five states.

The Doctrine and Discipline of the African Methodist Episcopal Church, Published by Order of the General Conference Held in Detroit, Michigan, May, 1940, by Rev. William K. Hopes. . . . Compiled by Bishop William Alfred Fountain, Chairman, Bishop David Henry Sims, Bishop Monroe Hortensius Davis, and others. . . . Philadelphia, PA: AME Book Concern, 1940.

Fountain, William A. *The Episcopal Address Presented by . . . to the Thirtieth General Conference of the African Methodist Episcopal Church. New York City, N.Y., May 6, of the General Conference.* Philadelphia, PA: AME Book Concern, 1936.

BAMEC, WWCA (38–40), *HAMEC, CEAMEC, WWCR, EWM, NYTO, WWWA* (vol. 3), *EAMEC, RLA, IBAW, AARS, HUBA.*

FOY, WILLIAM ELLIS (1818–November 9, 1893), a nineteenth-century Adventist minister, was born near Augusta, Maine, the son of Joseph and Elizabeth Foy, land owners and farmers. Little is known of his early life. In 1835 he had a conversion experience under the ministry of Silas Curtis, a white minister active in the anti-slavery cause and pastor of the Free Will Baptist Church in Augusta. Blacks had been encouraged to join the local Free Will congregation, and Foy eventually became a Free Will Baptist minister.

Foy married his wife Ann around 1836 and the following year they had their first child. About 1840 he moved to Boston and affiliated with the twelfth Baptist church on Southack Street. Though not a follower, he also began to associate with the Millerites, the followers of William Miller who were preaching the imminent return of Jesus Christ in October 1843. However, in 1842 at a gathering of Adventists at the Baptist church on Southark Street, he had a vision in which an angelic guide showed him the rewards of the faithful followers of Christ. The vision lasted for several hours. Three weeks later while at the nearby **African Methodist Episcopal Church** he had a second vision which concerned the fate of the wicked. He subsequently had two other visions, one occurring on October 23, 1844, the day Adventists call the Great Disappointment when Christ failed to appear as predicted. After the first two visions, Foy began to preach and relate their content.

In December 1844, Foy met Ellen G. White who would later found the **Seventh-day Adventist Church**. He found her vision confirmed his own and he gave her his support. About this time he also settled in Maine and remained there the rest of his life. There in 1845 he published an account of his experiences. Shortly afterward his wife passed away. He accepted a call to become pastor of a church in New Bedford, Massachusetts. In 1851 he married Caroline Griffin. In 1855 he returned to Maine as the pastor of the church at Chelsea. During his Chelsea years his second wife died. In 1860 he moved to Burham, Maine and served several small congregations in the area. During the 1860s he moved to Sullivan, Maine, and bought a farm. He also organized a church which he pastored for the rest of his long life. In the early 1870s he married Parcentia Rose. He died in Sullivan on November 9, 1893, in New England. He is remembered in Adventism as one of three people to whom God gave visions to confirm the Adventist message.

Baker, Delbert W. *The Unknown Prophet.* Washington, DC: Review and Herald Publishing Association, 1987. 160 pp.

FRANCIS, JOSEPH ABEL (b. September 30, 1923), a bishop of the **Roman Catholic Church**, was born in Lafayette, Louisiana, the oldest of five children in the family of Joseph Sr., a barber, and Mabel Ann (Coco) Francis. His parents were long-time members of the Catholic Church and the children were baptized in St. Paul's Church in Lafayette, run by priests of the Holy Ghost Fathers. The children attended St. Paul's parochial school, conducted by **Sisters of the Holy Family**, the second-oldest community of Black sisters in the United States.

At the age of twelve he made up his mind to become a priest and entered St. Augustine Minor Seminary, a Black school, at Bay St. Louis, Mississippi, in September, 1936. During the summers he went home to Lafayette and worked for tuition money. From 1941 to 1946 he attended St. Mary's Major Seminary in Techny, Illinois. At that integrated school he felt no race prejudice and excelled in all parts of his education. Over the course of time he made his religious vows with the Divine Word Society and was ordained priest on October 7, 1950.

His first assignment was at St. Augustine Seminary in Bay St. Louis as instructor and Assistant Dean of Students. From 1952 to 1959 he was Assistant Director and Instructor of French, English, and Religion at Holy Rosary Institute, a large co-educational high school in Lafayette, Louisiana. He also took time to study at the Catholic University of America in Washington, D.C., where he earned an M.A. in Education Administration in 1956. In 1959 he was administrator of the Immaculate Heart of Mary Parish in Lafayette, in 1960 he was pastor of Holy Cross Parish in Austin, Texas, and in 1960–61 he was an instructor at Pius X High School in Downey, California.

From 1961 to 1967 Francis was principal of the newly founded Verbum Dei High School in the ghetto of Watts in Los Angeles, California. He has described these years as among the best of his life because of the positive programs he was able to create in such a needful atmosphere. When the enrollment reached 350 students, 90 percent pursued college education, a tremendous achievement. In the 1966 Watts riots the school was not damaged at all. In 1967 he had major heart surgery, and upon recovery was elected superior of the Divine Word Fathers' Western Province, serving two consecutive three-year terms in that capacity. In 1973 he was elected superior of the Southern Province, and was reelected in 1976. Meanwhile he had become a member of the United States Catholic Conference and of the United States Advisory Committee on Priestly Ministry and Formation. From 1974 to 1976 he was president of the Conference of Major Superiors of Men, U.S.A. In November 1975 he was elected president of the **National Black Catholic Clergy Caucus**.

On May 3, 1976, Pope Paul VI named Francis Auxiliary (assistant) Bishop of Newark, New Jersey. After **James A. Healy** (1875), **Harold Perry** (1966), **Joseph Howze** (1972), and **Eugene Marino** (1974), he was the fifth Black American Catholic bishop in history. He was specifically assigned to Essex County, which includes Newark's large urban Black population and several upper-middle-class communities. He has served since that time also as trustee of a number of schools, including Mount St. Mary's Seminary in Baltimore, Maryland, and Harvard Divinity School in Boston, Massachusetts. He has been active in such organizations as the National Conference of Interracial Justice, Catholic Relief Services, Greater Newark Urban Coalition, Archdiocesan Commission on Justice and Peace, and the Advisory Board of the United Negro College Fund. He was a major force in the writing of the 1979 bishops' pastoral on racism, "Brothers and Sisters to Us."

"Joseph A. Francis, S.V.D., Auxiliary Bishop of Newark." *America* 164 (April 13, 1991): 402–406.

IBAW, WWABA (90–91), *WWA* (90–91), *GMOC, BDNM* (75), *OBS.*

FRANCISCAN HANDMAIDS OF THE MOST PURE HEART OF MARY. A religious order of the **Roman Catholic Church**. This third congregation of Black Catholic sisters, the Franciscan Handmaids of Mary as they are generally known, began as a necessity in Savannah, Georgia, in 1916. Proposed legislation in the Georgia legislature had been introduced to prevent white women from teaching Black children. This would have affected the Catholic parochial schools. In order to save the Catholic schools for Black children, Ignatius Lissner, a French priest and a member of the Society of African Missions, decided to found a community of Black sisters. Lissner was the superior of the missionaries working statewide among Blacks in the diocese of Savannah. With the approval of Bishop Benjamin Keiley of Savannah, plans were laid to create this community.

Lissner began a search for a woman to be the founder and director of the new community. He found **Elizabeth Barbara Williams** working as a receptionist at Trinity College in Washington, D.C. She was born in 1868 in Baton Rouge, Louisiana. As a young girl she had been a member of a community of Franciscan sisters that had been discontinued. It was a breakaway community from the Sisters of the Holy Family. She then tried to enter the **Oblate Sisters of Providence** in Baltimore but was advised that her vocation lay elsewhere. Lissner met Elizabeth Williams and persuaded her to become a co-founder of a new community of Black sisters. In October, 1916, she made her vows and took the name Theodore; the community began in 1917.

The new community had a difficult beginning. The proposed legislation regarding instruction of Blacks by Whites was never enacted. The result was that the White sisters continued to teach, leaving the new community with no ministry except for one school. The first days of the Handmaids were difficult. The sisters had little income and often knew hunger and privation. Lissner was unable to continue as director of the missions in Georgia. Mother Theodore accepted total responsibility. As a result, she decided to move from Savannah to New York in 1923. Cardinal Hayes of New York gave permission to the sisters to open a day-care center in Harlem. The sisters provided a day nursery for the poor women of Harlem who had no place and little funds to shelter their children while they worked. Mothers began to come with their children as early as 5:00 A.M. Some were infants less than a year old. Many mothers could pay little or nothing.

At the same time, the sisters began a soup kitchen which has continued its existence through the present. They operated a laundry to supply revenue for their other apostolates. They also began to teach in the parochial schools. Mother Theodore Williams was a remarkable leader. A tower of strength, she also set the direction for the congregation. She incorporated the community into the Franciscan Third Order in 1929. On July 14, 1931, she died.

The Franciscan Handmaids returned to the South with missions in North and South Carolina and the West Indies. They have a novitiate on Staten Island and in Harlem a home for working girls. The Franciscan Handmaids came to Harlem at the beginning of the Great Depression. As Black Catholic sisters they established a specific role for themselves in the Black metropolis. At the same time they made a specific contribution to the Catholic Church in New York. In 1991 they numbered some thirty members. In recent years the order has opened its membership to women other than African Americans.

Davis, Cyprian. *The History of Black Catholics in the United States.* New York: Crossroad, 1990.

Dehey, Elinor Tong. *Religious Orders of Women in the United States.* Cleveland, OH: The Author, 1930. 908 pp.

Guide to Religious Communities for Women. Chicago: National Sisters Vocational Conference, 1983. 445 pp.

Cyprian Davis

FRANCISCO, LESLIE, III (b. c.1940), the second Black bishop in the history of the **Mennonite Church** in North America, was born in Boone, North Carolina. He did not become a Christian until his sister took him to the Calvary Mennonite Church in Newport News, Virginia, in 1958. This was a new, intentionally interracial church, among the first in the denomination. Francisco became a deacon in 1960 and was ordained in 1966. He then assisted Pastor Nelson Burkholder, the White organizer of the Calvary Church, and preached every other Sunday.

In 1979 the Burkholders retired and Francisco became pastor of the church. This was also a time of some community transition and the congregation became almost entirely Black. The nature of worship and congregational life continued its change from a traditional Mennonite form to a form more compatible with the Black heritage in that community. In 1980 the national Mennonite Church had a total of about 1,650 Black members with 49 Black/integrated congregations; in 1988 there were 72 Black/integrated congregations.

In the early 1980s Francisco led in the building of the Calvary Community Church in Hampton, Virginia, which was dedicated in May, 1985. On December 15, 1984, the Virginia Mennonite Conference called him to become the second African American bishop (after **James Lark**) in the history of the denomination. He has remained as pastor of the new church in Hampton and oversees the two Black churches in that district, a Black church in the Chesapeake District, a Black church in Richmond, and five Black churches in North Carolina. There is now an Afro-American Mennonite Association within the Mennonite Church to serve the interests of the growing Black membership.

ME, BMC.

FRANKLIN, CLARENCE LAVAUGHN (January 22, 1915–July 27, 1984), Baptist minister, father of singer Aretha Franklin, and "the most imitated soul preacher in history," was born near Indianola, in Sunflower County, Mississippi, and grew up near Doddsville, Mississippi. His father left when Franklin was still a child, and when his mother remarried the family adopted the stepfather's surname of Franklin.

The family made a living by sharecropping, and bare survival was the normal order of things. Franklin went to a poor school in the off-seasons, held in a local Black church, and saw how the White children received all the good equipment and educated teachers. At about age nine he moved with the family near Cleveland, Mississippi, and shortly afterward he experienced conversion at St. Peter's Rock Baptist Church. As a teenager he began to feel a call to preach, and about age eighteen he was ordained as associate pastor of St. Peter's Rock Baptist Church. About age twenty he moved to Clarksdale to pastor some other churches, and married a woman named Barbara, with whom he had four children. About age twenty-one he began attending Greenville Industrial College and Seminary in Greenville, Mississippi, then accepted a call from two churches in Memphis, Tennessee. He moved there about 1940 and enrolled at LeMoyne College.

In Memphis, Franklin's previous fundamentalism began to give way to more varied interpretations of the Bible, and his sermons grew less emotional and more geared to reach people's minds. After about three years in Memphis he became pastor of the Friendship Baptist Church in Buffalo, New York. He preached at the National Baptist Convention in Detroit in 1945. In June 1946, he left Buffalo to pastor the New Bethel Baptist Church on Hastings Street in Detroit. He had had small radio programs in Memphis and Buffalo, and when he was having trouble completing a new church building for the Detroit congregation, he started another radio program over a Dearborn station. In 1952, the year his wife passed away, he got a better program over WJLB in Detroit, and this outreach greatly expanded the congregation. Sometimes there was standing room only for the Sunday night broadcasts.

In 1953 Franklin began recording his sermons, and the records became big hits. He began appearing in major cities, often with musicians to begin the program. No other preacher at the time had that kind of success with recorded sermons. Attendance at New Bethel Baptist Church peaked at about 10,000 in the late 1950s, the height of Franklin's popularity. His preaching style, sometimes called "soul preaching," developed into a pattern that began with several minutes of standard prose delivery, meant to capture the listener's intellect. In the latter, climactic part of the sermon, he would shift into a dramatic, poetic chant sometimes called "whooping." This was designed to capture the listener's emotions, and often followed certain melody lines. Some of his most famous sermons were "The Eagle Stirreth Her Nest," "A Mother at the Cross," and "Without a Song."

In 1963 the church moved to another location in Detroit and the congregation stabilized. That year he led a major civil rights march in Detroit, with an estimated two hundred thousand participants. He was an active leader in the **Southern Christian Leadership Conference** (S.C.L.C.), walked with **Martin Luther King, Jr.,** in the March on Washington, and preached at the Poor People's March in Washington, D.C., in 1968. He later became part of **Jesse Jackson**'s **Operation PUSH** (People United To Save Humanity), and preached Jackson's ordination sermon in 1968 at the Fellowship Missionary Baptist Church in Chicago. The last of Franklin's record albums, a total of over seventy, was made in 1974. In 1968 New Bethel had about 4,500 members, and in 1977–78 the church was down to about 2,000 members. On June 10, 1979, three men broke into Franklin's home, apparently to steal some lead glass windows. He was shot during the burglary and remained in a coma for the next five years, until his death. Jesse Jackson preached the eulogy, and the funeral was the largest Detroit had ever seen. Franklin's oratory combined contemporary learning and social awareness with the rich African American literary, cultural, and religious tradition. It has been said that "every African-American preacher either has imitated him or has tried to avoid doing so."

Bengston, Dale R. "The Eagle Stirreth Her Nest: Notes on an Afro-American Shamanistic Event." *The Journal of Religious Thought* 33 (Spring–Summer 1976): 75–86.

Titon, Jeff Todd, ed. *Give Me This Mountain: Rev. C. L. Franklin's Life History and Selected Sermons.* Urbana, IL: University of Illinois Press, 1989. 218 pp.

HUBA, IBAW.

FRANKLIN, MARTIN ROBERT (January 8, 1853– May 13, 1909), 31st bishop of the **African Methodist Episcopal Zion Church** (AMEZ), was born into slavery near Macon, Georgia. His parents were sold when he was still an infant, and he never saw or heard from them again. He followed Sherman's army in the Civil War, and reached the North in 1865. He settled in Chicago, Illinois, for several years, then moved to Washington, D.C. and entered Wayland Seminary there in 1879. He joined the Asbury Methodist Episcopal Church in Washington. In 1881 he left school, moved to Boston, Massachusetts, and joined the North Russell (Columbus Avenue) Street AMEZ Church. He was licensed to preach the same year.

His first church appointment was in 1884 in the Central North Carolina Conference, at Laurinburg, North Carolina, where he built a new building and expanded the membership. He was ordained deacon by Bishop **James W. Hood** on November 21, 1886, and ordained elder by Bishop **John J. Moore** on November 27, 1888. After other successful appointments at Manley, Carthage, and Statesville, he transferred in 1896 to the Allegheny Conference and pastored Avery Mission AMEZ Church in Allegheny City, Pennsylvania. In 1901 he was assigned to Mother Zion Church in New York City, and in 1906 became presiding elder of the New York Conference. In 1904 he was also elected Financial Secretary of the denomination.

At the 1908 General Conference he was elected bishop and was assigned to the Eighth Episcopal District (Georgia, South Carolina, and Palmetto Conferences). Although not required to do so, and despite the many hazards facing him in the South, he moved his residence from Brooklyn, New York, to Atlanta, Georgia. His presence in his district greatly improved the church situation, but he died within a year, before his many talents could be fully utilized in the episcopacy. He was remembered as an impressive preacher with a gentle, urbane, and pious character.

AMEZC, HAMEZC.

FRANKLINTON CHRISTIAN COLLEGE. A school sponsored by the Christian Church. The Christian Church (now a constituent part of the **United Church of Christ**) developed an African American membership in the states along the Eastern Seaboard from North Carolina to New York during the last half of the nineteenth century. As early as 1871, a White minister opened a school for Black children in the Christian Church at Franklinton, North Carolina. That same year the North Carolina Colored Christian Conference voted support for a plan to place a high school in Franklinton. They called for support through the Black congregations in both North Carolina and Virginia, where the bulk of the church's members resided. The high school opened in 1878.

With assistance from White Christians, a building was erected and opened in 1880. It was incorporated in 1883 as the Franklin Literary and Theological Christian Institute. Through the nineteenth century it was headed by a series of white principals. Under their guidance the school was improved and transformed in 1891 into Franklinton Christian College. Though never able to develop a full college curriculum, it was the training site for many Black Christian pastors and church workers.

In 1904, Henry E. Long became the first of three Black presidents who oversaw the school's life. He led in the purchase of land and the development of a new campus north of Franklinton. He was succeeded by F. S. Hendershot in 1917. The last president was James A. Henderson who began his tenure in 1922. The school served the denomination and the Black community for over 40 years, but was unable to survive the Depression and in 1930 was forced to close its doors. In 1931, the Christian Church merged with the Congregational Church which supported several predominantly Black colleges. The new denomination (now part of the United Church of Christ) did not reopen the school.

Taylor, J. Stanley. *A History of Black Congregational Christian Churches of the South.* New York: United Church Press, 1978. 175 pp.

FREE CHRISTIAN ZION CHURCH OF CHRIST. A Methodist church. The Free Christian Zion Church of Christ was formed by a group of ministers and lay leaders from a variety of different denominational backgrounds gathered under the leadership of E. D. Brown, a former conference missionary with the **African Methodist Episcopal Zion Church.** Methodists predominated at the meeting in Redemption, Arkansas, July 10, 1905, at which the new church was formed. A common opinion of the initial group was an objection to the "taxing" of churches for the support of denominational machinery. They believed that such money should be put into the service of the poor and those in more immediate need. The group retained the common Methodist doctrine and a modified episcopal polity.

There is an annual general assembly at which a presiding bishop is elected. They have charge of appointing the ministers to their respective congregations and naming the general church officers. Pastors and laity together administer the affairs of the local churches.

The small church grew slowly and by 1966 had only 5 congregations, but by 1988 had grown to 18 congregations and 3,800 members.

Piepkorn, Arthur C. *Profiles in Belief.* Vol. 2. San Francisco, CA: Harper & Row, 1978. 721 pp.

FREE GOSPEL CHURCH OF THE APOSTLE'S DOCTRINE.

An Apostolic Pentecostal church. The Free Gospel Church of the Apostle's Doctrine (also known as the Free Gospel Church of Christ and Defense of the Gospel Ministries) was founded in Washington, D.C., in 1962. Its founder, Bishop Ralph E. Green, was formerly a pastor in the **Way of the Cross Church of Christ**. Soon after founding the Church, Green began a radio ministry which is now heard on stations along the Atlantic coast.

The church is built around a large congregation in Washington, D.C. where it has developed an aggressive outreach ministry, including prison visitation and a publishing program. It publishes a periodical, *From Prison to Praise*, especially for the incarcerated, and a variety of gospel tracts. The Church choir has cut several albums, and Green has recorded over 1,000 sermons. An evangelistic outreach is carried on in the 1,000–seat tent owned by the Church. It also has a retreat center in King George, Virginia.

The church is headquartered in Washington, D.C., the lead church being a congregation of 2,500 members. There are five other congregations located in Maryland, Virginia, North Carolina, and Jamaica. A periodical, *Defense of the Gospel Newsletter*, is published.

Payne, Wardell J., ed. *Directory of African American Religious Bodies: A Compendium by the Howard University School of Divinity.* Washington, DC: Howard University Press, 1991. 363 pp.

FREE METHODIST CHURCH OF NORTH AMERICA.

A Holiness church. The Free Methodist Church of North America was founded in 1860, just as the Civil War was about to begin, by former members of the Genesee Conference (Western New York) of the Methodist Episcopal Church. Among the issues which isolated the early Free Methodists from their former colleagues was abolitionism. The Methodist Episcopal Church had adopted an anti-slavery policy, but was basically opposed to abolitionism. On the other hand, the Free Methodists were concentrated in New York and areas through the Midwest where few African Americans lived. They were not organized nor strong enough to contribute meaningfully to the Freedman's missions.

The church's attempt to minister to African Americans began in the 1920s when E. E. Shelhamer began an interracial ministry in the South though he was soon forced to close down by the local opposition. Shelhamer died in 1947, and his wife, Julia Shelhamer, and their son-in-law James Gilbert attempted to continue his work. She opened an interracial ministry in Washington, D.C., and he became head of the department of interracial evangelism for the denomination. In 1946 he founded a short-lived day school while pastoring in Shreveport, Louisiana, and later he taught at Asbury Theological Seminary, Wilmore, Kentucky. The department of interracial ministry was discontinued in 1960.

Jones, Charles Edwin. *Black Holiness: A Guide to the Study of Black Participation in Wesleyan Perfectionist and Glossolalic Pentecostal Movements.* Metuchen, NJ: American Theological Library Association/Scarecrow Press, 1987. 388 pp.

FREEMAN, AMOS (c.1810–c.1886), pioneer Congregational and Presbyterian minister, has been neglected in the published literature, and many details of his life remain in obscurity. In 1836 he enrolled in the Oneida Theological Institute in Whitesboro, near Utica, New York. The other three Blacks in the mostly white entering class were **Henry Highland Garnet**, **Alexander Crummell**, and **Amos Beman**. In about 1841, after graduation, Freeman was installed as the minister of the Black Congregational church in Portland, Maine, and stayed for eleven years. In 1852 he was installed as the minister of the Siloam Presbyterian Church in Brooklyn, New York City, founded by **James Gloucester** in 1849, and incorporated in 1850. Freeman became friends with the other leading Black clergy in the area, and was the one who introduced **Charles B. Ray** to **Theodore Wright**. In 1857 he was the moderator at the annual meeting, in Philadelphia, of the Evangelical Association of Colored Ministers of Congregational and Presbyterian Churches. By 1859, when the group met at Freeman's Siloam Presbyterian Church, there were twenty-seven Black churches belonging to the two denominations, twenty Black ministers, and nine vacant pulpits.

In 1860 he left the Siloam church for four years, perhaps to take part in the Civil War, and was replaced by a C. H. Thompson. In 1864 he returned to Siloam and remained as its minister until 1885, when he tendered his resignation. The congregation held him in such esteem that at first they refused to accept his resignation, and finally yielded only to his health considerations and after he promised to continue as Pastor Emeritus. It is thought that he passed away within the next year or two.

BPJ and information supplied by the Siloam Presbyterian Church, Brooklyn, New York.

FREEMAN, EDWARD ANDERSON (b. June 11, 1914), former vice-president of the Baptist World Alliance and former vice-president of the **National Baptist Convention, U.S.A., Inc.** (N.B.C.U.S.A.), was born in Atlanta, Georgia, the son of James Henry Watts and Ollie Watts Freeman. On March 17, 1938 he married Ruth Anthony, with whom he had three children. He received his B.A. in 1939 from Clark University in Atlanta, and his B.D. in 1949 and Th.D. in 1953 from Central Baptist Seminary in Kansas City, Kansas.

From 1939 to 1942 he was principal of a public school in Austell, Georgia, and from 1936 to 1942 pastored a Baptist church in Cornelia, Georgia. From 1942 to 1946 he was a chaplain in the U.S. Army. In 1946 he became pastor of First Baptist Church in Kansas City, where he remained for the rest of his career. He held many prominent posts during this pastorate. From 1949 to 1954 he was chaplain for the Kansas City chapter of the N.A.A.C.P., and from 1947 to 1955 he was chaplain of the Argonne Post of the American Legion. Beginning in 1954 he was a member of the City Planning Commission, and was its chair beginning in 1968.

Freeman was president of the Missionary Baptist State Convention of Kansas from 1957 to 1982 and was president of the National Sunday School and Baptist Training Union Congress from 1968 to 1983. From 1980 to 1985 he was vice-president of the Baptist World Alliance and has also been vice-president of the N.B.C.U.S.A. He has been active in **Jesse Jackson**'s **Operation PUSH** and in the National Council of Churches. He has served on the boards of the American Baptist Theological Seminary and the Greater Kansas City Baptist and Community Hospital. In 1950 he received the Man of the Year Award from the Wyandotte County Woman's Council of Churches and in 1955 received the Man of the Year Award from the National Baptist Convention of South India. He has published a number of writings, including *The Epoch of Negro Baptists and the Foreign Mission Board* (1953), *The Eighth Century Prophets* (1960), *Baptist Jubilee Advance* (1964), and *Baptist Relations with Other Christians* (1974).

Freeman, Edward A. *The Epoch of Negro Baptists and the Foreign Mission Board*. Kansas City, KS: Kansas Central Seminary Press, 1953. 301 pp.
EBA, WWR (77), WWABA (92–93), BDNM (75), AARS, HUBA.

FRIENDS (QUAKERS). Few religious organizations have the impressive record of opposition to slavery in America as do the Quakers. As early as 1671, George Fox, the Quaker founder, called upon Quaker slave-owners to protect them from cruelty and mistreatment, to educate them, and eventually to emancipate them. During the next generation, Quakers, while not yet abolitionists, made a number of protests related to the continuance of the slave trade. Then in the 1754, in response to Anthony Benezet's and John Woolman's exposés of the horrors of the slave trade, the Philadelphia Yearly Meeting made its strong condemnation of slavery. It added teeth to its condemnation in 1758 by appointing a committee to visit slaveholders and forbade the attendance at meetings of any who engaged in the slave trade. Woolman emerged as the first effective voice for abolition of slavery in America. Also, twelve years later, as a result of the Philadelphia Meeting's activist stance, the first Quaker school for African Americans was opened by Anthony Bezenet. In 1775 Quakers were leaders in the establishment of the first anti-slavery society in Philadelphia. In their efforts they were greatly encouraged by the British Quakers who had taken the lead in the abolitionist cause throughout the British Empire.

In the period from the Revolution until the Civil War, Quakers carried on an intense internal debate over the best means to achieve the end of slavery. A range of opinion was advocated by different leaders, through the movement provided prominent leadership to the abolitionist cause. Outstanding among the abolitionists were Elias Hicks, Benjamin Lundy (editor of *The Genius of Universal Emancipation*), the poet John Greenleaf Whittier, and the sisters Sarah and Angelina Grimké. **Paul Cuffe**, a Black sea captain, became the founder of the American Manumission and Colonization Society dedicated to returning freed Black people to Africa.

As a result of their anti-slavery leanings, Quaker growth was somewhat blocked in the South in the decades following the American Revolution. However, it has also been the case that Black membership, in spite of efforts to mobilize potential Black members, was never very large. As early as 1689 the Philadelphia meeting advised members to bring their Black servants and slaves to the meetings. Eleven years later, William Penn attempted to organize a special meeting for Black people to be held once a month, but with little success. A like attempt was made again in 1756, with more success, and other congregations around the country also established the practice.

Problems in mobilizing African Americans were present at both the group and individual level. As most Quakers did not own slaves and opposed the practice, they have no natural Black constituency from which to draw and increasingly they found it inappropriate to attempt to organize the Blacks associated with non-members. However, on the individual level, they found a great resistance to bringing Blacks into the fellowship. In the late 1700s the question of admitting individual Blacks to membership became a matter of continued debate and again and again the question was raised, referred from meeting to meeting without definitive resolution. Few Blacks jumped through the hurdles to full Quaker life.

And in spite of its notable efforts to educate African American children in the North, the Friends were unable to turn their efforts into a significant African American constituency. However, that small Black membership produced some outstanding Black leaders. Among the Blacks who either affiliated with the Society of Friends or were strongly influenced by it were **Sarah Douglas**, Duncan Freeland, Benjamin Bannecker, and **Sojourner Truth**. In more recent years the most outstanding Black Quaker has been Barrington Dunbar, who accomplished much as an interpreter of the Black revolution of the 1960s to contemporary Quakers. The only predominantly African American Quaker Meeting now active is the Chicago Fellowship of Friends.

Barbour, Hugh, and J. William Frost. *The Quakers*. New York: Greenwood Press, 1988. 407 pp.

Cadbury, Henry J. "Negro Membership in the Society of Friends." *Journal of Negro History* (1936): 151–213.
Fletcher, James A., and Carleton Mabree. *A Quaker Speaks from the Black Experience; The Life and Selected Writings of Barrington Dunbar*. New York: New York Yearly Meeting of the Religious Society of Friends, 1979. 67 pp.
Spann-Wilson, Dwight. *Quaker and Black: Answering the Call of My Twin Roots*. N.p.: The Author, 1980. 16 pp.

FULLER, THOMAS OSCAR (October 25, 1867–1942), state senator, educator, and executive of the **National Baptist Convention, U.S.A., Inc.** was born in Franklinton, North Carolina, the son of J. Henderson Fuller and Mary Eliza (Kearney). Both his parents were former slaves; his father after Emancipation was able to buy some property through his skills as carpenter and wheelwright and his ability to read and write. Fuller, the youngest of fourteen children, was an apt pupil, and after graduating from the local normal school attended Shaw University, where he received his B.A. degree in 1890 and his M.A. degree in 1893.

In April 1893, he was ordained a Baptist minister, and quickly became a leading force in his community. He pastored the Belton Creek Baptist Church in North Carolina from 1894 to 1898, adding the First Baptist Church in Warrenton from 1896 to 1898. He organized the Girls' Training School in Franklin County, assisted by a special legislative act, and was principal of the Shiloh Institute in Warrenton from 1895 to 1898. In 1898 he married Laura B. Faulkner. Also in 1898, the year of a tragic race riot in Wilmington, he ran successfully for a senate seat in the North Carolina legislature. The only Black legislator during his one-year (1899) term, he faced many obstacles of discrimination, yet managed to help pass several laws, including one which repealed the prohibition against outsiders recruiting Black labor in the state. Unfortunately, the legislature also passed a constitutional amendment which served to block political participation by Blacks, and Fuller's role as a government official came to an end.

In 1900 Fuller became pastor of the First Baptist Church in Memphis, Tennessee, where he remained the rest of his career. He was soon active again in education as the principal of Howe Institute in Memphis, a position he held for some thirty years, except for a period of several years beginning in 1931, when he took a leave for writing. In 1905 A&M College in Normal, Alabama, granted him an honorary doctorate. In 1906 he became assistant secretary of the National Baptist Convention, U.S.A., Inc. and served that office for twenty-five years.

From 1928 to 1942 he was a member of the executive committee of the Baptist World Alliance.

After he settled in Memphis, Fuller began supplementing his other activities with a steady stream of publications. His first work was a substantial autobiographical book, *Twenty Years in Public Life: 1890–1910, North Carolina—Tennessee* (1910). Two other valuable full-length books were *Pictorial History of the American Negro* (1933) and *History of the Negro Baptists of Tennessee* (1936). Further writings included *Bridging the Racial Chasms: A Brief Survey of Inter-Racial Attitudes and Relations* (1937), and *Story of Church Life Among Negroes in Memphis, Tennessee, for Students and Workers, 1900–1938.* (1938). He was a strong supporter of **Booker T. Washington**'s conservative approach to relations with White society, but also was known to voice support for the more activist policies of leaders like W. E. B. DuBois.

Edmond, Helen G. *The Negro and Fusion Politics in North Carolina, 1894–1901.* Chapel Hill, NC: University of North Carolina Press, 1951. 260 pp.

Fuller, Thomas Oscar. *Bridging the Racial Chasms: A Brief Survey of Inter-Racial Attitudes and Relations.* Memphis, TN: The Author, 1937. 73 pp.

———. *History of the Negro Baptists of Tennessee.* Memphis, TN: Haskins Print, 1936. 346 pp.

———. *Pictorial History of the American Negro.* Memphis, TN: Pictorial History, Inc., 1933. 375 pp.

———. *Story of Church Life Among Negroes in Memphis, Tennessee, for Students and Workers, 1900–1938.* Memphis, TN: n.p., 1938. 52 pp.

"Trying to be happy in worldly pleasure is like trying to fatten swine on pearls."

"I am not worried about the color of a chicken's feathers. I am concerned about the quality of its thighs."

"Put a spirit of reverence in the midst of your neighbors by honoring them whether they honor you or not."

Elder Lightfoot Solomon Michaux,
Founder, Gospel Spreading Church
1950

G

GAINES, ABRAHAM LINCOLN (May 8, 1866–August 22, 1931), 47th bishop of the **African Methodist Episcopal Church** (AME), was born in Washington, Georgia, the son of Stephen A. and Josephine (Andrews) Gaines. He attended public schools and Knox Institute in Athens, Georgia. He was converted in 1882 and the following year joined Bethel AME Church in Atlanta, Georgia. He joined the Georgia Annual Conference in 1887 and the same year was ordained deacon by his uncle, Bishop **Wesley John Gaines**. He was ordained elder in 1889. He received his B.A. in 1891 from Atlanta University and his B.D. the same year from Gammon Theological Seminary in Atlanta.

His first pastorates were in Rutledge, Georgia (1887–89) and St. James AME Church in Atlanta (1889–92). On June 6, 1890 he married Minnie Lillian Plant, with whom he had four children. In 1890 he was also principal of the Gray Street School in Atlanta. Further pastorates included St. John AME Church in Norfolk, Virginia (1892–96); Emmanuel AME Church in Portsmouth, Virginia (1896–1900); presiding elder, Virginia Conference (1900–03); Bethel AME Church in Baltimore, Maryland (1903–08); Trinity AME Church in Baltimore (1908–13); Waters AME Church in Baltimore (1913–18); presiding elder, Baltimore Conference (1918–19); and Trinity AME Church in Baltimore (1919–24).

He increased his national visibility by serving on the Church Extension Board from 1896 to 1904; the Sunday School Union Board from 1904 to 1908; and the Education Board from 1912 to 1916. During World War I he was treasurer of the Colored Division of the Maryland Council of Defense. He was secretary of the weekly periodical *Herald-Commonwealth* from 1922 to 1924 and in 1924 was president of the board of managers of the *Western Christian Recorder*.

Gaines was elected bishop on May 13, 1924 and was assigned to the Eighteenth Episcopal District (Louisiana, South America, and the British West Indies). Later that year, on the death of Bishop Coppin, he was assigned to the Fourth Episcopal District (Indiana, Illinois, Iowa, Minnesota, Michigan, Wisconsin, and the Dakotas). From 1928 to 1931 he headed the Second Episcopal District (Baltimore, Virginia, North Carolina, and Western North Carolina Conferences). Among others, a church in Kingston, Jamaica is named for him. He is said to have been an excellent executive.

EBA, HAMEC, EWM, WWCA (30–32), *BAMEC.*

GAINES, WESLEY JOHN (October 4, 1840–January 12, 1912), sixteenth bishop of the **African Methodist Episcopal Church** (AME), was born in Wilkes County, Georgia. He was the youngest of fourteen children born to William and Louisa Gaines, slaves of the well-known Toombs family. His mother was a Baptist, but he was brought up a Methodist, according to his father's church, the Methodist Episcopal Church, South. He was named after John Wesley, the founder of Methodism. He experienced conversion at the age of nine, and this apparently spurred his interest in education, especially for reading the Bible. He taught himself to read through the help of books he kept concealed from the Whites.

In 1855 he was moved to Stewart County, Georgia, and then to Muskogee County in 1856. He dated his call to the ministry to about this time, when he began preaching funeral sermons for dead birds and animals. He married another slave, Julia A. Camper, on August 20, 1863, with whom he had one daughter. He grew into a sizable figure, about six feet two inches in height and over 300 pounds. He later commented that he commanded $1,000 at one point when he was sold. At the end of the Civil War in 1865, he was licensed to preach in the Methodist Episcopal Church, South, by J. L. Davies. His brother, William Gaines, was ordained the same month into the AME Church, and later during a visit, convinced Gaines to join that church. He was ordained deacon in the South Carolina Conference of the AME Church in 1866, and an elder in the newly organized Georgia Conference the following year. His first appointment was to the Florence Mission, Atlanta, Georgia, from 1867 to 1869, then he spent a year at the church in Athens, where he studied theology with the local Episcopal minister. This was followed by appointments at the Cotton Avenue AME Church in Macon (1871–1873), St. James AME Church in Columbus (1874–1877), where he built a new sanctuary, and Macon again (1878–1880). From 1875 to 1878 he continued to further his education by studying with Joseph S. Key, a future bishop in the Methodist Episcopal Church, South. In 1881 he moved back to Atlanta as pastor of Bethel AME Church on Wheat Street. He built this church into the largest Black church in the South, with a membership of 2,000, and constructed a new sanctuary.

Gaines, who had never been to school himself, led in the founding of Morris Brown College in Atlanta, his most lasting legacy. That city already had three Black colleges—Atlanta University, Clark College, and Morehouse—with Spelman on the way. Gaines and his colleagues knew this, but wanted a college entirely financed and led by African Americans. He introduced the resolution to the North Georgia Annual Conference on January 5, 1881, trustees were elected (Gaines being the first), and the next month land was purchased. On November 26, 1885, the first wing of the school, Gaines Hall, was dedicated.

In 1885 Gaines became presiding elder of the Atlanta District of the North Georgia Conference, from which position he was elected bishop in May, 1888. Gaines presided over the Second Episcopal District from 1892 to 1896, the Sixth District from 1896 to 1900, the Seventh District from 1900 to 1904, and in 1906 he took over the First District on the death of Bishop **Benjamin Arnett**, and retained that position until his own death. During his time as bishop he continued to supervise the growth and building of Morris Brown College. He also wrote several books, his daughter serving as amanuensis. The most notable works were *African Methodism in the South* (1890) and *The Negro and the White Man* (1897). He presided over the organization of a number of new conferences, and served as vice-president of Payne Theological Seminary in Wilberforce, Ohio, after it was organized in 1891. Since his death, ten churches have been named for him in six different states.

Gaines, Wesley John. *African Methodism in the South; or, Twenty-Five Years of Freedom*. Atlanta, GA: Franklin Publishing House, 1890. 305 pp.

———. *The Gospel Ministry*. Atlanta, GA: n.p., 1899. 96 pp.

———. *The Negro and the White Man*. Philadelphia, PA: A.M.E. Publishing House, 1897. 218 pp.

Sewell, George. "Morris Brown College: Legacy of Wesley John Gaines." *Crisis* 88 (April 1981): 133–136.

HUBA, BAW, IBAW, EWM, BAMEC, HAMEC, DAB (vol. 4), *RLOA, BHAC, DNAADB, AARS, NCAB* (vol. 2), *CH, WWCR, CEAMEC.*

GALBREATH, GEORGE (March 4, 1799–1853), the 4th bishop of the **African Methodist Episcopal Zion Church** (AMEZ), was born in Lancaster County, Pennsylvania, to parents named Adam and Eve, who were slaves of Dr. Galbreath (sometimes spelled Galbraith). He was reared by Moses Williams of Hanover Township, Pennsylvania, who sent him to school with his own children. He learned the carpenter's trade and cabinetmaking from John Miller in Middletown, Pennsylvania. In 1825 he was among the first members of the new denomination (Church of God) founded by the former Reformed minister, John Winebrenner (1797–1860), experiencing conversion with that group. He later joined the Methodist Episcopal Church, and then about 1829 joined the AMEZ Church newly established by the Rev. J. D. Richardson in Middletown. He joined the Philadelphia Annual Conference in June, 1830, was ordained deacon in 1832 and elder in 1835. He was apparently both a husband and a father, but little else is known about those parts of his life.

He was appointed to the Harrisburg Circuit, and had conspicuous success in his several subsequent appointments, about which little information is available. He was consecrated bishop on May 30, 1848, and some dispute arose about whether he should be designated a full bishop or assistant only. The decision was for assistant, but many were not satisfied. At the 1852 General Conference he was re-elected (general superintendents at that time being elected only for four-year terms), but stated that he did not wish to serve again just as an assistant. A resolution passed which stated that for the time being the bishops would be on equal footing. He was satisfied, and assigned to the Southern Episcopal District, including the Philadelphia, Allegheny, and Baltimore Conferences. After a life plagued by hardships and poverty, he died in Philadelphia the following year from an asthma attack after a trip across the Allegheny Mountains. This left two remaining bishops, **George Spywood** and **William Haywood Bishop**, and Bishop decided to set aside the decision for episcopal equality, stating that he held a superior position to Spywood. This led to a schism which did not heal until 1860.

"Bishop George Galbreath." *The A.M.E. Zion Quarterly Review* 62, No.4 (1951): 224.

HNC, HAMEZC (vol. 1), AARS, AMEZC, EWM, HAMEZCIA.

GARDINER, THEOPHILUS MOMOLU (January 30, 1870–April 3, 1941), the fifth Black bishop consecrated by the **Episcopal Church** in the United States and the first native African so consecrated by American bishops, was born in Dearlah, Cape Mount, Liberia, the son of Momolu Fiker and Guarnyar (Tarweh) Gardiner. He was a member of the Vai tribe and at the age of ten entered the Mission School of St. John's in Cape Mount with the idea of learning English. He became attracted to Christianity and was baptized three years later. In the following years he became more and more interested in the church and refused a family offer to manage an estate of tribal lands and slaves. He received his B.A. in 1892 from Cuttington Collegiate and Divinity School in Cape Palmas, Liberia. That year he was confirmed in the church and became a candidate for Holy Orders.

After further studies at the Cuttington Collegiate and Divinity School in Cape Palmas he was ordained a deacon on August 30, 1896, and for the next nine years was assistant curate at St. Mark's Episcopal Church in Harper, Cape Palmas. On May 3, 1897 he married Miss F. R. Neal; after she passed away he married Danielette F. Wilson on May 13, 1903, and reared five children. From 1905 to 1913 he was assistant secretary and then secretary of the General Convention Missionary District of Liberia. He was responsible for overseeing the mission stations in the Sodeke and Cavalla River districts and elsewhere around the country. From 1902 to 1913 he was also rector of Mount Vaughan Episcopal Church in Cape Palmas. He was ordained priest on April 22, 1906, received his B.D. in 1912 from Liberia College and his D.D. in 1916, also from Liberia College. From 1913 to 1921 he was rector of St. James Episcopal Church in Cape Palmas. He also was a professor of History and assistant tutor in Theology at Cuttington College, and president of the Council of Advice for the bishop (1911–21). Apparently Gardiner was quite a topic of interest in Liberia as a Vai tribesman serving as a Christian minister, often among rival tribes.

In 1920 Gardiner was elected suffragan bishop of Liberia, and was consecrated for that office on June 23, 1921, at the Church of the Incarnation in New York City. The visit to New York was very disconcerting to him, and he reportedly at one point was lost in the subway for many hours. The previous Black priests consecrated bishops by the American Episcopal Church were **James T. Holly** (1874), **Samuel D. Ferguson** (1885), **Edward T. Demby** (1918), and **Henry B. Delany** (1918). Gardiner was the second Black bishop of the church to serve Liberia (after Ferguson) and was the first native African consecrated bishop by American bishops (the first Black bishop in the World-Wide Anglican Communion was Samuel A. Crowther, consecrated in 1864 for Africa). Gardiner made one more trip to the United States in October, 1928 to attend the church's General Convention in Washington, D.C.

NYTO, HAAG, WWWA (1), *WWCA* (38–40).

GARNET, HENRY HIGHLAND (December 23, 1815–February 13, 1882), Presbyterian minister, abolitionist, and diplomat, was born on a slave plantation in New Market, Kent County, Maryland. His grandfather, called Joseph Trusty, is said to have been a tribal ruler in the Mandingo Empire of West Africa before he was brought as a slave to the United States and sold to Col. William Spencer. Trusty's son George was Garnet's father. In 1824, when Garnet was about eight, Col. Spencer died, and rather than be parceled to relatives, George Trusty, his wife, Henrietta (who later changed her name to Elizabeth), their two children, and seven other slaves made a terrifying trek to freedom in New Hope, Pennsylvania. There Trusty made a living as a shoemaker, and the children were placed in public school. In 1826, after two years, the family took the name of Garnet and moved to New York City with the assistance of Thomas Garret, Quaker head of Pennsylvania's Underground Railroad.

Henry Garnet became a pupil at the African Free School No. 1 on Mulberry Street. At one point he took some time off from school to make two voyages to Cuba as a cabin boy, and in 1829 he became cook and steward on a ship running between New York and Washington, D.C. There was constant danger from slave hunters, who at one point that year temporarily seized his sister. Later in 1829 he apprenticed himself to Captain Epenetus Smith of Smithtown, Long Island, but a disease infected his right leg, which eventually, in December, 1840, had to be amputated (he then wore a wooden leg), and he returned to New York City. In 1831 he entered Curtis' Episcopal Collegiate School at Canal and Mercer, where he was allowed to sit in an area with two other Black boys, was occasionally received direct instruction. He was also in the high school for Blacks opened by **Peter Williams Jr.**, and in Phoenix High School opened in 1833 by **Theodore Wright**, **Samuel Cornish**, and Peter Williams, Jr., and others. In 1833 he joined the Sunday School of the First Colored Shiloh Presbyterian Church, led by Theodore S. Wright, and was baptized.

In the fall of 1834 Garnet, **Alexander Crummell**, and several other Blacks entered the previously all-White Noyes Academy in New Canaan, New Hampshire, in an experiment in integrated education. It went well for those in the school, but the townspeople became enraged and the following summer used oxen to tear the whole school down. The Black students then barricaded themselves in a house, and Garnet is credited with saving their lives by scaring off the attackers with a musket shot. In 1836 Garnet began studying for the ministry at the Oneida Theological Institute in Whitesboro, near Utica, New York. He finished his academic work at Oneida in the early fall of 1839 and settled in Troy, New York, where he taught a district school and succeeded **Daniel Payne** as pastor of the Liberty Street Presbyterian Church, the only Black Presbyterian church in the area. In December, 1839, he led the church in an eventually successful petition to have the Troy presbytery recognize it as a formally constituted Presbyterian church. Between 1839 and 1843, apparently in an effort to supplement his Oneida training toward eventual ordination, Garnet was tutored by Nathan S.S. Beman, a well-known White pastor of the First Presbyterian Church in Troy. In 1841 Garnet married Julia Williams, whom he had met in New Hampshire. In 1842 he was officially licensed to preach, and in 1843 he was ordained as the minister of the Troy church.

By this time he had also become a well-known abolitionist, and was quietly a major figure in the Underground Railroad in New York. In May, 1840 he made his first and only public speech with the American Anti-Slavery Society. Only a few days later he, Theodore Wright, Samuel Cornish, and others seceded from the American Anti-Slavery Society, objecting to the Garrisonian brand of radicalism, and formed the American and Foreign Anti-Slavery Society. Garnet quickly rose to pre-eminence among the Black abolitionists. He edited two short-lived weekly newspapers which addressed various social and religious issues, the *Troy National Watchman* (1842) and the *Troy United States Clarion* (1843). In 1843 he was the principal speaker at the important National Negro Convention in Buffalo, New York, where he delivered his famous "Address to the Slaves of the United States of America." He called for Blacks to resist slavery, even to the point of armed force, if necessary. This radical speech was buttressed by his belief that freedom was also spiritually necessary, that one cannot worship God authentically in slavery. The speech shocked many of the more conservative delegates, though it failed by only one vote of being named the official stance of the convention. The 1847 National Negro Convention at Garnet's church in Troy, New York, unanimously supported a similar speech given at that time by Garnet, and also approved his long-standing desire for the establishment of a national Black press. He worked with the Liberty party (predecessor of the Republican party)

for enfranchisement, and was associated with the land reform policies of Gerrit Smith.

In 1848, perhaps in frustration at Presbyterianism's ambivalence on slavery, he disconnected the Troy church from that denomination and renamed it the Church in Liberty Street. That same year he left Troy and went to Buffalo to do mission work with unchurched Blacks. In the early summer of 1850 he left that position to visit England under the auspices of the English Friends of Free Labor. From there, in August, he went as a delegate to the World Peace Congress in Frankfurt, Germany, and spent the following year addressing anti-slavery societies in various countries (he was fluent in French and German), especially England, Scotland, and Ireland. The United Presbyterian Church of Scotland was so impressed with him that it sent him in January, 1853 to Jamaica as minister of the Stirling Presbyterian Church. After three years there the entire family's poor health compelled him to return to the United States, though technically he faced the possibility of being returned to Maryland under the Fugitive Slave Law, passed in 1850. In 1855 he assumed the pastorate of the First Colored Shiloh Presbyterian Church in New York City, made vacant by the death of Theodore S. Wright. In 1858 he was elected president of the African Civilization Society. For some time he had been convinced that a strong Africa, especially one that would compete with the South in cotton production, could only benefit Blacks everywhere. Unlike many American Blacks, as early as 1848 he altered his earlier opposition and decided that some African emigration ideas were worthy of consideration. He said, "I would rather see a man free in Liberia than a slave in the United States." He insisted, however, unlike the American Colonization Society, that he was not in favor of wholesale emigration, and that Blacks who choose the United States as their true home be accorded all the rights of that society, and foresaw a time when this could happen. In August, 1861 he made another trip to England as a representative of the African Civilization Society.

Garnet was among the first to ask that Blacks be allowed into the Union Army. When this was authorized in late 1862, he volunteered as chaplain of the Black troops on Riker's Island and related to the 20th, 26th, and 31st regiments until they left for the field. This activity placed him in danger during the draft/race riots of 1863, when at one point he was chased down Thirtieth Street by an angry mob. A friendly Irishman saved his life by hiding him and misdirecting the mob, and his home was saved by his daughter's foresight in removing his nameplate from the door.

In March, 1864 Garnet was called to the prestigious Fifteenth Street Presbyterian Church in Washington,

D.C. On February 12, 1865, he became the first Black to speak before the House of Representatives, commemorating the passage of the Thirteenth Amendment. In July, 1865, the church permitted him to spend four months traveling in the South for the American Home Missionary Society. On July 22 he also became editor of the Southern Department of the *Anglo-African*. He resigned from the church in October, 1866, and was president of Avery College (founded in 1849 by Rev. Charles Avery) in Allegheny City (now Pittsburgh), Pennsylvania, for about four years before returning to the pastorate of Shiloh Presbyterian Church in New York City. His first wife had died, and about 1879 he married Sarah J. (Smith) Thompson, a widow. In 1881 President Garfield appointed Garnet minister and consul-general to the republic of Liberia. He set sail on November 12, arrived on December 28, and was accorded a gala welcoming dinner in Liberia in January, 1882. He died only one month later, and was survived by his second wife and two children from his first marriage; the daughter was an educator who married a Liberian planter, and the son went into business in South Carolina. He was also survived by a powerful legacy of ideas combining spiritual and physical liberation.

Campbell, Joan Salmon. "An Address to the Slaves of the United States of America." *American Presbyterians: Journal of Presbyterian History* 66 (Winter 1988): 251–253.

Garnet, Henry Highland. "An Address to the Slaves of the United States of America." In Dorothy B. Porter, ed. *Early Negro Writings, 1760–1837*. Boston: Beacon Press, 1971, 150–157.

———. "If You Must Bleed, Let It Come All At Once." In Thomas Wagstaff, ed. *Black Power: The Radical Response to White America*. Beverly Hills, CA: Glencoe Press, 1969, 32–40.

———. *A Memorial Discourse. Delivered in the Hall of the House of Representatives, Washington, D.C., on Sabbath, February 12, 1865*. Philadelphia, PA: J. M. Wilson, 1865. 91 pp.

———. *The Past and Present Condition, and the Destiny, of the Colored Race: A Discourse Delivered at the Fifteenth Anniversary of the Female Benevolent Society of Troy, N.Y., Feb. 14, 1848*. Troy, NY: Steam Press of J. C. Kneeland and Co., 1848. 29 pp.

———. *Walker's Appeal With a Brief Sketch of His Life*. New York: J. H. Tobitt, 1848.

MacMaster, Richard K. "Henry Highland Garnet and the African Civilization Society." *Journal of Presbyterian History* 48 (Summer 1970): 95–112.

Ofari, Earl. *Let Your Motto Be Resistance: The Life and Thought of Henry Highland Garnet*. Boston: Beacon Press, 1972. 221 pp.

Schor, Joel. *Henry Highland Garnet: A Voice of Black Radicalism in the Nineteenth Century*. Westport, CT: Greenwood Press, 1977. 250 pp.

HNC, HNRA, PP, NA, MBRL, NA, CH, MM, HNB, NBH, NG, BNA, NYTO, SBAA, ACAB, NCAB (vol.2), DAB (vol.4), DANB, BAW, HUBA, AARS, IBAW, GNPP, BPJ, SOTT, AAP, NYB (1912), BWTC, BWA.

GARNIER, LUC ANATOLE JACQUES (December 21, 1928–), a bishop of the **Episcopal Church**, was born in Maissade, Haiti. After attending a theological school in Haiti he was ordained deacon in April, 1956 and priest in November, 1956. He was appointed priest-in-charge of Gros-Morne and Gonaives in 1956, where he stayed for five years. On November 12, 1958 he married Marguerite Myrtil, with whom he had five children.

In 1961 Garnier was assigned to the Church of the Epiphany in Port-au-Prince and also covered churches in Thor and Taifer. The following year he became dean of the Cathédrale Ste. Trinité, where he remained for nine years, the last two of which he was also executive administrator of the diocese in the absence of the bishop. On April 20, 1971 he was consecrated as the first native bishop of the Eglise Episcopale D'Haiti, a missionary jurisdiction of the Episcopal Church in the United States. He is number 660 in the succession of bishops of the Episcopal Church.

ECA (1972), EBA.

GARVEY, MARCUS MOSIAH (August 17, 1887– June 10, 1940), one of the most famous exponents of Black nationalism and founder of the Universal Negro Improvement Association, was born in St. Ann's Bay, Jamaica, British West Indies, the youngest of eleven children in the family of Marcus M., Sr., and Sarah Garvey. His father was a stone mason descended from the Maroons. Garvey was brought up Roman Catholic, but attended the local Anglican grammar school.

At age fourteen the family's financial needs caused him to leave home to be a printer's apprentice, and in 1904, at age seventeen, he began practicing that trade in Kingston. Within two years he had become foreman of Jamaica's largest printing firm. In Kingston he began to exercise his considerable oratorical talents on behalf of better working conditions, but after a failed printers' strike in 1907 he was skeptical of the power of unions for Black workers. He then went into journalism and politics, and in 1910 founded the National Club and the *Watchman* paper to try to persuade the White and mulatto authorities to support labor reforms. When these officials proved uninterested, he concluded that seeking justice from Whites was a difficult prospect. He also worked variously on a United Fruit banana plantation in Costa Rica and on newspapers in Port Limón and Colón, Panamá, and elsewhere.

In 1912 he went to London, England, and was briefly a student at Birkbeck College. He became acquainted with the cause of African independence and wrote for Duse Mohammed Ali's *Africa Times and Orient Review*. He read Booker T. Washington's *Up from Slavery* and was energized by that vision of Black self-help. He returned to Jamaica and on August 1, 1914 (the 81st anniversary of emancipation in the West Indies) founded the Universal Negro Improvement and Conservation Association and African Communities League, usually shortened to the Universal Negro Improvement Association (U.N.I.A.). Its purpose was to draw Black people from around the world together through the development of self-image, education, and cooperative economic activity.

The first project was a Jamaican trades school modeled after Washington's Tuskegee Institute, but it needed more support and Garvey decided to take up Washington's invitation to visit in America. He arrived in New York on March 23, 1916, but Washington had died about four months previously. Knowing no one, he nevertheless introduced himself to Black churches and spoke in them throughout the United States on behalf of the U.N.I.A. and his vision of racial unity. In January, 1918 he began publishing a weekly newspaper, the *Negro World*. It soon had a circulation of 50,000, with subscribers in the West Indies, Latin America, and Africa. In 1919 he had enough money to purchase Liberty Hall, a large auditorium on W. 138th Street in Harlem, New York City, as headquarters for the U.N.I.A. His electrifying oratory brought followers in the thousands, mobilized in hundreds of U.N.I.A. chapters across the country and abroad.

Garvey's organization received a considerable boost on July 27, 1919, when he began the Black Star Line of ocean steamers. He advertised this as part of his economic self-help plan. Stocks in the company were sold only to Blacks at $5 per share and in only three months enough had been raised to buy the first ship. In one year the sum of $610,860 was raised and two more ships were purchased. The idea of a Jamaican running a Black-owned international shipping line connecting America with the African "motherland," complete with Black captains and crews, stirred the imaginations of Blacks around the world. Also in 1919 he established the Negro Factories Corporation, again with stock sold only to Blacks for $5 per share. Enough money was raised to help develop a chain of grocery stores, a restaurant, laundry, tailor/ dressmaking shop, millinery store, and publishing house, but in the long-term the enterprise was unsuccessful. In December, 1919 Garvey married his secretary, Amy Ashwood. He divorced her on June 15, 1922, and in July married his new secretary, Amy Jacques. He had two sons.

In New York in early August, 1920, he presided over the U.N.I.A.'s first international convention, staged at Liberty Hall, Madison Square Garden, and other locations, for which thousands of delegates came from around the world. This was the largest gathering of its kind in history, and revealed that Garvey was now the head of the biggest mass movement of Blacks America had ever seen. The convention adopted a Declaration of the Rights of the Negro Peoples of the World, called for the liberation of Africa, and named Garvey provisional president of the Republic of Africa, a sort of visionary government-in-exile. He tried to bolster the sense of racial pride with elaborate uniforms, parades, and ceremonials. This convention was termed his "hour of triumph."

The power of the Garvey movement was that it worked on many levels, and religion was a very important factor. He came to the poor Blacks of America as a Moses ready to lead them to the promised land. He argued that the possession of a homeland for Blacks was inseparable from redemption. In many ways he was as much a religious leader as a political one, and scholar Randall Burkett has even called him "the foremost Black theologian of the early 20th century." Despite the protests of many, the U.N.I.A. gathered the support of a surprisingly large number of the leading Black clergy of the day.

Garvey argued that participation in White religion and worshiping a White God was counterproductive and contended that God, Christ, and the Madonna were Black. He appointed **George Alexander McGuire** Chaplain-General of the U.N.I.A. and McGuire then formed a congregation called the Good Shepherd Independent Episcopal Church, with numerous branches. In 1921 McGuire wrote *The Universal Negro Catechism* and *The Universal Negro Ritual* for the U.N.I.A., both strongly influenced by Garvey. Garvey saw this explicitly religious work as an integral part of his program, and he proclaimed a motto of "One God! One aim! One destiny!" Garvey, however, was opposed to a single, "official" church of the U.N.I.A., and was forced to temporarily expel McGuire over this issue. McGuire then founded the **African Orthodox Church**, which was sympathetic to, but entirely separate from, the U.N.I.A. Garvey's concept of the role of religion was more broad in nature, with powerful sacred elements applied in a manner that could unite otherwise disparate elements in the process of nation building.

Late in 1920, thanks to encouragement from the government of Liberia, one of the two independent African states at that time, Garvey announced a campaign for a major new U.N.I.A. development project there. Within a few months $137,000 was raised, enough to send technicians to begin work. This development, part of the "redemption" of Africa, was to have both symbolic value and practical value, in the sense that it would form the basis of a Back-to-Africa colonization project. Garvey preached the separation of races and the building of the Black nation on African soil. He intended for at least some portion of American Blacks to emigrate to Africa. He believed this was the best place to repurify the race and solve what he considered the problem of mulattoes.

Unfortunately, the Black Star Line began to have trouble. He had initially paid high prices for old, poorly equipped ships in disrepair. On the first voyage of the Kanawha, a former pleasure yacht, the captain rammed a pier, the boiler exploded, and the ship was a total loss. On the first voyage of the Yarmouth, a $3,000,000 load of liquor was to be transported to Cuba. The ship foundered near Newport News and the cargo was a total loss. Garvey accused the crew of getting drunk on the cargo. There were insufficient resources to recover from this poor beginning. In 1921 membership fees in the U.N.I.A. yielded only $4,000, not nearly enough to support a venture of that size. By late 1921 two of the ships were inoperable and the third had been auctioned by the court for debts. Garvey kept funneling money to the company to try to reorganize and find more ships, but time ran out. With the urging of W. E. B. Du Bois of the N.A.A.C.P. and other critics, the authorities in early 1922 charged him and others with fraudulent use of the mails in selling the now-worthless Black Star Line stock.

The trial took place in the summer of 1923 and Garvey served as his own lawyer, taking the opportunity to expound on his philosophies. The three co-defendants were released, but Garvey was sentenced to the maximum term of five years in prison and a $1,000 fine. He was released on bail pending appeal, and his followers maintained a steady support. He began a new steamship line, the Black Cross Navigation and Trading Company and took further steps to construct settlements on land in Liberia. Liberia, however, under international pressure, reversed its former agreements, arrested the Garvey delegations, and confiscated all their equipment. In early 1925 the U.S. Supreme Court refused to reverse the judgment against him and on February 8, 1925, he entered the Atlanta Federal Penitentiary.

His supporters tried to keep the U.N.I.A. alive, but his image had fallen considerably, not only with the court problems, but also with controversial acts like visiting with Ku Klux Klan leaders in 1922 to stress the compatibility of the separatist views of the two groups. He agreed with the Klan that the United States was by right "a white man's country," and he opposed labor reforms as illusory. However, even some of his critics began to feel that Garvey's imprisonment on flimsy evidence represented an unequal application of justice. A campaign to free him was mounted, and in late 1927 President Calvin Coolidge pardoned him, but then deported him to Jamaica. There he tried to rebuild the movement, but with only minimal success. In 1930 he won a seat on the Kingston city council, but opponents had the election nullified on the basis that his campaign had been "libelous." The onset of the Depression did not help, changing the priority needs of Blacks who otherwise might have supported his ideas.

In 1935 Garvey moved to London, where he offered correspondence courses in the School of African Philosophy and published a periodical, the *Black Man*. He convened small U.N.I.A. conventions in Toronto in 1936, 1937, and 1938. Finally, struggling with bouts of pneumonia and asthma, his own poor health prevented further gatherings. A stroke in January, 1940 left him paralyzed on his right side and a second stroke in June killed him. He died without ever having visited Africa. His legacy largely was a change in the consciousness of millions of Blacks around the globe who participated in a mass movement toward freedom, self-respect, and unity.

Bennett, Lerone Jr. "Marcus Garvey's Day of Triumph." *Ebony* 32 (November 1976): 168–178.

Burkett, Randall. *Garveyism as a Religious Movement.* Metuchen, NJ: Scarecrow Press, 1978. 216 pp.

Clarke, John Henrik and Amy Jacques Garvey, eds. *Marcus Garvey and the Vision of Africa.* New York: Random House, 1974. 496 pp.

Cronon, Edmund David. *Black Moses: The Story of Marcus Garvey and the U.N.I.A.* Madison, WI: University of Wisconsin Press, 1969. 278 pp.

———, ed. *Marcus Garvey.* Englewood Cliffs, NJ: Prentice-Hall, 1973. 176 pp.

Davis, Lenwood G. and Janet L. Sims. *Marcus Garvey: An Annotated Bibliography.* Westport, CT: Greenwood Press, 1980. 192 pp.

Farajaje-Jones, Elias. *In Search of Zion: The Spiritual Significance of Africa in Black Religious Movements.* New York: P. Long, 1991. 213 pp.

Fax, Elton C. *Garvey: The Story of a Pioneer Black Nationalist.* New York: Dodd, Mead, 1972. 305 pp.

Garvey, Amy Jacques. *Garvey and Garveyism*. Kingston, Jamaica: Collier Books, 1963. 287 pp.

———. *The United States of America vs. Marcus Garvey: Was Justice Defeated?* New York: N.p., 1925. 36 pp.

Garvey, Marcus. *Aims and Objects of Movement for Solution of Negro Problem Outlined*. New York: Universal Negro Improvement Association, 1924. 8 pp.

———. *An Appeal to the Soul of White America*. N.p.: 1923? 10 pp.

———. *The Philosophy and Opinions of Marcus Garvey; or, Africa for the Africans*. 2 vols. Ed. Amy Jacques Garvey. New York: The Universal Publishing House, 1923–1926. Rpt. Dover, MA: Majority Press, 1986. 412 pp.

———. *The Tragedy of White Injustice*. New York: Amy Jacques Garvey, 1927. Rpt. New York: Haskell House Publishers, 1972. 22 pp.

Hill, Robert A., ed. *The Marcus Garvey and U.N.I.A. Papers*. 6 vols., in progress. Berkeley: University of California Press, 1983–.

———. *Marcus Garvey, Life and Lessons; a Centennial Companion to the U.N.I.A. Papers*. Berkeley: University of California Press, 1987. 451 pp.

Lewis, Rupert. *Marcus Garvey: Anti-Colonial Champion*. Trenton, NJ: Africa World Press, 1988. 301 pp.

Mackie, Liz. *The Great Marcus Garvey*. Hansib Publications, 1987. 157 pp.

Maglangbayan, Shawna. *Garvey, Lumumba, and Malcolm: National-Separatists*. Third World Press, 1972. 118 pp.

Martin, Tony. "Carter G. Woodson and Marcus Garvey." *Negro History Bulletin* 40 (November 1977): 774–777.

———. *Marcus Garvey, Hero: A First Biography*. Dover, MA: Majority Press, 1984. 179 pp.

———. *The New Marcus Garvey Library*. 5 vols. Dover, MA: Majority Press, 1983.

———. *Race First: The Ideological and Organizational Struggles of Marcus Garvey and the Universal Negro Improvement Association*. Westport, CT: Greenwood Press, 1976. 421 pp.

Nembhard, Len. *Trials and Triumphs of Marcus Garvey*. 1940. Rpt. Millwood, NY: Kraus Reprint Co., 1978. 249 pp.

Sewall, Tony. *Garvey's Children: The Legacy of Marcus Garvey*. Trenton, NJ: Africa World Press, 1990. 125 pp.

Stein, Judith. *The World of Marcus Garvey: Race and Class in Modern Society*. Baton Rouge, LA: Louisiana State University Press, 1986. 294 pp.

"The Ten Most Important Blacks in American History." *Ebony* 30 (August 1975): 130–134.

Vincent, Theodore G. *Black Power and the Garvey Movement*. New York: Ramparts Press, 1971. 299 pp.

BNA, AAE, GNPP, NYTO, NWAC, CH, HNB, HUBA, AARS, BAW, IBAW, BHBA, WWWA (4), CB (1940), DAB (supp.2), SBAA, NPT, EAB, DARB, WITW, TCSAPR, DANB, EBA, BLTC, BWA, ALNA, BRBR, BWASS, MBRL.

GAUDET, FRANCES JOSEPH (November 25, 1861– ?), president of the Woman's Christian Temperance Union (W.C.T.U.) of Louisiana and superintendent of its Prison Missionary Work, was born in a log cabin in Holmesville, Pike County, Mississippi, the daughter of James and Sylvia (Yancey) Thomas. Her father never returned from the Civil War and at age eight she went to live with her grandparents in Louisiana. She attended public schools to the fourth grade and for a time was a student at Straight University. She married a man named Joseph with whom she had three children, and joined the African Methodist Episcopal Church.

In 1894 she began work among prisoners in New Orleans, holding prayer meetings, carrying messages, providing clothing to released prisoners, and performing other services. She worked at first only with Black prisoners and later with White as well. She was the first woman, Black or White, to work with juvenile offenders and attended the courts with them even before the Juvenile Court was established in New Orleans. Her work was so exemplary that it gained the support of the governor, city authorities, and the Prison Reform Association.

In 1898 she became the president of the W.C.T.U. of Louisiana, holding that position until at least 1915. For six years she was also superintendent of that organization's Prison Missionary Work. In 1900 she was a delegate to the International Temperance Convention in Edinburgh, Scotland. In 1902 she founded and then managed the Colored Industrial Home and School in New Orleans. On July 11, 1905 she married again, this time to Adolph P. Gaudet. Over the years she built up the school to a complex of 105 acres and eight buildings, and cared for a total of about one thousand dependent children. In 1913 she wrote *He Leadeth Me: An Autobiography*.

Gaudet, Frances Joseph. *He Leadeth Me: An Autobiography*. New Orleans, LA: The Author, 1913. 144 pp.
WWCR, BWR.

GAYLES, GEORGE WASHINGTON (June 29, 1844– ?), Baptist official and state senator, was born into slavery in Wilkinson County, Mississippi, the son of Perry and Rebecca (Bowe) Gayles. He lived on the plantation of Emily Haile as a house servant, and gained a basic literacy from the private tutor of a nearby family. He grew very fond of reading the Bible and hymnbook. In 1863 he joined the Union Army and remained there until December, 1864. In December or 1865 he married Matilda Ross, with whom he had seven children. On November 21, 1867 he was ordained into the Baptist ministry. He then founded the Kindling Altar Missionary Baptist Church in Galesvill, Bolivar County, Mississippi, which he pastored for the rest of his career. In 1868 he also took on the pastorate of the New Morning Star Missionary Baptist Church in Egypt Ridge, and in 1869 added yet another church, the Jerusalem Missionary Baptist Church in Lake Bolivar.

On September 17, 1869 he was appointed a member of the Board of Police for District Three, Bolivar County, by Governor Ames. On August 2, 1870, Governor Alcorn appointed him Justice of the Peace for the District Five, Bolivar County, and on the 29th of that month also became supervisor of that district. In 1872 he was appointed missionary for Bolivar and Sunflower counties, later serving also in Coahoma County. From 1870 to 1873 he was a member of the House of Representatives in the Mississippi State Legislature. In 1874 he was elected corresponding secretary of the Baptist State Missionary Convention of Mississippi, where he stayed for two years. In July, 1876 he was elected president of that body, and held that position until 1895.

In 1877 he was elected state senator for the 28th Senatorial District, including Bolivar, Coahoma, and Quitman counties, and was re-elected several times, finally leaving office in 1887. He was during that time the only Black senator in the Mississippi State Legislature, there having been none since 1875. As a politician he was held in high esteem by most people, with never any hint of scandal. In 1880 he was a delegate to the Republican National Convention in Chicago, Illinois. He was similarly respected for his leadership in the state Baptist convention, which under his direction purchased a printing press in 1880 and bought Natchez College, which opened in 1885 for the education of Black children. He figured prominently in the National Baptist Convention in St. Louis in August, 1886, and was a delegate to the International Baptist Convention in Jerusalem in 1904. His first wife died on April 14, 1906 and on July 31, 1907 he married Ada Estelle Sessions. He founded and edited the *Baptist Preachers' Union*.

WWCR, HBB, MM, IBAWCB, IBAW, AAE, OBMS.

GEORGE, DAVID (1742–1810), pioneer Baptist minister, was one of nine children born to John and Judith George, slaves of the Chapel family in Essex County, Virginia. The owner was very cruel, and George ran away in 1762. He found work in Georgia for two years with a White man, John Green, but Chapel's son, George, caught up with him and he fled again. He was captured by the Creek Indians and made a slave of their chief, Blue Salt. George Chapel found him, but he once again escaped and found a life among the Natchez Indians.

George Galphin (or Gaulphin), a planter and merchant whose commerce with Indians was extensive, heard about George and purchased him from the Indians. George then was put to work with John Miller, Galphin's agent among the Indians. After a while he requested to live on Galphin's estate at Silver Bluff, South Carolina, about twelve miles from Augusta, Georgia. He became Galphin's personal servant and a few years later married another slave named Phyllis. He eventually had two children.

Galphin provided a mill barn as a church setting for his slaves, and George was converted by George Liele, a Black Baptist preacher, and Wait Palmer, whom some have identified as a White Baptist preacher from Connecticut. George was baptized by Palmer. Later, about 1774, when Liele and Palmer were unable to make regular visits because of war restrictions, they instructed George on procedures and placed him as the pastor of the Silver Bluff congregation, which then numbered eight and soon increased to as many as thirty-five. With the help of some White children, he learned to read enough to work with the Bible. Depending on the criteria, George's Silver Bluff group is usually considered the first Black Baptist church in America, and probably the first Black church of any denomination.

When the British took Savannah in 1778, Galphin fled to more secure areas, abandoning his slaves. George and the other slaves, probably responding to Lord Dunmore's standing offer of freedom to any slave that joined the British side, moved into occupied Savannah and joined George Liele in preaching among the Blacks. He supported himself by keeping a small butcher's stall. In 1780 he moved to occupied Charleston, South Carolina, and began a worshiping group there. In 1782, when the British pulled out, he sailed with a number of other Black Loyalists to Halifax, Nova Scotia, Canada, arriving in December. In June, 1783, he moved to Shelburne, Nova Scotia, and despite initial resistance from authorities, a chapel was built by mid-1784, with a congregation of fifty Blacks and some Whites. His missionary tours later led to other congregations in Saint John and Fredericton, New Brunswick, and in Preston, Nova Scotia. He had the largest following of any contemporary Baptist preacher in the region.

Especially in light of the limited fulfillment of land grants and support to which the Black Loyalists were entitled, George became enthusiastic over the proposal to create a British colony of freed slaves in Sierra Leone,

Africa. In January, 1792, he and about one-third of the Black Loyalist population in the region (1,196) left with recruiter John Clarkson for Sierra Leone. Once there, George established both an alehouse and the First African Baptist Church in Freetown, and gained a congregation of about two hundred. He thus shared pioneering missionary work in Sierra Leone with another Black preacher, Thomas Peters, and the Methodist preacher John Ball, both in the original company. Again, promises such as free land and self-government were not kept, and tensions ran high. George rallied his followers behind Clarkson and the other authorities, and spent from December, 1792 to August, 1793 in London with Clarkson garnering support for his mission work. While there he gave his memoirs to the *Baptist Annual Register*. On his return he continued to side with the authorities, and some of the more radical Baptists split away. He spent the rest of his life ministering to his church.

Brooks, Walter Henderson. *The Silver Bluff Church; A History of Negro Baptist Churches in America*. Washington, DC: Press of R. L. Pendleton, 1910. 47 pp.

George, David. "An Account of the Life of Mr. David George, from Sierra Leone in Africa; Given by Himself in a Conversation with Brother Rippon of London, and Brother Pearce of Birmingham." *Baptist Annual Register* 1 (1790–1793): 473–484.

ENB, DANB, HBB, SCA, SNB, IBAW, BPEAR, DCB (5).

GEORGE B. SMITH COLLEGE. A Methodist Episcopal Church school. George B. Smith College was a small school founded in 1894 in Sedalia, Missouri. It was begun on land donated by the daughters of General George B. Smith, who were themselves not Methodists, but who had been impressed by the efforts of the Methodist Episcopal Church to serve the interests of the Black community. They gave 28 acres to the Denomination's Freedman's Aid Society in 1888. Though remaining small, the school survived for a generation but was forced to close in 1925.

Stowell, Jay S. *Methodist Adventures in Negro Education*. New York: Methodist Book Concern, 1922. 190 pp.

GIBBES, EMILY V. (1915–), national executive of the **Presbyterian Church (U.S.A.)**, was born in Harlem, New York City. Her mother was an active member of the Salem Methodist Church in Harlem, but Gibbes was baptized by William Lloyd Imes of St. James Presbyterian Church in New York City, and became active in its youth program. After graduation from Wadleigh High School, she attended Hunter College, receiving her B.A. degree in 1937. Much of her extracurricular time was spent in service, either in the church in such capacities as Sunday School Superintendent and teacher, or in the community, in the New York Mission Society and Camp Minisink for underprivileged children.

Through these experiences, her original interest in a graduate degree in biology changed to religious education, in which she earned an M.A. from New York University. She supported herself for seven years as private secretary to Genevieve Earle, the first woman elected to the New York City Council. In 1944 she became secretary for the Field Director of Christian Education in the presbyteries of New York City, Brooklyn, and Nassau, and after two years stepped up to be Field Director herself, holding that position for six years.

In 1952 she was appointed Executive Secretary of the Women's Division of the Board of Christian Education, and served as the Field Director of the Eastern Area of the United States. In this capacity she also began to gain international experience. In 1953 she spent four months in a leadership training program with women in the churches of India and Pakistan. In 1966 she spent another four months on a Church Women United project working with international teams of women visiting women across Africa. From February 1969 to December 1972, she was employed by the United Presbyterian Commission on Ecumenical Mission and Relations to work with the churches in Kenya, the Cameroun, and Ethiopia as an ecumenical fraternal worker. During this time she also taught a course in Christian Education at St. Paul's Theological College in Limuru, Kenya. In 1973 she became Associate General Secretary of the National Council of Churches; Division of Education and Ministry, and contributed significantly to that work. She retired in 1981.

Wilson, Frank T., ed. "Living Witnesses: Black Presbyterians in Ministry, Part I." *Journal of Presbyterian History* 51 (Winter 1973): 347–391.

GIBBS, CAREY ABRAHAM (March 20, 1892–1972), 70th bishop of the **African Methodist Episcopal Church** (AME), was born in Madison, Florida, one of eleven children in the family of Jack and Lila Gibbs. Reared in a religious environment, he experienced conversion at age seventeen and became a full member of the local AME Church. He was immediately made

Sunday School superintendent, and also served as steward and class leader. His father died in 1909, and he helped support the family as a newsboy. His pastor arranged a scholarship for him to attend Edward Waters College in Jacksonville, Florida, from which he graduated with his B.A. in 1917.

In the fall of 1917 he enrolled in Howard University in Washington, D.C., earning money on the side with a hotel job. In the spring of 1918 he was drafted for World War I, and in less than three months was promoted to first sergeant, the highest position of a non-commissioned officer in the U.S. Army. While in the Army he experienced a call to the ministry, and after finishing his tour of duty entered Payne Theological Seminary at Wilberforce University in Ohio. He joined the North Ohio Annual Conference in October, 1921, and was pastor in Harveysburg in 1922–23. He married Pennie Ester Simmons in June, 1922. He graduated with his B.D. degree in June, 1923, and was ordained elder. After graduation he was assigned to Sabina, Florida, from 1923 to 1924, followed by Leesburg (1924–25), Ocala (1925–28), and Sanford (1928–29). In 1929 he was elected president of Edward Waters College, and kept the school afloat during the next three years, when the Depression made this a special feat. He then returned to the local church pastorate, serving four different AME churches in Jacksonville, four other churches elsewhere in Florida, and was a presiding elder for three years. In all his charges he experienced success, paying off mortgages and expanding the membership.

Gibbs was pastor of the Mt. Zion AME Church in Jacksonville when he was elected bishop in 1948, and was assigned to the Fourteenth Episcopal District (West Africa), and moved to Liberia. There they found a dismal situation, with no bishop in residence there for the past twenty years. Three weeks after their arrival Monrovia College was destroyed by fire, and other properties of the church, including the episcopal residence, were in the hands of others, and legal ownership had to be re-established. After one year setting things straight, Gibbs and his wife returned to the United States for eight months to tell the story and raise money, at which they were very successful. They also brought four students to attend Wilberforce University. The Gibbs then returned to Liberia and supervised the building of twelve new churches and the rehabilitation of the episcopal residence and Monrovia College. He and his wife had no children of their own, and they adopted a West Indian daughter.

In 1952 he was assigned to the Eighth Episcopal District (Mississippi and Louisiana Conferences), where he stayed only nine months. He then succeeded the late Bishop **John Gregg** in the Eleventh Episcopal District

(Florida). Among other accomplishments there, he paid Edward Waters College out of debt, completed its construction, and saw its accreditation by the Southern Association of Colleges. In 1956 Gibbs was assigned to the Ninth Episcopal District (Alabama), followed in 1960 by the Sixteenth Episcopal District (South America and the Caribbean islands). His first wife died on June 29, 1961, and on February 12, 1962, he married Alethia B. Frazier. The previous month he had been reassigned to the Seventh Episcopal District (South Carolina). Some years later he was assigned to the Thirteenth Episcopal District (Kentucky and Tennessee), his final office.

"Carey Abraham Gibbs." *A.M.E. Church Review* 105 (April–June 1972): 48–49.
"On the Cover." *A.M.E. Church Review* 78 (April–June 1963): 1.
BAMEC, WWWA (vol. 5), *HAMEC, EWM, BDNM* (70).

GIBBS, JONATHAN C. (c.1827–August 14, 1874), pioneer Presbyterian minister, educator, and state government official, was born in Philadelphia, one of four children in the family of Jonathan C. and Maria Gibbs. His father, a Wesleyan Methodist minister, died in 1831, when Gibbs was only about four, and his invalid mother was left to raise the family herself. Gibbs and his brother, Mifflin, apprenticed as carpenters, and along the way Gibbs converted to Presbyterianism. He managed to receive a basic schooling at Kimball Union Academy and was able, at age twenty-one, to enroll in Dartmouth College in Hanover, New Hampshire, with aid from the Presbyterian Assembly. One of only two Black students there, he graduated in 1852, and then did two years of study with theologians Hodge and Alexander at Princeton Theological Seminary in New Jersey.

After finishing at Princeton Gibbs applied for African mission work, but was turned down and about 1854 was ordained for a church in Troy, New York. After several years he transferred to a church in Philadelphia, Pennsylvania. During the Civil War he was active in the Negro Convention Movement and was present at the National Convention of Colored Citizens of the United States in October, 1864 at Syracuse, New York, out of which was born the National Equal Rights League. About that time the Old Style Presbyterian Church sent him to the South to open churches and schools. He attended the Colored People's Convention of South Carolina in November, 1865, and worked with Blacks in the Carolinas until 1867, when he moved to Florida.

In 1868 Gibbs was elected Florida's Constitutional

Convention, and was appointed secretary of state by the Republican governor, Harrison Reed, serving from November 6, 1868 until January 17, 1873 as the first and only African American cabinet member. His decorum, education, and oratorical abilities made him widely respected among White and Black alike, and during Reed's absences was acting governor. In 1870 he was one of four ministers in the newly organized East Florida Presbytery of the Northern Presbyterian Church. He was appointed superintendent of public instruction from 1873 to his death in 1874. During this brief period he established an orderly system of public schools with moves toward a standard curriculum, advocating integrated schools. He appeared on the program of the National Education Association at Elmira, New York, in August, 1873, and his speech gained him national acclaim from educators.

His death came in the midst of a campaign to send him to Congress, and there has been some speculation that his demise was not a natural attack of apoplexy, the official cause of death, but rather poisoning by his enemies. He was known to have received many death threats from the Ku Klux Klan, and was feared in other quarters as well. At one point he had testified before a Congressional committee that 153 Blacks had been murdered in Jackson County alone. Marriage information is unavailable, but he was the father of one child, Thomas Van Rensselaer Gibbs, who also became a Florida legislator. Named for him are a number of high schools, a junior college, and a hall on the Florida Agricultural and Mechanical University Campus in Tallahassee.

Gibbs, Jonathan C. *The Great Commission, a Sermon Preached Oct. 22, 1856, Before a Convention of Presbyterian and Congregational Ministers in the Shiloh Presbyterian Church, Corner Prince and Marion Streets, New York.* New York: Daly, 1857. 24 pp.

Gibbs, Mifflin W. *Shadow and Light: An Autobiography.* Rpt. New York: Arno Press and the New York Times, 1968. 372 pp.

Richardson, Joe M. "Jonathan C. Gibbs: Florida's Only Negro Cabinet Member." *Florida Historical Quarterly* (April 1964): 363–368.

———. *The Negro in the Reconstruction of Florida.* Tallahassee, FL: Florida State University, 1965. 255 pp.

CH, IBAW, AARS, HUBA, BAW, NIOY, NV, REAW, AAE, BR, BDAE, ESH, DANB, RLOA.

GILMORE, MARSHALL (January 4, 1931–), 41st bishop of the **Christian Methodist Episcopal Church** (CME), was born in Hoffman, North Carolina, and was reared from infancy by his great-aunt and uncle, Arthur Lonzo and Beulah Willis Sloan. After attending schools in Hoffman, he did a four-year tour of duty with the United States Air Force (1950–1954). He then enrolled in Paine College, Augusta, Georgia, graduating with a B.A. in 1957. He received his seminary training at Drew University School of Theology in Madison, New Jersey, graduating with an M.Div. in 1960 and named the "Best Preacher" of the graduating class. He married Yvonne Dukes, with whom he had two children.

His first pastorate was at the Rock of Ages CME Church in Augusta, while he attended college. After graduation from seminary, he pastored Bray Temple CME Church in Chicago, Illinois, from 1960 to 1962, followed by the W. Mitchell Street CME Church in Atlanta, Georgia (1962), the Allen Temple CME Church in Detroit, Michigan (1962–64), and Phillips Temple CME Church in Dayton, Ohio (1964–82), where he made his reputation. At the Phillips Temple Church he led in building a $1,000,000 structure, which was then paid in full. In 1971–72 he was president of the Dayton N.A.A.C.P. and in 1972–73 he was an instructor at Payne Theological Seminary in Wilberforce, Ohio. In 1966 he became a member of the board of trustees of Phillips School of Theology and in 1969 joined the trustees of Paine College.

At the General Conference in 1982 Gilmore was elected bishop on the first ballot and assigned to the Fourth Episcopal District (Louisiana and Mississippi Conferences), where he has since remained. He has been chair of the Human Relations Council of Dayton and has been a delegate to three World Methodist Council sessions, in Denver, Colorado, Dublin, Ireland, and Honolulu, Hawaii.

"Vitae of New Bishops: Bishop Marshall Gilmore." *The Christian Index* 115 (May 15, 1982).

WWABA (90–91), *WWR* (85), *BDNM* (75).

GLORIOUS CHURCH OF GOD IN CHRIST APOSTOLIC FAITH. An Apostolic Pentecostal Church. The Glorious Church of God in Christ Apostolic Faith grew out of the spread of non-Trinitarian Apostolic perspective in the **Church of God in Christ**, one of the early Pentecostal churches within the African American community. It was founded by H. Stokes who became its first bishop and led the church until his death in 1928. He was succeeded by Bishop S. C. Bass. Bass led the church for almost a quarter of a century during which time it grew and prospered. However, in 1952, the church ran into trouble.

Bass had for many years taught that remarriage after

divorce was wrong. Then following the death of his wife, he married a divorced woman. Bass met immediate opposition for a group of church leaders under the leadership of Bishop W. O. Howard. The resultant controversy split the church and approximately half of the 50 congregations left with the denomination's charter and reorganized as the original Glorious Church of God in Christ Apostolic Faith. Those loyal to Bass continued under the old name. Bass has been succeeded by Bishop Perry Lindsey.

Richardson, James C. *With Water and Spirit*. Martinsville, VA: The Author, n.d. 151 pp.

GLOUCESTER, JOHN (1776–May 2, 1822), founder of the first African American Presbyterian church, was born into slavery in Kentucky. As a young man he was converted by the preaching of Gideon Blackburn. Blackburn, a Presbyterian minister, recognized Gloucester's unusual abilities, bought him, took him back home to Tennessee, and gave him an education toward ministry. Gloucester tried out his preaching abilities as a missionary to the nearby Cherokees, under Blackburn's supervision. In 1807 Blackburn took Gloucester with him to the General Assembly in Lexington, Kentucky, and had the Presbytery of Union, Synod of Tennessee, present a motion to license him. A special committee to study the matter decided that, since Gloucester had been under the care of his presbytery for some time, had promising talents, and had been studying literature and theology (though apparently not yet up to regular ordination standards), he could be licensed if the presbytery so chose. The committee noted that "he may be highly useful in preaching the Gospel among people of his own color."

Archibald Alexander was at this time pastor of the 3rd Presbyterian Church in Philadelphia. In 1806 he had formed the Evangelical Society to help evangelize the city, and especially for work among the Blacks. He had a long-cherished idea of an African American Presbyterian church in Philadelphia. He met Blackburn and Gloucester at the 1807 General Assembly, and told them of his plans. At the end of the Assembly, Blackburn, and Gloucester traveled to Philadelphia with Alexander to look things over. Blackburn then agreed to free Gloucester to be an employee of the Evangelical Society as missionary to the Blacks.

At first Gloucester preached in houses, and then as the following grew, preached as early as 6 A.M. on Sundays at the corner of 7th and Shippen Streets. In poor weather they would retire to a nearby schoolhouse. In May, 1807, the First African Presbyterian Church was organized with 22 members, and accepted as such by the General Assembly's Committee on Missions. This was the first African American Presbyterian church in America, and met at this point at Keystone Hall on 16th and Lombard, Gloucester was said to have been an excellent preacher and an even better singer. Many leading citizens, including the physician Benjamin Rush, became regular hearers. He boarded with a sailmaker, Jacob Craig, and his wife.

On July 31, 1809, a joint committee of the church and the Evangelical Society published a plea for funds toward a meeting house. Within one year the cornerstone was laid on the lot at 7th and Shippen Streets, and the building was dedicated on May 31, 1811. The sermon on this occasion was preached by Archibald Alexander, now residing in Princeton, New Jersey, working to found Princeton Seminary. The church building was plain brick, 33' wide by 60' long, seating 370 on the main floor and 280 in the gallery. Money for the structure came largely from interested Whites, particularly Dr. Rush.

Meanwhile the matter of Gloucester's ordination was being resolved. On July 7, 1807, the Philadelphia Presbytery considered his case, and decided that the Presbytery of Union in Tennessee should make the decision, since they knew him better. This forced Gloucester to travel to Tennessee several times as the process continued. Finally, on April 30, 1810, the Presbytery of Union examined and ordained him. He then presented the Philadelphia Presbytery with the proper papers, and was accepted on April 16, 1811. (Gloucester was not the first Black Presbyterian minister, as John Chavis had been ordained as a home missionary in 1801). On October 16, 1811, the Philadelphia Presbytery took the church, now with 123 members, into its fold. Apparently because the church could not afford to pay him, Gloucester was never officially installed as the church's pastor, but remained in the hands of the Committee on Missions until his death.

Gloucester was fond of children and began a day school for their care and education, as an auxiliary to the Sabbath School. Although he was committed to this church work, he often had to be away from the pulpit, either because of visits to Tennessee, or because he was raising money for his family. His wife and four children were still slaves, and he needed $1,500 to free them. He visited most of the major cities, north and south, obtaining donations from sympathetic people, but was still short. In late 1818–early 1819 he went to England, where he achieved the remainder, and reunited his family upon his return. Funding for the church was also a problem, since the crucial outside support proved unstable, partly because other Black churches sprouted in the city, competing for money. Gloucester was forced to visit the various White Presbyterian churches himself and request money. He was, however, made a delegate to General Assembly in 1818.

The ministry of this church was enormously influential for many persons, including **Samuel Cornish**, who arrived in Philadelphia in 1815, joined the church, and was presented to the presbytery as a candidate for ministry about 1817. By the time Gloucester returned from England his health was failing, described variously as due to consumption or a ruptured blood vessel. Cornish preached regularly for him from early 1818 until October, 1819, when he left for missionary work, later founding the first Black Presbyterian church in New York City. On June 27, 1820, Gloucester requested that the presbytery help supply his pulpit. On April 18, 1821, he recommended son Jeremiah as a candidate for ministry. At the time of Gloucester's death the communicant members of the church numbered over 300.

Gloucester's sons continued in the ministry. Stephen founded the Central Presbyterian Church in Philadelphia in 1844, and James organized the Siloam Presbyterian Church in Brooklyn, New York in 1849. The presbytery of Gloucester's original church continued to supply the pulpit until May, 1823, when it was agreed to seek a settled pastor. Most voted for Samuel Cornish, but a significant minority preferred Jeremiah Gloucester, who was not yet finished with his studies and could not be a formal candidate. This minority preferred the supply pastoring until he was ready. The dispute could not be resolved, and on March 9, 1924, 75 people signed a petition to form the 2nd African Presbyterian Church. Jeremiah had a successful pastorate there, with 200 members by 1840. The church was burned down in a riot in 1842.

The First African Presbyterian Church renewed its invitation to Cornish after the congregational split, but he declined, and Benjamin Hughes, another product of Gloucester's ministry, was selected. He was ordained and installed on May 4, 1824. He stayed only six months, as the income was insufficient, and went into business. Supply from the presbytery continued for years. Charles Gardner, a Methodist minister, preached from October, 1827 to April, 1830. They finally got Cornish from December 13, 1831 to June, 1832, when he resigned. In May, 1836, Gardner returned, now a Presbyterian. He was installed on July 5, 1836, and stayed until February 14, 1848. For another seven years they took presbytery supply, trying unsuccessfully in 1850 to hire **Amos Beman** from the Temple Street Congregational Church in New Haven, Connecticut.

William Catto was installed as the next minister on March 23, 1855. The church made several geographic moves, first to 17th and Fitzwater, and in 1943 to 18th and Christian. The present location is 42nd Street and Girard Avenue.

Catto, William Thomas. *A Semi-Centenary Discourse and History of the First African Presbyterian Church, Philadelphia, May, 1857, From Its Organization, Including a Notice of Its First Pastor, John Gloucester, Also Appendix Containing Sketches of All the Colored Churches in Philadelphia.* Philadelphia, PA: Joseph M. Wilson, 1857. 111 pp.

Drury, Clifford Merrill. *Presbyterian Panorama.* Philadelphia, PA: Board of Education, Presbyterian Church in the United States, 1952. 458 pp.

Gloucester, John. *A Sermon Delivered in the First African Presbyterian Church in Philadelphia on the 1st of January, 1830, Before the Different Coloured Societies of Philadelphia.* Philadelphia, PA: 1839. 8 pp.

Irvin, Dale T. "Social Witness Policies: An Historical Overview." *Journal of Presbyterian History* 57 (Fall 1979): 353–403.

Smylie, James H. "Part IV: Freedom's Ferment and the Evangelical Front." *Journal of Presbyterian History* 63 (Spring–Summer 1985): 53–80.

Swift, David. "Black Presbyterian Attacks on Racism: Samuel Cornish, Theodore Wright, and Their Contemporaries." *Journal of Presbyterian History* 51 (Winter 1973): 433–470.

HUBA, FFF, CH, IBAW, BPJ, NAH, NYB (1925–26).

GOD'S HOUSE OF PRAYER FOR ALL NATIONS. An Apostolic Pentecostal church. Periodically the non-Trinitarian Apostolic Pentecostal teachings penetrate the **Church of God in Christ**, the largest of the predominantly Black Pentecostal churches in America. In the early 1960s it found an advocate in COGIC pastor Tommie Lawrence of Peoria, Illinois. Also strongly influenced by White healing evangelist A. A. Allen, Lawrence has placed a strong emphasis on spiritual healing in the House of Prayer.

In 1964 he left the church and founded God's House of Prayer for All Nations. Lawrence has led the church as its bishop. Several additional congregations have been founded, all in Northern Illinois.

GOLDEN, CHARLES FRANKLIN (August 24, 1912–November 12, 1984), a bishop of the United Methodist Church, was born in Holly Springs, Mississippi, the son of J. W. and Mary P. (Tyson) Golden. He received his B.A. in 1936 from Clark

College in Atlanta, Georgia and his B.D. in 1937 from Gammon Theological Seminary in Atlanta. He was ordained a deacon in 1934 and elder in 1938. On May 24, 1937 he married Ida Elizabeth Smith.

Golden was summer assistant pastor at St. Paul Methodist Church in Birmingham, Alabama (1935–36); student assistant at Warren Methodist Church in Atlanta, Georgia (1936); supply pastor for the Cookeville Circuit, Cookeville, Tennessee (1937); pastor of the Haven Methodist Church in Clarksdale, Mississippi (1938); and pastor of Wesley Methodist Church in Little Rock, Arkansas (1938–42). From 1942 to 1946 he was a chaplain in the U.S. Army. From 1947 to 1952 he was director of field service, Department of Negro Work, Methodist Board of Missions. He then rose in the ranks of the Methodist Board of Missions as associate secretary for the Division of National Missions (1952–56) and a director in the Division of National Missions (1956–60).

On July 17, 1960 Golden was elected bishop by the Central Jurisdiction, the segregated, non-geographical structure (1939–68) within the Methodist Church. He was assigned to the Nashville-Birmingham Episcopal Area, where he remained until 1968. In that year the Central Jurisdiction was dissolved as part of the merger with the Evangelical United Brethren that created the United Methodist Church. Golden was then assigned to the San Francisco Episcopal Area until 1972, when he moved to the Los Angeles Episcopal Area, where he stayed until retirement in 1980. Golden was one of those pioneering Black bishops who faced the many difficulties of the transition to a fully integrated church. He bore the numerous racist actions and remarks from the primarily White San Francisco and Los Angeles Episcopal Areas with dignity. His final assignment to the Los Angeles Area was also his most difficult, as he had to deal with a major financial crisis over Pacific Homes, a church-run set of retirement facilities that faced bankruptcy and lawsuits. The problem set most other programs of the area into stasis and Golden's leadership was sternly tested. The pressure on the church from Pacific Homes was not eased until about 1988.

Golden provided leadership in many areas of the church. He chaired the division of Peace and World Order of the Board of Christian Social Concerns (1964–68) and chaired the joint committee on missionary personnel of the Board of Missions (1964–68). He was a representative to the World Council of Churches in 1965 and chaired the department of Renewal, Life and Mission of the National Council of Churches (1967–68), later serving on the governing board of the National Council of Churches (1972–80). In 1971 he was a delegate to the World Methodist Council meeting in Denver, Colorado. He was vice-chair of the Commission on Religion and Race (1968–72) and president of the council of bishops (1973–74). Beginning in 1968 he was president of the board of trustees for Gammon Theological Seminary, and was variously also a trustee of Rust College (1960–64), Claflin College (1964–68), Bennett College (1964–70), Scarrit College (1964–70), Morristown College (1962–68), and Pacific School of Religion (1969–72).

WWR (77), *EBA*, *BDNM* (75), *WWABA* (80–81), *WWMC*, *EWM*, *WWA* (84–85).

GOLDER, MORRIS ELLIS (1913–), a bishop of the **Pentecostal Assemblies of the World**, was raised in Indianapolis, Indiana, during the early years of the Pentecostal movement. He experienced salvation under the ministry of **Garfield T. Haywood**, the presiding bishop of the Assemblies and pastor of Christ Temple. His father, Earl Golder, was a deacon at the temple, and his grandfather, Francis Golder, had been an early member. In 1903, though still a teenager, Golder was called into the ministry. After his graduation from high school, he also attended Butler University from which he earned his B.A. and M.A. degrees and then finished his B.D. at Christian Theological Seminary. In 1934, at the first denominational National Youth Convention, Golder was elected the historian of the group.

Around 1934, Golder began his pastoral career at Bethesda Temple in St. Louis, Missouri, where he stayed for thirteen years. In 1947 he returned to Indianapolis to became pastor of Christ Temple in Indianapolis, considered by many the mother church of the denomination. During his six years at the temple, he initiated a radio ministry and purchased a farm which produced food for the parishioners. From 1949 to 1953, he also served as editor of the *Christian Outlook*, the denomination's magazine. After six years at Christ Temple, in 1953 he became the pastor of Grace Apostolic Church in Indianapolis, a congregation he organized, and with whom he has remained until the present.

While having an outstanding pastoral career, Golder will be most remembered for his work at the denominational level. He has emerged as the denominations prime historian and has authored and published three important books: the *History of the Pentecostal Assemblies of the World* (1973); *The Life and Works of Bishop Garfield Thomas Haywood* (1977); and *The Bishops of the Pentecostal Assemblies of the World* (1980). He has also served as the denomination's treasurer, a member of its board of directors, and vice-chairman of the board of Aenon Bible school. In 1972 he was elected to the bishopric and assigned duties over Episcopal District 11 which includes the states of Kentucky and Tennessee.

Christ Temple Church Souvenir Booklet. Indianapolis, IN: Christ Temple Church, 1974. 72 pp.

Golder, Morris E. *The Bishops of the Pentecostal Assemblies of the World.* Indianapolis, IN: The Author, 1980. 69 pp.

———. *Grace Gleanings.* Indianapolis, IN: The Author, 1977. 125 pp.

———. *History of the Pentecostal Assemblies of the World.* Indianapolis, IN: The Author, 1973. 195 pp.

———. *The Life and Works of Bishop Garfield Thomas Haywood.* Indianapolis, IN: The Author, 1977. 71 pp.

GOMES, PETER JOHN (May 22, 1942–), Harvard University chaplain, was born in Boston, Massachusetts and grew up in nearby Plymouth. He received his B.A. in 1965 from Bates College in Lewiston, Maine, and his S.T.B. in 1967–68 from Harvard University. He was ordained with the **American Baptist Churches in the U.S.A.** in 1968. From 1968 to 1970 he taught history and directed an experimental program for freshmen at Tuskegee Institute in Alabama. In 1970 he became an assistant minister at Harvard University Memorial Church, and has moved up the ranks since then, becoming acting minister and then in 1974 becoming senior minister. Since 1974 he has also occupied the Plummer Chair of Christian Morals at Harvard.

Gomes is a board member of the Pilgrim Society in Plymouth and brings to his widely respected preaching a wealth of historical and literary knowledge. Music is another major interest; he is a member of the Royal Society of Church Music and the Harvard Musical Association. He was national chaplain of the American Guild of Organists from 1978 to 1982. He is a trustee of many organizations, including Donation to Liberia, Bates College, Charity of Edward Hopkins, Boston Freedom Trail, Wellesley College, and the International Defense Fund and Aid in South Africa. In 1971 he published a booklet, *The Pilgrim Society, 1820–1970; An Informal Commemorative Essay*, and in 1975 he co-authored *The Books of the Pilgrims*.

"American Preaching: A Dying Art?" *Time* 114 (December 31, 1979): 64–67.

Geller, Laurence D., and Peter John Gomes. *The Books of the Pilgrims.* New York: Garland Press, 1975. 91 pp.

Gomes, Peter John. *Churches of the Not-So-Standing Order: 1809–1869.* Boston: The Pilgrim Society, 1966.

———. *The Pilgrim Society; 1820–1970; An Informal Commemorative Essay.* Boston: Nimrod Press, 1971. 36 pp.

WWABA (92–93), *WWA* (90–91).

GOMEZ, JOSEPH (November 26, 1889–April 18, 1979), 67th bishop of the **African Methodist Episcopal Church** (AME), was born in Trinidad, West Indies, the son of Emmanual and Elizabeth (Richardson) Gomez. He went to the United States as a youth, received some education in New York City, and joined the Bethel AME Church in New York City under Rev. **Reverdy C. Ransom**. He graduated from Wilberforce University, Ohio, with a B.A. in 1914, and was ordained a minister in the AME Church, becoming an elder in 1918. On June 18, 1914, he married Hazel Thompson, with whom he had two children.

His first church assignments were in the mission fields of Bermuda and Canada. While in Bermuda he was elected Secretary of the First Interdenominational Alliance, the first Black to hold this position in that country. He then pastored the Ebenezer AME Church in Detroit, Michigan, followed by the Bethel AME Church, also in Detroit. He was the youngest pastor ever sent to Bethel, and while there (1919–1927) he built the largest edifice in the denomination (dedicated on June 7, 1925), which remained that church's home until 1968, when the congregation moved to another location. From 1928 to 1932 he was assigned to Allen Chapel AME Church in Kansas City, Missouri. In the summer of 1930 he was a delegate to the World's Convention of Young People in Berlin, Germany. In 1932 he went to St. Paul AME Church in St. Louis, Missouri, where he enrolled in the Eden Graduate School of Religion. He was one of the first two Blacks to receive an M.A. from that institution.

He then went to St. James AME Church in Cleveland, Ohio, which had been destroyed by fire on January 1, 1938. He rebuilt it, and during two years occupying the main auditorium all debts on the new church were eliminated. He was director of the St. James Literary Forum, and taught for a time at Payne Theological Seminary at Wilberforce University. A candidate for bishop as early as 1932, he was elected in 1948 from the St. James Church and assigned to South Africa. Upon the death of Bishop **George B. Young** in February, 1949, he was assigned to cover his area, the Tenth Episcopal District (Texas), where he stayed for seven years. During that time he was also chancellor of Paul Quinn College in Waco, Texas.

At the 1956 General Conference he was assigned to the Thirteenth Episcopal District (Kentucky and

Tennessee), but after the death of Bishop **A. J. Allen** in November, 1956, he was reassigned to the Fourth Episcopal District (Canada, Michigan, Illinois, and Indiana Conferences), where he stayed for twelve years. He was a delegate to the World Conference of Methodism in 1956 and again in 1961, and was sent to the World Council of Churches meeting in New Delhi, India. He was president of the denomination's Council of Bishops in 1960–61. About 1969 he spent one year presiding over the Seventeenth Episcopal District (Central Africa), and was the first AME bishop admitted to Rhodesia (now Zambia) by its government. He then retired to his home in Cleveland, Ohio. He was very civic-minded, serving on many boards and commissions. He was a trustee of Wilberforce University, chair of the board of Payne Theological Seminary, on the board of directors of the Cleveland Church Federation, and for a time was on the executive committee of the Federal (now National) Council of Churches.

WWCA (30–32), *EWM, HAMEC, BAMEC, BDNM* (75), *EAMEC.*

GOODGAME, JOHN WASHINGTON (c.1898–), famous Baptist radio preacher, began as a professional baseball player. Later he went into the ministry and became pastor of the Sixth Avenue Baptist Church in Birmingham, Alabama. During the 1940s and 50s he had an audience of 750,000 for his hour-long Sunday radio program on WVOK. In 1953, after **Joseph H. Jackson** took over the leadership of the **National Baptist Convention, U.S.A., Inc.,** Goodgame was named one of the members of the denomination's Commission on Undergraduate Scholarships.

"Top Radio Ministers." *Ebony* 4 (July 1949): 56–61.
SCA.

GORDON, BUFORD FRANKLIN (August 24, 1893–January 19, 1952), 51st bishop of the **African Methodist Episcopal Zion Church** (AMEZ), was born in Pulaski, Tennessee, the son of Aaron V. and Matilda (Laird) Gordon. He received a basic education at home, and then enrolled in Fisk University in Nashville, Tennessee, where he earned the B.A. degree in 1917. He studied at Yale University in New Haven, Connecticut in 1917–18, and while there pastored his first church in Branford, Connecticut. In 1918–19 he attended Officers Training School for World War I. He received his B.D. degree in 1920 from Yale University, and received at the same time an M.A. from the

University of Chicago. On May 18, 1920, he married Thelma Ruth Pierce, with whom he had seven children.

He was ordained deacon on June 27, 1920, and elder on June 18, 1922. His assignment after ordination as deacon was at First AMEZ Church in South Bend, Indiana, where he built the church edifice. In 1926 he moved to Akron, Ohio, where he also built a church, John Wesley AMEZ Church (also called Greater Wesley Temple). In 1930 he established himself as an author with the publication of *Pastor and People, Dealing with the Problems of Church Administration.* From the Akron pastorate he was elected editor of Church School Literature in 1931, and moved to the literature headquarters in Charlotte, North Carolina. He held this position for thirteen years, building a church-wide reputation as one of the finest editors and workers in the church's history. His labors significantly elevated the quality of the church literature. In 1936 he published another book, this time on teaching, and wrote numerous articles and pamphlets.

Gordon was elected bishop at the 1944 General Conference (consecrated on May 14) and was assigned to the Ninth Episcopal District (Florida, South Florida, West Tennessee, Mississippi, South Mississippi, and West Alabama Conferences). From 1948 until his death he supervised the Seventh Episcopal District (South Alabama, Cahaba, Central Alabama, Alabama, and West Alabama Conferences). He became a trustee of Livingstone College in Salisbury, North Carolina, and chair of the board of trustees of Lomax-Hannon College in Greenville, Alabama. He was the denominational representative to the Federal (now National) Council of Churches, and was a member of the executive committee of both the Boy Scouts of America and the N.A.A.C.P. He traveled extensively around the world, including visiting the World Youth Council in Amsterdam in 1939. He was a member of the curriculum committee of the International Council of Religious Education. He died at the age of fifty-eight after a brief, unidentified illness.

"Bishop Buford Franklin Gordon." *Star of Zion* 75 (January 31, 1951): 4.
"Bishop Gordon Dies After Short Illness." *Star of Zion* 75 (January 24, 1952): 1, 5.
"In Memoriam." *A.M.E. Zion Quarterly Review* 62 (1951): 228.
"Slade, Gordon Elected Bishops." *Star of Zion* 68 (May 25, 1944): 1, 8.
Gordon, Buford Franklin. *Pastor and People, Dealing with Problems of Church Administration.* Akron, OH: Superior Printing Company, 1930. 173 pp.
———. *Teaching for Abundant Living; Teaching Through*

Sharing and Guiding Experiences. Boston: The Christopher Publishing House, 1936. 188 pp.
RLA, NYTO, HAMEZC, AMEZC, HUBA, AARS, BAW.

GORDON, NORA ANTONIA (August 25, 1866–January 26, 1901), Baptist founder of the African Missionary Movement, was born in Columbus, Georgia. Her parents had been the slaves of former Confederate General John B. Gordon, from whom came their surname. She grew up attending the county schools in La Grange, Georgia, where she was a student of **Elijah John Fisher**. He recommended her to representatives from the Woman's American Baptist Home Mission Society for a scholarship to the newly founded (1881) Spelman Seminary in Atlanta.

She entered the school in the fall of 1882, where she soon converted and joined a Baptist Church in Atlanta. While still a student she organized temperance societies and Sunday Schools, encouraging the building of family altars in the homes of her Sunday School students. In 1888 she graduated from Spelman's higher normal course as the class poet and became a teacher in the Atlanta public schools. The following year she accepted a mission position in the Belgian Congo (now Zaire) with the Society of the West, receiving a brief training at the Missionary Training Institute in London, England.

She worked in Palabala in the Congo and helped found the Congo Seminary. In 1891 she moved to Lukungu, about 220 miles from the mouth of the Congo River. In 1893 health problems forced her to return to the United States, but her health subsequently improved and in 1895 she married Rev. S. C. Gordon, a member of the newly organized English Baptist Mission at Stanley Pool. The two returned to Africa together in 1896. In the summer of 1900 they left the Belgian Congo after the death of their second child and after witnessing the brutal treatment of the people by the colonists. They stayed in the French Congo for a few months, but Protestants there were forbidden to preach and they eventually returned to the United States via Europe. They returned to Spelman, where she founded the African Missionary Movement.

PNW, AAE, BWR, IBAW, HBB, NBAW.

GORDON, QUINLAND REEVES (1915–January 3, 1990), a priest of the **Episcopal Church** and former dean of Absalom Jones Theological Institute, was ordained a priest in October 1949. He served as rector of the Church of the Atonement in Washington, D.C.

until 1966, when he was appointed to the Executive Council staff. He then served as executive secretary and as consultant to church groups for the General Convention Special Program.

In 1966 Gordon, a strong advocate of civil rights, joined twenty-seven other Episcopal clergy in a prayer pilgrimage throughout the South, ending at the Episcopal General Convention in Detroit, Michigan. In 1971 he became dean of the Absalom Jones Theological Institute at the Interdenominational Theological Center in Atlanta. The next year the University of the South awarded him an honorary D.D. degree, and he later received other degrees from St. Augustine's College and General Theological Seminary. In 1976 he became a part of the editorial board of *St. Luke's Journal of Theology*. In 1978 he returned to parish ministry at St. Luke's Episcopal Church in Fort Valley, Georgia. Later he was Deployment Officer for the Diocese of Atlanta and Canon for Outreach at the Cathedral of St. Philip.

Hayden, J. Carleton. "Quinland Reeves Gordon, 1915–1990." *St. Luke's Journal of Theology* 33 (March 1990): 83.

GOSPEL SPREADING CHURCH. A Holiness Church. The Gospel Spreading Church was one of several churches which grew out of the **Church of Christ (Holiness), U.S.A.** It was founded by Elder **Lightfoot Solomon Michaux** (1885–1968). Following his marriage, Elder Michaux settled in Newport News, Virginia and became a prosperous businessman. A devout man, he built a small mission in Hopewell, Virginia, where his wife taught and guest ministers preached. Around 1917 he began to preach. He was licensed and ordained in the Church of Christ (Holiness). In 1919 he preached a revival at Newport News, and 150 people were converted. He built a new congregation, but in 1921 suddenly left the Church of Christ and founded the Church of God and the Gospel Spreading Association. He initiated work in Hampton, Virginia, the following year. Other congregations were started in Baltimore (1923), Edenborn, Pennsylvania (1924); Washington, D.C. (1927); Philadelphia (1930); New York City (1932). These congregations became the backbone of the Church.

In 1927/28, Michaux moved to Washington, D.C. over the years of his ministry, Michaux had gained some sense of the power of the radio, stations of which were slowly being established across the United States through the 1920s. In 1929 he began broadcasting on WJSV, a fortunate selection, as soon after his show went on the air, CBS bought the station. Gradually, his show began to be carried on other CBS stations, and within five years he was heard on 50 stations nationwide and in Europe on shortwave. No African American had ever been allowed to accumulate such an audience.

Speaking to a nation recovering from the Depression he brought a positive upbeat message of happiness and joy. In 1933 he began to broadcast his live church services, still an innovative format in the early 1930s. From the height of fame and influence in the 1930s, through the 1940s his national coverage was cut back and his program was carried primarily along the East Coast from Virginia to New York. However, he was in place to make the jump to television. On September 12, 1947, he and his wife Mary initiated the first regular weekly religious television show on WTTG channel 5, with the Dumont Television System in Washington. The following year, on September 19, 1948, he held the first televised Baptism service. 100 people were baptized as 25,000 looked on at Griffith Stadium.

Michaux developed a wide-reaching social service program to the growing Black community in Washington. It included assistance to orphans, the aged, and unemployed. He started one of the first church-related housing projects, Mayfair Mansions. In the 1950s, his work caught the attention of President and Mrs. Eisenhower, and he became an honorary member of the Church of God.

Among his last acts before his death, Michaux reorganized the church corporation under the name Gospel Spreading Church. In the new constitution, a board of elders consisting of the pastors of the seven original churches. The board of elders appoints the general overseer. Michaux was succeeded in that capacity by Robert Calhoon and in 1976 Willie Edwards. There is also a board of directors of the Gospel Spreading Association, which guided the temporal affairs of the church. Rudolph Jones succeeded Michaux in that capacity. Headquarters of the Church is in Washington, D.C. There are 14 congregations.

Michaux, Lightfoot Solomon. *Sparks from the Anvil*. Comp. and ed. by Pauline Lark. New York: Vantage Press, 1950. 145 pp.

Victory in Jesus: The Seven Churches and Mission of the Church of God. N.p.: 1979. 279 pp.

Webb, Lillian Ashcraft. *About My Father's Business: The Life of Elder Michaux*. Westport, CT: Greenwood Press, 1981. 210 pp.

GOW, FRANCIS HERMAN (September 29, 1896–), 74th bishop of the **African Methodist Episcopal Church** (AME), was born in Cape Town, South Africa,

the son of Francis McDonald and Sarah Elizabeth Gow. His father was for over twenty-five years superintendent of the AME Church in South Africa, until his death in 1931. Gow attended Bethel Institute School of Industry in Cape Town, then at about the age of eight moved to the United States, where he eventually received his B.A. from Wilberforce University in Ohio and attended Lane Theological Seminary in Jackson, Tennessee.

He joined the Ohio Annual Conference and pastored at Lee Chapel AME Church in Cincinnati, Ohio, and St. Paul AME Church in Charleston, West Virginia, where he paid off the mortgage. In 1924 he married Louise Ballou of Richmond, Virginia, with whom he had one child. That same year, at the invitation of Bishop Gregg, he returned to Africa to pastor the Bethel AME Church at Wilberforce Institute in Evaton, Transvaal. He also served as principal of Wilberforce Institute for a brief time. His next pastorate was at Bethel AME Church in Cape Town, followed by serving as presiding elder of the Cape Town District and superintendent of the Cape and Natal Conferences. Beginning in 1936 he was a delegate to General Conference.

Gow was elected bishop in May, 1956, when the General Conference required that a native South African be elected for episcopal supervision in that area. He was assigned to the Fifteenth Episcopal District (West and South Africa), where he remained the rest of his career. Over the years he served on the Commission for Revision of the Discipline and the Education and Mission Committee of the church. He was president of the African People's Organization and chair of the Coloured Advisory Council. He was president of the African Students' Union and commandant of the Civilian Protective Services. He was known as an eloquent orator with a great interest in music as an accomplished singer and player of a number of instruments. He was a pioneer organizer of musical groups for regular radio appearances in South Africa and played a key role in introducing Black spirituals into South Africa.

BDNM (70), EWM, HAMEC, BAMEC.

GRACE, CHARLES MANUEL (January 25, 1881– January 12, 1960), better known as Sweet Daddy Grace, was the founder of the **United House of Prayer for All People**. He was born in Brava, the Cape Verde Islands off the West African coast, of African and Portuguese ancestry. His birth name was Marcelino Manoel da Graca, later anglicized, and he was one of six sisters and three brothers born to Delomba and Emmanuel de

Graca. His family moved to New Bedford, Massachusetts, shortly after 1900, and he worked variously as a short-order cook on a railroad line, sewing machine salesman, and grocer. He reportedly married Jennie J. Lombard on February 2, 1909, fathering a son and daughter, then left the family in 1913, obtaining a divorce in 1920. A niece later suggested that the reason for the divorce was that the wife did not want "a spiritual life." He opened the first House of Prayer mission in West Wareham, Massachusetts, about 1921. In 1923 he made a trip to the Holy Land, establishing a House of Prayer in Egypt. In 1926 he founded the United House of Prayer for All People in Charlotte, North Carolina. During the 1960s this was the largest single Black church structure in the city.

His church operated generally in the Holiness-Pentecostal tradition, worship services including Bible reading, exhortations, brass bands, ecstatic dancing, and shouting. Instead of a pool for baptisms, Grace was known to use a fire hose. Physical healings were the primary way of bringing people into church membership, and hundreds testified to Grace's seemingly miraculous powers. The figure of Grace was prominent in worship services, and though he did not ascribe deity to himself, he claimed such a powerful role that God tended to fade into the background. The church's theological language centered on word-play with Grace's name. He asserted that Grace had given God a vacation, and that Grace was necessary for salvation. Favorite hymns were "Amazing Grace" and "His Grace is Sufficient for Me."

As Grace's organization grew, he extended his charisma to include a number of products marketed with his name, including toothpaste, cold cream, soap, shoe polish, coffee, and eggs. Use of these goods was thought to increase one's connection with Grace and his power. The church's journal, *Grace Magazine*, if placed on one's body, was supposed to have curative powers not unlike Grace himself. Members were encouraged to give generously to the church, and they did. The church acquired a coffee plantation in Brazil, an egg hatchery in Cuba, and many other properties, in addition to the many churches (estimates range from 111 to 350) founded during Grace's lifetime. Estimates of the number of followers range from 27,500 to 3,000,000. All monies raised for the central organization were to be used by Grace "as he sees fit without bounds." His lifestyle was flamboyant; in 1953, though the church headquarters was in Washington, D.C., he bought a twenty-room mansion in Montclair, New Jersey, and had other houses elsewhere, including an eighty-five-room mansion in Los Angeles. He wore expensive jewelry, long hair, and one-to-three-inch fingernails.

Grace was in constant trouble with either personal lawsuits or with the Internal Revenue Service (I.R.S). In 1934 he faced a Mann Act charge in Brooklyn, New York, and after a three-day trial was found guilty and sentenced to a year and a day in jail. Upon appeal the ruling was overturned. That same year the I.R.S. brought suit against him in 1934, charging that he paid only $41 tax on $190,000 income. The case was dropped when the court ruled that voluntary offerings are tax-free, but another case was pending at his death, when total church holdings were valued at about $10 million (the church won a favorable ruling in March, 1963).

In 1957 a Mrs. Louvenia Royster claimed she had married Grace on September 26, 1923 in New York City, when he was known as John H. Royster. The suit was dropped when he showed documents proving he had been out of the country at the time. That same year a fourteen-year-old girl claimed he struck her after she resisted sexual advances; he was also cleared of these charges. Most of his followers, who stuck with him through the good and the bad, came from Black ghettos, though he himself generally denied being Black: "I am God's child, and God is colorless." He was succeeded by **Walter McCollough**.

"America's Richest Negro Minister." *Ebony* 7–8 (January 1952): 17–23.

Casey, Phil. "The Enigma of Daddy Grace: Did He Play God?" *Washington Post* (March 6, 1960): E1.

Poinsett, Alex. "Farewell to Daddy Grace." *Ebony* 15 (April 1960): 25–34.

Robinson, John W. "A Song, a Shout, a Prayer." In C. Eric Lincoln, ed. *The Black Religious Experience.* Garden City, NY: Doubleday, 1974. 213–236.

BSC, BGM, IBAW, BH, ERS, BDA-AHP, DARB, NYTO, NWAC, ONL, RLOA, TCSAPR.

GRANT, ABRAM (August 25, 1848–January 22, 1911), 19th bishop of the **African Methodist Episcopal Church** (AME), was born into slavery in Lake City, Florida. He was sold at auction for $6,000 in Columbus, Georgia, just before the close of the Civil War. After the war he returned to Florida and clerked in a grocery store while studying in one of the missionary schools. He later was a hotel steward and a night student at Cookman Institute in Jacksonville, Florida. He was converted in 1869 and licensed to preach on April 3, 1873. He was pastor of the Duval County Mission from 1872 to 1875 and of the Lavella Circuit from 1874 to 1876. He was ordained deacon in December, 1873 and elder on March 4, 1876. His major living during this time (1869–1877) was as inspector of customs, and was appointed by Governor Stearns to be county commissioner of Duval County.

In 1878 he transferred to Texas, where he pastored the San Antonio AME Church until 1881, moving to Austin, Texas, from 1881 to 1885. He was presiding elder of the Austin District from 1875 to 1876 and then returned to the San Antonio church. For a time he was vice-president of Paul Quinn College in Waco, Texas. He was elected bishop on May 24, 1888, and was assigned to the Ninth Episcopal District (Texas, Louisiana, Washington, and Oregon Conferences). At election he was 39 years old, the second-youngest bishop ever elected in the denomination. In 1892 he was assigned to the Sixth Episcopal District (Georgia and Alabama Conferences), followed in 1896 by the First Episcopal District (Philadelphia, New York, New Jersey, New England, Nova Scotia, and Bermuda Conferences). In 1900 he was assigned to the Fourth Episcopal District (Indiana, Illinois, Iowa, and Michigan Conferences), and in 1904 went to the Fifth Episcopal District (Missouri, Kansas, Colorado, California, and Puget Sound Conferences). Morris Brown College in Atlanta, Georgia, finished its new dormitory during his administration in the Sixth District and named Grant Hall in his honor. On the death of Bishop Embry in June, 1897, he also covered the South Carolina Conference.

Grant (who spelled his first name Abram rather than Abraham, as it is sometimes listed) visited Europe in 1895 where he addressed the conference of the Wesleyan Methodist Church at Plymouth and was entertained by such dignitaries as Gladstone and Canon Wilberforce. He was president of the Publication Board for four years, of the Missionary Board for twelve years, and of the Financial Board for several years. He was president of the board of trustees of Wilberforce University in Ohio, and also of Western University in Michigan. He organized the Central Alabama Conference at Demopolis on November 23, 1892. He was a member of the executive committee of the World Methodist Conference in London in 1900. He married Mrs. L. R. Armstrong on October 23, 1902.

Grant, Abram. *Deaconess Manual of the African Methodist Episcopal Church.* Philadelphia, PA: AME Book Concern, 1902. 32 pp.
HUBA, HAMEC, EWM, CEAMEC, TCBDA, WWWA (1), *BAMEC.*

GRANT, ROBERT ALEXANDER (December 25, 1878–February 1, 1939), 50th bishop of the **African Methodist Episcopal Church** (AME), was born in Tallahassee, Florida. After attending Lincoln High

School he went to Florida A&M College, graduating with his B.S. in 1908. Up to that point he had been interested in business, and was already successful as a merchant and owner of hacks and drays for transportation and hauling. About the time of his graduation, however, he was converted under the preaching of Rev. R. D. Lewis and joined the Bethel AME Church.

He soon decided to become a minister and received a preaching license. He enrolled in Gammon Theological Seminary in Atlanta, Georgia, and graduated valedictorian in 1911. He joined the Florida Annual Conference in November, 1911, was ordained deacon, and assigned to the Waukula Circuit. In 1912 he was ordained elder and transferred to the East Florida Conference, where he was placed at the St. Paul AME Church in Jacksonville. On June 24, 1912, he married Maud E. Brookins. In his three years at St. Paul he increased the giving and membership, burned the mortgage, and remodeled the church and parsonage. He then spent fifteen months at the Mt. Olive AME Church in Jacksonville, followed by three years at Mt. Zion AME Church.

In 1920 Grant was appointed presiding elder of the North Jacksonville District and elected treasurer of Edward Waters College in Jacksonville. For several years thereafter he was minister of Grant's Memorial AME Church in Jacksonville, where he again paid off a mortgage and had great success. From that pastorate he was elected bishop in 1928 and assigned to the Alabama area. In 1936 he was assigned to the Florida area, and soon raised a significant amount of money for the support of Edward Waters College. He was president of the Church Extension Board from 1932 to 1936. On January 28, 1939, while traveling from the Orlando Conference to Jacksonville, he was in an automobile accident and died from injuries a few days later. Named for him are churches in Fort Lauderdale, Florida, and Gadsden, Alabama.

EAMEC, EWM, HAMEC, BAMEC.

GRAVES, WILLIAM H. (June 19, 1936–), 42nd bishop of the **Christian Methodist Episcopal Church** (CME), was born in Brownsville, Tennessee, the eighth of nine children in the family of Johnnie and Leatha Graves. His parents were sharecroppers and active in the CME Church. Soon the family moved to Detroit, Michigan, where Graves grew up. He received his B.A. degree from Lane College in Jackson, Tennessee, and his M. Div. degree in 1963 from the Phillips School of Theology of the Interdenominational Theological Center of Atlanta, Georgia. He married Alfreda Burton, with whom he had three children.

His first church assignment was as assistant minister of the St. John CME Church in Detroit, Michigan, under the Rev. (later Bishop) Walter Hansel Amos, from 1953 to 1956. While in seminary he pastored the Greater Hopewell CME Church in Atlanta, from 1961 to 1963. He then went to the Carter Chapel CME Church in Gary, Indiana from 1963 to 1966, followed by the Wesley Chapel CME Church in Beloit, Wisconsin from 1966 to 1967. From 1967 to 1982 he pastored the prestigious Phillips Temple CME Church in Los Angeles, California, where he built his primary reputation.

During the years prior to his election to the episcopacy he filled many responsible positions in the church. For eight years he was chair of the Committee on the Episcopacy and was a delegate to General Conference beginning in 1962. He was a delegate to the World Council of Churches meetings in New Delhi, India and in Uppsala, Sweden; and to World Methodist Council meetings in London, England; Denver, Colorado; Dublin, Ireland; and Honolulu, Hawaii. While in Los Angeles he worked on a D. Min. degree at Claremont School of Theology. He was elected bishop on the first ballot on May 8, 1982, and assigned to the First Episcopal District (North Arkansas; South Arkansas; West Tennessee; and East Tennessee Conferences), where he has since remained. He also became chair of the General Board of Publication Services.

"Bishop William H. Graves." *The Christian Index* 115 (May 15, 1982): 11.
WWR (85).

GRAY, WILLIAM HERBERT, III (August 20, 1941–), Baptist (**Progressive National Baptist Convention**) minister, former Congressman, and now president of the United Negro College Fund, was born in Baton Rouge, Louisiana, the only son of Dr. William H. Gray, Jr. and Hazel (Yates) Gray. His father was a Baptist minister who in 1941 became president of Florida Normal and Industrial College in St. Augustine, Florida, in 1944 became president of Florida A&M College in Tallahassee, and in 1949 succeeded William Gray, Sr., as pastor of the Bright Hope Baptist Church in Philadelphia, Pennsylvania. His mother was dean of students at another college campus.

Gray graduated from Simon Gratz High School in Philadelphia in 1959, then received his B.A. in 1963 from Franklin and Marshall College in Lancaster,

Pennsylvania. At that school he was strongly influenced by a political science professor, Sidney Wise. Although attracted by politics, Gray decided to follow in his father's and grandfather's footsteps and become a minister. He earned an M.Div. in 1966 from Drew Theological Seminary in Madison, New Jersey and while there was assistant pastor of the Union Baptist Church in Montclair, New Jersey.

Upon graduation, Gray was installed as senior pastor of the Union Baptist Church by Dr. **Martin Luther King, Jr.**, and established a pattern of strong community involvement. He founded the Union Housing Corporation to build apartment buildings for low- and middle-income Blacks. In 1970 he brought suit against a Montclair landlord who did not rent an apartment to him on the grounds of race. The New Jersey Superior Court, in a landmark decision that set a national precedent, awarded Gray financial damages as the victim of racial discrimination. From 1970 to 1974 he was also assistant professor at St. Peter's College in Jersey City, New Jersey, for which he was director as well. He occasionally lectured for other schools, including Rutgers University in New Brunswick, New Jersey. On April 17, 1971 he married Andrea Dash, with whom he has had three sons.

Upon his father's death in 1972, Gray succeeded him as pastor of the Bright Hope Baptist Church in Philadelphia. His grandfather had arrived as pastor of that church in 1925 and now he continued the unbroken line of Gray family pastors there. He established more non-profit housing corporations and founded the Philadelphia Mortgage Plan, which allowed otherwise ineligible residents to obtain mortgages for their homes. He ran for a seat in the U.S. House of Representatives in 1976 and was defeated by only a small margin in the Democratic primary. He tried again in 1978 and convincingly defeated the ten-term incumbent, Robert Nix, in the primary and won the office in the general election 84% to 16%. This election marked the first time a Black defeated an incumbent Black member of Congress.

He took his seat in the House in January, 1979 and was appointed to the Foreign Affairs, District of Columbia, Budget, and Democratic Steering and Policy Committees. Unable to make an impact in the policies of the Budget Committee, he left it in 1981 for a seat on the Appropriations Committee. He opposed the Reagan administration's economic plan and attempted to find ways of putting more money into social programs. He returned to the Budget Committee in 1983 and helped arrange a budget compromise between the House and Senate. On January 4, 1985, he was elected chair of the Budget Committee, the result of much behind-the-scenes coalition-building. That year he struggled to negotiate a bipartisan budget compromise and though this failed, he reportedly came closer to that goal than at any time "since the Budget Act was written." The basic outline of the Gray budget proposal, however, was what was eventually adopted by Congress for fiscal 1986. In 1985 he received the Martin Luther King Jr. Award for Public Service.

As a member of the Foreign Affairs Committee he sponsored a bill in 1980 that established the African Development Foundation to funnel American aid directly to African villages. It was the first time in the 20th century that a program created by a freshman was passed by the Congress. Later in 1980 he attended ceremonies marking the new independence of Zimbabwe, an event he later called "probably the highest moment" of his life in politics. As vice-chair of the Congressional Black Caucus, Gray was a vocal critic of South Africa's apartheid policy, and played an important role in successfully obtaining an override vote in 1986 of President Reagan's veto of the Anti-Apartheid Act. Seeking to ease Black-Jewish tensions in his home district of Philadelphia, Gray established Project Understanding, which each summer takes Black and Jewish students on a several-week trip together to Senegal and Israel. During all this time in Congress he remained pastor of the Bright Hope Baptist Church and preached about two Sundays each month.

In 1988 Gray presided over the delegates that drafted the Democratic party platform for the 1988 presidential campaign. He himself was discussed as a possible vice-presidential candidate. He did become majority whip of the House of Representatives and thus the highest-ranking Black elected official in the country. He was in line to become Speaker of the House, but then he made a career move that surprised many people. In September, 1991 he left Congress to be president of the United Negro College Fund, still retaining his position as pastor. The move did increase his salary from $130,000 to $175,000, but he said his primary desire was to bolster Black higher education. His interest in this is a combination of concern for the future and his family's past leadership in Black colleges.

DePalma, Anthony. "Preacher and Ex-House Whit Enjoys New Pulpit." *New York Times* (October 9, 1991): B9.

"Fresh Faces for an Old Struggle." *Time* 122 (August 22, 1983): 32–33.

"Introducing Our New Congressmen." *Ebony* 34 (March 1979): 25–30.

WWABA (90–91), *BDNM* (75), *CB* (88), *IBAW*.

GREENE, SHERMAN LAWRENCE, SR. (June 15, 1886–July 25, 1967), 51st bishop of the **African Methodist Episcopal Church** (AME), was born in Vicksburg, Mississippi, the son of Henry and Delia (Wilson) Greene. He was a student at the public school in Warrenton, Mississippi, and was active in the local AME Church, serving as steward and trustee. He attended Alcorn College in Lorman, Mississippi, from 1900 to 1902. He was licensed to preach at Bourbon, Mississippi, in 1904, and joined the South Arkansas Annual Conference in November, 1906. He married Pinkie Beatrice Spencer on June 21, 1905, with whom he had two children.

He served as pastor in Sherrill, Arkansas from 1906 to 1909 and had great success, building both Mt. Zion AME Church in Sherrill (1907) and New Hope AME Church in Tucker (1908). He was ordained deacon in 1908 and elder in 1910. He was a student at Payne Seminary in Wilberforce University in Xenia, Ohio, in 1910–11, but was unable to remain. He then was assigned to Ward Chapel AME Church in Little Rock, Arkansas, where he also continued his theological education at Shorter College, receiving his B.D. in 1912. His next assignments were in Louisiana, at St. Matthew AME Church in Shreveport (1912–13), as presiding elder of Monroe District in the North Louisiana Conference (1913–15), and at St. James AME Church in New Orleans (1915–16). From 1913 to 1915 he was also president of Lampton College in Alexandria, Louisiana. During this time he was able to work on his B.A. degree with Campbell College in Mississippi, receiving it in 1916.

From 1916 to 1918 Greene was assigned to Big Bethel AME Church in Little Rock, Arkansas, from which he became president of Shorter College in North Little Rock, serving from 1918 to 1924. He was then presiding elder of the Little Rock District from 1924 to 1928. He was elected bishop in 1928 and assigned to the 18th Episcopal District (South America and West Indies Islands). From 1932 to 1936 he covered the Arkansas and Mississippi areas, and from 1936 to 1948 he covered the Mississippi and Louisiana areas. From 1948 to 1951 he was assigned to the Ninth Episcopal District (Alabama), followed by the Sixth District (Georgia) from 1951 to 1956; the Twelfth District (Arkansas) from 1956 to 1957; the Eleventh District (Florida) from 1957 to 1962; the Washington, D.C. area from 1962 to 1964; and finally was assigned to write the history and polity of African Methodism.

He had one of the longest tenures as bishop in the history of the AME Church, serving most of his years prior to the 1948 decision to retire bishops at the close of the quadrennium nearest their seventy-fifth birthday. He was also among the most active and honored bishops. He was a delegate to seven World Methodist Conferences and on its executive committee beginning from 1951 to his death, and vice-president from 1957 to 1961. He was on the executive committee of both the National Council of Churches and the World Council of Churches and chaired the committee for the 200th Anniversary Celebration of the birth of **Richard Allen**. He was president of the Council of Bishops from 1953 to 1957, the first president of the General Board of the AME Church from 1956 to 1960, and chair of the Minimum Salary Board from 1960 to his death. His first wife died in September, 1961, and on May 28, 1962, he married Mrs. Callie Colston Logan. He published numerous articles, and was president of the Mississippi State Church Cooperative Council, the Gulfside Interdenominational Ministers' Conference, and the National Conference of Church Leaders (1936–1940).

BAMEC, EWM, BDNM (65), AAE, HAMEC, WWC, EAMEC.

GREENVILLE COLLEGE. An **African Methodist Episcopal Church** school. Greenville College was founded in 1887 as Greenville High School in Greenville, Tennessee. Rev. B. M. Gruger is given credit, but he was greatly assisted by the labors of Bishop **Thomas H. Lomax** who had been assigned to the Tennessee Conference in 1886. In a short time the school had been upgraded to a college. It operated successful until the Depression, and was finally forced to close in 1932.

Walls, William J. *The African Methodist Episcopal Zion Church: The Reality of the Black Church.* Charlotte, NC: AMEZ. Publishing House, 1974. 669 pp.

GREGG, JOHN ANDREW (February 18, 1877–February 17, 1953), educator and 49th bishop of the **African Methodist Episcopal Church** (AME), was born in Eureka, Kansas, the son of Alexander and Eliza Frances (Allen) Gregg. After attending the public schools in Eureka he attended the Southern Kansas Academy (1896–97), focusing on the science department. In June, 1898, he enlisted into military service for the Spanish-American War, and was stationed as quartermaster-sergeant in Santiago, Cuba, serving six months with the 23rd Kansas Volunteer. After this service he went to the University of Kansas at Lawrence and graduated with his B.A. in 1902, the only Black in a class of 215. He was active in his local church, serving as choir director, Sunday School superintendent, and president of the A.C.E. League. He was licensed to preach in September, 1898, in preparation for a career in the ministry. He married Celia Ann Nelson on August 21, 1900; there were no children.

He joined the Kansas Annual Conference in September, 1902 and was ordained deacon in 1903, elder in 1906. In 1902–03 he was a school teacher as well as pastor of Mt. Olive AME Church in Emporia, Kansas. From 1903 to 1906 he was a missionary in South Africa, serving in 1904 as presiding elder of the Cape Annual Conference. Upon returning to the United States, he pastored the Bethel AME Church in Leavenworth, Kansas (1906–1908), followed by five years at Ebenezer AME Church in St. Joseph, Missouri (1908–1913).

In 1913 Gregg began a significant career in higher education, becoming president of Edward Waters College in Jacksonville, Florida. For a time he was president of the Florida State Teachers Association. In 1920 he left Florida to be president of Wilberforce University in Xenia, Ohio. From this position he was elected bishop in May, 1924, and assigned to the 17th Episcopal District (South Africa), where he built Bethel AME Church in Cape Town. In 1926 he was the first Black elected president of Howard University in Washington, D.C., but declined the honor in order to fulfill his duties as bishop. In 1930 he published his first pamphlet, *Christian Brotherhood*. From 1928 to 1936 he covered the Fifth Episcopal District, followed by the Fourth Episcopal District from 1936 to 1948, and then the Eleventh Episcopal District from 1948 to 1953.

During World War II Gregg visited all war fronts (except Alaska) by appointment of President Franklin Roosevelt as the representative of the **National Fraternal Council of Negro Churches**. On his return, he was welcomed by large crowds in Memphis, Chicago, and other cities, who were anxious to hear his news of the troops. His most well-known published work came as a result of these experiences, a pamphlet called *Of Men and Arms* (1945). His first wife died in 1941 and on December 31, 1945 he married Mrs. Melberta McFarland.

He was active in many capacities as bishop. He was a trustee of Wilberforce University from 1911 to 1953 and of the related Payne Theological Seminary from 1920 to 1953, at one time chair of its building committee. He was co-chair of the Race Relations Department of the Federal (now National) Council of Churches. He was known for his many personal virtues that made him a sought-after and reliable leader and friend.

Gregg, John Andrew. *Christian Brotherhood.* Nashville, TN: A.M.E. Sunday School Union, 1930.

———. *Of Men and Arms.* Nashville, TN: A.M.E. Sunday School Union, 1945.

———. *Superlative Righteousness.* Nashville, TN: A.M.E. Sunday School Union, 1944.

DAB (supp.5), *WWWA* (3), *RLA, EWM, HAMEC, NYTO, DANB, CEAMEC, EAMEC, BAMEC, WWCA* (38–40), *BAW, AMECMIM, IBAW, WWCR.*

GREGORY, LOUIS GEORGE (June 6, 1874–July 30, 1951), the first high-ranking African American in the Baha'i Faith in the United States, was born in Charleston, South Carolina, the son of a former slave, Ebenezer George. At the age of five his father died, and his mother married George Gregory, a successful man who was able to send Gregory to a private high school and then to Fisk University in Nashville, Tennessee, where he earned his A.B. degree in 1896. He then studied law at Howard University in Washington, D.C., and received his LL.B. degree in 1902. After working with various firms around Washington, D.C., he took a job with the law division of the Treasury Department in 1906.

Sometime after this he first heard about the Baha'i Faith, and officially became a member in 1909. The organization quickly recognized his leadership potential, and Abdu'l-Baha, the son of the founder, sent him a message asking him to help lead the way toward racial harmony. The next few years were momentous ones. In 1911 he was elected to the committee which oversaw Baha'i activities in the Washington area, and traveled to Egypt to meet Abdu'l-Baha in person. In 1912 Abdu'l-Baha came to Washington and singled Gregory out for the place of honor at the ceremonial banquet. He also introduced Gregory to a White woman, Louisa Mathew, and urged them to marry, which they did. That same year Gregory became part of the national office of the Baha'i Faith, and served on the committee to build the central temple in Wilmette, Illinois. He was the first Black in America to attain such prominence in the Baha'i Faith.

In 1914 Gregory spoke at a Conference for Amity and Unity, and subsequently became the Baha'i Faith's major spokesperson for positive race relations, fulfilling Abdu'l-Baha's wishes. He led or was a member of the Baha'i National Committee for Race Unity for the rest of his career. His office sent him around the country, speaking on race relations and introducing the Black community to the Baha'i Faith. When a new governing body for the faith in America, the National Spiritual Assembly, was formed in 1932, he was elected to it,

though Abdu'l-Baha's successor, Shoghi Effendi, urged him not to let the new position reduce his successful work in the field.

Ill health forced Gregory to retire in 1946, and he spent most of his remaining five years at his home in Eliot, Maine. His pioneering work was not forgotten, however, and an award for service to humanity was established in his memory in 1968 by the National Spiritual Assembly. In 1972 the Louis B. Gregory Baha'i Institute at Hemingway, South Carolina, was dedicated in his memory.

"Louis G. Gregory." *Baha'i World* 12 (1956): 666– 670.

Morrison, Gayle. *To Move the World.* Wilmette, IL: Baha'i Publishing Trust, 1982. 399 pp.

EBA, WWCR, RLOA.

GREGORY, WILTON D. (December 7, 1947–), a bishop of the **Roman Catholic Church**, was born in Chicago, Illinois, one of three children in the family of Wilton Daniel and Ethel D. (Duncan) Gregory. His grandmother had attended a Catholic school, but the family was not Catholic. The Catholic schools had a good reputation, and the Gregory children attempted to enroll in one, but it was already overcrowded. In 1958 the St. Carthage Grammar School began enrolling Black children to fill the vacancies left by departing White families, and Gregory became a student there. Soon he decided he wanted to be a Catholic and eventually a priest. He was baptized on March 29, 1959, and sometime later his mother and two younger sisters also became Catholic. His parents divorced in 1954, though his father maintained a supportive role in the family.

He graduated from Quigley Preparatory Seminary South (a high school) in 1965 and entered Niles College of Loyola University, where he earned the B.A. in Philosophy in 1969. In 1973 he received the S.T.B. and M.Div. degrees from St. Mary of the Lake Seminary in Mundelein, Illinois. He was ordained a priest on May 9, 1973, and worked for a time at Mary Seat of Wisdom Church in Park Ridge, Illinois, assisting also in the poorer parishes of Chicago's South and West sides. At his request to experience what White Catholic life was like, he was soon moved to be an associate pastor at Our Lady of Perpetual Help in Glenview, Illinois, a prosperous suburban parish.

His experience in Glenview was good, and in 1976 he was commissioned to study at the Pontifical Liturgical Institute in Rome, Italy. In Rome he received the Doctor of Sacred Liturgy degree in 1980 from San Anselmo University, part of the Liturgical Institute. He was then assigned to head the department of Liturgy and lecture in Systematic Theology at Mundelein Seminary in Illinois. He was also a member of the Formation Staff and was Spiritual Director for the seminarians. In 1982 he was Master of Ceremonies for the Cardinal Archbishop of Chicago. In October, 1983, he was appointed Auxiliary Bishop of Chicago, and was consecrated for that office on December 13, 1983. At age thirty-five he had just reached the canonical age required for the office of bishop, and was the youngest Catholic bishop ever in the United States, as well as the first Black Catholic bishop in Chicago and the ninth Black American Catholic bishop. He was specifically assigned to the ninety-three parishes of Southside Chicago and South Cook County.

"Wilton D. Gregory, Auxiliary Bishop of Chicago." *America* 164 (April 13, 1991): 411–415.

Gregory, Wilton D. "Liturgy and the Assembly." *Liturgy 80* 14 (1982): 2–4.

———. "We Your People and Your Ministers: Liturgical Spirituality and Law." *Chicago Studies* 20 (1981): 163–175.

WWABA (90–91), *WWA* (90–91), *OBS, WWR* (85).

GREY, (SISTER) M. MARTIN DE PORRES

(1943–), founder of the **National Black Sisters' Conference**, was born in Sewickley, Pennsylvania, the daughter of Edgar W. Grey, a steelworker. She graduated from Mount Mercy College in Pittsburgh and entered the Pittsburgh Sisters of Mercy in 1961. Her religious name is in honor of Martin de Porres (1579–1639), the illegitimate offspring of a Spanish nobleman and a freed Black woman, who later became a Dominican priest. About 1960 Pope John XXIII made him the first Black saint of the **Roman Catholic Church**.

Sister Grey became active in ecumenical activities made possible by the liberalized atmosphere after Vatican II (1962–65) and also identified with the Black community. She was the only Black in the 500–member Sisters of Mercy order, and began to feel that it was incumbent upon her and other Black religious women to help educate the church on racial issues. Spurred on by the first Black Catholic Clergy Caucus (for priests and religious brothers) in April, 1968, she thus organized in November, 1968 the first National Black Sisters' Conference at Mount Mercy College, attended by 150 Black nuns. Its success prompted her to organize the second conference in 1969 as well. She has since been president of the National Black Sisters' Conference and Coordinator of the National Office of Black Catholics. She has often been called upon as a consultant and

speaker on various aspects of race relations. In a 1970 article she noted that only in the previous fifteen years had one hundred out of six hundred orders of religious women in the Catholic Church in the United States had accepted Black members.

Grey, Sister M. Martin de Porres. "The Church, Revolution, and Black Catholics." *The Black Scholar* 2 (December 1970): 20–26.

BWR, CRACG, AAE.

GRIGGS, SUTTON ELBERT

(1872–January 2, 1933), author and executive of the National Baptist Convention, was born in Chatfield, Texas, the son of Allen R. Griggs, a prominent Baptist minister who at one point was president of the **National Baptist Convention, U.S.A., Inc.** and editor of the *National Baptist Bulletin*. He graduated from Bishop College in Marshall, Texas, in 1890, and then trained for the Baptist ministry at Richmond Theological Seminary (now a part of Virginia Union University). He graduated in 1893 and pastored a church in Berkley, Virginia for two years. In 1895 he moved to Tennessee, becoming simultaneously pastor of the First Baptist Church of East Nashville and Corresponding Secretary of the Education Department of the National Baptist Convention, a position he held until 1915. On May 10, 1897, he married Emma J. Williams, with whom he remained the rest of his days. He had no children.

Griggs decided to use his writing skills to counter the post-Reconstructionist anti-Black literature. In 1899 he published his first book, a novel titled *Imperium in Imperio*, describing a secret plot by a Black organization to take over Texas and create a Black empire. This was the first Black political protest novel, and its radical overtones did not attract a mass market, but he sought instead to establish a readership among the Southern Blacks. He printed and distributed his works almost entirely at his own expense and efforts, frequently losing money.

The National Baptist Convention requested him to write a response to the racist books of Rev. Thomas Dixon, Jr., and the result was *The Hindered Hand* (1905), a novel which revealed the injustices faced by Blacks and the resulting contemplation of either open rebellion or emigration to Africa. Also in 1905 the Niagara Movement was founded by W. E. B. DuBois and other northern Blacks to protest the evils of racism and demand equal rights. Griggs was one of the few Southern ministers to join, and in 1907 he published *The One Great Question: A Study of Southern Conditions at*

Close Range as an attempt to expose the repression of Blacks and argue that equality is the only hope for the future. Unfortunately, this book was another in a series of financial failures. He decided that his voice was not going to be heard unless he changed his tactics from directing a protest message to an unreceptive Black audience to directing an accommodation message to a White audience. His future writings emphasized for Blacks a conservative message of racial improvement by sobriety and hard work, and for Whites a picture of what they had to gain by dealing fairly with the Blacks.

In 1913 Griggs moved from Nashville to be the pastor of the Tabernacle Baptist Church of Memphis. His new strategy, combined with the Memphis need to court Blacks and slow the losses to northern migration, gave him great power in the community. The White elite gave large sums of money to his church and endorsed his ideas. Although this was temporarily good for his publishing abilities and his career (he was president of the American Baptist Theological Seminary from 1925 to 1926), he became unpopular in the Black community. When the 1929 financial crash hit, there was no longer enough support to keep the church open. He returned to Denison, Texas, to serve the Hopewell Baptist Church, once pastored by his father. He resigned in 1932 to found the National Religious and Civic Institute in Houston, Texas, but died shortly thereafter.

Fleming, Robert E. "Sutton E. Griggs: Militant Black Novelist." *Phylon* (March 1973): 73–77.

Gloster, Hugh M. "Sutton Griggs, Novelist of the New Negro." *Phylon* (Winter 1943): 335–345.

Griggs, Sutton E. *Guide to Racial Greatness or the Science of Collective Efficiency.* Memphis, TN: National Public Welfare League, 1923. 229 pp.

———. *The Hindered Hand.* Nashville, TN: Orion Publishing Co., 1905. 303 pp.

———. *Imperium In Imperio.* Cincinnati, OH: Editor Publishing Co., 1899. 265 pp.

———. *The One Great Question: A Study of Southern Conditions at Close Range.* Nashville, TN: Orion Publishing Co., 1907. 58 pp.

———. *The Story of My Struggles.* Memphis, TN: National Public Welfare League, 1914. 24 pp.

DANB, BPL, EBA, SBAA, BAWPP, WWCR, NV, TSW, IBAW, HUBA, HNB, RLOA.

GRIMES, LEONARD ANDREW

GRIMES, LEONARD ANDREW (November 9, 1815–March 14, 1873), prominent Baptist minister and member of the Underground Railroad, was born in Leesburg, Loudon County, Virginia, but grew up in Washington, D.C. He was so light-skinned that he often passed for White, but still experienced many racial obstacles. He spent his youth working at the butcher's trade and in an apothecary in Washington, D.C. He later became employed by a slave-holder and traveled with him to various parts of the South on business. This gave Grimes the opportunity to see all the evils of slavery and soon made a decision to work against it with every means available. He began aiding slaves toward freedom, and for this he was arrested and imprisoned in Richmond, Virginia, for two years.

At the completion of his jail sentence he returned to Washington, experienced conversion, and was baptized in 1840 by the Rev. William Williams. He associated with the **American Baptist Missionary Convention** and went to New Bedford, Massachusetts, where he engaged in missionary work for about two years. In 1846 he went to Boston, Massachusetts by invitation of a small group of Black Baptists there. On November 24, 1848 the Twelfth Baptist Church on Phillips Street was formally organized with twenty-three members and Grimes was installed as the pastor, a position he held for the rest of his life. The Twelfth Baptist Church was the result of a split in the congregation of the Joy Street Baptist Church, the first Black church in Boston, founded by **Thomas Paul** in 1805. Becoming an immensely popular figure in Boston among both Blacks and Whites, Grimes continued his anti-slavery activities, and literally hundreds of slaves passed under his care on their way to freedom in Canada. If someone was caught on the way, Grimes was known to pursue the captor and purchase the slave himself, then let him go.

He was not known for eloquence, but for his abilities and power as a pastor, and his strength of character. He is known to have had a wife and family, but little other information on that part of his life is available. In early 1849 the church had grown to require a new meeting place, and a lot was purchased. Funds were gathered and solicited, and the cornerstone for the new building was laid in August, 1850. During the Civil War Grimes was instrumental in raising up the 54th Regiment, but was unable to accept the position of chaplain to the group, due to his other responsibilities. For many years he was president of the American Baptist Missionary Convention and of the **Consolidated Baptist Convention**. By the end of the Civil War the church counted about 300 members, with an indebtedness of only $2,000. By the time of his death the church had more than six hundred members and no indebtedness.

HNRA, HNC, MM, IBAW, AAE, HUBA, AARS.

GRIMES, SAMUEL JOSHUA (January 3, 1884–June 13, 1967), a bishop of the **Pentecostal Assemblies of the World** (PAW), presided for over three decades over the Assemblies. In spite of his long leadership career, little is known of his life prior to his experiencing salvation under the ministry of an elder W. W. Rue. As a young man he moved to Indianapolis and was greatly influenced by the ministry of **Garfield T. Haywood**, the presiding bishop of the PWA and was among the earliest members of the new denomination. He attended the National Bible College in Philadelphia and the Philadelphia College of the Bible. Grimes and his wife Carolyn, were also among the first to receive the missionary call and travel to Liberia as ministers.

Returning from Liberia in 1923, Grimes became active in the Assemblies during the last years of Haywood's leadership. He settled in New York City and there founded and led the Eastern District Council. In 1930, at the last convention Haywood attended, Grimes was elected editor of the Christian Outlook, the denomination's magazine. He served as editor for 19 years. Following Haywood's death, not only was the church faced with the vacuum left by the absence of a strong leader to assume his duties, but was ravaged by an unsuccessful merger attempt with the predominantly White Apostolic Churches of Jesus Christ. The negotiations cost the previously interracial Assemblies much of its White membership. In 1932, as the organization began its reorganization, Grimes was elected as the new presiding bishop.

Among the first duties of the bishop was to oversee the formation of the Women's Federation and the National Pentecostal Young People's Union, both of which were begun in 1933. More importantly, Grimes resisted the move to have the Assemblies become an all-Black organization and led the attempt by the Assemblies to keep a racial balance. In the wake of this decision, the Assemblies have remained the only predominantly Black Pentecostal organization which has retained a small but measurable White membership and White people in leadership positions. Grimes also promoted the development of the episcopacy as a means of building the church's organization. This process was often abused and men were elected to the office as an honor apart from organizational needs.

Among the major accomplishments, above and beyond the spread of the organization, during Grimes lengthy period of leadership were the founding and development of **Aenon Bible School** (1940), over which he served as director for many years, and the emergence of a home missions board (1984). He also encouraged the education of Ellen M. M. Hopkins as a nurse and sent she and her husband, Bishop Easter Richard Hopkins, to Liberia, where they founded the Samuel Grimes Maternity and Welfare Center in Liberia. Grimes also opened mission fields in the British West Indies and the Leeward Islands.

In 1952 Grimes faced the only challenge to his leadership when Bishop **Samuel N. Hancock**, who had been elected to the bishopric fives years before Grimes, challenged Grimes in the election. Hancock had argued that he had been prevented from becoming presiding bishop in 1931 by a resolution to keep the office vacant for a year out of respect for Haywood. In the meantime, forces organized around Grimes and against him. Hancock was defeated in a close vote. In 1957 he left the Assemblies and formed the **Apostolic Faith Church of God**. Grimes continued in his leadership until his death in 1967. Grimes was succeeded by Ross Paddock, a White man who had served as the assistant presiding bishop under Grimes.

Golder, Morris E. *The Bishops of the Pentecostal Assemblies of the World.* Indianapolis, IN: The Author, 1980. 69 pp.

————. *History of the Pentecostal Assemblies of the World.* Indianapolis, IN: The Author, 1973. 195 pp.

Richardson, James C., Jr. *With Water and Spirit.* Washington, DC: Spirit Press, 1980. 151 pp.

DuPree, Sherry Sherrod. *Biographical Dictionary of African-American Holiness-Pentecostals, 1880–1990.* Washington, DC: Middle Atlantic Regional Press, 1989. 386 pp.

GRIMKE, FRANCIS JAMES (November 4, 1850–October 11, 1937), prominent minister of the Presbyterian Church in the U.S.A., was born into slavery in Charleston, South Carolina, one of three sons born to Henry and Nancy (Weston) Grimke. His mother was the slave of his father, whose wife, Selina, died in 1843. Upon his father's death in 1852 the children were freed and placed under the care of his father's eldest son by Selina, E. Montague Grimke. This guardian, when Grimke was about ten, tried to enslave them, and Francis ran off, becoming the valet of a Confederate Army officer. About two years later while visiting Charleston with the regiment, he was suddenly arrested by his half-brother and thrown in jail. Only after several months was he removed to his old home, by this time in poor health. Even as his mother nursed him back to health, he was sold to another officer in the army.

Upon the end of the Civil War he attended the Morris Street School in Charleston for a time, then went North with his brother Archibald, under the direction of Mrs. Parker Pillsbury, a White northern abolitionist and principal of the Morris Street School. She arranged for him to stay in Stoneham, Massachusetts, at the home of

Dr. John Brown, who was to teach him medicine. His treatment there was poor, however, and he became a shoemaking apprentice with Lyman Dyke instead. Mrs. Pillsbury was still working on his behalf, however, and arranged an opening for both him and Archibald at Lincoln University in Pennsylvania. Here Grimke's abilities were allowed to shine and he graduated in 1870 at the head of his class. The brothers were supported morally and materially by their well-known White aunts, Sarah M. Grimke and Angelina Grimke Weld, who publicly acknowledged them as members of the Grimke family. In 1871 he began studies in the Law Department of Lincoln University, stopping for a year in 1872 to support himself as financial agent for the school. In 1873 he returned to his studies, then in 1874 transferred to the Law Department at Howard University in Washington, D.C. About that time he became interested in the ministry, and in the fall of 1875 enrolled in Princeton Theological Seminary in New Jersey, graduating in 1878. He immediately went to Washington, D.C. as pastor of the Fifteenth Street Presbyterian Church, where he stayed until October, 1885. On December 19, 1878 he married Charlotte L. Forten of Philadelphia, a well-known figure in the literary world, with whom he had one daughter, who did not live beyond her first year.

His next pastorate, in Jacksonville, Florida, at the Laura Street Presbyterian Church, only increased his already large reputation as a powerful preacher and learned man. In 1889 the Fifteenth Street Presbyterian Church called him back, and there he remained for the rest of his career. In 1891 he was elected professor of Christian evidence and mental and moral philosophy at Biddle University in Charlotte, North Carolina, but did not accept the position. His church in Washington became renowned as the congregation of some of the most distinguished Blacks in the city.

Grimke was famous for exhorting his listeners to attain higher moral levels and social roles, and over the years became more and more of a social prophet in the mold of his predecessor at the church, **Henry Highland Garnet**. Many of his sermons were widely distributed as pamphlets, and he often strongly condemned the hypocrisy of religious and political leaders and institutions regarding the rights of Blacks. He was a charter member of the Afro-Presbyterian Council in 1893 and was an early officer of the N.A.A.C.P. He clearly sided with the more radical strategies of W. E. B. Du Bois, over against the conservative policies of **Booker T. Washington**. One of his most critical and famous essays was delivered on November 20, 1923, at the annual convocation of Howard University School of Religion, titled "What Is the Trouble with Christianity Today?" He joined **Alexander Crummell** in founding the American Negro Academy in 1897 in an effort to foster opportunities for Black leadership. His standards of ethical conduct for both Black and White leadership were extremely high, and he was sometimes called the "Negro Puritan." He retired in 1925 to the status of Pastor Emeritus and donated his large library to Lincoln University and Howard University.

Ferry, Henry Justin. "Patriotism and Prejudice: Francis James Grimke on World War I." *Journal of Religious Thought* 32 (Spring–Summer 1975): 86–94.

———. "Racism and Reunion: A Black Protest by Francis James Grimke." *Journal of Presbyterian History* 50 (Summer 1972): 77–88.

———. *Francis James Grimke: Portrait of a Black Puritan*. New Haven, CT: Ph.D. dissertation, Yale University, 1970. 377 pp.

Grimke, Francis James. *Character, the True Standard by Which to Estimate Individuals and Races and by Which They Should Estimate Themselves and Others*. Washington, DC: R. L. Pendleton, 1911. 15 pp.

———. *What is the Trouble with the Christianity of Today?* Washington, DC: N.p., 1923.

Kerr, Hugh T., ed. *Sons of the Prophets: Leaders in Protestantism from Princeton Seminary*. Princeton, NJ: Princeton University Press, 1963. 227 pp.2

Moses, Wilson J. "Civil Religion and the Crisis of Civil Rights." *The Drew Gateway* 57 (Winter 1986): 24–42.

Weeks, Louis B. III. "Racism, World War I and the Christian Life: Francis J. Grimke in the Nation's Capital." *Journal of Presbyterian History* 51 (Winter 1973): 471–488.

Woodson, Carter G., ed. *The Works of Francis James Grimke*. 4 vols. Washington, DC: The Associated Publishers, 1942.

EBA, BA, WWCR, TCNL, HNB, NBH, PATN, IBAW, IBAWCB, BAW, HUBA, AARS, DANB, WWCA (38–40), AAE, MM.

GUILLORY, CURTIS J. (September 1, 1943–), a bishop of the **Roman Catholic Church**, was born in Mallet, Louisiana. He received his collegiate training at the Divine Word College in Epworth, Iowa; the Chicago Theological Union; and Creighton University in Omaha, Nebraska. He was ordained priest on December 16, 1972, and was consecrated Auxiliary Bishop of Galveston-Houston on February 19, 1988.

CAA.

"I remember Father [James A.] Healy. He was a colored man, and I remember it was quite well known and talked about that he was one. But if he had any such thing as an inferiority complex concealed about his person, his Irish congregation never discovered it, for he ruled them—and they were not easy to rule."

A member of Fr. Healy's congregation

H

HAMLETT, JAMES ARTHUR (April 10, 1882–February 17, 1962), 15th bishop of the **Christian Methodist Episcopal Church** (CME), then the Colored Methodist Episcopal Church, was born in Henderson, Tennessee, the son of Harry and Nannie (Bray) Hamlett. He was converted at age eleven and was licensed to preach at age fourteen. He was ordained deacon in 1900, at the age of eighteen. He married Lena A. Hercy in March 1904, with whom he had four children. His first pastorate of record was in Mason, Tennessee, from 1904 to 1905, followed by Dresden, Tennessee, from 1906 to 1907. He was ordained elder in 1906.

In 1908 he was assigned to a church in Topeka, Kansas, and took the opportunity to enroll in Washburn College in Topeka. That year he also established the *Western Trumpet*, and from 1910 to 1914, in addition to his church and school responsibilities, he was editor of *Western Index*. In 1914 he left Kansas and returned to Tennessee as editor of the CME Church's official organ, *The Christian Index*, maintaining that position until 1922. In 1914 he was also elected to the executive committee of the Federal (now National) Council of Churches. He received his B.A. from Lane College in Jackson, Tennessee, in 1916. He went on to Northwestern University and received both an M.A. from that institution and a B.D. from nearby Garrett Theological Seminary in 1922.

In 1922 he was elected bishop at age forty, one of the youngest people ever elected bishop in the denomination. His fame was won, not only as an able editor, but as a fine preacher and author of a number of books and pamphlets. As bishop he founded the Young People's Jubilees and was a delegate to the World Council of Churches "Faith and Order" Conference in Edinburgh, Scotland, in 1937. That same year he attended the World Conference on Life and Work in Oxford, England. One of his most lasting accomplishments was the founding of Phillips School of Theology at Lane College in Jackson, Tennessee, now a part of the Interdenominational Theological Center in Atlanta, Georgia. He retired from active service in May 1958.

"Bishop J. Arthur Hamlett in Final Retirement." *The Christian Index* 95 (March 8, 1962): 3.

"Death Comes to Bishop J. A. Hamlett." *The Christian Index* 95 (March 1, 1962): 1.

Hamlett, James Arthur. *Clean Water*. Jackson, TN: CME Publishing House, 1921. 80 pp.

———. *Our Church Problems and How to Meet Them*. Kansas City, MO: Punton Brothers Publishing Co., 1928. 244 pp.

CMECTY, WWCR, RLA, EWM.

HANAFI MADH-HAB CENTER, ISLAM FAITH. A Black Muslim group. The Hanafi Madh-hab Center, Islam Faith represents one of several thrusts within the African American community to find an orthodox Muslim faith within the midst of a variety of Islam-inspired groups such as the **Moorish Science Temple of America** and the **Nation of Islam**. The center was founded in New York City in 1958 by Hamaas Abdul Khaalis (born Ernest Timothy McGee) following his leaving the Nation of Islam, but dates to 1947 and the meeting of Khaalis with a Pakistani Muslim teacher, Dr. Tasibur Uddein Rahman. According to Khaalis, for three years Rahman taught him the sunnah (the tradition and practice of Islam) and then sent him into the emerging Nation of Islam with a mission to guide the group into orthodox Islam. The mission showed initial promise. By 1956, Khaalis had risen to become the Nation's national secretary. However, in the end he was unable to move the Nation's leader, **Elijah Muhammad**, from his unorthodox opinions. Frustrated, Khaalis left the Nation and opened an independent mosque.

In 1968, while still in New York, Khaalis met Kareem Abdul, a young Muslim convert, and became his teacher. He added the word Jabbar to the name of the rising basketball superstar who has remained a student of Khaalis' teachings. Shortly thereafter Khaalis moved to Washington, D.C., and in 1972 published his book, *Look and See*. He appeared to be the leader of a growing and possibly significant group. Then at the beginning of 1973 Khaalis picked up his special mission to the Nation of Islam by writing a series of letters to the leaders of the Nation of Islam. The letters were to initiate a series of dramatic events which were decisively to alter the fate of Khaalis and the center.

In the letters Khaalis called upon the Nation of Islam to drop their racial teachings and return to orthodox Sunni Muslim belief. Several days later, some men entered the Washington Center and murdered seven members of Khaalis' family and left his wife paralyzed for life. Subsequently five members of the Nation of Islam from Philadelphia were arrested and convicted of the murders.

In 1977 Khaalis and several of the members of his group, angered over the opening of a new motion picture on the life of Muhammad, took over three buildings in downtown Washington, D.C. People were held hostage for 38 hours and during the period one man, a reporter, was accidentally killed. Though the situation ended without further incident, those involved were given lengthy prison sentences, including Khaalis, who was sentenced to 41 to 120 years. The incident brought the growth of the movement to a halt.

The Hanafi Madh-Hab Center is headquartered in Washington, D.C. Khaalis remains the chief Imam (teacher) and is recognized as the official head of the organization. There are several mosques and a few hundred members. The group consider themselves as orthodox Sunni Muslims with a special mission to speak to the Black community to inform them that Islam is a religion without race or color distinctions.

Khaalis, Hamaas Abdul. *Look and See*. Washington, DC: Hanafi Madh-hab Center, Islam Faith, 1972. 113 pp.

HANCOCK, GORDON BLAINE (June 23, 1884–July 24, 1970), Baptist minister, journalist, and educator, was born in Ninety-Six, Greenwood County, South Carolina, one of two children in the family of Robert Wiley and Anna (Mark) Hancock. Anna Hancock died in 1886 and Robert Hancock later married Georgia Anna Scott, with whom he had six more children. Ninety-Six was a small rural town characterized at the time by an entrenched White racist leadership which often expressed itself in violence. In November of 1898 the Phoenix Riot in the vicinity of Ninety-Six saw White mobs executing Blacks who had signed up to vote. This incident had a lasting effect on Hancock. Four years later his father, a college graduate and pastor of the First Baptist Church in nearby Parksville, passed away.

In 1902 Hancock passed the county teacher examination and spent the next two years as schoolmaster in China Grove and Edgefield. In 1904 he enrolled in Benedict College in Columbia, South Carolina, working part-time to support himself. He received his B.A. in 1911 and B.D. in 1912, with highest honors. He was ordained in 1911 and became pastor of the 1,200–member Bethlehem Baptist Church in Newberry, near Columbia. On December 14, 1911, he married Florence Marie Dickson, whom he had met at college. In 1912 the South Carolina Negro Baptist Convention appointed him principal of Seneca Institute, a 300–student coed boarding school in Seneca, South Carolina. In six years there he successfully expanded the facilities and improved the curriculum. From 1914 to 1917 he was the statistician for the **National Baptist Convention, U.S.A., Inc.** He spoke often of the need to lift up the Black race and work against the "color prejudice" that held them down. In the spring of 1918 he received word that he was marked for lynching and soon left with his wife for Columbia.

His former professors helped him enter Colgate University in Hamilton, New York, an almost entirely White town. Despite having two degrees already, he entered Colgate as a junior and received another B.A. in 1919 and another B.D. in 1920. He was vice-president and valedictorian of his seminary class. He formed friendships with a number of White people and the experience changed his previous fear and hate of Whites. In 1920 he went to Harvard University in Massachusetts, where he earned an M.A. in 1921 in Sociology. In the years thereafter he did much of the work toward a Ph.D. but never finished the degree. Virginia Union did confer an honorary doctorate upon him in 1962, and Colgate followed suit in 1969.

In 1921 Hancock turned down a much higher paying position in the North to take a teaching position at Virginia Union University in Richmond, Virginia, strongly believing that he needed to return to the South to be a progressive force. That year he organized the Department of Economics and Sociology at the school, and his course in race relations is believed to have been the first of its kind offered anywhere in America. About this time he coined the term "Double-Duty-Dollar," meaning a dollar spent in a Black-run business, which not only purchased the necessary item but also helped provide employment for Black people. In 1925 he became pastor of the Moore Street Baptist Church in

Richmond, while remaining chair of the university's Department of Sociology. He led the church into sponsoring a day nursery, an employment center, and other community services. He preached on topics such as "The Gospel According to Hardworking Men and Women."

Hancock was a member of the Richmond Negro Welfare Survey Committee and a major writer of its 1929 report, *The Negro in Richmond, Virginia*. He joined the Associated Negro Press and wrote a regular article, "Between the Lines," which ran in 114 Black newspapers around the country. In 1931, thanks to philanthropic money from the Torrance family in Pennsylvania, he founded the Torrance School of Race Relations at Virginia Union. It promoted discussion and study of the possibility of Black/White reconciliation until it closed in 1934. He served on numerous boards and commissions, including the Virginia Commission on Interracial Cooperation, the Richmond N.A.A.C.P., the Crusade for Negro Voters, the **Lott Carey Baptist Mission Convention**, and the Council of Human Relations. In 1939 he delivered the famous "Color Challenge" address as the keynote speech of the Baptist World Alliance meeting in Atlanta, Georgia.

Hancock's work revolved around efforts to analyze race problems economically and sociologically, inspiring Blacks to look beyond their present circumstances, searching for ways to improve interracial relations, and promoting Black self-help and unity. In the depressed 1930s his "Double-Duty-Dollar" philosophy became widespread as a means of promoting Black solidarity. In 1935 he joined the Joint Committee on National Recovery meeting at Howard University in Washington, D.C. He became disenchanted with F. D. Roosevelt's "New Deal" because it did not do enough to meet Black needs. In 1940 he became dean of the seminary at Virginia Union, without leaving his church position. In 1942 he was part of the group of southern Blacks who issued the Durham Manifesto, opposing forced segregation and listing other grievances in a moderate manner. He cofounded the Southern Regional Council, which later became one of the leading organizations for peaceful change in the South, and published many articles on issues ranging from the state of African culture prior to the slave trade to the influence of advertising on criminal behavior.

In June 1952 he was unexpectedly retired from Virginia Union University. This came as such a shock to him that he had a physical breakdown and was hospitalized for several weeks. He tried to reshape his career focusing on the church, but he was never the same. In 1963 he retired from his pastorate, having built it from 600 members into a 2,500–member giant of the region. He left a strong legacy of pioneering efforts in sociology, interracial relations, and community service. He spent his remaining years offering his views as an elder statesman, despite the obstacles of a regional and generational obscurity. In 1968, suffering from terminal cancer, he stated that the Civil Rights era marked the most important change in race relations since Emancipation. His own work certainly helped pave the way.

Gavins, Raymond. "Gordon Blaine Hancock: A Black Profile from the New South." *The Journal of Negro History* 59 (July 1974): 207–227.

Gavins, Raymond. *The Perils and Prospects of Southern Black Leadership: Gordon Blaine Hancock, 1884–1970.* Durham, NC: Duke University Press, 1977. 221 pp.

Hancock, Gordon B. "The Challenge to Christianity Today." *Home Mission College Review* 1 (March 1928): 25–29.

———. "The Changing Status of Negro Labor." *Southern Workman* 60 (August 1931): 351–360.

Negro Welfare Survey Committee. *The Negro in Richmond, Virginia.* Richmond, VA: Richmond Council of Social Agencies, 1929. 136 pp.

IBAW, WWCA (38–40), EBA, BNA, BA.

HANCOCK, SAMUEL NATHAN (November 9, 1883–1963), for many years a bishop of the **Pentecostal Assemblies of the World** (PAW) and later founder of the **Apostolic Faith Church of God**, was born in Adair County, Kentucky, the son of John Wyatt and Lottie Winston Wheat Hancock. The family, which included six children, was poor. Hancock was raised in rural Kentucky and after 1888 in Norwood, Indiana. His father disappeared when he was thirteen and he had to get a job to help support the family. At the age of seventeen he was converted to Christianity and soon afterward began attending the church in Indianapolis, Indiana, pastored by **Garfield T. Haywood**, the head of the PAW. In 1908 he married Bertha Valentine.

The Pentecostal Assemblies of the World was an Apostolic Pentecostal church. It preached the possibility of believers receiving the baptism of the Holy Spirit which was initially evidenced by the person speaking in tongues. It also rejected the doctrine of the Trinity and believed that Jesus was the One God. It offered water baptism to members in the name of Jesus only. Hancock was baptized in 1914, and soon afterward received the baptism of the Holy Spirit and began preaching on the streets of Indianapolis. He became the assistant pastor of the Apostolic Faith Assembly in

Indianapolis for a period before moving to Detroit. He served a small mission which grew into the Greater Bethlehem Temple. Also in Detroit, he founded a home for unwed mothers.

In 1927 he was made a bishop and named to the original board of bishops of the PAW. His diocese consisted of Illinois, Iowa, Nebraska, and Wyoming, though he continued to serve the temple in Detroit which grew to 3,000 members. In 1932, following Haywood's death, **Samuel Grimes** was elected as the new presiding bishop. He held the post until 1967, his lengthy tenure preventing others of the original bishops from serving in that capacity. Hancock, on at least one occasion, in 1952, challenged Grimes for the position and lost in a close election.

In 1975 Hancock left the Assemblies and formed an independent denomination, the **Pentecostal Churches of Apostolic Faith**, built around the Detroit congregation.

Burgess, Stanley M., Gary B. McGee, and Patrick H. Alexander, eds. *Dictionary of Pentecostal and Charismatic Movements.* Grand Rapids, MI: Zondervan Publishing House, 1988. 914 pp.

Golder, Morris E. *The Bishops of the Pentecostal Assemblies of the World.* Indianapolis, IN: The Author, 1980. 69 pp.

———. *History of the Pentecostal Assemblies of the World.* Indianapolis, IN: The Author, 1973. 195 pp.

HANDY, JAMES ANDERSON (December 22, 1826–October 11, 1911), 22nd bishop of the **African Methodist Episcopal Church** (AME), was born in Baltimore, Maryland, one of five children in the family of Israel and Nancy Handy. His father was a slave, his mother was free. She died when he was about six and the children went to live with an uncle. The only formal schooling Handy ever received was three months in the winter of 1833. He was baptized in April 1833 and joined the Bethel AME Church in Baltimore in 1852, eventually filling almost every official position available.

In August 1860 he received a local preacher's license and in 1861 he was asked to fill in for a sick minister on a five-point circuit in Baltimore County, including Mt. Zion, Union, Camphane, Quaker Bottom, and Skullton. He would begin walking on Saturday and return to Baltimore on Tuesday, taking five weeks to visit the whole circuit. All the money he collected from the churches he had to give to the ailing preacher, and he supported himself by his cabinetmaking shop in which he worked the rest of the week. In 1862 Bishop **Daniel Payne** heard him preach and was not impressed, telling him to study a list of books if he were ever to think of attaining any proficiency. He did study those books and continued to study habitually the rest of his life.

In 1862 he was sent to Union Bethel AME Church in Washington City. He stayed there two years, his tenure being followed by several brief pastorates at Emmanuel AME Church in Portsmouth, Virginia (1864), St. Stephen's AME Church in Wilmington, North Carolina (1865), back to Union Bethel (1865–67), and then to Israel AME Church in 1868. He served only a few weeks in the Israel church, as he was elected missionary secretary for the denomination at the 1868 General Conference. On June 2, 1869 he married Mrs. Rachel S. Trives; there were no children. In 1871, while still missionary secretary, he filled an empty position as pastor of the Ebenezer AME Church in Baltimore.

In 1872–73 he was returned to the Ebenezer Church as its regular pastor, and from 1873–75 he was assigned to St. James AME Church in New Orleans, Louisiana. From 1875 to 1878 he returned to Maryland and pastored Bethel AME Church in Baltimore, and was presiding elder of the Baltimore District from 1878 to 1882. He then was pastor of Union Bethel (now Metropolitan Church) in Washington, D.C. for a few years, followed by appointment as presiding elder of the Potomac District. His first wife died, and in 1886 he married Mrs. Mary Frisby.

In 1888 Handy was elected financial secretary of the denomination. During his four years in that position the Financial Department Building on 14th Street in Washington, D.C. was purchased and furnished, with significant cash still left in the accounts.

In 1892 Handy was elected bishop and for his initial quadrennium assigned to the Fifth Episcopal District (Missouri, Kansas, and Colorado Conferences). From 1896 to 1900 he covered the Second Episcopal District (Baltimore, Virginia, Haiti, and San Domingo Conferences), followed by the Eleventh Episcopal District (Florida) from 1900 to 1904, and the Twelfth Episcopal District (Michigan, Canada, and Bermuda Conferences) from 1904 to 1908. He was a delegate to the World Methodist Conferences in 1891 and in 1911. In 1901 he published a significant book on church history, *Scraps of African Methodist Episcopal History.* He was the supporter of many charities, especially the Handy Old Folks' Home of Baltimore and the related cemetery. Churches are named for him in Joplin, Missouri, and Decatur, Alabama.

Handy, James Anderson. *Scraps of African Methodist Episcopal History.* Philadelphia, PA: AME Book Concern, 1901. 421 pp.

EWM, HAMEC, BAMEC, CEAMEC, IBAW, BAW, AARS, HUBA.

HANDY, WILLIAM TALBOT, JR. (b. March 26, 1924), a United Methodist bishop, was born in New Orleans, Louisiana, the son of William Talbot, Sr., and Dorothy Pauline (Pleasant) Handy. From 1943 to 1946 he was a staff sergeant with the U.S. Army. He received his B.A. in 1948 from Dillard University in New Orleans, Louisiana, and on August 11, 1948, married Ruth Odessa Robinson, with whom he had four children. He was ordained deacon in 1950 and elder in 1951. He received his M.Div. in 1951 from Gammon Theological Seminary in Atlanta, Georgia, and his S.T.M. in 1952 from Boston University School of Theology.

His first pastorate was at Newman Methodist Church in Alexandria, Louisiana (1952–59), followed by St. Mark Methodist Church in Baton Rouge, Louisiana (1959–68). Also from 1959 to 1968 he was chair of the subcommittee on Voting Rights of the U.S. Commission on Civil Rights. From 1968 to 1970 he was a publishing representative for the United Methodist Publishing House, and from 1970 to 1978 he was vice-president for personnel and public relations for the United Methodist Publishing House. From 1978 to 1980 he was district superintendent for the Baton Rouge District, where he served on the board of directors of Manpower Development, Inc. and on the Advisory Committee of the American Friends Service Committee.

He was elected bishop in 1980 and assigned to the Missouri Episcopal Area, where he served throughout his episcopal tenure. He was a trustee of Gammon Theological Seminary from 1970 to 1988 and became chair of the board of trustees in 1988. In 1980 he became chair of the board of trustees of St. Paul School of Theology in Kansas City, Missouri. In 1990 he became chair of the board of trustees of the Interdenominational Theological Center in Atlanta. From 1984 to 1988 he was on the Hymnal Revision Committee and during that same period was on the Council Committee on Episcopal Initiatives, which provided leadership for the well-known Episcopal Document, "In Defense of Creation." He is a life member of the N.A.A.C.P. He retired from the episcopacy in 1992.

WWR (85), *BDNM* (75), *WWMC, WWABA* (92–93), *WWA* (90–91), *BDUMB.*

HARBISON COLLEGE. A Presbyterian college. Harbison College began as Ferguson Academy in Abbeville, North Carolina, under the direction of Rev. and Mrs. Emory W. Williams. It received the support of the Board of Missions for Freedman of the Northern Presbyterians, now the **Presbyterian Church (U.S.A.).** Following a disastrous fire in 1890, the school began to grow as an elementary and high school. In 1901, the school moved into new facilities on twenty acres of land donated by Samuel P. Harbison, a member of the Board from Pittsburgh, Pennsylvania. The school's name was changed to Harbison College at that time. Harbison gave an additional 67 acres a few years later, and continued to generously support the school over the decades of its existence.

The college was closed in 1906 due to strong local racial antagonisms and when reopened in 1907 came under the leadership of Rev. Calvin M. Young, an African American graduate of Biddle University. In 1910, an incendiary bomb destroyed two main buildings. As a result the school moved to Irmo, South Carolina. It was also reorganized as an all-male agricultural college. Its name was changed to Harbison Agricultural College. The school prospered through the 1920s, its expansion being signaled by another name change in 1929 to Harbison Agricultural and Industrial Institute. That same year President Young ended his lengthy career.

While other schools suffered through the depression, Harbison experienced its best years due to the construction of a large dam in the county. Students were given jobs on the project, and its agricultural products had a new market. In 1933 the school became coeducational again.

A final decade of prosperity ended in 1941, however, when another fire destroyed a major portion of the school. It was closed for rebuilding and reopened in 1943 as a boarding school. It gradually upgraded it curriculum and in 1946 became Harbison Junior College. Over the next decade, however, the school fell behind in meeting the changing demands being made on it, especially the drive for accreditation. In 1958, the Church voted to close the school in favor of Barber-Scotia College.

Parker, Inez Moore. *The Rise and Decline of the Program of Education for Black Presbyterians of the United Presbyterian Church U.S.A., 1865–1970.* San Antonio, TX: Trinity University Press, 1977. 319 pp.

HARRIS, BARBARA CLEMENTINE (b. June 12, 1930), first woman bishop in the **Episcopal Church**, was born in Philadelphia, one of three children of Walter and Beatrice Waneidah Price Harris. She grew up attending the St. Barnabas Episcopal Church, and after graduation from high school entered the business world in the area of public relations, joining Joseph Baker Associates in 1958. She married Raymond Rollins in 1960, but divorced him in 1963. She has since remained single, and has no children.

In the 1960s she was active in the civil rights movement, helping register voters in the South, and participating in the 1965 march from Selma to Montgomery, Alabama, led by **Martin Luther King, Jr.** In 1966 she joined Sun Oil Company as a public relations executive, eventually becoming head of the department. As an adult she remained active in the St. Barnabas Episcopal Church, visiting prisoners as a volunteer with the St. Dismas Society. In 1968 St. Barnabas merged with St. Luke's, a predominantly White parish. Feeling that the new church was too staid, she joined the Episcopal Church of the Advocate in Philadelphia and soon was working towards the ordination of women and serving on the vestry board. On July 29, 1974, as crucifer, she led the procession at the Church of the Advocate, where eleven women were "irregularly" ordained into the Episcopal priesthood, two years before women priests were officially accepted by the Episcopal Church in America.

Shortly after the 1974 ordinations Harris told the rector, Paul Washington, of her own desire to become a priest. He told her to pray about it for a year, at which time her desire was still strong, and he supported her. For her college education and theological studies she mostly utilized correspondence courses with Metropolitan Collegiate Center in Philadelphia in 1976 and Villanova University in Pennsylvania from 1977 to 1979. She was ordained a deacon in September 1979, and a priest in October 1980.

She was assigned to serve as chaplain at Philadelphia County prisons, and also worked with a small parish, St. Augustine of Hippo, in Morristown. She became known in some circles for her powerful preaching and outspoken positions on such issues as South African apartheid. In 1984 the Episcopal Church Publishing Company's board of directors named Harris its executive director, her tasks including the oversight of a number of social justice programs and a leadership role in the production of the *Witness*, a liberal, Episcopalian social justice magazine. She began writing an ongoing article in the *Witness* titled "A Luta Continua," a Portuguese phrase meaning "the struggle continues." This forum made her a well-known and controversial figure in the denomination. She also served as interim pastor at the Church of the Advocate.

In August 1988, the Lambeth Conference of the Worldwide Anglican Communion voted, after heated debate, to allow national church bodies to consecrate women bishops. On September 24, 1988, the Diocese of Massachusetts elected Harris suffragan (assistant) bishop. After subsequent approval from the rest of the church, she was consecrated on February 11, 1989, at the Hynes Auditorium in Boston, Massachusetts, becoming the first woman bishop in the Worldwide Anglican Communion, 834th in the succession of American bishops. Opponents have threatened schism, and have criticized not only a woman as bishop, but also Harris's divorced state, her unorthodox higher education, and her liberalism. She nevertheless has remained a popular figure, and has been granted an honorary doctorate in Sacred Theology by Hobart and William Smith Colleges in Geneva, New York.

Barron, James. "Episcopal Diocese Chooses First Woman to Be a Bishop." *New York Times* (September 25, 1988): 1, 30.

Cuniberti, Betty. "The Bishop of Controversy." *Los Angeles Times* (February 15, 1989): Part V, 1–2.

Schmidt, Richard H. "It's Bishop Harris Now!" *The Episcopalian* 154 (March 1989): 1, 5–6.

Steinfels, Peter. "Advocate of Equality." *New York Times* (September 26, 1988): A-12.

Suhor, Mary Lou. "Cheers for the Bishop-Elect." *The Witness* 71 (October 1988): 5.

Walker, Richard. "Episcopalians Test Lambeth Ruling." *Christianity Today* 32 (October 21, 1988): 47, 49.

NA, NYTBS (89), *RLOA, NBAW.*

HARRIS, BRAVID WASHINGTON (January 6, 1896–October 21, 1965), the 6th Black bishop consecrated by the (Protestant) **Episcopal Church** in the United States, was born in Warrenton, North Carolina, the son of Bravid Washington and Margaret O. (Burgess) Harris. His father was a barber. After attending local parochial schools, Harris graduated in 1917 from St. Augustine's College in Raleigh, North Carolina. From 1917 to 1919 he was a 1st Lieutenant in the U.S. Army, serving in the 365th Infantry, 92nd Division. In November 1918 he received the Meritorious Service Citation for his actions in the Moselle section of France during World War I. On May 23, 1918, he married Flossie Mae Adams. He received his B.D. in 1922 from Bishop Payne Divinity School in Petersburg, Virginia.

Harris was ordained deacon in 1921 and priest in 1922. His first church assignment was as rector at All Saints Episcopal Church in Warrenton, North Carolina, from 1922 to 1924, and from 1924 to 1944 he was rector of Grace Episcopal Church in Norfolk, Virginia. From 1937 to 1944 he was also Archdeacon for Negro Work in the diocese of Southern Virginia, and from 1937 to 1943 he was a member of the Joint Commission of Negro Work of the General Conference. In 1933–34 he was president of the City Beach Corporation in Norfolk, which operated a city beach for Black residents. From 1934 to 1944 he was president of Norfolk Community Hospital, and for many years he was a trustee of Bishop Payne Divinity School. In 1937 he published a pamphlet, *A Study of Our Work*. In 1944–45 he was secretary for Negro Work in the Home Department, Division of Domestic Missions of the National Council of the (Protestant) Episcopal Church.

On April 17, 1945, Harris was consecrated Missionary Bishop of Liberia, the sixth Black bishop consecrated by the Episcopal Church in America, following **James T. Holly** (1874), **Samuel D. Ferguson** (1885), **Edward T. Demby** (1918), **Henry B. Delany** (1918), and **Theophilus M. Gardiner** (1920). Harris's nearly twenty years in Liberia were very successful. He built the B. W. Harris School, a new home for the treasurer, a new bishop's home, and made plans for a new cathedral, all in Monrovia. He remodeled the Bromley Girls' School and other schools in Cape Mount. Cuttington Collegiate and Divinity School had been closed since 1929, and Harris rebuilt it in Suacoco in 1948 and reopened it in 1949, serving as president of its board of trustees. He retired in 1964 and returned to the United States. For about a year he was acting director of the Foundation for Episcopal Colleges in New York City, which assisted students at Episcopal Church-related colleges with scholarships. He left that post early in 1965 when a permanent director was hired, Arthur Ben Chitty. On October 21, 1965, Harris was killed instantly when the car he was driving ran off Interstate 95 near Fredericksburg, Virginia. His wife and Arthur Chitty, also in the car, recovered from their injuries.

NYTO, WWWA (4), *ECA* (1946), *NCAB* (53).

HARRIS, CATHERINE (1809–1907), famous **African Methodist Episcopal Zion Church** (AMEZ) leader of the Underground Railroad, was born in Titusville, Pennsylvania. In 1831 she married John Harris and they were among the earliest settlers of Jamestown, New York. She became a member of the local AMEZ Church which today has its parsonage, built by her great-grandson, on the site of her home at 12 West Seventh Street. She was known in the community as a natural doctor, nurse, and midwife.

Although she had never personally experienced slavery, her sensitivity to human suffering made her interested in the plight of escaping slaves. In 1831 she began to use her home as a refuge for fugitive slaves and during the 1850s had as many as seventeen slaves in the house at any given time. She cared for their needs until such time as they could be sent on toward Canada in safety. This was one of the few Black-operated underground stations in the country. The most famous story about her concerns the ingenious way she found to get one fugitive slave into Canada. She placed him in a coffin-like box, by which means he was taken by wagon to Dunkirk and then ferried across Lake Erie to Canada. During all the time of her underground activities she felt obliged to mislead the agents hunting for the fugitives, yet morally called not to lie to them, both of which she managed.

Harris lived to the old age of 98, maintaining a keen mind and spirit. Her strong will is evidenced by the fact that she apparently was determined not to die before her youngest daughter, Mary Hall, who in her late 70s was in ill health. Harris felt that she had to be available to care for her as necessary. Harris passed away only two days after her daughter's death.

BRBR, HAMEZC.

HARRIS, CICERO RICHARDSON (August 25, 1844–June 24, 1917), 22nd bishop of the **African Methodist Episcopal Zion Church** (AMEZ), was born in Fayetteville, North Carolina, one of several children in the family of Jacob and Charlotte Harris. His father died when he was only three, and at age six the family moved to Chillicothe, Ohio, where he began attending public schools. At about the age of seven he had a narrow escape from drowning, which was interpreted as a providential act for his future. In 1854, when Harris was ten, the family moved to Delaware, Ohio, and three years later moved again to Cleveland, Ohio. He graduated from Cleveland High School in 1861 and took some additional training with an eye toward teaching. In 1863 he joined the American Wesleyan Church in Cleveland, led by the Rev. Adam Crooks.

In 1866 he returned to Fayetteville and began teaching with his brother, Robert, under the commission of the American Missionary Association. He joined the

AMEZ Church in 1867 and over the next several years became increasingly involved. He was licensed to preach in 1872 and joined the North Carolina Conference, leaving his teaching career. He served a number of small churches, was ordained deacon on January 4, 1874, and elder later the same year, on December 6, 1874. Because of his education and teaching experience, he was immediately found to be a valuable leader. In 1876 he was elected Assistant General Secretary of the denomination, and in this position he helped organize and write for the new periodical for the church, the *Star of Zion*. In 1878 he was appointed interim General Secretary. On December 17, 1879, he married Maria Elizabeth Guion, with whom he had six children.

About this time Zion Wesley Institute was being moved from its northern location to North Carolina, and Harris was heavily involved in this transaction. He was instrumental in having it located in Salisbury, North Carolina, and became its first principal in 1880. Also in 1880 he was elected General Steward of the church, filling both that and the office of General Secretary until 1884, when the offices were separated, and he continued on as General Secretary. In 1880 he also began a four-year term as business manager for the *Star of Zion*, but resigned in 1882 when he needed to reduced his load of responsibility. From 1882 to 1888, stepping down from the principal's position, he was professor of mathematics at the school, having returned to teaching after all.

In 1888 he was elected bishop (consecrated on May 22), and served in that capacity until his death. He was succeeded as principal of Zion Wesley Institute in 1882 by Joseph Charles Price, and the school was eventually renamed Livingstone College, one of the denomination's most important colleges. He authored several short works, the most well known of which was *Historical Catechism of the A.M.E. Zion Church*, first published in 1898. He was retired in 1916 and passed away the following year.

Harris, Cicero R. *Historical Catechism of the A.M.E. Zion Church*. Charlotte, NC: A.M.E. Zion Publishing House, 1922. 34 pp.
BAW, HUBA, AARS, WWWA (1), *ACAB* (vol.7), *EWM, WWCR, AMEZC, HAMEZC, OHYAMEZC.*

HARRIS, MARQUIS LAFAYETTE (March 8, 1907–October 7, 1966), college president and a bishop of the Methodist Church (now the **United Methodist Church**), was born in Armstrong, Macon County, Georgia, the son of William E. and Estelle M. (Glenn)

Harris. He received his B.S. in 1928 from Clark College in Atlanta, Georgia, his B.D. in 1929 from Gammon Theological Seminary in Atlanta, and his S.T.M. in 1930 from Boston University School of Theology. He supported himself as an instructor in physics, chemistry, and mathematics at Clark College from 1927 to 1929, and as instructor in physics and religion and football coach at Claflin College in Orangeburg, South Carolina, before moving to Ohio in late 1929.

He was ordained deacon in 1928 and elder in 1932. His first appointment was to Kinsman Avenue Methodist Church in Cleveland, Ohio, for a year beginning in April 1930. In April 1931 he was appointed to the Pennsylvania Avenue Methodist Church in Columbus, Ohio, where he stayed for two years. On September 6, 1931, he married Geneva M. Nelson, with whom he had one son. While in Ohio he was a student at Ohio State University, where he received his Ph.D. in philosophy in 1933. From 1933 to 1936 he was dean of Samuel Huston College in Austin, Texas. In 1936 he was elected president of Philander Smith College in Little Rock, Arkansas. Over the next twenty-four years he transformed the small, poverty-stricken school into a significant institution. By cultivating the Methodist constituency in the surrounding conferences, he was able to purchase more land, put up additional buildings, and increase the size of the student body.

Through service in a variety of arenas, Harris became a nationally known Methodist figure. He was a delegate to General Conference beginning in 1940 and was a delegate to the World Methodist Conference in Oxford, England in 1951. In 1952 and again in 1956 he was chair of the Committee on Education of the Jurisdictional Conference. He was on the denomination's General Board of Education from 1956 to 1960. In 1955 he was named Man of the Year in Race Relations in Little Rock and in 1957 received the Phi Beta Sigma Social Action Award. In 1955 he was vice-president of the Arkansas Council of Churches and founder and president of the Gulf Coast Inter-Collegiate Athletic Conference. He served on the general board of the National Council of Churches (1944–51) and the Committee on Church Union (C.O.C.U.). He was on the board of directors of Y.M.C.A. Colored Work, southwestern region. He variously chaired the trustee boards of Clark College, Claflin College, Bethune-Cookman College, and Gammon Theological Seminary. He published a number of books and pamphlets, including *The Voice in the Wilderness* (1941), *Our Tomorrow's World* (1945), *To Magnify Thy Power* (1948), and *Life Can Be Meaningful* (1951).

He was elected bishop in 1960 by the Central

Jurisdiction, the segregated, non-geographical structure within the Methodist Church (eliminated in 1968 with the merger that created the **United Methodist Church**). He was assigned to the Atlantic Coast Episcopal Area and served successfully until his death six years later. In 1961 he attended the World Methodist Conference in Oslo, Norway.

Harris, Marquis Lafayette. *Life Can Be Meaningful.* Boston: Christopher Publishing House, 1951. 195 pp.
———. *Some Conceptions of God in the Gifford Lectures During the Period 1927–1929.* Columbus, OH: The Ohio State University, 1933. 258 pp.
———. *The Voice in the Wilderness.* Boston: The Christopher Publishing House, 1941. 149 pp.
EWM, WWCA (38–40), *WWMC, BDNM* (70), *EBA, BAW, HUBA, AARS.*

HARRISON, SAMUEL (1818–August 11, 1900), pioneer Congregational minister, was born into slavery in Philadelphia, Pennsylvania, the son of William and Jennie Harrison. They belonged to the Bolton family of Savannah, Georgia, but soon gained their freedom. William Harrison died. Jennie Harrison remarried but chose to remain with the Boltons as a family servant. She moved with the Boltons to New York City, and Samuel Harrison remained there until the age of nine, when he returned to Philadelphia to learn shoemaking from an uncle. Jeannie Harrison joined him a few years later to escape his stepfather's alcoholism.

In Philadelphia he and his mother attended Second Presbyterian Church, where Harrison experienced conversion. He set his sights on gaining an education and then entering the ministry. In 1836 he enrolled in a manual labor school in Peterboro, New York. When the school closed in 1837, he had to transfer to Western Reserve College in Hudson, Ohio. There he followed a balanced program of scholarly study and manual skills such as shoemaking. In 1839, out of money, he returned to Philadelphia, where he established his own shoemaking business. He married Ellen Rhodes.

In the 1840s racial tensions with the Irish immigrants escalated, and in 1847 Harrison moved to Newark, New Jersey. Licensed to preach by the Newark Presbytery in April 1848, he assisted **Elymas P. Rogers**, a Black Presbyterian minister, at the Plane Street Presbyterian Church. He continued his studies toward ordination, and in January 1850 became the first regular pastor of the Second Congregational Church in Pittsfield, Massachusetts, the only Black church in town. He was ordained several months later by the Berkshire

Association of Congregational Ministers. His ministry there was successful, and he became a leader in a committee to chase slave catchers out of the county. In 1862, however, internal dissension at the church caused him to leave.

Harrison began recruiting Blacks to serve in the Union Army, and worked with the National Freedmen's Relief Society, a group helping emancipated Blacks in the South Carolina Sea Islands. Governor Andrew heard of Harrison's reputation and appointed him chaplain of the 54th Massachusetts Regiment. He reported for duty on November 12, 1863, but soon realized that for a Black officer to receive the pay due him, much less equal pay with Whites, was a problem. He joined other Black soldiers in lobbying for equal pay, and with the support of Governor Andrew and others, the requested congressional legislation was passed in 1864 and Harrison finally received his money.

Ill health forced Harrison to accept an honorable discharge on March 14, 1864, and for a time he worked again for the National Freedmen's Relief Society. In 1865–66 he shepherded the Union Congregational Church in Newport, Rhode Island, and from 1866 to 1870 he pastored the Sanford Street Congregational Church in Springfield, Massachusetts, a 29–member congregation he lifted to a high of 50. Internal conflicts, however, brought that pastorate to an end, and he went to the 22–member Fourth Congregational Church in Portland, Maine, for a brief stay. In 1872 he moved back to the Second Congregational Church in Pittsfield, where he stayed for the rest of his life. The congregation never numbered beyond about 60 members, but that was a sizable percentage of the Black population of the town. During the 1870s he authored a number of pamphlets denouncing racism and the failures of Reconstruction, though he consistently noted with approval those Whites who had proven themselves friends to Black people. From 1882 to 1884 he was chaplain of the W. W. Rockwell Post of the Grand Army of the Republic, and in 1896 he was recognized as one of the oldest Congregational ministers in western Massachusetts. In 1899 he published his autobiography, *Rev. Samuel Harrison—His Life Story as Told By Himself.* During his career he pastored four of New England's six Black Congregational churches, and another, the Talcott Street congregation in Hartford, Connecticut, tried to secure his services.

Harrison, Samuel. *Pittsfield Twenty-Five Years Ago. A Sermon. Delivered in the Second Congregational Church, Pittsfield, Mass., Jan. 11 and 18th, 1874.* Pittsfield, MA: Chickering and Axtell, 1874. 34 pp.

————. *Rev. Samuel Harrison—His Life Story as Told By Himself.* Pittsfield, MA: Eagle Publishing Company, 1899. 47 pp.

————. *"Shall a Nation be Born at Once?" A Centennial Sermon, Delivered in the Chapel of the Methodist Episcopal Church, July 2, 1876.* Pittsfield, MA: Chickering and Axtell, 1876. 25 pp.

BAHA, HUBA, BAW.

HATCHER, EUGENE CLIFFORD (September 2, 1902–1969), 73rd bishop of the **African Methodist Episcopal Church** (AME), was born in Eufala, Alabama, the son of Clarence George and Julia Ann (Watts) Hatcher. He spent his early years in Tuskegee, Alabama, and experienced conversion in December 1914 at the Cherry Street AME Church in Dothan, Alabama. He graduated from Booker T. Washington High School in Norfolk, Virginia, then was a student for a time at A&T College in Greensboro, North Carolina, before deciding to begin a career in the ministry.

He was licensed to preach on April 21, 1923, by his father, who at that time was presiding elder of the Florala District in Alabama. For a while he made his living as a bond and stock salesman with the Powell Realty Company in Jacksonville, Florida. He joined the South Alabama Conference in November 1923, was ordained deacon in 1924, and elder in 1925. His first pastorate was not in Alabama and was surprisingly large: the Wayman Chapel AME Church (105 members) in South Jacksonville, Florida, from 1924 to 1927. He was very successful in paying off a mortgage, and then was assigned to New Hope AME Church (236 members) in Jacksonville, Florida, from 1927 to 1929, where he also paid off a mortgage. From 1929 to 1930 he was assigned to South Street AME Church (300 members) in Dothan, Alabama. Meanwhile he was striving to complete his undergraduate work and received his B.A. in 1930 from Daniel Payne College in Birmingham, Alabama.

In 1930 Bishop **R. A. Grant** appointed him presiding elder, a position he held for the next eleven years, variously on the Florala and Ozark Districts. Also in 1930 he married Oretha May Tillman, with whom he had two children. For twelve years he was accountant for the six conferences in Alabama, and was known for his successful evangelistic meetings. At one point he served as professor of mathematics and chemistry at Bethel College in Montgomery, Alabama. In 1940 he was elected editor of the *Southern Christian Recorder*, holding that position until 1952 (being re-elected in 1944 and 1948).

In 1952 he was elected bishop and assigned to the Fourteenth Episcopal District (West Africa), where he became a close friend of President Tubman of Liberia, who gave him the honorary title of Knight-Commander. He built Hatcher Hall at Monrovia College, and several churches. In 1954, at the death of Bishop **John H. Clayborn**, he was assigned to the Thirteenth Episcopal District (Tennessee and Kentucky), and in 1956 was assigned to the Third Episcopal District (Western Pennsylvania, Ohio, and West Virginia). In Ohio he purchased the Episcopal residence in Cleveland and raised large amounts of money for Wilberforce University. He was president of the board of trustees of Wilberforce and was a trustee of Payne Theological Seminary at Wilberforce and of Daniel Payne College. For many years he was on the General Board of the National Council of Churches and was a delegate to the World Methodist Conference in Oslo, Norway, in 1961. He was famous for a hymn that he popularized throughout the connection, called "The Storm is Passing Over."

"Biography of Bishop Eugene Clifford Hatcher." *AME Quarterly Review* 96 (January–March 1969): 48–49.
EWM, BDNM (70), *BAMEC, HAMEC.*

HATZAAD HARISON. Hatzaad, literally "the First Step," was founded in 1964 as a meeting ground for members of the larger White Jewish community and **Black Judaism**. It was organized by Ya'akov Gladstone, a Canadian Jewish leader who was teaching in New York. He learned of a Black Jewish group in the Bronx and was very impressed by a visit he made to their center. They turned out to be immigrants from the West Indies whose families had been Jews for a number of generations. He arranged for a group of the center's children to sing at the 1964 celebration of Israel's Independence Day which resulted in a meeting at the Brotherhood Synagogue in Manhattan of those who desired to bring the Black Jews into closer contact with White Jews. The Brotherhood Synagogue's leader, Rabbi Irving J. Block, was already a supporter of the claims of the Black Jews and manifested his support by leading the synagogue to integrate over the next decade.

The organization gained a very favorable response from White Jewish leaders, and rabbis from Orthodox, Conservative and Reform traditions provided initial support. The American Zionist Youth Foundation provided secretarial help. Grants by the New York Federation of Jewish Philanthropies backed a program to relocate Black Jews within New York and New Jersey from African American areas to predominantly Jewish areas. The Lubavitch Hassidic community accepted the Black Jewish children in their schools.

However, after a burst of enthusiasm, the support for Hatzaad Harison became involved in a bitter debate over the necessity of the Black Jews ritually converting before being recognized by the White Jewish community. Whites argued that they had to go through the formal conversion process while Blacks, especially those in their third or fourth generation of Jewish practice, balked. The organization died in the midst of the unresolved differences. Its ideals continue to some extent in the Brotherhood Synagogue.

"The Black Jews." *Newsweek* (December 26, 1966): 44.

Block, Irving J. "The Black Jewish Community." *The Jewish Digest* (December 1966): 66–68.

Goldreich, Gloria. "Hatzaad Harison: First Step in the Integration of Black Jews." *Hadassah Magazine* 48, 5 (January 1967): 13, 31.

HAVEN INSTITUTE. A Methodist Episcopal Church school. Haven Institute began as the dream of Moses Adams, a Methodist preacher in Mississippi during the slave era. He began the school in his home in Meridian, Mississippi, in 1865, immediately after the Civil War. Organized by Blacks and always in their control, its work was included in the agenda of the Mississippi Mission Conference founded in 1865 by the Methodist Episcopal Church and for many years was in the Mississippi Conference created in 1869 by the division of the Mission Conference.

The school's most outstanding leader was J. B. F. Shaw, who after graduating from Rust College had studied at the University of Chicago. In 1916 he had become president of Central Alabama Institute, and moved to the presidency of Haven in 1921. At the time of Shaw's arrival, the school had just purchased a new campus, the former home of a girls' school, the Meridian College and Conservatory. Unfortunately, the school could not survive the financial pressures of the Depression, and it ceased to exist in the early 1930s.

Sowell, J. S. *Methodist Adventures in Negro Education*. New York: Methodist Book Concern, 1922. 190 pp.

HAWKINS, EDLER GARNETT (June 13, 1908– December 18, 1977), national Presbyterian leader and educator, was born in the Bronx, New York City, to Albert and Annie (Lee) Hawkins. He attended the public schools for a while, but when his father died in 1914 he went to work to help support the family. The family attended St. James Presbyterian Church in Manhattan. Hawkins attended night school, painted houses by day, and eventually went to Bloomfield College in New Jersey, where he received his B.A. in 1936. He then went to Union Theological Seminary, where he received his B.D. in 1938. He was ordained on June 19, 1938.

His first pastorate was at St. Augustine Presbyterian Church at Prospect Avenue and East 165th Street in the Bronx. This had formerly been Woodstock Presbyterian Church, with an all-White congregation that moved out as the Blacks moved in, leaving an almost deserted church. His initial congregation was nine Blacks, but support was provided by the St. James Church. He stayed at St. Augustine's until 1970, slowly building a multiracial congregation of more than one thousand, with three ministers and support staff. On January 30, 1944, he married Thelma Burnett, a nurse, with whom he had two children.

Hawkins was concerned with relating the church to the community, and founded Fellowship House (a community center) and helped establish Bohatom Camp to serve the inner-city youth. He began the Forest Community Committee, which in turn established a health center, several schools, and public and cooperative housing. He developed ties with the Hispanic community, and in 1959 hired Julio Garcia as minister for that population. He founded the Bronx Protestant Council. In 1948 he ran as a Democrat for the state assembly, the primary goal being, he said, not to win but to make the Black community more aware that they needed to organize politically. He was very active in the civil rights struggle, joining demonstrations and picket lines.

During this time he built a reputation in the denomination for tact and ability. In 1958 he was elected moderator of the Presbytery of New York City, the first Black in that position, and held the office for two years. In 1960 he narrowly missed election as moderator of the General Assembly of the United Presbyterian Church in the United States of America (which in 1983 merged with the Presbyterian Church in the United States to form the **Presbyterian Church U.S.A.**), and instead became vice-moderator. In 1963 he gave a powerful speech at the General Assembly which helped move the assembly to organize the Commission on Religion and Race, which he co-chaired from 1964 to 1972. He is given primary credit for keeping this commission afloat during its early years, despite its often controversial activities in support of civil rights. He was a guiding counsel behind Black Presbyterians United. In 1964, at the 176th General Assembly in Oklahoma City, he won the position of moderator by a vote of 465 to 368. He was the first Black to hold this highest position in the Presbyterian Church, a mostly White church, and was the first Black in any of the major White churches to hold the highest position.

In July and August 1964, Hawkins took a tour, traditional for the moderator, of countries around the world, including Africa, the Middle East, and Europe. He had a private audience with Pope Paul VI, the first moderator of the United Presbyterian Church to visit a pope. In 1968 he was a delegate to the World Council of Churches meeting in Uppsala, Sweden, at which time he was elected to the Central Committee of the World Council. The following year he played a key role in persuading the Central Committee to adopt the Programme to Combat Racism, which is still in operation.

In 1971 he retired from his pastorate and became a faculty member of Princeton Theological Seminary in New Jersey as professor of practical theology. He also became Princeton's first Coordinator of Black Studies and was the unofficial dean of Black students. He died of a heart attack the year of his anticipated retirement.

"Organizations and Leaders Campaigning for Negro Goals in the United States." *New York Times* (August 10, 1964): 16.
Edler G. Hawkins: Racial Justice and the Church. New York: Church and Society, 1987. 118 pp.
IBAW, WWABA (85), *NYTO, CB* (65), *BDNM*.

HAWKINS, JOHN RUSSELL (May 31, 1862–1939), educator and national officer of the **African Methodist Episcopal Church** (AME), was born in Warrenton, North Carolina, the son of Ossian and Christiana (Eaton) Hawkins. He grew up attending the local AME Church and attending school part-time, when it was possible to be absent from farm work. At age fifteen he scored the highest in a teaching exam and became assistant teacher in his local graded school. In 1881 he went to Hampton Normal and Agricultural Institute in Hampton, Virginia, where he spent one year in special study in preparation for business.

In 1882 he accepted a position as railway postal clerk on the line between Raleigh, North Carolina, and Norfolk, Virginia. He spent three years compiling an excellent record, then in 1885 returned to Warrenton and was made principal of the graded school. There he spent two years teaching and reading law under private tutors. In 1887 he went to Kittrell Normal and Industrial Institute in North Carolina as business manager and

treasurer. He so impressed everyone that in 1890 he became president of the school. On December 28, 1892, he married Lillian M. Kennedy, with whom he had two children. His wife was the granddaughter of **Richard Allen**, founding bishop of the AME Church.

Hawkins remained president of the school until 1896, traveling extensively to raise funds. He was successful in raising large amounts of money for the school and led the trustees into changing the nature of the curriculum to include a regular college course. He gained a reputation as one of the finest public speakers of his time. In 1896 he was elected commissioner of education for the AME Church, a position later changed to secretary of education. He was reelected every four years until 1912, when he was elected financial secretary, which position he held for the rest of his life.

His office as financial secretary was in Washington, D.C. and he took the opportunity to continue his education at Howard University, earning his law degree (LL.B.) in 1915. He was a trustee of Kittrell College, a trustee of Wilberforce University in Ohio, and a trustee (1925–39) of Howard University. He was a life member of the Association for the Study of Negro Life and History and was its president from 1921 to 1932. He was president of the Prudential Bank (later called the Industrial Bank of Washington) in Washington, D.C. and chair of the Colored Voters Division of the National Republican Committee in 1928. He was active in the N.A.A.C.P., and after President Woodrow Wilson presented his Fourteen Points for world peace in 1918 Hawkins presented to the N.A.A.C.P. his own Fourteen Points toward the implementation of true democracy in the United States. His major published writing was done as an associate editor under **Richard R. Wright** of the *Centennial Encyclopedia of the African Methodist Episcopal Church* (1916).

Wright, Richard R., Jr., and John Russell Hawkins, eds. *Centennial Encyclopaedia of the African Methodist Episcopal Church.* Philadelphia, PA: Book Concern of the AME Church, 1916. 387 pp.
Hawkins, John Russell. *What Does the Negro Want? Fourteen Articles as a Basis for Democracy at Home.* N.d.
DANB, WWCA (38–40), *EBA, WWCR, TCNL*.

HAYES, GREGORY WILLIS (September 8, 1862– ?), first president of the **National Baptist Educational Convention of the United States** and second president of Virginia Baptist Theological Seminary, was born into slavery in Amelia County, Virginia. He graduated in 1888 from Oberlin College in Ohio and was elected to the chair of pure mathematics in the Virginia Normal and Collegiate Institute. He also became the first president of the National Baptist Educational Convention of the United States and was commissioner-in-chief from Virginia for the Southern Inter-State Exposition.

On January 30, 1890, the first students were admitted to the Virginia Baptist Theological Seminary and College near Lynchburg, founded by the Virginia Baptist State Convention, though open to students of all denominations. Its first president, P. F. Morris, had already had to resign due to poor health, so Hayes, his immediate successor, was the real pioneer leader of the school. Starting with major obstacles of poor funding and few resources, Hayes nevertheless was able to construct a large building on the grounds. His philosophy was "self-help and spiritual independence," and the school became a major influence on Black Baptists in Virginia.

HBB.

HAYNES, GEORGE EDMUND (May 11, 1880– January 8, 1960), vice-moderator of the General Council of the Congregational Christian Churches (now an integral part of the **United Church of Christ**), an executive of the Federal (now National) Council of Churches, co-founder of the National Urban League, and sociologist, was born in Pine Bluff, Arkansas, the son of Louis and Mattie (Sloan) Haynes. Educational opportunities for Blacks in Pine Bluff and in Hot Springs (where the family later moved) were very limited. After a year at the Agriculture and Mechanical College in Normal, Alabama (1895), he transferred to Fisk University in Nashville, Tennessee, where he finished the high school department in 1899 and went on to receive his B.A. in 1903. He earned an M.A. in 1904 from Yale University in New Haven, Connecticut and then entered Yale University Divinity School, but dropped out after one year to help finance his sister's education. Although he was never ordained, he did pastor the small Congregational Church in Haverhill, Massachusetts in the summer of 1905. From September 1, 1905, to 1908 he was Secretary of the Colored Men's Department for the International Committee of the Y.M.C.A., for which he visited many Black colleges, and during the summers he took courses at Chicago University. From 1908 to 1910 he was a fellow of the Bureau of Social Research at the New York School of Philanthropy (later the New York School of Social Work at Columbia University). In 1910 he was the first Black

graduate of that institution, and that year founded the Social Science Department at Fisk University. Also in 1910 he co-founded with Mrs. William Henry Baldwin the Committee on Urban Conditions Among Negroes (now the National Urban League), a social service organization to improve the living conditions of urban Blacks. For the next seven years he served as its first executive director. On November 19, 1910, he married Elizabeth Ross, also a sociologist, with whom he had one son. In 1911 he was one of the founders and the first secretary (until 1916) of the Association of Colleges and Secondary Schools (Negro). In addition to those responsibilities he continued his research, and in 1912 received the Ph.D. in economics from Columbia University in New York. He was the first Black Ph.D. recipient at Columbia. His dissertation was published as *The Negro at Work in New York City: A Study in Economic Progress*. He was a charter member of the N.A.A.C.P. and the Association for the Study of Negro Life and History.

From 1918 to 1921 he took a leave from Fisk University to be special assistant to the U.S. Secretary of Labor as Director of Negro Economics. In 1920–21 he was Special Advisor on Negro Work for the Interchurch World Movement of North America. In 1921 he wrote *Negroes at Work During the World War and During Reconstruction* for the Department of Labor, and that year was a key organizer and the first executive secretary of the Department of Race Relations of the Federal (now National) Council of Churches. It is no wonder he gained a reputation for "always being first." He left Fisk and remained head of the Race Relations Department for sixteen years. From 1922 to 1924 he was co-executive of the Southern Interracial Commission and from 1925 to 1930 he administered the William E. Harmon Awards for Distinguished Achievement Among Negroes. He was a member of Grace Congregational Church in New York City and served as vice-chair of the Board of Home Missions and vice-moderator of the General Council of the Congregational Christian Churches.

In 1930 he took a brief leave from the Federal Council of Churches to make a social survey of Y.M.C.A. work in South Africa for the International Committee of Y.M.C.A.s. He wrote several books, including *Negro Newcomers to Detroit* (1918) and *The Trend of the Races* (1922). In the latter book he asserted his belief that the only solution to racial tensions was the application of good will as set forth in the Christian gospel. His views on Black/White relations were somewhere between those of **Booker T. Washington** and W. E. B. DuBois. He was co-author of the article on the American Negro in the *Encyclopedia Britannica* in 1929 and from 1941 to 1952. He became a trustee of both Dillard University and Fisk University and treasurer/director of the American Committee on Africa, Inc. In his work with the Federal Council of Churches he created Race Relations Sunday (the second Sunday of each February), now observed by at least sixteen national church bodies. He sponsored interracial clinics on the local, state, and national levels, wrote articles for the media, and pressed the religious community to work on race relations.

In 1947 he retired from his position with the Federal Council of Churches and made another survey of the Y.M.C.A. programs in Africa, which he presented at the World's Committee of Y.M.C.A.s Plenary in Edinburg, Scotland. In 1950 he published a result of his observations as *Africa—Continent of the Future.* From 1948 to 1955 he worked as consultant for Africa for the World's Committee of Y.M.C.A.s. He was a trustee of the State University of New York from its establishment in 1948 until 1953. In 1955 he was one of the New York State delegates to the White House Conference on Education in Washington, D.C. His first wife died in 1953 and on April 12, 1955, he married Olyve Love Jeter. From 1950 until the onset of illness in November, 1959 he taught a variety of courses at the College of the City of New York, including Negroes in American History, Africa in World Affairs, and Principles and Methods of Interracial Adjustment.

Haynes, George Edmund. *Africa, Continent of the Future.* New York: Association Press; Geneva, Switzerland: World's Committee of Young Men's Christian Associations, 1950. 516 pp.

———. *The Negro at Work During the World War and During Reconstruction.* Washington, DC: U.S. Department of Labor, 1921.

———. *The Negro at Work in New York City: A Study in Economic Progress.* New York: Longmans, Green & Co., 1912. 158 pp.

———. *Negro Newcomers in Detroit, Michigan; A Challenge to Christian Statesmanship.* New York: Home Missions Council, 1918. 42 pp.

———. *The Trend of the Races.* New York: Council of Women for Home Missions and Missionary Education of the United States and Canada, 1922. 205 pp.

Parris, Guichard and Lester Brooks. *Blacks in the City: A History of the National Urban League.* Boston, MA: Little, Brown, 1971. 534 pp.

Perlman, Daniel. *Stirring the White Conscience: The Life of George Edmund Haynes.* New York: Ph.D dissertation, New York University, 1972.

Weiss, Nancy J. *The National Urban League, 1910–1940.* New York: Oxford University Press, 1974. 402 pp.

DANB, NYTO, CH, EBA, AAE, WWWA (3), DAB (supp.6), NCAB (44), CB (1946), WWCA (38–40), HUBA,BAW, AARS, IBAW, IBAWCB, BA, WWCR.

HAYNES, LEMUEL (July 18, 1753–September 28, 1833), the first ordained Black Congregational minister, was born in West Hartford, Connecticut. He did not know his father, a Black man, and his mother was a New England White woman who later refused to have any connection with him. He was bound over while still a baby as an indentured servant to Deacon David Rose in Granville, Massachusetts. Rose treated him well, allowed him to attend public school, read books, and go to church with the family at the Middle Granville Congregational Church.

His period of indentureship ended in 1774, when he turned twenty-one, and he enlisted as a Minute Man at the siege of Boston. In 1776 he fought with Ethan Allen and the Green Mountain Boys at Ticonderoga. After his war service he returned to Granville and worked on a farm. He increased his own education as he could, turning down an offer to go to Dartmouth College and instead studying Greek and Latin with White pastors, Daniel Farrand of Canaan, Connecticut, and William Bradford of Wintonbury. He taught school for a time in Wintonbury. On November 20, 1780, he was rigorously examined and given a license to preach. He preached to the Congregational Church in Middle Granville for the next five years, becoming perhaps the first Black in America to lead a White congregation. On September 22, 1783, he married Elizabeth Babbit, a White schoolteacher in the town, with whom he had ten children.

On November 9, 1785, at the age of twenty-two, he was ordained by the Congregational Ministerial Association in Litchfield County, becoming the first ordained Black Congregational minister. His first official "call" was in Torrington, Connecticut, where he pastored in 1786–1787. There remained a heavy prejudice there against him, and in 1788 he left to pastor a Congregational church in Rutland, Vermont. This proved to be a good match, and he stayed there thirty years, bringing the church from 42 members to over 300. This was where he made his lasting fame, primarily in theological disputation with Hosea Ballou, the Universalist minister whose *Treatise on the Atonement* was published in 1804, and whose church was in the area. Haynes disagreed with Ballou's belief in universal salvation, and in 1805 published a satirical rejoinder, *Universal Salvation* (originally a sermon). This achieved a vast number of editions both in America and in England. Even before this attention, Middlebury College in Vermont was impressed enough to give Haynes an honorary M.A. degree in 1804, the first American Black so honored.

The last few years at Rutland were soured, however, by diehard racism and a clash of political views. Haynes opposed the War of 1812, but denounced the planned secession of New England, which had popular backing. Finally, he left in 1818 for a church in Manchester, Vermont. There he gained additional fame through involvement in the 1820 case of Russell Colvin, who had disappeared from Manchester in 1813. Colvin's two brothers-in-law were finally sentenced to death for his murder, but Haynes proclaimed their innocence. 37 days before the scheduled hanging, Colvin showed up, and Haynes became an instant sensation. His pamphlet on the case, *Mystery Developed*, which also included discussions of religion and prison conditions, was a bestseller for years.

In 1822 he left Manchester for Granville, New York, where he pastored until his death. He is known to have opposed slavery, but did not make much of an issue of it in his ministry.

Morse, W. H. "Lemuel Haynes." *Journal of Negro History* 4 (January 1919): 22–32.

Cooley, Timothy Mather. *Sketches of the Life and Character of the Rev. Lemuel Haynes.* New York: Harper & Brothers, 1837. 345 pp.

Haynes, Lemuel. *An Entertaining Controversy, Between Rev. Lemuel Haynes . . . and Rev. Hosea Ballou. . . .* Sag-Harbor, NY: Printed by Alden Spooner, 1810. 60 pp.

———. *The Influence of Civil Government on Religion.* Rutland, VT: Printed by John Walker, 1798. 17 pp.

———. *Mystery Developed, or Russell Colvin (Supposed to be Murdered) in Full Life.* Hartford, CT: William S. Marsh, 1820. 48 pp.

———. *The Nature and Importance of True Republicanism: With a Few Suggestions, Favorable to Independence.* Rutland, VT: William Fay, Printer, 1801. 24 pp.

———. *Universal Salvation, A Very Ancient Doctrine.* Brattleboro, VT: William Fessenden, 1806. 8 pp.

Newman, Richard. *Lemuel Haynes: A Bio-Bibliography.* New York: Lambeth Press, 1984. 138 pp.

DANB, BPEAR, NG, MM, HNB, NBH, CH, PHNA, NCAB (12), *ACAB, CP, BAW, AARS, HUBA, IBAW, NYB* (1925–26).

HAYWOOD, GARFIELD THOMAS

HAYWOOD, GARFIELD THOMAS (July 15, 1880–April 12, 1931), the first presiding bishop of the

Pentecostal Assemblies of the World (PAW), was born in Greencastle, Indiana, the third of eight children in the family of Benjamin and Penny Ann Haywood. When he was three years old the family moved to Haughville, Indianapolis, Indiana. His father worked in a local foundry and the family made do with very little income. Early on Haywood was drawn to church life; he became Sunday School superintendent for both the Methodist church and St. Paul Baptist Church in Haughville.

He was a gifted artist and after finishing two years of Shortridge High School was hired as a cartoonist for the Black weekly papers *Freedman* and *Recorder*. On February 11, 1902, he married Ida Howard, with whom he had one daughter. In 1906 **William Joseph Seymour**'s Azusa Street Mission in Los Angeles, California created the foundation of modern **Pentecostalism**, and in 1907 some visitors to that mission began to hold meetings in Indianapolis. In 1908 Haywood joined the newly founded Apostolic Faith Assembly on Michigan and Minerva Streets and received the Pentecostal signs of the Holy Spirit. In February 1909 he succeeded Elder Henry Prentiss as pastor of the thirteen-member congregation, and they moved to Twelfth and Lafayette Streets.

Over the following years the church grew in response to Haywood's inspired leadership. His preaching was not only informed by the Bible, much of which he had memorized, but by wide reading of secular magazines and books. In April 1910 he published the first issue of the *Voice in the Wilderness*, and thereafter he put out issues at irregular intervals, using a printing press he set up in his home. He also issued a number of pamphlets and used his artistic skills to create elaborate charts and biblical drawings. He published a hymnal, *The Bridegroom Cometh*, which contained many hymns of his own composition. In 1912 the church moved to Eleventh and Senate Streets. The congregation joined the Pentecostal Assemblies of the World (PAW) and in 1912 Haywood's new church hosted its annual meeting.

In 1914 the "Jesus Only" teaching worked its way through the PAW, identifying Jesus as the Jehovah of the Old Testament and denying the Trinity. Haywood was converted to this view and was rebaptized in the name of Jesus only. Soon the PAW made this the official doctrine. In 1918 Haywood was elected secretary-treasurer of the PAW and was the first editor of its periodical, the *Christian Outlook* (until 1930). In 1924 Haywood's congregation moved to a new, 1,200–seat sanctuary at Fall Creek Boulevard and Paris Avenue and renamed itself Christ Temple. This was now one of the largest Pentecostal churches in the world. In 1924 racial tensions within the PAW caused most of the White members to leave and form the Pentecostal Ministerial Alliance (now part of the United Pentecostal Church). The PAW reorganized, created the office of bishop, and elected Haywood as the first bishop. Under his leadership the PAW regained an even keel and a solid foundation for future growth. He remained as pastor of Christ Temple, and was known as a progressive thinker who pressed for musical instruments and choirs in the face of opposition to such "worldliness." During a 1929 trip to the Holy Land he used a motion picture camera to record his experiences, but opposition to motion pictures upon his return prevented him from sharing it with many people.

Dugas, Paul D., ed. *The Life and Writings of Elder G. T. Haywood*. Portland, OR: Apostolic Book Publishers, 1968.

Golder, Morris E. *The Bishops of the Pentecostal Assemblies of the World*. Indianapolis, IN: The Author, 1980. 69 pp.

———. *History of the Pentecostal Assemblies of the World*. Indianapolis, IN: The Author, 1973. 195 pp.

———. *The Life and Works of Bishop Garfield Thomas Haywood*. Indianapolis, IN: The Author, 1977. 71 pp.

Haywood, Garfield Thomas. *The Birth of the Spirit in the Days of the Apostles*. Indianapolis, IN: Christ Temple Book Store, n. d. 40 pp.

———. *Feed My Sheep*. Indianapolis, IN: Christ Temple Book Store, n. d. 62 pp.

———. *The Finest of the Wheat*. Portland, OR: Apostolic Book Publishers, n. d. 90 pp.

———. *A Trip to the Holy Land*. Indianapolis, IN: N.p., 1927. 77 pp.

———. *The Victim of the Flaming Sword*. Indianapolis, IN: Christ Temple Book Store, n. d. 71 pp.

BAW, BDACSL, BH, BDA-AHP, RLOA.

HEALY, ALEXANDER SHERWOOD (January 24, 1836–October 21, 1875), the second African American priest of the **Roman Catholic Church** (after his brother **James Augustine Healy** in 1854), was born on a plantation in western Georgia, one of ten children. His father, Michael Morris Healy, was the Irish owner of the plantation, and his mother, Mary Eliza Clark, was one of the mulatto slaves on the plantation. The two had been married in 1829, though such a marriage could not be legally recognized at the time. This family produced a host of Catholic leaders, including **James A. Healy**, who went on to become the first African American Catholic bishop.

In 1844 Healy was enrolled at Holy Cross College in Worcester, Massachusetts, there joining his older brothers. With them he was baptized in November 1844.

Healy showed great scholastic promise, but never graduated. When his brother Patrick left the school in 1850 for New York City so did he, finding a clerk's position in a wholesale warehouse. After two years he tired of this and entered the Sulpician Seminary in Montreal in September 1852. He learned French easily, but had some difficulties there, compounded by poor eyesight and general health. After a summer under a doctor's care in Boston he decided to join brother James at the Sulpician Seminary at Issy-les-Molineaux near Paris, France, departing from New York on September 1, 1853. This leave-taking was marred by the fact that his brother Hugh, on a small skiff in the harbor to wave goodbye to him, was capsized by another vessel, swallowed some contaminated water, contracted typhoid, and was dead within a few weeks.

Despite that tragedy, life in Paris was an excellent remedy for Healy, and he once again excelled in his studies. After two years he transferred to Apollonio College in Rome. He was ordained to the priesthood on December 15, 1858, received a D.D. degree, and in 1860 finished his doctorate in Canon Law. He was also a fine musician, and when he returned to the United States brought with him one of the best collections of classical sacred music in the country. He was such an impressive figure that in 1859, without his knowledge, he was considered for the post of rector for the new North American College in Rome.

Healy arrived in Boston, Massachusetts, in September 1860 and was assigned as assistant in the House of the Angel Guardian in Roxbury, a boys' school. In 1863, when his brother James was forced to take an extended leave for health reasons, Healy filled in for him as chancellor of the diocese and assistant at the cathedral. By the time James Healy returned in 1864, Alexander Healy was the one who needed a prolonged rest to recover his health. He was then assigned as a faculty member of the new provincial seminary in Troy, New York. He taught moral theology, church music, and rites and rubrics and was confessor and spiritual guide to the students. He put together a seminarians' *Manual of Plain Chant*, which was used for many years as a basic text in church music. He also composed a number of original works, including the popular Troy *Magnificat*.

In 1866 Bishop Williams chose him to be his personal theologian at the Second Plenary Council of Baltimore and again at the First Vatican Council in Rome in 1870. After that event Healy's health, especially his eyesight, had deteriorated to the point where he could not continue his teaching duties. Even while still in Rome, in March he fell so ill that he was given the Last Rites. He recovered, however, and once back in the United States was assigned as rector of the new cathedral on Washington and Malden Streets in Boston, still being built. This position was presumably to be less taxing on his health, but he became responsible for the tremendous fund-raising efforts required for the massive church. He even trained and conducted the Boston Choral Union for fund-raising concerts. He began a magazine, the *Cathedral*, that became a long-lived monthly. He was in great demand as an eloquent preacher and speaker. In March 1875 he was made priest of St. James Church, from which his brother James had just been made bishop, and began his duties there on April 5. He lived to attend his brother's consecration in June, but two lung hemorrhages on August 23 soon brought the end of his life. Thousands attended his funeral at St. James, paying tribute to him as a remarkable man and beloved priest.

HBCUS, IBAW, BMOC.

HEALY, ELIZA (December 23, 1846–September 13, 1919), the first Black convent superior, was born in Macon, Jones County, Georgia, one of ten children of Michael Morris Healy, an Irish plantation owner, and Mary Eliza Clark, his common-law wife and mulatto slave. The two considered themselves married in 1829, though such a marriage could never be officially sanctioned under Georgia laws. Besides Eliza Healy, the family produced other **Roman Catholic Church** leaders, including **Patrick Healy**, president of Georgetown University, and **James A. Healy**, the first Black American bishop.

When both mother and father died within a few months of each other in 1850, the three youngest children—Eliza, Amanda Josephine, and Eugene— were sent to New York to stay with their older brother, Hugh. The children were baptized as Catholics on June 13, 1851, and in September the two girls were sent to live with the Notre Dame sisters in St. Johns, Quebec, where an elder Healy sister, Martha, had just become a novitiate. Eliza's secondary education was at Villa Maria, in Montreal. In 1861 Eliza and Amanda Josephine joined Eugene and his foster family, the Hodges, in Boston. In 1864 older brother James, now a priest, was able to purchase a home in West Newton, near Boston, where the family members moved.

In 1874 Eliza decided to become a nun and entered the novitiate of the Congregation of Notre Dame in Montreal. She took her initial vows on July 19, 1876, and final vows on August 30, 1882. She took the name

Sister Mary Magdalene and was assigned to teach at St. Patrick's School in Montreal, and subsequently at other schools in Ontario and Quebec. In 1895 she went to Huntington School in Quebec, which she saved from financial insolvency while at the same time overseeing its community of French Canadian nuns. In 1898 she moved to the Mother House in Montreal to teach English studies, and from 1900 to 1903 she taught at the order's Normal School in Montreal.

In 1903 she moved to her most significant assignment at Villa Barlow at St. Albans, Vermont, a prestigious school where she was both principal of the school and superior of the convent. This high rank was a first for a Black American nun. As at the Huntington School, the Villa Barlow was in weak financial condition, and its physical plant was deteriorating. Healy managed, through dedicated leadership, to restore the school to top condition. Her devotional life, gracious bearing, and hard work were unstinting, and she gained the respect of the diocesan officials and the sisters with whom she worked. In 1918 her final assignment was as superior at the College of Notre Dame on Staten Island, New York. Unfortunately, an injury to her arm at the beginning of the school year resulted in an infection which soon took her life.

Fairbanks, Henry G. "Slavery and the Vermont Clergy." *Vermont History* 27 (October 1959): 305–312.
Foley, Albert S. *Bishop Healy: Beloved Outcast.* New York: Farrar, Straus, and Young, 1954. 248 pp.
DANB, OBS, RLOA, AAE, NBAW.

HEALY, JAMES AUGUSTINE (April 6, 1830– August 5, 1900), the first African American bishop of the **Roman Catholic Church**, was born on a plantation near Macon, Georgia, the first of ten children. His father, Michael Morris Healy, was an Irish plantation owner, and his mother, Mary Eliza Clark, was one of his mulatto slaves. They were married in 1829, though such a marriage could not be officially recognized. Several in this family, besides James, would become noted figures in Catholicism, namely brothers **Alexander Sherwood Healy**, **Patrick Francis Healy**, and sisters **Eliza Healy** and Josephine Healy.

To avoid Georgia's slavery laws, Healy studied in Quaker schools in Long Island and New Jersey. In 1844, thanks to the intervention of Bishop Fitzpatrick of Boston, Healy and several brothers were allowed to enroll in the program at the new Holy Cross College in Worcester, Massachusetts. They received religious instruction and were baptized on November 14, 1844.

In 1849 Healy was valedictorian of the first graduating class of Holy Cross.

Healy decided to become a priest and was accepted in 1849 at the Grand Séminaire at Montreal, Canada, managing to get by the problem of providing a copy of his parents' marriage certificate. In 1851 he returned to Holy Cross to receive his Master of Arts degree, and in 1852 he transferred to the Seminary of St. Sulpice in Paris, France, for continuing studies. He was ordained priest on June 10, 1854 in the Notre Dame Cathedral, the first Black American Catholic priest. Shortly afterward he returned to the United States and was assigned as assistant to Father Haskins at the Guardian Angel Orphanage in Boston. Late that year Bishop Fitzpatrick made Healy his personal secretary, and then diocesan chancellor. Due to declining health, the bishop relied heavily on Healy. From 1857 to 1866 Healy was rector of the Cathedral of the Holy Cross in Boston.

In 1866 Fitzpatrick's successor appointed Healy to St. James Church in South Boston, one of the largest churches in the diocese. Despite some initial resistance, the congregation, composed mostly of poor, immigrant Irish, came to accept and respect its new priest. During the typhoid and tuberculosis epidemics he administered his duties with no thought to his own health. He oversaw the building of a new basilica-style sanctuary that stands today. He became a champion of the poor, leading the development of the Home for Destitute Catholic Children, St. Ann's Foundling Home, and the House of the Good Shepherd for wayward girls.

In February 1875, Pope Pius IX appointed Healy bishop of Portland, a diocese including Maine and New Hampshire. Healy thus became the first African American Catholic bishop. During his tenure the Catholic population grew such that the diocese had to be divided in 1885. The remaining diocese of Maine added sixty churches and sixty-eight mission stations and doubled the number of communicants. He was loved by many as a friend of the poor and the children, building orphanages and battling child labor. Unlike many bishops, he related personally to his parishioners and was often seen performing deeds of kindness for them. On a national level, he was a significant participant in the Third Plenary Council of Baltimore in 1884, helped establish the Catholic University of America in Washington, D.C., and served on the Commission for Negro and Indian Missions. In June 1900, at the twenty-fifth anniversary celebration of his tenure as bishop, Pope Leo XIII sent word that he had appointed Healy Assistant to the Papal Throne, one step below the office of cardinal. He died two months later.

Foley, Albert S. *Bishop Healy: Beloved Outcast.* New York: Farrar, Straus, and Young, 1954. 243 pp.

Lucey, William L. *The Catholic Church in Maine.* Francestown, NH: M. Jones Co., 1957. 372 pp.

BHBA, HNB, IBAW, NA, DANB, EBA, NV, GMC,RLOA, GNPP, NCAB (10), *OBS.*

HEALY, PATRICK FRANCIS (February 27, 1834– January 10, 1910), pioneering Jesuit priest and president of Georgetown University, was born in Jones County, Georgia. His parents were Michael Morris Healy, an Irish plantation owner, and Mary Eliza Clark, his common-law wife and mulatto slave. Besides Patrick Healy, this family produced several Roman Catholic leaders, including **Eliza Healy**, the first Black convent superior, and **James Augustine Healy**, the first Black bishop. At the age of seven, Patrick Healy was sent to join a number of his nine siblings at a Quaker school in Flushing, Long Island, New York. In 1844 he transferred to Holy Cross College in Worcester, Massachusetts, in the footsteps of some of his brothers. He received his bachelor's degree in 1850, at the age of sixteen.

Upon graduation, he decided to enroll as a Jesuit novitiate in Frederick, Maryland. After his initial vows in 1852, he was assigned as teacher at St. Joseph's College in Philadelphia. In 1853 he was transferred to his former school, Holy Cross College, where he taught varied topics from rhetoric to bookkeeping. On November 17, 1858, he headed toward Rome for continued study, but for health reasons transferred the following year to the University of Louvain, Belgium. He was ordained a priest on September 3, 1864, and received a doctorate in philosophy on July 26, 1865, becoming the first Black American to receive a doctorate. In 1866 he returned to the United States as professor of philosophy at Georgetown University in Washington, D.C. He gave his final vows as a Jesuit on February 2, 1867, becoming the first Black American Jesuit priest. In 1868 he became dean of the university, then vice-president in 1869, vice-rector in 1873, and was inaugurated as president on July 31, 1874. He was the first Black president of a Catholic college.

Healy's imprint on Georgetown University was such that he has been called its "second founder." He was responsible for what became known as the Healy Building, a massive administration, classroom, and residential structure linking the Old North and Old South buildings. The cornerstone was laid in late 1877 and construction occupied the better part of the next five years. The burden of raising enough money to cover the construction was a heavy one, but he succeeded not only in that, but also in funding a number of new scholarships for student support. The key to this was the establishment and development of the alumni association. Healy also modernized the curriculum, centralized the library system, and incorporated the law school and medical school into the heart of university life. He was friends with Presidents Johnson, Hayes, and Grant, and participated in the highest social circles of the Washington, D.C. area. For a time he was head of the Catholic Commission on Indian Affairs.

The stress of Healy's many duties took a toll on his health, and he retired on February 16, 1882. In his remaining years, he spent a great deal of time visiting with his brother, Bishop Healy, in Maine, and accompanying him on his travels. When he was at home and physically able, he tended to duties at his official assignments in St. Joseph's Church in Providence, Rhode Island (1891–1894), St. Lawrence Church in New York City (1895–1906), and St. Joseph's Church in Philadelphia (1906–1908). His last years were spent in the infirmary, and he was buried on campus near the Healy Building.

IBAW, DANB, GMC, RLOA.

HEARD, WILLIAM HENRY (June 25, 1850–September 12, 1937), 35th bishop of the **African Methodist Episcopal Church** (AME), was born into slavery in Elbert County, Georgia, one of six children in the family of George W. and Parthenia (Galloway) Heard. His father lived on Thomas Heard's plantation three miles away, and was allowed to visit two nights a week. When his mother's master died, Heard, his mother, and two other children were sold at auction to Lindsay Smith, and stayed for three years at his farm in Rock Fence, Georgia. They were then sold again to Professor Trenchard, a high school principal in Elberton, Georgia. There Heard joined the Methodist Episcopal Church, South, and paid a White boy ten cents a lesson for a basic education. His mother died of typhoid fever when he was nine, and he continued to work the plantation until the Union Army troops came in 1865.

Over the next several years he worked variously on farms or in his father's blacksmith shop and continued to study as much as he could, sometimes formally in school, sometimes with a private tutor, or on his own. One of the farmers for whom he worked was named William Henry Heard, from whom Heard took his first two names. Finally he was able to assist teaching in the public school in Elberton. In January 1873 he obtained a teaching position at Mt. Carmel, South Carolina, for

$20 per month. For two years he studied at the University of South Carolina, and 1876 was elected to the state legislature from Abbeville County. During the 1876 election the Democrats tried to block Republican (Reconstruction) votes by force, and Heard himself was kidnapped and almost killed. In 1877, when he was a sophomore in the classics department, Reconstruction came to an end and all Black students were ejected from the university and from political offices.

He returned to Georgia and opened a school in the Athens AME Church. He spent a semester at Clark College in Atlanta, then entered Atlanta University. He was converted on May 16, 1879, and soon was a licensed exhorter in the AME Church. After a year at Atlanta University he was appointed railway postal clerk (1880), a position he held for two years as he became increasingly involved in the church. He joined the Georgia Annual Conference on July 12, 1880, and attended to pastoral charges as he was able, at the Johnstown Station (1880–81) and Markham Station (1882). His first wife died, and on January 22, 1882, he married Josephine Delphine Henderson; there were no children. He was ordained deacon in 1881 and elder in 1883. In 1883–84 he took his first full-time assignment at Aiken, South Carolina, where in only a short time he built a parsonage, renovated the church building, took in 160 members, and paid off the debt. By leaving the postal position his annual pay was cut from $1,150 to $355.

In 1885 Heard was assigned to Mt. Zion AME Church in Charleston, South Carolina, and in three years paid off a large debt, added a pipe organ, renovated the church, and received 1,100 people into the church. In August 1888 he went to Allen AME Church in Philadelphia, Pennsylvania, and while there took courses at the Reformed Episcopal Seminary. In 1889 he became presiding elder of the Lancaster District, and during that year brought his second suit against the Georgia Railroad for unequal treatment of Blacks. On May 8, 1889, the Interstate Commerce Commission ruled in his favor, but the conditions did not change. From 1890 to 1892 he pastored Mother Bethel Church in Philadelphia, where he finished building the church and raised large amounts of money. From 1892 to 1894 he was at Bethel AME Church in Wilmington, Delaware, where he received 460 new members. In 1894–95 he was appointed to the State Street AME Church in Harrisburg, Pennsylvania, where he again met with great success.

In February 1895, Heard was appointed by President Grover Cleveland as United States Minister Resident and Counsel General to Liberia, a position he held for four years. While there he built the first AME church in Monrovia, Liberia. On returning to America in 1899, he spent one year at Zion Mission AME Church in Philadelphia, one year as presiding elder of the Long Island District in the New York Conference, and then four months at the Phoenixville AME Church in Pennsylvania. In August 1901, he was appointed to the prestigious Allen Temple in Atlanta, Georgia, and that year published a book based on his experiences in Africa, *The Bright Side of African Life*. In 1904 he was elected secretary-treasurer of the Connectional Preachers' Aid and Mutual Relief Society, which he had long supported.

He was elected bishop in 1908 (consecrated on May 20) and assigned to the Thirteenth Episcopal District (Africa), staying there eight years. From 1916 to 1920 he was assigned to the Eighth Episcopal District (Mississippi and Louisiana), followed by the First Episcopal District (1920–1928), Third Episcopal District (1928–1932), and the First District again (1932–1937), which covered New York, New England, New Jersey, Pennsylvania, and Delaware. As bishop he was active in many civic institutions, and was one of the original directors of the Citizen and Southern Bank and Trust Company in Philadelphia. For a time he was president of the Colored National Emigration Association. In 1924 he published the story of his life, *From Slavery to the Bishopric in the AME Church: An Autobiography*. In August, 1937 he attended the World Faith and Order Conference in Edinburgh, Scotland, but the hotel where he had reservations would not accept him, stating that Blacks disturbed the American tourists. The Archbishop of York offered Heard his own home, but Heard found a more congenial hotel. He returned to the United States in apparent good health, but died a few weeks later. Churches are named for him in Pennsylvania, New Jersey, and Bermuda.

Heard, William Henry. *The Bright Side of African Life*. Philadelphia, PA: AME Publishing House, 1898. 184 pp.

———. *From Slavery to the Bishopric in the AME Church: An Autobiography*. Philadelphia, PA: AME Book Concern, 1924. 104 pp.

———. *The Missionary Fields of West Africa*. Philadelphia, PA: AME Book Concern, n.d. 28 pp.

AARS, HUBA, IBAW, IBAWCB, BAW, DNAADB, TCNL, WWCA (38–40), WWWA (1), AAE, EBA, HAMEC, NYTO, NCAB (vol.12), EWM, CEAMEC, WWCR, BAMEC.

HEDGEMAN, ANNA ARNOLD (July 5, 1899– January 17, 1990), executive for the Young Women's Christian Association (Y.W.C.A.) and the National

Council of Churches, was born in Mashalltown, Iowa and reared in Anoka, Minnesota, one of five children in the family of William James and Marie Ellen (Parker) Arnold. She grew up attending the Methodist Episcopal Church in an all-White neighborhood, and had little experience with racial tensions and little sense of her own "Blackness." She graduated from high school in 1918 and enrolled as the first Black student at Hamline University, a Methodist school in St. Paul, Minnesota. She received her B.A. in English in 1922. She wanted to be a schoolteacher in the South, and it did not occur to her that her color would prevent her from getting a position in most parts of the North. In her senior year she did her practice teaching in a Hamline freshman class, thinking it was an honor. She did not find out until years later that the local schools would not accept her as an intern because of her color.

From 1922 to 1924 she taught at Rust College in Holly Springs, Mississippi. In the South she learned about the cruelties of oppression and about the courage and sacrifices of the poor. She and most of the other faculty used some of their meager paychecks to provide glasses, books, tuition money, and other necessities for promising students struggling against all odds. She was outraged that such conditions of oppression were allowed in the United States, but realized that as a Northerner she could have only a limited impact in the South. She decided to do what she could in the North.

Discovering that teaching opportunities were unavailable, in 1924 she accepted an executive position with the Y.W.C.A. in Springfield, Ohio. She had charge of the "Negro branch," with inadequate staff and facilities, and discovered that even she as an executive could not eat in the cafeteria of the main Central branch. About the fall of 1926 she requested a move to the East, where she hoped she could find a freer atmosphere. She became the executive director of the Black Y.W.C.A. branch in Jersey City, New Jersey. Here she was again confronted with poor, segregated facilities and the realities of industrial workers dealing with humiliating conditions and few options. She began to distrust and reject White people as a whole. In the fall of 1927 she accepted a position with the large and successful Harlem Y.W.C.A. in New York City, where she stayed until 1933. In the fall of 1933 she became executive secretary of the Catherine Street branch of the Y.W.C.A. of Philadelphia. She went there because she knew it would involve ongoing relationships with White people, and she was ready to test those possibilities. A short time later, however, on November 1, 1933, she married Merritt Hedgeman and returned with him to New York City.

In the fall of 1934 she gained a supervisory post with the Emergency Relief Bureau of New York City. In 1936 she became Consultant on Race Problems of the City of New York. From 1938 to 1943 she was once again with the Y.W.C.A., aiding in developing community education programs for elementary and high school students. From 1942 to 1944 she was a regional representative with Civilian Defense, and was instrumental in getting Eleanor Roosevelt to help Black nurses find positions in military hospitals.

From February 1944 to 1948, Hedgeman was executive director of the National Council for a Permanent Fair Employment Practices Commission. On February 12, 1949, she became assistant to the head of the Federal Security Agency (now Health, Education, and Welfare) in Washington, D.C. She was the first Black person at the administrative level in that agency, and at $10,000 per year the highest-paid Black woman in government. In the fall of 1952 she went to India for several weeks as an exchange leader for the Department of State. When she returned she had to resign her agency position to make room for the appointees of the new Republican administration. On January 1, 1954, she joined New York Mayor Robert Wagner's cabinet, the first woman and the first Black to serve in the cabinet of a mayor of New York. She was responsible for contacts with welfare, libraries, air pollution control, and other departments.

In 1958 she left city hall to be a public relations consultant for a Black cosmetics firm. The firm soon bought the *New York Age*, one of the oldest Black newspapers in the country, for which she became full-time associate editor and columnist. She left the paper in 1960 and ran unsuccessfully for Congress. In July 1960 she was the keynote speaker for the First Conference of African Women and Women of African Descent in Accra, Ghana. On her return she became a consultant for the Division of Higher Education of the American Missionary Association (**United Church of Christ** Board for Homeland Ministries), particularly to help plan the centennial of six Black colleges which would begin in 1966. She served until 1963.

In August 1963 she was the only woman in the organizing group of the famous March on Washington. Just prior to the March, she was asked to serve as Coordinator of Special Events for the newly created Commission on Religion and Race of the National Council of Churches. Her first assignment was to help mobilize White Protestants across the country to participate in the March on Washington for civil rights. She traveled extensively, explaining the support of the National Council of Churches for the march. In 1964 she

wrote her autobiography, *The Trumpet Sounds*. She remained with the National Council of Churches until 1968, sometimes serving as director of Ecumenical Action. In 1967 she began the Hedgeman Consultant Service in New York City, which served her in active retirement. She was the recipient of numerous awards, including the Frederick Douglass Award from the New York Urban League in 1974. In 1977 she wrote another book, *The Gift of Chaos: Decades of American Discontent*, and in 1978 the National Conference of Christians and Jews honored her as one of the fifty Extraordinary Women of Achievement in New York City. She spent her final years at the Greater Harlem Nursing Home.

"Cabinet Has No Contact with President." *Ebony* 4 (August 1949): 16–18.

Hedgeman, Anna Arnold. *The Gift of Chaos: Decades of American Discontent*. New York: Oxford University Press, 1977. 249 pp.

————. *The Trumpet Sounds: A Memoir of Negro Leadership*. New York: Holt, Rinehart and Winston, 1964. 202 pp.

BWR, EBA, WWAW (74–75), *AAE, CA* (Perm. series), *IDAW, AARS, HUBA, IBAW, CH, IBAWCB, NBAW*.

HEIGHT, DOROTHY IRENE (b. March 24, 1912), civil rights activist, president of the National Council of Negro Women, and Young Women's Christian Association (Y.W.C.A.) executive, was born in Richmond, Virginia, the daughter of James Edward and Fannie (Burroughs) Height. When she was four the family moved to Rankin, Pennsylvania, where she attended integrated schools. Her father was a building contractor and a leader in the local Black Baptist church. Her mother was a nurse who was active in the church missionary society.

She graduated from high school with an excellent academic record and a $1,000 scholarship to college from winning a national oratorical contest sponsored by the Elks. Her speech was on the 13th, 14th, and 15th Amendments to the Constitution. She wanted to enter Barnard, but was told there were already two Blacks there and she would have to wait. Instead she went to New York University, where she helped organize the all-Black Rameses Club, received her B.S. in 1934 and M.A. in Social Work in 1935. She then worked for two years as a caseworker for the New York City Welfare Department. She was introduced to Rev. **Adam Clayton Powell, Sr.** (pastor of the large Abyssinian Baptist Church in Harlem) during that time, who had a great influence on her. She was also influenced by his son, Rev. **Adam Clayton Powell, Jr.**, and did some work on behalf of his Coordinating Committee for the Employment of Negroes. She was an officer of the Harlem Christian Youth Council.

In the summer of 1937 she was a delegate to an international church youth conference in Oxford, England, and returned with the conviction that her life work "must have a broader base." She left her job with the Welfare Department and joined the Harlem branch of the Y.W.C.A., the largest and most successful Black Y.W.C.A. in the country. In 1938 she gave testimony to the New York City Council with colleague **Anna Arnold Hedgeman** about the domestic "slave market" in the city, where desperate poor women would bargain for a day's housework with passing motorists for substandard wages. Over the years she served the Y.W.C.A. variously as director of the Emma Ransom House in New York City and of the Phillis Wheatley Y.W.C.A. in Washington, D.C. She began to devote considerable volunteer time to the National Council of Negro Women (N.C.N.W.), founded in 1935 by Mary McLeod Bethune as an umbrella organization for about thirty smaller groups with a combined membership of 4,000,000. She also did postgraduate work at the New York School of Social Work.

In 1952 Height was a visiting professor in the School of Social Work of the University of Delhi, India, and from 1952 to 1955 she was on the United States Department of Defense's advisory committee on women in the armed forces. In 1957 she became the fourth president of the N.C.N.W., which stressed interracial and inter-class cooperation in humanitarian and social action causes. She held this position concurrently with her Y.W.C.A. work. In 1958 the governor of New York appointed her to the state's Social Welfare Board, a position she held until 1974. In 1959 she and other leaders of private organizations toured South America under the sponsorship of International Seminars, with particular attention to the conditions of family life and children. In 1960 the Committee of Correspondence sent her to study women's organizations in Africa, and thereafter she served as African Affairs consultant to the U.S. Secretary of State. She helped win aid for new African countries and fostered a consciousness of the connections between the struggles of Blacks on both continents.

During the 1960s she worked closely with Rev. **Martin Luther King, Jr.** and other civil rights leaders through the United Civil Rights Leadership group, with representatives from different organizations. One civil rights project was her own organization. The Y.W.C.A. had gained an interracial charter in 1946, but its application had been minimal, and Black branches were still segregated with poor facilities. In 1963 the Y.W.C.A. assigned Height the task of improving the organization's integration of facilities and hiring programs. Her position was formalized as director of the Y.W.C.A. Office for Racial Justice. At the same time she directed the N.C.N.W. to contribute to the civil rights campaign through money, voter registration drives in the South, education in the North, workshops, and grass-roots communication.

She was at first reluctant to warm up to the "Black power" slogan of more militant Blacks, but by 1972 acknowledged that power relations between the races have to change as well as attitudes. She helped formulate the path-breaking 1970 public affairs priority statement of the Y.W.C.A. which stated that "the future health of mankind depends on uprooting the cancerous effects of White racism." She was the guiding force behind the establishment in 1974 of a national monument to **Mary McLeod Bethune** in Washington, D.C., the first monument to a Black person in a public park in Washington. She has received many awards, including the 1971 Distinguished Service Award from the National Conference on Social Welfare, and served on numerous committees, including the President's Committee for the Employment of the Handicapped; the Women's Committee of the Office of Emergency Planning; the President's Commission on the Status of Women; the President's Committee for Equal Opportunity; and the U.S.I.A.'s Advisory Council on Minority Groups.

In 1975 New York University gave her an honorary doctorate of humane letters. In 1977 she retired from the Y.W.C.A.; she never married. She has remained head of the N.C.N.W. and has led it to develop a wide range of human service programs involving food production, child care centers, housing initiatives, health care, career education, and alternatives to detention for young women. She has expanded the N.C.N.W. staff from three to over eighty-five.

"Women's Clubs: They Turn from Social Circles to Social Service." *Ebony* 32 (July 1977): 71–78.

Height, Dorothy Irene. *America's Promise, the Integration of Minorities.* New York: Woman's Press, 1946. 24 pp.

———, and J. Oscar Lee. *The Christian Citizen and Civil Rights; A Guide to Study and Action.* New York: Woman's Press, 1949. 71 pp.

———. *The Core of America's Race Problem.* New York: Woman's Press, 1946. 31 pp.

AARS, HUBA, IBAW, IBAWCB, CH, BAW, EBA, AAE, NYTBS (79), CB (1972), WWABA (90–91), WWAW (85–86), IDAW, NBAW, BWMH.

HEMINGWAY, LAWRENCE HENRY (June 5, 1884–November 30, 1954), 65th bishop of the **African Methodist Episcopal Church** (AME), was born in Conway, South Carolina, the son of John and Mary Frances (Demry) Hemingway. He attended the local public schools and served several positions in the Bethel AME Church in Conway. He married Hettie Gaddy, with whom he had four children, but she passed away in June 1909. He went to Allen University in Columbia, South Carolina, where he received the B.A. and B.D. degrees. He was licensed to preach in 1908 and joined the Northeast South Carolina Conference in 1910. He was ordained deacon in 1912 and elder a surprising thirteen years later, in 1923.

His pastorates were all in South Carolina and began with Pine Grove Circuit in Foreston (1911–12). Between 1912 and 1916 he apparently was building up the Union Premium Candy Company of Orangeburg, South Carolina, of which he was owner. He was widely recognized as an astute businessman and it made him financially very secure. He also gained a reputation for using his financial resources to help struggling congregations and preachers, and to extend the terms of public schools. He continued in the candy business until he became bishop. On August 25, 1915, he married Catherine Civilla Dingle, with whom he had three more children.

He returned to a pastorate with Laurel Hill Circuit in Davis Station, Wisacky (1916–18), followed by Western Chapel AME Church in Greenwood (1919–20); Beaufort Circuit in Beaufort (1921–23); Bethel Station in St. Matthews (1924–26); Felderville and Brown Chapel in Elloree and Cameron (1927–31); and presiding elder (1931–38) over a district. In each charge he paid off the mortgage and was very successful. He built the Cootoboro AME Church in Pine Grove, Foreston, and counted a total of 3,000 conversions over the years from his preaching. He was first elected a delegate to General Conference in 1928.

In 1938 he was elected secretary-treasurer of church extension for the denomination and held that position for ten years. He remodeled the church extension building and purchased $800,000 worth of church properties. He was elected bishop in May 1948 and was assigned to the Second Episcopal District. He served on the publication and educational boards of the church, was a trustee of Allen and Wilberforce universities, and published a number of articles in church periodicals. Although both of his parents were Black, by all appearances he seemed White. He was therefore able to travel freely on trains and stay in first-class hotels. He often used this to the advantage of Blacks, and no one ever accused him of being disloyal "to his race." At a conference session in Baltimore in late 1954 he fell down a stairway and was severely injured. He never recovered from his injuries and died a few weeks later. A church in Washington, D.C., is named for him.

HAMEC, EWM, BAMEC, AMSC.

HENDERSON, ALICE M. (b. 1947), the first woman U.S. Army Chaplain, was born in Indian Springs, Georgia, and as a young woman wanted to be a pop ballad singer. After freshman orientation at Clark University in Atlanta, Georgia, however, she changed her major from music to religion and philosophy. In her sophomore year she decided to become a minister, though she knew she faced many obstacles. Although she grew up a Baptist, she changed her membership to the **African Methodist Episcopal Church** (AME) because she felt it offered more opportunities for women in ministry. In college she was very involved in the issues of the day, and marched for civil rights and peace.

After graduating from Clark in 1968 with her B.A., she enrolled in Turner Theological Center of the Interdenominational Theological Center in Atlanta, Georgia. There, she was among the first women ever to attend some courses, and had to persevere through many barriers of attitude. While in seminary she was ordained in 1969 and served as an associate minister at the Cobb Bethel AME Church in Atlanta. Upon graduation from seminary no full-time appointment was forthcoming, and she was forced to return to teaching, something she had done part-time to support herself and her son (born in 1967) through school.

Finally, she decided to apply for a chaplain's job, and was surprised to find that the Army had not yet had any women chaplains. She attended the Army Chaplain School at Ft. Hamilton, New York, from July 1974 to September 1974 and was assigned as a full Captain to the 426th Signal Battalion at Ft. Bragg, North Carolina. With responsibility for 3,000 men and dependents, she was soon immersed in her duties, in particular the many counseling opportunities. She quickly overcame the initial surprise at her presence and became very popular.

"Woman AME Minister, Rev. Alice M. Henderson, Blazes Trail for Women Clerics in the Army." *Ebony* 3 (October 1975): 44–52.
AMECMIM, IBAW, NYTBS (1974).

HICKMAN, ERNEST LAWRENCE (b. June 8, 1903), 75th bishop of the **African Methodist Episcopal Church** (AME), was born in Fayetteville, Tennessee, the sixth of ten children in the family of Edgar and Lilla Ann (Bonner) Hickman. He was converted in August 1915, joined Brown Chapel AME Church in the Fayetteville Circuit, and over the years held most of the official church positions. On June 8, 1923, he married Cleopatra Watkins, with whom he had two daughters. Lack of money prevented him from attending college. He was licensed to preach in February 1924 and joined the Tennessee Annual Conference in 1925. He was ordained deacon in October 1926 and elder in October 1928.

His first pastorate of record was at Lee Chapel AME Church in Cleveland, Tennessee, from 1925 to 1928. During this time he was a student at Turner College, earning his B.D. degree in 1928. His next pastorates were at Allen Temple AME Church in Chattanooga (1928–30), New Tyler AME Church in Memphis (1930–32), Bethel AME Church in Knoxville (1932–35), Fayetteville AME Church (1935–37), Quinn AME Church in Paris (1937–40), and Warren AME Church in Chattanooga (1940–46). He had particular success at Warren, increasing the membership, remodeling the church, and paying off the mortgage, despite the attempt by a former pastor to start a rival church in town. He was president of the Chattanooga Interracial Committee and president of the Colored Ministers' Interdenominational Alliance in Chattanooga. In 1946 he was assigned to Quinn Chapel AME Church in Louisville, Kentucky, where he stayed for ten years and made his major reputation. At Quinn he bought the parsonage, received 521 people into membership, and remodeled the church. For a time, in addition to his pastoral responsibilities, he was presiding elder of the Louisville District.

Hickman was consecrated bishop on May 15, 1956, and was assigned to the Seventeenth Episcopal District (South Africa), maintaining his residence in Atlanta. In November 1956, after the death of Bishop **A. J. Allen**, he was reassigned to the Thirteenth Episcopal District. He stayed there until 1968, when he was assigned to the Sixth Episcopal District (Georgia), shifting in 1972 to the First Episcopal District (New York, New England, New Jersey, Pennsylvania). He was a member of the National Fraternal Council of Negro Churches and was on the board for the *Southern Recorder*. He was vice-president of Payne Theological Seminary in Wilberforce, Ohio, and of the Pension Board of the AME Church. For a time he was vice-chair of the board of the Interdenominational Theological Center in Atlanta. He retired in 1976.

EAMEC, EWM, EBA, BDNM (70), *BAMEC, HAMEC.*

HIGGINS, SAMUEL RICHARD (July 6, 1896–December 31, 1961), 76th bishop of the **African Methodist Episcopal Church** (AME), was born in Laurens, South Carolina, one of six children in the family of Levi and Adelia (Satterwhite) Higgins. After attending the local public schools he joined the U.S. Army for World War I. He then completed his normal training at Knoxville College in Tennessee in 1918. He received his B.A. degree in 1925 from Howard University in Washington, D.C., and the B.D. in 1928 from Union Theological Seminary in New York City. He was licensed to preach at Emanuel AME Church in New York City in 1926, joined the New York Annual Conference in 1927, and was ordained elder in 1928.

His first two appointments were at the 100–member Remly's Point AME Church in South Carolina (1928–31) and the 110–member Shiloh AME Church in Charleston (1931–35). While in Charleston he was principal of the well-known Burke High School. In 1931 he married Eugenia DeCosta, with whom he had one son. He pastored Johns Island AME Church (150 members) from 1935 to 1936 and Hanges Island AME Church (250 members) from 1936 to 1939. On July 6, 1937 he was elected president of Allen University in Columbia, South Carolina and remained in that position until 1956. He developed the largest student body of any of the AME Church colleges, enlarged the faculty, and built several buildings. He oversaw its accreditation by the Southern Association of Colleges. As president he was in great demand around the country as preacher and speaker.

Higgins was elected bishop in May 1956, the last of a line of Allen University presidents elected bishop, a line which included bishops **William D. Chappelle**, **William W. Beckett**, and **David M. Simms**. He was assigned to the Fourteenth Episcopal District (West Africa), where he organized the board of trustees of Monrovia College and started a rubber plantation. In 1960 he was assigned to the Seventh Episcopal District (South Carolina). He was a member of the special committee on the Coordination of Missionary Efforts for the church. Named for him is a church in Takonadi, Ghana, and a men's dormitory at Allen University. In the center of that campus is a monument to him.

HAMEC, EWM, BAMEC, AMSC.

HIGHER EDUCATION, CHURCH-SPONSORED AFRICAN AMERICAN INSTITUTIONS OF.

Church-sponsored African American institutions of higher education refers to those African American colleges and universities founded or supported by major Christian denominations in the United States. Any assessment of the African American religious presence in the United States must necessarily consider education. Education has been the "touchstone" of African American growth and progress. If education has been the touchstone of growth and progress in the African American community, then theological education has been important and will be even more significant in the future. Dr. Lawrence Jones has observed:

During [the] antebellum period, organized African American Christianity was in its infancy: the ranks of its members were very thin, and on the national level, the bulk of Black Christians belonged to predominantly White Methodist and Baptist bodies. The basic disability of the organized Black congregations was lack of qualified leadership. Few of the clergy were theologically trained, and most of their constituents possessed no formal education. Daniel A. Payne reported that in the Mother Bethel African Methodist Episcopal Church in Philadelphia, fewer than one hundred persons in a congregation of fifteen hundred could be found with a hymnbook in their hand.

Prior to the Civil War, there were only two institutions of theological education founded or sponsored by African Americans: Ashmun Institute and Wilberforce University. Ashmun Institute, now Lincoln University, was established by the Presbytery of New Castle, Pennsylvania, for "the scientific, classical, and theological education of the colored youth of the male sex." Following the subsequent approval of plans by the Synod in 1853, a charter was secured and the legislature incorporated the institution in 1854; its doors were opened in 1856.

In 1856 Wilberforce University was also organized. The **African Methodist Episcopal Church** denomination purchased this institution in 1862 from the Methodist Episcopal Church for $10,000. Having served on the Executive Committee of the Board of Trustees, and lived on the campus, Payne was selected as the first African American president of an institution of higher education in the United States in 1863 when he was elected president of Wilberforce University.

Early institutions like these struggled against great odds. Consequently, "The depth and quality of education offered varied from institution to institution. Some were hardly more than Bible Schools, training their students to know and interpret the Word with precision. Some were carbon copies of the White institutions of the North and reflected the pedagogy of the White missionaries who were instrumental in their founding." Biblical languages, exegesis, and rhetoric were among the staples of the curriculum in these schools. An indomitable spirit of freedom united these fledgling institutions.

Church-sponsored institutions of higher education included normal schools, colleges, and universities. Most such institutions were usually the product of White-Black cooperation or independent African American initiative, and most were established after the Civil War, and in the South. Because most religious-affiliating African Americans associated themselves with Protestantism, in general, and Baptist and Methodist religious bodies, in particular, schooling tended to develop along denominational lines.

The American Baptist Home Mission Society, an arm of Northern Baptists (now the **American Baptist Churches in the U.S.A.**), played a major role in the establishment of learning institutions for African Americans in the South, including Richmond Theological Seminary, Richmond, Virginia (1867); Shaw University, Raleigh, North Carolina (1865); Atlanta Seminary [originally founded at Augusta, Georgia (1867), moved to Atlanta (1879); Spelman Seminary [now Spelman College], Atlanta, Georgia (1881); Benedict College, Columbia, South Carolina (1887). African American Baptists were simultaneously establishing colleges by and for themselves. Among these independent colleges were: Guadalupe College, the first independent African American college (n.d); Houston College, Houston, Texas (1885); Virginia Theological Seminary and College at Lynchburg, Virginia (1888); Friendship Baptist College [now Friendship Junior College] (1891); and Morris College, Sumter, South Carolina (1905).

The Methodists brought into existence a host of African American colleges between 1865 and the early 1900s. With a history of independence, the African Methodists established several institutions of higher education. The African Methodist Episcopal Church has the distinction of inaugurating the first college for African Americans, Wilberforce University (1856). With the exception of R. R. Wright School of Religion in Johannesburg, South Africa, all African Methodist Episcopal colleges were founded prior to 1890 and include Edward Waters College, Jacksonville, Florida (1866); Allen University, Columbia, South Carolina (1870); Paul Quinn College, Waco, Texas (1872); Daniel Payne College, Birmingham, Alabama (1877);

and Shorter College, North Litte Rock, Arkansas (1886). The A**frican Methodist Episcopal Zion Church** founded and maintains Livingstone College (1879).

Continuing the effort to support Methodism even though divided in 1844 over the issues of slavery and the episcopacy, the Methodist Episcopal Church, South and the Methodist Episcopal Church (North) cooperated in the establishment of many colleges including three in 1869: Claflin College, East Orangeburg, South Carolina; Clark College (now Atlanta University); Dillard University, New Orleans, Louisiana. The **United Methodist Church** (1968) has nurtured into existence some fourteen institutions originally established as African American institutions of higher education.

Founded by former members of the Methodist Episcopal Church, South who separated into an independent organization in 1870, the Colored Methodist Episcopal Church (**Christian Methodist Episcopal Church**) founded five colleges including two in 1892: Lane College, Jackson, Tennessee and Paine College, Augusta, Georgia. In 1905, Miles College was established in Birmingham, Alabama.

The Presbyterian and Congregational denominations contributed greatly to the development of African American institutions of higher learning. Between 1867–1892, Presbyterians established, in addition to Ashmun Institute (Lincoln University) in Pennsylvania, five other colleges/universities which exist to the present. Those institutions include Barber-Scotia College, Concord, North Carolina (1867); Johnson C. Smith University (originally Biddle University) (1867); Knoxville College, Knoxville, Tennessee (1875); and Stillman College, Tuscaloosa, Alabama (1876).

The **United Church of Christ** (Congregational) also established several institutions including Atlanta University, Atlanta, Georgia (1867); Dillard University, New Orleans, Louisiana (1869); Howard University, Washington, D.C. (1867); Hutson-Tillotson College, Austin, Texas (1876); and Talladega College, Talladega, Alabama (1867). Many of the Presbyterian and Congregational educational establishments were founded in conjunction with the American Missionary Association (AMA), a major Northern interdenominational religious body which served as a collective Protestant missionary arm. Fisk University, Nashville, Tennessee (1866); Hampton University (formerly Hampton Institute), Hampton, Virginia (1868); and Tougaloo College, Tougaloo, Mississippi (1869) are representative results of AMA higher education activity.

While African American Episcopalians and Roman Catholics were small in number, their emphasis on higher education led them to establish several institu-

tions. The Protestant Episcopal Church initiated St. Augustine's College, Raleigh, North Carolina (1867) and St. Paul's College, Lawrenceville, Virginia (1888); they later assumed support for Voorhees College, Denmark, South Carolina (1897). The Roman Catholic Church established Xavier University, New Orleans, Louisiana (1915).

Several new and developing religious bodies have founded an institution for the purpose of educating their constituency and have one college. In this category are found Oakwood College (sponsored by the Seventh-day Adventists Church), Huntsville, Alabama (founded in 1896) and Disciples of Christ operate Jarvis Christian College in Hawkins, Texas (founded in 1912). The Church of God in Christ's Charles H. Mason Theological Seminary joined the Interdenominational Theological Center in 1970.

More than a hundred African American church-sponsored institutions of higher education have been identified. Many of these have been discontinued over the years (a large number unable to survive the Depression). Among the more prominent of these now closed institutions are Alabama Lutheran Academy and College, Selma, Alabama (1922); Daniel Payne College, Birmingham, Alabama (1877); and Mississippi Industrial College, Holly Springs, Mississippi (1905). The majority of these church-sponsored institutions have traditionally concentrated on providing training in the manual and liberal arts. Today, most of the institutions remain dominantly liberal arts and require or strongly encourage students to take religion/moral education courses. A very large number of historically African American church-sponsored colleges and universities may also be classified as Historically Black Colleges (HBC's). Historically Black Colleges are private, and public institutions formed after the Civil War to educate former slaves. Located mostly in the South, for over one hundred years, these schools have been a major source of African American college graduates.

Enrollment of students is a function of survival in African American educational institutions. African American institutions of higher education in general, and church-sponsored African American institutions of higher education, in particular, continue to receive a smaller percentage of African American students in higher education. For example, in 1964, more than 51 percent of all African Americans in college were enrolled in historically African American colleges and universities. In 1970 that percentage was 28 percent; in 1988, it was 17.2 percent, after a low of 16.5 percent in 1978. Clearly, this downward trend has serious implications for the church-sponsored African American colleges and universities. One result has been the closing of several institutions. On the other hand, some institutions have experienced increased enrollments through the matriculation of non-African American students. Consequently, historically African American colleges and universities may become beneficiaries of desegregation by developing a holistic curriculum, a curriculum which recognizes the interrelatedness of all areas of human experience and emphasizes ways in which the secular and the religious influence each other. A holistic perspective counters the charge of being narrow and exclusivistic which have been made by scholars like E. Franklin Frazier against African American colleges and universities.

African American Seminary Education. The lack of continued growth and development of African American colleges and universities may impact significantly African American seminaries. Because many African American graduate professional theological institutions are or were parts of African American colleges and universities, they have often been partners in coexistence. It has already been noted that most of the early institutions of higher learning included departments of theology or moral education; some were formed specifically to train persons for the ministry. Thus, they have indeed had mutual existences in terms both of geography and intellectuality. Although they were born in the same geographical territory, these institutions have often parted ways in contours of the mind. That is, while often remaining in the same area they have developed different foci in carrying out their respective missions, but united in their commitment of improving the condition of African Americans through education. That difference in emphasis may help account for the almost eighty-five church-sponsored African American institutions but relatively small number of African American seminaries.

There are eleven African American seminaries: Bay Ridge Christian College; Endich Theological Seminary; Hood Theological Seminary; Howard University School of Divinity; Interdenominational Theological Center; Payne Theological Seminary; Richmond Virginia Seminary; R. R. Wright School of Religion (Johannesburg, South Africa); Shaw Divinity School; Southern California School of Ministry; and Virginia Union University School of Theology. Only three, Howard University School of Divinity, Interdenominational Theological Center (ITC), and Payne Theological Seminary are fully accredited by the Association of Theological Schools.

African American Bible colleges are twelve in number and range from the American Baptist College of the American Baptist Theological Seminary in Nashville Tennessee (1924) with about one-hundred-sixty students and fifteen faculty to the Crenshaw Christian Center School of Ministry, Los Angeles, California (1985) with a large number of students instructed by ministerial assistants of the church.

Five widely acclaimed historically African American theological schools are Howard University School of Divinity, Interdenominational Theological Center, Payne Theological Seminary, Shaw Divinity School, and Virginia Union University School of Theology. Called "the School of Religion" until 1981, Howard was chartered for the general education of recently freedmen on March 2, 1867. Its education of "preachers and others looking forward to that work" began on January 6, 1868. The "Theological Department," established in 1870, has grown to a student body of more than two-hundred students, and over eighteen full-time and part-time faculty, along with fifteen adjunct faculty. With no formal denominational affiliation, the School's mission is threefold: 1) the preparation of professional religious leaders for service in religious or educational institutions and for service to underserved rural and urban African American communities; 2) inquiry into international, cross-cultural human values; and 3) preparation of student to pursue advanced studies in the theological disciplines and in the cultural and religious heritage of African Americans. A commitment to excellence in scholarship has been reflected in its highly respected *Journal of Religious Thought* (1943) and the *Directory of African American Religious Bodies* (1991) by its recently acclaimed Research Center on Black Religious Bodies. Dr. Clarence G. Newsome, the Dean of Howard Divinity School (Howard School of Religion until 1981), expects that the school will soon become the first "Ph.D.-granting department of religious studies to develop at a predominantly Black theological school."

The Interdenominational Theological Center (ITC) was established in 1958 and began operation in 1959. At that time, seventeen African American theological seminaries were operative. Initially ITC was comprised of four cooperating seminaries: Gammon Theological Seminary (United Methodist), Phillips School of Theology (Christian Methodist), Morehouse School of Religion (Baptist) and Turner Theological Seminary (African Methodist Episcopal). Since 1969, Johnson C. Smith Theological Seminary (Presbyterian), and Charles H. Mason Theological Seminary (Church of God in Christ) have joined. The ITC is now comprised of six participating seminaries. Its mission is "to provide quality theological education for the predominantly Black Christian churches." Although born more out of the desire for mutual survival of four struggling African American denominational seminaries than a commitment to Christian unity, the ITC provides an atmosphere in which ecumenicity can be seriously discussed and even actualized. The Center gives concreteness to African American ecumenicity by providing a much needed seminary and training center. The ITC also fosters economic cooperation in religion, a concept more often identified with social movements advocating community empowerment. Committed to excellence in scholarship, the ITC publishes the *Journal of the Interdenominational Theological Center* (1974). Although its students can receive the Ph.D. through the Atlanta Theological Association, the ITC long-range plan is to develop its own Ph.D. granting program.

Payne Theological Seminary bears the name of the first African American president of Wilberforce University, Bishop Daniel Alexander Payne. Bishop Payne established the theology department in the late 1860s which graduated its first class in 1871. Payne was present when the idea of a seminary was presented at the Ohio Conference of 1844 where the decision was made to erect a seminary. Today, Payne concentrates on preparing persons for ministry and service. With 25 students and six faculty members, the Seminary benefits from its proximity to and relationship with Wilberforce University and other institutions of higher education. Payne is fully accredited by the American Association of Theological Schools, a distinction held only by three African American theological institutions.

Virginia Union University School of Theology was founded in 1865 by the American Baptist Home Mission Society. After name changes reflecting several mergers, Virginia Union School of Theology has developed into one of the few church-sponsored schools for African Americans accredited by the American Association of Theological Schools. With an enrollment of 127 students, 22 percent women, this graduate professional school prepares persons for service in the African American context. The School of Theology is proud of its association with and support from six national multiracial Baptists organizations.

Among the first African American universities established immediately after the Civil War, the idea of Shaw University was nurtured by its founder, Rev. **H. M. Tupper** of the American Home Mission Society. Rev. Tupper taught his first class of religious instruction in 186. Shaw became a university in 1875, established a Graduate School of Religion in 1939, and renamed this division a School of Religion in 1969 to avoid the

University's loss of accreditation. Since 1987, a reunification of the School of Religion (now Shaw Divinity School) with the University has been underway. New facilities and academic restructuring have contributed to its becoming Associate Member of the Association of Theological Schools.

The Future of African American Seminary Education. The formal end of slavery paved the way for a new freedom: education. African Americans with unusual commitment responded to the new freedom. Just as they had been forced to establish their own churches which served the spiritual, socioeconomic and political needs, so African American religious bodies sponsored institutions necessary to accelerate progress toward greater freedom and independence. While many of the church-sponsored institutions no longer exist, they served as bridges to the twentieth century. Still more than a hundred strong today, those institutions still serve by providing access to and support for the achievement of spiritual and academic success. Carter G. Woodson once observed that "If you can control a man's thinking you do not have to worry about his action." African American religious education institutions continue to provide a place and opportunity for the development of thinking persons. The trend toward fewer educated men entering the professional ministry, the continuing impact of national economic fluctuations, and the perpetual struggle for excellence in the classroom and the concomitant demand for excellence in ministerial performance, church-sponsored institutions of higher education, especially seminaries, face great challenges as the twenty-first century approaches. According to Lincoln,

> If the Black Church is to have a viable future the need for professional seminary education appears to be critical. The educational issue is problematic for most Black churches because the historical evangelical background of the Baptists, Methodists, and Pentecostal did not have stringent educational demands but only required evidence of a personal call from God to the ministry. The anti-intellectual and fundamentalist strains of that tradition have made it difficult for innovative church leaders and bishops to make professional seminary education a requirement for the ministry.

Lincoln noted that the response to his survey of the educational level of ministers almost paralleled that of nineteen ministers by Walter and Brown in Washington, D.C.

Their median educational level was four years of college with 42 percent having had some level of college or postsecondary education, and 21.1 percent having attended graduate school. The clergy of the A.M.E. Church and the C.M.E. Church had the highest median levels of college graduates. The C.M.E. (51 percent) and the A.M.E. (48.2 percent) clergy had the highest reported rate of graduate study among the seven denominations.

Therefore, creating a tradition requiring a seminary educated ministry will be less than easy for evangelical-revivalist originated religious bodies. There has been a rather dramatic increase in the number of African Americans enrolling in seminaries. A recent study by Charles S. Rooks shows that the number of African Americans attending seminary has increased from 387 in 1959–60 to 3,379 in 1987–88. In 1988, African American institutions of higher learning enrolled 194,151 African American students of the 1,129,600 African American students enrolled in all institutions of higher learning in the United States, or 17.2 percent. In 1987, of the 3,379 African American students enrolled in seminaries, 731 (or 21.6 percent) were enrolled in six mostly African American seminaries. In the same year, women comprised 29.4 percent of students enrolled in seminaries which represents an increase of 982 percent over the number of women enrolled in the 1972 year. The dramatic change reflects a continually expanding role for Black women in African American religious life and leadership.

In spite of these dramatic increases, the trained personnel required by the 65,000 churches in the African American community is far from being met. African American churches are the "last frontier" of institutions controlled by African Americans. A major issue facing this community is the source and quality of future leadership. Data shows fewer African Americans choosing to enter the historically African American colleges and universities and more matriculating at predominantly White colleges and universities. Should this trend continue to escalate, the historic source of educated African American religious leadership (African American seminary graduates have been estimated at 10–20 percent) will be seriously diminished. Moreover, evidence shows that even a 982 percent increase of women enrolling in seminary can not fill the leadership need. Consequently, new innovative strategies will be required. Those strategies have historically come from church-sponsored African American institutions of higher education.

The influence of church-sponsored African American institutions extends far beyond the church and local community. These have and still reflect the potential impact of higher education upon the African American, the nation and the world. They necessitated, in the midst of both chaotic and organized opposition, a reconditioning of the American mind. These few extant institutions bear the future of over 35 million African American citizens, and as the American community moves into the twenty-first century, these institutions become greater bearers of responsibilities. They embody the past unborn and a future to be realized. Having served a marginalized people in the past, these institutions must prepare to serve both those who remain somewhat marginalized and the church universal in the future.

[*Editor's note*: More information on the institutions discussed above may be found in separate entries on the individual schools located throughout this volume.]

Baumgaetner, William L. *Fact Book on Theological Education, 1987–88.* Vandalia, OH: Association of Theological Schools in the United States and Canada, 1988.

Costen, James. "Black Theological Education: Its Content and Conduct." *Journal of the Interdenominational Theological Center* 12, 1/2 (Fall/Spring 1984–85).

Jones, Lawrence N. "The Organized Church: Its Historic Significance and Changing Role in Contemporary African American Experience." In Wardell J. Payne, ed. *Directory of the African American Religious Bodies: A Compendium by the Howard University School of Divinity.* Washington, DC: Howard University Press, 1991. 361 pp.

Lincoln, C. Eric, and Lawrence H. Mamiya. *The Black Church and the African American Experience.* Durham, NC: Duke University Press, 1990.

Ploski, Harry, ed. *The Negro Almanac: A Reference Work on the Afro-American.* New York: John Wiley and Sons, 4th ed., 1983.

Rooks, Charles S. *Revolution in Zion: Reshaping the African American Ministry.* New York: Pilgrim Press, 1919.

Woodson, Carter G. *The Education of the Negro Prior to 1861.* Washington, DC: Associated Publishers, 1919.

Herman E. Thomas

HIGHWAY CHRISTIAN CHURCH OF CHRIST. An Apostolic Pentecostal church. The Highway Christian Church of Christ was an early schism from the **Pentecostal Assemblies of the World** (PAW). It developed in Washington, D.C., when Elder James Thomas Morris left and began the Highway Christian Church of Christ in 1929. In 1941, PAW Bishop **J. M. Turpin**, who was in and out of the church over the years, consecrated Morris as a bishop. As the church grew, Morris moved to New York City to pastor. He died in 1959 and was succeeded by Bishop J. V. Lomax who had left the **Church of Our Lord Jesus Christ of the Apostolic Faith** to join Morris.

The Highway Christian Church follows the traditional Apostolic Pentecostal position. It rejects the doctrine of the Trinity and believes in one God whose name is Jesus. It baptizes in the name of Jesus rather in the more common formula of "Father, Son and Holy Spirit." Within the Apostolic community, the church is distinctive in its dress code which encourages members to limit their dress to black and white. Colored clothes are considered ostentatious. A similar position was adopted by the Methodists in the eighteenth century and was still popular in the nineteenth. The church does not ordain women, but has accepted female pastors from other denominations.

In 1980 the church had 13 congregations and some 3,000 members.

Richardson, James C., Jr. *With Water and Spirit: A History of Black Apostolic Denominations in the U.S.* Martinsville, VA: The Author, n.d. 151 pp.

HILDEBRAND, RICHARD ALLEN (b. February 1, 1916), 88th bishop of the **African Methodist Episcopal Church** (AME), was born in Winnsboro, South Carolina, the son of Benjamin F. and Agnes L. (Brogdon) Hildebrand. His father, grandfather, and uncle were all AME clergy. He experienced conversion in August 1926, and joined the Live Oak AME Church in Vance, South Carolina. He was licensed to preach in 1934 and joined the Central South Carolina Conference in November 1934. He was ordained deacon in November 1936, and given his first assignment of record at Sandy Run Circuit in St. Matthews, South Carolina, from 1936 to 1937, followed by Union Station AME Church in Sumter, South Carolina from 1937 to 1938. Meanwhile he attended Allen University in Columbia, South Carolina, and received his B.A. in 1938. Following graduation he was ordained elder and assigned to Ross Chapel AME Church in Jamestown, Ohio, from 1938 to 1941. While there he attended Payne Theological Seminary at Wilberforce University in Xenia, Ohio, and received his B.D. in 1941.

Following graduation from seminary, he went to St.

Paul AME Church in Akron, Ohio (1941–45), where he had his usual success, paying off the mortgage, renovating the church, and purchasing additional property. On December 3, 1942, he married Anna Beatrix Lewis, with whom he had one daughter. At Bethel AME Church in Providence, Rhode Island (1945–48), he paid off another large mortgage. He was assigned to Bayshore AME Church in New York from 1948 to 1949, and went on to Wilmington AME Church in Delaware (1949–50), Bethel AME Church in New York City (1950–65), and Bridge Street AME Church in Brooklyn, New York City (1965–72).

He made his primary reputation in New York City, and while at Bethel became the first Black president of the Manhattan Division of the Protestant Council of New York. He was also president of the New York City chapter of the N.A.A.C.P. In 1964 he was profiled in the *New York Times* as one of the major Black leaders working for social change. At that time he was chair of the Joint Committee for Equal Opportunity in Employment, a powerful civil rights organization. He was particularly interested in having the building trade unions opened fully to qualified minority workers.

In 1972 Hildebrand was the second of eight men elected bishop in the historic class of 1972, and was assigned to the Sixth Episcopal District (Georgia). From 1976 to 1984 he covered the First Episcopal District (Pennsylvania, New England, New York, New Jersey), from 1984 to 1988 the Tenth Episcopal District (Texas), and then the Third Episcopal District (Ohio). In 1982–83 he was chair of Religion in American Life, Inc., an interreligious educational group focusing on morality in business and the general belief that religion in a free society can be a means of channeling energies for the good of society. Hildebrand has been president of the Council of Bishops of the AME Church and chair of the board of directors of Morris Brown College in Atlanta, Georgia, Turner Theological Seminary in Atlanta, and Payne Theological Seminary in Ohio. He retired from the episcopacy at the general conference meeting in Orlando, Florida, in 1992.

"Bishop Hildebrand New Head of Religion in American Life, Inc." *The Christian Recorder* 132 (May 2, 1983): 1–2.
"Organizations and Leaders Campaigning for Negro Goals in the United States." *New York Times* (August 10, 1964): 16.
IBAW, WWABA (88), *AMSC, EBA, BDNM* (70), *EAMEC, HAMEC.*

HILL, EDWARD VICTOR (b. 1934), prominent Baptist (**National Baptist Convention of the U.S.A.,**

Inc.) preacher, gained his first pastorate at the Friendly Will Baptist Church in Austin, Texas, in 1954, while in school. In 1955 he received his B.S. in Agronomy from Prairie View A & M College in Texas. He then pastored the Mt. Corinth Baptist Church in Houston, Texas, from 1955 to 1960. In 1961 he moved to the Mt. Zion Missionary Baptist Church in Los Angeles, California, where he has since remained. He married Jane Edna Coruthers, with whom he has had two children.

In California he has made a name for himself as an outstanding preacher and community activist. He has been a leader in a number of anti-discrimination and integration efforts and is president of Mount Zion Towers and E. Victor Villa, Inc., housing projects related to the church. He has served as president of the Los Angeles City Housing Authority and the Los Angeles City Fire Commission. In 1970 he established the World Christian Training Center (W.C.T.C.) in south central Los Angeles, which seeks "the salvation of the city." It offers a ten-week program in Christian doctrine and personal evangelism, then sends graduates out to win a neighborhood block for Christ.

One W.C.T.C. program, the Work Experience Program, is funded by the government to evaluate, train, and place young people from 16 to 21 years old who are high school dropouts, ex-offenders of the law, gang members, or physically handicapped. This program was instituted in 1978 and very soon boasted a higher success rate than most other C.E.T.A. (Comprehensive Employment and Training Act) programs. The staff for the program are forbidden to evangelize, but claim that their Christian attitudes towards the youth make a real difference. Another W.C.T.C. program is the Volunteer Action Center, a referral service that allows offenders to do community service instead of prison time. Numerous other programs include Operation Looking Good (sprucing up neighborhoods), ministries in convalescent homes, on skid row, and in prisons, and work with the deaf and youth gangs. The center also operates as an extension of Fuller Theological Seminary in Pasadena and Biola University, which offer college-credit Bible courses there at reduced prices.

Hill has proven difficult for many observers to pin down philosophically. On the one hand, he personally nominated **Martin Luther King, Jr.**, for leadership of the **Southern Christian Leadership Conference** (S.C.L.C.), but on the other hand he led Black Clergy for Reagan. In return, Reagan offered him the post of chair of the U.S. Civil Rights Commission, but Hill turned it down, feeling he could be more effective where he was. He defends his conservative bent by suggesting that "white liberals have used us more than they have helped us." He has also said that "capitalism is the right way, the biblical way," and he has been associated with the Moral Majority.

He was raised to hate White conservatives as "bigots and ku-cluckers," but found that this was not necessarily so. He has noted that Jerry Falwell's congregation and the associated Liberty University have many Black students, a number of whom have spent summers working with Hill's evangelization program in the ghetto. He has served as president of the California State Baptist Convention; a board member of the Billy Graham School of Evangelism; chair of the National Concerned Clergy for Evangelism; and vice-president of the **National Baptist Convention of the U.S.A., Inc.** In 1984 *Ebony* magazine named him one of America's fifteen best Black preachers.

"America's Fifteen Greatest Black Preachers." *Ebony* 39 (September 1984): 27–33.

Billingsley, Lloyd. "WCTC Sends in Christians, Not Government, to Save City." *Christianity Today* 25 (October 2, 1981): 57, 65.

Hill, Edward V. "White Liberals Behind Black Militancy." *Christian Economics* 23 (February 11, 1970): 2 ff.

HUBA, AARS.

HILLERY, WILLIAM HENRY (January 19, 1842– July 22, 1893), 19th bishop of the **African Methodist Episcopal Zion Church** (AMEZ), was born in Virginia. He grew up in Wilkes Barre, Pennsylvania, was converted in 1856 and received his license to preach in 1860, at age eighteen. He joined the Genesee (Western New York) Conference of the AMEZ Church on September 6, 1862, and was sent as missionary to eastern Tennessee. There he was successful in establishing a number of societies with hundreds of members, despite the terror and violence of those Civil War days. He was ordained deacon on November 10, 1864, and elder on November 16, 1866.

He later labored for a time in Washington, North Carolina, and in 1868 transferred to the West Coast and became presiding elder. He was consecrated a bishop on July 4, 1876, and spent eight years leading several conferences in Kentucky and on the West Coast. At the General Conference of 1884 Hillery was brought up on several charges of immorality and intemperance. Although the Kentucky Annual Conference had decided that the charges against him could not be sustained, the General Conference took upon itself the consideration of the matter, and on May 12, 1884, voted to disrobe him, removing him from the episcopacy. The matter was then sent to the Genesee Conference (his "home" conference) for the trial of his Christian character. Little else is known of his life after this point.

HAMEZC, AMEZC.

HILLIARD, WILLIAM ALEXANDER (b. September 12, 1904), 67th bishop of the **African Methodist Episcopal Zion Church** (AMEZ), was born in Greenville, Texas, the son of John H. and Carrie Deloris (Hicks) Hilliard. When he was very young the family moved to Kansas City, Kansas, and then on to Des Moines, Iowa, where he went to elementary school. He went to high school back in Kansas City, then received his B.A. from Western University in Quinders, Kansas. He remained at the related Shaeffer Theological Seminary, receiving his B.D. in 1927. On September 12, 1927, he married Edra Mae Estelle.

He joined the Missouri Annual Conference in 1922 and was assigned to St. Matthew AMEZ Church in Kansas City. He was ordained deacon on July 8, 1924, and elder on September 7, 1927, and was assigned to Mt. Zion AMEZ Church in Argentine, Kansas, from 1927 to 1931. His next pastorate was at Metropolitan AMEZ Church in Kansas City, Missouri, from 1931 to 1936, followed by Metropolitan AMEZ Church in Chester, South Carolina (1936–41), St. John AMEZ Church in Wilson, North Carolina (1941–47), and St. Paul AMEZ Church in Detroit, Michigan (1947–60). In Detroit he built the membership to the point where it could split and start another congregation, and led them to purchase a large building on Dexter Street.

Hilliard was elected bishop in 1960 (consecrated on May 15), and was assigned to the Twelfth Episcopal District (Ghana, Liberia, and Nigeria) in Africa. While there he was declared a knight great band of the Order of Liberian and African Redemption. From 1964 to 1972 he served the Eleventh Episcopal District (Missouri, Colorado, and Western Regions), followed by the Third Episcopal District (Michigan, Ohio, Central North Carolina, Guyana, and Virgin Islands). In 1970 he received a certificate from the mayor of Oakland, California, and in 1971 he received an honorary plaque from the City of Los Angeles. He was president of the Board of Bishop in 1977–78, and was chair of the Board of Overseas Missions for the denomination from 1964 to 1980. He retired in 1980.

"Bishop and Mrs. Hilliard Retiring." *Star of Zion* 104 (May 1, 1980): 1, 4.

"Retired Bishop and Mrs. Hilliard Honored by St. Paul AMEZ, Detroit." *Star of Zion* 115 (January 10, 1991): 1–2.
WWW (80–81), *WWABA* (85), *AMEZC, HAMEZC, EWM*.

HOGGARD, JAMES CLINTON, SR. (b. August 9, 1916), 70th bishop of the **African Methodist Episcopal Zion Church** (AMEZ), was born in Jersey City, New Jersey, the son of Jeremiah Matthew and Symera (Cherry) Hoggard. His father was a minister with the AMEZ Church. Hoggard received his B.A. from Rutgers University in New Brunswick, New Jersey, in 1939, and joined the New York Conference that June. He married Eva Stanton, with whom he had two children. He enrolled in Union Theological Seminary in New York City, and while a student pastored the St. Francis AMEZ Church in Mt. Kisco, New York (1940–42). He was ordained deacon on November 4, 1940, and elder on June 21, 1942. He received his B.D. in 1942 and was assigned to the Institutional AMEZ Church in Yonkers, New York, from 1942 to 1951. He then was appointed to the Little Rock AMEZ Church in Charlotte, North Carolina, but only spent one year there since the General Conference of 1952 elected him secretary-treasurer of the Department of Foreign Missions. Among many other responsibilities, this also involved being editor of the *Missionary Seer*.

In twenty years serving in the Department of Foreign Missions (with the exception of interim pastorates in Washington, D.C. in 1953–56 and in Mount Vernon, New York in 1967–68), Hoggard gained an international reputation as a diligent and dedicated churchman. In 1956 he was elected to the executive council of the World Methodist Conference. From 1945 to 1951 he was vice-chair of the Municipal Housing Authority of Yonkers, New York. At the 1972 General Conference he was elected bishop, and consecrated on May 12. He was assigned to the Sixth Episcopal District (Kentucky, Indiana, Tennessee, Virginia, and North Alabama). He became a member of the Division of World Mission and Evangelism of the World Council of Churches, and was a delegate to the 5th Assembly of the World Council of Churches in Nairobi, Kenya, in 1975. In 1984 a restructuring made the Sixth District the Fourth Episcopal District (adding London-Birmingham and Jamaica), and he remained in place until his retirement in 1988.

"J. Clinton Hoggard." *Star of Zion* 83 (January 7, 1960): 5.
"One of Zion's Charming Teams: Bishop J. Clinton Hoggard

and Mrs. Eva Stanton Hoggard." *Star of Zion* 111 (November 5, 1987): 7–8.

BDNM (75), NA, AMEZC.

HOLLIDAY, JEHU (December 25, 1827–March 2, 1899), 26th bishop of the **African Methodist Episcopal Zion Church** (AMEZ), was born in Goshen Township, Columbia County, Ohio. He was converted in November 1860, by the work of Rev. Joseph Armstrong, and joined the Allegheny Conference in July, 1861. A year later, he was ordained both deacon and elder in one day, July 27, 1862. Over the next fourteen years he pastored a number of churches, including the Fifteenth Street AMEZ (Hughlett Temple) Church in Louisville, Kentucky; the AMEZ church in Russellville, Kentucky; and the AMEZ church in Bedford, Pennsylvania.

In 1876 he was appointed for the second time to the Fifteenth Street Church in Louisville. After one year he left to found the Twelfth Street (Broadway Temple) AMEZ Church in the same city. After only one year there he was able to purchase property, pay most debts, and take in more than two hundred members. In 1878 he was appointed to Blackford Street (Jones Tabernacle) AMEZ Church in Indianapolis, Indiana, staying until 1880, when he moved to John Wesley Chapel AMEZ Church in Pittsburgh, Pennsylvania. There he purchased a very large building for the church, in which the General Conference of 1892 was held.

In about 1888 he went to Avery Mission in Pittsburgh for one year, then was assigned to the church in Johnstown, Pennsylvania, where the flood of 1889 had washed the building away. In 1890 he was appointed presiding elder of the Allegheny Conference, and in 1892 was elected General Agent of the Book Concern, succeeding Bishop Walters. Later that year, in September, with the consent of the bishops, he added to his responsibilities by returning to the Twelfth Street Church in Louisville to save a deteriorating situation.

At the 1896 General Conference Holliday was elected bishop, though he only served a few years before his death. He was remembered as a zealous worker, warm friend, and persuasive preacher.

AMEZC, HAMEZC.

HOLLY, JAMES THEODORE (October 3, 1829– March 13, 1911), the first Black priest consecrated a bishop by the **Episcopal Church** (in the United States), was born in Washington, D.C. His father, James Holly, was a worker in the construction of the Capitol building, and was also a shoemaker. The family moved North in 1844 to escape the disabilities for Blacks in the South, living variously in New York City, Buffalo, and Detroit. Holly learned his father's shoemaking trade, doing that work while obtaining as much schooling as possible, only a few years of which was in a formal setting. In 1850 he and his brother Joseph opened their own bootmaking shop in Burlington, Vermont. About that time he married a woman named Charlotte, with whom he had six children.

In 1851 he moved to Detroit as associate editor of the *Voice of the Fugitive*, published in Windsor, Canada, and used the paper as a platform for his belief that emigration to another country was the ultimate answer to the plight of Blacks in America. In 1854 he was a public school principal in Buffalo, New York, and was among those who called the National Emigration Convention of Colored Men, meeting in Cleveland, Ohio, August 24–26, 1854. He led the section of the convention which favored emigration to Haiti over other locations in Africa or Central America. In 1851, although his parents had raised him as a Roman Catholic, he joined St. Matthew's Episcopal Church in Detroit, Michigan, and was ordained deacon in that church on June 17, 1855.

Soon after his ordination Holly went to Haiti, both to ascertain the feasibility of the church establishing a mission there and to advance his emigration ideas. He met with the leadership there and returned to report to the 1856 National Emigration Convention that Haiti was indeed a likely site for emigration. He was ordained a priest on January 2, 1856, passing the same rigorous exams given to others normally trained in college and seminary, and thus became the fourteenth African American Episcopal priest. He served as rector of St. Luke's Episcopal Church in New Haven, Connecticut, until 1861. During this time he continued to pursue the possibilities of emigration, and in 1857 published *A Vindication of the Capacity of the Negro Race for Self-Government, and Civilized Progress*. In this lecture he argued that Haiti was a living example of the ability of Blacks to organize a fine society with, he thought, more freedom and general welfare than in the United States. At that time, Haiti was the only nation outside Africa under Black control, and was the only nation where enslaved Blacks had successfully overthrown White domination and established an independent nation.

A combination of internal feuds in Haiti and lack of strong organization at home prevented any concrete emigration for a time. Meanwhile Holly co-founded with William Charles Munroe the Convocation of the

Protestant Episcopal Society for Promoting the Extension of the Work Among Colored People, which both brought Blacks into the church and into Holly's emigration movement. In 1859 President Geffrard of Haiti appointed James Redpath commissioner of emigration in the United States, with the understanding that he would work with Holly, who tried to convince the Episcopal Church to fund him as a missionary to Haiti.

In May 1861, Holly took 110 people, mostly members of his own church, to Haiti, one of the few emigration leaders (perhaps the only one) to follow through on rhetoric and leave the country. There he founded Holy Trinity Episcopal Church in Port-au-Prince, the nation's capital. The first year in Haiti proved to be a disaster, with his mother, wife, two children, and 39 other group members dying of malaria and yellow fever. After the return of many surviving people to the United States, Holly was left with only a handful of followers. He became a Haitian citizen and in 1862 obtained financial support from the American Church Missionary Society for a mission station. He married again in November 1862 to Sarah Henley, with whom he had eight more children. From 1864 to 1874 he served as consul for Liberia at Port-au-Prince. In 1865 the Episcopal Church finally agreed to provide a small amount of funding, which was continuous until 1911, though grudgingly given and never equal to the amounts given to other missionaries.

In 1874 an agreement was reached between the Episcopal Church in America and the fledgling Episcopal organization in Haiti, called the Eglise Orthodoxe Apostolique Haitienne, in which the latter was recognized as a foreign church under the "nursing care" of the American church. As a result, on November 8, 1874, Holly was consecrated Episcopal Missionary Bishop of Haiti in Grace Episcopal Church in New York City, the first Black so consecrated in the Episcopal Church (in worldwide Anglicanism the first Black bishop was Samuel A. Crowther, consecrated in 1864 for Africa). Because of the independent nature of the church in Haiti, Holly was not a member of the House of Bishops of the American Episcopal Church (although in later years the church in Haiti became a missionary jurisdiction of the American Episcopal Church and its bishops, like Luc Garnier, have since been a part of the Episcopal Church succession). For this reason, Samuel D. Ferguson is generally considered the first Black bishop of the Episcopal Church (in the United States).

In 1878 Holly went to England as a member of the second Lambeth Conference, and preached an eloquent sermon in Westminster Abbey on St. James Day. He spent the remainder of his life building up the church in Haiti, with only rare visits to the United States. By 1911 the church counted 2,000 members. At his death, his legacy was the first Anglican church in a French-speaking country, the first Anglican church in a Roman Catholic country, sixteen clergy, eighteen lay readers, 685 communicants, 54 schools, one seminary, and one hospital.

Hayden, J. Carleton. "Afro-Anglican Linkages, 1701–1900: Ethiopia Shall Soon Stretch Out Her Hands Unto God." *Journal of Religious Thought* 44 (Summer–Fall 1987): 25–34.

———. "James Theodore Holly (1829–1911) First Afro-American Episcopal Bishop: His Legacy to Us Today." *Journal of Religious Thought* 33 (Spring–Summer 1976): 50–62.

Dean, David M. *Defender of the Race: James Theodore Holly, Black Nationalist Bishop.* Boston, MA: Lambeth Press, 1979. 131 pp.

Holly, James Theodore, and J. Dennis Harris. *Black Separatism and the Caribbean, 1860.* Ed. with an introduction by Howard B. Bell. Ann Arbor, MI: The University of Michigan Press, 1970. 184 pp.

———. *Facts About the Church's Mission in Haiti: A Concise Statement.* New York: Thomas Whittaker, 1897. 27 pp.

———. *A Vindication of the Capacity of the Negro Race for Self-Government, and Civilization Progress, as Demonstrated by Historical Events of the Haytian Revolution, and the Subsequent Acts of That People Since Their National Independence.* New Haven, CT: W. H. Stanley, 1857. 48 pp.

———. *The Word of God Against Ecclesiastical Imperialism.* N.p., 1880.

BA, BGWC, WWWA (1), NBH, CH, HNC, BHAC, ACAB (vol.3), EBA, NYTO, TCBDA, DANB, DAB (vol.5), IBAWCB, AARS, HUBA, IBAW, BAW.

HOLLY, JOHN SILAS (1901–1979), a bishop of the **Pentecostal Assemblies of the World**, was born in Monroe, Louisiana. He joined the great migration north after World War I. He married and he and his wife Effie had five children. He also met Assemblies minister (later bishop) **A. R. Schooler**, pastor of the church in Cleveland, Ohio. He was called to the ministry in 1920 and studied with Schooler. Ordained in 1921, he was the youngest man ever ordained as a minister by the church. Three years later he became the youngest person named a district elder. In 1931 he became the pastor of the Apostolic Faith Assembly (which had been pastored by Schooler in the 1920s.) He would remain in Chicago for the rest of his life. He was elected bishop in 1952 and assigned as the episcopal head of the Illinois District, which like his church he would serve for the next quarter century.

Golder, Morris E. *The Bishops of the Pentecostal Assemblies of the World*. Indianapolis, IN: The Author, 1980. 69 pp.

HOLSEY, LUCIUS HENRY (July 3, 1842–August 3, 1920), 4th bishop of the **Christian Methodist Episcopal Church** (CME), then the Colored Methodist Episcopal Church, was born into slavery near Columbus, Georgia, the son of James and Louisa (Wynn) Holsey. His mother was the slave of his father, who died when he was about seven years old. At that point Holsey was sold away from his mother, but was reunited with her some years later when his new owner, T. L. Wynn (his father's cousin), brought her onto the plantation in Hancock County, Georgia. Wynn died in 1857, and Holsey was sold to Col. Richard Malcolm Johnstone, a professor who lived on the campus of the University of Georgia. About this time he was converted by the preaching of Rev. W. H. Parks of the Methodist Episcopal Church, South (MECS), and became very interested in things religious. He did not receive any formal education, but applied himself to learn as much as he could as the opportunity presented itself. On November 8, 1863, he married one of the servants of Bishop George F. Pierce of the MECS, named Harriet A. Turner, with whom he had nine children.

When Emancipation came in 1865 he obtained a position managing a farm near Sparta, and received private lessons from Bishop Pierce, toward the goal of church leadership. He was licensed to preach in February 1868 and was assigned to the Hancock Circuit, succeeding in his work despite concerted opposition from Whites. On January 9, 1869, he was sent to work in Savannah, Georgia. The following year he was a delegate to the first General Conference of the CME Church, formed after the MECS decided to help its Black membership set up its own separate organization. In 1871 he became pastor of the well-known Trinity Church in Augusta, Georgia, and from there was elected bishop in March 1873. Not quite thirty-one, he was the youngest person ever elected bishop in the history of the church.

As a youthful and creative bishop, Holsey had a great influence in the formative years of the church, and is considered the "father" of education in the church. At the first General Conference he offered the resolution that led to the founding of a publishing house for the denomination. He was also instrumental in raising the seed money for and founding Paine College in Augusta in 1882, for which he served as the first vice-president of its interracial board of trustees. He was also crucial in founding Lane College in Jackson, Tennessee, the Holsey Industrial Institute in Cordele, Georgia, and the Helen B. Cobb Institute for Girls in Barnesville, Georgia.

For many years he served as commissioner of education for the church, and edited the church paper, the *Gospel Trumpet*, for four years. He was a delegate to the World Methodist Conference in London in 1881 and again in Washington, D.C., in 1891. In 1891 he published *The Hymn Book of the Colored M. E. Church in America*, and in 1894 published *A Manual of the Discipline of the Colored Methodist Episcopal Church in America*. In 1898 he published his own story, called *Autobiography, Sermons, Addresses, and Essays of Bishop L. H. Holsey, D.D.*, and the following year wrote *The Race Problem*. In 1904 he was an honored delegate at the Sociological Congress meeting in Washington, D.C., and was at the center of sociological discussions of the issue of segregation and race. For 25 years he was Secretary of the College of Bishops, and was thus the spokesman for the denomination.

Cade, John B. *Holsey, the Incomparable*. New York: Pageant, 1963. 221 pp.
Holsey, Lucius Henry. *Autobiography, Sermons, Addresses, and Essays of Bishop L. H. Holsey, D.D.* Atlanta, GA: Franklin Printing and Publishing Co., 1898. 288 pp.
———. *Little Gems*. Atlanta, GA: Franklin Printing and Publishing Co., 1905. 55 pp.
———, ed. *A Manual of Discipline of the Colored Methodist Episcopal Church in America*. Jackson, TN: CME Church, I. H. Anderson, agent, 1894.
———. *The Racial Problem*. Atlanta, GA: The Author, 1899. 23 pp.
———. "Race Segregation." In National Sociological Society, *How to Solve the Race Problem*. Washington, DC: Bersford, Printer, 1904, pp. 40–66.
HUBA, AARS, BAW, IBAW, IBAWCB, WWCR, TCNL, EWM, WWWA (4), *NBH, CMECTY, HCMEC, HCMECA, DAB* (vol.5).

HOLY AFRICAN CHURCH. An Eastern Orthodox church. The Holy African Church emerged from the chaotic period following the death of Archbishop **George Alexander McGuire**, the founder of the **African Orthodox Church** (AOC). In 1935 Bishop **Reginald Grant Barrow** established the African

Orthodox Church of New York. He was soon joined by **Arthur Stanley Trotman** and **Robert Arthur Valentine**, two other former AOC bishops, and together they founded the **African Orthodox Church of New York and Massachusetts**. Meanwhile, a court suit over the use of the name began. While the suit was being adjudicated, Barrow suspended Trotman who proceeded to establish a third group, the African Orthodox Church, Inc. (the AOC had incorporated in Florida, not New York).

In 1938 the courts ruled against both Barrow and Trotman, forbidding their use of the names "African Orthodox Church" in any form. Trotman's jurisdiction reorganized as the Holy African Church which eventually absorbed the substance of Barrow's jurisdiction. Trotman consecrated **Frederick Augustus Toote**, formerly vicar general of the New York branch of the AOC, in 1938 and **Gladstone St. Clair Nurse** in 1939. Valentine succeeded Trotman, who died in 1945. Valentine was succeeded by Toote in 1954, and Nurse succeeded Toote in 1959. Nurse was finally able to work out an agreement with the AOC to unite the two jurisdictions once again in 1964, and the Holy African Church merged into the African Orthodox Church.

Terry-Thompson, A. C. *The History of the African Orthodox Church.* N.p.: 1956. 139 pp.

Trela, Jonathan. *A History of the North American Old Roman Catholic Church.* Scranton, PA: The Author, 1979. 124 pp.

HOLY FAMILY, CONGREGATION OF THE SISTERS OF THE.

A religious order of the **Roman Catholic Church**. This second religious congregation of African American Catholic sisters was founded in 1842 in New Orleans by two women of color, **Henriette Delille** (1813–1862) and Juliette Gaudin (1808–1887). The Free People of Color in Louisiana were descendants of French and Spanish soldiers and settlers and Indian and African women. They were French in language and culture and formed a category apart in the pre-Civil War period. Many women of color occupied a social position with White men unprotected by the marriage vows. It is from this background that Henriette Delille emerged. Very early in her youth she worked with several religious women in social service among the slaves and indigent Blacks. Juliette Gaudin, originally from Cuba, joined her in her works of charity and service to the poor. Two attempts to create a religious community failed because Black and White women were not permitted to live together.

Finally, in 1842, with the help of the vicar general of New Orleans, Étienne Rousselon, a priest from France, Henriette and Juliette became a community of two. The Sisters of the Holy Family was established on the Feast of the Presentation of the Blessed Virgin, November 21. In 1843, Josephine Charles (1812–1885), also a free woman of color, joined them. In 1852 the sisters made their first canonical religious vows.

From the beginning the sisters nursed the sick and cared for the indigent Blacks and slaves. They taught catechism and other subjects both to children of the Creoles of color and to the slaves. In 1853 they did heroic work in nursing the sick during the Yellow Fever epidemic. It was this action that finally brought them grudging public acknowledgement as a religious community in New Orleans. But it was not until 1872, ten years after Henriette's death, that the sisters received the right to wear the religious habit on the streets of New Orleans.

The spirituality of the Holy Family sisters was that of nineteenth-century France. Their rule of life, which was fairly severe, was based on the Rule of St. Augustine. It was Rousselon who named the community in honor of the Holy Family. Originally, Henriette Delille desired the title "Sisters of the Presentation." November 21st, the Feast of the Presentation of Mary, became their patronal feast. The Holy Family Sisters remained a diocesan congregation until 1949 when they petitioned and received official approval by Rome.

The work of the sisters has been in the area of education and nursing care. For a long time their ministry was confined to Louisiana. Today the sisters have schools in California, Texas, Oklahoma, and in Belize in Central America. They are also working in the African nation of Nigeria.

The Holy Family Sisters had a major role in the history of the Catholic Church in New Orleans and southern Louisiana. They were a major factor in the evangelization of the African American community in many places in the South. At the same time, their existence as an African American community in a southern, slaveholding city in the first part of the nineteenth century is a statement about the faith and the fervor of African American Catholics in Louisiana at that time. In recent years, the cause for the canonization of Henriette Delille has been introduced at Rome. In 1991 the community numbered some 200 members.

Baudier, Roger. *The Catholic Church in Louisiana.* New Orleans: A. W. Hyatt Stationery Manufacturing, 1939. 605 pp.

Davis, Cyprian. *The History of Black Catholics in the United States*. New York: Crossroad, 1990. 347 pp.

Dehey, Elinor Tong. *Religious Orders of Women in the United States*. Cleveland, OH: The Author, 1930. 908 pp.

Detiege, Sister Audrey Marie. *Henriette Delille: Free Woman of Color*. New Orleans: Sisters of the Holy Family, 1976.

Hart, Sister Mary Francis Borgia. *Violets in the King's Garden: A History of the Sisters of the Holy Family of New Orleans*. New Orleans: The Author, 1976. 137 pp.

Cyprian Davis

HOMER COLLEGE. A **Christian Methodist Episcopal Church** (CME) school. Homer College began with the desire of CME Church members in Louisiana to have a school for the training of their youth. Discussion were held at the 1878 and 1879 annual conferences and the town of Homer chosen as the site. Eighty acres were purchased the next year, but plans were scrapped in disagreements over the location. In the meantime, Isaac Bullock, a leading minister in the conference, obtained the cooperation of some of Homer's leading citizens to open a private school. Homer Seminary opened with M. L. Coleman as principal. In 1893 Homer Seminary came under the care of the Louisiana Conference and at the CME General Conference the next year, the school was adopted as a denominational educational facility.

In 1910 the name of the school was changed to Homer College, a sign of the changing emphasis of the school away from elementary and high school education. The years immediately after the adoption of the school by the General Conference saw two significant pressures placed on Homer. First, public education for African Americans in northern Louisiana improved to the point that its elementary and secondary schools (which had the bulk of the students) were not as necessary. On an average, of the 200 students at Homer annually, 10 to 12 were in the college department.

Then in 1910 **Monroe F. Jamison** was elected to the episcopacy and assigned to preside over the Texas and Louisiana Conferences. He was an advocate of Texas College, also a CME school. Rather than develop Homer as a college, he wanted to use Homer as a feeder school for Texas College. The conflict raised by Jamison contributed substantively to the decision to close the school in 1918.

Lakey, Othal H. *The History of the C.M.E. Church*. Memphis, TN: CME Publishing House, 1985. 683 pp.

HOOD, JAMES WALKER (May 30, 1831–October 30, 1918), 17th bishop of the **African Methodist Episcopal Zion Church** (AMEZ), was born in Chester County, Pennsylvania, the son of Levi and Harriet (Walker) Hood. His father was a tenant farmer and preacher who helped found a Methodist church in Wilmington, Delaware, where the family moved in about 1841. Hood received only a few years of formal schooling, but was a quick learner. At the age of eighteen Hood became assured of his Christian faith, and at age twenty-one received a call to preach. He did not receive a preacher's license, however, until 1856, because of several intervening circumstances. He married Hannah L. Ralph in September, 1852, and moved to New York, where she died of consumption in 1855. In 1857 he moved again, this time to New Haven, Connecticut, where he joined the local AMEZ Church. In May 1858, he married Sophia J. Nugent, with whom he had seven children.

Hood's career in the church began in June 1858, when the pulpit of the local church became vacant and the bishop placed him in charge. The following year he joined the New England Annual Conference on trial and was appointed as missionary to Nova Scotia. There was no money to fund such a venture, and Hood returned to New York City, where he worked in a hotel for thirteen months before he could afford to undertake the assignment. He was ordained deacon in September 1860, and sailed for Halifax. After a year of hard work, he managed to establish a small congregation in a community hostile to Methodists. He was ordained an elder in 1862. In 1863 he moved to Bridgeport, Connecticut, but after only six months was transferred to mission work in North Carolina among newly freed Blacks behind the advancing Union Army lines. He worked variously at New Berne, Fayetteville, and Charlotte. He is given the primary credit for the subsequent strength of the church in that state. In 1868 he took a prominent part in the North Carolina Reconstruction Constitutional Convention, and for three years thereafter served as Assistant Superintendent of Public Instruction.

On July 3, 1872, he was consecrated bishop in the AMEZ Church and headquartered in Fayetteville, North Carolina, where he remained the rest of his days. His second wife died on September 13, 1875. On June 6, 1877, he married a third time, to Keziah (or Katie) P. McCoy, with whom he had three children. During his lengthy forty-four years as bishop, Hood's accomplishments were many. He was one of the founders of Zion Wesley Institute in Salisbury, North

Carolina, in 1879, later renamed Livingstone College, and chaired its board of trustees for thirty-six years. He was an invited speaker at both the first Ecumenical Methodist Conference in London, 1881, and the second in Washington, D.C., in 1891. He helped found two major denominational journals, the *Church Weekly*, and the *Star of Zion*. He was the first Black American minister to publish a volume of sermons, *The Negro in the Christian Pulpit* (1884), a book which the General Conference of the church later adopted as a standard work. He had several other publications, the most well known being *One Hundred Years of the African Methodist Episcopal Zion Church* (1895), which appeared in time for the centennial of the church in 1896. He was known for his temperance work, and was a consultant to President Theodore Roosevelt from 1901 to 1909. He retired in 1916 and died at his home two years later.

Hood, James Walker. *The Negro in the Christian Pulpit; or The Two Characters and Two Destinies as Delineated in Twenty-One Practical Sermons.* Raleigh, NC: Edwards, Broughton & Co., 1884. 363 pp.
———. *One Hundred Years of the African Methodist Episcopal Zion Church.* New York: AME Zion Book Concern, 1895. 625 pp.
———. *The Plan of the Apocalypse.* York, PA: Anstadt & Sons, 1900. 192 pp.
———. *Sermons.* York, PA: P. Anstadt & Sons, 1908. 154 pp.
———. *Sketch of the Early History of the African Methodist Episcopal Zion Church with Jubilee Souvenir and an Appendix.* N.p.: The Author, 1914. 125 pp.
"Zion's Senior Bishops During the Twentieth Century." *Star of Zion* 104 (March 27, 1980): 1–2.
MM, NBH, HUBA, BAW, IBAW, EWM, HAMEZC, WWCR, ACAB, DNAADB, AMEZC, RLOA, IBS, HAMEZCH.

HOOD THEOLOGICAL SEMINARY. An **African Methodist Episcopal Zion Church** (AMEZ) school. When Livingstone College was founded by the African Methodist Episcopal Zion Church in 1882, its original task was the preparation of ministers for the denomination. However, it soon developed a full college curriculum and its theological task was accordingly deemphasized. Pressure emerged to form a separate department of theological studies. The denomination's general conference pledged $6,000 annually to the support of such a department. Future bishop **George Lincoln Blackwell**, a Livingstone graduate who had attended the School of Theology at Boston University, was selected as the first dean of the theological department, a task he fulfilled until his election as bishop in 1908. The department was named in honor of Bishop **J. W. Hood** who had worked so hard to establish the college originally.

The theological department quickly evolved into Hood Theological Seminary. In 1910 the new building that was to house the theological school was finished and opened for classes. The General Conference of 1912 voted to set Hood apart as a graduate school of religion under the general sponsorship of Livingstone College. William O. Carrington was named the first dean.

The seminary prospered for a decade. However, in 1917 Dr. Daniel Cato Suggs had been elected president of Livingstone College. Though personally a wealthy man, Suggs proved unable to accomplish the needed tasks of the school, and it suffered financially. Before he was fired in 1925 the school was in such financial trouble that the seminary was discontinued. Before the school could recover, it was overtaken by the Great Depression. It did not reopen until 1934. Since then it has remained the major theological training institution for the training of AMEZ ministers.

Walls, William J. *The African Methodist Episcopal Zion Church: Reality of the Black Church.* Charlotte, NC: A. M. E. Zion Publishing House, 1974. 669 pp.

HOOKS, BENJAMIN LAWSON (b. January 31, 1925), Baptist (**Progressive National Baptist Convention**) minister and head of the National Association for the Advancement of Colored People (N.A.A.C.P.), was born in Memphis, Tennessee, the son of Robert Britten and Bessie (White) Hooks. His father ran a photography studio and was opposed to organized religion, but even so Hooks found himself drawn to it. Upon graduation from Booker T. Washington High School in Memphis he attended LeMoyne College in Memphis from 1941 to 1943, until he was drafted into World War II. In the U.S. Army he found himself in the strange position of guarding Italian prisoners who would have been allowed to eat in the same Georgia restaurants that were off limits to him as a Black man.

When he left the military he enrolled in De Paul University in Chicago, Illinois, where he gained his J.D. degree in 1948. He returned to Tennessee as a lawyer determined to eliminate segregation. In Memphis he was excluded from the White bar associations and called "Ben" or "boy" in court. Nevertheless he persisted, and slowly gained recognition. On March 21, 1951, he married Frances Dancy, with whom he adopted a daughter. The pull toward the church finally became too much to resist and he was ordained in 1956 to the pastorate of the Middle Baptist Church in Memphis, in addition to his law practice. He co-founded the Mutual Federal Savings and Loan Association of Memphis in 1956 and served it as vice-president and treasurer until 1964. He joined the N.A.A.C.P. and in the late 1950s participated in some of its earliest restaurant sit-ins. He joined the board of directors of Rev. **Martin Luther King Jr.'s Southern Christian Leadership Conference** (S.C.L.C.).

In 1961 Hooks became assistant public defender of Shelby County, about the highest position available to him at the time. He ran once for the Tennessee State Legislature (1954) and twice for juvenile court judge (1959, 1963), losing each time, but continuing to build a constituency among Whites as well as Blacks. As a public defender he took on a number of civil rights cases, and more than once was in danger of losing his life to angry mobs. In 1964 he added the pastorate of the Greater New Mount Moriah Baptist Church in Detroit to his other pastorate and his law duties. He generally took an airplane on alternate Sundays to conduct services. In 1965 he became the first Black criminal court judge in Tennessee history when Governor Frank Clement appointed him to fill a vacancy in the Shelby County criminal court, and in 1966 he won election to a full term in that position.

On December 31, 1968, he resigned from the judgeship in order to devote more time to his ministries and to assume the presidency of Mahalia Jackson Chicken Systems, Inc., a shortlived fast-food chain that went out of business after only two years. He also became involved in Memphis television, producing and hosting the program "Conversations in Black and White" and co-producing "The 40 Percent Speak," referring to the fact that 40 percent of the Memphis population was Black. On April 12, 1972, President Richard Nixon announced his nomination of Hooks as the first Black member of the Federal Communications Commission (F.C.C.), and he was sworn in on July 6, 1972. About this time he became famous for identifying himself as just a "poor little ol' country preacher." As an F.C.C. commissioner he was concerned about the image of minorities in the media, and by 1977 had contributed substantially to the lifting of the minority employment figure in broadcasting from 3 percent to almost 15 percent. During his tenure he was generally characterized as an "activist, liberal, and a consumer advocate." While a member of the Commission, he still tried to preach in either the Detroit or the Memphis church at least once a month, but had to give up being the pastor.

On August 1, 1977, he left the F.C.C. to succeed Roy Wilkins as head of the N.A.A.C.P. There he stressed the importance of "affirmative action" hiring policies, especially for the government, corporations, and print media. He continued the battle for justice on other fronts as well, pushing for quality education for Black students and pressing the government to withhold investments from South Africa's apartheid system. He was perceived by many to reenergize the N.A.A.C.P. as a catalyst for social change. During the 1980s, however, the power and influence of the organization seemed to slip away in the midst of lower Black college enrollment, a larger gap between White and Black family income, and other losses. In February 1992, after fifteen years at the helm, Hooks announced that he would retire from the N.A.A.C.P. at the end of the year.

DeLaney, Paul. "A Purge at the Top, Confusion in the Ranks." *New York Times* (March 29, 1992): p.2, sec.4.

Douglas, Carlyle C. "Watchdog of the Air Waves." *Ebony* 30 (June 1975): 54–62.

IP, AAE, EBA, HBB, BDNM (75), *WWABA* (90–91), *CB* (1978), *NYTBS* (1976), *IBAW.*

HOSIER, HARRY (c.1750–May 1806), colleague of Francis Asbury and the first Black licensed to preach in Methodism. He was born into slavery in the south but manumitted. There is no real evidence for his birthplace, sometimes listed as Fayetteville, North Carolina. At some point he was converted to Methodism. The first clear reference to him is by Francis Asbury (1745–1816), the father of American Methodism, in his journal entry for June 29, 1780, in North Carolina, near the Virginia border. At that point Asbury already thinks of Hosier, sometimes called "Black Harry," as a potential partner in evangelical missions, and indeed we next find him preaching with Asbury at the Fairfax Chapel in Falls Church, Virginia, on May 13, 1781.

Hosier was an instant sensation among both White and Black audiences, with tremendous preaching abilities that earned almost universal praise. Dr. Benjamin Rush (1745–1813), famous Philadelphia physician, remarked of him that, "Making allowances for his illiteracy he was the greatest orator in America." Another Philadelphian, Dr. Sargent, said that Hosier was "the greatest natural orator he ever heard." Thomas Coke (1747–1814), who visited America in 1784 as John Wesley's representative, declared Hosier "one of the best preachers in the world." Asbury acknowledged that the best way to attract a large audience was to announce that Hosier would speak. Because Hosier could not read, his preaching was derived from an impressive memory of biblical texts, powers of observation, and large store of illustrations. He in fact avoided literacy, as he found that reading seemed adversely to affect his preaching. Described as small of stature and coal black, he traveled for months at a time on horseback with Asbury and others as a circuit rider.

He was present at the founding of American Methodism with the famous Christmas Conference in Lovely Lane Chapel in Baltimore, Maryland, meeting from December 24, 1784, to January 2, 1785. It is likely that he knew **Richard Allen**, eventual founder of the **African Methodist Episcopal Church**, though we have little knowledge of their relationship. In 1786 he accompanied Asbury to New York City and preached in the John Street Church in September. From 1786 to 1788 he toured with soon-to-be bishop Richard Whatcoat in Delaware, Maryland, and Pennsylvania, and in 1787, 847 new Black members were reported for that region.

Beginning in 1789 Hosier traveled with Freeborn Garrettson in New York and New England, with great success. In Boston in the summer of 1790 Hosier boarded for a time with Prince Hall (1735–1807), the founder of the first Masonic Lodge for Africans who had become a Methodist in 1774. In 1791 charges of an unknown nature were brought against Hosier by a Sally Lyon, and a full hearing was held in October. He was declared not guilty, and there were apparently no further repercussions. For a time in the 1790s he went with Jesse Lee (1758–1816), virtually founding Methodism in New England. He is credited with helping to found the Zoar Methodist Church in Philadelphia in 1796, said to be the oldest Black congregation in the denomination. In 1803 he was assigned to the Trenton Circuit with John Walker (1764–1849), and in the following years was found variously in Maryland and Pennsylvania.

Although Richard Allen was ordained a deacon in 1799, there is no evidence that Hosier was among those ordained, even after the Methodists formally approved such ordinations in 1800. He died in Philadelphia in May of 1806. Methodist preacher Christopher Atkinson, fellow African American, preached his funeral sermon on May 18. Decades later, rumors circulated that Hosier, whose career was soon forgotten, slid into alcoholism, but there is no evidence to that effect. During the last years of his life he is mentioned frequently in the journal kept by William Colbert, a White Methodist circuit rider who itinerated in and around Philadelphia and was present at Hosier's funeral. On May 1, 1805, just a year before his death, nineteen preachers signed a petition which seems to have been a request to have him ordained. This was not done, however, and he passed away as a faithful lay disciple. His life and ministry were extraordinary and of great impact, not only for the growth of the Methodist Church among both Whites and Blacks, but for the crossing of racial barriers and the reduction of prejudice.

Licorish, Joshua E. *Harry Hosier: African Pioneer Preacher.* Philadelphia, PA: Afro-Methodist Associates, 1967. 12 pp.

Melton, J. Gordon. "A Footnote to Black Methodist History—The Death of Black Harry Hosier." *Methodist History* 8, 1 (October 1969): 88–89.

Raybold, G. A. *Methodism in West Jersey.* New York: Lane & Scott, 189. 202 pp.

Smith, Warren Thomas. "Harry Hosier: Black Preacher Extraordinary." *Journal of the Interdenominational Theological Center* 7 (Spring 1980): 111–128.

Smith, Warren Thomas. *Harry Hosier: Circuit Rider.* Nashville, TN: The Upper Room, 1981. 64 pp.

HNRA, EWM, NYB (1912).

HOUSE OF GOD, HOLY CHURCH OF THE LIVING GOD, THE PILLAR AND GROUND OF THE TRUTH HOUSE OF PRAYER FOR ALL PEOPLE (HEBREW PENTECOSTAL). A Holiness Pentecostal church. The House of God, Holy Church of the Living God, the Pillar and Ground of the Truth House of Prayer for All People (Hebrew Pentecostal) was founded in Beaufort, South Carolina, in 1914 by R. A. R. Johnson, formerly associated with the **Church of the Living God, the Pillar and Ground of the Truth** headed by **Mary Lewis Tate**. From the Church of the Living God, Johnson received a Holiness Pentecostal doctrinal perspective and an acceptance of women in the ministry. From other sources he absorbed some Jewish emphases. The group strongly identifies with the ancient Hebrews and keeps some of the Jewish Festivals, especially Passover.

Johnson was succeeded in 1950 as by Bishop Simon Peter Rawlings (1914?–January 1, 1991). Rawlings had been a member of the church since the 1930s. He became a pastor for the Church in Lexington, Kentucky, in 1935 and remained there for the rest of his life. Rawlings has been succeeded by Bishop F. C. Scott.

Headquarters of the church is in Lexington, Kentucky.

HOUSE OF GOD, WHICH IS THE CHURCH OF THE LIVING GOD, THE PILLAR AND GROUND OF TRUTH, INC. A Holiness Pentecostal church. In

1919 the **Church of the Living God, the Pillar and Ground of Truth** founded by **Mary Lewis Tate** experienced its first major schism when Bishop Archie H. White led the Philadelphia congregation into an independent organization. The new church was like its parent organization in belief and practice, there being no doctrinal issues in the split. Bishop White led the church as its spiritual and temporal leader for many years and has been succeeded by his son Bishop Jesse J. White, the present leader.

Headquarters is located in Philadelphia. In 1990 there were approximately 110 congregations and 26,000 members.

HOUSE OF GOD, WHICH IS THE CHURCH OF THE LIVING GOD, THE PILLAR AND GROUND OF THE TRUTH WITHOUT CONTROVERSY. A Holiness Pentecostal church. **Mary Lewis Tate**, the founder of **Church of the Living God, the Pillar and Ground of the Truth**, died in 1930. Church leaders were unable to reach agreement on naming a successor. Instead, in 1931, they divided the country into three regions, each comprising 16 states. One of three overseers was Mary Frankie Lewis Tate, the widow of Mother Tate's son, W. C. Lewis. Over the years the region she led became was separated for the other two regions and became informally known as the Keith Dominion, and officially as the House of God, Which is the Church of the Living God, the Pillar and Ground of Truth Without Controversy. Keith was succeeded by Bishop J. W. Jenkins, the present Chief Overseer. He is assisted by a Supreme Executive Council.

Melton, J. Gordon. *The Encyclopedia of American Religions.* Detroit, MI: Gale Research Company, 1989. 1100 pp.

HOUSE OF JUDAH. Black Jewish sect. The House of Judah was founded in the 1960s in Chicago by William Alexander Lewis. Lewis had moved to Chicago from his native Alabama and had encountered a street preacher who introduced him to **Black Judaism**. Lewis' son became a preacher himself, taking the title Prophet, and gathered a small following in a storefront church on Chicago's south side. In 1971, he moved his followers to a rural communal site near Grand Junction, Michigan.

The group was little noticed in Michigan for over a decade. Then in 1983 a young boy in the group died and it was determined that he had been beaten to death. The death launched an investigation into possible child abuse within the community. As the investigation heated up and members of the group were arrested, the group moved its headquarters to Wetumpka, Alabama. The mother of the dead boy was convicted on manslaughter. In 1986, Lewis, who had ordered children beaten to teach obedience, and seven of his followers were convicted on child slavery charges. The convictions were upheld on appeal. In 1989, the woman convicted of manslaughter was released and rejoined the group in Alabama.

HOWARD, EDWARD J. (1871–1941), 58th bishop of the **African Methodist Episcopal Church** (AME), was born in Brownsville, Missouri. He experienced conversion in 1882 in Paola, Miami County, Kansas, where he went to high school. He later attended Paul Quinn College in Waco, Texas, was licensed to preach in 1895 and joined the Central Texas Annual Conference in 1897. He served a number of charges in Texas, and was pastor of Wesley Chapel AME Church in Houston when he was elected bishop in May 1936, on the fourth ballot.

He was assigned to the Fourteenth Episcopal District (West Africa), but because of the episcopal shifting after the death of Bishop **W. D. Johnson** was soon shifted to the Thirteenth Episcopal District (Kentucky and Tennessee). Bishop **Reverdy C. Ransom** had already closed Turner College in Tennessee and Howard sold it for $9,000. In 1940 he was assigned to the Twelfth Episcopal District (Oklahoma and Arkansas).

BAMEC, HAMEC, EWM.

HOWARD, M. WILLIAM, JR. (b. March 3, 1946), former president of the National Council of Churches and now president of New York Theological Seminary, was born in Americus, Georgia, the son of M. William, Sr., and Laura Turner Howard. He received his B.A. in 1968 from Morehouse College in Atlanta, Georgia, and his M.Div. in 1972 from Princeton Theological Seminary in New Jersey.

In 1972 he became executive director of the **Black Council** of the **Reformed Church in America**, although he is not a Reformed Church minister, but was ordained in 1974 with the **American Baptist Churches in the U.S.A.** He maintained his position with the African American Council until the spring of 1992. From 1976 to 1978 he was also moderator of the Program to Combat Racism of the World Council of Churches, and from 1979 to 1981 he was president of the National Council of Churches, its youngest president ever.

Howard has served on many boards and committees, including the boards of trustees of the National Urban League (1981–88), Independent Sector (1981–86), and Children's Defense Fund (1981–86). He is president of the American Committee on Africa and chaired the ecumenical delegation that went with Rev. **Jesse Jackson** in January 1984, to obtain the release of Lt. Robert Goodman in Damascus, Syria. He serves on the Human Rights Advisory Group of the World Council of Churches. He has received numerous honors and awards, including the Distinguished Alumnus Award from Princeton Seminary in 1982.

In December 1991, he was elected the ninth president of New York Theological Seminary, the first Black to occupy that position. He assumed the presidency in the spring of 1992 and immediately launched a capital funds campaign. The school is the city's largest seminary, with 490 students, an increase of almost 100 percent over the decade of the 1980s. The student body is about 41 percent Black, 21 percent Korean, 20 percent White, and 18 percent Hispanic, and the seminary has a tradition of active social involvement with the surrounding community.

Brozan, Nadine. "Chronicle." *New York Times* (December 11, 1991): D-26.
IBAW, WWABA (90–91).

HOWARD UNIVERSITY.

HOWARD UNIVERSITY. An interdenominational school. Though now a private secular university, Howard University began as part of the response of the Congregational Churches to the Freedmen following the Civil War. The idea of Howard seems to have arisen at First Congregational Church in Washington, D.C. The initial intention of starting the school was to provide for the training of ministers and teachers to lead the African American community. The charter was issued in 1867. From the beginning Howard differed from the other schools associated with the Congregationalist's American Missionary Association (AMA). From the beginning government money supplied a significant amount of the school's support. The AMA did, for obvious reasons, pay the salary of the first teacher and underwrote the expenses of the theological department since the government would not support the training of ministers. The ministerial training course began in 1868 and the theological department was formally established in 1870. That theological department grew into the

University's School of Religion (renamed School of Divinity in 1981).

Slowly the Congregationalists relinquished control of Howard which has grown into one of the most important African American institutions in the nation. The School of Divinity keeps a loose association with the **United Church of Christ** (of which the former Congregationalist Church is now a constituent part), which lists it among its officially approved schools for ministerial education.

In 1985 the School of Divinity instituted the research center on Black Religious Bodies under the direction of Dr. Wardell J. Payne. Its major product to date has been the *Directory of African American Religious Bodies: A Compendium by the Howard University School of Religion*, edited by Wardell J. Payne.

Holmes, Dwight O. W. "Fifty Years of Howard University." *Journal of Negro History* 3 (October 1918).
Payne, Wardell J., ed. *Directory of African American Religious Bodies: A Compendium by the Howard University School of Divinity.* Washington, DC: Howard University Press, 1991. 363 pp.
Richardson, Joe M. *Christian Reconstruction: The American Missionary Association and Southern Blacks, 1861–1890.* Athens, GA: University of Georgia Press, 1986. 348 pp.

HOWZE, JOSEPH LAWSON (b. August 30, 1923), the bishop of Biloxi, Mississippi for the **Roman Catholic Church**, was born in Daphne, Alabama, the oldest of four children in the family of Albert Otis and Helen Artemesia (Lawson) Howze. His father was an ice cream maker in a drugstore in Mobile and a strong Methodist. His mother sang in the Baptist Church. Their next-door neighbors were Catholic and suggested that Howze be sent to kindergarten at the nearby Most Pure Heart of Mary School, conducted by the Sisters of the Holy Ghost from San Antonio, Texas. His mother died in 1928 after the birth of her fourth child and the children were moved back to the Lawson farm in Daphne and were reared by their maternal grandparents. His father found new work in Mobile and later married Sammie L. Jones, with whom he had three more children.

Howze went to the Turkey Branch School where his aunt was the teacher and at age sixteen joined the Baptist Church in Saraland, Alabama. He taught himself how to play the piano and accompanied the Sunday School choir. About age sixteen he and a brother were sent to live with his paternal grandparents in Plateau, so they could attend the Mobile County Training School. Howze missed his entire junior year because of an operation to correct debilitating fallen arches, but still graduated as valedictorian in 1944 (the painful condition in his feet was never completely corrected). He then resided with a cousin, Susie Norris, who helped him move through Alabama Junior College and Alabama State University in Montgomery. He was president of his senior class and earned his B.S. in science in 1948.

In 1948, as he found a teaching position in biology and chemistry at Central High School in Mobile, he met the Josephite assistant pastor of Most Pure Heart of Mary Church in Mobile, Father Benjamin Horton. Under Horton's influence and direction, Howze decided to become a Catholic and was conditionally baptized on December 4, 1948. He took the religious name of Joseph. From 1951 to 1953 he taught at St. Monica's Catholic School in Tulsa, Oklahoma. By 1952 he had a desire to become a priest and received encouragement from Bishop Waters of Raleigh, North Carolina. In September 1953, when most Catholic seminaries still would not accept Blacks, he entered Epiphany Apostolic College in Newburgh, New York, a Josephite school. He later transferred to the Diocesan Preparatory Seminary in Buffalo, New York, then to Christ the King Seminary at St. Bonaventure University in New York, from which he graduated. He was ordained priest on May 7, 1959, and offered his first Mass on May 10.

From 1959 to 1972 Howze was parish priest at several Roman Catholic churches in North Carolina, including Our Lady of Consolation in Charlotte; Our Lady of Victory in Southern Pines; Our Lady of Lourdes in Sanford; St. Teresa of Avila in Durham; St. Anthony in Asheville; and St. Lawrence in Asheville. During these years he was also a high school teacher, chair of the Diocesan Liturgical Commission, and Director of the Propagation of the Faith. In the turbulent 60s he and other priests were forbidden to take part in public demonstrations; thus, his civil rights role was a quiet one. On November 8, 1972, Pope Paul VI appointed him Bishop of Maxita and Auxiliary Bishop of the Diocese of Natchez-Jackson (Mississippi), and he was consecrated for that task on January 28, 1973. He was the third Black American Catholic bishop in history, following **James A. Healy** (1875) and **Harold Perry** (1966). About 1974 he became president of the National Black Catholic Clergy, a caucus group within the church.

On March 1, 1977, Pope Paul VI appointed Howze Bishop of Biloxi, Mississippi, a newly established diocese covering the southeastern part of the state, with over 47,000 Catholics at the time, including about 5,000 Blacks. He was officially installed on June 6, 1977. By this time two other Black bishops had been consecrated, **Eugene Marino** (1974) and **Joseph Francis** (1976), but they and Perry were all auxiliary (assistant) bishops. Howze thus became the first Black bishop to head a diocese since Bishop Healy in the 19th century. At the time of Howze's appointment there were approximately one million Black Catholics in the America and 250 Black priests. Those numbers have since increased considerably, and the Roman Catholic Church currently has about the sixth largest Black membership of religious groups in America.

Poinsett, Alex. "God's Mississippi Servant." *Ebony* 35 (March 1980): 110–115.
"Ten Religious Groups with Biggest Black Membership." *Ebony* 39 (March 1984): 140–144.
OBS, OTSB, NA, IBAW, WWR (85), *WWABA* (90–91), *NYTBS* (1977).

HUDLUN, ANNA ELIZABETH (February 6, 1840–November 21, 1914), **African Methodist Episcopal Church** (AME) member and social worker, was born in Uniontown, Pennsylvania. Her mother, whose last name was Lewis, had just recently been set free by the Quaker family that had owned her; her father is unknown. After a few years Hudlun was placed with another Quaker family while her mother traveled as a personal servant to a prominent family. Hudlun was significantly influenced by the pious atmosphere of her Quaker surroundings.

At about the age of twelve she was rejoined with her mother and together they moved westward, stopping for a time in St. Louis, Missouri, then ending up in Chicago, Illinois, in 1854. There they joined Quinn Chapel AME Church and in 1855 she married Joseph Henry Hudlun. Her husband earned a good living working at the Chicago Board of Trade, and they built a five-room cottage on Third Avenue near the Dearborn Station, reportedly the first house in the city contracted for and built by Black people. Their home soon became a center of community social life. She was very active in the Quinn Chapel AME Church, and created programs to serve the poor through those auspices and worked to keep the Chicago integrated schools open.

In the terrible Chicago fire of 1871 the Hudluns took in many homeless families, Black and White, and cared for them until they could be reestablished. She sought out the distressed and gave them comfort, earning her the titles "Mother Hudlun" and "Fire Angel." In the midst of that fire her husband went to the Board of Trade, opened the vaults, and saved many valuable papers and books. In the second Chicago fire of 1874 she again was conspicuous for her work among those hardest hit, supplying food and clothing insofar as she was able. Another title was soon bestowed upon her by a grateful community, "Chicago's Grand Old Lady."

Her husband, Joseph Hudlun, was so honored by the Chicago Board of Trade for his heroic deeds that an oil portrait of him was hung in its "Hall of Celebrities," and upon his death Joseph Henry, Jr., was hired to take his place. Hudlun's daughter, Joan, worked with her to perpetuate the various efforts among Chicago's poor. On weekends they supervised activities for several dependents of the Juvenile Court and Joan helped Hudlun found and organize the Home for the Aged and Infirm, which claimed the major part of Hudlun's attention for the remainder of her life.

HH, PNW, IBAW, AAE.

HUGHES, (JAMES) LANGSTON (February 1, 1902–May 22, 1967), poet, playwright, author, and lecturer, was born in Joplin, Missouri, the son of James Nathaniel and Carrie Mercer (Langston) Hughes. His father was a businessman and rancher who spent years studying law on the side. Frustrated by color-based obstacles in the United States, he angrily left his family shortly after Hughes was born and moved to Mexico, where he gained some wealth. His mother traveled around looking for decent jobs. Hughes grew up in a number of cities, and spent some time in Lawrence, Kansas, living with a grandmother whose first husband, Sheridan Leary, had died with John Brown at Harper's Ferry. By 1914 it was clear that his father was not coming back. His mother then married Homer Clarke, and Hughes joined them in Lincoln, Illinois. There he finished grammar school in 1916 and was elected class poet because he was Black; he had not yet written any poems. He then wrote a poem and delivered it at graduation. He attended Central High School in Cleveland, Ohio, and was elected editor of the class yearbook.

Hughes spent the summer of 1919 in Mexico with his father, but they did not get along. His father promised, however, to give him a college education and in 1921 Hughes entered Columbia University in New York City. He felt lost and lonely there and quit at the end of the first year, but still published his first piece, "The Negro Speaks of Rivers," in *Crisis* magazine. He moved briefly to Harlem and then began to travel. He was a seaman on ships that took him to Africa and Paris,

and he worked variously as a cook, waiter, and doorman. He spent time in Italy and Spain before finally rejoining his mother in Washington, D.C. He found a job in a local hotel as a busboy and began adding to his early corpus of poetry, blues, and spirituals. Soon he was "discovered" by Vachel Lindsay, who brought him to the attention of the literary world. His poem, "The Weary Blues" won first prize in a contest sponsored by *Opportunity* magazine.

A wealthy New York woman "patron" helped him enroll in Lincoln University in Pennsylvania in 1926, from which he graduated with a B.A. in 1929. In the meantime, on weekends and holidays, he became the toast of the New York elite, along with other Black artists then in vogue, such as Paul Robeson, Florence Mills, and Roland Hayes. His first book of poems, *The Weary Blues*, came in 1926, and the second, *Fine Clothes to the Jew*, arrived in 1927. The White critics generally applauded these works, but the Black critics tended to feel that they focused too much on the imperfections and failures of Black life and did not put the traditional "best foot forward" for Blacks. Hughes identified strongly with the common people and felt that all of Black life needed to be expressed. His novel *Not Without Laughter* (1930) won the Harmon Prize of $400 and a gold medal.

Hughes realized the artistic "Harlem Renaissance" could not last when a satirical poem of his on the opening of the Waldorf Hotel in the midst of hundreds of the poor and hungry angered his patron. His autobiographical book, *The Big Sea* (1930), marked the beginning of an independent path. His works often portrayed the plight of the working oppressed, as in the poems of *Scottsboro Limited* (1932), and showed with humor and wisdom White society as seen by Blacks, as in *Ways of White Folks* (1934). In 1934 Dr. Charles Austin Beard selected him as one of America's twenty-five most interesting, socially conscious people. In 1935 he received the Guggenheim Fellowship for Creative Work. He continued traveling as much as possible and in 1936 was in Spain covering its civil war as correspondent for the Baltimore *Afro-American*. In 1936 his play, *Mulatto*, ran for a year on Broadway. For a Black person to make a living as a writer and lecturer in the Depression years was a major accomplishment, and in fact he was the first in America to so make his living at any time. He greatly boosted Black theater by founding the Suitcase Theater in Harlem, the Negro Art Theater in Los Angeles, and in 1940 the Skyloft Players in Chicago.

During the 1940s in a regular *Chicago Defender* column Hughes created the character Jesse B. Semple (or Simple), a ghetto dweller whose life is painful, but who nevertheless is not on welfare or drugs, is always looking ahead, and consistently reveals basic insights about life. This epitomized Hughes' identification with the common person, and Simple was the main character in five books published from 1950 to 1965. In 1947–48 he was visiting professor of creative writing at Atlanta University and in 1948 he accomplished his sixth cross-country tour. In 1949–50 he was poet in residence at the Laboratory School of the University of Chicago. In 1951 he wrote *Montage of a Dream Deferred*, with the lines, "What happens to a dream deferred? / Does it dry up / like a raisin in the sun?," which later inspired the famous play, *Raisin in the Sun* by Lorraine Hansberry.

In 1956 he published his second autobiography, *I Wonder as I Wander*. Over the years his output was prolific, with ten volumes of poetry, sixty-six short stories, more than one hundred essays, twenty theatrical works, eleven books on Black life and history (such as *Fight for Freedom: The Story of the N.A.A.C.P.*, 1962), two novels, and two autobiographies. He kept abreast of social change with such publications as *Ask Your Mama: 12 Moods for Jazz* (1961) and *The Panther and the Lash: Poems of Our Times* (1967). In 1960 he won the coveted Spingarn Medal as "Poet Laureate of the Negro Race," and in 1961 was elected to the National Institute of Arts and Letters. He never married.

Although critics, both Black and White, sometimes treated him harshly, his work has had among the greatest public response of any American writer. His poems have been translated into many languages and a number have been set to music. A large part of his artistic appeal stems from his sense that "we possess within ourselves a great reservoir of physical and spiritual strength." Some of his writing was specifically religious, such as the "gospel song-play" *Black Nativity*, which played on Broadway in 1961 and the similar *Tambourines to Glory* in 1963 (based on the 1958 novel of the same title), and *The Prodigal Son* (1964). He tried to express "his unshakable conviction that mankind is possessed of the divinity of God" in terms understood by almost everyone who could read.

Dickinson, Donald C. *A Bio-Bibliography of Langston Hughes, 1902–1967*. 2nd ed. Hamden, CT: Archon Books, 1972. 273 pp.

Emanuel, James A. *Langston Hughes*. New York: Twayne Publishers, 1967. 192 pp.

Hughes, (James) Langston. *The Big Sea, An Autobiography*. New York: A. A. Knopf, 1940. 335 pp.

———. *Fight for Freedom: The Story of the N.A.A.C.P.* New York: Norton, 1962. 224 pp.

———. *I Wonder as I Wander: An Autobiographical Journey*. New York: Holt, Rinehart & Winston, 1956. 405 pp.

———. *Montage of a Dream Deferred*. New York: Holt, Rinehart & Winston, 1951. 75 pp.

———. *Simple Speaks His Mind*. New York: Simon & Schuster, 1950. 231 pp.

Meltzer, Milton. *Langston Hughes: A Biography*. New York: T. Y. Crowell, 1968. 281 pp.

Mikolyzk, Thomas A. *Langston Hughes: A Bio-Bibliography*. New York: Greenwood Press, 1990. 295 pp.

Miller, R. Baxter. *Langston Hughes and Gwendolyn Brooks: A Reference Guide*. Boston: G. K. Hall, 1978. 149 pp.

Myers, Elisabeth P. *Langston Hughes, Poet of His People*. Champagne, IL: Garrard Publishing Co., 1970. 144 pp.

O'Daniel, Thermon B., ed. *Langston Hughes: Black Genius, a Critical Evaluation*. New York: Morrow, 1971.

Rampersad, Arnold. *The Life of Langston Hughes*. New York: Oxford University Press, 1986.

NYTO, DANB, EAB, WWWA (4), BHBA, HNB, TAO, BWASS, ALNA, CB (1940), BWA, IP, GNPP, GBA, PIC, WWCA (38–40), CH, NPT, IBAWCB, SBAA, BAW, AARS, HUBA, IBAW, AAE, EBA.

HUGHES, WILLIAM ALFRED CARROLL (June 19, 1877–July 12, 1940), the fourth Black non-missionary bishop of the Methodist Episcopal Church (now the **United Methodist Church**), was born in Westminster, Maryland, the son of Singleton R. Hughes, Jr. (mother's name unavailable). His father was the first African American appointed as a teacher in Carroll County, Maryland. His grandfather, Singleton R. Hughes, Sr., was a slave who organized and built the first Methodist church for Blacks in Maryland, and purchased freedom for himself and his family.

William A. C. Hughes received his B.A. from Morgan College in Baltimore, Maryland, and attended Gammon Theological Seminary in Atlanta, Georgia. In school he won several oratorical contests, and this ability brought him recognition throughout his career. He married Mary Butler of Baltimore, with whom he had four children. Hughes was licensed to preach at age seventeen and was ordained deacon in 1897 in the Washington Conference, a Black conference in the Methodist Episcopal Church. He attended school for the next two years, and in 1899 was transferred to the Delaware Conference to pastor a church in Hudson, New York. In 1901 he transferred back to the Washington Conference and was assigned to Leigh Street Methodist Episcopal Church in Richmond, Virginia (1901–02). Other pastorates included Lynchburg, Virginia (1903–

04), and the Sharp Street Methodist Episcopal Church in Baltimore, Maryland (1905–11).

In 1912 Hughes became district superintendent of the Baltimore District, and from 1913 to 1916 he was district superintendent of the Washington District. Beginning in 1916 he was a delegate to General Conference. From 1917 to 1940 he was Secretary for Negro Work, Board of Home Missions and Church Extension, Methodist Episcopal Church. During these years he became one of the best-known Black leaders of the denomination, and is credited with originating the Schools of Practical Methods. In 1939 the Methodist Episcopal Church merged with the Methodist Episcopal Church, South and the Methodist Protestant Church to form The Methodist Church. As part of the restructuring the nineteen Black conferences, regardless of location, became part of the Central Jurisdiction. The Central Jurisdiction elected him bishop on June 23, 1940, the first bishop elected by that new body. The previous non-missionary Black bishops of the Methodist Episcopal Church had been **Robert Elijah Jones** (1920), **Matthew Wesley Clair, Jr.** (1920), and **Alexander Preston Shaw** (1936). Unfortunately, Hughes was already in poor physical condition when elected bishop and immediately after his consecration entered Johns Hopkins Hospital. He passed away less than one month later.

EWM, MB.

HUNTER, JOHN ELLSWORTH (November 23, 1917–January 14, 1985), 101st bishop of the **African Methodist Episcopal Church** (AME), was pastoring the St. Stephen AME Church in Detroit, when elected bishop in 1980. He was assigned to the 15th Episcopal District in South Africa, and in 1984 became the first bishop of the newly created 19th Episcopal District of Southern Africa, maintaining his office in Southville, Mississippi. He passed away the following year, leaving behind his widow, Delorez A. Hunter.

Reid, Robert H., Jr. "African Methodism Mourns Bishop John E. Hunter." *AME Christian Recorder* 133 (January 28, 1985): 1.
WWR (85).

HUNTLEY, THOMAS ELLIOTT (June 28, 1903–c.1984), author and prominent Baptist minister, was born in Wadesboro, North Carolina, the son of John P. and Lula (Brewer) Huntley. He was ordained a Baptist minister in 1928. On December 21, 1933, he married Kiffie Elizabeth Esther Maddox. He received his B.A. in 1934 from Morehouse College in Atlanta, Georgia, and did some graduate work at Atlanta University.

From 1933 to 1938 he was pastor of Hall Street Baptist Church in Montgomery, Alabama, followed by pastorates at Mt. Zion Baptist Church in Pensacola, Florida (1938–41) and Spruce Street Baptist Church in Nashville, Tennessee (1941–42). In 1942 he became pastor of Central Baptist Church in St. Louis, Missouri, where he remained for the rest of his career. During that pastorate he gained an international reputation as a social activist and author.

In 1947 Huntley founded the Mobile Church Ministry, Church-on-Wheels. From 1948 to 1952 he was a member of the Social Service Committee of the **National Baptist Convention, U.S.A., Inc.** (N.B.C.U.S.A.), and from 1956 to 1958 served on its Historical Committee. In 1948 he was an organizer of the Ministers' Prayer March on Washington and in 1958 he received a citation from the St. Louis Metropolitan Church Federation. In 1956 he founded the National Baptist Publishing House of South India and the following year chaired the editorial staff of the *Bharath Social and Cultural Trust of South India*. He was active in Americans United for Separation of Church and State, the N.A.A.C.P., the Urban League, and the Society for the Scientific Study of Religion. In 1963 he founded the Family Fireside Institute for Citizenship and Baptist Doctrine. In 1964 he was a leader of the St. Louis Bank Protest Movement, which led to the establishment of the Gateway National Bank. His first book was *As I Saw It, Not CommUnism but CommOnism* (1955), and his 1963 book, *Manual for Every Baptist*, was adopted by the N.B.C.U.S.A. as a standard guide to Baptist church administration. Other writings included *A Baptist Manifesto in Three Epistles* and *Sense and Common Sense in a World of Non-Sense*. He retired in 1983 and passed away shortly thereafter.

Huntley, Thomas E. *As I Saw It, Not CommUnism but CommOnism; A Prophetic Appraisal of the Status Quo, a Message for Our Times and for All Times, for America and for All Nations.* New York: Comet Press Books, 1955. 146 pp.
———. *When People Behave Like Sputniks (As I Saw Them).* New York: Vantage Press, 1960. 112 pp.
———. *Manual for Every Baptist.* St. Louis, MO: Central Service Publications, 1963. 53 pp.
BDNM (75), *WWR* (85), *HUBA, AARS.*

HUNTON, ADDIE D. WAITES (June 11, 1875–June 21, 1943), national officer of the Young Women's Christian Association (Y.W.C.A.) and the National Association for the Advancement of Colored People (N.A.A.C.P.), was born in Norfolk, Virginia, the oldest of three children in the family of Jesse and Adelina (Lawton) Waites. Her father ran a wholesale oyster and shipping business, was part-owner of an amusement park for Blacks, was a founder of the Black Elks (I.B.P.O.E.W.), and was a prominent member of the **African Methodist Episcopal Church** (AME). Her mother passed away a few years after her birth and Hunton was reared by a maternal aunt in Boston. She attended the Boston Girls Latin School and the Spencerian College of Commerce in Philadelphia, where she was the first Black graduate (1889).

She then taught in a public school in Portsmouth, Virginia, for one year, until she was offered a position of "lady principal" and teacher at the State Normal and Agricultural College of Alabama (now Alabama A & M College), where she stayed until 1893. On July 19, 1893 she married William Alphaeus Hunton, who had courted her while she was in Portsmouth. They had four children, of whom only two survived infancy. Her husband was the first Black professional secretary in the International Y.M.C.A. In 1899 he was transferred to the Y.M.C.A. in Atlanta, where she became a secretary and bursar of Clark University. She became well-acquainted with the work of the "Y" and did pioneering organizing among Black women for that group. Her religious affiliation was Episcopalian.

In December 1906 the family moved to Brooklyn, New York, and Hunton was hired the following year by the National Board of the Y.M.C.A. as advisory secretary for work with Black students. She also served from 1906 to 1910 as national organizer for the National Association of Colored Women, the founding convention of which she had attended in 1895 as representative of the Woman's League of Richmond, Virginia. In the winter of 1907–08 she toured the South and Middle West for the "Y," and took a leave during 1909 as she and the children went to live in Switzerland and Strasbourg, where she took classes for three semesters at Kaiser Wilhelm University. She was already quite adept in French and German. In 1910 she returned to "Y" work and took more courses at the College of the City of New York. Her husband became fatally ill with tuberculosis in 1914, and the family moved to Saranac Lake, New York. She left her "Y" position in 1915 to care for him, and he passed away in 1916.

Hunton now volunteered her services to the Y.M.C.A. for World War I and worked with Helen Curtis in the canteens which had been established for Black soldiers in Brooklyn. Their real desire was to go overseas, which was finally permitted in the summer of 1918. Hunton was assigned by the Paris headquarters of the Y.M.C.A. to the Services of Supplies (S.O.S.) work in St. Nazaire, near the Loire River. By this time there were a number of "Y" huts for the 200,000 Black soldiers scattered in various camps, and Hunton, Curtis, and Kathryn Johnson were the only three Black women working among them. Hunton took charge of the canteen at St. Nazaire and added a literacy course and popular Sunday evening discussion to the usual activities. Her presence meant a great deal to the men as they struggled with loneliness and the multitude of indignities heaped upon Blacks in the service.

Her many labors took their toll, and in November 1918 she collapsed from exhaustion and was bedridden for several days. After the Armistice was signed that month the work continued, and in January 1919 she was transferred to direct "Y" work at Calles-les-Eaux in southern France. She arranged the full schedule of activities for more than one thousand Black soldiers who arrived there for leave each week. Not until the spring of 1919 did sixteen other Black women arrive in France to help with the "Y" work. Her most difficult assignment was in May 1919, when she went to the military cemetery at Romagne, where Black soldiers were reburying Americans killed in the Meuse-Argonne battle. She had to deal with the barely contained anger that the Black soldiers were always given the least desirable tasks in addition to countless other means of discrimination. In the fall of 1919, after closing the last hut at Camp Pontanezen, Brest, she returned to the United States.

In 1920 Hunton and Kathryn Johnson published a book about their experiences called *Two Colored Women with the American Expeditionary Forces*. In 1921 Hunton became a vice-president of the N.A.A.C.P. and a field secretary. Again and again she risked her life going into southern communities to speak of the work of the N.A.A.C.P. She took on numerous other duties as well. She was president of the International Council of the Women of Darker Races and of the Empire State Federation of Women's Clubs. She was also president of the Circle for Peace and Foreign Relations. She was a member of the Women's International League for Peace and Freedom and joined its committee which visited Haiti in 1926 to observe the United States occupation. The committee's report, *Occupied Haiti* (1927), included a chapter on race relations by Hunton.

She was a principal organizer of the Fourth Pan-African Congress in New York City, 1927. From 1930 to 1933 she was parliamentarian for the National Association of Colored Women, and she was a member of the Brooklyn Equal Suffrage League. In 1938 she published her last book, a biography of her husband. Her last public appearance was at the 1939 New York World's Fair when she presided over a ceremony honoring outstanding Black women.

Hunton, Addie D. Waites. *Two Colored Women with the American Expeditionary Forces.* Brooklyn, NY: Brooklyn Eagle Press, 1920. 256 pp.

———. *William Alphaeus Hunton, A Pioneer Prophet of Young Men.* New York: Association Press, 1938. 176 pp.

BAW, IBAW, IBAWCB, PNW, WWCR, WWCA (38–40), NAW, DANB, NBAW.

HUNTON, WILLIAM ALPHAEUS, SR.

HUNTON, WILLIAM ALPHAEUS, SR. (October 31, 1863–1916), the first Black national secretary of the Young Men's Christian Association (Y.M.C.A.), was born in Chatham, Ontario, Canada, the sixth son of Stanton and Mary Ann (Cooper) Hunton. His mother died when he was four and all the parental responsibilities then went to his father. His father had purchased his own freedom about 1840 and made his way to Chatham, an end station on the Underground Railroad, in 1843. In 1858 John Brown visited Stanton Hunton to consult about the proposed raid on Harper's Ferry Rebellion. After finishing high school in Chatham, Hunton went to the Wilberforce Institute of Ontario, where he graduated in 1884. He taught public school in Dresden, Canada for a year, and in May 1885 became a probationary clerk in the Department of Indian Affairs, Ottawa. He joined the Y.M.C.A. there as perhaps its only Black member.

In Norfolk, Virginia, there had been a Black Y.M.C.A. since 1875. By 1888 they had a solid enough organization to look for their first executive secretary, and they hired Hunton on January 1, who thus became the first Black employed by any branch of the Y.M.C.A., though there were at that time about fourteen other Black Y.M.C.A.s in the United States. It was surprising for Hunton to take this new position, considering the security of his previous government job and the insecurity of the new position, offered at a hoped-for $800 per year. He also gave up the freedom that Blacks had in Canada as well as a cherished notion of a career in the ministry. Nevertheless, Hunton felt this move was "God's leading," and he had little choice.

His leadership at Norfolk was very successful and the branch grew into rented rooms, acquiring a library, choral club, Bible study groups, educational classes, and more. In January 1891, he was invited by the International Committee of the Y.M.C.A. to be its first Black national/international-level secretary, in charge of "Colored Work." His job basically was to travel the country raising money, organizing Black branches, speaking to White branches, visiting schools and colleges, and holding conferences. In 1893 he wrote a pamphlet, *The First Step*, describing how to establish new "Y" branches. On July 19, 1893, he married Addie D. Waites, with whom he had four children, only two of whom survived infancy. His wife also became a well known "Y" executive. In 1895 the family moved to Atlanta, where Hunton based his work. In 1894 he was a delegate to the Golden Jubilee of the Y.M.C.A. in London.

Hunton's efforts yielded significant results. By 1896 there were about sixty Black Y.M.C.A.s in the country, including forty-one on college campuses. Also by that time the Black Y.M.C.A.s in New Haven, Philadelphia, Baltimore, Washington, Richmond, Norfolk, and Louisville all had paid secretaries. Recognizing the discrimination that faced Black applicants to White branches, Hunton favored the establishment of separate Black branches, and in 1896 he helped organize the Colored Men's Department of the Y.M.C.A. He prayed, however, for the time when there would be no judgments or separations by color. In 1898 Jesse Moorland was hired as the second Black national secretary, and this allowed Hunton to focus on developing branches on college campuses, while Moorland worked in the cities. During the Spanish-American War in 1898 Hunton was assigned to special duty among Black troops at facilities provided at three southern centers.

Hunton contracted malaria during one of his trips to the South, and the 1906 riot in Atlanta aggravated the problem into a severe attack of colitis. That year the family moved to Brooklyn, New York, for his health. In 1907 Hunton addressed the World's Student Christian Federation Conference in Tokyo, Japan, and visited other cities in the Far East. In 1913 he gave his last public address at the World's Student Christian Federation Conference in Lake Mohonk, New York. In 1914 he was stricken with tuberculosis and the family moved to Saranac Lake, New York. The peaceful environment slowed, but did not stop the disease, and he passed away two years later. His wife later wrote a book about his life, using a description of Hunton that W. E. B. DuBois once used, calling him a "Pioneer Prophet of Young Men."

Hopkins, C. Howard. *History of the Y.M.C.A. in North America*. New York: Association Press, 1951. 818 pp.

Hunton, Addie D. Waites. *William Alphaeus Hunton, A Pioneer Prophet of Young Men*. New York: Association Press, 1938. 176 pp.

Hunton, William A. "Women's Clubs: Caring for Young Women." *The Crisis* 2 (July 1911): 121–122.

DANB, IBAW, HUBA, WWCR.

HURST, JOHN (May 10, 1863–May 6, 1930), 36th bishop of the **African Methodist Episcopal Church** (AME), was born in Port-au-Prince, Haiti, one of five children in the family of Thomas and Sylvanie (Gordon) Hurst. He was educated at the combined grammar and high school Lycée National de Port-au-Prince, and was converted in 1877. He was licensed to preach in 1883, and at that time spoke only French. In 1884 the AME Church missionary in Haiti, Rev. Charles W. Morselle, took him to the United States to be a student at Payne Theological Seminary at Wilberforce University in Ohio, where he received his B.D. in 1886. He was ordained deacon that year and assigned to St. Paul's AME Church in Port-au-Prince from 1886 to 1889, and from 1888 to 1889, in addition to his church assignment, he was superintendent of missions in Haiti. He was ordained elder in 1887. In 1889 he was appointed First Secretary of the Haitian Legation at Washington, D.C. by President Hyppolite of Haiti, remaining in that position until 1893. On October 29, 1890, he married Kathrine Bertha Thompson, with whom he had one son.

In 1893 he joined the Baltimore Conference and was assigned to the Crowdensville Circuit, where he built Gaines Chapel. In 1894 he moved to Waters AME Church in Baltimore, where he stayed until 1898. From 1898 to 1903 he was at Bethel AME Church in Baltimore, and from 1903 to 1908 he was once again the pastor of the Waters AME Church. In 1908 he was elected financial secretary of the denomination, remaining in that office until May 1912, when he was elected bishop and assigned to the Eleventh Episcopal District (Florida).

As bishop, Hurst was chancellor of Edward Waters College in Jacksonville, Florida, and a member of the board of trustees for Payne Theological Seminary, Wilberforce University, and Howard University in Washington, D.C. He was a delegate to the World Faith and Order Conference in Lausanne, Switzerland, in 1927, and was a delegate to the World Methodist Conferences in London (1901), Toronto (1911), and London (1921). He served as the National Director of the National Association for the Advancement of Colored People (N.A.A.C.P.). At the death of Bishop Derrick in 1913 he was assigned to the Third Episcopal District (Ohio, Pittsburgh, West Virginia, Nova Scotia, West Indies, and South America). In that capacity he organized the AME Church in Jamaica, receiving nine congregations with 1,100 members.

In 1916 he was reassigned to Florida, where he remained for the next twelve years. In Florida he organized the Ministers Institute for the continuing education of the clergy. He made it both compulsory and possible for each of his ministers to spend one month gaining additional knowledge at Edward Waters College. From 1928 to 1930 he was assigned to the Seventh Episcopal District (South Carolina). He was president of the North Eastern Board, Federated Charities, based in Baltimore, for twelve years. At least eleven churches in Florida are named for him.

AME Year Book. Philadelphia: AME Book Concern, 1918.

———. "Christianity and Women." *The Crisis* 10 (August 1915): 179–180.

HUBA, AARS, CEAMEC, EBA, HAMEC, EWM, WWWA (1), *WWCA* (30–32), *BAMEC.*

HURSTON, ZORA NEALE (January 7, 1903(?)–January 28, 1960), author and folklorist, was born in Eatonville, Florida, one of seven children in the family of John and Lucy Ann (Potts) Hurston. Her birth year is variously given as 1889, 1891, 1901, 1903, and 1907. The *New York Times* obituary in 1960 listed her age as 57 and supported the 1903 date; Hurston herself used several birthdates. Eatonville was the first incorporated Black town in America, with a population of about three hundred. Her father was a carpenter and an itinerant Baptist preacher and her mother was a seamstress. At the age of seven she began to have visions of twelve "scenes" of life that she felt were portents of the future, and indeed over the years she saw each one fulfilled.

Her mother died when she was nine and her father remarried a woman Hurston did not like. Hurston spent the next five years moving among relatives and friends, with only occasional schooling. At the age of thirteen a brother invited her to his home, ostensibly to go back to school, but in reality she was only there to care for his children. She then found a job working as a maid for a White woman, a member of a traveling Gilbert and Sullivan troupe, and stayed with her eighteen months. She was only paid occasionally, however, and she left to waitress in a restaurant. She began attending a night high school in Baltimore, then finally registered at the high school department of Morgan College in Baltimore, Maryland, where she entered as a junior.

After graduating from high school she entered Howard University in Washington, D.C., in 1921, supporting herself as a manicurist. She wrote her first short story for *Stylus*, the college literary magazine. She became ill in the last part of her second year and could not earn enough money for tuition. She dropped out and tried her hand as a freelance writer in New York City. In 1925 a short story, "Spunk," won second prize in a contest sponsored by *Opportunity* magazine. This recognition brought her a job as secretary to the White novelist Fannie Hurst and a scholarship to Barnard College in New York City, where she was admitted as a junior. In New York she became part of the "Harlem Renaissance," with other Black artists such as Paul Robeson and **James Langston Hughes**. She became enamored of anthropology studying under Franz Boas, and upon graduation in 1928 was given a Rosenwald Foundation fellowship for two years' graduate work in anthropology at Columbia University in New York City. She became a member of the American Ethnological Society, the American Anthropological Society, and the American Folk-Lore Society. On May 19, 1927, she married Herbert Sheen.

Thanks to additional funding she was able to stay at Columbia until 1932, conducting Black folklore research both in New York and in Florida. In the winter of 1932 she produced a program of Black spirituals and work songs at the John Golden Theater in New York City, and in May 1934 took that troupe to the National Folklore Festival in St. Louis. Her purpose was to show that there was an audience for naturally performed spirituals, rather than just highly arranged songs. Her success had a large impact on the performance of Black songs and dances in the United States. In 1934 she published her first book, a novel about a Black preacher, called *Jonah's Gourd Vine*. It received very high critical acclaim, and thereafter she was kept busy with commissions for stories and articles. Most of her stories took place in a locale patterned after (if not actually identified as) Eatonville, Florida. Her second book, *Mules and Men* (1935), was a folklore study resulting from the material from Florida she had gathered while at Columbia. She was sometimes criticized for ignoring racial tensions and Black oppression, but she was "thoroughly sick" of the subject and chose instead to present the literary possibilities of day-to-day life in a different focus. She said that she had not had much experience in her own life of the kind of blatant discrimination reported by many of her contemporaries.

From 1936 to 1938, financed by a Guggenheim Fellowship, Hurston traveled in Jamaica and Haiti. The trip supplied the data which led to her writing *Tell My Horse* (1938), a combination of travelogue and anthropology, later reworked as *Voodoo Gods; An Inquiry into Native Myths and Magic in Jamaica and Haiti* (1939). Her first marriage had ended in divorce in 1931 and on June 27, 1939, she married Albert Price III, whom she also later divorced (finalized in November, 1943). She was a staff writer for Warner Brothers/Paramount Studios in Hollywood, California, in 1941, and in 1942 she published her autobiography, *Dust Tracks on a Road*. Her last major work was the novel *Seraph on the Suwanee* (1948), a result of folklore collecting in Honduras from 1946 to 1948.

She was briefly a professor of drama at North Carolina College for Negroes (now North Carolina Central University), but in the 1950s lost touch with most of her friends. This was partly because of a loss of financial support for publishing and research and partly because she withdrew from society after a devastating morals charge relating to an emotionally retarded sixteen-year-old boy. She was cleared, but the pain of the media sensationalism remained. She was also hurt socially by articles she wrote in such far-right publications as the *American Legion* magazine, voicing her dissent against the struggle for Black voting rights and against school desegregation.

She was a maid in 1950, a librarian at the Patrick Air Force Base in Florida in 1956–57, and a part-time teacher at Lincoln Park Academy in Fort Pierce, Florida, in 1958–59. She passed away the following year after a stroke in poverty and obscurity. Religiously, her primary importance is as the first major investigator and reporter of "**voduo**" and/or "hoodoo" practices, both in the United States and in the West Indies. Her novel, *Moses, Man of the Mountain* (1939) is also noteworthy because of its placing Moses and his law-giving activity in a traditional African context. This has been described by Robert Hemenway as an attempt to "kidnap Moses from Judeo-Christian tradition, claiming that his true birthright is African and that his true constituency is Afro-American."

Cannon, Katie G. "Resources for a Constructive Ethic in the Life and Work of Zora Neale Hurston." *Journal of Feminist Studies in Religion* 1 (Spring 1985): 37–51.

Williams, Delores S. "Women's Oppression and Lifeline Politics in Black Women's Religious Narratives." *Journal of Feminist Studies in Religion* 1 (Fall 1985): 59–71.

Hemenway, Robert E. *Zora Neale Hurston: A Literary Biography*. Urbana, IL: University of Illinois Press, 1977. 371 pp.

Hurston, Zora Neale. *Dust Tracks on a Road*. Philadelphia. PA: J. B. Lippincott Co., 1942. 294 pp.

———. *Jonah's Gourd Vine*. Philadelphia, PA: J. B. Lippincott Co., 1934. 316 pp.

———. *Moses, Man of the Mountain*. Philadelphia, PA: J. B. Lippincott Co., 1939. 351 pp.

———. *Mules and Men*. Philadelphia, PA: J. B. Lippincott Co., 1935. 342 pp.

———. *Voodoo Gods: An Inquiry into Native Myths and Magic in Jamaica and Haiti*. London: J. M. Dent & Sons, 1939. 290 pp.

Nathiri, N. Y. *Zora!: Zora Neale Hurston, A Woman and Her Community*. Orlando, FL: Sentinel Communications Co., 1991. 134 pp.

Newson, Adele S. *Zora Neale Hurston: A Reference Guide*. Boston, MA: G. K. Hall, 1987. 90 pp.

NG, ALNA, IBAWCB, BAW, BWR, CH, HNB, CA (85–88), SBAA, FAW, WWWA (3), LW, NAWMP, DANB, EBA, AAE, DAB (supp.6), NYTO, PNW, BWASS, BWA, CB (1942), AARS, HUBA, IBAW, BAWPP.

HUSTON-TILLOTSON COLLEGE. A school jointly sponsored by the **United Methodist Church** and the **United Church of Christ**. Huston-Tillotson College, Austin, Texas, was founded in 1952 by the merger of the Samuel Huston College and Tillotson College. Tillotson College was founded in 1877, one of a string of schools serving Black people created by the Congregational Church's American Missionary Association following the Civil War. Samuel Huston College was distinct among the schools for Black students of the Methodist Episcopal Church, most of which had been founded in cooperation with the Church's Freedman's Aid Bureau. It was founded in 1900 by the West Texas Conference, a Black conference in the Southwest.

At the time of the schools' merger the Methodist Episcopal Church had merged to create the Methodist Church (1939–1968) (now a constituent part of the United Methodist Church) and the Congregational Church had merged with the Christian Church (which are now constituent parts of the **United Church of Christ**.)

Harmon, Nolan B. *The Encyclopedia of World Methodism*. 2 vols. Nashville, TN: United Methodist Publishing House, 1974.

"We are often tossed and driven on the restless sea of time,
Somber skies and howling tempests oft succeed a bright sunshine,
In that land of perfect day, when the mists have rolled away,
We will understand it better by and by.

By and by when the morning comes
When the saints of God are gathered home,
We'll tell the story, how we've overcome,
For we'll understand it better by and by."

Charles A. Tindley, Methodist minister

I

IMES, WILLIAM LLOYD (December 29, 1889–January 13, 1986), a leading Presbyterian minister, was born in Memphis, Tennessee, the youngest of three sons in the family of Benjamin Albert and Elizabeth Rachel (Wallace) Imes. His father was a graduate of Oberlin College in Ohio and a missionary with the American Missionary Association. Imes attended Emerson Institute in Mobile, Alabama, then Knoxville College in Tennessee from 1906 to 1908. He moved to Fisk University in Nashville, and there received his B.A. in 1910 and an M.A. in sociology in 1912. His thesis was *The Negro in Tennessee Before the Civil War: A Sociological Study.*

He went on to Union Theological Seminary in New York City, studying concurrently at Columbia University, and obtained both his B.D. from the former institution and another M.A. (again in sociology) from the latter in 1915. He worked his way through by playing the organ at the Labor Temple, leading boys' clubs, and being a supply student minister. Shortly after his graduation, on September 9, 1915, he married Grace Virginia Frank, with whom he had three children.

He was ordained a Presbyterian minister in 1915 and pastored the Bethel Chapel in Plainfield, New Jersey, from 1915 to 1919. From 1919 to 1925 he was at Lombard Central Presbyterian Church in Philadelphia, Pennsylvania, and during these years a parsonage was bought, church debts eliminated, and a building fund begun. He served on the Interracial Committee of Philadelphia (organized by the Society of Friends), which tried unsuccessfully to prevent the segregation of state normal schools. From 1925 to 1943 he was the minister of the St. James Presbyterian Church in New York City (founded in 1895). During this pastorate he built a wide reputation, and doubled as a visiting lecturer to the Howard University School of Religion in Washington, D.C. from 1940 to 1943. The church made successive moves uptown until it arrived at West 141st Street and St. Nicholas Ave., and the membership was built up to more than one thousand. During part of

World War II he was on leave of absence for Y.M.C.A. work at Camp Merritt. At that point he was named president of Knoxville College in Tennessee, holding that position until 1947. From 1947 to 1955 he served with the New York State Council of Churches as Director of the Department of Social Education and Action and Field Service.

During his career he was known for active social engagement on behalf of the poor and oppressed. He supported labor leader A. Philip Randolph in the struggle of the Brotherhood of Sleeping Car Porters in the 1920s, and joined in protests and demonstrations against unjust practices of businesses in Harlem in the 1930s. In both Philadelphia and New York City he was in the forefront of movements for nondiscrimination and quality education in the public schools. In 1933 the New York Presbytery presented to the St. James Church the Award for Distinguished Service in Race Relations. In 1935 he helped found and was the first president of Harlem's Own Cooperative, Inc., which was designed to make inexpensive milk available to the community. His leadership on racial issues included his service on the boards of the N.A.A.C.P., the New York Urban League, and the Race Relations Department of the Federal (now National) Council of Churches.

He published a number of books, including *Integrity: Meditations of the Book of Job* (1939); *The Way of Worship in Everyday Life: A Course of Studies in Devotion* (1947); *The Black Pastures; An American Pilgrimage in Two Centuries; Essays and Sermons* (1957). His sermons were included in a number of collections of sermons. After retirement to his home in Dundee, New York, he kept busy with two interim years as Visiting Dean of Chapel at Fisk University (1956–57) and Dillard University in New Orleans, Louisiana (1958–59). In 1971 he published a new book, *The Hills Beyond the Hills.* His wife passed away in October 1972.

Imes, William Lloyd. *The Black Pastures; An American*

Pilgrimage in Two Centuries; Essays and Sermons. Nashville, TN: Hemphill Press, 1957. 146 pp.

———. *The Hills Beyond the Hills.* N. County Books, 1971.

———. *Integrity: Meditations of the Book of Job.* Philadelphia, PA: Westminster Press, 1939. 32 pp.

———, and Liston M. Oak. *The Plunder of Ethiopia.* New York: American League Against War and Fascism, 1935. 12 pp.

———. *The Way of Worship in Everyday Life: A Course of Studies in Devotion.* Winona Lake, IN: Light and Life Press, 1947.

Jenness, Mary. *Twelve Negro Americans.* New York: Friendship Press, 1936. 180 pp.

Wilson, Frank T., ed. "Living Witnesses: Black Presbyterians in Ministry, Part I." *Journal of Presbyterian History* 51 (Winter 1973): 347–391.

AARS, BDNM (75), *RLA, HUBA, IBAW, BAW, WWCA* (38–40).

IMMANUEL LUTHERAN COLLEGE. A Lutheran school. At the 1877 Synodical Conference, a confederation of conservative Lutheran denominational bodies, a plan was submitted for the training of Black pastors to serve the Black Lutheran churches in the South. One early suggestion was for the establishment of a school in the South expressly for that purpose, rather than send Black ministerial candidates to the older seminaries in the East and Midwest (some of which had yet to convert to English as a primary language). However, it was not until 1902 that the convention of the conference resolved to establish a high school. Rev. N. J. Bakke volunteered to become the instructor at the school which opened the next year in Concord, North Carolina. Bakke was joined the next year by Frederick Wahlers.

In 1904, the conference voted Immanuel its full support in the form of a substantial gift for its own campus in the city of Greensboro, North Carolina. The school moved into its new facilities the next year. As the school developed over the next decades, three departments emerged: a high school, a normal school for training school teachers, and a theological seminary for training ministers. After 1926, a more general liberal arts curriculum was designed.

The initial Lutheran venture in higher education for Black people operated successfully for several generations but was finally closed in 1961. Its work is continued in the Selma, Alabama, campus of Concordia College.

Drewes, Christopher F. *Half a Century of Lutheranism Among Our Colored People.* St. Louis, MO: Concordia Publishing House, 1927. 111 pp.

INDEPENDENT AFRICAN AMERICAN CATHOLIC RITE. A church in the Roman Catholic tradition. The Independent African American Catholic Rite grew out of the movement led by Rev. **George A. Stallings**, who in January 1990 established the **African American Catholic Congregation** in Washington, D.C. During the years immediately prior to his excommunication by the Roman Catholic Church and his organizing of his following in an independent jurisdiction, Stallings had developed a network of support which included Fr. Bruce E. Greening. Greening formed the second congregation of the African American Catholic Congregation, the Umoga Temple, also in Washington, D.C.

In February 1990, Greening and the Umoja Temple left Stallings' jurisdiction and attempted to reconcile with the Roman Catholic Church. They asked only that they be allowed a five-year period to experiment with the liturgy and that their pastor, Fr. Greening, be reinstated in the church's priesthood. They were unable to obtain a response to their overtures.

The Umoja Temple then changed its name to the Church of St. Martin de Porres, the Black saint from Peru canonized in 1963. On June 15, 1990, it declared its independence from Rome, and elected Fr. Greening its bishop. He was consecrated on September 28, 1990 by Archbishop Stafford Sweething, the present patriarch of the **African Orthodox Church**.

The church is committed to the empowerment of African Americans through the development of institutional ownership, the nurturance of an indigenous clergy and lay leadership, and the encouragement of Black-owned businesses. The church sees itself as redressing the inability of the Roman Catholic Church to be inclusive by ministering to those who have been neglected.

Payne, Wardell J., ed. *Directory of African American Religious Bodies: A Compendium by the Howard University School of Divinity.* Washington, DC: Howard University School of Divinity, 1991. 363 pp.

INTERDENOMINATIONAL THEOLOGICAL CENTER (ITC). The Interdenominational Theological Center, Atlanta, Georgia, grew out of "The Crusade for Christ" quadrennial program adopted by the Methodist Church (now the United Methodist Church) in 1944. One aspect of the program focused upon improving education for African American ministers, then concentrated at Gammon Theological Seminary. The study, initiated in the early 1940s, continued for a decade and began to point toward an interdenominational theological complex. In 1957, application for funds was made to the Sealantic Foundation, and with the grant ITC was founded the following year. Initially four seminaries relocated to adjacent campuses and created a graduate school of theology which would allow them to share programs, faculty, and library without losing their separate identity or denominational distinctiveness, which they might wish to pass on to their students.

At its founding ITC included Gammon Theological Seminary, Morehouse School of Religion (Baptist), Phillips School of Theology (**Christian Methodist Episcopal Church**), and Turner Theological Seminary (**African Methodist Episcopal Church**). More recently Johnson C. Smith Theological Seminary (Presbyterian) and the Charles H. Mason Theological Seminary (**Church of God in Christ**) have joined. There are approximately 300 students enrolled annually. ITC is also home to the "Black Women in Church and Society" program, a leadership program founded in 1981.

ITC is part of the Atlanta University Center (which includes a number of African American colleges) and the Atlanta Theological Association, through which it is able to offer a doctorate.

Harmon, Nolan B. *The Encyclopedia of World Methodism*. 2 vols. Nashville, TN: United Methodist Publishing House, 1974.

Payne, Wardell J., ed. *Directory of African American Religious Bodies: A Compendium by the Howard University School of Divinity*. Washington, DC: Howard University School of Divinity, 1991. 363 pp.

INTERNATIONAL EVANGELICAL CHURCH. A Pentecostal church. The International Evangelical Church is a fellowship of Pentecostal churches formed in 1964 as the International Evangelical Church and Missionary Association. As originally constituted the association was a corporation designed to legalize the Italian mission of John McTernan. Very early, McTernan became associated with John Levin Meares (b. 1920), the pastor of an independent Pentecostal church in Washington, D.C. Though still largely a foreign movement, the United States branch of the church has become an important structure within the African American Pentecostal community. The origin of the church in the United States can be traced directly to Mears' decision in the mid-1950s to establish a ministry within the Black community of Washington, D.C.

Mears was a promising young minister in the **Church of God (Cleveland, Tennessee)**, the nephew of the general overseer. He was in the midst of a successful pastorate in Memphis, Tennessee in 1955,

when he decided to resign and go to Washington to assist independent evangelist Jack Coe in a series of revival meetings. He liked the city and decided to stay and build a church, the Washington Revival Center. He also started a radio show, "Miracle Time." From the beginning, the major response to his ministry was from African Americans. He thus found himself as the White minister of an integrated congregation in which the majority of members were Black-affiliated, with a White-controlled denomination with very Southern attitudes about the races. He was forced to choose between his ministry and his denomination. He left the Church of God. The congregation grew, and in 1957 settled in an abandoned theatre as the National Evangelistic Center.

The center faced a series of problems which were increased by the tumultuous social changes going on around it. Meares changed the emphasis of his ministry from an emphasis on miracles to one of teachings. Several evangelists raided the membership. All of the problems climaxed in the riots following the assassination of **Martin Luther King, Jr.** in 1968. Almost all of the remaining White members left the congregation at this time. While the changes were going on around him, Meares became the vice-president of the International Evangelical Church and Missionary Association.

In the early 1970s, the several hundred remaining members reorganized and decided to build a new $3 million facility. The renewed congregation opened Evangel Temple in 1975. As the building was being completed, McTernan died in 1974 and Meares inherited the corporation which at some point became simply the International Evangelical Church (IEC). Since then the story of the International Evangelical Church has been the story of its international development and its expansion within the African American community. Internationally, the IEC began with some Italian churches and then reached out to include a group of Brazilian churches under Bishop Robert McAleister, and churches in Nigeria led by Bishop Benson Idahosa. Today over half the congregations associated with the church are in Africa. In 1972 the church joined the World Council of Churches.

In 1982 the church also became the instrument of the founding of a new Pentecostal ecumenical organization, the International Communion of Charismatic Churches. It includes the various branches of the International Evangelical Church, and several other church groups such as the Gospel Harvesters Church, founded by Earl P. Paulk in Atlanta. That same year, the bishops of the Communion, McAleister, Paulk, and Idahosa consecrated Meares as a bishop.

In the United States, Evangel Temple expanded and a ministry of people ordained by Meares emerged. Other independent Pentecostal congregations affiliated with the church. Through the 1980s, Meares emerged as a leader in a mediating position between the Black and White Pentecostal communities which for several generations had gone their separate ways. In 1984 he began the annual Inner-City Pastor's Conferences which draw together the pastors (primarily African American) of the many churches of the association. Meares has also become a major voice raising the issue of the White Pentecostal churches' role in the African American community.

The IEC has approximately 500 congregations worldwide, of which over 400 are in Africa. There are approximately 50 in South America, 20 in Italy, 20 in the United States and one in Jamaica.

Burgess, Stanley M., and Gary B. McGee, eds. *Dictionary of Pentecostal and Charismatic Movements*. Grand Rapids, MI: Zondervan Publishing House, 1988. 911 pp.

Evangel Temple's 30th Anniversary Historical Journal. Washington, DC: Evangel Temple, 1985. 61 pp.

Meares, John L. *Bind Us Together*. Old Tappan, NJ: Chosen Books, 1987. 159 pp.

———. *The Inheritance of Christ in the Saints*. Washington, DC: Evangel Temple, 1984. 109 pp.

INTERRELIGIOUS FOUNDATION FOR COMMUNITY ORGANIZATION. An ecumenical organization. The Interreligious Foundation for Community Organization (IFCO) was founded in 1967 by representatives of nine religious organizations and one civic foundation. It quickly picked up an additional thirteen members, including all of the social action agencies of the major Protestant denominations associated with the National Council of Churches, several Roman Catholic and Universalist Unitarian agencies, and the American Jewish Committee. IFCO functioned as a funding agency which channels money from the member groups to a variety of community organization/action projects around the United States.

IFCO became the center of intense controversy in 1969 when **James Forman** presented the "**Black Manifesto**" at its National Black Economic Development Conference (BEDC) in Detroit on April 26. The manifesto called for the White churches and synagogues to pay $5 million in reparation for their centuries of exploitation and oppression of Black people. Forman went on to lead an organization which took the name of the conference and which he hoped would be funded through the reparation money channeled by IFCO. However, within a matter of months, IFCO, which had initially looked with favor on the document though it had not formally adopted it as a policy statement, backed away from its alignment with it and with Forman. Over the next two years, most of the major IFCO members reallocated large sums of money in a response to the manifesto. However, only a percentage of that money went to IFCO and very little made its way to Forman's BEDC.

As the issue of the manifesto has faded, IFCO has continued to funnel the funds of its member agencies to a wide variety of causes. At any given time in the last decade it had over 100 projects in which it had taken an interest. In 1983 it launched the Central America Information Week Project, a decentralized but coordinated program to inform people about the problems inherent in U.S. government intervention in the area. To fund its many programs it has built an additional base of membership among individual clergy and laity, currently numbering about 5,000.

Headquarters is in New York City. It publishes the quarterly *IFCO News*.

"Manifest(o) Destiny: IFCO and the Churches." *Christianity Today* 13, 18 (June 6, 1969): 42–43.

ISAAC, TELÉSFORO ALEXANDER (b. 1929), a bishop of the **Episcopal Church**, was born in San Pedro de Macoris, Dominican Republic. He attended San Esteban's Episcopal Day School, completed high school at José Joaquin Pérez Liceum, then graduated from business school and worked as an office clerk. He married Juana María Rosa, with whom he had three children.

In 1954 Isaac entered the Episcopal Seminary in Haiti and graduated in 1958. That year he was ordained both deacon and priest. He became chaplain of San Esteban's Episcopal Day School and vicar-in-charge of the missions around the sugar plantations in San Pedro de Macorís. From 1961 to 1965 he was vicar-in-charge of Santa Cruz Episcopal Church in San Francisco de Macorís. From 1965 to 1970 he served the San Andrés Episcopal Church in Santo Domingo and took additional course work at the Universidad Autónoma de Santo Domingo. From 1966 to 1970 he conducted a fifteen-minute weekly religious program on the radio. In 1970 he earned a Divinitatis Magister at El Seminario Episcopal del Caribe and the following year was placed at San Esteban's Episcopal Church.

On March 9, 1972, Isaac was consecrated bishop for the Dominican Republic, becoming number 678 in the succession of bishops listed for the Episcopal Church in the United States. He is a trustee of El Seminario Episcopal del Caribe and has served as vice-chair of the IX Province and of the Church World Service in the Dominican Republic. He has authored a booklet: *The History of the Schools of the Episcopal Church in the Dominican Republic.*

ECA (1973).

ISEM, BENNIE G. (b. December 3, 1924) was the presiding bishop of the **Pure Holiness Church of God**. Isem joined the Pure Holiness Church as a young man. In 1948 he married Mattie Haynes, with whom he had four children. Six years later he was ordained as a minister and became the assistant pastor of the mother congregation of the denomination in Anniston, Alabama. In 1955 he became pastor of the Saint Timothy Pure Holiness Church, the headquarters church in Atlanta, Georgia.

In the early 1960s he succeeded Charles Frederick Fears as presiding bishop of the church. At the time Isem was ordained, the church had a rule against married presiding bishops, but over the years the rules had been rescinded. Isem served as presiding bishop for twenty years, the longest term of any of the church's bishops. He promoted the cause of education and led in the development of the Pure Holiness School of Theology under the presidency of Elder Judson Ringer. He encouraged the development of a denominational periodical, the *Triumph of Truth Newsletter*, under the editorship of Wilma Ringer. He also further developed the role of the ministers. Under his predecessors, pastors had for the first time received salaries. In 1966 Isem led in granting them the ability to officiate at ordinations, weddings and funerals.

In 1976 Isem's wife died. Two years later he married Wilma Ringer. He retired in 1984 and was succeeded by Stephen Edward Ackley.

DuPree, Sherry Sherrod. *Biographical Dictionary of African American Holiness-Pentecostals, 1880–1990.* Washington, DC: Middle Atlantic Regional Press, 1989. 386 pp.

ISLAM AS AN AFRICAN AMERICAN RELIGION.

During the last half of the twentieth century, Islam has emerged in strength in American society. Its challenge to Judaism's role as the second faith among the citizens of the United States has also led to a recovery of its long history in North America and its intimate connection with the African American community.

The Introduction of Islam in North America. Islam was introduced to North America by slaves brought from West Africa. The earliest documents date from the early eighteenth century. During the 1730s, among the Muslims taken into slavery were three who became well-known: **Job ben Solomon**, Yarrow Mamont, and Lamine Jay. Later in the century, **Abdul Rahahman**, Muhammed Kaba, Salih Bilali, Bilali, and Benjamin Cochrane arrived. These men stood out from the host of their fellow slaves, including the other Muslim slaves for their training and aristocratic bearing. They had all traveled widely as members of the elite of African society. Some were traders, other warriors. Rahahman was captured as he was returning home following a successful battle.

Most of these men were literate prior to their capture and several had learned to read and write Arabic. Job ben Solomon left the most complete literary record, including three copies of the *Qur'an* he wrote out from memory. In several cases they were sold to illiterate masters, and their literacy generally worked to their favor, and they tended to rise to the top of the very limited system in which they were entrapped. Several were finally able to gain their freedom and even make their way back home. These men, and a number of others discovered during the nineteenth century, became known because they kept Muslim religious practices which were noticed by their masters, neighbors, and or visitors. Some, like Rahahman, were seen to regularly say the required prayers five times daily. Job ben Solomon, who spoke no English, was "discovered" to be a Muslim by his refusal to drink wine.

It also seems to be the case that the several Muslims, including those who fathered children, were unable to perpetuate their faith into the next generation. At least we have no record of people who followed any practices or kept a self-identification as Muslims in the face of the intense sanctions against continuing African religious practices (or in many cases any religious practices) across the South in the decades prior to the Civil War. Yet it remains a tempting speculation that something might have survived.

Writing in 1964, Morroe Berger, one of the first to give systematic consideration to the Muslim slave accounts, suggests, "It is quite possible that some of the various American groups of the past half century or so had their roots in these vestiges, that the tradition was handed down in a weak chain from generation to generation."

The Second Emergence of Islam. Islam began to make a reappearance in the United States in the late nineteenth century with the arrival of individual Muslim immigrants from the Middle East Asia. The first prominent advocate was Alexander Russell Webb, the American consul in the Philippines. Converted during his stay in the Islands, Webb resigned his post and worked his way home by lecturing on his new found faith. He arrived in Chicago in time to be the only Muslim speaker at the 1893 World's Parliament of Religions that summer.

In the early twentieth century, Islam reappeared within the African American community through several movements which had drawn significant inspiration from Muslim themes. Among the first was the **Moorish Science Temple of America** founded in 1913 by **Noble Drew Ali** (1886–1929). Ali developed a myth of the origins of Black people whom he considered Moors whose homeland was Morocco. He claimed that the Moors had been systematically stripped of their identity by Whites during the eighteenth century. Their actions culminated in George Washington's cutting down the cherry tree, their bright red flag, which he had hidden away in Independence Hall in Philadelphia. During the first decade the Temple spread across the African American communities of the urban North and Midwest.

To Ali, the national religion of Black people was Islam. In 1927 he introduced Temple members to a new volume, *The Holy Koran*, which laid out Ali's beliefs about the origin of Black people and the problems created by their acceptance of Christianity. This *Koran*, however, was not the orthodox Islamic sacred text, the *Qur'an*, but a small book he had put together from, among other sources, *The Aquarian Gospel of Jesus Christ*, a Spiritualist text authored by one Levi Dowling.

Ali was still a relatively young man when he died in 1929. His movement continued (and is still in existence), but had peaked. The thrust initiated by the Temple was picked up within a few months by a former Temple member, Wallace Fard Muhammad. Making his appearance in Detroit, Muhammad claimed to be Noble Drew Ali reincarnated. He claimed that he had come all the way from Mecca, Saudi Arabia, to lead the Black people of America to freedom, justice, and equality. He called his new movement, the Nation of Islam.

Fard attracted a small following, among whom was his most capable lieutenant, Elijah Poole, soon reborn as Elijah Muhammad. Like Ali, Wallace F. Muhammad, taught a myth to explain the condition of the African American. He attributed it to Yakub, a mad scientist, who created White people. In return, Allah has allowed the White beast to reign for six thousand years, a period which ended in 1914. It was now time for Black people to regroup, reorganize, and regain their ascendant position.

Less heralded, but possibly more successful in its first generation, was the Muslim Mission of America established by Sheikh Daa'wud Faisal in Brooklyn, New York, in 1920. Shaikh Daa'wud moved to the United States from Bermuda in that same wave which brought so many West Indians to the New York area in the early decades of the twentieth century. His more orthodox form of Islam, though later overshadowed by the Nation of Islam, also took root in the African American communities, and mosques were founded across the Eastern half of the United States as far away as Ft. Worth, Texas.

Wallace F. Muhammad sent Elijah Muhammad to Chicago to begin a second temple of the Nation of Islam. After only a brief period, however, Elijah Muhammad was forced to return to Detroit and quiet a disturbance which threatened to split the Temple. In the process he moved his teacher to Chicago and soon emerged as the visible authority. Wallace Muhammad faded into obscurity and to this day his eventual fate is unknown. Elijah Muhammad began the long process of growing a national movement whose time was yet to come.

Meanwhile, among the Asian immigrants to America, a third Islamic movement had appeared. The Ahmadiyya movement had been founded by Hazrat Mirza Ghulam Ahmad in the nineteenth century. From India (present-day Pakistan) Ahmad saw himself as leading a revival of true Islam. Welcomed at first as an energetic teacher of the faith, Ahmad gradually departed from a number of orthodox Muslim teachings. He, for example, taught in contradiction to the *Qur'an* that Jesus had not died on the cross, but had survived his ordeal and retired quietly to India where he lived a long life and where he was eventually buried. More importantly, he began to assume the prerogatives of the "Madhi," the promised Prophet who would come to revive the faith when it was at a low ebb. In that regard, he seemed to be placing himself in the same level as Muhammad, a position angrily rejected by Muslims.

The followers of Ahmad differed from other Muslims in that they initiated a mission to proselytize Europe and North America. Thus while orthodox Muslims were moving to the American Midwest and creating cultural ghettos, the Ahmadiyyas sent missionaries. The first to arrive was Dr. Mufti Muhammad Sadiq who settled in Chicago in 1921 and who published a small magazine, *Muslim Sunrise*.

As the Ahmadiyya movement began to grow, it attracted primarily African Americans. Comparative religions scholar Charles Braden, who tracked the Ahmadiyyas for a generation, noted that one of its most appealing aspects was its message of racial brotherhood. Braden noted in 1959, after a quarter of century of evangelizing, that the majority of Ahmadiyyas were

Black people, and that Islam was demonstrating a much greater ability to handle the racial question than was Christianity. In any case, over its first generation, the Ahmadiyya version of Islam spread through the Black communities of the Northern United States.

Since World War II. Through the 1920s and 1930s, Islam, though of a unorthodox variety, established itself with the African American world. Not yet ready to challenge the Christian hegemony, it offered African Americans an alternative and saw the formation of a core group through which it could reach a mass following in future decades. The last World War proved a trauma for the Nation of Islam. With membership then numbering in the thousands, Elijah Muhammad planned to purchase property and establish permanent headquarters in Chicago. However, in 1942, he was arrested for preaching sedition and avoiding the draft. Convicted, he sat out the rest of the War in the Federal Penitentiary in Marion, Indiana. There was some compensation for the disaster of the early 1940s by the acquisition of Malcolm Little, later to be known as Malcolm X, as a member. Malcolm soon proved to be the Nations' most effective evangelist-spokesperson. Sent to New York, he built one of the strongest temples in the organization and through his travels was responsible for the founding of a number of other centers.

The Nation of Islam grew steadily through the 1950s. With the exception of a few scholars of religious and/or fringe groups in the African American community, the movement was virtually unknown in the White community. Then in 1959 Black journalist Louis Lomax initiated a television documentary on the Nation. It introduced its racial teachings to the American public. It was soon followed by two books, one by Lomax and one by scholar C. Eric Lincoln. While White people were concerned, if not horrified, the bad publicity made them famous and attracted many African Americans to the movement. The next fifteen years were ones of unexpected growth.

By 1970, as the flow under the new immigration law stabilized, the Nation of Islam was the voice of Islam within the Black community. It became the center of controversy as the White media attacked the anti-White teachings, and Blacks argued the degree of its correctness. The Nation's membership surpassed the 100,000 mark, and many suggested it was even larger. It challenged the Christian church members to leave the White man's religions and some did.

While it departed from Muslim orthodoxy to a large extent, it held the major Islamic symbols before its members, and provided a context in which some would begin to explore and accept orthodox Islam. Data has yet to be assembled detailing the openings provided by the Nation of Islam for the development of both orthodox and unorthodox forms of Islam among African Americans. Not the least of the sources of change within the movement was its insistence upon study of the *Qur'an*, which brought many up against the many statements which contradicted the Nation's racialist teachings.

Among the people attracted to orthodox Islam was Elijah Muhammad's own son, Wallace Muhammad (now known as Warith Deen Muhammad). Raised within the movement, as early as 1961 he questioned the teachings and on two occasions left the movement altogether. However, he was reinstated as a minister in 1974 and the following year assumed control as his father's successor. Within the first year he began to change the movement's teaching on race, an initial step that would over the next decade lead to the integration of the Nation into the larger orthodox Islamic community.

Other people initially attracted to Islam by the Nation could not wait for Wallace to gradually make the transition to orthodox Muslim life. They left the Nation (or never joined) and affiliated with orthodox Islamic centers. The emerging Muslim Student Association, annually adding new chapters on college campuses, provided the conduit through which African Americans could find their way to other orthodox Muslims. Islam welcomed all converts.

A few left to found rival movements. Malcolm X soon paid with his life for founding the competing Muslim Mosque, Inc. in New York. Haamas Abdul Khaalis was not at home the day the assassins arrived, but he lost several children, and his wife was permanently crippled. However, through the 1970s and into the 1980s, the majority of Black Muslims discovered the orthodox center of the faith.

While the great majority of African American Muslims slid over into the orthodox camp, new heterodox movements appeared. Several years after the changing of leadership in the Nation of Islam, Louis Farrakhan, possibly the most gifted speaker/leader with the movement, rejected the changes initiated by Wallace Muhammad and left the organization and reorganized the several thousand who left with him as the reconstituted Nation of Islam. Since his becoming independent in the late 1970s, Farrakhan has become the most notable of the several revived Nation of Islam groups (such as those led by John Muhammad or Silis Muhammad). An excellent orator, Farrakhan has attracted large crowds and his anti-White and anti-Jewish remarks, bordering on overt racism, have been widely reported. Though having the support of only a relatively small membership (5–10,000), Farrakhan has forced one Black leader after another (from Jesse Jackson to Mayor Tom Bradley of Los Angeles) to choose between him and solidarity with the African American community and their ties with the White power base they must have to survive as viable political voices.

The Future of Islam in the African American Community. As the 1990s begin, Islam has become an established minority voice within the African American community. It shows no signs of challenging the overwhelming support still given to the several large Christian denominations. It has also lost much of the controversial focus which carried it through the Civil Rights/Black Power era, and has been able to find common cause with the larger multiracial American Muslim Community, now numbering in the millions and growing.

Austin, Allan D. *African Muslims in Antebellum America: A Sourcebook.* New York: Garland Publishing, 1984. 759 pp.

Davis, Charles H., Jr. *Black Nationalism and the Nation of Islam.* 4 parts. Los Angeles: The John Henry and Mary Louisa Dunn Bryant Foundation, 1962. 167 pp.

Diara, Agadem I. *Islam and Pan-Africanism.* Detroit: AGASCA Productions, n.d.

Essien-Udom, E. U. *Black Nationalism: A Search for an Identity in America.* University of Chicago Press, 1962. Rept.: New York: Dell, 1964. 448 pp.

Goldman, Peter Louis. *The Death and Life of Malcolm X.* Urbana, IL: University of Illinois Press, 1979. 146 pp.

Lee, Martha F. *The National of Islam, An American Millenarian Movement.* Lewiston, NY: Edwin Mellen Press, 1988. 163 pp.

Lincoln, C. Eric. *The Black Muslims in America.* Boston, MA: Beacon Press, 1961. 276 pp.

Lomax, Louis. *When the Word is Given. . .* Cleveland, OH: World Publishing Company, 1964. 223 pp. Rept.: New York: New American Library, 1964.

Marsh, Clifton E. *From Black Muslims to Muslims: The Transition from Separation to Islam, 1930–1980.* Metuchen, NJ: Scarecrow Press, 1984. 149 pp.

al-Talal, Faissal Fahd, and Khalid Abdullah Tariq al-Mansour. *The Challenges of Spreading Islam in America.* San Francisco, CA: The Authors, 1980. 213 pp.

ISOM, DOTCY IVERTUS, JR. (b. February 18, 1931), 43rd bishop of the **Christian Methodist Episcopal** (CME) Church, was born in Detroit, Michigan, the son of Dotcy Ivertus, Sr., and Laura (Jones) Isom. After graduating from a Detroit high school, he enrolled at Wayne State University in Detroit, graduating with his B.S. in 1956. He married Esther Ladon Jones, with whom he had three children. For two years he taught special education in the Detroit public school system, followed by some time in the Saginaw, Michigan public school system.

After military service in Korea (winning five Bronze Stars), he decided to become a minister, and his first full-time pastorate was at Allen Temple CME Church in Paris, Tennessee. He then went to St. Luke CME Church in Saginaw, Michigan, followed by Carter Chapel CME Church in Gary, Indiana, and Pilgrim Temple CME Church in East St. Louis, Illinois. While at Pilgrim Temple he attended Eden Theological Seminary in nearby Webster Groves, Missouri, receiving his masters of Christian education and his M.Div. in 1966–67. In about 1972 he was assigned to the St. Paul CME Church in Chicago, Illinois, where he stayed for the next decade and made the major part of his reputation. He has been vice-chair of the Chicago chapter of the **Southern Christian Leadership Conference** (S.C.L.C.), and active in the N.A.A.C.P., the Urban League, and C.O.R.E.

On May 9, 1982, he was elected bishop and assigned to the Fifth Episcopal District (Alabama, Florida, and Haitian Mission Conferences). In 1986 he shifted to the Third Episcopal District (Michigan-Indiana, Southeast Missouri, Illinois, Wisconsin, and Kansas-Missouri Conferences). He also became chair of the General Board of Lay Activities.

"Bishop Dotcy Ivertus Isom." *Christian Index* 115 (May 15, 1982).

WWR (85), *WWABA* (85), *BDNM* (75).

"To the Black Revolution we bring the stabilizing influence of the religion of the Black Messiah, Jesus Christ. The Black Revolution is not going any farther than the Black Church enables it to go, by giving it a foundation, a philosophy, and a direction."

Jaramogi Abebe Agyeman, Founder
Pan African Orthodox Christian Church
1968

J

JACKSON, JESSE LOUIS (b. October 8, 1941), a Baptist minister internationally known for his social activism and political aspirations, was born in Greenville, North Carolina, the son of Helen Burns and Noah Louis Robinson. His parents never married each other, and the taunts he endured as a child about his illegitimacy made him only that much more determined to make something of himself. While he was still a child his mother married Charles Henry Jackson; she worked as a maid in a local hospital and he was a janitor. Together they made enough to keep bread on the table for the five children and the three-room house that was little more than a shack.

He was raised in a very religious and family-oriented home environment, and the poverty was no barrier to the gaining of strong moral values. He got his first job at age six, helping deliver wood from his grandfather's woodyard to local houses. At age eleven he had completed fourth grade and had more education than any of the grown men employed at the woodyard. He was then put in charge of the business, handling the payroll and the hiring and firing of employees. At Greenville's all-Black Sterling High School he was an athletic star on the football, basketball, and baseball teams, and was even offered a contract by the New York Giants upon graduation in 1959. He rejected the offer and accepted an athletic scholarship at the University of Illinois, hoping to be a starting quarterback. He only spent one year there after being told that Blacks are not supposed to be quarterbacks in football.

In 1961 he entered the mostly Black Agricultural and Technical College in Greensboro, North Carolina, and became not only an excellent quarterback, but honor student and president of the student body. He first made headlines in 1963 by leading the successful ten-month-long sit-in demonstration in downtown Greensboro to integrate the theaters and restaurants. In his senior year he married Jacqueline Lavinia Brown, with whom he had five children. When he graduated in 1964 with a B.A. in sociology, he worked for Terry Sanford, then

governor of North Carolina, organizing Young Democrat clubs across the state. At this point he was still uncertain about future directions. He had always been active in the Baptist Church, but had held sharp disdain for the traditional Black preachers who focused on the next world to the exclusion of this world.

In 1965, after seeing other options for a minister's role in the community, he enrolled in Chicago Theological Seminary. He wasted no time in creating his activist vision of ministry, and that same year marched in Selma with **Martin Luther King, Jr.** In Chicago he joined the Coordinating Council of Community Organizations (C.C.C.O.), a coalition of civil rights organizations, and was active in its programs. When Martin Luther King, Jr. began the Chicago branch of Operation Breadbasket later in 1966, he chose Jackson to head it. He left seminary one semester short of graduation in order to pursue this opportunity, but was ordained a Baptist minister on June 30, 1968. The seminary awarded him an honorary doctorate in 1969, one of over thirty-five honorary degrees since bestowed upon him. For most of the years since his ordination he has been co-pastor (on leave) of the Fellowship Missionary Baptist Church in Chicago.

Operation Breadbasket in Chicago was a quick success under Jackson's leadership. Basically it targeted businesses in the Black community that did not hire or train Blacks and if these practices were not changed, a boycott was the result. In August 1967 Jackson was appointed national director of Operation Breadbasket. In 1968 the grocery store A&P was the subject of a fourteen-week boycott of forty of its stores. In the end, an agreement was signed that led not only to the hiring of hundreds of Blacks, but the display of Black-manufactured products and the use of Black firms in business transactions. Every Saturday morning Jackson would conduct a three-hour rally/worship service at the South Side's Capitol Theatre, complete with the Breadbasket Gospel Choir and radio coverage.

Jackson was at the motel with Martin Luther King,

Jr., when he was assassinated on April 4, 1968, and for a time worked with King's successor, **Ralph D. Abernathy**, the new head of the **Southern Christian Leadership Conference** (S.C.L.C.). Jackson was prominent in the Poor People's Campaign later that year, and for a while was manager of the shantytown built in Washington, D.C. In December 1971 however, amidst tensions with Abernathy and other S.C.L.C. leaders, he withdrew from S.C.L.C. He took most of the Chicago chapter with him and founded **Operation PUSH** (People United to Save Humanity—since revised to People United to Serve Humanity) to continue and expand the programs begun by Operation Breadbasket. The new organization soon emerged as a national campaign to recover Black pride and gain access for Blacks to a greater share of the nation's political and economic power. He was famous for leading crowds in chants along the lines of: "I am somebody. I may be poor, but I am somebody. I may be uneducated, but I am somebody. Nobody can save us for us but us."

In 1976 he founded PUSH for Excellence, a program to encourage students to stop mindless and destructive activities and start taking pride in being students with a future in mind. Despite criticisms that his motivational tactics were insufficient for the problem, United States Education Commissioner Ernest L. Boyer stated that "it works with kids." Target schools reported much lower absentee rates and improved conduct.

In 1979 Jackson became an international figure, visiting South Africa and urging his audience there to work toward a non-segregated future. He then went on a widely publicized tour of Israel, the West Bank, Lebanon, Syria, and Egypt, meeting with leaders in an attempt to find peaceful resolutions to some of the long-term conflicts of the region. While many Israelis saw him as pro-Arab, embracing the Palestine Liberation Organization leader Yasir Arafat, many Arabs criticized him for his call for official recognition of Israel and its right to exist.

On November 3, 1983, Jackson formally entered the race for the Democratic nomination for President of the United States, taking a leave of absence from PUSH for the campaign. His gifts as an electrifying orator and his grassroots connections dubbed the "Rainbow Coalition" made up for the lack of a traditional high-budget organization. He also rose in the public's estimation with his diplomatic coup in January 1984, when he secured the release from Syria of captive United States Navy pilot Lieutenant Robert O. Goodman, Jr., whose plane had been shot down on December 4, 1983. This brilliant achievement was later tarnished when he admitted referring to Jews in a private conversation as "Hymies,"

and when **Louis Farrakhan**, head of the Nation of Islam and a close supporter of Jackson's campaign, made several problematic remarks about Judaism. Jackson apologized for his own remarks and condemned those of Farrakhan.

Jackson ended the primary campaign in third place, behind Walter Mondale and Gary Hart, with almost four million votes, still an historic accomplishment for the first substantial presidential campaign by an African American candidate. (There were two previous Black presidential candidates. Abolitionist Frederick Douglass received one vote at the 1888 Republican National Convention and in 1972 New York Democratic Congresswoman Shirley Chisholm won fourteen delegates in fourteen primaries). He could also take credit for many thousands of additional Blacks registered to vote. For the next year and a half he returned to Operation PUSH and continued his international appearances, including meeting with Soviet leader Mikhail Gorbachev in 1985 on behalf of the plight of Soviet Jews. In February 1986, he resigned from Operation PUSH, turning it over to Hycel Taylor, and established the National Rainbow Coalition as a multi-ethnic progressive force related to the Democratic party. In 1988 he again ran for president from the popular base of the National Rainbow Coalition, and with the slogan, "Keep Hope Alive." His strength increased with this primary and he received almost seven million votes, a significant second to Michael Dukakis' ten million votes. He has since maintained his social and political activism, and in the 1992 election he did not run, but served as a power-broker with the ability to throw major support to the candidate of his choice.

"America's Fifteen Greatest Black Preachers." *Ebony* 39 (September 1984): 27–33.

Kelly, James. "Looking for a Way Out: Jackson's Coup Creates an Opening in Lebanon." *Time* 123 (January 16, 1984): 10–13.

Poinsett, Alex. "PUSH for Excellence." *Ebony* 32 (February 1977): 104–111.

Candidates '84. Washington, DC: Congressional Quarterly, Inc., 1984. 135 pp.

Clemente, Frank, and Frank Watkins, eds. *Keep Hope Alive: Jesse Jackson's 1988 Presidential Campaign*. Chicago: South End Press and Keep Hope Alive PAC, 1989. 235 pp.

Drotning, Philip T., and Wesley W. South. *Up From the Ghetto*. New York: Cowles Book Co., 1970. 207 pp.

Hatch, Roger D. *Beyond Opportunity: Jesse Jackson's Vision for America*. Philadelphia, PA: Fortress Press, 1988. 165 pp.

Jackson, Jesse L. *Straight From the Heart*. Eds. Roger D. Hatch and Frank E. Watkins. Philadelphia, PA: Fortress Press, 1987. 324 pp.

Landess, Thomas H., and Richard M. Quinn. *Jesse Jackson and the Politics of Race*. Ottawa, IL: Jameson Books, 1985. 269 pp.

Reynolds, Barbara A. *Jesse Jackson: America's David*. Washington, DC: JFJ Associates, 1985. 489 pp.

RLOA, BLA, NA, IP, OTSB, EBA, WWABA (92–93), *WWR* (77), *CRS, BDNM* (75), *CB* (1970), *CB* (1986), *IBAW, HUBA, AARS, MBRL.*

JACKSON, JOSEPH HARRISON (September 11, 1900–August 18, 1990), long-time president of the **National Baptist Convention, U.S.A., Inc.**, was born in Rudyard, Mississippi, the son of Henry and Emily (Johnson) Jackson. He was ordained a Baptist minister in 1922 and pastored in rural Mississippi from 1922 to 1924. He was at Flowery Mount Baptist Church in McComb City, Mississippi while in school, and received his B.A. in 1927 from Jackson College in Mississippi. He married Maude Thelma Alexander on January 28, 1927, with whom he had one child.

He pastored Bethel Baptist Church in Omaha, Nebraska, from 1926 to 1934 and in 1933 he received an M.A. degree from Creighton University in Omaha, Nebraska. He led the Monumental Baptist Church in Philadelphia, Pennsylvania, from 1934 to 1941. On December 12, 1934 he became executive secretary of the Foreign Mission Board of the National Baptist Convention of the U.S.A., Inc. (N.B.C.U.S.A) and held that position for nineteen years, also becoming a regional vice-president. He soon visited Africa and subsequently published a pamphlet, *Voyage to West Africa and Some Reflections on Modern Missions*. In 1937 he was a delegate to an ecumenical conference in Oxford, England. In 1941 he succeeded L. K. Williams as pastor of the prestigious Olivet Baptist Church in Chicago, Illinois, where he remained until his death. In 1947 he lost a heated battle for vice-president-at-large with E. W. Perry. In 1950 he wrote his first book, *Stars in the Night*.

In 1953 Jackson succeeded **David V. Jemison** as president of the N.B.C.U.S.A., the largest Black religious group in the United States. He was re-elected each year for the next twenty-nine years. In 1954 *Ebony* magazine named him one of America's ten greatest Black preachers. His tenure was not without significant controversy, however. Early on the issue of length of tenure for officers arose and a practically deadlocked constitutional committee in 1956 recommended that beginning that year no official retain a position for more than four consecutive years. This had been the intent of changes which were made in the constitution in 1952, but which had since come to be regarded by many as

illegal changes. A heated debate ensued and finally in 1957 the decision was made that there was no limit to tenure, since the 1952 changes had been made contrary to constitutional rules. As the years passed Jackson continued to be re-elected and to solidify his power.

Another troublesome issue was the organization's relation to civil rights. In 1954 the U.S. Supreme Court ruled that segregation of public schools was unconstitutional and in 1956 the N.B.C.U.S.A. held a symposium entitled, "National Baptists Facing Integration—Shall Gradualism Be Applied?" A number of prominent activists, including **Thomas Kilgore** and **Martin Luther King, Jr.**, spoke strongly against a conservative, gradualistic approach, but Jackson's conservative position is what governed the policies of the organization. In 1961 the issues of civil rights and length of tenure combined to cause a faction to split from the group and form the **Progressive National Baptist Convention**. Jackson opposed public demonstrations for civil rights, including the March on Washington in 1963. He said "We must not sacrifice constructive human relations in a meticulous contention for the letter of the law." He preferred the use of lawsuits to civil disobedience. Jackson also opposed the trend toward developing a "black theology," as propounded by theologians such as **Joseph R. Washington** and **James H. Cone**. He feared that this would merely "make a god out of blackness."

Despite these controversies, Jackson continued to be the popular and strong leader of the N.B.C.U.S.A., and gave the denomination a high profile. In the fall of 1955 he became the first prominent African American to visit the Soviet Union since 1919, and made headlines around the world. He wrote campaign literature for President John F. Kennedy, and attended the 1962 meeting of the Second Vatican Council in Rome. One of his most ambitious ventures was a Liberian land investment program in which the denomination began to develop farms on 100,000 acres in Liberia. The proceeds from this agriculture would be funneled into African missionary work. The government there responded by naming him a Royal Knight of the Republic of Liberia.

In 1976 he published a book on his views of the Fifth Assembly of the World Council of Churches in Nairobi, Kenya, and in 1980 he published *A Story of Christian Activism: The History of the National Baptist Convention, U.S.A., Inc.*, a large and significant review of the denomination's growth. He conducted numerous preaching tours across Europe, Africa, Asia, and South America. In 1982 he was succeeded as head of the denomination by **Theodore J. Jemison**, but continued to pastor the Olivet Baptist Church in Chicago until his death. He was succeeded there by Dr. Michael A. Noble, Sr.

"The Baptists." *Ebony* 4 (October 1949): 28–33.

"Great Negro Preachers." *Ebony* 9 (July 1954): 26–30.

Jackson, Joseph H. *The Eternal Flame: The Story of a Preaching Mission in Russia.* Philadelphia, PA: Christian Education Press, 1956. 125 pp.

————. *Many But One: The Ecumenics of Charity.* New York: Sheed & Ward, 1964. 211 pp.

————. *Nairobi—A Joke, a Junket, or a Journey?: Reflections upon the Fifth Assembly of the World Council of Churches.* Nashville, TN: Townsend Press, 1976. 130 pp.

————. *A Story of Christian Activism: The History of the National Baptist Convention, U.S.A., Inc.* Nashville, TN: Townsend Press, 1980. 790 pp.

————. *Unholy Shadows and Freedom's Holy Light.* Nashville, TN: Townsend Press, 1967. 270 pp.

"Negro Minister Visits Russia." *Ebony* 11 (November 1955): 46–50.

"Organizations and Leaders Campaigning for Negro Goals in the United States." *New York Times* (August 10, 1964): 16.

Ostling, Richard N. "Moving Into the Mainstream." *Time* 122 (September 19, 1983): 62.

AARS, HUBA, IBAW, IBAWCB, RLA, HBB, EBA, NA, OTSB, CH, WWABA (90–91), SBAA, AAE, WWR (77).

JACKSON, MAHALIA (October 26, 1911–January 27, 1972), gospel singer, was born in New Orleans, Louisiana, the third of six children in the family of John Andrew and Charity (Clark) Jackson. Her father was a longshoreman, barber, and local Baptist preacher. He allowed only sacred music in the home, and she came to love it above all other kinds of music. She was strongly influenced, however, by listening at the homes of friends and elsewhere to the music of blues singer Bessie Smith and operatic tenor Enrico Caruso. She dropped out of school after the eighth grade and worked in a laundry and as a maid, singing in the church choir on Sundays.

At age sixteen she moved to Chicago, where she hoped eventually to become a beautician or nurse. She worked as a hotel maid and in a factory packing dates. She joined the Greater Salem Baptist Church in Chicago and soon became a soloist in its choir. The choir director formed a quintet featuring her that traveled from church to church giving concerts. She saved enough money to study at a beauty culture school and open her own small beauty shop in Chicago. In 1934 she made her first record for the Decca label called "God Gonna Separate the Wheat from the Tares." In 1936 she married Isaac Hockenhull, but divorced him in 1943; there were no children. Jackson did not move beyond a regional, church-oriented popularity until the 1945 recording of "Move on Up a Little Higher" on the Apollo label. This showcased her pathbreaking jazz- and blues-style of rendering the gospel song, and she attracted the attention of a wide audience. That recording eventually sold over one million copies and solidified her career. She denied that she was a blues singer, noting that she was "making a joyful noise to the Lord" rather than expressing sadness. She refused to perform in nightclubs or anywhere liquor was served, feeling that the environment was not appropriate to the music, and turned down lucrative contracts to sing secular songs.

In 1950 she made the first of what became annual Carnegie Hall performances in New York City. It was the first all-gospel concert in Carnegie Hall. In 1952 she made her first tour of Europe, which was critically acclaimed. In September 1954 she began her own weekly radio program called "Mahalia," which lasted until February 1955. She moved to Columbia Records, producing a number of albums, including "Mahalia Jackson," "Sweet Little Jesus Boy," "Bless This House," and "The World's Greatest Gospel Singer." She had a total of eight albums that sold more than one million copies. She became the official vocalist of the **National Baptist Convention, U.S.A., Inc.** (N.B.C.U.S.A.), and in 1948 co-founded with Theodore Frye the National Baptist Music Convention as an auxiliary to the N.B.C.U.S.A. She appeared many times on television shows, and her performance at the 1957 Newport (Rhode Island) Jazz Festival (in an afternoon devoted to gospel music) was said to be electrifying. In 1964 she married Sigmund Galloway, and they were divorced in 1967.

She sang for President Eisenhower at the White House, at the inauguration of President Kennedy in 1961, at the March on Washington in 1963, and at the funeral of **Martin Luther King, Jr.** in 1968. She was active in the civil rights movement beginning in 1955, when she went to Montgomery, Alabama, to support the bus boycott. In her later years, despite declining health, she was as active in the civil rights movement as possible, wanting very much to "heal the divisions" between people. She was known for her generous spirit, and she often donated her time and voice to worthy causes. In 1966 she wrote her autobiography, *Movin' On Up.* In the last two decades of her life she was acknowledged as a national treasure and sang for heads of state around the world. Her version of "Silent Night" was one of the all-time best-selling records in Denmark. She was called the "Queen of Gospel Singers" and the "Greatest Gospel Singer of All Time." Her most famous songs were "I Believe," "He's Got the Whole World in

His Hands," "I Can Put My Trust in Jesus," "Just Over the Hill," "When I Wake Up in Glory," "Precious Lord," "How I Got Over," and "Just a Little While to Stay Here." She is a member of the Gospel Music Hall of Fame, and her success paved the way for the popularity of later performers such as Aretha Franklin.

Jennings, Willie J. "When Mahalia Sings: The Black Singer of Sacred Song as Icon." *Journal of Black Sacred Music* 3 (Spring 1989): 6–13.

Terkel, Studs. "Mahalia, Songbird for God." *Negro Digest* 10 (July 1961): 8–12.

"Two Cities Pay Tribute to Mahalia Jackson." *Ebony* 27 (April 1972): 63–72.

Goreau, Laurraine R. *Just Mahalia, Baby.* Waco, TX: Word Books, 1975. 611 pp.

Jackson, Jesse. *Make a Joyful Noise Unto the Lord: The Life of Mahalia Jackson, Queen of Gospel.* New York: T. Y. Crowell, 1974. 160 pp.

Jackson, Mahalia, with Evan Mcleod Wylie. *Movin' On Up.* New York: Hawthorne Books, 1966. 212 pp.

NYTO, BWR, NAWMP, IBAW, EBA, AAE, AARS, HUBA, FAW, BDA-AAM, IP, WWWA (5), *LW, BHBA, CB* (1957), *NBAW, BWMH.*

JACKSON, MARY E. (1881– ?), 4th bishop of the Mt. Sinai Holy Church of America, lived a life mostly shrouded in obscurity. In 1924 **Ida Robinson** founded the Mt. Sinai Holy Church of America, Inc. in Philadelphia, Pennsylvania, and soon afterwards Jackson joined the group, becoming secretary of the corporation and third-highest ranking official. Church membership is limited to those who show evidence of sanctification and gifts of the Holy Spirit, particularly speaking in tongues. Behavior codes are very strict, with prohibitions against such activities as swearing, smoking, drinking, chewing gum, attending motion pictures, athletic events, or dances, and gambling in any form. In 1969, at the age of eighty-eight, Jackson became the fourth bishop of the church, maintaining that position at least into the mid-1970s. Throughout the history of the church, all of the bishops of this church have been women.

WRA, BGM.

JACKSON, RAYMOND S. (b. March 20, 1892), a minister of the **Church of God (Anderson, Indiana),** was born in Cass County, Michigan, the son of a slave, Abraham Isaac Jackson. During the Civil War he escaped into Union lines and was assisted in escaping to Canada. He returned to the United States after the war and married Jackson's mother, Sarah Ash. They settled in Cass County. Abraham Jackson became a Baptist minister and executive secretary of the Chain Lake Baptist Association. However, in the late 1870s he was converted to Holiness and left the Baptists to found an independent Holiness church in Vandalia, Michigan. Raymond was Abraham and Sarah's fourteenth child. Having his own conversion experience in 1916, he afterward affiliated with the **Church of God (Cleveland, Tennessee),** a Holiness Pentecostal group, and later came into contact with the Church of God (Anderson, Indiana) and in 1918 began to attend the annual camp meetings in Anderson. There he was introduced to the movement and met some of its Black leaders, especially **J. D. Smoot,** of whom he became a close friend.

Returning to Vandalia, he organized a Church of God congregation, the second African American Church of God congregation in the state. He also began to preach in nearby Three Rivers and organized a second congregation. In 1922 he started a church in the African American community in Kalamazoo. In 1923, he was finally ordained by the General Ministerial Assembly of the Church of God. By this time he had already become known as one of the outstanding preachers in the whole church. He was invited to preach at the annual camp meeting every year. He followed his pastorate in Kalamazoo with equally successful tenures in Gary, Indiana, Topeka, Kansas, and St. Louis, Missouri.

In 1938 he was invited as the first African American to serve on the denomination's board of publication. He served 16 years. In 1943 he followed J. D. Smoot as pastor of the Church of God of Detroit. He was further able to revive the church, which had fallen on hard times during the Depression. While at the church he also served as the chairman (1943–1955) of the General Ministerial Assembly of the National Association of the Church of God, the national organization for Black members of the Church of God. Like his predecessor, in 1954 Jackson left the congregation and began a new Church of God congregation in the expanding African American community in Detroit. He would remain at the Joseph Campau Church of God (named for the street on which the church relocated in 1959) until his retirement in 1967. In 1970 he received a D.D. from Anderson College.

Throughout his career Jackson had worked first to stop the segregation of the church, and then to heal it. He supported the move in 1951 to unite the Michigan Ministerial Assembly with the Ministers and Gospel Workers Association (the Black ministerial assembly that had been formed in 1934), and as head of the association, served on the merger committee. The merger was accomplished in 1954.

Hetrick, Gale. *Laughter among the Trumpets*. Anderson, IN: Ministerial Assembly of the Church of God of Michigan, 1980. 250 pp.

JACKSON, REBECCA COX (February 15, 1795– May 24, 1871), religious visionary and founder of the first African American community of the United Society of Believers in Christ's Second Appearing (Shakers), was born in Hornstown, Pennsylvania, the daughter of a woman named Jane (maiden name unknown) and an unknown father. Her father either left or died about the time of her birth, and her mother later married a sailor named Wisson (or Wilson), who died at sea. Her mother died when she was thirteen, and her elder brother, Joseph Cox, a local pastor at the Bethel **African Methodist Episcopal Church** (AME) in Philadelphia, took her in.

She remained in her brother's household for many years, and when she married Samuel S. Jackson the two settled into her room in the house. Rebecca Jackson earned her keep by taking care of her brother's four children (she had none of her own) and taking in sewing. In 1830 she had a dramatic conversion, soon followed by a sanctification experience, and became a leader in a Covenant Meeting, a group composed largely of AME Church members who gave each other support in a sanctified or Holiness interpretation of the Christian life. She refused to join the AME Church unless the Holy Spirit explicitly told her to do so, and the church leadership began to view her as a "loose cannon." Bishop Morris Brown came to one of her meetings to see for himself, and declared that "if ever the Holy Ghost was in any place it was in that meeting."

Throughout most of her adult life Jackson kept a journal of her religious experiences, and recorded a variety of remarkable experiences, including the ability to heal by prayer, numerous prophetic dreams, startling and complex visions, and an ever-present "inner voice," to which she referred all decisions and questions. At one point, aware of her limitations in being unable to read, she prayed for the gift of literacy, which was reportedly immediately granted. In 1833 the inner voice told her that she had a preaching mission and she began a career traveling around the Northeast as an evangelist. In the course of doing so she encountered still more opposition from the AME clergy, her brother, and her husband, who thought it inappropriate for women to evangelize. She was also accused of spreading heresy and in Philadelphia in 1837 she sought to put an end to this accusation once

and for all by demanding a formal heresy trial from both Methodist and Presbyterian clergy in the presence of "three or four mothers of the church." They refused to comply, and Jackson thereby cut all remaining ties with the AME Church, her brother, and also her husband. She was willing to forsake everything to follow her calling.

She continued to call people to a celibate, sanctified life, and became attracted by the celibate, visionary Shaker community at Watervliet near Albany, New York. She and her close disciple and friend, Rebecca Perot, joined the group in June 1847 and lived there until July 1851. Shaker theology not only supported her visionary life, but allowed her to picture a female spiritual guide for the first time. She preached frequently at the public meetings and seemed to have found a permanent home. She was occasionally depressed, however, over the loss of her previous missionary work, and also began to be critical of the failure of the Shakers to establish connections with the African American community. She was not able to come to an understanding with the leadership on this issue, and left with Perot in 1851. They spent several years in Philadelphia spreading the Shaker philosophy in the Black community there and returned to Watervliet in 1858–59 to rehash the issue. This time Jackson received the right to establish an official Shaker "out family" in Philadelphia. She did so, founding a mostly Black, mostly female group of believers centered on a core group of women who lived in one house, the only known urban Shaker family. Nonresident believers took part in the evening religious meetings with them. After Jackson's death in 1871 Rebecca Perot took over the leadership and the title of Mother Rebecca Jackson. The community basically ended in 1896, though remnants remained for many years beyond that. Her writings were slowly collected and anthologized, and her legacy of spiritual autobiography has, since about the beginning of the 1980s, finally been discovered and become a part of scholarly discourse and public heritage.

Humez, Jean McMahon, ed. *Gifts of Power: The Writings of Rebecca Jackson, Black Visionary, Shaker Eldress*. Amherst, MA: University of Massachusetts Press, 1981. 368 pp.

Williams, Richard E. *Called and Chosen: The Story of Mother Rebecca Jackson and the Philadelphia Shakers*. Metuchen, NJ: The Scarecrow Press and the American Theological Library Association, 1981. 179 pp.

BWR, IBAW, NBAW.

JACKSON STATE UNIVERSITY. A former Baptist school. Jackson State University, Jackson, Mississippi, today a state supported liberal arts college, was founded in 1877 as the Natchez Seminary by the American Baptist Home Missionary Society. It was established to train African American ministers, teachers and farmers in the Mississippi Valley. In 1882 it moved to Jackson, Mississippi, and continued as a small church-supported school. In 1911 Zackary Taylor Hubert became the school's first African American president. Under his administration the college curriculum was developed and the first B.A. degree offered (1924). In 1938 the school's maintenance was taken over by the state. In 1953 the graduate program was organized, a major step in the transition from a college to a university.

Rhodes, Lelia G. *Jackson State University: The First Hundred Years, 1877–1977.* Jackson, MI: University of Michigan, 1979. 340 pp.

JACOBS, FREDERICK MILLER (July 15, 1865–December 30, 1931), 46th bishop of the **African Methodist Episcopal Zion Church** (AMEZ), was born in Camden, South Carolina. He entered Jackson College, the preparatory school for South Carolina University, in 1873, remaining until 1877 when the end of Reconstruction meant the ejection of African Americans from the university. In 1880 he engaged in private study with tutors at Charleston Military College, supporting himself variously with photography, butchering, barbering, and brick masonry. While in Charleston he experienced conversion.

In 1882 he went to Charlotte, North Carolina, where he joined the Clinton Chapel AME Zion Church. That fall he was licensed to preach and joined the Central North Carolina Conference. In 1884 he enrolled in Howard University in Washington, D.C., in 1886 transferring his membership to the Philadelphia and Baltimore Conference, where he was ordained deacon on May 24, 1886. In 1887, in his senior year, he was appointed city missionary for Washington, D.C. A few months later he was sent to Baltimore, Maryland, where he reorganized the Clinton AME Zion Mission, and developed a Sunday School in the western part of the city of over forty children. He graduated with his B.A. in 1888 and was ordained elder on May 20, 1888. On June 17, 1888, he married Laura Etta Lomax, with whom he had six children.

He was then appointed to Wesley Union AME Zion Church in Harrisburg, Pennsylvania, followed shortly by a pastorate in Chattanooga, Tennessee. In about 1890 he was sent to Hopkins Chapel AME Zion Church in Asheville, North Carolina, where he had great success and organized a number of churches in the general area.

After several years there he moved to Loguen Temple AME Zion Church in Knoxville, Tennessee. In 1895 he was professor of Latin, Greek, literature, and higher mathematics at Greenville College in Greenville, Tennessee. In 1896 he attended Illinois Wesleyan College in Bloomington, Illinois. In 1897 he returned for one year to Hopkins Chapel, and in 1898 was appointed to Fleet Street AME Zion Church in Brooklyn, New York. He took the opportunity to enroll in New York Medical College, receiving his M.D. in 1901.

From that time Jacobs began to develop his medical/surgical practice along with his pastoral responsibilities. He oversaw the congregation's move to a new location on Bridge Street and in 1901 was a delegate to the Second World Methodism Conference in London. In 1909 he left the local church and became presiding elder within the New York Conference, by that time being one of the most prominent physicians of Brooklyn. In 1918 he was elected General Secretary-Auditor of the denomination, serving in that capacity until May 20, 1928, when he was consecrated bishop. He was assigned to the Twelfth Episcopal District and also became chair of the Publication Board, but his life ended before a full quadrennium had passed.

"Bishop F. M. Jacobs Dead." *Star of Zion* 56 (December 31, 1931): 4.
HAMEZC, WWCA (30–32), *AMEZC.*

JAMES, FREDERICK CALHOUN (b. April 7, 1922), 93rd bishop of the **African Methodist Episcopal Church** (AME), was born in Prosperity, Newberry County, South Carolina, the son of Edward and Rosa (Lee) James. After graduating from Drayton High School he went to Allen University in Columbia, South Carolina, where he earned a B.A. in 1943. He was ordained deacon in 1945 and elder in 1947. He earned a B.D. in 1947 at Howard University in Washington, D.C. On December 30, 1944, he married Theresa Gregg.

His pastorates were all in South Carolina and included Friendship AME Church in Irmo (1945); Bishop's Memorial AME Church in Columbia (1946); Wayman AME Church in Winnsboro (1947–50); Chappelle Memorial AME Church in Columbia (1950–53); and Mt. Pisgah AME Church in Sumter (1953–72). Prior to the Sumter pastorate, from 1949 to 1953, he was also dean of Dickerson Seminary at Allen University. He was president of the Sumter branch of the N.A.A.C.P. from 1959 to 1972 and was instrumental in desegregating the city.

At the Mt. Pisgah church James built a program of

heroic proportions. The old building was torn down and a large, new structure was built along historic lines. The membership was built up until the church was recognized as one of the foremost in the connection. He led the church into creating Mt. Pisgah Apartments (now called James Village), one of the first church-supported housing projects in South Carolina. In 1960 he authored the Social Action Bill, which created the first Commission on Social Action of the AME Church, and he was chosen its first director. In 1966 he was a delegate to the World Council of Churches Church and Society Conference in Geneva, Switzerland. He worked closely with several South Carolina governors, and from 1969 to 1972 he was president of the Wateree Community Actions Agency.

At the 1972 General Conference James was elected bishop, the first bishop in the denomination elected from a pulpit in South Carolina. He was assigned to the Eighteenth Episcopal District (Botswana, Lesotho, Swaziland, Mozambique, South Africa, and Namibia). He built the James Center in Maseru, Lesotho, as a community service organization, and enabled a number of African students to go to America for their education. From 1976 to 1984 he was assigned to the Twelfth Episcopal District (Arkansas and Oklahoma), during which time Shorter College in North Little Rock, Arkansas, became accredited.

From 1984 to about 1992 he was assigned to the Seventh Episcopal District (South Carolina). There he instituted the Economic Fund for the district, aimed at improving Allen University endowment, providing below-market-rate loans, offering business venture capital for approved businesses, and gaining leverage capital for higher levels of Black financial participation in South Carolina. He reopened Dickerson Seminary and established a fund for theological education. He founded the James Square Shopping Center on the campus of Allen University, which leases retail space and serves the surrounding community while funneling profits to the university. He founded the James Human Resource Center at Shorter College and the Theresa James Manor, an 89-unit living complex for the elderly and handicapped in Little Rock. He has served as vice-chair of the service and development agency of the Urban League, a trustee of Shorter College, and chair of the trustees of Allen University. In 1979 he became a member of the board of the National Council of Churches and in 1981 he was a delegate to a World Methodist Council meeting in Honolulu, Hawaii, and in 1986 to another meeting in Nairobi, Kenya. In 1986 he became president of the South Carolina Coalition of Black Church Leaders, and in 1989 was co-chair of the reapportionment committee of the South Carolina

Legislative Black Caucus. In 1992 he was assigned to the denomination's Ecumenical Office.

HAMEC, BDNM (75), *WWR* (85), *WWA* (90–91), *WWABA* (90–91), *AMSC.*

JAMISON, MONROE FRANKLIN (November 27, 1848–May 16, 1918), 9th bishop of the **Christian Methodist Episcopal Church** (CME), then known as the Colored Methodist Episcopal Church, was born near Rome, Georgia, the son of George and Olivia (Shorter) Jamison. He grew up in poverty, and never attended school, but applied himself to attain a remarkable command of the written word. He experienced conversion and joined the CME Church in Newbern, Alabama, in October 1867, and was licensed to preach in 1870. On February 24, 1874, he married Martha A. Flournoy.

He joined the East Texas Conference in 1874 and served CME churches in Marshall and Longview. During his career he pastored many of the leading charges in Texas until 1890, when he was elected extension secretary of the denomination, a position he held until 1893. Also in 1890 he was elected to complete the unexpired term of F. M. Hamilton as editor of the *Christian Index*, the church's journal. He remained as editor until May 1910, when he was elected bishop. He maintained his residence in Leigh, Texas, and served for eight years, until his death.

EWM, WWCR, WWWA (1), *CMECTY.*

JARVIS CHRISTIAN COLLEGE. A **Christian Church (Disciples of Christ)** school. Jarvis Christian College, Hawkins, Texas, began in 1912 through the efforts of the Woman's Board of Mission of the Disciples of Christ to provide educational opportunities for Black students in Texas. Virginia Hearne, the Board's state secretary for Texas, convinced Ida Van Zandt Jarvis and her husband to donate land upon which to build a college. Hearne chose a local educated Black man, J. N. Erwin, as the first president. Erwin mixed freely with White people and was liked by the members and leaders of the Disciples in Texas who supported the school over the years. It began as an elementary school and gradually became a high school, junior college and finally a senior college.

Garrison, Winfred Ernest, and Alfred T. DeGroot. *The Disciples of Christ: A History.* St. Louis, MO: Bethany Press, 1948. 592 pp.

JASPER, JOHN (July 4, 1812–March 30, 1901), pioneer Baptist preacher, was born in Fluvanna County, Virginia, a slave on the plantation of the Peachy family, and one of many children of Philip and Nina Jasper. His father was a preacher within the slave community. In 1834, at age twenty-two, he was sent to the home of John Blair Peachy near Williamsburg, Virginia, where after some years he married Elvy Weaden. Shortly after the wedding, however, he was compelled to go to Richmond, where he worked in Samuel Hargrove's tobacco factory. The marriage could not survive the separation, and soon they were divorced. He experienced conversion on July 25, 1839 and Hargrove, a pious member of the First Baptist Church of Richmond, gave him the day off to spread the news. He joined the First African Baptist Church and began to preach. With the church's blessing he married Candus Jordan in 1844, with whom he had nine children.

His desire to read the Bible for himself led him to spend many hours studying it with another slave, William Jackson, until he reached a basic literacy. Jasper's lack of refined grammar and learning was no barrier to a startling eloquence that soon made him famous, and crowds both Black and White quickly gathered everywhere to hear him. Admiration of him was often not shared by the new generation of educated and trained Black ministers that arose, and Jasper was often derided as an anachronistic antebellum preacher whose emotionalism and unlettered presentation epitomized the stereotypes of Black clergy which they were trying to avoid. Nevertheless, his appeal to the poor masses was strong, and his fame began as a specialist in funeral sermons. In those days Black funerals were often all-day events in a grove, and a Black could preach with a White minister present.

Even before the outbreak of the Civil War he was allowed to pastor the Third Baptist Church in Petersburg two Sundays each month, finally leaving his factory position in 1859 or 1860. During the Civil War he preached in Confederate hospitals and comforted the wounded soldiers. When Richmond fell on April 3, 1865, the social disruption cost him the pastorate in Petersburg, and he had to clean bricks in the street for about a year, returning to the Third Baptist Church in December 1866. Shortly after the end of the war, apparently due to infidelity, he divorced his wife, and married his third wife, Mary Anne Cole. In 1877 he began to preach to a small group on an island in the James River in Richmond, and baptized many people in the river. He formally organized the new church in September 1877, with 9 members. As the crowds grew the meeting place shifted to a location in the northern part of Richmond, where a building was purchased at Duval and St. John Streets for a church home. This became the Sixth Mount Zion Baptist Church, which he built to a congregation of over 2,000, remaining there until his death.

In 1874 his third wife died and he married an unnamed woman who survived him. In about 1880 he developed his most famous sermon, "The Sun Do Move," which he is supposed to have delivered some 250 times. His contention was that the literal word of Scripture which describes the sun moving, rather than the earth revolving around it, is correct at its face value. It is testimony to his oratorical power that the sermon increased his stature rather than the opposite. At the time of his death the *Richmond Dispatch* devoted significant editorial space to recounting his virtues.

Smith, H. H. "John Jasper: 'The Unmatched Negro Philosopher and Preacher.'" *Methodist Quarterly Review (South)* 72 (July 1923): 466–480.

Day, Richard Ellsworth. *Rhapsody in Black: The Life Story of John Jasper*. Philadelphia, PA: The Judson Press, 1953. 149 pp.

Hatcher, William E. *John Jasper: The Unmatched Negro Philosopher and Preacher*. New York: Fleming H. Revell Co., 1908. 183 pp.

Jasper, John. *"The Sun Do Move!" The Celebrated Theory of the Sun's Rotation Around the Earth, as Preached by Rev. John Jasper of Richmond, Virginia. With a Memoir of His Life*. New York: Brentano's Literary Emporium, 1882. 15 pp.

Randolph, Edwin A. *The Life of Rev. John Jasper*. Richmond, VA: R. T. Hill & Co., 1884. 167 pp.

BAW, AARS, HUBA, IBAW, ENB, GNPP, MM, ESB, NYB (1912), *NBH, DANB, HBBUS*.

JEFFRIES, ELMIRA (c.1890–c.1966), 2nd bishop of the Mt. Sinai Holy Church of America, lived a life little known to the world at large. Sometime after **Ida Robinson** founded the Mount Sinai Holy Church of America, Inc. in Philadelphia in 1924, Jeffries was appointed vice-bishop. The church has a very strict code of behavior, disallowing such things as attendance at the movie theater or athletic events, chewing gum, use of alcohol or tobacco, etc. Church membership is limited to those who give evidence of sanctification and the gifts of the Holy Spirit, especially speaking in tongues. When Bishop Robinson died in 1946, Jeffries succeeded her as head of the organization. In 1966 the church reported 92 congregations with an estimated membership of 7,000.

BH, BGM.

JEMISON, DAVID VIVIAN (1875–February 20, 1954), long-time president of the **National Baptist Convention, U.S.A., Inc.** (N.B.C.U.S.A.), was born near Marion, in Perry County, Alabama, the son of Perry and Tyresa (Carlysle) Jemison. The family lived on a 250–acre plantation where his father once worked as a slave but eventually came to own. At the age of sixteen Jemison converted from Methodism to the Baptist Church, which angered his Methodist parents, but he held firm to his convictions.

He graduated from the high school department of Selma University in 1899 and had already been ordained a Baptist preacher (in 1898). In 1900 he pastored both El Bethel Baptist Church in Selma and Mt. Olive Baptist Church in Marion. From 1901 to 1903 he pastored Bethany Baptist Church in Suttles, while also serving as principal of the Marion Baptist Academy in 1901–02. On June 18, 1902, he married Henrietta Phillips, with whom he had nine children, of whom only six survived to maturity.

From 1903 to 1929 he pastored the Tabernacle Missionary Baptist Church in Selma, Alabama, and in 1916 was elected president of the Alabama State Baptist Convention, remaining president for the rest of his life. He moved to the St. Louis Street Baptist Church in Mobile, Alabama, from 1929 to 1936. In 1931 he was elected vice-president-at-large of the N.B.C.U.S.A., representing the city of Atlanta, a position he retained for nine years. In 1936 he returned to the Tabernacle Missionary Baptist Church, where he led in building a new $85,000 colonial-style church structure, complete with a $6,000 pipe organ, thus fulfilling a lifelong dream.

On December 4, 1940, he was elected to succeed Lacey **Kirk Williams** as president of the N.B.C.U.S.A. Like his predecessor and like his successor, **Joseph H. Jackson**, Jemison took a conservative stance on race relations. He was a very popular leader and efficient administrator, and on December 10, 1942, he was able to burn the mortgage of the denomination's new publishing house in Nashville, Tennessee, which had been built in 1923–24 and dedicated in 1926. After more than twelve years of capably leading the denomination, Jemison was in poor health, nearly blind and hard of hearing, and voluntarily resigned the presidency in January of 1953, effective in September, 1953. He passed away the following year, leaving behind a significant legacy of service. One of his sons, **Theodore Judson Jemison**, succeeded Joseph H. Jackson in 1982 as president of the N.B.C.U.S.A., further enlarging the family legacy.

"The Baptists." *Ebony* 4 (October 1949): 28–33.
RLA, IBAW, WWWA (3), *SCA.*

JEMISON, THEODORE JUDSON (b. August 1, 1918), president of the **National Baptist Convention, U.S.A., Inc.** (N.B.C.U.S.A.), was born in Selma, Alabama, the son of David Vivian and Henrietta (Hillips) Jemison. His father was a prominent Baptist minister who was president of the N.B.C.U.S.A. for a number of years. Jemison received his B.S. in 1940 from Alabama State University and his B.D. in 1945 from Virginia Union University in Richmond. On August 4, 1945, he married Celestine Catlett, with whom he had three children.

From 1945 to 1949 he pastored the Mt. Zion Baptist Church in Staunton, Virginia, and in 1949 he became pastor of the Mt. Zion First Baptist Church in Baton Rouge, Louisiana, where he has since remained. In 1953, when **Joseph H. Jackson** succeeded Jemison's father as president of the N.B.C.U.S.A., Jemison was elected general secretary of the denomination. The two were reelected in tandem every year until 1982, even though they did not always agree on policies. Joseph Jackson believed that it was counterproductive to use public demonstrations and civil disobedience to achieve civil rights, and preferred lawsuits and other lower-key measures in a "gradualist" approach. Jemison, on the other hand, in 1953 had organized in Baton Rouge the nation's first bus boycott, achieving integration in only eight days. **Martin Luther King, Jr.** therefore consulted him before beginning the famous bus boycott in Montgomery, Alabama, in 1955.

The lack of support for the activists of the civil rights movement was a major reason for the creation in 1961 of the **Progressive National Baptist Convention** as a split from the N.B.C.U.S.A. It was very difficult for Jemison to watch happen, but out of loyalty to Jackson and the denomination he remained quiet and bided his time. Finally, at the annual convention in September 1982, with no signs of Jackson stepping down, Jemison launched a counter-candidacy and won the presidency. While maintaining his pastorate, Jemison has considerably changed the look and posture of the denomination, moving it, in his words, "into the mainstream." For the first time in years full delegations were dispatched to the National and World Councils of Churches. He launched an evangelistic crusade to win three million new members, each of whom would also be registered to vote. **Jesse Jackson** and other Black leaders hailed Jemison's presidency as the beginning of a new era for African American Baptists. Jemison has served on the Louisiana Rights Commission, is a member of the board of the National Council of Churches, and in 1976 was a city councilman in Baton Rouge.

One of Jemison's major accomplishments has been

the building of a national headquarters for the N.B.C.U.S.A., which traditionally has had its headquarters in the church office of the president. He said such an arrangement was a continual embarrassment to him and decided that a national headquarters would signal the willingness on the part of the denomination to begin a new period of accepting and asserting the prestige and power that goes with being the world's largest Black organization with the world's largest Black religious publications department, the Sunday School Publishing Board. Soon after becoming president he began an enthusiastic effort to establish such a center. Finally, in June 1989, the $10 million Baptist World Center was dedicated in Nashville, Tennessee, with a 160-foot-high steeple, offices, and 2,000–seat auditorium. The key to maintaining this complex and paying off its $7 million debt will be to encourage the churches and ministers to make larger and more regular contributions to the convention, which in 1989 had a budget of about $15 million to run foreign and home missions and an educational mission. The N.B.C.U.S.A. has not had a tradition of systematic giving to a national body, partly because of its strong commitment to local church autonomy. In 1984 *Ebony* magazine named Jemison one of the one hundred most influential African Americans.

"The One Hundred Most Influential Black Americans." *Ebony* 39 (May 1984): 29–34.

Ostling, Richard N. "Moving into the Mainstream." *Time* 122 (September 19, 1983): 62.

"The Religious Groups with the Biggest Black Membership." *Ebony* 39 (March 1984): 140–144.

Waddle, Ray. "National Baptists Build a Headquarters." *Christian Century* 106 (September 13–20, 1989): 805–807.

HBB, WWR (85), *WWA* (78–79), *WWABA* (90–91), *SCA*.

JERNAGIN, WILLIAM HENRY (October 13, 1869– ?), head of the Congress of Christian Education, vice-president of the **National Baptist Convention, U.S.A., Inc.** (N.B.C.U.S.A.), and president of the **National Fraternal Council of Negro Churches**, was born in Mashulaville, near Macon, Mississippi, the son of Allen and Julia (Ruth) Jernagin. After attending Meridian Academy he became a teacher in Mississippi public schools for five years. On October 15, 1889, he married Willie A. Stennis, with whom he had four children, of whom only two lived into maturity. He was licensed to preach in 1890 by the Bush Fork Baptist Church and was ordained in 1892 to pastor the New Prospect Baptist Church, near Meridian, Mississippi.

In about 1896 he moved to pastor in Oktiba, Mississippi, and further pastorates included Scooba; Okolona (where he united the Missionary Union Baptist Church and Second Baptist Church); the First Baptist Church in Winona; the First Baptist Church in Mound Bayou; the First Baptist Church in Brandon; and Tabernacle Baptist Church in Oklahoma City, Oklahoma (1906–1912). He organized and was president of the Young People's Christian Educational Congress of Mississippi, and while in Oklahoma he was president of the Oklahoma General Baptist Convention. He also served a couple of years as business manager of Alcorn College in Lorman, Mississippi. He was instrumental in establishing the Winona-Grenada Baptist College, the Meridian Baptist Seminary in Meridian, Mississippi, and the Woman's Baptist College in Mound Bayou, Mississippi. In 1912 he accepted the pastorate of Mt. Carmel Baptist Church in Washington, D.C., where he remained the rest of his career.

From his Washington pastorate Jernagin built a nationwide reputation for leadership. He was elected the first president of the National Race Congress in 1916, and was its representative to the Pan-African Congress in Paris, France, in 1919. At the same time the Peace Conference following World War I was in session, and he was part of a committee from the Federal Council of Churches (now the National Council of Churches) that presented a Memorial to the Peace Conference. In 1921 he attended the Pan-African Conference in London and Brest and the same year was host to President King of Liberia on his visit to Washington, D.C.

In 1926 Jernagin was elected president of the National Sunday School and Baptist Young People's Union Congress of America (sometimes called the Congress of Christian Education), a position he held for the rest of his career. In 1928 Jernagin was elected president of the Consolidated National Equal Rights League and Race Congress, and in 1932 was a delegate to the Republican National Convention in Chicago. In 1937 he was a speaker at the International Youth Conference of the Baptist World Alliance in Zurich, Switzerland, and that year was elected president of the National Fraternal Council of Negro Churches in America. In 1938 he was again a speaker at the Baptist World Alliance when it met in Atlanta, Georgia. He was president of the General Baptist Convention for ten years, and was vice-president of the N.B.C.U.S.A. for twelve years. During World War II he was a chaplain in the U.S. Army and visited the front lines in the Pacific in 1945. In the late 1940s he sued the Southern Railroad for bias and won.

"The Baptists." *Ebony* 4 (October 1949): 28–33.

Jernagin, William H. "Annual Address of Rev. W. H. Jernagin,

President of the National Sunday School and B. T. U. Congress, U.S.A." Delivered in Cleveland, Ohio, June 24, 1948.

————. *Christ at the Battlefront: Servicemen Accept the Challenge.* Washington, DC: Murray Brothers, 1946. 132 pp.

————. "President's Address to the Fraternal Council of Negro Churches in America, Washington, D.C., 1938." *Negro Journal of Religion* 4 (July 1938): 8ff.

WWCA (38–40), *RLA, SCA, HUBA, BAW, IBAW, AARS, WWCR.*

JOHNNIE COLEMON INSTITUTE. A Universal Foundation for Better Living school. The Johnnie Colemon Institute, Chicago, Illinois, is named after its founder, **Johnnie Colemon**, a former minister from the Unity School of Christianity who founded the Institute in 1974 in Chicago. She had previously founded the **Universal Foundation for Better Living**, a fellowship of New Thought metaphysical congregations for which the Institute serves as the educational arm. At the institute, which prepares both lay and religious persons to serve as channels for God's messages, students can obtain Master certificates, counselor and teacher training, ministerial training, leadership training and correspondence courses. Many of the graduates have become pastors of congregations of the Universal Foundation.

Isotta Poggi

JOHNS, VERNON (April 22, 1892–1968), Baptist minister, seminary president, and civil rights pioneer, was born in Darlington Heights, Prince Edward County, Virginia, the son of William and Sally Branch (Price) Johns. His father was a farmer and Baptist preacher, and Johns soon pictured himself following in those ministerial footsteps. He graduated from Virginia Theological Seminary and College in Lynchburg in 1915 and three years later completed work for a B.D. at Oberlin College Graduate School of Theology in Ohio.

He was ordained a Baptist (**National Baptist Convention of the U.S.A., Inc.**) minister in 1918 and his first pastorate of record was at Court Street Baptist Church in Lynchburg, from 1920 to 1926. From 1926 to 1929 he was director of the Baptist Educational Center in New York City. On December 21, 1927, he married Altona M. Trent, with whom he had six children. He quickly became legendary for his preaching prowess and scholarly abilities. In 1929 he accepted the position of president of Virginia Seminary and College,

where he remained for four years. During that time he organized the Farm and City Club and the Institute for Rural Preachers of Virginia.

From 1933 to 1937 Johns pastored the Holy Trinity Baptist Church in Philadelphia, Pennsylvania, followed by First Baptist Church in Charleston, West Virginia (1937–41); a return to Court Street Baptist Church in Lynchburg (1941–48); and Dexter Avenue Baptist Church in Montgomery, Alabama (1948–53). He was a man of the soil, as was his father, and at least in the Charleston pastorate he ran a farm as well as the church. He even tried to establish a set of farm products retail outlets. His business and ministerial ventures were often marred by a tendency to brash and tactless behavior. One of his sermons bore the title, "Some Virginians that Ought to Vanish."

His blunt passion had its positive effects in electrifying sermons and a willingness to face down the White racist system. He is considered the instigator of civil rights activity in Montgomery long before **Martin Luther King, Jr.**, succeeded him at the Dexter Avenue church. This is part of what made King's activism there palatable to the congregation, composed of the "cream of Montgomery's Black bourgeoisie." It was Johns' niece who filed the first suit to integrate the county's schools. He publicly berated anything that smacked of oppression, but almost never made the headlines. After he left Dexter Avenue he worked for a time as editor of *Second Century* magazine. He might have become better known had not a fire destroyed the complete manuscript of a book he had written called *Human Possibilities*, and reportedly also destroyed another manuscript called *Immorality*. A number of his sermons, however, did make it into print.

Johns, Vernon. Religion and the Open Mind, A Sermon. N.d.
————. Rock Foundation, A Sermon. N.d.
————. "Transfigured Moments." In Newton, Joseph Fort, ed. *The Best Sermons of 1926.*
————. *What Ails the World? A Sermon Delivered January, 1927.* New York: Religious Education Center, 1927.
ALNA, BAW, HUBA, BDNM (70), *IBAW, HBB, RLA, GBB.*

JOHNSON, HARVEY ELIJAH (August 4, 1843–1923), prominent Baptist minister, was born into slavery in Fauquier County, Virginia, the son of Thomas and Harriet Johnson. He was educated at the Free Negro School of Alexandria and at a Quaker school in Philadelphia. He was converted and baptized sometime after he was twenty years old. The baptizing minister, S. W. Madden, then enrolled him in Wayland Seminary in Washington, D.C., in 1868, and he supported himself while in school as a teacher and missionary under the American Baptist Home Mission Society. He graduated from the seminary in 1872 and that fall accepted the pastorate of the Union Baptist Church on North Street in Baltimore, Maryland. By 1885 he had taken the membership of the church from 250 to 2,200.

Johnson took a leading role in fighting for civil rights for Blacks and succeeded in having Blacks allowed to the Maryland state bar. When a member of his church was refused first-class passenger service on a steamship out of Baltimore, he helped file suit and won the case, setting an important precedent. He also led the forces which gained the acceptance of Black physicians and teachers in Maryland. He helped establish the Clayton Williams Academy in Baltimore for the training of Black preachers. On April 17, 1877, he married Amelia E. Hall, with whom he had three children.

He became pessimistic about the possibility of Whites changing their attitudes toward Blacks, and in the early 1890s proposed a plan to separate the races. Known as the "Texas Movement," the idea was to set aside the state of Texas for Black residents. It did not gain much acceptance, but he did succeed in getting the Black Baptists in Maryland to separate from the White Baptists. The result was the first Black Baptist convention in the state, the Colored Baptist Convention of Maryland, and Johnson was its first president. Johnson's sermons were filled with sociopolitical ideas, unusual for the time, but he was still highly respected among Black Baptists nationally. He was a constant advocate of self-help and freedom programs in all aspects of Black life, including within the National Baptist Convention, U.S.A., Inc. and its predecessors. He was not afraid to challenge the White supremacy ideologies with sermons like "The Hamite—The Only Historical Nation."

Johnson, Harvey Elijah. *The Nations from a New Point of View*. Nashville, TN: National Baptist Publishing Board, 1903. 289 pp.

———. *The Question of Race*. Baltimore, MD: Printing Office of J. T. Weishanipel, 1891. 31 pp.

———. *The White Man's Failure in Government*. Baltimore, MD: Press of Afro-American Company, 1900. 49 pp.

MM, AARS, HUBA, BAW, AAE, HBB, HNB, IBAW, OBMS.

JOHNSON, HENRY THEODORE (October 10, 1857–1910), educator, **African Methodist Episcopal Church** (AME) minister, and long-time editor of the *Christian Recorder*, was born in Georgetown, South Carolina. At the age of fifteen, after attending public schools, he was apprenticed to learn the printer's trade and worked for three years on the *Georgetown Planet* and the *Charleston Independent*. He then taught school for a time and saved enough money to enter the State Normal School and then the State University. He was compelled to leave the university in the fall of 1876 when the Democrats regained control and ended Reconstruction. He returned to teaching and was licensed to preach in the AME Church in 1877.

In the fall of 1878 Johnson entered Howard University School of Religion and graduated in the spring of 1880. He also studied mathematics and classics in the college department. He served churches in South Carolina until 1882, when he enrolled in Lincoln University in Pennsylvania, where he finished his undergraduate work in the spring of 1883. While at Lincoln he served a number of churches in the area and was ordained elder in June, 1883. He transferred to the New England Conference and placed at the Chelsea AME Church. He also studied for three years in Boston University.

About 1886 Johnson's deteriorating health caused a move to Tennessee, where he pastored until winter of 1889, when he transferred to Visitor's Chapel AME Church in Hot Springs, Arkansas. In 1891 he became presiding elder in Arkansas for a year. At the 1892 General Conference he was elected editor of the denomination's official organ, the *Christian Recorder*. By this time he was already known as an outstanding author, and some books, such as *Divine Logos* (1890), became a part of the standard ministerial course of studies in the church. He was the first course lecturer at Payne Theological Seminary at Wilberforce University in Ohio and was annual lecturer at Phelps Bible School at Tuskegee Institute in Alabama. Several of his publications, including *Pulpit, Pew, and Pastorate* (1902), were originally composed as Tuskegee lectures. He was president of the National Association of Educators of Colored Youth, treasurer of Douglas Hospital in Philadelphia, and trustee of the New Jersey Industrial School at Bordentown before it was incorporated by the State Board of Education. He lost a bid for the episcopacy in 1900, although some claimed he was the popular choice, and maintained his editorship for the remainder of his career. He was known as a man of progressive ideas and strong character.

Johnson, Henry Theodore. *The Divine Logos; or, Wonderful Word of John*. Boston, MA: The Author, 1890. 117 pp.

———. *Johnson's Gems, Consisting of Brief Essays and Dissertations of Literary, Ethical, Religious, and Current Topics*. N.p., 1901. 154 pp.

———. *Key to the Problem; or, Tale of a Sable City*. Philadelphia, PA: AME Book Concern, 1904. 66 pp.

———. *Lux Gentis Nigrae.* Philadelphia, PA: AME Book Concern, 1903. 30 pp.

———. *Pulpit, Pew, and Pastorate.* N.p., 1902. 139 pp.

———. *Wings of Ebony.* Philadelphia, PA: AME Book Concern, 1904. 51 pp.

IBAWCB, HUBA, BAWPP, BAW, AARS, TCNL.

JOHNSON, JAMES WELDON (June 17, 1871–June 26, 1938), novelist, historian, diplomat, and educator, was born in Jacksonville, Florida, the son of James and Helen Louise (Dillette) Johnson. His father was a headwaiter at a resort hotel and his mother was a schoolteacher. After attending Stanton Public School for Blacks in Jacksonville (where his mother taught), Johnson enrolled in Atlanta University in 1887, where he finished his high school education. He graduated from the college department in 1894 and became principal of the Stanton school, which at that point had one thousand pupils.

He was an able administrator and added high school grades to the school while founding a short-lived newspaper, the *Daily American*, the first Black daily newspaper in the country. In the fall of 1896 he began studying law on his own and passed the Florida bar, the first Black to do so, in 1898. He and his younger brother, John Rosamond Johnson, were both musically talented and together they wrote *Toloso*, a satirical comic opera about United States imperialism in the Spanish-American War. In the summer of 1899 they traveled to New York to try to find a producer and made many contacts, but failed to get backing. In 1900 Johnson composed a poem, "Lift Ev'ry Voice and Sing," which was set to music by his brother and first performed at a Jacksonville celebration of Lincoln's birthday. By the 1920s it had become so widespread and popular that it was called the "Negro National Anthem (or Hymn)."

In 1901 Johnson left Jacksonville for New York City and formed a musical partnership with Bob Cole. They produced a series of hit songs, including "The Maiden with the Dreamy Eyes," "My Castle on the Nile," "Under the Bamboo Tree," and "The Congo Love Song." They were successful enough to travel across the United States and Europe. From time to time between 1903 and 1906 he took graduate courses in English and drama at Columbia University in New York. In 1904 he did some campaigning on behalf of the Republican party and was rewarded in 1906 with the position of United States Consul in Puerto Cabello, Venezuela. By this time the glamour of show business had worn off and he was happy to accept the change. His duties in Venezuela (1906–09) and Nicaragua (1909–12) allowed him time for literary pursuits, and he began to write poetry. On February 10, 1910, he married Grace Nail; there were no children. In 1912 he completed a novel, *The Autobiography of an Ex-Coloured Man*, about a light-skinned man with ambivalent feelings concerning his racial identity. It did not gain much notice until it was reissued in 1927.

In 1912, with the Democrats in the White House, Johnson felt obliged to leave the consular service. He returned to Jacksonville for a year and a half, then went back to New York City, where he became an editorial writer for the Black weekly, the *New York Age*. At the end of 1916 he joined the newly formed (in 1910) National Association for the Advancement of Colored People (N.A.A.C.P.) as its first field secretary. He investigated racial incidents across the country and organized new branches. In 1917 he published his first book of poetry, *Fifty Years and Other Poems*. That year he also led a silent march through New York City to protest lynchings. From 1916 to 1920 he increased the N.A.A.C.P. membership from 9,000 to 90,000. In 1920 he became the first Black general secretary of the N.A.A.C.P., a position he held for the next ten years.

Johnson's leadership of the N.A.A.C.P. was invaluable during this critical period after the First World War, when the social and economic gains of the previous decade were threatened by the rise in lynchings and the terrorist activities of the Ku Klux Klan. It was a dangerous time to represent the nation's foremost Black advocate organization. His on-site investigation of the abuses of Haiti citizens by U.S. Marines during the American occupation of that country in 1920 led to a Congressional probe and helped turn the tide of public opinion away from the expansionism of President Wilson toward the more isolationist position of the next president, Warren Harding. The N.A.A.C.P.'s first Supreme Court case was Nixon v. Herndon in 1924, the first in a string of victories that led the Court in 1944 to declare, not just the Texas form, but all forms of the White-only primary elections, unconstitutional. One of the N.A.A.C.P.'s most widely distributed pamphlets was the very graphic *30 Years of Lynching in the United States, 1889–1919*. Johnson's leadership wrought large gains in N.A.A.C.P. membership and influence.

During this period he was also a key figure in the "Harlem Renaissance" of arts and letters. He was editor of several important anthologies, including *The Book of American Negro Poetry* (1922), *The Book of American Negro Spirituals* (1925), and *The Second Book of American Negro Spirituals* (1926). In 1925 he won the coveted Spingarn Award from the N.A.A.C.P. for his many contributions to Black life. Perhaps his most famous work was *God's Trombones: Seven Negro Sermons in Verse* (1927), which won the Harmon Award for Literature. Though Johnson himself was an agnostic, this is one of the most moving expressions yet produced of the profound depths of Black religious feeling. His song, "Lift Ev'ry Voice and Sing," similarly touched strong religious sentiment and has over the years found its way into many denominational hymnals.

In 1930 he left his position with the N.A.A.C.P. for the Adam K. Spence Chair of Creative Literature at Fisk University in Nashville, Tennessee. In 1933 he published his autobiography, *Along This Way: The Autobiography of James Weldon Johnson*. In that same year he won the W. E. B. Du Bois Prize for Negro Literature. In 1938 he was killed in a traffic accident while on vacation in Maine.

Fleming, Robert E. *James Weldon Johnson and Arna Wendell Bontemps: A Reference Guide*. Boston, MA: G. K. Hall, 1978. 149 pp.

———. *James Weldon Johnson*. Boston, MA: Twayne Publishing Co., 1987. 123 pp.

Johnson, James Weldon. *Along This Way: The Autobiography of James Weldon Johnson*. New York: The Viking Press, 1933. 418 pp.

———. *The Book of American Negro Poetry*. New York: Harcourt, Brace & Co., 1922. 217 pp.

———. *The Book of American Negro Spirituals*. New York: Viking Press, 1925. 187 pp.

———. *Fifty Years and Other Poems*. Boston, MA: Cornhill Co., 1917. 92 pp.

———. *God's Trombones: Seven Negro Sermons in Verse*. New York: Viking Press, 1927. 56 pp.

Kostelanetz, Richard. *Politics in the African-American Novel: James Weldon Johnson, W. E. B. Du Bois, Richard Wright, and Ralph Ellison*. New York: Greenwood Press, 1991. 180 pp.

Levy, Eugene D. *James Weldon Johnson, Black Leader, Black Voice*. Chicago: University of Chicago Press, 1973. 380 pp.

NBH, HNB, BHBA, WWCA (38–40), *SBAA, IBAWCB, NPT, CH, IP, GBA, DANB, AAE, EBA, EAB, DAB* (supp. 2), *BNA, BLTC, WWWA* (1), *IBAW, HUBA, AARS, BAW, BWA, BWASS, ALNA, BAW pp.*

JOHNSON, JOHN ALBERT (October 29, 1857– November 22, 1928), 34th bishop of the **African Methodist Episcopal Church** (AME), was born in Oakville, Ontario, Canada, one of four children in the family of John Garrison and Mary (Mackay) Johnson. His father was a quartermaster in the British merchant marine service and his mother was the daughter of a Chippewa chief of Dalhousie, Canada. He was educated in Canada, receiving both an M.A. and M.D. from the University of Toronto. While a student there, in 1874,

he left the Anglican Church, joined the African Methodist Episcopal Church, and was licensed to preach the same year. He joined the Canada Annual Conference in 1875, was ordained deacon in 1876, at Halifax, Nova Scotia, and became elder in 1880. On January 16, 1881, he married Minnie S. Goosley, with whom he had two children.

He was considered one of the ablest preachers of his day, with strong intelligent appeal, and his first assignment in 1875 was as itinerant minister in Nova Scotia, with charges in Oakville, Chatham, St. Catherine, and Hamilton, Ontario. In 1887 he went to Hamilton, Bermuda, to rebuild St. Paul's AME Church and parsonage there. Upon return to the United States about 1892 he became pastor of Union AME Church in Philadelphia, staying three years. While there he studied at the Philadelphia Divinity School, and in 1895 was the second Black graduate of that institution. He then went to Bethel AME Church in Germantown, Pennsylvania; Metropolitan AME Church in Washington, D.C.; St. John's AME Church in Baltimore, Maryland; and again at Union in Philadelphia. In 1891 and 1901 he was a delegate to the World Methodist Conferences.

At the General Conference of 1908 he received 437 of 445 votes cast for bishop, the highest percentage of votes ever given any one bishop. He was assigned to South Africa, where he lived for the next eight years. He established many schools and churches, from Capetown to the Limpopo River. His medical expertise also enabled him to treat the physical needs of the people, training several Zulus and others to continue the work after he left.

In 1916 he was assigned to the Second Episcopal District (North Carolina, Virginia, Washington D.C., and Maryland Conferences), succeeding Bishop **Levi Coppin**. In 1921 he was again a delegate to the World Methodist Conference. Johnson was one of the founders of the American Negro Academy in Washington, D.C., and was its vice-president from 1918 to 1920. In Philadelphia, where he resided, he was a director of Douglass Hospital, Citizens and Southern Bank, and the Pioneer Building and Loan Association. He was chair of the board of trustees of Kittrell College in North Carolina, and was a trustee of Wilberforce University in Ohio. He remained in the Second District until 1928, when all the bishops were moved, and he was assigned to the Thirteenth Episcopal District. He passed away, however, before the year was out.

Johnson, John Albert. *Private Journal*. Bermuda: N.p., 1889. *AARS, HUBA, NCAB* (21), *WWWA* (1), *EWM, HAMEC, BAMEC, CEAMEC.*

JOHNSON, JOHN HOWARD (b. 1897), prominent priest of the **Episcopal Church**, was born in Richmond, Virginia. He was educated at Columbia University and Union Theological Seminary, both in New York City, and then served on the New York City Mission Society staff for six years. In about 1928 he was assigned to St. Martin's Episcopal Church in Harlem, where he remained the rest of his career.

Under his leadership St. Martin's gained the most significant urban ministry of any Episcopal church in the country. He transformed it from a small mission church to a powerful institution with thousands of members. The Depression hit the Black community with greatest force, and it became more and more of a problem that the 125th Street White merchants in Harlem would not hire Blacks to help run the stores. In 1933 he helped organize the Harlem Citizens' League for Fair Play and its first mass meeting was held in St. Martin's. Represented were 62 of Harlem's social, religious, and business groups.

Johnson was elected chair of the committee to approach the merchants. The large Blumstein store was targeted first, but Mr. Blumstein refused to do more than hire Blacks as maids, porters, and elevator operators. Johnson had hoped that simple realization of the amount of money Blumstein took in from the Black community would cause him to reconsider, but this was not the case. Reluctantly, the Harlem Citizens' League resorted to picketing. After business seriously declined, Mr. Blumstein agreed to hire 35 Blacks as clerical and sales help. Eventually several hundred jobs were opened in Harlem, but the bad feelings with the merchants continued and led to the 1935 riot.

For twenty-five years Johnson was a chaplain in the New York Police Department and was also the chaplain of the Negro Actors Guild. He was the first Black to run for Harlem City Council. He was a trustee of the Cathedral of St. John the Divine from 1947 and 1965. In 1942 he published *Harlem, the War, and Other Addresses*, and in 1955 he published *A Place of Adventure*, a collection of sermons. He retired as rector emeritus in 1965, but continued an active ministry in the community into the 1980s.

Johnson, John Howard. *Folk-Lore from Antigua, British West Indies.* Lancaster, PA, 1921. 88 pp.

———. "Folk-Lore from Antigua, British West Indies." *Journal of American Folklore* 34 (January–March 1921): 40–88.

———. *Harlem, the War, and Other Addresses.* New York: W. Malliet & Co., 1942. 163 pp.

———. *A Place of Adventure: Essays and Sermons.* Greenwich, CT: Seabury Press, 1955. 130 pp.

IBAW, AARS, HUBA, BAW, NPT, CH, BGWC.

JOHNSON, JOSEPH ANDREW, JR. (June 19, 1914–September 26, 1979), educator and 34th bishop of the **Christian Methodist Episcopal Church** (CME), was born in Shreveport, Louisiana, the son of Rev. Joseph A., Sr., a well-known CME minister, and Rosa B. Johnson. From early on Johnson admired his father, and determined to be a minister himself. He was ordained a deacon in 1936 and elder in 1937, while attending Texas College in Tyler, Texas, where he received his B.A. in 1938. Also in 1938 he married Grace Leon Johnson, with whom he had three children.

His first full pastoral assignment was in 1938 at Mays Chapel and St. Mary Chapel CME Churches in Ruston, Louisiana. His next assignments were Phillips Chapel CME Church in Nashville, Tennessee, and Cleaves Memorial CME Church in Denver, Colorado. While in Denver he attended Iliff School of Theology, receiving his M.Th. in 1943 and D.Th. in 1945. Hethen went to Capers Memorial CME Church in Nashville, Tennessee, and while there was a student at Vanderbilt University. In 1951 he made his first trip abroad as delegate to the Eighth World Methodist Conference in Oxford, England. In 1952 he attended the Third World Conference on Faith and Order in Lunn, Sweden. He was the first Black to be admitted to Vanderbilt, the first to graduate, and the first to receive a Ph.D. from that institution, in 1958.

While both a student and a minister, he served as President and Professor of Christian Theology at Phillips School of Theology in Jackson, Tennessee, from 1943 to 1953. Upon receiving his Ph.D. he gained a position as Professor of Religion at Fisk University in Nashville, where he stayed until 1960. Then for seven years (1959–1966) he was Professor of New Testament and Director of Religious Services at the Interdenominational Theological Center in Atlanta, Georgia.

In 1966 he was elected bishop and assigned to the Fourth Episcopal District (Louisiana and Mississippi Conferences), where he remained the rest of his career. He also served variously as the chair of the College of Bishops, of the Board of Christian Education, and of the Board of Finance. In August 1971, he attended the Fifth World Conference on Faith and Order in Louvain, France, and in 1973 was a part of the Commission on Faith and Order in Zagorsk, Russia. In 1971 he published the first of six books (after his dissertation), *The Soul of the Black Preacher*. His final trip abroad was in November 1975, to the Ninth Assembly of the World Council of Churches in Nairobi, Kenya. He was very prolific in his final years, publishing *Proclamation Theology* in 1977 and *Basic Christian Methodist Beliefs* in 1978. He was widely revered as a significant theologian. He was instrumental in founding the Robert

400

S. Williams Theological Institute in Louisiana and the Elias Cottrell Theological Institute in Mississippi. He died unexpectedly while recovering from an operation; at the time he was working on two more books, including a twenty-year project of translating the New Testament from Greek to English.

Lakey, Othal Hawthorne. "The Thought of Joseph Andrew Johnson, Jr." *Christian Index* 110 (August 25, 1977): 4ff.

"The Obituary: Bishop Joseph Andrew Johnson, Jr." *Christian Index* 112 (September 27, 1979): 5.

Johnson, Joseph A. *Basic Christian Methodist Beliefs.* Shreveport, LA: Fourth Episcopal District Press, 1978. 268 pp.

———. *Christology and Atonement in the Fourth Gospel.* Ann Arbor, MI: University Microfilms (Vanderbilt University Dissertation), 1958. 396 pp.

———. "Jesus the Liberator." In James J. Gardiner and J. Deotis Roberts, Sr., eds. *Quest for a Black Theology.* Philadelphia, PA: United Church Press, 1971, pp. 97–111.

———. "The Legitimacy of Black Theology." *Christian Index* 103 (April 9, 1970): 3–4.

———. *Proclamation Theology.* Shreveport, LA: Fourth Episcopal District Press, 1977. 329 pp.

———. *The Soul of the Black Preacher.* Philadelphia, PA: Pilgrim Press, 1970. 173 pp.

EWM, CA (vol.89–92), *WWABA* (80–81), *AARS, HUBA, IBAWCB.*

JOHNSON, MORDECAI WYATT (January 12, 1890–September 10, 1976), Baptist minister and the first Black president of Howard University, was born in Paris, Tennessee, the son of Wyatt J. and Carolyn (Freeman) Johnson. His father was a millworker during the week and a preacher at Mount Zion Baptist Church on Sundays. Johnson attended local public schools and the high school department of Roger Williams University in Nashville, Tennessee (1903–04), until it was destroyed by fire. He finished his high school education at Howe Institute, a Baptist school in Memphis, Tennessee, graduating in 1905. In the fall of 1906 he entered Atlanta Baptist College (later called Morehouse College), but was expelled in 1907 for playing cards on Sunday. He worked in Chicago for a year, resolved never to fail again, reentered the school in the fall of 1908, and received his B.A. in 1911.

He was a professor of English, economics, and history at Morehouse College from 1911 to 1913, studying sociology in the summers and thus earning another B.A. in 1913 from the University of Chicago. During this time his mother passed away and he was forced to rethink his life and purpose. He decided to enter the ministry, and in the fall of 1913 he enrolled at Rochester Theological Seminary in New York, where he was strongly influenced by Walter Rauschenbusch, the major proponent of "Social Gospel" theology. He soon became a student pastor of the Second Baptist Church in Mumford, New York. He was ordained in 1916, left the seminary, and for a year was student secretary for the International Committee of the Young Men's Christian Association (Y.M.C.A.). On December 25, 1916, he married Anna Ethelyn Gardner, with whom he had five children. He served the First Baptist Church in Charleston, West Virginia, from 1917 to 1926. While pastoring in Charleston he finally wrote the required thesis and earned the B.D. in 1919 from Rochester Theological Seminary.

In 1921 Johnson's health was failing and the congregation urged him to take a rest. Instead, he simply shifted gears and enrolled in Harvard University Divinity School in Boston, Massachusetts. In 1922 he earned the S.T.M. and represented the Graduate Schools at the commencement program. He attracted wide attention for his speech on that occasion entitled, "The Faith of the American Negro." He returned to Charleston, where he founded the Charleston branch of the N.A.A.C.P. and organized a cooperative society and grocery.

On June 20, 1926, he was unanimously elected the first Black president of Howard University in Washington, D.C. At the time the school had a budget of $700,000, an enrollment of about 2,000 students, and consisted of a cluster of unaccredited departments instead of colleges. In 1928 he accomplished a major feat of securing the passage of a Congressional Act which allocated annual funds to the school for the purpose of building it into a first-class university. The funding increased previous federal monies and started with the 1931–32 budget with $2,179,469, and after ten years provided a total of $15 million. He received the coveted Spingarn Medal in 1929 for his accomplishments. By the time of his retirement in 1960 the school had constructed twenty buildings, worked with a budget of $8 million and counted ten distinct schools and colleges, all accredited, with more than 6,000 students. He was a powerful orator, and in 1954 *Ebony* magazine named him one of America's top ten Black preachers.

Johnson was a member of advisory councils for the Virgin Islands, the National Youth Administration, and the National Youth Commission. At various times he was a member of the national council of the United Negro College Fund, the National Conference of Christians and Jews, the executive board of the National Religion and Labor Foundation, and was vice-chair of the National Council for the Prevention of War. From

1962 to 1965 he was a member of the District of Columbia Board of Education. He was decorated by the governments of Ethiopia, Haiti, Liberia, and Panama, and was the recipient of numerous honorary degrees. He gained near-legendary status in his own lifetime. In 1973 an administration building at Howard University was named in his honor.

"Great Negro Preachers." *Ebony* 10 (July 1954): 26–30.

Johnson, Mordecai Wyatt. "America's Great Hour." In Paul Butler, ed. *Best Sermons*. New York: McGraw-Hill Book Co., 1955, 225–230.

———. "The Faith of the American Negro." *The Crisis* 24 (August 1922): 156–158.

———. *Inaugural Address of Mordecai Wyatt Johnson, 11th President of Howard University, June 10, 1927.* Washington, DC: Howard University Press, 1927. 15 pp.

TAO, WWWA (7), *CB* (1941), *NYTBS* (1976), *AAE,GNPP, BDNM* (65), *RLA, BDAE, EBA, CH, NBH, WWCA* (38–40), *HNB, IBAW, BAW, HUBA, AARS, IBAWCB, MBRL.*

JOHNSON, SHERROD C. (November 24, 1899–February 22, 1961), founder of the **Church of the Lord Jesus Christ of the Apostolic Faith**, was born in Pine Tree Quarter, Edgecomb County, North Carolina. He grew up in a sharecropping family, but he eventually left the farm and became a building contractor and musician. Then in 1919 he began preaching from the back room of his Philadelphia home on South 17th Street. He affiliated with the **Church of Our Lord Jesus Christ of the Apostolic Faith**, founded in 1919 by Robert C. Lawson. Lawson, though very strict in most of the usual Pentecostal injunctions against such things as divorce and remarriage, had showed some leeway in allowing women to wear bright colors and some makeup. Johnson rebelled against this liberalism and in 1930 left the organization to found the Church of the Lord Jesus Christ of the Apostolic Faith, a change of only one word from the other church title.

After some time of preaching out of a small storefront in Philadelphia rented for $45 a month, Johnson had a vision of himself as a radio preacher. He began two Sunday broadcasts, one on Philadelphia's WIBC and the other on Washington D.C.'s WOOK. He gained a significant audience, despite the severity of the message. He condemned Christmas, Lent, and Easter as pagan festivals and did not allow members to see motion pictures, smoke, drink, watch television, or listen to the radio (with the exception of his own programs). He insisted that women members wear opaque cotton stockings and long, plain dresses. Taped broadcasts eventually spread to over seventy church-owned radio outlets in the United States and abroad. The radio broadcasts attracted large numbers of followers to the headquarters church in Philadelphia, which became part of Apostolic Square, including housing for members. By his death affiliate churches had been established in about eighteen states and a number of foreign countries. His successor was **S. McDowell Shelton**.

"Top Radio Ministers." *Ebony* 4 (July 1949): 56–61.

Johnson, Sherrod C. *The Christmas Spirit is a False Spirit.* Philadelphia, PA: Church of the Lord Jesus Christ of the Apostolic Faith, n.d. 6 pp.

———. *Church Yearbook and Radio History.* Philadelphia, PA: Church of the Lord Jesus Christ of the Apostolic Faith, 1957. 47 pp.

———. *False Lent and Pagan Festivals.* Philadelphia, PA: Church of the Lord Jesus Christ of the Apostolic Faith, n.d.

———. *Let Patience Have Her Perfect Work.* Philadelphia, PA: Church of the Lord Jesus Christ of the Apostolic Faith, 1964. 12 pp.

———. *21 Burning Subjects: Who is This That Defies and Challenges the Whole Religious World on These Subjects?* Philadelphia, PA: Church of the Lord Jesus Christ of the Apostolic Faith, 196?. 24 pp.

BH, RLOA, NYTO, BDA-AHP.

JOHNSON, WILLIAM DECKER (November 15, 1869–June 17, 1936), 42nd bishop of the **African Methodist Episcopal Church** (AME), was born in Glasgow, Thomas County, Georgia, the son of Andrew Jackson and Mattie (McCullough) Johnson. His father was a migrant laborer and AME minister, founder of Gaines AME Church in Waycross, Georgia. He died when Johnson was thirteen years old. Johnson experienced conversion at the age of ten and joined the AME church in Wingham, Georgia. He was licensed to preach in 1887 and was admitted to the Georgia Conference in 1889. On December 3, 1891, he married Winifred E. Simon, with whom he had eleven children, only five of whom reached maturity.

His appointments included Westonia Mission (1889); Sunday School superintendent of the Thomasville District (1890); Dawson Mission (1891–92); Cuthbert Circuit (1893); Blakely Station (1894–97); Albany Station (1898–99); presiding elder of the Bainbridge District (1900–03); Americus Station (1904–05); presiding elder of the Thomasville District (1906–07); presiding elder of the Columbus District (1908); St. James Station in Columbus (1909–11); and presiding elder of the Cuthbert District (1911–c.1915). He signed his name with "Jr." added to differentiate himself from another William Decker Johnson (b.1842), who was secretary of the Georgia Conference in 1872 and Secretary of Education for the AME Church from 1884 to 1896.

Johnson was elected bishop in 1920 while serving as presiding elder of the Blakely District in Georgia. He was assigned to California and the Far West from 1920 to 1924, then Texas from 1924 to 1928, Mississippi and Louisiana from 1928 to 1936, and South Carolina in 1936. He was known as a hard worker and eloquent preacher. He published three songbooks and two volumes of "Marching Orders." A number of writings that are attributed to Johnson the bishop are by Johnson the Secretary of Education. He founded the Johnson Home-Industrial College in Archery, Georgia, a small town also founded by him. He was the organizer and Supreme Archer of the Sublime Order of Archery. Named for him are churches in Santa Ana, California, and Houston, Texas, and a building at Paul Quinn College in Waco, Texas. A son, William Decker Johnson, Jr., also became a well-known leader in the denomination.

Johnson, William Decker. *Biographical Sketches of Prominent Men and Woman of Kentucky.* Lexington, KY: Standard Print, 1897. 130 pp.

———. *Precious Jewels.* 1896.

EWM, BAMEC, HAMEC, WWCR.

JOHNSON C. SMITH UNIVERSITY. A Presbyterian school. Johnson C. Smith University, Charlotte, North Carolina, was founded in 1867. It originated in an idea to create a school to train ministers, teachers, and church lay leaders for the emerging African American church in the South. The plan was developed by the Revs. S. C. Alexander, Stanley S. Murland, and Willis L. Miller, members of the Presbyterian Church in the U.S. (the Southern branch of presbyterianism). Their idea of a school, however, was receiving the support of the North Presbyterians. As a result the Southern Presbyterians asked them to either break their relations with the Northern church or leave the southern Church. They chose to leave and in 1866 organized the Catawba Presbytery affiliated with the Presbyterian Church, U.S.A. The new Presbytery began with two churches made up of African American members and served by the White ministers.

When opened a short time later, the school was named Biddle Memorial Institute for the late husband of Mary Biddle of Philadelphia who had picked up the idea for the school and raised a substantial amount for its opening. In 1876 the name was changed to Biddle University.

George E. Davis was the first African American professor. His impressive work as the instructor in natural science changed many opinions about the abilities of Black people and paved the way for the appointment of Dr. Daniel Sanders as the first African American president in 1891.

The natural progress of the school was accelerated in 1921 by a large gift of Jane Berry Smith and the school was renamed for her husband, Johnson C. Smith. She continued to be a generous benefactor through the decade and eventually underwrote the cost of five new buildings. In 1932 the school, as part of a massive reconsideration of its African American schools by the Presbyterian Church, became coeducational and a year later reorganized as an independent Presbyterian college. At first women were admitted only to the senior class, but in 1941 were accepted as freshmen.

The school, which annually serves approximately a thousand students, is a four-year liberal arts college.

Parker, Inez Moore. *The Rise and Decline of the Program of Education for Black Presbyterians of the United Presbyterian Church, U.S.A., 1865–1970.* San Antonio, TX: Trinity University Press, 1977. 319 pp.

JONAS, MARK E. (October 30, 1885–February 26, 1973), a bishop of the **Church of God in Christ** (COGIC), was born in Edwardsville, Alabama. As a young man he migrated to California, and was among the people attracted to the small gathering on Azuza Street where **Pentecostalism** began. He was also one of the first to experience the baptism of the Holy Spirit as evidenced by his speaking in tongues, which occurred on April 20, 1906, just days after the revival began. He stayed in Los Angeles to help found the Apostolic Faith Mission. He remained in Los Angeles through the rest of the year, but in October received a call to preach. In May 1907, he left Los Angeles for Georgia and pioneered the Pentecostal message within the African American community of Atlanta.

Meanwhile, **Charles H. Mason**, who had also received the baptism of the Holy Spirit at Azusa, had founded the Church of God in Christ in Memphis and Jonas began to associate with Mason's movement. He attended the COGIC convocation in 1909, and brought his independent mission into the church. He was ordained by Mason and appointed overseer of the state of Georgia. After a decade in Georgia, he moved to Ohio and founded the first COGIC congregation in Cleveland. He was appointed overseer (later bishop) of the state of Ohio and remained in that post for the next 14 years. He retired as bishop in 1931 and was succeeded by

Riley F. Williams, but remained active as a pastor through the 1960s.

DuPree, Sherry Sherrod. *Biographical Dictionary of African-American Holiness-Pentecostals, 1880–1990.* Washington, DC: Middle Atlantic Regional Press, 1989. 386 pp.

Patterson, J. O., German R. Ross, and Julia Mason Atkins. *History and Formative Years of the Church of God in Christ with Excepts from the Life of Its Founder—Bishop C.H. Mason.* Memphis, TN: Church of God in Christ Publishing House, 1969. 143 pp.

JONES, ABSALOM (November 6, 1746–February 13, 1818), the first African American priest of the (Protestant) **Episcopal Church**, was born into slavery in Sussex, Delaware. He taught himself to read, and at age sixteen was separated from his mother and siblings and brought to Philadelphia to work in his owner's store as handyman and clerk. There, one of the other workers taught him to write. He received permission to attend Anthony Benezet's school at night beginning in 1766, and married a slave woman in 1770. With the help of his father-in-law, John Thomas, and some Friends (Quakers) in Philadelphia, he was able to purchase his wife's freedom and then finally his own in 1784. He was also able to purchase a lot, on which he built two houses that he rented. He continued to work for his former owner.

In February 1786, **Richard Allen** came to town, and joined Jones and some other Blacks in the worship at St. George's Methodist Church, all of them being seated along the outside wall of the sanctuary. Jones and Allen began preaching in the Black community, greatly increasing the Black attendance at St. George's. A separate Black church was proposed by Jones and Allen, but both Blacks and Whites expressed opposition. Instead, they organized the Free African Society on April 12, 1787. It was the first independent Black society in the United States, and was dedicated to mutual aid, moral betterment, and the abolition of slavery.

On a Sunday in November 1787, the church decided to restrict the Blacks to the upstairs gallery, without telling them that they could not use the front seats even up there. Jones and others were pulled from their knees during the opening prayer and told they were in the wrong place. They walked out of St. George's never to return. The Free African Society then provided the major gathering place, holding Quaker-like times of silence as part of their meetings. As they began building a sanctuary in late 1792 they had to decide upon a religious affiliation. Jones and Allen voted for Methodist, but most members, disappointed in Methodism, voted for Episcopalian, probably because of friendly associations with Episcopalians through the mission group Thomas Bray Associates and individuals such as Benjamin Franklin, Dr. Benjamin Rush, and Bishop William White. Allen chose to begin another church that later became the first **African Methodist Episcopal Church**. The construction on both churches was interrupted in 1793 with a yellow fever epidemic, in which Jones, Allen, and others worked tirelessly around the city tending to the sick and the dead, often in the face of abusive treatment.

Jones' church was dedicated on July 17, 1794, by two Episcopal rectors as the St. Thomas African Episcopal Church. It was formally received into the Diocese of Pennsylvania on October 17, 1794, with a guarantee that its members could control their local affairs. It was, however, denied a political voice in the denomination until 1863. Jones had accepted the position of leader, and was licensed as a lay reader. After the decision was made to waive the usual Greek and Latin requirements (not an uncommon occurrence in those times), Jones was ordained deacon on August 6, 1795, by Bishop William White, as the first ordained Black in the Episcopal Church. He was ordained a priest in 1804, and a rectory was built in 1809.

The St. Thomas church became a cornerstone of the African American community, with a membership of 427 by 1795. Jones saw that it organized schools for education, and such groups as the Female Benevolent Society and the African Friendly Society for mutual aid. Jones and Allen continued to work closely together, founding the African Masonic Lodge in Philadelphia in 1798. Jones was elected worshipful leader and Allen treasurer. In 1799 and 1800 they petitioned the state legislature and Congress to end slavery. In 1809 they founded the Society for the Suppression of Vice and Immorality. In the War of 1812, after the burning of Washington, D.C., the Vigilance Committee of Philadelphia asked James Forten, Allen, and Jones to pull Blacks together to build city defenses, and a group of about 2,500 was organized. Jones helped consecrate Allen on April 11, 1816, as the first bishop of the African Methodist Episcopal Church, and worked with Allen on a January 1817, convention of Blacks against the American Colonization Society. Jones died the following year, and Bishop White himself served the church for the next six years, until the next rector came. Jones' feast day, now on the calendar of the Episcopal Church, is February 13, honoring the day of his death.

Lammers, Ann C. "The Rev. Absalom Jones and the Episcopal Church: Christian Theology and Black Consciousness in a

New Alliance." *Historical Magazine of the Protestant Episcopal Church* 51 (June 1982): 159–184.

Bragg, George Freeman. *The First Negro Organization, the Free African Society, Established on April 12, 1787.* Baltimore, MD: The Author, 1924. 29 pp.

———. *History of the Afro-American Group of the Episcopal Church.* Baltimore, MD: Church Advocate Press, 1922. 319 pp.

———. *Richard Allen and Absalom Jones.* Baltimore, MD: The Church Advocate Press, 1915. 16 pp.

———. *The Story of the First of the Blacks, The Pathfinder Absalom Jones, 1746–1818.* Baltimore, MD(?): n.p., 1929. 16 pp.

Douglass, William. *Annals of the First African Church, in the U.S.A., Now Styled The African Episcopal Church of St. Thomas, Philadelphia.* Philadelphia, PA: King & Baird, Printers, 1862. 172 pp.

Jones, Absalom. *A Thanksgiving Sermon, Preached January 1, 1808, in St. Thomas' (or the African Episcopal) Church, Philadelphia.* Philadelphia, PA: Fry and Kammerer Printers, 1808. 24 pp.

Jones, Absalom, and Richard Allen. *A Narrative of the Proceedings of the Black People, During the Late Awful Calamity in Philadelphia in 1793, and a Refutation of Some Censures, Thrown Upon Them in Some Late Publications.* Philadelphia, PA: William W. Woodard, 1794. 28 pp.

DANB, WRF, CH, PHNA, NBH, HNB, IBAW, HUBA, AARS, BAW, BPEAR, NEA, NYB (1925–26), BGWC, IAAH.

JONES, CHARLES PRICE (December 9, 1865–January 19, 1949), founder of the **Church of Christ (Holiness) U.S.A.**, was born near Rome, Georgia. He grew up as a Baptist and as a young man settled in Crittenden County, Arkansas. He joined the Locust Grove Baptist Church in 1885 and soon felt the call to the ministry. He was licensed to preach in 1887 and entered Arkansas Baptist College. He became pastor of Pope Creek Baptist Church in July 1888 and was ordained in October. The following month, in November, he became pastor of St. Paul Baptist Church in Little Rock, Arkansas.

Upon graduation from college in 1891 he married Fannie Brown, and spent a year pastoring Bethlehem Baptist Church in Searcy, Arkansas. He then moved to the Tabernacle Baptist Church in Selma, Alabama, where in 1893 he encountered the Holiness movement and experienced sanctification in 1894. In 1895 he became the pastor of Mt. Helm Baptist Church in Jackson, Mississippi and began propounding the Holiness doctrine. He associated with **Charles Harrison Mason**, another African American Holiness

Baptist who was already forming an independent group, the Church of Christ (in 1897 changed to the **Church of God in Christ**). In 1896 Jones began a Holiness magazine, *Truth*, and published a booklet, *The Work of the Holy Spirit in the Churches*. Despite these efforts and those of a small number of like-minded Baptists, Baptists in general were not receptive to these new ideas.

In June 1897, Jones called a conference of other Black Holiness Baptists and they decided that the shift outside of the Baptist orbit was likely. Though already active in Mason's group, Jones did not formally withdraw from the Jackson Missionary Baptist Association until 1900. Concurrently he tried to remove "Baptist" from the Mt. Helm Baptist Church name, but the association would not allow it and forced him out by 1902. Jones then founded Christ Temple Church and associated it with the Church of God in Christ. This new denomination opened what would become a significant new field for African American religious participation, which previously had been largely channeled through Baptist and Methodist organizations. The Church of God in Christ grew rapidly, and Jones served as president of the annual convention.

In 1907 Mason visited **William J. Seymour** and the Azusa Street Mission in Los Angeles and was converted to **Pentecostalism**. This brought a split in the Church of God in Christ and a court case ensued, which lasted until 1909. At that point, Jones brought the non-Pentecostal members into a new denomination, the Church of Christ (Holiness) U.S.A., which he led for the rest of his life. In 1916 his first wife died and in 1918 he married Pearl E. Reed. In 1917 Jones organized the Christ Temple Church in Los Angeles and pastored that congregation until his death. In 1927 his position in the denomination was changed from president to senior bishop, and four other bishops were elected to assist him. Over the years Jones wrote over one thousand hymns, many of which were put into the church's official hymnal, *Jesus Only, Songs and Hymns.*

Cobbins, Otho B., ed. *History of the Church of Christ (Holiness) U.S.A., 1895–1965.* Chicago, IL: National Publication Board of the Church of Christ (Holiness) U.S.A., 1966. 446 pp.

Jones, Charles P. *An Appeal to the Sons of Africa.* Jackson, MS: Truth Publishing Co., 1902. 131 pp.

———. *His Fulness; Anthems, Songs, and Hymns.* Jackson, MS: Truth Publishing Co., 1906. 119 pp.

———. *The History of My Songs.* Los Angeles: N.p., n.d.

———. *Jesus Only, Songs and Hymns.* Jackson, MS: Truth Publishing Co., 1901. Unpaged.

BH, BAW, BDA-AHP, BDACSL, RLOA.

JONES, EDWARD (1808?–May 14, 1865), pioneer missionary with the **Episcopal Church**, was born in Charleston, South Carolina, the son of Jehu (or John) and Abigail Jones. His parents were free and owned the most prestigious hotel in the city, on Broad Street. The relatively liberal atmosphere of Charleston allowed Jones to receive a basic education, and the standing of his parents enabled Jones to be sent in 1822 to Amherst College in Massachusetts as its first Black student. He was not an honors student, but performed satisfactorily and apparently was treated as any other student. He helped run a Sunday School for some of the Black population around Amherst. He graduated on August 23, 1826, about two weeks before John Brown Russwurm graduated from Bowdoin College. Russwurm was long thought to have been the first African American college graduate in the United States, and for a time the same was thought of Jones, but now it appears that an Alexander Twilight received a B.A. from Middlebury College in 1823.

From 1828 to 1830 Jones studied at Andover Theological Seminary in Massachusetts, and then briefly at the African Mission School in Hartford, Connecticut. In August 1830 he became a deacon in the Protestant Episcopal Church, and in September he was ordained a priest. He was unable to return to South Carolina because of a law that prevented the return of free Blacks who had migrated North. Instead, he went as a missionary to Sierra Leone, arriving in 1831, and worked both there and in the Banana Islands as a schoolteacher. In a short time he married Hannah Nyländer, the daughter of a German missionary, with whom he had several children. After Hannah passed away he had a second marriage to the daughter (or sister) of another German missionary, Frederick Bultmann, and had two children with her. He was hampered for a long time in his church work because his American ordination was not recognized as allowing him to perform marriages and other services.

In January 1841, he became principal of Fourah Bay Christian Institution, a school founded in 1827 by the British Church Missionary Society. He led the school for the next seventeen years and was an effective money-raiser in England and an able administrator. By a special naturalization ordinance in 1845, the first of its kind in Sierra Leone, he was considered to be a British subject while in Sierra Leone. This went a long way toward removing obstacles to his acceptance. The school expanded until, in 1848, it took the name "college" and offered a unique program in African languages. For a long time it was the only school in all of West Africa offering education to Africans beyond the primary level. In 1853 he led a futile project to establish a mission among the Ibo people. He became a leading figure in the country and even a rumored candidate for the bishopric.

By 1858 the fortunes of the college had taken a downturn and that year Jones was called to England to account for "matters of a personal character." The school was temporarily closed during his absence, and upon his return he was relegated to a pastorate in Freetown at the Kissy Road Anglican Church. The college was not reopened until the early 1860s. He was also secretary and accountant for the Sierra Leone Mission and assistant editor of the *African and Sierra Leone Weekly Advertiser*. Briefly in 1861 he was editor of the *Sierra Leone Weekly Times and West African*, until he offended the colonial governor. In 1862 he married a third time, to a Miss Shuff. He had seen five of his children (perhaps all of them) as well as his first two wives, die. Soon his own health failed and he spent his last days in Chatham, England.

Contee, Clarence G. "The Reverend Edward Jones, Missionary-Educator to Sierra Leone and 'First' Afro-American College Graduate, 1808? to 1865." *Negro History Bulletin* 38 (February–March 1975): 356–357.

Hawkins, Hugh. "Edward Jones: First American Negro College Graduate?" *School and Society* 89 (November 4, 1961): 375–378.

Wade, Harold, Jr. *Black Men of Amherst*. Amherst, MA: Amherst College Press, 1976. 127 pp.

CH, IBAW, DANB.

JONES, EDWARD DERUSHA WILMOT (September 11, 1871–June 16, 1935), 41st bishop of the **African Methodist Episcopal Zion Church** (AMEZ), was born in Washington, D.C., the son of **Mary Jane Talbert Jones** and **Singleton Thomas Webster Jones**. His father was an AMEZ minister who became bishop in 1868. Jones experienced conversion at age eighteen, joined the John Wesley AMEZ Church in Washington, D.C., and decided to become a minister like his father. He graduated with his B.A. from Livingstone College in Salisbury, North Carolina, in 1893, working at masonry and plastering to support himself. On June 21, 1893, he married Maggie Cecil Davis, with whom he had two children.

In 1891, while still in college, he joined the Western North Carolina Conference, was licensed to preach, and later the same year, on October 6, was ordained deacon. In 1892 he was given his first pastoral assignment at Moore's Sanctuary AMEZ Church near Charlotte, North Carolina. His following appointments were at Logan Temple AMEZ Church in Knoxville, Tennessee; in

Maryville, Tennessee; Jacob Street Tabernacle AMEZ Church in Louisville, Kentucky; and Avery Memorial AMEZ Church in Allegheny City, Pennsylvania.

By this time Jones was stepping up to major churches, and his next pastorate was at Metropolitan AMEZ Church in St. Louis, Missouri, where he hosted the 1904 General Conference. This was followed by Walters Memorial AMEZ Church in Chicago, Illinois, Price Memorial AMEZ Church in Rochester, New York, Wesley AMEZ Church in Harrisburg, Pennsylvania, and First AMEZ Church in San Francisco. In 1920 he was appointed to Union Wesley AMEZ Church in Washington, D.C., from which he was elected bishop in 1924. He thus became the first of only a handful of people in the denomination to be a bishop who is the son of a bishop.

Jones was assigned to the Seventh Episcopal District, where he remained for the rest of his career. When Bishop **J. S. Caldwell** died in April 1935, Jones also took over the Philadelphia and Baltimore Conferences, the same conferences where his father had presided years earlier. This particular circumstance was a first for the AMEZ Church. He was a personal friend and admirer of Dr. Mordecai Johnson, the first Black president of Howard University in Washington, D.C. He published the *Comprehensive Catechism*, which was used by the church for years afterward, and had planned to write a full history of the denomination, but did not live to accomplish it.

Alleyne, C. C. "Obituary of Bishop Jones." *Star of Zion* 59 (June 27, 1935): 1, 5.

"The Anthology of the AME Zion Bishops." *Star of Zion* 57 (September 28, 1933): 1, 6.

"Bishop E. D. W. Jones." *Star of Zion* 59 (June 20, 1935): 1.

"New Era of Zion Methodism." *Star of Zion* 48 (August 7, 1924): 1, 5.

HAMEZC, AMEZC.

JONES, JAMES FRANCIS MARION (1907–August 13, 1971), famous evangelist and founder of the **Church of Universal Triumph/the Dominion of God**, was born in Birmingham, Alabama, the son of a railroad brakeman and a school teacher. He reportedly made his first prophecy at the age of two and grew up belonging to a group called **Triumph the Church and Kingdom of God in Christ**. He preached to that congregation regularly after his eleventh birthday, and had very little schooling. Later he said that God had forbidden him to read any human book. In 1938 the church sent him to Detroit, Michigan, as a missionary.

Jones rapidly became very successful in Detroit, and

followers began showering him with expensive gifts. The church headquarters claimed ownership of that wealth, but Jones claimed it was rightfully his. Within a year he broke away after being told to do so by a "voice" preceded by a fanning sound in his right ear. The same voice told him to go to Belle Island and take the first word from each of the first three freight boats that came down the river. These words were "universal," "triumph," and "dominion." Thus was founded the Church of Universal Triumph/the Dominion of God. It was organized as a corporation in which citizens (not members) register (not join), and everyone was given a royal title. In 1940 he began a radio broadcast on WKMH, which included a strong patriotic prologue. His charismatic style soon brought him a large following.

He became known as "the Prophet," and his birthday was celebrated in place of Christmas. Jones laid down very strict rules for the behavior of followers, who were forbidden to smoke, drink, play games of any kind, attend another church, or marry without the consent of Jones. Women had to wear girdles and men had to wear health belts. The "voice" in his ear was supposed to enable Jones to see into the future, and a major tenet of the church was that in the year 2000 history would come to an end and all persons then living would become immortal and live in heaven on earth. Jones also claimed healing powers, and much of his wealth came from people grateful for a successful healing. Three children were given to him by grateful mothers.

In 1944 he purchased a 54–room mansion in Arden Park, a wealthy neighborhood in Detroit, and staffed it with twelve salaried servants. His lavish lifestyle included almost 500 suits, three cars, $200,000 in furniture, and expensive jewelry. The first "thankful center," or church branch, was chartered in 1945, and at the peak of his popularity in the early 1950s he claimed to have 425 thankful centers and 6.5 million followers. He preached that death was not a necessary event and refused to hold funerals in the thankful centers. In 1951 his mother, Lady Catherine, passed away, and this affected him strongly. They had been very close, and she had lived in the mansion with him. He was not able to explain why he had not predicted her death or why he could not prevent it.

This event marked the beginning of his troubles. Over the next few years the F.B.I. was called in to solve an extortion plot against him, his Cadillac was peppered with buckshot, and in February 1956, he received several death threats, including one personally delivered by a man who burst into the home with an automatic weapon. Some considered that these problems really stemmed from his publicized proposal to move his headquarters to the exclusive suburb of Grosse Pointe, the residents of which had expressed their disapproval at that prospect.

In about September of 1956 the police raided his home and found Jones dressed in pajamas in his bedroom with two young boys who were there, he said, to discuss singing lessons. He was charged with gross indecency and attempted gross indecency. Soon after being released on bond he was rushed to the city hospital with ulcer problems. He claimed he was too poor to go to a private hospital, and indeed his mansion was soon sold to religious competitor "Sweet Daddy" Grace. The court trial acquitted him of all charges and he announced plans for a nationwide "soul-saving" tour, but his empire was already crumbling. He did not lose everything, and was able to maintain a viable, but low-profile ministry in Detroit until the end of his life. He suffered a stroke in October 1970, which paralyzed him, and he passed away ten months later. His successor as head of the organization was James Schaffer.

Cartwright, Marguerite. "Observations on Community Life." *Negro History Bulletin* 18 (January 1955): 88–89.

"Prophet Jones." *Ebony* 5 (April 1950): 67–72.

"The Prophet Threatened?" *Newsweek* 47 (February 13, 1956): 90–91.

"The Rise and Fall of Prophet Jones." *Ebony* 12 (October 1956): 63–66.

Thompson, Era Bell. "Black Astrologers Predict the Future." *Ebony* 24 (April 1969): 62–70.

IBAW, NYTBS (1971), *EBA*.

JONES, JOSHUA H., SR. (June 15, 1856–November 24, 1932), 38th bishop of the **African Methodist Episcopal Church** (AME), was born into slavery in Pine Plains, Lexington County, South Carolina, the son of Joseph and Sylvia Jones. His father was White and had another family with a White woman. He was reared on the estate of Asbury Hurley, outside of Orangeburg, South Carolina. He was converted at age ten, shortly after Emancipation, and joined the Shady Grove AME Church. By the time he was eighteen he had served in all the major offices of the church and was licensed as a local preacher. His slave mistress had given him the equivalent of an elementary education, and after Emancipation began to teach young and old in his neighborhood, as well as continuing his own education at night by a pine torchlight. He was ordained in 1873, and at about age twenty he married Elizabeth P. Martin.

In 1877, at age twenty-one, he and his wife both entered the Normal and College Preparatory Course of Claflin University in Orangeburg, South Carolina, finishing in 1880. He left to teach and preach for a year, then returned for the College Course, graduating with a B.A. in 1885. He studied briefly at Howard University in Washington, D.C., then transferred to Wilberforce University in Ohio, graduating with a B.D. in 1887. His first wife died in 1885, just before his graduation, giving birth to their fourth child, and he remarried in October 1886, to Augusta E. Clark; there were no further children.

When he reached the college rank he began to be given regular church assignments, and served in Branchville, Fort Motte, Elloree, Hickory Grove, and Ninety-Six while at Claflin University. His first appointment after the B.D. degree was at Lynn, Massachusetts, followed shortly, in February 1888, by the Meeting Street (Bethel) AME Church in Providence, Rhode Island. In 1890 he transferred to the Ohio Conference and was assigned to St. Paul's AME Church on Long Street in Columbus, Ohio. He was very successful here, and even was the first Black elected to the Columbus Board of Education, which he served from 1892 to 1900. Under his influence the board hired Black teachers for the first time. In 1893 he added to his duties the position of secretary of the combined Normal and Industrial Department at Wilberforce University, and was instrumental in getting state aid for the school. In 1894 he further added to his church and school duties as a presiding elder for the Columbus District, serving in that capacity until 1899. In 1899 he was assigned to the Zanesville AME Church.

At the 1900 General Conference he was elected president of Wilberforce University and served in that position for eight years. In 1908 he was succeeded by W. S. Scarborough and became a presiding elder again. At the General Conference in 1912 he was elected bishop and assigned to the Ninth Episcopal District (Tennessee and Alabama Conferences), but soon was shifted to the Texas area, where he did much to put Paul Quinn College in Waco on a steady footing. On the death of Bishop **Cornelius T. Shaffer** in 1919 he went to the Third Episcopal District, which included Ohio, and he immediately organized Wilberforce University to pay its debt and build Shorter Hall and other buildings.

In 1928 he was assigned to the First District (Philadelphia, New England, New Jersey) and despite the ravages of the Depression he raised $40,000 for Wilberforce, bought a new home for the Book Concern after its bankruptcy in 1930, organized Jones Tabernacle AME Church in Philadelphia, and saved many churches by the intervention of his personal funds. His achievements brought opposition, and at the 1932 General Conference there was an orchestrated accusation of misuse of funds leveled against him. He was suspended and forcibly retired, without being allowed the opportunity to defend himself, even though later investigation would show him completely guiltless. He passed away heartbroken less than a year later, closing a chapter that has been called the saddest in AME history. At least six churches in five states are named for him. One of his sons, Gilbert H. Jones, became the first African American to receive a Ph.D. from a German university (Jena, 1909), and another son, Alexander Jones, was the first Black to receive a Th.D. from Drew University in Madison, New Jersey.

Childers, Oliver W. H. "Bishop Joshua H. Jones, D.D., LL.D." *The A.M.E. Quarterly Review* 80 (April–June 1964): 38–42.
WWCR, AMSC, CEAMEC, BAMEC, WWWA (1), IBAWCB, TCNL, EWM, HAMEC.

JONES, LAWRENCE NEALE (b. April 24, 1921), **United Church of Christ** minister and long-time dean of Howard University Divinity School, was born in Moundsville, West Virginia, the son of Eugene Wayman and Rosa L. (Bruce) Jones. He received his B.S. in education in 1942 from West Virginia State College, then joined the U.S. Army, becoming a quartermaster captain. On March 29, 1945 he married Mary Ellen Cooley, with whom he had two children. In 1946 he was discharged and spent a year as a teacher at Dunbar High School in Fairmont, West Virginia. He reentered the Army in 1947, and until 1951 was a professor of military science and tactics. For the first two years he also studied at the University of Chicago, where he received an M.A. in history in 1948. He was discharged in 1953, having decided to enter the ministry.

He entered the Oberlin University School of Theology in Ohio, where he received his B.D. in 1956. While in school he pastored the West Salem Evangelical and Reformed Church. In 1957 that denomination merged with the Congregational-Christian Churches to form the United Church of Christ, into which he was ordained. From 1957 to 1961 he was a regional staff member of the Student Christian Movement for the Middle Atlantic Region. During this time he was a student at Yale University, where he received his Ph.D. in religion in 1961 on a Rockefeller scholarship. From 1961 to 1965 he was dean of the chapel at Fisk University in Nashville, Tennessee, and was chair of the Civil Rights Coordinating Committee of Nashville from 1962 to 1964. From 1965 to 1971 Jones was dean of students at Union Theological Seminary in New York City, becoming the school's first Black administrator, and apparently the first Black administrator of any mostly White seminary. In 1968–69 he was interim minister at Grace Congregational Church in New York City.

In 1970 Jones became professor of Afro-American Church History at Union Theological Seminary, and he was acting president of Union from July to December of 1970, among the first Blacks to serve in any fashion as president of a primarily White seminary (**Charles Rooks** was the first Black *elected* president of a primarily White seminary in 1974). In 1972 he was named William E. Dodge Professor of Applied Christianity, a position he held with the deanship until 1975. In the early 1970s he was the only Black faculty member at Union Theological Seminary, and successfully recruited more African American students and faculty members. In 1974 he succeeded Charles S. Rooks as the second president of the Society for the Study of Black Religion (S.S.B.R.), remaining in that office until 1977. In 1975 he left Union Theological Seminary to be professor and dean at Howard University's Divinity School in Washington, D.C., where he stayed for the next sixteen years.

Jones made a major impact at Howard University, where fewer than 75 students were enrolled at the School of Religion and the program was on a downward slide. During his tenure the school grew to 240 students and 22 faculty members. He persuaded the university to change the name of the School of Religion to the Divinity School and engineered the move in 1986 off campus to a 22–acre facility about a mile away that had been owned by the Friars Minor of the Franciscans. Since then the Divinity School has built a new library and will gain a new Islamic Institute in 1993. Jones was secretary of the Association of Theological Schools in 1981–82. He remained active denominationally, serving as a member of the United Church Board for World Ministries from 1975 to 1981. He has been on numerous other boards and agencies, including the National Committee of Black Churchmen (now the **National Conference of Black Churchmen**) and the Sheltering Arms and Children's Service of New York City. He retired from Howard University Divinity School at the end of the school term July 1991.

Collison, Michele N-K. "A Dean Leaves His Mark on Howard's Divinity School." *The Chronicle of Higher Education* 37 (July 17, 1991): A3.
Jones, Lawrence N. "Black Churches in Historical Perspective." *Christianity and Crisis* 30 (November 2 and 16, 1970): 226–228.
———. "They Sought a City: The Black Church and Churchmen in the Nineteenth Century." *Union Seminary Quarterly Review* 26 (Spring 1971): 253–272.

———. "To Seize the Times." *Theological Education* 9 (Summer 1973): 333–339.

AARS, BDNM (75), HUBA, WWABA (92–93), WWA (90–91), IBAW.

JONES, MARY JANE TALBERT (1831–July 18, 1895), founding president of the Woman's Home and Foreign Missionary Society of the **African Methodist Episcopal Zion Church** (AMEZ), was born in Brownsville, Pennsylvania. She married Singleton T.W. Jones on November 29, 1846, with whom she had twelve children. Her husband became a bishop in the AMEZ Church in 1868, but she made a name for herself through her own abilities in the church. Despite the many barriers to women taking on significant projects in the church, she worked steadily for an independent women's mission organization. At the 1880 General Conference she was successful and elected the first president of the Woman's Home and Foreign Missionary Society. She served in this position for fifteen years, until her death, and skillfully established the organization as an efficient and formidable power in the denomination.

AMEZC, HAMEZC.

JONES, OZRO THURSTON, JR. (1924–), a bishop of the **Church of God in Christ**, was born in Oklahoma, the son of Neanza Zelma and **Ozro Thurston Jones, Sr**. His father was a minister in the Church of God in Christ and assistant to the church's overseer for Oklahoma. In 1925 he became pastor of what became Holy Temple Church of God in Christ in Philadelphia, and his infant son moved with the family to Pennsylvania. Page grew up in the church in Philadelphia and, as a youth of twelve, experienced salvation under his father's ministry. The next year he felt a call to the ministry and preached his first sermon the next year during a youth gathering at Holy Temple. At the age of eighteen he was ordained to the ministry and for the next nine years served as Holy Temple's youth minister. During these years he attended Temple University where he earned a B.S. in Education, an M.A. in sociology (1946) and an S.T.B in 1949 from the School of Theology. He married Regina Shaw and they became the parents of twin sons.

In 1949 he left Philadelphia for the very different life as a missionary for the Church in Liberia. After four years he returned to pastor the Memorial Church of God in Christ in Haverford, Pennsylvania. He also completed his requirements for his S.T.M. (1953) from Temple's School of Theology and his S.T.D. (1962) from Temple's School of Religion and Philosophy. That same year his father became the second senior bishop of the church and resigned his parish. In the various changes in the transition of national leadership, Bishop A. B. McEwen resigned his position as head of the youth work to assume new duties and Jones was named to succeed him.

In 1964 he became associate pastor of Holy Temple Church of God in Christ and also became the president of the International Youth Congress of the church. While in that office he initiated the "Youth Seeks You" youth rallies which were held in local congregations throughout the church. In 1973 Jones was consecrated as the jurisdictional bishop for the state of Pennsylvania and in 1980 elected as a member of the general board.

DuPree, Sherry Sherrod. *Biographical Dictionary of African-American Holiness-Pentecostals, 1880–1990.* Washington, DC: Middle Atlantic Regional Press, 1989. 386 pp.

JONES, OZRO THURSTON, SR. (March 26, 1891–September 23, 1972), the former presiding bishop of the **Church of God in Christ**, the largest Pentecostal denomination in the United States, was born in Fort Smith, Arkansas, the son of Merion and Mary Jones. He was raised as a Baptist. As a young man, in 1912, he experienced salvation, was baptized with the Holy Spirit (the definitive religious experience of Pentecostals), and had a call to the ministry, all under the ministry of Elder Justus Bowe, then an evangelist for the Church of God in Christ. Soon afterwards, he, his older sister and a brother became an evangelist team in northwest Arkansas and the surrounding states. Over the next few years 18 congregations were established as a direct result of their evangelistic endeavors. In 1914 Jones organized the youth department of the Church of God in Christ and served as its first president. Two years later he founded and edited the *Y. P. W. W. Quarterly Topics*, an education-oriented journal. In 1920 he was appointed assistant to the state overseer in Oklahoma.

In 1925 Jones' career took a decisive turn when he became pastor of a small congregation of Pentecostal believers in Philadelphia. He moved to Philadelphia, where he would reside for the rest of his life. The congregation grew into Holy Temple Church of God in Christ. In 1926 he became state overseer for Pennsylvania. Not forgetting his work with youth, in 1928 he founded the International Youth Congress of the Church of God in Christ.

In 1933 **Charles Harrison Mason**, the founder of the Church of God in Christ, selected Jones as one of five men to be consecrated as the denomination's first bishops. He was later selected to serve on the executive commission created by Mason to assist him during his last years in office. Following Mason's death in 1961, the commission administered the affairs of the church for a year, and then the board of bishops moved to select a new senior bishop. They chose Jones and placed his name before the church's general assembly, which approved the motion. He resigned his work with the Y.P.W.W. and his parish to devote full time to the new office.

Events moved smoothly for several years, but opposition began to appear in 1965. Voices rose demanding regular elections for the office of presiding bishop. The situation threatened to split the denomination, and a lawsuit was filed. The courts finally ordered an election, and in 1968 a constitutional convention held its first session on January 30. The convention established clear guidelines for the election of leaders, and in the fall the elections were held. **James Oglethorpe Patterson** became the new presiding bishop. Jones moved into retirement and died a few years later.

Cornelius, Lucille J. *The Pioneer History of the Church of God in Christ.* N.p.: The Author, 1975. 102 pp.

JONES, RAYMOND LUTHER (April 7, 1900–May 12, 1972), 55th bishop of the **African Methodist Episcopal Zion Church** (AMEZ), was born in Chattanooga, Tennessee, the son of Rev. James and Callie Victoria (Bradford) Jones. He was converted at age six in Logan Temple AMEZ Church in Knoxville, Tennessee. After attending schools in Knoxville, in 1917 he went to Livingstone College in Salisbury, North Carolina, receiving first his B.A., then in 1924 his B.D. from the related Hood Theological Seminary. That same year he married Carrie L. Smith, with whom he had three children.

He was ordained deacon on November 12, 1922, and began serving churches while still in college, starting with the Second Creek Circuit in Salisbury, and then Marable Memorial AMEZ Church in Kannapolis, North Carolina. He was ordained elder on November 16, 1924, and appointed to Johnson City, Tennessee. His fourth pastorate was Grace AMEZ Church in Charlotte, North Carolina, followed by Hopkins Chapel AMEZ Church in Asheville, North Carolina. After ten successful years in Asheville he was assigned to the historic Broadway Temple AMEZ Church in Louisville, Kansas. There he found a $13,000 debt which he wiped

out by Easter 1944, and became dean of the Ministerial and Laymen Institute at Atkinson College.

In 1948, while hosting the General Conference at his church, he was elected bishop, and was consecrated on May 16. He maintained his residence in Salisbury, and his home was a haven of help and understanding for the many students at Livingstone College. He was a delegate to World Methodist Conferences in Oxford, England, Lake Junaluska, North Carolina, and Oslo, Norway. He was founder and editor-in-chief of an AMEZ meditation booklet called "The Strength of My Life." His first wife died in 1955 and on December 14, 1956 he married Mabel L. Miller, with whom he had one daughter. He served as trustee of Livingstone College, Clinton College in Rock Hill, North Carolina, and Lomax-Hannon Junior College in Greenville, Alabama. He became senior bishop in 1968 upon the retirement of Bishop W. J. Walls. He covered several episcopal areas, and at the time of his death was assigned to the First Episcopal District (New England, Philadelphia, New Jersey).

Flack, F. Z. "Bishop R. L. Jones As I Knew Him." *Star of Zion* 95 (June 29, 1972): 1, 8.

Lovell, Walter Raleigh. "Miss Miller and Bishop Jones Married." *Star of Zion* 80 (December 20, 1956): 1, 2.

"Obituary: Raymond Luther Jones." *A.M.E. Zion Quarterly Review* 84 (Summer 1972): 94–96.

"Raymond Luther Jones." *Star of Zion* 82 (June 25, 1959): 5.

Webb, Frank Mann. "Rev. Raymond L. Jones for Bishop." *Star of Zion* 72 (March 25, 1948): 6, 13.

"Zion's Senior Bishops During the Twentieth Century." *Star of Zion* 104 (March 27, 1980): 1, 2.

AMEZC, EWM, HAMEZC.

JONES, ROBERT ELIJAH (February 19, 1872–May 18, 1960), one of the first two Black (non-missionary) bishops elected in the mostly White Methodist Episcopal Church (MEC), now part of the **United Methodist Church**, was born in Greensboro, North Carolina, the son of Sidney Dallas and Mary Jane (Holley) Jones. He received his B.A. in 1895 and M.A. in 1898 from Bennett College in Greensboro. He was ordained deacon in 1893 and elder in 1896. The only local churches he pastored were during his schooling, and included Leaksville MEC (1891); Lexington and Thomasville (1892); Lexington MEC (1893); and Reidsville MEC (1894).

In 1897 he became assistant manager of a church periodical, *Southwestern Christian Advocate*, remaining until 1901. On January 2, 1901, he married

Valena C. MacArthur. From 1901 to 1904 he was Field Secretary of the Sunday School Board of the MEC. From 1904 to 1920 he was editor of the *Southwestern Christian Advocate*, and gained a wide reputation through that forum. As editor he lived in New Orleans, Louisiana, and was president of the Black Y.M.C.A. branch in that city. He was also vice-president and a trustee of New Orleans University, and a trustee of Bennett College and Gammon Theological Seminary. He was president of the Colored Travelers' Protective Association, first vice-president of the National Negro Press Association, and chair of the executive committee of the National Negro Business League. His first wife died on January 14, 1917, and on February 4, 1920 he married H. Elizabeth Brown. He was the father of five children. He was a delegate to General Conference beginning in 1904.

At the 1920 General Conference both Jones and **Matthew W. Clair, Sr.**, were elected bishops. Although four African Americans had been elected bishop in earlier years (**Francis Burns**, **John W. Roberts**, **Isaiah B. Scott**, and **Alexander P. Camphor**), they were designated specifically for overseas service. Therefore to Jones and Clair belongs the honor of being the first African Americans elected as bishops in the MEC for service in the United States. Both were full traveling superintendents, although both were assigned only to the Black conferences.

In 1923 Jones organized and became president of the Gulfside Association in Waveland, Mississippi. He was awarded the Harmon Foundation Bronze Medal in 1927 and the gold medal in 1929. In 1931 he was a delegate to the Ecumenical Methodist Conference. He served on every committee leading up to the 1939 merger with the M.E. Church, South, that created the Methodist Church. This merger also created the Central Jurisdiction (1939–1968), which moved all the nineteen Black conferences of the M.E. Church into one jurisdiction, regardless of geographical location. This sort of segregation, despite its limitations, gave the Black membership the ability to elect their own bishops and other officials without having to deal with the White majority. He served on the Committee on Negro Churches of the Federal (now National) Council of Churches and was a vice-president of the International Y.M.C.A. Jones retired in 1944.

Darrow, Clarence, and R. E. Jones. "The Religions of the American Negro." *Crisis* 38 (May 1931): 190–192.

Jones, R. E. "Qualifications of the Minister." In Arcadius S. Trawick, ed. *The New Voice in Race Adjustments*. New York: Student Volunteer Movement, 1914, 96–99.

EWM, IBAWCB, WWCR, RLA, AAE, MB, AARS, HUBA, WWCA (38–40).

JONES, SINGLETON THOMAS WEBSTER

(March 8, 1825–April 18, 1891), 16th bishop of the **African Methodist Episcopal Zion Church** (AMEZ), was born in Wrightsville, York County, Pennsylvania, the son of William H. and Catherine Jones. At the age of ten he was apprenticed to Thomas Kelly, a lawyer at York, Pennsylvania. For four years he served as house, farm, and cart servant. In 1839 he was released from that service and walked to Philadelphia in midwinter, looking for work. He eventually found a position in Harrisburg attending the dining room at the Temperance House Inn. For several years later he was a hod carrier in Harrisburg and then worked on a boat on the Ohio River.

He experienced conversion in February 1842, at the Wesley Union AMEZ Church in Harrisburg, was licensed to preach in 1846, and joined the Allegheny Conference on August 23, 1849. He was reared with almost no formal education, and realized that his duties as a minister required him to have command of the English language. He therefore dedicated himself to personal study, and became one of the most impressive and eloquent preachers in the denomination. He even learned to speak French, German, and Latin. He was ordained deacon on August 12, 1850, and elder on August 15, 1851.

He served AMEZ churches in Brownsville, Blairsville, and Bedford, all in Pennsylvania, then in May, 1853, he transferred to the Baltimore Conference and was assigned to South Howard Street AMEZ Church in Baltimore, Maryland. In 1857 he transferred to the New York Conference and pastored a church in Newark, New Jersey. In 1859 he moved to the Philadelphia Conference to pastor Wesley AMEZ Church in Philadelphia, followed by churches in Harrisburg and Chambersburg. In 1864 he went back to the New York Conference, to serve Mother Zion Church in New York City. There he was one of the founders and editors of *Zion's Standard and Weekly Review*, published in New York City for several years.

Jones was consecrated bishop on May 31, 1868, and continued his history of excellent leadership. That year he was Zion's representative to the Methodist Episcopal General Conference in Chicago, Illinois, where he attempted to negotiate affiliation between the two bodies. In 1884 he was a delegate to the Centennial Methodist Conference in Baltimore. In 1890, in ill health, he finished a disciplinary handbook for the church.

Jones, Singleton Thomas Webster. *Handbook of the Discipline of the AME Zion Church, for the Use of Ministers and Laymen.* New York: Hunt and Eaton, 1890. 46 pp.

————. *Sermons and Addresses of the Late Rev. Bishop Singleton T. Jones, D.D., of the AME Zion Church, with a Memoir of His Life and Character.* York, PA: P. Anstadt & Sons, 1892. 302 pp.

HAMEZC, OHYAMEZC, ACAB (supp.), *AMEZC, AMEZCH, BAW, AARS, HUBA.*

JONES, WILLIAM AUGUSTUS, JR. (b. February 24, 1934), former president of the **Progressive National Baptist Convention**, was born in Louisville, Kentucky, the son of William Augustus Sr. and Mary Elizabeth (Gill) Jones. From 1953 to 1956 he was First Lieutenant in the U.S. Army. He received his B.A. in 1958 from the University of Kentucky and his B.D. in 1961 from Crozer Theological Seminary. On June 14, 1958, he married Natalie Barkley Brown, with whom he had four children.

His first pastorate was at First Baptist Church in Philadelphia, Pennsylvania, from 1959 to 1962. In 1962 he became pastor of Bethany Baptist Church in Brooklyn, New York, where he has since remained. From 1965 to 1967 he was board chair of Bedford Stuyvesant Youth in Action. From 1967 to 1972 he was founder and chair of the Greater New York **Southern Christian Leadership Conference** (S.C.L.C.) Operation Breadbasket. From 1968 to 1970 he was president of the Eastern region of the newly founded Progressive National Baptist Convention, and in 1972–73 he was national chair of Operation Breadbasket. From 1970 to 1977 he was chair of the community board of Kings County Hospital Center in Brooklyn.

In addition to his pastoral duties, Jones has served as a teacher at a number of schools. During the 1970s in particular he served variously as visiting professor at Colgate Rochester Divinity School in New York, Union Theological Seminary in New York, Crozer Theological Seminary in Pennsylvania, Princeton Theological Seminary in New Jersey, and Wesley Theological Seminary in Washington, D.C. From 1978 to 1980 he was national president of the Progressive National Baptist Convention. He has been the recipient of numerous awards, including the Black Heritage Association Award (1971) and the Frederick Douglass Award of the New York Urban League (1972).

Since 1975 he has been a member of the general council of the Baptist World Alliance, and at its assembly in Toronto in 1980 he was the keynote preacher. In 1980 he was elected president of the National Black Pastors Conference. In 1984 *Ebony* magazine named him one of the top fifteen Black preachers in America. He has published a number of books and articles, including *God in the Ghetto* (1979).

"America's Fifteen Greatest Black Preachers." *Ebony* 39 (September 1984): 27–33.

Carter, Harold A., Wyatt T. Walker, and William Augustus Jones, Jr. *The Black Church Looks at the Bicentennial.* Elgin, IL: Progressive National Baptist Publishing House, 1976. 134 pp.

Jones, William Augustus, Jr. "Freedom of Conscience, the Black Experience in America." In *Religious Liberty in the Crossfire of Creeds.* Philadelphia, PA: Ecumenical Press, 1978.

————. *God in the Ghetto.* Elgin, IL: Progressive Baptist Publishing House, 1979. 164 pp.

————. *The Gospel and the Ghetto.* Rochester, NY: n.p., 1975. 125 pp.

————. "The Negro Church." *Foundations* 10 (April–June 1967): 108–110.

HBB, BDNM (75), *HUBA, WWA* (82–83), *WWABA* (90–91).

JORDAN, FREDERICK DOUGLASS (August 8, 1901–December 16, 1979), 72nd bishop of the **African Methodist Episcopal Church** (AME), was born in Atlanta, Georgia, the son of Professor D. J. and Carrie (Thomas) Jordan. As a youth he was active in the Bethel AME Church in Greensboro, North Carolina. After attending Kittrell College in North Carolina, A&T College in North Carolina, and Howard University in Washington, D.C., he entered Garrett Biblical Institute (now Garrett-Evangelical Theological Seminary) in Evanston, Illinois. He received his B.D. in 1925. While at Garrett, he also did work at nearby Northwestern University, from which he earned his masters degree in 1924. He did two additional semesters of post-graduate work at Northwestern and over two years of post-graduate work at the University of Chicago.

He joined the Chicago Annual Conference in September 1922, and was ordained deacon the same year. In 1923–24, while in college he pastored St. Paul AME Church in Chicago, and starting with only nine members he purchased three lots for the future church. In 1925 he was at St. Paul AME Church in Moline, Illinois. From 1925 to 1928 he was assigned to Bethel AME Church in Leavenworth, where he rebuilt the church edifice, preserving its Underground Railroad cellar. On September 2, 1925, he married Artishia Gilbert Wilkerson; there were no children. In 1927–28 he was also dean of the college at Western University. He was at Carey Temple AME Church in Chicago from 1929 to 1931, followed by the First AME Church in

Gary, Indiana, from 1932 to 1934, where despite the Depression he very nearly paid off a large mortgage.

In 1935 he served at St. Mary AME Church in Chicago, from which he was called in 1936 to be president of Western University. During his tenure he organized the Bishop Williams School of Religion. From 1939 to 1940 he pastored Bethel AME Church in Kansas City, Missouri, and in that short time significantly reduced the mortgage. In 1940 he was assigned to the First AME Church in Los Angeles, where he stayed for the decade. While there he burned the mortgage, built a $100,000 Youth Center, added 2,000 new members, built Emanuel AME Church, began St. Peter AME Church, and was significant in developing St. James AME Church, Second AME Church, and several other congregations. From 1950 to 1952 he pastored Ward AME Church in Los Angeles, where he purchased their meeting location, renovated the structure, and added 500 members. He was on the executive board of the N.A.A.C.P. in both Kansas City and Los Angeles, and was invited to be on the National Advisory Committee of C.O.R.E. In 1951 he was a delegate to the World Methodist Conference in Oxford, England.

In 1952 Jordan was elected bishop, and over the years became one of the most celebrated and internationally recognized bishops of his time. He was first assigned to the Seventeenth Episcopal District, soon adding the Fifteenth District, both in Africa. In 1956 he was shifted to the Fifth Episcopal District (Western United States), moving in 1957 to the Eighth District (Louisiana and Mississippi). In April 1962 he was assigned to the Fourteenth District (West Africa). From 1964 to 1968 he was assigned to the Thirteenth District (Tennessee and Kentucky). From 1968 to 1976 he was assigned to Urban Ministries and Ecumenical Relations, an office created at his request. As bishop he served as chancellor of the trustees of Campbell College in Buies Creek, North Carolina, during which time the student body was greatly increased and a new science department and new dormitory were built. Jordon himself donated the Chapel of Meditation as an "Act of Thanksgiving." He was a delegate to the World Council of Churches meetings in 1954, 1961, 1968, and 1975, and in the 1970s served on the Central Committee of the W.C.C. He was chair of the Commission on Union of Black Methodist Churches, and from 1969 to 1972 he was first vice-president of the National Council of Churches. He served as chair of the Consultation on Church Union (1973–1976, and was vice-president of the World Methodist Historical Council (1970–1975). He retired in 1976.

Brandon, John E. "In Memoriam: Frederick Douglass Jordan (1901–1979)." *Mid-Stream: An Ecumenical Journal* 20 (April 1981): 215–217.

Jordan, Frederick D. "Marching Orders." *The African Methodist Episcopal Church Review* 94 (July–September 1968): 8–10.

BAMEC, OTSB, WWR (77), *WWABA* (92–93), *AMECMIM, EWM, HAMEC, BDNM* (75), *EAMEC, HUBA*.

JORDAN, JOSEPH FLETCHER (June 6, 1863– ?), an early Universalist minister, was born in Gates County, North Carolina, in an area of the state known as the Dismal Swamp. He was the son of William and Anne Jordan, both former slaves. Though raised a Baptist he never joined the church. Around 1877 he was apprenticed to a member of the **African Methodist Episcopal Church** from whom he learned bricklaying and plastering. However, he found himself religiously inclined and he became a preacher for the African Methodists. During this time he attended the state normal school from which he graduated in 1885.

After twelve years in the ministry he took up the practice of law. He was residing in Durham, North Carolina, when he had occasion to hear Quillen Hamilton Shinn, a White Universalist minister who worked as a missionary among African Americans. As a result of his meeting Shinn, Jordan converted to Universalism. He attended Canton Theological School at St. Lawrence University, and then joined the Black Universalist congregation in Norfolk, Virginia, pastored by **Joseph H. Jordan** (no relation). He was licensed to preach in 1903 and ordained the following year. He was assigned to the Suffolk (Virginia) Mission. The school attached to the mission had fallen on bad times as the previous minister had left Universalism to join the Methodists. Jordan was able to quickly rebuild the school and revive the congregation. By 1912 the school offered a full curriculum of kindergarten through first year of high school.

Jordan stayed in Suffolk for the rest of his life. Besides managing the school and pastoring at the church, he served as a probation officer for Black youths who got in trouble with the law. Following his death, the church disbanded, but the school continued through the 1930s at the end of which it was absorbed by stages into the public school system.

Miller, Russell E. *The Larger Hope: The Second Century of the Universalist Church in America, 1870–1970.* Boston: Unitarian Universalist Association, 1985. 766 pp.

JORDAN, JOSEPH H. (1842–June 3, 1901), a Universalist minister, was born in West Norfolk, Norfolk County, Virginia. After the Civil War, his readings led him to the writings of Thomas Whittemore, Alonzo A. Miner, and Thomas B. Thayer and he was converted to a Universalist perspective, though he had had no contact with the church. In the 1880s, however, he made his way to Philadelphia where he attended the Church of the Messiah and heard the preaching of Edwin C. Sweetser. In 1889 he joined the church and later that same year was ordained to the ministry, the first Black minister in the Universalist Association. He had already gathered a small Black congregation which was also accepted into the fellowship.

Following his address to the 1893 general convention, he was able to raise enough money to construct a chapel in the Huntersville section of Norfolk. The chapel opened in 1894 as the First Universalist Church of Norfolk. It became Jordan's headquarters and he soon built a large congregation. The success of the Norfolk congregation prompted the establishment of a second church in Sulfolk, a suggestion of Thomas E. Wise, an early convert who became Jordan's assistant. The mission, when opened in 1898, included a school for 200 pupils.

Jordan continued to pastor the church in Norfolk for the rest of his life. He died there on June 3, 1901. Jordan is often confused with **Joseph Fletcher Jordan**, another Black Universalist minister who also worked in Norfolk. However, they were two different people and not related to each other.

Miller, Russell E. *The Larger Hope: The Second Century of the Universalist Church in America, 1970–1970.* Boston: Unitarian Universalist Association, 1985. 766 pp.

JOSEPHINE ALLEN INSTITUTE. An **African Methodist Episcopal Zion Church** school. The Josephine Allen Institute was founded in Mobile, Alabama, in 1900, as Zion Institute. That year, Jones University in Tuscaloosa, Alabama, had been merged into Lomax-Hannon Junior College. The 1900 denominational general conference voted to send monies previously earmarked for Jones to assist this new venture in southern Alabama. In 1909 Josephine Allen became the school's principal, a post she held for the next quarter of a century, though the school was discontinued soon after her retirement. Today it is primarily remembered for one of its graduates, baseball great Hank Aaron.

Walls, William J. *The African Methodist Episcopal Church: Reality of the Black Church.* Charlotte, NC: A.M.E.Z. Publishing House, 1974. 669 pp.

JOSEPHITES. *See*: **ST. JOSEPH'S SOCIETY OF THE SACRED HEART**.

"For more than two centuries our forebears labored in this country without wages; they made cotton king; they built the homes of their masters while suffering gross injustice and shameful humiliation— and yet out of a bottomless vitality they continued to thrive and develop. If the inexpressible cruelties of slavery could not stop us, the opposition we now face will surely fail. We will win our freedom because the sacred heritage of our nation and the eternal will of God are embodied in our echoing demands."

Martin Luther King, Jr.
Letter from Birmingham Jail
1963

K

KARENGA, RON NDABEZITHA (b. July 14, 1941), nationally known social activist and founder of the **Kawaida** faith, was born in Maryland as Ronald Everett. He was the youngest of fourteen children born to a Baptist minister. He was the first Black elected student body president at a California community college, and received an M.A. in political science at the University of California at Los Angeles (U.C.L.A.). He married Tiamoyo, with whom he had three children.

He first gained public attention in the aftermath of the Watts riots of 1965, when he turned from moderate to militant and took the Swahili name of Karenga, meaning "nationalist," or "keeper of tradition." He decided that no liberation movement could succeed until "Negroes" began to think "black" and develop pride in their own heritage. He founded a cultural nationalist organization called US (as opposed to THEM). Its purpose was to create a revolutionary African American culture to pull American Blacks together as a people. His principle was the combination of "tradition and reason," that is, placing traditional African culture in a new synthesis with the American experience.

Based on that principle he created the Kawaida religion as the foundation of the US organization and the formal statement of purpose and value. Kawaida is a Swahili word meaning "customary, or traditionally adhered to by African American people." Karenga was its chief *Imamu*, or "spiritual leader," and often was referred to by the title of "*Maulana*," meaning "master teacher," or "great leader." He wrote the *Kitabu*, or book of Kawaida doctrine, which was based upon Seven Principles, or *Nguzo Saba*. These principles are *Umoja* (Unity), *Kujichagulia* (Self-Determination), *Ujima* (Collective Work and Responsibility), *Ujamaa* (Cooperative Economics), *Nia* (Purpose), *Kuumba* (Creativity), and *Imani* (Faith). Followers were to learn the Swahili language and take a Swahili surname. Karenga created what was said to be the first African American wedding in the United States, called an "Arusi." Another popular Kawaida observance was the

Kwanzaa celebration, seen by many as an alternative to Christmas. It begins on December 26 and extends seven days, until January 1, one day for each of the Seven Principles.

The US organization quickly took a high profile in Los Angeles, working with a strong discipline and a confrontational stance and language ("When it's 'burn,' let's see how much you can burn. When it's 'kill,' let's see how much you can kill."). Karenga looked the role of the revolutionary leader, with armed guards, shaven head, Genghis Khan mustache, and dark glasses. The guards were part of a security force called "Simba Wachuka," meaning "young lions." Karenga was one of the main organizers of the National Conference on Black Power held in Newark, New Jersey, in July 1967. This brought together militant and moderate groups to promote an over-arching unity. Despite the incendiary atmosphere surrounding him, Karenga was credited with keeping Los Angeles calm after the assassination of **Martin Luther King, Jr.,** in 1968, meeting secretly with the chief of police. On the whole, Karenga maintained a policy against working with Whites. In August 1968, he was again a main organizer for the second National Black Power Conference in Philadelphia, Pennsylvania.

About that time the Black Panthers began to organize in Los Angeles, and sought an alliance with the Black Congress, the umbrella organization of Black groups in Los Angeles, of which Karenga was a key leader. Although there was initial agreement, relations between the Panthers and US deteriorated. The problems came to a head over the issue of control over student input into the new Black studies program at U.C.L.A. Finally, three members of US shot and killed two members of the Black Panthers on January 23, 1969. They were sentenced to life in prison on September 17, 1969.

After this incident both the Black Panthers in California and US lost membership and prestige. In 1971 Karenga was arrested for assaulting a female member of his group, and was sentenced to a six-month-to-ten-year prison term. Soon the organization was reduced to a handful of people, and he lost the support of his most influential protégé, writer **Amiri Baraka**. In 1974 US formally disbanded. He was released on parole in May 1975 and announced plans to finish a Ph.D. While in prison he published a number of articles in *Black Scholar* magazine. He helped the Kawaida faith gain a new organizational carrier in the NIA Cultural Organization, Inc. He eventually finished his degree and for a time was a professor of Afro-American Studies at San Diego State University. He is currently in the Department of Black Studies at California State University at Long Beach.

Poinsett, Alex. "Should Black Men Speak Swahili?" *Ebony* 24 (December 1968): 163–169.

"Whatever Happened to Ron Karenga?" *Ebony* 30 (September 1975): 170.

Karenga, Ron. *Beyond Connections: Liberation in Love and Struggle*. New Orleans, Ahidiana, San Diego: New Afro-American Movement, 1978. 23 pp.

———. *In Love and Struggle: Poems for Bold Hearts*. San Diego, CA: Kawaida Publications, 1978. 56 pp.

———. *Introduction to Black Studies*. Inglewood, CA: Kawaida Publications, 1982.

———. *Kwanzaa: Origin, Concepts, Practice*. Inglewood, CA: Kawaida Publications, 1977. 56 pp.

———. *The Quotable Karenga*. Clyde Halisi and James Mtume, eds. Los Angeles: US Organization, 1967. 30 pp.

IBAW, CRACG, PBP.

KEEBLE, MARSHALL (December 7, 1878–1968), an evangelist who brought many African Americans into the Churches of Christ (Non-instrumental), was born in Rutherford County, Tennessee, the son of former slaves, Robert and Minnie Keeble. When he was four years old his family moved from the farm to Nashville, Tennessee, where his father obtained work with the city. The family joined a congregation of the Christian Church (Disciples of Christ) during the years when the issues which were to split the Disciples were coming to the fore. Keeble was baptized at the age of fourteen but soon afterward joined with a group under the leadership of Preston Taylor who formed a separate congregation which would eventually identify with the Church of Christ (Non-instrumental) after the split became formalized in 1906.

Finishing what little formal school he was able to obtain, Keeble went to work in a soap factory. At the age of 18 he married Winnie Womack, the daughter of Christian minister S. W. Womack. Together they opened a grocery which Winnie tended while Keeble sold produce door to door. Around the turn of the century Keeble began to preach occasionally and showed himself to be a capable orator. By 1980 he was preaching regularly at a mission on Dozier Street. His fame spread, and he was invited to preach at various locations around the state. In 1914 he became a full-time evangelist and began to travel the country and speak. Saturdays would usually find him on the streets in a town where Black people had gathered for their weekly shopping. As was a common practice by ministers of the Churches of Christ, he also periodically engaged in public religious debates.

In 1918 Keeble had his first great success at Oak Creek, Tennessee, where following a three-week revival a church was organized. Other similar successes followed. In 1924 he made his first trip to the West Coast to speak at Oakland, California. The next decades of evangelistic activity were marked by the publication of the *Biography and Sermons of Marshall Keeble* (1931) edited by B. C. Goodpasture, owner of the Gospel Advocate Company, the leading Churches of Christ publishing center. The next year Minnie Keeble died and in 1934 Keeble married Laura Catherine Johnson.

The need for education for Black people, a continuing problem, led Keeble to participate in the reopening of the Nashville Christian Institute in 1940. Keeble sat on the board of trustees and led in the effort to have the school, accredited as an elementary and high school, which was accomplished in 1942. He worked on behalf of the school for the next 25 years and served as its president from 1942 to 1958.

Keeble remained active through the 1950s and became the only Black to participate in the development of the Churches of Christ on a national level. In the 1960s he was hobbled by cataracts, but was able to make his first overseas trip to the Holy Land and to Nigeria in 1962. In 1964 he culminated a long career with a round-the-world tour. He died in Nashville, Tennessee.

Choate, J. E. *Roll Jordan Roll: A Biography of Marshall Keeble*. Nashville, TN: Gospel Advocate Company, 1986. 143 pp.

Keeble, Marshall. *From Mule Back to Super Jet with the Gospel*. Nashville, TN: Gospel Advocate Press, 1962. 36 pp.

Goodpasture, B. C., ed. *Biography and Sermons of Marshall Keeble, Evangelist*. Nashville, TN: Gospel Advocate Company, 1931. 102 pp.

Hill, Samuel S., ed. *Encyclopedia of Religion in the South*. Macon GA: Mercer University Press, 1984. 878 pp.

Rhodes, F. N. *A Study of the Sources of Marshall Keeble's Effectiveness as a Preacher.* Carbondale, IL: Southern Illinois University, Ph.D. dissertation, 1970.

KELLY, EDWARD WENDALL (December 27, 1880–July 28, 1964), a bishop of the Methodist Church (now the **United Methodist Church**), was born in Mexia, Texas, the son of Taylor and Laura Kelly. He attended Wiley College in Marshall, Texas, and Gammon Theological Seminary in Atlanta, Georgia. On December 25, 1906 he married Oma A. Burnett, with whom he had one son. He taught for a time in the Texas public schools, then was ordained in 1917 at the age of thirty-seven.

His first pastorate was at Ebenezer Methodist Episcopal Church in Marshall, Texas. Further pastorates included Wesley Tabernacle Methodist Episcopal Church in Galveston, Texas; St. Paul Methodist Episcopal Church in Dallas, Texas; Scott Methodist Episcopal Church in Detroit, Michigan; and Union Memorial Methodist Episcopal Church in St. Louis, Missouri. In 1939 the Methodist Episcopal Church merged with the Methodist Episcopal Church (South) and the Methodist Protestant Church to form The Methodist Church. As part of the restructuring the nineteen Black conferences of the former Methodist Episcopal Church, regardless of location, became part of the all-Black Central Jurisdiction.

Kelly was elected bishop in 1944 by the Central Jurisdiction and assigned to the St. Louis Episcopal Area, where he remained for the rest of his career. He also taught evangelism in the Schools of Practical Methods conducted by the Board of Missions. He retired in 1952 to a home in Detroit.

EWM, MB.

KELLY, LEONTINE TURPEAU CURRENT (b. March 5, 1920), the first African American woman elected bishop of a major denomination (United Methodist), was born in Washington, D.C., the seventh of eight children in the family of David De Witt, Sr., and Ila (Marshall) Turpeau. Her father was pastor of the Mount Zion Methodist Episcopal Church in Washington and by the late 1920s moved to a church in Cincinnati, Ohio, where Kelly grew up.

Kelly learned as a child that the basement of the Cincinnati parsonage had been used as a station on the Underground Railroad, with a tunnel connecting it with the church. Her father's teaching reinforced this kind of social involvement of the church, saying that such politically charged action for justice was the duty of Christians. Part of her father's practice of this was serving four terms in the Ohio legislature as a Republican between 1939 and 1947. Her mother was a co-founder of the Cincinnati Urban League in September 1948, and was the first Black person to serve on the Cincinnati Camp Fire Girls Committee. Kelly also learned as she grew up the answer as to why they remained in a mostly White denomination that maintained separate local church and administrative structures to keep the races apart. As she put it in *I Dream a World*, "Our whole concept was that we were in mission to the church. Where the church saw us as objects of mission, we saw the major church as a mission field for us, knowing that if you ever got the major churches of this country straight, then you were working on the country at the same time."

She attended West Virginia State College from 1938 to 1941, but left after her junior year to start a family. She married Gloster Bryant Current, with whom she had three children. Current at that time was executive secretary of the Detroit branch of the N.A.A.C.P. and later was a Methodist minister. By the mid-1950s that marriage had ended in divorce, and Kelly was devastated. She met this crisis with disciplined Bible study and prayer that produced a more mature faith. In 1956 she married James David Kelly, pastor of the East Vine Avenue Methodist Church in Knoxville, Tennessee. In June 1958 he was transferred to the Leigh Street Methodist Church in Richmond, Virginia, and with his encouragement, Kelly became a certified lay speaker in the church. She also returned to college and received her B.A. in 1960 from Virginia Union University.

Kelly was a social studies teacher from 1960 to 1966, when her husband was transferred to the Galilee Methodist Church in Edwardsville, Virginia. When her husband died in 1969, the congregation, with the district superintendent's permission, asked her to fill the pulpit temporarily. She did so, even though she had previously not had any thoughts about being a minister. Once she was serving as a minister she found it much to her liking and began the Conference Course of Study, moving to summer courses at Wesley Theological Seminary in Washington, D.C. (1970 and 1971), and then to the full theological course at Union Theological Seminary in Richmond, Virginia. She remained at Galilee Methodist Church during this time and was ordained deacon in 1972. In addition to these responsibilities she adopted her late husband's great-granddaughter, Pamela Lynne Kelly. She graduated with her M.Div. in 1976.

In 1975 she left Edwardsville to be Director of Social Ministries for the Virginia Conference Council on Ministries. After her ordination as elder in 1977 she was appointed pastor of Asbury-Church Hill United Methodist Church in Richmond, where in six years she doubled the membership to four hundred. She also directed a cooperative urban ministry and outreach program and for four years served on the Richmond School Board. In 1983–84 she was Assistant General Secretary of the General Board of Discipleship, in charge of Evangelism. By this time, Kelly was widely known and respected in the denomination, especially among the clergywomen, who had seen for the first time one of their own, Marjorie S. Matthews, elected bishop in 1980. She was going to retire in 1984 and the clergywomen decided to mobilize to have Kelly elected that year.

Usually one is elected bishop by one's home jurisdiction, but it became clear that Kelly's Southeast Jurisdiction would not provide sufficient support. Focus was then placed on the Western Jurisdiction meeting in Boise, Idaho, where she was elected on the seventeenth ballot on July 19. She and other newly elected bishops were consecrated on July 20. She was assigned to the San Francisco Episcopal Area and in her four years as bishop worked to increase the church's social involvement, particularly in African-American communities. She was elected to the executive committee of the Council of Bishops and served on the Health and Welfare Ministries Division of the General Board of Global Ministries. She gained an international reputation as a brilliant preacher, and was the featured preacher at the Fifteenth World Methodist Conference in Nairobi, Kenya, in July 1986. She was very active in the issue of farmworker rights and formed the Methodist Selective Boycott Task Force to identify particular companies to target in the marketplace. Since her retirement on August 31, 1988, Kelly has served as president of the AIDS National Interfaith Network and as visiting professor of Evangelism and Witness at the Pacific School of Religion in Berkeley, California. She has received many awards and honors, including the highest honor of the **Southern Christian Leadership Conference** (S.C.L.C.), the Drum Major for Peace Award, in 1987.

Hoffman, Pat. "UMC Grape Boycott: Too Selective By Far." *Christian Century* 105 (June 22–29, 1988): 597–598.
NBAW, IDAW, WWA (90–91), *WWABA* (92–93), *BDUMB*.

KELLY, OTHA MIEMA (September 12, 1897– September 16, 1982), a bishop of the **Church of God in Christ** (COGIC), was raised in Mississippi. In 1914 he encountered Church of God in Christ preacher I. E.

Macfadden under whom he had the three experiences of salvation, sanctification, and the baptism of the Holy Spirit. COGIC is a Holiness Pentecostal church which believes that Christians should have a developed relationship with God that includes successively an accepting of his saving power, a cleansing from outward sin, and a filling of the Holy Spirit which is evidenced by speaking in tongues.

A short time later he moved to Chicago and joined the congregation headed by COGIC overseer/bishop **William M. Roberts** under whom he worked for fourteen years. He was ordained by Roberts and served churches at various locations in Illinois. At one point he was the president of the youth work for Illinois and Indiana.

Eventually Kelly moved to New York as an evangelist. Two years later he was appointed district superintendent for Eastern New York and several years later became State Overseer for Eastern New York. He retained his position as overseer/bishop for the rest of his life, but in 1976 also became Assistant Presiding Bishop for the denomination, a position he also retained for the rest of his life. His new responsibilities entailed his leading many of the national church extension and education programs, and he became a key guide to the ongoing national "Saints Center Building Project" at the world headquarters in Memphis, Tennessee.

To assist him in New York, he called Bishop F. D. Washington as his assistant and in the early 1980s as his health failed let it be known that he hoped Washington would succeed him in that position.

"COGIC Bishop Dies—Funeral Held in Brooklyn." *Star of Zion* 106 (October 7, 1982): 2.
DuPree, Sherry Sherrod. *Biographical Dictionary of African American Holiness-Pentecostals, 1880–1990.* Washington, DC: Middle Atlantic Regional Press, 1989. 386 pp.
International Annual Holy Convocation Diamond Jubilee [Souvenir Program]. Memphis, TN: Church of God in Christ, 1982. 428 pp.

KELSEY, GEORGE DENNIS SALE (b. July 24, 1910), well known professor of religion and Christian ethics, was born in Columbus, Georgia, the son of Andrew Z. and Marie H. (Jones) Kelsey. In 1930 he married Leola B. Hanks, with whom he had two children. He received his B.A. in 1934 from Morehouse College in Atlanta, Georgia, his B.D. in 1937 from Andover Newton Theological Seminary in Andover, Massachusetts, and his Ph.D. in 1945 from Yale University in New Haven, Connecticut.

While working on his Ph.D. he was also a professor

of religion and philosophy at Morehouse College from 1938 to 1945. From 1945 to 1948 Kelsey was director of the Morehouse College School of Religion, and from 1948 to 1952 he was associate director of the Field Department of the National Council of Churches. He was a guest lecturer in 1950–51 at Drew University in Madison, New Jersey, and from 1952 to 1957 was associate professor at Drew. From 1957 to retirement in 1976 he was Henry Anson Butts Professor of Christian Ethics at Drew. He was a member of the Association of Professors of Christian Ethics, the Morris County Urban League, the Fellowship of Southern Churchmen, and the Society of Religion in Higher Education. His major publications have been *Racism and the Christian Understanding of Man* (1965) and *Social Ethics Among Southern Baptists, 1917–1969* (1973). In 1970 he addressed the World Baptist Alliance in Rio de Janeiro, Brazil. He is credited with being a significant influence on **Martin Luther King, Jr.**, while he was at Morehouse College from 1944 to 1948.

Kelsey, George D. "The Christian Way in Race Relations." In William S. Nelson, ed. *The Christian Way in Race Relations*. New York: Harper & Brothers, 1948, 29–48.

———. "Churches and Freedom." *Journal of Religious Thought* 14 (Autumn–Winter 1956–57): 17–26.

———. "The Ethico-Cultural Revolution in American Race Relations." *Religion in Life* 26 (Summer 1957): 335–344.

———. *Racism and the Christian Understanding of Man.* New York: Scribner, 1965. 178 pp.

———. *Social Ethics Among Southern Baptists, 1917–1969.* Metuchen, NJ: Scarecrow Press, 1973. 274 pp.

BDNM (70), EBA, WWABA (90–91), SBAA, HUBA, AARS, IBAW, IBAWCB, OTSB.

KELSEY, SAMUEL (b. 1906), a bishop in the **Church of God in Christ**, was born in Sandville, Georgia, the son of Samuel and Ella Kelsey. In 1915, as a nine-year-old boy in rural Georgia, Kelsey attended services led by a Pentecostal minister. The services were being held in the Pentecostal Firstborn Church, a house church which met in a home of a nearby Black farmer. On May 16, 1915, Kelsey experienced sanctification (or cleansing from sin) and the baptism of the Holy Spirit (evidenced by his speaking in tongues). In 1920 Kelsey worked his way north to Philadelphia, Pennsylvania. In Philadelphia, Kelsey met Henry McCrary who had also been a member of the Firstborn Church in Georgia, but who had discovered the Church of God in Christ in Detroit. Under McCrary's influence Kelsey affiliated with the Church of God in Christ, as did most of the members of the Firstborn churches in Georgia. Also,

shortly after his arrival in Philadelphia, Kelsey met Jeanette Cooper, whom he married in December of that year.

Kelsey settled in Philadelphia and became an active member and preacher for the local Church of God in Christ congregation. Then in 1923 he was invited by W. C. Thompson, an overseer in the church, to accompany him to Washington, D.C., and assist in a tent revival. This revival resulted in the organization of a local congregation over which Kelsey presided. As winter approached, the group moved out of the tent into a storefront. In 1923 Kelsey also founded the Temple Church of God in Christ, a second congregation in Washington, D.C. The work in the area expanded through the 1930s, and in 1940 he was appointed overseer for Delaware and Washington, D.C.

In 1941 Kelsey began a radio show which included both his music and sermons. The broadcast was to continue into the 1980s. It also led to his cutting some records. Two men who heard him on the radio became his distributors. Later, when he had the opportunity to travel to Europe, he discovered that his music had preceded him. In 1949 his first wife died and in 1950 he married Annie Ruth.

In 1950 Kelsey was named a bishop in the church and invited to sit on the board of bishops for the church. He continued as pastor of Temple Church, which grew to over 1,000 members, and during the next decades oversaw the development of the Church of God in Christ in his area, which had 23 congregations in the 1980s. In 1972 the Samuel Kelsey Housing Complex was dedicated. For many years, in addition to his pastoral duties he served as a parole officer working with delinquent youth.

In recent years, Kelsey, as one of the senior ministers in Washington, D.C., has been frequently honored for his lifetime of service to the community. In 1976 the U.S. Congress published a "Salute." In 1977 the Committee of 100 Ministers cited him for his leadership.

In 1988 failing health forced Kelsey to retire, and he was succeeded as bishop by George W. Crudup.

Cornelius, Lucille J. *The Pioneer: History of the Church of God in Christ.* N.p.: The Author, 1975

DuPree, Sherry Sherrod. *Biographical Dictionary of African American Holiness Pentecostals, 1880–1990.* Washington, DC: Middle Atlantic Regional Press, 1990. 386 pp.

KILGORE, OSCAR THOMAS, JR. (b. February 20, 1913), the first African American president of the **American Baptist Churches in the U.S.A.**, was born in Woodruff, South Carolina, the son of Thomas, Sr. and Eugenia Kilgore. He received his B.A. in 1935 from Morehouse College in Atlanta, Georgia. He married Jeannetta M. Scott, with whom he had two children.

His first pastorate was New Bethel Baptist Church in Asheville, North Carolina (1936–38), during which time he was also principal of a local public school (1935–38). He pastored Friendship Baptist Church in Winston-Salem, North Carolina from 1938 to 1947 and Rising Star Baptist Church in Walnut Grove, North Carolina from 1941 to 1947. He was executive secretary of the General Baptist State Convention of North Carolina from 1945 to 1947. He pastored Friendship Baptist Church in New York City from 1947 to 1963, and while there he enrolled at Union Theological Seminary and received his B.D. in 1957.

In 1963 he accepted a call to the Second Baptist Church in Los Angeles, California, the oldest African-American Baptist church in Los Angeles, where he remained for the rest of his career. He was for a time Western Regional Director of the **Southern Christian Leadership Conference** (S.C.L.C.) and on the executive board of the N.A.A.C.P. On May 17, 1969, he was elected the first Black president of the American Baptist Churches in the U.S.A., and during his one-year tenure did what he could to raise the issues of war, hunger, and racism. He initiated the Fund of Renewal project, a joint effort with the Progressive National Baptist Convention to raise $7 million to revive America's Black colleges. Beginning in 1973 he was Advisor to the President and Director of the Office of Special Community Affairs at the University of Southern California (U.S.C.). From 1980 to 1982 he was adjunct professor at the U.S.C. School of Religion. He has served as president of the L.A. Black Agenda and chair of the trustees of Morehouse College. In 1984 *Ebony* magazine named him one of the top fifteen Black preachers in the United States.

"America's Fifteen Greatest Black Preachers." *Ebony* 39 (September 1984): 27–33.

Bennett, Lerone, Jr. "Black Firsts." *Ebony* 37 (March 1982): 128–133.

Kilgore, Thomas, Jr. "The Black Church: A Liberating Force for All America." *Ebony* 25 (August 1970): 106–110.

———. "In the Days Ahead." *Sepia* 28 (January 1979): 17.

HBB, AAE, EBA, WWABA (88), BDNM (75), AARS, IBAW, HUBA, OTSB.

KILLINGSWORTH, FRANK RUSSELL (November 28, 1878–April 20, 1976), founder of the **Kodesh Church of Emmanuel**, was born near Winnsboro,

South Carolina, the son of Frank and Sarah R. (Pool) Killingsworth, both former slaves. His father was a minister in the **African Methodist Episcopal Zion Church** (AMEZ). He received his basic education at the denominational school, Livingstone College in North Carolina (1894–99), then received his B.A. in 1907 from State College in York, South Carolina. He worked his way through school as principal of Jefferson Graded School in York. On October 7, 1908, he married Laura A. Penn, a physician, with whom he had one daughter (d. 1965).

From 1907 to 1917 he was a teacher and administrator of the Manassas Industrial Institute in Manassas, Virginia. From 1918 to 1926 he was pastor of the Lomax AMEZ Church in Arlington, Virginia, where he oversaw the building of a new edifice. From 1927 to 1929 he pastored the Varick Memorial AMEZ Church in Philadelphia, Pennsylvania. In 1929 he left the AMEZ with 120 followers to found the Kodesh Church of Emmanuel. He apparently left the AMEZ because he was frustrated by the appointive and financial powers of the bishops, and his new church did not have bishops. He was also influenced by the Holiness movement, and his new church included a doctrine of entire sanctification. The word "Kodesh" is derived from a Hebrew word meaning "holiness," and "Immanuel" is a title of Christ; therefore the name of the church could roughly be translated as "Holy Church of Jesus."

Killingsworth established churches in Washington, D.C. and Pennsylvania, and in 1934 his Church absorbed the Christian Tabernacle Union, a holiness body with headquarters in Pittsburgh. In 1936 the Kodesh Church of Emmanuel claimed nine congregations and 582 members. After World War II the church gained 300 acres in Liberia, West Africa, and began the Killingsworth Mission there. Killingsworth maintained his residence in Washington, D.C. and cordial relations with the AMEZ. After he turned 100 in 1973 the AMEZ newspaper, *Star of Zion*, made annual reports on him.

"Dr. Killingsworth, Marvelous Man." *Star of Zion* (February 6, 1975): 4.

Killingsworth, Frank R. *Doctrines and Discipline of the Kodesh Church of Immanuel.* Philadelphia, PA: Westminster Press, 1934. 74 pp.

———. *Theologic Questions and Answers on Christian Perfection or Sanctification.* Philadelphia, PA: Westminster Press, 1949. 93 pp.

WWCA (38–40), BH, BDA-AHP, CA (65–68), RLOA.

KINCHLOW, HARVEY BEN (b. 1936), televangelist and minister in the **African Methodist Episcopal**

Church, was born in Uvalde, Texas. After high school, he joined the U.S. Air Force. He married Vivian Jordan in 1959. His years in the service became a time of increasing growing Black consciousness of the racist environment in which he was forced to live to the point that he became a disciple of the teachings of **Malcolm X**, though he never officially joined the Nation of Islam.

He left the Air Force after thirteen years and returned to school. He earned his associate's degree from Southwest Texas Junior College. While there, John Corcoran, a White minister with whom Kinchlow had several intense racial confrontations, became the instrument of his converting to Christianity in 1968. He founded His Place, a ministry for teenage runaways, and later joined Christian Farms, a drug-alcohol rehab ministry, as their executive director. While there in the early 1970s, he was ordained as a minister in the African Methodist Episcopal Church.

While at Christian Farms, he met Pat Robertson, the founder of the Christian Broadcasting Network (CBN). He was hired to direct CBN's counseling center in Dallas, Texas. Then in 1977 he was invited to appear on the 700 Club, CBN's anchor program, as a guest. Invited back a few months later, he found himself the host of the show. The reaction was so favorable that he became Robertson's cohost. Over the next decade he became a celebrity. Kinchlow announced his retirement in January 1988, at which time Robertson was in the midst of his bid for presidential nomination. He has entered a more private phase of his life.

Harrell, David Edwin. *Pat Robertson*. San Francisco, CA: Harper & Row, 1987. 246 pp.

Hazard, David. "Ben Kinchlow: Off Camera and Off-the-cuff." *Charisma* 11, 8 (March 1986): 20–24.

Kinchlow, Ben. *Plain Bread*. Waco, TX: Word Books, 1985. 225 pp.

"Kinchlow Leaves '700 Club.'" *Charisma & Christian Life* 13, 8 (March 1988): 24.

KING, CHARLES H., JR. (b. c.1925), prominent Baptist minister and leader of workshops on racism, was born in Pottsville, Pennsylvania, one of nine children in the family of Charles Sr. and Esther (Dickerson) King. His father had killed a White man about 1905 in Louisiana and had fled to New York, changing his name from Richard Rembert to Charles H. King. He eventually settled in Pottsville as minister of the Mount Zion Baptist Church.

After King Jr. graduated from high school in 1943 he tried to enlist in the Marines, but was turned down because of his color. He shifted to the Navy, and was trained as a "captain's boy," waiter, and kitchen hand on a troop transport ship. By talking to Blacks from the South, he learned of the oppression of Blacks that had been mainly hidden from his experience in Pottsville. He slowly became aware of his blackness. This awareness was sealed when he hit a White, non-commissioned officer for calling him a "black nigger," and at the trial the captain said, "What else do you think you should be called?" King was sentenced to seven days on bread and water in the brig.

Discharged in 1945 he found a waiter's job at the Harrisburg Hotel near Steelton, Pennsylvania, where his family had moved. Searching for a prideful identity, he entered Virginia Union University in Richmond in the fall of 1945. He was not interested in the classwork and in 1948 dropped out to join the Air Force. While at Smoky Hill Air Force Base in Salina, Kansas, he took courses at Kansas Wesleyan University on and off for several years. He regained his academic confidence and won the annual McGurk oratorical contest. In 1951 he married a woman named Annese. He remained in the military for about six years.

Finally he felt called to the ministry and his first pastorate was the Fifth Ward Baptist Church in Clarkesville, Tennessee. In 1956 he went to the Liberty Baptist Church in Evansville, Indiana. He began to feel inner turmoil about merely preaching Jesus in the face of oppression. He was galvanized to action in the late 1950s by a barber who threatened him with a gun if he didn't leave the chair of a Whites-only shop. He had only stopped in to speak to a parishioner, the bootblack. King refused to leave and the police came and arrested him. He was charged with being drunk and disorderly. After that incident he became president of the local chapter of the N.A.A.C.P. and preached almost entirely a social gospel. He launched successful actions against an annual "blackface" minstrel show and against a large company that did not employ African Americans. In the spring of 1963 he was arrested in Nashville, Tennessee, for picketing for passage of the Civil Rights Bill. He was put in a 20 x 40 foot cell with 38 other people, with no toilet, ventilation, or water. Later he was present in Selma, Alabama, to protest its "wall" of segregation.

In 1966 King left the Liberty Baptist Church and left the ministry altogether, feeling too tied to the institution at a time when the civil rights movement demanded first priority. He then became the first executive director of the Human Relations Commission in Gary, Indiana. This position gave him the power to bring and prosecute suits against racial discrimination, and made him one of the most powerful men in the city. In 1967 he took a leave of absence to serve on the Kerner Commission on Civil Disorders. He became frustrated with the apparent intent of the commission to "whitewash" events and resigned on November 6, 1967. His resignation caused an upheaval among the directors and the commission's final report was clearly informed by the material King had tried to place in its hands.

In about 1970 King left Gary and obtained a position at Hamma School of Theology at Wittenberg University in Springfield, Ohio. His job was to teach half-time in Black history and Black theology, and half-time conducting race relations programs in White Lutheran churches throughout the state. Over time he felt unable to penetrate the wall of White ignorance among the students, until one day he simply exploded with Black anger in class and discovered that this was the thing that pierced the veneer of racism and led to real understanding. Both his classes and his racial awareness programs became vehicles for cleansing confrontational encounters with racism.

The Lutheran Church in America (L.C.A.) created a program called "Justice and Social Change" and asked King to administer it. He did, on his own terms, changing the name to "Black and White Encounter," and became famous for his biting "tell it like it is" six-hour sessions for getting Whites to acknowledge their own racism. He later added a second day for reconciliation. He tried the method on prominent citizens of Middletown, Ohio, which was experiencing a racial crisis, and found success. After further successes the L.C.A. voted to establish an Urban Crisis Center on the Wittenberg campus with King as director. That year, 1970, he received the Louis Brownlow Award from the American Society of Public Administrators and was selected by *Nation's Cities*, the magazine of the League of Cities, as the year's most effective contributor to urban affairs.

Lutheran support for the center ended after only one year, and in 1971 King opened the Urban Crisis Center, Inc., in an office in Dayton, Ohio. He managed to do an encounter with some Navy officials, and was on the verge of having his program adopted throughout the Navy when, in one seminar, King and his White woman colleague kissed each other as a technique to release hidden emotions in the participants. The admiral at that base heard about it and said, "No black man is going to kiss a white woman in my command." His influence caused the program to shut down. Still, King has since continued to conduct seminars across the country and in various branches of the military. In 1973 he moved the Urban Crisis headquarters to Atlanta, Georgia, where he has trained many leading citizens and corporate leaders. The well-known Black educator, Dr. **Benjamin Mays**, attended a course and afterward spoke strongly in favor of it.

King, Charles H. *Fire in My Bones*. Grand Rapids, MI: William B. Eerdmans Publishing Co., 1983. 230 pp.
———. "Growing Rebellion in the Negro Church." *Negro Digest* 12 (March 1963): 38–45.
———. "Negro Ministers Have Not Failed. Have Sociologists?" *Negro Digest* 13 (November 1963): 43–44.
AARS, HUBA.

KING, CORETTA SCOTT (b. April 27, 1927), civil rights activist and head of the Martin Luther King, Jr. Center for Nonviolent Social Change, was born in Marion, Alabama, the daughter of Obadiah and Bernice (McMurry) Scott. Her father was a pulpwood dealer and the family lived in moderate poverty on a farm. They were active in the Mount Tabor **African Methodist Episcopal Zion Church** (AMEZ). King attended an all-Black, one-room school in Heiberger, followed by Lincoln High School. At Lincoln she began a serious study of music and determined to make it her life's career. She went to Antioch College in Yellow Springs, Ohio, as one of its six Black students.

She discovered that in a northern state such as Ohio the more blatant and brutal forms of racism were replaced by subtler forms that could be just as damaging. As a major in elementary education with a specialty in music, she needed to have practice teaching experience in the local schools, but the schools did not want her, and Antioch College officials did not press the matter on her behalf. She fulfilled the requirement by teaching at the Antioch private school. She graduated in June 1951 with the strong realization that her color did not make her inferior and that the major faults rather lay with a racist system that prevented her from equal opportunities.

From Antioch she won a scholarship to the New England Conservatory of Music, where she studied for a concert career as a singer. She helped support herself with various jobs, including one in a mail-order house found through the local Urban League. A mutual friend matched King up with **Martin Luther King, Jr.**, who was studying at nearby Boston University. Although she was not interested in becoming serious with a clergyman, she felt Martin was different and continued to see him. When Martin took her to visit his parents in Atlanta, his father, Rev. **Martin Luther King, Sr.**, did not immediately warm up to her, but she held her ground and let him know that she was no mean catch and had a lot to offer. King, Sr. performed the wedding ceremony for them on June 18, 1953.

They found an apartment in Boston while Martin finished his thesis and she handled a schedule that included thirteen courses. In the spring of 1954 he finished his thesis and accepted a call to the Dexter Avenue Baptist Church in Montgomery, Alabama, beginning in September. She earned her Mus.B. degree in June 1954, but dropped her own career plans to support him in his church work. She was his secretary, served on several committees, was hostess of the parsonage, and sang in the choir. She continued to accept the occasional singing concert, mostly out of town, and the family eventually grew to four children.

After Rosa Parks was jailed on December 1, 1955, for refusing to give up her bus seat to a White man, E. D. Nixon, **Ralph D. Abernathy**, and Martin Luther King, Jr. decided to call a bus boycott. Coretta King made and answered the hundreds of phone calls necessary to make the operation a success. While her husband thereafter became an internationally known figure in the civil rights movement and often either in jail or on a trip, she held the household together and often fulfilled speaking engagements her husband was unable to keep. In 1960 they moved to Atlanta's Ebenezer Baptist Church, where King, Jr. copastored with King, Sr. Although her life was busy enough already, she began to move into leading positions of her own. In 1962 she went to Geneva, Switzerland as a delegate to the Women's International League for Peace and Freedom, and met with both American and Soviet representatives on the issue of a nuclear test-ban treaty. When her husband was held incommunicado in a Birmingham jail for several days, she placed a call to Attorney General Robert Kennedy that got quick results. That year she received the Distinguished Achievement Award from the National Organization of Colored Women's Clubs, and in 1963 received both the Women's Strike for Peace citation for work in peace and freedom and the Louise Waterman Award from the American Jewish Congress Women's Auxiliary.

On November 14, 1964, she performed the first of a series of Freedom Concerts, an eight-part performance combining songs and narration describing the African American struggle for freedom from 1955 to 1965. The concerts were well received and contributed more than $50,000 to the **Southern Christian Leadership Conference** (S.C.L.C.) and related causes. She grieved over the deaths of civil rights activist Medgar Evers, President John F. Kennedy, and many other lesser-known people whose lives were taken in the violence and hatred of the times. Then on April 4, 1968, her own husband, Martin Luther King, Jr., was assassinated, and the devastating loss might have crushed other people. She, however, resolutely picked up his work and moved ahead. Only four days after his death, one day before his nationally televised funeral, she personally led the scheduled march in Memphis on behalf of striking sanitation workers. Soon thereafter, in June in Washington, D.C. she led the Solidarity Day March for the Poor Peoples' Campaign. In her speech on that occasion she called upon American women to "unite and form a solid block of women power" to fight racism, poverty, and war.

By the end of 1968 Coretta King had gained a new stature in the nation's consciousness. That year she received the Women of Conscience Award from the National Council of Women, was named in a national college student poll as the most admired woman, and was selected the Woman of the Year by the National Association of Radio and T.V. Announcers. In January 1969 she founded the Martin Luther King, Jr., Federal Holiday Commission and announced plans for the Martin Luther King, Jr., Memorial Center for Nonviolent Social Change. While also speaking out against the war in Vietnam and lending her voice to other issues, she focused her efforts on these two projects. In 1969 she published the autobiographical book, *My Life with Martin Luther King, Jr.* She traveled around the world to proclaim the message of nonviolence, and in 1969 was the first woman to preach in St. Paul's Cathedral in London. She joined the boards of directors of the National Organization for Women and the S.C.L.C. In 1970 alone she received honorary doctorates from seven different colleges and universities.

The first major project to see realization was the Memorial Center, which was dedicated in Atlanta, Georgia, in 1981. The $8.4 million center includes exhibit areas, a 250–seat auditorium, a 90–seat theater, administrative offices, a library, archives, and the Martin Luther King, Jr., gravesite. As its president/chief executive officer, she has overseen the training of thousands of people through programs and workshops in the philosophy and strategy of nonviolence. The library and archives draw about 5,000 scholars annually to view many personal King items and over one million documents related to the civil rights movement. The center served as the clearing house for the six million signatures collected in support of a Martin Luther King, Jr., national holiday, which Congress passed for official observance beginning in January 1986. Coretta King has also led the center to work as an instigator of working coalitions, as with the National Committee for Full Employment (which she co-chairs) and the 1983 mobilization of 500,000 people for the 20th Anniversary March on Washington. Since 1980 she has been a news commentator for the Cable News Network in Atlanta. In 1984 *Ebony* magazine named her one of the one hundred most influential Black Americans. In 1986 she visited South Africa to meet with businessmen and anti-apartheid leaders. She chairs the Church Women United Commission on Economic Justice for Women.

King, Coretta Scott. "How Many Men Must Die?" *Life* 64 (April 19, 1968): 34–35.

———. "The Legacy of Martin Luther King, Jr." *Theology Today* 27 (July 1970): 129–139.

———. *My Life with Martin Luther King, Jr.* New York: Holt, Rinehart, and Winston, 1969. 372 pp.

———, ed. *The Words of Martin Luther King, Jr.* New York: Newmarket Press, 1983. 112 pp.

"The 100 Most Influential Black Americans." *Ebony* 39 (May 1984): 29–34.

Vivian, Octavia. *Coretta: The Story of Mrs. Martin Luther King, Jr.* Philadelphia, PA: Fortress Press, 1970. 111 pp.

WWA (90–91), *AAE, CB* (1969), *CA* (con.rev.series vol.27), *WWR* (85), *BWR, EBA, WWABA* (90–91), *SBAA, IBAWCB, AARS, HUBA, IBAW, NA, OTSB, CBL, LBAA, BWASS, IDAW, IP, RLOA, OS, NBAW, BWMH.*

KING, LORENZO HOUSTON (January 2, 1878–December 17, 1946), the fifth (non-missionary) African American bishop of the Methodist Church, now a part of the **United Methodist Church**, was born in Macon, Mississippi, the son of Houston Carlton and Leah (Frazier) King. His father died when he was an infant, and the rest of his life King helped support his mother and put himself through school. He received his B.A. in 1902 from Clark College in Atlanta, Georgia, and his B.D. in 1903 from Gammon Theological Seminary in Atlanta. On December 13, 1903, he married Louise Marie Watts, with whom he had three children.

His first pastorate was in Elberton, Georgia (1902), followed by Covington, Georgia (1903–04); South Atlanta, Georgia (1905–08); and Newman, Georgia (1909–10). In 1910–11 he studied at Columbia University Teachers College in New York City and at Union Theological Seminary in New York City, where he received his D.D. in 1911. In 1911–12 he taught English at Clark College in Atlanta, then pastored Central Methodist Episcopal Church in Atlanta from 1912 to 1920. From 1920 to 1930 he edited a denominational paper, the *Southwestern Christian Advocate*, gaining a national reputation as a campaigner for the rights of Blacks. From 1930 to 1940 he pastored the large and prestigious St. Mark's Methodist Episcopal Church in Harlem, New York City.

In 1939 the Methodist Episcopal Church merged with the Methodist Episcopal Church, South, and the Methodist Protestant Church to form the Methodist Church. As part of the restructuring the nineteen Black conferences of the former Methodist Episcopal Church, regardless of location, became part of the Central Jurisdiction. In 1940 King was elected bishop by the Central Jurisdiction, the second bishop (after **William A. C. Hughes**) elected by that new structure. Other preceding (non-missionary) Black bishops were **Robert E. Jones** (1920), **Matthew W. Clair, Sr.** (1920), and **Alexander Preston Shaw** (1936). King was assigned to the Atlantic Coast Episcopal Area, which included Atlanta, Central Alabama, Florida, Savannah, South Carolina, and South Florida Conferences. He was president of the board of trustees of both Gammon Theological Seminary and Claflin College in Orangeburg, South Carolina. He was vice-president of the board of trustees of both Clark College and Bethune-Cookman College in Daytona Beach, Florida. He was very effective in his six years as bishop, and passed away after a year-long illness.

MB, WWWA (2), *WWCA* (38–40), *EWM, NYTO.*

KING, MARTIN LUTHER, JR. (January 15, 1929–April 4, 1968), a Baptist minister with the **Progressive National Baptist Convention** and an internationally known civil rights leader, was born in Atlanta, Georgia, the son of **Martin Luther King, Sr.,** and Alberta Christine (Williams) King. His first name was actually Michael until about age five, when his father chose Martin as the name for both of them. His father was the second generation of King pastors of the Ebenezer Baptist Church in Atlanta. King, Jr. attended the local public schools for Blacks, was very bright, skipped several grades, and enrolled in Morehouse College in Atlanta at age fifteen, in 1944. He was deeply impressed by the president of Morehouse, **Benjamin Mays**, and theologian **George Kelsey**, and for the first time considered that he might become a minister.

He received his B.A. in 1948 and entered Crozier Theological Seminary in Chester, Pennsylvania. He was the first African American student body president there his senior year and graduated with a B.D. as valedictorian in 1951. While at Crozier he was introduced to the nonviolent resistance philosophy of Mahatma Gandhi (1869–1948), and embraced it, combined with a Christian philosophy of love, as the strategy of choice for the struggle against oppression. On a scholarship, he then entered Boston University School of Theology, where he was influenced by theologian Reinhold Neibuhr and the Boston school of theological personalism. He married Coretta Scott on June 18, 1953, with whom he had four children.

In September 1954, after he finished his thesis (he

received his Ph.D. in Systematic Theology in 1955), they moved to Montgomery, Alabama, where he succeeded **Vernon Johns** as pastor of the Dexter Avenue Baptist Church. He was scarcely settled in when Rosa Parks was arrested on December 1, 1955, for refusing to give up her bus seat to a White man. Within a week a bus boycott was begun, and despite his short tenure in the city, King was elected president of the Montgomery Improvement Association (M.I.A.), organized to maintain the boycott. He led its year-long operations, during which time he and his family endured harassment and the bombing of their home on January 30, 1956. The U.S. Supreme Court judged Montgomery's bus segregation laws illegal on November 13, 1956, and the buses were integrated on December 20, 1956.

The **Southern Christian Leadership Conference** (S.C.L.C.) was then organized in January 1957 to carry the tactics of the M.I.A. to other parts of the South, and King was elected its president. He was now becoming a national and international spokesperson for civil rights. In March 1957 he spoke at the ceremonies marking the independence from Great Britain of the new African republic of Ghana. In 1958 he published *Stride Toward Freedom: The Montgomery Story*, the first of six books. His career was nearly ended on September 20, 1958, when he was autographing books in Blumstein's Department Store in Harlem, New York. A mentally unstable woman named Izola Ware Curry stabbed him with a letter-opener. After delicate surgery he spent several days on the critical list, then slowly recovered.

In 1959 King and his wife visited India and met with those who had personally known Gandhi. This trip deepened his commitment to nonviolence. In November, 1959 he resigned from the Dexter Avenue Baptist Church and moved to Atlanta, where he co-pastored the Ebenezer Baptist Church with his father and was able to spend more time at the S.C.L.C. headquarters in that city. In 1961 King and a number of other Baptist clergy and churches seceded from the **National Baptist Convention, U.S.A., Inc.** (N.B.C.U.S.A.), and formed the Progressive National Baptist Convention. A major issue in this move was support for the growing civil rights movement. The historic position of the N.B.C.U.S.A. was conservative on racial issues, and the president of the denomination, **Joseph H. Jackson**, felt that demonstrations, marches, boycotts, and the like were harmful. King and others, however, no longer accepted a "gradualism" approach to civil rights and felt that frequent jail sentences for nonviolent protests against injustice were acceptable and even honorable.

In late 1962 King decided to focus on Birmingham, Alabama, "the most segregated city in America." The S.C.L.C.'s Leadership Training Committee led workshops to prepare volunteers for nonviolent response to brutal treatment. King told followers to follow **Booker T. Washington**'s admonition not to let anyone "drag them so low as to hate." The demonstrations and marches to end segregation brought much resistance, but in May 1963, media photographs of fire hoses and police dogs being set upon unarmed men, women, and children brought sympathetic outcries from around the nation. President Kennedy sent a Justice Department representative to help negotiate a settlement, and within a week many facilities in the city were desegregated. King spent much of the time during the demonstrations in prison, and wrote the now-classic "Letter from a Birmingham Jail," included in his 1964 book, *Why We Can't Wait.*

A second major event of 1963 was the S.C.L.C.-organized March on Washington, which brought 250,000 people, White and Black, of various religious beliefs, to the Lincoln Memorial to protest racism and its effects. At that even King gave his "I Have a Dream" speech, which has been termed the most eloquent of his career and "one of the most moving orations of our time." On January 3, 1964, he became the first Black to be honored by *Time* magazine as "Man of the Year." In December 1964, King became the third Black, twelfth American, and youngest person (at age thirty-five) to receive the Nobel Peace Prize. He donated the $54,600 award to the S.C.L.C. and several other civil rights groups, and rose to a still higher level of international prestige.

King's "finest hour" came as a result of the voter registration drive in Selma, Alabama, in early 1965. After demonstrators met with beatings and other harassment, he called for a "ministers march," and 1,500 clergy from all over the country showed up. Later on that same day, after the march, several of the White ministers were brutally beaten by some Whites and one was killed. Within a few days President Johnson asked the Congress to pass a voting rights bill, and federal troops were provided to oversee the safety of a five-day march from Selma to Montgomery to present demands to Governor Wallace. Later in 1965 the Voting Rights Act was signed into law; among other things it made illegal all literacy tests as a requirement for voting. The Act was universally recognized as having been the direct result of King's Selma campaign.

After 1965 King turned his attention to the Black ghettoes of the North. Chicago was the first target, and King moved his family into a slum apartment in the Lawndale section in January 1966. But Mayor Daley was intractable and riots broke out which threatened the whole enterprise. The S.C.L.C. seemed out of its environment. A largely symbolic open housing agreement was signed with city leaders on August 26, 1966, and King and the S.C.L.C. soon left; there were no further campaigns in the North. Some within the African American community, both North and South, began to feel that more radical means were necessary for change, and the "Black power" slogan became a rallying cry for these people. In King's 1967 book, *Where Do We Go From Here: Chaos or Community?* he answered these critics with his own critique of what he saw as their separatism, negativism, and atmosphere of violence. He added a new issue to his platform by voicing his opposition to the war in Vietnam, despite strong opposition even from his close advisors who felt it would alienate the supportive Johnson administration and spread the resources of the civil rights movement too thin. His first speech entirely devoted to the war was on April 15, 1967, at a large antiwar rally at the United Nations building in New York City. At the same time he was also turning his attention to the issue of poverty.

King was assassinated on the balcony of his motel room in Memphis in the midst of working for striking sanitation workers there and planning for the June Poor People's Campaign in Washington, D.C. James Earle Ray was convicted of the shooting and is still in prison. A number of people, however, including King's widow, have questioned Ray's involvement and raised the prospect of a conspiracy. After King's death **Coretta Scott King** took a highly visible role in the Poor People's Campaign and became a major civil rights leader on her own. In 1981 she dedicated the Martin Luther King, Jr., Memorial Center for Nonviolent Social Change in Atlanta, Georgia. The $8.4 million center includes exhibit areas, a 250–seat auditorium, a 90–seat theater, administrative offices, a library, archives, and the Martin Luther King, Jr., gravesite. Under her leadership the center has become the headquarters for promoting his vision of social action and progress.

King's impact on the United States was monumental. Even within his lifetime the social landscape in much of the South changed dramatically. The movement he led played a role in creating a new denomination, and both White and Black churches across the country were jolted into new perspectives through his work. Though his widow and others continue to remind the nation of the long road yet to travel, the first official recognition in January 1986 of his birthday as a national holiday is one indication of his influence in charting the direction and dimensions of that road.

Ansbro, John J. *Martin Luther King, Jr.: The Making of a Mind.* Maryknoll, NY: Orbis Books, 1982. 352 pp.

Baldwin, Lewis V. *There is a Balm in Gilead: The Cultural Roots of Martin Luther King, Jr.* Minneapolis, MN: Fortress Press, 1991. 348 pp.

Bennett, Lerone, Jr. *What Manner of Man: A Biography of Martin Luther King, Jr.* Chicago: Johnson Publishing Co., 1968. 251 pp.

Colaiaco, James A. *Martin Luther King, Jr.: Apostle of Militant Nonviolence.* New York: St. Martin's Press, 1988. 238 pp.

Collins, David R. *Not Only Dreamers: The Story of Martin Luther King, Sr. and Martin Luther King, Jr.* Elgin, IL: Brethren Press, 1986. 256 pp.

Cone, James H. *Martin & Malcolm & America: A Dream or a Nightmare.* Maryknoll, NY: Orbis Books, 1991. 358 pp.

Davis, Lenwood G. *I Have a Dream: The Life and Times of Martin Luther King, Jr.* Westport, CT: Negro Universities Press, 1969, 1973. 303 pp.

Downing, Fred L. *To See the Promised Land: The Faith Pilgrimage of Martin Luther King, Jr.* Macon, GA: Mercer University Press, 1986. 297 pp.

Fisher, William Harvey. *Free At Last: A Bibliography of Martin Luther King, Jr.* Metuchen, NJ: Scarecrow Press, 1977. 169 pp.

Garrow, David J. *Bearing the Cross: Martin Luther King, Jr. and the Southern Christian Leadership Conference, a Personal Portrait.* New York: William Morrow and Co., 1986. 800 pp.

————. *The F.B.I. and Martin Luther King, Jr.: From 'Solo' to Memphis.* New York: W. W. Norton, 1981. 320 pp.

————. *Martin Luther King, Jr.: Civil Rights Leader, Theologian, Orator.* 3 vols. Brooklyn, NY: Carlson Pub., 1989.

King, Coretta Scott. *My Life With Martin Luther King, Jr.* New York: Holt, Rinehart and Winston, 1969. 372 pp.

King, Martin Luther, Jr. *The Measure of a Man.* Philadelphia, PA: Christian Education Press, 1959. 34 pp.

————. *Strength to Love.* New York: Harper and Row, 1963. 146 pp.

————. *Stride Toward Freedom: The Montgomery Story.* New York: Harper and Brothers, 1958. 230 pp.

————. *The Trumpet of Conscience.* New York: Harper and Row, 1968. 78 pp.

————. *Where Do We Go From Here: Chaos or Community?* New York: Harper and Row, 1967. 209 pp.

————. *Why We Can't Wait.* New York: Harper and Row, 1964. 159 pp.

Lewis, David L. *King: A Biography.* Urbana, IL: University of Illinois Press, 1978. 468 pp.

Lomax, Louis E. *To Kill a Black Man.* Los Angeles, CA: Holloway House Publishing Co., 1968. 256 pp.

Oates, Stephen B. *Let the Trumpet Sound: The Life of Martin Luther King, Jr.* New York: Harper and Row, 1982. 560 pp.

Reavis, Ralph. *The Meaning of Martin Luther King, Jr. for*

the Black Experience. New York: Vantage Press, 1976. 132 pp.

Reddick, Lawrence D. *Crusader Without Violence: A Biography of Martin Luther King, Jr.* New York: Harper and Brothers, 1959. 243 pp.

Smith, Kenneth L. and Ira G. Zepp, Jr. *Search for the Beloved Community: The Thinking of Martin Luther King, Jr.* Valley Forge, PA: Judson Press, 1974. 159 pp.

Washington, James M., ed. *A Testament of Hope: The Essential Writings of Martin Luther King, Jr.* San Francisco: Harper and Row, 1986. 676 pp.

Witherspoon, William Roger. *Martin Luther King, Jr.: To the Mountaintop.* Garden City, NY: Doubleday, 1985. 244 pp.

DARB, SBAA, IBAWCB, CH, IBAW, HUBA, AARS, BWA, BLTC, BLA, NA, TCSAPR, BWASS, GBB, GNPP, GBA, BP, NPT, HNB, BHBA, WITW, EBA, ERS, DANB, WWWA (4), NCAB (54), EAB, CB (1965), CA (new rev. series, vol.27), AAE, RLOA, MBRL.

KING, MARTIN LUTHER, SR. (December 19, 1899–November 11, 1984), nationally known Baptist minister, was born in Stockbridge, Georgia, the second of nine children in the family of James Albert and Delia (Lindsay) King. His father was a sharecropper, and King grew up on the farm. His mother was very pious and saw to it that the children were close to the church. Schooling was very erratic. His father was a hard man, and at age fourteen, after a run-in with him, King left home briefly and found a job working in a train yard and shoveling coal on trains. At age fifteen he became a licensed preacher in Floyd Chapel Baptist Church. Religion was a great release from the harsh life for Blacks in the South. Whites hardly considered them human, and Blacks lived in constant danger. King witnessed a lynching and was himself beaten as a youngster for refusing to fetch water for a passing mill-owner.

At age eighteen he left the farm and went to Atlanta, working at a number of jobs until he became the first pastor of the East Point Baptist Church. In 1920 he founded the Second Baptist Church of College Park, and for many years pastored both congregations. He began to feel the need for more education, and enrolled at the Bryant School, starting at the fifth grade level. In 1926, after graduating from Bryant School, King felt the need to increase his education still further. He applied to Morehouse College in Atlanta, but was turned down for lack of proper educational preparation. He went directly to the president, John Hope, pleaded his case, and was allowed in. On November 25, 1926, after a six-year courtship, he married Alberta Christine Williams, with whom he had five children, only three of whom reached maturity. His father-in-law, A. D. Williams, was the pastor of the Ebenezer Baptist Church in Atlanta, one of the most prestigious churches in the area.

All these years King was known by the first name of Michael, which was his mother's preference. His father had always insisted that he had named him Martin, after one brother, and Luther, after another brother. There was no birth certificate available to consult. In 1933 King's father died, and in his last hours asked King to make official a change to Martin Luther. King agreed, made out the necessary legal papers, and changed both his and his namesake son's names to Martin Luther King. It also seemed fitting in that Martin Luther was the name of the founder of Protestantism.

In the summer of 1930, after a tremendous struggle, King graduated from Morehouse with a bachelor's degree in theology. At about that time he dropped the College Park church and added the Traveler's Rest Baptist Church. In 1931 his father-in-law passed away and King was asked to succeed him as pastor of Ebenezer Baptist Church. He did, and over the years the church grew significantly in membership (to about 3,500). In 1934 he visited the Holy Land, Europe, and a World Baptist Convention in Berlin, Germany. He began to feel that one of the responsibilities that went with his privileged position was that of working for better conditions for others. In 1935 he organized a march to city hall for voter registration, the first such demonstration in the city's history. In 1936 he stood with Black teachers for pay equal to the White teachers, a goal that was not won for eleven years, during which time his life was constantly threatened. He joined the N.A.A.C.P. and was a board member of its Social Action Committee. Almost singlehandedly he desegregated the elevators in the Atlanta Court House. He became a major figure in Black business and educational circles in Atlanta.

In the 1950s King watched with pride his son, **Martin Luther King, Jr.,** become a Baptist minister and leap into the public limelight leading the Montgomery bus boycott in 1956. King, Jr. soon became a national and international figure, leading the emerging civil rights movement. In 1960 King, Jr. moved to Atlanta to be near the headquarters of the **Southern Christian Leadership Conference** (S.C.L.C.) and to co-pastor Ebenezer Baptist Church, a long-cherished dream of King, Sr. For a time King, Sr. was moderator of the Atlanta Missionary Baptist Association. On April 4, 1968, tragedy struck when King Jr. was assassinated, and then again on July 21, 1969, when another son, Alfred Daniel Williams, drowned in his swimming pool.

In the 1970s "Daddy King" became something of an elder statesman. In 1972 he was voted Clergyman of the Year by the Georgia region of the National Conference of Christians and Jews. He traveled a great deal as a popular speaker. Tragedy struck again on June 30, 1974, when his wife was shot and killed by a psychopath named Marcus Chenault while she was playing the organ during a worship service in Ebenezer. Although most other people would have been crushed and embittered by such multiple tragedies, King Sr. came through it still maintaining his firm counsel that "God wants us to love one another and not hate." On September 14, 1975, he retired from Ebenezer Baptist Church and was succeeded by Joseph Lawrence Roberts, Jr. King, Sr. maintained an active schedule, and in the fall of 1975 was the first Black in history to address a joint session of the Alabama State Legislature. In the summer of 1976 he gave Jimmy Carter a crucial endorsement for president and delivered the benediction at the Democratic National Convention in New York City. In 1978 he was named National Father of the Year in Religion. In 1980 he again delivered the benediction at the 1980 Democratic National Convention and published the story of his life, *Daddy King: An Autobiography*.

Bims, Hamilton. "'He Never Gives Us More Than We Can Bear.'" *Ebony* 29 (October 1974): 37–44.

Kaiser, Charles. "No Time to Hate." *Newsweek* 96 (September 15, 1980): 92.

Collins, David R. *Not Only Dreamers: The Story of Martin Luther King, Sr. and Martin Luther King, Jr.* Elgin, IL: Brethren Press, 1986. 256 pp.

King, Martin Luther, Sr., with Clayton Riley. *Daddy King: An Autobiography*. New York: William Morrow and Co., 1980. 220 pp.

WWABA (80–81), *ERS, WWR* (85), *IBAW, OTSB, IP, NYTBS* (1984), *BWASS, RLOA*.

KING, WILLIS JEFFERSON (October 1, 1886–June 17, 1976), college president and a bishop of the **United Methodist Church**, was born in Rose Hill, Texas, the son of Anderson William and Emma (Blackshear) King. He received his B.A. in 1910 from Wiley College in Marshall, Texas and his S.T.B. in 1913 from Boston University School of Theology. On June 4, 1913 he married Permella J. Kelly, with whom he had three children.

He was ordained deacon in the Methodist Episcopal Church in 1908 and elder in 1913. While in school he pastored a church in Greenville, Texas (1908–10). In 1911 he was associate pastor of St. Mark's Methodist Church in New York City, while he began his seminary work in Boston. He then pastored Fourth Methodist Church in Boston (1912–1915); St. Paul's Methodist Church in Galveston, Texas (1915–1917); and Trinity Methodist Church in Houston, Texas (1918).

In 1918 he became professor of Old Testament Literature at Gammon Theological Seminary in Atlanta, Georgia. He also began work on his Ph.D., which he earned in 1921 from Boston University School of Theology. In 1922 he represented Black students at the World Student Christian Federation meeting in Peking, China. In 1926 he published his major work, *The Negro in American Life; An Elective Course for Young People on Christian Race Relations*. In 1929–30 he took a leave of absence from Gammon as a fellow under the Julius Rosenwald Fund to study at Oxford University and in Palestine with the American School of Oriental Research. In 1930 he became president of Samuel Huston College in Austin, Texas, serving until 1932, when he returned to Gammon as its president, where he stayed until 1944. In 1936–37 he was a member of the National Preaching Mission Staff. In 1937 he was a delegate to the Conference on Life and Work in Oxford, England. He was a member of the Fellowship of Reconciliation and the Commission on Interracial Cooperation. He was a member of the commission which worked out the merger with the Methodist Episcopal Church, South, in 1939, which created The Methodist Church (1939–1968). In 1943 he wrote an essay, *Personalism in Theology* and also contributed an essay to *Christian Bases of World Order* (1943). His first wife passed away in February 1943, and on June 28, 1944, he married Emma Clarissa Arnold.

In 1944 King was elected bishop in the Central Jurisdiction, the all-Black structure within The Methodist Church created by the 1939 merger. He served in Liberia, West Africa from 1944 to 1956, when he was shifted to the New Orleans area, where he remained until retirement in 1960.

King, Willis Jefferson. *The History of the Methodist Church Mission in Liberia*. Monrovia, Liberia: N.p., 1955. 77 pp.

———. *The Negro in American Life; An Elective Course for Young People on Christian Race Relationships*. New York: The Methodist Book Concern, 1926. 154 pp.

———. "The Negro Membership of the (Former) Methodist Church in the (New) United Methodist Church." *Methodist History* 7 (April 3, 1969): 32–43.

———. "The Negro Spirituals and the Hebrew Psalms." *Methodist Review (Bimonthly)* 114 (May 1931): 318–326.

———. "Personalism and Race." In Edgar Sheffield Brightman, ed. *Personalism in Theology*. Boston, MA: Boston University Press, 1943, 204–224.

———. *The Spiritual Pilgrimage of Two Christian Leaders ... Saul of Tarsus and John Wesley.* Monrovia, Liberia: N.p., n.d.

BDNM (75), MB, RLA, WWCA (38–40), BAW, AARS, HUBA, WWWA (7), RLOA, EWM, WWMC.

KINGSLEY, HAROLD MERRYBRIGHT (March 1, 1887–197?), a national-level officer of the Congregational Church (now the United Church of Christ), was born in Mobile, Alabama, the fourth of twelve children born to William and Mary Susan (Merrybright) Kingsley. His father was a White Episcopalian and his mother was a member of the oldest Black Baptist church in Mobile. The admitted ruler of the family was the maternal grandmother, a pillar of the same Baptist church. She urged that the Kingsley children attend the Black Episcopal church in town and receive education in the private Emerson School run by the Congregational Church. After graduating from Emerson School Kingsley went to Talladega College in Alabama, another Congregational institution. He received his B.A. there in 1908, then earned his B.D. in 1911 from Yale Divinity School. He was a founding member of the N.A.A.C.P. in 1909. On December 25, 1911, he married Mattie Satyra Jackson, with whom he had three children.

At Yale he decided to enter the ministry, but was disenchanted with what he saw as the classism of the Episcopal Church. He joined the African Methodist Episcopal (A.M.E.) Church and pastored the Bethel A.M.E. Church in Bridgeport, Connecticut for something less than a year in 1911. He was not comfortable there, either, and entered the Congregational ministry. From 1912 to 1914 he pastored Union Congregational Church in Newport, Rhode Island, the oldest Black Congregational church in the United States. From 1914 to 1917 he did field work for the denomination among Blacks in Texas and Oklahoma, with headquarters in Tillotson College in Austin, Texas.

In 1917 Kingsley was named Director of the Central District Congregational Field Work Among Negroes. In that position he served a year and a half at a mission church in Detroit, Michigan, then in 1918 moved to the Mount Zion Congregational Church in Cleveland, Ohio, where he stayed for four and a half years. From 1917 to 1919 he was Assistant Moderator of the National Council of Congregational Churches. In 1920 he was named Director of Northern Congregational Field Work Among Negroes, with headquarters in Chicago. From 1923 to 1925 he served a pastorate in Detroit, Michigan, and from 1925 to 1927 he served a church in Chicago, Illinois.

In 1927 he became the first pastor of the Good Shepherd Congregational Church in Chicago, and in less than two years he increased its membership from sixty-six to four hundred. At that church he did away with the traditional prayer meeting service, saying that theological pietism was dead anyway and needed to be replaced with a more socially oriented ministry. He preached against social evils, such as economic starvation, rather than individual evils such as card-playing and dancing. In 1944 he moved to Los Angeles, California, where he pastored the Church of the Christian Fellowship. He authored a number of articles and pamphlets and was one of the leading Black Congregationalists of his day.

Kingsley, Harold M. "The Negro Goes to Church." *Opportunity* 7 (March 1929): 90–91.
———. *The Negro in Chicago.* Chicago: Chicago Congregational Missionary and Extension Society, 1930. 16 pp.
WWCR, BA, BAW, HUBA, AARS, WWCA (38–40), RLA.

KINNEY [KINNY], CHARLES M. (1855–1951), the first African American ordained in the ministry of the Seventh-day Adventist Church, was born a slave in Richmond, Virginia. As a youth he left home for the West. In 1878 in Reno, Nevada, he attended a service conducted by Adventist evangelist John N. Loughborough. As a result, he became a charter member of the Reno congregation. He also served as secretary of the Nevada Tract and Missionary Society. In 1883 he moved to California to attend Heraldsburg College and after two years of schooling was assigned to Kansas as a colporteur (an evangelist who sells church literature from house to house) and later worked in St. Louis. In 1889 he was ordained by the church and assigned to Louisville.

During this period the church was engaged in an intense debate over the necessity of separated structures for Blacks in their southern work. Kinney favored separate structures for African Americans. He saw such separation as a great sacrifice for Black people, but one that had to be made rather than have Blacks segregated in the back of White congregations.

In the 1890s Kinney moved to Edgefield Junction, Tennessee, as pastor of a Black SDA congregation, the first of its kind, which had been organized in the early 1870s by E. B. Lane. He continued to pastor until his retirement in 1911, an event occasioned by the illness of his wife. He lived into his nineties, dying in 1951.

Schwarz, R. W. *Light Bearers to the Remnant.* Mountain View, CA: Pacific Press Publishing Association, 1979. 656 pp.

Seventh-day Adventist Encyclopedia. Washington, DC: Review and Herald Publishing Association, 1966. 1454 pp.

KIRKENDOLL, CHESTER ARTHUR, II (b. June 3, 1914), 35th bishop of the **Christian Methodist Episcopal Church** (CME), was born in Searcy, Arkansas, the son of Chester Arthur and Mattie (Wyatt) Kirkendoll. He grew up in Kansas City, Missouri, and was active in the Jamison Memorial Temple CME Church. In 1926 the General Conference was held in Kansas City and he served as altar boy, performing such errands as fetching water for the bishops. In 1935, while a student at Lane College in Jackson, Tennessee, he became Director of Youth Work under the Board of Religious Education of the denomination.

He graduated in 1938 with his B.A. and was assigned as pastor of the Clover Chapel (St. Paul) CME Church in Bolivar, Tennessee, still retaining his position with the Board of Religious Education. In 1939 he was Youth Delegate to the World Council of Churches in Amsterdam, Holland, and pastored Lane Chapel CME Church in Whiteville, Tennessee. That year he also married Alice Elizabeth Singleton, with whom he had three children. In 1940 he was appointed Director of Leadership Education and Sunday School Lesson Writer of Church School Publications under the General Board of Religious Education of the CME Church. He moved to Evanston, Illinois while working at this position and earned his M.A. in 1941 at Northwestern University. He retained his denominational position until 1950, though in 1949 he also pastored Walls Chapel AME Church in Chicago, Illinois, and taught mathematics in the Chicago public school system. In 1949 he authored *Improving the Educational Program of the Local Church.*

In 1950 he became the sixth president of Lane College, a position he held for twenty years. During this time the college was improved in numerous ways. In 1953 the I. B. Tigrett Science Building was purchased and renovated; in 1954 the Isaac J. Berry Music Hall was renovated and the first faculty residence was completed; in 1959 the J. T. Beck Faculty Apartments were completed; in 1961 the college was voted full membership in the Southern Association of Colleges and Schools; in 1963 the B. Julian Smith Residence Hall was completed; in 1965 the C. A. Kirkendoll Student Center was completed; in 1968 the Jubilee Men's Residence Hall was completed; in 1969 a new science education building was completed; and in 1970 the Women's Residence Hall was completed. From 1950 to 1970 he was also on the board of directors of the United Negro College Fund, and from 1961 to 1970 was a member of the Tennessee Council of Human Relations.

In 1970 Kirkendoll was elected bishop and assigned to the Third Episcopal District with offices in St. Louis, Missouri. He was a delegate to World Methodist Conferences in 1966, 1971, 1976, and 1981. He was chair of the board of trustees of Miles College in Birmingham, Alabama, from 1970 to 1982 and was a trustee of the Phillips School of Theology at the Interdenominational Theological Center in Atlanta, Georgia. He was a delegate to the Fifth Assembly of the World Council of Churches in 1975 and served on the Governing Board of the National Council of Churches from 1978 to 1981. In 1982 he became senior bishop of the denomination, retaining that status until his retirement in 1986. In 1984 *Ebony* magazine named him one of the one hundred most influential Black Americans.

"Bishop Kirkendoll Honorably Retired." *Christian Index* 119 (May 1, 1986): 3, 4.

"A Chronological Sketch: Chester Arthur Kirkendoll." *Christian Index* 110 (October 13, 1977): 5.

The Lane College Family. "A Tribute to Dr. C. A. Kirkendoll." *Christian Index* 110 (October 13, 1977): 4.

"The One Hundred Most Influential Black Americans." *Ebony* 39 (May 1984): 29–34.

"Ten Religious Groups with Biggest Black Membership." *Ebony* 39 (March 1984): 140–144.

Kirkendoll, Chester Arthur. *Improving the Educational Program of the Local Church.* Jackson, TN: C.M.E. Publishing House, 1949.

WWABA (92–93), BDNM (70), IBAW, WWR (85).

KITTRELL COLLEGE. An **African Methodist Episcopal Church** school. Kittrell College, Kittrell, North Carolina, grew out of the missionary efforts of Louisa Dorr, an African Methodist teacher who had moved to Raleigh, North Carolina, from the North in the 1880s and began teaching a Bible training class. Some of the young men who studied with her wished to see the work grow and petitioned the North Carolina Conference for better facilities. The suggestion grew quickly into a proposal for the conference to sponsor a school. Land was secured in nearby Kittrell and opened in 1886. Leading in the effort to create the school were the Rev. R. H. W. Leak and Bishop **William F. Dickerson**, who had earlier promoted and overseen the establishment of **Allen University** in South Carolina. The school received an early boost when in 1888 the Virginia Conference voted to support it rather than having a school in that state.

The school has grown in size and standing over the years, though it suffered a setback in the wake of the

Depression and was closed for three years (1934–37). In more recent years it has been the beneficiary of grants from the Duke Foundation that have provided it with some degree of financial stability.

Smith, Charles Spencer. *A History of the African Methodist Episcopal Church*. Philadelphia, PA: Book Concern of the AME Church, 1922. 570 pp.

Wright, Richard R., and John Russell Hawkins, eds. *The Centennial Encyclopedia of the African Methodist Episcopal Church*. Philadelphia, PA: Book Concern of the AME Church, 1916. Rev. 1947. 387 pp.

KNIGHTS OF PETER CLAVER. A **Roman Catholic Church** fraternal organization. The Knights of Peter Claver, a fraternal order analogous to the Knights of Columbus, was founded on November 7, 1909, in Mobile, Alabama, by four priests of the Society of St. Joseph: Fr. John H. Dorsey and three White colleagues, Frs. Conrad F. Rebeshier, Samuel J. Kelly, and Joseph P. Van Baast. They were joined by three African American laymen, Gilbert Faustina, Frank Collins and Frank Trenier. The organization sponsors educational, recreational and athletic events, and is designed to support the participation of its members in their local congregation.

The organization was named for a seventeenth-century association of followers of Peter Claver, a Spanish Jesuit priest who had been canonized twenty years previously in 1888. Clavier (1580–1654) had been sent to Cartegena, Columbia, in 1610. Here he met Alonso de Sandoval who aroused Claver's interest in assisting the slaves. Cartegena was at the time a major entry port for slaves in the Americas. He began to meet the ships as they came into the ports. He would often be the first person the newly arrived slaves saw as he came into the stinking holes where they were chained to care for their wounds and immediate needs. He is remembered as carrying many of the disabled and sick ones off the ship on his shoulders. He is said to have converted hundreds of thousands of slaves by his example. He organized a group to assist him in his work, the original Knights of Peter Claver. In his later life, he became paralyzed and the object of the hatred of a slave who was assigned to take care of him.

The Knights developed slowly over the century. A boy's division, the Junior Knights, was created in 1917. The ladies' auxiliary was initiated in 1922 and recognized formally as a division of the Knights in 1926. A Junior Daughters division was started in 1930. The organization began to expand rapidly in the 1970s as it became involved in the civil rights struggle. It has been a steady supporter of the **Southern Christian Leadership Conference**, the Urban League, and the N.A.A.C.P. They support a development fund at Xavier University and have created their own scholarship program.

Headquarters of the Knights is in New Orleans, where in 1976 it dedicated a new headquarters building. It claims over 100,000 families as members.

Payne, Wardell J., ed. *Directory of African American Religious Bodies: A Compendium by the Howard University School of Divinity*. Washington, DC: Howard University Press, 1991. 363 pp.

KNOXVILLE COLLEGE. A **Presbyterian Church (U.S.A.)** school. Knoxville College, Knoxville, Tennessee, was founded in 1875 by the United Presbyterian Church of North America, now a constituent part of the **Presbyterian Church (U.S.A.)**. It began with a need's survey made by Dr. J. W. Witherspoon at the denomination's direction. The church had been involved since 1863 in Nashville where Joseph G. McKee had founded the first free school for Blacks in the South. In 1865, however, the McKee school was closed and its assets moved to Knoxville. It originally offered an elementary school curriculum. A normal (teacher training) and college curriculum was added in the 1870s.

In 1901 the school was chartered by the state of Tennessee as a land grant school, and for the next eleven years received significant state support. However, in 1912 the land grant portion of the school was withdrawn and transferred to what is today Tennessee State University. Continuing without state support, Knoxville developed into a liberal arts college. The college evolved steadily until the Depression introduced a period of instability characterized by the continual overturn in the president's office. During this time, the first African American president, Dr. J. A. Cotton, served for two years (1940–1942). The period of instability continued until 1950 when James A. Colston began his lengthy tenure as president. During his 27 years in office, the school recovered its pre-Depression years stability and the student body greatly expanded. It now serves approximately 1,100 students annually.

Parker, Inez Moore. *The Rise and Decline of the Program of Education for Black Presbyterians of the United Presbyterian Church U.S.A., 1865–1970*. San Antonio, TX: Trinity University Press, 1977. 319 pp.

KODESH CHURCH OF EMMANUEL. A Holiness church. The Kodesh Church of Emmanuel developed as a Holiness movement in the **African Methodist Episcopal Church** in Philadelphia in the early twentieth century. In the summer of 1929, Rev. **Frank Russell Killingsworth** and 120 members left and organized an independent congregation who saw themselves as a body of saved people, called from worldliness and sin to a consecrated life of spiritual union and fellowship with God. Five years later they were joined by a like-minded congregation, the Christian Tabernacle Union in Pittsburgh, Pennsylvania. Subsequently churches were founded in Washington, D.C., and Virginia. By 1936 there were nine congregations.

The church had been formed on a Wesleyan concept of holiness. Members sought a work of the Holy Spirit in their hearts which would make them perfect in love and free from outward sin. Members agree to refrain from alcohol and tobacco, worldly amusements, prideful dress, and membership in secret societies. Members believe in the efficacy of divine healing, but are quick to add that they do not therefore boycott physicians. The church is headed by the quadrennial general assembly which passes on the content of the church manual, the church's law book, and appoints the supervising elders to oversee the church's work.

Headquarters of the church is in Bethel Park, Pennsylvania. In 1980 there were five churches and a mission in Liberia.

KWANZAA. An African American cultural festival. Kwanzaa is a festival originated in 1966 by Dr. **Maulana "Ron" Karenga** as an expression of the emerging African American culture. The term Kwanzaa is a Swahili term which means "the firstfruits of the harvest," and is celebrated December 26–January 1 of each year. While generally seen as a non-political and non-religious festival in which anyone can participate, it developed as an expression of the new Kawaida religion which in turn serves as the theoretical foundation of US, the organization Karenga created to put together a new revolutionary Black culture to unite African Americans.

The Kawaida religion is built upon seven principles termed *Nguzo Saba*. They are *Umoja* or unity; *Kujichagulia* or self-determination; *Ujima* or collective work and responsibility; *Ujamaa* or cooperative economic; *Nia* or purpose; *Kuumba* or creativity; and *Imani* or faith. Kwanzaa was created in part to serve as a substitute for the Christians' Christmas for followers of the Kawaida faith. As the celebration of Kwanzaa has spread it has primarily been presented and adopted by many thousands of people as a non-religious practice to honor the cultural roots of African Americans.

The celebration of Kwanzaa includes the seven basic symbols: *Mazao*, fruits and vegetables; *Mkeka*, a place mat; *Kinara*, a candle holder; *Vobunzi*, ears of corn; *Zawadi*, gifts; *Kikimbe Cha Umoja*, a community unity cup; and *Mishumaa Saba*, the seven candles. Proponents of the festival are quick to draw a distinction between the Kinara and the Jewish Minorah which it superficially resembles. The Kinara has a place for seven, not eight, candles. The seven candles include one black, three green, and three red candles. During the festival a different candle is lighted each day. The candles stand for the seven principles, the black one symbolizing Umoja. The week of celebration includes feasting and gift giving and concludes with an African feast and unity celebration, the Kwanzaa Karumu, on December 31.

Barashango, Ishakamusa. *Afrikan People and European Holidays: A Mental Genocide.* Washington, DC: IV Dynasty Publishing Co., 1980. 106 pp.

McClester, Cedric. *Kwanzaa: Everything You Always Wanted to Know But Didn't Know Where to Ask.* New York: Gumbs & Thomas, 1985. 36 pp.

KYLES, LYNWOOD WESTINGHOUSE (May 3, 1874–July 8, 1941), 34th bishop of the **African Methodist Episcopal Zion Church** (AMEZ), was born in Ivy Depot, Albermarle County, Virginia, the tenth child of Burrell and Mary (Wormley) Kyles. His early education was received in a log cabin country school house and the other seven months of the year he worked on a farm for twenty-five cents per day. At age fourteen he heard a Baptist preacher give an address on the importance of education, and he made his way to the Hampton Normal and Industrial Institute in Hampton, Virginia. He finished the English course and graduated from the Industrial Department as a wheelwright and blacksmith.

He worked these trades for a number of years first in Paterson, New Jersey, then in Somerville, followed by Flemington, and finally Ridgewood, New Jersey. About that time he shifted from the Baptist affiliation of his youth and joined the Ridgewood AMEZ Church. He became heavily involved, filling most of the offices available. Soon he decided to enter the ministry and joined the New Jersey Conference in September 1895 as a local preacher. His first appointment was to the AMEZ church in Englewood, New Jersey, in April 1896. He was ordained deacon on May 2, 1897, and that year also married Jenny V. Smith, with whom he had three children. About this time he moved to Pennsylvania and enrolled in Lincoln University, where he was a student for seven years. He also pastored the AMEZ church in Media, Pennsylvania from 1898 to 1902. Despite many hardships and privations, he graduated from the College Department in 1901 and from the Theological Department in 1904 with his B.D. He was ordained elder on May 20, 1901.

In 1902 he was appointed to John Wesley AMEZ Church in Washington, D.C., followed by Center Street AMEZ Church in Statesville, North Carolina (1904–06); Goler Memorial AMEZ Church in Winston-Salem, North Carolina (1906–08); and Big Zion AMEZ Church in Mobile, Alabama (1908–14). His first wife died in August, 1905, and on December 18, 1908, he married Louella Marie Bryan, with whom he had four children. While serving at the prestigious Big Zion, he built the largest parsonage owned by Blacks in the United States at that time, and added 1,600 members. In 1908 he was elected associate editor of the *A.M.E. Zion Quarterly Review*. In 1912 he became its third editor. In 1913 he added to those duties that of secretary-treasurer of the Ministerial Brotherhood and Relief. In both positions he was very successful, permanently establishing the Ministerial Brotherhood Department and enhancing the reputation of the journal. From 1914 to 1916 he was able to work those positions full time.

From these two offices he was elected bishop in 1916, with the highest vote up to that point in the history of the church. For eight years he was assigned to the Pacific Coast and organized churches in several western states. He then served the Arkansas, Missouri, and Indiana area for four years, later serving North Carolina and then New York. Shortly after World War I he became chair of the Tercentenary Campaign, which raised $300,000 for the denomination, one of his outstanding achievements. In 1922 his second wife died and on June 16, 1926, married Josephine Humbles, with whom he had two children. In 1921 he was a delegate to the World Methodist Conference in London. In 1932

he held the first of the Leadership Training Schools in Asheville, North Carolina, an event which later became an institution in the church.

In 1935 he was one of two American speakers at the World Christian Endeavor Convention in Budapest, Hungary. He helped found and in 1939 served as president of the **National Fraternal Council of Negro Churches of America**, and was on the executive committee of the Federal (now National) Council of Churches. He was a trustee of Walters Institute in Warren, Arkansas, and beginning in 1935 he served on the board of trustees of Livingstone College in Salisbury, North Carolina. His support and care for Livingstone College knew no bounds, and at one point he borrowed heavily against his life insurance to meet the faculty payroll, a loan that was never repaid. He reenergized Founder's Day celebrations for the college with fundraising and a motorcade pilgrimage. In 1935 he succeeded Bishop **Josiah S. Caldwell** as senior bishop.

"Anthology of the A.M.E. Zion Bishops." *Star of Zion* 57 (September 28, 1933): 1, 6.

"Bishop Lynwood Westinghouse Kyles." *A.M.E. Zion Quarterly Review* 77 (Fall 1965): 135–139.

"Bishop Lynwood Westinghouse Kyles Passes." *A.M.E. Zion Quarterly Review* 51 (July 1941): 55–56.

"Lynwood Kyles Remembered." *Star of Zion* 97 (October 3, 1974): 3, 6.

"New Era of Zion Methodism." *Star of Zion* 48 (August 7, 1924): 1, 5.

Kyles, Lynwood W. "The Contribution of the Negro to the Religious Life of America." *Journal of Negro History* 11 (January 1926): 8–16.

Wallace, Paris W. "He Fell Asleep: Eulogy to the Late Bishop L. W. Kyles." *Star of Zion* 65 (July 17, 1941): 1, 8

"Zion's Senior Bishops During the Twentieth Century." *Star of Zion* 104 (March 27, 1980): 1, 2.

HUBA, AARS, WWCR, WWCA (38–40), RLA, AMEZC, HAMEZC.

"About this time I had a call to preach at a place about thirty miles distant, among the Methodists, with whom I remained one week. . . . Here by the instrumentality of a poor coloured woman, the Lord poured forth his spirit among the people. Though, as I was told, there were lawyers, doctors, and magistrates present to hear me speak, yet there was mourning and crying among sinners. For the Lord scattered fire among them of his own kindling."

Jarena Lee, preacher
African Methodist Episcopal Church
1836

L

LAKEY, OTHAL HAWTHORNE (b. April 6, 1936), 44th bishop of the **Christian Methodist Episcopal Church** (CME), was born in Shreveport, Louisiana, the seventh child of Clarence John and Zandree (Ashley) Lakey. He was licensed to preach on May 31, 1948, at age twelve, at the Warren Chapel CME Church in San Pedro, California. He was admitted on trial to the California Annual Conference in 1951, ordained deacon in 1953, and elder in 1956.

In 1957 he graduated with his B.A. from Whitman College in Walla Walla, Washington, and while a student there had pastored at St. James CME Church in Pasco, Washington. From there he went to Drew Theological Seminary in Madison, New Jersey, graduating with his M.Div. in 1960. He married Narsis Beard, with whom he has had at least one child.

He was appointed to Allen Temple CME Church in Portland, Oregon, from 1960 to 1963, where during those years he was also chair of the Educational Committee of the Portland Urban League. From 1961 to 1963 he was vice-president of the Oregon Council on Alcoholic Problems. He then went to the Williams Memorial Temple CME Church in Shreveport, Louisiana, from 1963 to 1966. In 1966 he was a delegate to the World Methodist Conference in London, England. That year he transferred to the Dallas-Ft. Worth Annual Conference and was appointed to the Cedar Crest CME Church of Dallas, Texas.

While in Dallas, Lakey published a significant historical study, *The Rise of "Colored Methodism": A Study of the Background and Beginnings of the Christian Methodist Episcopal Church* (1972). In 1974 he was elected editor of the *Christian Index*, the official church magazine, holding that office for eight years. On May 9, 1982, he was elected bishop on the second ballot. He was assigned to the Second Episcopal District (Kentucky, and Ohio-Central Indiana Conferences), where he has since remained. He also became chair of the General Board of Christian Education. He has most recently completed a much expanded historical volume, *The History of the C.M.E. Church* (1985).

"Bishop Othal L. Lakey." *Christian Index* 115 (May 15, 1982): 13.
Lakey, Othal Hawthorne. *The History of the C.M.E. Church*. Memphis, TN: CME Publishing House, 1985.
———. *The Rise of "Colored Methodism": A Study of the Background and Beginnings of the Christian Methodist Episcopal Church*. Dallas, TX: Crescendo Book Publications, 1972. 128 pp.
BDNM, WWR (85), *HUBA.*

LAMPTON, EDWARD WILKINSON (October 21, 1857–July 16, 1910), 31st bishop of the **African Methodist Episcopal Church** (AME), was born in Hopkinsville, Kentucky, the son of Albert R. Lampton. He grew up in Bowling Green, Kentucky and experienced conversion on September 18, 1874. He joined the North Mississippi Annual Conference in 1886 and was ordained deacon the same year. He was ordained elder in 1888, held pastorates in Mississippi and Kentucky, and for a time was presiding elder in Mississippi. In 1902 he succeeded Phillip A. Hubbard as financial secretary of the denomination, a powerful office which had on occasion been used as a stepping-stone to the episcopacy. In 1907 he published two significant books that further enhanced his reputation, *Analysis of Baptism* and *Digest of Rulings and Decisions of the Bishops of the African Methodist Episcopal Church from 1847–1907.*

In 1908 he was elected bishop over the protests of those who objected to his divorced status. By this time he was already remarried and had fathered four children. Since 1908 no other financial secretary has been elected bishop. He was assigned to the Mississippi and Louisiana area and maintained his residence in Greenville, Mississippi. He engaged in a major controversy with the local phone company, asking the operators to address his family members with "Miss" or "Mrs." or "Mr.," instead of their first names. The company remained with its policy of not using respectful titles with any Black subscriber. The company removed his phone and so many threats were made against the family that they had to move to Chicago. This episode may have been a factor in his death not long afterward. Named for him were Lampton College in Louisiana, Lampton Theological Seminary in Jackson, Mississippi, and the AME Church in Canton, Mississippi.

Lampton, Edward Wilkerson. *Analysis of Baptism.* Washington, DC: Record Publishing Co., 1907. 76 pp.
———. *Digest of Rulings and Decisions of the Bishops of the African Methodist Episcopal Church from 1847–1907.* Washington, DC: Record Publishing Co., 1907. 334 pp.
BAW, EWM, BAMEC, HAMEC, CEAMEC.

LANE, ISAAC (March 3, 1834–December 6, 1937), 5th bishop of the **Christian Methodist Episcopal Church** (CME), then known as the Colored Methodist Episcopal Church, was born into slavery five miles north of Jackson in Madison County, Tennessee, the son of Joe Rodgers and Rachel Lane. Although on the plantation he was not allowed an education, he nevertheless was able to read and write by age eighteen. He married Frances Ann Boyce on December 24, 1853, with whom he had twelve children, of whom only five survived past 1929. He experienced conversion on September 11, 1854, and the next month, on October 21, joined the Methodist Episcopal Church, South (MECS) in Jackson. He received a lay exhorter's license in the fall of 1856, but the law forbade issuing preacher's licenses to Blacks, and he had to wait until the end of the Civil War for that.

After the Civil War there was a movement in the MECS to create a separate church for its Black members. While this was being organized, Lane was ordained deacon in 1866 and elder in 1867. That year he was appointed presiding elder of the Jackson District of the newly created Memphis Colored Conference, where he served for four years. He was also pastor of Jackson Station, later called the Mother Liberty Church, in Jackson, Tennessee. The first General Conference of the CME Church was held on December 15, 1870, and Lane played a prominent part in its proceedings. Rapid growth and unforeseen problems led to a special called session of the General Conference in 1873, at which he was elected bishop, along with **Lucius Holsey** and **J. A. Beebe**. Even after election to the episcopacy his annual salary was well under two hundred dollars a

year, and he had to raise cotton to help support his family.

As bishop, Lane was known for his deep piety, calm disposition, and commitment to education. On January 15, 1880, he oversaw the purchase of the four-acre site in Jackson, Tennessee, that would become Lane College, his most lasting legacy. He later personally raised $9,000 to start building the school. The college would slowly grow in size and quality until it was voted full membership in the Southern Association of Colleges and Secondary Schools on December 7, 1961. For many years he was president of the board of trustees, and one of his sons, James F. Lane, served as president of the college in the 1930s. On May 11, 1895, his first wife passed away, and later that year he married Mrs. Mary E. Smith. He was instrumental in the expansion of the church in such cities as Cleveland, Ohio; Chicago, Illinois; St. Louis, Missouri; Kansas City, Kansas; Oklahoma City, Oklahoma; and Tulsa, Oklahoma. He retired in May 1914, and when he died he was the oldest bishop in the world, at 103 years, nine months, and three days.

Lane, Isaac. *Autobiography: With a Short History of the C.M.E. Church in America and of Methodism.* Nashville, TN: Publishing House of the M. E. Church, South, 1916. 192 pp.
Savage, Horace C. *Life and Times of Bishop Isaac Lane.* Nashville, TN: National Publication Company, 1958. 240 pp.
DNAADB, HUBA, AARS, IBAW, NA, EBA, EWM, HNB, HCMEC, WWWA (1), WWCA (38–40), HCMECA, CMECTY, BTFTMC.

LANE COLLEGE. A **Christian Methodist Episcopal Church** (CME) school. Lane College, Jackson, Tennessee, had its beginning in 1878 and the vote of the Tennessee Conference of the CME Church to purchase land for a church school. In 1880 four acres in Jackson, Tennessee, were purchased. In 1882 the Methodist Episcopal Church, South (MECS) general conference established an education committee and fund. Though the bulk of the financial support of the MECS would go to Paine College, a significant amount of MECS funds went to Lane as well.

In the fall of 1882, an initial building was erected and the first classes opened for what was called the High School. Bishop **Isaac Lane**'s daughter, Jennie E. Lane was the first teacher. In January 1883, J. H. Harper, a MECS minister, became the principal of the school. Harper served in an interim until **Charles Henry Phillips**, a young minister of the CME Tennessee

Conference and one of the most educated ministers in the church, was able to take charge. At his suggestion, the name of the school was changed to Lane Institute. He stayed at the school for two years.

In the years after Phillips left, the MECS offered more financial help, but demanded that a MECS person be placed in charge. Thus, in 1887 T. F. Saunders became president of the Institute. At the same time Bishop Lane was made president of the school. He remained in office for 15 years during which time the MECS paid his salary. In 1903 the first African American president, James A. Bray, a graduate of Paine College, became president of the Institute. He was succeeded in 1907 by James F. Lane, Bishop Lane's son. Lane stayed at the school until 1944. Lane was succeeded by D. S. Yarborough (1944–1950), **Chester A. Kirkendoll** (1950–1970), and Herman E. Stone.

Over the years Lane developed an elementary and secondary school, a normal department and a college curriculum. As public education in the area emerged, the elementary and secondary schools were closed, and early in the twentieth century the college emerged as the central feature of the school.

Lakey, Othel H. *The History of the CME Church*. Memphis, TN: CME Publishing House, 1985.

Lane, Isaac. *Autobiography: With a Short History of the C.M.E. Church in America and of Methodism*. Nashville, TN: Publishing House of the M. E. Church, South, 1916. 192 pp.

Savage, Horace C. *Life and Times of Bishop Isaac Lane*. Nashville, TN: National Publication Company, 1958. 240 pp.

LANEY, LUCY CRAFT (April 13, 1854–October 23, 1933), pioneer Presbyterian educator, was born in Macon, Georgia, the seventh of ten children born to David and Louisa Laney, both former slaves. Her father was a carpenter and also pastored a Savannah church affiliated with the "Old School" Northern Presbyterians. At age fifteen, Laney graduated from Lewis High School (later called Ballard Normal School) in Macon, a private school established by the American Missionary Association. That association had recently opened Atlanta University, and she was chosen to be part of the first class of the Higher Normal Department, graduating in 1873.

She then taught in public schools around Macon, Milledgeville, Augusta, and Savannah, until 1883, when she gained the approval of the Presbyterian Board of Missions for Freedmen to start a private school for Blacks in Augusta. She was the first Black appointed by the board to head one of its major institutions. Virtually without funds, the school was opened in the basement of Christ Presbyterian Church in Atlanta. By the time it was chartered by the state on January 6, 1886, the enrollment had reached well over two hundred, and classes had moved to a two-story house on Calhoun Street. In May 1886, she traveled at great expense to Minneapolis to speak at the General Assembly of the Presbyterian Church in the United States (which merged in 1983 with the United Presbyterian Church in the U.S.A. to form the Presbyterian Church U.S.A.), with the aim of gaining financial backing for her school. But the Board of Missions for Freedmen only promised moral support. The trip was not wasted, however, because she did gain two strong Presbyterian woman allies, Francina E. H. Haines, secretary of the Women's Executive Committee of Home Missions, and a Mrs. Marshall.

School buildings were constructed on Guinnett Street in Augusta beginning in 1889, with a $10,000 contribution from Mrs. Marshall, and other money and support coming from Mrs. Haines, for whom the school, Haines Normal and Industrial Institute, was named. The Presbyterian Church gradually did assume some of the ongoing financial burden, and Northern benefactors contributed McGregor Hall (1906) and the Cauley-Wheeler Memorial Building (1924). Mrs. Anson Phelps Stokes helped expand the school grounds to include the whole city block. Money was still scarce, and Laney was always on the move, soliciting support. The school survived numerous calamities, and by World War I had 900 students, both high school and elementary, and more than thirty teachers. **Mary McLeod Bethune**, founder of Bethune-Cookman College in Florida, began her teaching career at the school in 1896–1897.

This achievement is all the more startling when one considers that public high schools for Blacks were virtually unknown in the South before World War I, and elementary schools for Blacks were few in number and poorly staffed. Laney went against the standard grain by offering, in addition to the industrial arts, a full humanities curriculum. She strove to unlock the potential in all of her students, and would not accept preset limits to their achievement. In the early 1890s she began the city's first kindergarten as well as a nurses' training department, which eventually became the Lamar School of Nursing at Atlanta University Hospital. She herself took summer courses at the University of Chicago when possible, and lent her political weight towards getting better public services in the Black areas of Augusta. She never married.

The Depression of the 1930s cut off the support of the Presbyterian Church, and for a time the school survived on alumni contributions and the largesse of other donors. Finally, especially without Laney's presence, this was not enough, and the school was closed and razed in 1949. Today, a modern school, the Lucy C. Laney High School, stands on the site.

Griggs, Augustus C. "Lucy Craft Laney." *Journal of Negro History* (January 1934): 97–102.

Wilson, Frank T., ed. "Living Witnesses: Black Presbyterians in Ministry." *Journal of Presbyterian History* 51 (Winter 1977): 347–391.

HUBA, IBAW, PIC, NAW, FAW, NNW, WWCA (30–32), BDAE, DANB, BWNCAL, PNW, NBH, PATN, NBAW.

LANGE, ELIZABETH (c.1787–1882), superior of the first African American religious order in the **Roman Catholic Church**, was born in Cuba of Haitian parents. She arrived in the United States about 1817, perhaps in response to a general invitation from Roman Catholics in Maryland to Catholics in the West Indies and Latin America to help bolster the Catholic population in Maryland, or perhaps as one of the large number of Haitian refugees from political unrest. She settled in the Fell's Point section of Baltimore, where many Black Haitians lived. Frustrated by finding Black children barred from the public schools, Lange and another woman founded a free school in her home.

The Haitians worshipped each Sunday in the lower chapel of St. Mary's Seminary on Paca Street, and in August 1827 a new Sulpician priest, Jacques Hector Nicolas Joubert de la Muraille, took charge of the chapel. He also was frustrated by the fact that Haitian children had trouble learning their catechism because they could not read. He discovered Lange's school and found that both Lange and the other teacher at the school had already considered the possibility of consecrating their lives to God. He decided to found a religious order, and the **Oblate Sisters of Providence** was founded in June 1828, with three women, eleven girl boarders, and nine day students.

The creation of this Black religious order was not without opposition, but Archbishop Whitfield of Baltimore saw the group as reflecting the will of God and gave it his full support. The three women made their first vows on July 2, 1829, at the celebration of the Feast of the Visitation. They renewed their vows each year on that date and did not make perpetual vows until later. This was the first Black American Catholic religious order. Lange took the name Mary Elizabeth when she made her vows; the other women of the early community were Marie Madeleine Balas, Rosine Boegue, and Almeide Duchemin Maxis. After the

Blessed Virgin the group honored St. Benedict the Moor (d.1589) as a secondary patron saint, who had been canonized in 1807 as a statement of opposition to the slave trade. In 1831 they were approved by Pope Gregory XVI and received a number of privileges, such as permission to reserve the Blessed Sacrament in their convent. Father Joubert remained a strong presence as chaplain for the community, as well as protector, spiritual director, and spokesperson.

In 1832 a number of the sisters risked their lives to tend to the victims of the cholera epidemic in Baltimore. About 1833 Lange received an inheritance of about $1,400 which she donated towards a chapel for the community, with the understanding that her mother could join the group later, and she did. The St. Francis Chapel of the Oblates was the first church in the United States built for Black Catholics. In 1837 a White mob attacked the convent, a sharp reminder of the harsh racism faced by this pioneer group of women. The amount of physical damage is unknown, but the emotional effects were severe, and for several years attendance fell at the school. A new archbishop was not supportive of their work. Joubert died on November 5, 1843, and was replaced in October 1847 by a Redemptorist priest, Thaddeus Anwander (1823–93), whose fresh enthusiasm made a significant difference. The school for girls became again very successful and a boys' school opened in 1852.

In 1863 the Oblate Sisters opened a day school for Black children and a night school for Black women in Philadelphia, a project which lasted until 1867, and over the following years other, more lasting projects were undertaken in other cities. In 1865 they opened an orphanage in Baltimore to care for Black orphans of the Civil War. Lange was superior of the order until the time of her death in 1882. The order was certainly placed on a strong footing, and by 1900 the sisters were conducting schools and orphanages in rural Maryland, Washington, D.C., Missouri, Kansas, and Cuba.

NBAW, BWMH, CCAN, HBCUS, IBAW.

LARK, JAMES H. (May 4, 1888–January 10, 1978), the first Black bishop in the **Mennonite Church**, was born in Savannah, Georgia, the only child of Lela and James Lark. He was orphaned at the age of six and was reared with the help of friends and relatives. He was baptized as a Baptist at age sixteen, but after a few years no longer attended. In 1916, at the age of twenty-eight, he graduated from the Quaker Institute for College Youth (later called Cheyney State College) in Pennsylvania. He taught for a time at Florida Baptist

Academy in Jacksonville, Florida, then studied some more at the Washington D.C. Normal School. During World War I he was a sergeant in the medics of the U.S. Army, and served in France for two years. In 1918, the day before he shipped out to France, he married Rowena, with whom he had six children.

After his discharge they lived a number of places and Lark dabbled in real estate. In 1927 they moved to a farm near Quakertown, Pennsylvania, where in 1931 the Rocky Ridge Mennonite Mission was founded. Rowena, who was teaching in Washington, D.C. and was only home on weekends, soon joined and after several years convinced her husband to join as well. In 1935 they moved to Washington, D.C. and joined the Brentwood Mennonite Church in Cottage City, Maryland. In 1936 they began helping with summer Bible school work in Harrisonburg, Virginia, and began to lead summer Bible schools in a number of communities. In 1944 they were called to teach a summer Bible school program in Chicago, and the response was so great that eventually the Bethel Mennonite Church was founded. On February 18, 1945, both Lark and his wife entered work as full-time superintendents of the Mennonite mission work among African Americans in the Chicago area. That year he founded the Dearborn Street Mission in Chicago to fight juvenile delinquency, and the mission lasted into the 1950s. The Franconia Conference ordained Lark a minister on October 6, 1946, the first Black minister in the Mennonite Church. His pastorate was the Bethel Mennonite Church.

The work of the Larks continued to meet with great success. In 1949 they established what came to be called Camp Rehoboth near Hopkins Park, Illinois. He was ordained the first Black Mennonite bishop on September 26, 1954, the same day that the new building for the Bethel Mennonite Church was dedicated. In 1956 the church opened a day-care center. In about 1955 Lark left the church in the hands of Paul O. King and moved to Camp Rehoboth to establish the St. Anne Congregation. His dream was to plant a Mennonite church in every Black community across the country. In 1956 they moved to St. Louis, Missouri, where they founded the Bethesda Mennonite Church.

In about 1960 they retired to California, and Lark served as interim pastor at Calvary Mennonite Church in Los Angeles when the community was shifting from White to Black, staying until Le Roy Bechler was installed as the regular pastor in January, 1961. They then moved to Fresno, where they began a church, but when the Southwest Mennonite Conference could not come up with a regular pastor for it the church closed. In 1970 his wife passed away, and Lark had a difficult period of readjustment. He went to Wichita, Kansas, as interim pastor of the Zion Mennonite Church, and developed a strong program for renewal and community outreach, but was blocked by people who did not share that vision. His last years were spent struggling with illness in the Veterans Hospital in Chicago. His legacy of building up the Black witness in the Mennonite Church is a major one.

Bechler, Le Roy. *The Black Mennonite Church in North America, 1886–1986.* Scottdale, PA: Herald Press, 1986. 196 pp.

Brown, Hubert L. *Black and Mennonite.* Scottdale, PA: Herald Press, 1976. 124 pp.

Ruth, John L. *Maintaining the Right Fellowship.* Scottdale, PA: Herald Press, 1984. 616 pp.

ME, BMC.

LARTEY, SOLOMOM DORME (September 12, 1898–August 3, 1969), 66th bishop of the **African Methodist Episcopal Zion Church** (AMEZ), was born in Christiansborg, Accra, Ghana, the son of Dorme and Amelia (Arhuma) Lartey. He was educated at the Presbyterian Mission School in Accra and majored in mathematics. As a young man he became a well-known accountant in the community and occasionally served as stated supply for Presbyterian churches. In August 1928, he moved to Liberia and after a few years became a naturalized citizen there.

Soon he was appointed Inspector of Internal Revenues, Treasury Department, of the Liberian government, then in 1932 became Accountant of the Bureau of Internal Revenues, serving in this position for fourteen years. In 1939, during the administration of Bishop **James Walter Brown**, he left the Presbyterian Church and joined the AMEZ Church. He was ordained elder in 1940 and made presiding elder also. Zion's work was previously limited to Montserrado County, and Lartey led the campaign to build the very first AMEZ church in Monrovia, Brown Memorial AMEZ Church on Benson Street, and served as its pastor for many years. During World War II he was the denomination's representative in Liberia. From 1946 to 1952 he was appointed bishop's deputy and oversaw the church's work in the bishop's absence. His first marriage, to Caroline Lewis, was dissolved and on September 12, 1945, he married Alicia Ethel Smith, daughter of the vice-president of Liberia, James S. Smith. The family eventually numbered eight children. He was known to have mortgaged his own property to raise $25,000 to advance the work of the church. In 1946 President Tubman of Liberia commissioned him as postmaster of the Monrovia Post Office, a post he remained at until 1960.

On the basis of this solid record, Lartey was consecrated bishop on May 15, 1960, the first native African to become bishop in the history of the denomination. He was assigned to the Ninth Episcopal District (Liberia, West and East Ghana, and the Federal Republic of Nigeria). He extended the work of the Mt. Coffee Mission to Sinoe County and built and managed Zion Academy in conjunction with Brown Memorial Church. He opened the Po-River Station where an institution was later built. He built the Cartwright Memorial AMEZ Church in Brewerville and several other churches and schools in Liberia and Ghana. He served as a trustee of Livingstone College in Salisbury, North Carolina and was chair of the International Justice and Goodwill Committee and the Worship and Ritual Committee of the church. He was on the executive board of both the World Methodist Council and the World Council of Churches. At his death the Liberian flags in Monrovia were flown at half-mast.

"Bishop S. Dorme Lartey: May He Rest In Peace." *Star of Zion* 92 (September 25, 1969): 4.
AMEZC, EWM, HAMEZC.

LASHLEY, JAMES FRANCIS AUGUSTINE, founder of the American Catholic Church, Archdiocese of New York (now known as the **Orthodox Catholic Church in America**), organized the church in 1927. Little is known of him prior to this date. In 1932 he was brought into the shadow of the **African Orthodox Church** when Bishop William F. Tyarcks, a White priest who had been consecrated by Archbishop **George Alexander McGuire** of the African Orthodox Church, laid his hands on Lashley and consecrated him to the episcopacy. At the time, Tyarcks had left McGuire and formed the independent American Catholic Orthodox Church. He served his small jurisdiction until his death in the mid 1980s, and was succeeded by Michael Edward Verra. During his career he had consecrated three men to the episcopacy—Verra, Sydney J. Ferguson, and Samuel T. Garner. Under Verra, the church adopted its present name.

Ward, Gary L. *Independent Bishops: An International Directory.* Detroit, MI: Apogee Books, 1990. 526 pp.

LATTER HOUSE OF THE LORD FOR ALL PEOPLE AND THE CHURCH OF THE MOUNTAIN, APOSTOLIC FAITH. A Pentecostal church.

The Latter House of the Lord for All People is a trinitarian Pentecostal church founded in 1936 by a former Baptist minister, L. W. Williams, who served as its bishop and chief overseer. The church grew out of a rich season of prayer in which Williams felt a spiritual enlightenment and spiritual blessing. Out of his experience the church began, with headquarters in Georgia. Among its unique doctrines is the use of water instead of grape juice or wine in the Lord's supper. There is also a belief that war is contrary to the expressed will of God, and members are conscientious objectors.

The present status of the church is unknown. In 1936 the church had six congregations and in 1947 reported 4,000 members. No sign of it has been reported in recent years.

LAVEAU, MARIE (1794–June 16, 1881), the great **Vodou** (or Voodoo) Queen of New Orleans, was born in New Orleans, the illegitimate daughter of Charles Laveau and Marguerite Darcantel. Little is known about Marie's childhood, and even an account of her adult life is difficult to separate from the legends which have grown up about her. She was raised Catholic and was a free person of color. In August 1819 she married Jacques Paris, also a free Black, at ceremonies officiated by the popular Roman Catholic priest Pere Antoine. For a short period the couple lived in the 1900 block of Rampart Street in a house given to Laveau by her father as part of her dowry. Yet only a few years after their marriage her husband vanished and was presumed dead. In order to support herself, Laveau, now called the Widow Paris, became a hairdresser. She later lived with and had fifteen children by her lover Louis C. Duminy de Glopion. Among them was her daughter, Marie Glopion, born February 2, 1827, who later played a significant role in Laveau's Vodou cult.

It is unclear how Laveau became involved in Vodou. The major folk religion of Haiti, Vodou was brought to America by Haitian slaves in the late 1700s. In its American setting it became a complex mixture of French Catholicism overlaying the African religion of the Ibos, Magos, and Dahomeans. Also integrated into New Orleans Vodou were the *root-man*, a conjurer who possessed magical healing powers; *gris-gris*, charms or potions for protection or to cross another; and ritual dancing to honor the snake god Zombi (or Damballah). Before the Civil War, Vodou was practiced secretly in various places. It was during the Emancipation period that this religion experienced a significant increase in popularity and became an organized secret society in New Orleans. Meetings were held at night and presided over by a king and queen. Elected to her position for life, the queen was the dominant figure in the ceremony. All we know is that by 1830 Laveau had become a Vodou queen. A number of Vodou queens "reigned" at any one time, but Laveau soon managed to oust her rivals (allegedly aided by the strategic use of gris-gris). By the mid-1830s she was the most powerful Vodou figure in New Orleans.

Vodou was one of the few ways for African American women to gain personal and economic power in a racist and sexist world, and Laveau used it effectively. Her beauty, charisma and theatrical talent, her business acumen, and her knowledge of personal secrets acquired during her years as a hairdresser helped propel her to prominence. In 1830, she acquired a house on St. Ann Street, a gift from a client whose son was acquitted from criminal charges following Laveau's intercession. Adjacent to Congo Square (today Louis Armstrong Park), the house became her base of operation until she died. Laveau transformed Vodou into a profitable business. Besides selling gris-gris and advice, she began charging curious Whites $10 to attend mass rituals she presided over at the riverfront. By 1850, when Vodou was at its height, the annual St. John's Eve celebrations at the banks of the Bayou had become large and show-like events. She also built Maison Blanche, a brothel near Milneburg that catered mainly to White men seeking colored women. Yet Laveau was socially involved in her community. She regularly visited the prisons to minister to Blacks on death row and spent years nursing yellow fever victims.

Laveau retired from her position as queen in 1869. While she no longer presided over rites and dances, she continued to exert considerable influence in the Vodou community. To a large extent this was because her daughter, Marie Glopion, who strongly resembled her, had gradually been taking over Laveau's functions in the cult. The substitution of the younger Marie added to Laveau's mystique of eternal youth and even immortality. Around 1875, the elder Laveau publicly renounced Vodou and returned to the Catholic church. Her daughter, however, continued to serve clients at the house on St. Ann Street and conducted ceremonies at the "Wishing Spot" near Lake Pontchartrain. Although the arrival of Jim Alexander, known as "Doctor Jim," a root-man with remarkable healing powers, provided her with stiff competition, Marie successfully carried on her mother's legacy until the late 1880s. When the Widow Paris died on June 16, 1881, her daughter continued to be known as Marie Laveau to many illiterate Black people and retained her power as supreme ruler over the other Vodou queens and witch doctors. The younger Marie Laveau is said to have died on June 11, 1897,

although many adherents of Vodou do not accept that date. The Vodou society, relatively unified and open under the leadership of the Laveaus, became fragmented and far more secretive after their passing.

Bodin, Robert. *Voodoo Past and Present.* Lafayette, LA: Center for Louisiana Studies, University of Southwestern Louisiana, 1990. 101 pp.

Martinez, Raymond J. *Mysterious Marie Laveau, Voodoo Queen, and Folk Tales along the Mississippi.* Jefferson, LA: Hope Publications, n.d. 96 pp.

Prose, Francine. *Marie Laveau.* New York: Berkley Publishing Corporation, 1977. 342 pp. A novel.

Tallant, Robert. *Voodoo in New Orleans.* New York: Collier Books, 1962. 252 pp.

Christel Manning

LAWLESS, ALFRED E., JR. (b. July 16, 1973), a Congregational Church minister, was born in Tribodaux, Louisiana, the son of Serena Ledet and Alfred Lawless, Sr. On May 19, 1892, he married Harriet O. Dunn, with whom he had three children. In 1895 he began a five-year tenure as principal of the public schools in Tribodaux. He entered Straight College (now Dillard University), New Orleans, from which he graduated in 1902. Two years later he was granted his B.D. He was ordained as a minister with the National Council of Congregational Churches (now a constituent part of the **United Church of Christ**). Shortly after graduation he founded Beecher Memorial Church in New Orleans and pastored it for the next ten years. While trying to organize Beecher, he also assumed duties at University Church adjacent to Straight College for a year (1904–05) and then in 1910 left Beecher to become University Church's full-time pastor. From 1904 to 1914 Lawless also served as the statistical secretary of the Louisiana State Conference of Congregational Churches.

Since the end of the Civil War, the predominantly Black Congregational churches in the South had been under the American Missionary Association (AMA). In 1914 the AMA reorganized the work into four districts. At the time of the reorganization, Lawless was selected as one of the field representatives to travel among the approximately 165 congregations, the majority of which had less than 100 members. He thus saw at first hand the changes wrought by World War I. As the war progressed, young men were pulled out of their communities to serve in the war, and immediately after the war, the exodus north began. The movement led to the closing of many of the churches and many of those that survived had no pastors and/or biweekly services.

In 1919 the work was reorganized again and a superintendent for the South who reported directly to the AMA was appointed. Lawless was selected. In spite of a reduced budget in the early 1920s, Lawless entered into his task with enthusiasm, and began to emphasize a program built around a modern interpretation of the teachings of Jesus. He encouraged the formation of women's groups and the extension of the church into neglected areas of life. He developed church school, stewardship, and evangelism programs. In 1924 he initiated the first Vacation Summer School programs. He actively enlisted young people for church work, and one of his recruits, Kathlyn Turrentine, would later become the first Black person appointed as a Church Extension Service worker by the denomination.

The last years of his tenure presented Lawless with an increasing number of problems. Evangelism was never able to compensate for the continued migration of members to the North. Then his health began to decline, and he was unable to contribute his energy to his work. The situation was helped when **Henry S. Barnwell**, one of the district superintendents, was called to Atlanta as an assistant. Lawless finally gave up all administrative duties in 1927, and Barnwell succeeded him. Among his last official actions was an address to the National Convention of Congregational Workers Among Negroes in Detroit, Michigan, in 1926. He lived to see the 1931 merger of the Congregational and Christian Churches but died a brief time afterward in Atlanta, Georgia, on September 9, 1931. He was buried in the cemetery adjacent to Dillard University.

Stanley, J. Taylor. *A History of Black Congregational Christian Churches of the South.* New York: United Church Press, 1978. 175 pp.

LAWSON, JAMES MORRIS, JR. (b. September 22, 1928), civil rights activist and prominent United Methodist minister, was born in Uniontown, Pennsylvania, the son of James Morris and Philane May (Cover) Lawson. His father was a militant United Methodist minister who had once worn a .38–caliber pistol on his hip while pastoring in the South, founding N.A.A.C.P. and Urban League chapters where none existed. Though his father was not a pacifist, even as a young man growing up in Ohio, Lawson was drawn to the vision of nonviolence he saw depicted in the New Testament. He committed himself to the Methodist ministry and received a local preacher's license in 1947, the year he graduated from high school.

He enrolled in the mostly White, Methodist-related Baldwin-Wallace College in Berea, Ohio, and maintained his activity in church programs. In 1948–49 he was chair of the National Methodist Youth Fellowship Commission, and in 1950–51 was a fieldworker for the International Christian University of Japan. He served as pastor of Turner Chapel Methodist Church from 1950 to 1951. At the college he became acquainted with the campus chapter of the Fellowship of Reconciliation, America's oldest pacifist organization. He became convinced that nonviolent resistance was the most effective and Christ-like means of combatting injustice, and joined the group. He was soon faced with a test of his beliefs. The draft was in force for the Korean War, and although he could easily have obtained a clergy deferment, he chose to not cooperate with the system. Some Blacks had called for a boycott of the draft until the military's policies of racial segregation were ended, and Lawson's objections to the military in itself only made the issue more clear. In 1951 he was sentenced to three years in prison for violation of the Selective Service Act, and ended up serving thirteen months before being paroled. He managed to graduate with his B.A. in 1952, and sought a missionary position in Africa. None was available, and he became director of athletics and campus minister at Hislop College in Nagpur, India, for three years.

He was still in India when he read of the Montgomery bus boycott, and was ecstatic that the day of organized resistance to racism had finally arrived. He returned to the United States in 1956 and enrolled in Oberlin's School of Religion in Ohio, but soon became impatient with theory rather than action. A dinner conversation with **Martin Luther King, Jr.** and the school desegregation crisis of 1957 galvanized him to drop out of school in the winter of 1957–58 and gain a position as southern secretary for the Fellowship of Reconciliation (F.O.R.). He opened an office in Nashville and worked with **Ralph Abernathy** of the Montgomery bus boycott and Glenn Smiley, a White minister from Texas. The team held seminars and workshops on nonviolence on campuses throughout the South. They used as a main text *The Power of Nonviolence* by Richard B. Gregg, a study of Gandhi's methods revised with a chapter on the Montgomery movement and an introduction by King.

In the fall of 1958 Lawson enrolled in Vanderbilt Divinity School to continue his studies, and pursued his F.O.R. duties part time. On July 3, 1959, he married Dorothy Dolores Wood, with whom he had three sons. In November 1959, he led a handful of divinity students in a series of lunch counter sit-ins in Nashville. These were low-key, non-confrontational events which did not receive the publicity given the Greensboro, North Carolina lunchcounter sit-ins two months later, which were credited with starting the sit-in movement. Lawson stepped up his sit-in encounters on February 13, 1960, bringing 100 divinity students to rush-hour lunch counters at the Woolworth, Kress, and McClellan department stores. After two Saturdays of simply closing the counters, arrests began on February 27, but by then there were 500 volunteers, far beyond the capacity of the jails.

White outrage at the incidents was directed against Lawson, and pressure was put on Vanderbilt to expel him. When this was done, even more support for the movement was created, as the dean and fourteen of the sixteen professors of the Divinity School resigned in protest of the expulsion. National attention was then focused on the issue and in this larger context Vanderbilt was forced to reinstate Lawson and urge the community to accept integration. Energized by this concrete example of the power of nonviolent resistance, Lawson and others organized the Student Nonviolent Coordinating Committee (S.N.C.C.) to extend nonviolent action to other locations in the South. At the founding convention in Raleigh, North Carolina, in the spring of 1960, Lawson delivered the opening speech. Instead of then taking the leadership position, as expected, he chose to finish his degree, but remained an official advisor until 1964. Boston University School of Theology agreed to honor his previous work and gave him the S.T.B. degree in 1960 after a summer's residence.

Later in 1960 he took an appointment at Scott Methodist Church in Shelbyville, Tennessee, where he led in the construction of a new building. In 1962 he was moved to Centenary Methodist Church in Memphis, a large and historic Black congregation. He joined the local N.A.A.C.P. and urged it to join him in more demonstrations, but it was largely unwilling to take that step. Instead he helped Martin Luther King, Jr. as a staff member with the **Southern Christian Leadership Conference** (S.C.L.C.), helping train volunteers for Birmingham actions. Back in Memphis, he organized 600 demonstrators against public school segregation inequities and became chair of the Memphis Area Project—South, a part of the federal war on poverty, finding jobs for many of the unemployed.

On February 12, 1968, 1,300 Memphis garbage collectors went on strike for better pay and recognition of their union. Thanks to prejudicial actions by the mayor and police, the racial aspects of the situation became clear, and the Black community rallied in protest as never before. Businesses were targeted for boycott and money was raised in the churches for the union. When union officials were prohibited by the courts from participating in strike activities, the clergy took their

place, with Lawson as the major spokesman and chair. He brought in leaders such as Roy Wilkins, Bayard Rustin, and King to rally the crowds and focus national attention. King led a march of 5,000 on March 28, 1968, which was turned violent by the presence of fringe groups that thought violence was the only way toward effective change. Despite these problems the strikers soon won their points. On the evening before King's assassination, he called Lawson "the leading theorist and strategist of nonviolence in the world."

When King was assassinated in Memphis the following month, Lawson formed a new organization, Community on the Move for Equality, designed to keep the movement going and systematically create an atmosphere for widespread progress. In 1968 he began many years as a member of the Church and Society Commission of the World Council of Churches, and remained Southern Region Field Secretary for the Fellowship of Reconciliation until 1969. In 1969 he began many years as a member of the Theological Committee of the National Committee of Negro Churchmen (now the **National Conference of Black Churchmen**), and from 1968 to 1971 was chair of **Black Methodists for Church Renewal**.

In 1974 he left Memphis to be senior minister of the prestigious Holman United Methodist Church in Los Angeles, California, the largest United Methodist Church in that metropolitan area with, at that time about 2,100 members and currently with about 2,700 members. In 1977, as part of an effort to reopen the investigation into King's assassination, Lawson entered into correspondence with James Earl Ray, the man convicted of the killing, eventually meeting both him and his girlfriend, Anna Sandhu. On October 13, 1978, he performed the wedding for them at the Brushy Mountain State Prison in Tennessee. This brought national headlines and an interview on "Good Morning, America." Although many were surprised that a Black person would willingly perform such a service for Ray, Lawson explained that it was part of his Christian ethic to care for sinners as well as saints, and that he believed Ray was innocent of this particular crime anyway. Lawson has remained at Holman United Methodist Church to the present time, taking a leading role in social justice issues in the community and in the denomination.

Young, A. S. Doc. "Why a Black Minister Married James Earl Ray." *Sepia* 28 (January 1979): 63–66.
WWABA (92–93), *IBAW, NPT, WWMC, BDNM* (75), *BPL*.

LAWSON, ROBERT CLARENCE (May 5, 1883– July 2, 1961), founder of the **Church of Our Lord**

Jesus Christ of the Apostolic Faith, was born in New Iberia, Louisiana. His parents passed away when he was still a child and he was reared by his aunt, Peggy Frazier. He left home in his teen years to pursue a nightclub singing career. In Indianapolis in 1913, at the age of thirty, he was stricken with tuberculosis, a fatal disease at the time. He was healed and converted by a woman member of an Apostolic Faith congregation.

He soon joined **Garfield T. Haywood**'s church in Indianapolis, Indiana, part of the **Pentecostal Assemblies of the World** (PAW), of which Haywood was the first presiding bishop. Lawson became a minister of the PAW and established congregations in St. Louis, Missouri, and San Antonio, Texas. He married Carrie Fields, with whom he had four children, and settled down at a church in Columbus, Ohio.

In 1919 he left the PAW over several issues, particularly divorce. Haywood was more lenient in the matter of divorce than Lawson, allowing for it on occasion, especially if the divorce occurred prior to a Christian conversion. Haywood accepted women ministers, but Lawson did not. Lawson moved to New York City in July 1919, where he founded the Refuge Church of Our Lord, the mother church of the Church of Our Lord Jesus Christ of the Apostolic Faith, which name was officially adopted in 1933. In 1923 Lawson began a radio ministry and founded the R. C. Lawson Institute in Southern Pines, North Carolina. Soon he had opened funeral homes, a day care center, a book store, a realty firm, a record store, a grocery, and a small publishing company which printed the church's periodical, *Contender for the Faith*. In 1926 he founded the Church of Christ Bible Institute.

Over the years the church grew steadily, and in 1935 began international outposts in the Caribbean. In August, 1945 the mother church in New York moved into new quarters in a refurbished theater. By 1949 he claimed to have baptized over 40,000 people. His first wife passed away on August 2, 1948, and in 1951 he married Evelyn Burke. He adopted an African daughter, Meatta, in 1949, and adopted another daughter, Japthahlyn, in 1951. In 1954 Lawson received the Star of Ethiopia from Emperor Hailé Selassié. His last years were marred by a 1957 schism, which took part of the membership away to form the **Bible Way Church of the Lord Jesus Christ World Wide**, and by trouble with New York City housing authorities. In 1959 an agent of Lawson's was fined $525 for violations of the multiple dwelling law in a building Lawson owned on West 124th Street. The problems were not corrected, and at the time of his death a warrant was out for Lawson's arrest. In 1961 the church claimed 70,000 members in 125 churches in the United States, West Africa, the Dominican Republic, the West Indies, and London. Lawson was succeeded by **Hubert Spencer**.

"Top Radio Ministers." *Ebony* 4 (July 1949): 56–61.
Lawson, R. C. *The Anthropology of Jesus Christ Our Kinsman.* New York: Church of Christ, n.d.
NYTO, BH, RLOA, BAW, HUBA, AARS, BDA-AHP.

LAYNE, AUSTIN AUGUSTINE (April 2, 1891–1967), a bishop of the **Pentecostal Assemblies of the World** (PAW), pioneered the Assemblies' work in St. Louis, Missouri. Layne was born on the island of Barbados in the West Indies. He later moved to New York City where he found salvation at King's Chapel under the ministry of Mother Susan G. Lightford, the pastor, an early Pentecostal minister in New York. He married, and he and his wife Selena had eight children. He was called to the ministry in 1914 and later accepted the non-Trinitarian Apostolic theology which became distinctive of the Pentecostal Assemblies of the World after its first articulation in 1915. While in New York he attended Columbia University and later moved to Chicago for a brief period to attend Moody Bible Institute. Around 1918 he moved to St. Louis where he founded the Temple Church of Christ, which he pastored for the rest of his life.

Through the years he served as a district elder and as chairman of the Midwestern District Council. He remained a member of the PAW during the 1930s when the majority of Black members went into union with the former White members of the PAW in the short-lived integrated organization, the Pentecostal Assemblies of Jesus Christ. He drafted the letter welcoming the schismatic brethren back to the PAW in 1937, when the majority of them returned. He was elected to the bishopric in 1950. In 1951 he was assigned to the Missouri-Southern Illinois diocese which he served for 27 years. A strong supporter of the National Pentecostal Young Peoples Union, he served as auxiliary bishop for the union after his elevation to the episcopacy.

Golder, Morris E. *The Bishops of the Pentecostal Assemblies of the World.* Indianapolis, IN: The Author, 1980. 69 pp.
———. *History of the Pentecostal Assemblies of the World.* Indianapolis, IN: The Author, 1973. 195 pp.

LAYTEN, MRS. S. WILLIE (? –January 14, 1950), the first president of the Women's Convention Auxiliary of the **National Baptist Convention, U.S.A., Inc.** (N.B.C.U.S.A.), was elected to that position at the formation of the Auxiliary in September 1901. She held that position until 1948, and during that time firmly established the work of women within the life of the N.B.C.U.S.A. Among other things, the Women's Convention Auxiliary supported the pioneering National Training School for Women run by **Nannie Helen Burroughs**.

SCA.

LEAKE, GEORGE JUNIUS, III (November 21, 1929–June 15, 1981), 75th bishop of the **African Methodist Episcopal Zion Church** (AMEZ), was born in Wilson, North Carolina, the son of David and Elsie Mae (Barnes) Leake. He graduated from Darden High School in Wilson and in 1950 entered the traveling ministry. He was ordained deacon in November, 1951, and elder on November 15, 1953. On September 7, 1953, he married Vilma Louise Dew, with whom he had two children. He soon enrolled in Livingstone College in Salisbury, North Carolina, and received a B.A. in sociology in 1957. He then entered the related Hood Theological Seminary and gained the M.Div. degree in 1960.

His first formal appointments were while he was in school, pastoring the church in Shelby, North Carolina, and the Pleasant Ridge AMEZ Church in Gastonia, North Carolina. In 1958 he was appointed to Durham Memorial AMEZ Church in Buffalo, New York. In 1962 he was moved to Little Rock AMEZ Church in Charlotte, North Carolina, where he stayed for ten years and made his primary reputation.

Deeply concerned about social injustices, he led the Little Rock church to acquire federal funding for the construction of 240 apartments for low income housing. In 1966–67 he was a consultant to the City of Charlotte Redevelopment Committee. In 1966 he ran for a seat in the North Carolina House of Representatives, and in 1969 ran for mayor of Charlotte. He was well known for courageous leadership given during the difficult days of school desegregation. From 1968 to 1972 he was director of a job motivation program called Opportunities Industrialization Center (O.I.C.).

On May 12, 1972, he was consecrated bishop, the ninth youngest bishop in the history of the denomination. He was assigned to the Eleventh Episcopal District (Missouri, Southwest-Rocky Mountain, Colorado, California, and Cape Fear Conferences), where he remained the rest of his career. His community involvement did not slow down, and in 1973 he helped found Pride, Inc., a counseling firm for helping Blacks find better jobs and encouraging businesses to hire them. In 1974 he founded Innovative and Concentrated

Approaches to Combating Drug Use, Inc., which recruited alcoholics to receive treatment. In the denomination he filled many roles, and organized the Alaska Conference. On January 8, 1981, he was in a serious car accident, and when he was released from the hospital in February, it seemed as though all would be well. On June 14, however, he had to be readmitted to the hospital for heart surgery, from which he did not recover, and his bright career was cut tragically short.

"Bishop George J. Leake, III." *Star of Zion* 105 (July 2, 1981): 4, 5.
"Bishop Leake Remains Hospitalized." *Star of Zion* 105 (January 22, 1981): 1.
Buie, George C. "A Tribute to Bishop George J. Leake, III." *A.M.E. Zion Quarterly Review* 93 (October 1981): 44.
"Death of Bishop George J. Leake Leaves Church in Mourning." *Star of Zion* 105 (June 25, 1981): 1.
Satterwhite, John H. "Bishop George Junius Leake III." *A.M.E. Zion Quarterly Review* 93 (June 1981): 52.
AMEZC.

LEE, BENJAMIN FRANKLIN (September 18, 1841–1926), 20th bishop of the **African Methodist Episcopal Church** (AME), was born in Gouldtown, New Jersey, the son of Abel and Sarah (Gould) Lee. His father died when he was only ten, and he was then placed with a relative. His mother was a schoolteacher who assisted him in gaining a solid early education. He stopped attending school when he was fourteen and worked full-time in farms and mills in Cumberland County, New Jersey, until age twenty-three. In 1862 he experienced conversion and joined the AME Church. In 1864, he left New Jersey to seek an education.

In November 1864 he enrolled at Wilberforce University in Xenia, Ohio, as a night student. He became a regular student in 1865, and that same year had a second conversion experience. He supported himself by working in the stables and doing other tasks on neighboring farms. While a student he was licensed to preach in 1868, ordained deacon in 1870, and ordained elder in 1872. He served churches in Lebanon, Salem, Springfield, Marietta, and Toledo, all in Ohio; and churches in Bridgewater and Williamsport, Pennsylvania. He graduated from Payne Theological Seminary at Wilberforce in 1872 and on December 30, 1872, married Mary E. Ashe, with whom he had nine children, only four of whom survived into adulthood. After graduation he was appointed to mission stations in Danville and Frankfort, Kentucky. He was appointed professor of pastoral theology and church history at Wilberforce in 1873, and in 1876 succeeded Bishop

Daniel Payne as president of Wilberforce University. In 1880 he published his major writing, *Wesley, the Worker*. In 1881 he was a delegate to the Ecumenical Methodist Conference in London. In 1883 he was elected editor of the *Christian Recorder*, a position he held until 1892, when he was elected bishop.

As bishop he served the Tenth Episcopal District (British Columbia, Louisiana, and the Western states) from 1892 to 1896; the Third District (Ohio, Pittsburgh, Demerara, Ontario, and St. Thomas) from 1896 to 1900; the Twelfth District (Baltimore, Virginia, North Carolina) from 1900 to 1904; the Seventh District (Arkansas and Tennessee) from 1904 to 1908; the Second District (South Carolina) from 1908 to 1912; the Fourth District from 1912 to 1916; and the Ninth Episcopal District (Alabama and Tennessee) until 1924. He was secretary of the Council of Bishops from 1906 to 1915, when he became senior bishop.

In 1911 he organized the Palmetto, South Carolina Conference, and was a delegate to the Ecumenical Methodist Conferences again in 1901 and 1911. He was the first bishop of the church to visit Demerara, South America, in 1899. In 1924 he was the first bishop to that point to retire voluntarily. Named for him are the B. F. Lee Theological Seminary in Jacksonville, Florida, and churches in Ohio, Arkansas, Louisiana, Tennessee, and Texas.

Lee, Benjamin Franklin. *Some Statistics of the AME Church, 1916*. Xenia, OH: Aldine Publishing House, 1916. 24 pp.
————. *Sketch of the History of Wilberforce University*. Xenia, OH: n.p., 1884. 16 pp.
————. *Wesley, the Worker*. 1880.
IBAW, HUBA, AARS, BAW, IBAWCB, MM, AAE,HAMEC, EWM, DAA, NCAB (5), *NNW, WWCR, BAMEC, CEAMEC, TCBD, ACAB, WWWA* (1).

LEE, JARENA (February 11, 1783–c.185?), the first woman licensed to preach in the **African Methodist Episcopal Church** (AME), was born in Cape May, New Jersey. At the age of seven she became a household servant some sixty miles away from her family. She had no religious training, yet often during her growing up years she felt trapped by sin. In 1804, when she was about twenty-one, she was profoundly moved by a Presbyterian missionary, but became so distraught that a few days later contemplated suicide. She did not attempt it, but her emotional condition reduced her to a sickbed for three months. Having recovered, but still spiritually seeking, she moved to Philadelphia for another housekeeping job and soon joined the Methodists after hearing the preaching of **Richard Allen**, who would found the AME Church in 1816. She experienced conversion three weeks after joining the Methodists on trial.

Still, however, for four years thereafter she struggled with depression and was again tempted toward suicide. A conviction of being justified by God, capped by baptism, broke this emotional state, and about six months later she experienced the gift of complete sanctification. For about four years afterwards she continued in her life, a stalwart member of the African Methodist Society in Philadelphia. She then had a vision which so clearly told her to preach that she was compelled to visit Richard Allen and ask permission for a preacher's license. He denied her request on the basis that the Methodist *Discipline* did not allow women preachers, and she accepted this judgment for the time being.

Shortly after this time, in 1811, she married Joseph Lee, a pastor of the African Methodist Society in Snow Hill, about six miles from Philadelphia. The following years were hard on her; she was in a new community and unable to preach as she desired, and only occasionally was allowed to exhort. In addition, four members of her family died during that time, and her husband also passed away in about 1818, leaving her alone with a two-year-old and six-month-old. For a time, now-Bishop Allen gave her permission to hold prayer services in a home and exhort freely. In about 1819, during a worship service at Bethel AME Church in Philadelphia, she felt compelled to stand and give her own testimony, to declare that she, like Jonah, had fled from what God asked of her, and that she knew she needed to heed the call to preach. Bishop Allen was in the congregation and declared that he now knew she was as truly called to preach as anyone.

Lee began to hold services in homes around town, preaching with great effect. She soon dropped her regular job and became famous as a traveling evangelist in the Northeast. In 1827 alone she traveled 2,325 miles and delivered 178 sermons. She later described herself as "the first female preacher of the First African Methodist Episcopal Church," and is generally acknowledged to have been the first woman in the AME Church to be licensed to preach. Her death date is unknown; she published her autobiography first in 1836, and revised it in 1849. She was at that time about 66, and passed away in the 1850s.

Lee, Jarena. *Religious Experiences and Journal of Mrs. Jarena Lee, Giving an Account of Her Call to Preach the Gospel. Revised and Corrected from the Original Manuscript, Written by Herself*. Philadelphia, PA: Published for the Author, 1849. 97 pp.

SS, BWNCAL, BWR, IAAH, BAW, AARS, HUBA, IBAW, NBAW.

LEE, WILLIAM LEONARD (August 8, 1866–October 3, 1927), 36th bishop of the **African Methodist Episcopal Zion Church** (AMEZ), was born near Canton, in Madison County, Mississippi. He attained a basic education in a log cabin school and supplemented this with diligent study on his own, while working in the cotton fields and on the railroad. He joined the Middleton Grove AMEZ Church in Madison County in 1888, and joined the West Tennessee and Mississippi Conference the following year.

In 1891 he married Amelia Aurilla Dunn, with whom he had one son before her premature death. After serving several small charges, he was ordained deacon on November 12, 1893, and appointed to the Batesville and Coffeeville Circuit in Mississippi, followed by Monroe and Wadesboro in North Carolina. He was ordained elder on November 10, 1895. On September 19, 1900 he married a second time, to Nettie E. Tillman, with whom he had seven children. From 1904 to 1905 he was stationed at the Rock Hill AMEZ Church in South Carolina, and from 1906 to 1908 was pastor of the Wilmington AMEZ Church in North Carolina. In 1908 he was appointed to the large John Wesley AMEZ Church in Pittsburgh, Pennsylvania, and was very successful. In 1914 he transferred to the New York Conference to pastor the prestigious Fleet Memorial (First) AMEZ Church in Brooklyn, New York.

Lee was elected bishop on May 16, 1916, and consecrated on May 19. A very large man, he was known for his courageous leadership, his remarkable rise from humble beginnings, and for stressing the importance of a living wage for all pastors. He served as trustee of Livingstone College in Salisbury, North Carolina, and of Walters Institute in Warren, Arkansas. At the time of his death he had been assigned to the Fourth Episcopal District.

Allen, Cleveland G. "Bishop W. L. Lee's Funeral." *Star of Zion* 51 (October 13, 1927): 5.
"New Era of Zion Methodism." *Star of Zion* 48 (August 7, 1924): 1, 5.
Wall, William J. *The African Methodist Episcopal Church: Reality of the Black Church.* Charlotte, NC: A.M.E. Zion Publishing House, 1974. 669 pp.
HAMEZC, WWWA (4).

LELAND UNIVERSITY. A Baptist school. Leland College was founded in 1870 in New Orleans, Louisiana. It grew out of the education endeavors of Revs. J. W. Horton and Jeremiah Chaplin of the American Baptist Home Mission Society and Holbrook Chamberlain of the Baptist Free Mission Society. The school was named for John Leland, an early Baptist minister in the South and an ancestor of Chamberlain's wife. The school was created to educate Black ministers but soon developed a broad curriculum including a strong industrial department. Slowly the school passed into the control of the **National Baptist Convention, U.S.A., Inc**. The school survived through the Depression and World War II but in more recent years it has closed.

Fitts, Leroy. *A History of Black Baptists.* Nashville, TN: Broadman Press, 1985. 368 pp.

LeMOYNE-OWEN COLLEGE. A United Church of Christ school. LeMoyne-Owen College, Memphis, Tennessee, was founded in 1863 by the American Missionary Association. It was named after Julius LeMoyne. During the nineteenth century it specialized in the training of African American teachers, but in 1924 was able to add a junior college curriculum. In 1968 it merged with Owen Junior College, which had been founded in 1954 by the Tennessee Baptist Missionary and Educational Convention, affiliated with the **National Baptist Convention, U.S.A., Inc.**

Today the school is primarily supported by the United Church of Christ. It continues its emphasis upon teacher training and serves over 1,000 students annually.

LEWIS, FELIX L. (September 4, 1888–August 10, 1965), 23rd bishop of the **Christian Methodist Episcopal Church** (CME), was born in Homer, Clayborn Parish, Louisiana, the son of Henry L. Lewis and wife (name unknown). He grew up related to the Pleasant CME Church near Athens, Louisiana, and joined the church in 1894. He was licensed to preach in 1901 and joined the Louisiana Conference on trial in 1906. He finished the Normal Course at Homer College in Homer, Louisiana. In 1912 he married Della Elizabeth Dunbar; there were no children.

His first appointment was at Mays Chapel CME Church in Ruston, Louisiana, and had significant success. While there he attended the Ruston Normal and Theological Institute, working through the Theological Course. He later attained the B.S. degree from Wiley College in Marshall, Texas, and took courses at Garrett Biblical Institute in Evanston, Illinois. His church appointments included the Williams Memorial Temple CME Church and Lane Chapel CME Church, both in

Shreveport, Louisiana, and the Mount Pisgah CME Church in Memphis, Tennessee. He was presiding elder in the Louisiana Conference for fifteen years.

In May 1934, he was elected General Secretary of the Kingdom Extension Department and served in that office until elected bishop on May 7, 1946. He was assigned to the West Coast, where he is credited with reviving a disintegrating presence, reclaiming hundreds of members and buildings. In particular, the existence of Missionary Temple CME Church in San Francisco is due to his labors. He later served the Louisiana episcopal area, and retired because of poor health in January 1960.

Carter, G. H. "Death Claims Bishop Felix L. Lewis (Retired)." *Christian Index* 98 (August 19, 1965): 1.
CMECTY, EWM.

LIELE, GEORGE (c. 1750–1820), perhaps the first licensed African American Baptist preacher, was born into slavery in Virginia, to parents remembered only by their first names, Liele and Nancy. The owner, Henry Sharp, a Baptist deacon, took George Liele to Burke County, Georgia, in about 1773, where he was converted by a White minister, Matthew Moore, at the Buckhead Creek Baptist Church. He expressed the desire to preach, and the White Baptists licensed him to do so. He began to preach to various Black plantation audiences, including one at nearby Silver Bluff, South Carolina. There **David George** was converted and the second Black Baptist church in America was organized. He was ordained on May 20, 1775.

Sharp manumitted Liele just prior to the Revolutionary War; possibly as a pious man he wanted to give Liele more opportunity to preach. Sharp died as a Tory officer in 1778, and his heirs tried to reenslave Liele, finding him in Savannah. The intervention of British officials prevented this from being successful. For three years the British occupied Savannah, and Liele continued his preaching there, converting and baptizing many, including **Andrew Bryan**, who later was able to organize what became known as the First Bryan Baptist Church of Savannah. Liele also baptized his own wife in Savannah. Because of this work, Liele is claimed as the founder of both today's First African Baptist Church of Savannah and the First Bryan Baptist Church.

When the British pulled out of Savannah in December 1782, Liele joined them, and paid his family's way to Jamaica by becoming an indentured servant to Colonel Kirkland. He arrived in Jamaica in January 1783, and Kirkland bound him over to the service of General Campbell, Governor of Jamaica. He worked off his indentureship by 1784 and was a free man. He immediately began to preach, and the government permitted it, despite protests from parts of the Anglican Church. Beginning with four friends from America, he built a congregation in Kingston of 350 members, mostly slaves, by December 1791. At first he preached in the open air at the local race course; then a lot was obtained and a sanctuary was completed in 1793, on the corner of Victoria Avenue and Elletson Road. This was the first Baptist church for Blacks in Jamaica. He also founded a free school, and supplemented his living as a farmer and hauler of goods. His work in Jamaica made him the first Black missionary from the United States of any denomination. John Rowe, the first British missionary to Jamaica from the Baptist Missionary Society, did not arrive until February 23, 1814.

Although Liele was careful to permit the authorities to inspect all aspects of his ministry, and reportedly allowed no one to join without the permission of their owners, as leader of so many Black slaves he was suspect, and so was often persecuted. He was jailed about 1801 on the charge of preaching sedition. He was freed for lack of evidence, but soon jailed again for failure to make payments on his church building. He had to remain in prison until the full debt was paid. One prayer meeting leader was beheaded by White slave owners. In 1805 a law was passed against preaching to slaves, but it was not strongly enforced, and Liele's church work continued to flourish. At his death he was survived by his wife and four children, and Black Baptists since then have remembered him as a spiritual father.

Davis, John W. "George Liele and Andrew Bryan, Pioneer Negro Baptist Preachers." *Journal of Negro History* 2 (April 1918): 119–127.
Holmes, Edward A. "George Liele: Negro Slavery's Prophet of Deliverance." *Foundations* 9 (October–December 1966): 333–345.
Clarke, John. *The Voice of Jubilee, A Narrative of the Baptist Mission, Jamaica, from the Commencement, With Biographical Notices of Its Fathers and Founders.* London: J. Snow, 1865. 359 pp.
Gayle, Clement. *George Liele, Pioneer Missionary to Jamaica.* Kingston, Jamaica: Jamaica Baptist Union, 1982. 47 pp.
SNB, HBBUS, HBB, SCA, PBGB, HNC, ENB, PHNA, ERS, DANB, BPEAR, NYB (1925–26).

LINCOLN, CHARLES ERIC (b. June 23, 1924), author, educator, and a minister of the **United Methodist Church**, was born in Athens, Alabama, the grandson of Less and Mattie (Sowell) Lincoln. He grew up attending the Village View Methodist Church and drew strength from this association, which helped to sustain him through the trials of a racist society. At age nine, waiting to receive inoculations with other school children, he was angrily told, "All niggers have to wait!" At age thirteen he was beaten by the manager of the local cotton gin when Lincoln protested the unfair price being given for the cotton he and his grandmother had picked to pay for schoolbooks. At the age of sixteen he lost his after-school job when he editorialized in the school paper against the segregated seating in the school auditorium.

He received his B.A. in 1947 from LeMoyne College in Memphis, Tennessee, and did postgraduate work in law at the University of Chicago in 1948–49. In 1950–51 he was Director of Public Relations at LeMoyne College. He received his M.A. in 1954 from Fisk University in Nashville, Tennessee. That year he was ordained a Presbyterian minister, and pastored the John Calvin Presbyterian Church in Nashville from 1953 to 1955. From 1954 to 1957, while pastoring the church and then while working on another degree, he was assistant personnel dean and assistant professor of religion and philosophy at Fisk University. He received his B.D. in 1957 from the University of Chicago and the following year was ordained a Methodist minister. He has since remained with the (now) United Methodist Church, but disliked the local church ministry and decided instead to pursue the scholarly life. In 1958–59 he was resident chaplain of Methodist-related Boston University School of Theology while working on his final degree. He received his Ph.D. in 1960 from Boston University. He had two children by a first marriage, and on July 1, 1961 he married again, to Lucy Alma Cook, with whom he had two more children.

In 1961 Lincoln published his thesis as his first book, *The Black Muslims in America*, the first major work on that group and the originator of the term "Black Muslims." From 1961 to 1963 he was associate professor and assistant to the president of Clark College in Atlanta, Georgia, where he had taught for a time prior to his doctoral work. From 1963 to 1965 he was professor and director of the Institute for Social Relations at Brown University in Providence, Rhode Island. From 1965 to 1967 he was professor of sociology at Portland State University in Oregon, and from 1967 to 1973 he was professor of religion at Columbia University in New York City. In 1973 he returned to Fisk University as the head of its department of Religious and Philosophical Studies, where he remained for three years. He said that one reason for accepting a position in the South was to reverse the "brain drain" to the North. Another reason was his love of the open

country, and he bought a 21–acre cattle ranch that he renamed "Kumasi Hill" after the capital of the Ashanti Kingdom in Ghana. In 1976 he was appointed professor of religion and culture at Duke University in Durham, North Carolina, where he has since remained.

Since his pioneering first book, Lincoln has written or edited about twenty-one books and numerous articles. Included among the books are *My Face is Black* (1964), *Sounds of the Struggle* (1967), *Martin Luther King, Jr.: A Profile* (1970), and *Race, Religion, and the Continuing American Dilemma* (1984). In 1974 he published *The Black Church Since Frazier*, which grew out of the James Gray Lectures he presented at Duke University in 1970. Lincoln is viewed by many as E. Franklin Frazier's successor as the leading sociologist of African American religion. Frazier did not live to see the rebellions of the 1960s, and Lincoln points out the rebirth the Black church experienced as a result of those struggles for civil rights. His book, *The Negro Pilgrimage in America* (1967) was commissioned by the Anti-Defamation League of B'nai B'rith and became a standard training resource for human relations departments and commissions across the country.

During the 1980s Lincoln received grants from the Lilly and Ford Foundations to study the seven largest Black churches, resulting in his most recent book, *The Black Church in the African American Experience* (1990). This major work provides the most complete and up-to-date information on the Black church in America since the 1930s. Creative writing was Lincoln's first love, and in 1988 he published his first novel, *The Avenue, Clayton City*. He is a recognized poet as well: the United Methodist Church commissioned him to write a new hymn for its 1989 hymnal, and the result was "How Like a Gentle Spirit." 1989 also saw the publication of Lincoln's first book of poetry, *This Road Since Freedom*.

Lincoln, C. Eric. *The Black Church in the African American Experience*. Durham, NC: Duke University Press, 1990. 519 pp.

———. *The Black Experience in Religion*. Garden City, NJ: Anchor Books, 1974. 369 pp.

———. *The Black Muslims in America*. Boston, MA: Beacon Press, 1961. 276 pp. Revised ed., 1973.

———. *Is Anybody Listening to Black America?* New York: Seabury Press, 1968. 280 pp.

———. *The Negro Pilgrimage in America*. New York: Bantam Books, 1967. 184 pp.

———. *Race, Religion, and the Continuing American Dilemma*. New York: Hill and Wang, 1984. 282 pp.

IBAW, IBAWCB, OTSB, SBAA.

LINSEY, NATHANIEL L. (b. July 24, 1926), 39th bishop of the **Christian Methodist Episcopal Church** (CME), was born in Atlanta, Georgia, the son of Samuel Linsey and L. E. (Forney) Linsey. He received his B.A. from Paine College in Augusta, Georgia, in 1948, and his B.D. from Howard University School of Religion in Washington, D.C., in 1951. While in seminary he took his first pastorate on the Halifax Circuit in Virginia, from 1949 to 1951. In 1951 he married Mae Cannon Mills, with whom he had four children.

From 1951 to 1952 he was national director of Youth Work for the CME Church, and pastored the Walterboro Circuit (Rock of Ages and St. Peter's CME Churches) in South Carolina, from 1952 to 1953. In 1953–54 he was presiding elder of the Greenville District in South Carolina, followed in 1954–55 by the pastorate of Vanderhorst Memorial CME Church in Charleston, South Carolina. In 1955 he was assigned to the Mattie E. Coleman CME Church in Knoxville, Tennessee, and in seven years transformed it from a mission charge to a self-supporting congregation, adding over 300 members. He was president of the Knoxville Branch of the N.A.A.C.P. in 1957 and at one point was arrested with an Episcopal minister in Knoxville for refusing to move from an all-White line at a movie theater. He also led a prayer-march in Knoxville to break down the walls of segregation. From 1960 to 1962 he served on the Mayor's Bi-Racial Committee.

From 1962 to 1966 Linsey was appointed to the Thirgood CME Church in Birmingham, Alabama, and led the congregation in a relocation to a new facility, also purchasing a new parsonage. In Birmingham he was again arrested, this time with **Martin Luther King, Jr.**, for violating a federal injunction not to march on city hall. In 1966 he was elected General Secretary of Evangelism for the denomination, where he served for twelve years. In this capacity he founded Contact-Atlanta, a 24–hour phone ministry for the troubled, staffed by 175 volunteers, each with at least fifty hours of training. He also founded Power Pool, a personal growth group, and published "The Power Pool Guide." From 1974 to 1982 he was chair of the Board of Lay Activities for the CME Church.

On May 2, 1978, Linsey was elected bishop and assigned to the Ninth Episcopal District (Muskogee, Oklahoma; Arizona-New Mexico; North and South California; and Alaska-Pacific Conferences), with headquarters in Los Angeles, California. In 1984 he was president of the Southern California Ecumenical Council of Churches. His assignment for 1990–94 is the Tenth Episcopal District (Liberia; Ghana; Nigeria; and Lagos Conferences). He is a member of the World Methodist Council and chair of the Department of Evangelism, Missions, and Human Concerns for the denomination.

"Our 39th Bishop—Nathaniel L. Linsey." *Christian Index* 111 (May 11, 1978): 6.
WWABA (92–93), *WWR* (85), *BDNM* (70).

LIVINGSTONE COLLEGE. An **African Methodist Episcopal Zion Church** (AMEZ) school. The rapid expansion of the African Methodist Episcopal Zion Church in the years immediately after the Civil War created a demand for a denomination school to train ministers and church leaders. Through the quadrennium 1876–1880, the North Carolina Conference struggled with plans for a college and the problem of financial support. It was through the efforts of Bishop **J. W. Hood** and A. S. Richardson, finally able to open a school, Zion Wesley Institute, in 1879. The school was accepted by the denomination's general conference in 1880, but lack of financial support hindered it.

In 1881 a unique opportunity was posed by the holding of the meeting of the Ecumenical Methodist Conference (which assembled every ten years). The 1881 gathering was to be held in England, and Bishop Hood was one of the delegates. During the trip to London, he convinced **Joseph Charles Price** to present the cause of the school to the conference and remain in England to raise money for its support. He stayed a year and raised $10,000 with which the school was able to purchase land for a permanent campus in Salisbury, North Carolina. Price was elected president of the school, which reopened in the fall of 1882. In 1885 the school was renamed in honor of David Livingstone, the explorer.

The school made great advances under Price, who was able to secure some large gifts for new buildings. However, he died in 1893 after a brief illness. He was succeeded by W. H. Goler, who led the school for 23 years. Goler was able to obtain both a substantial grant from the Rockefeller Foundation and a Carnegie Library for the school.

Livingstone quickly moved into a position as one of the leading African American schools in the South and its graduates were soon being accepted in graduate and professional schools. It continues to serve the denomination and the African American community. In 1903 a theological school was started at the college which later became Hood Theological Seminary.

Wall, William J. *The African Methodist Episcopal Zion Church: Reality of the Black Church.* Charlotte, NC: AMEZ. Publishing House, 1974. 669 pp.

LOGUEN, JERMAIN WESLEY (c.1813–September 30, 1872), 13th bishop of the **African Methodist Episcopal Zion Church** (AMEZ), was born near Nashville in Davidson County, Tennessee. His mother, originally called Jane, had been born free in Ohio but was kidnapped at age seven and sold into slavery to a Tennessean, David Loguen, who ran a whisky distillery. This man became Loguen's father, but after a few years sold both him and his mother, now known as Cherry, to a brother named Manasseth, who treated them with much brutality. In about 1834 Loguen escaped with two others and, with the help of some Quakers, made his way to Hamilton, on Lake Ontario, Canada, where he found work as a farmer and learned to read.

In the fall of 1837 he left Canada and found a job as a porter at the Rochester House in Rochester, New York. In about 1839 he enrolled at the Oneida Institute in Utica, New York, and remained as a student for three years. He supported himself by opening a school for Black children. In November 1840 he married Caroline Storum, with whom he had two daughters. About this time he discovered the Colored People's Church (AMEZ) in Utica, and joined. In 1841 he began preaching for the AMEZ Church. By this time he had added an "n" to his last name to better suit his taste, and showed his Methodist allegiance by adding Wesley as his middle name. He was popularly known as "Jarm." He joined the New York Conference in May 1842, was ordained deacon on May 21, 1843, and elder on May 23, 1844.

After ordination he served AMEZ charges successively in Bath, Ithaca, Syracuse, Troy, and then Syracuse again, all in Central New York, founding a number of churches. In Syracuse he founded what was known as the Abolition Church. He soon gained the love and respect of a large number of the citizens of the region, and the town of Cortland, where he had preached occasionally, even employed a negotiator in a failed attempt to purchase Loguen's mother from slavery. Loguen often risked his life to rescue runaway slaves, and gained the title of "Underground Railroad King." His own home became known as the Underground Railroad Depot at Syracuse, and it has been estimated that he aided over 1,500 slaves to escape during his lifetime, including Harriet Tubman. He had a very close relationship with abolitionist Frederick Douglass, and his daughter, Amelia, married Douglass' son, Lewis.

The Fugitive Slave Law of 1850, requiring northern states to return escaped slaves, increased the threat to those freedom seekers and those who would assist them. In particular it threatened Loguen, a well-known escaped slave, but he refused to go into hiding, and instead redoubled his anti-slavery efforts. In October, 1851,

Loguen and several others used crowbars and a battering ram to break into the Syracuse courthouse and rescue a runaway slave named Jerry McHenry. Loguen was among those due to be arrested in the following days, and to prevent being returned to slavery he made his way to Canada. There he found refuge among friends from years past, and preached among them with great effect.

After a few months he returned to Syracuse to face whatever consequences might come. With thousands in Syracuse watching out for his well-being, he was never placed in jail, and the indictment against him was never tried. Several others were tried in Albany, but the jury failed to agree on a verdict. Another trial was arranged in Canandaigua, but again there was no settlement, and all prosecution was abandoned. This was a major victory for the Underground Railroad and its supporters, and soon thereafter an open advertisement appeared in the local Syracuse paper saying that Loguen had agreed to devote himself full time to the aid of slavery fugitives, dependent only on the contributions of friends of this work. Syracuse became the first "open city" for fugitive slaves, where by law these persons could not be seized or returned to slavery. In 1859 Loguen published his autobiography, *The Rev. J. W. Loguen as a Slave and as a Freeman: A Narrative of Real Life.*

He was consecrated a bishop on May 30, 1864, but when he discovered he was likely to be sent to a post in the South he resigned, thinking it too soon for an escaped fugitive to return there. He was reelected bishop at the next General Conference, and consecrated on May 29, 1868. He was assigned to the Fifth Episcopal District (Allegheny and Kentucky Conferences plus surrounding mission fields). In his native state he founded the first AMEZ church in Tennessee, the famous Loguen Temple AME Zion Church in Knoxville. In 1870 he was moved to the Second Episcopal District (Genesee, Philadelphia, and Baltimore Conferences). In 1872 he was assigned to the Pacific Coast, but died in Saratoga Springs, New York, before he could leave for his post.

DeSisti, Carolann. "The Rev. Jermain Wesley Loguen." *A.M.E. Zion Quarterly Review* 82 (Fall 1970): 138–157

Loguen, Jermain Wesley. *Correspondence Between the Rev. H. Mattison and Rev. J. W. Loguen, on the Duty of Ministers to Allow Contributions in the Churches in Aid of Fugitive Slaves and the Obligation of Civil Government and the Higher Law.* Syracuse, NY: J. E. Masters, 1857.

———. *The Rev. J. W. Loguen, as a Slave and as a Freeman: A Narrative of Real Life.* Syracuse, NY: J. G. K. Truair & Co., 1859. 454 pp.

———. *Samuel Joseph May.* Syracuse, NY: Journal Office, 1871. 75 pp.

Merrill, Arch. *The Underground, Freedom's Road, and Other*

Upstate Tales. New York: American Book-Stratford Press, distributed by Seneca Book Binding Co., 1963. 181 pp.

Miller, Basil William. *Ten Slaves Who Became Famous.* Grand Rapids, MI: Zondervan Publishing House, 1951. 71 pp.

BAW, HUBA, IBAWCB, DNAADB, AARS, IBAW, DAB, WWWA (1), *HAMEZC, AAE, DANB, OYHAMEZC, AMEZC, HNB.*

LOMAX, THOMAS HENRY (January 15, 1832– March 31, 1908), 20th bishop of the **African Methodist Episcopal Zion Church** (AMEZ), was born in Cumberland County, near Fayetteville, North Carolina, the seventh son of Enoch and Rachel (Hammons) Lomax. His grandfather, William Lomax, arrived in America with General LaFayette from the French Colony in Africa, and fought in the Revolutionary War. Lomax joined the Methodist Episcopal Church, South, at age fourteen. In 1850, at age eighteen, he enrolled in night school and learned to read and write. He helped build the first brick church in the AMEZ denomination in the South, in Fayetteville, and became a member. It was named Evans Chapel after **Henry Evans**, the pioneer Methodist preacher in the area.

At the end of the Civil War he and his brothers employed a Dr. Sanford to teach them privately, and he was licensed to preach in 1867. He was ordained deacon on November 25, 1867, and elder on December 1, 1868. His first appointment was to the Whitesville Mission, where he built a church. He organized and built churches at Flemington, Swamp, and Christian Plains, and reorganized churches at Shady Grove, Brown's Chapel, and Goose Creek. He was presiding elder for a year in the Cape Fear area of North Carolina, during which time he organized five churches in the Marlboro District just across the border in South Carolina. He then spent a year reorganizing the church at Laurinburg, North Carolina, followed by three years at the well-known AMEZ church in Charlotte, North Carolina. In Charlotte he added seven hundred members to the congregation and organized the Little Rock church.

At the 1876 General Conference Lomax was elected bishop, and was consecrated on July 4. Maintaining his residence in Charlotte, he was appointed to the mission field in Ontario, Canada, and organized the Michigan and Canada Conference on September 11, 1879, bringing twenty-eight congregations into the fold. In 1878 he was given another assignment and organized the Texas Conference, ordaining eighteen deacons and elders and bringing $18,000 worth of property into the connection. In 1880 he was appointed to the Seventh Episcopal District (West Alabama, Louisiana, and California Conferences), followed by the Fifth Episcopal District. During three years there he organized the Missouri and South Georgia Conferences. In 1892 he went to the Fifth Episcopal District, and organized the East Tennessee Conference, also known as the East Tennessee, Virginia, and North Carolina Conference. He was on the committee which selected the site for Livingstone College in Salisbury, North Carolina, and paid the first $10 on college certificates. He helped lay the first brick for the first dormitory, and then served as one of the trustees. He was known as an earnest preacher, honest beyond reproach, and an astute businessman. At the time of his death he was financially well-to-do.

HAMEZC, AMEZC, HAMEZCIA, NYTO, ACAB (supp.), *OHYAMEZC.*

LOMAX-HANNON JUNIOR COLLEGE. An **African Methodist Episcopal Zion Church** (AMEZ) school. What today has become Lomax-Hannon Junior College is the result of the merger of two separate educational thrusts begun by the AMEZ Church in the nineteenth century in Alabama. The first was initiated by Bishop **Charles C. Pettey** and the North Alabama Conference, who in 1890 moved to found a school in Tuscaloosa (the home of the University of Alabama). Jones University was named for AMEZ Bishop **Singleton T. W. Jones**. The school opened in December 1890 and, under the leadership of its first president David Williams Parker, within the first two years purchased its own property and attracted 175 students.

Meanwhile the East Alabama Conference also had hopes of creating a school and in 1889 appointed a committee. Active in planning the school were Bishop **Thomas H. Lomax** and presiding elder Allan Hannon. The school finally was opened in Greenville, Alabama, in 1893, the first high school in Butler County. In 1900 Jones University was merged into the Greenville school.

The high school greatly benefited from the lengthy tenure of **John Wesley Alstork**, elected bishop and assigned to Alabama in 1900. Alstork took a personal interest in the school. For most of those years he also served as president of the school's board of trustees. He mobilized the church members in the state to support the school financially, secured an additional 200 acres of land upon which it could grow, and upgraded its curriculum to that of a junior college. He left his home to the school in his will. During the remaining years of the century, the school has been served by a number of outstanding AMEZ leaders including presidents

Solomon S. Seay, who saw it through the difficult years of the Depression, and T. M. Patton, whose two terms as president lasted over 25 years.

Walls, William J. *The African Methodist Episcopal Zion Church: Reality of the Black Church.* Charlotte, NC: AMEZ Publishing House, 1974. 669 pp.

LOTT CAREY BAPTIST FOREIGN MISSION CONVENTION. A Baptist organization. The Lott Carey Baptist Foreign Mission Convention was organized in 1897 at the Shiloh Baptist Church, Washington, D.C. It is the only Baptist convention designed exclusively for foreign missionary enterprises. It is the result of a controversy within the National Baptist Convention regarding the primacy of foreign missions and cooperation with White Baptists. A significant number of delegates from North Carolina, Virginia, the District of Columbia, Maryland, Pennsylvania, New Jersey and New York withdrew from the **National Baptist Convention, U.S.A., Inc.,** in order to form the Lott Carey Baptist Foreign Mission Convention.

Rev. H. L. Barco, of Portsmouth, Virginia, led the delegation of Baptist leaders in formulating plans for the operational structure of the new convention. The convention elected Rev. P. H. Morris of Lynchburg, Virginia, to serve as its first president. Soon thereafter, Morris declined from serving the office and was succeeded by Rev. **Calvin S. Brown**. Further, the convention elected Rev. William Alexander, founder and developer of the Sharon Baptist Church of Baltimore, to serve as its first corresponding secretary. Rev. W. T. Johnson, pastor of the First African Baptist Church, Richmond, Virginia, was chosen as the first chairman of the executive board.

Having formulated the basic structure, the founding fathers of the Lott Carey Baptist Foreign Mission Convention proceeded with the development of a constitution. They were careful to develop a document that would provide for and maintain the foreign mission motif. The constitution was in part a protest against the practice of the National Baptists which, at that time, were using approximately 75 percent of these funds on operating expenses. Consequently, the Lott Carey Baptist Foreign Mission Convention's constitution required that no more than 25 percent of the total income could be used for operating expenses while the remaining 75 percent must be sent to the foreign fields.

Having manifested its commitment to an independent foreign mission enterprise, the Lott Carey Baptist Foreign Mission Convention proceeded to charter its course in the cooperative world mission of the Christian church. On August 31, 1900, President C. S. Brown called a meeting during the annual session held in Shiloh Baptist Church, Alexandria, Virginia, for the purpose of organizing an official woman's auxiliary to the new convention. This new auxiliary was especially instrumental in the enlistment of youth to work for the cause of foreign missions. In 1920, the young people of the convention were officially organized as the Junior Department of the Lott Carey Baptist Foreign Mission Convention.

The last group to be organized in the convention was the laity. In 1943, Deacon R. L. Hollomon of the First Calvary Baptist Church, Norfolk, Virginia, addressed the convention in Union Baptist Church, East Orange, New Jersey, and recommended that the laymen be organized to assist their ministers in carrying out the great objectives of the convention. His recommendation was adopted and the Lott Carey Laymen's League was officially organized. Each auxiliary made special contributions to the financial program of the convention.

The foreign mission enterprise of the Lott Carey Baptist Foreign Mission Convention has been remarkably widespread. Beginning missionary work in the Republic of Liberia (1897), the convention expanded its work into the following areas: Russia (ca. 1900), South Africa (1899), Zaire (1901), Haiti (1916), India (1926), Nigeria (1961), and Guyana, South America (1964). Currently, the convention is extending its work into Kenya, East Africa. One of the outstanding features of the convention's work in these foreign fields is the policy of using "nationals" to administer its foreign programs. This policy has been highly acclaimed by the political and church officials in these foreign countries.

Fitts, Leroy. *A History of Black Baptists.* Nashville, TN: Broadman Press, 1985. 331 pp.

————. *Lott Carey: First Black Missionary to Africa.* Valley Forge, PA: Judson Press, 1978. 148 pp.

Leroy Fitts

LOUISVILLE BIBLE COLLEGE. A **Christian Church (Disciples of Christ)** school. The Louisville Bible College was opened in 1873 by Winthrop H. Hopson, a minister with the Disciples of Christ and a former chaplain in the Confederate Army. His effort grew out of efforts of the General Christian Missionary Society of the Disciples to initiate schools for the Freedmen in the South. Hobson served as the chairman of the board of trustees, which hired a Black minister, Patrick A. Morse, as the teacher. There were twelve students the first year studying for the ministry. Unfortunately, the Disciples were unable to raise the funds to sustain the effort and after four years the school closed. In part, it fell victim to efforts to initiate work in Mississippi which many Disciples felt to be a more fruitful territory.

During its brief life, the school graduated a small number of students, among them H. Jackson Brayboy, the most well-known African American evangelist during the next generation.

Harrell, David Edwin. *The Social Sources of Division in the Disciples of Christ.* Athens, GA: Publishing Systems, Inc., 1973. 458 pp.

McAleister, Lester G., and William E. Tucker. *Journey in Faith: A History of the Christian Church (Disciples of Christ).* St. Louis, MO: Bethany Press, 1975. 506 pp.

LOUISVILLE CHRISTIAN BIBLE COLLEGE. A **Christian Church (Disciples of Christ)** school. Among several short-lived attempts by the Disciples of Christ to provide educational opportunities for African Americans in Kentucky in the nineteenth century was the Christian Bible College, the spiritual heir of the older Louisville Bible College which had briefly existed in the 1870s. It opened around 1886 in New Castle, Kentucky, under the leadership of J. M. Maimuring and J. Augustus Reed. It had the backing of key Kentucky Disciples such as J. W. McGarvey, but was able to sustain itself for only five years. It was forced to close in 1891. However, by this time the newly formed Board of Negro Education and Evangelism had been created by the denomination and the stock given to the new board which had located its headquarters in Louisville, Kentucky. Before the year was out it opened a school which it called the Louisville Christian Bible College. Adoniram Judson Thompson was named principal. The school prospered through the 1890s and was able to survive for a generation.

Harrell, David Edwin. *The Social Sources of Division in the Disciples of Christ.* Athens, GA: Publishing Systems, Inc., 1973. 458 pp.

Garrison, Winfred Ernest, and Alfred T. DeGroot. *The Disciples of Christ: A History.* St. Louis, MO: Bethany Press, 1948. 592 pp.

LOVE, EDGAR AMOS (September 10, 1891–May 1, 1974), a bishop of the **United Methodist Church**, was born in Harrisonburg, Virginia, the son of Julius C. and Susie (Carr) Love. He received his secondary education at the Academy of Morgan College in Baltimore,

Maryland, from 1905 to 1909. He received his B.A. in 1913 from Howard University in Washington, D.C., his B.D. in 1916 from Howard University School of Religion, and his S.T.B. in 1918 from Boston University School of Religion.

He was ordained a deacon in 1916 and assigned to Grace Methodist Episcopal Church in Fairmount Heights, Maryland. From 1917 to 1919 he was a chaplain in the U.S. Army. He served with the 368th Infantry and the 809th Pioneer Infantry, and fourteen months of his twenty-seven months of duty were overseas. From 1919 to 1921 he was an instructor at Morgan College and principal of its academy. From 1921 to 1926 he pastored John Wesley Methodist Episcopal Church in Washington, Pennsylvania, and on June 16, 1923 he married Virginia Louise Ross, with whom he had one son. From 1926 to 1929 he pastored the Asbury Methodist Episcopal Church in Annapolis, Maryland, followed by the Simpson Methodist Episcopal Church in Wheeling, West Virginia (1929–31) and the John Wesley Methodist Episcopal Church in Baltimore, Maryland (1931–33).

In 1933 Love became district superintendent of the Washington District, part of an all-Black annual conference, and remained in that position for seven years. In 1939 the Methodist Episcopal Church merged with the Methodist Episcopal Church, South, and the Methodist Protestant Church to form the Methodist Church. As part of the restructuring the nineteen Black conferences of the former Methodist Episcopal Church, regardless of location, became part of the Central Jurisdiction. From 1940 to 1952 Love was Superintendent of Negro Work for the Board of Missions and Church Extension of the Methodist Church. In June 1952 he was elected bishop by the Central Jurisdiction and assigned to the Baltimore Episcopal Area, where he remained for the rest of his career.

Love was active in the National Council of Churches, the Y.M.C.A., the N.A.A.C.P., and was president of the Methodist Federation for Social Action for ten years. He served a term as president of the College of Bishops of the Central Jurisdiction and was president of the **National Fraternal Council of Negro Churches**. He was vice-president of the Board of Evangelism and served on the General Commission on Chaplains and the Board of Christian Social Concerns. For a time he was on the Maryland Interracial Commission and in October/November 1954 he visited Methodist work in Malaysia. He was a trustee of Bennett College, Morgan College, Gammon Theological Seminary, Wesley Theological Seminary, and the Gulfside Assembly in Waveland, Mississippi. In June

1964 he retired to his home in Baltimore, but was called back to active service from November 1966 to June 1967, in the Atlantic Coast Episcopal Area. In 1968 the Methodist Church merged with the Evangelical United Brethren to form the United Methodist Church.

Love, Edgar Amos. "Role of the Church in Maintaining the Morale of the Negro in World Wars I and II." *Journal of Negro Education* 12 (Summer 1943): 502–510.

HUBA, AARS, WWMC, WWCA (38–40), *WWWA* (6), *BDNM* (75), *EWM*.

LOVE, EMANUEL KING (July 27, 1850–April 24, 1900), four times president of the **Baptist Foreign Mission Convention**, was born into slavery near Marion, Perry County, Alabama, the son of Cumby Jarrett and Maria Antoinette Love. His early life was filled with hard farm work, but he was so desirous of an education that after Emancipation in 1865 he obtained private instruction from various Whites on the farm and studied at night by torchlight. He was converted and baptized in July, 1868 and was soon licensed to preach. He entered Lincoln University in Marion in 1871, but dropped out after six months after he mastered most of what it had to offer. With his church's help he entered Augusta Institute in Georgia in November 1872, where he led all his classes and graduated in 1877. While in school he endured tremendous hardships, was often without food and money, and slept on a bench at night in the classroom.

He was ordained a Baptist minister on December 12, 1875, and served his church in Marion for six months, then returned to Augusta to finish school. Upon graduation he was appointed missionary for Georgia under the joint supervision of the American Baptist Home Mission Board and the Georgia Mission Board, both being White groups. On July 1, 1879, he resigned to be pastor of the First African Baptist Church in Thomasville, Georgia. In two years there he rebuilt the sanctuary and baptized 450 converts. On October 30, 1879 he married Josephine Carter Leeks.

From October 1881 to October 1885 he was supervisor of Sunday School mission work among the Blacks of Georgia, under the auspices of the American Baptist Publication Society of Philadelphia. He was very successful in this position, but left it on October 1, 1885, to pastor the First African Baptist Church of Savannah, Georgia, where he remained the rest of his life. This church competes with the Bryan Baptist Church in Savannah for the honor of being the oldest Black Baptist church in the United States. In any case the First African Baptist Church in 1885 was the largest Black church of any denomination in the country. It was suffering from severe internal dissension, but Love was able to reunite it and over the years increased the membership from 4,313 to 6,389.

Love was one of the founders of the Baptist Foreign Mission Convention, and served one-year terms as its president in 1889, 1890, 1891, and 1893. In 1892 he and the church hosted its national meeting. In 1895 this organization joined with others to form the **National Baptist Convention, U.S.A., Inc.** For many years, until his death, Love was president of the Georgia Negro Baptist Convention and was founder and editor of its periodical, the *Baptist Truth*. He was also editor of the *Centennial Record* of the Black Baptists of Georgia, prepared for the centennial celebration in 1888, and associate editor of the *Georgia Sentinel*, a Baptist paper based in Augusta. He published a number of works, the most notable being the *History of the First African Baptist Church, From its Organization, January 20, 1788 to July 1, 1888* (1888).

Love was intensely interested in higher education for Blacks and was instrumental in the founding of the Georgia State Industrial College in Savannah. He was also a founder in 1899 of Central City College. Although he was a regular writer for the American Baptist Publication Society, and felt affection for the American Baptists, he supported the National Baptist Convention, U.S.A., Inc. when it decided to sever those ties and create its own Black-run publication house. Upon his early death in 1900, Love was succeeded at the church by James Wesley Carr.

Martin, Sandy D. "The Debate Over Interracial Cooperation Among Black Baptists in the African Mission Movement, 1895–1905." *Journal of the Interdenominational Theological Center* 13 (Spring 1986): 291–303.

Love, Emanuel King. *A Christian Seeking Work*. Baltimore, MD: Weishampel, 1880. 12 pp.

———. *History of the First African Baptist Church, From its Organization, January 20, 1788 to July 1, 1888*. Savannah, GA: The Morning News Printing Co., 1888. 360 pp.

———. *A Sermon on Lynch Law and Raping Preached by Rev. E. K. Love, D. D., at First African Baptist Church, Savannah, Georgia, of Which He is Pastor, Nov. 5, 1893*. Augusta, GA: Georgia Baptist Printers, 1894. 19 pp.

SCA, MM, AAE, WWWA (H), *DAB, NCAB* (7), *BAW, AARS, HUBA, OBMS*.

LOVELL, WALTER RALEIGH (June 7, 1890–November 16, 1968), long-time editor of the *Star of Zion*, was born in Pilot Mountain, Surry County, North Carolina, the seventh of eight sons and four daughters in the family of Jesse and Lightford (Pace) Lovell. He was converted at age nine and joined the **African Methodist Episcopal Zion Church** (AMEZ) in Little Rock, North Carolina. He was licensed to preach on July 12, 1912, joined the Western North Carolina Conference in November 1914, was ordained deacon in 1915 and elder in 1917.

His pastorates in that conference included Bethesda and Huntersville (1914–1916), and St. John's Chapel and Hopewell (1916–1917), while he was also a student at Bennett College in Greensboro, North Carolina. In 1917 he transferred to the Blue Ridge Conference as pastor of the Varick Chapel in Asheville, North Carolina. Further appointments were at Union Mills and Swannanoa (1919–1921), and Black Mountain (1921–1922). During this time he was also a teacher, beginning in the public schools of Mecklenburg County in 1914, then on to Stevens Lee High School in Asheville. In 1921 he published a book of poetry, *Lyrics of Love and Other Poems*.

In 1922 he transferred to the California Conference and was assigned to the Cooper AMEZ Church in Oakland. His next appointment was at Kyles Temple AMEZ Church in Vallejo, California, from 1924 to 1928. There he married Coretha Maize Flack on June 7, 1926, with whom he had four children. From 1928 to 1932 he pastored in Portland, Oregon, while a student at the University of Oregon in Eugene. From 1928 to 1932 he was also secretary-treasurer of the Oregon-Washington Conference. From 1932 to 1935 he was a presiding elder, followed by four years at the prestigious First AMEZ Church in Los Angeles, California.

In 1939 Lovell was selected to complete the unexpired term of W. A. Blackwell as editor of the *Star of Zion*, the official organ of the denomination. Lovell remained in that position for most of the next three decades, the longest editorship in the history of the denomination. In this powerful post, through lectures, editorials, and frequent travels, he was a major shaper of opinion throughout the church. In early 1952 the Board of Bishops relieved Lovell of his position and appointed a committee in his place, stating that "a climate had arisen around the *Star of Zion* where such loose freedom obtained that the church and its officials could be easily attacked and libeled to the dismay of us all, high and low, and to our disparagement before the world." The 1956 General Conference, however, disregarded this judgment and by a large margin re-elected Lovell to the editorship, where he stayed for the rest of his life. His first wife having died, he married Hera Drusilla Blakey on March 8, 1963. He attempted to streamline the administrative functions of the church

by editing the "Lovell Series" of "Standard Report Forms for Use in the AMEZ Church."

"Obituary." *Star of Zion* 92 (January 2, 1969): 3.
Lovell, Walter Raleigh. *Lyrics of Love and Other Poems.* Asheville, NC: Inland Press, 1921. 46 pp.
HAMEZC, RLA, WWWA (5).

LOWERY, JOSEPH E. (b. October 6, 1924), United Methodist minister and president of the **Southern Christian Leadership Conference**, was born in Huntsville, Alabama, where his father and mother, LeRoy and Dora (Fackler) Lowery, ran a small store and poolroom. Lowery received his A.B. degree from Knoxville College in Tennessee and his B.D. degree from Payne Theological Seminary in Alabama, also attending a number of other schools. He supported himself as editor of a small newspaper in Birmingham, Alabama, called the *Informer* (now the *Mirror*). In March, 1947, he married Evelyn Gibson, with whom he had three daughters.

He was ordained into the Methodist Church, and in 1948 received his first pastorate, St. James Methodist Church in Birmingham, Alabama. This church was part of the Black Central Alabama Conference within the Central Jurisdiction of the Methodist Church, a segregated structure that was dismantled when the United Methodist Church was formed in 1968. In 1949 he moved to the Alex City Church, and from 1952 to 1961 was at the Warren Street Methodist Church in Mobile. In 1955 he received the Outstanding Citizen Award from the city of Mobile. In 1961 he moved to Nashville, Tennessee, where for three years he served as administrative assistant to bishop Charles F. Golden. In 1964 he was assigned to St. Paul's Methodist Church in Birmingham, and in 1968 he moved to Central United Methodist Church in Atlanta, Georgia. This pastorate has been very successful; some two thousand members were added and the church built a 240–unit housing complex called Central Methodist Gardens for low- and moderate-income families. In 1985 he was assigned to the Cascade United Methodist Church in Atlanta.

When **Martin Luther King, Jr.** and **Ralph D. Abernathy** formed the Southern Christian Leadership Conference (S.C.L.C.) in early 1957, Lowery was elected vice-president. The S.C.L.C. carried King's nonviolent civil disobedience tactics beyond the original Montgomery bus boycott to cities throughout the South, and Lowery was a key leader on many fronts. In Birmingham he exposed police brutality and led the fight to hire Black police officers, and helped elect the first

Black mayor of Birmingham. In Nashville he fought against discrimination in restaurants and hotels, and in Louisiana revealed the oppressive conditions on sugar cane plantations. In 1967 he was elected chair of the board of directors of the S.C.L.C.

In 1968, after the assassination of King, Abernathy took over the S.C.L.C., but the group fell on hard times. Abernathy resigned in February 1977, and Lowery served as interim president until officially elected on August 18, 1977. By that time the organization was $10,000 in debt and was down from 11,000 chapters to 400. Lowery attempted to regain support by a renewed activism, marching on issues in addition to courting political support. A turning point was a 1979 March in Decatur, Alabama, for Tommie Lee Hines, a retarded youth accused of murdering and robbing a White woman. The Ku Klux Klan opened fire on the marchers, wounding several and just missing Lowery and his wife. This galvanized support for protest, and a second march under police protection drew 4,000 marchers. Also in 1979 Ambassador Andrew Young was forced to resign after an unauthorized meeting with the Palestine Liberation Organization (P.L.O.), and Lowery responded by taking a fact-finding delegation to the Middle East and meeting with Yasir Arafat, head of the P.L.O. The results included tensions with Jewish leaders and a new international profile for the S.C.L.C. In 1984 *Ebony* magazine named him one of the one hundred most influential Black Americans, and also named him one of America's fifteen top Black preachers. He retired from the pulpit in June 1992, but has remained president of the S.C.L.C.

"America's Fifteen Greatest Black Preachers." *Ebony* 39 (September 1984): 27–33.

Harris, Ron. "Dr. Joseph Lowery: The Man Who's Reviving SCLC." *Ebony* 35 (November 1979): 53–56.

"The One Hundred Most Influential Black Americans." *Ebony* 39 (May 1984): 29–34.

BDNM (75), *WWR* (77), *WWMC, WWABA* (88), *IBAW, CB* (82), *NA, RLOA.*

LUTHER COLLEGE. A Lutheran school. Luther College, New Orleans, was opened by Rev. F. J. Lankenau, who had been called to New Orleans in 1891 to succeed Rev. N. J. Bakke as a missionary for the Synodical Conference, an early Lutheran ecumenical organization, within the Black community. He also pastored St. Paul's Lutheran Church. In 1903 he opened Luther College using the facilities at St. Paul's as an initial home. New facilities were constructed and opened the next year. With the help of two assistants, Lankenau established a high school, a normal school, and a theological seminary. The seminary was closed in 1910. Only one student, Calvin Peter Thompson, had finished the course. The school was closed in 1925 when the Synodical Conference concluded that Alabama was a more promising field of endeavor and it transferred the monies being used in New Orleans to Alabama Luther College.

Drewes, Christopher F. *Half a Century of Lutheranism Among Our Colored People*. St. Louis, MO: Concordia Publishing House, 1927. 111 pp.

LUTHERANS, AFRICAN AMERICAN. The Lutheran Church emerged as a reformist movement within the **Roman Catholic Church** of Germany in the sixteenth century. It spread northward into Scandinavia and emerged as the dominant state church in many of the several German states, Denmark, Finland, Sweden, Norway, and Iceland. Lutheranism began in what is today the United States with the establishment of a Swedish colony on the Delaware River in 1638. Later in the century, Lutherans joined settlers in New York and Pennsylvania, and in 1734 a group of Lutheran Salzburgers settled in Georgia. From these three centers, Lutheranism dispersed throughout the country. They would eventually come to dominate in the upper Midwest, roughly in a strip from Chicago across Wisconsin and Minnesota into the Dakotas.

At one time separated into over 100 synods, divided geographically and ethnically, by the 1990s, there were some 20 Lutheran denominations, with the overwhelming majority in two churches, the Evangelical Lutheran Church in America and the Lutheran Church-Missouri Synod.

Lutherans early came into contact with the emerging African American community and began to welcome them as members into the church. The very first person baptized in the Lutheran Church in New York City, when it was finally allowed to organize and call a pastor in 1669, was a Black man remembered today only by his Christian name **Emmanuel**. As the predominantly German church spread into communities north and west of the city, it gathered a diverse membership that included a number of Blacks, both slave and free.

Through the eighteenth century, an original antislave stance among the small band of Lutherans in the South slackened, and some Lutherans, including the Lutheran ministers, joined the ranks of the slaveowners. In 1803, the North Carolina Synod was formed. That same year the first baptism of African Americans, presumedly slaves, took place at Gibsonville and they became members of the Frienden's Lutheran Church. Six years later the North Carolina Synod authorized ministers to baptize slaves when their owners allowed, and the following years instructed them to baptize the children of slaves if the master agreed to see to their religious training. That a number of Black people had become members and that their presence had become a problem to some is indicated by the 1814 legislation ordering pastors to create a special place in the church buildings for Black members since it was inexpedient for them to sit among the White members. The following year a more detailed report was adopted which dealt with a wide variety of issues from marriage to the reception of communion.

Practices initiated in North Carolina were transferred to synods through the South as a Black membership emerged in the congregations. Slaves were catechized orally (as it was illegal to teach them to read and write). There were also a number of special rules for Black members, such as their being allowed to receive communion only at the church of their White master. These rules were made in spite of the strong presence of antislavery sentiments among Southern Lutherans (only a minority of whom owned slaves).

Notable among the White Lutheran ministers was John Bachman of St. John's Church in Charleston, South Carolina. He carried on a ministry to Africans in the city and discovered a capable young man by the name of **Daniel Payne**, whom he quietly tutored. He facilitated Payne's attendance at the Lutheran Theological Seminary in Philadelphia. Unfortunately, after Payne's graduation in 1823, the Lutherans had no position for him and he left to join the **African Methodist Episcopal Church** in which he had an extraordinary career as a bishop and college president. It would not be until after the Civil War that the church would make a place for Black ministers.

The Lutheran Church was a minority church in the South through the decade prior to the Civil War. By the time the War broke out, the Synod of Georgia (with only 312 total members) counted 54 African American members, and the Synod of South Carolina had 954 Black members. The largest number was in North Carolina, where over 800 slaves had been baptized between 1821 and 1865.

After the War. Following the Civil War, the Tennessee Synod was the first to react to the new status of the Freedmen. In 1866 it passed legislation recommending that independent Black Lutheran churches be formed and that Black ministers be ordained to serve them. That same year the Synod licensed Thomas Fry, the first African American Lutheran preacher. The North Carolina Synod followed suit in 1868 and licensed Michael Coble who proceeded to gather a congregation in the area of Concord, North Carolina. After 1868, the only organized work among African Americans in the South was to be found in North Carolina.

Coble, like Payne and many Lutheran lay people, later joined the Methodists, but his place was taken by others such as David Koonts. Koonts was first licensed to preach and in 1880 became the first ordained Black Lutheran minister. Two other men, Samuel Holt and Nathan Clapp, were ordained in 1884. In 1888 the Synod established the Committee on Work among the Freedman. Koonts sat on the committee, the first Black person to serve on a synodical committee among the Lutherans.

In 1889 the committee recommended the formation of an African American synod. The Alpha Synod was founded in May 1889 and Koonts was elected president. He was joined by three other pastors, Holt, Clapp, and W. P. Phifer. They served five congregations and 180 members. Unfortunately, Koonts died suddenly in 1890 leaving his three colleagues to carry on without him.

Meanwhile, the Synodical Conference, which had been founded by several Lutheran synods in the Midwest, decided to launch a mission to the Freedmen at its meeting in 1877. A mission board was selected and it commissioned John Frederick Doescher as a first missionary. Following a missionary tour of the south, he settled in Baltimore, awaiting the end of a yellow fever outbreak in New Orleans. The following year Frederick Berg was sent as a missionary to Little Rock, where he organized St. Paul's Colored Lutheran Church. Before the year was out he dedicated a chapel and opened a parochial school.

By the end of 1878, Doescher was able to move to New Orleans, where he had previously started a Sunday school that would grow into Zion Lutheran Church. He later began a second congregation, St. Paul's. New Orleans became a major center of the Freedman's mission and by the 1920s eight congregations had been founded. Single additional stations were added in Virginia and Illinois, but progress was slow. Then in 1891, the members of the Alpha Synod, having heard of the Synodical Conference's effort, petitioned it for support. After investigation, the conference sent Rev. N. J. Bakke to Concord to assist with the work. With synodical support, the old Alpha Synod became the center of a vital work which led to the founding of over 20 congregations during the next forty years. In 1903 Bakke opened Immanuel Lutheran College, as a theological-normal-industrial school, and settled into permanent quarters in Greensboro.

There was an unhappy result of Bakke's movement to North Carolina. He was unable to accept two of the three pastors of the Alpha Synod whom he found unable to write and unqualified to pastor. He forced Sam Holt and Nathan Clapp to resign. He also ran into trouble with the third pastor W. P. Phifer (who could read and write). Phifer broke with Bakke and took most of his congregation's members under the support of the Ohio Synod.

Apart from the Synodical Conference's work in North Carolina and New Orleans, work to evangelize African Americans and bring them into the fellowship of the different synods of the Lutheran Church was scattered and left to a few local initiatives. The next breakthrough came in Wilcox County, Alabama, where in 1912 Rosa J. Young had begun a small school. The school soon had more than 200 pupils, and then hard times hit the area. Young appealed first to the Methodists and then in 1915 to the Lutherans. Bakke was sent to investigate and eventually was appointed mission superintendent of what became a vital missionary outreach. Not only were more than 25 congregations started in the surrounding counties, but, in 1925, Alabama Lutheran College (now one of the campuses of Concordia College) was begun with an all-Black faculty in Selma, Alabama.

Through the Twentieth Century. Apart from the missionary work of the Synodical Conference, no systematic attempt to evangelize in the Black community was carried out by the several Lutheran synods. However, predominantly Black congregations did emerge, and by the time of the major mergers of Lutheran synods to become the American Lutheran Church and the Lutheran Church in America in the 1960s, a modest number of Black churches and pastors had appeared. As did African Americans in other denominations, African American Lutherans organized in response to the call for Black Power and the assassination of Martin Luther King, Jr. The Coalition of Black Lutherans was founded by Black leaders in the American Lutheran Church (ALC), and the Association of Black Lutherans was founded by leaders in the Lutheran Church in America (LCA). Following the merger of the ALC and LCA with the Association of Evangelical Lutheran Churches in 1988, the association and coalition merged to form the African American Lutheran Association in the newly created Evangelical Lutheran Church in America (ELCA). The association works with the Commission for Multicultural Ministries, an agency founded by the merging churches in 1987, to develop programs for African Americans and other ethnic groups to ensure their full participation in the life of the ELCA.

Anderson, Hugh George. *Lutheranism in the Southeastern States, 1860–1886: A Social History.* The Hague, Netherlands: Mouton, 1996. 276 pp.

Drewes, Christopher F. *Half a Century of Lutheranism among Our Colored People.* St. Louis, MO: Concordia Publishing House Print, 1927. 111 pp.

Eisenberg, William Edward. *The Lutheran Church in Virginia.* Roanoke, VA: Trustees of the Virginia Synod, Lutheran Church in America, 1967.

A History of the Lutheran Church in South Carolina. South Carolina Synod of the Lutheran Church in America, 1971.

Kreider, Harry Julius. *Lutheranism in Colonial New York.* New York: Ph.D dissertation, Columbia University, 1942.

Luecke, Jessie Rayne. *Twenty-Eight Years in Negro Missions.* Fort Dodge, IA: Joselyn Press, 1953. 85 pp.

Moore, Robert, Jr. *A Brief History of Black Lutherans in North Carolina.* Greensboro, NC: The Author, 1974. 15 pp.

LYKE, JAMES PATTERSON (b. February 18, 1939), the second African American archbishop of the **Roman Catholic Church**, was born in Chicago, Illinois, the youngest of eight children in the family of Amos and Ora (Sneed) Lyke. His father was a factory worker and his mother worked as a domestic. They lived in a public housing project in a neighborhood filled with violence and despair. His mother felt that he was not being challenged at the McGosh Grammar School, and though she was Baptist, enrolled him in St. George School when he was ready for the fourth grade. Lyke was the only child in the family to attend a Catholic school, and his mother paid for it by taking another job doing laundry for the St. George parish.

Within a year, Lyke was so enthusiastic about the school and the teachers that he insisted on being baptized, and soon most of the rest of the family was baptized as well. In high school he expressed an interest in becoming a priest and went to visit Rollins A. Lambert, a Black priest who was at St. Malachy Church in Chicago. Seeing a real African American priest convinced him that his vocational goal was possible. He went to St. Joseph's Minor Seminary in Westmont (now Oak Brook) Illinois, where he completed his last two years of high school and first two years of college. He then entered the Franciscan novitiate at Teutopolis, Illinois, and in 1959 took his initial vows and became Brother Seth.

Immediately after those vows he went to Our Lady of Angels House of Philosophy in Cleveland, Ohio, and earned his B.A. in 1963 through Quincy College in Quincy, Illinois. Already he was active in programs to educate for human rights and engage in social action. He got his fellow brothers involved in the Interracial

Home Visiting Program in the Black section (Glenville) of Cleveland. In 1963 he moved to the Theological Seminary in Teutopolis, Illinois, and later that year, on June 21, 1963, made his final Franciscan vows. In the summer of 1965 he and two White classmates went to Grambling State University in Louisiana to work in a Newman ministry. They became involved in the struggle for civil rights and as a result were ejected from public places, followed, and threatened. He also had to cope with the sudden death of his mother in 1964 and the lingering illness of his father, who died of cancer in 1966. In 1967 he received his M.Div. degree.

On June 24, 1966, Lyke was ordained a priest and assigned to the Padua Boys' High School in Cleveland, serving also at St. Thomas Aquinas Church on weekends. Among many other activities, he worked there with **Martin Luther King, Jr.**'s Operation Breadbasket, and helped organize the picketing of an inner city branch of a national supermarket chain. Feeling that King's assassination in 1968 held a message for his own ministry, that year he requested a move to the city where King's death took place. Lyke became associate pastor of St. Thomas Catholic Church in Memphis, Tennessee, and was promoted to pastor in January, 1970. He also administered the Father Bertrand School, the only experimental elementary school in the Diocese of Memphis. In 1971 he was elected superior of the Franciscan Friary, an office he held in addition to his other responsibilities until 1977.

In Memphis Lyke worked with other leaders to create a model African American Catholic parish. He remodeled the church to reflect African American interests and culture. The same was done with liturgical celebrations and in the innovative educational offerings. Community centers were begun to meet the needs of the neighborhood poor. Professionals in the membership were encouraged to provide free services and consultation. Lyke chaired a federally funded anti-poverty agency called MAP-South, and also headed the police committee of the N.A.A.C.P.

In 1977 he was assigned to pastor St. Benedict, the Black parish in Grambling, Louisiana, and to direct the Newman Center at Grambling State University. In May and June of 1979 he made a pilgrimage to Europe, especially Italy, the birthplace of St. Francis, and to Africa, the motherland of African Americans. From 1977 to 1979 he was president of the **National Black Catholic Clergy Caucus**. On June 30, 1979, the announcement was made of Lyke's appointment as Auxiliary Bishop of Cleveland, and he was consecrated for that task on August 1, 1979. He became the youngest bishop in the American hierarchy, and was specifically assigned to the Urban Region of the Diocese of Cleveland.

Lyke has served on numerous boards and agencies, and is a member of the National Urban League, a founding member of the Association for the Study of Afro-American Life and History, a member of the **National Black Evangelical Association**, Bread for the World, and Pax Christi, U.S.A. In the mid-1980s he was the coordinator of the three-year project which created *Lead Me, Guide Me* (1987), the first African American Catholic hymnal. In the summer of 1990 Archbishop of Atlanta **Eugene Marino** stepped down from his office because of a revealed affair with a woman parishioner, and Lyke became Apostolic Administrator, sede vacante, Atlanta. On April 30, 1991, Lyke was named the new Archbishop of Atlanta, and was installed on June 24, 1991. He is currently the nation's highest-ranking African American Roman Catholic.

"James P. Lyke, O.F.M." *America* 164 (April 13, 1991): 397–401.

"Lyke Installed as Atlanta Archbishop." *Jet* 80 (July 15, 1991): 30.

Poinsett, Alex. "A Poor People's Bishop." *Ebony* 35 (October 1980): 78–84.

Lyke, James P. "Black Liturgy/Black Liberation." *Freeing the Spirit* 1 (August 1971): 14–17.

BDNM (75), WWABA (90–91), OBS, IBAW, HUBA, WWA (90–91).

LYNCH, JAMES D. (January 8, 1839–December 18, 1872), Presbyterian, African Methodist Episcopal, and Methodist Episcopal minister and the first Mississippi Black man elected to statewide office, was born in Baltimore, Maryland. His father, Benjamin Lynch, had purchased his mother from slavery, and worked as a merchant and part-time **African Methodist Episcopal Church** (AME) minister.

Lynch grew up attending the Bethel AME Church in Baltimore, where legendary future bishop **Daniel Payne** was appointed in 1845. Lynch became one of the students in Payne's school, and when Payne was transferred away in 1852, Lynch continued his schooling at the Kimball Union Academy in Meriden, New Hampshire. His father's business failed in 1855, and Lynch had to leave school. He moved with the family to Jamaica, Long Island, where he taught school for a year. He came in contact with **Amos Freeman**, well-known African American minister of Brooklyn's Siloam Presbyterian Church. He became Freeman's assistant in 1858, and Freeman began to tutor him towards the ministry.

In 1859, perhaps anticipating Freeman's departure from Brooklyn the following year, Lynch moved to the Bethel AME Church in Indianapolis, Indiana, where the minister, Elisha Weaver, licensed him to preach and further developed his skills. He was soon placed as pastor of a small AME church in Galena, Illinois, where he met his future wife, Eugenia Rice. In 1860 Bishop Payne helped him transfer to the Baltimore Conference, where he was assigned to the Ebenezer AME Church in Georgetown, Washington, D.C. He was ordained deacon in 1861, and on September 2, 1862 he married Eugenia Rice. In 1862 he was assigned to the Waters Chapel AME Church in Baltimore, a church struggling with heavy debt. By this time he was also an editor for the *Repository of Religion and Literature, and of Science and Art*, a church literary periodical, and was a regular writer for the denominational organ, the *Christian Recorder*. He was praised for his oratorical abilities and was standing on the verge of a promising ecclesiastical career.

In April 1863, concerned about the pressing needs of the freed Blacks of the South, he joined the newly founded National Freedman's Relief Association. On May 17, with Bishop Payne's blessing, he set sail from New York for work in South Carolina and Georgia, where for the next two years he organized churches, schools, and relief activities. After Blacks were admitted to the military in 1863, he became an informal chaplain to the troops. In January 1865, Lynch was the only freeborn Black in a delegation of twenty ministers who met with General Sherman, Secretary of War Stanton, and others to discuss the conditions of emancipated people. He experienced competition with White ministers of the Methodist Episcopal Church (North) and defended the idea of at least temporarily separate Black churches. He did, however, strongly believe that the future held one integrated national Methodist body. He thought the AME Church should look to that future by eliminating "African" from its title, a suggestion that did not sit well with church officials.

In the fall of 1865 he finally returned to his family and for six months was an assistant to Bishop Payne. In February 1866 he became editor of the *Christian Recorder*, the official newspaper of the AME Church, and moved to Philadelphia with his family in June. For the next year his leadership of the paper was exemplary, and he made it a center of information and discussion of all the pertinent issues of the day. In 1866 he took a four-month leave from the paper, ostensibly to travel to raise funds and subscribers. He returned to editorial duties in January 1867, but did not stay long. He was deeply concerned about whether Black churches now needed to maintain separate existences. He believed that interracial movements were necessary in religion as well as politics, and in May resigned from both the editorship and as an AME minister. Just as he did so, he found out he was being assigned to Mother Bethel AME Church in Philadelphia, one of the most prestigious positions in the denomination.

In June 1867, Lynch joined the Erie Conference of the Methodist Episcopal Church, from which he was transferred to the Mississippi Mission Conference as a presiding elder. He began a grueling schedule of travel across Mississippi, preaching and organizing the Black Methodists. Within one year he tripled the Black membership in the region, using to good advantage the oratorical skills that caused him later to be called "the Henry Ward Beecher of the colored race." On September 10, 1867, the Republican State Convention met, with one-third of the Black delegates. Lynch's popularity rose to new heights and he was elected vice-president. In June 1868, Lynch was Mississippi's only Black delegate to the Republican National Convention in Chicago. He attended the Methodist Episcopal Church general conference that year, but was not a formal delegate. He also ran for a state senate seat that year, but lost, along with most other moderate Republicans. After the election of President U.S. Grant in November 1868, however, his momentum returned. He began publishing the *Colored Citizen's Monthly*, which he printed until his death and used to build a popular base of support. At the Republican State Convention of July 1869, he helped fashion a platform of universal amnesty, universal suffrage, free schools, and free speech.

From July to September 1869, Lynch was assistant superintendent of education for the state, and in November won the election as secretary of state, despite fierce opposition and one apparent murder attempt. He served in office from 1870 to 1872 and established a popular reputation for fairness and efficiency. In 1872 he was again a delegate to the Republican National Convention, and was reelected secretary of state. He had hoped to become a congressman, but was defeated in that nomination, largely by charges that he was an alcoholic and had raped a local woman. A jury overturned the rape charge, but the damage was done. In 1872 he was a delegate to the Methodist Episcopal Church's general conference in Brooklyn and made an impressive appearance. He died unexpectedly later in 1872 from pneumonia and a kidney infection, cutting short a brilliant career. Tributes to his character and skills were presented at his funeral from across the country.

Gravely, William B. "A Black Methodist on Reconstruction in Mississippi: Three Letters by James Lynch in 1868–1869." *Methodist History* 11 (July 1973): 3–18.

———. "The Decision of AME Leader, James Lynch, to Join the Methodist Episcopal Church: New Evidence at Old St. George's Church, Philadelphia." *Methodist History* 15 (July 1977): 263–269.

Harris, William C. "James Lynch: Black Leader in Southern Reconstruction." *Historian* 34 (November 1971): 40–61.

HUBA, EWM, BAHA, IBAW.

"If a man can rejoice over the finding of his lost or strayed animal, or a piece of silver, or a son who had a desire to leave home to practice the evil habits of strangers, how much more should Allah and the Nation of Islam rejoice over finding us, who have been lost [from Allah and the Nation of Islam] for 400 years and following others than our own kind?"

Elijah Muhammad, Messenger
Nation of Islam

M

McALPINE, WILLIAM H. (June, 1847–c.1890), first president of the **Baptist Foreign Mission Convention of the U.S.A.** and president of Selma University, was born into slavery in Buckingham County, Virginia. At the age of three he, his mother, and younger brother were sold to a Presbyterian minister in Alabama named Robert McAlpine, whose surname he was given. This owner died five years later, and McAlpine came into the care of the son, a physician, whose wife saw to it that he was given a basic education. Their sponsorship also brought him into baptism and membership in 1864 at the mostly White Baptist church in Talladega, Alabama.

In 1866, after the Civil War, McAlpine worked as a carpenter and teacher in nearby Mardisville, and in 1868 began attending Talladega College. He was licensed as a preacher in 1869 and was ordained in 1871, when he began pastoring the Black Baptist church in Talladega. Besides his church work, he taught in the public schools for a time and organized several Baptist associations in the region, including Rushing Springs, Mount Pilgrim, and Snow Creek. His second pastorate was at the church in Jacksonville in Cannelton County. During this time he continued part time in his studies at Talladega College, and in 1873 was only six months short of graduation when his other duties forced him to end the program.

In 1868 McAlpine was present for Alabama's first Colored Baptist Missionary State Convention. In 1873 he caused quite a stir when, in the face of the advice of delegates from the White Baptists, he stated that the Black Baptists needed to found their own school. The convention accepted his proposal, and the following year asked him to spend some time raising money for the project. He was successful enough that the convention hired him full time for 1876 as a traveling and financial agent. By 1877 the convention had enough money to put a down payment on the old fairgrounds in Selma, Alabama, and McAlpine became the pastor of the Marion Baptist Church.

In 1878 he was chosen as the editor of the new church periodical, *Baptist Pioneer*, a position he held until 1882. On November 24, 1880, about 150 Black Baptist leaders from eleven states met to organize the Baptist Foreign Mission Convention, and McAlpine was elected president. He served for two terms, the maximum allowed by the convention's constitution. During that time the new organization established itself as a major avenue for Black Baptist activity, later becoming one of the predecessor bodies of the National Baptist Convention. Meanwhile the school which he had helped call into existence, Alabama Baptist Normal and Theological School (later changed to Selma University), slowly grew and in 1881 called McAlpine to be its president. Under his leadership its reputation was enhanced, and it became prominent in the education of Black leaders. Feeling that the position needed to be filled by someone with greater scholarly standing, he resigned after two years in favor of **E. M. Brawley**, who also became the editor of *Baptist Pioneer*.

In his final years, which are little known, he returned to serve the Marion Baptist Church, and for six years was the only Black on the Board of Trustees of Lincoln Normal University at Marion.

AARS, IBAW, RLOA, SNB, HBB, MM, ENB, OBMS.

McCARY, WILLIAM, a prophet who appeared among the Latter-day Saints in the mid-nineteenth century, joined the **Church of Jesus Christ of Latter-day Saints** as the members were leaving the Midwest for Utah in the winter of 1846–47. Little is known of him prior to his appearance at the Winter Quarters, Nebraska, where Brigham Young had established a camp, but he seems first to have associated with the Mormons in Cincinnati in 1846. Initially accepted as a musician, McCary fell from favor when he began to claim extraordinary powers of transfiguration, i.e., the ability to assume the identity of biblical figures. He was expelled from the camp and Mormon leader Orson Hyde preached a sermon against his ideas.

McCary settled a short distance away and in the summer of 1847 began to attract Mormon followers away from Winter Quarters. He introduced a system of polygamy (the practice of which among the Mormons had slowly become public knowledge), and like the Mormons established a sealing ceremony, by which his wives were married to him for all eternity. The idea of McCary having relationships with his White converts angered the Mormons and McCary took his small following to Missouri. There were reports that he joined one of the other small factions which had separated from the church, but after his highly charged encounter with the Mormons returned to the obscurity from which he first emerged.

McCary had an important role in pushing the Mormon leadership into an anti-Black position. McCary seems to have provided the occasion for Brigham Young first to articulate prohibition on Black members participating in Temple ceremonies and to cut them off from the priesthood, a position that would become Mormon policy for over a century.

Bringhurst, Newell G. *Saints, Slaves, and Blacks: The Changing Place of Black People within Mormonism.* Westport, CT: Greenwood Press, 1981. 254 pp.

McCOLLOUGH, WALTER (May 22, 1915–March 21, 1991), head of the **United House of Prayer for All People**, was born in Great Falls, South Carolina, the son of Robert and Janie Bell. Little has been written about his life prior to his association with the United House of Prayer for All People, an organization made famous by its charismatic leader, **Charles Manual Grace**, commonly known as "Sweet Daddy" Grace. McCollough married Clara Bell Price, with whom he had three children.

From 1941 to 1956 McCollough pastored the United House of Prayer Anacostia Mission, and from 1956 to 1960 he was the pastor of the church's national headquarters in Washington, D.C. He also served from 1956 to 1960 as state chair of the church's activities in Washington, D.C. and Maryland. He became owner of a dry cleaning establishment in Washington, D.C. After Bishop Grace died on January 12, 1960, there was no clear successor and a struggle for control of the church ensued. Although McCollough was an early favorite, he was not able to take office on a permanent basis until April 8, 1962, after the intervention of the courts.

Another problem was the $6 million tax suit by the

Internal Revenue Service, which claimed that Grace's estate did not belong to the church, but to Grace personally, and thus was subject to long-due taxes. The church finally won this argument when, in March, 1963, U.S. District Court Judge George L. Hart, Jr. ordered that frozen assets of $4.6 million be turned over to the United House of Prayer for All People. In the years after this was settled, McCollough slowly unified the church under his control and was able to expand the church into new cities. It assumed a more traditional Pentecostal stance and in 1974 launched a $1.5 million housing project in Washington, D.C. That year McCollough claimed a membership of four million, but this is difficult to verify. In 1985 he received the Distinguished Community Service Award from the National Urban Coalition.

"Walter McCollough." *Christian Century* 108 (April 24, 1991): 456.
WWABA (90–91), *TCSAPR, IBAW.*

McCOY, ALBERT BYRON (1881–September 2, 1951), national executive of the Presbyterian Church in the United States of America, today a constituent part of the Presbyterian Church (U.S.A.), was born in Cotton Plant, Arkansas. His mother died when he was five, and he went to live on a farm with foster parents. He later earned his way through Lincoln University and Seminary in Oxford, Pennsylvania, by doing clothing repair and being an agent for a shoe repairman. After graduation, about 1900, he went to Americus, Georgia, as a Sunday School missionary, frequently walking over ten miles between assignments. He supplemented his income as Grand Lecturer of the Knights of Pythias.

In 1904, at age twenty-three, he married Albertha H. Roseborough, with whom he had two children. Albertha died some years later, and he married Kate Dickson, with whom he had one child. McCoy's service was well regarded, and after several years he was appointed Superintendent of Sunday School Missions in ten southern states. During this time he published *Handbook for Missions.* He organized "Sunday School Bands," out of which came the first Daily Vacation Bible Schools among Blacks in the South. At one point an insurance company recognized his organizational abilities and offered him a job with a salary eight times what he was currently getting, but he stayed with the church.

In 1926 he moved the superintendent's headquarters to Atlanta, Georgia, where he set up a book depository to encourage and facilitate reading among the missionaries. He founded and supervised annual training events called Schools of Methods, which provided Christian nurture for Black Presbyterian youths in the Atlantic, Blue Ridge, Canadian, and Catawba Synods. In 1926 he represented the Presbyterian Church at an international conference on Christian work in Africa, held at LeZoute, Belgium.

In 1938, after almost forty years' service in Sunday School missions, he was appointed Secretary of the Unit of Work for Colored People of the Presbyterian Church in the U.S.A. This made him the first Black member of the Executive Cabinet of General Assembly agencies representatives. His accomplishments during the next thirteen years were many. He organized larger parishes in order to provide more services to poor churches. He organized summer conferences for Black Presbyterian leaders. He revitalized the Workers' Conference, a southeast training event for Black Presbyterians. He established a recruitment program with scholarship incentives, and increased the number of self-supporting Black churches. He opened lines of communication between racial and ethnic groups, and sponsored one of the first interracial conferences in the Presbyterian Church. His service was one which firmly established Blacks among the accepted leadership in the highest ranks of the Presbyterian hierarchy, while strengthening the ongoing ministry of Black Presbyterians. He retired in 1950, and died the following year. He was succeeded in that office by **Jesse Belmont Barber**.

Wilson, Frank T., ed. "Living Witnesses: Black Presbyterians in Ministry, Part II." *Journal of Presbyterian History* 53 (Fall 1975): 187–222.
NYTO.

McGEE, LEWIS ALLEN (November 11, 1893– October 10, 1979), Unitarian pioneer, was born in Scranton, Pennsylvania, the son of an **African Methodist Episcopal Church** (AME) minister. He graduated from high school in 1912, spent one year at the University of Pittsburgh, then entered Payne Theological Seminary at Wilberforce University, Ohio. He graduated with his B.D. in 1916, and the following year was ordained an elder in the AME Church, following in his father's footsteps. In 1918 he joined the 92nd Infantry Division of the U.S. Army as a chaplain, and after the war ministered in a number of small AME churches in Ohio and West Virginia. He married Ruth Lewis, with whom he had a son.

In 1927 he went to Chicago to meet Unitarian minister Curtis Reese, whose book, *Humanist Sermons*, had impressed him. McGee ended up staying in Chicago, and identified himself with the Humanist

faction of the Unitarian Church. He worked for a number of social service agencies while attending classes, and in 1936 received a B.A. in social science from Carthage College in Carthage, Illinois. Still not in a position to pursue a Unitarian ministry, he went back to Iowa for two years to serve an AME Church, and then returned to the Chicago area, ministering to a succession of other churches. In 1941, while still an AME minister, he began ten years on the board of the American Humanist Association. It is likely he was very guarded, within the church, in discussing his various associations.

In 1943 he reenlisted in the Army, and was chaplain to the 95th Engineer General Services Regiment, a Black engineers' battalion, at the Battle of the Bulge in Bastogne, Belgium. He left the Army in 1945 with the rank of captain, and, his first wife having died, married Marcella, with whom he had a daughter. McGee, more determined than ever to follow his own convictions, wherever they might lead, in September, 1946, he entered Meadville Theological School in Chicago to prepare for the Unitarian ministry.

In early 1947 McGee met Harry I. Jones at a Chicago Ethical Society meeting, and they began to hold meetings to see if any other Black Chicagoans would be interested in Unitarianism. A core group was developed, and the first regular Sunday worship of the congregation, called the Free Religious Fellowship (later the Free Religious Association), was held on October 5, 1947, with 125 persons attending. McGee was officially installed as the minister on June 13, 1948, with the full support of the denomination, as opposed to the earlier project of **Egbert Ethelred Brown** in Harlem.

By June 1953, the congregation had 75 members, and McGee felt it was strong enough to turn over to someone else. He moved to Yellow Springs, Ohio, to be the administrative assistant of the American Humanist Association. In 1958 he became the associate minister at the First Unitarian Church of Los Angeles, and in 1961 became the senior minister of Chico Unitarian Fellowship in California, the first time a Black had headed a White Unitarian church. His final pastorates were at Anaheim Unitarian Church (1962– 1963), Throop Memorial Church in Pasadena (1963– 1965), and Humboldt Unitarian Fellowship in Bayside, California (1965–1966). He retired in 1966.

Morrison-Reed, Mark D. *Black Pioneers in a White Denomination.* Boston: Beacon Press, 1984. 217 pp.
NYTO.

McGLOTHEN, MATTIE CARTER (b. 1897?), leader in women's work for the **Church of God in**

Christ, was born Mattie Carter near Dallas, Texas, the daughter of E. T. Carter and his wife. She grew up in Sapulpa, Oklahoma. At the age of fourteen she contracted tuberculosis, at the time considered an incurable disease. She was kept home for a year and a half, but was then able to go away to school at Quintaro, Kansas. She experienced a healing of her tuberculosis and was saved at a Pentecostal revival. She continued her studies at Quintero College and graduated in 1922. She then taught school in Depew, Oklahoma, for four years.

In the fall after her graduation she met George McClothen, a minister with the Church of God in Christ. They were married in 1924. Later in the decade they moved to California and founded the McGlothen Temple Church of God in Richmond, California. Quite apart from their work for the church, they both became active leaders in Contra Costa County, and Mother McGlothen was honored in 1989 for her lifetime of civil service as a community builder. By the time she had settled in Richmond, she had already become a leader in the church's missionary work and assisted Mother **Lizzie Roberson** in organizing the women on the West Coast. In 1983 she founded a home for missionaries in the Bahama Islands.

In 1951 she hosted the first women's National Convention which had been organized by Mother **Lillian B. Coffey**. Her faithful service over the years was rewarded in 1976 when she was named to succeed Mother **A. Penny Bailey** as the International Supervisor of Women in the Church of God, the highest office the church bestows on a woman. In 1984 she led in the establishment of a pavilion in Port-au-Prince, Haiti, to accommodate senior citizens and unwed mothers. She also led in the development of a senior citizens home in Memphis, Tennessee, where the church is headquartered.

DuPree, Sherry Sherrod. *Biographical Dictionary of African American Holiness Pentecostals, 1880–1990.* Washington, DC: Middle Atlantic Regional Press, 1989. 386 pp.

McGUIRE, GEORGE ALEXANDER (March 26, 1866–November 10, 1934), founder of the **African Orthodox Church** (AOC), was born in Sweets, Antigua, West Indies, the son of an Anglican father and Moravian mother. He graduated in 1886 from the Antigua branch of Mico College for teachers, and entered the new Moravian Theological Seminary at Nisky, St. Thomas. In 1888 he moved to pastor a church at St. Frederickstead in St. Croix, but was not ordained until January 17, 1893. He married Ada Eliza Roberts in 1892.

In 1894, along with many other West Indians of the time, he emigrated to the United States. Not finding a compatible Moravian group, he joined the (Protestant) **Episcopal Church** on January 2, 1895. He was ordained priest on October 22, 1897, was assigned to St. Andrew's Church in Cincinnati from 1897 to 1899, and was in Richmond, Virginia, from 1899 to 1901. At that point he became rector of St. Thomas First African Protestant Episcopal Church in Philadelphia, the church founded by **Absalom Jones**. While there he may have taken some courses at Jefferson Medical College in Philadelphia, though he did not graduate.

In 1905 McGuire became archdeacon for the Commission for Work Among the Colored People under William Montgomery Brown, the Bishop of Arkansas. Ironically, Brown had no interest in sharing the church with Blacks, and advocated that they create their own Episcopal church. Despite this conflict, McGuire managed to increase the number of missions from one to nine. In 1909 he became the first priest of St. Bartholomew's Church in Cambridge, Massachusetts. While there he obtained a degree from the Boston College of Physicians and Surgeons, a non-accredited school.

In 1911 he became Field Secretary of the American Church Institute for Negroes, which enabled him to visit Black Episcopalians across the country. In 1913, perhaps out of frustration, perhaps to see a sick mother, he went back to Antigua and stayed for five years as rector of St. Paul's in Falmouth and two other charges. Although he was happy there, and a person of significant prestige, he apparently heard about the work of fellow West Indian **Marcus Garvey**, and returned to the United States in 1918 in order to participate in his New York organization, the Universal Negro Improvement Association (UNIA).

Garvey was not interested in assimilation, and sought rather to claim equal and independent status with White culture. McGuire was named Chaplain-General of the UNIA, cut his ties with the Episcopal Church in 1919, and formed a congregation called the Good Shepherd Independent Episcopal Church. In his travels for the UNIA, he established similar groups in many places. In 1921 he produced two significant books for the UNIA, *The Universal Negro Catechism and The Universal Negro Ritual*. His aim was a worldwide Black church organically connected with the UNIA. This was not Garvey's vision, and McGuire was temporarily expelled from the UNIA.

McGuire organized the African Orthodox Church on September 2, 1921, and was elected its first bishop. After seeking consecration from several churches, he finally obtained it on September 28, 1921, from Joseph

René Vilatte of the American Catholic Church, an Old Catholic body. The beliefs of McGuire's Church were like most traditional Catholic beliefs, but the Church was explicitly geared to Black needs, and used representations of a Black Christ and a Black Madonna. By the time of his death, the Church counted 30,000 members in several countries.

Cronon, Edmund David. *Black Moses: The Story of Marcus Garvey and the Universal Negro Improvement Association*. Madison, WI: University of Wisconsin Press, 1962. 278 pp.

McGuire, George Alexander. *The Universal Negro Catechism*. New York: Universal Negro Improvement Association, 1921. 35 pp.

————. *The Universal Negro Ritual*. New York: Universal Negro Improvement Association, 1921. 138 pp.

Newman, Richard. "The Origins of the African Church." In *The Negro Churchman*. Millwood, NY: Kraus Reprint Co., 1977.

Terry-Thompson, Arthur C. *History of the African Orthodox Church*. New York: The Author, 1956. 139 pp.

White, Gavin. "Patriarch McGuire and the Episcopal Church." *Historical Magazine of the Protestant Episcopal Church* 38 (June 1969): 109–141.

RLOA, BA, DANB, GRM, IBAW, BDACSL, BRBR, IB.

McINTYRE, B. BARTON (b. March 24, 1910), **Salvation Army** officer, entered the work of the Army in 1931 in Waterbury, Connecticut. He attended Malone College in Canton, Ohio, from which he received a Th.B. degree and later studied at Oberlin College, the Cleveland Bible College, the Stauffer school of Social Sciences, and the College of the City of New York. In 1938 he married Lt. Mildred Bowen. Over the years he served appointments in Brooklyn, New York, Cleveland, Ohio, and in Harlem. He also served in several cities as a counselor on minority relations. While in Cleveland in 1949, McIntyre, then a major in charge of the "colored corps," made a formal request that his unit's name be changed to the Central Area Corps. That change, which was quickly granted, spearheaded the discontinuance of the word "colored" and of other racial designations for Army units. The name change was soon followed by new policy statements on discontinuing segregated facilities. In 1960 the two Army hospitals (one Black and one White) were merged into a single facility.

During the 1960s McIntyre moved to New York as a brigadier in charge of the Harlem Temple Corps. He became divisional secretary for metropolitan New York, which included 30 army units under his supervision. In 1969 he was promoted to lt. colonel, the highest rank ever obtained by an African American, and joined the territorial staff as the territorial evangelist for eleven states in the Northeast. He retired in 1975 after over 40 years of active service.

Garrett, Romeo B. *Famous First Facts About Negroes*. New York: Arno Press, 1972. 212 pp.

McKinley, Edward H. *Marching to Glory: The History of the Salvation Army in the United States of America, 1880–1980*. San Francisco, CA: Harper & Row, 1980. 286 pp.

McKINNEY, JOHN WESLEY (? –August 28, 1946), 16th bishop of the **Christian Methodist Episcopal Church** (CME), then known as the Colored Methodist Episcopal Church, was born in Texas. He was educated at Prairie View Normal School and Austin College. He joined the church in 1877 and began preaching in 1883. He served as a local pastor for several years before joining the West Texas Conference as an itinerant minister.

He pastored many churches over the years and was presiding elder and secretary of Church Extension before being elected bishop at the May 1922 general conference in St. Louis, Missouri. One of his accomplishments was the establishment, with the help of Bishop **Robert Turner Brown**, of a church in Trinidad, West Indies. Known as a person of conviction and high moral standards, he served as bishop for twenty years before retiring at the May 1942 general conference in Chicago, Illinois.

EWM, CMECTY.

McNEIL, JESSEY JAI (February 24, 1913–July 9, 1965), educator, ecumenical leader, and prominent Baptist (**National Baptist Convention, U.S.A., Inc.**) minister, was born in North Little Rock, Arkansas. He was baptized at the age of nine and at age thirteen started preaching. He was ordained a Baptist minister at age nineteen and began pastoring the Tabernacle Baptist Church in East Alton, Illinois. He attended the nearby Shurtleff College (since closed), but soon felt called to a larger ministry. He then moved to Virginia Union University's Graduate School of Religion, where he earned his B.D., followed by studies at Columbia University in New York City, where by 1943 he had earned a B.S., M.A., and a Doctorate of Education. While in New York he pastored the Salem Community Church. He married Pearl Lee Walker, with whom he had four children. His wife later became a well-known person in her own right as Dean of Students at Bishop College in Marshall, Texas.

In 1944 McNeil became Dean of the School of Religion at Bishop College, an American Baptist institution in Marshall, Texas. He was a lecturer in 1943 at the International Conference on Christian Education in Mexico City, and again in Toronto in 1950. He soon became known for his interest in the ecumenical dialogue. His first book, *Things That Matter* (1946), explored the stance for Christian unity. From 1947 to 1961 he pastored the Tabernacle Baptist Church in Detroit, Michigan, but this did not slow his growing international work. In 1947 he attended the Second World Conference of Christian Youth in Oslo, Norway, and in 1949 he spent the summer studying at the World Council of Churches Ecumenical Institute at Chateau de Bossey, Celigny, Switzerland, earning a Certificate of Ecumenical Studies. Also in 1949 he was the keynote speaker at the Baptist World Alliance Third World Congress of Baptist Youth in Stockholm, Sweden.

McNeil led the Detroit congregation into interracial and ecumenical involvements and sponsored music education programs to explore the stories behind the gospel hymns and spirituals. He founded the Tabernacle Lyceum to promote evangelism and the Christianization of the social order. This was an educational forum held every Sunday evening for nine months out of the year. The year was divided into segments which were devoted to a particular topic, such as Human Rights and Peace; the United Nations; Economic and Social Justice; Family Life; and so on. The church took an active role in the Detroit Council of Churches and the Michigan Council of Churches. In 1951 and 1953 McNeil took other leaders in the National Baptist Convention, U.S.A., Inc. on travel-study seminars to Europe. In 1955 he took a group of 35 Tabernacle members to the Fiftieth Anniversary Congress of the Baptist World Alliance in London. As vice-chair of the Michigan Correctional Commission, he helped design and implement a tri-faith prison chapel. For many years he was the Director of Publications for the National Baptist Convention, U.S.A., Inc., and was on the denomination's Commission on International and Intercultural Relationship.

From 1961 until his death McNeil was professor of Christian education at California Baptist Theological Seminary (now the American Baptist Seminary of the West, Covina Campus). With **George Kelsey** and others, he was among the first Blacks to hold professorships in a predominantly White theological seminary. In 1963 he helped mediate interracial meetings of religious leaders in strife-torn Detroit, Michigan. The 1960s were his most productive writing

times, and he authored several well-received books: *As Thy Days, So Thy Strength* (1960), which described his theories on Christian education; *The Preacher-Prophet in Mass Society* (1961); and *Mission in Metropolis* (1965), which called for a new mission emphasis on the needs of the city. His death at the young age of 52 was mourned as a great loss to the church.

McNeil, Jesse Jai. *As Thy Days, So Thy Strength*. Grand Rapids, MI: William B. Eerdmans Publishing Co., 1960. 167 pp.

———. *Men in the Local Church, a Manual for the Enlistment and Organization of the Christian Men Who Desire to Promote Fellowship and Brotherhood in the Local Church.* Detroit, MI: Tabernacle Baptist Brotherhood, 1951. 119 pp.

———. *The Minister's Service Book for Pulpit and Parish.* Grand Rapids, MI: William B. Eerdmans Publishing Co., 1961. 212 pp.

———. *Mission in Metropolis*. Grand Rapids, MI: William B. Eerdmans Publishing Co., 1965. 148 pp.

———. *Moments in His Presence*. Grand Rapids, MI: William B. Eerdmans Publishing Co., 1962. 98 pp.

———. *The Preacher-Prophet in Mass Society*. Grand Rapids, MI: William B. Eerdmans Publishing Co., 1961. 116 pp.

McNeil, Pearl L. "Baptist Black Americans and the Ecumenical Movement." *Journal of Ecumenical Studies* 17 (Spring 1980): 103–117.

GBB, AARS, HUBA, SCA.

MADISON, ELIJAH LOVETTE (May 20, 1876–June 26, 1946), 47th bishop of the **African Methodist Episcopal Zion Church** (AMEZ), was born in Madison Park, near Montgomery, Alabama. He attended Lomax Industrial Institute at Greenville, North Carolina, then in 1898 entered Livingstone College in Salisbury, North Carolina, graduating about 1902 with his B.A. degree. He was ordained deacon in the Western North Carolina Conference on November 6, 1898, and elder on November 11, 1900. In 1903 he married Julia F. C. Moseley, who in 1902 was the second woman graduate of the College Department of Livingstone College; with her he had eight children.

His pastorates included Cedar Grove and Second Creek Circuit; Hopkins Chapel AMEZ Church in Asheville; Clinton Chapel AMEZ Church in Charlotte; St. Stephens AMEZ Church in High Point; Trinity AMEZ Church in Greensboro; and St. Luke AMEZ Church in Wilmington, all in North Carolina. In 1920 he transferred to the Allegheny Conference to take the pastorate of John Wesley AMEZ Church in Pittsburgh, Pennsylvania. About this time, his first wife having passed away, he married Lucy Coleman, with whom he had one more child. He stayed at Pittsburgh for twelve years and established his reputation with great success there. He led in the establishment of an additional congregation and built the Wesley Center Church, dedicated on July 8, 1928.

At the 1932 General Conference Madison was elected Financial Secretary for the AMEZ Church, and served with distinction until 1936, when he was elected bishop. He was assigned to the Ninth Episcopal District (Alabama), where he again experienced success, especially in the rehabilitation of Lomax-Hannon College. He was known as a fair and generous leader, and on one occasion gave all the money on his person to help a church obtain a lamp that had none. In January 1941, after the death of Bishop **J. W. Brown**, he was assigned to the Sixth Episcopal District (North Carolina). On July 21, 1945, he suffered a paralytic stroke and was bedridden until he passed away almost one year later.

Allen, Laura V. "A Brief Sketch of Bishop E. L. Madison." *Star of Zion* 65 (July 31, 1941): 1, 8.

"Bishop Madison Succumbs." *Star of Zion* 70 (June 7, 1946): 1.

Chambliss, J. S. "Bishop Madison as a Christian Leader." *Star of Zion* 61 (August 5, 1937): 1.

HAMEZC, AMEZC.

MALCOLM X (May 19, 1925–February 21, 1965), Muslim minister and social activist, was born in Omaha, Nebraska, the seventh of thirteen children in the family of Earl and Louise Little. His father was a traveling Baptist preacher whose work was inspired by and connected with **Marcus Garvey**'s United Negro Improvement Association (U.N.I.A.). Earl Little's activist approach to Black rights placed him in some danger from White hate groups, but dealing with this was nothing new for him. Three of his four brothers had been killed by White men, and he himself had already lost an eye in violent confrontations.

The Littles moved from Omaha to Milwaukee, Wisconsin, then to Lansing, Michigan, where they bought a small house in a White section of town. This immediately created a problem with the Black Legion, a local White terrorist group. When Malcolm was four, two White men burned their house to the ground, but no one was injured. When he was six, his father was killed, reportedly in a trolley car accident, but the incident was commonly understood to have been in reality a murder by Whites. The insurance company called it suicide and refused to pay. His mother held the family together for a number of years, until a promising

relationship with a man ended and she suffered a complete breakdown. For the rest of her life she was confined to the State Mental Hospital at Kalamazoo, Michigan.

All the children in the family except the two oldest were sent to foster homes. Malcolm was thirteen and was placed in the home of a local Black family, the Gohannas. He was rebellious and was soon expelled from school, causing a transfer to a detention home run by the Swerlins, a White couple. They grew to like him "as a mascot" and placed him in Mason Junior High School, where he was accepted in a similar way. In the second semester of the seventh grade he was elected president of his class, but despite his popularity the students thought nothing of telling "nigger jokes" in his presence.

That summer, when he was fourteen, his oldest sister Ella brought him for a visit to her home in Boston. He appreciated her comfortable life amid many other Black people and decided that was for him. The eighth grade back in Mason went well until one of his favorite teachers, from whom he had earned very high grades, responded to his statement that he wanted to be a lawyer one day. He said, "A lawyer— that's no realistic goal for a nigger . . . Why don't you plan on carpentry?" From this point on Malcolm began to distrust Whites and withdraw from them. The change was noticeable and officials decided to move him to another family. He wanted to move to Boston and live with his sister, and the arrangements were made for that move immediately upon completion of the eighth grade.

In Boston, despite his sister's best efforts, he soon fell in with a crowd of street-wise hustlers and gained a hard city edge. He held a number of jobs and sold marijuana cigarettes on the side. He never got beyond a formal ninth-grade education, though he later educated himself. He found a job selling sandwiches on the New Haven railroad line running between Boston and New York, which introduced him to the New York night life that made Boston pale in comparison. When he lost that job in 1942 he moved to New York and found a job in a bar, Small's Paradise. When that job ended he became a full time marijuana pusher, mainly working the musicians and nightclubs. When pressure from the narcotics police became too great he reactivated his railroad passes and followed the musicians as they traveled. He avoided the draft for World War II by acting crazy for the examining psychiatrist. He got into heavier hustles and began using harder drugs like cocaine.

He moved back to Boston to cool off for a time, but eventually he began stealing from wealthy homes as the head of a burglary ring. Finally he was arrested at a jewelry store picking up a repaired stolen watch. In February 1946, he was sentenced to ten years in prison. A fellow inmate named Bimbi, respected by the others for his knowledge, awakened Malcolm's intellect and encouraged him to use the prison library and start correspondence courses. In 1948 his sister Ella managed to have him transferred to Norfolk Massachusetts Prison Colony, a progressive place with a less oppressive atmosphere.

By this time his brother Reginald had been converted to the **Nation of Islam** then led by **Elijah Muhammad**, as had some other members of the family, and under his influence through prison visits Malcolm slowly moved away from a long-held atheism to be a believer also. He obeyed the injunctions against tobacco, narcotics, liquor, and pork, and the teaching that the White man was the devil, descended from a shameless race created by a mad Black scientist, made sense in his experience. He began reading everything he could get his hands on, even at night in dim light, to the point where he needed glasses. His eyes were opened to the evils committed by Whites over history, and he felt he was finding verification of Muhammad's teachings. When Malcolm X was released from prison in August 1952, he joined his oldest brother, Wilfred, who found him a job at the Ford Motor Plant in Detroit. At about this time, in accordance with Muhammad's teachings, he formally dropped the last name of Little and replaced it with an "X," symbolizing his true African name now long-lost through generations of theft by the White slavemasters.

Malcolm X was successful in proclaiming the message of the Nation of Islam to the Black ghetto in Detroit, and the membership of the temple grew quickly. The entire membership of the Nation of Islam at this time was about 400. Elijah Muhammad saw his potential and in the summer of 1953 named him Assistant Minister to Detroit Temple Number One. By March 1954, he had founded Temple Eleven in Boston, and Muhammad sent him to Philadelphia, where in three more months he had founded Temple Twelve. In June 1954, he was sent to head Temple Seven in Harlem, New York City, where he remained for the next nine years. His former friends there were surprised to see the change in him, that he sincerely followed the strict moral code against gambling, attending movies or sporting events, lying, stealing, or fornication. He had no money and few possessions of his own; all his expenses were provided for by the temple. He urged Blacks to reject White society and unite under Muhammad and the Muslim faith, the only true path to dignity.

In 1956 Sister Betty X, an intelligent, college-educated woman who attracted his attention, joined the Temple. After receiving Elijah Muhammad's approval, they were married on January 14, 1958. Shortly after the wedding the Nation of Islam gained wide attention through an incident of police brutality involving one of the members. Malcolm X and a troop of the Fruit of Islam guards went to the precinct house and pressed the police to take the victim, Johnson Hinton, to the hospital for treatment. A metal plate had to be placed in his skull and the Nation of Islam later helped him sue the police. A jury awarded him over $70,000, the largest such judgment awarded up to that time. Soon **C. Eric Lincoln**, a Black scholar, asked permission to study the Nation of Islam for his doctoral dissertation, Alex Haley did an article for *Reader's Digest*, and a profile of the Nation of Islam was done for the Mike Wallace Show.

Malcolm X was now a major news figure and began speaking before national radio and television audiences, speaking on college campuses, and debating opponents. White intelligence agencies infiltrated the Nation of Islam and tapped its phones, but sometimes the Black agents would be converted and confess their roles. In 1963 Elijah Muhammad made Malcolm X the Nation of Islam's first national minister, but there were tensions growing within the organization over Malcolm's high public profile. On July 3, 1963, a news story broke that two former secretaries of Elijah Muhammad were filing paternity suits against him. This confirmed suspicions that had been circulating in the organization for many years, but Malcolm X found it difficult to believe that the person he had respected and even idolized for so long could be capable of such betrayal. He spoke to Elijah Muhammad himself, who essentially confirmed the story. Malcolm was devastated. He tried to recover by developing an argument that one's accomplishments outweigh one's weaknesses, and by suggesting that it was in some way a fulfillment of prophecy. He spoke with several other leaders in the organization to prepare them for the possible need for this approach, but it was interpreted as undermining Muhammad's authority. By this time the membership of the Nation of Islam had grown to as many as 40,000.

Immediately after President John F. Kennedy was assassinated on November 22, 1963, Elijah Muhammad placed a three-day moratorium on any Muslim comments on the event. During that time Malcolm X filled in for Muhammad at a speaking engagement at New York's Manhattan Center. When asked afterwards by reporters how he felt about Kennedy's assassination he said he thought it was a case of the "chickens coming home to roost," that the country's climate of hate had created the conditions for the assassination. The media reported this comment with an ominous slant; thus not only did he break Muhammad's moratorium, but the

Nation of Islam was receiving negative publicity. Muhammad silenced him for ninety days, and other Muslims began to shun him. Soon Malcolm X found out that orders had been placed in the organization to kill him.

Finally he made a complete break from the Nation of Islam and on March 8, 1964, founded the **Muslim Mosque, Inc.**, with temporary headquarters in the Hotel Theresa in Harlem. He announced its purpose would be to act as a spiritual force behind social action to eliminate the oppression of African Americans. Before moving fully with this new organization Malcolm X decided to make a pilgrimage to Mecca, something every Muslim tries to do at least once. Borrowing some money from his sister, Ella, now a Muslim herself, he left for Egypt on April 13, 1964. Thanks to references from Dr. Mahmoud Youssef Shawarbi, the Director of the Federation of Islamic Associations in the United States and Canada, whom he had met in New York, Malcolm X was shown great hospitality by powerful people during his visit. Prince Faisal, the ruler of Arabia, made him a guest of the state. Malcolm X was impressed by the genuine warmth expressed in Egypt among people of all colors and nationalities, and was forced to change his previous belief that all White people are evil. He wrote the "Letter from Mecca" to this effect, that was published in the United States. He also became acutely aware of the distance between the teachings of the Nation of Islam and the historic, orthodox Muslim faith. In Mecca he took the name El-Hajj Malik El-Shabazz—"Hajj" referring to the pilgrimage to Mecca, and "Shabazz" referring to an ancient Black tribe.

Malcolm X returned to the United States in May 1964, and on June 28, 1964, he founded the Organization of Afro-American Unity (O.A.A.U.) as a nonsectarian, nationalist movement designed to recruit those Blacks who desired to work toward similar goals of civil rights, but who would not accept Islam. White people were not allowed to join, but those who sincerely wished to help rid the country of hate and discrimination were supported and urged to work as they could in their own communities. The media continued to portray Malcolm X as someone who advocated violence. He kept trying to clarify that what he was for was Blacks defending their rights as human beings, even if that meant carrying weapons. He made another trip abroad from July 19 to November 24, 1964, and had extended audiences with seven heads of state in Africa. As a speaker at the Second Organization of African Unity Conference, he made an appeal for African delegates to raise the issue of Black oppression in the United States before the United Nations.

In late 1964, a court order was issued to force him and his family to move from the house previously provided by the Nation of Islam. He was under a great deal of stress as he tried to promote the O.A.A.U., and he felt his life was in constant danger from disaffected Black Muslims, though he did not rule out other forces at work. On February 13, 1965, his home was fire-bombed, but no one was injured. Finally, on February 21, 1965, as he addressed a crowd in the Audubon Ballroom in Harlem, he was assassinated. On March 10, Talmadge Hayer, Norman 3X Butler, and Thomas 15X Johnson, all members of the Nation of Islam, were indicted for the murder, and later convicted.

Neither the O.A.A.U. nor the Muslim Mosque, Inc. survived long after his death. Because of all the years in the Nation of Islam without any private income, Malcolm X left behind a pregnant wife and four daughters with no savings, no income, and no insurance. What became the Malcolm X Daughters' Fund was founded to help that situation. The life and work of Malcolm X has left a significant imprint around the world, and particularly upon the Black population of the United States. His autobiography, first published in 1964 and then in finished form posthumously, revealed to a wide public the details of his complex and moving personal journey. Ossie Davis, the actor who did the eulogy for him, has said that even when Blacks disagreed with Malcolm X, they took pride in his courage and his ability to be his own man.

Goldman, Peter. "Who Killed Malcolm?" *Newsweek* 93 (May 7, 1979): 39.

Hatch, Roger D. "Racism and Religion: The Contrasting Views of Benjamin Mays, Malcolm X, and Martin Luther King, Jr." *The Journal of Religious Thought* 36 (Fall–Winter 1979–80): 26–36.

Krieg, Robert A. "Malcolm X—Myth and Truthfulness." *The Journal of Religious Thought* 36 (Fall–Winter 1979–80): 37–44.

"Organizations and Leaders Campaigning for Negro Goals in the United States." *New York Times* (August 10, 1964): 16.

Breitman, George. *The Last Year of Malcolm X: The Evolution of a Revolutionary.* New York: Merit Publishing, 1966. 169 pp.

Clarke, John Henrik, ed. *Malcolm X: The Man and His Times.* New York: Macmillan, 1969. 360 pp.

Cone, James H. *Martin & Malcolm & America: A Dream or a Nightmare.* Maryknoll, NY: Orbis Books, 1991. 358 pp.

Curtis, Richard. *Life of Malcolm X.* Philadelphia, PA: Macrae Smith Co., 1971. 160 pp.

Davis, Lenwood G. *Malcolm X: A Selected Bibliography.* Westport, CT: Greenwood Press, 1984. 146 pp.

Goldman, Peter Louis. *The Death and Life of Malcolm X.* Urbana, IL: University of Illinois Press, 1979. 470 pp.

Hurst, Charles G. *Passport To Freedom: Education, Humanism, and Malcolm X.* Hamden, CT: Linnet Books, 1972. 242 pp.

Lomax, Louis E. *To Kill a Black Man.* Los Angeles: Holloway House Publishing Co., 1968. 256 pp.

Malcolm X. *The Autobiography of Malcolm X.* With the assistance of Alex Haley. New York: Ballantine Books, 1964, 1965. 460 pp.

———. *Malcolm X Speaks: Selected Speeches and Statements.* George Breitman, ed. New York: Merit Publishers, 1965. 242 pp.

———. *The Speeches of Malcolm X at Harvard.* Archie Epps, ed. New York: William Morrow, 1968. 191 pp.

Miah, Malik, ed. *Assassination of Malcolm X.* New York: Pathfinder Press, 1976. 190 pp.

Wolfenstein, Eugene V. *The Victims of Democracy: Malcolm X and the Black Revolution.* Berkeley: University of California Press, 1981. 432 pp.

NYTO, PBP, AAE, LV, DANB, EBA, EAB, NPT, BNA, CA (111), CH, IBAW, BHBA, SBAA, BP, GBA, CBL, IP, BLTC, BWA, MBRL, TCSAPR.

MALLORY, ARENIA CORNELIA (December 28, 1905–May 8, 1977), college president and leader in the **Church of God in Christ**, was born in Jacksonville, Illinois, the daughter of James Edward and Mazy Gay (Brooks) Mallory. Her parents were entertainers who toured the country with various other acts before settling in Jacksonville, the father as a successful merchant. Mallory attended the Whipple Academy of Music from 1918 to 1922 with the idea of becoming a concert pianist, but this was not to be.

About the time she was in the music academy she had a conversion experience during a Pentecostal revival meeting and became heavily involved in the Church of God in Christ. She continued her education at Newton Baton College in Jacksonville, Illinois, supporting herself as recreational director of the Butler Community Center in Chicago (1923) and as recreational director of the Lincoln Colored Home in Springfield, Illinois. In 1926 she went to teach at the only school then operated by the Church of God in Christ, then called the Industrial and Literary School, in Lexington, Mississippi. Almost immediately she inherited the administrative charge of the institution, which was little more than a small building with some homemade benches and a debt of several thousand dollars. Her beginnings there were made all the more difficult when she married A. C. Clemmons on June 4, 1927. He was not a member of the church, and marrying outside the faith was forbidden. She was ostracized and forced to take a leave of absence. She returned two years later and was readmitted to the church; it is not known what happened to her husband, who is not mentioned in connection with later events in her life. They had one daughter, Andrea Mazy E. Clemmons.

Once settled in charge of the school, Mallory turned it around, despite many obstacles and few resources. By the mid-1930s she oversaw 350 acres with $50,000 in buildings, fifteen teachers, and 400 students. It had twelve grades of study, a Home Economics Department, and a Class A rating. This was the first high school for Blacks in Holmes County, and it gained the first school band in the county. About 45 of the students boarded at the school, and only 12 of the 400 students could afford to pay full tuition. Mallory regularly solicited clothing for her students and for their parents as well, and during a 1934 nationwide tour collected some 25,000 garments. She arranged for the first bus transportation for Black students in the county, and created the first integrated faculty in the county. These formidable achievements began to bring some recognition, and in the late 1930s she was the first president of any school in Mississippi to represent her work at the White House.

Anxious to increase her capabilities, Mallory continued her own education without interrupting her responsibilities as president of the school. She received a B.A. in education in 1936 from Jackson College in Jackson, Mississippi, and a master's degree in business administration in 1950 from the University of Illinois. She was a charter member of the National Council of Negro Women (N.C.N.W.) and was named by that group in 1940 and again in 1945 as one of the nine outstanding women of America. She was first vice-president of the N.C.N.W. from 1954 to 1958, and in 1954 was its representative at the Convention of Women in Helsinki, Finland. She served in the Women's Army for National Defense (W.A.N.D.) and in 1956 the Utility Club of New York City named her "Woman of the Year." From 1956 to 1959 she was vice-president of the National Council of Women of the United States.

During this time also she was very active in the Church of God in Christ, and was its only female delegate to the World Pentecostal Convention in London in 1952. She served on the executive board of the Women's Department, was a member of the board of directors of the National Board of Education, and served on the Charles Harrison Mason Foundation. Honors continued to flow to her from all quarters. In 1960 she founded the Friends of Liberian Youth. In 1961 she was a delegate to the Conference for African Women and Women of African Descent, held in the newly founded nation of Ghana. From 1961 to 1963 she was on the

Educational Committee of the International Council of Women. In 1962 her school finally became Saints Junior College.

In 1963 she received the Sojourner Truth Award for Meritorious Service in the Development and Advancement of the Status of Women from the National Negro Business and Professional Women's Clubs. In 1965 she received the N.C.N.W.'s Tribute Award and Scroll of Honor. In November 1968, she became the first person of color and the first woman to be elected to the Holmes County Board of Education. She was cited for her outstanding work by the Church of God in Christ International meeting in 1969 and again in 1973. On April 19, 1974, she received the Governor's Outstanding Mississippian Award from Governor Waller, and that day was proclaimed Arenia Cornelia Mallory Day for the entire state. The Holmes County Board of Supervisors responded by naming a Lexington thoroughfare Arenia C. Mallory Road. She retired from Saints Academy and Junior College in June 1976, and the school remained in operation until May 1983.

WWCA (38–40), *WWAW* (77–78), *NBAW, BH, EBA, BDA-AHP, IBAW.*

MARCHENNA, RICHARD ARTHUR (March 17, 1911–September 2, 1982), founder of the Old Roman Catholic Church (in North America), was born in Jersey City, New Jersey. He first became a public figure as a priest in the New York Metropolitan Area for the **North American Old Roman Catholic Church** (N.A.O.R.C.C.). He was consecrated as a bishop for the Province of New Jersey by Archbishop Carmel Henry Carfora on April 16, 1941. The consecration of Marchenna, an African American, by Carfora, an Italian American, was part of an overall strategy by the Archbishop to build a rival organization to the **Roman Catholic Church** through the mobilization of ethnic Catholics dissatisfied with Roman Catholic attempts to disregard ethnicity at the episcopal level and assign bishops with no regard to the ethnicity of the churches in their diocese.

Marchenna worked in Harlem and was instrumental in convincing **Hubert Augustus Rogers**, who had left the **African Orthodox Church**, to join the North American Old Roman Catholic Church. Rogers would eventually become the church's primate. First, however, he reconsecrated Rogers and elevated him to the rank of archbishop. Then, in an attempt to woo the various factions of the African Orthodox Church which had splinters in the mid-1930s, Carfora established the African Independent Catholic Church, and placed

Rogers in charge of it, while allowing Rogers to retain his seat in the House of Bishops of the NAORCC. Marchenna strongly disapproved of Carfora's manipulations, and in response excommunicated Rogers. Carfora sided with Rogers and on September 22, 1948, deposed Marchenna from the office of bishop. During this period of independence, Marchenna continued to function as a bishop, and on March 25, 1950, consecrated British Bishop Gerard Shelley for the Old Roman Catholic Church in England.

The experiment with Rogers ended in 1950 when the NAORCC and the African Orthodox Church worked out a statement of intercommunion. That same year, the church's synod reinstated Marchenna. Marchenna's new status was short-lived. Carfora again deposed and excommunicated him in 1952 "for cause." Marchenna turned to British Archbishop Shelley of the Old Roman Catholic Church in England and, with the four parishes and several clergy who left the NAORCC with him, moved to establish the North American branch of his jurisdiction.

Through the 1960s Marchenna built a relatively substantial movement with congregations in the East and Midwest. He separated from Shelley in 1963, but the church continued to grow slowly in spite of defections by independent-minded bishops who left to found rival jurisdictions. Then in 1974 he made what many consider a strategic mistake. On October 4 of that year, he consecrated Robert Clement, a White man, as bishop for the Eucharistic Catholic Church. Clement, a practicing homosexual, was the head of a homosexual ministry. Many of the priests and bishops revolted and left Marchenna's jurisdiction.

Marchenna led the now decimated jurisdiction until his death in 1982. He was succeeded by Derek Lang-Rossi who moved the headquarters to Los Angeles and changed the church's name first to the American Prefecture and more recently to Church of Utrecht in America.

Trela, Jonathan. *A History of the North American Old Roman Catholic Church.* Scranton, PA: The Author, 1979. 134 pp.
Ward, Gary L. *Independent Bishops: An International Directory.* Detroit, MI: Apogee Books, 1990. 526 pp.

MARINO, EUGENE ANTONIO (b. May 29, 1934), the first African American archbishop of the **Roman Catholic Church**, was born in Biloxi, Mississippi, the sixth of eight children in the family of Jesus Maria and Irnen (Bradford) Marino. The family came from a long line of Catholics and Marino was baptized when he was nine days old. Marino's father was a baker and his mother worked part time as a domestic. All the children attended Our Mother of Sorrows School, related to the Josephite Parish of the same name. In school Marino was strongly affected by the **Divine Word Society**, an organization working to attract southern Blacks to church vocations.

When Marino graduated from high school in 1952 he entered Epiphany Apostolic College in Newburgh, New York, the minor seminary of the Society of St. Joseph of the Sacred Heart (the Josephites), a group which had labored in the United States since 1871 with a ministry solely to Blacks. He entered the novitiate on August 11, 1955, and made his first profession on August 12, 1956. That year he entered St. Joseph's Major Seminary in Washington, D.C., where he earned his B.A. in 1960. He had also, during the previous several summers, studied at the Edmundite College of St. Michael in Winooski, Vermont, and after graduation did additional studies at Loyola University in New Orleans, Louisiana. He made his final profession to the Josephites on May 1, 1961.

Marino was ordained a priest on June 9, 1962, and was assigned to teach various classes ranging from history to biology at Epiphany Apostolic College in Newburgh, New York. In 1967 he earned an M.A. in religious education from Fordham University in New York City. In 1968 he became Spiritual Director of St. Joseph's Major Seminary in Washington, D.C. On July 31, 1971, he was elected the first Black Vicar General of the Josephite Society. In that position he became a member of the General Council and Director of Spiritual and Educational Formation for the Josephite Society.

On July 16, 1974, the announcement was made of his appointment as Auxiliary Bishop of Washington, D.C. and he was consecrated for that office on September 12, 1974. After **James A. Healy** (1875), **Harold Perry** (1966), and **Joseph Howze** (1972), Marino was the fourth Black American bishop in the Roman Catholic Church. Described as theologically moderate to conservative, he became known in Washington as an advocate for the poor, homeless, unborn, and oppressed, and often testified at Congressional hearings on those topics. He was a significant force in increasing the self-identity of Black Catholics, encouraging liturgical changes to include the Black heritage, such as having choirs sing spirituals in worship. He appeared in a series of Catholic-sponsored television shows to educate people about Black Catholics, and joined in the 1984 pastoral letter produced by the African American bishops entitled "We Have Seen and We Have Heard," which urged increased attention to the needs of Black Catholics.

On November 12, 1985, Marino was elected secretary of the National Conference of Catholic Bishops, the first Black to hold that office. In 1987 Pope John Paul II visited the United States, and Marino played a key role in arranging for the Pope to meet with Black Catholics in a large celebration at the New Orleans Superdome. This successful event likely played a part in his appointment on March 15, 1988, as America's first Black archbishop. He was appointed to the Atlanta archdiocese, which includes 69 counties and 165,000 Catholics, of whom about 10,000 are Black. Because of the illness and death of his predecessor, the archdiocese had been without effective leadership for about a year. Marino quickly became popular as he firmly tackled a number of festering issues. In particular, he investigated the case of a priest whom a grand jury had indicted on charges of child molestation. Catholic officials had let him retreat to his native England, where he disappeared, and the families involved were very angry. Marino met the families personally and later announced tough new guidelines on the handling of sexual misconduct charges.

Ironically, in June 1990, Marino was forced to resign his office because of the revelation that he had been involved in an intimate relationship with a woman named Vicki Long since shortly after his arrival in Atlanta. Ms. Long was also implicated in relationships with other priests, and in 1987 had filed a $2.3 million paternity suit against a priest in Columbus, Ohio. An agreement was reached with church authorities and she received child support payments. Marino agreed to church-directed counseling, and observers noted that the tragedy at least had the benefit of bringing the issue of clerical struggles with celibacy into the open. Marino was succeeded by another African American bishop, **James Lyke**.

"All for Love." *Time* 136 (August 13, 1990): 61.

"An Intimate Relationship." *Christian Century* 107 (August 8–15, 1990): 729–730.

"Archbishop Eugene Marino Resigns after Relationship with Young Georgia Woman." *Jet* 78 (August 20, 1990): 4–6.

"Archbishop Marino's Resignation." *Origins* 20 (August 16, 1990): 169, 171.

Harris, Michael P. "A First for Black Catholics." *Time* 131 (March 28, 1988): 71.

Parker, Anthony A. "Black Catholic Archbishop." *Sojourners* 17 (June 1988): 13.

Treadwell, David. "Black Archbishop in Pioneer Role Again." *Los Angeles Times* (July 9, 1988): Part II, 6–7.

OBS, IBAW, NA, NYTBS (1988), *WWABA* (90–91), *RLOA, BDNM* (75).

MARRANT, JOHN (June 15, 1755–April 15, 1791), pioneer missionary related to the Methodist movement, was born in New York, but when his father died in 1759 the family moved to St. Augustine, Florida. He was able to attend school there, and then in Georgia, where the family moved eighteen months later. When he was about ten, they moved to Charleston, South Carolina, and he was urged to continue learning a trade he had begun in Georgia. Instead, he studied music for two years, learning the violin and French horn, and only then did he return as apprentice to an unknown trade.

At the age of thirteen, in 1768, Marrant experienced conversion through the preaching of George Whitefield, but his family was not pleased. He left home and wandered in the forest until he was found by an Indian hunter and made a home among the Cherokee for two years. He made enemies among them by his preaching, and was in danger for his life until the chief and his daughter were converted. He then spent six months trying to convert other tribes, without success, and decided to return to Charleston. He was among the first Methodists to do mission work among Native Americans, but because his successes were not followed up by a long-term effort, credit for being the "Father of Missions" to the Native Americans is generally given to another African American, **John Stewart** (1786–1823).

At the start of the American Revolution he was impressed into the British forces as a musician, serving almost seven years. In 1781 he was wounded off the Dogger Bank in the North Sea, was discharged, and made his way to London. There he worked for three years with a cotton merchant and joined the Countess of Huntingdon's Connexion, an evangelical group related to the Whitfield branch of Methodism. Marrant's brother, who had joined the 3,500 Black Loyalists moving to Nova Scotia after the war, wrote and urged him to come preach there. Marrant determined to do that, and was ordained in the Connexion on May 15, 1785. Before he left for Canada he published a review of the first thirty years of his life, *A Narrative of the Lord's Wonderful Dealings with John Marrant, a Black. . . .* This became an amazingly successful story, going through about twenty printings by 1835.

The reasons for the great popularity of this book are many. Although he was never a slave, the narrative has been seen as part of the classic slave story pattern of oppression, escape, and journey to the promised land. His recounting of his life among the Cherokees is considered to be among the three most popular Indian captivity tales ever told. Finally, the book had great appeal as a story of Christian conversion and success. His aim was not so much to give a history of his life as to portray a religious journey filled with miraculous incidents and providential design.

In Nova Scotia, he organized his first Huntingdonian congregation at Birchtown, Shelburne, and visited most of the Black loyalist settlements, where **David George** had already established some Baptist congregations. He married Elizabeth Herries at Birchtown on August 15, 1788. In the winter of 1789, he travelled to Boston, where he joined the first African American Masonic Lodge, founded in 1784 by Prince Hall, and became its chaplain. In his eloquent sermons he urged Blacks to have pride in their abilities and heritage. He left for England on February 5, 1790, and soon published his other major work, *A Journal of the Rev. John Marrant, From August the 18th, 1785, to the 16th of March, 1790.* After his death the following year, new editions of the *Narrative* omitted the reference to his color in the title and altered his picture to appear more White. This helps account for his neglect by the early biographers of Black pioneers.

Schomburg, Arthur Alfonso. "Two Negro Missionaries to the American Indians, John Marrant and John Stewart." *Journal of Negro History* 21 (October 1936): 394–415.

Marrant, John. *A Journal of the Rev. John Marrant, from August the 18th, 1785, to the 16th of March, 1790.* London: The Author, 1790. 106 pp.

———. *A Narrative of the Lord's Wonderful Dealings with John Marrant, a Black. . . .* Ed. Rev. Mr. Aldridge. 2nd ed. London: Gilbert and Plummer, 1785.38 pp.

———. *Sermon Preached on the 24th Day of June 1789, Being the Festival of St. John the Baptist, at the Request. . . Prince Hall, . . . of the African Lodge of the Honorable Society of Free and Accepted Masons. . . .* Boston: Bible and Hearts, 1789. 24 pp.

DCB (4), *DANB, BPEAR, BAWPP, IBAW, HUBA, BW, NEA.*

MARSHALL, ANDREW COX (c.1755–December 8, 1856), perhaps the preeminent African American minister of the antebellum South, was born into slavery in South Carolina, to a pure African mother and an English father. He grew up as the slave of John Houston, colonial governor of Georgia. At one point Marshall saved his life and in gratitude Houston freed him in his will. The executors of the will refused to grant this freedom, and sold Marshall again. He soon ran away, and while at large was purchased by Judge Joseph Clay as his coachman. In this capacity he travelled many times to the North, frequently seeing George Washington. During the Revolutionary War and the embargo of Savannah, Marshall was paid $225 by merchants of the city to carry word of the embargo to several American vessels in a bay on the lower seaboard. When George Washington visited Savannah as president, Marshall was appointed his body servant.

At about the age of fifty Marshall was converted by the preaching of a White minister and joined the Second Colored Baptist Church in Savannah. He was baptized by its Black minister, Henry Cunningham. At about this time Richard Richardson, business partner of his current owner, Robert Bolton, advanced him $200. This money, combined with what Marshall had saved over the years, allowed him to purchase his freedom. Soon thereafter he also purchased the freedom of his wife, four children, father-in-law, and stepfather. In 1806 his uncle, **Andrew Bryan**, who was pastor of the large First Colored Baptist Church in Savannah, ordained him as assistant pastor.

When Bryan passed away in October 1812, Marshall did not immediately succeed him as pastor of the church. The pulpit had no permanent occupant until 1815, when Marshall was finally called. Marshall was adept in business and during the interim kept busy with his large portage and draying business in Savannah, which used both teams and slaves. From 1818 to 1821 he built a two-story brick home, an undertaking unheard of for Blacks at that time. His prestige and wealth led a number of Whites to think he needed to be dropped in status. He was brought up on charges of stealing building supplies, found guilty, and sentenced to be whipped in public. Richard Richardson and other sympathetic Whites were able to intervene to the extent that the whipping was only simulated, and did not really hit his skin.

In 1823 the local Baptist association (Sunbury), in which Blacks had no real voice, changed the names of the Black churches, substituting "African" for "Colored." In 1832 Alexander Campbell, founder of the Christian Church (Disciples of Christ), visited Savannah and Marshall invited him to be a guest preacher at the First African Baptist Church. This controversial decision might have passed with no incident except that after Campbell's message Marshall said he thought that with further study he might even subscribe to Campbell's ideas. This ignited a riot in which the city police had to be called to restore order. The problem was compounded in that, since **Nat Turner**'s Rebellion in 1831, Black churches were already suspect and their activities were limited and persecuted.

The result was an unamendable split in the congregation and a strong reaction from the White community. Marshall and many of the members moved to a former White Baptist church building in Franklin Square that then became the First African Baptist Church. Other members went to Second African or Ogeechee Baptist Churches, leaving about two hundred at the original church, led at first by Deacon Adam Johnson and then by Rev. Thomas Anderson. Anderson reapplied to the Baptist Association for membership and his church was given the name Third African Baptist Church. For the next five years Marshall was silenced by the association, and his Sunday meetings could only engage in "prayer," not in a full preaching service. A number of people thought this would be the end of the church and Marshall, but in fact the congregation grew during this time. Finally Marshall and the First African Baptist Church were readmitted into the Baptist Association in 1837, when it had become clear that Marshall was not going away and that he was not, after all, going to subscribe to Campbellite ideas. Marshall then tried through the courts to reclaim the original church at Lot 7, called at that point the Third African Baptist Church, but failed in that effort. He continued to pastor the First African Baptist Church without further incidents until his death. His mile-long funeral procession was "unequalled by anything of the kind in that city or region where a colored person was concerned."

In 1865, after Emancipation, the Third African Baptist Church renamed itself the First Bryan Baptist Church. Both it and the First African Baptist Church have since claimed primacy as "the" church founded by **George Liele** and Andrew Bryan. A committee of the African Missionary Baptist State Convention in 1888 decided that "the church organized at Brampton Barn, three miles Southwest of Savannah, Jan. 20, 1788, is the First African Baptist Church of today." On the other hand, the First Bryan Baptist Church is still on Lot No. 7, the lot on which Bryan built his church in 1795.

Love, Emanuel King. *History of the First African Baptist Church, From Its Organization, January 20, 1788 to July 1, 1888*. Savannah, GA: The Morning News Printing Co., 1888. 360 pp.

Simms, James Meriles. *The First Colored Baptist Church in North America; Constituted at Savannah, Georgia, Jan. 20, A.D. 1788. With Biographical Sketches of the Pastors*. Philadelphia, PA: J. B. Lippincott Co., 1888. 264 pp.

ACAB, PBGB, ERS.

MARSHALL, ARTHUR, JR. (March 2, 1914–April 3, 1987), 73rd bishop of the **African Methodist Episcopal Zion Church** (AMEZ), was born in High Point, North Carolina, the son of Arthur and Nellie (Kindle) Marshall. He grew up serving in most of the offices at his home church, St. Stephen AMEZ Church in High Point. He joined the West Central North

Carolina Conference in 1933, at the age of nineteen, and was assigned to the St. Phillip Circuit in Greensboro. He was ordained deacon on November 25, 1934 and elder on November 15, 1936. While on the St. Phillip Circuit he attended Livingstone College in Salisbury, North Carolina, earning his B.A. degree in 1937.

In 1938 he became dean of Walters Southland Institute in Lexa, Arkansas, serving also as presiding elder of the Pine Bluff District of the Arkansas Conference. In 1939 he moved to the Wadsworth Street AMEZ Church in Providence, Rhode Island, during which time he also was a student at Boston University in Massachusetts, earning both his S.T.B. and M.A. in 1941. From 1941 to 1944 he was assigned to the Clinton AMEZ Church in Ansonia, Connecticut. From 1944 to 1947 he was appointed to the First AMEZ (Peoples) Church in Syracuse, New York, followed by a pastorate at John Wesley AMEZ Church in Pittsburgh, Pennsylvania, from 1947 to 1955. On May 3, 1952, he married Mary Ann Stotts, with whom he had one son.

From 1955 to 1961 he pastored Metropolitan AMEZ Church in Kansas City, Missouri, where in 1957 he initiated and led the civil rights movement to integrate public facilities. He was a member of the executive board of the Paseo Y.M.C.A., and received an award for leading the most fruitful membership drive in history in 1957–58. In 1960 he was a candidate for the Missouri State Legislature. In 1961 he transferred to Washington Metropolitan AMEZ Church in St. Louis, Missouri, where he stayed for eleven years. In 1961 he was a member of the executive committee of the Missouri Council of Churches, and in 1963 joined the general board of the National Council of Churches. He served on the Citizens Committee for Social Action and was president of the local chapter of the N.A.A.C.P. He was a leader in the fight against de facto segregation in the public school system of St. Louis.

At the 1972 General Conference Marshall was elected bishop and was consecrated on May 12. He was assigned to the Episcopal District which included the Louisiana, Alabama, and South Carolina Conferences. In 1984 he was assigned to the Sixth Episcopal District (West Central North Carolina, Pee Dee, Palmetto, South Carolina, Georgia, and South Georgia Conferences), where he stayed for the remainder of his career. As bishop he was chair of the National Board of Publications and vice-chair of the National Board of Church Extension for the denomination. He was president of the Consultation on Church Union from 1982 to 1984 and was on its executive committee from 1972 to 1984. He served as a trustee for Livingstone College in Salisbury, North Carolina, and was chair of the board of trustees for Clinton Junior College in Rock

Hill, South Carolina, during which time student enrollment doubled, major improvements were made in the facilities and the curriculum was revised. He was a member of the General Assembly and Council of the World Methodist Conference, and an honorary member of the legislative assemblies of the states of Alabama and Louisiana.

"Bishop Marshall New Consultation Head." *Star of Zion* 105 (April 16, 1981): 1.
Hoggard, J. Clinton. "Fifty Years on the Pilgrimage." *A.M.E. Zion Quarterly Review* 97 (January 1987): 11–13.
Hopkins, Samuel L. "Support Grows for Dr. Marshall to Bishopric." *Star of Zion* 95 (March 2, 1972): 1, 2.
Johnson, Dorothy S. "Bishop Marshall Will Celebrate 50 Years in Ministry." *Star of Zion* 110 (October 2, 1986): 2.
Satterwhite, John H. "A Tribute to Bishop Arthur Marshall, Jr., March 2, 1914–April 3, 1987." *A.M.E. Zion Quarterly Review* 98 (July 1987): 47.
"Zion Mourns Death of Bishop Marshall." *Star of Zion* 111 (April 16, 1987): 1, 3.
BDNM (70), *AMEZC*, *WWR* (85).

MARTIN, JOHN SELLA (September, 1832–August, 1876), Baptist, Congregationalist, and Presbyterian minister, editor, and abolitionist, was born into slavery in Charlotte, North Carolina. His mother, Winnifred, was a mulatto slave forced into a relationship with a Mr. Martin, the nephew of her owner, a Mrs. Henderson. John Martin and his sister, Caroline, the two children of that short-lived union, were sold to a slave trader along with their mother, and lived together on an estate in Columbus, Georgia. Three years later the family members were separated, and Martin was sold to Edward Powers, also of Columbus. Over time, with occasional help, Martin learned to read and write, and was of particular help to his owner in the latter's senior years with failing eyesight. When Powers died in 1850 he freed Martin in his will, but the family contested the will and Martin was sold to a succession of other people.

Martin's final owner had him working on various riverboats, and he used this transportation opportunity to escape in 1856 to Chicago, Illinois. He soon became an agent of the *Provincial Freeman* newspaper in Chicago, grew active in abolitionist circles, and immediately made a wide impression as an eloquent and earnest speaker. In later 1856 he moved to Detroit to study for the ministry under a local Baptist preacher. After nine months, in the spring of 1857, he did a lecture tour across Michigan, and was hailed as a "prodigy" and a "natural orator." Later in 1857 he was ordained and called to pastor the Michigan Street Baptist Church in

Buffalo, New York. Buffalo had a small Black population at that time, and quickly seemed too much away from the mainstream of action for which Martin yearned. He married a woman named Sarah in late 1858 and moved to Boston in the spring of 1859. Later that year, impressed by Martin as a guest speaker, the largest White Baptist church in Lawrence, Massachusetts, made him "permanent supply" minister. He also filled in regularly at Tremont Temple in Boston and was a popular abolitionist speaker. In October and November 1859, he toured Massachusetts, Connecticut, and New York speaking on **Nat Turner** and the destiny of African Americans. He often recited his own, often lengthy poetry, and his first published poem, "The Sentinel of Freedom," was printed in the *Anglo-African* magazine in 1859.

At the end of November 1859, Martin accepted the pastorate of the Joy Street Baptist Church, the oldest Black church in Boston, founded by **Thomas Paul** in 1805. Martin represented a minority of his colleagues in advocating emigration as a real option for a large number of Black Americans. For a time he was supportive of the African Civilization Society, with a program apparently similar to the **American Colonization Society**, and was a lifelong friend of **Henry Highland Garnet**, a major spokesman for emigration ideas. Martin came to believe, however, that the vast majority of Blacks would prefer to remain in the country of their birth. He spent most of his energies fighting slavery, and the Joy Street church became a central gathering point for countless meetings and petitions. In August 1861, he went to England on a speaking tour to gain support for the Union cause; at that point England was neutral on the gathering hostilities, as President Lincoln had refused to suggest that slavery was the central issue of the conflict. Martin was successful in England, and returned to the United States in February, 1862, with $2,500 to purchase the freedom of his sister, Caroline, and her two children.

Martin suffered from periodic illnesses, ranging from urinary tract infections to pleurisy, and he decided a change of climate would be good. In January 1863 he moved to fill the pulpit of the Congregationalist hall of the Harper Twelvetrees factory in London, England, where he had been so welcomed on his earlier visit. He quickly moved to the forefront of pro-North forces rallying in England, an important means of preventing European nations from entering the fray or working on behalf of the South. In early April 1864, he sailed back to the United States, again seeking a change that would help his sagging health. He accepted the pastorate of the historic Shiloh Presbyterian Church in New York, following such illustrious figures as Garnet and **J. W. C.**

Pennington. He did not actually settle in the pulpit until 1865, and he was frequently away at speaking engagements.

On May 10, 1865, he went to England again to raise money for the American Missionary Association (A.M.A.) and its work with newly freed Blacks. The Shiloh Presbyterian Church finally forced him to return in November, just when his patient work throughout the United Kingdom was beginning to bear fruit. The A.M.A. began to lose income from England without him, and induced him to leave his pastorate in April 1866 and return to England as a special secretary for the A.M.A. There he maintained as hectic a schedule as his fragile health would allow, and addressed the Paris Anti-Slavery Conference in August 1867. After experiencing general success in his fundraising efforts, Martin and his wife, whose health was also in question, sailed back to the United States in August 1868. By this time Martin was apparently addicted to laudanum and/or opium, widely prescribed drugs at the time. Martin and his wife lived for a time in Washington, D.C., and he accepted the pastorate of the Fifteenth Street Presbyterian Church. In 1869 he tried unsuccessfully to enroll his daughter in a White public school. He became active in the Colored National Labor Convention, which had its first meeting in December 1869, and in January 1870 he was appointed editor of the newly founded *New Era* magazine, the official organ of the Colored National Labor Union. He resigned from the church to focus his attention on the editorial duties, but the paper's success was short-lived. Later that year he left the paper to be a "special agent" at the Mobile, Alabama post office. In about late 1870 he moved his family to New Orleans, where he struggled to make a living as a lecturer. He became a known political figure and was rewarded for his support of Governor Warmoth by being appointed superintendent of public education for the fourth division. The Republican party did not support his appointment, however, and after a few months he left for Boston, and then for New Orleans. He shifted his support to the Liberal Republican party, led by editor Andrew Greeley. In 1872 he moved back to Washington, D.C., and rejoined the Republican party, which relieved him of the charge of betraying the "party of Black America." For a few months in 1873 he co-edited the *New National Era*, but depended upon the lecture circuit for most of his income. By late 1874 he was back in New Orleans and was a founder of the New Orleans Athenaeum Club, a Black self-help group. For perhaps a year he was an agent for the Treasury Department in Shieldsboro, Mississippi, near New Orleans. He finally died without having achieved the lasting security and recognition for which he had hoped.

He was, however, fondly remembered by Frederick Douglass and others as a courageous and gifted fighter for freedom and dignity.

BAB, DANB, AARS, IBAW.

MARTIN, JOHN WILLIAM (June 30, 1879–October 16, 1955), 43rd bishop of the **African Methodist Episcopal Zion Church** (AMEZ), was born in Russell County, near Lebanon, Virginia, one of more than twelve children in the family of Cornelius and Nancy (Martin—the same maiden name) Martin. He attended Langston High School in Johnson City, Tennessee, then enrolled at Lincoln University in Pennsylvania, where he received his B.A. and B.D. degrees. While in school he joined the Philadelphia and Baltimore Conference, and was ordained deacon on May 21, 1905, and elder on September 8, 1907. His first pastoral assignment was the Wooderville Circuit in the Washington District.

After graduation, in about 1905 he transferred to the Kentucky Conference and was appointed to St. Mark (now Walters Chapel) AMEZ Church in Indianapolis, Indiana. In Indianapolis he met and married Ola M. Ecton, with whom he had one daughter. Also while at this church he began teaching at Atkinson College some two hundred miles away in Madisonville, Kentucky. Bishop **George Clinton** soon insisted that he become president of the college, where he remained for the next ten years.

At the 1916 General Conference Martin was elected Secretary of Education for the denomination, and was so successful in this position that at the 1924 General Conference he was elected bishop by acclamation, with two other bishopric candidates moving and seconding the nomination. He was consecrated on May 20, 1924, and assigned to the Pacific Coast and Demerara, South America. He was the first resident bishop on the Pacific Coast, moving to Los Angeles, and added many congregations to the connection in that region. In 1928 he was assigned Missouri and Michigan along with the Pacific Coast, and the South American work was given to another Episcopal District. In 1932 Missouri was placed in another Episcopal District, and South Carolina was added to his work. In 1944 he was assigned to Ohio, Cape Fear, and Michigan, and in 1948 was transferred to North Carolina.

Other than California, his major achievements were in Michigan, where many churches were strengthened or founded under his direction. He was a trustee of both Livingstone College in Salisbury, North Carolina, and Clinton Junior College in Rock Hill, South Carolina, where a new gymnasium was named in his honor. He was known as an honest, thoughtful, and devoted servant of the church.

"The Anthology of A.M.E. Zion Bishops." *Star of Zion* 57 (September 28, 1933): 1, 6.
"Bishop John William Martin." *A.M.E. Zion Quarterly Review* 59 (1949): 104.
"Bishop John W. Martin Passes." *A.M.E. Zion Quarterly Review* 66 (1955): 56.
"The Magnificent Qualities of Our Bishops: The Jovial, Rugged, Philosophic, Fair-Minded Bishop John William Martin." *Star of Zion* 70 (June 20, 1946): 1, 8.
"New Era of Zion Methodism." *Star of Zion* 48 (August 7, 1924): 1, 5.
AMEZC, HAMEZC.

MARTIN, JOSEPH C. (February 8, 1865–February 6, 1939), 14th bishop of the **Christian Methodist Episcopal Church** (CME), then known as the Colored Methodist Episcopal Church, was born in Trenton, Gibson County, Tennessee, the son of Willis and Clara (Penn) Martin. After attending public schools in his home town he went to Howe Institute in Memphis, Tennessee, for a Bible course, and then to Roger Williams University in Nashville, Tennessee. He was converted in 1878, joined the church in 1879, and began preaching in 1887. He never married.

His first pastoral assignment was in West Tennessee from 1890 to 1892. He then transferred conferences to pastor Miles Memorial CME Church in Washington, D.C., from 1892 to 1896. He again transferred conferences, this time to the South Carolina Conference, and was appointed to Sydney Park CME Church in Columbus, from 1896 to 1901. In 1901 he was a delegate to the Third Ecumenical Methodist Conference in London. From 1901 to 1905 he was assigned to Collins Chapel CME Church in Memphis, Tennessee, and from 1905 to 1912 he was presiding elder of the Memphis District. He was president of the Solvent Savings Bank and Trust Co. in Memphis from 1911 to 1912.

In 1912 he was elected Publishing Agent for the denomination, staying in that position for ten years. He was very successful, showing great business acumen, and established a credit rating for the publishing house comparable to that of other significant publishing interests. He was a trustee of Lane College in Jackson, Tennessee. At the General Conference at St. Louis, Missouri, in May 1922, Martin was elected bishop, and served faithfully until his death seventeen years later.

EWM, CMECTY, WWCR.

MARTIN, RICHARD BEAMON (b. February 23, 1913), a bishop of the **Episcopal Church**, was born in Peak, South Carolina, the son of Benjamin and Viola Martin, both prominent educators. Martin received his B.A. in 1937 from Allen University in Columbia, South Carolina. He taught languages and social studies at Georgetown High School before entering Bishop Payne Divinity School in Petersburg, Virginia, where he earned his B.D. in 1942.

Martin was ordained deacon on June 8, 1942, and priest in February 1943. At that time he was assigned to Good Shepherd Episcopal Church in Sumter, South Carolina, and St. Augustine's Episcopal Church in nearby Wedgefield. He also taught English and philosophy at Morris College in Sumter. In June 1943 he married Annelle Hoover, with whom he had two sons. From 1944 to 1963 he was rector of Grace Episcopal Church in Norfolk, Virginia, and also served as Archdeacon of Southern Virginia. He continued his own education and received his D.D. in 1955 from Allen University. From 1963 to 1967 he was rector of St. Philip's Episcopal Church in Brooklyn, New York, and from 1965 to 1967 was Archdeacon of Brooklyn. He was chair of the Body of Christ Commission, a member of the Christian-Jewish Relations Commission, and a member of the Committee on Relations with Catholic-Orthodox-Protestant Churches. On February 2, 1967, he was consecrated suffragan bishop of Long Island.

ECA (1968).

MARTIN, ROBERTA (February 12, 1907–January 18, 1969), one of the pioneers of gospel music, was born in Helena, Arkansas. The family moved to Chicago, Illinois, when she was ten years old. She was greatly influenced by music teacher Mildred Byrant Jones at Wendell Phillips High School, and became a musician. In about 1931 she went to Ebenezer Baptist Church in Chicago to be the accompanist for the newly formed Gospel Choir, led by **Thomas A. Dorsey**.

In 1933 Martin and Theodore Frye organized a junior gospel choir at Ebenezer Baptist Church. Out of this group came the Martin-Frye Singers and then, in 1936, the Roberta Martin Singers. In 1939 she established the Roberta Martin Studio of Music in Chicago. For a short time in the 1940s she joined with **Sallie Martin** (unrelated) to form the Martin and Martin Singers, but then returned to the Roberta Martin Singers. This group toured the United States and Europe, and in 1964 performed at the Festival of Two Worlds in Spoleto, Italy. From 1956 to 1968 she was minister of music at the Mount Pisgah Baptist Church.

She wrote about one hundred songs in her career, the first being "Try Jesus, He Satisfies," in 1943. Her most popular songs are "God Is Still on the Throne" (1959), "Let It Be" (1962), and "Just Jesus and Me" (1966). She helped define the style of the gospel music pianist, and her pupils included **James Cleveland**, Alex Bradford, and Joe Washington. She accompanied such artists as **Mahalia Jackson** and Willie Ford Smith, and was a major influence in the field. In February 1981, the Smithsonian Institute in Washington, D.C., honored her with a series of lectures and recitals.

BDA-AHP, BDA-AAM, IBAW, BWR.

MARTIN, SALLIE (November 20, 1896– ?), with **Thomas A. Dorsey** the principal founder of Black gospel music, was born in Pittfield, Georgia. Orphaned at age sixteen, she did not start singing until 1931, when she joined Thomas Dorsey's newly founded gospel choir at the Ebenezer Baptist Church in Chicago, Illinois. In 1932 she helped Dorsey and others found the National Convention of Gospel Choirs and Choruses.

For years Martin as singer and Dorsey as pianist toured as a duet, promoting gospel music. Martin was responsible for organizing at least one hundred gospel choirs. In 1940 the two split up when Dorsey began touring with **Mahalia Jackson**. That year Martin formed the Martin and Morris Music Company with Kenneth Morris, in Chicago. It became one of the largest gospel music publishing houses in the world. In 1940 she also founded the Sallie Martin Singers and with them toured the United States and Europe. A strong supporter of **Martin Luther King, Jr.**, she represented him at the ceremony marking the independence of Nigeria in 1960. A building in Issluuka was named in her honor.

Banks, Lacy J. "Gospel Music: A Shout of Black Joy." *Ebony* 27 (May 1972): 161–168.
BDA-AHP, BWR, IBAW, BDA-AAM.

MARY ALLEN BAPTIST COLLEGE. A Baptist school. Mary Allen Baptist College, Crockett, Texas, began with the efforts of Rev. S. M. Tenny, a Confederate Army veteran, who after the war dedicated himself to the complete liberation of the freedmen. He raised the money to found a school which opened in 1870 in his church in Crockett. The school developed slowly over the next fifteen years, and in 1885 Tenny applied for funding from the Board of Missions for Freedmen of the Presbyterian Church U.S.A., now a constituent part of the **Presbyterian Church (U.S.A.).**

The board took the school under its care in 1886 as a boarding school for girls. Tenny also gained the attention of Mary Esther Allen who began organizing Presbyterian women to support the school. Allen died in 1886, and spoke of the school as she passed from this life. Her final words captured the imagination of many. Three days after her death on March 3, the school was named Mary Allen Seminary.

The school progressed steadily until the winter 1910–1911. Smallpox broke out in the student body. Then in January 1912 one of the main buildings was destroyed by fire. These two events were followed by a period of lessening commitment by the school's supporters and a decreasing student body. The downward turn was not reversed until 1924 when Rev. Byrd Randall Smith, the first African American president, assumed leadership of the school. He revitalized the school, developed the junior college curriculum, and saw the first junior college students graduate in 1927. In 1932 the school became the first college with a Black president recognized with an "A" rating by the Southern Association of Colleges and Secondary Schools. The following year the school became coeducational and was reorganized as Mary Allen Junior College. The high school was discontinued in 1936.

A decade of prosperity was followed by some interaction with the state of Texas, which wished to see the school expand into a four year college. The school's board, however, felt that it could not support such development. Therefore, in 1943 the school was sold and its records moved to Harbison College. The school reopened under Baptist auspices as Mary Allen Baptist College, a four-year institution.

Parker, Inez Moore. *The Rise and Decline of the Program of Education for Black Presbyterians of the United Presbyterian Church U.S.A., 1865–1970.* San Antonio, TX: Trinity University Press, 1977. 319 pp.

MARY HOLMES JUNIOR COLLEGE. A **Presbyterian Church (U.S.A.)** school. Mary Holmes Junior College, West Point, Mississippi, was founded in 1892 by the Board of Missions for Freedmen of the Presbyterian Church in the U.S.A., now a constituent part of the **Presbyterian Church (U.S.A.).** It was originally named Mary Holmes Seminary, in honor of the wife of Rev. Mead Holmes, who had worked with the Board of Missions for a number of years.

The school opened as a girl's school in Jackson, Mississippi, with an emphasis in domestic arts and Christian service. Two years later it was destroyed by

fire and reopened in West Point on some land donated by a group of citizens. Several additional plots of land, including some prime farm land were obtained at a later date. In 1932 the school opened its junior college department. In 1935 male students were initially admitted, though as day students only. Over the years the students worked the farm land which in more recent times has been given over to trees as a cash crop.

In 1941 the school was renamed Mary Holmes Junior College. In 1959 the high school was dropped, and the school has since continued as a junior college.

Parker, Inez Moore. *The Rise and Decline of the Program of Education for Black Presbyterians of the United Presbyterian Church U.S.A., 1865–1970.* San Antonio, TX: Trinity University Press, 1977. 319 pp.

MASON, CHARLES HARRISON (September 8, 1866–November 17, 1961), co-founder of the **Church of God in Christ**, was born in Shelby County, near Memphis, Tennessee. His parents, Jerry and Eliza Mason, former slaves, were tenant farmers and active members of the Missionary Baptist Church. In November 1878 the family moved to Plumersville, Arkansas, and that same year Mason experienced conversion. In 1879 a yellow fever epidemic claimed his father's life, and looked as though it might claim Mason's the following year, but a miraculous recovery occurred near the first Sunday in September 1880, when he was suddenly cured. This brought him to an even stronger religious conviction, and he was baptized, beginning to preach at revivals throughout Arkansas.

He was ordained in 1891, but refrained from full-time ministry when his fiancée, Alice Saxton, protested against his plans to be a preacher. After two years she divorced him, and Mason went into a deep depression. That year (1893), however, the autobiography of Black Holiness evangelist **Amanda Smith** was published, and Mason was reenergized, claiming sanctification and preaching the Holiness gospel. He then received a preacher's license from the Mt. Gale Missionary Baptist Church and on November 1, 1893, entered Arkansas Baptist College. After three unhappy months he concluded that the education offered there was of no use to him and left.

He soon met **Charles Price Jones**, pastor of the Mt. Helms Baptist Church in Jackson, Mississippi, who had also become involved in the Holiness movement. Their joint work then caused a split in the Baptist churches, which expelled them from fellowship. They then founded the Church of Christ in 1894, the name changing in 1897 to the Church of God in Christ, according to a revelation received by Mason. This new church significantly broadened the context for Black Christian experience, which heretofore had been generally channelled through the Methodist and Baptist churches. In 1903 he married Lelia Washington, with whom he had several children; she died in 1936.

In early 1907, Mason traveled to Los Angeles, California, to experience the Azusa Street Pentecostal revival under **William J. Seymour**, and received that new spiritual blessing in March. Upon his return to Mississippi, however, Mason discovered that speaking in tongues and other such Pentecostal marks were not universally accepted by the church. Some of the membership followed Jones in the formation of the Church of Christ (Holiness). Those who followed Mason reorganized the Church of God in Christ in September, 1907, electing Mason general overseer and his close colleague, D. J. Young, editor of the church's journal, *The Whole Truth.*

Somewhat unexpectedly, Mason's position as one of the few Pentecostal leaders in a legally incorporated body (chartered in Memphis in late 1897) made him a sought-after ordainer of other Pentecostals, both Black and White. Between 1909 and 1914, when the White Assemblies of God was formed, there were as many White congregations of the Church of God in Christ as Black. Mason maintained close ties with the Whites and in 1952 was the elder statesman at the Pentecostal World Conference in London, England.

The Church of God in Christ expanded rapidly, and soon became internationally known, although Mason's pacifism during World War I led to a brief arrest in 1918 and the maintenance of an FBI file on him. In 1943 he married a third time, to Elsie Washington. The church today is the largest Pentecostal denomination in America, and is second only to the **National Baptist Convention of the U.S.A., Inc.**, as the largest Black religious group.

Courts, James, ed. *The History and Life Work of Elder C. H. Mason, Chief Apostle, and His Co-Laborers.* Memphis, TN: Howe Printing Dept., 1920. 97 pp.

Patterson, J. O., German R. Ross, and Julia Mason Atkins. *History and Formative Years of the Church of God in Christ with Excerpts from the Life and Works of Its Founder— Bishop C. H. Mason.* Memphis, TN: Church of God in Christ Publishing House, 1966. 143 pp.

RLOA, BPL, BDACSL, ERS, DARB, BH, BSC, BDA-AHP, DPCM, PHCGC, HCGCH, TP, HPM.

MATTHEW, WENTWORTH ARTHUR (June 23, 1892–1973), founder of the **Commandment Keepers Congregation of the Living God**, was born in Lagos, Nigeria. His father died while Matthew was still young, and his mother took him back to her native West Indies. In 1913, at age twenty-one, Matthew moved to New York City, working odd jobs. He became a minister with a Black Pentecostal group, **Church of the Living God the Pillar and Ground of the Truth**. He became a follower of **Marcus Garvey**'s Universal Negro Improvement Association, and also encountered another West Indian, **Arnold Josiah Ford**, who claimed that all Blacks were by heritage Jewish. This idea took hold of Matthew, who began acquiring information about the Hebrew language and Jewish practices. Claims that he attended at various times Hayden Theological Seminary, Bishop Ecclesiastical School, Rose of Sharon Theological Seminary in Cincinnati, and the University of Berlin have been dismissed by some investigators.

In 1919 Matthew began his own group, the Commandment Keepers, Holy Church of the Living God, which combined Christian and Jewish elements. An inscription in the meeting room asserted that "Jesus Saves!" In the early 1920s Matthew discovered the existence of the **Falashas**, Black Jews in Ethiopia, and began emphasizing Ethiopian connections. He later claimed to have been ordained by the chief rabbi of the Ethiopian Falashas as well as by the Ethiopian National Church, which is Coptic Christian. In 1930 A. J. Ford moved to Ethiopia and left his congregation in Matthew's care. Matthew then opened a synagogue on 131st Street in Harlem and incorporated the group as the Commandment Keepers Congregation of the Living God.

By the 1930s the group had abandoned any Christian references, although a number of Protestant elements, such as testimonials, spontaneous sermons, foot-washing, healing, and even hymns with Old Testament themes were maintained. Christianity was denigrated as the religion of the White Gentiles, who stole the Jewish religion from Blacks through enslavement and oppression. Matthew maintained strict control over the organization, not only mandating the observance of kosher food laws and other Jewish practices, but enforcing a code of behavior designed to eliminate juvenile delinquency and sexual improprieties. Matthew founded the Ethiopian Hebrew Rabbinical College, with classes in Talmud, Jewish history, and other relevant topics. He also taught "Cabalistic Science," a mystical blend of Black traditions in conjure and **voodoo**, which Matthew used in the healing ministry of the synagogue.

In Matthew's lifetime the Commandment Keepers grew to be a solid group with many thousands of adherents. Relationships with White Jewish groups were complex, with some friendly and some in opposition. Matthew was succeeded by his grandson, David M. Dore, who in 1977 became the second Black to receive a degree from Yeshiva University.

"America's Black Jews." *Ebony* 11–12 (May 1957): 97–100.

Ehrman, Albert. "Black Judaism in New York." *Journal of Ecumenical Studies* 8 (Winter 1971): 103–113.

———. "The Commandment Keepers: A Negro 'Jewish' Cult in America Today." *Judaism* 8 (Summer 1959): 266–270.

Landes, Ruth. "Negro Jews in Harlem." *Jewish Journal of Sociology* 9 (December 1967): 175–189.

BDACSL, NWAC, BJH, RLOA, BDA-AHP, BSC, IBAW.

MATTHEWS, WILLIAM WALTER (October 28, 1871–March 15, 1962), 45th bishop of the **African Methodist Episcopal Zion Church** (AMEZ), was born in Batesville, Mississippi, the son of Thomas Augustus and Eliza Caroline (Bobo) Matthews. He attended Branch Normal College in Pine Bluff, Arkansas, from 1890 to 1900, and New Orleans University (now called Dillard University) in Louisiana from 1898 to 1901. He joined the Arkansas Conference in 1904 and was ordained deacon later that year, on December 12. In 1908 he married Alice Johnson, with whom he had six children, of whom only two survived him.

His first pastoral assignment was at Payne Chapel AMEZ Church in Little Rock, Arkansas, followed by Cherry Street AMEZ Church in Pine Bluff, Arkansas; Pettys Chapel AMEZ Church in New Orleans, Louisiana; Cooper AMEZ Church in Oakland, California; First AMEZ Church in San Francisco, California; First AMEZ Church in Portland, Oregon; Zion Temple AMEZ Church in McCloud, California; and Old Ship AMEZ Church in Montgomery, Alabama.

In 1920 Matthews was elected General Secretary of the Board of Foreign Missions, which also made him editor of the *Missionary Seer*, the board's official publication. He held that post until 1928, when he was elected bishop. He was consecrated bishop on May 20, 1928, and assigned to the West Coast of Africa. In his eight years there he built four school buildings and organized the Liberia Conference with eleven ministers and 2,500 members. In 1936 he was transferred to the Arkansas area, where he focused his energies on Walters-Southland Institute. He moved the school from Warren to Lexa, near Helena, Arkansas, and rebuilt it into one of the denomination's best secondary schools. After the death of Bishop George Clement in 1934, Matthews was assigned to the West Central North Carolina Conference and in 1941, after the death of Bishop **Lynwood W. Kyles**, he was assigned to the

Central North Carolina Conference. He eventually also served conferences in Texas, Oklahoma, Louisiana, Alabama, and Florida.

His first wife having passed away, on January 28, 1947, he married Etoria Dryver. His career came to an abrupt end at the General Conference of 1948, where formal charges were brought against him. He was charged with deceiving the church as to the date of his birth, stating it to be 1876 instead of 1871, so as to continue longer in the active episcopacy and not yet come under the rule of retirement at age 72. He was also charged with consorting with Etoria Dryver prior to his wife's demise, and marrying Dryver despite her previous two divorces. He denied the validity of the charges, but was found guilty, forcibly retired, and divested of his episcopal status. At the 1952 General Conference Matthews again tried to clear his name, but his petition was dismissed. He was allowed a pension of one-half his previous salary for the remainder of his life, and he spent his last years at his home in Washington, D.C.

"The Anthology of the A.M.E. Zion Bishops." *Star of Zion* 57 (September 28, 1933): 1, 6.

Lewis, Charles. "Crusading AMEZ Head Retires." *Star of Zion* 72 (September 16, 1948): 7.

"The Magnificent Qualities of Our Bishops: The Shrewd, Pioneering, Enterprising, and Skillful Bishop William Walter Matthews." *Star of Zion* 70 (August 8, 1946): 1, 8.

"Obituary and Program, Bishop W. W. Matthews." *Star of Zion* 85 (March 29, 1962): 3.

HAMEZC, AMEZC, WWCA (38–40).

MAY, FELTON EDWIN (b. April 23, 1935), a bishop of the **United Methodist Church**, was born in Chicago, Illinois, the son of James Albert and Florine Felton Caruthers. He attended the Chicago Teachers College from 1952 to 1956 while assistant to the executive director of the Chicago Sinai Congregation (1952–57). From 1957 to 1959 he was a laboratory technician with the U.S. Army at Fort Leonard Wood in Missouri.

Upon discharge from the Army, May worked as a clerk in the U.S. Postal Service in Chicago, then finished his college work at Judson College in Marion, Alabama, receiving his B.A. in 1961. From 1961 to 1963 he was assistant minister at St. James Methodist Church in Chicago, Illinois, and was ordained deacon in 1962. From 1963 to 1968 he pastored Maple Park Methodist Church. While at that church, on June 22, 1963, he married Phyllis Henry, with whom he had two children. In 1968 the Methodist Church merged with the Evangelical United Brethren to form the United Methodist Church. As part of the restructuring the all-

Black Central Jurisdiction was dissolved and the Black clergy and bishops were integrated into the new structure.

From 1968 to 1970 May was associate executive director of the Methodist Action Program in Wilmington, Delaware. While there he worked on his M.Div. at Crozier Theological Seminary in Chester, Pennsylvania. After he received the degree in 1970 he was ordained elder. From 1970 to 1975 he pastored the Ezion-Mt. Carmel United Methodist Church in Wilmington, and led the congregation in the building of a new church. He was district superintendent of the Easton District of the Peninsula Conference, and was based in Easton, Maryland, from 1975 to 1981. From 1981 to 1984 he was Conference Council Director of the Peninsula Conference. In 1984 he was elected bishop and assigned to the Harrisburg (Pennsylvania) Episcopal Area. Since 1990 he has been on special assignment in Washington, D.C., for the Council of Bishops, developing substance abuse programs. He has had a special concern for church growth in Africa, and has made six trips to fourteen countries in Africa to support the churches there. In 1979 he wrote a Developmental Evangelism Workbook for the Sierra Leone Annual Conference. He has been active in many organizations, including **Black Methodists for Church Renewal** and Americans for Democratic Action. He was vice-chair of the Dover branch of the American Red Cross and was a member of the Delaware Civil Rights Commission (1970) and the Delaware Health and Social Services Commission (1972).

BDNM (75), *WWA* (90–91), *BDUMB.*

MAYO, JAMES HASKELL (? –), 100th bishop of the **African Methodist Episcopal Church** (AME), was born in Springfield, Ohio, the son of Mark and Estelle Mayo. After attending high school in Springfield he enrolled in Wilberforce University, where he received his B.A. He earned his B.D. at Payne Theological Seminary at Wilberforce. He married Theodora Mayo, with whom he had three children.

In 1942 he was assigned to First AME Church in Xenia, Ohio, followed by further pastorates at St. John AME Church in River Rouge, Michigan; Ward AME Church in Washington, D.C.; St. James AME Church in St. Louis, Missouri; Shorter AME Church in Denver, Colorado; and Coppin AME Church in Chicago, Illinois. In the St. Louis pastorate he built James House for the elderly, and in Chicago he raised $100,000 to renovate the church, operated a day care center, and began a weekly radio broadcast.

In 1980 Mayo was elected bishop and assigned to the Fourteenth Episcopal District, covering Liberia and Sierra Leone in Africa. While there, he dedicated the new Richard Allen School in Sierra Leone. From 1984 to 1988 he headed the Sixteenth Episcopal District, then briefly was assigned to the Tenth Episcopal District, with headquarters in Dallas, Texas. More recently he has been assigned to the Fourth Episcopal District, with headquarters in Chicago, Illinois.

FEDHR.

MAYS, BENJAMIN ELIJAH (August 1, 1894–March 28, 1984), Baptist minister and nationally known educator, was born in Epworth, South Carolina, the last of seven children born to S. Hezekiah and Louvenia (Carter) Mays. He was valedictorian of his high school class in 1916 and decided to go on to college. His father, a farmer, felt this was an unwise move, "aiming too high." Nevertheless, working summers as a Pullman porter, he received his B.A. degree from Bates College in Maine in 1920, where he excelled scholastically and was a star debater. He married Ellen Harvin on July 31, 1920, but she died within a few years.

He was ordained a Baptist minister in 1922 and took his first pastorate at the Shiloh Baptist Church of Atlanta. The church was near Morehouse College, a Baptist institution where he taught part-time until 1924. In 1925 he received his M.A. degree from the University of Chicago, and became an English teacher at the State College of South Carolina at Orangeburg. He married Sadie Gray, a teacher, on August 9, 1926. He was executive secretary of the Tampa Urban League in Tampa, Florida, from 1926 to 1928, and national student secretary of the Y.M.C.A. from 1928 to 1930.

The turning point in his career came in 1930, when he was hired by the Institute of Social and Religious Research in New York City to direct a major study of Black churches in the United States. The study took two years, and resulted in a book, *The Negro's Church* (1933), which Mays cowrote with J. W. Nicholson. This was a landmark book in the study of Black religion, and later attained among scholars the status of a classic. He was thus brought in 1934 to the position of Dean of the School of Religion at Howard University in Washington, D.C. He held this position for six years, during which time the program was sufficiently upgraded to receive a Class A rating by the American Association of Theological Schools. In addition, he received his Ph.D. from the University of Chicago in 1935. Still a leading figure in the Y.M.C.A., he attended its World

Conference in Mysore, India, in 1937, and the Plenary Session of the World Committee in Stockholm in 1939.

In 1940 he was named president of Morehouse College, where he remained for twenty-seven years. One of his first acts as president was to appoint students to all major committees, a practice that later became standard on other college campuses. During his tenure the status of the college grew such that it was called the "Black Oxford of the South." His many publications extended his influence, with over seventy articles and many books, including *The Negro's God as Reflected in His Literature* (1938), *Seeking to be Christian in Race Relations* (1957), and *Born to Rebel: An Autobiography* (1971). Among many other positions, he became the first Black vice-president of the Federal Council of Churches in December 1944, headed the **National Baptist Convention, U.S.A., Inc.**, delegation to the World Council of Churches in 1948, and was leader of the Baptist World Alliance Assembly in 1950. In 1954 he was named by *Ebony* magazine as one of the top ten Black preachers in America.

He was a courageous supporter of civil rights and a foe of racial discrimination. To him belongs the famous quote that "eleven o'clock on Sunday morning is the most segregated hour in America." After his retirement in 1967, he expanded still further his public profile, becoming in 1969 the first Black on the Atlanta Board of Education, serving until 1981. **Martin Luther King, Jr.**, a former student at Morehouse College, called Mays "my spiritual mentor and my intellectual father."

Bennett, Lerone, Jr. "Benjamin Elijah Mays: The Last of the Great Schoolmasters." *Ebony* 33 (December 1977): 72–80.
"Great Negro Preachers." *Ebony* 9, 10 (July 1954): 26–30.
Mays, Benjamin E. *Born to Rebel: An Autobiography*. New York: Charles Scribner's Sons, 1971. 380 pp.
———. *Disturbed About Man*. Richmond, VA: John Knox Press, 1969. 143 pp.
———. *The Negro's Church*. New York: Institute of Social and Religious Research, 1933. 321 pp.
———. *The Negro's God as Reflected in His Literature*. Boston: Chapman & Grimes, Inc., 1938. 269 pp.
———. *Seeking to be Christian in Race Relations*. New York: Friendship Press, 1946. 48 pp.
WWCA (38–40), RLOA, BAA, BDA-AHP, ERS, RLA, BDNM (75), EBA, CA (45–48), NYTBS (84), CB (45), GNPP, IBAW, SBAA, BAW, HUBA, ONL, MBRL, LBAA, BHAC, BDAE, BLW.

MAYSON, HENRY IRVING (b. February 1, 1925), a bishop of the **Episcopal Church**, was born in Cleveland, Ohio, the son of Edwin Lawson and Josephine Bell (Hill) Mayson. He received his B.A. in 1948 from St. Augustine's College in Raleigh, North Carolina, and for a time fulfilled his musical talents as an oboist with the Cleveland Philharmonic Orchestra. In 1951 he married Alma Marie Harris, with whom he had two children.

He received his B.D. in 1951 from Bexley Hall Divinity School. In June 1951 he was ordained deacon and for several months was chaplain at Cleveland State Psychiatric Hospital. He was ordained priest on December 22, 1951, and founded St. Philip's Episcopal Church in Akron, Ohio. Within six years the church sponsored Akron's first Black debutante cotillion. Mayson was active in the community on the executive boards of the Akron chapter of Congress of Racial Equality (C.O.R.E.), of the Akron chapter of the N.A.A.C.P. (1960), and of the local branch of the Urban League (1957–61). He was also a leader in the Y.M.C.A. and in the Antipoverty Program in Summit County. He was a founding member of the Union of Black Clergy and Laity, later renamed the **Union of Black Episcopalians**.

In November 1969, Mayson was appointed Director of Christian Social Relations and thus became the first Black staff member of the Diocese of Ohio. In 1970 he was appointed Archdeacon of the Michigan Diocese. There he continued his community activities and extended them into a job training program in downtown Detroit. He was also a representative to the assembly of the Christian Communication Council of Metropolitan Detroit; a deputy to the General Convention in 1973; a member of the executive council of the Diocese of Michigan; and a trustee of Bexley Hall. On October 9, 1976, he was consecrated suffragan bishop of Michigan.

"Bright Young Men of God." *Ebony* 11 (March 1956): 17–23.
IBAW, ECA (1978), *BDNM* (70).

MEACHUM, JOHN BERRY (May 3, 1789–February 19, 1854), educator and influential Baptist minister in pre-Civil War Missouri, was born into slavery in Goochland County, Virginia, the son of Thomas and Patsy, and the property of Paul Meachum. Meachum grew up quite fond of his owner, but also desirous of his freedom. After they had moved to Kentucky, Meachum proposed purchasing his own freedom through extra work, and a deal was struck. It is unclear how long it took to collect the necessary money, but it is known that he spent some time laboring in a "saltpetre cave." He was finally emancipated in November 1812.

His father was still a slave in Hanover County,

Virginia, and a part time Baptist preacher. Meachum purchased his father's freedom and his father, in turn, saw to his conversion and baptism into the Baptist Church. They journeyed back to Kentucky, where his father was reunited with his mother. Eventually they settled in Harrison County, Indiana. Meanwhile, Meachum's former owner, Paul Meachum, now over one hundred years old, offered to give him his remaining seventy-five slaves if he would take them out of the state at his own expense and emancipate them. A caravan was formed and Meachum, in a situation likened to that of Moses, led the slaves across the Ohio River to federal land in Harrison County, Indiana, where his parents had settled. Such a large group raised the ire of the settlers already present, and an angry mob formed to chase them away. Fortunately there was no violence, and the group was able to depart intact. They were able to find other land on which to settle.

Soon afterward Meachum returned to Kentucky in search of his still-enslaved wife and children, only to find that they had been moved to Missouri. He made his way to St. Louis and arrived with almost no money. He had plenty of expertise as a carpenter and cooper (barrelmaker), and was soon able to make enough money to purchase his wife and children. They remained in St. Louis and he settled into the lucrative cooper business. They joined a Baptist mission run by White missionary John Mason Peck, and Meachum became the recognized leader of St. Louis' African Baptists. He helped found the mission's Sunday School, the first of its kind west of the Mississippi River. Although it was against the law to educate Blacks, Peck and Meachum ran a secret day school in the basement for that purpose, and the Sunday School also educated under the label of religious training. The basement school was the first recorded school for Blacks in Missouri.

Peck decided to move on, and helped ordain Meachum in February 1826, to carry on the mission, later called the First African Baptist Church. The church grew under his leadership and became the dominant Black church of any denomination in St. Louis. By 1846 the membership had grown from about two hundred (in 1826) to more than five hundred. Most of the members were slaves, and permission from the masters to attend services had to be carefully guarded. Despite constant restrictions on education for Blacks, Meachum maintained his clandestine school until it was finally closed and he was arrested and charged with inciting sedition. After his release from that charge, Meachum decided upon a most ingenious course of action. He purchased a steamboat and renovated it to function as a school. The Mississippi River was governed by federal law, not Missouri law, and thus Black students could be taught upon it during the day without legal retribution. He called his floating school the "Freedom School," and it became famous across the country. The existence of that school and the stout-hearted and creative resistance it symbolized was of tremendous value for the future of Black education in Missouri.

Meachum was generally successful in business, and was dedicated to using his success to help others. He regularly purchased slaves and taught them a marketable skill. Once they were earning wages they paid back to him their purchase price and he moved on to another slave. He was not altogether a success story, however, for he suffered at some point a reversal of fortune that left him with close to nothing. He passed away on a Sunday morning while conducting worship, and the obituaries noted that his legacy was very rich indeed.

Meachum, John Berry. *An Address to All the Colored Citizens of the United States.* Philadelphia, PA: King and Baird, 1846. 62 pp.

BAHA, HBB, BAW, HUBA, AARS.

MEDFORD, HAMPTON THOMAS (January 29, 1885–September 14, 1964), 56th bishop of the **African Methodist Episcopal Zion Church** (AMEZ), was born in Marion, North Carolina, the son of Charles Greenlee and Cecilia (Godfrey) Medford. He grew up in extreme poverty and was unable to obtain any education until he was fourteen. Then he took a job doing chores on a farm where he could board and have only a four-mile walk to school each day. He was a quick study and soon absorbed an elementary school education. This enabled him to become a public school teacher in his home county, McDonald. With his $20-a-month salary he bought a horse, buggy, and wagon, and established a grocery business. He began to gain his reputation as one who had the boundless energy and drive to succeed in many ventures at once. He was converted and joined the Doggette Grove AMEZ Church, later feeling the call to preach. On March 20, 1904, he married Mary Elizabeth Camp, with whom he had five children.

At the age of twenty-one, in 1906, he left his home town and joined the Western North Carolina Conference, and enrolled in 1909 in Livingstone College in Salisbury, North Carolina. He was ordained deacon on November 17, 1907, and elder on November 13, 1910. He earned his B.A. in 1912 and B.D. from the related Hood Theological Seminary in 1915, all while pastoring local churches. His pastorates included the Cherryville Circuit; Sandy Ridge and China Grove AMEZ Churches (1907–1910); Cleveland Circuit (1911–12); Moore's Chapel AMEZ Church in Salisbury

(1912); and Grace AMEZ Church in Charlotte (1913–1916), all in North Carolina. He then transferred conferences to pastor the Jacob Street Tabernacle AMEZ Church in Louisville, Kentucky (1916–21), followed by Loguen Temple AMEZ Church in Knoxville, Tennessee (1921–24). From 1924 to 1928 he was at the prestigious John Wesley AMEZ Church in Washington, D.C.

From this last pastorate Medford was elected General Secretary-Treasurer of the Department of Foreign Missions, which made him editor of the *Missionary Seer*, the official publication of that department. He supplemented these duties as an instructor at the School of Religion of Frelenghuysen University in Washington, D.C., and was dean in 1934. In 1931 he was a delegate to the Ecumenical Methodist Conference in Atlanta, Georgia. In 1934 he was the spokesman for the denomination at the Sesqui-Centennial of American Methodism in Baltimore, Maryland. In 1937 he published *Zion Methodism Abroad*. In 1941 he was a delegate to the International Council of Christian Educators in Mexico City, Mexico. In 1948 he published another book, *From the Depths*.

At the 1948 General Conference he was elected bishop and was consecrated on May 16. He was assigned to work in Africa and served with distinction there until 1952, when he was assigned to the Eighth Episcopal District (North Carolina, Virginia, and Albermarle Conferences). His first wife died in 1951, and on May 6, 1952 he married Mrs. Savannah Jones. He was known as a knowledgeable businessman who managed money and real estate well, becoming very wealthy. He was a trustee of Livingstone College in Salisbury, North Carolina. At the 1960 General Conference he retired to his home in Washington, D.C.

Barnes, Alexander. "Final Rights Held for Bishop Medford." *Star of Zion* 87 (October 22, 1964): 1.

"The Fabulous Bishop Medford." *Star of Zion* 75 (October 9, 1952): 1–2.

Medford, Hampton Thomas. *From the Depths*. Washington, DC: 1948.

———. *Zion Methodism Abroad*. 1937. 152 pp.

BAW, AARS, HUBA, WWCA (38–40), *BDNM* (70), *HAMEZC, AMEZC, RLA*.

MEHARRY MEDICAL COLLEGE. A **United Methodist Church** school. Meharry, one of the most important schools in America for the training of African American physicians and pharmacists, began in 1876 as the medical department of central Tennessee College (later Walden University). The department was organized by Dr. George W. Hubbard, who remained its head until his retirement in 1921. Hubbard had arrived in Nashville in 1864 on his way to Atlanta to take up duties with the Christian Commission in connection with the army of the Potomac. The Confederate army had cut the rail lines and he was stranded. Caught in Nashville, he began to teach African American youth. After the war he attended the University of Tennessee, earned his medical degree and settled down as a physician. Meanwhile, R. S. Rust of the Methodist's Freedman's Aid Society had interested the Meharry family of Indiana in the idea of starting a medical school for the Freedmen. Their initial gift made possible the opening of the school and thus, in the mid-1870s, Hubbard was asked to return to Nashville and, with the aid of an ex-Confederate surgeon, begin the department. In 1886 a dental school was added and in 1889 a pharmaceutical school.

The success of Meharry inspired the founding in 1889 of a similar school attached to New Orleans University, due to the gift of John D. Flint. A pharmacy department was soon added and a successful program managed for a quarter of a century. Then in 1911, the Flint Medical School was transferred to Nashville, and merged into Meharry. The pharmacy school was transferred four years later.

Hubbard retired in 1921 and was succeeded by John J. Mullowney. By that time the school had graduated 1,704 African American physicians, 479 dentists, and 284 pharmacists. Through the 1950s, Meharry graduated almost half of the Black physicians in the United States. Though that percentage has decreased with the lowering of racial barriers at the nation's other medical colleges, it remains the single most important medical school serving the African American community.

Stowell, Jay S. *Methodist Adventures in Negro Education*. New York: Methodist Book Concern, 1922. 190 pp.

MENNONITES. German-American Free Church Pietist Christians, a product of the radical phase of the sixteenth-century Reformation in Switzerland. Persecuted for their opposition to the authority of the state church and their doctrinal dissent from the Lutheran and Reformed Church, those who were not killed migrated westward. In Holland they found some protection and a new leader, former Roman Catholic priest Menno Simons, for whom they are presently named. They first arrived in the American colonies in the middle of the seventeenth century.

From Pennsylvania Mennonites spread westward and established many centers in the Western Plains. As they did so they split into numerous factions. A second wave of immigrants began to arrive in the nineteenth century from Russia where their ancestors had been welcomed a century earlier by Catherine the Great. Persecution began when later rulers demanded that Mennonites drop their pacifism and serve in the Russian Army.

Once in America, a few Mennonites, like their Quaker neighbors, became slaveowners, but as a group Mennonites generally opposed it. As early as 1688 some Mennonites joined with Quaker neighbors to protest slavery in Pennsylvania. Rarely activists in the anti-slavery cause, they were well known for their opposition to the practice and were frequently cited as an example of a community who refrained from participation in it. However, it was also the case that Mennonites themselves were a small minority, German-speaking in an English-speaking land, who still remembered their treatment in Europe before arriving in America. Because of their pacifism, they were under constant pressure from their neighbors and from the government.

For several reasons, including their opposition to slavery, Mennonites did not spread into the South, where most Blacks lived, prior to the Civil War, and Black people did not join the Mennonite Church. Living mostly in northern rural areas, Mennonites were least likely to encounter Black people in their daily life. It was also not until after the Civil War that any real attempts to proselytize outside of the Mennonite community developed within the movement. The first Black members came as a result of the Mennonite Brethren Church, one of the factions which had developed among the Russian Mennonites. The development of a Black membership began in 1896, after one Emily Pruden established several schools in the Appalachian Mountains. Pruden issued a general call for help from the Christian community, and among those who answered the call were Heinrich V. Weibe and his wife. The Weibes settled in Elk Park, North Carolina, and, overcoming local opposition, built a successful program. The work continued until the mine closed and then moved (along with much of the community) to Lenox, North Carolina. A generation later, in 1925, the work was joined by Peter H. Siemens and his wife. They spread the work along the mountain country in North Carolina and Tennessee and were instrumental in the founding of eleven churches and a high school. Ten Black ministers arose during Siemens' tenure, including Rondo Horton, who succeeded Siemens as the leader of the District, the only district in the Mennonite Brethren Church east of the Mississippi River.

The Mennonite Church, the oldest of the several Mennonite bodies in America, is credited with receiving the first Black people into Mennonite church membership. In 1897, Robert and Mary Elizabeth Carter and their son Cloyd Carter joined the Lauver Mennonite Church in Cocolamus, Pennsylvania. The following year, the Lancaster Conference opened the Welsh Mountain Industrial Mission for Black people living in Lancaster, Burks, and Chester Counties, Pennsylvania. The school was discontinued in 1924, but the mission continued. It was joined in 1933 by the Lancaster Colored Mission. Over the next two decades a dozen similar missions were established across Pennsylvania and in New York. There were also missions opened in Tampa, Florida, and Freemanville, Alabama. New missions were started in the 1970s and 1980s. By 1980 there were 1,600 members.

THE METROPOLITAN SPIRITUAL CHURCHES OF CHRIST. Bishop William F. Taylor, a former Colored Methodist minister, and Elder Leviticus L. Boswell, a former **Church of God in Christ** minister, established the mother congregation of the Metropolitan Spiritual Churches of Christ (MSCC) in Kansas City, Missouri, on September 22, 1925. By 1937, MSCC had grown to thirteen congregations nationwide, including the national headquarters in Kansas City, two congregations in Chicago, one in Gary, two in St. Louis, one in East St. Louis (Illinois), one in Detroit, one in Tulsa, one in Oklahoma City, one in Omaha, and two in Los Angeles. In 1942 MSCC merged with the Divine Spiritual Churches of the Southwest, based in New Orleans under the leadership of Bishop B. Watson, to form the United Spiritual Churches of Christ.

About the same time, a succession crisis occurred in the new association following the death of Bishop Taylor. One version of the events indicates that, prior to this departure for California in 1942 for a period of rest, Taylor placed Boswell in charge of the mother church in Kansas City and appointed the Rev. **Clarence Cobbs** his successor. Cobbs, who had started the First Church of Deliverance on the South Side of Chicago in 1929, apparently now regarded Chicago as the national headquarters of MSCC. As a result, a schism developed between the Midwestern and Louisiana factions. Watson's United Metropolitan group experienced yet another schism in 1951, resulting in the establishment of the Israel Universal Spiritual Churches of Christ with Bishop E.J. Johnson as its head. The original Metropolitan group prospered and grew under the astute leadership of Cobbs, who symbolized the "gods of the black metropolis" with his dapper mannerisms and love of the "good life." After a fire destroyed the Wabash facility in 1945, the First Church of Deliverance built a modern, flat-roofed sanctuary with a seating capacity of 1,200 on the same site. This church served for many years as the site of MSCC's annual convocation.

MSCC reportedly had somewhere between 80 and 125 congregations during the 1960s. While much smaller in size than various Black Baptist, Methodist, and Holiness-Pentecostal (or Sanctified) associations, MSCC has been and continues to be the largest of the many Spiritual associations and even has several congregations in West Africa. Since Cobbs's death in 1979, MSCC has declined somewhat due to a succession crisis. Many pastors pulled their congregations out of MSCC and some established their own associations. Dr. Logan Kearse, the founder of the Cornerstone Church of Christ (a congregation formerly affiliated with the **National Baptist Convention, U.S.A., Inc.** in Baltimore, became the new head of MSCC. At one point, two prominent trustees of the First Church of Deliverance filed an unsuccessful lawsuit to sever it from MSCC. Given the tensions between Kearse and various pastors in the Chicago area, MSCC relocated its national headquarters to Indianapolis, which was believed to be a more neutral site. While MSCC has congregations in many parts of the United States, most of them are concentrated in the Midwest, particularly in cities such as Chicago, Detroit, Gary, Indianapolis, and Kansas City.

Baer, Hans A. *The Black Spiritual Movement: A Religious Response to Racism.* Knoxville, TN: University of Tennessee Press, 1984. 220 pp.

Baer, Hans A. "The Metropolitan Spiritual Churches of Christ: The Socio-Religious Evolution of the Largest of the Black Spiritual Associations." *Review of Religious Research* 30, 4 (1988): 140–150.

Hans Baer

MICHAUX, LIGHTFOOT SOLOMON (November 7, 1884–October 20, 1968), founder of the **Gospel Spreading Church**, was born in Buckroe Beache, near Newport News, Virginia. His father was a seafood merchant, and as a young man Michaux expanded the business to service nearby military establishments. He was a successful businessman when he met Mary Eliza Pauline, whom he married in 1906. Under her influence, he shifted from a Baptist orientation, and became active in a **Church of Christ (Holiness)** congregation (St. Timothy's). In 1917 he had a vision that he was to lead a new church, and began one called Everybody's Mission. Soon he was ordained in relation to the Church of Christ (Holiness). In 1919 he began broadcasting a religious show over a small radio station in Newport News.

By 1921 his church was successful enough that **Charles P. Jones**, head of the Church of Christ (Holiness), wanted him to move and build up another congregation. Michaux was determined not to move, and instead, on February 26, 1921, independently incorporated the Gospel Spreading Tabernacle Building Association and purchased the building across the street from the former Church of Christ meeting house. In 1922 he was arrested in Newport News for holding racially integrated baptismal services, but he was able to successfully defend himself in court.

In 1928, already with a number of congregations in his association, Michaux moved to Washington, D.C., where the name changed to the Church of God and Gospel Spreading Association. His fame spread rapidly when he gained air time in 1929 at the WJSV radio station. He crafted the radio program Radio Church of God into one of the most entertaining on the air, with a 156–voice Cross Choir, which at one time included **Mahalia Jackson** and **Clara Ward**. The meeting would always start with his theme song, "Happy Am I," and he was known as the "Happy Am I Evangelist" who declared "war on the devil." By 1934, after CBS bought the station, Michaux was heard nationwide Saturday evenings on fifty stations by over 25 million people, the largest audience for any American Black in history. His once-a-year mass baptisms became famous; the crowd would parade through the streets until it reached the Potomac River, or after 1938 Griffith Stadium, where thousands would watch the ceremony in a festival atmosphere.

He established a monthly periodical called *Happy News*, which advertised the church activities. Michaux believed that the church should be relevant to ordinary lives, and it was church policy to provide food and shelter to evicted persons, help find jobs for the unemployed, and support orphanages and other social services. In 1932 Michaux supported Franklin Roosevelt for president, and is credited with shifting large numbers of Blacks from the Republican to the Democratic party. He founded the Good Neighbor League in 1933 to help the Depression poor, which among other things took a failed lunchroom and created the popular penny Happy News Cafe, which fed thousands. The church helped create one of the largest privately owned housing developments for Blacks in the United States. The 594 apartments of the Mayfair project were completed on July 4, 1946, in Washington, D.C.

By the mid-1940s Michaux's audience had declined to only a few radio stations on the East Coast, where some congregations remained. Still, in 1948 he accomplished another first by becoming the nation's first television preacher when his sermons were broadcast over Capitol City station WTTG. In 1964, before his death from a heart attack, he reorganized the church as the Gospel Spreading Church.

"Biggest Baptism." *Ebony* 3 (February 1948): 35–39.

"Top Radio Ministers." *Ebony* 4 (July 1949): 56–61.

Green, Constance McLaughlin. *Washington*. 2 vols. Princeton, NJ: Princeton University Press, 1963.

Lark, Pauline, ed. *Sparks from the Anvil of Elder Michaux*. Washington, DC: Happy News Publishing Co., 1950. 139 pp.

Lewis, Roscoe. *The Negro in Virginia*. New York: Hastings House, 1940. 380 pp.

Michaux, Lightfoot Solomon. *Spiritual Happiness Making Songs*. Washington, DC: The Author, n.d.

Webb, Lillian Ashcraft. *About My Father's Business*. Westport, CT: Greenwood Press, 1981. 210 pp.

BDACSL, RLOA, ONL, BDA-AHP, BH, IBAW, HUBA, CH, DANB, NWAC, NYTO, IP.

MILAN BIBLE AND INDUSTRIAL INSTITUTE. A Second Cumberland Presbyterian Church school. The Second Cumberland Presbyterian Church (now the **Cumberland Presbyterian Church of America**) tried on three occasions to create a school which would serve as a training facility for its ministers. In 1885 a short-lived effort was begun in Bowling Green, Kentucky, but closed heavily in debt. It was followed by a second effort in Springfield, Missouri, in 1895 and a third effort, the Cumberland Presbyterian Institute, in Huntsville, Alabama, in 1898. The Institute lasted until shortly after the turn of the century.

Finally, following the closing of the Institute in Huntsville, the most successful education effort opened in Milan, Tennessee. The Milan Bible and Industrial Institute lasted for several decades but closed at some time during the 1920s.

Campbell, Thomas D. *One Family Under God: A Story of Cumberland Presbyterians in Black and White*. Memphis, TN; Huntsville, AL: Federated Board of Christian Education of the Cumberland Presbyterian Church and the Second Cumberland Presbyterian Church, 1982. 237 pp.

MILES, WILLIAM HENRY (December 26, 1828–November 14, 1892), founding bishop of the **Christian Methodist Episcopal Church** (CME), then known as the Colored Methodist Episcopal Church, was born into slavery in Springfield, Kentucky. His owner, Mary Miles, freed him in her will in 1854, but a contest of the will postponed his freedom for two years. Even then, until Emancipation, his freedom was restricted under Kentucky laws. Meanwhile, he married Frances Ellen Arnold on December 24, 1849. They had eight children, four of whom survived their father. On October 30, 1855, he experienced conversion and joined the Methodist Episcopal Church, South (MECS) in Lebanon, Kentucky. Drawn toward the ministry, he was licensed to preach in August 1857 and ordained a deacon in October 1859 by Bishop James Andrew in Bardstown, Kentucky.

He preached for a time locally, but in 1865 he moved to Ohio. Soon he was informed that the MECS would likely remove its Black members, and he left the church and returned to Kentucky in 1867. He joined the **African Methodist Episcopal Zion Church** in Louisville, and was assigned to pastor the Center Street Church, the largest church of that denomination in Kentucky. He was instantly well known enough to be elected a delegate to General Conference in 1868. In that same year, however, he turned down Bishop **Jermain W. Loguen**'s appointment as general missionary and organizer, as no provision was made for his support.

Hearing of the new Kentucky Colored Conference of the MECS, he returned to that church to help organize that conference and pastor the congregation in Lexington. His work in Lexington encountered strong White resistance, and at one point a mob was organized to kill him, but a friend alerted him and he escaped. At the 1870 Kentucky Annual Conference, Miles was elected one of the delegates to the first General Conference of the CME Church, the new independent body being created by the MECS, for its Black members. Greatly impressed by his preaching ability, the conference elected William H. Miles the first bishop of the CME Church on December 21, 1870. He was consecrated the same day by Bishops Robert Paine and Holland N. McTyeire of the MECS.

The early years of the new church were very difficult as it tried to establish itself among newly freed Blacks, many of whom saw the CME Church as too connected with the religion of slaveholders. Miles was able to respond to these concerns while also welcoming a partnership with the MECS, which aided the young church by donating money, land, and general support. Miles helped organize the church into fifteen annual conferences serving 75,000 members. A publishing house was established, and a periodical, the *Christian Index*, which had actually begun in 1868, was officially adopted.

In 1874 Miles proposed the establishment of a

denominational school, and was chosen as the educational agent of the church. In this capacity he traveled around the country to raise money and interest in the project, scheduled to be located in Louisville, Kentucky. It never came to pass, but in 1898 Miles was honored for his 22 years of leadership in the church by the founding of Miles Memorial College in Birmingham, Alabama.

Lane, Isaac. *Autobiography of Bishop Isaac Lane, with a Short History of the CME Church in America and of Methodism.* Nashville, TN: Printed for the Author by the Publishing House of the Methodist Episcopal Church, South, 1916. 192 pp.
RLOA, NHM, EWM, NCAB (14), *CMECTY, HCMECA, EBA.*

MILES COLLEGE. A **Christian Methodist Episcopal Church** (CME) school. In 1887 the CME periodical the *Christian Index* carried an announcement that Alabama CMEs were planning to build a school, Beebe Theological Institute, in Greensboro, Alabama. However, those plans never came to fruition. Then several years later, Thomasville High School was started in Thomasville, Alabama under the leadership of W. M. Perkins. In 1895 the Thomasville school was adopted by the Alabama CME conferences.

In 1898 the two Alabama conferences voted to establish a college and appointed a board of trustees. They founded a second school, the Booker City High School, in Booker City (now Docena), Alabama. It replaced the Thomasville school as the major institution supported by the CME in Alabama. Mattie Welch gathered the first group of students. In 1907 the Booker City school was chartered as Miles Memorial College, in memory of **William H. Miles**, the pioneer CME bishop. That fall, **James A. Bray** became president of the school. He was able to create outside financial support. Bray began to build the school on its campus in Birmingham, Alabama. During his years the first dormitories were created for boarding students and the college department finally initiated.

In 1910 **George W. Stewart** became bishop of the Alabama conferences. No friend of Bray, he persuaded the board to fire him. Bray's removal proved a significant setback, as his successor was not as capable of raising the necessary funds to keep the school going. **William Augustus Bell**, at the time a mathematics instructor at Miles, was appointed interim president. He served only a year before moving to Paine College as dean. After a year, Bell was replaced with G. A. Payne (1911–1915) and later **R. T. Brown** (1918–1922). Finally, in 1922 G. W. Word became president and was

able to revive the school and turn it into a stable institution of higher education.

Miles had a series of strong presidents in the middle of the twentieth century. In 1932 William Augustus Bell was tempted back to Alabama from Paine College to resume the presidency of the school. He served for almost thirty years until his death in 1961. He was succeeded by Lucius H. Pitts (1961–1971) and W. Clyde Williams. During the 1960s, Miles became an organizing center for the civil rights demonstrations led by **Martin Luther King, Jr.**

Lakey, Othel H. *The History of the CME Church.* Memphis, TN: CME Publishing House, 1985. 683 pp.

MILLER, JOHN HENRY, SR. (b. December 3, 1917), 74th bishop of the **African Methodist Episcopal Zion Church** (AMEZ), was born in Ridgeway, South Carolina, the son of Fletcher and Frances Miller. Even while attending Dudley High School in Greensboro, North Carolina, he knew he wanted to be a minister. After one year at Agricultural and Technical College of North Carolina in Greensboro, in 1937 he headed toward Livingstone College in Salisbury, North Carolina, for his college and seminary training. He received his B.A. in 1941 and his B.D. from the related Hood Theological Seminary in 1945. He married Bernice Frances Dillard, with whom he had two children.

While in school he joined the West Central North Carolina Conference on November 30, 1938, was ordained a deacon on November 7, 1939, and elder on December 3, 1940. After pastoring a number of churches in North Carolina, he went to Peoples AMEZ Church in Syracuse, New York, followed by Seventh Street AMEZ Church in Troy, New York; New Britain AMEZ Church in Connecticut; Mt. Olive AMEZ Church in Waterbury, Connecticut; Goler Metropolitan AMEZ Church in Winston-Salem, North Carolina; and Broadway Temple AMEZ Church in Louisville, Kentucky. In Louisville he was president of the Louisville Area Council of Churches and a member of the City Crime Commission.

From Broadway Temple he was elected bishop in 1972, and consecrated on May 12. For eight years he was assigned to the Tenth Episcopal District (Arkansas, Cahaba, Oklahoma, North Arkansas, and Texas Conferences), and from 1980 to 1984 he was assigned to the Eighth Episcopal District (Blue Ridge in North Carolina, Central Alabama, Cahaba, and South Alabama Conferences). In 1984 he was shifted to the Seventh Episcopal District (Blue Ridge, Central North Carolina, Colorado, and Missouri Conferences). He has served as chair of the Christian Education Home and Church Division and chair of the Publication Board. He is a member of the World Methodist Council and on the Governor's Committee for Advocacy on Children and Youth. He has published a number of booklets, including *Leadership Training in the AMEZ Church* (1945); *Right Hand of Fellowship* (1963); *Trustees and Stewards: Power Struggle* (1973); and *Church Worker* (1983).

"Bishop John H. Miller Celebrates 50 Years in Ministry." *Star of Zion* 112 (March 3, 1988): 6–7.

"Vignettes of Our Bishops: Bishop John H. Miller, Sr." *Star of Zion* 111 (November 19, 1987): 7.

BDNM (75), WWABA (92–93), AMEZC.

MILLER, WILLIAM (August 23, 1775–December 6, 1845), 3rd bishop of the **African Methodist Episcopal Zion Church** (AMEZ), was born in Queen Ann County, Maryland. As a young man he moved to New York City, where he made a living as a cabinetmaker and joined the Methodist Episcopal Church. After a time he recognized a call to the ministry and in 1808 received a local preacher's license. Soon thereafter he was ordained deacon by Bishop Francis Asbury, but about that time he made a shift to **Richard Allen**'s AME Church, where he was again ordained deacon, on April 27, 1808. The one extant writing of his dates from 1810, an anti-slavery sermon. On January 17, 1817, the New York African Bible Society was founded at his home on Mulberry Street, and he served as its first president.

A successful minister for many years in the AME Church, he was ordained elder in 1823. In 1826, for unknown reasons, he left that denomination and joined the AMEZ Church. About that time he moved from New York City to Philadelphia, Pennsylvania, and served in AMEZ churches there. By the General Conference of May 1840, Miller was the oldest elder and had enough backing to run for bishop. He was elected "The Associate Pastor of Superintendent Rush," which left no ambiguity about who was the senior superintendent (as the bishops were called then). He is generally understood to have been consecrated on May 25, 1840, but some evidence points to his election as early as 1836. He discharged his duties with ability until September 1845, when illness made him bedridden, and he passed away about six months later.

"Bishop William Miller." *A.M.E. Zion Quarterly Review* 62 (1951): 233.

Miller, William. *A Sermon on the Abolition of the Slave: Delivered in the African Church, New York, on the First of January, 1810.* New York: John C. Totten, 1810. 16 pp.

BAW, HUBA, EWM, HAMEZC, AMEZC, HAMEZCIA.

MILLER, WILLIAM RUSSELL (b. March 2, 1900), a bishop of the **African Orthodox Church**, was born on the Island of Tobago in the British West Indies, the son of Catherine Turner and James Thomas Miller. He lived on Tobago for the first nine years of his life, and then the family moved to Trinidad where his father taught at the Toco Anglican Church School. He graduated from that school as a pupil teacher and in 1919, his father having died, became acting head master. The next year he became assistant master of a school in Port-of-Spain.

In 1921 he moved his family (mother, brothers and sisters) to Brooklyn, New York. There he continued his education at the New York School of Music, where he became most proficient at the organ. In 1925 Miller became aware of the African Orthodox Church through Canon Hugh H. Henry and Bishop **Reginald G. Barrow**, who introduced him to Archbishop **George Alexander McGuire**, the church's founder. He entered Endich Theological Seminary and began to be advanced through priestly orders. He was ordained as a priest in December 1927.

Several months after his ordination, Miller was placed in charge of the recently founded Church of Saint Simon the Cyrenian in Brooklyn. Two years of work led to his being named the congregation's first rector in 1930. The congregation met at several locations over the next fifteen years, but in 1945 was able to purchase permanent facilities. In 1950, Miller was elected bishop and consecrated Archbishop **William E. J. Robertson**, on August 6, 1950, at St. Simon's.

After many years of faithful service to the church, in 1976 Miller succeeded **Gladstone St. Clair Nurse** as primate of the African Orthodox Church. He held that position until his retirement in 1981. He was succeeded by **Stafford James Sweething**, whom Miller had consecrated.

Terry-Thompson, A. C. *The History of the African Orthodox Church.* New York: The Author, 1956. 139 pp.

Ward, Gary L. *Independent Bishops: An International Directory.* Detroit, MI: Apogee Books, 1990. 526 pp.

MILLS, CEDRIC EARL (b. December 17, 1903), a bishop of the **Episcopal Church**, was born in Hartford, Connecticut, the son of Patrick Henry and Sophronia (Blount) Mills. He received his B.A. in 1926 from Lincoln University in Pennsylvania, and on June 20, 1926 he married Rebecca Esther Taylor, with whom he had one son. He received his S.T.B. in 1929 from Philadelphia Divinity School, and his M.A. also in 1929 from the University of Pennsylvania.

He was ordained deacon in May 1929 and six months later was ordained priest. In June 1929 he was appointed vicar of the Chapel of the Ascension in West Chester, Pennsylvania, covering also St. Cyril's Mission in Coatesville and St. Mary's Church in Chester. During the same period (1929–37) he was chaplain for Episcopal students at Lincoln University, Cheyney State Teachers' College, and Downingtown Industrial School, where he was also dean of boys and teacher of math and science. From 1937 to 1940 he was priest-in-charge of St. Mark's Episcopal Church in Plainfield, New Jersey, and he cleared up the church's indebtedness.

From 1940 to 1963 Mills was rector of St. James Episcopal Church in Baltimore, Maryland. He was a member of the executive council of the Diocese of Maryland from 1944 to 1950 and from 1954 to 1957. During World War II he was secretary of the diocese's Army and Navy Commission. He was vice-president of the board of directors of the Baltimore Urban League and of the board of the Citizens Planning and Housing Association. He was on the board of directors of the N.A.A.C.P. and served on the Governor's Committee on Problems Affecting the Colored Population. He was a deputy to the General Convention in 1961.

In October 1962 he was elected bishop of the Missionary District of the Virgin Islands and was consecrated for that office on April 19, 1963, at St. James Episcopal Church in Baltimore. He arrived in the Virgin Islands on May 11, 1963, and remained there for nine years. From 1963 to 1970 he was a member of the Joint Committee on Ecumenical Relations. He retired on May 1, 1972, to his home in Southern California, but has remained active in a number of organizations.

BDNM (75), *ECA* (1964), *EBA*.

MING, DONALD GEORGE KENNETH (b. July 6, 1930), 97th bishop of the **African Methodist Episcopal Church** (AME), was born in Devonshire, Bermuda, the son of C. E. and Mable D. (Woolridge) Ming. He went to the United States in 1949 and was naturalized as a citizen in 1962. He attended Elliot School and Howard Academy. He earned his B.S. in 1954 from Wilberforce University in Ohio and his B.D. in 1955 from Payne Theological Seminary at Wilberforce. On July 6, 1957, he married Edith White.

His first pastorate was at Bethel AME Church in Beverly, New Jersey (1955–57), followed by Mt. Zion AME Church in Dover, Delaware (1957–60), where he built a new church; Murphy AME Church in Chester, Pennsylvania (1960–64); and Allen AME Church in Jamaica, New York (1964–76). He built a new church in Jamaica and paid for it in half the required time. In 1971 he organized the Allen Community Day Care Center, and in 1974 founded the Allen Community Senior Citizens Center. In 1973 he became program chair for the Jamaica Center for Older Adults. From 1965 to 1971 he was a member of the Jamaica Anti-Poverty Board, and in 1966 he joined the board of directors of Queens Shelter. In 1970 he received the Special Achievement Award from the AME Church and in 1973 and 1975 he received the New York City Board of Education Award for Special Dedication.

In 1976 Ming was elected bishop and assigned to the Episcopal District covering South Africa and Namibia. There he built an astounding forty-five new churches and developed an insurance and pension program for the clergy. In 1980 he was shifted to the Sixteenth Episcopal District (Haiti), where he built apartments for missionaries and classrooms for students. In 1984 he was shifted to the Eighth Episcopal District, with headquarters in New Orleans, Louisiana, where he has since remained. He has served as chair of the denomination's Commission on Missions and as president of the Bishop's Council. He is a member of the executive board of the World Methodist Council.

FEDHR, WWABA (92–93), *WWR* (85).

MINISTERS FOR RACIAL AND SOCIAL JUSTICE. A **United Church of Christ** organization. During the late 1960s, Black caucuses began to appear in all of the major predominantly White denominations, in large part flowing from the organization of the ecumenical National Committee of Negro Churchmen (now the **National Conference of Black Churchmen**). Black clergy within the United Church of Christ held an initial gathering in 1966 as an informal African American clergy coalition which formally organized the following year as the Ministers for Racial and Social Justice. Their immediate goal was the establishment of the **Commission for Racial Justice** as an official agency of the United Church of Christ to involve the church in the ongoing Civil Rights struggle. A second early goal was the creation of a similar organization for laity. United Black Churchmen (later **United Black Christians**) was founded in 1970 as a sister association.

The Ministers campaigned for the election of Dr. Arthur D. Gray, a leading Black minister/educator from the church-sponsored Talladega College, for president of the United Church of Christ. The effort, which would have made Gray the first president of a major predominantly White American denomination, failed, but it significantly raised the profile of the group and its program within the denomination.

Ministers for Racial and Social Justice meets biennially in a national convention with United Black Christians. Its headquarters is in Washington, D.C.

MISSISSIPPI INDUSTRIAL COLLEGE. A **Christian Methodist Episcopal Church** (CME) school. Mississippi Industrial College, Holly Springs, Mississippi, first appeared as the idea of Bishop **Elias Cottrell**, who believed that it was necessary that African Americans demonstrate their ability to help themselves and to build their own institutions. In 1900 he led in the establishment of a board of trustees which worked for the next three years to raise money and plan for the school. In 1903 land was purchased at Holly Springs, Mississippi, just south of Memphis, Tennessee, and the Mississippi Theological and Industrial Seminary opened. F. H. Rogers was the first president. In 1906 the present name was chosen.

By 1908, by which time Charles M. Newell had succeeded Rogers as president, the school had 450 pupils attending its elementary, secondary, agricultural, and industrial departments. Its teacher training department was especially strong and the majority of the school's graduates went on to take jobs as school teachers. The stability of the school was due in large part by the effectiveness of Cottrell, who lived to 1937, in raising money. He was, for example, able to obtain a large grant from philanthropist Andrew Carnegie.

During the middle of the twentieth century the presidency of the school was held by a set of outstanding educators, William McKinley Frazier, E. E. Rankin, and Theodore H. Debro.

Lakey, Othel H. *The History of the CME Church.* Memphis, TN: CME Publishing House, 1985. 683 pp.

MITCHELL, HENRY HEYWOOD (b. September 10, 1919), theologian and member of the **American Baptist Churches in the U.S.A.**, was born in Columbus, Ohio, the son of Orlando Washington (a post office letter carrier) and Bertha (Estis) Mitchell. He received his B.A. in 1941 from Lincoln University in Pennsylvania, and his B.D. in 1944 from Union Theological Seminary in New York City. On August 12, 1944, he married Ella Muriel Pearson, with whom he had four children.

He was assistant pastor of the Concord Baptist Church in Brooklyn, New York, in 1943–44 and was acting dean of the chapel and instructor at North Carolina College at Durham in 1944–45. From 1945 to 1959 he was an executive with the Northern California American Baptist Convention and from 1959 to 1966 he pastored the 2nd Baptist Church in Fresno, California. He was president of the Northern California Baptist Convention in 1961–62 and in 1966 he became president of the Fresno County Economic Opportunities Commission. From 1960 to 1971 he was a trustee of the Berkeley Baptist Divinity School in Berkeley, California, and from 1966 to 1970 he was a trustee of the National Committee of Black Churchmen. In 1966 he earned his M.A. from California State University at Fresno. From 1966 to 1969 he pastored the Calvary Baptist Church in Santa Monica, California.

In 1969 Mitchell began a new phase of his career by becoming the **Martin Luther King, Jr.** Professor of Black Church Studies at Colgate Rochester/Bexley Hall/Crozer Divinity School in Rochester, New York, an institution of the American Baptist Churches in the U.S.A. In 1970 he published his first major book, *Black Preaching.* He spent a year in residence at the School of Theology in Claremont, California, in 1972–73, where he received his Th.D. in 1973. In 1974 he left Rochester to be the director of the Ecumenical Center for Black Church Studies in Los Angeles, California, where he stayed until 1982. He also served during that time as adjunct professor at Fuller Theological Seminary in Pasadena and the American Baptist Seminary of West, Berkeley and LaVerne College. In 1974 he was the Lyman Beecher Lecturer on Preaching at Yale Divinity School in New Haven, Connecticut. In 1975 he published his second book, *Black Belief: Folk Beliefs of Blacks in America and West Africa,* and in 1977 he published *The Recovery of Preaching.* In 1981–82 he was visiting professor of Religion and Pan-African Studies at California State University, Northridge.

From 1982 to 1986 Mitchell was dean of the School of Theology at Virginia Union University, and later taught Homiletics there. He is now a professor of homiletics at the Interdenominational Theological Center. He is the author of: *Soul Theology: The Heart of American Black Culture* (1986); *Celebration and Experience in Preaching* (1990); and *Black Preaching: The Recovery of a Powerful Art* (1990).

Cooper-Lewter, Nicholas and Henry Mitchell. *Soul Theology: The Heart of American Black Culture.* San Francisco, CA: Harper & Row, 1986. 176 pp.
Mitchell, Henry Heywood. *Black Belief: Folk Beliefs of Blacks in America and West Africa.* New York: Harper & Row, 1975. 171 pp.
———. *Black Preaching.* Philadelphia, PA: J. P. Lippincott Publishing Co., 1970. 248 pp.

———. *Black Preaching: The Recovery of a Powerful Art.* Nashville, TN: Abingdon Press, 1990. 143 pp.

———. *Celebration and Experience in Preaching.* Nashville, TN: Abingdon Press, 1990. 155 pp.

WWABA (92–93), *CA* (new rev. series 10), *BDNM* (75), *WWR* (77), *HUBA, AARS.*

MOORE, BENJAMIN THOMAS (1929–December 15, 1988), a bishop of the **Pentecostal Assemblies of the World,** was born in Toledo, the son of Elder Curtis L. Moore. His father was a minister and he grew up in the church. He married Willa Mae Lee and they had four children. He attended Highland Park Junior College (A.A.), Wayne University (B.A.), Butler University, the University of Washington, and the American Bible College (D.D.). He was called to ministry through the instrument of his father and became the pastor of Bethel Christian Church in Seattle. During his years in Seattle he quickly emerged as a talented and energetic leader. For eight years he was the State Youth Leader and also developed a daily radio show. He was consecrated as a bishop in 1961 and named suffragan bishop of the 17th District which covers the states of Washington, Oregon, Utah, Montana, Alaska, and Western Canada. He was made bishop over the district two years later.

While in Seattle Moore served in a number of regional and national positions. Prior to being made a bishop he served as district council chairman. On the national level he served a term as assistant chairman of the Committee for the Propagation of the Faith, director of Public Relations, and auxiliary director of the National Pentecostal Young People's Union. He also became chairman of the board of directors of Aenon Bible College.

In 1977 Moore became the pastor of Christ Temple in Indianapolis, Indiana, the "Mother Church" of the denomination, originally pastored by **Garfield T. Haywood.** The previous pastor, James E. Tyson, had left to found Christ Church Apostolic, a second parish in the growing African American community in Indianapolis. During Moore's first six years there, he raised the money to pay off the large mortgage which had slowed the progress of the congregation and to institute new building projects. He enlarged the church's printing/publishing facilities, which keep Bishop Haywood's books in print as well as publish the several volumes authored by Moore, including *A Handbook for Saints* (1981) and *A Handbook for Soul Winners* (1981). He remained the pastor of the church until his death in 1988.

Christ Temple Jubilee. Indianapolis, IN: Christ Temple, 1983. 76 pp.

DuPree, Sherry Sherrod. *Biographical Dictionary of African American Holiness-Pentecostals, 1880–1990.* Washington, DC: Middle Atlantic Regional Press, 1989. 386 pp.

Golder, Morris E. *The Bishops of the Pentecostal Assemblies of the World.* Indianapolis, IN: The Author, 1980. 69 pp.

Moore, Benjamin T. *A Handbook for Saints.* Indianapolis, IN: Christ Temple Publications, 1981. 77 pp.

———. *A Handbook for Soul Winners.* Indianapolis, IN: Christ Temple Publications, 1981. 23 pp.

MOORE, EMERSON JOHN (b. May 16, 1938), a bishop of the **Roman Catholic Church,** was born in New York City, the oldest of three children in the family of Emerson and Dorothy (Williams) Moore. His father was a subway motorman and his mother was a practical nurse; they belonged to no particular denomination, but did not object when the children began to seek a religious identity. Moore was attracted by the Catholic ritual and discipline he saw at the nearby St. Augustine Catholic Church. Emerson and the other two children were baptized on April 4, 1950. As early as junior high he wanted to become a priest, and after his sophomore year at Benjamin Franklin High School in the Bronx he transferred to Cardinal Hayes High School, also in the Bronx, where he could get the required Latin credits.

He graduated from high school in 1956, spent the next two years at Cathedral College in New York City, and the two years after that in St. Joseph's Seminary at Dunwoodie in Yonkers, New York, graduating with a B.A. in Philosophy in 1960. While he was at St. Joseph's his parents were baptized. He was ordained a priest on May 30, 1964 and his first assignment was a four-month stay at St. Augustine Catholic Church in Ossining, New York. He then spent five years as assistant pastor of the Holy Family Catholic Church in Manhattan, New York, where he was involved with the Catholic Interracial Council and the Urban League. In 1965 he coordinated Pope Paul VI's visit to the United Nations.

In 1968 Moore was appointed director of Dunwoodie Camp for inner city children, and remained there for about eight years. Beginning in 1970 he was also director of the Central Office of Catholic Charities and executive director of the Lieutenant Joseph F. Kennedy Memorial Community Center. In the fall of 1975 he became pastor of St. Charles Borromeo Church in Harlem, New York City. This large, 1,500–member church has often been known as the "Cathedral of Harlem," and Moore quickly became a leader in the Central Harlem Head Start Program and the Harlem Urban Development Corporation. He founded the Office of Black Ministry within the New York Archdiocese.

On December 10, 1978, Moore was the first

American Black priest to be named Prelate of Honor to Pope Paul VI, which gave him the title of Reverend Monsignor. On October 2, 1979, Pope John Paul II visited St. Charles Borromeo Church. Shortly afterward, Moore was named Episcopal Vicar for Central Harlem and for Black community development in the Archdiocese of New York. On July 3, 1982, he was named Auxiliary Bishop of New York and was consecrated for that office on September 8, 1982. He has a reputation as a social justice activist.

"Emerson J. Moore, Auxiliary Bishop of New York." *America* 164 (April 13, 1991): 407–410.
WWABA (92–93), *BDNM* (75), *OBS, IBAW.*

MOORE, JERRY A., JR. (b. June 12, 1918), prominent Baptist minister, was born in Minden, Louisiana, the son of Jerry A., Sr. and Mal Dee Moore. He received his B.A. in 1940 from Morehouse College in Atlanta, Georgia and his B.D. in 1943 from Howard University in Washington, D.C. On January 14, 1946, he married Ettyce H. Hill, with whom he had two children.

In 1943 he was assistant director of the New Orleans U.S.O., and from 1944 to 1946 he was secretary for Boys Work for the Y.M.C.A. From 1946 to the present he has been pastor of the 19th Street Baptist Church in Washington, D.C. While there he furthered his education, receiving his M.A. in 1957 from Howard University. He has served on the executive committee of the Baptist World Alliance and on the National Committee for Support of Public Schools. From 1970 to 1984 he was a member-at-large of the Washington, D.C., City Council. Since 1985 he has been executive secretary of the Home Mission Board of the **National Baptist Convention, U.S.A., Inc.**, and is vice-president of the International Society of Christian Endeavor. He is active in many community groups, including the Urban League and the N.A.A.C.P.

BDNM (70), *WWABA* (92–93).

MOORE, JOHN HENRY (August 9, 1876–January 27, 1957), 19th bishop of the **Christian Methodist Episcopal Church** (CME), then known as the Colored Methodist Episcopal Church, was born in Huntsville, Alabama, the son of Turner and Savannah (Pettis) Moore. After a few years the family moved to Mississippi and Moore was educated in the schools of Chicasaw and Pontotoc counties. He received additional training at Rust College in Holly Springs, Mississippi,

supporting himself as a brick mason. On December 23, 1896, he married Julia Augusta McCorkel, with whom he had two children.

In 1899 he entered the ministry of the CME Church and pastored in local churches until 1906, when he was appointed presiding elder of the Meridian District, Mississippi. In 1909 he was shifted to the Durant District, staying until 1914. On May 22, 1914, at the General Conference, he was elected General Secretary of Missions. He was a powerful preacher and used that gift with great effectiveness as he traveled widely in the spread of the faith. He went to the British West Indies and established a mission there. Under his administration more than $200,000 was raised to help mission preachers.

He was elected bishop in May 1934, and his humble, congenial disposition made him one of the most generally loved bishops of the church. He presided mostly over Mississippi and helped Mississippi Industrial College in Holly Springs eliminate its heavy indebtedness as well as improve its facilities. He inaugurated a church extension program and supported the construction of more than thirty-eight churches in Mississippi and Oklahoma. He suffered a stroke just prior to the East Mississippi Annual Conference in December 1950, and was confined to his bed for the next year, before he passed away.

"Bishop John Henry Moore Dies." *Christian Index* 83 (February 1, 1951): 6, 14.
Harris, Eula W., and Maxie H. Craig. *Christian Methodist Episcopal Church Through the Years.* Jackson, TN: Christian Methodist Church Publishing House, 1965.
EWM, CMECTY, WWCR.

MOORE, JOHN JAMISON (October 19, 1814–December 9, 1893), 15th bishop of the **African Methodist Episcopal Zion Church** (AMEZ), was born in Martinsburg, Berkeley County, Virginia (now West Virginia). His date of birth has been questioned, and other accounts place it variously in 1804, 1811, or 1818. His mother, whose maiden name was Riedoubt, was a free Black in Maryland, but at the age of fifteen was kidnapped into slavery in Virginia. There she eventually married another slave named Hodge, with whom she had six children. A change of owners led to the surname change of the children to Moore. When Moore was about six, the family attempted to escape their condition with the help of some **Quakers**, but were recaptured and the oldest four children were sold South. A later attempt by the parents and two remaining children, including

Moore, was more successful, and after great hardship and trial they eventually reached Bedford County, Pennsylvania.

In Pennsylvania Moore was bound out as an indentured servant to a farmer, who taught him to read and write at a minimal level. His parents were obliged to travel on in order to elude the bounty hunters. The last part of his time was served with the farmer's brother-in-law, who kept him far beyond the appointed time and did not provide any of the goods required by law upon final release. After working on another farm for six months, Moore saved some money and walked the one hundred or so miles to Harrisburg, where he found employment first as a hod carrier, then as a hotel waiter, then as a bank messenger.

In 1833 he experienced conversion, left Harrisburg, and returned to Bedford County, where he obtained a job as a store porter. After about one year he recognized a call to the ministry, returned to Harrisburg, and received an exhorter's license, followed in 1835 by a preacher's license. For two years, in 1836–37, he attempted to overcome his lack of education by hiring teachers to instruct him in English grammar, Hebrew, geography, arithmetic, and other subjects. In 1839 he joined the Philadelphia Conference of the AMEZ Church, and was ordained deacon on June 10, 1842, and elder on June 12, 1843. He traveled widely in the Allegheny Mountains, preaching to fugitive slaves and coal and iron miners. In 1844 he was elected secretary of the Philadelphia Conference. In the late 1840s he was pastor of Big Wesley AMEZ Church in Philadelphia.

In 1852 he left for California, where he established churches in Napa and San Jose. He concentrated his efforts in San Francisco, where in 1852 he founded the first Black church in that city, which soon became the largest AMEZ church on the West Coast. On May 22, 1854, the first school for Black children in California opened in San Francisco in the basement of the newly founded St. Cyprian AME Church on Jackson Street between Stockton and Powell. Moore was its first teacher, and taught this group of between twenty and sixty-five children of various ages for five years. When a teachers' convention was called in 1855, Moore was the only Black teacher present, causing some commotion among the White teachers who attended. San Francisco City Assessor Stillman told the delegates that Moore's presence absolved them from having to remain at the conference, but there is no evidence that anyone left.

In June 1857, Moore was officially appointed by the board of education as principal of the Negro Children's School, and received a salary from city funds, something he had sought for some time. He was also a delegate to three state conventions called to abolish the "Black Laws," which disqualified Blacks as witnesses against Whites in criminal cases. In about 1858 he followed a large Black migration to the mining fields around Victoria in British Columbia. He settled in the Cariboo region and although he attempted to hold religious services, they were poorly attended. He had to support himself as a woodcutter and charcoal burner, and invested money in a mining company owned by both Whites and Blacks. At the end of the Civil War he returned to California and resided for a period in San Francisco.

Elected a bishop in 1868, Moore was assigned to a district back East. In about 1880 he made a long-sought trip to England, where he preached on behalf of the needs of the newly freed Blacks in America. In 1884 he published a major work, *History of the A.M.E. Zion Church in America*. He served as bishop for twenty-five years and lived to a ripe old age, despite the many dangers of his life, including being shipwrecked three times. During his episcopate he had charge of California, Canada and Michigan, Florida, Arkansas, New York, New England, Philadelphia and Baltimore, Virginia, West Tennessee and Mississippi, Georgia, and the Carolina Conferences. He was acknowledged to be one of the greatest preachers of his time.

"Bishop J. J. Moore." *A.M.E. Zion Quarterly Review* 61 (1951): 187.

Moore, John Jamison. *History of the A.M.E. Zion Church in America. Founded in 1796, in the City of New York*. York, PA: Teachers' Journal Office, 1884. 392 pp.

———. *A Scripture Catechism for Bible Scholars and Sunday Schools for the A.M.E. Zion Church*. Salisbury, NC: Livingstone College Printers, n.d. 14 pp.

BGRC, AMEZC, ACAB (supp.), *HAMEZC, EWM, OHYAMEZC, HAMEZCIA, IBAW, BAW, HUBA, AARS.*

MOORE, MORRIS MARCELLUS (November 15, 1856–November 23, 1900), 27th bishop of the **African Methodist Episcopal Church** (AME), was born in Quincy, Florida. He was converted in 1861 and licensed to preach in 1876 in Quincy by Rev. **J. H. Armstrong**. He joined the Florida Annual Conference in 1878 as an itinerant minister, was ordained deacon in 1880 and elder in 1881. He was assistant secretary of the General Conference in Philadelphia in 1892.

After serving at a number of local churches, Moore was elected Financial Secretary of the AME Church in 1896. After serving successfully in that position for four years, he was elected bishop in May 1900, and assigned to Africa. He was the first candidate for the bishopric who had ever been divorced, and he was elected over great opposition. Information about his marriage and family is not available. He died after only six months, at the age of forty-four, without ever presiding over an annual conference. Many in the church expressed the opinion that his short term was punishment for the divorce. He was buried in Jacksonville, Florida, where his former wife was still living. Named for him are churches in Jacksonville and St. Petersburg, Florida.

EWM, HAMEC, BAMEC, CEAMEC.

MOORE, NOAH WATSON, JR. (b. March 28, 1902), a bishop of the **United Methodist Church**, was born in Newark, New Jersey, the son of Noah Watson Sr. and Eliza A. (Boyce) Moore. He received his B.A. in 1926 from Morgan State College in Baltimore, Maryland, and his B.D. in 1931 from Drew University in Madison, New Jersey. On November 27, 1926, he married Carolyn W. Lee, with whom he had one daughter. He was ordained deacon in 1930 and elder in 1932.

His first pastorate was at New Rochelle, New York (1930–31), followed by Upper Hill, Maryland (1931–35); Fairmount Circuit and Upper Hill, Maryland (1935–37); Camphor Memorial Methodist Church in Philadelphia, Pennsylvania (1937–41); Zoar Methodist Church in Philadelphia (1941–43); and St. Daniels Methodist Church in Chester, Pennsylvania (1943–47). From 1947 to 1949 he was district superintendent of the Easton District in Maryland, and from 1949 to 1960 he pastored Tindley Temple Methodist Church in Philadelphia. This pastorate was very successful: he became a regular delegate to General Conference and a widely known figure. From 1954 to 1960 he was variously director or a board member of the Philadelphia Housing Authority, and from 1950 to 1960 he was trustee and vice-president of Morgan College. From 1952 to 1960 he was a member of the Methodist General Committee on Overseas Relief. From 1956 to 1960 he was a trustee of Morristown College in Morristown, Tennessee. In 1959 he was one of nine clergy from the United States to be part of a study tour of West Germany and Berlin.

Moore was elected bishop on July 14, 1960, by the Central Jurisdiction and consecrated on July 17. He was assigned to the New Orleans Episcopal Area, which included the Louisiana, Texas, and West Texas Annual Conferences. In 1962 he was president of the College of Bishops of the Jurisdictional Conference. In 1968 the Methodist Church merged with the Evangelical United Brethren to form the United Methodist Church. As part of this union the all-Black Central Jurisdiction was dissolved and the Black clergy and bishops were integrated into the new structure. Moore was then assigned to the Nebraska Episcopal Area, where he stayed until retirement in 1972. He was on the board of directors of the Philadelphia branch of the Urban League and the N.A.A.C.P. He was a member of the executive committee of the World Methodist Council. He was president of the board of trustees of both Philander Smith College (1964–68) and Wiley College (1964–68), and was a trustee of Dillard University (1960–68). From 1968 to 1972 he was on the denomination's General Board of Education and was president of the General Board of Evangelism.

EWM, WWA (74–75), EBA, WWABA (92–93), WWMC, BDNM (75), BDUMB.

MOORISH SCIENCE TEMPLE DIVINE AND NATIONAL MOVEMENT OF NORTH AMER-ICA. An Islamic organization. There presently exist two groups which trace their beginnings to the original movement founded by **Noble Drew Ali** (Timothy Drew), one being the **Moorish Science Temple of America** and the other the Moorish Science Temple Divine and National Movement of North America. The latter movement relates a much different history of the Moorish Science movement following the death of Noble Drew Ali in 1929. According to its records, Ali was succeeded by Sheik Timothy Givens-El, considered the second reincarnation of the author. Givens-El, Drew's chauffeur, assumed the title Prophet Noble Drew Ali Reincarnated Mohammad III. He led the movement through the 1930s and passed authority to Sheik Richardson Dingle-El.

Grand Sheik Richardson Dingle-El became the leader of a movement. He began to work for financial compensation and restoration of land, and the restoration of names, to Black people. These were concerns addressed in the original text of the Thirteenth Amendment to the U.S. Constitution (though dropped from the final text). In 1975 he formally incorporated the Moorish Science Temple Divine and National Movement of North America (a for-profit corporation) in Maryland. In his work, Richardson Dingle-El was assisted by his brother Timothy Dingle-El (d. 1982), who authored a chronicle of the movement, *The Resurrection of the Moorish Science Temple.*

The teachings of the movement derive from the writings of Noble Drew Ali and *The Holy Koran* first published by Noble Drew Ali, known as *The Holy Koran of the Moorish Science Temple Circle Seven.* The Circle Seven refers to the book of seven seals mentioned in the Biblical book of Revelation. Ali taught that Blacks were Asiatics, i.e., Moors, whose identity had been taken from them by White Americans. He saw the Moorish Science Temple returning the true identity to Black people and working for the restoration of all that had been stolen from them.

The movement continued to be led by Grand Sheik Louis Richardson Dingle-El who is known in the movement as Prophet Noble Drew Ali II, Reincarnated. Headquarters is in Baltimore, Maryland. The center in Chicago publishes a periodical, *Moorish Guide*.

MOORISH SCIENCE TEMPLE OF AMERICA. An Islamic group. The Moorish Science movement was founded by **Noble Drew Ali** (1886–1929), an African American born Timothy Drew among the Cherokee Indians of North Carolina. As a young man he began to explore the problem of being Black in America. His search led him to the conclusion, contrary to **Marcus Garvey** and other voices operating in the African American community, that Black people were not Ethiopians. They were Moors, i.e., descendants of the ancient Moabites of the Middle East. Their true homeland was Morocco and they were really Moors.

The present situation of African Americans can be traced to the Continental Congress, which stripped Black people of their nationality and forced them into slavery. George Washington had cut down the cherry tree (i.e., the bright red Moorish flag) and hidden it in Independence Hall. Islam was the true religion of the Moors. Only Islam could unite African Americans and return their identity again to them. The Christians' Jesus was also a Black man who tried to redeem his people, but was executed by the Whites, i.e., the Romans.

Ali formed the first temple in Newark, New Jersey. Over the next decade other temples were opened in African American communities across the Northeast and Midwest. In 1925 Ali relocated to Chicago, and in 1926 the movement was incorporated as the Moorish Holy Temple of Science (a not-for-profit corporation). Two years later he issued *The Holy Koran*, the movement's scripture. The temple's scripture should not be confused with the *Qur'an* of Islam, their sharing little beyond their name. *The Holy Koran* was written by Ali, who drew heavily from *The Aquarian Gospel of Jesus Christ*, an obscure Spiritualist text which was the result of automatic writing by Levi Dowling. That same year the temple was reincorporated as the Moorish Science Temple of America, a for-profit corporation. Ali died in 1929. He was succeeded by R. German Ali.

Ali provided for his followers a complete new identity as Moors. To indicate the new self-understanding, each person added the suffix "El" or "Bey" to their name. He also gave them cards which stated this new role. Some members followed Ali in donning a fez.

At the time of its founding, the Moorish Science movement was somewhat unique in offering African Americans both a new religious and a new national identity as a means of overcoming the inferior status assigned to them by the White-dominated culture. However, the temple was soon competing with the Garveyite movement (which may have underlain the move to Chicago, a community in which Garvey found little support). Following Ali's death, his temple became the seedbed of further competition. Within a few months of his death, a former temple member, Wallace Fard Muhammad, appeared in Detroit and began to suggest that he was Noble Drew Ali returned. He gained some following, which grew to be the Nation of Islam.

The temple seems to have peaked in the 1940s, at which time it had active centers across the Midwest and Northeast and into the South (Richmond, Virginia, and Chattanooga, Tennessee). In more recent years, while continuing to exist, it has not shown a great deal of vitality. In 1981 headquarters were moved to Baltimore and several active centers are located in the Baltimore/Washington, D.C. area. There is also a small center in Chicago.

Ali, Noble Drew [Timothy Drew]. *The Holy Koran of the Moorish Science Temple of America*. [Baltimore, MD]: Moorish Science Temple of America, 1978.
———. *Moorish Literature*. The Author, 1928.
Fauset, Arthur Huff. *Black Gods of the Metropolis*. Philadelphia, PA: University of Pennsylvania, 1971.

MORAVIAN CHURCH. A German Pietist church. The Moravian Church grew out of the non-Roman Catholic Christianity in Czechoslovakia. They found their great champion in John Hus, martyred at the Council of Constance in 1414. The church was all but destroyed in the religious wars of the sixteenth and seventeenth centuries, and a few members fled to Saxony, in East Germany, on the estate of Count Zinzendorf. Zinzendorf took an active interest in the Czech Brethren and at a communion service in his castle led in a reorganization and renewal of the United Brethren, or Unitas Fratrum. From that time on he became one of their most important leaders. The encounter with Zinzendorf also brought the Brethren into contact with German Lutheran Pietism, much of which they absorbed in their reconstituted life.

In 1737, Zinzendorf was in London negotiating Brethren concerns with the Archbishop of Canterbury.

The archbishop suggested that the Moravian Brethren begin a mission to the Black slaves in the British American colonies. Peter Böhler was selected to carry out the mission, and Zinzendorf's first official function as a Brethren bishop was the ordination and the commissioning of Böhler to his task. After spending some time in England with John Wesley to perfect his English, Böhler traveled to the colonies and landed in Savannah, Georgia, on October 16, 1738. He moved on to Purysburg, South Carolina, an old German settlement which became his headquarters. In spite of his negative reaction to the climate, he continued the mission for over a year until the threat of Spanish invasion drove him out.

While traveling north with evangelists George Whitefield, Böhler and some of his Moravian colleagues were commissioned to build the school for African Americans which had become a mission project for Whitefield. However, the project came to naught as Böhler and Whitefield came to loggerheads over their theological disagreements. Böhler sailed for Europe in 1741 and ended the first attempt by Moravians at a mission to African Americans. The Moravians, while occasionally preaching to Black people as opportunity afforded, turned their major energy to Native Americans and never again launched a denominational activity at either the slave or freedman community in North America.

The Moravians did have a successful mission among the slaves in the West Indies. One result of that mission, which would later have its effects in North America, was the founding of a theological school in Nisky on St. Thomas Island. Several graduates of that school would later leave both the West Indies and the Moravians for the United States. Possibly the most famous alumni, in that respect, was **George Alexander McGuire**, founder of the **African Orthodox Church**.

Hamilton, J. Taylor, and Kenneth G. Hamilton. *History of the Moravian Church: The Renewed Unitas Fratrum, 1722–1957*. Bethlehem, PA/Winston-Salem, NC: Interprovincial Board of Christian Education, Moravian Church in America, 1983. 723 pp.

MOREHOUSE COLLEGE. A Baptist school. Morehouse College, Atlanta, Georgia, was started in 1867 in Augusta, Georgia, by the American Baptist Home Missionary Society. It was opened by Edmund Turney, Richard Coulter, and William Jefferson. Originally known as Augusta Institute, it began with three teachers and 37 African American students who gathered for their work in the Springfield Baptist Church. In 1879 the school moved to Atlanta and was renamed the Atlanta

Baptist Seminary. In 1913 the school was renamed in honor of Henry L. Morehouse, for many years the corresponding secretary of the American Baptist Home Missionary Society.

Through the twentieth century Morehouse has become somewhat of a standard for African American colleges. Over the years approximately ten percent of its graduates have gone on to earn graduate degrees and approximately five percent of all African Americans with Ph.D.s attended the school at some point during their academic career. Among its illustrious alumni is **Martin Luther King, Jr.**

Today the school is part of the Atlanta University complex and is sponsored by the **National Baptist Convention, U.S.A., Inc**.

MORE-MORENO, JOHN (d. 1958), a bishop of the **Eastern Orthodox Catholic Church in America**, was born in the Danish West Indies early in this century. Little is known of him until 1931 when he appears in New York City as one of the first members of the Society of Clerks of St. Basil. The society had been founded by Bishop William Albert Nichols, a former Episcopal priest who had converted to Eastern Orthodoxy. Nichols had accepted episcopal orders from the Holy Eastern Orthodox Catholic and Apostolic Church in North America, the attempt to found a non-ethnic Orthodox church in North America originally conceived by Syrian Archbishop Aftimious Ofeish. In 1932 More-Moreno incorporated the Church of the Redeemer, a mission parish on Lenox Avenue in Harlem. In November 1933 Bishop Sophronios Bishara, who has succeeded Ofeish, consecrated More-Moreno. He was assisted by independent Russian Bishop Benjamin Fedchenkov.

More-Moreno worked his mission for the next year. Then in 1934, following the death of Bishara, he became the ruling bishop of the slowly shrinking Holy Eastern Orthodox Catholic and Apostolic Church in North America. It is difficult to assess how much of a following remained in the church at the time of More-Moreno's movement into the leadership. He attempted to carry on the church, and to that end he ordained several African American priests who were set to work in the New York metropolitan area.

Through the years, More-Moreno came into contact with John Thomas Beckles, another African American bishop who had founded the Eastern Orthodox Catholic Church in America, and accepted reconsecration from him. He assumed the ecclesiastical title Mar Chrysostomos and joined his work with Beckles's jurisdiction, which had an agenda very much in accord

508

with Ofeish's vision. In 1948 Beckles died. More-Moreno succeeded him as patriarch of the church, and united in his person the thrusts of both Ofeish's and Beckles's lifework.

At about the same time he came into contact with the Apostolic Episcopal Church (a predominantly White organization) and in 1946 assisted Archbishop Arthur Wolfort Brooks in the consecration of Dutch Bishop Herman P. Abbinga. In 1948 Brooks died and was succeeded by two bishops who served only a short time before resigning. In October 1949, by default, More-Moreno became the ruling bishop of the Apostolic Episcopal Church. Within a few months he had consecrated two bishops for the Apostolic Episcopal Church, Harold F. A. Jarvis (October 30) and Perry N. Cedarholm (December 6). After leading the church for over a year, in 1951 he turned it over to Cederholm who soon moved to Sweden.

More-Moreno now concentrated all of his attention on the Eastern Orthodox Catholic Church in America. He led the church until his death in 1958. Shortly before his death in June 1958 he consecrated Gregory R. P. Adair, who succeeded him as patriarch, and John Adair.

Persson, Bertil. *The Apostolic Episcopal Ministry, Archbishop Arthur W. Brooks and Christ's Church by the Sea: In Memory and Appreciation.* Solna, Sweden: The Author, 1989. 117 pp.

MORGAN, ROBERT, a priest of the Russian Orthodox Greek Catholic Church of America, was born in Jamaica. He went to Africa as a young man, attended Fourah Bay College in Sierra Leone and became an Anglican missionary in Liberia. He then traveled to England and studied at St. Aiden's College in Birkenhead, and King's College, London. He was ordained in England and subsequently migrated to America where he affiliated with the **Episcopal Church**. He was assigned to a parish in Wilmington, Delaware.

While in Wilmington he was converted to Eastern orthodoxy and at some point during the first decade of this century left the Episcopal Church and traveled to Constantinople, where he was rebaptized and reordained as a subdeacon and priest. He was assigned as a missionary to African American people. He returned to the United States and placed himself under the Russian Orthodox Church, the only Orthodox body in the United States at that time. He worked as a missionary in Philadelphia, but little is known of the results of his work.

MORGAN STATE UNIVERSITY. A Methodist school. Morgan State University, Baltimore, Maryland, began as Centenary Biblical Institute and for the first five years of its existence met in the facilities of Sharp Methodist Episcopal Church. Its primary purpose was to train ministers for the African American community. In 1872 the school was able to move into its own facilities, which it soon outgrew. A new building, in which it held classes for many years, became available in 1880. In 1890, through the generous gift of Dr. Lyttleton F. Morgan, it was able to make a substantial step forward and develop its college curriculum. In return, the school became known as Morgan College. The school continued as a Methodist school for the next half century, but in 1939 was taken over by the state and renamed Morgan State College. It became a university in 1975.

MORRIS, ELIAS CAMP (May 7, 1855–September 2, 1922), founding president of the **National Baptist Convention, U.S.A., Inc.**, was born into slavery in Springplace, Murray County, Georgia, the son of James and Cora C. Morris. While he was still a young boy, the family moved to Chattanooga, Tennessee, then to Stevenson, Alabama. After the death of both parents, Morris lived in the home of a relative, Robert Caver, a minister, while apprenticing to a shoemaker. He was converted in 1874, baptized in the Star Baptist Church in Stevenson, licensed to preach the same year, and determined to become a minister. He was a student at Nashville Institute (later called Roger Williams University) in Tennessee from 1874 to 1875. In 1877 he moved to Arkansas. In 1879 he was ordained and called to pastor the Centennial Baptist Church in Helena, Arkansas, where he remained the rest of his career. He married Fannie E. Austin on November 27, 1884, with whom he had five children.

Morris established himself as a significant figure in Arkansas. In 1880 he was elected secretary of the Arkansas Baptist State Convention. In 1882 he was elected president of the convention, and that same year founded, and for two years edited, the *Arkansas Times* (also known as the *Baptist Vanguard*), the first religious periodical for Blacks in the state. His church also published a weekly paper, called the *People's Friend*, which had a wide circulation. In 1884 he almost singlehandedly founded Arkansas Baptist College, and chaired its board of trustees for years afterward. This was the first Black-run college ever created by a state Baptist group. Beginning in 1884 Morris was a regular delegate to the Arkansas Republican State Convention, and was several times a delegate to the Republican National Convention.

Morris was also a rising star in two of the major Black Baptist organizations, the **Baptist Foreign Mission Convention** and the **American National Baptist Convention**, which elected him president in the early 1890s. In 1895 these two groups joined with the National Education Convention to form the National Baptist Convention, and Morris was elected its first president. He retained this position for the next 27 years, guiding the convention through its turbulent beginnings.

The most momentous issue Morris faced was the control of the National Baptist Publishing Board, run by **Richard Henry Boyd**, who was also corresponding secretary of the Home Mission Board. The board was incorporated in Tennessee in 1897 without any mention of the National Baptist Convention, and was legally set up and run as Boyd's business. Moreover, the convention was not incorporated, and thus had no legal life between its formal gatherings by which to control the boards informally associated with it. There was an inevitable clash as the convention sought to incorporate and establish control over the board, the result being that in 1915 Boyd and his followers established the National Baptist Convention of America and Morris's organization eventually restructured as the **National Baptist Convention, U.S.A., Inc.**

The courts gave most tangible assets to Boyd, and the National Baptist Convention, U.S.A., Inc. had to begin almost from scratch. Instead of relying on other Baptist material, a new publishing house was built, since Morris and others were adamant about Blacks controlling their own literature. Morris directed this process until his death.

Morris, Elias Camp. *Addresses to the Twenty-Fifth Annual National Baptist Convention, September 10–15, 1919.* Helena, AR: Royal Messenger Printing, 1919. 16 pp.

———. *Sermons, Addresses and Reminiscences and Important Correspondence.* Nashville, TN: National Baptist Publishing Board, 1901. 322 pp.

———. "Is the Young Negro an Improvement, Morally, on His Father?" 1902. Rpt. in Daniel W. Culp, ed. *Twentieth Century Negro Literature.* Miami, FL: Mnemosyne Publishing Co., 1969, 259–264.

RLOA, SNB, SCA, HNB, WWCR, HBBUS, NBH, IBAW, HUBA, BAW, HBB, ENB, OBMS.

MORRIS, SAMUEL SOLOMON, JR. (November 1, 1916–March 26, 1989), 89th bishop of the **African Methodist Episcopal Church** (AME), was born in Norfolk, Virginia, the son of Samuel Solomon Sr. and Mayme (Lawson) Morris. His father was a well-known AME minister, who for twenty years (1920–1940) was General Secretary of the Allen Christian Endeavor League, and then became General Secretary of the Christian Education Department. Morris Jr. attended Pearl High School in Nashville, Tennessee, received his B.S. from Wilberforce University in Ohio in 1937 and his B.D. from Yale University Divinity School, in New Haven, Connecticut, in 1940.

He was licensed to preach in Xenia, Ohio, in 1937, joined the Virginia Annual Conference in 1938, and was ordained deacon that same year and elder in 1940. His first major appointment after graduation was at St. Luke AME Church in Gallatin, Tennessee, from 1940 to 1941, serving at the same time St. John AME Church in Springfield. From 1941 to 1943 he was professor of Church History at Payne Theological Seminary at Wilberforce University. On November 30, 1942, he married Ermine Smith, with whom he had three children. His next station was St. Paul AME Church in Nashville, Tennessee, from 1943 to 1946.

From 1946 to 1948 Morris was president of Shorter College in North Little Rock, Arkansas, then returned to the local church in 1948–49 as associate pastor of Bethel AME Church in Detroit, Michigan. From 1949 to 1956 he was appointed to First AME Church in Gary, Indiana, followed by Coppin AME Church in Chicago, Illinois, from 1956 to 1972, where he firmly established his reputation. The church grew under his ministry, and he built the Copping Youth Center to accommodate a new emphasis on the needs of young people. In 1961 he was a delegate to the World Council of Churches Assembly in New Delhi, India, and the 1968 meeting in Sweden. He was president of the Chicago branch of the N.A.A.C.P. from 1960 to 1962 and served in a number of other major organizations, including the Chicago Urban League, Chicago Conference on Religion and Race, and Church Federation of Greater Chicago. He organized and chaired Clergy for Quality and Equality in Education. From 1969 to 1972 he was secretary of the board of directors of the Lake Grove Village Housing Complex.

At the General Conference in 1972 Morris was elected bishop and assigned to the Twelfth Episcopal District. He was chair of the board of trustees of Shorter College from 1972 to 1976. From 1972 to 1974 he was chair of the Social Action Committee of the AME Church. In 1974 he was a delegate to the World Council of Churches Assembly in Nairobi, Kenya. From 1976 to 1984 he was assigned to the Eleventh Episcopal District (Florida), during which time he was chair of the board of trustees of Edward Waters College in Jacksonville, Florida. From 1984 to 1989 he presided over the Fourth Episcopal District. In 1984 he was president of the general board of the denomination and *Ebony* magazine named him one of the one hundred most influential Black Americans. His funeral was attended by many dignitaries, including **Jesse Jackson**.

"AME Bishop Samuel S. Morris, Jr. Funeral Held in Chicago, Illinois." *Star of Zion* 113 (April 27, 1989): 6.

Coleman, J. C. "A Tribute to Bishop Samuel S. Morris, Jr." *The AME Church Review* 104 (April–June 1989): 5–6.

"The One Hundred Most Influential Black Americans." *Ebony* 39 (May 1984): 29–34.

Morris, Samuel Solomon. *An African Methodist Primer: A Digest of the History, Beliefs, Organization, and Operation of the African Methodist Episcopal Church.* Gary, IN: Harris Printing Co., n.d.

WWR (75–76 and 85), *EBA, WWABA* (88), *EAMEC, BDNM* (75), *HUBA, AARS, HAMEC.*

MORRIS BROWN UNIVERSITY. An **African Methodist Episcopal Church** (AME) school. The beginnings of Morris Brown University, Atlanta, Georgia, can be traced to a resolution approved by the North Georgia Conference of the AME Church in 1881. Bishop **William F. Dickerson** had been assigned to the conference following his election in 1880 and he promoted the establishment of the college (as he was at the same time working to establish **Allen University** in South Carolina). Dickerson served as the first chairman of the school's board of trustees but unfortunately died (1884) before the school, originally named Morris Brown College, actually opened in 1885.

For many decades the school operated as both college and high school, but the high school was discontinued in 1932. Turner Theological Seminary was started at Morris Brown in 1894. In recent years the growth of the school has prompted the adoption of its current name. Early in this century Morris Brown also absorbed the interests of Payne College, a small AME school which had been founded in 1879 in Cuthbert, Georgia.

Gregg, Howard D. *History of the African Methodist Episcopal Church: The Black Church in Action.* Nashville, TN: AMEC Sunday School Union, 1980. 535 pp.

Wright, Richard Robert, ed. *Encyclopedia of African Methodism.* 2nd ed. Philadelphia, PA: The Book Concern of the AME Church, 1947. 688 pp.

MORRIS COLLEGE. A Baptist school. Morris College, Sumpter, South Carolina, is a four-year liberal arts college founded in 1908 by the Baptist Educational and Missionary Convention of South Carolina, affiliated with the **National Baptist Convention, U.S.A., Inc.** It originally offered elementary, high school, and college classes, but over the years dropped the elementary and high school departments. It serves approximately 600 students annually.

MORRISTOWN COLLEGE. A **United Methodist Church** school. Morristown College began as a combination elementary and high school in Morristown, Tennessee, in the Eastern Tennessee Appalachian Mountains area, in 1881. It was founded by Judson S. Hill, a Methodist Episcopal Church minister from New Jersey, in cooperation with the denomination's Freedman's Aid Bureau. The original building which housed the school had been a slave market.

The school evolved into a junior college in 1923 at which time it became known as Morristown Normal and Industrial College. It assumed its present name in 1960.

Harmon, Nolan B., ed. *The Encyclopedia of World Methodism.* 2 vols. Nashville, TN: United Methodist Publishing House, 1974.

MOSS, OTIS, JR. (b. February 26, 1935), social activist and Baptist minister, was born in La Grange, Georgia, the son of Otis Sr. and Magnolia R. Moss. He received his B.A. in 1956 from Morehouse College in Atlanta, Georgia, and his B.D. from the Morehouse School of Religion in 1959. He married Edwina Hudson Smith, with whom he has had three children.

From 1956 to 1959 he pastored the Old Mt. Olive Baptist Church in La Grange, Georgia, and concurrently also pastored the Providence Baptist Church in Atlanta, Georgia, from 1956 to 1961. He was during that time vice-president of the Atlanta branch of the N.A.A.C.P. and in 1961, was voted Man of the Year in Religion in Atlanta. In 1960–61 he did additional graduate studies at the Interdenominational Theological Center in Atlanta. From 1961 to 1975 he pastored the Mt. Zion Baptist Church in Lockland, Cincinnati, Ohio. For one year, 1971, he co-pastored the Ebenezer Baptist Church in Atlanta with **Martin Luther King, Sr.** From 1970 to 1975 he wrote a regular column for the *Atlanta Inquirer* newspaper. The 1972 book, *Best Black Sermons*, included one of his sermons, "Going from Disgrace to Dignity." From 1975 to the present he has pastored the Olivet Institutional Baptist Church in Cleveland, Ohio.

He has long been a leader in the struggle for civil

rights and is on the board of directors of Morehouse School of Religion, the Martin Luther King, Jr. Center for Non-Violent Social Change, and **Jesse Jackson**'s **Operation PUSH**. He has been a part of clergy missions and delegations to Hong Kong, Japan (1970), Israel (1977–78), and Taiwan (1984). In 1983 he was named Black Professional of the Year by the Black Professional Association in Cleveland, Ohio. That year he also received the Governor's Award in Civil Rights. In 1984 *Ebony* magazine named Moss one of America's top fifteen Black preachers.

"America's Fifteen Greatest Black Preachers." *Ebony* 39 (September 1984): 27–33.

Moss, Otis, Jr. "Between Symbol and Substance." *Home Missions* 43 (April 1972): 28–29.

———. "Foundations for Thanksgiving." *Freeing the Spirit* 11 (Fall–Winter 1972, Spring 1973): 29–32.

———. "Going from Disgrace to Dignity." In William M. Philpot, ed. *Best Black Sermons*. Valley Forge, PA: Judson Press, 1972, pp. 50–57.

EBA, BDNM (75), *WWR* (85), *WWABA* (92–93), *HUBA, OTSB, IBAW*.

MOSSELL, MARY ELLA (May 22, 1853–1886), pioneer missionary to Haiti for the **African Methodist Episcopal Church** (AME), was born in Baltimore, Maryland as Mary Ella Forrester. She graduated from the Baltimore Normal School and received three scholarship prizes. She continued the study and practice of music until in 1874 she married C. W. Mossell, a minister in the AME Church. He was appointed as a missionary to Haiti, and the two in 1876 traveled together to that country.

Already versed in Latin, German, and Greek, Mossell successfully faced the challenge of mastering the language and customs of a Spanish and French culture. Although she might not have been the "official" missionary in the eyes of the church, she fully shared the missionary labors, trials, and successes with her husband. Using her skill with brightly colored yarn as an attention-getter, she won over the local women and was able to bring many of them and their families to the church and school. Her skills at the piano and in composing special songs for occasions were used to win over many of the more cultured leaders. She and her husband were instrumental in pulling together mainland support to send five Haitian boys to school at Wilberforce University.

Mossell struggled against the ravages of the climate and disease to bring faith and education to the people. Her most dangerous enemy was the instability of the government, and the Bazelias Revolution of September 1883, witnessed mass slaughter and destruction in the main city of Port au Prince. Her own house was burned to the ground, citizens who had sought safety there were shot, and her husband was marched off to meet the same fate. Her impassioned pleas, nobility, and courage in the face of this terror prevailed, however, and her husband's life was spared. The trauma, however, caused the premature birth of a daughter, who survived only a short while, but their remaining daughter remained well. Only a few years after the revolution, while she was still a young woman, Mossell's health finally gave out. President Solomon, on hearing of her death, asked, "How shall we estimate our loss when we recall that, perhaps, no one among us has accomplished larger labors in this field of dignified, useful, and indispensable service, and who has been more successful?"

HH, PNW, NNW, IBAW.

MOUNT CALVARY HOLY CHURCH OF AMERICA. Mount Calvary Holy Church of America is a Holiness denomination organized in 1928 in Boston, Massachusetts under the leadership of Bishop Broomfield Johnson. It is currently headed by Bishop Harold I. Williams (husband of famous evangelist and gospel singer, **Shirley Caesar**). Churches are located along the Eastern seaboard.

Payne, Wardell J. *Directory of African American Religious Bodies: A Compendium by the Howard University School of Divinity*. Washington, DC: Howard University Press, 1991. 363 pp.

Isotta Poggi

MOUNT CALVARY PENTECOSTAL FAITH CHURCH, INC. The Mount Calvary Pentecostal Faith Church, Inc., also known as Emmanuel Temple Pentecostal Faith Church, Inc., or Mount Assembly Hall of the Pentecostal Faith of All Nations, was founded in 1932 in New York City by Bishop Rosa Artemus Horne. Present work in the church is currently led by Mother Horne's adopted daughter, Bishop Gladys Brandhagen.

Payne, Wardell J. *Directory of African American Religious Bodies: A Compendium by the Howard University School of Divinity*. Washington, DC: Howard University Press, 1991. 363 pp.

Isotta Poggi

MOUNT HEBRON APOSTOLIC TEMPLE OF OUR LORD JESUS OF THE APOSTOLIC FAITH.

An Apostolic Pentecostal church. Mount Hebron Apostolic Temple of Our Lord Jesus of the Apostolic Faith dates to 1957 and the founding of the Yonkers, New York, congregation of the **Apostle Church of Christ in God**. During its first five years, founding pastor George H. Wiley, III, built one of the strongest and most vital Apostle Church congregations. Then in 1963, Wiley left the denomination and incorporated separately as a new denomination. Wiley suggested that the new arrangement gave him the freedom to develop ministries in fresh directions. He developed a vital multistate outreach aimed at youth, and began a radio program in New York that soon had outlets in the Carolinas. He also directed his ministry beyond the Black community to Whites and Puerto Ricans.

The Mount Hebron Temple follows the Apostolic Jesus Only doctrine of its parent body, there being no doctrinal issues in the 1963 split. As new congregations have been added, Wiley has given focus to his youth- and education-oriented emphases. In each congregation he has started a youth forum designed to give the youth input in church programming. He has also started a Bible school in each church. By 1980 there were 10 congregations and approximately 3,000 members.

Richardson, James C. *With Water and Spirit: A History of Black Apostolic Denominations in the U.S.* Martinsville, VA: The Author, n.d. 151 pp.

MT. ZION SPIRITUAL TEMPLE.

King **Louis H. Narcisse**, D.D., who died in the late 1980s, was one of the most colorful of the Spiritual leaders. In 1943 he established the Mt. Zion Spiritual Temple, which was incorporated in 1945. King Narcisse maintained his "International Headquarters" in Oakland, California, and his "East Coast Headquarter" in Detroit. In addition to these two temples, the association has seven other congregations, including a second temple in Detroit and temples in Sacramento, Richmond (California), Houston, Orlando, New York City, and Washington, D.C.

During his reign, King Narcisse often appeared before his followers dressed in a golden toga, a cape with a White surplice, a White crown with glitter and a golden tassel, eight rings on his fingers, and a ring on his left ear. He was chauffeured in a shiny Black Cadillac limousine with his title and name inscribed on the door. Officers in his kingdom bore titles such as "Reverend Queen," "Reverend Prince," "Reverend Princess," "Reverend Father," "Reverend Mother," and "Reverend Lady," "Professor," and "Madam."

For those occasions when King Narcisse could not be with his flock at the King Narcisse Michigan State Memorial Temple, a large picture of "His Grace" faced the congregation, reminding its members of their spiritual leader. A sign below the picture reads as follows:

GOD IS GREAT AND GREATLY TO BE PRAISED IN THE SOVEREIGN STATE OF MICHIGAN IN THE KINGDOM OF "HIS GRACE KING" LOUIS H. NARCISSE, DD/WHERE "IT'S (sic) NICE TO BE NICE, AND REAL NICE TO LET OTHERS KNOW THAT WE ARE NICE."

Baer, Hans A. *The Black Spiritual Movement: A Religious Response to Racism.* Knoxville, TN: University of Tennessee Press, 1984. 220 pp.

Hans Baer

MUHAMMAD, ELIJAH

MUHAMMAD, ELIJAH (October 7, 1897–February 25, 1975), head of the **Nation of Islam**, was born Elijah (possibly Robert) Poole, the seventh of thirteen children in the family of Wali, an ex-slave who was a sharecropper and part-time Baptist preacher, and Marie Poole. He grew up near Sandersville, Georgia, without much apparent future, his share of farm work preventing the progress of formal schooling beyond the age of nine. At age sixteen he left home and made his way doing odd jobs and working on the railroad. He married Clara Evans in 1919 and in 1923 they moved to Detroit, where he got a job on a Chevrolet plant assembly line. They had eight children (six sons and two daughters). Like so many others, especially Blacks, Muhammad was laid off in the 1929 Depression year and remained on relief for two years. Clara helped support the family by doing domestic work.

Muhammad's (Poole's) life changed in 1930 when he met **Wallace D. Fard**, who taught that Islam is the true heritage and destiny of Blacks. Fard (known as the Prophet) founded Temple No. 1 of the Nation of Islam in Detroit, and Muhammad was one of its first members, known by the name given him, Elijah Muhammad. Muhammad became chief assistant to the Prophet, who disappeared mysteriously in 1934. Muhammad claimed the right of succession as the Messenger of Allah, but rival factions forced him to move to Chicago, where he had founded Temple No. 2 in 1932. He founded other temples around the East Coast, constantly clashing with rival groups, until he was arrested in 1942 for sympathizing with the Japanese and encouraging young Black men not to serve in the military. Cleared of sedition charges, he was ultimately jailed for not having himself, at the age of forty-five, registered according to the Selective Service Act. His four-year stay at the federal penitentiary in Milan, Michigan, gained him a martyr status that placed him as undisputed head of the Black Muslims.

Muhammad taught that Blacks were the original people of creation, and Whites were later, evil mutations. The appearance of the Prophet signalled the beginning of the end of the 6,000–year domination by Whites and the time of preparation by Blacks to learn to control their own destiny. Muhammad was very critical of the civil rights movement led by **Martin Luther King, Jr.**, and the Black Christian church in general, thinking it at best ineffectual. Muhammad's goal was a separate Black Muslim nation, established in its own territory, if possible, but at least operating as a self-sufficient unit. To this end, members typically changed their last names, which had often come from owners during slavery, either to an Islamic name, or to "X," signifying an unknown past identity. In keeping with Muhammad's slogan, "Build Black, buy Black," they created, operated, and patronized a wide range of businesses. Members also submitted to strict disciplines, partly derived from Orthodox Islamic practices. Alcohol, tobacco, and narcotics were forbidden, as were adultery, dancing, gambling, and criminal activity. Those otherwise critical of the movement expressed admiration for the sometimes radical change in behavior achieved by followers.

Muhammad's teachings were spread through the periodical *Muhammad Speaks*, and several books, including *The Supreme Wisdom* (1957), *Message to the Black Man* (1965), and *The Fall of America* (1973). The conversion of heavyweight boxing champion Muhammad Ali (Cassius Clay) in the 1960s was a major event, but the biggest boost to the growth of the Nation of Islam came from **Malcolm X**, who was converted in prison. After his release in 1952 he rose through the ranks, becoming Muhammad's chief spokesperson and a major media figure. His charisma and militancy brought thousands into membership, and his departure from the group in 1964 was Muhammad's biggest disappointment. Nevertheless, Muhammad's following grew, with a membership at his death of around 100,000 in 70 temples in the United States. In his later days he lived in Phoenix, Arizona; his wife died in 1972. After his death, he was succeeded by his son, **Warith Deen Muhammad**, who changed the name of the organization

to American Muslim Mission and redirected it into the Sunni Muslim mainstream.

Alexander, E. Curtis. *Elijah Muhammad on African American Education*. New York: ECA Associates, 1989. 120 pp.

Ansari, Zafar Ishaq. "W. E. Muhammad: The Making of a 'Black Muslim' Leader (1933–1961)." *American Journal of Islamic Social Sciences* 2 (December 1985): 245–262.

Cushmeer, Bernard. *This Is the One: Messenger Elijah Muhammad*. Phoenix, AZ: Truth Publications, 1971. 160 pp.

Davis, Charles H., Jr. *Black Nationalism and the Nation of Islam*. 4 vols. Los Angeles: The John Henry and Mary Louisa Dunn Bryant Foundation, 1962.

Lincoln, C. Eric. *The Black Muslims in America*. Boston, MA: Beacon Press, 1961. 276 pp.

Lomax, Louis. *When the Word is Given*. Cleveland, OH: World Publishing Co., 1963. 223 pp.

Muhammad, Elijah. *The Fall of America*. Chicago: Muhammad's Temple of Islam No. 2, 1973. 265 pp.

———. *How to Eat to Live*. Chicago: Muhammad Mosque of Islam No. 2, 1967. 132 pp.

———. *Message to the Black Man in America*. Chicago: Muhammad Mosque of Islam No. 2, 1965. 355 pp.

———. *Our Saviour Has Arrived*. Chicago: Muhammad Mosque of Islam No. 2, 1974. 226 pp.

———. *The Supreme Wisdom*. 2 vols. Brooklyn: Temple of Islam, 1957.

"The Nation of Islam Mourns Elijah Muhammad." *Ebony* 30 (May 1975): 74–81.

"Organizations and Leaders Campaigning for Negro Goals in the United States." *New York Times* (August 10, 1964): 16.

Stewart, Ted. "Who Will Inherit the $80 Million Black Muslim Empire?" *Sepia* 24 (May 1975): 18–23.

Wintle, Justin, ed. *Makers of Modern Culture*. London: Routledge & Kegan Paul, 1981. 605 pp.

RLOA, IBAW, BDACSL, BHBA, HNB, NYTBS (75), ONL, CH, BSC, NSE, CB (71), NA, DARB, EBA, OTSB, SBAA, BRBR, AARS, BN, MBRL.

MUHAMMAD, WARITH DEEN (b. October 30, 1933), successor to **Elijah Muhammad** as leader of the **Nation of Islam**, was born in Hamtrack, Michigan, the seventh of eight children in the family of Elijah and Clara (Evans) Muhammad. His father was the leader of the Nation of Islam, a Black nationalist, Muslim-influenced religious organization. In 1934 the family moved to Chicago, where Elijah Muhammad founded Temple #2 of the Nation of Islam. The early years, until E. Muhammad's release from prison in 1946, were difficult ones of insecurity and poverty. W. D. Muhammad was not particularly groomed to be his father's successor, as others seemed more likely to take that role. His formal education was at Muhammad University of Islam in Chicago, an elementary and secondary school (renamed in 1976 the Sister Clara Muhammad Elementary and Secondary Schools). In high school he took Arabic classes, and through that avenue began to realize that the teachings of the Qur'an were different from those of the Nation of Islam. He married a woman named Shirley, with whom he had four children.

He wanted to become an electrical engineer, but his father discouraged any further education or pursuits outside the boundaries of the Nation of Islam. He worked at various positions within the Nation of Islam and became a lieutenant in the Fruit of Islam, the paramilitary security force. In 1958 he was appointed minister of the Philadelphia Temple. He was drafted shortly afterward and his father had him apply for conscientious objector status. This was granted, and he was assigned to Elgin State Hospital for alternative duty. He looked forward to this as a chance to become a lab technician, but his father told him to refuse the assignment, resulting in a three-year jail sentence (October 31, 1961–January 10, 1963). After his release it seemed that his relationship with the Nation of Islam had changed. He was probably the number three person in the organization, after his father and Raymond Sharrieff, the Supreme Captain of the Fruit of Islam, but he began to express serious differences with various programs and policies. He broke away from the group in 1964, about the same time that **Malcolm X** left, and was apparently in sympathy with Malcolm. He then supported himself as a house painter, welder, upholsterer, and other occupations. There were a few temporary readmissions into the Nation of Islam until finally, in 1974, he mended the relationship with his father and permanently rejoined the Nation of Islam.

When Elijah Muhammad passed away in February 1975, the Nation of Islam had a membership of about 100,000 in at least seventy temples across the United States. Wraith Muhammad took over the leadership, to the surprise of many, and immediately began to make major changes. In April 1975 he set up various committees such as Ways and Means, Child Interest, and Public Information to facilitate the administration of internal affairs. In May 1975, he began the first national fourth Sunday telephone broadcast from Chicago to followers across the country. In June 1975 he stunned the organization and outside observers by lifting the color ban on membership and allowing Whites to join. In about August of 1975 the Fruit of Islam, the paramilitary defense organization, was disbanded.

In September 1975 Warith Muhammad instituted the orthodox Muslim practice of fasting in the month of Ramadan, and began the practice of identifying Blacks in the western hemisphere of African American descent as Bilalians. Bilal was a Black Ethiopian whom Prophet Muhammad, the founder of Islam, chose as the first muezzin, or caller to prayers. As contemporary Black people are called to bring the world back to God, W. D. Muhammad said that it was appropriate to name them after such an honorable ancestor. In November 1975, the *Muhammad Speaks* newspaper was renamed the *Bilalian News*. In March 1976, W. D. Muhammad announced that W. D. Fard would no longer be considered Allah and that Elijah Muhammad would no longer be considered his messenger; they were simply divinely inspired men. In October 1975 the formal Muslim prayer service of Salat was instituted for the Nation of Islam. Despite these various changes, the vast majority of the membership remained loyal, and the withdrawal of **Louis Farrakhan** and his followers was one of the few notable schisms. Even with Farrakhan, it has been reported that most of his recruits were new and only a small number actually left Muhammad's group, but this kind of membership information is difficult to determine.

In January 1976, Warith Muhammad asked all followers to reject names with a slavery heritage and adopt Muslim or African names. He himself substituted Warith for his given first name of Wallace (after Wallace D. Fard). He encouraged the membership, once forbidden to be politically involved, to vote and act patriotically. He also renamed all of the organization's temples as mosques. Muhammad's Temple #1 in Detroit became Wali Muhammad Mosque #1; Muhammad's Temple #2 in Chicago became the Elijah Muhammad Mosque #2; Muhammad's Temple #3 in Milwaukee became the Sultan Muhammad Mosque #3; and Muhammad's Temple #7 in New York became the Malcolm Shabazz Mosque #7. To thus name a mosque after Malcolm X was symbolic of the philosophic shifts formulated by W. D. Muhammad. Malcolm X had left the Nation of Islam in 1964 and later advocated much the same move toward orthodox Islam that Muhammad was now accomplishing. In March 1976, Muhammad said, "We're trying to get away from a lot of spiritual spookiness so we can deal with reality the way it is." Previous teachings, such as the Yakub story of the origin of the races, were now to be treated symbolically.

Muhammad continued the process of reforming the Nation of Islam, in November 1976, changing its name to the World Community of Al-Islam in the West (W.C.I.W.). In March 1977, he substituted the term "Masjid" for "Mosque," and in November 1977, led a group of over two hundred on a Hajj or pilgrimage to

Mecca. In April 1978, he changed the name of the organization again, from the World Community of Al-Islam in the West to the American Muslim Mission, a name which seemed to speak more directly to the group's identity and aspirations. In September 1978, at an historic meeting in Atlanta, Georgia, Muhammad resigned from all administrative duties in favor of leadership by a more traditional seventeen-member National Council of Imams.

The American Muslim Mission (A.M.M.) continued to expand its activities, especially into education, and experienced more and more acceptance by the mainstream Muslim world. In February 1979, a $22 million contract was signed for A.M.M. food services to package foods for the Department of Defense. This was said to be the largest government contract ever awarded a minority-owned firm. In December 1980, the A.M.M. purchased the Palmer Memorial Institute in Sedalia, North Carolina, and later (1982) reopened it as the American Muslim Teachers College. In May 1981, another school, the American Muslim Mission Teachers College, was established in Chicago. In October 1981, the American Muslim Mission Library was opened in Chicago. In June 1982, 4,600 acres were purchased in Terrell County, Georgia, for a new project to be named Elijahville. In July 1983, Elijahville hosted the First A.M.M. National Convention, with about 10,000 delegates.

A sign of yet further changes, in January 1984, Muhammad demoted himself from head imam to simply the leader of Chicago's Elijah Muhammad Masjid, though he continued to function as an ambassador-at-large for the A.M.M. Then in 1985 Muhammad made the final step when, with the approval of the A.M.M.'s leadership, he disbanded its national structure. This change has allowed the former mosques and members of the Nation of Islam to integrate themselves into the larger Muslim community which is built around autonomous locally controlled centers.

As of the beginning of the 1990s, Muhammad remains the imam of the mosque in Chicago and regularly writes for the *Muslim Journal* (the continuing *Muhammad Speaks*) which now functions as an independent voice within the larger orthodox American Muslim community.

Ansari, Zafar Ishaq. "W. D. Muhammad: The Making of a 'Black Muslim' Leader (1933–1961)." *American Journal of Islamic Social Sciences* 2 (December 1985): 245–262.

"Black Muslims: Back to Allah." *Newsweek* 92 (September 25, 1978): 44.

"Black Muslim Leader Resigns." *The Christian Century* 95 (September 27, 1978): 881.

Gates, David and Tracey L. Robinson. "The Black Muslims: A Divided Flock." *Newsweek* 103 (April 9, 1984): 15.

Lee, Martha and Thomas Flanagan. "The Black Muslims and the Fall of America: An Interpretation Based on the Failure of Prophecy." *Journal of Religious Studies* 16 (1989): 140–156.

Mamiya, Lawrence H. "From Black Muslim to Bilalian: The Evolution of a Movement." *Journal for the Scientific Study of Religion* 21 (1982): 138–152.

Muhammad, Warithuddin. *Imam W. Deen Muhammad Speaks from Harlem, New York.* Chicago: W. D. Muhammad, distributed by M. M. Shabazz, 1984. 131 pp.

———. *Imam W. Deen Muhammad Speaks from Harlem, New York, Vol. II: Challenges That Face Man Today.* Chicago: W. D. Muhammad, distributed by M. M. Shabazz, 1985. 154 pp.

Nurriden, Aquil. "Why Wallace Muhammad Resigned." *Sepia* 28 (January 1979): 18–23.

Whitehurst, James Emerson. "The Mainstreaming of the Black Muslims: Healing the Hate." *The Christian Century* 97 (February 27, 1980): 225–229.

Williams, Dennis A. and Elaine Sciolino. "Rebirth of the Nation." *Newsweek* 87 (March 25, 1976): 33.

Woodward, Kenneth L. and Nolan Davis. "Second Resurrection." *Newsweek* 90 (August 20, 1977): 67.

WWABA (92–93), *WWR* (85), *IBAW*.

MURCHISON, ELISHA (b. June 18, 1907), 29th bishop of the **Christian Methodist Episcopal Church** (CME), was born in Fort Worth, Texas, the son of Elisha P. Sr. and Gertrude (Moore) Murchison. His father was a CME minister and a physician, and baptized Murchison himself in the Morning Chapel CME Church in Fort Worth. He was preaching in Texas as early as 1920, at age thirteen. He later began pastoring churches and was ordained an elder in the CME Church in 1926. He received his B.A. in 1929 from Clark College in Atlanta, Georgia, while serving churches in the area, and in 1930 earned his B.D. from Gammon Theological Seminary in Atlanta. He married Imogene Ford on August 15, 1930, with whom he had two daughters. He then went on to Boston University in Massachusetts, earning his M.A. there in 1932 while serving a church in Springfield, Massachusetts.

From 1932 to 1936 he was a professor and head of the Department of Religion at Texas College in Tyler, Texas, and from 1936 to 1939 he was Director of Leadership Training Department of the General Board of Religious Education. He then was assigned as district superintendent for the Chicago District, staying from 1939 to 1946. In 1939–40 he completed the classroom requirements for the Ph.D. at the University of Chicago.

From 1946 to 1958 he was editor of the *Christian Index*, the official organ of the CME Church, and established thereby a national reputation. He was a delegate to the First Assembly of the World Council of Churches in Amsterdam, Holland, in 1948.

At the 1958 General Conference Murchison was elected bishop with the largest number of first ballot votes up to that point in the history of the church. He was assigned to the Fifth Episcopal District (Alabama and Florida and mission work in Africa), where he stayed until 1970, when he was switched to the Second Episcopal District (Ohio, Kentucky, and parts of Indiana and West Virginia). In 1978 he was assigned to the Missouri, Mississippi, Illinois, and Kansas Conferences. In the 1960s he organized several churches in Ghana and Nigeria, essentially establishing the CME presence there. He served on the executive committee of the Consultation on Church Union (C.O.C.U.) and was the driving force in the CME Church for union with the AMEZ Church. In 1964 he was president of the **National Fraternal Council of Negro Churches**, and was vice-president-at-large of the National Council of Churches from 1970 to 1972. He was chair of the board of trustees of Miles College in Birmingham, Alabama from 1958 to 1970, and was also chair of the trustees at Phillips School of Theology in Atlanta, Georgia. He was a delegate to the World Council of Churches Assembly in Nairobi, Kenya, in 1975. In 1974 he became senior bishop and thus the executive head of the denomination. He retired at the April 1982 General Conference after serving one of the longer episcopal tenures in denominational history.

"Bishop Elisha P. Murchison, the Man." *Christian Index* 110 (July 28, 1977): 4, 6, 9.
"Our Retiring Bishops." *Christian Index* 115 (April 1, 1982): 3, 10.
EBA, WWABA (80–81 and 88), *EWM, WWR* (77), *BDNM* (75), *OTSB, CMECTY.*

MURPH, HENRY WENDELL (b. 1916), 86th bishop of the **African Methodist Episcopal Church** (AME), was born in Charleston, South Carolina, the son of Rev. and Mrs. J. W. Murph. He earned a B.A. from Allen University in Columbia, South Carolina and a B.D. from Oberlin Graduate School of Theology in Ohio. He married Rebecca Geraldine Stiles, with whom he had four children.

He had occasion to serve as professor of theology and philosophy and had a number of significant pastorates, including eight years at St. Philips AME Church in Savannah, Georgia, and eighteen years at

Grant AME Church in Watts, Los Angeles, California. His leadership at Grant was especially important during the difficult days of the Watts riots in the 1960s. He was chair of the O.I.C. in Los Angeles for four years. Murph was elected bishop in 1968 and was assigned to the Seventeenth Episcopal District. In 1972 he was assigned to the Second Episcopal District, based in Washington, D.C. In the 1980s he headed the Fifth Episcopal District, based in Los Angeles, California, and was senior bishop. He served as chair of the Program Committee of the General Conference Commission, and retired at the general conference of 1988.

James, Frederick C. *African Methodism in South Carolina: A Bicentennial Focus.* Tappan, NY: Custombook, 1987.
AMSC, HAMEC, WWR (85).

MURRAY, PAULI (November 20, 1910–July 1, 1985), lawyer, civil rights activist, poet, and the first female African American priest of the **Episcopal Church**, was born Anna Pauline Murray in Baltimore, Maryland, the fourth of six children in the family of William Henry and Agnes (Fitzgerald) Murray. Her heritage included Black slaves, White aristocrats, and Cherokee Indians. Her father was a principal in the Baltimore public schools and her mother was a nurse. Her mother passed away in 1914 and her father was soon committed to Crownsville State Hospital with typhoid fever effects. Murray went to live with her aunt, Pauline Dame, a schoolteacher, and her maternal grandparents, Robert and Cornelia Fitzgerald, in Durham, North Carolina. They brought her up in the Episcopal Church, where she was confirmed at age nine.

She graduated from Hillside High School in Durham in 1926, at the age of fifteen, but discovered that she did not have enough credits from her eleven-grade curriculum to enter Hunter College in New York City. To meet the problem she moved in with cousins Maude and James, enrolled in Richmond Hill High School in New York City and graduated with honors in 1927. She also by this point had the New York City residence requirements so she would not have to pay tuition at Hunter, a city school. She earned money in Durham for a year before entering Hunter College in the fall of 1928. The next year the stock market crashed, she lost her part-time jobs, and she was forced to leave school. In 1930 she married a man identified as "Billy," and kept it secret so that she would not lose her room at the "Y." They had no means of living together, and after several months they gave up in despair. Some years later the marriage was annulled.

In the spring of 1931 Murray helped a friend drive

to California to look for work, but was called back to North Carolina to look after her Aunt Pauline, who was ill. Since she had no money to travel across the country, Murray was forced to travel on trains as a hobo, dressed as a teenage boy. After her aunt recovered, Murray returned to Hunter College and graduated with a B.A. in English in January 1933, one of four Blacks in a class of 247. For a time she sold subscriptions to *Opportunity*, the magazine of the National Urban League. In the fall of 1935 she found a job with the Works Progress Administration (W.P.A.), first as a teacher in the Remedial Reading Project in the New York City public schools and then in 1936 in the W.P.A. Workers' Education Project.

Concerned about her own further education and wanting to be near Aunt Pauline, Murray applied to the University of North Carolina (U.N.C.) graduate school in the fall of 1938. The response, that Blacks were not allowed, arrived on December 14, 1938, two days after the U.S. Supreme Court had ruled, in Gaines v. Canada, that every state had to provide graduate and professional training to residents of the state based on equality of right. Murray thus unintendedly became a much-discussed figure, first in North Carolina, and then across the country. She was not admitted and the pattern at U.N.C. did not change until the 1950s, but Murray's role as a pioneer was widely recognized.

In 1939 she developed a friendship with Pulitzer Prize-winning poet Stephen Vincent Benét, who encouraged her in her first love, writing. Already she had written a novel, *The Angel of the Desert*, at age fifteen, published an article, "A Working Student," in the Hunter College magazine *Echo*, and had published a poem, "Song of the Highway," in an anthology called *Color* (1934). During this time she wrote other poems and articles and became acquainted with a number of the "Harlem Renaissance" authors, such as Countee Cullen and **Langston Hughes**. In 1939 she also began a correspondence with First Lady Eleanor Roosevelt and in their friendship over the following years became "a central figure in Mrs. Roosevelt's conscience on race."

In March 1940, while on a trip, Murray and a friend, Adelene McBean, were arrested for refusing to move further back in the bus to a broken seat. They were jailed for three days, found guilty, and fined. She found herself able to follow the legal arguments in the case and decided to become a lawyer and eradicate Jim Crow laws. She worked for the next two years for the Workers Defense League raising funds for the defense of Odell Waller, a Black sharecropper accused of killing a White landowner in a dispute over Waller's crops. In the fall of 1941 she entered Howard University Law School in Washington, D.C. She continued to try to help Waller,

but the appeals failed and he was executed in 1942. While at Howard she expanded her efforts into leading sit-ins to integrate local restaurants. In addition to the N.A.A.C.P. she joined the Congress of Racial Equality (C.O.R.E.), a Gandhi-inspired civil rights organization. In 1943 she published her most famous poem, *Dark Testament*, about the struggle for racial equality.

In her senior year at Howard, Murray was president of her class and chief justice of the Court of Peers. Her senior thesis argued that the "separate but equal" doctrine did violence to the personality of the minority individual, an argument used successfully later in the landmark 1954 Brown v. Board of Education of Topeka case. She graduated in May 1944, the only woman in her class, with a Rosenwald Fellowship for graduate study in law at Harvard University, only to find that Harvard did not admit women. Instead she entered the Boalt Hall of Law at the University of California, Berkeley, and received her LL.M. degree in 1945. Her master's thesis, "The Right to Equal Opportunity in Employment," was the first definitive published law review article on that issue. In January, 1946 she was appointed the first Black deputy attorney general of California, but had to give it up shortly because of her own illness and that of her Aunt Pauline. In 1946 the National Council of Negro Women named her Woman of the Year and in 1947 *Mademoiselle* magazine named her Woman of the Year.

Murray settled in New York City in late 1946, brought her aunts, Pauline and Sallie, to live with her, and worked as a law clerk because most law firms would not hire a woman. She was able to open her own law office in April 1949, and that year ran for a city council seat in the tenth senatorial district, representing the Liberal party. Despite her newcomer status, she came in second out of four candidates. In 1951 she published her first book, *States' Laws on Race and Color*, which she had written on retainer of the Women's Division of Christian Service of the Board of Missions of the Methodist Church. Supreme Court Justice Thurgood Marshall later stated that this book was the Bible for civil rights lawyers working against segregation. When it was published there was no other work with comprehensive coverage of segregation laws in the South. About this time Murray and James Baldwin became the first Black authors admitted to the McDowell Colony for artists in Peterborough, New Hampshire. In 1956 she published *Proud Shoes: The Story of an American Family*, recounting the life of her grandparents. With this book, the African American family history became a new literary genre, to be made famous by Alex Haley's *Roots* many years later.

In 1956 Murray became an associate attorney and

the only female in the prestigious law firm of Paul, Weiss, Rifkind, Wharton, and Garrison in New York City. The 1959 lynching of Mack Parker in Poplarville, Mississippi strongly affected her and she felt the need to leave the United States for a while. In February 1960 she resigned from the law firm and went to Ghana for eighteen months. While there she was a senior lecturer in the Ghana School of Law and coauthored *The Constitution and Government of Ghana*. In the fall of 1961 she entered the graduate school of law at Yale University in New Haven, Connecticut, on a scholarship. In 1962 she was selected to be a member of the Committee on Civil and Political Rights, a study group of the President's Commission on the Status of Women. Her paper, "A Proposal to Reexamine the Applicability of the Fourteenth Amendment to State Laws and Practices Which Discriminate on the Basis of Sex *Per Se*," was used as the basis of the committee's final report.

In 1965 Murray was the first Black to receive the Doctor of Juridical Science from Yale Law School. Despite the prestigious degree she was unable to find a teaching position and survived by writing "Human Rights U.S.A.: 1948–1966" for the Women's Division of the Methodist Church. In the fall of 1965 she was appointed to the board of directors of the American Civil Liberties Union (A.C.L.U.), a position she held for the next eight years. Also in 1965 she met with Betty Friedan and others to discuss the idea of an independent civil rights organization for women, and in October, 1966, Murray was one of the thirty-two women who met in Washington, D.C. to found the National Organization for Women (N.O.W.). For seven months in 1966–67 Murray was a consultant to the Equal Employment Opportunity Commission. In 1967–68 she was vice-president and professor of political science at Benedict College in Columbia, South Carolina.

In 1968 she served as a consultant on racism to the Fourth Assembly of the World Council of Churches in Uppsala, Sweden, and was energized into a recommitment to the church and religious service. She had all along maintained a relationship with the Episcopal Church, but had a running feud with it because of its refusal to include women in leadership roles in worship. From 1968 to 1970 she served on the Church Women United's Commission on Women in Today's World. From 1968 to 1972 she was professor of American Studies at Brandeis University in Waltham, Massachusetts, and in 1972 was named Louis Stulberg Professor of Law and Politics at Brandeis. At Brandeis she was treated harshly by many of the new generation of Black activists who considered her an outdated sellout. She in turn was put off by their lack of

intellectual rigor and often blatant sexism. In 1970 she published her only collection of poetry as *Dark Testament and Other Poems*. From 1970 to 1973 she was on the board of directors of the N.O.W. Legal Defense and Education Fund.

In 1973 her long-time friend Renee Barlow died in New York, and the experience of tending to her final needs galvanized her desire to be in religious service. She entered General Theological Seminary in New York City in September 1973, as the only Black woman and the oldest student. At this time women still were not allowed to be priests in the Episcopal Church, a position which did not officially change until the 1976 General Convention, effective January 1, 1977. She graduated in 1976 with an M.Div. and was ordained a deacon. On January 8, 1977, she was ordained the first Black woman priest in the history of the Episcopal Church, and one of the first three women of any color. Over the next seven years she served variously at the Episcopal Church of the Atonement in Washington, D.C.; as priest of a "floating parish" for the hospitalized and homebound in Alexandria, Virginia; and as priest of the Church of the Holy Nativity in Baltimore, Maryland. She retired in January 1984 and moved to Pittsburgh, Pennsylvania, where she died of cancer a little more than a year later. Her nearly finished autobiography was published posthumously as *Song in a Weary Throat: An American Pilgrimage* (1987), and reprinted in 1989 as *Pauli Murray: The Autobiography of a Black Activist, Feminist, Lawyer, Priest, and Poet*. In 1990 the University of North Carolina, with which she had been in an adversarial relationship for so long, honored her by establishing the Pauli Murray Scholarship for the financially needful undergraduate student who has done the most to improve race relations on campus. Despite a lifetime of disappointments and obstacles, Murray was a woman who never stopped seeking justice and refused to hate.

Haney, Elly. "Pauli Murray: Acting and Remembering." *Journal of Feminist Studies in Religion* 4 (Fall 1988): 75-79.

Hiatt, Suzanne R. "Pauli Murray: May Her Song Be Heard At Last." *Journal of Feminist Studies in Religion* 4 (Fall 1988): 69–73.

"Lady Lawyers." *Ebony* 3 (August 1947): 18–21.

Montgomery, Nancy S. "Song in a Weary Throat." *The Christian Century* 104 (September 30, 1987): 828–829.

Murray, Pauli. *"All for Mr. Davis." The Story of Sharecropper Odell Waller*. New York: Workers Defense League, n.d.

———. *Dark Testament and Other Poems*. Norwalk, CT: Silvermine Publishers, 1970. 106 pp.

———. *Proud Shoes: The Story of an American Family*. New York: Harper, 1978. 280 pp.

———. *Song in a Weary Throat: An American Pilgrimage.* New York: Harper & Row, 1987. 451 pp.

———. *States' Laws on Race and Color, and Appendices Containing International Documents, Federal Laws and Regulations, Local Ordinances, and Charts—1955 Supplement.* Cincinnati, OH: Woman's Division of Christian Service, Board of Missions of the Methodist Church, 1955. 256 pp.

"Rev. Dr. Pauli Murray." *Ebony* 34 (September 1979): 107–112.

SBAA, BAW, NYTBS (1974), *NBAW, WWWA* (8), *WWABA* (85), *OS, EBA.*

MUSIC IN THE AFRICAN AMERICAN CHURCH. Since the seventeenth century, Black Americans have participated in two culturally distinct religious traditions, differentiated by ideology, worship style, repertoire, and musical practice. The first replicates the ritual of White Protestant denominations. Items drawn from its musical repertoire—psalms, hymns, and spiritual songs—fill set places in the order of the service, according to Euro-American liturgical requirements and aesthetic principles. The second, independently developed by Black Americans, in keeping with a heritage that recalls African rituals, turns music itself into an act of worship. White Protestant hymns, especially those of Isaac Watts and the Wesley brothers, continue to be mainstays of its repertoire; but in performance, these songs undergo changes that bring them into line with African American aesthetic principles. The parallel evolution of these traditions reflects the duality of the Black experience in America. At the core of this experience was the struggle to maintain an African cultural identity, while meeting the expectations of American society at-large. Black people responded to the struggle by developing a repertoire of folk spirituals and gospel music, which now make up the foremost musical idiom of autonomous Black churches.

Spirituals, Gospels, and Hymnody: Use and Performance in the Black Church. Two related issues come to the fore in the consideration of Black hymnody: the ways the performance of music in Black American churches supported the struggle to preserve African cultural identity, and the factors—historical events, social issues, religious tenets, cultural practices—that encouraged the foundation of autonomous Black churches.

The Conversion of Slaves to Christianity During the Seventeenth and Eighteenth Centuries. During the seventeenth century, before slavery became a dominant institution in the United States, northern Blacks became familiar with most aspects of White culture. They lived in the homes of or in close proximity to their masters, and worked beside them—on farms, in kitchens, and in stores. Within these contexts, Blacks conformed to the cultural expectations of Whites. On Sundays, holidays, and other occasions, however, they demonstrated their cultural independence by participating in African rituals and other exercises. The clergy objected to these activities, which they interpreted to be incompatible with the teachings of Christianity. For example, in 1680, the Reverend Morgan Godwin was moved to express his disapproval:

> Nothing is more barbarous, and contrary to Christianity, than their ... Idolatrous Dances, and Revels, in which they usually spend the Sunday .... And here, that I may not be thought too rashly to impute Idolatry to their Dances, my Conjecture is raised upon this ground ... for that they use their Dances as means to procure Rain; some of them having been known to beg this Liberty upon the Week Days, in order thereunto.

In New England, clergymen believed that a knowledge of Christian principles would encourage slaves to abandon their African mode of life and adopt Western ideals. To create acceptable alternatives, they encouraged slaveholders, or required them by law, to provide their servants and slaves with religious instruction.

Conversion to Christianity involved a familiarity with the established musical repertoire of White Protestants. Missionaries, therefore, instructed slaves and free Blacks in psalm-singing and hymn-singing. Their pedagogical method centered on the English practice of "lining-out," where each line would be read or intoned by the minister or song leader, after which the line would be sung by the congregation. This practice, refracted through an African lens, later became standard in the worship of Black congregations. Whitelaw Reid, a journalist who, in 1866, attended a service on a Louisiana plantation, wrote that after the sermon,

> a young man, wearing the caped, light-blue army overcoat, rose and started a quaint chant. The congregation struck in and sung the line over. The young man chanted another line, and the congregation sang it after him; another was chanted, then sung; then another and so on. It was exactly the old Scotch fashion of "lining out," except that instead of reading the line which the congregation was to sing, the leader

delivered it in the oddest, most uncouth and sense-murdering chant ever conceived.

As Christians, Blacks became active participants in religious exercises, both at church and at home. Psalm-singing and hymn-singing became mainstays in some northern all-Black religious assemblies. In one instance, a group of slaves living in Boston in 1693 agreed always to sing a psalm between two prayers during their Sunday worship. By the end of the eighteenth century, many Blacks had established reputations for their musical skills; and in northern colonies, some even served as singing-school masters in all-White settings.

Whether attending White churches or conducting their own services, Blacks knew others expected them to sing songs from the established repertoire of Protestant hymnody, according to prescribed musical norms. For this reason, northern Blacks did not develop a distinct body of religious music before the founding of independent Black churches.

In contrast to the system of slavery in the North, many slaves in southern colonies lived on farms and plantations, located some distance from their owners' houses. The master's home life, therefore, had little influence on the religious education of his slaves. The sectarian affiliations of the country were different too: in the North, Congregationalism held sway; in the South, the Church of England (Anglican) enjoyed the highest prestige. In 1724, the Bishop of London initiated the first surveys of religious conditions among slaves in the United States. Responses from southern missionaries showed that cultural differences, language barriers, and slaveholders' resistance, interfered with their efforts at proselytizing the slaves. In the latter part of the century, Presbyterian and Methodist evangelists, inspired by the Great Awakening, intensified their efforts: they held camp meetings—emotionally charged assemblies, which attracted a sizeable number of Blacks, both slave and free. The informality of these meetings allowed Blacks to respond in a manner that was more open than Anglican etiquette required. Furthermore, these services bore some resemblance to African rituals. In spite of the appeal the meetings had for Blacks, the proportion converted to Christianity in the eighteenth century was small.

The system of slavery in southern colonies prevented slaveholders and other Whites from defining the slaves' cultural and spiritual frame of reference. Isolation from mainstream society due to limited contact between slaves and Whites enabled Blacks to retain ideals and traditions from their African past. Missionaries constantly complained about "barbaric" cultural practices and sought to impose their own values

by converting slaves to Christianity. But toward the end of the eighteenth century, missionaries conceded that slaves were unwilling to abandon their African worldview and musical practices. This realization forced them to relax the strictness by which they applied their religious tenets, and to incorporate into their instruction and services the slaves' musical practices. In 1784, Bishop Porteus of London even recommended that the clergy compose new songs in the slaves' musical tradition. The Bishop also encouraged the insertion of religious elements in the recreational activities of slaves, by providing "the help of a little sacred melody adapted to the peculiar taste and turn of the Africans." He and other members of the clergy conceded that religious songs with an African flavor would increase church attendance, prevent slaves from participating in "heathenish Sunday recreations," and provide them with an "instrument of moral and religious improvement" in the home.

The musical compromises the missionaries made in the eighteenth century set up the conditions from which a distinctly Afro-American religious musical tradition evolved.

The Nineteenth-Century Revival Movement and the Slaves' Musical Tradition. The nineteenth-century revival movement shaped the religious expression of both slaves and southern Whites. Descriptions of revival meetings reveal practices similar to those of African rituals. Witnesses noted that loud cries and groans punctuated the service. Men and women leaped out of their seats, screamed, jerked, shouted, fell into convulsions, spoke in tongues, and engaged in holy dancing. By fostering a highly charged atmosphere, music played an emotionally liberating role. Hymn performances, which were an integral part of services, incorporated elements from the Black music tradition. Many songs, executed in a call-response format or a verse-chorus structure, invited the congregation to join in on familiar phrases or choruses. Slaves responded to these and other familiar performance styles by participating with "exuberance and excitement."

Many nineteenth-century accounts of singing at camp meetings give special attention to the Black sections of the meeting areas. One observer recalled that:

> Their shouts and singing were so very boisterous that the singing of the White congregation was often completely drowned in the echoes and reverberations of the colored people's tumultuous strains.

J. D. Long reported that:

At every service the negroes were present in large numbers in a special section reserved for them, and many of them made professions of religion. Their singing was inspiring and was encouraged and enjoyed by the White congregation, who would sometimes remain silent and listen.

After the service at a camp meeting, when the people had dispersed to segregated lodging tents, Blacks continued singing, often throughout the night. One witness noticed that, when services lasted past midnight, Blacks seldom went to sleep; instead, they would sing hymns until half-past five in the morning.

John Watson, a Methodist minister, censured these activities. He was particularly critical of the original songs Blacks sang:

> Here ought to be considered too, a most exceptional error, which has the tolerance at least of the rulers of our camp meetings. In the Blacks' quarter, the coloured people get together, and sing for hours together, short scraps of disjoined affirmations, pledges, lengthened out with repetition [sic] choruses.

> We have too, a growing evil, in the practice of singing in our places of public and society worship, *merry* airs, adapted from old *songs*, to hymns of our composing: often miserable as poetry, and senseless as matter, and most frequently composed and first sung by the illiterate *Blacks* of society.

Watson also expressed his disapproval of what he considered the negative influence Blacks had on the musical practices of Whites:

> The example has already visibly affected the religious manners of some Whites. From this cause, I have known in some camp meetings, from 50 to 60 people crowd in one tent, after the public devotions had closed, and there continue the whole night, singing tune after tune, scarce one of which were in our hymn books.

The comments of Watson, and the observations of his contemporaries, provide evidence for the existence of a unique Black religious music tradition in the nineteenth century. Under the supervision of Whites, Blacks adopted customs that met the expectations of those in charge; however, away from Whites, in their own quarters, Blacks reverted to familiar customs, drawn from African cultures. These customs merged with elements of Protestant traditions, to lay the groundwork for the establishment of a Black religion and a corresponding tradition of Black religious music.

The Establishment of a Black Musical Tradition. The musical form referred to as the Negro folk spiritual evolved in praise-houses (plantation chapels built by some masters to house slave worship) and in northern independent Black churches. The slave preachers, whose chanted sermons and improvised songs motivated sung responses from the congregation, established the foundation for this form. These preachers, when unsupervised by Whites, set the musical standards, structured the services, and interpreted biblical passages from the cultural perspective of their congregations.

The Negro folk spiritual tradition struck various missionaries, European visitors, and American witnesses as a fount of "wild hymns," "barbaric songs," and "nonsensical chants." These accounts prove how radically Negro folk spirituals differed from White Protestant hymns. White eyewitnesses interpreted Black spirituals as "strange" and "weird" strains of disjointed and meaningless texts, not sung but "yelled," "hooted," and "screamed." These terms prove the need for extreme interpretive caution. Negro spirituals arose from, and developed within an African aesthetic, which defies characterization and qualitative assessment in a purely European frame of reference. The performance style of Negro spirituals, therefore, deserves description from an African American cultural and musical perspective. The aesthetics that govern the singing of Black Americans derive from a key cultural value, one that emphasizes free expression and group participation.

The features that distinguish Negro folk spirituals are: (1) call-response structure; (2) extensive melodic ornamentation (slides, slurs, bends, moans, shouts, wails, grunts); (3) complex rhythmic structures; and (4) the integration of song and movement. Each of these elements involves improvisation.

Call-response structure promotes both individual expression and congregational participation. The soloist, who presents the call, is free to improvise at will, and the congregation provides a stable, repetitive response.

Melodic ornamentation enables singers to embellish and intensify performances. Rhythmic patterns of handclapping and footstamping add to the effect: they create complexly layered metrical structures, which provide the rhythmic underpinning for gestures and dance-movements. In turn, spontaneous displays dictate other aspects of performance: the tempo and length of a spiritual often depend on the degree to which a congregation becomes physically involved.

Both Black and White observers recorded the integration of song and movement. James Lindsey

Smith, a slave who preached to Black assemblies during the 1830s later wrote:

> The singing was accompanied by a certain ecstasy in motion, clapping of hands, tossing of heads, which would continue without cessation about half an hour; one would lead off in a kind of recitative style, others joining in the chorus.

Blacks applied the same norms and aesthetics to songs from White Protestant traditions. They frequently transformed these songs beyond recognition, into folk spirituals. An English musician who toured the United States from 1833 to 1841 witnessed the transformative process while visiting a Black church in Vicksburg, Virginia:

> When the minister gave out his own version of the Psalm, the choir commenced singing so rapidly that the original tune absolutely ceased to exist—in fact, the fine old psalm tune became thoroughly transformed into a kind of negro melody; and so sudden was the transformation, by accelerating the time, that for a moment, I fancied that not only the choir but the little congregation intended to get up a dance as part of the service.

In 1853, Frederick Law Olmstead encountered a similar situation. He observed a hymn changed into a "confused wild kind of chant." Elizabeth Kilham, a schoolteacher in the South, expressed a widely held viewpoint: "Watts and Newton would never recognize their productions through the transformations they have undergone at the hands of their colored admirers."

Richard Allen, pioneer in the independent Black church movement, also led in providing the northern counterpart to the worship developments among southern slaves. He established a form of worship based on the aesthetic and cultural perspective of his Philadelphia congregation, Bethel African Methodist Episcopal (AME) Church. In doing so, he gave his services something of the character of those conducted by slave preachers on southern farms and plantations. He also reshaped the AME musical tradition. Addressing his congregation on Methodist and other denominational hymnals, he stated: "Having become a distinct and separate body of people, there is no collection of hymns we could with propriety adopt." In 1801, he solved this problem by publishing a hymnal, *A Collection of Spiritual Songs and Hymns Selected from Various Authors* by Richard Allen, African Minister. This book contains fifty-four hymn texts, including those of Isaac Watts, the Wesleys, and other composers popular among the Methodists and Baptists. In the second edition, also printed in 1801, Allen added ten hymns, including some of his own composition. This edition differed from standard hymnals in one important respect: Allen edited some texts. He replaced complex words and phrases with simpler ones, so the songs "would have a special appeal to the members of his congregation. . . ." To the orthodox hymns, he added easily memorized refrains and choruses. By making these changes, he ensured the full participation of all church members.

Further evidence that the singing in Allen's church followed the aesthetic principles and musical norms of Black people can be deduced from an account by Pavel Svinin, a Russian, who visited Allen's congregation in 1811:

> At the end of every psalm, the entire congregation, men and women alike, sang verses in a loud, shrill monotone. This lasted about an hour. When the preacher ceased reading, all turned toward the door, fell on their knees, bowed their heads to the ground and set up an agonizing, heartrending moaning. Afterwards, the minister resumed the reading of the psalter and when he had finished, sat down on a chair; then all rose and began chanting psalms in chorus, the men and women alternating, a procedure which lasted some twenty minutes.

The White Methodist clergy condemned these practices; they objected to the editorial alteration of orthodox hymns, to the use of original songs, and to the nature of the singing style. Nevertheless, Allen's innovations set a precedent, and his musical practices became commonplace in other Black Methodist churches.

Diversity in the Tradition. While some northern Black ministers, such as Allen, changed the structure of traditional Protestant services to meet the needs of their congregations, others chose to structure their worship around the doctrines, literature, and musical practices of White denominations. One of the first major conflicts that divided the membership of independent Black churches involved musical practices. **Daniel A. Payne**, who later became a bishop in the **African Methodist Episcopal Church**, campaigned to change the style of worship in this church. Influenced by his training at a Lutheran seminary and by his tenure as pastor in a Presbyterian church, Payne concluded:

> The time is at hand when the minister of the A.M.E. Church must drive out this heathenish mode of worship or drive out all the intelligence, refinement, and practical Christians.

Payne opposed the singing of spirituals, which he called "cornfield ditties." He also objected to the handclapping, footstamping, and "voodoo dances" that accompanied the spirituals. He preached the "right, fit, and proper way of serving God."

Bishop Payne initiated a change in the service of AME's by seeking to replace the practice of lining-out (a holdover from seventeenth century British tradition) with choral singing and instrumental music. He instituted these changes in Philadelphia in 1841–42, and in Baltimore in 1848–49. Many members responded by complaining: "You have brought the devil into the Church, and therefore we will go out." According to Payne, when choirs were introduced in the church, "many went out of Bethel, and never returned."

The adoption of choral singing in northern AME churches resulted in some congregational splits and withdrawals from membership. Amid controversy, Payne defended his innovations:

> The moral and religious effects of choral singing have been good, especially when the whole or a majority of the choir were earnest Christians. I have witnessed spiritual effects produced by Bethel choir in Philadelphia, and by Bethel choir in Baltimore, equal to the most unctuous sermons from the lips of the most eloquent and earnest of preachers, so that Christians did rejoice as though they were listening to the heavenly choir which the shepherds heard on the plains of Bethlehem announcing the advent of the Savior.

> In a musical direction what progress has been made within the last forty years! There is not a church of ours in any of the great cities of the republic that can afford to buy an instrument which is without one; and there are but few towns or villages where our Connection exists that are without an instrument to accompany the choir.

Yet along with Payne's innovations there is evidence that many AME churches retained an exuberant, perhaps African-derived, congregational singing style. In 1850, Fredrika Bremer, who visited an African Methodist Church in Cincinnati, gave this account of the musical practices she saw:

> I found in the African Church African ardor and African life. The church was full to overflowing, and the congregation sang their own hymns. The singing ascended and poured forth like a melodious torrent, and the heads, feet, and elbows of the congregation moved all in unison with it, amid evident enchantment and delight in the singing, which was in itself exquisitely pure and full of melodious life.

It would appear that the approach of Richard Allen and southern Black slave-preachers had a greater impact on the musical tradition of pre-twentieth-century Black religious groups than did that of Payne. While the use of choirs and instruments (mainly pianos and organs) did find increasing acceptance, most Blacks attended churches where the styles of worship reflected their daily experiences and cultural perspectives.

Music in the Twentieth-Century Black Church. In 1863, President Abraham Lincoln proclaimed the abolition of slavery in the United States; and in 1865, the Civil War came to a close. These events symbolically marked the freedom of slaves. In reality, however, many Blacks remained effectively enslaved, under a new system called sharecropping. This system, defined by an inequitable economic arrangement between landlords (former slaveholders) and share-croppers (former slaves), kept Blacks in debt and subjugated by southern Whites. Because most Blacks lived in the same shacks and worked on the same farms and plantations as they had as slaves, they remained isolated from mainstream society. Blacks, therefore, continued to rely on their own cultural norms as a basis for self-identification, social interaction, and group solidarity. These values found their fullest expression in the Black church, an institution that became the focal point of the Black community.

At the turn of the twentieth century, the music of the earliest autonomous Black churches consisted of spirituals and lined-out hymns, sung to the accompaniment of handclapping and footstamping. The addition of tambourines, drums, piano, horns, and (later) guitar and Hammond organ, created an original body of Black religious music known as gospel. The first gospel songs derived from spirituals, but the use of instruments in gospel singing separates the two musical traditions. In its developing stages, gospel music emerged only in the Black "folk church" (associated with Holiness, Pentecostal, and Sanctified sects). By ideology and worship style, this church stands apart from independent Methodist, Baptist, and other mainline denominations (e.g. Presbyterian, Episcopalian, Lutheran). Black mainline churches evolved from their White Protestant counterparts, but Black "folk churches" developed when dissatisfied members of the independent churches sought their ecclesiastical independence. The doctrines of the Black "folk church" encouraged free expression, which unveiled itself in spontaneous testimonies, prayers, and music. Describing the distinctiveness of the musical tradition in this church, Pearl Williams-Jones, gospel-music scholar and performer, draws these conclusions:

> The traditional liturgical forms of plain chant, chorales, and anthems do not fulfill the needs of traditional Black folk religious worship and ritual. They are unrelated and inappropriate as vehicles for folk-styled religious worship services because liturgical musical forms do not represent the dominant cultural values of the Black community. These values encompass the whole gamut of Black expressiveness—which is relevant to the ritual of Black folk-style worship—singing and preaching, linguistics, testifying, and praying. They are unique, personal, and highly valued within the community for their aesthetic values.

Holiness groups did not allow their members to interact with those belonging to non-Holiness churches. Therefore, until Black Methodist and Baptist songwriters introduced gospel compositions into their churches, most Black Americans did not hear gospel music. The first attempt to capture in religious song the urban Black experience came from a Methodist Episcopal Church minister, Charles Albert Tindley, who composed his first songs between 1900 and 1906. These pieces incorporate melodic and rhythmic elements of gospel singing from the Black "folk church." Under Tindley's influence, Thomas Dorsey, a Baptist, developed a gospel style that decisively differed from the more-familiar hymn tradition. Dorsey based his tonalities on the blues; performed with a ragtime-derived, boogie-woogie piano accompaniment, the music radiated an urban religious spirit and started a tradition of composed Black gospel songs.

Because of the cultural identities it evoked, gospel music moved beyond the boundaries of the Holiness-Pentecostal churches into many independent and mainline Black churches, ranging from Baptist and Methodist churches to Catholic parishes. Mellonee Burnim sums up the importance of gospel music in present-day Black religion: "In the same way that the Negro spiritual was fundamental to the religion of the Black slave, so is gospel music the backbone of contemporary Black religion."

The use and performance of gospel music varies within the Black religious denominations. In Holiness-Pentecostal churches, gospel, sung by both the choir and congregation, is intrinsic to the worship. Pre-1950s gospel styles (known as "traditional gospel") dominate congregational singing, while choirs frequently draw on the musical traits of the commercial and contemporary repertoires. Independent and mainline churches sing gospel music alongside songs from their official hymnals. Gospel selections take prescribed places in the worship. Hymns, frequently accompanied by gospel harmonies and rhythms on the piano and organ, form the basic repertoire for congregational singing.

In all Black churches, gospel music follows the musical norms and aesthetic principles that defined the spiritual tradition. Just as improvisation typifies Negro folk spirituals, it underlies the interpretation of the skeletal outlines—melodies, harmonies, rhythms, accompaniment—in the printed scores of gospel music. Renditions of gospel songs therefore vary remarkably from the music notation, and the performers rarely perform a song the same way twice. Though each performer interprets gospel songs differently, the musical vocabulary, technical devices, and performance practices dictate the basics of the style. Research conducted by Burnim on the gospel tradition reveals three primary areas of significance in gospel-music performance: (1) quality of sound; (2) style of delivery; and (3) mechanics of delivery.

The quality of sound hinges on the manipulation of elements of timbre, range, and shading, which contribute to the overall tonal "complexity sought for and desired in this tradition." Such manipulations result in (1) sudden changes in timbre, which extend from lyrical to raspy and percussive; (2) extreme, and often sudden, dynamic and tonal contrasts; (3) the use of the falsetto voice; and (4) the juxtaposition of different vocal and instrumental textures.

The style of delivery in gospel music mirrors Black cultural customs and behavior. Audiences expect performers to communicate through both musical and physical means. They expect a display of involvement that uses the whole body: head, hands, torso, feet. They further expect to see gospel choirs execute synchronized movements—during a processional, when the choirs march into the church; and during the worship, when they clap, "step," and "shout" to the music.

The quality of the sound, and the style of the delivery, intensify the performance. This intensity, however, depends on the mechanics used for delivery. By employing a variety of technical and improvisatory devices, performers manipulate time, text, and pitch. According to Burnim, time has both rhythmic and structural aspects. Performers can expand rhythmic structures from simple to complex by "gradually adding layers of handclaps, instrumental accompaniment, and/or solo voices." Similarly, by repeating phrases and entire sections of a song, and by adding a vocal or instrumental cadenza at the end, they can expand the length of the performance. When they do, the intensity builds, because each repetition brings in more rhythmic activity and new textual and melodic variation.

The manipulation of pitch results from a desire for melodic improvisation. To change or expand the melody, performers employ a variety of technical devices, including repetition, and the extensive use of melismas, shouts, slides, slurs, moans, and grunts. A successful performance depends on a performer's ability to manipulate time, text, and pitch, while affirming cultural concepts identified with the Black musical tradition. These elements, operating in conjunction with one another, are subject to constant interpretation and reinterpretation by individual performers. Through cultural immersion, one learns how to determine which structural, rhythmic, textual, and melodic units are potentially expandable, then demonstrates the knowledge in his or her own personal way during performance.

In the Black church, performances of gospel and spirituals reflect many of the cultural values Black Americans cherish and embrace. In relying on a conceptual framework that emphasizes freedom of expression and group participation, the Black religious tradition stands out from the rest.

Performances of spirituals and gospel music employ styles and features found in non-Black musical traditions, but they employ these traits in ways that both reflect the musical criteria, and meet the cultural expectations of Black Americans. Musical performance in the Black church incorporates a variety of techniques that mirror cultural values while accommodating traditional customs and behavior. In the mix of cultural traditions, a democratic approach to music making has given rise to an original body of authentic religious music. Spirituals and gospel music uniquely enhance the African American religious heritage, and their incorporation into the act of worship tends to distinguish the black church from all others.

Burnim, Mellonee. *The Black Gospel Music Tradition: Symbol of Ethnicity*. Bloomington, IN: M.A. thesis, Indiana University, 1980.

Chase, Gilbert. *America's Music from the Pilgrims to the Present*. 2nd ed. rev.: New York: McGraw-Hill, 1966.

Epstein, Dena. *Sinful Tunes and Spirituals*. Urbana, IL: University of Illinois Press, 1977.

Fisher, Miles. *Negro Slave Songs in the United States*. Ithaca, NY: Cornell University Press, 1953.

Godwin, Morgan. *The Negro's and Indians Advocate, Suing for their Admission into the Church: or A Persuasive to the Instructing and Baptizing of the Negros and Indians in our Plantations*. London: J. D., 1680.

Jones, Charles Colcock. *Religious Instruction of the Negroes in the United States*. Savannah, GA: T. Purse, 1842.

Long, John Dixon. *Pictures of Slavery in Church and State*. 3rd ed.: Philadelphia: The Author, 1857.

Maultsby, Portia K. "Afro-American Religious Music: A Study in Musical Diversity." *The Papers of the Hymn Society of America* 35 (1981).

Russell, Henry. *Cheer! Boys, Cheer!: Memories of Men and Music*. London: J. Macqueen, 1895.

Smith, James Lindsay. *Autobiography, Including also Reminiscences of Slave Life, Recollections of the War, Education of Freedmen, of the Exodus, Etc.* Norwich, CT: Press of the Bulletin, 1881.

Southern, Eileen. The *Music of Black Americans*. 2nd. ed.: New York: W. W. Norton, 1983.

Stevenson, Robert. *Protestant Church Music in America*. New York: W. W. Norton, 1970.

Svinin, Pavel P. *Picturesque United States of America, 1811, 1812, 1813*. Ed. by Avrham Yarmolinsky. New York: W. E. Rudge, Inc., 1930.

Williams-Jones, Pearl. "The Musical Quality of Black Religious Folk Ritual." *Spirit* 1 (1977).

Portia K. Maultsby

MUSLIM MOSQUE, INC. An Islamic center. In 1963 **Malcolm X** was heading for a showdown with the **Nation of Islam** and its leader **Elijah Muhammad**. The occasion for the split became a speech he gave in December, just a week following the assassination of President Kennedy. He spoke of the incident as a case of "chickens coming home to roost." He was summoned to Chicago and silenced for 90 days and then ordered isolated from the faithful. He decided that the conflicts with the Nation had become so severe that he must permanently separate. On March 8, 1964, he announced his leaving and the formation of a new center, the Muslim Mosque, Inc. The Mosque was soon joined by a second political-cultural entity, the Organization of Afro-American Unity.

The Muslim Mosque would differ from the Nation in that while it would be based upon Black nationalism, and demand a national home for African Americans, it would develop programs in which Black nonmembers and even White people could participate. He also began to separate from the nonviolent position which to that point had carried the day in the civil rights movement. He suggested arming the Black community and the formation of gun clubs.

Having formed both organizations Malcolm X began the development of a broad program which included a lengthy stay in Africa later in the year. During his time away the organizations suffered a split between the older following which had come from the Nation of

Islam and the newer members who had no attachment to it at all. While he put time into quelling the bickering, his energy was placed into the development of a broad base of support within the African American community. In the midst of his still putting together his program, on February 12, his home was firebombed. Two days later he was assassinated. Neither of his organizations, already weakened by inattention, survived very long without him.

Breitman, George. *The Last Year of Malcolm X: The Evolution of a Revolutionary*. New York: Schocken Books, 1969. 169 pp.

Goldman, Peter. *The Death and Life of Malcolm X*. New York: Harper & Row, 1974. 482 pp.

Jamal, Hakim A. *From the Dead Level: Malcolm and Me*. New York: Random House, 1972. 272 pp.

"After four hundred years here among the Caucasians, we are absolutely convinced that we can never live together in peace, unless we are willing to remain subservient to our former masters. Therefore, immediate and complete separation is the only solution."

Malcolm X, Spokesperson
Nation of Islam
1961

"It's time for martyrs now. And if I am to be one, it will be in the cause of brotherhood. That's the only thing that can save this country."

Malcolm X, Spokesperson
1965

N

NARCISSE, LOUIS HERBERT (1921–February 3, 1989), founder of the **Mt. Zion Spiritual Temple**, was born in New Orleans, Louisiana. His father, Jesse Narcisse, a shipyard worker, was killed in an accident before he was born. His mother raised the family as devout Baptists, and Narcisse was baptized in Mt. Zion Baptist Church. As a teenager, his singing abilities made him a choir soloist and a winner of five radio auditions. During World War II he migrated to San Francisco, California, and found an $85–a-week job as an electrical worker in a shipyard. He also spent some time as a bank janitor, living in the Hunter housing project in south San Francisco.

In 1945 Narcisse had a vision which impelled him to found the Mt. Zion Spiritual Temple, which began as a simple prayer meeting among a handful of people. It soon grew to a large church on 14th Street in Oakland, through a combination of his personal charisma and the success of his radio program, "Moments of Meditation," which developed a national audience of as many as 1.5 million. He further increased his visibility with a number of single records, such as "Without the Lord," or "Jesus, I Can't Forget You," cut for such labels as Jaxyson, Modern, Hollywood, Music City, Veltone, and Peacock. His signature theme song and church motto was, "It's Nice to be Nice."

Narcisse established churches in Sacramento, Detroit, Houston, New Orleans, and Orlando on a general Baptist format, but with other elements as well. He suggested burning incense at home to drive away evil spirits, and emphasized the power of blessed oils and waters. Sunday worship services were ecstatic experiences with shouting and dancing in the aisles. He preached a gospel that included the need for both heavenly and earthly nurture. He spoke of Black pride, and urged his followers to spend their money on building up their lives, rather than wasting it on gambling or drugs. He insisted that they practice doing good, not just in their families, as in honoring their parents, but in all aspects of life.

On March 9, each year, he held a mass prayer meeting in Oakland Park with city officials and citizens, and the mayor of Oakland proclaimed it Prayer Day. In September 1955 a coronation ceremony was performed at the municipal auditorium by the Right Reverend Frank Rancifer in which he was officially given the title "His Grace, the King of the Spiritual Church of the West Coast."

Part of his appeal was his flamboyant style; he was literally treated as royalty. He wore a crown, diamond rings and other jewels, and wherever he went in his Rolls Royce a red carpet was rolled out in front. He lived in a 24–room mansion in Oakland's Piedmont district, known as "The Light on the Hill," with numerous personal attendants. He often received followers in a "throne room," with a copy of federal income tax regulations sitting nearby. Narcisse explained that all the finery was not just for himself, but was a means of attracting those who are not yet ready for the purely spiritual. It also served as a symbol of the earthly achievements and prizes to which he called his followers. His church was also known for its many charity functions in the community.

"His Grace King; the West Coast's Most Colorful Religious Leader." *Sepia* 9 (February 1961): 42–47.

Robinson, Louie. "The Kingdom of King Narcisse." *Ebony* 18 (July 1963): 112–118.

RLOA, IBAW, AARS, BDA-AHP.

NATION OF ISHMAEL. An Evangelical Christian organization. The Nation of Ishmael was founded in 1975 by Jacob Smith as a service organization to help improve the economic, educational, spiritual, and social potential of African American communities in the United States. Headquartered in East Point, Georgia (an Atlanta suburb), it holds quarterly seminars for business owners, and works actively to assist in the procurement of loans for minority-owned businesses. The Nation also conducts a variety of programs for senior citizens and youth.

NATION OF ISLAM. An early Black Muslim group. The original Nation of Islam can be traced to 1929, the year of the death of Timothy Drew (**Noble Drew Ali**), the founder of the **Moorish Science Temple of America**. Shortly after his death, there appeared in Detroit, Michigan, a man named **Wallace D. Fard**. The mysterious Fard worked as a peddler in the Black community and gradually introduced people to as set of religious teachings which continued Noble Drew Ali's message that Black people were the true Muslims. In 1930 Elijah Poole, who had moved from Georgia to Detroit seeking work, met Fard and became his follower. Poole would later claim that he was the first one to recognize Fard's true nature as the returned Jesus which soon developed into the understanding that Fard was in fact Allah in person who had appeared to awaken Black people to their position as the Chosen People of Allah. Fard would later give Elijah Poole the name by which he would become famous, **Elijah Muhammad**. Under that name he became the Nation's leading minister.

The 1930s proved a tumultuous time for the new movement. It became successful enough to attract police attention and Fard was arrested on several occasions. In 1933, following a third arrest, he left Chicago and in effect disappeared from the scene. His eventual fate is unknown. Elijah Muhammad emerged as his successor. In 1934 he too left Chicago for a period though he eventually returned to make it the movement's headquarters. In 1942 he was arrested and sentenced to prison for his activity in encouraging young Black men to avoid the draft. He was released at the end of the war and came back to Chicago to revive the movement. After the purchase of a center, a growth phase began.

In 1947 Malcolm Little, soon to be known as **Malcolm X**, joined the Nation. He would emerge as the Nation's leading minister, and as he traveled across the Nation speaking on its behalf, he founded many of its temples. The Nation's growth through the 1950s brought new signs of prosperity in the founding of a number of Muslim-supported businesses by the Nation's members and in 1959 the founding of a periodical, *Islamic News* (superseded by *Muhammad Speaks* in 1961).

The rather quiet growth of the Nation within the Black community was ended in 1959 when a television documentary focusing upon the organization and emphasizing its racial doctrines brought it to the attention of the larger White society. Several books by **C. Eric Lincoln**, E. U. Essien Udom, and Louis E. Lomax further documented the group's life and belief. Attention focused upon the group's racial myth, the story of Yakub.

Elijah Muhammad taught that Black people, Earth's original human inhabitants, had come to earth from another planet. At the time their planet had exploded, members of the tribe of Shabazz were able to travel to this planet and settle in the Nile Valley. After centuries of peaceful living, some 6,600 years ago, one ambitious man, Yakub, began genetic experiments to produce White people. The product of his work was a genetically inferior race whose troublesome presence led to their banishment to Europe. Morally corrupt, the Whites spread their evil wherever they went. The height of their evil was the enslavement of Black people. Elijah Muhammad spoke of Whites as devils and equated them with the beast described in the biblical book of Revelation.

The period of White supremacy was coming to an end as Black people rediscovered their true history and nature. As steps along the way to a new millennium of peace, members of the Nation adopted a rigid behavior code that included a diet free of many traditionally Southern Black foods (especially pork) and a family-centered culture in which women were assigned a role as the progenitors of the next generation. The Nation also demanded the setting aside of a part of the United States in the South as territory in which they could build a Black national state. While bringing an angry response from both Blacks and Whites who were trying to alleviate racial tension, the controversy attracted many Black people to the movement, which continued its growth and business development.

In the mid-1960s the movement suffered one serious setback when Malcolm X, following a period of conflict with Elijah Muhammad, defected. After leaving the Nation, Malcolm X went on to found the independent **Muslim Mosque, Inc.** Later that year he made the pilgrimage to Mecca, a requirement upon all Muslims. During his trip he was profoundly impressed with the lack of racial discrimination among the pilgrims and he returned having been converted to orthodox Islam. Changing his name to El Hajj Malik El-Shabazz, he began to speak frequently of his new insights. Then on February 21, 1965, he was shot. The people later convicted of the murder were members of the Nation of Islam.

By the 1970s, the Nation was riding a crest of popularity within the Black community. It was also affected by internal power struggles, defections by disappointed leaders, and a wave of violence. The more important incidents include the shooting of Raymond

Sharrieff, the president of the Nation of Islam, on October 21, 1971. This event was tied to the killing of two former Muslims who had joined a small splinter group a short time later. In January 1972, a shootout in Baton Rouge, Louisiana, was tied to war-ring Muslim factions. In January 1973, several men later identified as members of the Nation of Islam killed seven members of the family of former Nation leader Hamaas Abdul Khaalis, who had founded a competing orthodox Islamic center in Washington, D.C. The violence peaked in 1973 and gradually died as the aging Elijah Muhammad, possibly in response to the violence, moved to soften his rhetoric toward the White community and began to reach out to various groups beyond the Muslim community.

From Nation of Islam to American Muslim Mission: Elijah Muhammad died in 1975. He was succeeded by his son, Wallace D. Muhammad (now generally referred to as **Warith Deen Muhammad**). Very soon after taking over, he began to lead the organization toward orthodox Islam. He initiated a reappraisal of the role of White people, who were no longer seen as devils but as fully human. He dropped the demand for land to create a national state and he also changed the name of the organization's periodical from *Muhammad Speaks* to *Bilalian News* (a reference to Bilal, a Black man who was close companion of the prophet Muhammad). Possibly the most dramatic change of all was the reduction of the status of Wallace D. Fard to merely the founder of the movement and Elijah, Fard's Messenger, to a "wise man" who brought many people to the *Qur'an*. These changes were capped in 1976 by a change of name as the Nation of Islam became the World Community of Al-Islam in the West.

Changes continued through the decade. A six-member Council of Imams was created to guide the organization administratively. In 1980 Wallace changed his name to Warith Deen Muhammad, a Muslim name. That change was quickly followed by the change of the organization's name to the American Muslim Mission and the periodical's name to the *American Muslim Journal*. These three changes represent a transition in the thinking of the movement's leadership to an understanding of the organization as just one segment of the larger Muslim presence in North America.

A final significant change occurred in 1985, when, with the approval of the organization's leadership, the national structure of the American Muslim Mission was formally disbanded and the various mosques assumed their place as autonomous centers within the larger movement. Since that time Warith Deen Muhammad has taken his place as a prominent world Muslim leader and serves as Imam of a masjid in Chicago. The *American Muslim Journal* continued as the *Muslim Journal*, providing coverage of the far-flung travels of Warith Deen Muhammad, news coverage of the centers of the former American Muslim Mission, and the spread of Islam among African Americans in general.

While Warith Deen Muhammad led the integration of the great majority of the Nation of Islam into the orthodox Muslim community, there were some losses along the way. At least four independent splinters of former members of the Nation were established, each assuming the name Nation of Islam and claiming to continue the thought and work of Elijah Muhammad. Of these four, the most important was established by **Louis Farrakhan**. Other organizations have been founded by Emmanuel Abdullah Muhammad, John Muhammad, and Silis Muhammad, though only Farrakhan has been able to draw together a national following.

Lee, Martha F. *The Nation of Islam, An American Millennarian Movement*. Lewiston, NY: Edwin Mellen Press, 1988. 163 pp.

Lincoln, C. Eric. *The Black Muslims in America*. Boston, MA: Beacon Press, 1961. 276 pp.

Muhammad, Warith Deen. *Al-Islam, Unity and Leadership*. Chicago: The Sense Maker, 1991. 175 pp.

———. *As the Light Shineth from the East*. Chicago: WDM Publishing Co., 1980. 242 pp.

Nu'Man Muhammad Armiya. *What Every Muslim Should Know About Islam and the Muslims*. Jersey City, NJ: New Mind Productions, 1985. 68 pp.

NATION OF ISLAM (FARRAKHAN). A Black Muslim organization. During the years following the death of **Elijah Muhammad** in 1975, with the change of the name of the organization he led from Nation of Islam to World Community of Al-Islam in the West (1976), and the dropping of many of the distinctive beliefs of the Nation of Islam, Minister **Louis Farrakhan** emerged as a prominent voice opposing the direction the organization was taking. Farrakhan had initially become prominent in the years after the defection and death of **Malcolm X** (1965) when he was appointed to become the head of the Nation of Islam's New York mosque. An excellent orator, Farrakhan was able to maintain a large membership at the center and was often cited as a possible successor to the Nation's founder.

Wallace D. Muhammad (now known as **Warith Deen Muhammad**), after succeeding his father as head of the Nation of Islam, requested Farrakhan's move to Chicago to assume a national post at the movement's headquarters. Many interpreted this move as an attempt to keep Farrakhan from speaking out on the changes which were soon to occur. Farrakhan remained quiet for three years, but in 1978 finally broke with his colleagues and founded a revived Nation of Islam with the beliefs and programs as they were in the early 1970s. He also began a periodical, *The Final Call*, modeled upon *Muhammad Speaks*.

Initially, several thousand followers responded to his recreation of the Nation. He reinstituted the former disciplines in relation to diet and dress. He also reestablished the Fruit of Islam, the elite internal security force, which had been associated with some of the violence connected with the organization and which had been disbanded by Wallace D. Muhammad. Farrakhan also continued the harsh appraisal of White people as "devils" which had been articulated by Elijah Muhammad throughout his life.

The revived Nation of Islam grew slowly for several years and Farrakhan was little noticed until 1984 when he publicly endorsed the campaign of **Jesse Jackson** for president of the United States. His association with Jackson led to some scrutiny of his remarks. He was accused of both anti-Semitic and racist statements and critics called upon Jackson to distance himself from Farrakhan. The publicity from the campaign has served to keep Farrakhan in the news as he has traveled the country. He has created programs within the Black community which under normal conditions would be welcomed by civic leaders, many of whom have been forced to withdraw support due to the controversy surrounding Farrakhan.

Farrakhan's general stance in opposition to Israel and alignment with Arab causes has led to an alignment with some Muslim leaders who see him as a valuable ally. He has often traveled to the Middle East in his quest to find support for the Nation of Islam he heads. He has purchased the former lead temple of the Nation of Islam in Chicago which served as its headquarters under Elijah Muhammad and now resides in a nearby mansion once owned by Elijah Muhammad.

Barboza, Steven. "A Divided Legacy." *Emerge* 3, 6 (April 1992): 26–32.

Farrakhan, Louis. *Back Where We Belong: Selected Speeches by Minister Louis Farrakhan*. Philadelphia, PA: PC International Press, 1989. 302 pp.

———. *Seven Speeches*. Newport News, VA: Ramza Associates and the United Brothers Communications Systems, n.d. 151 pp.

———. *Warning to the Government of America*. Chicago: Hon. Elijah Muhammad Educational Foundation, 1983. 55 pp.

NATION OF ISLAM (JOHN MUHAMMAD). An Islamic organization. Among the people who rejected the changes made in the **Nation of Islam** following the death of its longtime leader **Elijah Muhammad** was his younger brother John Muhammad. John Muhammad had joined the Nation of Islam in 1930 soon after his older brother had accepted **Wallace Fard Muhammad** as Allah in the flesh. Detroit was the founding place of the movement, and in that city John Muhammad has made his headquarters. In the 1980s he began *Muhammad Speaks Continues*, a reborn *Muhammad Speaks*, the periodical begun by Elijah Muhammad.

The branch of the Nation of Islam led by John Muhammad is one of the smaller branches of the continuing Nation of Islam movement, with only one center in the Detroit suburb of Highland Park.

Jones, Linda. "John Muhammad Preserves Islam's Old Ways." *Detroit News* (October 5, 1990).

NATION OF ISLAM (SILIS MUHAMMAD). An Islamic organization. Silis Muhammad joined the Nation of Islam in the 1960s and soon became known for his promotion of the Nation's tabloid, *Muhammad Speaks*. He was invited to Chicago to manage the national circulation of *Muhammad Speaks*, and assumed a role close to the Nation's leader, **Elijah Muhammad**, as his spiritual son (there was no familial relationship).

Following Elijah Muhammad's death in 1977, he rejected the changes instituted by the Nation's new leader, **Warith Deen Muhammad**, the son of Elijah Muhammad. In 1977 he charged Warith Muhammad with being a false prophet and demanded that he turn the property of the Nation back to his father's genuine followers. Soon afterward he left to reorganize the Nation of Islam under his own leadership with headquarters in the South. In 1982 he started a new edition of *Muhammad Speaks*. In 1985 he published an expanded version of his attack upon Warith Deen Muhammad and an alternative program for the reorganized Nation.

Soon after Silis attempted to resurrect the Nation of Islam, another prominent leader, **Louis Farrakhan**, also left and founded a rival Nation of Islam. Silis Muhammad and Farrakhan disagreed on the role of Elijah Muhammad in regard to Jesus. Farrakhan had interpreted some of Elijah Muhammad's statements as meaning that Elijah Muhammad had claimed to be the fulfillment of some of Jesus' prophecies. Silis Muhammad rejected such an interpretation. In the wake of the disagreement, as each developed their own constituency, the two have gone their separate ways.

The Nation of Islam headed by Silis Muhammad has established headquarters in Atlanta. In 1991 21 temples could be found across the United States. The Nation has reaffirmed that Allah appeared in the person of **Wallace D. Fard** (Muhammad) in 1930 and spoke face to face with Elijah Muhammad from 1931 through 1933. Hence Elijah Muhammad is Moses, the biblical account (and the account in the Qur'an) being prophetic and symbolic of today's African American.

Muhammad, Silis. *In the Wake of the Nation of Islam.* College Park, GA: The Author, 1985. 191 pp.

NATION OF THE FIVE PERCENT.

The Nation of the Five Percent was founded in 1964 by **Clarence Jowars Smith** (1929–1969). In 1961, Smith joined the Nation of Islam and affiliated with the temple in Harlem. He dropped his family name in favor of "X," an indication that Smith was a "slave" name he had been given in place of his forgotten real name. He was popularly known as Clarence 13X. Over the next three years he developed several distinct differences with the teaching of Elijah Muhammad, then head of the Nation. The most important divergence of views concerned the identification of Allah. The Nation of Islam taught that Allah had appeared in 1930 in Detroit in the person of **Wallace D. Fard** (Muhammad). Clarence 13X began to teach that all Black people are Allah.

In 1964 Clarence 13X was expelled from the Nation of Islam and founded the Nation of the Five Percent, the name derived from the belief that only five percent of Black people know the Truth and hence are capable of leading the African American community. He attracted a number of young African Americans to his teachings that the Black man is Allah and the Black woman is the Earth (and frequently his organization is also called the Nation of Gods and Earths). The woman's task, to raise a nation and its children, was viewed as the salvation of the Nation.

The Nation expanded quickly and soon had centers in Connecticut and New Jersey. In 1967 headquarters was established on 126th Street in Manhattan at what became known as the Allah School of Mecca. Then tragedy struck when in 1969 Clarence 13X was assassinated. The movement reorganized with a collective leadership and has attempted to continue its founder's program.

Headquarters of the group is in New York City. It publishes two periodicals, *The Word* and *The Five Percenters*. In 1988 the Nation faced a major crisis when the school, which had been its main center, burned.

As Sayyid Issa Al Haadi Al Mahdi. *The Book of Five Percenters.* Montecello, NY: Original Tents of Kedar, 1991. 627 pp.

NATION OF YAHWEH (HEBREW ISRAELITES).

Black Jewish movement. The Nation of Yahweh was founded in the 1970s by **Yahweh ben Yahweh**, born in 1935 as Hulon Mitchell, Jr., the son of a Pentecostal minister. As a young adult, Mitchell briefly associated with the Nation of Islam and was the leader of one of their affiliated mosques. However, he came to believe that he had a special role as the son of Yahweh and he left to found the Nation of Yahweh. Headquarters was established in Miami, Florida, where several hotels and apartment buildings were purchased and over 40 business ventures were initiated. The Florida work is centered upon the Temple of Love, the group's major worship facility. During the 1980s, the group spread rapidly through the Afro-American community in North America.

Members of the Nation of Yahweh affirm the One God whom they believe is Black and has woolly hair. Yahweh has in this generation sent his son (Yahweh ben Yahweh) to his people, the true lost tribe of Judah, and those who believe in his son have attained immortality.

Members reject their given slave name when they join and take a new name with the surname Israel. They see themselves as beginning to assume the leadership role for which they were destined. They commonly wear White robes. While the Nation of Yahweh is primarily a Black movement, ideally anyone of any race who believes in Yahweh ben Yahweh could join and attain salvation. In like measure, while Whites are seen as the major enemy of Yahweh's people, any who oppose Yahweh's work, of any race, are also of the devil.

The community saw itself as a moral community whose work would benefit not only its members but everyone. It articulated strong support for education, business opportunities, and improved health care in the Black community. It also worked for a strong family life. However, along the way problems developed as the group attempted to build a strong internal community and squelch any dissent. As early as 1985 reports of violence both within the community and against members who left the community began to circulate. Periodically arrests were made. Then in 1990 Yahweh ben Yahweh and 16 leaders of the Nation of Yahweh were arrested for murder. In 1992 Yahweh ben Yahweh and six of the other defendants were found guilty on a series of charges growing out of the murders. The state has moved for a new trial on matters about which the jury failed to reach a verdict.

NATIONAL ASSOCIATION OF BLACK CATHOLIC ADMINISTRATORS. Organization for Black **Roman Catholic Church** leaders. The National Association of Black Catholic Administrators was founded in 1976 by Fr. Jerome Robinson. Its membership includes vicars (administrators) of African American parishes and institutions, directors of diocesan Offices of Black Ministry, and staff of diocesan agencies concerned with African American ministries. Within the larger goals of ministering to Black Catholics and eradicating racist oppression both within the church and in the larger world, the association functions as a professional group and regularly offers programs to assist its members (especially the lay members) to become more proficient in their jobs and in their ability to function within the dictates of the Church's Canon Law system.

The association is headquartered in Rockville Center, New York. It is governed by a board of directors. Meetings are held twice a year in the spring and fall. It actively supports the work of the **National Black Catholic Congress**.

NATIONAL BAPTIST CONVENTION OF AMERICA. A Baptist organization. Organized in 1915, the National Baptist Convention of America grew out of a legal dispute with reference to the ownership and management of the National Baptist Publishing Board. The dispute centered on the fact that the National Baptist Publishing Board was incorporated before the **National Baptist Convention, U.S.A., Inc.** Hence, the Publishing Board felt the leave to act independently of the convention's leadership. Rev. **R. H. Boyd**, a powerful leader in the National Baptist Convention, U.S.A., Inc. was the primary leader who pursued this course of action.

The failure of the publishing board to obey the orders of the convention led ultimately to the question: Does the publishing board belong to the convention? This question gave birth to the "popular policy of convention control boards." A lawsuit was filed to decide between those who followed Boyd's claim of

independence for the publishing board and the popular policy of conventional ownership of all boards. In 1915, Judge Smith of Chicago, Illinois, in open court, pronounced the Boyd group a "rump" convention and dissolved an injunction which they had taken out against President **Elias Camp Morris** and other officers of the National Baptist Convention, U.S.A., Inc. Shortly after this unfavorable decision, the Boyd group rallied themselves together at Salem Baptist Church and on Thursday night, September 9, 1915, organized the National Baptist Convention of America (initially, the National Baptist Convention, Unincorporated).

In 1916, the new convention published a document entitled, "The Rightful and Lawful Ownership of the National Baptist Publishing House" in which it was argued that the publishing house did not belong to any convention; hence, it had the right to affiliate with any convention it so desired. This was done to counter the opinion of a few delegates to the new convention who were still doubtful of the ethics of the publishing board's leadership. Nevertheless, harsh feelings pre-vailed between the leadership of the new convention and the National Baptist Convention, U.S.A., Inc. for several years.

In 1924, the National Baptist Convention of America negotiated a compact with the **Lott Carey Baptist Foreign Mission Convention** in which it was agreed that the latter body would take care of the foreign mission work of the new denomination. How-ever, the next two decades witnessed a decline in the strength and vitality of both the Lott Carey Baptist Foreign Mission Convention and the National Baptist Convention of America. Eventually, both conventions decided to terminate their cooperative relationship. Consequently, the National Baptist Convention decided to organize its own foreign mission work. But its foreign mission work always remained much smaller in scope than the mission programs of either the National Baptist Convention, U.S.A. or the Lott Carey Baptist Foreign Mission Convention.

Throughout the history of the National Baptist Convention of America, the National Baptist Publishing Board exercised strong leadership in all the affairs of the convention. To be sure, it has been the focal point in the life of the denomination. This strong leadership role caused problems later on in the life of the convention. In 1989, a split within the National Baptist Convention of America erupted. Again, the National Baptist Publishing Board was a key factor in the split. The new convention called itself a "rebirth" of the ideals of the founding fathers and named itself the **National Missionary Baptist Convention of America** during its first annual session in Chicago. Among the leadership of the NMBCA include: Rev. S.M. Lockridge, president; Rev. F. Benjamin Davis, vice president of ecumenical affairs; and Dr. T. B. Boyd III, chief executive officer of the National Baptist Publishing Board. Hence, a new denomination has emerged out of the National Baptist Convention of America.

Fitts, Leroy. *A History of Black Baptists*. Nashville, TN: Broadman Press, 1985. 331 pp.

Leroy Fitts

NATIONAL BAPTIST CONVENTION, U.S.A., INC. A Baptist organization. Founded on September 24, 1895, the National Baptist Convention, U.S.A. Inc., is the largest body of organized African American Christians in the world (ca. 7,500,000), and the fourth largest denomination in the United States. The development of this denomination separate from White Baptists has deep roots in the cooperative efforts of African American Christians in antebellum America. The cooperative spirit among these Christians stands out especially in the milieu of social and political oppression.

Initially, African American Baptist churches maintained their affiliation with the established bi-racial associations, state conventions and the national denomination. But in 1834, a new spirit of independence, self-determination and cooperation among the local African American churches emerged. The Baptists of Ohio were first to manifest this new spirit with the organization of the Providence Baptist Association. Subsequently, other separate organizations emerged on the local, state, and regional levels of cooperation, resulting in the gradual development of an independent African American Baptist denomination. The Tripartite Union, consisting of the **New England Baptist Missionary Convention**, the African Foreign Mission Convention and the Foreign Mission Convention of America, was the earliest manifestation of this trend towards a new denomination. The new denomination became a reality in 1895 with the merger of the Foreign Mission Convention (1880), the **National Baptist Educational Convention** (1893), and the **American National Baptist Convention** (1886), to form the National Baptist Convention, U.S.A., Inc.

The constitution and program development of the National Baptist Convention, U.S.A., Inc. reflected the determination of the leadership to develop a denomination uniquely relevant to the needs of African American Baptists. Again, freedom and self-determination were creative factors. However, the new

denomination did not radically differ in organizational style and beliefs from the White Baptists. In fact, doctrinally, Black and White Baptists continued to share the same beliefs.

Specialized boards were organized in the new denomination, such as the Foreign Missions Board, Home Missions Board, and the Educational Board. These boards were designed to foster the specific ministries of the denomination. Similarly, the new denomination continued to support local Baptist church covenants, articles of faith and worship styles inherited from the pioneer days of African American Baptists.

In 1897, internal disturbances regarding foreign missions and cooperation with White Baptists led to the first major split from the National Baptist Convention, U.S.A., Inc. The majority of the leadership, inspired by Rev. **Harvey Johnson** of Baltimore, desired complete self-determination for African American Baptists apart from White Baptists. But those who argued for cooperation with White Baptists and the privacy of foreign missions as a denominational objective withdrew to form the Lott Carey Home and Foreign Mission Society (now known as the **Lott Carey Foreign Mission Convention**) specializing in foreign missions. However, this new body was never designed to take the place of the National Baptist Convention as a new denomination.

In 1915, a second major problem erupted in the National Baptist Convention regarding the National Baptist Publishing Board which led to the deliberate establishment of a new denomination. This new development was more significant than the first split of the convention. Rev. **Richard H. Boyd** and Rev. C. H. Clark were the leading spirits in the organization of the new **National Baptist Convention of America**. To be sure, the National Baptist Publishing Board became central to the life of the new denomination. Nevertheless, other boards were organized to rival those of the National Baptist Convention, U.S.A., Inc.

Notwithstanding these splits among the National Baptists, the convention remained the majority denomination among African Americans. Its scheme of operating through specialized boards remained intact after the splits from the fellowship. This was due largely to the skills and dynamic leadership of Rev. **Elias Camp Morris**, national president of the majority denomination. He led the convention through the turbulent years of its early development. During the long-time leadership of Morris, the basic denominational structure of the convention was completed with the organization of the Women's Auxiliary Convention (1900); Sunday School and Baptist Training Union Congress (1905); and, the Church Extension Board (1916). Also, the Women's

Auxiliary Convention founded the National Training School for Women and Girls in Washington, D.C. (1909), during the Morris era.

The Morris era in National Baptist development ended in 1922 with his death. Morris was succeeded as president of the convention by Rev. W. G. Parks. The new president, previously vice-president at large, served the convention for several months before the rise of Dr. **Lacey K. Williams** to the leadership of the denomination in December of 1922.

Williams, a native of Alabama, served as president of the National Baptist Convention from 1922 to 1940. The basic theme that motivated his administration was cooperation. In his 1924 Annual Presidential Address, he developed a plan entitled "Tentative Program of Cooperation between the National Baptist Convention Inc., American Baptist Publication Society, and Woman's American Baptist Home Mission Society." In 1924, this spirit of cooperation resulted in a cooperative venture with the Southern Baptist Convention in the founding of the American Baptist Theological Seminary, Nashville, Tennessee. The development of this school and stronger support of foreign missions were among the greatest accomplishments of the Williams administration.

In 1940, Rev. **D. V. Jemison** succeeded to the presidency of the National Baptist Convention. Basically, Jemison continued the program of the previous administration. Perhaps the greatest singular achievement of his administration was the liquidation and burning of the mortgage on the publishing house building in Nashville, Tennessee in 1942. During Jemison's administration (1940–53), the convention experienced growth through a period of relative calm. Jemison was succeeded by Rev. **Joseph H. Jackson**, who would lead the convention for several decades.

By 1961, another serious problem erupted in the National Baptist Convention, U.S.A., Inc. over issues related to leadership. The long-term presidency of Rev. Joseph H. Jackson was the center of the controversy. He sought re-election to the office of president beyond the tenure established by the convention in 1956. Rev. **Gardner C. Taylor** of New York and his "Taylor Team" led a strong movement to capture the office. However, the attempt failed and Jackson was re-elected to the presidency.

Jackson's philosophy on civil rights provided the second major divisive issue. His approach to civil rights was based on "gradualism". He felt that African American leaders should continue the struggle through the N.A.A.C.P. and the courts of America. American political theory and institutions were viewed with some sense of reverence by Jackson. On the other hand, a new philosophy expressed by Rev. **Martin Luther King, Jr.** was capturing the attention of the masses. He launched a Civil Rights Revolution based on civil disobedience and nonviolent direct action. The two philosophies clashed and played a key role in the organization of the **Progressive National Baptist Convention** in 1961. To be sure, the period between 1956 and 1961 was a time of lively debate and sometimes violent conflict within the convention. Much of the controversy lasted throughout the period of the Civil Rights Revolution.

Not withstanding the tensions within the convention, Jackson's administration experienced significant progress. He was a recognized leader among African American Christians nationally. The only successful challenge to Jackson's influence was in the area of socio-political matters. But his religious influence remained intact. Moreover, he set the moral and spiritual tone for the rapidly growing denomination for almost three decades (1953–1982).

In 1982, Rev. **Theodore Judson Jemison**, long-time general secretary of the convention, succeeded to the presidency of the National Baptist Convention. The major accomplishments of the new administration to date are the construction of the Baptist World Center in Nashville, Tennessee, and the shift of the civil rights stance from "gradualism" to a more liberal philosophy. The latter has resulted in greater dialogue with both the National Baptist Convention of America and the Progressive National Baptist Convention. Currently, there is a gradual return to the convention of those leaders who had rejected the socio-political perspective and leadership role of the late Rev. Joseph H. Jackson.

Fitts, Leroy. *A History of Black Baptists*. Nashville, TN: Broadman Press, 1985. 368 pp.

Jackson, J. H. *A Story of Christian Activism. The History of the National Baptist Convention, U.S.A., Inc.* Nashville, TN: Townsend Press, 1980. 591 pp.

Pelt, Owen D., and Ralph Lee Smith. *The Story of the National Baptists*. New York: Vantage Press, 1960. 272 pp.

Leroy Fitts

NATIONAL BAPTIST EDUCATIONAL CONVENTION. A Baptist organization. In view of the increasing need for an educated ministry, the National Baptist Educational Convention (NBEC) was founded in Washington, D.C. in 1893. National in scope, the NBEC had as its major goal the implementation of a unified educational policy for the Black Baptist churches. W. Bishop Johnson, who had organized the

Sunday School Lyceum in America in 1865, directed the NBEC. With the help of P. F. Morris, Johnson worked to strengthen ties between Black Baptist schools and member churches. The activities of the NBEC were directed primarily at coordinating educational programs, gathering pertinent data and publishing statistics on the relative strengths of the denomination's educational resources. The NBEC also raised large sums of money to help fund new as well as existing educational programs. In its brief two-year existence, however, little was actually accomplished by the NBEC. The NBEC joined with the **American National Baptist Convention** and the **Baptist Foreign Mission Convention** in 1895 to form the **National Baptist Convention, U.S.A., Inc**.

Fitts, Leroy. *A History of Black Baptists*. Nashville, TN: Broadman Press, 1985. 368 pp.

Jackson, Joseph H. *A Story of Christian Activism: The History of the National Baptist Convention, U.S.A., Inc*. Nashville, TN: Townsend Press, 1980. 790 pp.

Martin, Sandy D. *Black Baptists and African Missions*. Macon, GA: Mercer University Press, 1990. 242 pp.

Pelt, Owen D., and Ralph Lee Smith. *The Story of the National Baptists*. New York: Vantage Press, 1960. 272 pp.

Jon R. Stone

NATIONAL BAPTIST EVANGELICAL LIFE AND SOUL SAVING ASSEMBLY OF THE U.S.A.

A Baptist church. The National Baptist Evangelical Life and Soul Saving Assembly of the U.S. grew out of a schism in the National Baptist Convention of America. It dates its beginning to a mission founded in 1920 in Kansas City, Missouri, by "Captain" Arthur Allen Banks, Sr. The mission was to some extent modeled on the **Salvation Army**, both in its emphasis upon charitable self-help activities and a military-like structuring. After operation for many years within the context of the **National Baptist Convention of America**, internal organization problems led to a break in fellowship in 1936–37. By this time the mission had spread across the United States.

The leadership of the assembly moved quickly to provide the uniting structure previously assumed by the National Baptist Convention. It developed and for a number of years offered a series of correspondence courses in a variety of subjects from evangelism to the pastoral ministry, and granted non-academic diplomas upon completion.

The church is non-creedal, but generally follows the perspective of the National Baptist Convention, there being no doctrinal issues involved in the split. In fact, many of the churches affiliated with it are also affiliated with the National Baptist Convention of America as well. In 1951 the assembly reported 264 congregations and more recently has noted that its membership has changed little in the intervening decades. There are over 50,000 members in the affiliated congregations.

Piepkorn, Arthur C. *Profiles in Belief*. Vol. 2. San Francisco, CA: Harper & Row, 1978. 721 pp.

NATIONAL BLACK CATHOLIC CLERGY CAUCUS.

Organization of the African American priests, brothers, seminarians, and deacons of the **Roman Catholic Church**. The National Black Catholic Clergy Caucus was founded on April 18, 1968, in Detroit, Michigan, at a meeting of 58 Black Catholic priests just two weeks after the assassination of **Martin Luther King, Jr.** The formation of the caucus resulted both from the expansion of the number of Black priests in the preceding decades and the sense of urgency produced by the civil rights movement.

The caucus was organized as a fraternal association of Black men following religious vocations, which set as its goal the recruitment and support of Black men in seeking and living their vocation. In this regard it sponsors the Institute of Black Catholic Studies at **Xavier University**, New Orleans, Louisiana. Through Xavier, the only Black Catholic institution of higher learning, the institute offers a master's degree program. In conjunction with the **National Office for Black Catholics**, the caucus speaks to the entire church in an effort to inform it of the contributions of its African American members and as it attempts to invite the church to join the fight against racism in its many forms.

The caucus is headquartered in Washington, D.C. It meets annually in the summer at the same time and place as the **National Black Sisters' Conference**. It publishes a newsletter and annually updates its directory of Black clergy. It contributed to the effort to publish *The African American Catholic Hymnal*.

Lead Me, Guide Me: The African American Catholic Hymnal. Chicago: GIA Publications, 1987.

Smithson, Sandra O. *To Be the Bridge: A Commentary on Black/White Catholicism in America*. Nashville, TN: Winston-Derek Publishers, 1984. 128 pp.

NATIONAL BLACK CATHOLIC CONGRESS.

Organization of African Americans of the **Roman Catholic Church**. The National Black Catholic

Congress, incorporated in 1986, grew out of the felt need of many Black Roman Catholics for greater fellowship and communication among each other nationally. It grew out of a call for a national gathering of Black Catholics made in 1985 by Very Rev. **John H. Ricard**, a Black priest of **St. Joseph's Society of the Sacred Heart** (the Josephites), who the previous year had been named auxiliary bishop of Baltimore, Maryland. Ricard called attention to a set of five national meetings of African American Catholics which had occurred between 1889 and 1894, and suggested the revival of these congresses. One of these early gatherings had been in conjunction with the **World's Parliament of Religions** in Chicago in 1893. The nineteenth century congresses were held in:

1889, Washington D.C.
1890, Cincinnati, Ohio
1892, Philadelphia, Pennsylvania
1893, Chicago, Illinois
1894, Baltimore, Maryland

The idea found an immediate response and the National Black Catholic Congress was organized with support from the Josephites and a number of national Black Catholic organizations. The first of the new series of congresses (dubbed the sixth congress) was convened on May 21, 1987, at the Shrine of the Immaculate Conception in Washington, D.C. The key-note address was delivered by Very Rev. **Eugene A. Marino**, another Josephite priest who had become an auxiliary bishop for the Archdiocese of Washington (D.C.). In the process of preparing for the congress, groups of Black Catholics in 108 dioceses had met to prepare reports on their ideas for future ministry. These reports were edited into the conference working document, *Our Pastoral Vision*. Women were selected to fill seven of the twelve of the congress's major speaking assignments.

The congress was the largest national gathering of Black Catholics and others entered in ministry within the Black community. Its work has received the endorsement of the Black Catholic bishops, and it has formal ties to the **Secretariat for Black Catholics**, the official office on African American Catholic affairs for the National Conference of Catholic Bishops, founded the year after the Washington gathering. The secretariat offers the congress administrative over-sight. Headquarters for the congress is located in Baltimore, Maryland. Bishop Ricard, who is also on the Bishops' Committee of the secretariat, serves as the congress' national coordinator. The next congress gathering was planned for 1992.

Braxton, Edward K. "The National Black Catholic Congress of 1987: An Event of the Century." *The Josephite Harvest* 89, 2 (1987): 8–17.

NATIONAL BLACK CATHOLIC SEMINARIAN ASSOCIATION. Organization of African American men of the **Roman Catholic Church** preparing for the priesthood. The National Black Catholic Seminarian Association was founded in 1969 by Fr. Clarence Williams, a priest of the Congregation of the Most Precious Blood, and is one of several organizations created in the aftermath of the assassination of **Martin Luther King, Jr.** The association emphasizes its fraternal role and attempts to serve as a support group for African American students who are preparing for the priesthood and brotherhood in the Roman Catholic Church. The need of such an organization grew out of the situation of Black seminarians, the overwhelming majority of whom are being educated in predominantly White schools.

The association has developed a nurturance program for its members which encourages them to become somewhat self-directed in their seminary studies as a means of coping with curriculum which often provides little insight into their particular concerns and requirements. The program was produced with the assistance of church authorities in an effort to improve the Black seminarians' education and aid them in maintaining their vocational commitment.

The association is headquartered in Beaumont, Texas. It publishes a *Newsletter*. Its annual meeting is held in conjunction with the **National Black Catholic Clergy Caucus**. It has over 300 members.

NATIONAL BLACK EVANGELICAL ASSOCIATION. A Christian ecumenical organization. The National Black Evangelical Association was founded in 1963 as the National Negro Evangelical Association. It was conceived originally as an umbrella group of conservative African American Protestants, though during its early years it was overwhelmingly Baptist in representation. In 1970, the association sponsored the first inter-denominational conference on evangelism organized and led by African Americans. It was held in St. Stephen Baptist Church in Kansas City, Missouri and attracted over 1,500 delegates. The association has worked to introduce African American Evangelicals from a variety of denominational backgrounds to each other and to assist them in developing evangelical programs in their home communities.

The association gathers for an annual convention each April. It publishes a monthly periodical, the *NBEA Outreach*, and an annual *Journal*. In 1988 it initiated the Institute of Black Evangelical Thought and Action. Headquarters of the association is in Portland, Oregon. There are a number of local units scattered around the country.

"Many Whites Attend Black Conference." *Christianity Today* (October 9, 1970): 43–44.

NATIONAL BLACK LAY CATHOLIC CAUCUS.

An organization for African American lay people of the **Roman Catholic Church**. The National Black Lay Catholic Caucus was founded in 1970 with the purpose of providing support for lay people in Catholic parishes across the United States. It seeks to provide lay leaders, both men and women, with leadership training tools to improve their skills both in their local congregations and as organizers in their community.

The caucus is headquartered in Washington, D.C. It is affiliated with the **National Office for Black Catholics**.

NATIONAL BLACK PRESBYTERIAN CAUCUS.

The National Black Presbyterian Caucus was founded in 1983 by the merger of African American organizations within the two wings of the Presbyterian Church. In 1968 the organization in the Northern Church, Black Presbyterians Concerned, reorganized as Black Presbyterians United. It joined the several other African American support groups founded in the major predominantly White Christian denominations in response to the formation of the National Committee of Negro Churchmen (now the **National Conference of Black Churchmen**) and its attempt to speak to the issues raised under the label of Black Power. In the case of the United Presbyterian Church, however, there already existed a long tradition of an organized African American caucus which stretched back to 1894 and the formation of the Afro-American Presbyterian Council. In 1947 the council became known as the Presbyterian Council of the North and West. Finally in 1964, in response to the civil rights movement, Presbyterians Concerned was organized.

In 1969 among Southern Presbyterians, the small African American constituency organized as the Black Leadership Caucus. In 1983 the Northern and Southern Presbyterians merged to form the **Presbyterian Church (U.S.A.)** and the two African American organizations merged to form the National Black Presbyterian Caucus.

The National Black Presbyterian Caucus serves as an advocacy group for African Americans within the Presbyterian Church (U.S.A.). It has developed programs in African American history, and provides guidance to the church in creating a community in which African Americans can fully participate at all levels. The caucus coordinates its activity with the church through the Racial Ethnic Ministry Unit of the national denominational staff.

Payne, Wardell J., ed. *Directory of African American Religious Bodies: A Compendium by the Howard University School of Divinity.* Washington, DC: Howard University Press, 1991. 363 pp.

NATIONAL BLACK SISTERS' CONFERENCE.

Organization of Black women religious in the **Roman Catholic Church**. The National Black Sisters' Conference was founded in August 1968 as a fraternal organization of women in the Roman Catholic Church order. Its formation came just six months after the organization of the **National Black Catholic Clergy Caucus**, an additional expression of the growing emergence of Black members within Roman Catholicism.

The conference has attempted to create a network of support for Black Catholic Sisters which includes efforts to improve their education, spiritual life, and leadership. It also calls the attention of the Catholic Church to the contribution of Black people, especially Black sisters, to the Christian community, and encourages the church's promotion and use of Black leaders. To further its goals, in 1983, the conference established Sojourner House in Detroit, Michigan, as a spiritual life center for Catholic women and a resource center for Roman Catholic orders wishing to initiate a ministry within the Black community.

The conference is headquartered in Washington, D.C. It issues a newsletter, *Signs of Soul*, and has published a didactic text, *"Tell It Like It Is"—Catechetics from a Black Perspective*. It holds an annual meeting in conjunction with the National Black Catholic Clergy Caucus each summer.

NATIONAL COLORED SPIRITUALIST ASSOCIATION OF CHURCHES.

As Spiritualism grew in the decades following the organization of the National Spiritualist Association in 1893, Afro-Americans were attracted to the movement and some emerged as talented mediums (persons believed able to contact the spirits of the dead and bring messages from the other side). Black members were organized into auxiliary societies attached to the association. Racial tension erupted in the years after World War I, and in 1924 the NSA voted to call a meeting of representatives of the societies composed of "colored" members to create a separate Spiritualist organization for Black people. The NSA appointed a committee headed by its president, Joseph P. Whitwell, to organize and lead the meeting. It was held April 21, 1925, at the Labor Temple on Euclid Avenue in Cleveland.

Twenty delegates initially arrived for the meeting. A temporary organization was formed and fourteen of the delegates seated. Six withdrew in protest of the format of the proceedings. The convention, as the gathering had designated itself, then elected officers: Rev. John R. White, president; Sarah Harrington, vice-president; Mrs. C. W. Dennison, secretary; and a Mr. Smith as treasurer. A constitution and by-laws were adopted at its meeting in 1926, and a periodical, the *National Spiritualist Reporter*, begun.

The association modelled itself on the NSA as a loose association of churches, mediums, and healers. The association charters member churches, ordains ministers (mediums), and licenses healers. Belief is that common to Spiritualism. God is described as Infinite Intelligence. Nature is an expression of Infinite Intelligence. The heart of the faith, however, is the belief in communication with the so-called dead, a possibility actually proven to happen through the phenomenon of mediumship. Mediumship also demonstrates the principles of prophecy. Mediumship teaches the survival of individuals after death. Happiness comes from obeying the natural and spiritual laws of nature.

The association is currently headquartered in Phoenix, Arizona, under the leadership of the Rev. Nellie Mae Taylor.

One Hundredth Anniversary of Modern Spiritualism. Chicago: The National Spiritualist Association of United States of America, 1948. 253 pp.

NATIONAL CONFERENCE OF BLACK CHURCHMEN (NCBC). An ecumenical Christian organization. The National Conference of Black Churchmen (formerly the National Committee of Negro Churchmen) was founded in 1966 by Black Christian church leaders who felt the necessity to respond positively to the issue of Black Power which had been raised by Stokely Carmichael during the demonstration surrounding the admittance of James Meredith as the first Black student at the University of Mississippi. It

was both a demand for Black economic power as essential for the rise of Black people in America and a movement away from commitment to nonviolence as espoused by **Martin Luther King, Jr.**, and the **Southern Christian Leadership Conference**.

The NCBC was called together by Benjamin Franklin Peyton, a Baptist minister serving with the Commission on Religion and Race of the National Council of Churches. On July 31, 1966 the original committee issued a lengthy statement, "Black Power," which was published in a full-page ad in the *New York Times*. The statement gave a qualified endorsement of the Black Power perspective. It both called Black people to recognize the power they already possessed but often failed to use and demanded further power in order to more fully participate in American life. While a few ministers of Black denominations signed the statement, the majority of its support came from Black leaders within the large predominantly White liberal Protestant denominations affiliated with the National Council of Churches. They were also overwhelmingly from the North and Midwest, rather than the South, where King had built his support. During the first years of its existence, the conference's major accomplishment was to serve as a catalyst for the organization of Black caucus groups in most of the major White denominations.

While the conference had understood the critique Carmichael was offering of King's ideals and the loss of support for integration as a goal, it faced serious obstacles in attempting to implement a program. The conference leadership was somewhat distrusted by the rank and file of the Black denominations as it was led by men largely operating from a White power base. It soon found an avenue of expression in the person of **James Forman**. In April 1969 Forman presented a document entitled the "**Black Manifesto**," to a meeting of the Interreligious Foundation for Community Organization, in which a number of NCBC leaders were active. The manifesto demanded $500 million in reparations from the White church and Jewish synagogues and called upon Black people to disrupt White religious organizations until the demand was met. The following Sunday Forman made the demands public by interrupting the services at Riverside Church in New York City and reading the manifesto.

While the churches and synagogue associations did not fully accept either the philosophy underlying the manifesto or fund its demands, a number of denominations attempted to make a positive response. The primary recipients of the funds delivered to Black concerns were the various denominational caucuses whose formation the NCBC had encouraged, and the continued work of these groups its major legacy.

The conference was headquartered in Harlem for many years, but has more recently moved to Atlanta, Georgia.

Lincoln, C, Eric. *The Black Church Since Frazier*. New York: Schocken Books, 1974. 116 pp.

NATIONAL FRATERNAL COUNCIL OF NEGRO CHURCHES. An ecumenical organization. The National Fraternal Council of Negro Churches was founded in 1934 in Chicago as the Negro Fraternal Council of Churches, a cooperative organization among several African American denominations. It quickly grew to encompass twelve Protestant groups—the **African Methodist Episcopal Church**, the **African Methodist Episcopal Zion Church (AMEZ)**, the **African Orthodox Church**, the **Bible Way Church of Our Lord Jesus Christ World Wide**, the Central Jurisdiction of the Methodist Episcopal Church, the **Christian Methodist Episcopal Church**, the **Church of God in Christ**, the **Church of God and Saints of Christ**, the **United American Free Will Baptist Church**, the Metropolitan Community Church of Chicago, the **National Baptist Convention, U.S.A.**, and the **National Baptist Convention of America**. The founding president was Bishop **Reverdy C. Ransom** of the African Methodist Episcopal Church.

The council had a priority of coordinating matters of mutual concern and building cooperative structures. In this regard, it divided itself into twelve work areas with committees on: evangelism and worship, education, health and housing, race relations, industrial and economic relations, urban life, agricultural and rural life, family life, recreation and amusements, publication and publicity, program, Africa and peace, labor, and business. It also established a Washington office to act as a vigilance committee on national legislation and public issues which affected the African American community. The council provided a united voice for the African American community into the 1960s, but began to fade in importance as the civil rights movement gained momentum and the number of African American Christian organizations such as the **National Conference of Black Churchmen** and the **Southern Christian Leadership Conference** expanded. The major permanent product of its activity is the **Interdenominational Theological Center** in Atlanta, a coalition of seven theological seminaries for comparative graduate theological education.

Guzman, Jessie Parkhurst. *Negro Year Book.* Tuskegee, AL: Department of Records and Research, Tuskegee Institute, 1947. 708 pp.

Walls, William J. *The African Methodist Episcopal Zion Church: Reality of the Black Church*. Charlotte, NC: AME Zion Publishing House, 1974. 669 pp.

NATIONAL MISSIONARY BAPTIST CONVENTION OF AMERICA. A Baptist organization. The National Missionary Baptist Convention was founded in 1988 as the result of a schism in the **National Baptist Convention of America**. The crux of the conflict was the National Baptist Publishing Board. The board, which had been established in the 1890s by **Richard H. Boyd**, had operated as an independent corporation headed by Boyd and his descendants. In 1915, a disagreement over the relationship of the board to the National Baptist Convention led to a split and to the formation of the **National Baptist Convention, U.S.A., Inc.**, which wished to have a publishing concern under its own control, and the National Baptist Convention of America, which continued the relationship with the Boyd family's National Baptist Publishing Board.

Over the years, the board supplied many services to the convention. Among these has been an annual summer Sunday School congress, a teacher training school which has drawn more than 20,000 students. However, the board made no accounting of the profits from such activities, nor did the convention share in the revenues.

In the mid-1980s, voices began to rise within the convention calling for a reordering of the relationship between it and the publishing board. At a meeting in the summer of 1988, a majority of the attendees at the annual meeting of the National Baptist Convention of America voted to break ties with the publishing board and to begin conducting an independent Sunday School congress. As a result, those who disagreed with the decision met in Dallas, Texas, in November 1988, and organized the National Missionary Baptist Convention. They have remained loyal to the publishing house and will continue to support its annual Sunday School congress. Rev. S. M. Lockridge of San Diego, California, was elected as the first president of the convention.

Organizers of the new convention claim their share of the history of the National Baptists for the last century. It is too early yet to see what percentage of the 5 million-plus members will adhere to the continuing National Baptist Convention of America or to the new National Missionary Baptist Convention, though the majority has seemed to favor the new convention.

Waddle, Ray. "Baptists' Split Intensifies Over Rival Publishing Boards." *Nashville Tennessean* (March 11, 1989).

NATIONAL OFFICE FOR BLACK CATHOLICS.

Organization for Black members of the **Roman Catholic Church**. The National Office for Black Catholics was established in 1970, the culmination of both a generation of rapid growth on Black membership in the Catholic Church and concerns for eliminating racist structures in the church which had been building through the 1960s. The two years following the death of **Martin Luther King, Jr.**, had seen the formation of the **National Black Catholic Clergy Caucus**, the **National Black Sisters Conference** and the **National Black Lay Catholic Conference**. The new National Office became a coordinating agency for these prior organizations and provided them with a united voice for addressing the Roman Catholic hierarchy.

The Office set as its goals both the positive task of educating the church concerning the contributions of Blacks and Black culture to the church, and the more negative task of alerting the church to its racist practices in the hopes of its taking steps to eliminate them. It also keeps the church aware of opportunities for service in and to the Black community. Through the 1970s it promoted the National Black Catholic Collection (now the Black Catholics Concerned Appeal) to support the Office's work, a practice which many dioceses adopted. Besides its advocacy for Blacks within the church, it has also regularly lobbied to various government agencies on civil rights and other issues of relevance to the Black community.

By the time of its first national conference in 1980, there were over one million Black Catholics in the United States, but only 285 priests (the result of active discouragement of Black men wishing to enter the priesthood) and five Black bishops (the first, **Harold R. Perry**, having been appointed in 1965). From its headquarters in Washington, the Office has promoted work on the development of Black liturgical expressions and in recruiting men and women into religious vocations. It has also spearheaded efforts at evangelization within the Black community.

McCloy, Robert. "Black Catholics: Souls on Ice?" *U. S. Catholic* (April 1981): 23–28.

Smithson, Sandra O. *To Be the Bridge: A Commentary on Black/White Catholicism in America*. Nashville, TN: Winston-Derek Publishers, 1984. 128 pp.

Thus Far by Faith: American Black Worship and Its African Roots. Washington: National Office for Black Catholics/ The Liturgical Conference.

NATIONAL PRIMITIVE BAPTIST CONVENTION OF THE U.S.A.

A Baptist association. Primitive Baptists arose in the 1820s as a reaction to the spread of missionary societies and other organizations among Baptists which seemed to usurp the principle of local church autonomy, a basic Baptist principle. Primitive baptists were concentrated in the South, and African Americans became members during antebellum days. After the Civil War, Black Primitive Baptists churches began to form and by the end of the 1870s the first associations were created. Through the 1880s, almost total separation from the White associations was completed.

The Primitive Baptists have been the least organized of the Baptists, but within the Black Primitive Baptist associations, a move to build a national organization began around the turn of the century. The major advocate of some level of organization was Rev. Clarence F. Sams, pastor of Zion Primitive Baptist Church in Key West, Florida. The church, formed in 1870, had become one of the largest and most progressive in the movement.

An initial gathering of Colored Primitive Baptists convened at St. Bartley's Primitive Baptist Church in Huntsville, Alabama, in 1907. Sams preached on the "Divine Plan of Organized Government." Other talks were given on the need for unity and for printed materials for Primitive Baptists. A constitution was adopted and Elder James H. Carey of Charlotte, North Carolina, elected as the convention's first president. The convention voted to found a school, the Industrial and Theological College at Winston-Salem, North Carolina, and to support the Thomaston Academy, Thomaston, Alabama. Mrs. Elizabeth Bradford was elected president of the National Women's Auxiliary Convention. Following the convention, Sams, elected recording secretary, began to publish Sunday school literature and managed the Sunday School Union and Publishing Board.

The convention had no doctrinal argument with the primitive Baptist movement; it follows a strict Calvinist theology and adheres to a doctrine of election and predestination of a particular number of the human race to be saved, from the foundation of the world. It practices foot washing. The convention retains its congregational government, but through the convention the churches support a Sunday school board and a publishing concern. Headquarters is in Tallahassee,

Florida. Over the century, the great majority of African American Primitive Baptists have affiliated with the convention. In 1975, the last occasion when figures were released, the convention claimed 606 affiliated churches and 250,000 members.

Discipline of the Primitive Baptist Church. Tallahassee, FL: National Primitive Baptist Publishing House, 1966. 128 pp.

NATIONALISM, BLACK. Black nationalism is a generic term that accounts for a wide variety of ideas, actions, values and commitments; it includes perspectives ranging from the "simplest expressions of ethnocentrism and racial solidarity to the comprehensive and sophisticated ideologies of Pan-Negroism or Pan-Africanism." Black nationalist thought is predicated on the idea that Africans of the diaspora area united both by their common ancestry and their historical experiences of suffering. Moreover, Black nationalists in America also affirm the idea that they comprise a "nation within nation." Nationalists emphasize a variety of different perspectives as the basis of their claims about Black unity, such as culture, religion, economics, revolutionary idealism, bourgeois reformism, and emigrationism (which includes the famous "back to Africa" motif). Approaches range from the revolutionary philosophy of Denmark Vesey to the accommodationist ideology of **Booker T. Washington**, and the separatism of Black Muslims.

This essay traces the development of Black nationalist thought from its origins up to the end of its "golden Age," as symbolized in the demise of one of its most noble interpreters, **Marcus Garvey**, and focuses specifically upon the connections between various forms of Black nationalist thought and African American religious perspectives. From the beginning, Black nationalist thought has been rooted in the religious experiences of its strongest proponents and their communities. This has, indeed, been one of its principal strengths.

Black Religion and the Origins of Black Nationalist Thought. From its inception, Black nationalist thought has been based on the idea of the uniqueness and solidarity of Black Americans' history and culture. This point has been accented as the foundation of their sense of group consciousness and socio-political identity. Particular emphasis has been especially grounded in the religious experiences of the African American community, Christian and non-Christian. This point is clearly demonstrated, with varying points of emphasis, in the writings of some of the leading interpreters of African American life and thought, such as Eugene Genovese, Sterling Stuckey, Wilson Jeremiah Moses, **Gayraud Wilmore**, and a host of others.

Genovese, for example, proposes that Black nationalist consciousness emerged within the context of the paternalistic and exploitative system of American slavery. The paternalistic nature of the slave system forced the slaves to identify more with the values and beliefs of their oppressors than with each other. Genovese argues that it placed an inherent limit on the sense of revolutionary class consciousness that might have developed among the slaves. Yet the religious ethos of the slave community provided a vision and context wherein slaves could begin to value love and care for each other, as well as the things which are central to their own culture. Religion, particularly Christianity, provided the spiritual and psychological resources wherein slaves could envision and fashion a world that was different from what they experienced on the plantations. In this new worldview they were depicted as sons and daughters of God, children of the King, with golden slippers, mansions in which to live, and streets paved with gold. White slaveowners be-came the object of the slaves' spiritual satire as they sang, within an eye's gaze of the master's mansion, "Everybody talkin bout heaven aint goin there."

Genovese goes on to say that there was an element of paradox in what happened as a result of the perpetuation of the paternalistic system. Paternalism:

> . . . unwittingly invited its victims to fashion their own interpretation of the social order it was intended to justify. And the slaves, drawing on a religion [Christianity] that was supposed to assure their compliance and docility, rejected the essence of slavery by projecting their own rights and value as human beings.

The slaves' espousal of the Christian faith, a symbol of cultural assimilation to Whites, became the source of a new sense of political consciousness within the slave community. Thus Black political consciousness in the antebellum South emerged out of the religion of the slave quarters (which has its roots in West African religion).

Genovese's thesis about the subservice power of slave religion, however, does not, in his view, alter his thesis about the nature of the system of class exploitation and oppression in the antebellum South. He insists that despite the positive influence of religion, the system of slavery itself, thwarted the revolutionary potentials of the emerging Black nation. Nevertheless, for our purposes, the fact remains that the religious experiences of Black slaves provided the context for the emergence of African American socio-political visions.

Sterling Stuckey offers a different interpretation of the origins and content of Black nationalist thought. His central contention is that all forms of Black political consciousness (to include Black nationalism) have their roots in West African religious traditions in general and specifically the "ring shout." The ring shout is a religious ceremony in which participants sing religious "shout songs" and move in rhythmic step in a counterclockwise circle until they are possessed by the spirit. Widespread among Blacks during and beyond the antebellum period, it provided, asserts Stuckey, the principal foundation for the formation of a unified culture among the various tribes of Africans represented in the larger slave community. It provided a context wherein they could consciously draw upon and nurture some of the key aspects of their African cultural and religious heritage. The perpetuation of the ring shout was one aspect of the slaves' attempt to synthesize West African culture with their Christian and indigenous African beliefs. It represented a conscious defiance on the part of slaves and some free Blacks as they refused to succumb to all of the influences of Western culture.

Thus Stuckey proposes that Black nationalism in the nineteenth century and the twentieth century "was essentially African nationalism." This nationalism was born in the womb of the African religious experiences and expressed with Christian and non-Christian symbols.

The Institutional Bases of Black Nationalist Idealism: The Independent Black Churches. Independent Black churches began to emerge in America as early as the 1750s with the establishment of the plantation mission church in a region of what is now known as Mecklenburg, Virginia. Later in the 1770s there were plantation missions in Silver Bluff, South Carolina, and others in Petersburg and Williamsburg, Virginia. The independence movement among Black Methodists began to take shape in 1787 when **Richard Allen** and **Absalom Jones**, two free Black men in the city of Philadelphia, led a withdrawal from St. George's Methodist Episcopal Church in that city in response to abusive treatment in worship. Soon thereafter they began to work with an organization known as the Free African Society, a forerunner to the establishment of the **African Methodist Episcopal Church** (AME). The clergy and lay persons from these newly formed organizations would later become the leading exponents of Black nationalist idealism. Richard Allen, who became the first bishop of the African Methodist Episcopal Church, is a primary example of this fact.

The independent Black church movement began at a very significant time in the development of strong commercial routes and connections between the United States, Great Britain and Africa. As these trade routes, fueled by the barbarous realities of the slave trade and the production and sale of rum, continued to develop, many free Blacks became inspired by the idea of being able to return to Africa as business people and as missionaries. They saw the expanding trade routes as God's means of providing them with an opportunity for cultural, spiritual, and intellectual exchange between themselves and their African brothers and sisters. The idea of spreading the gospel and the notion of expanding their commercial interests were both key elements in the emergence of Black nationalist thought.

Paul Cuffe was one of the first African Americans to espouse this idea. He was a member of a chapter of Richard Allen's Free Africa Society in New Bedford, Massachusetts. Moreover, he was also instrumental in establishing several independent Black congregations in the New England region. Cuffe was a shipbuilder by trade and he ran a successful business. The culmination of his vision as a Black "Christian" businessman took place in 1815 when he took 38 free Blacks to Sierra Leone on a joint missionary and commercial venture. Thus he began the movement of free Blacks returning to Africa for religious and commercial purposes which would later culminate with the full-fledged spread of Pan-Africanist and emigrationist ideologies. Moveover, the Black church, of which Cuffe's work was an extension, provided Black nationalist thinkers with an institutional model of Black progress and control. This was the first institution that they controlled, owned and principally supported. In fact, institutional Black churches such as the AME, under the leadership of Richard Allen, were founded as a nationalist response to institutionalized White racism. As such, the Black church helped to foster both the quest toward independence and the support of emigrationist ideals, both of which were so crucial to Black nationalists.

The American Colonization Society. The idea of repatriating Blacks was originally proposed by Samuel Hopkins in 1759 and it was later institutionalized in the work of the American Colonization Society (ACS), founded in 1816. The organization was supported both by northern White abolitionists and White Christians of the South. It was dedicated to the task of supporting wholesale repatriation of Blacks back to Africa for the purpose of spreading the gospel and the benefits of western civilization. The ACS, modeled after what the British did in colonizing Sierra Leone, was instrumental in helping to establish Liberia as an American colony. It helped to provide the economic and philosophical support for the practice of repatriation. Thereby it provided strength to the Black emigrationists and later Pan-Africanists among whom this idea was so popular. Nonetheless, the ACS never claimed the support of a majority of Black leaders, particularly those who were northern abolitionists.

Some Black leaders espoused the philosophy of the ACS but withheld support from it because of suspicion of the racist White Southerners who supported it. Frederick Douglass vehemently opposed both the philosophy and the attitudes of ACS supporters. Douglass insisted that the emigrationist philosophy would distract African Americans from the goal that he deemed to be absolutely essential: the quest for inclusion, justice and integration in America. Douglass publicly debated with noted nationalists such as **Henry H. Garnet** and **Martin Delany** on this very issue. The staunch resistance of Black abolitionists, coupled with financial, logistical and morale problems, led to the ineffectiveness and eventual demise of the ACS. But it did, without question, help to influence the future course of Black nationalist movements, providing both a theological framework and the ethos for Black emigrationist philosophy, which was anchored in the belief that this would provide a context for Black self-rule. Black nationalist thought continues to draw upon particular religious experiences.

Nationalist Themes. The connection between Black religion and Black nationalism can be understood even more clearly if examined in greater detail in light of several themes around which Black nationalist thinking converged. This is particularly true of nationalists during the period extending from 1850–1925. Wilson Jeremiah Moses has called this period in one of his more noted writings, "The Golden Age of Black Nationalism," a time which begins with the passage of the Fugitive Slave Law and ends with the imprisonment of Marcus Garvey.

1. *Christianity and the Doctrine of European Superiority.* Most nationalists during this period were committed to the Western doctrine of "racial uplift." They believed that their total program for Black liberation included a moral mandate to lift the least of their fellow Africans and African descendants from their ignorance, poverty, and cultural deprivation. Despite their affirmation of the doctrine of Black pride, uniqueness and unity, these nationalists operated with the eurocentric assumption that Africa was the "dark continent." This dark continent was in need of the light of Western culture, the fire of Western religion, and the fuel of Western capitalism if there was to be any hope

for its survival. No Black nationalist expresses this idea more forcefully than does **Alexander Crummell**, the Anglican priest and missionary, who spent time in Europe and later served for more than 20 years as a missionary in Sierra Leone. He believed that African Americans were called upon to introduce Africans to true "civilization." He describes civilization as:

> . . . .the clarity of the mind from the dominion of false heathen [unchristian and superstitious] ideas. . . the conscious impress of individualism and its desire and appetites and passions as a sacred gift, and as under the law of divine obligation.

Civilization to Crummell clearly referred only to Western civilization. Crummell was also of the definite opinion that the Christian religion was a superior religion to African traditional religion. In fact, the notion of the superiority of the Christian faith provided an ideological foundation for the doctrine of Western elitism in general. This bias against non-Western culture is also expressed in terms of attitudes towards certain forms of behavior, particularly as it pertains to Christian worship.

As an example of this, Wilson cites an incident in the life of the famed AME leader, Bishop **Daniel A. Payne**. Payne was an ardent educator, churchman, civil rights advocate, and promoter of the doctrine of racial uplift. As such, he was an ardent critic of all forms of worship and doctrine which did not fit within the mainstream of the Christian tradition. He was incessant to the point of tyranny in his demand that all forms of "heathenism" be removed from worship services of AME congregations. One of the practices that he opposed most passionately was the ring shout, which was very popular among Black parishioners in his conference.

Payne provides the following description of his first encounter with this practice during an attendance at a "bush meeting." The members "formed a ring, and with coats off sang, clapped their hands and stamped their feet in a most ridiculous and heathenish way." The behavior was "disgraceful to themselves, the race, and the Christian name." The shouting reminded Payne of those aspects of Black culture that he found to be most troubling and retarding to the progress of the race. Thus, he deemed it an insult to the self, race, and, to the Christian religion. Preserving a sense of Black pride and unity, in his opinion, had nothing to do with perpetuating such distinctive religious practices. Payne was a true Anglophile.

Payne was not alone in sharing these opinions; even such a celebrated twentieth century pan-Africanist as

Marcus Garvey held similar views. No leader in the twentieth century was a greater promoter of the doc-trine of Black pride and the nationalist demand for justice. Yet Garvey's radical vision for Africans of the diaspora and for the motherland was essentially euro-centric in its view of Africans. His self-defined goal was to achieve the "general uplift of the Negro people of the world . . . civilizing backward tribes of Africans." Garvey's nationalism was limited by his inability to see beyond all of the trappings of Anglophilia. This is true, notwithstanding his progressive theological affirmation of the idea of the Blackness of God.

If Black nationalism is designed to do what we have suggested above, that is, to promote unity, self-respect, and solidarity, it is difficult to understand how this can be done without the simultaneous celebration of aspects of African American culture which seem to be so *sui generis*. At any rate, Moses is correct in noting that the issues that were discussed in this first theme present serious problems for persons who are committed nationalists. Indeed, there is a contradiction in any form of Black nationalism which celebrates Black pride and rejects the cultural foundations upon which it is established.

2. *The Doctrine of African Restoration.* One of the other key themes uniting Black nationalists was this doctrine, drawn largely from the Hebrew Bible, of the restoration of Africa and the messianic calling of all Africans of the diaspora. This doctrine further holds that Africa is a centerpiece in God's plan of universal redemption. Nationalists of various types have attached a kind of Zionist significance to Africa, linking the destiny of all Africans of the diaspora to the rise and restoration of their motherland. **Henry McNeal Turner**, the South Carolina born AME emigrationist, affirmed this conviction, as did Garvey and others. They were convinced that a strong Africa would be the strength of Blacks around the world. But behind this conviction was a very strong theological conviction about the socio-political and religious significance of Africa. This is evidenced in their reference to the prophetic promise of Psalm 68:31, which they adhered to with creedal certainty. One writer describes it as follows:

> But the promise is that princes shall come out of Egypt, and that Ethiopia shall soon stretch forth her hands unto God. . . the Negro Church stands forth as unquestionable evidence [of the fulfillment of Psalm 68:31]. It is the first fruit of the countless millions of that race who shall be found in the army. . . .

While it is certain that the doctrine of African redemption always had direct socio-political

implications, it is also important to grasp how this idea is grounded in a religious idea which is drawn from the Judeo-Christian tradition.

3. *Black Nationalism and the Shaping of a Black Theological Tradition.* This third and final theme in Black nationalist thought focuses on its contributions to the transformation of African American religious thought. Black nationalists of the periods that we have studied belonged primarily to mainline denominations, both Black and White. Moreover, we have noted their general intolerance to religious ideas that are unacceptable to the mainstream of the Christian tradition. A full-fledged non-Christian, nationalist project did not emerge until the flowering of the Black Muslims in the 1950s and 1960s. Notwithstanding this fact, these nationalists challenged some of the common theological assumptions of their religious communities. Nationalists, both clergy and laypersons, were radical and visionary in their interpretation of the Christian Gospel.

Robert Young's "Ethiopian Manifesto," in which he proclaimed the Blackness of God, began a tradition of interpretation that continues unto this day in various African American theological projects. He insists that the salvation of Black people could only come from a Black Messiah, born of a Black woman. In this he is consonant with Henry McNeal Turner and Marcus Garvey, both of whom affirm that a "Black" God was an essential component to any program of Black liberation. Turner says it best: "We do not believe that there is any hope for a race of people who do not believe they look like God." Garvey affirms this a very similar notion in his declaring that: "We believe in the God of Ethiopia," a Black God. That is to say, all of these writers believed and advocated that Blacks should have the right and power to create and affirm their own ideas about God and about Christian images, just as they have the right to control their own political destinies. Therefore, Garvey supported the creation of the **African Orthodox Church**, complete with a Black bishop, Black saints, relics, etc.

This same call for a Black God and Black Christ was echoed in the twentieth century in the literary works of Black cultural nationalists of the Harlem Renaissance period such as Countee Cullen and **Langston Hughes**. These members of the Black literati demanded a Black Christ who could identify with the plight of oppressed Blacks. Cullen declares: "Lord, I fashion dark gods, too, Lord, forgive me if my need sometimes shapes my human creed." Even more emphatic are the words of Hughes: "Christ is a Nigger, Beaten and Black."

If the nationalism of Turner, Young, Garvey, Hughes, and Cullen challenges the theological claims of

Western Christendom, other nationalists were even more vociferous in their critique of the lack of activism in the organized churches. Martin Delany, for example, challenged the tendency of the Black church to identify with the conservative evangelical theology of White evangelicals. He, a devout layperson and physician, called the church to a self-help, activist program of action. As he notes, "The time has now fully arrived, when the colored race . . . being made for the redemption of the world . . . God himself . . . has presented these measures to us." Alexander Crummell was another Black nationalist who called for a gospel of self love and self-aggrandizement. He challenged the Black church to promote a "diffusive" religion, a religion that flows outward, and is designed to change the affairs of the world. These nationalists used Christianity to produce a rational system of liberation for their people. In this sense they were prototype theologians who prefigured much of what would come in the twentieth century with the onset of the Black theology movement. They called for a liberating theology that demanded of the church a higher level of faithfulness to the Gospel. This is a tradition of radical African American religious thought that extends back to the very beginning of the Black religious development in the United States.

The interplay between Black religion and Black Nationalism through the early twentieth century established a motif which would be developed in greater detail through the twentieth century in movements such as the Black Muslims, Black theology, and the civil rights movement.

Bracey, John H., August Meier, Elliott Rudwick. *Black Nationalism in America.* Indianapolis, IN: Bobbs-Merrill Company, 1970.

Genovese, Eugene. *Roll Jordan Roll.* New York: Vintage Books, 1976.

Johnson, Alonzo. *Good News for the Disinherited: The Meaning of Jesus of Nazareth in the Writings of Howard Thurman.* New York: Ph.D. dissertation, Union Theological Seminary, 1990.

Moses, Wilson Jeremiah. *Alexander Crummell.* New York: Oxford University Press, 1989.

———. *The Golden Age of Black Nationalism.* Hamden, CT: Archon Books, 1978.

———. *The Wings of Ethiopia.* Ames, IA: Iowa State University Press, 1990.

Stuckey, Sterling. *Slave Culture.* New York: Oxford University Press, 1987.

Alonzo Johnson

NAZARENE BIBLE INSTITUTE. A **Church of the Nazarene** School. During World War II, the Church of the Nazarene became conscious of its neglect of African Americans and began a program to bring its Black churches and pastors into the life of the church and to give some priority to both evangelism and education in the African American community. In 1948 the church established the Nazarene Bible Institute in Institute, West Virginia on property adjacent to the West Virginia State College for the Colored. There was already a Black Nazarene congregation there.

Edwin E. Hale, a White man, became the first president, and R. W. Cunningham, a Black pastor, doubled as the institute's chaplain and an instructor. In 1955 Cunningham succeeded Hale as the president of the school. The school continued until 1970 when, as part of a move to discontinue segregated structures in the church, the school was merged into the Nazarene Bible College in Colorado Springs, Colorado.

Purkiser, W. T. *Called Unto Holiness II; The Story of the Nazarenes, the Second Twenty-five Years, 1933–1958.* Kansas City, MO: Nazarene Publishing House, 1983. 356 pp.

NAZREY, WILLIS (March 5, 1808–August 22, 1875), 5th bishop of the **African Methodist Episcopal Church** (AME), was born in the Isle of Wight, Virginia. He had no formal schooling, and all the education he acquired was on his own. He was converted in New York City in 1837 and licensed to preach that same year at Bethel AME Church on Sullivan Street by Rev. William Cornish. He joined the New York Conference as an itinerant minister in 1840, and was ordained deacon in 1841. He then transferred to the Baltimore Conference, and soon transferred again to the Philadelphia Conference, where he was ordained elder in 1843.

He was pastor of the AME church in Pennington, New Jersey, from 1842 to 1843, followed by Cook's Mill AME Church in 1843. In 1844–45 he covered charges in both New Brunswick and Princeton, New Jersey, then going to Morristown in 1845 and Bethel AME Church in Philadelphia from 1846 to 1848. In 1851 at the Baltimore Conference Bishop **William P. Quinn** appointed him assistant bishop. The following year Nazrey was elected bishop with **Daniel Payne** and was consecrated on May 13, 1852. He was assigned to the Second Episcopal District (Baltimore and New York Annual Conferences). He introduced the practice of examining the finances of the conference before the passage of probationers' character, and this practice was adopted by the 1856 General Conference. He urged greater attention to African and West Indian missions, and supported the newly organized *Christian Recorder* as a means of spreading information and connecting everyone in the church.

Soon after his election he moved to Canada to work with the churches there. In 1856 these churches, which had been connected with the AME Church for about seventeen years, separated and formed the independent British Methodist Episcopal (B.M.E.) Church. They also elected Nazrey bishop, and he served both areas from 1856 to 1864. On May 17, 1864, he resigned from his AME position and spent the rest of his career solely with the B.M.E. Church, residing in Chatham, Canada. The Canadian churches later reunited with the AME Church in 1884.

HAMEC, EWM, CEAMEC, BAMEC.

NEW BETHEL CHURCH OF GOD IN CHRIST. An Apostolic Pentecostal Church. The New Bethel Church of God in Christ emerged as the non- Trinitarian Jesus Only doctrine spread through the **Church of God in Christ**, the largest of the trinitarian Pentecostal churches in the Black community. Rev. A. D. Bradley became one of its advocates and was on several occasions admonished to desist from preaching the doctrine in COGIC gatherings. Finally, in 1927, with his wife and a colleague Lonnie Bates, Bradley left COGIC and founded the New Bethel Church.

The church follows the common Apostolic position and emphasizes the One God whose name is Jesus and in whose name believers are baptized. It is distinctive for its pacifist stance. Church members may meet their armed forces responsibilities with alternative noncombatant service. The church practices foot washing.

The New Bethel Church is led by its presiding bishop who is assisted by a board of bishops (judiciary) and a general assembly (legislative).

NEW ENGLAND BAPTIST MISSIONARY CON-VENTION. A Baptist organization. Organized in August, 1874, the New England Baptist Missionary Convention constitutes the oldest regional convention among African Americans Baptists. Initially an affiliated district convention of the **Consolidated American Baptist Convention**, this regional convention is currently affiliated with the **National Baptist Convention, U.S.A., Inc**.

The New England Baptist Missionary Convention was part of the general trend among African American Baptists of the post-Civil War era to seek greater cooperation among Baptist churches beyond state lines. Leading clergy from New England, New York, New Jersey, and Pennsylvania met in the Cogdon Street Baptist Church of Providence, Rhode Island to organize a regional convention designed to meet the needs of Baptist churches in New England and nearby states. Among the pioneer leaders of the new convention were: Rev. William Jackson, president; Rev. Spencer Harris of New York, vice-president; Rev. William A Burch of New Bedford, Massachusetts, recording secretary; Rev. Edmond Kelly, corresponding secretary; and William M. Green of Providence, Rhode Island, treasurer. These pioneers did not constitute the convention as a separate denomination, but as a regional body to undergird and intensify the broader ministry of the emerging denominational movement.

By the turn of the century, most of the principal leadership among African American Baptists were from the rank and file of the New England Baptist Convention. Their influence was felt in both the National Baptist Convention, U.S.A., Inc. and the **Lott Carey Baptist Foreign Mission Convention**. During this period of growth, various churches from as far south as Virginia affiliated with the convention. Moreover, the convention developed strategies for planting new churches in these areas.

The program development of the convention reflected the progressive spirit of its leadership. Provisions were made for the convention to foster and maintain home and foreign missionary work, establish and maintain educational institutions, and to establish other agencies necessary for the development of the broader Baptist ministry in the region. Perhaps its greatest contributions to the cooperative ministry of African American Baptists have been the planting and support of new churches in the region and the support of African missions. The convention has also given substantial support to educational institutions operated by the National Baptist denomination. The support of an educated ministry through these educational institutions was a primary concern of the convention's leadership.

During the early days of the New England Baptist Missionary Convention, the leadership recognized the need to organize the women of the convention into an effective working unit. In 1892, the Women's Auxiliary to the convention was organized in New Haven. This auxiliary was very supportive of missions and education. Moreover, the Women's Auxiliary became very influential in the development of the Women's

Convention of the National Baptist Convention, U.S.A., Inc.

In 1903, the convention adopted its first educational institution to be supported—the Virginia Seminary and College, Lynchburg, Virginia. This school became representative of the convention's emphasis on an educated ministry. Subsequently, other schools were adopted for support from the convention. Among these schools were such colleges and specialized schools as Northern Baptist University, Rahway, New Jersey; Lee and Hayes University, Baltimore, Maryland; Clayton Williams University, Baltimore, Maryland; National Training School, Washington, D.C.; and Virginia Union University, Richmond, Virginia. Similarly, the convention supported Good Samaritan Orphanage, Newark, N.J. and the Standard Theological and Industrial College, Pittsburgh, Pennsylvania. By 1921, the Northern Baptist University was actually owned and operated by the convention.

Again, the New England Baptist Missionary Convention was known for its strong leadership. In 1919, Rev. John C. Jackson was elected to the presidency of the convention. His leadership covered most of the progressive years of the convention's development. Jackson served the convention in concomitance with his long-time pastorate at the Union Baptist Church, Hartford, Connecticut. In his first annual address to the convention, he launched a Five Year One Million Dollar Campaign: $100,000 for Foreign Missions; $50,000 for needy churches; $750,000 for education; $425,000 for Widow's Fund; and, $75,000 for Aged Ministers.

Like other organized African American church bodies, the New England Baptist Missionary convention was in the forefront of the civil rights struggles of the race. Most of the great reform issues of the twentieth century were addressed by the leadership of the convention. As early as 1919, the convention went on record favoring women's suffrage and national prohibition and condemning lynching.

In 1921, the convention, under Jackson's strong inspiration, launched plans for the organization of the New England Baptist Pastors' Conference and Relief Association composed of pastors of the local churches represented in the convention. The purpose of the conference was to consolidate the work of the pastors and to enhance their effectiveness in the local churches. The leadership sought as much consensus as possible in the areas of doctrine and polity. Also, attention was given to some of the stress experienced by some of the local churches, especially a growing tendency to take problem matters to civil courts.

During the first half of the twentieth century, the convention remained strong in the programs and representation of local churches and associations. However, the last two decades have witnessed a decline in growth. Many churches in the region have developed a tendency to do all their denominational work directly through the National Baptist Convention, U.S.A., Inc. and other Baptist bodies operative in the region. Currently, the new president, Rev. O. B. J. Burson, is attempting to revitalize the convention by building a relevant mission in a new setting.

Fitts, Leroy. *A History of Black Baptists*. Nashville, TN: Broadman Press, 1985. 368 pp.
Journal, Golden Jubilee Session of The New England Baptist Missionary Convention, June 10–15, 1924. 130 pp.

Leroy Fitts

NEWMAN, ERNEST WILBUR (b. April 9, 1928), a bishop of the **United Methodist Church**, was born in Kingstree, South Carolina, the son of Meloncy and Serena (Hamilton) Newman. He was ordained deacon in 1946 and received his B.A. in 1948 from Claflin College in Orangeburg, South Carolina. He finished much of the theological program at Gammon Theological Seminary in Atlanta, Georgia, then took the Summerville Charge in Summerville, South Carolina (1950–52), followed by the Rockmill Charge in Anderson, South Carolina (1952–53); Kelley Chapel in Miami, Florida (1953); and the Talladega Charge in Talladega, Alabama (1954–55). On August 12, 1955 he married Thelma Heard, with whom he had two children.

In 1955 he returned to Florida to pastor St. Joseph Methodist Church in Jacksonville (1955–57), and in 1956 finally received the M.Div. from Gammon Theological Seminary. From 1957 to 1964 he pastored Zion Methodist Church in Ocala, Florida, followed by Ebenezer Methodist Church in Jacksonville from 1964 to 1972. From 1972 to 1977 he was district superintendent of the Melbourne District in the Florida Conference, and pastored the 2,000–member Plantation United Methodist Church in Plantation, Florida, from 1977 to 1982. This pastorate made Newman the first Black pastor in that conference to be assigned to a major, mostly White congregation. In 1982–83 he was associate Council Director for the Florida Conference, and in 1983 he was district superintendent of the Deland District. From 1976 to 1984 he was a member of the General Commission on Religion and Race.

Newman was elected bishop in 1984, the first African American bishop elected by the Southeastern Jurisdiction since the formation of the United Methodist

Church in 1968 (by the merger of the Methodist Church with the Evangelical United Brethren and the dissolution of the all-Black Central Jurisdiction). He was assigned to the Nashville Episcopal Area, where he has since remained. He is active in the SEJ Urban Workers Network and serves on the General Commission on Communications. He is a member of the board of trustees of many institutions, including Martin Methodist College, Rust College, Lambuth College, Emory University, Scarrit Graduate School, Lake Junaluska Assembly, and Gammon Theological Seminary. In 1989 he was named president of the College of Bishops of the Southeastern Jurisdiction. He retired in 1992.

WWABA (92–93), *BDUMB.*

NICHOLS, DECATUR WARD (b. October 15, 1900), 59th bishop of the **African Methodist Episcopal Church** (AME), was born in Charleston, South Carolina, the twelfth of thirteen children in the family of Lewis Ruffin and Anna Elizabeth (Cotton) Nichols. His father was an AME minister and builder of the Emanuel AME Church on Calhoun Street in Charleston, South Carolina. After attending the public schools of Charleston, he went to Avery Normal Institute in Charleston, graduating in 1919. He then enrolled in Howard University in Washington, D.C., where he received his B.A. in 1923. From there he moved to Drew Theological Seminary in Madison, New Jersey, where he received an M.A. in Missions in 1924 and B.D. in 1926.

He was licensed to preach by his father, joined the New Jersey Conference in 1922, was ordained deacon in 1922, and elder in 1925. For a time in 1925 he was supply minister for the Jamestown AME Church in Rhode Island, but after ordination he was appointed to the Emanuel AME Church on West 52nd Street in New York City, which had eighteen members at the time. He remained for the next fifteen years, during which he transformed it into a major church of 2,400 members. In 1926 a new $100,000 building was purchased at 119th Street and $56,000 in improvements were made. On March 2, 1927, he married Susan Bailey, with whom he had two children. She died in 1931, and in 1937 he married her sister, Sarah Katherine "Kay" Bailey. In 1936 his church hosted the General Conference.

Nichols was elected bishop in 1940, at the time the youngest bishop ever elected in the AME Church. He was assigned to the Ninth Episcopal District (Alabama) and supervised many accomplishments. Debt was decreased at Daniel Payne College in Birmingham, while property was renovated. An episcopal residence

was built at the college, plus a president's home, boys' cottage, teachers' cottage, luncheonette, girls' dormitory, and library. The chapel was remodeled, a lighting system was installed, and roadways were completed. In 1948 he was assigned to the First Episcopal District (New England, New York, New Jersey, Delaware, Pennsylvania, and Bermuda Conferences), where he stayed until 1956. In 1948 he bought the AME Book Concern building in Philadelphia to save it from a sheriff's sale. He used his own money and loans from friends to pay the $56,000. The 1952 General Conference promised to reimburse him, but never did so. He was instrumental in the organization of the Pension Department and was its first president. He was a delegate to the First Assembly of the World Council of Churches in Amsterdam in 1948 and the Second Assembly in Evanston, Illinois, in 1954. In 1951 he attended the Ecumenical Methodist Conference in Oxford, England. He was the first Black to serve as vice-president of the National Council of Churches. He was president of the board of trustees of both Daniel Payne College in Alabama and Allen University in Columbia, South Carolina, and was also a trustee of Wilberforce University in Ohio. From 1956 to 1957 he served on the Eleventh Episcopal District (Florida). In 1956 *Ebony* magazine did an article on his luxurious lifestyle, noting his homes in Long Island, Harlem, and Philadelphia, plus extensive real estate holdings in South Carolina and New York. His father had gained some wealth in real estate, and Nichols built upon his family resources.

In 1957 Nichols was brought to ecclesiastical trial on charges of violating the *Discipline* (provisions of the church's rulebook) with regard to financial matters, was found guilty, and suspended. He appealed the matter to the 1960 General Conference, which upheld the suspension. He was also taken to civil court on several charges, including mishandling of church funds, and the case moved slowly through the court system for a number of years. Meanwhile, in 1958 Nichols organized a new church called the Reformed AME Church. He pulled together a new congregation and in 1965 founded Christ Cathedral Reformed AME Church. On April 16, 1964, a jury convicted Nichols on twelve counts of embezzling $100,000 from the church. On October 27, 1964, the majority of a three-judge panel overturned this verdict, saying the prosecution had "failed utterly" to prove its case. The District Attorney then appealed to the New York State Supreme Court, which dismissed the appeal.

At the next General Conference, in 1968, Nichols was reinstated as bishop and assigned to the Twelfth Episcopal District (Arkansas and Oklahoma). In 1970 he became a member of the General Board of the

National Council of Churches. He attended the World Methodist Conference in Denver, Colorado, in 1971, and was on the executive committee for the World Methodist Conference in Accra, Ghana, in 1975. He was also a delegate to the World Council of Churches meeting in Nairobi, Kenya, in 1975. From 1972 to 1976 he presided over the Seventh Episcopal District (South Carolina). During this time he was able to save Allen University from possible government sale for nonpayment of taxes. He officially retired in 1976, but maintained the title of presiding bishop of Liberia and chancellor of Monrovia College in Liberia. Also in 1976 he became senior bishop of the denomination. He was known as an entertaining preacher with two trademarks—a long, towel-like handkerchief that he would wave in the air by its middle and use to dry his face, and the "Nichols whoop," a "broad, gullahish scream that [sent] thrills of emotion throughout the audience," usually in conjunction with the waving of the handkerchief. In 1988 he published an auto-biographical book, *Up to Now*. In 1990 the fiftieth anniversary of his election to the episcopacy was celebrated, and it was noted that he has become the oldest living and longest tenured Methodist bishop in the world.

"Bishop D. Ward Nichols Honored in South Carolina." *The AME Christian Recorder* 139 (August 20, 1990): 8.

"Bishop Nichols Out Forever 'No Matter What!' Says Norris." *The AME Quarterly Review* 82 (January-March 1965): 40–41.

"D.A. Appeals Judges' Rule Freeing Bishop Nichols." *The AME Quarterly Review* 82 (January-March 1965): 41.

"The Life of a Bishop Can Be Pleasant." *Ebony* 12 (August 1956): 23

Nichols, Decatur Ward. *The Episcopal Addresses Presented to the Thirty-Fourth Quadrennial Session of the General Conference of the African Methodist Episcopal Church at Chicago, Illinois, May 1952.* General Conference, 1952.

———. *Up To Now.* Nashville, TN: AME Sunday School Union, 1988. 112 pp.

HUBA, AARS, HAMEC, EWM, IBAW, AMSC, WWR (77), *EAMEC, WWE* (77–78), *BAMEC.*

NICHOLS, ROY CALVIN (b. March 19, 1918), a bishop of the **United Methodist Church**, was born in Hurlock, Maryland, the son of Roy and Mamie (Waters) Nichols. He received his B.A. in 1941 from Lincoln University in Pennsylvania, and his B.D. in 1947 from the Pacific School of Religion in Berkeley, California. On July 23, 1944 he married Ruth Richardson, with whom he had three children.

His first pastorate was the South Berkeley Community Church, from 1943 to 1947. He helped found this church, one of the first interracial churches with biracial co-pastors. He was ordained deacon in 1949 and elder in 1951. From 1949 to 1964 he was assigned to Downs Memorial Methodist Church in Oakland, California, where he developed a popular radio program called "The Christian Answer." In his last year there, 1963–64, he was also president of the Berkeley Board of Education. He was a General Conference delegate beginning in 1960. From 1964 to 1968 he pastored the 2,800–member Salem Methodist Church in Harlem, New York City, and he led the congregation into a deep commitment to community service. The church built a million-dollar, four-story community center as the base for its social services. From 1964 to 1968 he was on the Board of Managers of the Methodist Hospital of Brooklyn.

In 1968 the Methodist Church merged with the Evangelical United Brethren to form the United Methodist Church, and as part of the restructuring the Central Jurisdiction, the all-Black administrative structure of the Methodist Church, was dismantled and the Black clergy and bishops were integrated into the rest of the system. That year Nichols was elected bishop, the first Black bishop elected after the dissolution of the Central Jurisdiction. He was assigned to the Pittsburgh Episcopal Area until 1980, when he was moved to the New York Episcopal Area. In 1968 he was the Frank S. Hickman lecturer on the Ministry at Duke University in Durham, North Carolina. From 1968 to 1975 he served on the Executive and Central Committees of the World Council of Churches. He was active on numerous boards and commissions, for instance, chairing the section on Project Development of the Board of Evangelism of the United Methodist Church. In 1980 he published a book of sermons, *Footsteps in the Sea*. He retired in 1984 and has since been active in local church revitalization. His most recent book, *Doing the Gospel: Local Congregations in Ministry* (1990), is directed to this revitalization concern.

Nichols, Roy C. *Doing the Gospel: Local Congregations in Ministry.* Nashville, TN: Abingdon Press, 1990. 191 pp.

———. *Footsteps in the Sea.* Nashville, TN: Abingdon Press, 1980. 126 pp.

WWABA (92–93), *WWA* (84–85), *EWM, WWR* (77), *EBA, BDNM* (75).

NORTH AMERICAN OLD ROMAN CATHOLIC CHURCH (N.A.O.R.C.C.). An Old Catholic church. The North American Old Roman Catholic Church was not intended to be a predominantly African American organization. For its first generation it was led by a White archbishop and its membership was predominantly White. Its emergence as an African American body occurred in the 1950s at the time of the transition of power.

The founding of the N.A.O.R.C.C. was occasioned by the confinement of the Duc de Landas Berghes, an Austrian citizen and an Old Catholic bishop, in America for the duration of World War I. Old Catholicism emerged in 1870 among former Roman Catholics who rejected the changes made by the First Vatican Council. They differ from Roman Catholics in rejecting the infallibility of the Pope and in allowing priests to marry. In 1916 Landas Berghes consecrated Carmel Henry Carfora, an Italian-born former Roman Catholic priest, to the episcopacy. Carfora set about the task of building a multi-ethnic church by absorbing independent Catholic parishes and consecrating priests of various ethnic backgrounds as bishops for the various segments of the church. Among his consecrations were several of Black priests, most of whom were first-generation West Indian immigrants. As early as 1941 he consecrated **Richard A. Marchenna** and the following year **Hubert A. Rogers**. He also accepted into the church **Cyrus A. Starkey**, who had originally been consecrated in the African Orthodox Church.

Bishop Rogers came to the N.A.O.R.C.C. in 1940 during a period of tension in the **African Orthodox Church**. He brought two parishes in New York City with him and in 1942 was reconsecrated by Carfora, who hoped that more of the former African Orthodox would follow Rogers's example. To further that goal, in 1946 he elevated Rogers to be Archbishop of New York and gave the archdiocese a semi-independent status as the African Apostolic Catholic Church, though Rogers remained in the N.A.O.R.R.C. House of Bishops. In the meantime, however, Carfora reached an agreement with the African Orthodox Church placing it in full communion, and in 1950 Rogers' archdiocese was fully integrated back into the N.A.O.R.C.C.

After building a rather large and integrated fellowship in the late 1940s, the church began to fall apart as several bishops left to found independent jurisdictions of their own. The largest loss came between 1950 and 1952 when the many Ukrainian parishes left to join the Ukrainian Orthodox Church. In 1952, Carfora, now aged, appointed Rogers as his primate-coadjutor. As Carfora's health failed, Rogers gradually assumed all of the church's administrative business. Then late in 1957, following an intense disagreement on church policy, Carfora removed Rogers and replaced him with Cyrus Starkey.

Carfora died a few months later in January 1958. Starkey succeeded him, but at the meeting of the church's synod in 1958 they reversed Carfora's decision and installed Rogers as the new primate of the North American Old Roman Catholic Church. Starkey left in 1960 and established a rival jurisdiction with the same name. Meanwhile, Marchenna had also left and established a rival church.

Rogers accepted the action of the synod. When the dust settled in the early 1960s, only five parishes remained in the jurisdiction. He began to rebuild the work by initiating new missionary activity in northern Black communities and in Hispanic areas of New York City. Hopeful of new life through the 1960s, the effort began to fall apart and by the 1971 synod only a couple of churches remained. At that synod, the term of primate was limited to ten years, an obvious reflection on Rogers's leadership, though he was specifically excluded from the new rule. He took it as a rejection, the following year resigned from the primacy and a few weeks later, on the thirtieth anniversary of his consecration, resigned from the church and returned to the Dutch West Indies.

Rogers was succeeded by his son, **James Hubert Rogers**. Rogers attempted to pump new life into the work and before the decade ended had jurisdiction over five parishes with a combined membership of almost a thousand. Rogers has continued to lead the church through the 1980s. Headquarters are in St. Albans, New York.

Trela, Jonathan. *A History of the North American Old Roman Catholic Church.* Scranton, PA: The Author, 1979. 124 pp.

NURSE, GLADSTONE ST. CLAIR (–1976), the primate of both the **Holy African Church** and the **African Orthodox Church** (AOC), was a member of the very first class of the African Orthodox Church's Endich Theological Seminary which opened in 1922. He was subsequently ordained as a priest. At a later date, he left the AOC and affiliated with the Holy African Church, a schism of the African Orthodox Church founded in the 1930s. He was consecrated as a bishop by **Arthur Stanley Trotman**, the church's founder, on January 9, 1939. He served as a bishop under Trotman's successors, **Robert Arthur Valentine** and **Frederich Augustus Toote**, and in 1959 succeeded Toote.

Nurse attempted to build the church in several ways. He nurtured the efforts of **G. Duncan Hinkson**, a physician who had built a congregation in Chicago. He consecrated Hinkson as a bishop in 1959. He also hoped to develop a mission among White people and to that end in 1962 consecrated Francis Anthony Vogt. Nurse is remembered most of all, however, as the one who worked out a union of the Holy African Church with the African Orthodox Church. The latter absorbed the Holy African Church in 1964. At that time, **Richard Grant Robinson** (Peter IV) was the primate of the African Orthodox Church. When Robinson died in 1967, Nurse became the new primate of the African Orthodox Church and served until his death in 1976.

"Before I came to the Christian country, my religion was the religion of 'Mohammed, the Apostle of God—may God have mercy upon him and give him peace.' I walked to the mosque before daybreak, washed my face and head and hands and feet. I prayed at noon, prayed in the afternoon, prayed at sunset, prayed in the evening. I gave almost every year, gold silver, seeds, cattle, sheep, goats, rice, wheat, and barley. I gave tithes of all the above-named things. I went every year to the holy war against the infidels. I went on pilgrimage to Mecca, as all did who were able. —My father had six sons and five daughters, and my mother had three sons and one daughter. When I left my country I was thirty-seven years old; I have been in the country of the Christians twenty-four years."

Omar ibn Said
slave
1831

O

OAKWOOD COLLEGE. A **Seventh-day Adventist Church** school. Oakwood College is a privately controlled higher education institution in Huntsville, Alabama, owned and operated by the General Conference of Seventh-day Adventists. It was founded in 1896 by the General Conference following the direction of church prophetess Ellen G. White. Influenced by Booker T. Washington's Tuskegee Institute, it was suggested by conference administrator George Irwin that the school adopt a vocational training program. The institution was first named Oakwood Industrial School with the purpose of training Black graduates of the "Morning Star" elementary schools which the Seventh-day Adventist Church operated in various southern states. It was placed under the management of S. M. Jacobs from Iowa.

In 1917 the institution introduced a two-year college program and was elevated to junior college status; hence the name was changed to Oakwood College. By 1943 senior college status had been achieved. The year 1945 saw the installation of J. L. Moran as the college's first Black president. It also marked the first year that the college awarded degrees. Oakwood was granted accreditation by the Southern Association of Colleges and Schools in 1958, an action that was approved by the Seventh-day Adventist Board of Regents. The college became a member of the United Negro College Fund in 1964.

Oakwood College today offers a diversified program. The various departments include Behavioral Sciences; Biology; Business and Information Systems; Chemistry; Education; English, Communications, Foreign Languages, and Art; History; Home Economics; Mathematics and Physics; Music; Nursing; Physical Education; and Religion and Theology. It serves as the preferred pre-seminary college for Black Adventist preachers and ranks exceptionally high among national schools for the preparation of medical professionals. The college is also involved in cooperative programs with Howard University, Alabama A & M University,

Andrews University, and the University of Alabama in Huntsville. The student body of 1,200 is composed of people from all over the United States and a number of foreign countries.

Reynolds, Louis B. *We Have Tomorrow: The Story of Seventh-day Adventists with an African Heritage.* Washington, DC: Review and Herald Publishing Association, 1984.

Schwarz, R. W. *Light Bearers to the Remnant.* Mountain View, CA: Pacific Press Publishing Association, 1979. 656 pp.

Seventh-day Adventist Encyclopedia. Washington, DC: Review and Herald Publishing Association, 1966. 1454 pp.

Keith A. Burton

OBERLIN COLLEGE. An early Congregational school and underground railroad station. Oberlin College, the first college in America to admit students irrespective of race or gender, was founded in the 1830s as two radical social movements made common cause. One movement began at Lane Theological Seminary, the new revivalist-oriented school which opened in Cincinnati in the fall of 1833. Among the first schools to admit African Americans, Lane could be said to adhere to a general anti-slavery sentiment, but held back from either an abolitionist position or condemnation of slavery as sin. Many were advocates of colonization. However, Theodore Weld, an abolitionist, joined the first class of entering students and by the spring of 1834 promoted a major debate on abolitionism.

The 18–day debate won most students to the abolitionist cause. They established an abolitionist society and became immediately involved in a variety of activist issues. Much of their activity would have been tolerated had they not also taken the next logical step. They began to treat the Black residents of Cincinnati as social equals. Their visible interaction with African Americans led White leaders in Cincinnati to turn against the school. Over the summer of 1834 the board of trustees moved to stop the activism. Some forty students withdrew in protest and organized a free seminary across town.

Meanwhile, in Lorian County, Ohio, John J. Shepherd, and Philo P. Stewart were founding a school and communal experiment. While continuing to hold private property, they were going to live as if "we held a community of property." They dedicated themselves to a plain and simple life, free of bad habits, and oriented upon charity, education, and evangelism. In need of financial support, Shepherd traveled to Cincinnati where he met Asa Mahan, one member of the board of trustees who defended the students at Lane. The visit brought together the Oberlin colony with the needs of the Lane rebels. Shepherd soon reached an agreement which brought Mahan to Oberlin as the new president of the school and won the support of businessman Arthur Tappan, whose money followed the dissenting seminary students. Evangelist Charles G. Finney joined the faculty as professor of theology, and he and Mahan demanded that African Americans be admitted as students.

The emergence of Oberlin came just as a conservative response to abolitionism was sweeping the colleges of the United States. Over 300 students, many pushed out of their former school, arrived for the first year. By 1835 it had grown beyond its capacity to physically house the student body. Ten to twenty percent of the student body was Black and included both men and women. Classes, boarding, and eating facilities were completely integrated. The college became a stop on the underground railroad and a Fund for Fugitives was established to pay for the needs of escaped slaves. Finney led in the development of a position of civil disobedience as the school rejected new measures aimed at the return of slaves found in the state. Symbolic of the school's attitude was its refusal to celebrate July 4 (which acknowledged the freedom of Whites only) and its substitution with a celebration on August 1, the date of the emancipation of the slaves in the West Indies.

Oberlin's influence on the Black community was immense. A number of African Americans owed their freedom to the college. Many of its graduates went on to become leaders in the post-Civil War African American community. Two Oberlinites, Lewis Sheridan Leary and John A. Copeland, would join John Brown at Harper's ferry and give their life in the struggle. Oberlin also became the inspiration for other efforts at education for African Americans, most notably Wilberforce University.

Dayton, Donald W. *Discovering an Evangelical Heritage.* New York: Harper & Row, 1976. 147 pp.

Fairchild, Jams H. *Oberlin: The College and the Colony, 1833–1883.* Oberlin, OH: E. J. Goodrich, 1883.
Henry, Stuart C. "The Lane Rebels: A Twentieth Century Look." *Journal of Presbyterian History* (Spring 1971): 1-14.

OBLATE SISTERS OF PROVIDENCE. A religious order of the **Roman Catholic Church.** The Oblate Sisters of Providence is a community of Roman Catholic nuns founded in 1829 in Baltimore, Maryland. It is the oldest community of Black sisters in the United States, and one of the first religious communities of strictly American origin.

By 1829 there was a community of Blacks, most of whom were of Haitian origin, worshipping in the basement of the St. Mary's Seminary chapel. Jacques Joubert, S.S., a French Sulpician priest who had served in Haiti as a government official until the revolution, was appointed to minister to the needs of this Black community. Concerned about the education of the children of the community, Joubert learned that three Haitian women had begun a free school for the children in their home. **Elizabeth Lange** was the leader. She had been born in Cuba of Haitian parents of some means and came to the United States by way of the Carolinas about 1817. Assisting Elizabeth Lange were two other Haitian women, Marie Madeleine Balas and Rosine Boegue. Later they were joined by a young girl who had been with them as a student, Almaide (Therese) Maxis Duchemin, whose Haitian mother subsequently joined the community, as did the mother of Elizabeth Lange. Therese Duchemin would also become one of the founders of the Sister Servants of the Immaculate Heart of Mary in Monroe, Michigan. For these women becoming a part of a sisterhood was a considered step which they took eagerly.

On July 2, 1829, they made their vows as sisters. They had the approval of Archbishop James Whitfield, who supported them despite the hostility of many in Baltimore to the idea of Black nuns. In 1831 the Oblate Sisters of Providence were approved by Pope Gregory XVI. In the beginning the sisters renewed their vows annually on the Feast of the Visitation of the Blessed Virgin (July 2nd, at that time). Only later did they take perpetual vows.

Much of the original rule was written by Joubert himself. One of the patron saints of the new community was St. Frances of Rome (1384–1440), who had established a community of religious women in Rome who were not cloistered nuns but worked among the poor of Rome and were known as oblates. Another patron was the African Sicilian, St. Benedict the Moor (1526–1589), a Franciscan friar who had been canonized in 1807. The spirituality afforded the sisters, however, was the French spirituality of the eighteenth and nineteenth century.

As early as 1830 Black American women began entering the community. Some were freed slaves who came into the novitiate with their manumission papers. The religious habit was a White bonnet, black cape, and black dress. Only in 1906 did they begin to wear the veil.

The sisters adopted at the outset the task of the education of Black children. As soon as they became a religious community, they opened a school for girls. At a time when little was provided for the education of Black children, their contribution was very important. In 1852 they began a school for boys. From the beginning, orphan girls had lived with the community. In 1865 they opened an orphanage for Black children in Baltimore, many of them the children of African Americans orphaned by the Civil War.

After the death of Joubert in 1843, the community was neglected by the hierarchy. Archbishop Samuel Eccleston, who succeeded Whitfield as archbishop in 1834, had little sympathy for the sisters. Thanks to a young Bavarian priest, Thaddeus Anwander, C.S.S.R. (1823–1893), pastor of a German parish in Baltimore, the sisters received renewed support. In 1847, Anwander went to Eccleston and received permission to become chaplain. He was encouraged in this initiative by his superior, St. John Neumann (1811–1860), later the bishop of Philadelphia. The Oblates were rejuvenated and a period of growth began.

The Oblate Sisters of Providence opened schools on the east coast, in the Midwest, and in the South. Before the Cuban revolution, they had convents in Cuba and are presently in Costa Rica. These religious women played an important role in the growth of Catholicism among African Americans from the second quarter of the nineteenth century to the present day. At the same time their presence in pre-Civil War Baltimore, which as a religious community attracted so many young Black women from all parts of the east coast, stands as a silent witness to the depth of religious conviction among African American Catholics of the time. In recent times, a formal investigation into the possibility of making Elizabeth Lange (+1882) a saint has begun.

Mother Lange was succeeded by Mother Mary Francis Fielders and Mother M. Consuella. Today the order is headed by Sister Mary Alice Chineworth. In the 1960s the order had over 300 sisters under vows. Today (as other orders have begun to welcome African Americans into their membership), the number has shrunk to around 150. Headquarters is at the Motherhouse in Baltimore.

Davis, Cyprian. *The History of Black Catholics in the United States*. New York: Crossroad, 1990.

Dehey, Elinor Tong. *Religious Orders of Women in the United States*. Cleveland, OH: The Author, 1930. 908 pp.

Gerdes, Sister M. Reginald. "To Educate and Evangelize: Black Catholic Schools of the Oblate Sisters of Providence (1828–1880)," *U. S. Catholic Historian* 7 (1988): 183–199.

Lord, Daniel A. *Our Nuns*. New York: Benziger Brothers, 1924. 280 pp.

Sherwood, Grace. *The Oblates' Hundred and One Years*. New York: Macmillan Company, 1931.

Cyprian Davis

ODEN, DANIEL FELIX, a minister of the **Church of God (Anderson, Indiana)**, was born and raised in Alabama, where he encountered the Church of God (Anderson, Indiana), a predominantly White, but, at the time, integrated Holiness church. He was ordained in 1892 by two White ministers, Joseph F. Lundy and C. C. Collins, who were working to spread the church's teachings in the South. In 1895 Oden began a 22-year pastorate in Bessmer, Alabama, west of Birmingham. He emerged as one of the leading pastors in the Church of God and was frequently invited to speak at the annual national camp meeting.

Oden pushed the developing missionary program of the church and in 1909 was named as a charter member of the missionary board. Among his first contributions was an article on African missions in the first issue of the board's periodical, the *Missionary Herald*. In 1911, on behalf of the board, he took a missionary tour to Europe, Africa, and the Holy Land. While in Africa he became ill and it was thought that he would probably die, but he experienced a sudden recovery. It was later reported that his recovery occurred simultaneously with the prayers of his wife Rosa, home in Alabama. His experience did not stop his travels, and the following year he visited Cuba and Mexico.

In 1917 Oden moved to Detroit to become the pastor of a new congregation which had been formed by the split of Bethany Church of God, the original Church of God congregation in the city. It had been founded in 1900 by T. J. Cox, a White man. In 1910 he had been succeeded by Christina Janes, a Black woman, under whom the congregation had measurable growth. However, in 1914 the church experienced the emerging controversy over the advisability of interracial congregations of the Church of God that had split churches throughout the country. Janes resigned rather than give in to a segregated church. In 1915 the African

American members reluctantly formed a second congregation with Sarah A. Foster as the transition minister. The new congregation retained the name of the original church, the Church of God of Detroit.

Beginning with twelve members, by 1920 there were 50 members, and during the 1920s the church had been able to purchase property upon which to erect permanent facilities. The new building was well under way when the Depression hit and they were unable to finish until the 1940s. Meanwhile, Oden developed pneumonia and on December 17, 1931, died.

Callen, Barry L., ed. *The First Century: The Church of God Reformation Movement.* 2 vols. Anderson, IN: Warner Press, 1979.

Hetrick, Gale. *Laughter among the Trumpets.* Anderson, IN: Ministerial Assembly of the Church of God of Michigan, 1980. 250 pp.

OLIVIER, LEONARD JAMES (b. October 12, 1923), a bishop of the **Roman Catholic Church**, was born in Lake Charles, Louisiana, the son of James Lawrence and Mathielde (Rochon) Olivier. He attended St. Augustine's Seminary (1939–42), St. Mary's Seminary in Techny, Illinois (1942–46), and St. Augustine's Major Seminary in Bay St. Louis, Mississippi (1946–52). He was ordained a priest on June 29, 1951, associated with the **Society of the Divine Word** (S.V.D.). He received his M.A. in 1961 from Catholic University of America in Washington, D.C.

Olivier was assistant dean of students at St. Augustine's Major Seminary from 1952 to 1956 and head dean from 1956 to 1967. In 1967 he became rector of the seminary. On December 20, 1988, he was consecrated Auxiliary Bishop of Washington.

BDNM (75), *CAA*.

OPERATION PUSH. An ecumenical organization. Operation PUSH developed from Operation Breadbasket, a program established in the mid-1960s by **Martin Luther King, Jr.**, and the **Southern Christian Leadership Conference** (SCLC). In 1965 King introduced the program to Chicago and chose a young seminarian, **Jesse L. Jackson**, to lead it. Jackson made a success of it quickly, and in 1967 was made the national director.

The program was simple. Business operating in the Black community which did not hire and/or train African Americans were approached to reverse their policies. If they did not they were subject to an organized boycott.

The most successful boycott was directed at the A&P Food Stores. The program was in full swing when King was killed in 1968. **Ralph D. Abernathy** succeeded King, and over the next three years, Jackson developed a number of disagreements with his leadership. In 1971 he left SCLC and took most of the Chicago chapter with him. On Christmas Day, he reorganized as Operation PUSH (People United to Serve Humanity).

PUSH continued the program which had worked so well for Operation Breadbasket. It initially developed three emphases. It sought a betterment of the life of African Americans economically, especially in relation to corporate business structures. It championed political empowerment, especially as it related to their voter rights. Finally, it picked up on King's concern with the international escalation with the arms race. From these three beginning points it developed a multifaceted program looking toward Black liberation.

PUSH is oriented on the moral traditions of Judaism and Christianity and with the nonviolent approach of Henry Thoreau, Gandhi, and King. It seeks to spread moral values in the Black community, and has developed self-esteem programs for the schools. However, systemic economic changes which bring the African American community into the mainstream of American business life remain a primary focus.

Headquarters of Operation PUSH is in Chicago, with some 20 affiliates around the country. Through the 1980s, as Jackson's presidential aspirations blossomed, he gradually severed his ties to the organization. He was succeeded by Rev. Willie T. Burrow, who retired as executive director in 1989. The position was filled by Rev. Tyron Crider from 1989–91.

Hatch, Roger D. *Beyond Opportunity: Jesse Jackson's Vision for America.* Philadelphia, PA: Fortress Press, 10988. 165 pp.

Poinsett, Alex. "PUSH for Excellence." *Ebony* 32 (February 1977): 104–111.

ORGANIZATION OF BLACK EPISCOPAL SEMINARIANS. An **Episcopal Church** group. The organization is a fraternal and support group for the Black students training for the ministry. It is headquartered in New York City.

ORIGINAL CHURCH OF GOD (OR SANCTIFIED CHURCH). A Holiness church. The Original Church of God (or Sanctified Church) was formed in 1927 but continues the previous work of Elder Charles W. Gray (1861–1945) in Nashville, Tennessee. Gray originally founded a congregation in Nashville, affiliated with the Holiness movement begun by **Charles Price Jones** and **Charles H. Mason**. After Harrison and Jones split, Jones incorporated the **Church of Christ (Holiness), U.S.A.** with an episcopal polity. Gray agreed doctrinally with Jones, but did not wish to incorporate and preferred a congregational church polity. He kept the Nashville work out of Jones's church and began to build the **Church of God (Sanctified Church)**.

In 1927 a move developed to incorporate the Church of God and to place it under the guidance of a board of elders. The move succeeded and the church of God incorporated. At that time, Gray and those who opposed the incorporation left and reorganized on the older pattern under the name Original Church of God (or Sanctified Church).

The 1927 break did not involve doctrine, and the Original Church of God continued to teach the holiness doctrine common to the Church of Christ (Holiness) and the Church of God (Sanctified Church). Headquarters is in Nashville. In the early 1970s there were 85 churches and approximately 4,500 members.

ORIGINAL GLORIOUS CHURCH OF GOD IN CHRIST APOSTOLIC FAITH.

An Apostolic Pentecostal church. The Original Glorious Church of God in Christ emerged from a controversy in 1952 in the **Glorious Church of God in Christ Apostolic Faith**. In that year, presiding bishop S. C. Bass, who had for many years preached against the remarriage of divorced persons, married a divorcee. Opposition to Bass's continued leadership came from a group of ministers and laity led by Bishop W. O. Howard. Taking possession of the group's charter, Howard's following reorganized at the Original Glorious Church of God in Christ Apostolic Faith. Since no doctrinal issues were at stake, the beliefs and practice follow that of the parent body.

Howard led the group until 1972 when he retired due to poor health. He is credited with keeping together a group which had appeared ready to fly apart. Beginning with around 25 congregations, he saw another 15 added to the fellowship. Howard was succeeded by Bishop I. W. Hamiter, under whose leadership the church has shown spectacular growth. By 1980 the church had added an additional fifteen congregations and membership had grown to approximately 25,000. The real growth has been overseas, where over a hundred congregations were built. Hamiter also led in the development of a convention center in Columbus, Ohio, where the headquarters is currently located.

ORIGINAL HEBREW ISRAELITE NATION.

Black Jewish group. The Original Hebrew Israelite Nation began in the mid-1960s in Chicago following a vision received by Ben Ammi Carter. Carter had been given a bleak picture of the future of Black people in America, partially a result of the unrest of the 1960s. Through his vision he began to see a way out. He taught that Black people were the true Hebrews, the present-day Jews being impostors. He also believed that the Holy Land was the true home for the Black Hebrews. The first believers were gathered by Carter and Shaleah Ben-Yehuda at the A-Beta Hebrew Center on Chicago's South Side.

As early as 1967, the first group of his followers began to leave America. Unable to enter Israel, they settled in Liberia. In 1969 the first group finally arrived in Israel. Over 300 migrated over the next two years, until strict immigration restrictions were placed upon them by the Israeli government. In spite of restrictions and several deportations, some 1,000 had migrated by 1980. Many came on tourist visas and simply never went home. Carter settled with the group in Israel. To prevent their return to the United States, a number of the group renounced their American citizenship. Meanwhile, the movement was spreading through the Black communities in the United States. The American branch of the movement was led by Prince Asiel Ben Israel (born Warren Brown), one of the council of twelve princes who with Carter lead the movement.

The followers in Israel ran into a number of problems. Not really welcomed, they were able to obtain only the barest of necessities and inadequate housing. The government has questioned the legality of some members' migration and has refused to assign housing to them. While keeping many Jewish practices, the followers abandoned the synagogue structures and installed a system of polygamy (by which men could have up to seven wives).

Serious trouble emerged around 1980 as charges were made of the group's involvement in illegal activity, primarily fraud and the theft of credit cards and plane tickets to facilitate the movement of members to Israel. The FBI launched a raid. The first arrest was made the following year. Over the next five years a number of arrests were made. In 1986 Prince Asiel Ben Israel and 31 other leaders were tried on a variety of racketeering charges. Prince Asiel was convicted (along with several other leaders) and was given a sentence of ten to thirty years. Members of the group are still active in both Israel and America.

[Carter], Ben Ammi. *God and the Law of Relativity*. Washington, DC: Communicators, 1991. 131 pp.

———. *God, the Black Man, and Truth.* Chicago: Communicators Press, 1982. 242 pp.

———. *The Messiah and the End of the World.* Washington, DC: Communicators Press, 1991. 164 pp.

Gerber, Israel J. *The Heritage Seekers: Black Jews in Search of Identity.* Middle Village, NY: Jonathan David Publishers, 1977. 222 pp.

Whitfield, Thomas. *From Night to Sunlight.* Nashville, TN: Broadman Press, 1980. 189 pp.

Yehuda, Shaleak Ben. *Black Hebrew Israelites from America to the Promised Land.* New York: Vantage Press, 1975. 357 pp.

ORIGINAL UNITED HOLY CHURCH INTERNATIONAL.

A Holiness Pentecostal church. The Original United Holy Church International resulted from a split in the United Holy Church of America in 1977. Through the 1970s, Bishop **James A. Forbes** of the Southern District Convocation had a running feud with the church's president, Bishop W. N. Strobhar. The Southern District Convocation was the parent body of the national church. It had been organized in 1894 in North Carolina. As the church grew into a national body, the Southern District remained the largest district, encompassing almost half of the denomination. In the 1970s, Bishop Forbes complained of unfair treatment toward the district by the general church.

A hint of the future split occurred in 1972 when the Southern District reincorporated. Their action had the added effect of disincorporating the national church, and threw the denomination into a constitutional crisis. Attempts to reconcile the two groups were made over the next five years, but failed. In 1977, the general church disfellowshipped the Southern District which reorganized under its present name. The new church carried all but seven of the congregations in the district into the new organization. In addition, the denomination's mission field in Liberia aligned itself to the southern group. Two years after its formation, the Original United Holy Church International worked out an agreement of affiliation with the International Pentecostal Holiness Church. As part of the agreement, the International Pentecostal Holiness Church publishes the United Holy Church's periodical, *Voice of the World*, at its publishing concern in Franklin Springs, Georgia.

As there was no doctrinal dispute in the controversy, the Original United Holy Church adheres to the same doctrinal position as the United Holy Church in America. Headquarters of the church are in Goldsboro, North Carolina. A school, United Christian College, is also located there.

Jones, Charles Edwin. *Black Holiness: Guide to the Study of Black Participation in Wesleyan Perfectionist and Glossolalic Pentecostal Movements.* Metuchen, NJ: American Theological Library Association/Scarecrow Press, 1987. 388 pp.

Payne, Wardell J., ed. *Directory of African American Religious Bodies: A Compendium by the Howard University School of Divinity.* Washington, DC: Howard University Press, 1991. 363 pp.

ORTHODOX CATHOLIC CHURCH IN AMERICA.

An Eastern Orthodox group. The Orthodox Catholic Church was founded in 1927 as the American Catholic Church, Archdiocese of New York, by **James Francis Augustine Lashley**. The church received its orders from the **African Orthodox Church** through Bishop William Frederick Tyarcks, a White bishop who had been consecrated by Archbishop **George Alexander McGuire**.

Lashley described the American Catholic Church as being like the Old Catholic Church in Europe but not in direct contact with it. It followed pre-Vatican I Roman Catholic belief and practice. It denies the infallibility of the Pope and allows priests to marry. In recent years it has moved more into the Eastern Orthodox beliefs and practice, though it practices a western rite.

During his lengthy tenure as head of the church, Lashley consecrated a number of bishops including Sydney James Ferguson, Samuel T. Garner, Joel N. Ashby, W. G. Almeida, and **Michael Edward Verra**. In 1941 Lashley reported four churches and by 1947 there were twenty, nine in the United States and eleven in the West Indies. This number remained somewhat stable for the next three decades. In 1980, the church reported seven churches and approximately 700 members in the United States. In the mid-1980s, Lashley was succeeded by Archbishop Verra, who changed the name of the church to that presently used, a name more reflective of its Orthodox life.

Ward, Gary L. *Independent Bishops: An International Directory.* Detroit: Apogee Books, 1990. 524 pp.

OTTLEY, JAMES HAMILTON

(b. June 27, 1936), a bishop of the **Episcopal Church**, was born in Colón, Republic of Panama. He received his M.Div. in 1964 from the Seminario Episcopal del Caribe and his B.S. in psychology in 1968 from the University of Panama. He married Lillian García, with whom he has had four children.

Ottley was ordained a deacon and a priest in 1964. From 1964 to 1969 he was an assistant at St. Paul's Episcopal Church in the Republic of Panama. In 1970–71 he was priest-in-charge of St. George's Episcopal Church and St. Mary's Episcopal Church in Boca del Toro, Republic of Panama. From 1969 to 1972 he was a member of the executive council of the (Protestant) Episcopal Church of the U.S.A., and was a delegate to General Convention in 1970 and 1973. In 1971–72 he was assigned to St. Alban's Episcopal Church in Paraiso and St. Simon's Episcopal Church in Gamboa, both in the Republic of Panama, and was chaplain of the Corozal Mental Health Institute. In 1973 he finished an M.A. in psychology at the Centro Caribeno de Estudio de Postgrado, Puerto Rico.

From about 1973 to 1976 Ottley was chaplain of the Bella Vista Children's Home and the Episcopal University Center. He edited two provincial periodicals, *Conciencia* and *Mundo Episcopal*. From 1977 to 1984 he was rector of St. Paul's Episcopal Church. From 1974 to 1983 he was also professor of Developmental Psychology and Personality at the University of Panama in Panama City. On January 21, 1984, he was consecrated bishop of the Diocese of Panama. He has served as a member of the Theological Education Commission for Latin America and the Caribbean, a member of the Standing Commission on Ecumenical Affairs, a member of the Joint Commission on Autonomy for Province IX, and as Coordinator of the Christian Education Commission for Province IX.

ECA (1985).

"The Holy Ghost through me was teaching men to look to God, for He is the only help. I told them not to trust in the power of the United States, England, France or Germany, but to trust in God. The enemy (the devil) tried to hinder me from preaching the unadulterated word of God. He plotted against me and had the white people to arrest me and put me in jail for several days. I thank God for the persecution. 'For all that live godly must suffer persecution.' 2 Tim. 3:12."

Charles Harrison Mason, Founder
Church of God in Christ

P

PACKARD, SOPHIA B. (January 3, 1824–June 21, 1891), co-founder of Spelman College and a founder of the Woman's American Baptist Home Mission Society, was born in New Salem, Massachusetts, the fifth child of Winslow and Rachel (Freeman) Packard. She grew up on a farm, and the family was very pious. At the age of fourteen she began to teach in rural schools, and thereafter studied and taught in alternate years. In 1845 she briefly attended the New Salem Academy and in 1850 she graduated from the Charleston Massachusetts Female Academy, where she became a teacher. In 1855 she returned to New Salem Academy to teach.

At the New Salem Academy Packard met Harriet E. Giles, who became a lifelong friend. In 1856 the two moved to Orange, Massachusetts, where they taught for three years. They then tried briefly to open their own school in Fitchburg, Massachusetts, but in the fall of 1859 both accepted positions at the Connecticut Literary Institution in Suffield, Connecticut. In the fall of 1864 they moved together to the Oread Collegiate Institute in Worcester, Massachusetts, where Giles taught music and "ornamentals," and Packard taught metaphysics and literature and was co-principal. In 1867 a poor relationship with a new principal caused them to leave, and they spent the next twelve years in Boston.

In 1870, after a stint with the Empire Life Insurance Company, Packard became assistant to Rev. George C. Lorimer of the Shawmut Avenue Baptist Church. He held her in very high regard and willingly paved the way for this unusual position. When he moved to the Tremont Temple Baptist Church in Boston in 1873, she also moved and maintained her position there. She was responsible for conducting the women's prayer meeting, teaching Bible class in the Sunday School, and visiting the sick. In 1877 she helped organize the Woman's American Baptist Home Mission Society as an auxiliary to the American Baptist Home Mission Society. The new group was dedicated to the needs of the newly freed Blacks of the South. She presided at the first meeting and in 1878 became the corresponding secretary.

In February 1880 Packard traveled to the South to see in person where help was most needed, and returned determined to establish a school for Black women in Georgia. The Woman's American Baptist Home Mission Society finally decided to back the idea in March 1881 and soon Packard and Giles moved to Atlanta, Georgia. On April 11, 1881, they opened the Atlanta Baptist Female Academy in the basement of the Friendship Baptist Church, pastored by Rev. Frank Quarles. By that summer the enrollment had reached eighty girls and women of all ages, but the society dropped its support. Packard and Giles gamely continued their work, and the following January the support was renewed. Packard and Giles not only taught the regular classes, they also led Bible studies, held prayer meetings, conducted Sunday schools, and taught sewing.

In December 1882 the American Baptist Home Mission Society made a down payment on nine acres of land in Atlanta with five former Union Army buildings, and the school gained new quarters. John D. Rockefeller helped pay off the mortgage in 1884 and the school was renamed Spelman Seminary in honor of Mr. and Mrs. Harvey Buel Spelman, the abolitionist parents of Mrs. John D. Rockefeller. In 1888 the school was granted a charter by the state, and Packard became treasurer of the board of trustees as well as president of the school. She became ill in 1890 and took an apparently refreshing trip to the Holy Land, but died the following year of a cerebral hemorrhage. At her death the school counted 464 students and 34 faculty, and Giles succeeded her in the presidency. In 1924 the school became Spelman College, and in 1929 both it and its men's counterpart, Morehouse College, affiliated with Atlanta University.

NAW, FAW, EBA, LW, BDAE, NCAB (2), *NNW.*

PAGE, EMMETT MOORE (May 9, 1971–January 4, 1944), a bishop of the **Church of God in Christ**, was born on a farm near Yazoo, Mississippi, and lived there until he was 23. He was a member of the **African Methodist Episcopal Church** and had an experience of conversion as a youth of thirteen. In 1894 he left the farm and moved to Jackson, Tennessee, where he worked his way through Lane College. He was employed by the Illinois Central Railroad for many years. During these years he had been an active Methodist, but in 1902 was converted to Holiness by a traveling evangelist. In 1903 he traveled to Memphis where he met and was immediately impressed by **Charles H. Mason**, founder of the Church of God in Christ. He joined the Holiness church then headed by Mason.

In 1907 Mason traveled to Los Angeles where he experienced the Pentecostal baptism of the Holy Spirit as evidenced by speaking in tongues. Later that year he called an assembly of those who had accepted his new departure from standard Holiness belief and practice. Page was among those who gathered in Memphis, Tennessee, to elect Mason the first Chief Apostle of the Church of God in Christ.

Page was holding down a job and preaching and calling together new churches on the weekend. He attended the first Holy Convocation in November 1909 following the settling of all matters with the Holiness brethren who did not accept the baptism of the Holy Spirit. The Church of God in Christ was formally organized at that meeting. By 1911 the work had grown to the point that Page was able to quit his job and become a full-time minister. At the convocation in 1914, Page was appointed overseer for the state of Texas and he moved to Dallas.

Under Page's leadership, the work in Texas blossomed. At the time Page arrived in Dallas, there were 25 missions and few buildings. By 1919 there were 80 congregations and missions and some 35 buildings. By 1925 there were 135 congregations. Page's accomplishments were recognized in 1935 by his selection as one of the five original bishops of the church and his consecration to that office by Mason. His original territory included ten states across the Southwest from Mississippi to California and the state of Wisconsin. During the remaining years of his life, Page traveled widely and took an active role in his domain. Active for many years in the Ministerial alliance in Dallas, at one point he served as vice president of the Interdenominational Ministerial Alliance in Oklahoma City. He died in Dallas in 1944.

Cornelius, Lucille J. *The Pioneer History of the Church of God in Christ.* [San Francisco]: The Author, 1975. 102 pp.
DuPree, Sherry Sherrod. *Biographical Dictionary of African-American Holiness-Pentecostals, 1880–1990.* Washington, DC: Middle Atlantic Regional Press, 1989. 386 pp.
Mason, Mary Esther. *The History and Life Work of Elder C. H. Mason and His Co-Laborers.* N.p.: n.d. 93 pp.

PAINE COLLEGE. A **Christian Methodist Episcopal Church**, (CME) school. Paine College, Augusta, Georgia, grew out of the continuing cooperation between the CME Church and the Methodist Episcopal Church, South (MECS), from which it had been separated in 1870. In 1882, the MECS established an education commission under the leadership of Bishop George F. Pierce and a fund to establish a CME school. That summer in Atlanta Pierce and the commission met with the CME bishops **Lucius Holsey**, **William H. Miles**, **Joseph A. Beebe**, and **Isaac Lane**. They chose Augusta, Georgia, as a site. The MECS agreed to long-term support for Paine, which is continued to the present by the **United Methodist Church** into which the MECS merged.

Early in 1883 Holsey met with Morgan Calloway of Emory College and George Williams Walker, a presiding elder of the MECS in South Carolina, to organize the school. Walker was named president of the new venture. Holsey had recruited approximately 30 students. A board drawing members from both churches was created. During the first decades of its existence Paine was headed by a member of the MECS. Walker's 30-year tenure as president provided a much-needed stability. In 1971 the first African American president, Lucius Henry Pitts, was named.

Lakey, Othel H. *The History of the C.M.E. Church.* Memphis, TN: CME Publishing House, 1985. 683 pp.

PAN AFRICAN ORTHODOX CHRISTIAN CHURCH. A Black nationalist Christian church. The Pan African Orthodox Christian Church was founded by former members of the predominantly Black St. Mark's Presbyterian Church in Detroit, Michigan. In 1953, under the leadership of their pastor, Albert B. Cleage, Jr., they walked out of their sanctuary into new facilities and formed the Central Congregational Church. During the heated years of the civil rights movement, the church assumed a leadership role on issues of social change for Black people.

In 1967 Cleage preached a famous sermon calling

for a new Black theology and a responsive Black church ready to articulate it and act upon it. The sermon became the manifesto for a Black Christian Nationalist Movement. To dramatize the work, Cleage displayed for the first time a large painting of the Madonna as a Black woman. The Central Congregational Church became known as the Shrine of the Black Madonna. Cleage's first book, *The Black Messiah*, was published the following year and in 1969 his biography, *Prophet of the Black Nation*, appeared. Eventually the organization broke with the United Church of Christ, with which it had previously been associated.

Cleage changed his name to **Jaramogi Abebe Agyeman**, Swahili for "Liberator, blessed man, savior of the nation." He developed the ideas only hinted at in his sermon. He centered his thought on Jesus, whom he described as a Black revolutionary leader. Jesus was sent by God to free Black people from their exploitation and oppression at the hands of a White-dominated world. He called upon his followers to forsake individualism for the sake of the struggle. This perspective was enlarged upon in his second book, *Black Christian Nationalism* (1972).

Through the 1970s Agyeman led in the expansion of the movement, which assumed the corporate name of Pan African Orthodox Christian Church, and established three new centers in Detroit and one each in Atlanta, Georgia, Kalamazoo, Michigan, and Houston, Texas. He ordained ministers to serve the new congregations. They were given the title "Mwalimu," Swahili for teacher.

The seven centers have remained the base of Agyeman's efforts to aid the liberation of Black people. The work has included a major effort to teach Black history and instill pride in Black people through contact with their African heritage. The centers have also launched a number of social services designed to benefit the economically deprived.

Cleage, Albert B., Jr. "A Black Man's View of Authority." In Clyde L. Manchereck, ed. *Erosion of Authority*. Nashville, TN: Abingdon, 1971, pp. 59–91.

———. *Black Christian Nationalism: Directions for the Black Church*. New York: William Morrow, 1972. 312 pp.

———. *The Black Messiah*. New York: Sheed and Ward, 1968. 278 pp.

Ward, Hiley H. *Prophet to the Black Nation*. New York: Pilgrim Press, 1969. 222 pp.

PARIS, HAILU MOSHE, a Black Jewish rabbi, was born in Ethiopia among the **Falashas**, or Ethiopian Jews. In 1936, during the invasion of Ethiopia by Mussolini, he was adopted by an African American Jew, Eudora Paris, an immigrant to America from the West Indies, who had originally been converted to Judaism by **Arnold Josiah Ford**. After Ford left for Ethiopia, she attended the **Commandment Keepers Congregation of the Living God** led by Ford's disciple Rabbi **Wentworth A. Matthew**. Matthew took the boy under his tutelage and prepared him for bar mitzvah. The family also attended B'nai Israel, a synagogue in Harlem which derived from Matthew's work. After finishing high school, Paris attended New York City College for a period and later spent two years in Israel at Yeshiva Daraoma in Rehovot. He completed his A.B. at Yeshiva University in New York in 1968. In 1968 he completed his M.A. in Jewish education. He then joined the staff of the Horace Mann High School in Manhattan.

Ordained by Matthew upon his return from Israel, he became the rabbi at B'nai Israel in 1958. While at Yeshiva he attended the Orthodox Mount Horeb Congregation in the South Bronx where he assisted Rabbi Albert J. Moses. When Moses died in 1971, he succeeded him as rabbi. Because of the changing neighborhood, he led the congregation to move into new quarters in Queens in 1976.

Paris has been called upon to articulate the role of the Black Jews to both the White Jewish community and African Americans. During the 1960s he was especially active in attempts to bring reconciliation between the Black Jews and those of like faith in the White community, but eventually became discouraged of making any alliance with them. On the other hand he has had to defend his position to African Americans who do not understand the small Black Jewish community and its identification with Judaism, whose followers many African Americans have come to view as oppressors of Black people.

Rudin, Marcia R., and A. James Rudin. "Black Jews in America: Rabbi Hailu Moshe Paris and His People." *Present Tense* 7, 1 (Autumn 1979): 37–41.

PARKS, HENRY BLANTON (c.1856–February, 1936), 32nd bishop of the **African Methodist Episcopal Church** (AME), was born in Georgia. He was converted at an early age and joined Bethel AME Church in Atlanta, Georgia. He was educated at Atlanta University and became a minister in the AME Church. After serving a number of local churches, in 1896 he was elected Missionary Secretary for the denomination, and in that capacity edited the *Voice of Missions*. In 1896 he helped establish a friendship with the Ethiopian Church of South Africa, which enabled Bishop **Henry M. Turner** in 1898 to go to South Africa and organize the Cape and Transvaal Conferences.

After twelve years as missionary secretary, Parks was elected bishop in 1908 and assigned to Alabama and Tennessee. After the death of Bishop **Abram Grant** in 1911 he was given the additional work of the Fifth Episcopal District, comprising most of the western United States. In 1911 he was a delegate to the Ecumenical Methodist Conference in Toronto, Canada, and delivered one of the welcome addresses. He served the Fifth District exclusively from 1924 to 1936, and organized the Southern California Conference in September, 1925. He then bought a home in Oakland, California, becoming the first bishop to establish his episcopal residence on the West Coast. He was president of the Financial Board from 1912 to 1916 and was head of the Missionary Board at the time of his death. He was widely regarded as one of the finest preachers in all of Methodism, and delivered the Quadrennial Sermon at the Centennial General Conference in 1916. Churches are named for him in California, Missouri, Alabama, Nebraska, and Illinois.

Parks, Henry Blanton. *Africa. The Problem of the New Century. The Part the AME Church is to Have in Its Solution.* New York: Board of Home and Foreign Missionary Department of the AME Church, 1899. 66 pp.

———. "Bishop Henry McNeal Turner as Missionary and Promoter of Missions." In Henry McNeal Turner, ed. *Quarto-Centennial.* N.p.: N.p., 1905, pp. 149–155.

———. *The Redemption of Africa.* N.p.: N.p., n.d.

CEAMEC, BAMEC, WWCR, HUBA, AARS, BAW.

PATTERSON, JAMES OGLETHORPE, SR. (July 21, 1912–December 29, 1989), presiding bishop of the **Church of God in Christ**, was born in Derma, Mississippi, one of six children born to William Marion and Mollie Edwards Patterson. When he was eleven, the family moved to Memphis, Tennessee, the headquarters of their church, the Church of God in Christ, the largest Pentecostal church in the United States. Patterson decided to pursue a ministerial career, and attended the Howe School of Religion in Memphis, Tennessee, where he received his Th.M. degree. In 1934 he married Deborah Indiana Mason, daughter of **Charles H. Mason**, founder of the Church of God in Christ. He and Deborah had two children.

After some time in the dry cleaning and coal retailing business, he was ordained in 1936, and assigned to an eight-member church in nearby Gates. After serving a series of West Tennessee churches, he built a new headquarters church, the Pentecostal Temple Church of God on Wellington Street in Memphis, Tennessee, where he remained the rest of his career. In 1952 he became a part of the denomination's executive board, and in 1953 Mason consecrated him as a bishop of the church. He served as jurisdictional supervisor and bishop in Tennessee. Bishop Mason died in 1961, touching off a bitter debate within the church about the process of succession for that office. **Ozro Thurston Jones, Sr.,** was selected presiding bishop in 1962 by the executive board, but a powerful faction believed that a general election was necessary. Finally, at the 61st International Convocation in 1968, a restructuring was accomplished, and Patterson was elected presiding bishop on November 15. He retained this office for the rest of his life, being reelected every quadrennium.

During the 1960s Patterson had gained the respect of the younger generation in the church by being one of the few Pentecostal leaders willing to support the civil rights movement. While his colleagues felt that clergy should avoid political action, Patterson was a leader in the Memphis Ministers and Citizens League and supported sit-in demonstrations. As the new presiding bishop, he founded the church's first graduate school of religion, the Charles Harrison Mason Theological Seminary, which joined four other Black schools in Atlanta's Interdenominational Theological Center. He also founded a denominational bookstore and publishing house, the C. H. Mason System of Bible Colleges, the Historical Museum and Fine Arts Center, and the Charles Harrison Mason Foundation.

Under Patterson's direction the church's financial condition improved greatly. In 1970 he ran the first thorough census of church membership, revealing a far stronger following than had been anticipated, reaching three million in the 1980s. He founded the Chisca Hotel and Motel to provide additional income. He invested in the future with the Presiding Bishop's Benefit Fund, which gave scholarships to needy students, and supported clergy needs through the Good Shepherd Fund. In 1984 *Ebony* magazine named him one of the one hundred most influential Black Americans. In his last years, he dreamed of establishing a World Outreach Center, an All Saints University, and a multilingual publishing house. His wife, Deborah, died on June 2, 1985, and he married Mary Peat in April, 1989. That same month he was diagnosed as having pancreatic cancer, but he refused chemotherapy, preferring the ministry of prayer. He died eight months later and was succeeded as presiding bishop by **Louis Henry Ford**.

"COGIC Leader Patterson Dies." *Charisma and Christian Life* 15 (March 1990): 24.

"The One Hundred Most Influential Black Americans." *Ebony* 39 (May 1984): 29–34.

"Ten Religious Groups with Biggest Black Membership." *Ebony* 39 (March 1984): 140–144.

Tinney, J. S. "Black Pentecostals: Setting Up the Kingdom." *Christianity Today* 20 (December 5, 1975): 42–43.

Patterson, James O., German R. Ross, and Julia Mason Atkins. *History and Formative Years of the Church of God in Christ.* Memphis, TN: Church of God Publishing House, 1969. 143 pp.

BPL, RLOA, BH, NYTBS (89), WWABA (88), BDA-AHP, DPCM, PHCGC.

PATTON, GEORGIA E. LEE (April 16, 1864–November 8, 1900), pioneer physician and missionary, was born into slavery in Grundy County, Tennessee. Her father died shortly after she was born, and her mother, newly freed, struggled to care for the sizable family. Patton managed to attend the local school whenever it was offered during the winter months, but by the time she was seventeen only counted twenty-six months of education. Her mother passed away when she was sixteen, and Patton moved to the home of her oldest sister.

In 1886, at the age of twenty-two, she managed to scrape enough money together to go to Nashville, Tennessee, and enroll in Central Tennessee College. She lived at a brother's house and walked the two miles to the school every day. During the summer months she earned money by teaching in a rural school, and in this manner completed the senior normal course in 1890. She then entered the Meharry Medical Department of Central Tennessee College and completed her studies quickly, graduating in February 1893. She was the first Black woman to graduate from Meharry Medical College.

A strongly religious woman, Patton decided to offer her services as a physician in Africa, despite the fact that her church (Methodist Episcopal) would not officially back her. By this Christian witness, she hoped that "Ethiopia shall soon stretch out her hand unto God." She set sail on April 5, 1893, and worked for two years in Monrovia, Liberia, entirely self-supporting. She was the first graduate of Meharry to serve as a medical missionary in Africa. The conditions of her medical practice were very crude, and her supplies were endemically short and outdated. In 1895 her health gave out and she had to return to the United States.

She settled in Memphis, Tennessee, and built up a practice there. She was the first Black woman licensed as a physician and surgeon in Tennessee, and the first to practice medicine in Memphis. On December 29, 1897, she married David W. Washington, a well-respected letter carrier. He attended the Avery Chapel **African Methodist Episcopal Church**, while she attended the Centenary Methodist Episcopal Church. She continued to be renowned for her charity work and was a strong contributor to such causes as the Freedman's Aid Society. Unfortunately, the tuberculosis she contracted in Africa slowly grew worse, and she had to give up her medical practice. Her first child died shortly after birth on February 14, 1899. Her second child, born on July 11, 1900, survived her own death by about two weeks. This was a poignant ending for someone who had selflessly given of herself in so many ways.

NBAW, NNW, IBAW.

PAUL, NATHANIEL (c.1793–July 17, 1839), abolitionist and Baptist minister, was born in Exeter, New Hampshire, the son of a Black veteran of the Revolutionary War. He and his three brothers, including the well-known **Thomas Paul, Sr.**, entered the Baptist ministry. In Albany, New York, he helped organize the Albany African Church Association in 1820. In 1822 he became the founding pastor of the First African Baptist Church in Albany, the only Black church in the city. Strongly committed to education, he started the Adult African Sunday School on May 12, 1822. He helped found the Wilberforce School, the only school for Black children in Albany until 1873, which met weekdays at his church. He married a woman named Eliza, who died on December 2, 1827.

Paul became a major Black leader in the Northeast and was one of the original committee which organized *Freedom's Journal* in early 1827, edited by **Samuel Cornish**. On July 5, 1827, Paul delivered a stirring address at the celebration of the official end of slavery in the state of New York. He was always outspoken in his quest for racial justice, and in articles in *Freedom's Journal* and its successor, *Rights for All*, he denounced the American Colonization Society and the churches that supported it. He was founder and first president of the Union Society of Albany for the Improvement of the Colored People in Morals, Education, and the Mechanic Arts.

In 1830 he moved to the Wilberforce Community near Ontario, Canada, newly founded by Blacks fleeing from the anti-Black riots of Cincinnati, Ohio, in 1829. Paul established a Baptist church and school at Wilberforce Community and was a proposer of a manual-labor school designed to function on the collegiate level. In 1831 he was commissioned to go to England to raise funds for the school and sailed from New York on December 31, 1831. He was the first of many Black Americans to go to England to raise funds and promote the abolitionist cause. In 1832 he testified before a committee of Parliament investigating slavery.

When slavery was ended in the British West Indies on August 1, 1833, Paul decided to remain in England to help British abolitionists form societies for further victories. This did not sit well with those in Canada anxious for his return with the collected funds, and a William Nell was sent to bring him back, but Nell did not return either. Paul married an English woman named Ann and finally returned to Wilberforce Community in April 1835. He reported that he had collected $8,015.80, had spent $7,019.80 in expenses, had loaned William Lloyd Garrison $200, and was owed $1,600 in back salary. This report did not go over well, and he was nearly lynched. In 1838 he resumed his pastorate in Albany and passed away the following year. He is remembered as a pioneer in making the church and its theology relevant to the contemporary social needs of the Black community. For him, the promotion of God's work and the emancipation of Blacks were one and the same.

Paul, Nathaniel. *An Address, Delivered at Troy, on the Anniversary of the Abolition of Slavery in the State of New York, July 6, 1829.* Albany, NY: Printed by John B. Van Steenbergh, 1829. 16 pp.

————. *An Address, Delivered on the Celebration of the Abolition of Slavery, in the State of New York, July 5, 1827.* Albany, NY: John B. Van Steenbergh, for the Trustees of the First African Baptist Society in the City of Albany, 1827. 24 pp.

————. *Reply to Mr. Joseph Phillips' Enquiry, Respecting "The Light in Which the Operations of the American Colonization Society are Viewed by the Free People of Color of the United States."* London: J. Massedor, Printer, 1832. 8 pp.

MBRL, DANB, BPJ, HUBA, AARS, IBAW.

PAUL, THOMAS, SR. (September 3, 1773–April 13, 1831), pioneer Baptist minister and missionary, was born in Exeter, New Hampshire. His father fought in the Revolutionary War and three of his brothers, Benjamin, Nathaniel, and Shadrach, also became Baptist ministers. He was baptized in 1789 by the Rev. Locke. He received a basic education in a Baptist school in Hollis, New Hampshire, and began preaching in 1801. He was ordained into the Baptist ministry on May 1, 1805, in West Nottingham, New Hampshire.

He then moved to Boston, Massachusetts, at a time of increased Black population growth in that area and the beginning of significant Black social institutions. The African Masonic Lodge, African Society, and African School all existed, meeting in private homes. He organized a congregation on August 8, 1805, of those who felt alienated by the White churches, and on February 26, 1806, a committee was formed to raise funds for the purchase of a lot and building of a Baptist church. With some help from a group of White businessmen who advanced large loans and held the mortgage papers, a three-story brick structure was completed on Beacon Hill on Belknap (later Joy) Street, at a cost of $7,230. It was the first building in Boston constructed entirely by Black craftsmen, and the only building thereafter controlled by Blacks. The sale of pews was restricted to "Africans and people of color." Paul was installed as pastor on December 4, 1806, and remained there for almost the entirety of the remainder of his life. He is credited with beginning the movement toward the establishment of independent Black Baptist churches in the United States. On December 5, 1805, he married Catherine Waterhouse, with whom he had three children.

When Prince Hall, the founder of the African Masonic Lodge, died in 1807, Paul, the only Black minister in Boston, emerged as the major leader of the African American community. He was chaplain of African Grand Lodge No. 459, and the church was the focal point of Black community activities. The first floor of the church was occupied by the African School taught by Prince Saunders. Paul was also respected by the Whites and participated regularly with minimal discrimination in the Boston Baptist Association. He was known to be a spellbinding preacher. In 1820 he was its representative to a nearby New Hampshire Baptist Association.

Paul's fame spread such that in 1808 he conducted a lecture series among mostly White Baptist churches in New York City. When that was completed the First Baptist Church of New York City decided that a separate Black congregation could be organized. Sixteen Blacks of that church were honorably "discharged," and they invited Paul to help them establish a new congregation. This he did, and on July 5, 1809, they founded the Abyssinian Baptist Church in New York City, which later became (and remains today) the largest Black church in America. He did not remain there, however, but soon returned to Boston. In 1815 he traveled to England under the auspices of the Baptist Missionary Society of Massachusetts, and preached to very enthusiastic anti-slavery supporters.

In 1823 he presented to the Baptist Missionary Society of Massachusetts a plan for mission work in Haiti, and requested to be sent there as a missionary. With passage paid for by William Gray, the Boston shipping magnate, and accompanied by Prince Saunders, he set sail on May 31, 1823. They arrived on July 4, 1823, and were warmly greeted by President Jean Pierre Boyer. The strong Catholic presence and Paul's inability to speak French thwarted his progress, and he returned to Boston in about October 1823. He therefore follows **David George**, **Daniel Coker**, and **Lott Carey** as among the earliest Black American missionaries.

Paul carefully evaluated the appeal of Haiti and decided that conditions were not yet appropriate to recommend any general Black emigration there, and thereafter placed all of his efforts toward the abolition of slavery and the general uplift of Black life in America. He was friends with lay theologian **David Walker**, who lived near the African (Joy Street) Baptist Church. In late 1827 Walker and Paul agreed to be agents for the soon-to-be-published *Freedom's Journal*, edited by John B. Russworm and **Samuel Cornish**. He retired from the church in 1829, but his last years were marred by a serious and painful illness that dominated his existence until his death two years later. One of his children, Thomas Paul, Jr., became one of the first Black graduates of Dartmouth College. The African Baptist Church (later called the Joy Baptist Church) served as a Jewish synagogue from 1904 to 1972, and later became the Museum of Afro-American History.

DANB, ENB, HBB, AAE, IBAW, BPJ, NA, GNPP, HNC.

PAUL QUINN COLLEGE.

An **African Methodist Episcopal Church** (AME) school. Paul Quinn College began in the reflection of the AME ministers of the state of Texas. Realizing the handicap placed upon them by their lack of education, they were determined to provide such opportunities for the children then growing up in the church. Pooling their resources, they were able to open a college at Waco, Texas, in 1881. Originally named Waco College, the school was later renamed after one of the church's early bishops. Among the founders of the school was **Richard H. Cain**, who in 1880 was elected a bishop of the church and assigned to Texas. He served as the school's first president.

Wright, R. R., Jr., ed. *The Encyclopedia of the African Methodist Episcopal Church*. Philadelphia, PA: Book Concern of the AME Church, 1947. 688 pp.

PAYNE, CHRISTOPHER HARRISON

(September 7, 1848–December 5, 1925), Baptist minister, journalist, and the first Black state legislator in West Virginia, was born near Red Sulphur Springs, Monroe County, Virginia (now part of West Virginia). His father, Thomas Payne, was a cattle driver who died of smallpox when Payne was two years old. His mother was the daughter of slavemaster James Ellison, who saw to her education and then set her free. She in turn gave Payne, her only child, a basic education. During the Civil War Payne was forced to serve in the Confederate Army as a valet, but returned in 1864 to work on a farm near Hinton, West Virginia. In 1866 he married Delilah Ann Hargrove (or Hargro/Hargo), with whom he had six children.

He worked briefly on an Ohio River steamboat, then settled in Charleston, West Virginia, where he worked in the daytime and went to school at night. In 1868 he earned a teaching certificate, found a teaching position near Hinton in Summers County, and for a number of years taught in the winter months and worked a farm in the summer. In 1875 he was converted and on February 22, 1876, was licensed to preach. He was ordained a Baptist minister on May 29, 1877, and later that year in September entered Richmond Institute (now Virginia Union University), where he completed his secondary education in 1877–78. Financial need then led him to return to West Virginia, and he engaged in missionary work for the next two years.

In 1880 Payne returned to Richmond as the pastor of the Moore Street Baptist Church. He also studied in the theological department of Richmond Institute for three years, graduating in 1883. He was then appointed by the American Baptist Publications Society to travel through the Virginias as a Sunday School missionary. He later estimated that in this work he converted 500 people, delivered 1,500 sermons, founded nine churches and two Sunday Schools, and supported dozens of other churches and Sunday Schools. Pastorates that he held briefly during this time included Baptist churches in Norfolk, Virginia and Huntington, West Virginia, and the First Baptist Church of Montgomery, West Virginia. To educate people about the achievements of Black people and blunt the effects of prejudice, he began several weekly papers, beginning with the *Pioneer* in Montgomery. Both his preaching and his writing were well regarded.

In 1884 ill health compelled him to stop his traveling labors and in April he settled to pastor the First Baptist Church of Coal Valley, West Virginia. He founded the West Virginia Enterprise in 1885 and later founded the *Mountain Eagle*, his final weekly paper. He worked to establish a school with an industrial department, and organized and was the first president of the West Virginia Baptist State Convention. By this time he had developed a far-ranging reputation for leadership and clear thinking among both the Black and White populations and began to enter politics, helping the Republican party in its campaigns. In 1889 he was rewarded for his work by being appointed deputy collector of internal revenue at Charleston, West Virginia, a position he held until 1893. In 1891, thanks largely to his influence, the state legislature passed a bill for a land-grant college near Charleston, to be called West Virginia Colored Institute (later West Virginia State College).

Payne took the opportunity in Charleston to study law and was admitted to the West Virginia bar in 1896. That year he was also elected to the lower house of the state legislature, the first Black in the state to gain that position. He served a two-year term. Three times he was a delegate to the national Republican convention. In 1898–99 he was an internal revenue agent, and may at that point have returned to church work and/or the practice of law for a time. On May 1, 1903, he was appointed U.S. Consul to St. Thomas, Danish West Indies (Virgin Islands), remaining in that position until the United States purchased the islands in 1917. At some point his first wife passed away, and he married A. G. Viney of Gallipolis, Ohio. He continued to live in St. Thomas, where he worked as police, judge, and prosecuting attorney until his death. **Irving Garland Penn** called Payne "the most representative Negro in the state of West Virginia, both in religion and politics."

"Notes." *Journal of Negro History* 11 (January 1926): 225–227.

AARS, MM, AAE, CH, HNB, WWWA (4), WWCR, DAB, DANB, IBAW, AAP.

PAYNE, DANIEL ALEXANDER (February 24, 1811–November 29, 1893), 6th bishop of the **African Methodist Episcopal Church** (AME) and the first African American Black college president, was born in Charleston, South Carolina, to free parents, London and Martha Payne. Martha was from the Catawba Indians of South Carolina. As soon as possible, they taught him to read, and took him to Methodist class meetings at the Cumberland Street Methodist Episcopal Church in Charleston. His father, however, died when he was four and his mother when he was nine, and he went to live with his great-aunt, Sarah Bordeaux. He received two years of formal schooling at the Minor's Moralist Society School, but learned mostly through his own reading and the help of a tutor, studying Latin, Greek, history, various sciences, and the Bible. He was converted and joined the Cumberland Street Church in 1826. He was a carpenter for a while, then in 1829 established the Tradd Street School for Black children in Charleston. This was a great success until an 1834 bill against teaching Blacks caused the school to close on April 1, 1835, when the bill became law.

Deciding on the ministry, Payne entered Gettysburg Theological Seminary (Lutheran), Pennsylvania, in 1835, sometimes assisting at an AME church in Carlisle, some miles away. Always concerned about the education of children, he began a Sunday School in an old building near the seminary. In 1837, deteriorating eyesight forced him to cut short his program, and he accepted the pastorate of the Liberty Street Presbyterian Church in Troy, New York. He was ordained by the Franckean Synod (western New York) of the Lutheran Church in 1839. Soon, however, he injured his throat and was unable to speak for a year. He was succeeded in the Troy pastorate in the fall of 1839 by **Henry Highland Garnet**. Toward the end of 1840, as his voice returned, Payne made his way to Philadelphia and followed through on his educational concerns by starting began a high school. He renewed a relationship the AME Church, and in 1841 joined the Bethel AME Church in Philadelphia, the mother church of the denomination. He was soon licensed as a local preacher, and was ordained an elder in 1844. While at Bethel, he helped organize its first choir, countering the objections of many members.

In May 1843, while wanting to remain at his school, he followed Bishop **Morris Brown**'s request to be the pastor of Israel Bethel AME Church in Baltimore, Maryland. He began writing a series of articles advocating an educated ministry, and as a delegate to General Conference in 1844, caused great excitement and controversy with this idea. He was selected as the chair of the Committee on Education, and secured adoption of a course of study for young ministers. During his years at Israel Bethel, he introduced instrumental music for the first time in any AME congregation, and made it clear he was not comfortable with what he considered noisy or vulgar forms of worship. In 1847 he married Julia A. Farris, but she died within a year.

In 1848 the General Conference agreed to his proposition to allow him to write a history of the denomination. This task allowed him an exit from an awkward situation at his new appointment at the Ebenezer church in Baltimore, which considered his religious practices too genteel and refused to accept him. He spent most of the next four years traveling, collecting information for the book, which was carefully done and instantly authoritative, although publication was delayed until 1891. On May 13, 1852, he was consecrated bishop, the first bishop in the church to have systematic theological training. In 1854 he married Eliza J. Clark.

As bishop, he promoted literary societies, lyceums, and other means of increasing the level of education. He organized the New England Conference in 1852, the Missouri Conference in 1855, and the Kentucky Conference in 1868. In 1863, he arranged for the church to purchase Wilberforce University near Xenia, Ohio, which had been founded in 1856 by the Methodist Episcopal Church to educate Blacks. The cost was $10,000, and he signed the papers on the church's behalf, even though the church could not at the time see how to make the payments. Payne himself became Wilberforce's first president, indeed the first Black president of any college in the United States, serving in that capacity from 1863 to 1876. During this time he wrote another important historical treatise, *Semi-Centenary and the Retrospection of the AME Church in the United States of America* (1866). He made Wilberforce solvent, a highly regarded school and the intellectual heart of the AME Church. A moment of personal triumph for Payne was when he returned to Charleston in 1865, thirty years after it had forced him to close his school, and as bishop organized the South Carolina Conference of the AME Church. This conference then provided the base for the spread of AME congregations throughout the southern states.

After his retirement in 1876, Payne continued as chancellor and dean of the theological school at Wilberforce, and continued his writing, including finishing *The History of the AME Church from 1816 to 1856* (1891), and his autobiographical *Recollections of Seventy Years* (1888). He attended the World Methodist Ecumenical Conference in London in 1881, and presided over it on September 17, the first Black to do so. His tenure as bishop, forty-one years, was the longest of any to date, and he was senior bishop for over twenty years. His importance as a bishop in the AME Church is considered by many second only to **Richard Allen**, the founder.

"Bishop Daniel A. Payne—A Symposium." *AME Church Review* 10 (January, 1894): 393–414.

Bragg, George Freeman. *Men of Maryland*. Baltimore, MD: Church Advocate Press, 1914. 135 pp.

Brown, William Wells. *The Rising Son; or, the Antecedents and Advancement of the Colored Race*. 1874; Rept. Miami, FL: Mnemosyne Publishers, 1969. 552 pp.

Coan, Josephus Roosevelt. *Daniel Alexander Payne, Christian Educator*. Philadelphia, PA: AME Book Concern, 1935. 139 pp.

Payne, Daniel Alexander. *History of the AME Church from 1816 to 1856*. Nashville, TN: Publishing House of the AME Sunday School Union, 1891. 502 pp.

———. *Pleasures and Other Miscellaneous Poems*. Baltimore, MD: Sherwood, 1850. 43 pp.

———. *Recollections of Seventy Years*. Nashville, TN: Publishing House of the AME Sunday School Union, 1888. 335 pp.

———. *Semi-Centenary and Retrospective of the AME Church in the United States of America*. Baltimore, MD: Sherwood, 1866. 189 pp.

———. *Treatise on Domestic Education*. Cincinnati, OH: Cranston & Stowe, 1885. 184 pp.

Smith, Charles S. *The Life of Daniel Alexander Payne*. Nashville, TN: Publishing House of the AME Sunday School Union, 1894. 57 pp.

Wentz, Abdel Ross. *History of Gettysburg Theological Seminary, 1826–1926*. Philadelphia, PA: United Lutheran Publishing House, 1927. 624 pp.

RLOA, BDAE, ACAB, HNB, EWM, MM, BHBA, NG, NBH, NCAB (14), DARB, DAB (7), HNC, CH, DANB, MBRL, HAMEC, ERS, BAMEC, GNPP, IBAW, BHAC, BAW, HUBA, AARS, BAA, NAH, NEA, AMSC, NYB (1925–26), AMECMIM, CEAMEC, BTFTMC.

PAYNE THEOLOGICAL SEMINARY. An **African Methodist Episcopal Church** (AME) school. Payne Theological Seminary grew out of the vision of Bishop **Benjamin W. Arnett**, who had been elected to the episcopacy in 1888 after a lengthy career with the church in various capacities. He was able to secure an initial financial grant from the Rev. John G. Mitchell and then the approval of his episcopal colleagues for the idea of a seminary on the campus of Wilberforce University. The plan called for a school which would be a part of Wilberforce but controlled by a separate board of trustees. The school opened in 1891.

With the final approval of the Wilberforce board

to establish the seminary came the selection of the name of the school in honor of **Daniel A. Payne**, then the senior bishop of the church. Payne was chosen as the school's first dean, a post he held until his death two years later in 1893. The school has continued to serve the interest of the denomination through the twentieth century.

Wright, Richard Robert. *Encyclopaedia of African Methodism.* 2nd ed. Philadelphia, PA: The Book Concern of the AME Church, 1947. 688 pp.

HAMEC

PEACE MISSION MOVEMENT. The Peace Mission Movement, founded by Father Divine, grew up in the years immediately after World War I. It can best be seen as the extension of the man himself, the embodiment of his racially neutral and economically empowering religious vision for American society.

Though little is known about the early life of **Father Major Jealous Divine** (1877?–1965), it is generally accepted that during the early decades of the twentieth century, he lived as an itinerant preacher throughout the Southeast until finally settling down in Sayville on Long Island with his first wife, Peninah, in 1919. Not formally educated or ordained by any religious group, Father Divine preached a gospel of responsible living to the poor and needy Blacks of urban New York during the hard economic times prior to and during the Great Depression. The Mission began as daily informal gatherings at his home where people would come for work and free meals and then later for spiritual guidance and mental and physical healing.

During the Mission's first period, 1919–1931, Father Divine's following grew slowly, numbering from 30 to 40 members in 1924. By 1926, however, the movement had begun to integrate as poor Whites from metaphysical and Holiness groups, attracted by Divine's spiritually vibrant message and by his reported healings, began to join. Even so, it was not until 1930 that Whites began to join the Mission in any measurable way. Those who did join with Father Divine came mostly from outside mainline Protestant churches. Four major religious ideologies converged during this first period: New Thought, Holiness, Perfectionist, and Adventist streams.

During this dynamic early period, Divine's movement received an added boost when, in 1930, Eugene Del Mar, Walter Clemow Lanyon, and J. Maynard Mathews endorsed Father Divine. So impressed was Lanyon that he returned home to spread Father Divine's message in his native England and throughout Europe and as far as Australia. Mathews joined the movement, changing his name to Brother John Lamb, and became executive secretary to Father Divine. In 1931, Del Mar, an erstwhile New Thought divine, claimed that between 400 and 800 individuals visited Father Divine's home every day for meals.

The defining point of this period was also the movement's first major crisis. In November 1931, Father Divine and eighty of his followers, who had traveled to Sayville to attend a communion feast hosted by Divine, were arrested for disturbing the peace. Divine and twenty-five others pleaded not guilty and were brought to trial. Divine charged that the complaints against him were racially motivated and violated his constitutional rights. The case received national exposure from both African American papers and the White press. On May 25, 1932, Father Divine was found guilty and was sentenced on June 5, 1932, to one year in the county jail and a five hundred dollar fine—the maximum penalty allowed by law. Two days after sentencing, the judge died suddenly and unexpectedly of a heart attack, Divine claiming to have willed it. This incident gained national attention to the movement and gave Father Divine added stature among his followers who believed he was God.

During its second period, 1932–1941, Father Divine's movement began to consolidate its base and to define in greater detail its mission of social equality and racial harmony. In 1932, Divine moved his headquarters to Harlem, where the Mission began to expand through the purchase of housing projects (called "heavens") and through the publication of Father Divine's thoughts and speeches in its official organ, *New Day*, first printed in 1937. The movement was legally incorporated in 1941 and 1942 as the Peace Mission Movement.

In 1936, some of Father Divine's followers organized the Righteous Government Movement to fight racial discrimination. At the 1936 convention in New York City, delegates adopted the "Righteous Government Platform of Father Divine's Peace Mission Movement" which had as its central planks a call for the equal treatment of all races and persons in the United States and for laws against segregation, race hate crimes, and racially abusive language.

The third period, 1942–1965, is characterized by two defining events. The first is the move to Philadelphia, the movement's present headquarters, in 1942, where it began to build up its property holdings. In 1953, a large Philadelphia estate was given to the Mission. Named Woodmont, it became the home of

Father and Mother Divine as well as the final resting place of Father Divine at his death in 1965.

The second, and most profound, is the marriage of Father Divine to Edna Rose Ritchings (Sweet Angel), a twenty-one year old blonde Canadian, on April 29, 1946 (his first wife, Sister Penny, having died in 1940). To reassure his stunned followers, Divine told them that this marriage was symbolic of the birth of the Church United and would not be physically consummated. This day, he said, marked the beginning of the new era of Father Divine and is celebrated annually as the Peace Mission's most sacred day.

The death of Father Divine in 1965 initiated the fourth and current period in the history of the International Peace Mission Movement. When in 1960, Father Divine ceased to speak, Mother Divine began to take on more and more responsibility and importance, becoming its chief spokesperson. Since the dedication of the Shrine of Life at Woodmont in 1968, Father Divine's tomb, most of Mother Divine's time is spent overseeing the administration of the Peace Mission Movement and hosting its central sacramental banquets and ceremonies.

The main tenets of the movement include the belief that God's kingdom has come to earth, the conviction that God has appeared in human form as Father Divine, the belief that the church age has ended, and the view that church hierarchical structures and divisions between clergy and laity are no longer warranted—one now has direct access to God and his power in the person of Father (and Mother) Divine. A noticeable inner circle/outer circle division does exist, however, with the inner circle consisting of those who have given over their possessions to the Mission and the outer circle made up of those still engaged in worldly employment.

Aside from its belief in the divinity of Father Divine and its focus in spiritual and physical healing, the mission's strongest emphasis lies in its strong denouncement of racial prejudice and economic inequalities and in its prohibition of lust, primarily by shunning marriage, sexual intercourse, and dancing.

The Peace Mission does not claim to be one Christian movement among many but *the* Christian movement in a wholly new dispensation. In that the movement seeks to put Jesus' Sermon on the Mount into practical application for these troubled times, it is in great way a theology of "realized eschatology"—the Kingdom of God is within you and among you. Divine's teachings address very real life concerns offering practical prescriptions. In many ways, his Peace Mission Movement was a modified form of the Protestant ethic: work hard; keep both your mind and body healthy; eat right; dress properly; keep good company; and avoid all forms of evil and vice.

Burnham, Kenneth E. *God Comes to America*. Boston, MA: Lambeth Press, 1979. 167 pp.

Divine, Mother. *The Peace Mission Movement*. Philadelphia, PA: Imperial Press, 1982. 191 pp.

Melton, J. Gordon. *Encyclopedia of American Religions*. Detroit, MI: Gale Research, 3rd ed. 1989. 1100 pp.

———. *Religious Leaders of America*. Detroit, MI: Gale Research Inc., 1989. 1100 pp.

Weisbrot, Robert. *Father Divine and the Struggle for Racial Equality*. Urbana, IL: University of Illinois, 1983. 241 pp.

Jon R. Stone

PEGUES, ALBERT WITHERSPOON (November 15, 1859–July 28, 1929), Baptist minister, author, and educator, was born into slavery in McFarlan, North Carolina. His father is unknown and was never a part of his life. His mother helped him attend a Freedman's Aid Society school from 1867 to 1869, but then he had to go to work on a farm to support himself. He carefully saved his earnings and studied at night in order to fulfill his dream of attending college. In October 1876 he entered Benedict Institute (later Benedict College) in Columbia, South Carolina, and studied there for three years. In March 1877 he experienced conversion and was baptized into the Baptist Church that July. In the fall of 1879 he entered Richmond Institute (later Richmond Theological Seminary), a part of Virginia Union University. He was licensed to preach in 1881 and graduated in May 1882. That September he enrolled at the University at Lewisburg (later Bucknell University) in Lewisburg, Pennsylvania, where he received his B.A. in 1886. He was third in his class and the only Black student.

During 1887 Pegues was principal of Summer High School in Parkersburg, West Virginia, and in 1888 was called to the chair of philosophy and languages at Shaw University in Raleigh, North Carolina. That year he was also ordained a Baptist minister. In 1889 he received an M.A. from Bucknell and in 1890 he received the Ph.D. from Selma University, both apparently honorary degrees. On February 18, 1890, he married M. Ella Christian, with whom he had two children. In 1892 he published his major work, *Our Baptist Ministers and Schools*, which has preserved for posterity a good deal of hard-to-find information, including facts about his own life. In 1893 he left Shaw to be the principal of the North Carolina State School for the Deaf and Blind, where he remained until 1897. He then returned to Shaw University as a professor in the Theology Department.

Pegues was meanwhile very active in the still-young **Baptist Foreign Mission Convention**. At its 14th Annual Convention in 1894, he proposed that the Foreign Mission Convention merge forces with the **American National Baptist Convention** and the **Baptist National Educational Convention**. This in fact came to pass the following year, with the formation of the **National Baptist Convention, U.S.A., Inc.**

In 1897, however, this group experienced a split which created the **Lott Carey Baptist Foreign Mission Convention**. Pegues was elected its recording secretary at the founding meeting in December in Washington, D.C. For several years he was president of the Baptist State Convention of North Carolina, and was corresponding secretary of the Baptist State Sunday School Convention for twenty-seven years. In 1907 he left Shaw to once again be principal of the North Carolina State School for the Deaf and Blind, this time staying for twelve years. In 1919 he returned once more to Shaw University as dean of the Theology Department, which post he held until his death. During his career he was also director of the Mechanics and Farmers Bank in Raleigh, and president of the Eagle Life Insurance Company.

Pegues, Albert W. *Our Baptist Ministers and Schools.* Springfield, MA: Wiley & Co., 1892. 622 pp.

SNB, SCA, EBA, WWCA (30–32), *OBMS, HUBA, AARS, BAW, WWCR, IBAW.*

PENN, IRVINE GARLAND (October 7, 1867–July 22, 1930), educator and national-level leader in the Methodist Episcopal Church, now a constituent part of the **United Methodist Church**, was born in New Glasgow, Amherst County, Virginia, the son of Isham and Maria (Irvine) Penn. At age five he moved with the family to Lynchburg, Virginia, where he graduated from high school in 1886. He was a year late graduating from high school because he dropped out for a year to teach a school in Bedford County in order to support himself.

In 1886–87 he was superintendent of a school in Amherst County, then moved to teach in a Lynchburg school, soon becoming principal. On December 26, 1889, he married Anna Belle Rhodes, with whom he had seven children. An active writer even in high school, Penn began writing for the *Richmond Planet* and the *Virginia Lancet.* In 1889 he was a correspondent for the *Knoxville Negro World* and the *New York Age.* He was twice voted a commissioner of the Petersburg Industrial

Association in Lynchburg, and was secretary of the board of directors of the Lynchburg Real Estate Loan and Trust Company. In 1891 he published his best-known work, *The Afro-American Press and Its Editors,* which describes most of the nineteenth-century Black-run periodicals and offers short biographical sketches of over seventy editors.

In 1895 Penn left his principal's position to concentrate on his task as head of Negro Exhibits at the Cotton States and International Exposition in Atlanta, held in September 1895, and received a gold medal for his efforts. This was the exposition at which Booker T. Washington gave perhaps his most famous speech, and Penn is reportedly the one who issued Washington the invitation to speak. Also in 1895 Penn published a large, inspiration-by-example book called *The College Life; or, Practical Self-Educator.* In 1897 Penn became assistant general secretary of the Epworth League of the Methodist Episcopal Church. The Epworth League had been established in 1889 as the organization to carry youth and young adult programs within the church.

In 1912 Penn left the Epworth League to be corresponding secretary for Educational Institutions for Negroes, a division of the Board of Education of the Methodist Episcopal Church. In the many years he was with the Board of Education he was an advocate for the Black colleges connected with the church, and was a trustee for a number of them, including Wiley College in Marshall, Texas; Clark University in Atlanta, Georgia; Gammon Theological Seminary in Atlanta, Georgia; and Walden College in Nashville, Tennessee. In 1925 he shifted to be secretary of endowments and field activities for the Board of Education, and kept that position until his death. From 1916 to 1928 he served on the Joint Commission on Unification of the Methodist Episcopal Church (which happened in 1939). He was a delegate to General Conference from 1892 to 1928, and at the time of his death was senior member of the General Conference in point of service.

Northrop, Henry Davenport, Joseph R. Gay, and I. Garland Penn, eds. *The College Life; or, Practical Self-Educator; a Manual of Self-Improvement for the Colored Race.* Chicago: Chicago Publication and Lithograph Company, 1895.

Penn, I. Garland. *The Afro-American Press and Its Editors.* Springfield, MA: Wiley & Co., 1891. 365 pp.

———. "Negro Religious and Social Life." *Missionary Review* 45 (June 1922): 447–453.

———. *The Reasons Why the Colored Man is Not in the World's Columbian Exposition, The Afro-American's Contribution to Columbian Literature.* 1893. 81 pp.

Penn, I. Garland, and John W. E. Bowen, eds. *The United Negro; His Problems and His Progress.* Atlanta, GA: D. E. Luther Publishing Company, 1902. 600 pp.

DANB, EBA, WWWA (1), *IBAW, WWCR, WWCA* (30–32), *BAW, HUBA, AARS.*

PENNINGTON, JAMES WILLIAM CHARLES

(1807 or 1809–October 20 or 22, 1870), minister, educator, author, and abolitionist, was born into slavery on the eastern shore of Maryland. At the age of four he, his mother, and an older brother were sold to his first master's son, Frisbie, Tilghman, in Hagerstown, Maryland. He worked variously as a Blacksmith and stonemason until he ran away, at about age twenty-one. A dangerous journey which included a brief recapture brought him to the home of a friendly Quaker, William Wright in Pennsylvania, who took him in for about six months and started him on a course of basic education. During this time he took on the new surname of Pennington, perhaps because of its Quaker associations, and eventually also added the name William, after his benefactor.

He then moved to another Quaker farm near Philadelphia for seven months. In the spring of 1829 he moved to Brooklyn, New York, and soon joined Samuel Cox's Presbyterian Church in Manhattan. He found work to support taking night classes and tutoring by private teachers. His advance into literacy and even eloquence was exceedingly rapid, and as early as June of 1831 he was a major spokesman for Brooklyn Blacks. That month he was a speaker at the first national Black convention and condemned the **American Colonization Society** (A.C.S.). This was especially courageous considering that his employer was president of the Brooklyn chapter of the A.C.S. Fortunately his employer was convinced by Pennington and his many supporters, and dissolved that A.C.S. chapter.

In about 1833 Pennington was accepted as the teacher of a newly opened school for Black children in New Town, Long Island, some seven miles away. This new task strongly appealed to him as a means of elevating the aspirations and abilities of people, like himself, long bound by ignorance. During this time he felt a call to the ministry, and in about 1835 moved to New Haven, Connecticut, where he found another teaching position and applied to Yale Divinity School. He was not admitted as a student, but was allowed to audit classes and to make use of the library. He also took some leadership at the Temple Street African Congregational Church in New Haven, now without a pastor since his good friend Simeon Jocelyn had recently resigned.

After three years, in the summer of 1837, Pennington returned to the school in New Town and a few months later a Black church was pulled together with Pennington as preacher. He was ordained in May 1838, and in 1839 the congregation officially identified itself as Congregational in affiliation. In September, 1838, he performed the marriage ceremony in New York City for Frederick Douglass and his fiancée. Pennington was commissioned a home missionary by the American Home Missionary Society, and soon reported to them a flourishing Sabbath school as well as a growing church. A larger field of duty awaited him, however, and in the spring of 1840 he became the first Black pastor of the Colored Congregational Church in Hartford, Connecticut, later called the Fifth Congregational Church or the Talcott Street Congregational Church, where he remained until 1847. In 1841 he helped found and was named president of the newly organized Union Missionary Society, a forerunner of the American Missionary Association. This society denounced the A.C.S. and urged people not to purchase slave-produced goods, while urging evangelization work in Africa. Also in 1841 he published the *Textbook of the Origin and History (etc., etc.) of the Colored People*, designed to abolish the notion that Blacks are an inferior people.

Pennington's leadership abilities, education, and gifted oratory made him an increasingly known and respected figure. He had kept the fact that he was an escaped slave a secret even from his wife, Harriet (about whom we know little). He was a delegate to five different national Black conventions (General Convention for the Improvement of Free People of Colour). In 1843 he represented the Connecticut Anti-Slavery Society at the World's Anti-Slavery Convention in London, England. While there he also served as delegate of the American Peace Society to the World's General Peace Convention. He lectured and preached at prestigious locations in London, Paris, and Brussels. In about 1844 and 1845 he served twice as moderator of the otherwise all-White Hartford Central Association of Congregational Ministers, which twice placed him in the position of examining White candidates for the pastoral office. Despite this appearance of acceptance by his White colleagues, the office was not that meaningful and the other clergy tended to be absent when he presided.

In August 1845, he requested a two-year leave of absence without pay from his church, which was granted, beginning in November. He told them for the first time of his fugitive status and fears of recapture.

He wanted to change locations for a time and perhaps work on a college education. Not able to find a welcoming college venue, he ended up sailing to Jamaica on behalf of the Union Missionary Society. After about seven months word reached him of the death of his wife in June 1846, and he returned to the United States. He spent the rest of his two-year leave of absence studying on his own. He tried various means to secure the release from slavery of his parents and siblings, apparently helping his father and two brothers escape to Canada. His mother and a sister were sold to Missouri.

In 1847 he returned only briefly to the Talcott Street Church and in the spring of 1848 he accepted the pastorate of the First Colored (Shiloh) Presbyterian Church on Frankfort and William Streets in New York City, succeeding Theodore Wright, where he remained until about 1855. Within a month the church building was sold and a move was made to Prince Street. The church was already the largest Black Presbyterian church in the country at 413 members, and in Pennington's first year another forty members were added. In 1849 the Glasgow Female Anti-Slavery Society sponsored another voyage abroad, where he gave talks in England and Scotland and attended the World Peace Conference in Frankfurt, Germany, in the summer of 1850. While in England he wrote an autobiographical account titled, *The Fugitive Blacksmith; or, Events in the History of James W. C. Pennington*, and within one year the book, first published in London in 1849, went through three editions. This story clearly revealed the brutality of his early years and served as a harsh criticism of slavery in the United States. On December 19, 1849, the University of Heidelberg awarded him an honorary Doctor of Divinity degree, the first Black person to receive that degree from a European university.

In 1850 the Fugitive Slave Law was passed, and he decided that remaining abroad for a while was a prudent protection of his freedom. Eventually, $150 was paid to the estate of his former master, thus allowing for his return to the United States and formal manumission on June 5, 1851. Between then and 1855 Pennington's career was buffeted by a problem with alcohol and a declining reputation among other abolitionists who were suspicious of his position in a denomination which was not moving against slavery. He also bankrupted himself to purchase the freedom of a brother. In early 1855 he helped found the New York Legal Rights Association, an early civil rights group, which sued the Sixth Avenue Railroad Company for equitable Black access. The legal expenses of this action

also helped ruin him financially, and it was little help at the time to think that although the suit was legally unsuccessful, the social result of the next four years of agitation by others would be a significant improvement in the situation.

In September of 1855 Pennington, now remarried and with a family, left New York to pastor his old church in Hartford, Connecticut. This situation was not comfortable either, and he soon moved to pastor the Second Colored Presbyterian Church in New Town, Long Island. In 1861 he made another trip to England which ended ignominiously when he was arrested in June 1862, for stealing a book from a store, and sentenced to one month hard labor. In the fall of 1865, anxious to aid the newly freed slaves, he moved to New Orleans and was ordained for work by the Missouri Conference of the **African Methodist Episcopal Church** (AME). He taught and preached in Natchez, Mississippi, remaining for about a year and a half. From this location he contributed several articles to the *Anglo-African* magazine on the progress of Reconstruction.

In early 1867 he began pastoring at the Black Congregational church in Portland, Maine. Increasingly, ill health, possibly from alcoholism, limited his effectiveness. In late 1869, on appointment from the Presbyterian Committee of Missions for Freedmen, he moved to Jacksonville, Florida, hoping to restore his health. He founded a Black Presbyterian church and school there, but passed away a year later.

Bayliss, John F., ed. *Black Slave Narratives*. New York: Macmillan, 1970.

Pennington, James W. C. *Christian Zeal. A Sermon Preached Before the Third Presbytery of New York in Thirteenth Street Presbyterian Church, July 3, 1853*. New York: Zuille and Leonard, 1854. 15 pp.

———. *Covenants Involving Moral Wrong Are not Obligatory upon Man. A Sermon Delivered in the Fifth Congregational Church, Hartford, Connecticut, November 17, 1842*. Hartford, CT: J. C. Wells, 1842. 12 pp.

———. *The Fugitive Blacksmith; or, Events in the History of James W. C. Pennington*. 2nd ed. London: C. Gilpin, 1849. 87 pp.

———. *Textbook of the Origin and History, (etc., etc.) of the Colored People*. Hartford, CT: L. Skinner, Printer, 1841. 96 pp.

———. *Two Years' Absence; or, A Farewell Sermon, Preached in the Fifth Congregational Church, November 2nd, 1845*. Hartford, CT: H. T. Wells, 1845. 31 pp.

Washington, Joseph R., Jr. *The First Fugitive Foreign and Domestic Doctor of Divinity*. Lewiston, NY: The Edwin Mellon Press, 1990. 225 pp.

BPJ, MM, BH, HNB, CH, NG, HNC, DNAADB, BMIC, NCAB (14), ERS, AAE, WWWA (H), MBRL, DAB, DANB, BAW, IBAW, HUBA, AARS, IBAWCB, BAB.

PENTECOSTAL ASSEMBLIES OF THE WORLD (PAW). An Apostolic Pentecostal Church. The Pentecostal Assemblies of the World is the oldest of the Apostolic or "Jesus Only" Pentecostal churches. It began as a loosely organized fellowship in 1906 in Los Angeles among some of the first people affected by the revival on Azuza Street from which the Pentecostal movement spread around. Like all Pentecosts at the time the Assemblies was trinitarian in belief. Early centers appeared along the West Coast, and a second concentration began to appear in the Midwest within a few years. Beginning in 1913, the annual meeting was held in Indianapolis, Indiana, which was in the process of replacing Los Angeles as the chief center of the movement.

By the beginning of World War I, several Pentecostal organizations (**Assemblies of God, Church of God in Christ, Apostolic Faith Mission Church of God, Church of God [Cleveland, Tennessee]**) had been formed, and many independent ministers affiliated with one or the other as a means of dealing with the government. Then in 1915, PAW and the other Pentecostal associations were met with the "Jesus Only" issue. The issue had arisen in several stages in Southern California and is usually traced to the rediscovery of the power of the Name of Jesus in the working of healing miracles by John G. Scheppe. He shared his excitement with others such as Glenn A. Cook and Frank Ewart, who started the process of developing the idea into an alternative non-Trinitarian theology.

Briefly stated, the Apostolic position is anchored on the literal reading of several scriptures such as Isaiah 9:6, Acts 8:16, and Acts 19:5. The Isaiah passage, traditionally thought of among Christians as a prophecy referring to Jesus, suggests that Jesus is God the Father. The passages in Acts offer a baptismal formulary contrary to that in Matthew. The conclusion reached by Ewart and Cook was that the Trinity represents, in fact, a false theological construct, and was close to if not identical with tritheism. In response they began to emphasize the one God (and their followers were often labeled "Oneness" people) and suggested that God's name was Jesus. Jesus then appeared to humanity as Father, Son and Holy Ghost. Thus, in reading Matthew 28:19, in which the Risen Christ tells the disciples to baptize people in the *name* of the Father, and of the Son and of the Holy Spirit, the Oneness people concluded

that the *name* of the Father, Son, and Holy Spirit was Jesus. That rendering reconciled Matthew 28 with passages in the books of Acts such as Acts 19:5 which speaks of baptism in the name of Jesus. Thus the identification of Jesus as the name of the One God and the practice of baptism in the name of Jesus only came to be the distinguishing belief and practice of the movement initiated by Cook and Ewart.

Among the first people converted to the new perspective was a Black man, **Garfield Thomas Haywood**, a minister with the Pentecostal Assemblies of the World in Indianapolis. J. J. Frazee, a White man and the first general superintendent of the PAW, also accepted the Oneness doctrine. The juxtaposition of Frazee and Haywood indicates the integrated character of both the Pentecostal Movement in general and the PAW in particular during its first decades. By the end of the war, the movement began to segregate. The Church of God (Cleveland, Tennessee) and the Assemblies of God emerged as the primary White trinitarian group and the Church of God in Christ as the main Black trinitarian group. The Apostolic Faith Mission Church of God became the primary Black group spreading the Oneness faith in the South. The PAW tried to remain an integrated group operating primarily in the Midwest and far West, but quickly picked up a national following, including many White Southerners.

Following the acceptance of the Oneness theology by the majority of the PAW, it underwent a reorganization and began to expand. It gained an initial boost as the Oneness doctrine spread through the Assemblies of God and the Church of God in Christ and many shifted allegiance to the PAW. After the war, the growth of the Assemblies created a major problem. The development of an integrated fellowship was strongly supported by a belief that the heightened experience of the Holy Spirit was a sign that Jesus was about to return in a matter of a few years. By the 1920s it became evident to many that they were wrong. The social price being paid by Whites as members of an integrated church began to appear too high. Slowly whites began to withdraw individually, and then in 1924 the issue culminated in the majority of the remaining White pastors and members leaving and forming an independent White church (now an integral part of the United Pentecostal Church).

Compensation for the loss of some White members came as the church rapidly expanded and gained new leaders from the Black community. Among the outstanding early leaders were **Joseph M. Turpin**, P. J. F. Bridges, **F. I. Douglas**, and **Robert C. Lawson**.

Lawson also became the source of the first schism. Disagreeing with the PAW on the deployment of female ministers and its teachings on divorce and remarriage, Lawson left in 1919 to build what became the **Church of Our Lord Jesus Christ of the Apostolic Faith**.

In the wake of the schisms, the Assemblies underwent further reorganization and instituted an episcopal system of governance. An initial board of bishops included Haywood, Turpin, Douglas and **S. N. Hancock** (all Black) and G. B. Rowe, A. William Lewis, and R. G. Pettis (all White). PAW has consistently affirmed its goal of remaining an interracial fellowship by regularly electing men from the minority White membership to the bishopric, and even as presiding bishop.

In spite of the schisms, PAW prospered under Haywood's strong leadership. He was a writer and poet. His books, recently reprinted, helped spread the Oneness message, and his poem gave it a hymnology. A former missionary to Liberia, he also presented a missionary vision and during the 1920s PAW initiated work in not only in Africa, the traditional field for African American churches, but also in India and China.

Following the death of Haywood, in 1932 **Joshua Grimes** was elected presiding bishop. He would hold the office until his death in 1957 and leave a lasting stamp on the church. He led the church's expansion into the West Indies and established a strong organizational system as the church moved into all parts of the United States. His leadership was built off of his extensive travels to all parts of the church and his legendary teaching ability.

His holding the office for such a long period, of course, kept other worthy leaders from moving up, and his death precipitated another schism. S. N. Hancock had waited in the wings for almost four decades. However, in 1967 he was passed over for the office of presiding bishop, and Ross P. Paddock, a White man elected. At least part of the reason for the rejection of Hancock was his doctrinal deviation; He left to found the **Pentecostal Churches of the Apostolic Faith**. Paddock was succeeded in 1974 by Francis L. Smith, and Smith in 1980 by Lawrence E. Brisbin, a White man.

During Smith's administration, the PAW purchased a former shopping center in Indianapolis which it converted into its national headquarters. The building also houses Aenon Bible School, the church's seminary, and its publishing facility.

At present, the church is headed by James A. Johnson, its presiding bishop since 1986, and a board of bishops. The United States is divided into some 30 districts, each headed by one of the bishops. A missionary board oversees missions in Africa (Egypt, Ghana, and Nigeria), the United Kingdom, and Jamaica. In 1980 there were over 1,000 congregations and approximately 450,000 members. PAW is ultimately the source of almost all of the many Apostolic Pentecostal denominations.

Dugas, Paul P. comp. *The Life and Writings of Elder G. T. Haywood.* Portland, OR: Apostolic Book Publishers, 1968.

Golder, Morris E. *History of the Pentecostal Assemblies of the World.* Indianapolis, IN: The Author, 1973. 195 pp.

Richardson, James C. *With Water and Spirit: A History of Black Apostolic Denominations in the U.S.* Martinsville, VA: The Author, n.d. 151 pp.

Tyson, James L. *Before I Sleep.* Indianapolis, IN: Pentecostal Publications, 1976.

PENTECOSTAL CHURCH OF GOD. An Apostolic Pentecostal church. The Pentecostal Church of God dates to 1955 when independent evangelist Willie James Peterson of Meridian, Mississippi, accepted and began to preach non-Trinitarian Pentecostal doctrines. Previously, Peterson had gone through a series of events which began with a dream which found him in the presence of God and the angelic host. There followed a period of prayer and a call to preach. He formed congregations across the South and later moved into the Black communities in the North. During the next fourteen years he built a substantial denomination.

Throughout his life Peterson continued to have revelatory experiences through which his theological position was developed. His understanding of Christianity centered upon the kingdom of God. Through conversion one leaves the kingdom of this world ruled by Satan, and symbolized by worldly living, to the kingdom of God and a life of godliness. Both the **Roman Catholic Church** and Protestantism are very much a part of the kingdom of this world. They teach false Satanic doctrines such as the Trinity and the observance of holidays such as Christmas and Easter.

Joining the kingdom of God begins in turning away from the Babylonish churches to God's truths. One repents of one's sins and should be baptized by immersion in the name of Jesus Christ. Church members come to understand heaven as a place of God and his angels. They withdraw from participation in the government, which means adopting a pacifist position, not voting and not saluting the flag.

By the time of Peterson's death in 1969, he was succeeded by four bishops, William Duren, J. J. Sears,

C. L. Rawls, and E. Rice. Headquarters of the church is in Detroit, Michigan.

Faison, Jennell Peterson. *The Apostle W. J. Peterson*. Detroit, MI: The Pentecostal Church of God, 1980.

Richardson, James C. *With Water and Spirit: A History of Black Apostolic Denominations in the U.S.* Martinsville, VA: The Author, n.d. 151 pp.

PENTECOSTAL CHURCHES OF APOSTOLIC FAITH. An Apostolic Pentecostal church. The Pentecostal Churches of Apostolic Faith grew out of some longstanding conflicts in the **Pentecostal Assemblies of the World** (PAW), the oldest and largest of the Apostolic "Jesus Only" Pentecostal churches. From 1932 to 1967 PAW was headed by **Samuel Joshua Grimes** as presiding bishop. While providing able leadership, his holding the post for 35 years meant other leaders were unable to move upward. Among those most frustrated by the closed opportunities was **Samuel N. Hancock**, one of the original seven PAW bishops who was consecrated bishop five years prior to Grimes and had had an outstanding ministry in Detroit. In 1952 Hancock challenged Grimes for the presiding bishop's position, but was rebuffed by the general assembly. Thus in 1957 he left and with his supporters founded the Pentecostal Churches of Apostolic Faith.

As it turns out, there was a second issue involved in Hancock's rejection by the PAW and his leaving its ranks: he had himself moved from the Apostolic Pentecostal position. The Apostolic position had been hammered out in relation to the traditional Trinitarian doctrine which affirmed God as manifest in three persons, Father, Son and Holy Spirit. The Apostolic Oneness position taught that God was One, and His name was Jesus. Jesus was Father, Son, and Holy Spirit. Hancock moved to what was an old theology, usually called Arianism, which affirmed that Jesus was merely the Son of God. It seems that this understanding was tolerated in Hancock, who did not emphasize it, and that those opposed to Grimes left the PAW to join with Hancock in spite of it.

When Hancock died in 1963, his doctrinal deviation became the occasion of a split in the Pentecostal Churches of Apostolic Faith. Hancock was succeeded by Bishop Willie Lee. However, in 1964 the majority of the leaders of the churches coalesced around Bishop Elzie Young, who had possession of the original churches' charter and its corporate name. Charging that Lee held Hancock's heretical position, she assumed the presiding bishop's office and returned the church to the Apostolic position.

Bishop Young proved a strong leader. She established a system by which each congregation regularly contributes to the central church treasury, thus providing a stable central structure. Assisted by Bishop R. L. Little, who oversees foreign missions, she sold the cause of foreign missions and built an impressive mission program in Liberia and Haiti. By 1980 the church in the United States consisted of 115 congregations and some 25,000 members.

Richardson, James C. *With Water and Spirit: A History of Black Apostolic Denominations in the U.S.* Martinsville, VA: The Author, n.d. 151 pp.

PENTECOSTALISM. The African American community has given its primary religious allegiance to three Christian family groups, the Baptists, the Methodists, and the Pentecostals. In each it has assumed a unique role in originating new forms of the religious life and new ways of being religious. However, in the case of both the Methodists and the Baptists, African Americans received a prior form of the faith and developed their own variation on the tradition, while with Pentecostalism they assumed a leadership role at the beginning and helped to structure the tradition essentially from its point of origin.

Pentecostalism started as a movement within the Holiness churches, which, at the beginning of the twentieth century, had both Black and White denominations and a surprising number of interracial fellowships such as the **Church of God (Anderson, Indiana)**. John Wesley, the founder of Methodism, had taught the possibility of believers being sanctified, i.e., being made free from outward sin and perfected in love in this lifetime. The doctrine of Holiness was deemphasized in American Methodism, but a revival of the doctrine began in the decades before the Civil War by Methodists like Timothy Merritt and Phoebe Palmer, and the Congregationalists around Charles G. Finney, Asa Mahan, and **Oberlin College**. From Phoebe Palmer, these new Holiness advocates had picked up a novel twist. Palmer preached an immediate expectation of Holiness, even for the new believer. Holiness became not the expectation of a life of growing in grace but the normative experience for every church member.

It is the spread of Palmer's novel doctrinal emphasis that gave birth to the Holiness movement in the decades after the Civil War. Believers saw the Christian life marked by two experiences: justification, when a believer first accepts Christ, and sanctification, when a believer is made perfect in love. Holiness people often spoke of the latter experience as the baptism of the Holy Spirit.

The Holiness Movement originated among Methodists in the Northeast and found its greatest support among members of the Methodist Episcopal Church who carried it across the Midwest into the Far West. Within the African American community, Holiness teaching found its initial strength among Baptists in the Midsouth (Kentucky, Mississippi, Tennessee, and Arkansas). The original African American Holiness church began as the Christian Faith Band in the late 1870s in Kentucky. Founded by Thomas J. Cox, the Band would later become a Pentecostal church as the **Church of God (Apostolic)**.

The spread of the Holiness-Pentecostal movement within the African American community is to be traced to two moments in the history of African American Christianity: the Philadelphia Holiness Revival of 1877 and the Los Angeles Pentecostal Revival of 1906. While the Philadelphia Revival defines the contours of the Black Holiness movement, the Los Angeles Revival serves as the watershed, interjecting a Pentecostal faction in the movement which eventually became the dominant group. The Black Holiness-Pentecostal movement is united in its promotion of the Holiness doctrine and experience but divided over the place of Pentecostal elements.

Before the Black Holiness movement emerged in the 1870s, a number of African Americans espoused the Holiness doctrine and experience. **Jarena Lee**, a member of **Richard Allen**'s congregation and an early African Methodist preacher, testified to receiving the Holiness experience as early as 1808. She identified William Scott, an African American, as the person who introduced her to the Holiness message. Historians Catherine Albanese and Stephen Stein lodge Lee with **Zilpha Elaw** and **Julia Foote**, two other African American preaching women, within proto-Holiness and proto-Pentecostal movements. Other antebellum Holiness advocates included prominent African Americans, such as **Sojourner Truth** and **Daniel Alexander Payne**. Payne and **Amanda Berry Smith** served as a bridge between the antebellum preaching women and the Black Holiness movement of the late nineteenth century. The Holiness ministry of Amanda Berry Smith reached Europe, Asia, Africa in addition to United States during the late nineteenth century.

By this time the Holiness movement had entered Black Methodist and Baptist churches. The movement within African Methodism occurred from the Philadelphia Revival of 1877. Regionally, among African Methodists, the movement was centered in Philadelphia, western Pennsylvania, Missouri, and North Carolina. Among Black Baptists, the movement emerged in 1886 with centers in the Arkansas and Tennessee region, and North Carolina, and in 1895 with a center in Mississippi. During the 1880s Black Holiness congregations were formed in Michigan, South Carolina, and Alabama by African Americans associated with the Church of God (Anderson, Indiana), a bi-racial Holiness movement led by Daniel Warner, a Holiness minister. The Arkansas and Tennessee Black Holiness stream and the African American associates of Warner introduced into the Black Church a new phase, the nondenominational congregation which became the model for many Black Holiness congregations during late nineteenth century and throughout the twentieth century.

The Philadelphia Revival of 1877 started at Bethel **African Methodist Episcopal Church** (AME), the historic pulpit of Richard Allen, during the pastorate of George C. Whitefield. Whitefield commenced his appointment to Bethel in June of 1877, preaching Holiness sermons and scheduling an all-day Holiness conference for the 20th of that month. The all-day conference exemplified the tenor of the Philadelphia Revival by being bi-racial, interdenominational, and supporting female religious leadership. Represented at the conference were African Americans from the local Episcopal, Baptist, Presbyterian, and Methodist churches. Whitefield invited as conference speakers prominent local African American clergy, such as the Rev. Redding B. Johns, pastor of First African Presbyterian Church, and the Rev. Theophilus Gould, former pastor of Bethel AMEC. Also invited were Holiness clergy of national stature, such as John S. Inskip, president of the National Camp Meeting for the Promotion of Holiness; E. I. D. Pepper, editor of the *Christian Standard;* and William MacDonald. From Bethel, the Holiness meetings spread throughout the Black Christian community. According to Parker Smith, a contemporary of Whitefield, "several [Black] churches opened their doors to have [discussions of] the doctrine of the higher Christian life." Bethel sponsored Holiness meetings on Thursday night, had Holiness messages preached each Sunday, and organized "all-day meetings for the promotion of holiness." Union AME held regular Holiness meetings, some running all day. The Union American Methodist Episcopal Church, during the pastorate of Lorenzo D. Blackstone, sponsored Holiness meetings twice a week. Redding B. Johns and Lorenzo D. Blackstone joined Whitefield in receiving sanctification and preaching the doctrine. Some members of Johns' congregation were sanctified, professing the "blessings of a clean heart." Johns also organized all-day Holiness meetings at First African Presbyterian. Whitefield, Blackstone, and Johns led the interdenominational Holiness movement among African Americans in Philadelphia.

Among AMEC ministers in Philadelphia the Holiness message became the norm. At the August 1877, session of the local AMEC Preacher's Association, the Holiness experience became the topic of discussion. Each of the twelve ministers present defined himself in reference to the Holiness movement. These ministers included some of the leading AMEC clergy, such as **Jabez P. Campbell**, **Benjamin Tanner**, **Henry McNeal Turner**, and **Levi Coppin**. Nine ministers testified to having received the Holiness experience: Bishop J. P. Campbell, Benjamin Tanner, L. Patterson, Theophilus Gould, R. Barney, J. S. Thompson, W. H. Davis, W. H. Stiles, and H. H. Lewis. The two dissenters from the group were Henry McNeal Turner and Levi Coppin. Turner defined the Holiness experience as a "gradual work" in contrast to the majority which defined it as instantaneous, and Coppin acknowledged only the experience of conversion and "nothing else." C. C. Felts testified that he was seeking the Holiness experience. The involvement of Campbell, Tanner, and Whitefield gave the movement strong institutional support within AMEC in Philadelphia, given Campbell's status as bishop, Tanner's influence as editor of the national weekly the *Christian Recorder*, and Whitefield's position as pastor of the Bethel Philadelphia, Richard Allen's historic pulpit. Holiness meetings were being held in AME congregations in Chester, Germantown, other areas around Philadelphia, and in western Pennsylvania.

The Philadelphia Holiness Revival lasted from 1877 to 1879, when George Whitefield died. In addition to Whitefield's death, the leadership of the Philadelphia movement suffered by the removal of Blackstone from his pastorate and the resignation of Johns from First African Presbyterian Church. There were now no congregations holding Holiness meetings, not even Bethel, whose officers banned the meetings. The only Holiness meetings that continued were held in homes or at street rallies. And the leadership shifted from the prominent pastors to laypeople.

Public Holiness meetings slowly started reappearing after the near collapse of the movement. Under Whitefield's successor at Bethel, Levi Coppin, Holiness meetings were again permitted at the church. Zion Wesley AMEC initiated its first Holiness meeting ever with semi-monthly meetings. Holiness meetings were being sponsored weekly at Benezeb Hall, a public auditorium.

By 1881, the AMEC ministers in Missouri embraced the Holiness message. The two leaders of the Holiness movement within the AMEC in Missouri were Rev. James W. Taylor and Bishop **T. M. D. Ward**. Taylor received the Holiness experience at a camp meeting in 1877, and Ward publicly announced his support of the Holiness message by 1881.

Linking the Philadelphia Holiness movement and the AMEC in other regions were woman evangelists. A Sister Callund who had attended the school at Bethel returned in 1878 and preached a Holiness message to the congregation after an evangelistic tour in the West. Emma Williams, an AMEC Holiness preacher who relocated from the North to the South, returned North as part of a building fund campaign for a congregation in the South; she had already completed three church building projects. Thus these women intersected their Holiness ministries with the Philadelphia movement. Emily Calkins Stevens, a native of New Jersey, began serving as an AMEC evangelist in North and South Carolina in 1882. Stevens received the Holiness experience in 1853 and began preaching in 1868.

The Holiness message was also spread to Black congregations in Virginia and North Carolina during the early 1880s from the Boydton Institute in Boydton, Virginia, a town near the Virginia-North Carolina stateline. In 1881 nearly the entire student body of 104 African Americans sought the Holiness experience and large numbers received it. These students became school teachers and ministers throughout the region.

During the late 1880s and the early 1890s, Black Holiness congregations were formed in North Carolina around Raleigh, Wilmington, Durham, and Clinton. According to **Henry Fisher**, a later participant, in 1886 a Holiness revival began in a home in Method, located outside of Raleigh, North Carolina. A small but devoted number of African Americans embraced Holiness. In Wilmington, during November, 1892, Elijah Lowney of Cleveland, Ohio, an ex-Methodist minister, conducted a Holiness revival at First Baptist Church. Lowney attracted a bi-racial and interdenominational crowd. The Holiness meeting outgrew First Baptist and was transferred to the Sam Jones Tabernacle, which accommodated about four thousand people. From the revival a Black Holiness congregation was formed. At this place, a local AMEC preacher, received the Holiness experience and became the leader. By 1895, another Black Holiness congregation was formed by C. J. Wilcox, a member of the Lowney team, who returned to Wilmington. A few years later, W. H. Fulford, who belonged to the bi-racial Fire-Baptized Holiness Church, conducted a successful Holiness revival in Wilmington to a bi-racial audience. During the 1890s, Black Holiness congregations were also formed in Sampson County, around Clinton and Turkey, and in other areas, such as Durham. During October 1894, the Raleigh group joined with a Durham group to sponsor a convocation.

In September 1900, C. J. Wilcox, Joseph Silver, and John Scott, Holiness ministers in the Wilmington area, organized the Union Holiness Convention. By September 1900, P. N. Marable of Clinton and W. C. Carlton of Turkey, both local clergy and schoolteachers, organized the Big Kahara Holiness Association. Present at the meeting were persons who advocated that Holiness people attend congregations of established denominations, as opposed to forming separate congregations. On October 13, 1900, the Raleigh and Durham groups united to organize the Holy Church of North Carolina. On October 15, 1900, the Holiness groups clustered around Raleigh, Wilmington, and Durham united to form the Holy Church of North Carolina and Virginia, with W. H. Fulford serving as president from 1901 to 1916.

Historian Charles Edwin Brown recorded that during 1886 Jane Williams and other African Americans embraced the Holiness message in Charleston, South Carolina. They were instrumental in introducing the Holiness message, under the auspices of the Church of God (Anderson, Indiana), to African Americans in other parts of South Carolina and in Michigan and Alabama. Charles Oglesby, an African American Holiness preacher, licensed Beatrice Sapp as an evangelist in the Church of God in 1891 in South Carolina. Sapp moved to Alabama during the 1890s and was instrumental in establishing Holiness congregations among African Americans throughout the state. In 1895 she pastored a small congregation of 35 members in Bessemer.

Between 1900 and 1904, Ellen Mitchell conducted Holiness revivals in North Carolina. In South Carolina during the late 1890s, William E. Fuller organized Black Holiness congregations. Fuller was associated with the bi-racial Fire-Baptized Holiness Church which was organized in 1898 in Anderson, South Carolina, by Benjamin Irwin, a Holiness minister.

In 1902 a group withdrew from **William Christian**'s organization, forming the Church of the Living God (Apostolic Church), and in 1903 another withdrew under Magdalena Tate of Nashville, forming the **Church of the Living God, the Pillar and Ground of Truth**. The **Church of the Living God** began in

1888 near Wrightsville, Arkansas. William Christian, a Baptist preacher from 1875 to 1888 and pastor of a Baptist congregation in Ft. Smith, Arkansas, had a revelation in 1888 that, "he was preaching the doctrine of men and not of Christ." This revelation changed Christian's theology and preaching. It set him on a course of evaluating Christian faith and practice with scripture as the criteria and critiquing denominational Protestantism as a slave religion. Christian asserted that naming churches as Baptist, Methodist or Catholic was unbiblical. The church names selected should be taken from scripture. He critiqued the conversion process in most African American churches. He proposed substituting repentance for the Black Baptist emphasis on godly sorrow and "getting religion." Christian withdrew from the Baptist communion to establish his Bible-based fellowship, which by 1898 had approximately 90 congregations or ministries in eleven states, including the Indian Territory.

Christian's new biblical preaching included race consciousness. In response to the theory that Africans descended from beasts and not from the biblical Adam, Christian defended African humanity on biblical grounds. He taught that Adam was the father of the Hebrews, the Hebrews were the original Black people, and that from these Black people Jesus Christ descended. Christian also advocated an implicit critique of capitalism. He contended that the earth belonged to God. Land should be held in common under the control of the government, which should lease land to individuals.

Within the Kentucky and Tennessee area, George and Laura Goings were instrumental in spreading the Holiness message to African Americans. The Goings, an African American pastoral team affiliated with a Holiness church based in California, began their ministry to the region in 1897 in Slaughterville, Kentucky. There they discovered a significant Holiness movement, which emphasized fellowship and opposed forming congregations or denominations. They also discovered a small Black Holiness congregation in Slaughterville which was organized by four African Americans in 1893 and pastored by James A. Biglow.

George Goings' Holiness theology included a social dimension. He rebuffed ministry to African Americans which skirted the devastation of slavery and the injustice of their contemporary experience. He argued that the structures of the society systematically undermined all efforts of racial uplift. Furthermore the terrorism Whites employed to control African Americans deepened the crisis. The paucity of resources used to improve the plight exposed the lack of commitment of the society to African American progress.

The Black Holiness-Pentecostal movement in Mississippi took a variety of institutional forms: conferences, revivals, publications, itinerant evangelists of Holiness, the adoption of Holiness by established congregations, the organization of new congregations, and associations of Holiness congregations and clergy. The movement emerged during 1895 under the leadership of **Charles Price Jones** and **Charles Harrison Mason**. While Mason was an itinerant Baptist evangelist, Jones pastored Mt. Helm Baptist Church, a prestigious college church in Jackson, Mississippi. Jones began his pastorate at Mt. Helm in 1895 preaching Holiness sermons and conducting Holiness revivals. He sponsored his first Holiness convention in June 1897, at Mt. Helm Baptist Church. It was a regional convention with conferees drawn from Arkansas, Louisiana, Tennessee, Alabama, Missouri, Illinois, North Carolina, and Georgia.

Various Baptist congregations identified with the movement during the late 1890s. The most prominent congregation which embraced the Holiness doctrine was Mt. Helm Baptist Church in Jackson, the leader in the emerging movement. The other leading congregation was Damascus Baptist Church in Hazelhurst, a pastorate of Walter S. Pleasant.

Other congregations were established as Holiness churches. By 1905 twenty-nine new congregations, besides the ten established congregations, were associated with the movement, scattered throughout Mississippi, Arkansas, Tennessee, Louisiana, and Alabama. In October, 1901, Charles Price Jones and the majority of Mt. Helm lost possession of the church property to the anti-Holiness faction within Mt. Helm. From the loss of Mt. Helm, Jones organized Christ Temple. By 1906, Christ Temple built an edifice which had a seating capacity of 2,000 people. On Sundays, during this era, 800 to 1,000 worshiped at Christ Temple.

Among Black Methodists, the Colored Methodist Episcopal (later called **Christian Methodist Episcopal**) Bishop **Lucius Holsey** and others preached Holiness sermons in the late nineteenth century. During 1897 there were CME institutes in Missouri, Kentucky, and Arkansas that advertised discussions of the Holiness experience. In 1903, two separate groups withdrew from the CME Church. At West Lake, Louisiana, a group withdrew, forming **Christ's Sanctified Holy Church** (Colored). And at Jackson, Tennessee, a group withdrew under Robert E. Hart, a CME minister and former pastor of Liberty Temple, the CME mother church. In the

African Methodist Episcopal Zion Church (AMEZ), Bishop **Alexander Walters** preached Holiness messages during the 1890s and was involved in the Christian Holiness Association. D. J. Young, an AMEZ minister joined the Holiness movement in the early 1890s.

The Black Holiness movement entered the twentieth century with approximately two hundred congregations scattered throughout the United States. In addition to the Holiness congregations were individuals like Amanda Berry Smith and the AMEZ Bishop Alexander Walters who identified with the Holiness movement but remained in their original denominations.

William J. Seymour and the Los Angeles Revival. In 1906 a small Black Holiness congregation in Los Angeles, headed by Julia Hutchins, sponsored a revival led by **William J. Seymour**. It was here that Seymour introduced Pentecostalism to the Black Holiness movement as well as much of the American and the international Holiness movement. Hutchins invited Seymour to Los Angeles to preach at the new congregation she helped established. According to historian Cecil R. Robeck, Hutchins and the other members formed the new congregation after withdrawing from the Black Second Baptist Church, which refused to embrace the Holiness message. After hearing Seymour, Hutchins barred him from her pulpit because of his Pentecostal interpretation of the Holiness message. However other members of the congregation, first Edward Lee and later Richard Asberry, invited Seymour to resume preaching at their respective homes. The crowd continued to outgrow the sites until Seymour secured facilities at 312 Azusa Street, the former sanctuary of First African Methodist Episcopal Church. Seymour's meeting at Azusa Street attracted the attention of local Whites and Blacks, especially those involved in the Holiness community. Soon afterwards representatives of local and regional Holiness movements throughout the United States converged on the Azusa Street Mission to examine the new teaching.

Within twelve months the Azusa Street Mission spawned an international movement and started a journal, *The Apostolic Faith*. From 1906 to 1908, Seymour, the Azusa Street Mission, and the *Apostolic Times*, gave the movement a center and early leadership. Like its Holiness counterpart, the Pentecostal movement was basically local and regional. This local and regional leadership was headed by women and men. In many places the Pentecostalism assumed entire Holiness congregations and institutions. The Azusa Street Revival defined Pentecostalism, shaped its interracial relations, and gave it its multicultural character.

Seymour was introduced to the Pentecostal interpretation of the Holiness message by Charles Parham. Parham was the first proponent to link glossolalia with the biblical Pentecost event of Acts 2 and describe this experience as the baptism of the Holy Spirit instead of sanctification. The Holiness movement during the 1800s had read the Pentecost event in terms of sanctification. The Wesleyan wing of the Holiness movement described the experience in terms of cleansing, while the Reformed wing employed language of empowerment for Christian service. Each position located the experience as subsequent to justification; albeit the Reformed advocates accented the progressive dimensions while the Wesleyan advocates accented the instantaneous occurrence. Parham joined a shift in the late 1890s which sought a third definable experience which was subsequent to justification and sanctification. On January, 1901, Parham identified glossolalia with the third experience and linked this experience with Acts 2 instead of sanctification. He began preaching this new doctrine within the Holiness circles in the midwestern United States. In 1905 William J. Seymour "enrolled" in Parham's school in Houston, although Parham's enforcement of segregation prevented him from sitting with the students. In 1906 Seymour took this new message to Los Angeles.

African American Holiness leaders who embraced Pentecostalism along with all or some of their associated congregations included William Fuller, W. H. Fulford, Charles Harrison Mason, and Magdalena Tate. Among the leaders who rebuffed the Pentecostal addition were Charles Price Jones, William Christian, George and Laura Goings, Amanda Berry Smith, and Bishop Alexander Walters.

Azusa Street Mission provided the model of race relations. From 1906 to 1908, Blacks, Whites, Hispanics, and Asians worshipped together at the mission. Leaders such as Florence Crawford, Glenn Cook, R. J. Scott, and Clara Lum worked along with the pastor, Seymour, and other African Americans such as Jennie Evans Moore, Lucy Farrow, and Ophelia Wiley. Early Pentecostalism struggled with its interracial identity during an era in American Christianity and society when most institutions and movements espoused segregation. Pentecostal scholarship notes the insight of Frank Bartleman, an Azusa Street Mission participant, that, at the revival: "The color line was washed away in the blood [of Jesus Christ]." While Baptist, Methodist, Presbyterian, and Holiness communions marched into racially segregated congregations, associations, and denominational structures from 1865 to 1910, the Black and Pentecostals pastored and preached to, fellowshipped and worshipped with, each other between 1906 and 1914. In general, independent Pentecostal ministers declined to join the emerging Pentecostal denominations before 1914, yet many affiliated with the predominantly Black Pentecostal-Holiness group, the **Church of God in Christ**. The Pentecostal leadership was strongly anti-Klu Klux Klan and were often the targets of Klan terrorism because of their interracial ethic. Yet racism also countered the interracial ideal within early Pentecostalism. Parham exhibited racist behavior and a patronizing attitude toward his Black counterparts, especially Seymour. In 1908 Blacks withdrew from the Fire-Baptized Holiness Church (later called Pentecostal Holiness Church). In 1913 the Pentecostal Holiness Church dismissed the remaining Black congregations. In 1914 a large group withdrew from the Church of God in Christ. In 1920 a Black Florida group withdrew from the **Church of God (Cleveland)** to join the Church of God in Christ. And in 1924 the majority of Whites withdrew from the fifty-percent Black **Pentecostal Assemblies of the World**. While segregation among Pentecostals followed the pattern of American Christianity after the Civil War, there were exceptions. All Whites did not withdraw from the Church of God in Christ nor the Pentecostal Assemblies of the World. Blacks and Whites continued to struggle together to structure their interracial relationships during the height of segregation in the United States.

While many individual Black Holiness leaders declined to embrace Pentecostalism, the only organized Black Holiness groups to emerge from the Pentecostal watershed to be non-Pentecostal were congregations associated with the Church of the Living God headed by William Christian and those which sided with Charles Price Jones against Charles Harrison Mason, eventually organizing the **Church of Christ (Holiness), U.S.A.** From the Church of Christ (Holiness) emerged the other leaders of the non-Pentecostal Holiness wing. **Lightfoot Solomon Michaux**, a major religious radio personality in the Washington, D.C. area during the 1930s, separated from Jones's organization in 1917 to establish the Church of God (or **Gospel Spreading Church**). **William Washington** independently organized the **Associated Churches of Christ (Holiness)** in California in 1915. While he worked with Jones's group for over 30 years, in 1947, after the death of Jones, he claimed the autonomy of his organization. In 1920 King Hezekiah Burruss organized the Church of God Holiness after clashing with Jones.

The Pentecostal wing of the Black Holiness movement dominated the Black Holiness movement after the Azusa Street Revival. Under the leadership of Charles Harrison Mason, W. H. Fulford, Magdalena Tate, William Fuller, and William J. Seymour, the Black Holiness denominations combined Pentecostalism with their nineteenth-century Holiness beliefs.

While Pentecostal doctrine did divide the two wings of the Black Holiness movement, they still held in common many practices and beliefs. Carried over from the late nineteenth-century to the twentieth century by both wings of the movement was a prayer and healing tradition. From Elizabeth Mix, the first Black female serving full time as a healing evangelist, in the 1870s and 1880s, to **Frederick K. C. Price** in the 1970s and 1980s, Black Holiness-Pentecostal leaders have made the healing ministry central to the movement. Charles Price Jones, Charles Harrison Mason, and W. H. Fulford were all known for their healing ministries. During the early twentieth century, Lucy Smith, Rosa Artemus Horne, and Saint Samuel built their ministries as healing evangelists. In Chicago, Mattie and Charles Poole began a cluster of congregations modeled after their Bethlehem Healing Temple which stressed the healing ministry. Often prayer ministries served as the context for healing ministries. Charles Harrison Mason, St. Samuel, Elizabeth Dabney, and Elsie Shaw were known for their commitment to prayer. All-night prayer vigils called "shut-ins" or "consecrations," three-to-four hour prayer meetings, and periodic forty-day fasts distinguished the Black Holiness-Pentecostal prayer tradition along with practice of tarrying services, a prayer rite which prepared individuals for conversion, sanctification, and (in Pentecostal circles) the pentecostal experience. The prayer and healing tradition was a unifying force in the Black Holiness-Pentecostal movement, counterbalancing the divisive tensions over Pentecostal doctrine.

During the 1910s the Pentecostal movement split into two groups—trinitarian and "oneness"—over the interpretation of the doctrine of God. The Oneness doctrine critiqued the classic Christian doctrine of the Trinity as polytheistic. Oneness advocates claimed that consistent monotheism required the existence of only one God, not three persons in one as espoused by the doctrine of the Trinity. They argued that Jesus was the name of God and that while God expressed Godself in the form of the Father, Son, and Holy Spirit, God was only one person and not trinitarian. While the Black Pentecostal denominations, established as Holiness organizations in the late nineteenth century, remained trinitarian, such as the Church of God in Christ, United Holy Church, and Church of the Living God, many Black Pentecostal congregations rejected Trinitarianism. These congregations were located in the Midwest and often associated with **Garfield Thomas Haywood**. They emerged from groups which espoused a form of progressive sanctification instead of the instantaneous sanctification advocated by the Holiness people. Oneness denominations identified themselves as Apostolic churches.

Haywood and the Pentecostal Assemblies of the World are the parents of most Black Apostolic denominations in the United States. Significant leaders of the Black Oneness movement who originally served in the Pentecostal Assemblies of the World include **Robert C. Lawson** who organized **Church of Our Lord Jesus Christ of the Apostolic Faith** in 1919 and **Sherrod C. Johnson** who organized the **Church of the Lord Jesus Christ of the Apostolic Faith** in 1930. **Smallwood Williams**, who belonged to Lawson's group, organized the **Bible Way Churches of Our Lord Jesus Christ Worldwide** in 1957. From a separate trajectory, F. W. Williams, who had been to the Azusa Revival founded the Apostolic Faith Mission Church of God which became Apostolic in 1915. On of its ministers, William Phillips founded the Ethiopian Overcoming Holy Church (renamed the **Apostolic Overcoming Holy Church of God**) in Alabama two years later. The Black Oneness movement has grown to be a major faction within the Black Holiness-Pentecostal movement.

During the late 1910s, the Black Holiness-Pentecostal movement challenged the United States entry into World War I through adopting pacifism and engaging in anti-War preaching. According to historian Theodore Kornweibel, Jr., the Church of God in Christ, the Church of the Living God, and the Pentecostal Assemblies of the World articulated their opposition to the war. The most prominent Holiness-Pentecostal pacifist was Charles Harrison Mason. According to a Federal agent, Mason preached throughout the United States that World War I was "a rich man's war and a poor man's fight." Mason based his objection to the war on the biblical injunction against "shedding human blood or taking of human life." After Congress passed the draft act, Mason telegraphed President Woodrow Wilson to secure conscientious objector status for draft-age men in the Church of God in Christ. Mason also visited Washington to meet President Wilson to represent the pacifist stance of his denomination. Federal agents placed Mason and others under surveillance and had them arrested for obstruction of the draft in various states for their pacifist activities.

During the late 1910s, the Black religious

nationalism of Holiness leaders such as William Christian, George Goings, Alexander Walters, and James M. Webb found expression in the pan-Africanist movement of **Marcus Garvey** and the Universal Negro Improvement Association (UNIA). According to Randall Burkett, Black Holiness-Pentecostal clergy who supported UNIA included L. E. Hargrave of the Emmanuel Holiness Church, Sidney Solomon of the Pentecostal Church, **E. R. Driver** of the Church of God in Christ, and Prince C. Allen, Stephen I. Lee, R. H. Parker and Phillip Bishop from the Church of the Living God. Demonstrating their commitment to Black religious nationalism, the Church of the Living God officially endorsed UNIA in 1922, the only Black denomination to do so.

Black religious nationalism within black Holiness-Pentecostalism also shaped the mission emphasis of the movement. In 1902 the Rev. John Green, along with Dr. Harry Jones, Eli Lucas and A. C. Reeves, traveled to Liberia, representing the early Church of God in Christ led by Charles Price Jones and Charles Harrison Mason. In 1903 J. A. Jeter toured Liberia to ascertain the possibility of supporting a large missionary venture in the country. In 1904 Estelle Russell went to Liberia to support the other missionaries. The J. R. Ledbetters represented the Pentecostal Assemblies of the World in Liberia from 1914 to 1924. About 1918 the United Holy Church raised funds to sponsor its first foreign missionaries, Isaac and Annie Williams, who were sent to Liberia. In the 1920s the members of the Church of God in Christ went as missionaries to Black countries: Ms. January to Liberia in the early 1920s, Mattie McCauley to Trinidad in 1927, Joseph Paulceus, a Haitian, to Haiti in 1929. A group of Black congregations withdrew from the predominantly White Assemblies of God in 1924 because of its refusal to sponsor African American missionaries to Africa. In 1924 they formed the United Pentecostal Council of the Assemblies of God and sponsored two women, a Ms. Hathaway and a Ms. Wright, as missionaries to Liberia.

Coupled with Black religious nationalism within the Black Holiness-Pentecostal movement was the struggle for constructive interracial relations. In 1924 the Church of God in Christ adopted the Methodist model of establishing a minority conference, specifically a White conference, to unite the congregations across the United States which belonged to the predominantly Black denomination. This development was in response to the argument of the clergy who questioned the anomaly of White congregations in a Black denomination as being a racial minority within the larger system, but sought to maximize their presence by uniting under an administrative unit. The conference existed until the early 1930s when the predominantly Black leadership abolished the conference, accusing the leadership of forming a separate denomination. From 1919 to 1924 the Pentecostal Assemblies of the World was an interracial denomination which experienced a drastic increase in African American membership due to the appeal of Garfield T. Haywood, an African American minister who the interracial denomination elected as general secretary in 1919 and executive vice-chairman in 1922. Between 1924 and 1937, the denomination first lost a large group of Whites, later merged with a group, and eventually reorganized as a predominantly Black organization which slotted representation of the minority at all levels of its structures. The concern for interracial relations did not emerge again until the 1950s.

The cultural upheaval throughout the American society of the 1920s produced varied responses within the Black Holiness-Pentecostal movement. Women pastors came under attack from some quarters for "usurping authority over men." Some denominations limited the clerical authority of women. In various cities women pastored or headed the only Black Pentecostal congregations that existed. In Brooklyn there was only Eva Lambert's St. Mark Holy Church and Rosa Artimus Horn's Pentecostal Faith of Nations until the late 1920s. In Harlem, women pastored the Black Pentecostal congregations in the city until Robert Lawson arrived in 1919. In 1908 Mattie Thornton founded Holy Nazarene Tabernacle Apostolic Church, the first Black Pentecostal congregation in Chicago. Some denominations such as the Church of God in Christ, Church of Christ (Holiness), and the Church of Our Lord Jesus Christ, denied ordination to women. While ordination was denied in the Church of God in Christ, the denomination argued that women could be ministers of the Gospel. Women could be classified as evangelists and "teaching" missionaries. Other denominations such as the United Holy Church and the Pentecostal Assemblies of the World ordained women as ministers, allowed them to pastor, but denied them the office of bishop. Consequently, Black Pentecostal women have adopted the model established in 1903 by Magdalena Tate of women founding and heading denominations that promote full male-female equality in the church. In 1924 **Ida Robinson** withdrew her congregation from the United Holy Church because it denied women the office of bishop and founded the Mt. Sinai Holy Church to rectify this inequality. In 1944 Beulah Counts, the pastor of the Brooklyn congregation within Mt. Sinai Holy Church, withdrew from the Mt. Sinai Holy Church and organized the Greater Mt. Zion Pentecostal Church of

America. The same year, Magdalene Mabe Phillips, pastor of a United Holy Church congregation in Baltimore, withdrew from the United Holy Church and founded the **Alpha and Omega Pentecostal Church**. In 1947 **Mozella Cook** resigned from the Church of God in Christ and established the **Sought Out Church of God in Christ and Spiritual House of Prayer** in Brunswick, Georgia. During the next year, Florine Reed established the Temple of Christ, with her first congregation in Boston, Massachusetts. The House of the Lord founded by Alonzo Austin Daughtry in 1930 in Augusta, Georgia, was one of the few denominations not organized by women which elected a woman as its presiding bishop, Inez Conroy, who succeeded Daughtry in 1952 and served until 1960. Even in male-dominated denominations, Black Holiness-Pentecostal women played critical and progressive roles in women's departments and auxiliaries.

Black Holiness-Pentecostal women and men were also instrumental in the development of gospel music. The Black Holiness-Pentecostal movement itself was the major carrier of Black religious folk music associated with slave and West African culture, which was noted for its call-and-response, improvisation, polyrhythms, and diatonic harmonies. According Anthony Heilbut, a gospel music historian, the Black Holiness-Pentecostal movement was critical to the development of gospel music. Together with **Thomas Dorsey**, a Baptist and recognized father of the gospel music movement, Sallie Martin traveled across the country, individually and with Dorsey, organizing gospel choirs in Black congregations. **Sallie Martin** attended Black Pentecostal conventions presenting the new songs. Established Black Holiness-Pentecostal recording artists like Sallie Sanders, Ford McGee, Lightfoot Michaux, and Arizona Dranes added the new gospel songs to their repertoire. In their recordings of the 1920s Black Holiness-Pentecostal recording artists introduced to the broader religious community their religious music culture, which incorporated the New Orleans jazz style and ragtime-styled piano accompaniment and was impervious to distinctions between sacred and secular music. This music culture prepared the Black religious community for Dorsey's choral and solo compositions which he began distributing in the late 1920s. Finally, during the 1930s, the radio broadcasts of Eva Lambert in New York City and Lightfoot Michaux in Washington, D.C., along with **Lucy Smith**'s and **William Roberts**' in Chicago, introduced the new gospel compositions to thousands of homes.

During the 1930s and 1940s, Black Holiness-Pentecostal congregations could be found in most urban cities within the United States. This era also included the entry of the Black Holiness-Pentecostal movement into Black ecumenism. Black Holiness-Pentecostal denominations, according to historian Mary Sawyer, slowly joined the **National Fraternal Council of Negro Churches**. The Council was the major ecumenical thrust of Black denominations of the early twentieth century. It was founded in 1934, under the initiative of AMEC clergyman **Reverdy Ransom**, by the African Methodist Episcopal Church, African Methodist Episcopal Zion Church, Christian Methodist Episcopal Church, the **National Baptist Convention, U.S.A., Inc.**, **National Baptist Convention of America**, **Union American Methodist Episcopal Church**, and Black delegates of Community, Congregational, and Methodist Episcopal congregations. The Black Holiness-Pentecostal denominations which joined the Council were the Church of God in Christ, Church of God (Holiness), Church of Our Lord Jesus Christ of the Apostolic Faith, and The Pentecostal Church. Unfortunately, when White Pentecostals organized the Pentecostal Fellowship of North America in 1948, they denied membership to Black Pentecostals. Nonetheless, on the global level, Black Pentecostal denominations participated in the 1947 founding of the Pentecostal World Conference, a triennial, multi-racial, international assembly. In more recent years, the Church of God in Christ became a charter member of the Congress of National Black Churches, the major Black ecumenical organization of the late twentieth century. Pentecostal leaders such as William Bentley and George McKinney are active members of the National Association of Evangelicals, as well as the **National Black Evangelical Association**. During the 1980s, **J. O. Patterson, Sr.**, under the auspices of the Church of God in Christ, convened the first national assembly of Black Pentecostal denominations to begin the process of cooperation among Black Pentecostals.

Black Holiness-Pentecostal leaders also joined the ranks of religious social activists who engaged in campaigns for better race relations and upliftment of the race. William Roberts was a member of the delegation from the **National Fraternal Council of Negro Churches** which went to Washington, D.C. in 1941 to demand justice for African Americans. Robert Lawson joined **Adam Clayton Powell, Jr.**, and other Harlem clergy in campaigns for Black jobs. Along with Methodist college president **Mary McLeod Bethune**, **Arenia C. Mallory**, a leader in the Church of God in Christ, was a member of Eleanor Roosevelt's Negro Women's Cabinet which advised the first lady on issues from the Black woman's perspective. In the 1950s, **J. O.**

Patterson, a future presiding bishop of the Church of God in Christ, participated in local civil rights campaigns in Memphis, Tennessee, and Smallwood Williams led a legal battle against segregated public schools in Washington, D.C. During the 1960s, Holiness clergywomen **Willie Barrow** and Addie Wyatt, and Pentecostal bishops Arthur Brazier and **Louis Henry Ford**, were active in the civil rights efforts in Chicago. Barrows and Wyatt also worked with the Rev. **Jesse Jackson**, a Baptist minister, to organize **Operation PUSH**, a national civil rights organization headquartered in Chicago. Revs. Ithiel Clemmons and **Herbert Daughtry** in New York City were similarly involved in rights efforts. Included among the churches bombed during the civil rights movement were Black Holiness-Pentecostal congregations in Winnsboro, Louisiana, DeKalb, Mississippi, and Plainview, Texas.

During the 1950s a cadre of healing evangelists emerged who challenged the segregationist ethic of Pentecostals and other American Christians by rejecting segregated seating in their evangelistic crusades. These included Whites such as Oral Roberts and A. A. Allen. These ministers forged a new alliance between Black and Pentecostals against the social norm of race relations. The focus of these healing evangelists was a new accent on demonology, exorcism, and miracles. This new accent formed the core of a revival in Pentecostalism during the 1940s associated with William M. Branham, a healing evangelist, and identified by the 1950s as the deliverance movement. The deliverance movement among Black Pentecostals emerged from the ministry of Arturo Skinner who expanded the traditional Black Pentecostal emphasis on healing to include demonology and exorcisms, and heightened the accent on the miraculous. In 1956 he established the **Deliverance Evangelistic Centers**, with headquarters in Newark, New Jersey. While deliverance ministries emerged in traditional Pentecostal congregations, such as Chicago's Faith Temple Church of God in Christ under Harry Willis Goldsberry, new independent congregations emerged in urban centers which competed with traditional Black Pentecostals, such as the Deliverance Evangelistic Center in Philadelphia founded by Benjamin Smith in 1960 and Monument of Faith Evangelistic Center founded by Richard Henton in Chicago in 1963. The deliverance movement of the 1950s and early 1960s was the first national interracial experiment within American Pentecostalism since the interracial experiments of early Pentecostalism which ended by the early 1930s.

Relations between liberal Protestantism and Black Pentecostalism occurred on a number of levels. A significant number of Black Holiness-Pentecostals have been graduates of liberal seminaries from as early as the 1940s. By the 1960s and 1970s, Black Holiness-Pentecostals were graduates of such liberal seminaries as Interdenominational Theological Center (ITC), Howard, Yale, Princeton, Duke, Emory, and Harvard. This coupled with the presence of African American Pentecostals during the 1970s and 1980s on the faculties of liberal seminaries such as Union (NYC), Duke, Harvard, Howard, Emory, ITC, and McCormick. And the first accredited Pentecostal and only African American seminary, Charles Harrison Mason Theological Seminary, is a member of ITC, a consortium of African American seminaries affiliated with mainline denominations.

In the 1970s a number of Black Holiness-Pentecostal leaders began identifying with the Black theology movement associated with **James Cone**, Jacquelyn Grant, and **Gayraud Wilmore**. Different writers began to engage Black theology from a Pentecostal perspective. William Bentley and Bennie Goodwin, Jr., sought to incorporate the social critique of Black theology within Black Pentecostalism and infuse Black theology with Pentecostal spirituality and evangelical themes. Leonard Lovett and James Tinney sought to interject the liberationist agenda of Black theology into Black Pentecostalism. Cheryl Sanders placed Black theology in conversation with the Holiness tradition.

During the 1970s the "Word of Faith" movement intersected with Black Pentecostalism. Kenneth Hagin, a Pentecostal, led the Word of Faith movement with his message of healing, prosperity, and positive confession. **Frederick K. C. Price** emerged as the Word of Faith leader among Black Christians after establishing the **Crenshaw Christian Center** in Los Angeles in 1973. At the same time Pentecostalism emerged within the historic Black denominations, especially the African Methodist Episcopal Church. Neo-Pentecostal ministers began occupying major African Methodist Episcopal Church pulpits. The focal point for the movement during the early 1970s was St. Paul AMEC in Cambridge, Massachusetts, under the pastorate of **John Bryant**. By the 1980s the largest African Methodist Episcopal congregations were neo-Pentecostal: St. Paul in Cambridge, Bethel in Baltimore, Allen Temple in Queens (NY), Bridge Street in Brooklyn, Ward in Los Angeles. And two neo-Pentecostals, **Vernon Byrd** and John Bryant, were elected bishops of that denomination. Within the African Methodist Episcopal Zion Church, the center was John A. Cherry and his congregation, the Full Gospel AMEZ in Temple Hills, Maryland, a suburb of Washington, D.C. The focal point for the movement among Black Baptists was Pilgrim Baptist Cathedral pastored by Roy Brown. During this period some college campuses also became centers for the growth of Pentecostalism among Black students, particularly through the gospel choirs.

By the 1980s, according to Horace Boyer and Anthony Heilbut, Black Pentecostals such as **Andrae Crouch**, Edwin Hawkins, Walter Hawkins, **Shirley Caesar**, the Clark Sisters, The Wynans, and Richard Smallwood would dominate the gospel music movement. During the 1960s, Black Pentecostal musicians created a new sound within the gospel music movement which would later be called contemporary gospel music, in contrast to traditional gospel music, associated with Thomas Dorsey and Sallie Martin. As earlier Black Holiness-Pentecostal musicians borrowed from jazz, ragtime, and blues, the younger generation of Black Holiness-Pentecostal musicians would freely borrow from the soul music of the sixties, a style originally influenced by traditional gospel music. Andrae Crouch composed ballads and incorporated the melodies of soul and pop music. Edwin Hawkins wrote choral songs and borrowed from a variety of jazz and calypso sounds. Impervious to distinctions between sacred and secular music like their Holiness-Pentecostal predecessors, Andrae Crouch and Edwin Hawkins ushered in a new phase within Black religious music and the Black church.

Since its beginning during the late nineteenth century, Black Holiness-Pentecostalism has grown into the second largest religious movement among African Americans (second to the Baptists) and is one of the fasting growing religious movements in United States.

Anderson, Robert Mapes. *Vision of the Disinherited: The Making of American Pentecostalism.* New York: Oxford University Press, 1979. 334 pp.

Burgess, Stanley, et.al., eds. *Dictionary of Pentecostal and Charismatic Movements.* Grand Rapids: Regency Reference Library, Zondervan Publishing House, 1988. 914 pp.

Daniels, III, David Douglas. "The Cultural Renewal of Slave Religion: Charles Price Jones and the Emergence of the Holiness Movement in Mississippi." Ph.D. diss., Union Theological Seminary (NYC), 1992. 289 p.

DuPree, Sherry Sherrod, ed. *Biographical Dictionary of African-American Holiness-Pentecostals, 1880–1990.* Washington, D.C., Middle Atlantic Regional Press, 1989. 386 pp.

Heilbut, Anthony. *The Gospel Sound: Good News and Bad Times.* Rev. and Updated ed. New York, Simon and Schuster, 1971; repr., Limelight Editions, 1985. 370 pp.

Jones, Charles Edwin. *Black Holiness: A Guide to the Study of Black Participation in Wesleyan Perfectionist and Glossolalic Pentecostal Movements.* ATLA Bibliography Series, No. 18. Metuchen, N. J., & London, The American Theological Library Association and The Scarecrow Press, 1987. 388 pp.

Kornweibel, Jr., Theodore. "Bishop C. H. Mason and the Church of God in Christ During World War I: The Perils of Conscientious Objection." *Southern Studies: An Interdisciplinary Journal of the South* 26, 4 (Winter, 1987): 261–281.

Lovett, Leonard. "Black Origins of the Pentecostal Movement." In Vinson Synan, ed. *Aspects of the Pentecostal-Charismatic Origins.* Plainfield, NJ: Logos International, 1975, pp. 123–41.

Nelson, Douglas J. *For Such a Time as This: The Story of Bishop William J. Seymour and the Azusa Street Revival.* Birmingham, England; Ph.D dissertation, University of Birmingham, 1981. 346 pp.

Nickel, Thomas R. *Azusa Street Outpouring.* Hanford, CA: Great Commission International, 1979. 42 pp.

Richardson, James Collins. *With Water and Spirit: A History of Black Apostolic Denominations in the United States.* Martinsburg, VA: The Author, 1980. 151 pp.

Tinney, James S., ed. "The Black Origins of the Pentecostal Movement." *Christianity Today* (October 8, 1971): 4.

———. "The Blackness of Pentecostalism." *Spirit: A Journal of Issues Incident to Black Pentecostalism* 3, 2 (1979): 27–36.

———. *In the Tradition of William J. Seymour: Essays Commemorating the Dedication of Seymour House at Howard University.* Washington, DC: Spirit Press, 1978. 102 pp.

Turner, William C., Jr. "Movement in the Spirit: A Review of African American Holiness/Pentecostal/Apostolics." In Wardell J. Payne, ed. *Directory of African American Religious Bodies: A Compendium by the Howard University School of Divinity.* Washington, DC: Howard University Press, 1991. 363 pp.

David D. Daniels, III

PEOPLES COMMUNITY CHURCHES, NATIONAL COUNCIL OF THE. A liberal Protestant church association. The National Council of the Peoples Community Churches was founded in 1923 in Chicago, Illinois, by the coming together of several independent community-based liberal Protestant churches. Independent community churches began to emerge in the early twentieth century as Protestants responded to the ecumenical movement by forming what were seen as nonsectarian congregations based in a local community and often created in conjunction with a community center. The formation of such congregations proceeded at a vigorous pace during the decades immediately following the formation of the Federal Council of Churches in 1908. In May 1923 the leaders of the predominantly White community churches had organized as the Community Church Workers of the United States of America. This organization would continue for a decade, but eventually was discontinued.

The first permanent organization for community churches resulted from the call of the Rev. William D. Cook, pastor of the Peoples Church in Chicago, to his colleagues in the Black community to gather at a meeting to be held September 17–20, 1923. Four churches, two from Chicago and two from Detroit, responded and organized the National Council of the Peoples Community Churches. The council operated informally for a decade before its incorporation in 1933 as the Biennial Council of the Peoples Church of Christ and Community Centers of the United States and Elsewhere. By this time member churches could be found across the United States and in Canada. The 1929 annual meeting was hosted by the Rev. C. O. Greene, pastor of the Community Church of Chatham, Ontario.

Meanwhile, following World War II, the predominantly White churches were able to organize and in 1946 formed the National Council of Community Churches. In 1948 the Biennial Council voted to merge with the National Council, which was accomplished in 1950 and brought over 100 congregations to the new National Council. The congregations of the Biennial Council continue as an integral part of what is now the International Council of Community Churches. The council membership has remained almost evenly, Black and White, and over the years Black and White leaders have evenly shared the presidency and other leadership positions. It points with some justification at its ability to function as a fully integrated organization over the almost half a century of existence.

The council is very loosely organized as an association of autonomous congregations. It is headquartered in Homewood, Illinois.

Shotwell, J. Ralph. *Unity without Uniformity: A History of the Postdenominational Community Church Movement.* Homewood, IL: National Council of Community Churches, 1984. 64 pp.

PEOPLES TEMPLE. The Peoples Temple, a predominantly Black church which became infamous for the murder-suicide of hundreds of its members in November 1978, began in 1954 as the Community Unity Church, a multiracial Pentecostal-style congregation in Indianapolis, Indiana. The church was founded by a twenty-three-year-old white preacher, Jim Jones (1931–1978), who had made a name for himself in Pentecostal circles throughout the United States as a healer and prophet. By 1955, Jones's ministry had been renamed the Peoples Temple Full Gospel Church and was attracting large crowds for Sunday faith-healing services. Jones later insisted that the healing dramas of his early ministry were conducted mainly to draw people who could then be indoctrinated with his more important messages of apostolic socialism and racial equality. The young preacher's efforts to promote interracial harmony were heralded by the *Indianapolis Recorder*, a weekly Black newspaper, and earned Jones the position of director of the Indianapolis Human Rights Commission in 1961.

Jones was deeply impressed by the **Peace Mission Movement** of **Father Divine**, whom he visited in Philadelphia in 1956. The Mission's attempt to provide social services for the poor and a community life based on racial equality were copied by the young minister, who set up soup kitchens, distributed free groceries and clothing, and organized other community services through the Peoples Temple. During the early 1960s the Temple was accepted as a congregation in the **Christian Church (Disciples of Christ)**. Jones himself was ordained as a Christian minister in 1964.

Jones had a vision in 1961 in which the American Midwest was destroyed in a nuclear war and moved his congregation to Ukiah, California, shortly thereafter. This town in the Redwood Valley area north of San Francisco was believed by Jones to be one of nine safe places on the earth should nuclear war break out. The temple's services were initially held in homes and rented churches in Ukiah, but by 1969 a large complex—called "Happy Acres"—containing Jones's home, a meeting space, a swimming pool, a child care facility, and a senior citizen home had been opened.

Jones's ministry, which now claimed to have twenty thousand members, expanded into Los Angeles and into the predominantly Black Filmore district of San Francisco in the early 1970s. The city missions bused members to Ukiah for Jones's dramatic healing services, during which he claimed to resurrect members from the dead. Jones's message was also broadcast over KFAX in northern California. By mid-1972 the charismatic preacher, in imitation of Father Divine, was promoting himself as an embodied god was working to bring an end to poverty, racial prejudice, and injustice in the world. Jones was the recipient of several humanitarian awards during the mid-1970s and was appointed to the San Francisco Housing Authority after having worked on behalf of mayor-elect George Moscone.

In the wake of the defections of eight close aides in 1973 and an unfavorable series of articles on his movement in the *San Francisco Examiner*, Jones began making plans to move his congregation to the South American country of Guyana. At the time, Guyana was ruled by a Black, English-speaking, socialist regime who appeared sympathetic to the Peoples Temple's avowed socialism. By 1974, fifteen of Jones's followers had negotiated the lease of three thousand acres on Guyana's western border and begun clearing the jungle for what would become the Peoples Temple Agricultural Project. Jones referred to Guyana in his sermons as the "Promised Land" to which his people would make their exodus from the degradations and persecution of American society.

Just prior to the appearance of an August 1977 *New West* article that suggested the temple should be investigated for financial fraud, the mistreatment of members, and questionable dealings in San Francisco politics, Jim Jones fled to Guyana. By September, over one thousand California Temple members had joined him. The soon thriving communal village consisted of 75 percent Blacks, 20 percent whites, and five percent Hispanics, Asians, and Native Americans. Women composed nearly two-thirds of the community.

Jonestown advertised itself as a socialist utopia where racism, ageism, sexism, and classism had been eliminated and where the persecuted peoples of the United States could live in dignity and freedom. However, ex-members of the temple formed the Committee of Concerned Relatives in 1978 and published literature likening Jonestown to a concentration camp wherein armed guards subjected residents to torture, forced labor, and isolation from the world.

California congressman Leo Ryan took these charges seriously and initiated an official investigation of the Guyana community in November 1978. Ryan and several others visited Jonestown on November 17 and were on their way home with fourteen dissatisfied residents when Ryan was ambushed and killed by Jones's security forces. The next day, the entire community of 914 men, women and children committed mass suicide or were murdered rather than face the repercussions of Ryan's murder.

This tragic event sparked a strong reaction from the African American community. Black religious leaders like Dr. **Joseph E. Lowery** of the **Southern Christian Leadership Conference** commented that suicide was a relatively alien act to Black culture and the Black experience, and other Black spokespersons expressed alarm at the seeming historical receptivity of the Black lower class to messianic or cultic groups like the Peoples Temple. The Black Panther party issued a statement charging that the CIA and the U. S. Department of Defense had "quite possibly" used a neutron bomb to commit mass genocide against Jonestown. The reason given for this barbarous act was the embarrassment caused to the American government by a successful socialist settlement of emigre Blacks and other minorities near its southern border.

At a special two-day conference called "A Consultation on the Implications of Jonestown for the Black Church," Black leaders from around the country explored the meaning of the Guyana tragedy for the mission, history, and self-understanding of the Black church. The consensus of this conference was that Jonestown was a degradation perpetrated upon African Americans by an unscrupulous and exploitative white leadership. One speaker called Jim Jones a "new plantation boss" who had co-opted San Francisco civil rights groups by purchasing memberships for his followers. In the aftermath of the Guyana murders/ suicides, leaders in the Black community in the San Francisco Bay Area spearheaded efforts to aid the families of Jonestown survivors and to promote healing in the Black community.

The Assassination of Representative Leo J. Ryan and the Jonestown, Guyana Tragedy: Report of a Staff Investigative Group to the Committee of Foreign Affairs U.S. House of Representatives. Washington, DC: U.S. Government Printing Office, 1979.

Chidester, David. *Salvation and Suicide: An Interpretation of Jim Jones, the People's Temple, and Jonestown*. Bloomington, IN: Indiana University Press, 1988. 190 pp.

Hall, John R. *Gone from the Promised Land: Jonestown in American Cultural History*. New Brunswick, NJ: Transaction, 1987.

Feinsold, Ethan. *Awake to a Nightmare: Johnestown: The Only Eyewitness Account*. New York: W. W. Norton & Co., 1981.

Kilduff, Marshall, and Ron Jeaves. *The Suicide Cult: The inside Story of the Peoples Temple and the Massacre in Guyana*. New York: Bantam Books, 1978.

Klineman, George, and Sherman Butler. *The Cult that Died: The Tragedy of Jim Jones and the People's Temple*. New York: G. P. Putnam's Sons, 1979.

Lane, Mark. *The Strongest Poison*. New York: Hawthorn, 1980.

Melton, J. Gordon. *The Peoples Temple and Jim Jones: Broadening Our Perspective.* New York: Garland Publishing, 1990. 406 pp.

Moore, Rebecca. *In Defense of People's Temple—and Other Essays.* Lewiston, NY: Edwin Mellen, 1988.

Moore, Rebecca, and Fielding M. McGehee III, eds. *The Need for a Second Look at Jonestown.* Lewiston, NY: Edwin Mellen, 1989. 244 pp.

———. *New Religious Movements, Mass Suicide, and Peoples Temple: Scholarly Perspectives on a Tragedy.* Lewiston, NY: Edwin Mellen, 1989. 251 pp.

Reiterman, Tim, with John Jacobs. *Raven: The Untold Story of the Rev. Jim Jones and His People.* New York: Dutton, 1982. 622 pp.

Vee, Min S., and Thomas N. Layton. *In My Father's House.* Mew York: Holt, Rinehart and Winston, 1981.

Weightman, Judith Mary. *Making Sense of the Jonestown Suicides: A Sociological History of the Peoples Temple.* Lewiston, NY: Edwin Mellen, 1987.

Wooden, Kenneth. *The Children of Jonestown.* New York: McGraw-Hill, 1981.

Phillip Charles Lucas

PERKINS, JOHN M. (b. 1930), founder of the Voice of Calvary Ministries, was born in New Hebron, Mississippi, the son of sharecroppers Jap and Maggie Perkins. His mother died soon after his birth, and he and his brothers and sisters were raised by a grandmother. He experienced the oppression attendant upon living as a Black in the rural South of the time, including the 1947 death of a brother at the hands of a white policeman. Soon thereafter Perkins moved to California and in 1951 he married Vera Mae Buckley, with whom he had eight children. After he spent two years in the Army (1951–1953), he supported the family through a series of jobs.

Not very religious growing up, after his stint in the Army Perkins began to seek out experiences with a number of groups, including the Jehovah's Witnesses. In November 1957, in a **Churches of God (Holiness)** Bible study, he was converted, and began to re-evaluate his life. He decided he was too self-involved, and began sharing his new faith through the Child Evangelism organization and through visiting prisoners. In 1960 he moved back to Tennessee and found a job picking cotton. While continuing to testify to his faith whenever possible, he began to realize that he needed a different kind of evangelism, one that first encountered and dealt with the real needs of people.

In 1964, with the support of the Calvary Bible Church in Burbank, California, he began the Voice of Calvary Ministries in Mendenhall, Mississippi, a parachurch group combining evangelism with social services to the poor. He also founded and pastored the Berean Bible Church. Through the Voice of Calvary, he provided help with nutrition, education, and job skills. He joined in the growing civil rights activism by organizing a voter registration drive in 1966 and a leadership training program in 1968. The White community grew very hostile to Perkins, and he was arrested in December 1969. He was soon released, but continued to take part in marches and demonstrations. He and several other leaders were arrested on February 7, 1970, and were badly beaten. When they were released, a press conference was called and the welts and other marks of punishment were revealed to the public. After that, many of the White people were more sympathetic.

Over the years the Voice of Calvary Ministries expanded to include a housing co-op, a network of thrift stores, three Christian health care centers, and an International Study Center for leadership training. In 1976 he published the story of his ministry, *Let Justice Roll Down*, which further raised his profile in the evangelical community. In 1978 he began a new phase of the work in Jackson, about forty miles away from Mendenhall. In 1981 he resigned as president of the Voice of Calvary Ministries, and became minister-at-large, allowing him to begin other projects. He moved to Pasadena, California, and began the Harambee Christian Family Center in a high-crime neighborhood. The John M. Perkins Foundation for Reconciliation and Development was created to provide support for similar projects which have taken root in several other communities.

Norton, Will, Jr. "John Perkins, the Stature of a Servant." *Christianity Today* 26 (January 1, 1982): 18–22.

Aeschliman, Gordon D. *John Perkins: Land Where My Father Died.* Ventura, CA: GL Publications, 1987. 172 pp.

Perkins, John M. *Let Justice Roll Down.* Ventura, CA: GL Publications, 1976. 223 pp.

———. "Integration or Development." *Other Side* 10 (January–February 1974): 10–13.

———. *A Quiet Revolution.* Waco, TX: Word Books, 1976. 226 pp.

RLOA, WWABA (85), *HUBA.*

PERRY, HAROLD R. (b. October 9, 1916), the 2nd African American bishop of the **Roman Catholic Church**, was born in Lake Charles, Louisiana, the oldest of six children in the family of Frank and Josephine (Petrie) Perry. His father regularly commuted to work in the rice mills in Orange, Texas, and his mother was a part-time employee in the rectory of the Catholic church, of which they were loyal members. Perry thus grew up very close to the church and became aware of the possibility of Blacks becoming priests through the auspices of the **Divine Word Society**, based in Mississippi.

At age thirteen, in September 1930, with his parents' blessing, he left Lake Charles and entered the minor seminary of the Divine Word Society at Bay St. Louis, Mississippi. He was able to do this only because a Father Hannigan agreed to pay the tuition for the first four years. Perry moved through junior and senior high school, returning to Louisiana for occasional holidays and summer weeks. In 1937 he spent a year at the Society's novitiate in East Troy, Wisconsin, where he pronounced his first vows of poverty, chastity, and obedience. From 1938 to 1941 he completed his college studies at St. Mary's Seminary in Techny, Illinois, and from 1941 to 1944 engaged in theological studies at St. Augustine Seminary in Bay St. Louis.

Perry was ordained priest on January 6, 1944, the 26th Black American to become a priest. He was assigned as assistant pastor to Immaculate Heart of Mary Church in Lafayette, Louisiana. Further appointments included St. Peter's Catholic Church in Pine Bluff, Arkansas; Notre Dame Catholic Church in St. Martinville, Louisiana; and St. Gabriel's Catholic Church in Mound Bayou, Mississippi. In 1952 he was the founding pastor of St. Joseph Catholic Church in Broussard, Louisiana. Beginning with nothing, he led the building of a church, rectory, and school. In 1958 he was assigned as rector of St. Augustine Seminary in Bay St. Louis. For eight years he was national chaplain of the **Society of the Knights of Peter Clavier** and for six years was on the board of the National Catholic Council for Interracial Justice. He was very active in his support for greater Catholic attention to Black concerns, and in 1963 was invited by President Kennedy to participate in discussions on the peaceful desegregation of public accommodations. Soon thereafter he was the first Black clergyman to give the opening prayer of the 88th session of the U.S. House of Representatives.

In 1964 Perry was elected superior of the Southern Province of the Divine Word Society (S.V.D.), the first Black major superior of men in the United States. His jurisdiction included seventy-five priests and brothers, one minor and one major seminary, one high school, twenty parishes in Louisiana, four in Texas, and three in Arkansas. On September 29, 1965, Pope Paul VI appointed him Auxiliary Bishop of New Orleans. After **James A. Healy** (1875), Perry was the second Black American Roman Catholic bishop in history, and the first in the twentieth century. This appointment was understood to be a concrete expression of the new open spirit of Vatican II, the historic Catholic council that was just concluding. In 1962, at the beginning of Vatican II, Martin de Porres, a Black Dominican priest, was canonized as a saint. It was also helpful to the New Orleans archdiocese, which was experiencing unrest following the integration of its parochial schools in 1961. By February 1966, there were over 160 African American Catholic priests and about 725,000 African American Catholics.

Perry was consecrated for the office on January 6, 1966, and in addition to his episcopal duties was appointed as pastor of the New Orleans Little Flower of Jesus Church, a parish of four thousand members, one-fourth of them Black. He was also named rector of the National Shrine of Our Lady of Prompt Succor. Although he often spoke out in defense of civil rights, it was his desire mainly to carry out his duties in the archdiocese and not to be "the Catholic answer to Dr. **Martin Luther King**." On September 4, 1986, a major celebration was held in New Orleans to celebrate Perry's twentieth anniversary as bishop. By that time there were nine other Black bishops, who spoke of their gratitude for his pioneering role.

"Historic Bishop." *Time* 86 (October 8, 1965): 70.

"Louisiana Negro Priest Appointed Bishop." *Negro History Bulletin* 29 (December 1965): 65–66.

Thompson, Era Bell. "Bishop Harold Perry: Man of Many Firsts." *Ebony* 21 (February 1966): 62–70.

IBAW, CB (1966), *OBS, GMOC, WWABA* (90–91), *BDNM* (70), *AAE, NA.*

PERRY, RUFUS LEWIS (March 11, 1834–June 18, 1895), educator, editor, and Baptist minister, was born into slavery in Smith County, Tennessee, the son of Lewis and Maria Perry. His father was a Baptist preacher and such an accomplished mechanic and carpenter that he was able to negotiate some semblance of wages and freedom from his owner, Archibald W. Overton. The family was allowed to move to Nashville, where Perry attended a school for free Blacks. This came to an end when Perry was seven and his father fled to freedom in Canada. The remaining family was forced to move back to the plantation and Perry's small schooling gave him the reputation among Whites as being "dangerous."

In August 1852 Perry was sold to a slave dealer who intended to take him to Mississippi. After only three weeks Perry ran away to Canada and made it to Windsor, Ontario, where he dedicated himself to gaining more education and became a schoolteacher. In 1854 he experienced conversion and soon decided to enter the ministry. He graduated in 1861 from Kalamazoo Seminary in Michigan, and in about October 9, 1861, was ordained pastor of the Second Baptist Church of Ann Arbor, Michigan. Over the next several years he was also pastor in St. Catherine, Ontario, and Buffalo, New York. He married Charlotte Handy, with whom he had seven children.

In 1865 Perry began work as a general missionary and educator among the newly freed Blacks in the South, and for a time was superintendent of some schools. He was editor of the *Sunbeam* and of the *People's Journal*, both pioneering efforts to advocate moral, spiritual, and educational advancement in a general circulation paper along Baptist denominational lines. In 1866 the Northwestern Baptist Convention, **Southern Baptist Convention**, and American Baptist Missionary Convention, all Black groups, united to form the **Consolidated American Baptist Missionary Convention**. Perry, previously affiliated with the American Baptist Missionary Convention, was the first corresponding secretary for the new group, and served for ten years. In about 1869 he moved to Brooklyn, New York, and from 1869 to 1871 was co-editor of the *American Baptist* (later the *Baptist Weekly*). In 1871 the Consolidated American Baptist Convention held its annual gathering in Brooklyn.

From 1872 to 1895 Perry was co-editor, then editor-in-chief of the *National Monitor*, another Baptist periodical, and wielded great influence through this position. After his term as corresponding secretary with the **Consolidated American Baptist Convention** ended in 1876, he became corresponding secretary of the American Educational Association and of the American Baptist Free Mission Society. On May 16, 1887, he delivered a scientific lecture entitled "Light" at the State University in Louisville, Kentucky, and the following night the school officials presented him with an honorary Ph.D. His only known published book was *The Cushite; or, the Descendants of Ham as Found in the Sacred Scriptures, and in the Writings of Ancient Historians and Poets from Noah to the Christian Era* (1893), in which he demonstrated his remarkable knowledge of history and literature.

Perry, Rufus Lewis. *The Cushite; or, The Descendants of Ham as Found in the Sacred Scriptures, and in the Writings of*

Ancient Historians and Poets from Noah to the Christian Era. Springfield, MA: Willey and Company, 1893. 175 pp. AARS, HUBA, BAW, HBB, CH, AAE, MM, DAB, WWCR, IBAW, OBMS.

PETERSEN, ERNEST LEOPOLD (September 8, 1896–November 26, 1959), founder of the **American Catholic Church (Syro-Antiochian)**, was born in the Virgin Islands. After a short career as a machinist, he was ordained a priest in 1922 in the **African Orthodox Church**. He was sent to Miami where a small group of people had requested the formation of a parish. Within a few years Petersen had built a congregation of several hundred members. However, as complaints came into the church's headquarters, Archbishop **George Alexander McGuire** decided to remove Petersen and replace him with Bishop **William E. J. Robertson**. In response, Petersen resigned and, taking as many of the congregation as he could, formed a rival church which he also named St. Peter's. Peterson applied to Archbishop Frederick E. J. Lloyd of the American Catholic Church for jurisdiction, and Lloyd accepted him.

The American Catholic Church was a predominantly White organization which had direct responsibility for the founding of the African Orthodox Church, as its founder Archbishop Joseph René Vilatte had consecrated McGuire, and McGuire had retained his closest relationship with Lloyd, Vilatte's successor. Lloyd's quick acceptance of Petersen destroyed the communion between the two churches.

Lloyd further offended the African Orthodox on June 27, 1927, when Petersen was consecrated by Archbishop Lloyd. In 1932 Lloyd retired in favor of Daniel Cassel Hinton, who in turn stepped down in the late 1930s in favor of Percy Wise Clarkson. There was some controversy over this succession and Petersen left to form the American Catholic Church (Syro-Antiochian). He established his headquarters at St. Peter's in Miami, Florida. During the 1940s he had a Sunday morning radio broadcast over WMBM with a mixed Black and White audience of about 125,000.

"Top Radio Ministers." *Ebony* 4 (July 1949): 56–61.
IB.

PETTEY, CHARLES CALVIN (December 3, 1849–December 8, 1900), 21st bishop of the **African Methodist Episcopal Zion Church** (AMEZ), was born into slavery near Wilkesboro, North Carolina, the son of Jordan and Fannie Pettey. He became free with the end of the Civil War in 1865, then worked on his father's farm until age twenty-one. With only occasional assistance, he taught himself to read and write, and never went anywhere without Webster's blueback speller. At length he decided to save money to attend Biddle Institute (now called Johnson C. Smith University) in Charlotte, North Carolina, and made baskets, brooms, and shoes by night after farm work by day. At the end of August 1872, he left home, and studied at Biddle for seven years.

At the age of seventeen, he had already experienced conversion and joined the AMEZ Church, becoming a class leader. He received an exhorter's license on August 4, 1868, and a preacher's license in August, 1872. On December 11, 1872, his first year at Biddle, he was ordained deacon and from that point to graduation pastored country circuits in the area. In college he organized a literary society, helped a brother into Biddle, and sent a niece to Scotia Seminary. During the summers he taught school, sometimes having to walk fifty miles to his post. He graduated on June 5, 1878, with high honors for his B.A. degree, and was Latin salutatorian.

For four months thereafter Pettey was principal of the city school in Charlotte, North Carolina, at which point he went to pastor the AMEZ Church at the Lancaster Court House in South Carolina. In association with the church he founded Pettey High School (later called Lancaster High School) and was its principal for three years. He was ordained elder on November 10, 1878. At the 1880 General Conference in Montgomery, Alabama, he was recording secretary, and began to gain a higher profile in the denomination. In December, 1881 he transferred to the East Alabama Conference and was appointed to Clinton's Chapel (Old Ship) AMEZ Church in Montgomery, Alabama. In three years there he more than doubled the membership and paid off all church debts.

In May 1884, Pettey was elected general secretary of the denomination, and soon volunteered to go to Knoxville, Tennessee, to try to save a crisis situation, but contracted pneumonia and nearly died. He was on a sickbed until late 1885, when he went to the AMEZ Church in Chattanooga, Tennessee. In only four months he tripled its membership and paid off all debts, and then exchanged pulpits with Rev. A. Walters of San Francisco, California. For the next two years he was minister of the Stockton Street AMEZ Church in San Francisco, and was also presiding elder of California and Oregon as well as still being general secretary.

At the 1888 General Conference Pettey was elected

bishop and was consecrated on May 22. He was assigned to the Sixth Episcopal District (West Alabama, Louisiana, Texas, and California Conferences), and increased these four conferences to six. His first wife, about whom we know little, passed away, and on September 19, 1889, he married **Sarah E. C. Dudley Pettey**, a teacher. Immediately after the marriage they made a tour of the United States, Mexico, and Europe. He continued in the Sixth District for the rest of his career; he founded the Jones Institute of Tuscaloosa, Alabama, and served as its first president.

ACAB (supp.), *HAMEZC, AMEZC, OHYAMEZC, NNW, IBAW.*

PETTEY, SARAH DUDLEY (b. November 9, 1868), educator and general secretary of the Women's Home and Foreign Missionary Society of the African Methodist Episcopal Zion Church (AMEZ), was born in New Berne, North Carolina, the daughter of E. R. and Caroline E. Dudley. Both parents were former slaves, and her father gained considerable prominence during Reconstruction, serving in the state legislature. Pettey received a solid education, completing her grade school learning at the State Normal School. In 1880 she entered Scotia Seminary in Concord, North Carolina, from which she graduated with honors in 1883. She began teaching elementary school and after only one year was promoted to assistant principal, a position she held for six years. For two summers she was assistant professor in the Craven County Teachers' Institute. She was an accomplished musician and for several years was the organist at one of the New Berne churches.

On September 19, 1889, she married Charles Calvin Pettey, who the previous year had become a bishop in the AMEZ Church. Immediately after the marriage they embarked on a tour of the United States, Mexico, and Europe. She retired from teaching and became her husband's private secretary. In 1892 she was elected treasurer of the Woman's Home and Foreign Missionary Society of the AMEZ Church, and in about 1896 became its general secretary, a position she remained in for several years after her husband passed away in 1900.

Majors, Monroe A. *Noted Negro Women: Their Triumphs and Activities.* 1893. Rept.: Freeport, NY: Books for Libraries Press, 1971.
TCNL, PNW, NNW, HUBA, IBAW, IBAWCB.

PHILANDER SMITH COLLEGE. A United Methodist Church School. Philander Smith College, the first institution of higher learning serving the African American community of Arkansas, was founded in 1877 in a Black church in Little Rock as Walden Seminary. Then in 1883 the Philander Smith family of Oak Park, Illinois, donated $10,000 to construct the Main Building of the present campus. The school has prospered under the leadership of three outstanding presidents, each of whom served lengthy terms: Rev. Thomas Mason, a White man and first president who served until 1897; Rev. J. M. Cox, the first graduate of Gammon Theological Seminary, who served from 1897 into the 1920s; and **M. Lafayette Harris** (later bishop). Harris came to Philander Smith in 1936, when the school had yet to recover from the Depression, and over the next 24 years did a remarkable job of expanding the school and putting it on a firm financial footing. He left the school in 1960 when he was elected bishop and assigned to Atlanta.

Among the important facilities at the school for many years was the Adeline Smith Industrial Home which offered practical training for Black women. The Home survives in the B.S. degree in Home Economics presently offered by the school.

Stowell, Jay S. *Methodist Adventures in Negro Education.* New York: Methodist Book Concern, 1974. 180 pp.

PHILLIPS, CHARLES HENRY (January 17, 1858–April 11, 1951), 8th bishop of the **Christian Methodist Episcopal Church** (CME), formerly the Colored Methodist Episcopal Church, was born into slavery in Milledgeville, Georgia, the tenth of twelve children in the family of George and Nancy Phillips. Phillips experienced conversion in on December 26, 1874, at age seventeen and that same year entered Atlanta University, where he completed his basic education and continued through the position of college sophomore. He supported himself by cutting cordwood, carrying water for dormitories, and teaching in rural schools in the summer. He was licensed to preach in September 1878, and two months later entered Central Tennessee College in Nashville, from which he graduated in May 1880. He was ordained deacon in November 1879. On December 16, 1880, he married Lucy Ellis Tappan, a graduate of Fisk University, with whom he had five children.

After receiving his B.A. degree, Phillips stayed on at the related Meharry Medical College until he attained the M.D. in 1882. While attending school he was also working as a preacher in the Pine Knob Circuit in the West Tennessee Conference. He was ordained an elder in 1883, and instead of being appointed to a church as an elder, he became the principal of Jackson High School in Jackson, Mississippi, the name of which he changed to Lane Institute (later becoming Lane College). In 1885 he resigned to be the principal of the city school in Union City, Tennessee. After only a few months in that position, Bishop **William H. Miles** challenged him to devote full-time work to the church. The result was that in December 1885, he was appointed to Collins Chapel CME Church, Tennessee, and the following year was the youngest delegate ever sent to General Conference. He was also selected as the second fraternal delegate ever sent to the Methodist Episcopal Church, South, General Conference, the body which had given birth to the CME Church in 1870.

In December 1887, he was transferred to the Virginia Conference and its Israel Metropolitan CME Church in Washington, D.C. In his nearly four years there, he added well over one hundred members, reduced the debt, and gained a national reputation. In 1889 he spent two months in Europe as a delegate to the first World's Sabbath School Convention, preaching in many cities. When he left Israel Metropolitan Church later that year, luminaries such as Frederick Douglass spoke at a banquet in his honor.

In October 1891, he was assigned to the Center Street Church in Louisville, Kentucky, where as before, he added members, reduced the debt, repaired the buildings, and gained an outstanding reputation as a preacher. He used that prominence in a successful fight against additional Jim Crow (segregation) laws. In 1894 he became presiding elder of the Mt. Sterling District in Kentucky, and editor of the church's journal, the *Christian Index*, a position he held until 1902. In 1898 Phillips published the *History of the Colored Methodist Episcopal Church in America*, a major work.

He was elected bishop on May 15, 1902, and had as his territory most of the western United States. As people moved westward, he was able to organize the CME Church in their path, thus making it a national church. He was also known for his many close friendships with leaders in the other Black Methodist churches, thus raising the standing of the CME Church considerably, a body whose close relationship with the Methodist Episcopal Church, South, made it suspect among many African Americans. His first wife died in 1913 and he married Ella Cheeks on August 28, 1918; there was one daughter from this union, who later married Bishop **Rembert E. Stokes** of the AME Church. Phillips published his autobiography in 1932 and retired in 1946.

"Bishop C. H. Phillips Laid to Rest." *Christian Index* 83 (April 19, 1951): 5.

"Charles Henry Phillips: A 'Prince' Among Men." *Christian Index* 109 (April 8, 1976): 8–10.

Phillips, Charles Henry. *The Apostles' Creed.* Jackson, TN: Publishing House of the CME Church, 1938. 45 pp.

———. *From the Farm to the Bishopric: An Autobiography.* Nashville, TN: Parthenon Press, 1932. 308 pp.

———. *The History of the Colored Methodist Episcopal Church in America.* Jackson, TN: Publishing House of the CME Church, 1898. 247 pp.

RLOA, NYTO, RLA, EWM, WWCR, WWCA (38–40), HUBA, AARS, IBAW, BAW, BAA, CMECTY, HCMECA, BHAC, RCM, NV, HCMEC.

PLUMMER, HENRY VINTON (1844–February 8, 1905), temperance leader and perhaps the first African American chaplain (Baptist) of the post-Civil War Army, was born into slavery on the Calvert plantation in Prince George's County, Maryland. He was eventually sold into Howard County, Maryland, but escaped in late 1862 and enlisted in the Union Navy in 1864. He served for sixteen months, much of the time on the gunboat *Cordelion*, and learned to read. After discharge he went to Wayland Seminary in Washington, D.C., from which he graduated in 1879. He supported himself in school as a night watchman at the Washington post office and began preaching to several congregations. In 1867 he married Julia Lomax, with whom he had eight children.

After graduation he was ordained a Baptist minister and became a missionary for the Mount Carmel Baptist Church in Washington, D.C. On July 8, 1884, President Chester A. Arthur appointed him chaplain of the 9th Regiment of the U.S. Cavalry, and he became possibly the first Black chaplain of the post-Civil War Army. He served for ten years in Kansas, Wyoming, and Nebraska, during which time he consistently advocated temperance. This placed him in direct opposition to established military tradition and his broad popularity posed an additional threat to the white command structure.

In the summer of 1894 Plummer proposed to the War Department a plan to colonize central Africa, using himself in command of a company of volunteer Black soldiers. He thought this would help racial tensions in the United States, help meet the challenges of European expansionism, and build a positive climate for the colonists and their progeny. This apparently was an idea the military did not want spread around, and in three months Plummer was brought up on charges of drunkenness. He was convicted and dismissed in the fall of 1894 despite having only one prosecution witness with an admitted grudge and despite the testimony of defense eyewitnesses. He accepted the pastorate of the Rose Hill Baptist Church in Kansas City, Kansas, and the Second Baptist Church in Wichita, Kansas, and tried for years to be reinstated in the Army. In 1902 he was elected to the executive board of the Kansas Baptist Convention.

Plummer, Nellie Arnold. *Out of the Depths; or, The Triumph of the Cross.* Hyattsville, MD: N.p., 1927. 412 pp.

DANB.

POPE, DANIEL CARLETON (1887–March 4, 1964), 60th bishop of the **African Methodist Episcopal Zion Church** (AMEZ), was born in Theodore, Mobile County, Alabama, the son of Mr. and Mrs. Americus Pope. After attending the public schools in Mobile County he went to Tuskegee Institute, where he received his B.A., followed by the B.D. degree from Lincoln University in Pennsylvania.

He was ordained deacon on November 30, 1913 and elder on November 28, 1915, and served a number of charges, including Butler Chapel AME Zion Church in Tuskegee, Alabama. In 1924 he married Louise Hudson and a few months afterward they moved to Mt. Coffee, Liberia for mission work. During that time they educated and introduced to Christianity many children, though one of their own children died at age one and a half, and in 1930 Pope had to return to the United States due to his wife's poor health. She later passed away in November 1940. From 1930 to 1948 Pope pastored Wesley Union AME Zion Church in Harrisburg, Pennsylvania; Galbraith AME Zion Church in Washington, D.C.; Trinity AME Zion Church in Southern Pines, North Carolina; Evans Metropolitan AME Zion Church in Fayetteville, North Carolina; and Old Ship AME Zion Church in Montgomery, Alabama.

In 1948 Pope was elected Secretary of Foreign Missions and from that office was elected bishop in 1952. For the next eight years he served the Twelfth Episcopal District (West Africa, Liberia, Gold Coast, and Nigeria). He retired in 1960, but was recalled by the General Conference to serve the Sixth Episcopal District (Georgia, Pee Dee, South Carolina, East Tennessee, and Virginia Conferences).

"Bishop Daniel Carlton Pope." *Star of Zion* 101 (May 26, 1977): 5.

"Bishop Pope Translated." *Star of Zion* 87 (April 9, 1964): 5.

Coleman, Clinton R. "Bishop Daniel Carlton Pope Honored Posthumously." *Star of Zion* 101 (May 26, 1977): 1, 7.

"Final Rites for Bishop D. C. Pope." *Star of Zion* 87 (April 2, 1964): 1, 8.

Moncur, B. W. "Bishop Pope—Man of God." *Star of Zion* 87 (April 9, 1964): 1, 3.

Pope, Daniel Carlton. "Daniel Carlton Pope for Secretary of Missions." *Star of Zion* 71 (December 4, 1947): 7.

HAMEZC, AMEZC.

PORTER, HENRY PHILLIPS (March 15, 1879–May 8, 1960), 17th bishop of the **Christian Methodist Episcopal Church** (CME), was born near Kilgore in Rusk County, Texas, the son of George and Caroline (Mayfield) Porter. He experienced conversion and joined the CME Church on August 12, 1882, and was licensed to preach at an early age. He was educated in a local one-room school until 1883, when he entered the newly founded Texas College in Tyler, Texas, graduating from its preparatory course in 1903. In 1896, at age seventeen, he entered the ministry and while in school pastored several charges in the area. From 1898 to 1903 he also was a schoolteacher. On November 24, 1902, he married Elnora Brooks, with whom he had one daughter.

In 1912 he was assigned as presiding elder of the Beaumont District, where he served for nine years. During this time he was editor of the *Southwestern Christian Index* and a trustee of Texas College. In May 1922 he was elected Publishing Agent for the denomination, remaining in that position for twelve years. During that time an impressive new publishing building was built and the quality of the church literature was improved. In May 1934, he was elected bishop and assigned to Alabama, where he cleared the debts of many churches and the $135,000 debt of Miles College. He later presided over the Ohio, Kentucky, North Carolina, and South Carolina conferences. He spent eight years on the Eighth Episcopal District (Texas), where he led a successful $320,000 endowment for Texas College and completed several renovations of the campus. In 1961 he was a delegate to the World Methodist Conference in Oslo, Norway. He retired in 1958.

Cunningham, R. Theo. "He Sleeps with the Fathers." *Christian Index* 93 (July 21, 1960): 5.

"Rest, Soldier of Christ!" *Christian Index* 93 (May 19, 1960): 1.

EWM, CMECTY, WWCR.

POWELL, ADAM CLAYTON, JR. (November 29, 1908–April 4, 1972), pastor of the Abyssinian Baptist Church in New York City and United States congressman, was born in New Haven, Connecticut, the son of **Adam Clayton Powell, Sr.**, and Mattie (Fletcher) Powell. Shortly after his birth, the family moved to New York City, where his father was made pastor of the Abyssinian Baptist Church (unaffiliated with any denomination), with 12,000 members, the largest congregation in the country at that time. In 1923 the church and family moved to a new location in Harlem.

He graduated from Colgate University in 1930 and became business manager of his father's church. He continued his education, however, and obtained an M.A. from Columbia University in 1932. He married Isabel Washington on March 8, 1933. In 1937, when his father retired, Powell succeeded him as pastor of the Abyssinian Baptist Church, and was noted as a spellbinding orator. Already, Powell had shown a penchant for activist leadership; he had conducted picket demonstrations for issues ranging from fired workers to lower rents. He expanded the social service program of the church, adding a free soup kitchen and a relief structure to assist Depression-hit residents. In February 1936, after a Harlem race riot, he began a column in the *Amsterdam News* called "The Soap Box," in which he urged Blacks to work together to counter oppression. In 1938 he helped found the Coordinating Committee for Employment, representing 200 Black organizations, as a means of securing jobs for Blacks. Demonstrations resulted in Blacks being hired by the World's Fair, Harlem drugstores, the New York City bus line, and numerous other businesses.

In 1941 Powell won election to the New York City Council as its first Black member. In the final week of the campaign, his headquarters published an eight-page tabloid called *The People's Voice*, and the following year it became a national Black weekly, with Powell as editor. In 1943 a reapportionment bill made Harlem practically a separate Congressional district, and Powell announced he would run for Congress, winning the seat in 1944. He divorced his first wife in 1943 and married Hazel Scott in 1944. In 1945 he published *Marching Blacks: An Interpretive History of the Rise of the Black Common Man*, presaging the mood of the civil rights movement still years in the future. By this time the church's membership was in the 20,000 range.

In Congress, Powell was instantly controversial, with an independent and sensational style. He challenged racism by visiting traditionally white-only dining rooms, barber shops, and other establishments, often with his whole staff. He openly fought southern segregationist congressmen, and proposed many pioneer civil rights bills. His was the single most influential voice in integrating the military. His enemies made much of his lack of attention to regular congressional duties, missing many meetings, floor debates, and votes. There were questions of tax evasion and misuse of public funds, and he gained a reputation as a playboy whose irresponsible behavior placed his status in jeopardy. In typical forthright manner, he answered his critics by saying that he did in the open what other colleagues merely kept hidden. He divorced his second wife in 1960 and married Yvette Marjorie Flores Diago.

Despite continuous party efforts to oust him, his constituents in Harlem kept reelecting him, pleased with his conspicuous work on behalf of Blacks. In 1954 *Ebony* magazine named him one of the top ten Black preachers in America. In 1960 he became chair of the powerful Education and Labor Committee, which under his direction passed forty-eight major pieces of legislation, including the 1961 Minimum Wage Bill, the Manpower Development and Training Act, the Anti-Poverty Bill, and the Vocational Educational Act.

The unravelling of his career began in 1960 when a Harlem woman brought a libel suit against him. She won, but he refused to comply with the ruling. Finally, in 1966 he was convicted of criminal contempt, and to escape its consequences he moved to the Bahamian island of Bimini. The House of Representatives expelled him from Congress on March 1, 1967. In a special election to fill his seat two months later, Harlem residents still voted him back, feeling he was being unfairly singled out for errors less serious than those of other congressmen. He finally paid the court fines and was reseated in January 1969, but was stripped of his seniority. In June of that year the Supreme Court ruled that he had been expelled from Congress unconstitutionally. Later in 1969 he was finally defeated at the polls by another Black, Charles B. Rangel, after he had been diagnosed as having cancer. He retired to Bimini and spent some of his remaining time writing his autobiography, *Adam by Adam* (1971).

Alexander, E. Curtis. *Adam Clayton Powell, Jr. and the Harlem Renaissance.* New York: ECA Associates, 1988. 45 pp.

Dionisopoulos, P. Allen. *Rebellion, Racism, and Representation: The Adam Clayton Powell Case and its Antecedents.* Dekalb, IL: Northern Illinois University Press, 1970. 175 pp.

"Great Negro Preachers." *Ebony* 9, 10 (July 1954): 26–30.

Hamilton, Charles V. *Adam C. Powell, Jr.: The Political Biography of an American Dilemma.* New York: Macmillan, 1991. 448 pp.

Haskins, James. *Adam Clayton Powell: Portrait of a Marching Black.* New York: Dial Press, 1974. 174 pp.

Hickey, Neil, and Ed Edwin. *Adam Clayton Powell and the Politics of Race.* New York: Fleet Publishing Co., 1965. 308 pp.

Jacobs, Andy. *The Powell Affair, Freedom Minus One.* Indianapolis, IN: Bobbs-Merrill, 1973. 256 pp.

Jakoubek, Robert E. *Adam Clayton Powell, Jr.* New York: Chelsea House, 1988. 111 pp.

Levine, Richard M. "The End of the Politics of Pleasure." *Harper's Magazine* 242 (April 1971): 45–60.

"Organizations and Leaders Campaigning for Negro Goals in the United States." *New York Times* (August 10, 1964): 16.

Powell, Adam Clayton, Jr. *Adam by Adam: The Autobiography of Adam Clayton Powell, Jr.* New York: Dial Press, 1971. 260 pp.

———. "Can There Be Any Good Thing Come Out of Nazareth?" In A. L. Smith, ed. *Rhetoric of Black Revolution.* Boston, MA: Allyn and Bacon, 1969, 154–160.

———. *Keep the Faith, Baby!* New York: Trident Press, 1967. 293 pp.

———. *Marching Blacks: An Interpretive History of the Rise of the Black Common Man.* New York: Dial Press, 1945. 219 pp.

———. *The New Image in Education: A Prospectus for the Future by the Chairman of the Committee on Education and Labor.* Washington, DC: U.S. Government Printing Office, 1962. 12 pp.

Weeks, Kent M. *Adam Clayton Powell and the Supreme Court.* New York: Dunellen, 1971. 311 pp.

NYTO, CB (42), *ONL, HNB, CH, NWAC, BDA-AHP, EBA, CRS, HBB, PBP, BHBA, RLOA, BAA, IBAW, BAW, HUBA, AARS, SBAA, CA* (102), *BAC, BLW, BAC, BLTC, MBRL.*

POWELL, ADAM CLAYTON, SR.

POWELL, ADAM CLAYTON, SR. (May 5, 1865–June 12, 1953), author and pastor of the Abyssinian Baptist Church in New York City, was born in Franklin County, Virginia, of German, Indian, and African heritage. He grew up as one of seventeen children in the family of Anthony and Sallie Dunning Powell, former slaves. In March, 1885, he was working in an Ohio coal mine when he was converted in a revival meeting and determined to change his life. In 1887 he tried unsuccessfully to enter Howard University School of Law in Washington, D.C., and instead decided on the ministry. In 1888 he was admitted to both the normal/academic and theological departments of Wayland Seminary and College in Washington, D.C. (later a part of Virginia Union University), and graduated in 1892.

While at that school a Massachusetts visitor was so impressed with him that a $1,500 scholarship was offered if he would give up all other employment, work full-time on studies, and afterward settle in the South. Powell declined, and asked the school president for the one job for which there were no applicants, that of cleaning the college's privies. The astounded president, a White man, dismissed him abruptly, but called him back a few minutes later to give him the best student job on campus, that of dining-hall headwaiter. Powell married Mattie Fletcher Schaefer on July 30, 1889, with whom he had two children.

After a brief stay at Ebenezer Baptist Church in Philadelphia, Powell became the pastor of Emanuel Baptist Church in New Haven, Connecticut, in September 1893. He was successful in adding members, reducing indebtedness, and generally enhancing the standing of the church in the community. He had a tall, commanding presence, and was an impressive preacher. In 1895–1896 he was able to add a program of study at Yale University Divinity School. In 1900 he was a delegate to the World's Christian Endeavour Convention in London.

In December, 1908, Powell became the pastor of Abyssinian Baptist Church in New York, an old, established church with about 1,600 members and unaffiliated with any denomination. At that church his talents blossomed fully. He was theologically conservative, opposed to such diversions as dancing and theater-going, but was liberal and activist on many social questions. He also realistically understood the value of political contacts in accomplishing goals. His influence with local authorities was key in cleaning up the houses of prostitution in his neighborhood, one of his first priorities. He was a founder of the National Urban League and on the first board of directors of the National Association for the Advancement of Colored People (N.A.A.C.P.). His first book was *Patriotism and the Negro* (1918).

In 1923, at Powell's insistence, the church moved from West 40th Street to West 138th Street in Harlem. He saw that the future of New York's African American community lay in the formerly White neighborhood of Harlem. A large church and community house was built at a cost of $334,000, becoming the base of a significant religious and social education program. In 1926 a home for aged members was dedicated and named after Powell. During the Depression, the church supplied food and services for the poor, and Powell campaigned for more jobs and city support.

He retired in 1937, leaving the church as the largest congregation in America with 14,000 members, and was succeeded by his son, **Adam Clayton Powell, Jr.** His wife died in 1945, and he then married Inez Cottrell. He remained active as pastor emeritus, writing a number of books, including the autobiographical *Against the Tide* (1938), *Picketing Hell* (1942), and *Upon This Rock* (1949). After race riots erupted in 1943, he became co-chair of the City-Wide Citizens' Committee on Harlem. He was a regular lecturer at various universities, and was an editorial writer for the *Christian Review*. He was widely acknowledged to be one of the most famous and successful Black ministers of his time.

Hickey, Neil, and Ed Edwin. *Adam Clayton Powell and the Politics of Race*. New York: Fleet Publishing Co., 1965. 308 pp.

Powell, Adam Clayton, Sr. *Against the Tide: An Autobiography*. New York: R. R. Smith, 1938. 327 pp.

———. *Palestine and Saints in Caesar's Household*. New York: R. R. Smith, 1939. 217 pp.

———. *Picketing Hell: A Fictitious Narrative*. New York: W. Malliet and Co., 1942. 254 pp.

———. *Riots and Ruins*. New York: R. R. Smith, 1945. 171 pp.

———. *Upon This Rock*. New York: Abyssinian Baptist Church, 1949. 132 pp.

NBH, CH, NA, NV, GNPP, RLA, HNB, NYTO, WWCR, WWCA (38–40), EBA, NWAC, DANB, DAB (Supp.5), RLOA, BAA, HUBA, IBAW, BAW, AARS.

PREACHING AND THE PREACHER IN AFRICAN AMERICAN RELIGION. Though often caricatured as mere ritual ranting and raving, preaching is Black culture's most established mode of communication on matters of serious import. Almost every major African American personage in the Civil Rights Revolution of the 1960s was either a PK (Preacher's Kid) or a preacher's grandchild. This applies to everyone from **Martin Luther King, Jr.**, and James Farmer to Huey Newton, Bobby Seal, and Eldredge Cleaver. They not only struggled to establish their preacher-parents' biblically based ideals for society; they were fluent in their parents' oratory and idiom. Their charisma was related to the African American pulpit's best style of discourse, and, at times, to its undeniably worst. They succeeded in proportion to their capacity to appeal to the folk of the Black Church, the preeminent center of the African American community's life.

Description and Definition. Generally speaking, the preaching tradition of the masses of African American

Christians is to be distinguished from that of other ethnic traditions by its warmth and spontaneity, its graphic portrayals, and its **holistic** involvement of the entire personhood of preacher and audience (emotive and intuitive, as well as intellectual, or cognitive) in the preaching event. These characteristics are by no means unique, yet other ethnic and cultural groups, and other socioeconomic groupings with the same general characteristics, are easily distinguishable from African American culture. African Americans are equipped with innumerable sensitivities to subtleties of signal and substance, even in ordinary conversation.

In its involvement of the entire person, Black preaching not only communicates gut-level, sustaining core belief and motivation; it affirms the person and her/his culture, providing communion with God in the soul's "mother tongue." In other words, the preaching and worship traditions have survived amidst an alien majority culture precisely because they serve functions such as emotional support and affirmation of otherwise dehumanized personhood. In significant addition, it has been the instrument for the mobilization of membership clout for bringing about social change.

At its best, the Black Church's preachment is a synthesis of African culture (which lays great stress on the healing and instructive powers of possession by the Spirit), and Euro-American or Western tradition (which until recently has almost exclusively emphasized the enlightenment of the mind). The African tradition is and has been equally demanding of factual data and propositional truth, but prone to avoid abstraction, making the Word come alive in metaphors employing the concrete. This causes it to be more effective in the life of the hearer; hearing then becomes an **experience** of truth, as opposed to a mere understanding. The results are manifest in changed life, as well as changed ideas.

When the early Black preacher declared that he "saw John on the Isle of Patmos, early one Sunday morning," the hearer also "saw" or visualized John there. The result was an unforgettable experiential encounter, and not just an easily forgotten idea.

The saving and growth of persons comes from just such vivid encounters. No matter how stimulating and great one's abstract ideas may be, they are hard to remember and harder to implement. People are not saved and motivated by information and assent, but by faith, which is *not cognition (= sight)*. If the reverse were true, persons would be saved by wisdom, making salvation most available to those already best blest with intellectual gifts. This is manifestly untrue, but it is a strange fact that Western culture has been most reticent to embrace it. *Faith and hope and love are functions of intuitive and emotive consciousness*, with reason used only to monitor for self-contradiction and give coherent expression and application to holistic core (or "gut") belief. Reason may pave the way, but it cannot generate faith. The communication mode of the best of African American preaching has always sensed this, and has always spoken in vicarious experiences which were specific and concrete.

So what has been called Black Preaching for generations is, in fact, a most sophisticated and providentially healing and supportive tradition, taken at its best. It is often used by charlatans and simply insecure practitioners for selfish and manipulative purposes. But the African American style of preaching is, nevertheless, one of the main bases on which an unspeakably oppressed people have maintained a belief system which has helped them survive and remain creative. Preaching has been so important that the typical mass church will forgive a pastor for almost anything except the failure to communicate a moving, healing, empowering gospel message.

Roots of the Tradition. Given this recitation of benefits too long overlooked or taken for granted, the question of source rises irresistibly. How did such a marvelous tradition come to be? Who or what orchestrated this synthesis of African Traditional Religion and culture with the culture and faith of the Euro-American enslavers?

In the first place, it must be understood that cultures, including their belief systems, are not easily erased from group consciousness (as has been commonly and erroneously assumed with regard to the enslaved Africans). The only way to "strip" a people of indigenous culture and world view is to snatch all their babies from their mothers at birth, and rear them in an alien culture. In fact, if adults could be successfully stripped of their cultural "survival-kits," they would be shattered and in need of care in a mental institution. Indigenous culture persists. So when the slave masters outlawed African drums and medicine and meetings, they were only proving that African culture had indeed survived the Middle Passage and was alive and well in the colonies.

The evidence is impressive, causing wonderment as to why it was overlooked for so long. For instance, the well-known Morse code is **bi**nary, with only two signals: dot and dash. African drum code was **tri**naural, or three-noted (high, medium, and low). It was much more complicated, and therefore presumably far easier to destroy. Instead, it survived amazingly well, or it would not have had to be outlawed.

607

When African Religion's traditional medical remedies were outlawed, it was only among Whites, since it had seemed too often to fail to cure mean masters. It was still approved for practice among costly slaves, however. And African Traditional Religion's belief and worship, which were far less visible, were even harder to suppress. They just went underground and became "The Invisible Institution." The myth of Africans stripped of their heritage is manifestly false and long overdue for widespread correction.

Then it must be also understood that there was a great deal of overlap between ATR (African Traditional Religion) and O.T. (the Jewish Bible or Christian "Old Testament"). This well-established but oft-overlooked fact means that once they had been forced into English communication, and exposed to the English Bible (verbally and by stealing and reading), Africans could identify the commonalities and benefit from a kind of "head start" into the Christian faith.

This faith was not unlike their own ATR in pivotal doctrines, such as the omnipotence (cf. Olodumare of the Yoruba), omniscience (cf. Brekyirihunuade of the Ashanti), and omnipresence of their deity. The favorite folk doctrine of all the tribes was the providence of God, expressed in exquisitely symbolic proverbs: "God is the One who fans the flies for the cow who has no tail." It was not hard to embrace a Savior whose own religious roots were so like those of the ATR, and who was "'buked and scorned" like unto themselves. So their traditional religion/faith was like an African Old Testament, preparing them for Christ, to whom they were drawn with touching devotion. This is evidenced by Spirituals such as "Sweet Lil' Jesus Boy, they made you be born in a manger."

Now all of this leads up to the issue of preaching, because these commonalities between ATR and Christianity had to be shared in the form of legally acceptable gospel, through preaching. For their first century or so in the American colonies (1619 to the 1730s and 1740s), there had been two major barriers to the propagation of the Christian faith among the Africans. One had been fear on the part of owners that conversion to Christianity would mean freedom from slavery. The other had been unresponsiveness on the part of Africans to the formal and feelingless worship of the Virginia Anglicans (Episcopal) and even the New England Puritans (Congregational). The first barrier was moved by such legislation as the Virginia Assembly's decree (1667) that souls might be free while bodies were still in bondage. The second barrier was bridged by the providential coming of the First Great Awakening (1726–c.1750) and the Second Great Awakening (1800–

1850's). These were massive, nationwide religious revivals, and the preaching style and the dramatic response of the White participants turned out to be compatible with the religious responses of the Africans. Their ways of religious communication were "legitimated" by the powers that be. So they could hear Christ preached, accept salvation, and still be authentically and expressively African.

The most identifiable tracing of the bridging to African ways of preaching can be detected in the reaction of African Americans to the unprecedentedly sonorous, eloquent, profound, and emotionally powerful preaching of George Whitefield, an Anglican. When established pastors in the colonies opposed the emotional responses of his audiences, Whitefield was no longer welcome in "proper" sanctuaries. But the crowds far exceeded the capacities of the local churches anyway, so he preached in the open air. Ben Franklin (who was Whitefield's printer and personal friend) carefully computed audiences in Philadelphia to exceed 25,000. The unchurched Franklin also attested to the marvelous sonority or musicality of Whitefield's voice, which he said was like a great organ. The native African ex-slave and sailor, Gustavus Vassa, confirmed these characteristics and said that Whitefield made him think tearfully of home. It is not surprising that dozens of White preachers, if not indeed hundreds, fashioned their preaching after Whitefield, even to the tonality. The intonation (often called "whooping") of many African American preachers was shared in the beginning with Whites, under such rubrics as "the holy whine."

Unnumbered Africans now baptized their own native oratory, word-picture painting, and holy imagination, to produce a gospel that was authentically Christian and African at the same time. This pre-established culture-kit undoubtedly gave African American preachers a head start in the preaching arena. Much of what is taught even today is designed only to try to reach the levels of biblical clarity and dramatic power which these earliest Black preachers developed almost immediately.

This providential union has been widely accepted as a time-tested model of holistic preaching in recent years. But it has always had some strong support from Whites. An African American named **Harry Hosier** accompanied Bishop Asbury (1745–1816), often preaching after the bishop to audiences of Blacks. But these were known often to include many Whites, who considered Hosier's preaching far superior. The first pastor of many a Methodist or Baptist congregation in the South was a slave. And it was often only the fact that Black converts outnumbered the Whites that caused the churches to split and go their racially separate ways.

After the Civil War, preachers such as **John Jasper** (1812–1901), the ex-slave pastor in Richmond, Virginia, regularly drew huge numbers of Whites to hear such sermons as "De Sun Do Move." In Philadelphia, at the turn of the century, the hymn-writing United Methodist, **Charles A. Tindley**, had to accommodate hundreds of Whites. In that same era, in Augusta, Georgia, President Taft and John D. Rockefeller were often seen in the pews of the Tabernacle Baptist Church, where **C. T. Walker** held forth. Martin Luther King, Jr., was also a great preacher in this tradition, which took the Bible seriously, engaged in powerful rhetoric, and generated vivid word-pictures, moving hearers into an experience of the Gospel. This fusion of African beliefs and styles of communication, with aspects of the Euro-American Christian styles and content, has worked well.

Biblical and Theological Assumptions. An analysis of African American preachings also requires reference to its biblical and theological basis. Part of the caricature of Black preaching widely held among both African Americans and Whites associates its spontaneity and emotion (no matter how lofty) as the parent of empty utterance. Nothing could be further from the truth, in regard to the African American tradition at it best.

To start with, African Traditional Religion and culture know absolutely nothing about such Western culture habits as questioning the validity of the holy wisdom handed down by the ancestors. While never prone to rigid notions about biblical "inerrancy" and print literalness, African American oral culture carefully hands down the "story" with vivid portrayal and reverent care. Without a biblical text and serious attention to it, there is considered to be no preaching.

Scientific verifiability is never at issue; the perpetual concern has to do with how to use Scripture to save and maintain the group and its members. The process of handing it down was and is much like the purpose and reverence with which versions of portions of the Bible, especially the Old Testament, were handed down before they were ever written. From the beginning even until today, the mode of preaching is designed to find out what God was and is saying and doing in a particular situation to save God's people.

To do this kind of preaching properly, a variety of modes of preparation were and still are practiced. For the supposedly unlearned and often non-literate preacher of the early days, the first step was to memorize the biblical material. This was often accomplished by the oral tradition, which means that the preacher had no idea just when the Bible passage was first heard and committed to memory. At other times, especially among persons new to the faith, the prodigious memory common in the culture was employed after one or two hearings. With or without formal training as such, the African American preachers took personal ownership of the text and context. They started with living up to Deuteronomy 6:6, which declares that the Word shall first be in the teaching parent's heart.

Given this familiarity with the text, the preacher then sat on the porch or on a creek bank and mediated on that text. One saw and heard the Bible story, and then "wrote" and memorized the parts of the dialogue, learning each well enough to portray it in the sermon. What seemed like a leisurely life was in fact a rigorous process of disciplined preparation for making congregations see and hear John or Jesus or whoever it was. This mode of preparation is still advisable. One needs only the careful addition of the biblical data now available to assist toward the goal of greater vividness and fidelity to details. Whatever the level of scholarship, the preachers took ownership of the details added, just as they had taken the biblical account for their own.

Theologically speaking, the African American preaching tradition is strongly biblical and seldom likely to get argumentative or judgmental about abstract doctrine. If a concept is in the Bible and "backed up by the Holy Spirit," that's good enough. Only in recent years have appreciable numbers of African Americans allowed themselves to be party to the theological debates common to White Christendom. But this does not mean they have no theology. It simply means that their belief system is about supportive affirmations at the core of the Christian faith. Nobody argues about the providence or justice of God. In the mind common to the tradition, much of the rest of theology is irrelevant to the struggle of life.

Jesus is so prominent in the theology of the African American preaching tradition because Jesus is so relevant to and present in the struggle. Jesus is also the Incarnation of God, bringing within mind's grasp the infinite God of the Universe. Jesus said that whoever had seen him had also seen the Father, and the tradition was and is expert at vivid portrayals of Jesus. It is not easy to assign this tradition to high or low christology in Euro-American terms, but it is surely true that the gospel of this preaching tradition is Christ-centered.

Again, this preaching tradition strongly emphasizes the Holy Spirit, but not in abstract systems. The Holy Spirit is real and present in the worship service. One song puts it, "We're down here Lord, waitin' on you. We can't do nothin' 'til you come." Unlike the classic theological idea of worship as the *proper* preachment of the Gospel, and the *proper* administration of the sacraments, African American preaching anticipates the point at which propriety is transcended, and people are literally possessed by the Holy Spirit. The healing and empowerment of hearers which is mentioned above is the work of the Holy Spirit and not the preacher. While this work will remain safely within the parameters of African American cultural expectations, authentic preachers have no idea that they can or should control the Spirit.

The tradition is also very strong on the idea that a preacher should be called by God. The Holy Spirit works through divinely chosen and called preachers. This does not denigrate the work of the laity; huge churches thrive with just one professional clergy on staff. The rest of the supportive ministries in the extended family/church are carried on by laity. But the preacher/pastor may not be self-chosen for the task. Her or his work is far too taxing and complex for a mere mortal on his or her own. The pastor is guided by the Holy Spirit, who also guides the laity, even while dramatically possessing and healing and empowering them from time to time.

It is the Spirit which also confirms the Word delivered by the preacher with the dialogic response of the laity. Of the three persons of the seldom-mentioned Trinity, the Holy Spirit is the most concretely involved in the life and ministry of the preacher and the congregation as a whole.

Relevance to the Communal Life. With this emphasis on the supernatural and erstwhile otherworldly, one might expect this religion and its preaching to be "no earthly good." Quite to the contrary, the African American church and its preaching have been the catalysts for all the major liberating movements among African Americans, from the earliest slave rebellions to the present day. Martin Luther King, Jr., was only one in a long line of faithful preachers whose communication of the Word gave both hope and the motivation to bring dream to reality.

Prior to the Civil War, the chief African American proponents of the abolition of slavery were preachers, and their chief mode of motivation and mobilization was preaching. **Richard Allen**, father of the African Methodist Episcopal denomination, organized a convention of African Americans for the sole purpose of liberation in North as well as South. He led in launching a boycott of food produced by slave hands, and opposed recolonization as a ruse intended only for already freed Blacks. He set a militant precedent for AMEs in the years to follow.

Henry Highland Garnet, **Samuel Ringgold Ward**, and **J. W. C. Pennington** were powerful Presbyterian preachers on the abolitionist lecture circuit. It was Garnet who first used the militant phrase of the 1960s: "by any means necessary," referring to the methods of struggle for liberation. Baptists Josiah Bishop and **Thomas Paul** were also abolitionist orators. The Congregationalists included preachers such as **Amos Beman** and **Charles Bennett Ray**, who were greatly devoted to the abolitionist cause.

Perhaps the most outstanding denomination in opposition to slavery, however, was the AMEZ Church, even though not so closely associated with preachers and preaching, as such. There was Bishop **Jermain W. Loguen**, the abolitionist, but he was reluctant to fully embrace his high office. And the greatest orator of them all was Frederick Douglass, but he didn't desire to move in ministry past his AMEZ license to preach, conferred early in his life as a freeman. And the most heroic of them all was **Harriet Tubman**, a lay member of the AMEZ congregation at Auburn, N.Y.

In the Civil War, preachers recruited soldiers for the Union Army, and they called the churches to massive educational ministries in the South during Reconstruction. The funds given to start and operate schools and colleges were at a level which would shame today's support of those same schools. But it was "preached out" by men like **Joseph C. Price**, who founded Livingstone College (AMEZ), and **William J. Simmons**, who founded a Baptist college at Louisville (now Simmons Bible College).

During that same Reconstruction period, preachers had great political impact. It ranged all the way from the election of delegates to conventions for drafting new state constitutions, to actually serving in the U.S. Senate and House of Representatives. In the state constitutions, humanitarian influences for public education, universal suffrage (male) instead of only owners of property, female inheritance and even some forms of public welfare were adopted for the first time.

Later, it was the preaching of the hope of heaven, in the face of unbridled violence and death, that averted utter despair among Southern Blacks in the four decades just before and after the turn of the century. All too often this is misunderstood as "pie-in-the-sky" otherworldliness, but in an era of unchecked lynching in a completely closed society, the thought of heaven was all they had to keep them going here on earth. Far more credit is due these "down home" pastors, whose messages kept aflame the light at the end of the long, dark tunnel of massive oppression.

In the first decade of the twentieth century, the National Association for the Advancement of Colored People (1910) and the Urban League (1911) were organized. Each sought to better the condition of African Americans, and each had to depend heavily on preachers and their pulpit influence to gain the support needed in the Black communities. Preachers like **Reverdy Ransom** (AME) and Charles Satchell Morris (Baptist) were involved with the boards from the very beginning. (The current national Executive Director of the N.A.A.C.P. is both a Baptist preacher and a former judge and lawyer.)

Early in the twentieth century, Southern crop failures caused by floods and by boll weevils combined with economic opportunities created by the onset of World War I to draw thousands of African Americans from the rural South to the urban North. It was often the transplanted pastors from the South who made the disappointments of the "Promised Land" bearable. Their extended family congregations, often in store-front churches, were nourished, again with small credit, by the preached Word.

When, after World War II, the "Civil Rights Revolution" was launched, the preaching of persons like King and **Ralph David Abernathy** galvanized thousands into action. But this was not the preachers' only contribution. The very decision of the Supreme Court which launched it all was responding to cases filed by two AME pastors, one in Topeka, Kansas, and one in Colleton County, South Carolina, both on behalf of their own children. What these pastors did was not exceptional; many preacher/pastors have done the same sort of thing without the publicity.

Since 1944, there have been four African American preachers in the U.S. Congress: **Adam Clayton Powell, Jr.**, and Floyd Flake from New York; **Andrew Young**, from Georgia; and **William Gray, III**, from Pennsylvania. Dozens of pastors have served and are serving in political posts at the state and local levels.

The trend will be to increase such participation, as more and more African American preacher/pastors secure full professional training, thus equipping them to perform with confidence in these places of responsibility. This trend will be aided by the fact that good professional training now equips ministers to *function in African American culture*, whereas earlier training was always in the culture of the American majority. In other words, the preachers with adequate expertise will also have sufficient power bases in the churches of the masses, to whom they can now relate much more effectively.

Whatever may be said about the extremes and errors of many highly visible African American preachers, the vast majority are a part of the providential support system which has made it possible for an oppressed people to bear the unspeakable burdens heaped on them from the beginning. The "Black" preacher is sought out, even by the most ardent critics, in the major crises of the community. And this personage is expected to deliver whatever is needed, despite all previous oppositions. In this sense, the stature of African American preachers as the de facto leaders/ pastors of the whole community, even in the 1990s, is documented by the very expectations of their erstwhile enemies. The image of the "omni-competent" priest/ doctor of Africa is still alive and well.

Preachers, Preaching, and the Future. How long can this cultural heritage persist, when the rates of contemporary social change are so rapid? The answers lie as much in society at large as in the African American churches and communities themselves, and in aspects of the preaching tradition. The place of the church and preacher in the community is part and parcel of the separate and unequal existence of the African American. The church continues to be the serviceable adaptation of the African culture's extended-family society, and this grouping is supportive of existence in oppression in a way that no other group is or ever has been. In a word, whatever is second to the African American church and preacher in importance of role is so far behind that it is not profitable to try to identify it. Schools might be such a second, but they are not controlled by the African Americans who attend them. Lodges, sororities, fraternities, labor unions, and civic associations are all prone to help at times, but none of them is close to the effectiveness of the churches, except in rare local situations. The **Southern Christian Leadership Conference** (S.C.L.C.) purports to be an actual association of churches, and the National Association for the Advancement of Colored People is nearly as tied to the churches as S.C.L.C. The N.A.A.C.P.'s largest membership drives are in the churches. So one answer is that the churches will be at the center of community life as long as African Americans continue to be oppressed and separated from the rest of American life.

The answer with respect to the roles of preacher/ pastors is much the same. Inherent in the role of the church as an extended-family support unit is the need for a "parent" as leader. The trend in some cultures to make of the pastor a proper, distant professional is not likely to prevail among African Americans. This is true even though large urban churches have long since had to multiply professional staff. Call these staffers uncles and aunts, or even grandparents, but they will have a filial and therefore more permanent position in the church. Regardless of the high risk of investing too much trust in the priest ("parent") of the church/family, the pastor/preacher role is likely to survive as long as does the supportive network called the Black church.

The African American preaching tradition, however, has even more of a prognosis of permanence; its holistic approach is now the goal of scholarly homileticians everywhere. While it is not widely conceded that present trends take many of their cues from recent analyses of the African American tradition, the fact is that African American preachers and teachers of preaching are welcome, if not in actual demand, among seminarians everywhere. And it is all too obvious that the most *avant garde* thinking on preaching among Whites is full of parallels in the African American homiletical tradition. There is every reason to believe that this homiletical cross-fertilization could save the oft-thought-moribund art of preaching in today's world.

Ahlstrom, Sydney E. *A Religious History of the American People.* 2 vols. Garden City, NY: Image Books, Doubleday & Co., 1975.

Day, Richard Ellsworth. *Rhapsody in Black, The Life Story of John Jasper.* Valley Forge, PA: Judson Press, 1953. 149 pp.

Eerdmans' Handbook to Christianity in America. Grand Rapids, MI: William B. Eerdmans Publishing Co., 1983. 507 pp.

Frazier, E. Franklin. *The Negro Church in America.* New York: Schocken Books, 1963. 92 pp.

Franklin, John Hope. *From Slavery to Freedom.* New York: Alfred A. Knopf, Inc., 1967. 729 pp.

Harding, Vincent. *There is a River: The Black Struggle for Freedom in America.* New York: Harcourt Brace Jovanovitch, Publishers, 1981. 417 pp.

Lincoln, C. Eric, and Lawrence H. Mamiya. *The Black Church in the African American Experience.* Durham, NC.: Duke University Press, 1990. 520 pp.

Mitchell, Henry H. *Black Preaching: The Recovery of a Powerful Art.* Nashville, TN: Abingdon Press, 1990, 143 pp.

———. *Celebration and Experience in Preaching.* Nashville, TN: Abingdon Press, 1990. 155 pp.

Payne, Daniel A. *History of the African Methodist Episcopal Church.* Nashville, TN: Publishing House of the AME Sunday School Union, 1891. Rept.: New York: Arno Press & The New York Times, 1969. 502 pp.

Smith, Charles Spencer. *A History of the African Methodist Episcopal Church.* Philadelphia, PA: Book Concern of the AME Church, 1922. 571 pp. Rept.: New York: Johnson Reprint Corporation, 1968. 571 pp.

Walls, William J. *The African Methodist Episcopal Zion Church.* Charlotte, NC: AME Zion Publishing House, 1974. 669 pp.

Washington, James M. *Frustrated Fellowship: The Black Baptist Quest for Social Power.* Macon, GA: Mercer University Press, 1986. 226 pp.

Wilmore, Gayraud S. *Black Religion and Black Radicalism.* Maryknoll, N.Y.: Orbis Books, 1983. 288 pp.

Woodson, Carter G. *The History of the Negro Church.* Washington, DC: Associated Publishers (Association for the Study of Negro Life and History), 1972. 322 pp.

Woodson, Carter G., and Charles H. Wesley. *The Negro in Our History.* Washington, DC: Associated Publishers, Inc., 1966. 863 pp.

Henry H. Mitchell

PRESBYTERIAN CHURCH (U.S.A.). Formed in 1983 by the merger of the United Presbyterian Church in the U.S.A. and the Presbyterian Church in the U.S., the Presbyterian Church (U.S.A.) is the main body carrying the Presbyterian tradition in the United States. The first African American converts to Presbyterianism were slaves of Scotch-Irish immigrants who migrated into the Valley of Virginia during the 1730s. The earliest account we have of Blacks being evangelized by Presbyterians was in colonial Virginia after the First Great Awakening, when Rev. Samuel Davies reported baptizing some 150 in 1757. Slaves of devout Presbyterians received religious instruction. They memorized the Lord's Prayer and were taught to read or recite parts of the Bible, the Confession of Faith, and the Shorter Catechism.

According to W. H. Franklin, "slaves and servants coming from Presbyterian homes showed superior intelligence" because of the belief among the founders of American Presbyterianism that learning is essential to piety. We do not know the number of slaves who became Presbyterians in the eighteenth century. They were fewer than either Black Baptists or Methodists, but probably better educated. Presbyterian slave-holders sometimes permitted Black children to attend school along with their own, but more often taught them at Sabbath schools or in the home. **John Chavis**, born in 1763 in Granville County, North Carolina, was educated in this way and became the first Black Presbyterian preacher, serving as a missionary to slaves in Virginia from 1801 to 1808. He later opened a school and taught classical subjects to some of the leading white people of North Carolina.

More celebrated by African American Presbyterians today is **John Gloucester**, pastor of the earliest Black Presbyterian congregation—the First African Presbyterian Church of Philadelphia. Gloucester was taught by his master, Dr. Gideon R. Blackburn of Maryville, Tennessee. Blackburn brought him to the Presbyterian Evangelical Society in Philadelphia and released him for an urban ministry among Blacks in South Philadelphia. It was out of that work that the First African Presbyterian Church was founded in 1807.

John Gloucester's three sons followed him into the Presbyterian ministry. Jeremiah succeeded his father at First African in 1824; James organized Siloam in Brooklyn, N.Y., and served as its pastor from 1847 to 1851; Stephen was licensed as an evangelist by the Presbytery of Philadelphia and for a time served the Lombard Street Central Church of that city. Other early Black congregations were Shiloh in New York City (1822), Washington Street in Reading, Pa. (1823), Beaufort-Salem in Sheldon, S.C. (1828), Ladson in Columbia, S.C. (1828), Fifteenth Street in Washington, D.C. (1841), and Zion (now Zion-Olivet) in Charleston, S.C. (1846.)

Some White Presbyterian ministers were outspoken opponents of slavery, such as David Rice, who pastored those Blacks who had been evangelized by Davies. Another example is George Bourne, who accused the church of compromising on immediate emancipation and wrote a controversial volume, *The Book and Slavery Irreconcilable*. Nonetheless, both Northern and Southern Presbyterians took the conservative position that the church should be wary of interference in civil affairs. Hence, Presbyterians split over slavery in 1861 and at the end of the Civil War the Presbyterian Church in the United States (Southern) lost hundreds of its Black members to White Presbyterian missionaries from the North who claimed them for the Presbyterian Church in the U.S.A (Northern). In 1874 the Southern church attempted to create a Black Presbyterian church out of its 33 organized Black congregations and only twelve ordained clergy. This Black church began independent existence in 1898, but was abandoned in 1916, mainly because of apathetic support on the part of Whites. At that time Black Presbyterians in the South were organized as the segregated Snedecor Memorial Synod.

The Northern church created a Committee on Freedmen at the General Assembly of 1865 and launched a program of organizing churches and schools among the recently freed people. In 1882 this committee became the Board of Missions for Freedmen, located in Pittsburgh, Pennsylvania, and in 1923 could boast two universities: Lincoln, near Oxford, Pennsylvania, and Johnson C. Smith at Charlotte, North Carolina. It had also sponsored two colleges, five boarding schools and 138 parochial schools. These schools made an extraordinary contribution to Black education. Total enrollment reached 19,166 students and 494 teachers. Before the Second World War the Presbyterian Church, U.S.A., counted 438 Black churches and missions serving almost 28,000 communicants. In 1952 there were approximately 40,000 Blacks in the Northern church and fewer than 4,000 in the Southern church. When these two main branches of Presbyterianism reunited in 1983, Black Presbyterians, most in all-Black congregations, numbered about 60,000. In 1990 the new Presbyterian Church (U.S.A.) reported that 2.47 percent, or 64,841 of its 3 million members, were African Americans.

In the nineteenth century African American Presbyterians produced some of the most noteworthy of the Black abolitionist clergy. Among them were **Samuel Cornish**, **Theodore Wright**, **Henry Highland Garnet**, and **J. W. C. Pennington**. Black Presbyterians subsequently distinguished themselves as educators, overseas missionaries, and national staff persons. In 1883 **Lucy Craft Laney**, born a slave, established the famous Haines Normal Institute in Augusta, Georgia, and Daniel J. Sanders became the first Black president of J. C. Smith University in 1891. Over a score of Blacks served the Presbyterian Church in Africa during the nineteenth century, but Irving and Susan Underhill went to the Cameroons in 1928 as the first Black missionaries appointed after more than thirty years of discrimination by the Board of Foreign Missions.

Black Presbyterian and Congregational clergy organized the first Black caucus in a predominantly White church in 1859. In 1894 Northern Blacks created the Afro-American Presbyterian Council, which protested discrimination and fought for more control over home missions outside of the segregated Black synods in the South. Among the most outspoken leaders of this caucus were **Francis J. Grimke** of the Fifteenth Street Church in Washington, D.C., and Matthew Anderson of Berean in Philadelphia.

In 1938 **Albert B. McCoy** became the first Black executive of the Unit of Work for Colored People. He was followed by many outstanding leaders on the General Assembly and synod levels, such as Henry L.

McCrorey, Jesse Belmont Barber, G. Lake Imes, and Frank T. Wilson. Black Presbyterian women made an outstanding contribution to the church during this period and since. **Emily V. Gibbes** became a field director of the Board of Christian Education in 1950; Mable P. McLean served as president of Barber-Scotia, a Presbyterian college in Concord, North Carolina; and **Katie G. Cannon** was the first of many Black women clergy in the church. She was ordained in 1956 and became a seminary professor. In 1976 **Thelma Davidson Adair** was elected as the first Black woman moderator of the denomination, and Joan Salmon Campbell followed her in that office in 1989.

During the civil rights movement Black Presbyterians played a leading role in persuading the predominantly White churches to support Dr. **Martin Luther King, Jr**. Their caucus, Concerned Presbyterians, became radicalized as Black Presbyterians United in 1968. Led by Bryant George and **Edler G. Hawkins**, who was elected the first Black moderator of the General Assembly in 1964, Black clergy were influential in the creation of the national Commission on Religion and Race in 1963. **Gayraud Wilmore** of Philadelphia and J. Metz Rollins of Newport News, Virginia, were the first executives of this controversial thrust which brought the United Presbyterian Church into the middle of the struggle of the 1960s and 70s.

The Southern Presbyterians (Presbyterian Church in the U.S.) elected Lawrence W. Bottoms its first Black moderator in 1974. His election can be partly attributed to the rising militancy of its small African American constituency, which in 1969 organized the Black Leadership Caucus of the Presbyterian Church, U.S. Since the union of the two churches in 1983 a strong united front to monitor race relations in the denomination and support Black congregational development has been created as the **National Black Presbyterian Caucus** (NBPC).

Barber, Jesse B. *Climbing Jacob's Ladder*. New York: Board of National Missions, 1952. 103 pp.

Cave, Clarence, ed. *Black Presbyterians United: Report to the Session*. New York: Presbyterian Church, U.S.A., 1977.

Franklin, W. H. *The Early History of the Presbyterian Church in the U.S.A., Among the Negroes*. Pittsburgh: Board of Missions for Freedmen, n.d.

Murray, Andrew E. *Presbyterians and the Negro—A History*. Philadelphia: Presbyterian Historical Society, 1966. 270 pp.

Parker, Inez Moore. *The Rise and Decline of the Program of Education for Black Presbyterians of the United Presbyterian Church U.S.A., 1865–1970*. San Antonio, TX: Texas University Press, 1977. 319 pp.

Periscope I, II, and III. Essays on Black Presbyterianism published in 1982 and 1992. Available from Distribution Management Services, Presbyterian Church, U.S.A., 100 Witherspoon St., Louisville, KY 40202-1396.

Swift, David E. *Black Prophets of Justice: Activist Clergy Before the Civil War*. Baton Rouge: Louisiana State University Press, 1989. 384 pp.

Thompson, Ernest Trice. *Presbyterians in the South*. Vol. 3. Richmond, VA: John Knox Press, 1973.

Wilmore, Gayraud S. *Black and Presbyterian: The Heritage and the Hope*. Philadelphia: Geneva Press, 1983. 142 pp.

Gayraud S. Wilmore

PRICE, FREDERICK K. C. (b. 1932), founder of Ever Increasing Ministries and the Crenshaw Christian Center, was born in Santa Monica, California. His parents were Jehovah's Witnesses though they dropped out during his teen years. He attended Santa Monica Junior College. During his youthful years, he would go to church only to be with Betty Sue Stout, his future wife. In 1953, she invited him to a tent revival at which he had a conversion experience. Afterwards, they joined a Baptist church. At the time he joined the church, he heard a voice telling him, "You are to preach My gospel." He began by working around the church and preaching on occasion. He then became the part-time pastor of a series of different churches in different denominations until around 1966, when he became the pastor of the West Washington Community Church, a congregation of the Christian and Missionary Alliance. Over a four-year period the church went from 9 to 125 members. Price was able to begin pastoring full time.

About this time he was given some Pentecostal booklets. From these he learned of and then experienced, in part with the assistance of Pentecostal Lutheran minister Larry Christianson, the baptism of the Holy Spirit, evidenced by speaking in tongues. His ministry took on a new dimension, but he still felt something lacking. Then he was given some of the books of Kenneth Hagin, a Pentecostal televangelist from Tulsa, Oklahoma. Hagin's books taught Price about using faith to confess before God what one wants/ needs and then to operate out of trust that God will supply. He believed he had found the missing factor in his life. The first result of his preaching the "faith message" was that people were healed. His church quickly doubled in size.

He decided to move into an independent structure

and in 1973, the congregation purchased an abandoned church building on Crenshaw Boulevard in Inglewood, California, a Los Angeles suburb, and moved into what was called the Crenshaw Christian Center. The church grew rapidly and in the mid-1970s he released his first books, including *Is Healing For All?* (1976), *How Faith Works* (1976) and *How to Obtain Strong Faith* (1977). In more recent years he has authored a number of books and pamphlets and made numerous sermons and classes available on audio and video tapes. By 1977 the center had 130 members and kept growing. By the early 1980s it was holding three services each Sunday and in 1984 finally purchased the abandoned Los Angeles campus of Pepperdine University as a new home.

In 1978 Price's ministry took a significant boost when he went on television. His program was the work of Ever Increasing Faith Ministries, the church's outreach arm. Within a few years he had the largest audience of any African American minister on the air, and he quickly became a national leader among Charismatic Christians, especially those who were teaching the faith message. In 1979 he joined with a number of these leaders in founding the International Convention of Faith Churches and Ministries, an ecumenical organization called together by Tulsa minister/publisher Doyle Harrison. He began to hold crusades around the country and his ministry grew even more. His television program is carried on approximately 100 stations in the United States and other stations in Bermuda, Haiti, St. Croix, Nigeria, and South Africa.

By 1981 membership at the Center had risen above 9,000, and plans were underway to construct a 10,000–seat domed sanctuary for the congregation's services. By the time the new church was opened, in 1989, the 16,000 member church was the largest congregation in Los Angeles. Besides the early emphasis on healing, which continues as an important aspect of his ministry, Price has added an emphasis on prosperity and acting on faith that God will provide. The move also allowed space to develop a new **Crenshaw Christian Center School of Ministry** which opened in 1985.

In 1990 the Price took another expansive step with the first meeting of the Fellowship of Inner-City Word of Faith Ministries. The Fellowship conferences each summer bring African American pastors from around the country together to strategize on putting Price's teachings to work in other places.

Dart, John. "Low-Key Pastor Reaches for the Big Time." *Los Angeles Times* (December 7, 1981).

Price, Frederick K. C. *Faith: Foolishness, or Presumption?* Tulsa, OK: Harrison House, 1979. 148 pp.
———. *How Faith Works.* Tulsa, OK: Harrison House, 1976. 128 pp.
———. *How to Obtain Strong Faith (Six Principles).* Tulsa, OK: Harrison House, 1977. 184 pp.
———. *High Finance: God's Financial Plan, Tithes and Offerings.* Tulsa, OK: Harrison House, 1984. 180 pp.
———. *Is Healing for All?* Tulsa, OK: Harrison House, 1976. 127 pp.
———. *Prosperity on God's Terms.* Tulsa, OK: Harrison House, 1990. 107 pp.
Strang, Stephen. "The Ever-Increasing Faith of Fred Price." *Charisma* 10, 10 (May 1985): 20–26.

PRICE, HOLLIS FREEMAN (c.1900– ?), college president and the first African American moderator of the **United Church of Christ**, was born in Virginia. His father, William Gibbons Price, was principal at an American Missionary Association school and worked to obtain the best education possible for his son. Accordingly, at the age of sixteen, Price was sent to Williston Academy, in East Hampton, Massachusetts. Despite the difficult adjustments required, he was scholastically successful and he was able to enroll later at Amherst College, another mostly White school in Massachusetts.

When Price graduated with a degree in economics he went to Columbia University in New York City for his M.A. There he married Althea Banks. Upon achieving his degree they moved to Alabama, where he had a teaching position at Tuskegee Institute. Later he was appointed dean of LeMoyne College in Memphis, Tennessee. After only two years he became the first Black president of LeMoyne (now LeMoyne-Owen College) and remained in that position for the next 27 years. During that time he was a stabilizing force in a community divided by race and economics. He is credited with being one of the key organizers of the United Negro College Fund, and in 1965 became the first Black moderator of the United Church of Christ.

Walker, Sonia Louden. "A Tribute to Dr. Hollis F. Price." *The Cumberland Seminarian* 22 (Spring 1984): 23–26.

PRICE, JOSEPH CHARLES (February 10, 1854–October 25, 1893), minister of **African Methodist Episcopal Zion Church** (AMEZ), editor, and co-founder of Livingstone College, was born in Elizabeth City, North Carolina, the son of Charles Dozier and

Emily Paulin. His father was a slave and his mother was free, making the children also free. Dozier was soon sold away and his mother married David Price. During the Civil War they moved to New Bern, North Carolina. He grew up attending St. Peter's AMEZ Church and in 1866, as soon as possible, began as a student at the St. Cyprian Episcopal School.

Early on he was recognized as a bright child with exceptional abilities. From 1871 to 1873 he was principal and teacher in Wilson, North Carolina and then attended Shaw University in Raleigh, North Carolina, for about five months in 1873–74. He was converted during a campus revival and joined the AME Zion Church in New Bern. Soon he dropped earlier plans for a law career and moved instead toward the ministry. In 1875 he enrolled at Presbyterian-related Lincoln University in Pennsylvania, was licensed to preach in 1876, and soon thereafter was ordained deacon and elder in the AMEZ Church. He graduated as valedictorian in 1879 and during that senior year began studying in the junior theological department, graduating with his B.D. in 1881. He was a delegate to the 1880 General Conference of the AMEZ Church in Montgomery, Alabama.

His oratory and bearing so impressed the conference that with the help of Bishop **James W. Hood**, one of his benefactors in the church, he was designated a delegate to the 1881 World Methodist Conference in London. After a five-minute speech there he was dubbed by the *London Times* "the World's Orator." In various speaking engagements in Europe over a period of a year he raised $10,000 for the floundering Zion Wesley Institute in Concord, North Carolina. Upon his return he persuaded Bishop Hood and the trustees to close that enterprise and begin again at a new location in Salisbury, North Carolina. It was officially refounded in October 1882, with Price as the new president. The school was renamed Livingstone College in 1885, at the time of incorporation, after David Livingstone, the famous African explorer and missionary, and his son Robert Livingston, who died of gunshot wounds in a Confederate prison camp in Salisbury in 1864.

He married Jennie Smallwood in 1882, with whom he had five children. Price, a larger-than-life figure in many ways, being over six feet tall and almost 300 pounds, dedicated the rest of his life to making Livingstone College as substantial as possible. He also served as the driving force in the denomination on behalf of the benefits of education. In 1885 he visited California and obtained large grants from such philanthropists as William E. Dodge, Collis P. Huntington, and Leland Stanford. He traveled many other places across the country, and was the first Black preacher to occupy the pulpit of Henry Ward Beecher at Plymouth Church in Brooklyn. He was a delegate in 1884 to the Centennial Methodist Conference in Baltimore, and responded to the opening address by Bishop Andrews of the Methodist Episcopal Church.

In short order Price was a national-level leader and was compared to Frederick Douglass as an orator. In 1888 President Grover Cleveland offered to make him Minister Plenipotentiary to Liberia. Although Price turned it down, he was an early Pan-Africanist, before W. E. B. DuBois, the "Father of Pan-Africanism." He had a very strong interest in Africa and connections with African Americans. He felt African Americans had an obligation to bring education and Christianity to Africa, rather than exploit it as did the Europeans. From 1884 to 1892 Price was a popular choice for the bishopric in the AMEZ Church, but refused to be a candidate. He was a signer of the appeal by T. Thomas Fortune for a national convention to be held in Chicago on January 15, 1890, at which time Price was elected president of the newly founded National Afro-American League. In February, 1890, he was elected chair by acclamation of another new group, the Citizens' Equal Rights Association of the United States, but political infighting led to the demise of both these groups within three years. Price's strategy for Black advancement was to seek out and connect with the best traditions and people of the South. He was open to dialogue, but he was not submissive and did not offer such appeasing measures as did **Booker T. Washington** in the later 1890s.

Price's career was cut tragically short by his early death, at age 39, of Bright's disease. Many believe that had he lived longer he would have been an even greater international figure and that Livingstone College, in W. E. B. DuBois' words, would have become a "Black Harvard." As it was, he placed the school on such a solid foundation that it was one of the few of the early Black-owned and run colleges to survive into the present time, and it has played a significant role in education and in the AMEZ Church. One of the statements attributed to Price sums up the way he lived his life: "It matters not how dark the night, I believe in the coming of the morning."

Davis, Lenwood G. "Joseph Charles Price: An Early Black Pan-Africanist." *Negro History Bulletin* 43 (July–August–September 1980): 72.

———. "Joseph Charles Price: A Man for All Seasons." *A.M.E. Zion Quarterly Review* 92 (Spring 1980): 21–23.

———. "Joseph Charles Price's Rejection of Position as

Minister Resident and Consul General of the United States to Liberia." *Journal of Negro History* 63 (July 1978): 231–234.

Findley, J. W. "Biographical Sketch of Joseph Charles Price." *A.M.E. Zion Quarterly Review* 64 (1953): 144–153.

Sherrill, Josephine Price. "Section E: A Negro School-Master of the 1870s." *Journal of Negro Education* 30 (Spring 1961): 163–172.

Walls, William Jacob. *Joseph Charles Price: Educator and Race Leader.* Boston, MA: The Christopher Publishing House, 1943. 568 pp.

Yates, Walter L., ed. *He Spoke, Now They Speak.* Salisbury, NC: Rowan Printing Co., 1952. 167 pp.

IBAWCB, AARS, HUBA, IBAW, NBH, NAH, NG, BTFTMC, EBA, EWM, AAE, OHYNF, MM, DANB, AMEZC.

PRICE, JOSEPH L. (b. December 25, 1931), former **Church of God in Christ** bishop and currently founder and leader of the St. Jude Deliverance Centers of America, was born in Gary, Indiana. Not much is known of his early life. From 1951 to 1956 he was in the military service. He then attended East Los Angeles Junior College and pursued a number of occupations. He was a welder, photographer, real estate and insurance broker, and the owner of a furniture and appliance store.

In about 1960 he moved to Chicago, Illinois, and attended the Moody Bible Institute and the Chicago Baptist Bible Institute. In 1963 he became a minister in the Church of God in Christ, and gradually worked his way up through the ranks to become district superintendent and then bishop. In 1971 he left that denomination to found the St. Jude Deliverance Centers of America, with headquarters in Indianapolis, Indiana, where he had been living for several years.

BH, WWABA (92–93).

PRIMITIVE BAPTISTS. The Primitive Baptist movement emerged in strength as a reaction within the Baptist church to the organization of several boards to direct missionary and publishing activity rather than leaving the spreading of the Christian message to the direct efforts of the local churches. The issue came to a head in 1927 when the Kehukee Baptist Association withdrew its support from all missionary societies, Bible societies, and theological seminaries. As "Primitive" congregations identified themselves and associations ascribed to the Kehukee platform, a national movement (though concentrated in the South) emerged.

Black people became affiliated with the Primitive Baptist movement during the slave era and after the Civil War, independent Black Primitive Baptist churches began to appear. Possibly the most well-known congregation was Zion Primitive Baptist Church in Key West, Florida. It was formed in 1870, and by the beginning of the twentieth century owned its own building and ran a Bible school. Its pastor, Rev. C. F. Sams, was nationally known.

During the 1970s and 1880s the White associations debated the issue of the Black churches. In the years after the Civil War, Whites generally opposed the Black brethren organizing separately, but by the 1880s, by which time several associations had formed, favored a complete separation.

Around the turn of the century, C. F. Sams and others began to call for a national organization of Primitive Baptists. Supporters for such an organization met in 1907 and formed the **National Primitive Baptist Association**, however, some opposed the move as creating the very organization which called the Primitive Baptist movement into existence in the first place. These numerous Black Baptists refused to participate and have continued in almost invisible associations and churches ever since.

These independent Primitive Baptists emerged out of obscurity briefly in the 1950s when Elder E. J. Berry, who operated the Primitive Baptist Publishing House in Elon, North Carolina, agreed to publish a periodical on behalf of what at the time was called the "Colored Primitive Baptists." The first issue of the *Primitive Messenger* appeared in January 1953. Unfortunately, it ceased publication after four years from lack of support.

Because there is no central headquarters or even depository of information, it is very difficult to estimate the size of the Black Primitive Baptist movement today. In the early 1970s, 43 associations were known. They averaged five churches per association and 20 members per church. Thus it seems a reasonable estimate to assume that there are currently between 3,000 and 5,000 Primitive Baptists in unaffiliated associations.

PRIMM, HOWARD THOMAS (b. June 23, 1903), 71st bishop of the **African Methodist Episcopal Church** (AME), was born in Brentwood, Tennessee, the son of Zechariah and Addie (Curtis) Primm. The family soon moved to Nashville, Tennessee, where he attended Napier public school and then Pearl High School. He grew up attending Bethel AME Church in Nashville and as a young man served in most of the church's major offices. In high school he was captain of the football team and president of his class. He was licensed to preach in 1920, admitted to the Tennessee Annual Conference in 1921, and ordained deacon in 1922. He received his B.A. from Wilberforce University in Xenia, Ohio, in 1924, and his B.D. from the related Payne Theological Seminary in 1927. On October 3, 1926, he married Edythe Mae Hailey, with whom he had one child. He was ordained elder in 1928.

His first pastorate was at Trinity AME Church in Nashville, from 1926 to 1928, during which time he was also Secretary for Religious Work at the Nashville Y.M.C.A. His next pastorates were Gilchrist AME Church in Memphis (1928–29); Allen AME Church in Memphis (1929–31); Bethel AME Church in Alexandria, Louisiana (1931–32); St. Peter's AME Church in Port Gibson, Mississippi (1932–33); Union AME Church in Little Rock, Arkansas (1933–35); Visitor's Chapel AME Church in Hot Springs, Arkansas (1935–41); and Union Bethel AME Church in New Orleans, Louisiana (1941–52). While in Memphis he also taught at Turner College in Shelbyville, and while in Alexandria taught at Lampton College in the same town. While in Port Gibson he taught at Campbell College in Jackson, Mississippi, and then at Shorter College in Little Rock, Arkansas.

In all his pastorates Primm was very successful, adding a total of 5,000 new members and retiring the mortgages on four churches and three parsonages. In 1939 he was a delegate to the First World Youth Conference in Amsterdam, Holland, and was a delegate to the World Methodist Conference in Oxford, England, in 1951. At his final pastorate in New Orleans, where he firmly established his national reputation in that 2,000–member church, he built the Harvest Center, which included the Sarah Allen Child Care Center, Well Baby Clinic, Teen-Junction, and Sherman L. Green Four Freedoms Building. He received a special citation from the mayor for these major accomplishments.

In 1952 Primm was elected bishop and assigned to South Africa, but the death of Bishop Gregg caused several shifts and he was reassigned to the Eighth Episcopal District (North Carolina). There he oversaw the building of many new churches, a new episcopal residence, and the reduction of debt at Campbell College in Buies Creek. In 1956 he was assigned to the Tenth Episcopal District (Texas), where on Easter Sunday 1957, he baptized 1,700 persons, the largest number ever baptized at once in the history of the denomination. In 1958 another record was set with the ordination of 151 deacons and elders in one service. In 1960 he was sent to the Fifth Episcopal District (Puget Sound, California, Colorado, Kansas, Nebraska, and Missouri), where in 1964 he built the denomination's first home for senior

citizens in Kansas City, on the campus of Western University.

He was a trustee of Shorter College and Campbell College and was president of the General Board of the church from 1962 to 1964. He was active in the N.A.A.C.P. and the Urban League. In 1968 he was appointed to the Fourth Episcopal District, and in 1976 to the Thirteenth Episcopal District, from which he retired in 1980. He is the only bishop to have been elected president of the General Board two terms in succession. His first wife passed away, and in 1975 he married Mildred Elaine Nash. Churches have been named for him in New Orleans, Louisiana, Pomona, California, and Omaha, Nebraska.

EAMEC, BAMEC, HAMEC, EWM, RLA, EBA, BDNM (70).

PRIMO, QUINTIN EBENEZER, JR. (b. July 1, 1913), a bishop of the **Episcopal Church**, was born in Liberty County, Georgia, the son of Quintin Ebenezer Sr. and Alvira Wilhemenia (Wellington) Primo. His father was an Episcopal priest. After attending Fort Valley Normal and Industrial Institute in Fort Valley, Georgia, he received his B.A. in 1934 and S.T.B. in 1937 from Lincoln University in Pennsylvania. He earned his M.Div. in 1941 from Bishop Payne Divinity School, now part of Virginia Theological Seminary. On July 5, 1942, he married Winifred Priscilla Thompson, with whom he had three children.

He was ordained deacon in July 1941 and priest in June 1942. His first church assignment was as curate of St. Agnes' Episcopal Church in Miami, Florida (1941–42), after which he was vicar of a church in Rutherfordton, North Carolina (1942–44); priest-in-charge of St. Stephen's Episcopal Church in Winston-Salem, North Carolina (1944–45); St. Timothy's Episcopal Church in Brooklyn, New York (1945–47); and St. Simon's Episcopal Church in Rochester, New York (1947–63), where he built a longstanding mission station into a full parish and served as its first rector. He founded St. Simon's Community Center. He was a founding member of the Union of Black Episcopalians and was its first national president.

From 1963 to 1969 Primo served St. Matthew's Episcopal Church in Wilmington, Delaware, where he again built a mission station into a full parish, becoming its first rector in 1966. He founded St. Matthew's Tutorial and Job Training Program and was chair of the Transportation Committee for Wilmington's Poor People's Campaign. From 1969 to 1972 he was assigned to Detroit, Michigan, where he merged two inner-city parishes, St. Matthew's and St. Joseph's, and became rector of the combined congregations. On September 30, 1972, he was consecrated as suffragan bishop of the Diocese of Washington, where he remained until retirement in 1984. In 1985–86 he was interim bishop of Delaware. He has served as trustee of Rush-Presbyterian-St. Luke's Medical Center in Chicago, of St. Augustine's College in Raleigh, North Carolina, and of several other institutions. He was chair of the Diocese of Chicago Commission on Metropolitan Affairs, chaired the Committee on Urban Affairs of the House of Bishops, and has been active in the N.A.A.C.P. and Planned Parenthood. In 1988 he received a presidential citation from the National Association for Equal Opportunity in Higher Education.

BDNM (70), *WWABA* (92–93), *WWA* (90–91), *WWR* (85), *ECA* (1973), *OTSB*.

PRINCE, NANCY GARDNER (September 15, 1799–?), domestic servant and international missionary, was born in Newburyport, Massachusetts, the daughter of Thomas Gardner. Prince's grandmother was a Native American, and Prince's father died when she was only three months old. Her mother's first name is unknown; her maiden name was Wornton. Her mother worked as a domestic, remarried, and had six more children, making a total of eight.

Prince gained some amount of schooling and was trained in domestic work, especially as a seamstress. Her grandfather was a strong member of the Congregational Church, and Prince discovered early on an affinity for religion. After her stepfather passed away the family was in financial difficulty, and began to pick and sell berries. In April 1814, not quite fifteen years old, she moved to Essex to find new work. After various domestic positions she moved to Boston in April, 1816 to rescue her older sister, Silvia, from a house of "harlots," and stayed to work as a chambermaid. She was baptized on May 6, 1819, by **Thomas Paul**, pastor of the Joy Street Baptist Church, the only Black church in the city at that time.

After several more years of struggle and caring for various wayward family members, she met Mr. Prince, who arrived from Russia on September 1, 1823. He was born in Massachusetts, became a sailor, and had settled in St. Petersburg as a servant to one of the families related to the royal court. They married on February 15, 1824, and on April 14 they sailed for Russia via Europe. Back in St. Petersburg Mr. Prince became one of the twenty "colored men" serving as hall sentries in the palace of the Czar, and she ran a child boarding service. She also made fine children's clothes purchased by the Empress and other members of the nobility. This enterprise became so successful that she was able to hire a journeywoman and apprentices. She was active in the one Protestant chapel available and in the interdenominational Russian Bible Society, for which she passed out Bibles in the city and the royal palace. This society was suppressed in 1826.

The Russian winters hurt her health, and she left for the United States on August 14, 1833. Her husband, not quite so free to leave his position, was to follow within two years, but died before he could do so. Now a widow, Prince settled in Boston, began an orphanage for Black children, and became active in William Lloyd Garrison's Anti-Slavery Society. The orphanage was forced to close from lack of finances, and she eventually decided to go to Jamaica as a missionary. Slaves in the West Indies had been emancipated in 1833, and she hoped to bring them education and religion. She sailed on November 16, 1840 to work with Rev. Ingraham's mission station (presumably Baptist).

Once in Jamaica, she began working with a Mr. Abbott in a mission in Saint Ann, but her position there became tenuous when she spoke out against inappropriate conduct in the mission school. Within a few months her health began to break down, and she left to join Rev. Ingraham in Kingston. Ingraham had lost his position, however, and was no longer there. Determined to accomplish some good, Prince organized a society to create a Free Labor School for destitute girls. She sailed to the United States to raise money for this project, and spoke in Boston, New York, Philadelphia, and elsewhere. She returned to Kingston on May 6, 1842, and tried to set up the school, but found that the white supporters planned to take over the project, and she pulled out.

She sailed for New York on August 18, 1842, and arrived on October 9, after nearly losing her life to storms and her liberty to slave traders in Key West. She settled in Boston in August 1843 and engaged in unknown business enterprises that were not very successful. She published the first edition of *A Narrative of the Life and Travels of Mrs. Nancy Prince* in 1850 in an attempt to earn money. She published two more editions in 1853 and 1856, by which time her health was seriously compromised and she was dependent upon the care of friends. Events after 1856 are unknown.

Blakely, Allison. "The Negro in Imperial Russia: A Preliminary Sketch." *Journal of Negro History* 61 (October 1976): 352–361.

Prince, Nancy G. *A Narrative of the Life and Travels of Mrs. Nancy Prince.* 1850. 2nd ed.: Boston: The Author, 1853. 89 pp.

NBAW, BWR, BAW, IBAW.

PRIOLEAU, GEORGE W. (May 15, 1856–1927), educator and Army chaplain, was born in Charleston, South Carolina, the son of Lewis S. and Susan A. (Smith) Prioleau. His father was the minister of the St. Mathews African Methodist Episcopal (AME) Church just north of Orangeburg. Prioleau was educated at Avery Institute in Charleston and received his B.A. in 1875 from Claflin University in Orangeburg, South Carolina. He taught for a time in the public primary schools of Lyons Township in Orangeburg County.

In 1879 he was licensed to preach and joined the Columbia, South Carolina Conference of the AME Church. His first pastorate was the Double Springs Mission in Lawrence County, in 1879. In 1880 he enrolled in Wilberforce University in Ohio and received his B.D. in 1884. From 1881 to 1884, while he was in school, he was assigned to the AME church in Selma, Ohio. About this time he married Anna L. Scovell, who held two degrees from Wilberforce. After graduation he was appointed to Yellow Springs, Ohio (1885); Hamilton, Ohio (1885–87); and Troy, Ohio (1887–88). In 1889 he was professor of church history and homiletics in the Theological Department at Wilberforce as well as pastor of Trinity Chapel. In 1890, when the Theological Department became Payne Theological Seminary, he was given the chair in historical and pastoral theology, a position he held until 1894. From 1890 to 1892 he was also presiding elder of the Springfield District Superintendent of the Northern Ohio Conference, and from 1893 to 1895 he pastored in Xenia, Ohio.

In the spring of 1895 Prioleau became chaplain of the 9th Regiment of the U.S. Cavalry, with the rank of captain, and joined the unit at Fort Robinson, Nebraska. Just before the unit shipped out in 1898 for Cuba and the Spanish-American War, he contracted malaria and spent part of that year instead doing recruiting in Charleston. He advocated military careers to other Blacks as a means of gaining a bit more pay, security, and dignity than would normally be available in civilian life. He returned to the 9th Cavalry and spent most of his time for the next sixteen years in the Philippines. His first wife died in February, 1903 and in 1905 he married Ethel G. Stafford, during a brief stationing at Fort Riley in Emporia, Kansas; with her he had four children.

In 1915 he was transferred to the 10th Cavalry on the Mexican border. By 1917 he was senior chaplain in the Army, was promoted to major, and transferred to the 25th Infantry at Schofield Barracks near Honolulu, Hawaii. It has been claimed that he was the first Black Army chaplain for a mixed-race garrison. Since Henry V. Plummer was chaplain for the 9th Cavalry earlier (1884–94), the claim would have to apply to Prioleau's time with either the 10 Cavalry and/or the 25th Infantry. In 1917 he raised $3,200 for the N.A.A.C.P. to distribute to Black victims of the rioting in East St. Louis, Illinois. He retired in 1920 to his home in Los Angeles, California, and organized the Bethel AME Church.

DANB, WWCR.

PROCTOR, HENRY HUGH (December 8, 1868– May 12, 1933), prominent Congregational minister, was born near Fayetteville, Tennessee, the son of Richard and Hannah (Wetherley) Proctor. After studying in various public schools he became a teacher in Pea Ridge, Tennessee, then for a time was principal at a school in Fayetteville. After he experienced conversion in 1883 in a local church, his fondest hope was to get into a college. In 1884 he enrolled in Central Tennessee College in Nashville, but after one term transferred to Fisk University in Nashville, which he had heard was a better school. He went through the preparatory and college courses, supporting himself by working at various jobs around the campus, and earned his B.A. in 1891. It was at Fisk that his future course was set in the direction of the ministry. He was greatly influenced by Professor Henry S. Bennett, who organized the Congregational Church at Fisk. Proctor next went to the Yale University Divinity School, earning his B.D. in 1894. He was one of only twelve Black students at Yale, but felt no prejudice or ostracism. He wrote his senior thesis on the theology of the slave songs. On August 16, 1893, he married Adeline L. Davis, with whom he had six children.

He was ordained a Congregational minister on July 1, 1894, and began pastoring at the newly founded First Congregational Church in Atlanta, Georgia. He remained in that position for the next twenty-five years, becoming one of the most prominent ministers of his time. He weaned the church away from the support of the American Missionary Association and slowly increased the membership from 100 to 1,000. In 1903 Proctor and George W. Henderson, president of Straight University in New Orleans, founded the National Convention of Congregational Workers Among Colored

People, and Proctor was elected its first president (1906–08) and then its corresponding secretary (1908–33) This organization did much to support Black Congregational churches and increase their prominence in Congregationalism as a whole. From 1904 to 1906 Proctor was assistant moderator of the National Council of Congregational Churches.

On September 22, 1906, a terrible race riot rocked Atlanta, and in its wake Proctor was instrumental in creating the Interracial Committee of Atlanta, which did much to alleviate racial tensions and build understanding. He decided one of the problems was that the Black population did not have access to nice parks and other wholesome diversions. With the generous support of many people in and out of the church, he replaced the original church with the first Black institutional church in the South. Booker T. Washington spoke at the groundbreaking ceremonies in 1908. It held a Sunday School, gymnasium, kitchen, auditorium, offices, ladies' parlor, sewing room, library, employment bureau, and the first public kindergarten in Atlanta. The congregation began missionary activities among the poor and in the jails and pioneered a large number of social programs. It organized the first temperance society in Georgia and next door opened the first church-sponsored home for Black girls in the country, the Carrie Steele Orphanage. Through its various agencies the church served thousands of people and attracted the attention of such notables as Presidents Theodore Roosevelt and Taft. Proctor organized the Atlanta Colored Music Festival Association, which annually present the best of Black music. This was found to be in itself a powerful means of ameliorating racial tensions. He founded the *Georgia Congregationalist*, which later became the *Congregational Worker*, the national periodical for Black Congregationalists. From 1906 to 1909 he was vice-president of the American Missionary Association.

In 1919 Proctor went to France as a chaplain to the Black troops occupying that territory in the aftermath of World War I. He estimated that he traveled 4,000 miles and spoke to more than 100,000 troops. When he returned in 1920 he accepted the pastorate of the Nazarene Congregational Church in Brooklyn, New York, where he created another institutional church and became as prominent a leader as he had been in Atlanta. In 1926 he was elected moderator of the New York City Congregational Church Association, the first Black to hold that position. He was a famous lecturer and was especially known for his address, "The Burden of the Negro." In 1925 he published *Between Black and White: Autobiographical Sketches*. Before his death he had

lifted the membership of the Nazarene church from 160 to over 1,000. He conceived the idea of a concerted alumni giving program for Fisk University, and ran a financial campaign that netted $100,000, much of it in pennies, nickels, and dimes. From 1923 to 1930 he was a board member of the American Board of Commissioners for Foreign Missions.

Proctor, Henry H. *Between Black and White: Autobiographical Sketches*. Boston, MA: The Pilgrim Press, 1925. 189 pp.
———. *Sermons in Melody*. 1916.
———. "The Theology of the Songs of the Southern Slave, Part I." *Southern Workmen* 36 (November 1907): 584–592.
———. "The Theology of the Songs of the Southern Slave, Part II." *Southern Workmen* 36 (December 1907): 652–656.
TNA, BAW, HUBA, AARS, WWCR, EBA, TCNL, WWCA (30–32), WWWA (1), DANB, DAB, IBAW, IBAWCB.

PROGRESSIVE NATIONAL BAPTIST CONVENTION OF AMERICA. Organized in 1961, the Progressive National Baptist Convention grew out of a crisis within the **National Baptist Convention, U.S.A., Inc.** relative to the issues of tenure and civil rights strategies. Three key persons were dynamically involved in these issues: Rev. **Joseph H. Jackson**, president of the National Baptist Convention; Rev. **Gardner C. Taylor**, pastor of Concord Baptist Church of Brooklyn, N.Y. and an aspirant to the presidency of the National Baptist Convention; and Rev. **Martin Luther King, Jr.**, president of the **Southern Christian Leadership Conference**.

The initial crisis erupted in 1961 when Taylor challenged Jackson for the office of president of the convention. At issue was the question of tenure and Rev. J. H. Jackson's bid for reelection beyond tenure. The challenge was characterized by some physical violence, controversy, and a legal battle in court. The "Taylor Team" was determined to defeat Jackson and plan a new course for the convention. However, the tremendous popularity of Jackson prevailed in the vote for the presidency and his position was upheld in the civil court. But the Taylor Team did not accept this defeat. They were determined to lead African American Baptists in a new direction, especially in the area of civil rights.

On September 11, 1961, a national news release was issued which made concrete the determination of the Taylor Team to change the direction of African American Baptist denominational leadership to reflect the contemporary needs of the age. Rev. **LeVaughn V. Booth**, pastor of Zion Baptist Church of Cincinnati, Ohio, issued the official call to organize a new national convention. On November 14–15, 1961, about twenty-three Baptist clergymen convened the organizational meeting of the Progressive National Baptist Convention at the Zion Baptist Church, with twenty-three messengers registered, twelve states registered, and thirty-three messengers participating and fourteen states represented. The new convention was designed to represent the "progressive" leadership of the race in terms of theology and sociopolitical issues.

A comprehensive document relative to the rationale for the new convention was compiled by Rev. W. H. R. Powell, a former pastor of the Shiloh Baptist Church, Philadelphia, Pennsylvania. In this document, he offered a declaration of the organizational structure, principles, and aims of the new Progressive National Baptist Convention of America, Incorporated. The document was approved at Richmond, Virginia, Thursday morning, May 10, 1962. The document cited the internal disharmony within the National Baptist Convention, U.S.A., Inc. as one rationale for the new convention's existence. It also affirmed that the election of officers of the new convention should be limited by tenure and the true spirit of democracy should prevail throughout the entire denomination.

The following persons were elected to serve as the first officers of the Progressive National Baptist Convention of America, Inc.: Rev. **T. M. Chambers** of California, president; Rev. **L. V. Booth** of Ohio, vice-president; Rev. J. Carl Mitchell of West Virginia, secretary; Rev. Louis Rawls of Illinois, Treasurer; A. J. Hargett, director of publicity; and the Honorable William W. Parker, attorney. These men were able to lead the convention to a slow but significant progress.

In the area of civil rights, Rev. Martin Luther King, Jr. and Rev. **Ralph D. Abernathy** provided ready leadership within the Progressive National Baptist Convention of America. The leadership of the new denomination became strong in its moral, financial, and general support of the civil rights revolution. Moreover, many of the leaders who opted to remain within the National Baptist Convention still gave support to the new approaches to the civil rights struggle.

Again, the new "progressive" spirit of the denomination was manifested in a cooperative program between the **American Baptist Churches in the U.S.A.** (of which Abernathy was a member) and the Progressive National Baptist Convention of America. The new program, called the Fund of Renewal, was designed to give new life and vitality especially to African American Baptist schools and other special urban ministry projects. The new program offered a new spirit of cooperation between Black and White Baptists.

Fitts, Leroy. *A History of Black Baptists*. Nashville, TN: Broadman Press, 1985. 368 pp.

Leroy Fitts

PROUT, MARY ANN (February 14, 1801–1884), educator, member of the **African Methodist Episcopal Church** (AME), and founder of the order from which came the Independent Order of St. Luke, was born in South River, Maryland. In her childhood the family moved to Baltimore, Maryland. Some accounts indicate that the family was in slavery when Prout was born, but if so, it seems that after the move to Baltimore at least the children were free. Two of her older brothers, William A. (b.1790) and Jacob W. (b.1797), became leading citizens in Liberia, but she remained in the United States.

At the age of twelve she joined the Bethel AME Church on Saratoga Street in Baltimore, and was a loyal supporter of that denomination for the rest of her life. She always sought means to raise money for the church when it was burdened by debt. She founded a day school in about 1830 and taught there until 1867, when the school closed. At about that time she founded a secret order from which later evolved the Independent Order of St. Luke. She was very sensitive to the needs of the poor and saw the necessity of a Black organization to give financially to the sick and provide money to bury the dead. Prout led the organization for the rest of her life; she never married. After her death there was a split in the Order and a rival group formed in Richmond, Virginia, under the leadership of Maggie Lena Walker. She led the Independent Order of St. Luke to a national presence and an eventual high of 50,000 members. The stock market crash of 1929 apparently led to its demise in the 1930s.

NBAW, PNW, NNW, IBAW.

PRUITT, ROBERT LEE (b. 1935), 103rd bishop of the **African Methodist Episcopal Church** (AME), was born in Greenville, South Carolina, but grew up in Pennsylvania. He was converted at an early age and decided to enter the ministry. He received his B.A. from Wilberforce University and his M.Div. from Payne Theological Seminary at Wilberforce. He married Lola Arnetta Boxley, with whom he has had one son.

His pastorates have included North Hills AME Church in Philadelphia, Pennsylvania; Grant AME Church in Boston, Massachusetts; Metropolitan AME

Church in New York City; and Metropolitan AME Church in Washington, D.C. When he became pastor of the church in Washington, D.C., in about 1972, he was faced with a major dilemma. The church was listed as an historical landmark, and was the place where such luminaries as Frederick Douglass, Mary Church Terrell, and Paul Laurence Dunbar had worshipped. Presidents of the United States and other leaders had addressed literary society meetings there, and it had been the site of important civil rights meetings. Its founders had supported the Underground Railroad and Black craftsmen had completed the building in 1886 with self-made bricks. By the 1960s the church was surrounded by modern skyscrapers in the middle of a high-priced business district. City officials tried to pressure the church into selling and moving out. When Pruitt arrived as pastor, the offering prices for the church had reached over $4,000,000. The church, however, was still dynamic and active, and decided not to sell its heritage. After spending a half-million dollars to restore the exterior, it spent a similar amount on the interior, to maintain its service as a living church for years to come.

Pruitt was elected bishop from this congregation in 1984. He was assigned to the Seventeenth Episcopal District, covering Central Africa, Zambia, Zimbabwe, and Malwai. He successfully built many schools and churches in those regions. In about 1988 he was assigned to the Eighteenth Episcopal District, based in South Africa, moving to the Tenth Episcopal District in 1990, with headquarters in Dallas, Texas.

Booker, Simeon. "Washington Notebook." *Ebony* 34 (May 1979): 29.
AMSC, IBAW.

PURE HOLINESS CHURCH OF GOD. An Apostolic Pentecostal church. Rev. John Isaac Woodly was an early and outstanding leader of the **Church of God in Christ** (COGIC). Through the 1920s he had become the general evangelist for the states of Alabama, Georgia and Florida. During these years, the non-Trinitarian beliefs of the Apostolic Pentecostal movement spread through the South and Woodly and a number of the COGIC leaders associated with him accepted the new perspective in 1927. As a result, Woodly, Mother Lilla Pittman, Mother Mary Rowe, Elder Ed Lee Blackwell, and an Elder Brysen left to found the Pure Holiness Church of God with headquarters in Anniston, Alabama.

In addition to the acceptance of the Apostolic position on the Godhead, the group differed on several other concerns with COGIC. Most importantly, they ordained women, a practice opposed by COGIC founder **Charles H. Mason**. Pittman and Rowe became prominent ministers in the church. They also structured the church under the leadership of an unmarried presiding bishop and unsalaried pastors. Woodly led the church for the first five years, during which time it spread to Florida. He was succeeded by Bishop John Grayhouse who led the church through the difficult years of recovery from the Depression, but then left to the church to return to COGIC. He was succeeded by Bishop Charles White, who saw the church spread throughout the South.

Following White's death in 1947, Bishop Ed Lee Blackwell, one of the founders, became the presiding bishop. During his term, women's work expanded. The Women's Missionary Society was founded and Mother Luzole Tigner was selected as its first president. Mother Jessie Simms was appointed as the church's hymnal chairman, authoring 54 hymns which constitute the church's unique music. Blackwell also moved to develop a more democratic structure and for the first time ministers were permitted to vote in the church's convocations. He also supported the removal of the rule that presiding bishops must be unmarried.

In 1958 Charles Frederick Fears, the church's sunday school director, succeeded Blackwell as presiding bishop. During his term he promoted the system by which pastors became salaried. He was succeeded by **Bennie G. Isem**. During his term, in 1964, the church founded both the Pure Holiness School of Theology and a denominational periodical, the *Triumph of Truth Newsletter*, under the editorship of Sister Wilma Ringer. In 1978 Isem, a widower, married Ringer. He resigned in 1984 and was succeeded by Bishop Edward Ackley.

In 1990 the Pure Holiness Church of God reported 24 churches in the United States and four churches in Jamaica. Headquarters is in Atlanta, Georgia.

DuPree, Sherry Sherrod. *Biographical Dictionary of African-American Holiness-Pentecostals, 1880–1990*. Washington, DC: Middle Atlantic Regional Press, 1989. 386 pp.

"Hitler is alive! Yes, I mean very much alive in 'Constitution Hall' of the so-called 'Daughters of the American Revolution.' Crispus Attucks, a colored man, was among the first to die on the Boston Commons in 1776, fighting for the freedom of this Nation. Since that time Negro blood had been mingled with that of white patriots in defense of this Nation and the preservation of rights for others, but such rights are denied the Negro, even while in the uniform of this Country.

"During World War II, the colored soldiers had to fight two wars, the war against the Nazis, and the war against jim-crow. He helped to win the first, he lost the second."

Bishop Smallwood E. Williams, Founder
Bible Way Church of Our Lord
Jesus Christ World Wide

Q–R

QUINN, WILLIAM PAUL (April 19, 1788–February 3, 1873), 4th bishop of the **African Methodist Episcopal Church** (AME), was by some accounts born in Calcutta, India, of Roman Catholic parents. His origins are obscure, and others contend that he was born in the East Indies or Honduras, Central America. Most agree on the birth year of 1788. In any case, as a young man he made his way to the United States and was converted in 1808 in Bucks County, Pennsylvania. He was licensed to preach in the Methodist Episcopal Church in 1812 in Bucks County, and attended the formation of the AME Church in Philadelphia in 1816. He joined the new church that year and was ordained deacon in 1818.

He held pastorates in Bushtown, Gouldtown, Salem, and Springton, New Jersey, and in 1826, Bucks County, Pennsylvania. In about 1827 he had a disagreement with Bishop **Richard Allen** and left the denomination. In June 1828 he petitioned to be allowed to return, but the matter was not dealt with until June 1833, when the New York Conference admitted him. He was transferred to mission work in the West, around Ohio, where he had already been present for several years. He was the first itinerant minister for the AME Church to cross the Allegheny Mountains, and was present when the Western or Ohio Conference was organized in 1830. He finally was ordained elder in 1838 and about that time was assigned to the Pittsburgh Circuit, which included Pittsburgh, Washington D.C., and Uniontown, Pennsylvania. On October 2, 1840, he was a member of the newly formed Indiana Conference and was appointed pastor of the Brooklyn Circuit in Illinois, with all the other circuits also under his oversight.

At the 1841 Indiana Conference he was made assistant to Bishop **Morris Brown,** and became famous for his energetic travels and labors on behalf of the church's western outreach. Between 1840 and 1844 he helped organize 72 congregations, 47 churches, 40 temperance societies, 17 camp meetings, and 50 Sunday schools west of the Allegheny Mountains in Ohio, Indiana, Michigan, Illinois, Kentucky, and Missouri. The organization of churches in the slave states of Kentucky and Missouri meant defying the law and risking death. His amazing efforts earned him the title as the St. Paul of the AME Church, and the report he made to the General Conference in 1844 had such an impact that he was catapulted into the bishopric. He was consecrated on May 19, 1844.

At the 1848 General Conference Quinn presented the first full written report ever given by a bishop to a General Conference. He also recommended a presiding elder system, that was rejected at the time, but later became an integral part of the church's structure of ministry. He and Bishop **Willis Nazrey** oversaw the establishment of the British Methodist Episcopal Church as a separate entity in Canada on September 26,1856. These former AME churches later reunited with the AME Church in 1864. On May 9,1849, after the death of Bishop Morris Brown, Quinn became senior bishop and carried that office for 24 years and eight months, the longest tenure to that point of any senior bishop in the denomination's history. Named for him are Paul Quinn College in Waco, Texas, and churches in fifteen states.

Quinn, William Paul. *The Origin, Horrors, and Results of Slavery, Faithfully and Minutely Described, in a Series of Facts, and Its Advocates Pathetically Addressed.* Pittsburgh, PA: N.p., 1834. 24 pp.

HUBA, BAW, CEAMEC, BAMEC, RAM, EBA, CH, HAMEC, EWM.

RADIO AND TELEVISION MINISTRIES IN THE BLACK COMMUNITY. Religious broadcasting began soon after the the first radio station, KDKA, went on the air on November 1, 1920. The first religious broadcast was a worship service from Calvary Episcopal Church two months later. The experiment brought such a positive response from the listening audience that the church's weekly service was added to the station's schedule. Over the next five years approximately 600 radio stations were founded, about ten percent of which were licensed to various churches. Almost from the beginning the majority of religious broadcasts and the religious radio stations originated among conservative evangelical Christian groups, with a few being sponsored by various alternative groups such as the Unity School of Christianity.

African Americans were quick to make use of the new media. In 1924, Pentecostal minister **Samuel M. Crouch, Sr.** of the **Church of God in Christ** began the first known religious broadcast by an African American over a station in Fort Worth, Texas. Crouch went on to a successful ministry in Los Angeles beginning in the 1930s. At the end of the 1920s the first African American radio minister to gain a significant national audience went on the air. Having moved to Washington, D.C., in 1928, **Elder Solomon Lightfoot Michaux** of the Radio Church of God began his broadcast over WJSV the next year. He used a 150-member choir and a positive theme (happiness) to reach and hold his audience. In 1934 Michaux proved to be in the right place at the right time when CBS bought WJSV and began to carry the popular Washington-based show nationwide. He soon was heard over some fifty stations and his regular listening audience of 25 million was the largest audience of any African American to this day. He used his radio platform for such diverse programs as building political support in the Black community for Franklin Roosevelt to assistance for the Black urban poor.

Michaux seems also to have been a factor in expanding the Black community's access to radio during the 1940s, when a noticeable increase of broadcast ministries was seen. **John Washington Goodgame,** the prominent minister of Sixth Avenue Baptist Church in Birmingham, Alabama, who began a weekly program over WVOK just prior to World War II, led the way. He was soon joined by Atlanta colleague **William Holmes Borders,** and Chicago Baptist preacher **John L. Branham.** Adding some color to the era was radical Pentecostal minister, **James Marion "Prophet" Jones**, whose broadcast originated in Detroit.

In the intervening decades, the number of religious broadcasts by African American religious leaders had steadily expanded. Among the most notable were those of **Tom Skinner** (Baptist) and the late Pentecostal Bishop **Smallwood Williams.** In 1954 gospel singer **Mahalia Jackson** started a very successful radio show which introduced a musical format.

Religious broadcasting in the Black community follows much the same pattern as in the White community. The great majority originates among conservative evangelical Christians, especially Baptists and Pentecostals, with little programming coming from the more established Protestant groups. Also, a significant number of programs have been developed by groups and leaders from other religions. For example, one of the most successful programs in the 1950s and 1960s was that of **Clarence Cobbs,** a Spiritual church leader in Chicago with the **Metropolitan Spiritual Churches of Christ.** More recently metaphysical minister **Johnnie Colemon,** has built a growing broadcast ministry and Moslem leader **Warith Deen Muhammad** has a weekly national show which like Colemon's also originates in Chicago.

When television came on the scene, religious programming was originally dominated by mainline protestants. Then Pentecostal minister Oral Roberts developed his show which featured his ever-controversial healing ministry. The liberal Protestant dominance was curbed in the late 1960s when some FCC rulings opened the media to independent evangelicals who were prepared to make the most use of it. Black ministries were relatively much slower in making the move to what has proved a much more expensive ministry, but have gradually assumed a place, especially on the several cable television networks. A few have become popular superstars, most prominently **Ben Kinchlow** of Pat Robertson's 700 Club and **Fred Price**, whose Ever Increasing Faith Ministries sponsors the most popular current religious broadcast by a Black person.

Armstrong, Ben. *The Electric Church.* Nashville, TN: Thomas Nelson, 1975.

Schultze, Quentin J., ed. *American Evangelicals and the Mass Media.* Grand Rapids, MI: Zondervan Publishing House, 1990. 382 pp.

"Top Radio Ministers." *Ebony* 4 (1949): 56–61.

RAHAHMAN, ABDUL (1762–July 6, 1829), a nineteenth-century Muslim slave, was born in Timbo, Futa Jallon (in present day Guinea) of the Fulbe people. He was the son of Ibrahima Yoro Pate Sori. In the years 1776–78, his father conducted a series of wars which established a Muslim Kingdom in Futa Jallon. Rahahman was given a good education first at Timbo, his home town, and then at Masina and later at

Timbuctu. Being the second son he was assigned by his father to military duties.

In 1788 Rahahman was sent by his father to quell some unrest on the western edge of his kingdom. He successfully engaged the enemy, but on the way home was ambushed as he made his way through a narrow mountain pass. Captured, he was taken to Gambia and sold into slavery. He was subsequently taken to New Orleans and then up the Mississippi River to Natchez, Mississippi. Through a fellow slave he was able to communicate part of his story, and was given a nickname, "Prince." He fought his fate as best he could and at one point ran away. Unable to locate any compatriots of free Black people, he returned to the plantation. He seems to have reached some accord with the mistress of the plantation and he settled in to his life. Around 1794 he married. His wife, a Baptist, was also the plantation physician and midwife. They had nine children.

In 1807 while in Natchez selling vegetables, he encountered John Coates, the only White man to reside in Timbo during the years Rahahman was growing up. The two recognized each other. Cox attempted to obtain his freedom and widely publicized his story. However, Cox's owner would not sell him. It was not until 1826 that Rahahman wrote a letter to the U.S. Government explaining his plight. Two years later, Secretary of State Henry Clay arranged for his freedom and transport to Washington. People in Natchez raised the money for his wife's freedom. His owner may have relented in part due to Rahahman's age.

The pilgrimage from Natchez to Washington took a year. He frequently found himself the object of attention by representatives of the American Colonization Society and local groups of African Americans. In his attempt to raise money to return to Africa and to free his children left behind in Mississippi, he professed conversion to Christianity. He was often asked to write out the Lord's Prayer in Arabic. He graciously responded but wrote out the Fatiha, the introductory section of the Qur'an.

Finally in 1819 he sailed for Africa and landed in Liberia, south of his homeland. He had become ill and stayed in Liberia to improve his health. However, there he died several months later. Eventually, his children were freed and joined his widow in Liberia.

Rahahman is but one of a number of African Muslims who fell victim to the Atlantic slave trade. He most notable because of the extensive written record which documents his life in both Africa and America.

Alford, Terry. *Prince Among Slaves.* New York: Harcourt, Brace, Jovanovich, 1977. 284 pp.

Austin, Allen D. *African Muslims in Antebellum America: A Sourcebook.* New York: Garland, 1984. 759 pp.

RANDOLPH, FLORENCE (August 9, 1866–December 28, 1951), pioneer woman minister in the **African Methodist Episcopal Zion Church** (AMEZ), was born in Charleston, South Carolina, a daughter of John B. and Anna (Smith) Spearing. At the age of eight she was greatly impressed by the ministry of her blind grandmother. Randolph would lead her from house to house as she prayed with the sick and spoke to them about the Bible.

After attending a public school in Charleston, she went to Avery Normal School. She did much work on her own, hiring a private tutor to teach her Bible history, Greek, and Hebrew. She later (late 1920s) completed the "Synthetic Bible Course" at the Moody Bible Institute in Chicago, Illinois, and attended two terms at Drew Theological Seminary in Madison, New Jersey. On May 5,1886, she married Hugh Randolph, with whom she had one child.

In 1892, at the age of twenty-six, she became a lecturer and organizer with the Women's Christian Temperance Union (W.C.T.U.), and remained with that organization about forty years. She was licensed to preach in 1897 and ordained a deacon in Atlantic City, New Jersey, in May 1900. Her first pastorate was the Pennington Street (now Clinton Memorial) AMEZ Church in Newark, New Jersey, beginning in May 1901. That year she was a delegate to the World Methodist Conference in London, England. She was ordained elder in 1903. Later pastorates included the Little AMEZ Church in New York City; the AMEZ Church in Poughkeepsie, New York; and the Wallace Chapel AMEZ Church in Summit, New Jersey. In Summit she led in the building of an impressive new brick church, parsonage, and community.

For twenty-five years she was president of the Women's Home and Foreign Missionary Society of the New Jersey Conference of the church, and was national president of the society from 1916 to 1920. For two years she was the only Black member of the New Jersey State Christian Endeavor Society. In 1915 she founded the New Jersey State Federation of Colored Women's Clubs and was its president for twelve years. She was chaplain of the National Federation of Colored Women's Clubs for four years.

In 1922 Randolph again visited England on her way to a tour of the Gold Coast, British West Africa (now Ghana), Sierra Leone, and Liberia. She spent several months in the Quittah District of the Gold Coast, assisting the missionaries there. When she returned to the United States she brought with her an African girl, Charity Zombelo, whom she educated in Summit High School and Hampton Institute in Virginia. Zombelo later returned to Africa as a teacher. In 1931 Randolph made a trip to the Holy Land and various points in North Africa.

In June 1933 the AMEZ Livingstone College gave her an honorary Doctor of Divinity degree, the first woman in the AMEZ Church so honored. In July 1942, she was appointed by the New Jersey Federation to present Mrs. Eleanor Roosevelt to the convention at Bordentown Industrial School in New Jersey. The following month Randolph gave the invocation prior to Mrs. Roosevelt's address to the General Convention on Christian Education and Christian Youth Council at Livingstone College. In 1946, after over twenty years at the Wallace Chapel church, she retired, but remained active as a popular speaker.

"Rev. Florence Randolph." *A.M.E. Zion Quarterly Review* 69 (Fall 1959): 194–195.
IBAW, BWR, HAMEZC, EWM, WWCA (38–40).

RANDOLPH, PASCHAL BEVERLY (October 8, 1825–July 29, 1875), the pioneer Rosicrucian in nineteenth-century America and founder of the Fraternitas Rosae Crucis (Rosicrucian Fraternity), an occult Rosicrucian order, was born in New York City, the son of Edmund Randolph (of the famous Virginia Randolphs) and Flora Beverly, a Black woman whose heritage he later insisted included Madagascan royalty. Because of this background, Randolph has generally been classed as Black, though he did not see himself that way. Throughout his life, he insisted that he had so many blood strains in him that a regular classification would be impossible. His mother died when he was still a child, and he was reared by a friend of his mother's half-sister. In 1841, at the age of sixteen, he ran away to become a sailor, living that life until an accident five years later forced him into a new profession.

He became a barber and dyer and began to educate himself. By about 1850 he had learned enough medicine to make a living as a practicing "eclectic physician," or naturopath. He found a need for a physician willing to counsel people concerning sexual and marital problems, and specialized in the field through the remainder of his professional days. He became drawn to the works of Spiritualist Andrew Jackson Davis and seer Emanuel Swedenborg. It is difficult to construct a reliable history of Randolph's beginnings with Rosicrucianism. It is said

that in 1850 he traveled to Europe, where he encountered and joined the Rosicrucian Fraternity at Frankfort on Main, Germany. Upon returning to the United States, Randolph became active in politics in the Reform party, meeting Abraham Lincoln. In 1854 he returned to Europe where, it is claimed, he studied with many of the leading Rosicrucians, including Eliphas Levi, Kenneth MacKenzie, and Edward Bulwer-Lytton, and, while in Paris in 1858, he was made Supreme Grand Master of the Western World and a Knight of L'Ordre du Lis.

That year he returned to the United States and perhaps at that point began his own Rosicrucian activities. In September of 1861 he went to California for a two-month lecture tour, and while there, on November 5, founded the First Supreme Grand Lodge of the Rosicrucian Fraternity. He lived for several months in San Francisco. In 1862, he again went abroad, this time visiting the Middle East and Orient. He was reportedly initiated by the Ansaireh in Syria and the Order of the Rose in London. He returned to the United States in 1962 and settled in Boston. He worked for a year as a recruiter for Black soldiers for the Union Army. In 1864, at President Lincoln's request, he moved to New Orleans, Louisiana, where he spent two years educating the newly freed former slaves. He was the only African American to join the entourage accompanying Lincoln's body on the trip back to Illinois for burial, though color prejudice caused him to be removed from the train. In 1866 he was also a delegate to the Southern Loyalist Convention, an anti-Andrew Johnson gathering of support for more radical Reconstruction in the South.

His experiences in politics following the war drove Randolph out of the public sphere and back into his role as a doctor and a spiritual leader. He moved back to Boston, where he reopened his medical practice. He opened a center on Boylston Street, and in 1871 reorganized the Grand Supreme Lodge. He also continued to write about what he considered the heart of Rosicrucianism, the mystical function of sexuality. He published a summary statement of his findings in his most important book, *Eulis, the History of Love* (1874), a name he took from the Greek Eleusinian Mysteries, which he thought concerned sex. In February 1872, he was arrested in Boston on the charge of circulating books on free love. This was a well-publicized trial in which the prosecuting attorney said that Randolph was the most dangerous man in America. Randolph, though frail in appearance, was a powerful orator, and successfully defended himself. Out of the trial experience he published an autobiographical volume.

In November 1872, the Boston fire destroyed Randolph's home and belongings and he moved to Toledo, Ohio. He married in 1874 and had a son, Osiris Budha Randolph. Then, in 1875, he committed suicide. Though continuing to exist, the Rosicrucian Fraternity was largely dormant through the next several decades. It was finally reorganized in 1895 by R. Swinburne Clymer, and has been an active organization ever since.

Clymer, R. Swinburne. *Dr. Paschal Beverly Randolph and the Supreme Grand Dome of the Rosicrucians in France.* Quakertown, PA: Philosophical Publishing Co., 1929. 52 pp.

————. *The Rose Cross Order.* Allentown, PA: Philosophical Publishing Co., 1916. 208 pp.

————. *The Rosicrucian Fraternity in America.* 2 vols. Quakertown, PA: The Rosicrucian Foundation, 1935.

McIntosh, Christopher. *The Rosicrucians.* Revised ed. Wellingborough, Northamptonshire, UK: Crucible,1987.

Randolph, Paschal Beverly. *Eulis, the History of Love.* Toledo, OH: Randolph Publishing Co., 1874. Rept. as *Eulis, Affectional Alchemy.* Quakertown, PA: The Confederation of Initiates, 1930. 230 pp.

————. *P. B. Randolph . . . His Curious Life, Works, and Career.* Boston, MA: The Author, 1872. 96 pp.

————. *Ravalette. The Rosicrucian's Story.* Quakertown, PA: Philosophical Publishing Co., 1863, 1939. 283 pp.

————. *Seership: Guide to Soul Sight.* Quakertown, PA: Confederation of Initiates, 1868, 1930. 517 pp.

————. *Soul, the World Soul.* Quakertown, PA: Confederation of Initiates, 1932. 246 pp.

BDACSL, RLOA, BAW.

RANSOM, REVERDY CASSIUS (January 4, 1861–April 22, 1959), 48th bishop of the **African Methodist Episcopal Church** (AME), was born in Flushing, Ohio, the son of Harriet Johnson and an unnamed person. Sometime later George Warner Ransom married his mother and became a father to Ransom. At the age of four he went to live with George Ransom's parents, Louis and Betsy Ransom, in Washington, Ohio, where he attended a school in the local AME church. In 1869 the family moved to Cambridge, Ohio, where he was a student in a public school for Blacks, which also met in an AME church. He married Leanna Watkins in 1881, and had one son.

That year he entered Wilberforce University in Xenia, Ohio. He had saved money for college from a variety of jobs and his mother, who worked as a domestic servant, mortgaged her house for additional funds and took care of his infant son. In the fall of 1881

he experienced conversion at Wilberforce and joined the AME church. In 1882 he transferred to Oberlin College, where he was given a scholarship. Within a year, however, the scholarship was taken from him because he organized a protest against a new segregation policy at Oberlin separating the White and Black women in the dining hall. He returned to Wilberforce, scraping money together, and his mother even sold her cow. He was licensed to preach in October 1883, at Wilberforce and joined the Ohio Annual Conference in 1885. In 1885–86 he pastored the AME church in Selma, Ohio.

He graduated from Wilberforce with his B.A. in 1886, was ordained deacon, and assigned to Altoona, Pennsylvania, from 1886 to 1888. In 1886 he was divorced from his first wife, whom he had married under adverse circumstances, and on October 25, 1887, he married Emma Sarah Conner, with whom he had another son. He served in Manchester Mission in Allegheny City, Pennsylvania, from 1888 to 1890, where he transformed a ten-member, poverty-stricken congregation into a thriving church with well over one hundred people worshipping. This he did despite hostility from Whites, who stoned the house he had purchased. This pastorate was followed by the prestigious North Street AME Church in Springfield, Ohio (1890–93), where he organized the first men's club in the denomination in 1890. He was at St. John's AME Church in Cleveland, Ohio, from 1893 to 1896, and in 1893 he organized the first board of deaconesses in the denomination. In 1894 he was instrumental in having the first South African students enrolled in Wilberforce University in Ohio.

From 1896 to 1900 he was assigned to Bethel AME Church in Chicago, Illinois, where he became widely known as a great preacher and advanced social thinker. In 1900 he organized the Men's Sunday Club, which brought young men off the streets together with professionals and businessmen every Sunday afternoon for a cultural program. In 1899 he participated in the National Convention of the Afro-American Council in Chicago, Illinois. In 1900 he created what was known as the Institutional Church and Social Settlement on Dearborn Street near 39th Street, the first of its kind among Blacks. It was inspired by Hull House, founded by Jane Addams, with whom he had worked. He left Bethel and from 1900 to 1904 worked at the Institutional Church full time. In 1903 he preached a series of sermons against the crime and corruption in the area, naming names, and a dynamite explosion soon destroyed his office. He was successful, however, in closing down many of the gambling and racketeering houses.

He was assigned to New Bedford, Massachusetts, from 1904 to 1905, followed by the Charles Street AME Church in Boston, Massachusetts, from 1905 to 1907. While there he became one of the founding members of the Niagara movement organized by W. E. B. DuBois, and was an influential voice on behalf of Black dignity. In 1906, at the second annual meeting of the Niagara movement, Ransom delivered his famous speech, "The Spirit of John Brown," which electrified the audience. Du Bois' estimate was that the speech "led through its inspiration and eloquence to the eventual founding of the N.A.A.C.P."

Ransom's final pastorate was at Bethel AME Church in New York from 1907 to 1912. From 1912 to 1924 Ransom was editor of the *A.M.E. Church Review,* and under his leadership the journal expanded to include articles on a wide range of subjects. In 1913 he established a mission, the Church of Simon of Cyrene, to minister to the poor in the "Black Tenderloin" section of Manhattan, New York, and continued to lead it as a part-time pastor. In 1918 he was nominated by the United Civic League of New York as a candidate for the 21st Congressional District, but was defeated through a technicality that disallowed his name from even appearing on the ballot.

From the editorship he was elected bishop in 1924, and served first in the Thirteenth (Kentucky and Tennessee), then the Seventh, and from 1932 to 1952 in the Third (Ohio, Western Pennsylvania, and West Virginia) Episcopal Districts. He was a delegate to the World Methodist Conferences in London (1901), Toronto (1911), London (1921), and Springfield, Massachusetts (1947). From 1936 to 1940 he was the first Black commissioner of the Ohio Board of Pardon and Parole. In 1941 President Franklin D. Roosevelt appointed him a member of the Volunteer Participation Committee in the Office of Civil Defense. His second wife died in 1941, and in August 1943 he married Georgia Myrtle Teal Hayes. He was president of the board of trustees at Wilberforce University from 1932 to 1948, and was the first president of the **National Fraternal Council of Negro Churches** in 1934. From 1948 to 1956 he was the official historiographer of the denomination. He was a member of the executive committee of the Federal (now National) Council of Churches and was chair of its Race Relations Commission. In 1950 he published his autobiography, *The Pilgrimage of Harriet Ransom's Son.* He retired from the bishopric in 1952 at the age of 95, and was remembered as one of the most important Black religious leaders of the first half of the twentieth century.

Morris, Calvin S. *Reverdy C. Ransom: Black Advocate of the Social Gospel.* Lanham, MD: University Press of America, 1990. 203 pp.

Ransom, Reverdy C. "Confessions of a Bishop." *Ebony 5* (March 1950): 72–80.

———. *The Negro. The Hope or the Despair of Christianity.* Boston, MA: Ruth Hill Publisher, 1935. 98 pp.

———. *The Pilgrimage of Harriet Ransom's Son.* Nashville, TN: AME Sunday School Union, 1949. 336 pp.

———. *Preface to the History of the AME Church.* Nashville, TN: AME Sunday School Union, 1950. 220 pp.

———. *The Spirit of Freedom and Justice: Orations and Speeches.* Nashville, TN: AME Sunday School Union, 1926. 176 pp.

HAMEC, AMECMIM, NG, NV, AAP, BA, EWM, EBA, EAMEC, WWCR, WWCA (38–40), DANB, BAMEC, BAW, AARS, IBAW, HUBA.

RASTAFARIANISM. A Black nationalist movement which developed in Jamaica in the early twentieth century. Though the genesis of the Rastafari occurred in the twentieth century, its roots reach back to the seventeenth, to the settlement and colonization of Jamaica. The British attack and capture of Jamaica in 1655 allowed 1,500 Africans to escape to the interior of Jamaica. These "Maroons" became a force the British were never able to completely contain and successfully kept the British from inhabiting the interior of the island during their 307 years of occupation. Descendants of the original Maroons still exist in communities in central Jamaica, a living reminder of the only rebellion composed of slaves and ex-slaves which forced the British empire to offer a peace treaty (1738). Also in 1655, the Anglican Church was established on the island but made few attempts at missionary work among slaves until three Moravian missionaries arrived on December 7, 1754, and started preaching on the Bogue Estate in St. Elizabeth. In spite of the Moravians' zeal, Christianity was slow in developing until the end of the American Revolutionary period when several hundred loyalists, along with their slaves, left the United States for the British West Indies. **George Liele,** the freedman of a Baptist planter from Georgia, arrived in Kingston in 1783 and developed a successful ministry leading to the erection of a chapel for slaves. Subsequent ministry efforts by other African Americans and Jamaicans led to an emphasis that contrasted greatly with that of the White missionaries.

In addition to instruction in traditional Christian doctrine, these "Native Baptist" leaders prepared candidates for baptism by encouraging them to seek dreams and visions which came after many nights of praying and waiting in the woods. This pre-baptismal ritual resembled in form the inductions of initiates into Western African secret societies. The Spirit sought in these dreams was thought to be the highest divine power who could give the seeker faith, knowledge and life. Below this Spirit was the prophet John the Baptist. John baptized Jesus Christ, and therefore was higher in authority than him. Besides this reinterpretation of Christianity, the Native Baptist movement also developed its own system of organization. Religious leaders arose on the basis of their personal charisma, authority and conviction. The movement provided an opportunity for Afro-Jamaicans to gather outside of their work environment. Not surprisingly, the leaders of the two greatest political rebellions in Jamaica since the Maroons were both led by preachers in the Native Baptist Church.

During the Great Revival of 1860–61, White missionaries were elated with increased attendance at congregations, the demand for prayer meetings, and the desire for Bibles. But they were later dismayed to discover that *myalism,* or African-inspired rites to remove spells and evil influences, was mixed into the fervor to be cleansed from sin. Thus the Native Baptists ceased being seen by local clergy as an official Christian movement and became a competitor to the Euro-Christianity orthodoxy which they represented.

Other Influences: Besides the Native Baptists, several other movements substantively contributed to the environment in which Rastafarianism grew. In 1891, the Rev. Alexander Bedward received a special call to begin a public ministry of baptizing souls in the Mona River and dispensing the river water as medicine. Cures were reported as a result of drinking the water, and Bedwardite groups were organized throughout Jamaica. On December 31, 1920, he gathered his followers to witness his ascension into heaven. Bedward had declared that he was Jesus Christ, the Son of God, and prophesied that he would ascend like Elijah in a chariot of fire at 10 a.m. that morning. Bedward also told a White writer who had visited him on December 26th that in the new heaven and the new earth, he would be as White as she. He promised his followers that he would descend three days later and carry the elect with him into Heaven. Thrice more the ascension was announced only to be postponed, and finally Bedward proclaimed to the crowd that a "spiritual ascension" would occur. On April 27, 1921, he led eight hundred followers on a march toward the city of Kingston. After two miles, armed soldiers surrounded the group, some

of whom were arrested. Bedward was sentenced for the rest of his life to a lunatic asylum where he died ten years later. He left behind a settlement at August Town near University College where Bedwardites can still be found.

Marcus Mosiah Garvey called the attention of his fellow Jamaicans to Africa and Ethiopia as symbols of sacred space invested with a noble past and promising a glorious future. Garvey emphasized the long history of Africa before slavery and the promise it held for a future life free of the humiliations and limitations imposed upon Africans by Euro-American societies. In 1914, Garvey began organizing the Universal Negro Improvement Association (UNIA), whose purpose was to "take Africa, organize it, develop it, arm it, and make it the defender of Negroes the world over." After a decade in the United States, in 1927, he returned to Jamaica to preach his doctrine of Black racial pride and a return to Africa. In 1928, he founded the People's Political Party but in those days of limited suffrage, his political efforts against British colonialism were doomed due to a lack of support from an upper class who structured Jamaican society in the image of a tropical version of England. In 1935, after a series of election defeats, Garvey left Jamaica for England. He died abroad in 1940, reportedly at a time when he was making plans to return to Jamaica.

The Emergence of Rastafarianism. In 1930, Ras ("Prince") Tafari was crowned as His Imperial Majesty (HIM), the Emperor of Ethiopia, Haile Selassie I ("Power of the Trinity"), the King of Kings, the Lord of Lords, and the conquering Lion of the Tribe of Judah, 225th in the line of Ethiopian kings which began with the son of the Queen of Sheba and King Solomon. The *Kingston Daily Gleaner* featured the coronation of this Black king on the front page of its November 11th, 1930 issue. The Rastafarians saw in him a living representative of Garvey's "Black God" and Ethiopia, his kingdom, became their eschatological destination, their Promised Land.

The doctrine that Ras Tafari is the Living God was developed by several persons seemingly independent of each other. Leonard Percival Howell has been regarded as the first to preach the divinity of Ras Tafari in Kingston. Howell had returned to Jamaica in November 1932 from northeastern America where he had lived since 1918. It is known that he and Garvey knew of each other in New York. Joseph Nathaniel Hibbert was born in Jamaica in 1894, but went with his adopted father to Costa Rica in 1911. In 1924, he joined the Ancient Mystic Order of Ethiopia, a Masonic society, and upon returning to Jamaica, began to preach that Haile Selassie was the King of Kings, the returned Messiah and the Redeemer of Israel. Hibbert was originally in the Benoah District of St. Andrew, and when he moved to Kingston he found Howell preaching Ras Tafari as God at the Redemption Market.

Henry Archibald Dunkley, a seaman, quit the sea in 1930, moved to Kingston, and studied the Bible for two-and-a-half years on his own before deciding that Haile Selassie was indeed the Messiah. In 1933, Dunkley opened his own mission, preaching Ras Tafari as the "King of Kings, the Root of David, the Son of the Living God," but not the God Himself. Paul Erlington, Vernal Davis and Ferdinand Ricketts, secular leaders who led discussions on Garvey teachings, came under the influence of Howell, Hibbert, and Dunkley and sometime in 1934 recognized Haile Selassie as the Living God. Thus the first Rastafari missions originated independently, and from the beginning embodied significant diversity. For example, Dunkley's effort was the King of Kings Missionary Movement which had no headquarters, officers, or constitution and Dunkley, like most street preachers, was self-taught. Hibbert, on the other hand, took over Howell's ministry in Kingston when Howell went to preach at Port Morant in the St. Thomas Parish. With Howell gone, Hibbert persuaded the body of Howell's followers to join him in forming an organized group called the Ethiopian Coptic Faith. On returning, Howell rejected Hibbert's changes and left, taking his membership with him. Hibbert continued to preach and with his mystical orientation and Masonic discipline proceeded to develop the Ethiopian Coptic Church.

Leonard Howell was both the most successful and also the most controversial early Rastafarian preacher. On December 16, 1933, the *Kingston Daily Gleaner* reported that Howell was selling photographs of Emperor Haile Selassie in St. Thomas for one shilling each and informing buyers that this was their passport to Ethiopia. On January 5, 1934, Howell was arrested at Port Morant (after selling about 5,000 photos) and was sentenced to prison for two years for sedition. Once Howell was released from jail, he established the Ethiopian Salvation Society, which was said to be a local branch of an American organization. In May of 1940, he purchased a large abandoned estate and formed Pinnacle, a separatist Rastafarian community. Estimates of membership ranged from his report of 500 residents to police claims of more than 1,600. In the middle of 1941, 70 Rastafari followers of Howell who lived at the Pinnacle camp were arrested, mainly on charges of growing ganja (marijuana), of which 28 were sent to

prison. Howell was also arrested and again imprisoned for two years. Pinnacle continued to exist in a smaller form and in 1953, after a further term of imprisonment, Howell returned and implemented a new course for his community. Male Rastas became "locksmen," growing beards and long hair (dreadlocks) and calling themselves Ethiopians. Howell also began making claims to his own divinity. One deposition from a neighbor reveals this new dimension to Howell's ministry as he is reported to have said: "I will give you ninety-six lashes, I will beat you and let you know to pay no taxes. I am Haile Selassie, neither you nor the Government have any lands here." In 1954, Pinnacle was once more raided, and on this occasion was broken up. Howell was committed to Kingston Mental Hospital.

More Recent History. The first scholarly study of the movement appeared in 1955. George Eaton Simpson, a sociologist, depicted the early Rastafari as an anti-social, anti-White cult composed of unemployed urban transients. Despite the widespread public belief that Rastafari were primarily criminals and "bearded hoodlums," Simpson found no evidence of any substantial or organized illegal activity. This negative image of drug-crazed cult members terrorizing the populace which was promoted in the Jamaican media was echoed in American papers in the late 1970s and early 1980s. The study revealed the tension of the times as Simpson's report centered on racial issues, stating that the primary motive of the Rastafari's action is revenge ("Ras Tafari says: Death to the White man and to the Black traitors").

An equally important event that same year was the news that a land grant had been bestowed by Haile Selassie to "the Black people of the West." This had been facilitated by the Ethiopian World Federation, founded by Imperial charter, which had just formed a chapter in Kingston. The Emperor had made 500 acres of land near Addis Ababa available to the federation for settlement. At the same time, a mass migration to the United Kingdom (and later to Canada and the United States) was occurring as Afro-Jamaicans were encouraged to emigrate because of labor shortages in Britain. In the late 1950s as thousands were migrating, a social scientist who was conducting a house-to-house survey on employment conditions found that many householders assumed he was compiling a list of those who wanted to go to Africa.

In 1959, the Rev. Claudius Henry gained notoriety (and a jail sentence) by distributing 15,000 tickets to be used in place of passports in a repatriation he expected to occur on October 5th. One year after that, a cache of arms was discovered at his headquarters, along with two letters addressed to Fidel Castro notifying him of Henry's intention to take the country by force and hand it over to him, since the island's population would be returning to Africa. Henry, his wife and twelve followers were arrested for treason and Henry and two others were sentenced to ten years' imprisonment. Meanwhile, Henry's son Ronald was living in the hills, secretly training a small group for guerrilla warfare. After being surprised by British troops, there was a skirmish in which three Rastas and two soldiers were killed. The group retreated further into the hills, but were soon captured and hung. Rastas, who previously had been belittled and scorned, now represented to the ruling class a possible threat to national security.

In the aftermath of the Henry crisis and the sensational media coverage that occurred, several Rastafarians led by Mortimo Planno approached representatives of the major Jamaican university asking for assistance in achieving an equitable representation of the group which would hopefully put an end to their victimization. Three members of the University College of the West Indies (UCWI) spent two weeks surveying the Rastafari Movement and the resulting report was submitted to Prime Minister Norman Manley by UCWI Principal Arthur Lewis. Though hurriedly done, it presented a brief but fairly accurate portrait of the growth of the Rastafari, summarized their history, beliefs, goals and lifestyle, and made several recommendations for further action by the government to pursue their cause of repatriation to Ethiopia. *The Rastafari Movement* report stressed the strength, vitality and restlessness of the movement and urged the political authorities to address their case. The report acknowledged their diversity, "deep religiousness," lack of organization and the willingness of the more visible leaders to meet with government representatives to discuss issues of concern.

Despite vicious castigation in the press from many Euro-Jamaicans, Manley acted on the report's suggestion to send a delegation to Africa to investigate the possibility of resettlement there. The mission consisted of seven men, three of whom were Rastas (including Planno). On April 4, 1961 they left for five weeks in Africa amid much fanfare. The trip met with great success, touring Ethiopia, Nigeria, Ghana, Liberia and Sierra Leone, where the delegates were treated as foreign dignitaries. The group issued a report in 1961 outlining the emigration possibilities for each country. All five countries stated that repatriation was welcomed for skilled workers, those with agricultural ventures and others who met the suitable requirements.

A climactic event in the movement was the arrival in Jamaica in April 21, 1966 of their living God, Haile Selassie. For the Rastafari, this was not a state visit but the coming of Christ. The elated Rastafari took over the airport and completely disrupted the official welcoming ceremony, waving Ethiopian flags, lighting firecrackers and dancing in the rain. The Emperor was extremely moved at the crowd, estimated at 100,000, and their emotional adulation and he wept openly. The event had an uplifting effect on the Rastas, but it did not prevent the Jamaican government from bulldozing their homes in the center of Kingston in an attempt to upgrade the area.

On September 12, 1974, the Coordinating Committee of the Ethiopian Armed Forces deposed Emperor Haile Selassie I. He reportedly died at 83 while in confinement on August 27, 1975.

Rastafari Beliefs. The primary mode of communication and revelation in Rastafarianism is through its oral tradition. The Christian Bible is used to understand and interpret events of the world, but it is not considered infallible. Rastafarians view the Bible as the history of the African race, originally written in Amharic and given to the Israelites (Africans). It was later stolen by Europeans who mistranslated and corrupted it in order to deceive Africans to think they were inferior to them. Rastafarians, since they have the ability to see through the distortions created by their oppressors, can perceive the truth that still exists in the Bible.

Rastafarians consider His Imperial Majesty (HIM) Haile Selassie to be the Black Christ, Jah (Jehovah), the only living King, the incarnation of God on earth. His ascent to the throne was fulfillment of the prophecy that the Redeemer would be of the house of David. While to the world the Emperor is dead, Rastafarians note that there was no funeral, no grave, and no corpse; his death is a fictitious story and he is in hiding until the day of repatriation. Jah may have died in the flesh, but he is invincible and will rise again.

Jah's kingdom is Ethiopia, which is Zion, the Garden of Eden and the Promised Land flowing with milk and honey. Ethiopia symbolizes the entire African continent. It is the name Africa goes by in the Bible. The division of African countries is only a tragic remnant of their colonial past. Ethiopia has been the only continually sovereign African nation, a reflection of its divinity, holiness and power. Italy (the Beast) invaded Ethiopia in 1936 but was driven out in 1941 when HIM liberated his Kingdom, reentering it in glory. Both events were predicted in the biblical book of Revelation.

Africa is not the garden that it once was because Africans were taken into exile and have been forced to build up the kingdom of Babylon. Ethiopia is the divine heritage of African descendants the world over. Africa has withered but soon, when her children come home, her riches and glory will shine!

All Black people are Africans, the true children of Israel and descendants of the ancient Hebrews. At some point in the past, they were stubborn and disobeyed Jah, and were sent into exile. He allowed Europeans to take them captive, be put into bondage and taken to a foreign land. Africans are still suffering in this exile (Diaspora), but they will soon be delivered from Babylon. Babylon is the evil power, a country, a prison, and the source of all misfortune. Babylon is the slaver who sold human flesh, Babylon is the place of exile, Babylon is the colonial power who after emancipation still treats Africans as disposable servants and, above all, Babylon is *not Home*. To participate in Babylon, to work for one's oppressors, to vote, is to fool oneself that one is at home here. Who is Babylon? Babylon is Jamaica, who by its leaders and police enforce political and cultural oppression. Babylon is Italy, who invaded the Holy Land (Ethiopia) with the Pope as its agent. Babylon is Great Britain who took Africans and, with the United States, keeps them in economic and political subjugation.

Rastafarian Practice. Organized Rastafarianism is the exception, not the norm. Rastas create local communities, and they tend not to affiliate themselves with a Rasta organization beyond the local situation. There is no international organization of Rastas but the Twelve Tribes of Israel, formed in the late 1960s, is reportedly the most organized, and the Niyabinghi has a great deal of notoriety. Twelve Tribes is said to allow greater equality between the sexes than among other Rasta groups (women can wear pants) and they allow beards and dreadlocks to be optional.

Among the reported Rastafarian groups in Jamaica are the Twelve Tribes of Israel, the Niyabinghi, the Ethiopian World Federation, the Ethiopian Coptic League, the United Ethiopian Body, United Orthodox Rastas, the Ethiopian Zion Coptic Church, the Ethiopian Youth Cosmic Faith, the United Afro-West Indian Federation, and the African Cultural League.

The primary communal ritual of Rastafari are *groundings,* open discussions on the Bible and the state of the world. Here, newcomers are brought and exposed to the arguments, "reasonings" and oratorical skills of the more articulate brethren. Questions are raised and debated in a rhetorical free-for-all which can last hours.

This is not only an effective method of educating possible recruits but it also allows for greater creativity and flexibility than a formal creed would permit. By custom Rastafarianism grants much room for individual interpretation.

Ganja (marijuana), the "wise weed" is a sacramental gift from Jah and is the "herb" that grew out of King Solomon's grave. It is a medicine that cures disease when eaten, sniffed or drunk as a tea, offering comfort and strength. Ganja is shared communally in a pipe (chalice) or in spliffs. The sacred weed unites Rastafari with Jah, bringing new understanding of HIM and His creation. It also frees the mind from the bondage of Babylon, bringing divine inspiration.

Rastafarians plait their hair into "dreadlocks." It is considered the hairstyle of African warriors, and symbolizes both the lion's mane (a symbol of HIM) and Samson, whose virility and strength was in his hair. Rastafarianism became known internationally through its unique musical expression. Reggae, a form of rock music, attained popularity within the larger African American community and even with White youth. Bob Marley and Peter Tosh became international stars and significant forces in legitimizing Rastafarian life and belief.

Rastafarians in Diaspora. Jamaica has always had higher emigration than immigration, and a large-scale migration began in the years following the end of the second World War. West Indians in search of jobs moved to Canada (Toronto), to the United States (Miami, New York, Chicago, Philadelphia, Boston, Washington) and especially to Great Britain (London, Birmingham). Between 1954 and 1962, Britain encouraged migration with liberal immigration laws. Now it is estimated that more than half of the world's 4.4 million Jamaicans live outside Jamaica.

A group of West Indians did emigrate to Ethiopia, forming the settlement of Shashemane in the Shoa Province. It is one hundred and sixty miles from the capital city of Addis Ababa, between the Malcoda and Shashemane Rivers. There are other indigenous Rastafari groups in Africa including a commune of 200 at Kongo in Labadi. The largest is in Accra, the capital of Ghana. In New Zealand, the Rastafarian influence is said to be frequently seen among the Maori youth.

In the United States, Rastafarians can be seen in every African American community, though the number of people who consider themselves Rastas is difficult to estimate. The problem is further complicated by the diffusion of the symbols of both Jamaica and Rastafarianism through the youth culture far beyond the

African American community due to the popularity of Reggae music and the marketing of Rastafarian paraphernalia. Even White youth have been seen on many college campuses wearing dreadlocks.

There is no central organization of Rastafarians, and many who identify with the movement attend no formal gatherings apart from local Reggae concerts. Many will attempt to attend special events on the two main Rasta holidays: the anniversary of Haile Selassie's coronation (November) and Marcus Garvey's birthday (August). The significance of the Rastafarian movement, far beyond its size, is in its role as a symbol for African Americans in their struggle for liberation.

Barrett, Leonard E., Sr. *The Rastafarians.* Boston, MA: Beacon Press, 1988. 302 pp.

Bowrin, Leslie Arthur. *Black Resistance. An Interpretation of the Rastafarian Movement of Jamaica.* Los Angeles: Master's Thesis, UCLA, 1986.

Campbell, Horace. *Rasta and Resistance: From Marcus Garvey to Walter Rodney.* Trenton, NJ: Africa World Press, 1987. 236 pp.

Chevannes, Barry. "A Preliminary Rastafari Bibliography." *Caribbean Quarterly* 24: 3/4 (September/October 1978): 56–58.

Clarke, Peter B. *Black Paradise: The Rastafarian Movement.* Wellingborough, Northamptonshire, UK: Aquarian Press, 1986. 112 pp.

Faristzaddi, Millard. *Itations of Jamaica and I Rastafari.* New York: Rogner & Bernhard, 1982. Unpaged.

Jacobs, Virginia ed. *Roots of Rastafari.* San Diego, CA: Slawson Communications, 1985. 130 pp.

Kilgore, John Robert. *Rastafarian. A Theology for the African-American Church.* Claremont, CA: Th.D Dissertation, Claremont School of Theology, 1984.

Morrish, Ivor. *Obeah, Christ and Rastaman: Jamaica and its Religion.* Cambridge: James Clarke & Co., 1982.

Nagashima, Yoshika S. *Rastafarian Music in Contemporary Jamaica. A Study of Socioreligious Music of the Rastafarian Music in Jamaica.* Tokyo: Institute for the Study of Languages and Cultures of Asia & Africa, 1984.

Nettleford, Rex M. *Mirror, Mirror: Identity, Race and Protest in Jamaica.* London: Collins, Jamaica: William Collins, 1970.

Nicholas, Tracy, and Bill Sparrow. *Rastafari: A Way of Life.* Garden City, NY: Doubleday/Anchor Press, 1979. 162 pp.

Rodney, Walter. *Groundings With My Brothers.* London: Bogle-L'Ouverture Publications, 1969.

Simpson, George Eaton. "The Ras Tafari Movement in Jamaica: Study of Race and Class Conflict" *Social Forces* 34 (December 1955): 167–171.

Smith, M. G., Roy Augier and Rex Nettleford. *The Rastafarian Movement in Kingston, Jamaica.* Mona, Jamaica: University of the West Indies, 1960.

Elizabeth Pullen

RAY, CHARLES BENNETT (December 25, 1807– August 15, 1886), Congregational minister and journalist, was born in Falmouth, Massachusetts, the oldest of the seven children of Joseph Aspinwall and Annie (Harrington) Ray. He later boasted of carrying the blood of Native Americans, Africans, and early English settlers in his veins. His mother was a deeply religious (Methodist) woman who was widely read. His father was a mail carrier between Falmouth and Martha's Vineyard, and the children had access to decent schooling in the area. After completing a basic education, Ray worked at his grandfather's farm in Westerly, Rhode Island, for five years. He then went to Vineyard Haven, Massachusetts, and learned the trade of bootmaking. After a time, however, he decided to study for the Methodist ministry, and some abolitionists supported his study at Wesleyan Seminary in Wilbraham, Massachusetts, where he was the only Black, but felt accepted. After two years he went to the recently opened Wesleyan University in Middletown, Connecticut. A minority of students were angry at Ray's presence there and created a significant disruption. Wilbur Fisk, the president, made a firm appeal on Ray's behalf, and promised to protect him, but Ray decided to leave. The whole experience at Wesleyan University was a bitter and transformative one for Ray.

He moved to New York City that year, 1832, to visit his sister, and ended up opening a shoe and boot store in the Black district of lower Manhattan. In 1833 he joined the newly organized American Anti-Slavery Society and was a "conductor" on the Underground Railroad. He married Henrietta Green Regulus in 1834; she died in childbirth on October 27, 1836, as did the child. In 1837 he was named general agent and assistant editor for a new weekly Black newspaper founded by **Samuel Cornish** and Philip Bell called the *Colored American,* the fourth Black weekly in America. He traveled across the United States on its behalf, and was a regular columnist. Apparently to enlarge his traveling role and image, he was finally ordained a Methodist minister in 1837. After a time, however, he left Methodism and attended the mostly White Crosby Congregational Church in New York City. In 1838 he became part owner of the paper with Philip Bell, and soon was its sole owner, editor, and publisher. The quality of the paper was high, and he was an able manager, but the paper suffered the same lack of funding fate which so many other early Black papers encountered, and ceased publication in April, 1842.

In 1840 he married Charlotte Augusta Burroughs of Georgia, with whom he had seven children, though only three daughters survived his death. In 1843 he joined the New York Vigilance Committee, established in 1835 to assist escaped slaves, and in 1848 became its corresponding secretary. In 1845 he founded and became pastor of the Bethesda Congregational Church in New York City, a position he held for more than twenty years. In 1846 this was supplemented by the position of city missionary with the American Missionary Association, which provided him with grants until 1851. He was active in the New York Society for the Promotion of Education Among Colored Children, the African Society for Mutual Relief, and the Congregational Clerical Union. In 1847–1848, he helped organize a number of temperance societies. He retired from the church in 1868.

Penn, I. Garland. *The Afro-American Press and Its Editors.* 1891; reprint New York, 1969. 365 pp.

Ray, Charles Bennett. *Eighth Annual Report of City Missionary to the Destitute Colored Population.* New York: n.p., 1852. 8 pp.

Ray, Florence T., and Henrietta Cordelia Ray. *Sketch of the Life of Rev. Charles B. Ray.* 1887.

Work, Monroe N. "The Life of Charles B. Ray." *Journal of Negro History 4* (1919): 361–371.

DANB, DAB (vol. 8), *HUBA, IBAW, EBA, EAJ, CH, HNC, BPJ, SOTT.*

RAY, SANDY FREDERICK (February 3, 1898?), prominent leader in the **National Baptist Convention, U.S.A., Inc.** (N.B.C.U.S.A.),was born in Stranger, Texas. He received his B.A. from Morehouse College in Atlanta, Georgia and his D.D. in 1936 from Arkansas Baptist College. He married Cynthia (maiden name unknown), with whom he had two children. His pastorates included First Baptist Church in La Grange, Georgia; First Baptist Church in Macon, Georgia; St. Luke Baptist Church in Chicago, Illinois; and Shiloh Baptist Church in Columbus, Ohio. While in Ohio he was elected a member of the state legislature.

In 1944 he was called to the pastorate of Cornerstone Baptist Church on the eastern edge of the Bedford-Stuyvesant district in Brooklyn, New York, where he remained the rest of his career. The Cornerstone Baptist Church, a 5,000–member powerhouse congregation, became the base for his wide-ranging leadership. For many years he was the president of the Empire Baptist Missionary Convention, a regional collection of almost five hundred Baptist churches within the N.B.C.U.S.A., and was moderator of the Eastern Baptist Association of Brooklyn and Long Island. He chaired the Social Action Commission of the N.B.C.U.S.A. and was one of the leading nominees for the presidency of the denomination after the resignation of **David V. Jemison** in 1953. **Joseph H. Jackson** won that election, but Ray was able to remain a leading figure as one of the vice-presidents of the National Baptist Convention.

Ray was one of a small group of vocal liberals that stayed with the denomination after the **Progressive National Baptist Convention** broke away in 1961. In 1963 he was chair of the ministerial group that planned several demonstrations for more jobs for Blacks at the Downstate Medical Center. This group evolved into the Committee on Job Opportunities for Brooklyn. Ray was a delegate to the Republican National Convention in 1964, and refused to help make Barry Goldwater's nomination unanimous. Ray served on the New York State Commission on Human Rights and the State Commission on Discrimination. He was chair of the Brooklyn Advisory Committee of the New York Urban League, and in 1967 he was on the New York State Council on Youth. He was strongly ecumenical, participating in the National Council of Churches and the National Council of Christians and Jews. He was on the board of directors of a number of organizations, including the **Southern Christian Leadership Conference** (S.C.L.C.), Martin Luther King, Jr. Memorial Center for Social Change, Cornerstone Day Care Center, Morehouse College, and Andover-Newton Theological Seminary. In 1979 Ray published a book of sermons, *Journeying Through a Jungle.*

"Organizations and Leaders Campaigning for Negro Goals in the United States." *New York Times* (August 10, 1964): 16.

Ray, Sandy F. *Journeying Through a Jungle.* Nashville, TN: Broadman Press, 1979. 131 pp.

IBAW, OTSB, WWABA (85), *BDNM* (75), *SCA.*

REDEEMED ASSEMBLY OF JESUS CHRIST, APOSTOLIC. An Apostolic Pentecostal church. The lengthy reign of Bishop J. V. Lomax led to a schism within the **Highway Christian Church** in 1979. Two bishops, James Frank Harris and Douglas Williams, who pastored churches in Richmond, Virginia, and Washington, D. C., had been with the church through the 20 years of Lomax's leadership. They complained of his autocratic rule which had led to the church's stagnation. Another problem was Lomax's bypassing the general church executive board (primarily clergy), which had been established to oversee church affairs and make policy decisions. Lomax developed a habit of referring policy questions to the trustees (all lay persons) of the local church which he headed in Washington, D.C.

Harris and Williams saw Lomax's method of operating part of a structural flaw in the Highway Christian Church's structure in selecting bishops for life. They began the Redeemed Assembly of Jesus Christ with a much looser structure and without a presiding bishop elected for life. Harris was the first presiding bishop and Williams the first assistant presiding bishop. In the beginning, six churches, including Harris's church in Richmond, four churches in the Washington, D.C. metropolitan area, and one in New York affiliated with the new church. Three of these had been under Lomax's jurisdiction and three had been independent churches.

The church is headed by an executive council (the bishops) and an executive board (the bishops and all the pastors). Headquarters is in Washington, D.C.

Richardson, James C. *With Water and Spirit. A History of Black Apostolic Denominations in the U.S.* Martinsville, VA: The Author, n.d. 151 pp.

REFORMED CHURCH IN AMERICA. A Reformed/Presbyterian church.

The Reformed Church in America is derived from the Reformed Church in the Netherlands which arrived in what is now the United States in the early 1600s. The first congregation, The Collegiate Church of New York, now the oldest continuously existing congregation in the United States, was formed in 1628.

The Dutch were active participants in the slave trade and members of the Dutch Reformed Church had no problems with owning slaves. Some became members of the Church through their masters. In 1783, the Church, having given some consideration to the place of slaves in the church, agreed to take them into membership without the consent of their masters (there being no record that such consent was necessary for those slaves known to be members of the church of the first century).

The Church slowly acquired some African American members after the Civil War, but the first African American congregations seem to have been the result of the independent labor of Dr. W. L. Johnson (d. 1913), the first African American graduate of the

Church's New Brunswick Theological Seminary in New Jersey. Johnson organized two congregations in the late nineteenth century in South Carolina. They were accepted into the church in 1902, but then transferred to the Presbyterian Church in 1926. In 1919 the church assumed sponsorship of the Southern Normal School in Breton, Alabama which had been founded in 1911 by Mr. and Mrs. James Dooley. It has continued that support over the years and facilitated the graduates' entrance into the several senior colleges of the Church and New Brunswick Seminary.

Today approximately 45 congregations of the Church are African American, less than three percent. In 1969 they were encouraged to form the **Black Council**, a representative body for the African American membership.

REFORMED EPISCOPAL CHURCH.

On December 2, 1873, the assistant bishop of the **Episcopal Church's** diocese of Kentucky, George David Cummins, announced the organization of a new and separate Episcopal denomination, with its headquarters in New York City. Cummins had already resigned his position in the Episcopal Church on November 10, 1873, declaring his intention to "transfer my work and office to another sphere." The new denomination which was founded by Cummins and six other Episcopal priests on December 2 was introduced as the Reformed Episcopal Church. Behind Cummins' action lay a lengthy history of contention in the Episcopal Church between a powerful Evangelical party and the growing influence (since the 1840s) of Anglo-Catholicism. Cummins, as a leading Evangelical, eventually concluded that the Evangelical party was doomed to slow suffocation within the Episcopal Church, and his formation of the Reformed Episcopal Church as an Evangelical alternative was considered by Cummins to be the only solution to this conflict. The Evangelical convictions of Cummins and his followers were embodied in a *Declaration of Principles* which stated their belief in a limited notion of episcopal government ("not as of Divine right, but as a very ancient and desirable form of Church polity") and condemned as "erroneous and strange" such Anglo-Catholic tenets as a ministerial priesthood (Reformed Episcopal clergy would henceforth be known as *presbyters* rather than *priests),* baptismal regeneration, apostolic succession, and the corporeal or sacrificial presence of Christ in the Eucharist. Within one year, the Reformed Episcopal parishes had been organized, and by 1875 Cummins had been joined by 42 more presbyters and deacons.

Cummins' willingness to revise the structure of the Episcopal Church for Evangelicals opened his mind to the possibility of revising some deeply entrenched attitudes toward the participation of African Americans in the Episcopal tradition. The end of the American Civil War in 1865 brought an end to the system of slavery which had kept African Americans in bondage since colonial times. But in its place, southern Whites resorted to various forms of social and racial discrimination (in the form of "Jim Crow" laws) to drive the "freedmen" as far from their sight as possible. Most southern Whites were as prepared to apply the spirit of "Jim Crow" to their churches as to their laws. In 1875, St. Mark's Church in Charleston, South Carolina, whose membership was entirely composed of ex-slaves, applied for admission to the diocese of South Carolina, only to be refused on the ground that Black Episcopalians could never be considered the equals of White Episcopalians. The diocesan convention explained, "The Church is bound to recognize, in all its relations to the world, and its offices to mankind, that distinction between the races of men which God has been pleased to ordain, and to conform its polity and ecclesiastical organisms to his divine ordinance." The best that the diocesan bishop, W. B. Howe (who had bravely opposed the exclusion), could offer African American Episcopalians in South Carolina was the vague promise that a separate missionary jurisdiction could be set up for them.

The offer of a Jim Crow jurisdiction had little appeal to Black Episcopalians in South Carolina. It was also a blow to the handful of White Episcopal clergy who had put their energies into training the most gifted of the former slaves for ministry in the diocese of South Carolina. Chief among these was Peter Fayssoux Stevens, a "cradle" Episcopalian and one-time commandant of the South Carolina State Military Academy in Charleston. After brief service in the Confederate army in 1861 (he commanded Stevens' Battery during the bombardment of Fort Sumter), Stevens was ordained by then-Bishop T. F. Davis. While rector of Trinity Church, Pinopolis, Stevens established two "colored" chapels, Nazareth and Emmanuel, and astounded Bishop Howe there in 1879 when he presented the bishop with a confirmation class of 99 persons—95 of whom were "persons of color." In 1868, while still serving at Pinopolis, Stevens began preparing two ex-slaves, Frank C. Ferguson and Lawrence Dawson, for the ministry, even paying for Ferguson's education at St. Augustine's College in Raleigh out of his own pocket. But despite the bishop's encouragement, and a favorable examination by two examining chaplains, the diocesan standing committee refused to consider ordaining Blacks.

The news of the founding of the Reformed Episcopal Church offered a ray of hope to Ferguson and Dawson. On November 18, 1874, Ferguson called together representatives from four Black Episcopal missions in Charleston, Pinopolis, and Oakley, South Carolina, and "without one dissenting voice," Ferguson was authorized to establish contact with Cummins. Even though Cummins had been born and raised among slaveholders, and had favored colonization rather than emancipation as a solution to slavery, Cummins now responded eagerly to Ferguson's inquiry, sending one of his representatives, Benjamin Johnson, to meet with Ferguson. On June 6 and June 13, 1875, Johnson held two mass meetings with Ferguson and his loyalists, and was welcomed with a triumphant decision by Ferguson and his followers to join the Reformed Episcopalians. Then, in an equally strategic move, Johnson called on P.F. Stevens, who had moved to Anderson, South Carolina, in 1873, and persuaded Stevens to join him in the Reformed Episcopal Church and return to Pinopolis to give oversight to his "old field of labor."

Altogether, Johnson brought five Black churches—Redeemer, Emmanuel, Nazareth, Bethlehem, and St. James'—and 500 communicants into the Reformed Episcopal Church at one stroke, along with starting a new mission, Holy Trinity, in the heart of Charleston. In November, 1875, Cummins himself visited South Carolina, preaching beside Stevens and Johnson to overflow congregations in twelve different locations. Cummins also took the long-awaited step of ordaining Frank Ferguson a deacon on December 5, accompanied by Lawrence Dawson on December 19 and another Charleston leader, Edward A. Forrest, on December 17.

Of course, Cummins had not imagined that either he or the Reformed Episcopal Church would turn into pioneers of racial justice; and in the 1870s, he faced as much reluctance from northern Whites in his own new Church as from South Carolina Whites in their diocesan convention. So, when Cummins died suddenly in 1876, attention in the Reformed Episcopal Church shifted away from new initiatives and outreach to power struggles and debates over vestments and ritual by the Church's northern White leadership. National membership in the Reformed Episcopal Church stalled at the 10,000 mark until 1912; it then blipped upwards to just over 11,000 from 1915 until 1921, and then settled into a slow slide downward.

Over the same period, northern White Reformed Episcopalians retreated from Cummins' willingness to welcome African Americans. In 1919, the Reformed

Episcopal Church was approached by a Black West Indian Anglican priest, **George Alexander McGuire,** who offered to organize a series of missions for Black Americans and West Indians in New York City for the Reformed Episcopal Church. McGuire and his Church of the Good Shepherd were briefly received into the Reformed Episcopal Church. But McGuire was dreaming dreams of Black independence and self-determination which were a generation ahead of their time, and he soon found White northern Reformed Episcopalians indifferent to his Black nationalist aspirations. In January, 1921, McGuire withdrew from the Reformed Episcopal Church to organize what is now the **African Orthodox Church.**

In the same way, rather than seeing the Southern Reformed Episcopalians as full partners in the Reformed Episcopal movement, White Reformed Episcopalians interpreted the South Carolina churches and missions as a carefully controlled experiment in racial paternalism. While the northern White churches organized themselves into self-governing *synods* (the Reformed Episcopal equivalent of a *diocese),* the African American churches in South Carolina were only permitted to organize themselves as the "Special Missionary Jurisdiction of the South." In particular, African Americans in the "Jurisdiction" had no authority to elect their own bishop; instead, in 1879, Peter F. Stevens, the only White clergyman in the Jurisdiction, was appointed and consecrated by the General Council of the Reformed Episcopal Church as a "missionary bishop" for the Carolina parishes. With his undoubted devotion to the welfare of his churches and clergy, Stevens quickly emerged as the most capable and well-loved of all the Reformed Episcopal bishops after Cummins, notwithstanding his having been a former Confederate. But at the same time, Stevens never once seems to have challenged the civil *status quo* of Jim Crow legislation. He even suggested in 1894 that it would be a good idea if some of his "Afric-Americans" could be repatriated to Africa to "culminate in a colony of Reformed Episcopalians emigrating to Liberia."

On the other hand, the subordination of the South Carolina "jurisdiction" to White authority in the Reformed Episcopal Church had the unanticipated result of insulating African American Reformed Episcopalians from the debates and quarrels which divided and paralyzed their northern White counterparts. When Peter F. Stevens retired from his episcopal work in Charleston in 1909, he had built up the jurisdiction into 39 churches and 2,734 communicants, with over 1,100 children in 80 Sunday schools. He was briefly succeeded as bishop by a White Canadian, Arthur Pengelly, who had no prior pastoral or administrative experience, and who died of neglected appendicitis in 1922. Yet another White Canadian, Joseph Kearney, was appointed as "superintendent" of the Carolina churches in 1923. Kearney was eventually elected and consecrated missionary bishop for the South and served the second-longest episcopate in the Reformed Episcopal Church (28 years) until his retirement in 1958. But African American membership in the Reformed Episcopal Church, which at Kearney's consecration stood at 3,335, slowly ebbed out until by 1970, communicant membership in the Special Jurisdiction stood at only 2,177.

Even then, no one suggested that it was time that African American Reformed Episcopalians be given their own synodical organization. To the contrary, in 1960, yet another White superintendent from the North, William Henry Stuart Jerdan, was sent to Charleston to govern the African American parishes. In Jerdan, however, the Southern Reformed Episcopalians finally found their second Stevens: a relentless promoter and organizer, Jerdan identified himself deeply with the African American Reformed Episcopalians' patient wait for ecclesiastical autonomy. After his consecration as a missionary bishop in 1962, it was Jerdan who campaigned to have the Special Jurisdiction raised to the synodical level as the Charleston-Atlanta-Charlotte Synod, with its own constitution and canons. In 1987, Jerdan stepped aside to allow the election of the first African American Reformed Episcopal bishop in Charleston, Sanco King Rembert.

In 1990, overall communicant membership in the Reformed Episcopal Church stood at approximately 5,800, with 2,639 communicants in the Charleston-Atlanta-Charlotte Synod and 2,715 communicants in the New York-Philadelphia Synod. (The New York-Philadelphia Synod is mostly White in membership, with only three racially integrated congregations in New York City and Philadelphia). While the overall White membership of the Reformed Episcopal Church continues to decline, the African American membership of the church has been on the steady upswing since the 1960s. Nevertheless, the positions of leadership and authority in the church remain largely in White hands. The national church headquarters is in Baltimore. The current presiding bishop is the Rt. Rev. Franklin Henry Sellers, D.D.

Guelzo, Allen C. *Ritual, Romanism and Rebellion: The Irony of the Reformed Episcopalians, 1873–1930.* University Park, PA: Penn State University Press, 1993.

McCarrier, Herbert Geer, Jr., "A History of the Missionary

Jurisdiction of the South of the Reformed Episcopal Church." *Historical Magazine of the Protestant Episcopal Church* 41(1972): 197–220, 287–315.

Thomas, Albert Sidney. *A Historical Account of the Protestant Episcopal Church in South Carolina, 1820–1957.* Columbia, SC: R.L. Bryan, 1957.

Allen C. Guelzo

REFORMED METHODIST UNION EPISCOPAL CHURCH

REFORMED METHODIST UNION EPISCOPAL CHURCH. A Methodist church. The Reformed Methodist Union Episcopal Church emerged from a dispute within the **African Methodist Episcopal Church** (AME) in Charleston, South Carolina, in 1885. The trouble centered upon Rev. William E. Johnson. Johnson, a charismatic leader, joined with a group of former members who wished to claim the property of **Morris Brown AME Church** in Charleston. The South Carolina Conference, not wishing to lose their Charleston property, opposed Johnson in court and won. The court ruled that both factions of the congregations should have equal usage of the property as long as they remained adherents of the AME Church. Shortly thereafter, Johnson's followers left and founded the Reformed Methodist Union Episcopal Church.

In the beginning the church was decidedly against having a bishop, but by the turn of the century the call for a form of episcopal authority was being heard. After Johnson's death, in 1916 the church moved to reorganize as an episcopal organization and in 1919, the first bishop, E. Russell Middleton, was elected to office. He was consecrated by Rt. Rev. Peter F. Stevens of the Reformed Episcopal Church. Middleton died before a second bishop had been consecrated and his successor in office was consecrated by the laying-on-of-hands of seven elders.

The doctrine of the Reformed Church follows the common Methodist Articles of Faith originally produced by John Wesley and taken from the Church of England's articles. The church still follows the old Methodist practices of love feasts (a intimate members-only service which includes the Lord's supper and an informal time of prayer, singing, and testimony) and class meetings. Members of the congregations are organized in small groups for prayer, exhortation, discussion, and support. Headquarters of the church is in Charleston, South Carolina. In the early 1980s it had 18 congregations and approximately 3,800 members.

REFORMED ZION UNION APOSTOLIC CHURCH

REFORMED ZION UNION APOSTOLIC CHURCH. A Methodist church. The Reformed Zion Union Apostolic Church began in Mecklenburg, Brunswick and Lunenburg Counties in southeastern Virginia. Some of the Methodist freedmen found themselves no longer welcome at the worship services of the White churches, had no churches of their own, and had no educated ministers. While cut off by White racism, they did not particularly wish to associate with any of the several African Methodist churches which were organizing in the counties. On April 1, 1869, Rev. James R. Howell, a minister of the **African Methodist Episcopal Zion Church** from New York, had a revelation in which a solution to the problem was presented to him. Later that month, at Boydton, Virginia, he met with a group of the freedmen and proposed the formation of the Zion Union Apostolic Church.

In October 1869 an organizational convention was held, and Howell elected president. In 1874 the constitution was changed, and he was elected bishop for life. However, many members opposed the change and the controversy sent the church into a period of increasing disorganization. It was not until 1881 that one of the founders, Elder John M. Bishop, gathered the members and led in the reorganization of the church, at which time the present name was adopted. In 1882 he was elected bishop.

The church follows Methodist doctrine, and has published a catechism in which its beliefs are systematically presented. While generally agreeing with Methodist tradition, they go beyond in asserting, for example, a belief in angels and that Jesus ". . . changed the bread and wine into the substance of His body and blood by prayer and gave it to his disciples [at the Lord's Supper]." The church is organized episcopally. In 1922 a connectional council was formed which passes on matters of doctrine and disciple between the meetings of the general conference every four years. Headquarters is in South Hill, Virginia. Most of the members live in North Carolina and Virginia, with a few scattered in congregations in Michigan and New Jersey.

A Catechism: Reformed Zion Union Apostolic Church. Lawrenceville, VA: Johnson's Print Shop, 1958. 17 pp.

General Rules and Discipline of the Reformed Zion Union Apostolic Church. Norfolk, VA: Creecy's Good-Will Printery, 1966. 118 pp.

REID, FRANK MADISON, JR. (March 12, 1927– August 23, 1989), 94th bishop of the **African Methodist Episcopal Church** (AME), was born in Danville, Kentucky, the eldest son of Veatrice Victoria Andrews and **Frank Madison Reid, Sr.** His father became a bishop in the AME Church in 1940. Reid, Jr., attended public schools in Danville and St. Louis, Missouri, and decided to follow the calling of the church. At age seventeen he became the fourth generation AME preacher in his family. He received his B.S. in 1947 from Wilberforce University in Xenia, Ohio, then did additional work at the University of Chicago, from fall of 1947 to fall of 1951. Sometime later he enrolled at Garrett Theological Seminary in Chicago, Illinois, where in June 1956 he received his B.D. and the Kidder Award for creativity in preaching. He married Irene V. Bennett, with whom he had six children.

His first pastorate was at Young's Chapel AME Church in Irmo, South Carolina, followed by pastorates at Bethel AME Church in Evanston, Illinois; St. John's AME Church in Chicago, Illinois; St. James AME Church in St. Louis, Missouri; Bethel AME Church in Baltimore, Maryland; and Metropolitan AME Church in Washington, D.C. He developed a reputation as a courageous civil rights activist, and from this last pastorate he was elected bishop in 1972, the first bishop's son to become bishop in the history of the denomination. His father did not live to see the event, having passed away in 1962.

Reid was assigned to the Fourteenth Episcopal District (Liberia, Nigeria, Ghana, and Sierra Leone) until 1976, when he was transferred to the Seventh Episcopal District (South Carolina), where he remained until 1984. He served the Ninth Episcopal District (Kentucky and Tennessee) from 1984 to 1989, and the Fourth Episcopal District from March 1989 to August 1989. In 1984 he was president of the Council of Bishops and was pictured in *Ebony* magazine as administrative head of the AME Church, the denomination with the third largest Black membership in the United States. He was active in the National Council of Churches and the World Council of Churches. As president of Partners in Ecumenism he worked to bring a cooperative spirit and structure to the historically Black churches and ecumenical movement. He was a strong supporter of education and excellence as a way of life.

"Bishop Frank Madison Reid, Jr." *The A.M.E. Church Review* 105 (October–December 1989): 2.

"Funeral Services Held for AME Bishop Frank Madison Reid, Jr." *The Star of Zion* 113 (October 26, 1989): 1, 2.

"Ten Religious Groups with Biggest Black Membership." *Ebony* 39 (March 1984): 140–144.

WWR (85), HAMEC.

REID, FRANK MADISON, SR. (August 11, 1898– October 27, 1962), 61st bishop of the **African Methodist Episcopal Church** (AME), was born in Nashville, Tennessee, the son of S. R. and Parthenia (Douglas) Reid. His father was an AME minister, and Reid, Sr., grew up moving with the family from church to church. He was converted in 1904, and attended public schools in Paducah, Bowling Green, and Louisville, Kentucky, including Central High School in Louisville. Early on he decided on a career in the church and was licensed to preach in August, 1918. He received his B.A. from Wilberforce University in Xenia, Ohio, in 1921. He married Veatrice Victoria Andrews, with whom he had two children.

He joined the West Kentucky Annual Conference in October 1922, was ordained deacon the same year, and assigned briefly to Allen Chapel AME Church in Columbus, Kentucky. From 1922 to 1924 he pastored at St. John AME Church in Louisville, Kentucky, and in 1925 he was briefly at Asbury AME Church in Louisville. From 1925 to 1926 he was appointed to St. James AME Church in Louisville, followed by St. Paul AME Church in Lexington, Kentucky, from 1927 to 1931, where he built a parsonage in 1930. He pastored Quinn Chapel AME Church in Louisville from 1932 to 1936, and St. Paul AME Church in St. Louis, Missouri, from 1936 to 1940. In all these assignments he was very successful, taking in a total of 1,427 members and recording 216 conversions. He served on the board of the *Southern Christian Recorder* from 1928 to 1932, and during the same time was a trustee of Turner College.

In 1940 Reid was elected bishop at the very young age of forty-two, and assigned to the South Africa area, where he was reassigned in 1944, but after the death of Bishop **Joseph S. Flipper** on October 10, 1944, Reid moved to South Carolina, where he remained until 1956. He served on the board of trustees of Allen University in Columbia, South Carolina, and raised nearly half a million dollars for improvements in its facilities. He integrated the school with some White international students and teachers. During his administration church membership in South Carolina grew rapidly, many churches were built, and many debts were eliminated. The protest against school segregation began in one of those churches, and Reid supported the protest, despite much pressure to stifle it.

In 1956 he was moved to the Second Episcopal District (North Carolina, Virginia, Baltimore, and Washington, D.C.), where he stayed for the rest of his career. He was president of the Council of Bishops from 1958 to 1959 and was chair of the committee on the compilation of the *Book of Discipline* in 1960. He was a delegate to the World Methodist Conferences in 1951, 1956, and 1961. He was known as a gifted preacher, and was in constant demand as a public speaker. He did not live to see his son, **Frank Madison Reid, Jr.**, become the first bishop's son elected bishop in the history of the denomination, in 1972. Named for Reid, Sr., are the Reid Community House in Charleston, South Carolina, and Reid Hall at Allen University, as well as a church in Columbia, South Carolina.

BAMEC, HAMEC, EBA, EWM, EAMEC.

REORGANIZED CHURCH OF JESUS CHRIST OF LATTER DAY SAINTS. The Reorganized Church, one of the inheritors of the legacy of early Mormonism which developed a moderate theological position and coalesced as a recognizable group beginning in 1851, has never imposed official restrictions on Black members as did the **Church of Jesus Christ of Latter-day Saints** under Brigham Young. Instead, Reorganization leaders and members pragmatically accepted American middle-class racial concepts and reflected them back to the larger society. Currently, there are probably about 1,000 active African American Reorganized Latter Day Saints on the church's rolls, although no exact figures are available because statistics on race are not kept. This is probably the largest number of African Americans ever to be members in the church's history.

The Reorganized Church has pursued a two-pronged policy concerning Black members, one emphasizing the ideal and the other the practical. The first prong has remained unchanged since the church's organizational meeting: the gospel is offered to all humankind. This position, documented in restoration scriptures, asserts that the gospel of Jesus Christ is for all humanity, promoting universal Christian salvation without regard to race, color, or condition. The atonement of Christ is available for all. According to the *Book of Mormon* (II Nephi 11:113–15): "He inviteth them all to come unto him . . . black and white, bond and free, male and female, . . . all alike unto God." The *Doctrine and Covenants* (Section 1:1b) contains similar statements: "The voice of the Lord is unto all men, and there is none to escape, and there is no eye that shall not see, neither ear that shall not hear, neither heart that shall not be penetrated." A review of the Reorganized Church's General Conference Resolutions on race reveals a corresponding official position. A 1956 resolution said, as an example, "The gospel is for all mankind. It knows no distinction of race or color."

This official position tells only part of the story. The second prong of the church's racial policy suggests a wide divergence between the ideal and its implementation. The Reorganized Church has allowed practical considerations to impinge on its implementation of the official policy of complete racial equality. The Reorganization had mirrored those racial conceptions present in mainstream American society. There is cognizance in this discussion that the Reorganized Church has been since its inception in the 1850s and continues to be a White, American, Midwestern-based religious movement. It has also been a relatively conservative movement, in spite of whatever radical conceptions it might have inherited from early Mormonism. Its story is largely one of the American mainstream. Its leaders have been firmly incorporated into the American value system. Because they either were or aspired to be middle-class, they accepted, by and large, the racial attitudes of those Americans.

Joseph Smith III (1832–1914), son of Joseph Smith, the Mormon founder and president of the Reorganized Church between 1860 and his death, is a fine example of the embracing of middle-class racial ideas by a church leader. He was very much a product of his Midwestern society. Like others in antebellum Illinois, he became an early and vocal advocate of the abolition of slavery. As early as 1848, when he was not yet sixteen, Smith went out of his way to serve as the Nauvoo guide of Owen Lovejoy, an antislavery congressman from Illinois, so he could tell Lovejoy how he admired his stand against slavery. In 1858 he became a lifelong devotee of Abraham Lincoln and the antislavery politics of the Republican Party. At the same time, Smith was not interchangeable with a 1960s urban liberal campaigning for desegregation. He always held Blacks in an inferior position to Whites, and sometimes referred to them in derogatory terms. He commented during the Reconstruction era that Whites must not "sacrifice the dignity, honor and prestige that may be rightfully attached to the ruling races."

When the Reorganized Church first began to send missionaries into the South immediately following the Civil War, it planned to carry out an egalitarian racial policy. In 1865 the church agreed to ordain Blacks to the priesthood, on its face a courageous decision that stood up to the egalitarian ideal. There were at that time, however, no Black Reorganization members. Virtually the same was true in April 1866 when one of the ruling ecclesiastical bodies, the Quorum of Twelve Apostles, considered "whether Coloured Members should be organized by themselves into Branches or in connection with the White Brethren." After considerable discussion they "Resolved that as the Author of Life and Salvation does not discriminate among His rational Creatures on account of Colour neither does the Church of Jesus Christ of Latter Day Saints." In spite of good intentions, this resolution was enormously naive. The church hierarchy was largely ignorant of race realities in the South, and it misinterpreted the depth of racist ideology of most American southerners.

Although the Reorganization's official racial policy remained unchanged, as its missionaries gained experience in the South and made Black converts, and as conditions in the nation shifted during the latter nineteenth century, the implementation of policy shifted radically. From the outset, racism in the South made truly egalitarian policy toward Black members impossible. Virtually every letter from missionaries in the field complained of the difficulties of dealing with this issue. L. F. West, a church member in Alabama, wrote about this problem in April 1872: ". . . to break down the middle wall of partition from between the two races is beyond the power of mortal man, this can only be done by time." He sadly concluded, "To cultivate too much familiarity with the Blacks, offends the Whites, to neglect the Blacks, will offend the Lord." The dilemma of race relations forced the Reorganization to take a path less visionary than originally intended.

Practical concerns forced a rethinking of the *implementation* of the church's policy of complete racial equality, but not the overall position itself, and in ways that were important practical considerations, chipped away over time at the implementation of the ideal of racial equality among the Reorganized Latter Day Saints. This lead to the adoption of an informal policy of racial segregation of the races in Reorganized Church congregations in the South by 1881. It illustrated in graphic terms the acceptance of the racial *status quo*. From this expedient racial segregation sprang a whole series of compromises concerning race relations.

Between Reconstruction and World War II the church's official policy of racial equality remained unchanged. It was reaffirmed periodically in church publications and official correspondence, and if members raised the issue of racism in the church they were promptly told that none existed. If one scratched the surface of this official policy, however, they would find an unquestioning acceptance of the nation's racial caste system. This era was the most trying of any experienced by Black Saints of the Reorganization. Because of the lessened status of Blacks in larger society, they suffered in the church as well.

As racial consciousness in American society rose in concert with the changes of World War II, some Black Saints and a larger number of White members began to address the inconsistency between the official racial policy and its less than egalitarian implementation. Without the shifts in the larger society, however, Reorganization members probably would never have come to grips with this inconsistency. It was not, therefore, a move toward leadership in social issues but a natural following of the American mainstream. Always it was a cautious position, one which placed the church squarely in the middle of the social structure. At first hesitant to endorse the civil rights movement in 1960, by the end of the decade the church hierarchy had come out in favor of the nonviolent efforts of such Black activists as **Martin Luther King, Jr.**, again reflective of the larger society.

This aspect of the implementation of Reorganized Church policy resulted from some basic trends in the church. The church has never been able to transcend the society in which it resides. Even when the movement as a whole has wanted to do so—which has not usually been the case—any far-reaching commitment to racial equality would invite suspicion from outside the movement. The Reorganization's small size, its dissenting nature, and its membership's desire to fit in with neighbors have made it imperative for the church to reflect larger social ideals. Additionally, the basic practicality of the presidents of the church has also fostered this position. Committed to the preservation of the institution, they have sought to take positions that would not invite harsh criticism either internally or from outside. Without some semblance of church unity and relative peace with surrounding culture, the larger objectives of the church as a vehicle for converting humanity and establishing Zion could not be accomplished. The church has been willing to forego issues that had less support or were potentially divisive if they did not appear the most critical to the movement's overall welfare. F. Henry Edwards, a long-time church official during the twentieth century and member of the First Presidency between 1946 and 1966, offered this assessment of the position of the church hierarchy on the civil rights crusade of the 1960s: "Socrates was a gadfly, but gadflies don't build nests." Consequently, even if some members demanded that the church take a stand on an important and just issue, the First Presidency would refuse to do so until a consensus of support could be built at the grassroots level.

There has been, therefore, what can only be described as a push-pull relationship in the racial policy of the Reorganized Church. One part aims at lofty principles, the other recognizes the reality of human prejudices. The result is compromise. It is rather like the principles governing aeronautical flight. The lift component seeks to raise the aircraft off the ground, while the drag coefficient keeps it earthbound. Flight represents a compromise between the two principles. All of these factors have come together to form the two-pronged race policy of the Reorganized Church. One prong takes an officially egalitarian position; the other is an imperfect implementation of the official policy. The church has never satisfactorily overcome its relationship to society. Perhaps it never can overcome this relationship; perhaps it should not even attempt to do so. The result has been a small organization with a minuscule Black American membership throughout its history.

Edwards, Paul M. *Our Legacy of Faith: A Brief History of the Reorganized Church of Jesus Christ of Latter Day Saints.* Independence, MO: Herald Publishing House, 1991.

Launius, Roger D. *Invisible Saints: A History of Black Americans in the Reorganized Church.* Independence, MO: Herald Publishing House, 1988.

Love, Arlyn R. "The First Presidency's Response to the Civil Rights Movement." *John Whitmer Historical Association Journal* 4 (1984); 41–50.

Russell, William D. " A Priestly Role for a Prophetic Church: The RLDS Church and Black Americans." *Dialogue: A Journal of Mormon Thought* 12 (Summer 1979): 37–49.

Roger D. Launius

REVELS, HIRAM RHOADES (September 1, 1822–January 16, 1901), minister, educator, and first African American senator, was born in Fayetteville, North Carolina, to free parents of African and Croatian Indian descent. As a young man, he supported himself by working as a barber. Denied a regular education by North Carolina law, he attended a Quaker seminary in Liberty, Union County, Indiana, where he was the only Black student, and the Darke County Seminary for Negroes in Ohio. In 1845 he was ordained to ministry in the **African Methodist Episcopal Church** (AME), and spent the next eleven years teaching school and serving congregations in seven different states, mostly in the Midwest. Following a local church dispute in St. Louis, Missouri, Revels became a Presbyterian minister. In 1856 he entered Presbyterian-related Knox College in Galesburg, Illinois, as a scholarship student, and graduated two years later. He married Phoeba Bass.

From 1858 to 1863 he was the first Black pastor of the Madison Street Presbyterian Church in Baltimore, Maryland, and was also the principal of a school for African Americans. In 1861, at the outbreak of the Civil War, he organized the first two Black regiments in Maryland. In late 1863 he went to St. Louis, where he organized a school for newly freed Blacks, and in 1864 he organized a Black Missouri regiment, serving briefly as chaplain. He assisted the Freedmen's Bureau throughout Mississippi, mostly organizing schools. In Jackson, Mississippi, he returned to the AME Church and helped form several congregations. A loss of health then sent him to a quieter life of nearly two years of preaching and lecturing in Missouri and Kansas. In 1866 he was the minister of Bethel AME Church in Leavenworth, Kansas, the oldest AME church in that state.

Later in 1866 Revels moved to Natchez, Mississippi, where he served as presiding elder for the AME Church. In 1868 he joined the predominantly White Methodist Episcopal Church, and that same year was elected alderman and began his political career. He won the loyalty of many Whites as well as Blacks, and was elected to the Mississippi State Senate in 1869, which in turn elected him in January, 1870, to the United States Senate to fill the remainder of the term in Jefferson Davis' former seat. Some in the Senate were unwilling to recognize him, and only after bitter debate and a vote of forty-eight to eight was he officially seated on February 25, two days after Mississippi was readmitted into the Union. He thus became the first Black senator (Republican) in the history of the United States. His short tenure, characterized as conservative and dignified, ended on March 3, 1871. Among other things, he was proud to have arranged the hiring of Black mechanics for the first time in the United States Navy Yard.

Upon leaving the Senate, Revels helped Governor Alcorn found what would be called Alcorn University, and was named its president. The school opened its doors in February of 1872. He lost his presidency with a change in state leadership in 1874, and became minister of the M. E. Church in Holly Springs. In the 1875 elections, offended by Republican corruption, he campaigned for the Democrats. More difficult to explain is that he was the only prominent Black not to testify in Congress against the violence and intimidation used by the Democrats in those elections. He may have believed that this was the only way to hold on to the small gains made in a state rapidly reverting to a closed, racist society. His accommodationism helped restore him to the presidency of Alcorn University in 1876.

In 1876 he was a reserve delegate to the general conference of the M. E. Church, and was elected editor of the *Southwestern Christian Advocate*, but declined the position. From 1877 to 1880 he gave service in the Jackson District of the church, while still at Alcorn. From 1880 to July 1882, when he retired, he was full-time at Alcorn. From 1884 until his death he was district superintendent in what became the Upper Mississippi Conference, variously serving the Aberdeen, Holly Springs, and Greenwood Districts. He wrote a brief autobiography which was not formally published.

Lawson, Elizabeth. *The Gentleman from Mississippi.* New York: n.p., 1960. 63 pp.

Revels, Hiram Rhoades. *Autobiography of Hiram R. Revels.* N.p., n.d. 14 pp.

Smith, Samuel Denny. *The Negro in Congress, 1870–1901.* Chapel Hill, NC: University of North Carolina Press, 1940. 160 pp.

Wharton, Vernon Lane. *The Negro in Mississippi, 1865–1890.* Chapel Hill, NC: University of North Carolina Press, 1947. 298 pp.

RLOA, HNB, HNC, CH, DAB (8), *EWM, NBH, BR, HNRA, DANB, PHNA, NA, BAC, MM, HUBA, IBAW, BPUSA, RAM, AMECMIM.*

RICARD, JOHN HUSTON (b. February 29, 1940), a bishop of the **Roman Catholic Church**, was born in Baton Rouge, Louisiana, the second youngest of eight children in the family of Maceo and Albanie (St. Amant) Ricard. The family belonged to St. Francis Xavier Church in Baton Rouge, a Josephite parish. All the children attended the parochial schools run by the **Sisters of the Holy Family**. Ricard graduated from St. Francis Xavier High School in 1958 and entered Epiphany Apostolic College in Newburgh, New York. He studied there for three years and then spent a year at Mary Immaculate Novitiate in Walden, New York, where he made his initial vows to enter **St. Joseph Society of the Sacred Heart** on August 19, 1962. He received his B.A. in 1962, then studied philosophy and theology at St. Joseph's Seminary in Washington, D.C., receiving his M.A. in 1968. He made his final vows on May 31, 1967.

He was ordained priest on May 25, 1968, and in September was appointed associate pastor of St. Peter Claver Church in New Orleans, Louisiana. In 1968 he was instrumental in establishing the **National Office for Black Catholics**, and became a charter member of the board in 1970. While in New Orleans he studied at Tulane University and earned an M.A. in sociology in 1970. From 1970 to 1972 he was also adjunct professor at Tulane in Minority Studies. As part of his pastoral duties, he organized the Neighborhood Coordinating Council in 1971 as well as the Treme Child Development Center. He helped support Mid-City Enterprises, which teaches Black youth management skills through hands-on ownership and control of small businesses. He received a $25,000 grant from the Catholic Bishops Council to plan further programs to develop Black leadership.

In 1972 Ricard was appointed pastor of the Holy Redeemer Church in Washington, D.C., a 350–family church with a school conducted by the Sisters of the Blessed Sacrament. Ricard was also named spiritual director of St. Joseph's Seminary in Washington, D.C., and vicar of the Northwest Urban Vicariate. In 1975 he was named pastor of the Holy Comforter-St. Cyprian Church in Washington, D.C., a larger church with a 400–student school run by the **Oblate Sisters of Providence**. Having associate pastors allowed him to become an adjunct associate professor of Social Studies at the Catholic University's National Catholic School of Social Service. In 1978 he was elected Consulter General of the Society of St. Joseph, placing him on the executive committee.

In 1980 Ricard was appointed pastor of Our Lady of Perpetual Help in Washington, D.C., and in 1981 he began taking classes part-time at the Catholic University of America, working towards a Ph.D. in psychology and psychotherapy, which he received in 1985. On May 22, 1984, Pope John Paul named him Auxiliary Bishop of Baltimore, Maryland, and he was consecrated for that office on July 2, 1984.

CAA, WWABA (92–93), *WWR* (85), OBS.

ROBERSON, LIZZIE (April 5, 1860–November, 1945), founder and General Supervisor of Women's Work in the **Church of God in Christ**, was born into slavery in Phillips County, Arkansas. Little information is available about her early life; her father died during the Civil War and her mother saw that the children gained a basic literacy. Roberson (sometimes spelled Robinson) learned to read, as did many others of the time, using the Bible as textbook. She married Henry Holt in 1881, but he passed away shortly thereafter. She later married William Woods, with whom she had one daughter, Ida. Soon after that birth, Roberson experienced conversion and in 1892 joined the Baptist Church in Pine Bluff, Arkansas.

In 1901 she was strongly affected by reading a pamphlet called "Hope" by Joanna P. Moore, a white Baptist missionary. After some years Moore was able to use her influence to have Roberson sent to the Baptist

Missionary Society school in Dermott, Arkansas, for two years. While there she came into contact with the Church of God in Christ through the preaching of Elder D. W. Welk. In May, 1911, **Charles H. Mason**, General Overseer of the Church of God in Christ, held a meeting at the school, and she received the baptism of the Holy Spirit, evidenced by speaking in tongues. She then left the Baptists and worked with Elder R. L. Hart in Trenton and Jackson, Tennessee, for the Church of God in Christ.

In Tennessee, Roberson met another church evangelist, Lillian Brook, who told her of the first stirring of an organization for women in the church and urged her to attend the church-wide meeting later in 1911, in Memphis. At that convocation she met with Mason, who convinced her to accept the new position of Overseer for Women's Work. Under her direction, the organization grew rapidly, with women's prayer and Bible groups, sewing circles, home and foreign mission groups, and sunshine bands. In 1912 she was made General Supervisor of Women's Work. She strictly followed and taught the church's conservative position on women's apparel. Women had to wear shoes which did not reveal their toes, could not wear jewelry or feathers, and maintained hemlines well below the knees.

About this time, her second husband having passed away, she met and married Elder Roberson, with whom she traveled on evangelistic tours. They later moved to Omaha, Nebraska, where they founded the city's first Church of God in Christ. While Roberson continued to travel for the organization of the church women, her husband pastored the congregation in Omaha. Her successful work enabled her to give Bishop Mason $168.50 to start the denomination's first bank account. She was a leader in the plan to build the national headquarters in Memphis, Tennessee, and lived just long enough to see it and the hall named for her. She was succeeded by **Lillian Coffey**.

RLOA, BDA-AHP, PHCGC.

ROBERTS, JAMES DEOTIS (b. July 12, 1927), Baptist minister and theologian, was born in Spindale, North Carolina, the son of J. C. and Edith (Godde) Roberts. He received his B.A. in 1947 from Johnson C. Smith University in Charlotte, North Carolina, his B.D. in 1950 from Shaw University in Raleigh, North Carolina, his S.T.M. in 1952 from Hartford Theological Seminary in Connecticut, and his Ph.D. in 1957 from Edinburgh University in Scotland. On June 5, 1953, he married Elizabeth Caldwell, with whom he had four children.

While in school he supported himself as pastor of the Union Baptist Church in Tarboro, North Carolina (1947–50), and assistant pastor of the Union Baptist Church in Hartford, Connecticut (1950–52). In 1952–53 he was dean of religion at Georgia Baptist College in Macon, Georgia, and from 1953 to 1955 he was assistant professor of philosophy and religion and chaplain at Shaw University School of Religion. In 1956–57, while working on his dissertation, he was pastor-ad-interim at Radnor Park Congregational Church in Clyde Bank, Glasgow, Scotland. His dissertation topic was "The Rational Theology of Benjamin Whichcote: Father of the Cambridge Platonists." Roberts is a member of the International Neo-Platonic Association, a continuing interest reflected not only in his dissertation, but in his books *Faith and Reason: A Comparative Study of Pascal, Bergson, and James* (1962), an expansion of his B.A. thesis paper, and *From Puritanism to Platonism in Seventeenth Century England* (1968).

Upon completing his Ph.D., Roberts became instructor in philosophy of religion and Christian theology at Howard University School of Religion in Washington, D.C. He was promoted to assistant professor in 1963, to associate professor in 1966, and full professor of theology in 1970. From 1968 to 1977 he was a member of the Theological Commission of the National Committee of Negro Churchmen (now the **National Conference of Black Churchmen**). In 1971 his first major entries into Black theology came with *Liberation and Reconciliation: A Black Theology*, and *Quest for a Black Theology*. In 1973–74 he interrupted his time at Howard briefly by serving as dean of the School of Theology at Virginia Union University. He has been the recipient of numerous honors, fellowships, and grants, and has been the editor of the *Journal of Religious Thought*. In 1981 he left Howard to become the fourth president of the Interdenominational Theological Center in Atlanta, Georgia. Since 1984 he has taught theology at Eastern Baptist Theological Seminary in Philadelphia, Pennsylvania, except for 1986–88, when he was Commonwealth Professor at George Mason University in Fairfax, Virginia. He has continued a prodigious amount of writing, with at least ten books to date, including *A Black Political Theology* (1974), *Roots of a Black Future: Family and Church* (1980), *Black Theology Today: Liberation and Contextualization* (1983), and *A Philosophical Introduction to Theology* (1991).

Gardiner, James J. and James D. Roberts, eds. *Quest for a Black Theology*. Philadelphia, PA: Pilgrim Press, 1971. 111 pp.

"James Deotis Roberts." *Journal of the Interdenominational Theological Center* 8 (Spring 1981): 102–103.

Roberts, James D. *Black Theology in Dialogue.* Philadelphia, PA: Westminster Press, 1987. 132 pp.

———. *Black Theology Today: Liberation and Contextualization.* New York: Edwin Mellon Press, 1983. 217 pp.

———. *Liberation and Reconciliation: A Black Theology.* Philadelphia, PA: Westminster Press, 1971.

———. *Oppression and Liberation in World History.* Orbis, 1978.

———. *A Philosophical Introduction to Theology.* London: SCM Press; Philadelphia, PA: Trinity Press International, 1991. 182 pp.

———. *Roots of a Black Future: Family and Church.* Philadelphia, PA: Westminster Press, 1980. 152 pp.

IBAWCB, IBAW, CA (33R), WWR (77), WWABA (80–81), BDNM (75), MBRL.

ROBERTS, JOHN WRIGHT (September 8, 1812–January 30, 1875), the 2nd African American missionary bishop of the Methodist Episcopal Church (now the **United Methodist Church**), was born in Petersburg, Virginia, one of three sons born to free parents. His mother was reportedly a woman of strong character who had escaped from slavery, and his father died while he was a boy.

A branch of the American Colonization Society was established in Petersburg in 1825, and John's mother resolved to take up the offer of emigration to Liberia. The family sailed in 1829, the three boys having already experienced conversion and joined the Methodist Episcopal Church. One brother, Joseph, became Liberia's first president in 1848. John Roberts joined the Liberian Mission Conference of the Methodist Episcopal Church in 1838 and was ordained elder in 1841. By 1851 he was presiding elder of the Monrovia District (one of the two Liberia districts).

Following the death of Francis Burns the first missionary bishop of the Methodist Episcopal Church, in 1863 Roberts became the president of the Liberia Conference. In 1864 the General Conference authorized the consecration of a successor to Burns, and Roberts was elected to be that successor. He was consecrated in St. Paul's Methodist Episcopal Church in New York City on June 20, 1866, by Bishops Levi Scott and Edmund Janes. His years as bishop were marked by a fair and wise administration that enhanced the Liberian church's harmony and prosperity.

EWM, NYB (1925–26), IBAW.

ROBERTS, WILLIAM M. (1876–May 10, 1954), a bishop of the **Church of God in Christ**, was the son of Willie Roberts and his wife. In 1899 he married Mamie Hill and the following year moved to Memphis, Tennessee. There in 1904 he encountered Elder **Charles H. Mason**, pastor of the Church of God in Christ, then a Holiness church, but destined to grow into a large international Pentecostal denomination. He experienced salvation and joined the congregation. He was thus among the first to hear Mason after his return from Los Angeles in 1906 with the message of the baptism of the Holy Spirit evidenced by speaking in tongues. He accepted that message and later became a deacon and then the assistant minister in the Memphis congregation.

Several years later he was called by Sisters Mary Duncan, Mary Pierce, and Olina Leige and ten others to initiate COGIC work in Chicago. The women had been members of an Apostolic non-Trinitarian Pentecostal congregation, but had turned to the Church of God in Christ (a Trinitarian church). In 1917 he moved to Chicago with his family, which now included nine children. The church grew rapidly and in 1925 erected a permanent building with seating for a thousand people, the largest in the church at that time. The opening was saddened somewhat for Roberts by the death of his wife that same year. Roberts developed a pioneering radio ministry that further spread his ministry.

Soon after his arrival in Chicago, he was named overseer for Illinois and later for eight churches through the Midwest and Midsouth. As Mason developed the organization of the church, Roberts was one of the first group of five men who in 1933 were named as bishop. He continued to serve the Chicago congregation until his death in 1954.

DuPree, Sherry Sherrod. *Biographical Dictionary of African American Holiness-Pentecostals, 1880–1990.* Washington, DC: Middle Atlantic Regional Press, 1989. 386 pp.

International Annual Holy Convocation Diamond Jubilee [Souvenir Program]. Memphis, TN: Church of God in Christ, 1982. 428 pp.

ROBERTSON, WILLIAM ERNEST JAMES (February 29, 1875–1962), a bishop of the **African Orthodox Church** (AOC) was born in the Fair Prospect, Parish of Portland, Jamaica, the son of James and Angelina Roberts. He studied at an Anglican parochial school before entering Mico Training College for Teachers at Kingston, Jamaica, in 1896. He graduated two years later and for the next fifteen years taught in the public school. During his teaching years he took additional work at the London School of Technology which qualified him for a position at the Manual Training Centre at Porus. Four years later his health forced him to resign and he worked for the West India Electric Company until he departed for the United States in the summer of 1902.

In New York City, he met **George Alexander McGuire**, who was lecturing for the Universal Negro Improvement Association, whose meetings were popular gathering places for West Indians in the New York area. They became friends, and McGuire told him of his desire to found an independent Anglican church which would be controlled by African Americans. He aligned himself with McGuire and on September 25, 1921, at the church's first synod in Chicago, he was ordained as the first priest in the new church. He returned to New York with the newly consecrated bishop and performed the enthronement service on September 28, 1921.

Robertson's first post was to the work in Sydney, Nova Scotia, where he stayed a year and established the Congregation of St. Philip's. In 1922 he moved to Massachusetts and served both St. Michael's AOC in Boston and St. Luke's AOC in Cambridge. In 1923, in the midst of his residency in Massachusetts, he was elected auxiliary bishop of the church and consecrated at the annual synod on November 18, 1923, by McGuire and Archbishop Frederick E. J. Lloyd of the American Catholic Church. Following his consecration he returned to Massachusetts until May 1925, when he became head of the Southern Jurisdiction of the church and moved to Miami, Florida.

The work in Miami had been built up by **Ernest Leopold Petersen**, a priest who had been sent to Florida at the request of a group of lay people who wished to form a parish. However, problems had arisen and Petersen had been suspended, and among Robertson's duties was pastoring the Miami AOC. He had an immediate problem in that Petersen split the congregation when he left and remained in Miami as the priest of a rival group which he would eventually take into the American Catholic Church. Robertson rebuilt the congregation and was able to purchase property for a permanent church, St. Peter's Pro-Cathedral. He then turned to the establishment of other parishes along the east coast of Florida from Key West to Palm Beach and in the Bahamas.

In 1933 Robertson was named co-adjutor with right of succession to McGuire. In the summer of 1934, with McGuire very ill, Robertson was called north, arriving in time to be present with McGuire for the few days prior to his death. Robertson became the new primate as James I.

Robertson's immediate task was to guide the church through the chaotic years that followed McGuire's death. Several of the bishops including **Reginald G. Barrow**, **Arthur S. Trotman**, and **Robert A. Valentine** formed a rival organization and tried to assume control of the African Orthodox Church. They were defeated in court in 1938, though their organization survived as the **Holy African Church**.

Robertson served the church for almost three decades as its primate. He died in 1962 and was succeeded by Bishop **Richard Grant Robinson**, whom he had consecrated in 1937. At the time of his death, Robertson was in conversation with the leadership of the Holy African Church, which had broken with the AOC in the 1930s, possibly concerning reunion. That union was accomplished in 1964.

Terry-Thompson, A. C. *The History of the African Orthodox Church*. New York: The Author, 1956. 139 pp.

ROBINSON, GEORGE DEWEY (February 22, 1910–1972), a bishop of the **African Methodist Episcopal Church** (AME), was born in Sumter County, South Carolina, the son of Powell and Carrie (James) Robinson. He experienced conversion at an early age, and later decided to enter the ministry. He received his B.A. from Allen University in Columbia, South Carolina, and his B.D. from Howard University School of Religion in Washington, D.C. From 1941 to 1944 he was a chaplain in the U.S. Army. He married Dorris Mae Candler.

His pastorates included Young Chapel AME Church and Little Mountain Circuit, both in South Carolina; Burlington Circuit in North Carolina; Allen AME Church in Baltimore, Maryland; Ward Memorial AME Church in Washington, D.C.; Campbell AME Church in Washington, D.C.; Waters AME Church in Baltimore, Maryland; and Metropolitan AME Church in Washington, D.C. He was elected bishop from that pastorate in 1968 and assigned to the Fifteenth Episcopal District, with headquarters in Washington, D.C. He was an active member of the Y.M.C.A. and in Baltimore was part of the Christian Education Committee of the Urban League. He was a trustee of Kittrell College and was on the board of directors of the National Council of Churches and the World Council of Methodism. He wrote a denominational pamphlet called *What We Believe and Why We Believe It*. He served as bishop only four years before he passed away after the May 1972 General Conference.

BDNM (70), *AMSC*, *EBA*.

ROBINSON, HUBERT NELSON (b. April 28, 1912), 84th bishop of the **African Methodist Episcopal Church** (AME), was born in Urbana, Ohio, the son of John H. and Rovilla Ontario (Hill) Robinson. On October 15, 1929, he married Mary Magdalene Isley, with whom he had one daughter. He received his B.D. in 1934 from Hamma Divinity School and his B.A. in 1935 from Ohio State University.

He was ordained deacon in 1932 and elder in 1934. After serving various churches in school, upon graduation he pastored the Smithfield AME Church (1935); Jones Tabernacle AME Church in Cincinnati (1935–38); Steubenville AME Church (1938–40); St. Paul AME Church in Columbus, Ohio (1940–44); St. James AME Church in Pittsburgh, Pennsylvania (1944–48); St. James AME Church in Cleveland, Ohio (1948–55); and Ebenezer AME Church in Detroit, Michigan (1955–64), a 3,000–member church.

At the 1964 General Conference Robinson was elected bishop and assigned to the Eighteenth Episcopal District (South Central Africa), to which he made visits from his residence in Detroit. He edited hymnals in the Shangani and two other dialects for Mozambique, built three schools and seven churches. From 1968 to 1972 he was assigned to the Ninth Episcopal District (Alabama), and from 1972 to 1976 he headed the Eleventh Episcopal District (Florida and the Bahamas). From 1976 to 1984 he was assigned to the Fourth Episcopal District, with headquarters in Indianapolis, Indiana.

He was active in numerous organizations, including the N.A.A.C.P., **Operation PUSH**, and the Frontier Club of America. From 1962 to 1964 he was on the Governor's Commission on Morals and Ethics in Michigan. He was director of the Columbus, Ohio, Urban League and was on the board of directors of Children's Adoptive Agencies in Cleveland, Ohio and Detroit, Michigan. He was a trustee of Edward Waters College in Florida. He received numerous awards, including the 1974 Religion Award from the Jacksonville chapter of the **Southern Christian Leadership Conference**. He retired in 1984.

EBA, BDNM (75), *WWR* (77), *FEDHR, WWABA* (92–93), *HAMEC, EWM, HUBA.*

ROBINSON, IDA (1891–1946), founder of Mt. Sinai Holy Churches of America, Inc., was born in Florida and grew up in Georgia. In 1908, at the age of seventeen, she was converted and joined the **United Holy Church of America**. In 1917 she moved to Philadelphia and assumed the pastorate of a small mission called Mount Olive Holy Church. In 1924, while fasting and praying, she had a vision in which God called her to "come out on Mt. Sinai and loose the women." Later that year, following this directive, she organized the Mt. Sinai Holy Church of America.

As founding bishop she conducted revivals across the East Coast and established a significant network of churches with headquarters in Philadelphia. She gave full clerical and episcopal rights to women, based on several biblical passages, including God's creation of male and female in God's image (Genesis), the equality of male and female in the body of Christ (Galatians 3:28), and the role of women in announcing the resurrection of Jesus. Qualification for membership in the church included evidence of the Pentecostal gift of speaking in tongues. Discipline was very strict, and among the forbidden things were straightening the hair, athletic sports, fingernail polish, chewing gum, viewing movies, divorce, and remarriage. Robinson was succeeded in 1946 by **Elmira Jeffries** and beginning in 1969 the organization's fourth bishop was **Mary E. Jackson**.

Jones, P. "A Minority Report: Black Pentecostal Women." *Spirit* 1 (1977): 31–44.

Trulear, H. "There's A Bright Side Somewhere." *Journal of the Afro-American Historical and Genealogical Society* 2 (1987): 51–56.

DPCM, BGM, BH, IBAW, BWR, WRA (vol.3).

ROBINSON, JAMES HERMAN (January 24, 1907–November 6, 1972), Presbyterian minister and founder of Operation Crossroads Africa, was born in Knoxville, Tennessee, in a poverty-stricken area called the Bottoms, one of six children of Henry John and Willie Belle (Banks) Robinson. His father worked at a slaughterhouse and other jobs, but was often laid off, and found solace in Pentecostal religion. In 1917 the family moved to Cleveland, where there was supposed to be more opportunity. His father found work in another slaughterhouse and joined the Athens Fire Baptized Holiness and Sanctified Church. Robinson's mother died before long, and his father remarried in about 1921. Robinson attended Fairmount Junior High and then East Technical High School, working several odd jobs. His father wanted him to quit school and work full time, and he was forced to attend school in secret. He had to leave home after the secret was out.

In those difficult days he received important help from the Cedar Branch Hi-Y and its advisor, Ernest

Escoe. He graduated from high school in 1929 and the following year began classes at Western Reserve University, but had no money even for paper after the first year, and dropped out. About 1931 he went to Mount Zion Congregational Church and asked to organize gym activities for local boys. Soon he had seven additional clubs going, and the minister at St. Mark's Presbyterian Church took an interest in him. He said the church would pay for his college, and so Robinson became Presbyterian.

He went to Lincoln University in Oxford, Pennsylvania, but the church support was so low that living from term to term was still difficult. In the summers he pastored a church in Beardon. While at school he sought to end the brutal hazing of freshmen, and lobbied to add Black faculty. He graduated as valedictorian in 1935, and entered Union Theological Seminary in New York City. During these college and seminary years he struggled with the hatred of Whites he had developed through many bitter experiences. Over time, encounters with some Whites who helped him in crucial situations convinced him that Whites are not all alike, and that the skill lay in discerning friends from enemies. Despite constant barriers of prejudice, by his senior year he was president of the class at Union and director of the mostly White Morningside Community Center, a position he kept until 1961. Also while in seminary he began working on a new, multi-racial concept of ministry at a church on the edge of Harlem, where a previously all-White congregation had moved away. He graduated seminary in 1938, was ordained at St. Mark's in Cleveland, and in May, his new church officially opened with the name Church of the Master Presbyterian Church. In June, he married Helen Brodie.

Robinson sought to make the church relevant to all aspects of community life, and linked it with pioneering programs at the Community Center, which included a credit union, cooperative store, day nursery, and psychiatric counseling service. He was Youth Director for the National Association for the Advancement of Colored People (N.A.A.C.P.) from 1938 to 1940. A major focus of his ministry was the bridging of racial distrust and ignorance. In January, 1948, land was donated in Winchester, New Hampshire, and Camp Rabbit Hollow was founded for interracial experiences. He and a Congregational minister founded the Interracial Fellowship of Greater New York. He was a leader in founding Sydenham Interracial Hospital in Harlem. In 1950 he wrote his autobiography, *Road Without Turning*, though his most famous work was yet to come.

In 1951 the Presbyterian Board of Foreign Missions sent him on an eight-month tour of speaking to student groups in Europe, Africa, the Middle East, and Asia. In 1954 he followed this with another tour of eleven countries and territories in sub-Saharan Africa. He conceived the idea of bringing Black and White American students to Africa to facilitate communication and sharing between the cultures. This idea gave birth to Operation Crossroads Africa, with the first group of sixty persons visiting in the summer of 1958. With each year the project grew and gained a wide reputation. It is credited with being a forerunner of and inspiration for the Peace Corps, and ended up providing initial experiences for people who then fed into the Peace Corps.

Robinson also became known through his several books. His first book, *Tomorrow is Today* (1954), was based on his travels. In 1955 he was the first Black to give the Lyman Beecher lectures at Yale Divinity School, which were put together into *Adventurous Preaching* (1956). He wrote *Love of This Land*, about Black contributions to culture in the United States, and *Christianity and Revolution in Africa*, both in 1956. In 1962 he wrote perhaps his most well-known book, *Africa at the Crossroads*. In October 1962 he left the pastorate and the community center to be full-time director of Operation Crossroads Africa. He also became a member of the National Advisory Council of the Peace Corps and a consultant to the Africa Desk, State Department. He married a second time, to Gertrude Cotter; there were no children from either marriage. Ironically, given that he saw his organization as combatting the growth of Communism in Africa, he was the subject in the 1950s of numerous accusations of Communist ties. To clear up the matter, he requested a hearing before the Committee on Un-American Activities, which occurred on May 5, 1964. This apparently settled the issue, and he continued to direct Operation Crossroads Africa with success until his death.

Jefferson, Louise E. *Twentieth Century Americans of Negro Lineage.* New York: Friendship Press, 1965.

Lee, Amy. *Throbbing Drums: The Story of James H. Robinson.* New York: Friendship Press, 1968. 95 pp.

Plimpton, Ruth. O*peration Crossroads Africa.* New York: Viking Press, 1962. 142 pp.

Robinson, James H. *Adventurous Preaching.* Great Neck, NY: Channel Press, 1956. 186 pp.

———. *Africa At the Crossroads.* Philadelphia, PA: Westminster Press, 1962. 83 pp.

———. *Christianity and Revolution in Africa.* Chicago: Christian Century Foundation, 1956.

———. *Love of This Land: Progress of the Negro in the*

United States. Philadelphia, PA: Christian Education Press, 1956. 76 pp.

————. *Road Without Turning: The Story of Reverend James H. Robinson*. New York: Farrar, Straus and Co., 1950. 312 pp.

————. *Tomorrow is Today*. Philadelphia, PA: Christian Education Press, 1954. 127 pp.

Rowland, Stanley. *Men for Others*. New York: Friendship Press, 1965. 175 pp.

Testimony of Rev. James H. Robinson: Hearing Before the Committee on Un-American Activities, House of Representatives, May 5, 1964. Washington, DC: U.S. Government Printing Office, 1964.

Wilson, Frank T., ed. "Living Witnesses: Black Presbyterians in Ministry." *Journal of Presbyterian History* 51 (Winter 1973): 347–391.

BDNM (70), NYTO, MSB, HUBA, IBAW, SBAA.

ROBINSON, RICHARD GRANT, JR., (August 21, 1899–1967), a bishop of the **African Orthodox Church**, was born in Atlantic City, New Jersey, the son of Richard Grant and Florence D. Robinson. He grew up in Philadelphia and attended Temple University. He attended the Episcopal Church of Saint John the Divine for a number of years, but left in 1928 along with the church's rector (and later bishop) Frederick Alexander Garrett, and founded the African Orthodox Church of Corpus Christi. That same year he entered **Endich Theological Seminary**. While pursuing his education, he was elected rector of Corpus Christi in the spring of 1930. Later that year he received his Licentiate in Theology, and went on to complete his B.D. He was made an archdeacon the following year.

Robinson soon proved to be one of the most capable priests in the church, and his accomplishments were recognized in 1935 with the presentation of a Doctor of Canon Law degree. In 1937 he was elected auxiliary bishop of Pennsylvania and was consecrated by Archbishop **William E. J. Robertson**, the church's primate, on October 17, 1937, with Archbishop **Edmund R. Bennett** assisting. In 1940 he was designated Bishop of Philadelphia and two years later asked to assume duties over the Southern Jurisdiction as well. In 1947 he was named chancellor of the African Orthodox Church. In 1948 he was designated Archbishop of Philadelphia and the Southern Jurisdiction and formally elevated the following year.

In 1962, following the death of Archbishop Robertson, Robinson became the third primate of the African Orthodox Church. His tenure as primate was marked by the healing of the generation-old schism between the African Orthodox Church and the **Holy African Church**. Robinson completed the negotiation with Bishop **Gladstone St. Clair Nurse** and in 1964 welcomed the Holy African Church back into the AOC. When Robinson died in 1967, Nurse succeeded him as the new primate.

Terry-Thompson, A. C. *The History of the African Orthodox Church*. New York: The Author, 1956. 139 pp.

ROBY, JASPER, JR. (b. April 19, 1912) the presiding bishop of the **Apostolic Overcoming Holy Church of God** was born in Brooksville, Mississippi, the son of Jasper and Allie F. Horton Roby. He grew up in Alabama and in 1931 married Malinda Sanders (known throughout the church as Mother Roby) with whom he has had six children. He was ordained to the ministry of the Apostolic Overcoming Holy Church of God (which had just changed its name from Ethiopian Overcoming Holy Church of God). He became the founder and pastor of the Greater Seventeenth Street Church of God in Birmingham, Alabama, and has remained in the pastorate of that congregation throughout his career. He was consecrated to the episcopacy by the church's founder, Bishop William Thomas Phillips, in 1955.

During the years of his episcopacy Roby continued his education at the American Divinity School (Th.D., 1957) and Universal Bible Institute (D.D., 1964). Following the death of Bishop Phillips in 1973, Roby became the new presiding bishop. For many years Roby has had a television show, "His Word," on WVTM-TV in Birmingham.

ROGER WILLIAMS UNIVERSITY. A Baptist school. Roger William University began in 1865 as a class organized by Rev. D. W. Phillips, a missionary for the American Baptist Home Mission Society (supported primarily by White Baptists in the Northern United States) who settled in Nashville, Tennessee. He opened a class for Black youths in his home and then a second one in the First Colored Baptist Church. The next year he was able to obtain an abandoned government building into which he moved the classes and there organized the Nashville Institute. Beginning with 57 students, the school grew steadily and the name was later changed to Roger Williams University. As it emerged, it also accepted Native American students, one of the pioneering institutions in the South to so do. The school was largely White-led and supported until 1905, when a fire destroyed the principal buildings housing the school. The school was closed for three years, and when it reopened in 1908, African American leadership and financial support were quite evident. At that time control of the school was transferred to the Negro Baptist Missionary and Educational Convention of the State of Tennessee (affiliated with the **National Baptist Convention, U.S.A., Inc.**).

During the 1920s the university suffered some financial reverses and thus entered the Depression already in debt. It was closed in the early 1930s.

Fitts, Leroy. *A History of Black Baptists.* Nashville, TN: Broadman Press, 1985. 368 pp.

ROGERS, CORNISH ROMEO (b. December 3, 1929), seminary professor, former associate editor of the *Christian Century*, and prominent minister with the **United Methodist Church**, was born in New York City, the son of Neal and Mollie (Collins) Rogers. He received his B.A. in 1951 from Drew University in Madison, New Jersey and his S.T.B. in 1955 from Boston University School of Theology. On December 10, 1955, he married Elsie Virginia Daniels, with whom he had one son.

From 1953 to 1955 he was associate pastor of the Church of All Nations in Boston, Massachusetts. He then moved back to New York City, where from 1955 to 1957 he pastored the Metropolitan Community Methodist Church. In 1957–58 he pastored the Willis Avenue Methodist Church in the Bronx, New York. At that point he made a major move out to the West Coast and was assigned to Calvary Methodist Church in Los Angeles, California, where he stayed from 1958 to 1966. From 1964 to 1966 he was on the board of directors of the Welfare Planning Conference of Los Angeles. In 1966 he was Coordinator of Urban Ministries for the Pasadena District of the Methodist Church, and that year served a term as president of the Los Angeles County Federation of Community Councils. From February 1, 1967, to 1970 he pastored Wesley Methodist Church in Los Angeles, which has been called "The Mother Church of Negro Methodism on the West Coast." He was a member of the California State Advisory Committee on Children and Youth from 1966 to 1970. In the summer of 1969 he took a group of college students on a Latin American study seminar. He was a credentialed instructor in Black History for the Los Angeles Public Adult School Program and was a consultant in human relations for the Los Angeles Public School System.

In 1970 the prestigious *Christian Century* magazine added a new associate editorship with emphasis on the news, and named Rogers to fill that position. At that time he was also chair of the Black Methodist Caucus of Southern California, a member of the National Committee of Black Churchmen, and on the board of directors of **Black Methodists for Church Renewal**. He moved to Chicago to work on the magazine and became an occasional instructor at Garrett Theological Seminary. He joined the board of the Chicago Committee for Black Religious Studies, was vice-chair of the board of the Beacon Neighborhood House, and was vice-president of the board of the Chicago Federation of Settlements and Centers.

In 1974 Rogers returned to Southern California to pastor St. Paul's United Methodist Church in Oxnard. During this pastorate he became the first Black senior pastor of that conference of the United Methodist Church (now called the California-Pacific Annual Conference) to have a white associate pastor. In November 1977 he was assigned to the Claremont United Methodist Church, near the denomination's School of Theology at Claremont, about forty miles east of Los Angeles. In 1980 he became an associate professor of pastoral theology and in 1984 a full professor at that seminary, where he has since remained. His list of published articles is very long, and centers upon his editorial years at the *Christian Century*.

"News Editorship Established." *Christian Century* 87 (June 3, 1970): 684.
Rogers, Cornish R. "The Black Minister and His Family." *The Christian Ministry* 2 (July 1971): 19–20.
———. "The Caribbean Churches: Celebrating a Vital Unity." *Christian Century* 90 (November 28, 1973): 1166–67.
———. "The Politics of Holiness." *Christian Century* 89 (December 6, 1972): 1234–35.
———. "SCLC: Rhetoric or Strategy?" *Christian Century* 87 (September 2, 1970): 1032.
———. "Toward Tribalism?" *Christian Century* 89 (July 19, 1972): 769–70.
AARS, HUBA, WWMC, BDNM (75).

ROGERS, ELYMAS PAYSON (February 10, 1815–January 20, 1861), poet and pioneer Presbyterian minister, was born in Madison, Connecticut, the son of Abel and Chloe (Ladue) Rogers. At age nine he was sent by his poverty-stricken parents to live with strangers in a distant town. He returned at age fifteen to help his father on the farm and in the early 1830s moved to Hartford, working in the home of a Major Caldwell. He attended school and joined the Talcott Street (African) Congregational Church.

Already interested in the ministry, Rogers enrolled in 1835 in a school founded by **Gerrit Smith** in Peterboro, New York, but after eighteen months had to stop and earn money. He found a public school teaching job in Rochester, New York, and in the spring of 1837 was able to enter Oneida Theological Institute in Whitesboro, near Utica, New York. Each winter he would return for a teaching stint in Rochester, until he graduated in the spring of 1841. In 1838 he took on an illiterate fugitive slave, **Jermain Wesley Loguen**, as a student in Rochester, and enabled his admission to Oneida. Loguen later became an **African Methodist Episcopal Church** bishop.

Upon graduation, Rogers became principal of a public school for Blacks in Trenton, New Jersey, and married Harriet E. Sherman in August 1841. He continued to study theology, and on February 7, 1844, he was licensed by the New Brunswick Presbytery. That fall he became minister of the Witherspoon Street Presbyterian Church in Princeton, New Jersey, receiving full ordination in 1845. On October 20, 1846, he transferred to the Newark Presbytery and for the next fourteen years pastored the Plane Street (African) Presbyterian Church in Newark. Under his leadership the church grew from 23 members to 140 communicants and 130 Sabbath scholars. In 1856 Rogers was moderator of the Presbyterian and Congregational Convention.

During his time in Newark he published his abolitionist satires, *A Poem on the Fugitive Slave Law* (1855) and *The Repeal of the Missouri Compromise Considered* (1856). He became a member of the African Civilization Society, and on November 5, 1860, sailed from New York to Sierra Leone, the homeland of his great-grandmother. This visit deeply moved him, and he visited many areas, lamenting the evils done by slave-traders. He expressed the hope that many missionaries would bring the Gospel to the whole of Africa. Fifty days after his arrival, before he could return to the United States, he fell ill and died of a "disease of the heart."

Rogers, Elymas Payson. *A Poem on the Fugitive Slave Law.* Newark, NJ: A. Stephen Holbrook, 1855.

———. *The Repeal of the Missouri Compromise Considered.* Newark, NJ: A. Stephen Holbrook, 1856. 24 pp.

IPAA, BPJ, CH, EBAP, NA, IBAW, BAW, DANB.

ROGERS, HUBERT AUGUSTUS (March 9, 1887–August 25, 1976), primate of the **North American Old Roman Catholic Church** (N.A.O.R.C.C.), was born in the West Indies. He was raised a Methodist, and in 1916, at the age of twenty-nine, joined the many other West Indians migrating to the United States. In New York, he served as a lay-reader for the Harlem Christian Church, and became involved in **Marcus Garvey**'s Universal Negro Improvement Association (U.N.I.A.), which sought for Blacks a status equal to Whites and independent of White culture. He particularly associated with **George Alexander McGuire**, chaplain-general of the U.N.I.A. and founder in 1921 of the **African Orthodox Church**. Rogers was ordained in 1925 by McGuire, and became canon under McGuire at Holy Cross Cathedral. He later served for several years at the Chapel of the Messiah, also in New York.

McGuire's successor as primate of the African Orthodox Church was **William Ernest James Robertson**, who consecrated Rogers on November 7, 1937, as a bishop for the church. As with most other bishops in the African Orthodox Church, he continued to serve a local church, now at St. Leonard's in Brooklyn. In 1940, dissatisfied with the African Orthodox Church, Rogers took both the Chapel of the Messiah and St. Leonard's congregations with him into the North American Old Roman Catholic Church. This church was led by Carmel Henry Carfora, a White man who had brought a number of ethnic and racial groups together in his jurisdiction. Carfora consecrated Rogers on July 30, 1942, as a bishop for his church, and raised him on January 20, 1946, to the level of archbishop for New York.

Carfora's trust in Rogers continued to grow, and in 1953 Rogers was named Carfora's coadjutor, with right of succession. In 1957, however, this close relationship was marred by an argument resulting in Carfora naming **Cyrus Starkey** as successor instead. After Carfora died a few months later, the synod of the church decided that Rogers was the true successor, and voted him the new primate. With a West Indian as primate, racial tensions in the church came to the surface and there were large-scale separations, leaving a once-substantial organization with only a handful of mostly Black parishes.

Rogers struggled to rebuild the church by following Carfora's example of multi-cultural outreach. He initiated some Hispanic congregations in New York and New Jersey, and in 1969 consecrated three more bishops to help support the various ministries. Despite his best efforts the new ministries were lost and the church continued to decline. In 1971 the synod voted to limit the primate's term to ten years, meaning that Rogers would be forced to leave. He resigned as primate on April 30, 1972, and resigned from the church on July 30, 1972, on the anniversary of his consecration. He decided to return to his roots, and spent his few remaining years as minister of Trinity Methodist Church on St. Maarten's Island in the West Indies. His son, **James Hubert Rogers**, succeeded him as primate of the church.

Terry-Thompson, A. C. *The History of the African Orthodox Church.* N.p.: The Author, 1956. 139 pp.

Trela, Jonathan. *A History of the North American Old Roman Catholic Church.* Scranton, PA: The Author, 1981. 124 pp.

RLOA, IB.

ROGERS, JAMES HUBERT. (b. June 12, 1920) Primate of the **North American Old Roman Catholic Church** (N.A.O.R.C.C.). James Hubert Rogers was born in New York City on June 12, 1920. He was the first child of Octavia and **Hubert Augustus Rogers**. His father was one of the founders of the **African Orthodox Church**, and Rogers was raised in it. In 1940, along with his father who was now a priest, he left the African Orthodox Church and joined the North American Old Roman Catholic Church. He soon entered St. Francis Seminary in Chicago and in 1942 was ordained to the priesthood by Archbishop Carmel Henry Carfora, the Primate of the Church.

His first assignment was as pastor of St. Augustine's Cathedral in New York, which he was to serve for many years. A few months prior to his ordination, his father had been consecrated a bishop by Carfora. In 1948 Rogers was consecrated as a bishop by his father. During the next two decades, he operated quietly as the pastor of St. Augustine's and also had a weekday job at Cokesbury, the Methodist publishing concern.

In 1972, following the resignation of his father, then in his eighties, he was elected as the church's new primate. At this time the church was at a low point in it history and had been reduced to just a few congregations. He moved both to found new congregations and to align the church with other organizations through which it could have an outreach to the community. He was able to create several new congregations and by the end of his first decade in office, the church had almost doubled in size, though it did not continue to grow through the 1980s.

He attempted two experiments in cooperative endeavor. In 1973 he helped form the Middle Atlantic Catholic and Orthodox Conference, an ecumenical body of several independent Catholic and Eastern Orthodox jurisdictions, most small like the N.A.O.R.C.C. However, the association soon disbanded. He then turned to the Polish National Catholic Church and

attempted to gain communion with it, as the N.A.O.R.C.C. was at one in faith and practice with the Polish Church. The Polish Church is, however, the only Old Catholic body in North America in communion with the European Old Catholics, and has no relations with the numerous independent Old Catholic groups. The attempt at intercommunion failed.

During the 1980s, Rogers has led the church, which in spite of its ups and downs has continued to provide nurture to its small constituency.

Trela, Jonathan. *A History of the North American Old Roman Catholic Church.* Scranton, PA: The Author, 1979. 124 pp.

ROMAN CATHOLIC CHURCH. The Roman Catholic Church is both the largest ecclesiastical institution in the United States and the first Christian Church to establish parishes in North America. With a membership of over 50 million, it is not surprising that it includes a large number of African Americans even though the percentage is less than five percent. African American participation in the church goes back to its founding in what is now the United States.

The Spanish Influence. The history of African Americans in the Roman Catholic Church in North America begins with the settlement of St. Augustine in northern Florida. The Spanish-speaking Catholics who established the first parish in what is now the United States were both White and Black. The baptismal, marriage, and death registers identify Blacks by name and by whether the individual was slave or free. To weaken their adversaries the Spanish authorities encouraged the slaves in the English and French settlements to escape into Spanish territory. Those who converted to Roman Catholicism were granted their freedom. In 1738 the first Black town, Santa Teresa de Fort Mose, was established for the benefit of the freed slaves. They formed a militia and fought with the Spaniards against the British. The town was abandoned in 1763 when the Spanish were forced to quit Florida for some twenty years after losing the Seven Years' War.

In the period between 1784 and 1821, when Florida became an American territory, many of the soldiers garrisoned at St. Augustine were Blacks from Cuba or the African mainland. Although exact numbers are not easily determined, it would seem that by the end of the eighteenth century a third of the population was Black.

Black Spanish Catholics were among the settlers in what is now the Southwest of the United States. In 1781 eleven families made up the settlement of what was to become the city of Los Angeles. The census records list the settlers by both name and race. There were Native Americans, *mestizos*, Africans, and mulattoes.

Black Catholic Presence. During the colonial period Black Catholics were to be found along the Gulf Coast from Pensacola to Mobile to New Orleans, and along the Louisiana coast. Most were slaves to other Catholics. The slave codes for both the Spanish and the French stipulated that slaves were to be baptized, given religious instruction and the time for religious worship, and provided the opportunity to marry. The children of slaves were not to be sold away from parents. The practice often differed from the law. There arose in Louisiana and in the area around Mobile a third group who were mixed descendants of the white, Black, and Indian population. Known as "free people of color," they formed a group apart that was French in language, Catholic in religion, and at times financially independent.

Maryland was a center for English-speaking Black Catholics. Writing in 1785, John Carroll, who became the first American bishop in 1789, explained to the curial officials in Rome that there were three thousand Black Catholics, mostly slaves, out of a Catholic population of fifteen thousand in the state of Maryland. Some of these Catholic slaves would accompany the Maryland Catholics who settled in central Kentucky at the beginning of the nineteenth century.

Slavery. The Roman Catholic Church, like all of the major churches in pre-Civil War United States, was deeply implicated in slavery. Few Catholics were abolitionists, partly because the latter were often at the same time anti-Catholic in conviction and partly because they were viewed as extreme in their views and tactics. Not only were Catholic laypersons slave owners but priests and bishops, too, owned slaves. Religious orders like the Jesuits in Maryland and Missouri and the Vincentians in Missouri and Louisiana were also slave owners. Many communities of nuns like the Carmelites in Maryland, the Ursulines in New Orleans, the Dominicans, Sisters of Charity of Nazareth, and the Sisters of Loretto all in Kentucky were slaveholders.

Some defended slavery as not being contrary to the Scriptures or the teachings of the Catholic Church. In 1840 and 1841, Bishop John England of Charleston, South Carolina, published a series of eighteen letters to John Forsyth, who had been secretary of state in the Jackson administration. In these letters England sought to prove that neither Scripture, nor church councils, nor canon law forbade slavery. In 1839 Pope Gregory XVI had issued an apostolic letter which unequivocally condemned the slave trade. He also forbade any Roman Catholic to defend or teach anything that supported "the inhuman traffic in Negroes." Forsyth had attacked the Pope as an abolitionist; England sought to prove that he was not an abolitionist. In point of fact, it was fairly clear that Pope Gregory XVI, in condemning the slave trade had, by inference, condemned slavery itself. Subsequent church officials would interpret his writings in this way.

While White American Catholics were slow to condemn slavery, European Catholics were becoming increasingly and openly hostile. Daniel O'Connell (1775–1847), the Irish political leader, worked in Parliament to outlaw slavery in the British colonies in the Caribbean, and criticized his fellow Irishmen in the United States for their pro-slavery stance. Félix Dupanloup (1802–1878), bishop of Orléans in France and one of the most influential of the nineteenth-century bishops, wrote a pastoral letter in 1862 decrying the continued existence of slavery after some eighteen centuries of Christianity.

Black Catholic Initiative. The Black Catholic community itself, both slave and free, manifested a deep and vibrant faith. Black nuns appeared for the first time in the dark days of slavery. The earliest attempt at a community of Black sisters was in Kentucky in 1824. Charles Nerinckx (1761–1824), a Belgian missionary, gave the religious habit to three free Black women, who were to work in giving religious instruction to the slaves. This attempt did not succeed and the community was disbanded.

Five years later in 1829 the first permanent community of Black religious women was established in Baltimore. Five Black women from Haiti under the inspiration of **Elizabeth Lange**, a woman of color, and Jacques Joubert, a French Sulpician priest, began the **Oblate Sisters of Providence**. About thirteen years later in 1842, two women of color, **Henriette Delille** and Juliette Gaudin, established another religious community of Black women, the **Sisters of the Holy Family**, in New Orleans. The very existence of two religious communities of Black women devoted to the evangelization of the Black community is a sign of the vitality that existed among Black Catholics. In 1916 a third congregation, the **Franciscan Handmaids of the Most Pure Heart of Mary**, was founded in Savannah by a French priest, Ignatius Lissner, S.A.M., and Mother Theodore Williams, a dedicated Black woman who moved the community to Harlem in 1922.

The first Black priests in African American history were the three Healy brothers, the sons of Michael Morris Healy, who came from Ireland to Logan County in Georgia in about 1816. Healy worked the land with his slaves. Never married, he had nine surviving children by Mary Eliza, one of his slaves. Determined that his children not be slaves, he began sending them north. Three of the sons who went north, **James Augustine Healy** (1830–1900), **Patrick Francis Healy**, S.J. (1834–1910), and **Alexander Sherwood Healy** (1836–1875), became priests. James was ordained a priest in 1854 in Paris and Sherwood in 1858 in Belgium, both for the diocese of Boston. In 1875 James Augustine Healy became the second bishop of Portland (Maine and New Hampshire) and the first Black Catholic bishop in the United States. The growth during his tenure led to the separation of New Hampshire as a separate diocese in 1884. Patrick Healy became a Jesuit and in 1874 the president of Georgetown University. Although both James and Sherwood were recognized as African Americans, Patrick certainly was not. Blacks would not be admitted as students to Georgetown University until the 1960s. Nevertheless, Patrick Healy is rightly considered the second founder of the university. Two of the sisters of these priests became nuns in Canada, one serving for many years as superior in her congregation.

The first Black priest whom all recognized as Black was **Augustus Tolton** (1854–1897), born a slave near Hannibal, Missouri. His parents were Catholics. His father escaped in 1861 to join the Union Army in St. Louis, where he died. His mother fled slavery with her three children, crossing the Mississippi in a rowboat. The widow and her children found a home in Quincy, Illinois. There Augustus discovered his vocation to become a priest. No American seminary would accept him. Through the good offices of the Minister General of the Franciscan Order, he found a place in the seminary attached to the Roman Congregation of the Propaganda Fide. Tolton studied in Rome from 1880 to 1886, when he was ordained a priest. Originally slated to go to Africa as a missionary, the cardinal prefect of the Propaganda stated that America needed to see a Black priest and that Tolton would serve in the United States. As America's Black priest, he became an inspiration for the Black Catholic community. He served first in Quincy, but the actions of a bigoted priest forced him to seek a transfer to Chicago, where he built the first Black Catholic church, St Monica's. He died in 1897 and was interred in the cemetery in Quincy.

Efforts at Evangelization. At the end of the Civil War, the Second Plenary Council of Baltimore, 1866, discussed the question of appointing a bishop or a priest who would coordinate the efforts at evangelization on a nationwide basis. The Roman Curia favored this plan because of its efficiency. The bishops, however, rejected the notion as a derogation of their jurisdiction. This resulted in each diocese coordinating its own resources for work among the Black population.

The Mill Hill Fathers from England arrived in Baltimore in 1871 with the express purpose of working among the Black population. In 1893 the American priests separated from Mill Hill and formed **St. Joseph's Society of the Sacred Heart**, or Josephites. Their apostolate spread throughout the South. Other religious communities, such as the **Society of the Divine Word** and the Congregation of the Holy Ghost (now known as the Spiritans), also took up this ministry. In 1920 the Divine Word Fathers established the first seminary for Black priests in Mississippi.

Communities of sisters to educate Black children and minister to the Black community were established in many places in the South. One such was the Sisters of the Holy Spirit and Mary Immaculate, founded in San Antonio, Texas, in 1893. In 1891, the Philadelphia heiress Blessed Katherine Drexel had founded the **Sisters of the Blessed Sacrament** to work among the Native Americans and the African Americans. With her immense fortune she built schools, churches, and missions. Blessed Katherine Drexel established the first Black Catholic university, **Xavier University** of Louisiana, in New Orleans in 1931.

Black Catholic Congresses. The work of evangelization was a task that African American Catholics took on themselves. Daniel Rudd (1854–1933), born a slave in Bardstown, Kentucky, began a Black Catholic weekly newspaper in 1866 known as the *American Catholic Tribune.* Rudd was convinced that the Catholic Church was the natural home for American Blacks. He was convinced that Catholicism would be the agent for educating and transforming African Americans and bringing down the barriers of racism in the society. He also believed that there would be a massive conversion of Blacks to Catholicism. In his newspaper and on the lecture circuit, he expressed these views all over the country. He was responsible for the five lay-led **Catholic Afro-American Congress Movement** that met in the last decade of the nineteenth century: Washington, D.C. (1889); Cincinnati (1890); Philadelphia (1892); Chicago (1893); and Baltimore (1894). Rudd saw these congresses as a means of uniting Black Catholics and marshaling their strengths for concerted action. The delegates to the congress soon discovered a sense of unity and purpose. Always proclaiming a sincere loyalty and affection for the

Catholic Church, they also began to call for more action on the part of the Catholic Church for education and the elimination of racist barriers within the church. They spoke out against the social evils of the times. The congresses saw the emergence of an articulate, active laity proud of its faith but convinced that "whatever action is taken to thwart the racist practices of some members of the Church, it is done by those who both love and take pride in the Church," to use the words expressed at the fourth congress in 1893.

Roman Concerns. The Roman Curia began to take an active interest in the circumstances of Black Catholics at the end of the nineteenth century and the beginning of the twentieth. This was partly the result of reports about Blacks carried back to the Roman Curia. In 1903 a Belgian Josephite priest, Joseph Anciaux, S.S.J., wrote in Latin a short account of the harsh racial conditions of Blacks in the United States. The booklet described, with names and dates, the actions of officials within the church that demeaned or injured Blacks. Addressed to the Pope, it made its way into the hands of the Roman officials. In the following year, Girolamo Cardinal Gotti, prefect of the Congregation of the Propaganda (the United States had missionary status under this congregation until 1908) wrote a letter to the apostolic delegate to be passed on to the American bishops. The letter stated that it had been learned that in many places Black Catholics were treated by the clergy in a humiliating way. The letter went on to say that such was contrary to the "spirit of Christianity" for all "are equal before God." Little changed immediately, but the letter marked a renewed concern by the Roman curial officials.

The files of the apostolic delegation to the United States reveal that between 1912 and 1921 there was a great deal of correspondence between the Roman officials and the delegation regarding the efforts made by the American bishops to minister to the needs of Black Catholics. At the same time a biology professor at Howard University, **Thomas Wyatt Turner** (1877–1978), organized the **Federated Colored Catholics of the United States** in 1924. It was an action-oriented group within the church, prepared to fight racism and to take a leadership role on behalf of the Black Catholic community. It fought for the ordination of more Black priests, for the accession of Blacks to all levels of Catholic education, and for an end to racial discrimination within the church. Turner's movement eventually split. From it emerged the Catholic Interracial Councils which first began in New York in 1934. Unlike Turner's activist group, these councils became study

clubs and social centers for Catholic teaching on racial justice.

Civil Rights. The civil rights movement had its impact on the Black Catholic community. In 1968, as a result of the riots following the assassination of **Martin Luther King, Jr.**, Black Catholic priests met for the first time as a group in Detroit and formed the **National Black Catholic Clergy Caucus**. Shortly thereafter, Black religious women formed the National Black Sisters' Conference. Subsequently a National Black Catholic Seminarians Association was formed. An umbrella organization, the **National Office of Black Catholics**, was founded in 1970. In 1966 **Harold Perry**, S.V.D., was ordained auxiliary bishop for New Orleans, the second Black bishop in American history. And by the time of the death of Bishop Perry in 1991, there were thirteen Black bishops, one of whom, **James Lyke**, O.F.M., was archbishop of Atlanta.

Renewed Teaching. In 1979, the American bishops issued a pastoral letter entitled "Brothers and Sisters to Us," which was a teaching on social justice for all Catholics and a condemnation of racism as a sin. Five years later in 1984, the Black bishops issued a national pastoral letter, entitled "What We Have Seen and Heard," calling African American Catholics to responsible engagement in service and leadership within the church. Finally, in 1987 in Washington, D.C. the first Black Catholic congress in this century was held.

George A. Stallings, a charismatic Black priest of Washington, D.C., led a group of Black Catholics into schism when he rejected his ties with the church in 1989 and had himself ordained a bishop shortly thereafter. Subsequently, one of his colleagues, Bruce Greening, separated from Stallings, formed the **Independent African American Catholic Rite**, and was likewise ordained a bishop.

African American Catholics at the end of the twentieth century number almost two million members. There are close to three hundred clergy, priests and deacons. There are almost twice that number of sisters. Today African American Catholics rank fifth in size when compared to the Black Protestant churches. Despite neglect and setbacks, the Black Catholic community has become a vocal and active presence in most American dioceses.

Finally, sanctity has not been absent from the Black Catholic experience. Three Black Catholics have become candidates for sainthood. The first is a Haitian layman, **Pierre Toussaint**, who died in New York in 1853, leaving a reputation for holiness and practical charity that was never completely forgotten. The others are two nuns who founded the two religious communities of women, Elizabeth Lange of the Oblate Sisters of Providence, who died in 1882, and Henriette Delille, who founded the Sisters of the Holy Family and who died in 1852.

Davis, Cyprian. *The History of Black Catholics in the United States*. New York: Crossroad, 1990. 347 pp.

Foley, Albert Sidney. *God's Men of Color: The Colored Catholic Priests of the United States, 1854–1954*. New York: Farrar, Strauss, 1955. 322 pp. Rept.: New York: Arno Press, 1969. 322 pp.

Gillard, John T. *The Catholic Church and the American Negro*. Baltimore: St. Joseph's Society Press, 1929. 324 pp. Rept.: New York: Johnson Reprint Company, 1968.

Hart, Mary Francis Borgia. *Violets in the King's Garden: A History of the Sisters of the Holy Family of New Orleans*. New Orleans, LA: The Sisters of the Holy Family, 1976. 137 pp.

Hemesath, Caroline. *Our Black Shepherds*. Washington, DC: Josephite Pastoral Center, 1987.

Nickels, Marilyn. *Black Catholic Protest and the Federated Colored Catholics, 1917–1933: Three Perspectives on Racial Justice*. New York: Garland Publishing, 1988. 325 pp.

Ochs, Stephen. *Desegregating the Altar: The Josephites and the Struggle for Black Priests, 1871–1960*. Baton Rouge, LA: Louisiana State University Press, 1990. 500 pp.

Cyprian Davis

ROOKS, CHARLES SHELBY (b. October 19, 1924), **United Church of Christ** minister, educator, and seminary president, was born in Beaufort, North Carolina, the son of Shelby A. and Maggie (Hawkins) Rooks. His father graduated from Union Theological Seminary in New York City in 1934 and became pastor of the Nazarene Congregational Church in the Bedford-Stuyvesant section of Brooklyn, New York. Rooks was thus reared in a strong Christian environment. His parents, however, separated in 1939 and later divorced. Rooks moved with his mother to Norfolk, Virginia, where they joined the First Baptist Church. His father left Brooklyn to teach the Bible at Lincoln University in Oxford, Pennsylvania. In 1943 his father married famous soprano singer Dorothy Maynor and also became senior minister of the St. James Presbyterian Church in Harlem.

Rooks entered college in the fall of 1941 at the age of sixteen and was drafted at the end of his sophomore year. He spent thirty-one months in the U.S. Army in the South Pacific. During the last nine of those months he was the senior noncommissioned officer in a medical detachment and had enough time to do a lot of reading and reflecting. When he returned to college he had decided to train for the ministry. On August 7, 1946, he married Adrienne Rita Martinez, with whom he had two children. He received his B.A. in 1949 from Virginia State College and his B.D. in 1953 from Union Theological Seminary in New York City.

He was ordained a Baptist minister in 1951 so that he could co-pastor with a white seminary classmate at the Shanks Village Protestant Church in Orangeburg, New York. The two years, 1951 to 1953, spent in that unusual but successful environment were formative. In September, 1953, he was ordained as a minister of the United Church of Christ and accepted the pastorate of the Lincoln Memorial Congregational Temple in Washington, D.C. (1953–60). This church, with 800 members, was at the time the second-largest African American congregation in the denomination. His first year there he was elected moderator of the Washington Association of Congregational Christian Churches. Lincoln Memorial Congregational Temple was a very socially active congregation, and Rooks helped organize boycotts against segregation and was chair of the Housing Committee of the Washington Urban League. In 1958–59 he was chair of the Youth Marches on Washington organized by A. Philip Randolph, president of the Brotherhood of Sleeping Car Porters. These marches laid the groundwork for the more famous March on Washington in 1963, led by **Martin Luther King, Jr.**

Rooks' rise to national prominence was aided on September 1, 1960, when he was appointed as associate director of the Fund for Theological Education (F.T.E.), based in Princeton, New Jersey. The F.T.E. had been founded in 1954 with Rockefeller-related money. Rooks' job was to support African American students in graduate theological education toward the ministry. He discovered that in order to do that, major attitude changes were required on the part of the schools and on the part of Black Christians. He remained with the F.T.E. for the next fourteen years, and was its executive director from 1967 to 1974. In 1970 the F.T.E. began a program called Doctoral Scholarships for Black North Americans in an effort to produce more Black Ph.D.s in religion. The list of persons aided by this program reads like a who's who of African American religious leaders. Rooks was also involved about that time in the formation of the Society for the Study of Black Religion (S.S.B.R.), a scholarly organization, initially informally related to the American Academy of Religion (A.A.R.). Rooks was its first president (1970–74) and was succeeded by Lawrence Jones (Rooks was again president of the S.S.B.R. from 1980 to 1984).

In 1974 Rooks became the first Black president of Chicago Theological Seminary, a position he held for ten years. He was the first Black president *elected* to head any White seminary (Lawrence Jones, not elected, was acting president of Union Theological Seminary for much of 1970). From 1984 to the present he has been executive vice-president of the United Church Board for Homeland Ministries. His list of publications is very long, capped by *Revolution in Zion: Reshaping African American Ministry, 1960–1974* (1990), an autobiographical book focusing on his work with the F.T.E. and its impact on African American clergy.

Rooks, Charles Shelby. *Hopeful Spirit.* New York: Pilgrim Press, 1987. 170 pp.
———. *Rainbows and Reality.* Atlanta, GA: The I.T.C. Press, 1985.
———. *Revolution in Zion: Reshaping African American Ministry, 1960–1974.* New York: Pilgrim Press, 1990. 234 pp.
———. "Theological Reflections in an Uncertain Age." *Theology Today* 36 (July 1979).
———. *Toward the Promised Land.* Fort Worth, TX: Texas Christian University, Scott Lectures, 1972. 15 pp.
BDNM (75), WWABA (92–93), WWR (85), WWA (90–91), MBRL, IBAW, IBAWCB.

ROSE, JAMES EVERETT (January 3, 1883–May 14, 1942), civil rights leader and prominent Baptist minister, was born in Centralia, Virginia, the son of Richard and Matilda (Cheatham) Rose. He grew up in poverty and had little opportunity for schooling as a youth, but was determined to get an education. He graduated in 1902 from Virginia Normal and Industrial Institute in Petersburg, and finished his normal (high school) training at Howard University Academy in 1909, at the age of twenty-six. He supported himself during these years as a school teacher, and for one year was a letter carrier. He remained at Howard University in Washington, D.C. to receive his B.A. in 1913, and earned his B.D. in 1916 at Colgate Rochester Theological Seminary in New York.

On August 26, 1915, he married Mamie A. Reddy, and upon his graduation they worked together at a mission station in Leroy, New York. In four years' time the work grew into the Second Baptist Church of Leroy, and for part of that time, 1918 to 1920, Rose also pastored the Second Baptist Church in Mumford. His first wife passed away in December 1919, and on March 2, 1921, he married Carrie L. Duke, with whom he had two sons. In 1920 he accepted the pastorate of the Mount Olivet Baptist Church in Rochester, New York, where he remained the rest of his life. He succeeded Charles D. Hubert, the founder of Mount Olivet, in that pulpit. The congregation was educated and fairly well-to-do, an excellent environment for Rose's erudition and energies. He led the church in building a large, Gothic structure, one of the most impressive churches in the region despite the ravages of the Depression.

In his twenty-two years in the Olivet pastorate he gained a wide-ranging reputation as a an eloquent and stormy fighter against injustice and a dedicated ecumenist. He was the first Black to be elected moderator of the Baptist Union of Monroe County. He was also president of the Rochester Ministerial Association and vice-president of the Federation of Churches of Rochester and Monroe County. He was appointed to a number of Rochester housing groups. In 1940 Howard University recognized his accomplishments by awarding him an honorary Doctor of Divinity degree.

NYTO, WWC, GBB.

ROSS, ISAAC NELSON (January 22, 1856–1927), 41st bishop of the **African Methodist Episcopal Church** (AME), was born in Hawkins County, Tennessee. He was one of ten children in a pious farming family which moved to Bowersville, Green County, Ohio in 1861. Four of the five sons in this family became ministers in the AME Church. When farm work could spare him, Ross attended a local school for his early education. On January 1, 1879, he married Mary Robinson Fletcher, with whom he had six children.

He was converted at an early age, joined the Ohio Conference in 1880, was ordained deacon in 1882 and elder in 1883. His pastorates included the Oberlin Mission, Ohio; St. Paul's AME Church in Washington, Pennsylvania; Oil City and Titusville Circuit in Pennsylvania; Brown's Chapel AME Church in Allegheny City, Pennsylvania; Wiley Avenue AME Church in Pittsburgh, Pennsylvania; Warren Chapel AME Church in Toledo, Ohio; and St. Paul's AME Church in Columbus, Ohio, where he hosted the General Conference in 1900.

By this time he was a very popular and well-known pastor, with success following him wherever he went.

He reduced or eliminated the debt at many churches and remodeled others. In Columbus the church was renovated from top to bottom with the work paid for as it progressed. In 1901 he left Columbus and was appointed to Allen Temple AME Church in Cincinnati, Ohio, where he remained for five years. In 1906 he moved to Big Bethel AME Church in Atlanta, Georgia, where he again led in a major remodeling job on the church. In 1909, after about three and a half years, he was assigned to Metropolitan AME Church in Washington, D.C., where he greatly increased the congregation and made improvements in the church facilities. In 1912, even though he was not a delegate to the General Conference, he still received a large number of votes for the bishopric. In 1914 he moved to the historic Ebenezer AME Church in Baltimore, Maryland.

On May 18, 1916, Ross was elected bishop and assigned to the Fourteenth Episcopal District (West Africa). In spite of the possibility of dangerous submarine activity, he sailed to Africa to take his post. In 1920 he was moved to the Twelfth District (Arkansas), and remained there until his death. Named for him is a church in Jamestown, Ohio.

CEAMEC, BAMEC, HAMEC, EWM.

ROSS, MARY OLIVIA (b. c.1908), president of the Women's Convention and Auxiliary of the **National Baptist Convention, U.S.A., Inc**. (N.B.C.U.S.A), was born in Georgia, the daughter of Solomon and Beatrice (Taylor) Brookins. She graduated from Spelman College in Atlanta, Georgia, and from 1928 to 1930 was a teacher at the Walker Institute in Augusta, Georgia. On May 28, 1930, she married Solomon D. Ross, with whom she had three children.

After the marriage her husband became the pastor of the Shiloh Baptist Church in Detroit, Michigan, and she was a teacher in the Detroit public school system from 1934 to 1944. After 1944 she became more and more involved in Baptist activities and eventually was elected vice-president-at-large of the Women's Convention. When **Nannie Helen Burroughs**, founder of the Women's Convention and its second president, passed away in May 1961, Ross was elected to succeed her as its third president, and has since remained in that position.

Over the years, Ross has become a major Baptist and ecumenical leader. She was a delegate to the 6th Assembly of the World Council of Churches in Vancouver, British Columbia, in the early 1980s, and

has served as a member of the Central Committee of the World Council of Churches. She is a member of the board of managers of Church Women United and is on the executive committee of the North American Baptist Women's Union. She has been director of the Ministers' Wives Division of the National Baptist Congress of Christian Education, and is a life member of the N.A.A.C.P. She was a guest lecturer at the First Asian Baptist Congress in Hyberadad, India, and was Founder's Day speaker at Spelman College in 1983. She has received numerous awards and honorary degrees, including a Doctor of Divinity from the Interdenominational Theological Center of Atlanta in 1982 and the Living Legacy Award of 1986. She edits the *Mission*, a quarterly study guide for local mission societies, and has published many articles and longer works, the most recent being *From Crumbs to Gravy* (1990).

Ross, Mary O. *From Crumbs to Gravy*. Detroit, MI: Harlo Press, 1990.
WWABA (92–93), *SCA, IBAW.*

ROSS, PETER (1809–July 25, 1890), 11th bishop of the **African Methodist Episcopal Zion Church** (AMEZ), was born in New York City, and as a youth experienced conversion in the Mother Zion Church in that city. He received an exhorter's license soon after conversion, and apparently received a preacher's license in 1828. He joined the New York Conference in May 1834, was ordained deacon on May 22, 1840, and elder in 1842.

He spent a good part of his pastoral years in the mission field of Nova Scotia and New England. He gained a large reputation as an effective minister of unsullied character and was elected superintendent (as bishops were then called) in 1860 (consecrated on June 12, 1860). At that time superintendents were elected for four-year terms, and there was no set salary for them. Money was obtained through the "gleaning" system as they traveled through the various districts. Ross was assigned annually to the First, Second, and Third Districts.

At the May 1864 General Conference Ross resigned from his office, stating that his fields had already been gleaned to such an extent that he had barely secured $200 plus traveling expenses. Unable to support his family (about which we know little) on that income, he returned to his former trade as a shoemaker in his Providence, Rhode Island, home. He remained at least somewhat active as a part-time minister, serving thereafter as chaplain of the 14th Rhode Island Heavy Artillery group.

EWM, HAMEZC, AMEZC.

RUFFIN, GEORGE L. (b. c. 1868), Episcopal layperson and musician, was born in Boston, Massachusetts, in the middle of the nineteenth century, the son of Josephine St. Pierre and Judge George L. Ruffin. As a child he attended Trinity Episcopal Church and sang in the boys' choir under the direction of J. C. D. Parker. There as a child of eight, Ruffin was heard by Phillips Brooks, the pastor of the Church of the Advent and future bishop. Impressed with the "sweetness" of his voice, Brooks insisted upon Ruffin exercising his gift at his congregation's new sanctuary on Copley Square.

Riffin sang at the Church of the Advent for eight years, by which time his voice had matured, and he then returned to Trinity Church. During the next fifty years he was a leading member of the choir under the successive leadership of Horatio Parker, Wallace Goodrich, and Ernest Mitchell. While anchored in the choir, he became well known around Boston and the Northeast as a tenor. He was the first African American to join the Haydn Society and was a senior tenor with the Cecilia Society. He took roles in opera productions, possibly the most memorable one being as Amonasro in the 1903 production of *Aida* in New York. He also played the organ at St. Augustine's Church.

In 1890, Ruffin joined with his sister, Forida Ruffin Ridley, in founding the Society for the Collection of Negro Folklore, in Boston, the earliest group of Black folklorists (though previously Whites had organized for collecting Black folklore).

In 1934 Ruffin was honored for his 50 years of consecutive service at Trinity.

Cuney-Hare, Maud. *Negro Musicians and Their Music.* Washington, DC: Associated Publishers, 1936. 439 pp.

RUSH, CHRISTOPHER (February 4, 1777–July 16, 1873), 2nd bishop of the **African Methodist Episcopal Zion Church** (AMEZ), was born into slavery near New Bern, Cravens County, North Carolina. He experienced conversion in 1793, at the age of sixteen. Somehow, through escape, manumission, or other means, he was freed, and made his way to New York in 1798, at the age of twenty-one. He joined the Methodist Episcopal Church there in 1803, and was licensed to preach in 1815. After **James Varick** organized the AMEZ Church in 1820, Rush joined and was ordained both deacon and elder on the same day, July 23, 1822. He never married.

On May 18, 1828, after only six years in ordained ministry, he was elected superintendent (as bishops were called at that time), succeeding James Varick in that office. He was a very active leader on behalf of reform and abolition, and attended the various national conventions beginning with the first one in 1830. In 1833 he organized the Phoenix Society in New York City, an integrated group which worked for progressive and democratic goals based on peace, freedom, and equality for all persons. Most immediately, it was "to promote the improvement of the coloured people in morals, literature, and the mechanic arts." It established a high school for Black youth, conducted adult education classes, offered cultural and intellectual enrichment, and organized a center for training in the various manual trades. Phoenix Hall, on West Broadway, became the center of anti-slavery activities in New York City. Lewis Tappan provided most of the funds, and Rush remained as president for many years. With the support of the 1833 Convention of Colored People, similar societies were organized in many northern cities as branches of the Phoenix Moral and Reform Society.

Rush's work was monumental in spreading the AMEZ Church in the northeastern United States and increasing its esteem within the Black community. He was an exceptional speaker and his self-education was wide-ranging and profound. In 1831, 1,016 members were listed in the New York Conference and 673 members in the Philadelphia Conference. He worked alone until **William Miller** was elected to assist him in 1840. When Miller died in 1845 Rush was again alone in the episcopacy until **George Galbreath** was elected in 1848. In 1843 Rush published *A Short Account of the Rise and Progress of the AME Church in America.* He lost his eyesight in 1852, and retired that year from the episcopacy. The last several years of his long and eventful life were largely spent confined to his home.

Medford, H. T. "Christopher Rush." *Star of Zion* 70 (May 2, 1946): 5.

Payne, Daniel A. *History of the African Methodist Episcopal Church.* Nashville, TN: Publishing House of the A.M.E. Sunday School Union, 1891. 218 pp.

Rush, Christopher. *A Short Account of the Rise and Progress of the AME Church in America.* New York: The Author, 1843. 119 pp.

DNAADB, AARS, HUBA, BAW, HNC, HAMEZCIA, ACAB, HAMEZC, TCBDA, AMEZ, EWM, OHYAMEZC.

RUSSELL, CHARLES LEE (September 22, 1886–February 8, 1948), 21st bishop of the **Christian Methodist Episcopal Church** (CME), then known as the Colored Methodist Episcopal Church, was born in Campbell Clark County, Alabama. After attending public schools in his home area, he attended Miles College in Birmingham, Alabama. One source states that he received his B.A. degree from Frelinghusen College and both the Bachelor of Hebrew and S.T.B. degrees from Yeshiva College in New York City, but this cannot be confirmed. Another source indicates a B.A. in 1914 from Miles College in Birmingham, Alabama, and a D.D. in 1916 from Paine College in Augusta, Georgia. On December 4, 1918, he married Minnie L. Gardner.

He began his ministry serving several charges in Alabama, and later served four years as presiding elder of the Tallahassee District in Florida. He then was a pastor in Huntsville, Alabama, Thomasville, Georgia, and Israel CME Church in Washington, D.C. In 1926 he was elected General Secretary of the Epworth League and held that position for eight years. While in that office he enrolled in February 1930 in Dropsie University for Hebrew and Cognate Learnings (now called Annenberg Institute) in Philadelphia, Pennsylvania. He studied there for four years with a major in Egyptology and a minor in history. Before he could obtain a degree, however, he was assigned in 1934 to the prestigious Chestnut Street CME Church in Louisville, Kentucky.

Russell was elected bishop in 1938, and over the next ten years conducted a significant and successful rehabilitation and expansion campaign in his episcopal area around Washington, D.C. He published several pamphlets, but his most significant writing was *Light from the Talmud* (1943), which placed Hebrew and English on facing pages.

Russell, Charles Lee. *Light from the Talmud.* New York: Block Publishing Co., 1943.
EWM, AARS, BAW, HUBA, CMECTY.

RUSSELL, CLAYTON DONOVAN (c.1911–c.1980), radio preacher and at one time pastor of one of the largest churches in the United States, was once headed for a law degree. He left law school to be ordained in the People's Independent Church of Christ in Los Angeles, California. He stayed to pastor that church, a powerhouse church in the region with a membership of 11,000. He began a popular radio ministry over KFOX, and in 1949 had a reported audience of 75,000 for the Sunday morning broadcasts.

"Top Radio Ministers." *Ebony* 4 (July 1949): 56–61.
Russell, Clayton D. *America! This is Our Stand.* Los Angeles: N.p., 1942. 8 pp.
BAW.

RUSSELL, DANIEL JAMES (July 18, 1846– ?), head of the **African Union Methodist Protestant Church** (A.U.M.P.), was born in Delaware City, Delaware, the son of Rev. Daniel and Charles Anna Russell. He received four years of public school education in Marshalltown, New Jersey, and taught school in Summit Bridge, Delaware, for two years. He married Carrie Miller, with whom he had two children.

He studied medicine at Philadelphia Electoral Medical College and received his diploma in 1871. While in school he was ordained a deacon in the A.U.M.P. Church in 1868 and elder in 1870. In 1884 he was elected president (*Who's Who in Colored America* uses the term bishop through the denomination did not adopt that term until 1966).

In 1892 he became editor of the *Union Star.* In 1906 he became principal of the Bible and Training School of the A.U.M.P. Church, and in 1910 he became general manager of the publishing house of the denomination. He was also pastor of St. Matthew's A.U.M.P. Church, the location of which is unclear, but which may have been in Penns Grove, New Jersey. In 1920 he published the only major history of the denomination, *History of the African Union Methodist Protestant Church.*

Russell, Daniel James. *History of the African Union Methodist Protestant Church.* Philadelphia, PA: Union Star Book and Job Printing and Publishing House, 1920. 66 pp.
BAW, WWCA (38–40).

RUST COLLEGE. A **United Methodist Church** school. Rust College, Holly Springs, Mississippi, was founded in 1867 as Shaw University. Its original facilities were at the Asbury Methodist Episcopal Church in Holly Springs. Rev. A. C. Donald served as its first president. The Rev. A. P. Shaw assisted the school initially with a large donation. When first opened the school had an elementary, high school, and college section and served people of all ages. During most of the years the high school and elementary classes were opened, they were among the best, far superior to the state schools then available. In 1884 the Woman's Home Missionary Society opened the Elizabeth L. Rust Home on campus to teach domestic skills. In 1890 the school was renamed in honor of Richard S. Rust, who had been secretary of the Freedman's Aid Bureau.

During the late 1930s, the elementary and high school sections of Rust were discontinued in order for the school to apply for accreditation. It continues to emphasize the training of teachers for the public schools.

Harmon, Nolan B., ed. *The Encyclopedia of World Methodism*. 2 vols. Nashville, TN: The United Methodist Publishing House, 1974.

Stowell, Jay S. *Methodist Adventures in Negro Education*. New York: Methodist Book Concern, 1922. 190 pp.

"But from the stand point I look at it, I would move its [the Colonization Society] disbandment forthwith, and let the white people who wait for the Negro to emigrate to Africa so as to make more room for the great flood of foreigners who come to our shores, know that there is a place in the United States for the Negro.

"They are real American citizens, and at home. They have fought and bled and died, like men, to make this country what it is. And if they have got to suffer and die, and be lynched, and tortured, and burned at the stake, I say they are at home."

Amanda Smith, Evangelist
African Methodist Episcopal Church

S

SACRED HEART CATHOLIC CHURCH. An Eastern Orthodox church. The Sacred Heart Catholic Church grew out of the American Catholic Church, Archdiocese of New York (now the **Orthodox Catholic Church in America**). It was founded by Archbishop James Augustine Arrendale who had been consecrated to the episcopacy by Bishop Donald Anthony, assisted by William Wren and André Pinachio. The church is Orthodox in faith and practice.

Headquarters was established in New York City. Two years after its founding, the church reported three parishes and approximately 50 members. However, Arrendale died in 1985, and its present status is unknown.

SADLER, JAMES B. (1828–1911), a pioneer minister of the **Cumberland Presbyterian Church in America** (then known as the Second Cumberland Presbyterian Church in U.S.), was born in Tennessee, the son of a slave woman and a slave master. His father, it is believed, was a doctor named Sadler, and the same person who brought him and his mother to Bosque County, Texas, prior to the Civil War. At some point Sadler was converted to Christianity and affiliated with the Cumberland Presbyterian Church. In 1870 he organized the first African American congregation in Texas and oversaw the building of the first church sanctuary, the Rock Springs Cumberland Presbyterian Church. He became a minister and affiliated with the Waco Presbytery.

In the mid-1870s he joined with two other Black Cumberland ministers in requesting the organization of a separate African American presbytery. The Brazos River Presbytery first met in February 1877. It affiliated with the Second Cumberland Presbyterian Church which had been organized in 1874.

Sadler served with distinction through the rest of the century as pastor of the Rock Springs Church. He was elected moderator of the Brazos River Presbytery in 1878, 1884, and 1888. His son, G. W. Sadler, also had a long career in the ministry and served for many years as stated clerk of the Brazos River Presbytery and then, following three years as moderator of the church's general assembly, served eight years as stated clerk of the whole church, 1924–1931.

Campbell, Thomas D. *One Family Under God: A Story of Cumberland Presbyterians in Black and White*. Memphis, TN; Huntsville, AL: Federated Board of Christian Education of the Cumberland Presbyterian Church and the Second Cumberland Presbyterian Church, 1982. 237 pp.

Directory of Second Cumberland Presbyterian Church. Huntsville, AL: Second Cumberland Presbyterian Church, 1981. 78 pp.

ST. AUGUSTINE'S COLLEGE. An **Episcopal Church** school. St. Augustine's College, Raleigh, North Carolina, was founded in 1867 as St. Augustine's Normal and Collegiate Institute by Bishop Thomas Atkinson, the Episcopal Church bishop of North Carolina. Atkinson emerged from the smoke of the Civil War to call for the education of the freedmen. He issued an open invitation for ministers, both Black and White, to come to his diocese and assist in creating the school he was going to establish. He was joined in 1867 by Rev. J. Brinton Smith, who became the school's first principal. From its earliest years, the school specialized in the training of schoolteachers and ministers. In 1906 St. Augustine's came under the oversight of the American Church Institute for Negroes.

Today, St. Augustine's is a fully accredited four-year senior college.

Bragg, George F. *History of the Afro-American Group in the Episcopal Church*. Baltimore, MD: Church Advocate Press, 1922. 319 pp.

ST. AUGUSTINE'S SEMINARY. A **Roman Catholic Church** school. The idea of a seminary to train African Americas for the Roman Catholic priesthood seems to have originated with Fr. Aloysius Heick, a priest working in the Southern Province of the **Society of the Divine Word**. The Society had established a missionary work among Southern Black Catholics in 1905 in Mississippi. As the work grew and new parishes were formed, the appropriateness of having Black priests was noted, along with the fact that very few church schools would admit African Americans for college-level training. Hence, along with the provincial of the Order, in 1920 Heick approached the Bishop of Natchez (Mississippi), Mt. Rev. John E. Gunn, to seek his approval of the establishment of such a seminary. Gunn gave his endorsement to the project in June 1920. The preparatory seminary, providing a high school and junior college curriculum, opened in Greenville, Mississippi, in November.

The school, named for St. Augustine, the fifth-century bishop of Hippo, North Africa, remained in Greenville for three years, but in 1923 moved to Bay St. Louis, near Biloxi. The move occasioned a letter from Pope Pius XI commending the work of building a native clergy. In 1926, the first graduates of the preparatory seminary entered the novitiate of the society, and about the same time the senior seminary, which offered a three-year course in philosophy and a four-year course in theology, was opened.

The first graduates of the senior seminary were ordained May 23, 1934. They were Frs. Maurice Rousseve, Vincent Smith, Anthony Bourges, and Francis Wade. They each said their first masses the following day in what became the occasion for a gathering of hundreds of well-wishers at the seminary. St. Augustine's played a crucial role in the first generation of the development of an African American priesthood. Between 1920 and 1960, approximately two-thirds of all of the African American priests ordained in the United States received at least part of their training there. While that percentage has lowered as other Catholic seminaries have opened their doors to African American students, the school remains a vital center for the African American Catholic priesthood. The school produced its first bishop in the person of **Joseph Bowers**, consecrated in 1953 as bishop of Accra, Ghana, in Africa.

Gerow, Richard Oliver, comp. *Catholicity in Mississippi.* Natchez, MS: 1939.

Ochs, Stephen J. *Desegregating the Altar: The Josephites and the Struggle for Black Priests, 1871–1960.* Baton Rouge, LA: Louisiana State University Press, 1990.

ST. JOSEPH'S SOCIETY OF THE SACRED HEART. A religious order of the **Roman Catholic Church**. St. Joseph's Society of the Sacred Heart is one of several Roman Catholic orders associated with ministry to and by Black people in the United States in the decades since the Civil War. It was founded in England in 1866 by Fr. Herbert Vaughan (later a cardinal). It was brought to America in 1871 when Vaughan and four priests arrived to begin a mission to the freedmen. Vaughan quickly concluded that all-Black parishes were the best way to assure Black Catholics of some dignity, which they were denied in White-controlled congregations. The society chapter was officially organized in 1875 with James Noonan named as the first American provincial. The work did not prosper until John R. Slattery assumed duties as the new provincial in 1878.

Born in New York, Slattery finished seminary with the Society in England and was assigned to St. Francis Xavier Church in Baltimore in 1877. While there he worked with one of his Black church members, Elizabeth Herbert, in founding St. Elizabeth's Home for Colored Foundlings. The next year, with the order discouraged and in disarray, Vaughan appointed the young priest to lead the order. Slattery was enthusiastic for the work and revived it through his travels and his gaining of support for its endeavors.

Slattery also came to believe that a Black clergy was needed for the care of present Black members and absolutely necessary for the further evangelization of the large community of African Americans. A precedent had been set by the ordination of Blacks in other countries, though primarily for work in Africa. In 1883 he arranged for **Charles Randolph Uncles** to attend St. Hyacinth's College in Quebec. In 1887 Slattery received strong support from Francis A. Janssens, bishop of Natchez and future archbishop of New Orleans, who came out in favor of Black priests. In the fall of 1888, St. Joseph's Seminary opened in Baltimore with four students, including Uncles, in attendance. The following year Slattery opened Epiphany Apostolic College in the Baltimore suburb of Walbrook. Four Black students were in the first entering class. In 1891 Uncles was ordained and Slattery preached at his first mass.

With the development of the schools, reliance on England was unnecessary and Slattery moved to establish an independent American work. In 1893 the new St. Joseph's Society of the Sacred Heart was organized with Slattery in the leadership role. He began with a much-reduced organization as a number of the priests had decided not to remain with the new organization. In spite of those losses, the Josephites opened St. Joseph's Industrial School in Clayton,

Delaware, in 1895, modeled on Tuskegee. That same year three Black students entered Catholic University for the first time.

While Slattery promoted the cause of Black priests, he found himself in an increasingly hostile situation. In 1895, the Afro-American Congresses were discontinued. The church was involved in a liberal conservative controversy over the liberal "Americanist" attempts to build a truly indigenous church in the United States. The liberal bishops provided the main support for the Josephites. However, they lost the controversy when Rome condemned Americanism, and their subsequent loss of power meant a significant decrease of assistance from the church's hierarchy for a Black clergy. Slattery moved ahead with plans, however, and institutionalized his goals of employing Black catechists. To that end he opened St. Joseph's College of Negro Catechists near Montgomery, Alabama.

Two more priests nurtured by Slattery would soon be ordained, John Henry Dorsey (1902) and John J. Plantevigne (1907). But the effects of the changes wrought by the Americanist controversy eventually caught up with Slattery and after 25 years in his mission, he became at first discouraged and then convinced that the Roman Catholic Church had become too corrupt to reform. In 1904 he left the Josephites and two years later turned on the church as a severe critic. Slattery's defection also left his successors somewhat defenseless in the face of the growing opposition to Black priests. His successors quietly abandoned further recruitment of Black priests and during the first half of the twentieth century only a very few were admitted to the college and seminary. Though attacked by the **Federated Colored Catholics** in the 1920s, Josephite leader Louis B. Pastorelli refused to change his policy and the training of Black priests fell to the **Society of the Divine Word**.

It was not until 1941 that another Black priest, Chester Ball, would be ordained by the Josephites, and he left office the following year. Thus it was not until 1942 and the tenure of Edward V. Casserly as superior general of the order that Josephite policies began to change. Casserly benefitted from a church which had itself become more open to Black priests, and was especially aided by the support of bishops from the South who were ready to accept Black priests into their diocese. His major contribution was to open Epiphany Apostolic College and St. Joseph's Seminary to Black candidates to the priesthood. Under Casserly's successor, Thomas P. McNamara, the society began to bring Black men into the priesthood, and in 1954 dedicated itself to ridding the church of its segregated services. By that year the number of Black students at Epiphany for the first time exceeded that of Whites.

Through the 1960s and 1970s, the order experienced both celebrative and challenging events as the civil rights movements matured. The order worked in and for the civil rights movement and as students finished their education, ordained eleven Black priests. Some of these priests were among the 58 who met in Detroit in 1968 to form the **National Black Clergy Caucus**. The formation of the caucus signaled a new era of Black activism within the church and the Josephites soon found themselves on the receiving end of harsh criticism. They remained a predominantly White organization with what the new Black leadership saw as a poor record on racial concerns through the twentieth century. St. Joseph's Seminary became a focal point for debates on Black power and consciousness. As did the whole church, the society suffered greatly from the exodus of Black leadership who rejected their subordination in a predominantly White institution. However, the society responded positively. In 1971 Matthew O'Rourke, then the superior general, appointed a Black man, **Eugene Marino** as the vicar general (second in command) of the society. In 1974 **Carl A. Fisher** was named Director of Vocation.

By the mid-1970s, the high tensions between the church and the Black community lessened. The church established a set of Black structures throughout the country, and the number of Black priests steadily climbed. More Blacks were also admitted to the hierarchy, including three Josephites: Eugene Marino, **John H. Ricard**, and Carl H. Fisher. Marino would later become the first Black archbishop. Thus, recovering from their earlier paternalistic and racist patterns, the Josephites have emerged as one of the Catholic Church's major instruments for ministry within the Black community.

Ochs, Stephen J. *Desegregating the Altar: The Josephites and the Struggle for Black Priests, 1871–1960.* Baton Rouge, LA: Louisiana State University Press, 1990. 500 pp.

SAINT PAUL'S BIBLE INSTITUTE. A **Salvation and Deliverance Church** school. Saint Paul's Bible Institute is one of five Bible colleges founded by Apostle William Brown in the 1980s for the Salvation and Deliverance Church. The school is headed by its dean, Minister Jerome King.

Payne, Wardell J., ed. *Directory of African American Religious Bodies: A Compendium by the Howard University School of Divinity.* Washington, DC: Howard University Press, 1991. 363 pp.

ST. PAUL'S COLLEGE. An **Episcopal Church** school. St. Paul's College, Lawrenceville, Virginia, was founded in 1888 as St. Paul's Normal and Industrial School. It grew out of the labors of Rev. James Solomon Russell. Russell had attended Hampton Institute but left before graduation to become the first student at the new theological school in Petersburg, Virginia, later to be named Bishop Payne Divinity School. In 1882 he was ordained deacon and sent to Lawrenceville. Russell was able to collect enough money, through contacts in the North, to open the school six years later. The school grew steadily in quality of curriculum and number of students.

By the 1920s the student body numbered over 500. Today it is a four-year senior college with approximately 600 students.

SAINTS JUNIOR COLLEGE. A **Church of God in Christ** school. Saints Junior College grew out of the work in Mississippi of Bishop **Charles Mason Harrison**, founder of the Church of God in Christ, who promoted the ideals of education among church members. Not many years after the church was founded, Miss Pinkie Duncan began the Saints Home School of Negro Boys and Girls, an elementary school, in the basement of the Church of God in Christ in Lexington, Mississippi. In 1917 an education board was established to guide and support the project. As money was raised and more faculty hired, the school became the Saints Industrial School of Mississippi. Dr. James Courts became the school's principal.

In 1920 land for a permanent campus was purchased. Gradually the school, as it continued to grow and mature, became the Saints Industrial and Literary School, both an elementary and high school. In 1926 Courts died and was succeeded by **Arenia Cornelia Mallory**. Previously an instructor, Mallory made the school her life work. Starting with one two-story building, she built the campus, enlarged and upgraded the faculty, and gradually transformed the school which in 1954 was renamed Saints Junior College. Following her retirement in 1975, Mallory became the Church's Commissioner of Education. The school has been closed, but is expected to reopen.

Cornelius, Lucille J. *The Pioneer History of the Church of God in Christ*. [Sacramento, CA]: The Author, 1975. 102 pp.

SALTER, MOSES BUCKINGHAM (February 13, 1841–March 21, 1913), 21st bishop of the **African Methodist Episcopal Church** (AME), was born into slavery in Charleston, South Carolina, the son of Moses Buckingham and Mary M. Salter. He was converted in 1857, at the age of sixteen, and was class leader in the local Methodist Episcopal Church. In 1865, immediately after the Civil War, Bishop **Daniel Payne** organized the South Carolina Conference of the AME Church, the first formal AME presence in the South. Salter immediately joined and was licensed to preach. He became an itinerant member of the Annual Conference in 1866 and that year was ordained both deacon and elder, with a charge in Aiken, South Carolina.

From 1868 to 1870 he was presiding elder of the Aiken District, probably while remaining at his local church. From 1870 to 1874 he was a student at Wilberforce University in Xenia, Ohio. On September 2, 1874, he married Priscilla Smith; there were no children. In 1874 ill health forced him to cut short his academic pursuits and he was reappointed to his former Aiken charge for a year. In 1875 he went to Emanuel AME Church in Charleston, where he remained for some time with great success.

In 1892 Salter was elected bishop on the second ballot and was assigned to the Seventh Episcopal District (South Carolina) from 1892 to 1896, where he was a big supporter of Allen University in Columbia, South Carolina. His following assignments were in the Ninth Episcopal District (Kentucky and Tennessee) from 1896 to 1900; Tenth Episcopal District (Texas and Oklahoma) from 1900 to 1904; Eighth Episcopal District (Mississippi and Louisiana) from 1904 to 1908; and the Eleventh Episcopal District (Florida) from 1908 to 1912. He organized the Northeast South Carolina Conference at Marion in December 1892, and was a delegate to the World Methodist Conference in London in 1901. He retired in May 1912, and passed away the following year. Named for him are churches in Dyersburg and Henderson, Tennessee; Langston, Oklahoma; Bowling Green, Kentucky; and Miami, Florida.

Salter, Moses Buckingham. *The Seven Kingdoms; a Book of Travel, History, Information, and Entertainment*. Philadelphia, PA: AME Publishing House, 1902. 139 pp.
AMSC, TCBDA, EWM, HAMEC, NCAB (4), *CEAMEC, BAMEC, WWWA* (4), *BAW, HUBA*.

SALVATION AND DELIVERANCE CHURCH. The Salvation and Deliverance Church was begun in 1975 by Rev. William Brown as a ministry of the African **Methodist Episcopal Church**. Brown had been raised a Roman Catholic and become a businessman. He later entered the ministry. In the 1980s he separated from the African Methodist Episcopal Church in favor of developing an international, interracial, Holiness ministry. In a very short time the church has developed an enormous program which currently reaches to more than 40 countries. Emphasis in the membership is placed in nurturing holy living rather than doctrinal uniformity.

Apostle William Brown has led the church in the development of a multidimensional program. It includes an award-winning drug rehabilitation center in Harlem; a youth ministry, the International Youth Movement for Christ; schools (both elementary and bible schools); and work with the physically retarded. The church maintains a retreat center in the Catskill Mountains with special facilities for those involved in ministry to the retarded.

Headquarters of the church is in Manhattan. The more than 140 affiliated congregations include churches in Haiti, Nigeria, Jamaica, Liberia, India, and Canada. The church supports five Bible colleges, including Saint Paul's Bible Institute in New York.

Payne, Wardell J., ed. *Directory of African American Religious Bodies: A Compendium by the Howard University School of Divinity.* Washington, DC: Howard University Press, 1991. 363 pp.

SALVATION ARMY. A Holiness church. The Salvation Army was founded in England in the 1860s as a mission in the slums of London by William Booth. In stages it developed a military model, with its ministers designated by titles from the Army. Ministers begin as lieutenants and rise in rank and responsibility. The Army was brought to America in 1880 when Commissioner George Railton and seven female officers landed in New York City. It directed its program to social problems and established centers to aid those hurting because of poverty, illness or temporary disasters. Because of the very nature of its commitments, the Army quickly encountered the African American community. Among the early converts was W. S. Braithwaite, an immigrant from British Guinea, who had settled in Asbury Park, New Jersey. After an early setback in which the head of the American branch created a schism, evangelical and social work among African Americans began in the mid-1880s under the zealous new commander, Major Frank Smith, committed to the idea that the Army could break down the wall separating the races. In 1885 he announced the "Great Colored Campaign and Combined Attack on the South" for which he had been mobilizing the largely White corps for a year. He placed the new Captain Braithwaite, a West Indian who had experienced salvation at an Army meeting in New Jersey, in charge. Unfortunately, Braithwaite's conduct was not in accord with Army standards and he was dismissed from his

position shortly after the campaign started, but the effort continued. The first success was in Fredericksburg, Virginia, where a new unit was opened under a four-person team which included two African Americans, a Captain Johnson and an unnamed Black female officer. The audience who attended was also predominantly Black.

During these early years African Americans were welcomed to the officer's corps. Many were recruited as "Specials," the Army term for evangelist, and were included in interracial teams which went out to establish new units. In 1894 Ballington Booth, then in command in America, included five African Americans in his delegation to the International Convention in London as a official statement of the Army's policy of reaching out to the Black community. The extremes of the Army's efforts were demonstrated in 1895 by two officers in Frederick, Maryland, who risked their lives to save a Black man from a lynch mob. At the same time the work among Black people languished from lack of money and initiative, and racism raised its head in the units' in contradiction to the Army's official statements and directives. In the first decades of the twentieth century facilities in the South had to be either segregated or closed. They were segregated and work in the African American community largely abandoned.

While slowed, work within the Black community never died and there were periodic attempts to revive it. Just before World War I, two African American units were opened in Washington, D.C., and Charleston, South Carolina. The Washington unit under Brigadier and Mrs. James Roberts was the strongest of the Black units for many decades. Other new all-Black units appeared in the 1920s. As World War II began, the Army supported USO units for Black soldiers. The Washington unit, under the command since 1942 of Major and Mrs. Lambert Bailey, again led the effort. After World War II, the Army began a series of moves to desegregate, beginning with the fresh air camp operated by the Black unit in Washington. In 1952 the camp was closed and merged with the White camp under an African American director. In 1949 the word "colored" began its disappearance from Army unit titles. In 1960 the two army hospitals in Cleveland were merged. During the decade official policy on deliverance of Army services, recruitment policies to the officer's corps (ministry), and access to Army facilities reversed the segregation which had been imposed through the century. The Army was often in the crossfire as it attempted to serve those called into crisis situations, especially some of the urban riots.

In more recent decades, it has responded to the growing Black consciousness by putting budget into

Black ministries and empowering Black leaders. In 1969 it opened a new center in the midst of the area most affected by the Cleveland, Ohio riots. In 1969 it appointed **B. Barton McIntyre** as the first African American to hold the rank of Lieutenant Colonel, who served as a territorial revivalist over eleven states. Since that time, other African Americans have been promoted to the higher levels of the Army's leadership.

McKinley, Edward H. *Marching to Glory: The History of the Salvation Army in the United States of America, 1880–1980.* San Francisco: Harper & Row, 1980. 286 pp.

SAMPSON, FREDERICK GEORGE (b. August 9, 1925), prominent Baptist minister (**National Baptist Convention, U.S.A., Inc.**), was born in Port Arthur, Texas, the son of Frederick and Florence Sampson. He received his B.A. in 1946 from Bishop College in Dallas, Texas. In 1947 he was chaplain and instructor at Bishop and received his B.Th. In 1950 he earned a B.D. from Howard University School of Religion in Washington, D.C., in 1952 his M.Div. from Howard, and an M.A. in 1952 from Columbia University in New York City. He later did graduate work at the Episcopal Theological Seminary of Virginia. He married Earlene Zone Harrison, with whom he had two children.

His pastorates have included the Shiloh Baptist Church (1948–52); High Street Baptist Church in Roanoke, Virginia (1952–60); Mount Lebanon Baptist Church in Louisville, Kentucky (1960–1971); and Tabernacle Missionary Baptist Church in Detroit, Michigan (1971–present). He also developed an outstanding record of public service. While in Kentucky, he served as vice-president of the Louisville Branch of the N.A.A.C.P., and later in Detroit became the president of the Detroit Branch of the N.A.A.C.P. He was at one time chair of the board of the Y.M.C.A. in both Virginia and Kentucky, and was consultant to the governor of Kentucky on Human Relations. In 1984 *Ebony* magazine named Sampson one of the top fifteen Black preachers in the United States.

"America's Fifteen Greatest Black Preachers." *Ebony* 39 (September 1984): 27–33.
BDNM (70).

SAMS, JAMES C. (February 19, 1909–1985), long-time president of the **National Baptist Convention of America**, was born in Cochran, Georgia, the son of Lonnie and Charlotte Sams. On September 29, 1930, he married Cornelia Fleming. About that time he was ordained a Baptist minister and pastored in Jacksonville, Florida, for the next thirty-two years. He received his B.S. in 1946 from Florida A&M College. In 1961 he was elected first vice-president of the National Baptist Convention of America and remained in that office for six years. In 1967 he was elected president of the National Baptist Convention of America, the denomination with the second-largest Black membership in the country. He held the office of president until his death in 1985. During his years as president, *Ebony* magazine named him one of the one hundred most influential Black Americans. He was a trustee of Florida Memorial College and of Edward Waters College.

"Deaths: James C. Sams." *Christian Century* 102 (September 25, 1985): 826.
"Ten Religious Groups with Biggest Black Membership." *Ebony* 39 (March 1984): 140–144.
WWABA (85), *WWR* (77), *WWA* (84–85).

SANDERS, DANIEL JACKSON (February 15, 1847– March 6, 1907), pioneer Presbyterian minister and educator, was born into slavery near Winnsboro, South Carolina, the son of William and Laura Sanders. His owner was Thomas Hall, a Methodist preacher, who permitted him to learn to spell and read. At the age of nine he was apprenticed to a shoemaker. In 1866, after the Civil War, he moved to Chester, South Carolina, and struggled to gain more education while supporting himself as a shoemaker. For a time he was privately tutored by a Mr. W. B. Knox, and in 1869–70 he attended Brainerd Institute, a Presbyterian school, in Chester. He was such a quick study that he was soon made a tutor in the school, and in 1870 he was ordained a Presbyterian minister by the Fairfield presbytery.

In 1871 he entered Western Theological Seminary in Allegheny (now Pittsburgh), Pennsylvania, and graduated with honors in 1874. He became pastor that year of the Chestnut Street Presbyterian Church in Wilmington, North Carolina, where he stayed for the next twelve years. In 1875 he went to England and Scotland on behalf of the Presbyterian Board of Missions for Freedmen and raised a substantial sum of money. In addition, he raised $6,000 as an endowment for an African scholarship fund for students preparing for African mission work at Biddle University (now Johnson C. Smith), a Presbyterian school founded in 1867 in Charlotte, North Carolina. On January 1, 1879, he founded *Africo-American Presbyterian*, a journal which was influential in promoting Presbyterianism among Blacks, and served as the voice of Black Presbyterianism in the South. On September 16, 1880, he married Fannie T. Price, with whom he had nine children.

In 1891 he was appointed the first Black president of Biddle University, for which he had been trustee since 1877. Although some Blacks, like **Lucy C. Laney**, were already heading some smaller schools in the South, this was the first time the Board of Missions for Freedmen had selected a Black to run a major institution. The board had hoped to integrate the school's faculty, but with the arrival of Sanders all but one of the White faculty resigned, apparently not willing to work with a Black president. The board showed great courage in urging the faculty to remain while maintaining its support for Sanders. Sanders held the presidency until his death and became legendary for his many abilities used on behalf of the school, which improved and expanded under his leadership. In addition to administrative tasks he also taught theology and church government and was popular among the students, who nicknamed him "Zeus."

Sanders served as stated clerk in the Atlantic and Yadkin presbyteries and the Catawba Synod, and was the first Black moderator of both the Yadkin and Cape Fear presbyteries. His influence was also felt in Presbyterianism at the national and international levels. He was five times a member of the General Assembly and was three times a delegate to the Alliance of Reformed Churches Holding the Presbyterian System, in Toronto (1892), Liverpool, and Washington, D.C. (1899). He was a firm believer in the full citizenship rights of African Americans, and felt that Christian education was the best means for destroying racial animosities and prejudices.

DAB, BDAE, WWWA (1), *TCBDA, PATN, AAP.*

SANDERS, OSCAR HARWOOD

SANDERS, OSCAR HARWOOD (1892–1972), a bishop of the **Pentecostal Assemblies of the World** (PAW), was born in Lanoke, Arkansas. As a young man he had an experience of salvation under the ministry of **Garfield T. Haywood**, later the presiding bishop of the Assemblies. Haywood took him under his wing and trained him for the ministry. He became a charter member of the Apostolic Bible Students Association (later the Indiana State Council of the PAW). He married, and he and his wife Hattie became the parents of one child. They settled in Muncie, Indiana, where Sanders founded Christ Temple. He would pastor the church for over a half century.

When the majority of the leaders of the PAW followed the merger with the Pentecostal Ministerial Alliance, composed of the former White members of the PAW, Sanders remained loyal. The next year he emerged as a member of a PAW committee which attempted to work out a reconciliation between it and the new merged body, the Pentecostal Assemblies of Jesus Christ. At the national gathering of the Assemblies in 1947, someone noted that the corporate papers of the Assemblies called for a board of directors to govern the organization. Following discussion, it was agreed that the board of bishops continue to function in that regard but that four nonepiscopal members added to the board, Sanders being among them. The next year two of the four, including Sanders, were elected as bishops. He served for many years as diocesan for Indiana.

The same year Sanders was elected bishop, the PAW Home Missions Board was organized. Sanders became the treasurer of the new organization and helped guide its ever-expanding program.

Golder, Morris E. *The Bishops of the Pentecostal Assemblies of the World.* Indianapolis, IN: The Author, 1980. 69 pp.
———. *History of the Pentecostal Assemblies of the World.* Indianapolis, IN: The Author, 1973. 195 pp.

SATTERWHITE, JOHN H.

SATTERWHITE, JOHN H. (January 1, 1913–May 23, 1989), **African Methodist Episcopal Zion Church** (AMEZ) minister, educator, and long-time editor of the *A.M.E. Zion Quarterly Review*, was born in Newberry, South Carolina, the son of Modock and Lucretia Satterwhite. He spent his early years in Seneca, South Carolina, then received his B.A. at Benedict College in Columbia, South Carolina in 1934 and his B.D. in 1937 and S.T.M. in 1938 at Oberlin Graduate School of Theology in Ohio. He was ordained into the Philadelphia-Baltimore Annual Conference of the AMEZ Church.

In 1938 he gained a position as instructor of Religion and Philosophy at Livingstone College in Salisbury, North Carolina, staying for two years. While at Livingstone he met and married Lucille C. Mills, with whom he had two children (from 1958 to 1982 Lucille was organist and music director at Trinity AMEZ Church in Washington, D.C.). From 1940 to 1957 he was dean and professor of theology at Hood Theological Seminary, related to Livingstone College in Salisbury. During this time he worked on his doctorate, and in 1957 gained his Th.D. from the Boston University School of Theology in Massachusetts. In 1958 he became the first Black professor on the faculty of Wesley Theological Seminary in Washington, D.C., teaching systematic ecumenics. In 1966 he founded the Opportunities Industrial Center for Washington, and was on the executive board of the N.A.A.C.P. from 1963 to 1976.

He returned to Hood Theological Seminary from 1972 to 1974 as a visiting lecturer and dean of the Institute for Black Ministries.

From 1974 to 1977 Satterwhite was associate general secretary of the Consultation on Church Union (C.O.C.U.) in Princeton, New Jersey, and from 1977 to 1980 was executive secretary of the Center for Black Church Union. In 1980 he was elected editor of the *A.M.E. Zion Quarterly Review*, the denomination's more scholarly journal, and secretary of the church's Historical Society. His offices were at the publishing house in Charlotte, North Carolina, and at Heritage House on the Livingstone College Campus. He served impressively in that position until his death.

His extra activities in church and community were many. He was chair of the Board of Examiners for the Philadelphia-Baltimore Conference and president at one point of the American Society of Christian Ethics. He was active on the National Committee of Negro Churchmen (now the **National Conference of Black Churchmen**). He was a strong ecumenical advocate, and was a member of the Faith and Order Commission of the World Council of Churches and the Inter-Religious Committee on Race Relations. He was part of the World Methodist Council and the Division of Christian Unity of the National Council of Churches.

Satterwhite authored numerous publications. His first book was *The Bearing of Tillich's and Berdyaev's Philosophies of History Upon Theism* (1938), his master's thesis at Oberlin. His first article was "An Interpretation of History," in the *A.M.E. Zion Quarterly Review* (1939). Later writings included *Methodism: Confessional Guide for Doctrine and Life* (1947), *The Nature of Religion: A Theological Interpretation* (1956), *John Stewart and the Mission to the Wyandot Indians* (1966), and *Ecumenical Witness, Common Ground* (1976).

"Lucille C. Satterwhite Honored for 25 Years of Service." *Star of Zion* 106 (September 23, 1982): 1, 6.

Manning, Glenda. "Focus on Our General Officers: Dr. John H. Satterwhite, Editor, A.M.E. Zion Quarterly Review." *Star of Zion* 112 (June 16, 1988): 8.

Newby, Richard Lorenzo. "A Tribute to John H. Satterwhite: Gone But Not Forgotten." *A.M.E. Zion Quarterly Review* 102 (January 1990): 4–6.

"Newly Elected Bishops and Officers Begin Tour of Duties." *Star of Zion* 104 (June 19, 1980): 1, 2.

Satterwhite, John H. "African Methodist Episcopal Zion Theology for a Uniting Church." *Journal of Religious Thought* 29 (Autumn–Winter 1972): 61–67.

———. *The Bearing of Berdyaev's and Tillich's Philosophies of History upon Theism*. Oberlin, OH: Master's Thesis, 1938. 97 pp.

"Services Held for General Officer-Educator Dr. John H. Satterwhite." *Star of Zion* 113 (June 8, 1989): 1, 3.

WWABA (90–91), *BDNM* (75), *AARS, HUBA*.

SCANTLEBURY, VICTOR A. (b. March 31, 1945), a bishop of the **Episcopal Church**, was born in Colón, Republic of Panama. While growing up he served the Episcopal Church as an acolyte, church school teacher, and lay reader. As a young man he was a cameraman for the news department of Panama's first television station, RPC Channel 4. He was ordained deacon on October 29, 1973, and priest on August 6, 1974. In about 1975 he married Marcia V. Thomas, with whom he has had three children.

Scantlebury was vicar of San Juan Episcopal Church for ten years and rector of St. Paul's Episcopal Church for six years. He was twice president of the Standing Committee, chair of the Youth Department and of the Committee on Diocesan Property, and professor of religion for two diocesan schools. He was youth coordinator for Province IX from 1976 to 1986 and represented the province at the first synod of the Anglican Church of the South Cone in 1986, in Salta, Argentina. He was the Province IX representative to the denomination's executive council from 1986 to 1991 and was a delegate to the Partners in Mission Consultation of the Iberian Churches in March 1987, in Madrid, Spain. From 1988 to 1992 he was on the board of trustees of the Presiding Bishop's Fund for World Relief. On March 15, 1991, he was consecrated suffragan bishop of the Diocese of Panama, with special responsibility for missionary work in the western part of the country.

ECA (1992).

SCATES, LUCILLE MARIE SHERROD (December 8, 1914–October 13, 1977), a bishop of the **Church of the Living God, the Pillar and Ground of Truth**, was born in Joliet, Illinois, the daughter of Luke and Rosa Melton. After her mother passed away she was reared by her older sister, Bishop Helen M. Lewis. She experienced salvation and the Pentecostal gifts at age nine and was ordained a minister on April 18, 1939, at Belle Glade, Florida.

By this time she was already married and ran a small business. Her church calling led her to sell the business and move to Nashville, Tennessee, where she founded Youth for Christ. In 1954 she moved to Chicago, Illinois, to assist the new church work in that region. At first she and her six children lived with Bishop L. E. Shelton and her sister, Elder Georgia Harris, but after only one week their apartment building burned down and Scates found lodging only through the **Salvation Army**. Finally, Mother Bursey, a member of the **Church of God in Christ**, provided her with two unfurnished rooms. Scates healed Bursey's husband and began to hold church meetings in those rooms. As the congregation grew she moved to rented facilities for worship, and was enabled to move around Illinois building up other bands of worshipers. In 1968 she purchased a permanent center in Joliet, Illinois and opened the Less Fortunate Saints Home for poverty-stricken church members. By the time of her death the Illinois area was one of the strongest in the Church of the Living God, the Pillar and Ground of Truth. In 1984 the 81st Church Anniversary was dedicated in her honor.

SFAY, BDA-AHP, RLOA.

SCHOOLER, ALEXANDER R., a bishop of the **Pentecostal Assemblies of the World** (PAW), emerged out of obscurity as a leader in the Assemblies soon after it adopted the non-Trinitarian Jesus Only theology in 1915–16. Little is known of his early life, but in 1918 Schooler is one of four African Americans, including **Garfield T. Haywood**, on a list of field superintendents for the organization. Located in Cleveland as pastor of the Church of Christ, he shared responsibility for the state of Ohio with one of the other African Americans, **Robert C. Lawson** of Columbus, who would leave the PAW the following year to found the **Church of Our Lord Jesus Christ of the Apostolic Faith**. At this time the Assemblies consisted of a number of widely scattered churches, many White, some Black, a few integrated.

In 1920 Schooler is noted as being the vice-general overseer under Haywood (as general overseer), and in addition served on the national committee on evangelism. In 1921 he was elected Executive Vice Chairman of the PAW. In 1922 he moved to the publication committee charged with starting the Assemblies' new magazine, *The Christian Outlook*. He appears again amid the national leadership of the ever-changing organization in 1923 and 1924 as a member of the seven-person board of presbyters. At the annual convention in 1923 he was selected for the Committee on Resolutions.

In 1924 a resolution was offered to the convention in an attempt to head off the split in the organization. It proposed a reorganization of the PAW into two districts, an Eastern District composed primarily of the Black members and a Western District of the White members. Schooler was elected to the original council to head the Eastern District. While this change was adopted, it did not prevent the schism of the majority of the White members, who left to form the Pentecostal Ministerial Alliance. The Pentecostal Assemblies, now largely a Black group, reorganized at the national level without White members. It abolished all the legislation which had been made to accommodate White sentiments, and a national caretaker leadership was put in place. Schooler, now living in Chicago, Illinois, as pastor of the Apostolic Faith Church, was continued on the board of presbyters for 1924.

In 1925 the PAW went through its greatest organizational changes. The leadership of elders was replaced with an episcopal system and the first bishops elected. Schooler, now back in Cleveland, was one of the original five bishops.

As Schooler rose to prominence out of obscurity, by the end of the 1920s he returned to that obscurity. In 1929 he is missing without explanation from the roster of the board of bishops of the PAW. It is known that at some point Schooler moved to California. He was still a relatively young man, but nothing more is known of his career from this point.

Golder, Morris E. *The Bishops of the Pentecostal Assemblies of the World*. Indianapolis, IN: The Author, 1980. 69 pp.
———. *History of the Pentecostal Assemblies of the World*. Indianapolis, IN: The Author, 1973. 195 pp.

SCHULTZ, DAVID THURMAN (1889–1972), a bishop of the **Pentecostal Assemblies of the World**, was born and raised in Mayfield, Kentucky. Having experienced salvation in 1921, he was called to the ministry the following year. He served pastorates in Casper, Wyoming, and Joplin and Kansas City, Missouri. Then in 1929, the Assemblies' presiding bishop, **Garfield T. Haywood**, asked Schultz to fill the vacuum by the move of **Floyd I. Douglas** to California from Louisville, Kentucky. Thus, with his wife Grace and their two children, Schultz moved to Louisville as pastor of Bethel Temple where he would remain for the next four decades.

Schultz emerged into prominence on the national level soon after settling in Louisville. In 1932 he served on the committee which attempted to work out a merger agreement with the White former members of the PAW who had left to found the Pentecostal Assemblies of Jesus Christ. In 1933 the National Pentecostal Young

People's Union was formed to mobilize the youth of the church, and Schultz was the first national treasurer for the organization.

By 1935 the PAW settled into a period of relative stability as the lengthy administration of **Samuel J. Grimes** was set in place. Grimes led in the creation of a new national structure and in 1935 Schultz was elected as the fourth bishop of the growing church. During the long years of his service, he continued as pastor of the church in Louisville while giving episcopal guidance at different times over Alabama, Arkansas, Tennessee, Texas, and Kentucky. It should be noted that as a policy, PAW bishops regularly served over districts in which they did not reside, while other bishops served over districts in which another bishop pastored.

Golder, Morris E. *The Bishops of the Pentecostal Assemblies of the World.* Indianapolis, IN: The Author, 1980. 69 pp.

————. *History of the Pentecostal Assemblies of the World.* Indianapolis, IN: The Author, 1973. 195 pp.

SCOTT, ISAIAH BENJAMIN (September 30, 1854–July 4, 1931), college president and the third African American missionary bishop of the Methodist Episcopal Church (now the **United Methodist Church**), was born in Midway, Woodford County, Kentucky, the son of Benjamin and Polly (Anderson) Scott. His father was a carpenter and a worker in the Underground Railroad before the Civil War. Scott attended private schools in Frankfort, Kentucky, and then public schools in Austin, Texas. He attended Clark College in Atlanta, Georgia, from 1874 to 1877, and received his B.A. in 1880 from Central Tennessee College (later Walden University) in Nashville, Tennessee. He taught school in the summer months to support himself.

He stayed in Nashville briefly in 1880–81 to study theology, and joined the Tennessee Annual Conference of the Methodist Episcopal Church, pastoring the Nashville Circuit. He went to Texas in May 1881 to be professor of mathematics at Prairie View State Normal and Industrial College. On May 24, 1881, he married Mattie J. Evans, with whom he had six children. He transferred his ministerial credentials to the Texas Conference and in 1882 left his teaching post to work in the local church. He was assigned to Trinity Methodist Episcopal Church in Houston (1883), followed by St. Paul's Methodist Episcopal Church in Galveston (1884–85). In 1886 he pastored Ebenezer Methodist Episcopal Church in Marshall. From 1887 to 1890 he was district superintendent of the Marshall District, and from 1891 to 1892 he was superintendent of the Houston District. From 1893 to 1896 he was president of Wiley College in Marshall, Texas, and during that time freed the school from debt and placed it on a firm financial footing.

From 1896 to 1904 Scott was editor of the denominational paper, *Southwestern Christian Advocate*, based in New Orleans, Louisiana. His compelling writing and effective leadership brought a substantial increase in the circulation and influence of the paper, and he gained a respected national reputation. Five consecutive times, beginning in 1888, he headed his Texas Annual Conference delegation to General Conference. For four years he served on the Book Committee and for four years he served on the General Committee on Missions, Freedman's Aid, and Church Extension. He attended the Methodist Ecumenical Conferences in Washington, D.C. (1891) and in London (1901). In May 1904, Scott was elected bishop for service in Liberia. He was the third African American missionary bishop for the Methodist Episcopal Church, following **Francis Burns** and **John W. Roberts**. He stayed in Liberia, providing successful leadership, and in 1911 attended the Methodist Ecumenical Conference in Toronto, Canada. In 1916 he retired to his home in Nashville, Tennessee.

Scott, Isaiah Benjamin. *Four Years in Liberia: The Quadrennial Report to the General Conference of 1908.* New York: Africa Diamond Jubilee Commission, Board of Foreign Missions of the Methodist Episcopal Church, 1908. 13 pp.

————. *Official Journal of the Liberia Annual Conference Held at Clay-Ashland, Feb. 3–8, 1909.* Monrovia, Liberia: College of West Africa Press, 1909.

WWAM, MB, EWM, NCAB (14), WWWA (1), WWCA (30–32), BAW, WWCR.

SCOTT, MANUEL L., SR. (b. c.1927), Baptist minister, author, and former vice-president of the **National Baptist Convention, U.S.A., Inc.**, received his B.A. in 1949 from Bishop College in Dallas, Texas. He married Thelma Jean Scott, with whom he had six children. From 1950 to 1982 he pastored Calvary Baptist Church in Los Angeles, California, and since 1982 he has been at the historic Saint John Baptist Church in Dallas, Texas.

Over the years his fame as an outstanding preacher has grown, and he has been guest preacher at numerous Baptist state conventions, colleges, and universities. He has participated in the Billy Graham Evangelistic Association and attended the International Congress for World Evangelization in Lausanne, Switzerland. He is a member of the General Council of the Baptist World

Alliance and is a former vice-president of the National Baptist Convention, U.S.A., Inc. He has authored two books, *From a Black Brother* (1971) and *The Gospel for the Ghetto* (1973).

"America's Fifteen Greatest Black Preachers." *Ebony* 39 (September 1984): 27–33.

SCOTT, MARSHALL LOGAN (October 27, 1909– March 13, 1991), seminary president and first Black moderator of the United Presbyterian Church, since 1983 a constituent part of the **Presbyterian Church, (U.S.A.)**, was born in Greensburg, Indiana, the son of Robert Logan and Martha (McCall) Scott. He received his B.A. in 1931 from Muskingum College in New Concord, Ohio, and his B.D. in 1934 from McCormick Theological Seminary in Chicago, Illinois. On August 25, 1934, he married Carolyn Zoe Smith, with whom he had four children. He was ordained a minister in the United Presbyterian Church in 1934 and pastored a church in Prattsburg, New York, from 1934 to 1940. Most of that time, from 1935 to 1940, he also pastored a church in Pultney, New York. From 1940 to 1944 he pastored the First Presbyterian Church in Columbus, Ohio, and from 1945 to 1952 he was an instructor at the Biblical Seminary in New York as well as dean of the Presbyterian Institute of Industrial Relations in New York City. During this time he pursued additional degrees, receiving his M.A. in 1948 and Ed.D. in 1953, both from Columbia University in New York City. From 1949 to 1952 he also taught at Princeton Theological Seminary in New Jersey. From 1952 to 1970 he continued to be dean of the Presbyterian Institute of Industrial Relations after it moved to the McCormick Theological Seminary campus in Chicago. From 1945 to 1970 he was also assistant secretary of the Urban Church Department, Board of National Missions of the United Presbyterian Church.

On May 17, 1962 Scott was elected the first Black moderator of the United Presbyterian Church, serving a one-year term. He was a major figure in the denomination, serving from 1958 to 1966 as chair of the Committee to Study the Nature of the Ministry, and from 1963 to 1967 as chair of the Commission on Religion and Race. From 1963 to 1969 he chaired Chicago's Commission on Human Relations. In 1970 he was appointed president of McCormick Theological Seminary, where he remained until retirement in 1975. He was the author of one book, *The Christian and Social Action* (1948).

Bennett, Lerone Jr. "Black Firsts." *Ebony* 37 (March 1982): 128–133.
"Deaths." *The Christian Century* 108 (April 10, 1991): 394.
Scott, Marshall L. *The Christian and Social Action.* Philadelphia, PA: Westminster Press, 1948. 94 pp.
WWR (77), *WWA* (76–77).

SCOTT, NATHAN ALEXANDER, JR. (b. April 24, 1925), **Episcopal Church** priest, professor, and theologian, was born in Cleveland, Ohio, the son of Nathan A. and Maggie (Martin) Scott. He received his B.A. in 1944 from the University of Michigan, his B.D. in 1946 from Union Theological Seminary in New York City, and his Ph.D. in 1949 from Columbia University in New York City. On December 21, 1946 he married Charlotte Hanley, with whom he had two children.

He was dean of the chapel at Virginia Union University in 1946–47, and in 1948 became an instructor at Howard University in Washington, D.C. He was promoted to assistant professor in 1950 and associate professor of humanities in 1953. From 1953 to 1955 he was also director of the general education program in humanities. In 1955 he moved to the University of Chicago as assistant professor, was promoted to associate professor in 1958, and then in 1964 became full professor of theology and literature. In 1972 he was named Shailer Mathews Professor of Theology and Literature. He was ordained an Episcopal priest in 1960, and from 1966 to 1976 was canon theologian of the Cathedral of St. James in Chicago.

In 1976 he was named professor of English and William R. Kenan professor of religious studies at the University of Virginia at Charlottesville, where he has since remained. In 1980 he became chair of the Religious Studies Department. He has received numerous awards and honorary degrees, and is a trustee of Seabury-Western Theological Seminary in Evanston, Illinois. He has been an extremely prolific writer, with well over twenty books to his credit, beginning with *The Tragic Vision and the Christian Faith* (1957). Other major works have included *The Broken Center: Studies in the Theological Horizon of Modern Literature* (1966), *The Unquiet Vision* (1969), and *The Legacy of Reinhold Neibuhr* (1975). He has become a significant voice in the field of religion and literature, and in 1990 Mary Gerhart edited a book of essays in his honor, *Morphologies of Faith: Essays in Religion and Culture in Honor of Nathan A. Scott, Jr.*

Bims, Hamilton. "A Search for God in Contemporary Literature." *Ebony* 30 (April 1975): 44–52.
Scott, Nathan A., ed. *Adversity and Grace: Studies in Recent*

American Literature. Chicago, IL: University of Chicago Press, 1968. 269 pp.

———. *The Legacy of Reinhold Neibuhr.* Chicago, IL: University of Chicago Press, 1975. 124 pp.

———. *The New Orpheus: Essays Toward a Christian Poetic.* New York: Sheed and Ward, 1964. 431 pp.

———. *The Poetics of Belief: Studies in Coleridge, Arnold, Pater, Santayana, Stevens, and Heidegger.* Chapel Hill, NC: University of North Carolina Press, 1985. 198 pp.

———. *The Wild Prayer of Longing: Poetry and the Sacred.* New Haven, CT: Yale University Press, 1971. 124 pp.

IBAW, IBAWCB, OTSB, WWABA (92–93), *AARS, HUBA, BDNM* (75), *CA* (new revision, vol. 5), *WWA* (90–91), *WWR* (85), *EBA.*

SCOTT, SOLOMON TIMOTHY (August 20, 1790–January 4, 1862), 9th bishop of the **African Methodist Episcopal Zion Church** (AMEZ), was born in Smyrna, Delaware. He was converted there in 1830 and was licensed to preach the following year. He was ordained deacon on June 20, 1834, and elder on June 18, 1835. He was known as a preacher with a penchant for metaphors and was particularly famous for two sermons, one he called the "fish" sermon and the other an anti-slavery sermon. He was consecrated bishop on June 30, 1856, and served four very turbulent years. He had a tender and humble disposition and felt heavily the responsibility of his office. He retired in 1860 and passed away two years later.

AMEZC, EWM, HAMEZC.

SECOND CUMBERLAND PRESBYTERIAN CHURCH IN U.S. *See:* **CUMBERLAND PRESBYTERIAN CHURCH OF AMERICA.**

SECRETARIAT FOR BLACK CATHOLICS. The official **Roman Catholic Church** office concerned with Black members. Approval for a secretariat for Black Catholics was given by the National Conference of Catholic Bishops in 1986 and formally established in 1988. It is the conference's principal means of communicating with and listening to the Black constituency. It also serves as an information bureau for the national church on matters of concern to Black Roman Catholics. The office was created, in part, in response to the pastoral letter of the Black Catholic bishops, "What We Have Seen and Heard," issued in 1984 and the continued growth of Black membership (60 percent between 1975 and 1985). The secretariat is headed by the Bishops' Committee, the members of which are elected by the conference. The first committee consisted of Archbishop **Eugene A. Marino** and Bishops **Moses B. Anderson, Carl A. Fisher, Joseph Francis**, Joseph Florenza, Joseph Gozman, and **John H. Ricard**.

The secretariat is headquartered in Washington, D.C., at the conference's office. The Bishops' Committee meets three times a year.

SELMA UNIVERSITY. A **National Baptist Convention, U.S.A., Inc.** school. Selma University, Selma, Alabama, was begun by the Colored Baptist Convention of Alabama (later affiliated with the National Baptist Convention, U.S.A., Inc.). Initially turned down for assistance by White Baptists from whom it sought financial support, the convention proceeded to raise initial funds on its own and was finally able to open the school in Selma, Alabama, in 1878. In the beginning the Alabama Normal and Theological School met in the local African American Baptist church. Its name clearly identified its two priorities of training teachers for the public schools and ministers. A new campus was purchased several years later.

In 1880 the American Baptist Home Mission Society acknowledged the accomplishments of the school's founders and began to give it financial support. In 1881 **W. H. McAlpine**, one of the leading Black educators of the century, became president of the school. He built it into one of the leading African American schools in the country, and in 1895 the name was changed to Alabama Baptist Colored University. It became Selma University in 1908.

Through much of the century, the university operated as a junior college and only slowly developed into a full senior college, a process completed in 1979.

Fitts, Leroy. *A History of Black Baptists.* Nashville, TN: Broadman Press, 1985. 368 pp.

SENATLE, HAROLD BENJAMIN, 102nd bishop of the **African Methodist Episcopal Church** (AME), was born in Christiana, South Africa, the son of William and Anna Senatle. He was educated in Christiana and married Anna Gofengake, with whom he has had five children. He was ordained in 1950 and his pastorates have included Brandford AME Church in the Orange Free State; Mt. Sinnah AME Church in Edenburg; Mt. Pisgah AME Church in Bethlehem; Mt. Nebo AME Church in the Wilkom; Mt. Zion AME Church in Gloemfontein; and St. Peter AME Church in East

Transvaal, all in South Africa. He was administrative assistant to a number of bishops.

At the 1984 General Conference in Kansas City, Missouri, Senatle was elected bishop and for a time served both the Eighteenth and Nineteenth Episcopal Districts in Africa, since about 1988 covering just the Nineteenth. He has remodeled the R. R. Wright School of Religion, established a number of new congregations, purchased a new episcopal residence in Johannesburg, and remodeled the episcopal residence in Lesotho, South Africa. He founded the Self-Help Knitting Program in Lesotho and purchased the land for a new school in Mozambique. In Mozambique alone over five hundred new members have been added to church rolls. The only Black-owned piece of property in Johannesburg is the site of the new AME church headquarters, the construction of which Senatle supervised.

FEDHR.

SEVENTH-DAY ADVENTIST CHURCH. The Seventh-day Adventist Church is a worldwide Protestant denomination which came to birth after the Great Awakening of the late eighteenth and early nineteenth centuries. The direct roots of the church can be traced back to the Millerite Movement, which consisted of people from several denominations who were influenced by the teaching of the imminent return of Christ advocated by William Miller and other revivalists. When Christ did not return on the calculated day (an event known in Adventist circles as the Great Disappointment), the Millerites split into several groups. The most prominent of these groups officially organized in 1863 and assumed the name of Seventh-day Adventists. There were a number of people involved in the early formation of the group, but the names of the elected personnel responsible for the organization were James White, John H. Waggoner, John Loughborough, G. W. Amadon, Uriah Smith, George Lay, and Dan Palmer.

Doctrinal Development. In its early stages the church claimed the reformation principle of *sola scriptura*, and thus felt that a fixed set of doctrines was not necessary. However, in 1872 a set of 25 doctrinal statements were published, not to "secure uniformity," but "to meet inquiries," "to correct false statements," and "to remove erroneous impressions." By 1889 the denominational *Yearbook* listed an expanded list of 28 doctrines. Following a request from the African division of the church, the General Conference revised this list and in 1931 published a statement of 22 fundamental beliefs.

The latest stage in development took place in 1980 when the General Conference established 27 "Fundamental Beliefs of Seventh-day Adventists," summarized below under six headings:

1. THE DOCTRINE OF GOD. God who is the Father, Son, and Holy Spirit speaks to humans through his Word which is contained in the Holy Scriptures.

2. THE DOCTRINE OF MAN. The first man and woman were created by God on the sixth literal day of this earth's history. Humans can only exist with the breath of God which returns to Him after death. A person remains in an unconscious state after death until the resurrection.

3. THE DOCTRINE OF SALVATION. Before the world was created, a great controversy has been taking place between Christ and Satan. As a result of this controversy, Satan and the angels who allied with him were expelled from heaven and made their home on earth. Satan has succeeded in seducing the whole of humanity into sin which leads to eternal death. The perfect life, death, and resurrection of Christ has made it possible for worthy humans to escape this death.

4. THE DOCTRINE OF THE CHURCH. The church is comprised of all people who believe in the atoning sacrifice of Jesus Christ. The Seventh-day Adventist Church is the remnant church of Bible prophecy whose task it is to call people back to "true" worship. Consenting adults enter the church through the rite of baptism by immersion. Each church member is called to minister and receives at least one of the spiritual gifts. The identifying mark of the remnant church is the gift of prophecy, which the church believes was manifest greatly, though not uniquely, in the person of Ellen G. White.

5. THE DOCTRINE OF THE CHRISTIAN LIFE. The Christian will respond to God in faith and live obedient to His moral law. An important precept in God's law is the fourth commandment which calls for the observance of the seventh day of the week as a memorial of creation and redemption. God requires each person to return a faithful tithe and offering of all money earned. All Christians are also required to honor God in their bodies by abstaining from illegal narcotics, tobacco, alcohol, unclean foods, illicit sexual relationships, and attendance at "worldly" places.

6. THE DOCTRINE OF THE LAST THINGS. A number of events in nature, politics and society indicate that these are the final stages of this earth's history. Since October 22, 1844, Christ has moved into the Most Holy Place of the heavenly sanctuary

which signals the beginning of the "investigative judgment" of each person who has ever lived. When all the living and dead have been judged, their fates will be sealed. Christ will then return to the earth and the righteous dead will be resurrected, and together with the living will be transformed to immortal beings. All the living wicked will be slain at his appearing. The righteous will be taken to heaven for a millennium. At the end of the millennium, Christ and all the righteous will return to the earth, and the resurrected wicked along with the Devil and his angels will be consumed by a fire which will utterly cleanse the earth from sin.

The Early Development of the Work among Southern Blacks. True to their Millerite heritage, Seventh-day Adventists were very active in the anti-slavery campaign and published a large amount of literature to that effect. This stance made them unpopular in the South and hindered active proselytizing among any ethnic group. Also contributing to the unpopularity of the church in the South was its stress on a mandatory twenty-four hour break on the seventh day. This mandate was not pleasing to planters, who wanted maximum production from their workers.

The first known Adventist missionary to the South was Silas Osborn, a native of Kentucky, who had accepted the Adventist message in Iowa. He held meetings in Kentucky which resulted in the baptism of several Blacks, among others. One of his converts, W. K. Killen, a lawyer and a planter, brought many of his plantation laborers into the church. Killen soon started a self-supporting ministry, and consequently baptized a number of Blacks.

In 1871, E. B. Lane was appointed to work among the southern Blacks. He held evangelistic meetings between the segregated waiting rooms at the Edgefield Junction train station in Tennessee. As a result of these meetings the first recorded Seventh-day Adventist congregation which included Blacks was organized at Edgefield Junction in 1883. By 1886 southern pressure caused the segregation of the church, hence resulting in the first totally Black Seventh-day Adventist congregation.

Work was also taking place in Texas in the 1870s with Eddie Capman opening a freedman school which was operated by Mr. and Mrs. Joseph Clarke, both trained teachers. They soon felt a need for a trained minister, and in 1877 R. M. Kilgore, an ex-Union officer, responded to the call. Kilgore faced much opposition, especially from the Confederate contingency who called the Adventists "Yankees" come "to preach nigger equality."

Eventually, more Black churches were organized in the South. In 1890 A. Barry organized the Magazine Church in Louisville. Kentucky. Another was formed in 1891, at Bowling Green, Kentucky, a fourth in New Orleans, Louisiana in 1892, and a fifth in September 1894 at Nashville.

It was not until 1895 that a significant work was organized among Blacks. This was chiefly due to the commitment of James Edson White, the son of James and Ellen White. Edson gave up his business in Michigan and, along with Will Palmer of Battle Creek, started a "steamship evangelism" in the south. With limited support from the General Conference, the two men gathered enough funds to build a steamship which they christened the "Morning Star."

In January of 1895 the crew of the "Morning Star" headed down the Kalamazoo River for the Mississippi River. While travelling through Tennessee they were detained by the authorities and charged $500 for not having a licensed navigator. The fine was appealed and the crew waited in Memphis for a decision. While waiting they met a group of Black First-day Adventists who accepted the teachings of Seventh-day Adventism. Edson White used his own funds to provide a salary for the minister of this group. The fine was eventually dropped and the crew travelled on to Vicksburg, Mississippi which was to be the Morning Star's headquarters. White and Palmer started schools in some of the local Black churches, and held worship services in the ship on Saturdays. A number of the students joined the church, which created hostility between the Adventists and the local religious leaders. Consequently, the Adventists were barred from the local churches and had to construct a building of their own, which seated one hundred congregants.

White was soon to lose Palmer, who was asked by the General Conference to work on another project. White continued to work with the dedicated support of his wife and other concerned individuals. He organized the self-supporting Southern Missionary Society (SMS), incorporated in 1898, and chose Nashville for its headquarters. The task of the SMS was to administrate the educational and evangelical mission among southern Blacks. In 1901 the SMS became an official department of the Southern Union Conference of Seventh-day Adventists. Within eight years, the SMS was operating in ten southern states, sponsoring 55 primary schools with over 1,800 students. It also operated medical facilities for Blacks in the Nashville and Atlanta areas. In 1909, the SMS was assimilated into the General Conference Negro Department which had been recently formed.

Edson White's dedication portrays the greatest contribution to Adventist growth among southern Blacks in the nineteenth and early twentieth centuries. However, it would be unfair to overlook the work of one Brother Maxey, who in 1896 held meetings in Palatka, Florida, resulting in a Black company being formed. Maxey placed one of the converts, Charles Maynor, in charge of the company. Soon Black congregations were started all over Florida.

In 1896, the General Conference made a significant contribution to Black Adventists when, following the directions of Ellen White, they purchased an old 360–acre plantation in Huntsville, Alabama, upon which to begin a school. The school opened in 1896 with fifty students under the name Oakwood Industrial School. Its purpose was to accommodate the students who graduated from the "Morning Star" schools. By 1917, the school was promoted to junior college status and became known as **Oakwood College**. Among the products of the church's growing school system was Eva Dyke, the first Black woman to receive a Ph.D. (Harvard, 1921).

The Early Development of Work among Northern Blacks. Although many of the church's early resources and activities were in the North, a significant work among Blacks did not start there until 1902. When the work did start it was spearheaded by Blacks and pioneered by J. H. Carrol, a former Roman Catholic who made his headquarters in New York City. Carrol was soon overshadowed by one of his converts, James K. Humphrey.

James K. Humphrey was a former Baptist minister from Jamaica, West Indies. Humphrey, an excellent organizer, was chosen to pastor the first group of Black believers. By 1920, he had started four congregations, the largest being the First Harlem Church with a membership of 600. During this time, the White administration acted negligently towards the Black constituency. Although the Black membership made significant financial contributions to the church through tithes and freewill offerings, they were not allowed the full benefit of the growing Adventist system. Humphrey appealed for justice but was repeatedly ignored. He resolved that the only way that Blacks could get fair treatment was if they controlled their own affairs. With this conviction he organized an independent operation for Black retirees which was named the "Utopia Park Project." When the conference officials were informed of the project, they ordered him to cease operations. Humphrey refused, and as a result, he and the entire First Harlem congregation were cut off from the conference.

The Rise of Black Leadership in the Church. As the number of Blacks increased in the denomination, prominent leaders emerged from among them. One such leader was **Charles M. Kinney**, who was the first Black to be ordained into the Seventh-day Adventist ministry. He had shown promise while working for the Nevada Tract and Missionary Society, and was sent by conference leaders to Healdsburg College to study ministry. His first pastorate was at the Edgefield Junction Church in Tennessee. Another prominent leader was Harry Lowe, who is reputed to be the first Black convert. Records show that he also held the pastorate of the Edgefield Junction Church, and was the organizer of the first Black Seventh-day Adventist camp meeting in 1901. Other Blacks served as missionaries, with James Petterson being sent to Jamaica in 1892, Anna Knight to India in 1901 and Thomas Branch to East Africa in 1902.

Observing the ability and success of these Black leaders, Edson White was convinced that the success of the work among Blacks depended on the institution of Black leadership. In the early 1900s he extended a call to Frank G. Warnick, a former Baptist minister, to manage the Black work in Mississippi and its territories. Warnick received much opposition but led the work with much success.

Blacks were also given the opportunity to serve on the General Conference when in 1918 W. H. Green was nominated as the first Black secretary for the North American Negro Department. He was succeeded by George E. Peters in 1928. Anna Knight also had the opportunity to serve in a number of international capacities until her retirement. However, it was not until 1954, when Edward E. Cleveland was made a Ministerial Association associate secretary, that a Black was appointed to a position that placed him in charge of non-Blacks. Owen A. Troy followed in 1959 with an appointment to the secretariat of the Sabbath School Department. By 1962 the first Black general vice-president was elected in the person of Frank L. Peterson. Today, there are a large number of Blacks in top General Conference positions.

The Formation of Regional Conferences. James K. Humphrey, Charles M. Kinney and Edson White all saw the need for Blacks to administrate the work among Blacks. The General Conference had tried a compromise when they set up the North American Negro Department in 1909. It was not until 1918 that the department received its first Black field secretary in the person of W. H. Green. Within three years of Green's leadership, the Black membership doubled to 7,000. This statistic proved the reasoning behind Black leadership, but the conference administration still refused to accommodate the request for separate government.

In 1943 Lucy Byard, a seriously ill Black Adventist of light complexion, was refused treatment at the Adventist Hospital in Takoma Park after she had been admitted as a White patient and then discovered to be Black. She died before she could receive treatment at the Freedman Hospital across the state line. This incident, along with the fact that many other Adventist institutions actively practiced segregation, led to a meeting that was to change the face of Black Adventism in America.

The Birth of the Regional Conferences. Several laypersons met at the Ephesus Church in Washington, D.C., on October 16, 1943, and organized the National Association for the Advancement of Worldwide Work among Colored Seventh-day Adventists. Joseph Dodson was elected chairperson and Alma J. Scott vice-chairperson. John H. Wagner, who was secretary for the Black department of the Columbia Union, acted as advisor. The group aroused the awareness of the African American constituency around the country. They approached the General Conference President, J. Lamar McElhany, and asked for immediate action concerning the issue of separate conferences for African Americans. McElhany was sympathetic to the Black cause, and was able to persuade the General Conference to consider the proposition for separate conferences at its 1944 Spring Council. On April 10, 1944, the decision was made to allow Black conferences to be formed at the discretion of the Union conferences.

The Lake Union was the first to act, and on September 26, 1944, at the Shiloh Church on Chicago's South Side, the Black membership voted to organize the Lake Region Conference of Seventh-day Adventists, to be presided over by J. Gershon Dasent. The Atlantic and Columbia Unions followed suit, and the Northeastern and Allegheny Conferences emerged. They were soon joined by the South Atlantic, Southeastern, South Central, Central States, and Southwest Region Conferences. The Blacks along the Pacific coast and in the Northern Union opted to remain with the existing White conferences.

The "Regional Conferences" were faced with many obstacles in their infancy, as they were forced to govern large territories with extremely limited resources. In spite of the odds, they experienced remarkable success. The total Black membership at the time of the organization of Regional Conferences was 18,000, but by 1966 there were more than 60,000 Black Adventists in North America. The only other Protestant church in

North America growing more rapidly among African Americans was the Southern Baptist. More recent figures displayed in the October 1987 edition of the *North American Regional Voice* (the official paper of the Regional Conferences) show the remarkable way in which Black Seventh-day Adventism had developed in the United States of America by 1986. Membership had increased to 169,160, reflecting 24 percent of the total North American membership. Tithe income for the year had amounted to a massive $50,590,000. Black Adventists were controlling 91 primary schools, eight secondary schools, and one college. They also maintained 81 of the 9,861 beds in the North American Division Adventist Health system.

Through the twentieth century, the African American membership within Seventh-day Adventism has steadily increased, from 3,500 in 1918 to 18,000 in 1944. Following the separationist policies institutionalized at the beginning of the century, the church formed a variety of structures for Black members. In 1934, the *Message*, the church's periodical for Black members, was begun. In the last half of the twentieth century Black membership in the church has risen dramatically. By 1970 there were 74,000 members. Many White members became very conscious of them as the civil rights movement began and Black members began to move for a greater voice in the church. The General Conference called for a desegregation of the church's institutions in 1965. The first Black student entered a southern college in Cleveland, Tennessee, in 1968. In 1972, the first Black to hold the position of general vice-president of the General Conference, Frank L. Peterson, assumed office and in 1979 Charles Bradford became the first Black to serve as president of the North American Division of the church. A major product of this era of Black consciousness in the church was *Free at Last*, a Black interpretation of the Adventist message by E. E. Cleveland. The church has remained an attractive religious home for Blacks, who make up approximately 18 percent of its American membership.

Baker, Delbert. *The Unknown Prophet*. Washington, DC: Review and Herald Publishing Association, 1987. 160 pp.

Bull, Malcolm, and Keith Lockhart. *Seeking a Sanctuary: Seventh-day Adventism and the American Dream*. San Francisco, CA: Harper & Row, 1989. 319 pp.

Cleveland, E. E. *Free at Last*. Washington, DC: Review and Herald Publishing Association, 1970.

Dudley, Charles. "Statistics of the Regional Work—1986." *North American Regional Voice* (October 1987): 7–8.

Foy, William E. *The Christian Experience of William E. Foy*. Portland, ME: Pearson, 1845.

Graybill, Ronald D. *E. G. White and Church Race Relations*.

Washington, DC: Review and Herald Publishing Association, 1970.

———. *Mission to Black America.* Mountain View, CA: Pacific Press Publishing Association, 1971. 144 pp.

Mesar, J. & T. Dybdahl. "The Utopian Park Affair and the Rise of Northern Black Adventists." *Adventist Heritage* 1 (January 1974): 117–21.

Reynolds, Louis B. *We Have Tomorrow: The Story of Seventh-day Adventists with an African Heritage.* Washington, DC: Review and Herald Publishing Association, 1984. 480 pp.

Schwarz, R. W. *Light Bearers to the Remnant.* Mountain View, CA: Pacific Press Pub. Association, 1979. 656 pp.

Seventh-day Adventist Encyclopedia. Washington, DC: Review and Herald Publishing Association, 1966. 1454 pp.

Keith A. Burton

SEYMOUR, WILLIAM JOSEPH (May 2, 1870–September 28, 1922), a leading figure in the spread of **Pentecostalism** in the United States, was born in Centerville, Louisiana, to Phyllis Salabarr and Simon Seymour. His early life is marked by little formal education and several visions of God. In 1895 he moved to Indianapolis, Indiana, where he obtained a job as a waiter and joined the Methodist Episcopal Church. In 1900 he moved to Cincinnati, Ohio, where he was influenced by Martin Wells Knapp, a former Methodist minister who had founded an independent Holiness school and mission. He affiliated with the **Church of God (Anderson, Indiana)** which had an interracial membership nationally.

The next years were event-filled for Seymour. He became ill with smallpox and though losing his left eye, recovered. The illness broke down the resistance to the call to the ministry he had felt and in 1902 he was ordained as a Church of God minister. He moved South in 1903 as an evangelist and having reconnected with his family in Houston, Texas, he settled there. In the summer of 1905 he became the interim pastor of a Black Holiness church during the absence of its pastor, Lucy Farrow, the niece of Frederick Douglass. While at the church he met Neely Terry, who had come to Houston from Los Angeles to visit relatives who attended Farrow's church.

Meanwhile, Farrow had met Charles F. Parham, who first developed **Pentecostalism** in his Bible school in Topeka, Kansas. The essence of the movement is a belief in the baptism of the Holy Spirit as an in filling of spiritual power, accompanied and evidenced by the individual believer speaking in an unknown tongue. In December 1905, Seymour talked Parham into letting him audit classes at the Bible school he had opened in Houston. Seymour sat outside the door of the all-White class and listened. Though he understood the teachings he did not yet have the experience.

In 1906, Seymour began the most intense period of his life, a period which would alter the shape of religion in America through the twentieth century. In January, with some expense money from Parham, he moved to Los Angeles to pastor a new Black Holiness congregation (affiliated with the predominantly White Southern California Holiness Association) which was formed by some Baptists who had been kicked out of the Baptist church for accepting Holiness teachings. Neely recommended Seymour.

By the end of the first week, he was locked out of the church by those upset with the Pentecostal message. Through conversations with Seymour, the association's president and several leaders were converted and began attending the prayer meetings. On April 9 at a home on Bonnie Brae Street, in the midst of the evening meeting, in response to Seymour's preaching, people began to speak in tongues. The Pentecostal revival had begun. Seymour himself received the experience on April 12. A few days later the group rented larger facilities, an abandoned building on Azusa Street, formerly the home of First **African Methodist Episcopal Church** of Los Angeles.

Here meetings were attended by Blacks, Hispanics, and Whites, many of whom received the baptism of the Holy Spirit. The *Los Angeles Times* ran a feature article on the revival on April 18, the same day as the San Francisco earthquake. As word of the happenings circulated through the Holiness churches in Los Angeles and surrounding communities, Seymour's mission was crowded for three services daily.

By September, when Seymour began his periodical, *The Apostolic Faith*, he had ordained some ministers who had begun preaching on the street and raising up additional congregations. As those commissioned by Seymour and the tabloid periodical circulated around the country, people began to arrive from throughout the United States and Canada. Seymour began to call the movement generated at Azusa "Pentecostal." At the beginning of 1907 he formally incorporated the Azusa Street Apostolic Faith Mission of Los Angeles.

The years 1907 and 1908 marked the height of the revival in Los Angeles. Numerous people, both Black and White, who were to assume leading roles in the movement around the country arrived and received the baptism of the Holy Spirit. Among the African Americans was **Charles H. Mason**, founder of the **Church of God in Christ**. Already in 1906 F. W.

Williams had taken the revival message to Alabama where he founded the **Apostolic Faith Mission Church of God**.

The year 1908 started as if it were to be an even more expansive time, but it then saw the first of three major disasters which were to virtually destroy Seymour's ministry. On May 13 Seymour married Jennie Evans Moore, the first woman to speak in tongues under his preaching in April 1906. As a result of the marriage, Clara Lum, the administrative assistant for the newspaper, stole the mailing list and took it to Portland, Oregon, where Florence Crawford had begun an independent work and continued publishing *The Apostolic Faith*. From that point on, while the work in Los Angeles remained vital, the mission's influence around the country was lost.

In 1911 the next disaster hit when William H. Durham split the mission over both the racial issue (he was White) and a doctrinal dispute (he did not share Seymour's Holiness emphasis continued from the Church of God). The final disaster came in 1913 at the Pentecostal camp meeting at Los Angeles, at which the Trinity became the object of attack. As a result, over 300 people, including all of the Blacks (many of whom were regular attendees at Azusa) accepted the new non-Trinitarian theology. Almost overnight Seymour's following was reduced to about 20 people.

During the remaining nine years of his life, Seymour traveled around the country speaking to mostly African American audiences, a few of which became the seeds of new congregations. In 1915 he authored a handbook, the *Doctrines and Discipline*, to guide those associated with his mission. It made provision for leadership by a bishop who would be an African American. He died of a heart attack in 1922 and his wife succeeded him as pastor of the mission. She lost the mission in 1931 and at the time of her death in 1936 her home was in the midst of foreclosure proceedings. It was lost in 1938 and the work in Los Angeles discontinued. Some of the churches he started in the East have continued over the years and now form a set of Apostolic Faith denominations. They have recently formed an ecumenical association as the **United Fellowship of the Original Azusa Street Mission,** headquartered in Jefferson, Ohio.

Nelson, Douglas J. *For Such a Time as This: The Story of Bishop William J. Seymour and the Azusa Street Revival.* Birmingham, England; Ph.D. dissertation, University of Birmingham, 1981. 346 pp.

Nickel, Thomas R. *Azusa Street Outpouring.* Hanford, CA: Great Commission International, 1979. 42 pp.

Tinney, James S. *In the Tradition of William J. Seymour: Essays Commemorating the Dedication of Seymour House at Howard University.* Washington, DC: Spirit Press, 1978. 102 pp.

SHAFFER, CORNELIUS THADDEUS (January 3, 1847–March 27, 1919), 29th bishop of the **African Methodist Episcopal Church** (AME), was born in Troy, Ohio, the third son of John Shelby and Margaret (Otis) Shaffer. He attended public schools in Ohio and Indiana and was converted in Fountain City, Indiana, in 1860, joining the AME Church the following year. In 1864 he enlisted as a soldier in the Union Army and served in the 23rd Ohio Colored Infantry and the 100th U.S. Colored Infantry. After the war he was licensed to preach (1867) and enrolled in Berea College, Kentucky (1867–69). He joined the Kentucky Conference in 1870, and immediately transferred to the Ohio Conference, taking the AME church in Newark, Ohio. On October 26, 1870, he married Annie Marie Taylor, with whom he had three children. He was ordained deacon in 1872 and elder in 1874.

In 1871 he was moved to Delaware, Ohio, followed by Cadiz, Ohio (1873), where he was privately tutored by the superintendent of the public schools. From 1874 to 1877 he was appointed to Xenia, Ohio, and then he transferred to the New York Conference, taking the Fleet Street AME Church in Brooklyn. While there he took courses in Hebrew from a rabbi. In 1880 he was assigned to Allen Chapel AME Church in Philadelphia, and continued his education with tutoring from Dr. W. R. Harper, later president of the University of Chicago. In 1884 he was appointed to the Bethel AME Church in Baltimore, Maryland, serving there for two years. In 1886 he moved back to Philadelphia to pastor Union AME Church. This church was small enough to accommodate another educational challenge he had set for himself as a student in Jefferson Medical College in Philadelphia. He graduated with his M.D. degree in 1888 and the following year was sent to the prestigious Mother Bethel AME Church in Philadelphia.

In two short years (1889–91) at Mother Bethel, Shaffer paid off an old mortgage, purchased additional land, tore down the old church, and almost completed a new church. In 1892, on the basis of his many successful pastorates, he was elected the first Secretary-Treasurer of the Church Extension Society, holding that position for the next eight years. When he began, there was no money and he had to serve three years as presiding elder of the Philadelphia District for support. By the end of his tenure he had collected and disbursed for church purposes over $100,000, and had helped over 500 churches.

Shaffer was elected bishop in May 1900, and assigned to the Fifth Episcopal District, which stretched nearly 3,000 miles from St. Louis to Seattle, Washington. In his day he was the only bishop who was also a practicing physician. When Bishop **M. M. Moore** died in November 1900, his area of Africa was added to Shaffer's responsibilities. He visited Africa in 1902 and while there made arrangements to build a boys' industrial school near Arthington, Liberia, the first school of its kind for the AME Church in Africa. The school soon came to be called Shaffer Boys' High School. The national legislature of Liberia passed a bill providing some monetary support for the school for the first five years. Back in the Fifth District he improved the facilities at Western University in Quindaro, Kansas, and was president of its board of trustees from 1901 to 1903. From 1904 to 1912 he presided over the Fourth Episcopal District (Indiana, Illinois, Iowa, Michigan, Ontario, and Kentucky Conferences), and from 1912 to 1916 he was assigned to the Third Episcopal District (Ohio, West Virginia, and Pittsburgh Conferences). He was a delegate to the World Methodist Conference in 1911 and was president of the board of trustees of Wilberforce University in Ohio from 1912 to 1916.

Shaffer, Cornelius Thaddeus. *Pastors Visiting Companion and Diary.* 1885.
EWM, HAMEC, WWCR, BAMEC, WWWA (1), *CEAMEC.*

SHARPTON, ALFRED (b. 1954), a Pentecostal minister (**Church of God in Christ**) and prominent social activist, was born in New York City. His father, Alfred Sr., was a wealthy builder who soon deserted the family. His mother, a seamstress, then went on welfare, and the family moved from a two-family home in Hollis, Queens, to an apartment in Crown Heights, Brooklyn. Sharpton was preaching at the age of four and was ordained at age ten by the Rev. F. D. Washington, a Pentecostal minister. At age thirteen famous soul singer James Brown introduced him to the music world and became a father figure to him.

As a young man, Sharpton developed an organization called the National Youth Movement. For a time, it used the offices of Spring Records, owned by Julie Rifkin, an associate of James Brown. Though Rifkin has denied it, Sharpton has said that Rifkin introduced him to a number of people who later turned out to be organized crime figures, including Michael Franzese. The F.B.I. was conducting an undercover operation, and in 1983 one of its agents, posing as a colleague of Franzese interested in meeting the boxing promoter Don King, met with Sharpton. At the meeting

the agent turned the subject to drugs and although Sharpton said nothing incriminating, the F.B.I. later "bluffed" him into thinking they had a case against him. What the F.B.I. wanted was for Sharpton to provide information they could use to build a case against Daniel and Joseph Pagano, who reportedly ran Genovese family operations in Westchester and Rockland counties. In 1986 a successful case was brought against them, and the F.B.I. has said that Sharpton was a key "confidential source." Sharpton has denied providing that information, but has said he has voluntarily given information about other drug and organized crime investigations after being threatened by a mobster in the record industry. These murky episodes severely harmed Sharpton's credibility with a number of groups.

What Sharpton is most known for is serving as an advocate and advisor in racially charged cases such as the beating of Alfred Jermaine Ewell in June 1991 by White teenagers in Atlantic Beach, Long Island. In such cases a family member may call for him, the family's minister may suggest his services, or Sharpton may take the initiative in contacting the family. He will often pray with them and offer to cover funeral or other expenses for the victim. If his services are accepted, he supervises relations with the media and police and develops a strategy for keeping the issue in the forefront of public awareness. A major part of that strategy is a neighborhood march, and in some cases multiple marches. His trademark chant is "No Justice, No Peace!" Some of these families have become his strongest supporters, saying that he was there when they needed him.

Others have suggested that Sharpton's skill at handling the media and representing the downtrodden is overshadowed by general questions of motives and judgment. He has been criticized for rushing to the support of defendants without fully judging the merits or facts of the case. He himself has apologized for earlier years in which he used highly inflammatory language to express blanket condemnations of Whites and of Blacks who disagreed with him. In about 1990 he solidified a relationship with New Alliance, a controversial left-wing political group working for the rights of minority groups. Since then the group has provided as much as 50 percent of the marchers for his demonstrations, and through speaking engagements and other business enterprises has provided Sharpton with about $12,000 of his estimated annual $50,000 in income. Other income derives from other speaking engagements, consulting fees, and as an assistant to singer James Brown.

Early in 1992 Sharpton announced that he was going to enter the New York Democratic primary for the United States Senate. Observers give him little chance of winning, but that may not be his only objective. Sharpton has said that even if he only picks up about ten percent of the votes, it would be a boost to his legitimacy, and in the meantime he would be able to debate his opponents. One problem of the race is that he does not live in New York, but resides in an apartment in Englewood, New Jersey, with his wife, Cathy Lee Jordan, and their two daughters. The rules, however, only require that he be a resident of New York at the actual time of victory in the Senate race. Sharpton came in third in a field of four contenders, garnering fourteen percent of the votes cast. In spite of this loss, it is likely that he will continue to be a familiar and controversial figure in the life of New York for some time to come.

Gottlieb, Martin. "Sharpton Bidding to Draw Votes as Well as News." *New York Times* (January 26, 1992): 25.

Scott, Walter. "Personality Parade." *Parade: The Sunday Newspaper Magazine* (March 1, 1992): 2.

BH, NYTBS (1991).

SHAW, ALEXANDER PRESTON (April 18, 1879– March 7, 1966), the third non-missionary African-American bishop of the Methodist Episcopal Church (now the **United Methodist Church**), was born near Abbeville, Lafayette County, Mississippi, the fourth of seven children in the family of Duncan Preston and Maria (Petty) Shaw. Both parents were former slaves and his father was a Methodist minister of the Upper Mississippi Conference. Shaw was converted at age eleven at a revival conducted by his father. As a young boy his school classes were conducted on an irregular basis in church buildings, and he obtained the bare essentials of education. In 1893 he entered Rust College in Holly Springs, Mississippi on the fifth grade level, and there he completed his normal and college training, receiving his B.A. in 1902. He supported himself as a lineman for the new telephone company. He received his B.D. in 1906 from Gammon Theological Seminary in Atlanta, Georgia, then did about two years of postgraduate work at Boston University. He was ordained deacon in 1907 and elder in 1909.

His first church appointment was in Westminster, Maryland (1908–09), followed by Harrisburg, Pennsylvania (1909–11). In about 1911 he married Lottye B. Simon, with whom he had six children. At his next church, the John Mann Methodist Episcopal Church in Winchester, Virginia (1911–15), the parsonage was a one-and-a-half-story building, and Shaw, who was six feet four inches tall, could not stand upright in any room

upstairs. Repairs were begun to fix the situation, but he was moved before they were complete. He then pastored at Wesley Chapel in Little Rock, Arkansas (1915–17) and Wesley Methodist Episcopal Church in Los Angeles, California (1917–31). All of these pastorates were successful, and in 1931 he was elected a delegate to the Sixth Methodist Ecumenical Conference in Atlanta, Georgia.

In 1931 he became editor of the Southwestern edition of the denominational paper, the *Christian Advocate*. Such an editorship was often the stepping-stone to the bishopric for Black clergy, as had already been the case with Black clergy **Isaiah B. Scott** and **Robert E. Jones**. In May 1936 Shaw was elected bishop, the third Black, non-missionary bishop of the Methodist Episcopal Church, after Jones (1920) and **Matthew W. Clair, Sr.** (1920). Before that there had been four African-American bishops consecrated specifically for service in Liberia—**Francis Burns**, **John W. Roberts**, **Alexander P. Camphor**, and Scott.

Shaw was assigned to the New Orleans Episcopal Area, serving all-Black conferences. In 1939 the Methodist Episcopal Church merged with the Methodist Episcopal Church (South) and the Methodist Protestant Church to form the Methodist Church, and as part of the restructuring the nineteen Black conferences of the former Methodist Episcopal Church, regardless of location, became part of the Central Jurisdiction. The Central Jurisdiction remained in place until 1968, when another merger created the United Methodist Church, and for the rest of his career Shaw's episcopacy was always within the conferences of the Central Jurisdiction. From 1940 to 1952 he was assigned to the Baltimore Episcopal Area, where he became known for eliminating mortgages on old churches and starting new churches. He wrote a number of brochures, including *Thy Kingdom Come* (1944), *The Spirit of Abraham Lincoln*, and *What Must the Negro Do To Be Saved* (later published as an article). He wrote two books, *Christianizing Race Relations as a Negro Sees It* (1928). A brother wrote a book about Shaw, called *The Life and Work of Bishop Alexander P. Shaw* (1948). He retired in 1952, but was called back to active service in 1953 after the death of **Robert N. Brooks** and served the New Orleans Episcopal Area until 1956.

Shaw, Alexander P. *Christianizing Race Relations as a Negro Sees It*. Los Angeles: Wetzel Publishing Co., 1928. 88 pp.

———. "What Must the Negro Do To Be Saved?" *Religion in Life* 17 (Autumn 1948): 540–548.

Shaw, James Beverly Ford. *The Life and Work of Bishop Alexander P. Shaw*. Nashville, TN: Parthenon Press, 1948. 215 pp.

EWM, RLA, MB, BAW, AARS, HUBA.

SHAW, BENJAMIN GARLAND (August 26, 1878–April 14, 1951), 40th bishop of the **African Methodist Episcopal Zion Church** (AMEZ), was born in Pope, Panola County, Mississippi, the son of Charles and Bridget (Jackson) Shaw. He was ordained deacon on November 13, 1898, and elder on November 19, 1899. His first pastorate was at the AMEZ Church in Cotton Plant, Mississippi, in 1899, and the following year he pastored the Clinton Mission in Greenwood, Mississippi, while he attended Greenwood College in the same town. From 1901 to 1905 he was assigned to Payne Chapel AMEZ Church in Little Rock, Arkansas, while he was a student at Philander Smith College. He earned his B.A. degree from that school in 1904. In June 1905 he married Garnett Wilkins, with whom he had three children.

From 1905 to 1910 he was appointed to Hood Temple AMEZ Church in Evansville, Indiana. While there he completed a course (1907) at the Louisville Medical College, some 100 miles away. From 1910 to 1920 he built and pastored the Metropolitan AMEZ Church in St. Louis, Missouri. This was where he first gained national prominence, creating there the largest congregation in Zion Methodism. From 1920 to 1924 he was the first director of the Bureau of Evangelism for the denomination.

Shaw was consecrated bishop on May 20, 1924, the first person in the denomination to move from the mission field directly into the bishopric. He spent most of the rest of his career presiding over the Western North Carolina, North Alabama, Blue Ridge, South Georgia, and Georgia Conferences. At the 1936 General Conference charges were filed against Shaw concerning the placing of a Presbyterian minister in the pastorate of Metropolitan AMEZ Church in Birmingham, Alabama, and the misappropriation of certain funds. He was required to make restitution, but was not suspended.

Perhaps his single greatest achievement as bishop was the New Goler Metropolitan AMEZ Church at Winston-Salem, North Carolina, a division of the old Goler Memorial AMEZ Church. He was also responsible for the Clement Memorial AMEZ Church in Charlotte, North Carolina. He was considered the leading evangelist and preacher of the church. He was also a champion of labor unions and spoke often on behalf of the poor. His first wife passed away in about 1940 and he then married a woman named Maybelle. In 1941 he succeeded Bishop **Lynwood W. Kyles** as senior bishop and maintained that status until his death. He died of a heart attack in Salisbury, North Carolina, while tending to conference business.

"The Anthology of the AME Zion Bishops." *Star of Zion* 57 (September 28, 1933): 1, 6.
"Bishop Benjamin Garland Shaw." *A.M.E. Zion Quarterly Review* 59 (1949): 101.
"Bishop Benjamin Garland Shaw." *A.M.E. Zion Quarterly Review* 61 (1951): 50.
"In Memoriam." *A.M.E. Zion Quarterly Review* 62 (1951): 228–229.
"The Magnificent Qualities of Our Bishops: The Unique, Dynamic, Inimitable Evangelist, Bishop Benjamin Garland Shaw." *Star of Zion* 70 (May 16, 1946): 1, 8.
"New Era of Zion Methodism." *Star of Zion* 48 (August 7, 1924): 1, 5.
"Zion's Senior Bishops During the Twentieth Century." *Star of Zion* 104 (March 27, 1980): 1, 2.
AARS, AMEZC, WWCA (38–40), HAMEZC.

SHAW, HERBERT BELL (February 9, 1908–January 3, 1980), 57th bishop of the **African Methodist Episcopal Zion Church** (AMEZ), was born in Wilmington, North Carolina, the son of John Henry and Lummie Virginia (Hodges) Shaw. He attended public schools in Wilmington and St. Emma's Preparatory School in Castle Rock, Virginia. He was a student at Fisk University in Nashville, Tennessee from 1924 to 1926 and a student at Howard University School of Religion in Washington, D.C. from 1927 to 1928, but no degrees were recorded at either institution. He joined the Cape Fear Conference, North Carolina, in November 1927, and immediately transferred to the Philadelphia and Baltimore Conference, where he was ordained deacon in April 1928, as associate pastor of Union Wesley AMEZ Church in Washington, D.C. In 1929 he returned to his home conference and was ordained elder on November 16, 1930.

From 1929 to 1937 he was pastor successively at Bowen's Chapel AMEZ Church, St. Andrew's AMEZ Church, and Price Memorial AMEZ Church, all in the area around Wilmington, North Carolina. On September 1, 1931, he married Mary Ardelle, with whom he had two children. From 1937 to 1943 he was presiding elder of the Wilmington District, and from 1943 to 1952 served as secretary-treasurer of the Department of Home Mission, Pension, and Ministerial Relief. His able business administration of this office gained him national recognition, and in 1950 he was a delegate to the World Methodist Conference in England, making also a trip to AMEZ conferences in 23 countries.

On May 18, 1952, Shaw was consecrated bishop and assigned to the First Episcopal District. Later assignments were to the Sixth Episcopal District (Florida, West Alabama, and South Carolina) from 1956 to 1960, Third Episcopal District (1960–68), Second Episcopal District (1968–72), and First Episcopal District (New York, Cape Fear, New England, West Indian area, and London-Birmingham, England Conferences) from 1972 to 1980. He was a member of the General Commission on Army and Navy Chaplains and from 1967 to 1970 was president and chair of the board of directors of the National Committee of Negro Churchmen (now the **National Conference of Black Churchmen**). In 1969 he supported the **Black Manifesto**'s call for the payment of billions of dollars in "reparations" by Whites to Blacks, and also called for payments to be made to the Native Americans.

In 1959 he resurrected the Bahama Island Conference and supervised its growth for the rest of his career, formally presenting the Jamaica, West Indies Conference in May 1968. He was also responsible for creating an organized AMEZ presence in London, England, and for formally presenting the London-Birmingham Conference in May 1972. In May 1976, he formally presented the Trinidad-Tobago Conference. With these major accomplishments of church growth, he was considered one of the church's great expansionists.

He was vice-chair of the board of trustees of both Livingstone College in Salisbury, North Carolina, and Clinton College in Rock Hill, South Carolina, and was a trustee of Lomax-Hannon College in Greenville, Alabama. He was a vice-president of the World Methodist Council from 1961 to 1971, was a president from 1971 to 1976, and a vice-president again from 1976 to 1980. He was a delegate to the World Methodist Conferences in 1956 (Lake Junaluska, North Carolina), 1961 (Oslo, Norway), 1966 (London, England), 1971 (Denver, Colorado), and others. He was vice-president at-large of the National Council of Churches from 1970 to 1973 and was a delegate to the Third Assembly of the World Council of Churches in New Delhi, India, in 1961. In 1972 he succeeded Bishop **Raymond Luther Jones** as senior bishop and maintained that status until his death. He was twice named by *Ebony* magazine as one of the most influential Black leaders in America, and in 1978 the New York Council of Churches gave him its Martin Luther King Freedom Brotherhood Award.

"Celebration of the Life of Herbert Bell Shaw." *Star of Zion* 104 (February 7, 1980): 1, 2.

"Herbert Bell Shaw." *Christian Century* 97 (February 27, 1980): 224.

"Herbert Bell Shaw." *Christianity Today* 24 (January 25, 1980): 53.

"Senior Bishop Herbert Bell Shaw Honored Twice." *Star of Zion* 102 (June 22, 1978): 1.

"Senior Bishop Shaw Passes." *Star of Zion* 104 (January 24, 1980): 1.

"World Methodist Council Offers Congratulations." *Star of Zion* 101 (May 26, 1977): 1, 2.

"Zion's Senior Bishops During the Twentieth Century." *Star of Zion* 104 (March 27, 1980): 1, 2.

AARS, EWM, HAMEZC, WWR (75–76), WWABA (75–76), EBA, WWWA (7), NYTO, BDNM (75), AMEZC, OTSB.

SHAW DIVINITY SCHOOL. An **American Baptist Churches in the U.S.A.** school. Shaw Divinity School, Raleigh, North Carolina, traces its history to 1865 when Henry Martin Tapper began a school centered on religious instruction to the freedmen. The school evolved into Shaw University, and the religious instruction became a department of religion and then the Graduate School of Religion.

In 1969, the School of Religion became a factor in the possible loss of accreditation of Shaw University. To prevent that occurrence, the School of Religion was reorganized as an independent institution with a separate board of trustees. The relations between the two schools remained cordial, however.

In 1987, the accreditation issue being largely resolved, the two schools began conversations looking toward a reversal of the split. A decision was made to begin that process in stages, with an initial merger of administrative personnel and responsibilities. The possibility of a merger of the Divinity School back into the university is a real possibility for the 1990s.

Payne, Wardell J., ed. *Directory of African American Religious Bodies: A Compendium by the Howard University School of Divinity.* Washington, DC: Howard University Press, 1991. 363 pp.

SHAW UNIVERSITY. An **American Baptist Churches in the U.S.A.** school. Shaw University can be traced to the efforts of the Rev. **H. M. Tupper**, a Baptist minister from Massachusetts, to begin a school for Freedmen in Raleigh, North Carolina, under the auspices of the American Baptist Home Mission Society. He opened a theological class at the end of 1865, but had in mind a vision of a university. He was able to expand the next year with gifts from several acquaintances in Massachusetts, especially Elijah Shaw. With their money and the labor of several Black men in Raleigh, he built the Raleigh Institute. Instruction was provided at both the high school and college level with both day and night classes.

In 1870 a ten-acre tract of land was purchased for

the institute and a building program commenced. The expanded school was incorporated in 1875 as Shaw University. It soon was able to relinquish its high school work and concentrated entirely on college-level studies. It developed a normal and industrial department and over the next decades added a pharmacy, theology, law, and medical school. Financial problems forced the closing of the law and medical school in 1914, but by that time the medical school had graduated over 300 physicians.

Beginning in the early twentieth century, Black Baptists began to move for greater control of the university, whose faculty and administration were largely White. That control came only slowly. The school expanded greatly in the 1960s under the control of its Black president, James B. Cheek, who doubled the size of the faculty and greatly increased the size of the student body. He also moved to increase the financial support of North Carolina Baptists while separating the school from any direct control of the university's internal policies. Cheek left a legacy of academic excellence which those who have followed him have striven to maintain. In 1969 the Graduate School of Religion was set apart as an autonomous school, the **Shaw Divinity School**.

Fitts, Leroy. *A History of Black Baptists.* Nashville, TN: Broadman Press, 1985. 368 pp.

SHELTON, S. McDOWELL (April 18, 1929–October 13, 1991), apostle and general overseer of the **Church of the Lord Jesus Christ of the Apostolic Faith**, was born in Philadelphia, Pennsylvania. He received a B.S. degree from Rutgers University in New Jersey, and did graduate studies at the University of Lisbon in Portugal. He was also a student at the Berlitz School of Languages, and is known for speaking a number of languages fluently.

As a young man Shelton moved his way up the ranks as an evangelist for the Church of the Lord Jesus Christ of the Apostolic Faith. This church was founded by **Sherrod C. Johnson** in 1933 as a conservative break-off from the **Church of Our Lord Jesus Christ of the Apostolic Church**. When Johnson died in 1961, Shelton became his successor as bishop, apostle, and general overseer of the church. In this position, he has continued the program of strict guidelines laid down by his predecessor. Women in the church are not to wear jewelry or makeup, and must wear calf-length dresses, cotton stockings, unstraightened hair, and head coverings. Costly apparel is prohibited, as is remarriage after divorce. Salvation is understood to mean being

filled with the Holy Spirit and manifest in participation in the gifts of Pentecost, e.g. speaking in tongues. Juvenile delinquency among church families is almost unknown.

Shelton has wide fame as a radio preacher, and his radio program, "The Whole Truth," is carried on about fifty stations across the United States and abroad. In the United States the program is aired nightly, and the program in the Caribbean, Europe, Africa, and India is on a weekly basis. He is the editor of the church's monthly journal, also called *The Whole Truth*. He has traveled widely in the effort to build an international base for the church. Ironically, considering the church's guidelines on an austere lifestyle, Shelton has been criticized for living in opulent luxury. Although single, he is a family man, having adopted six sons. In 1972 he was the recipient of the Human Relations Award from the Philadelphia Commission on Human Relations.

Lear, Len. "Philadelphia's Bishop Shelton: Prophet or Profiteer?" *Sepia* 27 (January 1978): 56–61.
Shelton, S. McDowell. *Let Patience Have Her Perfect Work.* Philadelphia, PA: Church of the Lord Jesus Christ of the Apostolic Faith, 1964. 12 pp.
BH, IBAW, BDA-AHP, WWABA (90), *BDNM* (75), *RLOA.*

SHEPARD, MARSHALL LORENZO, SR. (July 10, 1899–February 21, 1967), politician and chair of the Board of Foreign Missions of the **National Baptist Convention, U.S.A., Inc.** (N.B.C.U.S.A.), was born in Oxford, North Carolina, the son of Robert and Pattie (Gilliam) Shepard. Early in life he experienced conversion and was baptized in the First Baptist Church of Oxford. He attended the Slater State Normal School in Winston-Salem, North Carolina, from 1912 to 1916, then received his B.A. in 1921 from Virginia Union University in Richmond, Virginia. He worked his way through school variously as a bootblack, porter, and waiter. In 1922–23 he was secretary for religious work of the West 135th Street branch of the Y.M.C.A. in New York City, and took some courses at Union Theological Seminary. On June 20, 1923, he married Willia Lucille Owens, with whom he had two sons.

From 1923 to 1926 Shepard was assistant pastor at the prestigious Abyssinian Baptist Church in Harlem, New York City. In 1926 he accepted the pastorate of Mount Olivet Tabernacle Baptist Church in Philadelphia, Pennsylvania, where he remained the rest of his life. There he developed a ministry of international scope. Three times, in 1934, 1936, and 1940, he was elected to the Pennsylvania State Legislature for two-year terms (1935–37; 1937–39; and 1941–43), and newspaper reporters named him Best Orator in the State House of Representatives. In 1936 he was one of the first Blacks to be named chaplain of the Democratic National Convention. When he rose to offer a prayer, former Senator Allison D. ("Cotton") Smith from South Carolina walked out of the convention hall. Shepard's comment later was, "It was just a sign the good brother needs more prayer."

In 1944 President Franklin D. Roosevelt rewarded Shepard for his political services by appointing him Recorder of Deeds for Washington, D.C. At that time Shepard and **Mary M. Bethune** were the only two Blacks in government service in the nation's capital. In November 1951 he resigned that position to run for Recorder of Deeds for the city of Philadelphia. He won, breaking a 67-year-old Republican hold on that office and a virtual Republican monopoly on Philadelphia municipal government. The Philadelphia office placed him as supervisor of 107 employees, many of them White, including his deputy and chief clerk. In 1953, when some departments were merged, he was named Commissioner of Records. In November, 1955 he left that post to run for Councilman-at-Large, which he won. He served consecutive terms in that office until his death.

Shepard was also very prominent in his denomination and in ecumenical circles. For many years he was chair of the Board of Foreign Missions of the N.B.C.U.S.A., and in 1947 was a delegate and speaker at the World Baptist Alliance meeting in Copenhagen, Denmark. He was a member of the Division of Christian Life and Work of the National Council of Churches as well. In all of these activities he continued to meet the needs of his congregation, especially the Sunday morning preaching. Famed preacher **Gardner C. Taylor** called Shepard probably the best extemporaneous preacher the Black race has produced. It was an unusual congregation that shared the time and abilities of their pastor to such an extent with the secular world. At the Eightieth Session of the N.B.C.U.S.A. in 1960, Shepard led the forces working against the reelection of **Joseph H. Jackson** as president of the denomination. The tactics of this opposition involved an unprecedented "sit-in" at the convention. Jackson was reelected despite this, and Shepard was one of several who were removed from their offices for their opposition efforts. Seven years later, on February 9, 1967, Shepard underwent brain surgery, from which he did not recover.

Smedley, Al. "The Preacher in City Hall." *The Crisis* 60 (February 1953): 98, 99, 130.
NYTO, GBB, BDNM (75), *WWCA* (38–40), *IBAW, SCA.*

SHERMAN, ODIE LEE (1897–April 19, 1983), 75th bishop of the **African Methodist Episcopal Church** (AME), was born in Jacksonville, Texas. He attended the public schools in his home town and experienced conversion in 1910. He was licensed to preach in 1919 in the Bethel AME Church in Keo, Arkansas, and served as a local pastor for two years. He joined the Little Rock (Arkansas) Annual Conference in 1921, was ordained deacon in 1923 and elder in 1925. He pastored the Sand Hill Mission with a membership of three, then returned to Keo, and spent three years on the Scott Circuit. While there and then at River View AME Church in Tie Plant, he was a student at Shorter College in North Little Rock, receiving his B.A. degree in 1927. In 1928 he was appointed to Lee AME Chapel in North Little Rock. He married Ruth Cindy Jones; there were no children.

In 1929 he became presiding elder, first covering the Augusta District for six years, then the Camden District for thirteen years, then the Hot Springs District for seven and a half years. His wife died in 1937 and in 1940 he married Edna Othenia Daniels, and the family came to include a stepson and an adopted daughter. Sherman was elected bishop on May 15, 1956, and was assigned to the Sixteenth Episcopal District (West Indies and South America).

In 1958 he was assigned to the Twelfth Episcopal District (Arkansas and Oklahoma), where substantial growth took place under his tenure. Many new churches were built and Sherman-Tyree Hall, a new administration-classroom building, was built at Shorter College. He was very active in the N.A.A.C.P. and was a courageous leader during the tension of integration of the public schools. He chaired a political campaign that drove out three segregation leaders from the school board in Little Rock, where he maintained his residence. He served as chair of the Little Rock Civil League for many years, and named for him is Sherman Park, filled with recreational facilities for the community of North Little Rock. He was later assigned to the Tenth Episcopal District (Texas), where he served as chancellor of Paul Quinn College in Waco, Texas. He retired at the 1972 General Conference.

"In Memoriam: O. L. Sherman." *The AME Christian Recorder* 132 (May 2, 1983): 1, 3.
EWM, HAMEC, OTSB, WWABA (85), *EBA, BDNM* (75), *BAMEC.*

SHILOH APOSTOLIC TEMPLE. An Apostolic Pentecostal church. Shiloh Apostolic Temple dates to 1948 when Robert O. Doub, Jr. moved to Philadelphia to begin the congregation of the **Apostle Church of**

Christ in God. Within a few years, he had not only founded a vital congregation, but had begun a home mission program which led to the founding of other congregations in nearby communities. He eventually ran into conflict with the area overseer, who was taking credit for Doub's work with presiding bishop J. W. Audrey. Doub wanted to be made bishop over the churches he had founded.

Thus in 1848 Doub left with his congregation. He tried to align with the **Church of God (Apostolic)**, but the agreement finally fell through. He decided to do it on his own. Throwing his energy into the new project, by 1980 he had established 23 congregations, including eight in England and two in Trinidad. He opened Shiloh Promised Land Camp in Montrose, Pennsylvania and initiated a periodical, *Shiloh Gospel Wave*. Headquarters remain in Philadelphia.

Richardson, James C. *With Water and Spirit: A History of Black Apostolic Denominations in the U.S.* Martinsville, VA: The Author, n.d. 151 pp.

SHIRLEY, LEMUEL BARNETT (b. July 23, 1916), a bishop of the **Episcopal Church**, was born in Colon, Republic of Panama, the son of Michael Barnett and Leanna Bricilla (Perry) Shirley. He attended the Canal Zone Elementary School at Gatun, the La Boca Normal Training School (1935–38), and the Bishop Payne Divinity School in Petersburg, Virginia, where he received his B.D. in 1941. He was ordained deacon in 1941 and priest in 1942. He was the first person born in Panama to be ordained in the Episcopal Church.

From 1942 to 1950 he was minister-in-charge of St. Christopher's, Rio Abajo, and St. Matthew's in Las Sabanas, all in the Canal Zone. From 1944 to 1952 he was also responsible for St. Peter's in La Boca. In 1946 he married Gwendoline Eastmond, with whom he had one daughter. In 1951–52 he was at St. Simon's in Gamboa. From 1952 to 1972 he was rector of St. Paul's Episcopal Church in Panama City and until 1970 was Archdeacon of Panama. In 1967 his first wife died and on April 17, 1969, he married Olga Gwendolyn Hinds. He was on the Council of Advice from 1945 to 1972 and was a deputy to General Convention in 1946, 1952, and 1967.

On February 19, 1972, Shirley was consecrated bishop for Panama, thus becoming the first person born in Panama to become a bishop in the Episcopal Church. In 1973 he was chair of the Ecumenical Commission of the denomination. From 1965 to 1974 he was president of the Bella Vista Children's Home and Child Day Care Center. For many years he was president of the Colegio Episcopal, Instituto San Cristobal, and was on the board of directors of the Balboa Y.M.C.A. and United Way from 1972 to 1979.

WWA (84–85), *ECA* (1973), *WWR* (77).

SHOCKLEY, GRANT S. (b. September 3, 1919), a minister of the **United Methodist Church**, college president, and author, was born in Philadelphia, Pennsylvania, the son of Andrew Caleb and Mattile Blanche (Sneed) Shockley. He received his B.A. in 1942 from Lincoln University in Pennsylvania, his B.D. in 1945 from Drew University in Madison, New Jersey, his M.A. in 1946 from Columbia University in New York City, and his Ed.D. in 1952, also from Columbia. He married Doris V. Taylor, with whom he had one daughter.

While in school Shockley was associate pastor of St. Mark's United Methodist Church in New York City from 1942 to 1946, and was ordained elder in 1944. From 1946 to 1949 he was associate professor of Bible and religion at Clark College in Atlanta, Georgia, and from 1949 to 1951 he was professor of religious education at Gammon Theological Seminary in Atlanta. In 1951 he returned to the pastorate at Whatcoat Memorial United Methodist Church in Dover, Delaware, where he stayed until 1953. From 1953 to 1959 he was assigned to Janes Memorial United Methodist Church in Brooklyn, New York City, and while there was instructor in the School of Education at New York University from 1957 to 1959.

From 1959 to 1966 Shockley was professor of religious education at Garrett Theological Seminary in Evanston, Illinois, and was very involved in the community. In 1961 he received the Merit Award for Distinguished Service in Promoting Better Intergroup Relations from the Northshore Human Relations Council, and he was a member of the Board of Education from 1963 to 1966. From 1966 to 1970 he was executive secretary of the Interboard Committee of Christian Education Overseas of the United Methodist Board of Global Ministries in New York City. From 1970 to 1975 he was professor of Christian Education at Emory University and Candler School of Theology in Atlanta, and from 1975 to 1979 he was president of the Interdenominational Theological Center in Atlanta, Georgia. From 1980 to 1983 he was president of Philander Smith College in Little Rock, Arkansas, and was professor of Christian education at Duke University Divinity School from 1983 until retirement in 1989. He was a contributor to a number of major publications, including the *Encyclopedia of World Methodism* (1968),

An Introduction to Christian Education (1966), *A History of American Methodism* (1964), and the *Westminster Dictionary of Christian Education*. He has also written several books, the most recent being *Heritage and Hope: The African-American Presence in United Methodism* (1991).

Foster, Charles R., and Grant S. Shockley, eds. *Working with Black Youth: Opportunities for Christian Ministry.* Nashville, TN: Abingdon Press, 1989. 126 pp.

Shockley, Grant S. *Heritage and Hope: The African-American Presence in United Methodism.* Nashville, TN: Abingdon Press, 1991. 350 pp.

———. "Jefferson on Religion in Public Education." *Journal of Religious Thought* 19 (Autumn/Winter 1963): 169–170.

———. *Understanding the New Generation in Africa: The Guide for Teachers and Leaders.* New York: Friendship Press, 1971. 100 pp.

HUBA, EBA, WWABA (92–93), *BDNM* (75), *IBAW*.

SHORTER, JAMES ALEXANDER (February 4, 1817–July 1, 1887), 9th bishop of the **African Methodist Episcopal Church** (AME), was born in Washington, D.C., the son of Charles and Elizabeth Shorter. He was apprenticed as a barber in Philadelphia, Pennsylvania, then went West, where he was converted in Galena, Illinois, in 1839, and joined the Methodist Episcopal Church. Returning eastward, he joined the Bethel AME Church in Philadelphia. Still in 1839 he married Julia Ann Stewart of Washington, D.C., with whom he had three children.

He was licensed to preach later that year by Rev. John Cornish in Washington, D.C., where he became a strong member of Israel Memorial (later Union Bethel) AME Church. He joined the Baltimore Conference in April 1846, was ordained deacon in April 1848, and elder in 1850. His wife died in 1850 and in 1851 he married Mrs. Maria Kerr, with whom he had two more children. Over the years from 1846 he pastored the Gettysburg and Lewiston Circuit, the Seningtonville Circuit, the Lancaster Circuit in Baltimore, Maryland, Israel Memorial AME Church in Washington, D.C., and Ebenezer AME Church in Baltimore.

In 1859, feeling the need to move to a strongly anti-slavery location with excellent educational opportunities for his children, he moved his family to a house on the campus of the newly opened Wilberforce University in Xenia, Ohio. He was appointed to the First AME Church in Xenia, about three miles away. In 1863 he was assigned to Allen Chapel AME Church in Cincinnati, Ohio, staying for three years. During this time he led the church in providing food and shelter for the thousands of Blacks making their way north from slavery. He added hundreds of members to the church through frequent revivals. In 1866 he became an agent for Wilberforce University and collected about $3,000 in one year for the school. In 1867 he was appointed to Wylie AME Church in Pittsburgh, Pennsylvania.

In 1868 Shorter was elected bishop and assigned to the Fifth Episcopal District (Kentucky, Tennessee, Mississippi, Arkansas, and Texas). He oversaw the tremendous work of the church of those areas in absorbing the thousands of Black former members of the Methodist Episcopal Church, South, who transferred into the AME Church. In 1872 he was assigned to the First Episcopal District (Philadelphia, New York, New Jersey, and New England), followed by the Fourth Episcopal District (Indiana, Illinois, Missouri, and Kansas) from 1876 to 1880; the Third Episcopal District (Ohio, Indiana, and Pittsburgh) from 1880 to 1884; and the Sixth Episcopal District (South Carolina and Georgia) from 1884 to 1887.

He organized the Mississippi Conference in October 1868, the Texas Conference in October 1868, the Kansas Conference in 1876, and the Tennessee Conference in September 1878. He also organized the Louisiana and Arkansas Conferences, while maintaining his residence in a home he built right next to Wilberforce University. He was president of the denomination's mission society and began an AME presence in Haiti and Africa. In 1881 he was a delegate to the First World Methodist Conference in London, England. Named for him are Shorter Hall at Wilberforce and Shorter College in Little Rock, Arkansas, as well as churches in six states.

HNRA, ACAB, HAMEC, BAMEC, EWM, CEAMEC.

SHORTER COLLEGE. An **African Methodist Episcopal Church** (AME) school. Shorter College was founded in 1886 in Little Rock, Arkansas, during the episcopacy of **T. M. D. Ward**. It was a joint project of the three Arkansas conferences and originally named Bethel University. The first facilities were located in the basement of Bethel AME Church in Little Rock, which accommodated an opening class of 108 pupils. In 1888 the school was renamed Bethel Institute, a more appropriate designation. Soon afterward the school accepted a generous offer of support which had been obtained by the presiding elder in the Arkadelphia District which included provision for the school to move to Arkadelphia. The change of residency occurred in 1891. The following year the school was renamed

Shorter University in honor of Bishop **James A. Shorter**, the bishop who had organized the church in Arkansas. The school adopted its present name in 1903.

During the early twentieth century, the school continued to grow. Eventually a second campus was opened in North Little Rock and subsequently, after the school attempted to operate two campuses, the Arkadelphia campus was abandoned.

Gregg, Howard D. *History of the African Methodist Episcopal Church: The Black Church in Action.* Nashville, TN; AMEC Sunday School Union, 1989. 523 pp.

Smith, Charles Spencer. *A History of the African Methodist Episcopal Church.* Philadelphia, PA: Book Concern of the AME Church, 1922. 570 pp.

SHRINE OF THE BLACK MADONNA. *See:* **Pan African Orthodox Christian Church**.

SHUTTLESWORTH, FRED LEE (b. March 18, 1922), minister in the **Progressive National Baptist Convention** and civil rights leader, was born in Muggler, Alabama, the son of Will and Alberta (Roberson) Shuttlesworth. He attended Cedar Grove Institute in Mobile, Alabama, received his B.A. from Selma University in Alabama and a B.S. from Alabama State Teachers College. He married Ruby Keeler, with whom he had four children.

His pastorates included the First Baptist Church in Birmingham, Alabama (1952–55); Bethel Baptist Church in Birmingham (1957–60); and Revelation Baptist Church in Cincinnati, Ohio (1960–66). In 1966 he left the 1,200–member Revelation Baptist Church because of internal dissent over his authoritarian style of leadership. He then founded and has since pastored the Greater New Light Baptist Church in Cincinnati. He was a strong advocate for civil rights; in 1956 he founded the Alabama Christian Movement for Human Rights (A.C.M.H.R.) and was its president until 1969. In January 1957, when **Martin Luther King, Jr.**, established the **Southern Christian Leadership Conference**, Shuttlesworth was elected its first secretary. He also served on the national advisory board of the Congress of Racial Equality (C.O.R.E.). In 1958 he received the Russwurm Award from the National Newspapers Publishers Association.

By the early 1960s, his activism had earned him the title of "the most abused and arrested minister in the nation." His move from Birmingham to Ohio was prompted by such virulent racist attacks in Birmingham that he felt he and his family were in danger for their lives. He received numerous awards and honors, including a 1963 award from the Cincinnati Business League for the display of self-sacrifice, gallantry, and bravery, the 1962 Award for Human Relations from the Capitol Press Club, and the 1963 Rosa Parks Award from the S.C.L.C. By November, 1965, Shuttlesworth had suffered four bad beatings, had his home bombed, and had been arrested twenty-two times for offenses ranging from speeding to parading without a permit. He decided to fight every arrest and injustice as far as possible, and the court cases took him to the U.S. Supreme Court at least eight times, more than any other individual in the Court's history. He first appeared at the Supreme Court in 1958 and lost his challenge to Alabama's pupil-placement law, even though the Court admitted it seemed designed to perpetuate segregation. In 1963 he was acquitted of the charge of aiding and abetting a Birmingham sit-in, a violation of the local trespass ordinance. Chief Justice Warren held that "there can be no conviction for aiding and abetting someone to do an innocent act."

In the late 1960s Shuttlesworth became president of the Southern Conference Educational Fund, a 17–state interracial civil rights group focusing on integration, with headquarters in Louisville, Kentucky. At the Greater New Light Baptist Church he helped create the Valid Christian Improvement Association, modeled on Chicago's Operation Breadbasket. He has continued to be recognized for his achievements, winning the Excellence Award from **Operation PUSH** (headed by **Jesse Jackson**) in 1974, the Martin Luther King, Jr. Civil Rights Award from the Progressive National Baptist Convention in 1975, and the Founder Award from the S.C.L.C. in 1977.

"The Benevolent Dictator." *Time* 86 (September 3, 1965): 71.

"Litigation." *Time* (November 26, 1965): 73–74.

"The Men Behind Martin Luther King." *Ebony* 20 (June 1965): 164–173.

EBA, BDNM (70), *AAE, CRACG, WWABA* (92–93), *IBAW*.

SHY, PETER RANDOLPH (b. May 10, 1898), 30th bishop of the **Christian Methodist Episcopal Church** (CME), was born in Kelly, Jasper County, Georgia. He joined the Annual Conference in 1918, was ordained deacon in 1921, and elder in 1925. On May 30, 1921, he received his B.A. in English from Paine College in Augusta, Georgia. He married Ira Lue Bonds of Northport, Alabama.

He pastored CME churches in Decatur, Athens, and Birmingham, Georgia, and was a professor at Miles College in Birmingham for ten years. On June 3, 1940, he received an M.A. in sociology from Fisk University in Nashville, Tennessee, and reportedly received another M.A. from Columbia University in New York City, but this has not been confirmed. He was assigned to Capers Memorial CME Church in Nashville, Tennessee, from 1940 to 1948, and also served as academic dean of Lane College in Jackson, Tennessee. Later he was the pastor of St. Paul CME Church in Jackson, Tennessee. On May 16, 1958, Shy was elected bishop. He retired in about 1972 to his residence in Atlanta, Georgia.

BDNM (65), *EWM, CMECTY.*

SIMMONS, JAMES (December 3, 1792–February, 1874), 8th bishop of the **African Methodist Episcopal Zion Church** (AMEZ), was born in Accomac County, Maryland. Little information is available about his early or family life. He joined the New York Conference on May 19, 1832, and was ordained both deacon and elder on May 22, 1833. He was plain in style and simple in preaching, of unsullied character and very strict in standards of duty and church discipline. He was consecrated bishop on June 30, 1856, at a time when bishops were elected for only four-year terms. He served only one term and went from there to give faithful service in the New York and New England Conferences until his death.

EWM, HAMEZCIA, HAMEZC, AMEZC.

SIMMONS, WILLIAM J. (June 29, 1849–October 30, 1890), author, educator, and founder of the **American National Baptist Convention** (a forerunner of today's **National Baptist Convention, U.S.A., Inc.**), was born in Charleston, North Carolina, to slaves Edward and Esther Simmons. While he was about ten, his mother fled with him and her two other children to the North. At the age of twelve, Simmons began an apprenticeship with a White dentist near his home in Bordentown, New Jersey. He applied to a dental school in Philadelphia, but was turned away. In 1864 he joined the Union Army's Forty-First Division of United States Colored Troops. After the war, he returned to Bordentown as a dental assistant, and joined a White Baptist church. The religious life soon took hold of him and he gained a new goal, that of becoming a minister. The congregation established a fund to help him get an education, and he attended Madison (later called Colgate) University in Hamilton, New York, then Rochester University in Rochester, New York. In 1871 he moved to Howard University in Washington, D.C., and graduated in 1873 with his B.A.

While at Howard he began a career in teaching at Hillsdale Public School, which he continued after graduation. On August 25, 1874, he married Josephine A. Silence, with whom he had seven children. After the marriage they moved to Ocala, Florida, where he soon became principal of Howard Academy. He was ordained and pastored a small church there, where he also held such offices as deputy county clerk and county commissioner. In 1879 he accepted the pastorate of First Baptist Church of Lexington, Kentucky.

His career took a turn toward national prominence in 1880 when he became president of the nearly defunct Normal and Theological Institution, a Baptist school in Louisville, Kentucky, which he turned into a vital center. In 1884 it was renamed Baptist State University. In 1882 he became editor of *American Baptist*, the magazine of the Northern Baptist Convention. He was active politically, often for the Republicans, but made a point of being independent. He was a leader in a number of conventions designed to help Black conditions in the South.

Racism caused Simmons and others to be ejected from their editorial positions with the White Baptists. He then decided to form a Black Baptist organization that would focus on the needs of religious education, presumably one that would complement the Foreign Mission Baptist Convention, formed in 1880. He put out the call on April 5, 1886, and at the first meeting on August 25, the American National Baptist Convention was founded. Simmons was elected president, a position he held for the few remaining years of his life. His skills and driving spirit gave the new organization a solid foundation.

In 1887 he published *Men of Mark*, a biographical dictionary of leading Black men, and a conscious effort to lift up Black accomplishments in the face of constant messages about the inferiority of Blacks. He was equally concerned about uplifting Black women. In 1883 he helped organize the first statewide convention of Black women, the Baptist Women's Educational Convention of the State of Kentucky. He appointed **Lucy Wilmot Smith** historian of the convention in 1886. In 1888 he began editing and publishing a magazine, *Our Women and Children*. He had planned to write a companion biographical volume on women, but a poor heart ended his life prematurely at the age of forty-one. In 1918 the school he gave so much to was renamed Simmons University, which flourished into the 1940s. It continues as Simmons Bible College.

DANB, RLOA, HBB, HBBUS, SCA, SNB, IBAW, BAW, AARS, EBA, ENB, MM, OBMS.

SIMMONS BIBLE COLLEGE. A Baptist school. What is now Simmons Bible College, Louisville, Kentucky, has had a long history under a variety of names. It was founded in 1879 as the Kentucky Normal and Theological School by the General Association of the Colored Baptists of Kentucky. The idea had been proposed as early as 1866 but lack of financial support had postponed the opening of the school. H. C. Marrs and Rev. E. P. Marrs managed the school during its early years. Significant financial contributions from William H. Steward, a local postal worker, provided some initial stability. The first president of the school was **William J. Simmons**, an outstanding Black educator and one of the founders of what is today the **National Baptist Convention, U.S.A., Inc.** He employed a number of early African American intellectuals on the faculty. During the Simmons era, the school became an important center in the struggle of Black Baptists to control their own institutions and provide employment for Black scholars and writers. The American Baptist Home Mission Society had been very slow to relinquish control of the many Black Baptist projects they had initiated immediately after the Civil War, even after ample competent Black leadership had emerged.

In 1884 the school changed its name to Baptist State University, the name by which it was known until 1818, when it became Simmons University. The school prospered through the 1920, but was devastated by the Depression. From a full college curriculum and hundreds of students, by the beginning of World War II the school had less than a hundred students, all enrolled in the theological program. The school survives as an independent Bible college.

Fitts, Leroy. *A History of Black Baptists.* Nashville, TN: Broadman Press, 1985. 368 pp.

SIMS, DAVID HENRY (July 18, 1886–1965), 55th bishop of the **African Methodist Episcopal Church** (AME), was born in Talladega, Alabama, the son of Rev. Felix Rice and Emma Eveline (Griffin) Sims. He completed the normal course at Georgia State College from 1900 to 1905, then received his B.A. in 1909 from Oberlin College in Ohio, earning four successive years of scholarships. He was licensed to preach in July 1909 and admitted that year to the Ohio Conference. He was known as an outstanding athlete and champion sprinter.

He earned his B.D. in 1912 from Oberlin Divinity School, and was elected by his mostly White class to deliver the "Mantle and Key" address at commencement. He went on to study at the University of Chicago, earning his M.A. there in 1916.

In 1910 Sims was appointed pastor of the Union AME Church in Painesville, Ohio, and about that time was ordained deacon. In 1911–12 he was assigned to the church in Narragansett Pier, Rhode Island, and during that time was ordained elder. From 1912 to 1917 he was pastor of the University Chapel at Morris Brown College in Atlanta, Georgia, and during that same period was professor of German and education at the college. For part of that time, 1914 to 1917, he was also vice-president of the college. From 1918 to 1924 he was dean and vice-president of Allen University in Columbia, South Carolina, and during that time was also pastor of the Mount Pisgah AME Church in Greenwood, South Carolina. In 1924–25 he was presiding elder of the Laurens District in South Carolina.

In 1924 Sims was elected president of Allen University and remained in that position for eight years. In July 1925, Governor McLeod appointed him a special messenger representing South Carolina to attend the National Educational Convention at Topeka, Kansas. Information about his first wife is unavailable; he married for a second time in 1932, to Mayme Anna Holden, with whom he had one daughter. In 1932 Sims was elected bishop and assigned to South Africa (1932–36); Alabama (1936–40); and the First Episcopal District (1939–46). In November 1946, he was expelled from the episcopacy by a special session of the General Conference for resisting (unspecified) orders of the Council of Bishops. He fought the action through the federal courts, but lost.

In 1956 the General Conference reconsidered his case and restored him to the episcopacy, though with no salary and no assignment. In 1960 he was finally restored to full salary and was assigned to the Fourteenth Episcopal District (West Africa). There he accomplished many things, including breaking ground on the ambitious Royesville Project, a mission station complete with schools, library, church, farm, and clinic. From 1962 until his death he headed the Eighth Episcopal District (Mississippi and Louisiana). He served on the board of directors of the *Philadelphia Tribune* newspaper as well as the Citizens and Southern Band and Trust Company of Philadelphia. The General Conference assigned him to write AME Church polity and history, and accordingly he published a number of works, including *History of the AME Church in the 14th District; The Function of the Presiding Elder; The Office of Presiding Elder; Religious Education in Negro Colleges;* and *The Function of Worship.*

EWM, BDNM (70), BAMEC, WWCA (38–40), EBA, AMSC.

SINGLETON, GEORGE ARNETT (June 4, 1894– November 7, 1970), educator with the **African Methodist Episcopal Church** (AME) and long-time editor of the *A.M.E. Church Review*, was born in Conway, Harry County, South Carolina, the son of George Congdon and Louzanne Taney (Moore) Singleton. In 1912 he saw military duty in the Philippine Islands. He received his B.A. degree in 1915 from Allen University in Columbia, South Carolina, and that year was ordained to ministry in the African Methodist Episcopal Church (AME). He married Ettie Ruth Cochran on August 15, 1916. During World War I he was 1st Lieutenant Chaplain in the U.S.Army with the A.E.F. in France, 1918–19.

From 1919 to 1923 he pastored the People's AME Church in Chelsea, Massachusetts, while a student at Boston University, where he earned an S.T.B. in 1922. From 1923 to 1929 he was a professor of history at Allen University and for part of that time (1924–26) he pastored the Mt. Pisgah AME Church in Greenwood, South Carolina, about sixty miles from Columbia. From 1929 to 1930 he was dean of Turner Theological Seminary at Morris Brown College in Atlanta, Georgia (since 1958 part of the Interdenominational Theological Center in Atlanta). During these two years he arranged to spend time as a student at the University of Chicago, where he earned an M.A. in 1929 and a B.D. in 1930.

In 1930–31 Singleton pastored St. John's AME Church in Paducah, Kentucky, while also a professor of history at West Kentucky College in Paducah. From 1931 to 1936 he was assigned to St. Paul's AME Church in Springfield, Illinois. In 1936 he was elected editor of the *Christian Recorder*, a denominational journal, a position he held until 1944. From 1944 to 1951 he pastored an AME church in Des Moines, Iowa, where he was president of the local branch of the N.A.A.C.P. Following his Iowa pastorate, from 1951 to 1967, he was editor of the *A.M.E. Church Review*, an influential position from which he influenced the thinking of the whole denomination. He wrote numerous pamphlets, and in 1952 he published a substantial historical study, *The Romance of African Methodism: A Study of the African Methodist Episcopal Church.* In 1964 he published the story of his life, *The Autobiography of George Arnett Singleton.* In 1967 he retired due to failing health and passed away a few years later.

Bright, John D., Sr. "Eulogy of Reverend George Arnett Singleton." *A.M.E. Church Review* 103 (January–February 1971): 25–28.

"The Late George A. Singleton." *A.M.E. Church Review* 103 (January–February 1971): 1.

Singleton, George Arnett. *The Autobiography of George Arnett Singleton.* Boston, MA: Forum Publishing Co., 1964. 272 pp.

———. "God, the Bible, and the African." *A.M.E. Church Review* 78 (July September 1962): 81–91.

———. *Religious Instruction of the Negro in the United States Before the Rebellion.* Chicago: Master's Thesis. University of Chicago, 1929.

———. *The Romance of African Methodism: A Study of the African Methodist Episcopal Church.* New York: Exposition Press, 1952. 251 pp.

Williams, Ethel. *Biographical Dictionary of Negro Ministers.* Boston: G. K. Hall, 1965.

RLA, HUBA, AARS.

SISTERS OF THE BLESSED SACRAMENT FOR INDIANS AND COLORED PEOPLE. A religious order of the **Roman Catholic Church.** The Sisters of the Blessed Sacrament for Indians and Colored People was founded in 1891 in Philadelphia by Katherine Drexel. Drexel was the daughter of Francis A. Drexel, a wealthy philanthropist. Though raised in luxury, young Katherine had a yearning for the religious life but could never find the right direction. She found each of the religious orders she investigated as not quite that for which she was looking. Then in 1800 Bishop Martin Marty, whose territory included parts of Minnesota and the Dakotas, appealed to her to assist his efforts on behalf of the Native Americans. She gave the money to erect five schools, which she later visited.

In 1887 she traveled to Rome and had a private audience with Pope Leo XIII. She asked him to send missionaries to the Native American people. He asked her to become the answer to her own request. She returned to America and entered the novitiate of the Sisters of Mercy, gathering around her others who shared her zeal for what had now become a mission not only to the Native Americans but the African Americans as well. They established a separate community within the Sisters of Mercy and took an additional vow to work solely for the people for which their community had been called together. Mother Katherine became the first superior. An initial motherhouse was located near Philadelphia and a novitiate opened in Torresdale. In 1892 they settled in a permanent location at Cornwall Heights in Bucks County.

The first projects of the order, undergirded with Drexel family money, were directed toward the Native Americans. Their first effort for African Americans began in 1899 when a boarding and industrial school for girls was opened in Rock Castle, Virginia. Shortly after the turn of the century a school was opened in Nashville, Tennessee, also for girls. The work spread throughout the country into the 1920s. In 1927 they opened the single institution for which they are most noted, Xavier College (now University) in New Orleans, still the only African American university for African American youth supported by the Roman Catholic Church.

Throughout the twentieth century the order has recruited African American and Native American women into membership, who now make up a substantial promotion of the order. Headquarters is in Bensalem, Pennsylvania. Mother Drexel headed the order until her death in 1955. The present president of the order is Sister Mary Juliana Haynes. It has 147 members under vows. Work is concentrated in the South and Southwest, with additional centers in several northern urban areas.

Dehey, Elinor Tong. *Religious Orders of Women in the United States.* Cleveland, OH: The Author, 1930. 908 pp.
Guide to Religious Communities for Women. Chicago: National Sisters Vocational Conference, 1983. 445 pp.

SKEETE, F. HERBERT (b. March 22, 1930), a bishop of the **United Methodist Church**, was born in Harlem, New York City, the son of Ernest A. and Elma I. (Ramsey) Skeete. From 1951 to 1955 he was in the military service at Sampson Air Force Base in Geneva, New York. On October 4, 1952, he married Shirley Clarissa Hunte, with whom he had two sons. He received his B.A. in 1959 from Brooklyn College, working his way through school as a door-to-door salesman (1955–58) and as a sales clerk (1958–59). In 1959 he was a social investigator for the New York City Department of Welfare.

He received his B.D. in 1962 from Drew University in Madison, New Jersey, and from 1960 to 1967 pastored Union Methodist Church in South Ozone Park, Queens, New York City. He was ordained deacon in 1960 and elder in 1962. He was very active in the community, on the executive board of the United Neighbors Civic Association and co-chair of the Queens Association for Integrated and Quality Education. From 1962 to 1964 he served on the church's New York Conference Board of Social Concerns, and in 1963 he was vice-chair of the New York chapter of **Black**

Methodists for Church Renewal. In 1967–68 Skeete was on the staff of the New York City Mission Society, and for the following twelve years pastored the large Salem United Methodist Church in Harlem, New York City. He maintained his high community involvement as treasurer of the Haryou-Act Board (1974–76) and was a board member of the Methodist Hospital in Brooklyn (1972–80) and the Federation of Protestant Welfare Agencies (1975–80). In 1969 he was a religious commentator for WINS radio. In 1971 he was a delegate to the World Methodist Conference in Denver, Colorado, and from 1972 to 1980 he was on the Board of Global Ministries, serving as vice-president of the National Division. He was a delegate to General Conference beginning in 1972. In 1975 he completed his D.Min. at Drew University in New Jersey.

In 1980 Skeete was elected bishop and assigned to the Philadelphia Episcopal Area, where he stayed until 1988, when he moved to the Boston Episcopal Area. As bishop he served eight years on the Board of Higher Education and Campus Ministry, chairing the Division of Higher Education the first four years and serving as president of the board for the next four years. He attended further World Methodist conferences in Dublin, Hawaii, and Nairobi, serving on the executive committee for the latter two meetings. In Philadelphia he moderated a monthly television program for a time. He is on the board of the American Bible Society and serves as a trustee of Union Theological Seminary in New York City, Drew University, and Gammon Theological Seminary in Atlanta.

Skeete, F. Herbert. *The Methodist Class Meeting as a Relevant Model for Urban Ministry.* Madison, NJ: D.Min. Thesis at Drew University, 1975. 129 pp.
WWA (90–91), *WWR* (85), *BDNM* (75), *BDUMB.*

SKINNER, TOM (b. June 6, 1942), prominent Baptist evangelist, was born in New York City to Alester J. and Georgia Robinson Skinner. His father was a Baptist minister, and Skinner grew up active in church life, a leader of the youth group. All was not, however, as it seemed. Skinner began to feel that the church was not relevant to his life as a Black person in Harlem. He started to lead a double life as a gang member.

By the young age of fourteen, he was already the leader of the Harlem Lords. Because he was bright and read the military tactics of famous generals, he was known as a brilliant leader of the gang "rumbles." For those who did not know this side of him, Skinner still seemed like the all-American boy. In high school, he was a good student, a multi-sport athlete, an actor in the Shakespearean Club, and was elected president of the student body.

After two years of leading the Harlem Lords, he was converted by listening to a radio evangelist. He quit the gang, a dangerous thing to do, and his witness led to the conversion of the gang's number two leader and later of other members as well. He began to preach on the streets of Harlem and enrolled in the Manhattan Bible Institute. On June 2, 1959, as he was about to turn seventeen, he was ordained by the United Missionary Baptist Association of Greater New York and Vicinity, a group related to the **National Baptist Convention, U.S.A., Inc.** His growing impact led to opposition among many of the established Harlem ministers. He said too many churches were more concerned with membership and offerings than with preaching the power of sin and the salvation of Jesus Christ. He also encountered resistance from some Black nationalists who believed that Christianity was a White religion. Skinner responded with his belief that salvation comes through Jesus the Christ, not through any human, Black or White.

In October 1961, Skinner met with a number of Harlem leaders at Emmanuel Chapel and decided to form the Harlem Evangelistic Association, dedicated to bringing the gospel to all of Harlem. Their first major event was a week-long crusade in July 1962, at the Apollo Theater. This was a great success, setting attendance records at the theater, and further crusades followed in Brooklyn, Guyana, Bermuda, Barbados, and elsewhere. The crusades abroad gave him a global vision of the needed work, and the necessity to reach as many people as possible. In 1964 a radio ministry was begun, and the organization Tom Skinner Radio Crusades was created to support it. In 1966 the name was changed to Tom Skinner Crusades, to correspond with the wide range of approaches besides radio that were being utilized.

In 1968 Skinner published his most well-known book, the autobiographical *Black and Free.* He followed this with *How Black is the Gospel?* (1970), *Words of Revolution* (1970), *If Christ is the Answer, What Are the Questions?* (1974), and numerous articles. He has been a major force among Black evangelical Christians, and has been among those urging evangelicals to be involved in urban/social issues.

"Preachers of an Active Gospel." *Time* 94 (September 19, 1969): 60.

Skinner, Tom. *Black and Free.* Grand Rapids, MI: Zondervan Publishing House, 1968. 154 pp.

———. *The Church and the Black Revolution; Message Delivered at the U.S. Congress on Evangelism.* Brooklyn, NY: Tom Skinner Associates, 1969. 48 pp.

———. "Evangelism, Racial Crisis, and World Evangelism." *The Message* 40 (September 1974): 40–48.

———. *How Black is the Gospel?* Philadelphia, PA: J. B. Lippincott Co., 1970. 128 pp.

———. *If Christ is the Answer, What Are the Questions?* Grand Rapids, MI: Zondervan Publishing House, 1974. 219 pp.

RLOA, HUBA, AARS, IBAW.

SKYLES, ROBBIN W. (July 28, 1911–June 18, 1981), a pioneer Lutheran minister, was one of only seventeen African American pastors of the Lutheran Church in America (now a constituent part of the Evangelical Lutheran Church in America) listed for June 1971. He graduated from Maywood Lutheran Seminary and was ordained in 1945. For the remainder of his life he pastored the St. James Lutheran Church on South Indiana Avenue in Chicago, Illinois, with an average membership during that time of about 250.

LCAY, EBA, LCAN.

SLACK, GEORGE (b. 1905?), bishop of the **Church of God in Christ Congregational**, arose out of obscurity in 1917 when as a teenager in Centerville, Mississippi, he experienced salvation and the baptism of the Holy Spirit as evidenced by speaking in tongues under the ministry of **Church of God in Christ** (COGIC) minister **Henry Feltus.** Six years later he moved to East St. Louis, Missouri and affiliated with the COGIC congregation at nearby Decatur, Illinois. In 1927 Elder A. W. Webb became the pastor of the church in Decatur.

Slack came into conflict with Webb over the issue of tithing, and Webb disfellowshipped Slack because he had come to feel that tithing was not a New Testament doctrine and hence refused to tithe. Slack and several others formed an independent congregation in East St. Louis. In 1934 a reconciliation between the independent congregation and the COGIC was worked out, and the church returned to the fold. However, the question of tithing soon rose again and in 1935 Slack and other turned to Elder Justus Bowe, former overseer of COGIC in Arkansas, who had left to found the Church of God in Christ Congregational. Slack affiliated with Bowe and for the next decade ministered in Bowe's jurisdiction.

In 1945 a crisis emerged. Bowe, one of the founding leaders of COGIC, came to feel that he should return to that church. Following a year of discussion, the Church of God in Christ Congregational refused to merge into COGIC. Bowe left the new church he had founded, and the church selected Slack as its new presiding bishop. Slack began a lengthy tenure which began with his presiding over the period of transition following the defection of its founder. He coauthored a new *Manuel* to guide the small denomination, directed its growth, including the development of affiliated congregations in England and Mexico, and was responsible for the founding of new churches. He also instituted a program to assist elderly members.

DuPree, Sherry Sherrod. *Biographical Dictionary of African-American Holiness-Pentecostals, 1880–1990*. Washington, DC: Middle Atlantic Regional Press, 1989. 386 pp.
Slack, George, William Walker, and E. Jones. *Manuel*. East St. Louis, IL: Church of God in Christ, 1948.

SLADE, WALTER WILLIAM (July 4, 1875–May 19, 1963), 50th bishop of the **African Methodist Episcopal Zion Church** (AMEZ), was born in Newton, North Carolina, the son of Rev. Mayfield Slade, a minister in the AMEZ Church who was a pioneer in the Western North Carolina and Blue Ridge Conferences. Slade followed in his father's footsteps, and it was his father who licensed him to preach in 1895. He joined the Blue Ridge Conference the following year, was ordained deacon at the conference session on November 10, 1896, and was ordained elder on November 13, 1898. He graduated from Livingstone College in Salisbury, North Carolina, in 1901. He married Mildred Burgen.

He first pastored the Lebaum Circuit in Greenville, Tennessee, then transferred to the Central and West Central North Carolina Conference, where he pastored several charges, including Evans Metropolitan AMEZ Church in Fayetteville, North Carolina. He then served many years as a presiding elder in the Central North Carolina Conference. His first wife passed away in 1927, and in 1931 he married Sallie Mae Blake. In 1928 he was elected Secretary of Evangelism, where he served admirably until 1932, when he was assigned to the prestigious Wesley Center AMEZ Church in Pittsburgh, Pennsylvania.

From that position he was elected financial secretary for the denomination in 1940, and moved to the church's headquarters in Charlotte, North Carolina. In four years as financial secretary Slade compiled a record unmatched by any previous person in that office, paying off longstanding debts from the Depression of more than $50,000. This accomplishment, plus his outstanding reputation as preacher and pastor, brought him election to the bishopric at the General Conference in 1944. He was consecrated bishop on May 14, 1944, and spent most of his tenure covering the North and South Carolina areas. He took a special interest in nurturing Clinton Junior College, the denominational school in Rock Hill, South Carolina. He retired in May 1960, and passed away a few years later.

"Slade, Gordon Elected Bishops." *Star of Zion* 68 (May 25, 1944): 1, 8.
Walls, William J. *The African Methodist Episcopal Zion Church: Reality of the Black Church*. Charlotte, NC: A.M.E. Zion Publishing House, 1974. 669 pp.
"Walter William Slade." *Star of Zion* 82 (May 28, 1959): 5.
"Walter William Slade." *Star of Zion* 86 (June 6, 1963): 4, 5.
HAMEZC.

SMALL, JOHN BRYAN (March 14, 1845–January 15, 1905), 27th bishop of the **African Methodist Episcopal Zion Church** (AMEZ), was born in Frazer, St. Joseph's Parish, Barbados, British West Indies. He grew up relating to the Church of England and had an excellent early education, first with private tutors and then as a student at St. John's Lodge. He graduated with honors from Codrington College in the West Indies in 1863 and then took a two-year trip to many points in Africa. In 1866 he accepted a clerkship in the consulate at Belize, British Honduras, and subsequently became a minister in the Wesleyan Methodist Church.

In 1871 he decided to visit Europe via the United States, but found a new career in the United States and apparently never made it to Europe. He preached as a guest at a number of prominent AMEZ churches on the East Coast and was so impressive that church leaders persuaded him to stay. Two weeks after his arrival he joined the AMEZ Church, and he was ordained deacon on May 26, 1872. In Bridgeport, Connecticut, he met Mary Jane Blair, whom he married on October 23, 1873. That year he met for the first time with the New England Conference, which promptly elected him secretary.

After serving several charges in New England he transferred to the Central North Carolina Conference to pastor at the Fayetteville AMEZ Church. After nine years in North Carolina he transferred to the Philadelphia and Baltimore Conference and was appointed to John Wesley AMEZ Church in Washington, D.C. In 1887 he was among the first group of four to receive an honorary Doctor of Divinity degree from Livingstone College in Salisbury, North Carolina. In 1895 he published the first of several books, *Practical and Exegetical Pulpiteer*.

Small was presiding elder of the Philadelphia and Baltimore Conference when he was elected bishop in 1896. He was consecrated on May 21, 1896, and assigned to the mission work of the church in Africa and the West Indies, in addition to the home conferences of North Alabama, West Alabama, and South Mississippi. He had long had a special interest in bringing the message of the church to Africa, and he made the building up of the African mission his primary career focus. In 1898 he was the first bishop of the denomination ever to make an official visit to Africa, arriving in Sierra Leone on July 16. In August he went to Liberia to inspect the work accomplished by Andrew Cartwright, the AMEZ Church's first missionary to Africa.

He arrived back in the United States in October 1898, and immediately began a campaign for the strengthening of the church's presence in Africa. In 1900 he was reassigned to the mission work, plus the home conferences of West Alabama, South Mississippi, Allegheny-Ohio, and Western New York. In 1902 he made his second trip to Africa, and upon returning home in August, 1903, made arrangements to send a recent seminary graduate, Rev. Frank A. Pinanko, to found the first AMEZ church on the Cape Coast. By 1908 there were fifteen churches on the Cape Coast, with over five hundred members, along with a school, Varick Memorial Institute. The contacts which Small personally made in Africa proved invaluable to the future possibilities of the church in that region, as he learned several African languages and listened carefully to the needs and ways of the people. The foundation he laid in that work as the "Pioneer Missionary Bishop" survived his death of heart failure in early 1905. He left behind his wife, who was president of the Woman's Foreign and Missionary Society and the second woman ever ordained in the denomination, and an adopted son of a relative.

Small, John Bryan. *A Cordial and Dispassionate Discussion on Predestination, its Scriptural Import*. York, PA: Dispatch Publishing Co., 1901. 230 pp.

———. *The Human Heart Illustrated by Nine Figures of the Heart, Representing Different Stages of Life, and Two Death-Bed Scenes; the Wicked and the Righteous*. York, PA: Dispatch Publishing Co., 1898. 257 pp.

———. *Practical and Exegetical Pulpiteer*. York, PA: Anstadt & Son, 1895. 312 pp.

"The Work of Bishop J. B. Small in Africa." *The Star of Zion* 55 (September 3, 1931): 1, 8.

HAMEZC, TCBDA, AMEZC, BAW, HUBA.

SMALL, MARY JANE (October 20, 1850–193?), pioneer woman minister in the **African Methodist Episcopal Zion Church** (AMEZ), was born as Mary Jane Blair in Murfreesboro, Tennessee. She grew up around the church and as a child had a dream of being a missionary overseas. As a young adult she worked for the finance department of the denomination, but did not experience conversion until October 26, 1873. Three days previously, on October 23, 1873, she had married Rev. **John Bryan Small**, who became bishop in 1896.

In about 1890 she began to feel a call to the ministry, but resisted it until January 21, 1892, when, while signing the Christian Endeavor pledge, she decided to follow that leading. Later that year she was licensed to preach by John E. Price, presiding elder of the Second District of the Philadelphia and Baltimore Conference. She was ordained deacon by Bishop **Alexander Walters** on May 19, 1895. She thus became the second woman ever ordained in the AMEZ Church, after **Julia A. Foote**, who was ordained deacon in 1884. Small was ordained elder by Bishop **Calvin C. Pettey** on May 23, 1898.

Her career seems largely to have focused on denominational-level work, rather than a position in a local church. In about 1900 she succeeded Mrs. K. P. Hood as the third president of the Woman's Home and Foreign Missionary Society of the AMEZ Church. She remained in that position until 1916, when she was succeeded by Rev. **Florence Randolph**. At that time she apparently retired to a residence in McKeesport, Pennsylvania. Her husband had passed away in 1905, but she was not alone, sharing her home with an adopted son, William W. Gittens, who was a relative of her husband. She was still there in September 1931, though it is said that her final years were spent in a nursing home in Pittsburgh.

"Cover Photograph." *A.M.E. Zion Quarterly Review* 90 (Fall 1978): 122.

"The Work of Bishop J. B. Small in Africa." *Star of Zion* 55 (September 3, 1931): 1, 8.

HAMEZC.

SMITH, AMANDA BERRY (January 23, 1837–February 24, 1915), internationally known evangelist, was born into slavery in Long Green, Maryland, one of thirteen children in the family of Samuel and Mariam (Matthews) Berry. Before the Civil War, her father was able to purchase the family's freedom and move them to a farm in York County, Pennsylvania, which became a station on the Underground Railroad. As a young girl, Smith helped earn money as a maid and washerwoman.

She had very little formal education, but her parents were both literate and taught her at home insofar as they could.

In September 1854, at the age of seventeen, she married Calvin M. Devine, with whom she had two children. One child died in infancy and the other, Mazie, lived into her twenties. Smith experienced conversion in March 1856, which gave her new strength to face a difficult marriage, the hard life of a domestic worker, and the painful loss of her child. In 1862 her husband joined the Union Army and was killed. In 1863 she and Mazie moved to Philadelphia, where she soon married James Smith, a coachman and ordained deacon in the Old Bethel **African Methodist Episcopal Church** (AME). In 1864 and again in 1865 she lost two more children in infancy. They moved to New York City in 1865, and her husband then found a better job in New Utrecht, New York, where he relocated. He visited when he could, and sent money to help support her and another infant, while she continued as a domestic worker.

Smith continued to nourish her religious needs by attending church and the Tuesday meetings of Methodist Phoebe Palmer, an early leader in the Holiness movement. She heard about the Holiness doctrine of entire sanctification, and prayed to experience it. This happened for her in September 1868, on hearing a sermon by Methodist minister John S. Inskip. The following year the tragedy of her family life continued with the death of her husband and infant. She began to spend most of her free time preaching to Black churches in the New York-New Jersey area, meeting with enough success to overcome opposition to women preachers.

An employer enabled her to go in the summer of 1870 to a Holiness camp meeting, where she preached to a large White audience for the first time, and again met with great success. In the fall she left her job to be a full-time evangelist, working the camp meeting circuit across the eastern United States, and guest preaching in both Black and White churches. She was a tall, striking woman with a beautiful contralto voice, and she would often break into a hymn, earning her the title "the Singing Pilgrim."

In 1878 she went to England, attending the annual Keswick Holiness Convention and filling numerous speaking engagements. The planned three-month trip stretched much longer, and in 1879 she was invited to India, where she conducted missionary work for nearly two years. At the end of 1881, after a brief return to England, she sailed for Liberia. For the next eight years she worked with the Methodist Episcopal Church, the AME Church, and other groups active in the region. She organized many temperance societies and took into her care a native boy and girl. She finally returned to the United States in September, 1890.

She continued to preach until October 1892, when she settled into the new Chicago temperance community of Harvey, where she wrote her autobiography, published the next year. In 1899 she opened a home for Black orphan girls and ran a newspaper, the *Helper*, to advertise its work. Although advancing rheumatism made it difficult, the home's need for money led her back to the preaching circuit. She finally retired in 1912 when the orphanage was given a state charter as the Amanda Smith Industrial School for Girls, and real estate magnate George Sebring offered her a retirement home in Sebring, Florida. The orphanage was destroyed by fire in 1918. Her career was a pathmaker for other women church leaders, particularly in the Methodist Episcopal and AME churches.

Brown, LeRoy Chester. *On Whom the Fire Fell: Testimonies of Holiness Giants*. Kansas City, MO: Beacon Hill Press of Kansas City, 1977. 56 pp.

Cadbury, M. H. *The Life of Amanda Berry Smith: The African Sybil, the Christian Saint*. Birmingham, England: Cornish Brothers, 1916. 84 pp.

McLeister, Clara (Orrell). *Men and Women of Deep Piety*. Syracuse, NY: Wesleyan Methodist Publishing Association, 1920. 512 pp.

Smith, Amanda Berry. *An Autobiography: The Story of the Lord's Dealing with Mrs. Amanda Smith the Colored Evangelist, Containing an Account of Her Life Work of Faith, Her Travels in America, England, Scotland, India, and Africa as an Independent Missionary*. Chicago: Meyer, 1893. 506 pp.

Taylor, Marshall W. *The Life, Travels, Labors, and Helpers of Mrs. Amanda Smith, the Famous Negro Missionary Evangelist*. Cincinnati, OH: Cranston and Stowe, 1886. 63 pp.

LW, FAW, WIWR, WWCR, NYTO, BDA-AHP, NNW, BWNCAL, FOWW, PNW, HH, BH, BWR, IBAW, BAW, AARS, BDA-AAM, NAW, RLOA, NYB (1925–26), NBAW.

SMITH, BENJAMIN JULIAN (December 27, 1899–August, 1977), 27th bishop of the **Christian Methodist Episcopal Church** (CME), was born in Barnesville, Georgia, the seventh child of John Benjamin and Martha Angeline (Thomas) Smith. He experienced conversion at an early age in White's Chapel CME Church in Barnesville. He was educated at the Helena B. Cobb Institute in Barnesville, Georgia and went on to receive a B.A. from Howard University in Washington, D.C., in 1924 and a B.D. from Garrett Biblical Institute in Evanston, Illinois, in 1927. On March 4, 1928, he married Hermion V. Jackson, with whom he had three children.

His first pastorate was during his college days, as assistant minister at Israel CME Church in Washington, D.C., from 1922 to 1924. He was ordained a deacon in 1924. While in seminary he pastored New Hope CME Church in Evanston, Illinois, from 1924 to 1928. He was ordained elder in 1926 as a member of the Southeast Missouri and Illinois Conference. From 1928 to 1929 he was acting pastor at Williams Institutional CME Church in New York City and Director of Religious Education for the Eighth Episcopal District (Illinois, Missouri, and Kansas). He pastored the Jubilee Temple CME Church in Chicago from 1929 to 1930 and the Jamison Temple CME Church in Kansas City, Missouri, from 1930 to 1935. In 1930 he published the first of several writings, *The Church at the Crossroads*.

In 1935 Smith was elected General Secretary of Christian Education for the denomination, and held that position for the next nineteen years. In 1936 he published *The Educational Opportunity of the Local Church*. In 1948 he was a delegate to the First Assembly of the World Council of Churches in Amsterdam. He was elected bishop in May 1954, and that year helped change the name of the church from the Colored Methodist Episcopal Church to the Christian Methodist Episcopal Church. He was assigned to the Eighth Episcopal District, then composed of Arkansas and Oklahoma. In 1958 the districts were altered and he was shifted to the First Episcopal District, composed of Arkansas and Tennessee, where he remained the rest of his career.

During his episcopal tenure 150 churches were built and that many more remodeled and improved. Six buildings were added to Lane College in Jackson, Tennessee, where he was chair of the board of trustees. Five housing projects were initiated at a cost of six million dollars, and one million dollars were secured for Collins Chapel Hospital. He was one of the founders of Phillips School of Theology, part of the Interdenominational Theological Center (I.T.C.) in Atlanta, Georgia, and served as chair of its board of trustees and vice-president of the I.T.C. He was on the Central Committee of the World Council of Churches, a vice-president of the National Council of Churches, and president of the Tennessee Council of Churches. He was a trustee of Mississippi Industrial College in Holly Springs, and director of the Rockefeller Brothers Fund for Theological Education. He was vice-president of the World Council Christian Education and Sunday School Association, and president of the denomination's Board of Christian Education. In 1970, the year of his retirement, he was recognized as senior bishop of the denomination.

"Fifty Years of Service." *Christian Index* 110 (September 15, 1977): 4, 5.

Smith, Benjamin Julian. *The Church at the Crossroads.* Quality Publishing Co., 1930.

———. *The Educational Opportunity of the Local Church.* Jackson, TN: C.M.E. Church Publishers, 1936.

WWA (74–75), *EWM, BDNM* (70), *CMECTY, RLA.*

SMITH, CHARLES SPENCER (March 16, 1852–February 1, 1923), 28th bishop of the **African Methodist Episcopal Church** (AME), was born in Colborne, Canada, the son of Nehemiah Henry and Catherine Smith. At age twelve he was apprenticed to learn furniture finishing, but a fire destroyed the furniture factory and his apprenticeship ended after about a year. In 1866, at age fourteen, he left Bowmanville, Canada, and found a job in a boarding house in Buffalo, New York. Two years later he moved to Chicago and worked there both as a porter in a barber shop and on boats of the Great Lakes.

In the fall of 1869 he decided that he had enough education to serve as a teacher to the newly freed Blacks in the South, and found a position at Payne's Station on the Lexington Branch of the Louisville and Nashville Railroad in Hopkinsville, Kentucky, where he also experienced conversion. In June 1870 he moved to Jackson, Mississippi, where he was licensed to preach in August 1871. He then moved to Greenwood, followed by Yazoo City, Meridian, West Point, and Dekalb County, all in Mississippi. He was ordained deacon in the Alabama Conference on December 6, 1873, and appointed to the AME Church in Union Springs, Alabama.

On November 3, 1874, Smith was elected to the State Legislature of Alabama for a two-year term. In 1876 he was a leader at the Colored Men's National Convention in Nashville, Tennessee. About that time he temporarily changed his religious affiliation to the Methodist Episcopal (MEC) Church in order to gain access to "favorable facilities for pursuing some special lines of duty." He was ordained elder in that denomination on October 22, 1876, and became a student at Central Tennessee College (now Walden University). He pastored M. E. churches during this time in both Nashville and Murfreesboro. In April 1876, he married Katie Josephine Black, with whom he had three children. In early 1878 he returned to the AME Church and was appointed to the AME Church in Brownsville,

Pennsylvania, moving in late 1878 to the Allen Chapel AME Church and East Liberty Circuit in Pittsburgh. He graduated from Central Tennessee College in 1880 with a medical degree, but never practiced medicine as a profession. In September 1880, he transferred to the Illinois Conference and pastored the AME Church in Bloomington. In 1881 he became an agent for the David C. Cook Sunday School Publishing House.

In 1882 Smith's plan for a Sunday School Union, based on what he saw in the MEC Church, was approved by the Council of Bishops and he was made corresponding secretary. In 1884, at the general conference, the plan was unanimously supported by the church and he was appointed the corresponding secretary and treasurer, holding those positions until 1900. His accomplishments as founder and head of the Sunday School Union were tremendous. He built the Sunday School Union Building on Public Square in Nashville and established Children's Day for the collection of funds for and promotion of the Union. He produced the first Sunday School literature ever published by a Black person in the United States. In 1884 the church adopted his resolution against the doctrine of apostolic succession, against ritualism, and against the wearing of robes by the clergy. His first wife died on July 28, 1885, and on December 31, 1888, he married Christine Shoecraft, with whom he had one more child. He was a delegate to the Second Ecumenical Methodist Conference in Washington, D.C., in 1891.

Smith was elected bishop in May 1900, and assigned to the Twelfth Episcopal District (Ontario, Nova Scotia, Bermuda, and West Indies), followed by the Thirteenth Episcopal District (South Africa) from 1904 to 1906; West Africa and Louisiana from 1906 to 1908; the Sixth Episcopal District (Georgia) from 1908 to 1912; the Tenth Episcopal District (Texas) from 1912 to 1916; and the Fourth Episcopal District (Michigan, Canada, and West Indies) from 1916 to 1920. He was a delegate to the Third Ecumenical Methodist Conference in London in 1901, the Fourth in Toronto, Canada, in 1911, and the Fifth in London in 1921. Victoria College in Toronto gave him an honorary D.D. degree in 1911, the first such degree it had awarded a Black person.

He was a frequent contributor of articles to newspapers and magazines, and was an orator of unusual power. His most famous addresses were "Ballots and Bullets," "The Conflict Between John and Tom—A Review of the Race Question," and "The Noachian Curse." In 1910, while heading the Georgia area, he organized a rally which raised $30,000 for Christian education, the most money for education raised up to that point in history at a single rally by African Americans. In Texas he restored Paul Quinn College in Waco to a sound financial footing and made major improvements in its facilities. From 1920 until his death he worked as official historiographer of the church, bringing Bishop **Daniel A. Payne**'s history up to date from 1890. Named for him are churches in Inkster, Michigan, Wichita Falls, Dallas, and Eastland, Texas.

Payne, Daniel Alexander. *History of the African Methodist Episcopal Church.* Ed. by Charles S. Smith. Nashville, TN: AME Sunday School Union, 1891. 502 pp.

Smith, Charles Spencer. *Glimpses of Africa, West and Southwest Coast, Containing the Author's Impressions and Observations During a Voyage of Six Thousand Miles from Sierra Leone to St. Paul de Loanda and Return.* Nashville, TN: AME Church Sunday School Union, 1895. 288 pp.

————. *A History of the African Methodist Episcopal Church, Being a Volume Supplemental to a History of the African Methodist Episcopal Church by Daniel Payne.* Philadelphia, PA: Book Concern of the AME Church, 1922. 570 pp.

————. *Liberia in the Light of Living Testimony: A Pamphlet Compiled by C. H. Smith.* Nashville, TN: AME Church Sunday School Union, 1895.

————. *The Life of Daniel Alexander Payne.* Nashville, TN: AME Church Sunday School Union, 1894. 57 pp.

————. *Race Question Reviewed, with Individual Comments and Press Notices.* Nashville, TN: N.p., 1889. 63 pp.

————. *The Relations of the British Government to the Natives of South Africa. Address of Bishop C. S. Smith, Resident Bishop of the African Methodist Episcopal Church in South Africa, 1904–1906, Delivered at the Negro Young People's Christian and Education Congress, in Convention Hall, Washington, D.C., Wednesday, August 1, 1906.* Washington, DC: N.p., 1906.

BAMEC, HAMEC, EWM, WWWA (1), EAMEC, CEAMEC, DNAADB, WWCR, IBAW, BHAC, BAW, HUBA, AARS.

SMITH, CLARENCE JOWARS (1929–June 13, 1969), also known as Clarence 13X, founder of the **Nation of the Five Percent**, a Black Muslim group, was born in Danville, Virginia. He was affectionately known by his four brothers as "Puddin." As a teenager he moved to Harlem where he met and in 1945 married his wife Dora, with whom he had four children. In 1961 Smith joined the **Nation of Islam**, where he received his new name, indicative of his being the 13th person named Clarence who joined the Harlem temple of the Nation. X was a common designation of Nation members to indicate their loss of identity in the White society.

As Clarence 13X, Smith began to develop his own variation of Muslim teachings. It was general belief that **Wallace Fard Muhammad**, the Nation's founder, was

Allah. Smith began to teach that all Black people were Allah and that they should begin an inner search for truth. As some were attracted to his teachings, in 1964, **Malcolm X**, then the leader of the Harlem temple, expelled Smith. Smith founded the Nation of the Five Percent. The group's name comes from a belief that only five percent of the people understand the truth that they are Allah, and these five percent are the rightful leaders of the community. Smith designated his early followers as the "First Born." The movement attracted a number of youth and soon centers were founded in New Jersey and other nearby states. It was slowed somewhat by Smith's arrest and confinement in a state hospital. Released in 1968, Smith was able to secure a home for the movement which became known as the Allah School of Mecca.

Smith was assassinated in 1969 in Harlem. He was shot seven times at the Martin Luther King Towers. His body was cremated. The movement he founded continues.

As Sayyid Issa Al Haadi Al Mahdi. *The Book of the Five Percenters.* Monticello, NY: The Original Tents of Kedar, 1991. 627 pp.

SMITH, ELIAS DEMPSEY (? –April 18, 1920), the founder of **Triumph the Church and Kingdom of God in Christ**, was born in Mississippi and as a young man joined the Methodist Church and eventually became a minister. Then on October 20, 1897, he received a revelation from God that he should start a new church. However, it was not until five years later that Triumph the Church and Kingdom of God in Christ was formally established with headquarters in Baton Rouge, Louisiana. During this formative period, Dempsey became acquainted with **Charles H. Mason**, founder of the **Church of God in Christ**, and carried on several doctrinal discussions with him. However, Dempsey did not accept Mason's Pentecostalism, though he came to teach what was termed fire baptism, an experience of empowerment by the Holy Spirit similar to the Pentecostal experience but not tied to speaking in tongues.

Smith was intensely dedicated to the uplift of his members and assisted them in becoming financially independent. In the months following World War I, he became involved in the Back to Africa movement and the Ethiopianism which had experienced a revival in the Black community. In 1919 Smith hosted **Marcus Garvey** at the church's national convention in Indianapolis, Indiana. As a result of that gathering,

Smith was inspired to move to Ethiopia. However, a short time after his arrival he was killed.

Clark, Elmer T. *Small Sects in America.* Nashville, TN: Abingdon, 1949. 256 pp.
DuPree, Sherry Sherrod. *Biographical Dictionary of African-American Holiness-Pentecostals, 1880–1990.* Washington, DC: Middle Atlantic Regional Press, 1989. 386 pp.

SMITH, EMORY BYINGTON (June 12, 1886–October 15, 1950), Congregational minister, educator, and judge, was born in Raleigh, North Carolina, one of three children in the family of George and Elizabeth Smith. His father was a Congregational minister and his mother was the first woman graduate of Atlanta University. In 1902 Smith moved to Philadelphia, Pennsylvania, and later studied at Hampton Institute in Virginia and the New York Evening School for Men in New York City. He graduated from Yale Divinity School in New Haven, Connecticut, in 1910 and moved to Washington, D.C.

In 1915 he accepted the pastorate of the Lincoln Temple Congregational Church in Washington, D.C., and while there studied at Howard University Law School. In 1919 he received his law degree and married Viola Harris. In 1920 he began to practice as a member of the District of Columbia bar. He resigned from the church in 1923 to become alumni and field secretary for Howard University, and later publicity director. From 1931 to 1941 he was a member of the faculty of Terrell Law School in Washington, D.C. He was a loyal worker for the Democratic Party, speaking for its candidates on many occasions, especially on behalf of Presidents Roosevelt and Truman. He was told as early as the first campaign for Roosevelt in 1932 that his efforts would be rewarded with a judgeship, but the appointment never happened. Finally President Truman appointed him judge of the Municipal Court for the District of Columbia, and the appointment was confirmed by the Senate on September 21, 1950. He was sworn in to his long-awaited post on October 2, but died of a heart attack two weeks later.

Lawson, Belford V., Jr. "Judge Emory B. Smith." *Journal of Negro History* 36 (January 1951): 118–119.
EBA, NYTO.

SMITH, FRANCIS L. (b. 1915), a bishop of the **Pentecostal Assemblies of the World** (PAW), was born in Ironspot, Ohio. He was the nephew of Bishop **Karl**

F. Smith, for many years pastor of the Church of the Apostolic Faith in Columbus, Ohio. Smith experienced salvation under his uncle's ministry in 1933. Two years later he felt a call to the ministry. He married, and he and his wife Natalie had five children. He attended Aenon Bible College and later Burton Seminary and Ohio State University. He began his ministry at the Church of Jesus in Springfield, Ohio, where he served for only six months before moving to Akron as the pastor of the First Apostolic Faith Church which he has served to the present.

During his many years in the pastorate, he served as vice-chairman and then chairman of the Ohio District Council and as the District Elder on the Committee for the Propagation of the Faith, and as a member of the Aenon board of directors. Smith was elected to the bishopric in 1972 and was assigned to Episcopal District No.10, which covers the states of Alabama, Mississippi, and Western Tennessee. In 1974 he succeeded Ross Paddock, a White bishop, as presiding bishop of the PAW, a position he held until 1980.

Golder, Morris E. *The Bishops of the Pentecostal Assemblies of the World*. Indianapolis, IN: The Author, 1980. 69 pp.

SMITH, JOHN WESLEY (January 27, 1862–October 14, 1910), 29th bishop of the **African Methodist Episcopal Zion Church** (AMEZ), was born in Fayetteville, North Carolina. At the age of three his mother died and he was reared by his grandmother. One of his teachers in the grade school of Fayetteville was **Cicero R. Harris**, later a bishop in the AMEZ Church. He graduated from the State Normal School at the head of his class in 1878.

He experienced conversion on March 4, 1880, became a full member of the AMEZ Church a few months later, and was licensed to preach on October 4, 1880. He was ordained deacon in the North Carolina Conference on November 21, 1881, and elder on September 4, 1882. His first major assignment was at the AMEZ church in New Haven, Connecticut, beginning in 1882. Other pastorates included Little Rock, Arkansas; Fifteenth Street AMEZ Church in Louisville, Kentucky; Baltimore, Maryland; John Wesley AMEZ Church in Washington, D.C.; Grace AMEZ Church in Charlotte, North Carolina; Wesley Union AMEZ Church in Harrisburg, Pennsylvania; and Carlisle, Pennsylvania. He married Emma Thompson in 1888, who later passed away, and then married Ida V. Thompson. From the Carlisle pulpit he was elected editor of the *Star of Zion* in 1896, remaining in that position for eight years. He was consecrated bishop on

May 19, 1904, but was able to serve only six years before his death.

"Bishop John W. Smith." *A.M.E. Zion Quarterly Review* 64 (1953): 105.
HAMEZC, AMEZC, AARS.

SMITH, KARL FRANKLIN (1892–1972), a bishop of the **Pentecostal Assemblies of the World** (PAW), was born in Zanesville, Ohio. He was brought into the Assemblies in 1915 just at the time the non-Trinitarian Apostolic theology was spreading through the church. A Methodist, Smith was converted by **Robert C. Lawson**, then serving the PAW as a pastor in Columbus, Ohio. He married, and he and his wife Josephine became the parents of nine children. Smith became Lawson's assistant pastor, a position he held until 1919 when Lawson left the PAW to found the **Church of Our Lord Jesus Christ of the Apostolic Faith** in New York City.

Smith succeeded Lawson as pastor of the Church of Christ of the Apostolic Faith in Columbus, and remained there for the next half century. Smith wavered in his loyalties between Lawson and the Assemblies, but during the 1920s became a strong leader in the Assemblies, especially in the cause of education. In 1927 he was appointed to the founding committee of the Church's National Sunday School Association. In 1929 he was elected general secretary of the church.

Smith's upward career in the Assemblies was interrupted in 1932 when he became involved in the merger attempt with the Pentecostal Assemblies of Jesus Christ. In the 1920s the majority of the White members of the PAW had left and reorganized. Following the death of **Garfield T. Haywood**, the presiding bishop and dominant leader in the Assemblies, they invited the PAW to consider a merger. Many of the leaders agreed to the plan of union and moved into the new predominantly White church in the hope of recreating the interracial fellowship which had been the reality of life in the PAW in its early years. The experience was to be a disappointing one. The White members perpetrated a number of racial incidents which culminated in the holding of the 1927 convention in Tulsa, Oklahoma, where all knew an integrated meeting could not be held. At that time, most of the Black members and leaders, including Smith, left and returned to the PAW. Smith, **Samuel N. Hancock**, and other pastors were welcomed back into the Assemblies and their seniority returned to them. Smith was elected to the bishopric in 1940.

Smith's great contribution to the PAW began in 1940. The same convention that selected him to be a bishop appointed him and L. H. Salisbury to initiate a school for the training of ministers. The fall of the following year Aenon Bible School opened in Smith's church in Columbus, Ohio. Permanent facilities were purchased in 1944. By 1950 Smith developed a four-year curriculum for Aenon. He continued to serve as president of the school through the remaining years of his pastorate. He had to continually motivate the support of the Assemblies, which has been slow to recognize the value of an educated ministry.

Smith passed away in 1972. Amid all his other duties, Smith authored one book, *The Christian Pastorate.*

Golder, Morris E. *The Bishops of the Pentecostal Assemblies of the World.* Indianapolis, IN: The Author, 1980. 69 pp.
————. *History of the Pentecostal Assemblies of the World.* Indianapolis, IN: The Author, 1973. 195 pp.

SMITH, KELLY MILLER (October 28, 1920–1984), civil rights leader, first Black faculty and administration member of the Vanderbilt University Divinity School, and prominent minister of the **American Baptist Churches in the U.S.A.**, was born in Mound Bayou, Mississippi, the son of Perry M. and Priscilla (Anderson) Smith. His father was a devout Baptist deacon who instilled pride in his Blackness. Mound Bayou was an all-Black town, and Smith was thus saved as a child from some of the daily features of racism. When he was twelve an armed lynch mob came to town and publicly threatened to shoot a doctor whom they suspected of treating the man for whom they were looking. Smith long remembered the way the doctor just stood there and said, "Well, shoot." The mob just drifted away. Smith received his B.A. in 1942 from Morehouse College in Atlanta, Georgia, and his B.D. in 1945 from Howard University School of Religion in Washington, D.C.

From 1946 to 1951 he pastored the Mount Heroden Baptist Church in Vicksburg, Mississippi, and during that time was also head of the Department of Religion at Natchez College (1946–48) and extension teacher at Alcorn College (1949–50). In 1951 he left Vicksburg to pastor the First Baptist Church, Capitol Hill (later called the First Baptist Church of Nashville), Tennessee, where he remained the rest of his life. At one point he did leave Nashville to try the pastorate of the Antioch Baptist Church in Cleveland, Ohio, but returned to Nashville after only six months. A brilliant orator, already in 1954 *Ebony* magazine named him one of the top ten African American preachers. In 1956 *Ebony* noted that he had been called "one of America's most persuasive ministers, young or old." In 1958–59 he edited the *Young Adult Quarterly,* published by the American Baptist Church, and was an instructor at the American Baptist Theological Seminary from 1959 to 1961.

Smith was president of the Nashville branch of the N.A.A.C.P. from 1956 to 1959 and became deeply involved in the civil rights struggle and the **Southern Christian Leadership Conference** (S.C.L.C.). In 1960 it was in his office that the police came to arrest Rev. **James Lawson** for his protests against segregation. His church was headquarters for the massive sit-in movement in Nashville, and he was constantly negotiating new social structures with merchants, mayors, police, etc. He was on the executive board of the Nashville Urban League and the Tennessee Council on Human Relations. He served on the board of managers of the American Baptist Church Foreign Mission Society, and from 1954 to 1961 was moderator of the Stone's River District Association. In 1965 he became the first Black faculty member of the Vanderbilt University Divinity School, and continued teaching until he was appointed assistant dean in 1969, becoming the school's first Black member of the administration. Over the years he contributed to two books, *The Pulpit Speaks on Race* (1964) and *Best Black Sermons* (1972), and edited another, *Racism, Racists, and Theological Education* (1971). In 1982 he gave the coveted Lyman Beecher Lectures at Yale University, which resulted in a book, *Social Crisis Preaching* (1984). The first copies of the book were issued on the day he passed away. He is remembered as an effective and courageous leader during difficult times. His papers are housed at the Jean and Alexander Heard Library at Vanderbilt University.

Campbell, Will D. "Freedom is. . . ." *Christianity and Crisis* 44 (September 17, 1984): 318.
"Church Attending Soars to New High." *Ebony* 11 (March 1956): 18–23.
"A Church That Belongs." *Time* 108 (September 27, 1976): 87.
"Great Negro Preachers." *Ebony* 9 (July 1954): 26–30.
Smith, Kelly Miller. *Social Crisis Preaching.* Macon, GA: Mercer University Press, 1984. 125 pp.
WWABA (80–81), *BDNM* (75).

SMITH, KENNETH BRYANT (b. February 19, 1931), **United Church of Christ** minister and seminary president, was born in Montclair, New Jersey. He received his B.A. in 1953 from Virginia Union University and his B.D. in 1960 from Bethany

Theological Seminary in Chicago, Illinois. He married Gladys Moran, with whom he has had three children.

While in school he was associate minister of the Park Manor Congregational Church in Chicago from 1957 to 1961. From 1961 to 1966 he pastored Trinity United Church of Christ in Chicago, and from 1966 to 1968 he was minister for the Urban Affairs Chicago Community Renewal Society. In 1968 he became senior minister of the Church of the Good Shepherd Congregational Church in Chicago, where he has served through the 1970s and 1980s. In 1984 he added to his church work by becoming president of Chicago Theological Seminary, a position he has retained to the present. He is the second Black president of that school, succeeding **Charles S. Rooks**, the first African American president (1974–1984).

He has served on the board of directors of the Chicago branch of the Urban League and on the board of trustees of Elmhurst College. In 1967 he joined the national executive council of the United Church of Christ, serving until 1973, and from 1971 to 1973 he was chair of the council. He has co-authored two significant studies of issues within the United Church of Christ.

Bass, Dorothy C. and Kenneth B. Smith. *The United Church of Christ: Studies in Identity and Polity*. Chicago: Exploration Press, 1987. 107 pp.
———. *The United Church of Christ: Issues in Its Quest for Denominational Identity*. Chicago: Exploration Press, 1985. 46 pp.
WWA (90–91), WWABA (92–93).

SMITH, LUCY (1874–1952), Pentecostal faith healer, was living with her husband and eleven children in Athens, Georgia, in 1910. When her husband deserted the family that year she moved to Chicago, Illinois. She found work as a dressmaker to support herself and the children and joined the Olivet Baptist Church. She was baptized in 1914 and in 1916 began faith healing in her apartment. Her first patient was a White man who was in the last stages of tuberculosis, but was reportedly miraculously cured by her ministry.

Her reputation began to grow, and she eventually became pastor of the 3,000–member All Nations Pentecostal Church in Chicago. In 1950 Elder Smith claimed to have healed some 200,000 people. She healed with various techniques, including "holy rubbing" and making the patient vomit. She held twice-daily healing meetings and had two weekly radio broadcasts that reached 100,000 people. Her church also saw itself as a mission church and conducted programs to feed the hungry and clothe the needy.

"Faith Healer." *Ebony* 5 (January 1950): 37–39.
BH, BWR, BDA-AHP.

SMITH, LUCY WILMOT (November 16, 1861– ?), Baptist evangelist and journalist, was born in Lexington, Kentucky, the daughter of Margaret Smith. Her early education was sketchy, but she obtained enough to serve as a local teacher as early as 1877, when she was only sixteen. In 1887 she graduated from the normal department of Kentucky State University.

Smith served for a long time as secretary to **William Simmons**, founder of the **American National Baptist Convention** and educator. In 1882 he became editor of the *American Baptist*, the periodical in Louisville, Kentucky, of the Northern Baptist Convention, and in 1884 he made Smith editor for the children's column. She later served on the staff of the *Baptist Journal* in St. Louis and freelanced with a number of other papers. She joined the Afro-American Press Convention and was greatly praised for her clear and dignified style. She wrote a number of articles on the rights of women and was a strong advocate of women's suffrage. She is most known for her work for *Our Women and Children* magazine in Louisville.

Dunningan, Alice E. "Early History of Negro Women in Journalism." *Negro History Bulletin* 28 (May 1965): 178–179.
AAP, NNW.

SMITH, NOEL KENNETH was a bishop of the **Holy African Church**. Little is known of Smith's early life. He appears in the 1950s as a priest of the Holy African Church, a schism of the **African Orthodox Church**. On December 14, 1956, Smith was consecrated as a bishop for the church by Bishop **Frederick Augustus Toote**, the church's primate. On January 21, 1962, he participated in the establishment of a church mission among White Americans as co-consecrator of Francis Anthony Vogt.

In 1964, **Gladstone St. Clair Nurse**, at the time the church's primate, worked out an agreement with the African Orthodox Church to reunite the two bodies. Smith went into the African Orthodox Church as a bishop when it absorbed the Holy African Church.

Ward, Gary L. *Independent Bishops: An International Directory*. Detroit, MI: Apogee Books, 1990. 526 pp.

SMITH, WILLIAM MILTON (b. December 18, 1915), 65th bishop of the **African Methodist Episcopal Zion Church** (AMEZ), was born in Stockton, Baldwin County, Alabama, the son of George and Elizabeth Smith. He completed his normal training at Lomax-Hannon High School/Junior College in Greenville, Alabama, then received his B.S. from Alabama State College in Montgomery. He later spent two summers at Tuskegee Institute in Alabama and received a B.D. from Hood Theological Seminary at Livingstone College in Salisbury, North Carolina. He also studied at Perkins School of Theology in Dallas, Texas. In 1925 he married Ida Mae Anderson, with whom he had one child.

He entered the ministry at an early age and joined the South Alabama Conference. He was ordained deacon on November 12, 1939. His pastorates were all in Alabama and included St. Thomas AMEZ Church in Perdido and Atmore Circuit (one year); Zion Star Church in Atmore and Zion Fountain Church in Brewton (three years); Ebenezer AMEZ Church in Montgomery (seven years); and in 1948 Big Zion Church in Mobile (twelve years). Throughout the church he was in constant demand as a speaker and his pastorates were very successful. For many years he had a weekly sermon column called "Safely Through Another Week" in the denominational journal, the *Star of Zion*. While in Montgomery he was president for four years of the Montgomery Civic and Improvement League, in which one of his later successors was **Martin Luther King, Jr.** In 1945 he was elected the Most Outstanding Citizen of Montgomery. At Mobile he added more than 500 members and led the city's first sit-in for integration.

From his Mobile pastorate Smith was elected bishop and consecrated on May 15, 1960. From 1960 to 1964 he was assigned to nine mission conferences, including South America and the Virgin Islands. From 1964 to 1972 he headed the Ninth Episcopal District (Alabama, Pee Dee, Palmetto, South Carolina, and Louisiana), then was shifted to the Second Episcopal District (Western North Carolina, New Jersey, West Alabama). In 1980 he was assigned to the First Episcopal District (New York, Western North Carolina, Bahama Islands, and India), where he has since remained.

He is chair of the board of trustees of Livingstone College and Hood Theological Seminary in Salisbury, North Carolina, and is a trustee of Alabama State University. He serves on the national board of directors of the N.A.A.C.P. and in 1986 was appointed by Dr. Benjamin Hooks, executive director of the N.A.A.C.P., as the organization's first national chaplain. In 1982 Smith, already chair of the Ecumenical Committee of the World Methodist Council, was elected to the seven-person Presidium of World Methodists as president of the North American Section of the World Methodist Council, was reelected in 1986, and remained in that post through 1991. In 1987 *Ebony* magazine listed him for the sixth time as one of the most influential Black Americans. He is chair of the denomination's Church Extension Board and vice-chair of the church's publishing house. He has been "White House Fellow," which allowed him to recommend persons to serve in significant government positions. In 1980 he succeeded Bishop **Herbert Bell Shaw** as the Church's senior bishop.

"Bishop Smith Elected Section President World Methodists." *Star of Zion* 106 (September 2, 1982): 1, 11.

Henry, Emmet J. "Portrait of Our Senior Bishop: William Milton Smith." *Star of Zion* 110 (July 3, 1986): 3.

"Senior Bishop Named by *Ebony* Among Top 100." *Star of Zion* 109 (June 20, 1985): 1.

"Ten Religious Groups with Biggest Black Membership." *Ebony* 39 (March 1984): 140–141.

"Vignettes of Our Bishops: Bishop William M. Smith." *Star of Zion* 111 (October 15, 1987): 7.

"Zion's Senior Bishops During the Twentieth Century." *Star of Zion* 104 (March 27, 1980): 1, 2.

EWM, WWR (85), *WWA* (88–89), *HAMEZC, AMEZC, WWABA* (90–91).

SMITH, WILLIE MAE FORD (b. June 23, 1904), the "Mother of Gospel" and an ordained minister, was born in Rolling Fort, Mississippi, the seventh of fourteen children in the family of Mary (Williams) and Clarence Ford. After a few years the family moved to Memphis, Tennessee; then when she was twelve they moved again to Saint Louis, Missouri. Her father was a railway brakeman and her mother started a restaurant in Saint Louis. Her father was a devout Baptist deacon and often sang duets in church with her mother. Smith also blossomed into a singer, and loved to sing the blues and all other styles. In 1921, after she experienced conversion, she decided to dedicate her life to gospel music, though, like **Thomas A. Dorsey**, she developed a gospel style much permeated by the blues.

In 1922 her father formed some family members into the Ford Sisters Quartet, with Smith as lead singer. In 1924 she married James Peter Smith (d.1950), who ran a hauling business. Together they had two children. They also later (in the 1930s) adopted Bertha Smith, her accompanist for many years. In 1924 the Ford Sisters sang at the **National Baptist Convention, U.S.A., Inc.** (N.B.C.U.S.A.), but the audience was not quite ready for this brand of lively gospel music. Smith was developing this new form of church music at the same time Dorsey was working independently in the same direction, and they finally met in 1932. Smith joined the gospel movement being created by Dorsey and **Sallie Martin** and agreed to organize choirs in St. Louis for Dorsey. For seventeen years she was also head of the N.B.C. U.S.A.'s Education Department.

In 1936 Smith became director of the Soloists Bureau of Dorsey's National Convention of Gospel Choirs and Choruses, related to the N.B.C.U.S.A. For many years she thus trained soloists from across the country. Her 1937 composition and interpretation of "If You Just Keep Still" is regarded as having "set the standard for solo singing" at the time. In 1939, on a trip to Ohio, she had a holiness experience with the Holy Spirit which caused her to leave the N.B.C.U.S.A. and join the **Church of God (Apostolic)**. She had a lively church career, as it is reported that in the 1940s (another source says the 1920s) she was ordained a minister in the **African Methodist Episcopal Zion Church** and in the 1950s she was ordained a minister in the Lively Stone Apostolic Church in Saint Louis, an affiliate of the **Pentecostal Assemblies of the World**.

In the 1930s and 40s "Mother" Smith was constantly on the road with her solo career. Her students included Myrtle Scott, Martha Bass, the O'Neal Twins, Edna Gallman Cooke, and Brother Joe May. She was an inspiration to **Mahalia Jackson**, who wanted to leave the beauty shop to "be like" her. Smith made only one "single" record during her prime years, but many of those who made numerous recordings used nearly exact replicas of her arrangements. Some of her arrangements made famous by others include Martha Bass's "I'm So Grateful;" Mahalia Jackson's "If You Just Keep Still;" **Roberta Martin**'s "What a Friend We Have in Jesus;" and Brother Joe May's "Search Me Lord," "Old Ship of Zion," and "He'll Understand." Smith apparently never received any compensation for these popular arrangements and depended solely upon the collections taken at her concerts. In the late 1940s Smith and Mahalia Jackson sang for an Easter Sunrise Service at the Hollywood Bowl in Southern California. Mahalia Jackson stated that "there was never a gospel singer better than Willie Mae Ford Smith."

Smith is given the credit for developing the "sermonette and song," whereby songs and preaching are variously combined. She viewed herself as an evangelist and was determined to save souls. Combined with a highly dramatic performance style, her sermonette and song created a powerful impact and was much imitated. Because she was not commercially oriented, she did not gain the prestige or income that could have been hers. By the 1970s she was living in a retirement home in St. Louis, working at a $40-a-week job in a mental health center. All of her spare time was spent instructing singers and giving the occasional concert. In 1982 she was featured in a film on gospel music, *Say Amen Somebody*, and in 1988 she received the Heritage Award from the National Endowment for the Arts.

Glassner, Barry. "Mother of Gospel." *Sepia* 24 (April 1975): 56–62.
NBAW, BDA-AHP, BH, IBAW.

SMOOT, J. D. (b. November 1, 1877), an early minister of the **Church of God (Anderson, Indiana)**, was born in Tuskegee, Alabama. Though raised in the Baptist church, he had encountered Holiness teachings and had had an experience of sanctification, of being cleansed and made perfect in love by the Holy Spirit, the definitive Holiness experience. Early in the century he became the pastor of a Free-Will Baptist Church in Chicago. Then in 1905, he and his wife encountered the Church of God through the ministry of George and Mary Cole who ran a missionary home in the city. They were immediately attracted and left the Baptists and affiliated with the Church of God. He worked with the Coles for several years and attended Moody Bible Institute.

In 1915 Smoot moved back to Alabama as the pastor of Mortimer Street Church of God. While there, in 1923, he became a charter member of the church's board of church extension. The board later called upon his services as a missionary in New Orleans. His success is attributed to his mixture of the fire of traditional African American preaching with the more tempered preaching style taught at Moody. He found himself called upon by both the Black and White congregations of the Church of God to fill their pulpits. Smoot also served for many years on the church's board of missions.

In 1939 Smoot moved to Detroit to become pastor of the Church of God of Detroit. This African American congregation, the oldest Church of God center in the city, had experienced problems since the Depression, which had caught it in the midst of a building program. During the next three years he was able to revive the congregation and finish the building. In 1942 he resigned as pastor to start a second African American congregation, the Zion Church of God, in the growing Black community. He remained at Zion until his death in 1947.

Hetrick, Gale. *Laughter among the Trumpets.* Anderson, IN: General Assembly of the Church of God of Michigan, 1980. 250 pp.

SOLOMON, JOB BEN (1702?–1776), an eighteenth-century Muslim slave in Maryland, was born in Bundu, a town in Galumbo (or Catumbo) in the kingdom of Fatu (now the eastern part of present-day Senegal), among the Fulbe people. He was born Hyuba, boon Salumena, boon Hibrahema (anglicized to Job, the Son of Solomon, the son of Abraham). Solomon's grandfather Hibrahim founded Bundu and was confirmed as its Lord Proprietor by Bubaker, the king of Fatu. Both Solomon's grandfather and father were high priests. As a teenager, he assisted his father as an Emaum, or sub-priest.

In 1730, he was sent by his father to sell slaves to an English dealer docked on the Gambia River and to purchase some paper. Not liking the deal he was offered by the Englishman, he sold the slave to the Mandingos. On his way home, however, he was himself captured by the Mandingos and sold into slavery. He was taken to Annapolis, Maryland, and sold to Vachell Denton and then to a Mr. Tolsey on Kent Island. Tolsey put him in charge of herd of cattle. It soon became known that he would leave the cattle and go into the nearby woods to pray.

In May 1831 he ran away, but was recaptured and imprisoned. Since he spoke no English, no one in America knew his story, but while in jail he met a White man named Thomas Bluett who recognized him as a Muslim because he spoke the names "Allah" and "Muhammad" and refused to drink wine. Bluett located another slave who spoke Solomon's language and through him was able to get an account of Solomon's story. Upon his return home, his owner set aside a place for him to pray without any hindrance.

In 1772 he wrote a letter to his father seeking assistance. The letter fell into the hands of James Oglethorpe, who posted a sum to cover Solomon's freedom. Thus in 1773 Solomon sailed for England. On board the ship he was taught English. He was allowed to kill the cows brought on board the ship so they could be prepared in the correct manner. While in England, he met the royal family. In the summer of 1774 he finally returned to Gambia. That same year Bluett published an account of his life to that point.

Little is known of his later years. When he returned to Africa, his people were involved in a war and it was some months before he was reunited with them. He seems to have lived a long life after his return and to have died in 1776.

Austin, Allen D. *African Muslims in Antebellum America: A Sourcebook*. New York: Garland Publishing, 1984. 759 pp.

Grant, Douglas. *The Fortunate Slave: An Illustration of African Slavery in the Early Eighteenth Century*. London: Oxford University Press, 1968.

SOUTHERN BAPTIST CONVENTION. The Southern Baptist Convention is the second largest Christian denomination in the United States. It was formed in 1945 when Baptists in America split along regional lines over the slavery issue. However, in the last half of the twentieth century it has become a national body with strength in all parts of the country. In 1991 it reported 14,907,826 members.

Southern Baptists and African Americans in the Nineteenth Century. The Southern Baptist Convention articulated its concern for Christianizing slaves from its inception in 1845 and, through its Board of Domestic Missions (later known as the Home Mission Board), made efforts to carry out the Convention's directive. Laws against teaching slaves how to read and write, the general acceptance by Southern Baptists of Black inferiority, as well as their acquiescence to the traditional views on race relations, however, combined effectively to limit the amount of work actually done among the slave population. For Blacks who were converted and became Baptists, the church membership patterns established prior to the formation of the Southern Baptist Convention continued between 1845 and 1865. The majority of slaves became members of White churches, but others attended services for Blacks conducted by White preachers or gathered together to hear approved Black preachers. As the Civil War began, Black and White Baptists in the South were involved with one another, even if the involvement was based on a master-slave relationship.

Almost immediately after the Civil War Black Baptists began to leave White churches. Although the evidence suggests that the parting was by mutual agreement, the split nevertheless reflected both Black Baptist determination to be able to participate fully and freely in their own religious organizations and White Baptists' inability to adjust to the freedpersons as equals in Christ. Blacks formed their first state convention in North Carolina in 1866 and continued to develop other state conventions into the 1870s. The impetus for a national structure culminated in the formation of the **Baptist Foreign Mission Convention** in 1880.

The major person behind the formation of the Baptist Foreign Mission Convention was **W. W. Colley**, a Virginia native who had served as a Southern Baptist missionary in Africa under appointment by the Foreign Mission Board. Upon his return to America in 1879, the Black Baptists of Virginia commissioned him to determine whether there was enough support among Blacks to establish a foreign mission agency under Black control. Colley himself was convinced of the need for Blacks to be more involved in the foreign mission enterprise and found enough support to hold a meeting in Montgomery, Alabama, on November 24, 1880, to establish a convention. Approximately 150 people, mainly ministers, attended the meeting and the Baptist Foreign Mission Convention was born. **William H. McAlpine**, a leading Baptist minister in Alabama, was elected president, and Colley was elected the corresponding secretary.

Despite Colley's involvement with Southern Baptists and the positive results of that involvement, Southern Baptists' involvements with Blacks between 1865 and 1900 were hampered by financial problems and by Southern Baptists' inability to rise above the racial attitudes of the South. The American Baptist Home Mission Society seized the initiative, especially in the establishment of schools for the education of the freedman, which eventually helped Southern Baptists engage more in educating Blacks. Though some leading Southern Baptists had serious doubts about the educability of Blacks, there was support from their Home Mission Board for the education of ministers who would be responsible for leading the religious development of Black people.

In order to accomplish this, the board sponsored short-term institutes for Black ministers, some in conjunction with Northern Baptists. The Board also helped sponsor some theology students at the Augusta Institute that had been established in 1867 in Augusta, Georgia, by the American Baptist Home Mission Society; and in 1884 the board appointed Robert T. Pollard, a Black Baptist minister in Alabama, to serve as a theological professor at Selma University in Alabama. The Home Mission Board also wanted Southern Baptists to begin a school for Blacks, but that was not accomplished in the nineteenth century.

While Black and White Baptists in the South continued their separate identity, their reaction to the American Baptist Publication Society's dominance in the field of religious literature also showed their kindred spirit, if not their actual involvement with one another. Following the Civil War, Southern Baptists once again began to feel that there was a need for them to begin publishing their own materials. After two failed attempts, in 1891 the Baptist Sunday School Board emerged again as an independent entity. Black Baptists made extensive use of materials from the American Publication Society, and many Black ministers worked as colporteurs. Increasing concern over the lack of materials designed to meet the needs of Black Baptists, however, led many leaders to conclude that they needed their own publication facilities. The leadership was also concerned that the publication society did not use

capable Black writers. These concerns alone did not lead to the formation of the **National Baptist Convention, U.S.A., Inc.** in 1895, but they were among the earliest concerns that the new convention tried to address. Both Black and White Baptists in the South felt that they needed to control the means of producing and distributing the materials used in their churches.

The Twentieth Century. A plan had been devised to help coordinate Northern, Southern, and Black Baptist efforts to aid Black Baptists in developing their own churches and their denominational structures as early as 1895. The plan, known as the New Era Plan, was modified in 1904 to include less Northern Baptist participation. Under the modified plan, missionaries were jointly appointed by the Southern Baptist Convention and the National Baptist Convention, U.S.A. By 1914, a total of forty-seven missionaries had been jointly appointed. This number was reduced by the split within the Black convention in 1915 and by the beginnings of a severe economic crunch that confronted the Home Mission Board of the Southern Baptist Convention, so that twenty fewer missionaries were jointly appointed in 1923. These missionaries worked with churches, Black associations, and conventions in a variety of capacities. Some of them served as teachers in institutes or in other teaching positions. This continued the earlier concern for the education of Black ministers. One of the most striking examples of this particular concern, which also demonstrates the continued involvement of Black and White Baptists, was the ongoing discussions between National and Southern Baptists regarding the establishment of a seminary for Black students. The discussions, which occurred over a period of twenty years, culminated in the founding in 1924 of the American Baptist Theological Seminary, which was jointly supported by the two conventions.

The financial problems of the Home Mission Board grew worse during the 1920s and necessitated further cuts in personnel. The cuts affected the number of missionaries that continued to serve under joint appointment. By 1932 only six missionaries remained in the program. Within five years, however, the future prospects for Black and White Baptist involvements improved. In 1937 Noble Y. Beall was appointed by Southern Baptists to direct the Home Mission Board's Department of Cooperative Work with Negroes. Under Beall the position of teacher-missionary was begun. Persons serving in this position were missionaries whose primary responsibilities were in the field of education as teachers in predominantly Black schools. Beall was also successful in cultivating relationships with the

Northern Baptists who provided support for him in return for his continued contact with Northern Baptist schools for Blacks.

Two other milestones in Black-White Baptist involvement in the South were achieved in the forties. The first was in Home Mission Board personnel, and the second was in the area of education. In 1942, during the time of Beall's leadership, the Home Mission Board employed its first Black staff person, Roland Smith, who was employed as an assistant secretary with responsibility to serve as a liaison between Black and White Baptists. Though he did not have office space in the Home Mission Board building, his employment as a professional staff person was a major advance for the Southern Baptist Convention. Smith served the board during the turbulent post-World War II years, resigning in 1949.

The second milestone occurred in the same year when Garlund Offutt became the first Black to receive a doctorate from a Southern Baptist school. Blacks had attended Golden Gate Baptist Theological Seminary, and Offutt himself had received a Th.M. from the Southern Baptist Theological Seminary only four years earlier, but no Black had received a doctorate. Because of the segregation laws, Offutt was unable to attend regular day classes at the Louisville school. Rather, several teachers permitted him to do his work in their offices, which allowed him the chance to complete the requirements for the Th.D. degree.

The period since 1950 has not been any more tranquil than the fifty years preceding, but the rays of hope have been much brighter in terms of Black involvement within the Southern Baptist Convention. Early events indicated that at least two different approaches to Black involvement with Southern Baptists might develop. On the other hand, the traditional ministries with and to Blacks continued. Guy Bellamy was elected by the Home Mission Board in 1949 to continue the work of relating to Blacks in National Baptist structures. Eight years later the board employed S. E. Grinstead to develop Baptist Student Unions on predominantly Black college campuses. The work was paternalistic in the sense that Southern Baptists determined what was needed and moved to meet the perceived need, often without much Black input and with little or no Black control. The work was also geared to provide a ministry to Blacks who were outside the Southern Baptist Convention.

On the other hand, a new thrust in the involvement of Blacks with the Southern Baptist Convention occurred in 1951 when the Community Baptist Church of Santa Rosa, California, and the Greater Friendship Baptist Church of Anchorage, Alaska, joined Southern Baptist associations. These were the first Black churches to become members of the Convention this century. Although not made without a good deal of controversy, these advances meant that Blacks were once again on the inside of Convention life and work.

By 1968 the number of Black Southern Baptist churches increased to 57, and in that same year the Home Mission Board elected Emmanuel McCall as an associate in the Department of Work with National Baptists, which was headed by Victor Glass. Earlier Glass had hired the first Black secretary to work at the board, Arvella Turnipseed, and now he employed the first Black staff person to have an office in the Home Mission Board building. While questions remain unanswered about how much authority Roland Smith had to act during the time he was related to the board, McCall had the same authority as any other staff associate. McCall worked to keep the respect he had among National Baptists while he cultivated the respect of Southern Baptists.

It was only in the last years of this century that there has been a large enough Black presence in the Convention to merit any meaningful statements about Black Southern Baptist involvement. Most of this involvement was at the state and associational levels. As early as 1969, Marion Wheeler served as a moderator of a Southern Baptist association in Michigan. In the seventies the Alaska Convention elected two Black presidents, Herb Cotton, a layman, and William Lyons, a pastor in Anchorage. Other state conventions, such as California and Michigan, elected Black vice-presidents. These positions of leadership were conferred to these people not because they were Black, but because their work had convinced their peers that they could do the job. Such was the case when Charles N. King, a pastor in Frankfort, Kentucky, was elected second vice-president of the Southern Baptist Convention in 1974.

Securing Black Southern Baptist involvement in the professional staff positions of Convention agencies has proven much more difficult. The Baptist Sunday School Board hired Bill Kelly to work as a Baptist Book Store manager and in 1979 employed Sid Smith to serve as a consultant in the Ethnic Liaison Unit which later became the Black Church Development Section. In 1983 the Foreign Mission Board employed Willie Simmons as manager of Black church relations to increase Black participation in foreign missions.

Throughout the seventies, the Home Mission Board continued to work with National Baptists primarily through the Department of Cooperative Ministries with National Baptists. The name of the department reflected the new fraternal attitude of the department. Rather than setting the agenda unilaterally, Southern Baptists began the long and sometimes painful process of working cooperatively with National Baptists. A third name change was effected in the mid-1980s and the Department of Cooperative Ministries became the Black Church Relations Department.

A shift in the focus of Black ministries at the HMB dispensed with the work of the Black Church Relations Department and renamed it the Black Church Extension Division. Its focus was to begin starting new Black SBC churches instead of cooperative ministries, although some cooperative ministries work is still very active in many states.

The Sunday School, Home Mission, and Foreign Mission Boards each have African American personnel assigned to work in and with Black churches. Some inroads have been made in hiring Blacks to work in areas not primarily concerned with Black churches.

Fitts, Leroy. A *History of Black Baptists*. Nashville, TN: Broadman Press, 1985. 368 pp.

Jordan, L. G. *Up the Ladder in Foreign Missions*. Nashville, TN: National Baptist Publishing Board, 1903. 269 pp.

Moore, William T. *His Heart Is Black*. Atlanta: Home Mission Board of the Southern Baptist Convention, 1978.

Rutledge, Arthur B. *Mission to America: A Century and a Quarter of Southern Baptist Home Missions*. Nashville, TN: Broadman Press, 1969.

Spain, Rufus B. *At Ease in Zion: A Social History of Southern Baptists, 1865–1900*. Nashville, TN: Vanderbilt University Press, 1961.

Torbet, Robert G. *A History of the Baptists*. Valley Forge, PA: Judson Press, 1950. 540 pp.

Olivia M. Cloud

SOUTHERN CHRISTIAN INSTITUTE. A **Christian Church (Disciples of Christ)** school. The most successful effort of the Christian Church (Disciples of Christ) to provide educational opportunities for its African American members was the Southern Christian Institute, opened in 1882 in Edwards, Mississippi. In 1873–74, a revival had broken out in the Black community in Mississippi. Among the prominent converts was a Black Baptist minister, Levin Wood. Wood oversaw five congregations with a total of 800 members. It is no surprise then that, among those Disciples most interested in the cause of education for Blacks, Mississippi became the focus of their attention. In 1874 Thomas Munnell, an agent with the American Christian Missionary Society, went to Mississippi and came away with the offer of 160 acres of land for a school from William T. Withers, a former general in the Confederate Army. A seven-person board, including Wood, was formed but both financial problems and opposition to the school prevented its opening. In 1880 Withers withdrew his offer of the land.

Determined to have the school, supporters made several efforts to open it even if underfunded. In 1880 a school was opened in Heminway, Mississippi, but closed four months later. In May 1881, J. M. Williams, a Black preacher, opened a school in Jackson, but it did not survive the year. Finally in 1882, a permanent site was purchased near Edwards, Mississippi. The board had been able to work out an arrangement with the county to pay the students' tuition. Jepthah Hobbs, a Disciples minister, was given the job of leading the school and raising the money for its support.

The Southern Christian Institute gained stability through the decade, and the American Christian Missionary Society bought up the stock which had been sold to provide the school's initial financial support. As it gained controlling interest in the stock, it began supporting the school. Then in 1890 the Disciples created the Board of Negro Education and Evangelism to guide and coordinate all of the work among African Americans. The support of the church for the college greatly improved over the next decade.

As with most of the church schools serving the African American community in the South, the Southern Christian Institute began as an elementary school and added high school and eventually college classes. Over the years the college enrollment was small. Thus in 1954, with the improvement of the public education system for Black people, the Disciples moved to close the school. The college was merged into **Tougaloo College**, the Congregational Church [now **United Church of Christ**] school at Tougaloo, Mississippi.

Harrell, David Edwin. *The Social Sources of Division in the Disciples of Christ*. Athens, GA: Publishing Systems, Inc., 1973. 458 pp.

McAleister, Lester G., and William E. Tucker. *Journey in Faith: A History of the Christian Church (Disciples of Faith)*. St. Louis, MO: Bethany Press, 1975. 506 pp.

SOUTHERN CHRISTIAN LEADERSHIP CONFERENCE. An interdenominational organization. The Southern Christian Leadership Conference (S.C.L.C.), remembered as the main organization through which **Martin Luther King, Jr.**, led the civil rights movement of the 1960s, was founded in 1957. It grew out of the Montgomery Bus Boycott of 1955–56 which gave focus to generations of racist policies and actions. While developed with a broad vision of supporting oppressed people everywhere and working for the liberation of all, S.C.L.C. was faced with the immediate problem of mobilizing the discontent which had become so visible through the boycott and of imposing King's nonviolent philosophy and tactics on the movement as protest swelled. Within the first year, chapters were formed across the South and a program centering on a voter registration drive was launched. In 1959 a major education effort was begun through the S.C.L.C. sponsored Institute of Nonviolent Resistance to Segregation.

By 1960 a noticeable movement had begun among students who had begun the era of the sit-ins. S.C.L.C. encouraged the formation of the Student Nonviolent Coordinating Committee which, initially at least, followed S.C.L.C.'s philosophy and tactics. Almost every year the organization broadened its thrust as new programs were created. In 1961 the Freedom Rides began and the next year King announced the beginning of Operation Breadbasket, a program to obtain new job opportunities through boycotts of businesses operating in the African American community. In 1963 the demonstrations in Birmingham, Alabama, culminated in the March on Washington, possibly the height of S.C.L.C.'s ability to mobilize public support. The following year the movement reached its first goal in the passing of the Civil Rights Bill.

Still possessed of tremendous momentum, S.C.L.C. moved from the civil rights legislation to voting rights. Joined by upwards of 50,000 people, King and the organization's leaders led a march from Selma to Montgomery, Alabama. The activity culminated in the passing of the Voting Rights Act later that year.

The passing of the two major pieces of legislation in 1964 and 1965 brought S.C.L.C. to the pinnacle of success, but a success that had the additional effect of largely killing a movement which had accomplished its goals. S.C.L.C. refocused its activity in Chicago. King pushed Operation Breadbasket on a youthful seminary student, Jesse Jackson, who emerged as S.C.L.C.'s most charismatic leader outside of the South.

One can only wonder how the development of S.C.L.C., and of African American history, would have differed if the event of April 4, 1968, had never occurred. By that time Martin Luther King, Jr., was under heavy attack on the ideological front from the advocates of Black Power who were challenging the adequacy of his non-violent tactics and program. Ministerial colleagues in the North had established the National Committee of Negro Churchmen (now the **National Conference of Black Churchmen**) to provide alternative directions.

Meanwhile, **Ralph D. Abernathy** succeeded King as leader of S.C.L.C. Amid some successes as the organization continued to engage in a wide variety of activities, internally it was in some chaos as many felt that Abernathy was not the right man to lead. Among those choosing to leave was **Jesse Jackson**, head of the Chicago S.C.L.C. Amid pressure, he stepped down in 1977 and was succeeded by **Joseph E. Lowery**, the present president.

The period of Lowery's leadership has been characterized as the passing of the times of the great demonstrations and the need to work more quietly and substantively for the implementation of the regulations passed in the 1960s. Demonstrations, when they have occurred, have tended to concern more local and short-term issues, though a massive push was mobilized for the extension of the Voting Rights Act in 1981. Also, since his death, Martin Luther King, Jr., has been increasingly recognized worldwide for his contributions to humanity.

Through the 1980s, the work of S.C.L.C. has been marked by number of celebrative occasions. In August 1982, Lowery, Abernathy and **Fred Shuttlesworth** led a march to mark the 25th anniversary of the organization's founding and open its convention. That convention was addressed by none other than former Alabama governor George Wallace, whose opposition played so important a role in the 1960s. In 1983 a march in Georgia on King's 54th birthday called for that day (January 15th) to be set aside as a national holiday. That holiday was established later that year. Lowery traveled to Germany in 1989 as the guest of the German government to celebrate King's 60th birthday.

The most substantive element of the expanded program of S.C.L.C. in the 1980s was its concern with the plight of the poor and homeless. In 1982, for example, the passing of the extension of the Voting Rights Acts caught many in Washington ready to lobby for what had quickly occurred. The group immediately reoriented, built Resurrection City II, and used the opportunity to call the public to an awareness of the nation's poor. In 1988 S.C.L.C. organized a demonstration at the Democratic Convention for the homeless. More recently the organization acquired a home which had been taken over in a foreclosure and, as a means of remembering the 25th anniversary of King's death, renovated it for occupancy by a homeless family.

The S.C.L.C. is headquartered in Atlanta, Georgia, and has affiliated chapters across the United States. Both **Coretta Scott King** and Martin Luther King, III, sit on the organization's board. The *Southern Christian*

Leadership Conference National Magazine is issued from the Atlanta headquarters.

Albert, Peter J., and Ronald Hoffman, eds. *We Shall Overcome: Martin Luther King, Jr., and the Black Freedom Struggle.* New York: Pantheon Books, 1980. 294 pp.

McGriggs, Lee Augustus. *The Odyssey of Martin Luther King, Jr.* Washington, DC: University Press of America, 1978. 195 pp.

Oates, Stephen B. *Let the Trumpet Sound: The Life of Martin Luther King, Jr.* New York: Harper & Row, 1987. 260 pp.

Patterson, Lillie. *Martin Luther King, Jr., and the Freedom Movement.* New York: Facts on File, 1989. 178 pp.

SPEAKS, RUBEN LEE (b. January 8, 1920), 76th bishop of the **African Methodist Episcopal Zion Church** (AMEZ), was born in Lake Providence, Louisiana, the son of Benjamin and Jessie Bell (Nichols) Speaks. He received his B.A. degree in 1946 from Drake University in Des Moines, Iowa, the B.D. in 1949 from Drew University in Madison, New Jersey, the S.T.M. in 1952 from Temple University in Philadelphia, and did further studies at Duke University in Durham, North Carolina. On August 31, 1947, he married Janie Angeline Griffin, with whom he had three children.

He was received into the New Jersey Conference of the AMEZ Church on credentials on May 20, 1946, and was ordained elder on June 8, 1947. His pastorates included St. Thomas AMEZ Church in Somerville, New Jersey (1947); Wallace Chapel AMEZ Church in Summit, New Jersey (1948–50); Varick Chapel AMEZ Church in Philadelphia, Pennsylvania (1950–56); St. Mark AMEZ Church in Durham, North Carolina (1956–64); and First AMEZ Church in Brooklyn, New York (1964–72).

In Durham he was on the board of directors of the Durham Committee on Negro Affairs from 1958 to 1963, and during the same period was chair of the executive committee of the N.A.A.C.P. In 1964 he was the recipient of the Citizens Award from the City of Durham. Under his leadership at First Church in Brooklyn an outreach program was developed in cooperation with Brooklyn College and Kingsboro Community College which helped many young people prepare for college admission through remedial work. He was on the board of directors of the New York Urban League from 1967 to 1972. In all his pastorates he was very successful and earned a reputation as one of the most effective administrators in the church, a reputation he has extended as bishop.

From his Brooklyn pastorate Speaks was elected bishop and consecrated on May 12, 1972. He was assigned to the Twelfth Episcopal District (West Ghana, Nigeria, Central Nigeria, Liberia, and East Ghana Conferences), where he stayed for eight years. In 1980 he was shifted to the Eighth Episcopal District (West Tennessee-Mississippi, South Mississippi, Cape Fear, Louisiana). In 1988 he was assigned to the Sixth Episcopal District (Pee Dee, South Carolina, Palmetto, Georgia, South Georgia, and West Central North Carolina Conferences). For his service in Africa the Republic of Liberia awarded him the honor of Knight of African Redemption. He has published a number of articles and pamphlets. He is a trustee of Livingstone College in Salisbury, North Carolina and the University of North Carolina in Wilmington. Among his many organizational affiliations, he is on the executive committee of the World Methodist Council and serves with the World Council of Churches, National Council of Churches, and N.A.A.C.P.

Speaks, Ruben Lee. "The Church and Black Liberation." *A.M.E. Zion Quarterly Review* 83 (Fall 1971): 138-148.
———. "Will the Negro Remain Protestant?" *Christian Century* 71 (June 2, 1954): 668–669.
———. "Zion! Africa is Calling." *A.M.E. Zion Quarterly Review* 8 (Spring 1973): 18–21.
"Vignettes of Our Bishops: Bishop Ruben L. Speaks." *Star of Zion* 111 (November 26, 1987): 7.
HUBA, AARS, WWR (75–76), *BDNM* (70), *WWA* (88–89), *WWABA* (85), *AMEZC.*

SPEIGNER, THEODORE ROOSEVELT (March 31, 1906–August 10, 1983), educator and pioneer Lutheran minister, was born in Montgomery, Alabama, the son of Edward and Sallie (Craig) Speigner. He attended Alabama State Teachers College in Montgomery from 1922 to 1926 and Wilberforce University in Ohio in 1926–27. He received his B.A. in 1931 from Talladega College in Alabama and his M.A. in 1933 from the State University of Iowa, Iowa City, Iowa. His master's thesis was "Economic Activities of the U.S. in Liberia, 1900–1930."

In 1931 Speigner became principal of Dobler Institute, a Lutheran primary and secondary school in Tuscaloosa, Alabama. The school had been founded about 1917 under the name St. Paul's Lutheran school and had been renamed in honor of Judge Dobler of Baltimore, who was on the mission board for twenty-eight years. Under Speigner's leadership Dobler Institute was renamed St. Paul Lutheran Academy, and then later Martin Luther Institute. Speigner and his wife (name unknown) did much to strengthen the school and the mission of which it was a part. He was ordained a minister in the American Lutheran Church (now a constituent part of the Evangelical Lutheran Church in America) in 1941. He became president of the Alabama Conference of the American Lutheran Church and from 1935 to 1939 was chair of the high school department of the Alabama State Teachers' Association. In September 1947 the high school was merged with the Alabama Lutheran Bible Institute and Speigner was granted a leave of absence to take a teaching post at North Carolina College in Durham, where he remained until retirement in 1979.

BDCALC, ALCY, LCAN, WWCA (38–40).

SPELMAN COLLEGE. A Baptist school. Spelman College is one of the early schools founded for the education of African American women. It opened in 1881 as the Atlanta Baptist Female Seminary in the basement of Friendship Baptist Church. The emergence of the seminary was the combined effort of the African American pastor of the church, Frank Quarles, and two White women from the Women's Baptist Home Missionary Society: Sophia Backard (1824–1891) and Harriet E. Giles (1833–1909).

The first class at the new school consisted of eleven women, all too old to attend public school. Soon the school picked up additional support from the American Baptist Home Missionary Society and from John D. Rockefeller, who gave money to complete the purchase of a campus. The school moved into its new home in 1883. In 1884 the school was renamed Spelman Seminary, in honor of Rockefeller's father-in-law. Over 500 pupils now attend the school.

Over the next generation, Spelman developed into a full four-year liberal arts college, and in 1924 it took its present name. It now serves over a thousand pupils annually.

Pegues, A. W. *Our Baptist Ministers and Schools.* Springfield, MA: Willey & Co., 1892. 643 pp. Rept.: New York: Johnson Reprint Corporation, 1970. 643 pp.

Read, Florence Matilda. *The Story of Spelman College.* Atlanta, GA: United Negro College Fund, 1961. 399 pp.

SPENCER, HUBERT J. (December 28, 1901–1964), presiding bishop of the **Church of Our Lord Jesus Christ of the Apostolic Faith**, was born in Marytown, West Virginia. Raised a Baptist, he experienced conversion at the age of nine. As a teenager he was influenced by the Pentecostal movement which was beginning to move into the area and at the age of

seventeen experienced the baptism of the Holy Spirit as evidenced by his speaking in tongues. He also felt a call to the ministry. Among his teenage friends was **Smallwood Williams.** At Williams's urging Spencer joined the Church of Our Lord Jesus Christ which had just been founded by **R. C. Lawson**. Lawson, a pioneer Apostolic or Oneness minister in Ohio with the **Pentecostal Assemblies of the World,** had left the Assemblies in 1919, moved to New York City, and founded an independent denomination.

Ordained by Lawson, Spencer served as an evangelist and pastor. In 1926 he became pastor of Rehoboth Church. In 1928 he was consecrated a bishop, one of the first and the few so honored by Lawson. Spencer had a long career assisting Lawson in the administration of the church. Then, in the 1950s, he had to face the issue raised by his longtime friend Smallwood Williams, who joined with other church leaders to complain that Lawson had become an autocrat and refused to share the leadership by naming further bishops. Williams had by that time become pastor of one of the largest churches in the denomination in Washington, D.C. Eventually, in 1957, Williams left and with others founded the rival **Bible Way Church of Our Lord Jesus Christ World Wide.** In the midst of the crisis, Spencer remained loyal to and supportive of Lawson.

Four years later, Lawson died. Spencer was chosen to succeed him. Spencer died after only three years in office as presiding bishop. He is credited with supplying the church with a period of transitional stability in the wake of two major crises. He was succeeded by **William Lee Bonner.**

DuPree, Sherry Sherrod. *Biographical Dictionary of African-American Holiness-Pentecostals, 1880–1990.* Washington, DC: Middle Atlantic Regional Press, 1989. 386 pp.

SPENCER, PETER (1782–July 25, 1843), founder of Union Church of Africans (or African Union Church) which survives to the present as two denominations, the **African Union First Colored Methodist Protestant Church** and the **Union American Methodist Episcopal Church,** was born in slavery in Kent County, Maryland. His master died when he was still relatively young, and Williams was given his freedom. In the 1790s he moved to Wilmington, Delaware. He was able to obtain an education, possibly in a Quaker school, and went to work as a mechanic. He married Anne Spencer. It would appear he also became a prosperous businessman and property owner in Wilmington.

Williams had become a Christian while still a slave. In Wilmington he affiliated with Asbury, a predominantly White congregation of the Methodist Episcopal Church. The congregation had a growing number of Black members. He became a class leader and lay preacher among the African members. Over the next few years as the proportion of African members increased, tension began to develop over the segregated seating and various actions by the Whites indicating their consideration of the Black members as inferior in status.

In 1805, Spencer and William Anderson led the Black members out and formed Ezion church. The members constructed their own church building, and the congregation remained a part of the Methodist Episcopal Church. Spencer served as one of the church's trustees. During the next seven years some degree of harmony existed. Then in 1812 the new elder appointed by the Methodists to Wilmington created a power struggle with the trustees at Ezion. He dismissed all of them. Spencer and Anderson again led the membership out, this time to found an independent congregation. In the summer of 1813 Spencer purchased a lot upon which a building was erected. It was incorporated as the Union Church of Africans, the first group of African American Methodists to organize separately from the Methodist Episcopal Church.

Shortly after incorporating, Spencer and Anderson were set apart as elders for the new church. Spencer was designated senior elder minister and pastor of the congregation in Wilmington. In forming the new church, Spencer decided against the addition of episcopal authority, a paid ministry, and the itinerancy (in which pastors regularly moved among the associated congregations rather than settling permanently in one location as a pastor). His church thus developed a rather loose structure.

Spencer led the church, which became a new denomination, for the rest of his life. Within a few years affiliated congregations appeared in Pennsylvania and New York, and some thirty had been founded by the time of Spencer's death. Spencer emerged as a champion of the causes of Black Americans. He opposed the work of the **American Colonization Society** and worked for the liberation of the slaves to a life in America. To that end he allowed his church to become a stop on the Underground Railroad.

He died in Wilmington in 1843.

Baldwin, Lewis V. *"Invisible" Strands in Methodism: A History of the African Union Methodist Protestant and Union American Methodist Episcopal Churches, 1805–1980.* Metuchen, NJ: Scarecrow Press, 1983.

———. *The Mark of a Man: Peter Spencer and the African Union Methodist Tradition.* Lanham, MD: University Press of America, 1987. 87 pp.

SPIRITUAL CHURCHES. The first prominent alternative religious community to develop in nineteenth-century America was Spiritualism. Taking elements from Swedenborgianism, and responding to Freethought's denial of spiritual realities and life after death, Spiritualism claimed to be able to demonstrate, scientifically, that individuals survive death into a spirit existence. Spiritualists, which had previously formed state associations across the country, in 1893 developed a national organization, the National Spiritualist Association (of Churches). Spiritualism had a ethic based upon a belief in universal brotherhood, and during its first generations, African Americans were welcomed into it and several emerged as mediums, i.e., movement leaders who claimed the ability to communicate with spirit entities. In spite of its ideals, in the early twentieth century the movement became the home to racist perspectives. In 1922 the National Spiritualist Association of Churches, forced its Black members out into the **National Colored Spiritualist Association of Churches**.

Through the 1920s, African American Spiritualists formed a variety of new denominations, generally taking the name "Spiritual" rather than "Spiritualist," a term which has come to distinguish them for their White counterpart. Among the early Black leaders was Leafy Anderson (1887–1927). Anderson emerged in Chicago where in 1913 she founded the Eternal Life Christian Spiritualist Association. Around 1920 she moved to New Orleans and organized the first Spiritualist congregation in the Black community in that city, the twelfth congregation of the Association. In Detroit, Willie Hurley founded **Universal Hagar's Spiritual Church** in 1923, and in 1925 William Frank Taylor and Leviticus L. Boswell of Kansas City founded the **Metropolitan Spiritual Churches of Christ**. About this same time, Derk Field organized the Church of God in David (a forerunner of **Spiritual Israel Church and Its Army**) in Alabama. In 1936, **Thomas Watson**, an Anderson student, founded the Divine Spiritual Churches of Southwest. Over the succeeding decades, a number of other denominations were formed and many independent spiritual congregations developed.

Beginning with Spiritualism, the new Spiritual denominations began an independent development, both in response to the unique situation within the African American community and the freedom presented to them once they stepped outside of the confinements of

Christian orthodoxy. The movement became quite diverse and eclectic, drawing upon a number of different religious sources. Leafy Anderson represents the more conservative wing of the early movement. After settling in New Orleans she followed a pattern familiar to White Spiritualist churches and she retained her contact with the White spiritualists, who frequently spoke at her churches. The Bible was used and familiar hymns (with offending passages altered) were sung. She made a point of denying any association with voodoo and denounced the popular magic with flourished in the African American community of New Orleans.

Mother Catherine Seals, a student of Mother Anderson, incorporated elements of popular folk magic, usually termed "hoodoo," into her group. In 1929 she built the Temple of the Innocent Blood in New Orleans. She also downplayed the giving of messages from the realm of spirits in place of spiritual healing.

The Spiritual movement basically mixed traditional Spiritualism with Christianity. In any given congregation or association of congregations, the exact nature of that mixture varies according to the background of the founding mediums. Thus in different churches, elements of Roman Catholicism, Protestantism, and/or Pentecostalism would be evident. Jacobs and Kaslow, for example, found that the Divine Spiritual Churches of the Southwest had taken the text of the Articles of Religion of the Methodist Episcopal Church (now the **United Methodist Church**) as the basis of its statement of belief. Additional material was added from a Roman Catholic source. Roman Catholic influence is especially evident in the Spiritual Churches of New Orleans where there is some identification of Roman Catholic saints and African deities.

In 1942 the Divine Spiritual Churches of the Southwest merged into the Metropolitan Spiritual Churches of Christ thus creating one of the largest national associations of Spiritual believers. This was the period of the rise of **Clarence Cobbs** as the national leader of the Churches, and Cobbs quickly came into conflict with Thomas Watson the first national president of the merged church. A schism ensued in 1945 with the Watson group continuing as the United Metropolitan Spiritual Churches of Christ with headquarters in New Orleans and Cobb's following continuing under the original name with headquarters in Chicago.

Since World War II, the older Spiritual churches have continued though frequently experiencing measurable ups and downs as prominent leaders have arisen and passed from the scene. Meanwhile the general process of fragmentation which has afflicted all of the religious communities in the United States, has also had its effect among the Spiritual churches as young talented mediums have left associations in which they received their early training and experiences to found their own independent churches.

Baer, Hans A. *The Black Spiritual Movement: A Religious Response to Racism.* Knoxville, TN: University of Tennessee Press, 1984. 221 pp.

Jacobs, Claude F., and Andrew J. Kaslow. *The Spiritual Churches of New Orleans: Origins, Beliefs, and Rituals of an African American Religion.* Knoxville, TN: University of Tennessee Press, 1991. 235 pp.

SPIRITUAL ISRAEL CHURCH AND ITS ARMY. A **Spiritual** church. The exact origins of the Spiritual Israel Church and Its Army remain obscure, but, as its name implies, it exhibits characteristics of two larger African American religious traditions, namely **Black Judaism** and Black Spiritualism. Several leaders of the Spiritual Israel Church, including Bishop Robert Haywood (the "King of All Israel") and Bishop George Coachman (the association's "Overseer"), have provided fragmentary data about the group's beginnings. One version traced the beginnings of the sect back to the 1920s, the other version placed its establishment in the late 1930s. The forerunner of the Spiritual Israel Church was the Church of God in David, which was established by Derk Field in Alabama. At some point, either in Alabama or Michigan, Field met W. D. Dickson, who had arrived at similar ideas. After Field's death, Dickson took on the title of the "King of All Israel" (a title also carried by his successors) and pulled Spiritual Israel "out of David" upon instructions from the Spirit.

Spiritual Israelites credit both Field and Dickson with "restoring" the teachings of the ancient Israelites. Apparently after the death of Derk (or Derks) Field, a power struggle for the leadership of the association occurred among Dickson and the surviving Field brothers, Doc and Candy. Each of the Field brothers established a separate organization, and several other groups, all containing the word "Israel" in their names, later broke away from the Spiritual Israel Church. Because of the severe Michigan winters, Dickson moved the sect to Virginia for a while, but returned to Detroit upon further instructions from the Spirit. Dickson was succeeded in his leadership by Bishop Martin Tompkin and Bishop Robert Haywood.

In 1982 the group reportedly had 38 temples and missions, with a concentration of them in southeastern Michigan (namely the Detroit metropolitan area, Flint, Ann Arbor, and Lansing). There were also congregations in New York City, the Chicago area, Milwaukee, Philadelphia, Minneapolis, Washington, D.C.,

Louisville, New Orleans, several cities in Indiana (Gary, Fort Wayne, and Muncie), a small city in Ohio, as well as five congregations in the Southeast (New Orleans, Florida, Georgia, Alabama, and Mississippi).

Members of Spiritual Israel Church and Its Army view themselves as spiritual descendants of the ancient Israelites or "Spiritual Jews," and their association as a restoration of the religion of the ancient Israelites. They maintain that "Ethiopian" is the "nationality" name of Black people whereas "Israel" is their "spiritual" name. The first human beings were Black people, starting with Adam, who was created from the "black soil of Africa." All of the great Israelite patriarchs and prophets were Black men. In time, however, with the sons of Isaac, a division in humanity developed. Jacob became the progenitor of the Ethiopian nation and Esau of the Caucasian nation. Spiritual Israelites maintain that most Whites who identify themselves as "Jews" are actually the descendants of Gentiles who intermarried with the original Jews or Israelites.

Spiritual Israelites maintain that they belong to the "one true Spiritual church" and that the Spirit dwells in all people. Like most other Spiritual groups, they believe that heaven and hell are projections of the human mind. The Christ Spirit, which is simply the "anointed power" of God, has occupied the bodies of many kings of Israel.

Baer, Hans A. *The Black Spiritual Movement: A Religious Response to Racism.* Knoxville, TN: University of Tennessee Press, 1984. 220 pp.

Baer, Hans A. "Black Spiritual Israelites in a Small Southern City." *Southern Quarterly* 23,3 (1985):103–124.

Hans A. Baer

SPIVEY, CHARLES SAMUEL, JR. (b. February 28, 1921), **African Methodist Episcopal Church** (AME) minister, seminary president, and prominent ecumenist, was born in Washington, Ohio, the son of Charles Samuel, Sr., and Ruth Elizabeth (McGee) Spivey. He received his B.S. in 1942 from Wilberforce University in Ohio, his B.D. in 1944 from Payne Theological Seminary at Wilberforce, and another B.D. in 1945 from Yale Divinity School in New Haven, Connecticut. In 1946 he was dean of Dickerson School of Theology at Allen University in Columbia, South Carolina, and from 1947 to 1957 he variously pastored Allen AME Church, Brown AME Church, and Bethel AME Church, all in Pittsburgh, Pennsylvania. On October 17, 1950, he married Ruth Elizabeth Everett, with whom he had three children.

From 1957 to 1967 Spivey was dean of Payne Theological Seminary in Wilberforce, Ohio, and in 1965 was a member of the Methodist Theological Study Conference at Oxford University in England. From 1967 to 1970 he was executive director of the Department of Social Justice of the National Council of Churches. From 1970 to 1973 he was program director of the Programme to Combat Racism with the U.S. office of the World Council of Churches. In 1973 he was appointed pastor of the Quinn Chapel AME Church in Chicago, and also served as executive director of the Church Federation of Greater Chicago. Beginning in 1968 he served many years on the executive committee of the Consultation on Church Union (C.O.C.U.). More recently he became pastor of Coppin Memorial AME Church in Chicago.

Spivey, Charles S., Jr. "The African Methodist Episcopal Church—Its Problems and Its Future." *The African Methodist Episcopal Church Review* 92 (January–March 1968): 27–36.

———. "COCU and the 'Black Problem.'" *The Black Church* 1 (1972): 79–82.

———. "Ecumenism and Racism." *Christian Century* 91 (April 24, 1974): 459–460.

HUBA, WWABA (80–81), *WWR* (77), *BDNM* (75).

SPOTTSWOOD, STEPHEN GILL (July 18, 1897–December 2, 1974), 58th bishop of the **African Methodist Episcopal Zion Church** (AMEZ) and head of the N.A.A.C.P. from 1961 to 1974, was born in Boston, Massachusetts, the only child of Abraham Lincoln and Mary Elizabeth (Gray) Spottswood. His parents were very pious and he early gained a sense of religious mission. He was educated in integrated schools, the Cambridge Latin School in Massachusetts and the Freeport High School in Maine. He graduated in 1917 with a B.A. in history from Albright College in Reading, Pennsylvania, working at many jobs to support his schoolwork.

On returning to Massachusetts he became assistant pastor of the First Evangelical United Brethren Church in Cambridge, then in 1918 was appointed assistant pastor of the Columbus Avenue AMEZ Church in Boston. Meanwhile he continued his education at the Gordon College of Theology in Boston, where he received his Th.B. in 1919. In 1919 he joined the itinerant ministry through the New England Conference and was assigned to West Newton and Lowell, Massachusetts, where he organized the First AMEZ Church of Lowell. On June 10, 1919, he married Viola

Estelle Booker, with whom he had five children. He was ordained deacon on February 5, 1920, and elder on June 20, 1920.

In 1920 he was assigned to Green Memorial AMEZ Church in Portland, Maine, the only Black church in the city, and in 1922 he became pastor of Varick Memorial AMEZ Church in New Haven, Connecticut. In 1922 he participated in a sit-in against segregation at a New Haven cinema and over the years participated in numerous sit-ins, boycotts, and pickets all over the East Coast, believing that the most effective form of protest is economic in nature. From 1925 to 1928 he pastored Goler Memorial AMEZ Church in Winston-Salem, North Carolina, followed by the Jones Tabernacle AMEZ Church in Indianapolis, Indiana from 1928 to 1932. From 1932 to 1936 he was appointed to St. Luke AMEZ Church in Buffalo, New York, and in 1936 he moved to the prestigious John Wesley AMEZ Church in Washington, D.C., where he stayed sixteen years. From 1947 to 1952 he was president of the Washington branch of the N.A.A.C.P. While in Washington he increased the church membership from 600 to more than 3,000 and paid off a $65,000 debt.

From his Washington pastorate Spottswood was elected bishop and consecrated on May 18, 1952. He was assigned to work in the areas of Ohio, Texas, Colorado, and then later in Michigan. In 1962 he was moved to the Fourth Episcopal District (North Alabama, East Tennessee-Virginia, Kentucky, Western New York, and Indiana Conferences), moving in 1968 to the Third Episcopal District (Allegheny, Philadelphia-Baltimore, Ohio, Barbados, and Guyana Conferences).

In 1959 Spottswood was elected vice-president of the national board of the N.A.A.C.P. and on April 10, 1961 he became president of the N.A.A.C.P., succeeding Robert C. Weaver. In July of that year he led the N.A.A.C.P.'s twenty-two car "Freedom Train" to Washington D.C. to encourage more civil rights legislation. In the 1960s his low-key leadership of the N.A.A.C.P. came under criticism from more militant factions, but he shifted from his behind-the-scenes negotiation stance when he felt the need. In 1969 he attracted much attention by labeling the Nixon administration "anti-black" and in 1970 he stated that "killing black Americans has been the 20th century pastime of our police."

As bishop he was on the executive committee of the World Methodist Council, a trustee of Livingstone College in Salisbury, North Carolina, and active in the National Council of Churches. He was also chair of the denomination's Board of Finance. His first wife passed away on October 24, 1953, and in 1969 he married Mattie Brownita Johnson Elliott. In May 1972 he retired from the bishopric but remained as head of both the N.A.A.C.P. and *The Crisis* magazine until his death.

"Bishop Stephen Gill Spottswood." *The Crisis* 82 (February 1975): 41.
"Bishop S. G. Spottswood Honored Posthumously." *Star of Zion* 101 (May 26, 1977): 1, 2
"Bishop S. G. Spottswood is New N.A.A.C.P. Chairman." *Star of Zion* 84 (May 4, 1961): 6.
"Bishop S. G. Spottswood is New N.A.A.C.P. Chairman." *A.M.E. Zion Quarterly Review* 73 (Fall 1961): 121.
"Bishop Spottswood Permanently Retired." *Star of Zion* 95 (June 1, 1972): 1, 8.
"Died: Bishop Stephen G. Spottswood." *Time* 104 (December 16, 1974): 69.
McFadden, Robert D. "Bishop Spottswood of N.A.A.C.P. Dies." *New York Times* (December 3, 1974): 1, 44.
Spottswood, Stephen Gill. "We Have Come This Far By Faith!" *The Crisis* 82 (February 1975): 43–49, 68.
"Stephen Gill Spottswood." *Star of Zion* 82 (November 12, 1959): 5.
Stringfield, J. A. "Dr. Spottswood for Bishop." *Star of Zion* 72 (January 8, 1948): 8.
Tillman, D. W. "What Shall We Do?" *Star of Zion* 71 (August 14, 1947): 6, 14.
"Transition: Bishop Stephen Gill Spottswood." *Newsweek* 84 (December 16, 1974): 77.
CB (1962 and 1975), *AMEZC, OTSB, EWM, BDNM* (70), *WWABA* (81–81), *EBA, HAMEZC, NA, WWW* (74–75).

SPYWOOD, GEORGE ALFRED (1802–January 15, 1875), 6th bishop of the **African Methodist Episcopal Zion Church** (AMEZ), was born in Mashpee, Mississippi, with an African and Native American background. Many details of his life are unknown, and sources differ on his birth information, some suggesting a date of January 5, 1798, in Providence, Rhode Island. He was converted in Providence on March 7, 1818, and licensed to preach in that city in 1831.

He joined the Annual Conference on June 20, 1842, was ordained deacon on May 24, 1843, and elder on May 23, 1844. He was consecrated a superintendent or general elder (as bishops were then called) on May 24, 1852. He was assigned to the Eastern Episcopal District, embracing New England, Nova Scotia, and British Guyana Conferences. Due to the death of Bishop **George Galbreath** and the trial of Bishop **William H. Bishop** during a turbulent political time in the denomination, Spywood was left as the only general elder of the church. On July 9, 1853, at a specially called

General Conference, he was consecrated a general superintendent, which apparently meant he was recognized as having senior status.

He retired in 1856 when there were more bishops than could be placed, and for the rest of his life was employed as an agent of the New England Mission Board, where he enjoyed great success. Other sources alternatively state his death date as March 9, 1876.

AMEZC, HAMEZC, EWM, HNC, AARS.

STALLINGS, GEORGE AUGUSTUS, JR. (b. March 17, 1948), founder of the **African-American Catholic Congregation**, was born in New Bern, North Carolina, the son of a convent housekeeper. His upbringing was very religious, and at the age of eight was already informally leading religious services for the neighborhood children. He attended parochial schools, received his B.A. in philosophy from St. Pius X Seminary in Garrison, New York, in 1970, and his M.A. in pastoral theology from Pontifical University of St. Thomas Aquinas in Rome in 1974, where he also received his S.T.L. in 1975.

He was ordained a priest in the **Roman Catholic Church** in 1974 at Our Lady Queen of Peace Church in Washington, D.C., where he was associate priest from 1974 to 1976. From 1976 to 1988 he was the priest of the St. Teresa of Avila Church in Washington, D.C., building up the church from 200 families to 2,000. He changed the atmosphere of the church by designing a liturgy which incorporated some elements of a traditional Black Protestant worship, including developing a gospel choir. He was active in the community, serving on the boards of MUSCLE, Inc. (Ministries United to Save Community Live Endeavors), a non-profit housing development corporation, and CONSERV, an association to help the homeless. During this time he also traveled a great deal, lecturing at Black churches and such places as the Washington Theological Union in Silver Spring, Maryland. He served a year as president of the **National Black Catholic Clergy Caucus**, continuing to build a national reputation. In 1988 he left St. Teresa's with the intention of studying in Rome for a year. He returned early and was not reappointed to St. Teresa's, as he wished, but was appointed by James Cardinal Hickey, Archbishop of Washington, as head of evangelism for the Archdiocese of Washington, D.C.

Stallings did not want the evangelism position, and eventually went public with his frustration. He accused the hierarchy of the church with racism, and claimed a lack of support for the models of Black Catholic ministry

he had been developing at St. Teresa's. After a series of responses back and forth, Stallings decided to venture out on his own. He established a new congregation with the name Imani Temple (Imani is Swahili for "faith"), holding the first service at Howard University Law School on July 2, 1989. The next day Hickey suspended his orders as a priest, but Stallings continued. He explained that he was not really leaving the Catholic Church, but only developing a new Black expression of it.

Within months four other temples were added to the new movement, and Stallings predicted many more would be added soon. In February 1990, Stallings announced a further break from Roman Catholicism by allowing the future ordination of women, permitting birth control and abortion, offering full communion to divorced and remarried Catholics, and instituting "optional celibacy" for priests. The Roman Catholic Church responded that by these actions he excommunicated himself. Stallings then acquired for his church an independent apostolic authority. He was consecrated a bishop for the African American Catholic Congregation on May 12, 1990, by Richard Michael Bridges of the American Independent Orthodox Church.

"Stallings Excommunicated." *Christian Century* 107 (February 21, 1990): 176.
RLOA, NM (90), IB.

STARKEY, CYRUS AUGUSTINE (d. December 1965), a bishop of the **North American Old Roman Catholic Church** (N.A.O.R.C.C.), emerged in the Old Catholic community on June 13, 1932, when he was ordained to the priesthood by Polish Old Catholic Bishop Francis Ignatius Boryszewski of the Independent Polish Catholic Church in Philadelphia. The next year finds him in New York City working as a priest under Arthur Wolfort Brooks of the Apostolic Episcopal Church. He was consecrated as a bishop of the **Holy African Church** (a splinter of the **African Orthodox Church**) in 1944 by Bishop **Reginald Grant Barrow**. He was assigned to work in the African American community in New York City.

In 1950 Starkey, supported by Bishop **Richard A. Marchenna**, applied for admission to the NAORCC and recognition of his Episcopal orders. His request was denied. Then in 1952 Archbishop **Hubert A. Rogers** petitioned the synod to accept him based upon the intercommunion between the N.A.O.R.C.C. and the church led by Barrow. The synod ordered Starkey reconsecrated which was done by Rogers on June 21, 1952. In 1853 Rogers was named Primate-Coadjutor, with right of succession to Archbishop Carmel Henry Carfora, the primate of the N.A.O.R.C.C. For the next five years Rogers and Starkey served as colleagues in the Church, then toward the end of 1957 and after a heated argument on the Church's policy, Carfora suddenly removed Rogers from his position and replaced him with Starkey. Carfora died a few months later in January 1958.

Starkey, as Primate-Coadjutor succeeded Carfora. Then at the meeting of the Church's synod later that year, the succession was set aside and Roger selected as the new Primate. For the moment, Starkey stepped aside. Then the next year he left the jurisdiction and aligned himself with Chicago Bishop John E. Schweikert, a White man formerly with the Old Roman Catholic Church which had been founded by Marchenna in 1952. The aging Starkey reasserted his right to Carfora's succession and proceeded to establish a new North American Old Roman Catholic Church. Two congregations voiced their allegiance to the reorganized church. Starkey died in 1965 and was succeeded by Schweikert who headed the church until his death in 1988. It is currently headed by Archbishop Theodore J. Rematt.

Trela, Jonathan. *A History of the North American Old Roman Catholic Church.* Scranton, PA: The Author, 1979. 124 pp.

STEIB, JAMES TERRY (b. May 17, 1940), a bishop of the **Roman Catholic Church**, was born in Vacherie, Louisiana, the oldest of five children in the family of Rosemond and Vivian (Jones) Steib. His father worked in the sugar cane fields, and both parents came from generations of devout Catholics. All the children were baptized at Our Lady of Peach Church in Vacherie, a segregated parish where the last seven pews in the back of the church were assigned to Blacks. He often expressed the desire to be an altar boy at church, but this position was denied to Blacks.

There was no parochial school, so Steib attended the all-Black Shell Mound Elementary School. In 1951 the Sisters of Mercy of the Holy Cross established a rural mission nearby called Our Lady of Peace Apostolate. They worked with priests in the area along the Mississippi River between Baton Rouge and New Orleans to evangelize and instruct, and made a big impression on Steib. In 1956 the Archbishop of New Orleans, Joseph Rummel, banished all forms of segregation in Catholic parishes, and Steib was finally able to become an altar boy. When he was in the sixth grade, a field trip to St. Augustine Minor Seminary in

Bay St. Louis, Mississippi, convinced him to become a priest. He enrolled at that school as a boarding student on September 8, 1953, and graduated from the high school department in 1957.

Steib was sent to the Divine Word Novitiate in Conesus, New York, where he gave his initial vows of poverty, chastity, and obedience on September 8, 1959. After finishing two years of college at Conesus, he transferred to St. Mary's Seminary in Techny, Illinois, where he earned his B.A. in 1963. He returned to Bay St. Louis for graduate work, made his final vows, and was ordained a priest on January 6, 1967. He was assigned to be assistant dean of students at St. Augustine Seminary and to teach English at the nearby St. Stanislaus High School. Meanwhile he studied at Xavier University in New Orleans, where he earned his M.A. in guidance and counseling in 1973.

In 1976 Steib left St. Augustine Seminary to serve as superior of the Divine Word Southern Province, covering about one hundred priests and brothers in Arkansas, Louisiana, Mississippi, and Texas. He was elected to an unprecedented three consecutive three-year terms in that office. He was praised for his consensus-seeking administration. In 1976–77 he was executive director of the **National Black Catholic Clergy Caucus** and remained on the board until 1981. He was also vice-president of the Conference of Major Superiors of Men and on the board of directors of the Divine Word College in Epworth, Iowa. On December 6, 1983, he was appointed an auxiliary bishop for the Archdiocese of St. Louis, and was consecrated for that task on February 10, 1984.

WWABA (92–93), *WWR* (85), *OBS.*

STEWARD, THEOPHILUS GOULD (April 17, 1843–1924), minister, educator, and author, was born in Gouldtown, Cumberland County, New Jersey, the son of James and Rebecca (Gould) Steward. He was licensed to preach in the **African Methodist Episcopal Church** (AME) in 1861, joined the Philadelphia Conference in 1864, and the following year transferred to the South Carolina Conference. There he worked with Bishop **Daniel Payne** to establish the AME presence in that state. On January 1, 1866, he married Elizabeth Gadschen of Charleston, South Carolina, with whom he had eight children.

Soon after that he moved to the state of Georgia, where he served as pastor and presiding elder. He organized the first school for Blacks in Macon, Georgia, and helped write the new Georgia State Constitution in

1868. He organized and built what is now called Steward Chapel AME Church on Cotton Street in Macon, leading that congregation from 1868 to 1871. He led a successful protest of freedmen in Americus, Georgia, against compulsory labor contracts, worked as a cashier in the Freedmen's Bank in Macon, and speculated in cotton.

In 1873 he went on a missionary journey to Haiti, where he established a church in Port-au-Prince. Upon return to the United States he served AME churches in Brooklyn, New York, and Philadelphia, Pennsylvania. While in Philadelphia he enrolled at West Philadelphia Divinity School, where he received his B.D. in 1880, followed by a D.D. in 1881 from Wilberforce University in Xenia, Ohio. While at Wilberforce he served an AME church in Wilmington, Ohio, some thirty miles away. In 1884 he nearly was chosen president of Wilberforce, but continued as pastor of a church in Washington, D.C. In 1885 he published his most famous book, *Genesis Re-Read*, which advocated an evolutionary theism, a position far in advance of most of his contemporaries and which established his reputation as a theologian.

In 1891 Steward became chaplain of the 25th Infantry Regiment, a position he retained for the next sixteen years. His first wife died in 1893 and in 1896 he married Susan Maria (Smith) McKinney, the widow of an Episcopalian minister. She was a graduate of the New York Medical School for Women and said to be the first Black woman in America to enter the medical profession. Steward received training at Fort Missoula, Montana, and managed to enroll as a student in the University of Montana for a brief time in 1898. On April 25, 1898, the United States declared war against Spain and Steward's regiment moved to Chickamauga, Georgia, and then to Cuba. In September 1898, he was the featured speaker at a Brooklyn peace jubilee sponsored by the Montauk Soldiers Relief Association. Steward then went to the Philippines and was stationed in Manila. He not only served as military chaplain but also was government superintendent of schools for the province of Luzon. In 1899 he wrote an excellent survey of Black soldiers in the Spanish-American War, *The Colored Regulars in the U.S. Army*. In the summer of 1902 the regiment returned to the United States and he spent the remainder of his Army career at Fort Niobrara, Nebraska.

After Steward's military retirement in 1907 he became a professor of history, French, and logic at Wilberforce University. He found the time to write more books, including an important study, *The Haitian Revolution 1791 to 1804 or Sidelights on the French Revolution* (1914) and his own autobiography, *Fifty Years in the Gospel Ministry, from 1864 to 1914* (1914). His experience in the military suggested to him that

victorious Black soldiers served to break down White prejudicial barriers. In 1911 Steward and his wife went as delegates of the AME Church to the First Universal Races Congress at the University of London, July 26–29.

Steward, Theophilus Gould. *A Charleston Love Story; or, Hortense Vanross*. London and New York: F. T. Neely, 1899. 245 pp.

———. *The Colored Regulars in the United States Army, With a Sketch of the Colored American, and an Account of His Services in the Wars of the Country, From the Period of the Revolutionary War to 1899*. Philadelphia, PA: AME Book Concern, 1904. 344 pp.

———. *Divine Attributes. The Tawawa Series in Systematic Divinity*. Philadelphia, PA: Christian Recorder Printing, 1884. 111 pp.

———. *Fifty Years in the Gospel Ministry, from 1864 to 1914*. Philadelphia, PA: AME Book Concern, 1914. 520 pp.

———. *Genesis Re-Read; or, The Latest Conclusions of Physical Science, Viewed in Their Relation to the Mosaic Record*. Philadelphia, PA: AME Book Rooms, 1885. 252 pp.

———. *The Haitian Revolution, 1791 to 1804; or, Sidelights on the French Revolution*. New York: T. Y. Crowell Co., 1914. 292 pp.

DANB, RAM, BHAC, WWCR, BAW, AARS, HUBA, IBAW, DNAADB, DAA.

STEWART, GEORGE WASHINGTON (February 3, 1858–September 20, 1915), 10th bishop of the **Christian Methodist Episcopal Church** (CME), then the Colored Methodist Episcopal Church, was born near Lynchburg, Ambours County, Virginia, the son of John and Charlotte (Caldwell) Stewart. The family soon moved to Courtland, Alabama, where Stewart experienced conversion, joined the CME Church, and was licensed to preach in 1880. In 1882 he joined the itinerant ministry through the Kentucky Conference and was sent to Indian territory, where he spent two years organizing missions and building two churches.

In 1884 he transferred to the Tennessee Conference and was appointed to Capers Chapel CME Church in Nashville. While there he attended Walden University (Central Tennessee College) in Nashville, receiving his B.A. in 1889. He later did some further studies at Gammon Theological Seminary in Atlanta, Georgia. On April 29, 1890, he married Jessie Lee Smyly, with whom he had six children. From 1894 to 1904 he was a presiding elder, and in 1901 was a delegate to the Ecumenical Methodist Conference in London, England. From 1903 to 1910 he was general secretary of the

Young People's Society of the denomination, and during the same period was Epworth League Secretary and editor of the *Epworth Courier*.

Stewart's successes in these positions brought him election to the bishopric on May 16, 1910, and he was assigned to the Alabama area. Unfortunately, he was only able to serve five years in that capacity before he passed away. His son, **Luther Caldwell Stewart**, was elected bishop in 1946, the first instance of a bishop's son becoming bishop in the history of the denomination.

EWM, CMECTY, WWCR.

STEWART, IMOGENE WILLIAMS BIGHAM (b. January 23, 1942), national chair of the American Women's Clergy Association and founder of the House of Imogene, was born in Dublin, Georgia, the daughter of Rev. and Mrs. Bigham. Her father was the pastor of a Baptist church in Dublin. After participating in many of the civil rights demonstrations of the 1960s, Stewart decided that she wanted to be a minister, but found that the Baptist Church was not partial to women ministers. She received some encouragement, however, from Julius Carroll, pastor of the East Calvary Baptist Church of Washington, D.C., and proceeded to establish what she called "The Church of What's Happening Now." This essentially consisted of a likely street corner on Washington's northeast side, where she would start preaching and singing to the gathering crowd. She received her A.A. in 1972 from the University of the District of Columbia. She married a Mr. Stewart, with whom she had two sons. In 1973 she became an inventory-management specialist with the U.S. Government Printing Office in Washington, D.C. That year she also entered Washington Inter-Met Seminary to receive formal training and ordination. As part of her training she was placed as an intern in a **United Methodist Church**, but left the church and the school after only six months. She felt she was being trained in keeping regular office hours or in answering the phone all day, rather than in addressing the needs of the community. She continued her Sunday morning street ministry. Information is not available concerning her eventual ordination.

Stewart was very sensitive to the problems of domestic violence, having seen her own mother a victim of it. Frustrated by the lack of places for these women to turn, in March 1977 she took her own funds and a few donations and founded the House of Imogene, a 24–hour emergency shelter for women and children who are victims of domestic violence. The shelter can accommodate up to twenty people and is affiliated with

Howard University Hospital's emergency unit for cases where medical treatment is necessary. Besides Stewart, the staff consists of two volunteers, and there is a board of directors. The House of Imogene gained partial funding from the United Black Fund of Greater Washington, and there is an occasional church grant. It is the only known domestic violence shelter founded and operated by African Americans which provides services to anyone. Stewart is also currently listed as the national chair of the American Women's Clergy Association.

Kinamore, Angela. "Essence Woman." *Essence* 15 (September 1984): 70.
White, Joyce. "Women in the Ministry." *Essence* 7 (November 1976): 62, 63, 104, 107, 108.
WWABA (92–93), IBAW.

STEWART, JOHN (1786–December 17, 1823), a pioneer Methodist missionary among Native Americans, was born in Powhatan County, Virginia, the son of free parents of mixed African/Indian ancestry. When he was still very young his parents moved to Tennessee and left him behind. When he reached the age of twenty-one he left Virginia and went westward in an effort to locate his parents. About 1811 he landed in Marietta, Ohio, where he had a difficult time. He was robbed, struggled with alcoholism, and contemplated suicide. He dried out briefly and regained his equilibrium while apprenticed to a sugar mapler in the same county (Washington), but when he returned to Marietta he returned to his former habits.

In September 1814 he experienced conversion at a camp meeting and joined the Methodist Episcopal Church in Marietta. He turned his life around in a more permanent manner and set up a blue-dying business. In the spring of 1815, after a near-fatal attack of tuberculosis, he decided to follow an earlier inclination to preach and focused on missionary work among the Indians. After stopping at the Moravian mission among the Delawares on the Tuscarawas River in Goshen, Ohio, he reached a White settlement where he preached with success and organized a church. He continued on until he reached the Wyandot Indians in the area of Upper Sandusky, Ohio. There he labored from November of 1816 until the following spring, using as interpreter Jonathan Pointer, a Black man taken prisoner by the tribe during his youth and who was now fluent in their language. During this brief time Stewart managed to convert Pointer, a number of Wyandot chieftains, and some tribe members to Christianity. Stewart was not the first Methodist to preach to Native Americans; in fact another African American, **John**

Marrant, may have been the first to do so in a substantive way among the Cherokee in the 1770s. Because that work was not followed up by a sustained effort of the institutional church, however, Stewart is generally the one given credit for founding the first prolonged and successful Methodist mission among Native Americans.

Some White traders who profited from the liquor traffic to the tribe tried to obstruct his work by encouraging alcoholism and inquiring about his lack of official status in the church. Frustrated, Stewart returned to Marietta from the summer of 1817 to the fall of 1818. Finding a renewed commitment, Stewart then returned to the Wyandot. In March 1819 he was licensed to preach at the quarterly meeting of the Mad River Circuit of the Methodist Episcopal Church, thus establishing some credentials for his work. On August 7, 1819, the Ohio Annual Conference established the first official Methodist mission to the Indians, based on Stewart's groundbreaking work. Rev. James B. Finley founded a missionary school at Big Springs and worked as a colleague with Stewart. In about 1820 Stewart married a woman named Polly, and Bishop William McKendree was instrumental in raising money to purchase a 53–acre tract near Sandusky for their home.

In the summer of 1822 Stewart was visited by representatives of the **African Methodist Episcopal Church** (AME), founded six years previously by **Richard Allen** in a break from the Methodist Episcopal Church. He felt this was the place for him to be, and joined the AME Church. Unfortunately his health began to fail, and by the fall of 1823 he was confined to his bed, passing away that winter. On October 16, 1916, a monument to his memory was unveiled at Upper Sandusky, with an inscription reading: "John Stewart, Apostle of the Wyandott Indians, Father of Missions of the Methodist Episcopal Church."

Barclay, Wade Crawford. *History of Methodist Missions*. 3 vols. New York: Methodist Board of Missions, 1949.

Finley, James Bradley. *History of the Wyandott Mission*. Cincinnati, OH: J. F. Wright and L. Swormstedt, 1840. 432 pp.

Mitchell, Joseph. *The Missionary Pioneer; or, A Brief Memoir of the Life, Labours, and Death of John Stewart, Man of Colour, Founder, Under God, of the Mission Among the Wyandotts, at Upper Sandusky, Ohio*. Ohio: The Author, 1827. 96 pp.

Schomburg, Arthur Alfonso. "Two Negro Missionaries to the American Indians, John Marrant and John Stewart." *Journal of Negro History* 21 (October 1936): 394–415.

DANB, HNC, NYB (1925–26), HUBA, IBAW, EWM.

STEWART, LUTHER CALDWELL (June 26, 1893–November 16, 1962), 22nd bishop of the **Christian Methodist Episcopal Church** (CME), then the Colored Methodist Episcopal Church, was born in Pleasant Hill, Alabama, one of six children in the family of Jessie Lee Smyly and **George Washington Stewart**. His father became a bishop in the CME Church in 1910. He attended Miles Memorial College in Birmingham, Alabama, and received his B.A. degree in 1914 from Paine College in Augusta, Georgia.

He was licensed to preach in 1914 and his first pastorate was at Pace Chapel CME Church in Pensacola, Florida. He was ordained a deacon in 1916 and an elder in 1917. From 1917 to 1919 he was a chaplain in the United States Army. On December 27, 1918 he married Marietta Wheatley, with whom he had two children. After leaving the chaplaincy he pastored CME churches in Opelika, Alabama, and in Owensboro, Elkton, and Winchester, Kentucky. In February 1925, he was assigned to Freeman Chapel CME Church in Hopkinsville, Kentucky, where he stayed for twelve years. He built a major reputation in this pastorate, erecting a new church building and strengthening the congregation. In 1937 he became presiding elder of the Hopkinsville District, remaining in that position for eighteen months.

At the 1938 General Conference Stewart was elected editor of the *Christian Index*, the official organ of the denomination, and remained in this influential position for eight years. He was elected bishop on May 7, 1946, the first son of a bishop to become bishop in the history of the CME Church. He was assigned to the Fifth Episcopal District, covering Alabama and Florida, then in 1950 was moved to the Fourth Episcopal District, covering Mississippi and Louisiana. About 1954 he was assigned to the Second Episcopal District (Kentucky and Ohio-Central Indiana Conferences), with his residence in Hopkinsville, where he spent most of the rest of his career.

He served as secretary of the College of Bishops for sixteen years, and was a trustee of Paine College. He was on the executive board of the American Bible Society and on the Kentucky Child Welfare Board. He was a member of the board of directors of the World Council of Churches and was a consultant to the National Council of Churches. In May 1962 he succeeded Bishop **W. Y. Bell** as senior bishop of the denomination. He passed away less than a year later, and over 3,500 attended his funeral.

Chapman, C. E. "Bishop Luther Caldwell Stewart, CME Church, Dies." *Star of Zion* 86 (January 31, 1963): 1, 2.

Merriweather, M. C. "Obituary." *Christian Index* 95 (November 29, 1962): 1, 14.
CMECTY, EWM.

STEWART, WILLIAM ANDREW

STEWART, WILLIAM ANDREW (August 20, 1890–August 5, 1984), 59th bishop of the **African Methodist Episcopal Zion Church** (AMEZ), was born in Burntcorn, Conecuh County, Alabama, one of four sons in the family of Eli and Allie Stewart. He was reared in a pious environment and at age sixteen became a class leader in the local AMEZ Church. He began in the public schools and when he was old enough enrolled in Tuskegee Normal and Industrial Institute. For some time he attended Phelps Hall Bible Training School in the morning, worked in the afternoon, and attended school at night.

This rigorous schedule took its toll, and by the time he finished the Bible course as valedictorian of his class his health was broken and he returned home. He married Sula Cunningham, with whom he had seven children, four of whom survived his long life. He was licensed as a local preacher and was chosen to give the address at a district meeting with Bishop **John Wesley Alstork** in attendance. Alstork was so impressed that he appointed Stewart to the Pineapple Circuit and set him on the road for a career in ministry. Within two years he was ordained and pastoring in Stockton, Alabama. He then decided he needed extra training and was next appointed to Butler Chapel AMEZ Church in Tuskegee, Alabama, where he could do more work at Tuskegee Normal and Industrial Institute. He graduated from the normal department in 1923 and remained to teach and pastor for one year.

In July 1924, Stewart was appointed to Varick Chapel AMEZ Church in Asheville, North Carolina, where he was elected principal of the Black Mountain School. He did not stay long, however, for Bishop **Lynwood W. Kyles** had promised to send him to a church close to Livingstone College in Salisbury, North Carolina, as soon as possible. In November 1924, Stewart was assigned to People's Choice AMEZ Church in Winston-Salem, North Carolina, and he immediately enrolled in Hood Theological Seminary at Livingstone College. His church work was successful, enabling him to burning the mortgage on the parsonage, and he was successful in his school work, graduating from the seminary with a B.D. in 1926.

He then moved to Center Street AMEZ Church in Statesville, North Carolina, where despite the distance he continued in the undergraduate program at Livingstone College, graduating with his B.A. degree in about 1929. In the fall of 1930 he left the newly

remodeled church to go to Old Ship AMEZ Church in Montgomery, Alabama, where in seven years he reduced the debt from $26,000 to $9,300 and reroofed the parsonage and part of the church. From October 1938 to May 1942 he was appointed to Logan Temple AMEZ Church in Knoxville, Tennessee, where he accomplished a major remodeling effort on both the parsonage and church. In May 1942 he was assigned to Union Wesley AMEZ Church in Washington, D.C., where he stayed for the next twelve years and led in building one of the finest church structures in the denomination.

Stewart was elected bishop at the General Conference on May 15, 1952, and consecrated on May 18. Over the next twenty years he presided over conferences from the West Coast to the South and Southeast, all with great success. From 1956 to 1960 he was vice-chair of the Home and Church Board of Christian Education Department, and during his tenure as head of the Board of Publication the AMEZ Publishing House was built. He was active in many civic areas and is given credit for reforming the attitudes and services of the L & N Railroad Company and the Western Railroad Company. He was a delegate to the 1966 World Methodist Conference in London, England. He retired in 1972.

"Bishop Stewart Dies in D.C." *Star of Zion* 108 (August 2, 1984): 2.
"Bishop W. A. Stewart Funeral Held in D.C." *Star of Zion* 108 (August 9, 1984): 1.
"Bishop William Andrew Stewart." *Star of Zion* 101 (May 26, 1977): 1, 2.
"Dr. W. A. Stewart A.B., B.D., Candidate for Bishopric." *Star of Zion* 67 (September 9, 1943): 1, 3.
Satter White, John H. "A Tribute to Bishop William Andrew Stewart." *A.M.E. Zion Quarterly Review* 96 (October 1984): 5.
Smith, William Milton. "God's Good Man." *A.M.E. Zion Quarterly Review* 96 (October 1984): 2–4.
"Some Notable Achievements." *Star of Zion* 75 (March 13, 1952): 4.
AMEZC, EWM.

STILLMAN COLLEGE

STILLMAN COLLEGE. A **Presbyterian Church (U.S.A.)** school. Stillman College, Tuscaloosa, Alabama, was the one venture into higher education within the African American community by the Presbyterian Church in the U.S., the Southern Presbyterian church. The school came into being through the vision and persistent effort of Rev. Charles A. Stillman, the pastor of First Presbyterian Church of Tuscaloosa, Alabama. The school opened in 1876 as the Tuscaloosa Institute.

Its primary task was to train ministers and missionaries for the Presbyterian Church. Several of the graduates had outstanding careers in Africa. The school was renamed in 1894 for its founder, and in 1924 Stillman Institute became Stillman College.

Stillman had remained a small school through the years, there being less than 60 African American congregations affiliated with the Southern Presbyterians, and most of the students attended the elementary and high school classes. Through the 1920s a diversified course of study had developed, the curriculum offering training in nursing, home economic, mechanical arts, and agriculture. There were approximately 150 students at any one time. During the 1930s, the elementary and high school courses were eliminated and the school emerged as a two-year junior college.

Stillman continued to evolve through the war years. A study completed in 1946 recommended, for example, the beginning of the process of the development of Black leadership through the addition of African Americans to the board of trustees. There had been Black faculty members for many years. Finally, in 1949 the school completed its transformation into a four-year liberal arts college.

Terry, Paul W., ed. *A Study of Stillman Institute: A Junior College for Negroes.* Tuscaloosa, AL: University of Alabama Press, 1946. 304 pp.

Thompson, Ernest Trice. *Presbyterians in the South.* 3 vols. Richmond, VA: John Knox Press, 1973. 636 pp.

STITH, FORREST CHRISTOPHER (b. May 18, 1934), a bishop of the **United Methodist Church**, was born in Marshall, Texas, the son of Forrest M. and Daisy L. (Haynes) Stith. He received his B.S. in 1955 from the University of Nebraska and his B.D. in 1958 from Drew Theological Seminary in Madison, New Jersey. He was ordained deacon in 1958 and elder in 1960. On June 19, 1960, he married Josephine Mitchell, with whom he had one daughter.

He stayed nine years at his first pastorate, the Douglas Memorial Methodist Church in Washington, D.C. (1958–67). There he served on the Commissioner's Youth Council and was chaplain for the Public Interest Civic Association. He was a charter member of **Black Methodists for Church Renewal.** From 1967 to 1970 he was the pastor of Sharp Street Memorial United Methodist Church in Maryland. From 1970 to 1978 he was executive secretary of the Baltimore Conference Board of Missions and Church Extension, then from 1978 to 1982 was Associate Council Director for Outreach. He was a delegate to General Conference

beginning in 1972. From 1982 to 1984 he was district superintendent of the Washington East District.

In 1984 Stith was elected bishop and assigned to the New York West Episcopal Area, where he has remained. He serves on the General Commission on the Status and Role of Women and is a trustee of Syracuse University. He has been on the General Board of Global Ministries and on the Africa Church Growth and Development Committee. He is known as a leader of hymn-sings.

BDNM (75), *WWR* (85), *WWMC, WWA* (90–91), *BDUMB*.

STOCKTON, BETSEY (c.1796–October 24, 1865), educator and the first single Black woman to serve as an American foreign missionary, was born into slavery, the property of Robert Stockton of Princeton, New Jersey. He later gave her as a gift to his daughter, Elizabeth, who married Ashbel Green, eventual president of the College of New Jersey (now Princeton University). Stockton served the Green family in Philadelphia for a number of years. Ashbel Green took an interest in her welfare and sent her to live for several years in the countryside with his niece's husband, in order that she would not be harmed by urban influences. When the Greens moved to Princeton she returned to live with them. He freed her when she was twenty years old, but she chose to stay with the family as a hired servant.

Surrounded by the Green family erudition, Stockton gained an education as well. In the winter of 1816–17 she experienced conversion and was baptized into the Presbyterian Church. She was one of thirty-eight Blacks to join the Presbyterian Church of Princeton during the pastorate of the Rev. William Schenck. She soon expressed a desire to be a missionary to Africa, but for a time her friends were able to persuade her to stay. In 1822 she received an invitation from the Rev. Charles Stewart to accompany his family in the first reinforcement to the Sandwich Islands (Hawaii) Mission sent by the American Board of Commissioners for Foreign Missions (A.B.C.F.M.). Stewart probably knew her from his student days at Princeton. Another source suggests that she sought him out and requested to join his family on the missionary voyage.

The A.B.C.F.M. accepted her presence because she gave evidence of the various qualities needed in a missionary, and did not even mention her color in its correspondence. Her color was, however, an underlying concern, and just before departure Green and Stewart worked out an arrangement with her for her exact duties. The A.B.C.F.M., not certain that she should be treated as any other missionary, decided that she would be under its supervision, but not a full missionary. The statement read that she was to be regarded "neither as an equal nor as a servant, but as a humble Christian friend," a situation without precedent. She was apparently the first single Black woman to serve as an American foreign missionary. She was not the first African American missionary, however, coming after **David George** (1792), **Daniel Coker** (1820), and **Lott Carey** (1821). The A.B.C. F.M. agreement protected her by noting that she could break the agreement at any time and still "remain under the care and superintendence of the Board, like any other missionary." Politically, the implication of this seemed to be that the board would accept her as a regular missionary once away from the shores of the United States and out of the sight of its constituency. Indeed, on board the ship Stockton experienced herself treated as an equal.

The ship left in about November 1822, the little band settled on Maui, and Stockton established a school, reportedly the first school ever on the islands. She instructed six Hawaiians and four English children in the English language. She also cared for the new infant of the Stewarts and served as unofficial doctor and nurse. After about a year they moved to Lahaina, where Stockton founded another school, this time to train and educate the chiefs' domestics and dependents. The A.B.C.F.M. kept the fact that it had a Black woman serving in one of its missions as a schoolteacher, as (almost) a *de facto* equal, in a low profile; thus, few back home were aware of her accomplishments. Over time her morale deteriorated. She became homesick, lonely, and tired of the awkwardness of her status, being partly a missionary and partly a Stewart servant. She chose, however, not to pull out of the agreement with the board. Mrs. Stewart's health necessitated a return to the United States in 1825, and Stockton took the opportunity to return as well. The ship left on October 17, 1825, and in some months she was in Cooperstown, New York, with the Stewarts.

She remained with the Stewarts for the next ten years, until 1836–37, when she went to Philadelphia to teach in an "infant school" for Black children. She later received an invitation from an English missionary in Canada to visit the Indian mission there and establish a similar infant school. By 1840 she was back in Princeton, New Jersey, where she taught until her death in a school for Blacks, probably in the Session House of the First Presbyterian Church. In Princeton she was active in the First Presbyterian Church, and in 1845 was part of a group urging the formation of a separate Black congregation. The church agreed to that on December 21, 1845, and the presbytery made it official on March 10, 1846. Ninety-two African Americans thus formed the First Presbyterian Church of Colour of Princeton, in 1848 renamed the Witherspoon Street Presbyterian Church. Stockton's name headed the list of petitioners at the formation of the church.

Andrew, John A. III. "A. D. Recalls: Betsey Stockton, Early Missionary to Hawaii." *A.D.* (March 1976): 30.

———. "Betsey Stockton: Stranger in a Strange Land." *Journal of Presbyterian History* 52 (Summer 1974): 157–166.

French, Thomas. *The Missionary Whaleship.* New York: Vantage Press, 1961. 134 pp.

BWR.

STOKES, REMBERT EDWARDS (b. June 16, 1917), 98th bishop of the **African Methodist Episcopal Church** (AME), was born in Dayton, Ohio, the son of W. O. and Hazel Stokes. He received a B.S. from Wilberforce University in Ohio, an S.T.B. from Boston University, and a Th.D. from Harvard Divinity School in Massachusetts. He married Nancy Phillips, with whom he has had three daughters.

He was ordained deacon in 1941 and elder in 1942. His pastorates have included Mt. Zion AME Church in Jamestown, Rhode Island, St. Paul AME Church in Cambridge, Massachusetts, and St. Paul AME Church in Canton, Ohio. He has served as dean of Payne Theological Seminary at Wilberforce and as president of Wilberforce University. Stokes was elected bishop in 1976 and assigned to the Eighteenth Episcopal District (South Africa). From 1980 to 1984 he was assigned to the Fourteenth Episcopal District, where he and his wife secured 10,000 books for Monrovia College, added clothing and school materials to orphanages, developed local leadership, and made other advances. From 1984 to 1988 he was assigned to the Tenth Episcopal District, with headquarters in Dallas, Texas, and since that time has been "located," outside a regular district assignment, in Dayton, Ohio.

FEDHR.

STREETS, FREDERICK J. (b. January 17, 1950), the first African American senior chaplain at Yale University, received his B.A. in 1972 from Ottawa University in Ottawa, Kansas, an **American Baptist Churches in the U.S.A.** school. He received his M.Div. in 1975 from Yale University Divinity School in New Haven, Connecticut. He married Annette, with whom he has had three children.

After graduation he became chaplain of Qunnipiac College in Hamden, Connecticut, a position he held for about a year. Also in 1975 he accepted the pastorate of the 700–member Mount Aery Baptist Church in Bridgeport, Connecticut. This church, and thus his ordained status, is affiliated with both the **Progressive National Baptist Convention** and the American Baptist Churches in the U.S.A. He has remained pastor of this church ever since, developing a wide range of programs appropriate to its urban setting. He also pursued his interest in social work, and from 1978 to 1980 was director of the Interfaith Friendly Visitation Program Amongst the Elderly, a program covering six cities around Bridgeport. In 1980 he received the Humanitarian Award from the National Council of Negro Women.

He received his M.S.W. in 1981 from the Wurzweiler School of Social Work at Yeshiva University, and served social work internships at Jewish Family Services in Bridgeport, Connecticut (1979–80) and Yale Psychiatric Institute in New Haven (1980–81). From 1982 to 1984 he was a psychiatric social worker at the Child Guidance Center of Greater Bridgeport, and from 1984 to 1989 he was a psychiatric social work associate at the Greater Bridgeport Community Mental Health Center. In 1987 he became assistant professor in pastoral theology at Yale Divinity School, a position he has maintained to the present. In 1990–91 he was visiting professor at Hartford Theological Seminary and in 1991–92 he was a Lilly Endowment Research Associate at Hartford Theological Seminary, studying alternative forms of theological education. Most recently he was appointed the first African American senior chaplain at Yale University, assuming the post on July 1, 1992.

Curriculum Vitae of Frederick Streets.

STROUD, W. F. GORDON

STROUD, W. F. GORDON (c.1880– ?), educator and pioneer lay missionary of the American Lutheran Church (now a constituent part of the Evangelical Lutheran Church in America), was born in Barbados, West Indies. He gained an excellent education, studying in Montreal and Baltimore, and in 1915 took charge of the newly founded St. Philip's Lutheran Mission School in Prattville, Alabama. In September, 1916 he was transferred to take charge of another new mission school, St. Paul's Lutheran School. He and his wife (name unknown) developed this school (later called Dobler Institute and then St. Paul Lutheran Academy) into a thriving elementary and high school with one hundred

and fifty students. He served the school until 1929, and information on his life after that time is unavailable.

LCAN.

SULLIVAN, LEON HOWARD

SULLIVAN, LEON HOWARD (b. October 16, 1922), prominent Baptist minister and founder of the Opportunities Industrialization Centers of America, was born into poverty and a broken home in Charleston, West Virginia. A gifted athlete with a strong interest in religion, he was ordained a Baptist minister at age seventeen and then went to West Virginia State University on an athletic scholarship. He played basketball and football until a knee injury ended his playing days. Without his scholarship he was forced to work nights in a steel mill in order to pay for his continued schooling.

Famous preacher and politician **Adam Clayton Powell, Jr.** met Sullivan on a trip to West Virginia, and was very impressed with his personality and abilities. After Sullivan finished his B.A. in 1943 Powell persuaded him to move to New York City and be the assistant pastor at his Abyssinian Baptist Church in Harlem while doing graduate studies. In 1944, when labor leader A. Philip Randolph threatened to bring 5,000 Blacks to a March on Washington, Sullivan was president of the organizing group. When President Roosevelt capitulated to the demands, Sullivan learned an important lesson in social action. He was also influenced by Father Divine, with whom he was close friends. He finished his B.D. at Union Theological Seminary in 1945 and left Abyssinia to pastor the First Baptist Church in South Orange, New Jersey. In August, 1945 he married Grace Banks, with whom he had three children. In five years at the First Baptist Church he earned an M.A. in sociology at Columbia University in New York City (1947) and was elected president of the South Orange Council of Churches.

In 1950 he accepted the pastorate of Zion Baptist Church in Philadelphia, Pennsylvania, where he remained for the next thirty-eight years. The church was located in a slum area, and he immediately set about establishing youth programs to combat delinquency. In 1955 the United States Junior Chamber of Commerce selected Sullivan as the outstanding young man of Philadelphia and one of the ten outstanding young men in America. In 1960 he founded and then chaired the Zion Home for the Retired. Noting that Blacks were being squeezed out of the job market by both racism and automation, he searched for a way to counter the problem. He organized four hundred other Black ministers in a boycott of some twenty businesses that refused to hire Blacks. The boycott lasted about three years, beginning in 1959, and began to take full effect in 1961. Almost overnight, thousands of jobs opened to Blacks in the Philadelphia area. In 1963 Sullivan received the Russworm Award from the National Publisher's Association and was named one of the one hundred outstanding young adults in the country. *Ebony* magazine placed him a number of times over the years on its list of the one hundred most influential Black Americans.

After the success of the boycott the next task was to train the unemployed in skills that were needed in the modern business environment. To emphasize this point, Sullivan coined such phrases as "Integration without preparation is frustration," and "Black power without brain power and green power is no power." The city donated an abandoned police station at Nineteenth and Oxford Streets in North Philadelphia, and the place was transformed into the Opportunities Industrialization Center (O.I.C.). The Philadelphia Council for Economic Advancement, a Ford Foundation agency, gave the money for a staff, and numerous other businesses donated equipment and support. The O.I.C. opened in January 1964, with courses in electronics, power sewing, drafting, cabinet making, and restaurant practices. Over the next five years seven branches of the O.I.C. were established, adding courses in commercial cooking, welding, department store sales, dry cleaning, and laundry work. Three federal agencies had financed O.I.C.s in ninety other cities by 1971. In its first ten years the O.I.C. trained some 150,000 poor Blacks, Whites, and Chicanos and placed about 35 percent of them in entry-level positions, a placement rate considered "very good" by the Labor Department.

In 1962 Sullivan founded Zion Investment Associates, Inc. He sold shares on the "10–36" plan ($10 a week for 36 weeks) to 650 members of his congregation. Within seven years the company was enabled to establish Zion Gardens (an apartment complex); Progress Plaza (the first Black-owned and operated shopping center in the United States); the Progress Garment Manufacturing Company; and Progress Aerospace Enterprises, Inc. This last project, begun in May 1968, particularly caught the imagination of the public. The U.S. Department of Labor gave a grant of $500,000 and General Electric provided contracts worth $2,575,000 to train one hundred hardcore unemployed as aerospace technicians. Sullivan has said that among the most important components of his program was the development, through special classes, of a new, positive self-image and attitude for the

trainees. In 1968 running the O.I.C.s became more than Sullivan could handle alone and he set up the National Industrial Advisory Council to guide the operation. In 1969 he published *Build, Brother, Build: From Poverty to Economic Power.*

By the 1970s Sullivan was established as a national figure. He received the coveted Spingarn Medal from the N.A.A.C.P. in 1971, and that same year became the first Black person ever elected to the board of directors of General Motors. Of this new position, he noted that he wanted to be "a voice from the outside on the inside." By 1976 General Motors was buying $50 million in parts from Black manufacturers, up from $2 million in 1971. It increased its advertising in Black periodicals from 66,000 lines annually to 1.3 million lines, and opened an account in every one of the nation's Black-owned banks. It also placed $2.5 billion of its insurance with Black underwriters. In 1976 the Leon Howard Sullivan Chair was established at the School of Social Welfare at the University of Wisconsin.

Over the years Sullivan did not neglect his church, and built it up from a membership of 600 to well over 5,000. His sermons were so popular that closed circuit television had to broadcast them to overflow crowds. The church developed a large-scale set of community programs, including a daycare center, credit union, community center, employment agency, literacy classes, athletic teams, counseling services, and a home for the aged. In 1987 Sullivan received the Franklin D. Roosevelt Four Freedoms Award and in 1988 the Leon Howard Sullivan Scholarship Fund was established at Bentley College in Massachusetts. Sullivan retired from the church in 1988.

"Black Church Launches Space Factory." *Ebony* 24 (November 1968): 33–44.

"The Black on GM's Board." *Time* 108 (September 6, 1976): 54–55.

"Church Attending Soars to New High." *Ebony* 11 (March 1956): 18–23.

Garland, Phyl. "The Unorthodox Ministry of Leon H. Sullivan." *Ebony* 26 (May 1971): 112–120.

"A Hand Up." *Newsweek* 82 (December 10, 1973): 105–106.

Poinsett, Alex. "O.I.C., Tutor of the Unemployed." *Ebony* 29 (June 1974): 43–48.

Sullivan, Leon H. *Alternatives to Despair.* Valley Forge, PA: Judson Press, 1972. 160 pp.

———. *Build, Brother, Build: From Poverty to Economic Power.* Philadelphia, PA: Macrae Smith, 1969. 192 pp.

IBAW, WWABA (92–93), *CB* (1969), *WWA* (90–91), *EBA, IP, CRACG, BDNM* (70).

SWIFT MEMORIAL COLLEGE. A Presbyterian school. Swift Memorial College was founded in 1883 as an elementary school for African American children in the Appalachian Mountain area near Rogersville, Tennessee. It was founded by Rev. William H. Franklin, an African American and graduate of Marysville College. It was named for Elijah E. Swift the president of the Board of Missions for Freedman which had been established that same year by the Northern Presbyterians, now part of the **Presbyterian Church (U.S.A.).** The school grew steadily through the rest of the century. Then in 1901 the Tennessee legislature passed a law which prohibited the instruction of Blacks and Whites in the same institution. The law directly affected Marysville College, a Presbyterian school which had begun admitting Black students following the war.

In order to cope with the new law, it was agreed to turn over funds given to Marysville for Freedmen to Swift. In 1904 Swift added a high school and a four-year college curriculum. Franklin became the first president of what was renamed Franklin Memorial College.

Franklin oversaw the school's development until his retirement in 1926. He was succeeded by Rev. C. E. Tucker. In 1928 the elementary school was dropped and over the next years Tucker saw to the development of the curriculum according to state standards. Unfortunately, in the 1940s the school was unable to keep up with the rapidly increasing standards for education and in 1952 the church decided to discontinue the school. A local committee tried to continue the school for several years, but in 1956 the property was sold to the local boards of education for use as a high school.

Parker, Inez Moore. *The Rise and Decline of the Program of Education for Black Presbyterians of the United Presbyterian Church U.S.A., 1865–1970.* San Antonio, TX: Trinity University Press, 1977. 319 pp.

"And about this time I had a vision,—and I saw white spirits and black spirits engaged in battle, and the sun was darkened—the thunder rolled in the heavens, and blood flowed in streams—and I heard a voice saying, 'Such is your luck, such you are called to see, and let it come rough or smooth, you must surely bare it.' I now withdrew myself as much as my situation would permit, from the intercourse of my fellow servants, for the avowed purpose of serving the Spirit more fully—and it appeared to me, and reminded me of the things it had already shown me, and that it would reveal to me the knowledge of the elements, the revolution of the planets, the operation of the tides, and changes of the seasons."

Nat Turner
Confession
1831

T

TALBERT, MELVIN GEORGE (b. June 14, 1934), a bishop of the **United Methodist Church**, was born in Clinton, Louisiana, one of seven children in the family of Nettles and Florence (George) Talbert. His father was a sharecropper, and the family was raised in relative poverty. Talbert attended public schools and was trained as a carpenter's helper. However, he managed to make it into college and received his B.A. in 1959 from Southern University in Baton Rouge, Louisiana. He then enrolled at Gammon Theological Seminary, the Methodist school in Atlanta, Georgia, where he earned his B.D. in 1962. In his middle year at Gammon he was student body president, even while also pastoring at Boyd Chapel Methodist Church in Jefferson City, Tennessee (1960–61) and Rising Sun Methodist Church in Sunrise, Tennessee (1960–61). In 1960–61 he was a member of the Student Non-Violent Coordinating Committee at the Atlanta University Center, and at one point spent three days and nights in jail with **Martin Luther King, Jr.** On June 3, 1961, he married Ethelou Douglas, with whom he had one daughter.

Talbert was ordained deacon in 1960 and elder in 1963 in what was then the Methodist Church. In 1961–62 he pastored St. John's Methodist Church in Los Angeles, California, followed by Wesley Methodist Church in Los Angeles (1962–64) and Hamilton Methodist Church in Los Angeles (1964–67). In 1967–68 he was associate council director of what at that time was called the Pacific and Southwest Annual Conference (now the California-Pacific Annual Conference). He was a delegate to the General Conference beginning in 1968, the year the Methodist Church merged with the Evangelical United Brethren to form the United Methodist Church. From 1968 to 1973 he was district superintendent of the Long Beach District, and in 1971 received the Special Achievement Award from the National Association of Black Business Women. From 1973 to 1980 he was general secretary of the General Board of Discipleship headquartered in Nashville, Tennessee.

In 1980 Talbert was elected bishop, the youngest bishop then serving the United Methodist Church. He was assigned to the Seattle Episcopal Area until 1988, when he moved to the San Francisco Episcopal Area. From 1980 to 1988 he was on the General Commission on Religion and Race, serving as its president from 1985 to 1988. From 1980 to 1984 he chaired the Missional Priority Coordinating Committee of the General Council on Ministries. He was on the executive committee of the World Methodist Council from 1976 to 1981 and again from 1984 to the present. Since 1980 he has been on the governing board of the National Council of Churches. From 1981 to 1984 he was on the African Church Growth and Development Committee, and has served on numerous other boards and commissions. He is a trustee of Gammon Theological Seminary, the University of Puget Sound in Tacoma, Washington, and the School of Theology at Claremont, California, where he was a visiting professor of evangelism in 1978.

BDNM (70), *WWR* (85), *WWABA* (92–93), *WWA* (88–89).

TALBOT, FREDERICK HILBORN (b. October 13, 1927), ambassador and 90th bishop of the **African Methodist Episcopal Church** (AME), was born in British Guiana (now Guyana), South America, the son of Simon E. A. and Helena Best (Adrian) Talbot. He grew up in the capitol city of Georgetown, and the family was active in the St. Peter AME Church. He received a scholarship to Allen University in Columbia, South Carolina, where he earned his B.A. in 1954. He received his B.D. in 1957 from Yale University Divinity School in New Haven, Connecticut, and his M.S.T. in 1959 from the Pacific School of Religion (P.S.R.) in Berkeley, California. In about 1959 he married Sylvia Ross, whom he met at Yale University.

His first pastorate was at the Little Mountain Circuit in South Carolina, from 1951 to 1954, while in school. He was ordained deacon in 1951 and elder in 1952.

Between 1954 and 1957, while in seminary, he pastored First AME Church in New Haven, Connecticut. In 1957–58 he was chaplain and English teacher at Shorter College in North Little Rock, Arkansas, and in 1958–59 he pastored the St. James AME Church in Colusa, California, while attending P.S.R. From 1959 to 1961 he was an instructor in practical theology at Payne Theological Seminary at Wilberforce University in Ohio, as well as pastor of Hickman Temple AME Church. During this time his wife was district health educator for the New York City Department of Health, working in the Bedford-Stuyvesant section of Brooklyn.

In 1961 Talbot returned home to Guyana to pastor the St. Peter AME Church in Georgetown, where he stayed until 1971. His wife came with him and for a time she was the Minister of Health for Guyana. From 1968 to 1971 Talbot was also Caribbean Consultant for the Family Life Church World Service division of the National Council of Churches, U.S.A. July of 1972 was an extraordinary month for Talbot. In that month he was appointed Permanent Representative with the rank of Ambassador, Extraordinary and Plenipotentiary, to the United States for Guyana, and was elected bishop in the AME Church. In 1973 he was also assigned High Commissioner to Canada.

His episcopal assignment for many years was in the Sixteenth Episcopal District, covering the Caribbean and South America area. He oversaw the founding of New St. Peter AME Church and Ebenezer AME Church, both in Georgetown, Guyana, and the Agape & Collins-Morris Community Centres in Georgetown. He was also chair of the Guyana Council of Churches. In about 1980 he was assigned to the Sixth Episcopal District, with headquarters in Atlanta, Georgia, and oversaw the building of a $2 million headquarters for Turner Theological Seminary. Since about 1988 he has been ecumenical officer for the church, stationed in Frederiksted, St. Croix, U.S. Virgin Islands.

Alexander, Royster. "Essence Woman: Sylvia Talbot." *Essence* 5 (June 1974): 14.
"Thanksgiving in Guyana for Bishop Fred Talbot's Election to Bishop of the AME Church." *Voice of Missions* 81 (September-October 1972): 110–112.
BDNM (75), HAMEC, HUBA, IBAW, FEDHR.

TALBOT, SAMSON DUNBAR (1819–1878), 14th bishop of the **African Methodist Episcopal Zion Church** (AMEZ), was born in West Bridgewater, Massachusetts. He was converted and called to preaching 1841, was ordained deacon in the New York Conference on May 21, 1843, and ordained elder on May 23, 1844. He married Sarah De Groat in 1844 and later, after her death, he married Sarah Gassaway in December 1865.

His pastorates included AMEZ churches in New York, New York; Boston, Massachusetts; Newark, New Jersey; Rochester, New York; Syracuse, New York; Washington, D.C.; and Troy, New York. For some years he was treasurer of the Book Concern. He was consecrated bishop on May 30, 1864, and assigned to the First Episcopal District (New York, New England, and Genesee Conferences). In 1866 he was moved to the Fourth Episcopal District (Georgia, Alabama, and Louisiana Conferences), where he stayed the rest of his career. He was considered one of the best preachers in the denomination and was respected by both Black and White, despite being a northerner working in the South during the difficult Reconstruction years.

AMEZC, OHYAMEZC, EWM.

TALLADEGA COLLEGE. An **United Church of Christ** school. Talladega College, Talladega, Alabama, was founded in 1866, by William Savery, a freedman. For a period it was the only school for African Americans in a ten-county area of the state. Savery began his efforts by convincing the Freedman's Bureau of Alabama of the need of such a school. The bureau then sought the additional support of the American Missionary Association (AMA), which purchased an unoccupied building of a former Baptist College. A carpenter, Savery joined the crew gathered to renovate the property. One hundred forty students were present for the first classes in 1867 under the leadership of Rev. Henry E. Brown. Beginning as an elementary school to train local teachers, the future college slowly moved toward a normal class. In 1869 a dormitory was built for female students. The school was chartered that same year.

Talladega suffered through the 1870s because of the AMA placing its emphasis and money on the development of Fisk University and Atlanta University. It suffered a major reverse in 1876 when funds were cut. By 1878 it had recovered slightly and began making plans for finally adding college work. It was not until the beginning of the 1890s that college work was actually offered. The first graduates received their diplomas in 1895. The school's central focus throughout this period, however, remained teacher training. During the 1876–77 school year, Edward P. Lord tried to institute an agricultural and mechanical program at the school. His unpopular approach, undergirded by a strong prejudice against Black people, soon cost the school the support of prominent African Americans in the state, and in 1879 he was fired. He was succeeded by Henry S. DeForrest. Under DeForrest, the school quickly regained its lost support and moved to become the college Savery originally envisioned.

Jones, Maxine D., and Joe M. Richardson. *Talladega College: The First Century.* Tuscaloosa, AL: University of Alabama Press, 1990. 340 pp.

Richardson, Joe M. *Christian Reconstruction: The American Missionary Association and Southern Blacks, 1861–1890.* Athens, GA: University of Georgia Press, 1986. 348 pp.

TALTON, CHESTER LOVELLE (b. September 22, 1941), a bishop of the **Episcopal Church**, was born in Eldorado, Arkansas. In August 1963 he married Karen Louise Warren, with whom he has had four children. He received his B.S. from California State University at Hayward, and his M.Div. in 1970 from the Church Divinity School of Pacific in Berkeley, California.

He was vicar of Good Shepherd Episcopal Church in Berkeley in 1970–71 and was ordained a priest in 1971. He was vicar of St. Matthias' Mission and curate of All Saints' Episcopal Church in Carmel, California (1971–73); vicar of Holy Cross Church in Chicago, Illinois (1973–76); and rector of St. Philip's Episcopal Church in St. Paul, Minnesota (1976–81). From 1981 to 1985 he was mission officer at Trinity Episcopal Church on Wall Street in New York City, and served as tutor at General Theological Seminary in New York City from 1982 to 1984. From 1985 to 1990 he was rector of the historic St. Philip's Episcopal Church in Harlem, New York City.

He was a member of the Standing Committee of the Diocese of New York, a member of the Diocesan Council, served on the Episcopal Housing Corporation, and was dean of the Manhattan North Clericus. He was active in Harlem Churches for Community Improvement, served on the Harlem Hospital Advisory Committee, was president of the Community Service Council of Greater Harlem, Inc., head of the Upper Manhattan Day Care and Child Development Center, Inc., and chair of the Peter Williams, Jr. Housing Corporation. On January 26, 1991, Talton was consecrated suffragan bishop of the Diocese of Los Angeles.

ECA (1992).

TANNER, BENJAMIN TUCKER (December 25, 1835–January 15, 1923), editor, author, and 18th bishop

of the **African Methodist Episcopal Church** (AME), was born in Pittsburgh, Pennsylvania, the son of Hugh S. and Isabel H. Tanner. His father passed away while he was still young, which made it more difficult for him to finish school. He supported himself at Avery College in Allegheny City (now Pittsburgh) from 1852 to 1857 by working as a barber. In 1856 he was converted and was licensed as a preacher in the AME Church. In 1857, after completing one year of the college-level program at Avery, he enrolled at Western Theological Seminary where he studied until 1860 and was ordained a deacon and elder the same year. On August 19, 1858, he married Sarah Elizabeth Miller, with whom he had seven children.

After Tanner declined a pastoral appointment to the Sacramento station in California for lack of means, Bishop **Daniel Payne** gave permission for him to be a temporary pastor of the 15th Street Presbyterian Church in Washington, D.C., for eighteen months. With the outbreak of the Civil War he organized a Sunday School for the freedmen of the Navy. In April 1862, he joined the Baltimore Conference and was installed as head of the Alexander Street Mission on E Street, the first of its kind in Washington, D.C., supported by the AME Church. He was appointed in 1863 to a church in Georgetown and in 1866 was moved to a larger pastorate in Baltimore. In 1865 he published his first book, *Paul versus Pius Ninth.* He resigned from this position to be the principal of the Conference school at Frederick, Maryland. In 1867 he published his second and most popular book, *An Apology for African Methodism.*

At the 1868 General Conference Tanner was chief secretary and was also elected editor of the *Christian Recorder,* a position he held for the next sixteen years. In 1870 Avery College gave him an honorary M.A. degree. In 1881 he was a delegate to the World Methodist Conference in London, England. Under his able leadership the *Christian Recorder* gained a reputation as one of the most reliable weeklies in America, carrying not only church news, but information and opinions about events of general interest. In 1884 he founded the *A.M.E. Church Review* and moved from the *Christian Recorder* to be its first editor. He set the tone for the new journal as a wide-ranging venue for high-quality literary, theological, and scientific expression for African Americans. It was immediately popular among the reading population of the church and gained a significant readership outside the church as well. In editorials he advocated economic support of Black-owned businesses as a means of combating the oppressive environment of racism.

In 1888 Tanner was elected bishop and was succeeded at the *AME Church Review* by Rev. **Levi J.**

Coppin, who later also became bishop. Tanner presided over the Eleventh Episcopal District (Ontario, Nova Scotia, Bermuda, St. Thomas, and Demerara Conferences) from 1888 to 1892; the First Episcopal District (New York, New England, New Jersey, and Eastern Pennsylvania Conferences) from 1892 to 1896; the Fifth Episcopal District (Missouri, Kansas, and Colorado Conferences) from 1896 to 1900; the Ninth Episcopal District (Tennessee and Kentucky Conferences) from 1900 to 1904; and the Eleventh Episcopal District (Florida Conferences) from 1904 to 1908. He organized the East Tennessee Conference in 1901 and the West Florida Conference on December 6, 1906.

In September 1901, he was a delegate to the Third World Methodist Conference in London and presented a paper entitled "Elements of Pulpit Effectiveness." That same year he served as dean of Payne Theological Seminary in Wilberforce, Ohio. He was a significant scholar and prolific writer with many books to his name, including a two-volume work, *The Dispensations in the History of the Church and the Interregnums* (1894) and *An Outline of Our History and Government for African Methodist Churchmen, Ministerial and Lay in Catechetical Form* (1884). He worked toward organic union of the three major Black Methodist churches, and in 1908 attended the first Tri-Council of Colored Methodist Bishops.

At the General Conference in May 1908, he was retired at his own request and was allotted half-pay, the first AME bishop to be given a pension. The *A.M.E. Church Review* continued to grow and flourish, and today is America's oldest Black magazine, just as the *Christian Recorder* is America's oldest Black weekly. One of Tanner's sons, Henry O. Tanner, became an internationally renowned artist.

Tanner, Benjamin Tucker. *An Apology for African Methodism*. Baltimore, MD: The Author, 1867. 468 pp.
———. *The Color of Solomon: What? "My Beloved is White and Ruddy."* Philadelphia, PA: AME Book Concern, 1895. 93 pp.
———. *The Dispensations in the History of the Church and the Interregnums*. 2 vols. Kansas City, MO: The Author, 1898–1899.
———. *A Hint to Ministers, Especially Those of the African Methodist Episcopal Church*. Wilberforce, OH: Industrial Student Printers, 1900. 96 pp.
———. *An Outline of Our History and Government for African Methodist Churchmen, Ministerial and Lay, in Catechetical Form*. Philadelphia, PA: Grant, Faires and Rodgers, Printers, 1884. 206 pp.
———. *Theological Lectures*. Nashville, TN: AME Sunday School Union Press, 1894. 185 pp.
DNAADB, BAMEC, ACAB, WWCR, CEAMEC, BHBA, MM, NCAB (3), BAW, IBAWCB, HUBA, AARS, DAA, IBAW, NYTO, CH, WWWA (1), DAB, DARB, AAE, TCBDA, HAMEC, EWM, DANB.

TAPPAN, JOHN (June, 1799–1870), 7th bishop of the **African Methodist Episcopal Zion Church** (AMEZ), was born into slavery in North Carolina. It is unclear how he obtained his freedom. In any case, he moved to New York, where he was converted on September 5, 1830. He began preaching in 1832 and joined the New York Conference on June 18, 1833. He was ordained deacon on May 20, 1834, and elder on May 15, 1835. He spent most of his ministry in that conference, and has been described as a plain but spirited and forceful preacher.

Tappan was elected superintendent (as bishops were then termed) and consecrated on July 9, 1853, a year which indicates a specially called General Conference. During these early years of the denomination, superintendents were not elected for life, but only for a quadrennial term. He failed to gain reelection in 1856 and continued as a regular preaching elder for the remainder of his career.

HAMEZC, HAMEZCIA, EWM, AMEZC.

TATE, MARY MAGDALENA LEWIS (January, 1871–December, 1930), founder of the **Church of the Living God, the Pillar and Ground of Truth**, probably grew up in Tennessee, though little is known about her family or early years. She married David Lewis as a teenager in the 1880s, and gave birth to her first child, Walter Curtis Lewis, in Vanlier, Tennessee, in 1890. Some years later the family moved to Clinton, Tennessee, where Tate had a religious experience which led her into preaching a Holiness gospel. She later moved to Dickson, Tennessee, which remained her home base for the rest of her life.

The beginning of the Church of the Living God, the Pillar and Ground of Truth, is generally dated to 1903, when Tate began her ministry in Steele Springs, Tennessee, moving quickly on to Paducah, Kentucky, Brooklyn, Illinois, and stops throughout the South. Her schedule forced her to leave the two boys with her two sisters in Paducah, Kentucky. She began to organize local Holiness groups while other Holiness preachers such as Charles Parham and **William J. Seymour** were spreading the news of the newly born Pentecostal movement. In 1908 Tate became seriously ill, and was given little hope of being cured. She was suddenly healed, however, and experienced the Pentecostal baptism of the Holy Spirit, speaking in tongues. Her ministry from this point was Pentecostal.

In June, 1908, she held a series of revival meetings in Greenville, Alabama. At the end of these meetings, the Church of the Living God, the Pillar and Ground of Truth was formally established. "Mother Tate" was ordained a bishop by the board of trustees, and she served as general overseer, president, and apostle elder until her death. She ordained the first ministers for the church, which quickly spread to the surrounding southern states. Ministry began in Georgia in 1910, also soon in Kentucky and Tennessee, and in Florida in about 1914. In 1914, she raised up four bishops for the growing church, including her two sons, Walter Curtis Lewis (d.1921) and Felix Early Lewis (d.1968). In 1919 a schism occurred, which led to the founding of the House of God, Which is the Church of the Living God, the Pillar and Ground of Truth, Inc., in Philadelphia. The rest of the organization survived intact, however, and in 1923 Tate opened the New and Living Way Publishing House in Nashville, Tennessee. She wrote much of the early literature of the church, including the *First Decree Book* (1914) and the *Constitution, Government, and General Decree Book* (1923) and subsequent revisions.

Tate's last preaching tour ended in wintertime in Philadelphia, where she caught frostbite in her foot and died of complications. The church was then reorganized with three general overseers, F. E. Lewis, M. F. L. Keith (the widow of W. C. Lewis), and B. L. McLeod. Their dominions of supervision eventually developed into separate denominations, with Lewis leading the group with the original name.

Tate, Mary M. Lewis. *The Constitution, Government, and General Decree Book of the Church of the Living God, the Pillar and Ground of Truth.* 2nd ed. Nashville, TN: The New and Living Way Publishing Co., 1924. 84 pp.
BDA-AHP, BH, RLOA, SFAY.

TAYLOR, DEON YVONNE WALKER (b. c.1916), first woman president of an **African Methodist Episcopal Church** (AME)-related college, was born in New Bedford, Massachusetts, the only child of Dougal Ormonde Beaconsfield and Eva Emma (Ravallion) Walker. Her father was an AME church minister who became a bishop in 1948. Taylor received an excellent education with a B.S. in 1936 from Wilberforce University in Ohio and an M.A. in English in June 1938 from Boston University. In 1950 she received an

honorary Doctor of Humanities degree from Monrovia University in Liberia, Africa. Upon return to the United States she worked on a degree at the University of Kansas. On August 28, 1963, she married R. Harvey Taylor.

From 1956 to 1964 Taylor was an assistant professor of English and administrative assistant to the president of Wilberforce University. From 1964 to 1967 she was associate professor of education and chair of the department at Wilberforce, a school related to the AME Church and the nation's oldest Black university. In 1967 she became assistant academic dean, moving to acting academic dean in 1968. During this time she became active in the National Association of Women Deans and Counselors, and from 1966 to 1968 she was president of Links Inc. From 1969 to 1972 she was dean of instruction and in this capacity introduced a number of new and innovative programs to the school. Among other achievements, she arranged for the introduction of a new engineering program to help fill the national need for Black engineers.

In 1973 she was named academic dean, the highest academic position. She was the first woman to hold this position at Wilberforce. On March 15, 1984, Taylor was inaugurated as the first woman president of Wilberforce, and the first woman president of any college related to the AME Church. Her father had also been president of Wilberforce from 1936 to 1941. She held that position until 1988, when she retired to a life of guest lecturing and some consulting for Central State University in Ohio.

"Wilberforce Names First Woman Dean." *College and University Business* 54 (June 1973): 24.
WWAW (75–76), *BAMEC, IAAH.*

TAYLOR, EGBERT DON (b. September 2, 1937), a bishop of the **Episcopal Church**, was born in Kingston, Jamaica, and grew up very active in St. Matthew's Episcopal Church in Kingston. He finished high school at Kingston College and then worked as a radio announcer for two years. He decided to enter the ministry and enrolled in St. Peter's Theological College. He was ordained deacon on September 21, 1960, and priest on October 29, 1961. He married Rosalie Ann French, with whom he has had one daughter.

Upon his ordination to the priesthood, he was assigned to organize and develop St. Mary's Parish in the western section of St. Andrew. He was also appointed headmaster of Kingston College. While serving in these two areas he furthered his education, receiving his B.A. in 1966 from the University of the

West Indies and in 1968 received his S.T.M. from Trinity College in Ontario. He was a popular preacher and retreat leader and was active in religious broadcasting. In 1972 he made a special study of evangelism among Blacks in the United States in an effort to ascertain the best approach to this ministry.

From 1973 to 1977 Taylor was rector of St. Philip's Episcopal Church in Buffalo, New York, and in 1977–78 was vicar of Holy Comforter Episcopal Church in Atlanta, Georgia. From 1978 to 1986 he was rector of Holy Cross Episcopal Church in Atlanta, Georgia. For six years he was a member of the Presiding Bishop's Committee on Evangelism. On February 24, 1987, he was consecrated bishop of the Virgin Islands.

ECA (1989).

TAYLOR, GARDNER CALVIN (b. June 18, 1918), former president of the **Progressive National Baptist Convention** and called one of the best preachers in the history of the United States, was born in Baton Rouge, Louisiana, the son of W. M. and Selma G. Taylor. He received his B.A. in 1937 from Leland College and was accepted at the University of Michigan Law School. Then an event occurred that changed the course of his life. As he was driving along a highway, two White men in an old Ford suddenly veered across the road and Taylor plowed into them, killing at least one of them. He feared that lynching was a distinct possibility, but two White witnesses testified that he was not responsible for the accident, and he was not detained. He believed that God was distinctly with him during the ordeal, and he turned his attention toward the meaning of his life. He was ordained a Baptist minister in 1939 and received his B.D. in 1940 from Oberlin School of Theology in Ohio. In 1940 he married Laura Scott, with whom he had one daughter.

His first pastorate was at a church in Elyria, Ohio, from 1938 to 1940, while he was in seminary. He then pastored in New Orleans from 1941 to 1943 and in Baton Rouge from 1943 to 1947. In 1948 he accepted the pastorate of the Concord Baptist Church of Christ in Brooklyn, where he remained for the rest of his career. During his pastorate there he was also a professor at Colgate-Rochester Divinity School in Rochester, New York, vice-president of the board of directors of the Urban League of Greater New York, and active in Job Opportunities for Brooklyn.

In 1958 Taylor became only the second African American since 1917 to be a member of the New York City board of education, and used that position to attack school segregation. He was a civil rights activist and was arrested with **Martin Luther King, Jr.,** during demonstrations in the 1960s. Taylor's strong support of such activities placed him in conflict with **Joseph H. Jackson,** the president of the **National Baptist Convention, U.S.A., Inc.,** who opposed the use of marches and demonstrations. The rivalry became so intense that Taylor was Jackson's main competitor for the presidency of the organization in the elections of September 1961. After a court-supervised vote, Jackson won reelection. Almost immediately thereafter, Rev. **L. Venchael Booth** called for the creation of a breakaway organization, the Progressive National Baptist Convention, which Taylor, Martin Luther King, Jr., and a number of others joined. Taylor later served as both vice-president and president of the Progressive National Baptist Convention.

The Concord Baptist Church burned to the ground in 1952, destroying everything except the membership roll, and a $1.7 million new building was dedicated in 1956. The mortgage was burned in November 1962. Taylor also led the church into operating a fully accredited elementary school, a 121-bed nursing home, a federal credit union, and a clothing exchange. Already a large church when Taylor arrived, it added some 8,000 members during the course of his ministry to reach a high of nearly 12,000 in the 1960s, making it one of the largest in the nation. In about 1962 he served a term as president of the Protestant Council of New York City, the first Black and the first Baptist ever to hold that position. He developed close relationships with Mayor David Dinkins and other city officials. He has been widely considered to be one of the premier masters of the art of preaching, listed as such by *Time* and *Ebony* magazines. He has preached or lectured all over the United States, Africa, Europe, China, and Australia. He has preached or spoken at five meetings of the World Baptist Alliance (Copenhagen, Cleveland, London, Miami Beach, and Tokyo), and has been the recipient of many awards and honors. He delivered the coveted Lyman Beecher Lectures at Yale University, which resulted in his one book to date, *How Shall They Preach?* (1977). On June 21, 1990, he introduced South African activist Nelson Mandela to a crowd of 2,000 at the Riverside Church in Manhattan. Nine days later he retired from his church position, but planned to continue preaching regularly around the country.

"American Preaching: A Dying Art?" *Time* 114 (December 31, 1979): 64–67.

"America's Fifteen Greatest Black Preachers." *Ebony* 39 (September 1984): 27–33.

"Church Attending Soars to New High." *Ebony* 11 (March 1956): 18–23.

Lorch, Donatella. "After King, Mandela and 42 Years, a Pastor Retires." *New York Times* (July 1, 1990): 26.

"Organizations and Leaders Campaigning for Negro Goals in the United States." *New York Times* (August 10, 1964): 16.

Taylor, Gardner C. *How Shall They Preach?* Elgin, IL: Progressive Baptist Publishing House, 1977. 148 pp.

————. "They Shall Ask the Way." *A.M.E. Church Review* 68 (April-June 1952): 56–58.

————. "Why I Believe There Is a God." *Ebony* 18 (February 1963): 86.

IBAW, HUBA, SCA, HBB, NA, BDNM (75).

TAYLOR, JAMES CLAIR (May 3, 1893–July 23, 1954), 54th bishop of the **African Methodist Episcopal Zion Church** (AMEZ), was born in Cambridge, Massachusetts, the oldest of four children in the family of James Madison and Harriette Ann Taylor. His father died when he was only four years old. He attended the public schools in that city through high school, and at the age of fifteen experienced conversion. He was baptized at St. Paul (now Peoples) Baptist Church in Boston and became leader of the youth group. In 1912 he married Alma Jackson of Boston, with whom he had one son.

Soon after this time they moved to Portland, Maine, where the only Black church around was AMEZ, and they became members. Taylor began to feel a call to the ministry and in preparation enrolled at Bates College in Lewiston, Maine. He later reportedly studied at Chicago Theological Seminary. He was ordained deacon on June 16, 1918, and elder on June 20, 1920. His first pastorate was Meriden, Connecticut, and other pastorates included Goldsboro, North Carolina; Moore's Chapel AMEZ Church in Salisbury, North Carolina; St. John's AMEZ Church in Rutherfordton, North Carolina; Memorial AMEZ Church in Rochester, New York; Wesley Union AMEZ Church in Harrisburg, Pennsylvania; and the Goodwin Street (First) AMEZ Church in Paterson, New Jersey.

In 1936 Taylor was elected editor of the *A.M.E. Zion Quarterly Review*, a position he held for the next twelve years, while also pastoring churches. His first wife passed away and while at the Rochester pastorate he married Anne Pate of Goldsboro, North Carolina. At the 1948 General Conference Taylor was elected bishop on the third ballot and was consecrated on May 16, 1948. He was assigned to the Alabama, Mississippi, and West Tennessee Conferences, but only served six years before his sudden death in Birmingham.

"Editorials." *A.M.E. Zion Quarterly Review* 65 (1954): 52.

"James Clair Taylor Elected Bishop." *Star of Zion* 72 (May 20, 1948): 5.

HAMEZC, AMEZC.

TAYLOR, MARSHALL WILLIAM (July 1, 1846–September 11, 1887), educator, the first Black editor of the *Southwestern Christian Advocate*, and one of the most prominent ministers of the Methodist Episcopal Church (now the **United Methodist Church**), was born in Lexington, Fayette County, Kentucky, the fourth of five children in the family of Samuel and Nancy Ann Boyd. His father was a rope maker, descended from the famous Boyd family of Scotland, and had bought his way out of slavery. His mother had gained her freedom in the will of her deceased master, and made a living in the millinery trade. Two of the five children were from a previous marriage of the mother to Albert Summers.

In 1854 the family moved to Louisville, Kentucky, looking for a school to which the children could go, but with little success. They variously attended Baptist, African Methodist, and Methodist Episcopal churches. For two years they lived in Ghent, Kentucky, near Vevey, Indiana. Taylor became a messenger in the law firm of J. B. Kincaid and John W. Barr, both of whom helped him with his education, and he was able to attend a series of private schools. From 1862 to 1865 he served in the Army of the Cumberland. By 1866 he had gained sufficient competence to open a Freedmen's School in Hardinsburg, Breckenridge County, Kentucky, using a former Methodist Episcopal Church, South building that had been given to the Black community for worship. This was the first school for Blacks the town had seen, and there was a great deal of animosity towards it from the Whites. Incidents of abuse directed at Taylor and the school escalated until the school was blown up on December 25, 1867. The apparent intent was to catch a large evening crowd gathered for a school exhibition, but by a stroke of luck the event was over early and the explosion only destroyed the building.

The Freedmen's Bureau helped build another schoolhouse, and by that time the Whites had become used to the idea, and some even sponsored it. Taylor became well-known in Kentucky educational circles and was elected president of an educational convention held at Owensboro in 1868. He married Kate Heston, with whom he had two children. He felt the call to the ministry and was licensed as a local preacher in 1869 by the Methodist Episcopal Church. He went to Arkansas for a year as a missionary teacher and preacher, then traveled through Texas, Indian Territory, and Missouri, returning to Kentucky in 1871. In 1872 he was ordained a deacon and assigned to both Coke

Chapel Methodist Episcopal Church in Louisville, Kentucky and the nearby Wesley Chapel Methodist Episcopal Church in Jeffersonville, Indiana. In his three years there he wrote regularly for the newspapers and published a monthly paper called the *Kentucky Methodist*. From 1875 to 1877 he pastored in Indianapolis, Indiana, and was ordained elder in 1876. In 1877–78 he was assigned to Union Chapel Methodist Episcopal Church in Cincinnati, Ohio. In 1878 he published *The Life of Rev. George W. Downing*, which spurred his reception, in 1879, of the honorary D.D. degree from Central Tennessee University (later Walden University) in Nashville, Tennessee.

In 1879 Taylor became district superintendent (or presiding elder) of the Ohio District of the Lexington Conference, where he stayed for four years. In 1880 he was the youngest delegate to the General Conference, and upon his motion fraternal delegates were sent to the various Black Methodist churches. In 1881 he was a delegate to the Ecumenical Methodist Conference in London, England. In 1883 he was appointed district superintendent of the Louisville District. At the 1884 General Conference he was the caucus nominee of the Black delegates for the one bishopric position available to Blacks, that in Liberia, West Africa. He declined the nomination, fearing the effects of such a move on his health, and instead he was elected editor of the *Southwestern Christian Advocate*, the first Black to hold that position. He held this influential position, based in New Orleans, Louisiana, for the few remaining years of his life.

Taylor wrote a number of books and pamphlets besides the one already mentioned, including *Handbook for Schools* (1871), *The Life of Rev. George W. Downing* (1878), *The Life, Travels, Labors, and Helpers of Mrs. Amanda Smith, the Famous Negro Missionary Evangelist* (1888); *A Collection of Revival Hymns and Plantation Melodies* (1883); and *The Negro in Methodism* (1887). Unfortunately, the editorial work of the *Southwestern Christian Advocate* put a great strain on his delicate health. This was aggravated by the controversy aroused when he upheld the church's ban on Blacks from a denominational school in Chattanooga. He urged African Americans rather to create their own destiny apart from Whites if necessary, and suggested that striving for social and religious equality with Whites was not the appropriate focus. He died at the young age of forty-one, cutting short a remarkable career. He has since sometimes been confused with a Black speed cyclist of the same name, born in Indianapolis in 1878.

Taylor, Marshall W. *A Collection of Revival Hymns and Plantation Melodies*. Cincinnati, OH: M. W. Taylor and W. C. Echols, 1883. 272 pp.

———. *Handbook for Schools*. Louisville, KY: 1871.

———. *The Life, Travels, Labors, and Helpers of Mrs. Amanda Smith, the Famous Negro Missionary Evangelist*. Cincinnati, OH: Pr. by Cranston and Stowe for the Author, 1886. 63 pp.

BAW, AARS, HUBA, BDSA, AAP, ACAB, WWWA (HS), *DAB, MM, AAE, HNRA, IBAW, IBAWCB*.

TAYLOR, PRINCE ALBERT, JR. (b. January 27, 1907), the first Black bishop of the Methodist Church (now **United Methodist Church**) to serve a predominantly White constituency, was born in Hennessey, Oklahoma, the fifth of fourteen children in the family of Prince Albert, Sr., and Bertha Ann (Littles) Taylor. His father was a Methodist minister in the (Black) Mississippi Conference, which included the Oklahoma territory. Taylor, Jr., completed his high school education in 1926 at Haven Teachers College, earlier known as Meridian Academy, in Mississippi. He then entered Clark College and Gammon Theological Seminary, both in Atlanta, Georgia, and did work in the two schools simultaneously. He supported himself by working in the school dining room. On July 18, 1929 he married Annie Belle Thaxton, with whom he had one daughter. He finished his work at Gammon in 1930, and thus could no longer hold the dining room job, but still had a year of college left. An arrangement was made with future bishop **Willis J. King**, the new president of Samuel Huston College (now Huston-Tillotson College) in Austin, Texas. Taylor spent a year as head of its sub-college department and finished his college work there. In 1931 he received both his B.A. from Samuel Huston and his B.D. from Gammon Theological Seminary. He was ordained deacon for the North Carolina Conference in 1929 and elder in 1931.

His first pastorate was in Kernersville, North Carolina (1931), followed by the Northwest Greensboro Charge, North Carolina (1931–34); St. John's Methodist Episcopal Church in Thomasville, North Carolina (1934–37); and East Calvary Methodist Church in New York City (1937–40). In 1939 the Methodist Episcopal Church merged with the Methodist Episcopal Church, South and the Methodist Protestant Church to create The Methodist Church. As part of the restructuring the nineteen Black conferences of the former Methodist Episcopal Church, regardless of location, became part of the Central Jurisdiction. Sixteen of the nineteen of the Black conferences opposed this new arrangement, which for the first time locked segregation into the constitution of the church. Taylor was one of those who expressed opposition to the plan.

While in New York he continued his own studies

and in 1940 received his M.A. from both Union Theological Seminary and Columbia University. From 1940 to 1943 he was assistant to the president (David Jones) at Bennett College in Greensboro, North Carolina, and from 1943 to 1948 he was professor and founding department head of Christian Education and Psychology at Gammon Theological Seminary in Atlanta, Georgia. During the summers of 1940–42 and 1945–48 he pastored the large St. Mark's Methodist Church in Harlem, New York City. Those summers allowed him to pursue further education, and in 1948 he received his Ed.D. from New York University. From 1945 to 1948 he also directed the Correspondence School for the Commission on Ministerial Training of the Central Jurisdiction.

In 1948 Taylor was elected editor of the *Central Christian Advocate*, the edition of the denominational paper, the *Christian Advocate*, that served the all-Black Central Jurisdiction. The editorship of the *Central Christian Advocate* or some other edition of the *Christian Advocate* has often been a stepping-stone for Black clergy into the bishopric, as in the cases of **Robert N. Brooks**, **John W. E. Bowen, Jr.**, **Alexander P. Shaw**, **Robert E. Jones**, **Lorenzo H. King**, **L. Scott Allen**, **Isaiah B. Scott**, and as was nearly the case with **Marshall W. Taylor**. From that editorship Prince Taylor was elected bishop by the Central Jurisdiction on June 16, 1956, and assigned to the Liberia Episcopal Area in West Africa, where he stayed for the next eight years. He was twice decorated by the Government of Liberia; he received the Decorated Star of Africa in 1948 and was the second private citizen to receive the Venerable Knighthood of the Pioneers in 1964.

On June 25, 1964, Taylor was named bishop for the New Jersey Episcopal Area, where he remained until retirement. He thus became the first Black bishop in the church to preside over a predominantly White part of the church. Taylor's appointment, essentially transferring part of the Central Jurisdiction (the Baltimore Episcopal Area) to a geographical jurisdiction (the Northeast Jurisdiction) was a landmark event, followed closely on July 10, 1964, by the appointment of **James Thomas** to the Iowa Episcopal Area. The reception accorded both bishops was reportedly overwhelmingly positive. In 1964 Taylor received the St. George's Award Medal from Old St. George's Church in Philadelphia, for distinguished service in the Methodist Church. In 1968 the Methodist Church merged with the Evangelical United Brethren to form the United Methodist Church, and the Central Jurisdiction was dissolved in a move toward integration.

As bishop, Taylor served in numerous positions of responsibility. From April 1965 through May 1966 he was president of the Council of Bishops, the first Black bishop to hold that position. For many years, beginning in 1967, he was chair of the board of directors of Religion in American Life. He was a member of the Commission on Ecumenical Affairs and was on the General Board of the National Council of Churches from 1966 to 1969. In 1967–68 he served on Governor Richard J. Hughes' Commission on Civil Disorder. From 1968 to 1972 he chaired the Commission on the Structure of Methodism Overseas. He was vice-president of the New Jersey Council of Churches and from 1971 to 1976 was chair of the executive committee of the World Methodist Council. From 1972 to 1976 he chaired the Division of Chaplains and Related Ministries. He has served as trustee of many institutions, including Drew University, Wesley School of Theology, Conwell School of Theology, Morristown College, Methodist Hospital of Brooklyn, Union Theological Seminary, and American University in Washington, D.C. He retired in 1976 and has since been a visiting professor at schools such as Drew University and Princeton Theological Seminary. He has also written an autobiography, *The Life of My Years*. In 1983 he was inducted into the United Methodist Communicators' Hall of Fame.

Bennett, Lerone, Jr. "Black Firsts in Politics, Entertainment, Sports, and Other Fields." *Ebony* 37 (March 1982): 128–133.

Harmon, Nolan B., ed. *The Encyclopedia of World Methodism*. 2 vols. Nashville, TN: United Methodist Publishing House, 1974.

"Move Toward Church Unity." *Ebony* 20 (February 1965): 54–60.

Taylor, Prince Albert, Jr. *A History of Gammon Theological Seminary*. New York: Doctoral Dissertation, New York University, 1948.

———. *The Life of My Years*. Nashville, TN: Abingdon Press, 1983. 160 pp.

BDUMB, EWM, BDNM (75), *HUBA, WWA* (76–77), *WWABA* (92–93), *WWMC, WWR* (77), *IBAW*.

TEISH, LUISAH (b. c.1948), author and priestess of the West African Yoruba religion, was born with the name Catherine in New Orleans, Louisiana. While her parents worked, she was raised, along with at least two sisters and one brother, by her grandmother, Catherine Mason Allen, for whom she was named. After some years the immediate family moved to Algiers, on the other side of the Mississippi, and then when she was seven they moved to the nearby town of Harvey. Her father's side of the family was active in the **African Methodist Episcopal Church**. Her mother tried to raise

Luisah as a Roman Catholic, but Luisah preferred to attend the local Sanctified Church. In her junior high years she was a student at the All Saints Catholic School in Algiers.

When she was fourteen her Aunt Cecilia took her to live in Palm Springs, California, moving to Los Angeles about 1963. In 1966 she graduated from Manual Arts High School with interests in journalism and dance. She spent a year at Pacific University in Forest Grove, Oregon, a school related to the United Church of Christ, where experiences with racism made her a political radical. She then transferred to Reed College in Portland, Oregon. In 1969 she got a scholarship to study dance with Madame Katherine Dunham at the Performing Arts Training Center in East St. Louis, Illinois. There she learned the dances of the Haitian Voudou (or **Voodoo**) and explored other parts of her African heritage. She also joined the Fahamme Temple of Amun-Ra in St. Louis, was initiated and given her current name, which means "adventurous spirit." In this temple she learned about the African mystery schools and the importance of that religious heritage.

By 1970 she was the choreographer for the Black Artists Group in St. Louis, but her personal life was not as successful. In the winter of 1973, she lost a baby and moved to Oakland, in the San Francisco Bay Area, to live with her younger sister, Safi. She tried to commit suicide, but came through it and became more involved in Voudou. A priest of the Yoruba tradition told her she was strongly connected with the love goddess Oshun, and a spirit guide became her constant companion. In 1977 she got a CETA job with the Berkeley Neighborhood Arts program. In that position she wrote and directed "The Deer Woman of Owo," a play based on a Yoruban folk tale. At about this time she returned to New Orleans for a visit and discovered that her grandmother's house was on the site of the former house of **Marie LaVeau**, the Voudou Queen of New Orleans in the 1800s. This helped her make sense of some of the psychic experiences she had had in the house, and to accept her connection with that tradition.

In about 1978 Teish wrote a letter to *Plexus*, a Bay Area magazine, to see if any women would be interested in talking with her about African goddesses, and received a surprising sixty calls. She began holding workshops at the Berkeley Women's Center, and about 1982 was formally initiated as a priestess of the Lucumi branch of the Yoruba tradition. In 1985 she wrote *Jambalaya: The Natural Woman's Book of Personal Charms and Practical Rituals*, in which she discusses her personal journeys and explains Voudou and the Yoruban traditions for the novice.

Albert, Mimi. "Out of Africa: Luisah Teish." *Yoga Journal* (January-February 1987): 32–35, 63–66.

Teish, Luisah. *Jambalaya: The Natural Woman's Book of Personal Charms and Practical Rituals*. San Francisco: Harper & Row, 1985. 268 pp.

RLOA.

TENNESSEE MANUAL LABOR UNIVERSITY. A **Christian Church (Disciples of Christ)** school. Tennessee Manual Labor University was a short-lived venture founded in Nashville in 1968 by Peter Lowery, an African American preacher with the Disciples of Christ. Lowery planned the school around a farm and mill, which would employ approximately 100 students who would work and earn money even as they were learning a trade. Though publicized and supported by the editors of several church periodicals, the school, having fallen into debt, failed after a short time.

Harrell, David Edwin. *The Social Sources of Division in the Disciples of Christ, 1865–1900: A Social History of the Disciples of Christ*, Volume II. Atlanta, GA: Publishing Systems, Inc., 1973. 458 pp.

TEXAS COLLEGE. A **Christian Methodist Episcopal Church** (CME) school. As early as 1884 CME Church members began to raise the issue of a CME school in Texas. Plans were laid over the next six years, and in 1894 Texas College opened in Tyler under the presidency of O. T. Womack. That same year the CME General Conference recognized it as a denominational institution. It had the support of the East Texas, Northwest Texas, and Texas Annual Conferences. It was initially an elementary and normal school, and in 1905, under the leadership of its new president, S. W. Broome, a college curriculum was added.

In 1902 Bishop **Charles H. Phillips** began his long tenure as CME bishop in the Western states. In 1908 the several Texas annual conferences voted to change the name of the school to Phillips University. However, two years later **Monroe F. Jamison** succeeded Phillips as bishop in Texas and Louisiana. No friend of Phillips, he strongly encouraged the change of the name back to Texas College. In spite of the controversy, the school prospered and became a stable educational facility in the early twentieth century.

During the 1930s Texas College absorbed Arkansas-Haygood Industrial College. That school had been founded in Washington, Arkansas in 1883, and over the next generation it grew and prospered. In 1910 a second school was started at Pine Bluff, Arkansas. Attempts to merge the two schools were blocked until 1915, when the buildings at Washington were destroyed in a fire. In 1916 the two schools finally merged as Arkansas-Haygood Industrial College. The new school prospered in the 1920s due to the support of Bishop **J. A. Hamlett**, but ran into the problems of the Depression and of a policy adopted by the Church leadership to support a single strong college west of the Mississippi. Thus the school merged into Texas College.

Lakey, Othel H. *The History of the C.M.E. Church*. Memphis, TN: C.M.E. Publishing House, 1985. 683 pp.

THARPE, ROSETTA NUBIN (March 20, 1921–October 9, 1973), a popular gospel singer, was born in Cotton Plant, Arkansas, the daughter of Katie Bell Nubin, an evangelist in a Holiness church. Tharpe traveled with her mother as a child, and as early as the age of six was working as a professional with evangelist P. W. McGhee. She learned to play the guitar to accompany her singing. She was still in her teens in 1938 when she became widely known because of her appearance at the famous Cotton Club in a show with Cab Calloway. That appearance led to a contract with Decca records and she became the first gospel singer to record with a major label. Her recording of Thomas A. Dorsey's "Hide Me in Thy Bosom," which came out under the more secular title "Rock Me," appeared later that year.

During the next decades Tharpe deviated from the common schedule of her contemporaries by not limiting her appearances to religious settings. She frequently sang on radio and television, in concert halls, and at theaters and even nightclubs. In 1943 she became the first gospel singer to perform at the Apollo Theater in Harlem. She toured with several of the more popular gospel music groups such as the Caravans, the James Cleveland Singers and the Dixie Hummingbirds. But she also associated with secular stars such as Muddy Waters, Lucky Millinder, and Sammy Blythe.

Following World War II, Tharpe emerged as the most popular gospel singer in the African American community. She was the first soloist to tour widely and she freely moved between church and stage. In 1946 she teamed up with Marie Knight as a Holiness gospel singer. Their first recording "Up Above My Head," was an immediate hit. They stayed together for the next few years. Later she utilized choirs and in 1960 teamed with the Sally Jenkins Singers of the **Church of God in Christ** to record "I Have Good News to Bring." Among Tharpe's most popular recordings were "Didn't It Rain," "End of My Journey," "This Train," and "I Looked Down the Line."

DuPree, Sherry Sherrod. *Biographical Dictionary of African-American Holiness-Pentecostals, 1880–1990*. Washington, DC: Middle Atlantic Regional Press, 1989. 386 pp.

Southern, Eileen. *Biographical Dictionary of Afro-American and African Musicians*. Westport, CT: Greenwood Press, 1982. 445 pp.

THEOLOGY, BLACK. Theology is essentially the Christian church's response to the autobiographical impulse. It grows out of the need to proclaim with authority and commitment the identity and mission of the church in the world. That is, in theology, the church both asks and answers the questions, "Who are we, and where are we going?" Theologians as theologians do not tell other Christians what they should believe; rather, their task is to help the community understand more clearly what they do believe, and to assess those beliefs in light of the major sources of Christian revelation.

Black theology differs from traditional theology in much the same way that African American Christianity differs from the Christianity of Europe and the North Atlantic. Since the first Africans set foot on this soil, people of African descent have had a singularly unique experience in the New World. They brought with them an inherent philosophical heritage, including a distinctive religious sensibility; they encountered the most brutal form of slavery in human history; and they were introduced to North Atlantic Christianity. Because there was no precedent for the experience of people of African descent, they created distinctive ways of conceptualizing and speaking about their ultimate concerns. Black theology is a continuation of that discursive tradition.

African American theological development can be best understood as the convergence of an African-derived world view with the complexities of the experience of slavery, oppression, survival, rebellion, and adjustment in the New World, and their encounter with the Biblical text. These realities shaped the African American intellect and spirit. Black theology reflects the passion, feeling, and expressiveness of African American Christianity. On the other hand, theological reflection is not synonymous with the sermon, the litany, or the testimony, although they all participate in the same ethos of religious expression. Black theology is also a formal, self-conscious, systematic attempt to interpret the faith of the church. The form need not always be linear, nor the system based on Western philosophy. Black theologians may employ explanatory and formal devices such as story or Biblical commentary. Black theology is passionate and incisive, reflecting what Paul Tillich called "ecstatic reason." The definitive factor, however, is that the resulting theology coherently interprets the experience of Black people and the gospel.

The need for theological acumen within the contemporary African American church grows directly out of both the attacks on the integrity of Black religion which must be resisted, and the continual evolution of religious life in America whose often surprising turns require a constant "testing of the waters" by Black theologians. Further, in a world where Black people, people of color, and poor people are continually frustrated in their attempt "to have life, and have it more abundantly," Black theologians speak to those systems, persons, and conditions which impede the worship and adoration of the God of the gospel, and the living of a just life.

Primary Agendas. In light of these factors, the first task of Black theology has become the *clarifying of the contexts—historical, socio-political, cultural, and intellectual—in which African American Christian faith is affirmed.* The historical context of the faith of Black Christians includes a shared legacy of slavery, the struggle to adapt to legal manumission, and the ongoing battle to be recognized as full human beings. The development of slave religion and its relation to the early freedom struggle among people of African descent is the historical source of contemporary Black Christian faith. African slaves who embraced Christianity also modified and shaped it to meet their existential needs and saw, even in the contorted presentations of the gospel by some White people, a continuity between what they knew of God in Africa and the God of the Bible. **Gayraud Wilmore** describes the essential relationship between faith and freedom in the development of Black religion.

> An exceedingly elastic but tenacious thread binds together the contributive and developmental factors of Black religion in the United States as one distinctive social phenomenon. It is the thread of what may be called, if properly defined, "Black radicalism." Black religion has always concerned itself with the fascination of an incorrigibly religious people with the mystery of God, but it has been equally concerned with the yearning of a despised and subjugated people for freedom—freedom from the religious, economic, social, and political domination that Whites have exercised over Blacks since the beginning of the African slave trade.

This thread can be traced through the public annals of professional historians, but is also present in the autobiographies, personal narratives, and journals of African American women and men who felt compelled to give testimony to the work of God in their lives.

The socio-political context for the reradicalization of African American Christianity in the twentieth century is the civil rights/Black Power movement. Scholars differ on which aspect of the substantively crucial period in American history is most directly responsible for the religious and theological revival in the Black community. Warner R. Traynham argues that the civil rights movement and its most visible leader, **Martin Luther King, Jr.**, were most responsible for the religious and theological re-awakening. Both **James H. Cone** and **J. Deotis Roberts** suggest that the radical critique of American racism inherent in the Black power movement is the source of contemporary Black theology and prophetic Black Christianity. Gayraud Wilmore argues that radical Black Christianity and Black theology in the twentieth century emerged after many of the leaders of the civil rights movement had been co-opted by the White power structure, and before the full measure of Black power had been seized. It seems clear that while there are differences in interpretation, the civil rights movement and the Black Power movement are part of a continuous tradition of protest and struggle in African American religious life. The civil rights movement was based on the notion that the equality of Black people was a function of their legal status in American society. Equality had been denied by the Fugitive Slave Law of 1850, the Dred Scott decision (1857) and the *Plessy* vs. *Ferguson* decision (1896) of the Supreme Court. These legal conscriptions were subsequently reversed or eliminated by the Brown vs. Board of Education of Topeka Supreme Court decision of 1954, and the Voting Rights laws passed in the 1960s. These advances were engineered by people and groups directly or indirectly related to the African American church. They were visible evidence of the reawakening of the Black church militant which had slumbered for decades. However, not since the end of slavery had the attitudinal and psychological dimensions of racism come to the forefront of discussion.

The Black power movement was, in part, the result of the failures and limitations of the early civil rights movement; especially its dependence on enfranchisement as a tool for liberation. Black power advocates asserted that control of the institutions that regulated *intellectual commerce* and *social values*, not legal prescriptions, were the most effective means for achieving the liberation of Black people. Racism was seen as an attitudinal, psychological, and structural aspect of American life. Therefore, it could not be eliminated simply through legislation because people tend to structure their behavior according to deep-seated values and not in strict accordance to extraneous norms. Thus, civil rights laws were widely ignored. The psychological, attitudinal, and structural aspects of racism also meant that racism was supported by the pseudo-Christian values prevalent in American society. The most profound contribution of the Black power movement to the development of Black theology was its challenge to Black people to show how they could be Black and Christian at the same time. This challenge was multidimensional. Black Muslims called Christianity a "White man's religion" which had nothing to do with the spiritual heritage of African Americans. Black secular Marxists argued that Christianity was an unscientific, irrelevant, and counter-revolutionary illusion which only hindered the liberation of Black people. Pan-Africanists eschewed Christianity to the extent that it obscured the reality that Black people were part of the African Diaspora. Black nationalists rejected Christianity on the grounds that it prevented Black people from seeing the necessity of separating themselves from White culture as a prerequisite for their liberation.

Black theology was, in part, a response to these objections. Black theologians were not willing to concede Christianity to its White abusers, and based their legitimacy on the fact that African American Christianity was the result of the encounter of Black people with the liberating essence of the gospel. Black theologians viewed the history of Black resistance to White oppression, and the fact that the leaders of that resistance were more often than not Black Christians, as evidence that the Black liberation struggle was rooted in Black religion. Black theologians stressed that the connection with Africa was more clearly evident in Black religious life than anywhere else. Further, they pointed to the identification of Black Christians with the biblical people of Israel as an example of an appropriate nationalist sentiment in the religious setting.

In addition to the historical and socio-political contexts, the cultural and intellectual contexts in which African American faith is affirmed are part of the focus of this first task of theology. Black religion was shaped in the midst of a profound cultural conflict between the inherited cosmology, value systems, and philosophical constructs which African slaves brought with them to the New World, and the protean culture of the colonies which was struggling to define itself over against the dominant European paradigm and in light of the ironic position of the colonies as an imperialist presence. (The colonists presumably came to the New World to escape

tyranny, but found themselves in the position of tyrants in relation to Amerindians and Africans.) The cultural matrix of the African tended to affirm the infinite worth of the African as a human being in relation to other human beings and under the auspices of a benevolent creator God. The community (the no longer living, the living, and the yet to be born) was affirmed as the basic social unit, and as the social framework in which the individual was defined. All creation, including nature, was seen as infused with the spiritual presence of God. The formative culture of the colonies demeaned the African as a human being by associating Blackness, and thus Black people, with evil; by denying the existence of an indigenous African culture and civilization; and by rejecting the notion that Africans had any idea of a Supreme Being, thereby condemning them to the state of God-forsakenness, and justifying their continued enslavement and exploitation. The culture of the colonies devalued community and idolized the individual, making the protection of private property and individual rights the basis for social and political organization. Further, nature and those living beings thought to be most closely related to it became, in the minds of the colonists, the "wilderness" and the "savages," both of which were to be tamed, subdued and domesticated. This cultural conflict has not been resolved in contemporary American life. As African Americans struggle with the pull of a secular, materialistic, hedonistic, narcissistic, and pessimistic culture, they also experience, to varying degrees, the magnetic hold of a spiritual, integrated, communal, and hopeful counterculture. African American Christian faith is in part a response to this cultural conflict, attempting to navigate, with varying degrees of success, a course between the old and the new, the familiar and the strange.

The intellectual context of Black faith is a similar struggle on the ideational and practical level. In the eighteenth century Gustavus Vassa, **Phillis Wheatley**, and Jupiter Hammon attempted to reconcile the African intellectual tradition with their crisis-ridden status as slaves in the New World. In the nineteenth century, **Henry Highland Garnet**, T. Thomas Fortune, **Martin R. Delaney**, and Maria Stewart attempted to resolve the problematic presence of African Americans and their relationship to Africa to the emerging national identity of the United States. In the first two-thirds of the twentieth century **Booker T. Washington**, W. E. B. DuBois, **Marcus Garvey**, **Mary McLeod Bethune**, **Martin Luther King, Jr.**, and **Malcolm X** attempted to relate the plight of African Americans to that of the insurgent liberation movements in Africa and the so-called Third World. The ideas generated in these historical moments owe much of their power and pertinence to the influence of African American Christianity. These attempts to orient people of African descent in an alien environment were shaped by the fundamental encounter with a sternly held faith and the fierce desire for freedom. Moreover, Black theology is the ideological progeny of these moments, and the work of Black theologians includes the serious encounter with these intellectual contexts and sources.

The Second Task. Black theology also has the task of *articulating, interpreting, and assessing the essential doctrinal affirmations of African American faith for the contemporary African American community of faith.* In spite of the unique history of the evolution of African American faith, this faith cannot be reduced to its contexts. That is, neither sociological reductionism, cultural reductionism nor ideological reductionism reach the spiritual essence of Black faith. Empathic intimacy with the heart of African American faith requires that we move beyond the *contexts* to the *content* of that faith.

Briefly stated, the content of African American faith is the story of God's dealings with God's people and the world. There are, in fact, two stories involved here. On one hand the Bible presents what I call "canonical stories." The canonical story is what we construe to be the message of the Bible and tradition. For African Americans that story has always been, in some paradigmatic form, the story of the liberation of the Hebrew slaves and Jesus' liberating mission in his time. The elements in that story are linked together by the providential will of God. That is, it is clear that God has been in control of events from the beginning and stands as the guarantor that, in the end, "everything will be alright." It is this guarantee which is the basis of faith. Yet, there is a danger of distortion here. It is also possible that this story can become a safe haven for those Christians who yearn for a return to the pristine past, or to create a religious subculture in which they might escape the demands of postmodern life.

On the other hand, African Americans bring their own stories to bear on the Bible and tradition. They bring what I call "folk stories." Because we are historical creatures, we suffer under the tragic limitations of human finitude, and folk stories are our way of expressing the fears, frustrations, struggles and the determination for freedom from existential anxiety, political oppression, and cultural exploitation which constitutes our experience. We live uncertain of whether our hopes will be vindicated, or whether the struggle for freedom will end; therefore we can only infer that given the faithfulness of God, one day "the wicked shall cease from troubling, and the weary shall be at rest." That is,

African American existence may be characterized by a rugged determination for freedom and not by any certainty that this freedom will be realized. There is a danger of distortion connected with this story as well. This existence may also portray a kind of pathos and despair in which anomie and disorientation in a mass-culture, secular society has all but extinguished the fires of will and determination. Black theology attempts to relate the "canonical" story, in its prophetic mode, with the "folk" story of a people who hope against hope. To accomplish this goal the Black theologian limits his/her immersion in the assurance, optimism, or myopia of the canonical story (the proclamation of the churches) so that s/he can see the challenge of the folk story. Conversely, the Black theologian resists enchantment with the pathos of the "folk" story, and/or the disillusionment with the tragic dimensions of African American experience, so that the hope expressed in the canonical story is not missed. That is to say, Black theologians tell a story which relates the hope of the biblical message to the realism of Black experience. Through the arrangement and explication of the basic Christian doctrines, from creation to consummation, Black theologians attempt to fashion a story that brings together the twin commitment of African American Christians to faith and freedom.

The Third Task. Finally, Black theology has the task of *examining the moral implications of that faith for Christian witness in the world.* African American Christian faith is shaped by a variety of *contexts*, has a distinctive and identifiable *content*, and matures through the fulfillment of its *intent*. The intent, goal, or telos of African American Christian faith is the moral ordering of personal and collective human existence through Christian witness in the world. Christian witness is here understood to involve three moral moments. First, Christians engage in moral discernment. They read the signs of the times, to look into the hearts of people, institutions, and social systems, to find the sources of impediments to justice and truth. Such discernment requires the employment of those modes of analytical discourse which can make plain the origins of human misery, especially a socio-economic and cultural analysis of our world and its inner workings. Human suffering in our time cannot be fully explained by looking at the cruelty which one individual inflicts upon another, but also as the result of conflicting economic interests and conflicting social values.

Second, moral discernment is guided by moral norms, a set of criteria by which one can determine whether or not the present social order is just. These norms are drawn from the content of African American

Christian faith, rather than any extraneous/ philosophical norms of good, evil, right or wrong. Therefore, any notion of justice, for example, as central to ethical behavior should also be one central to the theological affirmations of African American faith. In this manner, one begins to be able to act and empowered to live in a way that is consistent with one's beliefs.

Third, the moral norm eventually offers judgment on society, and the participation of African American Christians in that society, in such a way that one is forced to decide and moved to action. The theological task is not limited to the analysis of society and the announcement that injustice exists. Christian witness includes deciding for the victims and acting in solidarity with them. Christians act morally, but moral acts are grounded in a basic lifestyle and mind-set which itself is moral. Christians exist as moral people, but moral existence is buttressed by moral acts.

Black theologians contribute in a substantive and comprehensive way to authentic Christian witness. As "organic intellectuals" (Antonio Gramsci) their work involves social analysis, normative claims regarding the demands of the faith in the postmodern world, and actual engagement in communities of resistance. In this way, theology as a vocation becomes a form of authentic Christian witness.

A Future for Black Theology. The external and internal forces which shaped and continue to influence Black religious expression have brought faith and freedom into sharp relief. Doctrinal affirmations form the story or gestalt of Black Christianity around the twin elliptical centers of faith and freedom, the dialectic of which recasts and reinterprets the major sources of Christian revelation. The moral implications of this faith now guide and direct African American Christian witness in the world in a way that manifests the twin commitments of faithfulness to God and the struggle for freedom.

In general, the *contexts* of African American Christian faith are always in the background, and the *moral implications* of that faith always in the foreground, but the concern here is specifically the content of African American faith and its theological significance. Given the pressing nature of the faith/ freedom relationship, Black theology as introspection and as proclamation is a primary agenda item for the African American church. Faith seeks understanding; however, the point is not simply to understand the basis on which faith is affirmed, but to understand it in a way that makes the faithful a redeeming and transforming presence in the world. Faith seeks critical understanding. In like manner, freedom seeks expression; but the freedom is discernible in visible acts and modes of being

in the world. Christian freedom, is never simply a spiritual reality, or only a spiritual possession, but is realized in and among those who, even in our midst, struggle for liberation. Freedom seeks public expression.

Cone, James H. *Black Theology and Black Power.* New York: Seabury Press, 1969. 165 pp.
Roberts, J. Deotis. *Liberation and Reconciliation: A Black Theology.* Philadelphia, PA: Westminster Press, 1971.
Wilmore, Gayraud S. "Black Theology: Its Significance for Christian Missions Today." *International Review of Mission* 63 (April 1974): 211–31.

James H. Evans, Jr.

THOMAS, CORNELIUS EGBERTAN (b. May 4, 1923), 99th bishop of the **African Methodist Episcopal Church** (AME), was born in Marion, Alabama, the son of James A. and Serena A. Thomas. He was ordained deacon in 1942 and elder in 1944. He earned his B.A. in 1946 from Daniel Payne College in Birmingham, Alabama and his B.D. in 1949 from Gammon Theological Seminary in Atlanta, Georgia. He married Susie Jamar Thomas, with whom he had two children.

His pastorates have included St. Mark AME Church in Dora, Alabama (1943–49); Bethel AME Church in Ersely, Alabama (1949–52); and St. John's AME Church in Birmingham, Alabama (1952–76). At St. John's he paid off the mortgage, organized a credit union, established a scholarship fund, and purchased a new church and facilities. He was elected bishop in 1976 and assigned to the Seventeenth Episcopal District (in Africa), later moving to the Thirteenth Episcopal District. In Africa he redeemed a 50–acre farm in Zambia, established a building fund for future churches, and founded the Membe School of Religion on Wheels to train clergy at area centers. He accepted for the church the Sizane Secondary School, with eleven buildings and 800 students, from the National Christian Council of Women in Zimbabwe. Altogether, Thomas has built about twenty churches and schools. About 1990 he was assigned to the Ninth Episcopal District, with headquarters in Birmingham, Alabama, and in 1992 to the Eighth District (Mississippi, Louisiana).

FEDHR, BDNM (70).

THOMAS, FREEMAN N., a bishop of the **Pentecostal Assemblies of the World**, was born early in this century in Pelham, Georgia. After World War I he moved to Pennsylvania. He married and he and his wife Eunice had eight children. While residing in Pittsburgh, he encountered Assemblies minister P. W. Washington under whom he experienced salvation in 1925. Seven years later he had a call to the ministry. He later became the pastor of Bethlehem Temple in Pittsburgh, which he pastored for the rest of his life. He became the district elder and a member of the Home Missions Board created in 1948.

Thomas was elected to the bishopric in 1949 and in 1951 was assigned as bishop of District No. 2, Pennsylvania.

Golder, Morris E. *The Bishops of the Pentecostal Assemblies of the World*. Indianapolis, IN: The Author, 1980. 69 pp.

———. *History of the Pentecostal Assemblies of the World*. Indianapolis, IN: The Author, 1973. 195 pp.

THOMAS, JAMES SAMUEL (b. April 8, 1919), a bishop of the **United Methodist Church**, was born in Orangeburg, South Carolina, the son of James Samuel, Sr., and Dessie (Merks) Thomas. His father was a Methodist minister and among the few Blacks to have a college degree before 1900. His parents died before he was two years old and he was reared by foster parents, his mother's sister and her husband, also a Methodist minister. In 1923 he began school at Claflin College in Orangeburg, and stayed through fourth grade. Then the family moved 60 miles away to Sumter, South Carolina, but he later returned to Claflin, where he received his B.A. in 1939, and then spent one year as principal of a rural elementary school in Florence County, South Carolina. He was ordained deacon in 1942 and elder in 1944. He received his B.D. in 1943 from Gammon Theological Seminary, and his M.A. in 1944 from Drew University in Madison, New Jersey. On July 7, 1945, he married Ruth Naomi Wilson, with whom he had four daughters.

His first pastorate was on the Orangeburg Circuit (1942–43), after which he was chaplain at South Carolina State College from 1944 to 1946. From 1946 to 1948 he pastored in York, South Carolina, then from 1948 to 1953 was professor of Rural Church and Director of Field Work at Gammon Theological Seminary in Atlanta, Georgia. For a brief period he was acting president of Gammon. While at Gammon he also worked on his Ph.D., which he received in 1953 from Cornell University in Ithaca, New York. From 1953 to 1964 he was associate general secretary of the denomination's General Board of Education in charge of the church's thirteen Black colleges. He directed the program by which eleven of those colleges were accredited when the Southern Association of Schools and Colleges desegregated. It was from this position that the Central Jurisdiction elected him bishop in June 1964, after a record-breaking seventeen ballots. Thomas, at age forty-five, was one of the youngest bishops ever elected in the denomination.

Prior to 1964 all the African American bishops in the Methodist Church served only among the nineteen all-Black conferences, represented collectively from 1939 to 1968 by the Central Jurisdiction. On June 25, 1964, **Prince Albert Taylor** became the first Black bishop of the denomination to be appointed outside that structure, to a predominantly White constituency (New Jersey). Thomas was the second such bishop, assigned on July 10, 1964, to head the Iowa (or Des Moines) Episcopal Area. These two appointments were heralded as the beginning of a new era of integration in the Methodist Church, and helped pave the way for the dismantling of the Central Jurisdiction when the Methodist Church merged with the Evangelical United Brethren in 1968 to create the United Methodist Church. Both bishops were reportedly received with an overwhelmingly positive reaction.

Thomas remained in Iowa for twelve years, then moved to the Ohio East Episcopal Area in 1976, where he remained until retirement. He has served as president of the General Council on Ministries and as president of the General Council on Finance and Administration. He has also been vice-chair of the Methodist Commission on Christian Vocations. From April 1984 through March 1985 he was president of the Council of Bishops. He has been a trustee of numerous institutions, including Huston-Tillotson College, Simpson College, Claflin College, Clark College, Rust College, Wiley College, Paine College, Morningside College, and Gammon Theological Seminary. He retired in 1988 and has since served on the staff of Perkins School of Theology at Southern Methodist University in Dallas, Texas. In 1992 he published a long-awaited book, *Methodism's Racial Dilemma: The Story of the Central Jurisdiction*.

Bennett, Lerone, Jr. "Black Firsts in Politics, Entertainment, Sports, and Other Fields." *Ebony* 37 (March 1982): 128–133.

"Move Toward Church Unity." *Ebony* 20 (February 1965): 54–60.

"Ten Religious Groups with Biggest Black Membership." *Ebony* 39 (March 1984): 140–144.

Thomas, James Samuel. *Methodism's Racial Dilemma: The Story of the Central Jurisdiction*. Nashville, TN: Abingdon Press, 1992. 183pp.

———. "The Rationale Underlying Support of Negro Private

Colleges by the Methodist Church." *Journal of Negro Education* 29 (Summer 1960): 252–259.

————. *A Study of the Social Role of the Negro Rural Pastor in Four Selected Southern Areas.* Ithaca, NY: Doctoral Dissertation, Cornell University, 1952.

WWABA (92–93), BDUMB, EWM, BDNM (75), WWR (85), WWMC, AARS, HUBA, WWA (88–89), OTSB, NA, IBAW, MSB.

THOMAS, ROBERT, JR., a bishop of the **African Methodist Episcopal Church** (AME), was elected bishop about 1988 and has served since that time in the Fifteenth Episcopal District (South Africa).

YB (1988–92).

THOMPSON, HERBERT, JR. (b. 1933), a bishop of the **Episcopal Church**, was born in New York City and served in the United States Air Force. He graduated from Lincoln University in Pennsylvania in 1962 and from General Theological Seminary in New York City in 1965. During his student years he was a chaplain to migrant workers in Chester County, Pennsylvania. He was ordained both as deacon and priest in 1965, and for six years served St. Gabriel's Episcopal Church in Brooklyn, New York. For three of those years he was also executive director of Interfaith Services of Brooklyn, administering programs for 120 churches, agencies, and synagogues. In 1968 he married Russelle Cross, with whom he has had three children.

From 1971 to 1977 Thompson was rector of Christ Episcopal Church in Bellport, New York, a largely White parish. From 1977 to 1988 he was rector of historic Grace Episcopal Church in Jamaica, Long Island. In this very active parish he oversaw ministries that included a shelter for homeless men, tutorial programs, and various other services for needy families and individuals. In 1987 the church received $4.5 million from H.U.D. to build housing for elderly and handicapped persons. Thompson served as president of the diocesan Standing Committee, and has been a member of the Presiding Bishop's Commission on Black Ministries and the Coalition for Human Needs. For a time he was instructor at the Mercer School of Theology, and was active in the Queens Y.M.C.A. and the Jamaica Development Board. He was chaplain to the 69th General Convention that met in Detroit in 1988. On September 24, 1988, he was consecrated bishop coadjutor of the Diocese of Southern Ohio.

ECA (1990).

THOMPSON, JOSEPH PASCAL (December 20, 1818–December 21, 1894), 18th bishop of the **African Methodist Episcopal Zion Church** (AMEZ), was born into slavery in Winchester, Virginia. He ran away from his master as a youth and found a home with a gracious man in Pennsylvania, where he was nurtured religiously and educationally. At age fifteen he experienced conversion and at age twenty, in 1839, was licensed to preach.

Both medicine and the ministry attracted him as professions. He studied privately with a physician in Middletown Point (now Matawan), New Jersey, and also studied privately under Rev. Dr. Mills of Auburn Theological Seminary in Auburn, New York. He eventually combined the two callings. He joined the New York Conference of the AMEZ Church in May, 1844, was ordained deacon on May 17, 1846, and elder on May 2, 1847. He pastored a number of charges in that conference and in 1853 was sent as a missionary to Nova Scotia.

In Nova Scotia Thompson found great need and acceptance not only of his preaching but of his medical skill as well, and he resolved to make his medical knowledge more complete. He returned to the United States and enrolled at the University of Medicine in Philadelphia, where he graduated with his M.D. degree on April 1, 1858. After this time he fully combined ministry with medical practice. He served most of the charges available along the Hudson River and was three times pastor of Mother Zion Church in New York City. He centered his medical practice in Newburgh, New York, where he was one of its most prominent citizens. He married Catherine Gilchrist, the daughter of a conductor on the Underground Railroad, with whom he had one daughter. Thompson himself became one of the main leaders of the Underground Railroad, a link between his father-in-law in Williamsport, Pennsylvania and Jermain Wesley Loguen in Syracuse, New York. Thompson also was one of the prime organizers of the African Civilization Society, which sought the destruction of the slave trade and the Christianization of Africa.

Thompson was consecrated bishop on July 4, 1876, and became one of the most popular and honored ministers of his time. Officials in Washington, D.C. often conferred with him on public measures, particularly regarding the South, where he conducted most of his supervision. In 1878 he organized an Annual Conference in the Bahamas. In 1881 he was a delegate to the World Methodist Conference in London, England, and read a paper there.

HAMEZCIA, AMEZC, OHYAMEZC, HAMEZC.

THURMAN, HOWARD (November 18, 1900–April 10, 1981), theologian and founding co-pastor of the Church for the Fellowship of All Peoples in San Francisco, was born in Daytona, Florida, the son of Saul Solomon Thurman and Alice (Ambrose) Thurman. His father, a railroad worker, died when Thurman was still a young boy, and his mother then hired out as a cook. Until she remarried some years later, the daily rearing of the children was done by Thurman's grandmother. He grew up attending Mount Bethel Baptist Church. He attended high school at Florida Baptist Academy in Jacksonville (which later moved to St. Augustine and was renamed Florida Normal College), and worked at various jobs to help pay his way.

In 1919 he was licensed to preach, and entered Morehouse College, the Baptist-related Black college in Atlanta, Georgia. As valedictorian of Florida Baptist Academy, he received a tuition scholarship in the college. He graduated (again as class valedictorian) in 1923, with a B.A. in economics. He then entered Colgate-Rochester Divinity School in Rochester, New York. He was ordained a Baptist minister in 1925, and received his B.D. in June 1926. He married Kate Kelley one week later, on June 11, 1926, and accepted a position as pastor of Mount Zion Baptist Church in Oberlin, Ohio. He became aware of Rufus Jones, a Quaker theologian at Haverford College in Pennsylvania, and arranged to study with him. He resigned from the pastorate and arrived at Haverford in January 1929. In the fall of that year he left Haverford and became professor of religion and director of religious life at Morehouse College and its related school for women, Spelman College. In December 1930, his wife died, and the next summer he found renewal in a trip to Europe. He then returned for one more year at Morehouse.

In 1932 Thurman accepted the position of professor of systematic theology and later also as the first dean of the Andrew Rankin Chapel at Howard University in Washington, D.C., where he stayed for twelve years. On June 12, 1932, he married Sue E. Bailey, a writer and social historian. In 1935, as chair of the Delegation of Friendship on behalf of the World Student Christian Federation, he toured India, Burma, and Ceylon, and met Mahatma Gandhi. A conversation in which Gandhi was critical of Christianity's treatment of the dispossessed led Thurman to dedicate the rest of his career to making Christianity a living power for all people, especially the weak and disinherited. In 1944 he left Howard University and helped begin, with Albert Fisk, the Church for the Fellowship of All Peoples in San Francisco. For the next nine years he co-pastored this multi-ethnic, multi-cultural, ecumenical church, the first of its kind in the country. A number of his books date from this period, including *The Negro Spiritual Speaks of Life and Death* (1947), *Meditations for Apostles of Sensitiveness* (1948), *Jesus and the Disinherited* (1949), and *Meditations of the Heart* (1953).

In 1953 Thurman accepted the position of dean of Daniel L. Marsh Chapel and professor of spiritual resources and disciplines at Boston University, the first Black full-time professor ever hired at that institution. That same year *Life* magazine named him one of the twelve best American preachers of the twentieth century. In 1954 *Ebony* magazine named him one of the top ten Black preachers in the country. He had many honors and awards bestowed upon him throughout his career, including sixteen honorary doctorates. His service went far beyond his teaching and writing, such as being chair of the Student Christian Movements of India, on the board of directors of Meals for Millions, and a life member of the National Association for the Advancement of Colored People (N.A.A.C.P.), which gave him its Roy Wilkins Award in 1979. Even after his retirement in 1965, he continued to lecture and publish books, including *The Centering Moment* (1969), *The Search for Common Ground* (1971), and his autobiography, *With Head and Heart* (1980), which came out one year before his death.

"Great Negro Preachers." *Ebony* 9, 10 (July 1954): 26–30.

Thurman, Howard. *Deep River: An Interpretation of Negro Spirituals.* Revised ed. New York: Harper, 1955. 93 pp.

———. *Jesus and the Disinherited.* New York: Abingdon-Cokesbury Press, 1949. 112 pp.

———. *The Luminous Darkness.* New York: Harper & Row, 1965. 113 pp.

———. *The Search for Common Ground.* New York: Harper & Row, 1971. 108 pp.

———. *With Head and Heart.* New York: Harcourt, Brace, Jovanovich, 1980. 274 pp.

Yates, Elizabeth. *Howard Thurman: Portrait of a Practical Dreamer.* New York: John Day Co., 1964. 249 pp.

RLOA, CA (97–100), *ONL, ERS, LBAA, GNPP, NYTBS* (81), *HNB, BLW, BDNM* (75), *IBAW, BAW, MBRL, BLW.*

TINDLEY, CHARLES ALBERT (July 7, 1851–July 26, 1933), a minister of the Methodist Episcopal (ME) Church (now a constituent part of the **United Methodist Church**), was the son of Ester and Charles Tindley, two slaves who resided on the farm of Joseph Briddell near Berlin, Maryland. Unable to go to school, Tindley taught himself to read. After the Civil War, he married Daisy Henry and moved to Philadelphia. He obtained work as a hod carrier and later as sexton of

John Wesley Methodist Episcopal Church. Through the years he continued his education in night school, by correspondence courses and with the assistance of some acquaintances in Philadelphia. Over the years he decided to enter the ministry and in 1885 applied for admission to the Delaware Conference of the ME Church, an all-Black conference serving Maryland, New Jersey and Pennsylvania.

In spite of his lack of formal education, Tindley was admitted on probation and assigned as pastor to the church in Cape May, New Jersey. Two years later he was ordained as a deacon and sent to South Wilmington, Delaware. After a year as a special missionary among Black people in New Jersey (1888-89), he was ordained as an elder at the 1889 conference session. Over the next decade he served a succession of pastoral charges, culminating in his appointment as presiding elder of the Wilmington District in 1900. In 1901 he published the first collection of the many hymns he authored during his ministry. Some of these hymns became very popular among the different Black churches and a few, such as "Stand By Me" and "We'll Understand It Better By and By" found a larger audience within White churches.

In 1902 Tindley was appointed to Bainbridge Street MEC in Philadelphia. This was the old John Wesley Church now in a new sanctuary, and thus Tindley had now become the pastor of the church he once cleaned. He would remain at the church for the rest of his life. In 1906, under his leadership the congregation moved to Broad Street and was renamed East Calvary ME Church. Within a short time Tindley became one of the more powerful leaders in the Philadelphia Black community, and his church was a center of culture. The church's membership topped 5,000.

In 1908 Tindley was elected as a delegate to the Methodist general conference, an honor bestowed upon him every quadrennium for the rest of his life. In 1916 and 1920 he was nominated for bishop, an honor possibly denied him because of his lack of formal education. Even though not elected, he remained the dominant influence in the Delaware Conference. Following the 1920 general conference, he moved ahead with plans to build a cathedral-like church and with the help of philanthropist John Wannamaker secured the financing. The new 3,500-seat church was opened in 1925, the celebration of its completion being marred for Tindley by the sudden death of his wife. Eventually the church would be renamed Tindley Temple.

Tindley's last years were marked by his leadership of the largest Black congregation in the city and his popularity as a speaker before both Black and White audiences. He married Jenny Colton in 1927. While enjoying great prestige, he was never able to pull the church out of the debt incurred in the construction of the new building just before the great Depression. He died in Philadelphia.

Jones, Ralph H. *Charles Albert Tindley: Prince of Preachers.* Nashville, TN: Abingdon, 1982. 192 pp.

TOBIAS, CHANNING HEGGIE (February 1, 1882–November 5, 1961), national Young Men's Christian Association (Y.M.C.A.) leader and chair of the board of the National Association for the Advancement of Colored People (N.A.A.C.P.), was born in Augusta, Georgia, the son of Fair J. and Clara Belle (Robinson) Tobias. His father was a coachman and his mother, who passed away when he was twelve years old, worked as a household servant. He received his early education at Haines Normal and Industrial Institute in Augusta, founded by **Lucy C. Laney**. Relationships between the races in Augusta were generally amiable, and he grew up without racial bitterness. He did, however, possess a persistent drive to create a more democratic and egalitarian society. He received his B.A. in 1902 from Paine College in Augusta, and his B.D. in 1905 from Drew University in Madison, New Jersey. He was ordained by the **Christian Methodist Episcopal Church**.

Upon graduation he was offered a teaching post at Paine College, and was there from 1905 to 1911. On November 10, 1908, he married Mary Pritchard, with whom he had two children. In 1911 he was recruited by **William Hunton** to become secretary of the Student Department of the National Council of the Y.M.C.A., with headquarters in Washington, D.C. In September, 1921 he attended the Paris session of the Second Pan-African Congress. Also that year he was part of a Y.M.C.A. student deputation that studied the relief services of the Y.M.C.A. in most of the European countries. From 1923 to 1946 he was senior secretary of the Colored Men's Department of the National Council (founded by William Hunton), with headquarters in New York City.

During these years Tobias gained an international prominence. He served on the Inter-Racial Commission of the Federal (now National) Council of Churches. In 1926 he was a delegate and speaker at the World Conference of the Y.M.C.A.s at Helsingfors, Finland, and he visited numerous Y.M.C.A. centers across Europe. In 1931 he joined the board of trustees for Howard University in Washington, D.C., and remained with the board until 1953. In 1936–37 he was part of the U.S. delegation to the World Conference of the Y.M.C.A.s in Mysore, India, and did further traveling in the Near and Far East. He met Mahatma Gandhi and had a long discussion with him about strategies for helping oppressed minorities. During World War II he was a member of the National Advisory Committee on Selective Service and the Joint Army and Navy Committee on Welfare and Recreation. In 1943 he joined the board of trustees of the N.A.A.C.P. In 1946 and 1947 he was on President Truman's Committee on Civil Rights. He was a strong opponent of segregation and discrimination, and noted that "America and South Africa are practically the only countries in the world where racial exclusion is practiced in the Y.M.C.A.s." In 1946 he had to leave the Y.M.C.A. after exceeding its 60–year retirement age by three years, but remained on the 15–person International Committee.

From 1946 to 1953 Tobias was the first Black director of the Phelps-Stokes Fund in New York City, a foundation dedicated to improve the educational opportunities for African Americans. His first wife died in 1949 and on March 31, 1951, he married Eva Gassett Arnold. In 1951–52 he was an alternate delegate to the Sixth General Assembly of the United Nations in Paris, and made an address in which he denounced imperialism and colonial exploitation wherever it occurs. As with many others, he was groundlessly accused of being a communist.

From 1953 until his retirement in 1959 he was chair of the board of the N.A.A.C.P. By this time he was recognized by many as "the elder statesman of Negro America," and he moved with ease among national and international leaders. One Black newspaper editor observed about 1950 that Tobias "works quietly but manages to accomplish more for Negroes than any other single Negro leader in the country." He was chosen to deliver the N.A.A.C.P. Fiftieth Anniversary Keynote Address in New York City on July 13, 1959, one of his last major speeches. Under his leadership membership in the N.A.A.C.P. reached a new high (534,710) and many anti-discrimination goals were met under his program of "Free [of state-imposed segregation] by '63," the hundredth anniversary of the Emancipation Proclamation. He received many awards and honors, including the coveted Spingarn Medal in 1948. Three times he was a delegate to the C.M.E. Church General Conference. In 1950 he received the first honorary degree (Doctor of Laws) ever awarded an African American by New York University.

"Dr. Channing H. Tobias Receives Lane Bryant Citation." *Negro History Bulletin* 20 (May 1957): 182.

Finkelstein, Louis, ed. *Thirteen Americans: Their Spiritual Autobiographies*. Port Washington, NY: Kennikat Press, 1953, 1969. 296 pp.

Jenkins, Lenore. "The Forerunners." *The Crisis* 87 (December 1980): 559–567.

"Last Rites Held for Channing H. Tobias." *The Crisis* 68 (December 1961): 636–637.

"Milestones." *Time* 78 (November 17, 1961): 80.

"Mystery Man of Race Relations." *Ebony* 6 (February 1951): 15–21.

Tobias, Channing H. "A Decade of Student Y.M.C.A. Work." *The Crisis* 24 (October 1922): 265–267.

———. *Let Negroes Work; An Address Delivered at Hampton Institute, Founder's Day, 1940*. Hampton, VA: Hampton Institute, 1940.

———. "Negro Thinking Today." *Religion in Life* 13 (Spring 1944): 204–212.

———. "The Work of the Young Men's and Young Women's Christian Associations with Negro Youth." *The Annals of the American Academy of Political and Social Science* 140 (November 28, 1928): 283–286.

"Transition." *Newsweek* 58 (November 20, 1961): 70.

"The United Nations and the Negro." *Negro History Bulletin* 18 (March 1955): 134–135.

IBAW, IBAWCB, WWCR, NYTO, DANB, HNB, CH, WWWA (4), CB (1962), EBA, RLA, WWCA (38–40), BAW, AARS, HUBA.

TOLTON, AUGUSTUS (April 1, 1854–July 9, 1897), a pioneer African American priest of the **Roman Catholic Church**, was born into slavery near Brush Creek, Ralls County, Missouri. Augustine (or Augustus) was one of four children in the family of Peter Paul and Martha Jane (Chisley) Tolton. His father belonged to the Hager plantation and his mother to the Elliot plantation. In 1861 his father escaped to join the Union Army, only to die shortly thereafter. His mother then escaped with the children to the Mississippi River. They were almost recaptured, but were saved by federal soldiers passing by. Seven-year-old Tolton never forgot those fateful days.

They settled in Quincy, Illinois, and his mother found work at the Harris Tobacco Factory. Tolton also worked in the factory for twelve years, and during the winter shutdown attended the local public Lincoln School. His mother had been reared as a Roman Catholic, and so also were Tolton and the other children. They were among the few Blacks in St. Peter's Roman Catholic Church. Finally, Fr. P. B. McGirr admitted the Tolton children to the parish school, over the strong disapproval of many. Tolton attended that school for six years and tended the church furnace. In 1875 his mother found a job as housekeeper for a priest in northeastern Missouri, but racial relations were very difficult in that region and they only spent eleven months before returning to Quincy.

Now as a young man, Tolton worked variously in a horse collar factory and a soda firm, and did advanced studies with the Franciscans of the parish high school. From 1878 to 1880 he was a "special student" at Quincy College, a Franciscan school. He joined the parish Temperance Society and made known his desire to become a priest, despite the fact that no seminary in the United States would accept him. The Franciscans were impressed by him and secured his admission to the College of the Propagation of the Faith in Rome, Italy. He left Quincy on February 15, 1880, and enrolled at the college on March 12. After five years of study he was ordained on April 24, 1886, by Cardinal Parocchi in the Basilica of St. John Lateran. He offered his first Mass on Easter Sunday at the high altar of St. Peter's, a place usually reserved for the pope. After some discussion about whether he should be assigned to the United States or to some foreign mission station, Cardinal Simeoni said: "America has been called the most enlightened nation; we will see if it deserves that honor. If America has never seen a Black priest, it has to see one now." Actually, Tolton was not the first African American Roman Catholic priest, but was preceded by the Healy brothers, James Augustine (1854), Alexander Sherwood, and Patrick Francis (1864). The Healy family, however, was light enough to "pass" for White, and generally did so. They remained unknown to Tolton. Tolton was the first American Roman Catholic priest unmistakably recognizable as Black.

Tolton arrived in New York on July 6, 1886, and his first Mass in the United States was said at St. Mary's Hospital in Hoboken, New Jersey. He then made a triumphant appearance at St. Benedict the Moor Catholic Church in New York City. He returned home to celebrations in Quincy, and was assigned to the newly formed St. Joseph's Catholic Church for Negroes. They used a former Protestant Church, and the small congregation converted the basement into a school. The church was lively, but desperately poor. Its small size enabled him, now a famous figure, to travel often on speaking engagements. He was a featured speaker at the First Catholic Colored Congress in Washington, D.C., in 1889.

In 1889 philanthropist Anne O'Neill donated $10,000 to help establish St. Monica's Church for Negro Catholics in Chicago, Illinois, and Tolton transferred to that parish. His work in Quincy had been hurt by a growing racism among some of the priests, and he even feared for his safety. He was also very lonely, having no other Black priests to whom he could turn. St.

Monica's Chapel actually opened, still unfinished, in about 1893 on South Indiana Street, and Tolton was a successful, if low-key, pastor there for the rest of his life. Despite his disappointments in Quincy, he had converted nineteen people there who left their homes and followed him to Chicago. He continued to work under difficult conditions, without much diocesan support, and under constant scrutiny. In the summer of 1897, after returning from a diocesan retreat, he was stricken by the heat and died at the young age of forty-three. The funeral procession was one of the largest ever seen in Chicago.

Hemesath, Caroline. *From Slave to Priest: A Biography of the Rev. Augustus Tolton (1854–1897)*. Chicago: Franciscan Herald Press, 1973. 174 pp.
GNPP, IBAW, GMOC, HNB, AARS, HBCUS, MM, DANB, RLOA.

TOOKES, HENRY YOUNG (1882–June 8, 1948), 56th bishop of the **African Methodist Episcopal Church** (AME), was born in Madison, Florida, the son of Summer M. and Pennie M. Tookes. He was educated at Florida Memorial College and at Edward Waters College in Jacksonville, Florida. He experienced conversion at St. Thomas AME Church in 1897 and was licensed to preach in 1901. He joined the Florida Conference in 1904, was ordained deacon in 1906 and an elder in 1909. In 1906 he married Maggie Pearl Tookes, with whom he had one child.

His pastorates included Jasper Station (1903–06); New Bethel AME Church in Jacksonville (1906–08); Grant Memorial AME Church (1908–13); presiding elder of the North Jacksonville District (1913–17); presiding elder of the East Jacksonville District (1917–19); presiding elder of the South Jacksonville District (1919–24); Mt. Zion AME Church in Daytona (1924–26); Bethel AME Church in Chicago, Illinois (1926–28); and presiding elder again of the North Jacksonville District (1928–32).

From that last position Tookes was elected bishop in 1932 and assigned to West Africa, Kentucky, and Tennessee from 1932 to 1936. From 1936 to 1940 he covered Arkansas and Oklahoma, and from 1938 to 1948 he was assigned to Florida. Some of his most impressive accomplishments were in Florida, where he oversaw the accreditation of Edward Waters College and a major upgrading of the campus. The H. Y. Tookes Library was built, a 100–room girls' dormitory was built, the J. M. Wise Stadium was built, additional property was purchased, and the college was freed from debt. Tookes also raised the level of money brought in from Florida from seventh place in the denomination to first place. He had an imposing residence in Jacksonville, and a five-story apartment building in New York City, to which his family moved after his death.

BAMEC, EAMEC, HAMEC, EWM.

TOOTE, FREDERICK AUGUSTUS (? -1959), a bishop of the **Holy African Church**, first emerges out of obscurity in 1921 when he was assigned as the priest of the **African Orthodox Church** parish in New Haven, Connecticut. He later served at the Parish of St. Ambrose in New Bedford, Massachusetts. Nothing is known of his early life. By 1934, when Archbishop **George Alexander McGuire**, the church's founder, died, Toote was vicar general of the Manhattan jurisdiction of the church. During the next year disagreement arose over the manner in which Toote was administering the church's affairs. In the midst of this controversy, one of the church's bishops, **Reginald Grant Barrow**, formed a schismatic group. Barrow was joined by **Arthur Stanley Trotman**. The two soon disagreed and Trotman formed a second group. Toote aligned himself with Trotman. In 1938 the courts ruled against either Barrow or Trotman using the name of the African Orthodox Church. Trotman reorganized his following as the Holy African Church and later that year, on November 25, he consecrated Toote. The next year he consecrated **Gladstone St. Clair Nurse**.

Following Trotman's death in 1945, Trotman was succeeded by Robert Arthur Valentine, who had originally been consecrated by McGuire. Toote served under Valentine and in 1954 Toote succeeded him as Primate. In 1956 Toote consecrated **Noel Kenneth Smith**. In 1959 Toote was succeeded by Bishop Nurse.

Ward, Gary. *Independent Bishops: An International Directory.* Detroit, MI: Apogee Books, 1991. 524 pp.

TOUGALOO COLLEGE. A **United Church of Christ** and **Christian Church (Disciples of Christ)** school. Tougaloo College, Tougaloo, Mississippi, began in 1869 as a project of the American Missionary Association as a small school near Jackson, Mississippi. In 1871 it was chartered as Tougaloo University and for many years received government support of its teacher training program in cooperation with the state of Mississippi. The state withdrew its support in 1892. In 1897 the first college courses were offered. In 1916 the school adopted it present name. Tougaloo serves approximately 700 students annually under the joint sponsorship of the UCC and the Disciples.

TOUSSAINT, PIERRE (1766–June 30, 1853), a pre–Civil War social worker, currently a candidate in the early stages of the process to become the first African American designated a saint by the **Roman Catholic Church**, was born into slavery in St. Mark, Haiti. His mother was named Ursule, a chambermaid on the Plantation de Latibonite; nothing is known about his father. Jean Bérard, owner of the plantation, was one of the few in Haiti who treated his slaves with some decency. He assigned Toussaint to work in the house rather than in the fields and encouraged him to read and write and explore the estate's considerable library.

About 1787 Bérard and his new wife, a widow named Marie Elisabeth Bossard Roudanes, moved to New York City to wait out what they correctly predicted would be social unrest in Haiti. What in fact came was a revolution led by Toussaint-Louverture (no relation) that eliminated slavery and finally established a Black government in 1803. The retinue of servants that came to New York with Bérard included Toussaint and his sister, Rosalie. Bérard soon apprenticed Toussaint to Mr. Merchant, a leading hairdresser. Toussaint showed a gift for the intricate art of hairdressing, and this skill, combined with his quick wit and pleasing personality, brought him a long line of loyal customers. The old-fashioned powdered wigs were leaving the scene, and instead women sought highly stylized coiffures at extravagant cost. Toussaint soon was making a large income and conferring with some of the wealthiest women in New York City.

Bérard had anticipated that the troubles in Haiti would be over quickly, and had only brought to the United States enough cash to last one year. He was then forced to return to Haiti to attend to the plantation. He died there of pleurisy just before the most widespread and deadly of the revolts in August 1797. The Bérard plantation was destroyed and his investments in New York City became worthless when the principal firm collapsed. Madame Bérard, widowed now for the second time, was also destitute. Most thought that the French army would quickly restore order and that the properties would be restored. In the meantime, to prevent his mistress's social embarrassment, Toussaint began supporting her and the household with his own earnings, though few outside the family were aware of this. She apparently thought she could repay him at a later date, a date which would never come.

Although Toussaint would have had no problem gaining his freedom, he continued as her slave for all social appearances. A very devout Catholic, he began each day by attending the 6 A.M. Mass at St. Peter's Church on Barclay Street. During the day he would walk to his clients' homes; as a Black he was not allowed on the horse cars, but this reportedly did not stir any bitterness. He made it his personal goal to keep up Madame Bérard's spirits, though she gradually dropped into a deep depression. He spent nothing on himself until she and the household were seen to, and apparently took genuine joy in dressing her hair, bringing her flowers, and otherwise tending to her. He sometimes created social gatherings for her and after a hard day's work would serve as waiter, usher, and musician for the party at the Reade Street home.

Madame Bérard's fortunes seemed to take a turn for the better when she married Gabriel Nicolas, a refugee French planter who now made a decent living as a musician in New York's theaters. Misfortune again came her way, however, as religion-inspired laws closed most of the theaters and dried up his income. Once more she was completely dependent upon Toussaint. She returned to a state of depression and her health declined. On July 2, 1807, shortly before her death, she formally freed Toussaint. While she was alive, he put off marrying a young Haitian woman, Juliette Noel, whose freedom he purchased when she was fifteen. They were finally married in 1811 and took residence on the third floor of the Reade Street home, where Gabriel Nicolas and his servants occupied the first two floors.

Though he was already well-known for his faithfulness to Madame Bérard and his generosity to others, Toussaint's service to others now took on much broader proportions. He regularly visited the sick, the imprisoned, the friendless, and through his connections found employment for many who had fallen on hard times. His home functioned as a credit bureau, employment agency, emergency shelter, and visitor hospitality center. He was a primary supporter of an orphanage built on Prince Street in 1817. He often ventured into plague-infested parts of the city to look for ill people who had been abandoned. On one occasion he found a traveling priest ill with ship fever (typhus) and took him into his house until he was healthy again.

In particular Toussaint was concerned for the welfare of his niece, Euphemia. Her mother, Toussaint's sister Rosalie, had died of tuberculosis in 1815, and her father had abandoned the family. Toussaint adopted Euphemia and saw to her musical training and literary education. When she died of tuberculosis in 1829, at age fourteen, he was devastated. Instead of withdrawing, however, he became even more sensitive to suffering and more dutiful in his charitable activities. By this time he held a social position in New York such as no other Black before him. He was as honored among the rich as the poor, as much among the Protestants as the Catholics. One famous New Yorker, Mrs. Emma Cary, later wrote that she "used to hear Protestants speak with

reverence of two men—the great Fenelon and the humble Pierre Toussaint!"

He was a devoted supporter of the **Oblate Sisters of Providence**, a religious order for Black women, and was a benefactor of St. Vincent de Paul School on Canal Street, the first New York City Catholic school for Black children. The list of his other charitable efforts is almost endless. Among other things, he helped educate two priests and a number of poor Blacks, purchased the freedom of several slaves, supported other former slaves of the Bérard plantation, and financed the burial of the poor. Sometimes called "the Black St. Francis," he slowed down considerably after the death of his wife in 1851, and passed away two years later. His death was noted in the major papers as a great loss, and his life had a great effect on race relations in New York City. Revolutionary General Philip Schuyler noted: "I have known Christians who were not gentlemen, gentlemen who were not Christians. One man I know who is both and that man is Black."

Toussaint's gravesite on Mott Street was forgotten until a young seminarian, Charles McTague, searched it out in 1941. In 1951 Cardinal Spellman dedicated a plaque in Toussaint's honor and declared his grave a place of pilgrimage. In the early 1950s the John Boyle O'Reilly Committee for Interracial Justice, an Irish-American group devoted to social justice for Blacks, began researching his life and promoting that information. Later the Pierre Toussaint Haitian-Catholic Center was established in Miami, Florida, and a strong movement was begun to have him nominated for sainthood. In 1990 Cardinal O'Connor had his skeleton exhumed and moved it to a crypt in the modern-day St. Patrick's Cathedral. In June 1991 the archdiocese sent six boxes of documentation to Vatican City, including fifteen bound volumes of letters to and from Toussaint, and a collection of "Statements of Claimed Miracles and Favors Attributed to the Servant of God Pierre Toussaint." One of these miracles involved Gesner Lamonthe, a school principal in Haiti who was diagnosed with terminal stomach cancer in 1973. He and his priest prayed to Toussaint and the cancer reportedly vanished. One authenticated miracle is needed for beatification and generally a second miracle is needed for final canonization as a saint.

The movement to make Toussaint the first African American saint is controversial. While many, including Bishop **Emerson Moore**, an African American, think that he is an excellent choice for demonstrating "great sanctity," others think Toussaint is a poor role model. For these people, his charity is outweighed by his passivity and servility, an image associated with that of an "Uncle Tom." In Haiti he has some support, but is not a greatly popular figure, as many there feel that he could have stayed to help advance the revolution. He did not denounce slavery either there or in the United States, and apparently felt that the American abolitionists were in danger of instigating the same kind of blood bath he left in Haiti. Toussaint supporters suggest that his letters reveal a strength of character in transcending with grace the racism of his time that is indeed militant. Despite the controversy, his candidacy could well be on a fast track in Rome, since many see him as the perfect post–Vatican II candidate: a lay-person, married, native of a poor, troubled country, and non-White.

Hanley, Boniface. *Ten Christians*. Notre Dame, IN: Ave Maria Press, 1979. 269 pp.

Lee, Hannah Farnham Sawyer. *Memoir of Pierre Toussaint, Born a Slave in St. Domingo*. Boston: Crosby, Nichols, and Co., 1854. 124 pp.

Oliver, Vernell M. "Pierre: The Other Toussaint." *The Negro History Bulletin* 19 (February 1956): 114–115.

Sheehan, Arthur and Elizabeth Sheehan. *Pierre Toussaint: A Citizen of Old New York*. New York: P. J. Kennedy, 1955. 257 pp.

Sontag, Deborah. "Canonizing a Slave: Saint or Uncle Tom?" *New York Times* (February 23, 1992): 1, 32.

Tarry, Ellen. *The Other Toussaint: A Modern Biography of Pierre Toussaint, a Post-Revolutionary Black*. St. Paul Editions, 1981. 377 pp.

HBCUS, IBAW.

TOWNSEND, ARTHUR MELVIN (October 26, 1875–April 20, 1959), long-time corresponding secretary and virtual creator of the Sunday School Publishing Board of the **National Baptist Convention of the U.S.A., Inc.** (N.B.C.U.S.A.), was born in Winchester, Tennessee, the son of Anderson and Emma Alice (Singleton) Townsend. His father was a Baptist minister and director of the public schools for Blacks in Winchester. Townsend received his B.A. in 1898 from Roger Williams University in Providence, Rhode Island, and his M.D. in 1902 from Meharry Medical College in Nashville, Tennessee. On June 11, 1902 he married Willa Ann Hadley, with whom he had one son, who became a well-known physician.

After graduation he opened a medical practice in Nashville and taught materia medica and pathology at Meharry Medical College from 1902 to 1913. Always active in church, he served as organist for various Nashville congregations and was secretary of the Tennessee Baptist Missionary and Educational Convention from 1904–1921. He taught Sunday School classes and conducted missions to hospitals and jails. He

was elected cashier of the People's Bank and Trust Company at a time when the institution was on the verge of collapse. He was so highly regarded that his very presence pulled it through the crisis.

In 1913 Townsend resigned from his lucrative medical practice to accept the presidency of Roger Williams University, a training ground for many Baptist leaders. During his tenure the school built a new administration building and dormitory while strengthening its overall financial standing. He also was ordained and in 1917–18 pastored the Spruce Street Baptist Church in Nashville, Tennessee. In 1918 he left the presidency to pursue the ministry full time, and was pastor of the Metropolitan Baptist Church in Memphis, Tennessee from 1918 to 1921. He was chair of the Memphis Inter-Racial League in 1920–21.

In 1915 the **National Baptist Convention of America** broke away from the N.B.C.U.S.A. and took with it the publishing house. The N.B.C.U.S.A. had to create a new one from scratch, and a start was made by S. P. Harris and William Haynes. Between 1915 and 1920 small quarters had been rented and a staff of people assembled. The 1920 convention voted Townsend the new corresponding secretary, basically serving as the chief executive. He remained in that position for the next thirty-nine years, and the resulting Sunday School Publishing Board "is in the final analysis a monument to one man's devotion," that is, Arthur M. Townsend.

The 1920 convention authorized the building or buying of an appropriate headquarters in Nashville, but did not provide any money. Townsend's apparent genius for being able to do anything required of him came to the fore, and his personal prestige helped secure the financing for the $700,000 Morris Memorial Building. It was located, ironically, on the site of a former slave auction, a few blocks from the state capitol, and was designed by the Black architectural firm of McKissick and McKissick. At the time of its completion it was recognized as one of the finest Black-owned structures in the country. In its four floors were a bookstore, cafeteria, writing, editing, and production staffs, and giant printing plant. Townsend was instrumental in securing the charter for the publishing house and the passage of an enabling act in the Tennessee legislature to permit the chartering of non-profit Sunday School Board owned and controlled by parent corporations. Townsend also was a leader in the financial campaigns that later paid for the structure.

One of Townsend's first major publication challenges was a hymnal. Working with a committee appointed by the N.B.C.U.S.A., he put together the *Standard Baptist Hymnal*, a highly regarded hymnal with 755 songs, many of them newly arranged by

Townsend and his wife, also a musician. He then oversaw the creation of two supplemental volumes, *Gospel Pearls* and *Spirituals Triumphant, Old and New*. He carefully chose editors and staff support for the production of such denominational periodicals as the *Sunday School Informer* (now the *Baptist Teacher*), the *Star of Hope* (discontinued in 1960), and the *Baptist Voice*. He laid the foundations for what is now a major Baptist library of the Publishing Board. In addition to these labors, he was a member of the executive committee of the Inter-Racial League of Tennessee beginning in 1921 and the executive committee of the Federal (now National) Council of Churches, beginning in 1924. He served also on the boards of the World Baptist Alliance and the International Council of Religious Education of the World's Sunday School Association. By the time of his death, the Publishing Board counted assets of more than $4,200,000, and its yearly profits amounted to $70,000. His successor was Dennis C. Washington.

WWCA (38–40), SCA, SNB, WWCR.

TRIMM, TRUDIE (b. c.1915), the first woman pastor listed as a member of the **National Baptist Convention, U.S.A., Inc.**, was born in Spearsville, Louisiana, the last of fifteen children in the family. While her mother was pregnant with her, her father became very ill. Her mother made a vow to God that if her father's life was spared she would dedicate the child to the ministry. Her father did recover, but when Trudie was born a girl, her mother thought that the vow was fruitless, since women ministers were practically unknown at the time.

She did later marry Charles O. Trimm, a Baptist minister, and about 1944 they founded the New Testament Missionary Baptist Church in Chicago, Illinois. While her husband pastored the church, Trimm worked variously as a policewoman, political precinct captain, and later as a committee woman of the predominantly Black Second Ward. When her husband died in 1965 the church's board of directors chose her to take his place in the pulpit, and the congregation unanimously supported the decision. When word of this spread to the area ministers, there was an outcry against such a move. Opponents claimed it was against the will of God to ordain a woman, and it seemed for a time that she would not find anyone to ordain her. Then E. F. Ledbetter, pastor of the Metropolitan Missionary Baptist Church, one of the largest Black churches in Chicago, agreed to do it. He was influenced by the church's threat

to close its doors if she were not its pastor, and above all came to feel that she was called by God for the task.

When Trimm was ordained, she fulfilled her mother's wish that had seemed impossible, and the church did not regret the decision. In four years she increased the membership from 500 to 1,500, complete with a 300–member choir and a 320–pupil Sunday School. She also became the first woman minister recognized by the National Baptist Convention, U.S.A., Inc. Her daughter, Trudie Trimm Foote, and son-in-law, Lonnie Paul Foote, soon were serving the church as co-pastors under her authority. Her two sons, Cleophas and Charles Jr., became members of the Deacon Board. Trimm also served as president of the Illinois Baptist League and as president of the National Baptist Convention Women's Auxiliary.

"The Holy War of the Rev. Trudie Trimm." *Ebony* 24 (September 1969): 72–77.
IBAW, BWR.

TRIUMPH THE CHURCH AND KINGDOM OF GOD IN CHRIST. A Holiness church. Triumph the Church and Kingdom of God in Christ began in a divine revelation received by Father **E. D. Smith** in 1897. The impact of the revelation came in several stages, as it was "speeded to the earth" in 1902 and "opened to the world" in 1904. The church was organized in 1902 in Baton Rouge, Louisiana, but the content of the message was not released until 1904. Smith headed the church until 1920, when he moved to Addis Ababa, Ethiopia. However, prior to his move he had relocated the church's headquarters to Birmingham, Alabama.

The church is a fire-baptized body. It believes strongly in the spiritual experience of empowerment by the Holy Spirit, which in the second chapter of the biblical book of Acts is described as being accompanied by tongues of fire. As first described in the nineteenth century, fire baptism was similar to the Pentecostal experience, but was not associated with the experience of speaking in unknown tongues.

The church also has a unique doctrine of the church. It sees itself as superseding traditional Christianity, which has often spoken of itself as the church militant. The Church Triumphant has now received the Spirit which previously filled the church militant. That church was a church at war; the Church Triumphant is a church of peace.

Headquarters of the church is in Birmingham. In 1972 (its most recent report) the church claimed 475 churches and over 50,000 members. It is led by bishops and a hierarchy of state and local workers. Its International Religious Congress meets quadrennially.

Clark, Elmer. *Small Sects in America.* Nashville, TN: Abingdon-Cokesbury Press, 1949. 256 pp.

Hollenwager, Walter J. *Black Pentecostal Concept: Interpretations and Variations. Concept, #30.* Geneva, Switzerland: World Council of Churches, 1970. 70 pp.

TROTMAN, ARTHUR STANLEY (July 25, 1869–July 14, 1945) was the founder of the **Holy African Church**. Little is known of Arthur Stanley Trotman prior to the early 1920s, when he joined the **African Orthodox Church** founded by Archbishop **George Alexander McGuire**. In 1922 he was sent to Nova Scotia to succeed Fr. (later Bishop) **William E. J. Robertson**, as priest of St. Philip's Church. He stayed there for two years. In 1924 he became the third bishop of the church, and on September 10, 1924, was consecrated by McGuire. He was assigned to Massachusetts and again succeeded Robertson.

Following McGuire's death in 1934, Trotman left the African Orthodox Church and with his episcopal colleague **Reginald Grant Barrow**, who had formed a rival **African Orthodox Church of Massachusetts and New York**. The relationship lasted only a brief time as Barrow soon suspended Trotman who then founded the African Orthodox Church, Inc. The African Orthodox Church moved against both Barrow and Trotman, and in a 1938 court ruling, both were denied use of the name "African Orthodox Church" in any form. After the ruling Trotman reorganized his jurisdiction as the Holy African Church. Moving quickly to establish the church, in 1938 he consecrated **Frederick Augustus Toote**, and the following year he consecrated **Gladstone St. Clair Nurse**. He was succeeded by Bishop **Robert Arthur Valentine** who like Trotman had been consecrated by McGuire. In 1964 Nurse, who had emerged as primate, led the church back into the African Orthodox Church.

Anson, Peter. *Bishops at Large.* London: Faber, 1964. 593 pp.

Terry-Thompson, A. C. *The History of the African Orthodox Church.* N.p.: 1956. 139 pp.

Trela, Jonathan. *A History of the North American Old Roman Catholic Church.* Scranton, PA: The Author, 1979. 124 pp.

TRUE GRACE MEMORIAL HOUSE OF PRAYER. A Pentecostal church. Six months after **Walter McCollough** assumed control of the House of Prayer for All People, after the death of its founder,

Charles Manuel "Sweet Daddy" Grace, McCollough was relieved of his office under accusations of mishandling of church funds. Despite this, he was re-elected when a new vote for leader was held. Complaints against him continued, and he dismissed several of the church elders. Then, twelve members under the pastorship of Thomas O. Johnson, left the House of Prayer and formed the True Grace Memorial House of Prayer in Washington, D.C. In 1954 the True Grace Memorial House of Prayer adopted a new church covenant in 1964.

The church is currently led by Elder William G. Easton, Elder Johnson having been dismissed after 23 years as pastor.

Michael A. Köszegi

TRUE VINE PENTECOSTAL CHURCHES OF JESUS. An Apostolic Pentecostal church. The True Vine Pentecostal Churches of Jesus dates to a 1961 split in the **True Vine Pentecostal Holiness Church**, a trinitarian Pentecostal church. Robert L. Hairston, one of the church's founders, accepted the non-Trinitarian Jesus Only position of the Apostolic Pentecostal churches. Apostolic Pentecostals believe that there is one God whose name is Jesus. As a result, they baptize people in the name of Jesus Christ, rather than utilizing the traditional Trinitarian formula of "Father, Son, and Holy Spirit." Hairston split from long-time colleague Bishop Monroe Johnson and founded the True Vine Pentecostal Churches of Jesus.

Above and beyond the basic doctrinal split, the break with Johnson was also occasioned by two other factors. First, Hairston had also come to feel that Johnson's financial demand on the local churches to support the central headquarters was far too heavy. Second, in 1960, Hairston was divorced and subsequently remarried. The divorce also led to some coolness from the Apostolic leaders he had come to know. Thus, rather than simply joining one of the older Apostolic denominations, he founded a new one.

The new church began with the large congregation Hairston pastored in Martinsville, Virginia. In the intervening years new congregations have been founded and other independent churches have joined the fellowship. In 1976, several congregations headed by Bishop Thomas C. Williams aligned themselves with the True Vine Churches. As a result Williams was named senior bishop and Hairston remained presiding bishop.

The church is headquartered in Martinsville, Virginia, at New Bethel Apostolic Church. By 1980 it had ten affiliated congregations and approximately 900 members. The leadership of female ministers is encouraged by the church.

Richardson, James C. *With Water and Spirit: A History of Black Apostolic Denominations in the U.S.* Martinsville, VA: The Author, n.d. 151 pp.

TRUE VINE PENTECOSTAL HOLINESS CHURCH. A Holiness Pentecostal church. The True Vine Pentecostal Holiness Church was founded by Bishop William Monroe Johnson and Dr. Robert L. Hairston in the 1940. Its doctrine is similar to that of the Pentecostal Holiness Church International. Headquarters were established in Winston-Salem, North Carolina. In 1961 the tranquillity of the church was disturbed when Hairston accepted the non-Trinitarian Jesus only theology of the Apostolic Pentecostals. As a result he left the church and founded the **True Vine Pentecostal Churches of Jesus**.

Following Johnson's death, his son, Sylvester D. Johnson, became the new presiding bishop. Headquarters remains in Winston-Salem.

Richardson, James C. *With Water and Spirit: A History of Black Apostolic Denominations in the U.S.* Martinsville, VA: The Author, n.d. 151 pp.

TRUSTY, CHARLES H. (December 12, 1868–1946), pioneer Presbyterian missionary and denominational leader, was born in Cold Spring, New Jersey, the son of David M. and Keturah Seagraves Trusty. After he attended public schools in his hometown, a wealthy Quaker named Mrs. Cornelius Weatherby agreed to finance his ministerial education. In 1885 he thus enrolled in Lincoln University in Pennsylvania, a Presbyterian-related school with a mission to train Black preachers and teachers for work in the South. He graduated in 1889 with a B.A. degree and remained to study at Lincoln Theological Seminary, earning an M.A. and S.T.B. in 1892.

He affiliated with the Freedmen's Board (later called the Board of National Missions), an agency of the Presbyterian Church, U.S.A. supporting work among Blacks in the South, was ordained and sent to the Second Presbyterian Church in Maryville, Tennessee. In 1894 he married Kathlyn B. Wilson. In 1895 he opened a school and also organized another Black Presbyterian congregation in the neighboring town of Louisville. Later that same year he moved to the Leonard Street Presbyterian Church in Chattanooga, Tennessee, to pastor an eight-member church in a town with over 30 other Black churches. Despite these obstacles, in 1900 a new brick edifice was completed and about 200 new members had been added. In 1903 he led in founding the Newton Normal Institute, which soon had over 100 students. It was largely supported beginning in 1904 by the Newton Presbytery in New Jersey and focused on industrial education.

In 1898 there was an effort to merge the four separate Black presbyteries of the Presbyterian Church U.S.A. with the two separate Black presbyteries of the Presbyterian Church U.S. into an autonomous synod to be named the Afro-American Presbyterian Church. Trusty was a leader in this unsuccessful movement. What did happen was that in 1901 the Synod of Tennessee authorized the Black churches in the Kingston Presbytery to join with other Black congregations in the region to form the Presbytery of Birmingham. By 1902 it included not only its original five churches but eleven more in eastern Tennessee, Alabama, and Mississippi. While Trusty was in Tennessee, he was the chair of the Synod of Tennessee's Permanent Committee on Freedmen, with primary responsibility for making financial appeals for the work. He also oversaw (and was stated clerk of) the new Presbytery of Birmingham, the growth of which seemed to vindicate its existence. In 1905 this presbytery became part of the all-Black Synod of East Tennessee, which by 1913 included 34 congregations in Tennessee, Mississippi, Alabama, Virginia, and western North Carolina, plus some schools. Trusty was pivotal in the creation of both the Presbytery of Birmingham and the Synod of East Tennessee, which enhanced Black Presbyterian autonomy and prospects.

In 1907 Trusty moved to the 100–member Lafayette Presbyterian Church in Jersey City, New Jersey, which had been struggling since it separated from the First Presbyterian Church in 1900. His experience there, however, was not a happy one, and congregational discord led to his move in 1910 to the 200–member Grace Memorial Presbyterian Church in Pittsburgh, Pennsylvania. He remained there for fifteen years and capitalized on the northern migration of Blacks, increasing the membership to 488. He built a new brick building for the church and increased the church's visibility in the community by serving as president of the board of directors of both Coleman Industrial Home and Livingstone Memorial Hospital. He was one of the members of the Ministerial Advisory Board of the city's first Black bank, Steel City Banking Company. He helped found two new Black Presbyterian churches, People's Presbyterian Mission, later called Bethesda Presbyterian Church (1912) and Bidwell Street

Presbyterian Church a few years later, which began as a Free Methodist church in 1914. In 1922 he was president of the Afro-American Presbyterian Council (founded in 1893). In September, 1924 Trusty was voted moderator of the Pittsburgh Presbytery, filling a six-month unexpired term. Meanwhile, however, his own church had stagnated.

In June, 1925 Trusty left Pittsburgh to pastor St. Paul (later Hillside) Presbyterian Church in Omaha, Nebraska, a promising congregation less than five years old. In three years he doubled the membership to sixty and became director of the Anti-Saloon League. In 1928 he moved to his final pastorate at the 200–member Siloam Presbyterian Church in Elizabeth, New Jersey. There, despite the ravages of the Depression, the church managed to sponsor a day nursery, playground, and free employment agency. Trusty led in organizing a civic league. In 1934 the Elizabeth Presbytery chose him as a commissioner to the General Assembly. He retired in 1938 but continued his active participation in the Afro-American Presbyterian Council.

Dickerson, Dennis C. "Charles H. Trusty: Black Presbyterian Missionary and Denominational Leader." *American Presbyterians: Journal of Presbyterian History* 67 (Winter 1989): 283–296.

TRUTH, SOJOURNER (c.1797–November 26, 1883), evangelist, abolitionist, and reformer, was born in Hurley, Ulster County, New York. She was the next to the youngest child in the family of James (sometimes called Baumfree) and Elizabeth (Bett or Betsey), slaves of a Dutch farmer named Charles Hardenbergh. Her birth name was Isabella and her childhood language was Dutch. She was separated from her mother at age eleven and sold a number of times. From 1810 to 1826 she was in the household of John Dumont in New Paltz, New York, where she was treated cruelly and where she gave birth to at least five children of another slave named Thomas. Most of the four children who survived infancy were sold away from her.

In 1827, the year before all slaves were emancipated in New York State, she escaped to the home of Isaac and Maria Van Wagener. There she initiated successful legal proceedings with some Quaker friends to retrieve a son who had been illegally sold into Alabama, and in about 1829 she moved to New York City with son Peter and daughter Sophia, using the name Isabella Van Wagener. An intensely religious person who regularly had mystic visions, she first joined the John Street Methodist Church but soon encountered Elijah Pierson who called himself "The Tishbite," and his wife Sarah.

They had a mission among the prostitutes in the notorious "Five Points" area, a refuge called the Magdalene Asylum, and a group called the Retrenchment Society. She became part of the Pierson household, which encouraged much prayer and fasting, sometimes for as long as three days.

In the spring of 1832 Robert Matthews, who went by the name Matthias, appeared at the Pierson home and announced his divine mission, which the whole household readily joined. In 1833 he established a communal association in Sing Sing, New York, called "Zion Hill." All the members turned over to him all their money and worldly possessions, but the enterprise only lasted two years and the members lost everything. It ended with rumors of sexual improprieties by Matthews and the mysterious death of Elijah Pierson. Tried for murder, Matthews was found not guilty. Then Isabella was accused with having something to do with the death, and she fought back with a successful libel suit. She spent the next eight or nine years living quietly in New York City with her two children, earning a living as cook and maid. She began attending the **African Methodist Episcopal Zion Church** (AMEZ), which from that point on was her religious affiliation.

In 1843 the voices in one of her visions bade her take up the name "Sojourner Truth" and become an itinerant preacher. She started walking in June and moved apparently at random through Long Island and Connecticut, preaching a simple gospel of a good God and the need for people to love each other. In the winter of 1843 she joined a communal farm and silk factory in Northampton, Massachusetts, called the Northampton Association of Education and Industry, founded by George W. Benson, brother-in-law of abolitionist William Lloyd Garrison. This was her first encounter with the abolitionist movement, and she became an enthusiastic promoter of it. When the commune failed in 1946 she stayed in the Benson household and became a frequent lecturer for abolitionism around the state.

About 1850 she moved westward, and by this time her fame was already significant. She stood a lanky six feet tall, spoke in a guttural Dutch-accented voice, had a quick wit, often broke into song with a beautiful voice, and had a gift for engaging in successful debates with opponents. Her typical opening line, done with tremendous effect, was "Children, I talk to God and God talks to me!" She was altogether a remarkable presence. In 1850 she published the *Narrative of Sojourner Truth*, written for her by Olive Gilbert, the royalties from which helped support her, along with the sale of photographs of herself. In 1850 at a conference in Worcester, Massachusetts, she discovered the women's rights movement and began a long friendship with Lucretia

Mott, Elizabeth Cady Stanton, and other leaders. In later years she often spoke at women's rights conventions. In Akron, Ohio in 1851 she made one of the most famous speeches of the century, responding to the charge that women were too delicate for equal rights. She recounted her abilities and adventures with the recurrent refrain, "And ain't I a woman?"

Southern sympathizers often tried to break up her meetings, and her life was regularly threatened. She was clubbed in Kansas and mobbed in Missouri. There was a persistent rumor that she was really a man, and once in Indiana she opened her blouse and exposed her breasts to quiet and shame some of her male detractors. Her headquarters for touring the Midwest was the Salem *Anti-Slavery Bugle* in Ohio. She often shared a platform with Frederick Douglass and other abolitionist leaders. At one point she spent several days with Harriet Beecher Stowe in Massachusetts, who then wrote an article about her in the April, 1863 edition of the *Atlantic Monthly*, dubbing her the "Libyan Sibyl."

In the mid-1850s Sojourner Truth settled in Battle Creek, Michigan, but for many years it remained more of a home base for her frequent trips. During the Civil War she traveled many miles gathering food and clothing for volunteer Black regiments. In 1864 President Lincoln received her at the White House and in December of that year the National Freedmen's Relief Association appointed her "counselor to the freed people," and she remained at Freedmen's Village in Arlington Heights, Virginia, for about a year in that capacity. She did everything from nursing the wounded at Freedmen's Hospital, to distributing relief supplies, to teaching female former field hands housekeeping skills. Desiring to aid the crowded and destitute refugees, she came up with the idea of settling Blacks who wished to do so in a "Negro State," on public land in the Midwest. In 1870 she presented a petition to President Grant for this, and tried for years afterward to get still more names. Though her idea never came to fruition she is credited with influencing many of the Blacks who moved from the South into Kansas and Missouri.

In the early 1870s Sojourner Truth continued her lecture tours, covering many states with no set schedule or itinerary. Her messages frequently mixed the importance of Black rights, women's suffrage, and temperance with her own mystic vision of God's love. She was still able to draw some crowds, but her attraction was waning. In 1875 her grandson and traveling companion, Sammy Banks, became ill and they returned to Battle Creek, not to leave again. Until her death eight years later she continued to receive hundreds of visitors a year.

Bernard, Jacqueline. *Journey Toward Freedom: The Story of Sojourner Truth.* New York: Norton, 1967. 265 pp.

Fauset, Arthur Huff. *Sojourner Truth: God's Faithful Pilgrim.* Chapel Hill, NC: University of North Carolina Press, 1938. 187 pp.

Gilbert, Olive. *Narrative of Sojourner Truth, a Bondswoman of Olden Time.* 1850. Rept.: New York: Oxford University Press, 1991. 320 pp.

Lindstrom, Aletha Jane. *Sojourner Truth: Slave, Abolitionist, Fighter for Women's Rights.* New York: J. Messner, 1980. 124 pp.

Ortiz, Victoria. *Sojourner Truth: A Self-Made Woman.* Philadelphia, PA: Lippincott, 1974. 157 pp.

Vale, Gilbert. *Fanaticism, Its Source and Influence: Illustrated by the Simple Narrative of Isabella, in the Case of Matthias, Mr. and Mrs. B. Folger, Mr. Pierson, Mr. Mills, Catherine, Isabella, etc.* 2 vols. New York: The Author, 1835.

AAE, PP, AMEZC, BWNCAL, GNPP, NA, EBA, CH, BHBA, HNB, NBH, IBAWCB, BAW, BHONH, IBAW, WWF, NAH, HH, LW, FAW, DARB, DANB, NAW, BDBPC, EAB, NBAW, BWMH.

TUBMAN, HARRIET (c.1821–March 10, 1913), abolitionist, reformer, spy, and Underground Railroad conductor, was born in Dorchester County on the Eastern shore of Maryland, the daughter of slaves Benjamin Ross and Harriet Green. She was originally named Araminta by her master, but she later dropped that in favor of her mother's name. She performed many tasks around the estate, including woodcutting and working in the field, and she gained great strength and stamina. At about the age of thirteen an overseer struck her in the head with a two-pound weight thrown at a runaway slave she was protecting and fractured her skull. For the rest of her life she had to deal with occasional blackouts as a result of that injury. In 1844 her mother forced her to marry John Tubman, a free man; there were no children.

From 1847 to 1849 Tubman worked in the household of Anthony Thompson, a physician and Methodist minister whose father was the legal guardian of her legal master, who was not yet of age. In 1849 that legal master died and it was rumored his slaves were to be sold into the deep South. Tubman decided to take matters into her own hands and escaped to Philadelphia where she gained employment at a hotel. Having made it to freedom, however, she was still not satisfied while so many were still enslaved.

She made her first trip back to Maryland in December, 1850, and brought back on the Underground Railroad her sister and two children. Tubman's husband, who had refused to leave with her in 1849, by then had remarried and still had no wish to leave. Over the next decade she made approximately nineteen trips and rescued as many as 300, including her elderly parents. She became known as "the Moses of her people," and her courage and cleverness in avoiding capture made her legendary in both the North and South. At one point the reward for her capture amounted to $40,000, and yet she still eluded her enemies. She began to be a featured speaker at abolitionist meetings in the North and was revered by such leaders as Wendell Phillips and Frederick Douglass. She knew and met with Sojourner Truth on several occasions. She was very religious, affiliating with the **African Methodist Episcopal Zion Church** (AMEZ), and stated that her actions were guided by God through divine dreams and omens.

Through most of the 1850s Tubman made her home in St. Catherine's, Ontario, since the Fugitive Slave Act of 1850 made it unwise to stop short of the Canadian border. In 1858 she counseled with John Brown about his proposed raid on Harper's Ferry. She was unable herself to take her planned part as a bringer of reinforcements and conductor to freedom of the released slaves, thanks to a physical collapse that left her bedridden for weeks, and was deeply saddened by the venture's failure and Brown's subsequent hanging. In April 1860 in Troy, New York, she was a leader in a group that successfully overpowered officers to release a fugitive slave, although she was severely beaten in the process. In 1862 she offered her services to the Union Army and for the next three years worked mainly in South Carolina as a spy, scout, and nurse, supporting herself through the sale of chickens and eggs. The climax of her military career came on June 2, 1863, when she basically directed a covert gunboat expedition up the Combahee River near Beaufort. Confederate soldiers all along the river were so surprised that hardly a shot was fired. Dozens of mansions along the river, which provided food and shelter for the rebel soldiers, were burned to the ground, and almost 800 slaves were brought to safety. From that point she was recognized as a military hero and Union officers regularly tipped their caps to her. Toward the end of the war she worked at a freedmen's hospital in Fortress Monroe, Virginia.

After the war Tubman returned to her home, since about 1858, a farm near Auburn, New York, which had been sold to her on liberal terms by Senator William H. Seward. Her former husband was killed by a White man in 1867, and in 1869 she married Nelson Davis (who died in 1888). Also in 1869 she published *Scenes in the Life of Harriet Tubman*, written for her by Sarah H. Bradford. The income from this book helped support her, as did the voluntary gifts from her admirers. At her house she cared for her parents and a number of other people, orphans and elderly, whom she had brought from slavery but had no place to go. In 1896 she purchased a 25–acre plot adjoining her land as a permanent location for what became known as the Harriet Tubman Home for Indigent and Aged Negroes. Unable to secure enough funds to finish paying for the land, she soon deeded it to the AME Zion Church, which continued the Home a number of years past her death. She continued her travels on behalf of others, and spent a great deal of time in North Carolina trying to establish schools for newly freed people.

For over thirty years Tubman attempted to gain from the government some recompense for her war-time services, and Congress finally decided in 1898 to give her a mere $20 per month pension. She was active for many years in the fight for women's suffrage and temperance. She was a member of the AMEZ Church in Auburn, New York, now called the Thompson Memorial, and reportedly helped build it. Over time her image as a courageous leader in the struggle for justice has not dimmed. Many community houses and services have been named for her. In 1952 the Harriet Tubman Home on South Street was rebuilt and then maintained by the AMEZ Church, and the following year it was dedicated as a national shrine.

Bisson, Terry. *Harriet Tubman*. New York: Chelsea House, 1991. 112 pp.

Bradford, Sarah Elizabeth Hopkins. *Harriet, the Moses of Her People*. New York: For the Author by G. R. Lockwood & Son, 1886, expanded from the sketch of 1869. Rept.: Secaucus, NJ: Citadel Press, 1961, 1974. 149 pp.

Conrad, Earl. *Harriet Tubman*. Washington, DC: The Associated Publishers, 1943. 248 pp.

Petry, Ann. *Harriet Tubman, Conductor on the Underground Railroad*. New York: Crowell, 1955. 249 pp. (fiction)

DANB, DAB, BP, AMEZC, PP, NA, LW, TSW, GNPP, IP, BWNCAL, HNB, BHBA, CH, FNHA, HH, NBH, ESH, FAW, BDBPC, BHONH, IBAW, WWWA (4), ACAB, WWF, WITW, AAE, HAMEZC, EBA, WB, PNW, NAW, EAB, NBAW, BWMH.

TUCKER, CHARLES EUBANK (January 12, 1896– December 25, 1975), 61st bishop of the **African Methodist Episcopal Zion Church** (AMEZ), was born in Baltimore, Maryland, the son of William A. and Elivia (Clark) Tucker. His father was a minister of the Jamaica branch of the English Baptist Union. He attended Beckford and Smith's College in Jamaica, West Indies, and graduated in 1913, apparently from the High School Department. He then began ministry in the Baptist Union. In about 1915 he moved to the United

States and joined the Philadelphia and Baltimore Conference of the AMEZ Church. He was received on credentials as a deacon, then was ordained elder on July 2, 1916.

His first appointment was at the AMEZ church in Middletown, Pennsylvania (1916–17), followed by the AMEZ church in Delta (1917–19) and the Salem AMEZ Church in Williamsport, Pennsylvania (1919). While serving these churches he attended Lincoln University for a time, then from 1917 to 1919 was a student at Temple University in Philadelphia. He also studied law privately for a while under the Hon. Charles Gogg in Pt. Pleasant, Virginia. He then transferred south to pastor Hilliard's Chapel AMEZ Church in Montgomery, Alabama from 1920 to 1922. On March 29, 1922, he married Amelia Moore, with whom he had two children.

His next appointments included the AMEZ church in Sharon, Mississippi (1922–23); Mt. Zion Church in Augusta, Georgia (1923–27); Cornish Temple AMEZ Church in Key West, Florida (1927–29); Stoner Memorial AMEZ Church in Louisville, Kentucky (1929–30); and Jones' Temple AMEZ Church in New Albany, Indiana (1930–31). He was presiding elder of the South Georgia Conference from 1923 to 1927, while pastoring at Mt. Zion, and was made presiding elder again in 1931 for the Madisonville District in Kentucky.

In 1929 Tucker had begun the practice of criminal law in Louisville and in 1931 reestablished that practice in Louisville, where he made his residence while serving as presiding elder. In April 1931, he was defense counsel for Walter Duberry, who was being tried for murder at Elizabethtown, Kentucky. During a recess of the trial Tucker was set upon by a mob and beaten on the courthouse steps because he had insisted that the jury include Blacks, something almost unheard of in those days. He would have been lynched had it not been for the arrival of the National Guard, which had been alerted for possible trouble. In 1933 Tucker was a candidate for the state assembly. He remained as presiding elder in Kentucky into the 1940s, then at some point became presiding elder of the Indianapolis-Evansville District of the Indiana Conference, where he remained until 1956.

On May 13, 1956, Tucker was consecrated as bishop, the first person in the history of the denomination to be elected bishop directly from a presiding elder's position. From 1956 to 1960 he served the Tenth Episcopal District (Cahaba, Arkansas, North Arkansas, Oklahoma, and Texas Conferences); from about 1960 to 1964 the Seventh Episcopal District (Blue Ridge, Albermarle, Florida, and South Florida Conferences); from about 1964 to 1968 the Sixth Episcopal District (Kentucky, East Tennessee, Virginia, and Indiana Conferences); and from about 1968 to 1972

the Fifth Episcopal District (Philadelphia-Baltimore, Allegheny, and Virginia Conferences).

During this time he maintained his residence in Louisville and was episcopally very active in Mississippi as well. He was a leader in the fight for racial equality as chair of the Louisville branch of C.O.R.E. He was also director of the Southern Conference Educational Fund, an organization working to end discrimination and segregation. He started the protests that led to the resignations from the Louisville Commission on Human Relations of both Harold "Pee Wee" Reese (who managed a bowling alley which did not admit Blacks) and Albert J. Grisanti (who ran a restaurant which did not admit Blacks). Apparently because of his strong anti-segregation work, Tucker was severely beaten at his home by one or more White men in July 1962. He retired in 1972.

"Bishop Charles Eubank Tucker Laid to Rest." *Star of Zion* 100 (February 5, 1976): 1.

"Bishop Tucker Funeralized." *Star of Zion* 100 (February 5, 1976): 4.

"Bishop Tucker's Assault Protested." *Star of Zion* 85 (July 26, 1962): 1.

Hoggard, J. Clinton. "Eulogistic Message of Bishop Hoggard for Bishop Charles Eubank Tucker." *Star of Zion* 100 (February 26, 1976): 1, 2.

Polk, J. W. "Tucker for Bishop." *Star of Zion* 75 (March 13, 1952): 6.

BDNM (75), *AMEZC, HAMEZC, WWCA* (38–40), *EWM*.

TUPPER, HENRY MARTIN (May 28 [or April 11], 1831–November 12, 1892), Baptist minister and founder of Shaw University, was born in Monson, Massachusetts. As a teenager he attended Monson Academy, and there was converted to the Baptist Church; his parents were not churchgoers. During the summers he earned money teaching school in New Jersey. He received his B.A. in 1859 from Amherst College in Massachusetts, and received his B.D. in 1862 from Newton Theological Seminary (now Colby College) in Waterville, Maine. He was ordained a Baptist minister and immediately entered the Union Army, serving as a soldier and regularly performing chaplain's duties as well.

In 1865 he was discharged and went to Raleigh, North Carolina as a missionary for the American Baptist Home Mission Society. He reached Raleigh with his wife (name unknown) on October 10, 1865, and on February 17, 1866, he organized a Baptist Church. As the building went up he began to hold school classes as well as religious services. A charter was granted in 1866 for what would become Shaw University. For several years he taught from 7 A.M. to 5 P.M. and usually two or three hours at night. The school received some subsidy from the American Baptist Home Mission Society and from the Peabody Fund.

In 1870 the American Baptist Home Mission was so impressed by Tupper that it decided to help him build the school into a major institution. It financed a northern speaking tour for him, who succeeded in raising the necessary $13,000 for a new school site in only six weeks. In the spring of 1878 Tupper and his students began to make bricks for the school in their own crude kiln. A philanthropist in Brattleboro, Vermont, donated $8,000 to build a separate dormitory for women, and so the school grew. The normal, college, and theological departments existed from the beginning, and by the time of Tupper's death had trained over 4,000 students as teachers and clergy. The medical department opened in 1880–81, and still later Tupper oversaw the opening of the Law School and School of Pharmacy. In 1882 he recruited **C. S. Brown** to build Waters Institute in Winton, North Carolina to serve as a feeder school for Shaw. By 1885 the university's assets were more than $200,000.

SNB, NCAB (1), *ACAB* (supp.).

TURIYASANGITANANDA, SWAMI (b. August 27, 1937), founder of the Vedanta Center, Agura, California, was born Alice McLeod in Detroit, the daughter of Solon McLeod. The sister of famous jazz pianist Eddie Farrow, she was already a renowned musician and singer herself when she met in 1962 and eventually married jazz musician John Coltrane (author of "My Favorite Things" and "Love Supreme"). He introduced her to Eastern thought and music and at this time she also learned to play the harp. They had three boys (two of them, Oran and Ravi, are also jazz musicians) and a girl. After her husband's death, of a liver disease, at age of 40 in 1967, along with the suffering, the isolation, and the ascetic practices which followed, she experienced a spiritual awakening through the revelations of the Divine which culminated in an inner initiation to *sannyas*, the renounced life, directly from the Lord.

In 1970 she started to gather the revelations in a manuscript which was eventually published (in 1977) as the *Monument Eternal* and is now used as a textbook for the center. In the same year she also encountered Swami Satchidananda, the founder of Integral Yoga International, and with a few other students journeyed with him to India and Sri Lanka, thus completing what she described as "a most important part of my Sadhana

(spiritual struggle)." Upon her return and during the following years she created a series of records which express her spiritual development, such as "Journey in Satchidananda" (1970), "Universal Consciousness" (1971) and "World Galaxy" (1972), "Illuminations" (1974) (where she uses also her new name Turiya), and "Radha-Krsna Nama Sankirtana" (1977).

In 1975 she adopted her religious name, Swami Turiyasangitananda ("Transcendental Lord's highest song of bliss"), turned spiritual teacher and founded (and since then has directed) the **Vedantic Center** in Agoura, a Los Angeles suburb. She also authored in 1981 *Endless Wisdom* to continue the work started in *Monument Eternal*, here reporting the revelations of the most recent years.

Turiyasangitananda, Swami. *Monument Eternal*. Los Angeles: Vedantic Book Press, 1977. 53 pp.
———. *Endless Wisdom*. Los Angeles: Avatar Book Institute, 1981. 240 pp.

Isotta Poggi

TURKISH ORTHODOX CHURCH. An Eastern Orthodox church. The Turkish Orthodox Church emerged out of the same crises which accompanied the fall of the Ottoman Empire and the creation of the modern state of Turkey in 1923. In 1926 an excommunicated Greek Orthodox priest, Paul Eftymios Karahissaridis, appeared, claiming not only that he had his sentence of excommunication lifted, but also that he had been secretly consecrated a bishop by Bishops Cyril of Erdek and Aagthangelos of Prinkipo. Papa Eftim, as Karahissaridis became known, moved to take advantage of the new situation of the establishment of a secular state which happened to be in the land in which the Ecumenical Patriarch, the head of the Greek Orthodox Church resided. He in effect asked for a national Orthodox church (most Orthodox bodies being organized into national churches) free of the administrative control of the Ecumenical Patriarch. He introduced a Turkish-language liturgy and with some government support worked out an arrangement with the Patriarch. In 1962 Papa Eftim retired in favor of his son Eftim II.

The Turkish Orthodox Church came to the United States in 1966 when Eftim II appointed Most Rev. Civet Kristof (born Christopher M. Cragg) the metropolitan archbishop of New York and patriarch of a Turkish Orthodox Church in America. Archbishop Kristof was a well-educated African American who claimed some Ethiopian ancestry. The previous year he had been consecrated as a bishop in the American Orthodox Catholic Church, a small independent Orthodox body, by Christopher Maria Stanley. He edited the church's periodical, which he brought with him to the Turkish Orthodox Church as *Orthodoks Mustakil.*

The Church reported fourteen congregations and six missions by the end of the decade. However, in more recent years, there has been no sign of it, and it is presumed defunct.

Kristof, Most Rev. Metropolitan. *A Brief History of the Turkish Orthodox Church in America (Patriarchial Exarchate).* New York: Turkish Orthodox Church in America, Exarchal Office, [1967].

TURNER, FRANKLIN DELTON (b. July 19, 1933), a bishop of the **Episcopal Church**, was born in Norwood, North Carolina, the son of James and Dora S. Turner. He received his B.A. in sociology and history in 1956 from Livingstone College in Salisbury, North Carolina and his S.T.B. in 1965 from Berkeley Divinity School at Yale University in New Haven, Connecticut. He also took social work courses at West Virginia University in Morgantown, West Virginia in 1961–62. He married Barbara Dickerson, with whom he has had three children.

Turner was ordained deacon in June 1965 and priest in December 1965. He was vicar of the Church of the Epiphany and chaplain of Bishop College in Dallas, Texas, in 1965–66. For several years afterwards he was rector of St. George's Episcopal Church in Washington, D.C. For eight years he was an Army and National Guard chaplain. He has also served as executive for consultative services (1972–74); national staff officer for Black Ministries (1974–1988); and assistant to the bishop for congregations in the Diocese of Pennsylvania. He gained a reputation for expertise in urban ministry and congregational development.

As national staff officer for Black Ministries he worked out of the headquarters in New York City to coordinate publications, recruit ministry candidates, organize seminars, and otherwise provide leadership in every aspect of the church's work in the Black community. On the national level he has served on the Anglican Fellowship of Prayer, the Evangelical Education Society, the Council of the College of Preachers, the Church and City Conference, and as a trustee of the Berkeley Divinity School at Yale. On October 7, 1988, he was consecrated suffragan bishop of the Diocese of Pennsylvania.

Turner, Franklin D. "St. George's Episcopal Church; An Inner City Church, Washington, D.C." *Faith and Form* 3 (April 1970): 16–19.
ECA (1989), *BDNM* (70), *AARS, HUBA, BGWC.*

TURNER, HENRY MCNEAL (February 1, 1834–May 9, 1915), 12th bishop of the **African Methodist Episcopal Church** (AME) and first Black chaplain in the U.S. Army, was born in Newberry, Abbeville County, South Carolina, the oldest child of free parents Hardy and Sarah (Green) Turner. Turner's maternal grandfather had been manumitted because he was the son of an African king, and South Carolina upheld an English law forbidding enslavement of royalty. Turner's father died while he was still young. He worked in the cotton fields and as a blacksmith apprentice, gaining some basic reading skills in secret, as an 1835 law prohibited giving Blacks an education. His mother saw his potential and about 1846 moved to Abbeville, where she hired a White woman to teach him once a week. The authorities soon put an end to the lessons.

In 1849, at age fifteen, Turner got a job in a law firm at the Abbeville Court House doing various service tasks. His already acquired learning, plus his extraordinary memory abilities, made him a favorite among the lawyers. In defiance of law, they ended up teaching him in a number of subjects. He joined the Methodist Episcopal Church, South, in 1851, and received a preaching license in 1853. He began to travel throughout the South, preaching to crowds of both Blacks and Whites. He married Eliza Ann Peacher on August 31, 1856, with whom he had four children. In 1858, during a visit to New Orleans, he dropped his membership in the Methodist Episcopal Church, South, and joined the African Methodist Episcopal Church. Bishop Daniel Payne placed him in the Baltimore Conference and assigned him to a small mission in Baltimore. While there, to shore up a weak knowledge of grammar, he began a systematic study of English and other languages, including Latin, Greek, Hebrew, and German, taking some courses at Trinity College. He was ordained deacon in 1860 and elder in 1862, at which point he was appointed to Israel AME Church in Washington, D.C.

In 1863 President Lincoln appointed Turner chaplain to the 1st Regiment, U.S. Colored Troops, the first Black chaplain in the United States armed forces. Within ten days of leaving the Army in 1865, he was reappointed by President Andrew Johnson as a regular Army chaplain and assigned to the Freedmen's Bureau in Georgia. After a short time he resigned and, assigned by Bishop **Daniel Payne** as presiding elder of Georgia, traveled all over the state organizing schools and churches. When he began, there was only one AME church in the whole state, St. Phillip's AME Church in Savannah. He was a fiery orator and is given the primary credit for making Georgia an AME Church stronghold.

He organized the first Republican state convention in Georgia, and in 1868 was elected a senator in the Georgia legislature. He was not able to serve much of his term, as Georgia ejected Blacks from legislative seats in September 1868, and did not reseat them until forced by federal troops to do so in late 1869. He finished his term in 1870. Afterwards he served in local churches around Savannah and also was a U.S. customs inspector and a government detective.

In 1876 Turner was made manager of the AME Book Concern in Philadelphia, and editor of the *Christian Recorder*. He substantially built up the publishing department and became the first person from the deep South to gain wide recognition in the AME Church. He was elected bishop in 1880, and from that point the power in the AME Church began to shift to the southern states. While maintaining primary residence in Atlanta, Georgia, he served a variety of districts of the church during his tenure. He was assigned the Sixth District, Georgia and Alabama, from 1896 to 1908.

He was most productive as a bishop, publishing a catechism, a hymnal, and books such as *The Genius and Theory of Methodist Polity* (1885) and *The Black Man's Doom* (1896). In 1889 he founded the *Southern Christian Recorder*, in 1892 the *Voice of Missions* (which he edited until 1908), and in 1901 the *Voice of the People*. He inspired the organization of the Women's Home and Foreign Missionary Society in 1896, and helped begin the *Women's Christian Recorder*. For many years he edited *The Theological Institute*. He was president of the Board of Trustees of Morris Brown University in Atlanta from 1900 to 1908. He was historiographer of the denomination from 1908 to 1912. He always encouraged Black pride, and was a pioneer in stating, "God is a Negro." His first wife died in 1889, and he married Martha DeWitt in August, 1893. His third marriage was to Harriet A. Wayman on August 16, 1900, and his fourth marriage was to Laura Pearle Lemon on December 3, 1907.

Perhaps his most lasting legacy is in relation to Africa. He was a major advocate of African colonization, often expressing the hope that Africa would be the place where Blacks could finally flourish in peace. He went to Sierra Leone, West Africa, in 1891, and established the AME Church there, then doing the same thing in Liberia and South Africa. Although colonization never achieved widespread support among American Blacks, the church work he established in Africa has grown considerably. He has been called the "Apostle of Foreign Missions," and is considered to stand next to **Richard Allen** and Daniel Payne as one of the greatest bishops of the church. On August 11, 1974, his picture was hung in the hall of the State Capitol Building of Georgia.

Ponton, M. M. *Life and Times of Henry M. Turner*. Atlanta, GA: A. B. Caldwell Publishing Co., 1917. 173 pp.

Respect Black: The Writings and Speeches of Henry McNeal Turner. 1971.

Turner, Henry McNeal. *The Black Man's Doom*. Philadelphia, PA: The James B. Rogers Printing Co., 1896. 90 pp.

———. *Devotional Services for Annual Conferences and Churches*. Atlanta, GA: 1905. 106 pp.

———. *The Genius and Theory of Methodist Polity; or, The Machinery of Methodism*. Philadelphia, PA: AME Church, 1885. 342 pp.

RLOA, DANB, MM, DAB (vol.10), *BAMEC, EWM, HNB, MBRL, GNPP, HAMEC, RAM, BNA, CH, BR, WWCR, BAW, AARS, IBAW, ERS, BW, BRBR, BPUSA, AMSC, AAP, CEAMEC, AMECMIM.*

TURNER, NAT (October 2, 1800–November 11, 1831), preacher and leader of the most famous slave revolt in the history of the South, was born in Southampton County, Virginia, the son of an enslaved woman named Nancy on the plantation of Benjamin Turner. His father ran away while he was still small. Turner worked primarily as a field hand in cotton and tobacco production and was adept with mechanical devices. At some point he learned to read and write. He became deeply religious and served as a popular exhorter on Sundays, preaching to both Blacks and Whites, probably as a Baptist. He came to believe he was destined for some great purpose and was reportedly held in some awe by his peers for his judgment and comprehension. He spent many hours in fasting and prayer and was known as "the Prophet." In 1821 he escaped for thirty days, but religious compunctions reportedly brought him back to face the punishment of his owner and the criticisms of other slaves, who felt it was foolish to return. It is not clear whether he returned because he felt it wrong to leave his duty as a slave (later changing his mind regarding that duty) or because he already felt his destiny to be that of a liberator of a people and this he could not fulfill if he thought only of his own freedom.

In 1822 his owner died and Turner was sold to a neighbor, Thomas Moore. In 1825 he baptized a White man, Ethelred T. Brantley, and that same year had a vision of Black and White spirits contending in the skies. He began to see drops of blood on ears of corn and hieroglyphics in blood on leaves. In 1828 he had a vision in which he felt God instructed him to fight for the freedom of his people. For a time he kept the developing idea of a revolt mostly to himself, and in January 1830 he was moved to the home of Joseph Travis. While slaves were not permitted to marry, Turner had a partner he considered his wife, with whom he had a number of children.

An eclipse of the sun occurred in February 1831, and many across the country interpreted the event as an omen of something momentous and imminent. Turner decided it was a sign for action, and he began to gather a group to plot the means of insurrection. There seemed to be rebellion in the air, as the previous years had been marked by Denmark Vesey's plot (1822), **David Walker**'s inflammatory pamphlet (1829), revolts in the Caribbean Islands, and the appearance of Garrison's *Liberator* in January, 1831. Measures had already been taken throughout the South to tighten security. July 4, Independence Day, was selected as the best day to act, but Turner became ill and the day was postponed.

On August 13, 1831, another unusual phenomenon happened; the sun gained a peculiar bluish-green hue, and Turner accepted this as another sign that they should wait no longer. Shortly after midnight on August 22, 1831, Turner and six other slaves began the attack in the Travis household, killing three men, a woman, and a child. The rebellion spread quickly after that, with about seventy slaves taking part in actions across Southampton County. In a period of about forty hours approximately sixty Whites, men, women, and children, were killed in the antebellum South's bloodiest rebellion. Turner's plan was to head for the county seat, Jerusalem, for munitions supplies, but the police forces were able to suppress the rebels before this could happen.

The government was not able to capture Turner immediately. He initially hid in a cave some two miles from the Travis plantation for about six weeks and then at another location for two weeks after that. Meanwhile, Turner's wife was publicly whipped and tortured. A Benjamin Phipps captured Turner by accident on October 30, 1831. He was interviewed by an attorney, Thomas Gray, November 1–3, the text of which was later published as Turner's "Confessions." When Gray tried to get Turner to admit wrongdoing, Turner replied, "Was not Christ crucified?" On November 5, Turner was tried and sentenced to death by hanging, which was carried out on November 11, in Jerusalem (now called Courtland). Seventeen co-conspirators had already been hanged.

In the aftermath of the insurrection, measures for the control of Blacks were further intensified. Hundreds were arrested and dozens were killed, either in retaliation for Turner or in response to additional uprisings inspired by Turner. Religious activity among the slaves became more suspect. The South's fear of the influence of abolitionists in the North intensified, and any sentiments within the South for manumission were almost completely suppressed. The White population tended to think only of the violence done by Turner's group, ignoring the previously existing violence routinized by the slave system. For many Blacks, Turner became a symbol of the unquenchable human spirit struggling to assert itself against overwhelming odds. In later years, beginning with William Styron's historical novel, *The Confessions of Nat Turner* (1967), there has been an ongoing controversy over the assessment of Turner's character and deeds.

Aptheker, Herbert. *Nat Turner's Slave Rebellion*. New York: Humanities Press, 1966. 152 pp.

Clarke, John Henrik, ed. *William Styron's Nat Turner: Ten Black Writers Respond*. Boston, MA: Beacon Press, 1968. 120 pp.

Drewry, William Sydney. *The Southampton Insurrection*. Washington, DC: The Neale Co., 1900. 201 pp.

Duff, John B. and Peter M. Mitchell, eds. *The Nat Turner Rebellion: The Historical Event and the Modern Controversy*. New York: Harper & Row, 1971. 246 pp.

Foner, Eric, comp. *Nat Turner*. Englewood Cliffs, NJ: Prentice-Hall, 1971. 184 pp.

Gray, Thomas R. *The Confessions of Nat Turner*. Baltimore, MD: Lucas and Deaver, Printers, for T. R. Gray, 1831. 23 pp.

Johnson, Frank Roy. *The Nat Turner Slave Insurrection*. Murfreesboro, NC: Johnson Publishing Co., 1966. 248 pp.

Oates, Stephen B. *The Fires of Jubilee: Nat Turner's Fierce Rebellion*. New York: Harper & Row, 1975. 187 pp.

Styron, William. *The Confessions of Nat Turner*. New York: Random House, 1967. 428 pp. (historical novel)

Tragle, Henry Irving, comp. *The Southampton Slave Revolt of 1831: A Compilation of Source Material*. Amherst, MA: University of Massachusetts Press, 1971. 489 pp.

Turner, Lucy Mae. "The Family of Nat Turner, 1831–1954." *Negro History Bulletin* 18 (March-April 1955): 127–146.

PP, TSW, IBAW, WITW, EBA, HNB, AAE, MM, EAB, DANB, DAB, MBRL, GNPP, BMIC, HNRA, CH, BHBA, NBH, ESH, BAW, IBAWCB, BWA.

TURNER, THOMAS WYATT (November 16, 1877– April 21, 1978), founder of the **Federated Colored Catholics of the United States**, was born in Hughesville, Maryland, the son of Linnie Gross and Eli Turner. He was baptized in the **Roman Catholic**

Church and raised as a Catholic. He attended an Episcopal high school, and was offered a college scholarship if he would convert, but he chose to attend Howard University instead and majored in biology. Following his graduation he entered Catholic University but had to drop out from lack of funds. He taught at Tuskegee Institute for a brief time and settled down as a high school teacher in Baltimore. However, in his leisure time he pursued his graduate studies. He completed his M.S. at Howard in 1905. In 1907 he married Laura Elaine Miller. He was an early member of the N.A.A.C.P. and helped organize its Baltimore chapter. In 1913 Turner joined the staff of Howard University as an instructor in biology. Over the next eight years, he was finally able to complete his Ph.D. from Cornell University in 1921. Two years later he moved to Hampton Institute as the first chairman of the biology department. He stayed at Hampton until his retirement in 1945.

As a biologist, Turner became the first African American named as a research cytologist with the U.S. Department of Agriculture. He also worked for many years promoting the teachings of biology in the public schools. But Turner's contributions in biology are overshadowed by his work as a layman among African American Catholics. While pursuing his career as a biologist, he used the opportunities to travel and to attend scientific conventions to organize Black Catholics around the country.

Very soon after his appointment at Howard, he began to write articles on the problem of racial segregation in the church. The problem became acute during World War I when Black Catholic soldiers had no equivalent of the YMCA to care for their needs. He organized the Committee Against the Extension of Race Prejudice in the Church (later the Committee for the Advancement of Colored Catholics) which brought the concern to the National Catholic War Council, who soon met the need. In 1919, an era of unrest marked by a number of lynchings of African American men and violent racial riots, Turner authored a 20–page statement in the name of the committee calling the Church's hierarchy to the many needs of its African American members. It pointed out that Black people were excluded from the conferences in which the church made plans for ministry on their behalf.

The lack of response to the committee's document led to its more formal organization as the Federated Colored Catholics of the United States. The first convention met in 1925. Turner led the organization through the decade into the early 1930s. In 1932 Turner came into sharp conflict with two White priests, William Markoe and John LaFarge, both of whom wanted to move the federation away from concerns of African American rights into an interracial fellowship. The issue became a battle for Black lay control of the organization. Turner cut off federation support for the magazine published by Markoe, which had formerly been the federation's organ but which had been renamed *Interracial Review*. Turner was deposed from the presidency of the federation, and the organization split. Turner reorganized his support and continued to lead those who supported him. He addressed their 1933 convention on the topic "Does the Roman Catholic Church Need a National Federation of Colored Communicants?" However, what life remained in the organization was removed toward the end of the year when Turner was forced to resign the presidency due to the state of his health. While it continued to meet through the early 1950s, it was never again an effective voice for its constituency. The church entered an era of promoting the cause of interracialism. Turner died in Washington, D.C., shortly after his 101st birthday.

Davis, Cyprian. The *History of Black Catholics in the United States*. New York: Crossroad, 1992. 347 pp.

Nickels, Marilyn Wenzke. *Black Catholic Protest and the Federated Colored Catholics, 1917–1933: Three Perspectives on Racial Justice*. New York: Garland Publishing, 1988. 325 pp.

TURNER COLLEGE. An **African Methodist Episcopal Church** (AME) school. Turner College originated in the Tennessee Conference of the AME Church, which in 1895 passed a resolution to found a school. Bishop **Henry McNeal Turner** was the presiding bishop in the state at the time and the senior bishop in the church. The school was chartered in 1896 as the Turner Normal and Industrial Institute and later assumed the name Turner College. The school suffered through the Depression, and in 1934, after many years at Shelbyville, Tennessee, was forced to move to Memphis. In its new location, it used the facilities of St. Andrew's Church, but was able to survive only one more year and closed in 1935.

Wright, R. R. *The Encyclopedia of the African Methodist Episcopal Church*. Philadelphia, PA: Book Concern of the AME Church, 1947. 688 pp.

TURNER THEOLOGICAL SEMINARY. An **African Methodist Episcopal Church** (AME) school. Turner Theological Seminary began in 1894 as the theological department of **Morris Brown College** in

Atlanta, Georgia. In 1900 it was renamed for Bishop **Henry McNeal Turner**, who served as bishop in Georgia beginning in 1896 and who had become the church's senior bishop. Since 1957, the school has been an integral part of the **Interdenominational Theological Center**.

Wright, R. R. *The Encyclopedia of the African Methodist Episcopal Church*. Philadelphia, PA: Book Concern of the AME Church, 1947. 688 pp.

TURPIN, JOSEPH MARCEL (January 1, 1887–March 17, 1943) was one of the original bishops of the **Pentecostal Assemblies of the World**. He was born in Denton, Maryland. While in his youth, during the early days of Pentecostalism, he experienced salvation in a Pentecostal meeting, and he and his wife Ruth came to accept its belief in the baptism of the Holy Spirit. He settled in Baltimore, Maryland, founded the First Apostolic Church, and around 1919 affiliated with the Assemblies, at a time when it was fully integrated and the majority of ministers and members were White. However, the Assemblies was in the midst of the period of rapid organizational change which began with its acceptance of the non-Trinitarian Jesus Only theology in 1915 and continued through its loss of the majority of White members in 1924 and the establishment of an episcopacy in 1925. In 1920 he was listed as one of the church's general elders. At the time he was located in Baltimore, Maryland.

In 1923, the Assemblies reorganized under the leadership of an eight-member board of presbyters, among whom was Turpin. This was part of an attempt to head off the division of the Assemblies. In 1924 in a further attempt to head off the division, the church was reorganized into two districts, an Eastern district with most of the Black members and the Eastern with most of the White. Each district was to have its own offices, officers, and periodical. Turpin was chosen as one of the board of presbyters to lead the Eastern District. Within hours of the formation of the two districts, the White leaders had in fact withdrawn and formed the Pentecostal Ministerial Alliance. While still an integrated organization, it was now overwhelmingly Black.

In 1925 the church dropped the district structure and adopt an episcopal form of government. Five men were elected bishops, including **Garfield T. Haywood**, the acknowledged leader of the denomination, **A. R. Schooler**, A. F. Varnell, G. B. Rowe (a White man), and Turpin. Earlier, he and Schooler had founded the Eastern District Council which included the leaders and churches

on the East Coast and became a significant voice within the Assemblies.

In 1931 the Assemblies went through a period of turmoil following the death of Haywood. At their August meeting, an offer was made to unite with the predominantly White Pentecostal Ministerial Alliance. Many, including Turpin, wanted the merger. The PAW split into those who merged into what was called the Pentecostal Assemblies of Jesus Christ and those opposed to the merger who reorganized yet again as the continuing Pentecostal Assemblies of the World. Turpin appeared at the 1932 PAW meeting to propose a means by which it and the new Pentecostal Assemblies of Jesus Christ could reunite. The plan failed and Turpin remained with the Pentecostal Assemblies of Jesus Christ through the mid-1930s.

While a facade of interracial harmony existed in the Pentecostal Assemblies of Jesus Christ, from the time of its formation there had been a number of racial incidents. These culminated in 1937 when the White leaders moved to have the annual convention meet in Tulsa, Oklahoma, far enough South that the Black brethren would not be welcome. They were asked to not attend and wait out a year. Overwhelmingly, the Black members simply left. Many returned to the PAW. Turpin became an independent bishop. He had through the years remained pastor of the church he had founded in Baltimore. During the last years of his life he emerged in 1941 as the consecrator of James Thomas Morris as leader of the **Highway Church of Christ**.

Golder, Morris E. *The Bishops of the Pentecostal Assemblies of the World*. Indianapolis, IN: The Author, 1980. 69 pp.

———. *History of the Pentecostal Assemblies of the World*. Indianapolis, IN: The Author, 1973. 195 pp.

TYREE, EVANS (August 19, 1854–1921), 26th bishop of the **African Methodist Episcopal Church** (AME), was born into slavery in Tennessee, one of twelve children in the family of Harry and Winifred Tyree. He was converted in 1866 at Carthage and joined the Methodist Episcopal Church, South. He later joined the AME Church, for which he was licensed to preach in 1969. On January 12, 1871, he married Ellen Tompkins, with whom he had at least one child. He joined the Tennessee Annual Conference in 1872, was ordained deacon in 1875 and elder in 1876.

He began attending school in 1876 and received about ten years of schooling in all, mainly at Central Tennessee College (Walden University), where he received a B.A. degree, and Meharry Medical College in Nashville, where he received an M.D. degree. His pastorates included the Santa Fe Mission (1874–77); Alexander Mission (1872–74); Salem Station (1877–79); Franklin Station (1879–81); Payne Chapel AME Church (1881–85); Pulaski (1885–86); presiding elder (1886–87); St. Paul Chapel AME Church (1887–91); St. Paul AME Church in Columbia, Tennessee (1891–92); Quinn Chapel AME Church in Louisville, Kentucky (1892–97); and St. John AME Church in Nashville, Tennessee (1897–1900).

On the basis of his successful church ministries, Tyree was elected bishop and then consecrated on May 23, 1900. He was assigned to the Eighth Episcopal District (Mississippi and Arkansas) from 1900 to 1904, followed by the Tenth Episcopal District (Texas and Oklahoma) from 1904 to 1908; Texas from 1908 to 1912; First Episcopal District (Philadelphia, New Jersey, New England, and New York) from 1912 to 1920; and the Eighth Episcopal District (Mississippi) from 1920 to 1921.

He was a delegate to the World Methodist Conference in London in 1901. He served as chair of the Publications Board and was also chair of the General Conference Commission of 1916. Having grown up in the South he found it difficult to associate freely with White people and sometimes sent a substitute speaker to meetings where there would be many Whites. He was one of three AME bishops holding medical degrees in his generation. There are Tyree Halls at both Campbell College in Buies Creek, North Carolina, and Shorter College in North Little Rock, Arkansas. There are churches named for him in Philadelphia, Pennsylvania, Abilene, Texas, and Dumas, Arkansas.

WWAM, BAMEC, HAMEC, EWM, CEAMEC, WWWA (4), *WWCR.*

"I wonder if this is the world I was born in! For twenty years I was a slave on these streets. It was a penitentiary offense to educate a Negro. I have seen my fellow servants whipped for trying to learn; but, today, here I am on this great avenue in this great city with the bishops and elders and people of the Methodist Episcopal Church speaking at the breaking of ground where a building is to be erected for the education of my people. I wonder if this is the world I was born in!"

Rev. Emperor Williams, Trustee
New Orleans University
(now Dillard University)
1873

U

UNCLES, CHARLES JOSEPH (November 6, 1859–July 20, 1933), a pioneer African American priest of the **Roman Catholic Church**, was born in Baltimore, Maryland. His family was brought into an active relation with the church in the 1870s and Uncles was baptized in 1875 as a sixteen-year-old youth. He had earlier attended catechism classes conducted by the **Oblate Sisters of Providence**, who had opened work in the city. In 1878 he was confirmed and that same year entered Baltimore Normal School. Upon graduation he became a school teacher.

Uncles attended church at St. Francis Xavier Church, whose oversight was under the care of St. Joseph's Society, and through their encouragement he found a vocation as a priest. In 1883 he applied for admission to St. Hyacinthe's College in Quebec, there being no American Catholic seminary which would admit him. He graduated in 1888 at the head of his class. He then returned to Baltimore to the new Josephite seminary. In 1891 he became the first African American ordained in the United States (the few others previously having been ordained abroad). He was assigned to teach at the Epiphany Apostolic College, the Josephite minor seminary at Walbrook, Maryland. He taught Latin, Greek, and English. Except for one year as a missionary in the South, he taught at Epiphany for the rest of his life.

Not a writer, Uncles's major literary contribution was a lengthy article which appeared in *Colored Harvest* in 1909 entitled "The Catholic Church and the Negro," an apology for the ideals of the church over against the reality of the prejudice many felt.

In 1916 Uncles moved with the staff of the college to its new facilities in Newburgh, New York. He is remembered for attempting to keep the homely atmosphere that had pervaded the old college in its new expanded facilities. He lived there until his death in 1933.

Foley, A. S. *God's Men of Color: The Colored Catholic Priests of the United States, 1854–1954.* New York: Farrar, Straus & Co., 1955. 322 pp. Rept.: New York: Arno Press, 1969. 322 pp.

Ochs, Stephen J. *Desegregating the Altar: The Josephites and the Struggle for Black Priests, 1871–1960.* Baton Rouge, LA: Louisiana State University Press, 1990. 500 pp.

UNIFICATION ASSOCIATION OF CHRISTIAN SABBATH KEEPERS. Christian Adventist denomination. The Unification Association of Christian Sabbath Keepers was founded in 1956 as a movement to unite African Americans who observed the Sabbath (i.e., worshipped on Saturday rather than Sunday.) In 1941 Thomas I. C. Hughes, a former minister of the **Seventh-day Adventist Church**, has become pastor of the Advent Sabbath Church in New York City. Hughes wished to expand his congregation's outreach and in 1956 joined with the New York United Sabbath Day Advent Church to form the association. Having already founded missionary work in the West Indies, Hughes brought the missions into the association. It soon grew with the addition of the Believers in the Commandments of God.

The association's beliefs are similar to those of the Seventh-day Adventist Church. It is organized congregationally. The leading officer of the association is designated as bishop, but there is no assignment of traditional episcopal powers. Though the American work had dwindled to a single congregation in Elizabeth, New Jersey, member congregations can now be found in Africa and several West Indian islands.

Melton, J. Gordon. *Encyclopedia of American Religions.* Detroit, MI: Gale Research Company, 3rd edition, 1989. 1100 pp.

UNIFICATION CHURCH. The Unification Church (UC), is one of several so-called new religions which became prominent in the United States in the 1970s. It was founded in Korea in 1956 by the Rev. Sun Myung Moon and brought to the United States later in the decade. Like most of the new religious movements (NRMs) which became prominent during the 1970s, it appealed primarily to White, middle-class youth in the West. However, during the 1980s, the UC won converts in several African countries, especially Zaire, and actively engaged in ministerial outreach programs among Black clergy in the U.S. These initiatives generated controversy both within the UC and the Black religious community.

The UC sent its first missionaries to Africa in 1975. Although the church committed the bulk of its resources elsewhere, it did support mission activities in nearly all sub-Saharan countries. The missions to Zambia and Zaire were early successes. Missionaries also established viable bases in the Central African Republic and Ivory Coast. Still, their efforts had little impact outside local settings until, in 1987, a young Black Zimbabwean member gained recognition as the "returning resurrection" of Rev. Moon's deceased second son. Understood to have been specially prepared for his embodiment, the Zimbabwean's inhouse U.S. revival meetings and later apostasy created what one report referred to as a "theological uproar" within the UC.

In the U.S., the UC-funded Coalition for Religious Freedom (CRF) gained access to Black clergy who were predisposed to see Rev. Moon as a fellow victim of racial persecution. Several thousand Black clergy also participated in the UC's Interdenominational Conferences for Clergy (ICC) and in its CAUSA Ministerial Alliance. These meetings were controversial, in part, due to the involvement of high-profile 'celebrities.' Former Black Panther turned evangelical Christian Eldredge Cleaver, in a widely circulated statement, asserted that he'd "rather be with the littlest Moonie than with Billy Graham." More troublesome were the appearances at UC-sponsored meetings of prominent civil rights veterans **Wyatt Walker**, **Ralph D. Abernathy**, **Joseph Lowery**, and **James Bevel**—all once close associates of **Martin Luther King, Jr.** and strategists for the **Southern Christian Leadership Conference**. Some complained of a UC-influenced "rightward" shift among Black clergy. Others suggested that they had been "bought" off, citing Shaw Divinity School's 1985 acceptance of a reported $60,000 grant from the UC and its

subsequent award of an honorary doctorate to Rev. Moon. A final source of strain in the UC's dealings with the Black community was its practice of interracial marriage. With a reference to the Peoples Temple, under whose legacy all NRMs labored during the early 1980s, clergy opponents and even a few supporters complained that Black participation in UC mass marriages amounted to "racial suicide."

Murray, Virgie W. "Young Black College Students Work in Unification Church." *Los Angeles Sentinel* (August 26, 1976).

Michael L. Mickler

UNION AMERICAN METHODIST EPISCOPAL CHURCH. A Methodist church. The Union American Methodist Episcopal Church is one of two denominations which grew out of the movement led by **Peter Spencer** and William Anderson. They formed the African Union (also called the Union Church of Africans) in Wilmington, Delaware, in 1813. At some point, a schism occurred in the African Union Church. According to some accounts, around 1816, 30 congregations of the Union Church of Africans separated themselves from the other 24 congregations, and for a number of years the two groups existed side by side, each using the same name. Other accounts say the schism occurred in 1850, after Spencer's death. In any case, by the 1850s, two factions existed. In 1865, one faction united with the First Colored Methodist Protestant Church to become the **African Union Colored First Methodist Protestant Church**. That same year, the other group incorporated under the name African Union American Methodist Episcopal Church in the United States of America and Elsewhere (now the Union American Methodist Episcopal Church).

The church is Methodist in doctrine and episcopal in polity. There are two bishops who head four districts. The general conference meets quadrennially. The church not only allows but encourages female minsters. Headquarters of the church is in Camden, New Jersey. The church is led by Bishops Earl L. Huff and George W. Poindexter. The *Union Messenger* is its periodical. In 1990 the church had 55 congregations and over 12,000 members.

Baldwin, Lewis V. *The Mark of a Man: Peter Spencer and the American Union Methodist Tradition.* Lanham, MD: University Press of America, 1987. 87 pp.

UNION OF BLACK EPISCOPALIANS. An **Episcopal Church** group. The Union of Black Episcopalians was formed in 1968 as the Union of Black Clergy and Laity. It was one of a series of caucuses which were formed at the end of the 1960s in all of the major Christian denominations with a large Black minority membership. Among its early organizers were members of the National Committee of Negro Churchmen (now the **National Conference of Black Churchmen**), including Bishop **John M. Burgess**, and Revs. Kenneth Hughes, **Quinland R. Gordon**, Leon Modeste, Paul M. Washington, and Nathan Wright. The committee had tried to make a positive response to the issue of Black economic power raised by Stokely Carmichael.

The Union developed chapters across the church wherever there was a concentration of African American members. By the end of the 1980s, it had 20 chapters and ten interest groups which operate at the diocesan level. It encourages Black church members to participate in the total life of the church and work to shape its direction. It also targets lingering racism with the goal of eradicating it totally. It is headquartered in Washington, D.C.

Payne, Wardell J., ed. *Directory of African American Religious Bodies: A Compendium by the Howard University School of Divinity.* Washington, DC: Howard University Press, 1991. 363 pp.

UNITED AMERICAN FREE WILL BAPTIST CHURCH. A Baptist body. The Free Will Baptists began in North Carolina in the decades prior to the Revolutionary War. By the time of the Civil War, they had spread across the South and both free Blacks and slaves had become members. After the war, some African Americans began to organize separate congregations, among the first being the Shady Grove Free Will Baptist Church in Snow Hill, Greene County, North Carolina, formed in 1867. Inspired by this church, others formed. Most of these groups had no building and had to meet in what were called brush arbors. In 1870 an annual conference was created, the beginning of the United American Free Will Baptist Church, though the association was not incorporated until 1887. Through the natural process of growth, more congregations and other annual conferences were formed, and in 1901 a general conference was established.

The church follows a traditional Free Baptist position that emphasizes the common affirmations of Protestant Christianity such as the Trinity, the divinity of Christ, and salvation by faith. Like its White counterpart, it assumes an Armenian perspective on issues of salvation, emphasizing the free grace and salvation of God to all who will repent and in faith accept Christ. The church is opposed to traditional Calvinist emphases on election and predestination. The church is organized on a congregational system.

Headquarters of the church is in Kingston, North Carolina. The church sponsors Kingston College. In the mid-1970s the church reported 35,000 members in approximately 300 churches, a steep decline from 1952 when 826 churches and 100,000 members were reported to the *Yearbook of American Churches*.

UNITED BLACK CHRISTIANS (UBC). A **United Church of Christ** organization. United Black Christians was founded in 1970 as United Black Churchmen. The organization grew out of the desire of the Black ministers of the United Church of Christ, who in 1967 had formed themselves as the **Ministers for Racial and Social Justice**, to create a similar organization that would include the laity of the church. Shortly thereafter it was recognized as an official special interest group of the United Church of Christ for voicing concerns for the Black membership (approximately 50,000 strong). It includes within it the UBC Black Women's Caucus, the Black Seminary Student Network, and the Black Youth and Young Caucus.

UBC involves itself with all programs of the church which are deemed to have a direct impact upon the African American community. It also works closely with the Ministers for Racial and Social Justice and meets together with it every two years in a national convention. Headquarters is in Chicago, Illinois.

Payne, Wardell J., ed. *Directory of African American Religious Bodies: A Compendium by the Howard University School of Divinity.* Washington, DC: Howard University Press, 1991. 363 pp.

UNITED BLACK CHURCH APPEAL. An ecumenical organization. Growing out of the expressed need for economic empowerment of the African American community, in 1980 a group of Black church leaders from different denominations and independent congregations organized to provide leadership for the cause of community liberation and the raising of resources to fund empowering activities. The Appeal is based in part on a perceived abdication of leadership by pastors and other church leaders in guiding the future of the African American community, and the belief that ministers should reclaim that role.

The Appeal developed early programs to fight drugs, especially their spread among Black youth, and to distribute food to needy families, both in the United States and in Puerto Rico, Mexico, South America, and Africa. More recently it has launched an African American museum project dedicated to preserving the history of the Black church. Its headquarters is in the Bronx, New York. It holds an annual Black Empowerment and Leadership Conference.

Payne, Wardell J., ed. *Directory of African American Religious Bodies: A Compendium by the Howard University School of Divinity.* Washington, DC: Howard University Press, 1991. 363 pp.

UNITED CHRISTIAN COLLEGE. An **Original United Holy Church International** school. Even prior to World War I, the leaders of the **United Holy Church of America** planned for a school where ministers could be trained. A department of education was established, money was raised, and a plot of land purchased. However, during the war, plans were postponed, and the plot of land sold. It was not until 1936 that the idea of the school was revived. At the general convocation that year, a new board was constituted. It eventually found land in Goldsboro, North Carolina. It took several years and the full effort of the church to raise the money to construct the needed building, but in 1944 the school opened.

In 1977 the United Holy Church of America experienced a schism in which the Southern District Convocation was removed from the church. The school being in North Carolina went with the new body which reorganized in June 1977 as the Original United Holy Church of the World (since 1980, Original United Holy Church International).

Fisher, H. L. *The History of the United Holy Church of America, Inc.* The Author, n.d. 39 pp.
Jones, Charles Edwin. *Black Holiness: A Guide to the Study of Black Participation in Wesleyan Holiness and Glossolalic Pentecostal Movements.* Metuchen, NJ: American Theological Library Association/Scarecrow Press, 1987. 388 pp.

UNITED CHURCH AND SCIENCE OF LIVING INSTITUTE. A New Thought metaphysical church. The United Church and Science of Living Institute is a major thrust of New Thought in the African American community. It was founded in 1966 by former Baptist minister Rev. Frederick Eikerenkoetter II, who is more popularly known as Rev. Ike. Dedicated to evangelism and faith healing, he became influenced by New Thought soon after his graduation in Chicago, in 1956, from the American Bible School.

His teachings emphasize the prosperity theme typical of New Thought, the use of the power of the mind (developed through certain visualization techniques), the elimination of selfish attitudes and the focusing on God as the real man in the self who can insure prosperity.

Rev. Eikerenkoetter II is heard on over 89 radio and 22 television stations in the Eastern half of the country and in Hawaii. The Church publishes the periodical *Action.* There are two congregations, in New York and in Boston, but a large number of followers around the United States.

Frederick Eikerenkoetter. *Health, Happiness and Prosperity for You!* New York: Science of Living Publications, 1982.
Melton, J. Gordon. *Encyclopedia of American Religion.* 3rd ed. Detroit: Gale Research, Inc., 1989. 1102 pp.

Isotta Poggi

UNITED CHURCH OF CHRIST. The United Church of Christ (UCC) was created in 1957 by the union of Congregational Christian Churches and the Evangelical and Reformed Church. This union brought together churches of the "free church tradition," with roots in England, with those of a more presbyterial and reformed tradition having roots in Germany. It has been said that if one were predicting a union at the beginning of the twentieth century, one would not have selected these two bodies.

Of even more interest, it should be noted that both of these church bodies had experienced unions in the 1930s. The Congregational churches united with the Christian churches in 1931, resulting in the denomination known as Congregational Christian Churches (CC); the Evangelical Church united with the Reformed Church in 1936 and became known as the Evangelical and Reformed Church (E & R).

The UCC embodies both the free church, English/ early New England, and the German Evangelical/

Reformed traditions. It is trinitarian in belief and looks to the scripture as a source of authority. Though it functions within the framework of a national constitution it nonetheless is held together by the principle of "covenant" freely entered into by local churches. Each local church (about 6,000) is autonomous, as well as each of the 37 conferences (regional judicatories). Just as people covenant with one another to create local churches under the guidance of the Holy Spirit, so too do local churches covenant to create associations (mid-level judicatories which authorize ordination, clergy standing and recognition of local churches) and conferences (which create boundaries for associations, function as placement agencies for clergy and act as fiscal agents. They also are the link to the national instrumentalities).

The conferences elect delegates apportioned according to membership to the General Synod, which meets every two years. The chief officers of the Synod and the United Church of Christ are President, Secretary and Treasurer/Director of Finance. These officers are elected by the General Synod. The General Synod enacts policies which govern itself, the national program, and mission and service agencies. It also determines the ecumenical policies which include the UCC relationships with other denominations, the National Council of Churches of Christ, World Council of Churches, and other national and worldwide bodies. It addresses issues which face the nation and commends its actions to local churches, associations and conferences for their study.

African Americans and the UCC. The membership of the United Church of Christ is slightly more than 1.6 million members. African Americans constitute about three percent of that membership and are distributed among approximately three hundred churches.

We can trace African Americans' involvement in the UCC to a period before 1776. This involvement flows through the Congregational Christian tradition. The small numbers were a result of African American demographics in New England. There were, however, five clergy who served during the late eighteenth century. They were **Lemuel Haynes**, **Charles B. Ray**, **James W. C. Pennington**, **Amos G. Beman**, and **Samuel Ringgold Ward**. As there were no African American Congregational churches these men served primarily White congregations.

The career of the first recorded African American Congregational minister's career, Lemuel Haynes (1753–1833) is worth noting. Haynes served as a minuteman prior to the Revolutionary War, volunteered for service during that war and fought in the historic battle at Fort Ticonderoga in 1776. According to **Lawrence N. Jones**, Haynes was ordained in Torrington, Connecticut, on November 9, 1785. For three years he was an itinerant preacher before accepting a call to Rutland, Vermont, in 1788 and serving there until 1818. Subsequently, he served congregations in Manchester, New Hampshire (1819–22), and Granville, New York (1822–31). His sermons revealed careful theological scholarship, exegetical precision, and fervent evangelicalism. He passed away in 1833.

Charles B. Ray's service is also worthy of note. He served the Bethesda Church in New York City for twenty years prior to the Civil War. He was equally known for his activities in pursuit of racial justice and as an energetic participant in the anti-slavery movement. When the American Missionary Association was organized in 1846, Ray became a member of its executive committee and a city missionary under the auspices of the association. The breadth of his involvement included serving as secretary of the Nominating Committee of the Liberal Party Convention in Buffalo, New York, in 1844, and having been a participant in the "first national Black convention" called by Richard Allen in 1830 in Philadelphia.

These two men reflect the caliber of leadership provided by African Americans in early New England and New York Congregationalism.

Lawrence N. Jones points to several reasons why there was not greater African American participation in locations where early Congregationalism flourished. Let me identify three:

> The first was that the population pool of African Americans was quite small in comparison to the South.
>
> The second was the intellectual and experiential dimensions of Puritan religion which virtually assured that African Americans could not qualify for full membership.
>
> Third and perhaps the most damning was the prejudiced attitudes and customs of Whites with respect to African Americans, notwithstanding that in both New England and New York there existed passionate, though small, anti-slavery sentiment. The self respect of African Americans created in them an inability to reconcile the Christian

message with the practice of Christians some of whom were or had been their masters.

The Amistad Event. No event so galvanized many within the Congregational churches than that of the band of 53 Africans from the Mendi region of Sierra Leone when they revolted and seized command of the ship called Amistad. The ship was bound for the New World where these men, women and children would be sold. They had been kidnapped in 1839 while doing their farm work, resting in their homes or strolling along a road. With a stopover in Cuba, the ultimate destination was the colonies of the new world.

The revolt was led by a man named Cinque, acting on the Mendi tradition of freedom and democracy. The captain, commanding under a Spanish flag, was killed. The leaders of the revolt ordered two of the crewmen who survived to turn the ship towards Africa. Sailing eastward by day and northwest by night, the ship was seized off the coast of Long Island and the Africans arrested on charges of mutiny in August of 1839. Cinque never relented and encouraged his people to revolt against the new enslavers. Historian Diana McCain notes, "The Amistad incident raised fundamental moral, social legal, religious (theological), diplomatic, and political questions and had an impact upon American history. . . ."

Indeed, the event impacted the people of the churches. Many of the members, along with others, committed to the abolition of slavery, formed the Amistad Committee in September 1839. They embraced the case which ultimately found its way to the United States Supreme Court. The case was argued by Roger Sherman Baldwin and John Quincy Adams, President of the United States from 1824 to 1828. The Court rendered its decision on March 9, 1841, which completely vindicated the Amistad Africans. They were freed and were able to return to Sierra Leone.

Before sailing they were housed and boarded by the people of Farmington, Connecticut, most of whom were members of the Congregational Church. This experience, however, emboldened the abolitionists. The Amistad Committee merged with the Union Missionary Society in 1841. The society's first officers were the Rev. James W. C. Pennington of Hartford and the Rev. Amos Beman of New Haven, both freedmen and active abolitionists.

The **American Missionary Association** became the successor body of the Union Society in 1846. The association became one of the most powerful abolitionist organizations in the nation. It took on the task of educating millions of African Americans. It established several hundred elementary and secondary schools. Many of the major institutions of higher education established by the association continue to this day. Among them are Talladega College, Fisk University, LeMoyne-Owen College, Dillard University, Tougaloo College, Huston-Tillotson College, Berea College, Hampton University, and Atlanta University. The United Church of Christ continues to support all but the last three of these schools. These schools have produced major leaders of the African American community. They have produced clergy and denominational leaders in a continuous stream, even up to the present. The American Missionary Association continues under the umbrella of the United Church Board for Homeland Ministries.

The Afro-Christian Influence. Lawrence Jones reports, "it was inevitable that African Americans would be touched by the evangelical zeal of the Christian Church." The Christian churches, which united with the Congregational churches in 1931, developed out of the Cane Ridge Revivals of 1801. African Americans, both slave and free, became members of these Christian churches. There is no evidence, according to Jones, that they occupied official positions or exercised significant influence.

Following the Civil War, African American members broke from the Whites in the Christian Churches and established their own churches. They wanted to avoid White domination. By 1867 there were enough churches to organize the Western Colored Christian Conference. When the roll was called, it included twelve ministers and twenty churches. Within a decade, however, the number of conferences had grown to three: the North Carolina Colored Christian Conference (1866), the Eastern Atlantic Colored Christian Conference (1874), and the Virginia Colored Christian Conference (1873). Together they represented forty-one ministers and fifty-one churches. They (churches and clergy) organized the Afro-American Christian Convention in 1892, which was held in New Bern, North Carolina. By the 1895 convention they consisted of sixty-nine churches, thirty-three ministers, and eighteen licentiates. These churches and ministers were then grouped into five conferences, which reported a total membership of six thousand. In 1908 the Black Methodist Protestants joined the Afro Christian Convention. The Afro Christian Convention pioneered in the development of a school in Franklinton, North Carolina in 1878, and in 1891 the school was incorporated as Franklinton Christian College. Though it never became a full-fledged college, it nevertheless trained many clergy and laypersons, totally supported by the people of the churches. This college center became a rallying center for the Afro Christian Churches. The denomination also developed a women's department and foreign mission work in Monrovia, Liberia, and British Ghiana.

As one reviews the history of the Afro Christians, it is a wonder that they were willing to become a part of the union in 1931 between the Congregational churches and the Christian churches (White). That they did subscribe to the union added immeasurably to what is now the strength of the African American richness in the UCC. Of the approximately three hundred plus churches in the UCC, nearly two hundred can trace their origins to the Afro Christians principally located in Virginia and North Carolina.

The African American Heritage and the UCC. The UCC is one of the smaller old line/mainstream churches. Since the arrival of the Pilgrims in 1620 and the German immigrants into Pennsylvania and the Central Great Lakes Region, it has emphasized the importance of covenant, a people covenanting with God and with one another. The members have steadfastly believed that Jesus Christ was not only the head and "unseen presence" of the whole church, but of every local church. They have taken seriously the words of John Robinson, a father of British Congregationalism, that "the Lord always hath more truth and light to break forth out of his Holy word." They also relied more on the devoted leaders of irenic spirit and informed piety. With gentle, but persuasive, power they went about their tasks as ministers and teachers among the people as they guided the churches. As this was true among Whites, it was equally true among African Americans. Below is a partial list of the clergy who have influenced the early and present life of the UCC, in addition to those mentioned earlier in the text.

The Rev. **George W. Moore**, graduate of Fisk (about 1880), was the first Secretary for the South of the Home Missions Board for work among Negroes. He became a trustee of Fisk and remained on the board for several decades.

The Rev. **Henry Hugh Proctor**, long-time pastor of First Congregational Church, Atlanta, and of the Nazareen Congregational Church in Brooklyn, New York. Early proponent of "seven day a week church," an idea which spread across the country. Assistant moderator of the General Council of Congregational Churches in 1904.

The Rev. **Alfred E. Lawless, Jr.**, a graduate of Straight University (now Dillard) and pastor of Beacher Church in New Orleans, was Moore's successor. Assistant moderator, General Council of Congregational Churches, 1915.

The Rev. **Harold M. Kingsley**, a graduate of Talladega College and Yale. Reviver and founder of churches, sociologist on urban issues, was field secretary in the South under Moore and Lawless, and the first secretary of the Home Missions Board's work among Negroes in the North. Assistant Moderator of General Council in 1917.

The Rev. W. N. DeBerry, long-time pastor of St. John's Congregational Church, first African American church to organize a summer camp for youth (Camp Atwater), employment and recreational programs and home for young women. Assistant moderator of General Council, 1919.

The Rev. Henry C. McDowell, graduate of Talladega, principal of Lincoln Academy in North Carolina (AMA), pastor of Dixwell Avenue Congregational Church in New Haven, Connecticut, organizing minister, Church of the Open Door in Miami, Florida, established the Galenga Mission in Angola and directed it for thirty years.

The Rev. J. Taylor Stanley, a graduate of Talladega College, served as a pastor; however, he is remembered for his extended and distinguished ministry as an executive of the Convention of the South, which for two decades placed him in charge of all the African American Congregational and Christian churches in the Southern region.

The Rev. Arthur D. Gray, a graduate of Talladega College and the Chicago Theological Seminary, first African American President of Talladega, pastor in Chicago and Washington, D.C. Leader of the pro-union forces in the General Council of Congregational Churches as chair of that body's executive committee.

The Rev. William J. Faulkner, pastor in Chicago and Atlanta, Georgia, graduate of Springfield College (MA) and the Chicago Theological

Seminary. For twenty years he was dean of Chapel—Fisk University and in 1949 named assistant moderator of the General Council.

The Rev. Joseph H. Evans, graduate of Western Michigan University and Yale Divinity School; pastor, New York, Cleveland and Chicago. First African American to be a corporate officer in the church (secretary) and served as Interim President of the church before his retirement.

The Rev. Nicholas Hood, II, pastor in New Orleans and Detroit. Graduate of Purdue and Yale Divinity School. Became a leader in church-sponsored housing of all types in Detroit. Long-time member of Detroit City Council, shaped the Churches' Racial Justice Response in 1963.

The Rev. Charles Cobb, graduate of Howard University, Dean of Men at Kentucky State College. Long-time pastor of St. John's Congregational Church-Springfield, MA, was first full-time executive director of the Commission for Racial Justice. Served in this capacity for twenty years.

The Rev. **Charles Shelby Rooks**, graduate of Virginia State University and Union Theological Seminary in New York. Pastor in Washington, D.C., associate and then executive director of the Fund for Theological Education, which had major impact on theological training of African Americans, founder of Society for the Study of Black Religion, chair of the UCC Office of Communication for ten years, first African American president of a mainstream seminary (the Chicago Theological Seminary) and first African American to serve as executive vice president of the United Church Board for Homeland Ministries, the UCC's major domestic mission board.

All of the persons listed above are deceased, with the exception of Evans, Hood, Cobb and Rooks. These four have retired. Many more African Americans are currently serving strategically in local churches, in judicatory offices and at the national level. They give living testimony to the continuing influence of African Americans in the UCC.

Whatever the shape of the UCC in the years to come, we can be assured that African Americans will be sharing in the shaping and assisting this church in its response to issues of justice for all people. As A.

Knighten Stanley has reminded us, "The UCC may not prove to be the ultimate instrument through which the early Congregational spirit shall take on new life and move toward the full emancipation and liberation of all Americans, Black and White, but those who are true heirs of this legacy stand in a unique position to face the challenge of the new racial frontier. . . ."

Gunneman, Louis. *The Shaping of the United Church of Christ.* New York: Pilgrim Press, 1977.

Jones, Lawrence N. *From Consciousness to Conscience.* New York: United Church Press, 1976.

McCain, Diana R. *Free Men: The Amisted Revolt and the American Anti-Slavery Movement.* Hartford, CT: The Vernon R. Krieble Foundation, 1976.

Richardson, Joe M. *Christian Reconstruction: The American Missionary Association and Southern Blacks, 1861–1890.* Athens, GA: University of Georgia Press, 1986. 348 pp.

Stanley, A. Knighten. *The Children Is Crying.* New York: Pilgrim Press, 1979.

Stanley, J. Taylor. *A History of Black Congregational Christian Churches in the South.* New York: United Church Press, 1978. 173 pp.

Kenneth B. Smith

UNITED CHURCH OF JESUS CHRIST APOSTOLIC. An Apostolic Pentecostal church. The United Church of Jesus Christ Apostolic was founded in 1963 by Bishop James B. Thornton, formerly a minister of the **Church of Our Lord Jesus Christ of the Apostolic Faith**. During the early 1960s the Church of Our Lord Jesus Christ went through a significant period of turmoil due to the death of its founder and long-time leader **Robert C. Lawson**. Lawson was succeeded by **Hubert Spencer** who served during a two-year transition period prior to the election of **William Lee Bonner**.

The break was without doctrinal conflict, and the United Church follows the non-Trinitarian Jesus Only perspective of the parent body. It teaches the concept of the one God whose name is Jesus and baptizes members in the name of Jesus only rather than with the traditional baptismal formula of Father, Son, and Holy Ghost. Headquarters is in Baltimore, Maryland. In 1990 there were five congregations and approximately 1,000 members.

UNITED CHURCH OF JESUS CHRIST (APOSTOLIC). An Apostolic Pentecostal church. The

United Church of Jesus Christ (Apostolic) was founded in the mid-1960s when Monroe Saunders, the general secretary of the **Church of God in Christ (Apostolic)**, broke with the presiding bishop, Randolph Carr. Carr had remarried following a divorce, an action which contradicted what Carr had taught for many years. Saunders challenged Carr's authority. When Carr asked Saunders to leave, he did, along with the overwhelming majority of the church. The church members reorganized in 1965 and elected Saunders as the new presiding bishop.

Saunders, one of the few Apostolic Pentecostal leaders at the time to have a seminary education, set educational goals before the church, both ministers and laity. He founded the Institute of Biblical Studies adjacent to the headquarters church in Baltimore. The church soon became distinctive among Apostolic denominations for its trained ministry. Saunders has placed the education program beside an equally strong emphasis upon each congregation having an "atmosphere" conducive to the presence and activity of the Holy Spirit, a means of heading off criticism that education might go against the spirited life of Pentecostal churches.

In addition Saunders had founded the Center for More Abundant Living to address the life problems of members of the church and local community. The center services the aged, those in need of counseling, and alcoholics and drug addicts. It also operates a day care center and a baby clinic.

Prior to the founding of the United Church, the Church of God in Christ (Apostolic) had founded congregations in England and the West Indies. These congregations affiliated with the United Church and have had an expansive ministry that has extended throughout the Caribbean and into Mexico.

The church is led by its presiding bishop, who is assisted by a vice-bishop and other bishops. Saunders has developed an open policy with church leaders and promotes broad discussion of doctrinal, financial, and organizational issues. By 1980 the church had 52 churches and approximately 75,000 members.

UNITED FELLOWSHIP CONVENTION OF THE ORIGINAL AZUSA STREET MISSION. An ecumenical group of Holiness Pentecostal churches. The United Fellowship Convention of the Original Azusa Street Mission is an association of denominations which grew out of the missionary work in the East and South by **William J. Seymour.**

Pentecostalism began at the Azusa Street Mission in 1906. As the revival continued, grew locally, and spread around the country and into foreign fields, Seymour moved to incorporate and began to hold weekly meetings with the other pastors who had accepted the Pentecostal message. For the next six years, Seymour concentrated primarily on overseeing the Mission, which attracted hundreds to its daily activity.

As early as 1909 Seymour, accompanied by **Charles H. Mason**, held meetings in Washington, D.C. Among those affected by the meetings was Charles W. Lowe of Handsom, Virginia. He founded the **Apostolic Faith Church of God**. Over the years the church grew to include congregations along the eastern coast from South Carolina to New York. It also became the source for a number of new denominations which split from the original organization. These branches now include the **Apostolic Faith Churches of God**, the **Apostolic Faith Church of God Live On**, the Apostolic Faith Churches of God in Christ, the **Church of Christ Holiness Unto the Lord**, and the **Apostolic Faith Church of God and True Holiness**. In 1987 representatives of these churches assembled and reaffirmed their common heritage in William J. Seymour and organized the United Fellowship. They sponsor an annual fellowship convention.

DuPree, Sherry Sherrod. *The African American Holiness Pentecostal Movement: An Annotated Bibliography*. New York: Garland Publishing, 1993.

Payne, Wardell J., ed. *Directory of African American Religious Bodies: A Compendium by the Howard University School of Divinity*. Washington, DC: Howard University Press, 1991. 363 pp.

UNITED HEBREW CONGREGATION. A Black Jewish group. The United Hebrew Congregation was an association of approximately a half dozen Black Jewish centers in the Midwest. The association, founded by Rabbi Naphtali Ben Israel, was headquartered at the Ethiopian Hebrew Cultural Center on Chicago's Southside.

Naphtali Ben Israel taught that the children of the biblical Ham (Noah's son) and Abraham (the Chaldean) were Black. Hence, he concluded that the Hebrews discussed in the Jewish Bible (the Old Testament) were also Black people. For example, from the Song of Solomon 1:5, he also assumed that King Solomon was a Black man. Contemporary Black people could thus relate to the Bible as a Black person's book. The congregation's services were held on the Sabbath (Saturday).

No contact has been made with the congregation since the late 1970s, and it is assumed that it is now defunct. A lengthy description of the congregation appeared in the May 1968 issue of *Documents of Truth*, a tabloid devoted to Black history.

UNITED HOLY CHURCH OF AMERICA. A Holiness Pentecostal church. During the 1880s Holiness teachings spread among the African American community of North Carolina. One at Method, North Carolina, which began to meet in May 1886, included Rev. M. L. Mason, G. A. Mials, Isaac Cheshier, and H. C. Snipes. Six years later, the Method group organized the first large gathering of the state's Holiness groups in a convocation in Durham, North Carolina. Soon a loose network of churches emerged. In 1894 the Southern District Convocation, the parent organization of the church, was organized at Durham, North Carolina. Members of the convocation met October 15, 1900, at Durham, North Carolina, to create a more formal organization and adopt of set of rules for managing church affairs, a "discipline." The group took the name Holy Church of North Carolina. Later, as the church spread, the words "and Virginia" were added to the name.

In 1901 Elder W. H. Fulford was selected as president of the church and Elder W. C. Carlton was chosen vice-president. They served through 1915. In 1916 H. L. Fisher was chosen president and E. J. Branch was elected vice-president. In 1916 the name was changed to United Holy Church of America. It was incorporated two years later. In 1920 a second district within the church appeared as the Northern District Convocation. Branch was chosen as the district's first president. The Northwestern District was formed in 1924 followed by the New England, the Central Western, the Western and Pacific Coast, West Virginia, Florida, and Bermuda.

The church was founded as a Holiness church. It preached a second experience available to believers in which the Holy Spirit sanctifies them and makes them perfect in love. After the Pentecostal teachings entered the area in 1907, they were accepted by the membership and the church now believes in an additional experience available to the sanctified believer, the reception of the baptism of the Holy Spirit evidenced by speaking in tongues.

Over the years the church grew into a national body and headquarters were shifted to Pennsylvania. Fisher, after a lengthy tenure as president, was succeeded by G. L. Branch and later H. H. Hairston and W. N. Strobhar. In the mid-1970s, during Strobhar's presidency, a controversy developed with the southern district president Bishop J. **A.** Forbes. As a result, the Southern District Convocation was disfellowshipped from the rest of the body. The split resulted in the loss of about half the membership, the mission field in Liberia, and the college in Goldsboro, North Carolina.

The Church's current leader is Bishop **Joseph T. Bowens**, who succeeded Bishop Strobhar. The Church's headquarters in Philadelphia, where its periodical, the *Holiness Union* is published. In 1970 the Church had 470 churches and some 50,000 members.

Fisher, H. L. *The History of the United Holy Church of America.* N.P.: The Author, n.d. 55 pp.

Gregory, Chester W. *The History of the United Holy Church of America, Inc., 1886–1986.* Baltimore, MD: Gateway Press, 1986.

Standard Manual and Constitution and By-laws of the United Holy Church of America. Philadelphia, PA: United Holy Church of America, 1980. 221 pp.

Turner, William Clair. *The United Holy Church of America: a Study in Black Holiness-Pentecostalism.* Durham, NC: Ph.D. dissertation, Duke University, 1984.

UNITED HOUSE OF PRAYER FOR ALL PEOPLE, CHURCH ON THE ROCK OF THE APOSTOLIC CHURCH. A Pentecostal church. The United House of Prayer for All People was begun in Wareham, Massachusetts in 1919 by **Charles Manuel "Sweet Daddy" Grace** (1881–1960), born Marcelino Manoel de Graca. A native of Brava, Cape Verde Islands, Grace was a former railroad cook who had worked at several jobs while beginning his ministerial career. By 1927, his ministry had grown sufficiently for the formal incorporation of the House of Prayer. The United House of Prayer for All People rapidly became one of the most famous religious groups in the African American community, establishing centers in New York, Baltimore, Washington, D.C., and other major cities during the 30s and 40s.

The House of Prayer holds many similarities to Holiness Pentecostal groups in worship and doctrine. Central in the church tenets are the experiences of conversion, sanctification, and baptism of the Holy

Spirit. Even more central (and controversial), however, was the role of Sweet Daddy Grace himself. Veneration of Grace grew to the level of deification, as exemplified in his oft-repeated quote:

> Never mind about God. Salvation is by Grace alone . . . Grace has given God a vacation, and since God is on His vacation, don't worry Him . . . If you sin against God, Grace can save you, but if you sin against Grace, God cannot save you.

Until his death in 1960, Grace held autocratic authority in the Church. Bishop **Walter McCollough** emerged as his successor, soon causing a split when several congregations refused to acknowledge his authority (leading to the founding of the **True Grace Memorial House of Prayer**). Although McCollough did not inherit Grace's divine status, he did assume all of his worldly powers, and came to be known as "Sweet Daddy Grace" McCollough. McCollough, who has recently died (1991), led the Church into a more traditional Pentecostal stance.

Michael A. Köszegi

UNITED METHODIST CHURCH, METHODISM AND AFRICAN AMERICANS. African Americans were a part of the Wesleyan movement in North America from its very beginning. In the 1760s when a small band of persons gathered at Mud Creek in Frederick County, Maryland, to found the first Methodist society, a Black woman, Anne Sweitzer, was present and joined. When five persons gathered for services led by Philip Embury to form the John Street Church in New York City, another Black woman, known only to us as Bettye, was among them. And, in 1768, when the John Street Church was erected as the first meeting house for worship the names of several African Americans appeared as paid subscribers.

But even before these Black persons joined these societies in the United States, Methodism's founder, John Wesley, had authenticated the tradition of Black involvement by baptizing two Black Methodists at Bristol, England, in 1758. After hearing the preaching of an experiential faith through which people are brought into a redeeming conscious fellowship with God, these "Holy Nameless Two" became so imbued with such an evangelistic zeal that they went home and converted their owner, Nathaniel Gilbert. They soon returned with him to their native Antigua in the West Indies to establish the first Methodist chapel in the New World.

When the Methodist movement became a formally organized church at the Christmas Conference of 1784 at Lovely Lane Church in Baltimore, there was an African presence. Clearly seen in the painting of the ordination of Francis Asbury at that organizing conference is "Black" Harry Hoosier, who was to excel the Bishop in his popularity as a pulpit orator. Also present at that conference was Richard Allen, who was later to leave St. George's Methodist Episcopal Church in Philadelphia to found the African Methodist Episcopal Church. Within two years, Blacks represented more than twenty percent of Methodism's total membership.

In attempting to account for why the transplanted Africans were attracted to Methodism, *The Methodist Discipline* says: "Methodism won favor with the Black people for two main reasons: (1) its evangelistic appeal; (2) the Church's attitude toward slavery." While those reasons hold in summary, there were some other explicit factors: (3) the preaching and worship style appealed to Blacks; (4) Blacks were allowed to serve as lay preachers; and (5) Methodism was adaptable enough to fit their own unique situation so that they could make it their own.

And, indeed, some Black Methodists left and made *their own* branches of Methodism—finding their communion with the predominantly White Methodist Church untenable. The **African Methodist Episcopal Church** (AME) was formed under the leadership of **Richard Allen** and was legally constituted in 1816. The **African Methodist Episcopal Zion Church** (AMEZ) similarly was formed out of the John Street Church in New York City under the leadership of **James Varick**, and in 1820–1821 became incorporated. And the **Christian Methodist Episcopal Church** (CME) was comprised of those Black Methodists members who sought and secured a separate identification from the Methodist Episcopal Church, South, at its General Conference in New Orleans in 1866. They began their independent existence in 1870.

But a significant remnant declined to leave the church under any circumstances, clinging to a fragile faith that the church would do right on the issues of race and inclusiveness and return to the principles of its more radical beginnings. They took the view that, if there was freedom to leave, then there was also the freedom to stay. So they exercised that option, and in 1794 gathered in the African Zoar Church in Philadelphia to affirm their heritage and hope and their desire to remain in connection with the Methodist Episcopal Church. The descendants of this Black Remnant form the present African American presence within the United Methodist Church.

Even those who chose to leave did not leave the Methodist tradition; they merely left the structure. For they maintained the polity and theology and even the name, *Methodist*. Perhaps what Richard Allen had to say captured the spirit of these departing Black Methodists: "As for me, I could never be anything but a Methodist . . . and I am thankful that ever I heard a Methodist preacher!" For all of these Black Methodists—those who left, and those who stayed—Methodism was a sacred birthright not lightly to be eschewed. It represented an understanding of free grace and a social witness and discipleship which was part and parcel of their vision of the Kingdom of God.

These African American Methodist loyalists gathered themselves together in African Zoar Church in Philadelphia and remained a part of the connection. In spite of the racism and segregation, they were determined to claim the church as their own and to challenge these practices that were so antithetical to the church's earlier beginnings—either Methodism's beginnings at Baltimore or, perhaps more importantly, the Universal Church's beginnings at Pentecost. They were determined to be the primordial conscience of Methodism at every turn. They held a vision of a church that would, in time, transcend the accidents of race and the ephemerality of status and station. They were determined to make their witness *within* until the Methodist Church found that elusive place that surely would come when spiritual rhetoric and human practice were in compliance with each other. Until then, they lived in faith and hope. To some extent,

> this hope was probably based more on pride than reason, more on eager expectations than anything reality suggested. But it was nevertheless a hope, a faith, a gossamer anticipation that sometime, somewhere, somehow, their presence in the church would cease to be the great anomaly that it was.

And so, African Zoar was replicated as the Black Remnant left the White churches to establish their own churches and congregations. In the Northeast there was Mt. Hope in Salem, New Jersey (1801), Sharp Street in Baltimore (1802), Ezion in Wilmington, Delaware (1805). One of the first Black churches in New England and one of the earliest Methodist churches in Boston was Fourth Methodist (1818), where Prince Hall (the

African American father of Free and Accepted Masonry) and **David Walker** (later to write *The Appeal*) were communicants of its predecessor body. That church was renamed Union in 1949. In the South, Black Methodism was introduced by a local preacher named **Henry Evans** in Fayetteville, North Carolina, around 1800. That church was at first called "The African Meeting House" and later dedicated as Evans Chapel in 1802. It was for many years remarkably and ironically bi-racial because of the powerful preaching and effectiveness of this Black preacher's appeal to Whites as well as Black people in that town. The Gum Swamp Methodist Episcopal Church was established in Bolton (near Wilmington, North Carolina) in 1803. In Ohio, Wesley Chapel (Old Stone Church) was established in Cincinnati in 1805. When the White members objected to the emotional responsiveness of the Black members and proceeded to segregate them, these African American Methodists withdrew and established their own worship service and congregation at Deer Creek, in 1815. After several moves and name changes, they became Calvary Methodist Episcopal Church of Cincinnati. And, further south, in New Orleans in 1838, Wesley Church became the Mother Church for the birth of several other congregations in Louisiana and later extended its evangelistic influence to Texas and across to Mississippi.

In each region and in each place, these African Methodist loyalists preached, prayed, praised and practiced, in their own Methodist way, a warm heart, a social conscience to change society and the world, and a disciplined life of "holiness."

However, the vision of these loyalists of a totally inclusive church was not to be realized then, perhaps not now. For, while they remained in the church and a part of the connection, they became a "church within a church." Parallel institutions developed, talented preachers, teachers and leaders came forth, and their numbers grew among African Americans—slave and free. These souls of the Black diaspora of Africa responded to the Methodist message from the Black "sons of thunder": "Free grace and dying love was for all—available to all—even you!"

By the time the issues of racism and slavery split the communion into Northern and Southern fragments—a broken church, and eventually a broken nation—there were 207,000 African American Methodists, mostly in what was to become the Methodist Episcopal Church, South.

When the General Conference of the Methodist Episcopal Church (the Mother Church or sometimes commonly called "the Northern Church") met in 1864 in Philadelphia on May 2, the victory of the Union Army seemed imminent and the end of the war in view. As a result, one of the items that occupied the agenda of that conference was the need to develop a plan for the evangelization of the soon-to-be-freed Blacks in the South. Two options were present: (1) the establishment of separate missionary annual conferences in the overall structure of the Methodist Episcopal Church; and (2) the marshalling of teachers and missionaries to the South to aid Blacks in adjusting to their new status as citizens.

The first Black missionary conference to be established was the Delaware Conference, which convened at John Wesley Church in Philadelphia, currently Tindley Temple United Methodist Church (renamed after the Rev. **Charles A. Tindley**, pastor from 1902 to 1933 and famous hymn writer. Tindley penned such classic hymns as "When the Storms of Life Are Raging," "We'll Understand It Better By and By," and "Nothing Between." He has been called the father of African American Gospel Music). This conference included Black Methodists from the Delaware, the Eastern Shore of Maryland, and churches in New Jersey and Philadelphia. In the fall of the same year, the second conference, the Washington Conference, was formed at Sharp Street Church in Baltimore. It included churches in Maryland, the District of Columbia, West Virginia, and parts of Western Pennsylvania and Virginia. In 1869, the Lexington Conference was formed at Harrodsburg, Kentucky. It was later to include Black Methodists churches in Ohio, Illinois, Indiana, Michigan, Wisconsin, and Minnesota, as well as Kentucky. In succeeding years no fewer than twenty-five conferences were formed, generally along state lines, but sometimes dividing the state into two conferences. Among these were South Carolina, Florida, Mississippi, Alabama, Georgia, Texas, Tennessee, Arkansas, and Missouri.

Many of the conferences remained intact from the time of their organization to the end of structural segregation in the United Methodist Church in 1968, with the merger of The Methodist Church with the Evangelical United Brethren and the merger of the final conference in 1972. They represented segregated conferences on the one hand, but on the other hand, they provided these Black loyal Methodists a structure in which efforts of mission and self-direction took place. Indeed, segregation was the practice of the day. Nor had the Methodists been alone in their split over the issue of slavery. Virtually every major denomination had experienced the same kind of division. But at least now these loyal Black Methodists were granted status, security, and opportunity for ordination, Conference membership, eligibility for General Conference representation, appointments for service in the local church and beyond.

The second plan for evangelization was the establishment of schools and colleges for the education of Black people. The Freedmen's Aid Society was formed in Cincinnati, Ohio, in 1866, to work "for the relief and education of the Freedmen and people of color in general to cooperate with the Missionary and Church Extension Societies of the Methodist Episcopal Church." In this effort, the Methodist Episcopal Church far exceeded any other denomination. Within the first seventeen months of the operation of the Society, fifty-nine schools were established in ten States. Twelve of those schools exist today as some of the finest of educational institutions: Bennett College, Greensboro, North Carolina (1873); Bethune-Cookman College, Daytona Beach, Florida (1872); Claflin College, Orangeburg, South Carolina (1869); Clark Atlanta University, Atlanta, Georgia (1869); Dillard University, New Orleans, Louisiana (1869); Gammon Theological Seminary (the nucleus for the organization of Interdenominational Theological Center), Atlanta, Georgia (1883); Huston-Tillotston College, Austin, Texas (1878); Meharry Medical School, Nashville, Tennessee (1876); Morristown College, Morristown, Tennessee (1880); Paine College (sponsored jointly with the CME Church), Augusta, Georgia; Philander-Smith College, Little Rock, Arkansas (1877); Rust College, Holly Springs, Mississippi (1866); and Wiley College, Marshall, Texas (1873). Several other schools were established by the Methodists which later became state institutions, such as Morgan College (now Morgan State University, in Baltimore, Maryland) and Princess Ann, Maryland. In many cases, these schools and colleges were begun in the basements of local Black Methodist churches, as was the case, for instance, with Bennett College. They are testimony to the emphasis Black Methodists have placed on education for clergy and laity alike throughout their history.

These Black Methodist schools began to prepare persons for ministry, medicine, and missions as well as teaching and leadership—performing veritable miracles on meager resources. At the beginning of the last half of the twentieth century, Meharry Medical College had trained more than 50 percent of the Black doctors and dentists in the United States, with no regard for denominational affiliation. The same was true of

Gammon Theological Seminary in preparing persons for the ministry, which also provided the foundation and the original buildings, library and faculty for the development of the Interdenominational Theological Center in Atlanta, Georgia.

These schools and churches sent forth Black Methodist missionaries both in the United States and abroad: Africa, China, Malaysia, India, Pakistan, Sarawak, the Philippines and other places. Very significant is the Black Methodist mission to Liberia, where several missionaries served and where thousands of Liberians were made members of the Methodist Church—including the late President Tubman, who was a licensed minister of the Methodist Church. So successful was this missionary enterprise that it necessitated the first Black bishops to be elected by the Methodist Episcopal Church to serve as missionary bishops in Liberia. Between 1858 and 1916 four Black Americans served as bishops to superintend the work of Liberia: **Francis Burns** (1809–1863), a native of Albany, New York, was elected in 1858; **John W. Roberts** (1812–1875), of Petersburg, Virginia, in 1866; **Isaiah B. Scott** (1854–1931), of Midway, Kentucky, in 1904; and **Alexander P. Camphor** (1865–1919), of New Orleans, who had earlier served as a college professor of mathematics, a pastor, a college president, and for a period, United States vice-counsel in Liberia (selected in 1916 and served until his death.)

In an episcopal form of church government, the office of bishop is perceived as a signal of achievement and a position of power and prestige. The African Methodists (AME, AMEZ) had already established themselves and were electing their own bishops, while the loyalists in the Methodist Episcopal Church were superintended by White bishops. This added to their sense of urgency to achieve full African American representation at the episcopal level.

Notwithstanding the sentiment expressed by the founder of African Methodism that he "could never be anything but a Methodist," his well-meaning successors were expressing disgust, pity, and ridicule to the Black Remnant who remained in the Mother Church. The provocations and the enticements from the African Methodists who had left were many and often. The situation was exacerbated by the action taken by the Colored Methodists in 1866 to depart from the Southern Methodists. So the Black delegates to the General Conference of 1868 from the newly formed Black missionary Annual Conferences began to agitate for the election of Black bishops to serve in the United States. Building their case on the record of the Black

bishops serving in Africa, they argued that the church should act on its own principles.

One of the hollow arguments offered against the appeal for Blacks in the episcopacy was the familiar "there are none qualified." This was especially odious to these Black Methodists since among the several highly qualified persons offered for consideration was **John Wesley Edward Bowen, Sr.** (1855–1933), the second Black Ph.D. recipient in the nation. This distinguished scholar in historical theology from Boston University, then serving as Professor of Theology at Gammon Theological Seminary (and later its first Black president in 1906), was denied election in 1896, even though the church had compromised the Blacks' proposal in 1880 by voting to elect a "limited episcopacy," i.e., a Black bishop to superintend Black people.

It was not until 1920 that two distinguished and able Black bishops were selected on a separate ballot, but with all of the rights and privileges pertaining to that office. **Robert Edward Jones** (1872–1960) rose to the episcopacy from a brilliant career in the church as pastor, Sunday school field secretary, editor of the *Southwestern Christian Advocate*, and an outspoken leader of the church and civil rights. The other bishop elected was **Matthew Wesley Clair, Sr.** (1865–1943), an eloquent preacher, eminently successful pastor, administrator and presiding elder. In 1936 Clair retired and was replaced by the last of the Black bishops elected by the ME Church, **Alexander Preston Shaw** (1879–1966). An outstanding pulpiteer (known far and wide for his famous sermon, "Above the Snake Line"), Shaw was then editor of the *Southwestern Christian Advocate*. He served with distinction for almost two decades both in the ME Church and as bishop in The Methodist Church after the Southern Church and the Northern Church were reunified in 1939.

What the nation, North and South, was prepared to accomplish after the Civil War, the church was not, namely, to forgive and forget the grievances which people had created and gone to war for and the artificial contrivances of racialism and racial xenophobia. Attempts to bring together the two sections of the church in 1865 failed; the Southern Church was embittered and unwilling. Other attempts between 1916 and 1939 had also met with failure. It seems the main stumbling block and the all-pervasive problem for all concerned was this: *What do we do with these Black Methodists who never left the church?* Perhaps that is still an issue at the moment of this writing. As the Methodists struggled with it in the early part of the twentieth century, Bishop Earl Cranston of the Southern Church stated it correctly: "It was thought that if we could come to an agreement as to the status of the Negro, the other matters will adjust themselves to correspond to that understanding."

The year 1939 became the year to vote on the "solution" in Kansas City, Missouri. The Plan of Union devised called for the placement of all Black Methodists from Florida to New Jersey into one racially constituted jurisdiction and the division of all other church members into five geographical jurisdictions, thus giving *official* standing to segregation in the church for the first time in its history. Black Methodists vigorously opposed the Plan as "a stigma too humiliating to accept."

Black delegates came to the Reuniting Conference with hope that their vision of a church that knew no color line and a church that would put conscience above convention would be fulfilled: **the church would vote for no such pernicious plan.** But that outcome was not to be; their dream had to be deferred. As John Graham has put it: "The Negro became the 'sacrificial lamb' on the altar in order that union could be consummated." Of the forty-seven Black delegates to the General Conference, thirty-six voted against and eleven abstained. But the vote in favor of passage prevailed. In the time which followed as the Conference stood and sang "We're Marching Upward to Zion," the Black delegates demurred. For them it was no occasion to stand and sing; it was a time to sit and weep.

And some did, as the *Central Jurisdiction* came into being. This officially segregated structure lasted until 1968, when the Methodist Church merged with another body, the Evangelical United Brethren, and created a new name and denomination, the United Methodist Church. From that point, the churches and members in the former Central Jurisdiction were integrated into the geographical jurisdictional structure of the denomination. But from 1940 when the Central Jurisdiction was formally organized at St. Louis until its demise in Portland, Oregon, in 1968, Black Methodists took the advice of their oldest bishop, Robert E. Jones, who said in his Episcopal Address: ". . . it behooves us at the very beginning to recognize the gravity of our responsibility as well as the favorableness of our opportunity . . . it is an opportunity of which we should *hasten to take every advantage.*" During the period of the Central Jurisdiction, fourteen Black bishops were elected to serve five episcopal areas and Liberia. Many of them were outstanding national and regional leaders of the church, the Black community and ecumenical efforts, as well as ardent advocates for quality education, justice and racial inclusiveness in the church and society. Churches under their supervision showed growth in membership each quadrennium. They "hastened to take every advantage" of their separate existence and served Black Methodists and the community while they repeatedly and continually called on the church to be the church of its beginnings.

The Central Jurisdiction and the Plan must be assessed for what it was—a Machiavellian scheme and a contrived, demeaning, and disgraceful stratagem that placed convention above conscience and demonstrated the incapacity of the Methodist Church to be exemplary in its dealings with God's darker sons and daughters. But perhaps **C. Eric Lincoln** is correct: "[the Methodist Church] was probably considerably ahead of the efforts of its counterpart communions of the American mainline churches, who probably refrained from addressing 'the problem' at all."

The United Methodist Church has created a multi-ethnic church in which every ethnic group is represented in national positions, boards, agencies and working groups. Its *Hymnal* is probably the most inclusive hymnal ever produced by any church. All major ethnic groups are represented, including more than 100 sacred music selections out of the African American tradition: hymns, spirituals, gospel songs, prayers, etc. Many African Americans have been chosen by White majority jurisdictions to give episcopal leadership to predominantly White areas, even electing the first Black female bishop ever elected in the history of the Christian church in America, **Leontine T. C. Kelly**, who served the San Francisco Area. Several African Americans head national boards and agencies of the church, including Randolph Nugent, who heads the church's largest board (the Board of Global Ministries). And there are numerous examples of African Americans who serve predominantly White congregations; many Black professors of higher education in colleges, universities and seminaries across America, and leaders, both lay and clergy, in every conceivable part of the church and nation. The accomplishments of the United Methodist Church in this regard are to be celebrated, while care is taken not to lose sight of the fact that the vision of those first African American Methodists is yet to be fully realized at the local level in so many places, the vision of gathering in inclusive unity to worship and serve and reflect the will of God in our lives.

Brawley, James P. *Two Centuries of Methodist Concern: Bondage, Freedom and Education of Black People.* New York: Vantage Press, 1974. 606 pp.

Graham, John H. *Black United Methodists.* New York: Vantage Press, 1979. 162 pp.

McClain, William B. *Black People in the Methodist Church: Whither Thou Goest?* Nashville, TN: Abingdon Press, 1984. 159 pp.

Shockley, Grant, Karen Collier, and William B. McClain, eds. *Heritage and Hope: The African American Presence in United Methodism.* Nashville, TN: Abingdon Press, 1990. 350 pp.

William B. McClain

UNITED PENTECOSTAL COUNCIL OF THE ASSEMBLIES OF GOD.

A Trinitarian Pentecostal church. The United Pentecostal Council of the Assemblies of God is an early African American Pentecostal church which began in 1919 in Cambridge, Massachusetts. It was founded by George Allen Phillip with the original intent of supporting missionaries in Liberia. The year after its founding the council sent the Rev. Alexander and Margaret Howard to Africa as its first missionaries. They arrived in Liberia on December 21, 1920.

The church is a Trinitarian organization with beliefs similar to the Assemblies of God, but it notes that it is completely autonomous and has no connection with the Assemblies. Headquarters is in Milford, Connecticut. It is headed by Rev. Edgar L. Lashley, president, and Rev. Roderick R. Caesar, national bishop. Affiliated congregations are now found across the eastern half of the United States and in Panama and the West Indies.

Payne, Wardell J., ed. *Directory of African American Religious Bodies: A Compendium by the Howard University School of Divinity.* Washington, DC: Howard University Press, 1991. 363 pp.

UNITED WAY OF THE CROSS CHURCH OF CHRIST OF THE APOSTOLIC FAITH.

An Apostolic Pentecostal church. Following his becoming supreme bishop of the **Way of the Cross Church of Christ** in 1967, John Luke Brooks established a board of bishops to assist him. Among those chosen to sit on the board was Joseph H. Adams, whom Brooks consecrated as a bishop and assigned as diocesan of North Carolina. However, in 1974, Adams left the church and with Harrison L. Twyman, formerly of the Bible Way Church of Our Lord Jesus Christ World Wide, founded the United Way of the Cross Churches of Christ of the Apostolic Faith. The new denomination was the result of a vision received by Adams. Twyman had received a similar vision. He soon brought several other experienced pastors into the new church, including Bishop Preston Graves (from the **Bible Way Church of Our Lord Jesus Christ World Wide**), Elder James Pickard (from the **Apostle Church of Christ in God**), and Bishop S. David Neal (formerly with the Way of the Cross Church of Christ).

There being no doctrinal disagreement in Adams's break with the Way of the Cross Church, the new denomination follows similar teachings. It preaches the One God whose name is Jesus and baptizes members in the name of Jesus Christ, rather than following the traditional baptismal formula in the name of the Father, Son, and Holy Spirit.

By 1980 the church had 14 churches located in the Middle Atlantic states, and approximately 1,100 members. Headquarters is in North Carolina.

UNITED WESLEYAN METHODIST CHURCH OF AMERICA.

A Methodist church. The United Wesleyan Methodist Church of America traces its history to the beginning of Methodist missions in Jamaica and the other islands of the Caribbean in the eighteenth century. A strong Methodist movement spread throughout those islands, which were British possessions, and tended to follow the organizational patterns of British Wesleyanism, i.e., they had no bishops, but rather were led by conference presidents. During the late nineteenth century a small number of West Indian Methodists migrated to the United States. In 1905 they organized the United Wesleyan Methodist Church of America, but kept fraternal relations with the Methodist Church of the Caribbean and the Americas.

A small denomination of only four congregations, the church has gone almost unnoticed. However, in 1976 it entered into a concordant with the nine million member **United Methodist Church** with which it now cooperates on a number of projects in the Caribbean.

Bessil-Watson, Lisa, comp. *Handbook of the Church of the Caribbean.* Bridgetown, Barbados: The Cedar Press, 1982.

UNIVERSAL CHRISTIAN SPIRITUAL FAITH AND CHURCHES FOR ALL NATIONS.

The Universal Christian Spiritual Faith and Churches for All

Nations is a Pentecostal church formed in 1952 out of the merging of three denominations: the National David Spiritual Temple of Christ Church Union (Inc.) (U.S.A.), St. Paul's Spiritual Church Convocation, and King David's Temple of Truth Association. The National David Spiritual Temple of Christ Church Union (Inc.) (U.S.A.) originated in 1932 in Kansas City, Missouri under the leadership of former Baptist minister Bishop David William Short.

The merged church, differing from the mainstream Pentecostal churches, recognizes the presence of the Holy Spirit also in persons who do not experience speaking in tongues, although admits that a full and complete baptism of the Holy Spirit occurs along with speaking in tongues besides other gifts. The church reported in the mid-1960s work in 60 churches with 40,816 members. It publishes a monthly periodical called *The Christian Spiritual Voice* and created the St. David Christian Spiritual Seminary as its educational facility.

Hollenweger, Walter J. *Black Pentecostal Concepts*. Special issue of *Concept* 30 (1970).

Payne, Wardell J., ed. *Directory of African American Religious Bodies: A Compendium by the Howard University School of Divinity*. Washington, DC: Howard University Press, 1991. 363 pp.

Isotta Poggi

UNIVERSAL CHURCH OF CHRIST.

An Apostolic Pentecostal church. The Universal Church of Christ was founded in 1972 by Rev. Dr. Robert C. Jiggetts, Jr., with the assistance of Elders Nathaniel Kirton and Carl Winckler. The first center was in Orange, New Jersey. The church has been very service-oriented and in 1984 initiated a soup kitchen program which mobilized church volunteers, government grants of money and food surpluses, and donations from local businesses. By the beginning of the 1990s, it was serving 1,300 meals a month to the poor and homeless in its headquarters city.

The church accepted the Apostolic Pentecostal position which identifies Jesus as the one God of the Bible and denies the Trinity. It has three ordinances, baptism, the Lord's Supper, and holy matrimony. It affirms a belief in the infallibility of the Scripture and divine healing.

Jiggetts heads the church as its chief apostle, president, and overseer. Headquarters is in Orange, New Jersey, and in 1990 there were approximately 20 congregations in the northeast United States and in the West Indies.

Payne, Wardell J., ed. *Directory of African American Religious Bodies: A Compendium by the Howard University School of Divinity*. Washington, DC: Howard University Press, 1991. 363 pp.

UNIVERSAL CHURCH, THE MYSTICAL BODY OF CHRIST.

The Universal Church, The Mystical Body of Christ was formed in Saginaw, Michigan in 1970 by Bishop R. O. Frazer. Contact has not been made with the church in recent years. The periodical of the church is *The Light of Life Herald*.

Payne, Wardell J., ed. *Directory of African American Religious Bodies: A Compendium by the Howard University School of Divinity*. Washington, DC: Howard University Press, 1991. 363 pp.

Isotta Poggi

UNIVERSAL FOUNDATION FOR BETTER LIVING.

A New Thought metaphysical church. The Universal Foundation for Better Living grew out of the work of Rev. **Johnnie Colemon**, one of the first African American New Thought ministers. She was ordained minister with the Unity School of Christianity in Kansas City in 1956, after having experienced a healing from an incurable disease three years earlier. She moved to Chicago where she organized the Christ Unity Temple and was the first Black person to be elected president of the Association of Unity Churches.

After several decades of work with Unity, in 1974 she withdrew from her affiliation with both the Unity School of Christianity and the Association of Unity Churches, and renamed her congregation Christ Universal Temple. At the same time she also established the **Johnnie Colemon Institute** as the educational institution of her church. Through the Institute she began to train ministers, the first of which were ordained in 1978. As they moved out and founded new congregations, the Foundation emerged as an association of congregations.

In the early 1980s Colemon also began her broadcast ministry, now aired on thirteen stations across the United States. In 1985 the congregation completed the movement into a new sanctuary and headquarters complex on the far-Southside of Chicago, which now, in addition houses the UFBL bookstore and a 24-hour call-in service known as Prayer Ministry.

Johnnie Colemon's teaching is mainly in agreement with the Unity School of Christianity, with its emphasis on prosperity as attainable for everybody as the will of God, following the principles of Jesus, the Wayshower, and following right thinking with right action. Furthermore, Colemon's church focuses on those teachings that can help all persons to provide for themselves rather than provide support for needy people.

The foundation, which reported work in 1987 in seventeen churches and study groups across the country, also has established activity in Canada, Trinidad, and Guyana. The *Daily Inspiration for Better Living* is issued in Chicago. The church is also a member of the International New Thought Alliance, and Rev. Colemon has served as the district president for the Chicago area. She was chairperson of the sixtieth INTA congress which met in Chicago.

Colemon, Johnnie. *The Best Messages from the Founder's Desk.* Chicago: Universal Foundation for Better Living, 1987.

———. *It Works If You Work It.* 2 vols. Chicago: Universal Foundation for Better Living, n.d.

Harrel, Allison D. *Prosperity for Better Living.* Chicago: Universal Foundation for Better Living, n.d.

———. *Follow Me.* Chicago: Universal Foundation for Better Living, 1981.

Melton, J. Gordon. *Encyclopedia of American Religion.* 3rd ed. Detroit: Gale Research, Inc., 1989. 1102 pp.

Nedd, Don. *Practical Guidelines for Better Living.* Chicago: Lakemont, GA: CSA Press, 1983.

UNIVERSAL HAGAR'S SPIRITUAL CHURCH.

A Spiritual church. While Father Divine and his Peace Mission have received fairly extensive treatment, the Universal Hagar's Spiritual Church (UHSC) and its founder, Father Hurley, a contemporary of **Father Divine** and also a self-proclaimed god, have been almost entirely overlooked in the literature on African American religion. George Willie Hurley, who was born on February 17, 1884, in Reynolds, Georgia, received training as a Baptist minister, but later became a Methodist. After moving to Detroit with his wife in 1919, he joined a small Holiness sect called **Triumph the Church and Kingdom of God in Christ** and became its Presiding Prince of Michigan. In the early 1920s, Hurley became a minister in the National

Spiritual Church, probably a predominantly White organization. Shortly, thereafter, Hurley established UHSC in Detroit on September 23, 1923. In 1924 he established the School of Mediumship and Psychology, which eventually became a secret auxiliary in each congregation affiliated with UHSC. Father Hurley maintained that the school is a branch of the Great School of the Prophets, which Jesus attended during the eighteen years of his life that are not accounted for in the Bible. He also established the Knights of the All Seeing Eye, a Masonic-like auxiliary open to both men and women. By the eve of Hurley's death on June 23, 1943, UHSC had grown to an association of at least 37 congregations (eight in Michigan, eight in Ohio, six in Pennsylvania, seven in New Jersey, five in New York City, and single congregations in West Virginia, Delaware, and Illinois).

Like other Black Spiritual groups, UHSC contains elements from Spiritualism, Catholicism, African American Protestantism, and possibly **Voodoo** or hoodoo. Father Hurley also incorporated concepts from the *Aquarian Gospel of Jesus Christ*, astrology, Ethiopianism, and other belief systems in his church. Sometime around 1933 if not earlier, Father Hurley began to teach his followers that his "carnal flesh" had been "transformed into the flesh of Christ." He maintained that just as Adam had been the God of the Taurian Age, Abraham the God of the Arian Age, and Jesus the God of the Piscean Age, he was the God of the Aquarian Age. In contrast to the seemingly apolitical posture of many Spiritual groups, Father Hurley took unequivocal stands on a number of social issues, particularly the status of African Americans in the larger society, and urged his followers to vote for Franklin D. Roosevelt. Since Hurley's death the strongly nationalist and critical rhetoric of his church has been considerably tempered.

Father Hurley's successors as head of UHSC have included Prince Thomas Surbadger, Mother Mary Hatchett, Prince Alfred Bailey, and Rev. G. Latimer, a daughter of Hurley. The Wiseman Board, which has consisted primarily of women in recent decades, serves as UHSC's governing body. As is the case for many other Spiritual associations, there has been considerable turnover in congregations in UHSC. Over the years, the heaviest concentrations of Hagar's congregations have been in southeastern Michigan, the location of the association's headquarters, and the New York-New Jersey megapolis. Whereas in 1965 UHSC had 41 congregations in eight states, in 1980 it had 35 congregations in eleven states. Since the early 1960s,

UHSC has experienced not only fluctuations in the number of its congregations but also a pattern of geographical diffusion, particularly to California and the Southeast. While Father Hurley's association appears to have passed its zenith, it continues to thrive in various parts of the United States.

Baer, Hans A. *The Black Spiritual Movement: A Religious Response to Racism*. Knoxville, TN: University of Tennessee Press, 1984. 221 pp.

Hans A. Baer

"How did Marie Leveau do her work? I asked feeling that I had gotten a little closer.

"She go to her great Altar and seek until she become the same as the spirit, then she come out of the room where she listens to them that come to ask. When they finish she answer them as a god. . . . Marie Leveau is not a woman when she answer the one who ask. No. She is a god, yes. Whatever she say, it will come so."

Interview between Zora Neale Hurston,
folklorist, and devotee of Marie Leveau
1935

V

VALENTINE, ROBERT ARTHUR (May 2, 1890–1954), a bishop of the **African Orthodox Church** (AOC) and the **Holy African Church**, first emerges into the public light as a priest of the African Orthodox Church in the 1920s. On May 30, 1930, he was consecrated by Archbishop **George Alexander McGuire** with the assistance of Bishop **William E. J. Robertson**. Following McGuire's death in 1934, the AOC entered a period of turmoil and schism. Valentine joined with that section of the church aligned with Bishops **Reginald Grant Barrow** and **Arthur Stanley Trotman** which under Trotman's leadership became known as the Holy African Church. Valentine succeeded Trotman as primate in 1945. He served for nine years and was succeeded by Bishop **Frederick August Toote**.

VANDERHORST, RICHARD H. (December 15, 1813–July 17, 1872), 2nd bishop of the **Christian Methodist Episcopal Church** (CME), then known as the Colored Methodist Episcopal Church, was born into slavery in Georgetown, South Carolina, the oldest of five sons in the family of Charles and Diana Vanderhorst. His owners were two sisters, Betsy and Judith Wragg, who treated him rather well. Vanderhorst accompanied them as a body-servant to regular services at the Methodist Episcopal Church, South (MECS) which shaped his religious orientation.

At his parents' request he was apprenticed at about age seventeen to a Black carpenter named Sampson Dunmore and became skilled at that trade. Dunmore was himself an exhorter and class leader in the MECS. In 1833, at age twenty, Vanderhorst experienced conversion and joined the MECS at Georgetown. About two years after that he moved to Charleston, South Carolina, and joined the Trinity MECS in that city. Soon his strong Christian deportment brought him to the position of assistant leader of his class within the church. In about 1838 he moved his membership to Bethel M.

E. Church and became a class leader. He married Rosa Vanderhorst about this time.

He applied for a license to preach, but at that time it was not an office available to Blacks. Nevertheless, he carried forth a ministry as he was able. When Bishop **Daniel Payne** of the **African Methodist Episcopal Church** (AME) organized that work in South Carolina in 1865, Vanderhorst was one of the first to join. Payne quickly ordained him deacon and elder and sent him to Hilton Head, South Carolina, to do missionary work. In 1866 he was appointed to Augusta, Georgia, then in 1867 to Edisto Island, South Carolina. He began to be disappointed at Payne's treatment of him, and when he was approached in 1868 by members of the new CME Church in South Carolina, he was interested. He left the AME Church and helped organize the new CME Church as it separated from the ME Church. He was made a presiding elder of the Columbus District from 1868 to 1870 and is credited with organizing the Watchman's Banner and the Aid Society, charitable groups that existed for years in the Charleston area. He gained renown as a preacher of rare eloquence.

The first General Conference of the CME Church was held in Jackson, Tennessee, in December 1870, and the first bishop elected, on December 21, was **William H. Miles**. Vanderhorst was the second bishop elected, and like Miles was consecrated by MECS bishops Robert Paine and Holland N. McTyeire. Unfortunately he was only able to serve eighteen months before his death.

HCMEC, CMECTY, HCMECA, EWM.

VARICK, JAMES (c.1750–July 22, 1827), founding bishop of the **African Methodist Episcopal Zion Church** (AMEZ), was born near Newburgh, in Orange County, New York. His father, Richard Varick, was a free man baptized in the Dutch Church of Hackensack,

New Jersey, and his mother was a slave in the Varick (Van Varck) household, but later was manumitted. Varick grew up in New York City and may have attended the Free School for Negroes. At about the age of sixteen he joined the John Street Methodist Episcopal Church, the first Methodist congregation in the city, where he was later licensed to preach.

He apprenticed to a shoemaker and by the end of the Revolutionary War had his own shoemaking and tobacco cutting shop. In about 1790 he married Aurelia Jones, with whom he had seven children, four of whom survived to maturity. Over time the poor treatment of Blacks at the John Street Church, where they were forced to sit in the gallery or rear seats, became intolerable. The Blacks held some separate meetings as early as 1780, but not until 1796 did Methodist bishop Francis Asbury give official permission for the Black membership to meet separately when the building was not otherwise in use. This move, led by **Peter Williams, Sr.**, greatly strengthened the Black membership and they were enabled to build their own structure, dedicated on September 7, 1800, as Zion Church, at the corner of Church and Leonard Streets, near Wall Street. Peter Williams, Sr., laid the cornerstone of this, the only Black church in New York City at the time. The church was incorporated in 1801 in such a way that its basic independence was maintained and the property protected from White bishops through an all-Black board of trustees. It is true that White preachers still had the right to the pulpit, but some of the other problems **Richard Allen** later encountered in the use and control of property were avoided.

The problem of having no control over the White preachers was softened in 1806 when Francis Asbury ordained Varick a deacon as well as Varick's colleagues, Abraham Thompson and June Scott. They were the first ordained Blacks in the state of New York. Asbury had previously ordained other Blacks elsewhere, the first being Richard Allen in 1799. On January 1, 1808, the United States abolished the slave trade, and that day Varick celebrated by preaching his famous "Sermon of Thanksgiving on the Occasion of the Abolition of the African Slave Trade." Absalom Jones also preached on that subject that day, and the two sermons became the first sermons preserved for posterity preached by an African for an African audience. Varick organized educational classes in the church and became the chaplain of the New York African Society for Mutual Relief, organized in 1810. When the New York African Bible Society was organized on January 17, 1817, he was one of its vice-presidents. In 1818 he helped establish another African Methodist church in New Haven, Connecticut.

On July 16, 1820, William Stillwell, the White elder in charge of Zion Church and Asbury Church (another Black Methodist congregation), broke from the Methodist Church along with several hundred others over issues of congregational control and lay versus clergy power. The resulting uncertainty over future ministerial supervision was the catalyst for Zion to take a radical step. Some desired to become part of Richard Allen's **African Methodist Episcopal Church**, founded in 1816. Varick asked Allen if he would consecrate some Zion people as bishops in the New York area. Allen said he would do this only if they would be under his supervision within one overarching structure, and this Varick did not want to do. On July 21, 1820, the Asbury and Zion members held a conference to declare themselves a new autonomous entity called the African Methodist Episcopal Church ("Zion" was added to the name in 1848 to avoid confusion with Allen's organization). On October 1, 1820, Varick and Abraham Thompson were elected elders, lacking a more standard means of being ordained to that office. During this time the New Haven church, a group on Long Island, and two groups in Pennsylvania expressed a desire to join with Zion rather than with Richard Allen. The first yearly conference of the new group opened on June 21, 1821, and appointments were made for the now six congregations in association. Varick was assigned as "District Chairman," meaning presiding elder, but there was no provision for that office yet. Further overtures to the Methodist Episcopal Church for help in ordination and other matters were rebuffed. At one point the Zion people said they would return to the mother church if they could have an all-Black annual conference. The Philadelphia Conference agreed to this, but the New York Conference, still stung by the Stillwell loss, did not agree. Finally on June 17, 1822, James Covel, Sylvester Hutchinson, and William Stillwell, all former elders of the Methodist Episcopal Church, ordained as elders Abraham Thompson, James Varick, and Leven Smith. Varick was then elected the first superintendent (as bishops were then termed), and consecrated on July 30, 1822. When the Methodist Episcopal General Conference of 1824 failed to take any relevant action to retain Zion, the separation became complete and final.

In his years as superintendent, Varick labored to organize the new church in a way that would set it upon a firm foundation. He drafted a book of discipline and church government modeled after the Methodist Episcopal Church. In 1827 he worked with Samuel Cornish and others to found *Freedom's Journal*, the first Black newspaper in the United States. On July 4, 1827, just two weeks before his death, he was able to celebrate the final emancipation of all slaves in New York state.

He is revered as the founder of what has become a major religious organization in the United States. In 1925, when the new structure of the Mother Zion Church was completed in New York, his ashes were removed from Woodlawn Cemetery and placed in a crypt underneath the sanctuary. A bust and tablet honoring him were placed in the sanctuary.

"Historical Notes: James Varick." *A.M.E. Zion Quarterly Review* 81 (Spring 1969): 41–43.
HAMEZCIA, CH, IBAW, DAB, WWWA (H), HAMEZC, AMEZC, OHYAMEZC, DARB, EWM, DANB, HNB.

VEDANTIC CENTER. A Hindu group. The Shanti Anantam Vedantic Center is a 48–acre community located in Southern California which represents a major thrust to relate Hinduism to African Americans. It was founded in 1975 in Woodland Hills, California, by spiritual teacher **Swami Turiyasangitananda** (Alice McLeod Coltrane). Originally a famous jazz player and singer, upon her husband's death in 1967 she became a disciple for some years of yoga teacher Swami Satchidananda, the founder and director of Integral Yoga International (now headquartered in Buckingham, Virginia). Coltrane followed him in India and Sri Lanka and perhaps learned from him (who preaches the One Truth at the basis of all religions) to encourage interreligious dialogue, a tendency evident in the poetry of her music and in the revelations described in her books, *Monument Eternal* and *Endless Wisdom*. In her writings, the Christian God, Allah, and devotion to Hindu gods are all part of her spirituality. The Vedantic Center also reflects her tendency: its logo carries the symbols of all the major world religions and is "religiously and philosophically eclectic" as Shankari Carol G. Adams states in the introduction to *Endless Wisdom*.

In 1984 Swami Turiyasangitananda moved the center to Agoura, California, where an ashram has been established in a secluded valley. There she teaches courses on Eastern thought, as much as on the Bible and Islamic texts, even though lectures mainly focus on Vedantic texts and Hindu spirituality. She has incorporated jazz and rhythm and blues music into the singing of bhajans, the traditional Hindu devotional songs. The community members are vegetarian and practice daily hatha yoga. The center publishes quarterly *A Vedantic Center Information Service* and the *Center News*. In 1987 the community reported a membership of about 20 adults and 15 children, and additional support from adherents who live in the greater Los Angeles area.

Shanti Anantam Bhajan Songbook. Agoura, CA: The Vedantic Center, 1983. 96 pp.
Turiyasangitananda, A. C. *Monument Eternal.* Los Angeles: Vedantic Book Press, 1977. 53 pp.
———. *Endless Wisdom.* Los Angeles: Avatar Book Institute, 1981. 240 pp.

Isotta Poggi

VERNON, WILLIAM TECUMSEH (July 11, 1871– July, 1944), 45th bishop of the **African Methodist Episcopal Church** (AME), was born in Lebanon, Missouri, the son of Adam and Margaret Vernon. His father was an AME minister who helped organize the church in southwest Missouri. As a teenager he graduated from the high school department of Lincoln University in Jefferson City, Missouri, as class orator and valedictorian. He studied for a time at Wilberforce University in Ohio, then taught public school in Missouri.

He was converted in 1896, was licensed to preach, and the same year joined the Missouri Conference. He was assigned to be president of Western University in Quindaro, Kansas, which at the time had only one building and about a dozen students. He quickly gained fame as a great orator and platform speaker and made connections with politicians on the state and national levels. Through his influence the state of Kansas gave $250,000 to help Western University. On August 18, 1901, he married Emily Jane Embry; there were no children. By the time he left the school in 1906 it had four large buildings, four hundred students, and a reputation as one of the finest schools for Blacks in the nation. Though he never received a college degree himself he had a keen mind and the ability to move with ease among both the powerful and lowly.

On June 12, 1906, President Theodore Roosevelt appointed him Registrar of the United States Treasury, one of the highest offices held by a Black person up to that time. His specific duties were not that time-consuming, and he spent much of his time traveling all over the country delivering speeches on behalf of the Republican party and the church. He held this position through the election of another Republican, William Taft, in 1908, but Taft was not as supportive of Blacks in the government. Vernon resigned in 1911 to work as supervisor of government schools for Blacks in the South. From 1912 to 1916 he was president of Campbell College in Jackson, Mississippi, where he successfully raised large sums of money for the school, and from 1916 to 1920 was pastor of Avery Chapel AME Church in Memphis, Tennessee. In that pastorate his preaching was so popular that additions to the already large sanctuary had to be made to accommodate the overflow crowds.

At the 1920 General Conference Vernon made a moving speech on missions and the next day became a surprise winner in the bishopric elections. He was assigned to the Seventeenth Episcopal District covering South Africa, but did not wish to go, thinking it was a land of savages. Nevertheless he went and found a land much to his liking. He established the Emily Vernon Institute in Basutoland and made friends with many tribal chiefs. In Nyasaland he befriended a seventeen-year-old boy, Hastings Banda, and helped send him to the United States for an education. Banda became a physician and internationally known for leadership in the Rhodesia-Nyasaland Federation seeking equal rights for Africans.

From 1924 to 1928 Vernon was assigned to the Fourth Episcopal District (Bermuda, Nova Scotia, Ontario, Michigan, Illinois, and Indiana), then from 1928 to 1932 headed the Arkansas area. At the 1932 General Conference Vernon was suspended on charges ranging from misuse of church funds to infidelity. Some observers have labeled the expulsion politically motivated and undeserved, but it remained in force. From 1933 to the end of his career he was an administrator at Western University, the school he worked so hard to build into a major institution. Churches have been named for him in Oklahoma, Michigan, Arkansas, Florida, and Bermuda.

Vernon, William Tecumseh. *Democracy and the Negro and a Plea for Suspension of Judgment*. N.p., n.d.

————. *The Upbuilding of a Race; or, the Rise of a Great People, a Compilation of Sermons, Addresses, and Writings on Education, the Race Question, and Public Affairs*. Quindaro, KS: Industrial Students Printers, 1904. 153 pp.

HUBA, BAW, BAMEC, EWM, WWCA (38–40), WWCR, HAMEC, EBA, AMECMIM, WWWA (5), CEAMEC.

VERRA, MICHAEL EDWARD (b. February 21, 1848, archbishop of the **Orthodox Catholic Church in America (Western Rite)**, was born and raised in New York City. He attended Adelphi University, from which he received his M.Ed. degree. He was ordained a priest in the American Catholic Church, Archdiocese of New York by Archbishop **James Francis Augustine Lashley** in 1974 and three years later, on June 4, 1977, consecrated as a bishop in the church also by Lashley, assisted by Sydney J. Ferguson. On January 30, 1982, he was installed as the new primate of the church, and

a short time later changed its name to Orthodox Church in America (Western Rite).

VIRGINIA BAPTIST THEOLOGICAL SEMINARY. A Baptist school. The Virginia Baptist Theological Seminary grew out of initiatives within the Virginia Baptist State Convention in 1887 which established a committee to pursue the idea of founding a school for ministerial training. A site was selected in Lynchburg, and the school opened in 1890. It was originally called the Virginia Theological Seminary and College. The first president was Rev. P. C. Morris, one of the outstanding African American Baptist leaders of the era and a leading figure in the founding of the **National Baptist Convention, U.S.A., Inc.** Unfortunately, Morris was forced to resign due to poor health and **Gregory Willis Hayes** was president when the school opened. A graduate of Oberlin College, Hayes also became the first president of the **National Baptist Educational Convention of the United States**, one of the organizations which merged to form the National Baptist Convention in 1895.

The school developed out of the strong desire expressed during the last quarter of the nineteenth century by many Blacks for Black control of Black institutions. Within Baptist circles, the issue became Black control of the college and Black authorship of religious education material. The issues which led to the school's creation have stayed with the school over the years and have had a determining role to play in its life and relationship with the Black community as a whole.

During the 1960s, the school was led by Dr. M. C. Allen, who emerged as one of the early supporters of Black economic development. Already in the 1950s he had developed a concept of Black power and Black consciousness. The seminary's students moved on to leadership roles in the 1960s and 1970s.

Fitts, Leroy. *A History of Black Baptists*. Nashville, TN: Broadman Press, 1985. 368 pp.

VIRGINIA UNION UNIVERSITY. A Baptist school. Virginia Union University united several early attempts among Baptists to respond to the new conditions created at the end of the war and provide educational opportunities for the freedmen. The first such venture originated in 1864 by an independent organization, the National Theological Institute in Washington, D.C. The institute began to lobby for a national effort to provide education and religious nurture among African

Americans, and began holding classes in 1865. It was soon joined by Wayland Seminary founded by the American Baptists Home Missions Society (supported primarily by White Baptists in the northern states). The seminary opened in Washington, D.C., using the facilities of the Nineteenth Street Baptist Church. It was named for Francis Wayland, a powerful figure among Northern Baptists, who actively supported the new school. The Wayland seminary absorbed the National Theological Institute in 1869.

Meanwhile a third effort, a night school, the Richmond Theological Institute for Freedmen, was started in Richmond, Virginia, by Rev. J. B. Birney. He abandoned his effort the next year because of local opposition, but it was continued by Rev. Nathaniel Colver, an abolitionist from Chicago. Birney opened the Colver Institute in 1867. The American Baptist Home Mission Society assumed control of the new school and soon renamed it Richmond Theological Seminary. They appointed Rev. Charles Corey as president, who served for the rest of the century. In 1898 the society merged Wayland Seminary and Richmond Theological Seminary to form Virginia Union University. Still concerned with the education of ministers, the new school was additionally ready to develop a full liberal arts curriculum. Wayland Seminary became the men's school and Richmond Theological Seminary a graduate school of religion. The university was joined in 1932 by Hartshorn Memorial College, a women's school, and in 1964 by Storer College. Storer had been the oldest school for African Americans in West Virginia. It had actually closed in 1955 but officially closed by merging into the university.

During the early twentieth century, Black Baptists began to assume a more active role in teaching and administration of the university. In 1936 John M. Ellison became the first Black president of the institution. It became one of the first schools accredited by the Southern Association of Colleges and Secondary Schools, and its School of Religion seminary is accredited by the American Association of Theological Schools. It currently enjoys support from the several National Baptist Conventions, the **American Baptist Churches in the U.S.A.**, and the Southern Baptist Convention.

Fitts, Leroy. *A History of Black Baptists.* Nashville, TN: Broadman Press, 1985. 368 pp.

VODOU. "Voodoo" is a term used by outsiders for the African-based, Catholic-influenced religious practices of the people of Haiti, an impoverished, agricultural country occupying the western third of the island of Hispaniola in the Caribbean Sea. Scholars believe that the word voodoo itself is derived from *vodu* or *vodou*, which was used by the Fon-speaking people of Dahomey in West Africa (today called Benin) as a collective term for the deities that controlled the daily activities of people and that ruled the forces of nature such as fire and lightning. Haitians themselves have only recently begun to use *vodou* to refer to their religion and still prefer to speak of their ritual practices as "serving the spirits." Modern-day Haitians also use *vodou* to refer to particular ritual or dance styles among the many in their religious repertoire. The modern use of the term *vodou* rather than *voodoo* also emphasizes the observation that it is an African-based religion influenced by Catholicism, not an African-Catholic synthesis.

Sympathetic modern scholars like Karen McCarthy Brown counter the highly distorted and sensationalized depictions of Haitian religion (which many believe were propagated by fearful White slaveowners in the aftermath of Haiti's successful slave revolution in 1804) by describing it as a "repository for wisdom accumulated by a people who have lived through slavery, hunger, disease, repression, corruption, and violence." Brown also notes that vodou has been a source of empowerment for Haitians in general and for women in particular, both in Haiti itself and in the Haitian subcultures of New York City and Miami. In addition, she contends that the ritual prescriptions of vodou provide its participants with survival skills and a sense of self-respect in conditions of political and economic hardship.

The underlying foundations of the vodou world-view originated in the cultural traditions of eighteenth- and nineteenth-century West Africa. These traditions (especially those of the Fon-speaking and Ashanti peoples of Dahomey and of the Yoruba peoples of Nigeria) conceived of the universe as a large force field in which human beings interacted with the spirits of the soil, rocks, mountains, trees and rivers, and in which the ghosts of departed ancestors continued to affect the lives of their offspring in both positive and negative ways. The spirit beings were believed to be accessible to humans for guidance in making decisions and for healing and protection from harmful forces.

At the apex of the West African religious system was a supreme divine power, underneath which existed the deities responsible for the harmonious operation of the natural world. This group of spirits were known as the gods of war and peace, fire and iron, rivers and mountains, and disease and health. The ancestor spirits were the next step lower in this hierarchy and were believed to make certain that their earthly offspring properly carried out traditional moral precepts. The lowest level of divine power consisted of the heads of various clans, tribes, and families.

West Africans also believed in the dominant force of fate, which predetermined the outcome of each person's life. An individual's destiny could sometimes be foreseen through a system of divination based on the patterns in which seeds combined when thrown in a set number. The West African concept of fate taught that this force could be subverted or changed with the help of the divine trickster. This figure carried messages to the deity concerning the destiny of particular individuals and was believed capable of being persuaded to alter these messages so that an unhappy fate could be changed into a happy one.

The higher deities of West African religion could only be communicated with through a priestly intermediary. These priests or priestesses were the only ones who knew the proper way to perform the sacrificial rites. Sacrifices were offered to appease an angry deity, to prevent adversity, to purify individuals or a tribe, and to provide compensatory offerings for things a deity desired. The priest was also indispensable to the essential experience of West African religion, spirit possession. During rites of possession, a priest allowed a deity to take over his or her identity and to speak words of wisdom, guidance, or admonition to the community. These possession ceremonies were often accompanied by rhythmic clapping, singing, dancing, and drum-beating.

The West African worldview conceived of life as a continuous battle during which the life-force of individuals was constantly in danger of attack from hostile spirit beings. The medicine man was the person who was called upon to counteract such negative forces. This he was able to do through a combination of chanting, herbal medicine, magical practices, and rites of exorcism. A sorcerer was the negative counterpart of the medicine man. This powerful figure was called upon in times of war to attack the vitality of the enemy by magical spells and poisoning.

These elements of West African religion were brought to the West Indies and the American colonies by Africans who had been captured and sold as slaves. Although little is known of how exactly these traditions were formed into the vodou religious system, it is clear that vodou originated on the sugar plantations of Haiti during the height of the slave trade in the eighteenth century. Vodou helped provide continuity, identity, and self-empowerment to Africans who had been torn from their cultural matrix and forced to live in conditions of cruelty and hardship. Evidence supports the contention that vodou played a significant role in the successful Haiti slave rebellion of 1804.

The Roman Catholic overlay in vodou religion came about because of the French domination of Haiti during its pre-independence period. The church acknowledged that slaves were persons and sought to convert them to the Catholic faith. Many of the West African slaves were highly amenable to the Catholic conception of a supreme god and his angels and saints, who, like their own lesser deities, were honored with festivals and prayed to for practical assistance. In addition, it was not viewed as a betrayal of West African religious sensibilities to adopt a new god, provided this new god was efficacious in bringing a person practical benefits. Given the dominance of the White slaveowners, many slaves acknowledged the advantage inherent in honoring their gods.

In order to assist in the process of conversion, the Catholic authorities allowed for certain accomodations to African belief to occur. Thus, for instance, the Dahomean serpent-deity Da became identified with Saint Patrick, and the Dahomean god of entrances Legba was identified with the Catholic celestial gatekeeper Saint Peter. In the conditions of oppression and identity confusion brought about by slavery, West African medicine men and sorcerers thrived. Sorcerers in particular shrewdly disguised their practices with Catholic rites and traditions, and the resulting syncretistic system of mystical-magical practice and lore became the vodou of post-colonial Haiti. Today's vodou priests and priestesses regularly incorporate Catholic prayers and images into their practices, and vodou spirits often direct believers to undergo such Catholic rites as baptism, communion, and confession as part of their healing process.

Vodou practices were brought to the United States by Haitian slaves who were taken to Cuba by their French owners during the slave rebellion of 1804, and who subsequently migrated to New Orleans in 1809. Vodou rites and beliefs were also carried to New Orleans by Santo Domingan free Blacks, who had been forced to evacuate Hispaniola because they were identified with the White slaveowners. The Santo Domingan refugees and Haitian slaves began practicing their vodou ceremonies publicly in the second decade of the nineteenth century, though these practices were proscribed by various laws between 1820 and 1850. As a result of this repression, the rites went underground and contributed to a flourishing secret subculture of vodou religion that produced such prominent figures as the "voodoo queens" (free quadroon priestesses of vodou who became the focus and power of the cult)

Marie Laveau and her daughter Marie II in mid-century New Orleans. Vodou practices also came to the United States in the twentieth century with Haitian immigrants to New York City (where an estimated 450,000 Haitians are now ministered to by several hundred *manbos*—priestesses) and Miami.

A colorful 1825 ceremony in honor of the snake god Dambala was recounted to the journalist J. W. Buell in the late nineteenth century. This rite, which took place in New Orleans, began with rhythmic beating on various sized drums using the thigh bones of steers and smaller animals. Gourds filled with small pebbles were shaken to provide a counter beat. The ritual's participants then formed a semi-circle around the *manbo*, who in turn called four priests forward, sprinkled them with a ceremonial liquid, and pronounced a magical formula over them. Upon the *manbo's* signal, a priest removed a snake from a container, coaxed it to rise, and ceremonially passed it over the gathered participants. When the ritual meal was completed, the snake was again displayed, and then hurled into a fire. At this point, a woman dancer entered the ritual circle and began a dance that imitated the snake's characteristic movements. The other participants then reportedly entered into an ecstatic dance together which ended in an orgiastic celebration.

Male (*oungan*) and female (*manbo*) vodou functionaries conduct their rituals in both the cities and the countryside. In urban settings, the rituals take place in what is called an *ounfo*, or temple. This sacred space consists of a *peristil*—the central dancing and ceremonial area—and small adjoining rooms where altars are maintained (called *jevo*). In the countryside, small cult houses are set up on family land specially set aside for the spirits. Rural vodou differs from urban vodou in that the manner in which the spirits are served in the countryside is largely determined by ancestral inheritance and land tenure. Urban vodou is more institutionalized and complex than rural practice, and the urban initiates form a community that serves as a substitute for the extended kinship groups of the countryside.

The differences between rural and urban vodou also extend to the ceremonies themselves. The ideal in the countryside is to perform the rituals with simplicity and according to the ancient African traditions. When misfortunes hit, the inference is made that the family spirits have been angered in some way. At these times, special propitiatory ceremonies are held that may include energetic drumming and dancing as well as animal sacrifice.

The more routinized and elaborate urban rites are celebrated cyclically and honor the major vodou deities on the feast days of related Catholic saints. These rites, like those of their rural counterparts, usually include some form of animal sacrifice. Both urban and rural ceremonies are performed to serve such community needs as healing the sick, inaugurating new temples, initiating candidates for the vodou priesthood, and guiding the souls of the dead to the underworld.

The purpose of vodou communal rites such as drumming and dancing is to provide the proper atmosphere for the entrancement of the *oungan* or *manbo*. The entranced priest is believed to be possessed by a particular deity and to be used by this spirit to voice guidance and admonitions to the assembled believers. Offerings are made to the deity during this ceremony in order to assuage its anger and ensure its future beneficence.

The connotations of Black magic that surround the term vodou probably derive from the observed practices of vodou sorcerers who are believed to conjure spirits or powers to help people attain revenge, wealth, love, and power. These sorcerers also deal in *zombi*— either souls of the dead whose powers are manipulated for personal ends or the bodies of persons whose souls have purportedly left (which are used for menial labor). Less sinister vodou practices include divinatory rites, healing with herb compounds, the manufacture of talismans for the protection of land and family, and the concoction of love potions. All of these practices function to restore harmony in disrupted social systems.

In a significant recent development, nearly 100 *oungans* and *manbos* were killed by Haitian mobs following the ouster of the government of Jean Claude Duvalier in 1986. The main motive for these attacks appeared to be popular revenge against the Tontons Macoute militia that had served as the pillar of Duvalier's political power and had included vodou priests and leaders. These attacks were also spurred by the slander against vodou by fundamentalist Protestant and charismatic Catholic groups in Haiti that have long labelled vodou practices as Satanic. In the wake of this persecution, vodou practice has receded somewhat into the background. Haitian intellectuals have condemned this course of events as an attack on the foundations of Haitian culture, identity, and religious belief.

Anderson, John Q. "The New Orleans Voodoo Ritual Dance and Its Twentieth-Century Survivals." *Southern Folklore Quarterly* 23, 3 (Spring, 1959).

Brown, Karen McCarthy. *Mama Lola: A Vodou Priestess in Brooklyn.* Berkeley, CA: University of California Press, 1991.

Davis, Wade. *The Serpent and the Rainbow.* New York: 1985.

Haskins, Jim. *Voodoo and Hoodoo: Their Tradition and Craft as Revealed by Actual Practitioners.* New York: Stein and Day, 1978. 226 pp.

Metraux, Alfred. *Voodoo in Haiti.* London: Sphere Books, 1974. 368 pp.

Thompson, Richard Farris. *Flash of the Spirit: African and Afro-American Art and Philosophy.* New York: 1981.

Touchstone, Blake. "Voodoo in New Orleans." *Louisiana History* 13, 4 (Fall, 1972): 371–86.

Phillip Charles Lucas

VOORHEES COLLEGE. An **Episcopal Church** School. Voorhees College, Denmark, South Carolina, was founded in 1897, by Elizabeth Evelyn Wright, a young African American educator. Wright had previously attempted to found a school in two other locations but had been driven out by local hostility. In Denmark, she found assistance from S. G. Mayfield, a White man and state senator, who was impressed by the letter of support from **Booker T. Washington** which Wright had received. He helped her secure the land upon which the school opened with its original fourteen students.

The school functioned during its first five years as the Denmark Industrial School, but in 1902, Wright was placed in contact with the family of Ralph Voorhees, a blind philanthropist from New Jersey. He made a generous donation to the school which was renamed in his honor. Wright led the school until her death in 1906. For a number of years it stagnated, but in 1922 Joshua Blanton became its new principal. He revived the school by initiating a relationship with the Episcopal Church which has continued to this day. He also copied the earlier example of Fisk University and organized a singing group which toured the country raising money for the school.

Under Blanton's direction the program steadily improved. In 1929 the junior college curriculum was added and the name changed to Voorhees Normal and Industrial School. In 1947 the industrial department was discontinued. In 1967 the school became a senior four-year liberal arts college. The school now serves approximately 600 students annually.

"The portrayal of the universal God was such that an affirmation of this God meant a simultaneous negation of all others' cultural perceptions of divinity, as well as a negation of those very cultures. Nowhere was this more clear than in the area of Christian Foreign missions where conversion to Christianity implicitly meant deculturalization and acceptance of the western value system on the part of Asians, Africans, and Latin Americans."

Jacquelyn Grant, Theologian
Interdenominational Theological Center
1986

W

WACTOR, JAMES WESLEY (September 13, 1908–June, 1985), 71st bishop of the **African Methodist Episcopal Zion Church** (AMEZ), was born in Hoke County, North Carolina, the son of Henry Lee and Annie Bell (Campbell) Wactor. He grew up attending the Fair Promise AMEZ Church in Sanford, North Carolina. After finishing high school at Lee County Training School in Sanford, he went to Livingstone College in Salisbury, North Carolina, where he earned his B.A. degree in 1935. He was ordained a deacon on July 30, 1933, and elder on November 17, 1935. On July 3, 1934, he married Hildred Anita Henry; there were no children.

His pastorates before World War II included the Maineville Circuit near Salisbury, North Carolina; White Rock, Granite Quarry, and New Hope near Salisbury; Young's Chapel AMEZ Church in Morristown, Tennessee; Kesler Temple AMEZ Church in Henderson, North Carolina; Mattocks Memorial AMEZ Church in Fayetteville, North Carolina; St. James AMEZ Church in Red Springs, North Carolina; and Barry Avenue AMEZ Church in Mamaroneck, New York.

While in New York he did further study at Union Theological Seminary, then joined the war effort as a chaplain. He finished Chaplain's School at Harvard University in 1943, was briefly Assistant Post Chaplain at Fort Huachuca, Arizona, then saw overseas service with the 376th Engineer Regiment. After the war he and his wife continued in European military service, working in North Africa, Italy, France, and Germany. In 1946 he was cited for building the first American chapel on German soil, and for a time was on the board of directors of the German Youth Activities Program for Kaiser Wilhelm in Mannheim, Germany.

In 1948 Wactor returned to the United States to pastor Hood Memorial AMEZ Church in New York City, where he remained for twelve years. From 1960 to 1964 he pastored Big Zion Church in Mobile, Alabama, then from 1964 to 1972 was appointed to Metropolitan AMEZ Church in Birmingham, Alabama.

Each of his pastorates was marked by various standards of success, including reduction of mortgages, renovation of property, increase in community services, and increase in membership. At the 1972 General Conference Wactor was elected bishop and was consecrated on May 12, 1972. He was assigned to the Seventh Episcopal District (Blue Ridge, Albermarle, Florida, and South Florida Conferences), moving in 1980 to the Fifth Episcopal District (Philadelphia-Baltimore, Allegheny, and Virginia Conferences).

As bishop he supervised the construction of many new church buildings and was an active member and one-time director of both the Florida Council of Churches and North Carolina Council of Churches. He was a life member of the N.A.A.C.P. and served on both the World Methodist Conference and World Council of Churches. From 1954 to 1956 he was on the Evangelism Committee of the National Council of Churches. He was a trustee for a number of schools, including Lomax-Hannon Junior College in Greenville, Alabama, Clinton Junior College in Rock Hill, South Carolina, and Livingstone College in Salisbury, North Carolina. He was chair of the Board of Statistics and Records for the church and served in numerous other capacities in the denomination. In 1984 the church celebrated the Wactors' Golden Wedding Anniversary. This celebration was both joyous and poignant, since at the 1984 General Conference he had retired, stating honestly that with his illness doctors did not offer a good prognosis for the future.

"Biographical Sketch of Bishop James W. Wactor." *A.M.E. Zion Quarterly Review* 84 (Fall 1972): 162–163.

"Bishop James W. Wactor Funeral Held at Evans Metropolitan AMEZ." *Star of Zion* 109 (July 11, 1985): 1, 2.

"Retiring Prelate and Wife Honored on Golden Anniversary." *Star of Zion* 108 (September 20, 1984):1, 2.

Sawyer, Carrie W. "Brief Profile of Bishop and Mrs. J. W. Wactor." *Star of Zion* 95 (August 31, 1972): 1, 7.

Wactor, James W. "Dr. Wactor for Bishop." *Star of Zion* 83 (May 12, 1960): 7.

BDNM (75), *WWR* (75–76), *WWA* (84–85), *AMEZC*.

WADDLES, CHARLESZETTA LINA (b. October 7, 1912), Pentecostal minister and founder of Waddles Perpetual Mission for Saving Souls of All Nations, was born in St. Louis, Missouri, the oldest of seven children in the family of Henry and Ella (Brown) Campbell. Her father worked in a barber shop until he unknowingly serviced someone with impetigo, a contagious skin disease, and thereby lost his business. He never recovered from the ordeal, and Waddles saw him sink into poverty and depression. She also watched the church members shun him as he became more needy. This experience was formative for her. She attended public schools in St. Louis until age twelve, when her father's death forced her to leave school and work to help support the family. Her mother had a heart condition that severely limited her activity.

Waddles married a man named Clifford Walker when she was only fourteen, and was a widow at the age of nineteen. She married again at age twenty-one, and they moved to Detroit in 1937 where her husband found a job as a cook. That marriage ended in divorce, and she and her seven children returned to St. Louis to look after her ailing mother, until her mother's death. Waddles had a short, common-law relationship that gave her two more children. For years she lived on the edge of survival, the major money coming in being Aid to Dependent Children. Even so, she was ready to help someone else in need. When a friend with two children was about to lose her house, Waddles gave up her own house to live in her friend's basement, and the fresh income saved the house.

At age thirty-six, living in that basement, Waddles had a vision telling her to "create a church that had a social conscience, that would feed the hungry, clothe the naked, and take folks in from outdoors." Only gradually did this unfold. She held prayer meetings in her house and collected cans of food. In 1950 she opened a "thirty-five-cent restaurant," where every meal cost thirty-five cents. She did the cooking, laundry, and almost everything else for the enterprise. In 1956 she married Payton Waddles, whom she met at a church barbecue. The marriage took her off welfare, and she was enabled to do even more work for the poor.

About 1956 she gained access to a warehouse in the slums of Detroit's East Side, and founded Waddle's Perpetual Mission for Saving Souls of All Nations. In 1956 she was ordained a Pentecostal minister and the Mission was her own church and social services mission wrapped in one package. Ever since, in various Detroit locations, the Mission has provided spiritual succor as well as clothing, food, shelter, adult education, an employment bureau, medicine, transportation, and most anything else required by the poor. The Mission receives no federal money, and is constantly facing financial difficulties. Waddles depends upon a volunteer staff of up to 200 people, donations of items and money, radio and church fund-raising, and corporate sponsorship. She has also written a book on self-esteem, a book describing her personal philosophy of life, two cookbooks, and has produced the *Mother Waddles Christmas Album*. All proceeds, of course, go to the work of the Mission. Her husband passed away in 1980, but some of her children are regular workers at the Mission. The Detroit Mission is now headquarters for a network of ten urban missions across the country and two others in Africa. The Mission is working to provide a school to retrain people who have lost their jobs through plant closings and permanent layoffs.

"Mother Waddles" has been the subject of a Public Broadcasting Service (P.B.S.) documentary, "Ya Done Good" (1989) and numerous newspaper articles. She has been included in the Black Woman Oral History Project of the Schlesinger Library at Radcliffe College, and is depicted in the Smithsonian Institution Black Woman of Courage Traveling Exhibit. She has been the recipient of many awards and honors, including the Humanitarian Award presented by President Richard Nixon; the Volunteer Leadership Award presented by Governor William Milliken; the Humanitarian Award presented by Mayor Roman Gribbs; the Lane Bryant Citizens Award; the Sojourner Truth Award; and the Religious Heritage Award.

"Mother Waddles's Mission." *Newsweek* 79 (May 1, 1972): 123.

Smith, Vern E. "The Perpetual Mission of Mother Waddles." *Ebony* 27 (May 1972): 50–58.

BDA-AHP, NBAW, BH, BWR, BDNM (75), *WWABA* (92–93), *IBAW*.

WALDEN UNIVERSITY. A Methodist Episcopal Church school. Walden University was founded in 1865 in the basement of Clark Memorial Methodist Episcopal Church in Nashville, Tennessee. It was the first school organized by the newly created Freedman's Aid Society of the Methodist Episcopal Church. New facilities were secured on behalf of the society by Rev. John M. Walden at the close of the Civil War. These facilities served until a permanent campus site was purchased in 1867. Upon the move to the new site, the school was named Central Tennessee College. Through the 1870s and 1880s the school grew at a rapid pace through the addition of a medical (1876), industrial (1884), dental (1886) and pharmaceutical (1889) department. An African Training School was created in 1888 to train missionaries for Africa. The diversification of the program prompted the name change to Walden University.

The first decade of the twentieth century proved costly to the school. In 1900 Rev. John Braden, president since the school's founding, died. Three years later a fire took twelve lives. Several lawsuits tied up the school for a number of years and delayed its purchase of new equipment and the rebuilding of facilities. Walden never fully recovered and was closed in 1935. The medical, dental, and pharmaceutical school, however, survived as Meharry Medical College and remains an important institution within the Black community.

Stowell, Jay S. *Methodist Adventures in Negro Education.* New York: Methodist Book Concern, 1922. 190 pp.

WALKER, CHARLES THOMAS (February 5, 1858–July 29, 1921), vice-president of the **National Baptist Convention, U.S.A., Inc.** (N.B.C.U.S.A.) and founder of one of the largest Black churches in the United States, was born into slavery near Hephzibah, Richmond County, Georgia, the youngest of eleven children in the family of Thomas and Hannah Walker. His father died of pneumonia two days before Walker was born, and his mother died one year after the end of the Civil War, when Walker was eight years old. He moved around from relative to relative, and in 1873 settled as a farm hand for an uncle, Nathan Walker.

Nathan Walker and another uncle, Joseph T. Walker, were well-known Baptist ministers, as were many other relatives, and Walker was soaked in this environment. He experienced conversion and then was baptized in July 1873 into the Franklin Covenant Baptist Church, pastored by Nathan Walker. He plunged into every aspect of church life, and began to sense a call to the ministry. His education was weak, however, and in 1874 he entered the Augusta Institute (later Atlanta Baptist College and now Morehouse College), a major trainer of Black Baptist ministers. He could not afford the school, but managed to continue through the aid of friends and philanthropists. He finished the coursework in about 1877, but did not formally graduate because the school was not yet settled enough to offer diplomas.

Walker was licensed to preach in September 1876, and was ordained in May 1877. On October 1, 1877, he accepted the pastorate of the Franklin Covenant Baptist

Church, where he had been baptized, and actually began work there on January 1, 1878. Within one year he was also pastor of the Thankful Baptist Church in Waynesboro; McKinnie's Branch Baptist Church in Burke County; and Mount Olive Baptist Church in Augusta. He was at each about one Sunday per month. On June 19, 1879, he married Violet Q. Franklin, with whom he had four children, only one of whom reached maturity. In early 1880 he resigned from his churches to pastor the First Baptist Church of La Grange, Georgia. While at La Grange his exceptional preaching ability became apparent as he added 300 members through revival meetings and received many preaching invitations. He began a school that grew into La Grange Academy, a large Baptist high school. He also read law for two years under Judge Walker, but was not admitted to the bar.

In 1883 he left La Grange to pastor the Central Baptist Church in Augusta. This venerable church had been engaged in a vicious internal feud for some months prior to his arrival, and the animosities continued even afterward. Finally, the church was put up for auction in 1885 and the proceeds divided equally between representatives of the two factions. Walker was retained as the pastor of one faction that eventually organized as the Tabernacle Baptist Church, with 310 members. A new building on Ellis Street was dedicated on December 13, 1885, and its cost of $13,500 was covered within two years. Soon it was the leading black church in Augusta, and Walker had a wide reputation as a pulpit orator. By October 1, 1899, he had converted more than 2,000 people and added more than 1,400 to the membership rolls. From 1884 to 1896 he was business manager of the *Augusta Sentinel*, a weekly paper. In 1891 he was instrumental in moving a Baptist primary and high school from Waynesboro to Augusta, a move which greatly benefitted the school and the city. He founded the Tabernacle Old Folks' Home in Augusta. In 1891 the Tabernacle Baptist Church became the first Black church in the country to send its minister on a trip to the Holy Land.

In 1886 **William J. Simmons** convened the **American National Baptist Convention** in St. Louis, a forerunner of today's National Baptist Convention, U.S.A., Inc. Walker was one of three delegates from Georgia and served on the Committee on Permanent Organization. He became famous for speeches counseling moderation in race relations. During the 1890s his reputation as a compelling speaker made him a key preacher in revivals across the country, and he gained the title of the "Black Spurgeon," after Charles Haddon Spurgeon (1834–1892), a famous British Baptist preacher. In June 1898 he was appointed army chaplain with the rank of captain and assigned to Spanish-American War duty with the 9th Immune Regiment, which he joined in Cuba in November. After only two months he resigned his commission and returned to Augusta.

On October 1, 1899, Walker became the new pastor of Mount Olivet Baptist Church in New York City, much to the chagrin of the Tabernacle Baptist Church, which stipulated that he could return to his former position at any time. In less than three years the membership at Mount Olivet jumped from 430 to 1,800, and on one Sunday in March 1900 Walker baptized 184 people at once. Very quickly he organized the Colored Men's Branch of the Y.M.C.A., which was accepted as a regular branch, the first of its kind in New York City, soon after its formal application on December 18, 1900. In June 1901, the Tabernacle Baptist Church in Augusta once again requested his services as pastor. The New York church organized a spectacular series of events to express the desire that he remain with them. In December 1901, Walker decided to remain in New York with an associate minister, but to become also the nominal minister in Augusta and visit there several times a year, supplying other pulpit speakers the rest of the time.

In 1903 Walker finally left New York and returned to the Tabernacle Baptist Church, where he remained the rest of his life. By this time he was an international celebrity, and some called him the "greatest Negro preacher of his time." He held many high offices in the denomination, including secretary of the Missionary Baptist Convention of Georgia (eight years); vice-president of the Missionary Baptist Convention of Georgia (two years); treasurer of the Sunday School Workers' Convention of Georgia (several years); vice-president of the Georgia Interdenominational Sunday School Convention; treasurer of the N.B.C.U.S.A.; vice-president of the N.B.C.U.S.A. for the New York region; and vice-president of the N.B.C.U.S.A. for the Georgia region. He was a delegate to the Baptist World Alliance meeting in London in 1905 and was later a speaker at its meeting in Philadelphia. In 1910 he unsuccessfully challenged **Elias C. Morris** for the presidency of the N.B.C.U.S.A. In February 1918 he addressed 12,000 in Chicago on "The Nation's Call to Service and the Black Man's Answer," and on September 14, 1919 he addressed 8,000 delegates to the Walker Baptist Association on "The Duty of the Negro During the Reconstruction Period."

Floyd, Silas Xavier. *The Life of Charles T. Walker, D.D.* 1902. 193 pp.

Walker, Charles Thomas. *An Appeal to Caesar. Sermon on the Race Question by Rev. C. T. Walker.* New York: Pusey & Troxell, 1900. 32 pp.

————. *The Colored Man Abroad: What He Saw in the Holy Land and Europe.* Augusta, GA: J. M. Weigle, 1892. 148 pp.

————. *Fifty Years of Freedom for the Negro. Delivered at the Jubilee Celebration of the National Baptist Convention, Nashville, Tennessee, Friday, Sept. 19, 1913.* Augusta, GA: The Georgia Baptist, 1913. 15 pp.

————. "The Negro Church as a Medium for Race Expression." In Arcadius S. Trawick, ed. *The New Voice in Race Adjustments.* New York: Student Volunteer Movement, 1914, 50–54.

————. *Reply to William Hannibal Thomas, Author of The American Negro, the 20th Century Slanderer of the Negro Race.* N.p., 1901? 31 pp.

SCA, HUBA, AARS, NCAB (13), NYTO, BAW, WWWA (1).

WALKER, DAVID (September 28, 1785–June 28, 1830), abolitionist, author, and lay Methodist theologian, was born in Wilmington, North Carolina, to a free mother and a slave father. As the child's status always followed that of the mother, he was free. Though free, the circumstances of his childhood in the South were very harsh. He traveled widely in the South, observing the brutal treatment of slaves, and determined to move North. After many trials he reached Boston, Massachusetts, learned how to read and write, and in 1827 started a second-hand clothing business on Brattle Street. He joined the Methodist Church in Boston. In 1828 he married a woman named Eliza, with whom he had one child, born after Walker had died. That child, Edward G. Walker, in 1866 became the first Black elected to the Massachusetts State Legislature.

Walker's home became a refuge for fugitive slaves and he was always generous with the poor. He spent much of his spare time reading the history of slavery from the time of Egypt to his own time and began to speak and write on behalf of the people of color in America and around the world. One of his first articles, "Address Delivered Before the General Colored Association," was published in *Freedom's Journal* (December 1828). In it he denounced slaveholders and called for Black unity, but in a restrained manner. In 1829 he published his most famous work, *David Walker's Appeal in Four Articles Together with a Preamble to the Colored Citizens of the World, But in Particular and Very Expressly, to Those of the United States of America.* This essay exhibited none of the previous restraint, and very pointedly stated that the majority of Whites were the "natural enemies" of

Blacks. He appealed to slaves to take their destinies in hand and rise up against their oppressors.

Walker was intensely religious, and believed that through the action of rising up to claim justice Blacks could play a messianic role in God's plan for the world. The *Appeal* was filled with biblical imagery and prophecy, and has been called "one of the most remarkable religious documents of the Protestant era." Despite his relentless critique of the church he remained a sincere believer, and saw his mission as calling other true believers to defend the message of Christ against its misuse. His denunciations of generations of Whites who lived off the sweat of Black people were severe, and he framed any violence that might result from rebellion in terms of justifiable self-defense. He believed that not all Whites were enemies and willingly accepted the support of White allies. He also counseled forgiveness if slaveholders would repent of their sins and willingly release their slaves.

The publication of his *Appeal* brought strong reaction in the South. White officials in a number of states passed laws forbidding it and similar provocative literature, on pain of death, while Blacks smuggled copies from plantation to plantation. The pamphlet went through three editions very quickly, and after the introduction of the second edition William Lloyd Garrison, the famous White abolitionist, was accused of being connected with it and was forced to leave the country for a time. It became one of the most widely circulated books of the anti-slavery movement. Friends of Walker, fearing for his life, urged him to move to Canada, but he refused, saying, "I will stand my ground." A group of Georgia men offered a reward for Walker of $1,000 dead and $10,000 alive. They vowed to fast until he was taken, and many believe Walker died of poisoning. Although it is not known for certain that Nat Turner read the *Appeal*, its publication is counted as among the most powerful events leading to Turner's Rebellion in 1831.

Buckingham, Peter. "David Walker: An Appeal to Whom?" *Negro History Bulletin* 42 (January 1979): 24–26.

Diamond, John C., Jr. "David Walker's 'Appeal,' A Theological Interpretation." *Journal of the Interdenominational Theological Center* 3 (Fall 1975): 32–39.

Garnet, Henry Highland. *Walker's Appeal with a Brief Sketch of His Life*. New York: J. H. Tobitt, 1848.

Walker, David. *David Walker's Appeal in Four Articles Together with a Preamble to the Colored Citizens of the World, But in Particular and Very Expressly, to Those of the United States of America*. Boston: D. Walker, 1829. 76 pp.

BRBR, HNRA, BHBA, NA, NAHDA, PP, MBRL, NG, ESH, BNA, EBA, AAE, DAB, SBAA, WWWA (H), *HNB, NCAB* (14), *DANB, BAW, DNAADB, HUBA, IBAWCB, IBAW, BWA, BPJ*.

WALKER, DOUGAL ORMONDE BEACONS-FIELD (January 5, 1890–June 28, 1955), 66th bishop of the **African Methodist Episcopal Church** (AME), was born in Layou, St. Vincent, British West Indies, the son of George Oswald and Maria (Jeffers) Walker. After attending public schools in Layou, he attended the Latin School of Kingstown, then Howard University in Washington, D.C., from 1909 to 1911. He received his S.T.B. in 1914 from Boston University, and in 1914–15 was a student at Andover-Newton Theological School in Massachusetts. On April 21, 1915, he married Eva Revallion, with whom he had one daughter.

He pastored the People's AME Church in Chelsea, Massachusetts, from 1912 to 1915, where he increased the membership from 8 to 103. He was ordained deacon in 1913 and elder in 1915. His next pastorate was Bethel AME Church in New Bedford, Massachusetts (1915–20), where he rebuilt the church after a disastrous fire and then eliminated the entire indebtedness. He was next at St. James AME Church in Winston-Salem, North Carolina (1920–22), where he purchased land for a new parsonage. At St. Paul AME Church in Raleigh, North Carolina (1922–25), he purchased land and built a parsonage. While in Raleigh he took the opportunity to enroll in Shaw University, where he earned his B.A. in 1924. Next he pastored Bethel AME Church in Wilkes Barre, Pennsylvania (1925–26), where he built another parsonage and added 215 members. At St. James AME Church in Cleveland, Ohio (1926–36), he reduced the indebtedness and increased the membership from 486 to 1,267. While in Cleveland he continued his education at Western Reserve University, where he earned an M.A. in 1932.

In 1936 he was elected president of Wilberforce University in Ohio, and during his five-year tenure he increased the endowment, made many improvements to the campus, and oversaw its accreditation with the North Central Association of Colleges and Secondary Schools (1939). He was not known for his tact, and was outspoken in his criticism of Governor John W. Bricker, who finally forced his ouster from the presidency of Wilberforce. From 1941 to 1948 Walker pastored Bethel AME Church in Buffalo, New York, where he cleared a major debt. He was elected dean of Payne Theological Seminary at Wilberforce in June 1944, but refused the offer. He was elected bishop on the first ballot in 1948, but soon afterward had a physical breakdown. Upon recovery he served the Fifth Episcopal District, with headquarters in Wilberforce, Ohio, until his death in 1955. Named for him are churches in Los Angeles, California, St. Louis, Missouri, Long Beach, California, and St. Vincent's Island.

EWM, RLA, WWWA (3), *BAMEC.*

WALKER, GEORGE W., SR. (b. c.1935), a bishop of the **African Methodist Episcopal Zion Church** (AMEZ), began his ministry at the Rock Hill and Piney Grove charges in Pageland, South Carolina, in 1959–60. He married Geraldine Jackson Walker, a teacher. In 1960–61 he was assigned to Mt. Airy and St. James AMEZ churches in Cheraw, South Carolina. From 1961 to 1968 he pastored Foundation and Tabernacle AMEZ churches in Rock Hill, South Carolina, where he purchased a parsonage and completed major remodeling on the churches.

From 1968 to 1972 Walker was appointed to Jones Memorial AMEZ Church in Columbia, South Carolina, where he led a substantial renovation on the interior and exterior of the building. From 1972 to 1988 he pastored Greater Walters AMEZ Church in Chicago, Illinois. During that time the congregation moved to new quarters on South Damen Avenue with facilities and parsonage valued at one and a half million dollars. This whole indebtedness was paid off in May 1987, seven years ahead of schedule. He hosted the 1976 General Conference and introduced a new system of providing equal accommodations for lay and clergy delegates. At the August 1988 General Conference he was elected bishop and assigned to the Eleventh Episcopal District (western United States), while maintaining his residence in the Chicago area.

"Chicago District Ministerium Presents Bishop and Mrs. George W. Walker, Sr." *The Star of Zion* 113 (April 27, 1989): 1, 3.

"Dr. George Walker Announces for Episcopacy." *The Star of Zion* 112 (May 19, 1988): 5.

WALKER, JOHN THOMAS (July 27, 1925–September 30, 1989), the second African American bishop of the **Episcopal Church** to head a diocese in the United States, was born in Barnesville, Georgia, the son of Joseph and Mattie (Wyche) Walker. His great-grandfather had founded Barnesville's first **African Methodist Episcopal Church**. The family moved to Detroit, where Walker attended Cass Technical High School. His father worked as a janitor in the winter and

gardener in the summer. Walker received his B.A. in history in 1951 from Wayne State University and his B.D. in 1954 from Virginia Theological Seminary. He was the first black graduate of Virginia Theological Seminary. He married Rosa Maria Flores, with whom he had three children.

From 1954 to 1957 he was rector of St. Mary's Episcopal Church in Detroit, Michigan, which was about 80 percent White and 20 percent Black, reflecting the composition of the community. From 1957 to 1964 he taught history at St. Paul's School in Concord, New Hampshire, the first top Eastern boys' prep school to have an African American teacher on the faculty. In 1964–65 he took a leave of absence from the school to teach at the Bishop Tucker Theological College in Mukono, Uganda. From 1966 to 1971 he was canon of the Cathedral of Ss. Peter and Paul in Washington, D.C. In November 1970 he began hosting a weekly, half-hour television program called "Overview." On June 29, 1971, Walker was consecrated suffragan bishop of the Diocese of Washington D.C., becoming bishop coadjutor in 1976. In 1977 he succeeded Bishop William Creighton as head of the diocese, becoming only the second black bishop of the church (after **John Burgess** in Massachusetts in 1970) to head a diocese in the United States. He remained in that position, serving also as dean of the Washington Cathedral, for the rest of his career.

Walker was the first chair of the Metropolitan D.C. Urban Bishops Coalition in 1976. Beginning in 1977 he chaired the board of directors of Africare, and received that organization's Distinguished Service Award in 1981. He was chair of the Police Chief Citizen's Advisory Council and was active in a number of other Washington, D.C. organizations. He was a board member of Virginia Theological Seminary; the Black Student Fund; the Eisenhower Foundation; the Washington Hospital Center; Meridan House Foundation; Potomac School; Absalom Jones Theological Institute in Atlanta; Milton Academy in Massachusetts; and chaired the board of St. Paul's School in New Hampshire. He served on the Committee on the Placement of Negro Clergy and on the Standing Commission on Peace. In 1978 he received the Service Award from the National Conference of Christians and Jews, and in 1981 *Washingtonian Magazine* named him Washingtonian of the Year. He served as vice-president of the House of Bishops. He fought segregation whenever possible and was arrested in 1985 for protesting apartheid at the South African Embassy in Washington, D.C. He established the first full-time chaplaincy in the church to minister to AIDS patients.

He passed away in 1989 the day after triple-bypass heart surgery.

Bennett, Lerone Jr. "Black Firsts in Politics, Entertainment, Sports, and Other Fields." *Ebony* 37 (March 1982): 128–133.

"Church Attending Soars to New High." *Ebony* 11 (March 1956): 18–23.

"Deaths." *Christian Century* 106 (October 25, 1989): 953.

"John Walker, 64, 1st Black D.C. Episcopal Bishop, Dies." *Jet* 77 (October 16, 1989): 7.

"A Superior History Man." *Newsweek* 48 (December 31, 1956): 39–40.

IBAW, NA, EBA, WWABA (88, 92–93), *NYTBS* (1989), *ECA* (1972), *WWR* (85), *BDNM* (75).

WALKER, ORRIS GEORGE, JR. (b. 1942), a bishop of the **Episcopal Church**, was born in Baltimore, Maryland and grew up attending that city's public schools. He graduated in 1964 from the University of Maryland with a degree in political science and philosophy, and in 1968 received the S.T.B. from General Theological Seminary in New York City. He was ordained deacon in 1968 and priest in 1969. He married Norma Eloy McKinney, with whom he has had two children.

From 1968 to 1971 he was director of program and education at St. Mark's Ecumenical Church in Kansas City, Missouri. In 1971 he became associate rector for newly merged parishes now called St. Matthew's-St. Joseph's Episcopal Church in Detroit, Michigan. Within a year the rector, **Quintin Primo**, was elected bishop, and Walker succeeded him as rector, remaining in that position for the next seventeen years.

In this parish he established a national reputation for leadership. The church began spending about half its budget on various social programs. Walker served on the executive committee of the Detroit N.A.A.C.P., was president of the Cathedral Terrace, a senior citizen housing complex, and served on both the Highland Park Community Relations board and the Black Family Development board. He was named Archdeacon of Region V in the Diocese of Michigan and was five times a deputy to General Convention. He was a member of the Council of Advice and represented the Diocese at the Provincial Synod for ten years. He chaired the Episcopal Committee on Black Ministries and the Standing Commission on Constitution and Canons. In 1982 he was elected a trustee of General Theological Seminary. On April 9, 1988, he was consecrated bishop coadjutor of the Diocese of Long Island.

Carey, Joseph, Linda K. Lanier, Ron Sherer, Juanita Hogue, and Jack A. Seamonds. "New Shepherds to Lead Nation's Religious Flocks." *U.S. News and World Report* 97 (December 31, 1984/January 7, 1985): 86–87.

ECA (1989).

WALKER, WYATT TEE (b. August 15, 1929), civil rights leader and **Progressive National Baptist Convention** minister, was born in Brockton, Massachusetts, the son of John Wise and Maude (Pinn) Walker. He received his B.S. in 1950 from Virginia Union University and his B.D. in 1953 from that same institution's theological seminary. In 1950 he married Theresa Ann Edwards; they had four children.

His first pastorate was at Gillfield Baptist Church in Petersburg, Virginia, from 1953 to 1960. During those years he headed the Petersburg Improvement Association; was branch president of the N.A.A.C.P., state director of C.O.R.E., was a member of the **Southern Christian Leadership Conference** (S.C.L.C.) national board, was a trustee of Virginia Theological Seminary, and was president of the Virginia Council on Human Relations. From 1960 to 1964 he was vice-president and executive director of the S.C.L.C, working closely with **Martin Luther King, Jr.** In three years as head of the New York office, he raised the budget from $57,000 to $1,000,000. In 1964–65 Walker was associate minister with **Adam Clayton Powell, Jr.** at Abyssinian Baptist Church in Harlem, New York City, one of the largest Black churches in the United States. For a time considered a possible successor to Powell, Walker was dismissed from the church in September 1965, in a dispute over a visit by King. For several years thereafter he was vice-president, then president of American Education Heritage, Inc., publishers of the Negro Heritage Library, designed to provide information about African American history usually left out of textbooks. He also served as special assistant on urban affairs to the governor of New York State, Nelson Rockefeller.

Since about 1971 he has been pastor of the Canaan Baptist Church of Christ in New York City. Since 1975 he has also been president and chief executive officer of the Church Housing Development Fund, Inc. Since 1983 he has been closely associated with **Jesse Jackson** and has served as national coordinator of the church and clergy division of Jackson's National Rainbow Coalition. Walker is also chair of the Religious Action Network of the American Committee on Africa, and in that role works against South African apartheid. He has received more than one hundred awards and citations for his work in human relations and civil rights, including the Elks Human Rights Award (1963); National Alpha Award in Civil Rights (1965); and the Shriners National Civil Rights Award (1974). He is the author of several books, including *"Somebody's Calling My Name": Black Sacred Music and Social Change* (1979).

"The Men Behind Martin Luther King." *Ebony* 20 (June 1965): 164–173.

"King Advisor to Speak at State Tribute." *Newark Star-Ledger* (December 22, 1991): 43.

Carter, Harold A., Wyatt Tee Walker, and William Augustus Jones, Jr. *The Black Church Looks at the Bicentennial.* Elgin, IL: Progressive National Baptist Publishing House, 1976. 134 pp.

Walker, Wyatt Tee. *Road to Damascus: A Journey of Faith.* New York: Martin Luther King Fellows Press, 1985. 163 pp.

———. *The Scaffold of Faith: The Role of Black Sacred Music in Social Change.* Rochester, NY: N.p., 1975. 397 pp.

———. *"Somebody's Calling My Name": Black Sacred Music and Social Change.* Valley Forge, PA: Judson Press, 1979. 208 pp.

———. *Soul of Black Worship: A Trilogy—Preaching, Praying, Singing.* New York: Martin Luther King Fellows Press, 1984. 89 pp.

———. *Spirits That Dwell in Deep Woods: The Prayer and Praise Hymns of the Black Religious Experience.* New York: Martin Luther King Fellows Press, 1987. 82 pp.

IBAW, OTSB, EBA, BDNM (70), *CRACG, HUBA, WWABA* (92–93).

WALLACE, PARIS ARTHUR (April 17, 1870– February 21, 1952), 39th bishop of the **African Methodist Episcopal Zion Church** (AMEZ), was born near Maryville, Blount County, Tennessee, the third of nine children in the family of Tobias and Amanda Wallace. He worked on the farm and attended school in the winters until he was eighteen. At that time he enrolled in the Freedmen's Normal Institute, founded by Quakers in Maryville. He experienced conversion at that school and joined the local AMEZ church, serving in almost every office available.

He graduated from the institute in 1888 and in 1891 entered Maryville College, an interracial school. In 1894 he was licensed to preach and joined the Tennessee Conference later the same year. During his senior year he pastored the AMEZ church in Louisville, Tennessee. He graduated from Maryville College in 1895 and won a $25 prize for the best oration. While he was trying to decide on a career he was appointed principal of the school for Blacks in Maryville. He resigned after only a few months when he decided to enter the ministry, and enrolled in the Theological Department of Lincoln University in Pennsylvania. While there he was ordained deacon on September 20, 1896 and elder on May 23, 1897. He pastored the AMEZ church in nearby Oxford, Pennsylvania. He graduated with a B.A. and S.T.B. degree in 1898.

From 1898 to 1900 Wallace was appointed to Tompkins Chapel AMEZ Church in Chattanooga, Tennessee. During that time he met and married Ida Lorna Wallace, with whom he had two children. In the fall of 1900 he was transferred to Jacob Street Tabernacle AMEZ Church in Louisville, Kentucky, where he stayed for three years. In 1903 he was appointed to Metropolitan Zion in Washington, D.C., serving both there and in Gettysburg, Pennsylvania until 1908. From 1908 to 1916 he pastored Big Wesley AMEZ Church in Philadelphia, followed by Fleet Street Memorial AMEZ Church in Brooklyn, New York, from 1916 to 1920.

Wallace was consecrated bishop on May 20, 1920, and assigned to the area of Missouri, Indiana, Florida, and the Southwest. He later headed the First Episcopal District (New York, New Jersey, New England, and other conferences). He was an ardent supporter of education and was a pioneer leader of Minister's Institutes and Leadership Education schools. He purchased the Long Branch House for such educational ventures. He was a member of the Federal (now National) Council of Churches and the International Christian Endeavor, and was a trustee of Livingstone College in Salisbury, North Carolina. He was one of the most widely loved bishops, known for his sympathetic leadership, ready wit, and outstanding preaching. He retired in 1944, and most of his last years were spent struggling with deepening illness.

Allen, Cleveland G. "Impressive Tribute Paid the Late Bishop Wallace." *Star of Zion* 75 (March 6, 1952): 2, 3.

"The Anthology of the AME Zion Bishops." *Star of Zion* 57 (September 28, 1933): 1, 6.

"Historical Notes: Bishop Paris Arthur Wallace." *AME Zion Quarterly Review* 69 (Fall 1959): 192–193.

"In Memoriam." *A.M.E. Zion Quarterly Review* 62 (1951): 228–229.

"The Magnificent Qualities of Our Bishops: The Dignified, Modest, Princely Bishop Paris Arthur Wallace, Retired." *Star of Zion* 70 (May 2, 1946): 1, 8.

"New Era of Zion Methodism." *Star of Zion* 48 (August 7, 1924): 1, 5.

Walls, William Jacob. *The African Methodist Episcopal Zion Church; Reality of the Black Church.* Charlotte, NC: AME Zion Publishing House, 1974. 669 pp.

NYTO, HAMEZC.

WALLS, WILLIAM JACOB (May 8, 1885–April 23, 1975), historiographer and 42nd bishop of the **African Methodist Episcopal Zion Church** (AMEZ), was born in Chimney Rock, North Carolina, a son of Edward and Harriet (Edgerton) Walls. His father died when he was eight, and the family went to Asheville to live with his mother's parents. His mother worked in a laundry to support them. At a time when Sunday schools were a potent educational force, he was enrolled in four of them, of differing denominations, which met at different times. He attended Allen Industrial School in Asheville, North Carolina, and transferred to Livingstone College in Salisbury, North Carolina, where he completed his basic education. Funds to help at college came from his AMEZ local church, which had been impressed by his abilities as a boy-preacher. He was licensed to preach at Hopkins Chapel in Asheville in September 1899, when he was just fourteen. He joined the Blue Ridge Conference at Johnson City, Tennessee, on October 6, 1902, was ordained deacon on October 20, 1903, and elder on October 16, 1905. During this time he served as a traveling evangelist while continuing his education at Livingstone College, where he received his B.A. in 1908.

In 1905 he was appointed to his first regular pastorate, the Cedar Grove Circuit in Cleveland, North Carolina. In 1906 he was moved to the Miller's Chapel and Sandy Ridge Circuit in Landis, followed in 1908 by Moore's Chapel in Lincolnton. From 1910 to 1914 he pastored the Soldier's Memorial AMEZ Church in Salisbury. While there he took advantage of the presence of Hood Theological Seminary in Salisbury, and received a B.D. in 1913. From 1914 to 1920 he was at the Broadway Temple AMEZ Church in Louisville, Kentucky. In Louisville he led the congregation in a building campaign and created the present structure in 1915. He was a steadily rising figure in the denomination and in May 1918 was sent as a fraternal delegate to the General Conference of the Methodist Episcopal Church, South, in Atlanta, Georgia.

In 1920 Walls was elected the ninth editor of the *Star of Zion*, the denominational journal, and during the next four years tripled its circulation. In 1921 he was sent as a delegate to the Ecumenical Methodist Conference in London and extended the trip to tour five countries. Upon returning he took some courses in journalism and philosophy at Columbia University in New York City. On May 20, 1924, he was elected bishop at the General Conference in Indianapolis, the first single man elected bishop in the denomination for more than fifty years. He was made chair of the newly created Board of Religious Education, and held that position for the entire forty-four years of his bishopric.

His service extended in numerous directions. He was on the board of trustees of both Livingstone College and Gammon Theological Seminary. He was on the Executive Committee and the Race Relations Commission of the Federal (now National) Council of Churches, and chaplain of the National Negro Business League. In 1936 he gave an address at the 12th World's Sunday School Convention at Oslo, Norway. He received an M.A. from the University of Chicago in 1941, and two years later published a book about one of his heroes in the faith, **Joseph Charles Price**. In 1951 he succeeded Bishop **Benjamin Garland Shaw** as the senior bishop of the denomination.

In 1956, at the age of 71, Walls ended bachelorhood and married his secretary of five years, Dorothy Louise Jordan. She became pregnant the next year, but a miscarriage occurred and the couple remained childless. When Walls retired in 1968 to his home in Yonkers, New York, the General Conference commissioned him as historiographer to write a comprehensive history of the denomination. This was a task he had first proposed doing in 1946, and he produced a monumental work, *The African Methodist Episcopal Zion Church*, published in 1974, one year before his death. This remains the single most authoritative source on the history of the denomination and its people. Including retirement, he was a bishop for fifty-one years, longer than anyone in the history of the church. His image was so indelibly imprinted on the church that for years the AMEZ Church was known to many as "Walls' Church." He died in Yonkers, New York.

"The Anthology of the AME Zion Bishops." *Star of Zion* 57 (September 28, 1933): 1, 6.

"Bishop William J. Walls." *AME Zion Quarterly Review* 59, No. 3 (1949): 102–103.

Douglas, Carlyle C. "Fifty Years a Bishop." *Ebony* 30 (February 1975): 105–109.

Hoggard, J. Clinton. "Eulogy for Bishop William Jacob Walls." *AME Zion Quarterly Review* 87 (Fall 1975): 242–252.

"The Magnificent Qualities of Our Bishops: The Eloquent, Scholarly, Evangelistic, Historical-Minded Bishop William Jacob Walls." *Star of Zion* 70 (May 30, 1946): 1, 8.

"New Era of Zion Methodism." *Star of Zion* 48 (August 7, 1924): 1, 5.

"Zion's Senior Bishops During the Twentieth Century." *Star of Zion* 104 (March 27, 1980): 1, 2.

Walls, William Jacob. *The African Methodist Episcopal Zion Church; Reality of the Black Church*. Charlotte, NC: AME Zion Publishing House, 1974. 669 pp.

———. *Joseph Charles Price, Educator and Race Leader*. Boston: The Christopher Publishing House, 1943. 568 pp.

—————. *The Romance of a College.* New York: Vantage Press, 1963. 64 pp.

EWM, RLOA, NYTBS (1975), *WWCA, HUBA, AARS, IBAW, BAW, NV.*

WALTERS, ALEXANDER (August 1, 1858–February 2, 1917), 24th bishop of the **African Methodist Episcopal Zion Church** (AMEZ), was born in Bardstown, Kentucky, to slaves Henry and Harriet (Mathers) Walters. He was the sixth of eight children, four of whom died in infancy. As a young man he was employed in hotels and on steamboats around Louisville, Kentucky, and joined the AMEZ Church at age twelve. He was educated in private schools conducted by the area's Black churches, and graduated in 1875.

In 1876 he became a waiter with his brother Isaac in the Bates House in Indianapolis, Indiana. Both soon joined the Masons, Odd Fellows, and the United Brethren of Friendship. Walters began studying theology under private tutors. In March 1877, he was licensed to preach by the Quarterly Conference of the Blackford Street AMEZ Church in that city. On August 28, 1877, he married Katie Knox, with whom he had five children, and the following year was appointed to preach in the Corydon Circuit in Kentucky. He was ordained a deacon in the Kentucky Conference on July 3, 1879, and from 1880 to 1881 pastored in Cloverport, Kentucky. He was ordained elder on April 10, 1881, and appointed to the Fifteenth Street AMEZ Church in Louisville, which he served until 1883. During that time, in 1882, he was elected secretary of the Annual Conference and treasurer of the periodical *Zion's Banner.*

From 1883 to 1886 he was at the Stockton Street AMEZ Church in San Francisco, California, where he had great success as a spiritual leader and in paying off a burdensome mortgage. At the General Conference in New York City in May 1884, his rise in prominence was confirmed by being elected assistant secretary. After two brief but successful pastorates in Chattanooga and Knoxville, Tennessee, he was appointed in 1888, at the young age of thirty, to the prestigious "Mother Zion" Church in New York City. In his four years there he took in almost 700 members and raised over $32,000. In 1889 he was a delegate to the World's Sunday School Convention in London, and was also able to travel through Europe, Egypt, and the Holy Land. In the fall of 1889 he was appointed as the new general agent of the denomination's book concern, which he rejuvenated and developed.

On November 4, 1889, he joined T. Thomas Fortune's call for the organization of the Afro-American League, dedicated to the protection of Black rights.

Walters was keenly aware that after Reconstruction Blacks had been left to fend for themselves, and could not depend upon the government. The league disappeared after two years, but the issues remained alive. At the General Conference in Pittsburgh, on May 4, 1892, Walters was elected bishop, and was consecrated on May 18. At the age of thirty-three, he was one of the youngest people ever elected bishop. His first wife died on December 22, 1896, and he then married Emeline Virginia Bird, who died on February 27, 1902. His third wife was Lelia Coleman.

On September 15, 1898, after watching the civil rights of Blacks continue to erode, Walters and others reorganized the earlier league as the National Afro-American Council. This group was a direct ancestor of the National Association for the Advancement of Colored People (N.A.A.C.P.). Walters was elected president, a position he held for seven terms. In London in July 1900, he was elected president of the Pan-African Association. In 1908 he joined W.E.B. DuBois' Niagara Movement, dedicated to removing all barriers to the full participation of Blacks in American society. He believed that the United States had an obligation to support Liberia and keep it independent, and he visited the region in 1910. He served on the board of directors of the International Migration Society, which fostered Blacks' migration to Liberia.

Walters felt that the Republican party was not worthy of a taken-for-granted Black vote, and became the president of the National Colored Democratic League. He thus helped elect Woodrow Wilson president in 1912, and in 1915 Wilson offered him the post of minister to Liberia, which he declined. Among many additional commitments, he was an administrative council member of the Federal (now National) Council of Churches and a trustee of the United Society of Christian Endeavor. In 1916 he succeeded Bishop **James Hood** as senior bishop of the denomination. His autobiography, *My Life and Work,* was published the year of his death.

Mathurin, Owen Charles. *Henry Sylvester Williams and the Origins of the Pan-African Movement, 1869–1911.* Westport, CT: Greenwood Press, 1976. 183 pp.

Miller, George Mason. "The Life and Times of Alexander Walters." *AME Zion Quarterly Review* 82 (Winter 1970): 236–242.

Swain, B. W. "The Late Bishop Alexander Walters—Gone But Not Forgotten, An Appreciation." *Star of Zion* (February 5, 1920): 1.

Walters, Alexander. "Abraham Lincoln and Fifty Years of Freedom." In Dorothy Parker, ed. *Early Negro Writing, 1760–1837.* Boston: Beacon, 1971, pp. 554–561.

———. *Address*. New York: National Colored Democratic League, n.d. 12 pp.

———. *Frederick Douglass and His Work*. Nashville, TN: National Baptist Publishing Board, 1904.

———. *My Life and Work*. New York: Fleming H. Revell Co., 1917. 272 pp.

———. "Possibilities of the Negro in the Realm of Politics." In W. H. Ferris, ed. *The African Abroad*. New Haven, CT: Tuttle, Morehouse, Taylor, 1913, pp. 379–381.

"Zion's Senior Bishops During the Twentieth Century." *Star of Zion* 104 (March 27, 1980): 1, 2.

BRBR, RLOA, DANB, DAB, AMEZC, OYHAMEZC, WWCR, NYTO, BAW, IBAW, HUBA, AARS.

WARD, CLARA MAE (April 21, 1924–January 16, 1973), gospel singer, was born in Philadelphia, Pennsylvania, the daughter of George and Gertrude Mae (Murphy) Ward. The family attended Ebenezer Baptist Church, where at an early age Ward began showing signs of her exceptional gifts for singing and playing the piano. In 1931 Gertrude Ward began singing gospel music professionally, and in 1934 began to include daughters Willa and Clara, thus forming the Ward Trio. The Ward Trio toured for many years on the church and revival circuit, and did much to spread the pioneer gospel styles of **Sallie Martin** and **Thomas Dorsey**. In 1943 the group gained wide recognition for their performance for the **National Baptist Convention, U.S.A., Inc.** in Philadelphia.

In 1947 Marion Williams and Henrietta Waddy joined the group, which was renamed the Famous Ward Singers. They began recording, and the group's success jumped up another notch. In 1949 they began a fruitful relationship with preacher and songwriter W. Herbert Brewster, and popularized his song, "Surely God is Able," the first gospel song to use rhythmic triplets (12/8 meter). For a time in the early 1950s they toured with famous preacher Cecil L. Franklin, father of Aretha Franklin. Franklin later gave Ward credit for being her biggest inspiration and influence. Ward was married once, when she was seventeen, and it lasted only two years. In 1955 she almost married an unidentified minister in the western United States, whom she had dated for about six years, but those plans fell through.

During the 1950s the Famous Ward Singers were the most successful female gospel group. "Surely God is Able" is reported to have been the first gospel recording to sell one million copies. The group was also known for "Packin' Up," "Come in the Room," "Great is the Lord," and "The Day is Past and Gone." Ward's best-known solo was "How I Got Over," and her annual income stretched into $250,000. A consummate artist of vocal arrangements, Ward's clear alto voice and emotional delivery drew raves. She became known as the "Queen of the Moaners." She began to take more artistic control of the group and introduced the famous look of fabulous gowns, bare-backed slippers, and elaborate wigs, an innovation that helped make big business of gospel music. In 1955 the Ward Singers got another career boost with an appearance at the Apollo Theater in Harlem, New York City, but this was topped by the invitation to sing on an all-gospel matinee program at the 1957 Newport Jazz Festival. This was their first performance before a primarily White audience. The Newport Jazz Festival capped a very busy year which included "Big Gospel Cavalcade of 1957," where for one month the Ward Singers and seven other gospel groups appeared in a different city every night of the week except Saturday.

In 1958 Marion Williams and others left the group, and a succession of other singers took their place. In 1959 there was a very successful Scandinavian tour. In 1961 Mother Ward temporarily retired, and Clara Ward shifted the group into a whole new arena, that of nightclubs and theaters (following in the footsteps of Bessie Griffin, the first to make that move). They played at the Village Vanguard in New York City that year and were an instant hit. Later in 1961 they played a two-week engagement at the New Frontier Hotel in Las Vegas that was extended to forty weeks and repeated in 1962. At the time it was the longest consecutive booking for any performer in Las Vegas history. In 1962 the group, now known as the Clara Ward Singers, appeared for the first time at Disneyland in Anaheim, California, and thereafter were regulars. In 1963 they were the first gospel group to appear at Radio City Music Hall in New York City. Also in 1963 Clara Ward played a leading role in the gospel-song play by Langston Hughes, *Tambourines to Glory*, and the group appeared in the film, *It's Your Thing*. Later on Broadway, Ward co-starred with Lou Gossett, Jr. in another Langston Hughes production, *God's Trombones*.

Ward's shift of the traditional venue of gospel music from churches to nightclubs, Disneyland, and Broadway was very controversial. Further, she expanded the repertoire as well to include songs like "Born Free" and "America the Beautiful." She was constantly defending herself against charges that she had sold out to show business success. She pointed out that in nightclubs no alcohol was served while she performed, and many observers have agreed that her spiritual integrity did remain intact. She insisted that one did not have to look sad or dress in black to be religious, but rather, "you should live the life you sing about." She was certainly a major force in bringing gospel music to a wider audience around the world. In 1967 the Clara Ward Singers were the first gospel music group to sing at the Philadelphia Academy of Music. That year Ward suffered a stroke which temporarily retired her, but she soon returned to the nightclub circuit. In 1973, after two more strokes, she passed away at the age of forty-eight. In her lifetime she composed more than five hundred songs, many published by her own publishing company, Ward's House of Music. Her influences on individual performers and on the whole field of gospel music continue to be far-reaching.

"Clara Ward." *Newsweek* 81 (January 29, 1973): 45.

"Glamour Girl of Gospel Singers." *Ebony* 12 (October 1957): 24–28.

"Singing for Sinners." *Newsweek* 50 (September 2, 1957): 86.

NBAW, BDA-AAM, NYTBS (1973), *BDA-AHP, EBA, BWR, IBAW.*

WARD, SAMUEL RINGGOLD (October 17, 1817– c.1866), minister, author, and abolitionist, was born into slavery on the eastern shore of Maryland, the second of three children in the family of William and Anne Ward. His parents were very religious and believed that God was opposed to the system of slavery. His mother in particular exhibited an independent character that rankled the master, who would have sold her but for Ward's sickliness as a baby. In 1820 the family escaped and settled in Greenwich, New Jersey, among Quakers. In 1826 fear of recapture led to a move to New York City, where they arrived in August and stayed the first night with relatives, the parents of **Henry Highland Garnet**.

Ward attended the Mulberry Street School with such other future leaders as Garnet and **Alexander Crummell**. In 1833 he experienced conversion and about that time became a teacher in a school for Black children in Newark, New Jersey. In January, 1838 he married a Miss Reynolds, with whom he had a number of children, only a few of whom survived to maturity. For a time he was a student at the Oneida Institute in Whitesboro, New York, where he gained literary and rhetorical polish.

He began speaking on behalf of abolition, and his abilities drew the attention of abolitionist leaders such as Gerrit Smith and Lewis Tappan. This led in 1839 to an appointment as traveling agent for the American Anti-Slavery Society and then for the New York State Anti-Slavery Society. Also in 1839 (in May) he was licensed to preach by the New York Congregationalist (General) Association. In April 1841 he became the first pastor of an all-White Congregationalist church in South

Butler, New York. The church grew under his pastorate, yet he left in 1843 because of a threatening throat condition. He received successful treatment in Geneva, New York, and studied medicine for a few months. In 1845 he spent most of his time campaigning for the Liberty party candidates. He served as agent for the *Colored American* and as an editor of the *Farmer and Northern Star*. From 1846 to 1851 he pastored another all-White Congregationalist church in Cortland Village, New York. In 1850 he edited the *Impartial Citizen*, based in Boston, Massachusetts.

During this time Ward's fame as an orator grew, and after the passage of the Fugitive Slave Act in 1850 he stepped up his schedule of speeches throughout the North. He was often called "the Black Daniel Webster," and considered as a speaker second only to Frederick Douglass, the top Black abolitionist, who expressed great admiration for him. In October 1851, Ward joined future **African Methodist Episcopal Zion Church** bishop **Jermain Wesley Loguen** and others in freeing a fugitive slave named Jerry McHenry from the Syracuse county courthouse. Fearing recapture himself in the aftermath of that event, Ward fled to Canada where his family soon joined him.

He settled in Toronto and obtained a position as agent and orator for the Anti-Slavery Society of Canada. He organized branches of that society, gave speeches, aided refugees from the United States, and helped found newspapers. In early 1853 he co-edited the *Alienated American*, and for a time edited the *Provincial Freeman*. His father passed away in 1851 and his mother in September 1853. In April 1853 he left for England to raise money. He stayed for two years and raised a healthy sum for the Canadian work. He was a featured speaker at both the 1853 and 1854 meetings of the British and Foreign Anti-Slavery Society and spoke and traveled throughout England, Scotland, Wales, and Ireland.

On this trip Ward took time to reflect on his life and wrote *Autobiography of a Fugitive Slave* (1855). He enjoyed his experience abroad and had difficulty thinking about his return to the difficulties of North America. A Quaker philanthropist named John Candler presented him with fifty acres of land in the parish of St. George, Jamaica, and this seemed to solve the dilemma. Ward and his family moved to Jamaica in late 1855 and he became a Baptist minister at a small church in Kingston. For some years he is said to have exercised significant political influence in the area. Early in 1860 he left Kingston and settled on his land in St. George Parish. His fortunes, however, went steadily downhill, and in 1866 he published *Reflections Upon the Gordon Rebellion*, perhaps with an eye to additional income.

Sometime shortly afterward, though, he is reported to have passed away in poverty.

Ward, Samuel Ringgold. *Autobiography of a Fugitive Negro: His Anti-Slavery Labours in the United States, Canada, and England.* London: John Snow, 1855. 412 pp.

———. *Reflections Upon the Gordon Rebellion.* N.p., 1866. 8 pp.

HNC, AAE, HNB, EBA, SBAA, WWWA (H), MBRL, DANB, DAB, BAW, HUBA, AARS, IBAWCB, IBAW.

WARD, THOMAS MARCUS DECATUR (September 28, 1823–June 10, 1894), 10th bishop of the **African Methodist Episcopal Church** (AME), was born in Hanover, Pennsylvania. He experienced conversion in 1838, at age fifteen, and joined Bethel AME Church in Philadelphia. He was licensed to preach in 1843 and joined the New England Conference in 1846. He was ordained deacon in 1847 and elder in 1849.

In 1854 he left a charge in Massachusetts, arrived in California, and took over the leadership of St. Cyprian AME Church on Jackson Street between Stockton and Powell in San Francisco. A daily elementary school operated in its basement. In 1856 he was succeeded by Barney Fletcher, who had founded St. Cyprian in early 1854, and became missionary superintendent of the Pacific Coast. There were only 134 members and eight preachers in the whole region. He set about his task in earnest, though travel and every other aspect of life there was very difficult. Because the membership was small and poverty-stricken, Ward had to work at odd jobs to feed and support himself and his wife, a woman from Gorica, California. Among other things he reportedly drove a four-horse team and opened a laundry. Nevertheless his work was successful and on April 6, 1865, Bishop **Jabez P. Campbell** was able to organize the California Conference at the Union Bethel AME Church in San Francisco.

At the 1868 General Conference Ward's report of California's church growth was so captivating that it catapulted him into the bishopric and he was consecrated on May 25, 1868. From 1868 to 1872 he was assigned to the Pacific Coast, where he continued the work he had begun. From 1872 to 1876 he was assigned to the Georgia, Alabama, Florida, and Mississippi conferences. He then headed the Fifth Episcopal District (Louisiana, Texas, and Arkansas) from 1876 to 1880, followed by the Fourth Episcopal District (Kansas, Missouri, and Illinois) from 1880 to 1884; the Eighth Episcopal District (Mississippi, Arkansas, and Indian Missions)

from 1884 to 1888; the Colorado area from 1888 to 1892; and Florida from 1892 to his death.

Ward was a key builder of the church, and organized many new annual conferences, including the North Georgia Conference (1874), the South Arkansas Conference (1876), the Missouri Conference (1882), the Southeast Texas Conference (1879), the Indian Territory Mission Conference in Oklahoma (1879), the Iowa Conference (1883), the South Kansas Conference (1883), the West Arkansas Conference (1885), and the South Florida Conference (1893). He married a second time, in June 1884, to Rachel Smith of Baltimore, who passed away only three years later, in 1887. Ward liked to express himself in eloquent poetry, and gained a reputation as a pulpit orator of the first class. He was called "the old man eloquent" and "the golden mouthed," and had this ability and broad vocabulary despite his never having had a formal education. Churches are named for him in at least fourteen states.

IBAW, EWM, BGRC, HAMEC, RAM, CEAMEC, BAMEC.

WARNER, ANDREW JACKSON (March 4, 1850–May 31, 1920), 33rd bishop of the **African Methodist Episcopal Zion Church** (AMEZ), was born into slavery in Washington, Kentucky, the son of Reuben and Emily (Payne) Warner. In 1863, at age thirteen, he ran away from his owners and made his way to Ripley, Ohio, where he enlisted as a drummer boy in the 27th Ohio Colored Volunteers of the Union Army. By the end of the Civil War he had advanced to the rank of sergeant. He returned to Ohio where he worked during the day and attended high school at night in Cincinnati, graduating in 1867. He then studied for a time at Wilberforce University in Xenia, Ohio, and worked with private tutors in theology. He married Alice McNeil, with whom he had two children.

He experienced conversion in 1870 and joined the AMEZ Church. He was licensed to preach in 1874 and joined the Kentucky Conference in 1876. He was ordained deacon and elder on the same day, September 9, 1877. His first assignment was at Wesley Chapel AMEZ Church in Greenville, Kentucky. In two and a half years there he added more than one hundred to the membership. In about 1879 he was transferred to Little Rock, Arkansas, where he built the first AMEZ church in Arkansas (St. Paul). He then was appointed to Russellville, Kentucky, followed by the Washington Street Metropolitan AMEZ Church in St. Louis, Missouri. He stayed five years in St. Louis, during which time he founded the St. John AMEZ Church in East St.

Louis, Illinois, considered one of his most significant achievements.

From there Warner went to Knoxville, Tennessee, where he built the Loguen Temple AMEZ Church. He then pastored Big Zion Church in Mobile, Alabama, where he completed a remodeling program. In 1888 he was appointed to Tuscaloosa, Alabama, then in 1889 went to Birmingham, Alabama, where he built Thompson Temple AMEZ Church (now known as Metropolitan AMEZ Church). In about 1891 his first wife passed away and he married Mary Eliza Delmor, with whom he had another four children. In seven years at Birmingham he created a 1,000–member congregation and one of the finest appointments in the denomination. His fame as a leader and orator were such that he was given in 1890 an unsought nomination for Congress in the first Alabama District. He was twice chosen Presidential Elector and in 1898 ran for governor of the state. In 1896 he helped organize the Board of Church Extension and for two years served as its secretary, keeping his residence in Alabama. In 1898 he was assigned to Clinton Chapel AMEZ Church in Charlotte, North Carolina, where he stayed for ten years with great success.

At the 1908 General Conference his achievements as pastor were crowned with election to the bishopric, and he was consecrated on May 20, 1908. In his tenure as bishop he presided over the conferences in Mississippi, Louisiana, Tennessee, North Carolina, South Carolina, and Florida. His second wife passed away in 1908 and on July 6, 1910, he married Annie Weddington, with whom he had one more child. He was a trustee for Livingstone College in Salisbury, North Carolina, and director of a reform school in Charlotte, North Carolina.

"Famous Churchman Dies—Four Bishops and Hundred Preachers in Weeping Throng." *Star of Zion* (June 23, 1920): 1, 5, 8.
"They'll Live On." *Star of Zion* 104 (March 27, 1980): 3.
WWCR, AMEZC, HAMEZC, AARS, E pp.

WASHINGTON, BOOKER TALIAFERRO (April 5, 1856–November 14, 1915), Baptist educator and author, was born into slavery at Hale's Ford, Franklin County, Virginia. His father was believed to have been a White man from a neighboring plantation, and his mother, Jane Ferguson, was a cook for the James Burroughs plantation. Washington, his mother, and two siblings lived in a one-room cabin with a dirt floor and ate mostly scraps.

After Emancipation in 1865 his mother took the family to Malden, West Virginia, to join her husband, Washington Ferguson, whom she had married sometime after Washington's birth. Ferguson had gone on before to find work in the salt mines. Washington also worked packing salt for about a time, then worked in a coal mine. During this time he learned to read, and finally was able to attend school for a few hours every morning. Asked by the teacher for a name, he invented the surname of Washington, only later discovering that his mother had thought of giving him the name of Taliaferro.

In 1871 he worked in the household of Lewis Ruffner, owner of the mine and salt-works. Encouraged by Mrs. Ruffner, he continued to study as much as possible, and developed work habits based on her strict Puritan notions of responsibility, order, and cleanliness. His family began attending the African Zion Baptist Church in Tinkersville. In 1872, at the age of sixteen, having heard of Hampton Normal and Agricultural Institute in Virginia, he set off on foot for that school. He was accepted as a student and given a janitorial position to pay for room and board. The White head of the school, Samuel Chapman Armstrong, arranged for donors to pay his tuition. Hampton's curriculum was based on Armstrong's belief that the best education for Blacks was a combination of academic and practical (or industrial) subjects, and this strongly influenced Washington's later educational philosophy. Washington also gained there a love of daily Bible reading which he maintained for the rest of his life.

Washington graduated from Hampton with honors in 1875, with particular skills in brick masonry, and returned to Malden to teach school. In 1878–79 he spent eight months as a student at Wayland Seminary in Washington, D.C., a Baptist school where he contemplated a life in the ministry and for a time was a licensed Baptist preacher. He became disenchanted with the purely intellectual character of the studies, with no grounding in practical living skills. He then returned to the Hampton Institute to teach in a program for American Indians and serve as secretary to Samuel Armstrong. In 1881 the Alabama State Legislature authorized the establishment of a school to be situated in Tuskegee for the training of Black teachers. Armstrong was asked to recommend a White principal; he recommended Washington instead, and the recommendation was accepted.

When Washington arrived in Tuskegee he found that the state's funding was limited to $2,000 for salaries, and there was no provision for land, buildings, or equipment. The school had to open in a shack owned by a local Black Methodist church, and Washington worked to recruit students, faculty, and financial support.

He borrowed money through the Hampton Institute to purchase an abandoned plantation, and the students provided much of the labor of building facilities as part of their industrial training. In 1882 he married Fannie N. Smith, with whom he had one child. Fannie passed away in 1884 and in 1885 he married Olivia A. Davidson, with whom he had two more children. As early as 1888 the school owned 540 acres of land, had 400 students of both sexes, and offered classes in a wide variety of subjects. The academic classes focused on topics directly related to the lives of the students, such as personal hygiene, manners, and character building. The faculty was all-Black at a time when most schools for Blacks were still run by White missionaries.

The school was established on a nondenominational basis, but students were required to attend chapel daily and a number of religious services on Sundays. Washington himself gave moral exhortations on Sunday evenings. He continued his membership in the Baptist church and spoke several times at gatherings of the National Baptist Convention. Over time, however, his personal feelings became more eclectic and nondenominational, with a certain appreciation of Unitarianism. His theology was as pragmatic as the rest of his orientation, and he believed that the church should emphasize the needs of daily life rather than the supernatural. He built Phelps Hall, a nondenominational chapel, on campus, and the Phelps Hall Bible Training School for the basic education of clergy.

As Tuskegee Normal and Industrial Institute progressed, so also did Washington's reputation as a speaker and leader. His first major address was in 1884 for the National Education Association meeting in Madison, Wisconsin. His addresses emphasized the importance of character, an education fitted to one's life and the development of mutual respect between White and Black. His wording was often subtle and ambiguous, as he was working out a public stance that could satisfy the often conflicting views of his three major audiences—Blacks, northern Whites with money, and the southern Whites among whom he and his graduates worked. On October 12, 1893, his second wife having passed away in 1889, he married Margaret Murray, the principal of girl students at Tuskegee.

On September 18, 1895, he made a speech for the Cotton States and International Exposition in Atlanta, Georgia, that clearly lifted him to the height of national recognition. In it he expressed his philosophy of race relations succinctly: "In all things that are purely social we can be as separate as the fingers, yet one as the hand in all things essential to mutual progress." The effect of this speech was immediate and powerful, and from that point on Washington was widely considered the

successor of abolitionist Frederick Douglass (d.1895) as the leader of American Blacks.

Washington began to spend a portion of each year on the lecture circuit, and White audiences loved his illustrative stories, which tended to portray Blacks as lovable, ignorant, and harmless, but shrewd. The first of three autobiographies, *The Story of My Life and Work*, was published in 1900, and another one, *Up From Slavery*, was published the following year after appearing in serial form in *The Outlook*. *Up From Slavery* in particular soon became a bestseller, and attracted more White philanthropy to Tuskegee Institute from people like Andrew Carnegie, who appreciated the persistence and self-reliance in Washington's story. Washington's general philosophy was accommodating to the White establishment, and his publicly expressed views rarely went against the grain of prevailing White opinion. He spoke more of Black responsibilities than of Black rights, and gave the impression that the burden of improving race relations lay more with Blacks than Whites.

His philosophy did not sit well with the more educated, radicalized Black leaders, and his leadership was attacked as fatally conservative. Among his sharpest critics were William Monroe Trotter, editor of the *Boston Guardian*, and Atlanta University professor W. E. B. DuBois. They thought his system of industrial education, which greatly reduced standard academic expectations, had the practical effect of keeping Blacks in a manual labor class and preventing them from accessing the realm of intellectual achievement and prestige. Washington was denounced for ignoring the issues of segregation and disenfranchisement, and for surreptitiously suppressing criticism through a large network of loyalists. Critics noted that while outwardly preferring to work outside the political arena, Washington carefully cultivated political influence in secret. The extent of his control of Black media was suspected, but provable only much later when his personal papers were opened to the public. In 1905 DuBois and others founded the Niagara Movement to promote a more activist and militant philosophy.

The first decade of the twentieth century was the time of Washington's greatest power. He wrote some ten books during these years, the majority of his corpus. From 1901 to 1908 he had ready access to the Roosevelt White House, where he was consulted on a wide range of issues and appointments. He was a visitor to the Taft White House from 1908 to 1912 to a somewhat lesser degree. He was responsible for Blacks obtaining a number of prestigious government positions. He was instrumental in founding the National Negro Business League in 1900 and was its president until his death.

This group worked to encourage the development of Black-owned and operated businesses. Washington strongly influenced the National Afro-American Council, conspicuously attending its national conventions after 1902. In 1901 Dartmouth College gave him an honorary D.Litt. degree (Harvard University had presented him with an honorary M.A. in 1896), and he later had a personal audience with Queen Victoria on a visit to England. In 1903 Andrew Carnegie gave him $150,000 to ensure his personal financial security.

During the last five years of his life his influence began to wane. The emergence of the N.A.A.C.P., founded in 1909 as a rival organization, and the election of 1912 which put Woodrow Wilson in the White House sharply reduced his political force. His image was not helped by an awkward incident in March 1911, when he was beaten by a White man in New York City, Albert Ulrich, who accused him of looking through the keyhole of a White woman's apartment. Ulrich was later acquitted of assault. Though Washington's personal power had passed its zenith, Tuskegee Institute had entered its prime. At his death in 1915 from overwork and arteriosclerosis, Tuskegee owned 2,000 acres of local land plus 25,000 acres in northern Alabama, had a $2,000,000 endowment with an annual budget of $290,000, counted over 1,500 students, and had 197 faculty members teaching thirty-eight trades and professions. On its faculty were such renowned scientists and inventors as George Washington Carver. A college department was added in 1927.

Assessments of Washington's legacy still vary widely. He believed that earning a living and acquiring property were more important than the right to vote or getting a Ph.D., because gaining economic clout would necessarily eventually bring these and every other opportunity. Many still feel that this pragmatic philosophy was the most effective approach, at least for his day. Further, studies have shown that he accomplished much behind the scenes that was not known before. He secretly financed, for example, a number of legal battles against discrimination. On the other hand, many believe that he did not appreciate the power of the vote and civil rights to defend the very business interests he was emphasizing, and that his tactic of progress through appeasement was counterproductive, in the end delaying the achievement of the level playing field that was his own ultimate goal.

Bontemps, Arna. *Young Booker: Booker T. Washington's Early Days.* New York: Dodd, Mead & Co., 1972. 196 pp.

Harlan, Louis R. Booker T. *Washington in Perspective: Essays of Louis R. Harlan.* Jackson, MI: University Press of Mississippi, 1988. 210 pp.

———, ed. *The Booker T. Washington Papers.* 14 vols. Urbana, IL: University of Illinois, 1972–1989.

———. *Booker T. Washington: The Making of a Black Leader, 1856–1901.* New York: Oxford University Press, 1972. 379 pp.

———. *Booker T. Washington: The Wizard of Tuskegee, 1901–1915.* New York: Oxford University Press, 1983. 548 pp.

Hawkins, Hugh, ed. *Booker T. Washington and His Critics: The Problem of Negro Leadership.* Boston, MA: Heath, 1962. 113 pp.

Mathews, Basil Joseph. *Booker T. Washington, Educator and Interracial Interpreter.* Cambridge, MA: Harvard University Press, 1948. 350 pp.

Meier, August. *Negro Thought in America, 1880–1915: Racial Ideologies in the Age of Booker T. Washington.* Lansing, MI: University of Michigan Press, 1963. 336 pp.

Scott, Emmett Jay and Lyman Beecher Stowe. *Booker T. Washington, Builder of a Civilization.* Garden City, NY: Doubleday, Page, & Co., 1916. 331 pp.

Spencer, Samuel R., Jr. *Booker T. Washington and the Negro's Place in American Life.* Boston, MA: Little, Brown, & Co., 1955. 212 pp.

Stokes, Anson Phelps. *A Brief Biography of Booker T. Washington.* Hampton, VA: Hampton Institute Press, 1936. 42 pp.

———. *Tuskegee Institute, The First Fifty Years.* Tuskegee, AL: Tuskegee Institute Press, 1931. 99 pp.

Thornbrough, Emma Lou, ed. *Booker T. Washington.* Englewood Cliffs, NJ: Prentice-Hall, 1969. 184 pp.

Washington, Booker T. *Character Building: Being Addresses Delivered on Sunday Evenings to the Students of Tuskegee Institute by Booker T. Washington.* New York: Doubleday, Page, & Co., 1902. 291 pp.

———. *Frederick Douglass.* Philadelphia, PA: George W. Jacobs & Co., 1906. 365 pp.

———. *The Future of the American Negro.* Boston, MA: Small, Maynard & Co., 1899. 244 pp.

———, and R. E. Park. *The Man Farthest Down.* Garden City, NY: Doubleday, Page, & Co., 1912. 390 pp.

———. *My Larger Education: Being Chapters from My Experience.* New York: Doubleday, Page, & Co., 1911. 313 pp.

———. *The Negro in Business.* Boston, MA: Hertel, Jenkins, & Co., 1907. 379 pp.

———. *The Story of My Life and Work.* Toronto: J. L. Nichols & Co., 1900. 423 pp.

———. *The Story of the Negro: The Rise of the Race from Slavery.* 2 vols. New York: Doubleday, Page, 1909.

———. *Up From Slavery, An Autobiography.* New York: A. L. Burt, 1901. 330 pp.

———. *Working with the Hands.* New York: Doubleday, Page, & Co., 1904. 246 pp.

Weisberger, Bernard A. *Booker T. Washington.* New York: New American Library, 1972. 142 pp.

BRBR, LV, NPT, NAHDA, BNA, HNB, AAE, EBA, ACAB, BDAE, NCAB (7), *DAB, DANB, BR, BHAC, WWCR, NA, TSW, WGMC, BLTC, NAH, CH, TCNL, NSE, BHBA, MM, NG, NBH, AARS, EAB, ESH, BDSA, DNAADB, BAW, DARB, IBAWCB, HUBA, SBAA, BWA, ALNA, BWASS.*

WASHINGTON, DENNIS COMER (b. August 15, 1905), long-time head of the Sunday School Publishing Board of the **National Baptist Convention, U.S.A., Inc.** (N.B.C.U.S.A.), was born in Hale County, Alabama, the son of William H. and Mary (Scott) Washington. He received his B.S. from Alabama State Teachers College in Montgomery, Alabama. He married Bessie Randall, with whom he had four children.

From 1924 to 1939 he pastored various Baptist churches in Alabama, and from 1939 to 1959 he pastored the 17th Street Baptist Church in Anniston, Alabama. In Anniston he was a leader in the local branch of the N.A.A.C.P. and was on the executive board of the Alabama State Baptist Convention. At one point he was moderator of the Snow Creek Baptist District Association. In 1956 he was a member of the White House Conference on Civil Rights. In October, 1959 he succeeded **Arthur M. Townsend** as executive director of the Sunday School Publishing Board of the N.B.C.U.S.A., a powerful position that placed him in charge of one of the world's major religious publishing houses. He held this office for the rest of his career.

His task was to continue and expand the excellent establishment created by Townsend. Washington opened the library of the Publishing Board on November 27, 1959, with a resident librarian, Mrs. Hazel Thompson. The library has since proved an invaluable source of archival material for historians. He replaced the *Sunday School Informer* with the *Baptist Teacher*, and discontinued the *Star of Hope* in 1960 to avoid duplication of material in the *Worker*, a quarterly put out by the Women's Convention. In 1960 he brought **Jesse Jai McNeil** on as Director of Publications. Washington was a trustee of Selma University, the American Baptist Theological Seminary, and the Anniston Federation of Colored Women's Clubs.

BDNM (75), *SCA, SNB.*

WASHINGTON, JOSEPH REED, JR. (b. October 30, 1930), Baptist minister and theologian/sociologist, was born in Iowa City, Iowa, the son of Rev. Joseph R. Sr. and Susie (Duncan) Washington. He received his B.A. in 1952 from the University of Wisconsin. On February 13, 1952 he married Sophia May Holland, with whom he had two sons. From 1952 to 1954 he was a first lieutenant in the U.S. Army. He received his B.D. in 1957 from Andover-Newton Theological Seminary in Massachusetts, and his Th.D. in social ethics in 1961 from the Boston University School of Theology.

He assisted at a Baptist church in Woburn, Massachusetts from 1954 to 1956 and pastored a Congregational church in West Newfield, Maine, in 1956–57. He was ordained a Baptist minister in 1957 and in 1957–58 was minister to students at the First Baptist Church in Brookline, Massachusetts. From 1958 to 1961 he was assistant Protestant chaplain at Boston University and from 1961 to 1963 was dean of the chapel and assistant professor of religion and philosophy at Dillard University in New Orleans, Louisiana. From 1963 to 1966 he was chaplain and assistant professor of religion at Dickinson College in Carlisle, Pennsylvania. From 1966 to 1969 he was chaplain and associate professor of religion at Albion College in Albion, Michigan. In 1969–70 he was chaplain and professor of religion and sociology at Beloit College in Beloit, Wisconsin.

In the 1960s Washington began a steady stream of publications, including *Black Religion: The Negro and Christianity in the United States* (1964); *The Politics of God* (1967); and *Black and White Power Subreption* (1969). In 1970 he moved to the University of Virginia, where he was a professor of religious studies and chair of the Afro-American Studies department. He stayed there until 1975, during which time he wrote *Marriage in Black and White* (1971) and one of his most well-known books, *Black Sects and Cults* (1972). Since 1975 he has been a professor of religious studies and chair of the Black Studies department at the University of California at Riverside. In his prolific writings he has covered a broad range of disciplines, from theology to history to sociology to ethics. Recent works include *Anti-Blackness in English Religion, 1500–1800* (1984) and a two-volume work, *Race and Religion in Early 19th-Century America, 1800–1850* and *Race and Religion in Mid-19th-Century America, 1850–1877* (1988).

Washington, Joseph R., Jr. *Anti-Blackness in English Religion, 1500–1800.* Lewiston, NY: E. Mellon Press, 1984. 603 pp.

———. *Black Sects and Cults.* Garden City, NY: Doubleday & Company, 1972. 176 pp.

———. *The Moral of Molliston Madison Clark: The Adverse Atavisms Antiabolitionists Adored and an American African Methodist Moved to Abort.* Lewiston, NY: E. Mellon Press, 1990. 161 pp.

———. *Race and Religion in Early 19th-Century America, 1800–1850: Constitution, Conscience, and Calvinist Compromise*. Lewiston, NY: Edwin Mellon Press, 1988.

———. *Race and Religion in Mid-19th-Century America, 1850–1877: Protestant Parochial Philanthropists*. Lewiston, NY: E. Mellon Press, 1988.

IBAW, IBAWCB, HUBA, AARS, EBA, BDNM (70), *WWR* (77), *CA* (vol. 9–12), *SBAA, WWABA* (92–93).

WASHINGTON, WILBUR THORNTON (b. January 19, 1924), a minister in the **Reformed Church in America**, was born in Palmyra, New Jersey. He attended Tuskegee Institute for a year (1942–43) before entering West Virginia State College (1943–44). He completed his B.A. degree in 1949 at Rutgers University. He went on for ministerial training at New Brunswick Theological Seminary and earned his B.D. in 1952. He was licensed by the Presbytery of Cleveland in 1953 and ordained to the ministry the following year. Following his ordination he became pastor at Penbroke Community Church in St. Anne, Illinois. In 1959 he moved to Oakland, California as pastor of Community Reformed Church. Then in 1969 he moved as a counselor to Pella College in Pella, Iowa. His first year there he also served as president of the Church's Synod of the West. Also while at Pella, he continued his education with a year of post-graduate work at the University of Chicago (1970–71).

More recently he has served as pastor at First Reformed Church in Jamaica, Queens, Long Island, New York. In 1988 Washington was the first African American to be elected vice president of the Reformed Church in America and the following years became the first African American president of the synod. There are 45 predominantly African American congregations in the Reformed Church, less than three percent of the membership.

Vandenberge, Peter N. *Historical Directory of the Reformed Church in America, 1628–1978*. Grand Rapids, MI: William B. Eerdmans Publishing Company, 1978. 385 pp.

WASHINGTON, WILLIAM A. (October 30, 1883–1949?), a bishop of the **Church of Christ (Holiness), U.S.A.**, was born in Holmes County, near Lexington, Mississippi. He was raised in the Baptist Church, in which he was converted at the age of nine. However, he soon affiliated with the **Church of God in Christ** (COGIC) and at the age of twelve experienced sanctification, a cleansing from sin by the Holy Spirit. He was licensed to preach in 1895 at the age of sixteen.

In 1902 he began his first pastoral assignment in Edwards and Tougaloo, Mississippi. He then moved to Selma, Alabama, where he led the congregation in erecting a new sanctuary. While there he met his future wife, Tennessee Morgan. In 1905 he moved to Montgomery, Alabama, and later to Dyersburg, Tennessee, where again he led in building a new church.

Washington did not accept the new teachings on the Pentecostal experience introduced into the Church of God in Christ by **Charles H. Mason** in 1906. Over the next two years, as Mason consolidated his leadership of COGIC, Washington separated and affiliated with the predominantly White Holiness Church, one of a number of small Holiness denominations which had formed in the late nineteenth century. He attended the 1908 convention of the Holiness at Slaughterville, Kentucky, following which he organized a new congregation at Madison, Kentucky. He then moved to Seco, Kentucky, and organized a church at that location. He continued to operate in Kentucky and Tennessee until 1913, when he moved to Los Angeles, California. He worked in predominantly White congregations for several years, but in 1915 founded the Bethel Church for African American Holiness believers.

Over the next few years he founded several more congregations which were incorporated separately as an independent denomination. In the early 1920s, Elder **C. P. Jones** came to Los Angeles and held a revival. Jones and Washington had a natural affinity as each had been part of the pre-Pentecostal Church of God in Christ; Jones had been one of original founders of that church. He negotiated an agreement with Washington which brought his work into the Church of Christ (Holiness), U.S.A. In 1926 the Church of Christ's school, Christ Missionary and Industrial College, conferred a D.D. degree on Washington.

The agreement between Jones and Washington lasted through World War II, but around 1946, the two parted company, and Washington reorganized his congregations on the West Coast under the original corporation as the **Associated Churches of Christ (Holiness)** under which title they continue to this day. Washington died in Los Angeles a few years later.

DuPree, Sherry Sherrod. *Biographical Dictionary of African-American Holiness-Pentecostals, 1880–1990*. Washington, DC: Middle Atlantic Regional Press, 1989. 386 pp.

WATERS, CHARLES EMORY ROGERS (January 5, 1917–December 12, 1986), the founder of the **True Fellowship Pentecostal Church of God of America**, was born and raised in Baltimore, Maryland. He

Baptist Church and experienced salvation in the First Baptist Church of Fairfield at the age of twelve. As a young man he went to work as a salesman and at the age of twenty-one was able to purchase a confectionery store. His business success enabled him to expand the store into a grocery and meat market.

He was a prosperous businessman when he experienced sanctification and the baptism of the Holy Spirit as evidenced by his speaking in tongues, experiences which led him out of the Baptist Church into the Church of God in Christ. Then in 1947 he joined the **Alpha & Omega Pentecostal Church of America**, a new denomination which had been organized just two years previously by Magdalene Mabe Phillips. He became a minister and evangelist and later served as presiding elder of the board of directors and assistant overseer. In 1960 he became pastor of the Faith Tabernacle Alpha & Omega Pentecostal Church.

In 1964 Waters broke with the Alpha & Omega Church and founded the True Fellowship Pentecostal Church of America, the Faith Tabernacle becoming the first congregation. His major disagreement with the Alpha & Omega Church was over the role of women in the ministry. The next year he was consecrated as bishop of the new denomination.

DuPree, Sherry Sherrod. *Biographical Dictionary of African-American Holiness-Pentecostals, 1880–1990.* Washington, DC: Middle Atlantic Regional Press, 1989. 386 pp.

WATERS, EDWARD (March 15, 1780–June 5, 1847), 3rd bishop of the **African Methodist Episcopal Church** (AME), was born into slavery at West River, Maryland. He was converted in Baltimore, Maryland, in 1798 and joined the AME Church. He was licensed as a local preacher in 1810, was ordained deacon in 1818, and an elder in 1820. It is not known how he exited from slavery. He is known to have had a daughter, but other information about his family life is unavailable.

At the Fifth General Conference in May 1836, Waters was elected bishop. At the time bishops were not elected on an equal basis and Waters was considered a junior or assistant bishop. After an initial tour of almost all the conferences he remained primarily in Baltimore, with once-a-year visits to the Philadelphia and New York conferences.

As bishop he never presided over an Annual Conference nor did he ever ordain anyone, being only an assistant to Bishop **Morris Brown**. During much of his bishopric, at his own request, he even served as a local pastor. For a time he was at the Ellicott Mills Circuit and for a time at Bethel AME Church in Baltimore. In 1844 he resigned from the episcopacy and worked as an elder the rest of his career. In the spring of 1847 he was knocked down by a carriage and never recovered from his injuries. In 1883 the first school of higher education for Blacks in Florida, previously called Brown University, adopted the name Edward Waters College in his honor.

HAMEC, EWM, CEAMEC, BAMEC.

WATERS, ETHEL (October 31, 1896–September 1, 1977), singer, actress, and evangelist, was born in Chester, Pennsylvania, the daughter of John Wesley and Louisa Tar (Anderson) Waters. She was conceived when her father raped her mother at age twelve, and her mother later ignored her in favor of the legitimate daughter of a subsequent marriage. She was reared mostly by her maternal grandmother in such poverty that she was often forced to steal food. She attended an interracial Catholic school for a time, but spent much of her time on the streets. She was married to Merritt Purnsley at the age of thirteen, a relationship that lasted less than a year. About 1914 she got her first job as a chambermaid in a Philadelphia hotel, and soon was persuaded to try singing in a local club.

By age seventeen, Waters was singing with a vaudeville act at the Lincoln Theatre in Baltimore for $9 per week. With permission from W. C. Handy, she became the first woman to sing his jazz classic, "Saint Louis Blues," on stage. She went on some tours and made some recordings, and then got a big break in 1925, when she substituted for Florence Mills at the Plantation Club in Harlem and was a hit singing "Dinah." She then began to receive offers, not only for more singing engagements, but for theater work as well. She was in the 1927 Broadway production of *Africana*, followed by *Blackbirds* (1930), *Rhapsody in Black* (1931 and 1932), *As Thousands Cheer* (1933), and *At Home Abroad* (1935). In the 1933 season she was the highest-paid performer on Broadway, with $5,000–per-week earnings combined from the play, a nightclub act, and as a permanent guest on a radio network program. In 1938 and 1939 she played her first straight, non-singing, dramatic part as Hagar in *Mamba's Daughters*, and received strong praise from such stars as Tallulah Bankhead and Oscar Hammerstein. That role made her the first Black woman to star in a Broadway drama. Her second marriage was to Clyde Edward Matthews, a musician who also ran a restaurant in Harlem called Fat Man's Place. This marriage also ended in divorce.

In 1940–41 Waters starred in the Broadway production of *Cabin in the Sky* and received further critical acclaim. In 1942 she bought her first house, in Los Angeles. In 1942–43 she was on the executive council of the Actors Equity Association and was vice-president of the Negro Actors Guild. In those years she appeared in a number of films, but between 1943 and 1949 her bookings dropped off and then mysteriously almost disappeared. She nearly went bankrupt, and was reduced to appearing in small, unknown places. Finally, she portrayed the grandmother of the heroine in a 1949 film, *Pinky,* a performance that earned her an Academy Award nomination and an achievement plaque from the Negro Actors Guild. She returned to Broadway in 1950 in the play *The Member of the Wedding,* in the role of a cook giving counsel to a motherless child. This has been called her greatest dramatic success. In 1950 she starred in a short-lived television program called "Beulah." In 1951 she published her first autobiography, *His Eye is on the Sparrow,* the title of a song she sang in *The Member of the Wedding.* The book related in straightforward language her rough-and-tumble life, and was a best-seller. She was in such tax debt, however, that all her royalties went to the Internal Revenue Service.

In the late 1950s her career again went downhill, but she turned it around. This time she did not return to the theater, but became a member of evangelist Billy Graham's traveling revival team. Waters had always been known for being very devout, with an entire room of her home set aside for devotional purposes. She at first refused the role of Berenice the cook in *The Member of the Wedding,* because the woman was portrayed as someone who had lost faith in God. She only accepted when the script was rewritten to her satisfaction. Although she grew up as a Catholic, she had no denominational prejudices and often dropped in to the closest church when she felt the need. She toured with Graham from 1957 to 1976. In 1972 she published a second autobiography, *To Me It's Wonderful.* Regarded as one of the all-time great blues and jazz singers, Waters performed and recorded with such performers as Duke Ellington and Benny Goodman. She was particularly identified with songs such as "Dinah," "Am I Blue," "Stormy Weather," which she introduced at the Cotton Club in the 1930s, and "Heat Wave," a song from Irving Berlin's musical *As Thousands Cheer.*

"The Member of the Wedding." *Ebony* 8 (December 1952): 47–51.
"Miss Waters Regrets." *Ebony* 12 (February 1957): 56–60.
Waters, Ethel. *His Eye is on the Sparrow.* Garden City, NY: Doubleday & Company, 1951. 278 pp.
———. "The Men in My Life." *Ebony* 7 (January 1952): 24–38.
———. *To Me It's Wonderful.* New York: Harper and Row, 1972. 162 pp.
"Where Are They Now?" *Newsweek* 70 (July 17, 1967): 14.
NYTO, CB (1977), *CA* (vol. 81–84), *BWR, WWR* (77), *EBA, BDA-AAM, FAW, CH, HNB, BHBA, CB* (1941 and 1951), *LW, GNPP, IBAW, IBAWCB.*

WATSON, EDGAR BENTON (February 7, 1874–January 17, 1951), 53rd bishop of the **African Methodist Episcopal Zion Church** (AMEZ), was born in Chatham County, North Carolina, the son of Louis and Nanie (Rieves) Watson. After attending Hamilton High School in Carthage, North Carolina, he was a student for a time at the Agricultural and Technical College in Greensboro, North Carolina. He joined the Central North Carolina Conference of the AMEZ Church in 1905, then the West Central North Carolina Conference when it was organized in 1910. He earned the B.A. degree from Livingstone College in Salisbury, North Carolina, in 1911. On June 22, 1911, he married Margaret Morrow, with whom he had one child. He received the B.D. degree from Hood Theological Seminary at Livingstone College in 1915.

He was ordained deacon on November 24, 1907, and was assigned to the Mt. Pleasant Circuit while at Livingstone, from 1907 to 1911. He was ordained an elder on November 21, 1909. From 1911 to 1913 he pastored the Norwood Station, followed by the Zion Hill AMEZ Church in Concord, North Carolina, from 1913 to 1916. Other pastorates included Trinity Zion AMEZ Church in Greensboro, North Carolina (1916–20); Varick AMEZ Church in Philadelphia (1920–24); Metropolitan AMEZ Church in Washington, D.C. (1924–29); Metropolitan AMEZ Church in Birmingham, Alabama (1929–32); Oak Street AMEZ Church in Petersburg, Virginia (1932–c.1940); Hood Temple AMEZ Church in Richmond, Virginia; and Metropolitan AMEZ Church in Norfolk, Virginia.

From this last, very successful pastorate Watson was elected bishop and was consecrated on May 14, 1944. About this time, his first wife having passed away, he married Mary Jane Hedgepath. From 1944 to 1948 he was assigned to Texas, Oklahoma, Liberia, West Gold Coast, East Gold Coast, and Nigeria. From 1948 until his death he headed the Central North Carolina, Pee Dee, East Tennessee, and Virginia conferences. He was active in the N.A.A.C.P. and the Y.M.C.A. and was a trustee of Clinton Junior College. Twice he was elected chair of the Board of Bishops.

"Alstork, Watson Elected Bishops." *Star of Zion* 68 (May 25, 1944): 1.

"Bishop E. B. Watson Passes." *The A.M.E. Zion Quarterly Review* 60 (1950): 222.

"In Memoriam." *The AME Zion Quarterly Review* 62 (1951): 228–229.

"Last Rites for Bishop Watson." *Star of Zion* 74 (February 8, 1951): 1.

Lovell, Walter R. "Bishop Edgar Benton Watson." *The Star of Zion* 74 (February 1, 1951): 4.

Walls, William Jacob. *The African Methodist Episcopal Zion Church; Reality of the Black Church.* Charlotte, NC: AME Zion Publishing House, 1974. 669 pp.

AARS, WWCA (38–40), *AMEZC, HAMEZC.*

WATSON, THOMAS (1898–November 12, 1985), a pioneer leader among the **Spiritual churches** and the founder of both the Divine Spiritual Churches of the Southwest and the United Metropolitan Spiritual Churches of Christ, was raised in New Orleans. He was one of the early students of Xavier University (which had opened in the city in 1915) and following graduation attended Texas Christian University from which he obtained his master's degree. He became a teacher in the public school system. As the Spiritual movement emerged in the 1920s under Rev. Leafy Anderson, Watson associated with Anderson church and became one of its leaders.

In 1929, two years after Anderson's death, Watson left the church and founded the St. Joseph Helping Hand Church in Algiers, a suburb of New Orleans on the other side of the Mississippi River. Over the next five years, other Spiritual churches emerged in Algiers and neighboring communities, and in 1934, Watson organized them into the St. Joseph Helping Hand Missionary Association. This early organization emphasized the Christian nature of its beliefs which placed it in sharp distinction from other spiritual denominations and congregations.

In 1935 the association, having added congregations outside of the New Orleans metropolitan area, matured as the Divine Spiritual Churches of the Southwest. The Churches established an hierarchical polity and named Watson as its senior bishop. A woman, Bessie S. Johnson, was named junior bishop. Over the next four years Watson thought out his opinions on women in the ministry and the bishopric, and in 1940 demoted Johnson to Reverend Mother Superior. This occasioned the first major schism in the organization.

In 1942, Watson led the organization into a merger with the **Metropolitan Spiritual Churches of Christ**, a national Spiritual denomination. Watson was named president of the group. However, Watson soon came into conflict with **Clarence Cobbs**, a rising star from Chicago among the Metropolitan Churches. The conflict led to a schism in 1945. Cobb emerged as president of the Metropolitan Churches, and Watson reorganized his following as the United Metropolitan Spiritual Churches of Christ.

Watson led the United Metropolitan Churches for the rest of his long life. He was succeeded by his son, Bishop Aubrey Watson.

Jacobs, Claude F., and Andrew J. Kaslow. *The Spiritual Churches of New Orleans: Origins, Beliefs, and Rituals of an African-American Religion.* Knoxville, TN: University of Tennessee Press, 1991. 235 pp.

WAY OF THE CROSS CHURCH OF CHRIST. An Apostolic Pentecostal church. In 1926 **Henry Chauncey Brooks** felt a call to preach and the next year presented himself to Bishop **Robert C. Lawson**, the head of the church of Our Lord Jesus Christ of the Apostolic Faith, for a license. Not ready to respond to Brooks, Lawson suggested that he go to Washington and work with J. T. Morris, then a pastor with the **Pentecostal Assemblies of the World** (who would later leave and form the **Highway Christian Church of Christ**). Instead, Brooks went to Washington where he founded an independent congregation which he called the Way of the Cross Church. Brooks, having proven his ability, was given credentials by Lawson in 1928. A short time later, Brooks began a second congregation in Henderson, North Carolina, headed by his brother-in-law John Luke Brooks (1896–1980).

In the meantime, Lawson sent another minister to begin work in the African American community. In 1927 **Smallwood E. Williams** had founded the **Bible Way Church of Our Lord Jesus Christ World Wide**. In 1933 Lawson decided to put the two congregations in Washington, both of which were small, together. Rather than merge his work with Williams', Brooks dropped his affiliation with Lawson and became independent as the Way of the Cross Church of Christ. Other men came to Brooks for credentials, and under his lengthy tenure as supreme bishop, Brooks saw Way of the Cross churches spread up and down the East Coast. Following his death in 1967, he was succeeded by Bishop J. L. Brooks who was already in his seventies. Brooks served the headquarters church until 1979. At that time he retired from the pastorate but continued as supreme bishop until his death the next year. J. L. Brooks expanded the hierarchy of the church, consecrating 12 bishops during his first nine years in office. He also extended its outreach to Liberia.

In 1980, the Way of the Cross churches reported

48 congregations and approximately 50,000 members. Headquarters is in Washington, D.C. J. T. Brooks was succeeded by Alonzo D. Brooks, the son of H. C. Brooks.

JCR.

WAYMAN, ALEXANDER WALKER (September, 1821–November 30, 1895), 7th bishop of the **African Methodist Episcopal Church** (AME), was born in Caroline County, Maryland. As a young boy he worked with his parents, Francis and Matilda Wayman, on the family farm. His father taught him to read, and he gained the rest of his basic education on his own and from the children of Benjamin Kerby, to whom he was hired out in 1835. That same year Wayman was converted, though he did not join the Methodist Episcopal Church until March 19, 1837. In August 1839, he became convinced that God was calling him to preach, and in 1840 he left home for Baltimore, seeking more education. There he encountered the AME Church and visited its General Conference in May. He then moved to Philadelphia, where he joined the Bethel AME Church in June.

Wayman received an exhorter's license on October 16, 1840, and preached when he could, in addition to his private studying and his job as coachman. In May, 1842, he became assistant to Rev. Turner on the Princeton, New Jersey, circuit and taught at a small, primary school in New Brunswick. In 1843 he was assigned to the West Chester circuit, and in 1845 was ordained deacon in the Philadelphia Conference. In 1846 he pastored in Cape May, Springtown, Swedesboro, and Salem, New Jersey. In 1847 he was ordained elder and assigned to Trenton, New Jersey. In 1848 he transferred to the Baltimore Conference, and for the next fifteen years pastored churches in either Baltimore or Washington, D.C.

Wayman was a delegate to General Conference beginning in 1848, when he was elected a secretary. He served as chief secretary in 1856, 1860, and 1864. In 1860 he was appointed to a three-member committee to write a new edition of the *Discipline*, the church's polity book. This was also the year his wife died. On May 16, 1864, he received 84 out of 90 votes for the episcopacy, and was so elected. The following day he married Harriet Ann Elizabeth Wayman. He was assigned variously to the Second, Third, Fourth, Seventh, Ninth, and Tenth Episcopal District Areas, active until the time of his death. Many of the conferences over which he presided were conferences he had organized himself. He organized the Florida, North Carolina, Georgia, and Virginia Annual Conferences in 1867, the Pittsburgh Conference in 1868, the Illinois Conference in 1867, and the West Tennessee Conference in 1876.

On October 15, 1874, Wayman served as the chaplain at the unveiling of the Lincoln Memorial in Springfield, Illinois. He authored a number of works, the most important being *My Recollection of African M.E. Ministers, or Forty Years' Experience in the African Methodist Episcopal Church* (1881), and the *Cyclopedia of African Methodism* (1882). He became senior bishop upon the death of Bishop **Daniel Payne** in 1893. His tenure is well remembered for its many organizational and educational gifts to the denomination, and almost thirty churches in fourteen states are named after him.

Tanner, Benjamin Tucker. *An Apology for African Methodism.* Baltimore, MD: n.p., 1867. 468 pp.

Wayman, Alexander Walker. *Cyclopedia of African Methodism.* Baltimore, MD: Methodist Episcopal Book Depository, 1882. 190 pp.

———. *The Life of Rev. James Alexander Shorter, One of the Bishops of the African Methodist Episcopal Church.* Baltimore, MD: J. Lanahan, 1890. 50 pp.

———. *Manual, or Guide Book for the Administration of the Discipline of the African M. E. Church.* Philadelphia, PA: African Methodist Episcopal Book Rooms, 1886. 84 pp.

———. *My Recollections of African M. E. Ministers, or Forty Years' Experience in the African Methodist Episcopal Church.* Philadelphia, PA: A.M.E. Book Room, 1881. 250 pp.

RLOA, BAMEC, EWM, DAB (10), HAMEC, RAM, AARS, BAW, HUBA, CEAMEC.

WEIR, SAMUEL (April 15, 1812–February 15, 1884), an elder (minister) with the German Baptist Brethren (**Church of the Brethren**), was born into slavery in Bath County, Virginia, the son of James and Lucy Bird Weir. When he was twelve, he was purchased by Andrew McClure, a fortuitous event, as McClure eventually joined the German Baptist Brethren. The Brethren had a strong dislike of slavery and demanded new members free any slaves which they might own. Thus in 1843 Weir was freed, and he also joined the Brethren. A few months after his baptism he left Virginia for Ohio, where he affiliated with the Paint Creek Brethren congregation in Ross County. There he learned to read and write and later studied with Jacob Emmings, a Black Baptist minister in Highland County, Ohio.

In 1849 Weir was licensed to preach by the Paint Creek congregation and became the first Black to hold such a position among the Brethren. He established a ministry among the Black people of southern Ohio. He made his first converts at the end of the Civil War and formed the Frankfort congregation, of which he was named the minister. He also continued to work at other locations and in the 1870 organized the congregation at Circleville, Ohio, which soon outgrew the older congregation at Frankfort. In 1872 Weir was elected a minister by the Fairview congregation and that same year he saw his first convert, Harvey Carter, designated a deacon.

In 1881 Weir ordained an elder for the Scioto Valley of Ohio, and at the same meeting Carter was ordained to the ministry and succeeded the aging Weir as the minister at Frankfort. Weir gave his house and land to the church. He died a few years later following a prolonged illness. His work among Blacks continued into the early twentieth century but eventually died out, though the Circleville church still exists as a predominantly White congregation.

The Brethren Encyclopedia. 2 vols. Philadelphia, PA: The Brethren Encyclopedia, Inc., 1983.

WESLEYAN CHURCH. A Holiness church. The Wesleyan Church was formed in 1968 by a merger of the Wesleyan Methodist Church and the Pilgrim Holiness Church. The older of these two bodies, the Wesleyan Methodists, originated in 1843 and represented the abolitionist wing of the Methodist Episcopal Church. Relatively small, it began with only 6,000 members. Staunchly abolitionist in perspective, following the Civil War it began a variety of efforts for the freedmen, the most important one being a church and day school, Alabama Mission School, at Brent, Alabama. The school, founded in 1912, was managed by a Black staff and had a successful program until 1944 when it was turned over to the public school system.

Possibly the most lasting work by Wesleyan Methodist was in Ohio, where in 1894 the South Ohio Conference was organized. This all-Black conference had ten churches when carved out of the Miami and Central Ohio Conference. Rev. H. C. Pierce was the first president. The conference was carried into the merged church as the South Ohio district and included African American churches in Ohio, Indiana, West Virginia, Kentucky, and Tennessee. Several quadrennium later it was dissolved, and the churches merged into the geographical districts.

McLeister, Ira Ford, and Roy S. Nicholson. *History of the Wesleyan Methodist Church*. Marion, IN: The Wesley Press, 1959. 558 pp.

WESTERN UNIVERSITY. An **African Methodist Episcopal Church** (AME) school. Western University originated with a school begun at Quindaro, Kansas, by Rev. Eben Blatchley, a White Presbyterian minister during the Civil War. The school, Freedman University, was dedicated to the training of Black youth. Blatchley was able to keep the enterprise going for some fifteen years until his death in 1877. The land was donated to the AME Church. In 1880 Bishop **T. M. D. Ward** was assigned to preside over the Kansas Conference. He revived the school, but it was not until the 1890s, during the administration of Bishop **Henry McNeal Turner**, that the school showed signs of becoming a stable successful college. Then, under Bishop **Abram Grant**, who led the conference from 1904 to 1910, the school improved greatly. His work was assisted by the passing of the Bailey Bill by the Kansas State Legislature, which appropriated a large grant for industrial education in African American education, and the state established an industrial school in conjunction with the college.

During the tenure of Bishop **Henry B. Parks**, Ward Hall, the main campus building, burned down and remained abandoned for many years. In 1935 the state withdrew its support of the industrial department. The school reorganized under Bishop **Noah W. Williams** and pursued new directions. Ward Hall was reopened as the home of the Noah W. Williams School of Religion, the sign of a new emphasis on education for full-time Christian workers. The school continued through World War II but has since closed.

Smith, Charles Spencer. *A History of the African Methodist Episcopal Church*. Philadelphia, PA: Book Concern of the AME Church, 1922. 570 pp.

Wright, Richard R. *The Encyclopedia of the African Methodist Episcopal Church*. Philadelphia, PA: Book Concern of the AME Concern, 1947. 688 pp.

WHEATLEY, PHILLIS (c.1753–December 5, 1784), the first Black woman poet in America, was born probably on the west coast of Africa. She was carried on a slave ship to Boston, Massachusetts in 1861, where she was sold to John and Susannah Wheatley, from whom she took her name. She was trained as a personal lady's maid and perhaps partly because of her initial frailty was treated much better than the other slaves of the family. She was given a room in the main house, ate the same food as the family and often in the same room, and was taught to read and write. John Wheatley later noted that her intelligence was such that within sixteen months of her arrival she had mastered the speaking and reading of the English language to the extent of being able to comprehend the most difficult portions of the Bible. Proficiency in writing came shortly thereafter.

Over time it became clear that she had an innate interest in and ability with literature of all kinds. Her tasks were kept minimal in order to accommodate her gifts. She learned Latin in order better to read Virgil and Ovid and became thoroughly acquainted with the major English writers, especially the neoclassicist Alexander Pope, her favorite. She also quickly imbibed the strong religious atmosphere of the family, who in 1770 sponsored her as the first Black member in the Old South Church (Puritan, today Congregational). On August 18, 1771, she was baptized by the Rev. Samuel Cooper. Her writings centered on three major themes—learning, virtue, and redemption through Christ. Her first known poem, "To the University of Cambridge," written in 1767, exhorted the students to avoid sin and follow Christ. An early published work was "An Elegiac Poem on the Death of the Celebrated Divine. . . George Whitefield" (1770). She was one of only three Americans (and the first woman) able to publish writings while still in slavery, the other two being Jupiter Hammon (1711–179?) and George Moses Horton (1797–1883).

The fact that a high level of poetry was being achieved by a young Black woman with scarcely nine years' acquaintance with English was a cause of considerable wonder all along the eastern seaboard. Her work posed a stiff challenge to the accepted stereotype of Africans as sub-human and unable to appreciate any of the finer sensibilities. Wheatley began to live the life of a local celebrity as a frequent guest in various wealthy residences, composing verses of an evening. Her religious and political beliefs did not appear to range beyond the accepted bounds of her Massachusetts community, and later critics have chastised her for accepting a White mentality. Poems which, for instance, referring to Africa as "my Pagan land" provided the substance for this critique. Some recent commentators, however, have asserted that Wheatley used language, especially religious terminology, in subtle but powerful ways that undercut prejudices while still allowing her the freedom to write.

Her health, never good, began to deteriorate, and on the advice of a physician the Wheatleys sent her to England with their son, Nathaniel. Before the voyage they decided to free her; when the ship set sail in May 1773, Wheatley was no longer a slave. By this time she had published about a dozen poems and her reputation preceded her to England. She was received by the Countess of Huntingdon, a Methodist sponsor, and was celebrated across the country. She was universally deemed to have wit, modesty, and poise in abundance. Her one book, *Poems on Various Subjects, Religious and Moral*, was published in London later in 1773.

She returned alone to Boston in October 1773 and cared for her ailing former mistress, who died the following March. In 1776 she was invited to visit General George Washington, who received her with admiration. She remained at the Wheatley residence for several years, until John Wheatley and his daughter also passed away in 1778. Soon thereafter, on April 1, 1778, she married a man named John Peters, who had talent, good looks, and was variously employed as a baker, grocer, and lawyer. He also apparently was short on manners and showed little devotion to her. He seems to have wasted her money and was absent much of the time, either through neglect or imprisonment for debt. They moved to a small dwelling and she had three children by him, none of whom survived her. During the last couple of years of her life Peters was gone from the scene, leaving her poverty-stricken. Her spirit for writing, sporadic for some years, had disappeared after her last publication in September 1784, and she was forced to work in a boarding house in a poor section of Boston, where she and her third child passed away within hours of each other.

Wheatley's contributions were forgotten until Margaret Odell's *Memoir and Poems of Phillis Wheatley* was published in 1834, and Wheatley was subsequently cited by abolitionists as proof that Africans are as capable as anyone. Not until 1915 did she enter the scholarly dialogue with Charles F. Heartman's *Phillis Peters (Phillis Wheatley): A Critical Attempt.*

Graham, Shirley. *The Story of Phillis Wheatley.* New York: J. Messner, 1949, 1966. 176 pp.

Heartman, Charles Frederick. *Phillis Wheatley (Phillis Peters); A Critical Attempt and a Bibliography of Her Writings.* New York: The Author, 1915. 44 pp.

———, ed. *Phillis Wheatley . . . Poems and Letters; First Collected Edition.* New York: C. F. Heartman, 1915.

Mason, Julian D., ed. *The Poems of Phillis Wheatley.* Chapel Hill, NC: University of North Carolina Press, 1989. 235 pp.

Odell, Margaretta, ed. *Memoir and Poems of Phillis Wheatley, a Native African and a Slave.* Boston: G. W. Light, 1834. 155 pp.

O'Neale, Sondra. "A Slave's Subtle War: Phillis Wheatley's Use of Biblical Myth and Symbol." *Early American Literature* 21 (Fall 1986): 144–165.

Renfro, G. Herbert, ed. *Life and Works of Phillis Wheatley.* Miami, FL: Mnemosym Publishing Co., 1969. 112 pp.

Richmond, Merle A. *Bid the Vassal Soar: Interpretive Essays on the Life and Poetry of Phillis Wheatley and George*

Moses Horton. Washington, DC: Howard University Press, 1974. 216 pp.

Robinson, William Henry. *Critical Essays on Phillis Wheatley.* Boston, MA: G. K. Hall, 1982. 236 pp.

———. *Phillis Wheatley: A Bio-Bibliography.* Boston, MA: G. K. Hall, 1981. 166 pp.

———. *Phillis Wheatley and Her Writings.* New York: Garland Publishing, 1984. 464 pp.

Shields, John C., ed. *The Collected Works of Phillis Wheatley.* New York: Oxford University Press, 1988. 339 pp.

Wheatley, Phillis. *Letters of Phillis Wheatley, the Negro Slave Poet of Boston.* Boston, MA: J. Wilson & Son, 1864. 19 pp.

———. *The Poems of Phillis Wheatley, as They Were Originally Published in London, 1773.* Philadelphia, PA: R. R. and C. C. Wright, 1909. 88 pp.

———. *Poems on Various Subjects, Religious and Moral.* London: Printed for A. Bell, and sold by Messrs. Cox and Berry. Boston, MA: 1773. 127 pp.

CH, BHBA, NG, BAW, HUBA, IBAWCB, IBAW, SBAA, WWWA (H), ACAB, EBA, AAE, NAH, NBH, HH, BPEAR, NNW, FAW, DAB, NAW, DANB, BWA, ALNA, NBAW, BWMH.

WHITE, ALFRED EDWARD (b. April 29, 1921), 80th bishop of the **African Methodist Episcopal Zion Church** (AMEZ), was born in Pittsburgh, Pennsylvania, the son of John and Laura (Lewis) White. He received his B.A. degree in 1948 from Livingstone College in Salisbury, North Carolina and his B.D. degree in 1951 from Hood Theological Seminary at Livingstone College. On January 17, 1948, he married Mamie Williams, with whom he had one daughter.

He was ordained in 1944 and his first appointment was to the AMEZ Church in Derita, North Carolina, from 1945 to 1948, while a college student. Later pastorates included Gastonia, North Carolina (1948–52); Charlotte, North Carolina (1952–56); Salisbury, North Carolina (1956–62); and Hartford, Connecticut (1962–1984). While in Hartford he served as chair of the city's Human Relations Commission, was on the board of directors of St. Francis Hospital, and was a member of the National Board of Schools and Colleges of the AMEZ Church. He was also a trustee of the Hartford Conservatory of Music. In 1974 he was a member of the board of managers of the Central Branch Y.M.C.A.

White was elected bishop in 1984 and assigned to the Twelfth Episcopal District (Nigeria, Nigeria Rivers, Central Nigeria, West Ghana, and East Ghana Conferences), maintaining his residence in Hartford. On September 21, 1986, he received the Doctor of Ministry degree from Hartford Theological Seminary, writing a dissertation entitled, "The African Methodist Episcopal Zion Church in America and Africa: the Ministry of the Presiding Bishop of the Twelfth Episcopal District." This capped a long process of advancing his education which began when he earned the M.Div. from Hood Theological Seminary in 1974 and the D.D. in 1976.

In 1988 he was assigned to the Tenth Episcopal District (Alabama, Central Alabama, South Alabama, Cahaba, West Tennessee-Mississippi, and South Mississippi Conferences). He is a trustee of Livingstone College in Salisbury, North Carolina, and a trustee of Clinton Junior College. He has served on the Commission on Organic Union, the Commission on Family Life, and numerous other denominational boards.

"Bishop Alfred E. White Receives Doctorate Degree from Hartford." *Star of Zion* 110 (November 6, 1986): 1, 2.

"Vignettes of Our Bishops: Bishop Alfred E. White." *Star of Zion* 112 (January 7, 1988): 7.

WWR (77 and 85).

WHITE, WOODIE WALTER (b. August 27, 1935), a bishop of the **United Methodist Church**, was born in New York City, the son of Woodie W. and Elizabeth (Truitt) White. He graduated from DeWitt Clinton High School in New York in 1953, received his B.A. in 1958 from Paine College in Augusta, Georgia, and received his S.T.B. in 1961 from Boston University School of Theology. On June 3, 1961, he married Jennie May (Kim) Tolson. They had four daughters.

His first pastorate was at St. Andrew's Methodist Church in Worchester, Massachusetts, while in seminary (1960–61). He was ordained deacon in 1961 and elder in 1963. From 1961 to 1963 he was associate minister at East Grand Boulevard Methodist Church in Detroit, Michigan. With a white senior minister, this constituted the first bi-racial appointment in Michigan. He was a founding member of **Black Methodists for Church Renewal**, and was its vice-chair for some time beginning in 1963. From 1963 to 1967 he was senior pastor of the same church, and in 1967–68 he was Urban Missioner for the denomination in Metropolitan Detroit. There he was president of East Citizens for Action, president of the Churches on the East Side for Social Action, a member of Interfaith ACTION Council, Inc., and active in the N.A.A.C.P. For this work, in 1968, White received the Urban Award from the Office of Economic Opportunity for "outstanding work with the people of the Ghetto."

In 1968 the Methodist Church merged with the Evangelical United Brethren to create the United Methodist Church. As part of the restructuring the all-Black Central Jurisdiction of the former Methodist

Church was dismantled in a move toward integration. The denomination also established the Commission on Religion and Race, and White was its first general secretary, serving from 1968 to 1984. In 1972 he was part of a four-person task force to examine race relations in Australia and New Zealand for the Committee to Combat Racism of the World Council of Churches. In 1974 he received the Distinguished Service Award from the United Committee on Negro History. He was elected bishop in 1984 and assigned to the Illinois Episcopal Area. He has served on the General Board of Discipleship and participated in preaching missions in Chile, Argentina, and Brazil. He has been a part-time faculty member of Wesley Theological Seminary and Howard University School of Religion, both in Washington, D.C. He is the author of two books, *Racial Transition in the Church* (1980) and the devotional books, *Confessions of a Prairie Pilgrim* (1988) and *Conversations of the Heart* (1991).

Harmon, Nolan B. *Encyclopedia of World Methodism.* 2 vols. Nashville, TN: United Methodist Publishing House, 1974.

White, Woodie W. "Black and White Merger at Any Cost." *Christian Advocate* 13 (October 16, 1969): 9.

———. *Confessions of a Prairie Pilgrim.* Nashville, TN: Abingdon Press, 1988. 142pp.

———. *Conversations of the Heart.* Nashville, TN: Abingdon Press, 1991. 144pp.

———. *Racial Transition in the Church.* Nashville, TN: Abingdon Press, 1980. 142pp.

BDUMB, BDNM (75), WWABA (85), WWMC, HUBA.

WILBERFORCE UNIVERSITY. An **African Methodist Episcopal Church** (AME) school. The history of Wilberforce University can be traced to two separate educational ventures within the Black communities prior to the Civil War. First, in 1844 the Ohio Conference of the AME Church began Union Seminary, a secondary school which was located on land some twelve miles from Columbus. Second, a decade later, in 1853, the Ohio Conference of the predominantly White Methodist Episcopal Church appointed a committee on the "Elevation of the Colored People" under the chairmanship of John F. Wright. The committee mandate called upon the church to find a means of cooperating with the AME Church in promoting the "intellectual and religious improvement of the colored people." The idea of a new school for Black youth dominated the committee's discussions, and in 1855 the committee initiated steps to purchase Xenia Springs in Greene County, site of a popular resort. The necessary legislation to proceed was submitted to the Methodist Episcopal Church's general conference in 1856 and approved. The school opened later in the year.

The school grew steadily until the beginning of the Civil War. By 1962 it had so declined in both enrollment and support that it was closed. The following year, however, Bishop **Daniel A. Payne** negotiated the purchase of the campus by the AME Church. and in July of that year Wilberforce University was re-opened. Union Seminary was closed and merged into the new school. The expansion of the new school during its first generation was slowed only briefly by a fire which engulfed its main building in 1865 on the same day Lincoln was assassinated.

In the years after the Civil War, Wilberforce was both the most important of the AME schools, and the leading school for African American education in the country. It expanded steadily, and its significant educational role was underscored in 1887 by the state of Ohio's establishment and support of a normal and industrial department. **Payne Theological Seminary** was established on the campus in 1895.

In the late nineteenth century Wilberforce's future became entangled with the career of **Joshua H. Jones**. Jones was born a slave but following the war developed a thirst for education. He moved with his wife and family to Ohio to attend Wilberforce, from which he graduated in 1888. In 1900 he became the school's president. He sent his son there and then on to Germany where he became the first African American to obtain a German Ph.D. While at Wilberforce Jones began a series of reforms. The controversy surrounding the reforms led to his dismissal in 1908. However, four years later he was elected bishop and in 1919 assigned as bishop of Ohio, Western Pennsylvania and West Virginia. At that time he also became chairman of the board of Wilberforce.

Jones threw his energy into fundraising for his alma mater. His success was notable and led to some jealously on the part of his colleagues. In 1928 he was moved to New York. He continued to work for the school during the Depression. Then, at the 1932 General Conference, he was caught in the midst of what all now agree was one of the most tragic incidents in AME Church history. Charges were leveled that Jones had misappropriated monies, including some he had collected for Wilberforce. Before any defense could be mounted the conference voted to suspend him. Later it was discovered that he had been completely honest in his dealings. However, by that time he had passed away.

The next tragedy for the school occurred in 1947, when the state of Ohio withdrew its support from Wilberforce and established a separate competing institution adjacent to it. While hurt by the action,

Wilberforce has rebounded and continued on with its other programs. It has also established its own College of Education and Business Administration, which has substantively filled the vacuum created by the state's withdrawal.

Gregg, Howard D. *History of the African Methodist Episcopal Church: The Black Church in Action.* Nashville, TN: AMEC Sunday School Union, 1980. 523 pp.

Harmon, Nolan B. *The Encyclopedia of World Methodism.* 2 vols. Nashville, TN: United Methodist Publishing House, 1974.

WILEY COLLEGE. A **United Methodist Church** school. Wiley College, Marshall, Texas, was founded in 1973 by the Freedman's Aid Society of the Methodist Episcopal Church (now a constituent part of the United Methodist Church). The school was named for Bishop Isaac W. Wiley. Bishop John M. Walden and Society secretary R. S. Rust were particularly instrumental in securing the site for the college and the early fundraising. Headed by Whites during its first generation, Wiley received its first Black president in 1894 in the person of retired African Bishop **I. B. Scott**. In 1896 he was succeeded by Matthew W. Dogan, formerly mathematics professor at **Rust College**, who was to lead the school for the next quarter century. Under his leadership, the school grew into one of the largest of the Methodist-supported colleges for African Americans.

Stowell, Jay S. *Methodist Adventures in Negro Education.* New York: Methodist Book Concern, 1922. 190 pp.

WILKES, WILLIAM REID (b. April 10, 1902), 69th bishop of the **African Methodist Episcopal Church** (AME), was born in Eatonton, Putnam County, Georgia. At age five he began attending school in Bell Chapel Baptist Church in Putnam County, and over the next several years attended other rural schools in the vicinity. He grew up attending the Texas AME Church in Putnam County. He was licensed as a local preacher in 1919 and enrolled in Morris Brown College in Atlanta on a missionary scholarship. The money did little beyond pay his tuition and books, and he held a series of jobs throughout his college years. He was ordained deacon in 1925 and elder in 1928, the same year he received his B.A. By that time he was pastor of the Morris Brown College Chapel Church and operating a printing press on the side. In 1930 he married Nettie Julia Adams, with whom he had two sons.

From 1928 to 1930 he taught at Street Manual Training School in Minter, Alabama. Between 1930 and 1934 he successively served St. James AME Church, St. John AME Church, St. Peter's AME Church (all in Atlanta), and First AME Church in Athens, Georgia. In 1934 he was assigned to Allen Temple AME Church in Atlanta, where he settled in for almost fourteen years. In 1935 he received his B.D. from Morris Brown College. During the years at Allen Temple he was also Director of Leadership Education and Director of the Ministers' Institute for the Sixth Episcopal District. In that capacity he traveled with Bishop Fountain four times a year across the state, working with the clergy. At Allen Temple he built the first local church building of the denomination strictly dedicated to Christian education.

Wilkes was first a candidate for bishop in 1944, but had to wait four years for election in 1948. He was assigned to the Sixteenth Episcopal District, covering the Caribbean and South America. In 1951 he was assigned to the Twelfth Episcopal District, covering Arkansas and Oklahoma. In his work there he paid Shorter College in North Little Rock out of debt, increased the student body, established a scholarship fund, and raised faculty salaries. He built a new Jackson Theological Seminary building, paid for it, and equipped it. A church expansion fund was created to help support the poorer churches and mission points. In 1956 he was sent to the Sixth Episcopal District, with headquarters in his home town of Atlanta, Georgia. There he remained until 1968, when he was shifted to the Third Episcopal District, covering Ohio. There he supervised a great deal of new construction at Wilberforce University. In 1972 he was appointed to the Thirteenth Episcopal District (Kentucky and Tennessee), and he retired in 1976. He was president of the council of bishops for a time beginning in 1962. He was a trustee of Morris Brown College and the Interdenominational Theological Seminary in Atlanta.

EWM, NA, EBA, BDNM (70), *WWABA* (85), *OTSB, BAMEC.*

WILLIAMS, ALBERT CECIL (b. September 22, 1929), prominent minister of the **United Methodist Church**, was born in San Angelo, Texas, the second youngest of six children. As a young boy, he was deeply impressed by his maternal grandfather, Papa Jack, who had been a cowboy and carried three bullets in his body from that rough existence. Papa Jack was respected for the fact that he would stand up to the White folk. In the fall of 1938 he was buried in the Black part of the cemetery, a cluttered mess compared with the White section. This summed up the life expectancy of Blacks in that West Texas town, where even in death one's personhood was assaulted. One day Williams and his mother, holding her new light-skinned, blue-eyed infant son, tried shopping for groceries at a White store, which had better selection and quality than the store in their own neighborhood. In the store they were served last, and a woman stepped up to his mother, looked at the infant, and demanded, "Who you been foolin' with, nigger?" Once outside the store, two policemen stopped them, and in front of a laughing crowd, subjected them to insults and had them remove all the groceries to check against the receipt.

Williams had natural leadership ability, and even when he was young people called him "Rev." The family attended Wesley Methodist Church in San Angelo, a segregated church, but Williams imagined a time when he would be the minister of an integrated church. By age nineteen he already had an exhorter's license. At about that time his mother passed away from cancer and he determined not to let that stop his pursuit of an education and a future. In 1952 he received his B.A. from Sam Huston College (later Huston-Tillotson College) in Austin, Texas, where he had been class president and a member of a traveling quartet. He then became one of the first five Black students allowed to enroll at Perkins School of Theology at Southern Methodist University in Dallas, Texas. Amazingly, people went out of their way to make him feel at home and accepted, and generally he enjoyed his time there, though he struggled with the realization that the White church and his White friends still lived in a different world. From 1953 to 1955 he was assistant minister at St. Paul Methodist Church in Dallas, and seemed to be headed for a swift move up the church career ladder.

He received his B.D. in 1955 and was assigned to a church in Hobbs, New Mexico. Until 1968 the Methodist Church (now the United Methodist Church) had a Central Jurisdiction, a non-geographical structure for Black members and Black bishops, in which his appointment operated. Three weeks after his arrival in Hobbs he married Evelyn Robinson, with whom he had two children. (He and Evelyn divorced in about 1978.) Services were held in a schoolhouse, and this new congregation, he discovered, was apparently a means of keeping Black Methodists from attending the White Methodist church. He began with six members, but reached a high of 45 over the course of his year there. One lesson he learned there was to drop his manuscript sermons and preach more directly to the people. Another lesson was not to meekly accept the status quo.

In 1956 he became dean of men, chaplain, and an instructor at Huston-Tillotson College. He soon helped lead a successful student revolt against the lack of

decision-making power, and he began to get the reputation of a radical whom many of the powerful did not want to trust with mainstream power. He remained at the college until 1959, when he began postgraduate studies on a fellowship at the Pacific School of Religion at Berkeley, California. During this time he began to focus his theology on contextual ethics. In 1961 he was appointed to St. James Methodist Church in Kansas City, Missouri. He began with 35 members and four years later had 700 members.

In 1964 he was appointed director of community involvement at Glide Urban Center, a program of Glide Memorial Methodist Church in San Francisco, California. In 1966, in a move that surprised many people, he was appointed minister of Glide Memorial, a primarily White, middle-class congregation. He has retained this appointment ever since. In 1967 Williams began his transformation of that church by removing the giant cross from the rear wall of the sanctuary. He said, "As long as the cross is up there, we are not free to dramatize the bearing of the cross for ourselves," and added, "As long as we continue to crucify Jesus, we don't have to face our crucifixion of others, our crucifixion of ourselves." The rear wall was later covered with pictures of people in protest, struggling to remove injustice.

During the 1967 "Summer of Love," Glide sided with the protest movement, though Williams had ambivalent feelings toward the predominantly White "hippies." He appreciated their spirit of protest, but felt insulted by their artificial poverty and frustrated by their lack of focus. A seminary student sponsored the Artist's Liberation Front, an art event in the church parking lot, and then the staff agreed to host a three-day "happening" called the Invisible Circus. Almost immediately the event got out of control, with bodies so thick throughout the six-floor building that the carpet could not be seen. A woman dressed only in a G-string danced on the organ and a printing press on the second floor produced obscene leaflets. Many were unconscious from drugs or crying in corners. A deal was made to move the Saturday crowd to Ocean Beach, but to meet again at the church for Sunday worship. That Sunday turned a corner for the church. The traditional members were outraged by the dirt and obscenities still on the walls and floors, and by the unorthodox presentations during worship. Many of these members never returned, and neither did many of the hippies. What was left was a middle group that was open to creating a new kind of church.

The crisis did not kill the church, but gave it a new birth. Soon the average attendance rose from 125 a week to 2,200, with standing room only for both Sunday services, and with a wide variety of racial and economic groups. The pulpit, altar, and choir loft gave way to movable multimedia stagings and live rock music. Controversial figures like Angela Davis, Dick Gregory, Benjamin Spock, and Jane Fonda were often invited as speakers. The church sponsored a home for runaways, facilities for gay groups, and a Sex and Drug Forum, with its own library. In February 1972, for the first time since she had been arrested on charges of murder, kidnapping, and criminal conspiracy, Black militant Angela Davis agreed to a television interview, but only with Williams, her personal "spiritual advisor," on his weekly talk show. Although Williams was attacked in many parts of the church for his unusual ministry, his stature became such that he was one of seven key speakers at the 1972 General Conference of the United Methodist Church. To their credit, Rev. (later Bishop) Jack Tuell and others who had nominated him as a speaker refused to back down in the face of opposition. Six thousand people heard him speak at Atlanta Civic Auditorium, a sermon preceded by a young man who raced onto the platform and demanded that Williams repent from his support for the "Communist menace," and turn to Jesus Christ. The sermon Williams preached after that incident was considered by many to be one of his finest, a great success. That same year Glide Memorial hosted the First Annual Hookers' Convention, and got more mail on that event than on any other.

In 1974 the Symbianese Liberation Army (S.L.A.) designated Glide Memorial as one of the community organizations to oversee a free food program, one of the conditions for releasing kidnapped heiress Patty Hearst. For a time the F.B.I. and S.L.A. revolved so closely around the church that the staff felt in imminent danger. Over the years Williams has continued to capture the public's attention and imagination. He has served as chair of the Committee United for Political Prisoners, co-chair of the Congress of Racial Equality and is a trustee of the Martin Luther King, Jr. Center for Social Change. In United Methodist circles and elsewhere he has gained a near-legendary status. In 1980 he published *I'm Alive! An Autobiography*. In 1981 he began a movement called the New Moral Minority in an effort to combat the conservative political mood of the country, epitomized by Rev. Jerry Falwell's Moral Majority organization. Although the church has a large membership and a healthy income, it never needs to worry about money. About half of its budget is guaranteed by a trust established in 1930 by Elizabeth Glide in honor of her late husband, a California sheepherder who discovered oil. It is this money that helps the church continue its social outreach programs that serve about 600 people a week.

Ashley, Amelia A. "The Moral Minority vs. The Moral Majority." *Sepia* 30 (May 1981): 45–47.
"Fully Human." *Newsweek* 79 (February 21, 1972): 83.
Robinson, Louie. "Glide to Glory." *Ebony* 26 (July 1971): 44–52.
Williams, A. Cecil. "Black Folks Are Not For Sale." *The Black Scholar* 2 (December 1970): 35–42.
————. *I'm Alive! An Autobiography*. San Francisco, CA: Harper & Row, 1980. 214 pp.
WWABA (92–93), *BDNM* (75), *NA, AARS, HUBA, IBAW*.

WILLIAMS, ARTHUR BENJAMIN, JR. (b. June 25, 1935), a bishop of the **Episcopal Church**, was born in Providence, Rhode Island, the son of Arthur B. Sr. and Eleanor Williams. He received his B.A. in 1957 from Brown University in Providence and from 1957 to 1961 was an officer in the U.S. Navy. He received his M.Div. in 1964 from General Theological Seminary in New York City. He was ordained deacon in 1964 and priest in 1965. He married Lynette Irene Rhodes.

He was a Horner Fellow at Grace Episcopal Church in Providence (1964–65); assistant rector at St. Mark's Episcopal Church in Riverside, Rhode Island (1965–67); sub-dean of the Cathedral of St. John in Providence (1967–68); associate rector of Grace Episcopal Church in Detroit, Michigan (1968–70); Assistant to the Bishop of the Diocese of Michigan for Ministry, Deployment, and Urban Affairs (1970–77); and Archdeacon of Ohio (1977–86). He was on the board of directors of the Detroit Industrial Mission (1970–77) and was for a period co-director of New Perspectives on Race. He has served on the faculty of the University of Detroit (1969–70) and the New Directions School in Roanridge. For a number of years beginning in 1968 he was chair of the Michigan chapter of the **Union of Black Episcopalians**. He served on the executive council, the Anglican Fellowship of Prayer, the Executive Committee of Program, Budget, and Finance, and as trustee of General Theological Seminary. On October 11, 1986, he was consecrated suffragan bishop of the Diocese of Ohio.

ECA (1989), *BDNM* (75).

WILLIAMS, ELIZABETH BARBARA (1868–October, 1931), founder of the **Franciscan Handmaids of the Most Pure Heart of Mary**, a **Roman Catholic Church** religious order, was born in Baton Rouge, Louisiana. At age nineteen she entered a community of Black Franciscan sisters at Convent, Louisiana. This group had left the Sisters of the Holy Family in New Orleans in 1887 to form a more contemplative house following the Rule of St. Francis. When this group was suppressed by the church around 1900, Williams spent some time with the **Oblate Sisters of Providence**, then became a receptionist at Trinity College near Catholic University in Washington, D.C.

At some point she became acquainted with Ignatius Lissner from Georgia, who was very concerned about a proposed Georgia law that would prohibit the teaching of Black pupils by White teachers. This would imperil all the parochial schools that served Blacks, since the nuns were all White. With the backing of Bishop Keiley, Lissner proposed to establish a community of Black sisters to fill the staff of the schools. He convinced Williams to head and found this new group, to be called the Handmaids of Mary, which then was founded in 1916 on East Gordon Street in Savannah, Georgia, with a handful of members. The proposed law was never passed, which meant that the White nuns continued teaching, and the order had no mission. Those first years were filled with poverty and disappointment, but Williams was described as a courageous woman of strong faith who was able to hold the little band together.

In 1922 Williams moved the Handmaids of Mary to Harlem, New York City, at the invitation of Cardinal Hayes, where they ran St. Benedict's Day Nursery, kindergarten, and soup kitchen. There were more difficult years as the order coped with the trickle of financial aid from Catholic charities and the Christ Child Guild. The sisters numbered sixteen by 1925. In 1926 they took over the parochial school of St. Benedict the Moor parish in lower Manhattan, and later staffed the grammar school of St. Aloysius parish in Harlem. In 1929 the order affiliated with the Franciscan Third Order and expanded its official name to the Franciscan Handmaids of the Most Pure Heart of Mary. Also that year a separate novitiate was founded on Staten Island and a home for working girls was set up in Harlem. By the time of Williams's death the order numbered twenty members and included women from the West Indies and Virgin Islands.

HBCUS.

WILLIAMS, GEORGE WASHINGTON (October 16, 1849–August 4, 1891), historian, politician, and Baptist minister, was born in Bedford Springs, Pennsylvania, the second child of Thomas and Nellie (Rouse) Williams. The family moved several times in his youth as his father sought work in Johnstown and Newcastle, Pennsylvania. Williams had no opportunity for regular schooling (though some sources differ on this), and as a boy was placed in a home in western Pennsylvania for apprenticeship to the barbering trade.

When Blacks were permitted into the Union Army in 1863 Williams took the name of an uncle and enlisted. When he was discovered to be underage (fourteen) he was discharged, but after much pleading was allowed to reenlist. He was in a number of battles and was wounded near Fort Harrison, Virginia, in 1864. It is unclear what he did for the two years immediately after the Civil War; some sources say he became a lieutenant-colonel of artillery in the Republican Army of Mexico, and other sources say he went to Texas and became a colonel capturing munitions the Confederate Army had sold to Mexico. In August 1867 he enlisted in the Tenth Cavalry of the U.S. Army, but after one year received a gunshot wound in the chest and was medically discharged at Fort Arbuckle in September 1868.

Williams made his way to St. Louis, where, though his father was a Unitarian and his mother a Lutheran, he was baptized in the First Baptist Church by Rev. H. H. White. In 1869, in Quincy, Illinois, he heard of Howard University in Washington, D.C., and was admitted as a student in September of that year. After only a few months he decided on a career in the ministry, dropped out of Howard and entered Wayland Seminary in Washington, D.C. In September 1870, he tried to get into the theological program at Newton Theological Institution in Massachusetts, but was allowed only to enter the general studies program. Two years later he qualified to enter the theological department and graduated with honors in 1874. As a commencement speaker he chose the topic "Early Christianity in Africa." In June 1874 he married Sarah A. Sterrett, with whom he had one child.

He was ordained a Baptist minister on June 11, 1874, called to pastor the historic and prestigious 12th Baptist Church of Boston. While there he wrote an eighty-page history of the church. After fourteen months, however, he resigned and moved to Washington, D.C., where he founded a journal devoted to African American life, the *Commoner*. Despite support from such leaders as Frederick Douglass, the project was not a success, and he took a temporary job in the post office in December 1875. On March 2, 1876, he was installed as pastor of the Union Baptist Church in Cincinnati, Ohio. There he found law and Republican politics very attractive, and on December 1, 1877, soon after an unsuccessful run for the Ohio State Legislature, he resigned his position to study law at the Cincinnati Law School. He held a variety of jobs to support his schooling and contributed articles to the *Cincinnati Commercial* under the pen name "Aristides."

His political ambitions remained, and in 1879 he was elected in a close and bitter contest to the House of Representatives of the Ohio State Legislature. He served one two-year term during which he was busy as chair of the Committee on the State Library and as a member on several other committees. He proposed a number of bills, including one to repeal the statute against interracial marriage, none of which were passed. In 1881 he engaged full time in the writing of a history of African Americans, a project he had begun back in 1876. In 1883 he published a monumental two-volume work, *History of the Negro Race in America from 1619 to 1880*. No other Black American had ever undertaken a work of such scope. It was the first major history of African Americans ever written, and he reportedly consulted twelve thousand books and countless pamphlets and newspapers. Despite some defects, it remained the standard authority until the publication of John Hope Franklin's *From Slavery to Freedom* in 1947.

Williams was admitted to the Ohio bar on June 7, 1881, and was thus able to engage in a law practice when he finished his book. From 1880 to 1882 he was also judge-advocate general of the Grand Army of the Republic. For a time in Cincinnati he edited the *Southwestern Review*. In 1883 he moved to Boston and joined the bar in Massachusetts. His book brought lecture opportunities and other invitations. In 1884 he attended the World Conference on Foreign Missions in London and extended the trip to include a tour of Europe. At about this time he became interested in the situation of the Congo in Africa, and urged the Senate Committee on Foreign Relations to recommend recognition of the Congo Free State.

In March 1885 President Harrison appointed him minister to Haiti, but the incoming Democratic administration under Grover Cleveland prevented him from taking the position. He sued in the U.S. Court of Claims, but without success. In 1887 he published *A History of the Negro Troops in the War of the Rebellion*, another historical first that was received well by reviewers, cementing his reputation as a worthy historian of the African Americans. In 1889 readers of the *Indianapolis Freeman* voted Williams one of the ten greatest Blacks in history.

On trips to Europe after 1884 he met King Leopold of Belgium, who had jurisdiction over the Congo. Williams decided to support Congo development by urging some American Blacks to move there. In 1889 S.S. McClure commissioned him to write a series of articles on the Congo, and Collis P. Huntington asked him to report on the progress of the railroad there being built by the Belgians. He thus had a number of reasons to visit the Congo personally, but was discouraged from doing so by King Leopold. This raised his suspicions, and he spent four months in 1890 exploring the whole region. What he found was evidence of the brutal oppression of the Congo people by the Belgians. He expressed his condemnation of this in *An Open Letter to His Serene Majesty, Leopold II, King of the Belgians*. This letter was widely discussed, as were two subsequent reports, *A Report Upon the Congo-State and Country to the President of the Republic of the United States* and *A Report on the Proposed Congo Railway*.

By the late spring of 1891, after visiting other African territories and Egypt, he was in England working on a major book further detailing Belgian policies in the Congo. He passed away that summer of tuberculosis and pleurisy.

Franklin, John Hope. "Afro-American Biography: The Case of George Washington Williams." *American Philosophical Society Proceedings* 123 (June 18, 1979): 160–163.

——. "George Washington Williams, Historian." *Journal of Negro History* 31 (January 1946): 60–90.

Franklin, John Hope. *George Washington Williams, a Biography*. Chicago: University of Chicago Press, 1985. 348 pp.

Williams, George Washington. *History of the Negro Race in America from 1619 to 1880*. 2 vols. New York: G. P. Putnam's Sons, 1882.

——. *A History of the Negro Troops in the War of Rebellion, 1861–1865, Preceded by a Review of the Military Services of Negroes in Ancient and Modern Times*. New York: Harper and Brothers, 1888. 353 pp.

DANB, EBA, BHAC, DNAADB, BAW, HUBA, AARS, IBAWCB, IBAW, NG, SBAA, BWA, NAHDA, WWWA (H), DAB, NCAB (10), ACAB, HNB, MM.

WILLIAMS, LACEY KIRK (July 11, 1871–c.October 27, 1940), long-time president of the **National Baptist Convention, U.S.A., Inc.** (N.B.C.U.S.A.), was born on the Shorter Plantation in Eufaula, Alabama. His parents, Levi and Elizabeth (Hill), dropped the plantation name of Shorter for Williams, but remained on the plantation after the end of the Civil War, where work and a livelihood were certain. Lacey Williams was one of at least seven boys and several girls born to the Williams household, a pious household active in the Thankful Baptist Church.

After a number of years the family moved with others to Bryan, Burleson County, Texas and began sharecropping. Another Thankful Baptist Church was founded, and the children were placed in a public school as soon as one was established in 1880. In April 1884, Williams experienced conversion and was baptized into the Baptist church. That night he had a dream that seemed to portend a future in the Christian ministry. At the age of sixteen, when his father could no longer afford to keep him in school, Williams left home.

He made his way to Waco, Texas, where he met some relatives and worked a number of jobs. About 1889 he returned to Bryan and the following year passed the examination for a teaching certificate. He taught for a season in Hookersville, then moved to the River Lane School in his home community, where he was assistant teacher and then principal. In September 1893, he began four months as a student at Hearne Academy, in Hearne, Texas, on a scholarship. On August 15, 1894, he married Georgia A. Lewis, with whom he had two sons, one of whom died in infancy. Williams was licensed to preach in December 1894, and he was ordained a Baptist minister on February 11, 1895. His first pastorate was at College Station, near Prairie View State College, and at the end of August 1895, he became a traveling district missionary for the Sunday School Convention of the Old Landmark Association.

On February 10, 1895, Williams became pastor of Washington Chapel Baptist Church, and soon also of Pleasant Grove Baptist Church in nearby Wellborn. He then added his home congregation of Thankful Baptist Church in Bryan. In about 1896 he left these three churches to pastor Mt. Zion Baptist Church in Lyons and from there he moved to Lights Chapel Baptist Church in Cameron and Roan's Chapel Baptist Church in Bryan. In about 1897 he was called to Ebenezer Baptist Church in La Grange and still maintained regular teaching positions. This took a toll on his health, and after three months recuperation in Colorado, he took the pastorate of 8th Street Baptist Church in Temple. From there he went to Saint Emanuel Baptist Church in Hearne and Rock "Friendship" Baptist Church in Navasota.

In 1902 Williams fulfilled a dream and became a resident student at Bishop College in Marshall, Texas. That year he attended his first National Baptist Convention, in Birmingham, Alabama. While at Bishop College he took the pastorate of the Bethesda Baptist Church, called the College Church, and one Sunday a month preached at Saint John Baptist Church east of Marshall. In 1907 he went to Macedonia Baptist Church in Dallas, Texas, where he stayed for a little more than two years, while teaching in the Caroline Bishop Training School. In 1909 he became pastor of the Mount Gilead Baptist Church in Fort Worth. He graduated from Bishop College in 1912 with his B.Th. degree, and remained at Mount Gilead until 1916. He led the congregation in purchasing a new site on which ground was broken on March 3, 1912, and the first worship service conducted on August 31, 1913. From 1905 to 1916 he was also president of the Baptist Missionary and Educational Convention of Texas, the oldest and largest Baptist body in the state.

In June of 1916 Williams became the pastor of Olivet Baptist Church in Chicago, Illinois, where he would stay the rest of his life. He succeeded **Elijah John Fisher** in that pastorate, who had passed away, leaving behind a 3,900–member, national-level church. The membership grew still more after Williams' arrival, and in 1918 he led the congregation to purchase the old First Baptist Church (white) building on 31st and South Park Avenue. There Olivet settled and created a huge community service center that rendered invaluable assistance, especially during the Depression years. By the 1930s the church's membership stood at about 12,000 and was considered by many the largest Protestant church in the world. After the Chicago race riots of 1919 Governor Lowden appointed Williams to the new Illinois Race Commission.

Williams moved through the ranks of the N.B.C.U.S.A. and was a major figure in the efforts to keep **Richard H. Boyd** from removing the publishing house in the convention split of 1915. From about 1917 to 1922 Williams was president of the Illinois State Baptist Convention. In December 1922, Williams succeeded **Elias C. Morris** as president of the N.B.C.U.S.A. and held that position for the rest of his life. He oversaw the construction of the new publishing house that was completed in 1925, and established an interracial council with White Baptists, by which the latter contributed a great deal of financial support for the N.B.C.U.S.A. By this means the Southern Baptist Convention provided the building and equipment for the American Baptist Theological Seminary in Nashville, Tennessee, a school of the N.B.C.U.S.A. which opened in 1924.

In 1928 Williams was elected a vice-president of the Baptist World Alliance, another position he held for the rest of his life. Several times Williams wanted to leave the presidency and return to his regular pastoral duties, and he even formally resigned in 1930, but each time he was urged to maintain his leadership. In 1939 he introduced the first "Goodwill Tour," which carried the Convention to Baptists in out-of-the-way locations, and had the effect of rallying church forces wherever it went. In 1940 he was the second African American ever invited to speak at the University of Chicago Divinity School chapel. In late 1940 he was killed in a plane crash on the way to address a group in Flint, Michigan.

Fisher, Miles Mark. *The Master's Slave, Elijah John Fisher: A Biography.* Philadelphia, PA: The Judson Press, 1922. 194 pp.

Horace, Lillian B. *"Crowned with Glory and Honor": The Life of Rev. Lacey Kirk Williams.* Hicksville, NY: Exposition Press, 1978. 246 pp.

Williams, Lacey Kirk. *Address of Dr. L. K. Williams Delivered Before the World's Baptist Alliance, June 25, 1928.* Toronto: N.p., n.d.

———. *First Annual Address of Dr. L. K. Williams, President, National Baptist Convention, September 5–10, 1923.*

———. *"Lord! Lord!" Special Occasion Sermons and Addresses of Dr. L. K. Williams.* Edited by Theodore S. Boone. Fort Worth, TX: Historical Commission, National Baptist Convention, U.S.A., Inc., 1942. 188 pp.

———. *My Psalm, Series of Sermons.* Chicago: N.p., n.d.

———. *The Second Annual Address of Dr. L. K. Williams, President of the National Baptist Convention, Delivered Before the Forty-Fourth Annual Session of the National Baptist Convention, September 10th-15th, 1924, Nashville, Tennessee.* Nashville, TN: n.p., 1924. 31 pp.

HUBA, BAW, AARS, RLOA, SCA, HBB, WWWA (2), *WWCA* (38–40), *WWC.*

WILLIAMS, MILTON A. (b. c.1935), a bishop of the **African Methodist Episcopal Zion Church** (AMEZ), was elected bishop in 1988. He was assigned to the Twelfth Episcopal District (Nigeria, Nigeria Rivers, Central Nigeria, West Ghana, and East Ghana Conferences), where he and his wife have since been devoting their energies. Under his supervision a new secondary school is being added to the more than 280 schools in Ghana already sponsored by the AMEZ Church, and improvements are being made on a number of other properties as well.

"Twelfth Episcopal District Makes Strides in Education and Expansion." *The Star of Zion* 114 (June 7, 1990): 1, 2.

WILLIAMS, NOAH W. (December 25, 1876–February 12, 1954), 54th bishop of the **African Methodist Episcopal Church** (AME), was born in Springfield, Illinois, the son of Charles Henry and Harriett Williams. He was converted in February 1892 and was licensed to preach in 1894 at the St. Paul AME Church in Springfield. He joined the military service and went to Cuba in 1898 in the Spanish-American War as assistant chaplain with the Eighth Illinois Volunteer Regiment. He married Hallie C. Jacobs; there were no children.

He joined the Illinois Conference in 1899 and his first pastorate was in Tuscola, Illinois. He was a student for two years at Wilberforce University in Ohio (1901–02). He next was assigned to Greencastle, Indiana, where he also enrolled at De Pauw University. His schooling was interrupted by a later move to Terre Haute, Indiana. When he was assigned to Richmond, Indiana (1906–09), he took the opportunity to enroll at Earlham College in that town. His next pastorates were in Hannibal, Missouri, then Knoxville, Tennessee. At about this time he joined the Army again to serve as chaplain during World War I in France in 1917–18. Upon his return his assignments included Nashville, Tennessee (1918–19); Shelbyville,Tennessee (1919–20); Quinn Chapel AME Church in Louisville, Kentucky (1920–24); and St. Paul AME Church in St. Louis, Missouri (1925–32). His first wife passed away in July, 1924, and on December 16, 1925 he married Helen Rose Armstrong; there were again no children.

On the basis of his successful pastorates Williams was elected bishop at the 1932 General Conference. He was assigned to the Seventh Episcopal District (South Carolina) from 1932 to 1936, and the Fifth Episcopal District (Far West) from 1936 to 1948. He chaired the Financial Board of the church and the General Conference Commission. He was president of the board of trustees for both Allen University in Columbia, South Carolina, and Western University in Quindaro, Kansas. He also was the manager of Douglass Hospital in Kansas City, Kansas. He was famous for an oration called "The AME Church in World Assembly," in which he pictured one million members of the church all in one place praising God, and spoke of the mobilizing power of the bishops through the levels of communication with all those people. He retired in 1948. The Williams School of Religion in Kansas City, Kansas, was named in his honor, as were churches in Desoto, Missouri, and San Pedro, California.

EBA, HAMEC, BAMEC, EWM, WWC, EAMEC.

WILLIAMS, PETER, JR. (c.1780–October 18, 1840), abolitionist and Episcopal priest, was born in New Brunswick, New Jersey, to **Peter Williams, Sr.** and Mary (Durham). Williams, Sr., previously a slave, bought his freedom on November 4, 1785, and later opened a tobacco shop in New York City. Williams, Jr. received a good education through a combination of the Manumission Society's New York African Free School and private tutoring by the pastor of the John Street Methodist Church, Thomas Lyell. Williams, Sr. was a leader of the Blacks in that church, who began having separate meetings in 1796, built their own church in 1801, and eventually created a new denomination, the **African Methodist Episcopal Zion Church**.

Williams, Jr. did not go the way of his father,

however. When Lyell left the John Street Church to be an Episcopal priest, so also Williams, Jr. joined a group of Black Episcopalians who worshipped at Trinity Church in New York City on Sunday afternoons, led by an elderly Black lay reader named Thomas McCombs. Williams was tutored by a priest, Richard C. Moore, and by Bishop John Henry Hobart, who also officiated at his wedding. When the layreader died in 1812, Williams was elected to the position and licensed by the bishop. In 1818 he organized the Blacks into their own congregation, acquired a lot, and built a wooden church worth $8,000. It was consecrated on July 3, 1819, as St. Philip's African Church. It burned down in December 1821, but was fully insured and rebuilt in brick, dedicated by Bishop Hobart on December 31, 1822. Williams was ordained a deacon on October 20, 1820, and as an Episcopal priest on July 10, 1826, becoming the second Black Episcopal priest (the first was **Absalom Jones** in 1804). The ordination took place with the understanding that the congregation would not be admitted to the diocesan convention, but in 1845 the church made application for such admission, finally succeeding in 1853. This was the first Black Episcopal parish in the diocese of New York.

Williams, Jr. was a major Black leader in New York City. He was one of the primary backers of the first Black newspaper in the country, *Freedom's Journal*, edited by **Samuel Cornish** and John Russworm beginning in 1827. With **Richard Allen**, he was one of the leaders of the Convention Movement, beginning in Philadelphia in September 1830. In 1833 he worked with **Christopher Rush**, **Theodore Wright** and others to found the Phoenix Society, a mutual assistance group. He helped establish Phoenix High School in 1836.

He strongly opposed the American Colonization Society's plan to move all the free Blacks to Liberia, Africa. When the American Anti-Slavery Society was founded in December 1833, he was one of four Blacks (with Samuel Cornish, Theodore Wright, and Christopher Rush) on the first executive committee. The abolition issue was one of the instigating factors of a riot by White workers on July 7, 1834. For several days White mobs attacked areas of the Black community. A rumor that Williams had performed an interracial marriage led the mob to destroy St. Philip's Church and the rectory. Williams escaped unharmed, but Bishop Benjamin Onderdonk advised Williams to avoid such controversial issues and publicly withdraw from the Anti-Slavery Society. He complied reluctantly, with the full support of his congregation, but his image was somewhat tarnished among other New York Blacks. He continued, however, to be a key leader, and caused some

commotion, for example, in 1836, when he received a U.S. passport stating that he was a U.S. citizen.

Bishop, Shelton Hale. "A History of St. Philip's Church, New York City." *Historical Magazine of the Protestant Episcopal Church* 15 (1946): 298–317.

Williams Jr., Peter. *Discourse Delivered in St. Philip's Church for the Benefit of the Coloured Community of Wilberforce in Upper Canada, on the Fourth of July, 1830*. New York: G. F. Bunce, 1830. 16 pp.

———. *A Discourse, Delivered on the Death of Captain Paul Cuffee, Before the New York African Institution, in the AME Zion Church, October 21, 1817*. New York: B. Young and Co., Printers, 1817. 16 pp.

———. *An Oration on the Abolition of the Slave Trade; Delivered in the African Church, in the City of New York, January 1, 1808*. New York: Samuel Wood, 1808. 26 pp.

BAW, AARS, DANB, CH, ACAB, NCAB (10), NG, NEA, SOTT, BGWC.

WILLIAMS, PETER, SR. (175?–February, 1823), early Methodist sexton and founding member of the first **African Methodist Episcopal Zion Church** (AMEZ), was born into slavery in New York City, one of ten children born to George and Diana Williams. He was born in a barn in back of his owner's house on Beekman Street, and often remarked on the similarity of his birth setting with that of Jesus.

He was converted by the preaching of Captain Thomas Webb at the Rigging Loft on William Street, and became a member of the Methodist Society led by Webb and Philip Embury. In that group he met Mary (Molly) Durham, a slave (or perhaps indentured servant) from the West Indies, and they soon married. When the Rigging Loft became cramped, the Wesley Chapel was built in 1768 on John Street, and Williams became its sexton in about 1778, a first payment on the books to him listed for May 15. Williams was able to perform sexton duties while still a slave of James Aymar, a tobacco dealer. After only a short time, perhaps in the fall of 1778, Aymar moved the family, including Williams, to New Brunswick, New Jersey, participating in Tory activities. During this time others performed Williams's sexton duties. Williams re-appears on the books as sexton (and undertaker) on October 25, 1780. He and Mary at about this time began living in the parsonage, Mary serving as the housekeeper, and both attending to the visiting preachers.

At the end of the war Aymar decided to move to England, but Williams preferred to stay. An unusual arrangement was made whereby the trustees of the John

Street Church bought Williams from Aymar on June 10, 1783, for 40 British pounds. Williams saw this as purchasing his freedom, for he often mentioned that year as witnessing both his own freedom and that of New York from the British, who completed their evacuation on November 25, 1783. Williams agreed to pay back all the money out of his wages, which he did by November 4, 1785, and a Certificate of Emancipation was filed in court by the trustees the following month. Wakeley states that such a document was not filed until October 1796, but this may have been a supplemental document to fulfill some legal technicality.

It is not clear how long Williams was sexton. He and Mary apparently lived in the parsonage seven years, until about 1787, but he was on the record books as sexton until 1795, and may have served after that time. At any rate, he was at some point able to set up his own tobacco business on Liberty Street in New York City, and prospered so greatly that he could purchase the business's house and lot. He and his wife adopted an infant daughter, Mary, to be a sister to **Peter Williams, Jr.** Since Williams could not read or write, his son kept the books for the business.

Meanwhile the John Street Church was gaining many Black members, conditions became crowded, and some racial tensions became more manifest. In 1796 a number of Blacks, led by Williams, asked for a conference with Bishop Asbury about the possibility of holding separate meetings. He gave permission, and they met for a while in an old cabinetmaker's shop. In 1798 they purchased a lot on the corner of Leonard and Church Streets, and in 1800–01 a church was built, Williams having the honor of laying the cornerstone on July 30, 1800. For years it was popularly known as Zion Church, or the African Chapel. It was chartered as the African Methodist Episcopal Church, the first church exclusively for African Americans in New York City.

The Methodist General Conference of 1800 appointed elder John McClaskey to work with the congregation on some method of cooperation. They agreed to be a regular part of the Methodist Episcopal Church (MEC), with provisos such as the one which mandated that the property must be controlled by Black trustees. Up to that point the trustees of the John Street Church had controlled all Methodist property in town. Zion Church remained with the MEC until June 1821, when, after experiencing various obstacles in that denomination, they organized their own Annual Conference under the name African Methodist Episcopal Church in America ("Zion" was not added until 1848). Williams lived to see this, but his wife did not. Mary died on April 29, 1821, and Williams two years later.

John Street Methodist Episcopal Church: Centenary Memorial.... New York: n.p., 1868.

Wakeley, Joseph B. *Lost Chapters Recovered from the Early History of American Methodism.* New York: Carlton and Porter, 1858. 594 pp.

EWM, HAMEZC, PHNA, HUBA, IBAW, NNY, BPEAR.

WILLIAMS, RILEY FELMAN (May 1897–March 18, 1952), a bishop of the **Church of God in Christ**, was born on a farm at St. Francisville, Louisiana, the son of Albert and Vina Williams. His father died in the month before his birth and he was raised by his uncle, Frank Haywood, a deacon in the Mt. Olive Baptist Church. He was converted and called to the ministry in that same church twelve years later under the ministry of Rev. C. C. Richardson. A few years later, in New Orleans, he received the baptism of the Holy Spirit and at the age of 17 joined a Holiness church pastored by R. W. Clark. Three years later he married Sadie Williams, with whom he had five children.

Williams began preaching on the streets of New Orleans. Working with Clark, he helped establish churches in New Orleans and Algeris, Louisiana, and later served churches in Donaldsville and Burton, Louisiana. In 1918 he moved to Memphis, Tennessee, and the following year joined and was ordained as a minister by church founder **Charles H. Mason** in the Church of God in Christ. He founded the King Street Church later that year. He later moved to Grenada, Mississippi, and established a congregation there. Then, feeling called to Florida, he took what money he had and made his way to Monticello. Working out of a corn crib loaned by a local resident, he was able to lead 18 to receive the baptism of the Holy Spirit that first week. He then moved on to begin work in Lloyd and Jacksonville, Florida. Mason appointed him overseer of the state.

In 1920 he spoke at a Great Unity Council at which representatives of a number of independent Pentecostal churches gathered and out of which over a hundred decided to affiliate with the Church of God in Christ. Later that year he moved to Alabama as state overseer and initiated work at Sampson. Over the next several years he started churches in Dothan, High Bluff, Abbeville, Sapps, and East Birmingham, and settled in as pastor at the latter location. He soon moved on to Georgia and became overseer for the state.

In 1931 he was appointed overseer for Ohio and the following year moved to Cleveland to assume his duties. While there he was able to complete his college work at Cleveland Bible College from which he received a

B.D. In 1933 he became one of the group of five men chosen by Mason as one of the first bishops in the church.

In 1940 Williams received his most remembered assignment when Mason appointed him building commissioner for the new national temple to replace the one which had been destroyed by fire a few years before. Beginning with less than $3,000 in the bank, the project took five years. When the Mason temple was completed, however, it was the largest building constructed and owned by an African American religious group in the United States.

During his years in Cleveland, Williams led in the founding of over 25 congregations and the building of a number of church buildings. He died in 1952 of heart failure.

Clark, O. G., comp. *Life History of Bishop R. F. Williams.* Oakland, CA: The Author, n.d. 23 pp.

DuPree, Sherry Sherrod. *Biographical Dictionary of African-American Holiness-Pentecostals, 1880–1990.* Washington, DC: Middle Atlantic Regional Press, 1989. 386 pp.

Patterson, J. O. *History and Formative Years of the Church of God in Christ with Excerpts from the Life and Works of Its Founder, Bishop C. H. Mason.* Memphis, TN: Church of God in Christ Publishing House, 1969. 143 pp.

WILLIAMS, ROBERT SIMEON (October 27, 1858–January 13, 1932), 6th bishop of the **Christian Methodist Episcopal Church** (CME), then known as the Colored Methodist Episcopal Church, was born into slavery in Caddo Parish, Louisiana, the son of William J. and Edith Williams. He was converted at age sixteen, in 1872, and joined the CME Church in 1876. He joined the Louisiana Conference in November 1881 but transferred to the East Texas Conference, where he was appointed to the church in Longview. He was ordained deacon in 1881 and elder in 1883. At Longview he was one of the editors of *Christian Worker*, the Church's periodical for Texas. He also finished the normal course at Wiley College in Marshall, Texas, paying for tuition by working on farms and teaching school, in addition to his pastoral duties.

In 1884 he moved to the Virginia Conference and served at the Israel Metropolitan CME Church in Washington, D.C. He conducted a revival that converted more than one hundred people and raised money for remodeling the church. In addition, he studied for two years at Howard University. In 1887 he moved to the South Carolina Conference and was assigned to the Sydney Park CME Church in Columbia. In 1891 he transferred to the Georgia Conference and was appointed

to the Trinity CME Church in Augusta. On October 21, 1891 he married Willie A. Nichols, with whom he had six children.

At the May 1894 General Conference Williams was elected bishop and served several episcopal areas. In 1915 he covered the Second Episcopal District, which included Washington, D.C., Maryland, New Jersey, Pennsylvania, North Carolina, and South Carolina. He was a delegate to the World Methodist Conferences in 1891 and 1901. While in London he preached from one of John Wesley's pulpits. He was president of the board of trustees of Miles College and vice-president of the board of trustees of Paine College. In 1919 he became senior bishop of the denomination, remaining in that status until his death.

WWCR, EWM, HCMECA, CMECTY.

WILLIAMS, SMALLWOOD EDMUND (October 17, 1907–June 28, 1991), founding presiding bishop of the **Bible Way Church of Our Lord Jesus Christ World Wide, Inc.**, was born in Lynchburg, Virginia, the son of Edmund and Mary (Broadus) Williams. He was licensed to preach in 1923 in the **Church of Our Lord Jesus Christ of the Apostolic Faith**, founded by **Robert Clarence Lawson**. In 1925 he organized the Bible Way Church of Our Lord Jesus Christ in Washington, D.C. and was ordained, the youngest minister in the history of the denomination. He built that church into one of the premier churches of the denomination. He married Verna Lucille Rapley; they had four children. In a 1944 black newspaper poll he was picked as the most popular preacher in Washington, D.C., a popularity bolstered by his Sunday morning radio programs on WOOK with an audience of 500,000. He attended Howard University School of Religion, and received his B.Th. in 1948 from the American Bible College, also in Washington, D.C.

From 1934 to 1957 he was general secretary for the Church of Our Lord Jesus Christ of the Apostolic Faith, and from 1948 to 1952 was president of the Interdenominational Ministerial Alliance of Washington, D.C. In 1944 he founded and directed the Bible Way Training School for Ministers and Christian Workers. In 1948 he led in a survey for the most popular preacher in the city and won a six-week trip abroad. In 1950 he began ten years on the board of directors of the local branch of the N.A.A.C.P. The denomination was growing during this time, but R. C. Lawson refused to consecrate any other bishops. Finally, in 1957, Williams and 70 congregations broke away from the denomination to form the Bible Way Church of Our Lord Jesus Christ

World Wide, Inc. Williams was consecrated as presiding bishop and four others were also consecrated bishops.

In 1958 Williams founded a school and mission in Liberia, giving the new denomination an international presence. In 1960 he became a member of the District of Columbia Democratic Convention. In 1962 he was elected president of the Washington, D.C. branch of the **Southern Christian Leadership Conference**. In 1963–64 he was a member of the board of the Inter-Religious Committee on Race Relations. In 1963 he built the Bible Way Center and the following year served on the President's Committee on Religious Resources in Mental Retardation. In 1970 he became the president of Golden Rule Apartments, Inc., a non-profit housing corporation in Washington, D.C. In 1981 he published his autobiography, *This is My Story: A Significant Life Struggle*. He died in 1991 following heart surgery.

Richardson, James C., Jr. *With Water and Spirit: A History of Black Apostolic Denominations in the U.S.* Martinsville, VA: The Author, 1980. 151 pp.

Williams, Smallwood Edmond. *Brief History and Doctrine of the Bible Way Churches of Our Lord Jesus Christ World Wide*. Washington, DC: Bible Way Church, 1957. 24 pp.

———. *The Golden Jubilee Documentary*. Washington, DC: Bible Way Church, 1977. 130 pp.

———. *Significant Sermons*. Washington, DC: Bible Way Church Press, 1970. 164 pp.

———. *This Is My Story*. Washington, DC: Wm. Willoughby Publishers, 1981. 195 pp.

WILLIS, JOSEPH (1758–September 14, 1854), organizer of the first Baptist church west of the Mississippi, was born in Bladen County, North Carolina. He is typically described as a "free Negro," but the *Encyclopedia of Southern Baptists* states that he was of English and Cherokee Indian ancestry. He migrated to Mississippi in 1798 and labored as a missionary among the Natchez Indians. He moved to Louisiana in 1804 and preached in the Lafayette and Bayou Chicot regions to the Opelousa Indians.

Some sources say that Willis was ordained in 1804 and organized the first Baptist church west of the Mississippi in 1805. It does seem that the Calvary Baptist Church, with a mixed-race congregation located near Opelousas, was organized in 1805. Not until 1812, however, did the Mississippi Baptist Association send two ministers out to ordain him. By 1818 Willis had founded five churches in the state, and that year organized them into the Louisiana Baptist Association. In 1837 he was elected its moderator. At his death the Louisiana Baptist Association noted that "before the

church began to send out missionaries into destitute regions, he, at his own expense, and frequently at the risk of his life, came to these parts preaching the gospel of the Redeemer."

ESB, SNB, CH, SCA, HBB, NYB (1925–26).

WILMORE, GAYRAUD STEPHEN, JR. (b. January 20, 1921), minister with the **Presbyterian Church (USA)**, educator, and author, was born in Philadelphia, Pennsylvania, one of three sons of Gayraud, Sr., and Patricia (Gardener) Wilmore. His family attended the McDowell Presbyterian Church, part of the United Presbyterian Church in the USA, which in 1983 became part of the Presbyterian Church (USA), and he was influenced by the example of its minister, Arthur E. Rankin. During World War II Wilmore served in the 92nd Infantry Division of the U.S. Army in the Italian Campaign. In the midst of this first-hand look at human cruelty, he saw the need for a profound remedy, and made the decision to enter the ministry. He graduated from Lincoln University in Oxford, Pennsylvania, in 1947, and stayed on at Lincoln University Theological Seminary, earning a B.D. in 1950. Theologically, he began with a conception of revelation as akin to artistic insight in drama and literature, two of his other major interests. He married Lee Wilson, with whom he had four children.

Wilmore was a student pastor at Faith Presbyterian Church in York from 1948 to 1950, and from 1950 to 1953 ministered at Second Presbyterian Church in West Chester, Pennsylvania. He meanwhile did some graduate study at Temple University School of Religion in Philadelphia, earning an S.T.M. in 1952. In 1953 he became a member of the executive staff of the Student Christian Movement in the Middle Atlantic Region, with headquarters in Philadelphia. Here he provided leadership on the critical issues of the time in the intersection of faith and college life, including the Cold War, values in education, and civil rights. In 1956 he became associate secretary of the Social Education and Action section of the United Presbyterian Church Board of Christian Education. At this time he also founded the National Committee of Negro Churchmen (now the **National Conference of Black Churchmen**).

In 1960 he accepted a position on the faculty of Pittsburgh Theological Seminary as assistant professor of social ethics, while working for the next few years on a doctorate at Drew Theological Seminary in New Jersey. In 1963 he returned to a national church position as executive director of the United Presbyterian Commission on Religion and Race (later restructured as the Council on Church and Race). During the nine years in this office, he also spent some time as Cook lecturer in Asia under the sponsorship of the Commission on Ecumenical Mission and Relations. In 1962 he published his first book, *The Secular Relevance of the Church*. In 1970 he wrote his best-known book, *Black Religion and Black Radicalism*, which has been called the most important textbook on the history of Black religion and the Black church ever written.

In 1972 his accomplishments brought him to the position of Martin Luther King, Jr., Professor of Social Ethics at Boston University School of Theology. In 1974 he moved to be Martin Luther King, Jr., Memorial Professor of Black Church Studies at Colgate Rochester Divinity School/Bexley Hall/Crozer Theological Seminary in New York. In 1983 he became Dean of the M. Div. Program and Professor of Afro-American Studies at New York Theological Seminary.

Shannon, David T. and Gayraud S. Wilmore, eds. *Black Witness to the Apostolic Faith*. Grand Rapids, MI: William B. Eerdmans, for the Commission on Faith and Order, National Council of Churches, 1985. 104 pp.

Wilmore, Gayraud Stephen. *African American Religious Studies: An Interdisciplinary Anthology*. Durham, NC: Duke University Press, 1989. 468 pp.

————. *Black and Presbyterian: The Heritage and the Hope*. Philadelphia, PA: The Geneva Press, 1983. 142 pp.

————. *Black Religion and Black Radicalism*. New York: Doubleday & Company, 1972. 344 pp.

————, and James H. Cone. *Black Theology, A Documentary History, 1966–1979*. Maryknoll, NY: Orbis Books, 1979. 657 pp.

————. *Last Things First*. Philadelphia, PA: Westminster Press, 1982. 118 pp.

————. *The Secular Relevance of the Church*. Philadelphia, PA: Westminster Press, 1962. 89 pp.

Wilson, Frank T., ed. "Living Witnesses: Black Presbyterians in Ministry, Part I." *Journal of Presbyterian History* 51 (Winter 1973): 347–391.

WWABA (90–91), *SBAA, BDNM* (75), *AARS, HUBA*.

WILSON, FRANK THEODORE, SR. (January 1, 1900–February 11, 1988), national executive in the United Presbyterian Church in the U.S.A., now a constituent part of the **Presbyterian Church (USA)**, was born in Maxton, North Carolina, one of six children of James Jacob and Sudie Jane (Harris) Wilson. His father was a Presbyterian minister, and his mother was principal of the parochial school attached to the church in Wadesboro, North Carolina, where Wilson gained his early education.

At the age of twelve he entered Mary Potter Memorial School in Oxford, North Carolina, which prepared him for Lincoln University and Seminary in Oxford, Pennsylvania, where he received his B.A. in 1921 and S.T.B. in 1924. Upon graduation he became a regional secretary of the National Student Y.M.C.A., working with colleges in the Southeast, Southwest, and Middle Atlantic states. In about 1924 he married Anna Lucretia Dorsey, with whom he had two children. In 1928–29 he was in Mysore, India, as part of the General Commission of the World Student Christian Federation.

During his thirteen years with the Y.M.C.A.'s Student Christian Movement, Wilson prepared for the opening of future doors by taking courses at Columbia University in New York City, earning an M.A. in 1932 and Ph.D. in 1937 in education. In 1936, in the final stages of his Ph.D., which was on the development of religious education at Lincoln University, he was invited to become a faculty member at Lincoln University, where he stayed until 1949. In 1940 he became a member of the National Student Committee of the Y.M.C.A., a position he held for the rest of his career. From 1945 to 1948 he was director of the Young People's Summer Conferences in Blairstown, New Jersey.

In April 1949, he was surprised to hear that he had been elected Dean of the School of Religion at Howard University in Washington, D.C. He accepted, and moved there in August, teaching also in the field of religious education. In 1954 he was an accredited visitor at the World Council of Churches meeting in Evanston, Illinois. That year he also became a trustee of Lincoln University, serving in that capacity until 1960. In July 1957, he went to a national post in the United Presbyterian Church, that of Secretary of Education for the Board of Foreign Missions (later renamed the Commission on Ecumenical Mission and Relations). In his ten years in this position, he was widely acclaimed for his administrative excellence and Christian witness.

He retired in 1967 to the Lincoln University Village, but served until December 1968, as Consultant for Education with the commission in overseas assignments. He continued to be active in other respects until his death, serving as president of the trustees of the Interdenominational Theological Center in Atlanta, Georgia, vice-president of the Council of Theological Seminaries of the United Presbyterian Church, and chair of the Task Force on Improving Prospects of Minority Candidates for Church Ministry under the Vocation Agency of the United Presbyterian Church. In the 1970s he was editor of an important three-part series, "Living Witnesses: Black Presbyterians in Ministry," in the

Journal of Presbyterian History, which included his own biography in Part III.

United Church of Northern India. *Report of Survey Evaluation of Twenty-Eight Schools and Colleges Related to the United Church of Northern India, August 9–November 22, 1962.* Director Frank T. Wilson. New York: Office for Education, Commission on Ecumenical Mission and Relations, United Presbyterian Church in the U.S.A., 1963. 302 pp.

Wilson, Frank T. "The Black Revolution: Is There a Black Theology?" *The Journal of Religious Thought* 26 (Summer Suppl. 1969): 5–14.

———. "The Future of Missionary Enterprise in Africa South of the Sahara." *Journal of Negro Education* 30 (Summer 1961): 324–333.

———, ed. "Living Witnesses: Black Presbyterians in Ministry." Three Parts. *Journal of Presbyterian History* 51 (Winter 1973): 347–391; 53 (Fall 1975): 187–222; 55 (Summer 1977): 181–238.

———. "The Present Status of Race Relations in the United States." *Journal of Religious Thought* 2 (Autumn-Winter 1945): 30–41.

BDNM (75), AARS, HUBA.

WOMACK, ARTHUR WALTER

WOMACK, ARTHUR WALTER (July 10, 1885–July 31, 1961), 26th bishop of the **Christian Methodist Episcopal Church** (CME), was born in Halifax, Virginia, the eighth child of Guy and Hattie (Wood) Womack. His father died when he was three, and his mother moved the family to Philadelphia, Pennsylvania. Finding no CME Church there, she organized in her home what became the Hosley Temple CME Church. Womack went to the local public schools and the Institute for Colored Youth in Philadelphia. He was licensed to preach in 1896 at the young age of twelve.

About 1900, while he was still quite young, Bishop **R. S. Williams** arranged for him to attend Paine College in Augusta, Georgia, where he earned his B.A. He supported himself in school by serving numerous stations in South Carolina, including a few almost one hundred miles away. These charges were in Hodges, Allendale, Fairfax, Aiken, Graniteville, and Kathwood. In 1904 he joined the Washington Annual Conference and was appointed to Israel CME Church in Washington, D.C. Further pastorates included Bebee Chapel CME Church in Muskogee, Oklahoma and Mother Liberty CME Church in Jackson, Tennessee. In 1918–19 he was a chaplain in the military service. During World War I he also spoke all over Madison County, Tennessee and raised thousands of dollars for the Y.M.C.A. and the Red Cross.

He then pastored at Lane CME Church in Washington, D.C. (1919–21), where he also earned his B.D. at Howard University in 1921. He was then assigned to St. John CME Church in Detroit, Michigan, where he organized thirteen missions, all of which later became self-supporting churches. From 1928 to 1930 he pastored Lane Tabernacle CME Church in St. Louis, Missouri, where in 1929 he organized the first Mattie E. Coleman Circle of the Missionary Council. He was presiding elder of the Chicago District from 1930 to 1931. Later appointments included Greenwood and Collins Chapel CME Church in Memphis, Tennessee, Phillips Temple CME Church in Indianapolis, Indiana, and then Phillips Temple CME Church in Dayton, Ohio. During these years he served on the Commission on Evangelism of the Federal (now National) Council of Churches, was part of the National Speakers Bureau of the N.A.A.C.P., and wrote some pamphlets, including *The Question of Twelve Negroes* and *Heaven Bound Travelers*.

From the Dayton pastorate Womack was elected bishop on May 11, 1950, and assigned to the Georgia Conferences. In 1958 he was assigned to the Louisiana, New Orleans, and Mississippi Conferences. He was very interested in foreign missions and made two trips to Africa, helping to organize some of the CME Church's first stations there. He was instrumental in raising one-half million dollars in funding for Collins Chapel Hospital in Memphis, Tennessee. Three times he was a delegate to the Methodist Ecumenical Conferences, and was recognized as a champion of civil rights.

Carter, G. H. "Bishop Arthur Walter Womack." *Christian Index* 94 (August 10, 1961): 11.

"The Life and Works of the Late Bishop Arthur W. Womack." *Christian Index* 95 (April 5, 1962): 4–5.

WWCA (38–40), EWM, CMECTY.

WOMEN IN THE PULPIT, AFRICAN AMERICAN

WOMEN IN THE PULPIT, AFRICAN AMERICAN. The African American churches have a great record in matters of civil rights and socio-political activism, but that record is tragically flawed. Even while they proclaim racial justice and equality, they lag far behind in applying these values to women. And this applies most specifically to the professional options open to women. For instance, there are still rigid exclusions of women from ordination and from placement in the pulpits and pastorates of African American churches. In this area, equality is still the exception and not the rule.

Within the African American church, the acceptance of women into the pulpit can suitably be highlighted by dividing the churches into three categories: (1) African American denominations with episcopal governance, i.e., with bishops as the chief church officials; (2) African American denominations with congregational autonomy; and (3) African American congregations with membership in predominantly White denominations. However, some additional insight is gained by seeing women in the Christian traditions within the context of the place of women in the African traditions prior to the embracing of Christianity by a substantial percentage of African Americans.

Pre-Christian Practices. Careful observation of African Traditional Religion (ATR) today will reveal that women have a prominent place in the seamless garment of communal life and religious practice. Priestess/healers and seers loom large in the formal structures of society/ religion, and even larger in the impromptu or less hereditary incidence of local shrines and cult groups. While the top echelon of leadership seems not to include women, the qualms against female involvement in priestcraft, so common in the Black churches today, seem not to have any basis whatever in the African roots of Black religion.

The state of ATR today is relevant here because so little of it has changed since the ancestors of the slaves departed for the Western Hemisphere. There are sweeping industrial and commercial shifts, responding to external pressures. But worship patterns and inner spiritual life change much less readily. This is true in Africa, where persons affiliate with Islam or Christianity and still cling to the traditional African rites surrounding birth, marriage and death. It is also true that the same ATR practices and beliefs were transplanted to America and adapted, but certainly not eliminated. Much of the religious worship of the African American masses today is far more traceable to African roots than is widely known.

The question then arises as to how and when females lost their access to ordination and recognition as priestesses in African American religious practice. Even more important may be the question of *why* all of this took place, given the unashamed Africanness of the vast majority of practice in the churches which were not under White supervision. The most likely answer appears to be typified in the history of the **African Methodist Episcopal Church** (AME).

Women in the Independent Black Denominations (with Bishops). The African American Church became a reality at the point where the treatment accorded both slave and free members of a mixed church (*not really* integrated) became intolerable. Blacks also established separate churches in places where there was as yet no church for Whites, or where Blacks were not permitted in White congregations. In every case, however, some White model of doctrine and organization was used, since there were no ATR models of a congregation as such. White denominational difference is the source of African American denominationalism.

Thus were the African American churches in the strange position of standing over against racism in the White churches, while following their polity and doctrine in the most meticulous details. For instance, the AME hymnbook even today is far closer to the hymnal of John Wesley, literally, than is the United Methodist hymnbook—this even though the way hymns like "Amazing Grace" are *sung* is radically different.

The issue of women preaching and being ordained was first confronted by **Richard Allen**, father of the AME Church, on just such a basis as this. In 1809, **Jarena Lee** visited him, ". . . to tell him that I felt it my duty to preach the gospel." She reported that, ". . . he said that our *Discipline* knew nothing at all about it— that it did not call for women preachers." Years later, after a male preacher at an AME gathering suddenly found himself unable to complete his sermon, Jarena Lee took over the preaching event. When she finished, Lee reports, Richard Allen rose and recalled her request years before for permission to preach. On the earlier occasion he, says Lee, "had put me off; but . . . he now as much believed that I was called to that work, as any of the preachers present."

This strange contradiction is explained by the fact that the "African Society" did not become a denomination until 1816, and did not adopt a discipline of its own until 1817. In the interim, the AME's faithfully followed the White *Discipline*. In this case, it meant that Allen was more interested in denominational credibility based on a rule book, than in women's rights or God's call to women to use their gifts in ministry. Like many after him, Allen was a strong "Black Nationalist" in matters of power, but willing to concede to the White majority in many matters of ecclesiastical practice.

In 1830, **Rebecca Cox Jackson**, sister of a prominent AME clergyman, announced her call, only to be rebuffed on the basis of the *Discipline* (virtually identical to Wesley's), and her own radical Holiness (Wesleyan) leanings. She eventually left the AME church and became a Shaker, later establishing an all-Black Shaker sisterhood and commune.

Amanda Berry Smith (1837–1915) was another rebuffed AME woman of great preaching gifts. She, too, left her mother church and preached widely among Holiness movement churches in the United States, India,

England, and Liberia. She was regarded as one of the truly great itinerant preachers of the late nineteenth century.

In 1884, AMEs voted to give women license to preach locally, but without ordination. And again without ordination, they voted to create "deaconesses" in 1900, this despite the fact that deacons (men) were always ordained. The hold of the original *Discipline* against full ordination of women was not officially broken until 1948. And it is only within the last five years that women were appointed to what are considered major congregations in cities like Baltimore and Los Angeles.

Not organized as a denomination until 1870, the Colored Methodist Church (CME) (now the **Christian Methodist Episcopal Church**), like the AMEs, simply adopted the *Manual* of Bishop Holland McTyeire for their discipline. Thus they did not authorize full ordination until 1954. These former "Southern Methodists" kept cordial relations with their former masters, and shed their conservative ways only during and after the civil rights revolution. It is interesting to read Bishop **Lucius Holsey**'s *Manual*, copyrighted in 1894, and updated in 1984. [Note: Original pages refer to pastors using the male pronoun "he," but the interpretations which follow carefully speak of "s/he" and "her/him."]

The AMEZ Church was the third Methodist denomination to ordain women fully (earlier the Primitive Methodists and the Methodist Protestant Church had ordained women). Its decision to ordain females was due largely to the influence of two progressive bishops, **James Walker Hood** and **Alexander Walters**. In 1891, Hood had declared that "the word male was stricken out of our *Discipline* many years ago [1876], and at a more recent period, every restriction removed . . . there is one Methodist Episcopal Church that guarantees to women all rights in common with men."

Hood followed through with this declaration by ordaining **Julia A. J. Foote** as deacon in 1894, and as an itinerant elder in 1900. Meanwhile, in 1895, Bishop Walters had ordained **Mary J. Small**, wife of Bishop **John B. Small**, as a deacon. Bishop **Charles Calvin Pettey** ordained her an elder in 1898. Among the AMEZ today, female presiding elders are fairly common, and one could predict that they will be the first among independent Black Methodists to elect a female bishop.

Another African American denomination with bishops is the **Pentecostal Assemblies of the World** (PAW). Started after the great Azusa Street Revival (1906) in Los Angeles, with records dating back to 1912, PAW was racially integrated for many years. Its first "superintendent," a White man, J. J. Frazee, was followed in 1925 by its first "bishop," **Garfield Thomas Haywood**, an African American. It was at this point that the pressures of Southern congregations brought about a permanent division by race, with few Whites remaining in what is now the PAW.

Assuming that the return of Christ was imminent, this group was loosely organized and more literal about imitating the early church. Their emphasis on baptism in the name of Jesus won them the nickname "Jesus Only's." They still adhere to this emphasis.

In 1918, this body, often known as Apostolic Assemblies, held a convocation of merger with similar but formerly separate groups. Of the seventeen great preachers noted, one was a Mrs. M. G. Moise (a White woman) of St. Louis. Other records show considerable evidence of women as evangelists and missionaries, but not as elders over congregations, or as bishops. The records consulted did not include the present fact that there are a number of fully ordained and accepted women pastors, usually in smaller PAW churches. But this number is dwindling rather than growing.

The **Church of God in Christ** (COGIC), also stemming from the Azusa Street Revival, has taken a similar stand. Its episcopal structure and organizational rules are more detailed, however. The nationally binding rules outrightly prohibit women as pastors, but allow for female missionaries and evangelists. These often outnumber the male elders in any given congregation. And many revivals are conducted by nationally recognized women, thereby celebrating the gifts of women as preachers.

Fairly numerous exceptions have developed on the basis of various compelling circumstances, and in these cases the women have not been excluded from the national convocation. Some women have succeeded to the pastorate in churches "preached out" by their late husbands. Since such churches tend to be "kept in the family," this practice has been unofficially accepted. Other women have been *de facto* pastors while their husbands were the pastor of record. And still others have just gone ahead and "preached out" a church, afterward being accepted by certain bishops.

It is the personal initiative in starting churches which makes the rule of laws and bishops so problematic. If an "elder" and her (or his) congregation do not elect to transfer the title to their church property to the COGIC jurisdiction, bishops either accept them just as they are, or the new churches go where they are accepted, or go independent.

Originally COGIC was actually more congregational, with fatherly coordination by Bishop **Charles H. Mason**. Subsequent leaders pushed toward "episcopal" authority, apparently unaware that the rule of bishops in, for instance, the Methodist and Episcopal churches stems from the fact that their local congregations were originally sponsored with denominational funds. These denominations still hold property titles. It is this fact that gives their bishops the power to appoint pastors. This power of appointment, in turn, accounts for the larger number of women pastors (both Black and White) in episcopally administered denominations.

Among the COGIC bishops there are a tiny few who even now have transcended church laws and ordained women to full status and/or accepted them unconditionally into their jurisdictions. Bishop George D. McKinney of San Diego has fully accepted women. Bishop E. E. Cleveland of Oakland has accepted women pastors, even though his own daughter/pastor has elected not to affiliate.

One bishop-led pentecostal denomination, the **Mt. Sinai Holy Church**, originally organized as a congregation in Philadelphia in 1924, now includes churches from New England to Florida. The founding pastor of the church and the founding bishop of the denomination was Bishop **Ida Robinson**. Several area bishops have also been women.

Women in the Free Black Denominations (Autonomous Congregations). The clear majority of African American Christians are still in the self-governing ("free") congregations called Baptists. While a few are still independent of even the associations and conventions of Baptists, the vast majority have membership in one of the four national bodies: **National Baptist Convention, U.S.A., Inc.** (N.B.C.U.S.A., org. 1895); **National Baptist Convention of America** (org. 1915); **Progressive National Baptist Convention** (org. 1961); and **National Missionary Baptist Convention of America** (org. 1988). The only one of these on record as favoring ordination of women is the PNBC, and even its members are far from unanimous on the issue. The best known regional group officially favoring the ordination of women is the Baptist General Convention of Virginia. Elsewhere, church conventions and ministerial associations known to exclude members and congregations who recognize women are too numerous to mention.

Because there is no legal restriction on who can claim the name of Baptist or the right to ordain as such, it is impossible to arrive at any firm statistics on Baptist ordination of women. There are records of Baptist women preaching in the colonies as early as the First Great Awakening, but this does not involve ordinations or pastorates. There are also rare examples of women

serving as pastors throughout the memory of today's elderly. In Chicago, a woman succeeded her departed husband and served with distinction and the recognition of the N.B.C.U.S.A. until she died. The same has happened in Cleveland and elsewhere. While all the women who serve very large congregations seem to be nondenominational, or independent, there are respected "journeyman" women pastors here and there across the nation, with and without official recognition.

The one promising trend in the largest congregations can be seen in the ordination and appointment of women as critically important professional staff, such as associate pastor, handling the day-to-day details of ministry for senior pastors on the national circuit. This has been true with several Baptist pastors in Virginia and elsewhere. And in Virginia, women are even in the rotations to serve or already have served as presiding officers of city-wide ministerial alliances and conventions.

It is most ironic that ardent Baptist opponents of the ordination of women for local congregations are willing to seek a way to ordain trained women for military and other chaplaincies. The same could be said of persons in the Church of God in Christ. Thus many African American women are in the position of being forced out of the race, as it were, to practice ministry with recognition and support. So it is important to look at the next topic.

Black Women Preachers in "White" Denominations. It is a strange irony that African American women have always found their best reception in predominantly White denominations, whose acceptance of women generally was earlier. Congregationalists can boast of a trained female pastor as early as 1853, and Universalists as early as 1863. By 1900, Congregationalists (now the **United Church of Christ**) and Universalists had been joined by the **Christian Church (Disciples of Christ)**, **American Baptist Churches in the U.S.A.** (the "Northern" Baptists), the Unitarians, and the Cumberland Presbyterian Church in the ordination of women to full standing and pastorates.

The larger White denominations were slower, however. Like the AMEs, the Methodist Episcopal Church, now a constituent part of the **United Methodist Church**, voted to deny ordination to women in 1880, but authorized local preacher "orders," without ordination, in 1924. In 1939 the Methodist Episcopal Church merged with the Methodist Episcopal Church, South and the Methodist Protestant Church to form the Methodist Church (1939–1968). Women did not receive full ordination status in the Methodist Church until 1956. The United Presbyterian Church in the U.S.A. (the

"Northern" Presbyterians, now a constituent part of the **Presbyterian Church [U.S.A.]**), with a long history of controversy, had preceded the Methodists by just one year. The Presbyteran Church in the U.S. (the "Southern" Presbyterians) granted ordination to women in 1964. That same year, a congregation of the **Southern Baptist Convention** ordained a woman but without denominational approval.

The largest trend toward recognition of women was among the Holiness denominations which broke away from established Methodism in the late nineteenth century. The **Church of God (Anderson, Indiana)** was organized in 1880, with women pastors from the start. The first African American woman, Jane Williams, was ordained at a camp meeting in Augusta, Georgia, in 1885, and started a church across the river in South Carolina. The *Gospel Trumpet* of 1891 listed 88 women as active ministers. By the 1920s, a third of the pastors were women, but only a tenth or so are women today. Among these there has always been a proportionate number of African American women, although no statistics are available.

The Church of God has always taken literally the prophecy of Joel (2:28) that women would also prophesy in the last days. This has been evident in subtle but very important ways, such as the fact that printed ordination certificates have always used "he/she" to refer to the candidates.

Perhaps the most publicized election of an African American woman in a predominantly White denomination was that of **Barbara C. Harris** to the post of suffragan bishop in the **Episcopal Church** in 1988. Her denomination had been last of all major Protestant denominations to recognize women, having finally conceded officially, after much controversy, in 1976. It also agreed to regularize 11 previous ordinations done in a Black parish in Philadelphia in 1974. The first African American woman ordained to the Episcopal priesthood was attorney **Pauli Murray** in 1976, and the first ordination with appointment to a congregation went to the Rev. Sandra Wilson in 1978.

United Methodists elected an African American woman, the Rev. **Leontine T. C. Kelly**, as bishop in 1984. She had first been ordained and entered the pastorate in 1969, following the death of her pastor/husband. The date of the very first United Methodist ordination of an African American woman was 1958, when Sallie A. Crenshaw (1900–1986) was ordained an elder by the East Tennessee Conference. The number of African American pastors in both White and Black congregations of the United Methodist Church today is estimated at over 200. This number appears greatly to exceed that of the United Church of Christ, the

Presbyterians, and the Episcopalians, all of whom are now very open to appointment of African American women, and appears to be due in part to their active recruitment of young college-age women to church-related vocations.

The number of African American women pastors and staff in these denominations seems proportionately higher, and even numerically higher, than in the African American denominations, both with and without bishops. The question of how soon this flaw in the just exercise of power will be remedied is not easy to answer, especially among the congregational or free types.

Future Prospects. The progress of African American Methodism is easiest to predict. On the basis of the stellar performances of a number of AME, AMEZ, and CME women pastors in smaller charges, it seems logical that bishops will upgrade them before long, if only in the self-interest of the denomination.

Concerns of self-interest in the free churches work the other way. A Baptist pastor has no bishop and no guarantee of appointment, so that many without the security of professional preparation serve at all times in fear of sudden and permanent unemployment. The highly impressive gifts of so many second-career African American women often terrify these insecure men. Since they dare not be candid, the easiest defense is a rigid, surface biblical justification for the exclusion of women from the pulpit.

Future progress among Baptists on this issue will depend on several factors. One will be the networking of supportive male and female pastors in the placement of women, since official edicts mean nothing to an autonomous local congregation. Another will be the exposure of the talents of Baptist women to the churches, through the various professional and volunteer ministries open to them now. Still another will be the manifest tendency of opposing pastors to break down whenever a daughter of their own or a strong member hears the call. Finally, the percentage of seminary-trained clergy is growing, with the result that many enter training opposed, and leave changed, impressed by the capabilities of sizeable numbers of female classmates. With all of these factors, the future is not as dark as it might have been, and the huge reservoir of God-given gifts among female potential leaders may yet be utilized to save and enrich the African American churches.

Given the present indefinite prospects, the majority of the increasing numbers of Black women making the sacrifice to obtain full theological training would seem headed for disappointment. But when God calls and faith responds, human forecasts are transcended. It was with such a faith as prevails today that Black women like the author launched out four and five decades ago, with far fewer visible possibilities.

Golder, Morris A. *History of the Pentecostal Assemblies of the World*. Indianapolis, IN: The Author, 1973.

Humez, Jean McMahon. *Gifts of Power: The Writings of Rebecca Jackson, Black Visionary, Shaker Eldress*. Boston, MA: University of Massachusetts Press, 1981. 368 pp.

Hunter, Edwina, and David A. Farmer, eds. *And Blessed Is She*. New York: Harper & Row, 1990.

Lee, Jarena. "The Life and Religious Experience of Jarena Lee." In William L. Andrews, ed. *Sisters of the Spirit*. Bloomington, IN: University of Indiana Press, 1986.

Lincoln, C. Eric, and Lawrence H. Mayiya. *The Black Church and the African American Experience*. Durham, NC: Duke University Press, 1990. 280 pp.

Riley, Herman C. *Holsey's Manual, Updated with Commentary*. Oakland, CA: The Author, 1984.

Walls, William J. *The African Methodist Episcopal Church: Reality of the Black Church*. Charlotte, NC: A.M.E.Z. Publishing House, 1974.

Ella Pearson Mitchell

WOOD, JOHN WESLEY (May 10, 1865–April 17, 1940), 38th bishop of the **African Methodist Episcopal Zion Church** (AMEZ), was born in Talbot County, Georgia, the son of Isom B. and Amanda (Tignor) Burks. His parents died in his infancy and was eventually taken in by his grandfather, Levi Wood, from whom he took his name. His opportunities were very limited, and at age sixteen he still did not know the alphabet. He was able to attend public night school in Troup County, Georgia, in 1885–86, and was a student at La Grange Academy in La Grange, Georgia, from 1887 to 1889.

Having been named for the founder of Methodism, he was immersed in a religious atmosphere from the beginning of his life. He was licensed to preach in 1886, joined the West Tennessee and Mississippi Conference in 1888, was ordained deacon on December 17, 1888, and elder on December 14, 1890. About this time he married Janice Edmond, with whom he had five children. The date of this marriage has been listed variously as February 10, 1890, February 10, 1891, November 8, 1891, and January 20, 1891.

After pastoring several points in the conference, including Memphis, Tennessee, he transferred to the Virginia Conference and pastored in Norfolk and Berkeley. As early as 1900 he was a strong enough political force in the church to be elected a delegate to General Conference. After Berkeley he was assigned to Ahoskie in North Carolina, followed by three years as president of Edenton High and Industrial School, while also pastoring the AMEZ Church in Edenton, North Carolina. His last two pastorates were Jones Tabernacle AMEZ Church in Indianapolis, Indiana, and State Street AMEZ Church in Mobile, Alabama, and he also taught public school for three years in Lincoln, Alabama. In 1911 he traveled in Europe and Africa, beginning a lifelong study of the customs of the West Gold Coast tribes. Upon returning he spent several months as a student at Moody Bible School in Chicago, Illinois. He also made a lecture tour on the needs of Africa.

In 1912 Wood was elected missionary secretary for the denomination from his Mobile pastorate. He remained in this position for eight years, also editing the *Missionary Seer*. He was consecrated bishop on May 20, 1920 and served almost twenty years in that capacity. He was active in the Y.M.C.A. and N.A.A.C.P. and was a trustee of Livingstone College in Salisbury, North Carolina.

"The Anthology of the AME Zion Bishops." *Star of Zion* 57 (September 28, 1933): 1, 6.

"Bishop Wood." *Star of Zion* 64 (April 25, 1940): 4.

"Bishop Wood Translated." *Star of Zion* 64 (April 18, 1940): 1.

"New Era of Zion Methodism." *Star of Zion* 48 (August 7, 1924): 1, 5.

Wood, John Wesley. *Lyrics of Sunshine*. N.p., 1922.

WWCA (38–40), AMEZC, WWAM, WWCR, HUBA, AARS.

WOODBEY, GEORGE WASHINGTON (October 5, 1854–August 27, 1937), Baptist minister who for a time was the foremost Black proponent of Socialism, was born into slavery in Johnson County, Tennessee, the son of Charles and Rachel (Wagner) Woodbey. He was self-educated, except for two terms in common school. At some point he moved to Kansas, where on November 13, 1873 he married Annie R. Goodin, with whom he had five children.

He was ordained a Baptist minister in Emporia, Kansas in 1874 and became active in Republican Party politics. He soon moved to Nebraska, where in 1890 he ran for lieutenant governor and in 1894 for Congress on the Prohibition ticket. In 1896 he was elected a member of the Prohibitionist National Committee, but left the party and the following year joined the Populist Party. In 1900 he supported William Jennings Bryan on the fusion ticket, but heard Eugene V. Debs on the campaign trail and was so impressed that after the election he joined the Socialist Party. He resigned his pulpit, which apparently was the African Baptist Church in Omaha, Nebraska, and announced that he would thenceforth dedicate his life to Socialism.

In 1902 Woodbey went to San Diego, California to visit his mother, and lectured there and in Los Angeles. He had great skill as a speaker and the Socialist Party in California thought him a great asset. He accepted the pastorate of the Mount Zion Baptist Church in San Diego, which became the base from which he undertook his party organizing. He was the sole African American delegate to the Socialist National Convention in 1904, 1908, and 1912, and was a member of the California party's executive board. He wrote a pamphlet, *What To Do and How To Do It, or Socialism vs. Capitalism*, that was reprinted in the August, 1903 issue of *Wayland's Monthly*. It was heralded as an instant Socialist classic and by 1908 had been translated into three languages. In 1903 he wrote *The Bible and Socialism*, in which he made the case for the compatibility of Socialism and Christianity.

Woodbey's growing national and even international reputation brought some negative consequences. He became the target of conservative backlash and was regularly hounded by the police and vigilantes. In July 1905, he was attacked by a police officer and driven off a street corner where he was speaking. Woodbey led a group of protesters to the police station, where he was again attacked by the same officer. With the help of the County Attorney, he took the officer to court for assault and battery, but the jury found the officer innocent. This astounding verdict brought many more converts to Socialism, and Woodbey made the most of it. He wrote a four-page leaflet, *Why the Negro Should Vote the Socialist Ticket*, and for the 1908 presidential election toured the northern cities on behalf of the party. It was difficult to sell the Socialist Party to Black audiences, considering the fact that Eugene Debs' own American Railway Union banned Black members and the party did not wish to do anything special on the "Negro question."

His first wife having died in 1891, he married Mary E. Hart on November 14, 1908. Woodbey wrote another pamphlet in 1910, *The Distribution of Wealth*, which described what would happen after the capitalist system had been overthrown. In 1914 Woodbey was a candidate for state treasurer on the Socialist ticket, and at the time was still pastor of the Mt. Zion church and a member of the Western Baptist Association. Except for his death date, nothing further is known about his life after 1914.

Burkett, Randall K. *Black Socialist Preacher*, Book Review. *Church History* 54 (March 1985): 141–142.

Foner, Philip, S., ed. *Black Socialist Preacher: The Teachings of Reverend George Washington Woodbey and His Disciple, Reverend G. W. Slater, Jr.* San Francisco, CA: Synthesis Publications, 1983. 363pp.

———. "Reverend George Washington Woodbey: Early Twentieth Century California Black Socialist." *Journal of Negro History* 61 (April 1976): 136–157.

Woodbey, George Washington. *What To Do and How To Do It; or, Socialism vs. Capitalism*. Girard, KS: Press of Appeal Publishing Company, 1903. 44 pp.

IBAW, WWCR, BAW, BA.

WRIGHT, CORNELIA (b. c.1935), the first woman presiding elder in the United States in the history of the **African Methodist Episcopal Church** (AME), was appointed to that position on February 10, 1983 by Bishop **Vinton R. Anderson**. She was assigned to the Charleston District of the West Virginia Annual Conference. There was a previous woman presiding elder in the AME Church, but not in the United States, Dorothy M. Morris in 1973 in the Guyana Annual Conference in South America.

IAAH.

WRIGHT, HAROLD LOUIS (1929–June 11, 1978), a bishop of the **Episcopal Church**, was born in Boston, Massachusetts, the son of Mr. and Mrs. Harold L. Wright. He attended the New England Conservatory of Music and in 1952 married Edith C. Yancey, with whom he had four sons. He received his B.A. in 1954 from Boston University. He was told by a counselor at Boston University in 1952 that "there is no place for blacks in the Episcopal Church," but persevered in the church anyway. From 1949 to 1952 he was chair of the Commission on Youth, Province of New England. While in school he was organist-choirmaster of the Church of St. Augustine and St. Martin in Boston and of the Holy Trinity Church in Hicksville, New York. He received his S.T.B. in 1957 from General Theological Seminary in New York City, and that year was ordained a priest.

For the next seventeen years Wright served in a number of capacities in the Diocese of Long Island. For a time he was instructor in church history at the George Mercer School of Theology, and then was Coordinator for Training and Field Education of the Professional Leadership Development Section of the Executive Council of the Episcopal Church. For many years he was rector of the Church of the Resurrection in East Elmhurst, New York. At the time of his election to the bishopric he was assistant to the Bishop of New York for Ministries.

Wright was active in a number of capacities beyond his specific assignments. He was a founding member of the **Union of Black Episcopalians** and, from 1969 to 1975, was its national treasurer. Beginning in 1966 he was a trustee of the Protestant Episcopal Society for Promoting Religion and Learning in the State of New York. He was vice-chair of the New York City Local School Board #23 and on the Queensborough Advisory Committee to the New York City Youth Board. He founded the Resurrection Day Care Center in East Elmhurst and chaired its board of directors. On February 2, 1974 he was consecrated suffragan bishop of New York in the Cathedral Church of St. John the Divine. He was the first Black priest in the Diocese of New York to become a bishop and at the time of his consecration was one of six living Black Episcopal bishops, the other five being **John Burgess**, **Quintin Primo**, **John T. Walker**, **Richard B. Martin**, and **George D. Browne**. Wright was the seventeenth Black priest consecrated bishop by the Episcopal Church in America, beginning with **James T. Holly** in 1874. Wright was the seventh black Episcopal bishop to be assigned to work within the United States.

Dugan, George. "Episcopal Diocese Gets First Black Bishop." *New York Times* (February 3, 1974): 45.
IBAW, BGWC, EBA, NYTBS (1978), *ECA* (1975; 1979).

WRIGHT, NATHAN, JR. (b. August 5, 1923), a priest of the **Episcopal Church**, author, and educator, was born in Shreveport, Louisiana, the son of Nathan Sr. and Parthenia (Hickman) Wright. His father, an insurance salesman, moved the family to Cincinnati, Ohio, when Wright was six months old. Wright attended Walnut Hills High School and during World War II he was a Second Lieutenant in the U.S. Army. He participated in the first modern Freedom Ride in 1947 to test the laws regarding interstate travel and was field secretary for the Congress on Racial Equality (C.O.R.E.) for several years. In 1950 he was named Man of the Year by the New England C.O.R.E. He received his B.A. in 1947 from the University of Cincinnati; his B.D. in 1950 from the Episcopal Theological School in Cambridge, Massachusetts; and his S.T.M. in 1951 from Harvard Divinity School.

He was ordained an Episcopal priest in 1950 and from 1951 to 1964 was rector of St. Cyprian's Episcopal Church in Boston, Massachusetts. During this time he was also a research associate at the Center for Altruistic Studies at Harvard University (1951–52), the chaplain of the Children's Medical Center in Boston (1951–56), and the chaplain of the Boston Long Island Hospital

(1957–64). He continued his own education, receiving his Ed.M. in 1962 from the State Teacher's College in Boston and his Ed.D. in 1964 from Harvard University. His first significant book of more than a dozen books was published in 1952, *The Riddle of Life and Other Sermons*, followed by *The Nation America Founded— A Short History of Liberia's Beginnings* (1952) and *The Song of Mary* (1958), a collection of poems.

From 1964 to 1969 Wright was director of urban work for the Diocese of New Jersey, and during these years became nationally famous as an authority on urban unrest and as a powerful voice speaking from the black community. He was a founding member of the National Committee of Negro Churchmen (now the **National Conference of Black Churchmen**), in 1967 was chair of the National Conference on Black Power in Newark, New Jersey, and in 1968 was chair of the International Conference on Black Power in Philadelphia, Pennsylvania. The 1967 conference took place just after the Newark riots in July, and he gained wide recognition for his mediation of the different views represented at the meeting. His books gathered a number of honors: *One Bread, One Body* (1962) won First Prize from the Christian Research Foundation; *Black Power and Urban Unrest: The Creative Possibilities* (1967) won the Media Workshop Award; and *Let's Work Together* (1968) was nominated for a Pulitzer Prize. In 1968 he began a weekly editorial column in the Newark *Star-Ledger*.

From April 1969 to May 1981 Wright was professor of urban studies and African American studies at the State University of New York at Albany. On July 18, 1969, he married Carolyn Elliott May, with whom he has had five children. He considered himself "psychologically" close to such leaders as Stokely Carmichael and H. Rapp Brown, but placed their ideas within a pacifist approach. Wright's goal was understood to be not the destruction of America, but the fulfillment of its ideals through an assertive Black community that has taken its rightful place in society. He was chair of the two national conferences because of his abilities as a mediator. He said at one point that Blacks and Whites "don't need to like each other but need to respect each other" if the country is to survive. He was president of Empowerment Associates in New York City, on the Standing Liturgical Commission of the Episcopal Church, and a national syndicated columnist of "Black Empowerment." During the 1980s he took a position in Paterson, New Jersey. He is a noted lecturer and consultant, and since about 1990 has been one of the priests on staff at the 1,500–member Grace Episcopal Church in Jamaica, New York.

"Speaking of People." *Ebony* 14 (June 1959): 6–7.

"Speaking of People." *Ebony* 20 (May 1965): 6–7.

Wright, Nathan, Jr. *Black Power and Urban Unrest: Creative Possibilities.* New York: Hawthorn Books, 1969. 200 pp.

———. *Let's Face Racism.* Camden, NJ: Thomas Nelson, 1970. 92 pp.

———. *Let's Work Together.* New York: Hawthorn Books, 1968. 271 pp.

———. *One Bread, One Body.* Greenwich, CT: Seabury Press, 1962. 148 pp.

———. *Ready to Riot.* New York: Holt, Rinehart, and Winston, 1968. 148 pp.

———, ed. *What Black Educators Are Saying.* New York: Hawthorn Books, 1971. 286 pp.

IBAW, IBAWCB, OTSB, AAE, BGWC, SBAA, PBP, CA (37–40), *WWABA* (80–81), *BDNM* (75).

WRIGHT, RICHARD ROBERT, JR. (April 16, 1878–December 12, 1967), 57th bishop of the **African Methodist Episcopal Church** (AME), was born in Cuthbert, Georgia, one of nine children in the family of Major Richard Robert, Sr., and Lydia Elizabeth (Howard) Wright. In 1880 the family moved to Augusta, Georgia, where his father became principal of Ware High School. He attended the public schools and Haines Institute in Augusta. He experienced conversion in February 1892, at the age of fourteen, and joined Bethel AME Church. He held many positions in the church, and determined to enter the ministry.

In 1894 he entered Georgia State College in Savannah, where he managed the Georgia State College Journal from 1896 to 1898, and graduated in 1898 with his B.A. In April 1898, he received his exhorter's license, in April 1899 his preaching license, and in September 1900 he was ordained deacon. He earned his B.D. at the University of Chicago in 1901, and was ordained elder in September of that year. While continuing his studies, he was assistant pastor at the Institutional Church in Chicago under **Reverdy Ransom** from 1900 to 1901, and instructor of Hebrew and New Testament Greek in Payne Theological Seminary at Wilberforce University, Ohio, from 1901 to 1903. He studied at the University of Berlin in 1903 and the University of Leipzig in 1904, receiving his A.M. from the University of Chicago in 1904. He supported himself through these schools not only by pastoring, but by serving variously as dishwasher, janitor, farm hand, factory employee, book salesman, and laundry agent. He pastored the Trinity AME Church in Chicago in 1904–05.

From 1906 to 1908 Wright was a research fellow in sociology at the University of Pennsylvania. From 1908 to 1909, while continuing his doctoral studies, he pastored Conshohocken AME Church in Pennsylvania. He also entered the business of finance by founding the Eighth Ward Building and Loan Association in 1906. He was one of the founders and first field secretary of the Armstrong Association, the first affiliate of the National Urban League, and wrote its constitution, 1908–09. In 1909 he became editor of the *Christian Recorder*, a position he held until 1936, and also took over the AME Church Book Concern, a position he held from 1909 to 1912, and again from 1916 to 1920. In 1919 he burned the Book Concern's mortgage. On September 8, 1909, he married Charlotte Crogman, with whom he had three children. He finally received his Ph.D. from the University of Pennsylvania in 1911, one of the first Blacks to achieve such a degree.

On September 15, 1920, Wright co-founded the Citizen and Southern Banking Company, and in 1922 added the Citizen and Southern Building and Loan Association and the Citizen Southern Realty Company. He also kept busy with numerous church and community commitments. He was a delegate to the Methodist Ecumenical Conferences in 1911 (Toronto), 1921 (London), 1931 (Atlanta), 1947, and 1961 (Oslo). He served on the boards of the Association for the Protection of Colored Women; Spring Street Social Settlement, Philadelphia; Social Service Commission of the Federal Council of Churches, and others. From 1932 to 1936 he was president of Wilberforce University in Ohio. From that position he was elected bishop on May 16, 1936.

Wright held several distinctions as bishop. He was the first and so far only Ph.D. elected bishop in the denomination, and appears to have been the most prolific author. His sociological works include *Self-Help in Negro Education* (1909), *Social Work and the Influence of the Negro Church* (1907), and *A Study of the Industrial Conditions of the Negro Population of Pennsylvania...* (1914). His many religious works include *Outline of the Teaching of Jesus, or the Fundamentals of Christian Doctrine* (1911), *The (Centennial) Encyclopedia of the African Methodist Episcopal Church* (1916; revised 1947), and *The Bishops of the African Methodist Episcopal Church* (1963).

During his first four years as bishop he was assigned to South Africa, where he proceeded to found the Richard R. Wright, Jr. School of Religion, the W. H. Crogman Community Clinic, and over fifty churches and schools. On his way back to the United States in 1940, he appeared stranded in Liberia when the only steamship operating in wartime refused to book a Black; a phone call to President Roosevelt, however, soon brought results. He was bishop of Tennessee and

Kentucky from 1940 to 1946; from 1946 to 1948 of New York, New Jersey, New England, and Bermuda; from 1951 to 1952 of Arkansas and Oklahoma; from 1952 to 1957 of the West Indies and Guyana; from 1956 to 1957 of Louisiana and Mississippi; and from 1957 to 1960 of the Far West. In 1960 he hosted the first General Conference to be held in the Far West. At that conference he asked to be the historiographer of the church, and was given that position for the remainder of his life. The importance of his service to the church is hard to overestimate, and he must be ranked as one of the outstanding bishops of the denomination. His last publication, fittingly, was his autobiography, *Eighty-Seven Years Behind the Black Curtain* (1965).

Wright, Richard Robert, Jr. *The Bishops of the African Methodist Episcopal Church.* Nashville, TN: AME Sunday School Union, 1963. 389 pp.

———, and John Russell Hawkins, eds. *The Centennial Encyclopedia of the African Methodist Episcopal Church.* Philadelphia, PA: n.p., 1916. Revised, 1947. 387 pp.

———. *Eighty-Seven Years Behind the Black Curtain.* Nashville, TN: AME Sunday School Union, 1965. 351 pp.

———. *Social Work and the Influence of the Negro Church.* Philadelphia, PA: n.p., 1907. 93 pp.

———. *Who's Who in the General Conference, 1924.* Philadelphia, PA: AME Book Concern, 1924.

BAMEC, RLOA, WWCR, WWCA (38–40), EWM, NYTO, HAMEC, HUBA, AARS, BAW, IBAW, WWMC, DAB (Supp. 4), *BH, HNB, EBA, RLA, NV, EAMEC, CEAMEC.*

WRIGHT, THEODORE SEDGWICK (1797–1847), Presbyterian minister and first Black graduate of an American theological seminary, was born in New Jersey, but the family soon moved to Providence, Rhode Island, and then to Schenectady, New York. His father, R. P. G. Wright, was from Madagascar and was an early leader in the national Black conventions. Little is known about his mother. Wright was named for the Massachusetts jurist and legislator Theodore Sedgwick, who was well known for his support of Blacks.

Formal schooling was impossible for most of his childhood, except for a time when three Methodist teachers briefly opened their school to Blacks. In 1819, at the age of twenty-two, he enrolled in the New York African Free School, and after graduation tried to gain entrance to a college. After numerous failures, he was befriended by DeWitt Clinton, Arthur Tappan, and others, who helped him into Princeton Theological Seminary in 1825. He graduated in 1828 as the first Black graduate of an American theological seminary. Wright was by this time married; in this same year he

and his wife were traveling by boat up the Hudson towards Schenectady, and were denied a room for shelter from the elements. His wife died a few months later of complications from this exposure. It is not clear if he ever remarried.

In December 1828, a few weeks after his graduation, he was named as **Samuel Cornish**'s replacement as the pastor of the First Colored (Shiloh) Presbyterian Church in New York City, a position he held for the rest of his career. There were only 75 poverty-stricken members, and Wright's $500 annual salary was promised only on condition that it could be secured from donations from White churches. Wright brought a certain dynamism that quickly changed these circumstances. A schoolroom was rented for worship, and within one year the membership had risen to 120, and continued to rise. In late 1831 an old German Lutheran church close to the Bancker Street ghetto was purchased. A severe illness of Wright's slowed the church's progress, and he recuperated at his parents' home in Schenectady for about six months in 1832.

In May 1833, the American Anti-Slavery Society was founded, and Wright was one of four Blacks on its executive council (with Samuel Cornish, **Peter Williams, Jr.**, and **Christopher Rush**). He was vice-president of the Phoenix Society, a mutual aid group founded in 1833 with Williams, Jr., Cornish, and others, and was president of the trustees of the short-lived Phoenix High School, founded in 1836. In November 1835, he founded and chaired the New York Vigilance Committee, which aided fugitive slaves and protected free Blacks from kidnapping and other attacks. In May 1840, he joined Rush, Cornish, and others in withdrawing from that group and forming the American and Foreign Anti-Slavery Society, which separated itself from Garrisonian policies.

In 1841, Wright notified the Presbytery of New York of his withdrawal to join the Third Presbytery, founded in 1830 by liberal New York Presbyterian ministers and still a part of the Presbyterian Church. The Third Presbytery was willing to take a strong stance on abolition, as opposed to the Presbytery of New York, which invested its funds in the slave trade. In 1844 he was a member of the Liberty Party, and helped choose its presidential nominee. By this time the membership of his church had passed 400, making it the second-largest Black church in New York City, next to the 800–member mother church of the AMEZ denomination. He is well remembered for his accomplishments and courageous leadership.

Gross, Bella. "Life and Times of Theodore S. Wright, 1797–1847." *Negro History Bulletin* 3 (June, 1940): 133–138.

Pease, Jane H. and William H. *Bound With Them in Chains: A Biographical History of the Antislavery Movement.* Westport, CT: Greenwood Press, 1972. 334 pp.

Quarles, Benjamin. *Black Abolitionists.* New York: Oxford University Press, 1969. 310 pp.

Sorin, Gerald. *The New York Abolitionists: A Case Study of Political Radicalism.* Westport, CT: Greenwood Press, 1971. 172 pp.

Swift, David E. "Black Presbyterian Attacks on Racism: Samuel Cornish, Theodore Wright, and Their Contemporaries." *Journal of Presbyterian History* 51 (Winter 1973): 433–470.

Wesley, Charles H. *Neglected History, Essays in Negro History by a College President: Charles H. Wesley.* Wilberforce, OH: Central State College Press, 1965. 200 pp.

DANB, HNB, CH, IBAW, HUBA, PATN, BPJ, SOTT, BWA.

"But alas! the freedom to which we have attained, is defective. Freedom and equality have been 'put asunder.' The rights of men are decided by the color of their skin; and there is as much difference made between the rights of a free white man and a free colored man, as there is between a free colored man and a slave.

"We are natives of this country, we ask only to be treated as well as foreigners. Not a few of our fathers suffered and bled to purchase its independence; we ask only to be treated as well as those who fought against it. We have toiled to cultivate it, and to raise it to its present prosperous condition; we ask only to share equal privileges with those who come from distant lands to enjoy the fruits of our labour."

Peter Williams, Jr., Minister
Episcopal Church
1830

X–Y

XAVIER UNIVERSITY. A **Roman Catholic Church school**. Xavier University was founded by the **Sisters of the Blessed Sacrament for Indians and Colored People**. It began in 1915 when Archbishop James H. Blenk of New Orleans asked Mother Katherine Drexel, head of the Sister of the Blessed Sacrament, to launch an educational effort for African Americans in his archdiocese. She was able to purchase the abandoned campus of Southern University, and opened a high school. The same year the school began, Fr. John Henry Dorsey, a Black priest, visited the city and launched the parish Church of the Blessed Sacrament, originally located in the school auditorium. In 1917 she added a normal department. The school was chartered in 1918. The College of Liberal Arts and Sciences and the Teachers College were added in 1925, and the school of pharmacy was added two years later. The graduate school opened in 1933.

In 1932 the school was able to move onto a new campus, into what has become their permanent home. The new campus was dedicated by Cardinal Dennis Dougherty. The graduate school opened the next year, and the school continued to expand through the remainder of the decade. The school was named for St. Francis Xavier, considered to be one of the special patrons of the Sisters.

The university is the only university for African Americans sponsored by the Roman Catholic Church. From its modest beginnings, it has grown steadily through the twentieth century to the point of enrolling almost 1,500 students and employing over 100 faculty members. It serves the entire African American community of southern Louisiana, and approximately one-third of the student body is non-Catholic. In recent years, approximately ten percent of the student body has been White, and it also has many foreign students from Asia and Africa.

The university has also built a large collection in African American literary resources, and is home to a Roman Catholic Black Studies institute. It has become especially known for its fine arts department and the diversity and quality of its musical program.

BEN YAHWEH, YAHWEH (b. 1935) is the founder of the **Nation of Yahweh**. Yahweh Ben Yahweh is the religious name assumed in the early 1970s by Hulon C. Mitchell, Jr., at the time the founder of the Nation of Yahweh, a Black Jewish sect headquartered in Miami, Florida. He was born in 1935 in Enid, Oklahoma, where his father was a pastor in the **Church of God in Christ**, a large Pentecostal denomination. He sang with the Musical Mitchells, a traveling Gospel team his father created. His sister, Leona Mitchell, sings with the Metropolitan Opera.

Mitchell attended junior college in Texas and later served a period in the Air Force. Upon completion of his military service, he became the first Black student at Philipps University in Enid and graduated with a degree in psychology. While there, he was active in civil rights work and married his first wife, Nodie Mae. He attended **Atlanta University**, where he earned a master's degree in economics. He divorced his wife and shortly thereafter married Chloe Mitchell. He also joined the **Nation of Islam**. Assuming the name Hulan Shah, he became the leader of the Atlanta mosque. He later left the Nation of Islam, and in the early 1970s for a brief time headed the Modern Christian Church which he founded in Atlanta.

The Modern Christian Church disbanded after a few years and Mitchell reappeared as Yahweh Ben Yahweh. He moved his headquarters to Miami and under his guidance the new Nation of Yahweh grew and prospered. Businesses were started which provided work for members and apartment houses were purchased as residences. Through the 1980s, the organization sent missionaries out across America and centers were started in many Black communities.

Yahweh Ben Yahweh's work was disturbed by an ever-growing tension level with the community beginning with the discovery of the murdered body of a former temple member and vocal critic of Yahweh Ben Yahweh. Through the decade several members were arrested and their leader charged with creating a climate of fear among his followers. Then, in 1990, he and sixteen leaders were arrested on a number of charges, including murder. At the end of a five-month trial in 1992, Yahweh Ben Yahweh was found guilty of charges involving his connection in fourteen murders plus other crimes, and six of the other defendants were also convicted of related charges. Equally important were not guilty verdicts on charges of racketeering. He and the six members who were convicted began serving sentences while an appeal process was initiated by the defense and while the state moved to retry the defendants on charges upon which the jury was unable to reach a verdict.

"Black Sect Leader Gets 18-Year Term." *New York Times* (September 5, 1992).

Clary, Mike. "Cult Leader Convicted of Murder Conspiracy." *Los Angeles Times* (May 28, 1992).

Sach, Susan. "Cult Inspires Discipline, Fear." *Miami Herald* (December 8, 1985): 1, 22.

YAHWEH'S TEMPLE. An Apostolic Pentecostal Church. The **Church of God (Cleveland, Tennessee)**, the pioneering Pentecostal church in the South, developed a small African American membership through the first half of the twentieth century. Among the African American ministers was Samuel Officer. By 1947 Officer had accepted the non-Trinitarian Apostolic theology which identified Jesus with the God of the Old Testament. That year he left the Church of God and founded the Church of Jesus, changed in 1951 to the Jesus Church.

One of the central issues which prompted the formation of the Apostolic Pentecostal churches was the belief that they had discovered God's name, and that name was Jesus. This issue is very close to the one raised by the Sacred Name movement within Adventism in the early twentieth century. Sacred Name advocates believed that they had discovered the proper names of God and God's Sons by an examination of the Hebrew Bible, and that Yahweh was God's name.

In the 1970s, Officer absorbed elements of Sacred Name theology and as a result in 1981 changed the name of the church to Yahweh's Temple. He specifically rejected names such as "Church of God," "Pentecostal," and "Churches of Christ" as options for the name of the true church.

Officer also developed a unique organizational structure based upon Ezekiel 10:10, the vision of the angels with the four wheels. Officer suggested that each temple member has a special place to work together with others in a united body. Thus a system of wheels within a wheel has been constructed. Each wheel consists of a hub (the elders), spokes (helpers), and rim (members). The international bishop at the center exercises episcopal and theocratic leadership. Immediately under him in authority are national and state bishops.

The temple is headquartered in Cleveland, Tennessee. A periodical, *The Light of the World*, is published.

YOUNG, ANDREW JACKSON (b. March 12, 1932), **United Church of Christ** minister, former ambassador, former member of Congress, former mayor of Atlanta, and currently an organizer of the 1996 Olympic Games in Atlanta, was born in New Orleans, Louisiana, the son of Andrew J. and Daisy (Fuller) Young. His father was a dentist, and the family lived a comfortable existence. Young was the only Black child in a predominantly Irish and Italian, middle-class neighborhood. He attended a segregated elementary school and then Gilbert Academy, a private high school. He was a student at Dillard University in New Orleans in 1947–48, received his B.A. in 1951 from Howard University in Washington, D.C., and his B.D. in 1955 from Hartford Theological Seminary in Connecticut. In seminary he, like **Martin Luther King, Jr.**, was attracted to the nonviolence teachings of Mahatma Gandhi. On June 7, 1954, he married Jean Childs, with whom he had four children.

In 1955 Young was ordained a minister with the Congregational-Christian Churches, a denomination which merged with the Evangelical and Reformed Church in 1957 to form the United Church of Christ (U.C.C.). From 1955 to 1957 he pastored churches in Marion, Alabama; Thomasville, Georgia; and Beachton, Georgia. Despite threats from the Ku Klux Klan he helped church members organize a voter registration drive. From 1957 to 1961 he was associate director of the Department of Youth Work for the National Council of Churches, and worked out of New York City. During this time he administered a voter education and registration project funded by the Field Foundation of the United Church of Christ, and often collaborated with minister/activist Martin Luther King, Jr. In late 1961 he joined the staff of the **Southern Christian Leadership Conference** (S.C.L.C.) and for three years was in charge of the Citizen Education Program. From 1964 to 1967 he was executive director, a position subordinate only to King as president and **Ralph D. Abernathy** as vice-president-at-large/secretary-treasurer.

Young was responsible for creating community organizations to set up voter registration drives, strategize for legislation, and arrange for marches and demonstrations against segregation and discrimination. On May 3, 1963, after the police in Birmingham, Alabama had arrested King and Abernathy, Young stepped into the leadership position. He calmed the frightened crowd and focused them on an orderly demonstration march. The resulting confrontation with Public Safety Commissioner Eugene (Bull) Connor and the police was a turning point for the civil rights movement. Television screens across the nation vividly showed the unarmed men, women, and children knocked to the ground by fire-hoses and attacked by police dogs and police with nightsticks. Millions were outraged by this brutality and public opinion turned in favor of the movement. This enabled passage of the Civil Rights Act of 1964 and the Voting Rights Act of 1965, both of which Young helped to draft. After King was assassinated in 1968, Abernathy succeeded him as head of the S.C.L.C., and Young rose to the position of executive vice-president, a position he retained until 1970.

In 1970 he ran unsuccessfully for the Fifth Congressional Seat as a Democrat, then took a job as chair of Atlanta's Community Relations Commission. In 1972 he was successful in the race for the same office, and was reelected in landslides in 1974 and 1976. He was the first Black member of Congress from Georgia since Jefferson Long in the days of Reconstruction (1871). Young spent his years in Congress working on behalf of the poor and disadvantaged. He called for an end to the Vietnam War and for conservation measures to protect natural resources. He was a member of the Rules Committee and the Banking and Currency Committee, and his amendment to the National Mass Transportation Assistance Act of 1974 provided funding channels for the involvement of private citizens in the development of areas around bus and subway stations and corridors. In 1975 he was instrumental in having the Voting Rights Act of 1965 extended for another seven years and expanded to cover some language minorities. He broke from most of his Black colleagues in supporting Gerald Ford for president for pragmatic reasons, and later defended Ford's action in pardoning former president Richard Nixon. He continued to preach often in various churches.

Between 1970 and 1976 Young became close friends with Jimmy Carter and organized a massive voter registration drive in 1976 that brought 3,104,000 new,

mostly Democratic voters, a crucial factor in Carter's slim margin of victory over Ford in the presidential campaign that year. In November, Carter asked Young to represent the new administration in a meeting of American and African leaders in Lesotho, South Africa. The success of that meeting led Carter in December to nominate Young to be the American Ambassador to the United Nations (U.N.). After confirmation by the Senate, Young took office on January 31, 1977, and created a new, multi-ethnic U.N. staff. Almost immediately he gained a reputation for being outspoken and controversial; he felt it important to be able to speak his mind, whatever the immediate consequences. This approach, despite much success in relations with many "Third World" countries, led two years later to an incident that created an uproar of criticism that would not go away. The incident was a secret meeting that Young held with an official of the Palestine Liberation Organization (P.L.O.), a direct violation of United States policy, aggravated by the fact that he then seemed to mislead State Department officials about that meeting. The meeting was very brief, but it was enough, when the Israelis found out about it, to develop into a major diplomatic crisis.

Young tendered his resignation in August 1979, but stayed in office until January 1980. He then settled into a much quieter life of lecturing and preaching. In 1981 he ran successfully for mayor of Atlanta and was sworn into office in January, 1982, remaining there for two terms until 1989. In those two terms he reported 1,000 new companies located in Atlanta (300 from overseas), $70 billion invested ($11 billion from overseas), and 700,000 new jobs. In 1989 and 1990 he ran for the office of governor of Georgia and made it as far as a run-off in the primary with Lieutenant Governor Zell Miller, who defeated him by a two-to-one margin in August 1990. Following the campaign, Young took a position as consultant with Law Engineering, an international development company based in Atlanta. He continued as chair of the Atlanta Organizing Committee, working to bring the 1996 Summer Olympics to Atlanta. This effort was proved successful when the International Olympic Committee picked Atlanta over its competitors in September, 1990. Young is the recipient of many honors and awards, including the Spingarn Award from the N.A.A.C.P., the Pax Christi Award from St. John's University, the Medal of Freedom (1980), and the French Legion of Honor Medal (1982). He is a member of the board of directors of the Martin Luther King Jr. Center for Social Change.

Applebome, Peter. "Atlanta Seeks to Deliver City It Sold to Olympics." *New York Times* (September 23, 1990): 24.

Bims, Hamilton. "A Southern Activist Goes to the House." *Ebony* 28 (February 1973): 82–90.

"The Fall of Andrew Young." *Time* 114 (August 27, 1979): 10–16.

Gardner, Carl. *Andrew Young: A Biography*. New York: Drake, 1978. 232pp.

Johnson, Herschel. "A Close Encounter with Andrew Young." *Ebony* 33 (April 1978): 110–122.

Johnson, Robert E. "Ambassador Andrew Young's Last Official Visit to Africa." *Ebony* 35 (December 1979): 31-42.

"The Men Behind Martin Luther King." *Ebony* 20 (June 1965): 165–172.

Smothers, Ronald. "After Loss at Polls, Young Savors Role in Winning the Games." *New York Times* (September 23, 1990): 24.

———. "Georgia Democrats Pick Miller in Runoff for Governor." *New York Times* (August 8, 1990): A15.

Stone, Eddie. *Andrew Young: Biography of a Realist*. Los Angeles, California: Holloway House, 1980. 215pp.

Wills, Garry. "Georgia Is Much On His Mind." *Time* 136 (July 16, 1990): 66–68.

Young, Andrew J. *Andrew Young at the United Nations*. Salisbury, North Carolina: Documentary Publications, 1978. 189pp.

———. "The Church and Citizenship: Education of the Negro in the South." In Lewis S. C. Smythe, ed. *Southern Churches and Race Relations*. Lexington, Kentucky: The College of the Bible, 1963, 64–81.

———. "Demonstrations: A Twentieth Century Christian Witness." *Social Action* 30 (May 1964): 5–12.

———. "Speech at Thirtieth Anniversary Dinner of Christianity and Crisis." *Christianity and Crisis* 31 (May 3, 1971): 80–82.

HUBA, AARS, WWA (90–91), *EBA, WWABA* (88), *NYTBS* (1976, 1979, 1990), *CRACG, IP, AAE, CB* (1977), *BAC, IBAW*.

YOUNG, GEORGE BENJAMIN (? –February 3, 1949), 52nd bishop of the **African Methodist Episcopal Church** (AME), was born in Texas at an unknown time. He grew up on a farm, experienced conversion as a boy, and received some schooling. He married Lucy Young on August 6, 1881; there were no children. He went to Paul Quinn College in Waco, Texas, and then to Wilberforce University in Ohio, where he earned his B.D. degree in 1896.

He was ordained deacon and elder in Texas and served for a time as Dean of Theology at Paul Quinn College. He pastored a number of churches in Texas and was a presiding elder. In 1928 Young was elected bishop from the pastorate of the AME Church in Bethel, Texas. He was assigned to the Fifteenth Episcopal District (South Africa) from 1928 to 1932, and was very successful in that region. He extended the denomination into Swaziland and Rhodesia (today Zambia) and built churches in Bremersdorp, Swaziland and Salisbury, Rhodesia. He purchased a 3,000-acre tract near Bulawayos, Rhodesia, and inspired the formation of the South African Burial Society, which became one of the largest businesses conducted by the Bantu of South Africa.

From 1932 to 1936 Young was assigned to the Twelfth Episcopal District (Arkansas and Oklahoma), and from 1934 to 1948 covered the Tenth Episcopal District (Texas). He was chair of the board of trustees of Paul Quinn College, chair of the Missionary Board from 1936 to 1940, and chair of the Bureau of Evangelism from 1940 to 1944. He preached the Quadrennial Sermon at the 1944 General Conference. He retired in 1948 and passed away the following year. Named for him are AME churches in Bulawayo, Southern Rhodesia (now Zimbabwe), and in Malvern, Arkansas.

HAMEC, EAMEC, BAMEC, EWM.

YOUNG, ROY LEE (October 2, 1888–March 10, 1948), 24th bishop of the **Christian Methodist Episcopal Church** (CME), then the Colored Methodist Episcopal Church, was born in Whynot, Lauderdale County, Mississippi, the second of fourteen children in the family of E. Fred and Maggie (Harrison) Young. He attended Haven Institute, then received his B.A. from Paine College in Augusta, Georgia.

Upon graduation he was appointed to the Mt. Olive-Goodwater Circuit in Mississippi. On December 19, 1923, he married Estella Otis, with whom he had three children. He served a number of charges in Mississippi, including being presiding elder of the Meridian District. He gained a reputation as a church-builder and as an astute businessman. He was elected bishop on May 7, 1946, during the 20th General Conference in St. Louis, Missouri. He served only two years as bishop before he passed away in Nashville, Tennessee.

EWM, CMECTY, WWCA (38–40).

A Basic Bibliography
of
African American Religion

I. General Sources

1. Broderick, Francis and August Meier, eds. *Negro Protest Thought in the Twentieth Century.* New York: Bobbs-Merrill, 1965. 648 pp.

2. Burgess, John M. *Black Gospel/White Church.* New York: Seabury Press, 1982. 108 pp.

3. Burkett, Randall K. *Garveyism as a Religious Movement.* Metuchen, NJ: Scarecrow Press, 1978. 216 pp.

4. DuBois, W. E. B. *The Negro Church.* Atlanta Ga: Atlanta University Publications, 1968.

5. Frazier, E. Franklin. *The Negro Church in America.* Liverpool, England: University of Liverpool, 1963.

6. Fauset, Arthur Huff. *Black Gods of the Metropolis.* Philadelphia, PA: University of Pennsylvania Press, 1944. 128 pp.

7. Fuller, Thomas Oscar. *Story of Church Life Among Negroes in Memphis, Tennessee, for Students and Workers, 1900–1938.* Memphis, TN: n.p., 1938. 52 pp.

8. Lincoln, C. Eric. *The Black Church in the African American Experience.* Durham, NC: Duke University Press, 1990. 519 pp.

9. ———. *The Black Experience in Religion.* Garden City, NJ: Anchor Books, 1974. 369 pp.

10. ———, and Lawrence A. Mamiya. *The Black Church in the African American Experience.* Durham, NC: Duke University Press, 1990. 519 pp.

11. McCall, Emmanuel L., ed. *The Black Christian Experience.* Nashville, TN: Broadman Press, 1972. 126 pp.

12. Mays, Benjamin E., and Joseph W. Nicholson. *The Negro's Church.* New York: Institute of Social and Religious Research, 1933. 321 pp. Rept.: New York: Arno Press, 1969. 321 pp.

13. Melton, J. Gordon. *Encyclopedia of American Religions.* 1979. 3rd edition: Detroit, MI: Gale Research Company, 1989. 1100 pp. 4th edition: Gale Research, 1992. 1217 pp.

14. Nelsen, Hart M., Raytha L. Yokley, and Anne K. Nelsen, eds. *The Black Church in America.* New York: Basic Books, 1971. 375 pp.

15. Payne, Wardell J., ed. *Directory of African American Religious Bodies: A Compendium by the Howard University School of Divinity.* Washington, DC: Howard University Press, 1991. 363 pp.

16. Raboteau, Albert. *Slave Religion: The Invisible Institution in the Antebellum South.* New York: Oxford University Press, 1978. 382 pp.

17. Sernett, Milton C. *Black Religion and American Evangelicalism.* Metuchen, NJ: Scarecrow Press, 1975. 320 pp.

18. ———, ed. *Afro-American Religious History. A Documentary Witness.* Durham, NC: Duke University Press, 1985. 504 pp.

19. Sobel, Mechal. *Trabelin' On: The Slave Journey to an Afro-Baptist Faith.* Westport, CT: Greenwood Press, 1979. 454 pp.

20. Swift, David E. *Black Prophets of Justice: Activist Clergy Before the Civil War.* Baton Rouge, LA: Louisiana State University Press, 1989. 384 pp.

21. Washington, Joseph R., Jr. *Black Religion: The Negro and Christianity in the United States.* 1964. Rept.: Lanham, MD: University Press of America, 1984. 308 pp.

22. ———. *Black Sects and Cults.* Garden City, NY: Doubleday, 1972. 176 pp.

23. Wilmore, Gayraud S. *Black Religion and Black Radicalism.* Garden City, NY: Anchor Books, 1973. 344 pp. 2nd ed.: Maryknoll, NY: Orbis Books, 1983. 320 pp.

24. Woodson, Carter G. *The History of the Negro Church.* Washington, DC: Associated Publishers, 1921. 330 pp.

General Sources—Bibliographies

25. Davis, Lenwood G. *Daddy Grace: An Annotated Bibliography.* New York: Greenwood Press, 1992. 130 pp.

26. Richardson, Marilyn. *Black Women and Religion. A Bibliography.* Boston, MA: G. K. Hall & Co., 1980. 139 pp.

27. Williams, Ethel L., and Clifton L. Brown. *Afro-American Religious Studies: A Comprehensive Bibliography with Locations in American Libraries.* Metuchen, NJ: Scarecrow Press, 1972. 454 pp.

28. ———. *The Howard University Bibliography of African and Afro-American Religious Studies.* Wilmington, DE: Scholarly Resources, 1977.

General Sources—Biographies

29. "America's Fifteen Greatest Black Preachers." *Ebony* 39 (September 1984): 27–33.

30. "Bright Young Men of God." *Ebony* 11 (March 1956): 17–23.

31. Burkett, Randall, and Richard Newman, eds. *Black Apostles: Afro-American Clergy Confront the Twentieth Century.* Boston, MA: G. K. Hall & Co., 1978. 283 pp.

32. "Great Negro Preachers." *Ebony* 9, 10 (July 1954): 26–30.

33. "Top Radio Ministers." *Ebony* 4 (July 1949): 56–61.

34. Tucker, David M. *Black Pastors and Leaders: Memphis, 1819–1972.* Memphis, TN: Memphis State University Press, 1975. 158 pp.

35. Williams, Ethel. *Biographical Directory of Negro Ministers.* 1965. 2nd ed.: Metuchen, NJ: Scarecrow Press, 1970. 605 pp. 3rd ed.: Boston, MA: G. K. Hall, 1975. 584 pp.

36. Wills, David W., and Richard Newman. *Black Apostles at Home and Abroad.* Boston, MA: G. K. Hall & Co., 1982. 321 pp.

37. Young, Henry J. *Major Black Religious Leaders.* 2 vols. Nashville, TN: Abingdon Press, 1977–79.

II. Religious Life and Interpretation

Bible Interpretation

38. Barashango, Ishakamusa. *God, the Bible and the Black Man's Destiny.* Washington, DC: IV Destiny Publishing Co., 1982. 159 pp.

39. Dillard, William LaRue. *Biblical Ancestry Voyage: Revealing Facts of Significant Black Characters.* Morristown, NJ: Aaron Press, 1989. 244 pp.

40. Felder, Cain Hope. *Stony the Road We Trod: African American Biblical Interpretation.* Minneapolis, MN: Fortress Press, 1991. 218 pp.

41. Hopkins, Dwight N. *Black Theology, USA and South Africa: Politics, Culture, and Liberation.* Maryknoll, NY: Orbis, 1990. 249 pp.

42. McCray, Walter Arthur. *The Black Presence in the Bible.* Chicago: Black Light Fellowship, 1989. 48 pp.

43. McKissic, William Dwight, Sr. *Beyond Roots. In Search of Blacks in the Bible.* Wenonah, NJ: Renaissance Productions, 1990. 61 pp.

44. Merrill, Richard. *The Undeniable Case for a Black Bible Translation.* Camden, NJ: Revival Literature, 1885. 31 pp.

45. Mosala, Itumeleng T. *Biblical Hermaneutics and Black Theology in South Africa.* Grand Rapids, MI: William B. Eerdmans Publishing Company, 1989. 218 pp.

46. Moseley, William. *What Color Was Jesus?* Chicago: African American Images, 1987. 67 pp.

47. Rhoades, F. S. *Bible Characters and References of the Holy Bible.* N.p.: The Author, 1980. 94 pp.

Education

48. Jones, Maxine D., and Joe M. Richardson. *Talladega College: The First Century.* Tuscaloosa, AL: University of Alabama Press, 1990. 340 pp.

49. Richardson, Joe M. *Christian Reconstruction: The American Missionary Association and Southern Blacks, 1861–1890.* Athens, GA: University of Georgia Press, 1986. 348 pp.

50. Richardson, Joe M. *A History of Fisk University, 1865–1946.* University, AL: University of Alabama Press, 1980. 274 pp.

51. Stowell, Jay S. *Methodist Adventures in Negro Education*. New York: Methodist Book Concern, 1922. 190 pp.

Missions

52. Adams, C. C., and Marshall A. Talley. *Negro Baptists and Foreign Missions*. Philadelphia, PA: Foreign Mission Board of the National Baptist Convention, U.S.A., Inc., 1944. 94 pp.

53. Berry, Lewellyn L. *A Century of Missions of the African Methodist Episcopal Church, 1840–1940*. New York: Gutenberg Printing Co., 1942. 333 pp.

54. Boone, Clinton C. *Congo As I Saw It*. New York: J. J. Little and Ives Co., 1927. 96 pp.

55. ———. *Liberia As I Know It*. Richmond, VA: 1929. 152 pp. Rept.: Westport. CT: Negro Universities Press, 1970. 152 pp.

56. Bradley, David Henry. *A History of the AME Zion Church*. 2 vols. Nashville, TN: Parthenon Press, 1956, 1970.

57. Cade, John. *Holsey: The Incomparable*. New York: Pageant Press, 1964. 221 pp.

58. Calhoun, E. Clayton. *Of Men Who Ventured Much and Far: The Congo Quest of Dr. Gilbert and Bishop Lambuth*. Atlanta, GA: Institute Press, 1961. 153 pp.

59. Cannon, James. *History of Southern Methodist Missions*. Nashville, TN: Cokesbury Press, 1926. 356 pp.

60. Cauthen, Baker J., ed. *Advance: A History of Southern Baptist Foreign Missions*. Nashville, TN: Broadman Press, 1970. 329 pp.

61. Chirenje, J. Mutero. *Ethiopianism and Afro-Americans in Southern Africa, 1883–1916*. Baton Rouge, LA: Louisiana State University Press, 1987. 231 pp.

62. Colclough, Joseph C. *The Spirit of John Wesley Gilbert*. Nashville, TN: Cokesbury Press, 1925.

63. Coles, John J. *Africa in Brief*. New York: Freeman Steam Printing Establishment, 1886.

64. Coppin, Fanny Jackson. *Reminiscences of School Life and Hints on Teaching*. Philadelphia, PA: AME Book Concern, 1913. 191 pp. Rept.: New York: Garland Publishing, 1987. 191 pp.

65. Coppin, Levi J. *Observations of Persons and Things in South Africa, 1900–1904*. Philadelphia, PA: AME Book Concern, 1904. 205 pp.

66. Fitts, Leroy. *Lott Carey: First Black Missionary to Africa*. Valley Forge, PA: Judson Press, 1978. 159 pp.

67. Freeman, Edward A. *The Epoch of Negro Baptists and the Foreign Mission Board*. Kansas City, MO: Central Seminary Press, 1953. 301 pp.

68. Harvey, William J., III. *Bridges of Faith Across the Seas: The Story of the Foreign Mission Board, National Baptist Convention, USA, Inc.* Philadelphia, PA: Foreign Mission Board, National Baptist Convention, U.S.A., Inc., 1989. 523 pp.

69. Hervey, G. Winfred. *The Story of Baptist Missions in Foreign Lands*. St. Louis, MO: Chancy R. Barns, 1884.

70. Jacobs, Sylvia M., ed. *Black Americans and the Missionary Movement in Africa*. Westport, CT: Greenwood Press, 1982. 255 pp.

71. Jordan, Artishia Wilkerson. *The African Methodist Episcopal Church in Africa*. N.p., n.d.

72. Jordan, Lewis Garnett. *In Our Stead: Facts About Foreign Missions*. Philadelphia, PA: 1913.

73. ———. *Negro Baptist History, U.S.A*. Nashville, TN: Sunday School Publishing Board, 1930. 394 pp.

74. ———. *On Two Hemispheres*. Nashville, TN: The Author, 1935.

75. ———. *Pebbles From an African Beach*. Philadelphia, PA: Lisle-Carey Press, 1918?

76. ———. *Up the Ladder in Foreign Missions*. Nashville, TN: National Baptist Publishing Board, 1901. 269 pp.

77. Lambuth, Walter Russell. *Winning the World for Christ: A Study in Dynamics*. New York: Fleming H. Revell Company, 1915. 245 pp.

78. Martin, Sandy D. *Black Baptists and African Missions*. Macon, GA: Mercer University Press, 1989.

79. McAfee, Sara Jane. *History of the Woman's Missionary Society in the Colored Methodist Episcopal Church*. Jackson, TN: Publishing House C.M.E. Church, 1934.

80. Merriam, Edmund F. *A History of American Baptist Missions*. Philadelphia, PA: American Baptist Publication Society, 1900.

81. Pinson, William W. *Walter Russell Lambuth, Prophet and Pioneer*. Nashville, TN: Cokesbury Press, 1925. 261 pp.

82. Reeve, Thomas E. *In Wembo Nyama's Land, A Story of the Thrilling Experiences in Establishing the Methodist*

Mission Among the Atetela. Nashville, TN: Publishing House of the M.E. Church, South, 1923.

83. Rux, Mattie, and Ransome, Mary M. *History of the Woman's Auxiliary to the Lott Carey Baptist Foreign Mission Convention, 1900–1956.* N.p., n.d.

84. Tupper, Henry Allen. *Foreign Missions of the Southern Baptist Convention.* Philadelphia, PA: American Baptist Publication Society, 1880.

85. Williams, Walter L. *Black Americans and the Evangelization of Africa, 1877–1900.* Madison, WI: University of Wisconsin Press, 1982. 259 pp.

Preaching

86. Davis, Gerald A. *I Got the Word in Me and I Can Sing It, You Know: A Study of the Performed African-American Sermon.* Philadelphia, PA: University of Pennsylvania Press, 1985.

87. Mitchell, Henry H. *Black Preaching: The Recovery of a Powerful Art.* Nashville, TN: Abingdon Press, 1990, 143 pp.

88. ———. *Celebration and Experience in Preaching.* Nashville, TN: Abingdon Press, 1990. 155 pp.

Theology

89. Cleage, Albert B., Jr. *The Black Messiah.* New York: Sheed and Ward, 1968. 278 pp.

90. Cone, Cecil W. *The Identity Crisis in Black Theology.* Nashville, TN: AM.E. Church Press, 1975.

91. Cone, James H. *Black Theology and Black Power.* New York: Seabury Press, 1969. 165 pp.

92. ———. *A Black Theology of Liberation.* Philadelphia, PA: J. B. Lippincott, 1970.

93. ———. *For My People: Black Theology and the Black Church.* Maryknoll, NY: Orbis Books, 1982.

94. ———. *Speaking the Truth: Ecumenism, Liberation, and Black Theology.* Grand Rapids, MI: William B. Eerdmans Publishing Company, 1986.

95. Evans, James E., ed. *Black Theology: A Critical Assessment and Annotated Bibliography.* New York: Greenwood Press, 1987.

96. Gardiner, James A., and J. Deotis Roberts, eds. *Quest for a Black Theology.* Philadelphia, PA: Pilgrim Press, 1971.

97. Roberts, J. Deotis. *Black Theology in Dialogue.* Philadelphia, PA: Westminster Press, 1987. 132 pp.

98. ———. *Liberation and Reconciliation: A Black Theology.* Philadelphia, PA: Westminster Press, 1971.

99. ———. *Black Theology Today: Liberation and Contextualization.* New York: Edwin Mellon Press, 1983. 217 pp.

100. ———. *Oppression and Liberation in World History.* Maryknoll, NY: Orbis, 1978.

101. Wilmore, Gayraud S. "Black Theology: Its Significance for Christian Missions Today." *International Review of Mission* 63 (April 1974): 211–31.

102. ———, and James H. Cone, ed. *Black Theology: A Documentary History, 1966–1979.* Maryknoll, NY: Orbis, 1979. 657 pp.

III. The Religious Traditions

Adventists

103. Baker, Delbert W. *The Unknown Prophet.* Washington, DC: Review and Herald Publishing Association, 1987. 160 pp.

104. Bull, Malcolm, and Keith Lockhart. *Seeking a Sanctuary: Seventh-day Adventism and the American Dream.* San Francisco, CA: Harper & Row, 1989. 319 pp.

105. Cleveland, E. E. *Free at Last.* Washington, DC: Review and Herald Publishing Association, 1970.

106. Dudley, Charles. "Statistics of the Regional Work—1986." *North American Regional Voice* (October 1987): 7–8.

107. Foy, William E. *The Christian Experience of William E. Foy.* Portland, ME: Pearson, 1845.

108. Graybill, Ronald D. *E. G. White and Church Race Relations.* Washington, DC: Review and Herald Publishing Association, 1970.

109. ———. *Mission to Black America.* Mountain View, CA: Pacific Press Publishing Assn., 1971. 144 pp.

110. Mesar, J. & T. Dybdahl. "The Utopian Park Affair and the Rise of Northern Black Adventists." *Adventist Heritage* 1 (January 1974): 117–21.

111. Reynolds, Louis B. *We Have Tomorrow: The Story of Seventh-day Adventists with an African Heritage.* Washington, DC: Review and Herald Publishing Association, 1984. 480 pp.

112. Schwarz, R. W. *Light Bearers to the Remnant.* Mountain View, CA: Pacific Press Publishing Association, 1979. 656 pp.

113. *Seventh-day Adventist Encyclopedia.* Washington, DC: Review and Herald Publishing Association, 1966. 1454 pp.

Baptists

114. Banks, William L. *A History of Black Baptists in the United States.* Philadelphia, PA: Author, 1987. 160 pp.

115. Bacote, Samuel William, ed. *Who's Who Among the Colored Baptists of the United States.* Kansas City, MO: Franklin Hudson Publishing Co., 1913. 307 pp. Rept.: New York: Arno Press, 1980. 307 pp.

116. Boddie, Charles Emerson. *God's "Bad Boys."* Valley Forge, PA: Judson Press, 1972.

117. Boone, Theodore S. *Loyalty Unparalleled and Sacrifice Unstinted; Brother Branham with Dr. Williams.* Detroit, MI: N.p., 1948. 70 pp.

118. ———. *Negro Baptist Chief Executives in National Places.* Detroit, MI: N.p., 1948. 70 pp.

119. ———. *The Negro Baptist in Pictures and History; A Negro Baptist Historical Handbook.* Detroit, MI: Voice of Destiny, 1964. 54 pp.

120. ———. *"Old Chief," Alexander Lorenza Boone, D.D., LL.D.; A Biography by His Son, Theodore Sylvester Boone.* Houston, TX: The Western Star Publishing Co., 1927. 64 pp.

121. ———. *The Philosophy of Booker T. Washington.* Fort Worth, TX: Manney Printing Co., 1939. 311 pp.

122. ———. *A Social History of Negro Baptists.* Detroit, MI: Historical Commission, National Baptist Convention, U.S.A., 1952. 98 pp.

123. Booth, L.V. *"Crowned with Glory and Honor": The Life of Rev. Lacey Kirk Williams.* Hicksville, NY: Exposition Press, 1978. 246 pp.

124. ———. *Who's Who in Baptist America.* Cincinnati, OH: Western Printing Co., 1960.

125. Boyd, Richard H. *A Story of the National Baptist Publishing Board.* Nashville, TN: National Baptist Publishing Board, 1915. 145 pp.

126. Brooks, Walter Henderson. "The Evolution of the Negro Baptist Church." *Journal of Negro History* 7 (January 1922): 11–22.

127. ———. "The Priority of the Silver Bluff Church and Its Promoters." *Journal of Negro History* 7 (April 1922): 172–196.

128. ———. *The Silver Bluff Church; A History of Negro Baptist Churches in America.* Washington, DC: Press of R. L. Pendleton, 1910. 47 pp.

129. Davis, John W. "George Liele and Andrew Bryan, Pioneer Negro Baptist Preachers." *Journal of Negro History* 2 (April 1918): 119–127.

130. Dwelle, J. H. *A Brief History of Black Baptists in North America.* Pittsburgh, PA: Pioneer Publishing Company, n.d.

131. Fitts, Leroy. *A History of Black Baptists.* Nashville: Broadman Press, 1985. 368 pp.

132. Freeman, Edward A. *The Epoch of Negro Baptists and the Foreign Mission Board, National Baptist Convention, US.A., Inc.* 1953; Rept. New York: Arno Press, 1980. 301 pp.

133. Jackson, Joseph H. *A Story of Christian Activism: The History of the National Baptist Convention, USA., Inc.* Nashville, TN: Townsend Press, 1980. 790 pp.

134. Jordan, Lewis Garnett. *Negro Baptist History, USA 1750–1930.* Nashville, TN: The Sunday School Publishing Board, 1930. 394 pp.

135. Love, Emanuel King. *History of the First African Baptist Church, From Its Organization, January 20, 1788 to July 1, 1888.* Savannah, GA: The Morning News Printing Co., 1888. 360 pp.

136. Moses, W. H. *The Colored Baptists' Family Tree.* Nashville, TN: Sunday School Publishing Board of the National Baptist Convention of America, 1925.

137. Pegues, Albert W. *Our Baptist Ministers and Schools.* Springfield, MA: Wiley & Co., 1892. 622 pp.

138. Pelt, Owen D., and Ralph Lee Smith. *The Story of the National Baptists.* New York: Vantage Press, 1960. 272 pp.

139. Pius, N. H. *An Outline of Baptist History.* Nashville, TN: National Baptist Publishing Board, 1911. 154 pp.

140. Simms, James Meriles. *The First Colored Baptist Church in North America; Constituted at Savannah, Georgia, Jan. 20, A.D. 1788. With Biographical Sketches of the Pastors.* Philadelphia, PA: J. B. Lippincott Co., 1888. 264 pp.

141. Wagner, Clarence M. *Profiles of Black Georgia Baptists.* Atlanta, GA: Bennett Brothers Printing Co., 1980. 268 pp.

142. Washington, James M. *Frustrated Fellowships: The Black Baptist Quest for Social Power.* Macon, GA: Mercer University Press, 1986. 226 pp.

Congregationalists (United Church of Christ)

143. Jones, Lawrence N. *From Conscience to Consciousness: Blacks and the United Church of Christ.* Philadelphia, PA: United Church of Christ Press, 1976.

144. Stanley, A. Knighton. *The Children Is Crying: Congregationalism Among Black People.* New York: Pilgrim Press, 1979. 172 pp.

145. Taylor, J. Stanley. *A History of the Black Congregational Christian Church of the South.* New York: United Church Press, 1978. 175 pp.

Episcopalians

146. Bennett, Robert. "Black Episcopalians: A History from the Colonial Period to the Present." *The Historical Magazine of the Protestant Episcopal Church* 43, 3 (Sept. 1974): 231–245.

147. Bragg, George Freeman. *Richard Allen and Absalom Jones.* Baltimore, MD: The Church Advocate Press, 1915. 16 pp.

148. Bragg, George Freeman. *The History of the Afro-American Group of the Episcopal Church.* New York: Johnson Reprint Corp, 1968. 319 pp.

149. Burgess, John M., ed. *Black Gospel/White Church.* New York: Seabury Press, 1982. 108 pp.

150. Demby, Edward Thomas. *The Mission of the Episcopal Church Among the Negroes of the Diocese of Arkansas.* Little Rock, AR: N.p., [190–].

151. Hayden, J. Carleton. "Conversion and Control: Dilemma of Episcopalians in Providing for the Religious Instruction of Slaves in Charleston, South Carolina, 1845–1860." *The Historical Magazine of the Protestant Episcopal Church* 40, 2 (June 1971): 143–170.

152. ———. "After the War: The Mission and Growth of the Episcopal Church Among Blacks in the South, 1865–1877." *The Historical Magazine of the Protestant Episcopal Church* 42, 4 (Dec. 1973): 403–427.

153. Jackson, Irene. "Music Among Blacks in the Episcopal Church: Some Preliminary Considerations." In *Lift Every Voice and Sing: A Collection of Afro-American Spirituals and Other Songs.* New York: Church Hymnal Corporation, 1981, pp. xvii–xxvii.

154. *St. Luke's Journal of* Theology (proceedings of Black Theological consultation) 22 (Sept. 1979).

Friends

155. Barbour, Hugh, and J. William Frost. *The Quakers.* New York: Greenwood Press, 1988. 407 pp.

156. Cadbury, Henry J. "Negro Membership in the Society of Friends." *Journal of Negro History* (1936): 151–213.

157. Fletcher, James A., and Carleton Mabree. *A Quaker Speaks from the Black Experience; The Life and Selected Writings of Barrington Dunbar.* New York: New York Yearly Meeting of the Religious Society of Friends, 1979. 67 pp.

158. Spann-Wilson, Dwight. *Quaker and Black: Answering the Call of My Twin Roots.* N.p.: The Author, 1980. 16 pp.

Holiness

159. Cobbins, Otho B. *History of the Church of Christ (Holiness), USA., 1895–1965.* New York: The Author, 1966. 446 pp.

160. Hetrick, Gale. *Laughter Among the Trumpets.* Anderson, IN: Ministerial Assembly of the Church of God of Michigan, 1980. 250 pp.

161. Jones, Charles Edwin. *Black Holiness: Guide to the Study of Black Participation in Wesleyan Perfectionist and Glossolalic Pentecostal Movements.* Metuchen, NJ: The American Theological Library Association and Scarecrow Press, 1987. 388 pp.

162. *Victory in Jesus: The Seven Churches and Mission of the Church of God.* N.p.: 1979. 279 pp.

Independent Catholics/Orthodox

163. Newman, Richard. "The Origins of the African Orthodox Church." In *The Negro Churchman.* Millwood, NY: Kraus Reprint Co., 1977. Introductory essay for reprints of the AOC magazine.

164. Terry-Thompson, A. C. *The History of the African Orthodox Church.* N.p.: 1956. 139 pp.

165. Trela, Jonathan. *A History of the North American Old Roman Catholic Church.* Scranton, PA: The Author, 1979. 124 pp.

Islam

166. As Sayyid Isa Al Haadi Al Mahdi. *The Book of Five Percenters.* Montecello, NY: Original Tents of Kedar, 1991. 627 pp.

167. As Sayyid Isa Al Haadi Al Madhi. *Whatever Happened to the Nubian Islamic Hebrew Mission?* Brooklyn, NY: Original Tents of Kedar, 1989. 315 pp.

168. Austin, Allen D. *African Muslims in Antebellum America: A Sourcebook.* New York: Garland Publishing, 1984. 759 pp.

169. Davis, Charles H., Jr. *Black Nationalism and the Nation of Islam.* 4 parts. Los Angeles: The John Henry and Mary Louisa Dunn Bryant Foundation, 1962. 167 pp.

170. Diara, Agadem I. *Islam and Pan-Africanism.* Detroit, Ml: AGASCA Productions, n.d.

171. Essien-Udom, E. U. *Black Nationalism: A Search for an Identity in America.* Chicago: University of Chicago Press, 1962. Rept.: New York: Dell, 1964. 448 pp.

172. Hakim, Jameela A. *History of the First Muslim Mosque of Pittsburgh, Pennsylvania.* N.p., n.d. 21 pp.

173. Lee, Martha F. *The National of Islam, An American Millennarian Movement.* Lewiston, NY: Edwin Mellen Press, 1988. 163 pp.

174. Lincoln, C. Eric. *The Black Muslims in America.* Boston, MA: Beacon Press, 1961. 276 pp.

175. Lomax, Louis. *When the Word is Given. . . .* Cleveland, OH: World Publishing Company, 1964. 223 pp. Rept.: New York: New American Library, 1964.

176. Marsh, Clifton E. *From Black Muslims to Muslims: The Transition from Separation to Islam, 1930 -1980.* Metuchen, NJ: Scarecrow Press, 1984. 149 pp.

177. Marshall, William A. *Education in the Nation of Islam During the Leadership of Elijah Muhammad, 1935–1975.* Chicago: M.A. thesis, Loyola University of Chicago, 1976. 120 pp.

178. Nu'man, Muhammad Armiya. *What Every American Should Know About Islam & the Muslims.* Jersey City, NJ: New Mind Productions, 1985. 68 pp.

179. Phillips, Abu Ameenah Bilal. *The Ansar Cult in America.* Riyadh, Saudi Arabia: Tawheed Publications, 1988. 198 pp. An attack upon the Ansaaru Allah Community from a Sunni Muslim position.

180. al-Talal, Faissal Fahd, and Khalid Abdullah Tariq al-Mansour. *The Challenges of Spreading Islam in America.* San Francisco, CA: The Authors, 1980. 213 pp.

Judaism

181. Brotz, Howard. *The Black Jews of Harlem. Negro Nationalism and the Dilemmas of Negro Leadership.* New York: Schocken Books, 1964. 144 pp.

182. Ehrman, Albert. "Black Judaism in New York." *Journal of Ecumenical Studies* 8, 1 (Winter 1971): 103–114.

183. ———. "The Commandment Keepers: A Negro Jewish Cult in America Today." *Judaism* 8, 3 (Summer 1959): 266–70.

184. Ford, Arnold Josiah, ed. *The Universal Ethiopian Hymnal.* New York: Beth B'nai Abraham Pub. Co., n.d.

185. Kobre, S. S. "Rabbi Ford." *Reflex* (January 1929): 25–29.

186. Landes, Ruth. "Negro Jews in Harlem." *Jewish Journal of Sociology* 9 (December 1967): 175–189.

187. Gerber, Israel J. *The Heritage Seekers: Black Jews in Search of Identity.* Middle Village, NY: Jonathan David Publishers, 1977. 222 pp.

188. Yehuda, Shaleak Ben. *Black Hebrew Israelites from America to the Promised Land.* New York: Vantage Press, 1975. 357 pp.

Latter-day Saints

189. Bringhurst, Newell G. "Elijah Abel and the Changing Status of Blacks Within Mormonism." *Dialogue* 1 2 (Summer 1979). Rept. in: Lester E. Bush, Jr., and Armand L. Mauss, eds. *Neither White nor Black.* Medvale, UT: Signature Books, 1984. 249 pp.

190. ———. *Saints, Slaves, and Blacks: The Changing Place of Black People Within Mormonism.* Westport, CT: Greenwood Press, 1981. 254 pp.

191. Bush, Lester E., Jr., and Armand L. Mauss, ed. *Neither White nor Black: Mormon Scholars Confront the Race Issue in a Universal Church.* Midvale, UT: Signature Books, 1984. 249 pp. Contains an extensive bibliography on the debate over the status of African Americans in the Church.

192. Cherry, Alan Gerald. *It's You and Me, Lord!* Provo, UT: Trilogy Arts, 1970. 64 pp.

193. Lund, John Lewis. *The Church and the Negro.* Salt Lake City, UT: Paramount Publishers, 1967. 129 pp.

194. Martin, Wynetta Willis. *Black Mormon Tells Her Story: The Truth Sang Louder Than My Position.* Salt Lake City, UT: Hawkes Publishing, Inc., 1972. 94 pp.

195. Oliver, David H. *A Negro on Mormonism.* Salt Lake City, UT: The Author, 1963. 54 pp.

196. Stewart, John J. *Mormonism and the Negro.* Orem, UT: Bookmark, 1960. 54 pp.

197. Taggart, Stephen G. *Mormonism's Negro Policy: Social and Historical Origins.* Salt Lake City, UT: University of Utah Press, 1970. 82 pp.

Lutherans

198. Drewes, Christopher F. *Half a Century of Lutheranism Among Our Colored People.* St. Louis, MO: Concordia Publishing House, 1927. 111 pp.

199. Krebs, Ervin E. *The Lutheran Church and the American Negro.* Columbus, OH: Board of American Missions, American Lutheran Church, 1950.

200. Luecke, Jessie Rayne. *Twenty-Eight Years in Negro Missions.* Fort Dodge, IA: Joselyn Press, 1953. 85 pp.

201. Moore, Robert, Jr. *A Brief History of Black Lutherans in North Carolina.* Salisbury, NC: The Author, 1975. 15 pp.

Mennonites

202. Bechler, Le Roy. *The Black Mennonite Church in North America, 1886–1986.* Scottdale, PA/Kitchener, ON: Herald Press, 1986. 195 pp.

Methodists

203. Adams, E. A., Sr. *Yearbook and Historical Guide to the African Methodist Episcopal Church.* Columbia, SC: Bureau of Research and History, 1955.

204. Alexander, E. Curtis. *Richard Allen. The First Exemplar of African Methodist Education.* New York: ECA Associates, 1985. 172 pp.

205. Allen, Richard. *The Life, Experience, and Gospel Labors of the Rt. Rev. Richard Allen.* 1793; Rept.: Philadelphia, PA: Lee & Yeocum, 1888. 69 pp.

206. Anderson, Vinton R., ed. *A Syllabus for Celebrating the 200th Anniversary of the A.M.E. Church.* Nashville, TN: African Methodist Episcopal Church Sunday School Union, 1986.

207. Baldwin, Lewis V. *Invisible Strands in African Methodism.* Metuchen, NJ: Scarecrow Press, 1983. 288 pp.

208. ———. *The Mark of a Man: Peter Spencer and the African Union Methodist Tradition.* Lanham, MD: University Press of America, 1987. 87 pp.

209. Beck, Carolyn Stickney. *Our Own Vine and Fig Tree: The Persistence of the Mother Bethel Family.* New York: AMS Press, 1989. 327 pp.

210. *Biographical Directory of United Methodist Bishops, Spouses, and Widows.* Office of the Secretary of the Council of Bishops, 1988.

211. Boyd, Ruby Chappelle. *On This Rock . . . The Mother Church of African Methodism.* Philadelphia, PA: Princeton Press, 1982. 139 pp.

212. Bradley, David H., Sr. "Francis Asbury and the Development of African Churches in America." *Methodist History* 10 (October 1971): 3–29.

213. ———. *A History of the A.M.E. Zion Church.* 2 vols. Nashville, TN: Parthenon Press, 1956–1970.

214. Clair, Matthew W., Jr. "Methodism and the Negro." In William K. Anderson, ed. *Methodism.* Nashville, TN: The Methodist Publishing House, 1947, 240–250.

215. ———. *Sociological Origins of the Negro Ministry in the United States.* Denver, CO: Iliff School of Theology Thesis, 1927.

216. Crum, Mason. *The Negro in the Methodist Church.* New York: Board of Missions and Church Extension, The Methodist Church, 1957. 125 pp.

217. Dandridge, Octavia W. *A History of the Women's Missionary Society of the African Methodist Episcopal Church, 1874–1987.* The Author, 1975. 175 pp.

218. Doyle, Ruby Wilkins. *Twenty Daring Decades. An A.M.E. Church History/Textbook for Young Readers.* N.p.: 1987. 240 pp.

219. Foster, J. Curtis, Jr. *The African Methodist Episcopal Church Makes Its Mark in America.* Nashville, TN: African Methodist Episcopal Church Publishing House, 1976.

220. Gaines, Wesley J. *African Methodism in the South.* 1890. 305 pp. Rept.: Chicago: Afro-Am. Press, 1969. 305 pp.

221. George, Carol V. R. *Segregated Sabbaths: Richard Allen and the Emergence of Independent Black Churches 1760–1840.* New York: Oxford University Press, 1973. 205 pp.

222. Graham, J. H. *Black United Methodists: Retrospect and Prospect.* New York: Vantage Press, 1979. 162 pp.

223. Gravely, Will B. "African Methodism and the Rise of Black Denominationalism." In Russell E. Richey and Kenneth E. Rowe, eds. *Rethinking Methodist History: A Bicentennial Historical Consultation.* Nashville, TN:

Kingswood Books, An Imprint of the United Methodist Publishing House, 1985, 111–124.

224. Gregg, Howard D. *History of the African Methodist Episcopal Church: The Black Church in Action.* Nashville, TN: A.M.E. Sunday School Union, 1980. 523 pp.

225. Griffin, Paul R. *Black Theology as the Foundation of Three Methodist Colleges: The Educational Views and Labors of Daniel Payne, Joseph Price, and Isaac Lane.* Lanham, MD: University Press of America, 1984. 129 pp.

226. Handy, James Anderson. *Scraps of African Methodist Episcopal History.* Philadelphia, PA: AME Book Concern, 1901. 421 pp.

227. Harris, Eula W. and Maxie H. Craig. *Christian Methodist Episcopal Church Through the Years.* Revised ed. Jackson, TN: Christian Methodist Episcopal Church Publishing House, 1965. 121 pp.

228. Hood, James Walker. *One Hundred Years of the African Methodist Episcopal Zion Church.* New York: A.M.E. Zion Book Concern, 1895. 625 pp.

229. James, Frederick C. *African Methodism in South Carolina: A Bicentennial Focus.* Tappan, NY: Custombook, Inc., for the Seventh Episcopal District, A.M.E. Church, 1987.

230. Jenifer, John T. *Centennial Retrospect History of the African Methodist Episcopal Church.* Nashville, TN: AME Sunday School Union, 1916. 454 pp.

231. Jenkins, Warren M. *Steps Along the Way.* Columbia, SC: Socamead Press, 1967. 87 pp.

232. Jones, Absalom, and Richard Allen. *A Narrative of the Proceedings of the Black People During the Late Awful Calamity in Philadelphia in 1793, and a Refutation of Some Censures, Thrown Upon Them in Some Late Publications.* Philadelphia, PA: William W. Woodard, 1794. 28 pp.

233. Lakey, Othal Hawthorne. *The History of the CME. Church.* Memphis, TN: The C.M.E. Publishing House, 1985. 683 pp.

234. ———. *The Rise of "Colored Methodism"; a Study of the Background and the Beginnings of the Christian Methodist Episcopal Church.* Dallas, TX: Crescendo Book Publications, 1972. 128 pp.

235. McClain, William B. *Black People in the Methodist Church: Whither Thou Goest?* Cambridge, MA: Schenkman Publishing Co., 1984. 159 pp.

236. Mack, Edgar L. *Our Beginning: Introduction to the African Methodist Episcopal Church.* Nashville, TN: Christian Education Department, n.d.

237. Mathews, Donald G. *Slavery and Methodism: A Chapter in American Morality: 1780–1845.* Princeton, NJ: Princeton University Press, 1965. 329 pp.

238. Mathews, Marcia M. *Richard Allen.* Baltimore, MD: Helicon, 1963. 151 pp.

239. Moore, John Jamison. *History of the A.M.E. Zion Church in America.* York, PA: Teachers' Journal Office, 1884. 392 pp.

240. Payne, Daniel A. *History of the African Methodist Episcopal Church.* Nashville, TN: Publishing House of the A.M.E. Sunday School Union, 1891. 218 pp.

241. Phillips, Charles Henry. *The History of the Colored Methodist Episcopal Church in America.* New York: Arno Press, 1972. 247 pp.

242. Ransom, Reverdy C. *Preface to History of A.M.E. Church.* Nashville, TN: A.M.E. Sunday School Union, 1950. 220 pp.

243. Richardson, Harry V. *Dark Salvation.* Garden City, NY: Doubleday & Company, 1976. 324 pp.

244. Russell, Daniel James. *History of the African Union Methodist Protestant Church.* Philadelphia, PA: Union Star Book and Job Printing and Publishing House, 1920. 66 pp.

245. Shaw, J. Beverly F. *The Negro in the History of Methodism.* Nashville, TN: The Parthenon Press, 1954.

246. Singleton, George A. *The Romance of African Methodism: A Study of the African Methodist Episcopal Church.* New York: Exposition Press, 1952. 251 pp.

247. Smith, Charles Spencer. *A History of the African Methodist Episcopal Church.* Philadelphia, PA: Book Concern of the AME Church, 1922. 570 pp.

248. Walker, Clarence E. *A Rock in a Weary Land: The African Methodist Episcopal Church During the Civil War and Reconstruction.* Baton Rouge, LA: Louisiana State University Press, 1982.

249. Walls, William J. *The African Methodist Episcopal Zion Church.* Charlotte, NC: A.M.E. Zion Publishing House, 1974. 669 pp.

250. Wesley, Charles H. *Richard Allen: Apostle of Freedom.* 1935; 2nd edition, Washington DC: Associated Publishers, 1969. 303 pp.

251. Wright, Richard, Jr. *The Bishops of the African Methodist Episcopal Church.* Nashville, TN: A.M.E. Church Sunday School Union, 1963. 389 pp.

252. ———. *Centennial Encyclopedia of the African Methodist Episcopal Church.* Philadelphia, PA: Book Concern of the A.M.E. Church, 1916. Rev. ed. as: *Encyclopedia of the African Methodist Episcopal Church.* Philadelphia, PA: Book Concern of the A.M.E. Church, 1947. 688 pp.

New Thought Metaphysics

253. Eikerenkoetter, Frederick J. *Rev. Ike's Secrets for Health, Happiness, and Prosperity, for You: A Science of Living Study Guide.* 2nd ed. New York: Science of Living Publications, 1982. 280 pp.

254. Murray, Virgie W. "Rev. Ike." *Sepia* 1 (February 1981): 79–82.

255. "Rev. Ike Preaches About the Profits." *Newsweek* 100 (December 20, 1982): 16.

256. Sanders, Charles L. "The Gospel According to Rev. Ike." *Ebony* 32 (December 1976): 148–154.

Pentecostals/Charismatics

257. Arrington, Juanita R. *A Brief History of the Apostolic Overcoming Holy Church of God, Inc., and Its Founder.* Birmingham, AL: Forniss Printing Company, 1984. 18 pp.

258. Burgess, Stanley M. and Gary B. McGee, eds. *Dictionary of Pentecostal and Charismatic Movements.* Grand Rapids, MI: Regency Reference Library, Zondervan Publishing Co., 1988. 911 pp.

259. Clemons, Ithiel. "The Church of God in Christ." In Vinson Synan. *The 20th Century Pentecostal Explosion.* 1987.

260. Cornelius, Lucille J. *The Pioneer History of the Church of God in Christ.* N.p.: The Author, 1975. 102 pp.

261. Crews, Mickey. *The Church of God: A Social History.* Knoxville, TN: University of Tennessee Press, 1990. 260 pp.

262. DuPree, Sherry Sherrod. *African American Holiness Pentecostal Charismatic: Annotated Bibliography.* New York: Garland Publishing, 1993.

263. DuPree, Sherry Sherrod. *Biographical Dictionary of African-American Holiness-Pentecostals, 1880–1990.* Washington, DC: Middle Atlantic Regional Press, 1989. 386 pp.

264. Fisher, H. L. *The History of the United Holy Church of America.* N.p.: The Author, n.d. 55 pp.

265. Golder, Morris E. *The Bishops of the Pentecostal Assemblies of the World, Inc.* Indianapolis, IN: The Author, 1980. 69 pp. An unpublished updated addendum, circa 1988.

266. ———. *History of the Pentecostal Assemblies of the World.* Indianapolis, IN: The Author, 1973. 194 pp.

267. Gregory, Chester W. *The History of the United Holy Church of America, Inc., 1886–1986.* Baltimore, MD: Gateway Press, 1986. 275 pp.

268. Hollenweger, Walter J. *Black Pentecostal Concept: Interpretations and Variations.* Geneva, Switz.: World Council of Churches, 1970. 70 pp.

269. *An Introduction to the Church of God in Christ: History, Theology, and Structure.* N.p.: compiled by the Second Jurisdiction of Arkansas, Church of God in Christ., n.d. 66 pp.

270. Jones, Charles Edwin. *Black Holiness: A Guide to the Study of Black Participation in Wesleyan Perfectionist and Glossolalic Pentecostal Movements.* Metuchen, NJ: American Theological Library Association/Scarecrow Press, 1987. 388 pp.

271. Kelley, Frances Burnett, and German R. Ross. *Here Am I; Send Me: the Dramatic Story of Presiding Bishop J. 0. Patterson, Challenging and Bold Leader of the Church of God in Christ.* Memphis, TN: 1970.

272. Lewis, Helen M., and Meharry H. Lewis, eds. *Seventy-Fifth Anniversary Yearbook of the Church of the Living God, the Pillar and Ground of Truth, Inc., 1903–1978.* Nashville, TN: General Headquarters, Church of the Living God, the Pillar and Ground of Truth, 1978.

273. MacRobert, Iain. *The Black Roots and White Racism of Early Pentecostalism in the USA.* New York: St. Martin's Press, 1988.

274. Mason, Elise W. *From the Beginning of Bishop C. H. Mason and the Early Pioneers of the Church of God in Christ.* Memphis, TN: 1991.

275. Mason, Mary Esther. *The History and Life Work of Elder C. H. Mason, Chief Apostle and His Co-Laborers.* Memphis, TN: n.p., n.d. 93 pp.

276. Patterson, J. O., German Ross, and Julia Mason Atkins. *History and Formative Years of the Church of God in Christ with Excerpts from the Life and Works of Its Founder, Bishop C. H. Mason.* Memphis, TN: Church of God in Christ Publishing House, 1969. 143 pp.

277. Richardson, James C., Jr. *With Water and Spirit: A History of Black Apostolic Denominations in the U.S.* Martinsville, VA: The Author, 1980. 151 pp.

278. Simmons, Dovie Marie. *Down Behind the Sun: The Story of Arenia Conelia Mallory.* Lexington, TN: 1983.

279. Synan, Vinson. *The Holiness-Pentecostal Movement in the United States.* Grand Rapids, MI: William B. Eerdmans Publishing Company, 1971. 248 pp.

280. Turner, William Clair. *The United Holy Church of America: a Study in Black Holiness-Pentecostalism.* Durham, NC: Ph.D. dissertation, Duke University, 1984.

Presbyterians/Reformed

281. Barber, Jesse Belmont. *Climbing Jacob's Ladder: Story of the Work of the Presbyterian Church U.S.A. Among the Negroes.* New York: Board of National Missions, Presbyterian Church, U.S.A., 1952. 103 pp.

282. Cave, Clarence, ed. *Black Presbyterians United: Report to the Session.* New York: Presbyterian Church, U.S.A., 1977.

283. Erskine, Norl L. *Black People and the Reformed Church in America.* New York: Reformed Church Press, 1978.

284. Franklin, W. H. *The Early History of the Presbyterian Church in the U.S.A., Among the Negroes.* Pittsburgh, PA: Board of Missions for Freedmen, n.d.

285. Murray, Andrew E. *Presbyterians and the Negro—A History.* Philadelphia, PA: Presbyterian Historical Society, 1966. 270 pp.

286. Parker, Inez Moore. *The Rise and Decline of the Program of Education for Black Presbyterians of the United Presbyterian Church U.S.A., 1865–1970.* San Antonio, TX: Texas University Press, 1977. 319 pp.

287. Swift, David. "Black Presbyterian Attacks on Racism: Samuel Cornish, Theodore Wright, and Their Contemporaries." *Journal of Presbyterian History* 51 (Winter 1973): 433–470.

288. Wilmore, Gayraud S. *Black and Presbyterian: The Heritage and the Hope.* Philadelphia, PA: Geneva Press, 1983. 142 pp.

289. Wilson, Frank T., ed. "Living Witnesses: Black Presbyterians in Ministry, Part I." *Journal of Presbyterian History* 51 (Winter 1973): 347–391.

290. Wilson, Frank T., ed. "Living Witnesses: Black Presbyterians in Ministry, Part II." *Journal of Presbyterian History* 53 (Fall 1975): 187–222.

291. Wilson, Frank T., ed. "Living Witnesses: Black Presbyterians in Ministry, Part III." *Journal of Presbyterian History* 55 (Summer 1977): 180–238.

Roman Catholic

292. Davis, Cyprian. *The History of Black Catholicism the United States.* New York: Crossroads, 1990. 347 pp.

293. Foley, Albert Sidney. *God's Men of Color: The Colored Catholic Priests of the United States, 1854–1954.* New York: Farrar, Strauss, 1955. 322 pp. Rept.: New York: Arno Press, 1969. 322 pp.

294. Gillard, John T. *The Catholic Church and the American Negro.* Baltimore, MD: St. Joseph's Society Press, 1929. 324 pp.

295. Hart, Mary Francis Borgia. *Violets in the King's Garden: A History of the Sisters of the Holy Family of New Orleans.* New Orleans, LA: The Sisters of the Holy Family, 1976. 137 pp.

296. Hemesath, Caroline. *Our Black Shepherds.* Washington, DC: Josephite Pastoral Center, 1987.

297. Nickels, Marilyn. *Black Catholic Protest and the Federated Colored Catholics, 1917–1933: Three Perspectives on Racial Justice.* New York: Garland Publishing, 1988. 325 pp.

298. Ochs, Stephen. *Desegregating the Altar. The Josephites and the Struggle for Black Priests, 1871–1960.* Baton Rouge, LA: Louisiana State University Press, 1990.

299. Scally, Mary Anthony. *Negro Catholic Writers, 1900–1943.* Grosse Point, MI: Walter Romig, Publisher, 1945. 152 pp.

300. Smithson, Sandra O. *To Be a Bridge: A Commentary on Black/White Catholicism in America.* Nashville, TN: Winston-Derek Publishers, 1984. 128 pp.

301. Spaulding, David. "The Negro Catholic Congresses, 1889–1894." *Catholic Historical Review* 55 (1969): 337–57.

302. *This Far by Faith: Worship and Its African Roots.* Washington, DC: National Office for Black Catholics/Liturgical Conference, 1976. 104 pp.

Unitarian-Universalists

303. Morrison-Reed, Mark D. *Black Pioneers in a White Denomination.* Boston, MA: Beacon Press, 1984. 217 pp.

A Directory
of
African American Churches
and
Religious Organizations

[*Editors' note:* Included below are the current addresses and telephone numbers of the national headquarters of those churches and organizations discussed in the *Encyclopedia*. For a more detailed listings of names and addresses within the African American religious community, the reader is referred to the latest edition of the Directory of African American Religious Bodies, edited by Wardell J. Payne, published by the Howard University Press in Washington, D C.]

African-American Catholic Congregation
Pro-Cathedral of Our Lady of Africa
P.O. Box 91700
Washington, DC 20090-1700
Tel: (202) 371-0800
Fax: (202) 371-0808

African American Unitarian Universalist Ministry
25 Beacon Street
Boston, MA 02108
Tel: (617) 742-2100

Africa Islamic Mission
1390 Bedford Avenue
Brooklyn, NY 11216
Tel: (718) 638-4588
Fax: (718) 789-0530

African Methodist Episcopal Church
500 8th Avenue, S.
Nashville, TN 37203
Tel: (615) 242-6814 or 242-1420

African Methodist Episcopal Zion Church
P.O. Box 23843
Charlotte, NC 28232
Tel: (704) 332-3851

African Orthodox Church
112 West 129th Street
New York, NY 10027

African Orthodox Church of the West
St. Augustine's African Orthodox Church
5831 Indiana Street
Chicago, IL 60637
Tel: (312) 324-1096

African Theological Archministry
Oyotunji African Yoruba Village
P.O. Box 51
Sheldon, SC 29941
Tel: (803) 846-8900 or 846-9939

African Union First Colored Methodist Protestant Church
602 Spruce Street
Wilmington, DE 19801

African Universal Church, Inc.
2336 SW 48th Av.
West Hollywood, FL 33023
Tel: (305) 921-5392

The Afro-American Social Research Association
Box 2150
Jacksonville, FL 32203

Ahmadiyya Movement in Islam
2141 Leroy Place, NW
Washington, DC 20008
Tel: (202) 232-3737

Alpha and Omega Pentecostal Church of God of America, Inc.
1950 West North Avenue
Baltimore, MD 21216
Tel: (301) 366-2253

American Association for Ethiopian Jews
1836 Jefferson Place, NW
Washington, DC 20036
Tel (202) 223-6838

American Baptist Black Caucus— American Baptist Churches in the U.S.A.
34 W. Pleasant Street
Springfield, OH 45506
Tel: (513) 323-3504

Ansaaru Allah Community
716 Bushwick Avenue
Brooklyn, NY 11221
Tel: (718) 443-4414

Antioch Association of Metaphysical Science
Current address unavailable for this edition

Apostle Church of Christ in God
Current address unavailable for this edition

Apostolic Assemblies of Christ, Inc.
Current address unavailable for this edition

Apostolic Church of Christ, Inc.
2044 Stadium Dr.
Winston-Salem, NC 27107
Tel: (919) 788-2539

Apostolic Faith Church of God and True Holiness
c/o Bishop O. Key
825 Gregg Road
Jefferson, OH 44047

Apostolic Faith Church of God Live On
2300 Trenton Street
Hopewell, VA 23860
Tel: (804) 458-5688

Apostolic Faith Churches Giving Grace
c/o Bishop Geanie Perry
Rt. 3, Box 111
Warrenton, NC 27589
Tel: (919) 257-2120

Apostolic Faith Churches of a Living God
3416 Carver Street
Columbia, SC 29203

Apostolic Faith Churches of God, Inc.
700 Charles Street
Franklin, VA 23851

Apostolic Faith Mission Church of God
3344 Pearl Avenue N.
Birmingham, AL 36101
or
Bishop Houston Ward
P.O. Box 551
Cantonment, FL 32522
Tel: (904) 587-2332

Apostolic Holiness Church of America
P.O. Box 353
Fremont, NC 27830
Tel: (919) 242-6208

Apostolic Overcoming Holy Church of God, Inc.
Bishop Jasper C. Roby
1120 N. 24th Street
Birmingham, AL 35234
Tel: (205) 324-2202

Assemblies of God, General Council of the
1445 Boonville Avenue
Springfield, MO 65802
Tel: (417) 862-2781

Associated Churches of Christ (Holiness)
1302 E. Adams Blvd.
Los Angeles, CA 90011

Association of Black Directors of Christian Education
1439 West 103rd Street
Chicago, IL 60643
Tel: (312) 275-1430

Astrological, Metaphysical, Occult, Revelatory, Enlightenment (AMORE) Church
Current address unavailable for this edition

Ausar Auset Society
c/o Oracle of Truth
P.O. Box 281
Bronx, NY 10462

Bible Way Church of Our Lord Jesus Christ World Wide Inc.
1100 New Jersey Avenue NW
Washington, DC 20001
Tel: (202) 789-0700

Bible Way Pentecostal Apostolic Church
Current address unavailable for this edition

Black Affairs Council
25 Beacon Street
Boston, MA 02108

Black and White Action
25 Beacon Street
Boston, MA 02108

Black Concerns Working Group
25 Beacon Street
Boston, MA 02108

Black Council—Reformed Church in America
475 Riverside Drive
New York, NY 10115
Tel: (212) 870-2538

Black Methodists for Church Renewal, Inc.
601 W. Riverview Ave., Suite 325
Dayton, OH 45406
Tel: (513) 227-9460

Black Primitive Baptists
No central headquarters
For information contact:
Primitive Baptist Library
Rte. 2
Elon College, NC 27244

Catholic Negro-American Mission Board
Current address unavailable for this edition

Center of Being
Current address unavailable for this edition

Christ Holy Sanctified Church of America
5204 Willie Street
Fort Worth, TX 76105

Christian Church (Disciples of Christ)
222 S. Downey Avenue
P.O. Box 1986
Indianapolis, IN 46206
Tel: (317) 353-1491

Christian Methodist Episcopal Church
531 S. Parkway East
Memphis, TN 38106
Tel: (901) 947-3135

Christ's Sanctified Holy Church (Louisiana)
1310 S. Cutting Avenue at E. Spencer Street
P.O. Box 513
Jennings, LA 70546

**Church of Christ Holiness unto the
Lord**
1650 Smart Street
P.O. Box 1642
Savannah, GA 31401
Tel: (912) 857-3797

Church of Christ (Holiness), U.S.A.
329 E. Monument Street
Jackson, MS 39202
Tel: (601) 353-4033

**Church of God (Anderson,
Indiana)**
c/o Exec. Sec. Edward L. Foggs
P.O. Box 2420
Anderson, IN 46018
Tel: (317) 642-0256

Church of God (Apostolic)
1031 N. Highland Avenue
Winston-Salem, NC 27101
Tel: (919) 722-2285

Church of God (Black Jews)
Current address unavailable for this
edition

**Church of God (Cleveland,
Tennessee)**
P.O. Box 2430
Cleveland, TN 37320
Tel: (615) 472-3361

Church of God (Sanctified Church)
1044 Jefferson Street
Nashville, TN 37208
Tel: (615) 255-5579

**Church of God (Which He
Purchased with His Own Blood)**
1628 NE 50th Street
Oklahoma City, OK 73111
Tel: (405) 427-8264

Church of God in Christ
272 S. Main Street
P.O. Box 320
Memphis, TN 38103
Tel: (901) 578-3838

**Church of God in Christ,
Congregational**
918 Bond Avenue
East St. Louis, IL 62201
Tel: (618) 271-7780

**Church of God in Christ,
International**
c/o Rt. Rev. Carl E. Williams
584 Myrtle Avenue
Brooklyn, NY 11025
Tel: (718) 857-3444

**Church of Jesus Christ of Latter-Day
Saints**
50 E. North Temple
Salt Lake City, UT 84150

**Church of Our Lord Jesus Christ of
the Apostolic Faith, Inc.**
2081 Adam Clayton Powell Blvd.
New York, NY 10027
Tel: (212) 866-1700

Church of the Brethren
1451 Dundee Avenue
Elgin, IL 60120
Tel: (312) 742-5100

**Church of the Living God (Christian
Workers for Fellowship)**
Bishop F. C. Scott
801 NE 17th Street
Oklahoma City, OK 73105
Tel: (405) 427-3701

**Church of the Living God the Pillar
and Ground of the Truth**
4520 Hydes Ferry Pike
Box 5735
Nashville, TN 37208
Tel: (615) 255-0401

**Church of the Living God the Pillar
and Ground of the Truth
(General Assembly)**
Current address unavailable for this
edition

**Church of the Living God the Pillar
and Ground of the Truth of
Muskogee, Oklahoma**
Current address unavailable for this
edition

**Church of the Lord Jesus Christ of
the Apostolic Faith**
22nd & Bainbridge Sts.
Philadelphia, PA 19146
Tel: (215) 735-8982

Church of the Nazarene
6401 The Paseo
Kansas City, MO 64131
Tel: (816) 333-7000

**Church of Universal Triumph— the
Dominion of God**
c/o Rev. James Shaffer
8317 LaSalle Blvd.
Detroit, MI 48206

Churches of God, Holiness
170 Ashby Street N.W.
Atlanta, GA 30314

**Commandment Keepers
Congregation of the Living God**
Rabbi Mary M. Dore
1 E. 123rd Street
New York, NY 10035

**Commission for Catholic Missions
among the Colored People and
the Indians**
clo His Eminence John J. O'Connor
2021 H St., N.W.
Washington, DC 20006

Commission for Racial Justice
Executive Director:
Rev. Dr. Benjamin F. Chavis
700 Prospect Avenue
Cleveland, OH 44120
Tel: (216) 241-5400

Congress of National Black Churches
600 New Hampshire Ave., NW
Suite 650
Washington, DC 20037
Tel: (202) 333-3060

**Cumberland Presbyterian Church of
America**
226 Church Street, NW
Huntsville, AL 35801
Tel: (205) 536-7481

Deliverance Evangelistic Centers
Ms. Denise Holmes
621 Clinton Avenue
Newark, NJ 07108
Tel: (201) 824-7300

Deliverance Evangelistic Church
4732 N. Broad Street
Philadelphia, PA 19141
Tel: (215) 456-2151

Divine Word, Society of the
North American Province
1985 Waukegan Rd.
Teckny, IL 60082

**Eastern Orthodox Catholic Church
in America**
Most Rev. Dismas Markle
321 S. Magnolia Avenue
Sanford, FL 32771

**Emmanuel Tabernacle Baptist
Church Apostolic Faith**
329 North Garfield Avenue
Columbus, OH 43203
Tel: (614) 253-2535

**Episcopal Commission for Black
Ministries—Episcopal Church**
815 Second Avenue
New York, NY 10017
Tel: (212) 867-8400

**Ethiopian Orthodox Church in the
United States of America**
c/o His Eminence Abuna Yeshaq,
Archbishop
140-142 W. 176th Street
Bronx, NY 10451
Tel: (212) 299-2741
or
International Hq:
c/o His Holiness Abuna Tekle
Haimanot
Box 1283
Addis Ababa, Ethiopia

Ethiopian Orthodox Coptic Church
Diocese of North and South America
1255 Bedford Avenue
Brooklyn, NY 11216

Evangel Temple *See:* International
Evangelical Church and Missionary
Association

Faith Bible Church, Inc.
1350 Maryland Av. NE
Washington, DC 20002
Tel: (202) 398-4400

**Faith Tabernacle Council of
Churches, International**
7015 NE 23rd Avenue
Portland, OR 97211
Tel: (503) 282-8071

**Fire-Baptized Holiness Church of
God of the Americas**
556 Houston Street
Atlanta, GA 30312

**Franciscan Handmaids of the Most
Pure Heart of Mary**
15 W. 124th Street
New York, NY 10027

**Free Christian Zion Church of
Christ**
clo Chief Pastor Willie Benson
1315 Hutchinson
Nashville, AR 71852

**Free Gospel Church of The Apostle's
Doctrine**
Free Gospel Church of Christ
4702 Marlboro Pike
Coral Hills, MD 20743
Tel: (301) 420-9300

**Free Methodist Church of North
America**
901 College
Winona Lake, IN 46590
(219) 267-7656

**Glorious Church of God in Christ
Apostolic Faith**
Current address unavailable for this
edition

**God's House of Prayer for All
Nations, Inc.**
1801 NE Madison Street
Peoria, IL 61603

Gospel Spreading Church
1522 R Street, NW
Washington, DC 20009
Tel: (202) 387-8233

**Hanafi Madh-Hab Center, Islam
Faith**
7700 16th Street
Washington, DC 10012

Highway Christian Church of Christ
432 W Street NW
Washington, DC 20001
Tel: (202) 234-3940

Holy African Church *See:* African
Orthodox Church

**Holy Family, Congregation of the
Sisters of**
Supr. Gen.: Mother M. Rose de Lima
Hazeur, S.S.F.
6901 Chef Menteur Hwy.
New Orleans, LA 70126

**House of God, Holy Church of the
Living God, The Pillar and
Ground of Truth, the House of
Prayer for All People**
548 Georgetown Street
Lexington, KY 50608

**House of God Which is the Church of
the Living God, The Pillar and
Ground of Truth, Inc.**
Bishop Jesse J. White
7070 Whitney Street
Hartford, CT 06105

**House of God Which is the Church of
the Living God, The Pillar and
Ground of Truth without
Controversy (Keith Dominion)**
Chief Overseer: Bishop J. W. Jenkins
P.O. Box 9113
Montgomery, AL 36108

House of Judah
Current address unavailable for this
edition

**Independent African American
Catholic Rite**
Church of St. Martin de Porres
P.O. Box 41449
Washington, DC 20018
Tel: (202) 544-5234

**International Evangelical Church
(and Missionary Association)**
c/o Evangel Temple
610 Rhode Island Av. NE
Washington, DC 20002
Tel: (202) 635-8000

**Interreligious Foundation for
Community Organization**
402 W. 145th Street
New York, NY 10031
Tel: (212) 926-5757

Knights of Peter Claver
1825 Orleans Ave.
New Orleans, LA 70116

Kodesh Church of Emmanuel
Dr. Kenneth O. Barber
932 Logan Road
Bethel Park, PA 15102
Tel: (412) 833-1351

Latter House of the Lord for All People and the Church of the Mountain Apostolic Faith
Current address unavailable for this edition

Lott Carey Baptist Foreign Mission Convention
1501 11th Street, NW
Washington, DC 20001
Tel: (202) 667-8493

Mennonite Church
421 S. Second St., Ste. 600
Elkhart, IN 46516
Tel: (219) 294-7131

Metropolitan Spiritual Churches of Christ, Inc.
4315 S. Wabash Avenue
Chicago, IL 60653
Tel: (312) 373-7700

Ministers for Racial and Social Justice—United Church of Christ, Inc.
7223 16th Street, NW
Washington, DC 20012

Moorish Science Temple Divine and National Movement of North America, Inc.
P.O. Box 7213
Baltimore, MD 21218
Tel: (301) 366-3591

Moorish Science Temple of America
762 W. Baltimore St.
Baltimore, MD 21201

Moravian Church
Northern Province
1021 Center St.
Bethlehem, PA 18016
Tel: (215) 867-7566

Mount Calvary Holy Church of America
c/o Bishop Harold Williams
1214 Chowan Street
Durham, NC 27713

Mount Calvary Pentecostal Faith Church, Inc.
1204 Eutaw Place
Baltimore, MD 21217
Tel: (301) 728-9681

Mount Hebron Apostolic Temple of Our Lord Jesus of the Apostolic Faith
Mount Hebron Apostolic Temple
27 Vineyard Avenue
Yonkers, NY 10703
Tel: (914) 963-5372

Mount Zion Spiritual Temple
Current address unavailable for this edition

Nation of Ishmael
2696 Ben Hill Rd.
East Point, GA 30344
Tel: (404) 349-1153

The Nation of Islam (The Caliph)
Current address unavailable for this edition

The Nation of Islam (Farrakhan)
734 W. 79th Street
Chicago, IL 60620
Tel: (312) 994-5775

Nation of Islam (John Muhammad)
c/o Muhammad Temple #1
16187 Hamilton Ave
Highland Park, MI 48203

Nation of Islam (Silas Muhammad)
P. O. Box 50559
Atlanta, GA 30302

Nation of the Five Percent
Current address unavailable for this edition

Nation of Yahweh (Hebrew Israelites)
c/o Temple of Love
2766 NW 62nd Street
Miami, FL 33147
Tel: (718) 633-4861

National Association of Black Catholic Administrators
50 N. Park Ave.
Rockville Center, NY 11570
Tel: (516) 678-5800, x615 or 616

National Baptist Convention of America
1450 Pierre Avenue
Shreveport, LA 71103
Tel: (318) 221-2629

National Baptist Convention, U.S.A., Inc.
915 Spain Street
Baton Rouge, LA 70802
Tel: (504) 383-5401

National Baptist Evangelical Life and Soul Saving Assembly of the U.S.A.
441-61 Monroe Avenue
Detroit, MI 48226

National Black Catholic Clergy Caucus
1419 V Street, Ste. 400
Washington, DC 20009
Tel: (202) 328-0718

National Black Catholic Congress
320 Cathedral Street
Baltimore, MD 21201
Tel: (301) 547-5330

National Black Catholic Seminarian Association
St. Joseph's Seminary
1200 Varnum Street, NE
Washington, DC 20017
Tel: (202) 526-4231

National Black Evangelical Association
5736 North Albina Ave.
Portland, OR 97217
Tel: (503) 289-0143

National Black Lay Catholic Caucus
3015 4th Street, NE
Washington, DC 20017
Tel: (202) 635-1778

National Black Presbyterian Caucus
2923 Hawthorne Avenue
Richmond, VA 23222
Tel: (804) 321-3433

National Black Sisters' Conference
1001 Lawrence Street, NE, Ste. 102
Washington, DC 20017
Tel: (202) 529-9250

881

National Colored Spiritualist Association of Churches
Current address unavailable for this edition

National Conference of Black Churchmen (NCBC)
c/o Interdenominational Theol. Center
671 Beckwith Street, SW
Atlanta, GA 30314

National Missionary Baptist Convention of America
719 Crosby Street
San Diego, CA 92113
Tel: (619) 233-6487

National Office for Black Catholics
3025 4th Street, NE
Washington, DC 20017
Tel: (202) 635-1778

National Primitive Baptist Convention of the U.S.A.
P.O. Box 2355
Tallahassee, FL 32301
Tel: (904) 222-5218 or 5549

New Bethel Church of God in Christ (Pentecostal)
Current address unavailable for this edition

New England Baptist Missionary Convention
c/o Berean Baptist Church
924 Madison Street, NW
Washington, DC 20011

New Testament Church of God
P.O. Box 611
Mountain Home, AR 72653

North American Old Roman Catholic Church
c/o Most Rev. Edward J. Ford
200 Emerson Street So.
Boston, MA 02127
Tel: (617) 268-0511

Oblate Sisters of Providence
701 Gun Rd.
Baltimore, MD 21227

Operation PUSH
930 East 50th Street
Chicago, IL 60615
Tel: (312) 373-3366

Organization of Black Episcopal Seminarians
The Episcopal Church Center
815 Second Avenue
New York, NY 10017
Tel: (800) 334-7626

Original Church of God (Or Sanctified Church)
2214 E. 17th Street
Chattanooga, TN 37404

Original Glorious Church of God in Christ Apostolic Faith
Current address unavailable for this edition

Original Hebrew Israelite Nation
Communicators Press
P.O. Box 19504
Chicago, IL 60649

Original United Holy Church International
c/o Bishop H. W. Field
P.O. Box 263
Durham, NC 27702
Tel: (919) 682-3498

Orthodox Catholic Church in America
c/o Most Rev. Michael Edward Verra
238 Mott Street
New York, NY 10012
Tel: (212) 925-5238

Pan African Orthodox Christian Church
13535 Livernois
Detroit, MI 48238
Tel: (313) 491-0777

Peace Mission Movement
The Woodmont Estate
1622 Spring Mill Rd.
Gladwyne, PA 19035

Pentecostal Assemblies of the World
3939 Meadows Dr.
Indianapolis, IN 46205
Tel: (317) 547-9541

Pentecostal Church of God
9244 Delmar
Detroit, MI 48211
Tel: (313) 865-0510

Pentecostal Churches of Apostolic Faith
Current address unavailable for this edition

Presbyterian Church (U.S.A.)
100 Witherspoon Street
Louisville, KY 40202
Tel: (502) 569-5000

Progressive National Baptist Convention of America
601 50th Street NE
Washington, DC 20019
Tel: (202) 396-0558

Pure Holiness Church of God
c/o Saint Timothy's Pure Holiness Church
408 McDonough Blvd. SE
Atlanta, GA 30315
Tel: (404) 627-3791

Rastafarians
Current address unavailable for this edition

Redeemed Assembly of Jesus Christ Apostolic
c/o Bishop Douglas Williams
734 1st St., SW
Washington, DC 20024
Tel: (202) 646-0010

Reformed Church in America
475 Riverside Dr., Rm. 1811
New York, NY 10115
Tel: (212) 870-2841

Reformed Episcopal Church
4225 Chestnut Street
Philadelphia, PA 19104

Reformed Methodist Union Episcopal Church
Rt. Rev. Leroy Gethers
1136 Brody Avenue
Charleston, SC 29407
Tel: (803) 776-3534

Reformed Zion Union Apostolic Church
c/o Deacon James C. Feggins
416 South Hill Avenue
South Hill, VA 23970
Tel: (804) 447-3374

Reorganized Church of Latter Day Saints
The Auditorium
P.O. Box 1059
Independence, MO 64051

Roman Catholic Church
Apostolic Pro Nuncio
3339 Massachusetts Avenue NW
Washington, DC 20008
Tel: (202) 333-7121
See also: Secretariat for Black
   Catholics

Sacred Heart Catholic Church
Current address unavailable for this
   edition

St. Joseph's Society of the Sacred Heart
1130 N. Calvert St.
Baltimore, MD 21202

Salvation and Deliverance Church, Inc.
37 West 116th Street
New York, NY 10026
Tel: (212) 722-5488

Salvation Army
799 Bloomfield Ave.
Verona, NJ 07044
Tel: (201) 239-0606

Second Cumberland Presbyterian Church in U.S. *See:* Cumberland Presbyterian Church of America

Secretariat for Black Catholics
3211 4th Street, NE
Washington, DC 20017
Tel: (212) 541-3177

Seventh-day Adventist Church
6840 Eastern Av. NW
Washington, DC 20012
Tel: (202) 722-6000

Shiloh Apostolic Temple
1516 W. Master St.
Philadelphia, PA 19121
Tel: (215) 763-7335

Shrine of the Black Madonna
See: Pan African Orthodox
   Christian Church

Sisters of the Blessed Sacrament for Indians and Colored People
St. Elizabeth Convent
Box 8502
1663 Bristol Pike
Bensalem, PA 19020-5796

Southern Baptist Convention
901 Commerce
Nashville, TN 37203
Tel: (615) 244-2355

Southern Christian Leadership Conference
334 Auburn Avenue, NW
Atlanta, GA 30312
Tel: (404) 522-1420

Triumph the Church and the Kingdom of God in Christ (International)
c/o Chief Bishop Rt. Rev. A. J. Scott
1323 N. 36th St.
Savannah, GA 31404
Tel: (912) 236-2877

True Grace Memorial House of Prayer
911 6th Street, NW
Washington, DC 20001

True Vine Pentecostal Holiness Church
New Bethel Apostolic Church
931 Bethel Lane
Martinsville, VA 24112
Tel: (703) 632-7290

Unification Association of Christian Sabbath Keepers
255 W. 131st Street
New York, NY 10027
Tel: (212) 926-8694

Unification Church
4 W. 43rd Street
New York, NY 10036
Tel: (212) 768-7022

Union American Methodist Episcopal Church, Inc.
772-74 Pine Street
Camden, NJ 08103
Tel: (609) 962-4530 or 963-0434

Union of Black Episcopalians
Washington Cathedral
Mt. Saint Alban
Washington, DC 20016

United American Free Will Baptist Church
1011 University Street
P.O. Box 3303
Kinston, NC 28501
Tel: (919) 527-0120

United Black Christians—United Church of Christ
332 South Michigan, Ste. 1242
Chicago, IL 60604
Tel: (312) 786-9205

United Black Church Appeal
c/o Christ Church
860 Forrest Avenue
Bronx, NY 10456
Tel: (212) 665-6688

United Church and Science of Living Institute
Rev. Frederick Eikerenkotter II
Box 1000
Boston, MA 02103

United Church of Christ
105 Madison Avenue
New York, NY 10016
Tel: (212) 683-5656

United Church of Jesus Christ (Apostolic)
c/o Presiding Bishop Monroe Saunders
5150 Baltimore National Pike
Baltimore, MD 21229
Tel: (301) 945-0064 or 728-9679

United Fellowship Convention of the Original Azusa Street Mission
825 Gregg Rd.
Jefferson, OH 44047

United Hebrew Congregation
Current address unavailable for this
   edition

United Holy Church of America
312 Umstead Street
Durham, NC 27707
Tel: (919) 682-1819

United House of Prayer for All People, Church on the Rock of the Apostolic Church
1721 1/2 7th St. NW
Washington, DC 20001
Tel: (202) 289-1916

United Methodist Church
601 W. Riverview Avenue
Dayton, OH 45406
Tel: (513) 227-9460

United Pentecostal Council of the Assemblies of God
211 Columbia Street
P.O. Box 308
Cambridge, MA 02139
Tel: (617) 648-0808

United Way of the Cross Churches of Christ of the Apostolic Faith
c/o Bethel United Way of the Cross
Mount Cross Road
Danville, VA 24521

United Wesleyan Methodist Church of America
Rev. David S. Bruno
270 W. 126th Street
New York, NY 10027

Universal Christian Spiritual Faith and Churches for All Nations
Current address unavailable for this edition

Universal Church of Christ
19-23 Park Street
P.O. Box 146
Orange, NJ 07050
Tel: (201) 673-4424

Universal Church, the Mystical Body of Christ
Current address unavailable for this edition

Universal Foundation for Better Living
11901 Ashland Avenue
Chicago, IL 60643
Tel: (312) 568-2282

Universal Hagar's Spiritual Church
Current address unavailable for this edition

Vedantic Center
c/o Swami Turiyasangitananda
3528 N. Triunfo Canyon Rd.
Agoura, CA 91301
Tel: (818) 706-9478

Way of the Cross Church of Christ
332 4th St., N.E.
Washington, DC 20003
Tel: (202) 543-0500

Wesleyan Church
c/o Gen. Sec. Dr. Ronald R. Brannon
Box 50434
Indianapolis, IN 46250-0434
Tel: (317) 674-0444

Yahweh's Temple
Box 652
Cleveland, TN 37311

Biographical Cross-Index
by
Religious Tradition

ADVENTISTS

William Ellis Foy
Charles M. Kinney

AFRICAN METHODIST EPISCOPAL CHURCH

Bishops

John Hurst Adams
Alexander J. Allen
Richard Allen
Vinton Randolph Anderson
Josiah Haynes Armstrong
Benjamin William Arnett, Jr.
George Wilbur Baber
William Franklin Ball, Sr.
Harold Irvin Bearden
William Wesley Beckett
Henry Allen Belin, Jr.
George Wayman Blakely
Isaiah Hamilton Bonner
John Douglas Bright, Sr.
Hamel Hartford Brookins
William Samson Brooks
John M. Brown
Morris Brown
Harrison James Bryant
John Richard Bryant
Vernon Randolph Byrd
Richard Harvey Cain
Jabez Pitt Campbell
Archibald James Carey, Sr.
Richard Allen Chappelle, Sr.
William David Chappelle
John Henry Clayborn
Daniel Coker
Charles Cecil Coleman
George Napoleon Collins
James Mayer Conner
Levi Jenkins Coppin
Philip Robert Cousin

Frank Curtis Cummings
George Edward Curry
Monroe Hortensius Davis
William Benjamin Derrick
William Fisher Dickerson
Richard Randolph Disney
Samuel Chukukanne Ekemam
James Crawford Embry
Joseph S. Flipper
William Alfred Fountain
Abraham Lincoln Gaines
Wesley John Gaines
George Galbreath
Carey Abraham Gibbs
Joseph Gomez
Francis Herman Gow
Abraham Grant
Robert Alexander Grant
Sherman Lawrence Greene, Sr.
John Andrew Gregg
James Anderson Handy
Eugene Clifford Hatcher
William Henry Heard
Lawrence Henry Hemingway
Ernest Lawrence Hickman
Samuel Richard Higgins
Richard Allen Hildebrand
William Alexander Hilliard
James Clinton Hoggard, Sr.
Jehu Holliday
Edward J. Howard
John Ellsworth Hunter
John Hurst
Frederick Miller Jacobs
Frederick Calhoun James
Henry Theodore Johnson
John Albert Johnson
William Decker Johnson
Joshua H. Jones, Sr.
Frederick Douglass Jordan
Harvey Ben Kinchlow
Edward Wilkinson Lampton
Benjamin Franklin Lee
James Haskell Mayo

Donald George Kenneth Ming
Morris Marcellus Moore
Samuel Solomon Morris, Jr.
Henry Wendell Murph
Willis Nazrey
Decatur Ward Nichols
Henry Blanton Parks
Daniel Alexander Payne
Howard Thomas Primm
Robert Lee Pruitt
William Paul Quinn
Reverdy Cassius Ransom
Frank Madison Reid, Jr.
Frank Madison Reid, Sr.
George Dewey Robinson
Hubert Nelson Robinson
Isaac Nelson Ross
Moses Buckingham Salter
Harold Benjamin Senatle
Cornelius Thaddeus Shaffer
Odie Lee Sherman
James Alexander Shorter
David Henry Sims
Walter William Slade
Charles Spencer Smith
Rembert Edwards Stokes
Frederick Hilborn Talbot
Benjamin T. Tanner
Cornelius Egbert Thomas
Robert Thomas, Jr.
Henry Young Tookes
Henry M. Turner
Evans Tyree
William T. Vernon
Dougal Ormonde Beaconsfield Walker
Thomas Marcus Decatur Ward
Edward Waters
Alexander W. Wayman
William Reid Wilkes
Noah W. Williams
Robert R. Wright, Jr.
George B. Young

Ministers and Lay Members (AME)

William T. Anderson
Hallie Quinn Brown
James Russell Brown
Archibald James Carey, Jr.
James Hal Cone
Fanny Marion Jackson Coppin
William Howard Day
James William Eichelberger, Jr.
Frances Joseph Gaudet
Alice M. Henderson
John Russell Hawkins
Anna Elizabeth Hudlun
Addie D. Waites Hunton
Harvey Ben Kinchlow
Jarena Lee
James D. Lynch
Mary Ella Mossell
George W. Prioleau
Mary Ann Prout
Hiram Rhoades Revels
George Arnett Singleton
Amanda Berry Smith
Charles Samuel Spivey, Jr.
Theophilus Gould Steward
Deon Yvonne Walker Taylor
Cornelia Wright

AFRICAN METHODIST
EPISCOPAL ZION CHURCH

Bishops

Frank Wesley Alstork
John Wesley Alstork
Felix Sylvester Anderson
Herman Leroy Anderson
Cecil Bishop
William Haywood Bishop
George Lincoln Blackwell
John Delaware Brooks
James Walter Brown
John Mifflin Brown
Morris Brown
Robert Turner Brown
William Cornelius Brown
Robert Blair Bruce
Josiah Samuel Caldwell
Joseph Dixon Cauthen
George Clinton Clement
George Wylie Clinton
Isom Caleb Clinton
Joseph Jackson Clinton
Charles Cecil Coleman
Clinton Reuben Coleman
William Howard Day
Alfred Gilbert Dunston, Jr.
Richard Laymon Fisher
Joseph Simeon Flipper
Charles Herbert Foggie
Martin Robert Franklin

George Galbreath
Buford Franklin Gordon
Cicero Richardson Harris
William Henry Hillery
James Walker Hood
Edward Derusha Wilmot Jones
Raymond Luther Jones
Singleton Thomas Webster Jones
Lynwood Westinghouse Kyles
Solomon Dorme Lartey
George Junius Leake, III
William Leonard Lee
Jermain Wesley Loguen
Thomas Henry Lomax
Elijah Lovette Madison
Arthur Marshall, Jr.
John William Martin
William Walter Matthews
Hampton Thomas Medford
John Henry Miller, Sr.
William Miller
John Jamison Moore
Charles Calvin Pettey
Daniel Carleton Pope
Florence Randolph
Peter Ross
Christopher Rush
John H. Satterwhite
Solomon Timothy Scott
Benjamin Garland Shaw
Herbert Bell Shaw
James Simmons
John Bryan Small
John Wesley Smith
William Milton Smith
Ruben Lee Speaks
Stephen Gill Spottswood
George Alfred Spywood
William Andrew Stewart
Samson Cunbar Talbot
John Tappan
James Clair Taylor
Joseph Pascal Thompson
Charles Eubank Tucker
James Varick
John Wesley Wactor
George W. Walker, Sr.
Paris Arthur Wallace
William Jacob Walls
Alexander Walters
Andrew Jackson Warner
Edgar Benton Watson
Alfred Edward White
Milton A. Williams
John Wesley Wood

Ministers and Lay Members

Annie Walker Blackwell
David Henry Bradley, Sr.
Rufus Early Clement
Julia A. J. Foote
Catherine Harris

Mary Jane Talbert Jones
Walter Raleigh Lovell
Sarah E. C. Dudley Pettey
Joseph Charles Price
Florence Randolph
Mary Jane Small
Sojourner Truth
Harriet Tubman
Peter Williams, Sr.

AFRICAN ORTHODOX
CHURCH (and HOLY AFRICAN
CHURCH)

Reginald Grant Barrow
Edmund Robert Bennett
George A. Ford
George Alexander McGuire
William Russell Miller
Gladstone St. Clair Nurse
William Ernest James Robertson
Richard Grant Robinson, Jr.
Noel Kenneth Smith
Frederick Augustus Toote
Arthur Stanley Trotman

AMERICAN BAPTIST
CHURCHES IN THE U.S.A.

Ralph Abernathy
James Luther Bevel
Charles Emerson Boddie
James Timothy Boddie
William Sterling Cary
Peter John Gomes
Nora Antonia Gordon
Mordecai Wyatt Johnson
Thomas Oscar Kilgore, Jr.
Henry Heywood Mitchell
Sophia B. Packard
James C. Sams
Kelly Miller Smith
Frederick J. Streets

BAPTISTS

(*See also*: American Baptist Churches
in the U.S.A., National Baptist
Convention of America, National
Baptist Convention, U.S.A., Inc., and
Progressive National Baptist
Convention)

Duke William Anderson
Jared Maurice Arter
Augustus Allen Battle
John L. Branham
Andrew Bryan
Lott Carey

William W. Colley
Noah Davis
Richard De Baptiste
London Ferrill
Clarence Lavaughn Franklin
George Washington Gayles
David George
Leonard Andrew Grimes
Gregory Willis Hayes
Jesse Louis Jackson
John Jasper
Vernon Johns
Harvey Elijah Johnson
George Dennis Sale Kelsey
Charles H. King, Jr.
George Liele
Emanuel King Love
William H. McAlpine
Andrew Cox Marshall
John Sella Martin
Benjamin Elijah Mays
John Berry Meachum
Jerry A. Moore, Jr.
Nathaniel Paul
Thomas Paul, Sr.
Christopher Harrison Payne
Albert Witherspoon Pegues
Rufus Lewis Perry
Henry Vinton Plummer
Adam Clayton Powell, Jr.
Adam Clayton Powell, Sr.
James Deotis Roberts
James Everett Rose
William J. Simmons
Lucy Wilmot Smith
Leon Howard Sullivan
Howard Thurman
Henry Martin Tupper
Booker Taliaferro Washington
Joseph Reed Washington, Jr.
George Washington Williams
Joseph Willis

BRETHREN

Martha Cunningham Dolby
Samuel Weir

CHRISTIAN CHURCH/ CHURCHES OF CHRIST

Carnella Jamison Barnes
Marshall Keeble

CHRISTIAN METHODIST EPISCOPAL CHURCH

Bishops

John Claude Allen
Richard Oliver Bass
Joseph A. Beebe
William Augustus Bell
William Yancy Bell
James Albert Bray
Oree Broomfield, Sr.
Edward Lynn Brown
Robert Turner Brown
Henry Clay Bunton
Randall Albert Carter
Nelson Caldwell Cleaves
Caesar David Coleman
Joseph Carlyle Coles, Jr.
Elias Cottrell
Norris Samuel Curry
Bertram Wilbur Doyle
John Madison Exum
Marshall Gilmore
William H. Graves
James Arthur Hamlett
Lucius Henry Holsey
Monroe Franklin Jamison
Joseph Andrew Johnson, Jr.
Chester Arthur Kirkendoll, II
Othal Hawthorne Lakey
Isaac Lane
Felix L. Lewis
Nathaniel L. Linsey
John Wesley McKinney
Joseph C. Martin
William Henry Miles
John Henry Moore
Elisha Murchison
Charles Henry Phillips
Henry Phillips Porter
Charles Lee Russell
Peter Randolph Shy
Benjamin Julian Smith
George Washington Stewart
Luther Caldwell Stewart
Richard H. Vanderhorst
Robert Simeon Williams
Arthur Walter Womack
Roy Lee Young

Ministers and Lay Members

William Augustus Bell
Helena Brown Cobb
Mattie Elizabeth Coleman
Channing Heggie Tobias

CHURCH OF GOD IN CHRIST

Bishops

Virgil M. Barker
Charles Edward Blake
J. E. Bryant
Eddie R. Driver
Henry Feltus
Mark E. Jonas
Ozro Thurston Jones, Jr.
Ozro Thurston Jones, Sr.
Otha Miema Kelly
Samuel Kelsey
Charles Harrison Mason
Emmett Moore Page
James Oglethorpe Patterson, Sr.
Alfred Sharpton

Ministers and Lay Members

Anne Penny Lee Bailey
Singleton Robert Chambers
Lillian Brooks Coffey
Andrae Crouch
Samuel M. Crouch, Sr.
Mattie Carter McGlothen
Arenia Cornelia Mallory
Lizzie Roberson

EPISCOPAL CHURCH

Bishops

Dillard Houston Brown
George Daniel Browne
John Melville Burgess
Clarence Nicholas Coleridge
Henry Beard Delany
Edward Thomas Demby
Walter Decoster Dennis
Samuel David Ferguson
Theophilus Momolu Gardiner
Luc Anatole Jacques Garnier
Barbara Clementine Harris
Bravid Washington Harris
James Theodore Holly
Telésforo Alexander Isaac
John Howard Johnson
Richard Beamon Martin
Henry Irving Mayson
Cedric Earl Mills
James Hamilton Ottley
Quintin Ebenezer Primo, Jr.
Victor A. Scantlebury
Nathan Alexander Scott, Jr.
Lemuel Barnett Shirley
Chester Lovelle Talton
Egbert Don Taylor
Herbert Thompson, Jr.
Franklin Delton Turner
John Thomas Walker

Orris George Walker, Jr.
Arthur Benjamin Williams, Jr.
Harold Louis Wright

Ministers and Lay Members

Joseph Sandiford Attwell
Robert Wellington Bagnall
Robert Avon Bennett, Jr.
Hutchens Chew Bishop
Shelton Hale Bishop
George Freeman Bragg, Jr.
Tollie Leroy Caution, Sr.
Alexander Crummell
Quinland Reeves Gordon
Absalom Jones
Edward Jones
Pauli Murray
Peter Williams, Sr.

FRIENDS

Paul Cuffe

HINDU

Swami Turiyasangitananda
(Alice Coltrane)

HOLINESS

Willie B. Taplin Barrow
Bennie G. Isem
Raymond S. Jackson
Frank Russell Killingsworth
B. Barton McIntyre
Solomon Lightfoot Michaux
Daniel Felix Oden
John M. Perkins
J. D. Smoot

INDEPENDENT CATHOLIC/ ORTHODOX

James Francis Augustine Lashley
George Alexander McGuire
Richard Arthur Marchenna
John More-Moreno
Robert Morgan
Ernest Leopold Petersen
Hubert Augustus Rogers
James Hubert Rogers
George Augustus Stallings, Jr.
Cyrus Augustine Starkey
Federick Augustus Toote
Arthur Stanley Trotman
Robert Arthur Valentine

Michal Edward Verra

ISLAM AND ISLAMIC-INSPIRED GROUPS

Noble Drew Ali
Wallace D. Fard
Louis Farrakhan
Malcolm X
Elijah Muhammad
Warith Deen Muhammad
Abdul Rahahman
Clarence Jowars Smith

JUDAISM

Frank S. Cherry
William Saunders Crowdy
Arnold Josiah Ford
Wentworth Arthur Matthew
Hailu Moshe Paris
Yahweh ben Yahweh

LATTER-DAY SAINTS

Elijah Abel
William McCary

LUTHERANS

Daniel R. Braxton
Nathaniel Carter
Edward H. Dixon
P. C. Dumas
Emmanuel
Robbin W. Skyles
Theodore Roosevelt Speigner
W. F. Gordon Stroud

METHODISTS

(*See also*: African Methodist Episcopal Church, African Methodist Episcopal Zion Church, Christian Methodist Episcopal Church, and United Methodist Church)

Daniel James Russell (African Union Methodist Protestant Church)

MENNONITES

Leslie Francisco, III
James H. Lark

METAPHYSICAL

Johnnie Colemon
Father Major Jealous Divine
Frederick J. Eikerenkoetter, II

NATIONAL BAPTIST CONVENTION OF AMERICA

Henry Allen Boyd
Richard Henry Boyd
Calvin Scott Brown

NATIONAL BAPTIST CONVENTION, U.S.A., INC.

C. C. Adams
Charles G. Adams
Josephus Pius Barbour, Sr.
Russell Conwell Barbour
Edward Doyle Billoups
James Timothy Boddie
Theodore Sylvester Boone
William Holmes Borders
Edward McKnight Brawley
Walter Henderson Brooks
Nannie Helen Burroughs
Caesar A. W. Clark
James Cleveland
Thomas Andrew Dorsey
Ernest Coble Estell
Elijah John Fisher
Miles Mark Fisher
Edward Anderson Freeman
Thomas Oscar Fuller
John Washington Goodgame
Sutton Elbert Griggs
Gordon Blaine Hancock
Edward Victor Hill
James Clinton Hoggard, Sr.
Thomas Elliott Huntley
Joseph Harrison Jackson
Mahalia Jackson (Gospel Singer)
David Vivian Jemison
Theodore Judson Jemison
William Henry Jernagin
Vernon Johns
Mrs. S. Willie Layten
Jessey Jai McNeil
Elias Camp Morris
Sandy Frederick Ray
Mary Olivia Ross
Frederick George Sampsom
Manuel L. Scott, Sr.
Marshall Lorenzo Shepard, Sr.
Tom Skinner
Arthur Melvin Townsend
Trudie Trimm
Charles Thomas Walker
Clara Mae Ward

Dennis Comer Washington

PENTECOSTAL ASSEMBLIES OF THE WORLD

Floyd Ignatius Douglas
Morris Ellis Golder
Samuel Joshua Grimes
Samuel Nathan Hancock
Garfield Thomas Haywood
John Silas Holly
Austin Augustine Layne
Benjamin Thomas Moore
Oscar Harwood Sanders
Alexander R. Schooler
David Thurman Schultz
Francis L. Smith
Karl Franklin Smith
Willie Mae Ford Smith
Freeman N. Thomas
Joseph Marcel Turpin

PENTECOSTALS

(*See also*: Church of God in Christ and Pentecostal Assemblies of the World)

William Lee Bonner
Joseph Thomas Bowens
Henry Chauncey Brooks
Shirley Caesar
James I. Clark, Sr.
Herbert Daniel Daughtry
Henry Lee Fisher
James Alexander Forbes
Charles Manuel Grace
Samuel Nathan Hancock
Elmira Jeffries
Mary E. Jackson
Sherrod C. Johnson
James Francis Marion Jones
Robert Clarence Lawson
Walter McCollough
Frederick K. C. Price
Joseph L. Price
Lizzie Roberson
William M. Roberts
Ida Robinson
Jasper Roby, Jr.
Lucille Marie Sherrod Scates
William Joseph Seymour
S. McDowell Shelton
George Slack
Elias Dempsey Smith
Lucy Smith
Mary Magdalena Lewis Tate
Charleszetta Lina Waddles

PRESBYTERIAN/REFORMED

Thelma Cornelia Adair
Jesse Belmont Barber
Edward Wilmot Blyden
Eugene St. Clair Callender
Katie Geneva Cannon
John Chavis
John Francis Cook, Sr.
Samuel Eli Cornish
Amos Freeman
Saint Paul Langley Epps
Catherine Ferguson
Henry Highland Garnet
Emily V. Gibbes
Jonathan C. Gibbs
John Gloucester
Francis James Grimke
Edler Garnet Hawkins
M. William Howard, Jr.
William Lloyd Imes
Lucy Craft Laney
James D. Lynch
Albert Byron McCoy
James William Charles Pennington
James Herman Robinson
Elymas Payson Rogers
Daniel Jackson Sanders
Marshall Logan Scott
Betsy Stockton
Charles H. Trusty
Wilbur Thornton Washington
Gayraud Stephen Wilmore, Jr.
Frank Theodore Wilson, Sr.
Theodore Sedgwick Wright

PROGRESSIVE NATIONAL BAPTIST CONVENTION

Charles G. Adams
LaVaughn Venchael Booth
William Holmes Borders
Charles W. Butler
Timothy Moses Chambers
William Herbert Gray, III
Benjamin Lawson Hooks
William Augustus Jones, Jr.
Coretta Scott King
Martin Luther King, Jr.
Martin Luther King, Sr.
Otis Moss, Jr.
Fred Lee Shuttlesworth
Gardner Calvin Taylor
Walker Wyatt Tee

ROMAN CATHOLIC CHURCH

Bishops

Moses B. Anderson
Joseph Oliver Bowers
Carl Anthony Fisher

Joseph Abel Francis
Wilton D. Gregory
Curtis J. Guillory
James Augustine Healy
Joseph Lawson Howze
James Patterson Lyke
Eugene Antonio Marino
John Sella Martin
Emerson John Moore
Leonard James Olivier
Harold R. Perry
John Huston Ricard
James Terry Steib

Religious

Mathilda Beasley
Ann Marie Becraft
Thea Bowman
Mary Shawn Copeland
Henriette Delille
M. Martin De Porres Grey
Eliza Healy
Elizabeth Lange
Elizabeth Barbara Williams

Priests and Lay Members

Edward Kenneth Braxton
Alexander Sherwood Healy
Patrick Francis Healy
Augustus Tolton
Pierre Toussaint

UNITARIAN-UNIVERSALIST

Egbert Ethelred Brown
Joseph Fletcher Jordan
Joseph H. Jordan
Lewis Allen McGee

UNITED CHURCH OF CHRIST

Jaramogi Abebe Agyeman
Henry S. Barnwell
Amos G. Beman
Sterling Nelson Brown
Francis Louis Cardozo
William Nelson DeBerry
Amos Freeman
Samuel Harrison
George Edmund Haynes
Lemuel Haynes
Lawrence Neale Jones
Harold Merrybright Kingsley
Alfred E. Lawless, Jr.
John Sella Martin
James William Charles Pennington
Hollis Freeman Price
Henry Hugh Proctor
Charles Bennett Ray

Charles Shelby Rooks
Emory Byington Smith
Kenneth Bryant Smith
Samuel Ringgold Ward

UNITED METHODIST CHURCH

Bishops

Lineunt Scott Allen
Edsel Albert Ammons
Joseph Benjamin Bethea
John Wesley Edward Bowen, Jr.
Robert Nathaniel Brooks
Francis Burns
Alexander Priestly Camphor
Edward Gonzalez Carroll
Matthew Walker Clair, Jr.
Matthew Wesley Clair, Sr.
Ernest Thomas Dixon, Jr.
Charles Franklin Golden
William Talbot Handy, Jr.
Marquis Lafayette Harris
William Alfred Carroll Hughes
Robert Elijah Jones
Edward Wendall Kelly
Leontine Turpeau Current Kelly
Lorenzo Houston King
Willis Jefferson King
Edgar Amos Love
Felton Edwin May
Noah Watson Moore, Jr.

Ernest Wilbur Newman
Roy Calvin Nichols
John Wright Roberts
Isaiah Benjamin Scott
Alexander Preston Shaw
F. Herbert Skeete
Forrest C. Stith
Melvin G. Talbert
Prince Albert Taylor, Jr.
James S. Thomas
Woodie W. White

Ministers and Lay Members

Mary McLeod Bethune
John Wesley Edward Bowen, Sr.
Matthew Simpson Davage
Zilpha Elaw
Henry Evans
Harry Hosier
James Morris Lawson, Jr.
Charles Eric Lincoln
Joseph E. Lowery
John Marrant
Georgia E. Lee Patton
Irvine Garland Penn
Cornish Romeo Rogers
Grant S. Shockley
John Stewart
Charles Albert Tindley
David Walker
Albert Cecil Williams

UNCLASSIFIED

Amiri Baraka
Eva Del Vakia Bowles
B. H. Broadie
Clarence H. Cobb
Jennie Dean
James Forman
Marcus Mosiah Garvey
Louis George Gregory
Anna Arnold Hedgeman
Dorothy Irene Height
James Langston Hughes
William Alphaeus Hunton, Sr.
Zora Neale Hurston
Rebecca Cox Jackson
James Weldon Johnson
Ron Ndabezitha Karenga
Marie Laveau
Roberta Martin
Sallie Martin
Louis Herbert Narcisse
Nancy Gardner Prince
Pascal Beverly Randolph
Clayton Donovan Russell
Imogene Williams Bigham Stewart
Luisah Teish
Nat Turner
Ethel Waters
Phillis Wheatley

Index

[**Note**: Bold numbers refer to main entries in the text]

A

Abbinga, Herman P. 509
Abdu'l-Baha 313
Ibn Abdullah, Muhammad Ahmad 47
Abel, Elijah **1–2**, 169, 170
Abernathy, Ralph David **2–3**, 83, 386, 427, 448, 462, 463, 562, 611, 622, 716, 778, 863
Abyssinian Baptist Church 604, 606
Abyssinian Church 65
Ackley, Stephen Edward 379, 623
Adair, Gregory R. P. 245, 509
Adair, John 245, 509
Adair, Thelma Cornelia **3–4**, 614
Adams, C. C. **4**
Adams, Carol G. 801
Adams, Charles G. **4**
Adams, John Hurst **4–5**, 207
Adams, John Quincy 782
Adams, Joseph H. 792
Addams, Jane 631
Addison, Clarence C. 27
Adefunmi I, Oba Efuntola Oseijeman Adelabu 26
Adler, Cyrus 38
Adventist tradition 278–279, 777
Aenon Bible School **5**, 316
Africa 4, 8, 9, 10–23, 57, 63, 73, 76, 82, 85, 89, 98, 99, 101, 105, 107, 116, 119, 120, 124, 128, 130, 131, 137, 145, 148, 149, 154, 159, 166, 171, 175, 177, 178, 180, 188, 192, 201, 203, 204, 211, 212, 216, 218, 220, 226, 248, 261–262, 294, 298, 306, 307, 340, 352, 356, 387, 400, 406, 456, 473, 492, 517, 603, 616, 681, 687, 717, 758, 770, 778, 802, 804, 809, 864
African American Catholic Congregation **6**, 376, 723
African American Lutheran Association 465
African American Masonic Lodge 483
African American Unitarian Universalist Ministry **6**
African Apostolic Catholic Church 25, 554
African Civilization Society 292, 486
African Cultural League 636

African Independent Catholic Church 481
African Islamic Mission **6**
African Masonic Lodge 35, 404, 574
African Methodist Episcopal Church (AME) 3, 4, **6–8**, 9, 11, 18, 31–32, 33, 35, 43, 44, 46, 47, 52, 53, 61, 63, 73, 75, 85, 96, 100, 114–117, 119, 122–126, 130, 136, 137, 142, 144, 145, 147–148, 154, 155, 164, 179, 187, 190, 192, 203, 206–211, 213, 220, 225, 233–236, 245, 249, 251, 254, 271–272, 273–274, 276, 277–278, 289, 296, 298, 299, 304, 305, 307, 308, 309, 311, 312, 324, 330, 332, 339, 343, 344, 345, 350, 360, 361, 363, 366, 377, 390, 391–392, 397, 399, 402, 404, 408, 414, 424, 433, 436, 441, 451, 464, 466–467, 473, 492, 501, 505, 511, 512, 517, 523, 524, 543, 546, 549, 552, 570, 571, 573, 575, 576, 577, 582, 586, 587, 593, 617, 622, 627, 646, 650, 651, 655, 661, 672, 680, 685, 686, 692, 694, 697, 698, 701, 703, 704, 721, 724, 725, 730, 737, 739, 741, 745, 751, 753, 757, 769, 770, 773, 774, 787, 799, 800, 801, 813, 814, 821, 827, 830, 831, 834, 835, 841, 848, 853, 855, 864
African Methodist Episcopal Zion Church (AMEZ) 3, **8–10**, 13–14, 36, 37, 42, 44–45, 56, 75, 77, 78, 85, 87, 94, 95, 110–111, 116, 124, 127, 128, 143, 152, 180–185, 189, 227, 241–242, 246, 248, 251, 270, 273, 274, 282, 290, 305, 327, 328, 346, 351, 352, 353, 357, 391, 406–407, 410–413, 415, 424, 426, 436–437, 445–446, 451, 453, 456–458, 462, 476–477, 484–485, 487, 491, 494–495, 498, 499–500, 504, 543, 589, 593, 600, 601, 603, 615, 616, 629, 662, 675, 680, 689, 690, 696, 701, 702, 707, 710, 711, 717, 721, 722, 723, 727, 728, 738, 740, 743, 753, 764, 766, 767, 787, 799, 809, 814, 816, 817, 818, 820, 821, 828, 833, 841, 842, 851, 852
African Missionary Movement 306
African Missions and the African American Christian Churches **10–23**
African Orthodox Church (AOC) **23–25**, 25, 29, 72, 79, 80, 245, 250, 252, 276, 294, 355, 356, 376, 446, 474, 481, 500, 508, 543, 548, 554, 555, 564, 600, 641,